DICTIONARY OF MUSIC

DICTIONARY OF MUSIC

ERIC BLOM

BHARATIYA KALA PRAKASHAN
DELHI (INDIA)

First Edition : 1946 (London)
Indian Edition : 2007

Published by **C. P. Gautam**
BHARATIYA KALA PRAKASHAN
3421-A, IInd Floor Narang Colony, Tri Nagar,
Delhi-110035. Phone : 27393083, 32967505 (O)
E-Mail : bkp.3421@yahoo.co.in

ISBN : 978-81-8090-172-0

Laser Type Setting by
A-ONE GRAPHICS
Pitampura, Delhi-110088

Printed by :
BDH Printers at D. K. Fine Art Press, Delhi

PREFACE

Strictly speaking, this book is not a dictionary in every sense of the term. It includes biographical sketches, which it is no function of dictionaries to do; on the other hand, though it translates foreign terms, as a book of this kind should, it rarely attempts to offer guidance in the matter of pronunciation, for a reason to be explained presently. At the same time it could not have been called an encyclopaedia, for, although as comprehensive as possible within the small space allotted to the vast material, it does not contain long historical and critical articles, but contents itself with definitions, some of considerable length, yet all as brief as they could be kept without omitting essentials.

In order to keep within an amount of space permitting *Everyman's Dictionary of Music* to come within the reach of every man's pocket—and, it is hoped, every woman's handbag—and, more particularly, to make room for some special features that may claim to be both novel and useful, its scope had to be drastically restricted in some respects. There could be no pictures and no music-type examples, and no claim whatever is made that larger books containing a more or less lavish supply of both, as well as offering substantial articles, have now been superseded. This is not a manual for specialists: it is a book to be used for quick reference by anybody who is at all interested in music, and it may indeed be so used even by those who have no special learning and who may not be able to read musical notation. An attempt has been made to elucidate technical points without the aid of music-type. All the reader will need in some instances to grasp an explanation is to know the notes on the pianoforte keyboard.

Not everything that may conceivably be looked for will be found entered, and some subjects have been very briefly treated. References to ancient and oriental music and instruments have been excluded altogether. Western music of the Christian era alone—and not much of the early centuries of that—is dealt with. Little is said about the history and construction of instruments, and only what is essential about their character and functions. Few instrument makers or music printers and publishers appear, though the most important have been included. Birds, bells and other matters that barely reach the fringes of music as an art, though often found in other musical works of reference, have been ignored here. So, for pretty much the same reason, have ballet dancers, dead or alive.

The user of this book will be more forcibly struck, and sometimes inconvenienced, it is to be feared, by the absence of all living performers, even to cathedral organists, unless they happen to be composers with a reputation beyond their immediate sphere as well, or have some other claim to be mentioned. It is, of course, unfortunate that even such names as Beecham, Boult, Casals, Furtwängler, Kreisler, Kussevitsky, Lamond, Thibaud, Toscanini, and so on, cannot be looked up in this book; but to include any of them to the exclusion of others would have been dangerously invidious and necessarily unfair in many cases. In future editions many of those who may die in the meantime will, of course, be added. All the same, it is hoped that this announcement will not start an immediate wave of suicide among singers and players. Death will not be the only qualification for their future inclusion, for which many will remain ineligible in perpetuity; but those who have legitimate claims to remembrance may be assured of an eventual place in these pages. However, even the performers of the past who do appear will be found to have comparatively short entries allotted to them. Their biographies, sensational or otherwise, are not by any means told in full and will have to be looked up elsewhere by those whose interests stray in that direction.

The composers' lives are more fully told, though still with proportionate brevity. It is they who have built the art of music, whereas performers have at best graced it.

Another small saving of space has been made by disregarding entries that might have been convenient at times, but must really be regarded as superfluous. They are the ordinary dictionary words in foreign languages that find their way into the composer's vocabulary without becoming thereby universally recognized as specifically musical terms. Such words, which can be looked up in any ordinary dictionary, if indeed that is necessary at all, are not given here. It would have been absurd, for instance, to enter the French and German words indicating a quick tempo, although French and German composers do use *vite* and *schnell*, or *animé* and *geschwind*, or what not. The Italian *presto*, on the other hand, had obviously to be included as one of those universal musical terms. In fact a considerable number of quite ordinary Italian words are known to the world at large only in their musical sense, and for the sake of reasonable completeness they had to be entered as technical terms.

Foreign names of instruments, found in full scores and therefore worth knowing, are shown here only if they differ sufficiently from the English word to be unfamiliar or to lead to confusion. It would have been absurd to show that *flûte* is French for 'flute,' *Klarinette* German for 'clarinet' or *trombone* Italian for 'trombone.' On the other hand it is by no means useless to make sure that *clarino* is not taken to mean 'clarinet' or *tromba* confused with 'trombone.'

Phonetic transliterations showing, or pretending to show, the pronunciation of foreign names and terms have not been attempted, for the simple reason that they nearly always tend merely to substitute one mispronunciation for another. A few indications are nevertheless given here and there, as in the case of the Czech ˇ accent, the function of which is shown, under the letters with which it is used, in the proper alphabetical order. Also, accented syllables are pointed out for some current Italian terms which are commonly mispronounced by English-speaking people, even by some well-versed professional musicians (such as *cembálo* for *cémbalo, cantabíle* for *cantábile* or *piacevóle* for *piacévole*).

Something should be said about the order of the alphabetical entries adopted. All entries consisting of more than one word are ranged in such a way as to make the first word alone the key to their place in the alphabet. That is to say, the initial letter of the second word is not to be taken as part of the entry, though it does, of course, determine the place of that second word behind the first. To give a simple example, entries beginning with the letters W A R would be ordered thus (hyphens being disregarded):

War Aims		War Aims
War Babies		War Babies
War Damage		Warbling
War Ministry		War Damage
War-Monger		Warehouse
War Songs	*not*	Waring
Warbling		War Ministry
Warehouse		Warminster
Waring		War-Monger
Warminster		Warsaw
Warsaw		War Songs
Warwick		Warwick

Under the entries of proper names one or more of several Christian names will often be found in brackets. It was thought advisable to resort to this device in all cases where only one of these names is usually coupled with the surname. In Mozart's case there happen to be two: if he is given any fuller name than his surname alone we still think of him as Wolfgang Amadeus Mozart, and he accordingly appears so. But his father is never called anything but Leopold Mozart, and it would have been misleading to those unfamiliar with him to enter him as Johann Georg Leopold Mozart, for this would have looked as though he ought to be called Johann Mozart for short. The entry of '(Johann Georg) Leopold Mozart' gives his familiar name prominence while showing what his full baptismal name was. Such bracketed names are ignored from the point of view of the alphabet: '(William) Albert Smith' would stand before 'John Smith.'

Abbreviations are plentiful. Most of them will either be immediately intelligible or become so as soon as the reader is accustomed to the use of this book. No list of abbreviations is shown separately at the beginning or end of the volume; they are given their own entries, followed by explanations, in the main alphabet, where they can be turned up at least as quickly—and, after all, none need be looked up more than once, while many will require no key at all. Such a key is nevertheless given where there can be the least doubt; but in order to avoid insults to intelligence the most obvious abbreviations have been left without reference. It would have been worse than useless, for instance, to show even for the benefit of schoolboys that 'maths.' stands for 'mathematics'; and, in their particular contexts at any rate, such curtailed words as 'Revol.' or 'Restor.' could not possibly be mistaken for anything but 'Revolution' and 'Restoration.' On the other hand, some words had to be written out fully every time to avoid duplication of similar abbreviations. Thus 'lit.' stands for 'literal' and 'literally,' while 'literary' is spelt out.

The very numerous cross-references are not specifically indicated by any '(q.v.)' or other sign. The reader who comes across any word that seems to him to need further explanation will, as a rule, find it under its own entry in the alphabet as a matter of course, so long as it is a term with a musical connotation. Some help is offered, however, by the device of printing with capital initials many of the nouns to which cross-references will be found. This tells the reader nothing in the case of proper names, of course; but there it will generally be found that persons having their own entries are referred to by their surnames alone (with initials where the same surname occurs more than once), while others are shown in full. There is no need to remind the reader that this applies to musicians' names only.

Some matters of spelling and typographical style had perhaps better be briefly discussed here.

In Italian proper names the obsolete letter 'j,' which was never really a 'j,' but merely a long 'i,' has been discarded except where it is used as an initial for names that have become familiar in that form, such as that of 'Jommelli.' Nobody would think of looking him up under 'Iommelli,' though that spelling would be perfectly correct according to modern usage. But 'Araja,' 'Barbaja,' 'Majo,' etc., have been replaced by 'Araia,' 'Barbaia,' 'Maio,' etc.

For dates the Old Style has been discarded except for the English dates before the change to New Style in 1752, since the old dates have been fixed by musical history—those of the productions of Handel's operas before that year, for instance. On the other hand the old English legal year beginning on 25th March, found in seventeenth-century dates (Pepys, and so on) and often later, has been disregarded. For the purpose of this book 1st February 1669–70 is 1. II. 1670. Soviet Russia having now come into line with the rest of the western world in abandoning the old calendar, no useful purpose could have been served in retaining the now obsolete dates or in encumbering a book which aims at brevity of information with the double dates still to be found in many works of reference.

This brings us to the very difficult question of the transliteration of Russian names. It accords here as nearly as possible with what they would look like if spelt in the Latin alphabet according to the peculiarities of the English language. I have swept away German and French spellings like 'Tschaikowski' for 'Tchaikovsky' and 'Chaliapine' for 'Shaliapin,' even where the persons in question happened to use these spellings themselves whenever they used Latin script, as in these two cases. For the rest, I have followed more or less consistently (though with some slight deviations) the rules drawn up by the School of Slavonic Studies. The Russian letters for the sound 'ch' in the Scottish 'loch' is represented by the symbol 'kh'; that for the sound of the French 'j' is replaced by the symbol 'zh' (pronounced like 's' in 'pleasure') to avoid its being sounded like 'dj' in English. On the other hand, after some consideration, I decided to retain 'tch' for a sound which has one letter in Russian and for which the Germans use four ('tsch'), the reason being simply that we have adopted 'Tchaikovsky' and would never think of looking for that composer under 'Chaikovsky' in a reference book. On that analogy, I feel, we must also have 'Tcherepnin,' 'Tchekhov,' etc., and I have ventured also to insert the 't' in the middle of words, including the familiar patronymic endings such as that in 'Ivanovitch.' It is true that 'ch' would have done, at the cost of some inconsistency; but after all we have many English words ('itch,' 'witch,' etc.) retaining an equally superfluous 't.'

Not that consistency has been possible everywhere. It was simple enough to follow the same authority's rule about the very frequent 'ov' endings of surnames and rather a relief to do away with the formerly more common 'off' (again even in cases where it was used by the signatory himself, as with 'Rachmaninoff,' now spelt 'Rakhmaninov'). But the almost equally common 'eff' (now 'ev') ending was not so simple, and here I have deviated from authority in cases where this ending follows a vowel. In such cases I have ventured to insert the 'i' which is actually sounded in Russian in all such cases, the Russian letter 'e' being pronounced 'yé.' I felt I could not countenance such a spelling as 'Taneev,' which courts the wildest mispronunciation: the name appears in this book as 'Taneiev.' Indeed I hesitated between this and 'Taneyev,' and in fact wondered whether the double-vowel sound ought not to be shown in all such endings, e.g. 'Balakiriev' or 'Balakiryev.' However, I decided against such a course as being too much at variance with ordinary usage.

For the Russian 'y' the choice lay between using the freakish-looking 'oo,' the French 'ou,' which English readers might pronounce as in 'mouse,' or 'u,' which they might take for the vowel sound in 'mustard' or in 'music.' I decided to choose this last evil and spell 'Mussorgsky,' 'Glazunov,' etc.

Towns which have changed their names owing to political vicissitudes are, as far as possible, called by those of the period under notice. A musician may thus have been born at St. Petersburg in 1870, have worked at Petrograd in 1916 and have died at Leningrad in 1930; and it is hoped that the reader will have enough historical knowledge to realize that the place is always the same. Similar treatment has been given, for instance, to Christiania = Oslo and to Helsingfors = Helsinki. On the other hand towns in Czechoslovakia, Poland, etc., which ought never to have been called by German names, I have endeavoured to keep consistently to their native names. Brno is thus never called Brünn, Olomouc never Olmütz, Budějovice never Budweis, Lwów never Lemberg, and so on. I cannot guarantee, however, that my knowledge has always been sufficient not to forsake me in the more obscure cases of the kind, and there have been such perplexities as that of knowing when to give one and the same town the name of the Austrian Pressburg, the Hungarian Pozsony or the Slovak Bratislava. I can only hope that I have been reasonably accurate and that the reader will make such corrections as may occur to him. Sometimes the more familiar name is shown in brackets: few people would otherwise be aware that, for example, Jihlava is the place they may know better as Iglau. For the Alsatian capital, never certain for long whether it was French or German, I have avoided the spelling in either language and chosen, perhaps rather arbitrarily, the plausible and diplomatic compromise of 'Strasburg.'

The numerous references to literary works used by composers as a basis for operas, ballets, incidental music, concert overtures, symphonic poems, etc., which will be found entered under the authors' names, may, I hope, be regarded as useful and perhaps unique, at any rate in English publications, so far as I am aware. They show at a glance what musical works of various kinds have been founded on, for example, each of Shakespeare's plays, on the *Electras* of Sophocles, Hofmannsthal and Eugene O'Neill, on novels, epics, narrative poems, plays and other literature of many kinds, or, to change the point of view, on the miscellaneous works of any author who happens to have inspired composers. These authors are strangely various, and the Dictionary shows some interesting inclusions as well as rather astonishing exclusions. More musical works have come out of Rabelais, for instance, than one would have expected; none, on the other hand, seems to have proceeded from Jane Austen or the Brontës. No claim to completeness can be made, of course: the possible choice was endless and has been limited only by the entries of musical works under each composer's heading; these, however, will be found fully indexed under the entries given to literary references. Lyric poetry fares comparatively less well than epic or narrative, and incomparably less than drama, for it was obviously impossible to include references to many songs, lists of which would have run into tens of thousands. The important song-cycles, however, have been included to a considerable extent, and in some cases (as in those of Hardy and A. E. Housman) lists of settings that may make a fair claim to completeness are offered. There are also some summaries of the settings of poems by Goethe, Heine, Verlaine and others made by the greater composers.

Titles of foreign works were found to be a difficulty—too much so for consistency. As a rule those of French, German, Italian and Spanish works are given in the original (with translations where they appear as special entries under their own title-headings); those in languages less readily understood (or guessed) by the normally educated reader are usually given in an English equivalent of the foreign title. This applies to the entries under the composers' names as well as to the title-headings. The latter are sometimes given in the original, with cross-references to these originals from second entries of an English equivalent, and sometimes in English only where that is most familiar. Not consistency but consideration in each case of where the title of a work is most likely to be looked for by English-speaking people has been the guiding principle in the placing of these title-entries. Where the foreign title alone is familiar (e.g. *La Cigale, Les Cloches de Corneville, La Basoche*) no English entry appears at all, for the simple reason that nobody would know where to look for it. It would be absurd to give an entry to *Johnny and Meg* for *Hänsel und Gretel*, for instance, or to *Minstrel, The* for *Il trovatore*. The reader might, of course, guess what *Rustic Chivalry* or *The Lady gone astray* could stand for, but in that case he may just as well look at once for *Cavalleria rusticana* and *Traviata*.

The contents of the Dictionary are uncritical: the inclusion of any composer or work does not imply approbation any more than the exclusion of any subject, which may be due to one of a variety of other reasons, suggests disapproval. It may be asked why certain excessively popular but artistically valueless works are given prominence by special entries. The reason is precisely their popularity. Their titles may have acquired general currency, at any rate for a certain time, and this may induce some musical person to ask 'What *is* the so-and-so Concerto?' To such questions a dictionary should have an answer, even if the compiler happens to think that it was not worth asking.

Popular nicknames must be similarly treated, and for very similar reasons. The answer to 'What *is* the Victory Symphony?' must be given to those who in a few years may never have heard this title mentioned or even know what particular victory is referred to; and it is neither here nor there whether one thinks the use of the opening of Beethoven's fifth Symphony to spell the letter V in Morse code justified or not. A dictionary is concerned with information and must take facts as it finds them.

There being no such thing as infallibility, it is not impossible that discrepancies between this book and older works of reference may in isolated cases be due to a mistake or a misprint allowed to slip into the pages that follow. It may nevertheless be confidently asserted that as a rule the particulars given here are decisive. Dates and other details have been carefully checked by the results of recent research, whenever these were considered reliable. In an overwhelming number of cases, if not all, the information found here may thus be accepted as correct, even if it differs from that found in works hitherto accepted as reliable.

On the other hand it must be confessed that some of the information about living musicians, especially those in what were quite recently enemy or occupied countries, though reasonably accurate as far as it goes, cannot always be regarded as complete. Many things have happened in Europe of which no news had penetrated to England at the time of going to press. There is no doubt that the biographies of continental musicians will have to be subjected to many changes in future editions, and it is to be feared that some who have died in wartime obscurity will be found entered as though they were still alive. For such defects readers will, it is hoped, make due allowance. They will also bear the fact in mind that any work of reference is bound to go out of date to some extent during the many months it takes to produce.

There is one feature in this book which I may unblushingly claim to be valuable, since it is not my own contribution. It is the very full list of National Anthems found under that head. I am deeply indebted to Messrs. D. R. Wakeling and G. de Fraine, as well as to the editor of the *Music Review*, for their very kind permission to draw upon a compilation published in that periodical, vol. iii, Nos. 3 and 4, 1942, with musical quotations and some other particulars which it was not possible to reproduce here. On the other hand, Mr. Wakeling has put me under a further obligation, which nothing can repay, by placing at my disposal a revised manuscript list containing a number of valuable corrections and additions.

Operas which are still familiar or have some historical importance for their music or their librettos will be found under their titles as well as under their composers' entries, and in the title-entries details are given of the authors and sources of the librettos as well as, where ascertainable, place and date of first performances. To say that my work in this direction was greatly facilitated by Alfred Loewenberg's monumental *Annals of Opera* (Cambridge, 1943) would be a gross understatement: the fact is that without this invaluable book my efforts in this direction could never have been nearly as successful as they may now claim to be. I therefore wish to make a special point of explicitly and most gratefully acknowledging my indebtedness to Dr. Loewenberg. But this is not all: he has most generously assisted me further by offering to go through the proofs of this book and adding to them a number of details of recent events (the deaths of musicians abroad, the appearance of new works, etc.) not reported by the daily or even the musical press in this country during the war, but assembled and noted by him from a number of foreign publications to which his specialist work happens to have given him access. He has also made corrections in the dates and places of birth and death of numerous older musicians. All these are based on the records of recent research in various countries and may, so far as human fallibility and the possibility of misprints will allow, be confidently accepted as trustworthy, even where they differ from authoritiative works of reference published earlier. I hope that those who use this book will bear in mind that for a good deal of biographical information they are indebted, not to my efforts, but to Dr. Loewenberg's generous voluntary assistance.

Finally, I cannot forbear to say that by no means the least debt I owe to Messrs. Dent's learned and versatile reader, Mr. Charles Lee, who marked the proofs with a great variety of queries and suggestions nearly every one of which saved me from a pitfall or led to a valuable improvement.

ERIC BLOM.

9th January 1946.

A

A. The note bounding the range of the scales of A maj. and min. and of the Aeolian and Hypodorian (Gr. Mixolydian) modes.

A.B.A. A symbol, one of many possible ones, by which mus. forms can be conveniently demonstrated. It stands for a comp. in ternary form, e.g. a minuet or scherzo with trio or a *da capo* aria, A representing the section heard in the same form first and last, B for the contrasting middle section. Another such symbol frequently used is A.B.A.C.A., showing minuet or scherzo with 2 different trios; or A.B.A.C.A.B.A., standing for a rondo in which the 1st and 3rd episodes are the same theme, like a 2nd subject in so. form, while the middle one is different.

A battuta (It. = at the beat, with the beat). A direction indicating that after a free passage the strict time is to be resumed.

A cappella (It.), also **Alla cappella** (lit. at or in the chapel). A term used now only to designate unaccomp. voc. m.

A due (It.) = in 2 parts; gen. written '*a* 2.' The term is also used in the opposite sense in orch. scores where pairs of insts. are to play in unison.

A. E. (George William Russell) (1867–1935), Ir. poet. *See* **Busch** (songs).

A la manière de . . . (*In the Manner of . . .*), 2 sets of pf. pieces by Casella and Ravel imitating the styles of Wagner, Fauré, Brahms, Debussy, R. Strauss, Franck, Borodin, d'Indy, Chabrier & Ravel. Only the Borodin and Chabrier pieces are by Ravel.

A piacere (It. = at pleasure). A direction indicating that a passage may be played or sung in any way the perf. desires, esp. in regard to tempo.

A tempo (It. = in time). A direction indicating a return to the principal pace of a comp. after a temporary alteration.

Aaron, Pietro (b. Florence, ?; d. ?, before 1545), It. monk & ctptst. Wrote on hist. and science of m. and founded a school in Rome *c.* 1516.

Aavik, Juhan (b. Estonia, 29. I. 1884), Estonian cond. & comp. Studied at the St. Petersburg Cons. and became a cond. at Wanemuine in 1911, later dir. of the Dorpat Cons. and chor. cond. at Reval.

Works incl. cantata *Homeland*; unaccomp. chors.; pf. So. in C min.; songs, &c.

Abaco, Evaristo Felice dall' (b. Verona, 12. VII. 1675; d. Munich, 12. VII. 1742), It. vst. & comp. Worked at Modena, Munich and Brussels; wrote chiefly stg. m.

Abaco, Giuseppe Clemens Ferdinand dall' (b. Brussels, 1709; d. Verona, 1805), It.-Ger. cst. & comp., son of prec. Worked at Bonn and played in London, Vienna, &c. Comp. sos. for his inst.

Abacus. A diagram of the pf. or org. keyboard.

Abacus harmonicus. The disposition of the keyboard and pedals of an org.

Abba-Cornaglia, Pietro (b. Alessandria, Piedmont, 20. III. 1851; d. Alessandria, 2. V. 1894), It. comp. Studied at the Milan Cons. and later became a teacher and mus. historian.

Works incl. operas *Isabella Spinola*, *Maria di Warden*, *Una partita di scacchi*; Requiem; chamber m., &c.

Abbatino, Antonio Maria (b. Tiferno, now Città di Castello, *c.* 1598; d. Tiferno, 1679), It. comp. & church musn. Held various apps. at churches in Rome.

Works incl. 2 operas, masses, motets, psalms, madrigals, &c.

Abbellimenti (It. lit. embellishments) = Ornaments, esp. florid passages introduced into sacred voc. m.

Abbey, John (b. Whilton, Northants., 22. XII. 1785; d. Versailles, 19. II. 1859), Eng. org. builder. Worked in Paris from 1826 and built many orgs. in Fr. and S. America.

Abbott, Emma (b. Chicago, 9. XII. 1850; d. Salt Lake City, 5. I. 1891), Amer. sop. singer. Studied with Achille Errani in N.Y., later in Milan and Paris, with Mathilde Marchesi and others. She 1st appeared at Covent Garden in London, 1876, and formed an operatic company in Amer., managed by Eugene Wetherell, whom she married in 1878.

Abeille, Johann Christian Ludwig (b. Bayreuth, 20. II. 1761; d. Stuttgart, 2. III. 1838), Ger. comp., pfst. & orgst. In the service of the Duke of Württemberg.

Works incl. operettas *Amor und Psyche* & *Peter und Aennchen*; hpchd. concs.; songs, &c.

Abel, Carl Friedrich (b. Cöthen, 1725; d. London, 20. VI. 1787), Ger. hpchd. and va. da gamba player. Brought up under Bach at St. Thomas's School, Leipzig. Went to Dresden in 1748, to London in 1759, where he was app. chamber musn. to Queen

Charlotte. Made a name as a comp. and gave concerts jointly with Johann Christian Bach.

Abel, Christian Ferdinand (b. ?; d. ?), Ger. 17th–18th-cent. va. da gamba player & cst., father of prec. Worked in the court chapel at Cöthen.

Abel, Leopold August (b. Cöthen, 1717; d. Ludwigslust, 25. VIII. 1794), Ger. vst. & comp., son of prec.

Abélard, Pierre (b. Palet nr. Nantes, 1079; d. nr. Chalon-sur-Saône, 21. IV. 1142), Fr. scholar & musn. Comp. songs for his beloved, Héloïse, Lat. lamentations, &c.

Abell, John (b. London, 1650; d. Cambridge, 1724), Eng. counter-ten. singer & lutenist. Possibly a boy chorister at the Chapel Royal in London, of which he became a Gentleman in 1679. Married Frances Knollys, sister of the Earl of Banbury, travelled much abroad, was intendant at Cassel, 1698–9, and returned to Eng. as a stage singer. Pub. some collections of songs.

Abencérages, Les, ou L'Étendard de Grenade (*The Abencerrages, or The Standard of Granada*), opera by Cherubini (lib. by Victor Joseph Étienne de Jouy, based on a novel by Jean-Pierre de Florian), prod. Paris, Opéra, 6. IV. 1813.

Abendmusiken (Ger. = evening music[s]). Mus. evening perfs. of semi-sacred character estab. by Tunder at Lübeck in the 1640s and becoming so famous there that they were imitated by other north Ger. towns, esp. Hamburg. They were held mainly during Advent.

Abenteuer des Casanova (*Casanova's Adventures*), opera by Andreae (lib. by Ferdinand Lion, based on Casanova's memoirs), prod. Dresden, 17. VI. 1924.

Abert, Hermann (b. Stuttgart, 25. III. 1871; d. Stuttgart, 13. VIII. 1927), Ger. mcolst. of Cz. descent. Prof. of m. at Leipzig Univ. in succession to Riemann from 1920. Wrote many mcol. works, incl. a greatly enlarged ed. of Jahn's *Mozart*.

Abert, Johann Joseph (b. Kochovice, 21. IX. 1832; d. Stuttgart, 1. IV. 1915), Cz. db. player, cond. & comp., father of prec.

Abgesang (Ger. = after-song). The songs of the Ger. Minnesinger and Meistersinger were usually divided into 3 sections: 2 *Stollen* of equal length often sung to the same and always to very similar m., and an A. forming a concluding section of unspecified length and with different though relevant m. The 2 *Stollen* together were called *Aufgesang* (fore-song).

Abingdon, Henry. *See* **Abyngdon.**

Abondante, Giulio (b. ?; d. ?), It. 16th-cent. lutenist & comp. Pub. several books of lute pieces.

Abos, Girolamo (b. Malta, 1719; d. Naples, X. 1760), Maltese comp.
Works incl. operas *Artaserse* & others; church m., &c.

Abraham, Gerald (b. Newport, Isle of Wight, 9. III. 1904), Eng. mcolst. Apart from pf. lessons he is self-taught and studied Rus. in order to specialize in Rus. m. His 1st book was on Borodin, and others followed, incl. some collabs. with Calvocoressi, whose posthumous vol. on Mussorgsky he finished; other works incl. studies of Chopin and Wagner. Ed. of a series of books on comps. with chapters by var. authors.

Abramsky, Alexander (b. Moscow, 22. I. 1898), Rus. comp. Studied at the Moscow Cons. He turned to Soviet ideology by writing an opera on the subject of life on a collective farm.
Works incl. opera *Song of Friendship*; chor. works; chamber m., &c.

Ábrányi, Emil (b. Budapest, 22. IX. 1882), Hung. cond. & comp. Cond. of the Opera at Budapest since 1911. His operas, prod. there, incl. *Monna Vanna* (after Maeterlinck), *Paolo and Francesca* (after Dante) and *Don Quixote* (after Cervantes).

Ábrányi, Kornel (b. Hung., 15. X. 1822; d. Budapest, 20. XII. 1903), Hung. critic, father of prec. Part-founder of the mus. paper *Zenészeti Lapok*, 1860, and prof. at the Budapest Acad. of M. from 1875. Wrote the lib. for his son's *Monna Vanna.*

Abreise, Die, opera by d'Albert (lib. by Ferdinand von Sporck, based on a play by August von Steigentesch), prod. Frankfort, 20. X. 1898.

Absil, Jean (b. Péruwelz, Hainault, 23. X. 1893), Belg. comp. Studied at the Brussels Cons., where he became prof. in 1931, after being app. dir. of the Mus. Acad. at Etterbeek in 1923.
Works incl. opera *Peau d'âne*; chor. works; 2 syms.; pf. Conc., v. Conc.; *Petite Suite* for chamber orch.; 3 stg. 4tets; pf. m.; songs, &c.

Absolute Music. Broadly speaking, any m. not set to words and not based on any kind of literary, pictorial, descriptive or other extra-mus. subject or idea. Actually, however, much inst. m., even without such associations, cannot properly be described as A. M. if it suggests a definite mood or arouses strong emotion of any kind.

Absolute Pitch. Those who can identify by ear any note heard without ref. to printed m. are said to possess the faculty of A. P.

Abt, Franz (b. Eilenburg, 22. XII.

1819; d. Wiesbaden, 31. III. 1885), Ger. comp. & cond. Studied at St. Thomas's and Univ., Leipzig; later cond. at Bernburg, Zürich and Brunswick. Comp. an enormous number of songs and partsongs.

Abu Hassan, opera by Weber (lib. by Franz Carl Hiemer), prod. Munich, 4. VI. 1811.

Abyngdon, Henry (b. ?, *c.* 1418; d. ?, IX. 1497), Eng. comp. In the service of the Duke of Gloucester, 1445; app. succentor at Wells cath., 1447, and Master of the Children at the Chapel Royal in London, 1456.

Abzug (Ger.). *See* **Ornaments.**

Academic Festival Overture (*Akademische Fest-Ouvertüre*). An ovt. by Brahms, Op. 80, comp. in 1880 and 1st perf. at Breslau, 4. I. 1881. It was B.'s acknowledgment of the hon. degree of doctor of philos., conferred on him by Breslau Univ. in 1879. The thematic material consists of Ger. students' songs. The *Tragic Ovt.* was written as a companion-piece.

Academie (Ger., 18th cent., or **Akademie**) = a concert.

Académie de Musique. The official title of the Paris Opéra, though never actually called so after 1671. It was first so styled in letters-patent granted by Louis XIV, 28. VI. 1669. It became the Académie des Opera (*sic*) in 1671 and the Académie Royale de Musique in 1672 until the Revolution more than a cent. later; after that, at various times, according to the political situation: Théâtre de l'Opéra, Opéra National, Théâtre des Arts, Théâtre de la République et des Arts, Théâtre Impérial de l'Opéra, Théâtre de la Nation, Académie Nationale de Musique, Théâtre National de l'Opéra.

Acaen. *See* **Caen.**

Accelerando (It.) = accelerating; quickening of the pace.

Accelli, Cesare (b. Mantua, ?; d. ?), It. 16th-cent. comp. Wrote madrigals pub. between 1557–86.

Accent (Fr.). *See* **Ornaments.**

Accents. As. have much the same function in m. as in prosody, being the metrical or rhythmic stresses of m. Normally the main A. is on the 1st beat after the bar-line, and in any m. divided into bars of more than 3 beats there is usually a secondary A., less strongly stressed. But As. are frequently displaced by being marked on a weak beat, transferred by syncopation or omitted on the main beat by the replacement of a rest for a note or chord.

Acciaccatura (It., from *acciaccare* = to crush). An ornament in old keyboard m. consisting of a discordant note struck together with that immediately above, but at once released while the principal note is held on. The term is now generally used synonymously with Appoggiatura.

Accidentals. The signs by which notes are chromatically altered by being raised or lowered by a semitone or whole tone. The ♯ (sharp) raises and the ♭ (flat) lowers the note by a semitone: the × (double sharp) raises and the ♭♭ (double flat) lowers it by a whole tone; the ♮ (natural) contradicts a ♯ or ♭ in the key signature or restores a note previously sharpened or flattened to its orig. position.

Accomp. (abbr.). Accompanied, accompaniment, accompany.

Accompagnato. *See* **Recitativo accompagnato.**

Accompanied Recitative. *See* **Recitativo accompagnato.**

Accompaniment. The inst. part or parts forming a background to the melodic line of a solo voice or inst., generally played by a keyboard inst. or by the orch. The A. may also be improvised or ed. by the setting out of additional parts where the comp.'s harmony has been left incomplete or indicated only by a figured bass.

Accord (old Eng.). Harmony, harmoniousness, being in tune.

Accordance (old Eng.). The tuning of stg. insts. in certain intervals.

Accordatura (It.). The notes to which a stg. inst. is tuned.

Accordion. An inst. prod. its sound by means of tuned pipes through which wind is driven by pleated bellows opened and closed by the player's hands. The pipes speak when opened by the pressing of buttons and sometimes by the playing of one hand on a keyboard similar to that of the pf.

Achille, opera by Paer (lib., in It., by Giovanni de Gamerra), prod. Vienna, Kärntnertor Theatre, 6. VI. 1801. It was on hearing the funeral march in this work that Beethoven exclaimed 'How beautiful! how interesting! I shall have to compose that.' His pf. So. in A♭ major, Op. 26, containing a funeral march, was written at that time.

Achille et Polyxène, opera by Lully and Colasse (lib. by Jean Galbert de Campistron), prod. Paris, Opéra, 7. XI. 1687. Left unfinished at Lully's death and completed by his pupil Colasse.

Achille in Sciro, opera by Caldara (lib. by Metastasio), prod. Vienna, Burg Theatre, 13. II. 1736.

Opera by Naumann (lib. do.), prod. Palermo, 5. IX. 1767.

c. 25 other settings.

Achron. *See* **Akhron.**

Aci, Galatea e Polifemo, pastoral play with m. by Handel, comp. in It., 1708; revised version used with the Eng. *Acis and Galatea* of 1719 for a stage perf. in costume but without action, London, King's Theatre, 17. V. 1732.

Acis and Galatea, pastoral for solo voices, chor. and orch. by Handel (lib. by John Gay, with adds. by Dryden, Pope and John Hughes), perf. at Cannons nr. Edgware *c.* 1721 and prod. in costume but without action, London, King's Theatre, Haymarket, 17. V. 1732.

Acis et Galatée (*Acis and Galatea*), opera by Lully (lib. by Jean Galbert de Campistron), prod. at Anet at an entertainment given for the Dauphin by the Duke of Vendôme, 6. IX. and 1st perf. Paris, 17. IX. 1686.

Acoustic Bass. A 32-ft. org. stop, the tone of which is given by the beats produced from the playing of 5ths on 16-ft. pedals.

Acoustics. The physical science of all matters pertaining to sound, esp. the generation and reception of sound-waves; also, more loosely, the properties of sound-transmission in the interior of buildings.

Act Tune (obs.). A term used in 17th-cent. Eng. for a mus. Intermezzo or Entr'acte perf. between the acts of a play.

Action. The mechanism intervening between the player and an inst., esp. in stgd. keyboard insts., orgs. and hps. (in the last case pedals only).

Action musicale (Fr.). A term used by d'Indy for some of his operas, evidently on the model of Wagner's 'Handlung für Musik.'

Acute. *See* **Ornaments.**

Acute Mixture. An org. stop in which overtones are actually sounded by additional pipes, tuned slightly sharp.

Ad lib. (abbr. of Lat. *ad libitum* = at pleasure). A direction indicating that a passage may be played freely according to the perf.'s fancy. The term also applies to an inst. part that may be added or omitted in the perf. of a work.

Adagietto (It. lit. a little Adagio). A tempo direction indicating a pace slightly quicker than *adagio*.

Adagio (It. *ad agio* = at ease, comfortably) = at a slow pace. The word is also used as a noun for a slow piece or mvt.

Adam, Adolphe (Charles) (b. Paris, 24. VII. 1803; d. Paris, 3. V. 1856), Fr. comp. Allowed to study at the Paris Cons. only as an amateur. Prod. an operetta, *Pierre et Catherine*, at the Opéra-Comique in 1829 and his first opera, *Danilowa*, in 1830. Comp. a great deal for the stage and in 1847 started a new operatic venture, the Théâtre National. Member of the Institut, 1844, and prof. of comp. at the Cons., 1849.

Works incl. operas *Le Châlet, Le Postillon de Longjumeau, La Poupée de Nuremberg, Si j'étais roi, Falstaff,* &c.; ballets *Faust, Giselle,* &c.

Adam, Jean Louis (b. Mütterscholtz, 3. XII. 1758; d. Paris, 8. IV. 1848), Alsat. pfst. & comp., father of prec. App. prof. at Paris Cons., 1797.

Adam und Eva, opera by Theile (lib. by Christian Richter), prod. Hamburg, at the opening of the 1st estab. Ger. opera house, Theater am Gänsemarkt, 12. I. 1678.

Adamberger, Valentin (b. Munich, 6. VII. 1743; d. Vienna, 24. VIII. 1804), Ger. ten. singer. Studied and sang in It., appeared in London in 1777 and went to Vienna, becoming a member of the Ger. opera in 1780 and of the Imperial Chapel in 1789.

Adams, Charles (b. Charlestown, Mass., 9. II. 1834; d. West Harwich, Mass., 3. VII. 1900), Amer. ten. singer. Between 1867–76 1st ten. at the Opera in Vienna; made his 1st real success in U.S.A. in 1877.

Adams, Thomas (b. London, 5. IX. 1785; d. London, 15. IX. 1858), Eng. orgst. & comp. for his inst. Held various church apps. in London, but was known chiefly as a virtuoso.

Added Sixth, Chord of the. A common chord (maj. triad) with a maj. 6th added to it, used by some modern comps. (e.g. Delius) for the purpose of giving a certain vagueness to a final tonic chord, and by jazz and swing bands as one of their most conventional tricks.

Addinsell, Richard (b. London, 13. I. 1904), Eng. comp. Studied law at Hertford Coll., Oxford, but became interested in theatre m. and studied for a short time at the R.C.M. in London. In 1929–32 he studied abroad, mainly in Berlin and Vienna; in 1933 visited U.S.A. and wrote film m. at Hollywood.

Works incl. incid. m. for *Adam's Opera, Come of Age* & other plays by Clemence Dane, incl. her adapt. of Rostand's *L'Aiglon* and Max Beerbohm's *Happy Hypocrite*, Shakespeare's *Taming of the Shrew* & 2 adapts. of Lewis Carroll's *Alice in Wonderland*; m. for radio plays and Noel Coward's revue *Sigh no more*; film m. for *Fire over Eng., Good-bye Mr. Chips, Dangerous Moonlight* (incl. 'Warsaw' Conc. for pf. & orch.), *Blithe Spirit* (after Coward), *c.* 25 document. films; light & revue songs, &c.

Addison, John (b. London *c.* 1766;

d. London, 30. I. 1844), Eng. db. player & comp. His wife (*née* Willems) sang at Vauxhall Gardens in London; then both went to Liverpool and Dublin, returning to London in 1796 and proceeding to Bath, Dublin and Manchester. From 1805, when he wrote m. for Skeffington's *Sleeping Beauty*, he had a number of stage successes in London.

Addison, Joseph (1672–1719), Eng. essayist & poet. *See* **Conte Caramella** (Galuppi), **Festing** (*Ode for St. Cecilia's Day*), **Greene (M.)** (ode, *The Spacious Firmament*), **Paisiello** (*Tamburo*), **Rosamond** (Arne & Clayton), **Stanton** (*Spacious F.*).

Additional Accompaniments. Amplifying orch. parts added to old orats. and other works left by the comps. in an incomplete state, to be amplified orig. by the Continuo player at the org. or hpchd. The most familiar exs. are Mozart's A. A. for Handel's *Messiah.*

Adélaïde (ballet, Ravel). *See* **Valses nobles.**

Adelaïde, song by Beethoven to words by Friedrich von Mathisson, comp. in 1795 or 1796 and ded. to the poet.

'Adelaide' Concerto. A v. conc. ed. by Marius Casadesus in the early 1930s and alleged to have been taken from a v. part left by Mozart of a conc. ded. to one of the Fr. royal princesses, Mme Adélaïde de Fr., during his visit to Paris as a child in 1766. Its authenticity has never been definitely proved.

Adelboldus (b. nr. Liége, ?; d. ?), Flem. 10th-cent. ecclesiastic & musn. Bishop of Utrecht; wrote a treatise, *Ars musica,* between 990–1003.

Adenez (Adam Le Roy) (b. ?; d. ?), Fr. 13th-cent. minstrel. Lived at the court of Henry III, Duke of Brabant; sang troubadour romances, some of which are preserved.

Adhémar, Guillaume (b. ?; d. ?), Fr. 13th-cent. minstrel & juggler. Some of his troubadour songs are extant.

Adieux, l'absence et le retour, Les (*Farewell, Absence and Return*), Beethoven's own title for his pf. So. in E♭ maj., Op. 81a, comp. in 1809 and ded. to the Archduke Rudolph on his departure from Vienna during the occupation by the Fr.

Adler, Guido (b. Eibenschütz, Moravia, 1. XI. 1855; d. Vienna, 19. II. 1941), Cz.-Ger. mcolst. & ed. Studied in Vienna; app. prof. of mus. science at Prague Univ., 1885, and prof. in Vienna, 1898, in succession to Hanslick. Wrote many books on m. and ed. a *Handbuch der Musikgeschichte,* 1924.

Adlgasser, Anton Cajetan (b. Inzell, Bavaria, 3. IV. 1728; d. Salzburg, 23. XII. 1777), Ger. orgst. & comp. Went to Salzburg to become a pupil of Eberlin. Later orgst. at the cath. there.

Adlung, Jacob (b. Bindersleben nr. Erfurt, 14. I. 1699; d. Bindersleben, 5. VII. 1762), Ger. theologian, scholar and musn. Orgst. from 1727 and prof. from 1741 at Erfurt. Wrote several treatises on m.

Admeto, rè di Tessaglia (*Admetus, King of Thessaly*), opera by Handel (lib. by Nicola Francesco Haym or Paolo Antonio Rolli), prod. London, King's Theatre, Haymarket, 31. I. 1727.

Admetus. *See* **Alcestis.**

Adolfati, Andrea (b. Venice, 1711; d. ?), It. comp. Pupil of Galuppi at Venice. Held church apps. there and wrote several operas, incl. *Artaserse, Arianna, Adriano in Siria* and *La clemenza di Tito.*

Adrastus (b. Philippi, Macedonia, ?; d. ?), Gr. 4th-cent. B.C. philos. Pupil of Aristotle; wrote a treatise on m., *Harmonicon biblia tria.*

Adriaensen, Emmanuel (b. Antwerp, ?; d. ?), Flem. 16th-cent. lutenist. Pub. books of lute pieces. Also known as Hadrianus.

Adriana Lecouvreur, opera by Cilèa (lib. by Arturo Colautti, based on the play *Adrienne Lecouvreur* by Scribe & Ernest Legouvé), prod. Milan, Teatro Lirico, 6. XI. 1902.

Adriani, Francesco (b. Santo Severino, Ancona, *c.* 1539; d. Rome, 16. VIII. 1575), It. comp. Chapel master at St. John Lateran in Rome towards the end of his life. Wrote madrigals and other voc. works.

Adriano in Siria (*Hadrian in Syria*), opera by Pergolesi (lib. by Metastasio), prod. Naples, Teatro San Bartolommeo, with the intermezzi *Livietta e Tracollo*, 25. X. 1734.

Adson, John (b. ?; d. ?), Eng. 17th-cent. musn. & comp. He was a member of Charles I's household and pub. *Courtly Masquing Ayres* for var. insts. in 1611.

Aegyptische Helena (Strauss). *See* **Ägyptische Helena.**

Aeolian Harp. An inst. played by no human performer, but by currents of air blown across its stgs. when it is hung up in the open. It was first recorded in the 17th cent., but the principle dates back to antiquity.

Aeolian Mode. The scale represented by the white keys of the pf. beginning on the note A.

Aerophor (or **Aerophon**). A Ger. inst. invented by Bernhard Samuel and patented in 1912, with the aid of which wind insts. can sustain notes indefinitely. R. Strauss used it in the *Alpensinfonie* and *Festliches Praeludium.*

Aeschylus (525–456 B.C.), Gr. dramatist. *See* **Emmanuel** (*Prométhée & Salamine*), **Halévy** (*Prometheus*), **Hauer** (do.), **Lambert** (**L.**) (do.), **Leroux** (*Persians*), **Meyerbeer** (*Eumenides*), **Milhaud** (*Agamemnon, Choéphores & Euménides*), **Mulé** (*Choephorae & 7 against Thebes*), **Oresteia** (Taneiev), **Orestes** (Weingartner), **Parry** (**H.**) (*Agamemnon*), **Pizzetti** (do.), **Prométhée** (Fauré), **Schillings** (*Orestes*), **Siccardi** (*Prometheus*), **Stanford** (*Eumenides*), **Wallace** (**W.**) (do.), **Whittaker** (*Choephorae*).

Aesop (*c.* 620–*c.* 560 B.C.), Gr. fabulist. *See* **Reed** (**W. H.**) (symph. poem).

Aetherophone (from Gr.). An electrophonic inst. invented by Lev Theremin of Leningrad in 1924, producing notes from the air the pitch of which can be determined by movements of the hand but cannot be definitely fixed according to the normal chromatic scale, the transitions between the notes producing a sliding wail like that of a siren.

Affettuoso (It.) = affectionate, feeling (adv. *affettuosamente*).

Affilard, Michel d' (b. ?; d. ?), Fr. 17th-cent. ten. singer and teacher, app. to the Sainte Chapelle in Paris, 1679, and to the royal chapel, 1696–1708. In 1691 he pub. a treatise on sight-singing in which he used a system of regulating the speed of m. by a pendulum.

Affrettando (It.) = urging, hastening. The term is often used in m. to indicate emotional pressure as well as increase in speed.

Afranio (b. ?; d. ?), It. 16th-cent. priest. Canon at Ferrara, inventor of the Phagotus.

Africaine, L' (*The African Girl*; orig. title *Vasco da Gama*), opera by Meyerbeer (lib. by Scribe), prod. Paris, Opéra, 28. IV. 1865, after the comp.'s death.

Agazzari, Agostino (b. Siena, 2. XII. 1578; d. Siena, 10. IV. 1640), It. comp. Held various church apps. in Rome, but returned to Siena in 1630 as chapel master of the cath.

Works incl. pastoral *Eumelio*, madrigals, masses & other church m., &c.

Aggházy, Carolus (b. Budapest, 30. X. 1855; d. Budapest, 8. X. 1918), Hung. pfst. & comp. Pupil of Liszt, Bruckner and Volkmann.

Works incl. opera *Maritta*, cantata *Rakoczy*, &c.

Agincour, d'. *See* **Dagincourt.**

Agitato (It.) = agitated, precipitate, restless.

Agnelli, Salvatore (b. Palermo, 1817; d. ? Paris, 1874), It. comp. Pupil of Donizetti and Zingarelli at Naples. He worked at Marseilles and Paris in later life.

Works incl. operas, ballets, church m., &c.

Agnes von Hohenstaufen, opera by Spontini (lib. by Ernst Raupach), prod. Berlin, Opera, 12. VI. 1829.

Agnese di Fitz-Henry, opera by Paer (lib. by Luigi Buonavoglia, based on Amelia Opie's novel *Father and Daughter*), prod. Ponte d'Altaro nr. Parma, X. 1809.

Agnesi, Luigi (real name Louis Ferdinand Léopold Agniez) (b. Erpent, Namur, 17. VII. 1833; d. London, 2. II. 1875), Belg. bass singer. Made his 1st appearance in Merelli's It. opera company in Ger. and Hol. and went to the Théâtre Italien in Paris, 1864, and to London in 1865. After his successes in It. opera he also became a concert singer in Eng., 1871–4.

Agnew, Roy (b. Sydney, 1894), Austral. comp.

Works incl. Poem for voice & orch.; pf. sos. & pieces, &c.

Agostini, Ludovico (b. Ferrara, 1534; d. Ferrara, 20. IX. 1590), It. priest, comp. & poet. Chapel master to Alfonso II, Duke of Este. Wrote madrigals and other voc. works.

Agostini, Paolo (b. Valerano, 1593; d. Rome, IX. 1629), It. comp. Pupil and son-in-law of B. Nanini in Rome. After var. apps. in Rome, he became master of the Vatican chapel in 1627. Comp. many masses and other church m.

Agostini, Pietro Simone (b. Rome, *c.* 1650; d. ?), It. comp. Chapel master to the Duke of Parma. Wrote 5 operas, incl. *Il ratto delle Sabine*, orats., church m., &c.

Agrell, Johan Joachim (b. Löth, 1. II. 1701; d. Nuremberg, 19. I. 1765), Swe. comp. Studied at Linköping and Upsala, was app. court musn. at Cassel in 1723 and cond. at Nuremberg in 1746.

Works incl. concs., sos., &c.

Agréments (Fr. obs. *Agrémens*) = Ornaments.

Agricola, Alexander (b. Flanders, ?; d. Valladolid, *c.* 1506), Flem. comp. Pupil of Okeghem. In the service successively of Charles VIII of France, Lorenzo de' Medici at Milan and the ducal court of Mantua. Entered the service of Philip, Duke of Austria, in the Netherlands *c.* 1491 and followed him to Spa. in 1505.

Works incl. masses, motets, 4-part songs, &c.

Agricola, Johann Friedrich (b. Dobitz, Saxony, 4. I. 1720; d. Berlin, 1. XII. 1774), Ger. comp. Studied with Bach at Leipzig, afterwards with Hasse at Dresden and Graun in Berlin. Dir. of the royal chapel there from 1759 to his death. Married the singer Benedetta Molteni in 1751.

Works incl. operas, psalms, hymns and other church m., It. secular cantatas, &c.

Agricola, Martin (real name Sohr or Sore) (b. Schwiebus, 6. I. 1486; d. Magdeburg, 10. VI. 1556), Ger. mcolst. Wrote many theoret. treatises, some of which were printed by Rhaw of Wittenberg.

Agricola, Rudolph (real name Huessmann) (b. Baffeln nr. Groningen, 1442; d. Heidelberg, 25. X. 1485), Dutch lutenist, comp. & scholar. He returned from It. in 1477 and was sent to the court of the Ger. emperor. In 1479 he helped to build the great org. at Groningen and in 1482 he became prof. at Heidelberg.

Works incl. Dutch partsongs.

Agrippina, opera by Handel (lib. by Vincenzo Grimani), prod. Venice, Teatro San Giovanni Crisostomo, 26. XII. 1709.

Aguado, Dionisio (b. Madrid, 8. IV. 1784; d. Madrid, 20. XII. 1849), Spa. guitar player & comp. Wrote a method and studies for his inst.

Aguiar, Alexandre de (b. Oporto, ?; d. nr. Talavera, 12. XII. 1605), Port. lutenist & poet. In the service of King Sebastian and later of Philip II of Spa.

Works incl. lamentations for Holy Week.

Aguiar, Luiza Rosa d'. *See* **Todi.**

Aguiari, Lucrezia (old spelling Agujari) (b. Ferrara, 1743; d. Parma, 18. V. 1783), It. sop. singer. Made her 1st appearance at Florence in 1764. Mozart wrote down a remarkably high and florid passage he heard her sing in a letter of 24. III. 1770. She married Colla in 1780.

Aguilera de Heredia, Sebastián (b. Huesca, Aragon, ? 1570; d. ?), Spa. orgst. & comp. For many years from 1603 orgst. at the old cath. of Saragossa.

Works incl. magnificats and other church m.

Aguirre, Julián (b. Buenos Aires, 28. I. 1868; d. Buenos Aires, 13, VIII. 1924), Arg. pfst. & comp. Studied at the Madrid Cons. and became dir. of the Buenos Aires Cons.

Works incl. chamber m.; pf. works; songs, &c.

Ägyptische Helena, Die (*The Egyptian Helen*), opera by R. Strauss (lib. by Hugo von Hofmannsthal), prod. Dresden, 6. VI. 1928.

Ahle, Johann Georg (b. ? Erfurt, 1651; d. ? Mühlhausen, Thuringia, 2. XII. 1706), Ger. comp. Orgst. at the church of St. Blasius, Mühlhausen. Like his father, he wrote hymn tunes.

Ahle, Johann Rudolph (b. Mühlhausen, Thuringia, 24. XII. 1625; d. Mühlhausen, 9. VII. 1673), Ger. orgst. & comp., father of prec. App. orgst. at Erfurt in 1646 and held the same app. at Mühlhausen from or before 1654.

Ahlström, Olof (b. 15. VIII. 1756; d. 11. VIII. 1835), Swe. orgst. & comp. Orgst. at St. James's church at Stockholm and court accompst.; wrote pf. sos., cantatas and songs, and was co-ed. of a collection of Swe. folksongs.

Aiblinger, Johann Kaspar (b. Wasserburg, Bavaria, 23. II. 1779; d. Munich, 6. V. 1867), Ger. comp. & cond. Mus. dir. of the Munich opera, 1819–23, but as a comp. devoted mainly to church m.

Aichinger, Gregor (b. Ratisbon, 1564; d. Augsburg, 21. I. 1628), Ger. priest and musn. Orgst. to the Fugger family at Augsburg, pub. books of sacred m. at Venice in 1590 and 1603 and visited Rome for further mus. study in 1599.

Aida, opera by Verdi (lib. by Antonio Ghislanzoni, based on a scenario by François Auguste Ferdinand Mariette and outlined in French by Camille Du Locle), prod. Cairo, 24. XII. 1871; 1st perf. in It., Milan, Teatro alla Scala, 8. II. 1872.

Aiglon, L' (*The Eaglet*), opera by Honegger and Ibert (lib. by Henri Cain, based on Rostand's play), prod. Monte Carlo, 11. III. 1937.

Aimon (Pamphile Léopold) François (b. L'Isle nr. Avignon, 4. X. 1779; d. Paris, 2. II. 1866), Fr. cst. & comp. He cond. at Marseilles in his youth and in Paris from 1821.

Works incl. operas *Jeux floraux, Michel et Christine, Les Sybarites de Florence* and 4 others; chamber m., &c.

Air à boire (Fr.) = Drinking-Song, cultivated esp. in the 16th and 17th cents. and sung in parts.

Air de Cour (Fr. = court air). A courtly type of Fr. song orig. in the 16th cent., differing from earlier chansons by being for a single voice with lute or hpchd. accomp.

Akademie (Ger., 18th cent., or Academie) = a concert.

Akeroyde, Samuel (b. Yorkshire, ?; d. ?), Eng. 17th-cent. comp. Musn. in Ordinary to James II in 1687 and later to William and Mary. Contrib. many songs to var. collections and to the 3rd part of Durfey's *Don Quixote* in 1696, the m. to the first 2 of which had been written by Purcell the year before his death.

Akhron, Joseph (b. Lozdzeye, Lithuania, 1. V. 1886; d. Los Angeles, 29. IV. 1943), Rus. (Americanized) vst. & comp. Studied at Warsaw and at the St. Petersburg Cons., where Auer taught him v. and Liadov comp. Toured much as vst. and in 1913 joined the staff of the Kharkov Cons. In 1925 he settled in U.S.A.

Works incl. incid. & film m.; *Golem Suite* for small orch.; 3 v. concs.; *Sinfonietta* for stg. 4tet, &c.

Akimenko, Feodor Stepanovitch (b. Kharkov, 20. II. 1876; d. Paris, I. 1945), Rus. comp. Pupil of Balakirev and Rimsky-Korsakov in St. Petersburg. Taught in the court choir, where he had been a chorister, but lived in Fr. from 1903–6 and settled there after the Rus. Revol.

Works incl. opera, *The Queen of the Alps*; orch. and chamber m.; inst. sos.; numerous pf. works incl. *Sonate fantastique*, &c.

Al (It. masc. = 'at the,' in the manner of = Fr. *à la*). The word is used in var. combs. with nouns, as below.

Al fine (It.) = 'to the end.' The term is used in cases where an earlier portion of a comp. is to be repeated (*da capo*) and indicates that it is to be played over again to the end, not to some earlier place, which would otherwise be marked with a special sign, the appropriate direction being then

Al rovescio. *See* **Rovescio.**

Al segno. . . . (It.) = 'to the sign. . . .' Where some distinctive sign is placed after these words the comp. directs that an earlier portion of a piece is to be played over again to a place where that sign will be found later in the work.

Ala, Giovanni Battista (b. Monza, *c.* 1590; d. ?, *c.* 1620), It. comp. Orgst. of the church of the Servitori at Milan and comp. of canzonets, madrigals, &c.

Alabev, Alexander Alexandrovitch (b. Moscow, 15. VIII. 1787; d. Moscow, 6. III. 1851), Rus. comp. He was an army officer and cultivated m. as an amateur.

Works incl. opera *A Moonlit Night*; vaudevilles; *c.* 100 drawing-room songs incl. *The Nightingale*, &c.

Aladdin, opera by Bishop (lib. by George Soane), prod. London, Drury Lane Theatre, 29. IV. 1826. It was commissioned as a counter-attraction to Weber's *Oberon* at Covent Garden, but failed.

Alalá. A folksong of N.W. Spa.

Alaleona, Domenico (b. Montegiorgio, Piceno, 16. XI. 1881; d. Montegiorgio, 28. XII. 1928), It. comp. & orgst. Became orgst. in his native town at the age of 10, but later went to Rome for study, afterwards cond. chor. and orch. socs. at Leghorn and Rome.

Works incl. opera *Mirra*, Requiem, orch. works, a stg. 4tet and songs.

Alarcón, Pedro Antonio de (1833–91), Spa. novelist. *See* **Corregidor** (H. Wolf), **Manuel Venegas** (do.), **Rung** (*Three-Cornered Hat*), **Sombrero de tres picos** (Falla).

Alard, Delphin (b. Bayonne, 8. III. 1815; d. Paris, 22. II. 1888), Fr. vst. & comp. Student at the Paris Cons., where he succeeded Baillot as prof. Formed a stg. 4tet. Comp. mainly for his inst.

Albanesi, Carlo (b. Naples, 22. X. 1856; d. London, 21. IX. 1926), It. pfst. & comp. Settled in Eng. from 1882 and app. prof. of pf. at the R.A.M. in 1893, when he married the novelist E. Maria Albanesi. His daughter Meggie was a gifted actress in the 1920s, but died at an early age. Works incl. pf. pieces, chamber m. and songs.

Albani, Emma (b. Chambly nr. Montreal, 1. XI. 1852; d. London, 3. IV. 1930), Canad. sop. singer. Studied with Duprez in Paris and Lamperti at Milan. 1st stage appearance at Messina, 1870, and 1st in London, at Covent Garden, 1872. Lived and taught there, but toured widely. D.B.E. 1925.

Albéniz, Isaac (b. Camprodón, Catalonia, 29. V. 1860; d. Cambó, Pyrenees, 18. V. 1909), Spa. comp. He made his appearance as an infant prodigy, both as pfst. and comp. at Barcelona, a *Pasodoble*, written at the age of 7 being played by a military band there. Later he appeared in Paris as a child-pupil of Marmontel and afterwards studied at the Madrid Cons., where he received a grant from the king to enable him to go to Brussels. There he studied comp. with Gevaert and pf. with Brassin, and later went to Liszt at Weimar for pf. and to Jadassohn and Reinecke at Leipzig for comp. After touring successfully, he settled as pf. teacher first at Barcelona and then at Madrid, from *c.* 1880; but left before long and spent the rest of his life mainly in London and Paris. He had married in 1883. In London he prod. operas and began a trilogy on Arthurian legends to a libretto by Francis Money-Coutts (Lord Latymer), who financed him; but did not progress far.

Works incl. operas *The Magic Opal*, *Henry Clifford*, *Pepita Jiménez*, *San Antonio de la Florida*, *Merlin* (unfinished 1st part of Arthurian cycle); zarzuelas *Cuanto más viejo*, *Los Catalanes en Grecia*; contribution to Millöcker's operetta *Der arme Jonathan* for the London prod.; *Catalonia*, orch. with the aid of Dukas; *c.* 250 pf. pieces, incl. *Catalonia*, *La*

Vega, Navarra, Azulejos; the cycle of 12 entitled *Iberia*; 13 songs, &c.

Albéniz, Mateo (b. ?; d. ?), Spa. 18th-cent. comp. Wrote hpchd. sos.

Albéniz, Pedro (b. Biscay, *c.* 1755; d. *c.* 1821), Spa. monk & comp. Worked at the caths. of San Sebastián and Logroño and wrote church and other m.

Albéniz, Pedro (b. Logroño, 14. IV. 1795; d. Madrid, 12. IV. 1855), Spa. pfst. & comp., son of Mateo A. above. He was orgst. at var. towns from the age of 13 and in 1830 became prof. of pf. at Madrid Cons. and 1st orgst. at the royal chapel in 1834. App. pf. teacher to Queen Isabella and the Infanta Maria Luisa in 1841. Wrote a method for pf., *c.* 70 pf. works and some songs.

Albergati, Pirro Capacelli, Count (b. Bologna, 20. IX. 1663; d. Bologna, 22. VI. 1735), It. nobleman & amateur comp. In the service of the Emperor Leopold I from 1687.

Works incl. operas *Gli amici, Il principe selvaggio*; orats. *Giobbe, L'innocenza di Santa Eufemia, Il convito di Baldassare*; church m.; comps. for var. insts., &c.

Albert, Charles Louis Napoléon d' (b. Menstetten nr. Hamburg, 25. II. 1809; d. London, 26, V. 1886), Fr. dancer & comp. His father was a captain in the Fr. cavalry, after whose death in 1816 his mother took him to Eng.,where she taught him m. He became ballet master at the King's and Covent Garden Theatres, London, for a time, but afterwards taught dancing and wrote dance m. Later he settled at Newcastle-on-Tyne and married there in 1863.

Albert de Sisteron (b. Gapençois, ?; d. Sisteron, ?), Fr. 12th–13th-cent. troubadour, *c.* 20 of whose songs still exist.

Albert, Eugen (Eugène Francis Charles) d' (b. Glasgow, 10. IV. 1864; d. Riga, 3. III. 1932), Fr.-Eng. (later Germanized) pfst. & comp., son of C. L. N. d'A. Although born in Sco., he came from Newcastle-on-Tyne, and after being well taught by his father as a very precociously gifted child, he went as Newcastle scholar to the Nat. Training School in London (later the R.A.M.), where he learnt pf. from Pauer and theoret. subjects from Stainer, Prout and Sullivan. He appeared with great success as pfst. and comp. in London and later went to Vienna for further study, finishing with a course under Liszt. In 1892 he married Teresa Carreño, but they were divorced in 1895, and d'A. married 5 times more. In 1907 he succeeded Joachim as dir. of the Hochschule für Musik in Berlin.

Works incl. operas *Der Rubin* (after Hebbel), *Ghismonda, Gernot, Die Abreise, Kain, Der Improvisator, Tiefland, Flauto solo, Tragaldabas* (*Der geborgte Ehemann*), *Izeyl, Die verschenkte Frau, Liebesketten. Die toten Augen, Der Stier von Olivera, Revolutionshochzeit, Scirocco, Mareike von Nymwegen, Der Golem, Die schwarze Orchidee, Die Witwe von Ephesus, Mister Wu* (unfinished, completed by Blech); *Der Mensch und das Leben*, chor. work in 6 parts; Sym. in F maj.; ovts. *Esther* & *Hyperion*; 2 pf. concs., co. Conc.; 2 stg. 4tets; pf. Suite & So. &c.

Albert, Heinrich (b. Lobenstein, Saxony, 28. VI. 1604; d. ?, 6. X. 1651), Ger. poet, orgst. & comp. Studied m. at Dresden with Schütz, who was his uncle. His parents, however, compelled him to read law at Leipzig Univ.; but in 1626 he set out for Königsberg, was taken prisoner by the Swedes, and at last reached that city in 1628, resuming mus. studies with Stobäus. In 1631 he was app. orgst. at the Old Church there, and became member of the Königsberg school of poets.

Works incl. Te Deum, many hymns to words of his own, secular songs, &c.

Alberti Bass. A device of splitting up chords into figures, with the bass notes taking first place, frequently used in left-hand parts in classical keyboard m. It often occurs in the m. of Domenico Alberti, from whom it takes its name, but many more familiar examples are found in classics like Haydn and Mozart, e.g. in the opening of the latter's little C maj. So., K. 545.

Alberti, Domenico (b. Venice, *c.* 1710; d. Formia, 1740), It. comp., singer & hpchdst. Pupil of Lotti. The keyboard device known as the 'Alberti bass' is so called from his frequent use of it. Works incl. hpchd. m., &c.

Alberti, Giuseppe Matteo (b. Bologna, ? 1685; d. Bologna, II. 1751), It. vst. & comp. Wrote mainly for stg. insts.

Alberti, Innocenzo (b. Tarvisio, ?; d. ?), It. 16th-cent. comp. In the service of Alfonso, Duke of Ferrara. In 1568 he ded. a book of 46 madrigals to Henry, Earl of Arundel.

Works incl. madrigals, penitentia psalms, secular songs, &c.

Albertini, Gioacchino (b. ?, 1751; d. Warsaw, IV. 1812), It. comp. Chapel master to the Pol. court at the end of his life.

Works incl. 2 Pol. operas, *Don Juan* & *Kapelmaister Polski*, It. operas *Virginia, Scipio Africano*, Ger. opera *Circe und Ulysse*, &c.

Albicastro, Henrico (It. from Hainz Weissenburg), (b. ?; d. ?), Swi. 17th-cent. comp. He was a captain of the Swi. horse, serving in the Spa. war in the Nthlds. as a mercenary. Works incl. 8 op. nos. of solo and trio sos. and 1 of concs.

Albinoni, Tommaso (b. ?, ? 1674; d. ?, ? 1745), It. vst. & comp. Wrote over 50 operas and much inst. m. Bach used some of his themes.

Albion and Albanius, opera by Grabu (lib. by Dryden), prod. London, Duke's Theatre, 3. VI. 1685.

Alboni, Marietta (b. Città di Castello, 6. III. 1826; d. Ville d'Avray, 23. VI. 1894), It. con. singer. Pupil of Rossini; 1st appearance 1843, at the Scala, Milan. Sang with much success in Paris and London.

Alborada (Spa., pron. 'alvorada': from *alba* = dawn) = morning song, in the same sense that a serenade is an evening song; cf. Fr. *aubade*. Orig. the A. is a popular inst. piece of N.W. Spa., unusually played on bagpipes.

Alborada del gracioso (Spa. *The Jester's Morning Song.*) A pf. piece by Ravel in the set entitled *Miroirs*.

Albrechtsberger, Johann Georg (b. Klosterneuburg nr. Vienna, 3. II. 1736; d. Vienna, 7. III. 1809), Aus. theorist, comp. and teacher. Lived in Vienna. Beethoven studied ctpt. under him for a short time.

Works incl. Te Deum and much other church m.; syms., &c.

Albrici, Bartolomeo (b. Rome, *c.* 1630; d. ?), It. orgst. & comp. Orgst. at the court church of Dresden until 1663 and comp. to Charles II in London from 1664.

Albrici, Vincenzo (b. Rome, 26. VI. 1631; d. Prague, 8. VIII. 1696), It. comp., brother of prec. Attached to Charles II's court, together with his brother from 1664.

Albumblatt (Ger. = album leaf). The title often given to a short piece, usually for pf., suggesting an inscription in an autograph album.

Albuzzi-Todeschini, Teresa (b. Milan, 26. XII. 1723; d. Prague, 30. VI. 1760), It. con. singer. First sang in It., then at Dresden, and on the outbreak of the Seven Years war attempted to go to Warsaw, but died on the way.

Alceste. *See also* **Alkestis.**

Opera by Gluck (lib. by Ranieri Calzabigi), prod., in It., Vienna, Burg Theatre, 26. XII. 1767. Fr. version, revised by the comp. (lib. by François Louis Gand Lebland du Roullet), prod. Paris, Opéra, 23. IV. 1776.

Opera by Schweitzer (lib. by Wieland), prod. Weimar, at court, 28. V. 1773. The 1st Ger. opera in the manner of Metastasio.

Opera by Strungk (lib. by Paul Thiemich, based on Aurelio Aureli's *Antigona delusa da Alceste*), prod. Leipzig, 18. V. 1693. Written for the opening of the Leipzig opera-house.

Incid. m. by Handel to a play by Tobias Smollett based on Euripides, comp. for a prod. in London, Covent Garden Theatre, in 1750, which did not take place.

Alceste, ou Le Triomphe d'Alcide, opera by Lully (lib. by Quinault), prod. Paris, Opéra, 19. I. 1674.

Alchemist, The, incid. m. by Handel for a revival of Ben Jonson's play, prod. London, Drury Lane Theatre, 7. III. 1732.

Opera by Cyril Scott (lib. by comp.), prod. in Ger. trans., Essen, 28. V. 1925.

Alchymist, Der, opera by Spohr (lib. by Karl Pfeiffer, based on a story by Washington Irving), prod. Cassel, 28. VII. 1830.

Alcina, opera by Handel (lib. by Antonio Marchi), prod. London, Covent Garden Theatre, 16. IV. 1735.

Alcione, opera by Marais (lib. by Antoine Houdar de la Motte), prod. Paris, Opéra, 18. II. 1706.

Alcock, John (b. London, 11. IV. 1715; d. Lichfield, 23. II. 1806), Eng. orgst. & comp. Orgst. at var. parish churches in London and Warwicks., and for a time at Lichfield cath. Mus.D. Oxford, 1761.

Works incl. church m., glees & catches, hpchd. m., &c.

Alcôve, L', operetta by Offenbach (lib. by Philippe Auguste Alfred Pittaud de Forges and Adolphe de Leuven), prod. Paris, Salle de la Tour d'Auvergne, 24. IV. 1847. O.'s 1st operetta.

Aldomar (b. ?; d. ?), Spa. 16th-cent. comp. Contributed villancicos for several voices to var. collections.

Aldrich, Henry (b. London, 1647; d. Oxford, 14. XII. 1710), Eng. comp., theologian & architect. Educ. at Westminster School and Christ Church Coll., Oxford, where he became a canon in 1681 and dean in 1689. Vice-Chancellor of the Univ., 1692–5. He designed Peckwater quadrangle and All Saints' Church. Collected material for a large treatise on harmony.

Works incl. church and other m. (catch *Christ Church Bells*), &c.

Aldrich, Richard (b. Providence, Rhode Island, 31. VII. 1863; d. Rome, 2. VI. 1937), Amer. m. critic. After var. activities he became m. ed. of the *New York Times*. His work incl. 2 Wagnerian guide-books.

Aleko, opera by Rakhmaninov (lib. by Vassili Ivanovitch Nemirovitch-Danchenko, based on Pushkin's novel, *The Gypsies*), prod. Moscow, 9. V. 1893.

Alembert, Jean Le Rond d' (b. Paris, 16. XI. 1717; d. Paris, 29. X. 1783), Fr. author, philos. and mathematician. His books incl. many studies of mus. subjects, incl. acoustics, opera, the theories of Rameau, &c., and he contrib. mus. articles to the *Encyclopédie*. One of the adherents of Gluck against Piccinni.

Alessandrescu, Alfred (b. Bucharest, 14. VIII. 1893), Rum. cond. & comp. Studied at Bucharest and with Vidal and d'Indy in Paris. Later he became cond. of the Royal Opera at Bucharest and mus. dir. of the Rum. radio service. In 1926 he was app. cond. of the Bucharest Phil. Orch.

Works incl. Rum. Fantasy, symph. poem *Actéon*, ovt. *Didona* for orch.; *Crépuscule d'automne* for stg. 4tet & other chamber m.; songs, &c.

Alessandri, Felice (b. Rome, 24. XI. 1747; d. Casalbino, 15. VIII. 1798), It. cond. & comp. Studied at Naples and 1st worked at Turin and Paris; prod. his 1st opera at Verona in 1767 and went to London the following year, and in 1786 to St. Petersburg in search of a court app., which he failed to secure. From 1789–92 he was cond. at the Berlin Opera.

Works incl. *c.* 35 operas, an orat., several syms., sos., &c.

Alessandro, opera by Handel (lib. by Paolo Antonio Rolli), prod. London, King's Theatre, Haymarket, 5. V. 1726.

Alessandro della Viola. *See* **Merlo.**

Alessandro nell' Indie (*Alexander in India*). *See also* **Cleofide** and **Porc.**

Opera by Johann Christian Bach (lib. by Metastasio), prod. Naples, Teatro San Carlo, 20. I. 1762.

Opera by Francesco Corselli (? 1705–?) (lib. do.), prod. Madrid, Palacio Real Buen Retiro, at the wedding of Charles IV of Naples and Princess Maria Amalia of Saxony. The 1st It. opera prod. there.

Opera by Galuppi (lib. do.), prod. Mantua, Carnival 1738.

Opera by Pérez (lib. do.), prod. Genoa, Teatro Sant' Agostino, 26. XII. 1745.

Opera by Piccinni (lib. do.), prod. Naples, Teatro San Carlo, 12. I. 1774.

Opera by Sacchini (lib. do.), prod. Venice, Teatro San Salvatore, spring 1763.

Opera by Vinci (lib. do.), prod. Rome, Teatro delle Dame, 26. XII. 1729. (This was the 1st setting of the lib.).

Alessandro Romano. *See* **Merlo.**

Alessandro Severo, opera by Lotti (lib. by Apostolo Zeno), prod. Venice, Teatro San Giovanni Crisostomo, 26. XII. 1716.

Alessandro Stradella, opera by Flotow (lib., in Ger., by Friedrich Wilhelm Riese, pseud. 'W. Friedrich'), prod. Hamburg, 30. XII. 1844. It deals with doubtful incidents in the life of Stradella, and is based on a play with m., some by F., by Philippe Auguste Alfred Pittaud de Forges and Paul Dupert.

Alessandro vincitor di se stesso (*Alexander, Victor over himself*), opera by Cavalli (lib. by Francesco Sbarra), prod. Venice, Teatro Santi Giovanni e Paolo, prob. 20. I. 1651.

Alexander Balus, orat. by Handel (lib. by Thomas Morell), prod. London, Covent Garden Theatre, 9. III. 1748.

Alexander der Wilde (b. ?; d. ?), Ger. 13th-cent. Minnesinger, 6 of whose songs have been preserved.

Alexander's Feast. Dryden's ode set to m. by Handel (words arr. and added to by Newburgh Hamilton), prod. London, Covent Garden Theatre, 19. II. 1736.

Alexandrov, Alexander Vassilievitch (b. Plakhino nr. Riazan, 1884), Rus. cond. & comp. He came of peasant stock, was a choir-boy and later chor. cond. in St. Petersburg, where he studied under Rimsky-Korsakov and Glazunov at the Cons.; later with Vassilenko at the Moscow Cons., where he became prof.

Works incl. opera, *Water Nymph*; Sym. in E♭ maj., symph. poem *Death and Life*; patriotic cantatas, Red Army songs, &c.

Alexandrov, Anatol Nicolaievitch (b. Moscow, 25. V. 1888), Rus. comp. Studied under Taneiev and at the Moscow Cons., later comp. under Vassilenko and Ilyinski. Prof. at Moscow Cons.

Works incl. operas *Two Worlds* and *The Forty-First*; incid. m. for Maeterlinck's *Ariane et Barbe-bleue*, Scribe's *Adrienne Lecouvreur*, &c.; m. for film *Thirteen*; ovt. on popular Rus. themes and 2 suites for orch.; stg. 4tet; 8 pf. sos., pf. pieces; *Three Goblets* for bar. and orch.; songs, folk-song arrs., &c.

Alexis, Willibald (Georg Häring) (1798–1871), Ger. novelist. *See* **Leoncavallo** (*Roland*).

Alfano, Franco (b. Posilipo, 8. III. 1876), It. comp. Studied 1st at the Naples Cons. and afterwards at that of Leipzig under Jadassohn. He had some pf. pieces pub. in Ger. before the end of the cent. and in 1896 wrote his 1st opera, *Miranda*, on a subject from Fogazzaro. The ballet

Napoli and the 4th opera were both prod. in 1900; and his 1st Sym. was perf. by Ettore Panizza at San Remo. In 1919 he was app. dir. of the Liceo Musicale Rossini at Bologna and in 1923 of the Cons. at Turin. After Puccini's death in 1924 he completed the unfinished *Turandot*, finishing the final scenes from P.'s sketches.

Works incl. operas *Miranda*, *La fonte Enschir*, *Risurrezione* (based on Tolstoy), *Il principe Zilah*, *L'ombra di Don Giovanni*, *Sacùntala* (after Kalidasa), *L'ultimo Lord*, *Cyrano de Bergerac* (after Rostand); ballet *Napoli*; 2 syms., *Suite romantica* for orch.; stg. 4tet; So. for co. and pf.; songs incl. 3 settings of Tagore & a cycle *Dormiveglia*.

Alferaki, Achilles Nicholaievitch (b. Kharkov, 21. VI. 1846; d. Leningrad, 1920), Rus. comp. Wrote mainly pf. pieces and songs.

Alfieri, Pietro (b. Rome, 29. VI. 1801; d. Rome, 12. VI. 1863), It. priest & mcolst. For many years prof. of Gregorian m. at the Eng. Coll. in Rome; wrote a number of books on var. aspects of church m., ed. old masters and wrote a biog. of Jommelli.

Alfieri, Vittorio, Count (1749–1803), It. dramatist. *See* **Bazzini** (*Saul*), **Virginia** (Mercadante).

Alfonso und Estrella, opera by Schubert (lib. by Franz von Schober), comp. 1821–2, but never performed in S.'s lifetime; prod. Weimar, by Liszt, 24. VI. 1854.

Alford, John (b. ?; d. ?), Eng. 16th-cent. lutenist. He lived in London and in 1568 pub. a trans. of Adrien Le Roy's book on the lute, *A Briefe and Easye Instruction to learne . . . the Lute*.

Alfred, masque by Arne (words by James Thomson and David Mallet), perf. at Cliveden, Bucks, the residence of Frederick, Prince of Wales, 1. VIII. 1740. It contains 'Rule, Britannia.'

Alfvén, Hugo (b. Stockholm, 1. V. 1872), Swe. vst. & comp. Studied under Lindgren at the Stockholm Cons., and began his career as vst. in the court orch. In 1910 he became mus. dir. at the Univ. of Upsala.

Works incl. 3 syms., 2 symph. poems and Swe. rhapsody *Midsommarvaka* for orch.; *Sten Sture* for chor. and orch.; *The Bells* for solo voice & orch.; a cantata; 2 marches; pieces for pf. and for v.; songs, &c.

Algarotti, Francesco, Count (b. Venice, 11. XII. 1712; d. Pisa, 3. V. 1763), It. scholar. Among many learned works he wrote a treatise on the reform of opera, *Saggio sopra l'opera in musica*, pub. 1755.

Algarotti, Giovanni Francesco (b. Novara, ?; d. ?), It. 16th-cent. comp. Pub. books of madrigals at Venice in 1567 and 1569.

Alghisi, Paris Francesco (b. Brescia, 19. VI. 1666; d. Brescia, 30. III. 1733), It. comp. Studied under Polarolo and was engaged for some time at the Pol. court. Two operas were prod. at Venice: *Amor di Curzio per la patria*, 1690, and *Il trionfo della continenza*, 1691. He also wrote several orats. and other works.

Ali Baba, ou Les Quarante Voleurs (. . ., *or The Forty Thieves*), opera by Cherubini (lib. by Scribe and Anne Honoré Joseph Mélesville), prod. Paris, Opéra, 22. VII. 1833. A new version of *Koukourgi*, comp. 1793, but not perf.

Aline, Reine de Golconde, opera by Berton (lib. by Jean Baptiste Charles Vial and Étienne Guillaume François de Favières, based on Sedaine's older lib.), prod. Paris, Opéra-Comique, 2. IX. 1803.

Opera by Monsigny (lib. by Jean Michel Sedaine), prod. Paris, Opéra, 15. IV. 1766.

Alió, Francisco (b. ?, 1862; d. Barcelona, summer 1908), Spa. comp. Wrote many pf. pieces and songs in a conventional Spa. nat. idiom.

Aliquot Parts (from Lat. *aliquot* = some, so many). Parts contained by the whole, integral factors: in m. the parts of a fundamental note vibrating separately as Overtones.

Alkan (real name Charles Henri Valentin Morhange) (b. Paris, 30. XI. 1813; d. Paris, 29. III. 1888), Fr. pfst. & comp. He was so precocious as a player as to be admitted to the Paris Cons. at the age of 6. After a visit to London in 1833, he settled in Paris as teacher of the pf. In his comps. he cultivated an advanced, immensely difficult and often very modern technique.

Works incl. 2 pf. concs.; pf. Trio; pf. sos., numerous pf. studies (incl. 1 for the right hand and 1 for the left), characteristic pieces; 4 op. nos. of pieces for pedal pf., &c.

Alkestis, opera by Boughton (lib. taken from Gilbert Murray's Eng. trans. of the tragedy by Euripides), prod. Glastonbury, 26. VIII. 1922.

Opera by Wellesz (lib. by Hugo von Hofmannsthal, after Euripides), prod. Mannheim, 20. III. 1924.

All' ottava (It. = at the octave). A direction that a passage, so far as it is marked by a dotted line over it, is to be played an octave higher than it is written; it is usually represented by the symbol *8va*.

All' unisono (It.) = in unison.

Alla (It. fem. = 'at the,' in the manner

of, = Fr. *à la*). The word is used in var. ways in combs. with nouns, e.g. *alla marcia* = march-like, *alla francese* = in the Fr. manner, &c. (also abbr. *all'* with nouns beginning with a vowel).

Alla breve (It. = shortened). A term used for a tempo direction indicating that although the time is 4 in a bar, the tempo is so rapid that they must be counted at 2 beats to the bar. The *alla breve* time-signature uses the symbol ₵.

Alla cappella. *See* **A cappella.**

Allargando (It.) = becoming broader, slowing down.

Allegranti, Maddalena (b. ?; d. ?), It. 18th-cent. singer. Made her 1st appearance at Venice in 1771; went to Ger. in 1774, back to It. in 1779 and to Eng. in 1781.

Allegretto (It. dim. of *allegro*) = a little fast, i.e. not as fast as *allegro*.

Allegri, Domenico (b. Rome, 1585; d. Rome, 5. IX. 1629), It. comp. Chapel master at Santa Maria Maggiore in Rome, 1610–29. Works incl. motets and m. for voices and stgs.

Allegri, Gregorio (b. Rome, 1582; d. Rome, 17. II. 1652), It. priest & comp. Pupil of the Nanini brothers in Rome, where he sang ten. in the Papal Chapel from 1629. His famous *Miserere* is still sung there; Mozart, as a boy of 14, wrote it down from memory after hearing it in Rome. A. also wrote magnificats, motets and other church m.

Allegro (It. lit. cheerful, sprightly). In m. the term, although orig. doubtless describing the character of a piece, now indicates merely speed: a fast but not very fast pace.

Allegro, il Pensieroso ed il Moderato, L' (*The Cheerful, the Thoughtful and the Moderate*), orat. by Handel (lib. Parts i & ii by Milton, Part iii by Charles Jennens), prod. London, Lincoln's Inn Fields Theatre, 27. II. 1740.

Alleluia, a sym. by Haydn, No. 30, in C maj., comp. 1765.

Allemande (F. fem. = German). A dance in moderate 4–4 time, divided into 2 sections, each repeated, and usually beginning with a short upbeat. It occurs in most classical suites, where it takes 1st place unless they open with a prelude.

Allen, Henry Robinson (b. Cork, 1809; d. London, 27. XI. 1876), Irish bar. singer. He first became known in London *c.* 1842 and made a great reputation as an operatic artist, but retired early to devote himself to teaching and the comp. of songs, incl. 'When we two parted.'

Allen, Hugh P(ercy). (b. Reading, 23. XII. 1869; d. Oxford, 20. II. 1946), Eng. mus. scholar. He was orgst. at var. churches, went to Cambridge Univ. later and took the D. Mus. at Oxford in 1889. Orgst. at New Coll. there from 1901, from which time he took an active share in the Univ.'s mus. life. In 1918 he succeeded Parry as dir, of the R.C.M. in London and Parratt as Prof. of M. at Oxford. Knighted in 1920.

Allende, Humberto (b. Santiago, 29. VI. 1885), Chilean vst. & comp. Studied at the Nat. Cons. of Chile. Works incl. *Tres Toncdas, Escenas campesinas chilenas* & *La voz de la calle,* for orch.

Allison, Richard (b. ?; d. ?), Eng. 16th–17th-cent. comp. He first appeared as a contrib. to East's *Whole Book of Psalms* in 1592 and pub. a collection of church melodies set for voices and insts., *The Psalmes of David in Meter,* in 1599. Other works incl. lute m. and 24 songs for voices and insts., *An Howres Recreation . . .,* pub. in 1606.

Almahide, opera by ? Giovanni Bononcini (lib. by ?, after Dryden's *Almanzor and Almahide*, prod. London, Queen's Theatre, Haymarket, 10. I. 1710.

Almain (Middle Eng. adj. = German). One of the names given to the ' Allemande ' in the 16th cent. It makes a pretty Eng. word worth reviving.

Almand (old Eng.) = Allemande.

Almaviva (Rossini). *See* **Barbiere di Siviglia.**

Almeida, Fernando de (b. Lisbon, ? 1618; d. Thomar, 21. III. 1660), Port. monk & comp. Pupil of Lobo; entered the monastery of Thomar in 1638; wrote masses and other church m.

Almeida, Francisco Antonio de (b. ?; d. ?), Port. 18th-cent. comp. Prob. studied in Rome and was the 1st Port. to write It. operas, incl. *La Spinalba* & *La pazienza di Socrate.*

Almeida, Ignacio Antonio de (b. Guimarães, 18. II. 1760; d. S. Pedro de Penedono, 25. X. 1825), Port. priest & comp. His works incl. a Requiem, a *Stabat Mater* and other church m.

Almérie. A kind of lute invented in the 18th cent. by Jean Lemaire, on whose name its own is an anagram.

Almira, opera by Handel (lib. by Friedrich Christian Feustking), prod. Hamburg, Theater am Gänsemarkt, 8. I. 1705.

Almond (old Eng.) = Allemande.

Almorox, Juan (b. ?; d. ?), Spa. 15th–16th-cent. comp. Wrote villancicos for 4 voices and church m.

Alnaes, Eyvind (b. Frederiksstad, 29. IV. 1872; d. Oslo, 25. XII. 1932), Norw. orgst., cond. & comp. Studied at Christiania and Berlin and later became orgst. and chor. cond. at Drammen.

Works incl. syms.; pf. Conc.; songs, &c.

Alpenkönig und Menschenfeind (*Alpine King and Misanthrope*), opera by Blech (lib. by Richard Batka, based on Ferdinand Raimund's play), prod. Dresden, 1. X. 1903.

Alpensinfonie, Eine (*An Alpine Sym.*), sym. by R. Strauss, 1st perf. Berlin, 25. X. 1915.

Alphabetical Music. *See* **Letters.**

Alphorn (Ger. *Alpenhorn*). A primitive wind inst., often *c.* 8 ft. long, with a raucous and powerful tone, used by cowherds in Swi. and other mountainous countries. Having no keys, it can prod. only the natural harmonics.

Alpine Symphony (R. Strauss). *See* **Alpensinfonie.**

Also sprach Zarathustra (*Thus spake Zoroaster*), symph. poem by R. Strauss, based on Nietzsche, 1st perf. Frankfort o/M., 27. XI. 1896.

Alt, In (abbr. for It. 'in alto' = high up). A term used for notes above the stave in m. written in the treble clef.

Altenburg, Michael (b. Alach nr. Erfurt, 27. V. 1584; d. Erfurt, 12. II. 1640), Ger. theologian & church musn. Comp. hymn-tunes, psalms, motets, sacred pieces for voices & insts., intradas for insts., &c.

Alternativo (It.). A contrasting section, much the same as the trio in a minuet or scherzo, but often in a piece of a different character, and there may be more than one A. in a single piece. Familiar exs. appear in Schumann.

Althorn. *See* **Saxhorn.**

Altissimo, In (It. = at the highest). A term used for notes in the octave above that described as 'in alt.'

Altmann, Wilhelm (b. Adelnau, 4. IV. 1862), Ger. mus. critic & ed. Dir. of the mus. dept. of the State Library in Berlin, 1914–27. Ed. of classical m. and of mus. catalogues.

Altnikol, Johann Christoph (b. Berna, Silesia, XII. 1719; d. Naumburg, 25. VII. 1759), Ger. hpchd. player, orgst. & comp. Pupil of Bach at Leipzig from 1744. App. orgst. at Niederwiesa nr. Greifenberg, 1747, and at Naumburg, 1748. Married Bach's daughter Elisabetha Juliane Friederica (1726–81), 1749.

Alto (It. = high). An artificial extension of the highest male-voice register, prod. by Falsetto, used in Angl. church choirs and in male-voice 4tets and chor. socs., partic. in glees and partsongs.

Alto Bassoon. *See* **Dolcian.**

Alto Clef. The C clef so used as to indicate that middle C stands on the central line of the stave; now obs. in voc. m., but still in use for the va.

Alto Rhapsody (Brahms). *See* **Rhapsodie.**

Alwyn, William (b. Northampton, 7. XI. 1905), Eng. comp. Entered the R.A.M. in London as a student for fl., pf. & comp., studying the last under McEwen and obtaining the Costa Scholarship. Later he became prof. of comp. there, was elected to the Collard Fellowship of the Worshipful Co. of Musns. in 1937 and became an Hon. Freeman of that Co. in 1940.

Works incl. 5 **Preludes,** Conc. grosso and Ovt. to a **Masque for orch.**; pf. Conc., v. Conc., *Pastoral Fantasia* for va. & stgs.; m. for films *Desert Victory, World of Plenty, The Way Ahead,* &c.; stg. 4tets., Rhapsody for pf. 4tet.; So.-Impromptu for v. & va., Sonatina for va. & pf.; pf. pieces; Divertimento for solo fl., &c.

Alzira, opera by Verdi (lib. by Salvatore Cammarano, based on Voltaire's play *Alzire*), prod. Naples, Teatro San Carlo, 12. VIII. 1845.

Amadei, Filippo (b. Reggio, *c.* 1683; d. ?), It. comp. His 1st opera, *Teodosio il giovane,* was prod. in Rome in 1711. *See also* **Mattei (F.).**

Amadei, Michele Angelo (b. ?; d. ?), It. 16th–17th-cent. comp. 2 books of his motets were pub. at Venice in 1614–15.

Amadigi di Gaula (*Amadis of Gaul*), opera by Handel (lib. ? by John James Heidegger), prod. London, King's Theatre, Haymarket, 25. V. 1715.

Amadis, opera by Lully (lib. by Quinault), prod. Paris, Opéra, 18. I. 1684.

Amadis de Gaule, opera by J. C. Bach (lib. do., altered by Alphonse Marie Denis de Vismes), prod. Paris, Opéra, 14. XII. 1779.

Amadori, Giuseppe (b. ?; d. ?), It. 17th–18th-cent. comp. Chapel master in Rome, where his orat., *Il martirio di Sant' Adriano,* was prod. in 1702. He also wrote masses and other church m.

Amat, Juan Carles (b. Monistrol nr. Barcelona, ?; d. ?), Spa. 16th-cent. scientist & author. He wrote *Guitarra española . . .,* the earliest known treatise on the subject, pub. prob. 1586.

Amati. It. 16th–17th-cent. family of v. makers at Cremona:

Andrea A. (b. *c.* 1520; d. *c.* 1578).

Antonio A. (b. 1550; d. 1638).

Girolamo (or Geronimo) A. (b. 1551; d. 1635).

Nicolo A. (b. 3. IX. 1596; d. 12. VIII. 1684).

Girolamo A. (b. 1649; d. 1740).

Amati, Vincenzo (b. Sicily, 6. I. 1629; d. Palermo, 29. VII. 1670), It. priest & comp. Wrote masses, psalms, sacred concs. and an opera, *L'Isauro*, prod. at Aquila in 1664.

Amato, Pasquale (b. Naples, 21. III. 1878; d. Jackson Heights, Long Island, N.Y., 12. VIII. 1942), It. bar. singer. Made his 1st appearance in Eng. in 1904 and later had much success in opera in U.S.A.

Amber Witch, The, opera by Wallace (lib. by Henry Fothergill Chorley, based on Lady Duff-Gordon's trans. of Johann Wilhelm Meinhold's novel *Maria Schweidler, die Bernsteinhexe*), prod. London, Her Majesty's Theatre, 28. II. 1861.

Ambiela, Miguel (b. Aragon, 1665; d. Toledo, 23. III. 1733), Spa. priest & comp. Mus. dir. of the new cath. at Saragossa, 1700–7, and chapel master at Toledo, 1710–33.

Works incl. masses, *Stabat Mater* and other church m.

Ambleto (*Hamlet*), opera by Gasparini (lib. by Apostolo Zeno and Pietro Pariati), prod. Venice, Teatro San Cassiano, Carnival 1705.

Opera by D. Scarlatti (lib. do.), prod. Rome, Teatro Capranica, Carnival 1715.

Ambros, August Wilhelm (b. Vysoké Myto, 17. XI. 1816; d. Vienna, 28. VI. 1876) Cz. (Germanized) mcolst. Studied at Prague Univ. His life's work was a Hist. of M. which at his death reached only the 4th vol. and the early 17th cent. He also comp. a Cz. opera, *Bratislav and Jitka*, ovts. to Shakespeare's *Othello* and Calderón's *Mágico prodigioso*, &c.

Ambrosian Chant. The plainsong hymnody and psalmody introduced into the western Catholic church by St. Ambrose (340–97), Bishop of Milan from 374, differing from the Gregorian chant of Rome.

Ambrosio, Alfredo d' (b. Naples, 13. VI. 1871; d. Paris 31. XII. 1914), It. vst. & comp. Studied at Naples and Paris; wrote mainly light v. pieces.

Amer. (abbr.) = America, American.

American Organ. An inst. similar to the Harmonium, differing from the latter in some details, partic. in sucking in the wind through its pipes instead of expelling it. Its principle was discovered by a workman attached to Jacob Alexandre (1804–1876), an inst. maker in Paris, but he took it to Amer. and the 1st important insts. of the kind were made by Mason & Hamlin of Boston c. 1860.

Ames, John Carlovitz (b. Westbury-on-Trym nr. Bristol, 8. I. 1860; d. Torquay, 21. VII. 1924), Eng. pfst. & comp. Wrote an opera, *The Last Inca*, incid. m. to Shakespeare's *Richard II*, 2 pf. concs., chor. works and chamber m.

Ameyden, Christian (b. Oirschot, Brabant, c. 1534; d. Rome, 20. XI. 1605), Flem. priest & comp. Held var. church appts. in Rome; wrote church m. and madrigals.

Amicis, Anna Lucia de (b. Naples, c. 1740; d. Naples, 1816), It. sop. singer. Pupil (?) of Tesi-Tramontini, made her 1st appearance c. 1760 and went to London in 1762.

Amico Fritz, L', opera by Mascagni (lib. by P. Suardon, based on Erckmann-Chatrian's novel *L'Ami Fritz*), prod. Rome, Teatro Costanzi, 31. X. 1891.

Amid Nature (or *In Nature's Realm*) concert ovt. by Dvořák, Op. 91, comp. 1891 and forming, with *Carnival* and *Othello*, a cycle with thematic connections, orig. called *Nature, Life and Love*.

Amitié à l'épreuve, L' (*Friendship on Trial*), opera by Grétry (lib. by Charles Simon Favart & Claude Henri Fusée de Voisenon, based on a story by Marmontel), prod. Fontainebleau, at court, 13. XI. 1770; 1st Paris perf., Comédie-Italienne, 24. I. 1771.

Amleto (*Hamlet*), opera by Faccio (lib. by Boito, after Shakespeare), prod. Genoa, Teatro Carlo Felice, 30. V. 1865.

Ammon, Blasius (b. Imst, Tyrol, c. 1560; d. Vienna, VI. 1590), Aus. monk & comp. Studied in Vienna and entered the Franciscan monastery there. Wrote much church m.

Amner, John (b. ?; d. Ely, 1641), Eng. orgst. & comp. He became orgst. and choirmaster at Ely cath. in 1610; wrote services, anthems and *Sacred Hymns*.

Amon, Johann Andreas (b. Bamberg, 1763; d. Wallerstein, Bavaria, 29. III. 1825), Ger. hn. player. cond. & comp. Toured in Fr. and Ger. and had comp. lessons from Sacchini in Paris in 1781; became mus. dir. at Heilbronn in 1789 and chapel master to the Prince of Oettingen-Wallerstein in 1817.

Works incl. 2 operas, masses, syms., chamber m., &c.

Amor vuol sofferenza (*Love means Suffering*), opera by Leo (lib. by Antonio Federico Gennaro), prod. Naples, Teatro Nuovo, autumn 1739.

Amore artigiano, L' (*Love among the Artisans*), opera by Gassmann (lib. by Goldoni), prod. Vienna, Burg Theatre, 26. IV. 1767.

Opera by Latilla (lib. do.), prod. Venice, Teatro Sant' Angelo, 26. XII. 1760.

Amore di tre re, L' (*The Love of Three Kings*), opera by Montemezzi (lib. by

Sem Benelli, from his play of the same title), prod. Milan, Teatro alla Scala, 10. IV. 1913.

Amorevoli, Angelo (b. Venice, 16. IX. 1716; d. Dresden, 15. XI. 1798), It. singer. Spent most of his time at the court of Dresden, but sang in London in 1741.

Amoroso (It. =amorous). A direction indicating an emotional and tender manner of perf.

Amours d'Antoine et de Cléopâtre, Les (*The Loves of A. & C.*), ballet by R. Kreutzer (chgph. by Jean Pierre Aumer, based on Shakespeare), prod. Paris, Opéra, 8. III. 1808.

Amy Robsart, opera by Isidore de Lara (lib. by Augustus Henry Glossop Harris, based on Scott's *Kenilworth*), prod. in Fr. (trans. by Paul Milliet), London, Covent Garden Theatre, 20. VII. 1893.

An die ferne Geliebte (*To the Distant Beloved*), song cycle by Beethoven (6 songs), Op. 98, to poems by one A. Jeitteles, comp. 1816. It is prob. the 1st Ger. set of songs intended to form a connected cycle.

Ana, Francesco (b. ?; d. Venice, 1502), It. comp. At St. Mark's, Venice, 1490; comp. frottole, lamentations, &c.

Anacreon (*c.* 560–*c.* 476 B.C.), Gr. poet. *See* **Gostovac** (odes), **Maconchy** (*Garland*), **Renvoysy** (odes), **Roussel** (A.) (do.), Smyth (do.).

Anacréon, ou L'Amour fugitif, opera-ballet by Cherubini (lib. by R. Mendouze), prod. Paris, Opéra, 4. X. 1803.

Anacrusis. In prosody an unstressed syllable at the beginning of a verse or line; in m. the literary term is borrowed as a synonym for Upbeat.

Ancelot, Jacques (1794–1854), Fr. playwright. *See* **Puritani di Scozia** (Bellini), **Roberto Devereux** (Donizetti), **Roi malgré lui** (Chabrier).

Anches (Fr. = Reeds). The Fr. name for the reed stops of the org.

Anchieta, Juan de (b. Azpeitia nr. San Sebastián, ?; d. Azpeitia, 30. VII. 1523), Spa. comp. He became a court musn. in 1489 and a canon of Granada 10 years later. From 1504 he was rector of the parish church in his native place. Wrote church m. and secular songs.

Ancina, Giovenale (b. Fossano, 19. X. 1545; d. ? Saluzzo, 1604), It. priest & comp. He 1st studied medicine, then theology and became one of St. Philip Neri's oratorians. He wrote var. essays on m. and insts. and in 1599 compiled a collection of sacred songs, *Tempio armonico della Beata Vergine*, incl. some of his own.

Andamento (It.) = a fugue subject of more than usual length and often in 2 contrasted sections.

Andante (It. = going). A tempo direction indicating a 'walking pace,' i.e. a moderate tempo.

Andantino (It. dim. of prec.). Orig. intended to indicate a slower pace than *andante*, i.e. a dim. of 'walking'; but since *andante* is now taken to mean a slow pace, the dim. suggests an only moderately slow, i.e. slightly quicker tempo.

Ander, Aloys (b. Libitice, 10. VIII. 1821; d. Wartenberg. 11. XII. 1864), Boh. ten. singer. Made his 1st appearance in Vienna, 1845.

Andersen, Hans (Christian) (1805–75), Dan. poet & fairy-tale writer. *See* **Arregui, Bruden fra Lammermoor** (Bredal), **Enna** (*Little Match Girl*), **Farjeon, Françaix** (*Roi nu*), **Høffding** (*Emperor's New Clothes*), **Klenau** (*Lille Ida's blomster*), **Nightingale** (Stravinsky), **Rogers** (**Bernard**), **Rota** (**N.**) (*Principe porcaro*), **Toch** (*Prinzessin auf der Erbse*), **Travelling Companion** (Stanford), **Wagner-Régeny** (*Nackte König*), **Weissberg** (*Little Mermaid*).

Anderson (*née* **Philpot**), **Lucy** (b. Bath, 12. XII. 1797; d. London, 24. XII. 1878), Eng. pfst. Lived in London; teacher of Queen Victoria.

Anderson, W(illiam). R(obert). (b. Blackburn, 7. XII. 1891), Eng. mus. author, critic & ed. Trained as an orgst., took the B.Mus. at Durham and var. other mus. degrees, was ed. of the *Music Teacher* in 1920–5 and later broadcasting critic to the *Observer* and *Mus. Times*. Author of *M. as a Career*, with H. D. McKinney of *Discovering M.*, *M. in History* & *The Challenge of Listening*, &c.

Andrade, Francisco d' (b. Lisbon, 11. I. 1859; d. Berlin, 8. II. 1921). Port. bar. singer. Made his 1st appearance in 1882; sang all over Eur.

André, Johann (b. Offenbach o/M., 28. III. 1741; d. Offenbach, 18. VI. 1799), Ger. m. pub. & comp. Prod. his 1st comic opera in 1760 and set Goethe's *Erwin und Elmire* in 1775. Opened a m.-printing office in 1774. His opera *Belmont und Constanze* of 1781 preceded Mozart's *Entführung*, on the same subject.

André, Johann Anton (b. Offenbach o/M., 6. X. 1775; d. Offenbach, 6. IV. 1842), Ger. m. pub., vst., pfst. & comp., son of prec. He followed his father in business, acquired Mozart's MSS. from Constanze in 1799 and with Senefelder applied the principle of lithography to m. pub.

Andrea Chénier, opera by Giordano (lib. by Luigi Illica), prod. Milan, Teatro alla Scala, 28. III. 1896.

Andreae, Volkmar (b. Berne, 5. VII, 1879), Swi. comp. & cond. Studied at Berne and Cologne, in 1900 became asst. cond. at the Munich Opera, in 1902 chor. cond. at Zürich and Winterthur, later cond. of the Zürich sym. concerts and dir. of the Cons.

Works incl. operas *Ratcliff* (based on Heine's tragedy) & *Abenteuer des Casanova*; sym.; chor. works; chamber m., &c.

Andrée, Elfrida (b. Wisby, 19. II. 1841; d. Stockholm, 11. I. 1929), Swe. orgst. & comp. She was orgst. at Stockholm in 1861 and at Götaborg cath. in 1867; wrote a Swe. Mass, org. syms., chamber m., &c.

Andreiev, Leonid Nikolaievitch (1871–1919), Rus. novelist & playwright. *See* **Rebikov** (*Abyss*), **Sessions** (*Black Maskers*), **Tcherepnin (A.)** (*Ol-Ol*).

Andreozzi, Gaetano (b. Naples, 1763; d. Paris, 21. XII. 1826), It. comp. Pupil and relation of Jommelli; wrote 45 operas, 3 orats., chamber m. and songs.

Andrevi, Francisco (b. nr. Lérida, 16. XI. 1786; d. Barcelona, 23, XI. 1853), Spa. comp. of It. descent. He held var. church apps. in Spa. and Fr.; wrote 2 orats., a Requiem, a *Stabat Mater* and other church m.

Andrico, Michel (b. Bucharest, 22. IX. 1894), Rum. comp. Studied at the Bucharest Cons. and later became prof. at the Royal Acad. there, gaining the Enesco prize for comp. in 1924.

Works incl. ballet *Taina*; Sym. in B♭ maj., Suite, Serenade, 3 *Tableaux symphoniques, Suite pittoresque, Suite brève*, Poem, &c. for orch.; stg. 4tet, *Novellettes* for pf. 5tet & other chamber m.; Sonatina, *Suite lyrique* & other pf. works, &c.

Andriessen, Hendrik (b. Haarlem, 17. IX. 1892), Dutch orgst. & comp. Studied under Zweers at the Amsterdam Cons. Later became dir. of the Utrecht Cons. and choirmaster at the Rom. Catholic cath. there.

Works incl. 2 masses; 2 syms., Vars. for orch.; songs for voice & orch.; chamber m.; org. works, &c.

Andriessen, Willem (b. Haarlem, 25. X. 1887), Dutch pfst. & comp. Studied at the Amsterdam Cons., of which he became dir. in 1837 in succession to Dresden, after teaching at The Hague & Rotterdam.

Works incl. Mass for solo voices, chor. & orch.; Scherzo for orch.; pf. Conc.; pf. So., &c.

Andromaque (*Andromache*), opera by Grétry (lib. by Louis Guillaume Pitra, based on Racine's tragedy), prod. Paris, Opéra, 6. VI. 1780.

Androt, Albert Auguste (b. Paris, 1781; d. Rome, 19. VIII. 1804), Fr. comp. Student at the Paris Cons., where he was the 1st winner of the Prix de Rome at its institution in 1803 and was sent to It., making further studies with Guglielmi in Rome. There he wrote a Requiem and another sacred work with such success that he was asked to comp. an opera, but d. as soon as it was finished.

Anerio, Felice (b. Rome, *c.* 1560; d. Rome, 27. IX. 1614), It. comp. Chorister in the Papal Chapel as a boy, later chapel master at the Eng. Coll. in Rome, which he left for the service of Cardinal Aldobrandini. App. comp. to the Papal Chapel on the death of Palestrina in 1594.

Works incl. masses, motets, hymns and other church m.; madrigals, canzonets, &c.

Anerio, Giovanni Francesco (b. Rome, *c.* 1567; d. ?, 1621), It. comp., brother of prec. In the service of Sigismund III of Poland about 1609, then chapel master at the cath. of Verona and, about 1613, app. mus. instructor at the Seminario Romano and chapel master of the church of the Madonna de' Monti in Rome.

Works incl. masses, Requiem, Te Deum and other church m.

Anet, Jean-Baptiste (b. ?, *c.* 1661; d. Lunéville, 14. VIII. 1755), Fr. vst. & comp. He travelled in Fr. and It., studying with Corelli in Rome, and made a great reputation. He retired to the court of the ex-king of Pol., Stanislas Leczinski, at Lunéville. Wrote sos. and other works for his inst.

Anfossi, Pasquale (b. Taggia, nr. Naples, 25. IV. 1727; d. Rome, II. 1797), It. comp. Pupil of Piccinni at Naples. Prod. his 1st comic opera in Rome, 1763. Later prod. operas in Paris, London, Prague and Berlin. In 1792 he became chapel master to the Lateran in Rome.

Works incl. operas *La donna fedele, L'incognita perseguitata, La finta giardiniera, Il geloso in cimento, L'avaro, La vera costanza, Il curioso indiscreto, I viaggiatori felici, Le gelosie fortunate*, &c.

Angecourt, Perrin d' (b. ?; d. ?), Fr. 13th-cent. troubadour. He was at the court of Charles of Anjou. 53 of his songs have survived.

Angelina. An alternative title for Rossini's opera *La Cenerentola*, used esp. in Ger. and Aus.

Angiolina, ossia Il matrimonio per susurro (*Angiolina, or The Marriage by Noise*), opera by Salieri (lib. by Carlo Prospero Defranceschi, based on Ben Jonson's *Epicoene*), prod. Vienna, Kärntnertor Theatre, 22. X. 1800.

Anglebert, Jean Henri d' (b. ? Paris, 1635; d. Paris, 23. IV. 1691), Fr. hpchst. & comp. Pupil of Chambonnières. Became orgst. to the Duke of Orleans in 1661 and chamber musn. to **Louis XIV** in 1664. He wrote hpchd. and org. pieces and arr. many inst. pieces from **Lully's operas** for hpchd.

Anglès, Higini (b. Maspujols, Catalonia, 1. I. 1888), Spa. mcolst. Pupil of Pedrell at Barcelona. App. librarian of the m. dept. of the Catalan Library there, and after further studies in Ger., prof. of mus. hist. at the Cons. Has ed. and written on old Spa. m.

Ängstlich (Ger. =anxiously, apprehensively). Beethoven used the term as a direction for the singing of the recitative in the 'Agnus Dei' section of his *Missa solemnis.*

Animato (It. =animated). A direction orig. intended to suggest a spirited perf., but later generally the quickening of a passage.

Animuccia, Giovanni (b. Florence, *c.* 1500; d. Rome, III. 1571), It. comp. Studied under Goudimel in Rome; chapel master at the Vatican from 1555 until his death. A friend of St. Philip Neri, for whom he comp. a series of *Laudi.* He also wrote masses, other church m. and madrigals.

Animuccia, Paolo (b. ?; d. Rome, 1563), It. comp. brother of prec. Chapel master at the Lateran in Rome, 1550–2, before Palestrina. Wrote madrigals and church m.

Aniuta, opera by Fomin (lib. by Mikhail Vassilievitch Popov), prod. St. Petersburg, Tsarkoye Selo Palace, at court, 6. IX. 1772. The 1st opera by a Rus. comp.

Anna Bolena (*Anne Boleyn*), opera by Donizetti (lib. by Felice Romani), prod. Milan, Teatro Carcano, 26. XII. 1830.

Anna Karenina, opera by Hubay (lib., in Hung., by Sandor Góth, based on Tolstoy's novel), prod. Budapest, 10. XI. 1923.

Annibale (Il Padovano), (b. Padua, *c.* 1527; d. Graz, III. 1575), It. ctptst. & comp. Orgst. at St. Mark's, Venice, 1552–66, and then chapel master to the Archduke Carl at Graz. Wrote church and org. m., madrigals, &c.

Annibali, Domenico (b. ?, *c.* 1705; d. ?, 1779), It. male sop. singer. He came out at Venice in 1726 and went to Dresden in 1729, where he remained at court until 1764; but sang for Handel in London in 1736–7.

Annunzio, Gabriele d' (1863–1938), It. poet, novelist, dramatist & politician. *See* **Boulanger** (**N.**) (*Città morta*), **Fedra** (Pizzetti), **Francesca da Rimini** (Zandonai), **Franchetti** (*Figlia di Jorio*), **Leva** (*Gioconda*), **Martyre de Saint Sébastien** (Debussy), **Nave** (Montemezzi & Pizzetti), **Parisina** (Mascagni), **Pizzetti** (*Pisanella* & *Cabirio*), **Pugno** (*Città morta*), **Scontrino** (*Francesca da Rimini*), **Toselli** (*Fuoco*).

Ansani, Giovanni (b. Rome, 1744; d. Florence, 15. VII. 1826), It. 18th-cent. ten. singer. Sang with great success in Copenhagen and London, as well as It., and retired to Naples at the age of 50 to teach singing.

Anschlag }
Anschlagend } (Ger.). *See* **Ornaments**

Ansorge, Conrad (b. Buchwald, Silesia, 15. X. 1862; d. Berlin, 13. II. 1930), Ger. pfst. & comp. Studied at the Leipzig Cons. and under **Liszt** at **Weimar.** Wrote a Requiem, chamber m., pf. works, songs, &c.

Answer. In **Fugue** the 2nd entry of the subject, normally on Dominant harmony, brought in while the 1st voice, after bringing in the exposition of the subject in the **Tonic,** continues with ctptal. matter.

Antar. A programme sym. by Rimsky-Korsakov, based on Sankovsky's oriental story of that name, comp. 1868, revised 1875 and 1st perf. St. Petersburg, Rus. M. Soc., I. 1876.

Antheil, George (b. Trenton, N.J., 8. VII. 1900), Amer. comp. Pupil of Bloch, later studied in Eur., where he gave pf. recitals. In 1939 he became assoc. film prod. at Hollywood.

Works incl. operas *Transatlantic* & *Helen Retires*; ballets *Ballet mécanique* & *Dreams*; *Zingaresca, Capriccio* & *Archipelago* for orch.; 2 stg. 4tets; 3 v. & pf. sos., &c.

Anthem. A comp. for a church choir, with or without solo voices and accomp., sung in the course of a service in the Angl. Church, but not forming part of the liturgy. There are 2 kinds of A.: the Full A. is a species sung by the choir throughout, the Verse A. one consisting of chor. sections interspersed with passages for solo voices.

Anticipation. The occurrence of a single note from a chord before the rest of the chord is sounded.

Antigone, incid. m. to Sophocles's tragedy by Mendelssohn, prod. at the New Palace, Potsdam, 28. X. 1841, and repeated at the Berlin Opera, 13. IV. 1842.

Opera by Honegger (lib. by Jean Cocteau, after Sophocles), prod. Brussels, Théâtre de la Monnaie, 28. XII. 1927.

Opera by Zingarelli (lib. by Jean François Marmontel), prod. Paris, Opéra, 30. IV. 1790.

Antigono, opera by Gluck (lib. by Metastasio), prod. Rome, Teatro Argentina, 9. II. 1756.

Opera by Hasse (lib. do.), prod. Hubertusburg nr. Dresden, 10. X. 1743.

Antinori, Luigi (b. Bologna, c. 1697; d. ?), It. ten. singer. First appeared in London, 1725.

Antiphon. The psalmody in the Gr. Orthodox and Roman Catholic churches sung in the manner of responses between 2 choirs or between a single voice and the congregation. Portions of the Mass can also be sung antiphonally.

Antiquis, Giovanni d' (b. ?; d. ?), It. 16th-cent. comp. Mus. dir. at the church of San Niccolo at Bari; ed. 2 books of *Villanelle alla napolitana* by musns. of Bari, incl. himself, pub. at Venice, 1574.

Antoni, Antonio d' (b. Palermo, 25. VI. 1801; d. Trieste, 18. VIII. 1859), It. cond. & comp. Prod. a Mass at the age of 12 and became cond. at the Palermo theatre in 1817; settled at Trieste and founded the Società Filarmonica there, 1829.

Works incl. operas *Un duello a Palermo*, *Amina*, &c.

Antonii, Pietro degli (b. Bologna, 1648; d. Bologna, 1720), It. comp. Chapel master at var. Bologna churches. Wrote 3 operas, 3 orats., masses, motets and inst. works.

Antonio e Cleopatra, opera by Malipiero (lib. by comp., based on Shakespeare), prod. Florence, Teatro Comunale, 4. V. 1938.

Antony and Cleopatra. *See* **Amours d'Antoine et de Cléopâtre; Antonio e Cleopatra.**

Anzengruber, Ludwig (1839–89), Aus. novelist & playwright. *See* **Prohaska** (*Vierte Gebot*).

Aperto (It. lit. open, frank, straightforward). Mozart used the adj. in conjunction with *allegro* in some early works. The meaning is not clear, but may be taken to suggest an energetic delivery strictly in time.

Apollinaire, Guillaume (Wilhelm Apollinaris Kostrowitski) (1880–1918). Fr. poet of Pol. descent. *See* **Durey** (*Bestiaire*), **Poulenc** (do. & *Banalités*).

Apollo et Hyacinthus, Lat. intermezzo by Mozart (lib. by Rufinus Widl), prod. Salzburg Univ., 13. V. 1767.

Apollo Lyre. *See* **Lyre-Guitar.**

Apollonicon. A large organ playable both by hand and mechanically by barrels, built by Flight & Robson in London and exhib. by them in 1817.

Apostles, The, orat. by Elgar, Op. 49 (lib. compiled from the Bible by the comp.), Part I of a trilogy of which II is *The Kingdom* and III was never completed. Prod. Birmingham Festival, 14. X. 1903.

App. (abbr.) = Appoint, appointed.

Appalachia, vars. for orch. with chor. by Delius, comp. 1902, 1st perf. Elberfeld, 1904. The title is the old Red Indian name for N. Amer.; the theme is a Negro folksong.

Appassionata (It. = impassioned). The name commonly used for Beethoven's F min. pf. So. of 1804, Op. 57, but not authorized by himself.

Appassionato (It.) = impassioned, to be played or sung in a passionate manner.

Appenzeller, Benedictus (b. Oudenarde, ?; d. ?), Flem. 16th-cent. comp. (?) of Swi. origin. Pupil of Josquin des Prés. In the service of Mary of Hung., dowager regent of the Nthlds., with whom he went to Spa. in 1551; later (?) choirmaster at Lille.

Works incl. church m., a *Nenia* on the death of Josquin, &c.

Appleby, Thomas (b. ?; d. ? Lincoln, c. 1562), Eng. orgst. & comp. App. orgst. of Lincoln cath. in 1538, the next year orgst. at Magdalen Coll., Oxford, but returned to Lincoln in 1541; was succeeded by Byrd there in 1563. Comp. church m.

Applicatio (Lat.). A term formerly used for fingering in Ger.

Applicatur (Lat.-Ger.). Sometimes used for fingering in Ger.

Appoggiatura (It. der. from *appoggiare* = to lean). An ornament consisting of a short note inserted a whole tone or half a tone higher or lower than a note forming part of a chord without being an essential part of the melody. The double A. consists of 2 such short notes, one above and one below (or vice versa) the essential note.

Appt. (abbr). = Appointment.

Après-midi d'un faune (Debussy). *See* **Prélude à L'Après-midi d'un faune.**

Aprile, Giuseppe (b. Martina, Apulia, 29. X. 1732; d. Martinafranca, 11. I. 1813), It. male con. singer & teacher. Educ. at Naples and 1st appeared in 1763.

Arabella, opera by R. Strauss (lib. by Hugo von Hofmannsthal), prod. Dresden, 1. VII. 1933. Hofmannsthal's last lib. for S.

Arabeske (Ger.). }
Arabesque (Fr.). } Orig. a term applied to ornamentation in Arabic or Moorish architecture; used by some comps. (e.g. Schumann, Debussy) for pieces prob. meant to be regarded as decorative rather than emotionally expressive.

Arabian Nights, The (*Thousand and One Nights*), Arabian cycle of stories of (?) the 10th cent., partly of Persian and prob. Indian origin. *See* Dobroven (opera), Gerhard (*Sharazada*), **Mârouf** (Rabaud), **Sekles** (*Schahrazade*), Shahrazad (Rimsky-Korsakov), **Weisberg** (*Gulnara*).

Aragonaise (Fr.). A Spa. dance of Aragon, i.e. the *Jota aragonesa.*

Araia, Francesco (earlier spelling Araja) (b. Naples, *c.* 1700; d. Naples, *c.* 1770), It. comp. He was chapel master at the Rus. court in St. Petersburg from *c.* 1734 to 1759 and went back there in 1761. Wrote about a dozen operas, some in Rus. and most of them prod. at St. Petersburg. The very 1st opera in Rus. was his, a trans. of Metastasio's *La clemenza di Tito* by Feodor Grigorievitch Volkov, prod. 1751.

Aranaz, Pedro (b. Tudela, 1742; d. Cuença, 1821), Spa. priest & comp. App. chapel master at Saragossa cath. in 1766, having been a choirboy there. After a year at Zamora, he went to Cuença cath. in 1769.

Works incl. church m. with orch. accomp., secular songs (tonadillas and villancicos), &c.

Arbeau, Thoinot (anag. on real name of Jehan Tabourot) (b. Dijon, 1519; d. Langres, 1595), Fr. priest & author. Wrote a book on dancing, *Orchésographie,* pub. 1589, containing a large number of dance tunes current in 16th-cent. Fr.

Arbore di Diana, L' (*Diana's Tree*), opera by Martín y Soler (lib. by Lorenzo da Ponte), prod. Vienna, Burg Theatre, 1. X. 1787.

Arbós, Fernandez (b. Madrid, 25. XII. 1863; d. San Sebastián, 2. VI. 1939), Spa. vst. & cond. Studied at Cons. of Madrid and Brussels, also with Joachim; toured and returned to Madrid to teach at the Cons.; prof. of v. at R.C.M. in London, 1894–1916, when he returned to Spa. as cond. of the Madrid Sym. Orch.

Arbre enchanté, L', ou Le Tuteur dupé (*The Enchanted Tree, or The Tutor Duped*), comic opera by Gluck (lib. by Jean Joseph Vadé), prod. Vienna, Schönbrunn Palace, at court, 3. X. 1759.

Arcadelt, Jacob (b. ?, *c.* 1514; d. ?, *c.* 1575), Flem. comp. Became a singer at the court of the Medici at Florence before 1539, in which year he was app. singing-master to the boys at St. Peter's in Rome, entering the coll. of papal singers the following year. Many of his madrigals were pub. in his lifetime.

Works incl. masses, motets, madrigals, &c. (The *Ave Maria* attrib. to him is spurious.)

Arcadia in Brenta, L', opera by Galuppi (lib. by Goldoni), prod. Venice, Teatro Sant' Angelo, 14. V. 1749. The 1st comic opera by Galuppi written in collab. with Goldoni.

'Archduke' Trio. The name sometimes given to Beethoven's pf. Trio in B♭ maj., Op. 97, comp. in 1811 and ded. to the Archduke Rudolph of Aus.

Archlute. A large Lute of the theorbo type with 2 sets of stgs. the pegs of which were set at different distances in the double neck; the longer bass stgs. had no fingerboard and could therefore not be altered in pitch during perf.

Arco (It. = bow). A direction (sometimes **col arco**) in m. for bowed stg. insts. indicating that the bow is to be resumed after a passage of plucked notes.

Arditi, Luigi (b. Crescentino, 16. VII. 1822; d. Hove, 1. V. 1903), It. comp. & cond. Educ. at Milan Cons. Cond. in var. It. towns, went on tour with Bottesini in 1846, cond. in U.S.A. and settled in London in 1858. Of his comps. only the popular waltz song *Il bacio* is now remembered.

Arensky, Anton Stepanovitch (b. Novgorod, 11. VIII. 1861; d. Terioki, Finland, 25. II. 1906), Rus. comp. Pupil of Rimsky-Korsakov for a time, but belonged to the eclectic rather than the nationalist school. App. prof. at the Moscow Cons. in 1882.

Works incl. operas *A Dream on the Volga, Raphael, Nal and Damayanti*; ballet, *Egyptian Night*; incid. m. for Shakespeare's *Tempest*; 2 syms.; pf. Conc.; chamber m.; numerous pf. pieces; chors., songs, church m., &c.

Arg. (abbr.) = Argentine.

Argentine Composers. *See* **Aguirre, Berutti, Castro, Estrada, Faleni, Morillo, Paz, Siccardi, Ugarte, Williams (A.).**

Aria (It. = air). A vocal piece, esp. in opera or orat., formally more highly organized than a song: in the late 17th and early 18th cent. as a rule in 3 sections, the 3rd being a repetition of the 1st and the 2nd a contrasting strain (*da capo* A.); later often var. modifications of the inst. so. form. In the early 18th cent. arias were conventionally classified as follows:

A. all' unisono. An A. in which the voice and inst. parts have the tune in octave unison, without harmony, at any rate so far as the comp.'s writing went, though chords may have been added by the *continuo* player at the hpchd.

A. cantabile. An A. with a slow, sustained melody.

A. concertata. An A. making a feature of an elaborate inst. solo part in the accomp.

A. d'agilità = *A. di bravura.*

A. d'imitazione. An A. in which either the voice or some insts., or both, gave a more or less realistic imitation of some other mus. or non-mus. sounds.

A. di bravura. An A. containing a

more than usual amount of brilliant and difficult passages.

A. di mezzo carattere. An A. 'of indeterminate character' which could be almost anything that could not be classified under any other species, but had as a rule an elaborate accomp.

A. di portamento. An A. requiring a slow and full-toned delivery and laying great stress on the display of a beautiful voice at the expense of the accomp.

A. parlante. An A. of a declamatory kind, intended less to display the voice than the singer's verbal eloquence and dramatic expression.

A. senza accompagnamento. A wholly unaccomp. A., which was very rarely used.

See also **Parable Aria.**

Ariadne. *See also* **Ariane, Arianna.**

Ariadne auf Naxos, play with music (melodrama) by G. Benda (text by Johann Christian Brandes), prod. Gotha, 27. I. 1775.

Opera by R. Strauss (lib. by Hugo von Hofmannsthal), orig. a 1-act opera played after a shortened version of Molière's *Le Bourgeois gentilhomme,* with incid. m. by S., prod. Stuttgart, 25. X. 1912; 2nd version, with a new operatic 1st act, prod. Vienna, Opera, 4. X. 1916.

Ariadne in Crete, opera by Handel (lib., by Pietro Pariati, ascribed to Francis Colman), prod. London, King's Theatre, Haymarket, 26. I. 1734.

Ariane et Barbe-bleue (*A. and Bluebeard*), opera by Dukas (lib. Maeterlinck's play with slight alterations), prod. Paris, Opéra-Comique, 10. V. 1907.

Ariane, ou Le Mariage de Bacchus, opera by Cambert or Grabu (?) (lib. by Pierre Perrin), prod. London, Drury Lane Theatre, 30. III. 1674.

Arianna, opera by Marcello (lib. by Vincenzo Cassani), comp. 1727, never perf. in M.'s lifetime; ed. by Oscar Chilesotti, 1885, prod. Venice, Liceo Benedetto Marcello, 27. IV. 1913.

Arianna, L', opera by Monteverdi (lib. by Ottavio Rinuccini), prod. Mantua, at the ducal court, for the wedding of the Hereditary Prince Francesco Gonzaga with Margherita, Princess of Savoy, 28. V. 1608.

Arianna e Teseo (*Ariadne and Theseus*), opera by Porpora (lib. by Pietro Pariati), prod. Vienna, 1. X. 1714.

Arienzo, Nicola d' (b. Naples, 24. XII. 1842; d. Naples, 25. IV. 1915), It. comp. Studied law, and secretly m., at Naples. He first wrote operas in the Neapolitan dialect and later several others which gained a wider currency.

Arietta (It. =little air). A shorter and simpler kind of Aria, usually of a lighter character.

Arietto, Simone (b. Vercelli, ?; **d.** ?), It. 17th-cent. vst. He worked at the courts of Mantua and Savoy, and was perhaps the very 1st to play the v. as a virtuoso.

Ariodante, opera by Handel (lib. by Antonio Salvi, based on Ariosto's *Orlando furioso*), prod. London, Covent Garden Theatre, 8. I. 1735.

Arioso (It. =song-like). A vocal or inst. piece or passage of a declamatory or recitative character, to be sung or played in a melodic manner.

Ariosti, Attilio (b. Bologna, 5. XI. 1666; d. ?), It. comp. Prod. his 1st opera at Venice in 1686. Worked in Berlin, 1690–1715, but visited It., Vienna and prob. Fr. in between. Then he came to Eng. and remained until 1728.

Works incl. operas *La più gloriosa fatica d'Ercole, Amor tra nemici, La fede ne' tradimenti, Caio Marzio Coriolano, Vespasiano, Artaserse, Dario, Lucio Vero,* &c.; orat. *Nabucodonosor,* Passion orat. and others, cantatas, lessons for va. d'amore, &c.

Ariosto, Lodovico (1474–1533), It. poet. *See* **Ariodante** (*Orlando furioso,* Handel), **Holmès** (do.), **Orlando** (Handel), **Purcell (D.)** (*Orlando f.*), **Vivaldi** (do.).

Aristophanes (5th cent. B.C.), Gr. playwright. *See* **Auric** (*Birds*), **Bantock** (*Frogs*), **Broman** (*Lysistrata*), **Commer** (*Frogs*), **Delannoy** (*Peace*), **Diepenbrock** (*Birds*), **Glière** (*Lysistrata*), **Humperdinck** (do.), **Lajtha** (do.), **Leigh** (*Frogs*), **Ornstein** (*Lysistrata*), **Paine** (*Birds*), **Parry (H.)** (do., *Frogs, Clouds & Acharnians*), **Sabata** (*Lisistrata*), **Vaughan Williams** (*Wasps*), **Verschworenen** (Schubert), **Vögel** (Braunfels), **Walliser** (*Clouds*).

Aristoxenus of Tarentum, Gr. philos. of 4th cent. B.C. Wrote treatises on the elements of harmony (not in the modern, chor. sense) and rhythm.

Arkwright, Godfrey (Edward Pellew) (b. Norwich, 10. IV. 1864; d. Highclere, 16. VIII. 1944), Eng. mus. ed. and mcolst. Educ. at Eton and Oxford. Brought out a collection of early Eng. m., *Old Eng. Ed.,* 1889–1902; ed. Purcell's church m. for the complete ed., *The Mus. Antiquary* and the mus. catalogue of Christ Church Coll. library, Oxford.

Arlesiana, L' (*The Girl from Arles*), opera by Cilèa (lib. by Leopoldo Marenco, based on Daudet's play, *L'Arlésienne*), prod. Milan, Teatro Lirico, 27. XI. 1897.

Arlésienne, L' (*The Girl from Arles*), incid. m. by Bizet for Alphonse Daudet's play, prod. 1. X. 1872. B.

afterwards extracted 2 orch. suites from it.

Armida, opera by Anfossi (lib. by Jacopo Durandi, based on Tasso's *Gerusalemme liberata)* prod. Turin, Teatro Regio, Carnival 1770.

Opera by Dvořák (lib. by Jaroslav Vrchlický, based on his Cz. trans. of Tasso), prod. Prague, Cz. Theatre, 25. III. 1904.

Opera by Haydn (lib. by Jacopo Durandi), prod. Esterház, 26. II. 1784.

Opera by Mysliveček (lib. by Giovanni Ambrogio Migliavacca, an It. version of Quinault), prod. Milan, Teatro alla Scala, 26. XII. 1779.

Opera by Naumann (lib. by Giovanni Bertati, based on Tasso), prod. Padua, VI. 1773.

Opera by Rossini (lib. by Giovanni Schmidt, after Tasso), prod. Naples, Teatro San Carlo, 11. XI. 1817.

Opera by Sacchini (lib. by Giovanni de Gamerra), prod. Milan, Teatro Regio Ducal, Carnival 1772.

Opera by Salieri (lib. by Marco Coltellini, based on Tasso), prod. Vienna, Burg Theatre, 2. VI. 1771.

Opera by Traetta (lib. by Count Giacomo Durazzo, based on Quinault), prod. Vienna, Burg Theatre, 3. I. 1761.

Armide, opera by Gluck (lib. by Quinault, based on Tasso's *Gerusalemme liberata*), prod. Paris, Opéra, 23. IX. 1777.

Opera by Lully (lib. do.), prod. Paris, Opéra, 15. II. 1686.

Arminio, opera by Handel (lib. by Antonio Salvi), prod. London, Covent Garden Theatre, 12. I. 1737.

2 operas by Hasse: I. (lib. by Giovanni Claudio Pasquini), prod. Dresden, at court, 7. X. 1745; II. (lib. by Antonio Salvi), prod. Milan, 28. VIII. 1730.

Opera by A. Scarlatti (lib. by Salvi), prod. Villa Pratolino, IX. 1703.

Armourer of Nantes, The, opera by Balfe (lib. by John Vipon Bridgeman, based on Victor Hugo's *Marie Tudor*), prod. London, Covent Garden Theatre, 12. II. 1863.

Arne, Michael (b. ? London, 1740 or 1741; d. London, 14. I. 1786), Eng. singer & comp., illegitimate son of Thomas Augustine A. Went on the stage as a child and made his 1st appearance as a singer in 1750. When still a boy he pub. a collection of songs, *The Flow'ret*; in 1763 he prod. the mus. play *The Fairy Tale* and in 1764 the opera *Almena*, comp. with Battishill. He married the singer Elizabeth Wright on 5. XI. 1766, and the next year wrote incid. m. for Garrick's *Cymon*. He wrote several other dramatic pieces, incl. one on Sterne's *Tristram Shandy*, but was also interested in chemistry and alchemy, which pursuits twice ruined him.

Arne, Susanna Maria (b. London, II. 1714; d. London, 30. I. 1766), Eng. con. singer & actress, aunt of prec. First appeared on the stage in London, 1732; married Theophilus Cibber in 1734.

Arne, Thomas Augustine (b. London, 12. III. 1710; d. London, 5. III. 1778), Eng. comp., brother of prec. His father, an upholsterer, was against his taking up m., but had him educ. at Eton and wished him to take up law. But he practised secretly on a muffled hpchd. and learnt the v. from Festing. He also taught his sister, Susanna Maria, and she was so successful that in 1733 she succeeded in having his setting of Addison's *Rosamond* prod. He had frequent stage successes after that, and in 1740 the masque *Alfred* containing 'Rule, Britannia,' was perf. at the residence of Frederick, Prince of Wales, at Cliveden. He married the singer Cecilia Young in 1736. In 1742–4 he and his wife worked successfully at Dublin, which they twice revisited in the 1750s. In 1745 A. was app. comp. to Vauxhall Gardens. Mus.D. Oxford, 1759. In 1760, after a quarrel with Garrick, he gave up his app. as comp. to Drury Lane Theatre and went over to Covent Garden, and prod. there in 1762 his opera *Artaxerxes*, trans. by himself from Metastasio and set in the grand It. manner. Two years later he set that libst.'s *Olimpiade* in the orig. language.

Works incl. operas & plays with m.: *Rosamond, The Opera of Operas, or Tom Thumb the Great* (adapted from Fielding), *Love and Glory, The Fall of Phaeton, An Hospital for Fools, The Blind Beggar of Bethnal Green, Britannia, Eliza, The Temple of Dullness, King Pepin's Campaign, Harlequin's Incendiary, or Columbine, The Triumph of Peace, Don Saverio, The Prophetess, Thomas and Sally, Artaxerxes, Love in a Village, The Birth of Hercules, The Guardian Outwitted, L'Olimpiade, The Ladies' Frolic, The Fairy Prince, The Cooper, Squire Badger* (later *The Sot*), *The Rose, Henry and Emma* (after M. Prior), *Achilles in Petticoats, May Day, Phoebe at Court, Phillis*; masques *Dido and Aeneas, Comus* (Milton adapted by Dalton), *The Judgment of Paris, Alfred*; incid. m. to Aaron Hill's *Zara*, Shakespeare's *As You Like It, Twelfth Night, The Merchant of Venice, Cymbeline, The Tempest, Romeo and Juliet*, Mason's

Elfrida and *Caractacus*; orats. *The Death of Abel* and *Judith*; *Ode on Cheerfulness*, *Ode to Shakespeare*; c. 25 books of songs; masses and motets; 8 ovts. for orch.; 6 clav. concs.; 2 sos. for 2 v. and bass; 8 lessons (sos.) for hpchd.; org. concs., &c.

Arneiro, José Augusto Ferreira Veiga d' (b. Macao, China, 22. XI. 1838; d. San Remo, VII. 1903), Port. comp.
Works incl. operas *Elisir di giovinezza*, *La derelitta* (after Ann Radcliffe) & *Don Bibas*; ballet *Gina*; Te Deum & other church m., &c.

Arnold, F(ranck). T(homas). (b. Rugby, 6. IX. 1861; d. Bath, 24. IX. 1940), Eng. mcolst. Educ. at Rugby & Cambridge; app. lecturer in Ger. at Cardiff Univ. Made a special study of the practice of writing and playing from thorough-bass, on which he wrote for var. periodicals and pub. a large treatise in 1931.

Arnold, Matthew (1822–88), Eng. poet & critic. *See* **Somervell** (*Forsaken Merman*).

Arnold, Samuel (b. London, 10. VIII. 1740; d. London, 22. X. 1802), Eng. comp. Chorister at the Chapel Royal under Gates and Nares; was engaged by Beard as comp. to Covent Garden Theatre in 1765, where he prod. his 1st opera, *The Maid of the Mill*, that year. Ed. a collection of *Cath. M.* and the works of Handel. Mus.D., Oxford, 1773, and orgst. of the Chapel Royal, 1783. Founder of the Glee Club with Callcott in 1787.
Works incl. operas & plays with m.: *The Maid of the Mill*, *The Portrait*, *The Castle of Andalusia*, *Gretna Green*, *Peeping Tom of Coventry*, *Inkle and Yarico*, *The Enraged Musician*, *The Surrender of Calais*, *Harlequin Dr. Faustus*, *The Mountaineers*, *The Shipwreck*, *Obi, or Three-fingered Jack* and c. 25 others; orats. *Elisha*, *The Cure of Saul*, *The Resurrection*, *The Prodigal Son*; church m.; ovt. for orch.; odes for chor.; hpchd. m.; songs, &c.

Arnoldson, Sigrid (b. Stockholm, 20. III. 1861; d. Stockholm, 7. II. 1943), Swe. sop. singer. Daughter of the ten. Oscar A. Studied with Maurice Strakosch and Désirée Artôt-Padilla, made her 1st stage appearance at Moscow, 1886, and 1st appeared in London, 1887.

Arnould, Sophie (b. Paris, 13. II. 1740; d. Paris, 22. X. 1802), Fr. actress & sop. singer. Made her 1st stage appearance in 1757 and the last in 1778. She was a great wit and conversationalist.

Aron, Pietro. *See* **Aaron.**

Arpeggio (It. = harp-like). The playing of chords in a broken manner, giving out its notes in rapid succession instead of strictly together, usually beginning from the bottom.

Arpeggione. A 6-stgd. inst. invented by G. Staufer of Vienna in 1823; a hybrid between a co. and a guitar, played with a bow and with a fretted fingerboard. Schubert wrote a So. for it in 1824.

Arquimbau, Domingo (b. ?; d. Seville, 1829), Spa. comp. Mus. dir. of Seville cath., 1795–1829. Wrote a mass, motets and sacred villancicos.

Arr. (abbr.) = Arranged, Arrangement.

Arregui Garay, Vicente (b. Madrid, 3. VII. 1871; d. Madrid, 2. XII. 1925), Spa. comp. Studied at Madrid, Rome and Paris. Later m. critic of *El Debate* in Madrid.
Works incl. opera *Yolanda* (after Hertz's *King René's Daughter*); orat. *San Francisco*; symph. poem, *Historia de una madre* (after Hans Andersen) & *Sinfonia vasca* for orch.; stg. 4tet., pf. So., &c.

Arresti, Giulio Cesare (b. Bologna, 1630; d. Bologna, 1701), It. orgst. & comp. Pupil of Vernizzi at Bologna cath., where he was afterwards orgst. and chapel master. Wrote church and chamber m.

Arriaga y Balzola, Juan Crisostomo Antonio (b. Bilbao, 27. I. 1806; d. Paris, ? II. 1826), Spa. vst. & comp. Played and comp. as a child and was sent to the Paris Cons. in 1821. His early death cut short a remarkable comp.'s career.

Arrieta y Corera, Emilio (b. Puenta de la Reina, Navarre, 21. X. 1823; d. Madrid, 11. II. 1894), Spa. comp. Studied under Vaccai at the Milan Cons. and prod. his 1st opera there in 1845, returning to Spa. the following year. Prof. of comp. at the Madrid Cons. from 1857 and dir. from 1868.
Works incl. It. operas *Ildegonda*, *La conquista di Granada*, *Isabella la católica*; zarzuelas *El dómino azul*, *El grumete*, *La Estrella de Madrid*, *Marina* and c. 50 others, &c.

Arrigoni, Carlo (b. Florence, ?; d. ?), It. 18th-cent. lutenist & comp. Pub. *Cantate da camera* in London, 1732.

Arrigoni, Giovanni Giacomo (b. ?; d. ?), It. 17th-cent. orgst. & comp. Orgst. at the Viennese court under Ferdinand II and III. Wrote vocal chamber concs., madrigals and church m.

Arroyo, João (b. Oporto, 1861), Port. comp. Studied at Oporto and Coimbra and was minister of arts and public educ. under King Manoel. Works incl. operas *O amor de Perdição* & *Leonora Telles*; *Poème symphonique* for orch., &c.

Ars antiqua (Lat. = Old Art). The old m. cultivated before the introd. of the

Ars nova in the 14th cent., based melodically on Plainsong and harmonically on the Organum or Diaphony.

Ars nova (Lat. = New Art). The new mus. style that came into vogue in the 14th cent., partic. at Florence, tending to free itself harmonically from the stiffness of Organum and abandoning the rhythmic indefiniteness of Plainsong. Also cultivated in Fr. by Vitry, Machaut and others.

Arsinoe, Queen of Cyprus, opera or pasticcio ? by Clayton (lib. by Peter Anthony Motteux from the It. by Tommaso Stanzani), prod. London, Drury Lane Theatre, 16. I. 1705.

Arsis. *See* **Metre.**

Art nouveau (Fr. = New Art). *See* **Ars nova.**

Art of Fugue, The. *See* **Kunst der Fuge.**

Artamene, opera by Albinoni (lib. by Bartolomeo Vitturi), prod. Venice, Teatro di Sant' Angelo, 26. XII. 1740.

Opera by Gluck (lib. do.), prod. London, King's Theatre, Haymarket, 4. III. 1746.

Artaserse (*Artaxerxes*), opera by Abos (lib. by Metastasio), prod. Venice, Teatro di San Giovanni Crisostomo, Carnival 1746.

Opera by Gluck (lib. do.), prod. Milan, Teatro Regio Ducal, 26. XII. 1741. Gluck's 1st opera.

Opera by Graun (lib. do.), prod. Berlin, Opera, 2. XII. 1743.

Opera by Hasse (lib. do.), prod. Venice, Teatro San Giovanni Crisostomo, II. 1730.

Opera by Jommelli (lib. do.), prod. Rome, Teatro Argentina, 4. II. 1749.

Opera by Terradellas (lib. do), prod. Venice, Teatro San Giovanni Crisostomo, Carnival 1744.

Opera by Vinci (lib. do.), prod. Rome, Teatro delle Dame, 4. II. 1730.

Artaxerxes, opera by **Arne** (lib. by comp., trans. from Metastasio's *Artaserse*), prod. London, Covent Garden Theatre, 2. II. 1762.

Arteaga, Stefano (b. Madrid, 1747; d. Paris, 30. X. 1799), Spa. priest & author. On the suppression of the Jesuit order in Spa. he went to It., living at Padua and Bologna. There he wrote a treatise on the rhythm of ancient m. (lost) and another on It. opera, *Rivoluzioni del teatro musicale italiano*, pub. 1783–8.

Arthur, Fanny. *See* **Robinson, Joseph.**

Arthurian Legends, the epic 12th–13th-cent. cycle of Brit. tales, written in medieval Fr. *See* **Albéniz (I.), Boughton, Draeseke** (*Merlin*), **Ladmirault** (*Tristan et Iseult*), **Lancelot and Elaine** (MacDowell), **Martin (F.)** (*Vin herbé* on *Tristram and Yseult*). **Marty** (*Merlin enchanté*), **Steggall** (*Elaine*), **Tristan und Isolde** (*Wagner*).

Artôt, Désirée (b. Paris, 21. VII. 1835; d. Berlin, 3. IV. 1907), Belg. m.-sop. singer. Pupil of Pauline Viardot-García. First sang at concerts in Belg., Hol. and Eng., but joined the Paris Opéra in 1858. Later appeared in It., Ger. and Rus. Married Mariano Padilla in 1869.

Arts Council (of Great Britain). A nat. organization formed in 1940 as the Council for the Encouragement of M. and the Arts (CEMA), whose charter was renewed in 1945 under the new title, which is preferable, because it does not suggest that m. is no art.

Artsibushev, Nikolai Vassilievitch (b. Tsarskoie Selo, 7. III. 1858; d. Paris, 15. IV. 1937), Rus. comp. & lawyer. Pupil of Rimsky-Korsakov and from 1920 dir. of Belaiev's m. pub. firm.

Works incl. *Valse-Fantasia* for orch.; Serenade for stg. 4tet.; pf. m., songs, &c.

Artusi, Giovanni Maria (b. Bologna, *c.* 1540; d. Bologna, 18. VIII. 1613), It. mus. scholar. Wrote several treatises attacking modern m.

Asbjørnsen, Peter Christen (1812–85), Dan. folklore collector & author. *See* **Delius** (*Eventyr*).

Ascanio in Alba, opera by Mozart (lib. by Giuseppe Parini), prod. Milan, Teatro Regio Ducal, 17. X. 1771.

Ashton, Algernon (Bennet Langton) (b. Durham, 9. XII. 1859; d. London, 10. IV. 1937), Eng. comp. Son of a lay clerk at Durham cath. He entered the Leipzig Cons. in 1874 and studied with Raff at Frankfort in 1880–1. Prof. of pf. at the R.A.M. in London, 1885–1910. Comp. a vast amount, esp. chamber m.

Ashwell, Thomas (b. ?; d. ?), Eng. 15th–16th-cent. comp. Choirmaster at Lincoln cath., 1508–18. Wrote church m., songs, &c.

Asioli, Bonifacio (b. Correggio, 30. VIII. 1769; d. Correggio, 18. V. 1832), It. mus. scholar & comp. Worked in his native town at the beginning and end of his career, but in between was at Turin, Venice, Milan, London and Paris. Wrote much church, stage, voc. & inst. m. and several theoret. treatises.

Asola, Giovanni Matteo (b. Verona, ?; d. Venice, 1. X. 1609), It. priest & comp. Chapel master successively at Treviso and Vicenza. Wrote church m., madrigals, &c.

Aspiration (Fr.). *See* **Ornaments.**

Asplmayr, Franz (b. ?, *c.* 1721; d. Vienna, 29. VII. 1786), Aus. comp. He was attached to the Aus. court in Vienna.

Works incl. pantomime *Macbeth*, play with m. *Der Sturm* (after Shakespeare's *Tempest*); ballets; incid. m.; syms.; chamber m.; v. sos., &c.

Assafiev, Boris Vladimirovitch (b. St. Petersburg, 29, VII. 1884), Rus. comp. & critic. Studied philos. at St. Petersburg Univ. and m. at the Cons., where he later became prof. Author of numerous books on comps., incl. Glinka, Tchaikovsky, Scriabin & Stravinsky, on Rus. & Cz. m., &c., written under the name of Igor Glebov.

Works incl. 9 operas, e.g. *Cinderella The Treasurer's Wife* (after Lermontov), *The Storm* (after Ostrovsky), *A Feast in Time of Plague* (Pushkin), *The Brass Horseman* (Pushkin); 15 ballets incl. *Solveig* (based on Grieg), *The Fountain of Bakhchisserai* (after Pushkin), *Lost Illusions* (after Balzac), *The Beauty is happy* (after Gorky's story *Makar Chudra*), *Christmas Eve* (after Gogol); incid. m. to Shakespeare's *Macbeth*, *Merchant of Venice* & *Othello*, Tirso de Molina's *Seducer of Seville* (*Don Juan*), Sophocles' *Oedipus Rex*, Schiller's *Fiesco* & *Don Carlos*; 4 syms., Sinfonietta for orch., Suvarov Suite for wind insts.; pf. Conc.; stg. 4tet; va. solo So., So. for tpt. & pf.; 6 Arias for co. & pf.; pf. works; chors.; songs, &c.

Assai (It.) = much, very.

Assmayr, Ignaz (b. Salzburg, 11. II. 1790; d. Vienna, 31. VIII. 1862), Aus. orgst. & comp. Held several orgst.'s posts at Salzburg and Vienna, was cond. of the Vienna Mus. Soc. and wrote orats. and much church and other m.

Astaritta, Gennaro (b. Naples, *c.* 1749; d. ?), It. comp. Chapel master at Naples in 1770; wrote *c.* 40 operas, 1765–93, incl. *Circe ed Ulisse.*

Astarto, opera by G. Bononcini (lib. by Paolo Antonio Rolli, based on one by Zeno and Pietro Pariati), prod. London, King's Theatre, Haymarket, 19. XI. 1720.

Aston, Hugh (b. ?, *c.* 1480; d. ?, *c.* 1520), Eng. comp. Nothing is certainly known of his life; he wrote church and virginal m.

Astorga, Emanuele (Gioacchino Cesare Rincón), d' (b. Augusta, Sicily, 20. III. 1680; d. Lisbon or Madrid, *c.* 1756), Spa. comp. Although a nobleman, he had a passion for m. and prod. a pastoral opera, *Dafni*, at Genoa on 21. IV. 1709 and at Barcelona in the summer. He visited Mantua, Vienna, Moravia and London, but returned to Palermo, where he was senator in 1717–8, but spent the rest of his life in Port. and Spa.

Works incl. *Stabat Mater*, chamber cantatas, &c.

Astuzie femminili, Le (*Women's Wiles*), opera by Cimarosa (lib. by Giovanni Palomba), prod. Naples, Teatro del Fondo, 16. VIII. 1794.

At the Boar's Head, opera by Holst (lib. by comp., drawn from Shakespeare's *Henry IV*), prod. Manchester, 3. IV. 1925.

At the Old Bleaching-Ground (*Na Starém Bělidle*), opera by Kovařovic (lib. by Karel Šipek, based on Božena Němcová's novel *Babička*), prod. Prague, Cz. Theatre, 22. XI. 1901. An opera on the same subject, *Babička* (*Grandmother*), by Antonín Horák (1875–1910), was prod. at the same theatre, 3. III. 1900.

Atalanta, opera by Handel (lib. by ?), prod. London, Covent Garden Theatre, 12. V. 1736.

Atfield, John (b. ?; d. ?), Eng. 18th-cent. comp. Wrote songs pub. between 1735–50.

Athalia, orat. by Handel (words by Samuel Humphreys), prod. Oxford, 10. VII. 1733.

Athalie, incid. m. for Racine's tragedy by Mendelssohn, Op. 74; chors. comp. 1843, ovt. 1844–5, prod. Charlottenburg, 1. XII. 1845.

The chors. were also set by Moreau (Saint-Cyr, 5. I. 1691), Gossec (1785), Vogler (1786), J. A. P. Schulz (1786) & Boïeldieu (1836).

Atonality. A modern term for m. not written in definite keys. Also called Pantonality.

Attacca (It. imper. = attack, begin). A direction placed at the end of a mvt. indicating that the next mvt. is to be started without a pause.

Attacco (It. = attack). A short mus. figure or phrase treated by imitation.

Attaingnant, Pierre (b. ?; d. Paris, *c.* 1552), Fr. m. printer. He pub. many important m. books between 1525 and his death, and his widow (*née* Pigouchet), whose father he had succeeded, continued after 1553.

Attaque du moulin, L' (*The Attack on the Mill*), opera by Bruneau (lib. by Louis Gallet, based on Zola's story in *Soirées de Médan*), prod. Paris, Opéra-Comique, 23. XI. 1893.

Attenhofer, Karl (b. Wettingen, Aargau, 5. V. 1837; d. Zürich, 22. V. 1914), Swi. cond. & comp. Studied at the Leipzig Cons. and later became a chor. cond. at Rapperswil and Zürich and organizer of nat. singing festivals. Joint dir. with Hegar of the Zürich Cons. from 1896. Wrote numerous popular partsongs for male and mixed voices, also some church and chamber m.

Atterberg, Kurt (b. Göteborg, 12. XII. 1887), Swe. comp. & cond. First trained as a civil engineer, he studied m. at the R.A.M. in Stockholm under Hallén, and later at Munich, Berlin & Stuttgart. M. critic of *Stockholms Tidningen* since 1919. Has cond. much in Swe., Fr. & Ger.

Works incl. 3 operas; pantomime-ballet; incid. m. for plays; Requiem, *The Land of the Railway Porters*, for chor. & orch.; 6 syms. (1 in memory of Schubert), 8 suites, *Swe. Rhapsody*, symph. poem *Le Fleuve*, *Rondeau rétrospectif* & *The Song* for orch.; symph. poem for bar. & orch.; concs. for v., co., pf. & hn.; stg. 4tet; co. & pf. So., &c.

Atterbury, Luffman (b. ? London, ?; d. London, 11. VI. 1796), Eng. comp. Orig. a carpenter; became musn. to George III. He wrote many glees & catches, also an orat., *Goliah*, prod. in 1773.

Attey, John (b. ?; d. Ross, *c.* 1640), Eng. lutenist & comp. Pub. a *First Booke of Ayres* to the lute in 1622, later than all other similar pubs.

Attila, opera by Verdi (lib. by Temistocle Solera), prod. Venice, Teatro La Fenice, 17. III. 1846.

Attwood, Thomas (b. London, 23. XI. 1765; d. London, 24. III. 1838), Eng. orgst. & comp. Boy chorister in the Chapel Royal in London; studied at Naples and under Mozart in Vienna. Orgst. of St. Paul's cath. in London, 1796 to his death. One of the founders of the Phil. Soc. in 1813 and prof. at the R.A.M. from its foundation in 1823.

Works incl. *c.* 24 stage pieces; songs to a dram. version of Scott's *Guy Mannering*; sos. and lessons for pf.; songs; services, anthems, chants & other church m.; coronation anthems for George IV and William IV. He died when engaged on a 3rd for Queen Victoria.

Atys, opera by Lully (lib. by Philippe Quinault), prod. at Saint-Germain, 10. I., and 1st perf. Paris, IV. 1676.

Opera by Piccinni (lib. do., altered by Jean François Marmontel), prod. Paris, Opéra, 22. II. 1780.

Aubade (Fr. from *aube* = dawn) = morning song, in the same sense that a serenade is an evening song; cf. Spa. *Alborada.*

Auber, Daniel François Esprit (b. Caen, 29. I. 1782; d. Paris, 12. V. 1871), Fr. comp. Began to comp. early, but went to London as a young man to follow a commercial career. He attracted attention with his songs, however, and on his return to Paris in 1804 wrote co. concs. for the cst. Lamarre and a v. Conc. for Mazas. In 1805 he appeared with a comic opera, *L'Erreur d'un moment*, the lib. of which had previously been set by Dezède, but did not prod. an opera in public until 1813 (*Le Séjour militaire*) and had no real success until 1820 (*La Bergère châtelaine*). In 1842 he became dir. of the Paris Cons. and in 1857 of the imp. chapel.

Works incl. nearly 50 operas incl. *Emma, Leicester, Le Maçon, La Muette de Portici* (*Masaniello*), *La Fiancée, Fra Diavolo, Le Dieu et la Bayadère, Le Philtre, Le Serment, Gustave III, Le Cheval de bronze* (2 versions), *Actéon, L'Ambassadrice, Le Domino noir, Les Diamants de la couronne, La Part du diable, Haydée, Marco Spada* (with a later ballet version), *Jenny Bell, Manon Lescaut, La Circassienne,* &c.

Aubert, Jacques (b. ?, 1678; d. Belleville nr. Paris, 19. V. 1753), Fr. vst. & comp. Pupil of Senaillé; member of the king's 24 vs. from 1727 and of the Paris Opéra orch. from 1728. Wrote numerous v. concs., concert suites & other inst. works.

Aubert, Louis (b. Paris, 15. V. 1720; d. ? Paris, *c.* 1800), Fr. vst. & comp., son of prec. He was vst. and 2nd cond. at the Paris Opéra, 1731–74. Wrote sos. and other works for his inst.

Aubert, Louis (François Marie) (b. Paramé, Ille-et-Vilaine, 19. II. 1877), Fr. pfst., comp., critic & teacher. Studied at the Paris Cons., finally under Fauré.

Works incl. opera *La Forêt bleue*; ballets *La Momie* & *Chrysothémis*; incid. m. for Jean Bertheroy's *La Moisson*; some church m.; symph. poem *Habanera*; *Fantaisie* for pf. & orch.; *Suite brève* for 2 pfs. (later orch.); pf. suite *Sillages*; song cycle *Crépuscules d'automne,* &c.

Aubin, Tony (Louis Alexandre) (b. Paris, 8. XII. 1907), Fr. comp. Studied at the Paris Cons., where Dukas was his comp. master. Took the Prix de Rome in 1930. In 1939 he was app. head of the m. dept. of the Paris-Mondial wireless station.

Works incl. suite *Cressida* for solo voices, chor. & orch.; cantata *Actéon*; *Symphonie romantique* & *Le Sommeil d'Iskander* for orch.; stg. 4tet; So. & *Prélude, Récitatif et Final* for pf.; 6 Verlaine songs, &c.

Aubry, Pierre (b. Paris, 14. II. 1874; d. Dieppe, 31. X. 1910), Fr. mcolst. & orientalist. Lectured on mus. hist. at the École des Hautes Études Sociales in Paris; wrote several works on medieval m., esp. that of the troubadours.

Aucassin et Nicolette, ou Les Mœurs du bon vieux temps, opera by Grétry (lib. by Jean Michel Sedaine, based on a Fr. 13th-cent. tale), prod. Versailles, at court, 30. XII. 1779, 1st Paris perf., Comédie-Italienne. 3. I. 1780.

See also **Fickenscher, Le Flem, Lyon, Parker (C.), Rossellini.**

Aucassin og Nicolette, opera by Enna

(lib. in Dan., by Sophus Michaelis, based on the Fr. 13th-cent. tale), prod. Copenhagen, 2. II. 1896.

Auden, W(ystan). H(ugh). (b. 1907), Eng. poet. See **Britten** (*Paul Bunyan, Ascent of F.6, Ode to St. Cecilia, Our Hunting Fathers* & *On this Island*).

Audran, Edmond (b. Lyons, 11. IV. 1842; d. Tierceville, 17. VIII. 1901), Fr. comp. Studied at Niedermeyer's school in Paris and 1st made his mark as a church orgst. and comp. at Marseilles and Paris, prod. a mass; but later with operettas, the 1st of which, *L'Ours et le Pacha*, was prod. at Marseilles in 1862. The 1st prod. in Paris (1879) was *Les Noces d'Olivette*. Others incl. *La Mascotte, Gillette de Narbonne* (based on Boccaccio), *La Cigale et la Fourmi* (based on La Fontaine), *La Poupée, Monsieur Lohengrin*, &c.

Auer, Leopold (b. Veszprém, 7. VII. 1845; d. Loschwitz, 17. VII. 1930), Hung. vst. Pupil of Dont in Vienna and Joachim at Hanover. Prof. at the St. Petersburg Cons. from 1868. Went to U.S.A. after the Rus. Revolution. Teacher of many eminent vsts.

Aufforderung zum Tanz (*Invitation to the Dance*—not 'Waltz'). A pf. piece by Weber, Op. 65, which he calls a *rondeau brillant*, in waltz form with a slow introd. and epilogue, comp. in 1819.

Aufgesang (Ger. = Fore-song). *See* **Stollen.**

Auftakt (Ger.) = Upbeat.

Augenarzt, Der (*The Oculist*), opera by Gyrowetz (lib. by Johann Emanuel Veith), prod. Vienna, Kärntnertor Theatre, 1. X. 1811.

Augmentation. The enlargement of a mus. figure or phrase by lengthening, usually doubling, the note-values.

Augmented. Said of intervals which are normally 'perfect' (4ths, 5ths, 8ves) when they have been made wider by a semitone.

Aulin, Tor (b. Stockholm, 10. IX. 1866; d. Stockholm, 1. III. 1914), Swe. vst., cond. & comp. He founded a stg. 4tet in 1887 and became leader of the Royal Opera orch. at Stockholm in 1889. Wrote 3 v. concs., many smaller pieces for v. and misc. works.

Aulos (Gr.). An inst. usually described as the ancient forerunner of the fl., but played with a reed, and thus nearer the ob. or cl.

Aureliano in Palmira, opera by Rossini (lib. by Felice Romani), prod. Milan, Teatro alla Scala, 26. XII. 1813. The overture was afterwards used for *Elisabetta regina d'Inghilterra*, and later for *Il Barbiere di Siviglia*. Other parts of the m. also appear in the latter work.

Auric, Georges (b. Lodève, Hérault, 15. II. 1899), Fr. comp. Studied at the Paris Cons. and the Schola Cantorum. Member of the group of 'Les Six' and influenced by Satie and later by Stravinsky.

Works incl. comic opera *Sous le masque* (lib. by Louis Laloy); ballets *Les Noces de Gamache* (from *Don Quixote*), *Les Matelots, La Pastorale, La Concurrence, Les Imaginaires*; incid. m. to *Les Fâcheux* (Molière), *The Birds* (Aristophanes), *Volpone* (Ben Jonson), *La Mariage de Figaro* (Beaumarchais), *Le 14 Juillet* (Rolland, with 6 others); film m. *A nous la liberté* (René Clair), *Caesar and Cleopatra* (after Bernard Shaw), &c.; Sym., Suite, Ovt., *Fox-trot* & *Nocturne* for orch.; pf. Conc.; pf. So. & Sonatina, *3 Pastorales* for pf.; *Chandelles romaines* for pf. duet; Trio for ob., cl. & bn.; v. & pf. So.; several song cycles, &c.

Aus. (abbr.) = Austria, Austrian.

Aus Italien (*From Italy*), sym. by R. Strauss, Op. 16, comp. 1886 during and after a visit to It., 1st perf. Munich, 2. III. 1887. The 4 mvts. are entitled *On the Campagna, The Ruins of Rome, On the Shore of Sorrento* & *Neapolitan Folk Life*, and the last contains a quotation of Denza's *Funiculì, funiculà*, which S. took for a folksong.

Austin, Alfred (1835–1913), Eng. poet & dramatist. *See* **Pitt** (*Flodden Field*).

Austin, Ernest (b. London, 31. XII. 1874), Eng. comp. Did not take up comp. until he was 33.

Works incl. Vars. on *The Vicar of Bray* for stg. orch.; 12 tone-poems for org. on Bunyan's *Pilgrim's Progress*; numerous chamber & pf. works.

Austin, Frederic (b. London, 30. III. 1872), Eng. bar. singer & comp. Began his career as orgst. and m. teacher at Liverpool, but came out as a singer in 1902 and in opera at Covent Garden Theatre, London, in 1908. Artistic dir. of the B.N.O.C. from 1924. He arr. *The Beggar's Opera* for the revival at the Lyric Theatre, Hammersmith, London, in 1920, and the sequel, *Polly*, for that at the Kingsway Theatre in 1922.

Works incl. Sym. in E maj.; symph. poems *Spring* & *Palsgaard*; incid. m. to Čapek's *Insect Play*, Congreve's *The Way of the World*, Beaumont & Fletcher's *The Knight of the Burning Pestle*; *Pervigilium Veneris* for chor. & orch., &c.

Austin, Robert (b. Birmingham, 7. I. 1914), Eng. orgst., pfst. & comp. Studied mineralogy at Birmingham

Univ., later became an architect and is largely self-taught in m. Asst. orgst. at the Church of the Messiah in Birmingham from 1932 and app. orgst. and choirmaster in 1943. He married the singer Eileen Markham in 1939. In 1941 he became mus. dir. of the Midland Organization for Troop Entertainment and gave over 100 voluntary perfs. with it; also many 2-pf. broadcasts with Jane Minton in 1936–9.

Works incl. incid. m. for Molière's *Malade imaginaire*; m. for 2 revues; anthem, carols and Psalm cxxii for VE Day, 1945; Symph. Vars. & Suite for orch.; *Dream Dance* & Sketches for stg. orch.; Conc. for stg. 4tet & orch., Conc. & *Nursery Waltz* for pf. & stgs.; *The Night* for sop., chor. & chamber orch.; 3 fantasies and scherzo on folksongs for broadcast variety orch.; stg. 4tet, Elegy for stg. octet, pf. 5tet; *Introduction & Allegro moderato* for co. & pf.; pf. pieces; song cycles *The Hill* (Rupert Brooke) & *Al' on a summer's day* & many other songs, &c.

Australian Composers. *See* **Agnew, Benjamin, Clutsam, Glanville-Hicks, Grainger.**

Authentic Cadence. A cadence (full close) which moves to a conclusive common chord of the Tonic by way of Dominant harmony, as distinct from the Plagal C., which approaches the tonic through the Subdominant.

Authentic Modes. *See* **Modes.**

Auxcousteaux, Artus (or Arthur) (b. ?; d. ?, 1656), Fr. singer & comp. He was a singer in Louis XIII's chapel *c.* 1613–27 and (?) at Noyon; later m. master at the cath. of Saint-Quentin and singer in the Sainte-Chapelle in Paris, becoming chaplain, precentor and canon at later dates.

Works incl. masses, magnificats, *Noëls* & other church m.

Averkamp, Anton (b. Cabauw nr. Schoonhoven, 18. II. 1861; d. Bussum, 1. VI. 1934), Dutch cond., mcolst. & comp. Studied at Amsterdam, Berlin & Munich and later founded a chor. soc. at Amsterdam, for which he ed. much old Dutch and other m. Dir. of the Utrecht School of M.

Works incl. a Sym., many songs, &c.

Avison, Charles (b. Newcastle-on-Tyne, *c.* 1710; d. Newcastle, 9. V. 1770), Eng. orgst. & comp. Studied in It. and later with Geminiani in Eng. App. orgst. of St. Nicholas's church at Newcastle, 1736. In 1752 he wrote a book on mus. expression and in 1757 ed. Marcello's psalms with Eng. words and a biog. Comp. concs. for orch. & var. insts.

Avolio (or Avoglio). Signora (b. ?; d. ?), It. 18th-cent. sop. singer. Nothing is known of her career except that she sang for Handel. She was the sop. in the 1st perf. of *Messiah.*

Avondano, Pedro Antonio (b. Lisbon, ?; d. Lisbon, 1782), Port. vst. & comp. of It. descent.

Works incl. comic opera *Il mondo della luna*; sacred dramas *Il voto di Jefte* & *Adamo ed Eva*; *Sinfonia* for stgs.; ? church m. & hpchd. pieces destroyed in the Lisbon earthquake of 1755.

Axman, Emil (b. Ratay, Moravia, 3. VI. 1887), Cz. comp. Studied at Prague Univ. and was a comp. student of Novák.

Works incl. melodrama *Just Once*; cantatas & other chor. works; 5 syms., symph. poems *Sorrow and Hope* & *Light*, Suite, Sinfonietta, suite *From the Beskides*, Morav. Dances for orch.; v. Conc.; 3 stg. 4tets, pf. Trio; v. & pf. So., co. & pf. So.; 3 pf. sos., Sonatina & other pf. works, &c.

Axur (Salieri). *See* **Tarare.**

Aylward, Theodore (b. ?, 1730; d. London, 27. II. 1801), Eng. orgst. & comp. Orgst. at several London churches. Mus.D., Oxford; app. Prof. of M. at Gresham Coll., London, 1771.

Works incl. incid. m. for Shakespeare's *Cymbeline* & *Midsummer Night's Dream*; lessons for org.; canzonets for 2 voices; glees, catches & songs, &c.

Ayre (old Eng.). A 16th–17th-cent. song with predominantly melodic, as distinct from harmonic or ctptal, interest.

Ayrton, Edmund (b. Ripon, 1734; d. London, 22. V. 1808), Eng. orgst. & comp. Studied with Nares at York Minster, became orgst. & choirmaster at Southwell Minster in 1764, vicar-chor. at St. Paul's cath. in London, 1767, and lay clerk at Westminster Abbey in 1780, also Master of the Children at the Chapel Royal. Mus.D., Cambridge, 1784. Comp. services and anthems.

Ayrton, William (b. London, 24. III. 1777; d. London, 8. III. 1858), Eng. writer on m., son of prec. Lived in London. Ed. of the *Harmonicon,* mus. contrib. to the *Morning Chronicle* and the *Examiner,* married a daughter of Arnold; one of the founders of the Phil. Soc. in 1813.

Azione sacra (It. = sacred action). A 17th–18th-cent. term for a sacred drama with m. or acted orat.

Azione teatrale (It. = theatrical action). A 17th-cent. term for an opera or mus. festival play.

(Mark reference p. 15).

Amfiparnaso, L' (*The Amphi-Parnassus*), madrigal opera by Orazio Vecchi, prod. Modena, 1594, and pub. Venice, 1597, described as a *commedia harmonica.* It consists of 3 acts and a prologue, and the characters are the stock figures of the *commedia dell' arte,* but the mus. setting of their speech is in the form of madrigals for mixed voices. It has been supposed that the action was prod. in dumb-show while the madrigals were sung behind the scenes, but a passage in the text which says that 'the spectacle is to enter by the ear, not by the eye' gives good reason to doubt this. The same subject was treated earlier in a smaller form by Lassus.

(Mark reference p. 21)

Ariette (Fr. =little aria or air). Now the same as an *arietta,* but in 18th-cent. Fr. a song specially comp. for insertion into a spoken play or 'opera,' as distinct from the Vaudeville, which was a popular song introd. with new words forming part of the play.

B

B. The note bounding the range of the scales of B maj. & min., and of the Locrian or Hyperaeolian (rejected) and Hypophrygian (Gr. Hypodorian) modes. In Ger. the symbol for B♮ is H, B being B♭.

B.A.C.H. A mus. theme formed of the notes B♭, A, C, B♮, in Ger. nomenclature (*see* above) and used by var. comps. as a ref. to Bach, who was himself the 1st to use it. Here are some exs.:

Albrechtsberger, Fugue for org.

Bach, one of the subjects of the final fugue (unfinished) in *The Art of Fugue* (4 org. fugues are prob. spurious).

Barblan, Passacaglia for org.

Busoni, *Fantasia contrappuntistica* for pf.

Casella, *Ricercari sul nome di Bach* for pf.

Eisler, Trio on the 12-note scale.

d'Indy, *Beuron* in *Tableaux de voyage* for pf.

Karg-Elert, *Basso ostinato* in org. pieces *Semplice*, Op. 42.

Liszt, Fantasy & Fugue for org.

Nielsen (R.), Ricercare, Chorale & Toccata for pf.

Reger, Fantasy & Fugue for org.

Rimsky-Korsakov, Fugue in *Chopsticks* Vars. for pf. by var. comps.; 6 vars. for pf., Op. 10.

Schumann, 6 Fugues for org. or pedal pf.

B.B.C. *See* **British Broadcasting Corporation.**

B-la-F Quartet, a stg. 4tet on the name of Belaiev by Rimsky-Korsakov, Liadov, Borodin & Glazunov, perf. on M. P. Belaiev's 50th birthday, 22. II. 1886. It is constructed on the notes B♭, A, F.

B minor Mass. Bach's great Mass opening and concluding in that key, but with the key of D maj. predominating during its course, begun in 1733 with the 'Kyrie' and 'Gloria' only, designed as a Lutheran short Mass, and presented to the Elector Frederick Augustus of Saxony with a petition for the title of Court Comp.; completed later as a full Mass for the Rom. Catholic church, but on a scale too large for the normal service. Portions of it were taken from church cantatas Nos. 11, 12, 29, 46, 78, 120 & 171 and the secular cantata *Preise dein Glücke.*

B.Mus. *See* **Mus.B.**

B.N.O.C. *See* **British Nationa Opera Company.**

Babán, Gracián (b. ?; d. ?), Spa. 17th-cent. comp. Chapel master at Valencia cath. from 1657 for nearly 20 years. Comp. masses, psalms, lamentations & other church m.

Babbini, Matteo (b. Bologna, 19. II. 1754; d. Bologna, 22. IX. 1816), It. ten. singer. Began his career in the service of Frederick II of Prus. and Catherine II of Rus.; afterwards sang in Vienna, London, It. and again in Berlin.

Babell, William (b. ?, *c.* 1690; d. London, 23. IX. 1723), Eng. hpchdst., vst. & comp. Member of the royal band in London and for some years orgst. at All Hallows church.

Works incl. chamber m.; hpchd. pieces, airs from operas arr. for hpchd., &c.

Baby Grand (Piano). A grand pf. of the smallest size.

Baborácka. A Cz. folk dance in moderate 3–4 time.

Baborák. A Cz. folk dance in ternary form, the 1st and 3rd sections, in the tonic, and the 2nd, in the dominant, consisting of 8-bar phrases in 2–4 time, the whole being afterwards repeated in 3–4 time.

Bacarisse, Salvador (b. Madrid, 12. IX. 1898), Spa. comp. Studied at the Madrid Cons., Conrado del Campo being his comp. master. He became mus. dir. of the Unión Radio in Madrid, 1925.

Works incl. opera *Charlot*; Ballet *Corrida de feria*; *Tres marchas burlescas*, *Heraldos*, *Concertino*, *Música sinfónica*, *Serenata*, *Impromptu* for orch.; chor. sym. *La nave de Ulises*; pf. Conc., co. Conc.; 2 stg. 4tets; trio-so. for fl., co. & hp.; *Tres nanas* for voice & chamber orch.; *Ofrenda a Debussy*, *Tres canciones* & other songs; pf. pieces, &c.

Bacchantinnen, Die (*The Bacchantes*), opera by Wellesz (lib. by comp., based on Euripides), prod. Vienna, Opera, 20. VI. 1931.

Baccusi, Ippolito (b. Mantua, ?; d. Verona, 1609), It. comp. Worked at Ravenna, Mantua and Verona, being chapel master of the caths. of the last 2.

Works incl. masses, motets, psalms, madrigals, &c.

Bach. Ger. 16th–18th-cent. family of musns.:

1. Hans B. (b. ?, *c.* 1520; d. Wechmar nr. Gotha, ?).
2. Veit B. (b. ? Wechmar, ?; d. Wechmar, 8. III. 1619), ? son of prec.
3. Lips (Philippus) B. (b. Wechmar, ?; d. ? Wechmar, 10. X. 1620), son of prec.
4. Johannes (Hans) B. (b. Wechmar, ?; d. Wechmar, 1626), brother of prec.
5. Johannes B. (b. Wechmar, 26. XI. 1604; d. ? Erfurt, 13. V. 1673), son of prec.
6. Christoph B. (b. Wechmar, 19. IV. 1613; d. Arnstadt, 12. IX. 1661), brother of prec.
7. Heinrich B. (b. Wechmar, 16. IX. 1615; d. Arnstadt, 10. VII. 1692), brother of prec.
8. Johann Christian B. (b. Erfurt, 25. VIII. 1640; d. Erfurt, 11. VI. 1682), son of 5.
9. Georg Christoph B. (b. Erfurt, 6. IX. 1642; d. Schweinfurt, 24. IV. 1697), son of 6.
10. Johann Christoph B. (b. Arnstadt, 8. XII. 1642; d. Eisenach, 31. III. 1703), son of 7.
11. Johann Aegidius B. (b. Erfurt, 9. II. 1645; d. Erfurt, 1716), son of 5, brother of 8.
12. Johann Christoph B. (b. Erfurt, 22. II. 1645; d. Arnstadt, 25. VIII. 1693), son of 6.
13. Johann Ambrosius B. (b. Erfurt, 22. II. 1645; d. Eisenach, I. 1695), son of 6, twin brother of 12, father of 26.
14. Johann Michael B. (b. Arnstadt, 6. VIII. 1648; d. Gehren, V. 1694), son of 7, father of 25.
15. Johann Günther B. (b. Arnstadt, 17. VII. 1653; d. Arnstadt, 8. IV. 1683), son of 7.
16. Johann Nikolaus B. (b. Eisenach, 10. X. 1669; d. Jena, 4. XI. 1753), son of 10.
17. Johann Christoph B. (b. Erfurt, 16. VI. 1671; d. Ohrdruf, 22. II. 1721), son of 13, brother of 26.
18. Johann Christoph B. (b. Eisenach, 27. VIII. 1674; d. ? Eng., ? 1740), son of 10.
19. Johann Friedrich B. (b. Eisenach, *c.* 1675; d. Mühlhausen, 1730), brother of prec.
20. Johann Michael B. (b. Eisenach, *c.* 1676; d. ?), brother of prec.
21. Johann Bernhard B. (b. Erfurt, 23. XI. 1676; d. Eisenach, 11. VI. 1749), son of 11.
22. Johann Ludwig B. (b. ?, 1677; d. ? Meiningen, *c.* 1710), descendant of 3.
23. Johann Jakob B. (b. Eisenach, 9. II. 1682; d. ? Stockholm, ? 1722), son of 13, brother of 26.
24. Johann Ernst B. (b. Arnstadt, 8. VIII. 1683; d. Arnstadt, 21. III. 1739), son of 12.
25. Maria Barbara B. (b. Gehren, 20. X. 1684; d. Cöthen, VII. 1720), daughter of 14, 1st wife of 26.
26. Johann Sebastian B. (b. Eisenach, 21. III. 1685; d. Leipzig, 28. VII. 1750), son of 13, husband of 25 & 29.
27. Johann Christoph B. (b. Erfurt, 15. VIII. 1685; d. Erfurt, *c.* 1740), son of 11.
28. Johann Lorenz B. (b. ?, 10. IX. 1695; d. Lahm, 14. XII. 1773), grandson of 9.
29. Anna Magdalena B. (*née* Wilcken), (b. 22. IX. 1701; d. 27. II. 1760), 2nd wife of 26.
30. Johann Elias B. (b. ?, 12. II. 1705; d. Schweinfurt, 30. XI. 1755), grandson of 9, brother of 28.
31. Samuel Anton B. (b. Meiningen, *c.* 1710; d. ?, 1781), son of 22.
32. Johann Ernst B. (b. Eisenach, 1. IX. 1722; d. Eisenach, 28. I. 1777), son of 21.
33. Johann Michael B. (b. Schweinfurt, 1754; d. ?), son of 30.

Children of Johann Sebastian Bach (26) by 25:

34. Catharina Dorothea B. (b. Weimar, 29. XII. 1708; d. 14. I. 1774).
35. Wilhelm Friedemann B. (b. Weimar, 22. XI. 1710; d. Berlin, 1. VII. 1784).
36. Johann Christoph B. (b. & d. Weimar, 23. II. 1713). Twin.
37. Maria Sophie B. (b. & d. Weimar, 23. II. 1713). Twin.
38. Carl Philipp Emanuel B. (b. Weimar, 8. III. 1714; d. Hamburg, 15. XII. 1788).
39. Johann Gottfried Bernhard B. (b. Weimar, 11. V. 1715; d. Jena, 27. V. 1739).
40. Leopold Augustus B. (b. Cöthen, 15. XI. 1718; d. Cöthen, 28. IX. 1719).

Children of Johann Sebastian Bach (26) by 29:

41. Christiane Sophie Henrietta B. (b. Cöthen or Leipzig, 1723; d. Leipzig, 29. VI. 1726).
42. Gottfried Heinrich B. (b. Leipzig, 26. II. 1724; d. Naumburg, 12. II. 1763).
43. Christian Gottlieb B. (b. Leipzig, 14. IV. 1725; d. 21. IX. 1728).
44. Elisabetha Juliane Frederica B. (b. Leipzig, 5. IV. 1726; d. Naumburg, 25. VII. 1759), married Johann Christoph Altnikol.
45. Ernestus Andreas B. (b. Leipzig, 30. X. 1727; d. Leipzig, 1. XI. 1727).
46. Regine Johanne B. (b. Leipzig, 10. X. 1728; d. Leipzig, 21. IV. 1733).
47. Christiane Benedicta B. (b.

Leipzig, 31. XII. 1729; d. Leipzig, 4. I. 1730.)

48. Christiane Dorothea B. (b. Leipzig, 18. III. 1731; d. Leipzig, 31, VIII. 1732).

49. Johann Christoph Friedrich B. (b. Leipzig, 21. VI. 1732; d. Bückeburg, 26. I. 1795).

50. Johann August Abraham B. (b. Leipzig, 4. XI. 1733; d. Leipzig, 6. XI. 1733).

51. Johann Christian B. (b. Leipzig, 5. IX. 1735; d. London, 1. I. 1782).

52. Johanne Caroline B. (b. Leipzig, 30. X. 1737; d. 16. VIII. 1781).

53. Regine Susanna B. (b. Leipzig, 22. II. 1742; d. 14. XII. 1809).

Bach, Carl Philipp Emanuel (b. Weimar, 8. III. 1714; d. Hamburg, 15. XII. 1788), Ger. clav. player & comp. (38 above). Son of J. S. & Maria Barbara B. (26 & 25 above). Educ. under his father at St. Thomas's school, Leipzig. Entered the Univ. of Frankfort o/Oder in 1734, when he was already an accomplished hpdch. player and had written m. for his inst. He was engaged as domestic musn. by the crown prince Frederick of Prus. at Rheinsberg shortly before he succeeded to the throne as Frederick II in 1740, when B. remained attached to the royal household at Potsdam and Berlin. In 1744 he married Johanna Maria Dannemann and in 1747 he induced his father to visit the Prus. court. As a clav. comp. he progressed steadily in developing so. form and changing his style from the old hpdch. manner to one better suited to the modern pf., and in 1753 & 1762 he pub. the 2 parts of his treatise on keyboard playing, *Versuch über die wahre Art das Clavier zu spielen*. His servitude irked him because of the rigid discipline at court and Frederick's determination to direct the m. in his own conservative and wilful way; but it was not until 1767 that he succeeded in freeing himself and taking Telemann's place as cantor at the Johanneum at Hamburg and dir. of the m. at the 5 principal churches. He remained there to the end and gave many concerts.

Works incl. church m.; 2 passions, 2 orats., church cantatas; setting of Klopstock's *Morgengesang am Schöpfungstage*, sacred & secular odes; syms.; concs. for keyboard & other insts.; chamber m.; keyboard sos., rondos & other pieces; songs, &c.

Bach, Johann Ambrosius (b. Erfurt, 22. II. 1645; d. Eisenach, I. 1695), Ger. orgst. & comp. (13 above). Born as the twin of Johann Christoph B. (12 above) and taught by his father Christoph B. (6 above). He became town musn. at Erfurt in 1667, marrying Elisabeth Lämmerhirt there on 8. IV. 1668. In 1671 he was app. town musn. at Eisenach. His wife d. on 3. V. 1694, and he married Barbara Margaretha Keul on 27. XI, but d. himself 2 months later.

Bach, Johann (John) Christian (b. Leipzig, 5. IX. 1735; d. London, 1. I. 1782), Ger. clav. player & comp. (51 above). Son of J. S. & Anna Magdalena B. (26 & 29 above). Pupil of his father, and after 1750 prob. of Johann Elias B. (30 above), then at St. Thomas's school and of his brother Carl Philipp Emanuel (38 above) in Berlin. In 1756 he went to It., working at Milan, embracing Roman catholicism and writing m. for his adopted church. In 1761 he prod. his 1st opera at Turin. In 1762 he went to London, where he remained for the rest of his life. His 1st opera prod. there was *Orione*, 19. II. 1763. A year later he gave the 1st of the concerts he had organized with Abel, and the same year Mozart, at the age of 8, came under his influence. He married the singer Cecilia Grassi, *c.* 1773, visited Mannheim in 1772 and 1776 and Paris in 1778–9, prod. a Fr. opera there, 14. XII. 1779.

Works incl. operas *Artaserse, Catone in Utica, Alessandro nell' Indie* (all Metastasio), *Orione, ossia Diana vendicata, Zanaida, Adriano in Siria, Carattaco, La clemenza di Scipione, Temistocle, Lucio Silla, Amadis de Gaule*; orat. *Gioas rè di Giuda*; much Lat. church m.; anthem *Let the solemn organs blow*; songs for Eng. plays; many syms., ovts. and syms. with solo insts.; *c.* 40 pf. concs.; *c.* 20 stg. 4tets & other chamber m.; many pf. trios and v. & pf. sos.; *c.* 30 pf. sos. and a number of other works for pf.; some m. for military band; It. cantatas and arias; 3 books and some separate Eng. songs; 12 voc. duets, &c.

Bach, Johann Christoph (b. Arnstadt, 8. XII. 1642; d. Eisenach, 31. III, 1703), Ger. orgst. & comp. (10 above). Became orgst. at Eisenach in 1665 and remained there to the end of his life. Comp. motets, church cantatas, chorale preludes for org. and hpchd. m.

Bach, Johann Christoph (b. Erfurt, 16. VI. 1671; d. Ohrdruf, 22. II. 1721), Ger. orgst. (17 above). Pupil of Pachelbel at Erfurt. In X. 1694 he married Dorothea von Hof and the next year he took his young brother Johann Sebastian (26 above) into his house after their parents' death.

Bach, Johann Christoph Friedrich (b. Leipzig, 21. VI. 1732; d. Bückeburg, 26. I. 1795), Ger. comp. (49 above). Son of J. S. & Anna Magdalena B. (26 & 29 above). He was a student at Leipzig Univ. and in 1750 became chamber musn. to Count Wilhelm of Schaumburg-Lippe at Bückeburg, where he remained all his life. He married the court singer Lucia Elisabeth Münchhausen in 1755. Herder became court poet in 1771 and provided words for orats. and cantatas for him, also for an opera *Brutus*, perf. at Bückeburg, 1775. In 1778 he visited his brother Johann Christian in London.

Works incl. orats. (words by Herder) *Die Kindheit Jesu*, *Die Auferweckung Lazarus* & *Der Fremdling auf Golgatha*; secular cantatas (some with Herder); Passion *Der Tod Jesu* (words by Ramler); motets; 14 syms.; pf. concs. & sos; stg. 4tets & other chamber m., &c.

Bach, Johann Michael (b. Arnstadt, 9. VIII. 1648; d. Gehren, V. 1694), Ger. orgst., inst. maker & comp. (14 above). Orgst. and parish clerk at Gehren from 1673. Comp. motets, sacred arias, &c.

Bach, Johann Sebastian (b. Eisenach, 21. III. 1685; d. Leipzig, 28. VII. 1750), Ger. comp., orgst. & teacher (26 above). Learnt m. from his brother Johann Christoph B. from 1695, after the death of his parents. At 15 became a chorister at Lüneburg and took org. lessons from Böhm there. App. by the Duke of Weimar in 1703, but left for orgst.'s post at Arnstadt; refused the succession to Buxtehude's post at Lübeck in 1705, but left Arnstadt for Mühlhausen in 1707, when he married his cousin Maria Barbara B. Returned to Weimar in 1708 and remained until 1717, when he went into the service of Prince Leopold of Anhalt-Cöthen. His wife died at Cöthen in 1720, and he married Anna Magdalena Wilcken in 1721. Left for Leipzig in 1723, being app. cantor at St. Thomas's church and teacher at the school in succession to Kuhnau. With his eldest son, Wilhelm Friedemann B., he visited the court of Frederick II of Prus. at Potsdam, where his second son, Carl Philipp Emanuel B., held a post, in 1747. Two years later his eyesight failed seriously, and in 1750 he had an unsuccessful operation and became blind for a short time before his death.

Works incl. Passions according to St. John & St. Matthew; Mass, B min.; orats. for Ascension, Christmas & Easter; Magnificat, D maj.; over 200 church cantatas; 23 secular cantatas; 4 motets; 2 psalms; Funeral Ode; over 250 chorales harmonized; 6 orch. ('Brandenburg') concs.; nearly 20 concs. for solo insts. and stgs.; 12 sos. (partitas, suites) for unaccomp. v. & cc.: 21 sos. & other chamber works for var. insts. & clav.; 143 chorale preludes for org.; 26 preludes & fugues & 46 other works for org.; a large number of clav. comps., incl. *It. Concerto*, 7 partitas, 6 Eng. suites, 6 Fr. suites & *The Well-tempered Clavier* (48 preludes & fugues in all keys); *The Art of Fugue* (? for clav.); 5 songs, &c.

Bach Trumpet. A special brass wind inst. of the tpt. type invented by Kosleck of Berlin and improved by Walter Morrow of London, so devised as to be capable of playing the high Clarino parts in the works of Bach and his contemps. and forerunners, first heard at Eisenach in 1884.

Bach, Wilhelm Friedemann (b. Weimar, 22. XI. 1710; d. Berlin, 1. VII. 1784), Ger. orgst. & comp. (35 above). Eldest son of J. S. and Maria Barbara Bach (26 & 25 above); was taught by his father from the age of 10 and entered Leipzig Univ. in 1723. In 1733 he was app. orgst. at St. Sophia's church at Dresden and in 1746 succeeded Zachau as orgst. at the church of Our Lady at Halle. Married Dorothea Elisabeth Georgi in 1751. He resigned at Halle in 1764 and in 1770 went to live at Brunswick, but in spite of some efforts to secure a new app., he lived an unsettled life to the end, moving to Berlin in 1774, where he taught and gave org. recitals; but he fell into poverty.

Works incl. 21 church cantatas; 9 syms.; orch. concs.; pf. concs.; chamber m.; org. works; sos. & many other comps. for clav., &c.

Bache, Francis Edward (b. Birmingham, 14. IX. 1833; d. Birmingham, 24. VIII. 1858), Eng. pfst. & comp. Studied with Sterndale Bennett in London and came out early as a gifted player and comp.

Bache, Walter (b. Birmingham, 19. VI. 1842; d. London, 26. III. 1888), Eng. pfst., brother of prec. Lived in London. Pupil and disciple of Liszt.

Bachelet, Alfred (Georges) (b. Paris, 26. II. 1864), Fr. comp. Took the Prix de Rome at the Paris Cons. in 1890. Prod. the opera *Scemo* at the Paris Opéra in 1914, another, *Quand la cloche sonnera* at the Opéra-Comique in 1922 and *Un Jardin sur l'Oronte* at the Opéra in 1932.

Bachmann, Sixtus (b. Kettershausen, 18. VII. 1754; d. ? Marchtal, 1818), Aus. priest, orgst. & comp. Wrote syms., church and chamber m. when living in retirement at the monastery of Marchtal.

Bachofen, Johann Caspar (b. Zürich, 1697; d. Zürich, 24. VI. 1755), Swi. comp. Singing-master at the Lat. school and cantor at a church at Zürich. He compiled and partly comp. several books of hymns and psalms and set the Passion of Brockes to m. in 1759.

Bachrich, Sigismund (b. Zsambokreth, 23. I. 1841; d. Vienna, 16. VII. 1913), Hung. vst. & comp. Studied at the Vienna Cons. Played and cond. in Vienna & Paris, became prof. at the Vienna Cons. and played va. in the Phil. & Opera orch. and with the Rosé 4tet.

Works incl. operas *Muzzedin* & *Heini von Steier*, operetta *Der Fuchs-Major*; ballet *Sakuntala* (after Kalidasa), &c.

Backer-Grøndahl, Agathe (Ursula) (b. Holmestrand, 1. XII. 1847; d. Ormøen nr. Oslo, 4. VI. 1907), Norw. pfst. & comp. Pupil of Kjerulf and later of Kullak in Berlin and Bülow at Florence. She wrote many pf. pieces and songs.

Backer-Lunde, Johan (b. Le Havre, 6. VII. 1874), Norw. pfst. & comp. Pupil of Agathe Backer-Grøndahl at Oslo and Busoni in Berlin. Comp. much pf. m.

Backfall = Appoggiatura (taken from the note above).

Badajoz (? Garci Sánchez de) (b. ?, 1460; d. ?, 1526), Spa. orgst. & comp. Was for a time in the service of John III of Port. Wrote songs for several voices, incl. one in Gil Vicente's play *Dom Duardos*.

Badiali, Cesare (b. Imola, ?; d. Imola, 17. XI. 1865), It. bass singer. Made his 1st appearance at Trieste in 1827. Sang in Madrid, Vienna and London as well as It.

Badinage (Fr. lit. teasing, playfulness). *See* **Badinerie.**

Badinerie (Fr. lit. teasing, frivolity, playfulness). A title given, sometimes as *Badinage*, by Fr. & Ger. comps. of the 18th cent. to light, playful pieces in quick 2–4 time (e.g. the final mvt. of Bach's B min. Ovt. [suite] for fl. & stgs.).

Badings, Heink (b. Bandoeng, E. Indies, 17. I. 1907), Dutch comp. Began his career as a mining engineer, but studied m. with Pijper and in 1935 abandoned science entirely for m. Married the vst. Olly Folge Fonden. Prof. at the M. Lyceum, Amsterdam, and the Rotterdam Cons.

Works incl. incid. m. for plays; a cantata; 3 syms., symph. vars. & *Heroic Ovt.* for orch.; v. Conc., co. Conc.; recitations with orch.; 2 stg. 4tets; v. & co. sos.; pf. pieces, &c.

Bagatelle (Fr. = trifle). A short piece, generally of a light or humorous character.

Bagatelles. Short pf. pieces by Beethoven: 2 (C min. & maj.) comp. 1796; 7, Op. 33, comp. 1802; 11, Op. 119, comp. 1820–2; 6, Op. 126, comp. 1823–4.

Bagpipe. An inst. prod. its sound by wind stored up in a bag filled by the player through a mouthpiece; the melody is fingered on a pipe attached to that bag, called the chaunter, while a drone-bass is sounded continually by 2 or 3 additional pipes giving out fixed notes. In some types the wind was supplied by bellows.

Bai, Tommaso (b. Crevalcuore nr. Bologna, 1650; d. Rome, 22. XII. 1714), It. ten. singer & comp. Sang in the Vatican choir; wrote masses, motets and a famous *Miserere*.

Baildon, Joseph (b. ?, *c.* 1727; d. London, IV. 1774), Eng. singer, orgst. & comp. Lay-vicar at Westminster Abbey and orgst. at 2 other London churches. Wrote catches, glees and songs.

Bailey, Lilian (June) (b. Columbus, Ohio, 18. I. 1860; d. London, 4. XI. 1901), Amer. sop. singer. 1st appeared at Boston in 1876, where she married Henschel in 1881.

Baillot, Pierre Marie (François de Sales) (b. Passy nr. Paris, 1. X. 1771; d. Paris, 15. IX. 1842), Fr. vst. Studied in Rome and later under Catel, Cherubini and Reicha in Paris; joined Napoleon's private band, 1802, and began to give chamber concerts in 1814. Was prof. at the Cons. and comp. work for his inst. and chamber m.

Baines, William (b. Horbury, Yorks., 26. III. 1899; d. York, 6. XI. 1922), Eng. comp. Although self-taught, he developed remarkably early, but d. before he had attained full mus. maturity.

Works incl. Sym., Fantasy for stg. 4tet; pf. So., several sets of pf. pieces, &c.

Baini, Giuseppe (b. Rome, 21. X. 1775; d. Rome, 21. V. 1844), It. priest, singer & writer on m. Sang at the Pontifical Chapel in Rome; comp. a *Miserere*, prod. there, 1821. He wrote a biog. of Palestrina.

Bainton, Edgar L(eslie). (b. London, 14. II. 1880), Eng. comp. Studied at the R.C.M. in London and in 1901 was app. prof. of pf. and comp. at the Cons. of Newcastle-on-Tyne, of which he became principal in 1912. In 1934 he went to Australia as dir. of the State Cons. at Sydney.

Works incl. opera *Oithona* (after Ossian); *Before Sunrise* (Swinburne), for con. solo, chor. & orch.; *The Blessed Damozel* (Rossetti) for solo voices, chor. & orch.; Sym. in B♭ maj., symph. poem *Paracelsus* (after Browning); Conc.-Fantasia for pf. & orch.; stg. 4tet; va. & pf. So.; songs, part-songs, pf. pieces, &c.

Bairstow, Edward C(uthbert). (b. Huddersfield, 22. VIII. 1874), Eng. orgst., cond. & comp. After var. orgst.'s apps. he took the Mus.D. at Durham in 1901 and became orgst. and choirmaster at York Minster in 1913. Ed. *The Eng. Psalter* and wrote *The Evolution of Mus. Form* & (with Plunket Greene) *Singing learnt from Speech.* Knighted 1932.

Works incl. services, anthems; org. m.; Vars. for 2 pfs., &c.

Baiser et la quittance, Le (*The Kiss and the Receipt*), opera by Boïeldieu, Isouard, R. Kreutzer & Méhul (lib. by Louis Picard, Michel Dieulafoy & Charles de Longchamps), prod. Paris, Opéra-Comique, 18. VI. 1803.

Balakirev, Mily Alexeievitch (b. Nizhny-Novgorod, 2. I. 1837; d. St. Petersburg, 29. V. 1910), Rus. comp. He was taught m. by his mother, but learnt most of what he knew as a youth in the house of Ulibishev, on whose estate he was able to use the mus. library and gain experience with the private orch. At 18 he went to St. Petersburg, full of enthusiasm for nat. m., and won the approval of Glinka. In 1861 he began to form the group of nationalist musns. of which he became the leader, although he was not the eldest. Cui became his 1st disciple, Mussorgsky, Rimsky-Korsakov and Borodin following later, and he even influenced Tchaikovsky to some extent at first. In 1862 he estab. the Free School of M. with the help of the chor. cond. Lomakin and esp. of Stassov, and in connection with it cond. progressive sym. concerts. In 1871 he had a grave nervous breakdown and withdrew from public life, feeling that he had been defeated by the 'official' musns.; he was forced to become a min. railway official to earn a modest living and he turned to religious mysticism. Not till 1876 did he begin to take some interest in mus. life and comp. again, but only in 1883, when he was app. dir. of the Imp. Chapel, did he fully emerge once more. He retired in 1895 with a pension and took up comp. anew, but again lived in seclusion and was almost wholly forgotten by his former friends.

Work incl. 2 syms., symph. poems *Russia* & *Tamara*, ovts. on a Spa. march, on 3 Rus. themes, to *King Lear* & on Cz. themes; pf. Conc. (finished by Liapunov); many pf. works incl. So. in B♭ min., *Islamey* fantasy, scherzos, mazurkas, nocturnes, waltzes, &c.; 43 songs; 2 books of folksongs; 6 anthems for unaccomp. chor.; cantata for the unveiling of the Glinka monument.

Balalaika. A Rus. inst. similar to the guitar, but as a rule with a triangular body. It is made in var. sizes, so that bands of insts. ranging from treble to bass can be organized.

Balbi, Lodovico (b. Venice, ?; d. Venice, XII. 1604), It. monk, singer & comp. Pupil of Porta; singer at St. Mark's, Venice, c. 1570; later at Verona cath. Afterwards worked at Venice and Padua, and retired to the Minorite monastery at Venice.

Works incl. masses, motets & other church m.; madrigals, &c.

Baldassarri, Benedetto (b. ?; d. ?), It. 18th-cent. ten. singer. Appeared in London, 1720–2.

Baldwin, John (b. ?; d. 1615), Eng. singer & comp. At var. times singer in St. George's Chapel, Windsor, and a gentleman of the Chapel Royal in London. He copied out much m., esp. into a book for his own use, which preserves many valuable works and incl. inst. pieces and sacred and secular works for several voices.

Balfe, Michael (William) (b. Dublin, 15. V. 1808; d. Rowney Abbey, Herts., 2. X. 1870), Ir. comp. Son of a dancing-master, who removed to Wexford in 1810. There B. had v. lessons and he soon played for his father's classes; at 7 he comp. and scored a polacca. On the death of his father in 1823, he was sent to London as a pupil of C. E. Horn; there he appeared as a vst. and played in the orch. at Drury Lane Theatre. Next he studied comp. with C. F. Horn and came out as a singer in the 1st perf. in Eng. of Weber's *Freischütz* at Norwich. In 1825 Count Mazzara became his patron and took him to It., where he introduced him to Cherubini. He took comp. lessons from Paer in Rome and Federici at Milan, and improved his singing under Filippo Galli. A ballet, his 1st stage work, was prod. there. Next he went to Paris, met Rossini, and in 1827 appeared as Figaro in that master's *Barbiere* at the Théâtre Italien. Three years later he sang at Palermo and prod. his 1st opera there, *I rivali di se stessi.* At Milan he sang with Malibran and at Bergamo he met the Hung. singer Lina Rosa, whom he married. Early in 1833 he returned to London and appeared at concerts. His 1st Eng. opera, *The Siege of Rochelle*, was prod. at Drury Lane in 1835 and the next year Malibran sang in *The Maid of Artois.*

In 1842 he went to live in Paris for some years and worked there with great success, though in 1843 he returned for a time to prod. *The Bohemian Girl* in London. Triumphant visits to Berlin in 1849 and St. Petersburg in 1852 followed, and in 1854 he prod. *Pittore e Duca* at Trieste. That year he finally returned to Eng., though a Fr. version, with some new m., of *The Bohemian Girl* was brought out in Paris, 1869. He had bought a property in Hertfordshire, where he took to farming.

Works incl. 29 operas among which are *Un avvertimento ai gelosi, The Siege of Rochelle, The Maid of Artois, Joan of Arc, Falstaff* (It.), *Le Puits d'amour, The Bohemian Girl, Les Quatre Fils Aymon, The Bondman, The Maid of Honour, The Sicilian Bride, The Rose of Castile, Satanella, The Armourer of Nantes, Il Talismano*; operetta *The Sleeping Queen*; ballet *La Pérouse*; 3 cantatas, incl. *Mazeppa*; many songs, &c.

Balino. *See* **Fabri.**

Ballabene, Gregorio (b. Rome, 1720; d. Rome, *c.* 1803), It. comp. Lived a very retired life and wrote church m. in a very elaborate ctptal. style, incl. a Mass in 48 parts.

Ballabile (It. = in a dancing manner, accent on 2nd syll.). A term applicable to any piece in the form or character of a dance.

Ballad (Fr. & Ger. *Ballade*, It. *Ballata*). The It. sense, from *ballare* (to dance), is the orig. one, but it has acquired a different meaning in Eng., Fr. and Ger. In Eng., disregarding its meaning in poetry, we find that it has 3 different mus. connotations: (i) an old popular song, either a folk tune or an air by a known comp., set to words telling a story; (ii) a later but now old-fashioned species of light and sentimental song, generally about love, a garden or moonshine, or preferably love in a moonlit garden, the words of which are by a hack writer set to m. by a comp. of no merit but that of easy melodic invention; (iii) an inst. piece suggesting the character of (i). In Fr. definition (i) may also apply, but a *ballade* is more generally an inst. piece, sometimes in a kind of narrative, story-telling manner: e.g. Chopin, Fauré and others. In Ger. the same may be the case, but more often a Ger. *Ballade* is a lengthy song telling a romantic, frequently gruesome story: e.g. Schubert's *Erl King* and the numerous ballads by Loewe. Some Ger. ballads come from Scottish sources by way of Herder's trans.—*Tom the Rhymer, Archibald Douglas,* &c. The B. may also be a special type of narrative song in opera, esp. 19th-cent. Fr. (e.g. Auber's *Fra Diavolo*, Boïeldieu's *Dame blanche*, &c.), serving the double purpose of introd. a romantic mus. element and of conveying certain information about the plot to the audience. This device was adopted by other schools and later comps. (e.g. Senta's ballad in Wagner's *Flying Dutchman*).

Ballad Opera. An Eng. light operatic entertainment the fashion for which was set by *The Beggar's Opera* and Coffey's *The Devil to Pay* in 1728 and continuing its vogue until the 1760s. The most distinctive feature of its m. is that it consists mainly of short songs interspersed with dialogue and that they are not specially comp. for the piece, but chosen from well-known folksongs or, more particularly, popular songs of the day.

Ballade (Fr. & Ger.). *See* **Ballad.**

Ballamatia (It. obs.). A song in the style and mvt. of a dance.

Ballard. Fr. 16th–18th-cent. family of m. printers. The founder was Guillaume Le Bé, 1540, and the chief members were:

1. Robert B. (b. ?; d. Paris, 1606), son-in-law of Le Bé.
2. Lucrèce B. (*née* Le Bé), (b. ?; d. ?), his wife, who continued after his death.
3. Pierre B. (b. Paris, *c.* 1600; d. Paris, *c.* 1640), their son.
4. Robert B. (b. ?; d. Paris, 1679), son of 3.
5. Christophe B. (b. ?; d. Paris, 1715), son of 4.
6. Jean-Baptiste Christophe B. (b. ?; d. Paris, 1750), son of 5.
7. Christophe Jean François (b. ?; d. Paris, 1765), son of 6.
8. Pierre Robert Christophe B. (b. ?; d. Paris, ? 1788), son of 7.

Ballard (? Robert), Fr. 16th–17th-cent. lutenist. He taught the lute to the future Louis XIII and was (?) lute-player to Maria de' Medici.

Ballatella (It. = a little ballad). In m. either a small piece in the ballad style or a small dance piece.

Ballet (*see also* **Ballett**). A stage entertainment consisting entirely of dancing and therefore requiring exclusively inst. m. from the comp., although voc. features have been introd. by some modern musns. and were a feature in Fr. B. of the 18th cent., where the term was often short for *opéra-ballet* and the B. proper was called *ballet-pantomime*.

Ballet comique de la reine, Le (*The Queen's Comic Ballet*), stage entertainment perf. in Paris, 15. X. 1581, at the marriage of the Duc de Joyeux and Mlle de Vaudemont, with m. prob. by the bass singer Lambert de

Beaulieu, the It. vst. Baltasar de Beaujoyeulx (Baltazarini) and the singer and courtier Salmon.

Ballet de Cour (Fr. = court ballet). A 16th–17th-cent. Fr. stage entertainment with m. developing from the older tourneys and masquerades, containing voc. and dance mvts. specially comp. Guédron and Boësset were its chief exponents. The species developed later into the opera-ballet and the opera.

Ballet-pantomime. *See* **Ballet.**

Ballett (or Ballet). A type of 16th–17th-cent. comp. for several voices, resembling a madrigal, but in a lighter, more dance-like style.

Balletti (It.). Pieces of m. intended for dancing, esp. on the stage.

Balling, Michael (b. Heidingsfeld o/M., 29. VIII. 1866; d. Darmstadt, 1. IX. 1925), Ger. cond. Associated with the Wagner festivals at Bayreuth and cond. of the Hallé Orch., Manchester, 1912–14.

Ballo (It. = dance). Usually used in comb., e.g. *tempo di ballo.*

Ballo in maschera, Un (*A Masked Ball*), opera by Verdi (lib. by Antonio Somma, based on Scribe's *Gustave III* set by Auber), prod. Rome, Teatro Apollo, 17. II. 1859.

Balmer, Luc (b. Munich, 1898), Swi. comp. & cond., son of a painter, Wilhelm B., of Basle. Studied with Huber at the Basle Cons. and with Busoni in Berlin. Prof. of harmony at the Berne Cons., cond. of concerts at Lucerne and opera at Berne, where from 1935 he also cond. the popular sym. concerts.

Works incl. incid. m. for plays; Petrarch's Sonnet 103 for chor. & orch.; Sym., symph. fragment, Serenade and Symph. Vars. for orch.; pf. Conc., v. Conc.; stg. 4tets & other chamber m., &c.

Baltasar de Beaujoyeulx. *See* **Ballet comique de la Reine** *and* **Baltazarini.**

Baltazarini (Baldassaro da Belgioioso) (b. ?; d. *c.* 1587), It. vst. Was sent to France *c.* 1555 by the Maréchal de Brissac to lead Catherine de' Medici's stg. band. He took some share in the *Ballet comique de la Reine*, 1581.

Baltic Composers. *See* **Aavik, Erdmann, Lopatnikov, Medinš, Wihtol, Wilm, Wolfurt.**

Baltzar, Thomas (b. Lübeck, *c.* 1630; d. London, 1663), Ger. or Swe. vst. Went to Eng. in 1655 and was app. one of the king's 24 vs. in 1661.

Balzac, Honoré de (1799–1850), Fr. novelist. *See* **Assafiev** (*Lost Illusions*), **Leoncavallo** (*Serafita*), **Levadé** (*Peau de chagrin*), **Massimilla Doni** (Schoeck), **Shostakovitch** (*Human Comedy*).

Bamboula. A Negro drum and a Negro dance accomp. by it, orig. in the West Indies. Coleridge-Taylor's 'rhapsodic dance' for orch., Op. 75, is entitled *Bamboula.*

Banchieri, Adriano (b. Bologna, *c.* 1567; d. Bologna, 1634), It. orgst., theorist & comp. Learnt m. as a chorister at Lucca cath. Afterwards at St. Mark's, Venice; orgst. at Imola, 1600–7, and at the monastery of San Michele in Bosco (Monte Oliveto) nr. Bologna. He founded the Accademia Florida at Bologna, *c.* 1623, and wrote theoretical works, esp. on figured bass.

Works incl. masses; sacred syms. and concs.; comic intermezzi for the stage; org. works, &c.

Banda (It. = band). The brass section of the orch. in an opera or a special brass band used on the stage or behind the scene.

Bandora. *See* **Pandore.**

Bandurria (Spa. = Pandora). A stg. inst. of the Cittern or Mandoline type, with 6 stgs. which are plucked with the fingers or with a plectrum.

Banestre, Gilbert (b. ?; d. ?), Eng. 15th-cent. comp. Master of the Children in the Chapel Royal in succession to Abyngdon, 1478; wrote sacred and secular voc. m.

Banister, John (b. ?, 1630; d. London, 3. X. 1679), Eng. vst. & concert promoter. Lived in London; sent to France by Charles II in 1662. Comp. m. for Davenant's *Circe* & Wycherley's *Gentleman Dancing-Master* and contrib. songs to var. collections.

Banister, John (b. ?; d. London, 1735), Eng. vst., & teacher of his inst., son of prec. Comp. for the stage.

Banjo. An Amer. Negro stg. inst. of the Guitar type with a hollow body covered with stretched parchment and 5 to 9 stgs., which are plucked with the fingers; the neck is fretted.

Bánk-Bán, opera by Erkel (lib. by Béni Egressy, based on a play by József Katona), prod. Budapest, 9. III. 1861.

Bänkelsänger (Ger.). A singer of ballads, esp. at fairs, a chapman singing the songs he sold.

Banti (*née* **Giorgi**) **Brigitta** (b. Monticelli d'Ongina nr. Piacenza, *c.* 1756; d. Bologna, 18. II. 1806), It. singer. She sang in the streets of Venice and the cafés of Paris at first, but was engaged for the Paris Opéra in 1776 and had much success in London.

Bantock, Granville (b. London, 7. VIII. 1868), Eng. comp. Son of a doctor; educ. for the civil service, but entered the R.A.M. in 1889, where some of his earliest works were perf., and Lago prod. the opera *Cædmar* at the Olympic Theatre in 1892.

After some experience in theatrical cond., he gave a concert of modern Eng. m. in 1896. The next year he was app. cond. at the Tower, New Brighton, where he introd. much contemp. m. In II. 1900 he gave a concert of new Brit. m. at Antwerp and in IX. was app. principal of the Birmingham and Midland Inst. School of M. He remained in Birmingham until 1933, and became Prof. of M. at the Univ. in 1908, succeeding Elgar. Knighted in 1930.

Works incl. operas *Cædmar, Pearl of Iran, The Seal Woman*; incid. m. for Sophocles' *Electra*, Shakespeare's *Macbeth*, Wilde's *Salome*, &c.; orch. works: *Processional* & *Jaga-Naut* (from 24 projected symph. poems on Southey's *Curse of Kehama*), *Helena Vars.*, comedy ovt. *The Pierrot of the Minute* (after Ernest Dowson), orch. ballad *The Sea Reivers, Ovt. to a Gr. Tragedy*, symph. poem *Dante and Beatrice, Fifine at the Fair* (after Browning), ovt. to *The Frogs* (Aristophanes), *Hebridean Sym., A Pagan Sym.*; serenade *From the Far West, Scenes from the Scottish Highlands, The Land of Gael* for stg. orch.; *Elegiac Poem, Sapphic Poem, Celtic Poem* for co. & orch.; chor. & orch. (with or without solo voices): *The Fire-Worshippers, The Time-Spirit, Sea Wanderers, Christ in the Wilderness, Omar Khayyám* (setting of FitzGerald's trans. in 3 parts), *Gethsemane, The Great God Pan, Song of Songs*, orat. *The Pilgrim's Progress* (Bunyan); unaccomp. chor.: choral syms. *Atalanta in Calydon* (Swinburne) & *Vanity of Vanities* (Ecclesiastes), suite *A Pageant of Human Life* and many smaller works and partsongs; numerous songs incl. cycles *Songs of the East* (6 vols.), *Songs of the Seraglio, Six Jester Songs, Five Ghazals of Hafiz, Ferishtah's Fancies* (Browning), *Sappho, Songs from the Chinese Poets* (2 sets); sos. for v. & pf. and va. & pf.; *Poem* for co. & pf.; pf. pieces, &c.

Banville, Théodore de (1823–91), Fr. poet. *See* **Terrasse** (*Matinées poétiques*), **Vidal (P.)** (*Baiser*).

Bar. (abbr.) = Baritone.

Bar. Orig. the line drawn through the mus. stave or staves to indicate the metrical divisions of a comp., now called 'bar-line' in Eng., but still 'bar' in Amer., where 'bar' in the present meaning has become 'measure.'

Baranović, Krešimir (b. Šibenik, 25. VII. 1894), Yslv. cond. & comp. Studied at the Zagreb and Vienna Conss., and in 1915 became cond. at the Zagreb theatre. He was cond. of the Nat. Theatre at Belgrade in 1927–9, but returned to Zagreb as opera cond.

Works incl. operas *Clipped-mowed & The Turks go on*; ballets *The Cake Heart & Imbrek with the Nose*; Symph. Scherzo & *Poème balcanique* for orch.; *From my Mountains* for voice & orch.; chamber m.; songs, &c.

Barbaia, Domenico (old spelling Barbaja) (b. Milan, 1778; d. Posilipo, 16. X. 1841), It. impresario. Was 1st a waiter, then a circus proprietor and finally the most popular of operatic managers. In 1821–5, coming from the Teatro San Carlo at Naples, he managed the Kärntnertor Theatre and the Theater an der Wien in Vienna.

Barbarinus, Lupus Manfredus (Barberini) (b. Correggio, ?; d. ? St. Gall, ?), It. 16th-cent. comp. Went to live at the abbey of St. Gall in Swi. *c.* 1550. Comp. numerous songs and sacred pieces for several voices, incl. a set on tunes by Glareanus.

Barbe-bleue (*Bluebeard*), operetta by Offenbach (lib. by Henri Meilhac & Ludovic Halévy), prod. Paris, Théâtre des Variétés, 5. II. 1866.

Barbella, Emanuele (b. Naples, *c.* 1704; d. Naples, 1. I. 1777), It. vst. & comp. Studied at Naples and wrote duets and trios for stgs.; also an opera in collab. with Logroscino, *Elmira generosa*, prod. at Naples in 1753.

Barber of Bagdad, The (Cornelius). *See* **Barbier von Bagdad.**

Barber of Seville, The (Rossini). *See* **Barbiere di Siviglia.**

Barber, Samuel (b. Westchester, Pa., 9. III. 1910), Amer. comp. Studied at the Curtis Inst. of M., Philadelphia, and in 1935 won the fellowship of the Amer. Acad. in Rome.

Works incl. 2 syms., 2 Essays, Ovt. to Sheridan's *School for Scandal*, m. for a scene from Shelley for orch.; Adagio for stgs.; v. Conc.; *Capricorn Conc.* for fl., ob. tpt. & stgs.; Serenade for stg. 4tet & stg. 4tet in B min.; co. & pf. So.; *Dover Beach* for bar. & stg. 4tet; works for unaccomp. chor. to words by Helen Waddell, Emily Dickinson, James Stephens and Stephen Spender; song-cycle from James Joyce's *Chamber Music* and songs to words by James Stephens, A. E. Housman, Gerard Manley Hopkins, Yeats, &c.; *Excursions* for pf., &c.

Barberiis, Melchiore de (b. ?; d. ?), It. 16th-cent. lutenist. Lived at Padua and pub. several books of pieces in lute tablature, 1546–9.

Barberini. *See* **Barbarinus.**

Barbetta, Giulio Cesare (b. ?; d. ?), It. 16th-cent. lutenist. Lived at Padua and pub. 4 books of m. in lute tablature, 1569–1603.

Barbi, Alice (b. Modena, 1. VI. 1862; d. ?), It. m.-sop. singer & vst. Made her 1st appearance as singer in 1882 at Milan. She toured widely and became a favourite interpreter of Brahms.

Barbier von Bagdad, Der (*The Barber of B.*), opera by Cornelius (lib. by comp.), prod. Weimar, 15. XII. 1858.

Barbiere di Siviglia, Il, ossia La precauzione inutile (*The Barber of Seville, or Vain Precaution*; original title: *Almaviva, ossia L'inutile precauzione*), opera by Rossini (lib. by Cesare Sterbini, based on Beaumarchais's *Le Barbier de Séville*), prod. Rome, Teatro Argentina, 20. II. 1816.

Barbiere di Siviglia, Il, ovvero La precauzione inutile (*The Barber of Seville, or Vain Precaution*), opera by Paisiello (lib. by Giuseppe Petrosellini, based on Beaumarchais's *Le Barbier de Séville*), prod. St. Petersburg, Hermitage, at court, 26. IX. 1782.

Barbieri, Francisco (Asenjo) (b. Madrid, 3. VIII. 1823; d. Madrid, 19. II. 1894), Spa. comp. Studied pf. with P. Albéniz and comp. with Carnicer at the Madrid Cons. He made at 1st a poor living as clst. in a military band, pfst. in cafés, chorus singer, copyist, &c. Having deputized as an opera singer, he took to the stage and made his 1st success with the comic opera *Jugar con fuego* in 1851. As a scholar he did valuable work in ed. the *Cancionero musical* containing secular Spa. voc. m. of the 15th and 16th cents.

Comic operas incl. *Gloria y peluca, Tramoya, Jugar con fuego, Los diamantes de la corona, Pan y toros, El barberillo de Lavapiés*, &c.

Barbireau, Jacques (b. ?; d. Antwerp, 8. VIII. 1491), Flem. comp. Was choirmaster of Antwerp cath. until his death. Wrote masses and other church m., also songs for 3 and 4 voices.

Barblan, Otto (b. Scanfs, Engadine, 22. III. 1860; d. Geneva, 19. XI. 1943), Swi. orgst., cond. & comp. Studied at the Stuttgart Cons. After teaching and cond. at Chur, he became orgst. at Geneva cath. in 1887. Taught at the Cons. there and cond. the Société de Chant Sacré.

Works incl. m. for a festival play, *Ode patriotique* and cantatas for solo voices, chor. & orch.; Passion according to St. Luke; Psalm cxvii for double chor.; Passacaglia on B.A.C.H. for orch.; org. works, pf. pieces, partsongs, &c.

Barcarolle (Fr. from It. *barcaruola*). A boating-song, esp. of the type sung by the gondoliers at Venice. A piece or song in that style, generally in 6–8 time and a moderate tempo, with a swaying rhythm.

Barcroft, George (b. Ely, ?; d. Ely, ?), Eng. 16th–17th-cent. orgst. & comp. Studied at Cambridge and was min. canon and orgst. at Ely cath., 1579–1610. Comp. church m.

Barcroft, Thomas (b. ?; d. Ely, ?), Eng. 16th-cent. orgst. & comp., ? father of prec. Orgst. at Ely. Wrote church m.

Bardi, Giovanni, Count of Vernio (b. Florence, 1534; d. Rome, 1612), It. nobleman & amateur musn. Patron of the mus. *camerata* at Florence. Works by Caccini, Galilei, Peri and others were perf. at his house. He comp. madrigals himself.

Bärenhäuter, Der (*Bearskin*), opera by Siegfried Wagner (lib. by comp.), prod. Munich, 21. I. 1899.

Bargiel, Woldemar (b. Berlin, 3. X. 1828; d. Berlin, 23. II. 1897), Ger. comp. Studied under Dehn in Berlin and at Leipzig Cons. Later taught in Berlin, Cologne and Amsterdam, where he also cond.

Works incl. a Sym., orch. ovts.; psalm for chor. & orch.; much chamber m.; pf. pieces, &c.

Baring, Maurice (1874–1945), Eng. novelist & essayist. *See* **Edmunds** (*Blue Harlequin*), **Fête galante** (Smyth).

Bariolage (Fr.). The playing of high notes on stg. inst. in high positions on the lower stgs. to obtain a different tone-colour or to facilitate the perf. of rapid high passages without changing to lower positions.

Baritone. The male voice with a compass between that of a ten. and a bass; a brass inst. used in military bands; also a stg. inst. *See* **Barytone.**

Barkworth, John (Edmund) (b. Beverley, 20. V. 1858; d. Geneva, 18. XI. 1929), Eng. comp. Educ. at Rugby, Oxford and the R.C.M. His chief work is an opera on Shakespeare's *Romeo and Juliet*, prod. Middlesbrough, 7. I. 1916.

Bärmann, Heinrich Joseph (b. Potsdam, 14. II. 1784; d. Munich, 11. VI. 1847), Ger. clst. Member of the court orch. at Munich. Weber wrote several works for him.

Barnard, John (b. ?; d. ?), Eng. 17th-cent. musn. Min. canon at St. Paul's cath. in London; pub. the 1st printed collection of Eng. cath. m. in 1641.

Barnby, Joseph (b. York, 12. VIII. 1838; d. London, 28. I. 1896), Eng. cond., orgst. & comp. Held various orgst.'s posts in London; precentor at Eton Coll. 1875–92, then principal of G.S.M. Distinguished as chor. cond. Knighted 1892.

Barnett, John (b. Bedford, 15. VII. 1802; d. nr. Cheltenham, 16–17. IV. 1890), Eng. comp. of Ger. descent (orig. name Beer: Meyerbeer's family). Was a stage singer as a child and studied with C. E. Horn. In 1825 he prod. his 1st stage piece, which was followed by a large number of others, incl. *The Mountain Sylph*, prod. 25. VIII. 1834.

Barnett, John Francis (b. London, 16. X. 1837; d. London, 24. XI. 1916), Eng. comp. & pfst., nephew of prec. Studied in London and Leipzig, where he appeared at the Gewandhaus.

Works incl. Sym. in A min., ovt. to Shakespeare's *Winter's Tale*; cantatas *The Ancient Mariner* (Coleridge), *Paradise and the Peri* (Moore) & others; 2 orats.; chamber m.; pf. pieces, &c.

Baron, Ernst Theophilus (b. Breslau, 17. II. 1696; d. Berlin, 2. IV. 1760), Ger. lutenist & comp. Studied law and philos. at Leipzig, but later toured widely and worked at many courts; wrote a book on and many comps. for the lute.

Baroness, The (b. ?; d. ?), (?) Ger. 17th–18th-cent. singer whose name is unknown and who appeared in London under that nickname between 1706–15. She may be identical with Maria Gallia, the sister of Margherita de l'Épine.

Baroni. It. 17th-cent. family of singers and lutenists:

1. Adriana B. (b. ?; d. ?). She worked at Mantua and was eulogized in a book of verses in 1623.
2. Catarina B. (b. Mantua, after 1620; d. ?), daughter of 1. Also played the harp and wrote poetry.
3. Eleonora B. (b. Naples, ?; d. ?), sister of 2. Also played va. da gamba and comp. Milton met her in Rome in 1638 and wrote 3 poems on her and her mother.

Barré (Fr. lit. barred, actually ? cross-stopped). A chord on stg. insts. with fretted fingerboards is said to be played B. when a finger is laid horizontally across the whole fingerboard, thus raising all the stgs. in pitch by the same interval's distance from the fundamental tuning.

Barre, Antonio (b. ?; d. ?), It. 16th-cent. singer, m. printer and comp. Alto singer in the choir of St. Peter's in Rome in the middle of the cent. Wrote madrigals and pub. them, with those of many other comps., in 7 books printed by his own press, 1st in Rome and after 1564 at Milan.

Barré (or Barri), Léonard (b. Limoges, ?; d. ?), Fr. comp. Pupil of Willaert and singer in the Papal Choir in Rome, 1537–52. He attended the Council of Trent in 1545 to give advice on church m.

Barrel Organ. A popular mechan. inst. prod. m. by the mere turning of a handle, but sometimes actuated by clockwork. A cylinder (barrel) moves tongue-shaped keys by means of pins or studs arranged in such order that its turning prod. an ordered piece of m. The keys control pipes similar to those of the org., but restricted to a single range of tone-colour and limited in compass. B.O.s were formerly used in small village churches that could not maintain an org. and orgst., and they mechan. played a number of hymn tunes. The B. O. is often wrongly called Hurdy-gurdy, which is a totally different inst.

Barrett, John (b. *c.* 1674; d. *c.* 1735), Eng. orgst., teacher & comp. Wrote incid. m. for plays, many popular songs, &c.

Barrett, Thomas. *See* **Stuart, Leslie.**

Barrie, James (Matthew) (1860–1937), Sco. playwright & novelist. *See* **Bax** (*Truth about the Rus. Dancers*), **Davies (Walford)** (*Peter Pan* 4tet), **Mackenzie** (*Little Minister*), **O'Neill** (*Mary Rose* & *Kiss for Cinderella*), **Skilton** (*Mary Rose*).

Barrière, Théodore (1823–77), Fr. playwright. *See* **Offenbach** (*Gascon*).

Barrios, Angel (b. Granada, 1862), Spa. guitarist & comp.

Works incl. comic operas, *Granada mía*, &c., an opera with a Goya setting, *El Avapiés*, in collab. with C. del Campo, and works for his own inst.

Bartered Bride, The (*Prodaná Nevěsta*), opera by Smetana (lib. by Karel Sabina), prod. Prague, Cz. Theatre, 30. V. 1866. The current Eng. title is inaccurate; the heroine is not a bride, only betrothed. No doubt it is due to a lit. but inexact trans. of the Ger. *Verkaufte Braut.*

Barthélemon, François Hippolyte (b. Bordeaux, 27. VII. 1741; d. London, 23. VII. 1808), Fr. vst. & comp. Settled in London in 1764; 2 years later he prod. the opera *Pelopida* and married Mary Young, daughter of Charles Young and niece of Mrs. Arne and Mrs. Lampe. Comp. stage pieces for Garrick and visited Fr., Ger. and It. with his wife, who sang there.

Works incl. orat. *Jefte in Masfa*; syms., ovts. for orch.; sos., &c.

Bartholomew, Ann. *See* **Mounsey.**

Bartleman, James (b. ? London, 19. IX. 1769; d. London, 15. IV. 1821), Eng. bass singer. Educ. at Westminster school and abbey; sang as a boy and 1st came out as a bass in 1788.

Bartlet, John (b. ?; d. ?), Eng. 16th–17th-cent. lutenist & comp. Prob. in the service of Lord Hertford. Pub. a *Booke of Ayres* for voices and insts. in 1606.

Bartók, Béla (b. Nagyszentmiklós, 25. III. 1881; d. New York, 26. IX. 1945), Hung. comp. Son of a dir. of agriculture. His mother, a school-teacher, was a musn. and taught him from an early age. He appeared as public pfst. at the age of 10. Studied under Laszlo Erkel at Pozsony (Pressburg) until 1899 and then the pf. under István Thomán and comp. under Koessler at the Budapest Cons. About 1905 he began to collect folk tunes and to discover that the true Magyar m. differed greatly from that of the Hung. gypsies so far regarded as the only Hung. folk m. App. prof. of pf. at Budapest Cons. in 1907. After the war of 1914–8 he began to be known in Eur. and Amer., and in 1922 was made an hon. member of the I.S.C.M.

Works incl. opera *Bluebeard's Castle*; mime-plays *The Wooden Prince, The Miraculous Mandarin* (Lengyel); orch. m. incl. *Kossuth* Sym., 2 suites, *Two Portraits, Two Pictures, Dance Suite*, Conc.; 2 pf. concs., 2 rhapsodies for v. & orch., 1 for pf. & orch.; *Music for Stgs., Percussion and Celesta*; *Divertimento* for stgs.; So. for 2 pfs. & percussion; chamber m. incl. 6 stg. 4tets; 2 v. & pf. sos.; So. for unaccomp. v.; much pf. m. incl. 14 *Bagatelles, For Children*, 4 vols., 3 *Burlesques*, 2 *Elegies*, 2 *Rumanian Dances, Allegro barbaro*, Sonatina, So., Suite (Op. 14), *Microcosm* (153 progressive pieces); 2 sets of songs, 3 sets of folksongs; *Cantata profana* for solo voices, chor. & orch.; many arrs. of Hung., Slovak & Rum. folksongs, &c.

Bartoš, František (b. Mlatcov, Moravia, 15. III. 1837; d. Mlatcov, 10. VI. 1906), Morav. mcolst. Ed. 3 collections of Morav. folk m.

Bartoš, Josef (b. Vysoké, 4. III. 1887), Cz. critic. Author of biogs. of Dvořák, Fibich and J. B. Foerster.

Barytone. An obs. stg. inst. of the va. da gamba type with sympathetic stgs. It was cultivated mainly in Ger. and Aus. Haydn's patron, Prince Nicolas Esterházy, played it and H. wrote nearly 200 works for it.

Bas dessus (Fr. lit. low above). An obs. term for a m.-sop.

Base (Eng. obs.). The old Eng. word for Bass. It has been usefully revived, e.g. by Tovey, to denote a persistent bass figure used as a mus. foundation, as in vars. constructed on the bass rather than the tune of their theme or in mvts. built on a Ground. B. was also a colloq. term for the Bass Viol or Viola da gamba.

Basili (or Basily), Francesco (b. Loreto, 3. II. 1767; d. Rome, 25. III. 1850), It. singer & comp. Became dir. of the Milan Cons. in 1827. Chapel master at St. Peter's in Rome from 1837.

Works incl. operas *La locandiera, Achille nell' assedio di Troia, Ritorno d'Ulisse, Antigona, Achille, L'orfana egiziana*; orat. *Sansone*; Requiem for Jannaconi; several Misereres; syms., &c.

Basilius (*Der königliche Schäfer, oder Basilius in Arcadien: The Royal Shepherd, or Basil in Arcady*), opera by Keiser (lib. by Friedrich Christian Bressand), prod. Hamburg, Theater am Gänsemarkt, ? spring 1694.

Basoche, La (*The Corporation of Lawyers*), opera by Messager (lib. by Albert Carré), prod. Paris, Opéra-Comique, 30. V. 1890.

Basque Composer. *See* **Usandizaga.**

Bass. The lowest part in a comp.; the lowest male voice, with a compass from about F below the stave in the bass clef to about D above it.

Bass Clarinet. A cl. with a range an octave lower than the ordinary inst.

Bass Clef. The F clef indicating that F below middle C stands on the 4th line (from below) of the stave. It is one of the 2 clefs used in pf. m., also for bar. & bass voices and all insts. with bass range.

Bass Drum. The largest of the drums not prod. notes of definite pitch. It is placed upright and struck sideways, prod. a dull thud. It is used both in the orch. and in military bands, and in the latter it is played in conjunction with the Cymbals, one of which is placed on it while the other is held in the player's hand not used to hold the drumstick.

Bass Flute. A fl. with a range a fourth lower than that of the ordinary inst. It is a transposing inst. in G; also an 8-ft. org. pedal stop reproducing this.

Bass Horn. *See* **Ophicleide.**

Bass Trumpet. A tpt. in C with a range respectively a maj. sixth and a min. seventh lower than that of the insts. in A and B♭.

Bass Viol. *See* **Viola da gamba.**

Bassani, Giovanni Battista (b. Padua, *c.* 1657; d. Ferrara, 1. X. 1716), It. vst. & comp. Orgst. at Ferrara and later in charge of the cath. m. at Bologna; returned to Ferrara as cath. orgst. in 1685. Comp. 3 orats., prod. 5 operas and brought out a large amount of church and inst. m. Corelli was prob. his pupil.

Basse chantante (Fr. = singing-bass). A bass voice esp. suited to melodic delivery and lyrical parts.

Basse chiffrée (Fr.) = Figured Bass, Thorough-bass.

Basse-Contre (Fr.). A bowed stg. inst. of the v. family now obs., but used in the 17th cent., with a range from D below the stave in the bass clef.

Basse Danse. A Fr. dance of the 14th–16th cent. So called because the feet were kept low, not thrown up in the air as in some other dances.

Basse-Taille (Fr. lit. low cut). The orig. Fr. name for the bar. voice, derived from Taille, which was the name for the ten. voice.

Basset Horn. An inst. of the cl. type, with an extra key controlling 2 or 3 notes below the range of the ordinary A or B♭ cl. Mozart frequently wrote for it.

Bassetto. An obs. small bass viol with 4 stgs.; also a 4-ft. reed org. stop.

Bassi, Luigi (b. Pesaro, 4. IX. 1766; d. Dresden, 13. IX. 1825), It. bar. singer. Appeared in sop. parts at the age of 13 and went to Prague in 1784, where he made a great reputation. He was Mozart's 1st Don Giovanni there in 1787.

Basso cantante (It. = singing-bass). A bass voice esp. suited to melodic delivery and lyrical parts.

Basso continuo (It. = continuous bass). *See* **Thorough-Bass.**

Basso ostinato (It. lit. obstinate bass) = Ground Bass. A bass part in a comp. continually tracing the same melodic outline.

Basson Quinte (Fr.). An obs. small bn. transposing a 5th up.

Bassoon. An inst. with a double-reed mouthpiece, the bass of the wood-wind family in the orch. and sometimes used in chamber m. It has a compass of a little over 3 8ves above B♭ below the stave in the bass clef; also a 16-ft. org. pedal reed stop continuing the ob. or cl. stop in the bass.

Bastardella, La. The nickname given to the singer Lucrezia Aguiari, who was the illegitimate daughter of an It. nobleman.

Bastien und Bastienne, opera by Mozart (lib. by Friedrich Wilhelm Weiskern, based on Charles Simon Favart's parody of Rousseau's *Le Devin du Village*), prod. Vienna, in the garden theatre of Anton Mesmer, the hypnotist, ? IX. 1768.

Baston, Josquin (b. ?; d. ?), Flem. 16th-cent. comp. Prob. worked in It. Wrote motets and songs for several voices.

Bataille, Gabriel (b. ?; d. ?), Fr. 16th–17th-cent. lutenist & comp. Contrib. m. to ballets danced at the court of Louis XIII. Between 1608–23 he pub. many lute pieces and songs.

Bate, Stanley (b. Devonshire, *c.* 1910), Eng. comp. Studied with Vaughan Williams at the R.C.M. in London and later, with the aid of scholarships, with Hindemith in Ger., and Nadia Boulanger in Paris. On his return to London he was engaged in var. theatre and ballet activities. He married Peggy Glanville-Hicks, who had been his fellow student, in 1939, toured Australia with her in 1941, and both emigrated to U.S.A., settling in N.Y.

Works incl. incid. m. for *The Patriots*; ballets incl. *Dance Vars.*; m. for documentary film *The Fifth Year*; 3 syms., 2 Sinfoniettas, ballet suite *Perseus* for orch.; concs. for pf., 2 pfs., v. & 2 for va., Concertante for pf. & stgs., Concertino for pf. & chamber orch., *Haneen* for fl., gong & stgs.; *Incantations* for voice & orch.; stg. 4tet & 5 pieces for stg. 4tet, Trio for fl., co. & pf.; sos. for v. & pf. and fl. & pf., Sonatina for recorder & pf.; 3 pieces, ballet suite *Cap over Mill* and Ovt. for Rus. War Relief for 2 pfs.; So., 9 sonatinas, concert Suite, *Romance & Toccata & 6 Studies for an Infant Prodigy* for pf., &c.

Bates, Joah (b. Halifax, III. 1741; d. London, 8. VI. 1799), Eng. orgst., scholar & cond. Cond. the Concert of Ancient M. in London from its foundation in 1776.

Bates, William (b. ?; d. ?), Eng. 18th-cent. comp. Worked in London, where he prod. several stage pieces and wrote songs for the pleasure gardens, glees, catches, &c.

Bateson, Thomas (b. ? Cheshire, *c.* 1570; d. Dublin, III or IV. 1630), Eng. orgst. & comp. Prob. orgst. at Chester cath. until 1609, when he became vicar-choral and orgst. at Trinity cath., Dublin. 2 books of madrigals by him were pub. in 1604 and 1618.

Bath, Hubert (b. Barnstaple, 6. XI. 1883; d. Harefield, Middlesex, 24. IV. 1945), Eng. cond., educst. & comp. Studied at the R.A.M. in London.

Works incl. opera *Trilby* (on G. du Maurier) & others; incid. m. to Hauptmann's *Hannele*; film m. for *Love Story*, incl. *Cornish Rhapsody* for pf. & orch.; orch. vars. & suites; cantatas, songs, &c.

Bathe, William (b. Ireland, 2. IV. 1564; d. Madrid, 17. VI. 1614), Ir. priest & mus. scholar. In state service at first, he went to Spa. and became a Jesuit priest in 1599. He wrote *Briefe Introductions to the True Art of Musick* and *the Skill of Song*, also *Janua linguarum*.

Batistin. *See* **Stuck.**

Baton (Fr.). The stick used by the cond. in orch. and chor. perfs. It orig. from a roll of m. used in the 15th cent. and passed through a phase of a heavy stick beaten on the floor in the 17th (e.g. Lully).

Battaglia di Legnano, La (*The Battle of L.*), opera by Verdi (lib. by Salvatore Cammarano), prod. Rome, Teatro Argentina, 27. I. 1849.

Battement (Fr.) = Mordent.

Batten, Adrian (b. ?; d. London, 1637), Eng. orgst. & comp. Chorister at Winchester cath. as a boy. In 1614 he came to London as vicar-choral at Westminster Abbey and in 1624 became orgst. at St. Paul's cath.

Works incl. 11 services, *c.* 50 anthems and other church m.

Battery. A collective term for groups of perc. insts.

Battery (Eng. obs.) = Arpeggio.

Battishill, Jonathan (b. London, V. 1738; d. London, 10. XII. 1801), Eng. hpchdst., orgst. & comp. Choirboy at St. Paul's cath. About 1762 he became hpchdst. at Covent Garden Theatre, where he married a singer named Davies and prod. in 1764 the opera *Almena*, written jointly with M. Arne. About the same time he became orgst. of 3 city churches and began to write church m. He also wrote songs, glees and catches, but after 1777, when his wife ran away with the actor Webster, he ceased to comp.

Battistini, Mattia (b. Rome, 27. II. 1857; d. Colle Baccaro nr. Rieti, 7. XI. 1928), It. bar. singer. Made his 1st appearance in opera in Rome, 1878.

Battle of Prague, The. A descriptive pf. piece with v., co. & drum *ad lib.* by Franz Kotzwara, comp. 1788, of no mus. value, but very popular in the early 19th cent.

Battle of the Huns (Liszt). *See* **Hunnenschlacht.**

Battle of Vittoria, The. A classic ex. of inferior m. by a great composer: Beethoven's *Wellingtons Sieg, oder Die Schlacht bei Vittoria*, 1st perf. Vienna, 8. XII. 1813. It contains quotations of nat. tunes. The title should properly be *B. of Victoria.*

Batton, Désiré Alexandre (b. Paris, 2. I. 1798; d. Versailles, 15. X. 1855), Fr. comp. Studied at the Paris Cons. and gained the Prix de Rome in 1817; went to Rome and travelled after prod. his 1st comic opera, *La Fenêtre secrète*, in 1818.

Works incl. operas *Ethelwina*, *Le Prisonnier d'état*, *Le Champ du drap d'or*; church m.; Sym., &c.

Battuta (It.) = Beat. Often used loosely in the plur. (e.g. *ritmo di 3 battute*) to indicate a change in the metrical scheme of bars—not beats—grouped in unexpected numbers.

Baudelaire, Charles (1821–67), Fr. poet. *See* **Bréville** (*Cloche fêlée*), **Charpentier (G.)** (*Fleurs du mal*), **Debussy** (5 poems & *Préludes*, i. 4), **Dieren (van)** (recitations), **Morawski** (*Fleurs du m.*), **Sorabji** (songs), **Tommasini** (*Hymne à la Beauté*), 3 songs by **Fauré.**

Baudrier, Yves (b. Paris, 11. II. 1906), Fr. comp. He formed the group of 'La Jeune France' with Jolivet, Lesur and Messiaen in 1936.

Baulduin, Noël (b. ?; d. Antwerp, *c.* 1530), Flem. comp. Chapel master of Notre-Dame at Antwerp, 1513–8, ? living some time in It. Wrote motets and other church m.

Baumgartner, Wilhelm (b. Rorschach, 15. XI. 1820; d. Zürich, 17. III. 1867), Swi. pfst., cond. & comp. Studied in Swi. and Berlin, later settled at Zürich as pf. teacher and chor. cond.

Works incl. many songs, incl. the patriotic 'O mein Heimatland' to words by Gottfried Keller; pf. pieces, &c.

Bautista, Julián (b. Madrid, 21. IV. 1901), Spa. comp. Pupil of Conrado del Campo. He gained 2 nat. prizes for comp. in 1923 and 1926 and became prof. of harmony at the Madrid Cons. Some of his works were destroyed in the Spa. Civil War.

Works incl. opera *Interior* (lost); ballet-pantomime *Juerga; Tres Ciudades* for sop. & orch.; *La Flûte de jade* for voice & chamber orch.; 2 stg. 4tets (lost); *Colores* & *Preludio y danza* for pf.; songs, &c.

Bax, Arnold (Edward Trevor) (b. London, 8. XI. 1883), Eng. comp. Entered the R.A.M. in 1900, studying pf. with Matthay & comp. with F. Corder. Stayed frequently in Ir. and travelled in Rus. He never held any official mus. position until he was app. Master of the King's Music in 1942. Knighted in 1937.

Works incl. ballet *The Truth about the Rus. Dancers* (James Barrie); chor. works incl. *Enchanted Summer, Fatherland, I sing of a Maiden, Mater ora Filium, St. Patrick's Breastplate, This Worlde's Joie, To the Name above every Name*; m. for film *Malta G.C.*; Te Deum & Nunc Dimittis for chor. & org.; 7 syms., *Sinfonietta*, symph. poems *November Woods, The Garden of Fand, The Happy Forest, Tintagel*, ovt. *Work in Progress, Overture to a Picaresque Comedy, Legend* & other orch. works; concs. for v. & orch., and for co. & orch., Symph. Vars. & *Winter Legends* for pf. & orch.; chamber m, incl. Nonet, 8tet, 5tets for pf. & stgs., ob. & stgs., stgs. & hp., stgs., 3 stg. 4tets, pf. 4tet, trios for v., va. & pf. and fl., va. & hp.; 3 sos. for v. & pf., So. for va. & pf., So. for co. & pf., So. for cl. & pf.; 4 pf. sos. & numerous pf. pieces; So. & 5 other works for 2 pfs.; many songs and a number of folksong arrs., &c.

Bax, Clifford (b. 1886), Eng. poet & dramatist, brother of prec. *See* **Gibbs (C. A.)** (*Midsummer Madness*), **Shaw (M.)** (*Mr. Pepys*).

Bayer, Joseph (b. Vienna, 6. III. 1852; d. Vienna, 12. III. 1913), Aus. cond. & comp. Studied at the Vienna Cons., played the v. at the Court Opera and from 1885 was dir. of the ballet m. there.

Works incl. operettas *Der Chevalier von San Marco, Menelaus, Fräulein Hexe, Der Polizeichef* & others; ballets *Die Puppenfee* & many others, &c.

Bayreuth. The small town in Bavaria where Wagner built the festival theatre for the perf. of his works, opened in 1876 with the 1st prod. of the *Ring*.

Bazin, (Emmanuel Joseph) François (b. Marseilles, 4. IX. 1816; d. Paris, 2. VII. 1878), Fr. cond. & comp. Won the Prix de Rome at the Paris Cons. in 1840 and was later a prof. there. 7 of his operas were prod. at the Opéra-Comique between 1846–65.

Bazzini, Antonio (b. Brescia, 11. III. 1818; d. Milan, 10. II. 1897), It. vst. & comp. Toured in many countries, prod. an opera at Milan in 1867 and became prof. of comp. at the Cons. there in 1873; dir. in 1882.

Works incl. opera *Turanda* (after Gozzi's *Turandot*); concert ovts. to Alfieri's *Saul* and Shakespeare's *King Lear*; 2 cantatas; 6 stg. 4tets and other chamber m.; *Ronde des lutins* for v. & pf., &c.

Beach (*née* **Cheney), Amy Marcy** (b. Henniker, New Hampshire, 5. IX. 1867; d. New York, 27. XII, 1944), Amer. pfst. & comp., known as Mrs. Henry Beach.

Works incl. Mass in E maj.; *Christ in the Universe* for chor. & orch.; *Gaelic Sym.*; pf. Conc.; stg. 4tet, pf. Trio; numerous songs, &c.

Beale, William (b. Landrake, 1. I. 1784; d. London, 3. V. 1854), Eng. comp. Choir-boy at Westminster Abbey in London; joined the Navy; Gentleman of the Chapel Royal, 1816–20; orgst. of Trinity Coll., Cambridge, 1820–1, and of var. London churches later. Wrote glees and so-called madrigals.

Bear, The (*L'Ours*), the nickname of a Sym. by Haydn, No. 82 in C maj. (No. 1 of the 'Paris' syms.), comp. in 1786.

Bearbeitung (Ger. = working with or working upon). The process, either in playing or writing down, of developing given material, also that of arranging m. for another than its orig. medium.

Beard, John (b. London, *c.* 1717; d. Hampton, 5. II. 1791), Eng. ten. singer. Brought up as a chorister at the Chapel Royal in London under Gates; appeared 1st as a mature singer in works by Handel in 1736.

Beat. An ornament in old m. prob. similar to the mordent; the time-unit in m. indicated by the upper figure in the time-signature (e.g. a mvt. in 3–4 time has 3 beats to the bar); hence the cond.'s motion indicating each of these time units.

Beat (obs.) = Appoggiatura (taken from the note below).

Béatitudes, Les, orat. by Franck for solo voices, chor. & orch. (words from the Bible), comp. 1869–79, 1st perf. privately by the comp.'s pupils at his house, and in public only after his death, Paris, 1893.

Beatrice di Tenda, opera by Bellini (lib. by Felice Romani), prod. Venice, Teatro La Fenice, 16. III. 1833.

Béatrice et Bénédict (*Beatrice and Benedick*), opera by Berlioz (lib. by comp., based on Shakespeare's *Much Ado about Nothing*), prod. Baden-Baden, 9. VIII. 1862.

Beaucé, Delphine. *See* **Ugalde.**

Beaujoyeulx, Baltasar de. *See* **Ballet comique de la Reine** *and* **Baltazarini.**

Beaulieu, (Marie) Désiré (family name Martin-Beaulieu) (b. Paris, 11. IV. 1791; d. Niort, 21. XII. 1863), Fr. comp. & scholar. Won the Prix de Rome at the Paris Cons. in 1810 and settled at Niort, where he founded mus. socs. for the perf. of chamber and esp. chor. works. He wrote several theoret. books.

Works incl. operas *Anacréon* & *Philadelphie*; Requiem for Méhul; 3 orats.; masses and other church m.; orch. works, &c.

Beaumarchais, Pierre Augustin Caron de (1732–99), Fr. author & min. musn. He sang and played the fl. and hp., teaching the latter to the daughters of Louis XV. His comedy, *Le Barbier de Séville*, was at 1st to be a comic opera with m. arr. by B. from Spa. songs and dances. *See also* **Auric** (*Mariage de Figaro*), **Barbiere di Siviglia** (Paisiello & Rossini), **Benda (F. L.)** (*Barbier von Sevilla*), **Dittersdorf** (*Hochzeit des F.*), **Glière** (*Figaro*), **Morlacchi** (*Barbiere di S.*), **Nozze di Figaro** (Mozart), **Paer** (*Nuovo Figaro*), **Portugal** (*Pazza giornata*), **Ricci (L.)** (do. & *Nozze di F.*), **Schulz** (*Barbier de Séville*), **Shaporin** (*Marriage of F.*), **Tarare** (Salieri).

Beaumont, Francis (1584–1616) & **Fletcher, John** (1579–1625), Eng. poets & dramatists. *See* **Austin (F.)** (*Knight of the Burning Pestle*), **Confalonieri** (F.'s *Faithful Shep-*

herdess), **Cooper (J.)** (masque), **Glanville-Hicks** (Fletcher), **Grabu** (*Maid's Tragedy*), **Johnson (R. ii)** (F.'s *Valentinian & Mad Lover*), **Pastoral** (Bliss: F.), **Prophetess** (Purcell), **Purcell** (*Bonduca & Double Marriage*), F.'s *Fool's Preferment & Rule a Wife*), **Rawsthorne** (F., 2 songs).

Bebization. A 15th–16th-cent. Ger. system similar to Solmization, now obs.

Bebung (Ger. = Trembling). An effect of tone-vibration obtainable on the Clavichord by letting the finger oscillate on the key much as stg. players do in prod. *Vibrato.*

Bécarre (Fr.) = Natural: the sign ♮.

Beck, Conrad (b. Lohn, Schaffhausen, 16. VI. 1901), Swi. comp. After studying engineering, he became a student at the Zürich Cons. under Andreae and others; later in Berlin and Paris, where he lived in 1923–32 and was closely in touch with Roussel and Honegger.

Works incl. opera *La Grande Ourse*; incid. m. for Goethe's *Pandora* & other plays; orat. *Angelus Silesius*; Requiem; *Der Tod des Oedipus* for chor. & orch.; *Lyric Cantata* (Rilke) for female voices & orch.; chamber cantata (sonnets by Louise Labé); 5 syms., *Sinfonietta*, *Innominata* & *Ostinato* for orch.; Conc. for stg. 4tet & orch., *Konzertmusik* for ob. & stgs., Conc., Concertino & Rhapsody for pf. & orch., co. Conc.; 4 stg. 4tets; org. & pf. works; *Liederspiel* cycle & other songs, &c.

Beck, Franz (b. Mannheim, 15. II. 1723; d. Bordeaux, 31. XII. 1809), Ger. vst. & comp. At first a later member of the Mannheim school of early symsts., pupil of J. Stamitz. Fled to Fr. after a duel and settled at Bordeaux in 1761.

Works incl. incid. m.; *Stabat Mater*, syms. & ovts.; hpchd. sos., &c.

Becken (Ger., sing. & plur., lit. basin[s], bowl[s] = Cymbal[s].

Becker, Albert (Ernst Anton) (b. Quedlinburg, 13. VI. 1834; d. Berlin, 10. I. 1899), Ger. comp. Studied under Dehn in Berlin; later taught there and became dir. of the cath. choir in 1891.

Works incl. Mass in B♭ maj.; orat. *Selig aus Gnade*; psalms, motets & other sacred m.; Sym. in G min.; chamber m., songs, &c.

Beddoes, Thomas Lovell (1803–49), Eng. physiologist, poet & dramatist. *See* **Busch** (songs), **Dieren (van)** (do.), **Ireland (J.)** (*If there were dreams*), **Warlock** (*Sorrow's Lullaby*).

Bedford, Herbert (b. London, 23. I. 1867; d. London, 13. III. 1945), Eng. comp., author & painter. Largely self-taught in m. Married Liza Lehmann in X. 1894.

Works incl. opera *Kit Marlowe*; love scene from *Romeo and Juliet* for con., bar. & orch.; masque *The Daughters of Dawn*; many misc. works, incl. m. for military band and unaccomp. songs.

Bedyngham, John (b. ?; d. ?), Eng. 15th-cent. comp. Wrote masses, motets and other church m.; known on the Continent as well as in Eng.

Bee's Wedding, The. The Eng. nickname of Mendelssohn's Song without Words in C maj., Op. 67 No. 4, the Ger. being *Spinnerlied* (spinning-song). Neither title was the comp.'s own.

Beecke, Ignaz von (b. Wimpfen-im-Tal, 28. X. 1733; d. Wallerstein, 3. I. 1803), Ger. pfst. and comp. Officer in a Württemberg regiment, where he was adjutant and chapel master to Prince Oettingen-Wallerstein.

Works incl. opera *Claudine von Villa Bella* (Goethe), orat. *The Resurrection*, syms., concs., sos., &c.

Beer, Jakob Liebmann. *See* **Meyerbeer.**

Beerbohm, Max (b. 1872), Eng. essayist, novelist & caricaturist. *See* **Addinsell** (*Happy Hypocrite*), **Elwell** (do.).

Beethoven, Ludwig van (b. Bonn, 16. XII. 1770; d. Vienna, 26. III. 1827), Ger. comp. of Flem. descent. Son and grandson of musns. at the court of the Elector of Cologne at Bonn. Was taught by var. local musns. and pub. a pf. work at the age of 12. Became cembalist in the orch. and accompst. at the theatre in 1783, court orgst. in 1784 and played va. in the opera orch. from *c.* 1787. Having met Haydn twice at Bonn, he went to Vienna to study under him in 1792, but soon passed on to Schenk, Albrechtsberger, Salieri and Aloys Förster. Remained in Vienna and made his 1st public appearance as pfst. in 1795. Began to make a living by publishing his m. and giving lessons in aristocratic houses. Began to be alarmed by the threat of deafness in 1801 and wrote a suicidal document ('Heiligenstadt Testament') in 1802. Prod. his only opera in 1805. He fell deeply in love several times, e.g. with Countess Therese von Brunswick in 1809, but never married; nor did he travel much, either for pleasure or professionally. In 1812 he was seriously ill and his deafness increased disastrously. On the death of his brother Karl, his nephew, also named Karl, fell to his charge, then aged 9, and caused him endless trouble for the next 10 years. Meanwhile his fame became international. Invitation from the Phil. Soc. in London,

1824, but he was too ill to go; in 1826 Karl's attempt at suicide caused B.'s health to break down completely. He was quite deaf by that time, and his death the following year was due to dropsy.

Works incl. opera *Fidelio*; ballet *The Creatures of Prometheus*; incid. m. to Goethe's *Egmont* & to *The Ruins of Athens* & *King Stephen*; orat. *Christ at the Mount of Olives*; 2 Masses (incl. *Missa solemnis*); 9 syms.; 6 concert ovts.; 5 pf. concs.; v. Conc.; Conc. for pf., v. & co.; 16 stg. 4tets; *Great Fugue* for stg. 4tet; 8 pf. trios; 7tet; misc. chamber m.; 10 v. & pf. sos.; 5 co. & pf. sos; 32 pf. sos.; many sets of vars., 3 sets of *Bagatelles* & misc. pieces for pf.; numerous songs, incl. *Adelaide* and the cycle *An die ferne Geliebte*, &c.

Beffroy de Reigny, Louis Abel (b. Lâon, 6. XI. 1757; d. Paris, 17. XII. 1811), Fr. playwright & comp. Known as 'Cousin Jacques,' under which name he wrote satirical operettas popular during the Revolution, incl. *Nicodème dans la lune*, *Les Deux Nicodèmes* & *La Petite Nanette*.

Beggar's Opera, The, ballad opera with tunes arr. by Pepusch (lib. by John Gay), prod. London, Theatre in Lincoln's Inn Fields, 29. I. 1728. The tunes are for the most part not folksongs, but popular tunes of the day, chiefly opera and theatre songs, chosen mainly from Durfey's *Wit and Mirth, or Pills to Purge Melancholy*.

Begleiten (Ger.) = Accompanying.

Begleitung (Ger.) = Accompaniment.

Begnis (*née* **Ronzi**), **Giuseppina de** (b. Milan, 11. I. 1800; d. Florence, 7. VI. 1853), It. sop. singer. Studied at the Paris Cons. and (?) appeared at Bologna in 1816, where she married Giuseppe de B. Made her 1st appearance in Paris in 1819 and in London in 1822.

Begnis, Giuseppe de (b. Lugo, 1793; d. New York, VIII. 1849), It. singer, husband of prec. Choir-boy at Lugo; made his 1st operatic appearance at Modena in 1813, and went to Paris and London with his wife, 1819 and 1822.

Behn (*née* **Johnston**), **Aphra** (1640–89), Eng. dramatist & novelist. *See* **Courteville** (*Oroonoko*), **Paisible** (do.), **Purcell** (do. & *Abdelazer*).

Beiden Freunde von Salamanka, Die (*see* **Freunde von Salamanka**). The correct title of Schubert's operetta is *Die Freunde von Salamanka*: the word 'beiden' was erroneously inserted later, and the story is not about 2 friends, but 3.

Beisser (Ger. obs.) = Mordent.

Bekker, Paul (b. Berlin, 11. IX. 1882; d. New York, 7. III. 1937), Ger. writer on m. Studied in Berlin and was at 1st a vst. in the Phil. Orch. there. In 1906 he began to devote himself to mus. journalism and became critic to several papers, later operatic manager at Cassel and Wiesbaden. The Nazi regime drove him to U.S.A. Wrote on Beethoven, Wagner, Mahler, opera and modern comps.

Beklemmt (Ger. = oppressed). A term used by Beethoven in the Cavatina of the stg. 4tet, Op. 130.

Bel canto (It. lit. beautiful song). Singing in the traditional It. manner, with beautiful tone, perfect phrasing, clean articulation, &c. The art of B. c. culminated in It. in the 19th cent., but has now sadly declined there.

Belaiev, Mitrofan Petrovitch (b. St. Petersburg, 22. II. 1836; d. St. Petersburg, 10. I. 1907). Rus. timber merchant & mus. amateur. Founded a pub. firm for the propagation of Rus. m. in 1885.

Belaiev, Victor Mikhailovitch (b. Uralsk, 5. II. 1888), Rus. critic. Has written mainly on m. in var. Soviet countries, esp. Turkmenistan and Uzbekistan.

Belasco, David (1859–1931), Amer. playwright. *See* **Fanciulla del West** (**Puccini**), **Madama Butterfly** (do.)

Belcari, Feo (1410–84), It. poet & dramatist. *See* **Pizzetti** (*Sacra rappresentazione di Abraam ed Isacco*).

Beldemandis, Prosdocimo de (b. Padua, ?; d. ?), It. 14th–15th-cent. mus. scholar. Prof. at Padua in 1400. Wrote treatises on m. pub. between 1404–13. His name was playfully adopted by Philip Heseltine to catch his critics who had never heard of it before and took it for his own invention.

Belenoi, Aimeric de (b. Lespare, Bordelais, ?; d. Catalonia, ?), Fr. 13th-cent. troubadour, 22 of whose songs have been preserved.

Belfagor, opera by Respighi (lib. by Claudio Guastalla, based on a comedy by Ercole Luigi Morselli), prod. Milan, Teatro alla Scala, 26. IV. 1923.

Belg. (abbr.) = Belgian, Belgium.

Belgian (excl. earlier Flemish) Comps. *See* **Absil, Benoît, Bériot, Blockx, Campenhout, Dupuis** (2), **Eeden** (**van den**), **Franck, Gevaert, Gilson, Goovaerts, Gossec, Gregoir** (2), **Grétry, Grisar, Hasselmans, Hullebroek, Huybrechts, Jongen, Lassen, Le Borne, Lekeu, Lemmens, Maleingreau, Mathieu, Mermet, Quinet, Radoux** (2), **Ryelandt, Servais** (**F.**), **Timmermans, Tinel, Urhan, Verheyen, Vieuxtemps, Vreuls, Ysaÿe** (2).

Beliczay, Julius von (b. Komorn, 10. VIII. 1835; d. Budapest, 30. IV.

1893), Hung. theorist & comp. Trained for an engineer at first, but studied m. in Vienna and became prof. at the Nat. M. Acad. at Budapest. Pub. a book on comp. in Hung., 1891.

Works incl. Mass in F maj., *Ave Maria* for sop., chor. & orch.; 2 syms., pieces for stg. orch.; 3 stg. 4tets; pf. pieces; songs, &c.

Belin, Julien (b. Le Mans, *c.* 1530; d. ?), Fr. lutenist & comp. Pub. a book of lute pieces in tablature, 1556.

Belisario, opera by Donizetti (lib. by Salvatore Cammarano), prod. Venice, Teatro La Fenice, 4. II. 1836.

'Bell Anthem.' The familiar name of Purcell's anthem, *Rejoice in the Lord alway,* comp. *c.* 1682–5. The inst. introd. contains descending scales resembling the ringing of church bells.

Bell Gamba. An 8-ft. org. stop similar to the Gamba stop, but with the pipes surmounted by a 'bell' or cone.

Bell, W(illiam). H(enry). (b. St. Albans, 20. VIII. 1873), Eng. comp., cond. & teacher. Studied at the R.A.M. in London and under Stanford. In 1912 became principal of the S. African Coll. of M. at Capetown.

Works incl. operas *Hippolytus* (after Euripides), *Isabeau* and Japanese Noh-play *Tsuneyo*; incid. m. for Ben Jonson's masque *A Vision of Delight*; *Maria Assumpta* for chor.; 2 syms., *Walt Whitman Sym.*, Symph. Vars. for orch., several symph. poems; v. & va. sos., &c.

Bella, Jan Levoslav (b. Liptovsky Svaty Mikuláš, 1843; d. Bratislava, 25. V. 1936), Slovak priest & comp. Studied at Levoča and entered the priesthood. Wrote masses on Slovak folk tunes and other religious works. Prod. an opera, *Veland the Smith,* based on Wagner's sketched lib. for *Wieland der Schmied,* at Bratislava in 1926. Other works incl. a symph. poem, a stg. 4tet and Slovak folksong arrs.

Bellaigue, Camille (b. Paris, 24. V. 1858; d. Paris, 4. X. 1930), Fr. critic & pfst. Attached to the *Revue des Deux Mondes* from 1885. Author of an early biog. of Verdi and many other books on m.

Bellanda, Lodovico (b. ? Verona, ?; d. ? Verona, ?), It. 16th–17th-cent. comp. Lived at Verona; wrote sacred voc. pieces, madrigals, canzonette for 3 voices and songs.

Bellasio, Paolo (b. Verona, ?; d. ? Bologna, *c.* 1595), It. comp. Lived in Rome for a time and wrote 5 books of madrigals.

Bellazzi, Francesco (b. Vigevano, ?; d. ? Venice, ?), It. monk & comp. Pupil (?) of G. Gabrieli at Venice. 6 books of his masses, motets and other sacred works of his were pub. between 1618–28.

Belle Hélène, La (*The Fair Helen*), operetta by Offenbach (lib. by Henri Meilhac & Ludovic Halévy), prod. Paris, Théâtre des Variétés, 17. XII. 1864.

Bellermann. Ger. family of mus. scholars:

1. Johann Joachim B. (b. Erfurt, 23. IX. 1754; d. Berlin, 25. X. 1842). Wrote on Rus., incl. m.

2. Johann Friedrich B. (b. Erfurt, 8. III. 1795; d. Berlin, 4. II. 1874), son of prec. Wrote on ancient Gr. m.

3. Johann Gottfried Heinrich B. (b. Berlin, 10. III. 1832; d. Potsdam, 10. IV. 1903), son of prec. Wrote on mensural notation and ctpt. He was also a comp.

Bellerofonte, Il, opera by Mysliveček (lib. by Giuseppe Bonechi), prod. Naples, Teatro San Carlo, 20. I. 1767.

Opera by Terradellas (lib. by Francesco Vanneschi), prod. London, King's Theatre, Haymarket, 24. III. 1747.

Bellérophon, opera by Lully (lib. by Thomas Corneille with (?) Bernard de Fontenelle and Boileau), prod. Paris, Opéra, 31. I. 1679.

Belletti, Giovanni (b. Sarzana, 1813; d. Sarzana, ?), It. bar. singer. Studied at Bologna and made his 1st stage appearance at Stockholm in 1838 under the patronage of the sculptor Byström, and then sang with Jenny Lind, who was also coming out just then.

Belli, Domenico (b. ?; d. ?), It. 16th–17th-cent. comp. Prob. in the service of the Duke of Parma, and teacher at the church of San Lorenzo at Florence, 1610–3. Pub. a book of airs for 1 & 2 voices with chitarrone accomp. and another of 5 interludes for Tasso's *Aminta.*

Belli, Girolamo (b. Argenta nr. Ferrara, *c.* 1550; d. ?), It. comp. Pupil of Luzzaschi; in the service of the Duke of Mantua; in Rome in 1582. Pub. several books of madrigals as well as masses, psalms and *Sacrae cantiones.*

Belli, Giulio (b. Longiano, *c.* 1560; d. ? Imola, ?), It. monk & comp. Held var. church apps. at Imola, Venice, Montagnana, Osimo, Forli and Padua. He returned to Imola in 1611. Wrote madrigals and other secular voc. works at first, but (?) only church m. later, incl. numerous masses, motets, psalms, &c.

Bellini, Vincenzo (b. Catania, Sicily, 1. XI. 1801; d. Puteaux nr. Paris, 23. IX. 1835), It. comp. His father, an orgst., was enabled with the help of a Sicilian nobleman to send him to study with Zingarelli at the

Naples Cons., where he met Donizetti and Mercadante. In 1825 his 1st opera was prod., while he was still a student, and attracted the attention of Barbaia, who commissioned him to write a 2nd, which he prod. at the San Carlo Theatre in 1826. Its success induced Barbaia to ask for another opera for the Scala Theatre at Milan, which was prod. there in 1827 with Rubini in the cast. It was also successfully perf. in Paris, and 3 other operas followed, at Milan, Parma and Venice, before he attained full maturity in *La sonnambula*, brought out at Milan in 1831. *Norma* followed in XII of the same year, with Pasta in the title-part. In 1833 B. went to London and Paris, where Rossini advised him to write a work for the Théâtre Italien. This was *I puritani*, prod. there in 1835, with Giulia Grisi, Rubini, Tamburini and Lablache in the cast. It was brought to London the same year for Grisi's benefit perf. B. went to stay with an Eng. friend at Puteaux, at whose house he was taken ill and died.

Works incl. operas *Adelson e Salvini, Bianca e Gernando, Il pirata, La straniera, Zaira, I Capuletti ed i Montecchi* (based on Shakespeare's *Romeo and Juliet*), *La sonnambula, Norma, Beatrice di Tenda, I puritani*, &c.

Belloc, (Joseph) Hilaire (Pierre) (b. 1870), Eng. man of letters of Fr. descent. *See* **Williams (G.)** (songs).

Belloc, Teresa Giorgi (b. San Benigno Cavanese, 2. VII. 1784; d. San Giorgio Cavanese, 13. V. 1855), It. sop. singer of Fr. descent. Made her 1st appearance at the Teatro Regio, Turin, in 1801.

Belly. The body of stg. insts., also sometimes the Sound-board of the pf.

Belmont und Constanze, oder Die Entführung aus dem Serail, opera by André (lib. by Christoph Friedrich Bretzner, based on Isaac Bickerstaffe's *The Captive*), prod. Berlin, 25. V. 1781.

Opera by Christian Ludwig Dieter (1757–1822) (lib. do.), prod. Stuttgart, 27. VIII. 1784.

For Mozart's opera on this subject *see* **Entführung.**

Belshazzar, orat. by Handel (words by Charles Jennens), prod. London, King's Theatre, Haymarket, 27. III. 1745.

Belshazzar's Feast, cantata by William Walton (words from the Bible arr. by Osbert Sitwell), prod. Leeds Festival, 8. X. 1931.

Belyi, Victor. *See* **Biely.**

Bemberg, Herman (b. Buenos Aires, 29. III. 1861), Fr. comp. Pupil of Dubois and Massenet at the Paris Cons.

Works incl. operas *Le Baiser de Suzon* & *Elaine*; cantata *La Mort de Jeanne d'Arc*; recitation with accomp. *La Ballade du désespéré*; many songs incl. *Aime-moi* & *Chant hindou*, &c.

Bémol (Fr.) = Flat: the sign ♭.

Benda. Boh. 17th–18th-cent. family of musns.:

1. Jan Jiři B. (b. ? Staré-Benatky, ?; d. ? Staré-Benatky, ?). Weaver and wandering perf. on several insts.

2. František (Franz) B. (b. Staré-Benatky, 25. XI. 1709; d. Potsdam, 7. III. 1786), vst. & comp., son of prec. Choir-boy at Prague; went to Dresden as a vst., where Quantz heard him and engaged him for the service of the Crown Prince of Prus. at Rheinsberg in 1732. In 1771, on the death of J. G. Graun, he became concert master to the same patron, now Frederick II. His daughter Juliane married Reichardt.

Works incl. concs., trios, solos and studies for v., &c.

3. Jan B. (b. Staré-Benatky, 1713; d. Berlin, 1752), brother of prec. Entered the royal band in Berlin in 1740 and became chamber musn.

4. Jiři Antonín (Georg), (b. Staré-Benatky, 30. VI. 1722; d. Köstritz, Thuringia, 6. XI. 1795), comp., clav. & oboe player, brother of prec. He entered the royal band in Berlin, 1742, and became chapel master to the Duke of Gotha, 1748, whence he went to It. for a time. On his return to Gotha he wrote a melodrama, prod. in 1775. It was followed by a 2nd the same year. In 1778 he went to live at Hamburg, and in the end he retired to Köstritz.

Works incl. operas *Der Dorfjahrmarkt, Romeo und Julie, Walder, Der Holzhauer* & *Philon und Theone*; melodramas *Ariadne auf Naxos* & *Medea*; masses; church cantatas; syms.; concs.; sos., &c.

5. Josef B. (b. Staré-Benatky, 7. III. 1724; d. Berlin, 1804); vst., brother of prec. He was concert master to Frederick Willliam II in Berlin.

6. Anna Františka B. (b. Staré-Benatky, 1726; d. Gotha, 1780), singer, sister of prec. She joined her brother (4 above) at the court of Gotha, where she married a musn. named Hattasch.

7. Friedrich Wilhelm Heinrich B. (b. Potsdam, 15. VII. 1745; d. Potsdam, 19. VII. 1814), vst. & clav. player, son of 2. Played in the Prus. court band from 1782.

8. Friedrich Ludwig B. (b. Gotha, 1746; d. Königsberg, 27. III. 1792), comp., son of 4. Lived at Hamburg,

1780–2, and became mus. dir. at Königsberg in 1789.

Works incl. opera *Der Barbier von Sevilla* (based on Beaumarchais's play) & 2 others; orat.; 5 church cantatas; 3 v. concs.; v. & pf. So., &c.

9. Ernst Friedrich B. (b. Berlin, 1747; d. Berlin, 1785), son of 5. One of the founders of the Berlin amateur concerts.

10. Carl Hermann Heinrich B. (b. ?, 1748; d. ?), vst., son of 2. Taught m. to Frederick William III of Prus.

Works incl. v. So. and 6 adagios for pf.

Bendix, Victor Emanuel (b. Copenhagen, 17. V. 1851; d. Copenhagen, 5. I. 1926), Dan. cond. and comp. Pupil of Gade. Cond. chor. and orch. concerts.

Works incl. 4 syms.; pf. Conc.; Psalm with orch.; pf. Trio; pf. So.; songs, &c.

Bendl, Karel (b. Prague, 16. IV. 1838; d. Prague, 20. IX. 1897), Boh. comp. Spent some of his life in Fr., Belg. and It., but was a nationalist of the school of Smetana. Wrote operas, chor. and orch. works, church and chamber m.

Benedict, Julius (b. Stuttgart, 27. XI. 1804; d. London, 5. VI. 1885), Ger. (anglicized) cond. & comp. Pupil of Hummel and Weber, with the latter of whom he met Beethoven in Vienna in 1823, when he was app. cond. at the Kärntnertor Theatre. Next he went to Naples, where he prod. his 1st It. opera in 1829. In 1834 he went to Paris and in 1835 to London, where he remained for the rest of his life. He cond. a great deal in London, both opera and concerts, and was cond. of the Norwich Festival, 1845–78, and of the Liverpool Phil. Soc., 1876–80. Knighted in 1871.

Works incl. operas *Giacinta ed Ernesto, I Portoghesi in Goa, Un anno ed un giorno, The Gypsy's Warning, The Brides of Venice, The Crusaders, The Lily of Killarney, The Bride of Song*; 2 syms.; 2 pf. concs.; 5 cantatas, &c.

Benelli, Antonio Peregrino (b. Forli, 5. IX. 1771; d. Börnichen, Saxony, 16. VIII. 1830), It. ten. singer & comp. Studied under Mattei at Bologna and made his 1st stage appearance at Naples in 1790. Comp. church m. and wrote a treatise on singing.

Benet, John (b. ?; d. ?), Eng. 15th-cent. comp. Wrote masses and other church m.

Benevoli, Orazio (b. Rome, 1602; d. Rome, 17. VI. 1672), It. comp. Held apps. at the churches of San Luigi de' Francesi and Santa Maria Maggiore in Rome, the former with an interruption in 1643–5, when he was at the Aus. court in Vienna. In 1646 he became chapel master at the Vatican.

Works incl. masses, motets and other church m., much of it for several choirs in a large number of parts, up to 56 voices.

Benjamin, Arthur (b. Sydney, 18. IX. 1893), Austral. pfst. & comp. Educ. at Brisbane and studied m. at the R.C.M. in London, where later he became prof. After fighting in the 1914–8 war, he returned to Austral. to teach pf. at the Sydney Cons. in 1919–21, but having developed as a comp., settled in London, but from 1937 lived at Vancouver.

Works incl. operas *The Devil take her* & *Prima Donna*; film m., Sym., Suite *Light M.* & *Ov. to an It. Comedy* for orch.; *Romantic Fantasy* for v., va. & orch., v. Conc., Concertino for pf. & orch., *Elegy, Waltz and Toccata* for va. & orch.; *Pastoral Fantasy* for stg. 4tet, cl. 5tet; Sonatina for v. & pf.; Suite & pieces for pf.; songs, &c.

Bennet, John (b. ?, *c.* 1570; d. ?), Eng. 16th–17th-cent. comp. Pub. a book of madrigals in 1599 and contrib. others to collections, incl. *The Triumphes of Oriana*; he also left an anthem and 5 hymn tunes.

Bennett, (Enoch) Arnold (1867–1931), Eng. novelist & dramatist. See **Don Juan de Mañara** (Goossens), **Judith** (do.).

Bennett, Joseph (b. Berkeley, Glos., 29. XI. 1831; d. Purton, 12. VI. 1911), Eng. critic & author. Lived in London and was for many years m. critic of the *Daily Telegraph*. Wrote libs. for J. F. Barnett, Bottesini, Cowen, Mackenzie and Sullivan (*The Golden Legend*).

Bennett, Robert Russell (b. Kansas City, 15. VI. 1894), Amer. pfst., cond. & comp. Studied with his parents and later with Nadia Boulanger in Paris. He played in his father's orch. as a youth and earned a living as arranger and orchestrator.

Works incl. opera *Maria Malibran*; film m. *Sights and Sounds, Abraham Lincoln*; Sym., *Charleston Rhapsody*, &c. for orch.; March for 2 pfs. & orch., &c.

Bennett, William Sterndale (b. Sheffield, 13. IV. 1816; d. London, 1. II. 1875), Eng. pfst. & comp. Chorister at King's Coll., Cambridge and student at the R.A.M. in London. Pupil of Mendelssohn at Leipzig, where Schumann ded. his *Études symphoniques* for pf. to him. Prof. of M. at Cambridge Univ., 1856–75. Knighted 1871.

Works incl. incid. m. to Sophocles' *Ajax*; cantata *The May Queen*, odes for the Internat. Exhib. (Tennyson) & the Cambridge Installation of a Chancellor (Kingsley); anthems; Sym. in G min., ovts. *The Naiads* & *The Wood-Nymphs*, fantasy-ovt. on Moore's *Paradise and the Peri*; 4 pf. concs.; pf. pieces, songs, &c.

Benoît, Camille (b. Roanne, Loire, 7. XII. 1851; d. Paris, 1. VII. 1923), Fr. writer on m. & comp. Pupil of Franck. On the staff of the Louvre museum and curator from 1895.

Works incl. opera *Cléopâtre*; symph. poem *Merlin l'enchanteur*; *Eleison* for solo voices, chor. & orch.; Epithalamium for Anatole France's *Noces corinthiennes*, &c.

Benoît, Pierre (Léopold Léonard) (b. Harlebeke, 17. VIII. 1834; d. Antwerp, 8. III. 1901), Belg. comp. Pupil of Fétis at the Brussels Cons. He became cond. at a Flem. theatre and was keenly interested in Flem. nat. m. as distinct from that influenced by Fr. comps. He travelled in Ger. and visited Paris, but tended more and more towards an indigenous type of m. His 1st opera was prod. in 1857.

Works incl. Fr. opera *Le Roi des aulnes* (on Goethe's *Erl King*), Flem. operas *The Mountain Village*, *Isa*, *Pompeja*; incid. m. to Flem. plays; Te Deum, *Messe solennelle*, Requiem; orats. *Lucifer* & *The Scheldt*; *Petite Cantate de Noël* and many Flem. cantatas, &c.

Benserade, Isaac de (1612–91), Fr. poet & dramatist. *See* **Festes de l'Amour** (Lully).

Bentzon, Jørgen (b. Copenhagen, 14. II. 1897), Dan. comp. Studied law at first, but became a comp. pupil of Nielsen in 1915 and in 1920–1 was at the Leipzig Cons. President of the Dan. school of m.

Works incl. ovt. and vars. for orch.; 5 stg. 4tets, *Racconti* & *Variazioni interrotti* for wind & stgs., Sonatina for wind insts., Intermezzo for fl., cl. & v., &c.

Benucci, Francesco (b. ?, c. 1745; d. Florence, 5. IV. 1824), It. bass singer. He was engaged for Vienna in 1783, and was Mozart's orig. Figaro there in 1786.

Benvenuto Cellini, opera by Berlioz (lib. by Léon de Wailly & Auguste Barbier, based on Cellini's autobiog.), prod. Paris, Opéra, 10. IX. 1838.

Béranger, Pierre Jean de (1780–1857), Fr. poet. *See* **Monpou** (*Si j'étais petit oiseau*).

Berceuse (Fr.) = Cradle Song. Although strictly speaking a song, a B. may just as well be an inst. piece.

Berchem, Jachet (b. ?; d. ?), Flem. 16th-cent. comp. Prob. orgst. to the ducal court at Ferrara in 1555. Wrote church m., madrigals, capricci for 4 voices, Fr. chansons, &c.

Berenice, opera by Handel (lib. by Antonio Salvi), prod. London, Covent Garden Theatre, 18. V. 1757.

Opera by Perti (lib. do.), prod. Villa Pratolino nr. Florence, IX. 1709.

Berenstadt, Gaetan (b. ?; d. ?), It. bass singer of Ger. descent. The 1st record of his appearing in London dates from 1717.

Berezovsky, Maximus Sosnovitch (b. Glukhov, 1745; d. St. Petersburg, 1778), Rus. comp. Studied at Kiev and under Martini at Bologna. He had been a singer in the Imp. Chapel before, and when he returned after 9 years, he hoped to obtain the post of singing-master there and shot himself on being refused.

Works incl. opera *Demofoonte*; Lord's Prayer for solo voices & chor.; songs, &c.

Berezovsky, Nikolai (b. St. Petersburg, 17. V. 1900), Rus. (Americanized) vst. & comp. Learnt m. in the Imperial Chapel at St. Petersburg, became vst. in the opera orchs. at Saratov and Moscow and cond. at the School of Modern Art there; but emigrated to U.S.A. in 1922, continued his studies there, played in the N.Y. Phil. Orch., became a member of the Coolidge 4tet and appeared as concert and broadcasting cond.

Works incl. 4 syms., *Sinfonietta* & *Hebrew Suite* for orch.; waltzes for stg. orch.; v. Conc., Fantasy for 2 pfs. & orch., *Concerto lirico* for co. & orch., *Toccata, Vars. & Finale* for stg. 4tet & orch.; 2 stg. 4tets, 2 woodwind 5tets, 6tet for cl., pf. & stgs., suite for 7 brass insts., &c.

Berg, Alban (b. Vienna, 9. II. 1885; d. Vienna, 24. XII. 1935), Aus. comp. Began to teach himself at the age of 15 and in 1904 became a pupil of Schoenberg. In 1911 he married Helene Nahowski and in 1915–8 he served in the Aus. army. From 1918 to his death he taught privately in Vienna and travelled occasionally for the prod. of his works.

Works incl. operas *Wozzeck* & *Lulu* (unfinished); v. Conc.; stg. 4tet; Chamber Conc. for pf., v. & 13 wind insts.; *Lyric Suite* for stg. 4tet; *Der Wein*, concert aria for sop. & orch.; 5 orch. songs; 3 orch. pieces; 4 pieces for cl. & pf.; pf. So.; 11 songs, &c.

Berg, Natanael (b. Stockholm, 9. II. 1879), Swe. comp. Studied at the Stockholm Cons. and in Paris and Vienna.

Works incl. operas *Leila* (after

Byron's *Giaour*), *Engelbrekt* & *Judith* (after Hebbel's drama); 7 symph. works for orch.; v. Conc.; 2 stg. 4tets, pf. 5tet, &c.

Bergamasca. An It. dance from Bergamo, at least as old as the 16th cent., called Bergomask by Shakespeare.

Berger, Arthur (b. New York, 15. V. 1912), Amer. comp. Studied with Piston at Harvard Univ., with Pirro at the Sorbonne in Paris, also with P. Lalo and Paul Valéry there, and comp. with Nadia Boulanger. He became m. ed. of the N.Y. *Sun*.

Works incl. *Slow Dance* for stgs.; Serenade for chamber orch.; 3 pieces for stg. 4tet, wind 4tet, 2 mvts. for va. & co.; ballet *Entertainment Piece* & other works for pf.; *Words for Music, Perhaps* (Yeats) & other songs, &c.

Bergère châtelaine, La (*The Shepherdess as Lady of the Manor*), opera by Auber (lib. by François Antoine Eugène de Planard), prod. Paris, Opéra-Comique, 27. I. 1820.

Bergerette (Fr. from *berger* = shepherd). A light Fr. song of an artifically pastoral character fashionable in the 18th cent. when society, misunderstanding Rousseau's exhortation to return to nature, affected the simple life of shepherds and shepherdesses without incurring its discomforts or cutting itself off from an existence of leisured culture.

Berggreen, Andreas Peter (b. Copenhagen, 2. III. 1801; d. Copenhagen, 9. XI. 1880), Dan. orgst., teacher & comp. He prod. the opera *Billedet og Busten* (*The Picture and the Bust*) in 1832. Among his pupils was Gade.

Works incl. collections of nat. songs, psalm tunes, &c.

Bergknappen, Die (*The Miners*), opera by Umlauf (lib. by Paul Weidmann), prod. Vienna, Burg Theatre, on the opening of its career as a nat. Ger. opera, 17. II. 1778.

Bergman, Valentina Semenovna. *See* **Serov.**

Bergmann, Carl (b. Ebersbach, Saxony, 1821; d. New York, 16. VIII. 1876), Ger. cond. Went to U.S.A. in 1850 and did much to estab. orch. m. there. He was cond. of the N.Y. Phil. Soc. in the end.

Bergomask. *See* **Bergamasca.**

Bergonzi. It. family of v. makers:

1. Carlo B. (b. Cremona, *c.* 1683; d. Cremona, 1747). He began to work independently about 1716.

2. Michelangelo B. (b. Cremona, 1722; d. Cremona, *c.* 1770), son of 1.

3. Nicola B. (b. Cremona, ?; d. ?), son of 2.

4. Zosimo B. (b. Cremona, ?; d. ?), brother of 3.

5. Carlo B. (b. Cremona, ?; d. ?), brother of 4.

Bériot, Charles (Auguste) de (b. Louvain, 20. II. 1802; d. Brussels, 8. IV. 1870), Belg. vst. & comp. Played in public at the age of 9, but 10 years later went to Paris to perfect himself under Viotti and Baillot. He had a brilliant success in Paris and was app. chamber musn. to the king. In 1826 he visited London for the 1st time. He travelled much in the company of Malibran, whom he married after her divorce from her 1st husband; but after her early death in 1836 he retired to Brussels until 1840, when he travelled again and married Marie Huber in Vienna. Prof. of v. at the Brussels Cons., 1843–52.

Works incl. 7 v. concs., vars. & studies for v., pf. trios, &c.

Berkeley, Lennox (Randal Francis) (b. Oxford, 12. V. 1903), Eng. comp. Did not study m. until he left Oxford (Merton Coll.) in 1926, when he went to Paris until 1933 as a pupil of Nadia Boulanger. Works of his were heard at the I.S.C.M. festivals at Barcelona and London, 1936 and 1938, and at the Leeds and Worcester festivals, 1937–8.

Works incl. ballet *The Judgment of Paris*; m. for film *Hotel Reserve*; orat. *Jonah*; psalm *Domini est terra* for chor. & orch.; Ovt. & Divertimento for orch.; pf. Conc.; stg. 4tet; v. & pf. So.; pf. pieces; *Polka* for 2 pfs., &c.

Berlijn, Anton (b. Amsterdam, 2. V. 1817; d. Amsterdam, 16. I. 1870), Dutch comp. Wrote 9 operas, 7 ballets, orat. *Moses*, syms., &c.

Berlin, Irving (real name Balin) (b. Rus., 11. V. 1888), Amer. comp. of Rus. origin.

Works incl. m. for plays and revues, incl. *Music Box Revues*; popular songs, e.g. *Alexander's Ragtime Band*, &c.

Berlioz, (Louis-) Hector (b. Côte-Saint-André, Isère, 11. XII. 1803; d. Paris, 8. III. 1869), Fr. comp. Son of a doctor who taught him the fl., but wished him to study medicine. As a boy he also learnt the guitar and picked up theoret. knowledge from books. Sent to the École de Médecine in Paris, 1821, he found the studies so distasteful that he decided to give them up for m. His parents made great difficulties, but Lesueur accepted him as a pupil in 1823, when he at once set to work on an opera and an orat., a mass following the next year. Entered the Cons. in 1826, but failed several times to gain the Prix de Rome, obtaining it at last in 1830. In the meantime he had fallen in love with the Ir. actress Harriet Smithson and expressed his disillusion in her in the *Fantastic Sym.* Then, on the point of going to Rome, he became engaged to the pfst., Marie Moke, who during his absence married Camille Pleyel. He wrote much in Rome and returned to Paris in 1832, this time meeting Harriet and marrying her in X. 1833. To add to his income he became a m. critic. In 1838 Paganini sent him 20,000 francs to enable him to devote all his time to comp. Separation from Harriet in 1842 and liaison with the singer Marie Recio. Much travelling with her during the next few years, to Ger., Vienna, Prague, Budapest, Rus. and London. Death of Harriet and marriage to Marie, 1854; meanwhile he had resumed his journalistic work. Death of Marie, 1862. He suffered much ill health during the 1860s and was greatly depressed by the death of his son Louis in 1867. After another visit to Rus., he had a bad fall at Nice, where he had gone for his health in 1868, and he grew gradually worse. He wrote 7 books, incl. *Traité de l'instrumentation* and *Mémoires.*

Works incl. operas *Benvenuto Cellini*, *Les Troyens* (2 parts) & *Béatrice et Bénédict* (after Shakespeare's *Much Ado about Nothing*); the programme syms., *Symphonie fantastique*, *Harold en Italie* (with solo va.), *Roméo et Juliette* (with voices) & *Symphonie funèbre et triomphale* (for military band, stgs. and chor.); 6 concert ovts.; 2 marches for orch.; 25 chor. works incl. *Messe des morts* (Requiem), *La Damnation de Faust*, *Te Deum* & *L'Enfance du Christ*; 6 smaller voc. works with orch. or pf.; 28 songs incl. the cycle *Nuits d'été*; *Lélio, ou Le Retour à la vie,* a lyric monodrama intended as a sequel to the *Fantastic Sym.*, &c.

Bermudo, Juan (b. Ecija nr. Seville, ?; d. ?), Spa. 16th-cent. friar & mus. theorist. Friend of Morales. He wrote 2 mus. treatises, pub. 1549–50.

Bernabei, Ercole (b. Caprarola, *c.* 1620; d. Munich, XII. 1687), It. comp. Pupil of Benevoli in Rome, where he worked successively at the Lateran chapel, the church of San Luigi de' Francesi and the Julian chapel. In 1674 he entered the service of the Elector of Bavaria at Munich, where he was chapel master for the rest of his life.

Works incl. 16 operas; masses, motets & other church m., &c.

Bernabei, Gioseffo Antonio (b. Rome, *c.* 1649; d. Munich, 9. III. 1732), It. comp., son of prec. He went to Munich as asst. to his father in 1677 and succeeded him in I. 1688.

Works incl. 16 operas; masses, motets & other church m., &c.

Bernacchi, Antonio (b. Bologna, VI. 1685; d. Bologna, III. 1756), It. male sop. singer & teacher. 1st heard in London in 1716.

Bernal, Antonio (b. ?; d. ? Seville, ?), Spa. 16th-cent. comp. Worked at Seville, (?) at the church of San Salvador. Wrote church m., madrigals, songs, &c.

Bernard, Robert (b. Geneva, 1900), Swi. critic & comp. Studied at Geneva, where he founded the Nouvelle Société d'Art in 1918, but settled in Paris in 1926 and later became prof. at the Cons. Internat. and the Schola Cantorum. Became asst. ed. to Prunières of the *Revue musicale* and in 1935 ed. and wrote several works on modern Fr. m.

Works incl. *Hymne à la divinité* for solo voices, chor. & orch.; *Psalm CL* for chor., stgs. & org.; incid. m. to plays, incl. Samain's *Polyphème*; orch. works; pf. Conc., Divertissement for v. & orch., &c.

Bernard, Tristan (actually Paul) (b. 1866), Fr. playwright. *See* Terrasse (*Femme de Loth*).

Bernardi, Bartolomeo (b. Bologna, *c.* 1670; d. Copenhagen, 1732), It. vst. & comp. Left It. *c.* 1700 and prod. an opera, *Libussa*, at Prague in 1703. Later entered the service of the Dan. court at Copenhagen.

Works incl. v. sos. (some with org.) & trio sos.

Bernardi, Francesco. *See* Senesino.

Bernardi, Steffano (b. Verona, *c.* 1578; d. ? Salzburg, 1638), It. priest & comp. Chaplain at Verona cath., studied in Rome later and became chapel master of the church of the Madonna dei Monti. In 1611 he became chapel master at Verona cath., and in 1622 went into the service of the Archduke Karl Josef, Bishop of Breslau, and soon afterwards to Salzburg cath., which he helped to inaugurate by cond. Benevoli's 52-part Mass and prod. a Te Deum for 12 choirs of his own. He also wrote a stage work and many masses, motets, psalms, madrigals and inst. works.

Bernasconi, Andrea (b. Marseilles, 1706; d. Munich, 29. I. 1784), Fr. comp. of It. descent. Was chapel master at Munich from 1755. He married a widow of a member of the ducal household at Stuttgart, whose daughter Antonia he taught.

Works incl. *c.* 25 operas; sacred comps., &c.

Bernasconi, Antonia (b. ? Stuttgart, *c.* 1745; d. ?), Ger. sop. singer, stepdaughter of prec. She 1st appeared in Vienna, 1764, and sang the title-part in the prod. of Gluck's *Alceste* in 1767.

Berneker, Constanz (b. Darkehmen, E. Prus., 30. X. 1844; d. Königsberg, 9. VI. 1906), Ger. cond. & comp. Studied in Berlin and cond. there and later at Königsberg, where he also lectured at the Univ. and taught at the Cons.

Works incl. orat. *Judith; The Song of Solomon* for chor. & orch.; incid. m. to Schiller's *Bride of Messina*; church m., songs, &c.

Berners, Lord (Gerald Hugh Tyrwhitt-Wilson) (b. Arley Park nr. Bridgnorth, 18. IX. 1883), Eng. comp., painter & author. In the diplomatic service at first, he studied m. at Dresden and Vienna, also sought the advice of Stravinsky and Casella. His operatic setting of Mérimée's comedy, *Le Carrosse du Saint-Sacrement*, was prod. in Paris in 1924, and the ballet *The Triumph of Neptune* in London in 1926; another, with words by Gertrude Stein, *The Wedding Bouquet*, at Sadler's Wells Theatre, London, in 1937, with settings designed by himself.

Works incl. opera *Le Carrosse du Saint-Sacrement*; ballets *The Triumph of Neptune, Luna Park, The Wedding Bouquet* (words by Gertrude Stein), *Cupid and Psyche*; 3 Pieces (*Chinoiserie, Valse sentimentale, Kasatchok*), *Fantaisie espagnole* & *Fugue* for orch.; *Vars., Adagio & Hornpipe* for stg. orch.; *Le Poisson d'or, Trois Petites Marches funèbres* & *Fragments psychologiques* for pf.; *Valses bourgeoises* for pf. duet; songs incl. 3 sets in the Ger., Fr. & Eng. manners, &c.

Bernhard, Christoph (b. Danzig, 1627 or 1628; d. Dresden, 14. XI. 1692), Ger. comp. The son of a poor sailor, he picked up mus. instruction precariously, but was sent to Schütz at Dresden by a patron and there sang so well that the Elector of Saxony sent him to It. in 1649. He made friends with Carissimi and attracted attention by his comps.; returned to Dresden in 1655 and became vice chapel master; was ousted by the Its. at court and went to Hamburg as cantor, 1664–74, but returned to Dresden as chapel master.

Works incl. masses & other church m., some in many elaborately ctptal. parts, &c.

Berni, Francesco (1497–1536), It. poet. *See* **Malipiero** (sonnets).

Bernier, Nicolas (b. Mantes, 28. VI. 1664; d. Paris, 5. IX. 1734), Fr. comp. Studied in Rome. Chapel master at Chartres and at the church of Saint-Germain-l'Auxerrois in Paris; then m. master at the Sainte Chapelle there, 1704–26.

Works incl. 7 books of cantatas, 3 of motets, church m., &c.

Berselli, Matteo (b. ?; d. ?), It. 18th-cent. ten. singer. Went to London with Senesino in 1720.

Bertali, Antonio (b. Verona, III. 1605; d. Vienna, 1. IV. 1669), It. vst. & comp. Played in the court chapel in Vienna from 1637 and became chapel master in 1649. His opera *L'inganno d'amore* was prod. at the diet of Ratisbon in 1653.

Works incl. several operas; equestrian ballet; 3 orats.; masses & other church m., &c.

Berté, Heinrich (b. Galgócz, 8. V. 1858; d. Vienna, 25. VIII. 1924), Aus.-Hung. comp.

Works incl. operettas *Die Schneeflocke, Die Millionenbraut, Der Märchenprinz, Das Dreimäderlhaus* (*Lilac Time*, on m. by Schubert) & others; ballets *Das Märchenbuch, Amor auf Reisen* & others, &c.

Bertheaume, Isidore (b. Paris, *c.* 1752; d. St. Petersburg, 20. III. 1802), Fr. vst. & comp. Appeared at the Concert spirituel in Paris, 1761, and became cond. in 1783, but left at the Revol., going 1st to Eutin and then to St. Petersburg, where he joined the imp. band.

Works incl. 2 syms.; v. Conc. & several for 2 vs.; sos. for pf. with v. accomp.; v. duets, &c.

Bertin, Louise Angélique. *See* **Fausto.**

Bertini, Henri (b. London, 28. X. 1798; d. Meylan, 1. X. 1876), Fr. pfst. & comp. Pupil of his brother, Benoît Auguste B. (b. 1780). Went on a continental tour at the age of 12, lived in Eng. and Sco., but settled in Paris in 1821. Wrote much for his inst., incl. studies.

Bertoldo, Bertoldino e Cacasenno (also **Bertoldo** or **Bertoldo alla corte**), comic opera by Ciampi (lib. by Goldoni), prod. Venice, Teatro San Moisè, 27. XII. 1748.

Bertoletti, Gasparo di. *See* **Salò.**

Bertolli, Francesca (b. ?; d. ?), It. 18th-cent. con. singer. 1st heard in London in 1729.

Berton, Henri-Montan (b. Paris, 17. IX. 1767; d. Paris, 22. IV. 1844), Fr. vst. & comp. Vst. at the Paris Opéra from 1782, prof. at the Cons. from 1795 and cond. at the Opéra-Comique from 1807. His 1st opera was prod. in 1787.

Works incl. operas *La Dame invisible, Les Promesses de mariage, Les Rigueurs du cloître, Le Nouveau d'Assas, Ponce de Léon, Montano e Stéphanie, Le Délire, Aline Reine de Golconde, Ninon chez Madame de Sévigné, François de Foix, Roger de Sicile*; ballets incl. *L'Enlèvement des Sabines*; orats. incl. *Absalon*; cantatas for the Revol. and the 1st Empire; syms.; stg. 4tets; church m., &c.

Berton, Pierre-Montan (b. Maubert-Fontaines, 7. I. 1727; d. Paris, 14. V. 1780), Fr. comp. & cond., father of prec. App. cond. at the Paris Opéra in 1759.

Bertoni, Ferdinando Giuseppe (b. Salò nr. Venice, 15. VIII. 1725; d. Desenzano nr. Brescia, 1. XII. 1813), It. comp. Pupil of Martini at Bologna. Orgst. at St. Mark's, Venice, from 1752 and choirmaster at the Cons. dei Mendicanti from 1757. He prod. his 1st opera at Florence, 1745. In 1776, when he prod. *Orfeo*, a setting of the lib. already used by Gluck, he used an air from that comp.'s work claiming that it had already appeared in his own *Tancredi* in 1766 and suggesting that Gluck had stolen it; but it occurred already in Gluck's *Parnaso confuso* in 1765, and the theft was thus B.'s. In 1778–80 and 1782–3 he visited London to prod. operas. In 1785 he succeeded Galuppi as cond. at St. Mark's.

Works incl. operas *Cajetto, Orazio e Curazio, Tancredi, Orfeo, Quinto Fabio* & over 40 others; orats.; stg. 4tets; pf. sos., &c.

Bertrand de Born. *See* **Born.**

Berutti, Arturo (b. San Juan, 27. III. 1862; d. Buenos Aires, 3. I. 1938), Arg. comp. Studied at the Leipzig Cons. and in Paris and Milan, settling at Buenos Aires in 1896.

Works incl. operas *Vendetta, Evangelina, Taras Bulba* (after Gogol), *Pampa, Yupanki, Khrysé, Horrida nox* & *Los heroes*.

Berwald, Frans Adolf (b. Stockholm, 23. VII. 1796; d. Stockholm, 30. IV. 1868), Swe. vst. & comp. Comp. several works before he studied in Berlin. He twice visited Vienna, where he had more success than at home, but settled at Stockholm in 1849.

Works incl. opera *Estrella di Soria*; incid. m. to plays; 6 syms.; v. Conc.; orch. works incl. *Recollections of the Norw. Alps* and *A Rustic Betrothal in Swe.*; 2 stg. 4tets and other chamber m.; songs, &c.

Besard, Jean-Baptiste (b. Besançon, *c.* 1567; d. ? Augsburg, ?), Fr. lutenist & comp. Studied law at the Univ. of Dôle, then the lute with Lorenzini in Rome. Later lived at Cologne and Augsburg. Pub. theoret. works and collections of lute m. incl. his own.

Besseler, Heinrich (b. Hörde nr. Dortmund, 2. IV. 1900), Ger. mcolst. Studied at Freiburg i/B., Vienna and Göttingen, where later he became lecturer at the Univ., succeeding H. J. Moser as prof. at Heidelberg in 1928. Has written on medieval and Renaissance m. and ed. old works.

Best, William Thomas (b. Carlisle, 13. VIII. 1826; d. Liverpool, 10. V. 1897), Eng. orgst. Studied at Liverpool, where he lived most of his life as orgst. at St. George's Hall, where he gave recitals that made him famous all over the world. He made many org. arrs. of famous works.

Bettelstudent, Der (*The Beggar-Student*), operetta by Millöcker (lib. by F. Zell and Richard Genée), prod. Vienna, Theater an der Wien, 6. XII. 1882.

Betterton, Thomas (*c.* 1635–1710), Eng. actor & playwright. *See* **Prophetess** (Purcell).

Betz, Franz (b. Mainz, 19. III. 1835; d. Berlin, 11. VIII. 1900), Ger. bar. singer. Made his 1st appearance at Hanover in 1856 and was Wagner's 1st Hans Sachs at Munich in 1868.

Bevin, Elway (b. ?; d. ?), Eng. 16th–17th-cent. orgst. & comp. of Welsh descent. Pupil of Tallis. Vicar-chor. at Wells cath., 1575–84, and orgst. at Bristol cath. after that. He wrote a *Brief and Short Introduction to the Art of Musicke*. Comp. services, anthems & other church m.

Bevis (or **Beves**) **of Hampton** (or **Hamtoun**), Anglo-Norman 13th-cent. romance. *See* **Buovo d'Antona** (Traetta).

Bexfield, William Richard (b. Norwich, 27. IV. 1824; d. London, 29. X. 1853), Eng. orgst. & comp. Pupil of Buck at Norwich cath. Orgst. at Boston, Lincs., and London. Prod. the orat. *Israel Restored* at the Norwich Festival in 1852. He also wrote anthems & org. fugues.

Beydts, Louis (Antoine Hector Désiré) (b. Bordeaux, 29. VI. 1895), Fr. comp. Studied at Bordeaux.

Works incl. operettas *Moineau, Canards Mandarins, La S.A.D.M.P.* & *Le Voyage de Tchong-Li* (both libs. by Sacha Guitry); incid. m. to Musset's *Il ne faut jurer de rien*; suite for 14 insts. *A travers Paris*; film m. incl. *La Kermesse héroïque*; many songs with orch. & with pf.; inst. pieces; pf. works, &c.

Bianca e Falliero, ossia Il consiglio di tre (. . ., *or The Council of Three*), opera by Rossini (lib. by Felice Romani, from Manzoni's tragedy *Il conte di Carmagnola*), prod. Milan, Teatro alla Scala, 26. XII. 1819.

Bianca e Fernando, opera by Bellini (lib. by Domenico Gilardoni), prod. Naples, Teatro San Carlo, 30. V. 1826. B.'s 1st opera heard in public.

Bianca und Giuseppe, oder Die Franzosen vor Nizza (. . ., *or The French before Nice*), opera by Johann Friedrich Kittl (lib. by Wagner), prod. Prague, 19. II. 1848. Wagner had written the lib. for himself in 1836; it is based on a novel by Heinrich König.

Bianchi, Francesco (b. Cremona, *c.* 1752; d. Bologna, 24. IX. 1811), It. comp. He became cembalist in Paris under Piccinni in 1775 and prod. 2 operas there. In 1779 he prod. *Castore e Polluce* at Florence with Nancy Storace in the cast. He afterwards held posts at Milan and Venice. In 1790 Brigitta Banti sang in his *La vendetta di Nino* at Naples (later given as *Semiramide* in London), and the following year Mrs. Billington appeared at Naples in his *Inez de Castro.* Haydn heard his *Aci e Galatea* in London in 1795. In 1796 he went to London, where he prod. 7 operas until 1802.

Works incl. *c.* 60 operas & orats., also inst. m.

Bianciardi, Francesco (b. Siena, *c.* 1572; d. Siena, *c.* 1607), It. orgst. & comp. Chapel master at Siena cath. Wrote masses, motets and a book of rules on playing from figured bass.

Biber, Heinrich Johann Franz von (b. Wartenberg, Boh., 12. VIII. 1644; d. Salzburg, 3. V. 1704), Boh. vst. & comp. He was high steward and cond. at the archbishop's court at Salzburg.

Works incl. opera *Chi la dura la vince*; church m.; several sets of v. sos., partitas for 3 insts.; vespers for voices, stgs. & trombs., &c.

Bibi. *See* **Pianette.**

Bicinium (Lat.) = a song in 2 parts. (The term is obs.)

Bickerstaffe, Isaac (*c.* 1735–?1812), Eng. playwright & libst. *See* **Belmont und Constanze** (André & Dieter), **Entführung** (Mozart), **Ephesian Matron** (Dibdin), **Judith** (Arne), **Lionel and Clarissa** (Dibdin), **Love in a Village** (Arne), **Maid of the Mill** (Arnold), **Padlock** (Dibdin), **Thomas and Sally** (Arne).

Bie, Oscar (b. Breslau, 9. II. 1864; d. Berlin, 21. IV. 1938), Ger. writer on m. Studied at Leipzig and Berlin. Taught at the Berlin Hochschule für Musik from 1921. Wrote books on opera, dance music, history of the pf., R. Strauss, &c.

Biely, Victor (b. Berditchev, Ukraine, 14. I. 1904), Rus. comp. Studied v. & comp. at the Kharkov and Moscow Conss., pupil of Miaskovsky at the latter. Later prof. at Moscow Cons. and folksong expert. In 1925 he organized the Procoll soc. for the promotion of Soviet M. with Davidenko and Shekhter.

Works incl. incid. m. for *Salute to Spain* & other plays & films; suite on Tchuvash themes for orch.; Poem for va. & pf.; 3 pf. sos., Sonatina, preludes & other pf. works; orat. for 25th anniversary of the Oct. Revol., *Hunger March* for chor. & orch., chor. works, mass songs, &c.

Bierbaum, Otto Julius (1865–1910), Ger. poet & playwright. *See* **Mottl** (*Pan im Busch*), **Thuille** (*Lobetanz* & *Gugeline*).

Bierey, Gottlob Benedict (b. Dresden, 25. VII. 1772; d. Breslau, 5. V. 1840), Ger. comp. Succeeded Weber as cond. at the opera of Breslau in 1806. He wrote numerous operas, operettas and mus. plays, incl. *Rosette, das Schweizer Hirtenmädchen* and *Wladimir, Fürst von Novgorod.*

Bigot (*née* **Kiene**), **Marie** (b. Colmar, 3. III. 1786; d. Paris, 16. IX. 1820), Alsat. pfst., wife of the librarian to Count Rasumovsky in Vienna and a friend of Haydn and Beethoven. In 1809 she and her husband went to Paris, but he was taken prisoner at Milan in the war of 1812 and she had to give poorly paid lessons. Mendelssohn was her pupil in 1816.

Bilhon, Jean de (b. ?; d. ?), Fr. 15th–16th-cent. comp. Singer (?) in the pontifical chapel in Rome. Wrote masses on the tunes of Fr. songs, motets and other church m.

Billet de loterie, Le (*The Lottery Ticket*), opera by Isouard (lib. by Augustin François Creuze de Lesser and Jean François Roger), prod. Paris, Opéra-Comique, 14. IX. 1811.

Billings, William (b. Boston, Mass., 7. X. 1746; d. Boston, 29. IX. 1800), Amer. tanner & amateur comp. Wrote many hymn tunes and patriotic songs.

Billington (*née* **Weichsel**), **Elizabeth** (b. London, *c.* 1768; d. St. Artien nr. Venice, 25. VIII. 1818), Eng. sop. singer, daughter of Carl Weichsel, a Ger. obst. settled in London. She came out as a prodigy pfst. and singer while still a child. Married the db. player James B. She appeared with great success in Paris and It., and on her return to London in 1801 was engaged by Covent Garden and Drury Lane theatres at the same time and also sang at the It. opera in the King's Theatre. She died on the estate of her 2nd husband, Félissent.

Binary. A song or piece in 2 distinct sections is said to be in B. form. The sections are dependent on each other because the 1st does not close and the 2nd does not open in the principal key, so that each by itself would fail to give an impression of completeness. They are also usually based on the same or similar thematic material—alike but not identical. The dances in Bach's suites are exs. of B. form.

Binchois, Gilles (or Egidius) (b. ? Mons, *c.* 1400; d. Lille, 20. IX. 1460), Flem. comp. Chaplain to Philip, Duke of Burgundy, until 1437, when he became a canon at Mons. In 1452 he returned to the Burgundian court. Wrote masses and other church m., and esp. songs.

Binenbaum, Janco (b. Adrianople, 28. XII. 1880), Bulg. comp. Studied at Munich and cond. opera at var. Ger. theatres, but later retired to Chevreuse in Fr. and comp. much m. which he wished to see neither perf. nor pub.

Works incl. an opera; a ballet; 3 syms.; 2 v. concs.; 5 stg. 4tets & other chamber m.; sos., &c.

Binet, Jean (b. Geneva, 17. X. 1893), Swi. comp. Studied at the Jaques-Dalcroze Inst. at Geneva and with Barblan, Templeton Strong, Bloch & others. Lived in U.S.A. and Brussels for a time, but returned to Swi. in 1929.

Works incl. 3 Psalms for chor. & orch., *Cantate de Noël* for chor. & org.; ballet *Die Strasse*; suites on Swi. & Eng. themes and dances for orch.; Concertino for chamber orch.; stg. 4tet & other chamber m.; songs, partsongs, &c.

Biniou (Fr.). A small bagpipe used in Brittany.

Binyon, (Robert) Laurence (1869–1943), Eng. poet. *See* **Rootham** (*For the Fallen*), **Shaw (M.)** *Sursum corda*), **Spirit of England** (Elgar), **Stanford** (*Attila*).

Bioni, Antonio (b. Venice, *c.* 1698; d. ?), It. comp. Pupil of Porta. Prod. his 1st opera at Chioggia in 1721; worked at Breslau and Prague, 1726–34.

Works incl. *c.* 25 operas, e.g. *La pace fra la virtù e la bellezza* (lib. by Metastasio), *Climene, Endimione, Issipile*, &c.

Birch, Charlotte Ann (b. ?, *c.* 1815; d. London, 26. I. 1901), Eng. sop. singer. Studied at the R.A.M. in London and made her 1st appearance in 1834.

Birmingham, George (James Owen Hannay) (b. 1865), Eng. novelist. *See* **Nicholson (S.)** (*Mermaid*).

Birthday Odes. 6 cantatas by Purcell comp. as offerings to Queen Mary on her birthday, 30. IV, from the beginning of her joint reign with William III to the year of her death: 1. *Now does the glorious day appear* (1689), 2. *Arise my Muse* (1690), 3. *Welcome, welcome, glorious morn* (1691), 4. *Love's goddess sure was blind* (1692), 5. *Celebrate this festival* (1693), 6. *Come ye sons of art away* (1694).

Bis (Lat. = twice). *See* **Encore.**

Bisbigliando / **Bisbigliato** (It. = whispering, whispered). A direction used esp. for the hp., where it indicates a rapid, soft repetition of notes.

Bishop (*née* **Rivière**), **Ann** (b. London, 9. I. 1810; d. New York, 18. III. 1884), Eng. sop. singer. Taught singing by her father and pf. by Moscheles, also studied at the R.A.M., where she met Bishop, whom she married in 1831. She made her 1st public appearance that year, but in 1839 went on a tour with Bochsa and soon afterwards eloped with him, never to return to her husband.

Bishop, Henry (Rowley) (b. London, 18. XI. 1786; d. London, 30. IV. 1855), Eng. comp. Studied under Bianchi and prod. *Angelina* (comp. with Lanza) at Margate in 1804 and the ballet *Tamerlan et Bajazet* at the King's Theatre in London, 1806 From that time on he brought out one or more stage pieces almost each year until 1840. In 1813 he was one of the founders of the Phil. Soc. and became one of its conds. Knighted in 1842; D.Mus. at Oxford in 1853. He was twice married to singers: Sarah Lyon on 30. IV. 1809 and Ann Rivière on 9. VII. 1831.

Works incl. over 100 pieces for the stage, e.g. *The Corsair, The Circassian Bride, Guy Mannering* (after Scott), *The Burgomaster of Saardam, The Heart of Midlothian* (after Scott), *Montrose* (after Scott), *The Law of Java, Maid Marian, Clari, Cortez, Faustus, Aladdin, The Fortunate Isles*; incid. m. for 3 tragedies, for adapts. of Scott's *Kenilworth* & *Waverley*, for Byron's *Manfred* and for Shakespeare's *Midsummer Night's Dream, Comedy of Errors, Twelfth Night, 2 Henry IV, Two Gentlemen of Verona, As You Like It, Hamlet, Love's Labour's Lost*; orat. *The Fallen Angel*; cantata *The Seventh Day*; *Triumphal Ode* and Installation Ode for the chancellor of Oxford Univ.; 3 vols. of nat. melodies with words by Moore & other collections of arrs., &c.

Bispham, David (Scull) (b. Philadelphia, 5. I. 1857; d. New York, 2. X. 1921), Amer. bar. singer. Studied with Vannuccini and Lamperti at Milan and with Wm. Shakespeare in London, where he made his 1st concert appearance in 1890, and his 1st on the stage in 1891. 5 years later he 1st came out in N.Y., at the Metropolitan Opera.

Bisser (Fr. verb from Lat. *bis* = twice). *See* **Encore.**

Bitonality. The writing of m. in 2 keys at once. The fanfare in Stravinsky's *Petrushka*, played simultaneously in C maj. and F♯ maj., is a well-known ex.

Bittner, Julius (b. Vienna, 9. IV. 1874; d. Vienna, 19. I. 1939), Aus. comp. A lawyer at first, studied m. with Josef Labor and Bruno Walter.

Works incl. operas *Die rote Gret*, *Der Musikant*, *Der Bergsee*, *Der Abenteurer*, *Das höllisch Gold*, *Die Kohlhaymerin*, *Das Rosengärtlein*, *Mondnacht*, *Das Veilchen*; ballets *Der Markt der Liebe*, *Die Todestarantella*; *Missa Austriaca* for solo voices, chor. & orch.; chamber m.; pf. pieces; songs, &c.

Bizet, Georges (really Alexandre César Léopold) (b. Paris, 25. X. 1838; d. Bougival nr. Paris, 3. VI. 1875), Fr. comp. His father, a teacher of singing, gave him his 1st instruction in m. and at the age of 9, being exceptionally gifted, he was admitted to the Paris Cons., studying pf. under Marmontel, org. under Benoist and comp. under Zimmermann. In 1853, when Zimmermann d., he became a pupil of Halévy, having already taken a 1st prize for pf. In 1857 he won the Prix de Rome, but before he went to Rome he had already gained a prize in a competition for an operetta, *Le Docteur Miracle*, sponsored by Offenbach. He tied with Lecocq, whose setting was prod. alternately with his own at the Théâtre des Bouffes-Parisiens. He wrote several works in Rome and on his return to Paris in 1860 he set out to capture the operatic stage; but although the Opéra-Comique accepted his 1-act opera, *La Guzla de l'Émir*, he was not satisfied with it and withdrew it, destroying it later. But the Théâtre Lyrique prod. his next work, *Les Pêcheurs de perles*, in 1863; on the other hand, *Ivan le Terrible*, written in 1865, was never perf., and he was said to have burnt the score (which is reported to have been recovered by the Nazis in Paris, 1944). In 1869 Pasdeloup for the 1st time gave him the chance to appear with an orch. work, *Souvenirs de Rome*, perf. 28. II, which he later augmented to 4 mvts. and entitled *Roma*. The same year he married Geneviève Halévy, his former master's daughter. In 1872 he was commissioned to write incid. m. for Daudet's play, *L'Arlésienne*, and he had to do it very hastily before the prod. at the Vaudeville on 1. X. In 1874 Pasdeloup prod. his ovt. to Sardou's *Patrie*, but he had set to work on *Carmen* before that and given great care to the excellent lib. based on Mérimée's story. It was prod. at the Opéra-Comique, with spoken dialogue, on 3. III. 1875 and received 37 perfs., but on the day of the 23rd B. d., long before the work had won through prejudice to a decided success. It was at first coldly received, mainly because the conventional audience and critics regarded the character of Carmen as undesirable for an operatic heroine.

Works incl. operas *Don Procopio*, *Les Pêcheurs de perles*, *La Jolie Fille de Perth* (after Scott), *Djamileh*, *Carmen* (after Mérimée); operetta *Le Docteur Miracle*; incid. m. to Daudet's *L'Arlésienne*; cantatas *David* & *Clovis et Clothilde*; completion of Halévy's opera *Noë*; Sym. in C maj., suite *Roma*, ovt. *Patrie*, *Petite Suite* (*Jeux d'enfants*) & *Marche funèbre* for orch.; *Vasco da Gama*, symph. ode with chor.; pf. pieces: *La Chasse fantastique*, *Les Chants du Rhin*, *Trois Esquisses*, *Marine*, *Premier Nocturne*, *Variations chromatiques*; *Jeux d'enfants* suite for pf. duet; *Chanson du rouet* for voc. solo & chor., *Le Golfe de Bahia* for solo voices & chor.; *Saint Jean de Pathmos* for unaccomp. male chor.; 4 voc. duets; a number of songs incl. cycle *Feuilles d'album*, &c.

Björkander, Nils (b. Stockholm, 28. VI. 1893), Swe. comp. Prof. of m. at Stockholm.

Works incl. for the most part numerous pf. pieces, also a concert fantasy for pf. & orch., &c.

Bjørnson, Bjørnstjerne (1832–1910), Norw. poet, novelist & dramatist. *See* **Grieg** (*Sigurd Jorsalfar*, *Bergliot* & songs), **Halvorsen** (*The King*), **Hulda** (Franck, C.), **Kjerulf** (songs), **Nordraak** (*Mary Stuart*, *Sigurd Slembe* & Norw. nat. anthem), **Olav Trygvason** (Grieg), **Svendsen** (*Sigurd Slembe*).

Black, Andrew (b. Glasgow, 15. I. 1859; d. Sydney, N.S.W., 1920), Sco. bar. singer. At first an orgst., but studied singing in London and Milan. Appeared in Sco. with success and 1st sang in London in 1887.

'Black Key' Study. Chopin's pf. Study in G♭ maj., Op. 10 No. 5, written c. 1831–2 and pub. in 1833. It is by no means entirely played on the black keys, but its main melodic outlines use them predominantly.

Black Knight, The, cantata for chor. & orch. by Elgar, Op. 25, a setting of Longfellow's trans. of Uhland's ballad *Der schwarze Ritter*, prod. Worcester Festival, 1893.

Blackmore, Richard (Doddridge) (1825–1900), Eng. novelist & poet. *See* **Nevin (A.)** (*Lorna Doone*).

Blackwood, Algernon (b. 1869), Eng. novelist. *See* **Elgar** (*Starlight Express*).

Blaise le savetier (*B. the Cobbler*), opera by Philidor (lib. by Jean Michel

Sedaine, after La Fontaine), prod. Paris, Opéra-Comique, 9. III. 1759.

Blake, William (1757–1827), Eng. poet & painter. *See* **Busch** (songs), **Fogg** (*Seasons*), **Poldowski** (songs), **Stevens** (**B.**) (chor. work), **Tippett** (*Song of Liberty*).

Blamont, François Colin de (b. Versailles, 22. XI. 1690; d. Versailles, 14. II. 1760), Fr. comp. Pupil of his father, who was in the royal band, and later of Lalande. In 1719 he became superintendent of the royal m. and after Lalande's death in 1726 master of the chamber m.

Works incl. stage pieces (mostly ballets and ballet-operas) *Les Festes grecques et romaines*, *Le Retour des dieux sur la terre* (for the marriage of Louis XV), *Le Caprice d'Érato*, *Endymion*, *Les Caractères de l'Amour*, *Les Amours du printemps*, *Jupiter vainqueur des Titans*, *Les Festes de Thétis*; cantata *Circé* & 3 books of *Cantates françaises* for solo voice; motets with orch. accomp., &c.

Blanchard, Esprit Joseph Antoine (b. Perne, Vaucluse, 29. II. 1696; d. Versailles, 10. IV. 1770), Fr. comp. Held a number of church and cath. apps. at Aix, Marseilles, Toulon, Besançon and Amiens and in 1738 was app. to one of the 4 subordinate m.-masters' posts at the royal chapel in Paris & Versailles. Wrote motets and other church m.

Blanchard, Henri Louis (b. Bordeaux, 7. II. 1778; d. Paris, 18. XII. 1858), Fr. vst., comp., m. critic & playwright. Studied v. under R. Kreutzer and comp. under Méhul and others. Was cond. and theatre dir. in Paris. Wrote chamber m. and airs for vaudevilles.

Blanchet, Émile (**Robert**) (b. Lausanne, 17. VII. 1877; d. Pully, Vaud, 27. III. 1943), Swi. pfst. & comp. Studied at the Cologne Cons. and with Busoni at Weimar.

Works incl. *Conzertstück* for pf. & orch., numerous pf. works, &c.

Bland (*née* **Romanzini**), **Maria Theresa** (b. ? Italy, 1769; d. London, 15. I. 1838), Eng. ballad singer of It. extraction. Sang with great success, esp. at Vauxhall and the other London pleasure gardens. Married Bland, a brother of Mrs. Jordan, the actress.

Blangini, Giuseppe (**Maria Marco Felice**) (b. Turin, 18. XI. 1781; d. Paris, 18. XII. 1841), It. ten. singer & comp. Sang at Turin cath. as a child and learnt m. there. In 1799 he went to Paris, where he finished an opera left incomplete by a comp. named Della Maria and prod. one of his own. In 1809 he was called to Cassel as mus. dir. to King Jérôme; but he returned to Paris in 1814 and 2 years later became prof. of singing at the Cons.

Works incl. over 30 operas, e.g. *La Fausse Duègne* (finished by him), *Chimère et réalité*, *Nephtali, ou Les Ammonites*, *Encore un tour de Caliphe*, *Inez de Castro*, *Les Fêtes lacédémoniennes*, *Le Sacrifice d'Abraham*; contrib. to *La Marquise de Brinvilliers*; cantata *Die letzten Augenblicke Werthers* (after Goethe); 174 songs, &c.

Blaník (Smetana). *See* **Má Vlast.**

Blankenburg, Quirijn (i.e. **Gerbrandt**) **van** (b. Gouda, 1654; d. ? The Hague, after 1739), Dutch orgst. & comp. Studied maths. at Leyden, but became orgst. at Gouda in 1684 and at The Hague in 1687. Wrote theoret. books, pub. hpchd. & org. accomps. to psalms and hymns, and in honour of the betrothal of the Prince of Orange in 1733 wrote pieces in 2 parts to be sung normally or upside down, forwards or backwards.

Blaramberg, Pavel Ivanovitch (b. Orenburg, 26. IX. 1841; d. Nice, 28. III. 1907), Rus. comp. Was a civil servant and amateur musn., but studied with Balakirev after his retirement in 1870.

Works incl. operas *Mary of Burgundy* (after Victor Hugo), *The Mummer*, *The Russalka Maiden*, *Tushino* (based on Ostrovsky's play); incid. m. to Ostrovsky's *The Voyevoda*; cantata on Lermontov's *The Demon*; Sym. in B min.; songs, &c.

Bläser (Ger. = blowers). Wind insts. and their players.

Blasinstrumente (Ger.) = Wind insts.

Blasmusik (Ger. = blown m.) = m. for wind insts.

Blas de Castro, Juan (b. Aragon, *c.* 1560; d. Madrid, 6. VIII. 1631), Spa. comp. In the 1590s he was private musn. to the Duke of Alba at Salamanca and in 1605 musn. and usher to Philip III. Lope de Vega and Tirso de Molina mentioned him in their works. Only 20 songs for 3 & 4 voices survive.

Blauwaert, Émile (b. St. Nikolaas, 13. VI. 1845; d. Brussels, 2. II. 1891), Belg. bass singer. Studied at the Brussels Cons.; made his 1st appearance in 1866.

Blavet, Michel (b. Besançon, 13. III. 1700; d. Paris, 28. X. 1768), Fr. flst., bnst. & comp. Comp. operas incl. *Le Jaloux corrigé*, prod. in 1752, ballets, fl. sos., fl. duets, &c.

Blaze. *See* **Castil-Blaze.**

Blech, Leo (b. Aachen, 21. IV. 1871), Ger. cond. & comp. Pupil of Bargiel and Humperdinck; cond. in his native town, 1892–8; later at Prague and in 1906–35 cond. of the Berlin Opera.

Works incl. operas *Aglaja, Cherubina, Versiegelt, Das war ich, Aschenbrödel, Alpenkönig und Menschenfeind* (after Raimund); 3 symph. poems; chor. works with orch., &c.

Blessed Damozel, The (Debussy). *See* **Damoiselle élue.**

Bleyle, Karl (b. Feldkirch, Vorarlberg, 7. V. 1880), Ger. comp. Studied at Stuttgart and Munich, last under Thuille. Comp. orch. and chor. works, a v. Conc., pf. pieces, &c.

Blind Octaves. A trick in pf. writing: figures in 8ves rapidly alternating between the 2 hands where the thumbs trace a continuous melodic line while the outer notes played by the little fingers fly off at broken intervals. The device is crudely effective and of no artistic value.

Bliss, Arthur (b. London, 2. VIII. 1891), Eng. comp. Educ. at Rugby and Pembroke Coll., Cambridge, where he studied m. under C. Wood. Entered the R.C.M. in London, 1913, studying with Stanford, Vaughan Williams and Holst, but joined the army in 1914, serving all through the war until 1918. Prof. of comp. at R.C.M. in 1921, but took wholly to comp. the next year, never holding any official post until he was app. mus. dir. of the B.B.C. in 1941, an appt. he resigned to Hely-Hutchinson in 1945.

Works incl. ballets *Checkmate* & *Miracle in the Gorbals*; incid. m. for Shakespeare's *Tempest*; film m. for *Things to Come* (H. G. Wells), *Conquest of the Air, Caesar and Cleopatra* (G. B. Shaw); *Morning Heroes* for orator, chor. & orch., *Pastoral* for m.-sop., chor., fl., stgs. & drums; *A Colour Sym., Introduction and Allegro, Hymn to Apollo* & other orch. works; march *Phoenix* for the liberation of Fr.; *M. for Stgs.*; *Serenade for* bar. & orch.; concs. for pf. & for 2 pfs.; Conc. for pf., ten. & chamber orch., *Rout* for voice & chamber orch., *Madam Noy* for voice and 6 insts.; *Conversations* for fl., v., va. & co.; ob. 5tet, cl. 5tet; sos. for v. & pf. and va. & pf.; several song cycles with var. insts. or pf., incl. 5 *Amer. Songs* (Edna St. Vincent Millay), &c.

Blitheman, William (b. ?; d. Whitsunday, 1591), Eng. orgst. & comp. Choirmaster at Christ Church Coll., Oxford, in 1564; became orgst. of the Chapel Royal in London in 1585. Bull was his pupil.

Works incl. motets and an *In Nomine* for virginal.

Blitzstein, Marc (b. Philadelphia, 2. III. 1905), Amer. pfst. & comp. Appeared as solo pfst. at the age of 15; studied comp. with Scalero in N.Y., Nadia Boulanger in Paris and Schoenberg in Vienna; also pf. with Siloti in Amer. His 1st great success was the light opera *The Cradle will rock*, prod. in N.Y., 1937.

Works incl. operas *Triple Sec, Parabola and Circula, The Harpies, The Cradle will rock*; ballet *Cain*; incid. m. for Shakespeare's *Julius Caesar*; film m. for *Surf and Seaweed, The Spanish Earth, No for an Answer, Chesapeake Bay Retriever*; chor. opera *The Condemned*; radio song-play *I 've got the Tune*, Children's Cantata; *Romantic Piece, Jigsaw* ballet suite & Vars. for orch.; pf. Conc.; stg. 4tet and Serenade for stg. 4tet; pf. So. & *Percussion Music* for pf., &c.

Bloch, Ernest (b. Geneva, 24. VII. 1880), Swi. (Americanized) comp. Pupil of Jaques-Dalcroze at first, then of Ysaÿe and Rasse at the Brussels Cons., and afterwds. at the Hoch Cons. at Frankfort o/M, where Iwan Knorr was his comp. master. His last teacher was Thuille at Munich, and he then went to live in Paris, where he began the opera *Macbeth* on a Fr. lib. by Edmond Fleg, having already written several important works. It was prod. in Paris in 1910, but he had in the meantime returned to Swi. to cond. subscription concerts at Lausanne and Neuchâtel. In 1915 he became prof. of mus. aesthetics at the Geneva Cons., but the following year he went to U.S.A. and settled in N.Y. as prof. at the David Mannes School of M. A second opera, *Jézabel*, begun there in 1918, remains unfinished. From 1920 to 1925 B. was dir. of the Cleveland Inst. of M. In 1930 he retired to Swi. and lived quietly in remote places, and his fame gradually spread. Some interest was shown in his work in Eng. and a good deal in It., where his *Sacred Service* was prod. (at Turin) and *Macbeth* was revived in an It. trans. at Naples, 5. III. 1938. But the anti-Semitic movement encouraged by the Fascists put an end to this appreciation. As an Amer. citizen he could no longer remain absent from U.S.A. without losing his adopted nationality, and he returned there at the end of 1938.

Works incl. opera *Macbeth*; *Sacred Service* (*Avodath Hakdesh*) for bar. solo, chor. & orch.; *Israel* sym. for 5 voices & orch.; Sym. in C♯ min., symph. poems *Hiver—Printemps, Trois Poèmes juifs* for orch., *America*, epic rhapsody for orch., *Helvetia*, symph. fresco, *Evocations*, symph. suite, Suite: *Ovt., Passacaglia & Finale*; *Schelomo* for co. & orch., *Concerto grosso* for pf. & stgs., *Voice in the Wilderness* for co. & orch.;

Four Episodes for chamber orch.; stg. 4tet in B min.; 2 v. & pf. sos., va. & pf. Suite, pf. 5tet, *Three Nocturnes* for pf. trio, *In the Mountains, Night, Three Landscapes* & *Recueillement* (prelude) for stg. 4tet; *Poèmes d'automne* & 3 Psalms for voice & orch.; *Enfantines*, 5 *Sketches in Sepia, In the Night, Nirvana, Poems of the Sea* and So. for pf.; *Baal Shem* (3 pieces), *Melody, Exotic Night* & *Abodah* for v. & pf.; *From Jewish Life* (3 pieces) & *Méditation hébraïque* for co. & pf.; song cycle *Historiettes au crépuscule* & other songs, &c.

Block Harmony. A term used for a type of harmonic accomp. in which all the notes of the chords move simultaneously in 'blocks' without being made to depart from one another by means of figuration or ctpt. The progressions are strictly vertical, not linear or horizontal.

Blockflöte (Ger. lit. block fl.; actually Fipple Fl.) = Recorder.

Blockx, Jan (b. Antwerp, 25. I. 1851; d. Antwerp, 26. V. 1912), Belg. comp. Learnt m. as a choir-boy and went to the Antwerp School of M., later to the Leipzig Cons. In 1886 he became prof. and in 1902 dir. of the Antwerp Cons., succeeding Benoît, whom he followed as a Flem. mus. nationalist. Most of his operas and all his cantatas for solo voices, chor. & orch. are set to Flem. words.

Works incl. operas *Jets vergeten, Maître Martin, Herbergprinses, Thyl Uylenspiegel, De Bruid der Zee, De Kapel, Baldie*; ballet *Milenka*; cantatas *Op den Stroom, Het Droom van 't Paradies, Vredesang, De Klokke Roelandt, De Scheldezang*; ovt. *Rubens*; Romance for v. & orch. &c.

Blodek, Vilém (b. Prague, 3. X. 1834; d. Prague, 1. V. 1874), Cz. flst., teacher & comp. Prod. the nat. operas *In the Well* and *Zitek* at Prague in 1867–8.

Blok, Alexander (1880–1921), Rus. poet & dramatist. *See* **Gnessin** (*Rose and the Cross* & songs), **Mossolov** (songs), **Weissberg** (*The Twelve*).

Blondel de Nesle (b. ?; d. ?), Fr. 12th-cent. trouvère. According to a legend he discovered the place of captivity of Richard Cœur de Lion in Aus. by singing outside the prison and being answered by R. in song. 22 of his songs are preserved.

Blow, John (b. ? North Collingham, Notts., 1649; d. London, 1. X. 1708), Eng. orgst. & comp. He became one of the children in the Chapel Royal in London as soon as it was re-established after the Restor. (1660) and was taught by Cooke. He wrote 3 anthems in 1663 and took a share with Humfrey and Turner in the 'Club Anthem' *c.* 1664. About the same time he set Herrick's 'Go, perjur'd man' in the style of Carissimi at Charles II's request. Hingston and C. Gibbons also had a share in B.'s mus. educ. In 1668 he became orgst. at Westminster Abbey in succession to Albert Byrne; in III. 1674 he was sworn a Gentleman of the Chapel Royal and the following VII became Master of the Children following Humfrey. In IX he married Elizabeth Braddock. Hon. Mus.D. at Canterbury, 1677. In 1679 he was followed in the Westminster orgst.'s post by Purcell, in whose favour he had (?) resigned or been dismissed, probably the former, since he was reinstated after Purcell's death in 1695. In 1687 he succeeded Wise as almoner and choirmaster at St. Paul's cath. (as yet unfinished). James II app. him a member of the royal band and confirmed a previous app. as Comp. in Ordinary. Towards the end of the cent. he bought a property at Hampton, but still retained a house at Westminster, where he d. His wife had predeceased him on 29. X. 1683.

Works incl. *c.* 12 services; over 100 Eng. anthems, 15 Lat. anthems; masque *Venus and Adonis*; Act Songs for Oxford Univ.; *c.* 10 odes for New Year's Day, 4 for St. Cecilia's Day, odes on the death of Queen Mary and of Purcell; 3 coronation anthems for James II, 1 for William and Mary; anthem for the opening service at St. Paul's cath. (1697); So. for 2 vs. & bass; hpchd. lessons, suites and pieces; some org. pieces; song collection *Amphion Anglicus*; songs and catches, &c.

Blue Bird, The (Maeterlinck). *See* **Oiseau bleu.**

Bluebeard. *See* **Ariane et Barbe-bleue; Barbe-bleue; Ritter Blaubart.**

Bluebeard's Castle (*A Kékszakállú Herceg Vára*), opera by Bartók (lib. by Béla Balázs), prod. Budapest, 24. V. 1918.

Blues. An Amer. dance stemming from the Foxtrot, the speed of which it reduced and into which it brought a deliberately contrived dismal atmosphere. When B. are sung their words seem to aim at attaining to the utmost depths of gloom and inanity.

Bluette (Fr. = flash, spark). In m. the equivalent of an epigram, a light, graceful short piece; a trifle.

Blumenfeld, Felix Mikhailovitch (b. Kovalevska, 19. IV. 1863; d. Moscow, 21. I. 1931), Rus. pfst., cond. & comp. Studied at the St. Petersburg Cons. and was app. prof. in 1885.

Works incl. Sym.; *Allegro de Concert*

for pf. & orch.; numerous pf. works incl. 24 Preludes & So.-Fantasy; songs, &c.

Blumenthal, Jacob (b. Hamburg, 4. X. 1829; d. London, 17. V. 1908), Ger. pfst. & comp. Settled in London in 1848 and became pfst. to Queen Victoria. Wrote many light pf. pieces and songs.

Blüthner, Julius Ferdinand (b. Falkenhain, 11. III. 1824; d. Leipzig, 13. IV. 1910), Ger. pf. manufacturer. Founded his firm at Leipzig in 1853.

Bn. (abbr.) = Bassoon.

Bnst. (abbr.) = Bassoonist.

Boabdil, der letzte Maurenkönig (*B., the Last Moorish King*), opera by Moszkowski (lib. by Carl Wittkowsky), prod. Berlin, Opera, 21. IV. 1892.

Boatswain's Mate, The, comic opera by Ethel Smyth (lib. by comp., based on a story by William Wymark Jacobs), prod. London, Shaftesbury Theatre, 28. I. 1916.

Bobization. A 16th-cent. Flem. system similar to Solmization, now obs.

Boccabadati, Luigia (b. Parma, *c.* 1800; d. Turin, 12. X. 1850), It. sop. singer. Made her 1st appearance at Parma in 1817.

Boccaccio, Giovanni (1313–75), It. poet & novelist. *See* **Delannoy** (*Ginevra*), **Delvincourt** (*Boccaccerie*), **Kreutzer** (R.) (*Imogène*), **Nakhabin** (*Burgess of Tuscany*).

Boccherini, Luigi (b. Lucca, 19. II. 1743; d. Madrid, 28. V. 1805), It. cst. & comp. Was first taught by his father, a db. player, who sent him to Rome in 1757, where he became known as a perf. and comp. In 1764–9 he played co. in the theatre and town orchs. at Lucca. He prod. 2 orats. and an opera there and later went on tour with the vst. Filippo Manfredi, visiting northern It., southern Fr. and at last Paris in 1768. There he was very fashionable, began to pub. his chamber m. and was invited to visit Spa. by the Spa. ambassador. He went to Madrid *c.* 1768–9, and came under the patronage of the Infante Don Luis, who died in 1785. After (?) a tour in Ger. in the 1780s he was app. chamber comp. to Frederick William II of Prus. in Berlin, where he remained until 1797, when the king d. and B. found himself stranded. He returned to Spa., but ill health soon compelled him to give up the co., and this, combined with domestic troubles, caused him to live in straitened circumstances. His position improved when Lucien Bonaparte arrived in Madrid as ambassador of the Fr. Republic and patronized him. But after 1801, when he prod. the *Stabat Mater*, he fell into greater poverty than ever, little relieved by the guitar arrs. he made of some of his works.

Works incl. Spa. opera *Clementina*; orats. *Gioas* & *Giuseppe riconosciuto*, *Stabat Mater*, Mass, Christmas cantata, motets for voices & orch.; concert arias and duets; 20 syms., Suite for orch.; 4 co. concs.; 102 stg. 4tets, 60 stg. trios, 125 stg. 5tets, 12 pf. 5tets, 18 5tets for wind & stgs., 16 6tets, 2 octets; 27 v. sos., 6 co. sos., 6 v. duets; *c.* 75 other unpub. inst. works, &c.

Bocedization. A 16th-cent. Flem. system similar to Solmization, now obs., in which the syllables given to the notes were Bo, Ci, Di, &c.

Bochsa, Robert Nicolas Charles (b. Montmédy, 9. VIII. 1789; d. Sydney, N.S.W., 6. I. 1856), Fr. hpst., cond. & comp. Began as a comp. of opera, orat. and ballet at Lyons and Bordeaux; entered the Paris Cons. in 1806; made a great name as hpst. and opera comp., but fled to Eng. in 1817 when discovered in forgeries. Although condemned, he was able to live in London, where he made the hp. extremely popular and became prof. of the inst. on the foundation of the R.A.M., but in 1827 had to leave owing to scandals. In 1839 he ran away with Bishop's wife, Ann Rivière, and they went on a world tour together, during which he d.

Works incl. opera *Trajan* & 8 comic operas; a ballet; orat. *Le Déluge universel*, 2 Requiems (1 for Louis XVI); method and many pieces for hp., &c.

Bocklet, Carl Maria von (b. Prague, 1801; d. ? Vienna, 15. VII. 1881), Boh. pfst. & vst. Settled in Vienna in 1820. Friend of Beethoven and Schubert.

Bockshorn, Samuel (b. Žeržice nr. Mlada Boleslav, 21. XII. 1628; d. Stuttgart, 12. XI. 1665), Boh. comp. Mus. dir. at Pressburg, Nuremberg and Stuttgart.

Works incl. dramatic cantata *Raptus Proserpinae*; sacred & secular works for voices and insts.; voc. table music; songs, &c.

Bockstriller (Ger. = goat's trill). A kind of voc. shake of no artistic value, prod. by a rapid, bleating repetition of a single note. Wagner asks this kind of shake from the tailors' chor. in the 3rd act of *The Mastersingers*.

Bodanzki, Artur (b. Vienna, 16. XII. 1877; d. N.Y., 23. XI. 1939), Aus. cond. Studied at the Vienna Cons. and after some min. apps. became asst. cond. to Mahler at the Imp. Opera. After several engagements at Ger. opera houses, he became cond.

of the Ger. operas at the Metro. Opera in N.Y., 1915.

Bodenschatz, Erhard (b. Lichtenberg, 1576; d. Gross-Osterhausen, 1636), Ger. theologian & musn. Ed. of var. collections of sacred m., notably the *Florilegium Portense*, pub. in 2 parts (1603 & 1621).

Boëllmann, Léon (b. Ensisheim, 25. IX. 1862; d. Paris, 11. X. 1897), Fr. (Alsat.) orgst. & comp. Pupil of Gigout at Niedermeyer's school in Paris, later orgst. at the church of Saint-Vincent-de-Paul there.

Works incl. Sym. in F maj.; *Fantaisie dialoguée* for org. & orch., *Vars. symph.* for co. & orch.; pf. 4tet, pf. Trio; co. & pf. So.; church m.; org. works incl. 2 suites (1st *Gothique*).

Boëly, Alexandre (Pierre François) (b. Versailles, 19. IV. 1785; d. Paris, 27. XII. 1858), Fr. pfst., orgst. & comp. Orgst. at the church of Saint-Germain-l'Auxerrois, 1840–51, where he cultivated Bach's org. m.

Works incl. chamber m.; org. works; v. & pf. sos.; numerous pf. works incl. sos., caprices, studies, preludes & fugues, &c.

Boelza, Igor Fedorovitch (b. Keltzy, Poland, 1904), Rus. mus. scholar & comp. Studied at the Kiev Cons., where he taught later, settled at Moscow in 1941; did much work for film m. in 1930–8, and in the 1940s began a hist. of Eng. m.

Works incl. film m.; 5 syms.; Ovt., *Lyric Poem*, &c. for orch.; concs. for pf. & for org.; stg. 4tet, pf. Trio; 5 pf. sos.; inst. pieces; songs, &c.

Boësset. Fr .16th–17th-cent. family of musns.:

1. Antoine B., Sieur de Villedieu (b. ?, *c.* 1585; d. Paris, 8–9. XII. 1643). Became Master of the King's Music to Louis XIII through his marriage to Guédron's daughter and held other important posts at court. Wrote 24 ballets and pub. many of them in several books of *Airs de cour* in 4 & 5 parts; also comp. masses & motets, &c.

2. Jean-Baptiste B., Seigneur de Dehault (b. ?, *c.* 1613; d. Paris, 27. XII. 1685), son of prec. Succeeded his father in 1644. Wrote ballets, incl. *La Mort d'Adonis*, with words by Perrin, *Ballet du Temps*, *Triomphe de Bacchus* & *Alcidiane*; also voc. chamber m., &c.

3. Claude Jean-Baptiste B., Seigneur de Launay (b. ?, VIII. 1664; d. ?), brother of prec. Held some of his father's posts and titles from 1686, but was replaced by 1696 by Lully's son Jean-Baptiste and by Colasse.

Works incl. *Fruits d'automne*, &c.

Bogatirev, Anatol (b. Vitebsk, 1913), Rus. comp. Studied at the Minsk Cons. under Zolotarev. Later studied folksong and became deputy dir. of the Cons. at Sverdlovsk.

Works incl. operas *The Two Foscari* (after Byron) & *In the Thick Woods of Polesye*; incid. m. for Romashev's *Stars cannot be dimmed*; *The Tale of a Bear* for solo voices, chor. & orch., cantata *To the People of Leningrad*; stg. 4tet, pf. Trio; *Manfred* suite (after Byron) and Vars. for pf.; choruses, songs, folksong arrs., &c.

Boh. (abbr.) = Bohemia, Bohemian.

Bohème, La (*The Bohemians*), opera by Leoncavallo (lib. by comp., based on Murger's novel *Scènes de la vie de Bohème*), prod. Venice, Teatro La Fenice, 6. V. 1897. Comp. at the same time as Puccini's work.

Opera by Puccini (lib. by Giuseppe Giacosa & Luigi Illica, based on Murger), prod. Turin, Teatro Regio, 1. II. 1896.

Bohemian (incl. Moravian) Composers. *See* (also Czech for later names) **Benda (2), Bendl, Biber, Brixi, Černohorsky, Dušek, Dussek, Finger, Foerster (J.), Gassmann, Gelinek, Gläser, Gluck (?), Gyrowetz, Kalliwoda, Kittl, Kotzwara, Kozeluch, Kraft (2), Krommer, Krumpholz (2), Moscheles, Mraczek, Mysliveček, Pichel, Reicha, Richter (F. X.), Schack, Sechter, Seegr, Škroup, Skuherský, Stamitz (4), Stich, Tomašek, Tuczek, Tuma, Walter (I.), Wanhal, Weber (D.), Worzischek, Wranitzky, Zelenka.**

Bohemian Girl, The, opera by Balfe (lib. by Alfred Bunn, based on a ballet-pantomime, *La Gypsy*, by Jules Henri Vernoy de Saint-Georges), prod. London, Drury Lane Theatre, 27. XI. 1843.

Böhm, Georg (b. Goldbach nr. Gotha, IX. 1661; d. Lüneburg, 18. V. 1733), Ger. comp. Orgst. at Hamburg before 1698, then at St. John's church, Lüneburg. As comp. and orgst. an important forerunner of Bach: his works incl. a Passion and chorale preludes.

Böhm, Theobald (b. Munich, 9. IV. 1793 or 1794; d. Munich, 25. XI. 1881), Ger. flst. and inventor. He wrote m. for his inst. and made important changes in its fingering and mechanism.

Boïeldieu, François Adrien (b. Rouen, 16. XII. 1775; d. Jarcy, 8. X. 1834), Fr. comp. Studied under Broche, the orgst. of Rouen cath., and in 1793 brought out his 1st opera, *La Fille coupable*, there, with a lib. by his father, who was secretary to the archbishop. He also wrote many songs at that time, some of which were pub. in Paris. Having failed to estab. a school of m. on the model of the Paris Cons. at Rouen, he left for the capital, where in 1797 he prod. his 1st opera away from home, *La Famille suisse*, which was so successful that he brought out 4 more within 2 years. He also became pf. prof. at the Cons. in 1789. Being reproached by Cherubini for having attained too easy a success on very slender gifts, he placed himself under that master for a course in ctpt. In 1802 he married the dancer Clotilde Mafleuray, with disastrous results, and in 1803 he left for St. Petersburg as cond. of the Imp. Opera. There he prod. 9 operas between 1804–10. He returned to Paris in 1811 and had a greater success than before because there was less competition and he did better work. He collaborated by turns with Cherubini, Catel, Isouard, R. Kreutzer, Hérold, Berton, Paer and Auber, also with some of these and Batton, Blangini and Carafa in *La Marquise de Brinvilliers* of 1831; but his best works are among those he did alone. In *La Dame blanche*, to match the lib. from Scott, he used some Sco. folksongs. Soon after he began to suffer from consumption contracted in Rus. and his fortune declined until he was granted a gvt. pension. In 1827 he was married for the 2nd time, to the singer Philis Desoyres, with whom he had long been living and by whom he had a son, Adrien Louis Victor, in 1815, who also became a comp. B. lived at Geneva for a time not long before his death.

Works incl. operas *Le Calife de Bagdad, Ma Tante Aurore, Aline, Reine de Golconde, La Jeune Femme colère, Télémaque, Rien de trop, Jean de Paris, La Fêie du village voisin, Le Petit Chaperon rouge, La Dame blanche, Les Deux Nuits* & others; incid. m. for Racine's *Athalie*; pf. Conc.; pf. Trio & other chamber m.; duets for v. & pf. and hp. & pf., 6 pf. sos., &c.

Boileau(-Despréaux), Nicolas (1636–1711), Fr. critic & poet. *See* (?) **Bellérophon** (Lully), **Dieren (van)** (songs).

Boisdeffre, Charles (Henri René Le Mouton) **de** (b. Vesoul, 3. IV. 1838; d. Vézelise, Meurthe-et-Moselle, 25. XI. 1906), Fr. comp. Gained a prize for chamber m. in 1883.

Works incl. Sym. in A min., *Scènes champêtres* for orch.; *Messe solennelle*, cantata *Cantique des cantiques*; pf. 6tet, 2 pf. 5tets, pf. 4tet, 2 pf. trios; pf. sos., &c.

Boismortier, Joseph Bodin de (b. Perpignan, *c.* 1691; d. Paris, *c.* 1765), Fr. comp. Wrote 4 opera-ballets, cantatas, over 50 inst. works incl. many for musette and vielle.

Boito, Arrigo (b. Padua, 24. II. 1842; d. Milan, 10. VI. 1918), It. poet & comp. Studied at the Milan Cons. and prod. his Faust opera, *Mefistofele*, at the Teatro alla Scala there in 1868. Dir. of the Parma Cons., 1889–97. Wrote libs. for several comps. as well as for himself, incl. those of Verdi's *Otello* and *Falstaff*. His *Nerone* was not prod. until after his death. He also comp. an opera, *Ero e Leandro*, but destroyed the m. later and handed the lib. to Mancinelli; and he wrote a lib. on *Hamlet* for Faccio.

Bolero. A Spa. dance in 3–4 with a characteristic rhythm that usually has a triplet on the 2nd half of the 1st beat.

Bolero. An orch. work by Ravel, prod. Paris, 1928, and more than once used for ballets, consisting entirely of a single theme of Spa. character, repeated over and over again with different orchn. and in a gradually rising *crescendo*.

Bolivian Composer. *See* **Velasco Maidana.**

Bombard. The bass inst. of the obs. family of the Shawm, a double reed wind inst. prec. the ob., the B. thus being a forerunner of the bn.

Bombarde. A 16-ft. reed org. pedal stop, similar to the Bombardon, but with more powerful tone.

Bombardino (It. dim. of Bombardo). A small Bombard, and thus the ancestor of the ob.

Bombardon (Fr.; *see also* **Saxhorn**). The name of a brass inst. of the Tuba variety, derived from Bombard (or Ger. *Pommer*), previously applied to var. insts. of the ob. and bn. family. The B. takes the lowest bass parts in military and brass bands. Also a bass org. stop for 16-ft. reed pipes.

Bomtempo, João Domingos (b. Lisbon, 28. XII. 1775; d. Lisbon, 18. VIII. 1842), Port. comp. Settled in Paris in 1795, but returned to Lisbon in 1820, founding a Phil. Soc. there, and became dir. of the Cons. in 1833.

Works incl. It. opera *Alessandro in Efeso*; Mass for the promulgation of the Port. Constitution (1821), Requiems for Maria I, Pedro IV and Camoens; vars. on a fandango and on *God save the King* for orch.; 4 pf. concs.; pf. 5tet, &c.

Bona, Valerio (b. Brescia, *c.* 1560; d. ? Verona, after 1619), It. comp. & Franciscan friar. Chapel master at var. churches, incl. Vercelli, Milan, Brescia and Verona.

Works incl. masses, motets and other church m.; madrigals, canzonets, &c.

Bondeville, Emmanuel (b. Rouen, 29. X. 1898), Fr. orgst. & comp. Studied at Rouen and was app. orgst. of the church of Saint-Nicaise there in 1915, but held important broadcasting apps. in Paris from 1935.

Works incl. operetta *L'École des maris*; *Le Bal des pendus, Lara, Ophélie, Marine* & *Triptyque* for orch.; pf. So.; songs, &c.

Boni, Guillaume (b. Saint-Flour, ?; d. ?), Fr. 16th-cent. comp. Chapel master at the church of Saint-Étienne at Toulouse. Comp. 2 books of sonnets by Ronsard, 1 of quatrains by Pibrac, *Psalmi Davidici*, &c.

Bonini, Severo (b. Florence, ?; d. ?), It. 17th-cent. comp. Pupil of Caccini. Orgst. at Forlì. Comp. Rinuccini's *Lamento d'Arianna* in recitative style and made a new departure by writing madrigals and spiritual canzonets for a single voice with inst. accomp. He also wrote 3-part motets with thorough-bass and *Affetti spirituali* for 2 voices in the new style.

Bonmarché, Jean (b. Ypres or Valenciennes, 1520; d. ?), Flem. comp. Canon and chapel master at Cambrai. In 1565 he went to Spa. as master of Philip II's chapel, but (?) retired to Valenciennes. Comp. masses & motets.

Bonnal, Joseph (Ermand) (b. Bordeaux, 1. VII. 1880), Fr. orgst. & comp. Studied at the Paris Cons. Held several orgst.'s apps. at Paris churches, and in 1921 at Saint-André at Bayonne where he became dir. of the school of m.

Works incl. 2 ballets; *Poèmes franciscains, Le Tombeau d'Argentina* & *Petite Suite basque* for orch.; 2 stg. 4tets & other chamber m.; Sym., *Paysages euskariens* & many other works for org., &c.

Bonne Chanson, La, cycle of 8 songs by Fauré, set to poems from Verlaine's vol. of that name, comp. 1891–2.

Symph. poem by Loeffler, on the same source, comp. 1901 and prod. Boston, 12. IV. 1902.

Bonner, Eugene (MacDonald) (b. Washington, N.C., 1889), Amer. critic, & comp. Studied at the Peabody Cons. of Baltimore and in Eng., where he lived in 1911–17. Having served in the war of 1914–8, he settled in Paris until 1927, studying with Albert Wolff. On his return to U.S.A. he became m. critic in N.Y.

Works incl. operas *Barbara Frietchie, Celui qui épousa une femme muette, The Venetian Glass Nephew* & *The Gods of the Mountain*; incid. m. to *The Young Alexander*; prelude *White Nights* for orch.; *Whispers of Heavenly Death* (Whitman) for voice & orch.; pf. 5tet; *Flutes* for voice & 4 insts.; *Suite sicilienne* for v. & pf., &c.

Bonno, Giuseppe (b. Vienna, 29. I. 1710; d. Vienna, 15. IV. 1788); Aus. comp. of It. extraction. Was sent to Naples to study and from 1738 continued at the court chapel in Vienna, of which he became chapel master in 1774, succeeding Gassmann.

Works incl. over 20 operas; orats., e.g. *Il Giuseppe riconosciuto*; numerous cantatas; masses, hymns, &c.

Bononcini (or **Buononcini**). It. 17th–18th-cent. family of musns.:

1. **Giovanni Maria B.** (b. Montecorone nr. Modena, IX. 1642; d. Modena, 18. XI. 1678), chief musn. to the Duke of Modena, chapel master there of the church of San Giovanni in Monte and later of the cath. He wrote a treatise, *Il musico prattico*.

Works incl. masses; cantatas; sos., &c.

2. **Giovanni B.** (not G. Battista) (b. Modena, 18. VII. 1670; d. ?, 1755), son of prec. Pupil of Colonna and of his father, whom he succeeded at San Giovanni in Monte at Modena. Attached to the court in Vienna, 1692, and in Berlin, 1696. He prod. his 1st opera in Rome in 1692. Lived in Vienna and It., 1706–20, in London, 1720–32.

Works incl. operas *Tullo Ostilio, Serse, Astarto, Crispo, Erminia, Farnace, Calfurnia, Astianatte, Griselda* & many others, incl. an act in *Muzio Scevola* with Handel and (?) Mattei; orat. *Il Giosuè*; funeral anthem for Marlborough; m. for the Peace of Aix-la-Chapelle; 4 masses, Te Deum, psalms, *Laudate pueri*; chamber cantatas and duets, &c.

3. **Antonio Maria B.** (not Marc' Antonio) (b. Modena, 18. VI. 1677; d. Rome, 8. VII. 1726); brother of prec. Became chapel master to the Duke of Modena in 1721.

Works incl. *c.* 15 operas, e.g. *Camilla*, &c.

Bontempi, Giovanni Andrea (real name Angelini) (b. Perugia, 1624; d. Perugia, 1. VI. 1705), It. male sop. singer, theorist & comp. He took the name of a patron, Cesare Bontempi, and sang in St. Mark's, Venice, from 1643. At the end of the 1640s he went to Dresden, where he became asst. cond. to Schütz in 1666, but devoted himself to science and architecture the next year. He returned to It. in 1669 and after another visit to Dresden in 1671 settled down in his birthplace. He wrote 3 theoret. books.

Works incl. operas *Paride, Dafne, Jupiter und Io*, &c.

Borck, Edmund von (b. Breslau, 22. IX. 1906), Ger. cond. & comp. Studied at the Hochschule für Musik in Berlin. After cond. at Frankfort o/M., he became prof. at the Berlin Cons. in 1939.

Works incl. opera *Napoleon* (based on C. D. Grabbe's play); 5 Pieces, Prelude & Fugue, Conc. & Theme, Vars. & Finale for orch.; 6tet for fl. & stgs. and other chamber m., &c.

Borde, Jean de la. *See* **La Borde.**

Bordes, Charles (b. La Roche-Corbon nr. Vouvray, 12. V. 1863; d. Toulon, 8. XI. 1909), Fr. pfst., comp. & scholar. Pupil of Marmontel for pf. and of Franck for comp. As chapel master 1st at Nogent-sur-Marne and from 1890 at the church of Saint-Gervais in Paris, he devoted himself to research into old polyphonic m. and gave perfs. with the Chanteurs de Saint-Gervais cond. by him. In 1889–90 he explored Basque folk m. and in 1894 was one of the founders of the Schola Cantorum.

Works incl. unfinished opera *Les Trois Vagues*; Fantasy on a Basque theme for pf. & orch.; motets & spiritual dialogues; pf. works; choruses; 33 songs, &c.

Bordes-Pène (*née* **Pène**), **Léontine Marie** (b. Lorient, Finistère, 25. XI. 1858; d. Rouen, 24. I. 1924), Fr. pfst. Studied at the Paris Cons. and married a brother of Charles Bordes. She took a great interest in contemp. Fr. m.

Bordoni, Faustina (b. Venice, 1700; d. Venice, 4. XI. 1781), It. m.-sop. singer. 1st appearance in Venice, 1716; went to London in 1726 and became famous under Handel's management. Married Hasse in 1730 and sang at Dresden.

Bore. The width of the tubing of wind insts., which affects the character of their tone.

Boree. One of the old Eng. names for the Bourrée, others being Borea, Bore and Borry. One of these words, preferably the last, would be worth reviving.

Borgomastro di Saardam, Il (*The Burgomaster of Saardam*), comic opera by Donizetti (lib. by Domenico Gilardoni, based on a Fr. play by Anne Honoré Joseph Mélesville, Jean Toussaint Merle and Eugène Cantiran de Boirie), prod. Naples, Teatro del Fondo, 19. VIII. 1827. The subject is that of Lortzing's *Zar und Zimmermann.*

Boris Godunov, opera by Mussorgsky (lib. by comp. based on Pushkin's drama and Nikolai Mikhailovitch Karamzin's *History of the Rus. Empire*), comp. 1868–9; enlarged and revised 1871–2; this later version cut and prod. St. Petersburg, Imp. Opera, 8. II. 1874, the orig. having been rejected in 1870. Rimksy-Korsakov's ed. prod. St. Petersburg, Imp. Opera, 10. XII. 1896. Further revision by R.-K., 1908. The orig. prod. Leningrad, 16. II. 1928.

Born, Bertrand de (b. ?; d. ?, *c.* 1215), Fr. troubadour. 46 poems and 1 tune of his songs have been preserved.

Borne, Fernand Le. *See* **Le Borne.**

Bornelh, Guiraut de (b. ?; d. ?, *c.* 1220), Fr. troubadour. He was regarded as the master of his calling. More than 80 poems and 4 tunes of his songs are extant.

Bornier, Henri, Vicomte (1825–1901), Fr. dramatist. *See* **Coquard** (*Agamemnon*).

Borodin, Alexander Porphyrevitch (b. St. Petersburg, 11–12. XI. 1883; d. St. Petersburg, 28. II. 1887), Rus. scientist & comp. Illegitimate son of Prince Gedeanov, who registered him as the son of one of his serfs. He tried to compose at the age of 9 and was given m. lessons. In his studies at the Acad. of Medicine he distinguished himself esp. in chemistry, and while studying at Heidelberg he met the pfst. Catherina Protopopova, whom he married in 1863. The prec. year, having so far been self-taught in comp., he began to take lessons from Balakirev, who cond. his 1st Sym. in 1869. He lectured on chemistry at the School of Medicine for Women from 1872 to his death and wrote important treatises on his subject.

Works incl. opera *Prince Igor* (unfinished); 3 syms. (3rd unfinished); *In the Steppes of Central Asia* & Scherzo for orch.; 2 stg. 4tets; *Petite Suite* for pf.; *Serenata espagnola* for pf. duet; *Sérénade de quatre galants à une dame* for male-voice 4tet; 13 songs, &c.

Borosini, Francesco (b. Bologna, *c.* 1695; d. ?), It. ten. singer. He sang at Prague in 1723 and went to London the following year, singing in Handel's and Ariosti's operas in 1724–5.

Borosini (*née* **d'Ambreville**), **Rosa** (b. Modena, *c.* 1693; d. ?), Fr. 18th-cent. con. singer, wife of prec. Made her 1st appearance in 1713 and went to London with her husband in 1724.

Borren, Charles (Jean Eugène) van den (b. Brussels, 17. XI. 1874), Belg. mcolst. Studied law and practised for 8 years, but later devoted himself to mus. hist., esp. of the old Nthld. school. App. librarian to the Brussels Cons. in 1920, succeeding Wotquenne. His works incl. many valuable studies, e.g. on Eng. virginal m., the Eng. madrigal, the origins of

Nthld. keyboard m., the beginnings of m. in Venice, Lassus, Dufay, &c.

Børresen, Axel (Einar Haakon) (b. Copenhagen, 2. VI. 1876), Dan. comp. Pupil of Svendsen, he took a comp. prize in 1901. Later he held many important administrative posts in the mus. life of Copenhagen.

Works incl. operas *The Royal Guest* & *Kaddara*; ballet *Tycho Brahe's Dream*; incid. m. for plays; several syms. & other orch. works; chamber m.; songs, &c.

Borry. Eng. corruption of the Fr. *bourrée* found in 17th-cent. m., e.g. Purcell. It is a pretty word and no greater perversion than many another good Eng. term that comes from Fr.; its re-adoption is therefore not undesirable.

Bortkievitch, Sergei Eduardovitch (b. Kharkov, 22. II. 1877), Rus. comp. Studied law at St. Petersburg and comp. under Liadov, later at Leipzig. Lived in Berlin until 1914, when he joined the Rus. army, and at Constantinople after the 1st world war.

Works incl. symph. poem *Othello*; 4 pf. concs. (1 for the left hand), 2 v. concs., co. conc.; pf. sos. & pieces; songs, &c.

Bortniansky, Dimitri Stepanovitch (b. Glukhov, Ukraine, 1752; d. St. Petersburg, 9. X. 1825), Rus. comp. Studied at Moscow and in St. Petersburg under Galuppi, whom he followed to It. in 1768 with a grant from Catherine II. He made further studies at Bologna, Rome and Naples. He wrote motets and operas at Venice in 1776 and at Modena in 1778. In 1779 he returned to Rus. and became dir. of the imp. church choir, which he reformed and turned into the Imp. Chapel in 1796.

Works incl. operas *Creonte* & *Quinto Fabio*; 35 sacred concs., 10 concs. for double choir, mass, chants, &c.

Borwick, Leonard (b. London, 26. II. 1868; d. Le Mans, 15. IX. 1925), Eng. pfst. Pupil of Clara Schumann in 1883–9 at Frankfort o/M., where he made his 1st appearance, playing in London for the 1st time in 1890, at a Phil. Soc. concert. He also appeared in Vienna, frequently played with the most eminent artists in chamber m. at the London St. James's Hall and gave many recitals with Plunket Greene.

Boschi, Giuseppe (b. ? Viterbo, ?; d. ?), It. 17th–18th-cent. bass singer. Member of St. Mark's, Venice; (?) sang Polyphemus in Handel's *Aci* at Naples in 1709. 1st appeared in London in 1711.

Boschot, Adolphe (b. Fontenay-sous-Bois, Seine, 4. V. 1871), Fr. critic. Has been attached to var. Paris newspapers and reviews and written a number of books on m., particularly a biog. of Berlioz in 3 vols.

Bösendorfer, Ignaz (b. Vienna, 28. VII. 1796; d. Vienna, 14. IV. 1859), Aus. pf. manufacturer. Founded his firm in Vienna in 1828 and was succeeded in it by his son Ludwig (1835–1919) in 1859.

Bosio, Angiolina (b. Turin, 22. VIII. 1830; d. St. Petersburg, 12. IV. 1859), It. sop. singer. Studied at Milan under Cataneo and made her 1st appearance there in 1846. After many tours she 1st went to London in 1852.

Bossi, (Marco) Enrico (b. Salò, 25. IV. 1861; d. at sea, 20. II. 1925), It. orgst. & comp. Studied at the Liceo Musicale of Bologna and at the Milan Cons. After var. orgst.'s and teaching apps. he became dir. of the principal m. schools at Venice, Bologna and Rome in succession. Meanwhile he had become very famous as a concert orgst., and it was when returning from a tour in U.S.A. that he d.

Works incl. operas *Paquita*, *Il veggente* & *L'angelo della notte*; orats. *Il Paradiso perduto* (after Milton) & *Giovanna d'Arco*; masses, motets & sacred cantatas; secular chor. works with orch. or org. incl. *Il cieco*, *Inno di gloria* & *Cantico dei cantici*; orch. works; Conc. for org. & orch.; chamber music; c. 50 org. works incl. suite *Res severa magnum gaudium*; pf. pieces; songs, &c.

Bossi, Renzo (b. Como, 9. IV. 1883), It. comp., son of prec. Studied under his father at the Liceo Benedetto Marcello in Venice and took a comp. prize in 1902, when he went to Leipzig, where he continued studying pf., org. and cond., the last under Nikisch. He was cond. of more than 1 Ger. opera house before he went to Milan as asst. cond. at La Scala. Prof. of comp. at Parma from 1913 and Milan from 1916.

Works incl. operas *Rosa rossa* (after Oscar Wilde), *Passa la ronda!*, *La notte del mille*, *Volpino il calderaio* (after Shakespeare's *Taming of the Shrew*) & *Proserpina*; Sym., *Sinfoniale*, *Fantasia sinfonica* & *Bianco e nero* for orch.; v. Conc.; chamber m., &c.

Bossuet, Jacques-Bénigne (1627–1704), Fr. bishop, orator & author. *See* **Thomson (V.)** (*Oraison funèbre*).

Botstiber, Hugo (b. Vienna, 21. VI. 1875; d. Shrewsbury, II. 1942), Aus. mcolst. Pupil of Adler, R. Fuchs and Zemlinsky. Held several important mus. administrative posts in Vienna, ed. old m., wrote books on the orch. ovt., on the sym. since

Berlioz, &c., and completed Pohl's biog. of Haydn.

Bottesini, Giovanni (b. Crema, 24. XII. 1822; d. Parma, 7. VII. 1889), It. db. player, cond. & comp. Was engaged at Havana, Paris, Palermo, Barcelona and Cairo.

Works incl. *Marion Delorme* (after Victor Hugo), *Ali Baba* & *Ero e Leandro*, db. concs. with orch.; much m. for db. & pf., &c.

Boucher, Alexandre Jean (b. Paris, 11. IV. 1778; d. Paris, 29. XII. 1861), Fr. vst. Appeared in public at the age of 6, was court vst. at Madrid, 1787–1805, and toured Eur. from 1820 to 1844 with sensational success.

Boucicault, Dion (1820–90), Ir. actor & playwright. *See* **Lily of Killarney** (Benedict).

Bouffons. *See* **Guerre des Bouffons.**

Boughton, Rutland (b. Aylesbury, 23. I. 1878), Eng. comp. Studied at the R.C.M. in London under Stanford and Walford Davies. But he left very soon, finding academic teaching irksome, and prod. some early orch. works, cond. for a time at the Haymarket Theatre, had a hard struggle and accepted a teaching engagement at the Midland School of M. in Birmingham in 1904, remaining there until 1911, at the same time lecturing and cond., and prod. the chor. work *Midnight* to words from Edward Carpenter's *Towards Democracy* at the Birmingham Festival of 1909. Idealizing Wagner, he determined to found an Eng. Bayreuth and began in a very modest way at Glastonbury with a series of m.-dramas on the Arthurian legends, in 1914, 1st prod., however, *The Immortal Hour*. A special theatre was to be built at Glastonbury, but the project had to be abandoned. In 1922 *The Immortal Hour* had a long run in London, and *Alkestis* was prod. there by the B.N.O.C. in 1924.

Works incl. m.-dramas *The Birth of Arthur, The Immortal Hour, Bethlehem, The Round Table, Alkestis, The Queen of Cornwall, The Lily Maid*; ballets *Choral Dances, Snow White, The Moon Maiden*; dramatic scene *Agincourt* from Shakespeare's *Henry V*; works for chor. & orch.: *The Skeleton in Armour* (Longfellow), *The Invincible Armada* (Schiller), *Midnight* (Edward Carpenter), *Song of Liberty*; unaccomp. chor.: *Chor. Vars.* on folksongs, motet *The City, 4 Festival Chors.* (Drinkwater); 2 stg. 4tets; songs with stg. 4tet; v. & pf. So.; songs, &c.

Bouhy, Jacques (**Joseph André**) (b. Pépinster, 18. VI. 1848; d. Paris, III. 1929), Belg. bar. singer. Studied at Liége and Paris, where he made his 1st appearance at the Opéra in 1872. Dir. of N.Y. Cons., 1885–9. Lived and taught in Paris from 1907. The 1st Escamillo in Bizet's *Carmen*.

Bouilly, Jean-Nicolas (1763–1842), Fr. writer. Administrator of a dept. nr. Tours during the Terror. Wrote libs. for a number of operas (*see* **Rescue Opera**) for var. comps., incl. Cherubini and Gaveaux. The lib. of Beethoven's *Fidelio* is a Ger. trans. of his book for Gaveaux's *Léonore*.

Boulanger, Lili (**Juliette Marie Olga**) (b. Paris, 21. VIII. 1893; d. Mézy, Seine-et-Oise, 15. III. 1918), Fr. comp. Pupil of her sister Nadia at first, then at the Paris Cons. Gained the Prix de Rome in 1913, but suffered much ill health.

Works incl. incid. m. for Maeterlinck's *La Princesse Maleine*; 2 poems for orch.; cantata *Faust et Hélène* (after Goethe); psalms with orch., &c.

Boulanger, Nadia (**Juliette**) (b. Paris, 16. IX. 1887), Fr. comp. & teacher, sister of prec. Student at the Paris Cons., where she taught later, as well as at the École Normale de Musique and the Amer. Cons. at Fontainebleau. She went to U.S.A. after the outbreak of war in 1939. Many distinguished comps. in var. countries were her pupils.

Works incl. incid. m. to d'Annunzio's *La città morta* (with Pugno); cantata *La Sirène*; orch. works; inst. pieces, songs, &c.

Bourdon (Fr. = Drone). An org. stop with 16-ft. tone, stopped diapason.

Bourgault-Ducoudray, Louis (**Albert**) (b. Nantes, 2. II. 1840; d. Vernouillet, 4. VII. 1910) Fr. comp. A lawyer at first, he entered the Paris Cons. late and took a comp. prize in 1862. In 1869 he founded a chor. soc. in Paris with which he gave perfs. of unfamiliar works. Collected and pub. Gr. and Breton folksongs. Lectured on hist. of m. at the Cons. from 1878.

Works incl. operas *L'Atelier de Prague, Michel Colomb, Bretagne, Thamara, Myrdhin*; satiric play *La Conjuration des fleurs*; *Stabat Mater, Symphonie religieuse* for unaccomp. chor.; *Fantaisie en Ut mineur, Carnaval d'Athènes, Rapsodie cambodgienne, L'Enterrement d'Ophélie* (after Shakespeare) for orch. &c.

Bourgeois gentilhomme, Le (*The Burgess as Gentleman*), comedy-ballet by Molière with m. by Lully, prod. Chambord, 14. X. 1670.

Incid. m. by R. Strauss to a shortened version of Molière's comedy trans. by Hugo von Hofmannsthal, preceding the 1-act opera *Ariadne auf Naxos*, prod. Stuttgart, 25. X.

1912. S. afterwards dropped it for a new operatic 1st act and made a concert suite for orch. of the incid. m., adding a minuet by Lully.

Bourgeois, Louis (b. Paris, *c.* 1510; d. Paris, *c.* 1561), Fr. musn. A Protestant, he went to Geneva to join Calvin's church, taking the place of Franc, who had gone to Lausanne, and working with Guillaume Fabri. He contrib. to the Genevan Psalter by selecting and harmonizing tunes.

Bourgeois, Louis Thomas (b. Fontaine l'Évêque, Hainault, ?; d. ? Paris, I. 1750), Flem. singer & comp. Singer at the Paris Opéra, but left in 1711 to become a comp. Chapel master at Toul and at Strasburg.

Works incl. ballets; motet *Beatus vir*; cantatas incl. *Cantates anacréontiques*, &c.

Bourges, Clémentine de (b. ?; d. ?, 30. IX. 1561 or 1562), Fr. comp. & poetess. Lived at Lyons.

Bournonville, Jean-Valentin de (b. Noyon, *c.* 1580; d. ?, *c.* 1640), Fr. orgst. & comp. Worked successively at Rouen, Évreux, Saint-Quentin, Abbeville and Amiens cath. Wrote masses & other church m.; org. m., &c.

Bourrée (Fr.). A Fr. or Spa. dance in quick 2–4 time beginning with an upbeat.

Boutique fantasque, La (*The Fantastic Toyshop*), ballet by Respighi, arr. from m. by Rossini (chgph. by Leonid Fedorovitch Massin), prod. London, Alhambra Theatre, 5. VI. 1919. The m. consists mainly of small pieces written by R. in his retirement for the amusement of his friends.

Bouvet, Charles (René Clément) (b. Paris, 3. I. 1858; d. Paris, 22. V. 1935), Fr. mcolst. He was at first a vst. in the Cons. orch., but from 1903–11 was in charge of the Fondation J. S. Bach, from 1924 of the library and museum at the Opéra and in 1920–7 he was sec. of the Soc. française de Musicologie. He ed. old m. and wrote books on the Couperin family, on Tartini, Massenet, Spontini, &c.

Bovy-Lysberg, Charles Samuel (b. Lysberg, Ct. Berne, 1. III. 1821; d. Geneva, 25. II. 1873), Swi. pfst. & comp. Son of Antoine Bovy, a stamp engraver. Studied at home at first, but at the age of 15 was sent to Paris to study the pf. with Chopin and comp. with Belaire. Later he became prof. at the Geneva Cons.

Works incl. opera *La Fille du carillonneur*; pf. So. *L'Absence*, studies, nocturnes, waltzes, barcarolles, caprices, &c., for pf., &c.

Bow. The stick with horsehair stretched across it with which insts. of the viol and v. family are played.

Bowen, York (b. London, 22. II. 1884), Eng. pfst., vst., hn. player & comp. Studied at the R.A.M. in London.

Works incl. Sym. in E min., *Symph. Fantasia* for orch.; 3 pf. concs., v. & va. concs.; So. for va. & pf.; numerous pf. works, &c.

Bowles, Paul (Frederic) (b. New York, 30. XII. 1911), Amer. comp. Pupil of Aaron Copland, Virgil Thomson and Nadia Boulanger. He lived by turns in Spa., Mexico, Guatemala and N. Africa, but later returned to U.S.A.

Works incl. operas *The Wind Remains* & *Denmark Vesey*; ballets *Patorela, Yankee Clipper, Colloque sentimentale, Dance Ballet* & *Johnny A.*; film m. for *Roots in the Earth* (for the Mex. Dept. of Agriculture), *Congo* (for the Belg. gvt.), *America's Disinherited, Bride of Samoa, Innocent Island* & *Venus and Adonis*; incid. m. for Marlowe's *Dr. Faustus*, Shakespeare's *Twelfth Night*, Wm. Saroyan's *My Heart's in the Highlands* & *Love's Old Sweet Song*, &c. 10 other plays; cantata *Par le détroit*; Suite for orch.; *Romantic Suite* for 9 insts., *Mediodia* for 11 insts., *M. for a Farce* for cl., tpt. pf. & perc., *Scènes d'Anabase* for ten., ob. & pf., pf. Trio; sos. for ob. & cl., fl. & pf. and v. & pf.; 2 Sonatinas, *Huapango* Nos. 1 & 2, 2 *Portraits, Aria, Chorale and Rondo, La Femme de Dakar, Café sin nombre* & other works for pf.; *El Bejuco, Sayula, Nocturne, Caminata* & Suite for 2 pfs.; song cycles *Memnon* (Jean Cocteau), *Green Songs*, 4 Spa. Songs, *Danger de mort*, 6 *Songs, Letter to Freddy* (Gertrude Stein) & a number of other songs; partsongs, &c.

Bowman, Henry (b. ?; d. ?), Eng. 17th-cent. comp. Lived (?) at Oxford.

Works incl. a Miserere and a vol. of songs for 1–3 voices to words by Cowley and others.

Boyarina Vera Sheloga (Rimsky-Korsakov). *See* **Pskovitianka.**

Boyce, William (b. London, 7. II. 1710; d. London, 16. II. 1779), Eng. comp. & orgst. Boy chorister at St. Paul's cath. in London and later a pupil of Greene, whom he succeeded in 1755 as Master of the King's Band. Orgst. of the Chapel Royal from 1758. Pub. a collection of Eng. *Cathedral Music*, 1760–78. Mus.D., Oxford, 1749.

Works incl. stage entertainments *The Chaplet* & *The Shepherd's Lottery*; masque *Peleus and Thetis* & songs to Dryden's *Secular Masque*; serenata *Solomon*; incid. m. for Shakespeare's *Tempest, Cymbeline*

Romeo and Juliet & *Winter's Tale*; orats. *Noah* & *David's Lamentation over Saul and Jonathan*; *Ode to Charity*, 2 odes for St. Cecilia's Day; ode and anthem for perf. at Oxford, 1749; 8 syms.; 12 sos. for 2 v. & bass; songs incl. *Heart of Oak*, &c.

Brabançonne, La. *See* **National Anthems**: Belgium.

Brace. A bracket connecting the 2 staves, e.g. in pf. & hp. m., or a greater number of staves in a score.

Brade, William (b. ?, *c.* 1560; d. Hamburg, 26. II. 1630), Eng. violist & comp. Worked by turns at the court of Christian IV of Den., in the service of the Margraves of Brandenburg and the Duke of Schleswig-Gottorp, and at Halle, Berlin and Hamburg. Pub. inst. m. in several parts, incl. pavans, galliards and other dances, canzone, concs. and fancies in 6 books at Hamburg, Lübeck, Antwerp & Berlin, 1609–21.

Bradford, Hugh (St. John) (b. St. John's, N.F., 10. III. 1900), Brit. comp. Studied with Charles Wood at the R.C.M. in London.

Works incl. ballet *The Jackdaw and the Pigeons*; *Paysage* & *Fugal March* for orch.; Vars. on a Popular Theme & 7 Charact. Pieces for pf., *Song without Words* for 2 pfs., &c.

Braga, Gaetano (b. Giulianova, 9. VI. 1829; d. Milan, 21. XI. 1907), It. cst. & comp. Studied at the Naples Cons., toured Eur. and lived mainly in Paris & London.

Works incl. opera *La Reginella* & 7 others; cantata; co. Conc.; inst. pieces incl. *Serenata*, &c.

Braham, John (real name **Abraham**) (b. London, 20. III. 1777; d. London, 17. II. 1856), Eng. ten. singer & comp. Being very poor, he was taught by the Jewish singer Leoni, 1st appeared at Covent Garden Theatre in 1787 and continued to sing children's parts. When his voice broke he taught the pf., but reappeared at Rauzzini's concerts at Bath in 1794 and in London in 1796. In 1798–1801 he appeared in Paris, It. and Ger. He then became attached to Covent Garden for many years and often interpolated his own songs, which became very popular, in operas. He also contrib. to operas prod. at the Lyceum and Drury Lane Theatres, incl. one on Shakespeare's *Taming of the Shrew*. Towards the end of his career he was the 1st Huon in Weber's *Oberon*.

Brahms, Johannes (b. Hamburg, 7. V. 1833; d. Vienna, 3. IV. 1897), Ger. comp. Son of a poor db. player, from whom he learnt the rudiments of m. as a child. Although intended for an orch. player, he made such progress on the pf. that his parents decided to make a prodigy perf. of him when about 11; but his teachers wisely opposed this. He soon afterwards began to comp., but had to play in sailors' taverns and dancing-saloons at night to supplement his parents' earnings. He gave 2 concerts in 1848–9, but did not free himself from drudgery of playing and teaching until he went on a concert tour with Reményi in 1853, when he met Joachim, Liszt and other musns. of importance, partic. Schumann and Clara S., who took much interest in him. He greatly helped Clara when Schumann had his mental collapse in 1854 and after his death 2 years later. In 1857–60 he was intermittently engaged at the court of Lippe-Detmold, travelled as pfst. and worked at Hamburg between, cond. a ladies' choir there. 1st visited Vienna in 1862 and settled there for good the following year. Entirely devoted to comp. from 1864, except for some concert tours, on which he played mainly his own works. His success as a comp. was firmly estab. during the 1860s, and he became known abroad; but he did not write his 1st sym. until 1875, aged 42. He wrote much during summer holidays in Aus., Ger. or Swi., but hardly visited other countries except It. In 1877 he refused the Cambridge Mus.D. because he did not wish to go to receive it in person, but accepted the Dr. phil. from Breslau in 1879. The later years were uneventful except for the growing importance of his work, and in 1896 he began to suffer seriously from cirrhosis of the liver, the disease from which he died.

Works incl. *A Protestant Requiem* (see *Deutsches Requiem*) for sop., bar., chor. & orch., *Schicksalslied* (Hölderlin), *Triumphlied*, *Nänie* (Schiller) & *Gesang der Parzen* (from Goethe's *Iphigenie auf Tauris*) for chor. & orch., *Rinaldo* (Goethe) for ten., male chor. & orch., *Rhapsodie* (Goethe) for con., male chor. & orch.; 4 syms., 2 Serenades, Vars. on a theme by Haydn (also 2 pfs.), *Academic Festival* & *Tragic* ovts. for orch.; 2 pf. concs., v. Conc., double Conc. for v. & co.; 3 stg. 4tets, 2 stg. 5tets, cl. 5tet, 2 stg. 6tets, 5 pf. trios (1 with cl., 1 with hn.), 3 pf. 4tets, pf. 5tet; 3 v. & pf. sos., 2 co. & pf. sos., 2 cl. & pf. sos., mvt. of a v. & pf. So. (with Schumann & Dietrich); 3 sos., 5 sets of vars. (1 with fugue on theme by Handel), Ballads, Rhapsodies, Capricci, Intermezzi, Scherzo, &c. for pf.; pf. duets incl. 2 sets of *Liebeslieder* with voc. 4tet *ad lib.*; So. (from pf. 5tet) and

Haydn Vars. for 2 pfs.; 12 chorale preludes & 2 fugues for org.; over 100 partsongs for chor. or solo 4tet; 25 voc. duets; 190 songs; 7 vols. of arrs. of Ger. folksongs, &c.

Brall. An old Eng. name for the Branle, a variant of 'Brawl.'

Branco, Luiz Freitas (b. Lisbon, 12. X. 1890), Port. comp. Studied at Lisbon, with Humperdinck in Berlin, and in Paris. Taught score-reading at the Lisbon Cons. from 1916 and in 1930 took charge of the master-class in comp.

Works incl. orat., cantata; 3 syms., 2 Port. suites for orch.; v. Conc., Ballad for pf. & orch.; songs with orch.; stg. 4tet; 2 v. & pf. sos., co. & pf. So.; pf. pieces; songs; madrigals to words by Camoens, &c.

Branco, Pedro Freitas (b. Lisbon, 31. X. 1896), Port. cond. & comp., brother of prec. Studied under his brother and others, founded a Port. opera company in 1926, sym. concerts at Lisbon in 1928 and has cond. the State Sym. Orch. since 1934. Married the Fr. pfst. Marie-Antoinette de Lévêque (b. 1903).

Works incl. 2 stg. 4tets, pf. Trio, songs, &c.

Brand, Max (b. Lwów, 26. IV. 1896), Aus.-Pol. comp. Settled in U.S.A.

Works incl. opera *Maschinist Hopkins*; scenic orat. *The Gate*, &c.

Brand, Michael. *See* Mosonyi.

Branden (Ger. plur.) = Branles.

Brandenburg Concertos. A series of 6 orch. concs. by Bach for var. inst. combs., ded. in 1721 to the Margrave Christian Ludwig of Brandenburg: I. F maj. for v. piccolo, 3 obs., 2 hns., bn. & stgs.; II. F maj. for v., fl., ob., tpt. & stgs.; III. G maj. for stgs. (3 pts. each for vs., vas. & cos.); IV. G maj. for v., 2 fls. & stgs.; V. D maj. for v., fl., hpchd. & stgs.; VI. B♭ maj. for stgs. without vs.

Brandenburgers in Bohemia, The (*Braniboři v Čechách*), opera by Smetana (lib. by Karel Sabina), prod. Prague, Cz. Theatre, 5. I. 1866.

Brandts-Buys, Jan (b. Zutphen, 12. IX. 1868; d. Salzburg, 8. XII. 1933), Dutch comp. He won a state prize as a youth and studied at Frankfort o/M. Most of his operatic successes were Ger. works prod. in Ger. & Aus.

Works incl. operas *Das Veilchenfest, Le Carillon, Die Schneider von Schoenau, Der Eroberer, Mi-carême, Der Mann im Mond, Traumland, Ulysses*; *Oberon Romancero* for orch.; 3 pf. concs.; Suite for stgs., hp. & hn., stg. 4tets, 5tet for fl. & stgs., pf. trios; pf. works; songs, &c.

Brandukov, Anatol Andreievitch (b. Moscow, 6. I. 1859; d. Moscow, X. 1930), Rus. cst. Studied at the Moscow Cons.; travelled much as a virtuoso.

Brangill (Eng. obs.) = Branle.

Branle. A Fr. round dance in 2–2 time, dating from the 15th cent. and cultivated until the 18th, called Brawl in Eng.

Brant, Jobst vom (b. ?; d. ?), Ger. 16th-cent. comp. Contrib. songs to var. collections and also wrote psalms and Ger. songs for several voices.

Brass Band. A band consisting of brass insts. only, as distinct from the milit. band, which contains woodwind and perc. insts. as well.

Brassart, Johannes (b. ?; d. ?), Flem. 15th-cent. singer & comp. Sang in the Papal choir in Rome until 1431 and later worked at Liége and Tongern. Wrote church m.

Bratsche (Ger.) = Viola, a corruption from the It. *va. da braccio*.

Braunfels, Walter (b. Frankfort o/M., 19. XII. 1882), Ger. pfst. & comp. Studied at the Hoch Cons. at Frankfort, later in Vienna and Munich.

Works incl. operas *Prinzessin Brambilla* (after a story by E. T. A. Hoffmann), *Till Eulenspiegel, Die Vögel, Don Gil von den grünen Hosen, Der gläserne Berg, Galatea*; incid. m. to Shakespeare's *Twelfth Night* & *Macbeth*; Mass, Te Deum; orch. Vars. & other works; pf. music; songs, &c.

Brautwahl, Die (*The Choice of a Bride*), opera by Busoni (lib. by comp., based on a story by E. T. A. Hoffmann), prod. Hamburg, 13. IV. 1912.

Bravo (It. lit. brave, excellent). An expression of approval of a perf. used in other countries than It., but usually in the masculine form only: the correct form for a woman's perf. is *brava* and for that of several people *bravi*.

Bravura (It. lit. courage, bravery, swagger). In m. the term refers to passages in a comp. or feats in a perf. calling for brilliance and virtuosity. The term may be accepted as an Eng. word.

Brawl (Eng. obs.) = Branle.

Brazilian Composers. *See* **Fernandez (O. L.), Gomes, Guarnieri, Huizar, Levy, Mignone, Nepomuceno, Siqueira, Villa-Lobos.**

Break. The change in tone-quality between different registers of voices and of wind insts., a natural defect which may be more or less successfully corrected by technical means.

Breaking. The 17th-cent. practice of varying a theme by dividing it into figurations of smaller note-values, as in Divisions (vars.). Breaking the Ground was the same process if the theme was on a ground-bass.

Brecht, Bert(olt) (b. 1895), Ger. poet & playwright. *See* **Lehrstück & Weill.**

Brechung (Ger.). *See* **Ornaments.**

Brehme, Hans (b. Potsdam, 10. III. 1904), Ger. comp. Pupil of Robert Kahn in Berlin, he 1st attracted attention at the Bremen mus. festival.
Works incl. *Triptychon* (vars. on a theme by Handel) & *Concerto sinfonico* for orch.; pf. Conc.; Partita for stg. 4tet, &c.

Breitkopf & Härtel. Pub. firm at Leipzig, founded 1719 by Bernhardt Christoph Breitkopf (1695–1777).

Brema, Marie (real name Minny Fehrmann) (b. Liverpool, 28. II. 1856; d. Manchester, 22. III. 1925), Eng. con. singer of Ger. descent. 1st appearance at Bremen, 1891. Sang at Covent Garden in London, Bayreuth, N.Y. and in many Eur. capitals, both in opera and concerts. Prof. of singing at Manchester R.C.M.

Brendel, Karl (Franz) (b. Stollberg, 26. XI. 1811; d. Leipzig, 25. XI. 1868), Ger. m. critic, ed. & author. Settled at Leipzig and ed. the *Neue Zeitschrift für Musik*, founded by Schumann, from 1845. He advocated modern m. and wrote several books.

Brenet, Michel (real name Antoinette Christine Marie Bobillier) (b. Lunéville, 12. IV. 1858; d. Paris, 4. XI. 1918), Fr. mcolst. Lived in Paris from 1871. Her books incl. studies of Okeghem, Palestrina, Handel, Haydn, Grétry & Berlioz, hists. of the sym., of the lute, of the musns. of the Sainte-Chapelle, and of concerts and m. libraries in Fr.

Brent, Charlotte (b. London, c. 1735; d. London, 10. IV. 1802), Eng. sop. singer. Pupil of Arne, in whose opera *Eliza* she made her 1st appearance, at Dublin in 1755.

Bret, Gustave (b. Brignoles, Var, 30. VIII. 1875), Fr. orgst., critic & comp. Studied at the Paris Cons. with Lavignac and Widor, also comp. with d'Indy and org. with Guilmant. He has done much work on behalf of Bach and Franck and cond. orchs. in Paris, Ger. & Cz. M. critic of *L'Intransigeant* since 1900.
Works incl. orat. *Les Pèlerins d'Emmaüs*; unaccomp. chor. works; org. m.; songs, &c.

Bretón, Tomás (b. Salamanca, 29. XII. 1850; d. Madrid, 2. XII. 1923), Spa. comp.
Works incl. operas *Guzman el Bueno, Garin, Raquel, Farinelli, El certamen de Cremona, Tabaré & Don Gil*, zarzuelas *Los amantes de Teruel, La Dolores, La verbena de la paloma* & c. 30 others; orat. *Apocalipsia*; *Las escenas andaluzas, Salamanca, En la Alhambra* for orch.; v. Conc.; 3 stg. 4tets, pf. 5tet, 6tet for wind, pf. Trio, &c.

Bréval, Lucienne (real name Berthe Agnès Lisette Schilling) (b. Berlin, 4. XI. 1869; d. Paris, 15. VIII. 1935), Fr. sop. singer of Swi. descent. Studied at the Conss. of Geneva and Paris. Made her 1st appearance at the Paris Opéra in 1892 and remained there for nearly 30 years. She excelled partic. in Wagner.

Breve. A square note equalling 2 semibreves in value, now rarely used.

Bréville, Pierre (Onfroy) de (b. Bar-le-Duc, 21. II. 1861), Fr. comp. Was intended for the diplomatic service, but allowed to study with Dubois at the Paris Cons. He decided to devote himself to comp. and became a pupil of Franck. Later became prof. at the Schola Cantorum, a m. critic and member of the committee of the Société Nationale de Musique.
Works incl. opera *Éros vainqueur*; incid. m. for Maeterlinck's *Sept Princesses* and ovt. for his *La Princesse Maleine*; Mass & motets; *La Cloche fêlée* (after Baudelaire) for orch.; 2 v. & pf. sos.; cc. & pf. So.; So. and other works, incl. *Portraits de Maîtres, Stamboul, Prélude et Fugue*, for pf.; inst. pieces; songs, &c.

Brewer, Thomas (b. London, 1611; d. ?), Eng. comp. In the service of Sir Nicholas Lestrange.
Works incl. fancies for viols, songs for several voices, rounds and catches.

Brian, Havergal (b. Dresden, Staffs., 29. I. 1877), Eng. comp. & writer on m. Mainly self-taught as a comp. Studied casually at Birmingham and wrote criticism at Manchester from 1905.
Works incl. opera *The Grotesques*; setting of Heine's *Pilgrimage to Kevlaar* for chor. & orch.; Sym.; 3 *English Suites, Hero and Leander*, ovts. *For Valour* & *Dr. Merryheart, Festal Dance, Fantastic Vars. on Old Rhymes*, symph. poem *In Memoriam* for orch.; *By the Waters of Babylon* and *The Vision of Cleopatra* for chor.; songs; partsongs, &c.

Bride of Dionysus, The, opera by Tovey (lib. by Robert Calverley Trevelyan), prod. Edinburgh, 25. IV. 1932.

Bride of Lammermoor. *See* **Bruden fra Lammermoor, Lucia di Lammermoor.**

Bride of Messina, The (*Nevěsta Messinská*), opera by Fibich (lib. by Otakar Hostinský, based on Schiller's drama *Die Braut von Messina*), prod. Prague, Cz. Theatre, 28. III. 1884.

Bridge. The support over which the stgs. are stretched and kept away from the belly of stg. insts.

Bridge, Frank (b. Brighton, 26. II. 1879; d. Eastbourne, 10. I. 1941), Eng. comp. Student at the R.C.M., where Stanford was his comp. master. He also learnt the v., va. and cond. Later played va. in var. 4tets and gained varied experience as operatic and concert cond. Won Cobbett prizes for chamber m. in 1905–15 and honourable mention for the E min. stg. 4tet at Bologna in 1906.

Works incl. symph. poem *Isabella*, suite *The Sea*, rhapsody *Enter Spring*, tone-poem *Summer* for orch.; Lament for stgs. *There is a willow grows aslant a brook* (on a passage in *Hamlet*); *Phantasm* for pf. & orch., *Oration* for co. & orch.; 4 stg. 4tets, 2 pf. trios, Fantasy 4tet and several smaller pieces for stg. 4tet, pf. 5tet, Fantasy Trio & 4tet for pf. & stgs., stg. 6tet, Rhapsody for 2 v. & va., *Divertimenti* for wind insts.; v. & pf. So., co. & pf. So.; numerous pf. works incl. So., 4 *Characteristic Pieces*, suite *A Fairy Tale*, 3 Improvisations for the left hand; v., va., co. & org. pieces; chors.; songs, &c.

Bridge Passage. A transitional passage in a comp., of no partic. thematic interest in itself (though it may be of high musical interest), esp. the transition between 1st and 2nd subjects in a so.-form mvt.

Bridges, Robert (1844–1930), Eng. poet. *See* **Holst** (*Chor. Fantasy*), **Parry (H.)** (*Invocation to M.*, *Song of Darkness and Light*, *Chivalry of the Sea* & *Eton Memorial Ode*), **Stanford** (songs), **Swain** (songs).

Bridie, James (O. H. Mavor) (b. 1888), Sco. dramatist. *See* **Davie.**

Bridgetower, George (Augustus Polgreen) (b. ?, c. 1779; d. London, 29. II. 1860), mulatto vst., son of an African father and Ger. or Pol. mother. Met Beethoven in Vienna and Teplice and played the 'Kreutzer' So. with him, 17. V. 1803.

Briegel, Wolfgang Carl (b. Nuremberg, 21. V. 1626; d. Darmstadt, 19. XI. 1712), Ger. comp. Orgst. at Stettin and Gotha, from 1670 to his death mus. dir. at Darmstadt. Wrote sacred works for several voices, pieces for 3 & 4 insts., convivial and funeral songs for several voices, hymns, &c.

Briganti, I (*The Brigands*), opera by Mercadante (lib. by Jacopo Crescini, based on Schiller's drama *Die Räuber*), prod. Paris, Théâtre Italien, 22. III. 1836.

Brigg Fair (i.e. the fair at Brigg, Lincs.), rhapsody for orch. by Delius on a Lincs. folksong, actually a set of vars., or a kind of passacaglia, comp. 1907, prod. London, 1908.

Brighenti, Maria. *See* **Giorgi-Righetti, Geltrude,** for the singer's correct name.

Bright, Dora (Estella) (b. Sheffield, 16. VIII. 1863), Eng. pfst. & comp. Studied at the R.A.M. in London. She was the 1st pfst. to give a recital of Eng. m. and the 1st woman comp. invited to write a work for the Phil. Soc. She also played in Ger.

Works incl. 3 operas; c. 12 ballets incl. *The Dryad*; 2 pf. concs.; inst. pieces; songs, &c.

Brillant (Fr.) } **Brillante** (It.) } = Brilliant. Used either as an adj. in titles or as a direction showing how a partic. passage is to be perf.

Brillenbässe (Ger. = spectacles basses). An abbr. in the notation of tremolos (not only in the bass) in pf. m., esp. pf. arrs. of orch. m., where white notes looking like minims are connected with quaver, semiquaver, &c., stems, thus looking like pairs of spectacles.

Brindisi (It. = a toast, drinking of someone's health). A drinking song, esp. in opera, e.g. in Donizetti's *Lucrezia Borgia*, Verdi's *Macbeth*, *Traviata* & *Otello* or Mascagni's *Cavalleria rusticana*.

Brio (It. = spirit, fire, brilliance). The word is often used in the direction *con* (with) *b.*

Bristol Musical Festival. Founded in 1873 and held triennially until 1888, afterwards less regularly until 1912.

Brit. (abbr.) = Britain, British.

British Broadcasting Corporation. Founded as the British Broadcasting Company Ltd. in 1922 and incorporated under a Royal Charter in 1927, when it took its present name, now always known by its abbreviation, B.B.C.

British Council, The. An organization estab. in 1935 to further nonmaterialistic Brit. interests in foreign countries, incl. educ. and the arts. During the 1st decade of its existence its m. dept. formed 57 libraries of Brit. printed and recorded m. in 44 countries, among the largest being those at Buenos Aires, Cairo, Stockholm and Trinidad. The B. C. also assists eminent Brit. artists to perf. abroad, and gramophone records of a number of important Brit. orch. and chor. works have been made under its auspices.

British National Opera Company. Founded in 1922 by members of the company that had previously appeared under the direction of Sir Thomas Beecham. It did much good work for opera in Eng. and Eng. opera, but went into liquidation in 1929.

Britten, (Edward) Benjamin (b. Lowestoft, 22. XI. 1913), Eng. comp. Educ. at Gresham School, Holt, and studied pf. with Harold Samuel and comp. with Frank Bridge; later, with a scholarship, at the R.C.M. in

London under Benjamin and Ireland. He was represented at the I.S.C.M. festivals of 1934, 1936 and 1938, and at the Salzburg Festival of 1937. The outbreak of war in 1939 found him in U.S.A., where he stayed for some time, but he returned to Eng. in 1942.

Works incl. operas *Paul Bunyan* (W. H. Auden) & *Peter Grimes* (after Crabbe); incid. m. for J. B. Priestley's *Johnson over Jordan* & Auden's *The Ascent of F.6*; film & radio m.; *Kermesse canadienne, Sinfonia da Requiem* for orch.; *Vars. on a Theme by Frank Bridge* for stg. orch.; *Diversions on a Theme* for pf. (left hand) & orch., pf. Conc., v. Conc., *Sco. Ballad* for 2 pfs. & orch.; *A Boy was born*, vars. for chor., *Ballad of Heroes* for solo voice, chor. & orch., *Ode to St. Cecilia* (W. H. Auden) for unaccomp. chor.; ballad for male voices *Little Musgrave and Lady Barnard*; Te Deum & *Rejoice in the Lamb* for chor. & org.; song cycles with orch. *Our Hunting Fathers* (Auden) & *Les Illuminations* (Rimbaud); Serenade for ten., hn. & stgs.; 2 stg. 4tets, Fantasy 4tet for ob. & stgs.; song cycles with pf. *Friday Afternoons* (for children), *On this Island* (Auden), *Seven Sonnets of Michelangelo*; *Holiday Tales* suite for pf.; *Introduction and Rondo alla burlesca* & *Mazurka elegiaca* for 2 pfs.; Suite for v. & pf.; partsongs & chors.; voc. duets; folksong arrs. for voice & pf., &c.

Britton, Thomas (b. Rushden nr. Higham Ferrars, 14. I. 1644; d. London, 27. IX. 1714), Eng. coal dealer & mus. amateur. Began very poorly as a hawker, but acquired much knowledge in m. and science and estab. weekly concerts in a room over his shop in London which soon had a great following.

Brixi, Franz Xaver (b. Prague, 1732; d. Prague, 14. X. 1771), Boh. orgst. & comp. Studied philos. at Prague Univ. and m. with a kinsman, Peter Simon B. After var. church apps. he became orgst. of the cath. in 1756 and wrote a *Probation Mass* for the occasion. He did much to reform Catholic church m.

Works incl. 76 masses, orats., Requiems (one on the death of Maria Theresa) & other church m.; operas & operettas; org. Conc.; many org. works, hpchd. pieces, &c.

Broadwood. Brit. family of pf. manufacturers & mus. eds.:

1. John B. (b. Cockburnspath, 1732; d. London, 1812), worked with Shudi, married his daughter Barbara in 1769 and was sole proprietor of Shudi & Broadwood from 1782.

2. James Shudi B. (b. London, 1772; d. London, 1851), son of prec., was taken into partnership in 1795, when the firm became John B. & Son.

3. Thomas B. (b. ?; d. ?), brother of prec., was taken into partnership in 1807 and the name became John B. & Sons.

4. Henry Fowler B. (b. London, 1811; d. London, 1893), son of 2.

5. John B. (b. ?; d. ?), brother of prec. One of the earliest folksong collectors.

6. Henry John Tschudi B. (b. ?; d. London, 8. II. 1911), grandson of 4.

7. Lucy B. (b. ?; d. 22. VIII. 1929), daughter of 4. Collector and ed. of folksongs.

Brockes, Barthold Heinrich (1680–1747), Ger. poet. *See* **Handel** (Passion), **Telemann** (do.).

Brockway, Howard (b. Brooklyn, 22. XI. 1870), Amer. pfst. & comp. Studied in N.Y. and Berlin, taught privately in N.Y. from 1895 and in 1903 joined the Peabody Cons. at Baltimore. Returning to N.Y. in 1910 he taught comp. there privately and at the David Mannes M. School.

Works incl. Sym. in D maj., Ballad, Scherzino, *Sylvan Suite* for orch.; *Cavatina and Romanza* for v. & orch., Suite in E min. for 'co. & orch.; v. & pf. Só. in G min.; pf. pieces, &c.

Brodsky, Adolf (b. Taganrog, 21. III. 1851; d. Manchester, 22. I. 1929), Rus. vst. Pupil of Hellmesberger in Vienna; successively cond. at Kiev, prof. at the Leipzig Cons., leader of the Hallé Orch. in Manchester and principal of the R.C.M. there.

Broken Consort. In old Eng. m. a mixed team of stg. and wind insts., playing together, as distinct from a consort (concert) of viols.

Broman, Sten (b. Upsala, 25. III. 1902), Swe. va. player, critic & comp. Studied in Prague, Stockholm, Fribourg (Swi.) and Berlin, and in 1927 took a degree in mus. hist. at Lund Univ.

Works incl. incid. m. to Aristophanes's *Lysistrata*; fantasy for chor. & orch.; Acad. Festival Ovt. & Conc. for orch.; Prelude & Litany for stg. orch.; suite for va. & stgs.; 2 stg. 4tets, suite for v., va. & pf.; unaccomp. chor. works, &c.

Brome, Richard (?–? 1652), Eng. playwright. *See* **Wilson (J.)** (*Northern Lass*).

Bronsart, Ingeborg von. *See* **Starck.**

Bronwen (Holbrooke). *See* **Cauldron of Annwen.**

Brooke, Rupert (Chawnor) (1887–1915), Eng. poet. *See* **Austin (R.)** (*The Hill*), **Hughes (G.)** (songs).

Broqua, Alfonso (b. Montevideo, 11. XII. 1876), Uruguayan comp. Studied at Montevideo and after 1900 in Belg. and under d'Indy at the Schola Cantorum in Paris. He 1st appeared as a comp. at Montevideo in 1910.

Works incl. opera *Cruz del Sur*; ballets *Thelen et Nagouëy* & *Isabelle*; *Tabaré* for voice & orch.; songs *Trois Chants de l'Uruguay* & *Chants du Paraná*; *Trois Préludes pampéens* for pf.; *Evocationes criollas* for guitar, &c.

Bros, Juan (b. Tortosa, 1776; d. Oviedo, 1852), Spa. comp. Mus. dir. by turns at the caths. of Málaga, León and Oviedo. Wrote church m.

Broschi, Carlo. *See* **Farinelli.**

Brossard, Sébastien de (b. c. 1654; d. Meaux, 10. VIII. 1730), Fr. comp. Studied philos. and theol. at Caen and was self-taught in m. He lived there until 1683, when he went to Paris and worked at Notre-Dame, later at Strasburg. In 1689 he became chapel master at the cath. there and in 1698 mus. dir. at Meaux cath.

Works incl. 2 books of *Élévations et Motets* & other church m.; lute pieces; *Air sérieux et à boire*; *Symphonie pour la nuit de Noël*; cantatas, sos. for 2 vs. & bass, &c.

Browne, John (b. ?, c. 1426; d. ?, 1498), Eng. comp. Scholar (?) at King's Coll., Cambridge.

Works incl. a madrigal *Margarit meke*; anthems & hymns, &c.

Browning. An Eng. form of fancy for viols, similar to the 'In Nomine,' but based on a folk-tune instead of a plainsong theme.

Browning, Elizabeth Barrett (1806–61), Eng. poetess. *See* **Carse** (*Lay of Brown Rosary*), **Castelnuovo-Tedesco** (*Sonnets from the Port.*), **Sea Pictures** (Elgar).

Browning, Robert (1812–89), Eng poet, husband of prec. *See* **Bainton** (*Paracelsus*), **Bantock** (*Ferishtah's Fancies*), **Davies (Walford)** (*Hervé Riel*), **Fifine at the Fair** (Bantock), **Franco** (songs), **Greenwood** (*Pippa passes*), **Morris (H.)** (*Prospice*), **Parry (H.)** (*Pied Piper of Hamelin*), **Somervell** (*James Lee's Wife* & *Broken Arc*), **Walthew** (*Pied Piper*).

Bruch, Max (b. Cologne, 6. I. 1838; d. Friedenau, 2. X. 1920), Ger. comp. Learnt m. as a child from his mother, a singer, later, with a scholarship, from Hiller, Reinecke and Breuning. He visited Leipzig, Munich and other mus. centres to gain further experience and in 1863 prod. his opera *Loreley* at Mannheim, having obtained permission from Geibel to use the lib. orig. written for Mendelssohn. After 2 apps. at Coblenz and Sondershausen, he lived 1st in Berlin and then at Bonn, wholly devoted to comp. From 1880–3 he was cond. of the Liverpool Phil. Soc., and in 1881 he married the singer Clara Tuczek. From 1883–90 he cond. at Breslau and in 1892 he became prof. of comp. at the Hochschule in Berlin, retiring to Friedenau in 1910.

Works incl. opera *Scherz, List und Rache* (Goethe), *Die Loreley* & *Hermione* (after Shakespeare's *Winter's Tale*); works for solo voices, chor. & orch.: *Frithjof-Scenen* (after Tegnér), *Schön Ellen*, *Odysseus* (after Homer), *Das Lied von der Glocke* (Schiller), *Achilleus* (after Homer), *Das Feuerkreuz* (after Scott), *Moses*, *Gustav Adolf*, *Damajanti*, *Die Macht des Gesanges* (Schiller); 3 syms.; 2 v. concs.; *Scottish Fantasia* for v., hp. & orch.; *Kol Nidrei* & *Ave Maria* for co. & orch.; Marfa's scene from Schiller's *Demetrius* for m.-sop. & orch.; 2 stg. 4tets, pf. Trio; many chors.; inst. pieces; pf. m.; songs, &c.

Bruck, Arnold von (b. ?; d. ?), ? Aus. 16th-cent. comp. 1st chapel master to the emperor & dean of the Abbey of Laibach. Wrote motets & other church m., sacred & secular songs, esp. Ger. songs, &c.

Brucken Fock, Gerard von (b. Middelburg, 28. XII. 1859; d. Heemstede, 15. VIII. 1935), Dutch comp. & painter. Studied m. at Utrecht and Berlin, but was mainly self-taught.

Works incl. Requiem, orat. *De wederkomst van Christus*, bibl. cantata; 2 syms., suites for orch.; many preludes & other works for pf.; songs, &c.

Bruckner, Anton (b. Ansfelden, 4. IX. 1824; d. Vienna, 11. X. 1896), Aus. comp. Son of a country schoolmaster intended for the same calling and receiving little mus. educ. On the early death of his father in 1837 he was taken in as a choir-boy by the monastery of St. Florian. There he learnt the org. and was app. orgst. in 1845. By this time he had begun to comp., but was dissatisfied with his poor technique and went to study ctpt. with Sechter in Vienna, 1855. Cath. orgst. at Linz, 1856–68, where he comp. much in his spare time and became an ardent Wagnerian on visiting Munich for the prod. of *Tristan* in 1865. App. prof. at the Vienna Cons. in 1868 and remained in the capital for the rest of his life, but visited Nancy, Paris and London as org. virtuoso in 1869 and 1871. He was pensioned in 1891 and received the hon. doctor's degree from the Univ.

Works incl. 9 syms. (last unfinished), 2 early syms.; Ovt. in G min.; 4

masses; Requiem; Te Deum, Psalm cl; 3 secular chor. works; stg. 5tet, &c.

Bruden fra Lammermoor (*The Bride of Lammermoor*), opera by Ivar Frederik Bredal (1800–64) (lib., in Dan., by Hans Christian Andersen, based on Scott's novel), prod. Copenhagen, 5. V. 1832.

Brudieu, Jean (or Joan) (b. nr. Limoges, *c.* 1515; d. Urgell, Catalonia, 1591), Fr. (Hispanicized) singer & comp. He visited Urgell in the Pyrenees to sing there at Christmas in 1538, and remained there as choirmaster until the 1570s, when he was at the church of Santa Maria del Mar at Barcelona, where he pub. a book of madrigals in 1585. He had returned to Urgell in 1578. Comp. church m. as well as madrigals, incl. a *Missa defunctorum* (Requiem).

Bruhns, Nikolaus (b. Schwabstädt, Slesvig, *c.* 1665; d. Husum, 1697), Dan. orgst., stg. player and comp. 1st employed in Copenhagen, then town orgst. at Husum, Slesvig-Holstein. Wrote cantatas, motets with orch. & org. m.

Brulé, Gace (b. ?; d. ?), Fr. 12th-cent. trouvère. 90 songs are attrib. to him, but only some 30 are accepted as authentic.

Brüll, Ignaz (b. Prossnitz, Moravia, 7. XI. 1846; d. Vienna, 17. IX. 1907), Aus. pfst. & comp. Studied in Vienna, where his family settled when he was 3, played there, toured, and prod. a no. of comps. Later he taught the pf.

Works incl. operas *Die Bettler von Samarkand, Das goldene Kreuz, Der Landfriede, Bianca, Königin Mariette, Gloria, Das steinerne Herz, Gringoire, Schach dem König, Der Husar*; ballet *Champagnermärchen*; Sym.; ovt to Shakespeare's *Macbeth*, Serenade for orch.; 2 pf. concs.; v. Conc.; pf. Trio & other chamber m., So. for 2 pfs.; pf. m.; songs, &c.

Brumel, Antoine (b. ?; d. ?), Fr. 15th–16th-cent. comp. Choirmaster at Chartres cath. in 1483, canon at Laon in 1498, and from that year to 1501 choirmaster at Notre-Dame in Paris. Went to the court of the Duke of Ferrara in 1505, where he may have died. Wrote masses, motets, Fr. chansons, &c.

Brun, Fritz (b. Lucerne, 18. VIII. 1878), Swi. cond. & comp. Studied under Mengelberg, who was cond. at Lucerne in 1892–5, later at the Cologne Cons. and in Berlin and London. In 1903 he became pf. prof. at the Berne School of M., at whose periodical students' concerts he showed himself as an exceptional cond. In 1909 he was app. cond. of both the male and mixed chor. socs. as well as of the sym. concerts.

Works incl. 7 syms.; *Verheissung* (Goethe) for chor., orch. & org.; *Aus dem Buch Hiob* for orch.; 3 stg. 4tets; v. & pf. So. in D min.; male-voice chors.; songs, &c.

Bruneau, (Louis Charles Bonaventure) Alfred (b. Paris, 3. III. 1857; d. Paris, 15. VI. 1934), Fr. comp. & m. critic. Son of a painter; learnt m., incl. co., from his parents, who played v. & pf., and took a co. prize at the Paris Cons. as a pupil of Franchomme. Afterwards studied comp. with Massenet and played in Pasdeloup's orch. In 1887 he prod. his 1st opera; the next 2 were based on works by Zola, with whom he thus became friendly and who himself wrote the libs. for the next 3 stage works. The 1st of these, however, failed in 1897 because B. and Zola were ardent supporters of Dreyfus. After Zola's death B. wrote his own libs., some still based on Zola's work.

Works incl. operas *Kérim, Le Rêve & L'Attaque du moulin* (after Zola), *Messidor, L'Ouragan & L'Enfant-roi* (libs. by Zola), *Lazare, Naïs Micoulin & Les Quatre Journées* (after Zola), *Le Tambour, Le Roi Candaule, Angelo, tyran de Padoue, Virginie*; ballets *Les Bacchantes* (after Euripides) & *Le Jardin de Paradis*; incid. m. to his dram. adapt. of Zola's *La Faute de l'Abbé Mouret*; Requiem; chor. syms. *Léda, La Belle au bois dormant & Penthésilée*; cantata *Geneviève de Paris*; *Ouverture héroïque* for orch.; voc. duets; songs *Chansons à danser* & 2 books of *Lieds de France* (all words by Catulle Mendès).

Brunelli, Antonio (b. Bagnorea nr. Orvieto, *c.* 1575; d. ?), It. orgst., mus. scholar & comp. Worked at Florence, both at churches and at the Tuscan court. Wrote 2 learned theoret. books.

Works incl. masses, requiems, sacred songs, psalms; a ballet; canzonets, madrigals, &c.

Brunette (Fr. lit. a dark-haired girl). A light love-song of a type current in 17th–18th-cent. Fr., orig. so called because of the association of the words with dark girls.

Brunetti, Gaetano (b. Pisa, *c.* 1740; d. Madrid, 1808), It. vst. & comp. Son (?) of Antonio B., chapel master at Pisa cath. He was a pupil of Nardini at Florence. Spent most of his life in Spa., at the court of the Prince of Asturias, later Charles IV, and there worked with Boccherini.

Works incl. syms., serenades for orch.; 6tets, 5tets; v. duets, &c.

Brunetti, Giovanni Gualberto (b. Pisa,

c. 1710; d. ?), It. comp., ? brother of prec. Chapel master of Pisa cath. in succession to Antonio B., (?) his father.
Works incl. 6 operas; masses & other church m., &c.

Brustad, Bjarne (b. Oslo, 4. III. 1895), Norw. vst., violist & comp. Studied at the Oslo Cons., later under Carl Flesch, and became active as vst. and cond. in the Norw. capital.
Works incl. symph. poem *Atlantis*, suite for orch.; *Nature morte* for stg. orch.; 2 v. concs., *Rhapsody* for v. & orch., Concertino for v. & chamber orch.; stg. 4tet; suite for unaccomp. v. Suite for va. & pf.; v., va. & pf. pieces, &c.

Brusselmans, Michel (b. Paris, 12. II. 1886), Belg. comp. Pupil of Gilson at the Brussels Cons. In 1922 he settled in Paris as a member of m. pub. house of Jamin.
Works incl. *Kermesse flamande*, *Rapsodie*, *Ouverture fériale*, *Hélène de Sparte*, *Les Néréides*; sos. for v. & pf. and co. & pf.; org. pieces; songs, &c.

Brussilovsky, Eugene (b. Rostov-on-Don, 12. XI. 1905), Rus. comp. Having lost both his parents he joined the army at 16, but was released in 1922 in order to develop his mus. talent at the Moscow Cons. He was expelled in 1924 for non-attendance, due to serious illness, but although very poor, managed to go to Leningrad and induced Steinberg to teach him at the Cons. there. In 1933 he was commissioned to do mus. research in Kazakh folk m. and went to live at Alma-Ata, the capital of Kazakhstan. There he wrote operas in the nat. idiom.
Works incl. operas *Kiz-Ji-Bek*, *Er-Targhin* & *Jalbir*; 3 syms.; inst. pieces; pf. pieces; songs, &c.

Bryan, Albert (or Albertus Byrne) (b. ? London, c. 1621; d. London, ? 1668), Eng. orgst. & comp. Orgst. of St. Paul's cath. in London from 1638 and again after the Restor. After the fire of London in 1666 he became orgst. of Westminster Abbey, a post in which he was succeeded by Blow in 1668. Wrote services, anthems, dances, &c.

Bryllupet ved Como-Søen (*The Wedding by Lake Como*), opera by Franz Gläser (1798–1861) (lib. by Hans Christian Andersen, based on Manzoni's novel, *I promessi sposi*), prod. Copenhagen, 29. I. 1849.

Bryson, (Robert) Ernest (b. Glasgow, 31. III. 1867; d. St. Briavels, Glos., 20. IV. 1942), Eng. amateur comp. living at Liverpool.
Works incl. opera *The Leper's Flute*; chor. comps. *The Cloak, the Boat and the Shoes* (Yeats) & *Drum Taps* (Whitman); 2 syms., *Voices* study for orch.; *Vaila* for stg. orch.; 2 stg. 4tets, &c.

Brzezinski, Franciszek (b. Warsaw, 6. XI. 1867), Pol. critic & comp. Studied at Leipzig with Reger and others and became m. critic to 2 Warsaw papers in succession.
Works incl. *Polonaise-Ballad*, Waltz, &c. for orch.; pf. Conc.; v. & pf. So.; pf. pieces, &c.

Buccina. An ancient brass inst. of the bugle type, chiefly Roman. Sometimes called Busine, Buysine or Buzine in Eng.

Bucenus, Paulus (b. Holstein, ?; d. ? Riga, II. 1586), Dan. comp. Worked as church musn. at Riga.
Works incl. a St. Matthew Passion, masses, motets, *Sacrae cantiones*, &c.

Buchanan, George (1506–82), Sco. histor. & trans. *See* **Olthoff** (psalms).

Büchner, Georg (1813–37), Ger. poet & playwright. *See* **Müller-Hartmann** (*Leonce und Lena*), **Syberg** (do.), **Weismann** (do.), **Wozzeck** (A. Berg & M. Gurlitt).

Buchner, Johann (b. Ravensburg, Württemberg, 26. X. 1483; d. ? Zürich, 1538), Ger. comp. Prob. pupil of Hofhaimer. Worked at Constance cath., but left in 1526 because of its growing Protestantism, (?) for Zürich. Wrote sacred & secular songs, org. pieces, &c.

Buck, Dudley (b. Hertford, Conn., 10. III. 1839; d. Orange, N.J., 6. X. 1909), Amer. comp. & orgst. Studied in his native town and at Leipzig and Dresden. Held many org. posts until 1903 and wrote a large variety of m. as well as some books on the art.
Works incl. opera *Deseret*; numerous chor. works incl. *Voyage of Columbus*, *The Golden Legend* (Longfellow), *The Light of Asia*, Psalm xlvi; symph. ovt. *Marmion* (after Scott); anthems & other church m., &c.

Buck, Percy (Carter) (b. London, 25. III. 1871), Eng. mus. scholar & educst. Studied at the R.C.M. in London; M.A. and Mus.D., Oxford, 1897; orgst. at Wells and Bristol caths., 1896–1901, then mus. dir. at Harrow School. Prof. of M. at Univ. of Dublin, 1910, and London, 1915. Knighted 1937. Author of several books on m.

Buckingham, Duke of. *See* **Villiers, George.**

Budashkin, Nikolai (b. Liubakhovka nr. Mosalsk, 6. VIII. 1910), Rus. comp. Pupil of Miaskovsky.
Works incl. Sym., Festival Ovt.; Sonatina for pf.; songs, &c.

Buffa. *See* **Opera buffa.**

Buffo (It. lit. 'whiff' or 'puff,' hence *buffone*, a comic actor). In m. a singer of comic parts, used esp. as adj.: *tenore buffo*, *basso buffo*.

Bugle. A treble brass inst. resembling the tpt. but more rudimentary. It can prod. only the natural harmonics in its primitive form; but a key-bugle (or Kent bugle) was invented *c.* 1820.

Bühnenweihfestspiel (Ger., from *Bühne* = stage, *Weihe* = consecration, *Fest* = festival, *Spiel* = play). The description given by Wagner to *Parsifal*, which he did not wish to call an 'opera' or even a 'm.-drama.'

Bulg. (abbr.) = Bulgaria, Bulgarian.

Bulgarian Composers. *See* **Binenbaum, Vladigerov.**

Bull, John (b. Somerset, 1563; d. Antwerp, 12–13. III. 1628), Eng. comp. He was a choir-boy in the Chapel Royal in London under Blitheman and became orgst. of Hereford cath. in 1582. On Blitheman's death in 1591 he became orgst. of the Chapel Royal. Mus.D. Cambridge, before 1592, and Oxford that year. In 1596 Queen Elizabeth insisted on his being app. Prof. of M. at Gresham Coll., although he could not write and deliver the lectures in Lat., according to custom. In 1601 he visited Fr. & Ger., Thomas Byrd, son of William B., acting as his deputy. Married Elizabeth Walter in 1607 and gave up his professorship, which could be held only by single men. In 1613 he left Eng., apparently to escape punishment for some misdemeanours, and became orgst. at the archducal chapel in Brussels. In 1617 he was app. orgst. at Antwerp cath., where he remained to his death.

Works incl. anthems, incl. the 'Star' anthem *Almighty Lord*; secular voc. works for several voices; canons; a laud for the Blessed Virgin in Flem.; numerous org. and virginal pieces; some works for viols, &c.

Bull, Ole (Borneman) (b. Bergen, 5. II. 1810; d. Lysø nr. Bergen, 17. VIII. 1880), Norw. vst. & comp. Was largely self-taught, his father insisting on his studying theol. In 1829 he visited Spohr at Cassel and in 1831 1st made his mark as a public player in Paris. He married a Fr. girl there, appeared with Chopin and Ernst, and visited It. with great success. Went to Brit. 1st in 1836 and to U.S.A. in 1843. Founded the Norse Theatre at Bergen in 1850. In 1870 he was married a 2nd time, to an Amer. Wrote 2 concs. and many other works for the v., &c.

Bülow, Hans (Guido) von (b. Dresden, 8. I. 1830; d. Cairo, 12. II. 1894), Ger. pfst. and cond. 1st husband of Cosima Wagner (*née* Liszt). Studied law at Leipzig Univ. and pf. with Wieck there. At first exclusively a Wagnerian as a cond., but after his divorce in 1869 became equally enthusiastic about Brahms without abandoning Wagner. Made many tours both as cond. and pfst.

Bumbass. *See* **Drone.**

Bungert, August (b. Mühlheim o/Ruhr, 14. III. 1846; d. Leutesdorf, 26. X. 1915), Ger. comp. Studied at Cologne Cons. and elsewhere. Prod. his 1st (comic) opera at Leipzig in 1884. His ambition was to build a special theatre for the prod. of his tetralogy on the model of Bayreuth.

Works incl. operas *Die Studenten von Salamanka*, trilogy *Homerische Welt* (*Kirke, Nausicaa* & *Odysseus' Heimkehr*), *Odysseus' Tod*, 'mystery' *Warum? Woher? Wohin?*; incid. m. to Goethe's *Faust*; Sym. *Zeppelins erste grosse Fahrt*; *Tasso, Hohes Lied der Liebe, Auf der Wartburg* for orch.; pf. 4tet; pf. pieces; songs, &c.

Bunning, Herbert (b. London, 2. V. 1863; d. Thundersley, Essex, 26. XI. 1937), Eng. cond. & comp. Educ. at Oxford and began a military career, but later studied m. in Fr. & It. In 1892 he became mus. dir. of the Lyric Theatre in London.

Works incl. opera *Princess Osra*; incid. m. for plays; ovts. for orch.; songs, &c.

Bunyan, John (1628–88), Eng. author. For works based on *The Pilgrim's Progress see* **Austin (E.), Bantock, Kelley, Shepherds of the Delectable Mountains** (Vaughan Williams).

Buona figliuola, La (*The Good Girl*), also *La Cecchina*, opera by Piccinni (lib. by Goldoni, based on Richardson's *Pamela*), prod. Rome, Teatro delle Dame, 6. II. 1760.

Buonamente, Giovanni Battista (b. ?; d. Assisi, 1643). It. vst. & comp. Imp. court musn., 1626–9; chapel master at the Franciscan monastery of Assisi in 1636. Wrote sos. for 2 vs. & bass, m. for mixed teams of insts. &c.

Buonamici, Giuseppe (b. Florence, 12. II. 1846; d. Florence, 18. III. 1914), It. pfst., cond. & mus. ed. Studied at home at first, then at the Munich Cons., pf. with Bülow and comp. with Rheinberger. Prof. there from 1870, but returned to Florence in 1873 as pf. prof., chor. cond. and founder of a pf. trio. He did much to cultivate serious m.

Buononcini. *See* **Bononcini.**

Buovo d'Antona (*Bevis of Hampton*), opera by Traetta (lib. by Goldoni, based on the Anglo-Norman 13th-cent. romance), prod. Venice, Teatro San Moisè, 27. XII. 1758.

Burbero di buon cuore, Il (*The Good-hearted Grumbler*), opera by Martín y Soler (lib. by Lorenzo da Ponte, based on Goldoni's Fr. comedy *Le Bourru bienfaisant*), prod. Vienna, Burg Theatre, 4. I. 1786. Mozart wrote 2 extra arias for it when it was revived, Vienna, 9. XI. 1789, and Haydn an addit. duet for its prod. in London, 1794.

Burbure de Wesembeck, Léon (Philippe Marie) de (b. Termonde, 16. VIII. 1812; d. Antwerp, 8. XII. 1889), Belg. mcolst. & comp. Graduated at Ghent Univ. and studied old Nthld. m., of which he wrote many studies. Comp. sacred voc. works, orch. m., &c.

Burchiello, Il (Domenico di Giovanni) (1404–49), It. poet. *See* **Malipiero** (sonnets).

Burck, Joachim à (Joachim Moller von Burck) (b. Burg, 1541; d. Mühlhausen, 24. V. 1610), Ger. orgst. & comp. Orgst. at var. towns in Thuringia.

Works incl. 3 Passions, psalms; odes, songs, &c.

Bürde-Ney (*née* Ney), **Jenny** (b. Graz, 21. XII. 1826; d. Dresden, 17. V. 1886), Aus. sop. singer. Made her 1st appearance on the stage of Olomouc in 1847 and became very famous as an opera singer, esp. at Dresden.

Burden. In old voc. m. the refrain sung at the end of each verse, always to the same words, which often have no literal meaning, e.g. 'hey, nonny, nonny.'

Bürger, Gottfried August (1747–94), Ger. poet. *See* **Chasseur maudit** (Franck), **Duparc** (*Lénore*), **Paradies** (*Lenore*), **Raff** (do.), **Zumsteeg** (do.).

Burgmein. *See* Ricordi.

Burgmüller, Norbert (b. Düsseldorf, 8. II. 1810; d. Aachen, 7. V. 1836), Ger. comp. Studied under his father, mus. dir. at Düsseldorf, later under Spohr and Hauptmann at Cassel. A weak constitution led to his early death.

Works incl. 2 syms., an ovt.; pf. pieces & studies, &c.

Burian, Emil František (b. Plzen), 11. IV. 1904), Cz. singer, actor, author, stage manager & comp. Studied at the Prague Cons., joined the Dada Theatre in Prague and was dir. of the dramatic studio of the Brno Nat. Theatre in 1929–30; also founded a voice band.

Works incl. operas *Alladine and Palomides* (after Maeterlinck), *Before Sunset, Bubu de Montparnasse, Mr. Ipokras, Fear*; ballets *Bassoon and Flute, Manège, Autobus*; chors.; chamber m.; songs, &c.

Burian, Karel (b. Rousinov nr. Rakovnik, 12. I. 1870; d. Senomaty, 25. IX. 1924), Cz. ten. singer. 1st appeared at Brno in 1891. Sang at Bayreuth and in many Eur. capitals, but chiefly at Dresden.

Burkhard, Willy (b. Évilard-sur-Bienne, 17. IV. 1900), Swi. comp. Studied at the Berne School of M., at Leipzig with Karg-Elert and Teichmüller and at Munich with Courvoisier, later in Paris. Became pf. prof. at the Berne Cons. and cond. choirs and an amateur orch. Settled at Davos in 1937 to devote himself entirely to comp.

Works incl. orats. *Musikalische Uebung* (Luther) and *Das Gesicht Jesajas*, Te Deum, chor. suite *Neue Kraft*, festival cantata *Le Cantique de notre terre*, cantata *Das Jahr* & others, Psalm xciii for chor. & org.; *Christi Leidensverkündung* for ten., chor. & org.; 2 syms., *Ulenspiegel* vars. for orch.; Fantasy, Little Serenade and Conc. for stg. orch.; v. Conc., org. Conc.; 3 stg. 4tets, pf. Trio, 2 trio-sos.; Vars. and Fantasy for org.; song-cycles *Frage* and one on poems by Rilke, &c.

Burla (It. = jest, trick, practical joke). In m. a humorous piece, rather more boisterous than a scherzo.

Burleigh, Cecil (b. Wyoming, N.Y., 17. IV. 1885), Amer. vst. & comp. Studied in U.S.A., Berlin and finally at Chicago. After touring frequently and teaching in var. places, he settled down as v. prof. at Wisconsin Univ.

Works incl. symph. poem *Evangeline, Mountain Pictures*, &c. for orch.; 3 v. concs.; 2 v. & pf. sos. *The Ascension* & *From the Life of St. Paul*; numerous v. pieces, &c.

Burleigh, Henry T(hacker). (b. Erie, Pa., 2. XII. 1866), Amer. Negro singer & comp. Pupil of Dvořák at the Nat. Cons. in N.Y, where he introd. Negro tunes to his master.

Works incl. arrs. of Negro tunes, songs, &c.

Burlesca (It.) = Burla.

Burlesque. Another name sometimes used for the Burletta in Eng.

Burletta (It. = a little joke). A form of light comic opera or operetta in 18th- & 19th-cent. Eng.

Burmester, Willy (b. Hamburg, 16. III. 1869; d. Hamburg, 16. I. 1933), Ger. vst. Pupil of Joachim, but afterwards a virtuoso who travelled extensively as an exponent of his inst. rather than an interpreter of great m. He wrote a few comps. and arr. m. for v.

Burney, Charles (b. Shrewsbury, 7. IV. 1726; d. London, 12. IV. 1814), Eng. mus. hist., orgst. & comp. Travelled extensively on the Continent to collect material for the *General Hist. of M.*, and so accumulated matter for two journals on the state of m. in var. countries. Father of Fanny Burney and friend of Johnson, Reynolds, Mrs. Thrale, Garrick and J. C. Bach. His works incl. mus. play *The Cunning Man* adapted from Rousseau's *Devin du village*.

Burns, Robert (1759–96), Sco. poet. *See* **Chadwick** (*Tam o' Shanter*), **Drysdale** (do. & *To Edinburgh*), **Goossens** (*Tam o' S.*), **Jensen** (songs), **Khrennikov** (songs), **Mackenzie** (*Cottar's Sat. Night & Tam o' S.*), **Scott (F. G.)** (songs), **Swain** (songs).

Burrasca (It.=tempest, hurricane). In m. a piece describing a tempest or thunderstorm, as for ex. in Rossini's *Barber of Seville* or in the ovt. to his *William Tell*.

Burton, Avery (b. ?; d. ?), Eng. 15th–16th-cent. comp. Prob. a Gentleman of the Chapel Royal under Henry VIII. Wrote masses, org. m., &c.

Burton, John (b. Yorkshire, 1730; d. London, 1785), Eng. hpchdst., orgst. & comp. Pupil of Keeble. Became a very famous player and had a great success in Ger. in 1754. Comp. concs. for both his insts., sos., It. canzonets, &c.

Busby, Thomas (b. London, XII. 1755; d. London, 28. V. 1838), Eng. orgst. & comp. Sang at Vauxhall as a boy with great success, later became a pupil of Battishill. Worked at a mus. dictionary with Arnold, was app. church orgst. in 1786. Mus.D. at Cambridge in 1801. Wrote several books on m.

Works incl. incid. m. for Cumberland's *Joanna of Montfaucon*, an Eng. version of Kotzebue's *Johanna von M.*, Holcroft's *Tale of Mystery*, Anna Maria Porter's *Fair Fugitives* & Lewis's *Rugantino*; orats. *The Prophecy* (from Pope's *Messiah*) & *Britannia*; settings of odes by Pope and Gay.

Busch, Wilhelm (1832–1908), Ger. comic versifier & cartoonist. *See* **Goldschmidt (A.)** (*Fromme Helene*), **Mraczek** (*Max und Moritz*).

Busch, William (b. London, 25. IV. 1901; d. Woolacombe, Devon, 30. I. 1945), Eng. pfst. & comp. Educ. in N.Y., London and Berlin, studied pf. with Backhaus, Petri and others, and comp. with Leichtentritt, Ireland and van Dieren. Made his 1st appearance as pfst. in London, 1927. Later he became m. master at Highgate School in London.

Works incl. Prelude for orch.; pf. Conc., co. Conc.; pf. 4tet, *Ode to Autumn* for voice & stg. 4tet; 4 pieces for co. & pf.; *Theme, Vars. & Fugue, Nicholas Vars., Allegretto quasi pastorale, Gigue, Relinquishment, Prelude & Fugue* for pf.; songs to poems by Campion, Blake, Beddoes, 'A.E.' & James Stephens, &c.

Bush, Alan (Dudley) (b. London, 22. XII. 1900), Eng. comp. Studied at the R.A.M. in London and Berlin Univ., later with John Ireland. He became prof. at the R.A.M., cond. of the London Labour Chor. Union and in 1936 chairman of the Workers' M. Assoc.

Works incl. Fantasy on Soviet Themes for orch.; pf. Conc. with final bar. solo and male chor.; *Dialectic* for stg. 4tet; *The Songs of the Doomed* for ten. & pf., &c.

Bush, Geoffrey (b. London, 23. III. 1920), Eng. comp. Became a choirboy at Salisbury cath. in 1928, went to Lancing Coll. in 1933 and later to Balliol Coll., Oxford, where he gained the Nettleship Scholarship in mus. comp. B.Mus., Oxford, 1940. His studies were interrupted by war service at a hostel for abnormal evacuee children. He is mainly self-taught in comp., but had much valuable advice from his masters at Salisbury and Lancing, also from John Ireland and others later.

Works incl. opera *Spanish Rivals*; *12th Night* entertainment for chor. & orch.; ovts. *In Praise of Salisbury* & *The Rehearsal* for orch., Divertimento for stg. orch.; Conc. for pf. & stgs., *Sinfonietta concertante* for co. & chamber orch.; Rhapsody for cl. & stg. 4tet; sos. for v. & pf. and tpt. & pf.; 2 pf. Sonatinas; *Portraits & La Belle Dame sans merci* (Keats) for unaccomp. chor.; songs, &c.

Busine. *See* **Buccina.**

Busnois, Anthoine (b. ?; d. Bruges, 6. XI. 1492), Fr. comp. Pupil of Okeghem and later in the service of the Burgundian court until 1481, when (?) he became mus. dir. at the church of Saint-Sauveur at Bruges.

Works incl. masses, motets, magnificats; secular voc. pieces; songs, &c.

Busoni, Ferruccio (Benvenuto) (b. Empoli, 1. IV. 1866; d. Berlin, 27. VII. 1924), It. pfst. & comp. Appeared as pfst. in public at the age of 7; studied at Graz and Leipzig. Taught at the Helsingfors Cons. in 1889 and there married the Swe. Gerda Sjöstrand; taught at Moscow in 1890 and in Amer., 1891–4. Settled in Berlin for good in 1894, but travelled widely as a pfst. and during the war of 1914–8 lived 1st at Bologna as dir. of the Cons. and then at Zürich. At Bologna he hoped to influence It. m. and to prove that he was himself an It. comp., but was disappointed.

Works incl. operas, *Die Brautwahl, Turandot, Arlecchino & Doktor Faust*; 4 suites for orch., *Nocturne symphonique, Rondo arlecchinesco, Comedy*

Ovt. and other works for orch; *Konzertstück*, *Indian Fantasy* and *Romanza e Scherzoso* for pf. & orch.; Conc. for pf., orch. & male-voice chor.; v. Conc.; several voc. works with orch.; 2 stg. 4tets; 2 v. & pf. sos.; many pf. solo works, incl. So. in F min.; *4 Ballettszenen*, 24 Preludes, 7 Elegies, *Indianisches Tagebuch*, *Fantasia contrappuntistica*, 6 sonatinas; songs, &c.

Büsser, (Paul) Henri (b. Toulouse, 16. I. 1872), Fr. cond. & comp. Pupil of Guiraud at the Paris Cons. Gained the Prix de Rome in 1893. Successively orgst. at Saint-Cloud, cond. of the chor. class at the Cons. and dir. of Niedermeyer's school. App. prof. of comp. at the Cons. in 1921.

Works incl. operas *Jane Grey*, *Daphnis et Chloé*, *Colomba* (after Mérimée), *Les Noces corinthiennes*, *La Pie borgne*, *Le Carrosse du Saint-Sacrement* (Mérimée); masses & motets; *Hercule au jardin des Hespérides*, *Suite funambulesque* & other orch. works; chors., songs, &c.

Bustini, Alessandro (b. Rome, 24. XII. 1876), It. comp. Studied at the Acc. di Santa Cecilia in Rome, where he became prof. later.

Works incl. operas *Maria Dulcis* (based on a story in Berlioz's *Soirées de l'orchestre*), *La città quadrata* & *L'incantesimo di Calandrino*; funeral Mass for Victor Emmanuel II; 2 syms., symph. poem *Le tentazioni*; stg. 4tet; sos. for v. & pf. and va. & pf., pf. pieces, &c.

Buths, Julius (b. Wiesbaden, 7. V. 1851; d. Düsseldorf, 12. III. 1920), Ger. pfst. & cond. Worked at Düsseldorf from 1890, dir. of the Cons. there and cond. of the Lower Rhine Festival, where he introd. Elgar's *Dream of Gerontius* in 1901.

Butler, Samuel (b. Langar nr. Bingham, Notts., 4. XII. 1835; d. London, 18. VI. 1902), Eng. author, critic, biologist, painter & amateur comp. He adored Handel and wrote 2 cantatas, *Narcissus* & *Ulysses*, in imitations of H.'s orat. style.

Butt, Clara (b. Southwick, Sussex, 1. II. 1873; d. North Stoke, Oxon, 23. I. 1936), Eng. con. singer. Studied at R.C.M. in London, and in Paris. Made her 1st concert and stage appearance in 1892. A great voice made her very popular, and having placed it at the disposal of war charities, she received the D.B.E. in 1920.

Butterfly (Puccini). *See* **Madama Butterfly.**

'Butterfly' (or **'Butterfly's Wing'**) Study. A nickname sometimes given to Chopin's pf. Study in G♭ maj., Op. 25 No. 9.

Butterworth, George (Sainton Kaye) (b. London, 12. VII. 1885; d. Pozières, 5. VIII. 1916), Eng. comp. Educ. at Eton and Oxford, studied m. briefly at the R.C.M. in London. He collected folksongs, cultivated folk dancing and comp., but enlisted on the outbreak of war and was killed in action.

Works incl. Rhapsody *A Shropshire Lad* & Idyll *The Banks of Green Willow* for orch.; 2 song cycles on Housman's *Shropshire Lad*; Sussex folksongs arr.; carols set for chor.; a few other chor. pieces and songs, &c.

Butting, Max (b. Berlin, 6. X. 1888), Ger. comp. Studied at Munich.

Works incl. unfinished Mass; chamber sym.; co. Conc.; 4 stg. 4tets & other chamber m.; songs with small orch. &c.

Buttstett, Johann Heinrich (b. Bindersleben nr. Erfurt, 25. IV. 1666; d. Erfurt, 1. XII. 1727), Ger. orgst. & comp. Pupil of Pachelbel. Orgst. of 2 Erfurt churches from 1684 and of the cath. from 1691. Wrote masses, org. m., a vol. for hpchd. *Musikalische Klavierkunst*, &c.

Buus, Jachet (Jacques) (b. ? Bruges. ?; d. ? Vienna, ?), Flem. 16th-cent. orgst. & comp. 1st pub. some work in Fr., but went to It. and in 1541 became orgst. at St. Mark's in Venice, succeeding Baldassare da Imola. He went to Vienna on leave in 1550, but never returned and became orgst. at the court of Ferdinand I.

Works incl. motets, madrigals; Fr. chansons; ricercari for org., &c.

Buxtehude, Dietrich (b. Helsingborg, 1637; d. Lübeck, 9. V. 1707), Swe. comp. & orgst. Settled in Den. and from 1668 orgst. of St. Mary's church, Lübeck. An important forerunner of Bach as org. comp. He was long thought to have been a Dane.

Works incl. concerted m., *Abendmusiken*; church cantatas; sos. for stgs.; org. m., incl. chorale preludes; set of hpchd. suites on the planets, &c.

Buysine
Buzine } *See* **Buccina.**

Byrd, William (b. ? Lincoln, 1543; d. ?, Stondon, Essex, 4. VII. 1623), Eng. comp. After prob. studying under Tallis as one of the children of the Chapel Royal in London, he was app. orgst. of Lincoln cath. in 1563, at an unusually early age. He married Juliana Birley there, 14. IX. 1568, and on 22. II. 1569 was elected a Gentleman of the Chapel Royal, but continued his duties at Lincoln until 1572, when he became orgst. of the

Chapel Royal jointly with Tallis. In 1575 Queen Elizabeth granted the 2 an exclusive licence for printing and selling m., and they dedicated to her their *Cantiones sacrae* pub. that year. He married a 2nd time about 1587. In 1593 he bought Stondon Place nr. Stapleford-Abbott, Essex, where he remained for the rest of his life, as often as his duties in town would let him. He was frequently involved in litigation and was several times prosecuted for recusancy as a Rom. Catholic, but remained in favour with the queen. He wrote impartially and with equal genius for his own and the Angl. church.

Works incl. 3 masses; 17 Lat. motets in the *Cantiones sacrae* by Tallis & B.; 61 Lat. motets in 2 books of *Cantiones sacrae*; 99 Lat. motets in 2 books of *Gradualia*; *c.* 50 motets in MS; 5 Anglican services (1 incomplete); 61 anthems; some misc. Eng. church m.; *Psalmes, Sonets & Songs* (18 Nos.); *Songs of Sundrie Natures* (47 Nos.); *Psalmes, Songs & Sonnets* (32 Nos.); 4 sep. madrigals (others are in those 3 books); 31 songs; 32 canons; 6 rounds; 14 fantasies fo stgs., 8 In Nomines for stgs., 9 pieces for stgs. on plainsong tunes, some misc. m. for stgs.; *c.* 120 virginal pieces, &c.

Byrne, Albertus. *See* **Bryan, Albert.**

Byron, George Gordon, Lord (1788–1824), Eng. poet. *See* **Berg** (N). (*Leila*), **Bishop** (*Manfred*), **Bogatirev** (*Two Foscari & Manfred*), **Corsaro** (Verdi), **Due Foscari** (Verdi), **Harold en Italie** (Berlioz), **Hedy** (*Don Juan*, Fibich), **Hiller (F.)** (*Hebrew Melodies*), **Holbrooke** (*Ode to Victory*), **Holstein** (*Marino Faliero*), **Lacombe** (*Manfred*), **Lebrun (P.)** (*Fiancée d'Abydos*), **Mackenzie** (*Manfred*), **Maillart** (*Lara*), **Manfred** (incid. m., Schumann; sym., Tchaikovsky), **Marino Faliero** (Donizetti), **Mussorgsky** (*Destruction of Sennacherib*), **Nathan** (*Hebrew Melodies*), **Novák** (*Corsair & Manfred*), **Parisina** (Donizetti), **Poniatowski** (*Sposa d'Abido*), **Praeger** (*Manfred*), **Reinecke** (*König Manfred*), **Roslavets** (*Heaven and Earth*), **Rytel** (*Corsair*), **Schoenberg** (*Ode to Napoleon*), **Starck** (*Manfred*), **Steinberg** (*Heaven and Earth*), **Tasso** (Liszt), **Vavrinecz** (*Bride of Abydos*), **White (M. V.)** (songs), **Williams (G.)** (do.). *See also* **Vampyr** (Lindpaintner & Marschner; subject attrib. to Byron, but actually from a story by John William Polidori).

(Mark reference p. 35)

Bairstow, Edward, d. York, 1. V. 1946.

C

C. The note bounding the range of the scales of C maj. and min., and of the Ionian and Hypolydian (Gr. Hypophrygian) modes.

C. In Cz. c is pronounced 'ts.'

Č. In Cz. č is pronounced 'tch.'

C Clef. The clef used in key signatures, now chiefly for the va., indicating that middle C stands on the line of the stave on which it is placed. In old m. it could appear on any line, but its use is now restricted. The Alto Clef, with C on the middle line, is predominantly used for the va.; the Tenor Clef, with C on the 4th line from the bottom, is still useful for the higher middle register of the co. and bn.; the Soprano Clef, with C on the bottom line, though still found in scores up to the time of Brahms, is now obs., or should be, since it serves no useful purpose.

C.E.M.A. *See* **Arts Council.**

Cabaletta (It. corrupt. from *cavatinetta*, dim. of *cavatina*). The quick and usually brilliant final section of an aria consisting of more than one mvt.

Cabell, James Branch (b. 1879), Amer. author. *See* **Taylor (Deems)** (*Jurgen*).

Cabezón, Antonio de (b. Castrillo de Matajudíos nr. Burgos, 30. III. 1510; d. Madríd, 26. V. 1566), Spa. orgst. & comp. Although (?) blind from birth, he studied with Tomás Gómez at Palencia and became chamber orgst. and hpdchst. to Charles V, remaining at court under Philip II, (?) accomp. him to Eng. on his marriage to Mary I. Comp. org., vihuela and other m.

Cabezón, Hernando (b. ? Madrid, ?; d. Valladolid, 1. X. 1602), Spa. orgst. & comp., son of prec. Studied under his father, whom he succeeded at court and whose works he ed. Wrote org. m.

Cable, George Washington (1844–1925), Amer. novelist. *See* **Gilbert (H. F.)** (*Dance in Place Congo*), **Koanga** (Delius).

Cabo, Francisco (b. Náguera, Valencia, 1768; d. Náguera, 21. XI. 1832), Spa. orgst. & comp. After some min. posts he was app. cantor at Valencia cath. in 1810, 1st orgst. in 1816 and chapel master in 1830, succeeding Andrevi.

Works incl. church m., vocal m. with org. or orch., org. pieces, &c.

Caccia (It. = Hunt). A light It. madrigal the subject of the words for which is hunting. C. was also a 14-cent. It. term for Canon, because the parts 'chase' each other.

Caccini, Francesca (b. Florence, 18. X. 1588; d. ?), It. singer and comp. Pupil of her father.

Works incl. opera, *La liberazione di Ruggiero*); ballets *Il ballo delle zigane* & *Rinaldo innamorato* (after Tasso); sacred and secular cantatas for 1 & 2 voices, &c.

Caccini, Giulio (b. Rome, *c.* 1545; d. Florence, 10. XII. 1618), It. singer, lutenist & comp., father of prec. Entered the service of the Grand Duke of Tuscany at Florence in 1578. Visited Paris with his daughter in 1605. He wrote short voc. pieces in recitative style and sang them to the theorbo, which led to larger essays of the kind, set to scenes by Count Bardi, and eventually to Rinuccini's lib. for the opera *Euridice*, 1st set by Peri and immediately afterwards by C. in 1600.

Works incl. operas *Euridice* & *Il rapimento di Cefalo*; *Nuove musiche* containing madrigals and canzone for voice and thorough-bass.

Cachucha (Spa.). An Andalusian dance in quick, energetic 3–4 time.

Cacophony. M. that is discordant without reason and ill organized; the opposite of Euphony. The term is often loosely applied to Jazz and Swing, without justification, since they make much less use of discord than does much serious modern m., and mere noise is not properly described as C.

Cadence. A closing phrase, either finishing a mus. comp., a section thereof or a passage or phrase, coming to rest on the tonic note. Conventionally, if that note is approached through dominant harmony, a 'perfect C.' results; if through subdominant harmony, a 'plagal C.'; if the tonic note is evaded, or at least sounded with the support of some other harmony than the common tonic chord, the result is an 'interrupted C.'; if a tonic chord is reached, but not that of the main key of the comp., and if an impression of finality is avoided (as often between mvts. in Handel's concs.), there is an 'imperfect C.' or 'half-close'; a C. whose arrival at the tonic is delayed past a strong beat and made to fall on a weak beat is called a 'feminine C.'

Cadence (Fr.) = Shake.

Cadence appuyée (Fr.). *See* **Ornaments.**

Cadence-Phrase. The final group in

the exposition of a so. mvt., leading to the close in another than the tonic key.

Cadence sans tremblement (Fr.). *See* **Ornaments.**

Cadent. *See* **Ornaments.**

Cadenza (It. = Cadence). Orig. the C. was simply a cadence; but the custom gradually estab. itself of creating a feeling of suspense between the chords of a cadence by interpolating brilliant passages of greater or less extent and at the same time giving the perf. a chance to display technical gifts and (formerly) inventiveness in improvisation. Cs. in concs. are now rarely improvised, but supplied either by the comp. himself or some other musn. In the 18th and down to the 19th cent. improv. ran riot, esp. in opera and orat. arias, but voc. Cs., even in old m., are now almost wholly obs.

'Cadet Roussel' Variations. A series of voc. vars. on the Fr. folksong by Arnold Bax, Frank Bridge, Eugene Goossens & John Ireland, comp. *c.* 1917.

Cadi dupé, Le (*The Cadi Duped*), opera by Gluck (lib. by Pierre René Lemonnier), prod. Vienna, Burg Theatre, XII. 1761.

Opera by Monsigny (lib. do.), prod. Paris, Opéra-Comique, 4. II. 1761.

Cadman, Charles Wakefield (b. Johnstown, Pa., 24. XII. 1881), Amer. comp. Studied at Pittsburgh and became orgst., chor. cond. & critic there. He explored Amer.-Indian m. and used it in some of his comps. After a visit to Eur. in 1910 he became orgst. at Denver and later settled at Los Angeles.

Works incl. operas *The Garden of Mystery, The Land of Misty Water, The Garden of Death, Shanewis* (*The Robin Woman*), *A Witch of Salem, The Willow Tree*; cantatas for mixed & male voices; *Thunder-bird* Suite, *Oriental Rhapsody, Dark Dancers of the Mardi Gras* for orch.; *Amer. Suite* & *To a Vanishing Race* for stg. orch.; stg. 4tet, pf. Trio; v. & pf. So.; So., suite *Omar Khayyám, Idealized Indian Themes* & other works for pf.; *Four Indian Songs*, song cycles, *From Wigwam and Tepee, Birds of Flame, White Enchantment, Sayonara* (Jap.), *The Willow Wind* (Chin.) & *c.* 300 separate songs, &c.

Cadmus et Hermione, opera by Lully (lib. by Philippe Quinault), prod. Paris, Opéra, 27. IV. 1673.

Caduta de' giganti, La (*The Fall of the Giants*), opera by Gluck (lib. by Francesco Vanneschi), prod. London, King's Theatre, Haymarket, 7. I. 1746.

Caen, Arnold (incorrectly called Acaen, from 'A. Caen') (b. ?; d. ?), ? Flem. 15th–16th-cent. comp. Lived in It. early in the 16th cent. Wrote motets &c.

Cafaro, Pasquale (b. San Pietro in Galantina nr. Lecce, 8. II. 1706; d. Naples, 25. X. 1787), It. comp. Studied under Leo at Naples and later became chapel master of the royal chapel and dir. of the Cons.

Works incl. operas *Ipermestra, La disfatta di Dario, Antigono* (2 versions), *L'incendio di Troia, Arianna e Teseo, Il Creso, L'Olimpiade*; orats. *Sant' Antonio di Padua, Il trionfo di Davidde*; *Stabat Mater*; masses, motets & psalms; sacred cantatas, &c.

Caffarelli (Gaetano Maiorano) (b. Bari, 16. IV. 1703; d. Santo Dorato nr. Naples, 3. XI. 1783), It. male con. singer. Made his 1st stage appearance in Rome, 1724; sang 1st in London in 1738.

Cagnoni, Antonio (Godiasco, Voghera, 8. II. 1828; d. Bergamo, 30. IV. 1896), It. comp. Studied at the Milan Cons., 1842–7. Chapel master at Vigevano, 1856–63, then at Novara cath., and from 1886 at the church of Santa Maria Maggiore at Bergamo.

Works incl. operas *Don Bucefalo, Il testamento di Figaro, Amori e trappole, Giralda, La valle d'Andorra, Il vecchio della montagna, La tombola, Un capriccio di donna, Papa Martin, Francesca da Rimini* (after Dante), &c.; motets and other church m.

Cahen, Albert (b. Paris, 8. I. 1846; d. Cap d'Ail, 23. II. 1903), Fr. comp. Pupil of Franck for comp.

Works incl. operas *Le Bois, La Belle au bois dormant, Le Vénitien, La Femme de Claude*; ballet *Fleur de neiges*; *Jean le Précurseur* & *Endymion* for chor. & orch.; song cycle *Marines*, &c.

Caine, Thomas Henry Hall (1853–1931), Eng. novelist & playwright. *See* **Mascagni** (*Eternal City*).

Caisse (Fr.) *See* Grosse Caisse.

Caisse claire (Fr.) = Side Drum.

Caisse roulante or **Caisse sourde** (Fr.) = Tenor Drum.

Caix d'Hervelois, Louis de (b. Paris, *c.* 1670; d. Paris, *c.* 1760), Fr. va. da gamba player. In the service of the Duke of Orleans. A son and 3 daughters of his were chamber musns. at court. Wrote many pieces for va. da gamba, duets for viols & fl. sos.

Calando (It. = lowering, decreasing, calming down). A direction similar to *diminuendo* and *rallentando*, capable of expressing both at once, i.e. weakening in tone as well as slowing down.

Caldara, Antonio (b. Venice, 1670; d. Vienna, 28. XII. 1736), It. comp. Pupil of Legrenzi at Venice. After travelling much and working in Rome and Madrid, he settled in Vienna as vice-cond. under Fux in 1716.

Works incl. c. 100 operas & other stage works, e.g. *Ifigenia in Aulide, Lucio Papirio, Gianguir, Don Chisciotte, La pazienza di Socrate con due moglie* (with Reutter), *Il Demetrio, Sancio Panza, Achille in Sciro*; church m., orats., cantatas, madrigals, canons; trio sos., 4tets, Septet, &c.

Calderón de la Barca, Pedro (1600–81), Spa. dramatist. *See* **Ambros** (*Mágico prodigioso*), **Casal y Chapí, Celos aun del ayre matan** (Hidalgo), **Courvoisier, Ferreira, Fierrabras** (Schubert), **Friedenstag** (R. Strauss), **Hidalgo, Křenek** (*Vida es sueño*), **Laserna, Lassen** (*Circe*), **Opienski** (*Príncipe constánte*), **Peyro** (*Jardin de Falerina*), **Raff** (*Dame Kobold*), **Reinecke** (do.), **Rheinberger** (*Mágico p.*), **Rietz (J.)** (incid. m. for plays), **Seyfried** (*Vida es s.*), **Soler** (incid. m. for plays), **Tommasini** (*Life is a Dream*), **Umlauf (I.)** (*Oberamtmann und die Soldaten*), **Weingartner** (*Dame Kobold*), **Wolfurt** (do.).

Calife de Bagdad, Le, opera by Boïeldieu (lib. by Claude Godard d'Aucour de Saint-Just), prod. Paris, Opéra-Comique, 16. IX. 1800.

Calinda (or **Calenda**). A Negro dance introd. into the W. Indies and later cultivated in the southern states of U.S.A., orig. an African ritual dance accomp. by drums, which remained a feature of its m. Delius makes use of it in *Koanga*.

Calino casturame (corrupt. from Ir. 'Cailinog a stuír me' = 'Maiden, my treasure'). A tune mentioned in Shakespeare's *Henry V* (IV. iv) and contained in the *Fitzwilliam Virginal Book*.

Callcott, John (Wall) (b. London, 20. XI. 1766; d. Bristol, 15. V. 1821), orgst. & comp. Son of a bricklayer, he had no regular mus. teaching, but picked up much knowledge from Arnold and Cooke. Having obtained a deputy orgst.'s post, he found time to comp. and in 1785 gained 3 of the 4 prizes offered by the Catch Club. Two years later he took part in founding the Glee Club. When Haydn came to Eng. he studied inst. writing under him, but he continued to write glees and catches with great success. Mus.D., Oxford, 1800. In 1809 he went insane.

Works incl. setting of Joseph Warton's *Ode to Fancy*; anthem for Arnold's funeral; scena on the death of Nelson; a book of psalms ed. with Arnold, with some new tunes; numerous glees, catches & canons, &c.

Calm Sea and Prosperous Voyage (Beethoven & Mendelssohn). *See* **Meeresstille**).

Calvé, Emma (Rose Emma Calvet) (b. Decazeville, 15. VIII. 1858; d. Millau, 6. I. 1942), Fr. sop. singer. 1st appeared at Nice and came out in Brussels in 1882 and Paris in 1884.

Calvisius, Seth (b. Gorsleben, Thuringia, 21. II. 1556; d. Leipzig, 24. XI. 1615), Ger. scholar and musn. Cantor of St. Thomas's school and mus. dir. of its church from 1594, and thus a predecessor of Bach. Wrote several learned books on m., compiled collections of voc. m. and comp. motets, hymns, &c.

Calvocoressi, M(ichael). D(imitri). (b. Marseilles, 2. X. 1877; d. London, 1. II. 1944), Eng. m. critic of Gr. descent. Studied in Paris, partic, m. and languages, lectured there on m. at the École des Hautes Études Sociales, 1905–14, and then settled in London, becoming naturalized. His books incl. studies of mus. criticism, Mussorgsky, &c.

Calzabigi, Ranieri da (1714–95), It. lit. critic and author. Lived in Paris and Vienna for a time. Wrote the libs. for Gluck's *Orfeo, Alceste* & *Paride ed Elena*. *See also* **Finta giardiniera** (Anfossi & Mozart), **Orfeo ed Euridice** (Bertoni) & **Orpheus og Euridice** (Naumann).

Cambert, Robert (b. Paris, c. 1629; d. London, 1677), Fr. comp. Studied hpchd. with Chambonnières, was orgst. at the church of Saint-Honoré in Paris and superintendent of the queen's m. He was ousted by Lully and went to live in London in 1672. His *Pomone*, the 1st Fr. opera to be staged in public in 1671, was given in Fr. in London, 1674, with alterations by Grabu. Most of his m. is lost.

Works incl. comedy with m. *La Muette ingrate*; a pastoral perf. at Issy & another, *Les Peines et les plaisirs de l'amour*; operas *Ariane, ou Le Mariage de Bacchus, Pomone*; a trio for Brécourt's *Jaloux invisible*; *Airs à boire*, &c.

Cambiale di matrimonio, La (*The Marriage Contract*), opera by Rossini (lib. by Gaetano Rossi, based on a comedy by Camillo Federici), prod. Venice, Teatro San Moisè, 3. XI. 1810. R.'s 1st opera to be perf.

Cambiare (It. = to change). The word is sometimes used in place of *mutare*, e.g. *cambia in Re* (it changes to D), *cambiano in La* (they change to A), &c.

Cambiata. *See* **Nota Cambiata.**

Cambini, Giovanni Giuseppe (b. Leghorn, 13. II. 1746; d. Bicêtre nr. Paris, 29. XII. 1829), It. vst. & comp.

Pupil of Martini at Bologna. In 1770 he settled in Paris, had some syms. prod. at the Concert Spirituel by Gossec and later became cond. at different theatres. Successful at first, he spoilt his chances by loose living and by forging chamber m. in the style of Boccherini. D. in a hospital for the poor.

Works incl. operas & ballets; 60 syms., 29 *Symphonies concertantes*, 7 concs.; 144 stg. 4tets; hundreds of inst. pieces; 2 orats.; church m., org. m., &c.

Camera, Concerto da } (It. = chamber
Camera, Sonata da } conc., or so.). A secular work written for perf. at home or at concerts, as distinct from a conc. or so. *da chiesa* = for the church.

Camerata (It. = society). The artistic set at Florence working together just before and after 1600 and evolving the form of opera, incl. the musns. Caccini, Cavalieri, V. Galilei and Peri, the poet Ottavio Rinuccini and the amateur patrons Counts Bardi & Corsi.

Cameriera (It. = chambermaid). A term used in It. opera, esp. of the 17th & 18th cents., in the same way as *servetta* (servant-girl), for Soubrette parts.

Camilla (Bononcini). *See* **Trionfo di C.**

Camoens (properly **Camões**), **Luis Vaz de** (1524–80), Port. poet. *See* **Branco (L. F.)** (madrigals), **Machado** (*Lusiads*), **Vianna da Motta** (do).

Campagnoli, Bartolomeo (b. Cento nr. Bologna, 10. IX. 1751; d. Neustrelitz 6. XI. 1827), It. vst. & comp. Pupil of Nardini; worked in It., Ger. and Paris; wrote concs., sos., duets, &c. for v.; fl. m., Caprices for va., &c.

Campane (It., plur.) = Bells.

Campanella, La. The 3rd of Liszt's *Études d'exécution transcendante d'après Paganini* for pf., comp. in 1838, already used by him in 1831–2 for the *Grande Fantaisie de bravoure sur la Clochette*. The theme is that of the finale of P.'s v. Conc. in B min., Op. 7, a rondo in which harmonics are combined with a bell.

Campanette (It., plur.) = Chime Bells, *Glockenspiel*.

Campanini, Cleofante (b. Parma, 1. IX. 1860; d. Chicago, 19. XII. 1919), It. cond. Made his 1st appearance at Parma in 1883 and the same year went to U.S.A., where he spent most of his life. Married Eva Tetrazzini, the sister of Louisa T.

Campenhout, François van (b. Brussels, 5. II. 1779; d. Brussels, 24. IV. 1848), Belg. ten. singer & comp. Sang in Belg., Hol. & Fr. until 1827. During the 1830 Revol. he wrote the Belg. nat. anthem, *La Brabançonne*.

Works incl. operas *Grotius*, *Le Passe-partout*, *L'Heureux Mensonge*; church m.; chors.; songs, &c.

Campian, Thomas. *See* **Campion.**

Campioli (Antonio Gualandi) (b. Ger., ?; d. ?), It. male con. singer. 1st appearance, Berlin, 1708; 1st went to London in 1731.

Campion, Thomas (or Campian) (b. London, 12. II. 1567; d. London, 1. III. 1620), Eng. physician, poet & comp. Was sent to Cambridge in 1581 and being a lawyer at 1st entered Gray's Inn in 1586; (?) took part in the siege of Rouen in 1591 and soon afterwards practised medicine in London. He pub. a 1st collection of airs to the lute with Rosseter in 1601 and 4 more followed between c. 1613–7, all the words of the songs being his own. In 1613 he pub. a book on ctpt. and wrote the poetry for *Songs of Mourning* on the death of Prince Henry, set by John Cooper. He also pub. poems and a book on poetry. His poem *Neptune's Empire* was comp. for chor. & orch. by Ernest Walker. Poems set as songs by Wm. Busch.

Works incl. 5 books of airs to the lute (over 100) and 3 separate earlier songs; songs for the prod. of 4 masques, 1607–13, incl. *The Mask of Flowers*.

Campioni, Carlo Antonio (b. Leghorn, c. 1720; d. Florence, 1793), It. comp. In the service of the Grand Duke of Tuscany at Florence and the King of Sardinia. Comp. a Requiem and other church m., trio sos., duets for v. & hpchd., &c.

Campo, Conrado del (b. Madrid, 28. X. 1879), Spa. comp. Student and later prof. at the Madrid Cons.

Works incl. operas *Dies irae*, *Los amantes de Verona* (*Romeo and Juliet*), *El final de Don Alvaro*, *La flor del agua* and (with Barrios) *El Avapiés*; chor. works *La dama de Amboto* & *La divina commedia* (after Dante); symph. poems *Ante las ruinas* & *Granada y Galicia*; 8 stg. 4tets; v. & pf. So.; *Paisajes de Granada* for pf.; songs, &c.

Camporese, Violante (b. Rome, 1785; d. Rome, 1839), It. sop. singer. Sang in Paris and Milan before she made her 1st stage appearance in London, in 1817.

Campra, André (b. Aix-en-Provence, 4. XII. 1660; d. Versailles, 29. VI. 1744), Fr. comp. of It. descent. He held var. provincial orgst.'s posts and settled in Paris in 1694, when he was app. mus. dir. at Notre-Dame, where his motets soon attracted large congregations; but he became equally famous as a stage comp.

Works incl. operas and opera-ballets *L'Europe galante*, *Le Carnaval de*

Venise, *Hésione*, *Tancrède*, *Iphigénie en Tauride* (with Desmarets), *Alcine*, *Hippodamie*, *Les Festes vénitiennes*, *Idoménée*, *Le Jaloux trompé*, *Achille et Déidamie*, &c.; pasticcios *Fragments de Lully* & *Télémaque* (the latter with pieces by Charpentier, Colasse, Desmarets, Marais & Rebel sen.); entertainments *Amaryllis*, *Les Festes de Corinthe*, *Le Génie de la Bourgogne*, *Les Noces de Vénus*, &c.; a mass, cantatas, motets & psalms.

Canadian Composers. *See* **Lavallée, Willan.**

Canary (Eng.), also Canarie or Canaries. A dance in quick triple time with a dotted rhythm, now obs., poss. originating from the Canary Islands.

Cancan. A dance of a rather disreputable nature fashionable in Paris from *c.* the middle of the 19th cent. It is in very animated 2–4 time.

Cancel (Amer.) = Natural, ♮.

Canción (Spa.) = Song.

Cancionero (Spa.). A song-book.

Cancrizans (from Lat. *cancer* = crab) = crab-wise. A term used for the device of repeating a mus. phrase or theme backwards, note for note. 'Canon cancrizans' is a canon in which one part or more proceed normally while another one or more go backwards.

Candeille, Amélie-Julie (b. Paris, 31. VII. 1767; d. Paris, 4. II. 1834), Fr. actress, singer, pfst., hpst. & comp. Made her 1st appearance as an opera singer in 1782 and 10 years later she prod. her 1st opera, for which she had written both lib. and m., and in which she sang.

Works incl. operas *La Belle Fermière*, *Ida*, *l'orpheline de Berlin*; chamber m.; pf. pieces; many popular songs, &c.

Candeille, Pierre Joseph (b. Estaires, 8. XII. 1744; d. Chantilly, 24. IV. 1827), Fr. singer & comp., father of prec. Wrote operas, incl. *Castor et Pollux*, ballets, pantomime, incid. m., &c.

Candia, Cavaliere di. *See* **Mario.**

Canis, Corneille (Cornelis de Hond) (b. ? Antwerp, ?; d. Prague, 15. II., c. 1561), Flem. comp. Choirmaster of Charles V's imp. chapel in the Nthlds. from 1548, later chaplain to the Emperor Ferdinand in Prague. Wrote church m., chansons, &c.

Cannabich, Christian (b. Mannheim, 28. XII. 1731; d. Frankfort o/M., 21. I. 1798), Ger. comp., vst. & cond. Worked as a member of the Mannheim school of early symphonists and later at Munich.

Works incl. operas, ballets, syms., stg. 4tets, &c.

Cannabich, Rosa (b. Mannheim, 1764; d. ?), daughter of prec. The slow mvt. of Mozart's pf. So., C maj. (K. 309, 1777), is supposed to be a mus. portrait of her.

Canon. A device in comp. whereby a melody is 1st introd. alone and then repeated by another voice, or by more voices in succession (or inst. parts) in such a way that the entries occur before the previous statement of the tune is finished. Cs. are usually in unison, i.e. the entries occur on the same notes; but they can also do so at different intervals, in which case the C. is more complex in texture but less discernible by the ear.

Cantabile (It. = song-like, songful, singable). The direction is usually placed against phrases in inst. rather than voc. m., where the comp. desires an expressive delivery.

Cantata (It. = a sung piece). The definition has become narrowed in modern times to short voc. works, sacred or secular and for single voices or chor., with inst. accompaniment.

Cantatore (It.) = male singer.

Cantatrice (Fr. & It.) = songstress.

Cante flamenco (Spa. lit. 'flamingo song' or 'Flem. song'). A form of *cante hondo* modernized in the 19th cent. by the gypsies in a rather debased form.

Cante hondo (or jondo) (Spa. lit. 'deep song'). A traditional form of Andalusian song with guitar accomp., ornate in melody, using intervals smaller than the semitone on some notes and expressing moods of dejection, misery or even tragedy.

Canteloube de Malaret, (Marie) Joseph (b. Anonnay, Ardèche, 21. X. 1879), Fr. comp. Studied with d'Indy at the Schola Cantorum in Paris. In 1900 he began to collect and study Fr. folksong, particularly of Auvergne, of which he pub. several collections. Lecturer on Fr. m. and folksong since 1923.

Works incl. operas *Le Mas* & *Vercingétorix*; symph. poems *Vers la princesse lointaine* & *Lauriers*; *Pièces françaises* for pf. & orch.; *Poème* for v. & orch.; *Dans la montagne* for v. & pf.; songs with orch. and with pf., &c.

Canterbury Pilgrims, The, opera by Stanford (lib. by Gilbert Arthur à Beckett, after Chaucer), prod. London, Drury Lane Theatre, 28. IV. 1884.

Cantilena (It.) = a sustained, flowing melodic line, esp. when sung *legato* or played in the manner of such singing.

Cantino (It.). The E stg. of the v.

Cantiones Sacrae (Lat. = Sacred Songs). Latin motets were often so entitled in the 16th cent. and thereabouts, esp. by pubs. of collections.

Canto (It. = Song). In inst. as much as in voc. m. usually the part of a comp. which has the chief melody. The direction *marcato il canto* indicates that such a melody is to be emphasized.

Canto carnascialesco (It. carnivalesque song). A Florentine partsong of the 15th–16th cents. with secular, often ribald words, sung in carnival processions, with the tune in the ten. part.

Canto fermo (It.). *See* **Cantus firmus.**

Cantor (Lat. = singer). A church singer, esp. the leader or dir. of a church choir in a Lutheran church (e.g. Bach at Leipzig) or a synagogue.

Cantoris. In Eng. caths. and in churches where the choir is divided, the C. side is that on the north of the chancel, near the stall of the cantor or precentor, the other being the *Decani* side.

Cantus figuratus (Lat. = figured song). Plainsong with more than one note to some of its syllables.

Cantus firmus (Lat. lit. 'fixed song'). A pre-existing melody chosen by a comp. to envelop in ctptl. parts of his own, either for exercise or for the prod. of a comp. In old masses popular tunes were commonly used in this way, being sung in long notes in the ten. part (hence *tenor* = the holder).

Canzone (It. = song, ballad). A partsong in the style of a madrigal but lighter in character and less elaborately polyphonic, or an inst. piece written in a similar style.

Canzonet (from It. *canzonetta* = little song). Light songs written in Eng. round about 1600, either for several voices with or without insts. or for a single voice with lute accomp. Later simply a song in Eng., e.g. Haydn's Eng. Cs.

Canzonetta (It. = little song). Often synom. with Canzone in 16th–17th-cent. It.; later a light song or short and simple air in an opera, &c.

Canzoniere (It.). A song-book.

Čapek, Karel (b. 1890), Cz. novelist & dramatist. *See* **Austin (F.)** (*Insect Play*), **Makropoulos Case** (Janáček).

Capell, Richard (b. Northampton, 23. III. 1885), Eng. critic. His career of m. critic to the *Daily Mail* in London was interrupted by the 1914–8 war, in which he served, but resumed until 1933, when he became chief m. critic of the *Daily Telegraph*. On the outbreak of the 2nd war in 1939 he volunteered to serve as correspondent, 1st in Fr., later in N. Africa and Gr. He has written a book on Schubert's songs and trans. songs by var. masters and R. Strauss's *Friedenstag*.

Capellmeister (Ger.). *See* **Chapel Master.**

Capet, Lucien (b. Paris, 8. I. 1873; d. Paris, 18. XII. 1928), Fr. vst. & comp. Studied at the Paris Cons. Formed a stg. 4tet in 1893. He left v., chamber and other m.

Caplet, André (b. Le Havre, 23. XI. 1878; d. Paris, 22. IV. 1925), Fr. cond. & comp. He was much influenced by Debussy, of several of whose works he completed the orchn.

Works incl. symph. study *Le Masque de la Mort rouge* (after Poe); *Épiphanie* for co. & orch.; Mass for unaccomp. voices; *Le Miroir de Jésus* for voices, stg. 5tet & hp.; *Le Pie Jésus* for voice & org.; *Suite persane* for 10 wind insts., *Conte fantastique* (after Poe) for hp. & stg. 4tet; *Sonata da chiesa* for v. & org.; children's suite for pf. duet; song cycles *Prières*, *La Croix douloureuse*, *3 Fables de La Fontaine*, *5 Ballades françaises*, &c.

Capocci, Filippo (b. Rome, 11. V. 1840; d. Rome, 25. VII. 1911), It. orgst. & comp. Studied under his father, whom he succeeded as master of the Lateran Chapel in Rome, 1898. Wrote 5 sos. and much other m. for the org.

Capocci, Gaetano (b. Rome, 16. X. 1811; d. Rome, 11. I. 1898), It. orgst. & comp., father of prec. After var. studies and appts. he became master of the Lateran Chapel in 1855. Wrote masses, motets, psalms and other church m.

Capriccio (It. = Whim). A name given to var. types of comp. at different times: in the 18th cent. to animated pieces in a fugal style, but not strictly fugues in form, and by Bach to a hpchd. piece in several mvts. on the departure of his brother Johann Jakob; c. from the middle of that cent. to studies for the v. (e.g. Paganini's); later still to fantasies for pf. on well-known themes; last of all to short pieces in a humorous or whimsical manner.

Capriccio, opera by R. Strauss (lib. by Clemens Krauss), prod. Munich, State Opera, 28. X. 1942.

Capriccio espagnol (*Spa. C.*), the hybrid It. & Fr. title of an orch. work by Rimsky-Korsakov, written as a display piece for the St. Petersburg Orch., finished 4. VIII. and prod. St. Petersburg, 17. XII. 1887. It contains brilliant solo parts for most of the principal insts. and for the brass in groups.

Capriccio italien (*It. C.*), the hybrid It. & Fr. title of an orch. work by

Tchaikovsky, comp. during a visit to Rome in 1880 and 1st perf. Moscow, 18. XII.

Caproli (or **Caprioli**), **Carlo** (b. ?; d. ?), It. 17th-cent. vst. & comp. Was brought to Paris by Cardinal Mazarin and prod. the opera *Le nozze di Peleo e Teti* there in 1654. He wrote the orat. *Davidde prevaricante* in 1683.

Capuleti ed i Montecchi, I (*The Capulets and Montagues*), opera by Bellini (lib. by Felice Romani, based on Shakespeare's *Romeo and Juliet*), prod. Venice, Teatro La Fenice, 11. III. 1830.

Cara, Marchetto (b. Verona, ?; d. Mantua, *c.* 1527), It. lutenist & comp. In service at the ducal court of Mantua, 1495–1525. Wrote frottole and other songs.

Caractacus, cantata for solo voices, chor. & orch. by Elgar, Op. 35 (lib. by H. A. Acworth), comp. in 1898 and prod. Leeds Festival, 1899.

M. by Arne for a dramatic poem by William Mason (pub. 1759), perf. London, Covent Garden Theatre, 6. XII. 1776.

Caradori-Allan (*née* **de Munck**), **Maria (Caterina Rosalbina)** (b. Milan, 1800; d. Surbiton, Surrey, 15. X. 1865). It.-Alsat. sop. singer. Was taught m. entirely by her mother, whose name she took, and after a tour in Fr. & Ger. made her 1st stage appearance in London in 1822. She married in Eng. and appeared also at concerts and festivals.

Carafa (di Colobrano), Michele Enrico (b. Naples, 17. XI. 1787; d. Paris, 26. VII. 1872), It. comp. Studied at Naples 1st, then in Paris under Cherubini. On the failure of his 1st opera he enlisted in the bodyguard of Murat, then king of Naples, took part in the Rus. campaign in 1812 and was decorated by Napoleon, after whose fall he returned to m. He prod. operas not only in It., but in Vienna and Paris, where he settled in 1827 and became very popular.

Works incl. *c.* 35 operas, e.g. *Il fantasma, Il vascello di occidente, Gabriella di Vergy, Ifigenia, Berenice, Le Solitaire, La Violette, La Fiancée de Lammermoor* (after Scott), *Masaniello* (competing with Auber's *Muette de Portici*), *La Prison d'Édimbourg, Jeanne d'Arc* (after Schiller), &c.

Cardillac, opera by Hindemith (lib. by Ferdinand Lion, based on E. T. A. Hoffmann's story *Das Fräulein von Scudéri*), prod. Dresden, 9. XI. 1926.

Cardoso, Manuel (b. Fronteira no Alemtejo, 1569; d. Lisbon, 29. XI. 1650), Port. monk, orgst. & comp. Studied at the seminary of Evora and became choirmaster at the cath. there. Joined the Carmelite monastery at Lisbon in 1589 and became its mus. dir.

Works incl. masses, motets, magnificats and other church m.

Carducci, Giosuè (1836–1907), It. poet. *See* **Pratella** (*Chiesa di Polenta*).

Cardus, Neville (b. ?, 2. IV. 1889), Eng. critic. Began to write for the *Daily Citizen* at Manchester in 1913 and in 1917 joined the *Manchester Guardian* as asst. critic to Samuel Langford, whom he succeeded in 1927. He wrote on cricket as well as m., ed. Langford's writings and pub. a book on *Ten Composers* as well as several on cricket. In 1939 he went to live in Australia.

Carestini, Giovanni (b. Ancona, *c.* 1705; d. ?, *c.* 1759), It. male sop. singer, later con. Came out in Rome, 1721, and made his 1st London appearance in 1733.

Carew, Thomas (?1598–?1639), Eng. poet. *See* **Georges** (songs).

Carey, Henry (b. ?, *c.* 1690; d. London, 4. X. 1743), Eng. poet, comp. & dramatist. Pupil of Roseingrave and Geminiani. Wrote libs. for Lampe's ballad operas, *The Dragon of Wantley, Margery* and *Amelia*; comp. a tune (not the familiar one) for his *Sally in our alley*. The attribution of *God save the King* to him is unfounded.

Comps. incl. numerous cantatas & songs set to his own words; songs for Vanbrugh & Cibber's *The Provoked Husband*; plays with m. of his own *The Contrivances, or More Ways than One, Betty, or The Country Bumpkins* (ballad opera), *Cephalus and Procris, Chrononhotonthologos* (burlesque), *A Wonder, or The Honest Yorkshireman* (ballad opera), *Nancy, or The Parting Lovers*, &c.

Carillon. A set of bells hung in a church steeple or specially built tower, controlled by a keyboard below and played like an org. on manuals and pedals. Cs. are found partic. in the Nthlds. Also an org. stop controlling steel bars, gongs or bells.

Carissimi, Giacomo (b. Marino nr. Rome, IV. 1605; d. Rome, 12. I. 1674), It. comp. Chapel master at Assisi about 1624–8; then went to Rome, where he held a similar post at the church of Sant' Apollinare attached to the Ger. Coll. He cultivated the orat. and cantata in their early stages.

Works incl. masses, motets; *Lauda Sion* & *Nisi Dominus* for 8 voices; orats. *History of Job, Baltazar, Abraham and Isaac, Jephtha, The Last Judgment, Jonah*; sacred cantatas; vocal duets, &c.

Carl Rosa Opera Company. Founded by Carl Rosa in 1873 for the perf. of opera in Eng.

Carlton, Richard (b. ?, *c.* 1558; d. ?, *c.* 1638), Eng. comp. Educ. at Cambridge; became vicar at St. Stephen's church, Norwich, and min. canon at the cath. Pub. a book of madrigals in 1601 and contrib. to *The Triumphes of Oriana.*

Carmen, opera by Bizet (lib. by Henri Meilhac and Ludovic Halévy, based on the story by Mérimée), prod. Paris, Opéra-Comique, 3. III. 1874.

Carmen, Johannes (b. ?; d. ?), ? Fr. 15th-cent. comp. (whose name is known only in its Lat. form). Wrote motets, &c.

Carmen Sylva (Queen Elizabeth of Rum.) (1843–1916), Rum. poetess of Ger. birth. *See* **Hallström** (*Neaga*), **Otesco** (*Ilderim*), **Sommer** (*Sappho*).

Carnaval (Schumann). *See* **Carnival.**

Carnaval romain, Le (*The Roman Carnival*), concert ovt. by Berlioz, Op. 9, written in 1844 on material from the opera *Benvenuto Cellini* of 1834–8, and 1st perf., Paris, 3. II. 1844.

Carner, Mosco (b. Vienna, 15. XI. 1904), Eng. critic & cond. of Aus. origin. Studied at the New Vienna Cons. and mcol. at the Univ. under Adler, taking a Ph.D. degree there in 1928. He then became opera cond. in Vienna, Troppau and Danzig until 1933, when he settled in London, later becoming naturalized. He has worked as critic, m. correspondent to foreign journals & cond. and has pub. books, incl. *A Study of 20th-Cent. Harmony, Of Men and M.*, &c., chapters on Schubert, Dvořák, Puccini, &c.

Carnicer, Ramón (b. Tárrega nr. Lérida, 24. X. 1789; d. Madrid, 17. III. 1855), Spa. comp. Choir-boy at Urgell cath., later went to Barcelona and in 1808 fled to Minorca when Spa. was invaded by Fr. Later managed the It. opera at Barcelona and wrote It. works for it. into which he introd. Spa. songs. In 1827 he was called by royal command to dir. the opera at Madrid.

Works incl. operas *Adele di Lusignano, Elena e Constantino, Don Giovanni Tenorio, ossia Il convitato di pietra, Elena e Malvina, Cristoforo Colombo, Eufemio di Messina, Ismalia*; *Missa solemnis*, 2 Requiems; syms., &c.

Carnival, concert ovt. by Dvořák, Op. 92, comp. 1891 and forming, with *Amid Nature* and *Othello*, a cycle with thematic connections orig. called *Nature, Life and Love.*

Suite of pf. pieces on the notes A. S. (Ger. Es = E♭) C. H. (Ger. = B♮) by Schumann, Op. 9, the letters representing the only mus. ones in S.'s surname and the town of Asch in Bohemia, whence came Ernestine von Fricken, with whom he was in love in 1834–5, when he wrote the work. She is alluded to in the piece entitled *Estrella*; other persons referred to are Clara Wieck in that called *Chiarina*, Chopin and Paganini in those so entitled, and S. himself in his 2 different imaginary characters of *Florestan* and *Eusebius*.

Ballet on S.'s m., orch. by Glazunov & others (chgph. by Mikhail Mikhailovitch Fokin), prod. Paris, Opéra, 4. VI. 1910.

Carol. A Christmas song dating mainly from the 14th & 15th cents. in Eng., but older on the Continent, esp. the Fr. *Noël*. Its chief characteristic is that although the words deal with the birth of Christ, they often have a secular tinge in their refs. to the material rewards expected by the waits who sang them outside well-to-do people's houses during the Christmas season.

Caron, Philippe (b. ?; d. ?), Fr. or Flem. 15th-cent. comp. ? pupil of Binchois and Dufay; ? chorister at Cambrai cath. Wrote masses & other church m., chansons, &c.

Caron (*née* **Meuniez**), **Rose-Lucile** (b. Monerville, Seine-et-Oise, 17. XI. 1857; d. Paris, 9. IV. 1930), Fr. sop. singer. Studied at the Paris Cons. where she became prof. of singing in 1920. Made her 1st stage appearance at Brussels in 1884.

Carpani, Giuseppe (Antonio) (b. Villalbese nr. Brianza, 28. I. 1752; d. Vienna, 22. I. 1825), It. poet & writer on m. Settled in Vienna. Friend and biog. of Haydn.

Carpenter, Edward (1844–1929), Eng. poet. *See* **Boughton** (*Midnight*).

Carpenter, John Alden (b. Chicago, 28. II. 1876), Amer. comp. Learnt m. privately and studied with Paine while a student at Harvard Univ., and with Elgar in Rome in 1895, later at Chicago with Bernard Ziehn. Although a business man, he has comp. much.

Works incl. ballets *Krazy-Kat, Skyscrapers* & *The Birthday of the Infanta* (after Wilde); *Song of Faith* for chor. & orch.; Sym., *Adventures in a Perambulator* & *Sea Drift* (after Whitman) for orch.; Concertino for pf. & orch., v. Conc.; stg. 4tet, pf. 5tet; many songs incl. *Gitanjali* cycle (Tagore).

Carreño, Teresa (b. Caracas, 22. XII. 1853; d. New York, 12. VI. 1917), Venez. pfst. Studied in N.Y. and Paris, later under A. Rubinstein; made her 1st public appearance in

N.Y. aged 9, later became an opera singer for a time, reappearing as pfst. in 1889. Meanwhile she had married Giovanni Tagliapietra as her 1st and d'Albert as her 2nd husband, separated and married her 1st husband's brother; cond. opera in Venez.

Carrillo, Julián (b. Ahualulco, 28. I. 1875), Mex. comp. Studied at the Mexico Cons. and at Leipzig. After working at Mexico he settled in N.Y. and comp. to a system dividing the 8ve into small fractional notes he called 'Microtones.'

Works incl. operas; masses; syms.; Concertino for microtone insts., &c.

Carroll, Lewis (Charles Lutwidge Dodgson) (1832–98), Eng. mathematician & children's author. *See* **Addinsell** (*Alice in Wonderland*), **Head** (*Jabberwocky*), **Kelley** (*Alice in W.*), **Taylor (Deems)** (*Through the Looking-Glass*).

Carrosse du Saint-Sacrement, Le (*The Coach of the Holy Sacrament*), opera by Lord Berners (lib. from Mérimée's play), prod. Paris, Théâtre des Champs-Élysées, 24. IV. 1924.

Carse, Adam (b. Newcastle-on-Tyne, 19. V. 1878), Eng. m. scholar & comp. Studied in Ger. and at the R.A.M. in London. Asst. m. master at Winchester Coll., 1909–22 and prof. at the R.A.M. from 1923. He made a special study of insts. and orchn., on which subjects he has written several books.

Works incl. ballad *Judas Iscariot's Paradise* for bar., chor. & orch., cantata *The Lay of the Brown Rosary* (E. B. Browning); Vars. on *Barbara Allen* for stg. orch. & other small orch works; *Norw. Fantasy* for v. & orch.; inst. pieces; songs, &c.

Cartan, Jean (Louis) (b. Nancy, 1. XII. 1906; d. Bligny, 26. III. 1932), Fr. comp. Studied at the Paris Cons., where his comp. master was Dukas.

Works incl. cantata *Pater* for solo voices, chor. & orch., *Hymne à Dante* for chor. & orch.; 2 stg. 4tets, *Introduction and Allegro* for wind insts. & pf., Sonatina for fl. & cl.; Psalm xxii for voice & pf. & other songs incl. *Trois Chants d'été* and settings of poems by Tristan Klingsor, Villon and Mallarmé, &c.

Carter, Charles Thomas (b. Dublin, 1734; d. London, 12. X. 1804), Ir. comp. Choir-boy at Christ Church cath., Dublin, and orgst. at St. Werburgh's church there, 1751–69. He became very popular as a song writer and settled in London in 1770. Prod. a comic opera, *Just in Time,* in 1792 and wrote lighter stage pieces, &c.

Carter, Elliot (b. New York, 1908), Amer. comp. Educ. at Harvard Univ., where he studied m. with Piston; later a pupil of Nadia Boulanger in Paris. He returned to N.Y.

Works incl. 2 operas; 2 ballets; incid. m.; orat. *The Bridge* & other chor. works; Sym.; Conc. for Eng. hn.; 2 stg. 4tets; So. for fl. & pf., &c.

Cartier, Jean-Baptiste (b. Avignon, 28. V. 1765; d. Paris, 1841), Fr. vst. & comp. Pupil of Viotti; held posts at court before and after the Revol., during which he played in the Opéra orch. Comp. m. for his inst. and some other works.

Cartwright, William (1611–43), Eng. playwright. *See* **Lawes (H.)**.

Caruso, Enrico (b. Naples, 25. II. 1873; d. Naples, 2. VIII. 1921), It. ten. singer. Made his 1st public appearance at Naples in 1894 and began to become famous when he sang in the prod. of Giordano's *Fedra* at Milan in 1899. He 1st sang in London, with Melba, in 1902, and in Amer. in 1903.

Caruso, Luigi (b. Naples, 25. IX. 1754; d. Perugia, 1822), It. comp. Pupil of Sala at Naples. Comp. *c.* 60 operas, masses, orats., cantatas, &c.

Carvalho, João de Sousa (b. Alemtejo, *c.* 1730; d. Lisbon, 1798), Port. comp. Studied at Naples; taught at Lisbon on his return.

Works incl. 15 It. operas, e.g. *Perseo, Testoride Argonauta, Penelope, L'Endimione*; masses & other church m. with orch.; hpchd. sos., &c.

Carvalho (*née* **Miolan**), **Marie (Caroline Félix)** (b. Marseilles, 31. XII. 1827; d. Puys, 10. VII. 1895), Fr. sop. singer. Studied under her father and at the Paris Cons.; 1st appeared in 1849 and was engaged by the Opéra-Comique in 1850. There she married in 1853 Léon Carvalho (1825–97), who later became manager of that theatre.

Carver, Robert (b. *c.* 1491; d. after 1546), Sco. monk & comp. Lived at Scone Abbey.

Works incl. masses (1 in 10 parts), motets (1 in 19 parts) & other church m.

Cary, Annie Louise (b. Wayne, Me., 22. X. 1842; d. Norwalk, Conn., 3. IV. 1921), Amer. con. singer. Studied at Milan and later with Pauline Viardot. Made her 1st appearance in London and the 1st important one in U.S.A. in 1870.

Caryll, Ivan (real name **Félix Tilkin**) (b. Liége, 1861; d. New York, 28. XI. 1921), Belg.-Amer. comp. Studied at the Liége Cons.

Works incl. operettas *The Duchess of Dantzig, The Earl and the Girl, Our Miss Gibbs,* &c.

Casal y Chapí, Enrique (b. Madrid, 15 I. 1909), Spa. comp., grandson of Chapí. Self-taught at first, he entered the Madrid Cons. in 1928, studying comp. under Conrado del Campo. App. cond. at the Teatro Escuela de Arte in Madrid in 1933, but in 1937 settled in Fr.

Works incl. incid. m. to plays by Lope de Vega, Calderón, Georg Kaiser, &c.; *Fantasía sinfónica*, *Final para una sinfonía imaginaria* & other works for orch.; several songs with orch.; Sonatina & other pf. works, &c.

Casali, Giovanni Battista (b. Rome, *c.* 1713; d. Rome, 6. VII. 1792), It. comp. Chapel master of St. John Lateran, 1759–92. Wrote 9 operas incl. *Candaspe* and *Antigona*; orat. *La benedizione di Giacobbe*; masses, motets, magnificats, &c.

Casanova, opera by Różicky (lib., in Pol., by Juliusz Krzewinski), prod. Warsaw, 3. V. 1923.

Casanova (de Seingalt), Giovanni Jacopo (1725–98) It. adventurer & author, son of an opera singer (Giovanna C.), author & trans. of some libs., acquainted with many singers & comps., friend of Lorenzo da Ponte, &c. *See* **Abenteuer des Casanova** (Andreae), **Casanova** (Różycky), **Pick-Mangiagalli** (ballet).

Casella, Alfredo (b. Turin, 25. VII. 1883), It. comp. Was sent to the Paris Cons. in 1896 to study pf. under Diémer and comp. under Fauré. He lived there until the 1914–18 war, when he went to Rome and taught pf. at the Accademia di Santa Cecilia. In 1924 he founded, with d'Annunzio and Malipiero, an assoc. for the propagation of modern It. m.

Works incl. operas *Il convento veneziano*, *La donna serpente* (after Gozzi), *La favola d'Orfeo*, *Il deserto tentato*; ballet *La giara* (after Pirandello); 3 syms., suite *Italia*, *Elegia eroica*, *Pagine di guerra*, *Introduzione, aria e toccata*, *Concerto* for orch.; *A notte alta*, *Partita* & *Scarlattiana* for pf. & orch.; concs. for v., co., org. & orch.; *Notte di maggio* for voice & orch.; Conc. and 5 pieces for stg. 4tet & other chamber m.; co. & pf. So.; many pf. works incl. Sonatina & *Sinfonia, arioso e toccata*; 2 suites for pf., duet; numerous songs, &c.

Casella, Pietro (b. ?; d. before 1300), It. comp. Friend of Dante, mentioned in the *Divina commedia.* Wrote madrigals.

Casimiri, Rafaele (Casimiro) (b. Gualdo Tadino, Umbria, 3. XI. 1880; d. Rome, IX. 1943), It. mcolst., cond. & comp. Studied at Padua and in 1899 became master of the Schola Cantorum in Rome, and after var. appts. as choirmaster, master at the Lateran there. He wrote a book on Palestrina, ed. the journal *Note d'archivio* and comp. much church m.

Cassa. (It.) = Drum.

Cassandra, opera by Gnecchi (lib. by Luigi Illica), prod. Bologna, Teatro Comunale, 5. XII. 1905. In 1909 the It. critic Giovanni Tebaldini created a sensation by pointing out that R. Strauss's *Elektra*, which did not appear until that year, contained passages strikingly resembling G.'s music.

Cassation (var. langs.). An 18th-cent. comp. of the serenade or divertimento type. The origin of the word is uncertain, the most prob. being its deriv. from the Lat. *quassare* = to shatter (ref. to its several mvts.). Its connections with 'cessation' (a final work) or the Ger. *Gasse* (street, alley) are unlikely.

Casse-Noisette (Tchaikovsky). *See* **Nutcracker.**

Castanets (from Spa. *castañetas*). A perc. inst., doubtless orig. made of chestnut wood (*castaña*), held between the fingers and made to strike against each other by motions of the hand. So used mainly by Spa. dancers, but a simplified form is made for use in orchs. and bands.

Castel, Louis Bertrand (1688–1757), Fr. scientist. He made a study of the relationships between the 7 notes of the mus. scale and the 7 colours of the spectrum, wrote on the subject and constructed a 'Clavecin oculaire.'

Castelnuovo-Tedesco, Mario (b. Florence, 3. IV. 1895), It. comp. Studied at the Istituto Musicale Cherubini at Florence and later with Pizzetti. At the age of 15 he wrote *Cielo di settembre* for pf. (later orch.) and in 1925 he gained a prize for his opera, *La Mandragola* (after Machiavelli). He settled in U.S.A. in 1939, at 1st at Larchmont, N.Y., and then at Los Angeles.

Works incl. operas *La Mandragola*, *Bacco in Toscana* & *Aucassin et Nicolette*; 7 Shakespearian concert ovts.: *The Taming of the Shrew*, *The Merchant of Venice*, *Twelfth Night*, *Julius Caesar*, *A Winter's Tale*, *A Midsummer Night's Dream*, *King John*; 2 pf. concs., *Concerto italiano*, Symph. Vars. and *The Prophets* for v. & orch., Conc. for co. & orch., conc. for guitar & orch.; Concertino for hp. & 7 insts., stg. 4tet, pf. Trio; *So. quasi una fantasia* & Suite on themes by Donizetti for v. & pf., co. & pf. So.; pf. pieces; settings of all the songs in Shakespeare's plays (in Eng.) for voice & pf., *Sonnets from the Port.* (Elizabeth Barrett Browning) & other songs, &c.

Castéra, René de (b. Dax, 3. IV. 1873), Fr. comp. Pupil of d'Indy at the Schola Cantorum in Paris. In 1902 he founded the Édition Mutuelle for the pub. of works by pupils and assocs. of the Schola.

Works incl. ballet-pantomime *Nausicaa*; 2 chors. for Shakespeare's *As You Like It*; *Jour de fête au pays basque* for orch.; Conc. for fl., cl., co. & pf., pf. Trio; pf. pieces; songs, &c.

Castil-Blaze (François Henri Joseph Blaze) (b. Cavaillon, 1. XII. 1784; d. Paris, 11. XII. 1857), Fr. critic, trans. of opera libs. and author of books on m. Critic of the *Journal des Débats* before Berlioz.

Castillon (de Saint-Victor, Marie) Alexis de, Vicomte (b. Chartres, 13. XII. 1838; d. Paris, 5. III. 1873), Fr. comp. After training for a military career at Saint-Cyr, he studied in Paris with Massé and Franck. He served in the war of 1870–1 and lost his health, but before his death served as the 1st secretary of the Société Nationale de Musique.

Works incl. a sym., *Esquisse symph.* & ovt. *Torquato Tasso* for orch.; pf. Conc.; Psalm for solo voices, chor. & orch.; stg. 4tet, pf. 4tet, 2 pf. trios; v. & pf. So.; pf. works; songs, &c.

Castor et Pollux, opera by Rameau (lib. by Pierre Joseph Justin Bernard), prod. Paris, Opéra, 24. X. 1737.

Castore e Polluce (*Castor and Pollux*), opera by Vogler (lib. based on one by Carlo Innocenzio Frugoni), prod. Munich, 12. I. 1787. Weber wrote vars. for pf. on an air from it, Op. 5.

Castrati (It.). Male singers of the 17th & 18th cents., mainly but not exclusively in It., who were mutilated in boyhood to prevent the breaking of their voices and to supply male sops. and cons. to the churches and theatres of the time. The barbarism was orig. committed only because women singers were not allowed in church and sops. & cons. were required to sing m. of greater difficulty than could be managed by boys; but they eventually became fashionable and made their greatest and most sensational successes on the operatic stage.

Castro, Jean de (b. Évreux, ?; d. ?), Fr. 16th-cent. comp. of Spa. or Port. descent. Worked at Antwerp, Vienna, Cologne, &c. Wrote masses, motets, madrigals, chansons.

Castro, Juan (José) (b. Buenos Aires, 7. III. 1895), Arg. cond. & comp. Studied at Buenos Aires and with d'Indy in Paris. On his return he became cond. at the Teatro Colón.

Works incl. ballet *Mekhano*; *Sinfonia Argentina* & *Sinfonía Biblica*, *Allegro, Lento e Vivace*, &c. for orch., &c.

Casulana. *See* **Mezari.**

'Cat's Fugue, The.' The familiar name of a hpchd. So. in G min. by D. Scarlatti. It has a subject rising in curious intervals, as though accidentally picked out by a cat walking over the keyboard; but whether it was suggested by an actual incident of the kind is uncertain.

Catalani, Alfredo (b. Lucca, 19. VI. 1854; d. Milan, 7. VIII. 1893), It. comp. Studied 1st with his father, an orgst., and prod. a Mass at the age of 14. Went to the Paris Cons. in 1871 and then taught at the Milan Cons.

Works incl. operas *La Falce*, *Elda*, *Dejanire*, *Edmea*, *Loreley* & *La Wally*; Mass; symph. poem *Ero e Leandro*, &c.

Catalani, Angelica (b. Sinigaglia, 10. V. 1780; d. Paris, 12. VI. 1849), It. sop. singer. 1st appearance, Teatro La Fenice, Venice, 1795. Went to Port. in 1804, to London in 1806 and became manager of the It. Opera in Paris, 1813.

Catch. A partsong, in vogue in Eng. from the Restor. to the 19th cent., in which the voices follow each other in the manner of a canon or round, with the difference in the most characteristic examples that the words, thus mixed up, acquire new and ludicrous meanings, often of a very indecent nature in the 17th cent.

Catch Club. A soc. named The Noblemen and Gentlemen's C. C., founded in London in 1761 for sociable gatherings and the singing of catches. It still exists.

Catel, Charles Simon (b. L'Aigle, Orne, 10. VI. 1773; d. Paris, 29. XI. 1830), Fr. comp. Pupil of Sacchini and Gossec in Paris. After working as teacher, he became chief musn. with Gossec of the Garde Nationale, for which he wrote much military m., and accompst. at the Opéra in 1790. App. prof. of harmony at the Cons. on its foundation in 1795, and pub. a treatise on the subject in 1802.

Works incl. operas *Sémiramis*, *L'Auberge de Bagnières*, *Les Bayadères*, &c.; *De Profundis*, *Hymn of Victory*; syms. for wind insts.; chor. pieces; chamber m.; songs, &c.

Catgut Strings. Although still often so called, such stgs. are not made of the bowels of cats, but of sheep.

Cath. (abbr.) = Cathedral.

Catleen } **Catling** } The old Eng. names for the top stg. of a lute, connected with cat (catgut).

Catoire, George Lvovitch (b. Moscow, 27. IV. 1861; d. Moscow, 21. V. 1926),

Rus. comp. (?) of Fr. descent. Pupil of Klindworth in Berlin for pf. and Liadov at St. Petersburg for comp. Later app. prof. of comp. at the Moscow Cons.

Works incl. sym. in C min., symph. poem *Mtsyri* (after Lermontov); pf. Conc. in A♭ maj.; chamber m.; sos. and other pf. works, &c.

Catterall, Arthur (b. Preston, Lancs., 1883; d. London, 28. XI. 1943), Eng. vst. Studied in Manchester, became a member of the Queen's Hall Orch. in London in 1909, later of the Hallé Orch. in Manchester and in 1929 of the B.B.C. Orch., which he left in 1936. He founded a stg. 4tet in 1910.

Cauldron of Annwen, The, operatic trilogy by Holbrooke (lib. by Thomas Evelyn Ellis = Lord Howard de Walden).

I. **The Children of Don,** prod. London Opera House, 15. VI. 1912.

II. **Dylan, Son of the Wave,** prod. London, Drury Lane Theatre, 4. VII. 1914.

III. **Bronwen,** prod. Huddersfield, 1. II. 1929.

Caurroy, François (Eustache) du, Sieur de Saint-Frémin (b. Gerberoy nr. Beauvais, 1549; d. Paris, 7. VIII. 1609), Fr. comp. Went to Paris *c.* 1569 as a singer in the royal chapel, where he became master of the children in 1583. He became a canon in the Sainte-Chapelle and the title of Surintendant de la Musique du Roy was created for him in 1599.

Works incl. Requiem, motets, psalms, noëls, 2 books of *Preces ecclesiasticae*; inst. fantasies on sacred and secular tunes, &c.

Causton, Thomas (b. ?; d. London, 28. X. 1569), Eng. comp. Gentleman of the Chapel Royal in London. Comp. services, anthems, psalms, and contrib. to Day's *Certaine Notes.*

Cavaccio, Giovanni (b. Bergamo, *c.* 1556; d. Bergamo, 11. VIII. 1626), It. comp. Chapel master at Bergamo cath. in 1581 and later at the church of Santa Maria Maggiore there. Wrote a Requiem, magnificats, psalms, madrigals, &c. and contrib. psalms to a collection dedicated to Palestrina.

Cavalieri, Catharina (b. Währing nr. Vienna, 19. II. 1760; d. Vienna, 30. VI. 1801), Aus. sop. singer. Pupil of Salieri in Vienna, where she appeared at the It. opera at the age of 14 and was transferred to the Ger. opera a year later.

Cavalieri, Emilio de' (b. Rome, *c.* 1550; d. Rome, 11. III. 1602), It. comp. He was long in the service of Ferdinando de' Medici at Florence, where he was in close touch with the *Camerata*, and with them worked towards the evolution of opera, though his own works were still dramatic pieces to be perf. in concert form. They are the following, all set to words by Laura Guidiccioni: *Il satiro, La disperazione di Fileno, Il giuoco della cieca* & *La rappresentazione di anima e di corpo*, a kind of mystery play prod. in 1600.

Cavalieri, Lina (b. Viterbo, 25. XII. 1874; d. Florence, I. 1944), It. sop. singer. Born of humble parents, she 1st sang in cafés, but later studied seriously and made her 1st appearance in opera at Lisbon in 1901. 1st visited Eng. in 1908, but made her greatest successes in U.S.A. She was killed in an air raid.

Cavalleria rusticana (*Rustic Chivalry*), opera by Mascagni (lib. by Guido Menasci & Giovanni Targioni-Tozzetti, based on Giovanni Verga's play), prod. Rome, Teatro Costanzi, 17. V. 1890.

Cavalli, Pietro Francesco (b. Crema, 14. II. 1602; d. Venice, 14. I. 1676), It. comp. Became a singer under Monteverdi at St. Mark's, Venice, in 1617, 2nd orgst. of that church in 1640, 1st orgst. in 1665 and chapel master in 1668. His 1st opera was prod. in 1639, and in 1660 he was called to Paris to perform his *Serse* at Louis XIV's marriage. He wrote operas for the 5 theatres of Venice.

Works incl. operas *Le nozze di Teti e di Peleo, Gli amori di Apollo e di Dafne, La Didone, L'Egisto, Il Giasone, L'Oristeo, Serse, Il Ciro, L'Erismena, L'Hipermestra, Ercole amante, Scipione Africano, Mutio Scevola, Il Coriolano* & *c.* 20 others; masses, motets, psalms, antiphons, vespers, a Requiem, &c.

Cavatina (It. poss. from *cavata* = a digging-out; in m. prod. sound). A tune, played by an inst. or sung, usually taking the form of a short, sustained piece or air.

Cavazzoni, Girolamo (b. ? Urbino, *c.* 1500; d. ? Venice, 1560), It. orgst. & comp. He worked at Venice and comp. org. m., e.g. that pub. in his *Intavolatura* in 1542. An early exponent of the inst. canzone.

Cavendish, Michael (b. ? Cavendish Overhall, Suffolk, *c.* 1565; d. London, ? VII. 1628), Eng. comp. Belonging to a noble family, he seems to have held no apps. He contrib. to East's *Whole Booke of Psalmes* in 1592 and pub. a vol. of his own comps., ded. to Lady Arabella Stuart, his 2nd cousin, in 1598, containing 20 airs to the lute, or with 3 other voices, and 8 madrigals. He also contrib. a madrigal to *The Triumphes of Oriana.*

Caverne, La (*The Cave*), opera by

Lesueur (lib. by P. Dercy, from an episode in Lesage's *Gil Blas*), prod. Paris, Théâtre Feydeau, 16. II. 1793.

Cavos, Catterino (b. Venice, 1776; d. St. Petersburg, 28. IV. 1840), It. comp. Assisted his father, who was cond. at the Teatro La Fenice, later cond. at Padua and taught at Venice. In 1797 he went to Rus. with Astaritto's opera co., and 2 years later became dir. of the It. and Rus. operas there, for which he had to write works in both languages, as well as some in Fr. His Rus. opera, *Ivan Susanin*, prod. in 1815, was very successful.

Cazzati, Maurizio (b. Guastalla, *c.* 1620; d. Mantua, 1677), It. orgst. & comp. Held successive posts at Mantua, Ferrara, Bergamo and Bologna. Comp. secular voc. and inst. m. as well as works for the church.

Ce qu'on entend sur la montagne (*What is heard on the Mountain*), symph. poem by Liszt, based on a poem by Victor Hugo, comp. 1848–9, 1st perf. Weimar, II. 1850.

Cebell. A dance occurring in Eng. 17th-cent. m., similar to the Gavotte.

Cecchina, La (Piccinni). *See* **Buona figliuola.**

Čech, Svatopluk (1846–1908), Cz. novelist & dramatist. *See* **Janáček** (*Excursions of Mr. Brouček*), **Kovařovic** (do.).

Cecilia, Saint (b. ?; d. Sicily, 176–80), the patron saint of m. and the blind. She is said to have suffered martyrdom under Marcus Aurelius with her husband and other friends she had converted to Christianity and to have praised God by voc. and inst. m. Her festival is 22. XI.

Cédez (Fr. imper. lit. cede, give, surrender) = hold back. A direction used by Debussy and some other Fr. comps. to indicate a *ritenuto*.

Celesta. A keyboard inst. brought out by Mustel of Paris in the 1880s. The tone is prod. by hammers struck upon steel plates.

Celestina. A 4-ft. org. stop of delicate tone.

Cellier, Alfred (b. London, 1. XII. 1844; d. London, Dec. 28, 1891), Eng. comp. Having been a choir-boy in the Chapel Royal, he held var. orgst.'s appts., was cond. at Belfast and theatre cond. at Manchester and London.

Works incl. numerous operettas, e.g. *The Sultan of Mocha, Nell Gwynne, The Foster-Brothers, Dorothy, The Mountebanks* (lib. by Gilbert); opera *The Masque of Pandora* (lib. by Longfellow); Gray's *Elegy* for chor. & orch.; *Suite symphonique* for orch.; pf. pieces; songs, &c.

Cellini, Benvenuto (1500–71). It. sculptor, craftsman & autobiog. *See* **Benvenuto Cellini** (Berlioz), **Lachner (F.).**

Cello (It. dim. ending). The colloquial name of the Violoncello, so generally current that it should be taken up into literary Eng., not with the apostrophe still sometimes used ('cello), which it does not require any more than 'bus' or 'phone' do. Strictly speaking the name is as absurd as is 'piano,' but then so are 'pianoforte' (soft-loud) and violoncello, which comes from *violone* (a big fiddle, *-one* being an augment. ending), modified over again by the dim. ending (a little big fiddle). It is a pity that a good Eng. word has never been adopted. Chamber-m. players sometimes call the inst. their 'bass,' but that has the disadvantage of having other connotations as well.

Cellone (It. lit. big Co.). A modern co. of large size made by Stelzner of Dresden, capable of being played seated and intended to supply a double bass inst. for chamber m. It has 4 stgs. tuned in perfect 5ths from E in the 3rd space of the stave in the bass clef downwards.

Celos aun del ayre matan (*Jealousy, even of the air, is deadly*), opera on the subject of Cephalus and Procris by Juan Hidalgo (lib. by Calderón), prod. Madrid, Buen Retiro, 5. XII. 1660. The 1st Spa. opera.

Cembalist. Hpchd. player. *See also* **Maestro al cembalo.**

Cembalo (It. abbr. for clavicembalo, accent therefore on 1st syll.) = Hpchd.; also used to designate a Thorough-bass *continuo* part.

Cendrillon (*Cinderella*), opera by Isouard (lib. by Charles Guillaume Étienne, after Perrault), prod. Paris, Opéra-Comique, 22. II. 1810.

Opera by Laruette (lib. by Louis Anseaume, after Perrault), prod. Paris, Opéra-Comique, 21. II. 1759.

Opera by Massenet (lib. by Henri Cain, after Perrault), prod. Paris, Opéra-Comique, 24. V. 1899.

Opera by Steibelt (lib. by Étienne), prod. St. Petersburg, 26. X. 1810.

Cenerentola (*Cinderella*), opera by Wolf-Ferrari (lib. by Maria Pezzè-Pescolato, after Perrault), prod. Venice, Teatro La Fenice, 22. II. 1900.

Cenerentola, La, ossia La bontà in trionfo (*Cinderella, or The Triumph of Goodness*), opera by Rossini (lib. by Jacopo Ferretti, based on Étienne's), prod. Rome, Teatro Valle, 25. I. 1817.

Céphale et Procris, opera by Grétry (lib. by Marmontel), prod. Versailles, at court, 30. XII. 1773; 1st Paris perf., Opéra, 2. V. 1775.

Cephalus and Procris, opera by Araia (lib., in Rus., by Alexander Petrovitch Sumarokov), prod. St. Petersburg, at court, 10. III. 1755.

Cercar la nota (It. = seeking the note). Anticipating a note in singing before it is due; scooping.

Černohorsky, Bohuslav Matěj (b. Nymburg, Boh., 1684; d. ?, 1742), Boh. comp., theorist and friar. Held church apps. at Padua and Assisi, where Tartini was his pupil. From about 1735 he was dir. of m. at St. James's church in Prague.

Certon, Pierre (b. ? Melun, ?; d. Paris, 23. II. 1572), Fr. comp. He was in the Sainte-Chapelle in Paris, 1532, and became choirmaster there before 1542 and chaplain in 1548. As a canon of Notre-Dame at Melun he founded an annual service there.

Works incl. masses, *c.* 50 motets, psalms, canticles, *c.* 200 chansons, &c.

Cervantes, Miguel de (1547–1616), Spa. novelist & dramatist. For operas, &c. based on *Don Quixote see* **Abrányi (E.), Akeroyde, Auric** (ballet), **Caldara** (*Don Chisciotte*), **Champein, Clay, Conti** (F. B.), **Courteville, Dittersdorf, Don Chisciotte** (2 operas), **Don Quichotte** (Massenet), **Don Quixote** (Kienzl & R. Strauss, symph. poem), **D. Q., The Comical History of** (Purcell & others), **Esplá, Generali, Gerhard** (ballet & radio play), **Hervé, Heuberger, Hochzeit des Gamacho** (Mendelssohn), **Ibert** (film), **Khrennikov** (incid. m.), **Lalande** (*Folies de Cardenio*), **Lattuada** (*Caverna di Salamanca*), **Leo** (*Fantastico*), **Macfarren (G.), Mackenzie, Martini (G. B.), Marawski** (symph. poem), **Paisiello, Pessard, Ravel** (*Don Quichotte à Dulcinée*), **Reeve** (*Harlequin Q.*), **Retablo de Maese Pedro** (Falla), **Rubinstein (A.)** (mus. portrait), **Sancho Pança dans son île** (Philidor), **Sancho Panza** (Jaques Dalcroze), **Sancio Panza** (Caldara), **Serrano y Ruiz** (*Primera salida*), **Treu, Weinberger** (orch. work).

Other works *see* **Padlock** (Dibdin), **Paumgartner** (*Höhle von Salamanca*), **Preciosa** (Weber).

Cervetto, Giacomo Bassevi (b. ?, 1682; d. London, 14. I. 1783), It. vst. & comp. Settled in London in 1728. Wrote m. for his inst. and chamber m.

Cervetto, James (b. London, 1747; d. London, 5. II. 1837), Eng. cst. & comp. of It. descent, son of prec. Pupil of his father. Comp. m. for his inst.

Cesti, Marc' Antonio (b. Arezzo, 5. VIII. 1623; d. Florence, 14. X. 1669), It. comp. Pupil of Carissimi; became a member of the Papal Choir in Rome, 1660, after having been chapel master at Florence, and was app. vice chapel master to the Aus. court in 1666.

Works incl. operas *L'Orontea, Il Cesare amante, Alessandro il vincitor di se stesso, L'Argia, La Dori, Tito, Nettuno e Fiora festeggianti, Il pomo d'oro, Semiramide, Le disgrazie d'Amore*; orat. *Judicium Salomonis* (?); motets; cantatas for sop., canzonets, &c.

Ch. The sound of the Rus. letter *ч* is reprod. in this book by **Tch.**, this form having been made familiar by the transliteration of 'Tchaikovsky.'

Chabrier, (Alexis) Emmanuel (b. Ambert, Puy-de-Dôme, 18. I. 1841; d. Paris, 13. IX. 1894), Fr. comp. Studied law and was employed at the Ministry of the Interior, but cultivated m. as a gifted amateur. Having prod. 2 operettas in 1877 & 1879, he devoted himself entirely to comp. After the prod. of *Le Roi malgré lui*, the run of which was interrupted by the fire of the Opéra-Comique, he came under the influence of Wagner. Towards the end of his life he became the victim of acute melancholia, bordering on insanity.

Works incl. operas *Le Roi malgré lui, Gwendoline* & *Briséïs* (unfinished); operettas *L'Étoile* & *L'Éducation manquée*; rhapsody *España* & *Joyeuse Marche* for orch.; *La Sulamite* for m.-sop., chor. & orch.; 10 *Pièces pittoresques, Habanera* & *Bourrée fantasque*, &c. for pf.; 3 *Valses romantiques* for 2 pfs.; songs, &c.

Chaccon (Eng., obs.) = Chaconne.

Chace (old Fr. = *chasse* = chase, hunt). A 14th-cent. term for Canon, because the parts 'chase' each other.

Chaconne (Fr.). Orig. a dance, prob. of Spa. provenance. Now a comp. on an unvarying ground-bass which goes on throughout the piece and over which, at each reappearance, the upper parts are freely varied in different ways. This definition applies truly even to Bach's Chaconne for unaccomp. v., for although there the bass cannot be always present, it is always implied even when not actually heard.

Chacony (Eng., obs.) = Chaconne. A pretty word worth reviving.

Chaccoon (Eng., obs.) = Chaconne.

Chadwick, George (Whitefield) (b. Lowell, Mass., 13. XI. 1854; d. Boston, 4. IV. 1931), Amer. comp. Studied at Boston, Leipzig and Munich, in the last place under Rheinberger. Returned to Amer. in 1880, became orgst. at Boston, then prof. at the New Eng. Cons. and its dir. in 1897.

Works incl. operas *Tabasco, Judith, The Padrone*, &c.; chor. & orch.

works *The Viking's Last Voyage, The Song of the Viking, Lovely Rosabel, The Lily Nymph, Phoenix expirans,* &c.; 3 syms., symph. poems *Cleopatra, Aphrodite, Angel of Death, Tam o' Shanter* (after Burns), ovts. *Rip van Winkle, Thalia, Melpomene, Adonis* (after Shelley), *Euterpe,* &c., *Symph. Sketches, Sinfonietta, Suite symphonique*; 5 stg. 4tets, pf. 5tet; songs with orch. & with pf.; pf. & org. works; church m.; partsongs, &c.

Chair Organ = Choir Organ.

Châlet, Le, opera by Adam (lib. by Eugène Scribe & Anne Honoré Joseph Mélesville), prod. Paris, Opéra-Comique, 25. IX. 1834.

Chaliapine. *See* **Shaliapin.**

Chalumeau (Fr. = chanter). The pipe of the bagpipes on which the melody is played. The Fr. name is also given to a single-reed wind inst., the forerunner of the cl., and sometimes to a double-reed one which preceded the ob. (shawm). C. is, moreover, the name for the lowest register of the cl.

Chamber Music. Domestic m. played in a private room, often by amateurs, and consisting of works assigning individual parts to a few players (more rarely singers), to be enjoyed by themselves rather than by an audience: but C. M. is perfectly capable of being transferred to the concert room, the radio or the gramophone, and is best done justice to by professional players.

Chamber Sonata. *See* **Sonata da camera.**

Chamberlain, Houston Stewart (b. Portsmouth, 9. IX. 1855; d. Bayreuth, 9. I. 1927), Eng. writer, mainly on Wagner. Educ. at Cheltenham and in Fr. Married Wagner's daughter Eva and became a naturalized Ger. Great champion of Wagner and propagandist of Pan-Ger. theories. Hitler's ideal Englishman.

Chambonnières, Jacques Champion de (b. ? Brie district, 1602; d. Paris, *c.* 1672), Fr. hpchdst. & comp. In the service of Louis XIII & XIV, also for a time in Swe. He taught several of the later hpchdsts. and pub. 2 books of hpchd. pieces.

Chaminade, Cécile (b. Paris, 8. VIII. 1857; d. Monte Carlo, 17. IV. 1944), Fr. pfst. & comp. Studied with var. masters, incl. Godard for comp. Began to comp. at the age of 8, and at 18 gave her 1st concert. Toured widely in Fr. and Eng.

Works incl. comic opera *La Sévillane*; ballet *Callirhoë*; *Symphonie lyrique* for chor. & orch.; suites for orch.; *Concertstück* for pf. & orch.; 2 pf. trios; numerous light pf. pieces; songs, &c.

Chamisso, Adelbert von (1781–1838), Ger. poet & novelist of Fr. descent. *See* **Frauenliebe und Leben** (Schumann), **Jensen** (*Tränen*), **Palmgren** (*Peter Schlemihl*), **Rezniček** (do.).

Champein, Stanislas (b. Marseilles, 19. XI. 1753; d. Paris, 19. IX. 1830), Fr. comp. Went to Paris in 1770 and prod. a comic opera in 1780, which was followed by some 50 other works for the stage, incl. (?) a setting of a Fr. prose trans. of Sophocles' *Electra,* rehearsed at the Opéra, but prohibited.

Works incl. operas *La Mélomanie, Le Nouveau Don Quichotte,* &c.; masses & other church m., &c.

Chandos Anthems. 12 anthems by Handel, comp. 1716–8 for the Earl of Carnarvon, later Duke of Chandos, for perf. in his private chapel at Canons nr. Edgware.

Chanson (Fr. = song). In a special technical sense the C. is an old Fr. partsong cultivated in Fr. before and during the period the madrigal occupied the comps. of the Nthlds., It. & Eng. It approximates, however, more closely to the lighter type of the canzonet.

Chansons de geste (Fr. = songs of deeds, epic or heroic songs). 11th–14th-cent. verse-chronicles written mostly by Trouvères and recited or sung by Jongleurs.

Chant. In Catholic church m. the singing of psalms, canticles, masses, &c. in plainsong to Lat. words; in Angl. church m. the singing of the psalms to harmonized and measured tunes, the rhythm of which may, however, be modified or obscured by the necessity to fit longer or shorter psalm verses.

Chant-Fable (Fr. = song-fable). A 13th-cent. narrative Fr. Trouvère song.

Chantavoine, Jean (François Henri) (b. Paris, 17. V. 1877), Fr. mcolst. Studied m. and philos. at the univs. of Paris & Berlin. M. critic of the *Revue hebdomadaire* 1903–20 and *Excelsior* 1911–20, and contrib. to mus. journals. Wrote books on Beethoven, Liszt, m. & poetry, Fr. m., &c., and trans. Beethoven's letters as well as a number of operas and songs by Mozart, Brahms, Wagner, R. Strauss, &c.

Chanter. The pipe of the bagpipes on which the melody is played.

Chanterelle (Fr. lit. the singing one). The E stg. of the v. or (less often) the highest stg. of any stged. inst.

Chanty. *See* **Shanty.**

Chapeau chinois (Fr. = Chin. hat) = Chinese Pavilion.

Chapel Master (Fr. maître de chapelle; Ger. Capellmeister or Kapellmeister;

It. maestro di cappella; Spa. maestro de capilla). Orig. the master of the choristers in any chapel, church or cath., and still so in Fr., It. and Spa.; but more loosely used in Ger. as meaning simply a cond. All the foreign uses of the title are trans. 'chapel master' throughout this book, unless cond. is meant.

Chapel Royal. The Eng. court chapel, incl. not only the building but the whole institution, dating back to the 12th cent. at the latest.

Chapí, Ruperto (b. Villena nr. Alicante, 27. III. 1851; d. Madrid, 25. III. 1909), Spa. comp. Studied at the Madrid Cons. and in 1872 was given a mus. post in the artillery. Lived in Rome for a time from 1873.

Works incl. operas *Margarita la Tornera, La serenata, Roger de Flor, Circe* & 4 others, 30 zarzuelas; orat. *Los Angeles, Veni Creator* for double chor. & orch. Sym. in D min., Moorish fantasy *La corte de Granada*, legend *Los gnomos de la Alhambra* & other orch. works; *Jota* for v. & orch.; 4 stg. 4tets, pf. Trio; pf. pieces; songs, &c.

Chaplet, The, mus. stage entertainment by Boyce (lib. by Moses Mendez), prod. London, Drury Lane Theatre, 2. XII. 1749.

Chapuis, Auguste (Paul Jean-Baptiste) (b. Dampierre-sur-Sâlon, 20. IV. 1858; d. Paris, 6. XII. 1933), Fr. orgst. & comp. Studied at the Paris Cons. under Dubois, Massenet & Franck. He became orgst. at 2 Paris churches and prof. of harmony at the Cons., also mus. inspector of schools and examiner of military bands and chor. cond.

Works incl. operas *Enguerrande* & *Les Demoiselles de Saint-Cyr*; *Tableaux flamands* for orch.; sos. for v. & pf. and co. & pf.; songs, &c.

Charakterstück (Ger. = character or characteristic piece). A short inst. piece outlining some definite mood, human character or literary conception.

Charles V (Křenek). *See* **Karl V.**

Charleston. An Amer. dance stemming from the Foxtrot, of which it is a debased form.

Charpentier, Gustave (b. Dieuze, Meurthe, 25. VI. 1860), Fr. comp. Went into business at Tourcoing at the age of 15, but studied m. at the Lille and Paris Conss., gaining at the latter the Prix de Rome as a pupil of Massenet in 1887. In 1902 he founded the Cons. de Mimi Pinson, providing free instruction in m. and an opera theatre for working-class girls.

Works incl. operas *Louise* & *Julien*; cantata *Didon*; symph. drama for solo voices, chor. & orch, *La Vie du poète* (afterwards used in *Julien*); orch. suite *Impressions d'Italie*; *Fête du couronnement de la Muse* (later used in *Louise*); *Impressions fausses* (Verlaine) and *Sérénade à Watteau* for voice & orch.; *Poèmes chantés* and 5 poems from Baudelaire's *Fleurs du mal* for voice & pf., &c.

Charpentier, Marc-Antoine (b. Paris, 1634; d. Paris, 24. II. 1704), Fr. comp. Pupil of Carissimi in Rome. On his return he became domestic musn. to Mlle de Guise and comp. to the Comédie-Française, where he worked with Molière and continued after M.'s death. In 1679 he was app. church comp. to the Dauphin; later m. master to a Jesuit coll. and comp. teacher to the Duke of Orleans. In 1698 he became chapel master at the Sainte-Chapelle.

Works incl. operas *Les Amours d'Acis et Galatée, La Descente d'Orphée aux enfers, Endimion, Médée* & c. 12 others; incid. m. for Molière's *La Comtesse d'Escarbagnas* & *Le Malade imaginaire*, for P. Corneille's *Polyeucte* & *Andromède*, T. Corneille's *La Pierre philosophale*, T. Corneille & Visé's *Circé* & *L'Inconnu* and Visé's *Les Amours de Vénus et d'Adonis*; ballets, &c.; c. 10 masses, Requiem, motets, psalms and other church m., some with orch.; orats., cantatas *Histoires sacrées, Tragédies spirituelles*; voc. chamber m., *Airs sérieux et à boire*; inst. pieces, &c.

Charton-Demeur (*née* Charton), **Anne Arsène** (b. Saujon, 5. III. 1824; d. Paris, 30. XI. 1892), Fr. sop. singer. Made her 1st appearance at Bordeaux in 1842.

Chartreuse de Parme, La (*The Carthusian Monastery of Parma*), opera by Sauguet (lib. by Armand Lunel, based on Stendhal's novel), prod. Paris, Opéra, 16. III. 1939.

Chase, Gilbert (b. Havana, 4. IX. 1906), Amer. m. critic. Studied in N.Y. and Paris, where he lived in 1929–35 as m. critic to the *Daily Mail*. In 1936 he settled in N.Y. Made a special study of Spa. m. and wrote *The M. of Spa.*

Chasse. *See* **Chace.**

Chasse, La (*The Chase*), the nickname of a Sym. by Haydn, No. 73, in D maj., comp. in 1781; also of his stg. 4tet in B♭ maj., Op. 1 No. 1, written c. 1755.

Chasseur maudit, Le (*The Accursed Huntsman*), symph. poem by Franck, based on a ballad by Bürger, comp. 1882.

Chateaubriand, François René, Vicomte de (1768–1848), Fr. poet &

novelist. *See* **Franck** (**C.**) (songs), **Lenepveu** (*Velléda*), **Pedrell** (**F.**) (*Último Abencerraje*).

Chaucer, Geoffrey (?1340–1400), Eng. poet. *See* **Canterbury Pilgrims** (Stanford), **Dyson** (*Canterbury Pilgrims*), **Fée Urgèle** (Duni), **Koven** (*Canterbury Pilgrims*), **Pleyel** (**I.**) (*Fée Urgèle*).

Chausson, Ernest (b. Paris, 21. I. 1855; d. Limay, 10. VI. 1899), Fr. comp. Pupil of Massenet at the Paris Cons., then of Franck. He never held an official app., but helped to found the Société Nationale de Musique and was its sec. 1889–99. He d. after a bicycle accident.

Works incl. operas *Le Roi Arthus*, *La Légende de Sainte Cécile*, &c.; incid. m. to Shakespeare's *Tempest*; Sym. in B♭ maj., symph. poem *Viviane*; *Poème de l'amour et de la mer* for voice & orch.; stg. 4tet (unfinished), Conc. for v. & pf. with stg. 4tet, pf. Trio, pf. 4tet, *Chanson perpétuelle* for voice, stg. 4tet & pf.; pf. & org. pieces; 10 op. nos. of songs, &c.

Chauvet, Charles (**Alexis**) (b. Marines, Seine-et-Oise, 7. VI. 1837; d. Argentan, Orne, 28. I. 1871), Fr. orgst. & comp. Studied org. under Benoist and comp. under A. Thomas at the Paris Cons. and after filling var. posts was app. orgst. at the church of the Trinité there, 1869. He wrote much for org. & pf.

Chávez, Carlos (b. Mexico City, 13. VI. 1899), Mex. comp. of mixed Indian and Spa. descent. He was taught m. as a child by his brother and 2 casual teachers, but later went to Eur. and N.Y. to gain experience. In 1928 he founded a Mex. sym. orch., of which he later became cond., and the same year he became dir. of the Nat. Cons. A post in the Dept. of Fine Arts enabled him to do still more for the country's mus. reorganization, and he did much to explore Mex. folk m.

Works incl. ballets *El fuego nuevo*, *Los cuatros soles* and *H.P.*; *Energía*, *Sinfonía de Antigona*, *Sinfonía proletaria* & *Sinfonía India* for orch.; concs. for hp. and for pf. & orch.; *El sol* for chor. & orch.; stg. 4tet; So. for 4 hns.; pf. pieces, &c.

Checkmate. Ballet by Bliss (chgph. by Ninette de Valois), prod. by Sadler's Wells Ballet, Paris, Théâtre des Champs-Élysées, 15. VI. 1937; 1st London perf., Sadler's Wells Theatre, 5. X. 1937.

Chef d'orchestre (Fr. = chief of the orch.) = Conductor.

Chekker. A 14th–16th-cent. keyboard inst. used in Eng., Fr. and Spa., in which latter countries it was called *échiquier* and *exaquir* (and similar names). It was an inst. akin to the Virginal, square in shape and (?) not unlike a chessboard.

Chelard, Hippolyte (**André Jean Baptiste**) (b. Paris, 1. II. 1789; d. Weimar, 12. II. 1861), Fr. cond. & comp. Studied at the Paris Cons., v. under R. Kreutzer and comp. under Gossec, Méhul and Cherubini. Gained the Prix de Rome in 1811, studied church m. in Rome under Baini and Zingarelli, afterwards opera with Paisiello and Fioravanti at Naples, where he prod. an It. comic opera in 1815. In 1818 he became vst. at the Paris Opéra, where he prod. *Macbeth* in 1827. After the 1830 Revol. he settled at Munich and remained in Ger. to the end of his life. In 1832 & 1833 he cond. Ger. opera in London, with Schröder-Devrient and Haitzinger as the chief singers. In 1836 he became court mus. dir. at Weimar.

Works incl. operas *La casa da vendere*, *Macbeth* (in Fr., lib. by Rouget de l'Isle), *La Table et le logement* (later Ger. version *Der Student*), *Mitternacht*, *Die Hermannschlacht*, &c.

Chemineau, Le (*The Tramp*), opera by Leroux (lib. by Jean Richepin), prod. Paris, Opéra-Comique, 6. XI. 1907.

Chénier, Joseph (1764–1811), Fr. poet & dramatist. *See* **Méhul** (*Timoléon*).

Cherubini, (Maria) Luigi (**Carlo Zenobio Salvatore**) (b. Florence, 14. IX. 1760; d. Paris, 15. III. 1842), It. comp. Studied 1st under his father, a musn. at the Teatro della Pergola at Florence, then under var. min. masters At the age of 16 he had written an orat., masses, &c. About 1778, with a grant from the Grand Duke, he went to study with Sarti at Venice and in 1780 he prod. his 1st opera, *Quinto Fabio*. In 1785 & 1786 he prod. *La finta principessa* and *Giulio Sabino* in London and was app. Composer to the King, but left for Paris in the latter year. After a brief return to It. he settled in Paris for good in 1788 and prod. his 1st Fr. opera, *Démophon*, there, to a lib. by Marmontel. He now became very busy cond. and comp. opera, but was not very successful, chiefly owing to Napoleon's dislike of him. In 1795 he married Cécile Tourette. In 1806 he prod. *Faniska* in Vienna, where it had been specially commissioned, and met Beethoven, who admired his work and whose *Fidelio* was influenced by it. On his return to Fr. he lived retired and embittered at the Prince de Chimay's country residence and there wrote church m. as well as more operas. In 1816 he and

Lesueur became attached to the royal chapel with large salaries and in 1822 he became dir. of the Cons.

Works incl. operas *Armida abbandonata, Alessandro nell' Indie, Demetrio, Artaserse, Ifigenia in Aulide, Lodoïska* (Fr.), *Médée, Les Deux Journées (The Water Carrier), Anacréon, ou L'Amour fugitif, Faniska, Pimmalione, Les Abencérages, Bayard à Mézières, Ali Baba, ou Les Quarante Voleurs*; ballet-pantomime *Achille à Scyros*; 7 masses and a coronation mass, 2 Requiems (1 for male voices); Sym. in D maj., 2 ovts. and a funeral march for orch.; 6 stg. 4tets, stg. 5tet, &c.

Chest of Viols. A set of (usually 6) viols of var. sizes in a cupboard or chest, an article of furniture almost as common in Eng. families of the 16th & 17th cents. as the pf. is in modern households.

Chest Voice. One of the so-called 'registers' in singing, used or said to be used for the lower notes of the singer's range, and so called because its resonance gives the sensation of being lodged in the chest, not in the head, as in the case of the Head Voice.

Chester Musical Festival. Opened in 1772 and continued irregularly until 1829; a 2nd series began in 1879 and was given triennially until 1900.

Cheval de bronze, Le (*The Bronze Horse*), opera by Auber (lib. by Eugène Scribe), prod. Paris, Opéra-Comique, 23. III. 1835.

Chevalet (Fr.). V. bridge.

Chevillard, (Paul Alexandre) Camille (b. Paris, 14. X. 1859; d. Chatou, 30. V. 1923), Fr. cond. & comp. Pupil of Chabrier and son-in-law of Lamoureux, whose concerts he cond. after L.'s retirement.

Works incl. incid. m. for E. Schuré's play *La Roussalka*; *Ballade symphonique*, symph. poem *Le Chêne et le Roseau* & *Fantaisie symphonique* for orch.; stg. 4tet, pf. 5tet, 4tet & Trio; sos. for v. & pf. and co. & pf.; Vars. & *Étude chromatique* for pf.; v. and co. pieces, &c.

Cheville (Fr.). V. peg.

Chevroté (Fr.). *See* **Ornaments.**

Chézy (*née* **von Klencke**), **Wilhelmine (or Helmina) von** (1783–1856), Ger. dramatist & novelist. Wrote the lib. of Weber's *Euryanthe* and the play *Rosamunde* for which Schubert provided incid. m.

Chgph. (abbr.) Choreographer, choreographic, choreography.

Chiavetta (It. lit. little key, actually little clef). Chiavette (plur.) were used by comps. before the 17th cent. to change the clefs in voc. m. temporarily when the voice-part threatened to go far above or below the stave, to avoid leger-lines. The practice has fallen completely out of use.

Child, William (b. Bristol, 1606; d. Windsor, 23. III. 1697), Eng. comp. & orgst. Educ. at Bristol cath. and app. one of the orgsts. at St. George's Chapel, Windsor, in 1632. At the Restor. he received a court appt. and in 1663 he took the Mus.D. degree at Oxford.

Works incl. *c.* 25 services, *c.* 50 anthems, motet *O bone Jesu*, 20 psalms for 3 voices with thorough-bass, chants, *Magnificat in Gamut*, Te Deum & Jubilate and other church m.; secular voc. pieces, catches and ayres; 2 suites of dances for viols, &c.

Childe, Ann. *See* **Seguin, Arthur.**

Childhood of Christ (Berlioz). *See* **Enfance du Christ.**

Children of Don, The (Holbrooke). *See* **Cauldron of Annwen.**

Children's Corner. A set of pf. pieces, with Eng. titles, by Debussy, comp. in 1906–8, ded. to his daughter Claude-Emma D. (Chouchou): 1. *Doctor Gradus ad Parnassum*; 2. *Jimbo's Lullaby*; 3. *Serenade for the Doll*; 4. *Snow is dancing*; 5. *The Little Shepherd*; 6. *Golliwog's Cake-Walk.*

Chilean Composer. *See* **Allende.**

Chilesotti, Oscar (b. Bassano, 12. VII. 1848; d. Bassano, 20. VI. 1916), It. mcolst. Studied law at Padua Univ. Ed. much old It. m. and wrote several learned books.

Chime-Bells. *See* **Glockenspiel.**

Chin. (abbr.) = Chinese.

Chinese Block (or **Temple Block**). A perc. inst. in the shape of a hollow wooden box on which a dry, rapping sound is prod. It is used in jazz bands rather than in orchs.

Chinese Pavilion. An inst. shaped like a tree or pagoda and hung with brass plates and small bells, shaken to make a jingling noise and used in military bands, esp. in the 18th cent. It was popularly called 'Jingling Johnny' or 'Turkish Crescent.'

Chiroplast. Logier's apparatus invented in the early years of the 19th cent. to facilitate pf. practice by mechanically making the hands flexible.

Chishko, Oles. *See* **Tchishko.**

Chisholm, Erik (b. Glasgow, 1904), Sco. pfst., orgst., cond. & comp. Studied comp. under Tovey and in 1934 took the Mus.D. degree at Edinburgh Univ. After touring in Canada he returned to Glasgow as orgst. & cond., founded a soc. for the propagation of modern m. in 1930 and became cond. of the Glasgow Grand Opera Co., with which he has given interesting perfs., partic. of Berlioz's operas.

Works incl. opera *Isle of Youth* (lib. by comp.); ballets *The Forsaken Mermaid* & *The Pied Piper of Hamelin*; 2 syms.; ovt. *The Friars of Berwick*; pf. Conc., *Straloch Suite* for pf. & stgs.; double Trio for wind & stgs., &c.

Chitarrone (It. lit. big guitar, from *chitarra* with augment. ending). A very large double-necked lute or theorbo, used as a bass to the lute family in It. in the 17th cent.

Chladni, Ernst (Florens Friedrich) (b. Wittenberg, 30. XI. 1756; d. Breslau, 3. IV. 1827), Ger scientist. After studying both law and medicine he devoted himself to physics, made important researches into acoustics and wrote numerous books on the subject.

Chlubna, Oswald (b. Brno, 22. VII. 1893), Cz. comp. Pupil of Janáček and later prof. at the Brno Cons.

Works incl. operas *Catullus's Vengeance, Alladine and Palomides* (after Maeterlinck), *Nura* & *The Day of Beginning*; cantatas *Lord's Prayer, Minstrel's Child* & others; *Sym. of Life and Love*, symph. poems *Dreams, Before I go dumb, Two Fairy Tales, Song of my Longing*; ovt. *Fairy Land*, 2 suites for orch.; Sinfonietta for chamber orch.; 3 stg. 4tets, Ballad for stg. 4tet, Andante & Scherzo for pf. trio; Elegy for co. & pf.; Sonatina & other pf. works; songs, partsongs, &c.

Chocolate Soldier, The (*Der tapfere Soldat*), operetta by Straus (lib. Leopold Jacobson & Rudolf Bernauer, based on Bernard Shaw's *Arms and the Man*), prod. Vienna, Theater an der Wien, 14. XI. 1908.

Choir Organ. Formerly often a small inst. set apart from the principal org. in a church and used separately to accomp. the choir, except for certain special effects. It is now usually incorporated in the main inst., but there is still a special keyboard for it.

Chopin, Frederic (Fryderyk Franciszek) (b. Zelazowa Wola, prob. 22. II. 1810; d. Paris, 17. X. 1849), Pol. comp. of Fr. descent. The family moved to Warsaw later in 1810, C.'s father becoming prof. of Fr. there. C. took pf. lessons at the age of 6, played at a mus. evening at 7 and in public at 8; took comp. lessons with Elsner from 1822, made great progress in comp. and improv., and 1st pub. a work, the Vars. on a Ger. song, at 14. Left Warsaw Cons. in 1827 and played in Vienna in 1829. On his return he fell in love with the singer Konstancja Gladkowska, who appeared at the 3rd of his public concerts in 1830; but he left Pol. that year, playing in Vienna and Munich and visiting Stuttgart, where he heard of the taking of Warsaw by the Russ. Went to Paris in X. 1831 and decided to remain there. He appeared frequently in public and gave private lessons, esp. in Fr. and Pol. aristocratic circles. Began to pub. pf. works in 1832. Met Marya Wodzinska at Dresden in 1835 and Marienbad in 1836, fell in love with and (?) became engaged to her, but she dropped correspondence after his return to Paris. In 1838 he visited George Sand at Nohant, where she held house-parties in the summer, and although she was 6 years older an intimacy developed between them. She took him to Majorca in XI for his health, but the stay, until II. 1839, was spoilt by bad weather and primitive living conditions. Most summers spent at Nohant until 1847, when a family quarrel between G. Sand and her children led to one with C., and they parted. He suffered from consumption of the throat and gave his last public concert in II. 1848, but continued to teach and play at private houses. His pupil Jane Stirling took him to Sco. in VIII. 1848 for a rest at the country house of her brother-in-law, Lord Torphichen. He afterwards played at Manchester, Glasgow, Edinburgh, and returned to London in XI. In I. 1849 he was back in Paris in a critical state of health and finance, but was supported by wealthy friends until his death.

Works (nearly all for pf. solo) incl. 2 concs.; 4 other works with orch.; 51 Mazurkas, 27 Studies, 25 Preludes (24 in all keys), 19 Nocturnes, 14 Waltzes, 10 Polonaises, 4 Ballades (on poems by Mickiewicz), 4 Impromptus, 4 Scherzos, 3 Rondos, 3 sos., Barcarolle, Berceuse, Bolero, Fantasy in F min., Tarantella & other misc. pf. pieces; pf. Trio; co. & pf. So. (with Franchomme).

'Chopsticks' Variations. A set of vars. for pf. (3 hands, the 2nd player playing the familiar childish theme with 1 hand) by Borodin, Cui, Liadov and Rimsky-Korsakov, written before 1880, when a 2nd ed. appeared and Liszt contrib. a new var. of his own.

Chor. (abbr.) = Choral, Chorus.

Choragus. The office of C. was estab. at Oxford Univ. in 1626, together with that of Prof. of M. While the latter's function was to be the teaching of theory and lecturing on the hist. and science of m., the C.'s duty was to conduct voc. and inst. practices twice a week. These fell into disuse, but were revived in 1926, on the tercentenary of the foundation.

Choral (Ger.). **Chorale** (Eng.). The

Ger. word for 'hymn,' adapted to Eng. for the spec. purpose of designating a Ger. hymn. The final 'e,' though inaccurate, is useful as disting. the noun from an adj., and the O.E.D. reluctantly accepts 'choral(e)' because the final e is supposed to lengthen and accentuate the 2nd syllable. It is certainly preferable in 'Chorale Prelude' (actually the only occasion for its use), because 'Choral Prelude' appears to mean a prelude sung by a choir. The orig. Ger. use of the word by Luther and Johann Walther applied to chor. plainsong; it was only later, when hymns became harmonized, that it transferred itself to hymns sung in parts.

'Choral' Symphony. The name commonly used for Beethoven's 9th Sym., in D min., Op. 125, but not very correctly, since it is not all choral, but has a chor. finale with a solo 4tet, a setting of Schiller's ode *To Joy* (*An die Freude*). Comp. 1817–23, 1st perf. Vienna, 7. V. 1824.

Chorale Prelude. A Ger. type of org. piece for church use current in the 17th–18th cent. and repres. with partic. distinction by Bach; introducing the tune of the hymn about to be sung by the congregation and artistically elaborating it in var. ways instead of merely playing a few bars of it, as in the Angl. church. Bach's C. Ps., however, have defeated their orig. object, being such great m. as to be better suited to concert than to church use nowadays.

Chord. The sounding together of several notes in such a way as to produce a mus. result, either in harmony or in dissonance. Strictly speaking a C. cannot consist of less than 3 notes, 2 being an interval rather than a C.

Chording. A term used either to designate the spacing of the notes in a chord in comp. or the perf. of them strictly in tune in relation to each other.

Choreography. The invention, design and stage management of the dancing in a ballet.

Chorley, Henry Fothergill (b. Blackley Hurst, Lancs., 15. XII. 1808; d. London, 16. II. 1872), Eng. m. critic, libst. & author, contrib. to the *Athenaeum* from 1830.

Choron, Alexandre (Étienne) (b. Caen, 21. X. 1772; d. Paris, 29. VI. 1834), Fr. mus. scholar & comp. Among his books are a mus. encyclopaedia and treatises on mus. study, part-writing, plainsong, &c.

Comps. incl. a Mass, a *Stabat Mater*, psalms, hymns, &c.

Chorton (Ger. lit. choir-tone). The pitch to which church orgs. in Ger. were tuned in the 17th–18th cent., also stged. keyboard insts. It was higher, usually by a whole tone, than the *Kammerton* (chamber-tone), and it is for this reason that Bach transposed his concs. by a tone whenever he transcribed for the clavier one orig. written for the v. The transposition applied only to the solo part: the orch. parts could be used as they stood.

Chouquet, (Adolphe) Gustave (b. Le Havre, 16. IV. 1819; d. Paris, 30. I. 1886), Fr. mcolst. Lived in N.Y. in 1840–56, settled in Paris in 1860 and became curator of the Cons. museum of mus. insts. in 1871. He pub. its catalogue and *Histoire de la Musique dramatique en France*.

Christmas Eve. *See also* **Tchere-vitchki; Vakula the Smith.**

(*Notch Pered Rozhdestvom*), opera by Rimsky-Korsakov (lib. by comp., based on Gogol's story), prod. St. Petersburg, 10. XII. 1895.

Christmas Oratorio. A chor. & orch. work with solo voices by Bach, consisting of 6 church cantatas suited to Christmastide, 1st perf. at that time on 6 successive Sundays at St. Thomas's church, Leipzig, 1734.

Christmas Symphony (Haydn). *See* **Lamentatione.**

Christophe Colomb (*Christopher Columbus*), opera by Milhaud (lib. by Paul Claudel, prod., in Ger., Berlin, Opera, 5. V. 1930. The work makes use of cinematographic films.

Christus, orat. by Liszt (words from the Bible and the Roman Catholic liturgy), comp. 1855–66, 1st perf. Weimar, 29. V. 1873.

Orat. by Mendelssohn (words by Chevalier Bunsen), begun 1844, resumed 1847, but left unfinished.

Christus am Oelberge (*Christ at the Mount of Olives*), orat. by Beethoven, Op. 85 (lib. by Franz Xaver Huber), prod. Vienna, 5. IV. 1803.

Chromatic. The C. scale is one proceeding entirely by semitones, i.e. taking in all the notes available in normal western m. C. m. is comp. in which much is made of the notes not included in the scale of the prevailing key and thus, in notation, involving the use of many accidentals.

Chromatic Fantasy and Fugue. A hpchd. work in D min. by Bach, written *c.* 1720–3 and doubtless intended to show the advantages of Equal Temperament in keyboard m. by exploiting the accidentals both as sharps and flats.

Chromatic Harp. A Fr. type of hp. which, instead of being tuned to the scale of C♭ maj., like the normal hp., where each stg. can be raised in pitch by a semitone or a whole tone with the aid of pedals, has stgs. for all the notes of the chromatic scale. They are not all strung parallel, but slightly crossed, so that except where they actually intersect they stand away from each other in 2 ranges, one repres. the diatonic scale of C maj., the other the sharps or flats, like the white and black notes on the pf.

Chrotta. *See* **Crwth.**

Chrysander, Friedrich (b. Lübtheen, Mecklenburg, 8. VII. 1826; d. Bergedorf nr. Hamburg, 3. IX. 1901), Ger. mus. scholar & ed. Lived in Eng. for some time to make research into material for his great biog. of Handel, pub. 1858–67, but never completed. He also ed. Handel's complete works. Other works of his on old m. are valuable, but he was violently opposed to all 'modern,' i.e. post-Handelian m.

Chueca, Frederico (b. Madrid, 5. V. 1846; d. Madrid, 20. VI. 1908), Spa. comp. Studied the m. of the Spa. people in var. parts of the country and reprod. it in many of his light operas. He organized a street band for his own amusement and attracted Barbieri's attention with a set of waltzes for orch., which B. conducted with success.

Works incl. light operas *Cadiz, Caramelo, La alegría de la huerta, La caza del oso Pobre chica, El caballero de gracia, La gran via* (with Valverde) & others; waltzes, &c.

Church Modes. *See* **Modes.**

Church Sonata. *See* **Sonata da chiesa.**

Churchill, Winston (Leonard Spencer), Rt. Hon. (b. 1874), Eng. politican, Prime Minister in 1940–5. *See* **Gundry** (passages from a speech).

Chute (Fr.). *See* **Ornaments.**

Chute de la Maison Usher, La (*The Fall of the House of Usher*), opera by Debussy (lib. by himself, based on Edgar Allan Poe's story), worked at between 1908–18, but never completed.

Chybinski, Adolf (b. Cracow, 29. III. 1880), Pol. mcolst. Studied at Cracow Univ. and Munich. App. prof. of harmony at the Lwów Cons., in 1916, lecturer at the Univ. there in 1917 and prof. of m. in 1921. He has ed. old Pol. m. and written on the subject and on others in Pol. & Ger.

Ciacona (It.). *See* **Chaconne.**

Ciaia, A. B. della. *See* **Della Ciaia.**

Ciampi, Legrenzio Vincenzo (b. Piacenza, 1719; d. Venice, 29. III. 1762), It. comp. Little is known of his life, except that he visited London in 1748 and prod. his last opera in 1762.

Works incl. operas *Adriano, Il trionfo di Camilla, Bertoldo, Bertoldino e Cacasenno; Didone, Catone in Utica, Il negligente*; mass; ovts. & concs.; 6 org. concs.; 12 stg. trios; It. songs, &c.

Cibber, Colley (1671–1757), Eng. actor & playwright of Dan. descent. *See* **Carey** (*The Provoked Husband*), **Finger** (*Love makes a Man*), **Franck (J. W.)** (*Love's Last Shift*), **Paisible** (2 plays), **Pepusch** (*Myrtillo*), **Purcell (D.)** (*Love's L. S.* & *Love makes a Man*), **Weldon** (*She would*).

Cibber, Susanna Maria. *See* **Arne.**

Cid, Der, opera by **Cornelius** (lib. by comp., based on Corneille's drama), prod. Weimar, 21. V. 1865.

Cid, Le, opera by **Massenet** (lib. by Adolphe Philippe d'Ennery, Louis Gallet & Édouard Blau, based on Corneille's drama), prod. Paris, Opéra, 30. XI. 1885.

Cifra, Antonio (b. Rome, 1584; d. Loreto, 2. X. 1629), It. comp. Pupil of Palestrina in Rome. He was chapel master of the Ger. Coll. there in 1609, at Loreto in 1610 and at the church of St. John Lateran, Rome, in 1623. From 1625–8 he was abroad in the service of the Archduke Charles.

Works incl. masses, motets, psalms, madrigals, &c.

Cigale et la Fourmi, La (*The Grasshopper and the Ant*: in Eng. known as *La Cigale*), operetta by Audran (lib. by Henri Charles Chivot & Alfred Duru, the title alluding to La Fontaine's fable), prod. Paris, Théâtre de la Gaîté, 30. X. 1886.

Cilèa, Francesco (b. Palmi, Calabria, 26. VII. 1866), It. comp. Studied at Naples and while still at the Cons., prod. his 1st opera there in 1889. The pub. Sonzogno then commissioned a second, prod. at Florence in 1892. Prof. at the Reale Istituto Musicale at Florence, 1896–1904.

Works incl. operas *Gina, La Tilda, L'Arlesiana* (after Daudet), *Adriana Lecouvreur* (after Scribe), *Gloria*; co. & pf. So.; numerous pf. works, &c.

Cimador(o), Giambattista (b. Venice, *c.* 1761; d. London, *c.* 1808), It. comp. Belonging to a noble family, he held no official mus. appt., but settled in London as singing teacher c. 1791. There he arr. 6 of Mozart's syms. for stgs. & fl., having heard that the orch. at the King's Theatre refused to play them as too difficult.

Works incl. lyrical scenes *Pimmaglione, Il ratto di Proserpina, Ati e Cibele*; db. Conc.; duets for stgs.; voc. pieces, &c.

Cimarosa, Domenico (b. Aversa nr. Naples, 17. XII. 1749; d. Venice, 11. I. 1801), It. comp. Studied at Naples, among his masters being Sacchini and Piccinni, and prod. his 1st opera there in 1772. Later lived in Rome and Naples by turns, became famous with several operas, travelled much and in 1787 went to the court of Catherine II at St. Petersburg. About 1790 the Emperor Leopold II invited him to Vienna, where he prod. his most famous opera, *Il matrimonio segreto*, in 1792. He had been court mus. dir., but on Leopold's death Salieri was re-app. and C. returned to Naples in 1793, becoming mus. dir. to the king and teacher to the princesses. In 1799, when the Fr. repub. army marched into Naples, he expressed his enthusiasm with their cause and was imprisoned and condemned to death by King Ferdinand; reprieved later, but sent out of the kingdom, he intended to return to Rus., but d. at Venice on the way.

Works incl. over 60 operas, e.g. *Le stravaganze del conte*, *L'Italiana in Londra*, *Il pittore parigino*, *La ballerina amante*, *L'Olimpiade*, *Artaserse*, *L'impresario in angustie*, *Cleopatra*, *Idalide*, *Il matrimonio segreto*, *Le astuzie femminili*, *L'amante disperato*, *L'impegno superato*, *Gli Orazi ed i Curiazi*, *Penelope*, *Achille all' assedio di Troia*; masses, orats., cantatas, &c.

Cimbalo (Spa.) = Cymbal.

Cimbalom. A Hung. nat. inst., descendant of the dulcimer, with stgs. stretched over a horizontal soundboard which are struck by hammers.

Cinderella. *See* **Cendrillon, Cenerentola.**

Cinelli (It.) = Cymbals (more often called *piatti*).

Cinesi, Le (*The Chinamen*), opera by Caldara (lib. by Metastasio), prod. Vienna, at court, Carnival 1735.

Opera by Gluck (lib. do.), prod. Schlosshof nr. Vienna, at court, 24. IX. 1754.

Cinquepace (from Fr. *cinq pas* = 5 steps; also colloq. 'Sink-a-pace'). A dance of the 16th cent. in quick 3–4 time and requiring movements in groups of 5 paces. The name was used both for the Galliard following the Pavan and for the Tordion concluding the Basse Danse. Shakespeare makes a pun on it in *Much Ado about Nothing*.

Cinquième (Fr. = fifth). A bowed stg. inst. of the v. family now obs., but used in the 17th cent., with a range from middle C.

Cinti-Damoreau, Laure (b. Paris, 6. II. 1801; d. Paris, 25. II. 1863), Fr. opera singer. Studied at the Paris Cons. 1st appearance at the Théâtre Italien at the age of 18 and at the Opéra in 1826. She remained there until 1835 and the following year joined the Opéra-Comique.

Ciphering. The escape of air from org. pipes by a fault in or damage to the mechanism.

Circassian Bride, The, opera by Bishop (lib. by Charles Ward), prod. London, Drury Lane Theatre, 23. II. 1809.

Circe & Penelope, 2 parts of a cyclic opera, *Ulysses*, by Keiser (lib. by Friedrich Christian Bressand), prod. Brunswick, II. 1696.

Circolo mezzo (It.) = **Turn.**

Circular Canon. A canon whose tune ends in a key a semitone above that in which it begins, so that after 12 repetitions it has passed through all the maj. or min. keys.

Ciro in Babilonia, o sia La caduta di Baldassarre (*Cyrus in Babylon, or The Fall of Balthasar*), opera by Rossini (lib. by Francesco Aventi), prod. Ferrara, 14. III. 1812.

Cirullo, Giovanni Antonio (b. Andria, ?; d. Andria, ?), It. 16th–17th-cent. comp. Lived at Andria nr. Bari. Pub. 6 books of madrigals and contrib. to Phalèse's collection *Il Helicone* in 1616.

Cithara. *See* **Lyre.**

Citole (Fr.) = **Cittern.**

Cittern (or Cithren, Cither, Cythern, Gittern, &c.). An obs. stg. inst. of the lute type, used at least as early as the 13th cent. and not superseded by other insts. of its kind until the 17th. Its modern descendant is the guitar. It usually had 4 wire stgs. tuned in an ascending 5th, 6th & 5th in var. pitches, but never below the treble clef. The finger-board was fretted and the stgs. were played with a plectrum. The back was flat. The modern Ger. and Aus. *Zither* derives its name from it, but is only distantly related.

Čiurlionis, Mikalojus Konstantinas (b. Varena, Gvt. of Vilna, 10. IX. 1875; d. nr. Warsaw, 28. III. 1914), Pol. comp. & painter. Studied at the Warsaw Cons. where Noskowski was his comp. master, later under Reinecke at the Leipzig Cons. He settled at Warsaw as lecturer on m. and was one of a group of painters there.

Works incl. opera *Queen of the Ocean* (unfinished); symph. poems *The Forest*, *Polonez*, *Ocean* (1st form of the opera); cantata *De profundis* & other chor. works; pf. m., &c.

Cl. (abbr.) = Clarinet.

Claflin, Avery (b. Keene, N.H., 1898), Amer. comp. Graduated at Harvard Univ. and went into business, but spent much of his time at comp.

Works incl. operas *The Fall of Usher* (after Poe) & *Hester Prynne* (after Hawthorne's *Scarlet Letter*); ballet; Sym. in D min. and *Moby Dick Suite* (after H. Melville) for orch.; stg. 4tet, pf. Trio; female chors., &c.

Clairon (Fr.) = Bugle.

Clang-Tint (lit. from Ger. ***Klangfarbe***). A term Tyndall endeavoured to introd. into Eng. for the Fr. word *timbre*, which has however remained in use, though Tone-colour has become current.

Clapisson, Antoine Louis (b. Naples, 15. IX. 1808; d. Paris, 19. III. 1866), Fr. vst. & comp. Vst. at the Paris Opéra, 1832–8, after which he made a great success with songs and slight operas.

Works incl. operas ***La Figurante, Le Code noir, Gibby la Cornemuse, La Promise, La Fanchonnette, Madame Grégoire***, &c.

Clapp, Philip Greeley (b. Boston, Mass., 4. VIII. 1888), Amer. comp. Graduated at Harvard Univ. and studied with Schillings at Stuttgart, and in London. After several scholastic apps. he became Prof. of M. at Iowa Univ.

Works incl. cantata *A Chant of Darkness* (Helen Keller); 11 syms., symph. poem *A Song of Youth*, prelude *Summer, An Academic Diversion, Overture to a Comedy, Prologue to a Tragedy* for orch.; *Norge* for pf. & orch., pf. Conc. in B min., Fantasy on an Old Plainchant for co. & orch., *Dramatic Poem* for tromb. & orch.; songs with orch.; Fanfare Prelude for 20 brass insts.; stg. 4tet in C min., Suite for brass 6tet, Concert Suite for 4 trombs., Prelude & Finale for woodwind 5tet; v. & pf. So.; Sonatina for pf.; 20 songs; anthem 'O Gladsome Light' with org.; partsongs, &c.

Clarabella. *See* **Claribel.**

Claretie, Jules (1840–1913), Fr. novelist & dramatist. *See* **Navarraise** (Massenet).

Clari, Giovanni Carlo Maria (b. Pisa, 27. IX. 1677; d. Pisa, 16. V. 1754), It. comp. Chapel master successively at Pistoia, Bologna and Pisa.

Works incl. opera *Il savio delirante*; masses, *Stabat Mater*, Requiem, psalms; voc. duets & trios, &c.

Clari, or The Maid of Milan, opera by Bishop (lib. by John Howard Payne, based on Marmontel's story, *Laurette*), prod. London, Covent Garden Theatre, 8. V. 1823. It contains the song *Home, sweet home*, not only as a song, but as a kind of *Leitmotiv* or theme-song occurring in var. forms.

Claribel (or Clarabella or Claribel Flute). An 8-ft. org. stop of wooden flues.

Clarichord (Eng., obs.). A corruption, prob. from Lat. *clarus*, of Clavichord.

Clarinet. A woodwind inst. with a single reed made in var. pitches, the most current being cls. in A and in B♭. It came into use later than the other woodwind insts. still current and did not estab. itself regularly in the orch. until after the middle of the 18th cent. It has a range of *c.* 3½ 8ves from C♯ or D below middle C. Also an 8-ft. reed org. stop reproducing the tone of the C., sometimes called Cremona.

Clarinet Quintet. The techn. term for a 5tet for cl. and stg. 4tet.

Clarino (It. = clarion). A tpt. with a small bore on which high parts were comparatively easy to play. It became obs. after the invention of the valve tpt., which however could not prod. the high and florid parts written by Bach and his contemps. and forerunners, and this led to the invention of the Bach Tpt. The term C. was often used in old scores, not to indicate the inst., which was obvious, but the compass, a 1st C.-part ranging from *c.* an 8ve above middle C to E above the treble-clef stave, a 2nd from *c.* G above middle C to an 8ve above it. A lower part was often called Tromba and the lowest Principal.

Clarion. *See* Clarino. C. may also be a 4-ft. reed stop on the org.

Clarion Mixture. An org. stop with Mixtures prod. by flue-pipes.

Clarionet (obs.). *See* **Clarinet.**

Clarionet Flute. A stopped diapason org. stop with 8-ft. tone.

Clarke, Jeremiah (b. ? London, *c.* 1659; d. London, 1. XII. 1707), Eng. comp. Pupil of Blow at the Chapel Royal, orgst. at Winchester Coll., 1692–5, and of St. Paul's cath. in London from 1695. Sworn Gentleman-extraordinary of the Chapel Royal in 1700 and orgst. in 1704. He fell unhappily in love with an unattainable lady and d. by his own hand.

Works incl. anthems; odes on the Assumption of the Blessed Virgin, in praise of Barbadoes & *O Harmony*; setting of Dryden's *Alexander's Feast*; operas *The Island Princess* (with D. Purcell and Leveridge), *The World in the Moon* (Settle, with D. Purcell); incid. m. for Shakespeare's *Titus Andronicus*, Sedley's *Antony and Cleopatra* & other plays; hpchd. lessons, many songs, &c.

Clarke, Rebecca (b. Harrow, 27. VIII. 1886), Eng. va. player & comp. Studied at the R.A.M. in London. In a competition in U.S.A. in 1919 for a work for va. & pf. she won the prize with a So., 2nd only to Ernest Bloch's Suite. She settled in N.Y. in 1944 and married James Friskin.

Works incl. Psalm for chor.; pf. Trio; va. & pf. So., Rhapsody for co. & pf., duets for va. & co.; songs for voice and v. and for voice & pf.; inst. pieces, &c.

Clarone (It.) = Bass Clarinet (also called *clarinetto basso*) or Basset Horn.

Clàrsach (Gael.). The old Celtic hp., formerly used in Ir., Wales & Sco. and revived in the last-named region early in the 20th cent. for the accomp. of the rediscovered Gaelic folksongs.

Classical. In its Lat. derivation the term is opposed to 'proletarian,' and broadly speaking its present vulgar use for any m. that is not light, popular, frivolous or utilitarian (e.g. dance m.) is correct; but if so, its equally current use as opposed to 'modern' is misleading. The most usual application, but one also open to objections, is that meaning a fancied opposite to 'archaic' on the one hand and 'romantic' on the other, i.e. the m. from the 17th cent. to the early 19th.

Claudel, Paul (b. 1868), Fr. poet & dramatist. *See* **Christophe Colomb** (Milhaud), **Homme et son désir** (do.), **Honegger** (*Danse des morts*), **Jeanne d'Arc au bûcher** (Honegger), **Milhaud** (*Protée, Annonce faite à Marie,* Aeschylus transs. & songs).

Claudin de Sermisy. *See* **Sermisy.**

Claudine von Villa Bella, play for m. by Goethe.

M. by Ignaz von Beeck (1733–1803), prod. Vienna, Burg Theatre, 13. VI. 1780.

M. by Johann Christoph Kienlen (1784–*c.* 1830), prod. Munich, 9. IX. 1810.

M. by Reichardt, prod. Charlottenburg, Schloss Theatre, at court, 29. VII. 1789; perf. Berlin, Opera, 3. VIII. 1789.

M. by Claus Schall (1757–1837) (lib. a Dan. translation of Goethe's play by Niels Henrik Weinwich), prod. Copenhagen, 29. I. 1787.

Claudio da Correggio. *See* **Merulo.**

Claudius, Matthias (1740–1815), Ger. poet. *See* **Schoeck** (*Wandsbecker Liederbuch*), **Siegl** (*Grosse Hallelujah*), 12 songs by **Schubert.**

Clav. (abbr.) = Clavier.

Clavecin (Fr.) = Harpsichord (old spelling sometimes *clavessin*).

Clavecin oculaire. *See* **Castel** & **Colour Music.**

Clavel, Antoinette. *See* **Saint-Huberty.**

Clavicembalo (It.) = Harpsichord. The abbr. *cembalo* is often used.

Clavichord. An obs. stged. keyboard inst. differing in its tone-production from the hpchd. The stgs. were not plucked, but struck by a tangent which pressed against them as long as the key was held down by the finger and prod. a very faint note which could be made to vibrate by a gentle shaking of the finger. The pitch of the note was determined by the place at which it was struck by the tangent, so that the same stg. could be used for 2 adjacent notes, which then could never be sounded simultaneously. Such insts. were called 'fretted' Cs.; those which had a separate stg. for each note were 'fretless.'

Clavicymbal (Eng., obs.). The name sometimes given in Eng. to the hpchd., from the It. *clavicembalo.*

Clavicytherium (Lat.). A hpchd. whose wing-shaped body stood upright instead of being placed horizontally as in a grand pf.

Clavier (Fr. = keyboard; Ger = pianoforte). In Eng. the word may be used to designate any stged. keyboard inst., esp. the hpchd., clavichord and early pf. in cases where it is doubtful which was used in perf. or where the choice was at the player's discretion.

Clavierübung. A work in 4 parts by Bach containing var. comps. for keyboard insts.—hpchd. or clavichord & org.—pub. 1731, 1735, 1739 & 1742, and incl. the *Italian Conc.* & 'Goldberg' Vars. for hpchd., the 21 'Catechism' chorale preludes, &c.

Clavilux. *See* **Colour Music.**

Claviorganum. An inst. combining hpchd. and org. mechanisms, dating from the late 16th cent. and made in var. forms until the 18th.

Clay, Frederic (b. Paris, 3. VIII. 1838; d. Great Marlow, 24. XI. 1889), Eng. comp. Pupil of Molique and of Hauptmann at Leipzig. He began by writing light operas for amateurs, 1859–60, but prod. *Court and Cottage* at Covent Garden Theatre in London in 1862.

Works incl. light operas *Princess Toto, Don Quixote, The Merry Duchess, The Golden Ring,* &c.; incid. m. for Shakespeare's *Twelfth Night*; cantatas *The Knights of the Cross* & *Lalla Rookh* (Moore), the latter incl. 'I'll sing thee songs of Araby'; songs 'She wandered down the mountain-side,' *The Sands of Dee,* &c.

Clayton, Thomas (b. ? London, *c.* 1670; d. ? London, *c.* 1730), Eng. comp. and adapter. He set Addison's opera lib. of *Rosamond,* which proved a complete failure, in 1707. *Arsinoë,* prod. as his own opera in 1705, was a pasticcio of It. songs. In 1711 he prod. a setting of an altered version of Dryden's *Alexander's Feast.*

Cleave (Eng., obs.) = Clef.

Clef. The sign in front of the key and time signatures at the beginning of a comp. and repeated on each stave, determining the position of the notes shown on the stave; e.g. the C clef placed on the 3rd line indicates that the note on that line is middle C.

Clemenceau, Georges (1841–1929), Fr. statesman & author. *See* **Fauré** (*Voix du bonheur*, incid. m.).

Clemens non Papa (Lat. = Clement not the Pope). *See* **Clément, Jacques.**

Clément, Félix (b. Paris, 13. I. 1822; d. Paris, 23. I. 1885), Fr. mcolst., ed. & comp. Wrote largely on and ed. church m. Comps. incl. incid. m. for Racine's *Athalie* & *Esther*.

Clement, Franz (b. Vienna, 17. XI. 1780; d. Vienna, 3. XI. 1842), Aus. vst. 1st appeared at the age of 9; app. cond. at the Theater an der Wien in Vienna. Beethoven wrote his v. Conc. for him.

Clément, Jacques (called **Clemens non Papa**) (b. ?; d. ?, before 1558), Flem. comp. Worked (?) at Antwerp cath. and (?) was chapel master in Vienna to Charles V and Ferdinand I. He may also have been in It., since his nickname was given him to distinguish him from Pope Clement VII.

Works (over 250) incl. masses, motets, psalms in Flem., chansons, &c.

Clementi, Muzio (b. Rome, 24. I. 1752; d. Evesham, 10. III. 1832), It. pfst., pf. manufacturer, pub. & comp. Studied with church musns. in Rome and had written a Mass and other works before he was 14. He was taken to Eng. for his further educ. by Peter Beckford, M.P., at whose house in Wilts. he worked until 1773, when he appeared in London as pfst. & comp. with enormous success. He travelled much on the Continent after 1781, met Haydn and played in competition with Mozart, but spent most of his time in London as teacher and cond. and as a partner in the firm of Longman & Broderip, later C. & Co., pf. makers and m.-dealers. Field became his apprentice and pupil there. While in Berlin in 1804 he married a Ger. named Lehmann, who died in 1805, and in 1811 Emma Gisburne became his wife in London. His last years were spent in retirement at Evesham.

Works incl. many syms.; over 60 pf. sos., 100 progressive pf. studies entitled *Gradus ad Parnassum*, Capricci and other pf. works; sos. for var. insts. & pf., chamber m., &c.

Clemenza di Scipione, La (*The Clemency of Scipio*), opera by J. C. Bach (lib. by ?), prod. London, King's Theatre, Haymarket, 4. IV. 1778.

Clemenza di Tito, La (*The Clemency of Titus*). *See also* **Tito Vespasiano.**

Opera by Gluck (lib. by Metastasio), prod. Naples, Teatro San Carlo, 4. XI. 1752.

Opera by Mozart (lib. do., altered by Caterino Mazzolà), prod. Prague, to celebrate the coronation of the Emperor Leopold II as King of Boh., 6. IX. 1791.

Cleofide, opera by **Hasse** (lib. by M. A. Boccardi, based on Metastasio's *Alessandro nell' Indie*), prod. Dresden, at court, 13. IX. 1731.

Cleopatra (*Die betrogene Staats-Liebe, oder Die unglückselige Cleopatra, Königin von Egypten*), opera by Mattheson (lib. by Friedrich Christian Feustking), prod. Hamburg, Theater am Gänsemarkt, 20. X. 1704.

Cleopatra e Cesare, opera by Graun (lib. by Giovanni Gualberto Bottarelli, based on Corneille's *La Mort de Pompée*), prod. Berlin, Opera, 7. XII. 1742. Written for the inauguration of that theatre.

Cleopatra's Night, opera by H. K. Hadley (lib. by Alice Leal Pollock, based on Théophile Gautier's *Une Nuit de Cléopâtre*), prod. N.Y., Metropolitan Opera, 31. I. 1920.

Cléopâtre, opera by Massenet (lib. by Louis Payen), prod. Monte Carlo, 23. II. 1914.

Clérambault, Louis Nicolas (b. Paris, 19. XII. 1676; d. Paris, 26. X. 1749), Fr. orgst & comp. Pupil of André Raison. Orgst. at var. Paris churches. Wrote cantatas and pieces for org. and for hpchd.

Cliff (Eng., obs.) = Clef.

Clifford, James (b. Oxford, 1622; d. ?, 1698), Eng. divine & musn. Chorister at Magdalen Coll., Oxford, 1632–42; app. min. canon at St. Paul's cath. in London, 1661. Pub. a collection of the words of *Divine Services and Anthems*, 1663.

Clive (*née* **Raftor**), **Catherine (Kitty)** (b. London, 1711; d. Twickenham, 6. XII. 1785), Eng. actress & stage singer. Attached to Drury Lane Theatre in London, 1728–41.

Cloches de Corneville, Les (*The Bells of C.*), operetta by Planquette (lib. by Clairville & Charles Gabet), prod. Paris, Folies-Dramatiques, 19. IV. 1877.

Clochette, La (*The Little Bell*), opera by Duni (lib. by Louis Anseaume), prod. Paris, Comédie-Italienne, 24. VII. 1766.

Clochette, La, ou Le Diable page (*The Little Bell, or The Devil as Page*), opera by Hérold (lib. by Emmanuel Guillaume Théaulon de Lambert), prod. Paris, Opéra-Comique, 18. X. 1817. Schubert wrote 2 songs for the Vienna prod. in 1821.

Clock, The. The nickname of Haydn's Sym. No. 101, in D min. & maj. (No. 11 of the 'Salomon' syms.), written for London in 1794. The name derives from the ticking motion of the accomp. figures in the slow mvt.

Close Shake. *See* Vibrato.

Closed Horn. An 8-ft. reed org. stop.

Closson, Ernest (b. Saint-Josse-ten-Noode nr. Brussels, 12. XII. 1870), Belg. mcolst. Attached to the Conss. of Brussels and Mons and m. critic to *L'Indépendance belge* from 1920. Wrote several books on m., esp. Belg. folksong.

Clough, Arthur Hugh (1819–61), Eng. poet. *See* Gatty (odes).

Clst. (abbr.) = Clarinettist.

Club Anthem. An anthem comp. jointly by Blow, Humfrey and Wm. Turner *c.* 1664, when they were choir-boys at the Chapel Royal. It is a setting of the words 'I will always give thanks.'

Club Works. *See* **Collective Works.**

Cluer, John (b. ?; d. London, *c.* 1730), Eng. m. pub. Worked in London early in the 18th cent. and was succeeded by his widow and later her 2nd husband, Thomas Cobb. He pub. some of Handel's operas.

Clutsam, George (b. Sydney, N.S.W., 26. IX. 1866), Austral. pfst. & comp. Settled in London after touring as pfst. in New Zealand and Asia, and was m. critic to the *Observer*, 1908–18.

Works incl. operas *A Summer Night* & *After a Thousand Years*; cantata *The Quest of Rapunzel*; symph. idyll *The Lady of Shalott* (Tennyson); mus. comedies, &c. He also prod. a Ger. opera, *König Harlekin*, in Berlin in 1912. He is responsible for the Eng. version of the Schubert pasticcio *Lilac Time* and other similar things.

Co. (abbr.) = Cello (Violoncello).

Coates, Albert (b. St. Petersburg, 23. IV. 1882), Eng. cond. & comp. (mother Rus.). Sent to school in Eng. and entered Liverpool Univ., returned to Rus. to enter his father's business, but was sent to the Leipzig Cons. on showing mus. gifts. Studied cond. with Nikisch and cond. opera at several Ger. theatres before he was engaged at St. Petersburg. He fled to Eng. during the Revol. in 1919 and settled in London for good.

Works incl. operas *Assurbanipal, Samuel Pepys, Pickwick, Gainsborough's Duchess*; symph. poem *The Eagle*, Rus. Suite for orch., pf. pieces, &c.

Coates, Eric (b. Hucknall, Notts, 27. VIII. 1886), Eng. comp. Studied at the R.A.M. in London and became a va. player in a 4tet and in the Queen's Hall Orch., but later devoted himself to the comp. of light and popular m.

Coates, Henry (b. London, 28. III. 1881), Eng. writer on m., teacher & lecturer. Took the degrees of M.A. (Cantab.) and Ph.D. (London); teacher in the Faculty of M., London Univ., fellow and member of the board of Trinity Coll. of M., where he is teacher and examiner, as also at the G.S.M., lecturer to the London County Council, &c. He is the author of books on Palestrina and Bruckner, and ed. of Franck's and other org. m.

Coates, John (b. Girlington nr. Bradford, 29. VI. 1865; d. Northwood nr. London, 16. VIII. 1941), Eng. ten. singer. He was trained for and began to make a career as a bar., but made his 1st appearance as a ten. in 1899. He became equally famous in opera and orat., and later in life was one of the finest song recitalists.

Cobbett, W(alter) W(illson). (b. Blackheath, 11. VII. 1847; d. London, 22. I. 1937), Eng. mus. amateur & ed. A wealthy business man, he did much valuable work for chamber m. by offering prizes for new works by Brit. comps., esp. 1-movt. fantasies, and he ed. a *Cyclopaedic Survey of Chamber M.* pub. in 1929.

Cobbold, William (b. Norwich, 5. I. 1560; d. Beccles, 7. XI. 1639), Eng. orgst. & comp. Orgst. at Norwich cath., 1599–1608. He was one of the 10 musns. who harmonized the tunes in East's Psalter of 1592 and he contrib. a madrigal to *The Triumphes of Oriana* in 1601. Another madrigal and an anthem are preserved.

Cocchi, Claudio (b. Genoa, ?; d. ?), It. 17th-cent. comp. Worked in Ger. for a time and later at Trieste cath. and San Francesco at Milan.

Works incl. masses; books of voc. m. entitled *Armonici concentus* & *Ghirlanda sacra*, &c.

Cocchi, Gioacchino (b. Padua, *c.* 1715; d. Venice, 1804), It. comp. Worked at Venice until 1757, when he went to London until 1773 as comp. to the Opera and cond. of Mrs. Cornelys's subscription concerts for 2 years.

Works incl. over 40 operas, e.g. *Adelaide, Bajazette, Il pazzo glorioso*, &c.

Coccia, Carlo (b. Naples, 14. IV. 1782; d. Novara, 13. IV. 1873), It. comp. Pupil of Paisiello. He prod. many operas in It. between 1807–20, when he went 1st to Lisbon and then to London. He became cond. of the Opera there, also prof. of comp. at the R.A.M., and stayed until 1828, returning in 1833, but eventually settling at Novara as chapel master in succession to Mercadante.

Works incl. *c.* 40 operas, e.g. *Il matrimonio per cambiale, Donna Caritea, Maria Stuarda, Il lago delle fate*, 2 cantatas, &c.

Coccia, Maria Rosa (b. Rome, 4. I. 1759; d. Rome, XI. 1833), It. comp. At the age of 16 she passed a sever[e] examination at the Accademia d[i] Santa Cecilia in Rome with brillian[t] success and an account of it was pub.; and in 1780 another eulogy of her was issued with letters from **Martini, Metastasio** and Farinelli.

Works incl. Magnificat for voices and org., written at 15, *Dixit Dominus* and a cantata, but most are lost.

Cochlaeus, Johannes (Johann Dobnek) (b. Wendelstein nr. Nuremberg, 10. I. 1479; d. Breslau, 10. I. 1552), Ger. cleric and mus. scholar. He was a Roman Catholic and an opponent of Luther, in office at Cologne, Worms, Mainz and Frankfort o/M. Wrote a treatise on m. and comp. odes, &c.

Cockaigne (In London Town), concert ovt. by Elgar, Op. 40, comp. 1900 and 1st perf. London, Phil. Soc., 20. VI. 1901.

Coclicus, Adrian Petit (b. Hainault, *c.* 1500; d. Copenhagen, 1563), Flem. comp. Pupil of Josquin des Prés. He was in Rome as a member of the Papal chapel, but was imprisoned for moral laxity, went to Wittenberg in 1545 and became a Protestant. After var. apps. in Ger. he went to the Dan. court at Copenhagen. Pub. books of voc. m. entitled *Compendium musices* & *Musica reservata*, &c.

Coda (It. = tail). The part of a mus. comp. which forms a peroration, where it can be regarded, from the structural point of view, as a distinct and separate section. It is thus most clearly marked, for ex., in so. form, where it appears as a 4th division after the exposition, working-out and recapitulation, or in a minuet or scherzo with trio, where it rounds off the mvt. after the restatement of the 1st section, usually with material based either on that or on the trio.

Codetta (It. = little tail). A small form of coda, not appearing as a rule at the end of a mvt., but rather rounding off a section of such a movt. or a theme or group of themes, thus assuming the function of a bridge-passage.

Cocteau, Jean (b. 1891), Fr. critic & author. *See* **Antigone** (Honegger), **Bowles** (*Memnon*), **Mariés de la Tour d'Eiffel** (Les Six), **Markevitch** (cantata), **Milhaud** (songs), **Poulenc** (*Cocardes*).

Coelho, Ruy (b. ?, 3. III. 1892), Port. comp. Studied at Lisbon and later with Humperdinck in Berlin. Became m. critic of the *Diario de Noticias* at Lisbon and in 1924 won a prize with his 2nd opera.

Works incl. operas *Ines de Castro, Belkiss, Crisfal, Entre gestas, Tá-Mar*; symph. poems *Sinfonia camoniana, Promenade d'été*, &c; chamber m., pf. pieces, songs, &c.

Coerne, Louis (Adolphe) (b. Newark, N.J., 27. II. 1870; d. Boston, Mass., 11. IX. 1922), Amer. cond. & comp. Studied in Ger., Fr. and at Harvard Univ. After filling an orgst.'s post at Buffalo and cond. there and at Columbus, he became assoc. prof. at Smith Coll., Northampton, Mass., and also taught at Harvard. Later he held other distinguished teaching posts and visited Ger., where some of his works were perf.

Works incl. operas *A Woman of Marblehead, Zenobia* & *Sakuntala* (after Kalidasa); incid. m. to Euripides' *Trojan Women*; 6-part Mass; symph. poem *Hiawatha* (after Longfellow) & other works for orch.; v. Conc.; stg. 4tet in C min., 3 pf. trios in canon; Swe. So. for v. & pf.; pf. pieces; songs, partsongs, &c.

Cœuroy, André (Jean Belime) (b. Dijon, 24. II. 1891), Fr. critic & mcolst. Studied m. privately with Reger in Ger. Became m. critic of *Paris-Midi* and founder, with Prunières, of the *Revue musicale* in 1920. He has ed. books on m. and written works on modern m., the relationships between m. and literature, trans. old and modern operas from Ger., &c.

Coffee Cantata ('Schweiget stille, plaudert nicht'). A secular cantata by Bach for solo voices, chor. & orch., comp. *c.* 1732.

Coffey, Charles (?–1745), Ir. playwright. Author of the early ballad operas *The Devil to pay* (1731) and *The Merry Cobbler* (1735).

Cohen, Jules (Émile David) (b. Marseilles, 2. XI. 1835; d. Paris, 13. I. 1901), Fr. comp. Studied at the Paris Cons., where he was prof. later.

Works incl. operas *Maître Claude, José Maria, Les Bluets*, &c.; incid. m. for Racine's *Athalie* & *Esther*, &c.

Coke, Roger Sacheverell (b. Derbyshire, 1912), Eng. comp. Educ. at Eton Coll., where he studied m. under Henry Ley, and learnt pf. from Mabel Lander.

Works (some withdrawn) incl. opera *The Cenci* (after Shelley); 2 syms., symph. poem *The Lotus Eaters*; 4 pf. concs., 2 voc. concs. for sop. & orch.; chamber m.; 3 co. & pf. sos.; 3 pf. sos., Vars. & other works for pf.; *c.* 50 songs, &c.

Col legno (It. = 'with the wood'). A direction indicating that a passage for a stg. inst. or a group of such insts. is to be played by striking the stgs. with the stick of the bow.

Colachon
Colascione } An obs. inst. of the lute type used esp. in S. It., very large in size, but having only 2 or 3 stgs.

Colasse, Pascal (b. Rheims, 22. I. 1649; d. Versailles, 17. VII. 1709), Fr. comp. Studied at the Maîtrise de Saint-Paul and the Collège de Navarre in Paris, and c. 1677 obtained an appt. at the Opéra from Lully, in whose works he wrote some of the subordinate parts. In 1683 he became one of the 4 superintendents of the royal chapel, each of whom had to direct the m. for 3 months in the year, and 2 years later he shared with Lalande the appt. of royal chamber musn.
Works incl. operas *Achille et Polyxène* (with Lully), *Thétis et Pélée, Énée et Lavinie, Jason, La Naissance de Vénus, Polyxène et Pyrrhus*, &c.; motets, *Cantiques spirituels* and other church m., &c.

Colbran, Isabella (Angela) (b. Madrid, 2. II. 1785; d. Bologna, 7. X. 1845), Spa. m.-sop. singer. Made her 1st appearance in It. in 1806; married Rossini in 1822; comp. songs.

Coleman, Charles (b. ?; d. London, before 9. VII. 1664), Eng. comp. Chamber musn. to Charles I and after the Civil War m. teacher in London. Mus.D. degree, Cambridge, 1651; app. comp. to Charles II, 1662. With Cooke, Hudson, H. Lawes and Locke he contrib. m. to Davenant's *Siege of Rhodes* (entertainment at Rutland House), 1656.

Coleman, Edward (b. ?; d. Greenwich, 29. VIII. 1669), Eng. singer, lutenist & comp., son of prec. Both he and his wife sang in *The Siege of Rhodes* in 1656. He became a Gentleman of the Chapel Royal on its re-estab. in 1660 and succeeded Lanier in the royal band in 1662. Comp. incid. m. to Shirley's *Contention of Ajax and Achilles* in 1653, contrib. songs to *Select Musicall Ayres and Dialogues* the same year, and pieces of his appeared in Playford's *Musical Companion* in 1672.

Coleridge, Samuel Taylor (1772–1834), Eng. poet, critic & philosopher. *See* **Barnett (J. F.)** (*Ancient Mariner*), **Coleridge-Taylor** (*Kubla Khan*), **Griffes** (do.).

Coleridge-Taylor, Avril (b. London), Eng. cond. & comp., daughter of Samuel C.-T. Studied at the G.S.M.
Works incl. *Wyndore* & *Hist. Episode* for chor. & orch.; *Sussex Landscape, The Hills, To April, In Memoriam R.A.F.* for orch.; pf. Conc.; inst. pieces; songs, &c.

Coleridge-Taylor, Samuel (b. London, 15. VIII. 1875; d. Croydon, 1. IX. 1912), Brit. comp., father of prec. Sang at a church at Croydon as a boy and entered the R.C.M. as a v. student in 1890, but also studied comp. under Stanford. He had works perf. while still at coll. and in 1899 he was represented at the North Staffordshire Festival at Hanley. App. cond. of the Handel Soc. in 1904, and visited U.S.A. that year, as well as in 1906 and 1910; but otherwise devoted all his time to comp. and private teaching, with some teaching activity at the G.S.M. in the last years of his life.
Works incl. opera *Thelma*; settings for solo voices, chor. & orch. of portions from Longfellow's *Hiawatha* (3 parts), Coleridge's *Kubla Khan*, Noyes's *A Tale of Old Japan*; 5 Chor. Ballads (Longfellow), *Sea Drift* (Whitman) for chor.; orat. *The Atonement*; incid. m. for Shakespeare's *Othello* and Stephen Phillips's *Herod, Ulysses, Nero* and *Faust* (after Goethe); Sym. in A min.; *Ballade, African Suite, Scenes from an Everyday Romance*, ovt. *Toussaint l'Ouverture*, concert march *Ethiopia saluting the Colours, Symph. Vars. on an African Air* & *Bamboula* rhapsody for orch.; v. Conc. in G min.; Nonet for stgs. & wind, pf. 5tet, cl. 5tet, stg. 4tet in D min. & other chamber m.; v. & pf So. in D min.; many pf. pieces; songs; anthems; partsongs, &c.

Colinda (Rum.). A Rum. Christmas folksong.

Coll. (abbr.) = College.

Colla, Giuseppe (b. Parma, 4. VIII. 1731; d. Parma, 16. III. 1806), It. comp. Chapel master to the Duke of Parma. He married Aguiari in 1780.
Works incl. operas *Adriano in Siria, Didone, Tolomeo* & 3 others, &c.

Colla parte (It. = 'with the part'). A direction indicating that the accomp. to a voc. or inst. solo part is to follow the soloist in a passage perf. without strict adherence to the tempo.

Collective Works. Mus. comps. in which more than one comp. had a hand. *See*

A la manière de . . .
Aiglon, L'
B-la-F Quartet
Baiser et la quittance, Le
Brahms, Dietrich & Schumann, v. & pf. So.
'Cadet Rousselle' Vars.
Chopsticks Vars.
Club Anthem
Don Quixote, The Comical History of
Ernst & Heller, Pensées fugitives
Éventail de Jeanne, L'
Franchomme & Chopin, co. So.
Franchomme & others, duos on operatic airs
Hexameron
Hillemacher brothers
Joyce Book
Leighton, Teares and Lamentacions
Mariés de la Tour d'Eiffel
Marquise de Brinvilliers, La

Collective Works—*continued*
Mlada
Muzio Scevola
Quatorze Juillet (Rolland)
Rebel and Francœur
Requiem for Rossini
Siege of Rhodes, The
Triumphes of Oriana, The
Triumphs of Peace, The
Vars. on a Rus. Theme
Vaterländischer Künstlerverein
Vendredis, Les

Collegium Musicum (Lat. = mus. fraternity). An assoc. for the perf. of chamber and orch. m. in var. Ger. towns in the 18th cent. Bach was a member of the C. M. at Leipzig.

Colles, H(enry). C(ope). (b. Bridgnorth, 20. IV. 1879; d. London, 4. III. 1943), Eng. m. critic and scholar. Educ. at Oxford and the R.C.M. in London. Asst. m. critic to Fuller Maitland on *The Times* until 1911, when he became chief critic, and lecturer at the R.C.M. from 1919. Pub. var. books on m., incl. *Brahms, The Growth of M., Voice and Verse* &c., the 7th vol. of the *Oxford Hist. of M.*, and ed. the 3rd & 4th eds. of Grove's *Dictionary of M. and Musns.*

Collet, Henri (b. Paris, 5. XI. 1885), Fr. mcolst. & comp. He made a special study of Spa. m. and wrote *Le Mysticisme musical espagnol au XVIe siècle, Victoria, Albéniz et Granados* & *L'Essor de la musique espagnole au XXe siècle.*

Comps. incl. symph. poem *El Escorial*; chamber m.; songs in the Spa. manner, &c.

Collin, Heinrich Joseph von (1771–1811), Aus. poet. His chief connection with m. is the drama *Coriolan* for which Beethoven wrote an ovt. Stadler wrote incid. m. for his tragedy *Polyxena.*

Collingwood, Lawrance (b. London, 14. III. 1887), Eng. cond. & comp. Chorister at Westminster Abbey and org. scholar at Exeter Coll., Oxford; lived in Rus. for a time and worked with Albert Coates at the St. Petersburg Opera; married there and returned to Eng. during the Revol. Principal cond. of the Sadler's Wells Opera.

Works incl. opera *Macbeth*, symph. poem for orch., 2 pf. sos., &c.

Collins, William (1721–59), Eng. poet. *See* **Cooke (B.)** (*The Passions*), **Cowen** (do.), **Sanderson (J.)** (*Ode to the Passions*), **Smith (A. M.)** (do.).

Colman, George, jun. (1762–1836), Eng. playwright. *See* **Inkle and Yarico** (Arnold), **Kelly** (*Love laughs at Locksmiths*), **Storace (S.)** (*Iron Chest*).

Colman, George, sen. (1732–94), Eng. playwright. *See* **Gast** (*Heimliche Ehe*), **Matrimonio segreto** (Cimarosa).

Colomba, opera by Mackenzie (lib. by Francis Hueffer, based on Mérimée's story), prod. London, Drury Lane Theatre, 9. IV. 1883.

Colombani, Orazio (b. Verona, ?; d. ?, after 1595), It. comp. Pupil of Porta; chapel master at Vercelli cath. and from 1584 at the monastery of San Francesco, Milan. Later at Venice, Padua and Urbino.

Works incl. magnificats, Te Deum, psalms; madrigals, &c.

Colombe, La (*The Dove*), opera by Gounod (lib. by Jules Barbier & Michel Carré, after La Fontaine), prod. Baden-Baden, 3. VIII. 1860.

Colombian Composer. *See* **Uribe-Holguin.**

Colonna, Giovanni Paolo (b. Bologna, 16. VI. 1637; d. Bologna, 28. XI. 1695), It. comp. Studied in Rome with Carissimi, Abbatini and Benevoli. Became orgst. of San Petronio cath. at Bologna in 1674.

Works incl. opera *Amilcare di Cipro* & some others; masses, motets, psalms, litanies; orats., &c.

Colonne, Édouard (really Judas) (b. Bordeaux, 23. VII. 1838; d. Paris, 28. III. 1910), Fr. vst. & cond. Founder of the Concerts Colonne. He was the 1st to popularize Berlioz and was well known for his perfs. of Wagner, Tchaikovsky and other comps. then unknown in Fr.

Coloratura (It. lit. colouring). Not used in It. as a mus. term, but current in other countries to designate florid singing, esp. in sop. parts containing elaborately decorative passages. There is no good reason why the old Eng. word 'Colorature' should not be revived for the purpose.

Colour. A word frequently used metaphorically for the different qualities of tone prod. by var. insts. and combs. of insts. There is no other Eng. word for what is called *timbre* in Fr., but this is sometimes used in Eng. and an unsuccessful attempt has been made to make up an Eng. word (*see* **Clang-tint**). 'Tone-colour' is now generally current.

Colour Music. Var. attempts have been made to trans. m. into colour effects, e.g. by Castel with his 'Clavecin oculaire,' Rimington with the 'Colour Org.,' Thomas Wilfrid with the 'Clavilux,' Skriabin with the 'Tastiera per luce' in the score of his *Prometheus* and Adrian Bernard Klein with an improved 'Colour Org.' exhib. in London in 1932. Comps. referring to or using colour (light):

Bantock, *Atalanta in Calydon*, during the perf. of which the concert-room is to be lighted in a different colour for each mvt.

Bliss, *Colour Symphony*, each mvt. of which bears the name of a colour as title.

Schoenberg, *Die glückliche Hand*, in which coloured light plays a part, as noted in the score.

Skriabin, *Prometheus*, which contains an optional part for the *tastiera per luce*, designed to throw differently coloured lights.

Colporteur, Le, ou L'Enfant du bûcheron (*The Pedlar, or The Woodcutter's Child*), opera by Onslow (lib. by François Antoine Eugène de Planard), prod. Paris, Opéra-Comique, 22. XI. 1827.

Coltellini, Celeste (b. Leghorn, 1764; d. Capodimonte nr. Naples, 1829). It. sop. singer. Made her 1st appearance at Naples in 1781 and was at the Court Opera in Vienna in 1783–90. Paisiello wrote *Nina* for her.

Colum, Padraic (b. 1881), Ir. poet. *See* **Hughes** (songs).

Combarieu, Jules (Léon Jean) (b. Cahors, 3. II. 1859; d. Paris, 7. VII. 1916), Fr. mcolst. Studied with Spitta in Berlin, settled in Paris, founded the *Revue musicale* in 1904 and ed. it until 1912. His books incl. a hist. of m. in 3 vols. and studies of the relations of m. to poetry, rhythm, &c.

Come prima (It. = as at first). A direction indicating that the opening section of a mvt. is to be played again exactly as before, or that a passage is to be treated in the same manner as before.

Come sopra (It. = as above). A direction asking the player to repeat the manner of perf. of a passage heard earlier.

Come, thou monarch of the vine, song by Schubert, from Shakespeare's *Antony and Cleopatra*, trans. by Ferdinand von Mayerhofer as *Trinklied*, '*Bacchus*' and comp. in Ger. in 1826.

Comédie lyrique (Fr.). An 18th-cent. Fr. name for comic opera.

Comes. *See* **Dux and Comes.**

Comes, Juan Bautista (b. Valencia, 1568; d. Valencia, 1643), Spa. comp. Chapel master at Lérida at first, later mus. dir. at Valencia cath. from 1613 and again from 1632, with an appt. at the royal chapel in Madrid and another at the Colegio del Patriarca at Valencia in between.

Works incl. much church m. on a large scale; sacred m. with Spa. words, &c.

Commedia per musica (It. = comedy for m.). A Neapol. term of the 18th cent. for comic opera.

Commer, Franz (b. Cologne, 23. I. 1813; d. Berlin, 17. VIII. 1887), Ger. orgst., ed. & comp. Orgst. at the Cologne Carmelite church, 1828–32, then in var. posts in Berlin. Ed. old voc. and org. m. and comp. a number of works incl. m. for Aristophanes' *The Frogs* and Sophocles' *Electra*.

Commodo (It.). *See* **Comodo.**

Common Chord. The non-technical term for the maj. or min. triad, usually that which determines the key of a comp.

Common Time. A loose but widely current term for 4–4 time.

Community Singing. A form of popular m.-making, in favour partic. during and after the war of 1914–8, which consists of the unrehearsed perf. by large gatherings of people of folk and popular songs familiar to all.

Comodo (It. = easy, convenient). As a mus. direction the word means leisurely; it is frequently misspelt *commodo* by non-It. comps.

Comp. (abbr.) = Compose, Composed, Composer, Composition.

Compass. The range of notes covered by a voice or inst. beyond which it cannot go any higher or lower.

Compère, Loyset (b. ?; d. Saint-Quentin, 16. VIII. 1518), Fr. comp. At first a chorister, later a canon and chancellor of Saint-Quentin cath. Pupil of Okeghem.

Works incl. motets and other church m.; sacred and secular voc. comps.; partsongs with It. words, &c.

Competition Festival. An institution in Eng. based on the Eisteddfod in Wales, begun by J. S. Curwen (London) and Mary Wakefield (Kendal) in 1882–5, giving opportunities to bodies of singers and players, or individual perfs., mainly amateurs or learners, to perf. in friendly rivalry and to be judged by professional adjudicators.

Complainte (Fr. = complaint, plaint). An ancient form of Fr. song, esp. a religious ballad.

Composer. The creative mus. artist who expresses himself through the medium of m. invented, constructed and written down by himself.

Composition. The act of writing down m. originated by his own imagination by the comp.

Compound Intervals. Any Intervals exceeding the compass of an 8ve, so called, as distinct from Simple Is., because they differ from the latter only in width, not in character: e.g. a maj. 10th is essentially the same as a maj. 3rd, &c.

Compound Time (or Triple Time). Any mus. metre governed by a key signature prescribing 3, 6, 9 or 12 beats, i.e. having a multiple of 3 as its unit. Actually abnormal metres not coming under Simple Time, such as 5–4

7–8, &c. are also in C. T., though not technically so called.

Comte Ory, Le (*Count O.*), opera by Rossini (lib. by Eugène Scribe & Charles Gaspard Delestre-Poirson), prod. Paris, Opéra, 20. VIII. 1828. The only Fr. opera by R. apart from *Guillaume Tell*.

Comus, masque by Milton, with m. by Henry Lawes, prod. Ludlow Castle, 29. IX. 1634.

The same with alterations by Dalton and m. by Arne, prod. London, Drury Lane Theatre, 4. III. 1738.

Con. (abbr.) = Contralto.

Con (It.) = with. The prep. is often used in directions indicating the manner of perf. of a piece or mvt., e.g. *con brio* = with dash, *con molto espressione* = with much expression, &c.

Con amore (It. = with love, with affection). A direction indicating an enthusiastic manner of perf.

Conc. (abbr.) = Concerto.

Concent (old Eng.) = Concord.

Concento (It. = union, agreement). The playing of the notes of a chord exactly together.

Concert. Orig., as in the Eng. 'consort,' the singing or playing together under any conditions; now a public perf. of m., except that of an opera or as a rule that given by a single perf., which is more often called a Recital.

Concert spirituel (never Concerts spirituels). A mus. institution founded in Paris by A. Philidor in 1725 for the prod. of sacred works, but afterwards widening its scope to incl. secular m., esp. syms. and concs. It lasted until 1791, but was later replaced by similar organizations. It was also imitated elsewhere, under the same name, e.g. in London and Vienna.

Concertante (It. = Concertizing). An adj. used to designate inst. or more rarely voc. parts in a comp. which are designed mainly for the display of virtuosity. A *sinfonia concertante*, for ex., is a work with a prominent and brilliant solo part or several such parts.

Concertato (It.) = concerted. A work or portion of a comp. written for several persons to be perf. together.

Concerted Music. Any m. written for several persons to be perf. together, but only so long as they are all solo perfs. Thus any chamber m. or a 4tet or other ensemble in an opera or orat. is C. M., but the opera or orat. itself is not, neither is, for ex., a sym. or a chor. partsong.

Concertgebouw (Dutch = Concert Building). A concert hall at Amsterdam opened in 1888.

Concertina. An inst., patented in 1829, similar to the Accordion, prod. its sound by means of tuned pipes through which wind is driven by pleated bellows opened and closed by the player's hands.

Concertino (It. = little concert or little conc.). In the former sense the C. is a group of solo insts. playing alternately with the orchestra (*ripieno*) in a work of the *Concerto grosso* type; in the latter a C. is a conc. for a solo inst. formally on a smaller scale.

Concertmaster (Amer.). The term used in U.S.A. for the Leader of an orch., derived from the Ger. *Konzertmeister*.

Concerto (It. = concert or consort). A comp. formerly for orch. with or without groups of solo insts.; now a work for 1 or more solo insts. with orch., designed for display of the individual perf.'s technical powers, but also, in the best exs. to be valuable as a work of art. From about the time of Mozart, who settled a special type of so.-sym. form for the C., with an organic function for the orch., Cs. have been almost invariably written in so. form or some recognizable variant of it. There is nearly always a slow mvt., very rarely a scherzo, and the finale is generally either in so. or rondo form.

Concerto grosso (It. = grand or big concert). A type of conc. of the 17th–18th cent. played by an orch. in which a group of solo insts., usually 2 vs. and co., take a more or less prominent but not outstandingly conspicuous or brilliant part. The group of soloists was called the *concertino* and the main orch. (*tutti*) the *ripieno*. Bach's Brandenburg Concs. are works of the C. g. type, although Nos. 3 and 6 contain no *concertino* parts.

Concertstück (Ger., also *Konzertstück* = concert piece). A title sometimes given to works of the conc. type for solo inst. and orch. which are not fully developed concs. C.'s are often in 1 mvt. or in several connected sections. Although Ger., the title has been used by comps. in other countries, e.g. Chaminade & Pierné in Fr., Cowen in Eng., &c.

Conchita, opera by Zandonai (lib., in Fr., by Maurice Vaucaire, trans. into It. by Carlo Zangarini, based on Pierre Louÿs's novel, *La Femme et le pantin*), prod. Milan, Teatro dal Verme, 14. X. 1911. The lib. was orig. written for Puccini.

Concitato (It.) = Excited, agitated.

Concone, Giuseppe (b. Turin, 1810; d. Turin, 1. VI. 1861), It. teacher of singing. Worked in Paris for a time, but returned to Turin during the 1848 Revol. He pub. numerous useful voc. exercises.

Concord. The opposite of discord: the

sounding together of notes in harmony that satisfies the ear as being final in itself and requiring no following chord to give the impression of resolution.

Conductorless Orchestra. *See* Persymfans.

Conductus. A part in 12th–13th-cent. voc. comp. similar to a *cantus firmus* round which other parts were woven, but not consisting of a plainsong melody. The C. was either a popular song or a tune specially comp. In the former case the C. might be said to have a modern counterpart in a familiar song to which a descant has been fitted by a comp.

Confalonieri, Giulio (Melian) (b. Milan, 1896),, It. comp. Studied at Milan and was a pupil of Alfano at Bologna.
Works incl. incid. m. to Fletcher's *Faithful Shepherdess*; symph. poem *Una notte sul monte Imetto*; 2 v. & pf. sos.; *Preludi al mattino* for pf.; 4 *Melodie per Cloti* for voice & pf., &c.

Congreve, William (1670–1729), Eng. dramatist & poet. *See* Austin (F.) (*The Way of the World*), Eccles (J.) (do., *Love for Love, Semele* & *Ode for St. Cecilia's Day*), Finger (*Love for Love* & *Mourning Bride*), Judgment of Paris (J. Eccles, Finger, D. Purcell & Weldon), Philidor (8) (*Ode for St. C.'s D.*), Purcell (*Double Dealer* & *Old Bachelor*), Sammartini (G.) (*Judgment of P.*), Semele (Handel).

Conjunct Motion. *See* Motion.

Conon de Béthune (b. ?; d. ?), Fr. 12th-cent. trouvère. 10 of his poems, 9 with m., are preserved.

Conradi, Johann Georg (b. ?; d. ?), Ger. 17th-cent. comp. Mus. dir. at Oettingen, Bavaria. One of the earliest comps. of Ger. operas, which incl. *Ariadne, Diogenes, Numa Pompilius, Der tapfere Kaiser Carolus, Jerusalem, Pygmalion*, &c.

Cons. (abbr.) = Conservatoire, Conservatorio, Conservatorium, Conservatory.

Consecration of the House (Beethoven). *See* Weihe des Hauses.

Consecutive. An adj. used to describe the progression of intervals in similar motion by degrees of whole or half tones. C. 5ths and 8ves are theoretically inadmissible as part of harmonic progressions because they prod. a bad effect, but have been used by responsible comps. for a long time, esp. the former, where they happened to do what was required.

Consequent. Another term for the Answer in a Fugue.

Conservatoire de Musique. The chief school of m. in Paris, opened in 1579 with Sarrette as dir., having grown out of the École Royale du Chant, estab. in 1784 under the dir. Gossec. Later dirs. were Cherubini, Auber, A. Thomas, Dubois, Fauré, Rabaud and Delvincourt.

Conservatorio (It.), later Conservatoire (Fr.), Conservatorium (Ger.), Conservatory (Eng., espec. Amer.). A school of m., orig. in It., espec. Venice and Naples, an orphanage where children were 'conserved' to become useful citizens and at the same time trained as musns.

Console. The part of an org. which is directly under the control of the player's hands and feet.

Consonance. The purely-intoned and agreeable sounding together of notes capable of prod. concord.

Consort (Eng., obs.). In m. formerly the equivalent of 'concert,' i.e. insts. playing together.

Consort-Viol. A bass viol of the largest size, so called because it was used only in consorts, not as a solo inst.

Constantinescu, Paul (b. Ploesti, 1909), Rum. comp. Studied at Bucharest and Vienna, and later became dir. of broadcasting at Bucharest.
Works incl. opera *The Stormy Night*; ballet *The Wedding in the Far End of Moldavia*; Liturgy in the Byzantine style; chor. works; Sinfonietta, Suite, *Four Fables* &c. for orch.; Sonatina for v. & pf.; Rum. song-cycle, &c.

Contano (It. = they count; accent on 1st syll.). A direction in a voc. or inst. part of a work where the perfs. have a prolonged rest, warning them to count bars during that rest in order to make sure of coming in again at the proper moment.

Conte Caramella, Il, opera by Galuppi (lib. by Goldoni, partly based on Addison's comedy *The Drummer, or The Haunted House*), prod. Verona, 18. XII. 1749.

Contes d'Hoffmann, Les (*The Tales of Hoffmann*), opera by Offenbach (lib. by Jules Barbier & Michel Carré, based on a play of their own and farther back on stories by E. T. A. Hoffmann), prod. Paris, Opéra-Comique, 10. II. 1881, after the comp.'s death. He did not finish it; the scoring is partly by Guiraud.

Contesa dei numi, La (*The Contest of the Gods*), opera by Gluck (lib. by Metastasio), prod. Copenhagen, at court, 9. IV. 1749, to celebrate the birth of Prince Christian, later Christian VII.
Opera by Vinci (lib. do.), prod. Rome, Cardinal Polignac's palace, 26. XI. 1729, to celebrate the birth of the Dauphin, son of Louis XV.

Conti, Carlo (b. Arpino, 9. X. 1796; d. Naples, 10. VII. 1868), It. comp. Pupil of Zingarelli, later prof. at the Naples Cons., where he deputized as dir. in 1862 when Mercadante became blind.

Works incl. operas *Olimpia* & *Giovanna Shore* (after Rowe); 6 masses, 2 Requiems, &c.

Conti, Francesco Bartolomeo (b. Florence, 20. I. 1681; d. Vienna, 20. VII. 1732), It. lutenist & comp. Theorbo player to the Aus. court in Vienna, 1701–5 and again from 1708; court comp. from 1713.

Works incl. operas *Alba Cornelia, Clotilda, Il trionfo dell' Amore, I satiri in Arcadia, Don Chisciotte in Sierra Morena, L'Issipile*, &c., stage serenades; orats., cantatas, &c.

Continental Fingering. The fingering of pf. m. now in universal use, with the fingers marked 1–5 from the thumb. This system has displaced the so-called Eng. Fingering, marked + for the thumb and 1–4 for the other fingers, which however was by no means in use throughout the whole hist. of Eng. keyboard m.

Continuo (It. abbr. for *basso continuo*). *See* Thorough-Bass.

Contra (Lat. = against). A prefix used for org. stops denoting that the stop indicated by the word following it plays an octave lower.

Contra Bass. *See* **Double Bass.**

Contra Bassoon. *See* **Double Bassoon.**

Contrabass (Ger.) } = Double Bass.
Contrabasso (It.) }

Contrafagotto (It.) = Double Bassoon.

Contralto. The lowest woman's voice, called *alto* in some other languages, which term in Eng. is however reserved for the highest (falsetto) male voice—quite properly, since the It. word *alto* means 'high.'

Contrapunctus (Lat.) = Counterpoint.

Contrapuntal. The adj. derived from 'counterpoint.'

Contrary Motion. *See* **Motion.**

Contrattempo (It.) = Syncopation.

Contrebasse (Fr.) = Double Bass.

Contredanse (Fr.). *See* **Country Dance.**

Conus. *See* **Konius.**

Converse, Frederick (Shepherd) (b. Newtown, Mass., 5. I. 1871; d. Westwood, Mass., 8. VI. 1940), Amer. comp. Although intended for a commercial career, he studied m. at Harvard Univ. under Paine. Later he studied pf. with Carl Baermann and comp. with Chadwick at Boston, and took a finishing course at Munich. After his return to U.S.A. he held var. teaching posts at Boston and Harvard until 1907.

Works incl. operas *The Pipe of Desire, The Sacrifice, The Immigrants* & *Sinbad the Sailor*; *Job* for solo voices, chor. & orch., Psalm for male voices, brass & org.; 3 syms., tone-poems *Endymion's Narrative, The Mystic Trumpeter* (after Whitman), *Ormazd, Ave atque vale, Song of the Sea, Euphrosyne* ovt.; Fantasy *Flivver Ten Million* & *The Festival of Pan* for orch.; *Night* & *Day* for pf. & orch. (after Whitman); *Hagar in the Desert* for con. & orch., *La Belle Dame sans merci* (Keats) for bar. & orch.; 2 stg. 4tets; pf. Trio; So. & Conc. for v. & pf.; pf. pieces; songs, &c.

Convitato di pietra, Il, opera by Fabrizi (c. 1765–?), prod. Fano, 1788.

Convitato di pietra, Il, o sia Il dissoluto, opera by Righini (lib. by ?), prod. Vienna, Kärntnertor Theatre, 21. VIII. 1777.

Cook, Thomas (Aynsley) (b. London, VII. 1831 or 1836; d. Liverpool, 16. II. 1894), Eng. bass singer. Studied with Staudigl at Munich and sang at var. Bavar. theatres before he made his 1st stage appearance in Eng., at Manchester in 1856. He is the maternal grandfather of Goossens.

Cooke, Arnold (b. Gomersal nr. Bradford, Yorks., 4. XI. 1906), Eng. comp. Educ. at Repton School and Caius Coll., Cambridge, where he took the B.Mus. degree in 1929. From that year to 1932 he was a pupil of Hindemith at the State High School for M. in Berlin, then succeeded Walter Leigh as mus. dir. to the Cambridge Festival Theatre and in 1933 was app. prof. of harmony and comp. at the Royal Manchester Coll. of M. In 1938 he settled in London and in 1941 joined the Royal Navy for the duration of the 2nd world war, serving as liaison officer on foreign ships.

Works incl. cantata *Holderneth* for bar., chor. & orch.; Concert Ovt. for orch.; Passacaglia, Scherzo and Finale for stg. orch.; pf. Conc.; 4 Shakespeare sonnets for voice & orch.; stg. 4tet, Vars. for stg. 4tet, pf. Trio, 4tet for fl., v., va. & co., 5tet for fl., cl., v., co. & hp., Duo for v. & va.; sos. for v. & pf., va. & pf., co. & pf.; So. for 2 pfs.; pf. So. & Suite, &c.

Cooke, Benjamin (b. London, 1734; d. London, 14. IX. 1793), Eng. orgst. & comp. Pupil of Pepusch, whom he succeeded in 1752 as cond. to the Academy of Ancient M. In 1757 he was app. choirmaster at Westminster Abbey in succession to Gates. Mus.D., Cambridge, 1775, and Oxford, 1782, when he became orgst. of St. Martin's-in-the-Fields in London.

Works incl. services, anthems (some for special occasions), psalms, chants & hymns; ode for Delap's tragedy *The Captives*; *Ode on the Passions* (Collins), odes for Christmas Day, on Handel, on Chatterton and for the king's recovery, ode *The Syrens' Song to Ulysses*; glees, catches and canons; orch. concs.; org. pieces; hpchd. lessons, &c.

Cooke, Henry (b. ? London, *c.* 1615; d. Hampton Court, 13. VII. 1672), Eng. bass singer & comp. Pupil of the Chapel Royal; was a captain in the Duke of Northumberland's army during the Civil War. App. singer and Master of the Children at the Chapel Royal at the Restor. With Charles Coleman, Hudson, H. Lawes and Locke he contrib. to Davenant's *Siege of Rhodes* (entertainment at Rutland House), 1656, and sang in it.

Works incl. coronation m., hymn for the installation of Knights of the Garter, anthems, songs for 1 and more voices, &c.

Cooke, Thomas (Simpson) (Tom), (b. Dublin, 1782; d. London, 26. II. 1848), Ir. ten. singer, vst. & comp. Learnt m. from his father, Bartlett C., an oboist, played a v. conc. in public at 7, learnt comp. from Giordani, was leader of the Crow Street Theatre orch. at 15 and kept a m. shop in 1806–12. In 1813 he appeared in London with great success and settled there. For *c.* 20 years he not only sang at Drury Lane Theatre, but led the orch., played 9 different insts., managed the house and provided mus. stage pieces for it. He also taught singing with success.

Works incl. stage pieces *Frederick the Great, The Wager, The Brigand, Peter the Great, King Arthur and the Knights of the Round Table*; songs for Shakespeare's *Midsummer Night's Dream*; songs, glees, catches, &c.

Cooper, Gerald M(elbourne). (b. 13. IX. 1892), Eng. mcolst., author & ed. Wrote numerous articles, mainly on old Eng. m., organized series of old and modern m. and of classical chamber m. in London in 1922–30, and again from 1942. Hon. sec. of the Purcell Soc. and ed. of a popular ed. of extracts from its complete ed. of Purcell's works. Hon. sec. of the Royal Phil. Soc. 1929–32. On the death of Edwin Evans in 1945 he succeeded him as chairman of the London Contemp. M. Centre (Brit. section of the I.S.C.M.).

Cooper, James Fenimore (1789–1851), Amer. novelist. *See* **Genée.**

Cooper, John (self-styled Giovanni Coprario or Coperario) (b. ?, *c.* 1570; d. ?, 1627), Eng. lutenist, violist & comp. Studied in It., and on his return *c.* 1604 kept to his Italianized name. He taught the children of James I and was the master of W. and H. Lawes.

Works incl. *The Masque of the Inner Temple and Gray's Inn* (Francis Beaumont), *The Masque of Flowers*; *Funeral Teares* on the death of the Earl of Devonshire, *Songs of Mourning* on the death of Prince Henry (words by Campion); anthems; works for viols and for viols and org.; fancies for the org. based on It. madrigals; lute m.; songs, &c.

Cooper, Martin (Du Pré) (b. Winchester, 17. I. 1910), Eng. writer on m. Educ. at Winchester Coll. and Oxford, studied m. with Wellesz in Vienna. His work incl. books on Gluck and Bizet.

Coperario, Giovanni. *See* **Cooper, John.**

Copland, Aaron (b. Brooklyn, N.Y., 14. XI. 1900), Amer. comp. Began to learn the pf. at the age of 13 and studied theory with Rubin Goldmark; later went to Fr. and became a pupil of Nadia Boulanger at the Fontainebleau School of M. In 1924 a Guggenheim scholarship enabled him to spend 2 more years in Eur. He was represented for the 1st time at an I.S.C.M. festival at Frankfort in 1927 and won a prize in Amer. with his *Dance Symphony* in 1930. He has since done much propaganda work for Amer. m., is a member of the League of Comps. and writes and lectures on m.

Works incl. ballets *Grohg, Billy the Kid, Appalachian Spring*; school opera *The Second Hurricane*; m. for films incl. *Of Mice and Men*; orch. works: sym. for org. & orch., 1st Sym., *M. for the Theatre, Symph. Ode, A Dance Sym., Short Sym., Statements, El Salón Mexico, M. for the Radio, An Outdoor Ovt., Quiet City, Letter from Home, Danzon Cabano*; *Portrait of Abraham Lincoln* for orator & orch.; Conc. for pf. & orch.; *The House on the Hill* & *An Immorality* for female chor.; 2 pieces for stg. 4tet; 6tet for cl., stgs. & pf.; v. & pf. So.; pf. So., pieces, &c.

Coppard, A(lfred). E(dgar). (b. 1878), Eng. poet & novelist. *See* **Swain** (songs).

Coppée, François (1843–1908), Fr. poet & dramatist. *See* **Hubay** (*Luthier de Crémone*), **Paladilhe** (*Passant*), **Svendsen** (do.), **Widor** (*Jacobites*).

Coppélia, ou La Fille aux yeux d'émail (*C., or The Girl with Enamel Eyes*), ballet by Delibes (scen. by Charles Nuitter & A. Saint-Léon; chgph. by Louis Mérante), prod. Paris, Opéra, 25. V. 1870.

Coppola, Pier Antonio (b. Castrogiovanni, Sicily, 11. XII. 1793; d. Catania, 13. XI. 1877), It. comp. Studied at Naples and prod. his 1st opera, *Il figlio del bandito*, there in 1816. He was at Lisbon in 1839–42 as cond. of the San Carlos Theatre and again in 1850–71.

Works incl. operas *Nina pazza per*

amore, *Eva* (in Fr.), *Gli Illinesi*, *Ines de Castro*, &c.; masses, litanies and other church m., &c.

Coprario, Giovanni. *See* **Cooper, John.**

Coq d'or (Rimsky-Korsakov). *See* **Golden Cockerel.**

Coquard, Arthur (b. Paris, 26. V. 1846; d. Noirmoutier, 20. VIII. 1910), Fr. comp. Studied law in Paris and took harmony lessons from Franck. He gave up the idea of becoming a musn. at first and in 1870 became secretary to a member of the Senate; but later Franck encouraged him to further mus. studies. He became a m. critic and lecturer at the Institution for the Blind.

Works incl. operas *L'Épée du roi*, *Le Mari d'un jour*, *La Jacquerie* (left unfinished by Lalo), *Jahel*, *La Troupe Jolicœur*; incid. m. for Racine's *Esther*, Bornier's *Agamemnon* & other plays; scenes for voice & orch. *Le Chant des épées*, *Cassandre*, *Héro et Léandre*, *Christophe Colomb*, *Andromaque*; symph. poem on Ossian; sacred trilogy *Jeanne d'Arc*, &c.

Cor anglais. *See* **English Horn.** Also an 8-ft. reed org. stop reproducing that inst.'s tone.

Cor-de-Nuit. An 8-ft. closed metal flue stop on the org.

Cor-Oboe. An 8-ft. flue org. stop.

Corant (Eng.) = Courante. The word, like the Fr. masc. Courant, is obs., but might be revived with advantage.

Coranto (It.). *See* **Courante.**

Corbett, William (b. ?; d. London, 7. III. 1748), Eng. vst. & comp. At var. times leader of the orch. at the King's Theatre, Haymarket, dir. of Lincoln's Inn Fields Theatre, member of the royal band; lived for some time in It., where he toured as a vst. and collected insts.

Works incl. incid. m. to plays, e.g. Shakespeare's *Henry IV*, orch. concs. and sos. for var. insts.

Corbiac, Piere de (b. ?; d. ?), Fr. 13th-cent. troubadour, uncle of Belenoi. Wrote a song to the Virgin Mary.

Cordatura (It.). The notes to which a stg. inst. is tuned, e.g. G, D, A, E for the v. Any change in the normal tuning made temporarily is called *scordatura*.

Corder, Frederick (b. London, 26. I. 1852; d. London, 21. VIII. 1932), Eng. teacher, cond. & comp. Studied at the R.A.M. in London and under F. Hiller at Cologne. Prof. of comp. at R.A.M. from 1888. 1st Eng. trans. of Wagner's *Ring*.

Works incl. opera *Nordisa*, cantatas *The Bridal of Triermain* (after Scott) & *The Sword of Argantyr*, ovt. *Prospero* (after Shakespeare's *Tempest*), Elegy for 24 vs. & org.; recitations with m.; songs, partsongs, &c.

Corelli, Arcangelo (b. Fusignano, Imola, 17. II. 1653; d. Rome, 8. I. 1713), It. vst. & comp. Studied at Bologna, was (?) at Munich between 1670–2 and (?) at Hanover between 1680–5, when he settled in Rome and pub. his 1st v. sos. He lived at the palace of his patron, Cardinal Pietro Ottoboni. Visited Modena and Naples, cond. at the Roman residence of Christina of Swe., collected pictures and taught many v. pupils, incl. Geminiani and Locatelli.

Works incl. a set of Concerti grossi; 5 sets of chamber sos., &c.

Coriolan. Beethoven's ovt. to the play of that name by Heinrich von Collin, Op. 62, comp. in 1807 and prod. with the play in XII of that year. Apart from its subject the play has no connection with Shakespeare's *Coriolanus*.

Corkine, William (b. ?; d. ?), Eng. lutenist & comp. Pub. 2 books of airs to the lute and bass viol, followed by dances and other inst. pieces; an anthem is also preserved. The 2nd book of airs contains settings of Donne's 'Go and catch a falling star'; *Break of Day:* ''Tis true, 'tis day'; *The Bait:* 'Come live with me, and be my love.'

Corneille, Pierre (1606–84), Fr. poet & dramatist. *See* **Charpentier** (**M.-A.**) (*Polyeucte* & *Andromède*), **Cid** (Cornelius & Massenet), **Cleopatra e Cesare** (Graun), **Dukas** (*Polyeucte* ovt.). **Flavio** (Handel), **Gouvy** (*Cid*), **Holmes** (**A.**) (do.), **Lully** (*Œdipe*), **Lunssens** (*Cid*, symph. poem), **Martyrs** (Donizetti), **Nottara** (*Polyeucte*), **Poliuto** (Donizetti), **Polyeucte** (Gounod), **Rieti** (*Illusion comique*), **Roberto Devereux** (Donizetti), **Sacchini** (*Gran Cid*), **Tiersot** (*Andromède*), **Tinel** (*Polyeucte*), **Tito Vespasiano** (Caldara & Hasse), **Wagenaar** (**J.**) (*Cid*).

Corneille, Thomas (1625–1709), Fr. poet & dramatist, brother of prec. *See* **Bellérophon** (Lully), **Charpentier** (**M.-A.**) (*Pierre philosophale* & 2 plays with Visé), **Médée** (M.-A. Charpentier), **Psyché** (Lully).

Cornelius, Peter (b. Mainz, 24. XII. 1824; d. Mainz, 26. X. 1874), Ger. comp. & author. Studied m. after failing as an actor, 1st with Dehn in Berlin, 1845–50, and from 1852 with Liszt at Weimar, where he joined the new Ger. group of musns. and wrote eloquently about them in Schumann's *Neue Zeitschrift*, without however succumbing to Wagnerian influence in his own work. But he sought out Wagner in Vienna in 1858 and followed him to Munich in 1865.

Works incl. operas *Der Barbier von Bagdad*, *Der Cid* & *Gunlöd* (unfinished); chor. works *Trauerchöre* & *Vätergruft*; duets for sop. & bar.;

songs incl. cycles *Liedercyclus*, *Weihnachtslieder*, *Brautlieder*; song on 1 note *Ein Ton*, &c.

Cornelys (*née* Imer), **T(h)eresa** (b. Venice, 1723; d. London, 19. VIII. 1797), It. singer, married to the dancer Pompeati, but assumed the name of C. when at Amsterdam. She made her 1st appearance in London in 1746 as Signora P., in Gluck's *Caduta de' giganti*, and in 1764 began to give mus. entertainments at Carlisle House in Soho Square, continuing until 1771, when she was indicted for keeping it for immoral purposes, poss. at the instigation of jealous rivals.

Cornemuse (Fr.) = Bagpipe.

Cornet. A brass wind inst. of the tpt. type, but with a less incisive tone, now fitted with valves to enable it to prod. all the chromatic notes within its compass. It is comparatively rarely used in the orch. (most often in Fr.), but is an important member of the military band and the treble inst. of the brass band. Cs. are usually in A or B♭ and transpose accordingly. Also an org. mixture stop.

Cornet à pistons (Fr. = C. with valves). The Fr. name of the Cornet.

Cornett (Eng., obs.). The name of an old wind inst. now in disuse. It was quite unlike the modern cornet, being made of wood or ivory in the shape of a long, thin, slightly tapering tube, either straight or slightly curved, and covered with leather. C.'s were often used as treble insts. with sackbuts (trombones), frequently in church, and the Serpent belonged to the same family.

Cornetto (It.). The It. name of the Cornet and Cornett.

Corno (It.) = Horn.

Corno di bassetto (It.) = Basset Horn. (In 1888–9 Bernard Shaw wrote mus. criticism for the *Star* under the pseudonym of C. di B.). Also an 8-ft. org. stop with cl. tone and a bass register.

Corno dolce. An 8-ft. metal org. stop with soft tone.

Corno inglese (It.) = English Horn.

Corno torto. *See* **Lyzarden.**

Cornopean. An 8-ft. reed org. stop.

Cornyshe, William (b. ?, *c.* 1465; d. ?, *c.* 1523), Eng. comp. Attached to the courts of Henry VII and Henry VIII, not only as musn., but as actor and prod. of interludes and pageants. Gentleman of the Chapel Royal from *c.* 1496; succeeded Newark as Master of the Children in 1509. He wrote m. for the court banquets and masques and officiated in Fr. at the Field of the Cloth of Gold in 1520.

Works incl. motets, magnificats, *Ave Maria*; secular songs, some with satirical words, for insts. & voices, incl. a setting of Skelton's *Hoyda, Jolly Rutterkin*.

Corona (It. = *Fermata*). A rarely used name for the pause indicated by the sign 𝄐.

Coronach (Gael. = 'crying together'). A funeral cry, or in its more cultivated mus. form a dirge.

Coronation Anthem, an anthem by Purcell, 'My heart is inditing,' comp. for the coronation of James II and perf. on that occasion in Westminster Abbey, 23. IV. 1685.

Coronation Anthems, 4 anthems by Handel comp. for the coronation of George II and perf. at the ceremony in Westminster Abbey, 11. X. 1727. 1. 'Zadok the Priest,' 2. 'The King shall rejoice,' 3. 'My heart is inditing,' 4. 'Let thy hand be strengthened.'

'Coronation' Concerto. The nickname of Mozart's pf. Conc. in D maj., K. 537, comp. II. 1788 and perf. by him at Frankfort o/M. at the coronation festivities for Leopold II, 15. X. 1790. As he played also the Conc. K. 459, there is no good reason for calling K. 537 alone by that name.

'Coronation' Mass. Mozart's Mass in C maj. K. 317, comp. in III. 1779. The application of its nickname is uncertain, but it has been conjectured that M. dedicated the work to an image of the Virgin Mary, crowned in 1751, or wrote it for a commemoration of that crowning.

Correggio, Claudio da. *See* **Merulo.**

Corregidor, Der (*The Magistrate*), opera by Wolf (lib. by Rosa Mayreder, based on Pedro Antonio de Alarcón's story *El sombrero de tres picos* = *The Three-cornered Hat*), prod. Mannheim, 7. VI. 1896.

Corrente (It.) = Courante.

Corri, Domenico (b. Rome, 4. X. 1746; d. London, 22. V. 1825), It. cond., pub. & comp. Pupil of Porpora. Settled at Edinburgh in 1771 as cond. of the Mus. Soc., pub. and singing-master. He failed in business and settled in London *c.* 1790, where he set up in partnership with Dussek, who married his daughter Sophia in 1792.

Works incl. operas *Alessandro nell' Indie* & *The Travellers*; inst. sos., rondos & other pieces; songs incl. *Six Canzones dedicated to Scots Ladies*, &c.

Corsaro, Il (*The Corsair*), opera by Verdi (lib. by Francesco Maria Piave, based on Byron's poem), prod. Trieste, 25. X. 1848.

Corsi, Jacopo (b. ? Florence, *c.* 1560; d. Florence, 1604), It. nobleman & amateur comp. Took part in the initiation of opera at Florence. Peri's *Dafne* and *Euridice* were prod. at his house and he took some share in the comp. of the former.

Corteccia, Francesco Bernardo di (b. Arezzo, ?; d. Florence, 7. VI. 1571), It. orgst. & comp. Orgst. at the church of San Lorenzo from 1531 and chapel master from 1539 to Cosimo I de' Medici, for the marriage of whose son Francesco to Joanna of Aus. in 1565 he wrote m., with Striggio, for Cini's intermezzo *Psiche ed Amore*.

Works incl. hymns in 4 parts, canticles and responses, madrigals, pieces for 4–8 voices and insts.

Cortellini, Camillo (b. Bologna, ?; d. Bologna, *c.* 1621), It. vst. & comp. Worked at Bologna from *c.* 1583. Wrote masses (incl. some concerted ones with prominent inst. parts), psalms, litanies, madrigals, &c.

Corthol (Eng., obs.). Another form of Curtal(l), the old name for the bn.

Cosa rara (Martín y Soler). *See* **Una cosa rara.**

Così fan tutte, o sia La scuola degli amanti (*They all do it, or The School for Lovers*), opera by Mozart (lib. by Lorenzo da Ponte), prod. Vienna, Burg Theatre, 26. I. 1790.

Costa, Michele (Michael Andrew Agnus) (b. Naples, 4. II. 1808; d. Hove, 29. IV. 1884), It. (anglicized) cond. & comp., of Spa. descent. Studied at the Real Collegio of Naples and prod. his 1st 2 operas there in 1826–7, and wrote a Mass, 3 syms. and other works. In 1829 he was sent to Birmingham by Zingarelli to cond. a work by that master at the Festival, but by a mistake was made to sing the ten. part instead. He then settled in London, comp. many ballets and operas and perfected the orch. at the Opera; in 1846 he was app. cond. of the Philh. Soc. and Covent Garden opera, and he became the most important festival cond. Knighted in 1869.

Works incl. operas *Il delitto punito*, *Il sospetto funesto*, *Il carcere d'Ildegonda*, *Malvina*, *Malek Adhel* (for Paris), *Don Carlos* (London); ballets *Kenilworth* (after Scott), *Une Heure à Naples*, *Sir Huon*; orats. *La passione*, *Eli*, *Naaman*; Mass for 4 voices, *Dixit Dominus*; syms.; voc. quartet *Ecco il fiero istante*, &c.

Costanza e Fortezza (*Constancy and Power*), opera by Fux (lib. by Pietro Pariati), prod. Prague, Hradžin Palace, at the coronation of the Emperor Charles VI as king of Bohemia, and birthday of the Empress Elizabeth Christina, 28. VIII. 1723.

Costeley, William (Guillaume) (b. ?, 1531; d. Évreux, 1. II. 1606), Sco. or Ir. orgst. & comp. Settled in Fr. at an early age and was orgst. to Henri II and Charles IX. 1st president of the St. Cecilia soc. at Évreux estab. in the 1570s. Wrote chansons for several voices, inst. pieces, &c.

Cosyn, Benjamin (b. ?; d. ?), Eng. orgst. & comp. Orgst. at Dulwich Coll., 1622–4 and afterwards at Charterhouse School. Wrote church m. and collected a book of virginal pieces by var. comps.

Cotton, John (b. ?; d. ?), Eng. 11th–12th-cent. mus. scholar. Author of a Lat. treatise on m. which seems to have been widely distributed in MS.; 6 copies are preserved in Fr., It., Belg., Ger. & Aus., but none in Eng.

Coulé (Fr.). *See* **Ornaments.**

Council of Trent. An eccles. council held at Trent (It. Trento, Ger. Trient) in S. Tyrol between 1545 & 1563 in 3 different periods each incl. a number of sessions. It was intended to introd. counter-reforms into the Roman Catholic church to make the Reformation appear superfluous to Catholics who inclined to embrace Protestantism. Mus. reforms were not discussed in detail until near the end, esp. at the meeting of 11. XI. 1563. They incl. the abolition of all Sequences except 4 (*Dies irae*, *Veni Sancte Spiritus*, *Victimae Paschali* & *Lauda Sion*), the expunging of all tunes with impious or lascivious associations used as *canti fermi*, the simplifying of polyphony to make the words clearly audible (some members advocating the use of plainsong alone), correspondence between the m. and the meaning of the words, &c. The opening of a Roman seminary for the training of priests was also decided, and this was opened in 1565 with Palestrina as m. master.

Counter (verb). To perf. improvised vars. on a tune in the 16th–17th cents.

Counter Subject. The name for a theme in a fugue which continues in the 1st voice at the point where the 2nd voice enters with the subject, provided that this 2nd, different strain is itself treated as a fugal subject in the subsequent course of the comp.

Counter-Tenor = Male Alto. *See* **Alto.**

Counterpoint. The art of combining melodies in such a way that they make a satisfying mus. texture prod. good harmony incidentally by the intersection of the parts, but not standing still on chords or letting them progress in blocks. Where a melody is added to another melody, one is called the other's C. The general practice of C. as a mode of comp. is called Polyphony. Double C. is the term used in cases where the top-and-bottom position of 2 melodies combined in C. can be reversed without making the m. ungrammatical; this is also called Invertible C.

Country Dance. An Eng. dance which became very popular in Fr. in the 18th cent. and was called *Contredanse* there, having appeared as *Contredanse anglaise* in a pub. as early as 1699. It spread to other countries, being called *Contratanz* or *Kontretanz* in Ger. and Aus. It lost not only its rustic name but also its rustic nature on the Continent, where it was used for ballroom dancing and cultivated by comps. of distinction, incl. Mozart and Beethoven.

Coup d'archet (Fr. =stroke of the bow). The bow attack in stg. playing.

Coup de glotte (Fr. =stroke of the glottis). A trick in singing whereby vowel sounds are preceded by a kind of click in the throat prod. by a momentary cutting off of the breath-stream. It is effective as an inflection and insisted on as a point of good technique by many singing-masters while others consider it harmful to the voice.

Couperin. Fr. 17th–18th-cent. family of musns.:

1. Louis C. (b. Chaumes-en-Brie, c. 1626; d. Paris, 29. VIII. 1661).
2. François C., Sieur de Crouilly (b. Chaumes-en-Brie, c. 1631; d. Paris, c. 1701), brother of prec.
3. Charles C. (b. Chaumes-en-Brie, 7–8. IV. 1638; d. Paris, 1679), brother of prec.
4. François C. (b. Paris, 10. XI. 1668; d. Paris 12. IX. 1733), son of prec.
5. Marguerite-Louise C. (b. Paris, 1676 or 1679; d. Versailles, 30. V. 1728), daughter of 2.
6. Marie-Anne C. (b. Paris, 11. XI. 1677; d. ?), sister of prec.
7. Nicolas C. (b. Paris 20. XII. 1680; d. Paris 25. VII. 1748), brother of prec.
8. Marie-Madeleine (Cécile) C. (b. Paris, 11. III. 1690; d. Maubuisson, 16. IV. 1742), daughter of 4.
9. Marguerite - Antoinette C. (b. Paris, 19. IX. 1705; d. ?, 1778), sister of prec.
10. Armand-Louis C. (b. Paris, 25. II. 1727; d. Paris, 2. II. 1789), son of 7.
11. Pierre-Louis C. (b. Paris, 14. III. 1755; d. Paris, 10. X. 1789), son of prec.
12. Gervais-François C. (b. Paris, 22. V. 1759; d. Paris, VII. 1826), brother of prec.
13. Nicolas-Louis C. (b. Paris, c. 1760; d. after 1817), brother of prec.
14. Céleste C. (b. Paris, 1793 or 1794; d. ?), daughter of 12.

Couperin, Charles (b. Chaumes-en-Brie, 7–8. IV. 1638; d. Paris, 1679), Fr. orgst. & comp. (3 above). Succeeded his brother Louis as orgst. at the church of Saint-Gervais in Paris in 1661.

Couperin, François (b. Paris, 10. XI. 1668; d. Paris, 12. IX. 1733), Fr. comp., hpchdst. & orgst., son of prec. (4 above). The greatest member of a large mus. family. Learnt m. from his father and from Jacques-Denis Thomelin, orgst. of the king's chapel. App. orgst. at the church of Saint-Gervais in 1685, where he remained until his death. In 1693 he succeeded Thomelin as orgst. to the king, and in 1717 received the title of Ordinaire de la Musique de la chambre du Roi. He had been connected with the court before and taught the royal children. In wider circles, too, he was famous as hpchd. teacher and laid down his system in the treatise *L'Art de toucher le clavecin*, pub. in 1716. He married Marie-Anne Ansault c. 1689, and they had 2 daughters, the 2nd of whom, Marguerite Antoinette (9 above), became a distinguished hpchdst.

Works incl. 4 books of hpchd. pieces (c. 230); 42 org. pieces; 4 *Concerts royaux* for hpchd., stgs. & wind insts.; 10 chamber concs. *Les Goûts-réunis*; 4 suites for stgs. & hpchd. *Les Nations*; chamber sos. *Le Parnasse, ou l'Apothéose de Corelli* & *L'Apothéose . . . de Lully*; 2 suites of pieces for viols with figured bass; some misc. chamber works; 12 songs for 1, 2 or 3 voices; church m. incl. *Laudate pueri Dominum*, *Leçons de Ténèbres*, a number of motets, &c.

Coupler. An appliance whereby 2 manuals of an org. or a manual and the pedals can be so connected that while only 1 is being played the stops controlled by the other are brought into action. Special C.'s can also be used to double the notes played automatically an octave above or below.

Couplet (Fr.). Lit. a verse or stanza in a poem, not as in Eng., a 'couplet,' i.e. 2 rhyming lines of poetry. In m. the Fr. term denotes a strophic song, generally of a light and often of a humorous type, in which the same m. recurs for each verse. Also the forerunner of the Episode in the Rondo form, occurring in the Fr. Rondeau as cultivated by Couperin and others, where a main theme returns again and again after statements of var. *couplets* between.

Coupleux Organ. An electrophonic org. prod. its notes from the air, 1st installed at the Paris wireless station and in one of the churches in 1932.

Courante (Fr.). A dance in 3–2 time

popular esp. in the 17th cent., whose name (' the running one,' from *courir* = to run) suggests some affinity with the Eng. 'running set.' It has 2 parts of equal length, each repeated, and its special feature is the rhythmic modification of the last bar of each section, where the notes appear in 2 groups of 3 instead of 3 groups of 2, as in the rest of the piece. There are, however, other types of C., in 3-4 or 3-8 time, without this rhythmic characteristic. The C. is one of the fixed mvts. appearing in old suites, where it stands normally after the Allemande.

Courteville. Eng. family of musns., (?) of Fr. descent:

1. Raphael C. (b. ?; d. ? London, 28. XII. 1675), Gentleman of the Chapel Royal under Charles I and again under Charles II after the Restor.

2. Ralph (or Raphael) C. (b. ? London, ?; d. ? London, *c.* 1735), son of prec. Educ. in the Chapel Royal. App. orgst. of the church of St. James, Westminster, in 1691.

Works incl. incid. m. for Southerne's dram. version of Aphra Behn's *Oroonoko* and for Part III of Durfey's *Don Quixote*; sos. for 2 fls., hymn-tune *St. James*; many songs.

3. Raphael C. (b. ? London, ?; d. ? London, VI. 1772), son of prec., whom (?) he succeeded at St. James's church, though he was active mainly as a political writer.

Courtly Style. *See* **Galant.**

Courtois, Jean (b. ?; d. ?), Fr. or Flem. 16th-cent. comp. Chapel master at Cambrai cath. Wrote masses, motets, chansons in several parts, canons, &c.

Courvoisier, Walter (b. Riehen nr. Basle, 7. II. 1875; d. Locarno, 27. XII. 1931), Swi. comp. Pupil of Thuille at Munich and later his son-in-law. He became teacher at the Munich Acad. of M. in 1910 and prof. in succession to Klose in 1919.

Works incl. operas *Lanzelot und Elaine*, *Die Krähen* & *Der Sünde Zauberei* (after Calderón); *Totenfeier* (*Auferstehung*) for solo voices, chor. & orch.; symph. prologue to Spitteler's *Olympischer Frühling*; chors., pf. pieces, songs, &c.

Cousin Jacques. *See* **Beffroy de Reigny.**

Coussemaker, Charles (Edmond Henri) de (b. Bailleul, 19. IV. 1805; d. Bourbourg, 12. I. 1876), Fr. mcolst. He was destined for the law, but played pf., v. & co. well at an early age and went to Paris to study comp. under Reicha in 1825, later turned to mus. research. He became a judge, but continued to cultivate mcol. and wrote more than a dozen learned books on old m.

Cousser (or Kusser), Johann Sigismund (b. Pressburg = Pozsony, 13. II. 1660; d. Dublin, 1727), Hung. cond. & comp. Pupil of Lully in Paris. He worked at the court at Stuttgart from 1682, but the following year went to Strasburg, later to Brunswick and Hamburg, and from 1698 to Stuttgart again, where he was chapel master from 1700-4. Soon afterwards, having paid 2 visits to It., he went to London and in 1710 to Dublin, where he was app. to Christ Church cath.

Works incl. operas *Erindo*, *Porus*, *Pyramus und Thisbe*, *Scipio Africanus*, *Jason* & *Ariadne*; Serenade for the king's birthday; Ode on the death of Arabella Hunt; suites (with ovts.) for stgs.; collections of opera ovts. and airs, &c.

Covent Garden Theatre, London. 1st house opened 7. XII. 1732, burnt down 19. IX. 1808; 2nd opened 18. IX. 1809, burnt down 5. III. 1856; 3rd opened 15. V. 1858. The theatre did not become a regular opera house until 1847, though opera had long been perf. in it (e.g. Handel's 1st season there in 1734 and Weber's *Oberon* in 1826). The 1st work in 1847 was Rossini's *Semiramide*. It became the Royal Opera in 1892 and ran annual seasons, wholly in It. at first, but later in Fr. and Ger. also, until 1914, and again between the 2 world wars from 1919 to 1939.

Coward, Henry (b. Liverpool, 26. XI. 1849; d. Woking, 10. VI. 1944), Eng. choir-trainer & chor. cond. Trained to become a cutler at Sheffield, he picked up what educ. he could, left his trade at the age of 22, became a schoolmaster and in 1876 founded the Sheffield Tonic Sol-fa Assoc. Took the Mus.D. at Oxford and was knighted in 1926. He cond. much at festivals and abroad.

Coward, Noel (b. 1899), Eng. actor, playwright & amateur comp. *See* **Addinsell** (1945 revue & *Blithe Spirit*).

Cowell, Henry (Dixon) (b. Menlo Park, Cal., 11. III. 1897), Amer. comp. & writer on m. Studied in N.Y., at California Univ. and in Berlin. Toured in Eur. and Amer. as pfst., lectured on m. at univs. and colls. in U.S.A. and contrib. to many mus. papers. With Lev Theremin he invented the Rhythmicon.

Works incl. ballets *The Building of Banba* & *Atlantis*; Sym., *Synchrony*, *Reel*, *Hornpipe*, *Sinfonietta*, *Scherzo*, &c. for orch.; *Hymn and Fuguing Tune*, *Exultation* & *Four Continuations* for stgs.; pf. Conc.; 4 stg. 4tets; Toccata for sop. (wordless), fl., co. & pf.; other chamber m.; many pf. works, &c.

Cowen, Frederic (Hymen) (b. Kingston, Jamaica, 29. I. 1852; d. London, 6. X. 1935), Brit. comp. & cond. Studied in London, Leipzig and Berlin. Cond. by turns of the London Phil. Soc., at Liverpool and Manchester. Knighted 1911.

Works incl. operas *Pauline, Thorgrim, Signa* & *Harold*; operettas and incid. m.; orats. *The Deluge, St. Ursula, Ruth, The Veil*, &c.; cantatas *The Corsair, The Sleeping Beauty, St. John's Eve, Ode to the Passions* (Collins), *John Gilpin* (Cowper); jubilee (1897) and coronation (1902) odes; cantatas for female voices, anthems, partsongs; 6 syms. (No. 3 *Scandinavian*, No. 4 *Welsh*, No. 6 *Idyllic*); 4 concert ovts, *Sinfonietta, Indian Rhapsody* & other works for orch.; Conc. & *Concertstück* for pf. & orch.; stg. 4tet, pf. Trio; many pf. pieces; *c.* 300 songs, &c.

Cowley, Abraham (1618–67), Eng. poet. *See* **King (W.)** (songs).

Cowper, William (1731–1800), Eng. poet. *See* **Cowen** (*John Gilpin*), **Dunhill** (do.), **Latrobe** (airs).

Cox and Box, operetta by Sullivan (lib. by Francis Cowley Burnand, based on John Maddison Morton's farce *Box and Cox*), prod. London, Adelphi Theatre, 11. V. 1867.

Crab Canon. *See* **Cancrizans.**

Crabbe, George (1754–1832), Eng. poet. *See* **Peter Grimes** (Britten).

Crackle (verb). To perf. on the lute in a special way, prob. by arpeggios.

Cracovienne. *See* **Krakowiak.**

Craigie (*née* **Roberts**), **Pearl Mary Theresa** (John Oliver Hobbes) (1867–1906), Amer. novelist & playwright. *See* **Parry (H.)** (*Repentance*).

Cramer, Johann Baptist (b. Mannheim, 24. II. 1771; d. London, 16. IV. 1858), Ger. (anglicized) pfst., cond. & comp. Was taken to London at the age of 1, taught by his father and later went to Clementi for pf. study; 1st appeared in public in 1781. In 1824 he estab. a m. pub. business and between 1813–34 he occasionally cond. the Phil. Soc. concerts.

Works incl. 7 pf. concs.; pf. 4tet & 5tet; 105 pf. sos., 2 vols. of 42 studies each, 16 later studies, 100 daily exercises, &c.

Cramer, Wilhelm (b. Mannheim, 1745; d. London, 5. X. 1799), Ger. vst., father of prec. Settled in London in 1772; leader of the royal band and of many important concert organizns.

Cras, Jean (Émile Paul) (b. Brest, 22. V. 1879; d. Brest, 14. IX. 1932), Fr. naval officer & comp. He never abandoned his sailor's career and reached the rank of rear-admiral, but after some comp. lessons from Duparc and org. from Guilmant, he went on comp. whenever time allowed.

Works incl. opera *Polyphème* (lib. by Albert Samain); *Le Songe d'Acis et Galathée*, suite *Âmes d'enfants* and *Journal de bord* for orch.; stg. 4tet, pf. 5tet, *La Flûte de Pan* for voice, fl., v. & co.; co. & pf. So.; *Élégies* & *Offrande lyrique* (Tagore) for voice & orch.; songs incl. several cycles; pieces for pf. and for harp, &c.

Crassia, B. de. *See* **Vacqueras.**

Creation Mass (Haydn). *See* **Schöpfungsmesse.**

Creation, The (*Die Schöpfung*), orat. by Haydn (lib. by one Lidell or Lidley, based on Genesis and Milton's *Paradise Lost*, trans. into Ger. by Gottfried van Swieten and comp. to the Ger. words), prod. Vienna, Schwarzenberg Palace, 2. IV. 1798.

Cremona. Another name for the Cl. org. stop, orig. a corrupt. of Cromorne.

Crequillon, Thomas (b. ?; d. ?, *c.* 1557), Flem. comp. Choirmaster in Charles V's imperial chapel in the Nthlds. Wrote masses, motets, lamentations, chansons, &c.

Crescendo (It. = growing). Increasing in loudness.

Crescentini, Girolamo (b. Urbania nr. Urbino, 2. II. 1762; d. Naples, 24. IV. 1846), It. male sop. singer. Made his 1st appearance in Rome in 1783; sang in London in 1785–7.

Cricket on the Hearth, The. *See also* **Heimchen am Herd.**

Opera by Mackenzie (lib. by Julian Russell Sturgis, based on Dickens's story), prod. London, R.A.M., 6. VI. 1914.

Cristofori, Bartolommeo di Francesco (b. Padua, 4. V. 1655; d. Florence, 27. I. 1731), It. hpchd. maker. Worked 1st at Padua and then at Florence. Inventor of the pf., the 1st specimens of which he made in the earliest years of the 18th cent.

Critic, The, or An Opera Rehearsed, opera by Stanford (lib. by Lewis Cairns James, adapted from Sheridan's play), prod. London, Shaftesbury Theatre, 14. I. 1916.

Crivelli, Gaetano (b. Bergamo, 1774; d. Brescia, 10. VII. 1836), It. ten. singer. Appeared in It. at a very early age and 1st went to Paris in 1811 and London in 1817.

Croce, Giovanni (b. Chioggia nr. Venice, *c.* 1558; d. Venice, 15. V. 1609), It. priest & comp. Pupil of Zarlino, at Venice, where he worked at St. Mark's and succeeded Donati as chapel master in 1703. Wrote motets, psalms, madrigals, capricci for voices, &c.

Croche (Fr.) = Quaver.

Croche, Monsieur. An imaginary character under whose name Debussy pub. a selection of his critical articles in 1917, the book being entitled *Monsieur Croche, antidilettante.*

Crociato in Egitto, Il (*The Crusader in Egypt*), opera by Meyerbeer (lib. by Giacomo Rossi), prod. Venice, Teatro La Fenice, 7. III. 1824.

Croesus (*Der hochmütige, gestürzte und wieder erhabne Croesus*), opera by Keiser (lib. by Lucas von Bostel after the It. of Niccolò Minato), prod. Hamburg, Theater am Gänsemarkt, ? Carnival, 1711.

Croft, William (b. Nether Ettington, Warwicks., 1678; d. Bath, 14. VIII. 1727), Eng. orgst. & comp. Pupil of Blow at the Chapel Royal in London; orgst. at St. Anne's, Soho, from 1700 and orgst., with Clarke, at the Chapel Royal from 1704; Master of the Children there from 1715. Succeeded Blow as orgst. of Westminster Abbey in 1708. Mus.D., Oxford, 1713.

Works incl. incid. m. for Farquhar's *Twin Rivals*; m. for Steele's *The Lying Lover*; many anthems, some for special occasions (e.g. victory of Blenheim), burial service, psalm tunes *St. Anne* & *St. Matthew*; 2 odes on the peace of Utrecht; incid. m. for plays; sos. for v. & for fl.; songs, &c.

Cromorne (Eng. corrupt. from Ger. *Krummhorn*, lit. 'crooked horn'). An obs. wind inst. made of wood and bent, played with a double reed, in use mainly in the 14th–16th cents.

Crook. A detachable piece of tubing that can be fitted into brass wind insts., esp. hns., to alter the length of the tube and thus change the tuning. A D crook, for ex., may be used to play a part for a hn. in D, &c.

Crooning. A reprehensible form of singing that estab. itself in light entertainment m. about the 1930s. It recommended itself at first to would-be singers without voices who were unable to acquire an adequate technique and later to a large public because anything, however inartistic, is likely to become popular if only it is done often enough by a large enough number of people. The principle of C. is to use as little voice as possible and instead to make a sentimental appeal by prolonged moaning somewhere nr. the written notes, but preferably never actually on those notes. The smallest voc. equipment is sufficient for the purpose of C., one of its admirers' delusions being that it does not become wholly satisfactory until it is amplified by a microphone, a device capable of turning the squeak of a mouse into the howl of a factory siren.

Crosdill, John (b. London, 1751; d. Eskrick, Yorks., X. 1825), Eng. cst. The best Eng. player of his time, attached to the Concert of Ancient M., the Chapel Royal, &c. Chamber musn. to Queen Charlotte.

Cross Fingering. Certain awkward fingerings on woodwind insts. called for by the necessity of prod. more than 1 note in rapid passages with the aid of the same finger.

Cross-Rhythm. The device in comp. of making the accentuation of a theme or melody conflict with (*a*) the normal strong beats of the bar or (*b*) the accents of another tune combined with it. For ex. a melodic shape in groups of 3 crotchets to the bar would be in C.-R. if it occurred in a piece with the key-signature of 6–8.

Crossley, Ada (b. Tarraville, Austral., 3. III. 1874; d. London, 17. X. 1929), Austral. con. singer. Studied at Melbourne, with Santley in London and Mathilde Marchesi in Paris; made her 1st London appearance in 1895.

Crotch, William (b. Norwich, 5. VII. 1775; d. Taunton, 29. XII. 1847), Eng. comp. Played the org. as a wonder-child in London at the age of 4, went to Cambridge at 11 to assist Randall at the orgs. of Trinity and King's Colls. and prod. an orat. *The Captivity of Judah* there in 1789, having removed the prec. year to Oxford for theolog. studies. He turned to m. finally in 1790 and was app. orgst. at Christ Church cath. there. Mus.D., Oxford, 1799, having already succeeded Hayes as prof. in 1797. On the estab. of the R.A.M. in London in 1822 he became its 1st principal.

Works incl. orats. *Palestine* & *The Captivity of Judah* (2 settings); *Ode to Fancy* (Joseph Warton) and ode for the installation of Lord Grenville as Chancellor of Oxford Univ., ode for the accession of George IV; funeral anthem for the Duke of York; anthems & chants, motet *Methinks I hear*; glees; concs. & fugues for org., &c.

Crotchet. A note or rest taking half the time of a minim and forming the unit of any time-signature of which the lower figure is 4, also that marked C (=4–4).

Crouch, Frederick (Nicholls) (b. London, 31. VII. 1808; d. Portland, Maine, U.S.A., 18. VIII. 1896), Eng. clst. & comp. Studied at the R.A.M. in London and held var. appts. after 2 years at sea. He went to U.S.A. in 1849 and worked in var. cities, incl. N.Y., Boston & Baltimore.

Works incl. operas *Sir Roger de Coverley* & *The Fifth of November*, songs *Echoes of the Lakes* cont. *Kathleen Mavourneen*, &c.

Crowd. *See* Crwth.

Crowder (obs.). A player on the Crwth.

Crowne, John (? 1640–1703), Eng. playwright. *See* **Humfrey** (*Charles VIII*), **King (R.)** (*Sir Courtly Nice*), **Purcell** (*Married Beau & Regulus*), **Staggins** (*Calisto*).

Crüger, Johann (b. Gross-Breese, Prus., 9. IV. 1598; d. Berlin, 23. II, 1662), Ger. theorist & comp. Cantor at St. Nicholas's church, Berlin, from 1622. Wrote several chorales afterwards used by Bach.

Works incl. *Praxis pietatis melica* cont. hymn-tunes with bass, *Geistliche Kirchen-Melodien* cont. hymn-tunes prescribed by Luther set for 4 voices with insts., 2 vols. of Ger. magnificats; secular songs, &c.

Cruvelli (Crüwell), Johanne (Jeanne) Sophie Charlotte (b. Bielefeld, 12. III. 1826; d. Monte Carlo, 6. XI. 1907), Ger. sop. singer. Made her 1st stage appearance at Venice in 1847; 1st sang in Paris in 1851 and was engaged for the Opéra in 1854.

Cruz, Ivo (b. Cidade de Corumba, Braz., 19. V. 1901), Port. cond. & comp. Studied m. and law at Lisbon, where later he founded the review *Renascimento musical*, resuming his mus. studied at Munich in 1924. On his return he founded a chor. soc. in 1930 and a chamber orch. in 1933. App. dir. of the Lisbon Cons. in 1938.

Works incl. *Nocturnos da Lusitania* & *Motivos lusitanos* for orch., *Vexilla regis* for sop. & orch., Sonatina for v. & pf., pf. m., songs, &c.

Crwth (Welsh = Crowd, also called Cruit, Crot, Crotta, Crotte or Rotte). An ancient bowed stg. inst., ancestor of the v. family.

Crystal Palace, London. The enormous iron and glass structure built in Hyde Park for the 1851 Exhibition and re-erected at Sydenham in 1854, 1st used for concerts in 1855, when Manns was engaged as cond. It was destroyed by fire in 1936.

Cst. (abbr.) = Cellist (Violoncellist).

Csárdás (Hung.). A Hung. dance consisting of a slow mvt. called *Lassú* and a quick one called *Friss*.

Ctpt. (abbr.) = Counterpoint.

Ctptal (abbr.) = Contrapuntal.

Ctptst. (abbr.) = Contrapuntist.

Cuban Composers. *See* **Roldán, Sánchez de Fuentes.**

Cuckoo. A toy inst. *See* **Toy Symphony.**

Cuclin, Demetre (b. Galatz, 1885), Rum. comp. Studied at the Bucharest Cons. and later with Widor at the Cons. and d'Indy at the Schola Cantorum in Paris. In 1922–30 he taught in N.Y., but returned to Rum. to become prof. at the Bucharest Cons.

Works incl. operas *Soria*, *Agamemnon*, *Trajan* & *Bellerophon*; ovt. for chor. & orch., sacred & secular chors.; Sym., symph. Scherzo for orch.; pf. Trio; v. & pf. sos., suites for v. & pf. and co. & pf.; pf. pieces; songs, &c.

Cucuel, Georges (b. Dijon, 14. XII. 1884; d. Grenoble, 28. X. 1918), Fr. mcolst. Made a special study of Fr. 18th-cent. m. Wrote books on Fr. chamber and orch. m. of that period, and on comic opera, also a number of learned articles.

Cue. A few notes printed in small m. type in inst. or voc. parts of a mus. work, serving as a guide to show where the perf. is to come in after a lengthy rest.

Cui, César Antonovitch (b. Vilna, 18. I. 1835; d. St. Petersburg, 24. III. 1918), Rus. comp. of Fr. descent. Educ. at the High School of Vilna, where his father, a Fr. officer left behind in the retreat from Moscow in 1812, was prof. of Fr. He had some lessons in m. from Moniuszko, but was sent to the School of Military Engineering at St. Petersburg in 1850, where he became sub-prof. in 1857. He became an authority on fortifications and remained an amateur in m. But he joined Balakirev's circle of Rus. nationalist comps. and became one of the 'Kutchka' group, though the least exclusively Rus. among them. He became a critic, however, in 1864 and did much lit. work for the cause.

Works incl. operas *The Mandarin's Son*, *The Captive in the Caucasus* (after Pushkin), *William Ratcliff* (after Heine), *Angelo* (after Hugo), *Le Flibustier* (lib. by Jean Richepin), *The Saracen* (after Dumas sen.), *A Feast in Time of Plague* (Pushkin), *Mam'zelle Fifi* (after Maupassant), *Matteo Falcone* (after Mérimée) & *The Captain's Daughter*; works for chor. with and without orch.; 4 suites and other works for orch.; stg. 4tet in C min.; 15 op. nos. of pf. pieces, 3 pieces for 2 pfs.; var. inst. pieces; *c.* 25 op. nos. of songs incl. settings of Pushkin, Lermontov, Nekrassov, Richepin & Mickiewicz.

Cuivré (Fr. lit. 'coppery') = brassy, brazen. A term used by Fr. and other comps. to indicate that the clanging tone prod. by stopped hns. is required.

Cumberland, Richard (1732–1811), Eng. novelist & playwright. *See* **Busby** (*Joanna of Montfaucon*).

Cundell, Edric (b. London, 29. I. 1893), Eng. cond. & comp. Studied at Trinity Coll. of M. in London, where he became a prof. later. Cond. amateur orchs. and founded a chamber orch. of his own, and in 1938 became principal of the G.S.M. in succession to Ronald. He won the *Daily Telegraph* prize with a stg. 4tet in 1933.

Works incl. *Hymn to Providence* for chor. & orch., Mass for unaccomp. chor.; Sym. in C min., symph. poem *Serbia*; 2 stg. 4tets, stg. 6tet; *Our Dead*, sonnet for ten. & orch., &c.

Cunningham, Allan (1784–1842), Sco. poet, novelist & biog. *See* **Jensen** (songs), **Scott (F. G.)** (songs).

Cupid and Death, masque by James Shirley with m. by Locke and C. Gibbons, perf. London, before the Port. ambassador, Leicester Fields, 26. III. 1653.

Curioso indiscreto, Il (*Indiscreet Curiosity*), opera by Anfossi (lib. by ?), prod. Rome, Teatro delle Dame, II. 1777. Mozart wrote 2 extra sop. arias for this when it was prod. in Vienna, 30. VI. 1783.

Curschmann, Karl Friedrich (b. Berlin, 21. VI. 1804; d. Langfuhr nr. Danzig, 24. VIII. 1841), Ger. comp. Pupil of Spohr and Hauptmann. Remembered only for his songs, of which 92 are pub. incl. 9 duets and trios.

Curtain Tune (obs.). An old term sometimes used in the place of 'Act tune' for an Intermezzo or Entr'acte in the incid. m. for a play.

Curtal(l). The 16th–17th-cent. Eng. name for the bn.

Curwen. Eng. family of mus. educsts. & m. pubs.:

1. John C. (b. Heckmondwike, Yorks, 14. XI. 1816; d. Manchester, 26. V. 1880), founded the Tonic Sol-fa method of m. teaching, estab. the Tonic Sol-fa Assoc. in 1853 and the pub. firm in London in 1863.

2. John Spencer C. (b. London, 30, IX. 1847; d. London, 6. VIII. 1916), son of prec., studied at the R.A.M. under Macfarren, Sullivan and Prout, carried on his father's work and began the competition festival mvt. in Eng. with the Stratford (E. London) Festival in 1882.

3. Annie (Jessy), *née* Gregg (b. Dublin, 1. IX. 1845; d. Matlock, 22. IV. 1932), wife of prec., studied at the R. Ir. A.M., married in 1877 and wrote a number of books on a m.-teaching method of her own.

Curzon, (Emmanuel) Henri (Parent) de (b. Havre, 6. VII. 1861; d. Paris, V. 1942), Fr. mcolst. M. critic to var. Paris papers, last of the *Journal des Débats*, and librarian at the Opéra-Comique. Trans. Mozart's letters into Fr. and wrote var. books on m.

Cusins, William (George) (b. London, 14. X. 1833; d. Remonchamps, Ardennes, 31. VIII. 1893), Eng. pfst., vst., orgst., cond. & comp. Studied under Fétis at the Brussels Cons. and at the R.A.M. in London. Was active in var. mus. organizations in London and at court. Knighted 1892.

Works incl. orat. *Gideon*; *Royal Wedding Serenata*; ovt. to Shakespeare's *Love's Labour's Lost*; pf. Conc. in A min., &c.

Cutting, Thomas (b. ?; d. ?), Eng. 16th–17th-cent. lutenist. In the service of Lady Arabella Stuart until 1607, then of Christian IV. of Den. at Copenhagen until 1611, when he returned and entered Prince Henry's private band.

Cuzzoni, Francesca (b. Parma or Modena, *c.* 1700; d. Bologna, 1770), It. sop. singer. 1st appeared in Venice, 1719, and in London, 1722.

Cycle of Songs. *See* **Song Cycle.**

Cyclic Form. The form of a mus. work in several mvts., usually a sym. or chamber work in so. form, in which one or more themes appear in at least 2 mvts. and lend organic unity to the whole. Franck's Sym. is a typical ex. of this form, which was partic. favoured by his school.

Cymbalom. *See* **Cimbalom.**

Cymbals. Plate-shaped brass percussion insts. a pair of which is struck together or 1 of which is made to sound in var. ways by being touched with hard or soft drum-sticks. They have no fixed sound, but there were ancient C.'s of smaller size and with a brighter tone which gave out definite notes.

Cymbel. An org. Mixture stop.

Cymon, opera by Michael Arne (lib. by David Garrick, based on Dryden's *Cymon and Iphigenia*), prod. London, Drury Lane Theatre, 2. I. 1767.

Cyrano, operà by W. Damrosch (lib. by William James Henderson, based on Rostand's play, *Cyrano de Bergerac*), prod. N.Y., Metrop. Opera, 27. II. 1913.

Cyrano de Bergerac, opera by Alfano (lib. by Henri Cain, based on Rostand's play), prod. in It. trans., Rome, Teatro Reale, 22. I. 1936.

Cythare (Fr.) = Cittern.

Cythère assiégée, La (*Cytherea Besieged*), opera by Gluck (lib. by Charles Simon Favart, based on Longus's *Daphnis and Chloe*), prod. Schwetzingen nr. Mannheim and Vienna, summer 1759.

Cythern. *See* **Cittern.**

Cz. (abbr.) = Czech, Czechoslovakia.

Czaar und Zimmermann (Lortzing). *See* **Zar und Zimmermann.**

Czakan. A woodwind inst., prob. originating from Transylvania but very fashionable in Vienna *c.* 1830, of the fl. type, but made in the shape of a walking-stick and often used as such.

Czanyi, Cornelia. *See* **Schmitt, Aloys.**

Czardas (incorrect spelling). *See* **Csárdás.**

Czech Composers. *See also* **Bohemian** for earlier names. **Bella, Blodek, Dreyschock, Dvořák, Ernst, Fibich, Figuš-Bystrý, Finke, Foerster** (J. B.), **Hába, Hoffmeister, Janáček, Jeremiaš, Jirák, Jiránek, Kafenda, Kaprálová, Karel, Klička, Kovařovic, Křicka, Kunc, Kvapil, Lichard, Mahler, Martinů, Nápravnik, Navrátil, Nedbal, Nešvera, Neumann, Novák, Ostrčil, Petyrek, Pick-Mangiagalli, Roskošný, Schulhoff** (2), **Škroup, Smetana, Štěpan, Stiastný, Stransky, Suk** (2), **Vomáčka, Vycpálek, Weinberger, Weiss** (K.), **Zich, Zvonař.**

Czernohorsky. *See* **Černohorsky.**

Czerny, Karl (b. Vienna, 20. II. 1791; d. Vienna, 15. VII. 1857), Aus. pfst., teacher & comp. He was 1st taught the pf. by his father, played brilliantly at the age of 10 and became a pupil of Beethoven about that time: he also took advice from Hummel and Clementi. Not liking to appear in public, he took to teaching and soon had an enormous following of pupils, among which he chose only the most gifted. This left him enough leisure for comp., which he cultivated so assiduously as to prod. almost 1,000 works.

Works incl. 24 masses, 4 Requiems, 300 graduals and offertories; many syms., ovts.; concs.; stg. 4tets & trios; chors.; songs and, most numerous of all, masses of pf. music, incl. studies, exercises, preludes & fugues in all the keys and endless arrs. of other comps.' works.

Czibulka, Alphons (b. Szepes-Váralya, 14. V. 1842; d. Vienna, 27. X. 1894), Hung. comp. He became a military bandmaster in Vienna and wrote 6 operettas and much dance & popular light m.

(Mark reference p. 99)

Chevreuille, Raymond (b. ?, 17. XI. 1901), Belg. comp.

Works incl. Sym. with voc. 4tet, *Évasions* for sop. and chamber orch., *Saisons* for bar. & chamber orch., Conc. for 3 woodwind insts., co. Conc.; 5 stg. 4tets, &c.

D

D. The note bounding the range of the scales of D maj. and min., and of the Dorian and Hypermixolydian (Gr. Hypolydian) modes.

d. The Tonic note in any key in Tonic Sol-fa notation, pronounced Doh.

d'. Fr. names with the prefix *de* abbr. to *d'* before a vowel appear under the principal surnames: **e.g.** Vincent d'Indy as Indy, Vincent d'.

D.C. (It. abbr.). *See* **Da capo.**

D.Mus. *See* **Mus.D.**

Da capo (It. =' again ') = from the beginning. A direction indicating that from the point at which it is marked the performer is to turn back to the beginning of the comp.

Da capo al fine (It. =' again to the end '). As with the simple *da capo*, the perf. is asked to go back to the beginning, but the comp. is not in this case to be repeated as a whole, but only to the point where the word *fine* (end) appears.

Da capo Aria. A distinctive type of voc. piece for a single voice (though duets and other ensemble pieces may be in the same form) consisting of 3 sections, the 3rd of which is a repetition of the 1st, while the middle section is a contrast based sometimes on similar and sometimes of wholly different thematic material. The D. c. A. was cultivated in the 2nd half of the 17th and 1st half of the 18th cent. (up to the earlier works of Gluck), notably by A. Scarlatti, Handel, Bach, Hasse, Jommelli, &c.

Da Ponte, Lorenzo. *See* **Ponte, Lorenzo da.**

Dafne, opera by Schütz (lib. by Martin Opitz, partly trans. from Rinuccini), prod. Torgau, Hartenfels Castle, at the wedding of Georg, Landgrave of Hesse, and Sophia Eleonora, Princess of Saxony, 23. IV. 1627.

Dafne, La, opera by Gagliano (lib. by Ottavio Rinuccini), prod. Mantua, at the ducal court, I. 1608.

Opera by Peri (lib. do.), prod. Florence, Palazzo Corsi, Carnival 1597. The 1st It. opera and 1st opera on record anywhere.

Dafni, opera by Astorga (lib. by Eustachio Manfredi), prod. Genoa, Teatro San Agostino, 21. IV. 1709.

Dagincourt (or d'Agincour), François (?Jacques André) (b. Rouen, ? 1648; d. Paris, 18. VI. 1758), Fr. orgst. & comp. App. orgst. to the roya chapel in Paris, 1714. Wrote org. & hpchd. pieces.

Dahn, Felix (1834–1912), Ger. historian & novelist. *See* **Scharwenka (X.)** (*Mataswintha*), **Strauss (R.)** (*Schlichte Weisen*).

Dal segno . . . (It. =' from the sign . . .'). A direction indicating that where a comp. is to be perf. over again from an earlier point, it is to be resumed, not at the beginning, as in an ordinary *da capo*, but from where a certain sign or ' signal ' has been placed by the composer. That sign is shown after the words D. s.

Dalayrac (or d'Alayrac), Nicolas (b. Muret, 13. VI. 1753; d. Paris, 27. XI. 1809), Fr. comp. He was 1st intended for the law, then for a military career, for which purpose he was sent to Versailles. He often walked to Paris to hear the operas of the day and to take harmony lessons from Langlé. He comp. stg. 4tets and had 2 small operas perf. privately in 1781, and the following year Marie Antoinette ordered the comedy *L'Éclipse totale* with songs by D. to be prod. at the Comédie-Italienne. During the Revol., being in sympathy with democracy, he changed the spelling of his name to remove the aristocratic prefix.

Works incl. over 50 operas, e.g. *Nina, Camille, ou Le Souterrain, Ambroise, ou Voilà ma journée, Adolphe et Clara, Maison à vendre, Les Deux Petits Savoyards, Tout pour l'amour* (*Romeo and Juliet*); stg. 4tets; songs, duets, &c.

Dale, Benjamin (b. London, 17. VII. 1885; d. London, 30. VII. 1943), Eng. comp. Studied at the R.A.M. in London, where he later became prof. of comp. and warden.

Works incl. cantata *Before the Paling of the Stars* and *Song of Praise* for chor. & orch.; v. & pf. So.; Suite & Fantasy for va. & pf.; *Introd. and Andante* for 6 vas.; pf. So. in D min.; 2 songs from Shakespeare's *Twelfth Night*, &c.

Dalibor, opera by Smetana (lib., in Ger., by Joseph Wenzig, trans. into Cz. by Ervín Špindler), prod. Prague, Cz. Theatre, 16. V. 1868.

Dall' Occa, Sophie. *See* **Schoberlechner.**

Dallapiccola, Luigi (b. Pisino, Istria,

3. II. 1904), It. comp. Studied at the Florence Cons., where he became prof.

Works incl. Partita for orch.; works for solo or chor. voices with var. large or small orch. combs.: *Dalla mia terra, Laudi* (Jacopone da Todi), 2 lyrics from the *Kalevala*, 3 Studies, Rhapsody, *I cori di Michelangelo Buonarroti il giovane, Tre laudi*; Partita for orch.; *Piccolo Conc.* for pf. & orch.; m. for 3 pfs.; *Liriche anacreontiche* & other songs, &c.

Dallier, Henri (b. Rheims, 20. III. 1849; d. Paris, 23. XII. 1934), Fr. orgst. & comp. Orgst. at Rheims cath. from 1865, but went to Paris in 1872 and studied under Franck and Bazin at the Cons. App. orgst. at Saint-Eustache there in 1879 and at the Madeleine in 1905, when Fauré left to become dir. of the Cons.

Works incl. much org. m.; stg. 4tet, pf. Trio, pf. 5tet; pf. pieces, songs, &c.

Daman (or Damon), William (b. Liége, ?; d. ? London, *c.* 1590), Walloon (anglicized) comp. He was brought to Eng. by Lord Brockhurst in the 1560s. Harmonized 2 books of psalm tunes and wrote anthems, motets, &c.

Damascene, Alexander (b. ?; d. London, 14. VII. 1719), ? Fr. comp. of ? It. descent. Settled in London, comp. to William III and Gentleman of the Chapel Royal after Purcell's death in 1695. Contrib. songs to several collections.

Dame blanche, La (*The White Lady*), opera by Boïeldieu (lib. by Scribe, based on Scott's *Guy Mannering* and *The Monastery*), prod. Paris, Opéra-Comique, 10. XII. 1825. It contains some Sco. tunes.

Damenization. An 18th-cent. system similar to Solmization, now obs., in which the syllables given to the notes were Da, Me, Ni, &c.

Damnation de Faust, La, dramatic cantata by Berlioz (words by comp. & Almire Gandonnière, based on Goethe's drama), comp. 1846, incorporating the *Huit Scènes de Faust* of 1828; 1st perf. Paris, Opéra-Comique, 6. XII. 1846; prod. as an opera, Monte Carlo, 18. II. 1893.

Damoiselle élue, La (*The Blessed Damozel*), cantata for solo voice, chor. & orch. by Debussy, set to a Fr. trans. by Gabriel Sarrazin of Rossetti's poem in 1887–8.

Damoreau, Laure Cinthie Montalant. *See* **Cinti-Damoreau.**

Dämpfer (Ger. = damper). *See* **Mute.**

Damping Pedal. The so-called 'soft' P. of the pf., which so shifts the hammers of the inst. that they touch only a single stg. for each note, instead of 2 or 3, for which reason its use is often indicated by the words *una corda* (1 stg.).

Damrosch, Leopold (b. Posen, 22. X. 1832; d. New York, 15. II. 1885), Ger. cond., vst. & comp. Studied medicine in Berlin, but gave it up for m. Appeared as vst. and became leader in the Weimar court orch. under Liszt. Having cond. at Breslau from 1850–71, he went to N.Y., where he did much to advance orch. m. and opera at the Metropolitan Opera House.

Damrosch, Walter (Johannes) (b. Breslau, 30. I. 1862), Ger. (Americanized) cond. & comp., son of prec. Studied in Ger. and settled in U.S.A. in 1871; became cond. of the N.Y. Orat. and Sym. Socs. in 1885.

Works incl. operas *The Scarlet Letter* (after Hawthorne), *Cyrano de Bergerac* (after Rostand), *The Dove of Peace, The Man without a Country*; incid. m. to Euripides' *Electra, Iphigenia in Aulis* & *Medea*; *Abraham Lincoln's Song* for bar. solo., chor. & orch.; Te Deum; v. & pf. So.; songs., &c.

Dan. (abbr.) = Danish.

Danae's Kiss (R. Strauss). *See* **Kuss der Danae.**

Danaïdes, Les, opera by Salieri (lib. by François Louis Lebland du Roullet and Louis Théodore de Tschudy, partly based on and trans. from Calzabigi's *Ipermestra* ? intended for Gluck, comp. by Millico), prod. Paris, Opéra, 26. IV. 1784.

Dancla, Jean Charles (b. Bagnères-de-Bigorre, 19. XII. 1817; d. Tunis, 8. XI. 1907), Fr. vst. Pupil of Baillot at the Paris Cons., where he later became v. prof. He comp. much m., incl. educ. works for v.

Dandelot, Georges (Édouard) (b. Paris, 2. XII. 1895), Fr. comp. Studied at the Paris Cons. and in 1919 became prof. of comp. at the École Normale de Musique there.

Works incl. orat. *Pax*; pf. Conc.; *Trio en forme de suite*, stg. 4tet; waltzes for 2 pfs.; *Bilitis*: 17 songs (Pierre Louÿs), &c.

Dandrieu (or d'Andrieu), Jean François (b. Paris, late 1681 or early 1682; d. Paris, 17. I. 1738), Fr. orgst. & comp. Became orgst. of the church of Saint-Barthélemy in Paris in succession to his uncle, Pierre D., and in 1704 of that of Saint-Merry; member of the royal chapel in 1721; wrote a book on hpchd. accomp.

Works incl. a set of syms. *Les Caractères de la guerre*; trios for 2 vs. & bass; v. sos.; org. pieces; 3 vols. of hpchd. pieces, &c.

Dane, Clemence (Winifred Ashton), (b. ?), Eng. playwright. *See* **Addinsell** (*Adam's Opera, Come of Age,* &c.).

Danican, Michel (b. Dauphiné, ?; d. Paris, *c.* 1659), Fr. obst. in the service of Louis XIII, who bestowed on him the name of Philidor after the great obst. Filidori of Siena. (For all other members of the family *see* **Philidor.**)

Daniel, John. *See* **Danyel.**

Danish Composers. *See* **Bendix, Bentzon, Berggreen, Børresen, Bruhns, Bucenus, Danning, Enna, Gade, Gram, Hamerik** (2), **Hartmann** (3), **Heise, Henriqués, Høffding, Horneman, Klenau, Kuhlau, Lange-Müller, Lassen, Lumbye** (3), **Malling, Nielsen** (3), **Paulli, Pedersøn, Riisager, Rung, Schytte, Siboni (E.), Syberg, Weyse.**

Dankerts, Ghiselin (b. Tholen, Zeeland, ?; d. ? Rome, ?), Nthld. 16th-cent. comp. Singer in the Papal Chapel in Rome, 1538–65. He acted as judge in the dispute between Vicentino and Lusitano. Wrote motets and madrigals.

Danning, Sophus Christian (b. Copenhagen, 16. VI. 1867; d. Odense, 7. XI. 1925), Dan. cond. & comp. Studied in Copenhagen, Sondershausen and Leipzig. Travelled in It., Fr. and Ger., lived for a time in Fin., then taught at Copenhagen and in 1899 went to Norw. as theatre cond. at Bergen. In 1907–11 he was cond. at Oslo.

Works incl. operas *Gustav Adolf*, *Elleskudt* & *Kynthia*, operetta *Columbine*; incid. m. to Oehlenschläger's *Aladdin* & other plays; syms. (incl. *Dante*) & ovts. for orch.; cantatas; v. Conc.; pf. pieces, songs, &c.

Dannreuther, Edward (George) (b. Strasburg, 4. XI. 1844; d. Hastings, 12. II. 1905), Ger.-Eng. pfst., teacher & critic. Studied at Leipzig and went to live in London in 1863.

Dante Alighieri (1265–1321), It. poet. *See* **Abrányi (E.)** (*Paolo and Francesca*), **Cagnoni** (*Francesca da Rimini*), **Campo** (*Divina commedia*), **Danning** (sym.), **Dante Symphony** (Liszt), **Davies (Walford)** (Fantasy), **Foote** (*Francesca da R.*), **Foulds, Francesca da Rimini** (operas, Goetz, Nápravník, Rakhmaninov, Zandonai; symph. fantasy, Tchaikovsky), **Françoise de Rimini** (opera, A. Thomas), **Frank** (*Francesca da R.*), **Galilei** (*Conte Ugolino*), **Generali** (*Francesca da R.*), **Gilson** (do.), **Klenau** (*Inferno*), **Liszt** (so. & sym.), **Lourié** (*Canzona*), **Morlacchi** (*Francesca da R.* & *Narration of Ugolino*), **Ollone** (*Amants de Rimini*), **Paolo e Francesca** (Mancinelli), **Tommasini** (chor. work), **Trittico** (*Gianni Schicchi*, Puccini), **Volbach** (*Hymne an Maria*), **Wallace (W.)** (*Passing of Beatrice*), **Wolf-Ferrari** (*Vita nuova*), **Woyrsch** (Prologue to *Divina commedia*).

Dante Sonata. A 1-mvt. so. by Liszt, entitled *Après une lecture du Dante*, in the It. vol. of his *Années de pèlerinage*, comp. 1837–9, revised 1849. L. called it a *so. quasi fantasia*.

Dante Symphony. A sym. by Liszt based on Dante's *Divina commedia*, comp., 1855–6, 1st perf. Dresden, 7. XI. 1857. There are 2 mvts., *Inferno* and *Purgatorio*.

Danyel (or Daniel), John (b. ? nr. Taunton, c. 1565; d. ? London, c. 1630), Eng. lutenist & comp., brother of the poet Samuel D. When his brother d. in 1619 he succeeded him as inspector of the Children of the Queen's Revels and later joined the royal company of musns. for the lutes. Pub. a book of 20 songs with lute and bass in 1606.

Danzi, Franz (b. Mannheim, 15. V. 1763; d. Carlsruhe, 13. IV. 1826), Ger. cst. & comp. Pupil of Vogler; was a member of the court band at Mannheim and, from 1778, at Munich. Chapel master of the court of Württemberg at Stuttgart, and from 1808 at Carlsruhe. A minor member of the Mannheim school of symsts.

Works incl. operas *Die Mitternachtsstunde*, *Turandot* (after Gozzi); church m.; syms.; chamber m., &c.

Daphne, opera by R. Strauss (lib. by Joseph Gregor), prod. Dresden, 15. X. 1938.

Daphnis et Alcimadure, pastoral by Mondonville (lib., in the Languedoc dialect, by the comp.), prod. Fontainebleau, at court, 29. X. 1754, 1st Paris perf., Opéra, 19. I. 1755.

Daphnis et Chloé, ballet by Ravel (chgph. by Mikhail Mikhailovitch Fokin), prod. Paris, Théâtre du Châtelet, 8. VI. 1912.

Daquin (or d'Aquin), Louis Claude (b. Paris, 4. VII. 1694; d. Paris, 15. VI. 1772), Fr. orgst., hpchdst. & comp. Godson and (?) pupil of Élisabeth Jacquet de la Guerre and (?) pupil of her husband, the orgst. Marin de la Guerre. He was a wonder-child and played before Louis XIV at the age of 6. Later he was org. pupil of Marchand. La Guerre was displaced by him at the Sainte-Chapelle in 1706, when he was 12. In 1727 he defeated Rameau in a contest for the orgst.'s post at the church of Saint-Paul, in 1732 he succeeded Marchand as orgst. to the convent of the Cordeliers and Dandrieu as orgst. of the royal chapel in 1739.

Works incl. cantata *La Rose*, many motets, org. pieces, fugues, trios and 2 books of hpchd. pieces, incl. *Le Coucou*.

Dardanus, opera by Rameau (lib. by Charles Antoine Leclerc de La

Bruère), prod. Paris, Opéra, 19. XI. 1739.

Opera by Sacchini (lib. do., altered by Nicolas François Guillard), prod. Versailles, at court, 18. IX. 1784; 1st Paris perf., Opéra, 20. XI. 1784.

Dargason. An Eng. country dance and folksong at least as old as the 16th cent. Holst used it in his *St. Paul's Suite.*

Dargomizhsky, Alexander Sergeievitch (b. Tula, 14. II. 1813; d. St. Petersburg, 17. I. 1869), Rus. comp. Studied m. as an amateur at St. Petersburg and after retiring from 4 years' govt. service in 1835, he led the life of a dilettante. In 1833 he met Glinka, who lent him his notes taken during his studies with Dehn in Berlin, and he set to work on his 1st opera. After the next stage attempt he devoted himself mainly to songs between 1856–60, incl. many of a satirical nature anticipating those of Mussorgsky. In 1864 he visited western Eur., but was able to gain a hearing only in Belg., where he perf. his orch. fantasies. On his return he assoc. himself with Balakirev's nationalist group, without actually joining it. He set Pushkin's *Stone Guest* as an opera word for word, but, leaving it unfinished, entrusted Rimsky-Korsakov with its completion.

Works incl. operas *Esmeralda* (after Hugo), *The Russalka* (after Pushkin), *Rogdana* (unfinished), *The Stone Guest* (Pushkin, unfinished); ballet *Bacchus's Feast*; a duet for an opera *Mazeppa*; orch. fantasies *Kazatchok, Baba-Yaga* & *Mummers' Dance*; *Tarantelle slave* for pf. duet; c. 90 songs, voc. duets, trios, 4tets, chors., &c.

Darke, Harold (Edwin) (b. London, 29. X. 1888), Eng. orgst. & comp. Studied org. with Parratt and comp. with Stanford at the R.C.M. in London. Orgst. at St. Michael's, Cornhill, since 1916.

Works incl. *The Kingdom of God* for sop., chor. & orch., *Ring out ye crystal spheres* (Milton) for chor., org. & orch., other chor. works incl. *O Lord Thou art my God, Hymn of Heavenly Beauty* (Spenser); church m.; org. works, songs, &c.

Darnton, (Philip) Christian (b. Leeds, 30. X. 1905), Eng. comp. Educ. at Cambridge. Studied m. with Rootham there, at the R.C.M. in London and under Butting in Berlin.

Works incl. Sinfonietta for chamber orch.; pf. Conc., va. Conc.; stg. 4tet, 8tet for wind and stgs., Suite for fl., va. & hp.; *Duo concertante* for 2 pfs.; duet for 2 vs.; *Swansong* (Robert Nichols) for sop. & orch., &c.

Daser, Ludwig (b. Munich, c. 1525; d. Stuttgart, 27. III. 1589), Ger. comp. He was chapel master to the Bavarian court at Munich, 1552–9, when Lassus succeeded him, and held a similar post at the court of Württemberg at Stuttgart from 1572 to his death. Wrote masses, motets, a Passion, org. m., &c.

Daudet, Alphonse (1840–97), Fr. novelist. *See* **Arlesiana** (Cilèa), **Arlésienne** (Bizet), **Pessard** (*Tartarin sur les Alpes*), **Porrino** (*Tartarin de Tarascon*), **Sapho** (Massenet).

Daughter of the Regiment (Donizetti). *See* **Fille du Régiment.**

Dauvergne, Antoine (b. Moulins, Bourbonnais, 3. X. 1713; d. Lyons, 12. II. 1797), Fr. vst. & comp. Pupil of his father, Jacques D.; played at Clermont-Ferrand and went to Paris in 1739 as vst. in the court chamber m. and in 1744 at the Opéra. In 1762 he became one of the dirs. of the Concert spirituel and later manager of the Opéra.

Works incl. over 20 operas & other stage works, e.g. *Les Troqueurs, Les Amours de Tempé*; motets; symph. concs., divertimenti; v. sos., &c.

Davenant (or D'Avenant), William (1606–68), Eng. poet & playwright. *See* **Banister** (*Circe*), **Lawes (W.)** (*Triumph of the Prince d'Amour* & *Unfortunate Lovers*), **Locke** (*Macbeth*), **Pepys** ('Beauty retire'), **Siege of Rhodes** (Locke, H. Lawes, H. Cooke, Coleman & Hudson).

Davico, Vincenzo (b. Monaco, 14. I. 1889). It comp. Studied at Turin and with Reger at Leipzig.

Works incl. opera *La dogaressa*; Requiem, orat. on Flaubert's *La Tentation de Saint Antoine*; orch. works *La principessa lontana, Impressioni romani, Poema erotico* & *Polifemo*, &c.

David, Félicien (César) (b. Cadenet, Vaucluse, 13. V. 1810; d. Saint-Germain-en-Laye, 29. VIII. 1876), Fr. comp. Entered the Paris Cons. in 1830. having been a chorister at Aix cath. and afterwards cond. at the theatre. In 1833 he travelled in the near east, returned in 1835, lived nr. Igny for a time on finding that Paris neglected him, but settled in the capital in 1841 and made a great success with his oriental descriptive sym. *Le Désert* in 1844.

Works incl. operas *La Perle du Brésil, La Fin du monde, Herculanum, Lalla-Roukh* (after Moore), *Le Saphir* & *La Captive* (withdrawn); orat. *Moïse au Sinaï*; mystery *Eden*; motets & hymns; descriptive syms. *Le Désert* & *Christophe Colomb*; 2 syms.; stg. 4tet, 24 stg. 5tets, 2 nonets for wind; *Mélodies orientales* for pf.; songs, &c.

David, Ferdinand (b. Hamburg, 19. VI. 1810; d. nr. Klosters, Swi., 18. VIII. 1873), Ger. vst. & comp. Studied with Spohr and Hauptmann and made his 1st appearance at the Leipzig Gewandhaus in 1825, where he became leader under Mendelssohn in 1836. Wrote 5 concs. and many other works for the v., chamber m., &c.

David, Karl Heinrich (St. Gall, 30. XII. 1884), Swi. cond. & comp. Studied at the Cologne and Munich Conss. Cond. at var. theatres, became prof. at the Basle Cons. in 1910 and settled at Zürich in 1917. Ed. of the *Schweizerische Musikzeitung*.

Works incl. operas *Der Sizilianer* (after Molière), *Traumwandel*; *Aschenputtel* play with m., Youth Festival Play; *Das hohe Lied Salomonis* for solo voices, chor. & orch.; festival drama for the Berne Exhib. of 1914; var. chor. works with solo voices; 3 syms., *Rome*, Partita & Serenade for orch.; Conc., Fantasy & *Andante and Rondo* for v. & orch.; 4 stg. 4tets, stg. 6tet; songs, &c.

Davidde penitente (*The Penitent David*), cantata by Mozart, K. 469 (lib. ? by Lorenzo da Ponte), made up in III. 1785, mainly from portions of the unfinished C min. Mass, K. 427, of 1782–3. Only 2 arias are new.

Davide, Giacomo (b. Presezzo nr. Bergamo, 1750; d. Presezzo, 31. XII. 1830), It. ten. singer. After many triumphs in It. he 1st sang in Paris in 1785 and London in 1791.

Davide, Giovanni (b. Naples, 15. IX. 1790; d. St. Petersburg, *c.* 1851), It. ten. & bass singer, son and pupil of prec. Made his 1st appearance at Brescia in 1810.

Davidenko, Alexander Alexandrovitch (b. Odessa, 1. IV. 1899; d. Moscow, 1. V. 1934), Rus. comp. Studied with Glière at the Moscow Cons.

Works incl. opera *The Year 1905* (with Shekhter); pf. So. *Tchetchensk*; mass songs; songs, &c.

Davidov, Charles (b. Goldingen, Courland, 17. III. 1838; d. Moscow, 15. II. 1889), Rus. cst. & comp. Made his 1st appearance at the Leipzig Gewandhaus in 1859 and later became 1st cst. in its orch. and prof. at the Cons. In 1862 he was app. to a similar post at the St. Petersburg Opera and was dir. of the Cons. there in 1876–86. Wrote 4 co. concs. and many other works for his inst., &c.

Davidsbund (Ger. = League of David). An assoc. formed in 1834 by Schumann and his friends to combat the mus. ' Philistines.'

Davidsbündler (Ger.). The members of the above. They appear in the title of Schumann's *Davidsbündlertänze* and in the finale of his *Carnival* in a ' marche contre les Philistins.'

Davidsbündlertänze (*Dances of the David Leaguers*). A set of 18 pf. pieces by Schumann, Op. 6, comp. in 1837, the title alluding to the above.

Davie, Cedric Thorpe (b. Blackheath, 30. V. 1913), Sco. orgst. & comp. Student at the Sco. Nat. Acad. of M., Glasgow, the R.A.M. in London and later the R.C.M. there, where he was a pupil of R. O. Morris, Vaughan Williams and Gordon Jacob, gaining the Cobbett and Sullivan Prizes in 1935. He also studied pf. with Egon Petri in Ger., and comp. with Kodály at Budapest and Kilpinen at Helsinki. App. teacher of theory and comp. and the Sco. Nat. Acad. of M. at Glasgow and orgst. of Queen's Park High Parish Church there.

Works incl. opera *Gammer Gurton's Needle*, ballad opera *The Forrigan Reel* (James Bridie); *Dirge for Cuchullin* (Ossian); 3 anthems for chor. & orch.; incid. m. for Bridie's *The Anatomist* and *The Switchback* and for Neil Gunn's *Sun and Moon*; *Fantasy on 4 Sco. Folk Tunes* for orch.; Conc. for pf. & stgs.; stg. 4tet; v. & pf. So., sonatinas for co. & pf. and fl. & pf.; 8 *Little Songs*, &c.

Davies, Ben(jamin **Grey**) (b. Pontardawe nr. Swansea, 6. I. 1858; d. Bristol, 28. III. 1943), Welsh ten. singer. Studied at the R.A.M. in London; made his 1st concert appearance at Dublin in 1879 and 1st sang in opera at Birmingham in 1881.

Davies, Cecilia (b. ? London, *c.* 1750; d. London, 3. VII. 1836), Eng. singer. Sang at Dublin in 1763 and 1st appeared in London in 1767. The following year she went to Paris & Vienna with her sister Marianne (1744–?), a fl., hpchd. and harmonica player, where they had a great success, Hasse writing an ode for them to words specially provided by Metastasio; and in 1771–3 they were in It., where C. became famous as 'L'Inglesina.'

Davies, Fanny (b. Guernsey, 27. VI. 1861; d. London, 1. IX. 1934), Eng. pfst. Studied at Leipzig and under Clara Schumann at Frankfort o/M., making her 1st London appearance in 1885.

Davies, (Henry) Walford (b. Oswestry, 6. IX. 1869; d. Wrington, Som., 11. III. 1941), Eng. orgst., educst. & comp. Educ. at St. George's Chapel, Windsor, under Parratt, and at the R.C.M. in London, where Stanford was his comp. master. Held var. orgst.'s apps., took the Cambridge Mus.D. degree in 1898, when he was app. orgst. and choirmaster at the Temple Church. Prof. of M.

at the Univ. of Wales, Aberystwyth, from 1919. Knighted 1922. He resigned from the Temple in 1923 and became orgst. at St. George's, Windsor, in 1927 and Master of the King's M. in succession to Elgar in 1934.

Works incl. comps. for solo voices, chor. & orch.: *Hervé Riel* (Browning), *Everyman, Ode on Time* (Milton), *Noble Numbers* (Herrick), *Dante Fantasy* (from the *Divine Comedy*), *High Heaven's King* (Spenser), *Christ in the Universe* (Alice Meynell); Sym. in G maj., *Festal Ovt.*, *Parthenia* and *Memorial* suites, Suite after Wordsworth for orch., *Solemn Melody* for org. & stgs.; *Conversations* for pf. & orch.; many services and anthems; *Peter Pan* suite for stg. 4tet; pf. 5tet, 2 v. & pf. sos.; several works for voices with chamber m. & with pf.; many songs, part-songs, &c.

Davies, W(illiam). H(enry). (1871–1940), Eng. poet. *See* **Head** (*Songs of the Countryside*).

Davis, J(ohn). D(avid). (b. Birmingham, 22. X. 1869; d. Estoril, Port., 20. XI. 1942), Eng. comp. Studied at the Raff Cons. at Frankfort o/M. and at the Brussels Cons. Taught at the Midland Inst. School of M., Birmingham, 1893–1904.

Works incl. opera *The Zaporogues*; symph. ballad *The Cenci* (after Shelley), prelude to Maeterlinck's *L'Intruse*, *Miniatures* for small orch.; chamber m.; pf. pieces; songs, &c.

Davison, James William (b. London, 5. X. 1813; d. Margate, 24. III. 1885), Eng. critic, attached to *The Times*, 1846–79. Married the pfst. Arabella Goddard.

Davy, John (b. Upton Helions nr. Exeter, 23. XII. 1763; d. London, 22. II. 1824), Eng. comp. Pupil of Jackson at Exeter. Played in the Covent Garden orch. in London and wrote m. for many plays, incl. Shakespeare's *Tempest*. His song *The Bay of Biscay* became famous.

Davy, Richard (b. ?; d. ?), Eng. 15th–16th-cent. comp. Educ. at Magdalen Coll., Oxford, where he was orgst. & choirmaster in 1490–2. Chaplain to Anne Boleyn's grandfather & father in 1501–15. Comp. over 90 motets, Passion m. for Palm Sunday, part-songs, &c.

Day, John (b. Dunwich, Suffolk, 1522; d. London, 23. VII. 1584), Eng. printer. Estab. in London *c.* 1547. He pub. several m. books, incl. *Certaine Notes* containing prayers and psalms and Sternhold's Psalter (both 1560).

db. (abbr.) = Double Bass.

De. The prefix ' De ' or ' de ' appears in this work as an initial only in the case of Eng. names, with some exceptions (e.g. De Lara). It is often so shown in It. works of reference where the prefix has a capital D (e.g. De Sabata, De Sanctis), but it is unlikely that such names would be looked for under D by Eng. readers. In Fr. the custom is to use the principal name as a key-word, unless the prefix is incorporated in it (e.g. Debussy). In Spa. the ' de ' is not used except when the name is mentioned in full (Spaniards say, e.g. 'Manuel de Falla' or 'Falla').

De la Mare, Walter (b. 1873), Eng. poet. *See* **Dyson** (*Won't you look out of your window?*), **Gibbs** (**C. A.**) (*Crossings* & songs).

De Quincey, Thomas (1785–1859), Eng. essayist. *See* **Dieren (van)** (*Murder as One of the Fine Arts* & songs).

'Death and the Maiden' Quartet. Schubert's stg. 4tet in D min., begun III. 1824, finished or revised I. 1826 and 1st perf. Vienna, 1. II. 1826. It is so called because the 2nd mvt. is a set of vars. on his song *Death and the Maiden* (*Der Tod und das Mädchen*), or rather on the 2nd half of that song alone, Death's quiet and reassuring answer to the maiden's agitated plea to be spared.

Death and Transfiguration (Strauss). *See* **Tod und Verklärung.**

Debora e Jaele (*Deborah and Jael*), opera by Pizzetti (lib. by comp.), prod. Milan, Teatro alla Scala, 16. XII. 1922.

Deborah, orat. by Handel (words by Samuel Humphreys), prod. London, King's Theatre, Haymarket, 17. III. 1733.

Debussy, (Achille) Claude (b. Saint-Germain-en-Laye nr. Paris, 22. VIII. 1862; d. Paris, 25. III. 1918), Fr. comp. Son of a shopkeeper, took his 1st pf. lessons at the age of 7, and from 1870 was taught for 3 years by Mme. Mauté de Fleurville, a former pupil of Chopin's. Entered the Paris Cons. in 1873, studying with Lavignac and Marmontel, later with Emile Durand. At 17 he failed to win a pf. prize, but entered a comp. class in 1880. For the next 2 summers became domestic musn. to Nadezhda von Meck, Tchaikovsky's former patroness, whose children he taught and who took him to Swi. and It. the 1st time and to Rus. the 2nd. Gained 1st Prix de Rome in 1884 and went to Rome the next year, but left in 1887 before the statutory 3 years were completed. Began to comp. seriously in the new manner for which he became known with a Fr. trans. of Rossetti's *Blessed Damozel*, finished 1888. Influenced by Satie in 1891 and perf. his 1st important mature work, the prelude to Mallarmé's poem *L'Après-midi d'un faune*, in 1894. Married a dressmaker, Rosalie (Lili) Texier, in 1899; became m. critic for the *Revue blanche* in 1901; prod. his only finished opera, a setting of Maeterlinck's *Pelléas et Mélisande*, 30. IV. 1902. Left his wife in 1904 for Mme. Emma Bardac; divorced 1905 and married to Mme. B. Growing success, abroad as well as in Fr., during the last 10 years, but *c.* 1909 he began to suffer from cancer.

Works incl. opera *Pelléas et Mélisande*; incid. m. to d'Annunzio's *Le Martyre de Saint Sébastien*; ballets *Jeux* & *Khamma*; cantatas *L'Enfant prodigue* & *La Damoiselle élue*; 3 *Chansons de France* (Charles d'Orléans) for unaccomp. chor.; *Printemps, Prélude à l'Après-midi d'un faune*, 3 *Nocturnes*, *La Mer* & 3 *Images* for orch.; *Fantaisie* for pf. & orch.; *Danse sacrée et danse profane* for hp. & stgs.; stg. 4tet; sos. for co. & pf., fl., va. & hp. and v. & pf., and some smaller chamber works for saxophone, cl. & fl.; many pf. pieces incl. *Suite bergamasque*, suite *Pour le Piano*, 3 *Estampes*, *Masques*, *L'Île joyeuse*, 2 sets of 3 *Images*, suite *Children's Corner*, 2 sets of 12 *Préludes* & 12 *Études*; *Petite Suite*, *Marche écossaise*, *Six Épigraphes antiques*, &c. for pf. duet; *Lindaraja* & *En blanc et noir* for 2 pfs.; *c.* 70 songs incl. sets *Cinq Poèmes de Baudelaire*, *Ariettes oubliées* (Verlaine), 2 sets of *Fêtes galantes* (Verlaine), *Proses lyriques* (Debussy), 3 *Ballades de Villon*, *Chansons de Bilitis* (Pierre Louÿs), *Le Promenoir des deux amants* (Tristan Lhermite), *Trois Poèmes de Stéphane Mallarmé*, &c.

Decani. In Eng. caths. and in churches where the choir is divided, the D. side is that on the south of the chancel, near the dean's stall, the other being the *Cantoris* side.

Deceptive Cadence (Amer. from Ger. Trugschluss). *See* **Interrupted Cadence.**

Declamation with Music. *See* **Recitations.**

Decrescendo (It. = waning, decreasing). Synon. of *diminuendo*, which is now more frequently used.

Ded. (abbr.) = Dedicated, dedication.

Dedekind, Constantin Christian (b. ? Reinsdorf, Anhalt, 2. IV. 1628; d. Dresden, IX. 1715), Ger. poet & comp. Studied at Dresden and in 1654 became a member of the Saxon court chapel there. He arr. words for sacred mus. dramas.

Works incl. psalms, sacred and secular voc. m., concs. for voices and insts. &c.

Dedekind, Heinrich (or Enricius) (b. Neustadt, Bavaria, ?; d. ? Lüneburg, 1619), Ger. clergyman & comp. Cantor at St. John's church, Lüneburg. Wrote psalms and other sacred voc. works.

Dedekind, Henning (b. ? Neustadt; d. ?, *c.* 1630), Ger. comp., brother of prec. Held posts as cantor and preacher at Langensalza and Gebsee in Thuringia.

Works incl. Mass; secular voc. m., &c.

Deering. *See* **Dering.**

Defesch, William (b. ?; d. ? London, *c.* 1758), Flem. orgst., vst. & comp. Orgst. and later choirmaster at Antwerp cath. until 1731, when he settled in London.

Works inc.. Mass; orats. *Judith* & *Joseph*; concs. & sos. for var. insts.; co. pieces; songs, &c.

Defoe, Daniel (? 1661–1731), Eng. novelist & journalist. *See* **Linley** (1) (*Robinson Crusoe*), **Rieti** (*Robinson & Friday*), **Robinson Crusoé** (Offenbach).

Degtiarev, Stephan Anikievitch b. ?, 1766; d. ?, 1813), Rus. comp. Pupil of Sarti at St. Petersburg.

Works incl. church m., chor. works *Minin and Pozharsky*, *The Liberation of Moscow* & *Napoleon's Flight* (unfinished), many concs., &c.

Dehmel, Richard (1863–1920), Ger. poet. *See* **Knab** (songs), **Melcer** (songs with orch.), **Verklärte Nacht** (Schoenberg), **Zilcher** (*Fitzebutze*).

Dehn, Siegfried (Wilhelm) (b. Altona, 25. II. 1799; d. Berlin, 12. IV. 1858), mus. author, ed. & teacher. Librarian of the mus. section of the Royal Library in Berlin, ed. of the periodical *Caecilia*, author of theoret. books, ed. of Lassus, Bach and other old masters and teacher of mus. theory.

Deidamia, opera by Handel (lib. by Paolo Antonio Rolli), prod. London, King's Theatre, Haymarket, 10. I. 1741. H.'s last opera.

Delage, Maurice (Charles) (b. Paris, 13. XI. 1879), Fr. comp. Pupil of Ravel.

Works incl. ovt. to a ballet *Les Bâtisseurs de ponts* (after Kipling), symph. poem *Conté par la mer* & other orch. works; piano pieces; songs, &c.

Delannoy, Marcel (François Georges) (b. Ferté-Alais, 9. VII. 1898), Fr. comp. A painter and architect at first, he was mainly self-taught in m.

Works incl. operas *Le Poirier de misère*, *Philippine*, *Fête de la danse*, *Ginevra*; ballet-cantata *Le Fou de la dame*, ballets *La Pantoufle de vair* & *L'Éventail de Jeanne* (with others); incid. m. for Aristophanes' *Peace* & other plays; Sym. & *Figures sonores* for orch.; *Sérénade concertante* for v. & orch.; stg. 4tets; many songs, &c.

Delbos, Claire. *See* **Messiaen.**

Deldevez, Édouard (Marie Ernest) (b. Paris, 31. V. 1817; d. Paris, 6. XI. 1897), Fr. vst., cond. & comp. Studied at the Paris Cons. Later played in and cond. var. orchs. Wrote several theoret. books.

Works incl. ballet *Lady Henriette* (with Burgmüller & Flotow, the latter's opera *Martha* being later based on it); 3 syms., concert ovts.; chamber m., &c.

Delibes (Clément Philibert) Léo (b. Saint-Germain-du-Val, 21. II. 1836; d. Paris, 16. I. 1891), Fr. comp. Studied at the Paris Cons., where Adam was his comp. master. He became accompst. at the Théâtre Lyrique in 1853 and was orgst. successively at 2 churches. Later he became accompst. and chor. master at the Opéra and in 1881 prof. of comp. at the Cons.

Works incl. operas *Maître Griffard, Le Jardinier et son seigneur, Le Roi l'a dit, Jean de Nivelle, Lakmé, Kassya* (unfinished); ballets *La Source* (with Minkus), *Coppélia, Sylvia, Le Pas des fleurs*; divertissement for Adam's ballet *Le Corsaire*; incid. m. for Hugo's *Le Roi s'amuse*; operettas *Deux Sous de charbon, Deux Vieilles Gardes, L'Omelette à la Follembûche, Le Serpent à plumes, L'Écossais de Chatou* and others; Mass; cantata *Alger*; dramatic scene *La Mort d'Orphée*; songs; children's chors., &c.

Delius, Frederick (b. Bradford, 29. I. 1862; d. Grez-sur-Loing, 10. VI. 1934), Eng. comp. of Ger. descent. His father was a well-to-do business man and wished him to follow a commercial career; but m. was cultivated in the home and although D. had little systematic teaching until he went to Florida as an orange planter in 1884 and came under the influence of Thomas Ward, orgst. at Jacksonville, he worked steadily at m. by himself. Only in 1886, after some teaching in U.S.A., he went to the Leipzig Cons. for a short time, but found its conservative teaching uncongenial. In 1887 he visited Norw. and made friends with Grieg, who persuaded his father to let him devote himself to comp. From 1889 he lived in Fr., mainly Paris, and in 1897 he married Jelka Rosen, a Ger. painter of Dan. descent, and they settled at Grez-sur-Loing nr. Fontainebleau. A concert of his works was given in London in 1899 and he became known here and there in Ger. In 1922 he was attacked by paralysis, which gradually increased until 4 years later he was helpless and totally blind. In 1928 Eric Fenby volunteered to live in his house and act as amanuensis.

Works incl. operas *Irmelin, The Magic Fountain, Koanga, A Village Romeo and Juliet, Margot-la-Rouge, Fennimore and Gerda*; incid. m. for Heiberg's *Folkeraadet* & Flecker's *Hassan*; orch. works: *Florida* suite, *Over the Hills and Far Away, Paris, Life's Dance, Brigg Fair, In a Summer Garden*, 2 *Dance Rhapsodies, On hearing the first Cuckoo in Spring & Summer Night on the River, North Country Sketches, Eventyr* (after Asbjørnsen's fairy-tales); concs. for pf., v., co. and v. & co.; 2 stg. 4tets; 2 v. & pf. sos.; So. for co. & pf.; works for chor. & orch.: *Appalachia, Sea Drift, A Mass of Life, Songs of Sunset, Arabesk, A Song of the High Hills*; *Requiem, A Song before Sunrise, A Poem of Life and Love*; some partsongs; songs with orch. incl. cycle from Tennyson's *Maud*, 7 Dan. songs, Dowson's *Cynara*; c. 40 songs; 2 pieces for pf. & 1 for hpchd., &c.

Della Ciaia, Azzolino Bernardino (b. Siena, 21. III. 1671; d. Pisa, I. 1755), It. orgst. & comp. He was a knight of the order of San Stefano and presented an org. to its church at Pisa, not only designed by himself but partly built by his own hands.

Works incl. masses, motets, *Salmi concertati*; *Cantate da camera*; hpchd. sos., &c.

Delle Sedie, Enrico (b. Leghorn, 17. VI. 1824; d. Paris, 28. XI. 1907), It. bar. singer. After fighting as a volunteer in the war against Aus. he studied singing with Orazio Galeffi at Leghorn and made his 1st appearance at Pistoia in 1851. In 1867 he became prof. at the Paris Cons.

Dello Joio, Norman (b. New York, 24. I. 1913), Amer. comp. Studied comp. at the Juillard Graduate School in N.Y., with Wagenaar, later with Hindemith at Yale School of M. He joined the teaching staff of Sarah Lawrence Coll.

Works incl. sym. *Western Star* for solo voices, narrator, chor. & orch.; Sinfonietta, ballet suite *Duke of Sacramento*, symph. mvt. *Silvermine* for orch.; concs. for pf., 2 pf., hp. & fl.; 4tet & Trio for woodwind, Trio for fl., co. & pf.; v. & pf. So., *Duo concertante* for co. & pf., Sonatina for co. solo; Suite & *Duo concertante* for 2 pfs.; 2 pf. sos., &c.

Delmas, Marc (Marie Jean Baptiste) (b. Saint-Quentin, 28. III. 1885; d. Paris, 30. XI. 1931), Fr. comp. Studied at the Paris Cons, and took the Prix de Rome in 1919.

Works incl. operas *Iriam, Camille,*

Le Dieu sans couronne, Le Masque, Cyrca, Le Giaour; symph. poem *Les Deux Routes*; chamber m.; pf. pieces; songs, &c.

Delvincourt, Claude (b. Paris, 12. I. 1888), Fr. comp. Studied at the Paris Cons. under Caussade and Widor. Took the Prix de Rome in 1913. He was wounded in the 1914–8 war and incapacitated for 8 years, but became dir. of the Versailles Cons. in 1932 and of the Paris Cons. in 1941 in succession to Rabaud. During the 2nd world war he helped the students to join the Maquis & to escape service in Ger.

Works incl. opera *La Femme à barbe*; *Boccacerie, L'Offrande à Siva, Bal vénitien* & *Prélude chorégraphique* for orch.; Trio for ob., cl. & bn.; v. & pf. So.; *Heures juvéniles* & *Images pour les contes du temps passé* for pf.; pf. duets & solo pieces; songs, &c.

Demelli, Francesco. *See* **Suppé.**

Demetrio (*Demetrius*), lib. by Metastasio.

Opera by Caldara, prod. Vienna, at court, 4. XI. 1731.

Opera by Gluck, prod. Venice, Teatro San Samuele, 2. V. 1746.

Opera by Hasse, prod. Venice, Teatro San Giovanni Crisostomo, I. 1732.

Opera by Jommelli, prod. Parma, Carnival 1750.

Opera by Pérez, prod. Venice, Teatro San Samuele, spring 1751.

Opera by Pescetti, prod. Florence, Teatro della Pergola, 26. XII. 1732.

Demeur. *See* **Charton-Demeur.**

Demi-Semiquaver. A note or rest of the value of a quarter of a quaver.

Demofoonte, rè di Tracia (*Demophoon, King of Thrace*), lib by Metastasio.

Opera by Caldera, comp. 1733.

Opera by Gluck, prod. Milan, Teatro Regio Ducal, 26. XII. 1742.

Opera by Graun, prod. Berlin, Opera, 17. I. 1746. 3 airs are by Frederick II of Prus.

Opera by Hasse, prod. Dresden, at court, 9. II. 1748.

Opera by Jommelli, prod. Padua, 13. VI. 1743.

Opera by Leo, prod. Naples, Teatro San Bartolommeo, 20. I. 1735.

Opera by Portugal, prod. Milan, Teatro alla Scala, 8. II. 1794.

Demon, The, opera by A. Rubinstein (lib., in Rus., by Pavel Alexandrovitch Viskovatov, based on Lermontov's poem), prod. St. Petersburg, 25. I. 1875.

Démophon, opera by Cherubini (lib. by Marmontel, based on Metastasio's *Demofoonte*), prod. Paris, Opéra, 5. XII. 1788, C.'s 1st Fr. opera.

Demuth, Norman (b. London, 15. VII. 1888), Eng. comp. Educ. as a choirboy at St. George's Chapel, Windsor, and at Repton School. Studied m. at the R.A.M. in London, where he became prof. of comp. in 1929.

Works incl. ballets *The Flame* & *Planetomania*, chgph. sym. *Night M. for a dancer*; 5 syms., *Introd. and Allegro*, Partita, nocturne *Paris, Serenata, Prelude for a Drama, Cortège, Notturno e Scherzo, The Dance of Life, Fantasy and Fugue* for orch.; *Pastoral* for stgs.; v. Conc., va. Conc.; 2 v. & pf. sos. & pieces; Sonatina for fl. & pf.; *Prelude, Air and Toccata* for hpchd.; *M. for Dancing* & other pf. works; part-songs, &c.

Den. (abbr.) = Denmark.

Dent, Edward J(oseph). (b. Ribston, Yorks, 16. VII. 1876), Eng. mcolst. & comp. Educ. at Eton and Cambridge, became Prof. of M. there in 1926. President of the I.S.C.M. from its foundation in 1922 until 1938. A governor of Sadler's Wells Opera, for which he has trans. many works. His books incl. works on A. Scarlatti, Mozart's operas, Eng. opera, Handel and Busoni, and his comps. polyphonic motets and a version of *The Beggar's Opera*.

Denza, Luigi (b. Castellamare di Stabia, 1846; d. London, 26. I. 1922), It. singing-teacher & comp. Studied at the Naples Cons. Settled in London in 1879, made a success with many of his light songs, esp. *Funiculì, funiculà*, and was prof. of singing at the R.A.M. from 1898.

Works incl. an opera on Schiller's *Wallenstein*, over 500 songs, &c.

Deprés. *See* **Josquin.**

Dering, Lady. *See* **Harvey, Mary.**

Dering (or Deering), Richard (b. ?; d. London, 1630), Eng. orgst. & comp. Studied in It. and made his reputation there before he returned to Eng. (?) soon after 1600. He went to Brussels in 1617 as orgst. to the convent of Eng. nuns, but returned again to become orgst. to Henrietta Maria on her marriage to Charles I in 1625.

Works incl. *Cantiones sacrae* for several voices, motets, anthems; canzonets for 3 & 4 voices, quodlibets on street cries; fancies & other pieces for viols, &c.

Des Prés. *See* **Josquin.**

Desbordes-Valmore, Marceline (1785–1859), Fr. poetess. *See* **Franck (C.)** (songs).

Descant. Formerly meaning ctpt., D. came later to mean the polyphonic combination of additional parts with a given melody, in measured m. as distinct from plainsong; and in modern terminology it is the addition of a treble part to a well-known tune, either by a comp. or by improvisation, not so much to enrich it harmonically as to decorate it melodically. In this sense the word has become synonymous with Faburden and Fauxbourdon.

Descant Viol. *See* **Treble Viol.**

Descartes, René (b. La Haye, 35. III. 1596; d. Stockholm, 11. II. 1650), Fr. philosopher. Wrote a book on m., *Compendium musicae.*

Deschamps, Émile (1791–1875), Fr. poet. *See* **Niedermeyer** (songs).

Déserteur, Le, opera by Monsigny (lib. by Jean Michel Sedaine), prod. Paris, Comédie-Italienne, 6. III. 1769.

Désir, Le (waltz attrib. to Beethoven). *See* **Trauerwalzer.**

Desmarets, Henri (b. Paris, *c.* 1662; d. Lunéville, 7. IX. 1741), Fr. comp. Educ. at the court of Louis XIV. At the end of the cent. he secretly married the daughter of a dignitary at Senlis and fled to Spa., becoming mus. superintendent to Philip V in 1700. In 1708 he became mus. dir. to the Duke of Lorraine at Lunéville.

Works incl. operas *Didon, Circé, Théagène et Chariclée* (on Heliodorus's *Aethiopica*), *Les Amours de Momus, Venus et Adonis, Les Fêtes galantes, Iphigénie en Tauride* (with Campra) & *Renaud, ou La Suite d'Armide*; motet and Te Deum for the marriage of Princess Élisabeth Thérèse to the King of Sardinia; church m. comp. early in his career under the name of Goupillier, &c.

Dessus (Fr. = above, top). A bowed stg. inst. of the v. family, now obs., but used in the 17th cent., with a range from E above middle C.

Dessus de viole (Fr. = top of the viols). Any inst. of the viol family taking the treble part in a consort.

Destinnova (*née* **Kittl**) (better known as **Destinn**), **Emmy** (b. Prague, 26 II. 1878; d. Budějovice, 28. I. 1930), Cz. sop. singer. Made her 1st appearance in Berlin in 1898; 1st visited London (Covent Garden) in 1904.

Destouches, André(-Cardinal) (b. Paris, 1673; d. Paris, 8. II. 1749), Fr. comp. A sailor at first, and then a musketeer, he studied with Campra and prod. his 1st stage work, *Issé,* in 1697. He held var. court apps. and was dir. of the Opéra in 1728–31.

Works incl. operas *Amadis de Grèce, Marthésie, Omphale, Callirhoé, Télémaque et Calypso, Sémiramis, Les Stratagèmes de l'Amour*; heroic pastoral *Issé*; comedy-ballet *Le Carnaval et la folie*; ballet *Les Éléments* (with Lalande); cantatas *Œnone & Sémélé,* &c.

Dettingen Te Deum, a Te Deum comp. by Handel to celebrate the victory of Dettingen won on 26. VI. 1743. 1st perf. London, Chapel Royal, 27. XI. 1743.

Deuteromelia. The 2nd part of a collection of canons, rounds and catches pub. by Ravenscroft in London in 1609, the 1st part being *Pammelia.*

Deutsch, Otto Erich (b. Vienna, 5. IX. 1883), Aus. mus. biog. and biblfog. Made a special study of 1st eds. and of Schubert and other classics. After the *Anschluss* he took refuge in Eng. and settled at Cambridge. His pubs. incl. the complete Schubert documents, much enlarged in the Eng. ed., a study of Mozart eds. (with C. B. Oldman), Leopold Mozart's later letters (with B. Paumgartner), the Harrow Replicas of var. old pubs., &c.

Deutsche Tänze (Ger. plur. = Ger. Dances). Not an equivalent of the Allemande, but a type of country dance in 3–4 (slow waltz) time, cultivated by Mozart, Beethoven, Schubert and others. The adj. 'Deutsche' was frequently used alone in titles.

Deutsches Requiem (Brahms). *See* **German Requiem.**

Deux Avares, Les (*The Two Misers*), opera by Grétry (lib. by Charles Georges Fenouillot de Falbère), prod. Fontainebleau, at court, 27. X. 1770; 1st Paris perf., Comédie-Italienne, 6. XII. 1770.

Deux Chasseurs et la Laitière, Les (*The Two Huntsmen and the Milkmaid*), opera by Duni (lib. by Louis Anseaume, after La Fontaine), prod. Paris, Comédie-Italienne, 21. VII. 1763.

Deux Journées, Les (*The Two Days*: better known as *The Water-Carrier*), opera by Cherubini (lib. by Jean Nicolas Bouilly), prod. Paris, Théâtre Feydeau, 16. I. 1800.

Deux Petits Savoyards, Les (*The Two Little Savoyards*), opera by Dalayrac (lib. by Benoît Joseph Marsollier), prod. Paris, Comédie-Italienne, 14. I. 1789.

Development. *See* **Working-Out.**

Devil and Kate, The (*Čert a Káča*), opera by Dvořák (lib. by Adolf Wenig), prod. Prague, Cz. Theatre, 23. XI. 1899.

Devil to Pay, The, or The Wives Metamorphos'd, ballad opera (lib. by Charles Coffey), prod. London, Drury Lane Theatre, 6. VIII. 1731

Devil's Opera, The, opera by Macfarren (lib. by George Macfarren, the comp.'s father, a satire on the diabolic elements in works like Weber's *Freischütz,* Meyerbeer's *Robert le Diable,* Marschner's *Vampyr,* &c.),, prod. London, Lyceum Theatre 10. IX. 1838.

Devil's Trill (Tartini). *See* **Trillo del Diavolo.**

Devil take her, The, opera by Benjamin (lib. by Alan Collard & John B. Gordon), prod. London, R.C.M., XII. 1931.

Devin du village, Le (*The Village Soothsayer*), opera by Rousseau (lib. by comp.), prod. Fontainebleau, at court, 18. X. 1752, with ovt. and recits. by Pierre de Jélyotte (1713–87) and Francœur; Paris, Opéra, 1. III. 1753, with m. all by R.

Devrient, Eduard (Philipp) (b. Berlin, 11. VIII. 1801; d. Carlsruhe, 4. X. 1877), Ger. bar. singer and actor.

Devrient, Wilhelmine. *See* **Schröder-Devrient.**

Dezède, Nicolas (b. ? Turin or Lyons, c. 1744; d. Paris, 1792), Fr. comp. (?) of It. descent. He did not know what his parentage was, but received a handsome allowance on condition that he should not try to find out, and it was stopped when he persisted in his inquiries. He then began to prod. light operas.

Works incl. operas *Julie, L'Erreur d'un moment, Les Trois Fermiers, Blaise et Babet, Alexis et Justine*, &c.

Diabelli, Anton (b. Mattsee nr. Salzburg, 6. IX. 1781; d. Vienna, 7. IV. 1858), Aus. m. pub. & comp. Educ. for the priesthood, but studied m. with M. Haydn. Went to Vienna as pf. & guitar teacher and joined Peter Cappi in his pub. firm in 1818; it became D. & Co. in 1824.

Works incl. operetta *Adam in der Klemme*; masses; many pf. pieces, incl. the little waltz on which Beethoven wrote the 33 vars., Op. 120, &c.

'Diabelli' Variations. *See above* & **Vaterländischer Künstlerverein.**

Diable à quatre, Le, ou La Double Métamorphose, ballad opera with airs arr. by Philidor (lib. by Jean Michel Sedaine, based on Coffey's *Devil to Pay*), prod. Paris, Opéra-Comique, 19. VIII. 1756.

Diable dans le beffroi, Le (*The Devil in the Belfry*), opera by Debussy (lib. by himself, based on Egar Allan Poe's story), worked at in 1903 but not completed.

Diabolus in Musica (Lat. = the devil in m.). A medieval warning against the use of the Tritone—the interval of the augmented 4th or diminished 5th (e.g. C–F♯ or B–F), which was not allowed to be used simultaneously in harmony and looked at askance as a melodic progression.

Diaghilev, Sergey Pavlovitch (b. Gvt. of Novgorod, 19. III. 1872; d. Venice, 19. VIII. 1929), Rus. impresario. Studied law and m. at St. Petersburg, founded an art review there in 1899, prod. Rus. m. in Paris from 1907 and in 1909 organized the Rus. Ballet there, which 1st visited London in 1911.

Dialogue. A type of 17th-cent. comp. for 2 voices where each represented a distinct personage.

Diamants de la Couronne, Les (*The Crown Diamonds*), opera by Auber (lib. by Scribe & Jules Henri Vernoy de Saint-Georges), prod. Paris, Opéra-Comique, 6. III. 1841.

Diamond, David (Leo) (b. Rochester, New York, 9. VII. 1915), Amer. comp. of Aus. descent. Studied at the Eastman School of M. at Rochester and later at Fontainebleau with Nadia Boulanger. After his return to Amer. he was awarded several comp. prizes.

Works incl. 2 syms., Sinfonietta, Serenade, Vars., *Psalm, Elegy in Memory of Ravel* & ballet suite *Tom* for orch.; Conc. for stg. orch.; v. Conc., *Hommage à Satie* & Ballade for chamber orch., concs. for pf. & for hpchd. with chamber orch.; *A Night Litany* (Ezra Pound) for chor. & 3 madrigals for unaccomp. chor. (James Joyce); stg. 5tet, stg. Trio; Sonatina for v. & pf., co. & pf. So., Partita for bn. & pf.; So. & Sonatina for pf., &c.

Diana, Paolo. *See* **Spagnoletti.**

Diapason (from Gr. = interval of an octave; Fr. = a tuning-fork and hence pitch). The normal modern Eng. use of the term designates the foundation stops of the org., which produce the inst.'s most distinctive and characteristic tone. There are 2 kinds of D. pipes: open and stopped.

Diapente (Gr.). The interval of the 5th. In old m. canons at the 5th were called Epidiapente when answered in the 5th above and Subdiapente when answered below.

Diaphone. A powerful Tremulant org. stop which may embrace 8-ft., 16-ft. and 32-ft. pipes.

Diaphony (or Lat. **Diaphonia**). In Lat. 'dissonance' as distinct from *symphonia* = 'consonance.' In Eng. the term is used to designate an old form of descant dating back to at least the 9th cent., sung chiefly in 4ths, but with exceptions where this would have resulted in tritones and usually bringing voices gradually together into unison at final cadences. To all intents and purposes D. is the same as Organum.

Diastole (from Gr. = distinction, differentiation). An old term, in use to the middle of the 18th cent., for the divisions of m. into sections or phrases.

Diatessaron (Gr.). The interval of the 4th.

Diatonic. D. m. is the opposite of chromatic m., using the notes proper to the prescribed maj. or min. scale only, without deviations to those marked with additional accidentals.

Diaz, Gabriel (b. ?, *c.* 1590; d. Madrid, after 1631), Spa. comp. Worked at the Spa. court and later at Larma, Granada and Córdoba.

Works incl. church m., a Requiem, secular voc. m., &c.

Dibdin, Charles (b. Southampton, III. 1745; d. London, 25. VII. 1814), Eng. singer, author & comp. He was a choir-boy at Winchester cath. and at the age of 15 went to London, where he soon appeared on the stage of Covent Garden Theatre. On the ten. Beard's advice he wrote the pastoral *The Shepherd's Artifice*, which was prod. there in 1764. After that he prod. innumerable stage pieces and many of the songs in them became very popular (e.g. *The Bells of Aberdovey* in *Liberty Hall*). In the 1780s he went into theatrical management with varying success and in 1787–8 he made a tour of Eng. to raise funds for a visit to India, which he attempted in 1788, only to be driven back by a tempest. In 1789 he began a long series of 'Table Entertainments,' at which he recited, sang and accomp. his own inventions. One of the most successful, *The Oddities*, contained the song *Tom Bowling*, and many others of his sea-songs appeared there. Later he became a pub., built a theatre of his own, wrote a *Hist. of the Stage* and other books, incl. novels.

Works incl. over 100 dramatic pieces, e.g. *Lionel and Clarissa, The Padlock, The Ephesian Matron, The Captive, The Ladle, The Trip to Portsmouth, The Seraglio, Rose and Colin, The Touchstone, The Milkmaid, Tom Thumb, Harvest Home*; over 30 table entertainments containing innumerable songs, &c.

Dichterliebe (*Poet's Love*), song cycle by Schumann, Op. 48 (16 poems by Heine), comp. in 1840.

Dickens, Charles (1812–70), Eng. novelist. *See* **Cricket on the Hearth** (Mackenzie), **Edwards (J.)** (*Dolly Varden*), **Gál** (*Pickwickian Ovt.*), **Heimchen am Herd** (Goldmark), **Holbrooke** (*Pickwick Club* 4tet), **O'Neill** (*Pickwick*), **Pickwick** (A. Coates), **Préludes** (Debussy, II. 9), **Schmidt (G.)** (*Christmas Carol*), **Village Coquettes** (Hullah), **White (F.)** (*D. Note-book*), **Wood (C.)** (*Pickwick Papers*), **Zandonai** (*Grillo sul focolare*).

Dickinson, Emily (1830–86), Amer. poetess. *See* **Barber** (chors.).

Diction. The popular but inaccurate term for enunciation of the words in singing. It has become so generally current that attempts to eradicate its use in this sense would be futile by this time, but it is worth remembering that properly D. means the use of words in speaking or writing grammatically.

Dido and Aeneas, opera by Purcell (lib. by Nahum Tate, after Virgil), prod. Chelsea, London, Josias Priest's boarding school ('by young gentlewomen'), ? XII. 1689.

Dido, Königin von Carthago, opera by Graupner (lib. by Heinrich Hinsch), prod. Hamburg, Theater am Gänsemarkt, spring 1707.

Didon (*Dido*), opera by Piccinni (lib. by Marmontel), prod. Fontainebleau, at court, 16. X. 1783, 1st Paris perf., Opéra, 1. XII. 1783.

Didone abbandonata (*Dido Forsaken*), lib. by Metastasio:

Opera by Hasse, prod. Hubertusburg nr. Dresden, 7. X. 1742.

Opera by Jommelli, prod. Rome, Teatro Argentina, 28. I. 1747.

Opera by Sarro, prod. Naples, Teatro San Bartolommeo, 5. II. 1724.

Opera by Traetta, prod. Venice, Teatro San Moisè, autumn 1757.

Didone, La (*Dido*), opera by Cavalli (lib. by Giovanni Francesco Busenello), prod. Teatro San Cassiano, Carnival 1641.

Diémer, Louis (b. Paris, 14. II. 1843; d. Paris, 21. XII. 1919), Fr. pfst. & comp. Studied with Marmontel, Bazin & A. Thomas at the Paris Cons. In 1888 he became pf. prof. there.

Works incl. pf. Conc., *Concertstück* for pf. & orch., another for v. & orch.; chamber m., &c.

Diepenbrock, Alphons (b. Amsterdam, 2. IX. 1862; d. Amsterdam, 5. IV. 1921), Dutch comp. At first a philologist, self-taught in m.

Works incl. *Stabat Mater*, Te Deum for solo voices, chor. & orch., Mass; incid. m. for Aristophanes' *The Birds*, Sophocles' *Electra*, Goethe's *Faust*, Vondel's *Gysbrecht van Amstel*; songs with orch.; chamber m.; songs, &c.

Dieren, Bernard van (b. Rotterdam, 27. XII. 1884; d. London, 24. IV. 1936), Dutch (anglicized) comp. Educ. for science, he had little mus. experience, apart from v. playing, before the age of 20, when he began to comp. In 1919 he settled in London as correspondent to foreign papers, after making serious mus. studies, which he continued in Ger. in 1912, when his real creative career began.

Works incl. opera *The Tailor* (Robert Nichols); Sym. on Chinese poems for solo voices, chor. & orch., *Les Propous des beuveurs* (Rabelais) for chor. & orch.; *Beatrice Cenci*, orch. epilogue to Shelley's drama,

Ovt. *Anjou*; **Serenade for small orch.**, **Ovt.** for chamber orch.; *Diafonia* for **17 insts.** & bar. (Shakespeare sonnets) *Fayre eies* (Spenser) for bar. & chamber orch.; 6 stg. 4tets; 3 unaccomp. chors.; So. & 3 Studies for unaccomp. v.; v. & pf. So.; songs for bar. & stg. 4tet (Shelley & De Quincey), 2 recitations with stg. 4tet (Baudelaire & Villon); *Marginalia* from De Quincey's *Murder as One of the Fine Arts* for bar., voc. 4tet & pf.; 6 Sketches, Toccata, 3 Studies, Prelude, 12 Vars. for pf.; songs to words by Shakespeare, Nash, Beddoes, Keats, Landor, Joyce, Goethe, Heine, Mörike, Verlaine, Charles d'Orléans, Ronsard, Boileau, Hugo, Villiers de l'Isle Adam, &c.

Dies irae. The 2nd section of the Requiem Mass, orig. assoc. with a distinct plainsong theme which has been frequently used or quoted by var. comps., e.g.:

Bantock, Witches' Dance in incid. m. to *Macbeth*.

Berlioz, Witches' Sabbath in *Fantastic Sym.* & Requiem.

Liszt, *Totentanz* for pf. & orch. & *Danté* sym.

Miaskovsky, Sym.

Mussorgsky, *Trepak* in *Songs and Dances of Death*.

Rakhmaninov, Rhapsody on a Theme by Paganini for pf. & orch.

Rakhmaninov, *The Isle of the Dead*, symph. poem.

Saint-Saens, *Danse macabre* for orch.

Schelling, *Victory Ball* for orch.

Sorabji, Vars. for pf.

Tchaikovsky, Theme & Vars. in Suite No. 3 for orch.

Vaughan Williams, *Five Tudor Portraits* for chor. & orch. (funeral of Philip the sparrow).

Diesis (Gr. = division). The name given by the Grs. to quarter-tones.

Dietrich, Albert (Hermann) (b. Golk nr. Meissen, 28. VIII. 1829; d. Berlin, 20. XI. 1908), Ger. comp. & cond. Court mus. dir. at Oldenburg from 1861. Wrote a v. & pf. So. jointly with Schumann and Brahms, 1853.

Works incl. opera *Robin Hood*; incid. m. to Shakespeare's *Cymbeline*; Sym. in D min.; chor. & orch. works; hn. concs.; chamber m., &c.

Dietrich, Sixt (b. Augsburg, *c.* 1491; d. St. Gall, 21. X. 1548), Ger. comp. Studied at the Univs. of Freiburg i/B. and Wittenberg, holding appts. at Strasburg and Constance between. Wrote magnificats, antiphons and other voc. m.

Dietsch, Pierre Louis Philippe (b. Dijon, 17. III. 1808; d. Paris, 20. II. 1865), Fr. cond. & comp. He comp. an unsuccessful opera to the orig. Fr. lib. of Wagner's *Flying Dutchman*, *Le Vaisseau fantôme*, prod. at the Paris Opéra in 1842. Cond. the disastrous perfs. of W.'s *Tannhäuser* in 1861. Works incl. church and org. m.

Dieupart, Charles (b. ?; d. ? London, *c.* 1740), Fr. vst., hpchdst. & comp. Settled in London at the end of the 17th cent. Taught hpchd. and gave concerts. Comp. suites for hpchd. and var. other insts.

Dièze (Fr.) = Sharp: the sign ♯.

Diferencias (Spa. lit. differences) = Variations.

Differential Tones. *See* **Resultant Tones.**

Dima, Gheorge (b. Brasov, 10. X. 1847; d. Cluj, 4. VI. 1925), Rum. comp. Studied at Carlsruhe, Vienna, Graz and Leipzig, and on returning to Rum. became chor. cond. at Brasov and mus. dir. of the church of St. Nicholas, also of the cath. at Sibiu.

Works incl. orat. *The Mother of Stephen the Great*; church liturgies; cantatas; songs, &c.

Diminished. Said of intervals which are normally 'perfect' (4ths, 5ths, 8ves) when they have been made a semitone narrower.

Diminished 7th Chord. A chord of 3 superimposed min. 3rds, e.g. C♯, E, G, B♭, very easy to modulate from on account of its indefinite tonality and often used in the 18th and 19th cents. for pathetic or dramatic suggestion, but now rather worn out both as a harmonic device and as an effect.

Diminuendo (It. = waning, lessening). A dir. to decrease the sound of a note, chord or phrase, synon. with *decrescendo* and now more frequently used.

Diminution. A shortening of a mus. figure or phrase by its reduction to smaller note-values.

Dimitri, opera by Dvořák (lib. by Maria Červinková-Riegerová), prod. Prague, Cz. Theatre, 8. X. 1882. The subject is the 'false Dimitri,' the pretender who also figures in Mussorgsky's *Boris Godunov*.

Dinorah (Meyerbeer). *See* **Pardon de Ploërmel.**

Dioclesian (Purcell). *See* **Prophetess.**

Direct. A sign used in plainsong notation and sometimes in old m. in staff notation, indicating at the end of the stave the position of the notes at the beginning of the following one, like a catchword in old books.

Diruta, Agostino (b. Perugia, ?; d. Rome, ?), It. 16th–17th-cent. orgst. & comp. Orgst. at Venice, 1617, Asolo, 1620–2, and Rome, 1630–46.

Works incl. masses, motets, psalms, *Sacrae cantiones*, canticles and other voc. m.

Diruta, Girolamo (b. Perugia, *c.* 1560;

d. ?, after 1628), It. Franciscan monk, orgst. & comp., relative and master of prec. Pupil of Zarlino, Porta and Merulo. Orgst. at Chioggia and Gubbio caths. He was a famous player and wrote a treatise of org. playing, *Il Transilvano*, ded. to the Prince of Transylvania, Sigismund Bathori. Comp. org. m.

Discant. *See* **Descant.**

Discord. The opposite of concord: the sounding together of notes that do not satisfy the ear as being final in themselves and require a following chord to give the impression of resolution.

Disjoint Motion. *See* **Motion.**

Dissoluto punito, Il (Mozart). *See* **Don Giovanni.**

Dissonance. The sounding together of notes which produces Discord.

Distler, Hugo (b. Nuremberg, 24. VI. 1908), Ger. orgst. & comp. Studied at Leipzig, became orgst. and cantor at Lübeck in 1921 and prof. of comp. at the Stuttgart Cons. in 1937.

Works incl. 52 motets entitled *Jahrkreis*, a Passion, orat. *Nativity*; org. works; hpchd. Conc., &c.

Distratto, Il (*The Distracted One, The Absent-Minded One*), the nickname of a Sym. by Haydn, No. 60, in C maj., arr. in 1775 from incid. m. to the comedy *Der Zerstreute*, a Ger. adapt. of Regnard's *Le Distrait*, prod. Pressburg, 22. XI. 1774.

Dital Harp. *See* **Harp Lute.**

Dittersdorf, Carl Ditters von (orig. Ditters) (b. Vienna, 2. XI. 1739; d. ?, 24. X. 1799), Aus. vst. & comp. Educ. in the household of the Prince of Hildburghausen in Vienna, studied comp. with Bonno. In 1761 he visited It. with Gluck and on his return competed successfully with Lolli as a vst., but left Vienna for Pressburg in 1764 to enter the household of the Bishop of Grosswardein, succeeding M. Haydn. In 1769 he went to the household of Count Schaffgotsch, the retired Prince Bishop of Breslau, at Johannisberg, where he remained until 1795; but he was frequently away for the prod. of his works, esp. in Vienna, where he was on good terms and played chamber m. with Haydn, Mozart, Wanhal, Storace, Kelly and others. In *c.* 1773 he married a singer named Nicolini. His last employment was in the household of Count Stillfried at Rothlhotta nr. Neuhaus in Boh. He dictated his autobiog. to his son shortly before his death.

Works incl, operas *Il viaggiatore americano, Doctor und Apotheker, Betrug durch Aberglauben, Democrito corretto, Die Liebe im Narrenhaus, Hieronymus Knicker, Das rote Käppchen, Don Quixotte der Zweite, Die lustigen Weiber von Windsor* (after Shakespeare), *Die Hochzeit des Figaro* (after Beaumarchais); orats. *Davidde, Esther, Isacco, Giobbe*; masses & motets; syms. incl. 6 on Ovid's *Metamorphoses*; concs., many for v. and 1 with 11 insts.; divertimenti; stg. 4tets; songs, &c.

Divertimento. An inst., mainly orch., type of work in several mvts. akin to the suite, but not containing dance mvts. as a rule, except minuets; the 1st mvt. is usually in so. form and the last generally a rondo. Solo insts. occur frequently and the whole work may be for a chamber comb. of such insts.

Divertissement. Mainly a term connected with ballet, where it means a set of varied dances with no partic. plot. In m. a suite, partic. of arrs. or pieces based on familiar tunes, an entertaining piece of any kind or a fantasy of a lighter sort, such as Schubert's *Divertissement à la hongroise*. In 18th-cent. Fr. usage a dance interlude, with or without songs, in a play or opera; also sometimes a short play with dances and songs.

Divisi (It. plur. = divided). A direction found in orch. scores where stg. parts are intended to be distributed in such a way as to play in 2 or more parts within a single group of insts. which would normally play in unison. Where several notes appear simultaneously such division would seem obvious even without any indication of 'divisi,' but it is often given in order to save the perfs. from attempting to play a passage of this kind in double stopping.

Division Viol. A bass viol of moderate size on which divisions were often played in the 17th cent. Simpson, for ex., wrote a work for it.

Divisions. A term used in 17th-cent. Eng. for vars. It became current because vars. were then usually divided by breaking up the melody of the given theme into notes of smaller value.

Djamileh, opera by Bizet (lib. by Louis Gallet, based on Musset's *Namouna*), prod. Paris, Opéra-Comique, 22. V. 1872.

Djinns, Les (*The Genii*), symph. poem by Franck for pf. & orch., based on verses from Hugo's *Les Orientales*, comp. 1884.

Dmitri (Dvořák). *See* **Dimitri.**

Do. The old name for the note C (*see* Solmization), still used in Lat. countries, and in Tonic Sol-fa notation the Tonic note in any key, represented by the symbol d, pronounced Doh.

Dobroven, Issay Alexandrovitch (b.

Nizhny-Novgorod, 27. II. 1894), Rus. cond. & comp. Studied with Taneiev and others at the Moscow Cons. and later took a pf. course with Godowsky in Vienna. He became prof. at the Moscow Cons. in 1917 and cond. of the Opera in 1919. Later he cond. Rus. opera on tour in Ger. and in 1927–8 he was cond. of the Bulg. State Opera at Sofia. In the 1930s he cond. extensively in U.S.A. and Palestine.

Works incl. opera *A Thousand and One Nights*; incid. m. to Verhaeren's *Philip II*; pf. Conc., v. Conc.; So. & *Fairy Tales* for v. & pf.; 2 sos., studies & pieces for pf.; songs, &c.

Dobson, (Henry) Austin (1840–1921), Eng. poet. *See* **Lutyens** (*Dying of Tanneguy du Bois*).

Doctor und Apotheker (*Doctor and Apothecary*), opera by Dittersdorf (lib. by Gottlieb Stephanie, jun.), prod. Vienna, Kärntnertor Theatre, 11. VII. 1786.

Dodecuple Scale. Another name for the Twelve-Note Scale.

Dog Waltz. One of the nicknames given to Chopin's Waltz in D♭ maj., Op. 64 No. 1, another being 'Minute Waltz.' It is supposed to illustrate George Sand's dog chasing its tail.

Doh. The name for the Tonic note in any key in Tonic Sol-fa, so pronounced, but in notation represented by the symbol d.

Dohnányi, Ernö (or **Ernst von**) (b. Pozsony = Pressburg, 27. VII. 1877), Hung. pfst. & comp. Studied under Carl Forstner, the cath. orgst. at his native town, until 1893, when he went to the R. Hung. A. M. at Budapest, where he studied pf. under Stephan Thomán and comp. under Koessler. In 1897 he had some lessons from d'Albert and appeared as pfst. in Berlin and Vienna. He visited Eng. in 1898 and U.S.A. in 1899, made many tours later, but eventually became better known as a comp.

Works incl. operas *Aunt Simona, The Tower of Voivod & The Tenor*; ballet *Pierrette's Veil*; Syms. in F min. & D min., Suite in F♯ min. for orch.; Conc. & *Vars. on a Nursery Song* for pf. & orch., v. Conc., *Concertstück* for co. & orch.; 2 stg. 4tets, pf. 5tet; Serenade for stg. trio; sos. for v. & pf. and co. & pf.; *c.* 10 op. nos. of pf. m., incl. a Passacaglia, 4 Rhapsodies, *Humoresques in form of a Suite, Ruralia hungarica*; songs, &c.

Doina (Rum. = lament). A Rum. type of folksong. The term was formerly used for var. kinds of songs, but is now properly restricted to laments.

Doktor Faust, opera by Busoni (lib. by comp., based on Goethe's drama), left unfinished at B.'s death and completed by Jarnach; prod. Dresden, 21. V. 1925.

Dolby, Charlotte. *See* **Sainton-Dolby.**

Dolcan. An 8-ft. metal org. stop of soft tone, also called Dolce.

Dolce (It. = sweet). A direction indicating a suave and ingratiating perf., unusually but not necessarily in a soft tone.

Dolce, Lodovico (1508–68), It. poet & playwright. *See* **Merulo** (*Troiano*).

Dolcian. An obs. inst. of the bn. type, standing an octave higher in pitch than the bn. and therefore sometimes called Alto Fagotto or Alto Bassoon.

Doles, Johann Friedrich (b. Steinbach, Saxe-Meiningen, 23. IV. 1715; d. Leipzig, 7. II. 1797), Ger. orgst. & comp. Pupil of Bach at Leipzig from 1739. Cantor of St. Thomas's School there from 1756 in succession to Harrer.

Works incl. 3 Passions, church cantatas, 2 masses, motets, psalms, hymn-tunes, &c.

Dollarprinzessin, Die (*The Dollar Princess*), operetta by Fall (lib. by Alfred Maria Willner & Fritz Grünbaum), prod. Vienna, Theater an der Wien, 2. XI. 1907.

Dolly, suite of 6 children's pieces for pf. duet by Fauré, Op. 56, comp. in 1893, orch. for a ballet by Rabaud in 1896. It is ded. to the daughter of Mme. Emma Bardac, later Debussy's 2nd wife. As in the case of Debussy's *Children's Corner*, written for his own daughter by that wife, the title and 2 of the sub-titles seem to suggest some Eng. association: 1. *Berceuse*; 2. *Mi-a-ou*; 3. *Le Jardin de Dolly*; 4. *Kitty-Valse*; 5. *Tendresse*; 6. *Le Pas espagnol.*

Dolmetsch, Arnold (b. Le Mans, 24. II. 1858; d. Haslemere, 29. II. 1940), Swi. (anglicized) mcolst., inst. maker and perf. on old insts. B. in Fr., he studied v. under Vieuxtemps at Brussels, but turned his interests to old m. and insts. Worked with the pf. firm of Chickering at Boston, 1902–9, and then with that of Gaveau in Paris until 1914, when he went to live in Eng. and set up his own workshop for hpchds., viols, lutes, recorders, &c. at Haslemere, where he arr. periodical festivals of old m. and brought up a family to take part in it with var. insts. He ed. old m. and wrote a treatise on ornament.

Domestic Symphony (R. Strauss). *See* **Symphonia domestica.**

Dominant. The 5th note of the maj. or min. scale above the tonic, or key-note, or the 4th below it. In classical harmony the D. is the most conspicuous note in the scale apart from the tonic and forms the basis of the predominant chord (hence its name) of the dominant 7th, which calls for a direct resolution on the tonic triad. Modes also had their Ds., but they varied in position according as to whether the mode was authentic or plagal.

Domino noir, Le (*The Black Domino*), comic opera by Auber (lib. by Scribe), prod. Paris, Opéra-Comique, 2. XII. 1837.

Domp(e). *See* **Dump.**

Don Carlos, opera by **Verdi** (lib. by François Joseph Méry & Camille Du Locle, based on Schiller's drama), prod. Paris, Opéra, 11. III. 1867. V.'s 2nd Fr. opera.

Don Chisciotte in corte della duchessa (*Don Quixote at the Duchess's Court*), opera by Caldara (lib. by Giovanni Claudio Pasquini, based on Cervantes), prod. Vienna, 6. II. 1727.

Don Chisciotte in Sierra Morena (*Don Quixote in the S. M.*), opera by Conti (lib. by Zeno and Pietro Pariati, based on Cervantes), prod. Vienna, 11. II. 1719.

Don Giovanni (*Don Juan*), opera by Lattuada (lib. by Arturo Rossato, based on a Spa. drama by José Zorilla), prod. Naples, 18. V. 1929.

Opera by Mozart (1st title: *Il dissoluto punito, o sia Il D. G.*: *The Rake Punished*, or *Don Juan*) (lib. by Lorenzo da Ponte), prod. Prague, 29. X. 1787. In Vienna, with additions, Burg Theatre, 7. V. 1788.

Don Giovanni Tenorio, ossia Il convitato di pietra (*Don Juan Tenorio, or The Stone Guest*); opera by Carnicer (lib. by ?) prod. Barcelona, Teatro Principal, 20. VI. 1822. The 1st Don Juan opera by a Spa. comp., but set to It. words.

Opera by Gazzaniga (lib. by Giovanni Bertati, based on Tirso de Molina), prod. Venice, Teatro San Moisè, 5. II. 1787.

Don Juan. *See also* **Convitato di pietra; Don Giovanni; Ombra di Don Giovanni; Stone Guest.**

Symph. poem by R. Strauss, based on Lenau's poem, 1st perf. Weimar, 11. XI. 1889.

Don Juan de Mañara, opera by Goossens (lib. by Arnold Bennett), prod. London, Covent Garden Opera, 24. VI. 1937.

Don Juan legend. For mus. treatments *see* **Albertini, Alfano** (*L'ombra di Don Giovanni*), **Assafiev** (*The Seducer of Seville*), **Carnicer, Convitato di pietra** (Fabrizi & Righini), **Dargomizhsky** (*Stone Guest*), **Don Giovanni** (Lattuada & Mozart), **Don G. Tenorio** (Carnicer & Gazzaniga), **Don Juan** (R. Strauss), **D. J. de Mañara** (Goossens), **D. Js. letztes Abenteuer** (Graener), **Enna** (*D. J. Mañara*), **Ferreira, Koreshtchenko, Lattuada, Ombra di Don Giovanni** (Alfano), **Purcell** (Shadwell's *Libertine*), **Salazar** (*D. J. en los infiernos*), **Schulhoff (E.)** (opera), **Shebalin** (*Stone Guest*). *See also* **Byron.**

Don Juans letztes Abenteuer (*Don Juan's Last Adventure*), opera by Graener (lib. by Otto Anthes), prod. Leipzig, 11. VI. 1914.

Don Pasquale, comic opera by Donizetti (lib. by comp. & ?, based on Angelo Anelli's *Ser Marcantonio*, comp. by Pavesi in 1810), prod. Paris, Théâtre Italien, 3. I. 1843.

Don Quichotte, opera by Massenet (lib. by Henri Cain, based on Cervantes & Jacques Le Lorrain's comedy, *Le Chevalier de la longue figure*), prod. Monte Carlo, 19. II. 1910.

Don Quixote. *See also* **Don Chisciotte; Retablo de Maese Pedro; Sancio Panza; Sancho Panza.**

Opera by Kienzl (lib. by comp., based on Cervantes), prod. Berlin, Opera, 18. XI. 1898.

Symph. poem by R. Strauss, based on Cervantes, 1st perf. Cologne, 8. III. 1898. The work is described as 'Fantastic Vars.' and contains important solo parts for co. (Don Q.) and va. (Sancho Panza).

Don Quixote, The Comical History of, play by Thomas Durfey, based on Cervantes, with m. by Purcell and others, comp. Parts i & ii, 1694, by Purcell & Eccles; Part iii, 1695, by Akeroyde, Courteville, Pack, Morgan & D. Purcell. i. prod. London, Dorset Gardens, V. 1694; ii. ib. VI. 1694; iii. London, Drury Lane Theatre, XI. 1695.

Don Sébastien, Roi de Portugal (*Dom Sebastian, King of Portugal*), opera by Donizetti (lib. by Scribe), prod. Paris, Opéra, 13. XI. 1843.

Donati, Ignazio (b. Casalmaggiore nr. Cremona, *c.* 1585; d. ? Milan, 1638), It. orgst. & comp. Chapel master and orgst. in succession at (?) Pesaro, Urbino, Ferrara, Casalmaggiore, Novara, Lodi and Milan.

Works incl. masses, motets, psalms, eccles. concs., &c.

Donato (or **Donati**), **Baldassare** (b. ? Venice, ?; d. Venice, 1603), It. orgst., singer & comp. App. to St. Mark's at Venice in 1550, he remained there in var. capacities all his life, becoming chapel master in succession to **Zarlino** in 1590. He also taught singing at the seminary attached to St. Mark's.

Works incl. motets, psalms; madrigals, villanelle, canzoni, &c.

Doni, Giovanni Battista (b. Florence, *c.* 1594; d. Florence, 1. XII. 1647), It. scholar, mcolst. & antiquarian. He travelled in Fr. and Spa. and held important secretarial and professorial posts in Rome and Florence; pub. treatises on ancient m.

Donizetti, Gaetano (b. Bergamo, 29. XI. 1797; d. Bergamo, 8. IV. 1848), It. comp. Grandson of a Scotsman, Donald Izett, settled in It. and son of a weaver. Studied at Bergamo and at the Liceo Filarmonico at Bologna. He entered the army to avoid following his father's trade and while at Venice in 1818 prod. his 1st opera, *Enrico di Borgogna*, there. After that, exc. in 1821, he prod. operas annually until 1844, when *Catarina Cornaro* came out as the last at Naples and his reason began to fail. In 1839–40 and 1843 he visited Paris and prod. operas there. He became paralysed in 1845.

Works incl. 62 operas, among them *Emilia di Liverpool, Olivo e Pasquale, Il burgomastro di Saardam, La regina di Golconda, Il castello di Kenilworth* (after Scott), *Anna Bolena, Fausta, L'elisir d'amore, Torquato Tasso, Lucrezia Borgia* (after Hugo), *Rosmonda d'Inghilterra, Buondelmonte* (*Maria Stuarda*), *Marino Faliero* (after Byron), *Lucia di Lammermoor* (after Scott), *Maria di Rudenz, La Fille du régiment, La Favorita, Linda di Chamounix, Don Pasquale, Maria di Rohan, Don Sébastien*, &c.

Donna ancore è fedele, La (*The Lady is still Faithful*), opera by Pasquini (lib. by Domenico Filippo Contini), prod. 19. IV. 1676.

Donna del lago, La (*The Lady of the Lake*), opera by Rossini (lib. by Andrea Leone Tottola, based on Scott's poem), prod. Naples, Teatro San Carlo, 24. IX. 1819.

Donna Diana, opera by Rezniček (lib. by comp., based on Moreto's comedy), prod. Prague, Ger. Theatre, 16. XII. 1894.

Donna serpente, La (*The Serpent-Woman*), opera by Casella (lib. by Cesare Lodovici, based on Gozzi's comedy, prod. Rome, Teatro Reale, 17. III. 1932. Wagner's *Die Feen* was on the same subject.

Donne curiose, Le (*The Inquisitive Ladies*), opera by Wolf-Ferrari (lib. by Luigi Sugana, based on Goldoni's comedy), prod. Munich, in Ger., 27. XI. 1903.

Donne, John (1571–1631), Eng. divine & poet. *See* **Corkine** (3 songs), **Hilton (J. ii)** (hymn from *Divine Poems*), **Křenek** (chors. & songs). **Maconchy** (motets).

Donneau de Visé, Jean. *See* **Visé.**

Donzelli, Domenico (b. Bergamo, 2. II. 1790; d. Bologna, 31. III. 1873), It. ten. Made his 1st appearance in It., 1816, in Vienna, 1822, in Paris, 1824, and in London, 1829.

Doppelschlag (Ger.) = **Turn.**

Dopper, Cornelis (b. Stadskanaal nr. Groningen, 7. II. 1870; d. Amsterdam, 18. IX. 1939), Dutch cond. & comp. Studied at the Leipzig Cons., cond. opera in Hol. and U.S.A. and became asst. cond. to Mengelberg at the Amsterdam Concertgebouw in 1908. Comp. operas, chor. works, 7 syms., &c.

Doppio (It.) = double.

Doppio movimento (It. = double movement). A direction indicating that a new tempo is to be exactly twice as fast as the one it displaces.

Doppler. Pol.-Hung. family of musns.:

1. **Albert Franz D.** (b. Lemberg, 16. X. 1821; d. Baden nr. Vienna, 27. VII. 1883), flst. & comp. Taught at Pest and comp. operas, incl. *Judith*, a ballet, ovts., fl. concs., &c.

2. **Karl D.** (b. Lemberg, 12. IX. 1825; d. Stuttgart, 10. III. 1900), flst., cond. & comp., brother of prec. Toured widely and became cond. at the Pest Nat. Theatre. Wrote operas, incl. *Erzébeth* with Albert D. and Erkel, ballets, fl. m., &c.

3. **Arpad D.** (b. Pest, 5. VI. 1857; d. Stuttgart, VIII. 1927), pfst. & comp., son of prec. Studied and taught at Stuttgart, and for a time in N.Y. Wrote a mus. play *Halixula*, orch. works, pf. m., songs, &c.

Doret, Gustave (b. Aigle, Vaud, 20. IX. 1866; d. Lausanne, 19. IV. 1943), Swi. comp. Studied v. in Ger. with Joachim and comp. in Paris with Massenet. App. cond. of the Société Nationale there, and lived alternately in Paris and nr. Lausanne.

Works incl. plays with m. *Henriette, Aliénor, La Nuit des Quatre-Temps, Tell, Davel, En Prison, Maedeli, Les Armaillis, Le Nain du Hasli, La Tisseuse d'orties*; incid. m. for Shakespeare's *Julius Caesar*; cantata *La Fête des vignerons* and hymns; orch. works; many songs, partsongs, &c.

Dorfbarbier, Der (*The Village Barber*), comic opera by Schenk (lib. by Joseph and Paul Weidmann), prod. Vienna, Burg Theatre, 30. X. 1796.

Dori, La, ovvero La schiava fedele (*Doris, or The Faithful Slave*), opera by Cesti (lib. by Apollonio Apolloni), prod. Florence, Teatro dei Sorgenti, Carnival 1661.

'Dorian' Fugue. The name given to the fugue in Bach's D min. org. Toccata and Fugue. It was so named because B.'s orig. notation was without a key-signature and, the fugue being in D, thus suggested the Dorian mode; but the accidentals proper to D min. are inserted throughout.

Dorian Mode. The scale represented

by the white keys on the pf. beginning on the note D.

Dorn, Heinrich (Ludwig Egmont) (b. Königsberg, 14. XI. 1804; d. Berlin, 10. I. 1892), Ger. comp., teacher & cond. Pupil of *Zelter* in Berlin, teacher of Schumann at Leipzig, opera cond. at Hamburg and Riga where he succeeded Wagner in 1839. Finally cond. at the Royal Opera and prof. in Berlin.

Works incl. operas, e.g. *Die Rolandsknappen, Die Nibelungen*, &c.; ballet *Amors Macht*; Requiem; cantatas; orch. works; pf. m.; songs, &c.

Dornel, Louis Antoine (b. ?, *c.* 1685; d. Paris, 1765), Fr. orgst., hpchdst. & comp. Worked in Paris and was famous as a keyboard player.

Works incl. motets, psalms, hpchd. pieces, trios, inst. sos., &c.

Dorothy, operetta by Cellier (lib. by Benjamin Charles Stephenson), prod. London, Gaiety Theatre, 25. IX. 1886.

Dorus-Gras. *See* Gras.

Dostoievsky, Feodor Mikhailovitch (1821–81), Rus. novelist. *See* **Janáček** (*From the House of the Dead*), **Jeramiáš** (*Brothers Karamazov*), **Maréchal** (*Crime and Punishment*), **Pedrollo** (*Delitto e castigo*), **Prokofiev** (*Gambler*).

Dot. A D. placed over a note indicates that it is to be played *staccato*.

Dot-Way. A 17th-cent. system of notation for recorders, with staves each line of which repres. a finger-hole, while dots placed over the lines showed which fingers were to be kept down for each note.

Dotted Notes. Notes with a dot placed on their right, with the effect of prolonging them by half their orig. value. A double dot has the effect of adding another half of the smaller value to the orig. note, which is thus lengthened by three-quarters of its value. Double dots were introd. by Leopold Mozart, before whose time their effect could not be precisely indicated in notation, though it was often prod. at will by the interpreter, esp. in slow mvts. written in singly dotted rhythm, such as the slow introds. in Lully's and Handel's ovts.

Dotzauer, (Justus Johann) Friedrich (b. Hildburghausen, 20. VI. 1783; d. ? Dresden, 6. III. 1860), Ger. cst. Played 1st in the court orch. at Meiningen, then at Leipzig, Berlin and Dresden. Wrote an opera, *Graziosa*, a sym., chamber m. and many co. works.

Double (Fr.). The old Fr. name for a type of var. that was merely a more highly ornamented version of a theme previously played in plainer notes; much the same as the Eng. Division.

Doublé (Fr.) = Turn.

Double Bar. A pair of bar-lines placed very close together and marking off a principal section of a comp., such as the end of the exposition and beginning of the working-out in a so. or sym. It may be prec. or followed by repeat signs, or both, in which case the m. before and/or after it must be repeated.

Double Bass. The largest inst. of the v. family, playing the bass of the stg. section in the orch. and occasionally in chamber m. It had 3 stgs. formerly, but now usually 4, and its normal written range is from E below the stave in the bass clef, which however sounds an 8ve lower. This can be artificially extended either by a temporary tuning down of the bottom stg. or by the addition of a 5th stg. In the latter case the range will go down to B, thus continuing the tuning of the stgs. in intervals of perfect 4ths.

Double Bass Viol. *See* **Violone.**

Double Bassoon. A bn. with a range an 8ve lower than that of the ordinary inst.

Double Cadence (Fr.) = Turn. *See* **Ornaments.**

Double Chant. A chant in 2 sections used in the Angl. church and covering 2 verses of a psalm.

Double Concerto. A conc. for 2 solo insts.: e.g. Bach's D min. for 2 vs., Mozart's E♭ maj. for 2 pfs., Brahms's B min. for v. & co., &c.

Double Counterpoint. *See* **Counterpoint.**

Double Dots. *See* **Dotted Notes.**

Double Flat. An accidental, 𝄫, lowering the note before which it stands by a whole tone.

Double Fugue. A fugue on 2 subjects which appear simultaneously and are both made to enter in the normal fugal manner. A theme which in an ordinary fugue appears at 1st as an episode may subsequently be used in this way, in which case the comp. becomes a D. F. only in the course of its development.

Double Sharp. An accidental, ×, raising the note before which it stands by a whole tone.

Double Stopping. Strictly speaking, the prod. of 2 notes together on any stg. inst., but the term is more loosely used also for any chords played on such insts., even if they contain more than 2 notes.

Doucemelle (Fr.). A keyboard inst. of *c.* the 15th cent.; a forerunner of the Clavichord and prob. similar to the Chekker.

Douglas, Roy (b. Tunbridge Wells, 1907), Eng. pfst. & comp. Assoc. as orch. pfst. with ballet, orch. and broadcast perfs. He has arr. much m. for dancing and films, &c.

Works incl. film m.; suites for orch.; 2 4tets with hp., Trio with fl., wind 5tet; songs, &c.

Dowland, John (b. ? London or Dublin, 1563; d. ? London, 20–21. I. 1626), Eng. or (?) Ir. lutenist & comp. He entered the service of the Eng. ambassador, Sir Henry Cobham, in Paris *c.* 1580, and was from 1583 in that of his successor, Sir Edward Stafford. He became a Rom. Catholic, returned to Eng. soon after and married. In the 1590s he sought a place at Elizabeth's court, but was not admitted and went to Ger. in the service of the Duke of Brunswick, then entered that of the Landgrave of Hesse and travelled to It., returning home towards the end of the cent. and turning to Protestantism again. But in XI. 1598 he went to Den. as court musn. to Christian IV, returning in 1601 to buy mus. insts. for the king and living in London again for a time in 1603, finally settling there in 1606 on being dismissed from Copenhagen. He complained of neglect after his successes abroad, but from 1612–8 he was employed in var. ways at court.

Works incl. 3 vols. of songs to the lute; a book of inst. pavans entitled *Lachrymae*; a book of songs with lutes and viols, *A Pilgrimes Solace*; lute, viol and voc. m. contrib. to Leighton's *Teares and Lamentacions*, East's Psalter and to a number of foreign collections, incl. Füllsack's and Fuhrmann's.

Dowlands, Robert (b. ? London, *c.* 1586; d. ? London, 1641), Eng. lutenist & comp., son of prec. App. lutenist to Charles I on his father's death in 1626. Comp. lessons for the lute, &c. and pub. a book of airs by Eng. Fr., It. & Spa. comps.

Down Bow. The mvt. of the bow in the playing of stg. insts. in the direction from the heel to the point.

Downbeat. The downward motion of the cond.'s baton indicating the 1st, stressed beat of any bar, but esp. the 1st of any comp. beginning on the 1st note of the bar, not with an Upbeat.

Dowson, Ernest (1867–1900), Eng. poet. *See* Bantock (*Pierrot of the Minute*), Delius (*Cynara*).

Drachman, Holger (1846–1908), Dan. poet & dramatist. *See* Halvorsen (*Gurre*), Rangström (*Medeltida*), Rung (*1001 Nights*).

Draeseke, Felix (August Bernhard) (b. Coburg, 7. X. 1835; d. Dresden, 26. II. 1913), Ger. comp. Studied at the Leipzig Cons. and with Liszt at Weimar, later taught at Dresden, Lausanne, Munich and Geneva, and finally settled at Dresden in 1876, becoming prof. of comp. at the Cons. in 1884.

Works incl. operas *Gudrun*, *Herrat* and *Merlin*; Requiem, trilogy of orats. *Christus*, Easter scene from Goethe's *Faust* for solo voices, chor. & orch.; 4 syms., ovts. for orch. incl. *Penthesilea* (after Kleist); concs. for pf., v. & co.; 3 stg. 4tets, stg. 5tet; many pf. works incl. a So., &c.

Draghi, Antonio (b. Rimini, 1635; d. Vienna, 18. I. 1700), It. comp. Went to Vienna to take up a court app. in 1674, and in 1682 he settled there for good. He was also a libst. for other comps., incl. Bertali, Ziani and the Emperor Leopold I.

Works incl. 67 operas, 116 smaller stage pieces, 37 orats., cantatas, hymns, &c.

Draghi, Giovanni Battista (b. ?, *c.* 1640; d. London, *c.* 1710), It. hpchdst. & comp. Settled in London; m. master to the Princesses Mary and Anne and orgst. to Catherine of Braganza, wife of Charles II. Set Dryden's Ode for St. Cecilia's Day, 1687, contrib. m. to Durfey's *Wonders in the Sun*, 1706, and comp. many hpchd. lessons and songs.

Dragon of Wantley, The, burlesque opera by Lampe (lib. by Carey), prod. London, King's Theatre, Haymarket, 16. V. 1737.

Dragonetti, Domenico (b. Venice, 7. IV. 1763; d. London, 16. IV. 1846), It. db. player & comp. He was admitted to the opera orchs. at Venice from the age of 13 and soon began to comp. concs., sos. and other works for his inst. His 1st appearance abroad was in 1794 in London, where he spent most of the rest of his life with the cst. Lindley as partner.

Dragons de Villars, Les (*The Dragoons of V.*), opera by Maillart (lib. by Joseph Philippe Lockroy & Eugène Cormon), prod. Paris, Opéra-Comique 19. IX. 1856.

Drame lyrique. A modern Fr. term for a serious opera.

Dramma giocoso (It. = jocular or playful drama). An It. name, mainly of the 2nd half of the 18th cent., for comic opera, of a type capable of sometimes accommodating serious or even tragic situations (e.g. Mozart's *Don Giovanni*).

Dramma (per musica) (It. = drama [for m.]), 18th-cent. It. terms for opera; actually plays written especially for the purpose of being set to m.

Drátenik (*The Tinker*), opera by Škroup (lib. by Josef Krasoslav Chmelenský), prod. Prague, 2. II. 1826. The 1st Cz. opera.

Drdla, František (b. Saar, Moravia, 28.

XI. 1868), Cz. vst. & comp. Studied at the Prague & Vienna Conss., played v. in the Vienna Court Opera orch. and toured Eur. as a virtuoso.

Works incl. operettas *The Golden Net* & *The Shop Countess*; many v. pieces; pf. pieces; songs, &c.

Dream of Gerontius, The, orat. by Elgar, Op. 38 (words selected from Cardinal Henry Newman's poem), prod. Birmingham Festival, 3. X. 1900.

Drei Pintos, Die (*The Three Pintos*), unfinished opera by Weber (lib. by Theodor Hell, based on Carl Ludwig Seidel's story *Der Brautkampf*), partly comp. 1821; prod. in an ed. completed by Mahler, Leipzig, 20. I. 1888.

Dreigroschenoper, Die (*The Three Groats' Opera*), operetta by Weill (lib. by Bert Brecht, based on Elisabeth Hauptmann's Ger. version of Gay's *Beggar's Opera*), prod. Berlin, Theater am Schiffbauerdamm, 31. VIII. 1928.

Dresden, Sem (b. Amsterdam, 20. IV. 1881), Dutch cond. & comp. Studied under Zweers at the Amsterdam Cons. and with Pfitzner in Ger. He became a chor. cond., cultivating particularly motets and madrigals in Hol. Dir. of the Amsterdam Cons., 1924–37, and then of that at The Hague, in succession to Wagenaar. He wrote a book on *Dutch M. since 1880*.

Works incl. *Chorus tragicus* for chor. & orch.; Vars. for orch.; v. Conc.; *Symphonietta* for cl. & orch.; stg. 4tet, 6tet for stgs. & pf., 3 6tets for wind & pf.; sos. for v. & pf., co. & pf. and fl. & hp.; Duo for 2 pfs.; pf. pieces; songs, &c.

Dressler, Ernst Christoph (b. Greussen, Thuringia, 1734; d. Cassel, 6. IV. 1779), Ger. comp. & singer. Member of the court chapels at Bayreuth and Gotha, later chapel master at Wetzlar, finally opera singer in Weimar and Cassel. Beethoven's 1st pub. work was a set of Vars. on a March by D., pub. 1783.

Dreyschock, Alexander (b. Žak, 15. X. 1818; d. Venice, 1. IV. 1869), Cz. pfst. & comp. Pupil of Tomašek in Prague. Travelled widely from 1838 and in 1862 was app. prof. of pf. at the St. Petersburg Cons. and court pfst. Comp. mainly for his inst.

Drigo, Riccardo (b. Padua, 30. VI. 1846; d. Padua, 1. X. 1930), It. cond. & comp. He became ballet cond. at the St. Petersburg Court Opera.

Works incl. ballet *Harlequin's Millions*; many drawing-room pieces, &c.

Drinkwater, John (1882–1937), Eng. actor, dramatist & poet. *See* **Boughton** (festival chors.), **Filippi** (*Robert E. Lee*).

Driving. A 17th-cent. Eng. term for Syncopation.

Drone. The 3 lower pipes of the bagpipe which prod. a fixed chord above which the melody is played on the chanter. The name was also given to a bowed inst. with a single stg. stretched on a stick over a bladder; this was also called Bumbass.

Drone Bass. An unvaryingly sustained bass in any mus. comp. resembling the drone of a bagpipe.

Drum Mass (Haydn). *See* **Paukenmesse.**

Drum-Roll Symphony (or ' Symphony with the Drum-Roll'). The nickname of Haydn's Sym. No. 103, in E♭ maj. (No. 8 of the ' Salomon ' syms.), written for London in 1795. The slow introd. opens with a drum-roll.

Drummond, William (1585–1649), Sco. poet. *See* **Scott (F. G.)** (songs).

Drums. Percussion insts. on which the sound is prod. by beating a skin stretched tightly over a hollow space left open by a framework of var. patterns. *See* **Bass Drum, Kettledrum, Side Drum, Tabor, Tambourine, Tenor Drum.**

Drumslade (Eng., obs., also ' dromslade '). A drum-beat, prob. a corrupt. from Ger. *Trommelschlag*, also used by false analogy for a drum in the 17th cent. and for a drummer in the 18th.

Dryden, John (1631–1700), Eng. poet, dramatist & satirist. *See* **Acis and Galatea** (Handel), **Albion and Albanius** (Grabu), **Alexander's Feast** (Handel), **Almahide** (G. Bononcini), **Boyce** (*Secular Masque*), **Clarke (J.)** (*Alexander's Feast*), **Clayton** (do.), **Cymon** (M. Arne), **Draghi (G. B.)** (*Ode for St. Cecilia's Day*), **Eccles (J.)** (*Spanish Friar*), **Humfrey** (*Conquest of Granada* & *Indian Emperor*), **Indian Queen** (Purcell), **King Arthur** (do.), **Marcello** (*Timoteo*), **Ode for St. Cecilia's Day** (Handel), **Purcell** (*Amphitryon, Aureng-Zebe, Cleomenes, Love Triumphant, Spanish Friar, Tyrannic Love* & *Oedipus*), **Staggins** (*Conquest of G.* & *Marriage à la Mode*).

Drysdale, Learmont (b. Edinburgh, 3. X. 1866; d. Edinburgh, 18. VI. 1909), Sco. comp. Studied at R.A.M.

Works incl. operas *Fionn and Tera, Red Spider, The Plague, Hippolytus* (Euripides, trans. by Gilbert Murray); cantatas *The Kelpie, Tamlane, To Edinburgh* (Burns), *The Lay of Thora, The Scottish Tribute to France, The Proud Damozel, Barbara Allen*; orch. works: concert ovts. *Tam o' Shanter* (after Burns) & *Herondean*, Ovt. to a Comedy, ballad *The Spirit of the Glen*, prelude *Thomas the Rhymer*, tone-poem *Border Romance*; pf. pieces; songs, partsongs, &c.

Du Mage, Pierre (b ?; d. ?), Fr. 17th-18th-cent. orgst. & comp. Pupil of Marchand in Paris, orgst. of the collegiate church at Saint-Quentin in 1703–13. He played at the inauguration of the new org. at Notre Dame in Paris. Pub. a vol. of org. pieces in 1708.

Du Maurier, George (Louis Palmella Busson) (1834–96), Eng. novelist & black-and-white artist of Fr. descent. *See* **Bath** (*Trilby*), **Holländer (V.)** (do.), **Peter Ibbetson** (Taylor, Deems).

Du Puy, Jean Baptiste (Édouard) (b. Corcelles, Neuchâtel, 1770–1; d. Stockholm, 3. IV. 1822), Swi. bar. singer, vst., pfst. & comp. Studied v. with Chabran and pf. with Dussek in Paris and became leader of the orch. of Prince Henry of Prus. at Rheinsberg in 1785. In 1793 he settled at Stockholm, but was expelled in 1799, when he went to sing in opera at Copenhagen and taught singing to the wife of the future Christian VIII, with whom he was exiled for a love affair in 1809. In 1811 he returned to Stockholm and became court cond. and prof.

Works incl. operas *Ungdom og Galskab* (a Swe. version of the lib. of Méhul's *Une Folie*) & *Felicie*; several ballets; incid. m. for plays; funeral m. for Charles XIII, &c.

Dub (Eng., obs.). The beat or sound of a drum; also another word for the Tabor.

Düben, Ger,-Swe. family of musns. :

1. Andreas D. (b. Lützen, 1558; d Leipzig, 19. IV. 1625), orgst. at St Thomas's church, Leipzig.

2. Andreas D. (b. ? Leipzig, *c.* 1590; d. Stockholm, 1662), orgst. & comp., son of prec. Pupil of Sweelinck at Amsterdam, 1614–20, went to Swe. in 1621, became orgst. at the Ger. church in Stockholm in 1625 and court mus. dir. in 1640. Comp. dances for viols, &c.

3. Gustaf D. (b. Stockholm, 1624; d. Stockholm, 19. XII. 1690), orgst. & comp., son of prec. Succeeded his father in both his posts.

Works incl. church m., concerti grossi, syms. and dances for stgs., &c.

4. Gustaf D. (b. Stockholm, 6. VIII. 1659; d. Stockholm, 5. XII. 1726), son of prec., whom he succeeded as court mus. dir.

5. Andreas D. (b. Stockholm, 1673; d. Stockholm, 23. VIII. 1738), son of prec., whom he succeeded.

Dubois, (François Clément) Théodore (b. Rosnay, Marne, 24. VIII. 1837; d. Paris, 11. VI. 1924), Fr. comp. Studied at Rheims and then at the Paris Cons., where he took the Prix de Rome in 1861. Returning to Paris in 1866, he was active as orgst. and teacher, at last succeeding Saint-Saëns as orgst. at the Madeleine in 1877. From 1896–1905 he was dir. of the Cons.

Works incl. operas *La Guzla de l'Émir*, *Le Pain bis*, *Aben-Hamet*, *Xavière*; ballet *La Farandole*; Requiem, *Messe de la Délivrance* and other masses, motets & other church m.; orats. *Les Sept Paroles du Christ* & *Paradis perdu*; orch. works: *Divertissement*, *Pièces d'orchestre*, *Suite d'orchestre*, *Scènes symphoniques*, ovt. *Frithjof* (after Tegnér), symph. poem *Notre-Dame de la mer*; &c.

Dubourg, Matthew (b. London, 1703; d. London, 3. VII. 1767), Eng. vst. Pupil of Geminiani, for many years living in Dublin and towards the end of his life in London.

Ducasse, Roger. *See* **Roger-Ducasse.**

Duchess of Dantzic, The, operetta by Caryll (lib. by Henry Hamilton, based on Sardou's comedy, *Madame Sans-Gêne*), prod. London, Lyceum Theatre, 17. X. 1903.

Ducis (Hertoghs), Benedictus (b. ?, *c.* 1480; d. ?), Flem. comp. He was orgst. at Antwerp cath. Visited Eng. (?) in 1515.

Works incl. motets; songs for several voices; elegies on the deaths of Josquin des Prés (1521) and of Erasmus of Rotterdam (1536), &c.

Due Foscari, I (*The Two Foscari*), opera by Verdi (lib. by Francesco Maria Piave, based on Byron's drama), prod. Rome, Teatro Argentina, 3. XI. 1844.

Due litiganti (Sarti). *See* **Fra due litiganti.**

Duenna, The, or The Double Elopement, opera by Linley (lib. by Sheridan), prod. London, Covent Garden Theatre, 21. XI. 1775. Sheridan was L.'s son-in-law.

Duet. A comp. in 2 parts for voices or insts. A duet may be strictly in 2 single melodic parts only, but they may be accomp. by insts. in fuller harmony or it may be itself for 2 harmonic insts. or a single such inst. for 2 players (e.g. pf. duet).

Duettino (It.)=little duet.

Dufay, Guillaume (b. ? Hainault, before 1400; d. Cambrai, 27. XI. 1474), Flem. comp. He learnt m. as a chorister at Cambrai cath., became a singer in the Papal choir in Rome, 1428–37, and afterwards became a canon both of Cambrai and of Mons, but (?) lived for some time in Savoy, and some time in the 1440s he was in the service of Philip the Good, Duke of Burgundy, as m. master to his son, Charles, Comte de Charolais.

Works incl. church m.; chansons for 3 voices, &c.

Dugazon. A type of character and voice in Fr. stage works taking its name from its 1st exponent, Louise Rosalie D.

Dugazon (*née* **Lefèvre**), **Louise Rosalie,** (b. Berlin, 18. VI. 1755; d. Paris, 22. IX. 1821), Fr. m.-sop. singer, daughter of a ballet master attached to the Prus. court. Trained as a dancer, she made her 1st appearance as a singer at the Comédie-Italienne in Paris in 1774. Married the actor Dugazon in 1776.

Dukas, Paul (b. Paris, 1. X. 1865; d. Paris, 18. V. 1935), Fr. comp. Studied at the Paris Cons., among his masters being Dubois and Guiraud. Prof. of comp. there from 1913 to his death.

Works incl. opera *Ariane et Barbe-bleue* (Maeterlinck); ballet *La Péri*; Sym. in C maj., ovt. to Corneille's *Polyeucte*, *L'Apprenti sorcier* (on Goethe's poem *Der Zauberlehrling*); So. in E♭ min., *Vars. on a theme by Rameau*, *Prélude élégiaque* on the name of Haydn & *La Plainte, au loin, du faune* in memory of Debussy for pf.; *Sonnet de Ronsard* & *Vocalise* for voice & pf.; *Villanelle* for hn. & pf., &c. (incl. unpub. ovts. to Shakespeare's *King Lear* and Goethe's *Götz von Berlichingen*).

Duke, Vernon. *See* **Dukelsky.**

Dukelsky, Vladimir (b. Parfianovka nr. Pskov, 10. X. 1903), Rus.-Amer. comp. Studied at Moscow and Kiev, Glière being among his masters. Went to live in Constantinople in 1920 and settled in N.Y. in 1922. Under the influence of Gershwin he wrote light m. under the name of Vernon Duke, but cultivated an advanced modern style under his own name. In 1924 Diaghilev heard his pf. Conc. and commissioned him to write a work for the Rus. Ballet.

Works incl. operetta *Yvonne*; ballets *Zéphire et Flore* & *Public Gardens*; orat. *The End of St. Petersburg*; 2 syms., *Dédicaces* for sop., pf. & orch., pf. Conc.; stg. 4tet; song cycle *Triolets of the North* (Feodor Sologub); 3 Chin. songs & other songs, &c.

Dulciana. An open Diapason org. stop of delicate tone. It may embrace 4-ft., 8-ft. and 16-ft. pipes.

Dulciana Mixture. An org. Mixture stop of Dulciana pipes.

Dulcimer. An inst. akin to the psaltery, with a set of stgs. stretched over a sound-board which are struck by hammers. The Hung. Cimbalom is a descendant of it.

Dulcitone. A keyboard inst. prod. its sound on a set of tuning-forks, similar to the Celesta.

Dulichius, Philipp (b. Chemnitz, 1562; d. Stettin, 25. III. 1631), Ger. comp. Took the D.Phil. degree at Chemnitz and went to Stettin as m. teacher at the Pädagogium in 1587.

Works incl. sacred & secular comps. for several voices, &c.

Dumanoir, Guillaume (b. Paris, 16. I. 1615; d. Paris, ?), Fr. vst. & comp. As 'Roi des Violons' he came into conflict with the dancing-masters, whom he wished to compel to contribute to the vsts.' guild of Saint-Julien, and being unsuccessful he wrote the abusive pamphlet *Le Mariage de la musique avec la danse* in 1664. He comp. dance m. which was liked by Louis XIV, who app. him ballet master of the royal pages.

Dumanoir, Guillaume (b. Paris, ?; d. ? Paris, 1697), Fr. vst. & comp., son of prec. Succeeded his father as head of the Confrérie de Saint-Julien and renewed the quarrel with the dancing-masters, resigning in 1685. Before that he had quarrelled with Lully over the privilege of training orch. musns. and lost a law-suit against him in 1673. Comp. dance m.

Dumas, Alexandre, jun. (1824–95), Fr. dramatist & novelist. *See* **Fauré** (*Caligula*), **Traviata** (Verdi), **Varney (P.)** (*Chant des Girondins*).

Dumas, Alexandre, sen. (1803–70), Fr. novelist. *See* **Cui** (*Saracen*), **Enna** (*Gloria Arsena*), **Franck (C.)** (songs), **Gemma di Vergy** (Donizetti), **Salvayre** (*Dame de Monsoreau*), **Trois Mousquetaires** (Lara).

Dumka (Rus. & Cz.). A lament, which in m. takes the form of a slow piece alternating with more animated sections, as e.g. in Dvořák's *Dumky* Trio.

Dumky (Rus. & Cz.), plur. of Dumka.

'Dumky' Trio. A pf. Trio by Dvořák, Op. 90, based on m. of the type of the above, comp. in 1891.

Dump (Eng., obs.). A name sometimes used for a doleful piece in the 17th & 18th cents. Also Domp or Dompe.

Dunaievsky, Isaac (b. Lokhvitsi nr. Poltava, 30. I. 1900), Rus. comp. Studied at the Kharkov Cons.

Works incl. incid. m. for plays; m. for many films; operettas, ballets *Rest of a Faun* & *Mursilka*; 2 suites for orch.; Rhapsody on People's Songs & *The Music Shop* for jazz-band; stg. 4tet; inst. pieces; songs for massed voices, &c.

Dunbar, William (? 1465–? 1530), Sco. poet. *See* **Dyson** (*In Honour of the City of London*), **Parry (H.)** (*Ode on the Nativity*), **Scott (F. G.)** (*7 Deadly Sins, Ballad of Kynd Kittok* & songs), **Walton** (*In Honour of the C. of L.*).

Dunhill, Thomas (Frederick) (b. London, 1. II 1877; d. Scunthorpe, Lincs., 13. III. 1946), Eng. comp. Entered the R.C.M. in 1893, Stanford being his comp. master. He was asst. m. master at Eton Coll. in 1899–1908 and organized concerts for chamber m. and for the promotion of contemp. Brit. m. in London during the early years of the cent. Prof. of comp. at the R.C.M. His 2nd ballet was prod. at Hamburg in 1937.

Works incl. operas *The Enchanted Garden, Tantivy Towers* (A. P. Herbert) & *Happy Families*; ballets *Dick Whittington* & *Gallimaufry*; Sym. in A min., *Elegiac Vars.* in memory of Parry & ovt. *Maytime* for orch.; *Triptych* for va. & orch.; pf. 4tet, 2 pf. trios, 5 5tets & other chamber m.; v. & pf. So. in D min., Vars. for co. & pf.; many songs incl. *The Cloths of Heaven* (Yeats); children's cantatas incl. *John Gilpin*, partsongs, incl. *Song of the King's Men* from Hardy's *Dynasts* for male voices, &c.

Duni, Egidio Romoaldo (b. Matera nr. Naples, 9. II. 1709; d. Paris, 11. VI. 1775), It.-Fr. comp. Studied at Naples, prod. his 1st opera in Rome, 1735, travelled much and settled in Paris in 1757.

Works incl. operas *Nerone, Le Caprice amoureux, Le Peintre amoureux de son modèle, L'Isle des fous, Le Milicien, Les Deux Chasseurs et la laitière, La Fée Urgèle, La Clochette, Les Moissonneurs, Les Sabots,* &c.

Dunstable, John (b. ?; d. ? London, 24. XII. 1453), Eng. mathematician, astrologer & comp. Prob. connected with St. Albans cath., (?) visited the Nthlds., Fr., Spa. and It., where he was certainly famous in his lifetime.

Works incl. motets, hymns & other church m.; 3-part songs incl. *O Rosa bella*, &c.

Duo (It.) = Duet.

Duodecuple Scale (from Lat. *duodecim* = 12). An Eng. term for the Twelve-note Scale in which the notes no longer have the functions of Tonic, Dominant, &c.

Duodrama. A mus. stage work for 2 solo singers, an opera with a cast of 2. The outstanding ex. is G. Benda's *Ariadne auf Naxos*, prod. in 1775, which is also a Melodrama, i.e. a spoken play with m.

Duparc, Elisabeth (b. ?; d. ?), Fr. 18th-cent. sop. singer. She appeared in It. in her youth, where she was given the nickname of La Francesina, and 1st came out in London in 1736.

Duparc, (Marie Eugène) Henri (Fouques) (b. Paris, 21. I. 1848; d. Mont de Marsan, 13. II. 1933), Fr. comp. Was taught the pf. as a child by Franck at the Jesuit Coll. of Vaugirard in Paris, and later became a comp. pupil of that master. He never took any share in official mus. life, but continued to comp. at intervals until 1885, when he began to suffer from an incurable nervous complaint and retired to Swi.

Works incl. symph. poem *Lénore* (on Bürger's poem) & nocturne *Aux Étoiles*; motet *Benedicat vobis Dominus*; 15 songs incl. *Phydilé* & *Invitation au voyage*; and several afterwards destroyed.

Duple Time. *See* **Simple Time.**

Dupont, Gabriel (b. Caen, 1. III. 1878; d. Vésinet, 3. VIII. 1914), Fr. comp. Son of the orgst. Achille D. of the church of Saint-Pierre at Caen and pupil of Widor at the Paris Cons. He took the Sonzogno prize at Milan with his 1st opera. Owing to ill health he never held an official mus. post.

Works incl. operas *La Cabrera, La Glu* (after Richepin), *La Farce du cuvier* & *Antar*; symph. poems *Hymne à Aphrodite* & *Chant de la destinée*; stg. 4tet; pf. pieces incl. *Les Heures dolentes*; songs incl. cycle *Poème d'automne*, &c.

Duport, Jean Louis (b. Paris, 4. X. 1749; d. Paris, 7. IX. 1819), Fr. cst. Made his 1st appearance at the Concert spirituel in Paris in 1768. He went to the Prus. court in Berlin at the outbreak of the Revol. and there Beethoven played with him (or with his brother) his 2 co. sos., Op. 5. He returned to Paris in 1806.

Duport, Jean Pierre (b. Paris, 27. XI. 1741; d. Berlin, 31. XII. 1818), Fr. cst., brother of prec. Made his 1st appearance at the Concert spirituel in Paris in 1761, visited Eng. in 1769 and Spa. in 1771, and in 1773 went to the court of Frederick II of Prus. in Berlin. Mozart wrote pf. vars. on a minuet of his (K. 573).

Dupré, Marcel (b. Rouen, 3. V. 1886), Fr. orgst. & comp. Played Bach from memory at the age of 10, in 1898 was app. orgst. of the church of Saint-Vivien at Rouen and prod. an orat. in 1901. After that he studied pf., org. and comp. at the Paris Cons. and gained the Prix de Rome in 1914 as a pupil of Widor. Orgst. at Notre-Dame in 1916–22 during the illness of Vierne. App. prof. of org. at the Paris Cons. in 1926 and orgst. at Saint-Sulpice in 1936, succeeding Widor.

Works incl. orat. *Le Songe de Jacob*, motets and *De Profundis*; 2 syms.; Conc. for org. & orch.; v. & pf. So.; co. pieces; songs; many org. works incl. *Symphonie-Passion*, 79 Chorales, *Le Chemin de la Croix*, &c.

Duprez, Gilbert (Louis) (b. Paris, 6. XII. 1806; d. Paris, 23. IX. 1896), Fr. ten. singer. 1st appeared at the Théâtre de l'Odéon in Paris, 1825.

Dupuis, Albert (b. Verviers, 1. III.

1877), Belg. comp. Studied at the Verviers m. school, under d'Indy and Guilmant at the Schola Cantorum in Paris and at the Brussels Cons., where he gained the Belg. Prix de Rome in 1903. Later he became dir. of the Verviers school of m.

Works incl. operas *L'Idylle, Bilitis, Jean-Michel, Martylle, Fidelaine, La Chanson d'Halewyn, Le Château de la Bretèche, La Passion, La Délivrance, La Victoire, Hassan,* biblical drama *La Captivité de Babylone*; cantatas *Les Cloches nuptiales, Œdipe à Colone* (after Sophocles); Sym. & other orch. works; concs. for pf., v., co. & hn.; stg. 4tet, pf. Trio; pf. So.; songs, &c.

Dupuis, Sylvain (b. Liége, 9. X. 1856; d. Bruges, 28. IX. 1931), Belg. cond. & comp. Studied at the Liége Cons., where he gained the Belg. Prix de Rome in 1881 and became prof. in 1886. He cond. chor. & orch. concerts there, became cond. of the Théâtre de la Monnaie in Brussels, 1900–11, and then returned to Liége as dir. of the Cons.

Works incl. operas *Coûr d'Oignon* & *Moïna* (after Ossian); cantatas; sym. poem on Shakespeare's *Macbeth*, ovt. & 2 suites for orch.; Concertino for ob.; pf., org., v. & co. pieces, &c.

Dur (Ger., from Lat. *durus* = hard). The Ger. word for Major, because it is based on the *hexachordum durum*.

Durand, (Marie) Auguste (b. Paris, 18. VII. 1830; d. Paris, 31. V. 1909), Fr. m. pub., orgst. & comp. Studied at the Paris Cons., was orgst. at var. churches and was a partner in the pub. firm of Durand & Fils. He wrote drawing-room m. for pf., incl. popular waltzes.

Durand (Duranowski), Auguste Frédéric (b. Warsaw, *c.* 1770; d. ? Strasburg, after 1834), Pol.-Fr. vst. & comp. He was sent to Paris to study under Viotti in 1787, travelled much in Ger. & It., joined the Fr. army and settled at Strasburg in 1814. Wrote much superficial concert m. for his inst.

Durante, Francesco (b. Frattamaggiore nr. Naples, 15. III. 1684; d. Naples, 13. VIII. 1755), It. comp. & theorist. Studied at one of the 4 Conss. of Naples and later became dir. successively of 2 others. Teacher of many famous comps., incl. Jommelli, Paisiello, Pergolesi, Piccinni, Sacchini, Traetta and Vinci.

Works incl. masses, motets, psalms, offertory *Protexisti me, Deus*; orats. *Abigaile* & *S. Antonio di Padova*, &c.

Durastanti, Margherita (b. ?, *c.* 1695; d. ?), It. sop. singer. Visited London in 1720 and again in 1733.

Durchführung (Ger. lit. through-leading). The Ger. term for the development or working-out section of a mvt. in so. form.

Durchkomponiert (Ger. lit. composed through or throughout). A song is said in Ger. to be *durchkomponiert* if the words are set to m. continuously, not strophically with the same m. repeated for each verse.

Durey, Louis (b. Paris, 27. V. 1888), Fr. comp. He did not study m. until the age of 22, and in 1914 he enlisted on the outbreak of war. In 1916, during leave, he came under the influence of Satie and joined the group of 'Les Six,' but was the 1st to secede from it in 1921, and in 1923 he went to live in seclusion in the south of Fr., writing very little.

Works incl. opera on Mérimée's *L'Occasion*; incid. m. to Hebbel's *Judith*; *Éloges* for solo voices, chor. & orch.; *Pastorale* for orch. (all these unpub.); 2 stg. 4tets, pf. Trio, stg. Trio; song cycles with chamber m. or pf. *Offrande lyrique* (Tagore), *Images à Crusoé, Épigrammes de Théocrite, Trois Poèmes de Pétrone, Le Bestiaire* (Guillaume Apollinaire); songs to words by Verlaine, Francis Jammes, André Gide; *Carillon* & *Neige* for pf. duet, &c.

Durfey (or D'Urfey), Thomas (1653–1723), Eng. playwright and poet. *See* **Akeroyde** (*Don Quixote*), **Courteville** (do.), **Don Quixote, The Comical History of** (Purcell & others), **Draghi (G. B.)** (*Wonders in the Sun*), **Eccles (J.)** (*Don Q.*), **Grabu** (*Squire Oldsapp*), **Locke** (*Fool turned Critic*), **Purcell (D.)** (*Cynthia and Endymion*), **Purcell** (*Fool's Preferment, Marriage-Hater Matched, Richmond Heiress, Sir Barnaby Whigg* & *Virtuous Wife*), **Turner (Wm.)** (*Fond Husband* & *Madam Fickle*).

Durón, Sebastián (b. Brihuega, Castile, ?; d. ? Cambó, Pyrenees, after VIII. 1716), Spa. comp. Was orgst. at Las Palmas, Canary Islands, and in 1691 became chapel master at the court of Madrid until 1700. Not having supported the Bourbon succession, he (?) went into exile to Fr. and made his will at Bayonne in 1715. He was an early exponent of Spa. opera.

Works incl. operas *Muerte en amor es la ausencia, Apolo y Dafne, Selva encantada de Amor, Las nuevas armas de Amor, La guerra de los gigantes, Salir el amor del mundo*; incid. m. for a comedy, *Jupiter*; 2 ballets, &c.

Duruflé, Maurice (b. Louviers, Eure, 11. I. 1902), Fr. orgst. & comp. Learnt m. in the choir-school of Rouen cath., 1912–8, and then studied at the Paris Cons. under Vierne, Tournemire & Dukas. App.

orgst. at the church of Saint-Étienne-du-Mont in 1929.

Works incl. chorale on *Veni Creator*, Suite and many other works for org.; *Prelude, Recitative and Vars.* for fl., va. & pf.; 3 dances for orch., &c.

Dušek. *See also* **Dussek & Tuczek.**

Dušek, Franz (František Xaver) (b. Chotěboř, 8. XII. 1731; d. Prague, 12. II. 1799), Boh. pfst. & comp. Pupil of Wagenseil in Vienna; taught in Prague, master of many famous pupils.

Dušek (*née* **Hambacher**), **Josefa** (b. Prague, 1756; d. Prague, ?), Boh. sop. singer, wife of prec. She travelled in Aus. and Ger. The 1st Donna Anna in Mozart's *Don Giovanni*, 1787. M. wrote the concert aria *Bella mia fiamma* (K. 528) for her.

Dusík. *See* **Dussek.**

Dusk of the Gods, The (Wagner). *See* **Ring des Nibelungen.**

Dussik (or **Dusik, Dušek**), **Jan Ladislav** (b. Časlav, 12. II. 1760; d. Saint-Germain-en-Laye, 12. III. 1812), Boh. pfst. & comp. Played the pf. from the age of 5 and the org. at 9, became a chorister at the Minorite church of Jihlav, where he studied m. with Father Ladislav Spinar and had a general educ. at the Jesuit Coll., later going to Kutna Hora as orgst. of the Jesuit church. After some theological studies in Prague, he went to the Nthlds. in the late 1770s, working as orgst. at Mechlin and Berg-op-Zoom, where he gave up the org. and went to Amsterdam to make his way as pfst. and comp. There and at The Hague, which he left for Hamburg in 1782, he wrote his 1st concs. and sos., and at Hamburg he continued studies with C. P. E. Bach. Next he travelled, staying in Berlin, St. Petersburg and on Prince Radziwill's estate in Lithuania, going to Paris in 1786 and playing before Marie Antoinette. After a visit to It. he returned to Paris in 1788, but the Revol. drove him to London, where he 1st appeared at one of Salomon's concerts in 1790. He met Haydn, married Sophia Corri, Domenico C.'s daughter, in 1792, gave concerts with her and estab. a m. shop with her father. It failed in 1800 and he had to fly, returning to Hamburg. In 1803 he met Prince Louis Ferdinand of Prus. at Magdeburg and lived with him until he was killed in the battle of Saalfeld in 1806, teaching him pf. and comp. He then entered successively the service of the Princes of Isenburg and Benevento (Talleyrand), but left Paris to recover from an illness at Saint-Germain, where he d.

Works incl. incid. m. for *The Captive of Spilburg* & Sheridan's *Pizarro* (both with Kelly); 3 ovts. & Serenade for orch.; (?) Mass; 3 stg. 4tets, 2 pf. 4tets, pf. 5tet, *c.* 20 pf. trios; *c.* 12 sos. for pf. duet, So. for 2 pfs.; pf. m.: *c.* 18 concs., *c.* 32 sos., *c.* 25 rondos, *c.* 20 sets of vars., var. misc. pieces; *c.* 65 sos. with v. or fl., &c.

Dussek (or **Dusík, Dušek**), **Sophia Giustina** (b. Edinburgh, 1. V. 1755; d. ? London, 1847), Eng. sop. singer of It. descent. Daughter of Domenico Corri and wife of prec. Pupil of her father, she appeared as a pfst. at Edinburgh at a very early age, and came out as a singer in London when the family moved there in 1788. She married in 1792.

Dutch (excl. early Netherland) **Composers.** *See* **Agricola (R.), Andriessen, Averkamp, Badings, Berlijn, Blankenburg, Brandts-Buys, Brucken-Fock, Diepenbrock, Dieren (van), Dopper, Dresden, Enthoven, Felderhof, Franco, Gilse (van), Hol, Hollander, Hondt, Hutschenruyter (2), Ingenhoven, Ketting, Koeberg, Landré (2), Lange (3), Lier (van), Mengelberg, Monnikendam, Nicolai (W.), Noordt, Otterloo, Pijper, Ruygrok, Ruyneman, Schäfer, Schwindl (?), Sigtenhorst-Meyer, Silas, Verhulst, Voormolen, Wagenaar (2), Zagwijn, Zweers.**

Duval, François (b. ?, *c.* 1673; d. Versailles, 27. I. 1728), Fr. vst. & comp. He was a member of Louis XIV's '24 violons du roi' and wrote v. sos. in the It. style, pub. as the 1st of the kind in 1794. Wrote numerous books of sos. for v. and bass & 2 vs. and bass.

Duvernoy, Victor Alphonse (b. Paris, 30. VIII. 1842; d. Paris, 7. III. 1907), Fr. pfst. & comp. Pupil at the Paris Cons. where later he became pf. prof.

Works incl. operas *Sardanapale* & *Hellé*; ballet *Bacchus*; lyric scene *Cléopâtre*; *La Tempête* for solo voices, chor. & orch.; ovt. to Hugo's *Hernani* and other orch. works; numerous pf. pieces, &c.

Dux and Comes (Lat. = leader & companion). The names formerly used for the subject in a fugue, at its 1st appearance and brought in by way of answer respectively.

Dvořák, Antonín (b. Nelahozeves, 8. IX. 1841; d. Prague, 1. V. 1904), Cz. comp. Son of a village innkeeper and butcher. He heard only popular and simple church m. as a child, but developed remarkable gifts. Sent to the org. school at Prague in 1857, began to comp. 2 years later and joined an orch. as vst.; later va. in the orch. at the Cz. nat. theatre, under Smetana. In 1873 he married

Anna Čermaková. The next year he received for the 1st time the Aus. state prize for comp. and became a friend of Brahms, who was on the committee and introd. him to his pub., Simrock. 1st visit to Eng. in 1884 to cond. the *Stabat Mater* in London. In 1885 he bought the country estate of Vysoká, which remained his home. Hon. Mus.D. at Cambridge in 1891, when he was app. prof. at Prague Cons., of which he became dir. in 1901. In 1892–5 he was dir. of the new Nat. Cons. in N.Y., and spent some holidays at the Cz. colony of Spillville, Iowa. In 1896 he paid the last of his many visits to Eng., where he had prod. several works at the mus. festivals.

Works incl. operas *Alfred* (unpub., lib. by Körner), *King and Collier, The Pigheaded Peasants, Wanda, The Peasant a Rogue, Dimitri, The Jacobin, The Devil and Kate, Russalka, Armida*; 9 syms. (incl. 2 unpub. & posthumously pub.); 5 symph. poems *The Water-Sprite, The Noonday Witch, The Golden Spinning-Wheel, The Wood-Dove, Hero's Song*; 7 concert ovts. incl. the cycle *Amid Nature, Carnival* & *Othello*; var. orch. works incl. *Czech Suite*, 3 *Slavonic Rhapsodies, Scherzo capriccioso, Symph. Vars.*, 2 sets of Slavonic Dances; *Serenade* and *Notturno* for stg. orch.; concs. for pf., v. & co.; 4 smaller pieces for solo insts. & orch.; 8 stg. 4tets and some early exs. pub. later; 3 stg. 5tets; stg. 6tet; 4 pf. trios; pf. 4tet; pf. 5tet; *Bagatelles* for 2 v., co. & harmonium; *Terzetto* for 2 v. & va.; works for chor. & orch. (some with solo voices): *Stabat Mater, The Spectre's Bride, St. Ludmilla*, Psalm cxlix, Mass in D maj., Requiem; *The American Flag*, Te Deum; smaller chor. works: *The Heirs of the White Mountain, Song of the Czechs, Hymn of the Czech Peasants, Hymnus, Festival Song*; several sets of partsongs; 4 sets of voc. duets; 68 songs; 14 op. nos. of pf. pieces, incl. Theme & Vars., *Poetic Tone-Pictures*, Suite & *Humoresques*, also some sep. pf. pieces; 6 sets of pf. duets, incl. Slavonic Dances, *Legends* & *From the Bohemian Forest*; So., Sonatina & smaller pieces for v. & pf.; Rondo, &c. for co. & pf., &c.

Dvorsky, Michel. *See* **Hofmann, Josef.**

Dyck, Ernest (Marie-Hubert) van (b. Antwerp, 2. IV. 1861; d. Berlaer-les-Lierre, 31. VIII. 1923), Belg. ten. singer. After studying law and working as a journalist, he learnt singing and made his 1st appearance in Paris in 1883. In 1887 he sang the 1st of the Wagnerian parts with which he was afterwards chiefly assoc., Lohengrin in Paris, and the following year he was 1st engaged as Parsifal at Bayreuth.

Dygon, John (b. ?, *c.* 1485; d. ?, 1560), Eng. cleric & comp. Took the Mus.B. at Oxford in 1512, (?) in 1521 went to Louvain to study with the Spa. humanist Juan Luis Vives, and became a prior at St. Austin's Abbey, Canterbury. A motet of his is preserved.

Dykes, John Bacchus (b. Hull, 10. III. 1823; d. St. Leonards, 22. I. 1876), Eng. church musn. Learnt m. from an orgst. at Hull, graduated at Cambridge, where he studied m. under Walmisley, and became a curate at Malton, Yorks, becoming precentor and min. canon at Durham cath. in 1849–62. Wrote services, anthems and esp. many hymn-tunes, and took part in the compilation of *Hymns A. & M.*

Dylan (Holbrooke). *See* **Cauldron of Annwen.**

Dynamics. The gradations of loudness and softness in m.

Dyphone. *See* **Mace, Thomas.**

Dyson, George (b. Halifax, 28. V. 1883), Eng. comp. Studied at the R.C.M. in London and became mus. dir. at Winchester Coll. in 1924, having already held the apps. of m. master at Osborne, Marlborough, Rugby and Wellington, serving in the 1914–8 war between. In 1937 he was app. dir. of the R.C.M. in succession to Hugh Allen. Knighted in 1941.

Works incl. comps. for solo voices, chor. & orch.: *The Canterbury Pilgrims* (setting of Chaucer's prologue), *St. Paul's Voyage to Melita, Nebuchadnezzar, Quo vadis*; chor. & orch.: *In Honour of the City of London* (Dunbar), *The Blacksmiths*; Sym., *Siena* & suite *Won't you look out of your window?* (after Walter de la Mare) for orch.; *Prelude, Fantasy and Chaconne* for co. & orch.; 3 Rhapsodies for stg. 4tet; church m., pf. pieces, songs, partsongs, &c.

Dzerzhinsky, Ivan (b. Tambov, 8. IV. 1909), Rus. comp. Studied at the Gnessin School of M. at Moscow and at the Leningrad Cons.

Works incl. operas *Quiet flows the Don, Ploughing the Fallows* (both after novels by Mikhail Sholokhov), *In the Days of Volochaiev, The Storm* (after Ostrovsky), *The Blood of the People*; incid. m. for plays; film m.; *Spring, Poem of the Dnieper* & *Rus. Ovt.* for orch.; 2 pf. concs., pf. pieces; song cycles, &c.

E

E. The note bounding the range of the scales of E maj. and min., and of the Phrygian and Hypoaeolian (Gr. Dorian) modes.
Ě. In Cz. Ě or ě is pronounced ' yé.'
E.N.S.A. *See* **ENSA.**
Ear Training. The development in mus. pupils of the sense of Absolute or at least Relative Pitch, the ready distinction of intervals, identification of var. types of chords, &c.
Early Reign of Oleg, The, Rus. ' opera ' or play with m. (lib. by Catherine II), m. by Pashkeievitch, Canobbio & Sarti, prod. St. Petersburg, at court, Hermitage Theatre, 22. X. 1790.
Easdale, Brian (b. Manchester, 10. VIII. 1909), Eng. comp. Educ. at the Westminster Abbey choir-school and the R.C.M. in London.
Works incl. operas *Rapunzel* & *The Corn King*; *Dead March*, *Tone Poem*, *Six Poems* for orch.; pf. Conc.; stg. Trio; pieces for 2 pfs.; song cycle, &c.
East, Michael (b. ? London, *c.* 1580; d. ? Lichfield, 1648), Eng. comp. He was (?) in the service of Sir Christopher Hatton and of his widow in London early in the 17th cent. and later orgst. of Lichfield cath.
Works incl. Evening Service, anthems; 6 books of madrigals (some with anthems) and a madrigal contrib. to *The Triumphes of Oriana*; m. for viols, &c.
East, Thomas (b. ?, ?; d. London, *c.* 1608), Eng. pub., ? father of prec. He worked in London and brought out several works by Byrd and the Elizabethan madrigalists.
Easter Music-Drama. *See* **Sepulchre Music.**
Ebeling, Johann Georg (b. Lüneburg, VII. 1637; d. Stettin, 1676), Ger. comp. Mus. dir. at the Nicolai church in Berlin in 1662 and prof. of m. at Stettin in 1668. He ed. the hymns of Paul Gerhardt and other m. Comp. church m., esp. chorales.
Eberl, Anton (b. Vienna, 13. VI. 1766; d. Vienna, 11. III. 1807), Aus. pfst. & comp. He had little training as a comp., but prod. his 1st opera as early as 1787. Chapel master at St. Petersburg, 1796–1801. He returned to Vienna to prod. another opera, but again visited Rus. in 1803 and in 1806 travelled all over Ger. as pfst.
Works incl. operas *La Marchande de modes* & *Die Königin der schwarzen Inseln*; melodrama *Pyramus und Thisbe*; wedding cantata *La gloria d'Imeneo*; syms.; pf. concs.; stg. 4tets, pf. trios & other chamber m.; pf. sos., vars., &c.; songs, &c.
Eberlin, Johann Ernst (b. Jettingen nr. Günzburg, 27. III. 1702; d. Salzburg, 21. VI. 1762), Ger. orgst. & comp. Went from his native Bavaria to Salzburg and became sub-orgst. at the cath. in 1725, chief orgst. in 1729 and court orgst. in 1754.
Works incl. masses & motets; orats. incl. *Componimento sacro*; preludes, toccatas & fugues for org.; m. for clav., &c.
Eberst, Jakob Levy. *See* **Offenbach.**
Eberwein, Traugott Maximilian (b. Weimar, 27. X. 1775; d. Rudolstadt, 2. XII. 1831), Ger. vst. & comp. Son of a member of the Weimar court band, in which he played as a child. Through Zelter's influence he was much esteemed by Goethe. He went into the service of the Prince of Schwarzburg-Rudolstadt in 1797 and became mus. dir. there in 1817.
Works incl. operas *Claudine von Villa Bella* & *Der Jahrmarkt von Plundersweilen* (libs. by Goethe), *Preciosa* (P. A. Wolff) & 8 others; Mass; 3 cantatas; concs., *Sinfonia concertante* for wind insts.; voc. 4tets; songs, &c.
Eccard, Johann (b. Mühlhausen, Thuringia, 1553; d. ? Berlin, 1611), Ger. comp. Pupil of David Köler in the choir-school attached to the Weimar court chapel, 1567–71, and (?) of Lassus at Munich. In the service successively of Jacob Fugger at Ausgburg, at Königsberg, of the Margrave of Brandenburg-Ansbach and of the Elector Joachim Friedrich of Brandenburg in Berlin and his successor, Johann Sigismund.
Works incl. motets, chorales (some harmonized, some newly comp. by him); sacred songs; secular Ger. songs for several voices, wedding songs, odes, festival songs, &c.
Eccles (Eagles), Eng. family of musns.:
1. Solomon E. (b. ?, 1618; d. London, 11. II. 1683), descendant of a mus. family, teacher of virginals & viols. He embraced Quakerism *c.* 1660 and burnt all his m. and insts., but in 1667 pub. a book arguing for

and against the moral justification of m. He went to the West Indies with George Fox to estab. Quakerism in 1671, was in New Eng. in 1672 and was prosecuted for sedition at Barbados in 1680. After his return he (?) resumed the mus. profession and contrib. to *The Division Violin*.

2. John E. (b. London, *c.* 1650; d. Kingston-on-Thames, 12. I. 1735), comp., son of prec. Pupil of his father. Began to write m. for the theatres *c.* 1681. He became a member of the King's Band in 1694 and its Master in 1700 on the death of Staggins, and the same year gained the 2nd prize in a contest for the best comp. of Congreve's masque *The Judgment of Paris*, Weldon being 1st and D. Purcell and Finger 3rd & 4th. For *c.* a quarter of a cent. he lived in retirement at Kingston, devoted mainly to fishing, though he continued to write odes for the royal household.

Works incl. m. for many plays, e.g. *The Spanish Friar* (Dryden), *Love for Love* (Congreve), *Don Quixote* (Durfey, with Purcell), *The Stage Coach* (Farquhar), *Macbeth* (Shakespeare), *Europe's Revels for the Peace, Rinaldo and Armida, The Way of the World* & *Semele* (both Congreve), *The Biter* (Rowe); m. for Queen Anne's coronation; Congreve's *Ode for St. Cecilia's Day*; many songs, &c.

3. Henry E. (b. London, *c.* 1652; d. ? Paris, ? 1742), vst. & comp., brother of prec. Member of the King's Band, 1674–1710, but went to Paris, considering himself neglected at home, and joined the royal band there. Wrote sos. for v. and for viol.

4. Henry E. (b. ?; d. ?), violist, ? uncle of 2 & 3, was a member of the King's Band in the last quarter of the 17th cent.

5. Thomas E. (b. London, *c.* 1655; d. ?), vst., son of 1. Pupil of his brother Henry (3), although highly gifted, secured no appt., being a wastrel, but made such a living as he could by playing at taverns.

Échelle de soie, L' (*The Silken Ladder*), opera by Gaveaux (lib. by François Antoine Eugène de Planard), prod. Paris, Opéra-Comique, 22. VIII. 1808. The orig. of Rossini's *Scala di seta*.

Échiquier. *See* **Chekker.**

Echo. An org. contrivance enabling the player to repeat a phrase more softly on a different set of stops or even on a separate inst. placed in another part of the building.

In comp. var. echo effects have been used in many ways at all times; e.g. Lassus's madrigal *Olà, che buon eco*, the witches' chor. in Purcell's *Dido and Aeneas*, the *Echo* piece in Bach's B min. clav. Partita, the *Scène aux champs* in Berlioz's *Fantastic Sym.*, the 2nd act of Humperdinck's *Hänsel and Gretel*, &c.

Écho et Narcisse, opera by Gluck (lib. by Louis Théodor de Tschudy), prod. Paris, Opéra, 24. IX. 1779.

Eck, Franz (b. Mannheim, 1774; d. Strasburg, 1804), Ger. vst. Pupil of his brother Johann. Played in the court band at Munich as a youth, then travelled much and took Spohr to Rus. with him as his pupil.

Eck, Johann Friedrich (b. Mannheim, 1766; d. Bamberg, 1809), Ger. vst., cond. & comp., brother of prec. In the court band at Munich, 1778–88, and later opera cond. there. He travelled much and became very famous, but in 1801 married a woman of wealth and retired to Paris and Nancy.

Works incl. 4 v. concs. and a *Concertante* for 2 vs., &c.

Eckardt, Johann Gottfried (b. Augsburg, *c.* 1735; d. Paris, VIII. 1809), Ger. pfst., comp. & miniature painter. Settled in Paris, 1758. Wrote sos., Vars., &c. for pf.

Eckert, Carl (Anton Florian) (b. Potsdam, 7. XII. 1820; d. Berlin, 14. X. 1879), Ger. pfst., vst., cond. & comp. Pupil of Mendelssohn at Leipzig. Accompst. at the Théâtre Italien in Paris and to Henriette Sontag in the U.S.A., then cond. at the same theatre in Paris, dir. of the Court Opera in Vienna, chapel master at Stuttgart in succession to Kücken, and successor of Dorn in Berlin.

Works incl. operas *Das Fischermädchen, Wilhelm von Oranien*; orats. *Ruth* & *Judith*; church m.; Sym.; co. Conc.; pf pieces; songs, &c.

École d'Arcueil. A group of Fr. comps. gathered round Satie in his later years at his home in the Arcueil suburb of Paris, formed in 1923 and incl. Henri Cliquet-Pleyel, Roger Désormière, Maxime Jacob, Henri Sauguet & others.

Écorcheville, Jules (Armand Joseph) (b. Paris, 17. III. 1872; d. Perthes-les-Hurlus, 19. II. 1915), Fr. mcolst. Pupil of Franck and Riemann, co-founder of the Fr. section of the I.M.S., whose publications he ed. He did much research, and pub. the results, on old Fr. lute and v. m., mus. bibliography, &c. He was killed in battle.

Écossaise (Fr. fem. = lit. Sco. one). A dance long supposed to be of Sco. origin, but no longer considered so. As a fashionable ballroom dance in the early 19th cent. it was in fairly animated 2–4 time, about halfway between the polka and the galop in speed. Among the comps. who cultivated it are Beethoven, Schubert and Chopin. The Ger. *Schottisch* (usually written (in the plur.), *Schottische*, in Eng.) is the same thing.

Ed. (abbr.) = Edited, edition, editor.

Edelmann, Johann Friedrich (b. Strasburg, 6. V. 1749; d. Strasburg, 17. VII. 1794), Alsat. pfst. & comp. His pupil, Baron Dietrich, took him to Paris and helped him to become famous as player and comp., and E. returned to Strasburg with him when he became mayor there, but denounced him, with many others, during the Reign of Terror. He was himself guillotined later.

Works incl. operas *Ariane dans l'île de Naxos, La Bergère des Alpes* & *Diane et l'Amour*; syms.; concs.; sos. & pieces for clav., &c.

Edgar, opera by Puccini (lib. by Ferdinando Fontana, based on Musset's *La Coupe et les lèvres*), prod. Milan, Teatro alla Scala, 21. IV. 1889.

Edgcumbe, Richard. *See* **Mount-Edgcumbe.**

Edmunds, Chris(topher Montague). (b. Birmingham, 26. XI. 1899), Eng. comp. & orgst. Pupil of Bantock at the Birmingham and Midland School of M., later prof. of comp. there, and in 1945 app. principal in succession to Allan K. Blackall. Mus.D., Manchester, 1935. Orgst. at Aston parish church.

Works incl. opera *The Blue Harlequin* (after Maurice Baring); Sym. in D maj. (No. 2), Sym. for stgs. (No. 1); Romance for pf. & orch.; many chamber works; pf. m., &c.

Eduardo e Cristina. *See also* **Odoardo e Cristina.**

Opera by Rossini (lib. by Giovanni Schmidt, written for Pavesi, altered by Andrea Leone Tottola and Gherardo Bevilacqua-Aldovrandini), prod. Venice, Teatro San Benedetto, 24. IV. 1819.

Edwards, Julian (b. Manchester, 11. XII. 1855; d. Yonkers, N.Y., 5. IX. 1910), Anglo-Amer. comp. Pupil of Oakley and Macfarren, became a theatre cond. in 1877 and in 1888 settled in U.S.A.

Works incl. operas *Jupiter, King René's Daughter* (on Hertz's play) & *The Patriot*, operettas *Brian Boru, Princess Chic, Dolly Varden* (on Dickens's *Barnaby Rudge*), *When Johnny comes marching home, Friend Fritz* (after Erckmann-Chatrian), *The Belle of London Town, The Maid of Plymouth, The Land of Heart's Desire* (W. B. Yeats) & others; 4 sacred cantatas, secular cantata *The Mermaid*; songs, &c.

Edwards, Richard (b. Somerset, c. 1523; d. London, 31. X. 1566), Eng. comp. Pupil of the musn., physician and Gr. scholar George Etheridge of Thame, (?) at Oxford, where he entered Corpus Christi Coll. in 1540, and passed on to Christ Church Coll. on its foundation in 1547. App. Master of the Children of the Chapel Royal in London in 1561. He was also a playwright, prod. *Palamon and Arcite* before Queen Elizabeth and also writing *Damon and Pithias*, &c., and a poet, compiling and contributing to a book of verse, *The Paradise of Dainty Devices.*

Works incl. m. to his own *Damon and Pithias*; madrigals *In going to my naked bed* & *O the silly man*, &c.

Eeden, Gilles (or Heinrich) van den (b. ?; d. Bonn, VI. 1782), ? Flem., Dutch or Ger. orgst. & comp. 2nd court orgst. at Bonn. One of Beethoven's early teachers.

Eeden, Jean (Baptiste) van den (b. Ghent, 24. XII. 1842; d. Mons, 7. IV. 1917), Belg. comp. Studied at Ghent and Brussels Conss. In 1878 he became dir. of the School of M. at Mons.

Works incl. operas *Numance* & *Rhéna*; orat. *Le Jugement dernier*; cantatas; orch. works; songs, part-songs, &c.

Egiazarov, Grigory (b. Ikdir, Rus. Armenia, 23. X. 1908), Rus. comp. After being an army bandsman, 1921–9, he studied at the Moscow Cons. under Glière, Miaskovsky and others.

Works incl. ballet *A Drop of Mead*; stg. 4tet; Scherzo for bn. & pf.; dances for pf., mostly based on Tartar, Armenian and Kurd folk m., &c.

Egisto, L' (*Aegisthus*), opera by Cavalli (lib. by Giovanni Faustini), prod. Venice, Teatro San Cassiano, autumn 1643.

Egk, Werner (b. Auchsesheim, Bav., 17. V. 1901), Ger. comp. Mainly self-taught and spent some time in It. He began to comp. to broadcasting commissions. Settled nr. Munich and succeeded Graener as head of the faculty of comp. in the Reichsmusikkammer.

Works incl. operas *Die Zaubergeige* & *Peer Gynt* (after Ibsen); ballet *Joan de Zarissa*; orat. *Columbus*; dance suite *Georgica* for orch.; v. Conc., &c.

Egli, Johann Heinrich (b. Seegräben nr. Zürich, 4. III. 1742; d. Zürich, 19. XII. 1810), Swi. comp. Pupil of Pastor Schmiedli at Wetzikon nr. Zürich & later m. teacher at Zürich.

Wrote many songs of which he pub. several books.

Egmont, incid. m. by Beethoven for Goethe's tragedy of that name, Op. 84, written in 1810 for a revival at the Burg Theatre in Vienna on 24. V.

Egyptian Helen, The (R. Strauss). *See* **Ägyptische Helena.**

Ehlert, Ludwig (b. Königsberg, 13. I. 1825; d. Wiesbaden, 4. I. 1884), Ger. pfst., critic & comp. Pupil of Mendelssohn at the Leipzig Cons. and afterwards studied in Vienna. Worked in Berlin, Florence and at the court of Meiningen. He wrote several books on comps. and mus. life in It. and Ger.

Works incl. *Spring Sym.*, ovt. *Hafiz* & *A Winter's Tale* (Shakespeare); Requiem for a child; Romantic So. & pieces for pf.; songs, &c.

Eichendorff, Joseph von (1788–1857), Aus. poet & novelist. *See* **Fröhlich (F. T.)** (song from *Aus dem Leben eines Taugenichts*), **Knab** (songs), **Lothar** (*Freier*), **Paumgartner** (*Aus dem Leben e. T.*), **Pfitzner** (*Von deutscher Seele*), **Schoeck** (*Schloss Dürande, Wandersprüche* & songs), **Schumann** (*Liederkreis*); 6 songs by **Brahms,** 16 by **Schumann,** 28 (incl. 8 early) by **H. Wolf.**

Eichheim, Henry (b. Chicago, 3. I. 1870; d. Montecito, Cal., 22. VIII. 1942), Amer. vst. & comp. Studied at the Chicago Mus. Coll. and became vst. in Theodore Thomas's orch., where his father was a cst. Later he played in the Boston Sym. Orch., 1890–1912. He then devoted himself to comp. and to travel in Asia, esp. Japan, where he studied eastern m.

Works incl. ballets *Chinese Legend, Burmese Pwe* & *The Moon, my Shadow and I*; *Oriental Impressions, Chinese Legend, Burma, Java* & *Malay Mosaic* for orch. with oriental insts., &c.

Eighteen-Twelve Overture (Tchaikovsky). *See* **Year 1812.**

Eighth Note (Amer.) = Quaver. The Amer. designation, derived from Ger., is logical if a semibreve can be regarded as a ' whole note,' but uses 2 words where 1 is enough.

Ein musikalischer Spass (Mozart). *See* **Musikalischer Spass.**

Eine kleine Nachtmusik (Mozart). *See* **Kleine Nachtmusik.**

(For other titles with the Ger. prefix ' Ein ' or ' Eine ' *see* under the following word.)

Einleitung (Ger.) = Introduction, Prelude.

Einstein, Alfred (b. Munich, 30. XII. 1880), Ger. mcolst. Pupil of Sandberger, took his doctor's degree in 1903. Became ed. of the *Zeitschrift für Musikwissenschaft* in 1918, was m. critic of the *Berliner Tageblatt* from 1929, in 1933 went into exile from Ger., settling 1st in London, then at Florence and lastly in Northampton, Mass., where he is prof. at Smith Coll. He revised Riemann's *Musiklexicon* and Köchel's Mozart catalogue and wrote works on Ger. va. da gamba m., on Gluck and Mozart, a short hist. of m. and in partic. specialized in the study of the It. madrigal, on which he wrote a chapter in Adler's *Handbuch* as well as a monumental book of his own.

Eisler, Hanns (b. Leipzig, 6. VII. 1898), Ger. comp. Studied with Schoenberg in Vienna and gained a comp. prize in 1924. In 1925–33 he taught in Berlin, but emigrated to U.S.A. when a price was put on his head for being interested in m. for the proletariat and in anti-Nazi activities. He was app. prof. at the New School of Social Research there.

Works incl. opera *Goliath*, didactic plays *Mother* (after Gorky's novel), *Hangmen also die, For whom the bell tolls, The Roundheads and the Pointed-heads* & others; m. for numerous films; *Ger. Sym.* for solo voices, chor. & orch., cantatas, chor. ballads, proletarian songs, &c.; orch. suites on Rus. & Jewish folksongs; wind 5tet; chamber cantata *Palmström* for speech-song, fl., cl., v. & co.; *Zeitungsausschnitte* for voice & pf., &c.

Eisteddfod (Welsh, plur. Eisteddfodau = a sitting of the learned). An annual gathering, now taking the form of a mainly mus. festival, but formerly a triennial assembly of Welsh bards, dating back to the 7th cent. at latest.

Eitner, Robert (b. Breslau, 22. X. 1832; d. Templin nr. Berlin, 2. II. 1905), Ger. mcolst. & bibliog. Founder of the Gesellschaft für Musikforschung in 1868, ed. of the *Monatshefte für Musikgeschichte*, compiler of the *Quellen-Lexicon* (a catalogue of the contents of m. libraries) and other bibliog. works, &c.

Electrochord. An electrophonic pf. invented by Vierling of Berlin in 1929–33, prod. its notes by the conversion of electrical waves into audible sounds.

Electronde. An electrophonic inst. invented by Martin Taubman of Berlin in 1929, prod. notes from the air graded according to the chromatic scale by means of a switch, not indeterminate in pitch like those of the Aetherophone or Theremin.

Electrone. An electrophonic org. brought out by the Compton Org. Co. of London in 1939, prod. its notes by electrostatic methods and capable of imitating the sound of var. org. stops and mixtures.

Electronic and Electrophonic Instruments. Modern insts. of var. kinds prod. their sound by high-frequency oscillations of radio vacuum tubes or by electro-magnetic agencies.

Elegy (from Gr. *elegos*). In poetry a piece of sorrowful and usually commemorative character; in m. either a voc. setting of such a poem or an inst. piece suggesting the mood awakened by it.

Elektra, opera by R. Strauss (lib. by Hugo von Hofmannsthal, a much modernized reinterpretation of Sophocles), prod. Dresden, Royal Opera, 25. I. 1909.

Elgar, Edward (b. Broadheath nr. Worcester, 2. VI. 1857; d. Worcester, 23. II. 1934), Eng. comp. Son of a Worcester m. dealer and orgst. at St. George's Rom. Catholic church. Learnt much from listening to his father and more from picking up m. and insts. in the shop, where he also taught himself theory from books. Began to comp. at 12, when he wrote m. for a little domestic play, *The Wand of Youth*. Sent to a solicitor's office at 15, but preferred to help at the shop; joined a wind 5tet as bnst. and the Worcester Glee Club, and at 17 became an orch. vst. Intended to go to London for study, but could not afford it, so never had any scholastic instruction; but for some v. lessons in London he was entirely self-taught. In 1879 he became cond. of the Worcester Glee Club and of the band at the county lunatic asylum, for which he arr. much m. Also played org. at his father's church and became member of Stockley's orch. at Birmingham, which gave the 1st public perf. of a work of his, the *Sérénade mauresque*. Married Caroline Alice Roberts in 1889 and went to live in London. In 1890 the Three Choirs Festival (at Worcester that year) for the 1st time played a work of his, the *Froissart* ovt. Gradually his m. was heard here and there, at provincial festivals and in London, e.g. *The Banner of St. George* written for Q. Victoria's diamond jubilee (1897) and the *Enigma* Vars. for orch., prod. by Hans Richter in VI. 1899. Setting of Cardinal Newman's *Dream of Gerontius* prod. at Birmingham Festival, 3. X. 1900 and, in Ger., at the Lower Rhine Festival, Düsseldorf, in 1901 & 1902. Elgar Festival at Covent Garden Theatre in London, III. 1904, brought him greater recognition, and he was knighted on 5. VII that year. Prof. of M. at Birmingham Univ., 1905–6. 1st Sym. prod. by Richter, Manchester and London, XII. 1908, and v. Conc. by Kreisler, XI. 1910. During the war of 1914–8 he wrote much topical m. and afterwards 3 chamber works, the 1st of his maturity. After the death of his wife in 1920 he only wrote some small pieces and incid. m., but at his death left unfinished a 3rd Sym. and an opera, *The Spanish Lady*, based on Ben Jonson's *The Devil is an Ass*.

Works incl. incid. m. for Yeats & George Moore's *Grania and Diarmid*, Algernon Blackwood's *The Starlight Express* & other plays; 2 Syms.; concert ovts. *Froissart, Cockaigne, In the South, Polonia*; many misc. orch. works, incl. 2 suites from *The Wand of Youth*, Serenade for stgs., *Enigma* Vars., *Introduction and Allegro* for stgs., symph. study *Falstaff, Dream Children* (after Lamb) for small orch., *Nursery Suite*; v. Conc., co. Conc.; cantatas *The Black Knight, King Olaf, The Banner of St. George, Caractacus, The Music Makers*; orats. *The Light of Life, The Dream of Gerontius, The Apostles, The Kingdom*; stg. 4tet, E min., pf. 5tet, A min., v. & pf. So., E min.; numerous smaller chor. pieces & partsongs; songs for solo voice, incl. cycle *Sea Pictures* with pf. or orch.; *Severn Suite* for brass band, &c.

Elijah (Ger. *Elias*), orat. by Mendelssohn (words from the Old Testament), prod. 1st in the Eng. version at the Birmingham Festival, 26. VIII. 1846; 1st Ger. perf., Hamburg, 7. X. 1847.

Eliot, T(homas). S(tearns). (b. 1888), Amer. (naturalized Eng.) poet. See **Porter** (**Q.**) (*Sweeney Agonistes*), **Shaw** (**M.**) (*Rock*).

Elisa, opera by Fux (lib., in It., by Pietro Pariati), prod. at court at Laxenburg Palace nr. Vienna, 25. VIII. 1719.

Elisabetta regina d'Inghilterra (*Elizabeth, Queen of England*), opera by Rossini (lib. by Giovanni Schmidt), prod. Naples, Teatro San Carlo, 4. X. 1815. The ovt. was taken from *Aureliano in Palmira* and afterwards used for *Il barbiere di Siviglia*.

Elision. A term used in poetry for the suppression of a vowel or syllable. In m. it may be used for similar effects of omission in the restatement of a theme by way of a var. that reduces instead of elaborating it: e.g. in the finale of Brahms's B♭ maj. stg. 6tet, Op. 18, 79 bars before the *animato* at the end, or in the 3rd mvt. of Tchaikovsky's 4th Sym., 50 bars before the end.

Elisir d'amore, L' (*The Love Potion*), opera by Donizetti (lib. by Felice Romani, based on Scribe's *Le Philtre*, comp. by Auber), prod. Milan, Teatro della Canobbiana, 12. V. 1832.

Elizalde, Federico (b. Manila, P.I., 12. XII. 1908), Spa. cond. & comp. Educ. at Stanford Univ., California, and Cambridge; studied m. with Pérez Casas in Madrid, Alfred Hertz and Bloch at San Francisco and E. Halffter in Paris.

Works incl. opera *Paul Gauguin*; ovt. *La pájara pinta*; Sinfonia concertante for pf. & orch.; m. for 15 solo insts., &c.

Ella, John (b. Thirsk, 19. XII. 1802; d. London, 2. X. 1888), Eng. vst. & writer on m. Estab. the chamber concerts of the Mus. Union in London and ran them for 35 years. M. critic of the *Morning Post*.

Elsner, Joseph Xaver (b. Grottkau, Silesia, 29. VI. 1769; d. Warsaw, 18. IV. 1854), Ger.-Pol. comp. Being intended for medicine, he had little mus. teaching in his youth, but learnt the v. and some harmony at Breslau and studied more assiduously on going to Vienna. In 1791 he became vst. at the Brno theatre and the next year cond. at Lwów. He went to Warsaw as theatre cond. in 1799, estab. a mus. soc. there in 1815 and became the 1st dir. of the Cons. opened in 1821. Among his pupils there was Chopin.

Works incl. 27 operas (22 in Pol., e.g. *Krol Lokietek*), ballets & melodramas, *Stabat Mater*, church m.; syms.; stg. 4tets; inst. pieces, &c.

Éluard, Paul (b. 1895), Fr. poet. *See* **Poulenc** (*Chansons villageoises* & *Figure humaine*).

Elvey, George (Job) (b. Canterbury, 27. III. 1816; d. Windlesham, 9. XII. 1893), Eng. orgst. & comp. Received his mus. educ. at Canterbury cath. and at the R.A.M. in London under Potter and Crotch. Orgst. at St. George's Chapel, Windsor, 1835–82; Mus.D., Oxford, 1840; knighted 1871.

Works incl. orats. *The Resurrection and Ascension* & *Mount Carmel*; services, anthems, festival anthems for Gloucester and Worcester; wedding march for Princess Louise; org. m., &c.

Elwart, Antoine (Aimable Élie) (b. Paris, 18. XI. 1808; d. Paris, 14. X. 1877), Fr. comp., mus. scholar & author of Pol. descent. Studied at the Paris Cons. under Fétis and Lesueur and gained the Prix de Rome in 1834. He taught at the Cons., cond. concerts, wrote books on var. subjects and gave much time to comp.

Works incl. opera *Les Catalans*; orats. *Noé* & *La Naissance d'Ève*; incid. m. for Euripides' *Alcestis*; *Omaggio alla memoria di Bellini*; masses and other church m.; syms., ovts.; chamber m., &c.

Elwell, Herbert (b. Minneapolis, 10. V. 1898), Amer. comp. Educ. at Minnesota Univ. and studied m. with Bloch in N.Y., Nadia Boulanger in Paris and at the Amer. Acad. in Rome. Settled at Cleveland on his return to U.S.A. in 1932 as critic and teacher.

Works incl. ballet *The Happy Hypocrite* (after Max Beerbohm); cantata; Sketches for orch.; stg. 4tet, pf. 5tet, Divertimento for stg. 4tet; v. & pf. So.; So. & other works for pf., &c.

Elwes, Gervase (Cary) (b. Northampton, 15. XI. 1866; d. nr. Boston, U.S.A., 12. I. 1921), Eng. ten. singer. Studied in Vienna, Munich, Paris and London. In Brit. diplomatic service, 1891–5. Made his 1st professional appearance in 1903.

Embouchure (Fr., but used in Eng.). The action of the lips on the mouthpiece in wind inst. playing.

Emerald Isle, The, unfinished operetta by Sullivan, completed by German (lib. by Basil Hood), prod. London, Savoy Theatre, 27. IV. 1901.

Emicon. An electrophonic inst. appearing in U.S.A. in 1931, prod. notes from the air graded according to the chromatic scale by means of a keyboard, not indeterminate in pitch like those of the Aetherophone or Theremin.

Emma di Resburgo (*Emma of Roxburgh*), opera by Meyerbeer (lib. by Gaetano Rossi), prod. Venice, Teatro San Benedetto, 26. VI. 1819.

Emmanuel, (Marie François) Maurice (b. Bar-sur-Aube, 2. V. 1862; d. Paris, 14. XII. 1938), Fr. mcolst. & comp. Student at the Paris Cons. and pupil of Gevaert at Brussels. After var. apps. as historian and musn. he became prof. of mus. hist. at the Cons. in succession to Bourgault-Ducoudray in 1909 and retained the post until 1936. He wrote several learned books on the mus. idiom, Gr. m., modal accomp., Burgundian folk-song, &c.

Works incl. operas *Prométhée enchaîné* & *Salamine* (both after Aeschylus); operetta *Pierrot peintre*; incid. m. for Plautus's *Amphitryon*; 2 syms., *Suite française*, *Ouverture pour un conte gai*, *Zingaresca* for orch.; *3 Odelettes anacréontiques* for voice, fl. & pf.; v. & pf. and co. & pf. sos.; *Sonate bourguignonne* and 6 sonatinas for pf.; *In memoriam matris* & *Musiques* for voice & pf., &c.

'Emperor' Concerto, nickname for Beethoven's E♭ maj. pf. Conc., Op. 73, known only in Brit. & U.S.A., prob. invented by J. B. Cramer. There is nothing to justify it, though it suits the majestic work well enough.

Emperor Jones, opera by Gruenberg (lib. by Kathleen de Jaffa, based on Eugene O'Neill's play), prod. N.Y., Metrop. Opera, 7. I. 1933.

'Emperor' Quartet. *See* **Emperor's Hymn.**

Emperor's Hymn. The former Aus. nat. anthem, words by Lorenz Leopold Hauschka written in 1796 and set for 4-part chor. in 1797 by Haydn, who used it afterwards for vars. in the stg. 4tet in C maj., Op. 76 No. 3.

En Saga (Sibelius). *See* **Saga, A.** The word 'saga' being accepted as Eng., there is no good reason for persisting in the use of the Swe. form of the title of this work, esp. as Sibelius is not a Swe. comp.

Encina, Juan del. *See* **Enzina.**

Encore (Fr. = again, still). In Eng. the request for a perf.'s repetition of a programme item that has pleased partic. or for the extra perf. of some additional matter not on the programme. Such an extra item is called by the noun of 'an E.' The word is not used in Fr. in that sense: the demand for an E. there is made with the Lat. word *bis* (twice), and out of this the anomalous verb *bisser* has been made. In 'Eng.' the verb is 'to encore.'

Énée et Lavinie (*Aeneas and Lavinia*), opera by Colasse (lib. by Bernard de Fontenelle, after Virgil), prod. Paris, Opéra, 16. XII. 1690.

Opera by Dauvergne (lib. do.), prod. Paris, Opéra, 14. II. 1758.

Enesco, Georges (b. Dorohoiû, 19. VIII. 1881), Rum. vst. & comp. Studied at the Vienna Cons., 1888–93, and then went to Paris to finish his v. studies with Marsick and comp. with Massenet, Gédalge and Fauré. In 1899 he began his career as a virtuoso vst. and teacher of the inst.

Works incl. opera *Œdipe* (after Sophocles); 3 syms., *Poème roumain*, *Rumanian Rhapsodies*, suites and intermezzi, &c. for orch.; m. for stg. and for wind combs.; v. & pf. sos.; suites and other works for pf.; songs, &c.

Enfance du Christ, L' (*The Childhood of Christ*), orat. by Berlioz, Op. 25, for solo voices, chor. & orch., comp. in 1850–4, 1st perf. Paris, 10. XII. 1854.

Enfant prodigue, L' (*The Prodigal Son*), lyric scene by Debussy (lib. Édouard Guinand), written for the Prix de Rome and pub. 1884; prod. as an opera, London, Covent Garden Theatre, 28. II. 1910.

Pantomime by Wormser (scen. by M. Carré, jun.), prod. Paris, Cercle Funambulesque, 14. VI, and Bouffes-Parisiens, 21. VI. 1890.

Engel, Carl (b. Thiedewiese nr. Hanover, 6. VII. 1818; d. London, 17. XI. 1882), Ger. mcolst. who wrote on m. in Eng. After studying the org. at Hanover and the pf. with Hummel, and being for some time attached to the household of a Pomeranian nobleman, he went to Eng. *c.* 1845, settling 1st at Manchester, then in London. He wrote on mus. archaeology, insts., folk m., &c. and compiled the catalogue of the mus. insts. in the Victoria & Albert Museum.

Engel, Carl (b. Paris, 21. VII. 1883; d. New York, 6. V. 1944), Amer. mcolst. of Ger. descent. Studied at Strasburg & Munich and settled in U.S.A. in 1905. App. chief of the m. division of the Library of Congress at Washington in 1922 and succeeded Sonneck as ed. of the *Musical Quarterly* in 1929. One of the organizers and in 1937–8 president of the Amer. Mcol. Soc. He pub. many articles and books on m., also some comps.

Engführung (Ger. lit. 'narrow leading') = Stretto.

English Fingering. An obs. system of fingering of pf. m. according to the principle that the human hand has 4 fingers and a thumb, the former being thus marked 1–4 and the latter +. E. F. has now been wholly displaced by Continental Fingering, where the thumb is marked 1, the numbering continuing to the little finger, which thus becomes 5. This system was, in fact, in use in early Eng. virginal m.; E. F. was a later fashion.

English Folk Dance and Song Society. An amalgamation of the Folksong Soc., founded in 1898, and the Eng. Folk Dance Soc., founded by Cecil Sharp in 1911 the aim of both being the collection, study and practice of old folksongs and dances, the pub. of a *Journal* and the holding of annual festivals with the collaboration of visiting foreign singers and dancers.

English Horn (from Fr. *cor anglais*, poss. but not prob. der. from *cor anglé* = angled horn). A woodwind inst. with double reed, belonging to the ob. family, played exactly like that inst. but standing a 5th lower in pitch and tuned in F, thus transposing a 5th down. Its tone is nasal, like that of the ob., but darker and more melancholy in quality.

English Suites. 6 suites for hpchd. by Bach, comp. *c.* 1725 and so called prob. because they have long preludes for 1st mvts., which seems to have been considered an Eng. fashion, perhaps because Purcell's suites have preludes. The Fr. Suites by Bach have none.

Enharmonic (adj.). In Gr. m. there were 3 genera: the diatonic, the chromatic and the E., and the last had divisions into degrees smaller than semitones. In modern usage the word E. is applied to modulations made by means of changes of a note or notes between sharps and flats, e.g. C♯ becoming D♭, E♭ becoming D♯, &c. On the pf. or other inst. using the tempered scale these notes actually remain the same, but in stg. insts. there is, at least to the player's feeling, a minute difference between them.

Enigma Canon. A Canon written down in a single part with no indication where the subsequent entries of the other parts are to occur, the perfs. being left to guess how the m. fits or to find it out by experiment.

'Enigma' Variations. A set of orch. vars. by Elgar, Op. 36, comp. 1898, 1st perf. London, 19. VI. 1899, presenting puzzles of 2 different kinds. (1) the theme was said by the comp. to go in ctpt. with another well-known tune, never divulged by him and so far never discovered; (2) each var. is a mus. portrait of some person indicated only by initials or by a nickname, all of whom have however been identified. *See also* **Potter.**

Enigmatic Scale (Verdi's). *See* **Scala enigmatica.**

Enimma (It. = enigma, riddle). The It. name for an Enigma Canon or Riddle Canon.

Enna, August (b. Nakskov, 13. V. 1860; d. Copenhagen, 3. VIII. 1939), Dan. comp. of It. descent. The son of a cobbler, he was almost entirely self-taught, although the family moved to Copenhagen in 1870, until 1888, when Gade helped him to study in Ger. for a year. He had already prod. an operetta by that time and become a provincial cond.

Works incl. operas *Heksen* (*The Witch*), *Cleopatra*, *Aucassin and Nicolette*, *The Little Match-Seller* & *The Princess on the Pea* (both after Andersen), *Komedianter* (*The Jesters*) (after Hugo), *Gloria Arsena* (after Dumas *père*), *Don Juan Mañara*, &c.; operetta, *A Village Tale*; ballets; chor. work *Mother-Love*; 2 syms., Festival Ovt., symph. pictures; v. Conc., &c.

ENSA (abbr.). Entertainments Nat. Service Assoc.: an organization estab. during the 2nd world war (1939–45) to provide entertainment for troops & factory workers.

Ensalada (Spa. lit. salad). A kind of burlesque madrigal cultivated in Spa. in the 16th cent., in dramatic form, like Vecchi's *Amfiparnaso*, not intended for stage perf. Also a Quodlibet.

Ensemble (Fr. = together). The word is used in Eng. for concerted singing or playing, esp. in critical descriptions of such singing or playing.

Entführung aus dem Serail, Die (*The Elopement from the Harem*, known in Eng. as *The Seraglio*). *See also* **Belmont und Constanze.**

Opera by Mozart (lib. by Christoph Friedrich Bretzner [*Belmont und Constanze*], altered by Gottlieb Stephanie, jun., based on Isaac Bickerstaffe's *The Captive*), prod. Vienna, Burg Theatre, 16. VII. 1782.

Enthoven, Henri Émile (b. Amsterdam, 18. X. 1903), Dutch comp. Pupil of Wagenaar at Amsterdam and Schreker in Berlin. Asst. to Weingartner at the Basle theatre and later lecturer and m. critic at Leyden and Amsterdam.

Works incl. incid. m. for plays; 3 syms., 4 suites & other orch. works; Fantasy for v. & orch.; Festival Prelude for wind insts. & org.; pf. m.; songs, &c.

Entr'acte (Fr.). *See* **Intermezzo.**

Entrata (It.). *See* **Intrada.**

Entrée (Fr. = entrance, entry). In the 18th cent. a piece of m. in march rhythm accomp. the entry of processions, &c. in ballets and other stage pieces; also, more generally, an introd. or prelude to any work, but more esp. a ballet or opera where it accomp. the rise of the curtain; an E. could also be the beginning of each new scene in a ballet.

Entry. A 17th–18th-cent. Eng. term for Prelude.

Enunciation. *See* **Diction.**

Enzina (or **Encina**), **Juan del** (b. nr. Salamanca, 1469; d. León, 1534), Spa. poet, playwright & comp. Studied at Salamanca Univ., entered the service of the Duke of Alba at Toledo, was app. archdeacon of Málaga in 1509, went to Rome in 1514 and to the Holy Land in 1519, and became prior of León. Prod. the *Farsa de Placida e Vittoriano* in Rome and comp. many songs for his own plays.

Éolides, Les, symph. poem for orch. by Franck, on a poem of the same name by Leconte de Lisle; comp. 1876, 1st perf. Paris, 13. V. 1877.

Ephesian Matron, The, comic serenata by Dibdin (lib. by Isaac Bickerstaffe), prod. London, Ranelagh House, 12. V. 1769.

Epidiapente (from Gr. *See also* **Diapente**). A 5th higher. The term is used esp. for canons in the 5th.

Epidiatessaron (from Gr.). A 4th higher.

Épine, Francesca Margherita de l' (b. ?; d. ?, 9–10. VIII. 1746), It. or Fr. singer. 1st came to London in 1692, remaining there until her death and marrying Pepusch in 1718.

Épinette (Fr.) = Spinet.

Episode. An incid. passage in a comp.

that may be described as a digression from the main theme or themes. It may or may not be derived from the chief thematic material: in a fugue it usually is so derived, whereas in a rondo it is as a rule an entirely new idea placed between 2 recurrences of the subject, but may assume the function of a 2nd subject, as in so. form.

Equal Temperament. The tuning of an inst., esp. the pf. or org., by dividing the 8ve into 12 semitones all divided by exactly the same ratio of vibrations, as distinct from Just Intonation, where the intervals vary slightly and the sharps and flats are not precisely the same in pitch.

Equal Voices. A voc. comp. written for more than 1 voice of similar compass, e.g. 2 sops. or 3 tens. (also, more loosely, for such combs. as 2 cons. and 2 basses—because they are all low voices), is said to be for E. V.

Equale (It., plur. *Equali* = equals). A term used for inst. pieces, esp. trombones (e.g. Beethoven's E.) written for a group of similar insts.

Equivoci, Gli (*The Doubles*), opera by Storace (lib. by Lorenzo da Ponte, based on Shakespeare's *Comedy of Errors*), prod. Vienna, Burg Theatre, 27. XII. 1786.

Equivoci nel sembiante, Gli (*Dissimilarity in Similarity*), opera by A. Scarlatti (lib. by Domenico Filippo Contini), prod. Rome, Teatro Capranica, II. 1679. S.'s 1st opera.

Érard, Pierre (b. Paris, 1796; d. Passy nr. Paris, 18. VIII. 1855), Fr. pf. & hp. maker. Joined his uncle Sébastien É. in business.

Érard, Sébastien (b. Strasburg, 5. IV. 1752; d. ?, 5. VIII. 1831), Fr. pf. & hp. maker, uncle of prec., founder of the firm, estab. *c.* 1777.

Erba, Dionigi (b. ?; d. ?), It. 17th-cent. comp. Chapel master at the church of San Francesco, Milan, in 1692. Wrote (?) a Magnificat for double choir from which (?) Handel borrowed for *Israel in Egypt*.

Erckmann-Chatrian (Émile E., 1822–99; Alexandre C., 1826–90), Fr. novelists. *See* **Amico Fritz** (Mascagni), **Edwards (J.)** (*Friend Fritz*), **Fourdrain** (*Rantzau*), **Juif polonais** (C. Erlanger), **Maréchal** (*Ami Fritz*), **Mascagni** (*Rantzau*), **Roland-Manuel** (*Ami F.*), **Walthew** (*Friend F.*), **Weiss (K.)** (*Polish Jew*).

Ercole amante (*Hercules as Lover*), opera by Cavalli (lib. by Francesco Buti), prod. Paris, Tuileries, 7. II. 1662. The only opera specially written for Paris by C. The ballet m. was by Lully. The title alludes to the marriage of Louis XIV.

Erdmann, Eduard (b. Wenden, Latvia, 5. III. 1896), Baltic-Ger. pfst. & comp. Educ. at Riga and studied pf. with Ansorge and comp. with Tiessen in Berlin. Toured as pfst. from 1919 and propagated modern m.; prof. of comp. at Cologne from 1925.

Works incl. 2 syms., pf. Conc.; So. for unaccomp. v.; pf. works; songs, &c.

Erdmannsdoerffer, Max von (b. Nuremberg, 14. IV. 1848; d. Munich, 14. II. 1905), Ger. cond. & comp. Studied at the Leipzig Cons. Became dir. of the Imp. Rus. Mus. Soc. in Moscow, 1882. Comp. chor. works, chamber m., &c.

Erk, Ludwig Christian (b. Wetzlar, 6. I. 1807; d. Berlin, 25. XI. 1883), Ger. orgst., cond. & ed. Studied under his father, orgst. at Wetzlar, and André at Offenbach. Became a mus. educst. and chor. cond., from 1836 in Berlin, and ed. a collection of old Ger. songs and so-called folksongs, *Deutscher Liederhort*.

Erkel, Ferencz (b. Békésgyula, 7. XI. 1810; d. Budapest, 15. VI. 1893), Hung. comp. As a pfst. and cond. he organized mus. life at Kolozsvar in his early days and in the 1830s went to Budapest as asst. cond. at the Ger. theatre, becoming cond. of the Nat. Theatre in 1837. In 1845 he gained the prize in a competition for a Hung. nat. anthem. He founded the Budapest Phil. Soc. in 1853 and was dir. of the royal High School of M. in 1875–89. His operas were very popular for their patriotic subjects and nat. m.

Works incl. operas *Báthor Mária*, *Hunyadi László*, *Bánk Bán*, *Dozsa György*, *Brankovics*, *Nóvtolen Hösök*, *Istvan Kiraly* (*King Stephen*); many songs, &c.

Erlanger, Camille (b. Paris, 25. V. 1863; d. Paris, 24. IV. 1919), Fr. comp. Studied at the Paris Cons. and gained the Prix de Rome in 1888.

Works incl. operas *Saint Julien l'Hospitalier* (after Flaubert), *Kermaria*, *Le Juif polonais* (after Erckmann-Chatrian), *Aphrodite*, *Bacchus triomphant*, *La Sorcière*, *Le Fils de l'étoile* & *La Forfaiture*; cantata *Velléda*; *Sérénade carnavalesque* for orch.; pf. pieces; *Poèmes russes* & other songs, &c.

Erlanger, Frédéric d' (b. Paris, 29. V. 1868; d. London, 23. IV. 1943), Fr. (anglicized) banker & comp. He had only private lessons in m. and was largely self-taught. Settled in London and became naturalized, but retained the Fr. title of Baron.

Works incl. operas *Jehan de Saintré*, *Inez Mendo* & *Tess* (after Hardy's *Tess of the d'Urbervilles*); Requiem;

Suite symphonique for orch.; *Concerto symphonique* for pf. & orch., v. Conc.: stg. 4tet, pf. 5tet; songs, &c.

Erlkönig (*Erl King*), one of Schubert's 1st great songs, a setting of a ballad by Goethe, comp. 1815 at the age of 18, 1st sung in public by Johann Michael Vogl, Vienna, 7. III. 1821, pub. as Op. 1 that year.

Ermelinda Talèa Pastorella Arcada. *See* **Maria Antonia Walpurga.**

Ernani, opera by Verdi (lib. by Francesco Maria Piave, based on Victor Hugo's drama *Hernani*), prod. Venice, Teatro La Fenice, 9. III. 1844. The 1st of V.'s operas prod. outside Milan.

Ernelinde, Princesse de Norvège, opera by Philidor (lib. by Antoine Alexandre Henri Poinsinet), prod. Paris, Opéra, 24. XI. 1767.

Ernst, Heinrich Wilhelm (b. Brno, 6. V. 1814; d. Nice, 8. X. 1865), Morav. vst. and comp. Pupil of Böhm, Seyfried and Mayseder in Vienna. Lived in Paris for 6 years and then travelled much.

Works incl. concs., fantasies, vars., an *Elégie*, &c. for v., also, with Heller, *Pensées fugitives* for v. & pf.

Ernste Gesänge (Brahms). *See* **Vier ernste Gesänge.**

Ero e Leandro (*Hero and Leander*), opera by Bottesini (lib. by Boito, at 1st intended for himself), prod. Turin, Teatro Regio, 11. I. 1879.

Opera by Mancinelli (lib. do.), 1st prod. as a cantata, in Eng., Norwich Festival, 8. X. 1896; 1st stage prod. Madrid, Teatro Real, 30. XI. 1897.

Eroe cinese, L' (*The Chinese Hero*), opera by Bonno (lib. by Metastasio), prod. Vienna, Schönbrunn Palace, at court, 13. V. 1752.

Eroica (It. fem. adj. = heroic). An adj. sometimes used in titles of mus. works, as for the

'Eroica' Symphony. Beethoven's 3rd Sym., in E♭ maj., Op. 55, written in 1803–4 and ded. to Prince Lobkowitz. The ded. was at first intended for Napoleon, but when B. heard of his assuming the title of emperor, he angrily changed his mind and called the work 'Sinfonia eroica composta per festeggiare il sovvenire di un grand' uomo' ('Heroic Sym. comp. to celebrate the memory of a great man.')

'Eroica' Variations. A set of pf. vars. in E♭ maj. by Beethoven, Op. 35, concluding with a fugue, comp. in 1802 and ded. to Count Moritz Lichnowsky. The theme is that used later (again for vars.) in the finale of the 3rd ('Eroica') Sym. and previously as a Country Dance and in the *Prometheus* ballet.

Errars, Jean (b. ?; d. ?), Fr. 14th-cent. troubadour, 24 of whose songs are preserved.

Erreur d'un moment, L', ou La Suite de Julie (*The Error of a Moment, or Julie Continued*), opera by Dezède (lib. by Jacques Marie Boutet de Monvel), prod. Paris, Comédie-Italienne, 14. VI. 1773.

Errico, Corrado (15th–16th cent.), It. poet. *See* **Pizzetti** (*Rappresentazione di Santa Uliva*).

Esclarmonde, opera by Massenet (lib. by Édouard Blau & Louis de Gramont), prod. Paris, Opéra-Comique, 15. V. 1889.

Escobar, ? (b. ?; d. ?), Spa. 16th-cent. comp. Chapel master at Seville early in the cent. Comp. church m. and secular pieces for 3 & 4 voices.

Escobar, João de (b. ?; d. ?), Port. 17th-cent. comp. Wrote a treatise on the theory and practice of m. (lost) and comp. motets pub. at Lisbon in 1620.

Escobedo, Bartolomeo (b. Zamora, *c.* 1515; d. Segovia, ? 1563), Spa. comp. Entered the Papal Chapel in Rome in 1536, acted as judge in a dispute between Vicentino and Lusitano in 1551. In 1554 he returned to Spa. as chapel master at Segovia. Wrote masses, motets, magnificats, Miserere, &c.

Escribano, Juan (b. ?; d. Rome, 1558), Spa. singer & comp. Sang in the Papal Chapel in Rome, 1507–39. Wrote church m., chansons for several voices, &c.

Escudier, Léon (b. Castelnaudary, Aude, 17. IX. 1821; d. Paris, 22. VI. 1881) and

Escudier, Marie (b. Castelnaudary, Aude, 29. VI. 1819; d. Paris, 18. IV. 1880), Fr. writers on m., brothers, who did most of their work jointly. It incl. biogs. of singers and of Rossini, a mus. dictionary, &c., and they ed. *La France musicale.* L. became dir. of the Théâtre Italien in 1876.

Eslava y Elizondo, Miguel Hilarion (b. Burlada, Navarre, 21. X. 1807; d. Madrid, 23. VI. 1878), Spa. vst., church musn., comp. & ed. App. chapel master at Borgo de Osma in 1828 and later at Seville, where he took holy orders. Ed. *Lira sacro-hispana,* a collection of Spa. church m. in 10 vols., and the *Gaceta musical de Madrid.* App. prof. at the Real Cons. de Música in Madrid, 1854.

Works incl. operas *Il solitario, La tregua di Ptolemaide* & *Pedro el cruel;* Miserere for Seville cath., masses, motets, psalms & other church m.; org. works.

Esmeralda, opera by Fabio Campana (1815–82) (lib. by Giorgio Tommaso Cimino, based on Victor Hugo's novel, *Notre-Dame de Paris*), prod. St. Petersburg, 30. XII. 1869.

Opera by Dargomizhsky (lib. by comp., trans from Victor Hugo's lib. based on his *Notre-Dame de Paris*, and written for Louise Angélique Bertin (1805–77) for her opera prod. Paris, 1836), prod. Moscow, 17. XII. 1847.

Opera by G. Thomas (lib. by Theophilus Julius Henry Marzials & Alberto Randegger, based on Hugo), prod. London, Drury Lane Theatre, 26. III. 1883.

España, rhapsody for orch. by Chabrier on Spa. tunes collected by the comp. during a visit to Spa. in 1882–3; comp. 1883 and 1st perf. Paris, XI. 1883.

Esplá, Oscar (b. Alicante, 5. VIII. 1886), Spa. comp. Studied civil engineering and took the degree of doctor of philosophy, but also worked at m. and took a prize for an orch. suite in Vienna in 1909. Settled at Brussels in 1936.

Works incl. ballets *El contrabandista* & *Ciclopes*; symph. poems *El sueño de Eros, La vela de armas de Don Quixote* & *Los Cumbres, Poema de niños, Ambito de la danza* & *Levantine Suite* for orch.; 5tet; v. & pf. So.; So., Scherzo & other works for pf., &c.

Esposito, Michele (b. Castellamare nr. Naples, 29. IX. 1855; d. Florence, 26. XI. 1929), It. pfst. & comp. Studied at the Naples Cons., lived in Paris in 1878–82 and was then app. prof. of pf. at R. Ir. A.M. at Dublin, where in 1899 he estab. the Dublin Orch. Soc., which he cond.

Works incl. operetta *The Postbag*; incid. m. for Douglas Hyde's *The Tinker and the Fairy*; cantata *Deirdre*; Ir. Sym., ovt. to Shakespeare's *Othello*; stg. 4tet; sos. for v. & pf. and co. & pf., &c.

Essential Discord. A chord which is dissonant according to acoustic theory, but whose notes belong to the key in which a comp. or passage is written and has become sufficiently current to be introd. without preparation.

Essipova, Anna Nikolaievna (b. St. Petersburg, 1. II. 1851; d. St. Petersburg, 18. VIII. 1914), Rus. pfst. & teacher. Studied at the St. Petersburg Cons., esp. under Leschetizky, whom she married in 1880, separating in 1892. She toured widely and taught many pfsts.

Estampes (*Engravings*), a set of 3 pf. pieces by Debussy, comp. 1903: 1. *Pagodes*, 2. *Soirée dans Grenade*, 3. *Jardins sous la pluie*.

Estampida (Provençal). A dance-song used by the Troubadours in the 13th–14th cents.

Esther, orat. by Handel (words by Samuel Humphreys, based on Racine's drama), prod. as a masque, entitled *Haman and Mordecai*, Cannons nr. Edgware, 29. VIII. 1720; as an orat. London, King's Theatre, Haymarket, 2. V. 1732.

Estinto (It. = extinct, dead). A direction indicating that a passage is to be perf. in a toneless manner.

Estompé (Fr. lit. stumped, shaded off) = damped, muffled. A direction frequently used by Debussy where he asks for a veiled or dull tone.

Estonian Composers. *See* **Baltic Composers.**

Estrada, Juan (García) (b. Buenos Aires, 8. XI. 1895), Arg. comp. Pupil of Ibert in Paris.

Works incl. *Tres aires argentinos* for orch.; pf. pieces; songs, &c.

Etheredge, George (1635–? 91), Eng. playwright. *See* **Staggins** (*Man of Mode*).

Étoile du Nord, L' (*The North Star*), opera by Meyerbeer (lib. by Scribe), prod. Paris, Opéra-Comique, 16. II. 1854.

Étouffé (Fr. = stifled, smothered). A direction to deaden the tone on insts. where it is liable to vibrate on after being sounded, as on the hp. or the kettledrums.

Étranger, L' (*The Stranger*), opera by d'Indy (lib. by comp.), prod. Brussels, Théâtre de la Monnaie, 7. I. 1903.

Ettinger, Max (b. Lwów, Pol., 27. XII. 1874), Ger. comp. Studied in Berlin and Munich and lived at both places until 1933, when he went into exile in It. Swi.

Works incl. operas *Clavigo* (after Goethe), *Judith* (after Hebbel), *Frühlingserwachen* (after Frank Wedekind), *Juana* (after Georg Kaiser), *Dolores*; *Old English Suite* (from virginal pieces), *Suite of Old Dances*, *3 Traumbilder*, *An den Wassern Babylons* for orch.; orat. *Moses*, *Weisheit des Orients* (from Omar Khayyám) for solo voices, chor. & orch.; stg. 4tet; sos. for v. & pf. and co. & pf., suite for va. & pf.; songs, &c.

Étude (Fr. = study). Strictly speaking an E. is a technical exercise for an inst. (more rarely a voc.) perf., but in practice it takes the form of a comp. of greater or lesser mus. value. Es. may be as much exercises in expression (e.g. many of Stephen Heller's) as in technique, and at their best (e.g. Chopin's) they will combine both purposes.

Études symphoniques, a set of 12 concert studies for pf. by Schumann, Op. 13, at first entitled *Études en forme de variations*, comp. in 1834. They are vars. on a theme by the father of Ernestine von Fricken, with whom S. was in love at that time, but they are ded. to Sterndale Bennett, in whose honour S. introd. into the finale a theme from **Marschner's** *Ivanhoe* opera *Der Templer und die Jüdin*: a song in praise of Eng.

Etwas (Ger. =somewhat, rather). Ger. comps. who give directions in their own language use the word to make sure that an indication of tempo or expression is obeyed in moderation.

Eugene Onegin, opera by Tchaikovsky (lib. by comp. & Konstantin S. Shilovsky, based on Pushkin's poem-novel), prod., by students of the Cons., Moscow, 29. III. 1879.

Eunuch Flute. A obs. wood-wind inst. with a mouthpiece containing a membrane vibrating when the player sang into it. It dates back to the 16th cent. at least, but was never much more than a toy.

Eunuch Singers. *See* **Castrati.**

Euphonium (*see also* **Saxhorn**). A brass inst. of the Tuba variety, but playing parts in the ten. range, used chiefly in military and brass bands.

Euphony. Suavity and harmoniousness of sound, the opposite of Cacophony.

Eur. (abbr.) = Europe, European.

Eurhythmics. A system of teaching mus., esp. rhythmic, perception by means of bodily mvts., invented by Jaques-Dalcroze.

Euridice, L', opera by Caccini (lib. by Ottavio Rinuccini), prod. Florence, Palazzo Pitti, 5. XII. 1602.

Opera by Peri (lib. do.), prod. Florence, Palazzo Pitti, 6. X. 1600.

Euripides (480–6 or 5 B.C.), Gr. dramatist. *See* **Alcestis** (Handel), **Alkestis** (Boughton & Wellesz), **Bacchantinnen** (Wellesz), **Bell** (*Hippolytus*), **Bruneau** (*Bacchantes*), **Coerne** (*Trojan Women*), **Damrosch (W.)** (*Electra, Iphigenia in Aulis, Medea*), **Drysdale** (*Hippolytus*), **Elwart** (*Alcestis*), **Enesco** (*Œdipe*), **Foulds** (*Trojan Women*), **Gray (C.)** (do.), **Ifigenia in Aulide** (Caldara, Cherubini, Graun & Zingarelli), **Ifigenia in Tauride** (Galuppi, Maio & Traetta), **Iphigénie en Aulide** (Gluck), **Iphigénie en Tauride** (Campra, Gluck & Piccinni), **Koreshtchenko** (*Trojan W.* & *Iphigenia in A.*), **Lloyd (C. H.)** (*Alcestis*), **Mulè** (*Bacchae, Medea, Cyclops, Hippolytus, Iphigenia in A.* & *in T.*), **Nottara** (*Hecuba*), **Pijper** (*Cyclops* & *Bacchantes*), **Riadis** (*Hecuba*), **Salviucci** (*Alcestis*), **Schürmann** (*Getreue Alceste*), **Senilov** (*Hippolytus*), **Slonimsky** (*Orestes*), **Taubert** (*Medea*), **Toch** (*Bacchantes*), **Walker** (*Rhesus* & *Hymn to Dionysus*), **Wood (C.)** (*Ion* & *Iphigenia in T.*).

Europe galante, L' (*Amorous Europa*), opera-ballet by Campra (lib. by Antoine Houdar de la Motte), prod. Paris, Opéra, 24. X. 1697.

Euryanthe, opera by Weber (lib. by Helmine von Chézy), prod. Vienna, Kärntnertor Theatre, 25. X. 1823.

Eusebius. One of the 2 imaginary characters, Florestan and E., used by Schumann as pseudonyms for his critical writings and also introd. into his m. (*Carnaval, Davidsbündlertänze*) to personify what he felt to be his dual character as an artist. F. repres. him as an impetuous romantic and E. as a dreamer.

Euterpe. The Muse of lyric poetry in Gr. mythology, and since such poetry was sung, also the Muse of m., which had no separate patroness among the 9 Muses, doubtless because in ancient Gr. it had no separate existence as an art.

Evangelimann, Der (*The Gospel Man*), opera by Kienzl (lib. by comp., based on a story by Leopold Florian Meissner), prod. Berlin, Opera, 4. V. 1895.

Evans, Edwin (b. London, 1. IX. 1874; d. London, 3. III. 1945), Eng. m. critic. App. critic to the *Pall Mall Gazette* in 1912 and the *Daily Mail* in 1933. President of the I.S.C.M. in succession to Edward Dent in 1938. He wrote much on behalf of modern m.

Eve of St. John, The, opera by Mackenzie (lib. by Eleanor Farjeon, based on Scott's ballad), prod. Liverpool, 16. IV. 1924.

Éventail de Jeanne, L' (*Joan's Fan*), ballet by Auric, Delannoy, Ferroud, Ibert, Milhaud, Poulenc, Ravel, Roland-Manuel, Roussel & Schmitt (chgph. by Alice Bourgat), prod. Paris, in private, 16. VI. 1927; Opéra, II. 1929.

Everyman, incid. m. for Hugo von Hofmannsthal's Ger. version of the 15th-cent. Eng. morality play, *Jedermann*, by Sibelius, Op. 83, comp. 1916.

Setting of the morality play for solo voices, chor. & orch. by Walford Davies, prod. Leeds Festival, 1904.

See also **Lehmann (L.)** & **Martin (F.).**

Evesham, Walter of. *See* **Odington.**

Evirati (It.). *See* **Castrati.**

Exaquir. *See* **Chekker.**

Exaudet, Joseph (b. Rouen, *c.* 1710; d. Paris, *c.* 1763), Fr. vst. & comp. Played at the Rouen Acad. concerts and joined the Paris Opéra orch. in 1749.

Works incl. sos. for v. & bass and trios for 2 vs. & bass; a minuet of his is still popular.

Eximeno, Antonio (b. Valencia, 26. IX. 1729; d. Rome, 9. VI. 1808), Spa. Jesuit & mus. theorist. Studied at Salamanca Univ. and became prof. of mathematics and m. at the military acad. of Segovia. Settled in **Rome**

when the Jesuits were expelled from Spa. Wrote a treatise *Dell' origine e delle regole della musica* and a novel *Don Lazarillo Vizcardi* dealing with a mus. adventurer on the model of Don Quixote.

Expert, Henri (b. Bordeaux, 12. V. 1863), Fr. mcolst. Studied, and later taught, at Niedermeyer's school in Paris, and was also a pupil of Franck and Gigout. Prof. of m. at the École des Hautes Études Sociales and librarian of the Cons. library. Ed. series of old Fr. m., *Les Maîtres musiciens de la renaissance française* and *Monuments de le musique française*, of settings of Ronsard's poetry, old songs, church & hpchd. m., &c.

Exposition. The 1st setting forth of thematic material in a comp. In a fugue the E. is the statement of the subject by its 1st entry in each voice; in a rondo the statement of the subject up to the 1st episode; in a so.-form mvt. the whole 1st section up to the double bar after which the working-out section begins.

Expression Marks. All the indications by which the comp. indicates his wishes as to the manner of perf. of a work, esp. from the dynamic point of view (*forte, piano, crescendo, diminuendo*); but they may extend also to matters of speed and rhythm (e.g. *rallentando, rubato, accelerando,* &c.). E. Ms. were little used before the 18th cent. and hardly at all before the 17th, but have often gone to fantastic lengths in the 20th.

Expressionism. A term properly belonging to painting, esp. in Ger. in the 1910s, but loosely applied to comps. who aimed at a similar kind of interpretation, not of outward and visible things, but of moods and states of mind, not by the accepted symbols of romanticism, but by abstractions which have no superficially perceptible connection with those moods and states, but are said to be their outward psychological manifestations.

Extemporization. *See* **Improvisation.**

Extravaganza (corrupt. from It. *stravaganza*). This hybrid word, Eng. with an It. ending, is sometimes used for a comp. of a freakish nature, esp. for a light and fantastic stage piece with m., e.g. Gilbert & Sullivan's *Trial by Jury*.

Eybler, Joseph von (b. Schwechat nr. Vienna, 8. II. 1765; d. Vienna, 24. VII. 1846), Aus. comp. Pupil of Albrechtsberger and, after holding var. apps. in Vienna, chief chapel master to the Aus. court in 1824.

Works incl. opera *Das Zauberschwert* and others; orat. *Die vier letzten Dinge*, Requiem in C min., cantata *Die Hirten bei der Krippe*, 2 Te Deums, 7 masses, offertories, graduals & other church m.; syms.; chamber m.; pf. pieces, &c.

Ezio (*Aetius*). Lib. by Metastasio:

Opera by Gluck, prod. Prague, Carnival 1750.

Opera by Handel, prod. London, King's Theatre, Haymarket, 15. I. 1732.

Opera by Hasse, prod. Dresden, at court, 20. I. 1755.

Opera by Jommelli, prod. Bologna, Teatro Malvezzi, 29. IV. 1741.

F

F. The note bounding the range of the scales of F maj. and min., and of the Lydian and Hypolocrian or Hyperphrygian (rejected) (Gr. Phrygian) modes.

f. The subdominant note in any key in Tonic Sol-fa notation, pronounced Fa.

f (abbr.). The symbol commonly employed in m. to indicate a loud (*forte*) tone. Progressively even louder dynamics are marked *ff*, *fff*, &c.

f **Holes** (or *ff* **Holes**). The sound-holes of insts. of the v. family, so called because of their shape.

Fa. The old name for the note F (*see* **Solmization**), still used in Lat. countries, and in Tonic Sol-fa notation the subdominant note in any key represented by the symbol f, pronounced Fa.

Fa-La. A light 16th–17th-cent. Eng. comp. for several voices of the ballet or canzone type. Its name derives from the syllables to which the refrain was sung.

Faa, Orazio (b. ?; d. ?), It. 16th-cent. comp. Pub. 2 books of madrigals in 1569 and 1571, set psalms to m. and comp. other church m.

Fabliau (old Fr. = fable). A Troubadour ballad with narrative words, distinct from the love songs sung by the Ts.

Fabre, Henri (1823–1915), Fr. entomologist & author. *See* **Festin de l'araignée** (Roussel).

Fabre (d'Eglantine), Philippe (François Nazaire) (1750–94), Fr. dramatist, revolutionist & amateur comp. (song 'Il pleut, il pleut, bergère'). *See* **Godard** (*Jeanne d'Arc*).

Fabri, Annibale Pio (b. Bologna, 1697; d. Lisbon, 12. VIII. 1760), It. ten. singer & comp. 1st went to Eng. in 1729. He was also known under the name of Balino.

Fabricius, Werner (b. Itzehoe, Holstein, 10. IV. 1633; d. Leipzig, 9. I. 1697), Ger. orgst. & comp. Studied under his father, Albert F., orgst. at Flensburg and under Selle and Scheidemann at the Hamburg Gymnasium. After pursuing other studies at Leipzig Univ., incl. law, he became mus. dir. at St. Paul's church there in 1656 and, in addition, at St. Nicolas' church in 1658. He was also public notary.

Works incl. motets, hymn tunes; sacred and secular songs for several voices; suites for viols & other insts., &c.

Fabritius, Albinus (b. ?; d. ?), Ger. 16th–17th-cent. comp. Lived (?) at Görlitz, Prus. Wrote motets, 25 of which were pub. in his lifetime in 1595, many of them re-issued in var. collections.

Faburden (Eng.). *See* **Fauxbourdon.**

Façade, diversion by Walton (poems by Edith Sitwell), privately prod. London, Chenil Gallery, Chelsea; 1st public perf. London, Aeolian Hall, 12. VI. 1923. 2 concert suites arr. later for enlarged orch. and for pf. duet. Prod. as a ballet (chgph. by Frederick Ashton), London, Cambridge Theatre, 26. IV. 1931.

Faccio, Franco (b. Verona, 8. III. 1840; d. Monza, 23. VII. 1891), It. cond. & comp. Studied at the Milan Cons., prod. his 1st opera there at the Cons. and the 2nd at the Teatro alla Scala in 1863. Boito was his friend and libst. App. prof. of harmony at the Cons. in 1868 and later cond. at the Carcano and Scala theatres. He was Verdi's cond. for *Aida* and *Otello* at Milan, 1872 & 1887.

Works incl. operas *Le sorelle d'Italia*, *I profughi fiamminghi*, *Amleto* (after Shakespeare's *Hamlet*); Symph. in F maj., &c.

Fackeltanz (Ger.) = Torch Dance.

Fading (Eliz. Eng.; obs.). A Burden or Refrain; also an Ir. dance.

Fage. *See* **La Fage.**

Fago, Nicola (b. Taranto, 19. I. 1676; d. Naples, 18. II. 1745), It. comp., nicknamed Il Tarantino from his birthplace. Studied at the Cons. de' Turchini at Naples under A. Scarlatti and Provenzale. Taught there later in succession to the latter.

Works incl. operas *Radamisto*, *Astarto*, *Masiello*, *Cassandra indovina* & others; an orat.; masses & other church m.; cantatas, &c.

Fagott (Ger.) = Bassoon.

Fagottino (It. lit. little bundle) = Tenoroon.

Fagotto (It. lit. fagot or bundle) = Bassoon also a 16-ft. reed org. stop prod. bn. tone.

Faignient, Noé (b. ?; d. ?), Flem. 16th-cent. comp. Wrote motets, madrigals, chansons, &c.

Fair Maid of Perth (Bizet). *See* **Jolie Fille de Perth.**

Fair Maid of the Mill (Schubert). *See* **Schöne Müllerin.**

Fair Melusina (Mendelssohn). *See* **Schöne Melusine.**

Fair of Sorotchintsy (Mussorgsky). *See* **Sorotchintsy Fair.**

Fairchild, Blair (b. Belmont, Mass., 23. VI. 1877; d. Paris, 23. IV. 1933), Amer. comp. Studied at Harvard Coll. under Paine and Spalding and later at Florence under Buonamici. Was in the U.S.A. diplomatic service 1901–3 and in the latter year settled in Paris for the rest of his life.

Works incl. ballet-pantomime *Dame Libellule*; symph. poems *East and West, Zál, Shah Feridoun*; *Légende & Étude symphonique* for v. & orch.; stg. 4tet, pf. 5tet, pf. Trio & other chamber m.; 2 v. & pf. sos.; chor. works; song cycle *Stornelli toscani* & others, &c.

Fairies, The, opera by John Christopher Smith (lib. by comp., based on Shakespeare's *A Midsummer Night's Dream*), prod. London, Drury Lane, 3. II. 1755.

Fairy Queen, The, opera by Purcell (lib. adapted from Shakespeare's *Midsummer Night's Dream* ? by Elkanah Settle), prod. London, Dorset Gardens Theatre, IV. 1692.

Faisst, Immanuel (Gottlob Friedrich) (b. Esslingen nr. Stuttgart, 13. X. 1823; d. Stuttgart, 5. VI. 1894), Ger. orgst. & comp. Studied theology at Tübingen Univ., but gave it up for m., in which he was self-taught according to Mendelssohn's advice. He travelled as orgst. and settled at Stuttgart, where he founded an org. school in 1847 and a soc. for the study of church m., and was one of the founders of the Cons. He wrote on and ed. m.

Works incl. cantata *Des Sängers Wiederkehr*, chor. setting of Schiller's *Die Macht des Gesanges*; double fugue for pf.; org. works; voc. 4tets, &c.

Falchi, Stanislao (b. Terni, 29. I. 1851; d. Rome, 17. XI. 1922), It. comp. Dir. of the Liceo Musicale di Santa Cecilia in Rome.

Works incl. operas *Lorhélia, Giuditta, Il trillo del diavolo*; Requiem; ovt. to Shakespeare's *Julius Caesar*; chamber m., &c.

Falcon, (Marie) Cornélie (b. ? Le Monastier nr. Le Puy, 28. I. 1814; d. Paris, 25. II. 1897), Fr. sop. singer. Student at the Paris Cons. and pupil of Nourrit for operatic acting. 1st appearance 1832, at the Opéra.

Falconi, Placido (b. Asola, *c.* 1530; d. Monte Cassino, after 1600), It. comp. He became a Benedictine at Brescia in 1549 and later a monk at Monte Cassino. Wrote church m.

Falconieri, Andrea (b. Naples, ?; d. Naples, 1656), It. comp. Lived at Florence in 1615.

Works incl. *Villanelle* for 1–3 voices with guitar, *Musiche* for 1–3 voices, inst. pieces, &c.

Faleni, Arturo (b. Chieti, It., 1877), Arg. comp. of It. descent. Studied at Genoa. In 1897 he settled at Buenos Aires and became an Arg. citizen. He founded a mus. acad. named after Verdi and wrote several educ. works on m.

Works incl. Ovt. in D maj., Fantasy, Fugue, symph. poem *The Earthquake* for orch.; pf. pieces; songs, &c.

Fall. A Cadence (e.g. 'dying fall') in Shakespeare; in the 17th cent. an **Appoggiatura.**

Fall, Leo (b. Olomouc, 2. II. 1873; d. Vienna, 16. IX. 1925), Aus. comp. Studied at the Vienna Cons. and became cond. at Berlin, Hamburg and Cologne. Wrote *c.* 25 works for the stage, chiefly operettas, incl. *Die Dollarprinzessin, Eternal Waltz, Die geschiedene Frau* (*The Girl in the Train*), *Der liebe Augustin* (*Princess Caprice*), *Madame Pompadour*, &c.

Falla, Manuel de (b. Cadiz, 23. XI. 1876), Spa. comp. Began to study the pf. in Madrid at the age of 8 and prod. a zarzuela, *Los amores de Inés*, written with very little tuition in comp. in 1902. This had no success, and he studied comp. with Pedrell, 1902–4. In 1905 he gained 2 prizes, for pf. playing and for his opera *La vida breve*. In 1907–14 he lived in Paris, but returned to Spa. and settled in Madrid on the outbreak of war. The prod. of *La vida breve* at Nice and Paris in 1913 and of the ballet *The Three-cornered Hat* in London in 1919 spread his reputation. In 1921 he moved to Granada and became more exclusively a nationalist comp. again; but had later works perf. in Eng., Paris and N.Y. During the Spa. Civil War he settled in S. Amer. and remained there.

Works incl. operas *La vida breve, Fuego fatuo* (based on Chopin's m.), *El retablo de maese Pedro* (for puppets, after Cervantes's *Don Quixote*); ballets, *El amor brujo, El sombrero de tres picos* (on Alarcón's story); *Noches en los jardines de España* for pf. & orch.; *Psyché* for m.-sop., fl., ob., clar., v., co. & hp.; Conc. for hpchd., fl., ob., clar., v. & co.; 4 Spa. pieces, *Fantasia baetica* & *Pour le tombeau de Paul Dukas* for pf.; *Homenaje: pour le tombeau de Debussy* for guitar; 3 songs (Gautier), 7 popular Spa. songs, *A Córdoba* (Góngora), for voice & hp., &c.

False Relations. The simultaneous or closely adjacent occurrence in a comp. in several parts of 2 notes a semitone apart, at least 1 of which must be foreign to the key of the passage in question. Such clashes, though harsh in sound and not normally accepted in good part-writing, may sound satisfactory if each part pursues a natural course of its own, and they can be used to make special points of expression. Byrd and the Eng. madrigalists cultivated F. Rs. deliberately with such ends in view.

Falsetto (It.). The tone-prod. of male singers resulting in notes above their normal pitch and sounding like those of an unbroken voice, and that normally cultivated by male altos. The voices of the Castrati in the 17th & 18th cents., however, were not F. voices, for they had never broken. F. notes are sometimes illegitimately prod. by tens. who are incapable of singing high notes softly in their normal register; they have also been used occasionally by comps. to prod. comic effects in opera, e.g. the phrase sung by Falstaff disguised as the Old Woman of Brentford in Nicolai's *Merry Wives of Windsor*.

Falsobordone (It.) = Fauxbourdon.

Falstaff. *See also* **At the Boar's Head; Lustigen Weiber von Windsor; Sir John in Love.**

Opera by Balfe (lib., in It., by S. Manfredo Maggioni, based on Shakespeare's *Merry Wives of Windsor*), prod. London, Her Majesty's Theatre, 19. VII. 1838.

Opera by Verdi (lib. by Boito, based on Shakespeare's *Merry Wives of Windsor* and *Henry* plays), prod. Milan, Teatro alla Scala, 9. II. 1893.

Symph. study by Elgar, Op. 68 (based on Shakespeare's *King Henry IV* & refs. to Falstaff in *King Henry V*), comp. 1913, prod. Leeds Festival, 2. X. 1913.

Falstaff, ossia Le tre burle (*Falstaff, or The Three Jests*), opera by Salieri (lib. by Carlo Prospero Defranceschi, after Shakespeare), prod. Vienna, Kärntnertor Theatre, 3. I. 1799.

Famintsin, Alexander Sergeievitch (b. Kaluga, 5. XI. 1841; d. St. Petersburg, 18. VII. 1896), Rus. critic & comp. Studied at St. Petersburg Univ. and m. under Hauptmann, Richter and Moscheles at Leipzig. App. prof. of mus. hist. at the St. Petersburg Cons. He wrote some valuable antiquarian books on m., but fiercely attacked the new nat. school headed by Balakirev.

Works incl. operas *Sardanapalus* & *Uriel Acosta* (after Gutzkow); *Rus. Rhapsody* for v. & orch.; 3 stg. 4tets, pf. 5tet, &c.

Fanciulla del West, La (*The Girl of the [Golden] West*), opera by Puccini (lib. by Guelfo Civinini & Carlo Zangarini, based on David Belasco's play), prod. N.Y., Metrop. Opera, 10. XII. 1910.

Fancy. The old Eng. term equivalent to the It. *fantasia*, used not in the modern sense for any comp. of a free or fantastic character (*see* **Fantasy**), but for a polyphonic comp. for a consort of viols or broken consort or keyboard inst. Fs. had no definitely determined form, but always made considerable use of ctpt. and were generally divided into a number of sections, played without a break but not thematically connected.

Fandango. A Spa. dance, prob. introd. from S. Amer. early in the 18th cent. It is in animated triple time, accomp. by several insts. among which only the guitar and castanets are obligatory. There is a slower Basque form, and it is this which Gluck used in the *Don Juan* ballet, and which Mozart closely copied from Gluck in *Figaro*, where it is the only piece attempting to suggest its Spa. setting.

Fandanguillo (Spa.). An Andalusian folksong.

Fanelli, Ernest (b. Paris, 29. VI. 1860; d. Paris, 24. XI. 1917), Fr. comp. Studied with Alkan and Delibes at the Paris Cons., but was too poor to make his way as a comp. and became perc. player in an orch.

Works incl. *Tableaux symphoniques* (on Gautier's *Roman de la momie*), *Suite rabelaisienne*, *Impressions pastorales*, *Les Humoresques* for orch.; stg. 5tet, &c.

Fanfare. A flourish of tpts., in Fr. also a brass band, in It. orig. the *toccata* (cf. 'tucket'). Fs. have also been written for other insts., though usually wind and mainly brass, or imitated in any medium (e.g. stgs. in Purcell's *Dido and Aeneas* or pf. in Debussy's *Feux d'artifice* prelude). In opera Fs. have frequently served as an excellent scenic effect (e.g. in Beethoven's *Fidelio*, Bizet's *Carmen*, Verdi's *Otello*, &c.).

Faniska, play with m. by Cherubini (lib., in Ger., by Josef Sonnleithner), prod. Vienna, Kärntnertor Theatre, 25. II. 1806.

Fantaisie (Fr.)
Fantasia (It.)
Fantasie (Ger.) } *See* **Fancy; Fantasy.**

Fantasiestück (Ger. = Fantastic Piece). A short inst. piece of a free or fantastic character, rather less extended as a rule than a fantasy and keeping to a single mvt. and mood, whereas the latter is usually in several connected sections.

Fantasio, opera by Ethel Smyth (lib. by comp. based on Musset's play), prod. in Ger., Weimar, 24. V. 1898.

Fantastic Symphony (Berlioz). *See* **Symphonie fantastique.**

Fantasy. An inst. comp. of a free or fantastic character, in no particular form, usually in a number of linked-up but not thematically connected sections. A F. may also be a comp. based on a chosen mus. theme from another comp.'s work, a folksong, a popular tune, an operatic air, &c.

Faramondo, opera by Handel (lib. by Apostolo Zeno, altered), prod. London, King's Theatre, Haymarket, 7. I. 1738.

Farandole (Fr.). A dance of Provence, prob. of Gr. orig. It is danced by large groups of people in procession through the streets and accomp. by pipe and tabor. The m. is in 6–8 time, so that the ex. in Bizet's *Arlésienne* m. is not traditionally correct, though very evocative.

Farce (Eng. & Fr., from Lat. *farcire* = to stuff, to lard). In earlier Eng. the verb had the meaning it still has in Fr. of stuffing food with seasoning, and in m. it was used for the practice of singing interpolations in liturgical m. (*see also* **Sequence & Tropes**). By the 9th cent. this had become habitual, and these intrusive passages were often frankly comic: hence the modern sense of the term.

Farewell, Absence and Return (Beethoven). *See* **Adieux, l'absence et le retour.**

Farewell Symphony. The nickname of a Sym. by Haydn, No. 45, in F♯ min., comp. in 1772 as a hint to Prince Esterházy that the private orch. at Esterház wished to obtain leave of absence. The finale was so scored that the players could drop out and leave the platform one by one until only 2 solo vs. were left.

Farinelli (real name Carlo Broschi) (b. Andria, 24. I. 1705; d. nr. Bologna, 15. VII. 1782), It. male sop. singer. Pupil of Porpora; made his 1st appearance in Rome, 1722, when he had already acquired some fame in southern It. Went to Vienna in 1724; first appeared in London in 1734 and had a great success there; then became attached to the Spa. court and retired to Bologna at an advanced age.

Farjeon, Harry (b. Hohokus, New Jersey, 6. V. 1787), Eng. comp. Pupil in London of Landon Ronald & others, and later at the R.A.M., where Corder was his comp. master. He taught harmony and comp. there later.

Works incl. operettas *Floretta, The Registry Office, A Gentleman of the Road*; *Hans Andersen* suite for small orch.; pf. conc.; stg. 4tets; v. & pf. sos.; suites, preludes & other works for pf.; song cycles & other songs, &c.

Farmer, Henry G(eorge). (b. Birr, 17. I. 1882), Ir. mus. scholar. Educ. at Glasgow Univ. He graduated as a scholar in Arabic and hist. and wrote much on Arabian m. and insts., ancient Sco. and Welsh m., &c.

Farmer, John (b. ?; d. ?), Eng. 16th–17th-cent. comp. He was (?) in the service of Edward de Vere, Earl of Oxford, and orgst. from (?) some time early in the 1590s of Christ Church cath. at Dublin until 1599, when he went to London. He wrote a treatise on the polyphonic setting of plainsong tunes.

Works incl. psalm tunes set for 4 voices contrib. to East's Psalter; madrigals, &c.

Farnaby, Giles (b. ? Truro, *c.* 1560; d. ? London, *c.* 1600), Eng. comp. He lived in London, where he married in 1587, and took the Mus.B. at Oxford in 1592.

Works incl. 20 canzonets for 4 and 1 for 8 voices, madrigals; psalm tunes set for 4 voices in East's Psalter; over 50 virginal pieces, &c.

Farquhar, George (1678–1707), Ir. dramatist. *See* **Croft** (*Twin Rivals*), **Eccles** (*Stage Coach*), **Finger** (*Sir Harry Wildair*), **Leveridge** (*Constant Couple, Recruiting Officer, Love and a Bottle*), **Purcell (D.)** (*Beaux's Stratagem, Constant Couple, Inconstant*).

Farrant, John (b. ?; d. ?), Eng. orgst. & comp. Orgst. of Ely cath., 1567–72, when he married Margaret Andras at Salisbury, where he became lay clerk and choirmaster at the cath. In 1587 he was app. orgst., but he was expelled in 1592 for an attack made on the dean. He then became orgst. of Hereford cath., but lost that post too in 1593 because of his ungovernable temper. Wrote church m.

Farrant, John (b. Salisbury, IX. 1575; d. Salisbury, 1618), Eng. orgst. & comp., son of prec. He became a choir-boy at the cath. under his father, and later orgst., holding the post in 1598–1606 and 1611–6, prob. without any interruption between. Wrote church m.

Farrant, Richard (b. ?; d. Windsor or Greenwich, 1581), Eng. orgst. & comp. Gentleman of the Chapel Royal in London until 1564, when he became orgst. and choirmaster at St. George's Chapel, Windsor.

Works incl. Service in A min. (usually sung in G min.), anthems *Call to remembrance* & *Hide not Thou Thy face* & other church m.; songs for plays prod. by him with the choir-boys before Queen Elizabeth, &c.

Farrenc (*née* Dumont), Louise (b. Paris, 31. V. 1804; d. Paris, 15. IX. 1875), Fr. pfst. & comp., wife of Jacques Hippolyte Aristide Farrenc (1794–1865), flst., writer on m. & pub. Pupil of Reicha, Hummel & Moscheles, she married in 1821, toured with her husband and was prof. of pf. at the Paris Cons. 1842–73. Ed. the *Trésor des pianistes* with her husband, and her pf. works were favourably noticed by Schumann.

Works incl. 2 syms., 3 ovts.; chamber m.; v. & co. sos.; studies, sos., &c. for pf., &c.

Farsa (or **Farsa per musica**) (It. = farce [for m.]). An It. term of the early 19th cent. for a type of comic opera after the Fr. style, i.e. with spoken dialogue.

Farwell, Arthur (b. St. Paul, 23. IV. 1872), Amer. comp. and educst. Studied engineering, but afterwards went to Ger. as a pupil of Humperdinck and Pfitzner and to Guilmant in Paris. On returning to U.S.A. in 1899 he began to collect Indian folk m., and became a mus. lecturer, critic and pub. After var. appts. in N.Y. he went to the m. dept. of the Michigan State Coll.

Works incl. masque *Caliban* for the Shakespeare tercentenary; Sym., Symbolistic Studies (1 based on Whitman), suite *The Gods of the Mountain, Prelude to a Spiritual Drama* & other orch. works; symph. song suite *Mountain Song* & other chor. works; stg. 4tet, pf. 5tet; sos. for v. solo and for v. & pf.; v. pieces; pf. works, &c.

Fasch, Carl Friedrich (Christian) (b. Zerbst, 18. XI. 1736; d. Berlin, 3. VIII. 1800), Ger. hpchdst. & comp. Pupil of his father and of Hertel at Strelitz. In 1756 he was app. accompst. to Frederick II of Prus. at Potsdam & Berlin on the recommendation of F. Benda. During the Seven Years War, 1756–63, he was reduced to giving lessons, but was reapp. at court and in 1774–6 was also in charge of the court opera. Later he devoted himself to church m.

Works incl. Mass for 16 voices, orat. *Giuseppe riconosciuto*, psalms & other church m.; canons, &c.

Fasch, Johann Friedrich (b. Buttelstedt nr. Weimar, 15. IV. 1688; d. Zerbst, 5. XII. 1758), Ger. orgst. & comp., father of prec. Pupil of Kuhnau at St. Thomas's school, Leipzig. He founded the 'Collegium musicum' at Leipzig, travelled after 1714, held var. posts at Gera, Zeitz and in the service of Count Morzin at Lukaveč, Boh., and in 1722 was app. chapel master at Zerbst.

Works incl. 3 operas; masses, a Requiem, church cantatas, motets, a Passion; ovts.; trios, sos., &c.

Fasolo, Giovanni Battista (b. Asti, ?; d. ?), It. 17th-cent. monk, orgst. & comp. He became a Franciscan *c.* 1645 and in 1659 was app. chapel master to the Archbishop of Monreale at Palermo.

Works incl. *Arie spirituali*, cantatas, ariettas, sacred & secular songs; org. works; guitar pieces, &c.

Fauré, Gabriel (Urbain) (b. Pamiers nr. Foix, 12. V. 1845; d. Paris, 4. XI. 1924), Fr. comp. Studied at Niedermeyer's school of m. in Paris, 1854–66, and became church orgst. at Rennes in the latter year. Returned to Paris in 1870, became orgst. 1st at Saint-Sulpice and then at Saint-Honoré, and choirmaster at the Madeleine in 1877, being app. orgst. there in 1896, a post he held until 1905, when he became dir. of the Cons., where he had been prof. since 1896. He resigned in 1920. He had many distinguished comp. pupils.

Works incl. m.-drama *Prométhée*, opera *Pénélope*; incid. m. *Caligula* (Dumas), *Shylock* (*Merchant of Venice*: Shakespeare), *La Voix du bonheur* (G. Clemenceau), *Pelléas et Mélisande* (Maeterlinck); *Pavane*, suite *Masques et bergamasques*, &c. for orch.; Sym. (unpub.); *Ballade* & *Fantaisie* for pf. & orch., *Romance* for v. & orch.; 2 pf. 5tets, 2 pf. 4tets; 2 sos. for v. & pf., 2 sos. for co. & pf.; pieces for v. & pf., co. & pf. and fl. & pf.; *Cantique de Racine* & *Les Djinns* (Hugo) for chor. & orch.; *La Naissance de Vénus* for solo voices, chor. & orch.; *Madrigal* for voc. 4tet; Requiem for solo voices, chor. & orch.; *Messe basse* for fem. voices & org.; 11 misc. religious voc. pieces; 34 op. nos. of pf. m. incl. 3 *Romances sans paroles*, 5 Impromptus, 13 Barcarolles; 4 Valses-caprices, 8 Nocturnes, Theme & Vars., 8 *Pièces brèves*, 9 Preludes; *Dolly*, 6 pieces for pf. duet; 96 songs incl. cycles *Poème d'un jour*, 5 *Mélodies de Verlaine*, *La Bonne Chanson* (Verlaine), *La Chanson d'Ève* (Charles van Lerberghe), *Le Jardin clos* (do.), *Mirages*, *L'Horizon chimérique*, &c.

Faure, Jean-Baptiste (b. Moulins, 15. I. 1830; d. Paris, 9. XI. 1914), Fr. bar. singer. Studied at the Paris Cons. Made his 1st appearance at the Opéra-Comique in 1852 and from 1861 was attached for many years to the Opéra.

Faust. *See also* **Arnold (S.)** (*Harlequin Dr. Faustus*), **Damnation de**

Faust (Berlioz), **Doktor Faust** (Busoni), **Goethe**; **Lenau**; **Marlowe**; **Mefistofele** (Boito), **Petit Faust** (Hervé), **Reutter** (H.) (*Doktor F.*), **Szenen aus Goethes ' Faust '** (Schumann).

Ballet by Costa, Panizza & Bajetti (chgph. by Jules Perrot), prod. Milan, Teatro alla Scala, 12. II. 1848.

Episodes from Lenau's *Faust*: 2 orch. pieces by Liszt, *Night Procession* & *Dance in the Village Inn* (1st *Mephisto Waltz*), comp. *c.* 1860, 1st perf. Weimar, 8. III. 1861.

Opera by Gounod (lib. by Jules Barbier & Michel Carré, based on Goethe's drama), prod. Paris, Théâtre Lyrique, 19. III. 1859.

Opera by Spohr (lib. by Joseph Karl Bernard, founded on the Faust legend without ref. to Goethe's work, not completed at that time), prod. Prague, 1. IX. 1816.

Opera by Zöllner (lib. by comp., based on Goethe's drama), prod. Munich, 19. X. 1887.

Ovt. by Wagner, not for Goethe's drama, but a kind of symph. poem on it, comp. Paris, XI. 1839 after hearing Beethoven's syms. at the Cons.

Faust-Symphonie, Eine, sym. by Liszt, based on Goethe's drama, 'in 3 character pictures': 1. *Faust*; 2. *Gretchen*; 3. *Mephistopheles*, with final chor. ' Alles Vergängliche ist nur ein Gleichnis '; finished, without the chor., 19. X. 1854, chor. added 1857 and revised 1880; 1st perf. Weimar, Court Theatre, 5. IX. 1857, on the occasion of the unveiling of the Goethe-Schiller monument. The work is ded. to Berlioz.

Fausta (i.e. Empress F., wife of Constantine I), opera by Donizetti (lib. by Domenico Gilardoni), prod. Naples, Teatro San Carlo, 12. I. 1832.

Fausto (*Faust*), opera by Louise Angélique Bertin (1805—77) (lib., in It., by comp., based on Goethe's drama), prod. Paris, Théâtre Italien, 8. III. 1831. The 1st It. *Faust* opera and the only one by a woman. B. was the daughter of Berlioz's ed. of the *Journal des Débats*: he may have had a hand in the work; at any rate he almost certainly suggested the subject.

Faut (=Fa ut). *See* **Gamut.**

Faux Lord, Le (*The False Lord*), opera by Piccinni (lib. by Giuseppe Maria Piccinni, the comp.'s son), prod. Paris, Comédie-Italienne, 6. XII. 1783.

Fauxbourdon (Fr. lit. false drone). The Fr. term is generally used in Eng., though Faburden is quite a good equivalent, and is used by Shakespeare. The forerunner of the Descant, dating back to the 14th cent. at latest, prob. of Eng. origin. The name is said to derive from the tendency in F. to place the melody in the treble part instead of keeping it in the lowest part, as in Organum or Diaphony, with the result that the bass (or ' drone ' or ' burden ') was not a real tune, but a ' false '. one. Later on, however, the melody reverted to the ten. part, and F. became merely a top-dressing, eventually growing indistinguishable from Descant.

Favart, Charles Simon (1710–92), **Fr.** playwright & libst. *See* **Bastien und Bastienne** (Mozart), **Cythère assiégée** (Gluck), **Lottchen am Hofe** (**J. A.** Hiller), **Moissonneurs** (Duni), **Rosina** (Shield), **Süssmayr** (*Soliman II*).

Favart (*née* **Duronceray**), **Marie Justine Benoiste** (b. Avignon, 15. VI. 1727; d. Paris, 21. IV. 1772), Fr. dancer, actress & singer, wife of prec. After making her début as a dancer in 1744, she married Favart in 1745 and in 1751 joined the Comédie-Italienne. In 1753 she appeared in her own *Bastien et Bastienne* (the direct model for Mozart's little opera), a parody of Rousseau's *Devin du village* with popular tunes in the style of a ballad opera.

Favola d'Orfeo, La (*The Fable of Orpheus*), opera by Casella (lib. by Angelo Ambrogini =Poliziano, prod. Mantua, ducal court, 18. 7. 1472, with m. by one Germi), prod. Venice, Teatro Goldoni, 6. IX. 1932.

Opera by Monteverdi (lib. by Alessandro Striggio), prod. Mantua, at the court of the Hereditary Prince Francesco Gonzaga, Carnival 1607.

Favola per musica (It. =fable for m.). An early It. term for opera of a legendary or mythological character: actually a story of that kind in dramatic form written for the purpose of being set to m.

Favorite, La, opera by Donizetti (lib., in Fr., by Alphonse Royer & Gustave Vaëz, with Scribe's assistance), prod. Paris, Opéra, 2. XII. 1840.

Faydit, Gaucelm (b. Uzerche, Limousin, *c.* 1150; d. ?), Fr. troubadour. He went to the Holy Land with Richard Cœur de Lion.

Fayrfax, Robert (b. ? Yorkshire, ?; d. St. Albans, 24. X. 1521), Eng. comp. Lived for a time (?) at Bayford, Herts., and became orgst. and choirmaster at St. Albans cath. before 1502, when he took the Mus.D. degree at Oxford. On the accession of Henry VIII in 1509 he was a Gentleman of the Chapel Royal, with which he attended at the Field of the Cloth of Gold in 1520.

Works incl. masses, motets, magnificats, *Stabat Mater*; songs for several voices, &c.

Feast at Solhaug, The, incid. m. for Ibsen's play by H. Wolf for a prod. of a Ger. trans. by Emma Klingenfeld, Vienna, 1891.

Fedele. *See* **Treu, Daniel Gottlieb.**

Federici, Camillo (1749–1802), It. actor & playwright. *See* **Cambiale di matrimonio** (Rossini).

Fedora, opera by Giordano (lib. by Arturo Colautti, based on Sardou's play), prod. Milan, Teatro Lirico, 17. XI. 1898.

Fedra (*Phaedra*), opera by Pizzetti (lib. Gabriele d'Annunzio's tragedy), prod. Milan, Teatro alla Scala, 20. III. 1915.

Opera by Romani (lib. by Alfredo Lenzoni), prod. Rome, Teatro Costanzi, 3. IV. 1915.

Fée Urgèle, La, ou Ce qui plaît aux dames (*The Fairy U., or What Pleases the Ladies*), opera by Duni (lib. by Charles Simon Favart, based on a story by Voltaire founded on Chaucer's *Tale of the Wife of Bath*), prod. Fontainebleau, at court, 26. X. 1765; 1st perf. Paris, Comédie-Italienne, 4. XII. 1765.

Feen, Die (*The Fairies*), opera by Wagner (lib. by comp., based on Gozzi's comedy, *La donna serpente*), comp. 1833 and not staged in W.'s lifetime; prod. Munich, 29. VI. 1888.

Feinberg, Samuel Evgenievitch (b. Odessa, 26. V. 1890), Rus. pfst. & comp. Studied at the Moscow Cons. under Skriabin and Miaskovsky.

Works incl. 8 pf. sos., 2 fantasies & other pf. pieces, songs, &c., to words by Pushkin & others, folksong arrs., &c.

Feis Ceoil. An Ir. mus. festival founded in 1897 on the model of the Welsh Eisteddfod, held annually, generally at Dublin.

Fel, Marie (b. Bordeaux, 24. X. 1713; d. Chaillot nr. Paris, 2. II. 1794), Fr. sop. singer. Made her 1st appearance at the Paris Opéra and at the Concert spirituel in 1734.

Felderhof, Jan (b. Zaandam, 27. IX. 1907), Dutch comp.

Works incl. opera *Serenade on St. John's Night*; *Dance Rhapsody* for orch.; Rhapsody for ob. & orch.; 2 stg. 4tets, 2 pf. trios; v. & pf. So., co. & pf. So., Suite for fl. & pf., &c.

Feldpartie or **Feldpartita** (Ger. lit. field party or field suite). An old Ger. term for suites written for wind insts. and played in the open on military or war-like occasions.

Félix, ou L'Enfant trouvé (*Felix, or The Foundling*), opera by Monsigny (lib. by Jean Michel Sedaine), prod. Fontainebleau, at court, 10. XI. 1777; 1st Paris perf., Comédie-Italienne, 24. XI. 1777. M.'s last opera.

Fellerer, Karl (Gustav) (b. Freising, Bavaria, 7. VII. 1902), Ger. mus. scholar. Studied at the Ratisbon School of Church M. and at Munich and Berlin. Lecturer at the Univ. of Münster in 1927 and prof. of m. at Fribourg (Swi.) Univ. Has written esp. on Catholic church m.

Fellowes, Edmund H(orace) (b. London, 11. XI. 1870), Eng. clergyman (Canon) and mcolst. Educ. at Winchester Coll. & Oxford. Attached to St. George's Chapel, Windsor, since 1900. Hon. Mus.D., Dublin, 1917 and Oxford, 1938. Author of books on the Eng. madrigal, Byrd and O. Gibbons; ed. of *The Eng. Madrigal School*, Eng. lutenist songs, Byrd's works and co-ed. of *Tudor Church M.*

Felszynski, Sebastian (b. *c.* 1490; d. ? 1543), Pol. comp. Studied at Cracow Univ. He compiled a hymn-book for Sigismund I in 1522. Comp. church m.

Female Cadence / **Feminine Cadence** A cadence in which the conclusive tonic chord is reached on a weak beat of the bar.

Fenby, Eric (William) (b. Scarborough, 22. IV. 1906), Eng. comp. Became an orgst. at the age of 12 and studied m. with A. E. Keeton. From 1928–34 he acted voluntarily as amanuensis to Delius, who was living blind and paralysed at Grez-sur-Loing, and helped him to commit his last works to paper until his death.

Works incl. Sym., ovt. *Rossini on Ilkla Moor*, &c.

Fénelon, François (de Salignac de La Mothe) (1651–1715), Fr. archbishop, moralist & author. *See* **Schürmann** (*Télémaque*).

Fenney, William (b. Birmingham, 21. V. 1891), Eng. comp. Pupil of Bantock at the Birmingham and Midland School of M.

Works incl. *Avon Romance*, *Dawn*, *In Shadow*, *Vision of Ancient Empire* for orch.; Suite for stgs.; 2 stg. 4tets, pf. Trio; Sonatina for v. & pf.; inst. pieces; songs, partsongs, &c.

Fennimore und Gerda, opera by Delius (lib., in Ger., by comp., based on Jens Peter Jacobsen's novel *Niels Lyhne*), prod. Frankfort, 21. X. 1919.

Fenton, Lavinia (real name Beswick) (b. London, 1708; d. Greenwich 24. I. 1760), Eng. sop, singer & actress. Made her 1st appearance at the King's Theatre in London in 1726 and was the 1st Polly in *The Beggar's Opera* in 1728. She retired at the end of the season and became the mistress of the Duke of Bolton, who married her on the death of his wife in 1751.

Feo, Francesco (b. Naples, *c.* 1685; d. in or after 1745), It. comp. Studied at Domenico Gizzi's private m. school at Naples and under Pitoni in Rome, where he prod. his 1st operas. App. dir. of the Cons. dei Poveri at Naples before 1730.

Works incl. operas *Ipermestra*, *Arianna*, *Andromaca*, *L'Amor tirannico*, *Siface* & others; orats., masses, &c.

Feramors, opera by A. Rubinstein (lib., in Ger., by Julius Rodenberg, based on Moore's *Lalla Rookh*), prod. Dresden, 24. II. 1863.

Ferguson, Howard (b. Belfast, 21. X. 1908), Ir. comp. Educ. at Westminster School and the R.C.M. in London as a pupil of R. O. Morris.

Works incl. Partita & *4 Diversions on Ulster Airs* for orch.; Octet; v. & pf. So., 4 pieces for cl. & pf.; So. & 5 Bagatelles for pf.; 2 Ballads for bar. & orch.; *3 Medieval Carols* for voice & pf., &c.

Ferlendis (*née* **Barveri**), ? (b. Rome, *c.* 1778; d. ?), It. con. singer. Made her 1st appearance at Lisbon, where she married the obst. Alessandro F.

Fermata (It.) = pause, indicated by the sign 𝄐, prolonging a note or rest beyond its normal length. For very short pauses a square sign was invented by Vincent d'Indy, but this useful device never found general acceptance. It is important that notes or rests over which the F. appears should not be lengthened in any mathematical relation to the basic time, which it must break. It should never suggest the insertion of an extra beat of the prescribed tempo. A good rule is to lengthen a note or rest by a little more than twice its value for an ordinary F. and a little less for the d'Indy F.

Fernand Cortez, ou La Conquête de Mexique (*Hernán Cortés, or The Conquest of Mexico*), opera by Spontini (lib. by Joseph Alphonse Esménard & Victor Jacques Étienne de Jouy, based on a tragedy by Piron), prod. Paris, Opéra, 28. XI. 1809.

Fernández de Castilleja, Pedro (b. *c.* 1490; d. Seville, 1574), Spa. comp. Chapel master at Seville, 1514–74. Wrote motets & other church m.

Fernandez, Oscar Lorenzo (b. Rio de Janeiro, 4. XI. 1897), Braz. comp. He studied pf. as well as comp. at Rio and won a comp. prize in 1924. App. dir. of the Braz. Cons. in 1936.

Works incl. opera *Malazarte*; Symph. Suite on popular themes, Indian poem *Imbapara* & *Reisado do pastoreio* for orch.; Suite for wind 5tet; *Trio brasileiro*; pf. pieces; songs, &c.

Fernando, operetta by Schubert (lib. by Albert Stadler), comp. 1815; never perf. in S.'s lifetime; prod. Magdeburg, 18. VIII. 1918.

Ferne Klang, Der (*The Far-off Sound*), opera by Schreker (lib. by comp.), prod. Frankfort, 18. VIII. 1912.

Ferrabosco. Eng. family of musns., later members:

1. Henry F. (b. ? Greenwich, *c.* 1618; d. ?, *c.* 1658), son of Alfonso, jun. Succeeded his father as comp. of the King's M. He was killed as a captain in the expedition to Jamaica.

2. Alfonso F. (b. ? Greenwich, *c.* 1620; d. ? London, before 1660), brother of prec. Violist & wind player at court.

3. John F. (b. ? Greenwich, 1626; d. ? London, 1682), brother of prec. Wind player at court; app. orgst. at Ely cath. in 1662. Comp. services and anthems.

4. Elizabeth F. (b. Greenwich, 1640; d. ?), singer, daughter of 1.

Ferrabosco, Alfonso (b. Bologna, I. 1543; d. Bologna, 12. VIII. 1588), It. comp. Settled in London before 1562; left the service of Queen Elizabeth in 1569 and returned to It. on leave, which he extended until 1572. In 1578 he left Eng. for good and entered the service of the Duke of Savoy at Turin.

Works incl. motets, madrigals, &c.

Ferrabosco, Alfonso (b. Greenwich, *c.* 1575; d. Greenwich, 11. III. 1628), Eng. comp. of It. descent, son of prec. He was left behind, being prob. illegitimate, when his father left Eng. in 1578. Trained in m. (?) at Queen Elizabeth's expense, he became one of James I's court musns.

Works incl. masques (Ben Jonson) *The Masque of Blackness, Hymenaei, The Masque of Beauty, The Hue and Cry after Cupid, The Masque of Queens, Love freed from Ignorance and Folly*; fancies for viols; lessons for lyra viol; ayres with lute and bass viol.; contribs. to Leighton's *Teares or Lamentacions*, &c.

Ferrabosco, Domenico Maria (b. Bologna, 14. II. 1513; d. Bologna, II. 1574), It. comp., grandfather of prec. Chapel master of the cath. of San Petronio at Bologna. App. to a similar post at the Vatican basilica in Rome, 1546; was a singer in the Papal Chapel there, 1550–5.

Works incl. motets, madrigals, &c.

Ferrarese del Bene (*née* **Gabrieli**), **Adriana** (b. Ferrara, *c.* 1755; d. ? Venice, after 1798), It. sop. singer. Pupil of the Ospedaletto at Venice, married to one Del Bene and called La Ferrarese. Appeared in London in 1785–6 and in Vienna in 1788–91. The 1st Fiordiligi in Mozart's *Così fan tutte*, 1790.

Ferrari, Benedetto (b. Reggio, *c.* 1597; d. Modena, 22. X. 1681), It. theorbist, playwright & comp. Lived at Venice, where he began to prod. mus. dramas with words and m. of his own in 1637. In 1645 he went to the court of Modena, where he remained until 1662, except for a visit to Vienna in 1651–3. He was then dismissed, but app. again in 1674.

Works incl. operas *Armida, La ninfa avara, Il pastor regio, Proserpina rapita* & others; orat. *Sansone*; 3 books of *Musiche varie a voce sola*, &c.

Ferrari, Domenico (b. Piacenza, ?; d. Paris, 1780), It. vst. Pupil of Tartini. Lived at Cremona at first, but began to travel in 1749, was partic. successful in Vienna and in 1753 joined the court band at Stuttgart under Nardini. He was (?) murdered during a visit to Paris. Pub. 6 v. sos.

Ferrari, Gustave (b. Geneva, 1872; d. London, 1944), Swi. pfst., writer on m. & comp. Settled in London in 1901. Accompst. to Yvette Guilbert. Wrote incid. m. for Shakespeare's *Hamlet* for Irving's prod. in 1905, songs, &c.

Ferreira, Manuel (b. ?; d. ?), Spa. 18th-cent. comp. & cond. Attached to a Madrid theatre for which he wrote incid. m. for plays and light operas which are early exs. of tonadillas.

Works incl. opera *El mayor triunfo de la mayor guerra*, numerous light operas, incid. m. to plays by Calderón, Moreto, &c., incl. Antonio de Zamora's Don Juan play.

Ferri, Baldassare (b. Perugia, 9. XII. 1610; d. Perugia, 8. IX. 1680), It. male sop. singer. In 1625 he went to the court of Pol. and later to that of the Emperors Ferdinand III and Leopold I.

Ferroud, Pierre (Octave) (b. Chasselay, Rhône, 6. I. 1900; d. Debrecen, Hung., 17. VIII. 1936), Fr. comp. & critic. Pupil of Ropartz and Florent Schmitt. He was killed in a motor accident.

Works incl. opera *Chirurgie*; ballets *Jeunesse* & *Le Porcher*; Sym. in A maj., *Foules, Au Parc Monceau* & *Types* for orch.; Trio for wind insts.; sos. for v. & pf. and co. & pf.; *Trois Chansons de fou* for voice & orch.; chors. for female voices; pf. pieces, songs, &c.

Fervaal, opera by d'Indy (lib. by comp.), prod. Brussels, Théâtre de la Monnaie, 12. III. 1897.

Fesca, Friedrich Ernst (b. Magdeburg, 15. II. 1789; d. Carlsruhe, 24. V. 1826), Ger. vst. & comp., ? of It. descent.

Works incl. operas *Cantemira* & *Leila*; *De profundis*; 2 syms.; 7 stg. 4tets, &c.

Fesch, Willem de (b. ? Amsterdam, *c.* 1700; d. London, *c.* 1760), Nthld. orgst. & comp. App. orgst. at Antwerp cath. *c.* 1725, but was dismissed in 1731 and settled in London.

Works incl. operettas *Love and Friendship* & *The London Prentice*; orats. *Judith* & *Joseph*; chamber m.; songs, &c.

Festa, Costanzo (b. Piedmont, 1490; d. ? Rome, 10. IV. 1545), It. comp. Became a member of the Papal choir in Rome, 1517, and later chapel master at the Vatican. Comp. masses, magnificat, litanies, motets, Te Deum; madrigals, &c.

Festa teatrale (It. = theatrical feast or festival). An 18th-cent. type of opera of a festive kind, esp. one expressly written for an occasion, such as a royal or princely patron's wedding. The subject of the lib. was usually mythological and allegorical.

Festes. *See also* **Fêtes.**

Festes de l'Amour et de Bacchus, Les (*The Feasts of Cupid and Bacchus*), opera by Lully (lib. by Quinault, with Molière and Isaac de Benserade), prod. Paris, Opéra, 15. XI. 1672. Lully's 1st opera.

Festes de Thalie, Les (*Thalia's Feasts*), opera-ballet by Mouret (lib. by Joseph de Lafont), prod. Paris, Opéra, 19. VIII. 1714.

Festes vénitiennes, Les (*The Venetian Feasts*), opera by Campra (lib. by Antoine Danchet), prod. Paris, Opéra, 17. VI. 1710.

Festin de l'araignée, Le (*The Spider's Feast*), ballet by Roussel (chgph. by Gilbert de Voisins, based on Henri Fabre's *Souvenirs entomologiques*), prod. Paris, Théâtre des Arts, 3. IV. 1913.

Festing, Michael (Christian) (b. ?; d. London, 24. VII. 1752), Eng. vst. & comp., ? of Ger. birth or descent. Pupil of Geminiani in London. Made his 1st appearance there about 1724 and became a member of the King's Band in 1735. Mus. dir. of the It. Opera in 1737 and of Ranelagh Gardens from 1742.

Works incl. Paraphrase of the 3rd chapter of Habakkuk, Milton's *Song on May Morning*, Addison's Ode for St. Cecilia's Day and other odes, cantatas, syms., concs. and sos. for var. insts.; songs, &c.

Fête galante, opera by Ethel Smyth (lib. by Edward Shanks, based on a story by Maurice Baring), prod. Birmingham Repertory Theatre, 4. VI. 1923.

Fêtes. *See also* **Festes.**

Fêtes d'Hébé, Les, ou Les Talens lyriques (*Hebe's Feasts, or The Lyrical Gifts*), opera-ballet by Rameau (lib. by Antoine Gautier de Montdorge), prod. Paris, Opéra, 21. V. 1739.

Fétis, François Joseph (b. Mons, 25. III. 1784; d. Brussels, 26. III. 1871), Belg. mcolst. App. prof. at the Paris Cons., 1821, and librarian, 1827. Author of a *Biographie universelle des musiciens*, an *Histoire générale de la musique* and many theoretical works. He also comp. several operas.

Feuermann, Emanuel (b. Kolomea, Galicia, 22. XI. 1902; d. New York, 25. V. 1942), Aus. cst. Made his 1st appearance as a boy in 1914, later travelled and studied with Klengel at Leipzig and became prof. at the Cologne Cons. at 17. In 1929–33 prof. in Berlin, in succession to Hugo Becker; driven to U.S.A. by the Nazi régime.

Feuersnot (*The Dearth of Fire*), opera by R. Strauss (lib. by Ernst von Wolzogen), prod. Dresden, 21. XI. 1901.

Fevin, Antoine de (b. ? Arras, *c.* 1485; d. Blois, 1512), Fr. comp. Wrote masses, motets, magnificats, lamentations, &c.

Fevin, Robert de (b. Cambrai, ?; d. ?), Fr. 15th–16th-cent. comp., (?) related to prec. In the service of the Duke of Savoy early in the 16th cent. Wrote masses, &c.

Février, Henri (b. Paris, 2. X. 1875), Fr. comp. Studied under Massenet and Fauré at the Paris Cons.

Works incl. operas *Monna Vanna* (after Maeterlinck), *Ghismonda, La Damnation de Blanchefleur, La Femme nue, L'Île désenchantée,* operetta *Sylvette* (with Delmas); comic operas *Le Roi aveugle, Agnès dame galante, Carmosine* (after Musset); songs, &c.

ff **Holes** (or *f* **Holes**). The Sound-holes of insts. of the v. family, so called because of their shape.

Ffrangcon-Davies, David (Thomas) (b. Bethesda, Carnarvon, 11. XII. 1856; d. London, 13. IV. 1918), Welsh bar. singer. Studied at G.S.M., London, and made his 1st appearance with the Carl Rosa Opera Co. in 1890, but later became mainly a concert singer.

Fiati (It., from *fiato* = breath). Wind insts.

Fibich, Zdeněk (b. Šebořice nr. Časlav, 21. XII. 1850; d. Prague, 15. X. 1900), Cz. comp. Very precociously gifted, he studied at the Leipzig Cons. under Carl Richter and Jadassohn, also Moscheles for the pf. Later in Paris and Mannheim. After teaching in Pol. for a time, he returned to Cz. in 1874, cond. at the Nat. Theatre in Prague and became a mus. nationalist to some extent. He soon retired to devote himself entirely to comp. and wrote over 600 works of var. kinds.

Works incl. operas *Bukovin, Blaník, The Bride of Messina* (after Schiller), *The Tempest* (after Shakespeare), *Hedy* (after Byron's *Don Juan*), *Šarka, Pad Arkuna*; melodramas *Christmas Eve, Eternity, The Water-Sprite, Queen Emma, Haakon* and the trilogy *Hippodamia*; incid. m. to Vrchlický's comedy *A Night at Karlstein*; 3 syms., ovts., symph. poems *Othello* & *The Tempest* (both after Shakespeare) & 4 others; 2 stg. 4tets, pf. 4tet, pf. Trio, 5tet for pf., v., co., cl. & hn.; pf. So., 350 pieces *Moods, Impressions and Memories* for pf.; songs, voc. duets, &c.

Fickenscher, Arthur (b. Aurora, Ill., 9. III. 1871), Amer. comp. Studied at the Munich Cons. Taught in Berlin, where he patented his Polytone in 1912, and settled at San Francisco in 1914. In 1920 he became head of the m. dept. of the Univ. of Virginia.

Works incl. *The Chamber Blue* & *Aucassin and Nicolette* for solo voices, chor. & orch.; *Willowwave and Wellaway, Day of Judgment* & *Out of the Gay Nineties* for orch.; *Visions* for voice & orch.; *Vars. on a Theme in Medieval Style* for stgs.; pf. 5tet; church m.; partsongs, songs, &c.

Fiddle. A colloq. generic term for insts. of the v. family.

Fidelio, oder Die eheliche Liebe (*Fidelio, or Wedded Love*), opera by Beethoven (lib. by Josef Sonnleithner, based on Bouilly's lib. of *Léonore, ou L'Amour conjugal* written for Gaveaux), prod. Vienna, Theater an der Wien, 20. XI. 1805, with the ovt. *Leonora No. 2*; revised version, with ovt. *Leonora No. 3,* same theatre, 29. III. 1806; ovt. *Leonora No. 1* written for perf. in Prague, 1807, which did not take place; 2nd revision prod. Vienna, Kärntnertor Theatre, 23. V. 1814, with *Fidelio* ovt. in E maj.

Field, John (b. Dublin, 26. VII. 1782; d. Moscow, 11. I. 1837), Ir. pfst. & comp. Son of a vst. at the Dublin theatre, he was taught m. and the pf. by his grandfather, an orgst. Having removed to Bath and then to London, his father apprenticed him to Clementi, who taught him and at whose pf. warehouse he was employed to show off the insts. by improvisation. He made his 1st public appearance at Giordani's concerts at Dublin in 1792 and in London in 1794. In 1802 Clementi took him to Paris, Ger. and Rus., leaving him behind at St. Petersburg in 1803, where he settled down as pf. teacher. He married Mlle Percheron in 1808. In 1822 he settled down at Moscow, where he had as great a success as he had had in the new capital. He travelled much as pfst., visited London in 1832, afterwards Paris, Belg., Swi. and It. At Naples he was taken ill and lay in hospital for months until a Rus. family took him back to Moscow, where he d. soon after his return.

Works incl. 7 pf. concs.; 20 nocturnes, 4 sos. & many rondos, fantasies, vars., &c. for pf.; pf. 5tet & other chamber m.; works for pf. duet, &c.

Fielding, Henry (1707–54), Eng. novelist & dramatist, author of ballad operas *The Intriguing Chambermaid, The Lottery, Miss Lucy in Town, Don Quixote in England* & others. *See* **Arne (T. A.), Monro** (*Temple Beau*), **Tom Jones** (German & Philidor, 8).

Fielitz, Alexander von (b. Leipzig, 28. XII. 1860; d. Salzungen, 29. VII. 1930), Ger. comp. Studied comp. under Kretschmer at Dresden and cond. under Nikisch at Leipzig. After 10 years spent in It. for his health he held posts as cond. and teacher in Berlin, Chicago from 1905, and Berlin again from 1908 as prof. and from 1915 dir. of Stern's Cons.

Works incl. operas *Vendetta* & *Das stille Dorf*; 2 suites for orch.; pf. pieces; song cycle *Eliland* & other songs, &c.

Fierrabras (Spa. *Fierabras = The Braggart*), opera by Schubert (lib. by Joseph Kupelwieser, after Calderón, taken from A. W. von Schlegel's *Spanisches Theater*), comp. 1823, but not perf. during S.'s lifetime; prod. Carlsruhe, 9. II. 1897. The 2 r's in the Ger. title are a mistake.

Fiesco, Giulio (b. Ferrara, *c.* 1519; d. ? Modena, *c.* 1586), It. lutenist & comp. In the service of the Dukes of Modena, Ercole II and Alfonso II. Wrote madrigals for 4 & 5 voices, *Musica nova* for 5 voices, songs, &c.

Fife. A simple and now obs. form of small transverse fl. with finger-holes and without keys, generally used in military bands in connection with drums. The name is now used for a military fl. in B♭ with six finger-holes and several keys, used in drum and fife bands.

Fifine at the Fair, orch. fantasy by Bantock on Browning's poem, comp. 1902, 1st perf. Birmingham, 1912.

Fifteenth. A 2-ft. org. stop prod. notes 15 diatonic degrees above those played on the keyboard.

Fifth. An interval covering 3 whole tones and a semitone, in which case it is a perfect F., e.g. D–A. If either of these notes is sharpened or flattened, the result is an augmented or a diminished F. D♭–A or D–A♯ is an augmented F., D♯–A or D–A♭ a diminished F.

Figaro (Mozart). *See* **Nozze di Figaro.**

Figlia del reggimento. *See* **Fille du Régiment.**

Figure. A short mus. phrase, esp. one that assumes a distinctive character in the course of a comp. by repetition or thematic use.

Figured Bass. *See* **Thorough-Bass.**

Figuš-Bystrý, Viliam (b. Banska, Bystrice, 28. II. 1875), Slovak comp. As the child of poor parents he made his way with difficulty, but taught at var. places until he returned to Banska in 1907 as teacher and orgst. He took great interest in the folk m. of his country, which was then under Hung. rule, and refused a prof.'ship at Budapest in order to collect folksongs at home, which he pub. in 5 books.

Works incl. opera *Detvan* (in Slovak); *The Cricket and the Glow-worm* & *Songs of Rest, Love and Peace* for women's voices & pf., cantata *Slovak Songs* for solo 4tet & chor.; pf. 4tet, &c.

Fileuse (Fr. fem. = spinner, from *filer* = to spin). The name of a special type of inst. piece with rapid figurations of var. kinds suggesting the motion of a spinning-wheel and often, in its melody, a spinning-song. There are familiar exs. by Raff and Fauré (in the latter's incid. m. for *Pelléas et Mélisande*), and Mendelssohn's Song without Words, Op. 67 No. 4, although not so entitled, conforms to the type, being in fact nicknamed *Spinnerlied* in Ger., though called *The Bee's Wedding* in Eng. The prototype of the F. was, of course, voc., e.g. the spinning-chors. in Haydn's *Seasons* (Winter) and Wagner's *Flying Dutchman*, Schubert's song *Margaret at the Spinning-Wheel*, &c.

Filippi, Amadeo de (b. Ariano, 1900), Amer. cond. & comp. of It. birth. Was taken to U.S.A. at the age of 5 and studied in N.Y. Later became theatre cond.

Works incl. operas *The Green Cockatoo* & *Malvolio* (on Shakespeare's *Twelfth Night*); ballets *Les Sylphides* & *Carnaval*; incid. m. for John Drinkwater's *Robert E. Lee*; m. for films; Sym., Suite, Conc. & *5 Arabian Songs* for orch.; Serenade for stgs.; Sonnet for con. & chamber orch.; chor. works; stg. 4tet, pf. 5tet; So. & Dance Suite for v. & pf.; So., 6 Sonatinas, *Prelude, Passacaglia & Toccata*, Partita for pf., &c.

Fille de Madame Angot, La (*Mme A.'s Daughter*), operetta by Lecocq (lib.

by Clairville, Paul Siraudin & Victor Koning, based on a vaudeville by Maillot, *Madame Angot, ou La Poissarde parvenue*, of 1796), prod. Brussels, Théâtre Alcazar, 4. XII. 1872.

Fille du Régiment, La (*The Daughter of the Regiment*), opera by Donizetti (lib. by Jules Henri Vernoy de Saint-Georges & Jean François Alfred Bayard), prod. Paris, Opéra-Comique, 11. II. 1840. D.'s 1st Fr. opera.

Film Music. Silent cinematographic films were variously accomp. by ready-made m. played on anything from a pf. to (esp. in U.S.A.) a full orch.; but the invention of the sound-track led to the mechanical reprod. of more elaborate m. and to the commission of special scores, often from the most distinguished comps. of the day. This kind of m. has been esp. cultivated in U.S.A., Fr., Ger., Rus. & Eng. from the 1930s onwards.

Filosofo di campagna, Il (*The Country Philosopher*), comic opera by Galuppi (lib. by Goldoni), prod. Venice, Teatro San Samuele, 26. X. 1754.

Filtz, Anton (b. ? Boh., *c.* 1725; d. ?, 1760), ? Boh. cst. & comp. Entered the orch. at Mannheim in 1754 and became one of the early symsts. attached to that court. Wrote *c.* 40 syms., ovts., a Mass, trios, &c.

Fin. (abbr.) = Finland, Finnish.

Final. The Tonic note of the Modes on which the scales of the authentic modes begin and end, whereas in the case of the plagal modes the F. is on the 4th above the starting-note.

Final (Fr.) = Finale.

Finale. The last mvt. of any inst. work in several mvts., more esp. one in so. form, incl. syms. and chamber m.; also the last number in any act of an opera where the m. is divided into more or less distinctly separated pieces, provided that this number is on a large scale (e.g. the great ensemble piece at the end of Act II of Mozart's *Figaro* is a F., but the aria at the end of Act I is not).

Finck, Heinrich (b. ? Bamberg, 1445; d. Vienna, 9. VI. 1527), Ger. comp. Educ. in the court chapel at Warsaw and (?) at Leipzig Univ. and held appts. at the Pol. court *c.* 1492–1506; then at the Court of Württemberg at Stuttgart until *c.* 1519. Later he lived at the Sco. monastery in Vienna.

Works incl. masses, motets, hymns & other church m., sacred & secular songs for several voices, songs to the lute, &c.

Finck, Henry T(heophilus). (b. Bethel, Mo., 22. IX. 1854; d. Rumford Falls, Me., 1. X. 1926), Amer. critic. Studied under Paine at Harvard Univ., also in Berlin, Heidelberg & Vienna. M. critic of the N.Y. *Evening Post* 1881–1924. Wrote books on Chopin, Wagner, Grieg, &c.

Finck, Hermann (b. Pirna, Saxony, 21. III. 1527; d. Wittenberg, 28. XII. 1558), Ger. comp. & theorist. Studied at the Univ. of Wittenberg, where he taught m. later. In 1557 he was app. orgst., but he d. the following year at the age of 31. He wrote a theoret. book, *Practica musica* in 5 vols. Comps. incl. motets, sacred songs and wedding songs for several voices, &c.

Findeisen, Nikolai Feodorovitch (b. St. Petersburg, 5. VIII. 1868; d. Leningrad, 20. IX. 1928), Rus. mcolst. & critic. Studied at the St. Petersburg Cons. and in 1894 founded the *Rus. Mus. Gazette.* He also ed. *Mus. Antiquity* in 1903–12 and collected much material on Rus. insts. and for the biogs. of the 19th-cent. Rus. comps., some of which he pub., as well as a hist. of early Rus. m.

Fine (It. = end). The word is often set by comps. at the close of a work, but serves no purpose unless that close does not occur at the end of the printed m., as for ex. in a piece where an earlier portion is to be repeated to form the closing section.

Fingal's Cave (also called **Hebrides**), concert ovt. by Mendelssohn, Op. 26, comp. in recollection of a visit to the Hebrides in 1829, Rome, XII. 1830; revised version, London, summer 1832. The 1st score was entitled *Die einsame Insel* (*The Solitary Island*).

Finger, Gottfried (or **Godfrey**) (b. Olomouc, ?; d. ?), Morav. 17th–18th-cent. comp. Nothing is known of his career until he went to London *c.* 1685, working under the patronage of James II. He left in 1702, piqued at having gained only the 4th prize after Weldon, Eccles and D. Purcell for the comp. of Congreve's masque, *The Judgment of Paris*, and went into the service of the Queen of Prus., Sophia Charlotte, in Berlin. Later he lived in the Palatinate & wrote some operas for Neuburg and Heidelberg.

Works incl. operas *The Virgin Prophetess* (Settle), *Sieg der Schönheit über die Helden*, *L'amicizia in terzo* (in part); masques *The Loves of Mars and Venus* (Motteux, with Eccles) & *The Judgment of Paris* (Congreve); incid. m. (some with D. Purcell) for Lee's *Rival Queens*, *The Wives' Excuse*, *Love for Love* & *The Mourning Bride* (both Congreve), *Love at a Loss*, *Love makes a Man* (Cibber), *The Humours of the Age* (Southerne), *Sir Harry Wildair* (Farquhar) & *The Pilgrim* (Vanbrugh);

concs. and sos. for var. insts.; pieces for v. & fl. (with Banister), &c.

Fingerboard. The part of the neck of a stg. inst. to which the stgs. are pressed by the fingers in order to change their length and thus prod. different notes.

Fingered Tremolo. *See* **Tremolo.**

Fingering. The use of the fingers on any inst. to prod. the notes in var. ways; also the figures written above the notes indicating which finger is to be used to prod. this or that note.

Finite Canon. A Canon sung through once, without repetition of its phrases.

Finke, Fidelio (b. Josefstal, Boh., 22. X. 1891), Ger.-Cz. comp. Studied at the Prague Cons., where Novák was his comp. master. He taught there from 1915, became inspector of the Ger. m. schools in Cz. in 1920 and dir. of the Ger. Acad. of M. in Prague in 1927.

Works incl. opera *Die Jakobsfahrt*; *Pan* sym., ovt. and other works for orch., Suite for stgs.; pf. Conc.; 2 stg. 4tets, pf. 5tet, pf. Trio & other chamber m.; sos. for v. & pf., co. & pf. and fl. & pf.; numerous pf. works; many pieces for recorder; chor. works with pf. and with wind insts., unaccomp. chor. works; songs, &c.

Finlandia, symph. poem for orch. by Sibelius, Op. 27 No. 7, comp. in 1894. It has become a work for nat. celebrations in Fin., being based on material sounding like Fin. patriotic songs, the whole of which, however, is the comp.'s own invention, not folk m.

Finney, Ross Lee (b. Wells, Minnesota, 23. XII. 1906), Amer. comp. Educ. at Carleton Coll., Minn., and studied m. at Minn. Univ. and later in Paris and Vienna with Nadia Boulanger and Alban Berg, also with Sessions at Harvard Univ. App. assoc. Prof. of M. at Smith Coll., Northampton, Mass.

Works incl. Ovt. to a Social Drama for orch.; pf. Conc., v. Conc.; *John Brown* for ten., male chor. & chamber orch.; 2 stg. 4tets, pf. Trio; v. & pf. So.; 2 pf. sos.; 8 Poems for sop., ten. & pf., &c.

Finnish Composers. *See* **Furuhjelm, Hannikainen, Järnefelt, Kilpinen, Klami, Klemetti, Krohn, Kuula, Launis, Linko, Madetoja, Melartin, Merikanto** (2), **Pacius, Palmgren, Raito, Rauta, Schantz, Sibelius, Törne, Wegelius.**

Finot, Dominique. *See* **Phinot.**

Finta giardiniera, La (*The Pretended Garden-Girl*), opera by Anfossi (lib. by Ranieri de Calzabigi), prod. Rome, Teatro delle Dame, Carnival 1774.

Opera by Mozart (lib. do.), prod. Munich, 13. I. 177?.

Finta semplice, La (*The Pretended Simpleton*), opera by Mozart (lib. by Marco Coltellini), comp. for Vienna, 1768, but not perf. there; prod. Salzburg, 1. V. 1769.

Finte gemelle, Le (*The Pretended Twins*), opera by Piccinni (lib. by Giuseppe Petrosellini), prod. Rome, Teatro Valle, 2. I. 1771.

Finto Stanislao, Il (*The False Stanislas*), opera by Gyrowetz (lib. by Felice Romani), prod. Milan, Teatro alla Scala, 5. VIII. 1818. The lib. was used by Verdi in 1840.

Opera by Verdi. *See* **Giorno di regno.**

Finzi, Gerald (b. London, 14. VII. 1901), Eng. comp. Private pupil of Bairstow and R. O. Morris; prof. of comp. at the R.A.M. in London, 1930–3, and afterwards went to live in the country to give his whole time to comp.

Works incl. *A Severn Rhapsody* for orch.; v. Conc. and *Introit* for v. & small orch.; *Requiem da camera* for chor. chamber orch.; *Farewell to Arms* (Traherne) for ten. & small orch.; Interlude for ob. & stg. 4tet, stg. Trio; 5 *Bagatelles* for cl. & pf.; 2 sonnets by Milton for ten. & small orch.; 3 Hardy song-cycles *By Footpath and Stile, A Young Man's Exhortation* & *Earth and Air and Rain*, 3 Shakespeare Songs, Children's Songs (Christina Rossetti); partsongs (Bridges), &c.

Fiocco. It.-Belg. family of musns.:

1. Pietro Antonio F. (b. Venice, ?; d. Brussels, 3. XI. 1714), cond. & comp. He went to Brussels late in the 17th cent. and was app. cond. of the court band. Comp. prologues for several of Lully's operas; masses, motets; *Sacri concerti*; cantata *Le Retour du printemps*, &c.

2. Jean Joseph F. (b. ? Brussels, ?; d. ?), cond., son of prec. Succeeded his father as cond. in 1714.

3. Joseph Hector F. (b. ? Brussels, ?; d. ? Brussels, ?), cond., hpchdst. & comp., brother of prec. He was cond. at Brussels in 1729, became choirmaster at Antwerp cath. in 1731 and chapel master at Sainte-Gudule at Brussels in 1737. Comp. hpchd. pieces.

Fioravanti, Valentino (b. Rome, 11. IX. 1764; d. Capua, 16. VI. 1837), It. comp. Pupil of Sala at one of the Naples Conss. Prod. his 1st opera in Rome in 1784. He was in Paris in 1806–7, returned to Naples and in June 1816 succeeded Jannaconi as chapel master at St. Peter's in Rome.

Works incl. operas *Le avventure di Bertoldino, Le cantatrici villane, I virtuosi ambulanti, Ogni eccesso è vizioso* & *c*. 50 others; church m., &c.

Fiorillo, Federigo (b. Brunswick, 1753; d. ?), It.-Ger. vst. & comp. Pupil of his father. He went to Pol. in 1780 and *c.* 3 years later became cond. at Riga. Visited Paris in 1785 and London in 1788, remaining there for some years and then going to Amsterdam, and again to Paris in 1823.

Works incl. v. concs., concertantes for 2 vs., duets for 2 vs., v. & pf. and v. & co., 36 Caprices for v.; stg. 4tets & 5tets and other chamber m., &c.

Fiorillo, Ignazio (b. Naples, 11. V. 1715; d. Fritzlar, Hesse, VI. 1787), It. comp., father of prec. Pupil of Leo and Durante at Naples. Prod. his 1st opera, *Mandane*, at Venice in 1736; became court cond. at Brunswick in the 1750s and at Cassel in 1762, retiring in 1780.

Works incl. 21 operas; orat.; Requiem, 3 Te Deums; syms.; sos., &c.

Fioriture (It. lit. flowerings, flourishes, decorations). Ornamental figures elaborating a plainer melodic passage, either according to the comp.'s notation or improvised according to the perf.'s fancy. The term 'coloratura' is often applied to F., but it is not a recognized It. designation.

Fipple Flute. A woodwind inst. of the fl. type, but held vertically and blown into through a mouthpiece in which the air is diverted by an obstructive block called the 'fipple.' The recorder (Ger. *Blockflöte*) is the chief member of the F. F. family.

Fire Symphony, the nickname of a sym. by Haydn, No. 59, in A maj., comp. *c.* 1775.

Firebird, The (*Zhar Ptitsa*), ballet by Stravinsky (chgph. by Mikhail Mikhailovitch Fokin), prod. Paris, Opéra, 25. VI. 1910.

Fireworks Music, a set of inst. pieces for wind band by Handel comp. in 1749 for perf. at the celebrations of the Peace of Aix-la-Chapelle, London, Green Park, 27. IV. 1749, which owing to an accident did not take place.

First Subject. *See* **Sonata.**

Fischer, Johann (b. Augsburg, 25. IX. 1646; d. Schwedt, Pomerania, *c.* 1721), Ger. vst. & comp. Studied with Bockshorn at Stuttgart and went to Paris, where he became copyist to Lully. Later he travelled, worked for a time at Ausgburg and Schwerin, in Den. and Swe., and finally became chapel master to the Margrave of Schwedt.

Works incl. *Feld und Helden Musik* describing the battle of Hochstadt, table m., ovts., dances and other pieces for v. and for viol.

Fischer, Jonann Caspar (Ferdinand) (b. ?, *c.* 1665; d. ? Rastatt, 27. III. 1746), Ger. comp. Mus. dir. to the Margrave Ludwig of Baden at the castle of Schlackenwerth, Boh.

Works incl. Vesper Psalms for 8 voices with stgs. & org.; *Le Journal du printemps* for insts. with tpts. ad lib.; several sets of hpchd. works incl. suite *Musikalisches Blumen-Büschlein, Ariadne musica neo-organoedum* containing 20 preludes and fugues in different keys, with ricercari on church tunes, *Musikalischer Parnassus* containing 9 suites named after the Muses; preludes and fugues entitled *Blumenstrauss* for org., &c.

Fischer, Johann Christian (b. Freiburg, Breisgau, 1733; d. London, 29. IV. 1800), Ger. obst. & comp. Employed as ob. player in the Saxon court orch. at Dresden from 1764; from *c.* 1771 in the service of Frederick II of Prus.; 1st visited London in 1768 and lived much there later, marrying Gainsborough's daughter Mary in 1780. He played much at J. C. Bach & Abel's concerts and at Vauxhall. He wrote concs. and pieces for ob., 4tets, &c. Mozart wrote pf. vars. on a minuet of his (K. 179).

Fischer, Ludwig (b. Mainz, 18. VIII. 1745; d. Berlin, 10. VII. 1825), Ger. bass singer. He became very famous in Ger. & Aus. and visited Paris and It. in 1783–4.

Fischer, Michael Gotthardt (b. Albach nr. Erfurt, 3. VI. 1773; d. Erfurt, 12. I. 1829), Ger. orgst. & comp. Pupil of Kittel at Erfurt and later orgst. of the Franciscan church there. Wrote org. m., syms., stg. 4tets, pf. sos., songs, &c.

Fischietti, Domenico (b. Naples, *c.* 1725; d. ?), It. comp. Pupil of Durante and Leo at Naples, became cond. in Prague, lived at Dresden in the same capacity, 1765–72, and was then mus. dir. at Salzburg cath. until 1783.

Works incl. operas *Lo speziale* (with V. Pallavicini), *Il signor dottore, Il mercato di Malmantile, La ritornata di Londra* (all on libs. by Goldoni) & *c.* 20 others; church m., &c.

Fisher, John Abraham (b. Dunstable or London, 1744; d. ? London, V. 1806), Eng. vst. & comp. Studied v. under Pinto and made his 1st public appearance at the King's Theatre, Haymarket, in 1765. Mus. B. & D., Oxford, 1777. He married the daughter of the actor Powell *c.* 1770, and after her death, after 1780, he went on a tour in Ger., Rus. & Aus. In Vienna in 1784 he married Ann Storace, but ill-treated her and was forbidden the country by the emperor. Later he lived for some years at Dublin.

Works incl. orat. *Providence*; incid. m. for Shakespeare's *Macbeth* & *The Tempest*, m. for pantomimes; syms., &c.

Fitelberg, Gregorz (b. Dinaburg, Livonia, 18. X. 1879), Pol. cond. & comp. App. cond. of the Warsaw Philh. concerts in 1908 and returned there after cond. at the Vienna Opera and at Leningrad, identifying himself with the nat. Pol. mus. mvt. His wife, Halina F., a singer, was killed in a Ger. raid on Warsaw in IX. 1939.

Works incl. Sym. in E min., *Pol. Rhapsody* for orch.; chamber m.; songs, &c.

Fitelberg, Jerzy (b. Warsaw, 20. V. 1903), Pol. comp., son of prec. He played perc. in his father's orch. as a boy and studied comp. under Schreker in Berlin; settled in Paris in 1933.

Works incl. Concert Piece and 2 suites for orch., Conc. for stgs.; 2 pf. concs., v. Conc., co. Conc.; 3 stg. 4tets; stg. Trio, woodwind 5tet; Suite for v. & pf., Sonatina for 2 vs., Duo for v. & co.; pf. So., &c., pieces, &c.

FitzGerald, Edward (1809–83), Eng. poet & translator. *See* **Omar Khayyám.**

Fitzwilliam, Viscount (Richard Wentworth) (1745–1816), Eng. collector & founder of the Fitzwilliam Museum at Cambridge, which houses his collection of MS. and printed m., among other things left by him, incl. the old It. church m. pub. as *Fitzwilliam Music* by Vincent Novello in 1825 and Eng. virginal m. ed. as the *Fitzwilliam Virginal Book* by J. A. Fuller-Maitland and W. Barclay Squire in 1899.

'Five, The.' *See* **Kutchka.**

Five Tudor Portraits, chor. suite by Vaughan Williams on poems by Skelton. I. Ballad, *The Tunning of Elinor Rumming*; II. Intermezzo, *My Pretty Bess*; III. Burlesca, *Epitaph on John Jayberd of Diss*; IV. Romanza, *Jane Scroop: her Lament for Philip Sparrow*; V. Scherzo, *Jolly Rutterkin.* For m.-sop., bar., chor. & orch. 1st perf. Norwich Festival, 25. IX. 1936.

Fl. (abbr.) = Flute.

Flageolet. A woodwind inst. similar to the recorder, with 2 of its finger-holes on the under side, to be stopped by the thumbs. It belongs to the Fipple Flute family. Also a soft 2-ft. flue org. stop.

Flageolets (Fr. plur.) } = Harmonics.
Flageolette (Ger. plur.) }

Flam. A single stroke, as distinct from a roll, on the Side Drum.

Flamenco. *See* **Cante flamenco.**

Flat. The sign ♭, which lowers a note by a semitone. Also an adj. describing out-of-tune intonation on the F. side.

Flatté (Fr.). *See* **Ornaments.**

Flatterzunge (Ger.). *See* **Flutter-Tonguing.**

Flaubert, Gustave (1821–80), Fr. novelist. *See* **Davico** (*Tentation de Saint Antoine*), **Erlanger (C.)** (*Saint Julien l'Hospitalier*), **Gilbert (H. F.)** (*Salammbô*), **Giuliano** (Zandonai), **Gray (C.)** (*Temptation of St. Anthony*), **Hauer** (*Salammbô*), **Hérodiade** (Massenet), **Kabalevsky** (*Mme Bovary*), **Navrátil** (*Salammbô*), **Salammbô** (Mussorgsky & Reyer), **Schmitt (F.)** (*Salammbô*), **Tiessen** (do.).

Flautando (It. = fluting). A flute-like, brittle tone prod. on the v. by drawing the bow lightly over the stgs. at the bridge end of the fingerboard.

Flautina. A 2-ft. org. stop like the Fifteenth, but with softer tone, prod. notes 15 diatonic degrees above those played. It continues the Gemshorn stop in a higher register.

Flautist. The Eng. word for flute-player, der. from It. *flauto* and *flautista*. There is no good reason why we should not revert to 'flutist,' the older and more truly Eng. word.

Flauto (It.) = Flute.

Flauto piccolo (It. = little flute). *See* **Piccolo.**

Flauto traverso (It.). The transverse fl., distinguished from the Recorders and similar fls. played vertically; also a 4-ft. org. stop with fl. tone.

Flautone (It. = big fl.) = Bass Flute.

Flavio, rè de' Longobardi (*Flavius, King of the Lombards*), opera by Handel (lib. by Nicola Francesco Haym, partly based on Corneille's *Cid*), prod. London, King's Theatre, Haymarket, 14. V. 1723.

Flavius Bertaridus, König der Longobarden (*F.B., King of the Lombards*), opera by Telemann (lib. by Christian Gottlieb Wendt), prod. Hamburg, Theater am Gänsemarkt, 23. XI. 1729.

Flebile (It.; accent on 1st syll.). Plaintive, mournful.

Flecha, Matéo (b. Prades, Tarragona, 1481; d. Poblet, *c.* 1554), Spa. monk & comp. Pupil of **Juan Castelló** at Barcelona, chapel master to the Infantas of Castile, later became a Carmelite and settled in the monastery of Poblet.

Flecha, Mateo (b. Prades, *c.* 1520; d. Solsona, Lérida, 1604), Spa. monk & comp., nephew of prec. Pupil of his uncle. In the service of the Emperor Charles V until 1558 and of Philip II, then in Prague in that of the Emperor Maximilian, after whose death in 1576 he remained there until 1599, when he went to the abbey of Solsona as a Franciscan monk. A stage work of his, *El Parnaso* (?) was perf. at Madrid in 1561.

Works by the 2 Fs. (not always distinguishable) incl. church m., madrigals, *ensaladas* (burlesque madrigals), &c.

Flecker, James Elroy (1884–1915), Eng. poet & dramatist. *See* **Delius** (*Hassan*), **Wood (T.)** (*Ballad of Hampstead Heath*).

Fledermaus, Die (*The Flittermouse, The Bat*), operetta by **J. Strauss,** jun. (lib. by Carl Haffner & Richard Genée, based on a Fr. vaudeville, *Le Réveillon*, by Henri Meilhac and Ludovic Halévy, taken from a Ger. comedy, *Das Gefängnis*, by Roderich Benedix), prod. Vienna, Theater an der Wien, 5. IV. 1874.

Flem. (abbr.) = Flemish.

Flem, Paul Le. *See* **Le Flem.**

Flesch, Carl (b. Moson, 9. X. 1873; d. Lucerne, 15. XI. 1944), Aus.-Hung, vst. & teacher. Studied in Vienna and Paris, where he was a pupil of Marsick's with Kreisler. Made his 1st public appearance in Vienna, 1895, toured widely and taught by turns at Bucharest, Amsterdam, Philadelphia and Berlin. In 1934 he settled in London. Wrote books on v. playing and comp. v. studies.

Fletcher, John. *See* **Beaumont & Fletcher.**

Flicorno. An It. brass inst. used in milit. bands correspond. to the Saxhorn and Flügelhorn.

Fliegende Holländer, Der (*The Flying Dutchman*), opera by Wagner (lib. by comp., based on Heine's *Memoiren des Herrn von Schnabelewopski*), prod. Dresden, 2. I. 1843.

Flood, William Henry Grattan (b. Lismore, Co. Waterford, 1. XI. 1859; d. Enniscorthy, 7. VIII. 1928), Ir. orgst. & mcolst. Educ. for the priesthood, he became a musn. and orgst. at Belfast, Thurles and Enniscorthy caths. successively. Comp. church m. and wrote a number of books on Ir. and early Eng. m.

Floquet, Étienne Joseph (b. Aix-en-Provence, 23. XI. 1748; d. Paris, 10. V. 1785), Fr. comp. He received his mus. educ. at the church of Saint-Sauveur at Aix, wrote a motet at the age of 10 and went to Paris *c.* 1769. In 1774, having come into conflict with Gluck's partisans, he went to Naples, where he studied under Sala, and to Bologna, where he sought further instruction from Martini, but returned to Paris in 1777.

Works incl. operas *Hellé*, *Le Seigneur bienfaisant*, *La Nouvelle Omphale* & *Alceste* (Quinault); opera-ballets *L'Union de l'Amour et des Arts* & *Azolan*; 2 Requiems, ode *La Gloire du Seigneur* (J. B. Rousseau), &c.

Florence, Evangeline (real name Houghton) (b. Cambridge, Mass., 12. XII. 1873; d. ?, 1929), Amer. sop. singer. Made her 1st appearance at Boston in 1891. Later continued her studies in London and appeared much in Eng.

Florestan. One of the 2 imaginary characters, F. and Eusebius, used by Schumann as pseudonyms for his critical writings and also introd. into his m. (*Carnaval*, *Davidsbündlertänze*) to personify what he felt to be his dual character as an artist, F. repres. him as an impetuous romantic and E. as a dreamer.

Florian, Jean-Pierre (Claris) de (1755–94), Fr. novelist & poet. *See* **Abencérages** (Cherubini), **Franck (C.)** (songs).

Florid. A term used for any decorative passages, but more partic. those which elaborate a theme or motif 1st stated in a simpler form. Vars. are most apt to use the device of F. writing.

Floridante, Il, opera by Handel (lib. by Paolo Antonio Rolli), prod. London, King's Theatre, Haymarket, 9. XII. 1721.

Florimo, Francesco (b. San Giorgio Morgeto, Calabria, 12. X. 1800; d. Naples, 18. XII. 1888), It. mus. historian & comp. Studied under Zingarelli and others at Naples and later became librarian of the Real Collegio di Musica there. Friend of Bellini and later of Wagner, on both of whom he wrote, also on the Neapol. school of comps.

Works incl. church m.; chor. works; Funeral Sym. on the death of Bellini; voc. 4tets & duets, songs, &c.

Flotow, Friedrich von (b. Teutendorf, Mecklenburg-Schwerin, 27. IV. 1812; d. Darmstadt, 24. I. 1883), Ger. comp. Son of a nobleman. Went to Paris in 1827 and studied m. under Reicha and others. Began to prod. operas at aristocratic houses and brought out a Fr. version of his later *Stradella* at the Palais-Royal in 1837. The next 2 years he contrib. mus. numbers to Grisar's operas *Lady Melvill* and *L'Eau merveilleuse*, and in 1839 he made his 1st public stage success with *Le Naufrage de la Méduse.* He was intendant of the court theatre at Schwerin in 1856–63. He then returned to Paris, but went to live nr. Vienna in 1868.

Works incl. Fr., Ger. & It. operas, e.g. *La Duchesse de Guise*, *L'Esclave de Camoëns*, *Stradella*, *L'Âme en peine*, *Martha*, *Rübezahl*, *L'Ombre*,

Il fior d'Harlem, Rob Roy (after Scott); ballets *Lady Henriette* (with Burgmüller & Deldevez, on which *Martha* was based later), *Die Libelle & Tannkönig*; incid. m. to Shakespeare's *Winter's Tale*; *Fackeltanz*, ovts. &c. for orch.; chamber m.; songs, &c.

Flourish. Lit., in old Eng., a Fanfare, but in modern mus. terminology a short figure used as an embellishment rather than as a theme.

Flst. (abbr.) = Flautist.

Flue Stops. Org. stops which control pipes resembling whistles and fls. in being mere tubes with an open mouthpiece, as distinct from the Reed Stops, which have vibrating metal tongues.

Flügel (Ger. lit. wing). The Ger. name for the grand pf., which is wing-shaped.

Flügelhorn (Ger. lit. wing horn). A brass wind inst. akin to the keyed bugle and alto Saxhorn, still called by its Ger. name in Eng. It is made in 3 pitches, sop., alto and ten., and used in military and brass bands.

Flute. A woodwind inst., descendant of the recorder, but played horizontally instead of vertically and now normally used only in its high-pitched varieties (*see also* Piccolo). It is played through an open mouth-hole without reeds and the notes are controlled by keys, many more being obtainable, however, by overblowing and cross-fingering. It has a compass of *c.* 3 8ves from middle C up. Also an org. stop of 4-ft. or 8-ft. open or stopped pipes with fl. tone.

Flûte à Bec (Fr. = beak fl.) = Fipple Fl., Flageolet, Recorder.

Flûte à Cheminée. An org. stop of metal pipes with 8-ft. tone with a tube or 'chimney' in the stopper.

Flute Bass. Sometimes the name of the Bass Fl. org. stop.

Flûte d'amour. A soft flue org. stop with 4-ft. or 8-ft. pipes; also an obs. fl. standing a min. 3rd lower than the common fl.

Flûte douce (Fr. lit. sweet fl.) = Recorder.

Flute Harmonic. A 4-ft. or 8-ft. org. stop of open metal pipes of double speaking length.

Flutist. *See* **Flautist.**

Flutter-Tonguing. A special kind of tone-prod. in fl. and cl. playing, i.e. rolling an R while playing rapid figures.

Flying Dutchman. *See* **Fliegende Holländer, Vaisseau-fantôme.**

Fock, Gerard van Brucken. *See* **Brucken Fock.**

Fodor-Mainvielle, Joséphine (b. Paris, 13. X. 1789; d. Saint-Genis nr. Lyons, 14. VIII. 1870), Fr. sop. singer, daughter of the vst. & comp. Joseph Fodor (1752–1828). 1st appeared at the Opéra-Comique in Paris, 1814.

Foerster. *See also* Förster.

Foerster, Josef (b. Osenice, 22. II. 1833; d. Prague, 3. I. 1907), Boh. comp. & orgst. Wrote mainly church m. Orgst. at Prague cath. from 1887 and prof. at the Cons.

Foerster, Josef Bohuslav (b. Dětenice, 30. XII. 1859), Cz. comp., son of prec. Studied at Prague Org. School. Mus. teacher and critic at Hamburg, 1893–1903, and Vienna, 1903–18. Returned to Prague and was app. prof. at the Cons., and dir. in 1922.

Works incl. operas *Deborah, Eva, Jessica* (on Shakespeare's *Merchant of Venice*), *The Invincibles, The Heart, The Fool*; incid. m. for Vrchlický's *Samson*, Strindberg's *Journey of Fortunate Peter*, Schiller's *Maria Stuart* & other plays; *Stabat Mater* & other works for chor. & orch.; 4 syms., 6 suites, 4 symph. poems & 2 ovts. for orch.; 2 v. concs.; 3 stg. 4tets, 3 pf. trios, 5tet for wind insts.; 2 v. & pf. sos., co. & pf. So.; works for pf., org. & harmonium; 10 recitations with pf. accomp.; songs, partsongs, &c.

Fogazzaro, Antonio (1842–1911), It. novelist. *See* Alfano (*Miranda*).

Fogg, Eric (b. Manchester, 21. II. 1903; d. London, 19. XII. 1939), Eng. comp. Studied m. with his parents and as choir-boy at Manchester cath., later with Bantock. Worked for the B.B.C. at Manchester and later in London.

Works incl. ballets *Hänsel and Gretel & The Golden Butterfly*; *The Hillside* (Tagore) & *The Seasons* (Blake) for chor. & orch.; suite *The Golden Valley & Sea-Sheen* for orch.; ovt. to Shakespeare's *Comedy of Errors* for small orch.; bn. Conc.; stg. 4tet in A♭ maj., *Dance Fantasy* for pf. 5tet; Poem for co. & pf.; pf. pieces; *Three Chinese Songs* & a song-cycle *Songs of Love and Life* (Tagore); songs, partsongs, &c.

Foggia, Francesco (b. Rome, 1604; d. Rome, 8. I. 1688), It. comp. Studied under Cifra, Nanini and Agostini; went into the service of the Elector of Cologne and Bavaria and the Archduke Leopold of Aus. in turn and after his return held var. church apps. in It., including St. John Lateran in Rome, 1636–61, and Santa Maria Maggiore there from 1677.

Works incl. masses, motets & other church m.

Foli (Foley), Allan James (b. Cahir, Tipperary, 7. VIII. 1835; d. Southport, 20. X. 1899), Ir. bass singer. Studied at Naples and made his 1st appearance at Catania in 1862; in London in 1865.

Folksong (*see also* **Volkslied**). A traditional song of often great but indeterminate antiquity the origins and comp. of which are unknown, but which has been preserved by being handed down aurally from generation to generation, often in several different versions or corruptions.

Folksong Society. *See* **English Folk Dance and Song Society.**

Folquet de Marseille (b. Marseilles, ?; d. Toulouse, 1231), Fr. troubadour. He entered the church at the end of the 12th cent. and d. as Bishop of Toulouse. 27 poems and 13 tunes of his songs are extant.

Fomin, Evstigney Ipatovitch (b. St. Petersburg, 16. VIII. 1761; d. St. Petersburg, IV. 1800), Rus. comp. Studied under Martini at Bologna and later became cond. of the public theatre at Moscow.

Works incl. operas *The Renaissance, The Miller who was a Wizard, a Deceiver and a Marriage-Broker, Vassily Boyeslavovitch, Orpheus, Clorida and Milo, The Americans, The Golden Apple,* &c.

Fontaine, Pierre (b. ?; d. ?), Fr. 15th-cent. singer & comp. Sang in the Papal Chapel in Rome *c.* 1420. Wrote songs.

Fontana, Giovanni Battista (b. Brescia, ?; d. Brescia, 1630), It. vst. & comp. Wrote sos. for his inst.

Fontanelli, Alfonso, Count (b. ?; d. ?), It. 16th–17th-cent. comp. Was in the service of the Duke of Modena at the end of the 16th cent. and in 1605 settled in Rome. Comp. madrigals and songs.

Foote, Arthur (William) (b. Salem, Mass., 5. III. 1853; d. Boston, 8. IV. 1937), Amer. comp. Studied at the New Eng. Cons. at Boston and later with Paine. For many years held org. appts. at Boston.

Works incl. cantatas on Longfellow's *The Farewell of Hiawatha, The Wreck of the Hesperus* & *The Skeleton in Armour*; ovt. *In the Mountains,* prologue to *Francesca da Rimini* & 3 suites for orch.; co. Conc.; 3 stg. 4tets, pf. 4tet, pf. 5tet, 2 pf. trios; chor. works; org. & pf. pieces; songs, &c.

Ford, Thomas (b. ?, *c.* 1580; d. London, XI. 1648), Eng. lutenist & comp. He was in the service of Henry, Prince of Wales, in 1611 and app. one of the musns. to Charles I in 1626.

Works incl. airs to the lute, also to be perf. in 4 voc. parts, catches and rounds; 2 anthems contrib. to Leighton's *Teares and Lamentacions* & others; dances for lute, &c.

Ford, Walter (Armitage Justice) (b. London, 20. III. 1861; d. Padworth, 21. VIII. 1938), Eng. bar. singer & teacher. Educ. at Repton & Cambridge. He taught at Wellington Coll. and then studied singing in Berlin & Milan. He sang much in London and was app. prof. of singing at the R.C.M. in 1895 and Reading Coll. in 1915.

Forefall = **Appoggiatura** (from below).

Forêt bleue, La (*The Blue Forest*), opera by Aubert (lib. by Jacques Chenevière, based on a tale by Perrault), prod. Geneva, 7. I. 1913.

Forkel, Johann Nikolaus (b. Meeder, Saxe-Coburg, 22. II. 1749; d. Göttingen, 17. III. 1818), Ger. writer on m. & orgst. Mus. dir. at Univ. of Göttingen. Bach's 1st biog.

Forlana (It.). An old It. dance in 6–8 time. A classical ex. of its use is in Bach's Ovt. (Suite) in C for orch. and a modern one in Ravel's *Tombeau de Couperin.*

Form. The F. of a mus. comp. is the course it is planned to take from beginning to end in such a way as to unfold itself logically, as for ex. by means of an exposition, working-out section, recapitulation and (optional) coda in 1st-mvt. so. F., or the periodical statement of a subject intersected by episodes in a rondo. Fugues, minuets or scherzi with their trios, var. old dances, &c., also have their recognized Fs., while fantasies, rhapsodies, &c. may be treated quite freely from the formal point of view, though they must not be allowed to fall into mere shapelessness. The Fs. more or less definitely shaped in the course of mus. hist., it is important to remember, have never become stereotyped. Mus. textbooks alone lay down rigid laws for them: comps. have always applied them freely. *See also* **Fugue, Rondo, Sonata, Suite, Symphony, Variations.**

Formé, Nicolas (b. Paris, 26. IV. 1567; d. Paris, 28. V. 1638), Fr. comp. He was a clerk and singer in the Sainte-Chapelle in Paris, 1587–92, then became a counter-ten. in the royal chapel and succeeded Eustache du Caurroy as choirmaster and comp. there in 1609. Although dismissed from the Sainte-Chapelle for not conforming to the ecclesiastical rules, he returned there in 1626 and, as a favourite musn. of Louis XIII, enjoyed special privileges.

Works incl. masses, motets, Magnificat & other church m.

Fornsete, John of. *See* **John of Fornsete.**

Forqueray, Fr. family of va. da gamba players:

1. Antoine F. (b. Paris, 1671; d. Nantes, 28. VI. 1745). Pupil of his father. He played before Louis XIV at the age of 5. In 1689 he became a royal chamber musn.

2. Jean Baptiste Antoine F. (b. Paris, 3. IV. 1700; d. ?), son of prec. His father's pupil. He also played to Louis XIV when he was 5 and later became chamber musn. at court. Wrote va. da gamba pieces.

3. Jean Baptiste F. (b. Paris, *c.* 1728; d. ?), son of prec. Pupil of his father, whose viol pieces he pub. and to which he added some of his own.

Förster, (Emanuel) Aloys (b. Niederstein, Glatz, Silesia, 26. I. 1748; d. Vienna, 12. XI. 1823), Ger. comp. Self-taught in m. as a youth; served in the Prus. army until 1776, when he settled in Vienna to cultivate m. He taught and wrote a treatise on thorough-bass. Beethoven took lessons in 4tet writing from him.

Works incl. 48 stg. 4tets; pfs. sos., pf. vars. on a theme from Sarti's *I finti eredi*, long attrib. to Mozart; preludes & fugues for org.; songs, &c.

Forster, Joseph (b. Trofaiach, Styria, 10. VIII. 1845; d. Vienna, 23. IV. 1917), Aus. comp.

Works incl. operas *Die Wallfahrt der Königin*, *Die Rose von Pontevedra*, *Evanthia* & *Der dot Mon* (Hans Sachs); 2 ballets; Sym. in C min., &c.

Forsyth, Cecil (b. Greenwich, 30. XI. 1870; d. New York, I. 1945), Eng. violist & writer on m. Studied at Edinburgh Univ. & the R.C.M. in London. Author of books on orchn., *M. and Nationalism* and, with Stanford, a hist. of m.

Forte (It. lit. strong) = loud. This dir. is generally abbr. by the symbol *f*.

Fortepiano (It. lit. loud-soft). The early It. name for the pf., given to the inst. because, unlike the hpchd., it was capable of having var. intensities of tone prod. by the player's touch.

Fortissimo (It. superl., lit. strongest) = loudest. A direction symbolized by *ff* or a larger number of *f*'s.

Fortner, Wolfgang (b. Leipzig, 12. X. 1907), Ger. comp. Pupil of Hermann Grabner and later teacher at the Inst. for Protestant Church M. at Heidelberg, where he founded and cond. a chamber orch

Works incl. *Deutsche Liedmesse*, *Marianische Antiphonen* for unaccomp. chor.; *Sinfonia concertante* for chamber orch.; concs. for var. insts. and small orch., &c.

Forty-Eight (Preludes and Fugues) (Bach). *See* **Well-tempered Clavier.**

Forza del destino, La (*The Force of Destiny*), opera by Verdi (lib. by Francesco Maria Piave, based on the drama by Angelo Pérez de Saavedra, Duke of Rivas, *Don Alvaro, o La fuerza de sino*), prod. St. Petersburg, 10. XI. 1862; 1st perf. in It., Rome, Teatro Apollo, 7. II. 1863.

Forza dell' amor paterno, La (*The Force of Paternal Love*), opera by Stradella (lib. by ?), prod. Genoa, Teatro del Falcone, Carnival 1678.

Foss, Hubert J(ames). (b. London, 2. V. 1899), Eng. pfst., writer on m., ed., & comp. Educ. at Bradfield Coll., joined the Oxford Univ. Press in 1921, formed a m. dept. and remained until 1941, when he became active in the nat. organization of mus. educ. He has written *Music in my Time* & ed. 2 vols. *The Heritage of Music*. Comps. incl. settings of poems by Thomas Hardy for voice & pf.

Foster, Arnold (Wilfred Allen) (b. Sheffield, 6. XII. 1898), Eng. comp. After serving in the 1914–8 war, he studied pf., hn. & comp. at the R.C.M. in London, the last under Vaughan Williams. M. master at Westminster School, 1926, and dir. of m. at Morley Coll. in 1929 in succession to Holst.

Works incl. folk-dance ballet *Midsummer Eve*; *Autumn Idyll* & other works for small orch.; suite on Eng. folk airs for stgs.; pf. Conc. on country-dance tunes; Fantasy pf. 4tet; v. & pf. pieces; pf. m.; many folksong arrs. for orch., pf., chor. and voice & pf., &c.

Foster, Muriel (b. Sunderland, 22. XI. 1877; d. London, 23. XII. 1937), Eng. con. singer. Studied at R.C.M., London, made her 1st appearance at Bradford in 1896, and sang extensively in Eng., on the Continent and in Amer. until her marriage in 1905.

Foster, Stephen (Collins) (b. nr. Pittsburgh, 4. VII. 1826; d. New York, 13. I. 1864), Amer. comp. He was almost wholly self-taught in m., but pub. his 1st song as early as 1842. He wrote *c.* 175 popular songs, incl. *Old Folks at Home*, *My Old Kentucky Home*, *Massa's in the cold, cold ground*, &c. &c.

Foulds, John (Herbert) (b. Manchester, 2. XI. 1880; d. Calcutta, IV. 1939), Eng. cond. & comp. He joined a theatre orch. in Manchester at the age of 14 and the Hallé Orch. in 1900. Later he worked at var. opera-houses abroad, gave concerts for the forces during the 1914–8 war, and later cond. var. mus. socs. in London.

Works incl. incid. m. for Kalidasa's *Sakuntala*, Euripides' *Trojan Women* & several others; *A Vision of Dante* (concert opera), *A World Requiem* for solo voices, chor. & orch.; *Epithalamium*, *Keltic Suite* & *Suite fantastique* for orch.; *Holiday Sketches*, *Suite française* & *Gaelic Dream Song* for small orch.; *Idyll* for stg. orch.; *Mood Pictures* for v. & pf.; Vars. & *Essays in the Modes* for pf., &c.

Fouqué, Friedrich (Heinrich Karl), Baron de la Motte (1773–1843), Ger. poet & novelist. *See* **Lvov** (*Undine*), **Perfall** (do.), **Strong** (*Sintram* & *Undine*), **Undine** (Girschner, **Hoffmann** [E. T. A.] & Lortzing).

Four Serious Songs (Brahms). *See* **Vier ernste Gesänge.**

Fourdrain, Félix (Alfred) (b. Paris, 3. II. 1880; d. Paris, 23. X. 1923), Fr. comp. Pupil of Widor at the Paris Cons.

Works incl. operas *La Légende du pont d'Argentan*, *La Glaneuse*, *Vercingétorix*, *Madame Roland*, *Les Contes de Perrault* & *La Griffe*; operettas *Cadet-Roussel*, *Le Secret de Polichinelle* & *Dolly*; incid. m. for Erckmann-Chatrian's *Les Rantzau*, George Sand's *Claudie* & *La Mare au Diable*, &c.

Fourestier, Louis (Félix André) (b. Montpellier, 31. V. 1892), Fr. cond. & comp. Pupil of Leroux, Gédalge, Vidal & d'Indy at the Paris Cons., and a follower of Dukas; took the Prix de Rome in 1925. He cond. much in Paris and also took charge of concerts at Angers, Cannes & Vichy, being app. cond. of the Paris Opéra in 1938.

Works incl. cantata *La Mort d'Adonis*; symph. poem *Polynice* & *À Saint-Valéry* for orch.; *Orchestique* (Paul Valéry), *Edward* and 4 poems by Tagore for voice & orch.; stg. 4tets, &c.

Fourniture. The Fr. name of the Furniture org. stop.

Fourth. An interval covering 2 whole tones and a semitone, in which case it is a perfect F., e.g. D–G. If either of the notes is sharpened or flattened, the result is an augmented or a diminished F. D♭–G or D–G♯ is an augmented F., D♯–G or D–G♭ a diminished F.

Fox Strangways, A(rthur). H(enry). (b. Norwich, 14. IX. 1859), Eng. mcolst., critic & ed. Educ. at Wellington Coll. and Balliol Coll., Oxford, and studied m. in Berlin. After teaching at Dulwich and Wellington Colls. until 1910, and visiting India, on the m. of which he wrote a book, *The Music of Hindostan*, he became asst. critic of *The Times* in London in 1911 and chief critic of the *Observer* in 1925. Founded *Music & Letters* in 1920 and ed. it until 1936. He also wrote a biog. of Cecil Sharp and trans. many songs (some with Steuart Wilson) by Schubert, Brahms, Wolf, &c.

Fox, The, dance scene by Stravinsky (lib. by comp., based on Rus. folk tales, Fr. trans., *Renard*, by Charles Ferdinand Ramuz), prod. Paris, Opéra, 2. VI. 1922.

Foxtrot. An Amer. dance dating from 1912 and cultivated mainly by the jazz bands. It gradually developed into 2 forms, quicker and slower, the former merging into the Charleston and the latter into the Blues.

Fr. (abbr.) = France, French.

Fra Diavolo, ou L'Hôtellerie de Terracine (*Brother Devil, or the Inn at Terracina*), opera by Auber (lib. by Scribe), prod. Paris, Opéra-Comique, 28. I. 1830.

Fra due litiganti il terzo gode (*Between Two Litigants the Third makes Profit*), opera by Sarti (lib. altered from Goldoni's *Le nozze*), prod. Milan, Teatro alla Scala, 14. IX. 1782. Mozart quotes a tune from it in the second-act finale of *Don Giovanni*: it was 1st perf. in Vienna 28. V. 1783.

Franc, Guillaume (b. Rouen, ?; d. Lausanne, VI. 1570), Fr. comp. Fled to Swi. (?) as a Protestant, settled at Geneva in 1541 and estab. a school of m., becoming master of the children and singer at the cath. the next year, and he ed. Calvin's Genevan Psalter, in which Bourgeois and Marot also had a hand; but in 1545 he left for the cath. of Lausanne. In 1565 he issued a new Psalter there with some tunes of his own.

Françaix, Jean (b. Le Mans, 23. V. 1912), Fr. comp. Studied under his father, dir. of the Mans Cons. and Nadia Boulanger in Paris.

Works incl. ballets *Beach* & *Le Roi nu* (after Hans Andersen); Sym., *Suite concertante* & *Le Diable boiteux* (after Lesage) for orch.; *Divertissement* for stg. trio & orch.; pf. Conc. & Concertino, fl. Conc., Fantasy for co. & orch.; 5tet for fl., hp. & stgs., &c.

France, Anatole (A. Thibault) (1844–1924), Fr. poet, novelist & essayist. *See* **Benoît** (C.) (*Noces corinthiennes*), **Jongleur de Notre-Dame** (Massenet), **Levadé** (*Rôtisserie de la Reine Pédauque*), **Thaïs** (Massenet).

Francesca da Rimini. *See also* **Françoise de Rimini; Paolo e Francesco.**

Opera by Generali (lib. by Paolo Pola, based on Dante), prod. Venice, Teatro La Fenice, 26. XII. 1829.

Opera by Nápravník (lib. by O. O. Paleček and E. P. Ponomarev, based on a play by Stephen Phillips, *Paolo and Francesca*, and farther back on Dante), prod. St. Petersburg, 9. XII. 1902.

Opera by Rakhmaninov (lib. taken from scenes of Pushkin's play, with additions by Modest Ilitch Tchaikovsky, based on Dante), prod. Moscow, 24. I. 1906.

Opera by Zandonai (lib. by Tito Ricordi, based on d'Annunzio's tragedy, and farther back on Dante), prod. Turin, Teatro Regio, 19. II. 1914.

Symph. fantasy by Tchaikovsky, Op. 32 (based on Dante), comp. 1876, 1st perf. Moscow, 9. III. 1877.

Unfinished opera by Goetz, completed by Ernst Frank (lib. by comp.), prod. Mannheim, 30. IX. 1877.

Francesco da Milano (b. ? Monza, 18. VIII. 1497; d. ?, c. 1573), It. lutenist & comp. In the service 1st of the Duke of Mantua, c. 1510, and then of Ippolito de' Medici, c. 1530. Pub. and contrib. to several books of lute pieces.

Francesina, La. *See* **Duparc, Élisabeth.**

Franchetti, Alberto (b. Turin, 18. IX. 1860; d. Viareggio, summer 1942), It. comp. Studied 1st in It., then with Draeseke at Dresden and at the Munich Cons. under Rheinberger.

Works incl. operas *Asrael, Cristoforo Colombo, Fior d'Alpe, Signor di Pourceaugnac* (after Molière), *Germania, La figlia di Jorio* (after d'Annunzio), *Notte di leggenda, Glauco* & (with Giordano) *Giove a Pompei*; Sym. in E min., &c.

Franchomme, Auguste (Joseph) (b. Lille, 10. IV. 1808; d. Paris, 21. I. 1884), Fr. cst. Studied at the Paris Cons. He played in var. theatre orchs. and had much success as solo and 4tet player. Chopin, whose friend he was, wrote the Polonaise for co. & pf., Op. 3, for him, and he collab. with that master, as well as with Bertini & Osborne, in duos on operatic airs, Chopin's choice being Meyerbeer's *Robert le Diable.* He was the cst. in Alard's 4tet.

Francis of Assisi (1181 or 2–1226), It. saint & author. *See* **Inghelbrecht** (*Cantique des créatures*), **Loeffler** (*Canticum*), **Pierné** (*Fioretti*), **Suter** (*Laudi*).

Francisque, Antoine (b. Saint-Quentin, c. 1570; d. Paris, 1605), Fr. lutenist & comp. He lived at Cambrai in 1596 and was married there, but went to Paris not long after, pub. a book of lute pieces, *Le Trésor d'Orphée,* some comp. by himself, others arr. from popular dances.

Franck, César (Auguste) (b. Liége, 10. XII. 1822; d. Paris, 8. XI. 1890), Belg. comp. Precociously gifted, esp. as a pfst., he made a concert tour in Belg. at the age of 11. Sent to Paris in 1835 to enable him to study there, and he entered the Cons. in 1837. There he won var. prizes each year until he left in 1842. He returned to Belg., but settled permanently in Paris in 1844. In 1848, in the midst of the Revol., he married a young actress, daughter of the tragedian, Mme Desmousseaux, 22. II, and was app. orgst. at the church of Saint-Jean-Saint-François in 1851. In 1853 he became choirmaster and in 1858 orgst. at Sainte-Clotilde. App. prof. of the org. at the Cons. in 1872. He became a chevalier of the Legion of Honour in 1885 and 2 years later, 30. I. 1887, a festival of his m. was held. 6 months before his death he was involved in a street accident.

Works incl. operas *Le Valet de ferme* (unpub.), *Hulda, Ghisèle*; Sym. in D min.; sym. poems *Les Éolides, Le Chasseur maudit* (after Bürger), *Psyché* (with chor.); *Les Djinns* & *Variations symphoniques* for pf. & orch.; 4 pf. trios, pf. 5tet, stg. 4tet; So. for v. & pf.; works for chor. & orch. (some with solo voices): *Ruth, La Tour de Babel, Les Béatitudes, Rédemption, Rébecca,* Psalm cl; *Paris: chant patriotique* for ten. & orch.; *Messe solennelle* for bass & org.; Mass for 3 voices, org., hp., co. & db.; 3 motets, 3 offertories & other small sacred voc. works; c. 16 works for pf., incl. *Prélude, Choral et Fugue* & *Prélude, Aria et Final*; 9 works for org., incl. 6 *Pièces pour Grand Orgue,* 44 *Petites Pièces,* 3 *Pièces pour Grand Orgue,* 3 *Chorals*; 5 works for harmonium; songs to poems by Chateaubriand, Hugo, Musset, Dumas, sen., Sully-Prudhomme, Joseph Méry, Jean-Pierre de Florian, Jean Reboul, Marceline Desbordes-Valmore, &c.

Franck, Johann Wolfgang (b. ?, c. 1641; d. ?), Ger. comp. Chapel master at Ansbach between 1673 and 1679, when he killed a musn. of the chapel and wounded his wife from jealousy and fled to Hamburg, where he prod. 14 operas in 1679–86. After 1690 he lived in London for some years, giving concerts with Robert King, contrib. songs to the *Gentleman's Journal* and writing one for Colley Cibber's *Love's Last Shift,* also m. for a masque by Motteux added to Shadwell's adapt. of Shakespeare's *Timon of Athens.*

Franck, Melchior (b. Zittau, 1573; d. Coburg, 1. VI. 1639), Ger. comp. Worked at Ausgburg and briefly at Nuremberg, and in 1603 became chapel master to the Duke of Coburg.

Works incl. *Melodiae sacrae* for 3 to 12 voices, *Paradisus musicus* for 4 voices, church m., hymn-tunes; songs with inst. accomp.; madrigals; inst. pieces, &c.

Franckenstein, Clemens von (b. Wiesentheid, Bavaria, 14. VII. 1875; d. Munich, 23. VIII. 1942), Ger. comp. Studied in Vienna and later at Munich with Thuille and at Frankfort with Knorr. After a visit to U.S.A. he cond. the Moody-Manners Opera Co. in Eng., 1902–7, then worked at the court theatres of Wiesbaden & Berlin, and in 1912 became general intendant of the Munich court theatres.

Works incl. operas *Griseldis*, *Rahab* & *Litaipe*; ballet *Die Biene*; orch. works: Vars. on a theme by Meyerbeer, Dance Suite, Serenade, Rhapsody, Praeludium, Symph. Suite, *Das alte Lied*, 4 Dances, *Festival Prelude*; chamber m.; pf. works; songs, &c.

Franco, Johan (b. Zaandam, 12. VII. 1908), Dutch comp. Pupil of Pijper.

Works incl. Sym., symph. poem *Peripetie*, Sinfonia for orch.; *In Memoriam* for stg. orch.; *Concertino lirico* for v. & orch., *Introduzione e scherzo* for cl. & orch.; songs with orch.; stg. Trio; 2 pf. sos.; songs to poems by Browning, &c.

Francœur, François (b. Paris, 28. IX. 1698; d. 6. VIII. 1787), Fr. vst. & comp. Played in the royal and Opéra orchs., the latter from 1710, managed the Opéra with Rebel from 1736 and was superintendent of the king's m. in 1760–78. His nephew, Louis Joseph F. (1738–1804), was a vst., cond. & opera comp. and managed the Opéra from 1792.

Works incl. operas (written jointly with Rebel), ballets, v. sos., &c.

Françoise de Rimini (*Francesca da R.*), opera by A. Thomas (lib. by Jules Barbier & Michel Carré, based on Dante), prod. Paris, Opéra, 14. IV. 1882.

Frangipani, Cornelio (16th cent.), It. poet & playwright. *See* Merulo (*Tragedia*).

Frank, Ernst (b. Munich, 7. II. 1847; d. Oberdöbling nr. Vienna, 17. VIII. 1889), Ger. cond. & comp. Studied at Munich Univ. and m. under Franz Lachner. Cond. successively at Würzburg, Vienna, Mannheim, Frankfort o/M. & Hanover. He finished Goetz's opera *Francesca da Rimini* and trans. operas by Stanford and Mackenzie.

Works incl. operas *Adam de la Halle*, *Hero* (after Grillparzer) & *Der Sturm* (after Shakespeare's *Tempest*); voc. duets from Kate Greenaway's *Under the Window*; songs, partsongs, &c.

Frankel, Benjamin (b. London, 31. I. 1906), Eng. comp. His father was a synagogue beadle and, unable to give him a mus. educ., sent him to the City to work at warehouses and as a watchmaker's apprentice. But Victor Benham insisted on giving him pf. lessons and he managed to secure 6 months' study in Ger. thanks to the favourable exchange after the 1914–8 war. At 17 he returned to London and picked up a precarious living as m. teacher, café pfst. & jazz-band vst. But he managed to attend the G.S.M. in the daytime and eventually gained a comp. scholarship there, studying with Orlando Morgan. He gradually improved his living as orchestrator and theatre cond., finally succeeding as cond. and comp. of film m.

Works incl. m. for many films, incl. some sponsored by the Ministry of Information; *Pezzo sinfonico* for orch., *Solemn Speech and Discussion* & *M. for Young Comrades* for stg. orch.; 2 stg. 4tets, *3 Sketches* for stg. 4tet, stg. Trio, Trio for cl., co. & pf.; v. & pf. So., sos. for unaccomp. v. & va., *So. ebraica* for co. & hp., *Élégie juive* for co. & pf.; Passacaglia for 2 pfs.; pf. pieces; songs, &c.

Franz, Robert (real name Knauth) (b. Halle, 28. VI. 1815; d. Halle, 24. X. 1892), Ger. comp. After much parental opposition he became a pupil of Schneider at Dessau in 1835, and after 2 years returned home, devoting himself to study and comp. without being able to secure a mus. post. He became one of the best exponents of Ger. songs, the 1st of which he pub. in 1843 and which attracted the attention of Schumann, Mendelssohn, Liszt and others. He then became a church orgst. and chor. cond., also lecturer at Halle Univ. Much troubled by increasing deafness and a nervous complaint, he had to retire in 1868, but did much work in ed. the older chor. classics.

Works incl. 257 songs, church m., partsongs, &c.

Frappé (Fr.). *See* **Ornaments.**

Fraschini, Gaetano (b. Pavia, 1815; d. Naples, 24. V. 1887), It. ten. singer. Made his 1st appearance as a church and opera singer at Pavia in 1837.

Fraser, Marjory Kennedy (b. Perth, 1. X. 1857; d. Edinburgh, 22. XI. 1930), Sco. singer & folksong collector, daughter of David Kennedy. Studied under her father and Mathilde Marchesi in Paris and began to visit the Hebrides to collect folksongs in 1905. Pub. several collections of these songs and wrote the lib. for Bantock's opera *The Seal Woman*.

Frasi, Giulia (b. ?; d. ?), It. singer. 1st appeared in London in 1743.

Frau ohne Schatten, Die (*The Woman without a Shadow*), opera by R. Strauss (lib. by Hugo von Hofmannsthal), prod. Vienna, Opera, 10. X. 1919.

Frauenliebe und Leben (*Woman's Love and Life*), song cycle by Schumann, Op. 42 (8 poems by Adelbert von Chamisso), comp. in 1840.

Fredegunda, opera by Keiser (lib. by Johann Ulrich König, from the It. by Francesco Silvani), prod. Hamburg, Theater am Gänsemarkt, III. 1715.

Frederick II (Frederick the Great) (b. Berlin, 24. I. 1712; d. Potsdam, 17. VIII. 1786), king of Prus., flst. &. comp. Learnt m. from Gottlob Hayn, the Berlin cath. orgst., and in 1728 had fl. lessons from Quantz. In 1734 he estab. a private band at his castle at Rheinsberg and on his accession in 1740 a court band at Berlin and Potsdam. Graun, Quantz and C. P. E. Bach were in his service.

Works incl. part of the opera *Il rè pastore* (Metastasio) and contribs. to others; 120 inst. works, many with prominent fl. parts, &c.

Frege (*née* Gerhard), Livia (b. Gera, 13. VI. 1818; d. Leipzig, 22. VIII. 1891), Ger. sop. singer. Made her 1st appearance at the Leipzig Gewandhaus in 1732 at a concert given by Clara Wieck.

Freischütz, Der (lit. *The Freeshooter*), opera by Weber (lib. by Friedrich Kind, based on a story in Apel and Laun's *Gespensterbuch*), prod. Berlin, Schauspielhaus, 18. VI. 1821.

Freitas, Frederico de (b. Lisbon, 1902), Port. cond. & comp. Studied at the Lisbon Cons. He visited Brazil, Fr. Spa. and Holl. as cond. and became broadcasting cond. at Lisbon.

Works incl. opera *Luzdor*; cantata *The Seven Words of Our Lady*; symph. poems *Lenda dos bailarins, Ribatejo, Nazaré* & *Suite colonial*; poem on an eclogue by Virgil and prelude on a Lisbon street-cry for stg. orch.; So. for v. & co.; inst. works; pf. pieces; songs, &c.

French Horn. *See* **Horn.**

French Overture. *See* **Overture.**

French Sixth. A form of the chord of the augmented 6th, which has a maj. 3rd with a maj. 2nd above it between its 2 extreme notes, e.g. D♭, F, G, B.

French Suites. A set of 6 hpchd. suites by Bach, comp. *c.* 1722 and cultivating a Fr. style. Unlike Bach's Eng. Suites, they have no preludes.

Frescobaldi, Girolamo (b. Ferrara, 1583; d. Rome, 1. III. 1643), It. comp. & orgst. Studied at Ferrara under the cath. orgst. Luzzaschi; was at Antwerp before 1608, when he was app. orgst. at St. Peter's in Rome. Left for the service of Ferdinand II, Duke of Tuscany, in 1628, but returned to Rome in 1633.

Works incl. ricercari, canzoni, toccatas, &c. for org. & for hpchd.; fantasies for insts. in 4 parts; madrigals, &c.

Frets. The small strips of wood or metal set across the fingerboard on certain stg. insts. not of the v. family (incl. the old va. da gamba and the modern guitar, mandoline, banjo, ukelele and the Rus. balalaika), enabling the player to play in tune with certainty, the stg. being stopped at exactly the right spot, not by the finger itself, but by the F.

Freunde von Salamanka, Die (*The Friends of Salamanca*), operetta by Schubert (lib. by Johann Mayrhofer), comp. 1815, but never perf. in S.'s lifetime; prod., with a new lib. by Günther Ziegler, Halle, 6. V. 1928.

Freytag, Gustav (1816–95), Ger. novelist. *See* **Vollerthun** (*Freikorporal*).

Frezzolini, Erminia (b. Orvieto, 1818; d. Paris, 5. XI. 1884), It. sop. singer. Made her 1st appearance in 1838, at Florence.

Friberth, Karl (b. Wullersdorf, Lower Aus., 7. VI. 1736; d. Vienna, 6. VIII. 1816), Aus. ten. singer, author & comp. Studied with Bonno and Gassmann in Vienna and in 1759 joined the Esterházy household under Haydn, for whom he wrote the lib. of *L'incontro improviso*. Returned to Vienna as chapel master to the Jesuits and Minorites in 1776. Comp. mainly church m.

Fricassée (Fr.). A term now used only in cookery, but in the 16th cent. for a Quodlibet of var. tunes sung together, often in different languages.

Friderici, Daniel (b. nr. Querfurt before 1600; d. Rostock, 23. IX. 1638), Ger. comp. Cantor at St. Mary's church of his native town from 1619 to his death. Pub. Morley's 3-part madrigals with Ger. words in 1624.

Works incl. madrigals, Ger. songs for 3–8 voices, &c.

Friedemann Bach, opera by Graener (lib. by Rudolf Lothar), prod. Schwerin, 13. XI. 1931.

Friedenstag (*Peace Day*), opera by R. Strauss (lib. by Joseph Gregor, who 1st suggested it to Stefan Zweig, based on Calderón's play *La redención de Breda* and Velazquez's picture illustrating that), prod. Munich, 24. VII. 1938.

Friedheim, Arthur (b. St. Petersburg, 26. X. 1859; d. New York, 19. X. 1932), Rus. pfst. of Ger. descent. Pupil of Liszt. He taught at Leipzig and at the R.C.M., Manchester, and settled in N.Y. in 1915.

Friedländer, Max (b. Brieg, Silesia, 12. X. 1852; d. Eichkamp nr. Berlin, 2. V. 1934), Ger. bar. singer and writer on m. Studied under García in London and Stockhausen at Frankfort. Taught in Berlin and at Harvard Univ. Ed. songs by Schubert & Schumann, Gluck's odes and Ger. folksongs and wrote books on Ger. song and Brahms's songs.

Friedländer, Thekla (b. ?; d. ?), Ger. sop. singer. Studied with F. Hiller and Schneider at Cologne and made her 1st appearance at Leipzig in 1873.

Went to Eng. in 1875 and remained c. 12 years.

Friskin, James (b. Glasgow, 3. III. 1886), Sco. pfst. & comp. Studied at the R.C.M. in London. In 1914 he went to N.Y. and became pf. prof. at the Inst. of Mus. Art. He married Rebecca Clarke in 1944.

Works incl. 2 motets on Sco. psalm tunes; Suite for orch.; pf. 5tet in C min.; Phantasy stg. 4tet; co. & pf. So., &c.

Friss. *See* **Csárdás.**

'Frog' Quartet. The nickname of Haydn's stg. 4tet in D maj., Op. 50 No. 6, the finale of which is supposed to have a 'croaking' theme.

Froberger, Johann Jacob (b. Halle, c. 1617; d. Héricourt nr. Montbéliard, 7. V. 1667), Ger. orgst. & comp. Studied under his father, who was cantor at Halle. App. court orgst. in Vienna on the accession of the Emperor Ferdinand III in 1637, remaining there until 1657, but spending 1637–41 in It. as a pupil of Frescobaldi. In 1662 he went to London, where he arrived destitute, having been twice robbed on the way, and was glad to accept the post of org.-blower at Westminster Abbey. On Charles II's marriage he overblew the org. and caused C. Gibbons's playing to break down, but although Gibbons abused him, he seized a chance to sit down at the org., whereupon a foreign lady who had been his pupil recognized his style and presented him to the king, who made him play the hpchd. and app. him court orgst. But he was dismissed later and took refuge in the house of Sibylla, Dowager Duchess of Württemberg, at her retreat at Héricourt.

Works incl. hpchd. suites, many pieces for org. and hpchd. incl. toccatas, ricercari, &c.

Fröhlich, Aus. family of musns., 4 sisters, friends of Schubert:

1. Anna (Nanette) F. (b. Vienna, 19. IX. 1793; d. ?), pfst. & sop. singer. Pupil of Hummel, Hauss and Siboni, singing teacher at the Vienna Cons. 1819–54. She gave the 1st perf. of several of Schubert's works.

2. Barbara F. (b. Vienna, 30. VIII. 1797; d. ?), con. singer & painter. Married Ferdinand Bogner, prof. of fl. at the Vienna Cons.

3. Katharina F. (b. Vienna, 10. VI. 1800; d. Vienna, 3. III. 1879), intimate friend of Grillparzer, who lived in the sisters' house until his death in 1872.

4. Josefine F. (b. Vienna, 12. XII. 1803; d. Vienna, 7. V. 1878), sop. singer. Pupil of her sister Anna, made her 1st appearance in 1821, later went to Copenhagen to study under Siboni and sang with success in Scand., also, c. 1829–31, in It.

Fröhlich, Friedrich Theodor (b. Brugg, 25. II. 1803; d. Aarau, 16. X. 1836), Swi. comp.

Works incl. pf. m.; popular songs, e.g. Eichendorff's 'Wem Gott will rechte Gunst erweisen,' &c.

Froissart, concert ovt. by **Elgar,** Op. 19, comp. in 1890 and prod. at the Worcester Festival of that year.

Froissart, Jean (1338–1404), Fr. historian. *See above.*

From Bohemia's Fields and Groves (Smetana). *See* **Má Vlast.**

Fromm, Andreas (b. ?; d. ?), Ger. 17th-cent. comp. He was cantor & prof. at the Pädagogium of Stettin in the middle of the cent.

Works incl. orat. (the 1st known in Ger.) *Vom reichen Mann und Lazarus*; *Dialogus Pentecostalis*, &c.

Frottola. An It. song for several voices, forerunner of the Madrigal and the Villanella in the 15th cent., less polyphonically elaborate than the former but rather more so than the latter, though like the villanella it was a popular type of song with comic or sentimental words divided into verses and often telling a long story.

Frumerie, Gunnar de (b. ?, 20. VII. 1908), Swe. pfst. & comp.

Works incl. 2 pf. concs.; Vars. & Fugue for pf. and many other pf. works, incl. Chaconne, Suite, *Six Pieces*; songs on Chin., Persian and gypsy poems, &c.

Fry, William Henry (b. Philadelphia, 10. VIII. 1813; d. Santa Cruz, Virgin Islands, 21. IX. 1864), Amer. comp. He was mainly self-taught. Lived in Eur. in 1846–52 as mus. correspondent of the *New York Tribune*, of which he later became m. critic.

Works incl. operas *Leonora* (after Bulwer-Lytton's *Lady of Lyons*) and *Notre-Dame de Paris* (after Hugo); *Stabat Mater*; cantatas; 4 programme syms., ovts.; pf. pieces, songs, &c.

Fuchs, Robert (b. Frauenthal, 15. II. 1847; d. Vienna, 19. II. 1927), Aus. comp. Prof. at the Vienna Cons. from 1875.

Works incl. 2 operas; Mass; Sym. in C maj., 5 Serenades for stgs.; pf. Conc.; chamber m., &c.

Fuenllana, Miguel de (Navalcarnero, Madrid, ?; d. ?), Spa. 16th-cent. lutenist & comp. Although blind, he became a great player, and in 1554 he pub. a book of m. for vihuela and similar insts., incl. comps. of his own and many arrs. of works by Guerrero, Morales, Arcadelt, Verdelot and others.

Fuentes, Pascual (b. Albaida, Valencia, ?; d. Valencia, 26. IV. 1768)

Spa. comp. Chapel master at the church of S. Andrea at Valencia and from 1757 of the cath. Wrote church and secular voc. m.

Fuga (It. = flight) = Fugue; in the 14th cent. one of the It. terms for Canon, another being Caccia.

Fuga ligata. *See* Ligata.

Fuga ricercata. *See* Ricercare.

Fugato (It. = fugued). A passage written in the manner of a fugue, occurring merely incidentally in a comp.; or a piece in fugal style that cannot be considered to be in the form of a fugue.

Fugère, Lucien (b. Paris, 22. VII. 1848; d. Paris, 15. I. 1935), Fr. bar. singer. Having failed as a sculptor and made a living as a commercial traveller, he appeared at the Ba-ta-clan café-concert in Paris in 1870 with Planquette's marching-song *Le Régiment de Sambre-et-Meuse* and made his 1st stage appearance at the Bouffes-Parisiens in 1874.

Fughetta (It. = little fugue). Unlike a *fugato*, a F. is formally a proper fugue, but much more condensed.

Fugue. A polyphonic piece of m. written in a definite number of parts from beginning to end (the parts being throughout indicated by rests wherever one or more happen to pause) and based on one or more subjects introd. at first by each part (called voice) in turn. There are as many entries with the subject as there are voices, and as the 2nd, 3rd, &c. voices enter those already brought in continue with other matter combining with the subject in satisfactory ctpt. After these 1st entries the mus. fabric may be woven in var. ways, mainly from the subject, portions or modifications of the subject or from episodes more or less relevant to it. A variety of devices may be introd., such as Augmentation or Diminution of the subject, Inversion (upside down or backwards: *cancrizans*), Stretto (the drawing of the entries closer together in time) and Pedals (the halting of one voice, usually the bass, on a single sustained note). The 1st time the 2nd (and 4th, if there is a 4th, and possible further even entries) occurs on a different degree of the scale from the 1st, 3rd (and more odd ones, if there are any), and these even entries are called answers. They usually appear in the dominant and thus tend to make the m. modulate into a neighbouring key, to prevent which the comp. may be compelled to alter some of the intervals of the subject in order to keep it in the tonic key. In such a case the F. is called a Tonal F., whereas if the comp. succeeds in keeping the subject in exactly the same shape for the answer without thus being drawn into modulation, the F. is called a Real F. Where a subject at once appears with a counter-subject at the 1st entry, and that counter-subject itself is made to behave fugally, the F. becomes a Double Fugue.

Fuhrmann, Georg Leopold (b. ?; d. ?) Ger. 16th–17th cent. lutenist, engraver & bookseller. Worked at Nuremberg, where in 1615 he pub. a book of lute pieces, *Testudo Gallo-Germanica*, incl. some by J. & R. Dowland.

Fulda, Adam of (b. ?, 1445; d. ?), Ger. monk, theorist & comp. Wrote a tract on m. and comp. motets, &c.

Fuleihan, Anis (b. Kyrenia, Cyprus, 2. IV. 1901), Amer. (naturalized) pfst. & comp. Educ. at the Eng. School in Cyprus and studied m. in U.S.A., where he settled in 1915. Toured much in U.S.A. and the East, and lived at Cairo for 2 years. After his return to Amer. in 1928 he cond. and comp.

Works incl. several ballets; a Sym., suite *Mediterranean* and *Preface to a Child's Story-Book* for orch.; 2 pf. concs., va. Conc.; suite for chamber orch., &c.

Full Anthem. *See* Anthem.

Full Score. *See* Score.

Fuller, Donald (b. Washington, D.C., 1. VII. 1919), Amer. comp. Graduated at Yale Univ. and studied m. in U.S.A. with Wagenaar, Copland and Milhaud.

Works incl. Sym.; Trio for cl., co. & pf., Sonatina for ob., cl. & pf.; So. for 2 pfs.; So., Sonatina & pieces for pf.; songs, &c.

Fuller-Maitland, J(ohn). A(lexander). (b. London, 7. IV. 1856; d. Carnforth, Lancs., 30. III. 1936), Eng. critic, ed. and writer on m. Educ. at Westminster School and Cambridge. Studied m. with Stanford, Dannreuther and Rockstro, became a m. critic in London and was from 1889–1911 chief critic of *The Times*. Ed. old m., esp. for the hpchd., incl. the *Fitzwilliam Virginal Book* with W. Barclay Squire, and was ed. of the 2nd ed. of Grove's Dict. Among his books is the 4th vol. of the *Oxford Hist. of M.*

Füllsack, Zacharias (b. ?; d. ?), Ger. 16th–17th-cent. lutenist and trombst. Worked at Hamburg until 1612 and later in the court chapel at Dresden. In 1607, with Christoph Hildebrand, he pub. a book of *Auserlesene Paduanen und Galliarden*, incl. many pieces by Eng. comps.

Fundamental Bass. An imaginary harmonic phenomenon expounded by

Rameau. The F. B. is the Root bass of any chord occurring in a comp., and according to Rameau no comp. was aesthetically satisfying unless that bass, either actually present or implied, was present in each chord used, proceeding from the one before it to the one after it in accordance with definite rules of mus. logic. Rameau's own harmonic procedures, however, are limited, and the F. B. is satisfying at most as a neat and tidy theory. It will not fit the bulk of the world's great m. in practice and has no value at all for any m. later than Rameau's.

Funeral March. *See* **March.**

Funeral Ode (Bach). *See* **Trauer-Ode.**

Furiant (Cz.). A lively Cz. dance in 3–4 time with a characteristic effect of cross-rhythm, often used in place of a scherzo by Dvořák and other Cz. comps. of the nat. school. (The name has nothing to do with 'fury.')

Furlana. *See* **Forlana.**

Furlong. An old Eng. name for the Forlana.

Furniture. An org. Mixture stop.

Fürstenau, Anton Bernhard (b. Münster, 20. X. 1792; d. Dresden, 18. XI. 1852), Ger. flst. & comp. In the court orch. at Dresden from 1820. Wrote 2 methods and many pieces for his inst. He accomp. Weber to London in 1826.

Furuhjelm, Erik (b. Helsinki, 6. VII. 1883), Fin. critic & comp. Studied at the Helsinki Cons. and later in Vienna, Munich and Paris. After his return to Fin. he became prof. at the Helsinki Cons. and m. critic to 2 newspapers. He wrote a biog. of Sibelius.

Works incl. Sym., ovt. & suites for orch.; *Concertstück* for v. & orch.; chamber m., &c.

Fux, Johann Joseph (b. Hirtenfeld nr. Graz, 1660; d. Vienna, 13. II. 1741), Aus. theorist & comp. Became orgst. to the Sco. monastery in Vienna in 1696, court comp. in 1698, 2nd chapel master at St. Stephen's cath. in 1705 and 1st in 1712, and vice chapel master to the court in 1713, advancing to chief in 1715. He wrote a treatise on ctpt., *Gradus ad Parnassum.*

Works incl. 18 operas, e.g. *Costanza e fortezza*; 50 masses, 3 Requiems, 22 motets, over 100 hymns and much other church m.; 10 orats.; *c.* 30 partitas and ovts.; *c.* 40 sos. in 3 parts for church use; clav. m., &c.

fz. (abbr. for It. *forzando*). A direction which, placed against a note or chord, indicates that it should be strongly accentuated. The more usual word is *sforzando*, marked ***sf.***

G

G. The note bounding the range of the scales of G maj. and min., and of the Mixolydian and Hypoionian (Gr. Lydian) modes.

G.P. (abbr.). General Pause. The abbr. is used in mus. notation where, in a comp. for a number of perfs., the m. temporarily ceases completely for a time specified by rests.

G.S.M. (abbr.). Guildhall School of Music (London).

Gabrieli, Andrea (b. Venice, *c.* 1510; d. Venice, 1586), It. comp. Pupil of Willaert at St. Mark's in Venice, where he became a member of the Doge's choir in 1536, 2nd orgst. in succession to Merulo in 1566 and later 1st orgst. He was a famous teacher and had many distinguished pupils, It. and foreign, incl. his nephew Giovanni G.

Works incl. masses, motets & other church m. with insts.; spiritual songs; madrigals, &c. for several voices; chors. for Sophocles' *Oedipus Tyrannus*; ricercari for org., &c.

Gabrieli, Giovanni (b. Venice, 1557; d. Venice, 12. VIII. 1612), It. comp., nephew of prec. Pupil of his uncle, musn. (?) to the Duke of Bavaria in his youth; became 1st orgst. at St. Mark's in Venice in 1585 in succession to Andrea G., like whom he had many famous It. and foreign pupils.

Works incl. church m. for voices and insts., often laid out antiphonally for chor. & orch. groups; *Sacrae symphoniae* in many voc. & inst. parts; inst. pieces of var. kinds; org. m., &c.

Gabrielli, Catterina (b. Rome, 12. XI. 1730; d. Rome, IV. 1796), It. sop. singer. Pupil of Garcia and Porpora, made her 1st appearance at Lucca in 1747.

Gabrilovitch, Ossip Salomonovitch (b. St. Petersburg, 7. II. 1878; d. Detroit, 14. IX. 1936), Rus.-Amer. pfst., cond. & comp. Studied pf. with A. Rubinstein, later at the St. Petersburg Cons., where Liadov and Glazunov were among his masters, and finished his pf. studies with Leschetizky in Vienna, 1894–6, making his 1st appearance in Berlin in the latter year. He toured much in Eur. and U.S.A., married the con. Clara Clemens (b. 1874), daughter of Mark Twain, in 1909 and settled in N.Y. as an Amer. citizen in 1914. App. cond. of the Detroit Sym. Orch. in 1918.

Works incl. Ovt.-Rhapsody for orch.; Elegy for co. & pf.; many pf. pieces; songs, &c.

Gade, Niels Vilhelm (b. Copenhagen, 22. II. 1817; d. Copenhagen, 21. XII. 1890), Dan. comp. Pupil of Berggreen, Weyse and others. He learnt var. insts. and became a vst. in the royal orch.; and having gained a comp. prize with the *Ossian* ovt. in 1841, was enabled to go to Leipzig for further study with a royal grant. There he came into touch with Mendelssohn, who prod. his 1st Sym. in 1843 and engaged him to cond. the Gewandhaus concerts in his absence. He returned to Copenhagen in 1848 and worked as orgst., cond. and teacher, becoming court mus. dir. in 1861.

Works incl. opera *Mariotta*; cantatas *Baldurs Drøm*, *Comala*, *Erl King's Daughter*, *Zion*, *The Crusaders*, *Den Bjaergtagne*, *Psyche*, &c.; 8 syms., ovts. *Echoes from Ossian*, *In the Highland*, *Hamlet* (after Shakespeare), *Michelangelo*, &c., suite *Holbergiana* for orch.; stg. 4tet, 5tet, stg. 8tet, pf. trios & other chamber m.; 4 v. & pf. sos.; inst. pieces; pf. So. in E min. & pieces for pf. solo & duet; songs, partsongs, &c.

Gadsky, Johanna (b. Anclam, Prus., 15. VI. 1872; d. Berlin, 23. II. 1932), Ger. sop. singer. Made her 1st appearance in Berlin in 1889.

Gadzhibekov, Uzeir Abdul Hussein Ogli (b. Adzhabedy nr. Shusha, Azerbaijan, 18. IX. 1885), Rus. (Azerbaijan) comp. Educ. at a teacher's training coll. at Gori, Georgia, later studied m. at Baku, Moscow & St. Petersburg. He became dir. of the Baku Cons. and studied Azarbaijan folk m., on which his work is based.

Works incl. 7 Azerbaijan nat. operas & 1 operetta; folksong arrs., &c.

Gafori, Franchino (b. Ospitaletto nr. Lodi, 14. I. 1451; d. Milan, 24. VI. 1522), It. priest & writer on m. Chapel master at Monticello and Bergamo, and from 1484 attached to Milan cath. Wrote several theoret. books, incl. *Practica musicae*.

Gagliano, Giovanni Battista da (real name Zenobi) (b. Gagliano nr. Florence, *c.* 1585; d. ? Florence, *c.*

1650), It. comp. Instructor at the church of San Lorenzo at Florence in 1613 in succession to his brother and later musn. to the Grand Duke of Tuscany.

Works incl. motets, psalms & other church m., &c.

Gagliano, Marco da (Zenobi) (b. Gagliano nr. Florence, *c.* 1575; d. Florence, 24. II. 1652), It. comp., brother of prec. Studied org. & theorbo under Luca Bati at the church of San Lorenzo at Florence, where he became instructor in 1602 and chapel master in 1608. In 1607 he founded the Accademia degl' Elevati for the cultivation of m. and *c.* 1610 became chapel master to the Grand Duke of Tuscany. He was also in touch with the ducal family of Gonzaga at Mantua, where his opera *Dafne*, a setting of Rinuccini's lib., was prod. *c.* I. 1608. He stayed till VI and wrote m. for the wedding of the duke's son.

Works incl. operas *Dafne, La Flora, Il Medoro* (m. lost); orat. *La regina Santa Orsola* (m. lost); masses, offices for the dead, *Sacrae cantiones*; madrigals, &c.

Gagliarda (It.) = Galliard.

Gaigerova, Varvara (b. Orekhovo-Zuevo, 4. X. 1903), Rus. comp. She was a pupil of Miaskovsky at the Moscow Cons.

Works incl. 3 syms., symph. suite on Caucasian themes; 2 stg. 4tets; pf. sos.; songs to words by Pushkin, &c.

Gailhard, Pierre (b. Toulouse, 1. VIII. 1848; d. Paris, 12. X. 1918), Fr. bar. singer. Studied at the Toulouse & Paris Conss. and made his 1st appearance in 1867, at the Opéra-Comique. In 1894–1908 he was intermittently joint and sole manager of the Paris Opéra at var. times.

Gaillard. *See* **Galliard.**

Gál, Hans (b. Brunn, 5. VIII. 1890), Aus. comp. & mcolst. Pupil of Mandyczewski in Vienna and lecturer at the Univ. there from 1918; later dir. of the Mus. Acad. at Mainz. After the *Anschluss* he took refuge at Edinburgh, where in 1945 he was app. lecturer at the Univ.

Works incl. operas *Der Fischer, Der Arzt der Sobeide, Ruth, Die heilige Ente, Das Lied der Nacht, Die beiden Klaus Der Zauberspiegel*; *Requiem für Mignon* (from Goethe's *Wilhelm Meister*), for chor. & orch. and other chor. works; *Sinfonietta, Ballet Suite, Pickwickian Ovt.* (after Dickens), &c. for orch.; Serenade for stgs.; pf. Conc., v. Conc.; 2 stg. 4tets, 5 Intermezzi for stg. 4tet, Serenade for stg. trio; pf. works, &c.

Galant (Fr. & Ger. = courtly). An adj. used to designate a special mus. style of the 18th cent., esp. that of C. P. E. Bach and the Mannheim school. Its main characteristics are elegance, a certain superficiality of feeling, formality (the 1st approaches towards so. form) and profuse ornamentation. The term must not be trans. into Eng. as 'gallant,' which has not the same meaning. 'Courtly Style' may be recomm. as a good Eng. term.

Galanterien (Ger.) } lit. courtesies).
Galanteries (Fr. }

The extra dances or other pieces added to those which are obligatory to the classical Suite or Partita (Allemande, Courante, Sarabande and Gigue). The most frequently used Gs. were Bourrées, Minuets, Passepieds, Chaconnes, and among pieces other than dances Airs.

Galatea, La, opera by Schürer (lib. by Metastasio), prod. Dresden, at court, 8. XI. 1746.

Galilei, Vincenzo (b. Santa Maria in Monte nr. Florence, 1520; d. Florence, VI. 1591), It. comp., lutenist & theorist. Studied under Zarlino at Venice. He took part in the discussions which led the Florentine *camerata* to opera after his death and wrote theoret. books, becoming involved in controversy with Zarlino. Father of the astronomer Galileo Galilei.

Works incl. cantata *Il Conte Ugolino* from Dante, a setting of the Lamentations of Jeremiah (both lost, and both among the earliest m. for a single voice with accomp.); 2 books of madrigals; pieces for 2 viols; a lute book in tablature, &c.

Galimat(h)ias (Fr. = gallimaufry, farrago, gibberish). In m. the term is found in Mozart's *Galimathias musicum* (K. 32) written by him at The Hague in 1766, at age of 10, for the coming of age of William of Orange. It contains the Dutch nat. air 'Wilhelmus van Nassouwe.'

Gallenberg, Wenzel (Robert) von, Count (b. Vienna, 28. XII. 1783; d. Rome, 13. III. 1839), Aus. amateur comp. Studied with Albrechtsberger and married Countess Giulietta Guicciardi, the pupil of Beethoven, who fell in love with her.

Works incl. over 40 ballets, 3 ovts., 8 pieces for wind band, dances for orch. & for pf., contributions to periodical pubs., &c.

Galli (?) (b. ?; d. ? London, 1804), It. m.-sop. singer. Settled in London, where she 1st appeared in 1743 and remained until her death.

Galli, Filippo (b. Rome, 1783; d. ? Paris, 3. VI. 1853), It. bass singer, at first a ten. Made his 1st appearance as a ten. at Bologna in 1804 and as a bass at Venice in 1812.

Galli-Marié, Marie (Célestine Laurence) (b. Paris, XI. 1840; d. Vence nr. Nice, 22. IX. 1905), Fr. m.-sop. singer. Pupil of her father; made her 1st appearance at Strasburg in 1859.

Galliard (Eng., from Fr. *Gaillarde* & It. *Gagliarda*). A sprightly dance of some antiquity (*c.* 15th cent.), usually in 3–2 but sometimes in 4–4 time; often used in m. as a contrast to the slower and statelier **Pavan** and frequently based on the same mus. material. Its special assoc. with Rome gained it the alternative name of Romanesca.

Galliard, Johann Ernst (John Ernest) (? orig. Gaillard) (b. Zell, Hanover, *c.* 1687; d. London, 1749), Ger. (anglicized) orgst., obst. & comp. Pupil of Steffani and others. Settled in Eng. *c.* 1706, became chamber musn. to Prince George of Den., later orgst. at Somerset House, obst. in the opera orch. under Handel and comp. of pantomimes, &c. to John Rich.

Works incl. operas *Calypso and Telemachus, Pan and Syrinx* & *Oreste e Pilade* (unfinished); several pantomimes and other stage entertainments; incid. m. for Lee's *Oedipus* and the Earl of Mulgrave's adaptation of Shakespeare's *Julius Caesar*; Morning Hymn from Milton's *Paradise Lost* for chor. & orch.; Te Deum & Jubilate, anthems; pieces for 24 bns. & 4 dbs. and other inst. pieces; songs, &c.

Galliculus (? Hähnel, Hähnlein), Joannes (b. ?; d. ?), Ger. 16th-cent. theorist & comp. Worked at Leipzig (?) as a teacher; wrote a theoret. work *Isagoge* (later *Libellus*) *de compositione cantus* and comp. a Passion accord. to St. Mark, 2 magnificats, a psalm, liturgical works for Easter and Christmas, &c.

Gallus, Jacobus. *See* Handl.

Galop (Fr. =gallop). A quick ballroom dance in 2–4 time 1st appearing under that name in Paris in 1829, but of older Ger. org., its Ger. name (now *Galopp*) having been *Hopser* (hopper) or *Rutscher* (glider).

Galoubet (Fr.). A small wind inst., the Pipe used with the accomp. Tabor (Fr. *tambourin*).

Galpin, Francis W(illiam). (b. Dorchester, 25. XII. 1858; d. Richmond, Surrey, 30. XII, 1945), Eng. clergyman & mus. scholar. Educ. at Sherborne School and Cambridge, where he picked up much mus. study and played the cl. in the Univ. orch. Canon of Chelmsford in 1917 and Lit.D. Cambridge, 1938. He made a collection of old mus. insts. and wrote several learned books and many articles on the subject.

Galsworthy, John (1867–1933), Eng. novelist & playwright. Made a trans. of Bizet's *Carmen*.

Galuppi, Baldassare (b. Burano island nr. Venice, 18. X. 1706; d. Venice, 3. I. 1785), It. comp. Son of a barber who was also a vst., and gave him his 1st mus. instruction. It was not until after he had prod. his 1st opera at Chioggia in 1722 that he entered the Cons. degli Incurabili as a pupil of Lotti. His next stage work, *Gli odi delusi dal sangue*, written with Pescetti, appeared in 1728, and thereafter he turned out a vast number of operas, often several in the same year. Goldoni became his librt., with the result that his operas were as distinguished from the literary as from the mus. point of view. In 1741–3 he was in London and in 1765–8 in St. Petersburg, prod. earlier and new works in both capitals. He was app. vice chapel master at St. Mark's in Venice in 1748 and became chief chapel master in 1762.

Works incl. operas *Alessandro nell' Indie, Issipile, Adriano in Siria, Penelope* (London), *L'Olimpiade, L'Arcadia in Brenta, Il Conte Caramella, Il mondo della luna, Il mondo alla roversa, La calamità de cuori, Il filosofo di campagna, Le nozze, L'amante di tutti, Le tre amanti ridicoli, Il Marchese Villano, Ifigenia in Tauride* (St. Petersburg), &c.; inst. works; hpchd. sos., &c.

Gamba (abbr., *see* **Viola da gamba**). Also an open metal org. stop imitating the tone of the va. da gamba, ranging over 4-ft., 8-ft. & 16-ft. pipes.

Gammer Gurton's Needle, Eng. comedy by ? (poss. John Bridges, Dean of Salisbury, or William Stevenson), written *c.* 1560, pub. 1575. *See* Davie (opera).

Gamut. The word is now loosely used in the sense of 'range' or 'compass.' Orig. it was derived from 'Gamma Ut,' the lowest note (G on the bottom stave of the bass clef), from which the Hexachords were reckoned, being marked with the Gr. letter Γ and called 'Ut,' which later became 'Do,' as in Tonic Sol-fa notation. Above this the scale was marked as now, A, B, C, &c. and side by side with these letters went the syllables Ut, Re, Mi, Fa, Sol, La, representing the hexachord of 6 notes. But these syllables could be so transferred that, for ex. C, which was Fa in the 1st hexachord, became Ut in the 2nd, the m. being now no longer in the Mixolydian mode starting on G, but in the Ionian starting on C. Similarly the Ut could be transferred to F and the series of syllables continued thence upwards, the m. thus changing to the Lydian mode. This was, in fact, a primitive system of Modulation, called Mutation, and it differed from modulation in making no use of accidentals, except that both B♮ and B♭ were used. The nomenclature of the G. persisted in mus. practice after the displacement of the modes by maj. and min. keys and up to the time of Purcell, in whose works are found such titles as *Ground in C fa ut* (sometimes spelt 'C faut'). Shakespeare puns on the terms of the G. in *The Taming of the Shrew* (III. i).

Gamut-Way. A 17th-cent. term for m. written in ord. notation, as distinct from tablature.

Ganascione (It.). A large It. lute.

Ganne, (Gustave) Louis (b. Buxière-les-Mines, Allier, 5. IV. 1862; d. Paris, 14. VII. 1923), Fr. comp. Pupil of Dubois & Franck. He cond. the Opéra balls in Paris and orchs. at Royan and Monte Carlo, and became very popular as a comp. of light m.

Works incl. operettas *Rabelais, Les Colles des femmes, Les Saltimbanques* & *Hans le joueur de flûte*; ballet *La Source du Nil* & several others; popular songs including *La Marche Lorraine* & *Le Père la Victoire*; dances *La Tsarine*, &c.

Gänsbacher, Johann (b. Sterzing, Tyrol, 8. V. 1788; d. Vienna, 13. VII. 1844), Aus. comp. Pupil of Vogler and Albrechtsberger. Became chapel master of St. Stephen's cath. in Vienna, 1823.

Works incl. incid. m. to Kotzebue's *Die Kreuzfahrer*; 35 masses, 8 Requiems & other church m.; a sym.; pf. m.; songs, &c.

Gänsbacher, Joseph (b. Vienna, 6. X. 1829; d. Vienna, 4. VI. 1911), Aus. teacher of singing & cst., son of prec. Prof. at the Vienna Cons.

Gapped Scales. Any scales containing less than 7 notes, e.g. Pentatonic, Whole-tone scales, &c.

Garat, Pierre Jean (b. Ustaritz, 25. IV. 1764; d. Paris, 1. III. 1823), Fr. ten.-bar. singer. Pupil of Beck at Bordeaux. He became the favourite singer of Marie Antoinette, went to Hamburg and London during the Revol. and in 1799 became prof. of singing at the Paris Cons. He wrote some popular songs.

Garay, János (1812–53), Hung. poet. *See* **Háry János** (Kodály).

Garborg, Arne (1851–1925), Norw. poet. *See* **Grieg** (*Haugtussa*).

García, Spa. family of singers:

1. Manuel (del Popolo Vicente) G. (b. Seville, 22. I. 1775; d. Paris, 2. VI. 1832). Ten. singer, teacher & comp. Was a chorister at Seville cath. and became well known as singer, cond. and comp. in his teens. In 1808 he made his 1st appearance in Paris and in 1811 in It. At Naples he prod. an opera, *Il Califfo di Bagdad*, not the 1st of a number of works for the stage. He now sang much in Paris and London, in 1825 brought the 1st It. opera co., incl. himself, his son (2) and elder daughter (3), to N.Y., and in 1826–8 was in Mex.

2. Manuel (Patricio Rodriguez) G. (b. Zafra, Catalonia, 17. III. 1805; d. London, 1. VII. 1906), singing teacher, son of prec. Pupil of his father and of Fétis in mus. theory. He appeared early in opera, but in 1829 retired to devote himself to teaching only. App. prof. at the Paris Cons. in 1842 and at the R.A.M. in London in 1848, where he remained to the end of his long life, retiring in 1895.

3. Maria Felicità G. (b. Paris, 24. III. 1808; d. Manchester, 23. IX. 1836), sister of prec. *See* **Malibran.**

4. (Michelle Ferdinande) Pauline G. (b. Paris, 18. VII. 1821; d. Paris, 17–18. V. 1910, sister of prec. *See* **Viardot-García.**

5. Gustave G. (b. Milan, 1. II. 1837; d. London, 12. VI. 1925), bar. singer, son of 2. Appeared as an opera singer in London and then sang at Milan, but settled in London as teacher, at the R.A.M. from 1880 and was prof. at the R.C.M. from 1883.

García Roblez, José (b. Olot, 1839; d. Barcelona, IV. 1910), Spa. comp.

Works incl. opera *Julio César* (after Shakespeare); *Catalonia* for chor. & orch. & other chor. works, &c.

Gardano, Antonio (b. ?; d. Venice, 1569), It. m. printer, estab. at Venice from 1538. His sons Cipriano and Annibale continued the business, as well as 2 other relatives, Angelo and Alessandro G., until 1619.

Garden of Fand, The, symph. poem by Bax, comp. 1913, 1st perf. Chicago, 29. X. 1920. (Fand is a heroine of Ir. legend, but in this work the garden of F. is simply the sea, charged with Ir. legendry.)

Gardiner, H(enry). Balfour (b. London, 7. XI. 1877), Eng. comp. Educ. at Charterhouse School and Oxford, and studied m. under Knorr at Frankfort. Became m. master at Winchester Coll. for a short time, then devoted himself wholly to comp.

Works incl. *News from Wydah* (Masefield) for chor. & orch.; Sym. in D maj., *English Dance*, Fantasy & *Shepherd Fennel's Dance* (after Hardy) for orch.; stg. 4tet, stg. 5tet & other chamber m.; *Noel*, 5 pieces, &c. for pf.; partsongs, &c.

Gardiner, William (b. Leicester, 15. III. 1770; d. Leicester, 16. XI. 1853), Eng. manufacturer, mus. amateur, writer & ed. Admirer of Haydn, to whom he sent 6 pairs of silk stockings with themes from H.'s works woven into them; in 1793 he became acquainted with Beethoven's work, some of which, as well as Haydn's and Mozart's, he adapted to Eng. words in var. ways. Wrote books on m. and comp. as an amateur.

Gare generose, Le (*The Generous Quarrels*), opera by Paisiello (lib. Giovanni Palomba), prod. Naples, Teatro dei Fiorentini, spring 1786.

Gargantua, opera by Mariotte (lib. by Armory, based on Rabelais), prod. Paris, Opéra-Comique, 17. II. 1935.

Garlandia, Johannes de (b. ?; d. ?), Eng. 13th-cent. scholar & writer on m. Studied at Oxford and Paris, where he later opened a school, *c.* 1215. In 1229 he helped to found the Univ. of Toulouse, where he remained until 1232, returning to Paris. Wrote treatises on plainsong, mensurable m. and (?) ctpt.

Garnett, Richard (1835–1906), Eng. essayist, biog. & poet. *See* **Sea Pictures** (Elgar).

Garrick, David (1717–79), Eng. actor & playwright. *See* **Cymon** (M. Arne), **Gast** (*Heimliche Ehe*), **Matrimonio segreto** (Cimarosa), **Vernon** (2 plays).

Garrigues, Malwina (b. ?, 7. XII. 1825; d. Carlsruhe, 8. II. 1904), Ger. sop. singer. Was engaged for the Opera at Carlsruhe, where she met the ten. **Ludwig Schnorr von Carolsfeld**, whom she married. In 1860 they were engaged by the Dresden Court Opera. In 1865 she was Wagner's 1st Isolde in the Munich prod. of *Tristan und Isolde*, to the Tristan of her husband, who d. the following month.

Gasco, Alberto (b. Naples, 3. X. 1879; d. Rome, 11. VII. 1938), It. comp. Pupil of Terziani and d'Indy. M. critic of *La Tribuna* in Rome.

Works incl. opera *La leggenda delle sette torri* (after Rossetti's watercolour *The Tune of Seven Towers*); orat. *San Francesco*; *Presso al Clitunno*, *Preludio pastorale*, *Preludio giocoso*, *Buffalmacco* & *Scherzo orgiastico* for orch.; stg. 4tet *Venere dormiente* (after Giorgione's picture); v. & pf. So. *La visione di Sant' Orsola* (after Carpaccio's picture); *Le danzatrici di Jodhpur* (after Besnard's picture) for pf., &c.

Gasparini, Francesco (b. Camaiore nr. Lucca, 5. III. 1668; d. Rome, 22. III. 1727), It. comp. Pupil of Corelli and Pasquini; chor. master at the Ospedale della Pietà, Venice; app. chapel master of St. John Lateran, Rome, 1725.

Works incl. over 50 operas, e.g. *Il più fedel fra i vassalli*, *La fede tradita e vendicata*, *Ambleto* (on Shakespeare's *Hamlet*); orats. *Mosè liberato dal Nilo*, *La nascita di Cristo* & *Le nozze di Tobia*; church m.; cantatas, &c.

Gasparini, Quirino (b. Bergamo, ?; d. Turin, 11. X. 1778), It. cst. & comp. Court chapel master at Turin in 1760–70.

Works incl. opera *Mitridate* (lib. later set by Mozart); *Stabat Mater* & other church m.; v. Conc.; trio sos., &c.

Gasparo da Salò. *See* **Salò.**

Gassenhauer (Ger. lit. street-beater). The term now means a popular song of a vulgar kind, but was formerly a Ger. equivalent of Passacaglia, from the Spa. *pasar* (to walk) and *calle* (street).

Gassier, Édouard (b. ? Paris, 30. IV. 1820; d. Havana, 18. XII. 1872), Fr. bar. singer. Studied at the Paris Cons. and made his 1st appearance at the Opéra-Comique there in 1845.

Gassier (*née* **Fernandez**), **Josefa** (b. Bilbao, 1821; d. Madrid, 8. XI. 1866), Spa. sop. singer, wife of prec. Made her 1st appearance in London in 1846.

Gassmann, Florian Leopold (b. Brüx, 4. V. 1723; d. Vienna, 22. I. 1774), Boh. comp. Studied with Martini at Bologna, was in the service of Count Leonardi Veneri at Venice and in 1762 went to Vienna as ballet comp. App. court chapel master on Reutter's death in 1772.

Works incl. *c.* 25 operas, e.g. *Gli uccellatori*, *L'amore artigiano*, *La notte critica*, *La contessina*, *I rovinati* (not by Umlauf); orat. *La Betulia liberata*, church m., &c.

Gast, Peter (real name Johann Heinrich Köselitz) (b. Annaberg, 10. I. 1854; d. Annaberg, 15. VIII. 1918), Ger. comp. Studied at the Leipzig Cons. and later went to Basle as a friend and disciple of Nietzsche. Afterwards he lived at Venice and Weimar.

Works incl. opera *Die heimliche Ehe* (based on the lib. of Cimarosa's *Matrimonio segreto* and farther back on Colman & Garrick's *Clandestine Marriage*); *Hosanna* for chor. & orch.; sym. *Helle Nächte* & other orch. works; stg. 4tet, 7tet, &c.

'Gastein' Symphony. A Sym. in C maj. supposed to have been written by Schubert during a visit to Gastein in VIII.–IX. 1825, of which no trace is left, unless it is identical with the Grand Duo for pf. duet, Op. 140. There are several refs. to the Sym., but if it was written at that time, or at all, it was probably begun at Gmunden before the visit to Gastein, where S. stayed only a short time and is known to have written the pf. So. in D maj., Op. 53.

Gastoldi, Giovanni Giacomo (b. Caravaggio, ?; d. Mantua, ?), It. 16th–17th-cent. comp. Chapel master at the church of Santa Barbara at Mantua from 1581 to his death.
Works incl. a Magnificat & other church m.; madrigals; balletti and canzoni for voices & insts., &c.

Gastoué, Amédée (b. Paris, 13. III. 1873), Fr. mcolst. & orgst. Prof. of plainsong at the Schola Cantorum and the Institut Catholique in Paris and author of several books on the subject, on old Fr. m., the hist. of the org., &c.

Gates, Bernard (b. London, 1685; d. North Aston nr. Oxford, 15. XI. 1773), Eng. theorist, singer & comp. Gentleman of the Chapel Royal from 1708 and Master of the Children some time before 1732.
Works incl. Service in F maj.; songs, &c.

Gatti, Guido M(aria). (b. Chieti, 30. V. 1892), It. critic. Founder of the review *Il Pianoforte* (later *La Rassegna Musicale*) in 1920 and promoter of concerts. His books incl. studies of Schumann, Bizet, Fr. m. and esp. modern It. m.

Gatty, Nicholas (Comyn) (b. Bradfield nr. Sheffield, 13. IX. 1874), Eng. critic & comp. Studied at Cambridge and at the R.C.M. in London, under Stanford.
Works incl. operas *Greysteel, Duke or Devil, Prince Ferelon, The Tempest & Macbeth* (both Shakespeare), *King Alfred and the Cakes*; *Ode on Time* (Milton) and 3 *Short Odes* (Clough & Shelley) for chor. & orch.; *King Cole Vars.*, comedy ovt. & other works for orch., *Haslemere Suite* for stg. orch.; Vars. for stg. 4tet, pf. Trio; v. & pf. So.; inst. pieces; songs, &c.

Gaul, Alfred (Robert) (b. Norwich, 30. IV. 1837; d. Birmingham, 13. IX. 1913), Eng. orgst. & comp. Studied under Z. Buck as a chorister at Norwich cath. and later became orgst. at var. churches at Birmingham.
Works incl. orats. *Hezekiah, Ruth, The Holy City, Joan of Arc, The Ten Virgins, Israel in the Wilderness, Una*; Psalms, Passion m., hymns, chants; partsongs; pf. pieces, &c.

Gaultier. Fr. family of lutenists:
1. Ennemond G. (b. ? Lyons, *c.* 1575; d. Villette, Dauphiné, 17. XII. 1651), taught Queen Marie de' Medici and Richelieu. Wrote lute pieces.
2. Jacques G. (b. ?; d. ?), ? son of prec. Fled to London *c.* 1617 and was attached to the court until 1647. Visited Hol. & Spa. and comp. lute pieces & songs.
3. Denis G. (b. ? Marseilles; d. Paris, I. 1672), nephew or cousin of 1. Wrote a large number of lute pieces.
4. Pierre G. (b. Orléans, ?; d. ?), ? unrelated to the prec. He was in Rome in 1638 and pub. lute pieces there.

Gautier, Théophile (1811–72), Fr. poet & novelist. *See* **Cleopatra's Night** (H. K. Hadley), **Falla** (songs), **Fanelli** (*Tableaux symphoniques*), **Giselle** (Adam), **Reyer** (*Sélam*), **Terrasse** (*Matinées poétiques*).

Gavazzeni, Gianandrea (b. Bergamo, 25. VII. 1909), It. comp. Studied in Rome and Milan, and later became a comp. pupil of Pizzetti and Pilati. He became both a cond. and a critic.
Works incl. opera *Paolo e Virginia* (after Saint-Pierre); orat. *Il canto di Sant' Alessandro*; chor. triptych; Symph. Prelude, *Three Episodes*, &c. for orch.; concs. for v. and for co.; interludes to Tasso's *Aminta* for bar. & orch.; pf. Trio; sos. for v. & pf. and co. & pf.; So. & other works for pf.; songs, &c.

Gaveau, Étienne (b. Paris, 7. X. 1872), Fr. pf. manufacturer. Followed his father, Joseph G. (?–1903) and built a factory at Fontenay-sous-Bois in 1896 and a concert hall (Salle G.) in Paris in 1907.

Gaveaux, Pierre (b. Béziers, VIII. 1761; d. Passy nr. Paris, 2. II. 1825), Fr. ten. singer & comp. Pupil of Beck at Bordeaux, where he came out as an opera singer.
Works incl. operas *Les Deux Suisses, L'Amour filial, La Famille indigente, Le Petit Matelot, Léonore, ou L'Amour conjugal, Un Quart-d'heure de silence, Le Bouffe et le tailleur, Monsieur Deschalumeaux, L'Enfant prodigue*; revol. hymn *Le Réveil du peuple*; It. canzonets & Fr. romances for voice & pf., &c.

Gaviniès, Pierre (b. Bordeaux, 26. V. 1726; d. Paris, 9. IX. 1800), Fr. vst. & comp. Made his 1st appearance in Paris in 1741, at the Concert spirituel, of which he was cond. in 1773–7. Prof. of v. at the Cons. from its foundation in 1794.
Works incl. opera *Le Prétendu*; v. concs.; sos. for v. & bass, v. & pf., 2 vs. & unaccomp. v., v. studies *Les Vingt-quatre Matinées*, v. pieces incl. the *Romance de G.*, &c.

Gavot. The old Eng. name of the Gavotte, obs. but worth reviving.

Gavotte (Fr.). A Fr. dance in moderately animated 4–4 beginning on the 3rd beat, in 2 sections, each of which is repeated, the 1st ending usually in the dominant. It often occurs in suites, but is not a regular constituent of them, and it may therefore have an alternative or trio section, sometimes in the character of a Musette.

Gay, John (1685–1732), Eng. poet & playwright. *See* **Acis and Galatea** (Handel), **Beggar's Opera, Busby** (odes), **Dreigroschenoper** (Weill), **Polly.**

Gay, María (b. Barcelona, 13. VI. 1879; d. New York, 29. VII. 1943), Spa. mezzo-sop. singer. Studied sculpture and v. as a girl, but was self-taught in singing. In 1902 Pugno engaged her to sing at his and Ysaÿe's concerts in Brussels and she appeared as Carmen at the Théâtre de la Monnaie at 5 days' notice. She 1st appeared in Eng. in 1906. In 1913 she married the ten. Giovanni Zenatello.

Gaztambide, Joaquín (b. Tudela, Navarre, 7. II. 1822; d. Madrid, 18. III. 1870), Spa. cond. & comp. Studied at Pamplona and the Madrid Cons. After a stay in Paris he became theatre manager and cond. in Madrid.

Works incl. 44 zarzuelas, e.g. *La mensajera, El estreno de una artista, El valle de Andorra, Catalina, Los Magyares, El juramento, La conquista de Madrid*, &c.

Gazza ladra, La (*The Thievish Magpie*), opera by Rossini (lib. by Giovanni Gherardini, based on the Fr. melodrama, *La Pie voleuse*, by Jean Marie Théodore Baudouin d'Aubigny & Louis Charles Caigniez), prod. Milan, Teatro alla Scala, 31. V. 1817.

Gazzaniga, Giuseppe (b. Verona, X. 1743; d. Crema, 1. II. 1818), It. comp. Pupil of Porpora and Piccinni. 1st at Venice and later at Naples, where his 1st opera was prod. in 1768. Later in life he became chapel master at Crema and devoted himself to church m.

Works incl. 50 operas, e.g. *Il barone di Trocchia, La locanda, L'isola di Alcina, La vendemmia, La moglie capricciosa, Il finto cieco, Don Giovanni Tenorio* (*Il convitato di pietra*); 3 orats.; church m., &c.

Gebel, Georg (b. Brieg, 25. X. 1709; d. Rudolstadt, 24. IX. 1753), Ger. orgst., hpchdst. & comp. Pupil of and later deputy orgst. to his father, Johann Georg G. at Breslau, where later he became orgst. at the church of St. Mary Magdalen. Afterwards he held appts. at Oels, Dresden and Warsaw and in 1747 went to the court of Rudolstadt.

Works incl. 8 operas, e.g. *Oedipus, Medea, Tarquinius Superbus, Sophonisbe, Marcus Antonius*; much church m., Christmas orats., Passions; syms.; hpchd. m., &c.

Gebel, Georg Sigismund (b. Breslau, 1715; d. Breslau, 1775), Ger. orgst., hpchdst. & comp., brother of prec. Orgst. of several churches at Breslau. Comp. org. m.

Gebel, Johann Georg (b. Breslau, 1685; d. Breslau, 1750), Ger. orgst. & comp., father of prec. Pupil of Tiburtius Winckler, cath. orgst. at Breslau, for whom he deputized later. App. orgst. at Brieg in 1709 and returned to Breslau in 1713, where he held org. appts. at var. churches.

Works incl. motets, church cantatas, psalms, Mass & Passion; org. works, &c.

Gebrauchsmusik (Ger. lit. utility m.). A term invented by Hindemith for a species of work written for special occasions, and best trans. as 'workaday m.,' since no work of art can be intended strictly for pure usefulness. Hindemith's pub. works of the kind (several are unpub.) are: *Spielmusik* for stgs., fls. & obs.; 4 3-part *Songs for Singing Groups*; an educ. work for concerted vs. in 1st position; *Music to Sing or Play* (5 Nos. for var. voc. or inst. combs.); *Lesson* for 2 male voices, narrator, chor., orch., a dancer, clowns and community singing; *Let's Build a Town*, a mus. game for children; *Plöner Musiktag* (4 Nos. for var. voc. & inst. combs.). Some other comps., e.g. Milhaud in Fr., and Weill in Ger., have done similar work.

Gedackt (sometimes Gedact, Ger. properly 'gedeckt' = covered). An adj. used for stopped Diapason org. stops prod. a muted 8-ft. tone.

Gédalge, André (b. Paris, 27. XII. 1856; d. Paris, 5. II. 1926), Fr. comp. Studied at the Paris Cons., where he became prof. of ctpt. & fugue in 1905.

Works incl. operas *Le Petit Savoyard, Pris au piège, Sita, La Farce du Cadi* & *Hélène*; 3 syms.; concs.; chamber m.; songs, &c.

Geibel, Emanuel von (1815–84), Ger. poet. *See* **Jensen** (*Spanisches Liederbuch*), **Loreley** (Bruch & Mendelssohn), **Schumann** (*Vom Pagen und der Königstochter*), **Spanisches Liederbuch** (H. Wolf), **Volbach** (*Vom Pagen und der K.*).

Geige (Ger. = fiddle). The familiar Ger. name of the v.

Geigen Principal. An 8-ft. open Diapason org. stop prod. an imitation of v. tone.

Geijer, Erik Gustaf (b. Ransæter nr. Karlstad, 12. I. 1783; d. Stockholm, 23. IV. 1847), Swe. historian, philos., poet & comp. As a musn. he became popular with many simple songs that have become the common property of the Swe. people.

Geisha, The, operetta by Sidney Jones (lib. by Owen Hall & Harry Greenbank), prod. London, Daly's Theatre, 25. IV. 1896.

Gelinek, Joseph (b. Selcz, 3. XII. 1758;

d. Vienna, 13. IV. 1825), Boh. secular priest, pfst. & comp. Studied m. & theol. in Prague, was ordained there and later had lessons in comp. from Albrechtsberger. He became famous as a pf. teacher and improviser and in 1795 entered the service of Prince Esterházy.

Works incl. vars., fantasies, &c. for pf.

Gellert, Christian Fürchtegott (1715–69), Ger. poet. *See* **Hiller (J. A.)** (odes & songs), **Quantz** (hymns).

Gelosie fortunate, Le (*The Fortunate Jealousies*), opera by Anfossi (lib. by Filippo Livigni), prod. Venice, Teatro San Samuele, autumn 1786. Mozart added an aria to it on its prod. in Vienna, 2. VI. 1788.

Gelosie villane, Le (*The Rustic Jealousies*), opera by Sarti (lib. by Tommaso Grandi, based on a comedy by Goldoni), prod. Venice, Teatro San Samuele, XI. 1776.

Gemel. *See* **Gymel.**

Gemellum (*see also* **Gymel**). In the 15th & 16th cents. the term G. ('twin-song') was used to indicate the division of a single voice-part temporarily into 2 parts, like the modern *divisi*; the return to a single part was marked *semellum.*

Geminiani, Francesco (b. Lucca, *c.* 4. XII. 1687; d. Dublin, 17. IX. 1762), It. vst. & comp. Pupil of Corelli in Rome; went to Eng. in 1714 and lived in London, Dublin, Paris and again in Ir. until his death. He taught the v. more progressively than it had been done before in Brit. and wrote several theoret. works.

Comps. incl. orch. concs., sos. and solos for v.; solos for co.; trios; hpchd. pieces, &c.

Gemma di Vergy, opera by Donizetti (lib. by Emanuele Bidera, based on the elder Dumas's play, *Charles VII chez ses grands vassaux*), prod. Milan, Teatro alla Scala, 26. XII. 1834.

Gemshorn (Ger. = chamois hn.). A 4-ft. open org. stop of soft, rather nasal tone.

Genée, Franz (Friedrich Richard) (b. Danzig, 7. II. 1823; d. Baden nr. Vienna, 15. VI. 1895), Ger. cond. & comp. Studied medicine at first, but took to m. and became cond. successively at Reval, Riga, Cologne, Aachen, Düsseldorf, Danzig, Mainz, Schwerin, Amsterdam, Prague and Vienna. He wrote or collab. in many libs. for operettas by other Viennese comps.

Works incl. operettas *Der Geiger aus Tirol, Der Musikfeind, Die Generalprobe, Rosita, Der schwarze Prinz, Am Runenstein* (with Flotow), *Der Seekadett, Nanon, Im Wunderlande der Pyramiden, Die letzten Mohikaner* (after Fenimore Cooper), *Nisida, Rosina, Die Zwillinge, Die Piraten, Die Dreizehn*; partsongs incl. the comic *Italienischer Salat,* &c.

Generalbass (Ger. lit. general bass) = Thorough-Bass.

Generali, Pietro (real name Mercandetti) (b. Masserano nr. Vercelli, 4. X. 1783; d. Novara, 3. XI. 1832), It. comp. Studied under Giovanni Massi in Rome and in 1800 prod. his 1st opera there. In 1817–21 he cond. opera at Barcelona, and later became chapel master at Novara cath.

Works incl. *c.* 60 operas, e.g. *Gli amanti ridicoli, Il Duca Nottolone, La villana in cimento, Le gelosie di Giorgio, Pamela nubile* (after Richardson, via Goldoni's comedy), *La calzolaia, Misantropia e pentimento* (after Kotzebue), *Gli effetti della somiglianza, Don Chisciotte* (after Cervantes), *Orgoglio ed umiliazione, L'idolo cinese, Lo sposo in bersaglio, Le lagrime di una vedova, Adelina, La moglie giudice del marito, I baccanti di Roma, Francesca da Rimini* (after Dante); masses & other church m.; cantata *Roma liberata,* &c.

Genet, Elzéar (b. ? Carpentras, *c.* 1470; d. Avignon, 14. VI. 1548), Fr. priest & comp. He was a singer in the Papal choir in Rome in 1508 and again from 1513, and also served at the court of Louis XII. In 1522 he became dean of Saint-Agricol at Avignon, where he remained until his death, paying a 3rd visit to Rome in 1524.

Works incl. masses, motets, magnificats, lamentations, psalms, hymns, &c.

Genlis, Stéphanie Félicité de, Countess (1746–1830), Fr. educst. & novelist. *See* **Siege of Rochelle** (Balfe).

Genoveva, opera by Schumann (lib. by comp. altered from one by Robert Reinick based on the dramas by Tieck and Hebbel), prod. Leipzig, 25. VI. 1850.

Gentle Shepherd, The, ballad opera (lib. by Allan Ramsay), prod. Edinburgh, Taylor's Hall, 29. I. 1729. It was published in 1725 as a pastoral comedy, and is therefore not, as is sometimes said, the 1st ballad opera, *The Beggar's Opera* having appeared earlier.

George, Stefan (1868–1933), Ger. poet. *See* **Knab** (songs), **Maler** (cantata), **Schoenberg** (*Buch der hängenden Gärten*), **Webern** (songs & chor.).

Georges, Alexandre (b. Arras, 25. II. 1850; d. Arras, 18. I. 1938), Fr. orgst. & comp. Studied at the École Niedermeyer in Paris and qualified as an orgst. & choirmaster.

Works incl. operas *Le Printemps,*

Poèmes d'amour, Charlotte Corday, Miarka (Jean Richepin), *La Passion, Les Chansons de Leïlah, Myrrha, Sangre y sol*; incid. m. for Villiers de l'Isle-Adam's *Le Nouveau Monde* & *Axël* & other plays; symph. poems *Léila, La Naissance de Vénus, Le Paradis perdu* (after Milton); *Chansons de Miarka* for voice & orch.; 3 *Chansons anglaises* (Carew), &c.

Ger. (abbr.) = German, Germany.

Gerarde, John Theodoricus (Derick Gerard) (b. ?; d. ?), Flem. 16th-cent. comp. Prob. lived in Eng. for some time.

Works incl. numerous motets; madrigals, chansons, carols; m. for viols, &c.

Gerber, Ernst Ludwig (b. Sondershausen, 29. IX. 1746; d. Sondershausen, 30. VI. 1819), Ger. mus. bibliog. Studied under his father and at Leipzig Univ. His chief work is a lexicon of musns.

Gerber, Heinrich Nicolaus (b. Weingen-Ehrich, Schwarzburg, 6. IX. 1702; d. Sondershausen, 6. VIII. 1775), Ger. orgst. & comp., father of prec. Studied at Leipzig Univ. and became a disciple of Bach there. Court orgst. at Sondershausen from 1731. Improved and invented insts., incl. the *Strohfiedel*.

Works incl. a hymn-book with figured basses; vars. on chorales for org.; m. for hpchd., org., hp., &c.

Gerbert von Hornau, Martin (b. Horb o/Neckar, 12. VIII. 1720; d. St. Blasien, 13. V. 1793), Ger. mus. historian. Studied at Ludwigsburg, entered the Benedictine monastery at St. Blasien in 1737, was ordained priest in 1744 and became abbot in 1764. He wrote much on church m., incl. a hist. of the subject.

Gerhard, Roberto (b. Valls, Catalonia, 25. IX. 1896), Spa. pfst. & comp. Although a choir-boy and a tentative pfst. & comp. from an early age, he began serious mus. studies late, owing to parental opposition. But after 2 years' commercial studies in Fr. Swi., he studied pf. with Granados and comp. with Pedrell at Barcelona in 1915–22 and then comp. with Schoenberg in Vienna in 1923–8. In 1929–38 he lived and taught at Barcelona, was in charge of the m. dept. of the Catalan Library, for which he ed. m. by 18th-cent. Catalan comps., trans. var. mus. treatises into Spa. and contrib. to the literary weekly *Mirador*. Pedrell introd. him as a comp. and he began to make his way in Spa. and Lat. Amer. After the downfall of the Spa. Repub. he emigrated to Eng. and in 1939 settled at Cambridge with a research scholarship from King's Coll.

Works incl. ballets *Ariel, Soirées de Barcelone, Don Quixote* (after Cervantes), *Alegrias* & *Pandora*; m. for radio plays *Cristobal Colón* & *Adventures of Don Quixote* (Eric Linklater, after Cervantes); Sym. *Hommage à Pedrell*; v. Conc.; *Cancionero de Pedrell, Serranillas* & *Cançons i Arietes* for voice & orch.; stg. 4tet, pf. Trio, wind 5tet; cantata for solo voices, chor. & orch.; song cycle *L'infantament meravellós de Shaharazada* & other songs; var. arrs. of old Spa. m., &c.

Gerhardt, Paul (? 1606–76), Ger. hymn-writer. *See* **Ebeling (hymns).**

Gerle, Hans (b. Nuremberg, ?; d. Nuremberg, ?), Ger. 16th-cent. lutenist, violist & lute-maker. Son of Konrad Gerle (d. 1521), also a lute-maker. He pub. a book on viol and lute playing and a collection of lute pieces in tablature.

German, Edward (real name Edward German Jones) (b. Whitchurch, Salop, 17. II. 1862; d. London, 11. XI. 1936), Eng. comp. Educ. at Chester. On his return home he organized and cond. a band and learnt the v. Later he studied at Shrewsbury and the R.A.M. in London. He became an orch. vst. and in 1888 mus. dir. of the Globe Theatre, writing incid. m. for Richard Mansfield's prods. In 1901 he completed *The Emerald Isle*, left unfinished by Sullivan. Knighted in 1928.

Works incl. light operas *The Rival Poets, Merrie England, The Princess of Kensington, Tom Jones* (after Fielding), *Fallen Fairies* (W. S. Gilbert); incid. m. for Shakespeare's *Richard III, Henry VIII, Romeo and Juliet, As You Like It, Much Ado about Nothing*, Anthony Hope's *Nell Gwynn*, &c.; 2 syms., Symph. Suite in D min., symph. poem *Hamlet*, symph. suite *The Seasons, Welsh Rhapsody, Theme and 6 Diversions* & other orch. works; Coronation March & Hymn for George V, &c.

German Flute. The name for the transverse fl. used in Eng. in the 18th cent.

German Requiem, A. Work for chor., sop. & bar. solo & orch. by Brahms, Op. 45, comp. in 1866–9. The orig. name, *Ein deutsches Requiem*, means simply that B. did not set the liturgical Lat. text, but a choice of his own from Luther's trans. of the Bible, approximating to the words of the Catholic Mass for the Dead. The exact meaning is 'a Requiem in Ger.,' and it becomes misleading when trans. into any other language. A proper title for the work in Eng. would be 'A Protestant Requiem.'

German Sixth. In harmony a chord, the 2 outer notes of which are an augmented 6th (e.g. D♭, B♮), resolving into a common chord with the tonic in 8ves, proceeding from the 6th by 2 semitonal steps, the lower downwards and the higher upwards. The intervening notes are a maj. 3rd with a min. 3rd above it (e.g. D♭, F, A♭, B).

Gernsheim, Friedrich (b. Worms, 17. VII. 1839; d. Berlin, 11. IX. 1916), Ger. pfst., cond. & comp. Studied at the Leipzig Cons. and in Paris. Cond. in var. cities, incl. Rotterdam, and later taught in Berlin.

Works incl. *Salamis*, *Hafis*, *Preislied*, *Nornenlied*, *Phöbus Apollo*, *Agrippina*, &c. for chor. & orch.; 4 syms. & other orch. m.; concs. for pf. & for v.; 2 stg. 4tets, stg. 5tet, pf. 4tets & trios & other chamber m.; 3 v. & pf. sos., &c.

Gero, Jhan (b. ?, *c.* 1518; d. ?, *c.* 1553), ? Flem. comp. Went to It. and became chapel master at Orvieto cath. Comp. motets & other sacred m., madrigals, canzoni, &c.

Gershwin, George (b. Brooklyn, New York, 26. IX. 1898; d. Hollywood, 11. VII. 1937), Amer. comp. Wrote a popular song at the age of 14, studied the pf. and had lessons in theory from R. Goldmark. From 1914–7 he worked as pfst. in a m. pub.'s office and wrote songs and a mus. comedy. Aged 20, he was commissioned to write incid. m. for George White's play *Scandals*, and in 1923, at the invitation of Paul Whiteman, he wrote the *Rhapsody in Blue*.

Works incl. opera *Porgy and Bess*; many mus. comedies incl. *Lady, be good* & *Of Thee I sing*; m. for several films; *An American in Paris* & *Cuban Ovt.* for orch.; *Rhapsody in Blue* and Conc. for pf. & orch.; a large number of popular songs.

Gerstenbüttel, Joachim (b.* ?; d. ?, 1721), Ger. church comp. Wrote a Passion according to St. Matthew in 26 parts.

Gerster, Etelka (b. Kassán, Hung., 25. VI. 1855; d. Pontecchio nr. Bologna, 20. VIII. 1920), Hung.-Ger. sop. singer. Studied with Mathilde Marchesi in Vienna and made her 1st stage appearance at Venice in 1876. She married the It. cond. Carlo Gardini.

Geschöpfe des Prometheus, Die (*The Creatures of Prometheus*), ballet by Beethoven (chgph. by Salvatore Viganò), prod. Vienna, Burg Theatre, 28. III. 1801.

Gervais. *See* **White, Terence.**

Gese (or **Gesius**), **Bartholomäus** (or **Barthel Göss**) (b. Müncheberg nr. Frankfort o/O., *c.* 1555; d. Frankfort o/O., 1613 or 1621), Ger. theologian & comp. Cantor at Frankfort o/O.

Works incl. masses (1 on themes by Lassus), motets, psalms, hymns, sacred songs, &c., all for the Lutheran church; Passion according to St. John; wedding & funeral m., &c.

Gesellschaft der Musikfreunde (Ger. lit. Soc. of the Friends of Music = Phil. Soc.). A soc. formed in Vienna in 1813 for the promotion, perf. & collection of m.

Gesius. *See* **Gese.**

Gestalt (Ger. = shape, formation). A word that has gained currency as a mus. term in Ger.-speaking countries recently, used in mus. analysis and in philos. or pseudo-philos. discussions on m. to designate a mus. idea as it comes from the comp.'s mind in what is supposed to be a kind of primeval or pre-existing form.

Gestopft (Ger. = stopped up, obstructed) = Muted, in the case of wind insts.

Gesualdo, Carlo, Prince of Venosa (b. Naples, *c.* 1560; d. Naples, IX. 1615), It. amateur comp. In spite of his position, he took his mus. studies seriously in his youth and became a very accomplished lutenist. He married a noble Neapolitan lady in 1586, but had her assassinated with her lover in 1590. In 1594 he went to the court of Ferrara and married Eleonora d'Este there, but returned to his estate at Naples soon after Duke Alfonso d'Este II's death in 1597.

Works incl. 7 books of madrigals (the last posth.); 2 books of *Sacrae cantiones*, responses for 6 voices, &c.

Getreue Alceste, Die (*The Faithful Alcestis*), opera by Schürmann (lib. Johann Ulrich König), prod. Brunswick, II. 1719.

Gevaert, François Auguste (b. Huysse nr. Oudenarde, 31. VII. 1828; d. Brussels, 24. XII. 1908), Belg. mus. historian, theorist & comp. Studied at Ghent and worked as orgst. there; later travelled in Spa., It. and Ger. Dir. of the m. at Paris Opéra, 1867–70; afterwards devoted mainly to the writing of hist. and theor. works; but he had prod. a number of operas and other m. before. Dir. of the Brussels Cons. from 1871. He wrote several mus. treatises.

Works incl. operas *Hugues de Zomerghem*, *La Comédie à la ville*, *Georgette*, *Le Billet de Marguerite*, *Les Lavandières de Santarem*, *Quentin Durward* (after Scott), *Le Diable au moulin*, *Château Trompette*, *La Poularde de Caux*, *Les Deux Amours*, *Le Capitaine Henriot*; Requiem for male voices & orch., Christmas cantata, psalm *Super flumina*, cantatas *De nationale verjaerdag* & *Le Retour de l'armée*; orch. *Fantasia sobre motivos españoles*, &c.

Gewandhaus (Ger. = Cloth Hall). Orig. the hall of the cloth makers' guild at Leipzig, used for concerts from 1781 and rebuilt espec. as a concert hall in 1884.

Gherardello (b. ?; d. ?), It. 14th-cent. comp. Lived at Florence; wrote madrigals, *caccie*, ballads, &c.

Gherardesca, Filippo Maria (b. Pistoia, *c.* 1738; d. Pisa, 1808), It. hpchdst. & comp. Pupil of Martini at Bologna. Prod. his 1st opera at Lucca in 1763. App. chapel master of the church of the Cavalieri at Pisa in 1769 and later of the grand-ducal chapel.

Works incl. operas, *I due gobbi* & 6 others; masses, Requiem; pf. So.; songs, &c.

Gheyn, Matthias van den (b. Tirlemont, 7. IV. 1721; d. Louvain, 22. VI. 1785), Flem. hpchdst., orgst., carillonneur & comp. Son of a bell founder. The family moved to Louvain in 1725 and in 1741 G. became orgst. at the church of Saint-Pierre there, having been (?) a pupil of Déodat Raick there. In 1745 he was app. carillonneur to the city. Wrote org., hpchd. & carillon m.

Ghimel. *See* **Gymel.**

Ghiselin, Jean (b. ?; d. ?), Flem. 15th–16th-cent. comp. Petrucci of Venice pub. several of his works between 1501–42. Comp. masses, motets, songs, &c.

Ghislanzoni, Antonio (b. Lecco, 25. XI. 1824; d. Caprino Bergamasco, 16. VII. 1893), It. bar. singer, novelist, mus. ed. & libst. He ed. the *Gazzetta musicale* of Milan and wrote the lib. for Verdi's *Aida* on a scenario by Mariette and a Fr. draft by Camille du Locle.

Ghittern. *See* **Cittern.**

Ghizzolo, Stefano. *See* **Pasino.**

'Ghost' Trio. The nickname given to Beethoven's pf. Trio in D maj., Op. 70 No. 1, on account of its slow mvt. in D min., which has a mysterious, gloomy and haunting theme, accomp. frequently by stg. tremolos.

Ghro (or **Groh**), **Johann** (b. Dresden, ?; d. ?), Ger. 16th–17th-cent. orgst. & comp. Orgst. at Meissen in 1604–12 and later mus. dir. at Wesenstein.

Works incl. intradas, pavans, galliards & other pieces for several insts., &c.

Giacobbi, Girolamo (b. Bologna, VIII. 1567; d. Bologna, II. 1629), It. comp. Chapel master at San Petronio cath. at Bologna.

Works incl. operas *Andromeda*, *L'Aurora ingannata*, *Amor prigioniero*, *La selva dei mirti*, *Il Reno sacrificante*; intermezzi, &c.; motets, psalms & other church m., &c.

Giacomelli, Geminiano (b. Parma, *c.* 1686; d. Parma, 19. I. 1743), It. comp. Pupil of Capelli at Parma and later of A. Scarlatti. Attached to the court of Parma and for some time to that of Aus. in Vienna.

Works incl. operas *Ipermestra*, *Cesare in Egitto* & 16 others; Psalm for 2 tens. & bass; concert arias, &c.

Giacometti, Giovanni Battista (b. ?; d. ?), It. 16th-cent. vst. Lived in Rome, 1571–86, and then became chapel master at the court of Mantua in succession to Soriano.

Giacometti, Paolo (1816–82), It. dramatist. *See* **Judith** (Serov).

Gianettini, Antonio (b. prob. Fano, 1648; d. Modena, 12. VII. 1721), It. comp. App. chapel master at the ducal court of Modena in 1686. Prod. his 1st opera, *Medea in Atene*, at Venice in 1675.

Works incl. operas, orats., cantatas, motets, psalms, &c.

Gianni Schicchi (Puccini). *See* **Trittico.**

'Giant' Fugue. The nickname of Bach's fugal chorale prelude on 'Wir glauben all'' in Part III of the *Clavierübung*, so named because of a striding figure in the pedals.

Giardini, Felice de (b. Turin, 12. IV. 1716; d. Moscow, 17. XII. 1796), It. vst. & comp. Choir-boy at Milan cath. and later pupil of Somis at Turin. Played in the opera orchs. at Rome and Naples, in 1748 visited Ger. and then settled in London, becoming leader of the opera orch. in 1752, succeeding Festing. He played and taught there until 1784, when he retired to It., but he reappeared in London in 1790 and d. during a tour in Rus.

Works incl. operas *Enea e Lavinia*, *Il rè pastore* & others; incid. m. for Wm. Mason's *Elfrida*; part of orat. *Ruth* (with Avison), 12 v. concs.; 18 stg. 4tets, 6 stg. 5tets, 7 sets of stg. trios; sos. for v. & pf.; v. duets, &c.

Giasone (*Jason*), opera by Cavalli (lib. by Giacinto Andrea Cicognini), prod. Venice, Teatro San Cassiano, prob. 5. I. 1649.

Gibbons. Eng. family of musns.:

1. William G. (b. Oxford, *c.* 1540; d. Cambridge, X. 1595), singer &/or player. Lived at Cambridge from 1567, but returned to Oxford *c.* 1579 and went back to Cambridge *c.* 1587.

2. Edward G. (b. ? Cambridge, *c.* 1570; d. ? Exeter, *c.* 1650), orgst. & comp., son of prec. Graduated B. Mus. at Cambridge and later (1592) at Oxford. Lay clerk at King's Coll. chapel, Cambridge, and from *c.* 1606 held an appt. at Exeter cath.

Works incl. anthems, Kyrie and Creed; In Nomine in 5 parts, &c.

3. Ellis G. (b. Cambridge, XI. 1573;

d. ? Cambridge, V. 1603), **comp.,** brother of prec.

Works incl. madrigals, &c.

4. Ferdinando G. (b. Cambridge or Oxford, c. 1579; d. ?), singer, brother of prec. Lived at Lincoln.

5. Orlando G. (b. Oxford, 1583; d. Canterbury, 5. VI. 1625), comp., brother of prec. Pupil of his father, who took him back to Cambridge at the age of *c.* 4 and entered him as a chorister at King Coll. chapel in 1596. He also learnt much from his brother Ellis. In 1605 he was app. orgst. of the Chapel Royal in London and *c.* 1606 married Elizabeth Patten, by whom he had 7 children. In 1619 he became virginal player at court in succession to Walter Earle and in 1622 received the hon. Mus.D. degree from Oxford. In 1623 he succeeded John Parsons as orgst. of Westminster Abbey. After cond. the m. for the funeral of James I in IV. 1625, he went to Canterbury for the reception of Henrietta Maria, who was married to Charles I by proxy in Paris on 1. V, the Chapel Royal having to be in attendance at Canterbury cath.; but G. d. of an apoplectic fit before her arrival.

Works incl. 2 services, 2 preces & psalms, motets, *c.* 40 anthems; madrigals for viols or voices, London street-cries for voices & viols; 30 fantasies, 4 In Nomines & several dances for stgs.; 16 fantasies, 6 sets of vars., 4 *Makes*, 2 In Nomines & *c.* 25 pieces for keyboard insts., &c.

6. Christopher G. (b. London, VIII. 1615; d. London, 20. X. 1676), comp., son of prec. Pupil of his father in the Chapel Royal, but (?) was adopted by his uncle Edward G. at Exeter on Orlando's death. App. orgst. at Winchester cath. in 1638. In 1646 he married Mary Kercher, who d. in 1662, and later Elizabeth Ball. On the Restor. in 1660 he was app. private orgst. to Charles II, also orgst. at the Chapel Royal and Westminster Abbey. Mus.D., Oxford, 1663.

Works incl. m. for Shirley's masque *Cupid and Death* (with Locke); anthems; many fantasies for stgs., &c.

Gibbs, C(ecil). Armstrong (b. Great Baddow nr. Chelmsford, 10. VIII. 1889), Eng. comp. Educ. at Winchester Coll. and Trinity Coll., Cambridge, where he studied m. with Dent, and later at the R.C.M. in London, where he became a prof. of comp.

Works incl. incid. m. to school play *Crossings* (W. de la Mare) & Maeterlinck's *The Betrothal*; comic opera *The Blue Peter* (A. P. Herbert); play with m. *Midsummer Madness* (Clifford Bax); Nativity play *The Three Kings*; cantata *The Birth of Christ*, chor. sym. *Odysseus*; *La Belle Dame sans merci* (Keats), *The Highwayman* (Alfred Noyes) & *Deborah and Barak* for chor. & orch.; 3 Psalm Motets for unaccomp. chor.; *Cantate Domino, Deus misereatur*, anthem *I, then the prisoner* & other church m.; Sym. in E maj., *A Westmorland Sym.* for orch.; Concertino for pf. & stgs.; stg. 4tet in A maj. & other chamber m.; songs (many to poems by Walter de la Mare), &c.

Gibbs, John (b. ?; d. ?), Eng. 17th-cent. comp. Worked (?) at Westminster Abbey in London. Wrote church m., In Nomines, &c.

Gibbs, Richard (b. ?; d. ?), Eng. 17th-cent. orgst. & comp. Orgst. at Norwich cath. *c.* 1622–35. Wrote services, anthems, &c.

Gide, André (b. 1869), Fr. novelist, essayist, poet & dramatist. *See* **Durey** (songs), **Honegger** (*Saül*), **Perséphone** (Stravinsky), **Reutter (H.)** (*Verlassene Sohn*).

Giga (It.). *See* **Jig.**

Gigault, Nicolas (b. ? Paris, *c.* 1625; d. Paris, *c.* 1707), Fr. orgst. & comp. App. orgst. to the church of Saint-Nicolas-des-Champs in Paris, *c.* 1652. Pub. a book of org. pieces in 1685.

Gigelira (It.) = Xylophone.

Gigg (obs.). *See* **Jig.**

Gigli, Giovanni Battista (b. ?; d. ?), It. 17th-cent. comp. He was in the service of the court of Tuscany at Florence and (?) that of Modena.

Works incl. 2 orats., a cantata, 6 trio sos., &c.

Gigout, Eugène (b. Nancy, 23. III. 1844; d. Paris, 9. XII. 1925), Fr. orgst. & comp. Studied m. at Nancy cath. and the École Niedermeyer in Paris. He was a pupil of Saint-Saëns there and often deputized for him as orgst. at the Madeleine. Married one of Niedermeyer's daughters and became prof. at his school. App. orgst. of Saint-Augustin church in 1863 and travelled much as org. virtuoso. In 1885 he founded an org. school.

Works incl. church m.; Meditation for v. & orch.; pf. So.; *c.* 50 org. works for concert use and *c.* 400 smaller org. pieces with pedals *ad lib.* for the church.

Gigue (Fr.). *See* **Jig.**

Gilbert, Henry F(ranklin). (Belknap) (b. Somerville, Mass., 26. IX. 1868; d. Cambridge, Mass., 19. V. 1928), Amer. comp. Studied m. and Fr. lit. at Boston and became a business man, but later devoted himself to comp. He often used Negro tunes for his thematic material.

Works incl. ballet *The Dance in Place Congo* (after G. W. Cable); symph. prologue to Synge's *Riders to the Sea*; *Salammbô's Invocation to Tanith* (after Flaubert) for sop. & orch.; *Indian Sketches* & *Hymn to America* for chor. & orch.; *Americanesque, Comedy Overture on Negro Themes*, 3 *American Dances, Negro Rhapsody, Legend* & *Negro Episode* for orch.; *The Island of Fay* (after Poe), *Indian Scenes* & *Negro Dances* for pf.; *Pirate Song* (Stevenson) for voice & pf.; ed. of 100 folksongs, &c.

Gilbert, W(illiam). S(chwenck). (1836–1911), Eng. playwright & libst. Libs. *see* **Cellier** (*Mountebanks*), **Gondoliers** (Sullivan), **Grand Duke** (do.), **H.M.S. Pinafore** (do.), **Iolanthe** (do.), **Mikado** (do.), **Patience** (do.), **Pirates of Penzance** (do.), **Princess Ida** (do.), **Ruddigore** (do.), **Sorcerer** (do.), **Thespis** (do.), **Trial by Jury** (do.), **Utopia Limited** (do.), **Yeomen of the Guard** (do.).

Gilchrist, Anne (Geddes) (b. Manchester, 8. XII. 1863), Eng. folksong expert. She collected and studied folksongs and in 1906 joined the ed. committee of the *Journal of the Folk Song Society*, to which she contrib. regularly.

Giles, Nathaniel (b. Worcestershire, *c.* 1558; d. Windsor, 24. I. 1633), Eng. orgst. & comp. Orgst. of Worcester cath., 1581–5, when he became orgst. and choirmaster of St. George's Chapel, Windsor, and also, in 1596, of the Chapel Royal in London, where he took the official titles of Gentleman and Master of the Children on the death of Hunnis in 1597. Mus.D., Oxford, 1622.

Works incl. 4 services, 32 anthems, 5 motets; madrigal *Cease now, vain thoughts*, &c.

Gilly, Dinh (b. ?; d. London, 19. V. 1940), Fr.-Algerian bar. singer. Pupil of Cotogni. Made his 1st appearance in London, at Covent Garden, in 1911. Married the con. Edith Furmedge.

Gilman, Lawrence (b. Flushing, New York, 5. VII. 1878; d. Franconia, N.H., 8. IX. 1939), Amer. critic. Self-taught in m., he wrote for var. papers at first and in 1923 became m. critic to the *New York Herald-Tribune* in succession to Krehbiel. Wrote books on MacDowell, Wagner, modern m., &c. and was a well-known programme annotator and wireless commentator.

Gilse, Jan van (b. Rotterdam, 11. V. 1881), Dutch cond. & comp. Studied at the Cologne Cons. and with Humperdinck. Cond. of the Utrecht Municipal Orch. 1917–22; app. dir. of the Cons. there in 1933.

Works incl. *A Mass of Life* & *Circle of Life* for chor. & orch.; 4 syms. & *Prologue brevis* for orch.; *Dansschetseis* for pf. & orch.; songs with orch, &c.

Gilson, Paul (b. Brussels, 15. VI. 1865; d. Brussels, 3. IV. 1942), Belg. comp. Pupil of Gevaert and others, he gained the Belg. **Prix de Rome** in 1889. App. prof. of harmony at the Cons. of Brussels in 1899 and of Antwerp in 1904. He was also m. critic of *Le Soir*, 1906–16, and then of *Le Midi*.

Works incl. operas *Prinsess Zonneschijn* & *Zeevolk*; ballets *La Captive* & *Daphne*; orat. *Le Démon* (after Lermontov); *Francesca da Rimini* (after Dante) for solo voices, chor. & orch.; cantata *Sinaï* and one for the Brussels Exhib. of 1897; *La Mer* for recitation & orch.; Fantasy on Canadian Themes, Sco. Rhapsody, &c. for orch.; *Humoresque* & other works for wind insts.; chamber m.; many songs with orch. or pf., &c.

Gimel. *See* **Gymel.**

Gines Pérez, Juan (b. Orihuela, X. 1548; d. Orihuela, 1612), Spa. comp. He held a church appt. in his native town at the age of 14, in 1581–95 was chapel master and dir. of the choir school at Valencia, and *c.* 1600 returned home as canon at Orihuela cath.

Works incl. motets, psalms; secular Spa. songs; m. contrib. to the Mystery play perf. annually at Elche nr. Alicante, &c.

Ginguené, Pierre Louis (b. Rennes, 25. IV. 1748; d. Paris, 15. XI. 1816), Fr. priest, author and lit. historian. Wrote on opera and m. in general, and was a partisan of Piccinni (whose biog. he wrote) against Gluck in the quarrel staged between the adherents of these two in Paris.

Gioconda, opera by Ponchielli (lib. by Boito, based on Victor Hugo's *Angelo*), prod. Milan, Teatro alla Scala, 8. IV. 1876.

Giocoso (It.) = Playful, joking, humorous.

Gioielli della Madonna, I (*The Jewels of the Madonna*), opera by Wolf-Ferrari (lib. by Enrico Golisciani & Carlo Zangarini), prod., in Ger., Berlin, Kurfürsten-Oper, 23. XII. 1911.

Giordani. It. family of musns.:

1. Carmine G. (b. Cerreto Sannita nr. Benevento, ?; d. Naples, 1758), singer & comp. Prod. an opera, *La vittoria d'amor coniugale* at Naples in 1712 and the family appeared there in opera until 1753, when he with his 2 daughters and elder son went to London. Other works incl. cantata for sop., *Versetti* for org., &c.

2. Tommaso G. (b. Naples, *c.* 1733; d. ? Dublin, II. 1806), comp., son of prec. Appeared in opera at Naples

with his family before 1753, when they went to London and he worked there & in Dublin, living alternately in the 2 capitals for long periods. In 1783 he married Miss Wilkinson, and their son Tommaso became a m. teacher at Dublin.

Works incl. operas *Love in Disguise, Phillis at Court* (after Lloyd's *Capricious Lovers*), *Artaserse, Antigono, Perseverance, Il bacio, The Siege of Gibraltar* & many others; incid. m. for Sheridan's *The Critic*; orat. *Isaac*; Te Deum; ode for the Viceroy of Ir.; ovts.; concs.; 4tets; songs, &c.

3. Giuseppe G. (called Giordanello) (b. Naples, *c.* 1744; d. Fermo, 4. I. 1798), comp., brother of prec. Studied m. at the Cons. di Loreto at Naples and brought out his 1st opera there in 1771, but followed his family to Eng. in 1772. Later he joined his brother Tommaso at Dublin, but returned to It. in 1779 and became choirmaster at Fermo cath. in 1791.

Works incl. many operas, e.g. *La vestale, La disfatta di Dario*, &c.; orats. *La fuga in Egitto, Le tre ore d'agonia di Nostro Signore Gesù Cristo*; masses, motets & other church m.; ovt.; concs.; 4tets; songs incl. 'Let not age' & (?) 'Caro mio ben,' &c.

Giordano, Umberto (b. Foggia, 27. VIII. 1867), It. comp. Son of an artisan, he was allowed to learn m. as best he could, but in the end studied at the Naples Cons. under Serrao. He attracted the attention of the pub. Sonzogno with the opera *Marina* and soon became very successful with a series of stage works.

Works incl. operas *Marina, Mala vita, Regina Diaz, Andrea Chénier, Fedora* (after Sardou), *Siberia, Marcella, Mese Mariano, Madame Sans-Gêne* (after Sardou & Moreau), *Giove a Pompei* (with Franchetti), *La cena delle beffe, Il rè*.

Giorgi-Righetti, Geltrude (or Righetti-Giorgi; not Maria Brighenti, as in some dictionaries) (b. Bologna, 1792; d. ?), It. m.-sop. singer. Made her 1st appearance at Bologna in 1814 and was Rossini's 1st Rosina in *Il Barbiere di Siviglia* in 1816.

Giorno di regno, Un, ossia Il finto Stanislao (*A Day's Reign, or The False Stanislas*), opera by Verdi (lib. by Felice Romani, used earlier by Gyrowetz, *see* **Finto Stanislao**), prod. Milan, Teatro alla Scala, 5. IX. 1840. V.'s only comic opera except *Falstaff*.

Giornovichi, Giovanni (Mane) (known as Jarnowick) (b. Palermo, *c.* 1740; d. St. Petersburg, 21. XI. 1804), It. vst. & comp. Pupil of Lolli, made his 1st appearance at the Concert spirituel in Paris in 1770. Having lived in Paris, Berlin, Aus., Pol., Rus. and Swe., he went to London in 1791, but left for Hamburg in 1796, whence he went to St. Petersburg in 1802. He wrote *c.* 20 v. concs., 3 stg. 4tets & much m. for the v.

Giovane, Joan Domenico del. *See* **Nola.**

Giovanelli, Ruggiero (b. Velletri nr. Rome, 1660; d. Rome, 7. I. 1725), It. comp. After holding var. church appts. in Rome, he followed Palestrina at St. Peter's in 1594 and became a member of the Sistine Choir in 1599. At the request of Pope Paul V he undertook a new ed. of the Gradual.

Works incl. masses, Miserere & other church m.; 6 books of madrigals, 1 of canzonette and villanelle, &c.

Giovanna d'Arco (*Joan of Arc*), opera by Verdi (lib. by Temistocle Solera, based on Schiller's drama *Die Jungfrau von Orleans*), prod. Milan, Teatro alla Scala, 15. II. 1845.

Giovanna de Guzman (Verdi). *See* **Vêpres siciliennes.**

Giovanni da Cascia (b. Cascia, ?; d. ?), It. 14th-cent. comp. Worked at the court of Mastino II della Scala at Verona, 1329–51. Comp. madrigals, caccie, canzonets, ballads for several voices, &c.

Giovannini, ? (b. ?; d. ? Berlin, ?), It. 18th-cent. vst. & comp. Pupil of Leclair. He lived mainly in Berlin from 1740. In 1745 he went to London, where he prod. the pasticcio *L'incostanza delusa* and pub. some v. solos under the name of Count of St. Germain. Bach describes the song 'Willst du dein Herz mir schenken' in one of the m. books for his wife as 'aria di Giovannini.'

Works incl. v. solos, songs, &c.

Giove in Argo (*Jove in Argos*), opera by Lotti (lib. by Antonio Maria Lucchini), prod. Dresden, Assembly Hall (Redoutensaal), 25. X. 1717, the new opera-house not being ready. This was opened with that work, 3. IX. 1719. (The same lib. was set by Handel in 1739: the only one of his operas which was never perf.).

Gioventù di Enrico V, La (*The Youth of Henry V*), opera by Pacini (lib. by Jacopo Ferretti, partly based on Shakespeare's *Henry IV*), prod. Rome, Teatro Valle, 26. XII. 1820.

Gipps, Ruth (b. Bexhill, 20. II. 1921), Eng. comp., pfst. & obst. She played the pf. in public at the age of 4 and pub. a pf. piece, *The Fairy Shoemaker*, when she was 8. Pupil of her mother, Mrs. Bryan Gipps, at the Bexhill School of M. and later at the R.C.M. in London. In 1944–5 she was in the City of Birmingham Orch. as 2nd ob. & Eng. hn.

Works incl. ballet *Sea Nymph*; Sym.

in F min., symph. poems ***Knight in Armour*** & *Death on the Pale Horse*, ovt. to Rostand's *Chantecler*, Vars. on a theme by Byrd for orch.; v. Conc., cl. Conc., ob. Conc.; stg. 4tet *Sabrina*; 5tet for ob., cl. & stgs., Trio for ob., cl. & pf., *Flax and Charlock* for Eng. hn., v., va. & co., *Brocade* for pf. 4tet; So. & suites for ob. & pf.; *Jane Grey* for va. & pf.; *Ducks* for sop., fl., co. & pf.; Rhapsody without words for sop. & small orch.; *Chamois* for 2 vs. & pf.; inst. pieces; pf. pieces; songs, &c.

Giraffe. An obs. 19th-cent. species of pf., like a grand pf. the body of which stands up on end, the bass stgs. on the left encased in an elongated box not unlike the neck of a giraffe in appearance. The inst. did not resemble that animal very closely, but it was a freak among its kind in much the same way.

Girardeau, (*née* ? **Calliari), Isabella** b. ?; d. ?), It. 17th–18th-cent. sop. singer, Fr. by marriage. Made her 1st appearance in London c. 1710.

Giraud, Albert (b. 1860), Belg. poet. *See* **Pierrot lunaire** (Schoenberg), **Vrieslander** (*Pierrot l.*).

Giraudoux, Jean (1882–1944), Fr. poet, novelist & dramatist. *See* **Honegger** (*Sodome et Gomorrhe*), **Rieti** (*Électre*).

Girdlestone, C(uthbert). M(orton). (b. Bovey-Tracey, 17. IX. 1895), Eng. scholar & mus. author. Educ. at the Sorbonne in Paris and Cambridge, where he became lecturer in Fr. Prof. of Fr. at King's Coll., Newcastle-on-Tyne since 1926. Author of *Mozart et ses concertos pour piano*.

Girelli Aguilar, Antonia Maria (b. ?; d. ?), It. 18th-cent. sop. singer. She sang in Mozart's *Ascanio in Alba* at Milan in 1771 and the following year appeared in London, succeeding Grassi.

Girl of the Golden West (Puccini). *See* **Fanciulla del West.**

Giroflé-Girofla, operetta by Lecocq (lib. by Albert Vanloo & Eugène Leterrier), prod. Brussels, Théâtre Alcazar, 21. III. 1874.

Giselle, ou Les Willis, ballet by Adam (chgph. by Jean Coralli, on a story by Heine, adapted by Théophile Gautier), prod. Paris, Opéra, 28. VI. 1841.

Gismondi, Celeste (b. ?; d. London, 28. X. 1735), It. m.-sop. singer. Made her 1st appearance in London in 1732. She married an Eng. named Hempson.

Gittern. *See* **Cittern.**

Giuliano, opera by Zandonai (lib. by Arturo Rossato, based on Flaubert's *Saint Julien l'Hospitalier*), prod. Naples, Teatro San Carlo, 4. II. 1928.

Giulietta e Romeo (*Juliet and Romeo*). Opera by Vaccai (lib. by Felice Romani, after Shakespeare), prod. Milan, Teatro della Canobbiana, 31. X. 1825.

Opera by Zandonai (lib. by Arturo Rossato, after Shakespeare), prod. Rome, Teatro Costanzi, 14. II. 1922.

Opera by Zingarelli (lib. by Giuseppe Maria Foppa, after Shakespeare), prod. Milan, Teatro alla Scala, 30. I. 1796.

Giulio Cesare, opera by Malipiero (lib. by comp., based on Shakespeare's *Julius Caesar*), prod. Genoa, Teatro Carlo Felice, 8. II. 1936.

Giulio Cesare in Egitto (*Julius Caesar in Egypt*), opera by Handel (lib. by Nicola Francesco Haym), prod. London, King's Theatre, Haymarket, 20. II. 1724.

Giulio Sabino, opera by Sarti (lib. by Pietro Giovannini), prod. Venice, Teatro San Benedetto, I. 1781.

Giuramento, Il (*The Vow*), opera by Mercadante (lib. by Giacomo Rossi, based on Victor Hugo's *Angelo*), prod. Milan, Teatro alla Scala, 10. III. 1837.

Giusti, Giuseppe (1809–50), It. poet. *See* **Nielsen** (satires).

Guistini, Lodovico (b. Pistoia, ?; d. ?), It. 18th-cent. comp. Pub. in 1732 a book of sos., prob. the 1st pub. m. specifically written for the pf., as distinct from m. for keyboard insts. in general.

Giustiniana (It.). A type of It. song similar to the villanella, but always set to a love poem, current in the 15th and 16th cents. and so named after Leonardo Giustiniani.

Giustiniani, Girolamo (17th–18th cent.), It. poet. *See* **Marcello** (psalms).

Giustiniani, Leonardo (*c.* 1385–1446), It. poet. He wrote love poems for mus. settings, some of which he provided himself, and they were called after him as late as the 16th cent.

Giustino, opera by Handel (lib. altered by ? from Nicolo Beregani), prod. London, Covent Garden Theatre, 16. II. 1737.

Giusto (It.=just, strict, suitable). A direction used, generally as an adj. with *tempo*, to indicate that a movt. is to be taken at a suitable or reasonable pace, or that it is to be perf. strictly in time.

Gizziello (so called after his teacher Domenico Gizzi, real name Gioacchino Conti) (b. Arpino nr. Naples, 28. II. 1714; d. Rome, 25. X. 1761), It. male sop. singer. 1st appeared in Rome, 1730, and in London, 1736.

Gjellerup, Karl (1857–1919), Dan. dramatist. *See* **Schjelderup** (*Offerildene*).

Glanville-Hicks, Peggy (b. Melbourne, 29. XII. 1912), Austral. comp.

Studied at the Melbourne Cons. and from the age of 19 under Vaughan Williams, Gordon Jacobs and R. O. Morris at the R.C.M. in London. She gained a scholarship in 1932 and another in 1935, which enabled her to travel and to study further with Wellesz in Vienna and Nadia Boulanger in Paris. In 1838 her chor. Suite was perf. at the I.S.C.M. festival in London and in 1939 she married Stanley Bate, with whom she went to U.S.A., settling in N.Y.

Works incl. opera *Cædmon*; Sinfonietta, *Prelude & Scherzo*, *Spa. Suite & M. for Robots* for orch.; chor. Suite (Fletcher) for women's voices, ob. & stgs.; pf. Conc., fl. Conc.; *Concertino da camera* for fl., cl., bn. & pf.; *Aria concertante* for ten., ob., gong, pf. & 4 women's voices; Sonatina for recorder (or fl.) & pf.; So. & Sonatina for pf.; 6 Housman songs, 5 modern Chin. songs & others, &c.

Glareanus, Henricus (real name Heinrich Loris) (b. Glarus, VI. 1488; d. Freiburg i/B., 28. III. 1563), Swi. theorist. Studied m. at Berne and Cologne, taught at Basle from 1515 and again from 1522, after holding a professorship in Paris from 1517 on the recommendation of Erasmus of Rotterdam. In 1529 he moved to Ger., settling at Freiburg. He studied the relationship between the Gr. and the church modes and wrote 2 treatises, *Isagoge in musicen* and *Dodecachordon*.

Glasenapp, Carl Friedrich (b. Riga, 3. X. 1847; d. Riga, 14. IV. 1915), Ger. biog. Author of the 1st large biog. of Wagner and of var. other works on him.

Gläser, Franz (b. Obergeorgental, 19. IV. 1798; d. Vienna, 29. VIII. 1861), Boh. comp. Studied in Prague; app. cond. at the Leopoldstadt Theatre in Vienna, 1817, at the Josephstadt Theatre, 1822, and at the Theater an der Wien, 1827. Later in Berlin and Copenhagen. Wrote mainly operas, e.g. *Des Adlers Horst*, *Bryllupet ved Como-Søen* (after Manzoni's *Promessi sposi*) & 2 other Dan. operas.

Glass Harmonica. *See* **Harmonica.**

Glastonbury. The mus. connection of the ancient town in Somerset is the festival theatre planned there and partly carried into practice by Rutland Boughton in 1914–27.

Glazunov, Alexander Konstantinovitch (b. St. Petersburg, 10. VIII. 1865; d. Paris, 21. III. 1936), Rus. comp. After being taught m. at home as a child, he studied with Rimsky-Korsakov from 1880 and finished his course in 18 months, having a 1st Sym. ready for perf. early in 1882. Belaiev arr. a concert of his works in 1884 and began to pub. them. App. dir. of the St. Petersburg Cons. in 1905 and wrote little after that to augment his enormous earlier output. He left Rus. in 1928 and settled in Paris.

Works incl. ballets, *Raymonda*, *Les Ruses d'amour* and *The Seasons*; incid. m. for Romanov's play, *The King of the Jews*; 8 syms.; 5 concert ovts. incl. 2 on Greek themes and *Carnival*, symph. poems *Stenka Razin*, *The Sea*, *The Kremlin*; suite *From the Middle Ages*, 2 serenades, fantasy *The Forest*, *Introduction and Salome's Dance* (after Oscar Wilde), many misc. orch. works; v. Conc., 2 pf. concs., Conc. for saxophone; 5 stg. 4tets, stg. 5tet, *Novelettes* and Suite for stg. 4tet; 17 works for pf. incl. 2 sos. and Theme & Vars.; Suite for 2 pfs.; var. small inst. pieces; 21 songs; 3 cantatas; *Hymn to Pushkin* for fem. voices, &c.

Glebov, Igor. *See* **Assafiev.**

Glee. A partsong, usually for male voices, in not less than 3 parts, much cultivated by Eng. comps. in the 18th and early 19th cents. Its style is loosely polyphonic, and it is in that sense a debased descendant of the madrigal, but it has at its best a character of its own. Its name is said to be derived from the Anglo-Saxon *gliw* = music: it does not indicate a cheerful style, which seems nevertheless to have been cultivated unconsciously because of its connotation. Webbe, Stevens, Callcott, Horsley, Attwood, Battishill, Cooke and others cultivated the G. Its manner has been familiar to large modern audiences by Sullivan's use of it, though he does not allow it to remain altogether unaccomp. The 'merry madrigal' in *The Mikado*, 'Brightly dawns our wedding-day,' is much more like a G.

Glee Club. A club formed in London in 1783 and existing until 1857, for the performance of glees, madrigals, motets, canons and catches at table after dinner at a member's house or in a tavern or coffee-house.

Gleichnisarie (Ger.) *See* **Parable Aria.**

Glière, Reinhold Moritzovitch (b. Kiev, 11. I. 1875), Rus. comp. of Belg. descent. Learnt the v. as a child, but soon began to comp. and was sent to the Kiev school of M. and later to the Moscow Cons., where he was a pupil of Arensky, Taneiev and Ippolitov-Ivanov. Taught at the Gnessin School of M. in Moscow and at the Kiev Cons., of which he became dir. in 1914, but settled at Moscow in 1920. He made research into Azerbaijan, Uzbek and Ukrainian folksong and based some of his later works on it. In 1939 he became chairman of the Organizing Committee of U.S.R. comps.

Works incl. operas *Shakh-Senem*, *Leili and Medjun* & *Rachel* (after Maupassant's *Mlle Fifi*); ballets *The Red Poppy*, *Gulsara, 1905*; incid. m. for Sophocles' *Oedipus Rex*, Aristophanes' *Lysistrata*, Beaumarchais's *Marriage of Figaro*, &c.; 3 syms. (No. 3, *Ilia Muromets*), 3 symph. poems, 5 concert ovts.; hp. Conc., Conc. for voice & orch.; Fantasy for wind insts.; 4 stg. 4tets, 3 stg. 6tets, stg. 8tet; many inst. pieces; 18 op. nos. of pf. m.; 22 op. nos. of songs, &c.

Glinka, Mikhail Ivanovitch (b. Novospasskoi, Gvt. of Smolensk, 2. VI. 1803; d. Berlin, 15. II. 1857), Rus. comp. The son of a wealthy landowner, he was sent to school at St. Petersburg, 1817–23. He took some pf. lessons from Field and others, also studied v. and theory. At his father's wish he worked in the Ministry of Communications in 1824–8, but not being obliged to earn a living and wishing to devote himself to m., he gave it up. He studied with an It., Zamboni, visited It., 1830–3, where he had lessons from Basili at Milan, and afterwards Vienna and Berlin, studying under Dehn in the latter city. On his father's death he returned to Rus., settled in St. Petersburg and married in 1835. There he worked at *A Life for the Tsar* and succeeded in having it prod. in 1836. *Russlan and Ludmilla* was delayed by domestic troubles and the separation from his wife in 1841. It was prod. in 1842. In 1844 he visited Paris and Spa., in 1848 Warsaw, and Fr. again in 1852–4. It was during his visit to Berlin, 1856–7, that he d.

Works incl. operas *A Life for the Tsar* (now *Ivan Sussanin*) & *Russlan and Ludmilla*; incid. m. to Count Kukolnik's *Prince Kholmsky*; orch. works: *Jota aragonesa*, *A Night in Madrid*, *Kamarinskaya*, *Valse-Fantaisie*; stg. 4tet in F maj.; Trio for cl., bn. & pf.; 6tet for pf. & stgs.; *c.* 40 pf. pieces; Pol. hymn and *Memorial Cantata* for chor.; *c.* 85 songs; some voc. duets & 4tets, &c.

Glissando (mock-It. der. from Fr. *glisser* = to glide, slide). A direction, never used in It. (where the proper term is *strisciando*), for rapid scales played on the pf. or hp., not by fingering, but by sliding over the keys or stgs. On the pf. only the C maj. and pentatonic scales can thus be played (on white and black keys resp.), and this applies also to the chromatic hp. with its crossed stgs., where however a chrom. scale can be played in addition if the stgs. are touched at the point of intersection. A G. effect can also be obtained on stg. insts. by sliding the finger along the stg. or by a voice by scooping, but in both cases the direction for this is more properly *portamento*. Trombs. can play G. passages by not interrupting the breath while the slide is brought to another position.

Glock, William (b. 3. V. 1908), Eng. pfst. and m. critic. Studied with Boris Ord and Edward Dent at Cambridge in 1926–30 and with Schnabel in Berlin in 1930–3. He joined the *Observer* in 1934 and succeeded Fox Strangways as chief m. critic in 1940, resigning in 1945. Author of books on Britten and Tippett.

Glockenspiel (Ger. = play of bells). A set of tuned steel bars played either with 2 hammers held one in each hand or with a pf. keyboard (e.g. Papageno's bells in Mozart's *Magic Flute*). In the former case not more than 2 notes can be struck together. The G. is generally called by its Ger. name in Eng., but Chime-bells is a good Eng. name for it.

Glosas (Spa. = glosses). Ornamentations by which passages in old voc. or inst. m. were elaborated.

Gloucester Festival. *See* **Three Choirs Festival.**

Gluck (*née* **Fiersohn**), **Alma** (b. Bucharest, 11. V. 1884; d. New York, 27. X. 1938), Rum.-Amer. sop. singer. Was taken to U.S.A. as a child and worked as a stenographer in N.Y. until her marriage to Bernard Gluck in 1906, when she began to study singing, making her 1st appearance in 1909 at the Metrop. Opera. In 1914 she married the vst. Efrem Zimbalist.

Gluck, Christoph Willibald (b. Erasbach, Upper Palatinate, 2. VII. 1714; d. Vienna, 15. XI. 1787), Boh.-Ger. comp. Son of a huntsman and forester in the services of Boh. noblemen, esp. at Kamenice. He had a good educ. which incl. m. Sent to a Jesuit coll. at the age of 12 and to Prague (? Univ.) at 18. There he learnt v. and co., being already a hpchd. player, orgst. and singer, and came under the tuition of Černohorsky. At 22 he became chamber musn. to Prince Lobkowitz in Vienna, although the prince was only 12, and in 1737 Prince Melzi took him to Milan, where he studied with G. B. Sammartini and heard many contemp. It. operas, which greatly influenced him. He prod. his 1st opera, a setting of Metastasio's *Artaserse*, 26. XII. 1741. After that he went on writing It. operas, even after leaving It. for Eng. in 1745, after a visit to Paris. Late in 1746 he went to Hamburg and then worked at Leipzig and Dresden, returning to Vienna at the end of 1747. Visits to Hamburg, Copenhagen and Hol. in 1748–9, and to Prague in 1750, the year he married the wealthy Marianne Pergin and settled down in Vienna for good, except for extensive travelling. In the 1750s he began a series of Fr. comic operas for the Aus. court and in 1761 prod. the ballet *Don Juan* at the Kärntnertor Theatre. He was 48 by the time his 1st It. opera appeared which no longer conformed to the current conventions: *Orfeo ed Euridice* was prod. in Vienna on 5. X. 1762; but he reverted to the older type before (and again after) the next 'reform' work, *Alceste*, appeared in Vienna, 16. XII. 1767, and *Paride ed Elena* on 30. XI. 1770. A serious Fr. opera, also of the new type, *Iphigénie en Aulide*, came out in Paris, 19. IV. 1774 before the new Fr. versions of *Orphée et Eurydice* and *Alceste* were heard there, 2. VIII. 1774 and 23. IV. 1776. *Armide* followed on 23. IX. 1777, but before that a furious quarrel had broken out between G.'s adherents and those of Piccinni, in spite of the fact that the 2 comps. admired each other. *Iphigénie en Tauride* was prod. on 18. V. and *Écho et Narcisse* on 24. IX. 1779. After that G. returned to Vienna and retired from public life, having had a stroke. He still wrote some smaller works, but had repeated seizures, from one of which he d.

Works incl. serious operas: *Alceste* (It. & Fr.), *Antigono*, *Armide* (Fr.) *Artamene*, *Artaserse*, *La caduta de' giganti*, *Le cinesi*, *La clemenza di Tito*, *La contesa de' numi*, *La corona*, *La danza*, *Demetrio*, *Demofoonte*, *Écho et Narcisse*, *Ezio*, *Le feste d'Apollo* (cycle of 4); *La finta schiava*, *L'innocenza giustificata*, *Ipermestra*, *Iphigénie en Aulide*, *Iphigénie en Tauride*, *Ippolito*, *Issipile*, *Le nozze d'Ercole e d'Ebe*, *Orfeo ed Euridice* = *Orphée et Eurydice*, *Paride ed Elena*, *Il Parnasso confuso*, *Poro*, *Il prologo*, *Il rè pastore*, *Semiramide riconosciuta*, *Sofonisba*, *Telemacco*, *Tetide*, *Tigrane*, *Il trionfo di Clelia*; comic operas and vaudevilles: *L'Arbre enchanté*, *Le Cadi dupé*, *La Cythère assiégée*, *Le Diable à quatre*, *La Fausse Esclave*, *L'Isle de Merlin*, *Isabelle et Gertrude*, *L'Ivrogne corrigé*, *La Rencontre imprévue*; ballets: *Don Juan*, *L'orfano della China*, *Semiramide*; *De profundis* for chor. & orch.; odes by Klopstock; syms (ovts.); 7 sos. for 2 v. & bass, &c.

Glückliche Hand, Die (*The Lucky Hand*), opera by Schoenberg (lib. by comp.), comp. 1913, prod. Vienna, Volksoper, 14. X. 1924.

Glyn, Margaret (Henrietta) (b. Ewell, Surrey, 28. II. 1865), Eng. mcolst. Pupil of C. J. Frost and Yorke Trotter. She specialized in Elizabethan keyboard m., ed. org. works by Byrd and virginal m. by Byrd, Bull and O. Gibbons; also wrote a book on this subject as well as one on *Theory of Musical Evolution*.

Glyndebourne Opera. A private opera theatre opened by John Christie on his estate of Glyndebourne, Sussex, in 1934, for the perf. of opera in beautiful surroundings and carefully prepared with an internat. company of singers. Until the 2nd world war brought the enterprise to a standstill in 1939, the repertory was devoted almost wholly to Mozart, the only exceptions being Verdi's *Macbeth* and Donizetti's *Don Pasquale*.

Gnecchi, Vittorio (b. Milan, 17. VII. 1876), It. comp. Studied m. at Milan. His 1st opera at Bologna in 1905 aroused great controversy in 1909, when Strauss's *Elektra* appeared and showed var. striking similarities to G.'s m.

Works incl. operas *Cassandra* (after Homer's *Iliad*) & *La Rosiera*; heroic poem for orch. *Notte nel campo di Holoferne*, &c.

Gnecco, Francesco (b. Genoa, 1769; d. Milan, 1810), It. comp. Pupil of Mariani and Cimarosa.

Works incl. c. 20 operas, e.g. *Carolina e Filandro* & *La prova d'un opera seria*, &c.

Gnessin, Mikhail Fabrianovitch (b. Rostov-on-Don, 4. II. 1883), Rus. comp. Studied with Rimsky-Korsakov and Liadov at the St. Petersburg Cons. and in Ger. from 1911–4. Settled at Rostov in 1914, at Moscow in 1923 and became prof. at the Leningrad Cons. in 1936. His work is influenced by Jewish m.

Works incl. operas *Youth of Abraham* & *The Maccabees*; incid. m. for plays, incl. Sophocles' *Antigone* & *Oedipus Rex*, Gogol's *The Revisor*, Blok's *The Rose and the Cross*, &c.; *1905–17* for solo voices, chor. & orch.; *Symphonic Fragment* (after Shelley), *The Conqueror Worm* (after Poe), *Song of Adonis* & *Fantasia in the Jewish Style* for orch.; *Requiem* for pf. 5tet, *Vars. on Jewish Themes* & *Azerbaijan Folksongs* for stg. 4tet, 6tet *Adygeya*; v. & pf. So. in G min., *So.-Ballade* for co. & pf.; songs with orch.; song cycles to words by Alexander Blok, Sologub, &c.; Jewish folksong arrs., &c.

God save the King (or Queen). The Brit. nat. anthem. A tune of possibly remote but uncertain ancestry, 1st appearing in its present form in 2 eds. of the *Thesaurus Musicus* in London, 1744–5. In the latter year it became very popular as a royalist song attacking the Young Pretender—hence the defiant words of the 2nd and 3rd verses (there was a 4th, even more topical, beginning 'God grant that Marshal Wade'). The song is sung throughout Gt. Brit. and some at least of the colonies and dependencies on all public occasions, incl. stage perfs. and concerts, at which all on the platform stand except csts. and hpsts., and all in the auditorium save poss. bath-chair invalids.

Godard, Benjamin (Louis Paul) (b. Paris, 18. VIII. 1849; d. Cannes, 10. I. 1895), Fr. comp. Studied v. and comp. at the Paris Cons. He became a va. player in chamber m. In 1878 he tied with Dubois in gaining the prize in a competition organized by the municipality of Paris with the dramatic sym. *Le Tasse* for solo voices, chor. & orch. In 1885 he estab. a series of 'modern concerts' without success.

Works incl. operas *Pedro de Zalamea, Jocelyn, Le Dante, La Vivandière, Les Guelfes*; incid. m. to Shakespeare's *Much Ado about Nothing* & Fabre's *Jeanne d'Arc*; Sym., *Scènes poëtiques*, dramatic poem *Diane*, *Symphonie-Ballet*, *Symphonie gothique*, *Symphonie orientale* & *Symphonie légendaire* for orch.; 2 v. concs., pf. Conc.; 3 stg. 4tets, pf. Trio; 3 v. & pf. sos.; pf. pieces; over 100 songs, &c.

Goddard, Arabella (b. Saint-Servan, Saint-Malo, 12. I. 1836; d. Boulogne, 6. IV. 1922), Eng. pfst. Pupil of Kalkbrenner in Paris and later of Thalberg in Eng. Made her 1st public appearance in London in 1850. She studied the classics with Davison, whom she married in 1859.

Godfrey, Dan(iel Eyers) (b. London, 20. VI. 1868; d. Bournemouth, 20. VII. 1939), Eng. cond. Son of the bandmaster Daniel Godfrey (1831–1903). Studied at the R.C.M. in London and 1st cond. a military band and opera, and in 1892 became cond. of a small seaside orch. at Bournemouth, which in time he raised to a full sym. orch. He was knighted in 1922 and retired in 1934.

Godowsky, Leopold (b. Vilna, 13. II. 1870; d. New York, 21. XI. 1938), Pol. (Americanized) pfst. & comp. Very precociously gifted, he appeared in public at the age of 9, made a tour in Pol. & Ger., and then entered the Hochschule für Musik in Berlin, studying with Bargiel and Rudorff. He 1st visited the U.S.A. in 1884, where he settled in 1901 and later became dir. of the Chicago Cons. In 1909–14 he taught in Vienna. He made many arrs. for pf. and comp. studies, concert pieces, &c.

Goedicke, Alexander Feodorovitch (b. Moscow, 4. III. 1877), Rus. pfst. & comp. Studied under Pabst, Arensky, Safonov and others at the Moscow Cons., where he became prof. in 1903.

Works incl. operas *Virinea, Driving the Railway Engine, The Jacquerie* & *Moving Through*; cantata *Glory of the Soviet Pilots*; 3 syms. & other orch. works; stg. 4tets, pf. 5tet, pf. Trio; v. & pf. So.; Rus. folksongs for voice, pf. & co.; pf. pieces; songs, &c.

Goehler, Karl Georg (b. Zwickau, 29. VI. 1874), Ger. cond. & comp. Studied under Kretzschmar at Leipzig Univ. Cond. the Riedelverein there in 1897–1913 and later was operatic, chor. & orch. cond. at Hamburg, Lübeck and Halle, but retired to devote himself to comp. in 1932. He is also a writer on m. and has trans. operas by Verdi.

Works incl. opera *Prinz Nachtwächter*; 3 syms., Suite & other orch. works; concs. for pf., v. (2) & co.; cantatas with orch. on poems by Leopardi; 2 stg. 4tets & other chamber m.; 24 Bagatelles for pf.; male voice chors.; *c.* 200 songs, &c.

Goes, Damião de (b. Alemquer, II. 1502; d. Lisbon, 30. I. 1574), Port. historian, explorer & musn.

Works incl. motets and songs for several voices, &c.

Goethe, Johann Wolfgang von (1749–1832), Ger. poet, novelist, dramatist and philosopher. *See* **André (J.)** (*Erwin und Elmire*), **Beecke** (*Claudine von Villa Bella*), **Benoît (P.)** (*Roi des aulnes*), **Blangini** (*Letzten Augenblicke Werthers*), **Brahms** (*Gesang der Parzen* & *Rinaldo*), **Brun** (*Verheissung*), **Claudine von Villa Bella** (4 comps.), **Dieren (van)** (songs), **Dukas** (*Apprenti sorcier* & *Götz von Berlichingen*), **Eberwein** (*Claudine von V. B.* & *Jahrmarkt von Plundersweilen*), **Egmont** (Beethoven), **Erlkönig** (Schubert), **Ettinger** (*Clavigo*), **Gál** (*Requiem für Mignon*), **Goldmark (C.)** (*Götz von B.* & *Meeresstille und glückliche Fahrt*), **Haydn** (*Götz von B.*); **Hoffmann (E. T. A.)** (*Scherz, List und Rache*), **Hüttenbrenner (A.)** (*Erlkönig*), **Istel** (*Satyros*), **Jery und Bätely** (Reichardt & Seckendorff), **Kienlen** (*Claudine von V. B.* & *Scherz, L. und R.*), **Koechlin** (*Nuit de Walpurgis classique*), **Křenek** (*Triumph der Empfindsamkeit*), **Lassen** (*Pandora*), **Loewe (K.)** (*Erlkönig*), **Marx (A. B.)** (*Jery und B.*), **Mathieu** (ballads), **Medtner** (songs)

Meeresstille (Beethoven & Mendelssohn), **Mendelssohn (A.)** (*Werther*), **Mendelssohn** (*Erste Walpurgisnacht*), **Mignon** (A. Thomas), **Moser (R.)** (*Fischerin*), **Pugnani** (*Werther* sym.), **Randegger** (*Werthers Schatten*), **Rauzzini (V.)** (*Werther*), **Reichardt** (*Claudine von V. B.*, *Erwin und E.* & *Jery und B.*), **Rhapsodie** (Brahms), **Rietz (J.)** (*Jery und B.* & incid. m. for plays), **Rinaldo** (Brahms), **Rubinstein (A.)** (*Wilhelm Meister*), **Scherz, List und Rache** (Bruch), **Schoeck** (*Erwin und Elmire*, *Dithyrambe* & songs), **Scholz** (*Iphigenie*), **Schröter (C.)** (*Fischerin*, *Neue Amadis* & *Erlkönig*), **Schumann** (*Requiem für Mignon*), **Schweizer** (*Clavigo* & *Erwin und E.*), **Starck** (*Jery und B.*), **Stegmann** (*Erwin und E.*), **Stiehl** (*Jery und B.*), **Streicher (T.)** (*Mignons Exequien*), **Suter** (*Erste Walpurgisnacht*), **Tasso** (Liszt), **Tomašek** (songs), **Trunk** (male chors.), **Unger (H.)** (*Gott und Bajadere*), **Valen** (songs), **Veilchen** (Mozart), **Vogler** (*Erwin und E.*), **Vrieslander** (songs), **Wallace (W.)** (*Anvil or Hammer*), **Webern** (2 chor. songs), **Wellesz** (*Scherz, L. und R.*), **Werther** (Massenet,) **Winter** (*Scherz, L. und R.* & *Jery und B.*), **Wolf (E. W.)** (*Erwin und E.*), **Zagwijn** (*Sorcerer's Apprentice*), **Zelter** (songs), **Zunsteeg** (*Clavigo*).

5 songs by Brahms, 1 by Mozart (*Veilchen*), 71 by Schubert, 19 by Schumann, 60 (incl. 9 early) by Wolf.

Faust see **Adam (A.)** (ballet), **Boulanger (L.)** (*F. et Hélène*), **Bungert** (incid. m.), **Coleridge-Taylor** (do.), **Damnation de Faust** (Berlioz), **Diepenbrock** (incid. m.), **Doktor Faust** (Busoni), **Draeseke** (*Easter Scene*), **Faust** (ballet, Costa, &c.; operas, Gounod & Zöllner; orch. works, Liszt & Wagner), **Fausto** (Bertin), **Gregoir (J. M. J.)** (cantata), **Gretchen am Spinnrade** (song, Schubert), **Lassen** (incid. m.), **Lazzari** (do.), **Lindpaintner** (do.), **Liszt** (sym.), **Lortzing** (incid. m.), **Mefistofele** (Boito), **Meyer-Lutz** (opera), **Mihalovich** (ovt.), **Paumgartner** (incid. m.), **Petit Faust** (parody-operetta, Hervé), **Pierson** (incid. m.), **Radziwill** (do.), **Rubinstein (A.)** (mus. portrait), **Salmhofer** (incid. m.), **Schillings** (do.), **Schulz-Beuthen** (2 scenes), **Streicher (T.)** (monologues), **Szenen aus Gs. F.** (Schumann), **Tomašek** (incid. m.), **Wagner** (ovt. & 7 songs), **Walter (I.)** (opera), **Weingartner** (incid. m.), **Wolfurt** (Rhapsody).

Separate settings of songs, &c. in 'Faust' incl. *Der König in Thule* by Schubert; *Gretchen* (prayer, 'Ach neige') by Schubert (unfinished); 'Song of the Flea' by Beethoven & Mussorgsky.

Goetz, Hermann (b. Königsberg, 7. XII. 1840; d. Hottingen nr. Zürich, 3. XII. 1876), Ger. comp. At first he studied m. only incidentally when a student at Königsberg Univ., but later went to the Stern Cons. in Berlin. In 1863 he went to Swi. as orgst. at Winterthur and in 1867 he settled at Zürich.

Works incl. operas *Der Widerspänstigen Zähmung* (on Shakespeare's *Taming of the Shrew*) and *Francesca da Rimini* (unfinished); *Nänie* (Schiller) & Psalm lxxxvii for solo voices, chor. & orch.; cantata for male voices & orch.; Sym. in F maj., *Spring* ovt. for orch.; v. Conc. in G maj., pf. Conc. in B♭ maj.; pf. 5tet, pf. 4tet, pf. Trio; So. for pf. duet; sonatina, *Genrebilder* & other works for pf.; songs, &c.

Gogol, Nikolai Vassilievitch (1809–52), Rus. novelist. *See* **Assafiev** (*Christmas Eve*), **Berutti** (*Taras Bulba*), **Christmas Eve** (Rimsky-Korsakov), **Gnessin** (*Revisor*), **Janáček** (*Taras B.*), **Kashperov** (do.), **Lissenko** (do.), **Marriage** (Mussorgsky), **May Night** (Rimsky-K.), **Rousseau (M.)** (*Taras B.*), **Serov** (*Christmas Eve Revels*), **Shostakovitch** (*Nose*), **Sokalsky (P.)** (*Night in May* & *Taras B.*), **Soloviev** (*Vakula the Smith*), **Sorotchintsy Fair** (Mussorgsky), **Vakula the Smith** (Tchaikovsky), **Weiss (K.)** (*Revisor*), **Zanella** (do.).

Goldberg, Johann Gottlieb (b. Danzig, III. 1727; d. Dresden, IV. 1756), Ger. clav. player & orgst. Pupil of W. F. Bach at Dresden and of J. S. Bach at Leipzig from 1741. It is for him that Bach wrote the so-called 'Goldberg Vars.' for hpchd. in 1742.

Goldberg Variations (Bach). *See above.*

Golden Cockerel, The (*Zolotoy Petushok*), opera by Rimsky-Korsakov, (lib. by Vladimir Ivanovitch Bielsky, based on Pushkin's satirical fairy-tale), prod. Moscow, 7. X. 1909, after R.-K.'s death. It is his last opera.

Golden Legend, The, orat. by Sullivan (on Longfellow's poem), prod. Leeds Festival, 1886.

'Golden Sonata,' the nickname given to the 9th (G min.) of Purcell's 10 *Sonatas of IV Parts* for 2 vs., co. & continuo, pub. posthumously in 1697.

Goldene Kreuz, Das (*The Golden Cross*), opera by Brüll (lib. by Salomon Hermann Mosenthal, based on a Fr. play, *Cathérine*, by Anne Honoré Joseph Mélesville & Nicolas Brazier), prod. Berlin, Royal Opera, 22. XII. 1875.

Goldmark, Carl (b. Keszthely, 18. V. 1830; d. Vienna, 2. I. 1915), Aus.-Hung. comp. Son of a poor Jewish cantor, who managed to enter him at the Sopron school of m. in 1842. He studied v. and made such rapid progress that he was sent to Vienna the next year and entered the Cons. in 1847. During the 1848 Revol. he played at the theatre at Györ in Hung. and was nearly shot as a rebel. In 1850 he returned to Vienna and gradually became famous as a comp.

Works incl. operas *Die Königin von Saba, Merlin, Das Heimchen am Herd* (after Dickens's *Cricket on the Hearth*), *Die Kriegsgefangene, Götz von Berlichingen* (after Goethe) & *Ein Wintermärchen* (after Shakespeare's *Winter's Tale*); syms. *Rustic Wedding* & E♭ maj., 2 Scherzos for orch. & ovts. *Sakuntala* (after Kalidasa), *Penthesilea* (after Kleist), *Im Frühling, Der gefesselte Prometheus, Sappho, In Italien* & *Aus Jugendtagen*, symph. poem *Zrinyi*; *Meeresstille und glückliche Fahrt* (Goethe) for male chor. & hns. & other chor. works; 2 v. concs.; stg. 4tet, pf. 5tet, 3 pf. trios & other chamber m.; 2 suites and So. for v. & pf.; co. & pf. So.; pf. pieces; songs, &c.

Goldmark, Rubin (b. New York, 15. VIII. 1872; d. New York, 6. III. 1936), Amer. comp. of Aus.-Hung. descent, nephew of prec. Studied at the Vienna Cons. and the Nat. Cons. in N.Y., where Dvořák was his comp. master. He was dir. of the Colorado Coll. Cons. in 1895–1901, but returned to N.Y. in 1902 and settled as private pf. and comp. teacher, until in 1924 he was app. to the Juilliard Graduate School there.

Works incl. *Hiawatha* (after Longfellow), *Samson, Requiem* (on Lincoln's address at Gettysburg), *Negro Rhapsody* & *The Call of the Plains* for orch.; stg. 4tet in A maj., pf. Trio in D min.; v. & pf. So.; v. pieces; pf. m.; songs; chors., &c.

Goldoni, Carlo (1707–93), It. playwright & libst. *See* **Amore artigiano** (Gassmann & Latilla), **Arcadia in Brenta** (Galuppi), **Buovo d'Antona** (Traetta), **Burbero di buon cuore** (Martín y Soler), **Conte Caramella** (Galuppi), **Donne curiose** (Wolf-Ferrari), **Filosofo di campagna** (Galuppi), **Fischietti** (4 operas), **Fra due litiganti** (Sarti), **Gelosie villane** (Sarti), **Generali** (*Pamela nubile*, after Richardson), **Isola disabitata** (G. Scarlatti), **Lottchen am Hofe** (J. A. Hiller), **Malipiero** (3 operas), **Mondo alla roversa** (Galuppi), **Mondo della luna** (do. & Haydn), **Paisiello** (*Ciarlone*), **Pallavicini (V.)** (*Speziale*), **Pescatrici** (Bertoni), **Piccinni** (*Vittorina*), **Quattro rusteghi** (Wolf-Ferrari), **Scarlatti** (6) (*Portentosi effetti*), **Scholz** (*Mirandolina*), **Sinigaglia** (*Baruffe chiozzote*), **Speziale** (Haydn), **Tigrane** (Gluck), **Uccellatori** (Gassmann), **Vendemmia** (Gazzaniga), **Wagenaar (J.)** (*Philos. Princess*), **Wolf (E. W.)** (*Dorfdeputierten*).

Goldschmidt, Adalbert von (b. Vienna, 5. V. 1848; d. Vienna, 21. XII. 1906), Aus. comp. He devoted himself as an amateur to the comp. of large-scale works, the 1st of which, prod. in Berlin in 1876, showed remarkable affinities with Wagner's *Ring*, not heard until later in the year at Bayreuth.

Works incl. m.-dramas *Die sieben Todsünden, Helianthus, Gaea* (trilogy), opera *Die fromme Helene* (after Wilhelm Busch); symph. poem; *c.* 100 songs, &c.

Goldschmidt, Hugo (b. Breslau, 19. IX. 1859; d. Wiesbaden, 26. XII. 1920), Ger. mcolst. Studied singing with Stockhausen at Frankfort, but later took up mus. hist. One of the dirs. of the Scharwenka-Klindworth Cons. in Berlin and later prof. of mus. hist. there. Wrote several works on the hist. of singing, one on 17th-cent. It. opera, &c.

Goldschmidt, Otto (b. Hamburg, 21. VIII. 1829; d. London, 24. II. 1907), Ger. pfst. & comp. Studied at the Leipzig Cons. under Mendelssohn and in 1848 went to Paris to study with Chopin, but found him too ill. In 1849 he settled in London. Accompst. and later husband of Jenny Lind. Founder of the Bach Choir.

Works incl. orat. *Ruth*; cantata *Music* for sop. and female voices; pf. Conc.; pf. Trio; 2 duets for 2 pfs.; studies & pieces for pf.; songs, &c.

Goldsmith, Oliver (1728–74), Eng. novelist, poet, dramatist & essayist. *See* **Lehmann (L. ii)** (*Vicar of Wakefield*), **She Stoops to Conquer** (G. Macfarren), **Torrance** (*Captivity*), **Vento** (*Threnodia Augustalis*), **White (F.)** (*Deserted Village*).

Golenishtchev-Kutuzov, Arseny, Count (1848–1913), Rus. amateur poet, distant relative of Mussorgsky. *See* **Songs and Dances of Death** (Mussorgsky), **Sunless** (do.).

Golestan, Stan (b. Vaslui, 26. V. 1875), Rum. comp. Studied at the Schola Cantorum and the Cons. in Paris under d'Indy, Roussel & Dukas. M. critic of *Le Figaro*. As a comp. he cultivated a Rum. nat. style.

Works incl. Sym., *Rapsodie Dambovitza* & *Rumanian Rhapsody*; *Concerto roumain* for v. & orch., *Concerto moldave* for co. & orch., pf. Conc., *Sur les cimes carpathiques, Intermezzo et Siciliennes* for hp. & orch., *Oriental Fantasy* for bn. & orch.; 2 stg. 4tets, *Divertissement* for ob., cl. & bn.; v. & pf. So., fl. & pf. Sonatina; Theme & Vars. for pf.; pieces for wind insts.; 10 Rumanian folksongs, &c.

Golinelli, Stefano (b. Bologna, 26. X. 1818; d. Bologna, 3. VII. 1891), It. pfst. & comp. Pupil of Benedetto Donelli for pf. and of Vaccai for comp. App. by Rossini pf. prof. at the Liceo musicale at Bologna.

Works (all for pf.) incl. 5 sos., 12 studies, 3 sets of 24 preludes, 3 toccatas & others in *c.* 200 op. nos.

Goltermann, Georg (Eduard) (b. Hanover, 19. VIII. 1824; d. Frankfort o/M., 29. XII. 1898), Ger. cst., cond. & comp. Studied at Munich and began to tour as a co. virtuoso in 1850. In 1853 he became 2nd and in 1874 1st cond. at the Frankfort theatre. Comp. a Sym.; a co. Conc. and many pieces for that inst.

Golubev, Evgeny (b. Moscow, 16. II. 1910), Rus. comp. Studied at the Moscow Cons. He went to the Ukraine in 1937 to study its folk m.

Works incl. orat. *The Return of the Sun*; 2 syms. & Double Fugue for orch.; stg. 4tet; Poem for v. & pf.; 3 sos. and *Ukrainian Rhapsody* for pf., &c.

Gombert, Nicolas (b. Bruges, *c.* 1505; d. ?), Flem. comp. Pupil of Josquin des Prés. He was in service at the Emperor Charles V's chapel in Flanders from 1520 and became chapel master in 1530; later he became a canon at Tournai and in 1537 went to Spa. with 20 singers and held a post in the imp. chapel in Madrid.

Works incl. masses, motets, psalms; chansons, &c.

Gomes, (Antonio) Carlos (b. Campinas, 11. VII. 1836; d. Belem, 16. IX. 1896), Braz. comp. of Port. descent. Studied at the Milan Cons. as a pupil of Lauro Rossi. In 1895 he was app. dir. of the Cons. at Pará, but he was delayed at Lisbon by illness and d. soon after his arrival.

Works incl. operas *A noite do castello*, *Joanna di Flandres*, *Il Guarany*, *Fosca*, *Salvator Rosa*, *Maria Tudor* (on Victor Hugo's play), *Lo schiavo*, *Condor*; revues *Se sa minga* & *Nella luna*; ode *Il saluto del Brasil* (Philadelphia Exhib., 1876) & cantata *Colombo* (Columbus Festival, 1892), &c.

Gómez Camargo, Miguel (b. Guadalajara, ?; d. Valladolid, ?), Spa. 16th-cent. comp. Choirmaster at Valladolid, then the capital of Spa. Comp. a hymn to St. James, &c.

Gomis, José Melchior (b. Onteniente, Valencia, 6. I. 1791; d. Paris, 26. VII. 1836), Spa. comp. Bandmaster at Barcelona, moved to Madrid *c.* 1817 and in 1823 went to Paris for political reasons. In 1826–9 he taught singing in London, where he pub. many Spa. songs, and then returned to Paris, where he prod. comic operas.

Works incl. Spa. monodrama *Sensibilidad y prudencia, ó La Aldeana*, Fr. comic operas *Le Diable à Séville*, *Le Revenant* (after Scott), *Le Portefaix* & *Rock le barbu*; *L'inverno* for 4 voices & orch.; songs, &c.

Gondoliers, The, or The King of Barataria, operetta by Sullivan (lib. by W. S. Gilbert), prod. London, Savoy Theatre, 7. XII. 1889.

Gong. An oriental bronze disc with turned-down rims, not strictly a mus. inst., but used in var. ways for signalling by means of a penetrating noise, and now a regular constituent of the percussion dept. of a full orch. It is struck with a mallet covered with var. materials according to the quality of sound required.

Góngora y Argote, Luis de (1561–1627), Spa. poet. *See* **Falla** (*A Córdoba*).

Gonzaga, Guglielmo, Duke of Mantua (b. Mantua, 1538; d. Mantua, 1587). He succeeded to the duchy in 1550, became a great patron of m. and was himself a comp., pub. anonymously a book of madrigals and 1 of *Sacrae cantiones*.

Good-Humoured Ladies, The, ballet by Tommasini on m. by D. Scarlatti (chgph. by Leonid Fedorovitch Massin), prod. Rome, Teatro Costanzi, 12. IV. 1917.

Goossens, Eugene (b. London, 26. V. 1893), Eng. cond. & comp. of Belg. descent, grandson of Eugène Goossens (1845–1906) and son of Eugène Goossens (b. 1867), both conds. of the Carl Rosa Opera Co. He was sent to the Bruges Cons. in 1903, to the Liverpool Coll. of M. in 1906 and later studied v. with Rivarde and comp. with Stanford at the R.C.M. in London, with pf. as 2nd study. He played v. in the Queen's Hall Orch., 1911–5, and then, until 1920, cond. some of Beecham's operatic prods. After that he formed an orch. of his own, which had a brief season in 1921, and cond. the Rus. Ballet and the Sym. Orch. at Rochester, U.S.A. In 1931 he was app. cond. of the Cincinnati Sym. Orch. and has continued to live there.

Works incl. operas *Judith* & *Don Juan de Mañara*; ballet *L'École en crinoline*; incid. m. to Verhaeren's *Philip II*, Somerset Maugham's *East of Suez* & Margaret Kennedy's *The Constant Nymph*; 2 syms., Sinfonietta, symph. poem *The Eternal Rhythm*, symph. prelude to a poem by Ossian, scherzo *Tam o' Shanter* (after Burns), Ovt. for Jubilee of Cincinnati Orch.; Miniature Fantasy & Concertino for stg. orch.; *Silence* for chor. & orch.; Fantasy Conc. for pf. & orch., ob. Conc.; 2 stg. 4tets, Fantasy & 2 Sketches for stg. 4tet, pf. 5tet, stg. 6tet, Suite for fl., v. & hp., *Impressions of a Holiday* for fl., co. & pf. & other chamber m.; v. & pf. So., Rhapsody for co. & pf.; *Kaleidoscope, Four Conceits, Nature Poems, Ships*, &c. for pf.; *The Cowl* (Barbor) for recitation & pf.; many songs in Eng. & Fr., &c.

Goovaerts, Alphonse (Jean Marie André) (b. Antwerp, 25. V. 1847; d. Brussels, 25. XII. 1922), Belg. comp. & writer on m. Studied at the Jesuit Coll. of Antwerp and at the age of 15 was obliged by financial losses to take to a commercial career; but he studied m. thoroughly by himself and in 1866 obtained a post at the Antwerp town library. He succeeded in having his motets perf. in the churches and in 1869 his *Messe solennelle*, and in pub. some Flem. songs. In 1874 he was app. mus. secretary to Antwerp cath. and he estab. a special choir for which he copied a vast quantity of old motets of var. schools. He began to write on the reform of church m. and in 1887 was app. keeper of the royal archives at Brussels.

Works incl. motets, *Petite Messe, Messe solennelle* & other church m.; songs, partsongs, &c.

Gopak (or Hopak). A Rus. folk dance with m. of a lively character in quick 2–4 time.

Gorczycki, Grzegorz (b. ?; d. Cracow, IV. 1734), Pol. comp. Chapel master at Cracow cath. Comp. motets & other church m.

Gordigiani, Luigi (b. Modena, 21. VI. 1806; d. Florence, 1. V. 1860), It. comp. Pupil of his father, Antonio G., who d. when he was 14, so that he had to make a living by writing pf. pieces under Ger. names. The Rus. Prince Nikolai Demidov and the Pol. Prince Joseph Poniatowski discovered his great gifts and patronized him, the latter providing him with the lib. for his opera *Filippo*, prod. at Florence in 1840.

Works incl. 10 operas; *Canzonette, Canti popolari* & other songs (c. 300 in all); duets for female voices; Tuscan airs with pf. accomp., &c.

Gordon, Adam Lindsay (1833–70), Austral. poet. *See* **Sea Pictures** (Elgar).

Gordon, Gavin (Muspratt) (b. Ayr, 24. XI. 1901), Sco. singer, actor & comp. Educ. at Rugby and studied m. at the R.C.M. in London.

Works incl. ballets *A Toothsome Morsel, Regatta, The Scorpions of Ysit* & *The Rake's Progress* (after Hogarth), &c.

Gorgheggi (It.). *See* **Solfeggio.**

Gorky, Maxim (Alexei Maximovitch Peshkov) (1868–1936), Rus. novelist. *See* **Assafiev** (*Makar Chudra*), **Eisler** (*Mother*), **Zhelobinsky** (do.).

Görner, Johann Gottlieb (b. Penig, Saxony, 1697; d. Leipzig, 15. II. 1778), Ger. orgst. & comp. at Leipzig. Founded a Collegium Musicum there in 1723. Orgst. at St. Paul's (Univ.) church, 1721; at St. Nicholas's and St. Thomas's, 1729. Comp. church m.

Göss, Barthel. *See* **Gese, Bartholomäus.**

Goss, John (b. Fareham, Hants, 27. XII. 1800; d. London, 10. V. 1880), Eng. orgst. & comp. Studied under his father, orgst. at Fareham, then under J. S. Smith at the Chapel Royal in London and finally under Attwood. After holding several org. appts., he succeeded Attwood as orgst. of St. Paul's cath. in 1838 and in 1856 became one of the comps. to the Chapel Royal in succession to Knyvett. Knighted in 1872 and Mus.D., Cambridge, in 1876.

Works incl. services, anthems, chants, psalms; orch. pieces; glees; songs, &c.

Gossec, François Joseph (b. Vergnies, Hainault, 17. I. 1734; d. Passy nr. Paris, 16. II. 1829), Belg. comp. Son of a farmer, became a choir-boy at Antwerp cath. which he left at the age of 15. In 1751 he went to Paris and at Rameau's recommendation became cond. of La Pouplinière's private orch. where he cond. Rameau's works and his own syms., the 1st of which he wrote in 1754. He also wrote stg. 4tets for the Prince de Conti, whose service he entered later. He founded the Concert des Amateurs in 1770, reformed the Concert spirituel in 1773 and in 1784 organized the École de Chant, which turned into the Cons. in 1795, of which he was made joint inspector with Cherubini, Lesueur and Méhul, and prof. of comp.

Works incl. operas *Le Tonnelier, Le Faux Lord, Les Pêcheurs, Toinon et Toinette, Le Double Déguisement, Sabinus, Alexis et Daphné, Philémon et Baucis, Hilas et Silvie, La Fête de village, Thésée, Rosine*, &c.; ballets *Les Scythes enchaînés, La Reprise de Toulon, Mirsa* & *Callisto*; incid. m. for Racine's *Athalie* & Rochefort's *Électre*; orats. *La Nativité, Saül* & *L'Arche d'alliance*; Requiem, *Dixit Dominus, Exaudiat, Dernière Messe des vivants*, motets, &c.; funeral m. for Mirabeau, *Le Chant du 14 juillet, L'Offrande à la liberté, Le Triomphe de la République* & other m. for the Revol.; over 30 syms., ovts. & other orch. works; 12 stg. 4tets, trios & other chamber m., &c.

Gostena, Giovanni Battista dalla (b.

Genoa, ?; d. Genoa, 1598), It. comp. Pupil of Philippe de Monte, chapel master at Genoa cath. from 1584 to 1598, when his nephew, Molinaro, succeeded him.

Works incl. motets & other church m.; 2 books of madrigals, 1 of canzonette; 25 fantasies for lute, &c.

Gostling, John (b. East Malling, Kent, c. 1650; d. London, 17. VII. 1733), Eng. cleric & bass singer. Became a Gentleman of the Chapel Royal in London, 1679, and later held var. clerical posts in and out of the capital.

Gotovac, Jakov (b. Split, 11. X. 1895), Yslv. cond. & comp. Studied at his home town, at Zagreb and in Vienna. In 1923 he became cond. of the Croat. Opera at Zagreb, also of a Balkan chor. soc., with which he travelled in Eur.

Works incl. operas *Morana* & *Ero from the Other World*; incid. m. for pastoral play *Dubravka*; chor. works; *Symph. Kolo* & *The Ploughers* for orch.; songs with orch. (incl. 2 odes by Anacreon); stg. 4tet; songs with pf., &c.

Götterdämmerung (*The Dusk of the Gods*, Wagner). *See* **Ring des Nibelungen.**

Gotthelf, Jeremias (Albrecht Bitzius) (1797–1854), Swi. novelist. *See* **Hauer** (*Schwarze Spinne*), **Mendelssohn (A.)** (*Elsi*); **Sutermeister** (*Schwarze S.*).

Göttin der Vernunft, Die (*The Goddess of Reason*), operetta by J. Strauss, jun. (lib. by Alfred Maria Willner & Bernhard Buchbinder), prod. Vienna, Theater an der Wien, 13. III. 1897. S.'s last operetta.

Götz, Hermann. *See* **Goetz.**

Goudimel, Claude (b. Besançon, c. 1505; d. Lyons, 27. VIII. 1572), Fr. comp. 1st appeared as comp. in Paris in 1549. About 1557, having become a Huguenot, he went to live at Metz with the Protestant colony there, but about 10 years later left for Besançon, and afterwards for Lyons, where he d. in the massacre of the Huguenots.

Works incl. masses, magnificats, psalms in motet form & other works for the Catholic church; psalms, incl. a complete psalter, for the Protestant church; sacred songs and numerous secular chansons for several voices, &c.

Gounod, Charles (François) (b. Paris, 17. VI. 1818; d. Saint-Cloud, 18. X. 1893), Fr. comp. Son of a painter. His mother, a good pfst., taught him m. from an early age and he was educ. at the Lycée Saint-Louis and in mus. at the Paris Cons., where his masters were Halévy, Paer and Lesueur. He gained the Prix de Rome in 1839 and spent the statutory 3 years in Rome, studying the old It. church comps. After a tour in Aus. and Ger. he returned to Paris and was app. orgst. at the church of the Missions étrangères. Intending to become a priest, he did not prod. any important m. until his opera *Sapho* appeared in 1851, his mus. inclinations having gained the upper hand. But he had no very great success until *Faust* was prod. in 1859, and he never quite attained that again. In 1852–60 he cond. the united chor. socs. named Orphéon, and in 1870–5 he lived in London, where he was driven by the Franco-Prus. war and was so popular that he wished to stay on. During the last years of his life he turned to religious mysticism.

Works incl. operas *Sapho*, *La Nonne sanglante*, *Le Médecin malgré lui* (on Molière), *Faust* (after Goethe), *Philémon et Baucis*, *La Reine de Saba*, *Mireille* (after Mistral), *La Colombe*, *Roméo et Juliette* (after Shakespeare), *Cinq-Mars* (after Alfred de Vigny), *Polyeucte* (after Corneille), *Le Tribut de Zamora*; incid. m. for Ponsard's *Ulysse*, Legouvé's *Les Deux Reines* & Barbier's *Jeanne d'Arc*; orats. *La Rédemption*, *Mors et Vita*, *Tobie*; 8 cantatas; 9 masses, 3 Requiems, *Stabat Mater*, Te Deum, *De profundis*, *Ave, verum corpus*, *Pater noster*, Magnificat & other sacred voc. pieces; 3 syms.; some pf. comps. incl. the *Funeral March for a Marionette*; *Méditation sur le Prélude de Bach* for sop.. v., pf. & org.; some smaller chor. works; many songs, &c.

Gouvy, Louis Théodore (b. Goffontaine nr. Saarbrücken, 2. VII. 1819; d. Leipzig, 21. IV. 1898), Ger. comp. of Fr. parentage. Studied law at Metz and Paris, but turned to m., which he learnt under Elwart in Paris and in Berlin and It. Settled in Paris in 1846, but making his success of Ger., went to live at Oberhomburg.

Works incl. opera *Der Cid* (after Corneille); *Missa brevis*, Requiem, *Stabat Mater*, cantatas and dramatic scenas; 7 syms., Sinfonietta, symph. paraphrases, ovts., &c. for orch.; 5 stg. 4tets, 8tet for wind, 6tet for fl. & stgs., pf. 5tet, 5 pf. trios; inst. sos.; pf. solos; songs, &c.

Gow. Sco. family of musns.:

1. Niel Neil G. (b. Inver nr. Dunkeld, 22. III. 1727; d. Inver, 1. III. 1807), vst. Intended to become a weaver, he made his fame by playing Sco. dance tunes at balls in Sco. cities and even in London.

2. Donald G. (b. Inver nr. Dunkeld, c. 1730; d. ?), cst., brother of prec.

3. William G. (b. Inver nr. Dunkeld,

1751; d. Edinburgh, 1791), vst., son of 1. Leader of the Edinburgh Assembly orch. until his death.

4. Nathaniel G. (b. Inver nr. Dunkeld, 28. V. 1763; d. Edinburgh, 19. I. 1831), tptr., vst. & pub., brother of prec. At 16, when living at Edinburgh, he was app. royal tptr., learnt the v. from Mackintosh, became leader of the Edinburgh Assembly orch. on the death of his brother and provided dance m. by playing, comp. and after 1796 pub. it. He wrote songs, pieces descriptive of Edinburgh street cries (incl. 'Caller Herrin',' at first an inst. piece and not fitted with words by Lady **Nairne** until *c.* 20 years later), &c.

5. Niel G. (b. Edinburgh, *c.* 1795; d. Edinburgh, 7. XI. 1823), comp., son of prec. He joined his father in the pub. business in 1818. Wrote songs, incl. 'Flora Macdonald's Lament,' 'Cam' ye by Athol,' &c.

Goward, Mary Anne (b. Ipswich, 22, XI. 1805; d. London, 12. III. 1899), Eng. sop. singer & actress. Made her 1st stage appearance at Dublin in 1823 and in London in 1825. In 1826 she sang the Mermaid in the prod. of Weber's *Oberon.* In 1829 she married the comedian Robert Keeley, under whose name she became a famous comedy actress.

Goyescas, opera by Granados (lib., in Spa., by Fernando Periquet y Zuaznabar), prod. N.Y., Metrop. Opera, 28. I. 1916. Much of the material is taken from G.'s pf. work below.

2 sets of pf. pieces by Granados inspired by etchings of Spa. scenes by Goya, 1st perf. Paris, 4. IV. 1914: I. *Los requiebros* (*The Compliments*), *Coloquio en la reja* (*Colloquy at the Grilled Window*), *El fandango del candil* (*The F. of the Lantern*), *Quejas,ó La maja y el ruiseñor* (*Plaints, or The Maja and the Nightingale*); II. *El Amor y la Muerte* (*Love and Death*), *Epílogo: la serenata del espectro* (*Epilogue: the Spectre's Serenade*). (A *maja* is the feminine counterpart of *majo* = a fop, a masher.) G. also wrote a separate *escena goyesca* for pf.: *El pelele* (a puppet or straw-man tossed in a blanket).

Gozzi, Carlo (1722–1806), It. dramatist. *See* **Danzi** (*Turandot*), **Donna serpente** (Casella), **Feen** (Wagner), **Hartmann (J. P. E.)** (*Ravnen*), **Himmel** (*Sylphen*), **Jensen** (*Turandot*), **Joachim (A.)** (ovt. on 2 comedies), **Lachner (V.)** (*Turandot*), **Liuzzi** (*Augellin bel verde*), **Love of Three Oranges** (Prokofiev), **Paumgartner** (*Turandot*), **Reissiger** (do.), **Romberg (A.)** (*Rabe & Blaue Ungeheuer*), **Romberg (B.)** (*Wiedergefundene Statue*), **Schweitzer** (*Segreto pubblico*), **Stenhammar** (*Turandot*), **Turanda** (Bazzini), **Turandot** (incid. m., Weber; operas, Busoni, Lovenskjold & Puccini), **Vesque von Püttlingen** (*Turandot*).

Gr. (abbr.) = Greece, Greek.

Grabbe, Christian Dietrich (1801–36), Ger. dramatist. *See* **Borck** (*Napoleon*), **Lortzing** (*Don Juan und Faust*), **Tiessen** (do.).

Grabu (or **Grabut, Grebus**), **Louis** (b. ?; d. ?), Fr. 17th-cent. vst. & comp. App. comp. to Charles II in 1665 and Master of the King's M. in 1666. Adapted the m. for London of Cambert's opera *Ariadne* in 1674 and wrote incid. m. for Shadwell's version of Shakespeare's *Timon of Athens*, 1678. Comp. m. for Dryden's 'opera' *Albion and Albanius* in 1685, also songs for Durfey's *Squire Oldsapp* and incid. m. for Waller's adapt. of Beaumont & Fletcher's *The Maid's Tragedy.*

Grace, Harvey (b. Romsey, 25. I. 1874; d. Bromley, Kent, 15. II. 1944), Eng. orgst., educst., mus. ed. & writer. Studied m. under the orgst. of Southwark cath. in London and later held var. orgst.'s posts, the last being that of Chichester cath. He often adjudicated at mus. festivals, succeeded W. G. McNaught as ed. of the *Mus. Times* in 1918 and wrote books on org. playing and chor. conducting & on Bach's and Rheinberger's org. m.

Grace Notes or **Graces** = **Ornaments**

Gracioso (Spa. = jester, buffoon). The word appears in the title of one of Ravel's *Miroirs* for pf., *Alborada del gracioso* (*The Jester's Morning Song*).

Gradus ad Parnassum. (I) a treatise on ctpt. by Fux, pub. in 1725; (II) a series of 100 instructive and progressive pf. pieces by Clementi, pub. in 1817. The 1st piece in Debussy's *Children's Corner* for pf. alludes to C.'s collection.

Graener, Paul (b. Berlin, 11. I. 1872; d. Berlin, 15. XI. 1944), Ger. comp. Was a choir-boy in Berlin cath. and at 16 entered Veit's Cons., but soon began to teach himself, leading a wandering life, cond. at var. theatres and comp. a number of immature works. In 1896–1908 he was in London as teacher at the R.A.M. and cond. at the Haymarket Theatre, and was then app. dir. of the New Cons. in Vienna and in 1910 of the Mozarteum at Salzburg. After some years in Munich he succeeded Reger as prof. of comp. at the Leipzig Cons., but resigned in 1925. In 1930 he became dir. of Stern's Cons. in Berlin and under the Nazi régime vice-president of the Reichsmusikkammer, being succeeded by Egk in 1941.

Works incl. operas *Der vierjährige Posten* (Körner), *Das Narrengericht, Don Juans letztes Abenteuer, Theophano* (*Byzanz*), *Schirin und Gertraude, Hanneles Himmelfahrt* (after Gerhart - Hauptmann), *Friedemann Bach, Der Prinz von Homburg* (after Kleist); chor. works; Sym. *Schmied Schmerz, Romantic Fantasy, Vars. on a Rus. folksong* & other orch. works; 3 stg. 4tets, 3 pf. trios & other chamber m.; So. & Suite for v. & pf., Suite for co. & pf.; pf. pieces; over 100 songs, &c.

Graf (or **Graff**), **Friedrich (Hartmann)** (b. Rudolstadt, 1727; d. Augsburg, 19. VIII. 1795), Ger. flst. & comp. Became chapel master at Augsburg in 1772. Later worked in Vienna and London for a time. Mus.D., Oxford, 1789.

Works incl. cantatas, syms., concs., chamber m., &c.

Grahame, Kenneth (1859–1932), Eng. author. *See* **Thompson (R.)** (*Wind in the Willows*).

Grainger, Percy (Aldridge) (b. Melbourne, 8. VII. 1882), Austral.-Amer. pfst. & comp. Studied under his mother and Louis Pabst at Melbourne, later in Ger. with Kwast, Knorr and Busoni. He lived in London in 1900–15 and became interested in Eng. folk m.; toured Scandinavia in 1909 and settled in U.S.A. in 1915, later becoming naturalized.

Works incl. comps. for chor. & orch. with and without solo voices: *Marching Song of Democracy, The Bride's Tragedy* (Swinburne), *Father and Daughter* (Faroe folksong), *Sir Eglamore, We have fed our seas* (Kipling), *Tribute to Foster, Bridal Song*, &c.; partsongs *Brigg Fair, Morning Song of the Jungle* (Kipling), &c.; pieces for small orch.: *Molly on the Shore, Colonial Song, Shepherd's Hey, Mock Morris, Irish Tune from County Derry* (Londonderry Air), clog dance *Handel in the Strand*; suite *In a Nutshell* for 2 pfs.; 4 Ir. dances on themes by Stanford, *Walking Tune*, &c. for pf.; songs, &c.

Gram, Peder (b. Copenhagen, 25. XI. 1881), Dan. cond. & comp. Studied at Copenhagen Univ. and m. at the Leipzig Cons., cond. under Nikisch. In 1908 he became cond. and prof. at Copenhagen. He visited Fr. & Ger. as cond., held var. official posts and in 1937 became dir. of m. of the Dan. broadcasting organization.

Works incl. 2 syms., ovts.; concs. for v. & for co.; songs, &c.

Gramophone (formerly Phonograph, and still so called in Amer.). An inst. invented in its primitive form by Edison and gradually developed into the most perfect inst. devised for mech. reproduction of m. The m. is now recorded on a disc of wax, afterwards transferred to a disc of some kind of hard shellac mixture. The sound-waves of the m. are reproduced thereon in a series of grooves. In perf. the disc revolves, a static needle is brought into contact with the grooves, and the 'frozen' sound-waves are released and amplified by a sound-box.

Gran Cassa (It. lit. great case, great box) = Bass Drum.

Gran Mass (' Graner Messe '). A mass by Liszt for solo voices, chor., orch. & org., comp. in 1855 for the inaug. of a church at Gran in Hung. and perf. there 31. VIII. 1856.

Granados, Enrique (b. Lérida, 29. VII. 1867; d. at sea, 24. III. 1916), Spa. comp. Studied comp. with Pedrell at Barcelona and pf. in Paris. Returning to Madrid in 1889, he became a well-known pfst. and in 1900 he founded the Sociedad de conciertos clásicos there, which he cond. After a visit to N.Y. for the prod. of *Goyescas* in the operatic version in I. 1916, he went down in the *Sussex*, torpedoed by a Ger. submarine in the Eng. Channel.

Works incl. operas *María del Carmen, Gaziel, Goyescas* (based on the pf. work), *Petrarca, Picarol, Follet, Liliana*; symph. poem *La nit del mort*, 4 suites &c. for orch.; *Cant de las Estrelles* for chor., org. & pf.; pf. Trio, *Oriental* for ob. & stgs.; *Goyescas* (2 vols.), 12 Spa. Dances, 6 pieces on Spa. folksongs, *Escenas románticas, Escenas poéticas, Libro de horas* Impromptus, children's pieces for pf.; songs *Escritas en estilo antiguo* & a collection of tonadillas, &c.

Grand Bourdon (Fr.). An org. ped. stop of 32-ft. tone.

Grand Chœur (Fr. lit. great choir) = Full Org., a direction that the org. is to be used with all the registers.

Grand Duke, The, or The Statutory Duel, operetta by Sullivan (lib. by W. S. Gilbert), prod. London, Savoy Theatre, 7. III. 1896. Gilbert's last lib. for S.

Grand Jeu (Fr. lit. great play) = Grand Chœur; also used for a harmonium stop that brings the whole inst. into play.

Grand Opera. Not properly a dictionary term and devoid of any definite meaning, but often used in Eng. to denote serious as distinct from comic opera or operetta.

Grand Piano. *See* **Pianoforte.**

Grand Prix de Rome. *See* **Prix de Rome.**

Grande-Duchesse de Gérolstein, La, operetta by Offenbach (lib. by Henri

Meilhac & Ludovic Halévy), prod. Paris, Théâtre des Variétés, 12. IV. 1867.

Grandi, Alessandro (b. ? Sicily, ?; d. Bergamo, *c.* 1630), It. comp. Pupil of (?) G. Gabrieli at Venice, chapel master of the church of the Santo Spirito at Ferrara, 1610–7, and then at St. Mark's, Venice, until 1628, when he became choirmaster at the church of Santa Maria Maggiore at Bergamo.

Works incl. masses, motets, psalms; madrigals; arias for solo voice, &c.

Grandioso (It. =grandiose). A direction asking for perf. in a dignified manner.

Graner Messe (Liszt). *See* **Gran Mass.**

Grania and Diarmid, incid. m. by Elgar, Op. 42, for the play by George Moore and William Butler Yeats, comp. in 1902.

Graphophone. Another name for the Gramophone.

Gras (or **Dorus-Gras**), **Julie Aimée Josèphe** (b. Valenciennes, 7. IX. 1805; d. Paris, 6. II. 1896), Fr. opera singer. Student at Paris Cons., pupil of Paer; 1st appeared at Brussels in 1825 and came out at the Paris Opéra in 1830. Married the vst. Gras, 1833.

Gräser, Wolfgang (b. Zürich, 7. IX. 1906; d. Nikolassee nr. Berlin, 13. VI. 1928), Swi. mathematician, physicist, philologist & writer on m. He wrote a book on Bach's *Art of Fugue* & scored it for orch.

Grassi, Cecilia (b. Milan, 1746; d. ?), It. sop. singer. Went to London in 1766, where she married J. C. Bach.

Grassi, Eugène (Cinda) (b. Bangkok, 5. VII. 1887), Fr. comp. Studied with d'Indy and Bourgault-Ducoudray in Paris, then returned to Siam to study native m., and settled in Paris in 1913.

Works incl. *5 Mélodies siamoises* & *Poème de l'Univers* for orch.; *3 Poèmes bouddhiques* for chor. & orch.; *Les Équinoxes* for pf.; *Chanson nostalgique* for voice & pf., &c.

Grassini, Giuseppina (b. Varese, 1773; d. Milan, 3. I. 1850), It. con. singer. Studied singing at Milan and made her 1st appearance there in 1794. She 1st sang in Paris in 1800 and London in 1804.

Graun. Ger. family of musns.:

1. August Friedrich G. (b. Wahrenbrück, Saxony, 1699; d. Merseburg, 5. V. 1765), cantor at Merseburg from 1729.

2. Johann Gottlieb G. (b. Wahrenbrück, 1703; d. Berlin, 27. X. 1771), vst. & comp., brother of prec. Pupil of Pisendel and, in It., of Tartini; played in the Dresden court orch. until 1726, when he became orch. leader at Merseburg. In 1728 he went into the service of the Crown Prince of Prus. at Rheinsberg and followed him to Berlin when he became Frederick II, becoming cond. of the court orch.

Works incl. concs. for hpchd. & for org.; trio sos. with 2 fls.; v. sos., &c.

3. Karl Heinrich G. (b. Wahrenbrück, 7. V. 1704; d. Berlin, 8. VIII. 1759), ten. singer & comp., brother of prec. Learnt m. as a boy sop. to the Dresden town council under var. masters and came under the influence of Lotti, who cond. his operas during a visit to Dresden. In 1725 he was engaged by the opera at Brunswick, cond. by Schürmann. He wrote arias of his own to replace those in his parts and was soon commissioned to comp. whole operas. In 1735 he joined his brother (2) at Rheinsberg and on the accession of Frederick II in 1740 became mus. dir. at Berlin and Potsdam. He was sent to It. to find singers for the opera, remained there more than a year and sang in var. places; on his return he resumed operatic comp. In 1755 his Passion orat. *Der Tod Jesu* to words by Ramler was 1st perf.

Works incl. operas *Sancio und Sinilde, Iphigenia in Aulis* (Ger.), *Polidorus, Scipio Africanus, Lo specchio della fedeltà, Pharao Tubaetes, Rodelinda, regina de' Longobardi, Cleopatra e Cesare, Artaserse, Demofoonte, Ifigenia in Aulide* (It.), *Silla, Montezuma, Merope,* &c.; several Passion cantatas incl. *Der Tod Jesu,* Te Deum; funeral m. for the Duke of Brunswick & for Frederick William I of Prus.; pf. concs.; trios, &c.

Graupner, Christoph (b. Hartmannsdorf, Saxony, 13. I. 1683; d. Darmstadt, 10. V. 1760), Ger. comp. Studied under Schelle & Kuhnau at St. Thomas's school, Leipzig. In 1706–9 he played hpchd. at the opera in Hamburg under Keiser, but went into the service of the Landgrave Ernst Ludwig of Hesse-Darmstadt in 1710, becoming chapel master on the death of Briegel in 1712. Although chosen as cantor at St. Thomas's in Leipzig in 1723, he preferred to stay at Darmstadt, and the post went to Bach.

Operas incl. *Dido, Königin von Carthago, Der angenehme Betrug* & *Die lustige Hochzeit* (both with Keiser), *Hercules und Theseus, Antiochus und Stratonice, Bellerophon, Simson, Berenice e Lucilla, Telemach, La costanza vince l'inganno*; over 1,000 church cantatas, chorales with org. or orch. accomp., &c.; 116 syms., 50 concs., 80 ovts.; trios & sos.; hpchd. works incl. sos., partitas & suites, &c.

Grave (It. =heavy, serious). A direction indicating a slow tempo.

Grave Mixture. A Mixture org. stop sounding the lower ranges of the harmonics with the fundamental notes, unlike the Sharp M., which sounds the higher partials.

Gravicembalo (It.) = Clavicembalo, of which it is a perversion.

Gray, Alan (b. York, 23. XII. 1855; d. Cambridge, 27. IX. 1935), Eng. orgst., educst. & comp. Studied with E. G. Monk, was mus. dir. at Wellington Coll., 1883–92, and orgst. at Trinity Coll., Cambridge, 1892–1912, also cond. of the Cambridge Univ. Mus. Soc.

Works incl. Festival Te Deum, Easter Ode, cantatas *Arethusa, The Vision of Belshazzar, A Song of Redemption* for chor. & orch.; Coronation March; chamber m.; org. pieces, &c.

Gray, Cecil (b. Edinburgh, 19. V. 1895), Sco. writer on m. & comp. Studied m. privately. In 1920 he became joint ed. of the *Sackbut* with Philip Heseltine, with whom he also wrote a book on Gesualdo, and whose biog. as a comp. (Peter Warlock) he pub. Other books are a *History of M.*, essays *Predicaments & Contingencies*, & 2 works on Sibelius.

Comps. incl. operas *Deirdre, The Temptation of St. Anthony* (after Flaubert) & *The Trojan Women* (after Euripides).

Gray, Thomas (1716–71), Eng. poet. *See* **Cellier** (*Elegy*), **Randall** (*Installation Ode*), **Stanford** (*Bard*).

Grazia, Con (It. = with grace) = *grazioso*.

Graziani, Tommaso (b. Bagna Cavallo, Romagna, ?; d. Milan, *c.* 1630), It. monk & comp. Pupil of Porta. Chapel master of Ravenna, Porto Gruaro (Lombardy) and several churches at Milan at var. times.

Works incl. masses, psalms & other church m.

Grazioli, Giovanni Battista (b. Venice, *c.* 1750; d. Venice, *c.* 1820), It. comp. Pupil of Bertoni. 2nd orgst. at St. Mark's, Venice, from 1782 and 1st from 1785.

Works incl. 3 vols. of hpchd. sos., sacred songs for 1 & more voices with insts., &c.

Grazioso (It. = graceful). An adj. sometimes used alone to indicate the character of a piece or passage and more often in combination with a tempo indication, e.g. *allegro grazioso, andantino grazioso*, &c.

Great Fugue (Beethoven). *See* **Grosse Fuge.**

Great Organ. The chief division of the org. containing the foundation stops, controlled by 1 of the keyboards.

Great Quint. Another name for the Quint org. stop.

Greaves, Thomas (b. ?; d. ?), Eng. 16th–17th-cent. lutenist & comp. In the service of Sir Henry Pierpoint, whose wife was a cousin of Michael Cavendish. In 1604 he pub. a book of *Songs of Sundrie Kindes* cont. 15 songs to the lute & 6 madrigals.

Greber, Jakob (b. ?; d. ?), Ger. 17th–18th-cent. comp. Went to London in 1692 with Margherita de l'Épine and stayed there until *c.* 1706. In Vienna or Innsbruck in the service of the Emperor Charles VI, *c.* 1708, and in the Palatinate (Heidelberg, &c.) in 1717–23.

Works incl. opera *The Loves of Ergasto* (*The Temple of Love* attrib. to him is by Saggione), shorter stage pieces, serenatas, &c.; cantata for solo voice & var. insts., &c.

Grebus. *See* **Grabu, Louis.**

Grechaninov. *See* **Gretchaninov.**

Greco, Gaetano (b. Naples, *c.* 1657; d. Naples, *c.* 1728), It comp. Pupil of A. Scarlatti at Naples, whom he succeeded in 1717 as comp. teacher at the Cons. dei Poveri di Gesù there. Later he went to that of Sant' Onofrio. Wrote hpchd. m., &c.

Greef, Arthur de (b. Louvain, 10. X. 1862; d. Brussels, 29. VIII. 1940), Belg. pfst. & comp. Pupil of Brassin at the Brussels Cons. and of Liszt at Weimar. He began his career about the age of 20 and became pf. prof. at the Brussels Cons. in 1885. He toured widely in Eur. and frequently visited Eng.

Works incl. Sym., *4 Old Flemish Folksongs* for orch., Ballad for stg. orch.; Conc. & Fantasy for pf. & orch., *Menuet varié* for pf. & stgs.; *Chants d'amour* for voice & orch.; So. for 2 pfs.; pf. pieces; songs, &c.

Greek Composers. *See* **Levidis, Petrides, Samara, Xyndas.**

Greenaway, Kate (Catherine) (1846–1901), Eng. painter & illustrator. *See* **Frank** (*Under the Window*).

Greene, Harry Plunket (b. Old Connaught House, Co. Wicklow, 24. VI. 1865; d. London, 19. VIII. 1936), Ir. bar. singer. Studied at Stuttgart, Florence & London, where he made his 1st appearance in 1888. Wrote *Interpretation in Song.*

Greene, Maurice (b. London, *c.* 1695; d. London, 1. XII. 1755), Eng. orgst. & comp. Son of a clergyman, he became a choir-boy at St. Paul's cath. under King. He studied the org. there under Richard Brind, on whose death, after holding 2 other church appts., the latter at St. Andrew's, Holborn, on the death of D. Purcell in 1717, he became orgst. of St. Paul's in 1718. On Croft's death he was also app. orgst. & comp. to the Chapel Royal. In 1730 he became prof. of m. at Cambridge Univ. in succession to Tudway and received the Mus.D. degree, and in 1735 he became Master of the King's Band in succession to Eccles. In 1750 an inheritance enabled him to take more leisure and he devoted it to the compilation of a collection of cath. m., which on his death he left to Boyce to complete.

Works incl. numerous anthems, Service in C maj., Te Deum; orats. *Jephthah* & *The Force of Truth*, setting of Pope's *Ode on St. Cecilia's Day* and a number of odes for royalty, Addison's ode *The Spacious Firmament*; pastorals *Love's Revenge, or Florimel and Myrtillo* & *Phoebe*, masque *The Judgment of Hercules*; 25 sonnets from Spenser's *Amoretti*, 12 songs *The Chaplet*, misc. songs, duets and trios; catches & canons; org. voluntaries, hpchd. lessons, &c.

Greenwood, John (b. London, 1889), Eng. comp. Learnt pf. and va. from his parents and at 18 entered the R.C.M. to study va. and hn., also comp. under Stanford.

Works incl. ballet; incid. m. for Shakespeare's *Merchant of Venice* & *Midsummer Night's Dream*; film m. for *Man of Aran* & many others; Psalm cl for chor. & orch.; 2 syms., symph. poems *Pippa passes* (after Browning) & *Punchinello, Salute to Gustav Holst* for orch.; *La Belle Dame sans merci* (Keats) for ten. & orch.; fl. & pf. So.; pf. So., &c.

Gregoir, Édouard Georges Jacques (b. Turnhout, 7. XI. 1822; d. Wyneghem nr. Antwerp, 28. VI. 1890), Belg. comp. & writer on m. Studied at Biberich together with his brother and later prod. works of his in London, Amsterdam & Paris. He settled at Antwerp in 1850. He wrote a hist. of the org. & other books.

Works incl. operas *Marguerite d'Autriche, Willem Beukels* & *La Belle Bourbonnaise*; incid. m. for *De Belgen in 1848* & *Leicester*; orats. *La Vie* & *Le Déluge*; histor. Sym. *Les Croisades*, &c.

Gregoir, Jacques Mathieu Joseph (b. Antwerp, 18. I. 1817; d. Brussels, 29. X. 1876), Belg. pfst. & comp., brother of prec. Appeared in public as a child pfst. and studied with Herz in Paris, later, together with his brother, under Rummel at Biberich. He taught at Brussels and for a year at Bruges and toured widely.

Works incl. opera *Le Gondolier de Venise*; *Lauda Sion*, cantata *Faust* (after Goethe); pf. Conc.; numerous pf. works; duets for v. & pf. (with Léonard and Vieuxtemps) and for co. & pf. (with Servais).

Gregorian Chant. The plainsong hymnody and psalmody prob. collected and supervised mainly by Pope (St.) Gregory (c. 540–604) and differing from the Ambrosian chant of Milan.

Gregorian Tones. The chants of the Gregorian psalmody sung in groups corresponding to the eight church modes (4 authentic and 4 plagal).

Gregory, William (b. ?; d. London, 20. VIII. 1663), Eng. singer & comp. Attached to the Chapel Royal in London between 1626 and 1649 and in the service of Cromwell during the Commonwealth.

Works incl. anthems, hpchd. pieces, songs, &c.

Greiter, Matthias (b. Aichach, Bavaria, c. 1500; d. ? Strasburg, ? 1552), Ger. singer, poet & comp. He was a monk and a chorister in Strasburg cath., but became a Lutheran in 1524. In 1549 he founded a Protestant choir school. He wrote words & (?) m. of hymns and comp. Ger. songs for 4 & 5 voices.

Grell, Eduard August (b. Berlin, 6. XI. 1800; d. Steglitz nr. Berlin, 10. VIII. 1886), Ger. orgst. & comp. Pupil of Zelter & others. Vice cond. under Rungenhagen of the Berlin Singakademie from 1832 and full cond. from 1853; orgst. of the court cath. from 1839.

Works incl. orat. *Die Israeliten in der Wüste*, unaccomp. Mass in 16 parts, Te Deum, psalms, motets; cantatas; songs, duets, &c.

Gresham, Thomas (1519–79). Founder of Gresham Coll. in London. Knighted 1559. The Coll. was provided for by his will and among the prof.-ships was one for m., which has continued to the present day. The 1st prof. app. in 1596 was Bull.

Gretchaninov, Alexander Tikhonovitch (b. Moscow, 25. X. 1864), Rus. comp. Although the son of small, semi-illiterate shopkeepers, he managed to study the pf. at the Moscow Cons. under Safonov, but in 1890 he went to that of St. Petersburg as a comp. pupil of Rimsky-Korsakov. He settled in Paris c. 1930 and later in U.S.A.

Works incl. operas *Dobrinya Nikititch* & *Sister Beatrice* (after Maeterlinck's play), incid. m. for plays; much m. for the Rus. church, incl. 2 complete liturgies, Catholic church m., incl. 3 masses & 6 motets; chor. works; 4 syms., Elegy for orch.; 3 stg. 4tets; *Mus. Pictures* for bass solo, chor. & orch.; v. pieces; pf. m., many songs, incl. 'The Dreary Steppe,' &c.

Gretchen am Spinnrade (*Margaret at the Spinning-Wheel*). Schubert's 1st great song, a setting of Gretchen's song in Goethe's *Faust*, Part I, comp. 1814 at the age of 17, pub. as Op. 2 in 1821.

Grétry, André Ernest Modeste (b. Liége, 11. II. 1742; d. nr. Montmorency, 24. IX. 1813), Belg. comp. Learnt m. from var. masters at a local church and some from his father, a vst. Before he was properly equipped, he prod. 6 short syms. in 1758 and a *Messe solennelle* in 1759. That year he was able to go to Rome, though on foot, and to study at the Collège de Liége there. He stayed until 1767, studying under Casali, who dismissed him as incompetent, yet contriving to prod. a small It. opera in 1765. For a year or so he stayed at Geneva on his way to Paris, and at last reached the Fr. capital, where he prod. an endless succession of operas from 1768 onwards. On the foundation of the Cons. in 1795 he was made one of the inspectors. He bought and retired to the former residence of J. J. Rousseau, L'Ermitage nr. Montmorency.

Works incl. operas *La vendemmiatrice, Isabelle et Gertrude, Le Huron, Lucile, Le Tableau parlant, Silvain, Les Deux Avares, L'Amitié à l'épreuve, Zémire et Azor, L'Ami de la maison, Le Magnifique, La Rosière de Salency, La Fausse Magie, Les Mariages samnites* (several versions), *Matroco, Le Jugement de Midas, Le Fausses Apparences, ou L'Amant jaloux, Les Événements imprévus, Aucassin et Nicolette, Thalie au Nouveau Théâtre, Théodore et Paulin* (later *L'Épreuve villageoise*), *Richard Cœur de Lion, Les Méprises par ressemblance, Le Comte d'Albert, Le Prisonnier anglais* (later *Claire et Belton*), *Le Rival confident, Raoul Barbe-bleue, Pierre le Grand, Guillaume Tell, Basile, Les Deux Couvents, Joseph Barra, Callias, Lisbeth, Le Barbier de village, Elisca*: all comic operas; prod. at the Opéra: *Céphale et Procris, Les Trois Âges de l'Opéra, Andromaque, La Double Épreuve, ou Colinette à la cour, L'Embarras des richesses, La Caravane du Caire, Panurge dans l'île des lanternes* (after Rabelais), *Amphitryon, Aspasie, Denys le Tyran, La Fête de la Raison, Anacréon chez Polycrate, Le Casque et les Colombes, Delphis et Mopsa*, &c. (some in MS.).

Grétry, Lucile (b. Paris, 1773; d. ?, 1793), Fr. comp., daughter of prec. At the age of 13 she prod. an opera, scored by her father, *Le Mariage d'Antonio*, in 1786, and the following year *Toinette et Louis*.

Greville, Fulke (Lord Brooke) (1554–1628), Eng. statesman & poet. *See* **Peerson** (*Caelica*).

Grew, Sydney (b. Birmingham, 13. VIII. 1879), Eng. writer on m. Studied at the Midland Institute School of M. and ed. the *British Musician* from 1926. Pub. books on the player-pf., on comps. & perfs. and, with his wife, Eva Mary G., a work on Bach.

Grieg, Edvard (Hagerup) (b. Bergen, 15. VI. 1843; d. Bergen, 4. IX. 1907), Norw. comp. of Sco. descent (orig. Greig). Son of a merchant and Brit. consul, was taught the pf. by his mother from 1849 and tried to comp. in 1855. Ole Bull persuaded his parents to send him to Leipzig for study in 1858, and he entered the Cons. there. Back home with his health permanently damaged in 1860, but returned the following year, completing his studies at the Cons. in 1862, when he finally settled at home and gave a concert at Bergen. In 1863 he went to live in Copenhagen and studied with Gade. In 1864 he met Rikard Nordaak, who fired his enthusiasm for Norw. nat. m., and became engaged to his cousin Nina Hagerup, whom he married in 1867, after a stay in Rome the prec. year. Settled as teacher and cond. at Christiania in 1867. The following year he received a govt. grant to revisit Rome, which he did in 1870, and the next year he founded the Christiania Mus. Soc. In 1874 Ibsen invited him to write incid. m. for his *Peer Gynt*, which was prod. on 24. II. 1876, and its success, together with a govt. life annuity granted him in 1874, enabled him to acquire a property at Lofthus in the Hardanger fjord, which remained his home for the rest of his life. He lived in the village at first, but built the villa of Troldhaugen in 1885. In 1888–9 he and his wife appeared in London, Paris and Vienna, and in 1894 he was in Eng. again to receive the hon. Mus.D. degree conferred on him by Cambridge Univ. He revisited London and Paris several times before his death.

Works incl. incid. m. for Ibsen's *Peer Gynt* and Bjørnson's *Sigurd Jorsalfar*; concert ovt. *In Autumn*; *Holberg Suite* for stg. orch.; pf. Conc. in A min.; works for solo voices, chor. & orch.: *Before the Cloister Gate, Land-sighting, Olaf Trygvason*; *Bergliot* (Bjørnson) for declamation and orch.; 4 Psalms for mixed voices unaccomp.; a set of partsongs for male voices; *Den bergtekne* (*The Solitary*) for bar. solo, stgs. & 2 hns.; stg. 4tet in G min.; 3 sos., for v. & pf.; So. for co. & pf.; 22 op. nos. of pf. pieces, incl. 10 vols. of *Lyric Pieces*, So. in E min., Ballad in var. form, arrs. of Norw. folk tunes; 4 works for pf. duet; old Norw. melody with vars. for 2 pfs.; 143 songs, incl. *Haugtussa* cycle (Garborg), settings of Ibsen, Bjørnson, &c.

Grieg (*née* **Hagerup**), **Nina** (b. Bergen, 24. XI. 1845; d. Copenhagen, 9, XII. 1935), Norw. singer, cousin & wife of Edvard Grieg, most of whose songs she was the 1st to sing both at home and on their tours abroad.

Griffes, Charles T(omlinson). (b. Elmira, New York, 17. IX. 1884; d. New York, 8. IV. 1920), Amer. comp. Studied in Berlin and taught there for a time. Returned to U.S.A. in 1907 and became m. teacher at a boys' school at Tarrytown, N.Y., until his early death, brought about by ill-health and overwork.

Works incl. Japanese mime play *Schojo*; dance drama *The Kairn of Koridwen*; *The Pleasure Dome of Kubla Khan* (after Coleridge) for orch.; Poem for fl. & orch.; *These things shall be* (J. A. Symonds) for unison chor.; Sketches on Indian themes for stg. 4tet; pf. So. & pieces; songs, &c.

Grigny, Nicolas de (b. Rheims, II. 1671; d. Rheims, 30. XI. 1703), Fr. orgst. & comp. Son of Louis de G. (c. 1646–1709), orgst. at Notre-Dame of Rheims. Studied under his father and in Paris, was orgst. of Saint-Denis abbey in 1693–5 and then of Rheims cath. Wrote org. m. which Bach knew and copied in his early years.

Grillparzer, Franz (1791–1872), Aus. poet & dramatist. Friend of Beethoven and Schubert. Wrote funeral oration for the former and sketched inscription for the latter's gravestone.

For works used by comps. *see* **Frank** (*Hero*), **Hummel (J. N.)** (*Ahnfrau*), **Mraczek** (*Traum*), **Sappho** (Kaun), **Schöne Melusine** (Mendelssohn & K. Kreutzer), **Schulz-Beuthen** (*Meeres und der Liebe Wellen*), **Seyfried** (*Ahnfrau & König Ottokar*), **Straus** (*Traum ein Leben*).

Grimaldi. *See* **Nicolini.**

Grimm, Friedrich Melchior von, Baron (1723–1807), Ger. littérateur. Lived in Paris from 1750 to the Revol. and during the 'Guerre des bouffons' in 1752 took the part of the Its. He wrote several pamphlets on mus. matters, incl. a satire on Stamitz, *Le Petit Prophète de Boemisch-Broda*.

Grimm, Jacob (Ludwig Carl) (1785–1863) & **Wilhelm (Carl)** (1786–1859), brothers, Ger. philols., mythols. & authors. *See* **Hänsel und Gretel** (Humperdinck), **Schoeck** (*Vom Fischer und syner Fru*).

Grimm, Otto Julius (b. Pernau, Livonia, 6. III. 1827; d. Münster, Westphalia, 7. XII. 1903), Ger. pfst. & comp. Studied at the Leipzig Cons. Worked at Göttingen at first and in 1860 was app. chor. cond. at Münster.

Works incl. ode for chor. & orch., *An die Musik*; Sym. in D min. & other orch. works; Suite in canon-form for stgs.; pf. works; songs, &c.

Grisar, Albert (b. Antwerp, 26. XII. 1808; d. Asnières, 15. VI. 1869), Belg. comp. He was intended for a business career and sent to Liverpool, but ran away to Paris to study m. in 1830; became a pupil of Reicha, but was driven to Antwerp by the Revol.; prod. *Le Mariage impossible* at Brussels in 1833, returned to Paris, where he made further operatic successes, studied with Mercadante at Naples in 1840 and remained there, but lived in Paris from 1848 to his death.

Works incl. operas *Sarah* (after Scott), *L'An 1000*, *Lady Melvill* & *L'Eau merveilleuse* (both with Flotow), *Le Naufrage de la Méduse* (with Flotow & Pilati), *Les Travestissements*, *L'Opéra à la cour* (with Boieldieu, jun.), *Gilles Ravisseur*, *Les Porcherons*, *Bonsoir, M. Pantalon*, *Le Carillonneur de Bruges*, *Les Amours du diable*, *Le Chien du jardinier*, *Voyage autour de ma chambre*, *La Chatte merveilleuse*, *Bégaiements d'amour*, *Douze innocentes*, &c.

Grisi, Giuditta (b. Milan, 28. VII. 1805; d. Cremona, 1. V. 1840), It. m.-sop. singer. Studied at the Milan Cons., and made her 1st appearance in Vienna in 1823.

Grisi, Giulia (b. Milan, 28. VII. 1811; d. Berlin, 29. XI. 1869), It. sop. singer, sister of prec. Pupil of her sister, Boccabadati, Guglielmi & others. Made her 1st appearance in 1828 and was engaged for Milan in 1829. In 1832 she 1st sang in Paris and in 1834 in London.

Grob, Therese (b. Vienna, 1800; d. ?), Aus. sop. singer. Sang in Schubert's F maj. Mass in 1814 and he is said to have been in love with her in 1815.

Groh, Johann. *See* **Ghro.**

Groll, Sophie. *See* **Tomasini, 3.**

Gröndahl, Agathe. *See* **Backer-Gröndahl.**

Groppo (It.) = **Turn.**

Grosse Caisse (Fr. lit. great case or chest) = Bass Drum.

Grosse Fuge (*Great Fugue*). A work for stg. 4tet by Beethoven, Op. 133, in a fugal form 'tantôt libre, tantôt recherchée,' written in 1825 as the finale of the B♭ maj. stg. 4tet, Op. 130, and 1st perf. with it, Vienna, 21. III. 1826, when B. realized that it was too long, difficult and abstruse for that purpose and wrote the new finale now part of Op. 130.

Grossi, Carlo (b. ?; d. ?), It. 17th-cent. singer & comp. Worked as singer and chapel master successively at Reggio, Vicenza, Venice and Mantua.

Works incl. 4 operas; masses & other church m.; sacred concs.; sos.; songs, &c.

Grossi, Giovanni Francesco. *See* **Siface.**

Grossi, Lodovico. *See* **Viadana.**

Grossvater-Tanz (Ger. = grandfather's dance). A Ger. dance dating from the 17th cent., with words referring to a grandfather's wooing, sung and danced at weddings and later used as the final dance at balls and therefore called 'Kehraus' (sweep-out). Schumann used it both in *Papillons*, Op. 2, and *Carnival*, Op. 9, in the latter to stand for the 'Philistines' in the finale.

Grosz, Wilhelm (b. Vienna, 11. VIII, 1894; d. New York, 10. XII. 1939), Aus. comp. Pupil of Adler for theory & Schreker for comp. Cond. at Mannheim Opera in 1921, but returned to Vienna in 1922 to make a living as pfst. & comp.; worked with a gramophone company in Berlin from 1927, cond. the Kammerspiele in Vienna, 1933–4, when he became a refugee in London & N.Y.

Works incl. operas *Sganarell* & *Achtung, Aufnahme*; play with m. *St. Peters Regenschirm*; ballets *Der arme Reinhold* & *Baby in der Bar*; incid. m. to Werfel's *Spiegelmensch* & Hauptmann's *Die versunkene Glocke*; m. for films & radio; Symph. Vars., Serenade, Suite, ovt. to an opera buffa, &c. for orch.; Symph. Dance for pf. & orch.; stg. 4tet; 2 v. & pf. sos.; 3 pf. sos., Vars. on a theme by Grieg & other pf. works; Suite for 2 pfs.; several song cycles, &c.

Ground. A title sometimes used by Purcell and other old Eng. comps. for pieces built on a Ground Bass.

Ground Bass. A melodic figure used as a bass in a comp., constantly repeated without change, except sometimes by way of transposition, while the upper structure of the m. is developed freely at the comp.'s will. A partic. ingenious way of using the G. B. (e.g. by Purcell) was to devise it so that its length did not occupy a number of complete bars, its 1st note thus appearing variously at different points of the bars.

Grove, George (b. London, 13. VIII. 1820; d. London, 28. V. 1900), Eng. civil engineer, biblical scholar & writer on m. Sec. to the Crystal Palace Co., 1852–75; dir. of R.C.M. 1883–94. Ed. of the famous *Dictionary of Music and Musicians* and author of a book on Beethoven's syms. Knighted in 1883.

Grovlez, Gabriel (Marie) (b. Lille, 4. IV. 1879; d. Paris, 24. X. 1944), Fr. cond., pfst. & comp. Studied at the Paris Cons., later taught pf. at the Schola Cantorum and in 1939 became prof. of chamber m. at the Cons. Cond. at Lisbon, Chicago and Paris, from 1914 at the Opéra.

Works incl. operas *Cœur de rubis* & *Le Marquis de Carabas*; ballet *Maïmouna*; symph. poems *Dans le Jardin*, *Madrigal lyrique*, &c.; co. & pf. So.; pieces for wind insts.; *Almanach aux images*, *Le Royaume puéril*, 2 Impressions &c. for pf.; 3 *Ballades françaises* & other songs, &c.

Gruenberg, Louis (b. Rus., 3. VIII. 1884), Amer. pfst. & comp. of Rus. descent. He was taken to U.S.A. at the age of 2. Studied in Berlin & Vienna, pf. pupil of Busoni; 1st appeared as pfst. in Berlin in 1912 and then began to travel, but from 1919 remained in U.S.A. to devote himself wholly to comp.

Works incl. operas *The Bride of the Gods*, *The Dumb Wife*, *Jack and the Beanstalk*, *Emperor Jones* (after Eugene O'Neill), *Helena's Husband*; children's opera *The Witch of Brocken*; radio opera *Green Mansions*; 2 syms., *Hill of Dreams*, *Enchanted Isle*, *Vagabondia*, *Jazz Suite*, *Moods*, *Serenade*, *Music to an Imaginary Pantomime* for orch.; v. Conc. *The Daniel Jazz* (Vachell Lindsay), *Animals and Insects* & *The Creation* for voice and chamber orch.; *4 Indiscretions* for stg. 4tet; 2 sos. and *Jazettes* for v. & pf.; Poem for co. & pf.; *Jazzberries* & *Impressions* for pf.; numerous songs, &c.

Grunewald, Gottfried (b. ?, 1673; d. Darmstadt, 10. XII. 1739), Ger. singer & comp. Sang at the Hamburg Opera in 1703 and prod. the opera *Germanicus* there in 1706 after bringing it out at Leipzig in 1704, having prod. another, *Der ungetreue Schäfer Cardillo*, there in 1703. He became cond. at Darmstadt in 1712.

Gruppo (It.) = **Turn.**

Grützmacher, Friedrich (Wilhelm Ludwig) (b. Dessau, 1. III. 1832; d. Dresden, 23. II. 1903), Ger. cst. & comp. Studied at Leipzig, where he became cst. at the Gewandhaus in 1849 and later teacher at the Cons. In 1860 he became chamber virtuoso to the King of Saxony at Dresden. Comp. mainly concs. & studies for co., but also orch. & chamber works, songs, &c.

Guadagni, Gaetano (b. Lodi or ? Vicenza, *c.* 1725; d. Padua, XI. 1792), It. male con. singer. Made his 1st appearance prob. at Parma in 1747 and went to London in 1748. Later sang in Dublin, Paris, Lisbon, It. and Vienna, where he was the 1st Orpheus in Gluck's *Orfeo* in 1762.

Guadagnini. It. family of v. makers:

1. Lorenzo G. (b. ?; d. Piacenza, c. 1750), ? pupil of Stradivari, worked at Piacenza.

2. Giovanni Battista G. (b. Piacenza, c. 1745; d. Turin, c. 1790), son of prec. Worked at Piacenza, Milan, Parma and Turin.

3. Giuseppe G. (b. ?; d. ?), son of prec. Worked at Como, Pavia and Turin.

Guajira. A Spa. dance in which the rhythm alternates between 6–8 and 3–4 time.

Guarducci, Tommaso (b. Montefiascone, c. 1720; d. ?), It. singer. Pupil of Bernacchi at Bologna. Made his 1st appearance c. 1745 and went to London in 1766.

Guarini, Giovanni Battista (1537–1612), It. poet. *See* **Pastor fido** (Handel), **Rossi (S.)** (*Idropica*), **Settle** (*Pastor fido*).

Guarneri. It. family of v. makers:

1. Andrea G. (b. ?, c. 1626; d. Cremona, 7. XII. 1698). Pupil of Amati.

2. Pietro Giovanni G. (b. Cremona, 18. III. 1655; d. Mantua, 26. III. 1720), son of prec. Worked at Mantua.

3. Giuseppe Giovanni Battista G. (b. Cremona, 25. XI. 1666; d. Cremona, c. 1740), brother of prec.

4. Pietro G. (b. ? Cremona, 14. IV. 1695; d. Venice, 7. IV. 1762), nephew of 2 & 3. Worked at Venice.

5. Giuseppe Antonio G. (b. Cremona, 21. VIII. 1698; d. Cremona, 17. X. 1744), son of 3. Worked at Cremona and is known as Giuseppe G. del. Gesù.

Guarnieri, Camargo (b. Tieté, 1. II. 1907), Braz. comp.

Works incl. syms.; chamber m.; co. & pf. So., &c.

Gudehus, Heinrich (b. Altenhagen nr. Celle, 30. III. 1845; d. Dresden, 9. X. 1909), Ger. ten. singer. Studied with Malwina Schnorr von Carolsfeld at Brunswick and Gustav Engel in Berlin; made his 1st appearance there in 1871, sang Parsifal at Bayreuth in 1882 and 1st went to London in 1884.

Gudenian, Haig (b. Caesaria, Asia Minor, 19. V. 1886), Armen. vst. & comp. Studied m. at Brussels and Prague, collected folksongs in the East, in 1918 visited the U.S.A. and married the pfst. Katherine Lowe, with whom he toured in Eur. and Amer., where he settled. His comps. are based on nr.-eastern m.

Guédron, Pierre (b. Beauce, 1565; d. Paris, 1625), Fr. singer & comp. He was a chorister in the chapel of the Cardinal de Guise and later of Henri IV. In 1601 he was app. comp. to the king in succession to Claude Le Jeune and held var. other posts at court, finishing as Surintendant de la Musique under Louis XIII in 1613. His daughter Jeanne married Boësset, with whom, as well as Bailly, Mauduit and Bataille, he collab. in the comp. of court ballets. He also contrib. airs with lute accomp. (*airs de cour*) to var. collections.

Guerre des Bouffons (Fr., lit. War of the Buffoons). The quarrel that broke out in Paris in 1752 between the adherents of Fr. m., esp. opera, and the imported art of the Its., who prod. or revived several exs. of *opera buffa* in the Fr. capital that year.

Guerrero, Francisco (b. Seville, V. 1527; d. Seville, 8. XI. 1599), Spa. comp. Pupil of his brother Pedro G. and of Fernández de Castilleja at Seville cath., where he was a chorister; he also had some lessons from Morales as a child. App. to the cath. of Jaén in 1545 and after the death of Morales to that of Málaga, though he never resided there, filling posts at Seville cath. until he succeeded Castilleja as chapel master in 1574. Visited Lisbon, Rome (twice), Venice and the Holy Land.

Works incl. masses, motets, psalms, vespers, magnificats, Te Deum, spiritual songs, &c.

Guerrero, Pedro (b. Seville, c. 1515; d. ?), Spa. comp., brother of prec. (?) visited It. early in life and (?) d. there. Wrote church m., lute songs, &c.

Guevara, Luis Velez de (1579–1644), Spa. novelist & dramatist. *See* **Hidalgo** (*Celos hacen estrellas*), **Una cosa rara** (Martín y Soler).

Guglielmi, Pietro (b. Massa di Carrara, 9. XII. 1727; d. Rome, 18. XI. 1804), It. comp. Studied under Durante at Naples and prod. his 1st opera at Naples in 1757, having already written one at the age of 11. After many successes in It. he went to London in 1767, staying intermittently and returning to It. in 1772. In 1793 he was app. chapel master at the Vatican in Rome.

Works incl. c. 100 operas, e.g. *Il ratto della sposa, La sposa fedele, La villanella ingentilita, La Quakera spiritosa, Le vicende d'amore, La virtuosa in Mergellina, Enea e Lavinia, L'inganno amoroso* (*Le due gemelle*), *La pastorella nobile, La bella pescatrice, La serva innamorata*, &c.; masses, motets & other church m.; orats.; m. for stg. insts.; hpchd. works, &c.

Guglielmi, Pietro Carlo (b. Naples, c. 1763; d. Massa di Carrara, 28. II. 1827), It. comp., son of prec. Studied at Loreto Cons. In 1810 he went to London and later became chapel master to the Grand Duchess of Massa di Carrara.

Works incl. operas *La scelta dello sposo*, *Amor tutto vince*, *Guerra aperta*, *Paolo e Virginia* (after Saint-Pierre), & over 40 others, &c.

Guglielmo Ratcliff (*William R.*), opera by Mascagni (lib. by comp., based on Heine's tragedy), prod. Milan, Teatro alla Scala, 16. II. 1895. An earlier work than *Cavalleria rusticana*, although prod. later.

Gui, Vittorio (b. Rome, 14. IX. 1885), It. cond. & comp. Student at the Liceo di Santa Cecilia in Rome. App. cond. at the Teatro Adriano there and later cond. opera at Turin, Naples and Milan. In 1928 he became dir. of the Stabile Orchestrale at Florence.

Works incl. opera *La fata Malerba*; symph. poems; chamber m., &c.

Guida (It. = guide). The leading part of a canon, into which the other voices subsequently drop with the same tune one by one.

Guidetti, Giovanni (b. Bologna, XII. 1530; d. Rome, 30. XI. 1592), It. priest. Pupil of Palestrina, whom he assisted in compiling the revised church services commissioned by Pope Gregory XIII, the *Directorium chori*, in 1576–81.

Guidiccioni, Laura (16th cent.), It. poetess. *See* Cavalieri (E.), *also* Rappresentazione di anima e di corpo.

Guido d'Arezzo (b. Arezzo, *c.* 990; d. Pomposa, *c.* 1050), It. Benedictine monk & mus. theorist. Went to Fr. and (?) Eng. and worked at the Abbey of Saint-Maur-des-Fossés. He returned to It. later. He greatly advanced Solmization and Mutation by adapting the syllables Ut, Re, Mi, Fa, Sol, La to the Hexachord and by demonstrating the hexachordal positions on the fingers by the use of the 'Guidonian hand.' He is also, rather doubtfully, credited with the invention of the mus. stave, the use of which he certainly encouraged.

Guignon, Jean-Pierre (Giovanni Pietro Ghignone) (b. Turin, 10. II. 1702; d. Versailles, 30. I. 1774), Fr. vst. & comp. of It. orig. He went to Paris in his youth, 1st studied the co., but gave it up for the v., on which he rivalled Leclair. In 1733 he was app. at court and in 1741 he became Roi des Violons et Ménétriers, the last to hold that title.

Works incl. concs., sos. and duets for v.

Guilbert, Yvette (b. Paris, 20. I. 1867; d. Aix-en-Provence, 3. I. 1944), Fr. diseuse. Trained as an actress and café singer, but cultivated Fr. folksong and popular songs of the past, of which she became a great exponent.

Guildhall School of Music. A m. school established in 1880 to serve the City of London and housed in a new building in 1887.

Guillaume Tell (*William Tell*), opera by Grétry (lib. by Jean Michel Sedaine), prod. Paris, Opéra-Comique, 9. IV. 1791.

Opera by Rossini (lib. by Victor Joseph Étienne de Jouy & Hippolyte Louis Florent Bis, based on Schiller's drama), prod. Paris, Opéra, 3. VIII. 1829. R.'s last opera.

Guillemain, (Louis) Gabriel (b. Paris, 15. XI. 1705; d. Paris, 1. X. 1770), Fr. vst. & comp. He became a member of the royal chapel in 1738 and wrote stg. 4tets, trio sos., v. sos., hpchd. pieces, &c.

Guilmant, (Félix) Alexandre (b. Boulogne, 12. III. 1837; d. Meudon, 29. III. 1911), Fr. orgst. & comp. Pupil of his father, an orgst. at Boulogne, where he afterwards held several church appts., studying with Lemmens briefly in 1860 and removing to Paris in 1871, where he was orgst. at the Trinité church until 1901. He toured widely with great success and was prof. of org. at the Schola Cantorum, which he had helped Bordes and d'Indy to found, and at the Cons.

Works incl. 2 syms. for org. & orch.; 8 sos. & 25 sets of pieces for org., org. m. for church use, &c.

Guimerá, Angel (1849–1924), Spa. (Catalan) dramatist. *See* Tiefland (d'Albert).

Guiraud, Ernest (b. New Orleans, 23. VI. 1837; d. Paris, 6. V. 1892), Fr. comp. Son of a musn., with whom he studied. His 1st opera, *Le Roi David*, was staged when he was 16. He then went to the Paris Cons. and gained the Prix de Rome in 1859. He became prof. at the Cons. in 1876, following Massé at the head of the advanced comp. class in 1880.

Works incl. operas *Sylvie*, *En Prison*, *Le Kobold*, *Madame Turlupin*, *Piccolino*, *Galante Aventure*, *Le Feu*, *Frédégonde* (unfinished, completed by Saint-Saëns); ballet *Gretna Green*; ovt. *Arteveld*, *Chasse fantastique* (after Hugo's *Beau Pécopin*), & Suite for orch.; Caprice for v. & orch., &c. Recitatives for Bizet's *Carmen* and orch. of Offenbach's *Contes d'Hoffmann*.

Guiraut de Bornelh. *See* Bornelh.

Guitar. A Spa. stg. inst. which remains the most important descendant of insts. of the lute and cittern type. Its back is flat, its belly has a waist, as though to allow for the playing with a bow, but the stgs. are plucked with the fingers. The sound-hole in the sound-board is often very decoratively carved. There are 6 stgs., tuned in 4ths, except that there is 1 interval of a 3rd between the 4th &

5th stg. counting from the bottom. The finger-board is fretted.

Guitar Violoncello. *See* **Arpeggione.**

Guitry, Sacha (b. 1885), Fr. actor & playwright. *See* **Beydts** (*La S.A.D.M.P.* & *Voyage de Tchong-Li*), **Hann** (*Mozart*).

Gumpeltzhaimer, Adam (b. Trostberg, Bavaria, *c.* 1559; d. Augsburg, 3. XI. 1625), Ger. comp. Studied at the monastery of St. Ulric at Augsburg and in 1575 went into the service of the Duke of Württemberg at Stuttgart. In 1581–1621 he was cantor at the church of St. Anna at Augsburg. He pub. a treatise, *Compendium musicae latinum-germanicum* in 1591.

Works incl. psalms, hymns, sacred songs, &c.

Gundry, Inglis (b. London, 8. V. 1905), Eng. comp. Educ. at Oxford, where he read law, but turned to literature, writing poems and a novel, *The Countess's Penny*, and studied m. at the R.C.M. in London under Vaughan Williams, Gordon Jacob and R. O. Morris. In 1940 he enlisted in the Navy, his ship, H.M.S. *Welshman*, was sunk, he was promoted warrant officer and went as schoolmaster to the Royal Marines at Chatham. In 1944 he became instructor Lieutenant and mus. adviser to the Admiralty educ. dept., for which he ed. a *Naval Song Book*.

Works incl. operas *Naaman: the Leprosy of War*, *The Return of Odysseus* (after Homer), *The Sleeping Beauty* & *Partisans*; ballet *Sleep*; naval suite *Five Bells* and *Choral Overture 1940* (words from a speech by Winston Churchill) for chor. & orch.; suite *Heyday, Freedom*, Vars. on an Indian theme & ovt. *Per mare, per terram* for orch.; Comedy Ovt. for small orch.; *Sostenuto and Vivace* for stgs.; Fantasy stg. 4tet, Duo for cl. & va.; 3 Chinese Pictures for bar., cl. & pf.; 5 Homeric songs & a duet, 3 *Songs from a Medieval Bestiary*, &c.

Gung'l, Joseph (b. Zsàmbèk, 1. XII. 1810; d. Weimar, 31. I. 1889), Aus.-Hung. bandmaster & comp. Entered the Aus. army and later made tours with a military band of his own. In 1849 he visited the U.S.A., becoming mus. dir. to the King of Prus. on his return and in 1858 to the Aus. Emperor. In 1864 he went to live at Munich and in 1876 at Frankfort. He wrote hundreds of marches and dances.

Gunn, Neil (b. 1891), Sco. dramatist. *See* **Davie.**

Günther von Schwarzburg, opera by Holzbauer (lib. by Anton Klein), prod. Mannheim, at court, 5. I. 1777.

Guntram, opera by R. Strauss (lib. by comp.), prod. Weimar, 10. V. 1894. S.'s 1st opera.

Gura, Eugen (b. Pressern nr. Saatz, 8. XI. 1842; d. Aufkirchen, Bavaria, 26. VIII. 1906), Boh.-Ger. bar. singer. After technical and art studies in Vienna, he studied singing at the Munich Cons. and made his 1st stage appearance there in 1865. In 1876 he appeared in the prod. of Wagner's *Ring* at Bayreuth.

Guridi, Jesús (b. Vitoria, 25. IX. 1886), Spa. comp. of Basque race. Studied at the Schola Cantorum in Paris, also at Brussels and Cologne. His m. is based on Basque themes.

Works incl. operas *Mirentxu* & *Amaya*, zarzuela *El caserio*; orch. & org. m.; settings of Basque folk-songs, &c.

Gurlitt, Cornelius (b. Altona, 10. II. 1820; d. Altona, 17. VI. 1901), Ger. pfst., orgst. & comp. App. church orgst. at Altona in 1864.

Works incl. opera *Scheik Hassan*, 2 operettas; numerous pf. pieces, mostly educational, &c.

Gurlitt, Manfred (b. Berlin, 6. IX. 1890), Ger. cond. & comp. Studied comp. with Kaun and Humperdinck, cond. with Muck and pf. with Breithaupt in Berlin. After var. operatic appts. he was general mus. dir. at Bremen in 1914–27. Later he appeared as guest opera cond. in Ger. and Spa.

Works incl. operas *Die Heilige*, *Wozzeck* (Georg Büchner's drama), *Soldaten*, *Nana* (after Zola), *Seguidilla bolero*, *Feliza*; incid. m. for 2 Spa. plays; m. for films; orch. works; concs. for pf., v. & co.; chamber concs.; pf. 5tet in C min.; pf. So.; songs with chamber orch., &c.

Gurlitt, Wilibald (b. Dresden, 1. III. 1889), Ger. mcolst., great-nephew of Cornelius G. above and son of Cornelius G., an authority on painting. Prof. at Freiburg i/B., 1920–37, and founded a Collegium Musicum there for the perf. of old m. on ancient insts. Has written works on M. Praetorius, Johann Walther, Schütz, Bach, &c. and ed. old Ger. m.

Gurney, Ivor (Bertie) (b. Gloucester, 28. VIII. 1890; d. Dartford, Kent, 26. XII. 1937), Eng. comp. & poet. He was a choir-boy at Gloucester cath. and later studied at the R.C.M. in London with a scholarship. He suffered much from ill-health and during the 1914–8 war was badly wounded and shell-shocked. He struggled for a time against poverty, but in 1922 lost his reason, and he d. of tuberculosis.

Works incl. *The Apple Orchard* & *Scherzo* for v. & pf.; 2 sets of pf.

pieces; song cycles *Ludlow and Teme* (A. E. Housman) & *The Western Playland*, many songs, some to his own poems (27 pub.). 2 vols. of poetry, *Severn and Somme* & *War's Embers*.

Gussly. A Rus. stged. inst. of the Psaltery type.

Gustave III, ou La Bal masqué (*Gustavus III, or The Masked Ball*), opera by Auber (lib. by Scribe), prod. Paris, Opéra, 27. II. 1833. *See also* **Ballo in maschera.**

Gutiérrez, Antonio García (1812–84), Spa. dramatist. *See* **Simon Boccanegra** (Verdi), **Trovatore** (do.).

Gutmann, Adolph (b. Heidelberg, 12. I. 1819; d. Spezia, 27. X. 1882), Ger. pfst. & comp. Pupil and friend of Chopin. Wrote numerous pf. works, incl. 10 *Études caractéristiques*.

Gutzkow, Karl (Ferdinand) (1811–78), Ger. novelist & dramatist. *See* **Famintsin** (*Uriel Acosta*), **Rathaus** (do.), **Serov** (do., by V. S. Bergman).

Guzla. A bowed stg. inst. of a primitive kind used in Dalmatia and Serbia. It has a single stg. made of horse-hair and played with a bow, stretched over a belly covered with skin or parchment and with a round back.

Gwendoline, opera by Chabrier (lib. by Catulle Mendès) prod. Brussels, Théâtre de la Monnaie, 10. IV. 1886.

Gymel (from Lat. *gemellum* = a 'twin-song'). Voc. m. of great antiquity in 2 parts, differing from the Faburden or Descant by having the tune in the upper voice, practised in Eng. before the Norman conquest and possibly of Celtic orig.

Gyrowetz, Adalbert (b. Budějovice, 19. II. 1763; d. Vienna, 19. III. 1850), Boh. comp. Learnt m. from his father, a choirmaster; later studied law in Prague, but continued to work at m. On becoming private secretary to Count Franz von Fünfkirchen, he was expected to take part in the domestic m. and so had much practice in the art. He then went to It. for study under Sala at Naples and later visited Paris, where syms. of his had been perf. under the name of Haydn. In 1789 the Revol. drove him to London, where the score of his opera *Semiramis* was burnt in the fire of the Pantheon in 1792. He returned to Vienna soon after, and in 1804 was app. cond. at the court theatres, where he prod. many works until 1831.

Works incl. It. operas *Federica ed Adolfo* & *Il finto Stanislao*, Ger. operas *Agnes Sorel*, *Ida die Büssende*, *Der Augenarzt*, *Robert, oder Die Prüfung*, *Helene*, *Felix und Adele*, *Hans Sachs*, *Die Junggesellen-Wirtschaft*, *Der Sammtrock*, *Aladin* (after Oehlenschläger), *Das Ständchen*, &c.; ballet *Die Hochzeit der Thetis* & others; melodramas *Mirina* & others; comic cantata *Die Dorfschule*; over 60 syms., serenades, ovts. & other orch. works; *c.* 60 stg. 4tets, 5tets, numerous trios; *c.* 40 v. & pf. sos.; inst. pieces, dances, &c.

Gyterne
Gythorne } *See* **Cittern.**

H

H. The Ger. symbol for the note B ♮.

H.M.S. Pinafore, operetta by Sullivan (lib. by W. S. Gilbert), prod. London, Opera Comique, 25. V. 1878. The 1st work by G. & S. to make a world-wide success.

Haas, Joseph (b. Maihingen, Bavaria, 19. III. 1879), Ger. comp. Pupil of Reger at Munich and then at the Leipzig Cons. Teacher of comp. at Stuttgart from 1911 and Munich from 1921.

Works incl. opera *Tobias Wunderlich*; chor. works; Serenade for orch.; 2 stg. 4tets. Divertimento for stg. trio, Trio for 2 cos. & pf. & other chamber m.; So. & Sonatina for v. & pf.; many pf. works; org. pieces; songs, &c.

Haas, Robert (Maria) (b. Prague, 15. VIII. 1886), Aus. mcolst. Took the D.Ph. at Prague Univ. and became assistant to Adler. Later lecturer at Vienna Univ. and dir. of the m. dept. of the State Library there. Part-ed. of the orig. versions of Bruckner's works, &c., author of books on baroque m., Gluck, Mozart, Bruckner, &c.

Hába, Alois (b. Vyzovice, Moravia, 21. VI. 1893), Cz. comp. Picked up a knowledge of folk m. before he studied at the Prague Cons. under Novák; later a pupil of Schreker in Vienna & Berlin. App. prof. at the Prague Cons. in 1924. He became interested in the division of the scale into quarter-tones, on which much of his later work is based.

Works incl. opera *Die Mutter*; Ovt. & Symph. M. for orch.; Fantasy for pf. & orch.; 5 stg. 4tets & other chamber m.; pf. So. & other works (some for quarter-tone pf.); works for stg. insts., &c.

Habanera. A dance, with words to be sung, introd. into Spa. from Africa via Cuba. It is in a moderate 2–4 time and has a basic rhythm of 4 quavers, the 1st of which is dotted. The most famous ex. by a comp. is that in the 1st act of Bizet's *Carmen*.

Habeneck, François Antoine (b. Mézières, 23. I. 1781; d. Paris, 8. II. 1849), Fr. vst. & cond. of Ger. descent. Pupil of Baillot. Founder of the Société des Concerts du Cons. in Paris; cond. at the Opéra 1824–47. The 1st cond. to cultivate Beethoven in France.

Haberbier, Ernst (b. Königsberg, 5. X. 1813; d. Bergen, Norw., 12. III. 1869), Ger. pfst. & comp. Pupil o his father, an orgst. He toured widely and lived for a time in St. Petersburg, settling at Bergen in 1866. Wrote numerous pf. works.

Haberl, Franz Xaver (b. Ober Ellenbach, Bavaria, 12. IV. 1840; d. Ratisbon, 5. IX. 1910), Ger. priest & mcolst. Worked at Passau, Rome & Ratisbon and devoted much time to the study of Catholic church m., about which he wrote extensively. Ed. Palestrina's complete works, &c.

Habermann, Franz Wenzel (b. Königswart [Lázně Kinžvart], 20. IX. 1706; d. Eger, 7. IV. 1783), Boh. comp. Pub. 6 Masses in 1747, which Handel drew upon for his *Jephtha* of 1751.

Hackbrett (Ger. lit. 'chopping-board'). The Ger. name for the Dulcimer.

Haddon Hall, operetta by Sullivan (lib. by Sydney Grundy), prod. London, Savoy Theatre, 24. IX. 1892.

Hadley, Henry (Kimball) (b. Somerville, Mass., 20. XII. 1871; d. New York, 6. IX. 1937), Amer. cond. & comp. Studied with his father, with Chadwick at Boston and Mandyczewski in Vienna. Cond. opera in U.S.A. and Ger., and in 1909 became cond. of the Sym. Orch, at Seattle, of that of San Francisco in 1911–5 and from 1920 lived in N.Y.

Works incl. operas *Safié, Azora, Daughter of Montezuma, Bianca, Cleopatra's Night* & *Mirtil in Arcadia*; *Music, The New Earth* & *Resurgam* for solo voices, chor. & orch.; 4 syms., ovts. *In Bohemia, Herod* and to Shakespeare's *Othello*, Symph. Fantasy, tone-poems *Salome, Lucifer* & *The Ocean*, &c.

Hadley, Patrick (Arthur Sheldon) (b. Cambridge, 5. III. 1899), Eng. comp. Educ. at Winchester Coll. & Cambridge Univ., and studied m. at the R.C.M. in London, where in 1925 he joined the teaching staff. Mus.D. Cambridge in 1938 and app. lecturer at the Univ.

Works incl. incid. m. to Sophocles' *Antigone*; Sym. for bar. & chor. *The Trees so high, La Belle Dame sans merci* (Keats) for ten., chor. & orch., *My Beloved spake* (Song of Solomon) for chor. & orch.; *Travellers* for orch.; *Ephemera* (Yeats) & *Mariana* (Tennyson) for voice & chamber orch.; stg. 4tet in C maj., Fantasy for 2 vs. & pf.; songs with orch. & with pf.; partsongs, &c.

Hadow, (William) Henry (b. Ebrington, Glos., 27. XII. 1859; d. London, 8. IV. 1937), Eng. educst. & mus. scholar. Educ. at Malvern Coll. & Oxford, where later he lectured on m., having studied at Darmstadt and under C. H. Lloyd. Having comp. some chamber m. & songs, he held important educ. posts at Newcastle-on-Tyne & Sheffield, but gave some of his time to writing on m. He ed. the *Oxford Hist. of M.* and wrote vol. v and other pubs., incl. *Studies in Modern M., Eng. M.*, &c. Knighted in 1918.

Hadrianus. *See* **Adriaensen.**

Haessler, Johann Wilhelm (b. Erfurt, 29. III. 1747; d. Moscow, 29. III. 1822), Ger. pfst., orgst. & comp. Pupil of the orgst. Kittel, a pupil of Bach. Travelled much, estab. concerts at Erfurt in 1780, visited London & St. Petersburg in 1790–4, when he settled at Moscow.

Works incl. pf. sos., *Grande Gigue* in D min. & many other works for pf., org. works; songs, &c.

'Haffner' Serenade. Mozart's Serenade in D maj., K. 250, written at Salzburg in VII. 1776 for the marriage of Elisabeth Haffner, daughter of the late burgomaster Sigmund Haffner, celebrated on 22. VII.

'Haffner' Symphony. Mozart's Sym. in D maj., K. 385, comp. in Vienna in VII–VIII. 1782 for the Haffner family, probably on the occasion of the ennoblement of Sigmund Haffner, jun., on 29. VII. 1782.

Hafiz (Shams-ud-din Mohammed) (14th cent.), Pers. poet. *See* **Bantock** (5 ghazals), **Gernsheim** (chor. work), **Henschel** (songs), **Huber** (do.), **Schoeck** (do.), **Szymanowski** (love songs).

Hageman, Richard (b. Leeuwarden, 9. VII. 1882), Dutch-Amer. cond. & comp. Studied at the Amsterdam Cons., of which his father was dir., and later at the Brussels Cons. He was app. cond. of the Amsterdam Opera and in 1907 settled in U.S.A., where he cond. opera and concerts in var. cities.

Works incl. opera *Caponsacchi*; many songs, incl. *At the Well*, &c.

Hahn, Reynaldo (b. Caracas, Venezuela, 9. VIII. 1875), Fr. cond. & comp. Was sent to the Paris Cons. at the age of 11, where he studied under var. masters, incl. Massenet. He cond. opera in Paris and became cond. at Cannes in 1919.

Works incl. operas *L'Île du rêve, La Carmélite, La Colombe de Bouddha, Nausicaa, Le Pauvre d'Assise, La Reine de Saba, Le Temps d'aimer, Brummell, Le Marchand de Venise* (after Shakespeare), many operettas incl. *Ciboulette*; ballets *La Fête chez Thérèse* & *Le Dieu bleu*; incid. m. for Shakespeare's *Much Ado*, Rostand's *Le Bois sacré*, Sacha Guitry's *Mozart*, &c.; ode *Promethée* for solo voices, chor. & orch.; symph. poem *Nuit d'amour bergamasque*; chamber m.; pf. pieces; songs incl. cycles *Chansons grises, Chansons latines, Chansons espagnoles*, &c.

Hahnebüchen (Ger. or *hanebüchen* = uncouth, clumsy, loutish). Schumann uses the word as a direction ('etwas hahnebüchen') in his *Davidsbündlertänze* for pf.

Hahnentrapp (Ger. obs. = cock's walk or tread). An old Ger. equivalent of Passacaglia, arrived at by the mistaken idea that the word came from the Spa. *pasar* (to walk) and *gallo* (cock), whereas the 2nd word more prob. comes from *calle* (street).

Hainlein, Paul. *See* **Heinlein.**

Hairpins. The colloq. word for *crescendo* and *diminuendo* marks shown by the conventional signs < and >.

Haitzinger, Anton (b. Wilfersdorf, Lichtenstein, 14. III. 1796; d. Vienna, 31. XII. 1869), Aus. ten. singer. Made his 1st appearance at the Theater an der Wien in Vienna in 1821.

Hale, Adam de la. *See* **Halle.**

Hale, Philip (b. Norwich, Vermont, 5. III. 1854; d. Boston, Mass., 30. XI. 1934), Amer. m. critic. Studied in U.S.A., Ger. & Paris, and settled as critic at Boston in 1889 and for many years wrote programme notes for the orch. concerts there.

Halévy (Lévy), Jacques François (Fromental Elias) (b. Paris, 27. V. 1799; d. Nice, 17. III. 1862), Fr. comp. Studied at the Paris Cons. under Berton and Cherubini from 1809 and after twice taking a 2nd prize, gained the Prix de Rome in 1819. He continued to study in It. and on his return to Paris tried to gain a foothold on the operatic stage, for which he had already written more than one work. He succeeded with *L'Artisan* in 1827, after which he prod. an enormous number of operas. He became prof. of harmony and accomp. at the Cons. in 1827, of ctpt. & fugue in 1833 and of comp. in 1840.

Works incl. *c.* 40 operas, e.g. *La Dilettante d'Avignon, Ludovic* (begun by Hérold), *La Juive, L'Éclair, Guido et Ginevra, Le Shérif, Le Guitarréro, La Reine de Chypre, Charles VI, Les Mousquetaires de la reine, Le Val d'Andorre, La Fée aux roses, La Tempesta* (in It., after Shakespeare), *La Dame de Pique* (after Mérimée), *Le Juif errant* (after Sue), *Jaguarita l'Indienne, La Magicienne*, &c.; ballets *Yella, Manon*

Lescaut (after Prévost); incid. m. to *Prométhée enchaîné* (trans. from Aeschylus); cantatas *Les Derniers Moments du Tasse, La Mort d'Adonis* & *Herminie*; funeral march & *De profundis* on the death of the Duc de Berry, &c.

Halewijn, opera by Pijper (lib., in Dutch, by Emmy van Lokhorst, based on a Flem. story by Charles de Coster), prod. Amsterdam, I.S.C.M. festival, 13. VI. 1933.

Half-Close. An imperfect Cadence, ending on a common chord, but in such a way as to evade the feeling that it is in the tonic and thus to lead the ear to expect something to follow. Familiar instances often occur between the movements of Handel's orch. concs., and there are 2 isolated chords between the 1st & 2nd mvts. of Bach's 3rd Brandenburg Conc. which may serve as a perfect ex. of a H.-C. The chief reason why the finishing triad sounds inconclusive is that it is approached through a flat 7th, not through a leading-note.

Half Fall. *See* **Ornaments.**

Half Note (Amer.) = Minim. The Amer. designation, derived from Ger., is logical so long as the semibreve, not the breve, is accepted as a 'whole' note; but it uses 2 words where one will do and is apt to be confused with Semitone.

Halffter Escriche, Ernesto (b. Madrid, 16. I. 1905), Spa. cond. & comp. Cond. of the Orquesta Bética de Cámera. After the Spa. war he settled in Port.

Works incl. *Dos retratos, Dos bocetos, Rapsodia portuguesa* for orch.; *Suite ancienne* for wind insts.; 2 stg. 4tets, &c.

Halíř, Karel (b. Hohenelbe, Boh., 1. II. 1859; d. Berlin, 21. XII. 1909), Cz. vst. Educ. at the Prague Cons. and under Joachim, of whose 4tet he became a member, besides leading one of his own.

Halka, opera by Moniuszko (lib., in Pol., by Wlodzimierz Wolski, based on a story by Kazimierz Wladyslaw Wójcicki), prod. Vilna, 16. II. 1854. The chief Pol. nat. opera. Wallek-Walewski's opera *Jontek's Revenge* is a sequel to it.

Hall, Henry (b. New Windsor, *c.* 1655; d. Hereford, 30. III. 1707), Eng. poet, orgst. & comp. He was a choir-boy in the Chapel Royal in London under Cooke. App. orgst. at Exeter cath. in 1674 and at Hereford cath. in 1688.

Works incl. Te Deum in E♭ maj., Benedicite in C min., *Cantate Domino* & *Deus misereatur* in B♭ maj., anthems & other church m.; songs, duets, catches, &c.

Halle (or **Hale**), **Adam de la** (b. ? Arras, *c.* 1230; d. Naples, before 1288), Fr. minstrel (*trouvère*). Educ. for the priesthood, but fell in love and married a young girl, whom he left to retire to Douai in 1263 (?) to rejoin the church. In 1282 he went to Naples with the Comte d'Artois.

Works incl. stage pieces *Le Jeu d'Adam, ou de la feuillée* & *Le Jeu de Robin et de Marion*; motets; chansons, &c.

Hallé, Charles (orig. Carl Halle) (b. Hagen, Westphalia, 11. IV. 1819; d. Manchester, 25. X. 1895), Ger.-Eng. pfst. & cond. Studied 1st under his father, an orgst., then at Darmstadt and Paris, where he had pf. lessons from Kalkbrenner. Settled in Eng. in 1848 and founded the Hallé concerts at Manchester. He cond. many concerts and festivals elsewhere in the country as well and frequently appeared as pfst. His 2nd wife was the vst. Wilma Neruda, whom he married in 1888, when he was knighted.

Hallé, Lady. *See* **Neruda.**

Hallé Orchestra. Founded by Charles Hallé at Manchester in 1857.

Hallén, Johan (**Andreas**) (b. Göteborg, 22. XII. 1846; d. Stockholm, 11. III. 1925), Swe. cond., critic & comp. Studied at Leipzig, Munich & Dresden and later worked mainly at Göteberg & Stockholm.

Works incl. operas *Harald der Wiking* (in Ger.), *Hexfällan* (later revised as *Valborgsmässan*) & *Valdemarsskatten*; ballads for solo voices, chor. & orch.; symph. suite *Gustav Wasa Saga*, symph. poems *The Island of the Dead* (after Böcklin's picture), *Sounds of the Spheres, Autumn* & *A Summer Saga*, 2 rhapsodies for orch.; inst. pieces; songs, &c.

Halling. A Norw. dance originating from the Hallingdal between Oslo and Bergen. It is usually in 2–4 time and goes at a moderately quick pace. In its primitive form, as distinct from that cultivated by Grieg and other comps., its m. is played on the Hardanger Fiddle.

Hallström, Ivar (b. Stockholm, 5. VI. 1826; d. Stockholm, 11. IV. 1901), Swe. pfst. & comp. Had private m. lessons and studied law at Upsala Univ. There he met Prince Gustaf, with whom he wrote an opera, which was prod. at Stockholm in 1847. After the prince's death he became librarian to Prince Oscar, later Oscar II, and in 1861 he was app. dir. of Lindblad's m. school, where he had taught the pf.

Works incl. operas *The White Lady of Drottningholm* (with Prince Gustaf), *Den Bergtagna, Duke Magnus and the Mermaid, The Vikings, Neaga* (lib. by Carmen Sylva); ballets *A Dream, An Adventure in Scotland, Per Svinaherde*; saga play with m.; cantatas; songs, &c.

Halvorsen, Johan (b. Drammen, 15. III. 1864; d. Oslo, 4. XII. 1935), Norw. vst. & comp. Pupil of Lindberg and Nordquist at the Stockholm Cons., later of Brodsky at Leipzig and César Thomson at Liége for v. and A. Becker in Berlin for comp. Became cond. of the sym. concerts at Bergen and later of the Nat. Theatre at Oslo. He married a niece of Grieg's.

Works incl. incid. m. for Bjørnson's *The King*, Drachman's *Gurre*, Hamsun's *Dronning Tamara*, &c.; coronation cantata for King Haakon; symph. poem; v. Conc.; 3 suites for v. & pf., &c.

Haman and Mordecai (Handel). *See* **Esther.**

Hamboys, John (b. ?; d. ?), Eng. 15th-cent. cleric & mus. scholar. Mus.D., Oxford. He wrote at least one treatise on m., *Summa super musicam continuam et discretam.*

Hamel, Margarete Luise. *See* **Schick.**

Hamerik, Asger (orig. Hammerich) (b. Copenhagen, 8. IV. 1843; d. Frederiksborg, 13. VII. 1923), Dan. comp. of Ger. descent. Pupil of Gade at Copenhagen, later of Bülow in Berlin for pf. and of Berlioz in Paris for orchn. In 1872–98 he was in U.S.A. as dir. of the Cons. of the Peabody Inst. at Baltimore.

Works incl. operas *Tovelille, Hjalmar og Ingeborg, La vendetta* & *Den Rejsende*; Requiem, 2 chor. trilogies; 6 syms., the last for stgs., 5 *Northern Suites* & other orch. works, &c.

Hamerik, Ebbe (b. Copenhagen, 5. IX. 1898), Dan. cond. & comp., son of prec. Pupil of his father and Frank van der Stucken. Cond. of the royal theatre at Copenhagen, 1919–22, and of the Musikforeningen there, 1927–30 He then went to live in Aus., but returned home in 1934.

Works incl. operas *Stepan, Leonardo da Vinci* & *Marie Grubbe* (after Jacobsen); syms. E maj. & *Cantus firmus, Quasi Passacaglia e Fuga*, Vars. on an old Dan. folk-tune; 2 stg. 4tets; Suite for con. & chamber orch.; pf. pieces; org. works; songs, &c.

Hamlet. *See also* **Ambleto; Amleto; Shakespeare.**

Incid. m. for Shakespeare's tragedy by Tchaikovsky, Op. 67a, incl. 16 numbers and an abridged version of the *Hamlet* fantasy-ovt., Op. 67, 1st perf. St. Petersburg, 17. XI. 1888; the play 1st perf. with T.'s m., St. Petersburg, 21. II. 1891.

Opera by Aristide Hignard (1822–98), (lib. by Pierre de Garal, after Shakespeare), pub. 1868, but not then prod. on account of A. Thomas's rival opera; prod. Nantes, 21. IV. 1888.

Opera by A. Thomas (lib. by Jules Barbier & Michel Carré, after Shakespeare), prod. Paris, Opéra, 9. III. 1868.

Symph. poem by Liszt, comp. 1858 as a prelude to Shakespeare's tragedy; 1st concert perf. Sondershausen, 2. VII. 1876.

Hammerclavier (Ger. lit. 'hammer keyboard' = Pianoforte). The Ger. name for the pf. which Beethoven was anxious to introd. *c.* 1816, and now attached as a nickname to his pf. So. in B♭, Op. 106, with no good reason, since he used the designation also for the So. in A maj., Op. 101.

Hammerich. *See* **Hamerik.**

Hammerschmidt, Andreas (b. Brüx, 1612; d. Zittau, 8. XI. 1675), Boh. comp. Taken to Freiberg, Saxony, in 1626. Became orgst. there, 1635, and at Zittau, 1639. Wrote much Lutheran church m.

Works incl. sacred concs. and madrigals for several voices, sacred dialogues for 2 voices, odes, motets and hymns, 17 short Lutheran masses; thanksgiving for 8 voices for the Saxon victory at Liegnitz; dances for viols, &c.

Hammond Organ. An electrophonic org. invented by Laurens Hammond of Chicago in 1934, prod. its notes by means of electro-magnets and capable of imitating var. org. stops more or less faithfully.

Hamsun, Knut (b. 1859), Norw. novelist & dramatist. *See* **Halvorsen** (*Dronning Tamara*), **Karel** (*Game of Life*).

Handel, George Frideric[1] (Georg Friedrich Händel) (b. Halle, 23. II. 1685; d. London, 14. IV. 1759), Ger.-Eng. comp. Showed mus. talent at 4, but his father, a barber-surgeon, did not wish him to become a professional musn. On finding the boy of 7 practising the hpchd. in secret, however, he allowed him lessons, and in 1694 H. learnt clav. and org. from Zachau and also took up the v. and ob. Began to comp. at 10. After his father's death he went to the Lat. school and at 16 began to deputize for the cath. orgst., being given the appt. in 1702, while he studied law at the Univ. But in 1703 he went to Hamburg and played v. at the Opera under Keiser. Prod. 2 operas there, a mixture of Ger. and It., incl. *Almira*, and wrote 2 more, but went to It. in

[1] The form of the name adopted by himself after settling in Eng.

1706, visiting Florence, Rome, Venice and Naples, and writing var. works, incl. an opera for Venice, *Agrippina*. In 1710 he went to the court of the Elector of Hanover with Steffani, but obtained leave to visit London, where he prod. the opera *Rinaldo* in II. 1711. Returned to Eng. in 1712 and, although only on leave, remained for the rest of his life, except for some visits to the Continent. Between that year and 1741 he prod. 1 or 2 It. operas each year, with varying success and often in the face of opposition and dangerous fashionable competition. Became attached to the household of the Earl of Burlington in 1713 and of the Earl of Carnarvon (later Duke of Chandos) at Canons nr. Edgware in 1718. Meanwhile, in 1714, the Elector of Hanover had succeeded to the throne as George I and H. was in disgrace for a time for having taken indefinite leave. From 1720 he directed the Opera at the King's Theatre, Haymarket, under the auspices of the newly formed Royal Acad. of M. Bononcini arrived that year and became a dangerous rival, opposing parties forming round him and H., and later 2 factions also formed round the rival singers Bordoni and Cuzzoni, who eventually quarrelled on the open stage, an incident exploited satirically by Gay in *The Beggar's Opera*, which in 1728 further undermined the success of It. opera. In 1726 H. became naturalized and the next year he wrote 4 anthems for the coronation of George II. The new king's quarrel with the Prince of Wales, who supported an opposition opera started by the singer Senesino and had most of the m.-loving society on his side, made matters worse still. H. therefore tried his luck with Eng. orat. from 1733, though he still prod. It. operas. The successes of Porpora and Hasse at the rival house, and still more that of the male sop. Farinelli, greatly worried H., who had a stroke in 1737 and went bankrupt more than once. But he rallied again and again, prod. the orats. *Saul* and *Israel in Egypt* in 1739. In 1741 followed *Messiah*, prod. at Dublin, 13. IV. 1742. Many orats. followed during the next years, usually perf. at Lent in the theatres, H. playing org. concs. between the parts. In 1751 his eyesight began to fail and, after an unsuccessful operation, he was almost totally blind by 1753. He still appeared as cond. and orgst., however, but his health deteriorated and he was seriously unwell for many months before his death.

Works incl. It. operas written for London: *Admeto, Alcina, Alessandro, Amadigi, Arianna, Ariodante, Arminio, Atalanta, Berenice, Deidamia, Ezio, Faramondo, Flavio, Floridante, Giove in Argo* (not prod.), *Giulio Cesare, Giustino, Imeneo, Lotario, Muzio Scevola* (1 act only by H.), *Orlando, Ottone, Partenope, Il pastor fido* (2 versions), *Poro, Radamisto, Riccardo primo, Rinaldo* (2 versions), *Rodelinda, Scipione, Serse, Silla* (not prod.), *Siroe, Sosarme, Tamerlano, Teseo, Tolomeo*; incid. m. to Ben Jonson's *The Alchemist* and Smollett's *Alceste*; orats. *Alexander Balus, Athalia, Belshazzar, Deborah, Esther* (orig. *Haman and Mordecai*), *Israel in Egypt, Jephtha, Joseph and his Brethren, Joshua, Judas Maccabaeus, Messiah*, Occasional Orat., *Samson, Saul, Solomon, Susanna, Theodora, The Triumph of Time and Truth* (3 versions, 2 It.); 2 Passions (in Ger. on Brockes's words); secular voc. works: *Acis and Galatea* (3 versions, 2 It.), *Alexander's Feast, L'Allegro, il Pensieroso ed il Moderato, The Choice of Hercules, Hercules, Hymen, Il Parnasso in festa, Praise of Harmony, Semele*; odes for the birthday of Queen Anne and for St. Cecilia's Day; church m. incl. 12 'Chandos' anthems, 4 coronation anthems, Dettingen Te Deum, Utrecht Te Deum and Jubilate, funeral anthem for Queen Caroline, wedding anthems for Princess Anne and for the Prince of Wales; voc. chamber m. incl. 79 It. cantatas, 20 It. duets, 2 It. trios; inst. chamber m. incl. 15 solos and 27 sos. for 1 or 2 insts. and continuo; 12 Concerti grossi for stgs.; 6 Concerti grossi for wind and stgs.; c. 10 other concs. for var. insts.; *Water Music* and *Fireworks Music* for orch.; 17 concs. for org. & orch.; misc. hpchd. m. incl. some 2 dozen suites, &c.

'Handel' Variations. Brahms's Variations and Fugue on a theme by Handel for pf., Op. 24, comp. in 1861. The theme is the Air in H.'s hpchd. Suite in B♭ maj., No. 1 of the 2nd set of Suites (or Lessons) pub. in 1733.

Handl, Jacob (Latinized Jacobus Gallus) (b. Reifnitz, Carniola, 31. VII. 1550; d. Prague, 18. VII. 1591), Aus. comp. Chapel master to the Bishop of Olomouc in 1579 and later cantor in Prague. Wrote masses, motets, Te Deum & other church m.

Handle-Piano. *See* **Piano-Organ.**

Handlo, Robert de (b. ?; d. ?), Eng. 14th-cent. writer on m. Wrote on notation.

Handlung (Ger. = action). Wagner called some of his operas from *Lohengrin* onward a H., or 'H. für Musik,' indicating that he was no longer satisfied with the term 'opera,' but evidently deriving the term from the old It. *azione teatrale*.

Hanebüchen. *See* **Hahnebüchen.**

Hannikainen, Ilmari (b. Jyväskylä, 19. X. 1892), Fin. pfst. & comp. Studied at the Helsingfors Cons., also in Vienna, Leningrad, Berlin, Paris, Antwerp and London. With his brothers Arvo and Tauna, a vst. and a cst., he founded a pf. trio and toured Eur. widely with them.

Works incl. opera *Talkoojuhla*; pf. Conc.; pf. 4tet; pf. m.; songs, &c.

Hans Heiling, opera by Marschner (lib. by Eduard Devrient, orig. written for Mendelssohn), prod. Berlin, Opera, 24. V. 1833.

Hans Sachs, opera by Lortzing (lib. by comp. and Philipp Reger, based on a play by Johann Ludwig Ferdinand Deinhardstein), prod. Leipzig, 23. VI. 1840. An earlier opera on the subject of Wagner's *Meistersinger,* which was also used before that by Gyrowetz.

Hänsel und Gretel, opera by Humperdinck (lib. by Adelheid Wette, H.'s sister, from a tale by the Brothers Grimm), prod. Weimar, 23. XII. 1893.

Hanslick, Eduard (b. Prague, 11. IX. 1825; d. Vienna, 6. VIII. 1904), Aus. m. critic. Wrote for the *Neue freie Presse* in Vienna and was lecturer on mus. hist. at the Univ. A fierce opponent of Wagner and ardent partisan of Brahms. His books incl. *Vom musikalisch Schönen* (*Of the Beautiful in Music*).

Hanson, Howard (b. Wahoo, Neb., 28. X. 1896), Amer. comp. of Swe. descent. Studied m. in N.Y. and at Evanston, Ill. Univ. After var. appts., he gained the Amer. Prix de Rome, and after his stay in It. was app. dir. of the Eastman School of M. at Rochester, N.Y.

Works incl. opera *Merry Mount* (after Hawthorne); chor. work *The Lament for Beowulf*; 4 syms., symph. poems *North and West, Lux aeterna* & *Pan and the Priest* for orch.; stg. 4tet, pf. 5tet, Conc. for pf. 5tet; pf. pieces; songs, &c.

Hardanger Fiddle (Norw. *Hardangerfelen*). A primitive Norw. v. with 4 stgs. and 4 sympathetic stgs., used for playing folk dances.

Hardy, Thomas (1840–1928), Eng. novelist & poet. *See* **Dunhill** (*Song of the King's Men* from *The Dynasts*), **Gardiner (H. B.)** (*Shepherd Fennel's Dance* from *Wessex Tales*), **Milford** (*Dark Thrush*), **Holst** (*Egdon Heath* from *The Return of the Native*), **Queen of Cornwall** (Boughton), **Shaw (M.)** (*Budmouth Dears*), **Tess** (d'Erlanger).

Poems set as songs by Austin (F.) (3), Bax (3), Cochran (Leslie) (1), Finzi (20: 2 cycles), Foss (7), Gardiner (H. B.) (1: m. arr. from Hardy's own), Gibbs (C. A.) (2), Hale (Alfred) (12: incl. 2 cycles), Harrison (Sydney) (1), Head (Michael) (2), Holst (2), Ireland (6, incl. cycle), Lane (Edgar) (2), Le Fleming (Christopher) (4), Milford (5), Parish (F. Wilson) (1), Sarson (May) (1), Scott (Cyril) (1), Serell (Alys F.) (1), Sheldon (Mary) (4), Slater (Gordon) (1), Speyes (Charles A.) (2), Stewart (D. M.) (1), Tate (Phyllis) (1).

Harington, Henry (b. Kelston, Som., 29. IX. 1727; d. Bath, 15. I. 1816), Eng. physician & amateur musn. Studied 1st theol. and then medicine at Oxford and settled in practice at Bath. Comp. glees, catches, rounds, songs, &c. The popular setting of Ben Jonson's ' Drink to me only with thine eyes ' is attrib. to him.

Hark, hark, the lark, song by Schubert from Shakespeare's *Cymbeline,* trans. by A. W. Schlegel as *Ständchen aus ' Cymbeline '* and comp., in Ger., in 1826.

Harmonic. A prefix denoting org. pipes prod. harmonic notes from pipes of double, triple or quadruple speaking-length.

Harmonic Bass. Another name for the Acoustic Bass org. stop.

Harmonic Flute. Another name for the Flute Harmonic org. stop.

Harmonic Minor. The min. scale conforming to the key signature, with the exception of the leading-note, which is sharpened casually at each appearance. The H. M. is one of the 2 forms of the min. scale, the other being the Melodic Min. *See also* **Minor.**

Harmonica. An inst. also called Glass Harmonica, the notes of which are prod. by friction on a series of tuned glasses, either with the fingers or mechanically.

Harmonics. The partials or secondary sounds prod. by any note played on an inst., more or less audibly and most distinctly on bells. On some insts. the fundamental note can be cut out and one of the H.'s made audible instead. Wind insts. do this normally by overblowing, but more artificially sounding H.'s can be prod. on stgs., both of the v. family and the hp.

Harmoniemusik (Ger.) M. for a combination of woodwind and brass insts., with or without perc., i.e. for military band. Mendelssohn wrote an ovt. ' für H.'

Harmonious Blacksmith, The. The name given to the air on which Handel wrote vars. in his Suite (Lesson) in E maj. pub. in 1720. It has been said to be a Fr. song and has also been attrib. to Wagenseil, who was aged 5 in 1720. The tradition is that Handel took refuge in a blacksmith's shop at Edgware during a storm, and that the blacksmith, Powell, sang the song while he hammered on the anvil. The story came into currency suspiciously late—in 1835—and the name of Powell did not appear until later still, when the anvil was mysteriously 'discovered' and sold by auction. But at the end of the 18th cent. the title was already current for quite another reason: one of the pubs. J. & W. Lintern, who brought out an ed. under that name, had been a blacksmith in his youth, and this is the only origin of the title that should be accepted as authenticated.

Harmonium. An inst. of the org. type, but much smaller and portable, the sound of which is prod. by reeds played by wind coming from bellows worked by the player's feet. The reeds are made to speak by playing on a keyboard similar to that of the pf. It dates from the early 19th cent. The American Organ is almost identical with it, except that the wind is sucked into instead of driven out through the reeds.

Harmony. The sounding together of notes in such a way that, whether they produce concord or discord, they make sense to the mus. ear; also the management of the succession or progression of chords in a way that does not offend against mus. grammar or, more broadly, against mus. reason.

Harold en Italie. A descriptive sym. by Berlioz, Op. 16, for solo va. & orch., based on Byron's *Childe Harold*, comp. in 1834 and 1st perf. Paris, 23. XI. It was suggested by Paganini, but not played by him.

Harp. An inst. dating from prehistoric times, so shaped that the stgs. stretched parallel across its frame are graded in length and thus prod. the different notes of a mus. scale. Old Hs. had comparatively few stgs. and their notes were fixed; the modern concert H. has a range of 6½ 8ves and the stgs. represent the diatonic scale of C♭ maj.; but each note can be raised individually throughout all the octaves at once by a semitone and by a whole tone at will by means of a set of pedals at the base of the inst. Thus the H. can be tuned in a moment to any diatonic scale. The chromatic scale is available only on the Chromatic Harp (q.v.).

Harp Lute. An obs. inst., sometimes called Dital Harp, invented early in the 19th cent. It was derived from insts. of the lute type, but had a larger number of stgs. held by pegs in the harp-shaped head, c. half of them changeable in pitch by a finger-board, the others remaining open and thus capable of playing only a single fixed note.

'Harp' Quartet. The nickname given to Beethoven's stg. 4tet in E♭ maj., Op. 74, comp. in 1809, because it contains several arpeggios divided between the insts., which however do not sound in the least like a hp.

Harpègement. *See* **Ornaments.**

Harpsicall, **Harpsicon** } Old Eng. terms, corruptions of 'Harpsichord.'

Harpsichord. The most important stgd. keyboard inst. before the pf., shaped usually in the wing form of a grand pf. and played by means of a similar keyboard, but prod. its notes by plucking the stgs. with plectra, not striking them with hammers. The Virginal and Spinet were insts. of the same type, but smaller and square in shape. Hs. usually had 2 keyboards, each controlling a different set of quills, harder and softer, and sometimes there were stops by which yet other ranges of quills could be set into action; but the tone could not be controlled by the player's fingers. The H. was universally used in the 16th–18th cents. and then gave way to the pf., but it has recently been revived for the perf. of old m., being a quite distinctive inst., not merely a primitive pf.

Harpway. The special tuning of the Bass Viol or Lyra Viol in the 17th cent., not in the usual way, but to the notes of a common chord, either maj. (H. sharp) or min. (H. flat).

Harrer, Johann Gottlob (b. Görlitz, 1703; d. Leipzig, 9. VII. 1755), Ger. comp. & collector of m. Succeeded Bach as cantor at St. Thomas's church, Leipzig, in 1750.

Works incl. orats., Passion m.; 24 syms.; inst. concs.; hpchd. sos., &c.

Harris, Augustus (Henry Glossop) (b. Paris, 1852; d. Folkestone, 22. VI. 1896), Eng. operatic manager. He began to prod. opera with Verdi's *Aida* in 1887, when he was manager of Drury Lane Theatre in London, and the following year he revived opera at Covent Garden. Knighted in 1891.

Harris, Clement (Hugh Gilbert) (b. London, 8. VII. 1871; d. Pentepigadia, 23. IV. 1897), Eng. pfst. & comp. Educ. at Harrow and studied m. at Frankfort o/M., Clara Schumann teaching him pf. He was travelling in Gr. when the Greco-Turkish war broke out, fought voluntarily on the Gr. side and was killed in battle.

Works incl. symph. poem *Paradise*

Lost (after Milton); Romances for v. & pf. and cl., co. & pf.; 4 concert studies, Ballade, *Il Pensieroso* & *L'Allegro* (after Milton), &c. for pf.; songs, &c.

Harris, Joel Chandler (1848–1908), Amer. author. *See* **Jacob** (G.) (*Uncle Remus*).

Harris, Renatus (b. ?; d. ?), Eng. 17th–18th-cent. org. builder. Worked in London. Built many famous orgs. and enlarged that made by his grandfather for Magdalen Coll., Oxford.

Harris, Roy (b. Lincoln Co., Okla., 12. II. 1898), Amer. comp. His father was a farmer who migrated to California during H.'s boyhood, and at 18 H. had a farm of his own. In 1916 he enlisted in the 1st world war, returning to U.S.A. in 1918 and becoming a m. student at the Univ. of California, driving a dairy cart to earn a living. Next he studied under Arthur Farwell for 2 years and prod. an Andante for stgs. with the N.Y. Phil. Orch. in 1926, when he went to Paris for a further 2 years' study with Nadia Boulanger with a Guggenheim scholarship. He returned to U.S.A. in 1929 and later became dir. of the comp. dept. at the Westminster Choir School at Princeton, N.J. and afterwards joined Cornell Univ.

Works incl. 6 syms., *Folksong Symphony*, *Farewell to Pioneers*, *Three Symph. Essays* & other works for orch.; *Chorale* & *Prelude and Fugue* for stg. orch.; Conc. for v. & orch.; Sym. for chor. & orch., *Whitman Suite* & *Second Suite* for women's chor. & 2 pfs., *Song for Occupation*, *Story of Noah* & *Symphony for Voices* for 8-pt. unaccomp. chor.; 3 stg. 4tets, 6tet & 5tet for wind & pf., stg. 6tet, pf. 5tet, pf. Trio, *Variations on a Theme* for stg. 4tet, *4 Minutes 20 Seconds* for fl. & stg. 4tet, Conc. for pf., cl. & stg. 4tet; v. & pf. So.; pieces for v. and va. & pf.; pf. works, incl. sos. & *Children's Suite*, &c.

Harrison, Julius (b. Stourport, Worcs., 26. III. 1885), Eng. cond. & comp. Studied under Bantock at the Midland Institute, Birmingham. Cond. opera under Beecham's management and with the B.N.O.C. and in 1930 became mus. dir. to the Hastings Corporation.

Works incl. suite *Worcestershire Pieces* for orch.; *Troubadour Suite* (on troubadour tunes) for stgs., hp. & 2 hns.; stg. 4tet *Widdicombe Fair* & other chamber m.; pf. works, inst. pieces; cycle *Cavalier Songs* & other songs, &c.

Harsanyi, Tibor (b. O-Kanizea, 27. VI. 1898), Hung. comp. Studied at the Budapest Cons.

Works incl. opera *Domestic Happiness*; ballet *The Last Dream*; Suite, 3 Dances & *Joie de vivre* for orch.; chamber m., &c.

Harte, Francis Bret (1839–1902), Amer. humorous writer. *See* **James** (ovt.), **Weinberger** (*Outcasts of Poker Flat*).

Hartleben, Otto Erich (1864–1905), Ger. poet & dramatist. *See* **Pierrot lunaire** (Schoenberg).

Hartmann. Ger.-Dan. family of musns.:

1. Johann Ernst H. (b. Glogau, Silesia, 24. XII. 1726; d. Copenhagen, 21. X. 1793), Ger vst., cond. & comp. Worked at Breslau and Rudolstadt before he settled in Copenhagen, where he became leader of the royal orch. in 1768.

Works incl. opera *The Fishermen*, containing the song *Kong Christian*, now the Dan. nat. anthem, &c.

2. August Wilhelm H. (b. Copenhagen, 1775; d. ?), orgst., son of prec. Orgst. at the Garrison church in Copenhagen, 1800–50.

3. Johann Peter Emilius H. (b. Copenhagen, 14. V. 1805; d. Copenhagen, 10. III. 1900), comp., son of prec. Became dir. of the Copenhagen Cons., 1840.

Works incl. operas *Ravnen* (after Gozzi), *Korsarerne* & *Liden Kirsten*; melodrama *The Golden Horns* (after Oehlenschläger); incid. m. for plays; cantata on the death of Thorvaldsen & other chor. works; Sym. in G min.; pf. pieces, &c.

4. Emil H. (b. Copenhagen, 21. II. 1836; d. Copenhagen, 18. VII. 1898), orgst. & comp., son of prec. Pupil of his father and Gade, who was his brother-in-law. Orgst. at var. churches in 1861–73 and cond. of the Mus. Soc. from 1895, succeeding Gade.

Works incl. operas *En Nat mellem Fjaeldene*, *Elverpigen*, *Korsikaneren* & *Ragnhild*; ballet *Fjeldstuen*; cantata *Winter and Spring*; 3 syms., *Northern Folk Dances* & ovt. *A Northern Campaign*; concs. for v. & for co.; Serenade for cl., co. & pf.; songs, &c.

Harty, (Herbert) Hamilton (b. Hillsborough, Ir., 4. XII. 1879; d. Hove, 19. II. 1941), Ir. cond. & comp. Studied pf., va. & comp. under his father and became an orgst. at the age of 12. Later orgst. at Belfast and Dublin, where he studied further under Esposito. In 1900 he settled in London as accompst. & comp. and married the sop. Agnes Nicholls. He then took to cond. and after much experience in London was app. cond. to the Hallé Orch. at Manchester in 1920, retiring in 1933. Knighted and Mus.D. Dublin, 1925.

Works incl. Ir. Sym., *Comedy Ovt.*, symph. poem *With the Wild Geese* for orch.; v. Conc.; cantata *The Mystic Trumpeter* (Whitman); *Ode to the Nightingale* (Keats) for sop. & orch.; many songs, &c.

Harvey, Mary (Lady Dering) (b. ?, VIII. 1629; d. ?, 1704), Eng. amateur comp. Daughter of Daniel Harvey of Folkestone and Combe (Surrey), married Sir Edward Dering, a member of a Kentish family, 1648. Pupil of H. Lawes, in whose *Second Book of Select Ayres and Dialogues* 3 of her songs appeared.

Harwood, Basil (b. Woodhouse, Olveston, Glos., 11. IV. 1859), Eng. orgst. & comp. Educ. at Charterhouse and Oxford, studied m. at Bristol, Oxford and the Leipzig Cons. Orgst. 1st in London, then at Ely cath., 1887–92, and Christ Church, Oxford, 1892–1909, also precentor at Keble Coll. there, orch. & chor. cond. and choragus of the Univ.

Works incl. psalms & motets with orch.; services, anthems & other church m.; *Ode on a May Morning* (Milton) for chor. & orch., cantata *Love Incarnate*; org. Conc. with orch.; 2 sos. & other works for org., &c.

Háry, János, ballad opera by Kodály (lib. by Béla Paulini & Zsolt Harsányi, based on a poem by János Garay), prod. Budapest, 16. X. 1926. It contains popular Hung. tunes and begins with an orch. imitation of a sneeze.

Hasse, Faustina. *See* **Bordoni.**

Hasse, Johann Adolph (b. Bergedorf nr. Hamburg, 25. III. 1699; d. Venice, 16. XII. 1783), Ger. comp. Pupil of his father, an orgst. & schoolmaster. He went to Keiser's Hamburg Opera as ten. and afterwards sang at Brunswick, where he prod. his 1st opera in 1721. In 1724 he went to Naples for more serious study under Porpora and later A. Scarlatti. A duet serenade sung by Tesi and Farinelli secured him the commission of the opera *Sesostrate* for Naples, and in 1727 he went to Venice, where he taught at the Cons. degl' Incurabili and married Faustina Bordoni in 1730. They went to Dresden together in 1731, she as singer and he as mus. dir. of the court Opera. In 1760 H. lost most of his m. in the fires caused by the siege of Dresden, and when the court m. was disbanded afterwards he went to Vienna and collab. with Metastasio in opposition to Gluck; but at Milan in 1771 he acknowledged the superiority of the boy Mozart, and he lived at Venice for the rest of his life.

Works (many destroyed) incl. operas *Antioco, Tigrane, Il Sesostrate, Artaserse, Cleofide, Caio Fabrizio, Il Demetrio, Siroe, rè di Persia. Tito Vespasiano, Lucio Papirio, Didone abbandonata, Antigono, Semiramide riconosciuta, Arminio, Leucippo, Demofoonte, Attilio Regolo, Il Ciro riconosciuto, Solimano, Ezio, Olimpiade, Alcide al Bivio, Il trionfo di Clelia, Partenope, Piramo e Tisbe, Ruggiero* & c. 70 more; masses, psalms, Miserere, Te Deum & other church m.; orats. incl. *I pellegrini al sepolcro*; inst. concs.; hpchd. works, &c.

Hasselbeck, Rosa. *See* **Sucher.**

Hasselmans, Alphonse (Jean) (b. Liége, 5. III. 1845; d. Paris, 19. V. 1912), Belg., naturalized Fr., hpst. & comp. Settled early in Paris and became hp. prof. at the Cons. in 1884. Appeared frequently as a virtuoso and comp. c. 50 works for the hp., incl. *Patrouille* & *L'Orientale*.

Hassler, Hans Leo (b. Nuremberg, 25–26. X. 1564; d. Frankfort o/M., 8. VI. 1612), Ger. orgst. & comp. Pupil of his father, Isaac H. and, after an appt. at Nuremberg, was sent to Venice for further study under A. Gabrieli. Orgst. to Octavian Fugger at Augsburg, 1585–1600. Having returned to Nuremberg as orgst. of the church of Our Lady, he married and went to live at Ulm in 1604, but soon went into the service of the Emperor Rudolph in Prague. In 1608 he became orgst. to the Elector of Saxony at Dresden, but suffered from consumption and d. during a visit with the elector to Frankfort o/M.

Works incl. masses, magnificats, hymn-tunes, motets (incl. 2 collections *Sacrae cantiones* & *Sacri concentus*), fugal psalms and Christian songs; It. canzonets for 4 voices, It. & Ger. madrigals, *Lustgarten neuer teutscher Gesäng* (32 Ger. songs for 4–8 voices); ricercari, toccatas, &c. for org., &c.

Hassler, Jacob (b. ? Joachimstal, Boh., 17–18. XII. 1569; d. ?, after 1618), Ger. orgst. & comp., brother of prec. Studied under his father and at Venice, became orgst. to Christoph Fugger at Augsburg and then to Prince Eitel-Fritz of Hohenzollern at Hechingen, and in 1602–12 was in the service of the imp. court in Prague.

Works incl. masses & other church m.; It. madrigals; org. works, &c.

Hassler, Kaspar (b. Nuremberg, VIII. 1562; d. Nuremberg, VIII. 1618), Ger. orgst. & comp., brother of prec. Studied under his father and (?) at Venice. Orgst. at the church of St. Laurence at Nuremberg. Ed. collections of motets, incl. some by his brother Hans Leo H.

Hauch, Johannes Carsten (1790–1872), Dan. poet & dramatist. *See* **Heise** (*Marsk Stig*).

Hauer, (Josef) Matthias (b. Wiener-Neustadt, 19. III. 1883), Aus. comp. Pub. a series of pamphlets on comp. according to a 12-note system of his own, different from that of Schoenberg, his mus. material being based on groups of notes he calls *Tropen*, derived from the combs. of the 12 notes of the chromatic scale allowed by the agreement of their overtones.

Works (all based on this system) incl. opera *Salammbô* (after Flaubert); play with m. *Die schwarze Spinne* (after Jeremias Gotthelf); Mass for chor., org. & orch.; cantata *Wandlungen*; m. for Aeschylus's *Prometheus Bound* & tragedies by Sophocles; *Vom Leben*, recitation with singing voices & chamber orch. for broadcasting; Sinfonietta, 8 Suites, 7 Dance Fantasies, Concert Piece, *Apocalyptic Fantasy*, *Kyrie*, &c. for orch.; Sym. for stgs., harmonium & pf.; v. Conc., pf. Conc., 3 stg. 4tets, 5tet for cl., v., va., co. & pf.; many pf. pieces, incl. 2 sets of Studies and pieces on Hölderlin titles; inst. pieces; 6 song-cycles to poems by Hölderlin & other songs, &c.

Haug, Hans (b. Basle, 27. VII. 1900), Swi. cond. & comp. Studied at Basle and Munich and became orch. and chor. cond. at var. Swi. towns and prof. at the Lausanne Cons.

Works incl. operas *Don Juan in der Fremde*, *Madrisa*, *Tartuffe* (after Molière), *E liederließ Kleeblatt* (in Swi. dialect), *Ariadne*; Te Deum; orat. *Michelangelo*; orch. works; v. Conc., pf. Conc.; chamber m.; partsongs, arrs. of Swi. folksongs, songs with pf.; film & radio m., &c.

Hauk, Minnie (b. New York, 16. XI. 1852; d. Triebschen, Lucerne, 6. II. 1929), Amer. m.-sop. singer of Ger. descent. Made her 1st stage appearance at Brooklyn in 1866 and her Eur. début in London, at Covent Garden, in 1868.

Haunted Tower, The, opera by Storace (lib. by James Cobb), prod. London, Drury Lane Theatre, 24. XI. 1789.

Hauptmann, Gerhart (b. 1862), Ger. dramatist. *See* **Bath** (*Hannele*), **Graener** (*Hanneles Himmelfahrt*), **Grosz** (*Versunkene Glocke*), **Krehl** (*Hannele*), **Tcherepnin (A.)** (do.), **Ullrich** (*Hanneles H.*), **Unger (H.)** (*Hannele*), **Versunkene Glocke** (Respighi & Zöllner), **Weisberg** (*Rautendelein*), **Zilcher** (*Goldene Harfe*).

Hauptmann, Moritz (b. Dresden, 13. X. 1792; d. Leipzig, 3. I. 1868), Ger. theorist, writer on m. & comp. Studied at Dresden and began to work there, lived in Russia in 1815–9, played v. in Spohr's orch. at Cassel from 1822 and was cantor at St. Thomas's church in Leipzig from 1842 to his death. Wrote on acoustics, harmony, fugue, &c.

Works incl. opera *Mathilde*; 2 masses, motets & psalms; chors. & partsongs; 3 sos. for v. & pf., v. duets; songs, &c.

Hausegger, Siegmund von (b. Graz, 16. VIII. 1872), Aus. cond. & comp. Studied under his father, a Wagnerian critic, and others. After cond. at Graz, he shared the cond.-ship of the Kaim Orch. at Munich with Weingartner. Later in charge of concerts at Frankfort o/M., Glasgow & Edinburgh (Sco. Orch.) and Hamburg, and at Munich again in 1920–36.

Works incl. opera *Zinnober*; syms. *Barbarossa* & *Natursinfonie*, *Dionysische Phantasie*, *Wieland der Schmied* & *Aufklänge* for orch.; Mass & Requiem; chor. works, partsongs, &c.

Hauser, Franz (b. Krasowice nr. Prague, 12. I. 1794; d. Freiburg i/B., 14. VIII. 1870), Boh.-Ger. bar. singer. Pupil of Tomašek and successful opera singer until 1837, when he began to teach in Vienna. In 1846 he became dir. of the Munich Cons.

Hauser, Miska (b. Pozsony, 1822; d. Vienna, 9. XII. 1887), Hung. vst. He studied in Vienna and made his 1st appearance on a tour undertaken at the age of 12. Travelled much and wrote *Lieder ohne Worte* for v.

Hausmann, Robert (b. Rottleberode, Harz, 13. VIII. 1852; d. Vienna, 19. I. 1909), Ger. cst. Studied at the Hochschule für Musik in Berlin and with Piatti in London and It. He joined the Joachim 4tet in 1879.

Haussman, Valentin (b. ?; d. ?), Ger. 16th–17th-cent. orgst. & comp. He was orgst. and town councillor at Gerbstädt nr. Merseburg. Ed. voc. pieces by Marenzio, Vecchi, Gastoldi and Morley with Ger. words.

Works incl. Ger. secular songs for 4–8 voices, inst. dances, incl. *Venusgarten* containing 100 dances, mostly Pol., &c.

Hautboy (from Fr. *hautbois* = lit. 'high wood': a high-pitched wooden inst.). The old Eng. name for the Oboe, sometimes spelt 'hoboy.' Also an 8-ft. reed org. stop reprod. the tone of the ob.

Haute-contre (Fr.). A bowed stg. inst. of the v. family now obs., but used in the 17th cent., with a range from A below middle C.

Hawaiian Guitar. *See* **Ukelele.**

Hawkins, John (b. London, 30. III. 1719; d. London, 21. V. 1789), Eng. mus. historian. Devoted at first to architecture and then to law, he gradually became interested in lit. and m. Having married a wealthy wife in 1753, he was able to retire and to undertake, among minor works, his *General History of the Science and Practice of Music*, pub. in 1776, the same year as the 1st vol. of Burney's similar work. Knighted in 1772.

Hawley, Stanley (b. Ilkeston, 17. V. 1867; d. Ilkeston, 13. VI. 1916), Eng. pfst. & comp. Studied at the R.A.M. in London and later became hon. sec. to the Phil. Soc.

Works incl. m. for Poe's *The Bells*, *The Raven* & other pieces for recitation with accomp., &c.

Hawthorne, Nathaniel (1804–64), Amer. novelist. *See* **Claflin** (*Hester Prynne*), **Hanson** (*Merry Mount*), **Scarlet Letter** (W. Damrosch).

Hay (Country Dance). *See* **Hey.**

Haydn, (Franz) Joseph (b. Rohrau, Lower Aus., 31. III.–1. IV. 1732; d. Vienna, 31. V. 1809), Aus. comp. (?) of Croatian descent. Son of a poor wheelwright. After some casual teaching he was sent to the cath. school of St. Stephen's in Vienna at the age of 8 and remained there until 1749. The following year, at 18, he wrote a mass and (?) his 1st stg. 4tets. He played in street bands and was discovered there by the comedian Kurz, who asked him to set a comic opera, *Der neue krumme Teufel*, prod. 1752. He taught Marianne Martinez in 1754 and met there Metastasio and Porpora, becoming the latter's valet-pupil. An appt. at Weinzierl in 1755 brought him into touch with an orch., for which he comp., but he returned to Vienna the next year, making a modest living by teaching. In 1759 Count Morzin invited him to Lukaveč, where he wrote the 1st sym. that has been preserved. The next year, at 28, he married Anna Maria Keller, a shrew with whom he lived as little as possible later on. He entered the service of Prince Paul Anton Esterházy at Eisenstadt in 1761, after whose death the following year he remained with Prince Nicholas, who was building the palace of Esterház by the Neusiedler lake inside the Hung. border, whither the household removed in 1766, H. remaining there off and on as mus. dir. until 1790, writing syms. and 4tets, &c. for home perf. and a number of operas for singers and for marionettes. His fame soon became international, works being pub. in Paris and Amsterdam as early as 1764–5. The Concert de la Loge Olympique in Paris commissioned 6 syms. in 1786, the London pub. Bland vainly invited him to Eng. in 1787 and he ded. 6 4tets to Frederick William II of Prus, that year. When he retired at the death of Esterházy in 1790, he did pay a visit to London, which lasted until VI. 1792. During this visit and the next he wrote 12 syms. for Salomon's concerts; in 1791 he also perf. one, written in 1788, at Oxford, where he rec'd the Mus.D. on 8. VII. The 2nd visit to Eng. was between II. 1794 and VIII. 1795. After that he lived wholly in Vienna, where he wrote the Aus. hymn (and the 4tet with vars. on it) in 1797, prod. the orat. *The Creation* in 1798 and another, *The Seasons*, in 1801.

Works (never properly classified in a complete ed.) incl. 104 syms.; c. 150 other orch. works; *c.* 50 concs., divertimenti, &c. with solo insts.; *c.* 200 solos for barytone (Esterházy's favourite inst.); 84 stg. 4tets, 38 pf. trios, *c.* 30 stg. trios, *c.* 30 misc. chamber works; 42 pf. sos.; *c.* 20 misc. pf. works; *c.* 24 works for the stage, incl. *Acide e Galatea*, *Lo speziale*, *Le pescatrici*, *L'incontro improviso*, *La vera costanza*, *Il mondo della luna*, *Dido* (for marionettes), *L'isola disabitata*, *La fedeltà premiata*, *Orlando paladino*, *Armida*, *Orfeo ed Euridice* (unfinished); incid. m. for Shakespeare's *King Lear* & *Hamlet*, Goethe's *Götz von Berlichingen*, also for Ger. adapts. of Alexander Bicknell's *The Patriot King* and Regnard's *Le Distrait*; a number of works for several voices, incl. settings of Sco., Ir. & Welsh airs, many for single voice; 24 songs, 12 Eng. canzonets and other works for 1 voice; 12 Masses, a *Stabat Mater* and some other church m.; orats.: *Il ritorno di Tobia*, *Die Schöpfung* (*The Creation*), *The Seven Words of the Saviour on the Cross* (arr. from a stg. version written for Cadiz cath.) & *Die Jahreszeiten* (*The Seasons*); some cantatas and chors., &c.

Haydn, (Johann) Michael (b. Rohrau, Lower Aus., 14. IX. 1737; d. Salzburg, 10. VIII. 1806), Aus. comp. & orgst., (?) of Croatian descent, brother of prec. Boy chorister at St. Stephen's cath. in Vienna; app. mus. dir. to the Bishop of Grosswardein in 1757; in 1762 became cond. to the Archbishop of Salzburg, where he was afterwards orgst. Married the singer Maria Magdalena Lipp in 1768.

Works incl. operas *Andromeda e Perseo*, *Die Hochzeit auf der Alm*; 24 masses, 2 Requiems, 4 Ger. masses, 114 graduals, 67 offertories, many litanies, vespers & much other church m.; orats. & cantatas; Ger. sacred songs; partsongs & canons; 30 syms. & partitas for orch., 12 orch. minuets; v. Conc.; 3 5tets, 6tet & other chamber m.; 50 org. preludes on the 8 church modes, &c.

' Haydn ' Quartets. The familiar name of Mozart's 6 stg. 4tets ded. to Haydn: G maj., K. 387 (1782), D min., K. 421 (1783), E♭ maj., K. 428 (1783), B♭ maj., K. 458 (1784), A maj., K. 464 (1785), C maj., K. 465 (1785).

' Haydn ' Variations. A set of vars. by Brahms for orch., Op. 56a, or for 2 pfs., Op. 56b, on a theme called the ' St. Anthony Chorale ' from a Divertimento for wind insts., by H., where it is also treated in var. form. 1st perf. of the orch. version, Vienna, 2. IX. 1873.

Hayes, Catharine (b. Limerick, 25. X. 1825; d. London, 11. VIII. 1861), Ir. sop. singer. Studied under Antonio Sapio at Dublin, where she made her 1st appearance in 1840. Later she studied with García in Paris and Ronconi at Milan, where she sang at the Scala in 1845, after a début at Marseilles. After many successes in It. and Vienna, she 1st appeared in London in 1849.

Haym, Nicola (Francesco) (b. Rome, *c.* 1679; d. London, 11. VIII. 1729), It. cst., libst. & comp. of Ger. descent. Settled in London in 1704, played 1st co. in Clayton's *Arsinoe* and then prod. var. operas and pasticcios much of the words and m. of which he unjustifiably claimed as his own. He wrote or adapted the lib. for Handel's *Teseo* in 1713 and for several other works of his as well as 2 each for Ariosti and Bononcini. His own works incl. a Lat. orat. and a serenata *Il reciproco amore di Tirsi e Clori*, an anthem, *The Lord is King*, (?) *Dixit Dominus* & 2 sets of sos. for 2 vs. & bass.

Head, Michael (b. Eastbourne, 28. I. 1900), Eng. singer, pfst. & comp. Gave up the study of mechanical engineering for m., which he studied at the R.A.M. in London, incl. comp. under Corder. In 1925 he became pf. prof. there. He has given many song recitals and broadcasts, playing his own accomps., and toured widely in the Brit. Empire.

Works incl. Tone Poem & Scherzo for orch.; *Jabberwocky* (Lewis Carroll) for chor.; pf. Conc.; *c.* 60 songs incl. cycles *Songs of the Countryside* (W. H. Davies), *Over the Rim of the Moon*, &c.

Head Voice. One of the so-called ' registers ' in singing, used or said to be used for the higher notes of the singer's range, and so called because its resonance gives the sensation of being lodged in the head, not in the chest, as in the case of the Chest Voice.

Heather (or Heyther), William (b. Harmondsworth, Middlesex, *c.* 1584; d. Oxford, VII. 1627), Eng. m. scholar. Lay vicar at Westminster Abbey in London and Gentleman of the Chapel Royal. In 1622 Camden, whose house he shared, sent him to Oxford with the deed of endowment for his Chair of Hist. He received the Mus.D. degree and in 1627 founded the Chair of M. there.

Hebbel, (Christian) Friedrich (1813–63), Ger. poet & dramatist. *See* **d'Albert** (*Rubin*), **Durey** (*Judith*), **Ettinger** (do.), **Genoveva** (Schumann), **Holofernes** (Rezniček), **Judith** (N. Berg), **Lassen** (*Nibelungen*), **Mottl** (*Agnes Bernauer*), **Rathaus** (*Herodes und Mariamne*), **Schillings** (*Moloch*), **Schoeck** (songs), **Stephan** (*Liebeszauber*).

Hebenstreit, Pantaleon (b. Eisleben, 1669; d. Dresden, 15. XI. 1750), Ger. dulcimer player. At 1st a vst. and dancing-master at Leipzig, he made his name as a virtuoso on the dulcimer towards the end of the 17th cent. and had such a success in Paris in 1705 that Louis XIV named his inst. after him, and it was long called ' Pantaleon.' In 1714 it was introd. into the court band at Dresden, with him as player.

' Hebrides ' Overture (Mendelssohn). *See* **Fingal's Cave.**

Heckelclarina (not Heckelclarind). The name of a special inst. invented by the firm of Heckel at Biberich for the playing of the shepherd's pipe part in Act III of Wagner's *Tristan*.

Heckelphone. An ob. of bar. pitch invented by the Ger. inst. maker Heckel. It stands an 8ve lower than the ob. R. Strauss used it in some scores, but it has not gained wide currency.

Heding (or Hedine), Jacques de (b. Picardy, ?; d. ?, *c.* 1270), Fr. troubadour, 2 of whose songs are preserved.

Hedy (*Haidée*), opera by Fibich (lib. by Anežka Schulzová, based on an episode in Byron's *Don Juan*), prod. Prague, Cz. Theatre, 12. II. 1896.

Hegar, Friedrich (b. Basle, 11. X. 1841; d. Zürich, 2. VI. 1927), Swi. cond. & comp. Studied at Zürich and at the Leipzig Cons. After working in Pol. and Alsace, he went to Zürich, where he did much useful work as concert, operatic and esp. chor. cond., and was given the hon. doctor's degree by the Univ. in 1885.

Works incl. numerous chor. works with and without solo voices or orch., many for male voices; v. Conc., co. Conc.; stg. 4tet; v. & pf. So.; pf. pieces; songs, &c.

Hegedüs, Ferencz (b. Pécs, 26. II. 1881; d. London, 12. XII. 1944), Hung. vst. Pupil of Hubay and others at the Budapest Cons. Began to tour Eur. in 1901, 1st visiting Eng. Later he lived at Zürich.

Heger, Robert (b. Strasburg, 19. VIII. 1886), Ger. cond. & comp. Studied at Zürich and Munich, Schillings being his chief master. He has cond. opera in many Ger. cities, also in Vienna and London.

Works incl. operas *Ein Fest zu Haderslev*, *Der Bettler Namenlos* (from Homer's *Odyssey*), *Der verlorene Sohn*; melodrama *Die Jüdin von Worms*; *Ein Friedenslied* for solo voices, chor., orch. & org.; Sym. in D min., symph. poem *Hero und Leander*; v. Conc. in D maj.; pf. Trio, &c.

Heiberg, Johan Ludvig (1791–1860), Dan. critic & poet. *See* **Delius** (*Folkeraadet*), **Kuhlau** (*Elverhoj*).

Heimchen am Herd, Das (*The Cricket on the Hearth*), opera by Goldmark (lib. by Alfred Maria Willner, based on Dickens's story), prod. Vienna, Opera, 21. III. 1896.

Heimkehr aus der Fremde, Die (*The Return from Abroad*, better known as *Son and Stranger*), operetta by Mendelssohn (lib. by Karl Klingemann), prod. Leipzig, 10. IV. 1851.

Heine, Heinrich (1797–1856), Ger. poet. *See* **Brian** (*Pilgrimage to Kevlaar*), **Dichterliebe** (Schumann), **Dieren (van)** (songs), **Fliegende Holländer** (Wagner), **Giselle** (Adam), **Guglielmo Ratcliff** (Mascagni), **Humperdinck** (*Wallfahrt nach Kevlaar*), **Jirák** (*Tragi-Comedy*), **Klose** (*Wallfahrt nach K.*), **Leroux** (*William Ratcliff*), **Lesur** (songs with stg. 4tet), **Medtner** (songs), **Meyer-Helmund** (*Heines Traumbilder*), **Ratcliff** (Andreae), **Schoeck** (songs), **Schumann** (*Liederkreis*), **Schwanengesang** (Schubert), **Shebalin** (songs), **Shtcherbatchev (N. V.)** (songs), **Silcher** (*Loreley*), **Stanford** (*Wallfahrt nach K.*), **Stucken** (*Wm. Ratcliff*), **Vavrinecz** (do.), **White (M. V.)** (5tet *Du bist wie eine Blume* & songs), **William Ratcliff** (operas, Cui, Dopper & Pizzi).

6 songs by Brahms, 6 by Schubert, 39 by Schumann.

Heinichen, Johann David (b. nr. Weissenfels, 17. IV. 1683; d. Dresden, 16. VII, 1729). Ger. comp. & theorist. Studied under Schelle and Kuhnau at St. Thomas's school, Leipzig, 1st practised as lawyer, then went to It. for further study, entered the service of Prince Leopold of Anhalt-Cöthen, where he was succeeded by Bach in 1717, when he became mus. dir. to the Saxon court at Dresden. He wrote 2 theoret. works.

Comps. incl. operas *Paris und Helena*, *Calfurnia*, *Le passioni per troppo amore*; 55 masses, 3 Requiems, many motets & over 100 other church works; 5 serenades; voc. solos and duets, &c.

Heinlein, Paul (b. Nuremberg, 11. IV. 1626; d. Nuremberg, 6. VIII. 1686), Ger. orgst., wind player & comp. Studied with a town musn. at Nuremberg and in 1646–9 in It. App. to var. Nuremberg churches in 1655–8, finishing as orgst. at St. Sebald's cath. Wrote church m. and set many sacred poems by contemp. authors.

Heinrich the Monk (**Henricus Monachus**) (b. ?; d. ?), Ger. or Swi. 10th–11th-cent. comp. of sequences.

Heinrich von Müglin (b. ?; d. ?), Ger. 14th-cent. song comp.

Heise, Peter Arnold (b. Copenhagen, 11. II. 1830; d. Ny Taarbaek, 12. IX. 1879), Dan. comp. Pupil of Berggreen at Copenhagen and Hauptmann at Leipzig.

Works incl. *Paschaens Datter* & *Drot og Marsk*; incid. m. for many plays, incl. Oehlenschläger's *Palnatoke* & Hauch's *Marsk Stig*; *Rusk Cantata* & cantata *Tornerose* (*Sleeping Beauty*); Sym.; pf. Trio; numerous songs, &c.

Hekking, André (b. Bordeaux, 30. XII. 1866; d. Paris, 14. XII. 1925), Fr. cst. Pupil of his uncle Charles H. Began his concert career with a tour in Spa., settled in Paris in 1909 and in 1919 became prof. of co. at the Cons.

Heldenleben, Ein (*A Hero's Life*), symph. poem by R. Strauss, comp. VIII.–XII. 1898, 1st perf. Frankfort o/M., 3. III. 1899. The work is autobiographical.

Heldentenor (Ger. = heroic ten.). One of the Ger. categories of operatic voices: a ten. capable of sustaining parts of a heroic as distinct from lyrical type; equiv. to the It. *tenore robusto*.

Hèle, Georges de la. *See* **La Hèle.**

Helicon. A brass wind inst. playing the bass in military bands, similar to the Bombardon, but made in a circular form so that it may be carried slung over the player's shoulder when marching.

Heliodorus (?–?), Gr. author. *See* **Desmarets** (*Théagène et Chariclée*).

Heller, Stephen (b. Pest, 15. V. 1814; d. Paris, 14. I. 1888), Hung. pfst. & comp. Studied with Anton Halm in Vienna and made his 1st public appearance at Pest in his teens and later went on tour in Ger. He lived at Augsburg in 1830–3 after a long illness, working quietly at comp., and settled in Paris in 1838. He visited Eng. in 1850 and 1862.

Works (nearly all for pf.) incl. 4 sos., a very large number of studies, vars. and fantasies on operatic tunes, 5 Tarantellas, Caprice on Schubert's *Trout*, several sets entitled *Im Walde*, *Promenades d'un solitaire* (after

Rousseau's letters on botany), *Blumen-, Frucht- und Dornenstücke* (after Jean Paul), *Dans le bois, Nuits blanches*, &c. With Ernst he wrote v. & pf. pieces entitled *Pensées fugitives*.

Hellertion. An electrophonic inst. invented by Lertes and Helberger of Leipzig in 1930, prod. notes from the air graded according to the chromatic scale by means of a keyboard, not indeterminate like those of the Aetherophone or Theremin.

Hellinck, Joannes Lupus (b. ?; d. ?, 1541), Flem. comp. (?) choirmaster at Cambrai and Bruges at different times.

Works incl. masses, motets; Ger. sacred songs; Fr. chansons, &c.

Hellmesberger. Aus. family of musns.:

1. Georg H. (b. Vienna, 24. IV. 1800; d. Neuwaldegg, 16. VIII. 1873), vst., cond. & comp. Studied in Vienna and became in 1821 asst. teacher and in 1833 prof. of the v. at the Cons. In 1829 he was app. cond. of the court Opera. Wrote many works for his inst.

2. Joseph H. (b. Vienna, 3. XI. 1828; d. Vienna, 24. X. 1893), vst. & cond., son of prec. Pupil of his father. Appeared as an infant prodigy and was app. v. prof. at the Cons. in 1851, and cond. of the Phil. Soc. He resigned the latter post to Herbeck in 1859, but retained that of dir. of the Cons. He also held posts at the Opera and the court concerts, and led a stg. 4tet from 1849–87.

3. Georg H. (b. Vienna, 27. I. 1830; d. Hanover, 12. XI. 1852), vst. & comp., brother of prec. Studied with his father and toured with him and his brother Joseph in Ger. & Eng. In 1850 he was app. leader of the opera orch. at Hanover, where he prod. the operas *Die Bürgschaft* (after Schiller, not prod.) and *Die beiden Königinnen*.

4. Joseph H. (b. Vienna, 9. IV. 1855; d. Vienna, 26. IV. 1907), vst. & comp., son of 2. Pupil of his father, in whose 4tet he played 2nd v. until 1887, when he succeeded him as leader. Solo vst. at the Opera and court chapel and v. prof. at the Cons. from 1878.

Works incl. 6 operettas & 6 ballets.

Helmholtz, Hermann (Ludwig Ferdinand) von (b. Potsdam, 31. VIII. 1821; d. Berlin, 8. IX. 1894), Ger. scientist. After holding 3 prof.-ships in physiology, he turned to physics, of which he became prof. at Berlin Univ. in 1871. He specialized in acoustics and in 1862 pub. his *Lehre von den Tonempfindungen als physiologische Grundlage für die Theorie der Musik*.

Hely-Hutchinson, Victor (b. Cape Town, 26. XII. 1901), Eng. pfst. & comp. Educ. at Eton and Balliol Coll., Oxford, and became lecturer in m. at Cape Town Univ. in 1922. In 1926 he returned to Eng. and joined the staff of the B.B.C., 1st in London and then as regional dir. of m. at Birmingham, where he became prof. of m. at the Univ. in 1934. He resigned in 1944 to take up the appt. of mus. dir. of the B.B.C.

Works incl. *A Carol Sym.* and Vars. for orch.; pf. 5tet, stg. 4tet; chor. works; songs, incl. settings of Edward Lear; film m., &c.

Hemans (*née* Browne), Felicia Dorothea (1793–1835), Eng. poetess. *See* **Jensen** (songs).

Hemiole. The change in triple time which turns the accentuation of 6 notes from groups of 3 into groups of 2. The device was used frequently by old church comps., but it survives e.g. in Handel's frequent habit of ending a mvt. in 3–4 time with 2 bars so accentuated as to sound like a bar of twice the extent divided into 3–2; also in cross-rhythms often found in Brahms, for ex.

'Hen' Symphony (Haydn). *See* **Poule.**

Henderson, W(illiam). J(ames). (b. Newark, N.J., 4. XII. 1885; d. New York, 5. VI. 1937), Amer. m. critic. After some general journalistic work he became m. critic to the *N.Y. Times* in 1887 and the *N.Y. Sun* in 1902. In 1904 he was app. lecturer at the Inst. of Mus. Art. in N.Y. His books incl. studies of the hist. and practice of singing, aesthetics, the evolution of m., Wagner, early It. opera, &c.

Henriqués, Fini (Valdemar) (b. Copenhagen, 20. XII. 1867), Dan. vst. & comp. Among his masters were Joachim for v. and Svendsen for comp. He played at the Dan. royal chapel and in the Copenhagen State Orch., where he was leader.

Works incl. several operas; ballets, e.g. *Den lille Havfrue*; incid. m. for plays; 2 syms., symph. poems; stg. 4tet & other chamber m.; v. & pf. Sc. in G min.; pf. pieces; songs, &c.

Henry VI (b. Windsor, 6. XII. 1421; d. London or Windsor, 21. V. 1471), King of Eng. He was an amateur comp. A Gloria and Sanctus of his is in the *Old Hall* MS.

Henry VIII (b. Greenwich, 28. VI. 1491; d. London or Windsor, 28. I. 1547), King of Eng. Received mus. instruction as part of an eccles. educ.

Works attrib. to him (some lost) incl. 2 masses, a Lat. motet, an anthem 'O Lord, the Maker of all things'; ballet for 3 voices, 'Passetyme with good companye,' partsongs for 3 & 4 voices; pieces for consorts of viols.

Henry VIII, opera by Saint-Saëns (lib. by Léonce Détroyat and Paul Armand Silvestre, based on Shakespeare), prod. Paris, Opéra, 5. III. 1883.

Henschel, (Isidor) Georg (later George) (b. Breslau, 18, II. 1850; d. Aviemore, Inverness, 10. IX. 1934), Ger. (naturalized Brit). bar. singer, cond., pfst. & comp. Appeared as pfst. in Berlin in 1862 and at Hirschberg as singer in 1866. After studying at the Leipzig & Berlin Conss. he appeared at the Lower Rhine Festival in 1874 and for the 1st time in Eng. in 1877. He remained there until 1881, when he married the Amer. sop. Lillian Bailey and became cond. of the new Boston Sym. Orch. In 1884 he settled in London and organized var. orch. and chor. concerts, also cond, the Sco. Orch. in 1893–5. His wife d. in 1901 and he married Amy Louis in 1907. He sang again, in Eng. and on the continent, often accomp. himself, until he gave his last recital in London in 1914, when he was knighted.

Works incl. operas *Friedrich der Schöne* & *Nubia*; operetta *A Sea Change*; incid. m. for Shakespeare's *Hamlet*; Eng. Mass for 8 voices, Te Deum, Stabat Mater, Requiem, Psalm cxxx, anthems; Festival March for orch.; Ballade for v. & orch.; stg. 4tet in B♭ maj.; many pf. works; numerous songs (some with orch.) incl. 2 cycles from Scheffel's *Trompeter von Säckingen*, 4 poems by Hafiz, 3 songs from Kingsley's *Water Babies*, ballad *Young Dietrich*; *Serbisches Liederspiel* for 1–4 voices; 5 voc. 4tets to poems from Rus.; partsongs, &c.

Hensel, (*née* **Mendelssohn-Bartholdy**), **Fanny (Cécile)** (b. Hamburg, 14. XI. 1805; d. Berlin, 17. V. 1847), Ger. pfst. & amateur comp., elder sister of Mendelssohn, with whom she was brought up musically. She married the painter Wilhelm Hensel in 1829.

Works incl. pf. Trio; 4 books of pf. pieces; 2 of songs; partsongs *Gartenlieder*, &c. (6 of her songs were pub. as her brother's.)

Henselt, Adolf von (b. Schwabach, Bavaria, 12. V. 1814; d. Warmbrünn, Silesia, 10. X. 1889), Ger. pfst. & comp. Pupil of Hummel at Weimar and Sechter in Vienna. He toured Ger. in 1836 and then settled in St. Petersburg. He was app. court pfst. and teacher to the imp. children.

Works incl. pf. Conc. in F min.; pf. Trio; much pf. solo m., comprising 2 sets of Studies (e.g. *Si oiseau j'étais*), *Frühlingslied*, *Wiegenlied*, Impromptu in C min., *La Gondola*, &c.; also transcriptions of Cramer, Weber, &c.

Heptachord (from Gr.). A scale of 7 notes.

Her Stepdaughter (*Její Pastorkyňa*; also called *Jenufa*), opera by **Janáček** (lib. by comp., based on a story by Gabriela Preissová), prod. Brno, 21. I. 1904.

Herbeck, Johann (Franz) von (b. Vienna, 25. XII. 1831; d. Vienna, 28. X. 1877), Aus. cond. & comp. Lived in Vienna; app. cond. to the Phil. Soc. in 1859 and dir. of the Court Opera in 1871.

Works incl. 2 masses; Sym. in D min., Symph. Vars. & other orch. m.; 2 stg. 4tets; songs, partsongs, &c.

Herbert, A(lan). P(atrick). (b. 1890), Eng. author & statesman. *See* **Dunhill** (*Tantivy Towers*), **Gibbs (C. A.)** (*Blue Peter*), **Toye (G.)** (*Red Pen*).

Herbert, George (1593–1633), Eng. poet. *See* **Vaughan Williams** (*5 Mystical Songs*).

Herbert, Victor (b. Dublin, 1. II. 1859; d. New York, 26. V. 1924), Ir.-Amer. cst., cond. & comp. Studied in Ger. and toured Eur.; settled in N.Y. in 1886 and remained there.

Works incl. operas *Natoma* & *Madeleine*, operettas *The Wizard of the Nile*, *Babes in Toyland* & over 30 others; cantata *The Captive*; symph. poem *Hero and Leander* & 3 suites for orch.; Serenade for stgs.; songs, &c.

Herbst, Johann Andreas (b. Nuremberg, 1588; d. Frankfort o/M., 26. I. 1666), Ger. comp. He was chapel master at var. places, incl. Darmstadt, Nuremberg and Frankfort. Pub. 3 theoretical works.

Works incl. Ger. & Lat. madrigals; 5-part settings of hymn-tunes; congratulation cantata *Beatus vir* for 5 voices & other occasional works, &c.

Hercules. Secular orat. by Handel (lib. by Thomas Broughton), prod. London, King's Theatre, Haymarket, 5. I. 1745.

Herder, Johann Gottfried von (1744–1803), Ger. philos., philol. & author. *See* **Bach (J. C. F.)** (*Brutus*, orats. & cantatas), **Jensen** (*Stimmen der Völker*), **Loewe (K.)**, **Prometheus (Liszt)**, **Reichardt** (*Morning Hymn*), **Schröter (C.)** (songs), **Wolf (E. W.)** (*Easter Cantata*).

Heredia, Pedro (b. ? Spa., ?; d. Rome, 1648), It. comp. of Spa. descent. Choirmaster at Vercelli in his early days and later in the service of the Vatican.

Works incl. masses, motets; a madrigal, &c.

Hereford Festival. *See* **Three Choirs Festival.**

Héritier, Jean l'. *See* **L'Héritier.**

Héritte-Viardot, Louise (Pauline Marie) (b. Paris, 14. XII. 1841; d. Heidelberg, 17. I. 1918), Fr. con. singer, teacher & comp. Daughter of Louis V. and Pauline V.-García. Studied with her mother and later taught at St. Petersburg Cons., the Hoch Cons. at Frankfort o/M. and in Berlin. She married the Fr. consul-general H. in 1862.

Hermannus Contractus (Hermann the Deformed) (b. Sulgau, 18. VII. 1013; d. Alleshausen nr. Biberach, 24. IX. 1054), Ger. mus. scholar & comp. Studied in Swi. at the monastery of St. Gall and became a Benedictine monk. He entered the monastery at Reichenau. Wrote mus. treatises and comp. hymns, sequences, &c.

Hermione, opera by Bruch (lib. by Emil Hopffer, based on Shakespeare's *Winter's Tale*), prod. Berlin, Opera, 21. III. 1872.

Hero and Leander. *See* **Ero e Leandro.**

Hero's Life (R. Strauss). *See* **Heldenleben.**

Hérodiade (*Herodias*), opera by Massenet (lib. by Paul Milliet & 'Henri Grémont' = Georges Hartmann, based on a story by Flaubert), prod. Brussels, Théâtre de la Monnaie, 19. XII. 1881.

Hérold, (Louis Joseph) Ferdinand (b. Paris, 28. I. 1791; d. Paris, 19. I. 1833), Fr. comp. Studied under his father, the pfst. François Joseph H. (1755–1802), and later under Fétis and Louis Adam, Adolphe A.'s father and his godfather. In 1806 he entered the Cons. as a pupil of Catel and Méhul, and took the Prix de Rome in 1812. In Rome and Naples, where he became pfst. to Queen Caroline, he comp. several inst. works, also a comic opera *La Jeunesse de Henri V*. Returning to Paris in 1816, he collab. with Boïeldieu in *Charles de France* and in 1817 began to prod. operas of his own. He was accompst. at the Théâtre Italien from 1820 to 1827, when he married Adèle Élise Rollet and became choirmaster at the Opéra. About this time he began to suffer seriously from consumption, from which he d.

Works incl. operas *Les Rosières*, *La Clochette*, *Le Premier Venu*, *Les Troqueurs*, *L'Amour platonique*, *L'Auteur mort et vivant*, *Le Muletier*, *Lasthénie*, *Le Lapin blanc*, *Vendôme en Espagne* (with Auber), *Le Roi René*, *Marie*, *L'Illusion*, *Emmeline*, *L'Auberge d'Auray* (with Carafa), *Zampa*, *Le Pré aux Clercs*, *Ludovic* (unfinished, completed by Halévy); ballets *Astolphe et Joconde*, *Le Sonnambule*, *Lydie*, *La Fille mal gardée*, *La Belle au bois dormant* (after Perrault); incid. m. for Ozaneaux's *Dernier Jour de Missolonghi*; 2 syms.; cantata *Mlle de la Vallière*, *Hymne sur la Transfiguration*; 3 stg. 4tets; 2 sos., vars., rondos, &c. for pf., &c.

Herrick, Robert (1591–1674), Eng. poet. *See* **Davies (Walford)** (*Noble Numbers*), **Horn (C. E.)** (*Cherry ripe*), **Hughes (G.)** (songs), **Lawes (H.)** (*Hesperides*), **Murrill** (songs), **Quilter** (*To Julia*), **White (M. V.)** (songs), **Williams (G.)** (do.).

Herrmann, Hugo (b. Ravensburg, 19. IV. 1896), Ger. orgst. & comp. Studied at Stuttgart and Berlin, Schreker being among his masters. Orgst. at Ludwigsburg 1919–23, then at Detroit until 1925, when he left the U.S.A., becoming chor. cond. at Reutlingen and in 1930 at Weimar; orgst. again from 1931.

Works incl. opera *Vasantasena*, chamber opera *Das Gazellenhorn*, 2 school operas; orat. *Jesus und seine Jünger* & several other chor. works; Sym. in C♯ min., Concert M. I & II, &c. for orch.; v. Conc.; Sym. for chamber orch., &c.

Hertoghs. *See* **Ducis.**

Hertz, Henrik (1797–1870), Dan. poet & dramatist. For works on *King René's Daughter see* **Arregui, Edwards (J.), Iolanta** (Tchaikovsky), **Smart** (H.).

Hervé (real name Florimond Ronger) (b. Houdain, Pas de Calais, 30. VI. 1825; d. Paris, 3. XI. 1892), Fr. comp. Studied m. as a choir-boy, then with Elwart and Auber. Orgst. at var. Paris churches, incl. Saint-Eustache; later theatre manager, operetta singer, libst., cond., &c.

Works incl. numerous operettas, e.g. *Don Quixote et Sancho Pança* (after Cervantes), *Le Hussard persécuté*, *La Fanfare de Saint-Cloud*, *Les Chevaliers de la Table Ronde*, *L'Œil crevé*, *Chilpéric*, *Le Petit Faust*, *Les Turcs*, *La Belle Poule*, *Le Nouvel Aladin* (parody of Racine's *Bajazet*), *Frivoli*; ballets *Dilara*, *Sport*, *La Rose d'Amour*, *Cléopâtre*, *Les Bagatelles*; sym. *The Ashanti War* for solo voices & orch.; many light songs, &c.

Hervelois. *See* **Caix d'Hervelois.**

Herz, Henri (Heinrich) (b. Vienna, 6. I. 1806; d. Paris, 5. I. 1888), Aus. pfst. & comp. Pupil of his father and of Hünten, entered the Paris Cons. in 1816 and settled there, becoming a fashionable teacher. App. pf. prof. at the Cons. in 1842. Toured U.S.A., Mexico and the W. Indies in 1845–51, making a fortune with which to begin a pf. manufacture, and built a concert hall.

Works incl. 8 pf. concs. & some 200 works for pf. solo: vars., studies, fantasies, &c.

Herzogenberg, Heinrich von (Baron v. H.-Peccaduc) (b. Graz, 10. VI. 1843; d. Wiesbaden, 9. X. 1900), Aus. comp. & cond. Studied at the Vienna Cons. and settled at Leipzig in 1872. Cond. the Bach soc. there in 1875–85 and then became prof. of comp. at the Berlin Hochschule für Musik. Husband of Elisabeth von H. (1842–92), a fine amateur pfst. and pupil of Brahms.

Works incl. Mass, Requiem, psalms; orats. *Die Geburt Christi* & *Die Passion*; cantata *Columbus*; syms. *Odysseus* (after Homer) & C min.; 3 stg. 4tets, 2 pf. trios, 2 stg. trios; 2 v. & pf. sos., c. & pf. So.; 2 sets of vars. for 2 pfs., many pf. pieces & duets; fantasies for org.; songs, voc. duets, partsongs, &c.

Hesdin, Pierre (b. ?; d. ?), Fr. 16th-cent. comp. Registrar of the brotherhood of Saint Julien in Paris in 1522 and singer in Henri II's chapel in 1547–59.

Works incl. masses, motets; chansons, &c.

Heseltine, Philip (Peter Warlock) (b. London, 30. X. 1894; d. London, 18. XII. 1930), Eng. mcolst. & ed. (under his own name) and comp. (as P. W.). Educ. at Eton, where he studied m. in partic., and later influenced by Delius and van Dieren. Founded the *Sackbut*, a combative mus. paper, wrote numerous articles, ed. old Eng. m., esp. of the lutenist school & pub. books on the Eng. ayre, Delius and (with Cecil Gray) Gesualdo.

For comps. *see* **Warlock.**

Hess, Willy (b. Mannheim, 14. VII. 1859; d. Berlin, 17. II. 1939), Ger. vst. Studied with his father, a pupil of Spohr's, was taken to U.S.A. as a child, played in T. Thomas's orch. there and made his 1st appearance as a soloist in Hol. in 1872. Later studied with Joachim in Berlin, became prof. at Rotterdam, leader of the Hallé Orch. at Manchester, and worked by turns at Cologne, London, Boston and Berlin.

Hesse, Adolf Friedrich (b. Breslau, 30. VIII. 1809; d. Breslau, 5. VIII. 1863), Ger. orgst. & comp. Studied org. & pf. at Breslau and was sent by the city authorities on a tour to play his own org. works. In 1831 he was app. orgst. to the church of the Bernhardins at Breslau, where he remained until his death, also cond. the sym. concerts. Wrote numerous org. works & much other m.

Heuberger, Richard (Franz Josef) (b. Graz, 18. VI. 1850; d. Vienna, 28. X. 1914), Aus. m. critic & comp. Studied engineering at first, but at the age of 26 devoted himself to m., becoming a chor. cond. in 1878 and a critic in 1881.

Works incl. operas *Abenteuer einer Neujahrsnacht, Manuel Venegas, Miriam* (later *Das Maifest*), *Barfüssele*; operettas *Der Opernball, Ihre Excellenz, Der Sechsuhrzug, Das Baby, Der Fürst von Düsterstein, Don Quixotte* (after Cervantes); ballets *Die Lautenschlägerin* & *Struwelpeter*, &c.

Heure espagnole, L' (*The Spanish Hour*), opera by Ravel (lib. by Franc-Nohain, based on his own comedy), prod. Paris, Opéra-Comique, 19. V. 1911.

Heuschkel, Johann Peter (b. Harras, Meiningen, 1773; d. Biberich, 5. XII. 1853), Ger. obst., orgst. & comp. In the service of the court chapel at Hildburghausen, later at Wiesbaden and Biberich. Wrote inst. works and songs.

Heward, Leslie (Hays) (b. Liversedge, Yorks, 8. XII. 1897; d. Birmingham, 3. V. 1943), Eng. cond. & comp. Began to learn m. from his father, an orgst., and became a chorister at Manchester cath., having been discovered at the Morecambe Festival by Sydney H. Nicholson. In 1914 he was given an orgst.'s post, but in 1917 he went as asst. m. master to Eton, studying at the R.C.M. in London at the same time. He then taught at Westminster School, became theatre cond., and coach and occasional cond. with the B.N.O.C. on its tours. In 1924 he went to Cape Town as mus. dir. to the S. African Broadcasting Corp. and cond. of the Cape Town Orch., but returned to Eng. in 1927 and rejoined the B.N.O.C. In 1930 he succeeded Boult as cond. of the City of Birmingham Orch.

Works incl. opera on Ibsen's *Peer Gynt* (unfinished); m. for film *The Loves of Robert Burns*; church m.; *South African Patrol, Revel, Quodlibet*, &c. for orch.; stg. 4tet in A min.; songs with orch. & with pf., partsongs, &c.

Hewlett, Maurice (1861–1923), Eng. novelist. *See* **Křička** (*Hypolita*).

Hexachord (from Gr. = six sounds). A system of dividing the mus. scale into groups of 6 notes, which Guido d'Arezzo in the 11th cent. named Ut, Re, Mi, Fa, Sol, La. They could begin on 3 different notes, the lowest starting from G on the bottom line of the bass clef, then marked with the Gr. letter Γ (*gamma*), the other 2 being C and F above; and these were repeated 4 times, starting on G, C, F and F counting upwards. The remaining notes were named by letters from A to G, as to-day, but the syllables remained the same in each hexachord, so that in the 1st Γ was

Ut, A was Re, &c.; in the 2nd C became Ut, D Re, &c.; in the 3rd F became Ut, G Re, &c.; and so on throughout the 7 hexachords. But each hexachord had to have its only semitone interval between the notes marked with the syllables Mi and Fa, so that in the 3rd and 6th the 4th note, which fell on B, had to be flattened. Thus the 1st accidental was introd. into the diatonic scale, and it was through this that the modes began to give way to the modern maj. and min. scales. Up to the time of Purcell the hexachordal system persisted in so far as the syllables of the Gamut (a word derived from ' Gamma Ut ') pertaining to it remained in use. Pieces are found described as being, for ex., in ' C fa ut ' (sometimes spelt ' C faut ').

Hexameron. A collective pf. work, pub. in 1837, consisting of bravura vars. on the march in Bellini's *Puritani* by Liszt, Thalberg, Pixis, Herz, Czerny and Chopin, with an introd., finale and connecting passages by Liszt.

Hexatone (from Gr. =6 notes). A ' gapped ' scale of 6 notes to the 8ve.

Hey. An old country dance similar to the Reel and prob. to the Canarie.

Heyse, Paul (Johann Ludwig) (1830–1914), Ger. poet & novelist. *See* **Italienisches Liederbuch** (H. Wolf), **Jensen** (*Spanisches Liederbuch*), **Spanisches Liederbuch** (H. Wolf).

Heyther, William. *See* **Heather.**

Hiawatha, 3 cantatas for solo voices, chor. & orch. by Coleridge-Taylor, a setting of parts of Longfellow's poem: I. *Hiawatha's Wedding Feast,* II. *The Death of Minnehaha,* III. *Hiawatha's Departure,* 1st perf. as a whole, London, 22. III. 1900.

Hichens, Robert (Smythe) (b. 1864), Eng. novelist. *See* **Ronald** (*Garden of Allah*).

Hidalgo, Juan (b. ?; d. Madrid, ?), Spa. 17th-cent. comp. (?) hpst. in the royal chapel at Madrid and inventor of an inst. called the *claviharpa.*

Works incl. operas *Celos aun del aire matan* (lib. by Calderón) & *Los celos hacen estrellas* (lib. by Guevara); incid. m. to var. plays by Calderón incl. *Ni Amor se libra de Amor,* &c.

Hidden Fifths
Hidden Octaves } Consecutive 5ths or 8ves made less apparent to the eye by the fact that they are concealed by a passing note in one of the offending parts, but none the less ungrammatical.

Highland Fling. A Sco. dance-step rather than the dance itself, although that is often so called. The m. is that of the Strathspey and the step is a kick of the leg backwards and forwards.

Hill, Aaron (1685–1750), Eng. playwright. *See* **Arne** (**T. A.**) (*Zara*), **Rinaldo** (Handel).

Hill, Edward Burlingame (b. Cambridge, Mass., 9. IX. 1872), Amer. comp. & teacher. Studied at Harvard Univ., where he became a teacher in 1908 and prof. of m. in 1928. Wrote a book on modern Fr. m.

Works incl. 2 ballets; 2 syms., 2 suites *Stevensoniana,* Sinfonietta, symph. poem *Lilacs* for orch.; Sinfonietta for stg. orch.; Concertino for pf. & orch., M. for Eng. hn. & orch; stg. 4tet in C maj., 6tet for wind & pf.; cl. & pf. So. & pieces; songs, &c.

Hill, Joseph (b. ?, 1715; d. London, 1784), Eng. v. maker. He worked in London, where the house of his descendants, W. E. Hill & Sons, still exists.

Hillemacher, Paul (Joseph Wilhelm) (b. Paris, 25. XI. 1852; d. Versailles, 13. VIII 1933) & **Lucien (Joseph Édouard)** (b. Paris, 10. VI. 1860; d. Paris, 2. VI. 1909), Fr. comps., brothers who wrote all their works in collab. Studied at the Paris Cons., where P. gained the Prix de Rome in 1876 and L. in 1880.

Works incl. operas *Saint-Mégrin, La Légende de Sainte Geneviève, Une Aventure d'Arlequin, Le Régiment qui passe, Le Drac, Orsola, Circé*; mimed dramas *One for Two* & *Fra Angelico*; incid. m. for Haraucourt's *Héro et Léandre* and for George Sand's *Claudie*; symph. legend *Loreley* & other orch. works; chamber m., songs, partsongs, &c.

Hiller, Ferdinand (b. Frankfort o/M., 24. X. 1811; d. Cologne, 10. V. 1885), Ger. pfst. cond. & comp. Was taught m. privately as a child and appeared as pfst. at the age of 10. In 1825 he went to Weimar to study under Hummel. After a brief return to Frankfort he lived in Paris from 1828–35, where he taught and gave concerts. He prod. his 1st opera at Milan in 1839 and his 1st orat. at Leipzig in 1840, then studied with Baini in Rome, lived at Frankfort, Leipzig and Dresden, became cond. at Düsseldorf in 1847 and at Cologne in 1850, where he remained and founded the Cons.

Works incl. operas *Romilda, Die Katakomben, Der Deserteur*; orats. *Die Zerstörung Jerusalems* & *Saul*; cantatas *Nala und Damajanti, Prometheus, Rebecca* & others, incl. one from Byron's *Hebrew Melodies*; 3 syms., 4 ovts. (e.g. to Schiller's *Demetrius*) & other orch. works; 5 stg. 4tets, 5 pf. 4tets, 5 pf. trios; v. & co.

So.; So., 24 studies, *Modern Suite* & many other works for pf.; songs, partsongs, &c.

Hiller, Johann Adam (b. Wendisch-Ossig nr. Görlitz, 25. XII. 1728; d. Leipzig, 16. VI. 1804), Ger. comp. Studied with Homilius at Dresden after some hard early struggles due to his father's death, and also came under the infl. of Hasse and Graun. He entered Leipzig Univ. as a law student in 1751, but did not neglect m. After a brief term in the service of Count Brühl at Dresden, he returned to Leipzig and made his way as fist., singer, author and comp. as best he could, cond. the amateur concerts from 1763 and founding a singing-school in 1771. In 1781 the Concert spirituel he had estab. on the Paris model moved into the new Gewandhaus. Adapting Eng. & Fr. mus. stage pieces, he founded the Ger. *Singspiel*. He succeeded Doles as cantor at St. Thomas's.

Works incl. plays with m. *Der Teufel ist los* (2 parts, based on Coffey's *The Devil to pay*), *Lisuart und Dariolette*, *Lottchen am Hofe*, *Die Muse*, *Die Liebe auf dem Lande*, *Der Dorfbarbier*, *Die Jagd*, *Der Erntekranz*, *Der Krieg*, *Die Jubelhochzeit*, *Das Grab des Mufti* (later *Die beiden Geizigen*), *Das gerettete Troja*; hymn-tunes to Gellert's odes and songs, Passion cantata, 100th Psalm, a hymn-book; sacred and secular songs; inst. works, &c.

Hillern, Wilhelmine von (1836–1916), Ger. novelist. *See* **Jaques-Dalcroze** (*Fille au vautour*), **Wally** (Catalani).

Hilton, John (b. ?; d. Cambridge, III. 1608), Eng. orgst. & comp. App. orgst. to Trinity Coll., Cambridge, in 1594, after (?) being a singer & asst. orgst. at Lincoln cath. Comp. anthems, madrigals, &c.

Hilton, John (b. ? Cambridge, 1599; d. London, III. 1657), Eng. orgst. & comp., (?) son of prec. Took the Mus.B. degree at Cambridge in 1626 and 2 years later became orgst. at St. Margaret's church, Westminster.

Works incl. services and anthems; madrigals, *Ayres, or Fa La's* for 3 voices; Elegy on the death of Wm. Lawes for 3 voices & bass; collection of catches, rounds & canons *Catch that catch can*; songs, fantasies for viols, hymn 'Wilt Thou forgive that sin where I begun' from Donne's *Divine Poems*, &c.

Himmel, Friedrich Heinrich (b. Treuenbrietzen, Brandenburg, 20. XI. 1765; d. Berlin, 8. VI. 1814), Ger. clav. player & comp. Studied theology at Halle, but played the hpchd. so well that Frederick William II of Prussia had him educ. in m. by Naumann at Dresden. In 1794 he was app. court chapel master in Berlin in succession to Reichardt. He prod. operas abroad, in It., Rus., as well as Ger., but retired in 1808.

Works incl. operas *Il primo navigatore*, *Semiramide*, *Alessandro*, *Frohsinn und Schwärmerei*, *Vasco di Gama*, *Fanchon, das Leiermädchen*, *Die Sylphen* (after Gozzi), *Der Kobold*; orat. *Isacco*, funeral cantata for the King of Prussia, Te Deum for his successor; masses, motets, psalms, &c.; anthem 'Incline Thine ear'; cantata *La Danza*; pf. sos. and other works; songs, incl. 'An Alexis,' &c.

Hindemith, Paul (b. Hanau, 16. XI. 1895), Ger. comp. He was taught the v. as a child and entered the Hoch Cons. at Frankfort o/M., where he studied under Arnold Mendelssohn and Sekles. Later he played in the Frankfort Opera orch. and was leader there in 1915–23; and in 1921 he founded a stg. 4tet with the Turkish vst. Licco Amar (Amar-Hindemith 4tet) in which he played va. Works of his were heard at the Donaueschingen festival in 1921 and at the I.S.C.M. festival at Salzburg in 1922, and from that time he became known abroad. From 1927 he taught comp. at the Berlin Hochschule für Musik, but the Nazis proscribed his works as degenerate art. His opera, *Mathis der Maler*, was therefore prod. in Swi., at Zürich, in 1938. For some years after 1933 he was at Ankara in an official capacity to reorganize Turkish mus. educ. In 1939 he emigrated to U.S.A., where he teaches at Yale Univ.

Works incl. operas *Mörder, Hoffnung der Frauen* (Kokoschka), *Das Nusch-Nuschi* (for marionettes), *Sancta Susanna*, *Cardillac* (after E. T. A. Hoffmann), *Neues vom Tage*, *Mathis der Maler*; revue sketch *Hin und zurück*; ballets *Der Dämon*, *Nobilissima Visione*, *Cupid and Psyche*, *Mirror before Me* (after Mallarmé's *Hérodiade*); incid. m. for Christmas play on Immermann's *Tulifäntchen*; orat. *Das Unaufhörliche*, for solo voices, chor., boys' chor. & orch.; Sym. in E maj., Concert M. for stgs. & brass, *Philharmonic Concerto*, sym. from *Mathis der Maler*, Conc. for orch., *Philharmonic Dances*, Symph. Metamorphosis on a Theme by Weber; concs. for co. & for pf. (unpub.); for chamber orch.: Chamber M. Nos. 1–6 for var. insts., *Merry Sinfonietta* (unpub.), Conc. for org. and chamber orch., *Der Schwanendreher* for va. & small orch., *Trauermusik* for va. & stgs.; *Concert Music* for wind orch. & for pf., brass & hp.; 5 stg. 4tets; 2 stg. trios; var.

other chamber works; 16 sos. for var. insts.; some pieces for solo insts. & pf.; 3 sos., *1922* Suite, *Ludus tonalis*: 12 fugues with prelude and postlude and some other works for pf.; 7 waltzes for pf. duet (unpub.); So. for 2 pfs.; 2 org. sos.; 8 songs and song-cycle, *Das Marienleben* (Rilke); *Die junge Magd*, 6 songs for con. with fl., clar. & stg. 4tet; *Die Serenaden* for sop. with ob., va. & co.; sos. for fl., ob., Eng. hn., cl. bn., hn., tpt. trb., hp., &c.; 3 sets of partsongs, Chansons (Rilke) for unaccomp. chor.; several works for 'workaday music' (*see* **Gebrauchsmusik**).

Hingston, John (b. ?; d. ?, 1683). Eng. orgst., vst. & comp. Pupil of O. Gibbons. Keeper of the orgs. at court, in which he was assisted and later succeeded by Purcell. Musn. to Charles I and later to Cromwell, in whose household he was orgst. at Hampton Court and played on the org. removed from Magdalen Coll., Oxford. He taught Cromwell's daughters. At the Restor. in 1660 he became vst. in the royal band.

Hinton, Arthur (b. Beckenham, Kent, 20. XI. 1869; d. London, 11. VIII. 1941), Eng. comp. Educ. at Shrewsbury School and later studied m. at the R.A.M. in London, afterwards with Rheinberger at Munich. Married the pfst. Katharine Goodson (b. 1872).

Works incl. opera *Tamara*; children's operettas *The Disagreeable Princess* & *St. Elizabeth's Rose*; 2 syms., fantasy *The Triumph of Caesar*, suite *Endymion* for orch.; pf. Conc. in D min., *Chant des vagues* for co. & orch.; pf. 5tet, pf. Trio; So. and Suite for v. & pf.; *Summer Pilgrimage in the White Mountains*, 4 Bagatelles, &c. for pf., &c.

Hippolyte et Aricie (*Hippolytus and Aricia*). *See also* **Ippolito ed Aricia.**

Opera by Rameau (lib. by Simon Joseph de Pellegrin), prod. Paris, Opéra, 1. X. 1733.

Hirschler, Žiga (b. Trnovica, 21. III. 1894), Yslv. critic & comp. Studied at Zagreb Cons., became a critic and mus. correspondent there and ed. a mus. review.

Works incl. opera *A Night at Florence*; operettas; incid. m.; *Croatian Rhapsody*, 2 ovts. & suites for orch.; chamber m.; pf. works, &c.

Histoire du soldat (*The Soldier's Tale*), action for a narrator, actors and dancers by Stravinsky (lib. by Charles Ferdinand Ramuz), prod. Lausanne, 28. IX. 1918.

Hlahol. A chor. soc. formed in Prague in 1861, by Zvonař and others, for the cultivation of nat. Cz. m.

Hn. (abbr.) = Horn.

Hobday, Alfred C(harles). (b. Faversham, 19. IV. 1870; d. Tankerton, Kent, 23. II. 1942), Eng. va. player. Studied at the R.A.M. in London, became principal va. in the Phil. and London Sym. Orchs. and excelled in chamber m. Married the pfst. Ethel Sharpe (b. 1872) in 1895.

Hoboe (Ger.). An earlier Ger. spelling of Oboe.

Hoboy. *See* **Hautboy.**

Hobrecht, Jacob. *See* **Obrecht.**

Hochzeit des Gamacho, Die (*Gamacho's Wedding*), opera by Mendelssohn (lib. by Carl August Ludwig von Lichtenstein, based on Cervantes's *Don Quixote*), prod. Berlin, Schauspielhaus, 29. IV. 1827.

Hocket. A word similar to 'hiccup' and derived from the Fr. equiv. *hoquet*. It is used for a device in medieval voc. m., a kind of ornamental passage consisting of phrases broken up by rests, regardless of the words, which may be interrupted in the middle.

Høffding, Nils (Finn) (b. Copenhagen, 10. III. 1899), Dan. comp. Pupil of Jeppesen in Copenhagen and J. Marx in Vienna. App. prof. at the Royal Dan. Cons. in 1931. Author of several theoret. books.

Works incl. operas *The Emperor's New Clothes* (after Andersen), &c.; 4 syms. (1 with chor.); 3 stg. 4tets; duet for ob. & cl.; pf. pieces; songs, &c.

Hoffheimer. *See* Hofhaimer.

Hoffmann, Ernst Theodor Wilhelm (b. Königsberg, 24. I. 1776; d. Berlin, 25. VI. 1822), Ger. novelist & amateur comp. He changed his 3rd name to Amadeus in homage to Mozart. He is the hero of Offenbach's *Tales of Hoffmann*.

Comps incl. operas (mostly lost) *Der Renegat*, *Faustine*, *Die lustigen Musikanten* (Brentano), *Der Kanonikus von Mailand*, *Liebe und Eifersucht* (after Calderón), *Der Trank der Unsterblichkeit*, *Das Gespenst*, *Aurora*, *Undine* (after Fouqué), *Julius Sabinus* (unfinished); ballet *Harlekin* (unfinished); incid. m. to Goethe's *Scherz, List und Rache* & other plays; Requiem; 2 syms., &c.

For mus. works based on his writings *see* **Braunfels** (*Prinzessin Brambilla*), **Brautwahl** (Busoni), **Cardillac** (Hindemith), **Contes d'Hoffmann** (Offenbach), **Kreisleriana** (Schumann), **Nutcracker** (Tchaikovsky) **Offenbach** (*Goldsmith of Toledo*).

Hoffmann, Karel (b. Smíchov, Prague, 12. XII. 1872; d. Prague, 30. III. 1936), Cz. vst. Studied at the Prague Cons. and founded the Boh. 4tet with Suk, Nedbal and Berger in 1892. App. v. prof. at the Cons. in 1922.

Hoffmann, Leopold (b. Vienna, *c.* 1730; d. Vienna, 17. III. 1793), Aus. comp. Chapel master at St. Stephen's cath. in Vienna from 1772. He belongs to the Viennese school of symphonists.
Works incl. church m., syms., concs., chamber m., &c.

Hoffmeister, Karel (b. Liblice, 1868), Cz. teacher, writer on m. & comp. Studied in Prague, where, after some years at Ljubljana, he was app. prof. at the Cons. in 1898. He was pfst. of the Cz. Trio and wrote books on Smetana, Dvořák and pf. m.
Comps. incl. song-cycles *At Twilight, Unhappy Love, Legend of May* and others, &c.

Hofhaimer (or Hoffheimer), Paul (b. Radstadt, 25. I. 1459; d. Salzburg, ? 1537), Aus. orgst. & comp. In the service of the Emperor Maximilian at Innsbruck, *c.* 1480–1519, and was orgst. to the Archbishop of Salzburg from 1526 to his death.
Works incl. setting of odes by Horace *Harmoniae poeticae* for 4 voices, Ger. songs for 3 & 4 voices, org. m., &c.

Hofmann, Heinrich (Karl Johann) (b. Berlin, 13. I. 1842; d. Berlin, 16. VII. 1902), Ger. pfst. & comp. Was a chorister at the cath. in Berlin and studied at Kullak's acad. He taught the pf. and played much in public.
Works incl. operas *Cartouche, Der Matador, Armin, Aennchen von Tharau, Wilhelm von Oranien, Donna Diana* (Moreto); *Hungarian Suite, Fritdjof* sym. (after Tegnér), suite *Im Schlosshof*, scherzo *Irrlichter und Kobolde*, &c. for orch.; cantatas *Die schöne Melusine, Aschenbrödel, Editha, Prometheus, Waldfräulein, Festgesang*; several works for voices & orch.; co. Conc.; pf. 4tet, pf. Trio, stg. 6tet, Octet; pf. pieces; songs, duets, &c.

Hofmann, Josef (Casimir) (b. Podgorze nr. Cracow, 20. I. 1876), Pol.-Amer. pfst. & comp. Studied early with his elder sister and his father, the pfst. & cond. Casimir H., and made his 1st public appearance at the age of 6. At 9 he toured Eur. and in 1887 paid his 1st visit to U.S.A., where after further study and success in Eur. he settled in 1898 and became naturalized in 1926. His comps. appeared for a time under the pseud. of Michel Dvorsky.
Works incl. Sym. in E maj., symph. narrative *The Haunted Castle*; 5 pf. concs. & *Chromaticon*, for pf. & orch.; numerous pf. works; Nocturne for v. & pf.; *God's Hand* for voice & pf., &c.

Hofmannsthal, Hugo von (1874–1929), Aus. poet & dramatist. *See* **Ägyptische Helena** (R. Strauss), **Alkestis** (Wellesz), **Arabella** (R. Strauss), **Ariadne auf Naxos** (do.), **Bourgeois gentilhomme** (do.), **Elektra** (do.), **Everyman** (Sibelius), **Frau ohne Schatten** (R. Strauss), **Legend of Joseph** (do.), **Reuss** (*Tor und der Tod*), **Rosenkavalier** (R. Strauss), **Tcherepnin (A.)** (*Hochzeit der Sobeide*), **Unger (H.)** (*Tod und der Tor*), **Wellesz** (*Lied der Welt & Leben, Traum und Tod*).

Hogarth, George (b. Carfrae Mill nr. Oxon, Berwickshire, 1783; d. London, 12. II. 1870), Sco. critic & writer on m. Studied law in Edinburgh, but learnt co. and comp. as an amateur. Settled in London in 1830 and became critic to the *Morning Chronicle*. In 1836 his daughter Catherine married Dickens, who became ed. of the *Daily News* in 1846 and engaged H. as m. critic. He wrote several books, mainly chronicles of opera, festivals and concerts.

Hohl Flute. An 8-ft. org. stop similar to the Claribel, but having the mouth on the wider side of the square pipes.

Hohlflöte (Ger. = hollow flute). The name sometimes used for the Hohl Flute.

Hol. (abbr.) = Holland.

Hol, Richard (b. Amsterdam, 23. VII. 1825; d. Utrecht, 14. V. 1904), Dutch orgst., cond. & comp. Studied at Amsterdam and became cond. of a male-voice chor. soc. there in 1856. In 1862 he went to Utrecht as mus. dir. to the town, became cath. orgst. in 1869 and dir. of the m. school in 1875. He wrote a book on Sweelinck.
Works incl. operas *Floris V & Uit de branding*; masses & cantatas; orat. *David*, 4 syms., ovts. & other orch. works; chamber m.; songs, &c.

Holberg, Ludvig (1684–1754), Norw. dramatist and satirist. *See* **Gade** (suite), **Grieg** (do.), **Nielsen (C.)** (*Maskarade*), **Riisager** (*Erasmus Montanus*), **Schoeck** (*Don Ranudo*), **Weismann** (*Pfiffige Magd*).

Holbrooke, Joseph (or Josef) (b. Croydon, Surrey, 6. VII. 1878), Eng. comp. Studied at the R.A.M. in London, but was dismissed for playing a work of his own without warning at a public function. After a hard struggle as pfst. & cond. he came under the patronage of Lord Howard de Walden, who wrote the libs. for his dramatic trilogy. He engaged in much militant propaganda on behalf of the Brit. comps. of whom he approved, incl. himself.
Works incl. operas *Pierrot and Pierrette, The Snob, The Wizard, The Stranger* & the trilogy *The Cauldron of Annwen* (*The Children of Don, Dylan & Bronwen*); ballets *The Red Mask* (after Poe), *The Moth and the Flame, Coromanthe*, &c.; *Dramatic Chor*

Sym. & *The Bells* for chor. & orch. (both after Poe); symph. poems *The Raven, Ulalume, The Masque of the Red Death* (all after Poe), *The Viking, Ode to Victory* (Byron), *The Skeleton in Armour* (Longfellow), *Queen Mab* (Shakespeare), *Apollo and the Seaman*, with chor. (Herbert Trench); vars. for orch. on *Three Blind Mice, Auld Lang Syne* & *The Girl I left behind me*; pf. Conc. *The Song of Gwyn ap Nudd*, v. Conc.; 6 stg. 4tets (incl. *Pickwick Club* after Dickens), 3 trios, 4 4tets, 5 5tets, 4 6tets for var. insts., Sinfonietta for chamber orch. & other chamber m.; pf. pieces; songs, &c.

Holcombe, Henry (b. ? Salisbury, *c.* 1690; d. London, *c.* 1750), Eng. singer, hpchd. player & comp. Choirboy at Salisbury cath., sang as a boy on the stage in London and later taught hpchd. & singing there.

Works incl. solos for v.; 2 books of songs, &c.

Holcroft, Thomas (1745–1809), Eng. playwright. *See* **Busby** (*Tale of Mystery*).

Holden, John (b. ? Glasgow, ?; d. Glasgow, ?), Sco.18th-cent.scholar&comp. Pub. an *Essay towards a Rational System of M.* and a collection of church m.

Holden, Smollett (b. ?; d. Dublin, ?), Ir. 18th–19th-cent. m. dealer, pub. & comp. He kept a m. shop at Dublin and pub. 2 vols. of Ir. airs, also Welsh m., &c., and wrote military m.

Hölderlin, Johann Christian Friedrich (1770–1843), Ger. poet. *See* **Hauer** (pf. pieces & songs), **Schicksalslied** (Brahms), **Strauss** (R.) (3 hymns).

Hole, William (b. ?; d. London, ?), Eng. 16th–17th-cent. m. engraver. He engraved *Parthenia* for Dorothy Evans in 1611.

Hollander, Benno (b. Amsterdam, 8. VI. 1853; d. London, 27. XII. 1942), Dutch (anglicized) vst. & comp. Studied at the Paris Cons. with Massart, later comp. with Saint-Saëns. After a tour in Eur. he settled in London in 1876. He played va. in Auer's 4tet and led several important orchs., later estab. one of his own.

Works incl. opera *Mietje*; sym. *Roland*, symph. poem *Pompeii*, orch. pieces *Drame* and *Comédie*; 2 concs. & *Pastoral Fantasy* for v. & orch.; 2 stg. 4tets, 7tet for pf., stgs. & hns., pf. Trio, stg. Trio; 2 v. & pf. sos.; pf. So., &c.

Hollander, Christian Janszon (b. ?; d. ?, before 1570), Flem. singer & comp. App. choirmaster at St. Walburg's church at Oudenarde in 1549 and from 1559 was a singer in the Imp. Chapel in Vienna.

Works incl. many motets, sacred songs for several voices, secular Ger. songs, &c.

Holländer, Gustav (b. Leobschütz, Silesia, 15. II. 1855; d. Berlin, 4. XII. 1915), Ger. vst., teacher & comp. Studied with David at Leipzig and Joachim in Berlin and became 4tet player, orch. leader and prof. of v. at Cologne and Berlin.

Works incl. 4 v. concs., 1 for students, &c.

Holländer, Victor (b. Leobschütz, Silesia, 20. IV. 1866; d. Hollywood, Cal., 24. X. 1940), Ger. pfst. & comp., brother of prec. Pupil of Kullak in Berlin, where he taught and cond. after var. appts. at Hamburg, Budapest, Marienbad, U.S.A. and London. Later he emigrated to California.

Works incl. operas *San Lin* & *Trilby* (on G. du Maurier's novel), comic operas *Die Primanerliebe, Carmosinella, The Bey of Morocco, Der Sonnenvogel* & *Der Regimentspapa*; pantomime *Sumurun*; pf. m., &c.

Höller, Karl (b. Bamberg, 25. VII. 1907), Ger. comp. Studied at Munich under Josef Haas.

Works incl. orch. and solo concs., symph. fantasy on a theme by Frescobaldi, *Gregorianische Hymnen*; stg. 4tets, &c.

Hollins, Alfred (b. Hull, 11. IX. 1865; d. Edinburgh, 17. V. 1942), Eng. orgst. & comp. for his inst. Although blind, held var. orgst.'s appts. and toured widely in Australia, S. Africa and U.S.A.

Holmes, Alfred (b. London, 9. XI. 1837; d. Paris, 4. III. 1876), Eng. vst. & comp. With very little regular instruction he became a famous vst., playing duets with his brother Henry and later touring widely with him in Eur. He settled in Paris in 1864.

Works incl. opera *Inez de Castro*; syms. *Jeanne d'Arc, The Youth of Shakespeare, Robin Hood, The Siege of Paris, Charles XII* & *Romeo and Juliet* (after Shakespeare); ovts. *The Cid* (after Corneille) & *The Muses*.

Holmès (Holmes), Augusta (Mary Anne) (b. Paris, 16. XII. 1847; d. Paris, 28. I. 1903), Ir., naturalized Fr., pfst. & comp. Although her Ir. parents were against her taking up m., she played the pf. and sang as a child prodigy and began to comp. under the name of Hermann Zenta. She then studied with the orgst. Lambert at Versailles and had already written much when in 1875 she went to Franck for more solid study.

Works incl. operas *Héro et Léandre, La Montagne noire, Astarté, Lancelot du Lac*; chor. works *Les Argonautes* (on Homer's *Iliad*), psalm *In exitu*, ode *Ludus pro patria* & *Ode triomphale*; syms. on Ariosto's *Orlando furioso, Lutèce* & *Pologne*, symph. poem *Irlande*; song-cycle *Les Sept Ivresses*, &c.

Holmes, George (b. ?; d. Lincoln, 1721), Eng. orgst. & comp. At 1st orgst. to the Bishop of Durham, he was app. orgst. of Lincoln cath. in 1704. Wrote anthems, burial sentences for Lincoln cath., Ode for St. Cecilia's Day, catches, &c.

Holmes, Henry (b. London, 7. XI. 1839; d. San Francisco, 9. XII. 1905), Eng. vst. & comp., brother of Alfred H., whose career he largely shared. After parting with Alfred in Paris in 1865, he went to Den. & Swe. and later gave chamber concerts in London and was v. prof. at the R.A.M., but retired to California in 1894.

Works incl. 4 syms.; v. Conc., &c.

Holmes, John (b. ?; d. ? Winchester, ?), Eng. orgst. & comp. He was orgst. at Winchester cath. Wrote church m. and contrib. a madrigal to *The Triumphes of Oriana* in 1601.

Holofernes, opera by Rezniček (lib. by comp., based on Hebbel's drama *Judith*), prod. Berlin, Deutsches Opernhaus, 27. X. 1923.

Holst, Gustav (Theodore) (b. Cheltenham, 21. IX. 1874; d. London, 25. V. 1934), Eng. comp. of Swe. descent. The family had been in Eng. since 1807. His father was a m. teacher and his mother a pfst., and he was intended to follow their career; he also had early experience as orgst. and chor. and orch. cond. in a small way. In 1893 he was sent to the R.C.M. in London, but disliked the keyboard insts. and wished to take to comp., which he studied under Stanford. Suffering from neuritis, he took up the trombone instead of the pf., and on leaving played in the orch. of the Carl Rosa Opera Co. and later in the Sco. Orch. In 1903 he became m. master at a school in south London, in 1905 at St. Paul's Girls' School, where he remained to his death, and in 1907 was app. mus. dir. at Morley Coll. for Working Men and Women. From 1919 he taught comp. at the R.C.M. and in 1919–23 at Reading Coll.

Works incl. operas *The Idea, The Wandering Scholar, Sāvitri, The Perfect Fool, At the Boar's Head* (on Shakespeare's *Henry IV*); ballets *The Golden Goose* & *The Morning of the Year* with chor. & orch.; Chor. Hymns from the *Rig Veda* with orch., 2 Psalms for chor. stgs. & org., *The Hymn of Jesus* for chor. & orch., Festival Te Deum, *Ode to Death* (Whitman) for chor. & orch., Chor. Sym. (Keats) for sop., chor. & orch., Chor. Fantasy (Bridges) for chor., org., stgs., brass & percussion; 2 motets for unaccomp. chor., *Ave Maria* for fem. voices, partsongs & arrs. of folksongs for unaccomp. chor.; *A Somerset Rhapsody, Beni Mora* suite, *The Planets, Japanese Suite, Fugal Overture, Egdon Heath* (after Thomas Hardy) for orch.; *St. Paul's* suite for stgs.; *Fugal Concerto* for fl., ob. & stgs., Conc. for 2 vs. & orch.; 2 suites for military band; *A Moorside Suite* for brass band; 9 Hymns from the *Rig Veda* for voice & pf., 12 songs (Humbert Wolfe) for voice & pf., 4 songs for voice and v.; a few pf. pieces, &c.

Holst, Imogen (b. London, 12. IV. 1907), Eng. pfst. & comp., daughter of prec. Studied with her father and at the R.C.M. in London and became m. mistress at several schools, did much work for the Eng. Folk Dance Soc. and wrote a book on G. Holst.

Works incl. Ovt. for orch., pf. pieces, folksong arrs., &c.

Holstein, Franz (Friedrich) **von** (b. Brunswick, 16. II. 1826; d. Leipzig, 22. V. 1878), Ger. comp. Although trained for the army, he studied m. under Griepenkerl. When he had written 2 operas, Moritz Hauptmann persuaded him in 1852 to take entirely to m. and gave him further instruction.

Works incl. operas *Zwei Nächte in Venedig, Waverley* (after Scott), *Der Haideschacht, Der Erbe von Morley, Die Hochländer* & *Marino Faliero* (after Byron); ovts. *Loreley* & *Frau Aventiure*; voc. scene from Schiller's *Braut von Messina* & another, *Beatrice*.

Holtei, Karl Eduard von (1798–1880), Ger. actor & dramatist. *See* **Rietz (J.)** (*Lorbeerbaum und Bettelstab*).

Hölty, Ludwig (Heinrich Christoph) (1748–76), Ger. poet. *See* **Tomašek** (*Elegie auf eine Rose*).

6 songs by Brahms, 21 by Schubert.

Holz (Ger. = wood). Sometimes used as an abbr. for woodwind insts.

Holz, Carl (b. Vienna, 1798; d. Vienna, 9. XI. 1858), Aus. vst. Lived in Vienna, where he became a member of Schuppanzigh's 4tet in 1824.

Holzbauer, Ignaz (b. Vienna, 1711; d. Mannheim, 7. IV. 1783), Aus. comp. Learnt m. as a choir-boy at St. Stephen's cath. in Vienna, but was intended for the law. He studied by himself, then briefly in It., and after var. engagements he was app. chapel master by the Elector Palatine at Mannheim. With Cannabich as leader he made the orch. he cond. famous. He prod. operas at Turin and Milan, but remained at Mannheim even when the court moved to Munich. Member of the

Mannheim school of early symphonists.

Works incl. operas *Il figlio delle selve, Nitteti, Alessandro nell' Indie, Günther von Schwarzburg,* &c.; masses & other church m.; 65 syms., &c.

Holzbläser (Ger. lit. woodblowers) = Woodwind insts.

Holzblasinstrumente (Ger.) = Woodwind insts.

Holztrompete (Ger. = wooden tpt.). An inst. designed for use in the 3rd act of Wagner's *Tristan,* actually a revival of the Cornett, but provided with a valve.

Homer (?–? B.C.), Gr. poet. *See* **Bruch** (*Achilles & Odysseus*), **Gnecchi** (*Cassandra*), **Gundry** (*Return of Odysseus* & songs), **Heger** (*Bettler Namenlos*), **Herzogenberg** (*Odysseus* sym.), **Holmes** (*Argonautes*), **Homerische Welt** (Bungert), **Morning Heroes** (Bliss).

Homer, Sidney (b. Boston, 9. XII. 1864), Amer. comp. Studied with Chadwick at Boston and Rheinberger at Munich. Became lecturer at Boston until 1900 and then moved to N.Y. Married the con. Louise Beatty (b. 1871) in 1895. Wrote many popular songs.

Homerische Welt (*Homeric World*), operatic trilogy by Bungert (lib. by comp., based on Homer's *Iliad* and *Odyssey*).

I. *Kirke* (*Circe*), prod. Dresden, 29. I. 1898.

II. *Nausikaa* (*Nausicaa*), prod. Dresden, 20. III. 1901.

III. *Odysseus' Heimkehr* (*The Return of Ulysses*), prod. Dresden, 12. XII. 1896.

B.'s attempt to create a Wagnerian cycle, but based, like Berlioz's *Troyens* and Taneiev's *Oresteia,* on classical Gr. subjects.

Homilius, Gottfried August (b. Rosenthal, Saxony, 2. II. 1714; d. Dresden, 5. VI. 1785), Ger. comp. & orgst. Pupil of Bach at Leipzig, app. orgst. of the church of Our Lady, Dresden, 1742, and mus. dir. of the 3 principal churches there, 1755.

Works incl. 32 motets, a Passion cantata, Christmas orat., several settings of the Passions, a book of 167 hymns; 6 Ger. arias; org. m., &c.

Homme armé, L' (Fr. = the armed man). The name of an old Fr. secular song the tune of which was often used by comps. of the 15th & 16th cents. as *cantus firmus* for their masses, which were then designated by that name.

Homme et son désir, L' (*Man and his Desire*), ballet by Milhaud (words, 'plastic poem,' by Paul Claudel, chgph. by Jean Borlin), prod. Paris, Théâtre des Champs-Élysées, 6. VI. 1921.

Homophonic (from Gr., lit. alike-sounding). Strictly speaking H. m. is single, unaccomp. melody, sung or played in unison (which is properly called Monophonic), but the term is generally used as the opposite of 'polyphonic' and indicates m. that does not move in several simultaneous melodic parts, but has a single tune accomp. by chords either in blocks or broken up into some kind of figuration.

Honauer, Leonzi (b. ?; d. ?), Ger. 18th-cent. comp. Settled in Paris c. 1760 and wrote chamber m., hpchd. sos. with and without v., &c.

Hond, Cornelis de. *See* **Canis.**

Hondt, Gheerkin (Gerard) de (b. ?; d. ?), Dutch 16th-cent. comp. Choirmaster at Hertogenbosch. Wrote motets, &c.

Honegger, Arthur (b. Le Havre, 10. III. 1892), Swi. comp. Was 1st taught by the orgst. R. C. Martin at his birthplace, then sent to the Zürich Cons., 1909–11, and, his parents still living at Le Havre, studied at the Paris Cons. 1911–3. After that he became a private pupil of Widor and d'Indy and in 1914 began to comp. Though always in touch with Swi., he belongs mainly to the Fr. school, and he joined the group which c. 1920 became known as 'Les Six.' He married the comp. Andrée Vaurabourg, who was also attached to it, though not as a member.

Works incl. operas *L'Aiglon* (with Ibert) & *Antigone* (after Sophocles), biblical operas *Le Roi David* & *Judith,* scenic work *Nicolas de Flue,* operettas, *Les Aventures du Roi Pausole* & *Le Petit Cardinal* (with Ibert); mimed sym. *Horace victorieux,* melodrama *Amphion* (Paul Valéry), ballet-pantomime *Sémiramis,* ballets *La Fée dans la montagne, Vérité? Mensonge?, Les Mariés de la Tour Eiffel* (with others of 'Les Six'), *Skating-Rink, Sous-marine*; much m. for films; incid. m. for Max Jacob's *La Mort de Sainte Alméenne,* Gide's *Saül,* Shakespeare's *Tempest,* Racine's *Phèdre,* Rolland's *Danton* & *Le 14 Juillet,* Claudel's *Jeanne d'Arc au bûcher* & *Le Soulier de satin,* Giraudoux's *Sodome et Gomorrhe* & other plays; orat. *Danse des morts* (on Holbein's *Dance of Death,* words by Claudel), cantata *Libération de Paris* (1944); Sym., *Le Chant de Nigamon, Pastorale d'été, Chant de joie,* 3 symph. mvts. *Pacific 231, Rugby* & No. 3; Sym. for stgs.; co. Conc., Concertino for pf. & orch.; stg. 4tet; 2 v. & pf. sos., va. & pf. So., co. &

pf. So., sonatinas for 2 vs. & for cl. & pf.; Partita for 2 pfs.; *Chanson de Ronsard* & *3 Chansons* for voice, fl. & stg. 4tet; 7 works for pf.; 2 org. pieces; *Danse de la chèvre* for fl.; *c.* 25 songs, &c.

Hook, James (b. Norwich, 3. VI. 1746; d. Boulogne, 1827), Eng. orgst. & comp. Studied under Garland, the Norwich cath. orgst. He made a success in London in early manhood and in 1769 became orgst. and comp. to Marylebone Gardens, and acted in the same posts at Vauxhall in 1774–1820. He married Miss Madden *c.* 1770 and wrote m. for her play, *The Double Disguise*, in 1784. In 1795 he did the same for his son James's *Jack of Newbury* and in 1797 for *Diamond cut Diamond* by his second son Theodore Edward, for whose plays he continued to write. Hundreds of his songs became very popular at the pleasure gardens.

Works incl. mus. plays *Love and Innocence*, *Country Courtship*, *The Lady of the Manor*, *Too civil by half*, *The Triumph of Beauty*, *The Peruvian*, *The Soldier's Return*, *The Siege of St. Quintin*, Hannah Moore's *The Search after Happiness*, &c.; odes, cantatas, catches; a vast number of songs, &c.

Hook, James (1772–1828), Eng. divine & author, son of prec. *See* **Hook** (J. i) (*Jack of Newbury*).

Hook, Theodore (Edward) (1788–1841), Eng. novelist, playwright & wit, brother of prec. *See* **Hook** (J. i) (*Diamond cut Diamond*, &c.).

Hooper, Edmund (b. Halberton, Devon, *c.* 1553; d. London, 14. VII. 1621), Eng. orgst. & comp. After being (?) a chorister at Exeter cath. he went to London and joined the Westminster Abbey choir, becoming a Gentleman of the Chapel Royal in 1604 and orgst. of the Abbey in 1606. He contrib. harmonizations of hymn-tunes to East's and Ravenscroft's Psalters, also 2 voc. pieces to Leighton's *Teares or Lamentacions* and 1 to Myriell's *Tristitiae remedium*.

Works incl. services & anthems; secular m. for several voices; virginal m., &c.

Hopak. *See* **Gopak.**

Hope, Anthony (A. Hope Hawkins) (1863–1933), Eng. novelist & playwright. *See* **German** (*Nell Gwynn*).

Hopkins, Edward John (b. London, 30. VI. 1818; d. London, 4. II. 1901), Eng. orgst. & comp. Learnt m. as a chorister in the Chapel Royal and after var. appts. became orgst. of the Temple church in 1843, remaining for 55 years. He received the degree of Mus.D. from the Archbp. of Canterbury.

Works incl. services, anthems, chants, hymns; voc. duets and trios, &c.

Hopkins, Gerard Manley (1844–89), Eng. poet *See* **Barber** (songs), **Tippett** (*Windhover*), **Wellesz** (*Leaden Echo and Golden Echo*).

Hopkinson, Francis (b. Philadelphia, 21. IX. 1737; d. Philadelphia, 9. V. 1791), Amer. lawyer, politician & amateur comp. He made several useful mechanical inventions connected with m. and wrote a number of songs, incl. the 1st Amer. secular song, 'My days have been so wondrous free'; also the 'oratorial entertainment' *The Temple of Minerva*.

Hopser. *See* **Galop.**

Hoquegan. *See* **Okeghem.**

Horace (Quintus Horatius Flaccus) (65–8 B.C.) Rom. poet. *See* **Moser** (R.) (odes), **Parry** (H.) (*Persicos odi*), **Philidor** (8) (*Carmensaeculare*), **Thompson** (R.) (odes), **Tritonius** (do.).

Horák, Antonín. *See* **At the Old Bleaching-Ground.**

Horizontal. Ctptal as distinct from harmonic m. is said to be written in a H. manner, the harmony being prod. by the coincidence of a network of melodic lines which the eye follows horizontally in a score, not, as in the case of blocks of chords, vertically.

Horn. A brass wind inst. with its tube bent in a circular form. In its early stages it could prod. only the natural harmonics and was used mainly for hunting fanfares. When comps. began to write for it they could use only those notes, usually in the key of F, in which it was pitched as a rule; but the invention of a series of crooks which could be inserted the length of the tube could be altered and the inst. played in a variety of keys. Some extra notes, of rather uncertain quality, could also be obtained by inserting the hand into the bell. It was only by the introd. of valves about the 1830s that the full chromatic scale could be played on a single inst. The compass is *c.* 3½ 8ves from (on the F hn.) B♮ below the stave in the bass clef.—Also an 8-ft. reed org. stop of powerful tone.

Horn, Charles Edward (b. London, 21. VI. 1786; d. Boston, Mass., 21. X. 1849), Eng. ten.-bar. singer & comp. of Ger. descent. He studied under his father, Karl Friedrich H. and had singing lessons from Rauzzini at Bath in 1808, making his 1st stage appearance in London in 1809. He then began to comp. theatrical pieces, starting with *The Magic Bride*. in 1810. In 1823 he visited Dublin and brought Balfe back with him as a pupil. Having been mus. dir. at the Olympic Theatre in 1831–2, he went to U.S.A. in 1833, became a m. teacher and pub. at Boston, where after a brief return to Eng. he settled for good in 1847, becoming cond. of the Handel and Haydn Soc.

Works incl. stage pieces *Lalla Rookh* (after Moore), *The Beehive, Rich and Poor, Peveril of the Peak* (after Scott), *Honest Frauds* and many others, some with Blewitt, Braham, T. Cooke or Reeve; ovt. to Thomas Moore's *M.P., or The Blue Stocking*; songs in Shakespeare's *Merry Wives of Windsor* (with Webbe, jun. & Parry); orats. *The Remission of Sin* (later *Satan*) & *Daniel's Prediction*; glees, canzonets & many songs, incl. 'Cherry ripe' (Herrick), &c.

Horn Diapason. An 8-ft. open Diapason org. stop.

Horn, Karl Friedrich (b. Nordhausen, Saxony, 1762; d. Windsor, 5. VIII. 1830), Ger. pfst., orgst. & comp., father of C. E. H. He studied m. in his home-town and went to London in 1782, (?) as a valet, where he was patronized by the Saxon ambassador, Count Brühl. He became a fashionable teacher and m. master to Queen Charlotte and her daughters until 1811. In 1810 he pub. with S. Wesley the 1st Eng. ed. of Bach's *Well-tempered Clavier*. In 1824 he became orgst. at St. George's Chapel, Windsor, in succession to William Sexton.

Works incl. sos. for pf. with & without fl. or v. accomp.; themes with vars., *Military Divertimentos*, for pf., &c.

Horn Signal, Symphony with the. The nickname of a Sym. by Haydn, No. 31, in D maj., comp. in 1765.

Hornbostel, Erich von (b. Vienna, 25. II. 1877; d. Cambridge, 28. XI. 1935), Aus. mcolst. Studied physics and philosophy at Vienna and Heidelberg, and in 1906 became head of the gramophone archives in Vienna for the recording of the m. of primitive peoples, on which he wrote several learned works. In 1923 he went to Berlin, in 1933 to N.Y. and the following year to London and Cambridge.

Horneman, Christian Emil (b. Copenhagen, 17. XII. 1841; d. Copenhagen, 8. VI. 1906), Dan. comp. Studied with his father and at the Leipzig Cons. On his return to Copenhagen he founded a concert soc. and in 1880 a m. school.

Works incl. opera *Aladdin* (Oehlenschläger); ovt. *A Hero's Life*; pf. pieces; songs, &c.

Hornpipe. An Eng. sailors' dance, so called because it was at first accomp. on a pipe of the same name, made from an animal's horn. It had not always nautical assocns. and up to the time of Handel, who has such an ex. in one of his Concerti grossi, it was in 3–2 time. The later form is in 2–4.

Horsley, Charles Edward (b. London, 16. XII. 1822; d. New York, 28. II. 1876), Eng. pfst., orgst. & comp. Studied under his father, William H., and Moscheles, later with Hauptmann at Cassel and Mendelssohn at Leipzig. In 1845 he returned to London and became orgst. at St. John's church, Notting Hill, comp. several works for provincial festivals, &c. In 1862 he went to Austral. and in the early 1870s to U.S.A.

Works incl. orats. *David, Joseph* & *Gideon*; setting of Milton's *Comus*; ode *Euterpe* for the opening of Melbourne Town Hall; pf. Trio, &c.

Horsley, William (b. London, 15. XI. 1774; d. London, 12. VI. 1858), Eng. orgst. & comp., father of prec. Studied m. privately, but had some advice from Callcott. He became orgst. of Ely Chapel, Holborn, in 1794, assisted Callcott as orgst. at the Asylum for Female Orphans and succeeded him in 1802. Later he held several other appts. He was one of the founders of the Phil. Soc. in 1813 and his family became very friendly with Mendelssohn.

Works incl. anthem *When Israel came out of Egypt*, hymn & psalm tunes; 3 syms.; many glees, &c.

Hostinský, Otakar (b. Martinov, 2. I. 1847; d. Prague, 19. I. 1910), Cz. critic & libst. Studied at Prague Univ. and became prof. of aesthetics there. Critic to several newspapers, author of books on Cz. & other m. and libst. of Fibich's *Bride of Messina* & Rozkošný's *Popelka*.

Hoteterre. Fr. family of wind inst. players:

1. Jean H. (b. ?; d. ?, 1678).
2. Nicolas H. (b. ?; d. Paris, 1694), son of prec.
3. Martin (b. ?; d. Paris, 1712), brother of prec.
4. Louis H. (b. Paris, ?; d. Paris, 1719 or 1720), son of 2.
5. Nicolas (Colin) H. (b. Paris, ?; d. 14. XII. 1727), brother of prec.
6. Jacques Martin H. (b. ? Paris, ?; d. Paris, c. 1761), son of 3.

Hothby, John (b. ?; d. ?, 6. XI. 1487), Eng. Carmelite, mus. scholar, comp. & doctor of theol. Graduated at Oxford and lectured there in 1435. Travelled (?) in Spa., Fr. & Ger., settled *c.* 1440 (?) at Florence and also (?) lived at Ferrara. He was called Giovanni Ottobi in It. and spent *c.* 1468–86 at Lucca. He taught there, but was recalled to Eng. by Henry VII. Wrote a number of theoret. treatises and comp. church m.

Housman, A(lfred). E(dward). (1859–1936), Eng. poet & Lat. scholar. Poems from *A Shropshire Lad* (S.L.) and *Last Poems* (L.P.) set to m.:

Barber, Samuel, S.L. LIV.
Bax, L.P. XXIII, S.L. XIII, LII.
Butterworth, S.L. II, VI, XIII, XV, XX, XXI, XXIII, XXV, XXVII, XLIX, LIV.
Cripps, A. Redgrave, S.L. V, XIII, XV, XVI, XXII, XXIII, XXVII, XXIX, XXXV, XL, XLIX, LII, LIV, LVII.
Douglas, Keith, L.P. XI.
Foss, S.L. XXXIV.
Gardiner, S.L. III, XIII.
Gibbs, Armstrong, S.L. XIII.
Glanville-Hicks, 6 songs.
Gurney, S.L. II, IV, VII, X, XIII, XVI, XVII, XXIII, XXVI, XXVII, XXIX, XXXV, XXXIX, XL, LII, LIV.
Hamilton, Janet, S.L. XXI, XXXIX, LIV.
Herbert, Muriel, S.L. II.
Ireland, X. XVII, XXII, XXIX, XXXIII, XXXIX, LI, LVII.
Johnson, Ora Agatha, S.L. XIII.
Lambert, Frank, S.L. XXII.
Ley, Henry G. S.L. XXXVI, LII.
Lutyens, Elisabeth, *The Deserter*.
Manson, Willie B., S.L. II, XLIX, LVIII.
Milvain, Hilda, S.L. XXIX.
Moeran, S.L. II, VII, VIII, XXIII, XXIV, XXXIX, LII.
Orr, C. W., S.L. II, V, VI, VII, VIII, XI, XII, XIII, XVIII, XX, XXIII, XXV, XXVI, XXVII, XXIX, XXXIX, XL, XLVII, LIV, LV, LIX, LXI.
Peele, Graham, S.L. II, IV, VI, XXI, XXII, XXIV.
Priestley-Smith, Hugh, S.L. XXXII, XXXVI, XL, XLIX.
Procter-Gregg, Humphrey, S.L. II, XL.
Rose, Edwin, C., S.L. XL.
Somervell, S.L. II, XIII, XIV, XXI, XXII, XXIII, XXXV, XXXVI, XL, XLIX.
Stewart, D. M., L.P. Pref., XXIII, XXVII, XXXIV.
Swain, S.L. XX, XXI, XXXVI, XXXIX, LII.
Taylor, E. Kendal, S.L. XXXVI.
Vaughan Williams, L.P. Pref., XXIII, XXVI, XXVII, LXI; S.L. XVIII, XXI, XXVI, XXVII, XXXI, XXXII, L, LIV.
Young, Dalhousie, S.L. XXI.

Housman, Lawrence (1865–1944), Eng. author. *See* **Lehmann (Liza)** (*Sergeant Brue*).

Hove, Joachim van den (b. Antwerp, ?; d. ?), Flem. 16th–17th-cent. lutenist & comp. Pub. a book of songs for 2 voices & lute, 1 of songs & dances arr. for lute and 1 of preludes for lute & viol.

Hoven. *See* **Vesque von Püttlingen.**

Howard, Robert (1626–98), Eng. playwright. *See* **Indian Queen (Purcell).**

Howard, Samuel (b. ?, 1710; d. London, 13. VII. 1782), Eng. orgst. & comp. Pupil of Croft at the Chapel Royal and later of Pepusch. App. orgst. at the churches of St. Clement Danes & St. Bride. Mus.D. Cambridge in 1769. He assisted Boyce in compiling his *Cathedral Music*.

Works incl. anthems & other church m.; pantomimes *The Amorous Goddess, or Harlequin Married* & *Robin Goodfellow, or The Rival Sisters*; cantatas; songs, incl. vols. *The British Orpheus*, &c.

Howell, Dorothy (b. Birmingham, 25. II. 1898), Eng. pfst. & comp. Studied comp. under McEwen and pf. under Tobias Matthay at the R.A.M. in London.

Works incl. ballet *Koong Shee*; symph. poem *Lamia* (after Keats), ovt. *The Rock*; pf. Conc.; chamber m.; pf. m., &c.

Howells, Herbert (b. Lydney, Glos. 17. X. 1892), Eng. comp. Pupil of Herbert Brewer at Gloucester cath. and later under Stanford at the R.C.M. in London, where he became prof. of comp. later, having been 1st sub-orgst. at Salisbury cath. and living a retired life in 1917–20 owing to poor health. Mus.Dir. at St. Paul's Girls' School from 1937, in succession to Holst. Mus.D., Oxford, 1937.

Works incl. *Sine Nomine* for 2 voices, org. & orch., *A Kent Yeoman's Song* & Requiem for solo voices, chor. & orch., Mass in the Dorian mode; *Procession, Pastoral Rhapsody, Paradise Rondel, Merry-Eye, Puck's Minuet, King's Herald* for orch.; Lady Audrey's Suite for stg. orch.; *Pageantry* for brass band; 2 pf. concs.; song cycle *In Green Ways* with orch.; Fantasy stg. 4tet, stg. 4tet *In Gloucestershire*, clar. 5tet; v. & pf. So. in E min., org. So.; *Lambert's Clavichord* for clavchd.; pf. pieces; songs, &c.

Howes, Frank (b. Oxford, 2. IV. 1891), Eng. m. critic. Educ. at St. John's Coll., Oxford. He joined *The Times* as asst. m. critic in 1925, became lecturer at the R.C.M. in 1938 and succeeded Colles in 1943 as chief *Times* critic. His books incl. a life of Byrd, studies of Vaughan Williams and Walton, of mus. appreciation, psychology, opera, the orch., &c.

Hp. (abbr.) = Harp.

Hpchd. (abbr.) = Harpsichord.

Hpchdst. (abbr.) = Harpsichordist.

Hpst. (abbr.) = Harpist.

Hubay, Jenö (orig. Eugen Huber) (b. Budapest, 14. IX. 1858; d. Budapest, 12. III. 1937), Hung. vst. & comp. Pupil of his father Karl Huber, he appeared as a prodigy at the age of 11, but later went to study with Joachim in Berlin. He travelled much, ed. and completed some of Vieuxtemps's works and became v. prof. at the Brussels Cons. in 1881 and at the Budapest Cons. in 1886.

Works incl. operas *Alienor*, *A Cremonai Hegedüs* (after Coppée's *Luthier de Crémone*), *A Falu Rossza*, *Karenina Anna* (after Tolstoy), *Az Âlarc*, &c.; 4 v. concs.; *Sonate romantique* for v. & pf.; many v. pieces, studies, &c.

Hubeau, Jean (b. ?, 1918), Fr. pfst. & comp. Gained a prize for pf. playing & comp. before he was app. dir. of the Versailles Cons. in 1942.

Works incl. v. Conc.; So. for tpt. & pf.; songs to words by Villon, &c.

Huber, Ferdinand (Fürchtegott) (b. St. Gall, 31. X. 1791; d. St. Gall, 9. I. 1863), Swi. tptr., orgst., cond. & comp. Studied m. at Stuttgart and held var. appts. as orgst., cond. & teacher at Berne and St. Gall. Studied Swi. folk m. and adapted some of it as partsongs.

Works incl. inst. works; pf. m.; songs, partsongs, &c.

Huber, Hans (b. Eppenberg, Solothurn, 28. VI. 1852; d. Locarno, 25. XII. 1921), Swi. comp. After attending an eccles. seminary at Solothurn, he studied m. under Carl Munzinger there and later at the Leipzig Cons. After teaching in Alsace, he settled at Basle in 1877. In 1889 he became prof. at the Cons. there and succeeded Selmar Bagge as its dir. in 1896, retiring in 1918.

Works incl. operas *Weltfrühling*, *Kudrun*, *Simplicius*, *Die schöne Bellinde*, *Frutta di mare*, *Der gläserne Berg* (unfinished); orat. *Mors et Vita* (unfinished); masses, cantatas, &c.; 8 syms. (No. 2 on pictures by Böcklin) & other orch. works *Sommernächte*, Serenade, *Carneval* & *Römischer Carneval*; pf. Conc., v. Conc.; much chamber m.; pf. m.; songs, incl. Hafiz cycle, &c.

Hubert, Anton. *See* **Uberti, Antonio.**

Hubert, Nikolai Albertovitch (b. St. Petersburg, 9. III. 1840; d. Moscow, 8. X. 1888), Rus. mus. scholar. Fellow-pupil with Tchaikovsky at the St. Petersburg Cons.; became prof. of theory at the Moscow Cons. and succeeded N. Rubinstein as its head.

Hucbald (b. ?, c. 840; d. ? Saint-Amand, 930), Fr. monk & musn. Lived at the monastery of Saint-Amand. Wrote the treatise *De harmonica institutione*, mainly on the Gamut and the Modes.

Hudson, George (b., ?; d. ?), Eng. 17th-cent. vst. & comp. Worked in London. Took part, with Coleman, sen., Cooke, H. Lawes and Locke, in providing m. for Davenant's *Siege of Rhodes* (entertainment at Rutland House) in 1656; member of the King's Band from 1661 and comp. to the king.

Hudson, W(illiam). H(enry). (1841–1922), S. Amer.-Brit. naturalist, traveller & author. *See* **Tippett** (*Boyhood's End*).

Hüe, Georges (Adolphe) (b. Versailles, 6. V. 1858), Fr. comp. Studied at the Paris Cons., where he obtained the Prix de Rome in 1879. Member of the Académie des Beaux-Arts in 1922 in succession to Saint-Saëns.

Works incl. operas *Les Pantins*, *Le Roi de Paris*, *Le Miracle*, *Titania* (after Shakespeare), *Dans l'ombre de la cathédrale*, *Riquet à la Houppe* (after Perrault); ballets *Siang Sin* & *Nimba*, pantomime *Cœur brisé*; incid. m. to Rostand's *Les Romanesques*, Kalidasa's *Sakuntala*, &c.; sym. *Rübezahl*, symph. legend & other orch. works; songs, &c.

Hueffer, Francis (orig. Franz) (b. Münster, 22. V. 1843; d. London, 19. I. 1889), Ger. (anglicized) m. critic. Studied in Ger., Paris and London, where he settled, became m. critic to several periodicals and wrote and lectured on the troubadours, Wagner and other subjects. Wrote libs. for Mackenzie and Cowen.

Hugh the Drover, or Love in the Stocks, opera by Vaughan Williams (lib. by Harold Child), prod. London, R.C.M., 4. VII. 1924.

Hughes, Anselm, Dom (b. London, 1889), Eng. mus. scholar & Angl. Benedictine. Prior of Nashdom Abbey. Part-ed. of the pub. of the Old Hall MS. of 15th-cent. Eng. church m., preserved at Ware.

Hughes, Gervase (b. Birmingham, 1. IX. 1905), Eng. comp. Studied under Frank Shera, Ernest Walker, W. H. Harris, Thomas Wood and Armstrong Gibbs, and took the B.Mus. at Oxford in 1927. In 1926 he joined the mus. staff of the B.N.O.C. and later cond. at var. theatres. In 1933 he left the mus. profession, but after the 2nd world war took to comp. again.

Works incl. opera *Imogen's Choice*, operettas *Castle Creevy* & *Venetian Fantasy*; Sym. in F min., *Ovt. for a Mus. Comedy* for orch.; inst. pieces; pf. m.; songs to words by Herrick, R. L. Stevenson & Rupert Brooke, &c.

Hughes, Herbert (b. Belfast, 16. III. 1882; d. Brighton, 1. V. 1937), Ir.

critic & comp. Studied at the R.C.M. in London, collected Ir. folksongs and was for many years attached as m. critic to the *Daily Telegraph.* Ed. *Irish Country Songs* and comp. *Rhymes, Parodies,* songs to poems by Padraic Colum, &c.

Hughes, John (1677–1720), Eng. playwright. *See* **Acis and Galatea** (Handel), **Pepusch** (*Alexis,* &c.).

Hugo, Victor (1802–85), Fr. poet, novelist & dramatist. *See* **Armourer of Nantes** (Balfe), **Blaramberg** (*Mary of Burgundy*), **Bottesini** (*Marion Delorme*), **Ce qu'on entend . . .** (Liszt), **Cui** (*Angelo*), **Dargomizhsky** (*Esmeralda: Notre-Dame de Paris*), **Delibes** (*Roi s'amuse*), **Dieren (van)** (songs), **Djinns** (Franck), **Duvernoy** (*Hernani* ovt.), **Enna** (*Komedianter*), **Ernani** (Verdi), **Esmeralda** (Campana, Dargomizhsky & G. Thomas), **Fauré** (*Djinns*), **Franck (C.)** (songs), **Fry** (*Notre-Dame de P.*), **Gioconda** (Ponchielli), **Giuramento** (Mercadante), **Guiraud** (*Chasse fantastique*), **Kashperov** (*Mary Tudor*), **Lange (D. de)** (*Hernani*), **Lucrezia Borgia** (Donizetti), **Maillart** (*Gastibelza*), **Maria Tudor** (Gomes), **Mazeppa** (Liszt), **Mazzucato (A.)** (*Esmeralda*), **Monpou** (songs), **Niedermeyer** (songs), **Nielsen (L.)** (*Lola*), **Pedrell (F.)** (*Quasimodo*), **Pedrollo** (*L'uomo che ride*), **Pedrotti** (*Marion Delorme*), **Ponchielli** (do.), **Poniatowski** (*Ruy Blas* & *Esmeralda*), **Prévost** (*Esmeralda*), **Rigoletto** (Verdi), **Ruy Blas** (Glover, Marchetti & Mendelssohn), **Schmidt (F.)** (*Notre-Dame*), **Simon (A.)** (*Esmeralda* & *Fishers*), **Strunz** (*Ruy Blas*), **Wagner-Régeny** (*Mary Tudor*), **White (M. V.)** (songs).

Huguenots, Les, opera by Meyerbeer (lib. by Scribe & Émile Deschamps), prod. Paris, Opéra, 29. II. 1836.

Huizar, Candelario (b. Jérez, 2. II. 1888), Mex. comp.

Works incl. 3 syms. on native tunes, &c.

Hulda, opera by C. Franck (lib. by Charles Grandmougin, based on a play by Bjørnson), not perf. in F.'s lifetime; prod. Monte Carlo, 8. III. 1894.

Hullah, John (Pyke) (b. Worcester, 27. VI. 1812; d. London, 21. II. 1884), Eng. cond., teacher & comp. Had m. lessons from Wm. Horsley in London and studied singing at the R.A.M. In 1836 he became known as the comp. of Dickens's opera, *The Village Coquettes.* After a stay in Paris he taught singing in London, esp. at a school opened at Exeter Hall in 1841 for the instruction of schoolmasters. In 1847 his friends opened St. Martin's Hall for him, and he gave concerts there until 1860, when the hall was burnt down. Later he held a number of mus. appts. and wrote several books, mainly on singing and voc. m.

Works incl. operas *The Village Coquettes, The Outpost* & *The Barbers of Bassora*; numerous songs, &c.

Hullebroeck, Emiel (b. Ghent, 20. II. 1878), Belg. pfst., singer & comp. A promoter of community singing in Flem. & Dutch, and comp. of a large number of Flem. songs that have become very popular.

Works incl. opera *Het Meisje van Zaventem*; orat. *Kunstvisionen*; cantatas; inst. m., &c.

Hüllmandel, Nikolaus Joseph (b. Strasburg, 1751; d. London, 19. XII. 1823), Alsat. hpchdst., pfst. & comp. Pupil of C. P. E. Bach. He appeared in London in 1771 and settled there in 1790 after a visit to It. and residence in Paris. Wrote a treatise on pf. playing.

Works incl. numerous sos. for hpchd. and later for pf., many with v. accomp., &c.

Hume, Tobias (b. ?; d. London, 16. IV. 1645), Eng. va. da gamba player & comp. He was an army captain and towards the end of his life a pensioner in the Charterhouse. Comp. dances for va. da gamba, songs to the lute, &c., pub. in *Musicall Humours* & *Poeticall Musicke,* &c.

Humfrey, Pelham (b. ? London, 1647; d. Windsor, 14. VII. 1674), Eng. comp. Entered the re-estab. Chapel Royal in London in 1660 under Cooke, joined Blow and Turner in the comp. of the so-called 'club anthem' and was sent abroad for study by Charles II in 1664. Returned in 1667 from Fr. and It. and became a Gentleman of the Chapel Royal, where he succeeded Cooke as Master of the Children in 1672. He taught Purcell there.

Works incl. incid. m. to Shakespeare's *Tempest,* Dryden's *Conquest of Granada* & *The Indian Emperor,* Crowne's *History of Charles VIII* & Wycherley's *Love in a Wood*; services, &c.; odes, sacred songs, airs for 1 & 2 voices, &c.

Hummel, Ferdinand (b. Berlin, 6. IX. 1855; d. Berlin, 24. IV. 1928), Ger. pfst., hpst. & comp. After playing pf. & hp. in public as a child, he studied at Kullak's Cons. in Berlin and later had a success with realistic operas.

Works incl. operas *Mara, Angla, Ein treuer Schelm, Assarpai, Sophie von Brabant, Die Beichte, Die Gefilde der Seligen*; incid. m. for 14 plays by Wildenbruch & others; Sym., ovt.; pf. Conc., Fantasy for hp. & orch.; chor. works; chamber m.; pf. pieces, &c.

Hummel, Johan Nepomuka (Johann

Nepomuk) (b. Pozsony, 14. XI. 1778; d. Weimar, 17. X. 1837), Hung.-Ger. pfst. & comp. Learnt m. at first from his father, the cond. Joseph H., who went to Vienna in 1785 as cond. of the Theater auf der Wieden. By that time he was already a brilliant pfst. and Mozart took him as a pupil for 2 years. In 1787 he went on tour in Ger., Hol., Sc. & Eng. and had further lessons from Clementi in London, where he stayed until 1792. In 1793 he was back in Vienna, studying comp. with Albrechtsberger, Haydn and Salieri. In 1803 he visited Rus. and from 1804–11 he was mus. dir. to Prince Esterházy. In 1816–20 he held a similar post at the court of Württemberg at Stuttgart and in 1820–2 and 1833–7 at that of Weimar, undertaking extensive concert tours in between, spending much time in London. He married the singer Elisabeth Röckl (1793–1883).

Works incl. operas *Die Rückfahrt des Kaisers* & *Mathilde von Guise*; ballets *Hélène et Paris*, *Das belebte Gemälde*, *Sappho*; pantomime *Der Zauberring*; incid. m. to Grillparzer's *Die Ahnfrau*; masses & other church m.; pf. concs.; chamber m.; sos. for pf. with another inst.; pf. sos., rondos, vars., &c.

Humoreske (Ger.) / **Humoresque** (Fr.) } A piece (or in Schumann a series of mvts.) of capricious or fantastic rather than humorous character.

Humperdinck, Engelbert (b. Siegburg, 1. IX. 1854; d. Neustrelitz, 27. IX. 1921), Ger. comp. Studied under F. Hiller at the Cologne Cons. and later with F. Lachner and Rheinberger at Munich. In 1879 he met Wagner in It. and acted as his asst. at Bayreuth in 1880–1. He is said to have scored and perhaps actually written a few bars for the transformation in *Parsifal*, where the m. was found to be too short for scenic requirements. Later he travelled in Fr., It. and Spa. and taught at the Barcelona Cons. in 1885–7. In 1890–6 he taught at the Hoch Cons. at Frankfort o/M. and was for a time m. critic of the *Frankfurter Zeitung*. In 1900 he became dir. of the Meisterschule for comp. in Berlin.

Works incl. operas *Hänsel und Gretel*, *Dornröschen*, *Die Heirat wider Willen*, *Königskinder*, *Die Marketenderin*, *Gaudeamus*; play with m. *Königskinder* (an earlier version of the opera); spectacular pantomime *The Miracle*; incid. m. to Shakespeare's *Merchant of Venice*, *Winter's Tale*, *The Tempest* & *Twelfth Night*, Maeterlinck's *The Blue Bird*, Aristophanes' *Lysistrata*; chor. works *Das Glück von Edenhall* (Uhland), *Die Wallfahrt nach Kevlaar* (Heine); *Humoreske* & *Maurische Rhapsodie* for orch.; partsongs, songs, &c.

Humphrey, Pelham. *See* Humfrey.

Humphries, John (b. ?, 1707; d. ?, c. 1730), Eng. vst. & comp. Pub. a book of solos for v. & bass and 2 books of concs. for 2 vs.

Humstrum. A primitive and now obs. v. with 4 wire stgs. and a tin canister for a soundbox.

Huneker, James (Gibbons) (b. Philadelphia, 31. I. 1860; d. New York, 9. II. 1921), Amer. critic. Studied the pf. in Paris and N.Y. and later became a teacher at the Nat. Cons. there. He wrote essays on the arts and became art and m. critic to var. newspapers in Philadelphia and N.Y., the last being the *N.Y. World*. His books incl. vols. on Chopin and Liszt and collected essays.

Hung. (abbr.) = Hungarian, Hungary.

Hungarian Composers. *See* **Abrányi, Aggházy, Bartók, Beliczay, Berté, Cousser, Czibulka, Dohnányi, Doppler, Erkel, Goldmark, Gung'l, Harsanyi, Heller, Hubay, Hummel, Jemnitz, Joachim, Kéler-Béla, Kodály, Lajtha, Lehár, Lendvai, Liszt, Mihalovich, Moor, Mosonyi, Novaček, Poldini, Radnai, Raimann, Seiber, Sucher, Szábados, Szabo, Szántó, Székely, Szendy, Vavrinecz, Veress, Wagner-Regeny, Weiner, Zador, Zichy.**

Hunnenschlacht (*Battle of the Huns*), symph. poem by Liszt inspired by Kaulbach's fresco, comp. 1857; 1st perf. Weimar, 29. XII. 1857.

Hunnis, William (b. ?; d. London, 6. VI. 1597), Eng. comp. Gentleman of the Chapel Royal in the reigns of Edward VI, Mary I and Elizabeth, though dismissed as a Protestant in Mary's time. He became Master of the Children in 1566.

Works incl. metrical psalms & other portions of the Bible versified by himself.

Hunt, Arabella (b. ?; d. London, 26. XII. 1705), Eng. singer and lutenist. M. teacher of Princess (later Queen) Anne and a favourite of Queen Mary. Blow and Purcell wrote many songs for her. Congreve wrote an ode on her and Kneller painted her portrait.

'Hunt' Quartet. The familiar nickname of Mozart's B♭ maj. stg. 4tet, K. 458, because the opening suggests hunting-hns.

Hünten, Franz (b. Coblenz, 26. XII. 1793; d. Coblenz, 22. II. 1878), Ger. pfst. & comp. Pupil of his father, the orgst. Daniel H., and later of Pradher for pf. and Reicha and Cherubini for comp. at the Paris Cons. Taught there for some years and made pf. arrs. of var. m. He wrote a method of pf. playing and comp. a *Trio concertante* for v., co. & pf., many pf. works, songs, &c.

Hunyady László, opera by Erkel (lib. by Béni Egressy), prod. Budapest, 27. I. 1844. The chief Hung. nat. opera.

Huon de Bordeaux, medieval Fr. romance. *See* **Oberon** (Weber & Wranitzky).

Hurdy-Gurdy (onomat.). The Eng. name, often wrongly used for the Barrel Organ, of the Fr. *vielle*, a rustic stg. inst. whose medieval name was *organistrum*. Its stgs., usually 6, are set vibrating by a wheel turned with a handle. The tune is played on the top stg. (G above middle C) by means of a keyboard, the lower stgs. remaining unchanged in pitch and thus acting as a drone.

Huré, Jean (b. Gien, Loiret, 17. IX. 1877; d. Paris, 27. I. 1930), Fr. orgst. & comp. He became orgst. at the church of Saint-Augustin in Paris in succession to Gigout in 1925 and ed. a journal *L'Orgue et les Organistes*.
Works incl. opera *Le Bois sacré*; incid. m. to Musset's *Fantasio*; Te Deum & other church m.; 2 stg. 4tets & other chamber m.; v. & pf. So., 3 co. & pf. sos.; org. works, &c.

Hurlebusch, Heinrich Lorenz (b. Hanover, 8. VI. 1666; d. Brunswick), Ger. orgst. & comp. Wrote org. works.

Hurlebusch, Konrad Friedrich (b. Brunswick, 1696; d. Amsterdam, 16. XII. 1765), Ger. orgst. & comp., son of prec. Travelled much as a virtuoso, visiting It. and Swe., holding brief offices at Brunswick and Hamburg, and finally settling at Amsterdam.
Works incl. operas, cantatas, hymns, overtures, hpchd. pieces, songs, &c.

Hurlstone, William (Yeates) (b. London, 7. I. 1876; d. London, 30. V. 1906), Eng. pfst. & comp. Studied at the R.C.M. in London, having already pub. waltzes for pf. at the age of 9. Prof. of ctpt. at the R.C.M. from 1905 to his early death.
Works incl. Fantasy-Vars. on a Swe. Air and suite *The Magic Mirror* for orch.; pf. conc. in D maj.; stg. 4tet in E min., pf. & wind 5tet, pf. 4tet, Fantasy stg. 4tet; sos. for v. & pf., co. & pf., bn. & pf. suite for cl. & pf., &c.

Huss, Henry Holden (b. Newark, New Jersey, 21. VI. 1862), Amer. pfst. & comp. 1st studied with his father and others at home, later at Munich, his comp. master being Rheinberger.
Works incl. pf. Conc. in B maj., Rhapsody for pf. & orch., v. Conc. in C min.; 2 stg. 4tets; v. & pf. So., co. & pf. So.; pf. pieces; songs, &c.

Hussey, Dyneley (b. Deolali, India, 27. II. 1893), Eng. m. critic. Educ. at Oxford, joined the staff of *The Times* and became critic 1st to the *Saturday Review* and then to the *Spectator*. During the 2nd world war he joined the Admiralty. His books incl. vols. on Mozart and Verdi & *Eurydice, or The Nature of Opera*.

Hutchings, Arthur (James Bramwell) (b. Sunbury-on-Thames, 14. VII. 1906), Eng. writer on m. & comp. Contrib. to mus. periodicals since the age of 19 and author of books on Schubert, Mozart's pf. concs. and Delius.
Works incl. *O quanta, or Heart's Desire* for double chor., orch., brass band & org.; motets & other church m.; works for stg. orch., &c.

Hutschenruyter, Wouter (b. Rotterdam, 28. XII. 1796; d. Rotterdam, 18. XI. 1878), Dutch vst., cond. & comp. Studied v. & hn., but later cond. var. mus. socs. at Rotterdam and Schiedam.
Works incl. opera *Le Roi de Bohème*; masses, cantatas & other chor. works; 4 syms., 2 ovts.; co. & pf. So.; songs, &c.

Hutschenruyter, Wouter (b. Rotterdam, 15. VIII. 1859), Dutch cond., comp. & writer on m., grandson of prec. Cond. at Amsterdam and Utrecht, and in 1917–25 dir. of the M. School at Rotterdam. His books incl. studies of Chopin, Wagner, Brahms, Mahler & R. Strauss, and his comps. orch. & chamber m.

Hüttenbrenner, Anselm (b. Graz, 13. X. 1794; d. Strasserhof nr. Graz, 5. VI. 1868), Aus. comp. Pupil of Salieri and friend of Schubert, whose unfinished Sym. he withheld from the world until 1865.
Works incl. operas *Die Einquartierung, Ödipus auf Kolonos* (Sophocles), *Armella & Lenore*; incid. m. for several plays; 6 masses, 3 Requiems & other church m.; 6 syms.; 2 stg. 4tets; songs incl. a setting of Goethe's *Erlkönig*, &c.

Huybrechts, Albert (b. Dinant, 12. II. 1899; d. Woluwé-Saint-Pierre, 21. II. 1938), Belg. critic & comp. Studied at the Brussels Cons., Jongen being among his masters.
Works incl. orch. poem *David*; stg. 4tet; v. & pf. So.; songs, &c.

Huygens, Constantin (b. The Hague, 4. IX. 1596; d. The Hague, 28. III. 1687), Dutch official, physicist, poet, writer, linguist & musn. He was military secretary at The Hague from 1625 to his death. He was a lutenist and also played viol and the keyboard insts., paying 3 visits to

Eng. and others to Ger., It. and Fr. He collected a mus. library and wrote on the use of the org. in church & other mus. subjects. One of his sons, Christian H. (1629–95), was also a musn. as well as a mathematician.

Hyde, Douglas (b. 1860), Ir. philol. & author, President of Eire. *See* **Esposito** (*Tinker and Fairy*).

Hydraulus. The water org. invented in Egypt by Ctesibius in the 3rd cent. B.C. The pipes were played by wind forced through them by the compression of water.

Hyllested, August (b. Stockholm, 17. VI. 1858), Swe. pfst. & comp. of Dan. descent. Studied at the Copenhagen Cons. and toured Scand. as a pfst., was cath. orgst. in Copenhagen, 1876–9, then went to finish his studies in Berlin and with Liszt at Weimar. In 1886 he settled at Chicago.

Works incl. symph. poem *Elizabeth* for chor. & orch.; *Suite romantique, Marche triomphale* & other works for orch.; 2 pf. trios; *Scand. Dances, Variations sérieuses, Suite de ballet,* &c. for pf., &c.

Hymn. A song in praise of Apollo in ancient Gr. and of God in the Christian churches, where it was at first sung in plainsong, and still is in the Rom. Catholic church, later, esp. in the Protestant churches, partic. the Lutheran and Anglican, a tune harmonized in 4 parts and so sung if there is an estab. choir, but by the congregation normally in 8ve unison with org. accomp. The chief distinction of the H. from the psalms is that the words are specially written, not taken from the Bible. The Ger. Choral(e) is simply the Lutheran H.

Hymn of Praise (Lobgesang). Mendelssohn's symph. cantata, Op. 52, in which a complete sym. precedes the chor. portion; prod. Leipzig, St. Thomas's church, 25. VI. 1840; in Eng., Birmingham Festival, 23. IX. 1840.

Hymn of the Nations (Verdi). *See* **Inno delle nazioni.**

Hypo- (prefix). *See* **Modes.**

(Mark reference p. 243)

Heming, Michael (Savage) (b. London, 14. I. 1920; d. E. Akkikir, 3. XI. 1942), Eng. comp. Educ. at Haileybury and at the Sorbonne in Paris, and studied m. at the R.A.M. in London, intending to become a cond. During the 2nd world war he became a lieut. and intelligence officer in the King's Royal Rifles and was killed in the battle of El Alamein.

Works incl. symph. poem on Marlowe's *Tamburlaine* (lost in transit) & *Threnody* for orch. (unfinished, completed by Anthony Collins as *Threnody for a Soldier Killed in Action*).

(Mark reference p. 254)

Hopekirk, Helen (b. Edinburgh, 20. V. 1856; d. Cambridge, Mass., XI. 1945), Sco.-Amer. pfst. & comp. Studied at Edinburgh, at the Leipzig Cons. and with Leschetizky in Vienna. Made her 1st appearance at the Gewandhaus, Leipzig, in 1878, and in 1882 married William Wilson, a Sco. merchant, with whom she settled in U.S.A. in 1883. She lived in Vienna, 1887–91, and taught at the New Eng. Cons. at Boston in 1897–1901, later at Brookline, Mass.

Works incl. orch. m.; Conc. and *Konzertstück* for pf. & orch.; 2 v. & pf. sos.; many pf. works; over 100 songs, &c.

I

I.S.C.M. (abbr.) = International Society for Contemporary Music.

Iberia, 4 sets of pf. pieces by I. Albéniz, representing different parts of Spa., comp. at var. times before 1909: I. *Evocación, El Puerto, Fête-Dieu à Séville*; II. *Triana, Almeria, Rondeña*; III. *El Albaicin, El Polo, Lavapiés*; IV. *Málaga, Jérez, Eritaña.*

Ibéria (Debussy). *See* **Images pour Orchestre.**

Ibert, Jacques (François Antoine) (b. Paris, 15. VIII. 1890), Fr. comp. Studied at the Paris Cons. and gained the Prix de Rome in 1919. He became dir. of the Fr. Acad. in Rome in 1937.

Works incl. operas *Angélique, Persée et Andromède, On ne saurait penser à tout, Le Roi d'Yvetot, Gonzague* & (both with Honegger) *L'Aiglon* (after Rostand), *Le Petit Cardinal*; radio opera *Barbe-bleue*; ballets *Les Rencontres, Diane de Poitiers* and contribution to *L'Éventail de Jeanne*; incid. m. to Labiche's *Le Chapeau de paille d'Italie* & other plays, also (with 6 others) for Rolland's *Le 14 Juillet*; film m. incl. *Don Quichotte*; cantata *Le Poète et la Fée*; symph. poem *La Ballade de la geôle de Reading* (after Wilde); suites *Escales* & *Paris, Scherzo féerique, Nationale* (for Paris Exhib., 1937), *Jeux, Donogoo, Ouverture pour une fête*, all for orch.; Divertimento for chamber orch.; concs. for pf., for saxophone & for co. & wind; stg. 4tet; pf. works, incl. *Pièces romantiques, Noël de Picardie, Le Vent dans les ruines, Matin sur l'eau, Le Petit Âne blanc*, &c.; 5 pieces for hp.; pieces for pipes & pf., &c.

Ibsen, Henrik (1828–1906), Norw. dramatist. *See* **Egk** (*Peer Gynt*), **Feast at Solhaug** (incid. m., H. Wolf), **Grieg** (songs), **Heward** (*Peer Gynt*), **O'Neill** (*Pretenders*), **Paz** (*Julian the Emperor*), **Peer Gynt** (Grieg), **Pfitzner** (*Feast at S.*), **Rangström** (*Brand*), **Schjelderup** (do.), **Steinberg** (do.), **Stenhammar** (*Feast at S.*), **Ullmann** (*Peer Gybt*), **Wallace (W.)** (*Lady from the Sea*).

Ideale, Die (*The Ideals*), symph. poem by Liszt, based on a poem by Schiller, comp. 1857, 1st perf. Weimar, 5. IX. 1857 at the unveiling of the Goethe-Schiller monument.

Idée fixe. Berlioz's term for a motto theme (e.g. in the *Fantastic Sym.*) which recurs several times in the course of a comp. as an allusion to some definite idea. It is an anticipation of the Wagnerian *Leitmotiv.*

Idoménée (*Idomeneus*), opera by Campra (lib. by Antoine Danchet), prod. Paris, Opéra, 12. I. 1712.

Idomeneo, rè di Creta, ossia Ilia ed Idamante (*Idomeneus, King of Crete, or Ilia and Idamantes*), opera by Mozart (lib. by Giovanni Battista Varesco, based on the Fr. lib. by Antoine Danchet), prod. Munich, 29. I. 1781.

Iernin, opera by George Lloyd (lib. by William Lloyd, the comp.'s father), prod. Penzance, 6. XI. 1934.

Ifigenia, L', opera by Jommelli (lib. by Mattia Verazi), prod. Rome, Teatro Argentina, 9. II. 1751.

Ifigenia in Aulide (*Iphigenia in Aulis*), opera by Caldara (lib. by Apostolo Zeno), prod. Vienna, 4. XI. 1718.

Opera by Cherubini (lib. by Ferdinando Moretti), prod. Turin, Teatro Regio, II. 1788.

Opera by Graun (lib. by Leopoldo de Villati, after Racine's *Iphigénie en Aulide*), prod. Berlin, Royal Opera, 13. XII. 1748. Frederick II of Prus. prob. collaborated.

Opera by Zingarelli (lib. by Ferdinando Moretti), prod. Milan, Teatro alla Scala, 27. I. 1787. (All libs. based ultimately on Euripides.)

Ifigenia in Tauride (*Iphigenia in Tauris*), opera by Galuppi (lib. by Marco Coltellini), prod. St. Petersburg, at court, 2. V. 1768.

Opera by Maio (lib. by Mattia Verazi), prod. Mannheim, at court, 4. XI. 1764.

Opera by Traetta (lib. by Marco Coltellini), prod. Vienna, Schönbrunn Palace, at court, 4. X. 1763. (Libs. based on Euripides.)

See also **Iphigénie.**

Ilyinsky, Alexander Alexandrovitch (b. Tsarskoye Selo, 24. I. 1859), Rus. pfst. & comp. Studied pf. under Kullak and comp., under Bargiel in Berlin. Returning to Rus. in 1885, he became prof. at the Phil. Soc.'s School of M. in Moscow.

Works incl. opera *The Fountain of Bakhchiserai* (after Pushkin); cantatas *Strekozi* & *Russalka*; incid. m. to Sophocles' *Oedipus Rex* and *Philoctetes*, ovt. to A. Tolstoy's *Tsar Feodor*;

Sym., 3 orch. suites (No. 2 *A Village Holiday*, No. 3 *Noor and Anitra*, Symph. Scherzo, Croatian Dances for orch.; stg. 4tet; v. pieces; pf. m.; songs, &c.

Images, 2 sets of pf. pieces by Debussy: 1st series, comp. 1905, *Reflets dans l'eau, Hommage à Rameau, Mouvement*; 2nd series, comp. 1907, *Cloches à travers les feuilles, Et la lune descend sur le temple qui fut, Poissons d'or.*

Images pour Orchestre, 3 symph. pieces by Debussy: *Rondes de printemps*, comp. 1909; *Ibéria* (*Par les rues et par les chemins, Les Parfums de la nuit & Le Matin d'un jour de fête*), finished 1908; *Gigues* (orig. *Gigues tristes*), comp. 1911.

Imareta, Tirso. *See* **Yriarte.**

Imbert, Hugues (b. Moulins-Engilbert, Nièvre, 11. I. 1842; d. Paris, 15. I. 1905), Fr. critic & writer on m. He had a general educ. and became an official, but did much mus.-lit. work. His books incl. sketches of var. comps. and special studies of Wagner, Brahms, Gounod, Bizet, &c.

Imbroglio (It. lit. intricacy). A term borrowed from drama, where it means a complicated plot in a play; in m., partic. in opera, it is a passage where the comp. suggests a confusion of parts or themes which are in fact combined with great skill to prod. such an effect (e.g. at the close of Acts I & II of Wagner's *Mastersingers*).

Imitation. A device in comp. whereby a mus. figure is repeated after its 1st statement, either exactly as before or with some change, such a displacement to a higher or lower position, augmentation, diminution, rhythmic distortion, elaboration, simplification, &c. Such an I. may either be deferred until the 1st statement has been completed or made to overlap with it.

Imitations. Mus. comps. or parts thereof where a comp. deliberately writes in the manner of some other comp. Here are some exs.:

Bréville, *Portraits de Maîtres* for pf. (Franck, d'Indy, Chausson, Fauré).

Casella & Ravel, *A la manière de . . .* for pf. (Wagner, Fauré, Brahms, Debussy, R. Strauss, Franck, d'Indy, Ravel, Borodin, Chabrier; only the last 2 by Ravel).

Grieg, *Gade* (*Lyric Pieces* for pf.).

Holbrooke, *Les Hommages* for orch. (Wagner, Grieg, Dvořák, Tchaikovsky).

Holst, Parodies of Wagner & Verdi, in *The Perfect Fool.*

d'Indy, *Schumanniana* for pf., Op. 30.

Mason, D. G., *Variations on Yankee Doodle* for pf. (Grieg, Tchaikovsky, Brahms, Debussy, MacDowell, Dvořák, Liszt).

Mozart, Ovt. (suite) in Handel's style for pf. (K. 399).

Mussorgsky, satirical song, *The Peepshow* (var. styles).

Ravel, *La Valse* for orch. (in the manner of Viennese waltzes of the J. Strauss period).

Ries, Sonata in Mozart's style for pf.

Rimsky-Korsakov, var. passages in the opera *Mozart and Salieri.*

Rossini, *Capriccio offenbachique* (orch. by Respighi for *La Boutique fantasque*).

Schumann, *Chopin* and *Paganini* mvts. in *Carnival* for pf.; *Erinnerung* (Mendelssohn) in *Album für die Jugend* for pf.

Spohr, 1st 3 mvts. of *Historical Symphony* (Haydn, Mozart, Beethoven).

Strauss, R., Waltzes in *Der Rosenkavalier* in the style of Johann Strauss; also ten. aria in Act I, imitating 18th-cent. It. opera style. S.'s *Ariadne auf Naxos* contains var. incidents in different styles.

Tchaikovsky, Divertissement in 2nd Act of *The Queen of Spades* in the style of Mozart; *Un poco di Chopin* & *Un poco di Schumann* for pf.; *Alla Schumann* in Vars. on an orig. theme for pf.

Vaughan Williams, *The Poisoned Kiss*, opera, parodies of var. styles.

Immermann, Karl Leberecht (1796–1840), Ger. novelist & dramatist. *See* **Hindemith** (*Tulifäntchen*), **Rietz (J.)** (incid. m. for plays), **Tiessen** (*Merlin*).

Immortal Hour, The, opera by Boughton (lib. by comp. adapted from plays and poems by Fiona Macleod), prod. Glastonbury, 26. VIII. 1914.

Imperfect Cadence. *See* **Half-Close.**

Impériale, L', the nickname of a sym. by Haydn, No. 53, in D maj., comp. c. 1773.

Impresario, The (Mozart). *See* **Schauspieldirektor.**

Impresario in angustie, L' (*The Impresario in Distress*), opera by Cimarosa (lib. by Giuseppe Maria Diodati, similar to that of Mozart's *Schauspieldirektor*), prod. Naples, Teatro Nuovo, X. 1786.

Impressionism. A term properly belonging to painting but transferred, more or less loosely, to comps. (esp. Fr.) contemporary with the school of impressionist painters. Debussy, although he disapproved, was designated as the leader of mus. I. One of the chief aims of I. is to interpret artistically a momentary glimpse of things rather than their permanent state.

Impromptu (from Lat. *in promptu* =

in readiness). A piece of m. suggesting, or intended to suggest, that it resembles an improvisation.

Improvisation (or **Extemporization**). The art of playing on any inst., but esp. keyboard insts., m. not written down by a comp. but proceeding straight from the player's imagination. Thorough-bass playing, from a figured bass, demanded a skill that was largely, though not wholly, improvisatory from the perf., who had only the bass line and a harmonic skeleton to guide him, but was expected to enrich the texture of the m. by more or less elaborate upper parts. In the 18th cent. I. flourished among keyboard players and was expected of them, and in cadenzas it was obligatory. These are now nearly always comp. beforehand, and altogether I. has fallen largely into disuse. It is still most frequently cultivated by orgsts., but often shown in its most debased form in their hands.

In Nature's Realm (Dvořák). *See* **Amid Nature.**

In Nomine. An inst. piece of the later 16th cent. for viols or virginal, similar to the Fancy or Fantasia, but based on one partic. plainsong tune used as a *cantus firmus*. The tune, however, is not one assoc. with the Benedictus in the Mass (' qui venit in nomine Domini '), but with ' Gloria tibi Trinitas ' from the antiphon for Trinity Sunday. The words ' in nomine ' may therefore have been merely a kind of déd. of the piece to God.

In the South, concert ovt. by Elgar, Op. 50, comp. during a visit to It. in 1903 and pub. in 1904.

Incid. m. (abbr.) = **Incidental music.**

Incidental Music. M. written for use in stage plays perf. by speaking actors, who may however be required to sing songs the words of which are provided by the author and set to m. by the comp. of the I. M., whose contrib. of voc. m. may also extend to chors., as for ex. in the I. M. to Gr. drama. The rest of the m., however, will be instrumental, e.g. an ovt., act-tunes or preludes to each act, accomps. to passages treated as Melodrama, descriptive pieces (for tempests, fires, battles, &c.), dances or whole ballets, processional marches, pieces for musns. appearing on the stage, fanfares, &c.

Incledon, Charles (Benjamin) (b. St. Keverne, Cornwall, I. or II. 1763; d. London, 18. II. 1826), Eng. ten. singer. He learnt m. as a choir-boy in Exeter cath., but became a sailor. He settled down in 1783 and the following year made his 1st stage appearance at Southampton. During an engagement at Bath he had lessons from Rauzzini, and in 1786 he 1st appeared in London, at Vauxhall.

Incontro improviso, L' (*The Unforeseen Meeting*), opera by Haydn (lib. by Karl Friberth, trans. into It. from Dancourt's *La Rencontre imprévue*, comp. by Gluck), prod. Esterház, 29. VIII. 1775.

Incoronazione di Poppea, L' (*The Coronation of Poppaea*), opera by Monteverdi (lib. by Giovanni Francesco Busenello), prod. Venice, Teatro SS. Giovanni e Paolo, autumn 1642.

Indes galantes, Les, opera-ballet by Rameau (lib. by Louis Fuzelier), prod. Paris, Opéra, 23. VIII. 1735.

Indian Queen, The, play by Dryden and Robert Howard, prod. 1664; adapted as an ' opera ' with m. by Purcell, prod. London, Drury Lane Theatre, 1695.

Indigo und die vierzig Räuber (*I. and the Forty Robbers*), operetta by J. Strauss, jun. (lib. by Maximilian Steiner), prod. Vienna, Theater an der Wien, 10. II. 1871. S.'s 1st operetta.

Indy, (Paul Marie Théodore) Vincent d' (b. Paris, 27. III. 1851; d. Paris, 2. XII. 1931), Fr. comp. Although b. in Paris, he belonged to a noble family of the Ardèche district in the Vivarais. His mother d. at his birth and he was brought up by his paternal grandmother, a good musn. At the age of 11 he was sent to Diémer for the pf. and Lavignac for theory, and later studied pf. under Marmontel. In 1870 he pub. his 1st comps. and served in the defence of Paris against the Prus. army. To please his family he studied law, but was determined to be a musn. and went for advice to Franck, who offered to teach him. He also joined Colonne's orch. as drummer to gain experience. Pasdeloup gave the 1st perf. of one of his works, the ovt. to Schiller's *Piccolomini*, afterwards part of his *Wallenstein* trilogy. Next to Franck he admired Liszt, with whom he spent several months at Weimar in 1873, and Wagner, whose 1st *Ring* cycle he attended at Bayreuth in 1876. In 1894 he joined Charles Bordes, together with Guilmant, in founding the Schola Cantorum; he taught there until his death and had many pupils of the highest distinction. From 1912 he also dir. the orch. class at the Cons.

Works incl. operas, *Attendez-moi sous l'orme*, *Le Chant de la cloche*, *Fervaal*, *L'Étranger*, *La Légende de Saint Christophe*, *Le Rêve de Cinyras*; incid. m. for Catulle Mendès's *Médée*; 2 syms. (the 1st entitled *Jean*

Hunyade), symph. trilogy *Wallenstein* (after Schiller), sym. vars. *Istar, Jour d'été à la montagne*; *Symphonie sur un chant montagnard français* (*Sym. cévenole*) for pf. & orch.; 3 stg. 4tets, stg. 6tet, pf. 4tet & pf. 5tet, trios for pf., clar. & co. and pf. v., & co., Suite for tpt., 2 fls. & stg. 4tet, and some other chamber works; sos. for v. & pf. and co. & pf.; 18 op. nos. of pf. works, incl. *Poèmes des montagnes, Tableaux de voyage*, So. in E maj., *Thème varié, Fugue et Chanson*; 3 org. works; 10 songs; 90 *Chansons populaires du Vivarais* arr.; 12 Fr. folksongs for unaccomp. chor.; var. voc. works with and without orch., &c.

Inez de Castro, opera by Persiani (lib. by Salvatore Cammarano), prod. Naples, Teatro San Carlo, 28. I. 1835. Written for Malibran.

Infantas, Fernando de las (b. Córdoba, 1534; d. ? Paris, after 1609), Spa. comp., descendant of the Fernández family of Córdoba, known by that name because one of his ancestors conveyed the infantas Constanza and Isabella to Bayonne, occupied by the Eng. in the 14th cent., before their marriage to John of Gaunt and Edmund Langley. His comps. attracted the attention of the Bishop of Córdoba, the Archduke Charles of Austria. He settled in Rome *c.* 1559, but took holy orders in 1584 and went (?) to Paris.

Works incl. motets, some for special occasions, such as the death of the Emperor Charles V (1558) and the battle of Lepanto (1571), a setting of Psalm xcix, &c.

Infante, Manuel (b. Osuna, 29. VII. 1883), Spa. comp.

Works incl. pf. solo comps.: *El vito*, Vars. on a popular theme, *Danse originale, Sevillana, Guadalquivir, Gitanerías*; 2 pfs.: *3 Danses andalouses, Ritmo, Gracia, Sentimiento*, &c.

Infinite Canon. A canon contrived to make the end overlap with the beginning, so that it can be repeated to infinity.

Inganno (It. = deception). The It. name for the Interrupted Cadence.

Inganno felice, L' (*The Happy Deceit*), opera by Rossini (lib. by Giuseppe Maria Foppa), prod. Venice, Teatro San Moisè, 8. I. 1812.

Ingegneri, Marc Antonio (b. Verona, *c.* 1545; d. Cremona, 1. VII. 1592), It. comp. Learnt m. from V. Ruffo at Verona cath. and *c.* 1570 became chapel master at Cremona cath. Monteverdi was his pupil there.

Works incl. 2 books of masses, 3 books of motets, 1 of hymns and 8 of madrigals; also 27 responses for Holy Week (long attrib. to Palestrina).

Ingenhoven, Jan (b. Breda, 19. V. 1876), Dutch cond. & comp. He was a chor. cond. before he had any systematic mus. educ., but studied later with Brandts-Buys and with Mottl at Munich, where he cond. both orch. & chor. concerts, as he did later both in Hol. and abroad. He also sang ten. and played the pf. & cl.

Works incl. 3 symph. pieces for orch.; symph. fantasy on Nietzsche's *Zarathustras Nachtlied* & ballad *Klaus Tink* for voice & orch.; 4 stg. 4tets; v. & pf. So. in C maj., co. & pf. So. in G maj.; chors. & voc. 4tets; songs, &c.

Inghelbrecht, D(ésiré-). **É**(mile). (b. Paris, 17. IX. 1880), Fr. cond. & comp. Cond. many concerts of modern m. in Paris, also the Swe. Ballet in Paris & London.

Works incl. ballet *El Greco*; *Cantique des créatures de Saint François* for chor. & orch.; 5tet for stgs. & hp.; So. for fl. & hp.; *Suite Petite-Russienne* & other pf. works; *La Nursery* for pf. duet (3 books); songs, &c.

Inglesina, L'. *See* **Davies, Cecilia.**

Inkle and Yarico, opera by Arnold (lib. by George Colman, jun., based on a story by Steele), prod. London, Little Theatre, Haymarket, 4. VIII. 1787.

Innig (Ger. = inwardly, intimately, heart-felt). A term, not translatable exactly, frequently used by Ger. romantic comps., esp. Schumann, where profound feeling is required in perf.

Inno delle nazioni (Hymn of the Nations), cantata by Verdi written for the Internat. Exhib. in London, but prod. at Her Majesty's Theatre, 24. V. 1862. It introd. nat. airs in ctptal comb.

Innocenza giustificate, L' (*Innocence Vindicated*), opera by Gluck (lib. by Giacomo Durazzo, with words for the airs by Metastasio), prod. Vienna, Burg Theatre, 8. XII. 1755.

Insanguine, Giacomo (b. Monopoli nr. Naples, *c.* 1742; d. Naples, *c.* 1795), It. comp. Studied at the Cons. di Sant' Onofrio at Naples and in 1774 became a prof. there. He was also known as Monopoli.

Works incl. operas *Didone abbandonata, Arianna e Teseo, Adriano in Siria, Le astuzie per amore, Medonte, Calipso* & over a dozen others; masses, motets, psalms, a Passion, &c.

Inscription. An indication written in words at the beginning of a canon to show the manner of its perf.: at what points the voices are to enter and/or at what intervals the different voices are to sing; also sometimes a mystifying clue given for the perf. of a Riddle Canon.

Inst. (abbr.) = Instrument, instrumental.

Instrumentation. The art of writing for insts. in a manner suited to their nature, also Orchestration.

Intendant (Ger.). The manager or dir. of an opera-house or other theatre in Ger., esp. one attached to a court in former times. The post was usually held by courtiers or high-born officials, whose interest in the arts was often amateurish and whose knowledge of them haphazard.

Interlude. A piece of m. played or (more rarely) sung between 2 others or forming a bridge between 2 distinct sections of a large-scale comp.; also a mus. piece perf. between parts of some other perf. or function, such as certain liturgical portions of a church service, acts or scenes of a play, dances at a ball or courses of a dinner, &c. Act-tunes (*entr'actes*) in a theatre are, properly speaking, Is.

Intermède (Fr.) = Interlude, Intermezzo.

Intermezzi (It. plur. = interludes). Comic operatic pieces, usually in 2 scenes and for 2 or 3 characters, 1 of whom could be a 'mute,' played as interludes between the acts of a serious opera in 18th-cent. It., esp. Naples. The most famous ex. is Pergolesi's *La serva padrona*. The orig. of the I. is earlier, but in the 16th cent. they were only songs or madrigals sung in costume.

Intermezzo (It. sing. =interlude). Orig. any mus. piece played between the parts of a larger work, mus. or theatrical; e.g. Purcell's 'act-tunes' serving as interludes to plays, the *entr'actes* in Schubert's *Rosamunde* or Bizet's *Arlésienne* m. Later a short concert piece, not necessarily designed for any purpose implied by the name, which means lit. 'in the middle' or 'in between'; e.g. Brahms's Intermezzi for pf. An I. may also be an inst. piece played during an act of an opera while the action is arrested or the stage left empty (e.g. in Mascagni's *Cavalleria rusticana*).

Intermezzo, opera by R. Strauss (lib. by comp.), prod. Dresden, 4. XI. 1924. The material of the lib. is autobiographical.

International Society for Contemporary Music. An organiz. formed after a mus. festival held at Salzburg in 1922 for the furtherance of modern m. and the holding of annual festivals in var. mus. centres.

Interpretation. The presentation of a mus. work to an audience according to the perf.'s idea of revealing what was in the comp.'s mind, an idea which may be right or wrong (a matter that can be decided only by comparison with another's idea), or which may, more ascertainably, be persuasive, indifferent or unacceptable.

Interrupted Cadence. *See* **Cadence.**

Interval. The distance in pitch between 2 notes, whether struck simultaneously or successively.

Intonation. The way in which m. is sung or played according to the ear's perception of what is or what is not in tune; also the act of Intoning.

Intoning. In Plainsong, the singing of the opening phrase by a singer in authority to ensure that the right melody will be sung and at the proper pitch.

Intrada (It.) = Introduction, Prelude.

Introduction. Usually a slow section preceding the 1st so.-form mvt. in a sym., so. or chamber work, with which it may or may not be thematically connected; also sometimes the 1st number of an opera following the ovt., esp. when it has a lengthy inst. passage preceding and accomp. the rise of the curtain.

Introit (from Lat. *introitus* = entrance). An antiphon or portion of a psalm sung in plainsong at the beginning of Mass in the Roman church. Sometimes also a mus. piece of introductory character, esp. at the head of a concert setting of a mass, requiem, &c.

Intrusive H. A bad habit in singing of aspirated words in order to produce a more striking effect at the beginning of a phrase; or, in rapid passages, inserting an aspirate before each note, thereby making the perf. very much easier. Modern It. singers, who have no aspirates in their language, cultivate it most extensively and offensively, saving themselves much trouble in acquiring a good technique by singing, for ex., 'Lusi-hinghe più-hù ca-hare' instead of 'Lusinghe più-ù ca-are.'

Inventions. The title given to Bach's 2 sets of short keyboard pieces written strictly in 2 and 3 parts respectively, and prob. designed as technical studies. He called the 3-part set 'symphonies,' but there is no essential difference between them and the 2-part Is. in character.

Inversion. A device in comp. whereby a mus. theme, esp. a fugue subject, may be differently presented in 2 ways: (1) by being turned upside down, so that the descending intervals now go up and vice versa; and (2) by being turned backwards (*cancrizans*), so that the last note appears 1st and the 1st last.

Invertible Counterpoint. *See* **Counterpoint.**

Invitation to the Dance (Weber). *See* **Aufforderung zum Tanz.**

Iolanta, opera by Tchaikovsky (lib. by Modest Ilitch Tchaikovsky, T.'s brother, based on Hertz's play *King René's Daughter*), prod. St. Petersburg, 18. XII. 1892.

Iolanthe, or The Peer and the Peri, operetta by Sullivan (lib. by W. S. Gilbert), prod. London, Savoy Theatre, 25. XI. 1882, and N.Y., Standard Theatre, same date.

Ione (old It. spelling *Jone*), opera by Petrella (lib. by Giovanni Peruzzini, based on Bulwer-Lytton's novel *The Last Days of Pompeii*), prod. Milan, Teatro alla Scala, 26. I. 1858.

Ionian Mode. One of the 2 church modes introd. much later than the fundamental ones: in the 16th cent. Represented by the white keys of the pf. beginning from C, it corresponds in fact exactly to the modern C maj. scale.

Ipermestra (*Hypermnestra*), opera by Gluck (lib. by Metastasio), prod. Venice, Teatro San Giovanni Cristostomo, 21. XI. 1744.

Iphigénie en Aulide (*Iphigenia in Aulis*), opera by Gluck (lib. by François Louis Lebland du Roullet, based on Racine and farther back on Euripides), prod. Paris, Opéra, 19. IV. 1774. Gluck's 1st opera for the Paris stage, though not his 1st Fr. work.

Iphigénie en Tauride (*Iphigenia in Tauris*), opera by Desmarets and Campra (lib. by Joseph François Duché and Antoine Danchet), prod. Paris, Opéra, 6. V. 1704.

Opera by Gluck (lib. by Nicolas François Guillard), prod. Paris, Opéra, 18. V. 1779.

Opera by Piccinni (lib. by Alphonse Du Congé Dubreuil), prod, Paris, Opéra, 23. I. 1781.

(All libs. based on Euripides.)

See also **Ifigenia.**

Ippolito ed Aricia (*Hippolytus and Aricia*), opera by Traetta (lib. by Carlo Innocenzio Frugoni, trans. from Simon Joseph de Pellegrin's lib. for Rameau's *Hippolyte et Aricie*, 1733), prod. Parma, 9. V. 1759.

Ippolitov-Ivanov, Mikhail (b. Gatchina nr. St. Petersburg, 19. XI. 1859; d. Moscow, 28. I. 1935), Rus. comp. Studied in the choir-school of Isaaky cath. and the Cons. at St. Petersburg, his comp. master being Rimsky-Korsakov. In 1882 he settled in the Caucasus, at Tiflis, where he cond. orch. concerts and taught at the school of m. Married the singer Varvara Zarudina, and both were app. profs. at the Moscow Cons. in 1893, of which he became dir. in 1905.

Works incl. operas *Ruth, Azra, Asia* (after Turgenev's story), *Treachery, Ole from Norland, The Last Barricade,* also completion of Mussorgsky's *Marriage*; *Hymn to Labour* for chor. & orch.; 2 syms., *Caucasian Sketches, Iberia, Armenian Rhapsody, Mtsyri* (after Lermontov), *From Ossian, Episode from Schubert's Life, Turkish Fragments, Musical Scenes from Uzbekistan, The Year 1917, Catalonian Suite,* &c. for orch.; 2 stg. 4tets, *An Evening in Georgia* for hp. & wind insts.; v. & pf. So.; pf. & other inst. pieces; cantatas for chor. & pf.; 116 songs, &c.

Ireland, Francis (real name Hutcheson) (b. Dublin, 13. VIII. 1721; d. Dublin, 1780), Ir. physician and amateur comp. Wrote madrigal 'Return, return,' glees, catches, &c.

Ireland, John (b. Bowden, Ches., 13. VIII. 1879), Eng. comp. Studied at the R.C.M. in London in 1893–1901, his comp. master being Stanford. His many early works up to 1908 he destroyed. Apart from 1 or 2 orgst.'s appts., and his later comp. prof.-ship at the R.C.M., he has been devoted entirely to creative work. In 1932 he received the hon. Mus.D. degree from Durham Univ.

Works incl. prelude *The Forgotten Rite,* symph. rhapsody *Mai-Dun, A London Overture, Epic March* for orch.; *Concertino pastorale* for stg. orch.; Conc. in E♭ maj. and *Legend* for pf. & orch.; *A Downland Suite* for brass band; 3 pf. trios; 2 v. & pf. sos., co. & pf. So., Fantasy-So. for cl. & pf.; *Greater Love hath no Man,* motet for chor., orch. & org., Morning & Evening Services; *These Things shall be* (John Addington Symonds) for chor. & orch.; So., Sonatina, *Decorations, Rhapsody,* 4 Preludes, *London Pieces, Leaves from a Child's Sketchbook, The Towing Path, Equinox, February's Child, Month's Mind, Green Ways* and many other pieces for pf.; some v. & pf. and org. pieces; song cycles *Songs of a Wayfarer, Marigold, The Cost, Mother and Child* (Christina Rossetti), *The Land of Lost Content* (A. E. Housman), 3 & 5 Thomas Hardy songs, 5 16th-cent. songs, &c.; *c.* 30 separate songs, incl. *Bed in Summer, Earth's Call, Hawthorn Time* (Housman), *Hope the Hornblower, If there were dreams to sell* (Beddoes), *Sea Fever* (Masefield), *Spring Sorrow, The Adoration, The Heart's Desire* (Housman); *c.* 20 part-songs, &c.

Ireland, William Henry (1777–1835), Eng. bookseller, author and Shakespeare forger. *See* **Linley (7)** (***Vortigern***).

Iris, opera by Mascagni (lib. by Luigi Illica), prod. Rome, Teatro Costanzi, 22. XI. 1898.

Irish Composers. *See* **Balfe, Carter, Cooke (T.), Costeley (?), Dowland (?), Ferguson, Field, Holden (S.), Holmès, Hughes, Ireland (F.), Kelly, Levey, Maconchy, Moorhead, O'Neill, Rooke, Stanford, Stevenson (J. A.), Stewart, Torrance, Wallace (V.), Wood (C.), Woodward.**

Irish Symphony, Stanford's 3rd Sym., in F min., Op. 28, comp. 1887 and 1st perf. London, 27. VI.

Irving, Washington (1783–1859), Amer. author. *See* **Alchymist** (Spohr), **Koven** (*Rip van Winkle*), **Planquette** (do.).

Isaac, Henricus (Heinrich) (b. ?, *c.* 1450; d. Florence, 1517), Flem. or Ger. comp. In *c.* 1484, when he seems to have been at Innsbruck and in touch with Hofhaimer there, he went via Ferrara to Florence as musn. to the Medici family. He became orgst. at the chapel of San Giovanni there, visited Rome in 1489 and married Bartolomea Bello, the daughter of a wealthy butcher. Lorenzo de' Medici having d. in 1492 and his successor, Pietro, keeping a less lavish household, I. accepted an invitation from the Emperor Maximilian, who visited Pisa in 1496, to join the imp. court, just then about to be transferred from Augsburg to Vienna; but he seems to have visited Innsbruck again to be formally app. and possibly Augsburg too. His duties were not arduous, so that he was able to live by turns in Vienna, Innsbruck, Constance (all connected with the court) and It. He also spent much time at the court of Ercole d'Este, Duke of Ferrara, and during his last years he remained at Florence.

Works incl. many masses, *c.* 50 motets, sequences, lamentation *Oratio Jeremiae*, 58 4-part settings of the offices; 4-part Monodia on the death of Lorenzo de' Medici (words by Poliziano); many Ger., It., Fr. and Lat. songs (incl. 'Innsbruck, ich muss dich lassen,' which may not be his own tune), 58 inst. pieces in 3–5 parts, 29 domestic pieces in 2–5 parts, &c.

Isis, opera by Lully (lib. by Quinault), prod. Saint-Germain, 5. I. 1677 and 1st perf. Paris, IV. 1677.

Isle de Merlin, L', ou Le Monde renversé, comic opera by Gluck (lib. by Louis Anseaume), prod. Vienna, Schönbrunn Palace, at court, 3. X. 1758.

Isola disabitata, L' (*The Desert Island*), opera by Bonno (lib. by Metastasio), prod. Aranjuez, at the Spa. court, spring 1754, and Schlosshof nr. Vienna, before the Aus. court, 23. IX. 1754.

Opera by Haydn (lib. do.), prod. Esterház, 6. XII. 1779.

Opera by G. Scarlatti (lib. by Goldoni), prod. Venice, Teatro San Samuele, 20. XI. 1757.

Opera by Traetta (lib. by Metastasio), prod. Bologna, Teatro Comunale, ? 26. IV. 1768.

Isorhythmic (from Gr. = equally rhythmic). Motets of the 14th & 15th cents. were called I. when they repeated certain phrases in which the rhythm remained the same although the notes sung were different.

Isouard, Niccolo (b. Malta, 6. XII. 1775; d. Paris, 23. III. 1818), Maltese comp. Studied engineering and artillery in Paris, learnt the pf. and passed an examination for the navy, but returned to Malta to engage in commerce, afterwards at Palermo, where he began to study m. seriously, and then went as a bank clerk to Naples, where he became a pupil of Sala and Guglielmi. In 1794 he prod. his 1st opera, *L'avviso ai maritati*, at Florence under the name of Niccolo. After prod. a setting of Metastasio's *Artaserse* at Leghorn, he became orgst. and later choirmaster to the order of St. John at Malta, and when the island was occupied by the Fr. he went to Paris, where he wrote the operas *Le Petit Page* and *Flaminius à Corinthe* with R. Kreutzer and afterwards prod. more than 30 of his own. He also appeared as pfst.

Works incl. operas *Le Tonnelier*, *La Statue, ou la Femme avare*, *Michel-Ange*, *Le Baiser et la quittance* (with Méhul, Kreutzer & Boïeldieu), *Léonce*, *Le Rendez-vous bourgeois*, *Cimarosa*, *Cendrillon*, *Le Billet de loterie*, *Lulli et Quinault*, *Bayard à Mézières* (with Cherubini, Catel & Boïeldieu), *Joconde*, *Jeannot et Colin*, &c.; masses, psalms, motets; cantatas & other voc. works; pf. pieces, &c.

Israel in Egypt, orat. by Handel (words from the Bible), comp. 1738, prod. London, 4. IV. 1739.

'Israel' Symphony, a sym. by Bloch, comp. 1913–6, 1st perf. N.Y., 3. V. 1916.

Issé, opera by Destouches (lib. by Antoine Houdar de la Motte), prod. Fontainebleau, at court, 7. X. 1679, 1st Paris perf., Opéra, 30. XII. 1697.

-issimo (It. superl. ending), e.g. *pianissimo* = softest; *fortissimo* = loudest, &c.

Istar, symph. vars. by d'Indy, Op. 42, 1st perf. Brussels, 10. I. 1897. The work is based on the Babylonian legend of Ishtar's descent into limbo and illustrates her disrobing at the 7 stations of her progress by the devices of presenting the vars. 1st, in diminishing complexity, and stating the theme only at the end, in bare 8ve unison.

Istel, Edgar (b. Mainz, 23. II. 1880), Ger. mcolst. & comp. Studied at Munich, comp. with Volbach and Thuille and mcol. with Sandberger. He lived and taught there until 1913, when he went to Berlin as lecturer on m. In 1920 he was in Madrid and later went to the U.S.A. His books incl. works on Wagner, Cornelius, Paganini and esp. on var. aspects of opera.

Comps. incl. operas *Der fahrende Schüler*, *Des Tribunals Gebot* & others; incid. m. for Goethe's *Satyros*, &c.; *Hymn to Zeus* & other chor. works; *Singspielouvertüre* for orch. &c.

Istesso tempo, L' (It. from *lo stesso tempo* = the same pace). A direction given where a change is indicated in the time-signature, but the comp. wishes the m. to continue at the same pace or beat in the new rhythm. The change is thus merely one of metre, not of mvt. (The adj. is ***stesso***, the *i* being merely a connecting interpolation, as in, for ex., *in Isvizzera* for *in Svizzera* [in Swi.]).

It. (abbr.) = Italian, Italy.

Italian Concerto, a hpchd. work in 3 mvts., in F maj., by Bach, pub. in 1735 as Part ii of the *Clavierübung* (keyboard exercise) and imitating the It. style, which B. knew from the work of such masters as Albinoni and Vivaldi. Changes between the 2 manuals of the hpchd., prod. alternate *forte* and *piano*, suggest the contrasting effects of the *concertino* and *ripieno* groups in a Concerto grosso.

Italian Overture. *See* **Overture.**

Italian Sixth. A form of the chord of the augmented 6th which has a maj. 3rd above its lowest note, e.g. D♭, F, B.

'Italian' Symphony. Mendelssohn's 4th Sym., Op. 90, in A maj. & min., begun in It. in 1831 and finished in Berlin, 31. III. 1833; 1st perf. London, 13. V. 1833, cond. by the comp.

Italiana in Algeri, L' (*The Italian Girl in Algiers*), opera by Rossini (lib. by Angelo Anelli), prod. Venice, Teatro San Benedetto, 22. V. 1813.

Italiana in Londra, L' (*The Italian Girl in London*), opera by Cimarosa (lib. by Giuseppe Petrosellini), prod. Rome, Teatro Valle, 28. XII. 1778.

Italienisches Liederbuch (*It. Song Book*), H. Wolf's settings of It. poems in Ger. trans. by Paul Heyse, comp. (22 nos.) IX. 1890–XII. 1891 and (24 nos.) III–IV. 1896.

Ivan le Terrible, opera by Bizet (lib. by Arthur Leroy & Henri Trianon, 1st offered to Gounod and refused by him), comp. in 1865 and accepted for prod. by the Théâtre Lyrique in Paris, but withdrawn by the comp., who is said to have burnt the score; this is, however, reported to have been recovered from the Paris Cons. library by the Nazis during their occupation of Paris in 1944 and prepared for prod. at Dresden with a new lib. under the title of *König Turpin*, with the scene laid in Fr. at the Merovingian court of the 6th cent.

Ivan Sussanin, opera by Cavos (lib. by Prince Alexander Alexandrovitch Shakhovskoy), prod. St. Petersburg, 31. X. 1815. The subject is that on which Glinka's *Life for the Tsar* was based in 1836.

The title given to Glinka's *Life for the Tsar* in Soviet Rus.

Ivan the Terrible (Rimsky-Korsakov). *See* **Pskovitianka.**

Ivanhoe, opera by Sullivan (lib. by Julian Russell Sturgis, based on Scott's novel), prod. London, Royal Eng. Opera House (now Palace Theatre), 31. I. 1891.

Ivanov, Mikhail Mikhailovitch (b. Moscow, 23. IX. 1849; d. Rome, 20. X. 1927), Rus. critic & comp. Studied with Tchaikovsky and others at the Moscow Cons., lived mainly in Rome in 1870–6 and then became m. critic to the *Novoie Vremya*.

Works incl. operas *Potemkin's Feast*, *Zabava Putiatishna*, *The Proud Woman* & *Woe to the Wise*; ballet *The Vestal*; Requiem; Sym., symph. prologue *Savonarola*, *Suite champêtre* for orch.; pf. pieces; songs, &c.

Ivanov-Radkevitch, Nikolai Pavlovitch (b. Krasnoyarsk, Siberia, 10. II. 1904), Rus. comp. He was exceptionally gifted as a child, but did not study until 1923, when he went to Vassilenko and Glière at the Moscow Cons. Later he became prof. of orchn. there.

Works incl. a ballet and incid. m. for plays; 3 syms. & *Dance Suite* for orch.; inst. sos., &c.

Ive (or **Ives**), **Simon** (b. Ware, VII. 1600; d. London, 1. VII. 1662), Eng. singer, orgst. & comp. Vicar-choral at St. Paul's cath. in London and orgst. at Christ Church, Newgate, there; singing-master during the Commonwealth, returned to St. Paul's in 1661. In 1633 he took part with W. Lawes in the comp. of Shirley's masque *The Triumph of Peace*. Other works incl. Elegy on the death of W. Lawes, catches & rounds; fancies & other inst. works, &c.

Ives, Charles Edward (b. Danbury, Conn., 20. X. 1874), Amer. comp.

Pupil of H. Parker and D. Buck. Engaged in business, but wrote much m., some in a polytonal idiom employing intervals smaller than the semitone.

Works incl. 5 syms., *3 Places in New England* for orch.; stg. 4tet; 5 v. & pf. sos.; *Aeschylus and Socrates* for voice, pf. & stg. 4tet; chor. works; 3 v. & pf. sos.; 2 sos. & other m. for pf.; org. works; over 200 songs; marches, dances, &c.

Ivrogne corrigé, L' (*The Reformed Drunkard*), opera by Gluck (lib. by Louis Anseaume on a fable by La Fontaine), prod. Vienna, Burg Theatre, IV. 1760.

Opera by Laruette (lib. do.), prod. Paris, Opéra-Comique, 24. VII. 1759.

Ivry, Richard d', Marquis (b. Beaune, 4. II. 1829; d. Hyères, 18. XII. 1903), Fr. amateur comp. who wrote under the name of Richard Yrvid.

Works incl. operas *Fatma, Quentin Matsys, La Maison du docteur, Omphale et Pénélope, Les Amants de Vérone* (on Shakespeare's *Romeo and Juliet*) & *Persévérance d'amour*.

J

Jaches de Wert. *See* **Wert.**

Jachet Buus. *See* **Buus.**

Jachet da Mantua (Jaquet ?) (b. ?; d. ?, *c.* 1559), Flem. singer & comp. Attached to San Pietro cath. at Mantua in 1527–58. Wrote masses, magnificats, motets, psalms, hymns, &c.

Jack. The mechanism in the virginal, hpchd. and similar insts. by which the stgs. are plucked.

Jackson, William (b. Exeter, 29. V. 1730; d. Exeter, 5. VII. 1803), Eng. orgst. & comp. Learnt m. as a choir-boy in Exeter cath., then studied in London, became m. teacher at Exeter and from 1777 held var. appts. at the cath. there.

Works incl. operas *The Lord of the Manor* & *The Metamorphosis*; a stage piece *Lycidas* (based on Milton); Te Deum, services, anthems & other church m.; setting of Pope's ode *The Dying Christian*; var. voc. pieces & songs; hpchd. sos., &c.

Jackson, William (b. Masham, Yorks, 9. I. 1815; d. Bradford, 15. IV. 1866), Eng. orgst & comp. Mainly self-taught, he was so gifted as to be app. church orgst. at the age of 16. Having been a tallow-chandler for some years, he went to Bradford as m. dealer, orgst. & choirmaster; later cond. the Bradford Festival.

Works incl. orat. *The Deliverance of Israel from Babylon*, Psalm ciii for solo voices, chor. & orch., cantata *The Year*; services, anthems, a mass, &c.; partsongs, glees; songs, &c.

Jacob, Gordon (Percival Septimus) (b. London, 5. VII. 1895), Eng. comp. & cond. Studied under Stanford and C. Wood at the R.C.M., where later he became prof. of orchn. D.Mus., London, 1935.

Works incl. ballets *The Jew in the Bush* & *Uncle Remus* (after J. C. Harris); m. for films; Sinfonietta, Vars. on an air by Purcell and on an orig. theme for orch., *Passacaglia on a Well-known Theme* (' Oranges and Lemons ') for orch.; Sym. & *Denbigh* suite for stgs., Divertimento for small orch.; concs. for pf., v., va. & ob.; Suite for military band; 4tet for ob. & stgs. and other chamber m.; inst. pieces, &c.

Jacob, Max (1876–1944), Fr. dramatist. *See* **Honegger** (*Mort de Sainte Alméenne*, **Poulenc** (*Bal masqué*).

Jacob, Maxime (b. Bordeaux, 13. I. 1906), Fr. comp. Pupil of Milhaud and later a member of Satie's ' École d'Arcueil.'

Works incl. comic opera; orch. m.; pf. pieces; songs, &c.

Jacobi, Frederick (b. San Francisco, 4. V. 1891), Amer. cond. & comp. Pupil of Bloch & others in U.S.A. and of Juon in Berlin. Asst. cond. at Metrop. Opera in N.Y., 1913–7, later studied m. of the Pueblo Indians in Mexico and Arizona. Prof. of comp. in N.Y. from 1924.

Works incl. Sym., *Indian Dances*, *The Eve of St. Agnes* (after Keats), &c. for orch.; concs. for pf., v. & co.; Sabbath Evening Service; *Two Assyrian Prayers* & *The Poet in the Desert* for voice & orch.; 2 stg. 4tets, pf. 5tet *Hagiographia*, Scherzo for wind insts., &c.

Jacobs, W(illiam). W(ymark). (1863–1941), Eng. novelist. *See* **Boatswain's Mate** (Smyth).

Jacobsen, Jens Peter (1847–85), Dan. poet & novelist. *See* **Fennimore und Gerda** (Delius), **Hamerik (E.)** (*Marie Grubbe*), **Schoenberg** (*Gurrelieder*).

Jacobson, Maurice (b. London, 1. I. 1896), Eng. pfst. & comp. Studied at the R.C.M. in London under Stanford and Holst. He is a dir. of the m. pub. house of Curwen and frequently adjudicates at mus. competition festivals.

Works incl. ballet *David*; incid. m. for Shakespeare's *Antony and Cleopatra*, *Hamlet*, *Julius Caesar* & *Macbeth*; m. for broadcast *The Woman of Samaria* (after Rostand's *La Samaritaine*); *The Lady of Shalott* (Tennyson) for chor. & orch.; Suite for fl., co. & pf.; Theme & Vars. and numerous pf. works; songs, &c.

Jacques, Gheert & **Jacques, Jean** } *See* **Turnhout.**

Jacquet, Élisabeth. *See* **La Guerre.**

Jadassohn, Salomon (b. Breslau, 13. VIII. 1831; d. Leipzig, 1. II. 1902), Ger. comp., cond. & teacher. Studied at the Leipzig Cons. and under Liszt at Weimar. Became cond. at Leipzig and later prof. at the Cons. He wrote several theoret. works.

Comps. incl. Psalms and cantatas; 4 syms., ovts. and serenades (1 in canon) for orch.; 2 pf. concs.; 2 stg. 4tets, pf. trios, 4tets, 5tets & 6tet, &c.

Jadin, Louis Emmanuel (b. Versailles, 2. IX. 1768: d. Paris, 11. IV. 1853), Fr. comp., son of the vst. & comp. Jean J. Worked at the Théâtre de Monsieur in Paris from 1789 and became pf. prof. at the Cons. in 1802.

Works incl. opera *Joconde* and *c.* 40 others; voc. & inst. works for the Revol. festivals; *La Bataille d'Austerlitz* for orch.; chamber m.; works for 1 & 2 pfs., &c.

Jagd, Die (*The Chase*), opera by J. A. Hiller (lib. by Christian Felix Weisse, based on Jean Michel's Sedaine's lib. for Monsigny's *Le Roi et le fermier*), prod. Weimar, 29. I. 1770.

Jahn, Otto (b. Kiel, 16. VI. 1813; d. Göttingen, 9. IX. 1869), Ger. philol., archaeol. & writer on art and m. Studied at Kiel, Leipzig and Berlin, became prof. at Greifswald and later at Bonn. His numerous writings on m. include the 1st large-scale work written on Mozart.

Jaleo. A Spa. dance in moderate 3–8 time, accomp. by Castanets.

James, Philip (b. Jersey City, N.J., 17. V. 1890), Amer. cond., orgst., teacher & comp. Studied in N.Y. and became prof. at Columbia and N.Y. Univs.

Works incl. *Missa imaginum*, *Stabat Mater* & other chor. works; ovts. on Fr. Noëls & *Bret Harte*, Welsh rhapsody *Gwallia*, *Station WGZBX*, for orch.; Suite for stg. orch.; pf. 4tet, woodwind 5tet, &c.

Jammes, Francis (1868–1938), Fr. poet & novelist. *See* **Durey** (songs).

Janáček, Leoš (b. Hukvaldy, Moravia, 3. VII. 1854; d. Prague, 12. VIII. 1928), Cz. comp. Son of a poor schoolmaster; became choir-boy at the monastery of the Austin Friars at Brno; later earned his living as m. teacher and went to the Org. School in Prague for study. Cond. var. chor. socs., made some desultory studies at Leipzig and Vienna, and in 1881 returned to Brno to found an Org. School there, where he taught until it was taken over by the state in 1920, when he became prof. of a master class at the Prague Cons. Made close studies of folksong and speech, which he applied to his voc. m.

Works incl. operas *The Beginning of a Novel*, *Fate*, *Her Stepdaughter* (*Jenufa*), *The Excursions of Mr. Brouček* (after Čech), *Káta Kabanová*, *The Cunning Little Vixen*, *Sárka*, *The Makropoulos Case* (on a play by Čapek), *From the House of the Dead* (after Dostoievsky); *The Eternal Gospel* for solo voices, chor. & orch., *The Wandering Madman* (Tagore) for sop. & male-voice chor., numerous chor. works, many for male voices; *Šumařovo Dítě*, rhapsody *Taras Bulba* (on Gogol), *The Ballad of Blanik*, Sinfonietta for orch.; stg. 4tet (on Tolstoy's *Kreutzer Sonata*), wind 6tet *Youth*, suite for 2 v., va., co. & db.; v. & pf. So.; pf. So., vars., &c.; org. works; *The Diary of a Vanished One* for voice & pf., Morav. folksongs for voice & pf., &c.

Janiewicz, Felix (b. Vilna, 1762; d. Edinburgh, 1848), Pol. vst. Studied in Vienna, where he met Haydn and Mozart, and in It. Appeared in Paris and London later and settled 1st at Liverpool and then at Edinburgh.

Janissaries. Turkish infantry forming a bodyguard for the sultan. Their m. made use of special percussion insts. incl. the Turkish Crescent or Jingling Johnny, imitated by western comps., as in Haydn's 'Military' Sym. (No. 100) and Mozart's *Entführung*. Brahms playfully called the 3rd mvt. of his 4th Sym. 'janissaries' m.'

Jannaconi, Giuseppe (b. Rome, 1741; d. Rome, 16. III. 1816), It. comp. Studied in Rome, where in 1811 he became chapel master at St. Peter's in succession to Zingarelli.

Works incl. 30 masses, 42 psalms, motets & other church m., some for several antiphonal choirs, &c.

Jannequin, Clément (b. ?, *c.* 1475; d. ?, *c.* 1560), Fr. comp. Pupil (?) of Josquin des Prés. He may have become a Huguenot in the course of his long life.

Works incl. masses on his own songs *La Bataille* & *L'Aveugle Dieu*, motet *Congregati sunt*, *Proverbes de Salomon*, *Psaumes de David* (both to Fr. rhymed versions); numerous chansons for 4 voices containing imitative and descriptive passages, &c.

Janotha, Nathalie (b. Warsaw, 8. VI. 1856; d. The Hague, 9. VI. 1932), Pol. pfst. Studied in Berlin, also with Clara Schumann, Brahms & others, and made her 1st appearance at Leipzig in 1874.

Jaques-Dalcroze, Émile (b. Vienna, 6. VII. 1865), Swi. teacher & comp. Studied with Delibes in Paris, with Bruckner and Fuchs in Vienna and at the Geneva Cons., where in 1892 he became prof. of harmony. There he invented a system of teaching m. by co-ordination with bodily mvt., known as Eurhythmics. In 1910 he founded an institute for this purpose at Hellerau nr. Dresden.

Works incl. operas *Le Violon maudit*, *Janie*, *Sancho Panza* (after Cervantes), *Le Bonhomme Jadis*, *Les Jumeaux de Bergame*, *La Fille au vautour* (after W. von Hillern's *Die*

Geier-Wally), festival play *La Fête de la jeunesse et de la joie*; chor. works *La Veillée*, *Festival vaudois*; suite for orch.; 2 v. concs.; 3 stg. 4tets; pf. pieces; many collections of popular and children's songs, *Chansons de route*, *Rondes enfantines*, *Chansons de gestes*, &c.

Jarnach, Philipp (b. Noisy, Fr., 26. VII. 1892), Franco-Spa. comp. Studied pf. with Risler and comp. with Lavignac in Paris, went to Swi. in 1914 and taught ctpt. at the Zürich Cons. in 1918–21, when he settled in Berlin and continued to study with Busoni, whose unfinished opera *Doktor Faust* he completed.

Works incl. prelude to *Prometheus*, Suite *Winterbilder*, *Prologue to a Tournament*, *Sinfonia brevis*, *Morgenklangspiel*, Prelude No. 1, *Musik mit Mozart* for orch.; stg. 4tet & 5tet; v. & pf. So., 2 sos. for unaccomp. v.; *Konzertstück* for org.; Sonatina & other works for pf.; songs with orch. and with pf., &c.

Järnefelt, Armas (b. Viborg, 14. VIII. 1869), Fin. cond. & comp. Studied at Helsingfors, Berlin and Paris, cond. at var. Ger. theatres and in 1898–1903 at Helsingfors. App. cond. of the Opera there in 1903 and at Stockholm in 1907.

Works incl. incid. m. to *The Promised Land*; chor. works; orch. m. incl. *Praeludium* & *Berceuse* for small orch.; songs, &c.

Järnefelt-Palmgren (*née* **Pakarinen**), **Maikki** (b. Joensuu, 26. VIII. 1871; d. Turku, 4. VII. 1929), Fin. sop. singer, wife, 1st of prec., then of Palmgren. Studied at Helsingfors and in Paris, Berlin and It. She married Järnefelt in 1893 and in 1895 began to appear in opera in Ger. After a divorce she married Palmgren in 1910 and went to live in U.S.A. with him for several years in 1923.

Jarnowick. *See* **Giornovichi.**

Jazz. Amer. dance m. of the early 20th cent. developed out of Ragtime and relying for its effects mainly on syncopations and rhythmic displacement of accents which do not, however, affect the regular metrical monotony of the beat; and on a special combination of insts., incl. plucked stg. insts. and saxophones, made to play abnormally for the most part, e.g. *pizzicato* db., muted brass, &c. J. has influenced certain comps., e.g. Stravinsky in *Ragtime*, Milhaud in *La Création du monde* and *Le Bœuf sur le toit*, Křenek in *Jonny spielt auf*, Gershwin in the *Rhapsody in Blue*, Copland in the ballet *Billy the Kid*, Blitzstein in his operas, &c., Hindemith in *Kammermusik No. 1*, Lambert in *The Rio Grande*, Weill in *Mahagonny* & *Dreigroschenoper*, &c.

Jean de Neuvellois (or **Neuville**) (b. Château-Neuville, Champagne), Fr. 12-cent. troubadour. 19 of his songs are still preserved.

Jean de Paris, opera by Boïeldieu (lib. by Claude Godard d'Aucour de Saint-Just), prod. Paris, Opéra-Comique, 4. IV. 1812.

Jean Paul. *See* **Richter, J. P.**

Jeanie Deans, opera by MacCunn (lib. by Joseph Bennett, based on Scott's *Heart of Midlothian*), prod. Edinburgh, 15. XI. 1894.

Jeanne d'Arc au bûcher (*Joan of Arc at the Stake*), dramatic orat. by Honegger (lib. by Paul Claudel), prod. Basle, 12. V. 1938.

Jeans, James (**Hopwood**) (b. London, 11. IX. 1877), Eng. astronomer & physicist. Wrote a book on acoustics, *Science and Music*. Knighted 1928.

Jeffries, George (b. ?; d. ?, 1685), Eng. comp. Steward to Lord Hatton of Kirby, Northants., member of the Chapel Royal, orgst. to Charles I at Oxford in 1643 during the Civil War.

Works incl. services, anthems, over 120 motets, sacred solos and duets, carols; m. for masques & plays; secular songs, duets, &c.; fancies for stgs. & virginals, &c.

Jeffries, Matthew (b. ?; d. ?), Eng. 16th–17th-cent. comp. Vicar-choral at Wells cath. Comp. services, anthems, &c.

Jelmoli, Hans (b. Zürich, 17. I. 1877; d. Zürich, 6. V. 1936), Swi. pfst., cond., critic & comp. Studied with Humperdinck and others at Frankfort o/M., and after cond. opera in Ger. settled at Zürich as teacher and critic.

Works incl. operas *Sein Vermächtnis*, *Prinz Goldhaar*, *Die Schweizer*, *Die Badenerfahrt*, *Das Gespenst auf dem Petersturm*; incid. m. to Wiegand's *Marignano* & other plays; cantata to words from *Des Knaben Wunderhorn*; pf. pieces; chors.; songs, &c.

Jélyotte, Pierre de (b. Lasseube, Basses-Pyrénées, 13. IV. 1713; d. Estos, Basses-Pyrénées, 11. IX. 1787). Fr. alto singer, guitar player, cst., hpchdst. & comp. Studied for the priesthood, but became a versatile musn. and 1st appeared as singer at the Paris Opéra in 1733 and at the Concert spirituel in 1734; later appeared at court and taught the guitar to the king. Comps. incl. m. to the comedy-ballet *Zelisca*.

Jemnitz, Alexander (b. Budapest, 9. VIII. 1890), Hung. comp. & critic. Studied at the Budapest Cons., then with Reger at Leipzig and lastly with Schoenberg in Berlin, where he also taught. Later he returned to Budapest.

Works incl. Prelude and Fugue for orch.; chor. m.; 2 stgs. trios, trios for var. other insts., Partita for 2 vs., 3 v. & pf. sos., sos. for va. & co., saxophone and banjo; Passacaglia and Fugue for org.; 3 pf. sos., unaccomp. sos. for v., co., db., harp & tpt., &c.

Jenkins, John (b. Maidstone, 1592; d. Kimberley, Norfolk, 27. X. 1678), Eng. comp., lutenist & stg. player. He lived under the patronage of the gentry and nobility, esp. Sir Hamon L'Estrange in Norfolk and Lord North, whose sons, incl. Roger, he taught m. His last patron was Sir Philip Wodehouse at Kimberley.

Works incl. fancies and *Rants* for viols; fancies for org.; other inst. pieces; anthems and psalms; Elegy on the death of W. Lawes, *Theophila, or Love's Sacrifice, A Divine Poem* for voices; rounds, songs; 12 sos. for 2 vs. & bass, &c.

Jensen, Adolph (b. Königsberg, 12. I. 1837; d. Baden-Baden, 23. I. 1879), Ger. pfst. & comp., grandson of the orgst. & comp. Wilhelm J. (d. 1842), prof. of m. at Königsberg Univ. A. J. studied under var. masters, visited Rus. and Copenhagen, where he made friends with Gade, was back at Königsberg in 1860–6, taught the pf. in Berlin for the next 2 years and then lived at Dresden, Graz & elsewhere for his health.

Works incl. opera *Die Erbin von Montfort* (adapted to a new lib. based on Gozzi's *Turandot* by Kienzl after his death); cantatas *Jephthas Tochter, Der Gang der Jünger nach Emmaus, Donald Caird* (Scott) & *Adonisfeier*; Concert Ovt. & *Geistliches Tonstück* for orch.; Ovt. & *Geistliches Tonstück* for orch.; c. 25 op. nos. of pf. m. incl. *Innere Stimmen, Romantische Studien*, So. in F♯ min., *Deutsche Suite, Erotikon, Ländler aus Berchtesgaden; Hochzeitsmusik, Abendmusik, Lebensbilder, Silhouetten, Ländliche Festmusik*, &c. for pf. duet; song for bar. & orch. *Alt Heidelberg*; c. 30 sets of songs incl. 2 from Geibel & Heyse's *Spanisches Liederbuch, Liebeslieder, Dolorosa* (from Chamisso's *Tränen*), *Gaudeamus* (Scheffel), *Romanzen und Balladen* & songs from Burns, Scott, Moore, Allan Cunningham, Tennyson, Mrs. Hemans and Herder's *Stimmen der Völker*; partsongs, &c.

Jensen, Johannes (Vilhelm) (b. 1873), Dan. poet, novelist & dramatist. *See* **Riisager** (*Darduse*).

Jenufa (Janáček). *See* **Her Stepdaughter.**

Jephta's Gelübde (*Jephtha's Vow*), opera by Meyerbeer (lib. by Alois Schreiber), prod. Munich, 23. XII. 1812. Meyerbeer's 1st opera.

Jephté (*Jephtha*), opera by Montéclair (lib. by Simon Joseph de Pellegrin), prod. Paris, Opéra, 28. II. 1732.

Jephtha, orat. by Handel (lib. by Thomas Morell), prod. London, Covent Garden Theatre, 26. II. 1752.

Jeppesen, Knud (b. Copenhagen, 15. VIII. 1892), Dan. mcolst. Studied with Nielsen and Thomas Laub at Copenhagen and later with Adler and Robert Lach in Vienna. App. dir. of the Cons. and prof. of mus. science at the Univ. of Copenhagen. His books incl. studies of Palestrina, voc. polyphony, the It. *laudi*, &c.

Jeremiáš, Bohuslav (b. Řestoky nr. Chrudim, 1. V. 1859; d. Budějovice, 18. I. 1918), Cz. orgst., chor. cond. & comp. Having held var. other posts, he was in 1906 app. dir. of the m. school at Budějovice.

Jeremiáš, Jaroslav (b. Písek, 14. VIII. 1889; d. Budějovice, 16. I. 1919), Cz. comp., son of prec. Pupil of Novák and others at the Prague Cons.

Works incl. opera *The Old King*; mystery play *Rimoni*; orat. *Jan Hus*; symph. idyll *A Summer's Day*, &c.

Jeremiáš, Otakar (b. Písek, 17. X. 1892), Cz. comp., brother of prec. Pupil of Novák at the Prague Cons. Succeeded his father at Budějovice.

Works incl. opera *The Brothers Karamazov* (after Dostoievsky), &c.

Jérusalem. The title of the Fr. version of Verdi's opera *I Lombardi alla prima crociata*.

Jervis-Read, H(arold). V(incent). (b. Powyke, Worcs., 14. III. 1883), Eng. comp. Prof. of comp. at the R.A.M. in London.

Works incl. Concertino da camera for 2 vs. & chamber orch.; chamber m.; So., Poems & pieces for pf., &c.

Jery und Bätely, play with m. by Reichardt (text by Goethe), prod. Berlin, Opera, 30. III. 1801.

Play with m. by Carl Siegmund von Seckendorff (text do.), prod. Weimar, at court, 12. VII. 1780.

Jessonda, opera by Spohr (lib. by Eduard Heinrich Gehe, based on Lemierre's tragedy *La Veuve de Malabar*), prod. Cassel, 28. VII. 1823.

Jeune France, La. A group of young Fr. comps. formed in 1936 by Baudrier, Jolivet, Lesur and Messiaen.

Jeune Henri, Le (*The Young Henry*), opera by Méhul (lib. by Jean Nicolas Bouilly, orig. intended for Grétry and called *La Jeunesse de Henri IV*), prod. Paris, Opéra-Comique, 1. V. 1797. The ovt. called *La Chasse du* *jeune Henri* was known as a concert piece long after the opera was forgotten.

Jeune Sage et le vieux fou, Le (*The Wise Youth and the Old Fool*), opera by Méhul (lib. by François Benoît Hoffman), prod. Paris, Opéra-Comique, 28. III. 1793.

Jeux, ballet by Debussy (chgph. by Vaslav Nizhinsky), comp. in 1912 and prod. Paris, Théâtre du Châtelet, 13. V. 1913.

Jew's Harp. An ancient and primitive inst. consisting of a metal frame held between the player's teeth and a vibrating metal tongue set in motion by the fingers and emitting a note which can be varied by changes in the cavity of the mouth.

Jewels of the Madonna (Wolf-Ferrari). *See* **Gioielli della Madonna.**

Jewess, The (Halévy). *See* **Juive, La.**

Jhan, ? (called Maître J.) (poss. identical with Gero) (b. ?; d. ?), ? Fr. or Flem. 16th-cent. comp. He was chapel master to Ercole d'Este, Duke of Ferrara. Comp. motets, psalms, sacred songs for several voices, madrigals, &c.

Jig. An old dance in binary form in some kind of animated triple time, usually 6–8 or 12–8; the It. *giga* and Fr. *gigue*. It is one of the dances regularly found in suites, where it forms the finale. Comps. of suites acquired a habit of building the 2nd part on an inversion of the theme of the 1st.

Jingling Johnny. *See* **Chinese Pavilion.**

Jirák, Karel Boleslav (b. Prague, 28. I. 1891), Cz. cond. & comp. Studied with Novák in Prague and was later influenced by J. B. Foerster. Cond. at the Hamburg Opera in 1815–8, but returned to Prague and cond. the Hlahol chor. soc. on a tour in Yslv., 1920–1.

Works incl. opera *Apollonius of Tyana*; 2 syms., ovt. to a Shakespearian comedy; stg. 4tet, stg. 6tet; sos. for v. & pf. and co. & pf.; song-cycles *Tragi-Comedy* (Heine), *Meditations, Brief Happiness, 3 Songs of Home, Evening and the Soul*; *Suite in the Old Style* for pf., &c.

Jiránek, Josef (b. Ledeč, 24. III. 1855), Cz. pfst., teacher & comp. Pupil of Smetana. Prof. of pf. at Kharkov in 1877–91 and from 1927 at the Prague Cons.

Works incl. Ballad and *Scherzo fantastique* for orch.; pf. Trio, pf. 5tet; songs, chors., &c.

Joachim, Amalie. *See* **Weiss.**

Joachim, Joseph (b. Kittsee nr. Pozsony, 28. VI. 1831; d. Berlin, 15. VIII. 1907), Hung. (Germanized) vst. & comp. Lived successively at Leipzig, Weimar, Hanover and Berlin; frequent visitor to Eng.; founder of the J. 4tet, 1869, and head of one of the mus. depts. of the Royal Acad. of Arts in Berlin.

Works incl. ovts. for orch. to Shakespeare's *Hamlet* and *Henry IV*, in commemoration of Kleist and on 2 comedies by Gozzi; 3 v. concs. (incl. 'Hung.'), Vars. for v. & orch.; Vars. for va. & pf.; v. & pf. pieces; Marfa's scene from Schiller's *Demetrius* for con. & orch., &c.

Joan of Arc. *See* **Giovanna d'Arco, Jeanne d'Arc au bûcher, Maid of Orleans.**

Job, masque for dancing by Vaughan Williams (chgph. by Ninette de Valois, settings by Gwendolen Raverat, based on Blake's illustrations to the Book of Job), prod. London, Cambridge Theatre, 5. VII. 1931.

Orat. by Parry (words from the Book of Job), prod. Gloucester Festival, 1892.

Jocelyn, opera by Godard (lib. by Paul Armand Silvestre & Victor Capoul, based on Lamartine's poem), prod. Brussels, Théâtre de la Monnaie, 25. II. 1888. It contains the popular *Berceuse de Jocelyn*.

Johansen, David Monrad (b. Vefsen, 8. XI. 1888), Norw. comp. & critic. Studied at Oslo and Berlin, Humperdinck being among his masters. He became m. critic of 2 Norw. papers in succession and ed. of the *Norsk Musikblad*, and has written a life of Grieg.

Works incl. Symph. Fantasy for orch.; large chor. works, unaccomp. chors.; v. & pf. So.; 5 suites for pf., &c.

John of Forsete (Forncett) (b. Forncett, Norfolk, ?; d. Reading, 19. I. 1239), Eng. monk & musn. Monk at Reading Abbey. Hitherto considered the prob. comp. of the rota 'Sumer is icumen in'; but this is now conjectured to be too late for his dates (*c.* 1280 at the earliest).

Johnny plays (Křenek). *See* **Jonny spielt auf.**

Johnson, Edward (b. ?; d. ?), Eng. 16th–17th-cent. comp. ? in the service of Lord Hertford at Elvetham, where (?) he contrib. m. to an entertainment given to Queen Elizabeth in 1591. Mus.B., Cambridge, 1594.

Works incl. madrigals, viol m., virginal pieces, &c.

Johnson, John (b. ?, *c.* 1540; d. ?, 1595), Eng. lutenist & comp. Attached to Queen Elizabeth's court and (?) to the household of Sir Thomas Kitson at Hengrave Hall, Suffolk, and in London, 1572–4. Took part in Leicester's entertainments at Kenilworth castle in 1575.

Wrote lute pieces, songs to the lute, &c.

Johnson, Robert (b. Duns, *c.* 1490; d. ?, *c.* 1565), Sco. priest & comp. Fled to Eng. as a heretic and (?) settled at Windsor. Wrote Lat. motets, Eng. services & prayers, In Nomines for insts., songs, &c.

Johnson, Robert (b. ?, *c.* 1583; d. ?, before 30. IV. 1634), Eng. lutenist & comp., son of John J. Was taught m. at the expense of Sir George Carey, husband of Sir Thomas Kitson's granddaughter, in whose household (? in Suffolk) he was brought up, and was app. lutenist to James I in 1604; taught Prince Henry and remained in his post under Charles I.

Works incl. songs for several voices; songs to the lute; catches; pieces for viols; also songs in Shakespeare's *Tempest*, in Fletcher's *Valentinian* & *The Mad Lover*, (?) Middleton's *The Witch* and (?) Jonson's *Masque of Gypsies*.

Joio, Norman dello. *See* Dello Joio.

Jókai, Mór (or **Maurus**) (1825–1904), Hung. novelist. *See* **Zigeunerbaron** (J. Strauss).

Jolie Fille de Perth, La (*The Fair Maid of Perth*), opera by Bizet (lib. by Jules Henri Vernoy de Saint-Georges & Édouard Adenis, based on Scott's novel), prod. Paris, Théâtre Lyrique, 26. XII. 1867.

Jolivet, André (b. Paris, 8. VIII. 1905), Fr. comp. Pupil of Le Flem and Varèse. He formed the group of 'La Jeune France' with Baudrier, Lesur and Messiaen in 1936.

Works incl. *Danse incantatoire* for orch.; *3 Chants d'hommes* for 3 bars. & orch.; *3 Poèmes* for Ondes Martenot & pf.; suite *Mana* for pf., &c.

Jommelli, Niccolò (b. Aversa nr. Naples, 10. IX. 1714; d. Naples, 25. VIII. 1774), It. comp. Pupil of Feo, Mancini and Leo at Naples. Prod. his 1st opera in 1737, became famous all over It. and in Vienna. In 1753 he was app. chapel master to the Duke of Württemberg at Stuttgart, where he remained 15 years, returning to Naples afterwards.

Works incl. c. 50 operas, e.g. *Ezio, Achille in Sciro, Didone, Ciro, Merope, L'Olimpiade, Artaserse, Ifigenia in Aulide, Fetonte, Armida, Demofoonte, Ifigenia in Tauride*; Requiem, Miserere & other church m.; Passion Orat., orats. *Betulia liberata* & *Isacco*; cantatas, &c.

Jonas, Émile (b. Paris, 5. III. 1827; d. Saint-Germain, 22. V. 1905), Fr. comp. Studied at the Paris Cons., prof. of Solfège there in 1847–65, dir. of m. at the Port. synagogue and bandmaster in the Garde Nationale. Prod. his 1st operetta, *Le Duel de Benjamin*, in 1855.

Works incl. numerous operettas, e.g. *Avant la Noce, Les Deux Arlequins, Le Canard à trois becs, Cinderella the Younger* (*Javotte*), *Le Premier Baiser*; collection of Hebrew tunes, &c.

Joncières, Victorin de (real name Félix Ludger Rossignol) (b. Paris, 12. IV. 1839; d. Paris, 26. X. 1903), Fr. comp. Began by studying painting, but set a friend's adapt. of Molière's *Le Sicilien* as a comic opera with such success that he entered the Cons. He left again after a disagreement about Wagner, whom he admired, and studied privately. In 1871 he became m. critic to *La Liberté*.

Works incl. operas *Sardanapale, Le Dernier Jour de Pompéi* (after Bulwer-Lytton), *Dimitri, La Reine Berthe, Le Chevalier Jean, Lancelot*, incid. m. to Shakespeare's *Hamlet*; *La Mer*, symph. ode for m.-sop., chor. & orch.; suite for orch. *Les Nubiennes, Sérénade hongroise*, ovt., marches & other orch. m.; v. Conc., &c.

Jone (Petrella). *See* **Ione**.

Jones, Edward (b. Llanderfel, Merioneth, 2. IV. 1752; d. London, 18. IV. 1824), Welsh harper & song collector. Taught the hp. by his father, he went to London in 1775 and was app. bard to the Prince of Wales in 1783. Pub. several collections of Welsh & other nat. airs.

Jones, John (b. ?, 1728; d. London, 17. II. 1796), Eng. orgst. & comp. App. orgst. of the Middle Temple in 1749, of Charterhouse, succeeding Pepusch, in 1753 and of St. Paul's cath. in 1755. Wrote chants, hpchd. lessons, &c.

Jones, Robert (b. ?; d. *c.* 1617), Eng. lutenist & comp. He worked for several patrons and took the Mus.B. degree at Oxford in 1597. In 1610, with Rosseter and others, he obtained a patent to train children for the queen's revels, and in 1615 they were allowed to erect a theatre in Blackfriars, but its opening was subsequently prohibited.

Works incl. madrigals, 5 books of songs to the lute, anthems, &c.

Jones, Sidney (b. Leeds, 1869; d. Kew, 29. I. 1946), Eng. cond. & comp. At first a bandmaster & cond. of a travelling opera, he became cond. of the Empire Theatre in London in 1905. Wrote a number of operettas, incl. *The Geisha, San Toy, The Greek Slave, My Lady Molly*, &c.

Jongen, Joseph (b. Liége, 14. XII. 1873), Belg. comp. Studied at the Liége Cons. Gained a prize from the Académie Royale in 1893 and the

Belg. Prix de Rome in 1897. After teaching for a short time at the Liége Cons., he went to Rome and later travelled in Ger. & Fr., taking up a prof.-ship at Liége in 1903. In 1914–8 he was in Eng. as a war refugee, but returned to Liége until 1920, when he became prof. at the Brussels Cons., of which he was later app. director.

Works incl. ballet *S'Arka*; *Fantaisie sur deux Noëls wallons*, symph. poem *Lalla Rookh* (after Thomas Moore), *Impressions d'Ardennes*, *Tableaux pittoresques*, *Passecaille et Gigue* for orch.; *Pièce symphonique* for pf. & wind orch., Suite for va. & orch., *Symphonie concertante* for org. & orch.; 3 stg. 4tets, 2 Serenades for stg. 4tet, pf. Trio; 2 v. & pf. sos., co. So.; *Sonata eroica* for org.; Introd. & Dance for va. & pf. and other inst. pieces; *Suite en forme de sonate* & other pf. works; songs. &c.

Jongleur (Fr. = juggler). A medieval wandering minstrel, one of whose accomplishments was juggling, but who also sang and played. Such a J. is the subject of Massenet's opera below.

Jongleur de Notre Dame, Le (*Our Lady's Juggler*), opera by Massenet (lib. by Maurice Léna on a story by Anatole France in *L'Étui de nacre*, based on a medieval miracle play), prod. Monte Carlo, 18. II. 1902.

Jonny spielt auf (*Johnny plays*), opera by Křenek (lib. by comp.), prod. Leipzig, Munic. Opera, 10. II. 1927.

Jonson, Ben(jamin) (1573–1637), Eng. poet & dramatist. *See* **Alchemist** (Handel), **Angiolina** (Salieri), **Auric** (*Volpone*), **Bell** (*Vision of Delight*), **Ferrabosco** (A. ii) (masques), **Harington** (' Drink to me only '), **Johnson** (R. ii) (*Masque of Gypsies*), **Lanier** (*Masque of Lethe* & *Vision of Delight*), **Lothar** (*Lord Spleen*), **Pastoral** (Bliss), **Schweigsame Frau** (R. Strauss), **Spanish Lady** (Elgar), **Vaughan Williams** (*Pan's Anniversary*).

Joseffy, Rafael (b. Hunfalu, 3. VII. 1852; d. New York, 25. VI. 1915), Hung. pfst. Studied at Budapest, Leipzig & Berlin, also with Liszt at Weimar; made his 1st public appearance in 1872, at Berlin; settled in N.Y. in 1879.

Joseph, opera by Méhul (lib. by Alexandre Duval), prod. Paris, Opéra-Comique, 17. II. 1807. Weber wrote pf. Vars., Op. 28, on a romance from it and Ethel Smyth used a tune in *Entente cordiale*.

Joseph and his Brethren, orat. by Handel (lib. by James Miller), prod. London, Covent Garden Theatre, 2. III. 1744.

Josephslegende (R. Strauss). *See* **Legend of Joseph.**

Joshua, orat. by Handel (lib. by Thomas Morell), prod. London, Covent Garden Theatre, 9. III. 1748.

Josquin (Josse) des Prés (or Deprés) (b. Condé, Hainault, *c.* 1445; d. Condé, 27. VIII. 1521), Flem. comp. Pupil of Okeghem. He became a singer in the Papal Chapel at Rome in 1486, having spent some time at var. It. courts before; later in the service of the Emperor Maximilian and became provost of the collegiate church at Condé, where he remained to his death.

Works incl. masses, motets, psalms, *Stabat Mater*, *Miserere*, *Ave Maria* & other church m.; chansons for several voices, &c.

Josten, Werner (b. Elberfeld, 12. VI. 1888), Ger.-Amer .comp. Studied in Munich, Geneva (with Jaques-Dalcroze) and Paris. In 1918 he became asst. cond. at the Munich opera, but in 1920 emigrated to U.S.A. App. prof. at Smith Coll., Northampton, Mass., in 1923.

Works incl. ballets *Jungle*, *Batouala*, *Joseph and his Brethren*, *Endymion*; *Crucifixion* for bass solo and chor., *Hymnus to the Quene of Paradys* for con. solo, women's chor., stgs. & org., *Ode for St. Cecilia's Day* for solo voices, chor. & orch.; Sym. in F maj., Serenade, &c. for orch.; 2 *Concerti sacri* for stgs. & pf., &c.

Jota. Spa. dance, esp. of Aragon and Navarre. It dates from the 12th cent. and may be connected with the Moor Aben Jot. It is in quick 3–4 time. The m. is played on insts. of the guitar type and usually accomp. by castanets & other percussion.

Joteyko, Tadeusz (b. Potsuiky nr. Kiev, 1. IV. 1872; d. Cieszyn, 19. VIII. 1932), Pol. comp., critic & teacher. Studied with Gevaert at Brussels & Noskowski at Warsaw. There he cond. the Phil. Orch. in 1914–8 and was app. prof. at the State Cons.

Works incl. operas *The Minstrel*, *Zygmunt August*, *The Fishermen*, *Queen Jadwiga*, *Kilinski*; *The Phantom*, *Peasant Wedding* & *Suite of the Legions* for chor.; Sym., Pol. Ovt., Pol. Suite, *Le Doute et la foi*, *Christmas*, *Esquisses maritimes* & *Tatra* suite for orch., &c.

Journet, Marcel (b. Grasse, 1870; d. Vittel, IX. 1933), Fr. bar. singer. Studied at the Paris Cons. and made his 1st appearance at the Théâtre de la Monnaie at Brussels in 1891. He was a well-known figure at the Paris Opéra, the Teatro alla Scala in Milan, Covent Garden Opera in London and the Metrop. in N.Y.

Joyce Book. A collection of settings of poems by James Joyce by George Antheil, Arnold Bax, Arthur Bliss, Edgardo Carducci, Bernard van Dieren, Eugene Goossens, Herbert Howells, Herbert Hughes, John Ireland, E. J. Moeran, C. W. Orr, Albert Roussel & Roger Sessions, ed. by Herbert Hughes, pub. in 1932.

Joyce, James (1882–1941), Ir. novelist & poet. *See* **Barber** (*Chamber M.*), **Diamond, Dieren** (van) (songs), **Joyce Book, Moeran** (songs), **Orr** (**C. W.**) (songs), **Roussel** (**A.**) (' A flower given to my daughter '), **Sessions** (songs), **Szymanowski** (songs).

Jubel-Ouvertüre (*Jubilee Ovt.*). A concert ovt. by Weber, Op. 59, comp. in 1818 as a companion-piece to the *Jubel-Cantate* for the 50th anniversary of the accession of the King of Saxony, Frederick Augustus. It cannot be perf. in Eng., except possibly at the end of concert, because it concludes with the tune of ' God save the King,' which would bring an audience to its feet.

Jubili (Lat. = jubilations). The Lat. name sometimes given to the Pneuma, voc. ornaments used in Plainsong, inserting long cadential phrases on the syllables of certain words. They developed later into Tropes and Sequences.

Judas Maccabaeus, orat. by Handel (lib. by Thomas Morell), comp. 9. VII.–11. VIII. 1746, prod. London, Covent Garden Theatre, 1. IV. 1747.

Judenkünig, Hans (b. ?; d. ? Vienna, c. 4. III. 1526), Ger. or Aus. lutenist. Lived in Vienna and wrote and arr. pieces for his inst.

Judgment of Paris, The, masque by Congreve, for the comp. of which a prize was advertised in the *London Gazette* in 1699, the 1st 4 prizes being won by Weldon, Eccles, D. Purcell and Finger in 1701. Eccles's setting prod. London, Dorset Gardens Theatre, 21. III. and Finger's 27. III. 1701. Purcell's was pub., Weldon's is lost. The lib. was later set by Arne, prod. Dublin, 31. V. 1744, and by G. Sammartini.

Judith. *See also* **Ettinger, Holofernes, Klughardt.**

Opera by Natanael Berg (b. 1879), (lib., in Swe., by comp., based on Hebbel's drama), prod. Stockholm, 22. II. 1936.

Opera by Goossens (lib. by Arnold Bennett), prod. London, Covent Garden Theatre, 25. VI. 1929.

Opera by Serov (lib., in Rus., by comp. & Apollon Nikolaievitch Maikov, based on Paolo Giacometti's drama *Giuditta*), prod. St. Petersburg, 28. V. 1863.

Orat. by Arne (lib. by Isaac Bickerstaff), prod. London, Drury Lane Theatre, 27. II. 1761.

Orat. by Parry (lib. from the Bible), prod. Birmingham Festival, 1888.

Play with m. by Honegger (lib. by René Morax), prod. Mézières, Swi., open-air Théâtre du Jorat, 13. VI. 1925; operatic version, Monte Carlo, 13. II. 1926.

Juif polonais, Le (*The Polish Jew*), opera by C. Erlanger (lib. by Henri Cain & Pierre Barthélemy Gheusi, based on Erckmann-Chatrian's novel) prod. Paris, Opéra-Comique, 11. IV. 1900. The subject is that of the play *The Bells,* in which Irving made his greatest popular success.

Juive, La (*The Jewess*), opera by Halévy (lib. by Scribe), prod. Paris, Opéra, 23. II. 1835.

Julie, opera by Dezède (lib. by Jacques Marie Boutet de Monvel), prod. Paris, Comédie-Italienne, 28. IX. 1772. Mozart wrote pf. vars. (K. 264) on the air 'Lison dormait' in 1778.

Julien, ou La Vie du poète (*Julian, or The Poet's Life*), opera by G. Charpentier, sequel to *Louise* (lib. by comp.), prod, Paris, Opéra-Comique, 4. VI. 1913.

Julius Caesar (Handel & Malipiero). *See* **Giulio Cesare.**

Jullien, (Jean Lucien) Adolphe (b. Paris, 1. VI. 1845; d. Chaintreauville, 30. VIII. 1932), Fr. critic. Studied law at first, and m. with a retired prof. of the Cons. He began to write for the mus. papers and to champion Berlioz, Wagner, Schumann and modern m. App. m. critic to *Le Français* in 1872 and the *Journal des Débats* in 1873. His books incl. studies of 18th-cent. opera, Berlioz, Wagner, Goethe and m., &c.

Jullien (orig. **Julien**), **Louis Antoine** (b. Sisteron, 23. IV. 1812; d. Paris, 14. III. 1860), Fr. cond. Son of a bandmaster, he studied unsuccessfully at the Paris Cons., became a cond. of dance m. and compiler of quadrilles on popular operas. Went to London c. 1840 and made sensational successes with promenade concerts, quadrille bands, &c., due as much to his eccentric behaviour as to his superficial mus. gifts.

Jungfernquartette (Ger. = Maiden 4tets). Another nickname for Haydn's 6 stg. 4tets, Op. 33, also known as 'Rus. 4tets' and more generally as ' Gli Scherzi.'

Juon, Paul (b. Moscow, 9. III. 1872; d. Swi., VIII. 1940), Rus. comp. Studied with Taneiev and Arensky in Moscow and with Bargiel in Berlin, where he settled and was later app. prof. at the Hochschule für Musik by Joachim.

Works incl. ballet *Psyche*; 2 syms.,

Serenade & other works for orch.; 2 v. concs., *Épisodes concertantes* for v., co. & pf. & orch.; chamber Sym., 5 pieces for stg. orch.; 3 stg. 4tets, 6tet for pf. & stgs., 2 pf. 5tets, 2 pf. 4tets, 3 pf. trios, Divertimento for wind & pf., do. for cl. & 2 vas.; inst. pieces; *Satyrs and Nymphs, Preludes & Capriccios*, &c. for pf., &c.

' Jupiter ' Symphony. The nickname given to Mozart's last Sym., in C maj., K. 551. It is not his own name and is not well suited to any but the last mvt. and to the 1st at a pinch. The work is the 3rd of the group of M.'s final syms., which form a kind of trilogy, though they were not so intended; E♭ maj., K. 543, finished 26. VI. 1788; G min. K. 550, finished 25. VII. 1788; C maj., K. 551, finished 10. VIII. 1788.

Just Intonation. The singing or inst. playing, esp. on stg. insts., in what is said to be the pure natural scale, not that artificially fixed on keyboard insts. by Equal Temperament. In J. I. the 12 semitones of the 8ve are not all divided by exactly the same ratio of vibrations and the intervals vary slightly, sharps and flats not having precisely the same pitch. But J. I. is ' just ' only in theory: there is no fixing the intervals in any invariable way in practice.

K

K. (abbr.) = **Köchel.** The thematic catalogue of Mozart's works ed. by Ludwig von Köchel. M.'s works are identified by the sign 'K.,' followed by catalogue numbers instead of by op. numbers.

Kabalevsky, Dimitri Borisovitch (b. Leningrad, 30. XII. 1904), Rus. comp. Entered the Skriabin School of M. at Moscow when the family settled there in 1918, studying pf. and becoming a comp. pupil of Vassilenko and Catoire, afterwards of Miaskovsky. Later became prof. of comp. there.

Works incl. operas *The Golden Spikes, The Craftsman of Clamecy* (after Romain Rolland's novel *Colas Breugnon*) & *Before Moscow*; incid. m. for Shakespeare's *Measure for Measure*, Sheridan's *School for Scandal* & an adaption of Flaubert's *Madame Bovary*; film m.; *Poem of Struggle, Our Great Fatherland* & *People's Avengers* for chor. & orch.; 4 syms. (No. 3, *Requiem*); 2 pf. concs.; stg. 4tet; So., 2 sonatinas & other pf. m.; songs, &c.

Kade, Otto (b. Dresden, 6. V. 1819; d. Doberan nr. Rostock, 19. VII. 1900), Ger. mcolst. Studied at Dresden and went to It. for research in old m., in which he specialized, esp. the Flem., Ger. & Spa. schools. He also cond. the ducal chapel choir at Mecklenburg-Schwerin.

Kafenda, Bedřich (b. Mošovce, 2. XI. 1883), Slovak comp. & cond. Studied at the Leipzig Cons. and in 1920 became prof. at the M. School at Bratislava.

Works incl. church m., chor. works, *Ave Maria* for sop. & org.; stg. 4tet; sos. for v. & pf. and co. & pf.; songs, &c.

Kahn, Robert (b. Mannheim, 21. VII. 1865), Ger. comp. Studied at Mannheim, Berlin and (with Rheinberger) at Munich. In 1890–3 he cond. a women's choir at Leipzig and then became prof. at the Hochschule für Musik in Berlin.

Works incl. stg. 4tet, pf. 5tet, 3 pf. 4tets, 3 pf. trios, cl. Trio; 3 sos. and Suite for v. & pf., 2 co. & pf. sos.; many fem. chors.; pf. pieces; songs, &c.

Kaiser, Georg (1878–1945), Ger. dramatist. *See* **Casal y Chapí, Ettinger** (*Juana*), **Wagner-Régeny** (*Bürger von Calais*), **Weill** (*Protagonist, Silbersee* & *Zar lässt sich photographieren*).

Kaiser Quartett (Haydn). *See* **Emperor Quartet.**

Kajanus, Robert (b. Helsingfors, 2. XII. 1856; d. Helsinki, 6. VII. 1933), Fin. cond. & comp. Studied at the Helsingfors and Leipzig Conss., also comp. with Svendsen in Paris. Founded the orch. of the Helsingfors Phil. Soc. in 1882, with which later he paid several important visits to foreign countries.

Works incl. Sym. *Aino* (on an incid. from the *Kalevala*), &c.

Kalafaty, Vassily Pavlovitch (b. Eupatoria, Crimea, 10. II. 1869), Rus. comp. Pupil of Rimsky-Korsakov. In 1900 he was app. prof. of comp. at the St. Petersburg Cons., where he had Stravinsky and Prokofiev among his pupils.

Works incl. Sym. & other orch. works; chamber m.; pf. pieces; songs, &c.

Kalbeck, Max (b. Breslau, 4. I. 1850; d. Vienna, 4. V. 1921), Ger. critic and writer on m. Worked in Vienna. Trans. opera libs. and wrote the 1st full Brahms biog.

Kalcher, Johann Nepomuk (b. Freising, Bavaria, 1766; d. Munich, 1826), Ger. orgst. & comp. Studied at Munich, where he became court orgst. in 1798. Wrote masses, syms., org. m., songs, &c.

Kalevala, The, Fin. nat. epic. *See* **Dallapiccola, Kajanus** (*Aino*), **Klami** (suite), **Launis** (*Kullervo*), **Lemminkainen's Home-Faring** (Sibelius), **Merikanto (A.)** (*Abduction of Kyllikki*), **Pohjola's Daughter** (Sibelius), **Schantz** (*Kullervo*), **Sibelius** (do.), **Swan of Tuonela** (Sibelius), **Tapiola** (do.).

Kalidasa (?–?), Indian (Sanskrit) dramatist. Works based on *Sakuntala, see* **Bachrich** (ballet), **Coerne, Foulds, Goldmark (C.), Hüe, Leggenda di S.** (Alfano), **Paderewski, Perfall, Sacountala** (Reyer), **Sakuntala** (Weingartner), **Scharwenka (P.).**

Kalinnikov, Vassily Sergeyevitch (b. Voni, 13. I. 1866; d. Yalta, 11. I. 1901), Rus. comp. He was educ. at a seminary, where he cond. the choir, but in 1884 went to Moscow and, in spite of great poverty, obtained a mus. educ. at the Phil. Soc. M. School. After cond. opera for the 1893–4 season, he was found to suffer from consumption and lived mainly in the Crimea, devoted to comp.

Works incl. incid. m. to Alexey

Tolstoy's *Tsar Boris*; cantatas *St. John Chrysostom* and *Russalka*; 2 syms., Suite, 2 Intermezzi & 2 Sketches for orch.; stg. 4tets; pf. pieces; songs, &c.

Kalisch, Alfred (b. London, 13. III. 1863; d. London, 17. V. 1933), Eng. critic of Ger. descent. Educ. at Oxford for law, but became a mus. journalist in 1894. Trans. of R. Strauss's operas.

Kalkbrenner, Friedrich (Wilhelm Michael) (b. on a journey between Cassel & Berlin, 1788; d. Enghien nr. Paris, 10. VI. 1849), Ger. pfst., teacher & comp. Studied under his father, Christian K. (1755–1806) and at the Paris Cons. Made his 1st public appearance in Berlin and Vienna in 1813. Lived in London as teacher and perf. in 1814–23 and then settled in Paris as a member of the pf. firm of Pleyel, but continued to teach and perf.

Works incl. 3 pf. concs., Conc. for 2 pfs.; pf. 7tet, 6tet & 5tet; pf. school with studies appended, sos., vars. & numerous other works for pf.

Kalliwoda, Johan Vaclav (b. Prague, 21. III. 1800; d. Carlsruhe, 3. XII. 1866), Boh. vst. & comp. Studied at the Prague Cons. in 1811–7 and played in the orch. in 1817–23. He then became mus. dir. to Prince Fürstenberg at Donaueschingen until his retirement in 1853.

Works incl. opera *Blanka*; 7 syms.; concertinos for v., for cl. and other insts.; stg. 4tets; v. duets, v. pieces; songs, &c.

Kamienski, Lucjan (b. Gniezno, 7. I. 1885), Pol. comp. & mcolst. Studied at Breslau and Berlin, became mus. ed. of a paper at Königsberg in 1909, was app. 2nd dir. of the Poznan Cons. in 1920 and prof. at the Univ. there in 1922.

Works incl. opera *Ladies and Hussars*; *Silesia sings* for orch.; *Symphonia paschalis* and 2 poems from *Des Knaben Wunderhorn* for chor. & orch.; v. & pf. So.; *Fantasy on Pol. Christmas Song, Early Pol. Suite*, &c. for pf.; songs with chamber orch., with co. & pf. & several song cycles with pf., &c.

Kamienski, Maciej (b. Sopron, 13. X. 1734; d. Warsaw, 25. I. 1821), Hung.-Pol. comp. Studied in Vienna and settled at Warsaw in *c.* 1760. He prod. the 1st Pol. opera there on 11. V. 1778.

Works incl. opera *Happiness in Unhappiness* & 5 others in Pol. & 2 in Ger.; church m.; cantata for the unveiling of the Sobieski monument, &c.

Kaminski, Heinrich (b. Tiengen nr. Waldshut, 4. VII. 1886), Ger. comp. Studied at Heidelberg and Berlin, then lived nr. Munich devoted to comp., which he later taught for a short time in Berlin. He emigrated to U.S.A. in 1939.

Works incl. opera *Jürg Jenatsch* (after Conrad Ferdinand Meyer); Psalm lxix, Magnificat and *Introit and Hymn* for solo voices, chor. & orch.; Conc. for orch., *Concerto grosso*; stg. 5tet; *Triptychon* for voice & org., &c.

Kammerton (Ger. lit. chamber-tone). The pitch to which hpchds. in Ger. were tuned in the 17th–18th cent. It was lower, usually by a whole tone, than the *Chorton* (choir-tone) used for church orgs., and it was for this reason that Bach transposed his concs. by a tone whenever he transcribed for the clavier one orig. written for the v. The transposition applied only to the solo part: the orch. parts could be used as they stood.

Kantele. A Fin. obs. inst. of the Psaltery type.

Kapelle (Ger. = chapel). Formerly the mus. estab. of a king's or prince's chapel in the religious sense, but later, by transfer, a Ger. name for an orch.

Kapellmeister (Ger.). *See* **Chapel Master.**

Kapellmeistermusik (Ger. = conductor's m.). A contemptuous term for a mus. work which betrays creative weakness and has no merit but that of a knowledge of rules and glib craftsmanship.

Kapp, Julius (b. Steinbach, Baden, 1. X. 1883), Ger. writer on m. Studied chemistry and then became a literary ed. In 1921 he ed. the paper of the Berlin State Opera and in 1923 he became dramatic dir. there and adapted a number of works for its stage. He ed. Wagner's letters and his books incl. studies of Liszt, Wagner, Berlioz, Weber, Meyerbeer, R. Strauss, &c.

Kaprálová, Vitězslava (b. Brno, 21. I. 1915, d. Montpellier, 16. VI. 1940), Cz. comp. Studied with her father, Vaclav Kaprál (b. 1889), Novák and others.

Works incl. *Military Sinfonietta*; pf. Conc.; stg. 4tet; pf. works; songs, &c.

Kapsberger, Johann Hieronymus (b. ?; d. ?, *c.* 1633), Ger. lutenist and comp. Lived in Venice and pub. 3 books of m. for chitarrone in tablature. He also wrote voc. villanelle with that inst., motets, an epithalamium, an apotheosis of Ignatius Loyola, &c.

Karamzin, Nikolai Mikhailovitch (1765–1826), Rus. histor., novelist & poet. *See* **Boris Godunov** (Mussorgsky).

Karatyghin, Viatcheslav Gavrilovitch (b. Pavlovsk, 17. IX. 1875; d. Leningrad, 23. XII. 1925), Rus. critic & comp. Wrote chiefly on Mussorgsky and pub. a number of his own songs.

Karel, Rudolf (b. Plzen [Pilsen], 9. XI. 1880; d. Theresienstadt, 6. III. 1945), Cz. comp. Studied comp. under Dvořák at the Prague Cons. In 1914, on holiday in Rus., he was interned as an Aus. subject, then taught at Taganrog and Rostov-on-Don, fled to Siberia and eventually escaped to Cz., where he became prof. at the Prague Cons. He d. tragically at a concentration camp.

Works incl. operas *Ilsa's Heart* & *Godmother Death*; incid. m. to Knud Hamsun's *The Game of Life*; *Awakening*, sym. for solo voices, chor. & orch.; *Renaissance* sym., symph. poems *The Ideals* & *Demon*, Suite, Fantasy, Slavonic Dances, &c. for orch.; v. Conc.; 2 stg. 4tets, pf. 4tet, pf. Trio; v. & pf. So.; So., *Tema con variazioni* & other pf. works; chors., &c.

Karg-Elert, Sigfrid (real name Karg) (b. Oberndorf-on-Neckar, 21. XI. 1877; d. Leipzig, 9. IV. 1933), Ger. orgst., pfst. & comp. Studied at the Leipzig Cons. and became prof. at those of Magdeburg and Leipzig, was a brilliant pfst., but was persuaded by Grieg to devote himself to comp.

Works incl. a Sym.; stg. 4tet; v. & pf. sos.; So. & other works for pf.; over 100 songs; pieces for harmonium & many org. works, incl. 66 Chorale Improvisations, 24 Preludes & Postludes, Sonatina, Passacaglia, Fantasy and Fugue in D maj., *Chaconne, Fugue-Trilogy and Chorale*, 10 Characteristic Pieces, 3 Symph. Chorales, 7 *Pastels from Lake Constance*, 6 *Cathedral Windows*, 54 var.-studies *Homage to Handel*, &c.

Karl V, opera by Křenek (lib. by comp.), prod. Prague, Ger. Opera, 15. VI. 1938.

Karlowicz, Miecyslaw (b. Wiszniezo, 11. XII. 1876; d. Zakopane, 8. II. 1909), Pol. comp. The son of a noble family, he travelled much as a child and learnt the v. in Prague, Dresden and Heidelberg, and soon played chamber m. with his parents, a cst. and a pfst. Later studied at Warsaw, where his comp. teacher was Noskowski, and afterwards with Urban in Berlin, also cond. with Nikisch at Leipzig. Settled at Zakopane in the Tatra mountains in 1908 and was killed by an avalanche there.

Works incl. incid. m. to *Biala Golabka*; Sym. in E min., symph. poems *Returning Waves, The Sad Story (Preludes to Eternity), Stanislas and Anna Osiwecim, An Episode of the Masquerade*, Serenade, *Lithuanian Rhapsody* for orch.; v.Conc.; songs,&c.

Kasanli. *See* **Kazanly.**

Kashin, Daniel Nikititch (b. Moscow, 1773; d. Moscow, 1844), Rus. comp. Pupil of Sarti.

Works incl. operas *Natalia, Fair Olga* & *The One-day Reign of Nourmahal* (on Moore's *Lalla Rookh*); cantatas & other chor. works; patriotic songs, &c.

Kashkin, Nikolai Dmitrievitch (b. Voronezh, 9. XII. 1839; d. Moscow, 1921), Rus. m. critic & teacher. Prof. at the Moscow Cons. from its foundation in 1864 to 1896. Critic of the *Russky Vedomosti* and author of a vol. of reminisc. of Tchaikovsky.

Kashperov, Vladimir Nikititch (b. Simbirsk, 1827; d. Romantsevo, 8. VII. 1894), Rus. comp. Studied with Henselt in St. Petersburg and later in Berlin and It. Prof. of singing at the Moscow Cons. in 1866–72.

Works incl. operas *The Gypsies, Mary Tudor* (after Hugo), *Rienzi* (after Bulwer-Lytton), *Consuelo* (after George Sand), *The Storm* (after Ostrovsky), *Taras Bulba* (after Gogol), &c.

Kashtchey the Immortal (*K. Bessmertny*), opera by Rimsky-Korsakov (lib. by comp.), prod. Moscow, 25. XII. 1902. Kashtchey is the wizard of Rus. fairy lore who appears also in Stravinsky's *Firebird* ballet.

Kasprowicz, Jan (1860–1926), Pol. poet. *See* **Szymanowski** (songs).

Kassern, Tadeusz Zygfryd (b. Lwów, 19. III. 1904), Pol. comp. Studied at the Poznan Cons. while reading law at the Univ. there, and settled there later.

Works incl. Children's Cantata for sop., chor. & orch.; symph. poem *Dies irae* in memory of Marshal Pilsudski, *Sinfonietta giocosa*; Conc. for stg. orch.; concs. for sop., for db. and for fl.; Concertino for fl., cl. & bn.; 2 sos., Sonatina, Mazurkas and Preludes for pf.; *Naïve Songs* & other songs; chors., &c.

Kastalsky, Alexander Dimitrievitch (b. Moscow, 28. XI. 1856; d. Moscow, 17. XII. 1926), Rus. comp. Studied under Tchaikovsky and Taneiev at the Moscow Cons. He taught the pf. at the Synodal School there from 1887 and became its dir. in 1900. After the Revol. he took part in the reform of Rus. church m. and wrote liturgical works; he also helped to estab. people's theatres and centres for the cultivation of Rus. folksongs, many of which he ed.

Works incl. opera *Clara Militch* (after Turgenev's tale); *Requiem for Fallen Heroes* & other chor. works: *Epic Tale, Glory, Russia, Hymn to the Proletariat, Hymn for the First of May*, cantata *1905*; *The Railway Train* for chor., pf., tpt. & perc.; *Sym. of the Tilling of the Soil, Georgian Suite*, &c. for orch., &c.

Kastner, Jean Georges (Johann Georg) (b. Strasburg, 9. III. 1810; d. Paris, 19. XII. 1867), Alsat. comp. and theorist. Studied theology at home, but prod. an opera *Die Königin der Sarmaten* and was sent by the Strasburg town council to study with Berton and Reicha at the Paris Cons. He wrote a treatise on orchn. and compiled an encyc. of m. (unfinished).

Works incl. operas *Die Königin der Sarmaten, Gustav Wasa, Oskars Tod, Der Sarazene, Beatrice, La maschera, Le Dernier Roi de Juda, Les Nonnes de Robert le Diable*; cantatas *La Résurrection, Sardanapale, Cantate alsacienne*; scenes for voice & pf.; songs, partsongs, &c.

Kastner, Santiago (Macario) (b. London, 15. X. 1908), Anglo-Port. mcolst. & comp. Studied at Amsterdam, Leipzig and with Anglès at Barcelona. He writes on Spa. & Port. m. and has ed. a collection of old Spa. & Port. keyboard m. Comps. incl. *Kraviastas portugueses*, 5 *Tentos* by Manoel Rodrigues Coelho, &c.

Káta Kabanová, opera by **Janáček** (lib. by Vincenc Červinka, based on Alexander Nikolaievitch Ostrovsky's play *Groza*), prod. Brno, 23. X. 1921.

Katona, József (1792–1830), Hung. dramatist. *See* **Bánk-Bán** (Erkel).

Katuar. *See* **Catoire.**

Kauer, Ferdinand (b. Znaim, Moravia, 18. I. 1751; d. Vienna, 13. IV. 1831), Aus. comp. Studied at Znaim and Vienna, where he was app. leader and 2nd cond. at the Leopoldstadt Theatre, for which he wrote m. for *c.* 100 pantomimes, farces, &c. as well as operettas & operas.

Works incl. operas *Das Donauweibchen, Das Waldweibchen*; orat. *Die Sündflut*; trio *Nelsons grosse See-Schlacht*, &c.

Kaún, Hugo (b. Berlin, 21. III. 1863; d. Berlin, 2. IV. 1932), Ger. comp. He had written over 100 works before he was 16 and studied with Kiel at the Berlin Acad. of Arts. In 1884 he went to U.S.A. as pfst., but had to give up that career owing to an injury; and in 1887 settled at Milwaukee, but returned to Berlin in 1901, teaching comp. 1st at the Acad. and from 1922 at the Klindworth-Scharwenka Cons.

Works incl. operas *Der Pietist, Sappho, Der Fremde & Menandra*; several chor. works; 3 syms., *Minnehaha und Hiawatha* (after Longfellow), symph. prologue *Marie Magdalene*, humoresque *Falstaff* (after Shakespeare) & other orch. works; 4 stg. 4tets, pf. 5tet, 2 pf. trios, 8tet; v. & pf. So., &c.

Kazanly, Nikolai Ivanovitch (b. Tiraspol, 17. XII. 1869; d. Petrograd, 15. VIII. 1916), Rus. comp. & cond. Studied with Rimsky-Korsakov at the St. Petersburg Cons.

Works incl. opera *Miranda*; Sym.; Sinfonietta, symph. poem *Villa by the Sea* (on Böcklin's picture); songs, &c.

Kazuro, Stanislaw (b. Teklinopol nr. Vilna, 1881), Pol. comp. & cond. Studied at the Warsaw Cons. and the Accademia di Santa Cecilia in Rome. App. prof. at the Warsaw Cons. and has trained and cond. several chor. socs.

Works incl. operas *The Fairy Tale & The Return*; orats. *The Sun, The Flight & The Sea*; misc. chor. works; symph. poem *Youth*; songs, incl. children's songs and It. & Pol. folksongs, &c.

Keats, John (1795–1821), Eng. poet. *See* **Converse** (*Belle Dame sans merci*), **Dieren** (van) (songs), **Gibbs** (C. A.) (*Belle Dame s. m.*), **Greenwood** (do.), **Hadley** (P.) (do.), **Harty** (*Ode to Nightingale*), **Holst** (*Chor. Sym.*), **Howell** (*Lamia*), **Jacobi** (*Eve of St. Agnes*), **MacDowell** (*Lamia*), **Mackenzie** (*Belle Dame s. m.*), **Paine** (*Realm of Fancy*), **Parry** (H.) (*Proserpine*), **Riegger** (*Belle Dame s. m.*), **Rubbra** (do.), **Scott** (C.) (do.), **Valen** (*To Hope*), **Walker** (*Ode to Nightingale*), **Walthew** (do.).

Keeley, Mary Anne. *See* **Goward.**

Keeners. Professional singers of lamentations for the dead in Ir.

Kehraus (Ger. = clear-out or sweep-out). *See* **Grossvater-Tanz.**

Keil, Alfredo (b. Lisbon, 1850; d. Hamburg, 4. X. 1907), Port. comp. (?) of Ger. descent. Studied at Munich and Nuremberg and prod. his 1st stage work, the operetta *Suzanna*, at Lisbon in 1883.

Works incl. operas *Donna Bianca, Irene, Serrana*; symph. poems *Uma caçada na corte & Orientães*; cantatas *Patria & Primavera*; song 'A Portugueza,' which became the nat. anthem in 1911, &c.

Keirnine. A small Ir. hp.

Keiser, Reinhard (b. Teuchern nr. Weissenfels, Saxony, 9. I. 1674; d. Hamburg, 12. IX. 1739), Ger. comp. Studied under Schelle at St. Thomas's school, Leipzig. Went to the court of Brunswick in 1692 and to Hamburg in 1694, where he made the opera in the Theater am Gänsemarkt the most distinguished then in Ger. and comp. 116 works for it.

Works incl. operas *Circe, Penelope, Der geliebte Adonis, L'inganno fedele,*

Orpheus, *La forza della virtù*, *Stoertebecker und Joedge Michaels*, *Masagniello furioso*, *Croesus*, *Ulysses*, *Der lächerliche Prinz Jodelet*, &c.; orats. *Der für die Sünde der Welt gemarterte and sterbende Jesus* & *Der verurteilte und gekreuzigte Jesus*, Passion according to St. Mark, histor. orats.; motets, psalms, &c.

Kéler, Béla (Adalbert von Kéler) (b. Bartfeld, Hung., 13. II. 1820; d. Wiesbaden, 20. XI. 1882), Hung. vst. & comp. Studied in Vienna, where he became a vst. at the Theater an der Wien. In 1854 he became cond. of Gungl's band in Berlin, but returned to Vienna and took over Lanner's band in 1855. The next year he became an infantry bandmaster and in 1870 cond. of the Spa. orch. at Wiesbaden. He wrote innumerable light pieces, esp. ovts., dances & marches.

Keller, Gottfried (1819–90), Swi. poet & novelist. *See* **Baumgartner** (' O mein Heimatland '), **Romeo und Julia auf dem Dorfe** (Delius), **Schoeck** (*Gesangfest im Frühling*, *Lebendig begraben*, *Gaselen*, *Unter Sternen* & songs), **Vrieslander** (songs), **Zemlinsky** (*Kleider machen Leute*).

6 of his poems set by Hugo Wolf.

Kelley, Edgar Stillman (b. Sparta, Wis., 14. IV. 1857; d. New York, 12. XI. 1944), Amer. comp. & writer on m. Studied at Chicago and Stuttgart, and on his return to U.S.A. became orgst. & critic in Cal., where he also made a study of Chin. m. He then taught at Yale Univ., Berlin and, from 1910, at the Cincinnati Cons.

Works incl. operetta *Puritania*; incid. m. for Shakespeare's *Macbeth* and for a dram. version of Wallace's *Ben Hur*; orch. suite on Chin. themes, *Aladdin*, *Gulliver* sym. (after Swift), *New England Sym.*, suite *Alice in Wonderland* (after Lewis Carroll); cantata *Pilgrim's Progress* (after Bunyan), *Wedding Ode* for ten., male chor. & orch.; *My Captain* (Whitman) & *The Sleeper* (Poe) for chor.; Vars. for stg. 4tet, stg. 4tet, pf. 5tet; pf. pieces; songs, &c.

Kellner, Johann Peter (b. Gräfenroda, Thuringia, 24. IX. 1705; d. Gräfenroda, 1788), Ger. orgst. & comp, Having been cantor at Frankenhain for 3 years, he returned home to take a similar post, which he kept to his death. When Bach visited his church he improvised a fugue on B.A.C.H.

Works incl. cantatas; org. m.; suites & sos. for hpchd., &c.

Kellogg, Clara Louise (b. Sumterville, S.C., 12. VII. 1842; d. New Hartford, Conn., 13. V. 1916), Amer. sop. singer. Studied in N.Y. and made her 1st stage appearance there in 1861.

Kelly, Michael (b. Dublin, XII. 1762; d. Margate, 9. X. 1826), Ir. ten. singer, actor & comp. Appeared at Dublin as a child actor and studied m. with M. Arne and others, also singing under var. It. masters, last with Rauzzini. In 1779 he went to It., where he made further studies with Fenaroli and Aprile, going to Vienna in 1783, where he was engaged at the Court Opera. He made friends with Haydn and Mozart, and was the 1st Basilio in the latter's *Figaro* in 1786, appearing on the prog. as ' Signor Ochelly.' In 1787 he went to London with Nancy and Stephen Storace and Attwood. He appeared successively at Drury Lane and the King's Theatre, and became manager of the latter. Early in the 19th cent. he also kept a m. shop and dealt in wines. In 1826 he pub. his *Reminiscences*.

Works incl. opera *The Gypsy Prince* (Thomas Moore); m. for *c.* 60 stage pieces, e.g. *The Castle Spectre* (M. G. Lewis), *Pizarro* (Sheridan), *Love laughs at Locksmiths* (Colman jun.), *Cinderella*, *The Forty Thieves*, *The Jew of Mogadore*, *The Lady and the Devil*, &c.

Kelway, Joseph (b. ?; d. London, ? V. 1782), Eng. orgst. & hpchdst. Pupil of Geminiani. App. orgst. at St. Michael's church, Cornhill, in London *c.* 1730 and of St. Martin's-in-the-Fields in 1736 in succession to Weldon. There he attracted much attention by his improv., even Handel coming to hear him, and as a hpchd. player he was a brilliant performer and teacher of Queen Charlotte.

Kelway, Thomas (b. ?; d. Chichester, 21. V. 1749), Eng. orgst. & comp., elder brother of prec. He was educ. in m. as chorister at Chichester cath. and became orgst. there in 1726. Wrote services and anthems.

Kemble, Adelaide (b. London, 1814; d. Warsash House, Hants., 4. VIII. 1879), Eng. sop. singer, daughter of the actor Charles K. She 1st appeared in London and at the York Festival in 1835, but went to Ger. and It. for further study, last with Pasta. In 1839 she appeared as Norma in Venice, toured widely in It. and returned to London for an appearance in the same part in 1841.

Kenilworth. *See* **Amy Robsart**; **Leicester.**

Kennedy, David (b. Perth, 15. IV. 1825; d. Stratford, Ont., 12. X. 1886), Sco. singer. He 1st sang in church as precentor and was an apprentice and later master house-painter, but in 1859 made his 1st concert appearance at Liverpool. He began to tour widely, 1st in Sco. and Eng. and later in the Brit. colonies and U.S.A. One of his daughters was Marjory K.-Fraser; another was Jessie, who married Tobias Matthay.

Kennedy-Fraser, Marjory. *See* **Fraser.**

Kent Bugle. *See* Bugle.

Keraulophon. An 8-ft. org. stop of the Gamba type.

Kerl (or Kerll), Johann Caspar (b. Adorf, Saxony, 9. IV. 1627; d. Munich, 13. II. 1693), Ger. orgst. & comp. Settled early in Vienna as a pupil of Valentini; then studied in Rome under Carissimi and prob. the org. under Frescobaldi (but was only 16 when F. d.). In the service of the Elector of Bavaria in Munich, 1656–74. Again went to Vienna, as private teacher, and was app. court orgst. there in 1677, but returned to Munich in 1684.

Works incl. operas *Oronte, Erinto, Le pretensioni del sole, I colori geniali*; masses, motets & other church m.; sos. for 2 vs. & bass; toccatas, ricercari & other works for org., &c.

Kerle, Jacob van (b. Ypres, c. 1531; d. Prague, 7. I. 1591), Flem. comp. He spent some time in It., partly in Rome in the service of Otto von Truchsess, Cardinal-Archbp. of Augsburg, in whose service he was in 1562–75, with whom he was also at Augsburg at times, and with whom he (?) attended the Council of Trent in 1562–3. Later he became canon of Cambrai, but was often in Vienna and Prague attending on the Emperor Rudolf.

Works incl. masses, motets, Te Deums, Magnificats, hymns, *Sacrae cantiones*, &c.

Kern, Jerome (David) (b. New York, 27. I. 1885; d. New York, 11. XI. 1945), Amer. comp. Pupil of Paolo Gallico and Alexander Lambert in N.Y. He turned to the comp. of mus. comedy and other light m.

Works incl. mus. comedies *Sunny, Show Boat, Music in the Air* & others; film m., &c.

Kersey, Eda (b. Goodmayes, Essex, 15. V. 1904; d. Ilkley, 13. VII. 1944), Eng. vst. Studied in London, but was partly self-taught, made her 1st appearance at the age of 16 and began to broadcast in 1925.

Ketting, Piet (b. Haarlem, 29. XI. 1905), Dutch pfst. & comp. Studied with Pijper and later became prof. at the Rotterdam Cons.

Works incl. Sym.; chor. m.; 3 stg. 4tets, Trio for fl., cl. & bn. & other chamber m., sos. for fl., bass cl. & pf. and fl., ob. & pf., Partita for 2 fls.; 4 Sonatinas, Fugue, &c. for pf.; songs, incl. Shakespeare sonnets, &c.

Kettledrums. Drums with a single head of skin stretched over a cauldron-shaped receptacle. They produce notes of definite pitch which can be altered by the turning of screws at the rim of the 'kettle,' thus tightening or relaxing the skin. At least 2 Ks. are used in the orch., and normally tuned to the tonic and dominant notes of the key of the work played; but the modern orch. usually has 3 Ks., and more may be demanded by the comp., in which case 1 player may not be sufficient. A variety of sticks covered with different materials can be used to prod. a harder or softer impact.

Keuchenthal, Johannes (b. ?; d. ?), Ger. 16th-cent. Lutheran clergyman & musn. Pub. *Kirchengesang, lateinisch und deutsch*, a collection of m. for the Lutheran church, incl. a setting of the Passion, at Wittenberg in 1573, &c.

Keussler, Gerhard von (Schwanenburg, 23. VI. 1874), Ger. comp. & cond. Orig. a botanist, he did not study m. until 1900, when he went to the Leipzig Cons. He became cond. and lecturer in Prague in 1906, and in 1918 cond. of the Hamburg Voc. Acad. Later he cond. in var. places, incl. Prague again and Austral. in 1932–5, and in 1939 he was app. head of the comp. class at the Berlin Acad. of Art.

Works incl. operas *Wandlungen, Gefängnisse* & *Die Geisselfahrt*; orats. *Jesus aus Nazareth, Die Mutter, Zebaoth, In jungen Tagen*; syms. in D min. & C maj., symph. works *Auferstehung und jüngstes Gericht, Morgenländische Phantasie, An den Tod, Das hohe Lied, Australia*; many songs, &c.

Key. The word has 2 meanings in m.: (1) The levers by means of which notes are prod. on keyboard insts. by being pressed down or struck by the finger are Ks.; also those on wind insts. stopping the note-holes which cannot be reached directly by the fingers. (2) The equivalent in modern m. of the modes; the tonal regions of the min. and maj. scales on which m. since the 17th cent. has normally been based. Any piece of m. in maj. or min. is said to be in the K. of whatever its Tonic or Keynote may be—any natural, sharp or flat note. Thus a piece with the K.-signature of 1 sharp is normally either in G maj. or in E min.; one with 3 flats either in E♭ maj. or C min., &c.

Key Bugle. *See* Bugle.

Key Relationships. In comps. constructed on the principle of maj. and min. keys (i.e. excepting old modal and modern atonal m.) the structure of a work depends to a very great extent upon the manipulation of K. Rs.: the distribution of var. passages not in the tonic key in such a way that they form logical connections with that key. A good comp. will so use a variety of keys as to create a satisfactory balance in the use of keys closer to and more remote from the tonic; for each tonality will stand in a different K. R. to that tonic. The key of the dominant (e.g. G maj. in relation to C maj.), that of the tonic min. (e.g. F min. in relation to F maj.) or that of the relative min. (e.g. E min. in relation to G maj.) are very closely related; others are progressively more and more remote.

Key Signature. The Sharps and Flats which occur in the key of a given comp. written at the beginning of each stave of that comp. and thus obviating the repeated notation of them throughout the piece. The signatures are the following:

Sharps	Flats	Major	Minor
–	–	C	A
1	–	G	E
2	–	D	B
3	–	A	F♯
4	–	E	C♯
5	–	B	G♯
6	–	F♯	D♯
7	–	C♯	A♯
–	7	C♭	A♭
–	6	G♭	E♭
–	5	D♭	B♭
–	4	A♭	F
–	3	E♭	C
–	2	B♭	G
–	1	F	D

Keys with 5 to 7 sharps or flats overlap enharmonically; in the tempered scale of the pf. they are identical as follows: B maj. & G♯ min.=C♭ maj. & A♭ min.; F♯ maj. & D♯ min.= G♭ maj. & E♭ min.; C♯ maj. & A♯ min.=D♭ maj. & B♭ min.

Keyboard. The array of levers on insts. of the pf. type and on the org., also, more primitively, on such insts. as the Hurdy-gurdy and the Concertina, by means of which the fingers, and on the org. also the feet, release the notes.

Keynote. The Tonic: the note on which the scale begins and ends, which determines the key of a piece of m. in maj. or min. and after which that key is named. D, for ex., is the K. of a piece in D maj. or D min., which will normally end on the note or common chord of D.

Khatchaturian, Aram Ilitch (b. Tiflis, 6. VI. 1903), Rus. comp. His father, a poor workman, was able to send him to Moscow only after the Revol.; he entered the Gnessin School of M. there and studied under that master in 1923; 3 years later he went to the Moscow Cons. as a pupil of Vassilenko and afterwards of Miaskovsky. Studied the folksongs of Rus. Armenia and other southern regions, which have influenced his comps.

Works incl. ballets *Happiness* & *Gayane*, incid. m. for Shakespeare's *Macbeth*, Lope de Vega's *Widow of Valencia*, Pogodin's *Kremlin Chimes*, Kron's *Deep Drilling*, &c.; *Song of Stalin* for chor. & orch.; 2 syms. & *Dance Suite* for orch.; pieces on Uzbek & Armenian themes for wind band; pf. Conc., v. Conc.; stg. 4tet in C maj., Trio for cl., v. & pf.; v. & pf. So. in D min.; pf. pieces; songs; partsongs; songs for the Rus. army. &c.

Khorovod (Rus.). A type of ancient Rus. folksong sung in chor. of 2 or more parts in a primitive kind of ctpt. It was sung mainly at religious and family festivals and on seasonal occasions.

Khovanshtchina, unfinished opera by Mussorgsky (lib. by comp. and Vladimir Vassilievitch Stassov), prod., as completed and scored by Rimsky-Korsakov after M.'s death, St. Petersburg, 21. II. 1886.

Khrennikov, Tikhon Nikolaievitch (b. Elets, 10. VI. 1913), Rus. comp. He was taught m. at home, but entered the Gnessin School of M. at Moscow in 1929 and the Cons. in 1932 as a pupil of Shebalin.

Works incl. operas *The Brothers* (*In the Storm*); incid. m. for Shakespeare's *Much Ado about Nothing*, an adaptn. of Cervantes's *Don Quixote*, &c., film m. for *The Pigs and the Shepherd*; 2 syms.; pf. Conc.; pf. pieces; songs to words by Pushkin and Burns; war songs, &c.

Kidson, Frank (b. Leeds, 15. XI. 1855; d. Leeds, 7. XI. 1926), Eng. mcolst. & folksong collector. He became an authority on Eng. folksong and dance, also on the popular m. of the 18th cent. Collected and pub. country dances and other trad. tunes and wrote on Eng. m. printers, engravers and pubs., on ballad opera, &c.

Kiel, Friedrich (b. Puderbach o/Lahn, 7. X. 1821; d. Berlin, 14. IX. 1885), Ger. comp. & teacher. He made his way as a vst. at first, but studied theory with Dehn in Berlin from 1843 and became attached to the court of Frederick William IV of Prus. In 1869 he joined the council of the Berlin Acad. of Arts, and he was app. prof. of comp. of the Hochschule für Musik there.

Works incl. *Missa solemnis*, 2 Requiems; orat. *Christus*; *Reise-*

bilder for co. & pf.; *Canons and Fugues, Vars. and Fugue*, &c. for pf., &c.

Kienlen, Johann Christoph (b. Ulm, 1784; d. Dessau, 1830), Ger comp. He appeared as singer and pfst. at the age of 7 and was later sent to Paris to study with Cherubini. After being mus. dir. at Ulm he went to Vienna in 1811, where he taught, and in 1823 he became singing-master to the Berlin opera.

Works incl. operas, e.g. *Claudine von Villa Bella* (Goethe: 2 versions); a Sym.; additions to E. T. A. Hoffmann's incid. m. for Goethe's *Scherz, List und Rache*; 2 pf. sos.; many songs, &c.

Kienzl, Wilhelm (b. Waizenkirchen, Styria, 17. I. 1857; d. Vienna, 3. X. 1941), Aus. comp. His father, a lawyer, became mayor of Graz in 1861 and the family settled there. He studied there under W. Mayer, who also taught Weingartner and Busoni, later went to the Prague Cons. and finally to Rheinberger at Munich. Jensen and Liszt encouraged him to comp. and he came into close touch with Wagner at Bayreuth for a time. He held no official posts and remained at Graz most of his life.

Works incl. operas *Urvasi, Heilmar der Narr, Der Evangelimann, Don Quixote, In Knecht Rupprechts Werkstatt, Der Kuhreigen, Das Testament, Hassan der Schwärmer, Sanctissimum*; orch., chor. and chamber works; *Dichterreise* and many other pf. works; *Tanzbilder* for pf. duet; over 100 songs, &c. He adapted Jensen's opera *Die Erbin von Montfort* to a new lib. based on Gozzi's *Turandot*.

Kiladze, Grigory Varfolomei (b. Batum or Tiflis, 1905), Rus. comp. He earned his living as a manual worker and later as a film mechanic, but studied v. and entered the Tiflis Cons., later that of St. Petersburg, returning to Tiflis to teach at the Cons. He studied the folk m. of Georgia.

Works incl. opera *Lado Ketskhovelli*; incid. & film m.; symph. poem *The Hermit* and suites for orch.; massed chors. incl. *Song of Stalin*, &c.

Kilpinen, Yrjö (b. Helsinki, 4. II. 1892), Fin. comp. Had a few lessons in theory at the Helsingfors Cons. and in Berlin and Vienna, but is otherwise self-taught. In receipt of a small gvt. grant, he devotes himself entirely to comp.

Works incl. co. So., va. da gamba So.; pf. sos.; over 500 songs on Fin., Swe. and Ger. poems, &c.

Kindertotenlieder (*Songs of Dead Children*), cycle of 5 songs by Mahler, with orch. or pf., to poems by Rückert, comp. 1902.

King and Collier (or **Charcoal-Burner**) (*Král a Uhlíř*), comic opera by Dvořák (lib. by Bernhard Guldener), prod. Prague, Cz. Theatre, 24. XI. 1874. D.'s 1st opera to be perf.

King Arthur, or The British Worthy, opera by Purcell (lib. by Dryden), prod. London, Dorset Gardens Theatre, V or VI. 1691.

King Charles II, opera by Macfarren (lib. by Michael Desmond Ryan, based on a play by John Howard Payne), prod. London, Princess's Theatre, 27. X. 1849.

King, Charles (b. Bury St. Edmunds, 1687; d. London, 17. III. 1748). He went to London as a chorister at St. Paul's cath., where he was taught by Blow and by Clarke, whose daughter he married later. He then became a supernumerary singer in the choir and, after taking the B.Mus. at Oxford in 1707, succeeded Clarke as almoner and choirmaster at St. Paul's, becoming vicar-choral there in 1830. He comp. services and anthems.

King Christian II, incid. m. for Adolf Paul's play by Sibelius, Op. 27, comp. 1898.

King Lear. *See also* **Re Lear.** Verdi worked at the Shakespearian subject for many years, but never brought the opera anywhere near completion, and his sketches were destroyed after his death, by his own wish.

Incid. m. for Shakespeare's tragedy by J. André, prod. Berlin, 30. XI. 1778.

Incid. m. by Haydn, written c. 1776–80, for a perf. at Esterhàz.

Incid. m. by Stegmann, prod. Hamburg, 17. VII. 1778.

King, Matthew (**Peter**) (b. London, 1773; d. London, I. 1823), Eng. comp. Studied under C. F. Horn.

Works incl. many stage pieces (some with Braham, Kelly and others); orat. *The Intercession*; 4 sets of pf. sos.; solo cantatas, glees, songs, &c.

'King of Prussia' Quartets (Mozart). *See* **'Prussian' Quartets.**

King Olaf, cantata for solo voices, chor. & orch. by Elgar, Op. 30, set to words by Longfellow altered by A. C. Acworth, prod. at the N. Staffs. Festival, Hanley, 1896.

King, Robert (b. ?; d. ?), Eng. 17th–18th-cent. comp. He joined the royal band in 1680 on the death of Banister, received a licence to give concerts in 1689 and took the Mus.B. at Cambridge in 1696.

Works incl. incid. m. for Crowne's *Sir Courtly Nice* & many other plays; Shadwell's Ode on St. Cecilia's Day, Motteux's Ode for John Cecil, Earl of Exeter; many songs for one and more voices, &c.

King, William (b. Winchester, 1624; d. Oxford, 17. XI. 1680), Eng. orgst. & comp., son of George K., orgst. of Winchester cath. (d. 1665). He went to Oxford as a clerk of Magdalen Coll. in 1648, took the B.A. there in 1649, became a chaplain at the Coll. in 1652, but went to All Souls' Coll. as probationer-fellow in 1654 and became orgst. of New Coll. in 1664.

Works incl. a service, a litany, anthems; songs to a thorough-bass for theorbo, hpchd. or bass viol to poems by Cowley, &c.

Kingdom, The, orat. by Elgar, Op. 51 (lib. compiled from the Bible by the comp.), Part II of a trilogy of which I is *The Apostles* and III was never completed. Prod. Birmingham Festival, 3. X. 1906.

King's Henchman, The, opera by **Deems Taylor** (lib. by Edna St. Vincent Millay), prod. N.Y., Metrop. Opera, 17. II. 1927.

Kingsley, Charles (1819–75), Eng. novelist & poet. *See* **Bennett (W. S.)** installation ode), **Henschel** (*Water Babies*), **Macfarren (G.)** (songs).

Kinkeldey, Otto (b. New York, 27. XI. 1878), Amer. mcolst. After a general academic educ. in N.Y. and Berlin, he studied m. with MacDowell in 1900–2 while he was a schoolmaster and chapel orgst. After further studies at the Univ. and Acad. for church m. in Berlin, he became org. teacher at a similar institution at Breslau, and later lecturer and prof. in mcol. Returning to U.S.A. in 1914, he was alternately chief of the m. division of the N.Y. Public Library and prof. at Cornell Univ. He wrote a dissertation on 16th-cent. keyboard m. and many valuable contribs. to mus. periodicals, ed. old m., &c.

Kinsky, Georg (b. Marienwerder, E. Prus., 29. IX. 1882), Ger. mus. scholar & ed. Self-taught in m., he worked at first at the Prus. State Library in Berlin and then became curator of the Heyer museum of mus. insts. at Cologne. He compiled a catalogue of it and in 1927 left to become prof. at Cologne Univ., retiring in 1932. His books, which incl. a *History of M. in Pictures*, are mainly on insts. and on orig. eds. of important works.

Kipling, Rudyard (1865–1936), Eng. poet & novelist. *See* **Delage** (songs), **Grainger** (*We have fed our seas* & *Morning Song of the Jungle*), **Koechlin** (*Course de printemps*), **Scott (C.)** (*Jungle Book*), **Sullivan** (*Absent-minded Beggar*), **Thompson (R.)** (*Solomon and Balkis*).

Kirbye, George (b. ? Suffolk, c. 1565; d. Bury St. Edmunds, X. 1634). He 1st appeared as the most copious contributor, except Farmer, to East's Psalter. In 1598 he married Anne Saxye, and he seems to have lived at that time at Rushbrooke nr. Bury St. Edmunds as domestic musn. at the residence of Sir Robert Jermyn, to whose daughters he ded. his book of 24 madrigals in 1597. In 1601 he contrib. a madrigal to *The Triumphes of Oriana*.

Works incl. motets, a hymn; madrigals; a pavan for viols, &c.

Kircher, Athanasius (b. Geisa nr. Fulda, 2. V. 1602; d. Rome, 28. XI. 1680), Ger. mathn., philos. and mus. scholar. He was prof. at the Jesuit Coll. of Würzburg, but was driven from Ger. by the 30 Years War in 1631, going to Avignon, Vienna and in 1635 to Rome, where he settled for the rest of his life. His chief mus.-literary work is *Musurgia universalis*.

Kirchhoff, Gottfried (b. Mühlbeck nr. Bitterfeld, 15. IX. 1685; d. Halle, 21. I. 1746), Ger. orgst. & comp. Pupil of Zachau at Halle, whom he succeeded, after some other appts., as orgst. of the church of Our Lady there in 1714. He comp. much for the org.

Kirchner, Theodor (b. Neukirchen nr. Chemnitz, 10. XII. 1823; d. Hamburg, 18. IX. 1903), Ger. comp. Studied under C. F. Becker at Leipzig and went to Swi. in 1843 to become orgst. at Winterthur. In 1862 he went to Zürich as cond. and teacher, but returned to Ger. in 1873 to become dir. of the m. school at Würzburg. In 1875 he moved to Leipzig, in 1883 to Dresden and in 1890 to Hamburg.

Works incl. a stg. 4tet, 3 works for pf. trio; v. and co. pieces; c. 100 op. numbers of pf. pieces; songs, &c.

Kirkby Lunn, Louisa. *See* **Lunn.**

Kirkman. Eng. family of hpchd. and later pf. makers:

1. Jacob K. (orig. Kirchmann) (b. ?; d. London, ?), was a Ger. by birth, settled in London early in the 18th cent., working for Tabel, a Flem. maker, whose widow he married.

2. Abraham K. (b. ?; d. London, ?), nephew of prec.

3. Joseph K. (b. ?; d. London, ?), son of prec.

4. Joseph K. (b. London, ?; d. London, 1877), son of prec.

5. Henry K. (b. London, ?; d. London, ?). brother of prec.

Kirnberger, Johann Philipp (b. Saalfeld, Thuringia, IV. 1721; d. Berlin, 27. VII. 1783), Ger. theorist, vst. & comp. Pupil of Bach, 1739–41, became vst. to Frederick II of Prus. in Berlin, 1751 and chapel master to Princess Amalie of Prus., 1758. Wrote a treatise, *Die Kunst des reinen Satzes* (*The Art of Pure Setting*).

Works incl. motets, cantatas; fugues, sos., &c.

Kiss, The (*Hubička*), opera by Smetana (lib. by Eliška Krásnohorská, based on a story by Karolina Světlá), prod. Prague, Cz. Theatre, 7. XI. 1876.

Kistler, Cyrill (b. Grossaitingen nr. Augsburg, 12. III. 1848; d. Kissingen, 2. I. 1907), Ger. comp. He learnt m. as a choir-boy and was taught the fl. as a child. After a period of schoolmastering, he went to the Munich Cons. in 1876, and F. Lachner taught him privately for a time afterwards. After teaching m. for 2 years at Sondershausen, he settled at Kissingen, where he ran a private m. school.

Works incl. operas *Kunihild, Eulenspiegel, Arm Elslein, Röslein im Hag, Der Vogt auf Mühlstein, Baldurs Tod, Die deutschen Kleinstädter*; orch. & chor. works; org. pieces; songs, &c.

Kit. A diminutive v., now obs., formerly used by dancing-masters, who on account of its small size and narrow shape were able to carry it in the long pockets of their tail-coats. Its Fr. name is therefore *pochette* and its Ger. *Taschengeige*.

Kitchen or **Kitchen Department** The popular and playful name for the perc. section of the orch.

Kitezh (Rimsky-Korsakov). *See* **Legend of the Invisible City of Kitezh.**

Kithara. A stg. inst. of ancient Gr., prob. a primitive forerunner of insts. of the Cittern and Guitar type.

Kitson, Charles Herbert (b. Leyburn, Yorks, 13. XI. 1874; d. London, 13. V. 1944), Eng. theorist. Studied theol. at Cambridge, but was also an org. scholar there and decided to devote himself to m. He took the Mus.D. at Oxford in 1902. In 1913–20 he lived at Dublin as orgst. & choirmaster of Christ Church cath. and prof. at Univ. Coll. He then returned to Eng. to become prof. of harmony and ctpt. at the R.C.M. in London, but also accepted the appt. of prof. of m. at Dublin Univ., which did not require continuous residence. He wrote many books on theoret. subjects.

Kittel, Johann Christian (b. Erfurt, 18. II. 1732; d. Erfurt, 18. V. 1809), Ger. orgst. & comp. Pupil of Bach in the last years at Leipzig, orgst. at Erfurt from 1756.

Works incl. preludes and other org. m.; 6 sos. for keyboard insts. and a fantasy, &c.

Kittel, Kaspar (b. ?; d. ?), Ger. 16th-cent. lutenist, orgst. & comp. Studied under Schütz and in 1624–8 in It. at the expense of the Elector of Saxony. He taught theorbo at Dresden from 1630 and 2 years later became inspector of insts. His later appt. as court orgst. he held till 1669. He wrote airs and cantatas for one or several voices with continuo.

Kittl, Johann Friedrich (b. Worlik, Boh., 8. V. 1806; d. Lissa, Pol., 20. VII. 1868), Boh. comp. Pupil of Tomašek in Prague, where he gave a 1st concert in 1836. In 1843 he succeeded Dionys Weber as dir. of the Prague Cons.

Works incl. operas *Bianca und Giuseppe, oder Die Franzosen vor Nizza* (lib. by Wagner, orig. written for himself), *Die Waldblume* & *Die Bilderstürmer*; *Jagdsymphonie* for orch., &c.

Kjerulf, Halfdan (b. Christiania, 15. IX. 1815; d. Grefsen nr. Christiania, 11. VIII. 1868), Norw. comp. At his father's desire he studied law at Christiania Univ., but on the death of his father in 1840 he decided to devote himself to m. He taught, and pub. some songs, even before he had done much in the way of theoret. study. About 1850 he received a gvt. grant to study at Leipzig for a year, and on his return he tried to estab. classical subscription concerts, with little success. He became a friend of Bjørnson's, who wrote many poems espec. for him to set.

Works incl. chors. and 4tets for male voices; pf. pieces; over 100 songs, &c.

Klafsky, Katharina (b. Szt. Janos, 19. IX. 1855; d. Hamburg, 22. IX. 1896), Hung. m.-sop., later sop. singer. Daughter of a poor shoemaker, she had to beg for her living at Sopron, but went to Vienna as a nursery maid, and her employers had her taught singing. After singing in an opera chor. she attracted Hellmesberger's attention by her voice and he induced Mathilde Marchesi to teach her free. After her 1st marriage at Leipzig she appeared in small parts there, but gradually made a repertory of the most important parts, esp. Wagner's, and she visited London, Paris and the U.S.A. with great distinction.

Klami, Uuno (Kalervo) (b. Virolahti, 20. IX. 1900), Fin. comp. Studied at the Helsingfors Cons., 1920–4, with Ravel in Paris, 1924–5, and Bruno Walter in Vienna. He became m. critic to the *Helsingin Sanomat* and in 1938 received a gvt. grant for comp.

Works incl. Psalm for solo voices,

chor. & orch.; Sym. in D maj., *Karelian Rhapsody, Pictures of the Sea, Kalevala* suite for orch.; pf. Conc., Fantasy for co. & orch.; pf. 4tet; pf. pieces, &c.

Klaviatur (Ger.) = Keyboard.

Klavier (Ger.) = Pianoforte (but *see also* Clavier).

Kleeberg, Clotilde (b. Paris, 27. VI. 1866; d. Brussels, 7. II. 1909), Fr. pfst. Studied at the Paris Cons. and made her 1st appearance in her early teens; 1st visited Eng. in 1883.

Klein, Bernhard (b. Cologne, 6. III. 1793; d. Berlin, 9. IX. 1832), Ger. comp. Studied in Paris, became attached to Cologne cath. on his return and settled in Berlin in 1819 as teacher at the Institute for Church M. and mus. dir. at the Univ.

Works incl. operas *Dido, Ariadne & Irene*; orats. *Job, Jephthah & David*; Mass in D maj., Magnificat and much other church m., &c.

Kleine Nachtmusik, Eine (*A Little Serenade*, lit. ' night m.'), a serenade for stgs. by Mozart, K. 525, comp. VIII. 1787. The title must not be taken as indicating a work noticeably smaller than M.'s other serenades; but it is unique among his comps., and may perhaps refer to the Ger. or rather Aus. character of the m., which is esp. striking in the finale.

Kleinknecht. Ger. 17th – 18th - cent. family of musns.:

1. ? K. (b. ?; d. ?), lutenist at (?) Augsburg.

2. Johann K. (b. ?; d. ?), mus. dir. & 2nd orgst. at Ulm cath., early 18th cent.

3. Johann Wolfgang K. (b. Ulm, 17. IV. 1715; d. Ansbach, 20. II. 1786), vst. & comp., son of prec. Was employed at Eisenach, Bayreuth, Stuttgart and Ansbach.

Works incl. a v. Conc., ? sos., &c.

4. Jakob Friedrich K. (b. Ulm, 8. VI. 1722; d. Ansbach, 4. VIII. 1794), vst., flst. & comp., brother of prec. In service at the court of Bayreuth.

Works inc.. *Sinfonie concertate*, fl. concs., trios for fls. & bass, sos. for var. insts., &c.

5. Johann Stephan K. (b. Ulm, 17. IX. 1731; d. Ansbach, *c.* 1803), flst., brother of prec. Studied under his father (2), toured in Ger. and was app. to the court chapel at Ansbach.

Kleinmichel, Richard (b. Posen, 31. XII. 1846; d. Charlottenburg, 18. VIII. 1901), Ger., pfst., teacher & comp. Studied under his father, the cond. Friedrich K. (1827–94), and at the Leipzig Cons., 1st settled at Hamburg, but was later operatic cond. at Leipzig, Danzig and Magdeburg.

Works incl. operas *Schloss de l'Orme* (after Prévost's *Manon Lescaut*), *Der Pfeifer von Dusenbach*; 2 syms.; much pf. m., &c.

Kleist, (Bernd) Heinrich (Wilhelm) von (1777–1811), Ger. poet, novelist & dramatist. *See* **Draeseke** (*Penthesilea* ovt.), **Goldmark** (**C.**) (do.), **Graener** (*Prinz von Homburg*), **Joachim** (commemoration ovt.), **Klenau** (*Michael Kohlhaas*), **Lux** (*Käthchen von Heilbronn*), **Marschner** (*Prinz von H.*), **Penthesilea** (Schoeck), **Pfitzner** (*Käthchen von H.*), **Reinthaler** (do.), **Unger (H.)** (*Penthesilea*), **Vesque von Püttlingen** (*Käthchen von H.*), **Wagenaar (J.)** (*Amphitryon*), **Wagner-Régeny** (*Zerbrochene Krug*), **Wolf (H.)** (*Penthesilea*).

Klemetti, Heikki (b. Kuortane, 14. II. 1876), Fin. comp. & cond. Studied at Helsingfors, Berlin and in Fr., It. and Scand. Cond. of the Helsingfors Univ. choir, 1907–32 and of the mixed choir Suomen Laulu.

Works incl. opera *Vallis gratiae*; *Lyric Ovt.* for orch.; church m.; chor. works; songs, &c.

Klenau, Paul von (b. Copenhagen, 11. II. 1883), Dan. cond. & comp., ? of Ger. descent. Studied v. and comp., the latter with Malling, at Copenhagen, and after 1902 with Bruch in Berlin and Thuille in Munich. When app. operatic cond. at Stuttgart in 1908 he studied further with Schillings. In 1914 he returned home and estab. the Phil. Soc., at which he introd. many modern orch. works; he also cond. orch. and chor. concerts in Vienna.

Works incl. operas *Shulamith, Kjartan and Gudrun* (revised as *Gudrun in Iceland*), *The School for Scandal* (after Sheridan), *Michael Kohlhaas* (after Kleist), *Rembrandt van Rijn*; ballet *Lille Ida's blomster* (after Andersen); 3 syms., 3 orch. fantasies on Dante's *Inferno, Bank Holiday-Souvenir of Hampstead Heath* for orch.; orat. *Job, The Song of the Love and Death of Cornet Christof Rilke* for bar. solo, chor. & orch.; *Dialogues with Death* for con. & orch., *Ebbe Skammelsen* for bar. & orch.; stg. 4tet in E min.; pf. pieces, &c.

Klengel, August (Alexander) (b. Dresden, 27. I. 1783; d. Dresden, 22. XI. 1852), Ger. orgst. & comp. Pupil of Clementi, with whom he travelled from 1803 onwards. He visited Rus., Paris and London, and in 1816 was app. court orgst. at Dresden.

Works incl. pf. concs.; pf. 5tet; much pf. m., incl. esp. canons and fugues, &c.

Klengel, Julius (b. Leipzig, 24. IX. 1859; d. Leipzig, 27. X. 1933), Ger. cst. & comp. Studied co. with Emil Hegar and comp. with Jadassohn, joined the Leipzig Gewandhaus orch.

at the age of 15, began to travel as virtuoso in 1875 and in 1881 became leading cst. in the orch. and prof. of co. at the Cons.

Works incl. co. concs., double concs. for v. & co. and 2 cos., *Hymnus* for 12 cos.; *Caprice in form of a Chaconne* for co. solo, many co. pieces & studies, &c.

Klengel, Paul (b. Leipzig, 13. V. 1854; d. Leipzig, 24. IV. 1935), Ger. vst., pfst., cond. & comp., brother of prec. Studied at the Leipzig Cons. and became chor. and orch. cond. in Leipzig, Stuttgart and N.Y.

Works incl. 2 suites for v. & pf.; songs, &c.

Klenovsky, Nikolai Semenovitch (b. Odessa, 1857; d. Petrograd, 6. VII. 1915), Rus. comp. & cond. Studied at the Moscow Cons., Tchaikovsky being among his masters, cond. the 1st perf. of the latter's *Eugene Onegin*; later cond. of the Univ. orch. and asst. cond. at the Imp. Opera. Collected and ed. folksongs with Melgunov. App. dir. of the school of m. at Tiflis, 1893, and asst. dir. of the Imp. Chapel at St. Petersburg, 1902.

Works incl. several ballets; incid. m. to Shakespeare's *Antony and Cleopatra* & other plays; *Georgian Liturgy* for unaccomp. chor.; cantatas, &c.

Klenovsky, Paul. A comp. invented by Sir Henry Wood to shoulder his orch. arr. of Bach's D min. Toccata & Fugue.

Klička, Josef (b. Klatovy, 15. XII. 1855; d. Prague, 28. III. 1937), Cz. orgst., cond. & comp. Studied at the Org. School in Prague, was asst. cond. at the Cz. Theatre, 1876–81, choirmaster of the Hlahol choir, 1890–7, and app. org. prof. at the Prague Cons. in 1920.

Works incl. masses; chor. cantatas and humorous chors.; So., concert fantasies & other works for org.; chamber m., &c.

Klindworth, Karl (b. Hanover, 25. IX. 1830; d. Stolpe, 27. VII. 1916), Ger. pfst. & cond. Pupil of Liszt; arranger of m. for his inst., incl. voc. scores of Wagner's works. He lived in London as pfst., cond. & teacher in 1854–68, then became pf. prof. at the Moscow Cons., but returned to Ger. in 1882 and opened a school of m. in Berlin, 1893.

Klingsor, Tristan (Léon Leclère) (b. 1874), Fr. poet. *See* **Cartan, Shéhérazade** (Ravel).

Klopstock, Friedrich (1724–1803), Ger. poet. *See* **Bach** (C. P. E.) (*Morgengesang am Schöpfungstage*), **Gluck** (odes), **Lesueur** (*Mort d'Adam*), **Schröter** (C.) (songs), **Schwenke** (odes), **Spohr** (*Vater unser*), **Stadler** (*Frühlingsfeier*), **Wolfrum** (*Grosse Hallalujah*).

13 songs by Schubert.

Klose, Friedrich (Karl Wilhelm) (b. Karlsruhe, 29. XI. 1862; d. Ruvigliana nr. Lugano, 24. XII. 1943), Swi. comp. Studied with V. Lachner at Karlsruhe, Adolf Ruthardt at Geneva and finally with Bruckner in Vienna. He lived in these 3 cities until 1906, when he was app. prof. at the Basle Cons., which he left in 1907 for a prof.-ship at Munich. In 1919 he retired to Swi., living 1st at Thun and then in the Ticino.

Works incl. Mass in D min.; orat. *Der Sonne-Geist*, *Ein Festgesang Neros* for ten. solo, chor., orch. & org., *Die Wallfahrt nach Kevlaar* (Heine) for recitation, chor., orch. & org.; dramatic sym. *Ilsebill*, symph. poem *Das Leben ein Traum*; Prelude and Double Fugue for org. & wind; stg. 4tet in E♭ maj.; male-voice chors.; songs, &c.

Klotz. Ger. 17th–18th-cent. family of v. makers:

1. Egidius K. (b. ?; d. Mittenwald, ?), the 1st to make vs. at Mittenwald in Bavaria.
2. Matthias K. (b. Mittenwald, 1653; d. Mittenwald, 1743), son of prec. He worked for a time at Florence and Cremona, but returned to Mittenwald *c.* 1683.
3. Sebastian K. (b. Mittenwald, ?; d. Mittenwald, ?), son of prec.
4. Joseph K. (b. Mittenwald, ?; d. Mittenwald, ?), brother of prec.
5. Georg K. (b. ?; d. ?), ? son of 4 or 5.
6. Michael K. (b. ?; d. ?) } ? sons
7. Karl K. (b. ?; d. ?) } of prec.
8. Egidius K. (b. ?; d. ?) }

Klughardt, August (Friedrich Martin) (b. Cöthen, 30. XI. 1847; d. Dessau, 3. VIII. 1902), Ger. cond. & comp. Began his career as a theatre cond. and became court mus. dir. at Weimar, 1869, Neustrelitz, 1873, and Dessau, 1882. At Weimar he came under Liszt's influence.

Works incl. operas *Miriam, Iwein, Gudrun, Die Hochzeit des Mönchs* (*Astorre*), *Judith* (after Hebbel's drama); incid. m. for Calderón's *La vida es sueño*; orats. *Die Grablegung Christi, Die Zerstörung Jerusalems, Judith*; 2 Psalms for solo voices and chor.; 5 syms., 5 ovts., 2 orch. suites; ob., v. & co. concs.; chamber m., &c.

Knab, Armin (b. Neu-Schleichach, Franconia, 19. II. 1881), Ger. comp. Studied at Würzburg and began his career as a lawyer, but devoted all his leisure to m. In 1934 he was app. prof. at the High School for Church M. in Berlin.

Works incl. Christmas play *Das Lebenslicht*; incid. m. to var. plays; cantatas, unaccomp. cycles of mixed, male & female chors., unison chors. with insts.; *c.* 12 song cycles incl. 2 of children's songs and others on poems from *Des Knaben Wunderhorn* and by Stefan George, Dehmel, Eichendorff, &c.

Knaben Wunderhorn, Des (*The Youth's Magic Horn*), Ger. anthol. of old folk poetry. *See* **Jelmoli** (cantata), **Kamienski (L.)** (chors.), **Knab** (songs), **Mahler** (songs, 9 with pf., 13 with orch.), **Trunk** (male chors.), **Vrieslander** (songs).

Knecht, Justin Heinrich (b. Biberach, 30. IX. 1752; d. Biberach, 1. XII. 1817), Ger. orgst. cond. & comp. He was prof. of literature at Biberach, but being mus. gifted, became mus. dir. in 1771 and cond. of the opera and court concerts at Stuttgart, 1807.

Works incl. several plays with m.; a sym. *Le Portrait musical de la nature* with a programme very similar to that of Beethoven's 'Pastoral' Sym.; church m.; voc. and inst. works of var. kinds, &c.

Kneisel, Franz (b. Bucharest, 26. I. 1865; d. New York, 26. III. 1926), Cz. vst., whose father, a bandmaster, came from Olomouc in Moravia. He studied at the Vienna Cons. and made his 1st appearance in 1882. In 1885 he went to U.S.A. as leader of the Boston Sym. Orch. and founded the K. 4tet there.

Knight, Joseph Philip (b. Bradford-on-Avon, 26. VII. 1812; d. Great Yarmouth, 2. VI. 1887), Eng. clergyman and comp. Studied under Corfe, orgst. of Bristol cath. and at the age of 20 began to write songs, at first under the name of Philip Mortimer. In 1839 he visited the U.S.A. and became almost as popular there as at home, and his songs were also known in Ger.

Works incl. numerous songs, e.g. 'Rocked in the cradle of the deep,' some to words written for him by Thomas Moore.

Knight, Robert (b. ?; d. ?), Eng. 16th-cent. comp. Only a 5-part motet *Propterea maestum* is certain to be his.

Knight, Thomas (b. ?; d. ?), Eng. 16th-cent. comp. Orgst. and vicar-choral of Salisbury cath. for 5 or 10 years from 1535.

Works incl. Magnificat and (?) Mass, motets, evening canticles, &c., some of which may be by Robert K.

Knipper, Lev Constantinovitch (b. Tiflis, 16. XII. 1898), Rus. comp. Self-taught as pfst. & comp. at first; but after 5 years' military service he entered the Gnessin School of M. at Moscow as a comp. pupil of Glière and others. About 1930 he made research into the folksongs of Tadjskistan, which has influenced his work, and in 1932 he became mus. instructor to the Red Army and Navy.

Works incl. operas *North Wind* & *Maria*; opera-ballet *Candide* (after Voltaire); ballets *Satanella* & *The Little Negro Sebi*; incid. & film m.; 8 syms., Sinfonietta, *The Legend of the Plaster Buddha*, *Miniatures* for children, *Maku*, *Vanteh* & other suites, studies and sketches for orch.; v. Conc.; *A Poem to Horses*, for chor. & orch.; songs; army songs, &c.

Knittl, Karel (b. Polná, 4. X. 1853; d. Prague, 17. III. 1907), Cz. cond. & teacher. Studied at the Org. School in Prague and became prof. at the Cons., of which he became the administrative dir. in 1901, acting in that capacity when Dvořák was nominal dir. He cond. the Hlahol chor. soc. and was also a critic.

Knorr, Iwan (b. Mewe, W. Prus., 3. I. 1853; d. Frankfort o/M., 22. I. 1916), Ger. comp. & teacher. Studied at the Leipzig Cons. after having lived in var. small Rus. towns in 1857–68. He returned to Rus. and became prof. at Kharkov in 1874, but settled at Frankfort in 1883, where he became dir. of the Hoch Cons. in 1908.

Works incl. operas *Dunja*, *Die Hochzeit* & *Durchs Fenster*; symph. fantasy for orch.; pf. 4tets, Vars. on a theme by Schumann for pf. trio; *Ukrainian Love-Songs* for voc. 4tet & pf.; pf. works for 2 & 4 hands; songs, &c.

Knot. The ornamental fretwork soundhole of many flat-bellied stg. insts. and keyboard insts., more generally called Rose.

Knüpfer, Paul (b. Halle, 21. VI. 1866; d. Berlin, 4. XI. 1920), Ger. bass singer. Studied at the Cons. of Sondershausen and made his 1st stage appearance there in 1885. He 1st sang at Bayreuth in 1901 and in London in 1904 and was leading bass at the Berlin Opera, 1898–1920.

Knyvett. Eng. family of musns.:

1. Charles K. (b. ? Norfolk, 22. II. 1752; d. London, 19. I. 1822), alto singer & orgst. App. Gentleman of the Chapel Royal, 1786, and one of the orgsts., 1796. Estab. the Voc. Concerts with Samuel Harrison in 1791.

2. Charles K. (b. London, 1773; d. London, 2. XI. 1852), orgst., teacher & comp., son of prec. Pupil of Samuel Webbe. App. orgst. of St. George's, Hanover Square, 1802, and pub. a *Selection of Psalm Tunes*, 1823.

3. William K. (b. London, 21. IV.

1779; d. Ryde, 17. XI. 1856), alto singer & comp., brother of prec. App. Gentleman of the Chapel Royal, 1797, and comp. to it in succession to Arnold, 1802. He sang and cond. much at concerts and festivals, and comp. anthems, glees, songs, &c.

4. Deborah K., *née* Travis (b. Shaw nr. Oldham, ?; d. ? London, 10. II. 1876), singer, wife of prec. Studied under Greatorex and made her 1st appearance in 1815.

Koanga, opera by Delius (lib. by Charles Francis Keary, based on George Washington Cable's novel *The Grandissimes*), prod. Elberfeld, in Ger., 30. III. 1904.

Koch, Erland von (b. Stockholm, 26. IV. 1910), Swe. comp. Studied at the Stockholm Cons. and later in London, Paris and Dresden.

Works incl. symph. poem *A Tale from the Wilderness, Symph. Episode, Symph. Dance*; pf. Conc., v. Conc.; suite for chamber orch.; stg. 4tet, stg. Trio; v. & pf. So.; pf. works; songs, &c.

Kochanski, Paul (b. Warsaw, 14. IX. 1887; d. New York, 12. I. 1934), Pol. vst. Studied with Mlynarski and at 14 joined the Phil. Orch. at Warsaw; later studied with Thomson at Brussels and became v. prof. at the Warsaw Cons. in 1907 and at that of St. Petersburg in 1913 in succession to Auer. In the 1920s he settled in U.S.A.

Köchel, Ludwig von, Ritter (b. Stein nr. Krems, 14. I. 1800; d. Vienna, 3. VI. 1877), Aus. naturalist & mus. bibliog. He lived at Salzburg in 1850–63 for the purpose of compiling his thematic catalogue of Mozart's works, pub. in 1862 (modern ed. revised by Alfred Einstein, 1937).

Koczwara. *See* **Kotzwara.**

Kodály, Zoltán (b. Kecskemét, 16. XII. 1882), Hung. comp. Learnt the v. in his childhood, sang in a cath. choir and tried to comp. without systematic instruction. In 1900, after living in small provincial towns, he entered the Univ. of Budapest for science, but also became a pupil at the Cons. Studied Hung. folksong and in 1906 wrote his Univ. thesis on it, afterwards collecting songs in collab. with Bartok. App. prof. at the Cons. that year and deputy dir. in 1919. He was often from the first (1923) repres. at the I.S.C.M. festivals.

Works incl. plays with m. *Háry János* & *Székely Fonó*; *Summer Evening, Ballet Music, Theatre Overture, Dances of Galánta, Marosszék Dances*, Vars. for orch.; 2 stg. 4tets; Duo for v. & co., Serenade for 2 vs. & va.; sos. for co. solo and for co. & pf.; *Meditation on a motif by Debussy, Valsette*, 9 pieces (Op. 3), 7 pieces (Op. 11) for pf.; 21 songs, *Énekszó* (16 songs on folk words); 57 folksong arrs.; 21 works for chor. with & without orch., incl. *Psalmus Hungaricus, Jesus and the Traders, Budavari Te Deum, Bicinia Hungarica* (60 children's songs), &c.

Koeberg, F. E. A. (b. The Hague, 15. VII. 1879), Dutch vst., pfst., cond. & comp. Studied at the Hague Cons. and in Berlin. Played v. in var. Ger. orchs. and toured as pfst., but returned to Hol. as comp. & cond. of a students' mus. soc. at Leyden and an orch. at The Hague, where he also became prof. of comp. at the Cons.

Works incl. opera *Bloemenkind*; open-air plays *Ydylle, Bloemensproke, Plato, Alianora, Middelburg's Overgang in 1574, Koninginne Kantate*; 3 syms., symph. poems *Zeelandia, Zevenzot, Zonneweg, Zotskap, Zelma, Minone, Kolma*, ovts.; chors.; stg. 4tet; v. pieces, pf. pieces; songs, &c.

Koechlin, Charles (b. Paris, 27. XI. 1867), Fr. (Alsat.) comp. Studied at the Paris Cons., finally under Fauré. He has never appeared as an executive musn. or held any official appt., but devoted himself wholly to comp. and the writing of some theoret. books as well as studies of Debussy and Fauré.

Works incl. ballet *La Divine Vesprée*; incid. m. to Rolland's *14 Juillet* (with 6 others); Sym., orch. cycles *La Forêt* & *Les Saisons, Seven Stars Sym.* (on film stars) and other orch. works: *En Mer la nuit, Études antiques, Nuit de Walpurgis classique* (after Goethe), *Rapsodie sur des chansons françaises, Les Heures persanes, La Course de printemps* (after Kipling's *Jungle Book*); 3 *Chorals* for org. & orch., *Ballade* for pf. & orch.; 3 stg. 4tets, pf. 5tet, Trio for fl., cl. & bn., pieces for pf., v. & hn., Suite for pf., va. & fl.; sos. for v., va., co., fl. ob., cl., bn. & hn., all with pf., So. for 2 fls.; Sonatinas, *Esquisses, Pastorales, Petites Pièces*, &c. for pf., suites & *Sonatines françaises* for pf. duet & 2 pfs.; chors., songs, &c.

Koessler, Hans (b. Waldeck, Bavaria, 1. I. 1853; d. Ansbach, 23. V. 1926), Ger. comp. & teacher. Studied with Rheinberger at Munich and at the Dresden Cons. After cond. at Dresden and Cologne, he went to Budapest as prof. of comp. at the Nat. Acad. of M., where Dohnányi, Bartók and Kodály were among his pupils.

Works incl. opera *Der Münzenfranz*; Mass & psalms; chor. works; Sym., Symph. Vars.; v. Conc.; 2 stg.

4tets, stg. 5tet, stg. 6tet; sos. for v. & pf. and co. & pf.; pf. Suite; songs with pf. & with chamber m., &c.

Koffler, Józef (b. Stryj, 28. XI. 1896), Pol. comp. Studied comp. with Grädener and mcol. with Adler in Vienna, where he came under the infl. of Schoenberg and began to cultivate the 12-note system. Later he became prof. at the Lwów State Cons.

Works incl. ballet *Alles durch M. O.W.*; 3 syms. & *Pol. Suite* for orch., 15 Vars. for stg. orch.; stg. 4tet, stg. Trio, cantata *Die Liebe* for voice, va., co. & cl.; pf. m. 40 *Pol. Folksongs, Musique de ballet, Musique quasi una sonata,* Sonatina, &c.; 4 Poems for voice & pf., &c.

Köhler (Christian) Louis (Heinrich) (b. Brunswick, 5. IX. 1820; d. Königsberg, 16. II. 1886), Ger. pfst., teacher & comp. Studied in Vienna and became a theatre cond. before he settled at Königsberg in 1847.

Works incl. opera *Maria Dolores*; ballet *Der Zauberkomponist*; numerous pf. works, incl. studies & other educ. m.

Kokoschka, Oskar (b. 1886), Ger. poet, playwright & painter. *See* **Hindemith** (*Mörder, Hoffnung der Frauen*), **Orpheus und Eurydike** (Křenek).

Kolb, Karlmann (b. Köstlarn, Bavaria, 1703; d. Munich, 15. I. 1765), Ger. priest, orgst. & comp. Studied and was ordained at the Abbey of Aschbach, where he became orgst., but later became m. tutor to a noble family at Munich. Wrote org. m. for church use.

Kolberg, Oskar (b. Przysucha nr. Radom, 1815; d. Warsaw, 3. VI. 1890), Pol. folksong collector & comp. Studied in Berlin and in 1840 began to collect Pol. songs. Comp. Pol. dances and an operetta *The Shepherd King.*

Kolenda (Pol.). A type of Pol. folksong (carol) sung at Christmas, some specimens dating back to the 13th cent.

Köler, David (b. Zwickau, ?; d. Zwickau, VII. 1565), Ger. comp. After working at Altenburg and Güstrow in Mecklenburg, he was recalled to Zwickau to become cantor at St. Mary's church.

Works incl. 10 Psalms for 4–6 voices, Mass on a motet by Josquin des Prés, sacred songs, &c.

Kollmann, August Friedrich Christoph (b. Engelbostel, Hanover, *c.* 1756; d. London, 19. IV. 1828), Ger. orgst., theorist. & comp. Was taught by his father, an orgst., and later held an appt. at Lüne nr. Lüneburg. He went to London in 1784 as chapel-keeper and teacher at the Ger. Chapel, St. James's. He wrote several theoret. books.

Works incl. 'syms.' for chamber m.; pf. Conc.; fugues for org. & pf. duet, &c., also a sym. *The Shipwreck.*

Kondracki, Michal (b. Poltava, 4. X. 1902), Pol. comp. Studied with Szymanowski at Warsaw and with Dukas and Nadia Boulanger in Paris, returning to Pol. in 1931.

Works incl. opera *Popieliny*; ballet *Legend of Cracow*; *Cantata ecclesiastica* and humorous cantata *Krasula*; orch. works *Little Mountain Sym.*, symph. action *Metropolis*, Toccata and Fugue, symph. picture *Soldiers march past, Match,* Partita for small orch., Nocturne for chamber orch.; pf. Conc., &c.

Königin von Saba, Die (*The Queen of Sheba*), opera by C. Goldmark (lib. by Salomon Hermann Mosenthal), prod. Vienna, Opera, 10. III. 1875.

Königskinder (*King's Children*), opera by Humperdinck (lib. by Ernst Rosmer), prod. as a play with accompanying m., Munich, 23. I. 1897; the operatic version prod. N.Y., Metrop. Opera, 28. XII. 1910.

Königsperger, Marianus (b. Roding, Bavaria, 4. XII. 1708; d. Prüfening nr. Ratisbon, 9. X. 1769), Ger. priest, orgst. & comp. He was educ. and took his vows at the Benedictine abbey of Prüfening, where he was orgst. and choirmaster all his life.

Works incl. masses, offertories, litanies, &c.; sym. and sos. for var. insts. with org.; preludes, fugues and other works for org., &c.

Konius. *See* **Conus.**

Kontrabass (Ger.) = Double Bass.

Kontrafagott (Ger.) = Double Bassoon.

Konzertmeister (Ger. = concert master). The leader of an orch.

Konzertstück. *See* **Concertstück.**

Kopylov, Alexander Alexandrovitch (b. St. Petersburg, 14. VII. 1854; d. St. Petersburg, 20. II. 1911), Rus. comp. He was educ. mus. in the imp. chapel and later became voc. instructor there.

Works incl. Sym. in C maj., Scherzo, Concert Ovt. for orch.; 2 stg. 4tets & Andantino for stg. 4tet; *Souvenir de Peterhof* for v. & pf.; pf. pieces; chors., songs, &c.

Koreshtchenko, Arseny Nikolaievitch (b. Moscow, 18. XII. 1870; d. Moscow, 1918), Rus. pfst. & comp. Studied pf. with Arensky and comp. with Taneiev at the Moscow Cons., where he later became a prof.

Works incl. operas *Belzhazzar's Feast, The Angel of Death* (after Lermontov), *The Ice Palace*; ballet *The Magic Mirror*; incid. m. to Euripides' *The Trojan Women* & *Iphigenia in Aulis* & Shakespeare's *Twelfth Night*; cantata *Don Juan*, var. chor. works; Sym., 2 *Symph.*

Sketches, Armenian Suite, Scènes nocturnes & other works for orch.; Concert Fantasy for pf. & orch.; stg. 4tet; pieces for v. and for co.; pf. pieces; *c.* 80 songs, &c.

Körner, (Karl) Theodor (1791–1813), Ger. poet. *See* **Dvořák** (*Alfred*), **Graener** (*Vierjährige Posten*), **Reinecke** (do.), **Vierjährige Posten** (Schubert).

Korngold, Erich (Wolfgang) (b. Brno, Moravia, 29. V. 1897), Aus. comp. Son of Julius K. (1860–1945), m. critic of the *Neue Freie Presse* in Vienna, thanks to whose influence he had his pantomime *The Snowman* prod. at the Court Opera at the age of 11. He studied with Fuchs, Grädener and Zemlinsky. App. cond. at the Hamburg Opera, 1919, and prof. at the Vienna State Acad., 1927. After the *Anschluss* he emigrated to U.S.A. Collab. with Max Reinhardt at his Theatre School at Hollywood.

Works incl. operas *Der Ring des Polycrates, Violanta, Die tote Stadt, Das Wunder der Heliane, Die Katrin*; ballet-pantomime *Der Schneemann*; incid. m. to Shakespeare's *Much Ado about Nothing*; film m. *Sea Hawk*; Symphonietta, Sym.-Ovt., Ovt. to a play; pf. Conc. for the left hand; stg. 4tet, pf. Trio, pf. 5tet, 6tet; v. & pf. So.; 3 pf. sos. & pieces; songs, &c.

Kortchmarev, Klementy Arkadievitch (b. Verkhni Udinsk, 3. VII. 1899), Rus. comp. Pupil of Malishevsky at the Odessa Cons.

Works incl. operas *Ivan the Soldier* & *Ten Days that Shook the World*; ballet *The Serf Ballerina*; incid. m. for plays; Voc. Sym. on his 2nd opera; 2 pf. sos., &c.

Kos. A Hung. dance.

Kossenko, Victor (b. St. Petersburg, 1896; d. Kiev, 3. X. 1938), Rus. comp. Studied pf. under his sister at first, but in 1914 entered the St. Petersburg Cons., continuing pf. studies and becoming a comp. pupil of Sokolov and Steinberg. In 1918 he went to live in the Ukraine, settling at Zhitomir, and in 1929 to Kiev as prof. at the Cons.

Works incl. *Heroic Ovt.* & *Moldavian Poem* for orch.; pf. Conc., v. Conc.; stg. 4tet, pf. Trio; sos. for v., va. and co. & pf.; 3 pf. sos. & other works for pf.; songs; Ukrainian folksong arrs., &c.

Kotzebue, August (Friedrich Ferdinand) von (1761–1819), Ger. playwright. *See* **Busby** (*Johanna von Montfaucon*), **Generali** (*Misantropia e pentimento*), **Lortzing** (*Graf Benjowsky* & *Schutzgeist*), **Reichardt** (*Kreuzfahrer*), **Ritter (P.)** (*Eremit auf Formentara*), **Ruins of Athens** (Beethoven), **Salieri** (*Hussiten vor Naumburg*), **Süssmayr** (*Wildfang*), **Teufels Lustschloss** (Schubert), **Walter (I.)** (*Spiegelritter*), **Wessely (C. B.)** (*Sonnenjungfrau*), **Wildschütz** (Lortzing), **Wolf (E. W.)** (*Eremit auf Formentara*), **Wranitzky** (m. for plays).

Kotzwara (Kočwara), Franz (b. Prague, ?; d. London, 2. IX. 1791), Boh. comp. Settled in London in the 1780s, visited Ir. in 1788 and played in the King's Theatre Orch. in London, 1790.

Works incl. *The Battle of Prague* for pf. with v., co. & drums ad lib.; songs, &c.

Koukourgi (Cherubini). *See* **Ali Baba.**

Koval, Marian (b. Pristan-Vosnessey nr. Olonezka, 17. VIII. 1907), Rus. comp. Studied at St. Petersburg and Nizhny-Novgorod. In 1925 he became a comp. pupil of Gnessin at the Moscow Cons. and in 1930 a private pupil of Miaskovsky.

Works incl. operas *The Manor House* (after Pushkin) & *Emilian Pugatchev*, children's opera *The Wolf and the Seven Goats*; incid. m.; 2 suites and symph. poem *Tale of a Partisan* for orch.; orats. *The People's Sacred War* & *Tchkalov*, cantata *Fighting in Moscow* for chor. & orch.; several song cycles to poems by Pushkin, Nekrasov, &c., Ballad for co. & pf.; battle songs, &c.

Kovařovic, Karel (b. Prague, 9. XII. 1862; d. Prague, 6. XII. 1920), Cz. cond. & comp. Studied cl. & hp. at the Prague Cons., became an orch. hpst. in 1885 and then studied comp. with Fibich. He toured as accompst. with the vst. Ondříček, 1886–8, afterwards cond. in the provinces, in 1895 was app. to cond. at the Ethnographic Exhib. in Prague, and in 1900 became chief cond. at the Nat. Opera there.

Works incl. operas *The Peasants' Charter, At the Old Bleaching-House*, comic operas *The Bridegrooms, The Way through the Window, The Night of Simen and Jude*; ballets *Hashish* and *A Tale of Luck Found*; incid. m. to Tyl's *Wood Nymph*, Čech's *The Excursions of Mr. Brouček* and other plays; symph. poem *The Rape of Persephone*, dramatic ovt. in C min.; pf. Conc. in F min.; 3 stg. 4tets; chor. pieces, songs, &c.

Koven, (Henry Louis) Reginald de (b. Middletown, Conn., 3. IV. 1859; d. Chicago, 16. I. 1920), Amer. comp. Graduated at Oxford in 1879 and then studied m. on the Continent.

Works incl. operas *The Begum, Robin Hood* (*Maid Marian*) & *Rob Roy* (both after Scott), *The Canterbury Pilgrims* (after Chaucer), *Rip van Winkle* (after Washington Irving), many operettas & ballets; orch. works; pf. So. & pieces; *c.* 400 songs, &c.

Kozeluch (Koželuh), Leopold (b.

Welwarn, 9. XII. 1752; d. Vienna, 7. V. 1818), Boh. comp. Studied with his cousin, Johann Anton K. (1738–1814). In 1765 he went to Prague and prod. a ballet there, 1771. In 1778 he settled in Vienna as pf. teacher and became pf. master to the Archduchess Elizabeth. He succeeded Mozart in the nominal post of Imp. Chamber Comp.

Works incl. operas *Judith*, *Mazet* & *Didone abbandonata*; orat. *Debora und Sisara*; 24 ballets & 3 pantomimes; orat. *Moses in Aegypten*, cantatas; *c.* 30 syms.; much pf. m.; settings of Brit. folksongs for Thomson's collection, &c.

Kraft, Anton (b. Rokitzen nr. Pilsen, 30. XII. 1752; d. Vienna, 28. VIII. 1820), Boh. cst. and comp. Studied law in Prague, but also cultivated the co., on which he had finishing lessons in Vienna, where Haydn engaged him as cst. in Prince Esterházy's band, 1778. On his patron's death in 1790 he entered the service of Prince Grassalkovitch and in 1795 that of Prince Lobkowitz.

Works incl. co. concs. and sos., duets for v. & co., trios for 2 barytones & co., duets for 2 cos., Divertimento for co. & db., &c. (It is prob. that the co. Conc. in D maj. attrib. to Haydn is by K., though very possibly scored by Haydn.)

Kraft, Nicolaus (b. Esterház, 14. XII. 1778; d. Stuttgart, 18. V. 1853), Boh. cst. & comp., son of prec. Pupil of his father, with whom he travelled. Settled in Vienna, 1790, and became chamber musn. to Prince Lobkowitz in 1796. In 1801 he had further lessons with Duport in Berlin and in 1809 he went to Stuttgart as a member 1st of the Court Opera and then of the Court Chapel.

Works incl. co. concs., *Scène pastorale* for co. & orch.; Fantasy for co. and stg. 4tet; duets and divertissements for 2 cos., &c.

Krakowiak. A Pol. dance from the region of Cracow, sometimes introd. into ballets and ballrooms in the 19th cent. under the name of *Cracovienne*. In its orig. form it was danced by all the assembled couples and sometimes words were sung to it. It is in quick 2–4 time.

Kraus, Joseph Martin (b. Miltenberg nr. Mainz, 26. VI. 1756; d. Stockholm, 15. XII. 1792), Ger.-Swe. comp. Studied law and philos. at Mainz, Erfurt and Göttingen, also comp. with Vogler. He accomp. a Swe. friend to Stockholm and remained there as theatre cond., becoming mus. dir. in 1781. In 1782–7 he travelled with a grant from the King of Swe., visiting Ger., Fr., It. & Eng. In 1788 he succeeded Uttini as chapel master.

Works incl. operas *Soliman II*, *Aeneas at Carthage* & 2 others; church m.; syms. & ovts.; stg. 4tets, &c.

Krauss, (Marie) Gabrielle (b. Vienna, 24. III. 1842; d. Paris, 6. I. 1906), Aus. sop. singer. Studied at the Vienna Cons. and with Mathilde Marchesi; after singing at concerts she made her 1st stage appearance at the Vienna Opera in 1859 and in Paris, at the Théâtre des Italiens, in 1867; in 1875–88 she was a member of the Opéra almost continuously.

Krebs, Johann Ludwig (b. Buttelstädt, Thuringia, 10. X. 1713; d. Altenburg, I. 1780), Ger. orgst., hpchdst. & comp. Pupil of Bach at Leipzig from 1726, orgst. at Zwickau, Zeitz and Altenburg.

Works incl. Magnificat, settings of Sanctus; trios; sos., suites, fugues, chors., with vars., &c. for clavier; fl. sos., &c.

Krebs, Johann Tobias (b. Heichelheim, 7. VII. 1690; d. Buttelstädt, after 1758), Ger. orgst., father of prec. Pupil 1st of Walther and then of Bach at Weimar; app. orgst. at Buttelstädt *c.* 1721.

Krehbiel, Henry Edward (b. Ann Arbor, Mich., 10. III. 1854; d. New York, 20. III. 1923), Amer. m. critic & author. After studying law at Cincinnati, he became m. critic to the *Cincinnati Gazette*, 1874, and to the *N.Y. Tribune*, 1880. He edited Thayer's life of Beethoven, collected and wrote on Negro folksongs and wrote many books incl. studies of opera, of Wagner and of Amer. mus. life.

Krehl, Stephan (b. Leipzig, 5. VII. 1864; d. Leipzig, 7. IV. 1924), Ger. theorist & comp. Studied at the Leipzig and Dresden Conss., taught at Carlsruhe & Leipzig, and became dir. of the Cons. at the latter in 1921. He wrote several theoret. books.

Works incl. cantata *Tröstung*; symph. prelude to Hauptmann's *Hannele*; stg. 4tet, suite for stg. 4tet, cl. 5tet; co. & pf. So., &c.

Krein, Alexander Abramovitch (b. Nizhny-Novgorod, 20. X. 1883), Rus. comp. Son of a vst. & folksong collector, went to the Moscow Cons. in 1897 to study co. and comp. He became prof. there in 1912.

Works incl. opera *Zagmuk*; ballets *Laurencia* (after Lope de Vega's *Fuente Ovejuna*) & *Tatiana*, chor. ballet *Othello and Desdemona* (after Shakespeare); incid. m. to many plays; film m.; *Kaddish* symph. cantata for solo voice, chor. & orch., trilogy *The Soviet Shock Brigade* for chor. & orch.; Sym. in F♯ min., symph. poem *Salome* (after Wilde) & other orch. works; *Poem* stg. 4tet, 2 suites of *Jewish Sketches* for cl. & stg. 4tet, *Elegy* for pf. trio; many inst. pieces; pf. So., *Dance Suite* & other pf. pieces; song cycle *From Balkaria's Mountains*, 16 op. nos. of songs; Jewish folksong arrs., &c.

Krein, Grigory Abramovitch (b. Nizhny-Novgorod, 4. VII. 1880), Rus. comp., brother of prec. Studied with Glière at Moscow and Reger at Leipzig.

Works incl. 3 symph. episodes *Lenin*; v. Conc.; stg. 4tet, pf. 4tet; So. and *Poem* for v. & pf., &c.

Krein, Julian Grigorievitch (b. Moscow, 5. III. 1913), Rus. comp., son of prec. Studied with Dukas in Paris. He returned to Rus. about 1930.

Works incl. *Spring Sym.*, Ballad for orch., symph. prelude *Destruction*; *Lyric Poem* for pf. & orch.; Suite for co. & pf.; v. pieces; *Tango, Nocturne et Bal* for pf., other pf. works, &c.

Kreisleriana. A cycle of pf. pieces by Schumann, Op. 16, comp. in 1838 and ded. to Chopin. The title is borrowed from the musn. Kreisler in E. T. A. Hoffmann's stories *Fantasiestücke in Callots Manier*.

Kreissle von Hellborn, Heinrich (b. Vienna, 1812; d. Vienna, 6. IV. 1869), Aus. lawyer and state official, 1st biog. of Schubert, on whom he pub. *F. Schubert: eine biographische Skizze*, 1861, and *Franz Schubert*, 1865.

Krejči, Iša (b. Prague, 10. VII. 1904), Cz. comp. Pupil of Novák and Jirák. After working for some time at Bratislava he returned to Prague and joined the wireless service.

Works incl. operatic scene *Antigone* (after Sophocles); Sinfonietta for orch.; *Little Ballet* for chamber orch.; stg. 4tet in D maj., Nonet, trios for ob., cl. & bn. and cl., db. & pf.; Sonatina for cl. & pf.; songs, &c.

Křenek, Ernst (b. Vienna, 23. VIII. 1900), Aus. comp. of Cz. descent. Pupil of Schreker in Vienna and Berlin. In the 1920s he appeared at several of the smaller festivals in Ger. and in 1925–7 he was cond. at the operas of Cassel, Wiesbaden and other smaller towns in order to gain experience in operatic stagecraft. He married 1st Anna Mahler, the comp.'s daughter, and then the actress Berta Hermann. After the prod. of *Jonny spielt auf* at Leipzig in 1927 his success was assured, but he later worked in 12-note m. as a disciple of Schoenberg. In 1933, when the Nazi régime gained the upper hand, he settled in Vienna and worked on behalf of progressive Aus. comps., but was interferred with by the Fascist party; left Aus. for U.S.A. in 1937, lived in London and settled in U.S.A. in 1938. App. prof. of m. at Vassar Coll., N.Y., in 1940. His book, *Über neue Musik*, is a defence of the 12-note system.

Works incl. operas *Der Sprung über den Schatten*, *Orpheus und Eurydike*, *Jonny spielt auf*, *Leben des Orest*, *Karl V*, *Tarquin*, also 3 1-act operas; cantatas *Die Jahrezeiten* & *Von der Vergänglichkeit des Irdischen*; ballets *Mammon*, *Der vertauschte Cupido*; incid. m. to Shakespeare's *Midsummer Night's Dream*, Goethe's *Triumph der Empfindsamkeit* & Calderón's *La vida es sueño*; chors. on poems by John Donne, *The Seasons* for unaccomp. chor.; 4 syms. & *Little Symphony*, 2 Concerti grossi, Vars. on *I wonder where I wander* for orch.; 2 pf. concs., v. Conc.; Theme & 13 Vars. for orch.; 7 stg. 4tets; 3 pf. sos.; c. 25 songs, song cycles *Reisebuch aus den österreichischen Alpen*, *Fiedellieder*, *Gesänge des späten Jahres*, *Poems by John Donne*, &c.

Kretschmer, Edmund (b. Ostritz, Saxony, 31. VIII. 1830; d. Dresden, 13. IX. 1908), Ger. orgst. & comp. Studied at Dresden, where he became church orgst. in 1854 and court orgst. in 1863. He founded and cond. chor. socs.

Works incl. operas *Die Folkunger*, *Heinrich der Loewe*, *Der Flüchtling*, *Schön Rohtraut*; 4 masses; cantatas *Die Geisterschlacht*, *Pilgerfahrt*, *Sieg im Gesang*; *Musikalische Dorfgeschichten* for orch., &c.

Kretzschmar, (August Ferdinand) Hermann (b. Olbernhau, Saxony, 19. I. 1848; d. Nikolassee nr. Berlin, 12. V. 1924), Ger. mcolst. Studied at Dresden and the Leipzig Cons., where he became a prof. in 1871. After several appts. elsewhere, he returned as mus. dir. to Leipzig Univ. and cond. var. organizns. there. In 1909 he succeeded Joachim as dir. of the Berlin Hochschule für Musik. He wrote on many subjects, incl. old notation, the hist. of opera and of Ger. song, and pub. a collection of analytical notes on a var. of works, *Führer durch den Konzertsaal*.

Kreusser, Georg Anton (b. Heidingsfeld, 1743; d. Frankfort o/M., c. 1810), Ger. vst. & comp. Studied at Amsterdam and in It., and in the 1780s became leader of the electoral orch. at Mainz. Later he was app. cond. at the Frankfort theatre.

Works incl. Passion *Der Tod Jesu* (Ramler); mus. prologue *Die Ausbreitung der Kunst*; syms.; chamber m.; songs, &c.

Kreutzer, Conradin (b. Messkirch, Baden, 22. XI. 1780; d. Riga, 14. XII. 1849), Ger. cond. & comp. He 1st learnt m. as a choir-boy, went to Freiburg i/B. to study medicine, but gave it up for m., travelled in Swi. as pfst. & singer and in 1804 went to Vienna to study comp. with Albrechtsberger. After cond. at the court of Stuttgart and Donaueschingen, he returned to Vienna and became cond. at the Kärntnertor Theatre for 3 periods between 1825–40 and of the Josefstadt Theatre in 1833–40. Later he worked at Cologne and Paris, and again in Vienna.

Works incl. operas *Conradin von Schwaben, Die Alpenhütte, Libussa, Melusina, Das Nachtlager von Granada, Cordelia* & c. 25 others; incid. m. to plays incl. Raimund's *Der Verschwender*; orat. *Die Sendung Mosis*; church m.; chamber m.; pf. works; male-voice partsongs; songs, &c.

Kreutzer, Rodolphe (b. Versailles, 16. XI. 1766; d. Geneva, 6. VI. 1831), Fr. vst. & comp. He was taught mainly by his father and at the age of 16 was app. by Marie Antoinette 1st v. in the royal chapel, where he learnt much from hearing Mestrino and Viotti. Later he became leader at the Théâtre Italien, where he began to prod. operas of his own. In 1798 he went to Vienna in the suite of Bernadotte and made friends with Beethoven. He toured much and became v. prof. at the Paris Cons., in 1795. He often played v. duets with Rode, on whose departure to Rus. in 1801 K. became leader at the Opéra, and later he held court appts. under both Napoleon I and Louis XVIII. He compiled a *Méthode de violon* with Baillot.

Works incl. operas *Jeanne d'Arc à Orléans, Paul et Virginie* (after Saint-Pierre), *Lodoïska, Imogène, ou La Gageure indiscrète* (after Boccaccio), *Astyanax, Aristippe, La Mort d'Abel, Mathilde* and many others; ballets *Paul et Virginie, Le Carnaval de Venise, Clari* and others; 19 v. concs., 3 *Symphonies concertantes*; 15 stg. 4tets, 15 trios; sos., caprices, studies, airs with vars. &c. for v., &c.

'Kreutzer' Sonata, the nickname of Beethoven's A maj. v. & pf. So., Op. 47, comp. in 1803 and ded. to R. Kreutzer. The work is the subject of Tolstoy's novel *The Kreutzer Sonata*, in which it has a disastrous effect on the characters.

Křička, Jaroslav (b. Kelč, Moravia, 27. VIII. 1882), Cz. comp. Studied at the Prague Cons., 1902–5, and came under the infl. of Novák, enlarged his experience in Berlin, and then went to Rus. teaching at the m. school of Ekaterinoslav. On his return to Prague in 1909 he became cond. of the Hlahol chor. soc.

Works incl. operas *Hypolita* (after one of Maurice Hewlett's *Little Novels of Italy*) and *The Gentleman in White* (after Wilde's *Canterville Ghost*); chor. works *The Temptation in the Wilderness* & many others with and without orch.; Sym. in D min., symph. poems *Faith*, ovt. to Maeterlinck's *Blue Bird, Polonaise* and *Elegy on the Death of Rimsky-Korsakov, Children's Suite* for small orch., *Nostalgia* for stg. orch.; stg. 4tet in D maj.; v. & pf. So.; *Intimate Pieces, Lyric Suite*, &c. for pf.; song cycles *Northern Lights, Of Love and Death, Songs of Parting, 3 Legends*, &c.

Krieger, Adam (b. Driesen, Prus., 7. I. 1634; d. Dresden, 30. VI. 1666), Ger. orgst., comp. & poet. Pupil of Scheidt and Schütz, orgst. of St. Nicholas's church at Leipzig and afterwards court orgst. at Dresden.

Works incl. arias for voice & bass, songs for 1–5 voices & insts., &c.

Krieger, Johann (b. Nuremberg, 28. XII. 1651; d. Zittau, 18. VII. 1735), Ger. orgst. & comp. Pupil of his brother; court orgst. at Bayreuth, 1671–7, and later orgst. and town mus. dir. at Zittau.

Works incl. plays with m.; sacred and secular songs for several voices with insts.; org. works; 6 partitas, preludes, fugues, &c. for clavier, &c.

Krieger, (Johann) Philipp (b. Nuremberg, 25. II. 1649; d. Weissenfels, 7. II. 1725), Ger. orgst. & comp., brother of prec. Travelled in It. and studied under Rosenmüller at Venice; entered the service of the Duke of Saxe-Weissenfels, was chamber musn. and orgst. at Halle from 1677 and mus. dir. at Weissenfels from 1712.

Works incl. opera *Der grossmütige Scipio* & others; plays with m.; church m.; arias for 1–4 voices with insts.; sos. for v. & va. da gamba; *Partien* for wind insts., &c.

Krilov, Ivan Andreievitch (1769–1844), Rus. fabulist. *See* **Rebikov** (*Fables*).

Krizhanovsky, Ivan Ivanovitch (b. Kiev, 8. III. 1867; d. Leningrad, 9. XII. 1924), Rus. comp. He took m. lessons at Kiev while studying medicine, and in 1896–1900 was a pupil of Rimsky-Korsakov in St. Petersburg. He returned to medicine and became prof. at St. Petersburg Univ., but continued to comp. in his spare time.

Works incl. cantata *Paradise and the Peri* (Thomas Moore); several orch. works; pf. Conc., v. Conc.; stg. 4tet, pf. Trio; v. & pf. So., co. & pf. So.; org. & pf. m.; songs, &c.

Křižkovský, Pavel (christened Karel) (b. Holasovice, 9. I. 1820; d. Brno, 8. V. 1885), Cz. monk & comp. His father was so poverty-stricken a musn. that he would not allow his son to take up m.; but he picked up much knowledge at the church of Opava and was eventually admitted to the choir-school; later he took a degree at Brno Univ. and entered the Augustinian community of St. Thomas, became prof. of divinity collected and arr. folksongs, and was sent to Prague for 6 months for mus. study. He succeeded Bohumir Rieger (1764–1855) as mus. dir. of the Austin Friars' church and cond. concerts of sacred m. at Brno.

Works incl. cantata *Two Stars from the East*, funeral song with tromb. accomp.; many chor. works for male voices, often based on folk material; songs, &c.

Krohn, Ilmari (b. Helsingfors, 8. XI. 1867), Fin. mcolst. & comp. Studied at Helsingfors and Leipzig Cons., app. lecturer in m. at Helsingfors Univ. 1900, and prof., 1918. He coll. and ed. Fin. folksongs and wrote several books incl. a study of old Fin. sacred songs and a theoret. handbook.

Comps. incl. opera *The Deluge*; orats. *Eternal Treasures* and *Victors*; church cantatas; org. & pf. m., &c.

Krommer, Franz (b. Kamenice, 17. V. 1760; d. Vienna, 8. I. 1831), Morav. vst., orgst. & comp. Having been an orgst. from 1776–84, he went to Hung. and later became mus. dir. to Prince Grassalkovitch in Vienna. In 1818 he succeeded Kozeluch as court mus. dir.

Works incl. masses; m. for wind band; syms.; 69 stg. 4tets & 5tets, fl. 4tets & 5tets, &c.

Kronke, Emil (b. Danzig, 29. XI. 1865; d. Dresden, 16. XII. 1938), Ger. pfst. & comp. Studied at the Leipzig and Dresden Conss. and settled at Dresden as concert pfst. and teacher. Ed. Chopin's works.

Works incl. Symph. Vars., *Carnival* Suite and *Ballad* for orch.; pf. Conc.; hn. 4tets & other chamber m.; suites for v. & pf., co. & pf., fl. & pf., &c.; var. inst. pieces; concert Vars. & numerous pieces for pf., &c.

Kroyer, Theodor (b. Munich, 9. IX. 1873), Ger. mcolst. Studied with Rheinberger and Sandberger at Munich. Prof. of m. at Munich, 1907, Heidelberg, 1920, at Leipzig, where he succeeded Abert, 1923, and Cologne, 1933, where he estab. an institute for mus. research. He has written on the It. madrigal and other subjects, and ed. works by Machault, Okeghem, Senfl, Aichinger, Marenzio, &c.

Krug, Arnold (b. Hamburg, 16. X. 1849; d. Hamburg, 4. VIII. 1904), Ger. comp. Studied with var. masters and at the Leipzig Cons. In 1872–7 he taught at Stern's Cons. in Berlin, then visited Fr. and It., and in 1878 settled at Hamburg, where he cond. chor. concerts and became prof. at the Cons. in 1885.

Works incl. a number of cantatas; Sym., suite *Aus der Wanderzeit*, prelude to Shakespeare's *Othello*, *Italienische Reiseskizzen* for orch.; *Liebesnovelle* & Serenade for stgs.; v. Conc.; stg. 4tet, pf. 4tet, pf. Trio, stg. 6tet; pieces for v. and for co.; pf. works, &c.

Krummhorn. *See* **Cromorne.**

Krumpholz, Johann Baptist (b. Zlonice nr. Prague, *c.* 1745; d. Paris, 19. II. 1790), Boh. hpst. & comp. His father became bandmaster of a Fr. regiment, so that he lived in Paris from his childhood. In 1772 he appeared in Vienna and in 1773–6 was in the orch. at Esterház under Haydn, from whom he took comp. lessons. After some travel, he settled in Paris for good, teaching and making improvements in his inst. His wife (*née* Meyer), also a hpst., played with him and introd. his works, but left him in 1788, and he drowned himself from grief at her desertion.

Works incl. syms. for hp. & small orch., 6 hp. concs., 32 sos. for hp. & v., 4tet for hp. & stgs. & many pieces for 1 and 2 hps.

Krumpholz, Wenzel (b. ? Paris, 1750; d. Vienna, 2. V. 1817), Boh.-Fr. vst., mandoline player & comp. He joined the Vienna court opera orch. in 1796 and became a friend of Beethoven's, who wrote a mandoline So. for him. His comps. incl. *Abendunterhaltung* and *Eine Viertelstunde* for v. alone, &c.

Krylov. *See* **Krilov.**

Kryzhanovsky. *See* **Krizhanovsky.**

Kubelik, Jan (b. Michle nr. Prague, 5. VII. 1880; d. Prague, 5. XII. 1940), Cz. vst. He was taught by his father, a gardener and good mus. amateur, and made his 1st public appearance in Prague in 1888. In 1892 he entered the Cons. as a pupil of Ševčik and began his real career with a concert in Vienna, 1898.

Kubik, Gail (b. Coffeyville, Okla., 1914), Amer. vst. & comp. Studied at the Eastman School of M., Rochester, N.Y., and gained several comp. prizes.

Works incl. *In Praise of Johnny Appleseed* (Vachel Lindsay) for bar., chor. & orch.; Suite for orch.; v. Conc., *American Caprice* for pf. & 32 insts.; 2 *Sketches* for stg. 4tet, pf.

Trio, wind 5tet, *Trivialities* for fl., hn. & stg. 4tet, &c.

Kücken, Friedrich Wilhelm (b. Bleckede, Hanover, 16. XI. 1810; d. Schwerin, 3. IV. 1882), Ger. cond. & comp. His father, a landed proprietor, was against his taking up m., but he was helped by his brother-in-law, Lührss, who was mus. dir. and orgst. at Schwerin, where he learnt a good deal and played var. insts. in the ducal orch. He began to comp. songs, some of which became very popular, but in 1832 he went to Berlin for further study, and later still he studied ctpt. with Sechter in Vienna and orchn. with Halévy in Paris. In 1851 he became court cond. at Stuttgart with Lindpaintner, and alone after the latter's death in 1856.

Works incl. operas *Die Flucht nach der Schweiz* & *Der Prätendent*; sos. for v. and for co. & pf.; a vast number of songs, some of which became so popular that the Gers. mistook them for folksongs, e.g. 'Ach, wie wär's möglich dann,' &c.

Kufferath, Hubert Ferdinand (b. Mühlheim o/Ruhr, 10. VI. 1818; d. Brussels, 23. VI. 1896), Ger. vst., pfst. & comp. Studied under his brother Johann K. at Utrecht, at Cologne and at the Leipzig Cons. In 1844 he settled at Brussels, where he founded chamber concerts with Léonard and Servais, became court pfst. to Leopold I and prof. at the Cons., 1872.

Works incl. Sym.; pf. Conc., Capriccio for pf. & orch.; stg. 4tet, pf. Trio; pf. pieces; songs, &c.

Kufferath, Maurice (b. Brussels, 8. I. 1852; d. Brussels, 8. XII. 1919), Belg. writer on m. Studied law and philol. at Brussels Univ. and was on the staff of *L'Indépendance belge* until 1900, when he became joint dir. of the Théâtre de la Monnaie with Guillaume Guidé. He wrote on Berlioz, Schumann, Vieuxtemps & Wagner, and made Fr. translations of some of Wagner's writings and operas.

Kugelmann, Hans (b. ? Augsburg, ?; d. Königsberg, 1542), Ger. tptr. & comp. He was tptr. in the service of the Emperor Maximilian at Innsbruck in 1519 and afterwards at the ducal court of Königsberg, where he became mus. dir. In 1540 he pub. a Lutheran service book, containing a Mass, a Magnificat and hymns, some comp. by himself.

Kuhlau, Friedrich (b. Uelzen, Hanover, 11. IX. 1786; d. Copenhagen, 12. III. 1832), Ger. comp. A child of poor parents, he picked up mus. knowledge at Brunswick and Hamburg. During the Fr. occupation he went to Den. to escape conscription and became flst. in the court orch. at Copenhagen. In 1825 he visited Vienna and met Beethoven, who comp. a punning canon on his name.

Works incl. operas *Røverborgen*, *Trylleharpen*, *Lulu* and several others; incid. m. for Heiberg's *Elverhøj*; pf. works; fl. pieces, &c.

Kühmstedt, Friedrich (b. Oldisleben, Saxe-Weimar, 20. XII. 1809; d. Eisenach, 10. I. 1858), Ger. orgst. & comp. Studied at Weimar Univ. and m. under Rinck at Darmstadt. His playing was marred by paralysis of the hand, but he became mus. dir. and prof. at the Seminary of Eisenach in 1836.

Works incl. operas; orats. *Die Auferstehung* & *Triumph des Göttlichen*; syms.; many org. pieces, incl. preludes, fugues, *Gradus ad Parnassum* preparatory to the works of Bach, *Fantasia eroica*, &c.

Kuhnau, Johann (b. Geising, Saxony, 6. IV. 1660; d. Leipzig, 5. VI. 1722), Ger. orgst. hpchdst., comp. & writer on m. Cantor at Zittau, went to Leipzig in 1682, became orgst. at St. Thomas's church in 1684, mus. dir. of the Univ. and the churches of St. Nicholas and St. Thomas in 1700, and cantor of St. Thomas's in 1701, in which post he preceded Bach. His Biblical Sos. for hpchd. are early exs. of programme m.

Other works incl. motets on hymn-tunes & other church m.; partitas and other pieces for hpchd., incl. 7 sos. entitled *Frische Clavier-Früchte*, &c.

Kühnel, August (b. Delmenhorst, 3. VIII. 1645; d. ?), Ger. va. da gamba player & comp. Pupil (?) of Steffani. He was in the court chapel of Zeitz, 1661–81, visited Fr. in 1665 to study the players there, played at var. Ger. courts on his return, visited London in 1685 and the following years went to the court of Cassel. He wrote sos. for his inst.

Kuhreigen or **Kuhreihen** } *See* **Ranz des Vaches.**

Kujawiak. A Pol. dance in 3–4 time, a variant of the Mazurka.

Kullak, Theodor (b. Krotoschin, Posen, 12. IX. 1818; d. Berlin, 1. III. 1882), Ger. pfst. & comp. He was intended for a lawyer and at some time studied medicine, but in 1842 decided definitely in favour of m. and went to Vienna to finish his pf. studies with Czerny. In 1846 he became court pfst. to the King of Prus. and settled in Berlin, founding a Cons. with Stern and Marx there, 1850, and one of his own in 1855.

Works incl. pf. Conc. in C min.; pf.

Trio; duets for pf. & v.; a vast number of pf. pieces, studies, &c.

Kummer, Friedrich August (b. Meiningen, 5. VIII. 1797; d. Dresden, 22. VIII. 1879), Ger. cst., obst. & comp. Pupil of Dotzauer at Dresden, where he hoped to enter the court orch. as a cst., but did so as an obst., finding no vacancy for the former post, 1814. In 1817, however, he changed to the co. again and also travelled as a virtuoso.

Works incl. concs., fantasies and numerous other works for the co.; interludes for the Dresden theatre, &c.

Kunc, Jan (b. Doubravice, Moravia, 27. III. 1883), Cz. cond., teacher & comp. Pupil of Janáček at the Org. School of Brno, and later of Novák and Kovařovic at the Prague Cons. He became a critic, toured with his wife, a singer, and in 1919–20 was cond. at the Cz. Theatre in Prague. Later he went to the Brno Cons., of which he became dir. in 1923.

Works incl. symph. poem *Song of Youth*; *Seventy Thousand* for chor. & orch., many other chor. works with and without orch.; Cz. Mass for sop. & org.; 2 stg. 4tets, pf. Trio; So. in C min., *Moods & Miniatures* for pf.; many songs, &c.

Kunst der Fuge, Die (*The Art of Fugue*). Bach's last work, left unfinished at his death in 1750. A series of exs. of the art of fugal and canonic writing, all based on the same theme.

Kunz, Ernst (b. Berne, 2. VI. 1891), Swi. cond. & comp. Studied at Munich and cond. at theatres there and at Rostock. In 1919 he returned to Swi. and became mus. dir. at Olten and to the canton of Solothurn, cond. chor. and orch. concerts, also a chor. soc. at Zürich.

Works incl. operas *Der Fächer, Vreneli ab em Guggisberg, Die Bremer Stadtmusikanten*; Christmas Orat., Requiem; *Huttens letzte Tage* (C. F. Meyer) for solo voices, male chor. & orch., other chor. works; syms.; concs.; stg. 4tet & other chamber m.; org. & pf. works; songs, &c.

Kunzen, Friedrich Ludwig Aemilius (b. Lübeck, 24. IX. 1761; d. Copenhagen, 28. I. 1817), Ger. cond. & comp. Pupil of his father, Adolph Karl K. (1720–81). Having given up legal studies, he went to the Copenhagen Opera, where he prod. his 1st work. After a period in Berlin, where he ed. a mus. journal with Reichardt, he went as cond. to Frankfort o/M., 1792, and Prague, 1794, prod. his only Ger. opera at the former city. But he returned to Copenhagen as dir. of the Opera.

Works incl. operas *Holger Danske, Ossians Harfe, Hemmeligheden, Dragedukken, Erik Ejegod, Min Bedstemoder, Kærlighed paa Landet, Stormen* (on Shakespeare's *Tempest*), &c.

Kurpinski, Karol (Kasimir) (b. Wloszakowice, 6. III. 1785; d. Warsaw, 18. IX. 1857), Pol. vst., cond. & comp. Taught by his father, a village orgst., he took part in private stg. 4tet perfs. and in 1810 succeeded in securing a post as vst. at the Boguslawski Theatre at Warsaw. He later became cond. and finally co-dir. with Elsner.

Works incl. operas *Two Huts, Jadwiga, The New Cracovians, The Castle of Czorsztyn* & many others; ballets; church m.; ovts., &c.

Kurth, Ernst (b. Vienna, 1. VI. 1886), Aus. mcolst. Studied under Adler in Vienna and after holding a post in Thuringia went to Swi., settling as teacher at Berne, 1912, and becoming prof. of m. at the Univ. in 1920. His books incl. studies of Gluck's operas, of harmonic theory, of linear ctpt. based on Bach's works and of romantic harmony based on Wagner.

Kurz, Selma (b. Biala, 15. XI. 1877; d. Vienna, 10. V. 1933), Aus. sop. singer. Studied with Pless and became the chief lyric sop. at the Vienna Court Opera. She 1st appeared in London in 1904.

Kuss der Danae, Der (*Danae's Kiss*), opera by R. Strauss (lib. by Josef Gregor), intended for prod. at the Salzburg Festival, 1. VIII. 1944, but postponed owing to war. The orig. title seems to have been *Die Liebe der Danae*.

Kusser. *See* Cousser.

Kutchka (Rus. = handful; short for *mogutchaya kutchka* = the mighty handful). The group of 5 Rus. comps. who under the leadership of Balakirev began a conscious campaign in favour of nationalist m. based on folk m. This was no new departure, for Glinka had already made a beginning, but it was the 1st organized attempt in this direction. The other members of the group were Borodin, Cui, Mussorgsky and Rimsky-Korsakov, and they all carried out its principles, with the exception of Cui, so far as their talents and temperaments would allow.

Kuula, Toivo (b. Vaasa, 7. VII. 1883; d. Viipuri, 18. V. 1918), Fin. comp. Studied with Wegelius, Järnefelt and Sibelius at the Helsingfors Cons., also with Busoni at Bologna and Labey in Paris. App. cond. of the orch. at Uleaaborg, 1910, and asst. cond. of the Helsingfors Munic. Orch. under Kajanus, 1911. In 1915 he became cond. of the orch. at Viipuri.

Works incl. *Stabat Mater, Song of*

the Sea for chor. & orch.; symph. poem *Son of a Slave*, 2 *East Bothnian Suites* for orch.; pf. Trio; v. & pf. So.; pf. pieces; songs, &c.

Kvapil, Jaroslav (b. 1868), Cz. poet & dramatist. *See* **Ostrčil** (*Orphan*).

Kvapil, Jaroslav (b. Fryštát, Moravia, 21. IV. 1892), Cz. comp. Studied with **Janáček** at Brno and was later app. prof. of org. and ctpt. at the Org. School there. In 1911–3 he continued studying at the Leipzig Cons., and on his return to Brno became prof. of pf. & comp. at the Cons. and cond. of the Phil. Soc.

Works incl. 3 Syms., Vars. & Fugue for orch.; cantata for bar. solo, chor. & orch.; stg. 4tet, pf. 5tet, pf. Trio; 2 v. & pf. sos., co. & pf. So.; pf. So. & pieces; songs, &c.

L

l. The submediant note in any key in Tonic Sol-fa notation, pronounced Lah.

L. H. (abbr.) = Left Hand, often used in pf. m., also in Ger. (*Linke Hand*).

La. The old name for the note A (*see* **Solmization**), still used in Lat. countries, and in Tonic Sol-fa notation the submediant note in any key, repres. by the symbol l, pronounced Lah.

La Borde, Jean Benjamin de (b. Paris, 5. IX. 1734; d. Paris, 22. VII. 1794), Fr. author & amateur comp. Pupil of Rameau for comp., chamberlain to Louis XV. He d. on the scaffold during the Revol.

Works incl. 32 operas, songs with v. & bass, songs with pf. He wrote books incl. an *Essai sur la musique ancienne et moderne*.

La Cruz, Ramón de (1731–94), Spa. dramatist. *See* **Rodríguez de Hita** (var. operas).

La Fage, Juste Adrien Lenoir de (b. Paris, ? 30. III. 1805; d. Charenton, 8. III. 1862), Fr. writer on m. & comp. Pupil of Choron in Paris and Baini in Rome. He travelled a good deal, held church appts. in Paris and paid 2 more long visits to It. Comp. a comic opera, *I creditori*, church m., inst. works, &c. and wrote books on plainsong hist., bibliog., &c.

La Fontaine, Jean de (1621–95), Fr. poet. *See* **Blaise le savetier** (Philidor), **Caplet, Cigale et la Fourmi** (Audran), **Colombe** (Gounod), **Deux Chasseurs** (Duni), **Gluck** (*Ivrogne corrigé*), **Laruette** (do.), **Pierné** (*Coupe enchantée*), **Poulenc** (*Animaux modèles*).

La Guerre (*née* **Jacquet**), **Élisabeth (Claude) de** (b. Paris, 1659; d. Paris, 27. VI. 1729), Fr. hpchdst. & comp. Pupil of her father, an orgst. and hpchd. teacher. She attracted attention as a player at the age of 5 and came under the patronage of Louis XIV and later, *c.* 1681, of Mme. de Montespan. In 1687 she left the court, where she had prod. a pastoral in 1685, to be married to Marin de La Guerre. After her husband's death she gave concerts and taught the hpchd.

Works incl. opera *Céphale et Procris*, (?) divertissement *La Musette, ou Les Bergers de Suresne*, opera-ballet *Les Jeux à l'honneur de la victoire*; Te Deum & other church m.; cantatas on biblical subjects and others on classical themes; inst. sos.; hpchd. pieces; *Airs sérieux*, comic duet for Le Sage's *La Ceinture de Vénus*, &c.

La Guerre, Michel de (b. Paris, *c.* 1605; d. Paris, 13. XI. 1679), Fr. orgst. & comp., father-in-law of prec. Orgst. of the Sainte-Chapelle in Paris, 1633–79. His 2 sons, Jérôme (*c.* 1654–?) and Marin (1658–1704) were both orgsts. & comps.; the latter married Élisabeth Jacquet.

Works incl. opera *Le Triomphe de l'Amour sur des bergers et bergères*; *airs de cour*; (?) motets, (?) org. works, &c.

La Halle, Adam de. *See* **Halle.**

La Hèle (or **Helle**), **Georges de** (b. Antwerp, after 1550; d. ? Madrid, 1589), Flem. comp. Chorister at the royal chapel in Madrid in his youth. Choirmaster at Tournai cath. in 1578, but prob. back in Spa. by 1580. He obtained 2 prizes at the Puy de Musique at Évreux in 1576.

Works (some destroyed in a fire at Madrid in 1734) incl. masses, motets; chansons, &c.

La Laurencie, Lionel de (b. Nantes, 24. VII. 1861; d. Paris, 21. XI. 1933), Fr. mcolst. While studying law in Paris he also attended the Cons. and in 1898 decided to devote himself entirely to m. and became lecturer at the École des Hautes Études Sociales. He wrote much for the mus. journals and pub. books on Rameau, Fr. v. m., lutenists, &c.

La Mara (**Marie Lipsius**) (b. Leipzig, 30. XII. 1837; d. Leipzig, 2. III. 1927), Ger. authoress & ed. Wrote, under the pen-name of L. M., var. books on comps., mainly of a romantically biog. character, and ed. letters of Liszt & Berlioz.

La Pouplinière (or **Poupelinière**), **Alexandre Jean Joseph le Riche de** (b. Chinon, 29. VII. 1693; d. Paris, 5. XII. 1762), Fr. mus. patron. He was farmer-general of taxes and amassed a huge fortune. He kept a private orch., had Rameau living in his house for several years and studied under him, and patronized a number of other comps. and perfs.

La Presle, Jacques (**Paul Gabriel Sauville**) **de** (b. Versailles, 5. VII. 1888), Fr. comp. Studied at the

Paris Cons. both before and after the 1914–8 war, in which he served. In 1921 he gained the Prix de Rome, in 1930 became mus. dir. of Radio-Paris and in 1938 prof. of harmony at the Cons.

Works incl. orat. *L'Apocalypse de Saint Jean*; cantata *Hermione* and *2 Chœurs de printemps* for chor. & orch.; *Album d'images* for orch.; *Le Vent* & *Impressions* for voice & orch.; Suite in G maj. for stg. 4tet; v. & pf. So.; *Parade fantasque* for pf.; songs, &c.

La Rue, Pierre de (b. Picardy, ?; d. Courtrai, 20. XI. 1518), Flem. comp. Pupil of Okeghem, in the service by turns of the court of Burgundy, Charles V and Margaret of Aus. when governor of the Nthlds. He was app. prebendary of Courtrai and later of Namur.

Works incl. 36 masses, 38 motets; chansons, &c.

La Tombelle, Antoine (Louis Joseph Gueyrand Fernand Fouant) de (b. Paris, 3. VIII. 1854; d. Château de Fayrac, Dordogne, 13. VIII. 1928), Fr. orgst. & comp. Began to study with his mother, a pupil of Liszt and Thalberg, later entered the Paris Cons. and finished his studies with Saint-Saëns. From 1878 he shared the org. concerts at the Trocadéro with Guilmant. In 1896–1904 he was prof. at the Schola Cantorum.

Works incl. operetta *Un Rêve au pays du bleu*; Mass, motets & other church m.; orat. *Crux, Les Sept Paroles de notre Seigneur*; suite *Impressions matinales* for orch.; stg. 4tet in E maj., pf. Trio; v. & pf. So.; org. & harmonium pieces; songs, &c.

Labé, Louise (*c.* 1525–66), Fr. poetess. *See* **Beck** (sonnets).

Labey, Marcel (b. Le Vésinet nr. Paris, 6. VIII. 1875), Fr. cond. & comp. Studied at the Schola Cantorum in Paris, d'Indy being among his masters. Later he cond. the orch. class there and in 1931 became vice dir., also pf. prof. 1907–14. Sec. and organizer of the Société Nationale de Musique.

Works incl. opera *Berengère*; 3 syms., *Fantaisie, Suite champêtre, Ouverture pour un drame* for orch.; stg. 4tet, pf. 5tet, 2 pf. trios; 2 v. & pf. sos.; chors.; pf. pieces; songs, &c.

Labialstimme(n) (Ger. lit. labial voice). The Flue Stop(s) of the org.

Labiche, Eugène (1815–88), Fr. playwright. *See* **Ibert** (*Chapeau de paille d'Italie*), **Shaporin** (*It. Straw Hat*), Thompson (R.) (do.).

Lablache, Luigi (b. Naples, 6. XII. 1794; d. Naples, 23. I. 1858), It. bass singer, of Fr. descent. Made his 1st stage appearance at the Teatro San Carlino, Naples; later became famous all over Eur.

Labroca, Mario (b. Rome, 22. XI. 1896), It. critic & comp. Pupil of Respighi and Malipiero. Critic of *Il Lavoro fascista* and *L'Idea nazionale*, superintendent of the Teatro Vittorio Emanuele at Florence and organizer of the *Maggio musicale* festivals there.

Works incl. *Stabat Mater, Il lamento dei mariti e delle mogli* for 6 voices & small orch.; Sym. for pf. & small orch.; 2 stg. 4tets, pf. Trio; Sonatina for v. & pf., Suite for va. & pf.; pf. pieces; songs, &c.

Labunski, Feliks Roderyk (b. Ksawerynowo, 27. XII. 1892), Pol. comp. Studied at Warsaw and with Dukas and Nadia Boulanger in Paris. He founded a soc. of Pol. musns. there and later went to live in U.S.A.

Works incl. *Pastoral Triptych* for orch; Concertino for pf. & orch.; stg. 4tet; Divertimento for fl. & pf.; *Olympic Hymn* for chor. & orch., *The Birds* for voice & orch., Pol. Cantata, for solo voices & chor.; pf. pieces; songs, &c.

Lac des cygnes (Tchaikovsky). *See* **Swan Lake.**

Lach, Robert (b. Vienna, 29. I. 1874), Aus. mcolst. & comp. Studied at the Vienna Cons. and graduated in Prague, 1902. In 1911 he was app. dir. of the m. dept. of the Vienna State Lib., in 1915 teacher and in 1920 prof. at the Univ. His writings incl. studies of folksong, oriental & western melody, the dance, Mozart, Schubert, Wagner & Brahms.

Comps. incl. 2 operas; 8 masses, Requiem, 3 cantatas; 10 syms.; chamber m.; chors.; songs, &c.

Lächerliche Prinz Jodelet, Der (*The Ridiculous Prince J.*), opera by Keiser (lib. by Johann Philipp Praetorius, based on Paul Scarron's comedy, *Jodelet, ou Le Maître valet*), prod. Hamburg, Theater am Gänsemarkt, 1726.

Lachmann, Robert (b. Berlin, 28. XI. 1892; d. Jerusalem, 1939), Ger. mcolst. Studied philol. in London & Berlin, and later, becoming interested in the exotic songs of African and Asiatic war prisoners, studied mus. science under Carl Stumpf & Johannes Wolf in Berlin. In 1927 he became an official in the m. dept. of the Prus. State Library, but emigrated to Palestine in 1934 as lecturer at the Hebrew Univ. at Jerusalem. He wrote several books on exotic m.

Lachner. Ger. family of musns.:

1. Theodor L. (b. Rain, Bavaria, 1798; d. Munich, 22. V. 1877), orgst. and cond. He was the eldest son

and pupil of an orgst. at Rain o/Lech and became orgst. at Munich, also chor.-master at the court theatre.

2. Thekla L. (b. Rain, *c.* 1800; d. ? Augsburg, ?), orgst., sister of prec. Pupil of her father, became orgst. at Augsburg.

3. Franz L. (b. Rain, 2. IV. 1803; d. Munich, 20. I. 1890), cond. & comp., brother of prec. Pupil of his father and later of Stadler and Sechter in Vienna, where he became a friend of Schubert's. App. asst. cond. at the Kärntnertor Theatre there, 1826, and succeeded Weigl as chief cond., 1827. In 1834 he went to Mannheim as opera cond. and in 1836 to Munich as court mus. dir.

Works incl. operas *Die Bürgschaft* (on Schiller's poem), *Alidia, Catarina Cornaro* & *Benvenuto Cellini*; orats. *Moses* & *Die vier Menschenalter*; Requiem, 3 masses; cantatas & other chor. works; 8 syms.; hp. & bn. concs.; 5 stg. 4tets, Nonet for wind insts., trios & other chamber m.; pf. pieces; songs, &c.

4. Christiane L. (b. Rain, 1805; d. Rain, ?), orgst., sister of prec. She studied under her father and succeeded him as orgst. at Rain o/Lech.

5. Ignaz L. (b. Rain, 11. IX. 1807; d. Hanover, 24. II. 1895), cond. & comp., brother of prec. Studied under his father and at Augsburg, joined his brother Franz in Vienna, 1824, became asst. cond. at the Kärntnertor Theatre there, 1825, app. court mus. dir. at Stuttgart, 1831, and at Munich, 1842, jointly with Franz. Later he filled var. posts at Hamburg, Stockholm and Frankfort o/M.

Works incl. operas *Der Geisterturm, Die Regenbrüder* & *Loreley*; ballets & melodramas; masses; syms.; stg. 4tets; pf. m.; songs, &c.

6. Vincenz L. (b. Rain, 19. VII. 1811; d. Carlsruhe, 22. I. 1893), cond. & comp., brother of prec. Studied with his father and at Augsburg. He became orgst. in Vienna, 1834, and was court mus. dir. at Mannheim, 1836–73. He retired to Carlsruhe, but still taught there at the Cons.

Works incl. incid. m. to Schiller's adapt. of Gozzi's *Turandot*; partsongs, songs, &c.

Lacombe, Louis (Trouillon) (b. Bourges, 26. XI. 1818; d. Saint-Vaast-la-Hougue, 30. IX. 1884), Fr. pfst. & comp. Studied at the Paris Cons. and, after a tour with his sister, with Czerny, Sechter and Seyfried in Vienna. He settled in Paris in 1839.

Works incl. operas *L'Amour, La Madone, Winkelried, Le Tonnelier de Nuremberg, Korrigane*; dram. syms. with solo voices & chor. *Manfred* (after Byron) & *Arva*, melodrama with chors. *Sapho*; 5tet for pf., v., ob., co. & bn., 2 pf. trios & other chamber m.; pf. pieces & studies, &c.

Lacombe, Paul (b. Carcassonne, 11. VII. 1837; d. Carcassonne, 5. VI. 1927), Fr. comp. Studied with the orgst. François Teysserre and from 1866 by correspondence with Bizet.

Works incl. 3 syms., *Ouverture symphonique*; Suite for pf. & orch.; stg. 4tet, 3 pf. trios; 3 sos. for v. & pf., So. for co. & pf.; numerous pf. works; songs, &c.

Lacy, John (?–1681), Eng. playwright. *See* **Purcell (D.)** (*Sawny the Scot*).

Lacy, John (b. ?; d. Devonshire, *c.* 1865), Eng. bass singer. Pupil of Rauzzini at Bath. He sang in London with success at an early age and went to It., settling in London afterwards, except for a period spent at Calcutta, 1818–26, with his wife.

Lacy, Michael Rophino (b. Bilbao, 19. VII. 1795; d. London, 20. IX. 1867), Ir. vst. Learnt m. as a child in Spa., was sent to school at Bordeaux, 1802, and in 1803 went to Paris to finish his training with R. Kreutzer. He 1st appeared in Paris, 1804, and London, 1805. He played with success for many years there as well as at Liverpool, Edinburgh, Glasgow, Dublin, &c. and made a number of tasteless adapts. of operas and orats. by var. comps.

Lacy (*née* Jackson), ? (b. London, 1776; d. London, 19. V. 1858), Eng. sop. singer, wife of John L. (ii) above. Made her 1st appearance in London, 1798, and married Bianchi, 1800, after whose death in 1810 she married L. in 1812.

Ladmirault, Paul (Émile) (b. Nantes, 8. XII. 1877), Fr. comp. Studied at home and later at the Paris Cons. He became prof. at the Nantes Cons.

Works incl. operas *Gilles de Retz* & *Myrdhin*; ballet *La Prêtresse de Korydwen*; incid. m. to *Tristan et Iseult*; *Messe brève, Tantum ergo* & other sacred works; symph. poems *En Forêt, La Brière, La Jeunesse de Cervantes* for orch.; Vars. on a chorale for pf. 5tet; v. & pf. So., modal fantasy *De l'ombre à la clarté* for v. & pf.; *Esquisses, 2 Danses bretonnes*, &c. for pf.; *Variations sur des airs de biniou trécorois, Rapsodie gaëlique* for pf. duet; *Triolets à Catherine, Chansons écossaises, Chansons bretonnes* & other songs; partsongs, &c.

Lady Macbeth of the Mtsensk District (*L.M. Mtsenskago Uyezda*), opera by Shostakovitch (lib. by A. Preis and comp., based on a novel by Nikolai

Semenovitch Leskov), prod. Moscow, 22. I. 1934. Very successful at first, but afterwards discountenanced as decadent by the Soviet govt.

Lafont, Charles Philippe (b. Paris, 1. XII. 1781; d. nr Tarbes, 23. VIII. 1839), Fr. vst., singer & comp. He was at first taught by his mother, a sister of the vst. Berthaume, and he travelled to Ger. with his uncle as a child, playing there with success. Later he studied with R. Kreutzer in Paris, appeared as a ballad singer at the Théâtre Feydeau, completed his v. studies with Rode and went on tour in 1801–8. In 1808–15 he was solo vst. to the tsar in St. Petersburg, and then received a similar appt. from Louis XVIII. In 1831–9 he made long tours with Herz, cut short by a carriage accident that caused his death.

Works incl. 2 operas; duets for v. & pf. written with Kalkbrenner, Herz & others; more than 200 songs, &c.

Lafontaine. *See* **La Fontaine.**

Lagerlöf, Selma (1858–1940), Swe. novelist. *See* **Vittadini** (*Nazareth*), **Zandonai** (*Cavalieri di Ekebù*).

Lah. The name for the submediant note in any key in Tonic Sol-fa, so pronounced, but in notation represented by the symbol l.

Lahee, Henry (b. London, 11. IV. 1826; d. London, 29. IV. 1912), Eng. orgst. & comp. Pupil of Sterndale Bennett, Goss and Potter. Orgst. of Holy Trinity Church, Brompton, 1847–74.

Works incl. cantatas *The Building of the Ship* (Longfellow) & *The Sleeping Beauty* (Tennyson); madrigals & glees, &c.

Lai (Fr., later Eng. *lay*). A medieval lyrical poem in 12 pairs of stanzas in different metrical forms; also the m. set to such poems.

Laidlaw, Robena Anna (b. Bretton, Yorks, 30. IV. 1819; d. London, 29. V. 1901), Eng. pfst. Pupil of Herz and L. Berger. Played with much success on the Continent. Schumann ded. his *Fantasiestücke*, Op. 12, to her.

Lajtha, László (b. Budapest, 30. VI. 1891), Hung. folksong expert & comp. Studied at the M. High School at Budapest, specialized in folk m. and joined the folklore dept. of the Nat. Museum in 1913. App. prof. at the Budapest Cons. in 1938.

Works incl. ballet *Lysistrata* (after Aristophanes); chor. works; stg. 4tet, pf. 4tet, pf. 5tet, stg. Trio, pf. Trio; So., *Des écrits d'un musicien, Contes* & other works for pf.; songs, &c.

Lakmé, opera by Delibes (lib. by Edmond Gondinet & Philippe Gille), prod. Paris, Opéra-Comique, 14. IV. 1883.

Lalande, Henriette-Clémentine. *See* **Méric-Lalande.**

Lalande, Michel (Richard) de (b. Paris, 15. XII. 1657; d. Versailles, 18. VI. 1726), Fr. orgst. & comp. He learnt m. as a chorister at the church of Saint-Germain-l'Auxerrois in Paris and taught himself the v., bass viol & hpchd. On being refused admission to Lully's orch., he took to the org. and secured orgst.'s appts. at 3 churches. He failed to obtain the post of court orgst., but was given charge of the princesses' mus. educ. and in 1683 was app. one of the superintendents of the royal chapel. In 1684 he married the court singer Anne Rebel, who d. in 1722, and in 1723 he married again, Mlle. de Cury, daughter of one of the court surgeons.

Works incl. ballets and opera-ballets *Ballet de la jeunesse, Le Palais de Flore, Adonis, Myrtil et Mélicerte, Les Fées, L'Amour fléchi par la Constance, L'Hymen champetrê, Ballet de la Paix, Les Folies de Cardenio* (from Cervantes's *Don Quixote*), *Ballet de l'inconnu, Les Élémens* (with Destouches), *L'Amour berger, Églogue, ou Pastorale en musique, Les Fontaines de Versailles*; 42 motets with orch. accomp.; cantata *Le Concert d'Esculape*; 3 *Leçons de Ténèbre*, Miserere for solo voice; m. for the royal table, &c.

Lalla-Roukh, opera by F. David (lib. by Hippolyte Lucas & Michel Carré, based on Moore's *Lalla Rookh*), prod. Paris, Opéra-Comique, 12. V. 1862.

Lallouette, Jean François (b. Paris, c. 1651; d. Paris, 31. VIII. 1728), Fr. vst. & comp. He studied v. with Guy Leclerc and comp. with Lully. In 1668–77 he was vst. and cond. at the Opéra, but Lully dismissed him for claiming collab. in his *Isis*, which may have been true, for he was said to have often assisted Lully. In 1677 he became chapel master at Rouen cath. and in 1695 of Notre-Dame at Versailles.

Works incl. dram. interludes and ballets; masses, motets, Misereres, &c.

Lalo, (Victor Antoine) Édouard (b. Lille, 27. I. 1823; d. Paris, 22. IV. 1892), Fr. comp. of Spa. descent. He 1st studied v. & co. at the Lille Cons. and then v. at that of Paris, taking comp. lessons privately at the same time. In 1855 he became va. in the Armingaud-Jacquard 4tet, but did not at once make his way as a comp. He wrote little until 1865, the year of his marriage to Mlle. Bernier de Maligny, who sang his songs in public. Gradually his success grew both in the opera-house and the concert-room.

Works incl. operas *Fiesque* (after Schiller), *Le Roi d'Ys, La Jacquerie* (unfinished, completed by Coquard); pantomime with chors. *Néron*; ballet *Namouna*; Sym. in G min., *Divertissement, Rapsodie norvégienne* & Scherzo for orch., 2 Aubades for small orch., Conc., *Symphonie espagnole, Fantaisie norvégienne, Romance-Sérénade* & *Concerto russe* for v. & orch., concs. for pf. & for co.; 2 stg. 4tets, 3 pf. trios; v. & pf. So. and a number of pieces, co. & pf. So. & pieces; *La Mère et l'enfant* for pf. duet; over 30 songs and 2 voc. duets; church m., &c.

Lalo, Pierre (b. Puteaux, 6. IX. 1866; d. Paris, VIII. 1943), Fr. m. critic, son of prec. He became m. critic to *Le Temps* in 1898 and also wrote for the *Journal des Débats*.

Laloy, Louis (b. Grey, Haute Saône, 18. II. 1874; d. ?, 1944), Fr. mcolst. & critic. Studied at the Schola Cantorum in Paris, became a m. critic, lecturer at the Sorbonne, 1906, sec. to the Opéra, 1914, and prof. of mus. hist. at the Paris Cons., 1936. His works incl. studies of ancient and Chin. m., Rameau, Debussy, &c.

Lamartine, Alphonse de (1790–1869), Fr. politician & poet. *See* **Jocelyn** (Godard), **Massé** (*Fior d'Aliza*), **Niedermeyer** (songs), **Préludes** (Liszt).

Lamb, Charles (1775–1834), Eng. essayist. *See* **Elgar** (*Dream Children*).

Lambe, Walter (b. ?; d. ?), Eng. 15th-cent. comp. Wrote church m.

Lambert, Constant (b. London, 23. VIII. 1905), Eng. comp., cond. & critic. Son of the painter George Washington L. Studied at the R.C.M. in London. Diaghilev commissioned a ballet from him when he was still a student and prod. it at Monte Carlo in 1926. He began to make his mark as a cond. of ballet with the Camargo Soc. and was later engaged to cond. ballet at Sadler's Wells Theatre, with which he appeared in Paris in 1937, having already cond. at the I.S.C.M. Festival at Amsterdam, 1933. He also became a concert cond., was for a time m. critic to the *Referee* and pub. a book of criticism, *Music Ho!*

Works incl. ballets *Romeo and Juliet, Pomona, Horoscope*; incid. m. for Shakespeare's *Hamlet*; m. for film *Merchant Seamen*; *Summer's Last Will and Testament* (Nash), masque for bar. solo, chor. & orch.; *The Rio Grande* for pf., orch. & chor.; *M. for Orch., Aubade héroïque* for small orch.; Conc. for pf. and chamber orch.; pf. So.; 4 poems by Li-Po for voice & pf., &c.

Lambert, Lucien (b. Paris, I. 1861), Fr. pfst. & comp. Studied pf. under his father and toured successfully in Eur. and U.S.A. He then studied comp. with Massenet and Dubois in Paris.

Works incl. operas *Brocéliande, Le Spahi* (lib. by Loti), *La Flamenca, Penticosa, La Sorcière, La Marseillaise*; ballet *La Roussalka*; incid. m. to A. Alexandre's *Sire Olaf*; lyric scene *Prométhée enchaîné* (after Aeschylus); *Tanger le soir*, Moorish rhapsody for orch.; *Andante et Fantaisie tzigane* for pf. & orch.; pf. pieces; songs, &c.

Lambert, Michel (b. Vivonne, Poitou, *c.* 1610; d. Paris, 1696), Fr. lutenist, singer & comp. He was master of the royal chamber m. and in 1663 became master of the children in the royal chapel. Lully married his daughter Madeleine. He wrote songs to the lute.

Lambertini, Giovanni Tommaso (b. Bologna, ?; d. ?), It. 16th–17th-cent. priest & comp. Singer at San Petronio cath. at Bologna, (?) 1556–1628, and some time treasurer there.

Works incl. penitential psalms & other church m.; madrigals, villote, &c.

Lamentatione (=Lat. *lamentatio* or It. *lamentazione*; also called *Christmas Symphony*), the nickname of a sym. by Haydn, No. 26, in D min., comp. *c.* 1765.

Lamentations. The Ls. of Jeremiah used in the Rom. Catholic service at matins on Thur., Fri. & Sat. of Holy Week; orig. sung in plainsong and still surviving in that form, but from the early 16th cent. also used in polyphonic settings.

Lamento (It.=lament). A plaintive aria in early 17th-cent. It. opera conventionally placed before the tragic culmination of the plot.

Laments. Pieces for bagpipes, and much more rarely for voices, perf. at burials in Sco., where each clan had a different L. reserved to itself; also sometimes in Ir.

Lamm, Pavel Alexandrovitch (b. Moscow, 27. VII. 1882), Rus. pfst. & mus. ed. Studied at the Moscow Cons. and began his career as pfst. Later became dir. of the Rus. State Pub. Dept., where among other things he ed. the critical ed. of Mussorgsky's complete works in the orig. form.

Lämmlein. *See* **Lemlin.**

Lamoureux, Charles (b. Bordeaux, 28. IX. 1834; d. Paris, 21. XII. 1899), Fr. vst. & cond. Studied v. and theory at the Paris Cons., joined a theatre orch., then played at the Opéra, in 1860 helped to found a chamber m. society for the introd. of new works, cond. chor. works by Bach, Handel & others in the 1870s became cond. at the Opéra and in 1881 founded the Concerts L., at which he made a great deal of orch. m., incl. Wagner, known to a wide public.

Lampe, Johann Friedrich (John Frederick) (b. Saxony, 1703; d. Edinburgh, 25. VII. 1751), Ger. bn. player & comp. Went to Eng. from Brunswick about 1725 and settled in London, but went to Dublin in 1748 and to Edinburgh in 1750. Married Isabella Young, sister of T. A. Arne's wife.

Works incl. burlesque operas *The Dragon of Wantley* & *Margery, or A Worse Plague than the Dragon* (libs. by Carey), mock opera *Pyramus and Thisbe* (from Shakespeare's *Midsummer Night's Dream*), masque *The Sham Conjurer*; m. for Carey's *Amelia*; *c.* 10 other stage works; cantata to celebrate the suppression of the Stuart rebellion; songs, &c.

Lamperti, Francesco (b. Savona, 11. III. 1813; d. Como, 1. V. 1892), It. teacher of singing. Master of many eminent singers and author of voc. studies and a treatise on singing.

Lampons (Fr. from imper. of *lamper* = to drink, to quaff, to swill). An old Fr. name for drinking-songs, often of a scurrilous char.: hence the Eng. 'lampoon.'

Lampugnani, Giovanni Battista (b. Milan, 1706; d. Milan, 1781), It. comp. He appeared as opera comp. in Rome before he went to London in 1743 to cond. opera in place of **Galuppi**. After his return to Milan he was hpchdst. at the Teatro alla Scala from 1779 to his death.

Works incl. operas *Semiramide*, *Rossane*, *Alfonso*, *Alceste*, *Siroe*, *L'Amore contadino* & *c.* 25 others: trio sos., &c.

Lancelot and Elaine, symph. poem No. 2 by MacDowell, Op. 25, based on the Arthurian legend, comp. 1888.

Lancers. *See* **Quadrille.**

Länderer. *See* **Ländler.**

Landi, Steffano (b. Rome, *c.* 1590; d. Rome, *c.* 1655), It. singer & comp. He was chapel master at Padua about 1620 and sang alto in the Papal Chapel in Rome about 1630.

Works incl. operas *La morte d'Orfeo* & *Il S. Alessio*; masses & psalms; madrigals & cantatas; arias for 1 voice, &c.

Landino (or Landini), Francesco (b. Florence, *c.* 1325; d. Florence, 2. IX. 1397), It. orgst., lutenist & comp. Although blind from early childhood, he perfected himself on var. insts. and became orgst. of the church of San Lorenzo at Florence. He is one of the chief exponents of the It. **Ars nova.**

Works incl. madrigals, ballads, canzoni, secular songs, &c.

Landino Sixth. A cadence in It. m. of the 14th & 15th cents. named after the prec., of whose voc. works it is a feature. Instead of proceeding melodically from the leading-note to the tonic, according to the most common cadential formula, it goes 1st from the leading-note to the note (6th) below and then rises to the tonic.

Ländler, or Ländlerischer Tanz (Ger. = 'of the Landel': Lower Aus.). An Aus. country dance, a slow waltz and the forerunner of that dance, in 3–4 time and played rather more slowly than the waltz. In its primitive form it has a regularly accented accomp. of a bass note on the 1st beat, followed by chords, and melodically it is square-cut into regular periods of 2 bars and very simply diatonic, with harmony alternating chiefly between tonic and dominant. L. (plur. same as sing.) were often called *Deutsche Tänze* (Ger. dances) or simply *Deutsche*. They were artistically cultivated by Mozart, Beethoven, Schubert & others, and Bruckner's and Mahler's scherzos are often in L. style.

Landor, Walter Savage (1775–1864), Eng. poet & man of letters. *See* **Dieren (van)** (songs).

Landormy, Paul (Charles René) (b. Issy, 3. I. 1869; d. ? Paris, 1943), Fr. mcolst. & critic. After teaching philos. at var. provincial schools, he went to Paris in 1892 to study singing and mus. science. He organized lectures with **Rolland** at the École des Hautes Études Sociales and dir. his own laboratory for the study of mus. physics, 1904–7. In 1918 he became critic to *La Victoire* and also wrote on m. for *Le Temps* and mus. journals. Sec. to the m. section of the Internat. Exhib. in Paris, 1937. His books on m. incl. studies of hist., the great masters, Schubert, &c.

Landowska, Wanda (b. Warsaw, 5. VII. 1877), Pol. hpchdst., pfst. & mus. research scholar. She toured widely and settled in Fr., where in 1927 she opened a school for the study of old m. at Saint-Leu-la-Forêt nr. Paris. Her lit. work incl. books and articles on var. aspects of that subject.

Landré, Guillaume (b. The Hague, 24. II. 1905), Dutch lawyer & comp. Studied law at Utrecht Univ. and m. under his father & **Pijper.**

Works incl. light opera *The Pike*; m. for the open-air play *Cortez*; Sym., Sinfonietta & other orch. works; chamber m.; partsongs, &c.

Landré, Willem (b. Haarlem, 12. VI. 1874), Dutch critic & comp., father of prec. Mus. ed. of the *Nieuwe Rotterdamsche Courant*, 1906–37.

Works incl. operas *De roos van Dekama* & *Beatrijs*; Requiem for solo voices, chor. & orch.; Nocturne & other works for orch.; Cantata for pf. & orch.; *Illegale Liederen* for bar. & orch.; chamber m., &c.

Láng, Paul H(enry). (b. Budapest, 28. VIII. 1901), Hung. mcolst., naturalized Amer. He emigrated to U.S.A. during the Nazi régime in central Eur. and became prof. of mcol. at Columbia Univ. in N.Y. In 1945 he became ed. of the *Mus. Quarterly*. Among his writings is a book on *M. in Western Civilization*.

Lang, Walter (b. Basle, 19. VIII. 1896), Swi. pfst. & comp. Studied in his native town at first and afterwards with Jaques-Dalcroze both at Hellerau nr. Dresden and at Geneva. Klose at Munich and Andreae and Walter Frey at Zürich were among his later teachers. As a pfst. he is chiefly interested in chamber m. and he founded a trio.

Works incl. *Sonata festiva* for stg. orch., *Bulgarian Folksongs* for chamber orch.; Vars. on a Siberian Convict Song for va. & orch.; stg. 4tet, stg. Trio; sos. for var. insts.; pf. sos. and pieces, &c.

Lange, de. Dutch family of musns.:

1. Samuel de L. (b. Rotterdam, 9. VI. 1811; d. Rotterdam, 15. V. 1884), orgst., teacher & comp. Orgst. at the church of St. Lawrence at Rotterdam and comp. of org. m.

2. Samuel de L. (b. Rotterdam, 22. II. 1840; d. Stuttgart, 7. VII. 1911), cond. & comp., son of prec. Pupil of his father and of Verhulst, and later studied in Vienna. He travelled in Pol., lived at Lwów in 1859–63 and then returned to Rotterdam as orgst., teacher & cond. Later he worked at Basle, Cologne, The Hague and Stuttgart, where he succeeded Faisst as prof. at the Cons., of which he became dir. in 1900.

Works incl. orat. *Moses*; 3 syms.; *Conzertstück* for co. & orch., pf. Conc.; 3 stg. 4tets, 5tet, pf. Trio; 4 v. & pf. sos., 2 co. & pf. sos.; 8 org. sos.; male-voice partsongs, &c.

3. Daniel de L. (b. Rotterdam, 11. VII. 1841; d. Point Loma, Cal., 31. I. 1918), cst., pfst., orgst. & comp., brother of prec. Studied under his father and Verhulst, also co. under Servais. He followed his brother at Lwów, 1860–3, then went to Paris for further study and remained there as orgst. until 1914, when he returned to Hol. and settled at Amsterdam, cond. chor. socs. and teaching at the Cons., of which he became dir. in 1895.

Works incl. opera *De val van Kuilenburg*; incid. m. to Hugo's *Hernani*; Psalm xxii for solo voices, chor. & orch., Mass, Requiem; cantatas; 2 syms., ovt. *Willem van Holland*; co. Conc., &c.

Lange-Müller, Peter (Erasmus) (b. Frederiksborg, 1. XII. 1850; d. Copenhagen, 25. II. 1926), Dan. comp. Studied at the Copenhagen Cons.

Works incl. operas *Tove*, *Spanske Studenter* & *Vikingeblod*; incid. m. to plays; orch. & chor. works; *c.* 200 songs, &c.

Langford, Samuel (b. Manchester, 1863; d. Manchester, V. 1927), Eng. m. critic. He was brought up to succeed his father as a nursery gardener, but turned to m. and studied with Reinecke at Leipzig, 1896–1900. In 1905 he became m. critic to the *Manchester Guardian*, a post he held until his death.

Lanier (or Laniere), Nicholas (b. ? Greenwich, IX. 1588; d. London, II. 1666), Eng. painter, flst., singer & comp. of Fr. descent (? Lanière). He was prob. a pupil of his father, John Lanier (or Lanyer), a sackbut player, and about 1604 was flst. at court; also musn. to Henry, Prince of Wales. In 1613, with Coperario and others, he comp. a masque for the marriage of the Earl of Somerset and in 1617 he not only set Ben Jonson's *Masque of Lethe*, but sang in it and painted the scenery. In 1625 he was sent to It. to collect pictures for the royal collection. App. Master of the King's M. in 1626. Lived in the Nthlds. during the Commonwealth, but resumed his post at the Restor.

Works incl. masques, e.g. *Masque of Lethe* & *The Vision of Delight* (Jonson); cantata *Hero and Leander*, New Years' songs; voc. dialogues, songs, &c.

Lanner, Joseph (Franz Karl) (b. Vienna, 12. IV. 1801; d. Oberdöbling nr. Vienna, 14. IV. 1843), Aus. vst. & comp. Son of a glove-maker, he taught himself the v. Anxious to cond. an orch. he began by getting together a stg. 4tet, in which J. Strauss, sen., played va. They played at var. taverns selections from favourite operas arr. by him, and he soon turned to the comp. of country dances and waltzes, in which he was to be Strauss's greatest rival. He was engaged to cond. the orch. at var. dances, visited the prov. cities with his own band and finally cond. the court balls in turn with Strauss.

Works incl. over 200 waltzes, country dances, quadrilles, polkas, galops, marches, &c.

Laoutari (Rum.). Gypsy lute players and singers to the lute in Rum. who appear at christenings, weddings, funerals, &c.

Laparra, Raoul (b. Bordeaux, 13. V. 1876; d. Paris, 4. IV. 1943), Fr. comp. Studied at the Paris Cons.
Works incl. operas *Peau d'âne*, *La Habanera*, *La Jota*, *Le Joueur de viole*, *Las Toreras*, *L'Illustre Fregona*; *Un Dimanche basque* for pf. & orch.; stg. 4tet; songs, &c.

Lara, Isidore de (Cohen) (b. London, 9. VIII. 1858; d. Paris, 2. VIII. 1935), Eng. amateur comp. Studied comp. with Mazzucato and singing with Lamperti at the Milan Cons., later went to Lalo in Paris. He returned to London and became well known in wealthy drawing-rooms as a song comp. and perf. Later he came under the patronage of the Princess of Monaco, which enabled him to have his operas staged in the grand manner.
Works incl. operas *The Light of Asia*, *Amy Robsart* (after Scott's *Kenilworth*), *Moïna*, *Messaline*, *Soléa*, *Sanga*, *Naïl*, *Les Trois Masques*, *The Three Musketeers* (after Dumas) & others; cantata *The Light of Asia* (1st version of the opera); many songs, &c.

Largamente (It. = broadly, spaciously). An indication that a mvt. or phrase is to be played in a broad manner.

Large. The largest note-value in the early system of measured notation. Its nearest division was into Longs, of which it could contain 2 or 3, according to the time-signature.

Larghetto (It. lit. little *largo*). A tempo indication for a slow mvt., but less slow than a Largo.

Largo (It. = large, broad, wide, spacious). A tempo indication for a slow mvt., generally slower than Adagio, but denoting a broad style as much as a slow pace.

'Largo.' The popular name for the aria 'Ombra mai fù' ('Shade never was') from Handel's opera *Serse* (*Xerxes*), more generally known as an inst. piece pub. in all kinds of arrs. The familiar title is merely the tempo indication, which is *Largo*; so is that of many similar arias in H.'s operas and orats.

Lark Ascending, The, romance for v. & orch. by Vaughan Williams, comp. 1914, 1st perf. London, Queen's Hall, 14. VI. 1921.

'Lark' Quartet. A nickname sometimes given to Haydn's stg. 4tet in D maj., Op. 64 No. 5, on account of the exposed high 1st-v. passage at the opening.

Laroche, Herman Augustovitch (b. St. Petersburg, 25. V. 1845; d. St. Petersburg, 18. X. 1904), Rus. m. critic. Fellow-student with Tchaikovsky at the St. Petersburg Cons.; prof. at the Moscow Cons. from 1867. Returned to the new capital in 1871. Critic of many leading Rus. newspapers.

Larsson, Lars-Erik (b. Aakarp nr. Lund, 15. V. 1908), Swe. cond. & comp. Studied at the R.A.M. at Stockholm, and later in Leipzig and Vienna, where he was a pupil of Berg. In 1937 he was app. to a mus. post in the Stockholm wireless service.
Works incl. opera *The Princess of Cyprus*; incid. m. to Shakespeare's *Winter's Tale*; 2 syms., 2 concert ovts., Lyric Suite for orch.; Sinfonietta for stgs., Divertimento for chamber orch.; saxophone Conc., &c.

Laruette, Jean Louis (b. Toulouse, 27. III. 1731; d. Toulouse, I. 1792), Fr. actor, singer & comp. He appeared at the Opéra-Comique and the Comédie-Italienne in Paris.
Works incl. operas *Cendrillon*, *L'Ivrogne corrigé* (after La Fontaine) & 8 others, operettas, &c.

Las Infantas, Fernando de. *See* **Infantas.**

Laserna, Blas (b. Corella, Navarre, 4. II. 1751; d. Madrid, 8. VIII. 1816), Spa. comp. He became official comp. to several Madrid theatres in 1779.
Works incl. numerous tonadillas, comic opera *La gitanilla por amor*; incid. m. for plays by Calderón, Lope de Vega, Moreto, Ramón de la Cruz's *El café de Barcelona* & others, lyric scene *Idomeneo*, &c.

Lassalle, Jean (b. Lyons, 17. XII. 1847; d. Paris, 7. IX. 1909), Fr. bar. singer. He was intended to follow his father in the business of a silk merchant, but went to Paris, 1st to study painting and then singing at the Cons. and privately. He made his 1st public appearance at Liége in 1868.

Lassen, Eduard (b. Copenhagen, 13. IV. 1830; d. Weimar, 15. I. 1904), Dan.-Belg. cond. & comp. Was taken to Brussels at the age of 2 and studied at the Cons. there, and took the Belg. Prix de Rome in 1851. Unable to get his 1st opera staged at Brussels, he took it to Liszt at Weimar, who prod. it in 1857. He became mus. dir. there, 1858, and succeeded Liszt as court opera cond., 1860.
Works incl. operas *Landgraf Ludwigs Brautfahrt*, *Frauenlob*, *Le Captif*; incid. m. to Sophocles' *Oedipus*, Goethe's *Faust* & *Pandora*, Calderón's *Circe*, Hebbel's *Nibelungen*; Festival Cantata, Te Deum; *Biblische Bilder* for voices & orch.; 2 syms., *Beethoven* & *Festival* ovts., &c.

Lasserre, Jules Bernard (b. Tarbes, 29. VII. 1838; d. Tarbes, 19. II. 1906), Fr. cst. & comp. Studied at the Paris Cons., became solo cst. in the Pasdeloup orch., later travelled in Spa. and settled in Eng., 1869. Wrote studies, fantasies & many other pieces for co.

Lasso, Orlando di (*see* **Lassus**). As he was a Flem. master and lived in It. a compar. short time, there is no good reason for keeping to the It. form of his name, familiar as it is.

Lassú. *See* **Csárdás.**

Lassus, Orlande de (or perhaps de Lattre or Delattre) (b. Mons, prob. 1532; d. Munich, 14. VI. 1594), Flem. comp. He seems to have gone to It. as a boy, and he travelled there and served in var. noble households, in Sicily, Naples and Milan. In 1553–4 he was choirmaster at St. John Lateran in Rome, after which he returned home, visited Eng. and Fr. and settled for 2 years at Antwerp, where in 1555–6 he began to pub. his 1st works. In 1556 he went to Munich and entered the service of the Duke of Bavaria. There he married Regina Weckinger in 1558, and in 1563 became chief chapel master in succession to Daser. Visit to Venice, 1567, to find musns. for Munich, and to Ferrara. In 1570 he was ennobled by the Emp. Maximilian. After a visit to Paris in 1571 Charles IX offered him a post as chamber musn., but he returned to Munich after the king's death in 1574. That year he went to Rome to present Pope Gregory XIII with a vol. of masses and received the order of the Golden Spur. In spite of an offer from Dresden, he remained attached to the Bavarian court to the end.

Works incl. some 1,250 comps.: masses, motets, *Sacrae cantiones*, psalms (incl. 7 penitential psalms); madrigals, It. canzoni, Fr. chansons, Ger. songs for several voices, &c.

Last Days of Pompeii. *See* **Ione** and **Ultimo giorno di Pompei.**

Last Judgment, The. The current Eng. title of Spohr's orat. *Die letzten Dinge*, prod. Cassel, 25. III. 1826.

Lat. (abbr). = Latin.

Latilla, Gaetano (b. Bari, 12. I. 1711; d. Naples, 1791), It. comp. Was a choir-boy at Bari cath. and later studied at the Cons. di Sant' Onofrio at Naples. Prod. his 1st opera in 1732 and was app. vice chapel master at Santa Maria Maggiore in Rome, 1738; returned to Naples, 1741, and went to Venice, 1756, where he became choirmaster at the Cons. della Pietà and in 1762 2nd chapel master at St. Mark's. Retired to Naples, 1772.

Works incl. operas *Li mariti a forza, Orazio, Madame Ciana, La finta cameriera* & over 40 others; church m.; 6 stg. 4tets; arias, duets, &c.

Latrobe, Christian Ignatius (b. Leeds, 12. II. 1757; d. Manchester, 6. V. 1836), Eng. clergyman & comp. Studied at the coll. of the Moravian Brethren at Niesky in Upper Lusatia and in 1795 became secretary of the Eng. branch. Ded. 3 sos. to Haydn, with whom he made friends during the latter's visits to Eng. Ed. Moravian hymn-tunes & 6 vols. of Ger. & It. church m.

Works incl. *Dies irae*, Te Deum, Miserere, anthems & other church m.; inst. sos.; airs to poems by Cowper & Hannah More, &c.

Lattuada, Felice (b. Caselle di Morimondo nr. Milan, 5. II. 1882), It. comp. Studied at the Milan Cons.

Works incl. operas *La Tempesta* (after Shakespeare), *Sandha, Le preziose ridicole* (after Molière), *Don Giovanni* (after Zorrilla's *Don Juan Tenorio*), *La caverna di Salamanca* (after Cervantes), *Follie d'amore* (on a comedy by Regnart); chor. works; orch. m., &c.

Latvian Composers. *See* **Baltic Composers.**

Laub, Ferdinand (b. Prague, 19. I. 1832; d. Gries nr. Bozen, 17. III. 1875), Cz. vst. Studied at the Prague Cons. and in Vienna. Travelled much and succeeded Joachim as leader of the court orch. at Weimar in 1853. Prof. at Stern's Cons. in Berlin and from 1866 at the Moscow Cons.

Lauber, Joseph (b. Ruswil, Lucerne, 25. XII. 1864), Swi. comp. Studied at Zürich and later with Rheinberger at Munich and Massenet in Paris. After teaching at the Zürich Cons. he became dir. of that of Geneva.

Works incl. opera *Hexe*, festival play *Neuchâtel Suisse*; orats. *Ad gloriam Dei* & *Weltendämmerung*, 4 cantatas; 5 syms., symph. poems *Sur l'Alpe, Chant du soir* & *Le Vent et la vague*, suites & ovts. for orch., Divertimento for small orch.; 2 pf. concs., 2 v. concs.; chamber m.; songs, &c.

Laúd (Spa.) = Lute.

Lauda Sion. A sequence sung at Mass on the Feast of Corpus Christi in the Roman church, words by St. Thomas Aquinas, *c.* 1264.

Cantata by Mendelssohn written for a festival at Liége and perf. there on 11. VI. 1846.

Laudi spirituali. It. sacred songs of the 13th cent. & later, with words in the vernacular, at first for single voice and later in parts. Their centre of origin was Florence.

Laudon Symphony, the nickname of a

sym. by Haydn, No. 69, in C maj., comp. *c.* 1778 in honour of Field Marshal Baron Gideon Ernst von Laudon.

Launis, Armas (Emanuel) (b. Tavastehus, 22. IV. 1884), Fin. mcolst. & comp. Studied at Helsingfors & Berlin, also mus. hist. with Krohn at Helsingfors Univ., where he lectured, 1918–22. Ed. Fin. folksongs.
Works incl. operas *The Seven Brothers*, *Kullervo* (from the *Kalevala*), *Aslak Hetta*, *The Song of the Magician*, &c.

Laurencie, Lionel de la. *See* **La Laurencie.**

Lautenclavicymbel. *See* **Lute-Harpsichord.**

Lauterbach, Johann Christoph (b. Culmbach, Bavaria, 24. VII. 1832; d. Dresden, 28. III. 1918), Ger. vst. Studied at the Brussels Cons. and later held appts. at Munich and Dresden.

Lavagne, André (b. ?, 1914), Fr. comp. Pupil of Roger-Ducasse in Paris.
Works incl. opera *Comme ils s'aiment*; ballet *Kermesse*; *Concert dans un parc* for orch.; *Concerto romantique* for co. & orch., &c.

Lavallée, Calixa (b. Verchères, Quebec, 28. XII. 1842; d. Boston, Mass., 21. I. 1891), Canad. pfst. & comp. Studied at the Paris Cons. and later toured as pfst. in North Amer.
Works incl. opera *The Widow*; syms.; stg. 4tets; nat. air ' O Canada,' &c.

Lavignac, (Alexandre Jean) Albert (b. Paris, 21. I. 1846; d. Paris, 28. V. 1916), Fr. mcolst. Studied at the Paris Cons., where he became prof. later on. Founder and 1st ed. of the *Encyclopédie de la musique*; also wrote many technical treatises, a study of Wagner, &c.

Lavoix, Henri (Marie François) (b. Paris, 26. IV. 1846; d. Paris, 27. XII. 1897), Fr. mcolst. Studied at the Sorbonne in Paris and in 1865 became librarian of the Bibliothèque Nationale. Wrote books on mus. hist., medieval m., Fr. m., Shakespeare & m., orchn., singing, &c.

Lavolta, or (It.) *Volta* or (Fr.) *Volte.* An old dance in 3–2 time, prob. of It. orig., since the jump that was a feature of it retained the It. word *volta.*

Lawes, Henry (b. Dinton, Wilts., 5. I. 1596; d. London, 21. X. 1662), Eng. comp. Pupil of Cooper (Coperario), app. gentleman of the Chapel Royal in 1626. Having supplied m. for Thomas Carew's masque *Coelum Britannicum*, prod. at court, 18. II. 1634, he was commissioned by the Earl of Bridgewater to set Milton's *Comus* for perf. at Ludlow castle, 29. XI. 1633. He was the subject of a sonnet by Milton, 1646. He was re-app. to the court service on the Restor. in 1660 and wrote a coronation anthem for Charles II.
Works incl. opera *The Siege of Rhodes* (with Locke, Cooke, Colman & Hudson); masques (as above); coronation anthem *Zadok the Priest*, anthems, psalm-tunes; Elegy on the death of his brother William; songs in plays by William Cartwright, Christmas songs in Herrick's *Hesperides*; airs, dialogues & songs for 1 and more voices, &c.

Lawes, William (b. Salisbury, IV. 1602; d. Chester, 1645), Eng. comp., brother of prec. Studied with Cooper (Coperario) and became a musn. at Charles I's court. He joined the Royalist army during the Civil War and was made a commissary by Lord Gerrard to keep him out of danger, but he was killed by a shot during the siege of Chester.
Works incl. m. for Shirley's masque *The Triumph of Peace* (with Ive) and Davenant's *The Triumph of the Prince d'Amour* & *The Unfortunate Lovers*; anthems & psalms; m. for consorts of viols; airs for v. & bass; catches & canons; airs and dialogues for 1 and more voices, &c.

Lawrence, D(avid). H(erbert). (1885–1930), Eng. novelist & poet. *See* **Williams (G.)** (songs).

Lay. *See* **Lai.**

Layolle, François de (Francesco dell' Aiolle) (b. ? Lyons, ?; d. ? Florence, ?), Fr. 16th-cent. orgst. & comp. Settled at Florence about 1540 and became Benvenuto Cellini's m. teacher. His son Aleman L. afterwards taught Cellini's daughter and became orgst. at Lyons for a time.
Works incl. masses, motets; canzoni, madrigals, &c.

Lays (or Lay, Laï or Lais), François (b. La Barthe-de-Neste, Gascony, 14. II. 1758; d. Ingrande nr. Angers, 30. III. 1831), Fr. singer. He learnt m. at the monastery of Guaraison, but left to become a public singer and made his 1st appearance at the Paris Opéra in 1780. He also sang at court, at the Concert spirituel, &c., and on the foundation of the Cons. in 1795 became prof. of singing there.

Lazarus, Daniel (b. Paris, 13. XII. 1898), Fr. pfst. & comp. Studied at the Paris Cons.
Works incl. 3 ballets; incid. m. for Rolland's *14 Juillet* (with 6 others); *Symphonie avec Hymne* for orch. & chor.; Fantasy for co. & orch.; v. & pf. So.; pf. pieces, &c.

Lazarus, Henry (b. London, 1. I. 1815; d. London, 6. III. 1895), Eng. clst. Studied under var. masters and after playing in theatre and concert orchs.

was app. 1st cl. at the Opera in London, 1840, prof. at the R.A.M., 1854, and at Kneller Hall, 1858.

Lazzari, Sylvio (b. Bozen, 31. XII. 1857; d. Paris, VI. 1944), Aus.-It. comp., later belonging to the Fr. school & naturalized Fr. Studied at Innsbruck, Munich and the Paris Cons., where Franck was one of his masters.

Works incl. operas *Armor, La Lépreuse, Le Sautériot, Melaenis, La Tour de feu*; incid. m. for Goethe's *Faust*; Sym. in E♭ maj., orch. Suite in F maj., symph. tableau *Effet de nuit* (after Verlaine), *4 Tableaux maritimes, Ophélie* (after Shakespeare), *Rapsodie espagnole, Impressions d'Adriatique*, &c.; *Concertstück* for pf. & orch., *Rapsodie* for v. & orch.; stg. 4tet, pf. Trio, Octet for wind insts.; v. & pf. So.; pieces for v., co., pf. &c.; *c.* 50 songs; chors., &c.

Le Bègue, Nicolas Antoine (b. Laon, *c.* 1630; d. Paris, 6. VII. 1702), Fr. orgst. & comp. Orgst. of 2 Paris churches and succeeded La Barre as orgst. to the king in 1678.

Works incl. 2 books of hpchd. and 3 of org. pieces.

Le Bel, Firmin (b. ?; d. ?), Fr. 16th-cent. cleric and musn. Worked in the diocese of Noyon, but in 1540 succeeded Mallapert as chapel master at Santa Maria Maggiore in Rome and later occupied a similar post at San Luigi dei Francesi, eventually becoming, in 1561, a singer in the Papal choir.

Le Borne, Fernand (b. Charleroi, 10. III. 1862; d. Paris, 15. I. 1929), Belg. comp. Pupil of Franck, Massenet and Saint-Saëns in Paris. He was later a m. critic.

Works incl. operas *Daphnis et Chloé, Hedda, Mudarra, Les Girondins, La Catalane, Cléopâtre, Néréa, Le Maître*; 2 ballets; incid. m.; Mass in A maj., motets; *Symphonie dramatique* and other orch. works; *Symphonie-Concerto* for pf., v. & orch.; stg. 4tet, pf. Trio; v. & pf. So.; pf. pieces; songs, &c.

Le Couppey, Félix (b. Paris, 14. IV. 1811; d. Paris, 5. VII. 1887), Fr. pfst. & teacher. Studied at the Paris Cons., where later he was pf. prof. He wrote many studies for his inst. and several books on its perf.

Le Fanu, Joseph Sheridan (1814–73), Ir. novelist & poet. *See* **Shamus O'Brien** (Stanford), **Stanford** (*Phaudrig Crohoore*).

Le Flem, Paul (b. Lézardieux, Côtes-du-Nord, 18. III. 1881), Fr. comp. & critic. Pupil of d'Indy and Roussel, among others, later prof. at the Schola Cantorum, chor. master at the Opéra-Comique, cond. of the Chanteurs de Saint-Gervais and critic for *Comoedia*.

Works incl. opera *Le Rossignol de Saint-Malo*; chgphic. drama on Shakespeare's *Macbeth*; cantata *Aucassin et Nicolette*; Sym. in A maj., *Triptyque symphonique* for orch.; Fantasy for pf. & orch.; chamber m.; v. & pf. So.; pf. works; chor. m., &c.

Le Franc, Guillaume. *See* **Franc.**

Le Jeune, Claude (or Claudin) (b. Valenciennes, *c.* 1523; d. ? Paris, *c.* 1600), Fr. - Flem. comp. Worked most of his life in Paris. Having turned Huguenot, he tried (?) to escape from Paris during the siege of 1588, and his MSS. were (?) saved from seizure by the Catholic soldiers by his colleague Mauduit, himself a Catholic. Later L. became chamber musn. to the king. Like Baïf and Mauduit, he was an exponent of *Musique mesurée.*

Works incl. motets, psalms set to rhymed versions in measured m. and also to tunes in the Genevan Psalter set for 3 voices; chansons, madrigals; instrumental fantasies, &c.

Le Maistre, Matthieu (b. ? Liége, ?; d. ? Dresden, *c.* 1577), Flem. comp. He succeeded Walther as chapel master to the Saxon court at Dresden in 1554, a post from which he retired with a pension in 1568.

Works incl. masses, motets; Lat. & Ger. sacred songs, setting of the Lutheran catechism in Lat.; Ger. secular songs, &c.

Le Roux, Gaspard (b. Paris, *c.* 1660; d. Paris, *c.* 1710), Fr. hpchd. player & comp. He was a m. master, but hardly anything is known of his career.

Works incl. motets; pieces for 1 or 2 hpchds. with or without v. & bass parts; *Airs sérieux et à boire*, &c.

Le Roy, Adrien (b. ?; d. Paris, ? 1589), Fr. singer, lutenist, m. pub. & comp. He worked in Paris and assoc. himself with Ballard (1) in 1552, having married his sister the prec. year. Lassus visited him in 1571 and he pub. some works of his. He pub. an instruction book for the lute and another for the cittern. Some of the airs with lute and chansons for 4 voices were comp. by himself.

Lead. *See* **Ornaments.**

Leader. The usual Eng. name for the principal 1st violin in an orch. or of a stg. 4tet or other chamber m. team. In Amer., esp. in journalism, the cond. is often called 'leader,' the usual term for the leading 1st orch. v. there being Concertmaster, from Ger. *Konzertmeister*. The L. is the spokesman and social repres. of an orch. and is also respons. for certain mus. matters, such as uniformity of bowing, intonation, &c.

Leading Motif. *See* **Leitmotiv.**

Leading-Note. The seventh note of an ascending maj. or min. scale 'leading' to the tonic by a semitonal step and, espec. when it is the top note in a chord of the dominant 7th, inducing the ear to expect the tonic.

Leading Seventh. The chord of the min. 7th on the leading-note in maj. keys (e.g. B D F A in C maj.), making a resolution of the commonest kind in 'concertina' harmony.

Lear, Edward (1812–88), Eng. artist & author. *See* **Hely - Hutchinson** (songs).

Leben des Orest (*The Life of Orestes*), opera by Křenek (lib. by comp.), prod. Leipzig, 19. I. 1930.

Lebrun (*née* **Danzi**), **Francesca** (b. Mannheim, 1756; d. Berlin, 14. V. 1791), Ger. sop. singer & comp. of It. descent, daughter of a cst. at the court of Mannheim, sister of Franz D. & wife of Ludwig L. She made her 1st appearance in 1771, was engaged by the court opera, and later sang in It. and Eng. Comp. sos.

Lebrun, Jean (b. Lyons, 6. IV. 1759; d. Paris, *c.* 1809), Fr. hn. player. Pupil of Punto in Paris. Played in the Paris Opéra orch., 1786–92, and later worked in London and Berlin. He is said to have invented the mute for the hn.

Lebrun, Louis (Sébastien) (b. Paris, 10. XII. 1764; d. Paris, 27. VI. 1829), Fr. ten. singer & comp. He sang at the Paris Opéra and Opéra-Comique and was Napoleon's chapel master.

Works incl. operas *Marcelin*, *Le Rossignol* & many others; a Te Deum, &c.

Lebrun, Ludwig (August) (b. Mannheim, *c.* 1746; d. Berlin, 16. XII. 1790), Ger. obst. & comp. of Fr. descent. He was obst. at the Mannheim court, which he followed to Munich in 1778, and toured all over Eur. with his wife, Francesca L.

Works incl. 7 ob. concs.; 12 trios with ob. parts, &c.

Lebrun, Paul (Henri Joseph) (b. Ghent, 21. IV. 1863; d. Louvain, 4. XI. 1920), Belg. comp. Studied at the Ghent Cons., took the Belg. Prix de Rome in 1891, became prof. at his school and in 1913 dir. of the m. school at Louvain.

Works incl. opera *La Fiancée d'Abydos* (after Byron); cantata *Andromède*, ode *Ons Belgie vrij*; Sym. in E min., symph. poem *Sur la Montagne*, *Marche jubilaire* for orch.; stg. 4tet, &c.

Lechner, Leonhard (b. Etsch valley, before 1550; d. Stuttgart, 9. IX. 1606), Aus. comp. Pupil of Lassus in the court chapel at Munich, became a schoolmaster at Nuremberg in 1570 and in 1579 began to pub. a revised ed. of Lassus's works. In 1584–5 he was mus. dir. to Count Eitel Friedrich of Hohenzollern at Hechingen and in 1587 was app. to a similar post at the court of Württemberg at Stuttgart.

Works incl. masses, motets, Magnificat, psalms, introits, wedding motet for the Elector Johann Georg I of Saxony; sacred & secular Ger. songs for 3–5 voices, &c.

Leclair, Jean-Marie (b. Lyons, 10. V. 1697; d. Paris, 22. X. 1764), Fr. vst. & comp. Began (?) his career as a dancer at Rouen and certainly went to Turin as ballet-master in 1722, where Somis took him in hand for the v., which so far he had prob. played only in the way of a dancing-master, and where he comp. dances for Orlandini's *Semiramide*. In 1728 he made his 1st appearance as vst. in Paris, at the Concert spirituel and at court. He now studied comp. seriously and played in the Opéra orch. until 1735. He then retired to devote himself to comp., but in 1743–4 visited the court of Don Felipe of Spa. at Chambéry; in 1748 became vst. in the Duc de Gramont's private orch. and at the end of his life visited Hol. to meet Locatelli. He was murdered at night in the street nr. his house.

Works incl. operas *Scylla et Glaucus* & *Le Danger des épreuves*; ballets & divertissements; 12 v. concs.; numerous trios and sos. for 2 vs. & bass; sos. for v. unaccomp. & with bass. &c.

Lecocq, Alexandre Charles (b. Paris, 3. VI. 1832; d. Paris, 24. X. 1918), Fr. comp. Studied at the Paris Cons., 1849–54, and prod. his 1st operetta, *Le Docteur Miracle*, in 1857, having tied with Bizet in a competition organized by Offenbach. He did not make a great success until he prod. *Fleur de thé* in 1868 and until then supplemented his income by teaching and org. playing. After that he made a fortune with his many operettas.

Works incl. opera *Plutus*, operettas *Les Cent Vierges*, *La Fille de Madame Angot*, *Giroflé-Girofla*, *La Petite Mariée*, *Le Petit Duc*, *Camargo*, *Ninette*, *Barbe-bleue* & about 40 others; orch. works; v. & pf. So.; sacred songs for women's voices *La Chapelle au couvent*; inst. pieces; pf. works; songs, &c.

Leçon. *See* **Lesson.**

Leconte de Lisle, Charles (1818–94), Fr. poet. *See* **Éolides** (Franck),

Massenet (*Érynnies*), **Préludes** (Debussy, I. 8).
5 songs by Fauré.

Ledger Lines (*see* **Leger Lines**). This is the correct spelling and the only one admitted by the *O.E.D.*, but Leger L. is very much more usual.

Leduc, Simon (b. Paris, *c.* 1748; d. Paris, I. 1777), Fr. vst., comp. & m. pub. Pupil of Gaviniés for the v. He appeared for many years as soloist at the Concert spirituel and in 1767 began to pub. his own works and those by eminent foreign comps.

Works incl. 3 v. concs., 2 *Symphonies concertantes*, 6 trios for 2 vs. & bass, v. sos. & duets, &c.

Ledwidge, William. *See* **Ludwig.**

Lee, Nathaniel (? 1653–92), Eng. playwright. *See* **Finger** (*Rival Queens*), **Galliard** (*Oedipus*), **Purcell** (*Oedipus*, *Massacre of Paris*, *Sophonisba* & *Theodosius*), **Staggins** (*Gloriana*).

Leeds Musical Festival. A triennial mus. festival estab. at Leeds, on the opening of the new Town Hall, in 1858 and continued uninterruptedly to the present day except during the 2 20th-cent. world wars.

Leero Viol. *See* **Lyra Viol.**

Lefébure-Wély, Louis (James Alfred) (b. Paris, 13. XI. 1817; d. Paris, 31. XII. 1869), Fr. orgst. & comp. Studied at the Paris Cons., but had already appeared as an infant prodigy before he entered it. He was orgst. of the Madeleine in 1847–58 and of Saint-Sulpice from 1863 to his death, but made his living mainly as a concert player.

Works incl. opera *Les Recruteurs*; masses, canticles, offertories & *O Salutaris*; much org. m.; pf. & harmonium pieces, &c.

Lefebvre, Charles (Édouard) (b. Paris, 19. VI. 1843; d. Aix-les-Bains, 8. IX. 1917), Fr. comp. Studied at the Paris Cons. and took the Prix de Rome in 1870. After his stay in Rome he travelled in the East and in 1895 succeeded Godard as prof. of the ensemble class at the Cons.

Works incl. operas *Le Trésor*, *Zaïre*, *Djelma* & 2 others; 4 cantatas; Sym. in D maj., *Ouverture dramatique* & *Toggenburg* ovt., orch. scenes *Dalila*; Suite for wind insts. & other chamber m., &c.

Left Hand, Pianoforte Works for. Such works have been written mainly as exercises for the L.H. The right hand has not been thus cultivated by comps. because the left is more in need of practice, and also because it has the advantage of commanding the bass region of the pf., the notes of which can be sustained by the pedal while the hand moves on to play passages above. The following are exs. of L.H. pf. m.:

Alkan, Study.
Bortkievitch, Conc., Op. 28
Brahms, arrs. of Bach's v. Chaconne & Presto.
Bridge (Frank), 3 Improvisations.
Britten, Diversion on a Theme, with orch.
Czerny, Studies, Op. 399.
Gál, pf. 4tet.
Korngold, Conc.
Ravel, Conc.
Reger, 4 Studies.
Saint-Saëns, 6 Studies, Op. 135.
Scriabin, Prelude & Nocturne, Op. 9.
Strauss (R.), Parergon to the *Sinfonia Domestica*, with orch.
Tappert, 50 Studies.
Walker (E.), Vars. with cl. & stg. trio.
Zichy, Conc. in E♭, So. & 6 Studies.

Legato (It. = bound, tied). In m. the word is used to designate a sustained manner of singing or playing, one note leading smoothly to the next.

Legend of Joseph, The, ballet by R. Strauss scen. by Hugo von Hofmannsthal & Harry Kessler, chgph. by Mikhail Mikhailovitch Fokin), prod. Paris, Opéra, 14. V. 1914.

Legend of the Invisible City of Kitezh and the Maiden Fevronia (*Skazkanie o nevidimom gradie Kitezh i dieve Fevronie*), opera by Rimsky-Korsakov (lib. by Vladimir Ivanovitch Bielsky), prod. St. Petersburg, 20. II. 1907.

Legend of Tsar Saltan, The (*Skazka o Tsarie Saltanie*), opera by Rimsky-Korsakov (lib. by Vassily Ivanovitch Bielsky, after Pushkin), prod. Moscow, 3. XI. 1900.

Légende de Saint Christophe, La, opera by d'Indy (lib. by comp.), prod. Paris, Opéra, 6. VI. 1920.

Legende von der heiligen Elizabeth, Die (*The Legend of St. Elizabeth of Hungary*), orat. by Liszt (words by Otto Roquette). 1st perf., in Hung., Budapest, 15. VIII. 1865; 1st prod. as an opera, Weimar, 23. X. 1881.

Leger Lines. The short strokes drawn through or between those notes which go above or below the stave in mus. notation and indicating their position by providing a kind of imaginary and momentary continuation of the stave. The usual spelling is as shown here, although Ledger L. is more correct and is the only form admitted by the *O.E.D.*

Leggenda di Sakuntala, La, opera by Alfano (lib. by comp., based on Kalidasa's play), prod. Bologna, Teatro Comunale, 10. XII. 1921.

Leggero. *See* **Leggiero.**

Leggiadro (It.) = elegant, graceful.

Leggieramente (It.). Adv. of *leggiero*.

Leggiero (It.) = light, swift.

Legno. *See* **Col legno.**

Legouvé, Ernest (1807–1903), Fr. playwright. *See* **Adriana Lecouvreur** (Cilèa), **Gounod** (*Deux Reines*).

Legrenzi, Giovanni (b. Clusone nr. Bergamo, VIII. 1626; d. Venice, 26. V. 1690), It. comp. Orgst. at his birthplace, then chapel master at Ferrara. Between 1664 and 1672 he became dir. of the Cons. dei Mendicanti at Venice and in 1685 chapel master of St. Mark's there.

Works incl. operas *Achille in Sciro, Eteocle e Polinice, La divisione del mondo, Germanico sul Reno, Totila, I due Cesari, Il Giustino, Pertinace* & c. 10 others; masses, motets, psalms & other church m.; orch. works; church sos., &c.

Legros, Joseph (b. Monampteuil, Laon, 7. IX. 1730; d. Rochelle, 20. XII. 1793), Fr. ten. singer & concert manager. Made his 1st appearance at the Paris Opera in 1764 and when Gluck visited Paris became his principal ten. He became too stout for the stage and in 1777–91 managed the Concert spirituel.

Lehár, Ferencz (Franz) (not Léhar) (b. Komárom, 30. IV. 1870), Hung. comp. Studied at the Prague Cons. and became a military bandmaster, but later devoted himself entirely to the very successful comp. of operettas.

Works incl. opera *Kukuška* (later called *Tajana*), operettas *The Merry Widow, The Count of Luxembourg, Gypsy Love, The Three Graces, Pompadour, Springtime, Frasquita, Clo Clo, The Blue Mazurka, Frederica, The Land of Smiles* & many others; symph. poem *Fieber*, 3 Comedy Scenes for orch., &c.

Lehmann, Lilli (b. Würzburg, 24. XI. 1848; d. Berlin, 17. V. 1929), Ger. sop. singer. Studied under her mother, the singer Marie L., appeared at Prague as the 1st genie in Mozart's *Magic Flute* at an early age, was engaged at Danzig in 1868, at Leipzig in 1870, and made her 1st appearance in Berlin in the latter year. In 1876 she 1st sang at the Wagner performances of Bayreuth and in 1880 1st visited London.

Lehmann, 'Liza' (Elizabetta Nina Mary Frederika) (b. London, 11. VII. 1862; d. Pinner, Middlesex, 19. IX. 1918), Eng. singer & comp. Studied 1st with her mother, Amelia Chambers, an accomplished amateur comp. and later at Rome, Wiesbaden and at home with MacCunn, also singing with Randegger. In 1885 she made her 1st appearance as a singer at St. James's Hall, where she sang for the last time in 1894, when she married Herbert Bedford.

Works incl. light opera *The Vicar of Wakefield* (after Goldsmith), mus. comedy *Sergeant Brue* (L. Housman); incid. m. for *Everyman* & other plays; ballads for voice & orch.; song cycles *In a Persian Garden* (Omar Khayyám), *In Memoriam* (Tennyson), *The Daisy-Chain, More Daisies, Songs of Love and Spring*; pf. pieces; songs, &c.

Lehrstück (Ger. = didactic piece, educational play). A small form of m. drama cultivated in Ger. in the 1920s–1930s by Eisler, Hindemith, Weill and other comps., the chief literary exponent being Bert Brecht. It was cultivated mainly by the working classes in Ger. at first, though later the influence spread to other Eur. countries and to U.S.A. The L. makes use of hist. material and dialectical discussion for the purpose of enlightening the masses, and it was for a time a counteragent to the Nazi movement until its exponents were forced to emigrate.

Leicester, ou Le Château de Kenilworth, opera by Auber (lib. by Scribe & Anne Honoré Joseph Mélesville, based on Scott's *Kenilworth*), prod. Paris, Opéra-Comique, 25. I. 1823.

Leich (Ger., obs. = lay). A medieval type of Ger. song similar to the Fr. Lai.

Leichtentritt, Hugo (b. Pleszew, Posen, 1. I. 1874), Ger. mcolst. Studied with Paine at Harvard Univ. and later at the Hochschule für Musik in Berlin, where he became prof. at the Klindworth-Scharwenka Cons. In 1933 he left Ger. as a refugee from the Nazi régime and returned to U.S.A. to join the staff of Harvard Univ. His books incl. studies of Keiser, Handel, Chopin, Busoni, the motet, &c.

Leigh, Walter (b. London, 22. VI. 1905; d. Libya, VI. 1942), Eng. comp. Studied at Cambridge and with Hindemith in Berlin. In 1932 a work of his was perf. at the I.S.C.M. festival in Vienna. He joined up during the war and was killed in action.

Works incl. comic operas *The Pride of the Regiment, The Jolly Roger*; pantomime *Aladdin*; revues *Nine Sharp* and *Little Revue, 1939*; incid. m. to Aristophanes' *Frogs*, Shakespeare's *Midsummer Night's Dream*; ovt. *Agincourt, M. for Stg. Orch., 3 Pieces for Amateur Orch.*; Concertino for hpchd. & stgs.; 3 movts. for stg. 4tet, Trio for fl., ob. & pf. & Sonatina for va. & pf.; songs, &c.

Leighton, Sir William (b. ?; d. ?, before 1617), gentleman pensioner under Elizabeth and James I. He pub. in 1614 a collection of airs for voices and insts. entitled *The Teares or Lamentacions of a Sorrowfull Soule* with contributions by Bull,

Byrd, Coperario, Dowland, Ferrabosco, Ford, O. Gibbons, Giles, Hooper, Robert Johnson, Robert Jones, Kindersley, Leighton, T. Lupo, John Milton (sen.), Peerson, Pilkington, John Ward, Weelkes & Wilbye.

Leila, opera by Bendl (lib., in Cz., by Eliška Krásnohorská, based on Bulwer-Lytton's novel), prod. Prague, Cz. Theatre, 4. I. 1868.

Leite, Antonio da Silva. *See* **Silva Leite.**

Leitgeb. *See* **Leutgeb.**

Leitmotiv (Ger. lit. leading motif, plur. *Leitmotive*). A short theme assoc. with a personage, object or idea in an opera or other work, quoted at appropriate moments or worked up symphonically. Its chief exponent is Wagner, but it was not his invention, for it occurs in earlier comps., e.g. Mozart (esp. *Così fan tutte*), Weber, Spohr, Berlioz, &c. *See also* **Clari.**

Lekeu, Guillaume (b. Heusy nr. Verviers, 20. I. 1870; d. Angers, 21. I. 1894), Belg. comp. Studied with Franck and d'Indy in Paris. In 1891 he obtained the 2nd Belg. Prix de Rome with the lyric scene *Andromède*.

Works incl. symph. study on Shakespeare's *Hamlet*, *Fantaisie sur deux airs populaires angevins* for orch.; Adagio for stg. 4tet and orch.; Introd. & Adagio for brass; *Chant lyrique* for chor. & orch.; pf. 4tet (completed by d'Indy), pf. Trio; v. & pf. So., co. & pf. So. (completed by d'Indy); 3 pf. pieces; *3 Poèmes* for voice & pf., &c.

Lélio, or Le Retour à la Vie (*L., or The Return to Life*), 'lyric monodrama' by Berlioz for an actor, solo voices, chor., pf. & orch., Op. 14bis, comp. in 1831 as a sequel to the *Symphonie fantastique* and 1st perf. with the latter, Paris Cons., 9. XII. 1832.

Lemare, Edwin (Henry) (b. Ventnor, Isle of Wight, 9. IX. 1865; d. Los Angeles, 24. IX. 1934), Eng. orgst. & comp. Studied at the R.A.M. in London and after var. church appts. became orgst. of St. Margaret's, Westminster. In 1900 he toured in U.S.A., having by that time become a very successful concert orgst., and he was attached to the Carnegie Inst. at Pittsburg in 1902–15 and in 1921–34 he was at Portland, Maine.

Works incl. 2 syms. for org. and a vast amount of other concert m. for his inst.

Lemierre, Antoine Marin (1723–93), Fr. poet & dramatist. *See* **Jessonda** (Spohr).

Lemlin (or Lämmlein), Lorenz (b. Eichstätt, Bavaria, ?; d. ? Heidelberg, ?), Ger. 16th-cent. singe & comp. He studied at Heidelberg Univ. and became singer and chapel master to the elector palatine there.

Works incl. Lat. motets, Ger. songs, e.g. 'Ein Gutzgauch auf dem Zaune sass,' &c.

Lemmens, Nicolas Jacques (b. Zoerle-Parwys, Waterloo, 3. I. 1823; d. Linterport nr. Malines, 30. I. 1881), Belg. orgst., pfst. & comp. Studied at the Brussels Cons. and with Hesse at Breslau. In 1849 he became org. prof. at the Brussels Cons., but after 1857, when he married Helen Sherrington, he lived much in Eng.

Works incl. So., offertories and other concert m. for org., a treatise for accomp. of plainsong, &c.

Lemmens-Sherrington, Helen (b. Preston, 4. X. 1834; d. Brussels, 9. V. 1906), Eng. sop. singer, wife of prec. Studied with Verhulst at Rotterdam and at the Brussels Cons., and made her 1st appearance in London in 1856.

Lemminkainen's Home-Faring, symph. legend by Sibelius, Op. 22, 1 of 4 on subjects from the *Kalevala*, only 2 of which were pub., the other being *The Swan of Tuonela*. L. was comp. in 1893–5.

Lemoyne, Jean Baptiste (b. Eymet, Périgord, 3. IV. 1751; d. Paris, 30. XII. 1796), Fr. cond. & comp. Having cond. in the provinces, he went to Berlin to study with Graun, Kirnberger & others. He cond. there and at Warsaw, but returned to Paris to prod. his 1st opera, in imitation of Gluck, whose pupil he called himself. When Gluck denied this, he wrote a 2nd opera in the style of Piccinni. Later he visited It.

Works incl. operas *Électre* (after Sophocles), *Phèdre* (after Racine), *Les Prétendus*, *Nephté* & c. a dozen others, &c.

Lenau, Nikolaus (Franz Niembsch von Strehlenau) (1802–50), Hung. poet who wrote in Ger. *See* **Don Juan** (R. Strauss), **Liszt** (*Faust*), **Rabaud** (*Procession nocturne*), **Schoeck** (*Postillon* & songs).

Lendvai, Erwin (b. Budapest, 4. VI. 1882), Hung. comp. Studied under Koessler at Budapest and with Puccini at Milan, where he gained a state prize. From 1913 he taught at Jaques-Dalcroze's school at Hellerau nr. Dresden and from 1919–22 at the Klindworth - Scharwenka Cons. in Berlin, later at Hamburg, Munich, &c.

Works incl. opera *Elga*; *Stimmen der Seele* for double chor., *Nippon* for female chor., cycle for male-voice chor. and bar. solo; Sym. in D maj., orch. scherzo *Masken*, *Archaic Dances* for small orch.; stg. 4tet in E min., 3 stg. trios. 5tet for wind insts.; 4

pieces for co. & pf.; pf. pieces; *Minnelieder* & other songs, &c.

Lenepveu, Charles (Ferdinand) (b. Rouen, 4. X. 1840; d. Paris, 16. VIII. 1910), Fr. comp. 1st studied law in Paris, but after a success with a cantata at Caen decided to enter the Cons., where he worked under A. Thomas. He took the Prix de Rome in 1865 and after his stay in Rome resumed studies with the orgst. Charles Chauvet. In 1880 he became teacher of harmony at the Cons. and in 1894 prof. of comp.

Works incl. operas *Le Florentin* & *Velléda* (after Chateaubriand's *Les Martyrs*), lyric drama *Jeanne d'Arc* (for perf. in Rouen cath.); 2 Requiems; cantatas for the Soc. d'Agriculture et de Commerce of Caen & *Renaud dans les jardins d'Armide* (after Tasso); funeral march for Henri Régnault, &c.

Lengyel, Menyhért (b. 1880), Hung. playwright. *See* **Bartók** (*Miraculous Mandarin*), **Szántó** (*Typhoon*).

Lenormand, René (b. Elbeuf, 5. VIII. 1846; d. Paris, 3. XII. 1932), Fr. comp. Intended for a commercial career, but studied m. with his mother and from 1868 with Damcke in Paris. He founded a soc. for the cultivation of songs of all nations and wrote a book on modern harmony (with almost exclus. Fr. exs.).

Works incl. opera *Le Cachet rouge*; mimed drama *La Nuit de juillet*; cantata *Souvenirs du Valais*; *Le Voyage imaginaire* & 2 *Esquisses* on Malay themes for orch.; *Le Lahn de Mabed* for v. & orch.; stg. 4tet, pf. Trio; v. pieces; pf. m.; *c.* 150 songs, &c.

Lento (It.) = slow.

Lenton, John (b. ?, 1656; d. ? London, ? *c.* 1719), Eng. vst. & comp. He was a musn. at court under Charles II, William & Mary and Anne, pub. an instruction book for the v. containing airs of his own, revised the tunes for Durfey's *Wit and Mirth* and contrib. songs to var. collections.

Works incl. incid. m. for Shakespeare's *Othello*, Otway's *Venice Preserved*, Rowe's *Tamerlane* & *The Fair Penitent* & other plays, &c.

Lenz, Wilhelm von (b. Riga, 1. VI. 1809; d. St. Petersburg, 31. I. 1883), Latvian statesman and writer on m. Councillor at St. Petersburg. Pub. 2 books on Beethoven, *B. et ses trois styles* & *B.: eine Kunststudie*, as well as studies of contemp. pf. virtuosi.

Leo, Leonardo ([Lionardo] Oronzo Salvatore de) (b. San Vito degli Schiavi nr. Brindisi, 5. VIII. 1694; d. Naples, 31. X. 1744), It. comp. Educ. (?) by the Dominican friars at San Vito, who discovered his mus. talent, he was sent to the Cons. della Pietà dei Turchini at Naples in 1703, studying under Provenzale and Fago, and remaining until 1715. His 1st orat., *Santa Chiara*, was perf. at the Cons. in 1712 and his 1st opera, *Pisistrato*, prod. in 1714. He became a teacher at the Cons. and orgst. at the royal chapel.

Works incl. operas *Sofonisba, Lucio Papirio, Caio Gracco, La mpeca scoperta* (in Neapol. dialect), *Timocrate, Il trionfo di Camilla, La semmeglianza di chi l'ha fatta, Il Cid, Catone in Utica, La clemenza di Tito, Demofoonte, Farnace, Siface, Ciro riconosciuto, L'amico traditore, La simpatia del sangue, L'Olimpiade, Vologeso, Amor vuol sofferenza* (*La finta Frascatana*), *Achille in Sciro, Scipione nelle Spagne, Il fantastico* (*Il nuovo Don Chisciotte*, after Cervantes) & *c.* 40 others; orats. *Il trionfo della castità di S. Alessio, Dalla morte alla vita, La morte di Abele, S. Elena al Calvario, S. Francesco di Paola nel deserto* & others; masses, motets, psalms & other church m.; Conc. for 4 vs., 6 co. concs.; hpchd. pieces, &c.

Léonard, Hubert (b. Bellaire, Belg., 7. IV. 1819; d. Paris, 6. V. 1890), Belg. vst. Studied at the Paris Cons. under Habeneck, made his 1st appearance on tour in Ger., 1844, later became v. prof. at the Brussels Cons. and retired to Paris in 1867.

Leoncavallo, Ruggiero (b. Naples, 8. III. 1858; d. Montecatini nr. Florence, 9. VIII. 1919), It. comp. Studied pf. privately at first and then entered the Naples Cons., which he left in 1876 with a master diploma. He went to Bologna to attend Carducci's lectures in literature. There he was on the point of prod. his 1st opera, *Chatterton*, but was swindled and found himself penniless. He made a precarious living by lessons and playing the pf. at cafés, but later managed to travel as café pfst. to Eng., Fr., Hol., Ger. and Egypt. He then began a trilogy on the It. Renaissance, *Crepusculum*, with *I Medici*, but never prod. the 2 following works, *Savonarola* & *Cesare Borgia*; but in the meantime he made an enormous success with *I Pagliacci* at Milan in 1892 and soon all over It. *La Bohème* at Venice in 1897 was ruined by the appearance of Puccini's work on the same subject, and in spite of a commission from William II for a Ger. opera for Berlin, *Der Roland von Berlin*, in 1904, he never repeated his *Pagliacci* success.

Works incl. operas *Chatterton* (after Alfred de Vigny), *I Medici, I Pagliacci, La Bohème* (after Murger), *Zaza, Der Roland von Berlin* (after Willibald Alexis), *Maia, I zingari,*

Goffredo Mameli, *Edipo rè* (after Sophocles), *Tormenta* (unfinished); operettas *A chi la giarettiera*, *Il primo bacio*, *Malbruk*, *La reginetta delle rose*, *Are you there?*, *La candidata* & *Prestami tua moglie*; ballet *La vita d'una marionetta*; symph. poem *Serafita* (after Balzac's novel), &c.

Leoni, Leone (b. ?; d. Vicenza, ?), It. 16th–17th-cent. comp. Chapel master of Vicenza cath. from *c.* 1588.

Works incl. masses, motets (some in many parts with insts.), *Sacrae cantiones*, psalms, magnificats & other church m.; sacred & secular madrigals, &c.

Leonora, ossia L'amore conjugale (*Leonora, or Wedded Love*), opera by Paer (lib. by ? Giacomo Cinti, based on Bouilly's lib. for Gaveaux), prod. Dresden, 3. X. 1804.

Leonora Overtures (Beethoven). *See* **Fidelio.**

Léonore, ou L'Amour conjugal (*Leonora, or Wedded Love*), opera by Gaveaux (lib. by Jean Nicolas Bouilly, based on a real event), prod. Paris, Théâtre Feydeau, 19. II. 1798. The forerunner and model of Beethoven's *Fidelio*.

Leonova, Daria Mikhailovna (b. Tver, 1825; d. St. Petersburg, 6. II. 1896), Rus. con. singer. Pupil of Glinka; made her 1st appearance at St. Petersburg in his *Life for the Tsar* in 1843. She helped Mussorgsky towards the end of his life by engaging him as pfst. on a tour in S. Rus. and at her singing-school at St. Petersburg.

Leopardi, Giacomo (1798–1837), It. poet. *See* **Goehler** (cantatas), **Malipiero** (*Commiato*).

Leopold I (1640–1705), emperor, comp. an opera, *Apollo deluso*, to a lib. by his court musn. Antonio Draghi, 1669, and contrib. to numerous other operas by the same comp.

Leopolita, Marcin (real name Lwowczyk) (b. ?, 1540; d. Lwów, 1589), Pol. comp. Member of the Coll. of Roratists and court comp. at Cracow from 1560.

Works incl. masses (e.g. *Missa Paschalis*), motets; secular songs for several voices, &c.

L'Épine, Francesca Margherita de. *See* **Épine.**

Lermontov, Mikhail Yurevitch (1814–41), Rus. poet & novelist. *See* **Assafiev** (*The Treasurer's Wife*), **Blaramberg** (*Demon*), **Catoire** (*Mtsyri*) **Cui** (songs), **Demon** (Rubinstein), **Gilson** (*Demon*), **Ippolitov - Ivanov** (*Mtsyri*), **Koreshtchenko** (*Angel of Death*), **Mossolov** (songs), **Nápravnik** (*Tamara* & *Demon*), **Rogowski** (*Tamara*), **Senilov** (*Mtsyri*), **Shebalin** (*Masquerade*), **Spendiarov** (*3 Palm Trees*), **Tamara** (Balakirev).

Lero Viol. *See* **Lyra Viol.**

Leroux, Xavier (Henri Napoléon) (b) Velletri, It., 11. X. 1863; d. Paris, 2. II. 1919), Fr. comp. Studied at the Paris Cons., among his masters being Massenet, and gained the Prix de Rome in 1885. He became harmony prof. there in 1896 and ed. the periodical *Musica*.

Works incl. operas *Evangeline*, *Astarté*, *La Reine Fiammette* (after Catulle Mendès), *William Ratcliff* (after Heine), *Théodora*, *Le Chemineau*, *Le Carillonneur*, *La Fille de Figaro*, *Les Cadeaux de Noël*, *1814*, *Nausithoé*, *La Plus Forte*, *L'Ingénu*; incid. m. to Sardou & Moreau's *Cléopâtre*, Aeschylus's *The Persians* & Richepin's *Xantho chez les courtisanes*; cantatas *Endymion* & *Vénus et Adonis*; ovt. *Harald*; Mass with orch.; motets; numerous songs, &c.

Lesage, Alain René (1668–1747), Fr. novelist. *See* **Caverne** (Lesueur). **Françaix** (*Diable boiteux*), **La Guerre** (E.) (*Ceinture de Vénus*), **Neue krumme Teufel** (Haydn), **Rencontre imprévue** (Gluck), **Satanella** (Balfe), **Semet** (*Gil Blas*).

Leschetizky, Theodor (b. Lancut, Pol., 22. VI. 1830; d. Dresden, 14. XI. 1915), Pol.-Aus. pfst., teacher & comp. He 1st appeared in Vienna in 1845, was pf. prof. at St. Petersburg Cons., 1852–78, and then settled in Vienna as an independent teacher of many famous pupils, incl. Paderewski.

Works incl. opera *Die erste Falte*, many pf. pieces, &c.

Leskov, Nikolai Semenovitch (1831–95), Rus. novelist. *See* **Lady Macbeth of the Mtsensk District** (Shostakovitch).

Lessel, Franz (b. Pulawy, *c.* 1780; d. Piotrkow, VIII. 1838), Pol.-Aus. comp. Studied medicine in Vienna, but became a pupil of Haydn, whom he looked after until his death, whereafter he went to Pol. and lived with Prince Czartoryski's family until they were driven away by the Revol. The rest of his life was unsettled.

Works incl. masses, Requiem & other church m.; syms.; pf. Conc.; chamber m.; pf. sos. & fantasies, &c.

Lesson. A keyboard piece or more often a set of pieces (' lessons ' were thus often synonymous with ' suites ') of the 17th & 18th cents., generally of an instructive character.

Lesueur, Jean François (b. Drucat-Plessiel nr. Abbeville, 15. II. 1760; d. Paris, 6. X. 1837), Fr. comp. He 1st learnt m. as a choir-boy at Abbeville, then held church appts. at Amiens and Paris picking up mus.

knowledge eagerly. After 1781 he became m. master successively at Dijon cath., at Le Mans and Tours, only to return to Paris as choir-master of the church of the Innocents in 1784. Having had some advice from Sacchini, he applied for the post of mus. dir. at Notre-Dame, which he obtained in 1786. He was allowed to use a full orch. at mass and to open the proceedings with an ovt. This aroused a controversy which led to his resignation, and he spent 1788–92 in the country, devoted to the comp. of operas. In 1793 he was app. prof. at the school of the Nat. Guard and in 1795 he was app. one of the inspectors at the newly opened Cons. In 1804 he succeeded Paisiello as chapel master to Napoleon, after whose fall he was app. superintendent and comp. to the chapel of Louis XVIII. In 1818 he became prof. of comp. at the Cons., where his pupils incl. Berlioz and Gounod.

Works incl. operas *Télémaque*, *La Caverne*, *Paulin et Virginie* (after Saint-Pierre), *Ossian, ou Les Bardes*, *Le Triomphe de Trajan* (with Persuis), *La Mort d'Adam* (after Klopstock) & some others; Mass & Te Deum for Napoleon's coronation, 3 solemn masses, *Stabat Mater*, motets, psalms & other church m.; orats. *Messe de Noël*, *Debora*, *Rachel*, *Ruth et Noémi*, *Ruth et Boaz*; cantatas, &c.

Lesur, Daniel (b. Paris, 19. XI. 1908), Fr. orgst. & comp. Pupil of Tournemire, Caussade & others. In 1938 he became prof. of ctpt. at the Schola Cantorum in Paris. He was also app. orgst. at the Benedictine abbey, and with Baudrier, Jolivet and Messiaen formed the group known as 'La Jeune France.'

Works incl. *Suite française* for orch.; *Passecaille* for pf. & orch.; 3 Heine songs for voice & stg. 4tet; suite *Le Carillon* for pf.; *La Vie intérieure* for org.; songs, &c.

Letters, Music based on. Comps. have sometimes amused themselves by turning names or other words into notes representing in mus. nomenclature the letters of which they are formed, or as many as can be thus used. In Eng. the letters A to G can be thus represented; in Ger. H (=B♮) and S (Es=E♭) can be added, and in Fr. & It. the syllables Do, Re, Mi, Fa, Sol, La, Si may be used. In Fr. a rather fantastic system was devised for the works on the names of Fauré and Haydn listed below, whereby the notes A to G were followed by further 8ves named from H onwards. Here are some exs.:

Abegg (friends of Schumann's): Schumann, *Vars. on the Name of A.* for pf., Op. 1.

Asch (the birthplace of Ernestine von Fricken): Schumann, *Carnival* for pf., Op. 9.

Bach. *See* **B.A.C.H.**, *also* Faber *below*.

Bamberg (the maiden name of Cui's wife): Cui, Scherzo for pf. duet (on B. A. B. E. G. & C. C. = César Cui).

Belaiev: Borodin, Glazunov, Liadov & Rimsky-Korsakov, stg. 4tet on 'B-la-F.'

Faber: Canon in 7 parts by Bach, dated 1. III. 1749, sung over a Ground or Pes on the notes F. A. B(♭). E. and marked 'F A B E Repetatur,' thus forming the name Faber, which may be a Lat. form of some Ger. surname derived from some kind of manual labour. The canon also bears an inscription in Lat. containing the following acrostics on the names of Faber and Bach: 'Fidelis Amici Beatum Esse Recordari' and 'Bonae Artis Cultorem Habeas.' *See also* **B.A.C.H.**

Fauré: Pieces by Aubert, Enesco, Koechlin, Ladmirault, Ravel, Roger-Ducasse & Schmitt contrib. to a Fauré number of the *Revue musicale* in 1924.

Gade: Schumann's pf. piece so entitled in *Album für die Jugend*.

Haydn: Ravel, *Menuet sur le nom d'Haydn* for pf.

Sacha: Glazunov, *Suite sur le thème du nom diminutif russe* for pf., Op. 2.

Schumann (letters S. C. H. A. only): Schumann, *Carnival* (inversion of the letters A. S. C. H.).

Leutgeb (or Leitgeb), Ignaz (b. ?; d. Vienna, 27. II. 1811), Aus. hn. player. Lived 1st at Salzburg, then in Vienna, where he kept a cheese-monger's shop. He was a friend of Mozart's who wrote his 4 hn. concs. and the hn. 5tet for him.

Leva, Enrico de (b. Naples, 19. I. 1867), It. comp. & singing-teacher. Studied at the Naples Cons. and in 1907 became dir. of the Istituto dei SS. Giuseppe e Lucia there.

Works incl. opera *La Camargo*; settings of poems from d'Annunzio's *Gioconda*; serenade *A Capomonte* & a very large number of light and popular songs in the Neapolitan folksong manner.

Levadé, Charles Gaston (b. Paris, 3. I. 1869), Fr. comp. Studied under Massenet at the Paris Cons.

Works incl. operas *L'Amour d'Héliodore*, *Les Hérétiques*, *La Rôtisserie de la Reine Pédauque* (after Anatole France), *La Peau de chagrin* (after Balzac); pantomime *Cœur de Mar-*

got; suites, *Prélude religieux* &c. for orch.; chamber m.; pf. pieces; songs, &c.

Levasseur, Marie (Claude Josèphe) (b. Valenciennes, 8. X. 1749; d. Neuwied o/Rhine, 6. V. 1826), Fr. sop. singer. She 1st appeared on the stage in Paris in small parts and under the name of Rosalie, using her own name from 1775. She was one of Gluck's artists in Paris. After the Revol. she twice left Fr. as a refugee.

Levasseur, Nicolas (Prosper) (b. Bresles, Oise, 9. III. 1791; d. Paris, 6. XII. 1871), Fr. bass singer. Studied at the Paris Cons. and made his 1st stage appearance in 1813.

Leveridge, Richard (b. London, *c.* 1670; d. London, 22. III. 1758), Eng. bass singer and song writer. Made his 1st appearance in London before Purcell's death in 1695 and sang until a few years before that of Handel in 1759, his last recorded appearance being in 1751.

Works incl. incid. m. for Shakespeare's *Macbeth*, Farquhar's *The Recruiting Officer*, *Love and a Bottle* & (with D. Purcell) *The Constant Couple*, Vanbrugh's *Aesop* & other plays; masque *Pyramus and Thisbe* (after Shakespeare); songs, e.g. 'The Roast Beef of Old England,' &c.

Levey, Richard Michael (actually O'Shaughnessy) (b. Dublin, 25. X. 1811; d. Dublin, 28. VI. 1899), Ir. vst., cond. & comp. He entered the orch. of the Theatre Royal at Dublin in 1826, for which he comp. 50 ovts. and arr. m. for 44 pantomimes. He was one of the founders of the R. Ir. A.M. in 1850.

Levi, Hermann (b. Giessen, 7. XI. 1839; d. Munich, 13. V. 1900) Ger. cond. Studied with V. Lachner at Munich and at the Leipzig Cons. After var. appts. he became dir. of the Munich court theatre, 1872–96. Cond. the 1st perf. of Wagner's *Parsifal* at Bayreuth.

Levidis, Dimitri (b. Athens, 1886), Gr. comp. Studied at the Athens Cons., at the Munich Acad. and with Dénéréaz in Swi. He settled in Fr. and became naturalized in 1829. Some of his comps. make use of the Ondes Musicales invented by Martenot.

Works incl. ballet *Le Pâtre et la nymphe*; *Roubayyat Persans* (after Omar Khayyám) & *Sirène* for orch.; *Poème* for pf., v. & orch.; symph. poem for O. M.; *De profundis* for voice & 2 O. M., &c.

Levitsky, Misha (b. Krementchug, 25. V. 1898; d. Avon-by-the-Sea, New York, 2. I. 1941), Rus. pfst. & comp. Studied at Warsaw, went to U.S.A. in 1906 and continued his studies under Stokowski in N.Y., later with Dohnányi in Berlin, 1911–5.

Works incl. many pf. pieces, cadenza for Beethoven's C min. pf. Conc., &c.

Levy, Alexandre (b. São Paulo, 10. XI. 1864; d. São Paulo, 17. I. 1892), Braz. pfst. & comp.

Works incl. *Suite brasileira* for orch., Vars. on a Braz. theme for pf., &c.

Lewis, C(ecil). Day (b. 1904), Eng. poet. *See* **Rawsthorne** (*Enemy Speaks*).

Lewis, Matthew Gregory (1775–1818), Eng. novelist & playwright. *See* **Busby** (*Rugantino*), **Kelly** (*Castle Spectre*).

Ley, Henry G(eorge). (b. Chagford, Devon, 30. XII. 1887), Eng. orgst. & cond. Studied at Keble Coll., Oxford, and was app. orgst. at Christ Church cath. there in 1900. Later taught org. at the R.C.M. in London and in 1926 became dir. of m. at Eton Coll.

Works incl. church m.; Vars. on a theme by Handel for orch.; chamber m.; org. m.; songs, &c.

L'Héritier, Jean (b. ?; d. ?), Fr. comp. Pupil of Josquin des Prés. Wrote masses, motets, &c.

Lhermite, Tristan (orig. François) (*c.* 1601–55), Fr. poet. *See* **Debussy** (*Promenoir des deux amants*).

L'Homme armé. *See* **Homme armé.**

Lhotka, Fran (b. Vožice, 25. XII. 1883), Yslv. comp. Studied at the Prague Cons. with Dvořák, **Janáček** and others, and went to Rus. as prof. at the Cons. of Ekaterinoslav. He then joined the Opera at Zagreb and later became prof. and in 1938 dir. of the Acad. of M. there, also cond. of a chor. soc.

Works incl. operas *Minka* & *The Sea*; ballets *The Devil at the Village* & *A Medieval Love*; Sym., Scherzo, Yslv. Capriccio & *Reveille of the Trenks Soldiers* for orch.; chamber m.; chors.; songs, &c.

Li-Tai-Po (or Li-Po) (705–62), Chin. poet. *See* **Lambert (C.)** (songs), **Lied von der Erde** (Mahler), **Morning Heroes** (Bliss).

Liadov, Anatol Constantinovitch (b. St. Petersburg, 10. V. 1855; d. Novgorod, 28. VIII. 1914), Rus. comp. Studied under his father and later with Rimsky-Korsakov at the St. Petersburg Cons., where he became a teacher in 1878, when he was also app. to the Imp. Chapel. The Imp. Geograph. Soc. commissioned him, with Balakirev and Liapunov, to collect folksongs in var. parts of the country.

Works incl. symph. poems *Baba Yaga*, *The Enchanted Lake*, *Kikimora*, 2 orch. Scherzos, *The Inn-Mazurka*, Polonaise in Memory of Pushkin for orch.; chor. settings from

Schiller's *Bride of Messina* and Maeterlinck's *Sœur Béatrice*, 3 chor. works for female voices; *c.* 40 op. nos, of pf. pieces, incl. *Birulki* (*Spillikins*). ballads *From Days of Old*, *Marionettes*, *Musical Snuff-Box*, Vars. on theme by Glinka & on a Pol. song, *From the Book of Revelation*, studies, preludes, mazurkas, &c.; songs, folksong settings, &c.

Liapunov, Sergey Mikhailovitch (b. Yaroslav, 30. XI. 1859; d. Paris, 11. XI. 1924), Rus. pfst. & comp. Studied at Nizhny-Novgorod and at the Moscow Cons. In 1893 the Imp. Geograph. Soc. commissioned him, with Balakirev and Liadov, to collect folksongs. In 1894–1902 he was asst. dir. of the Imp. Chapel. He took refuge in Paris from the Revol.

Works incl. 2 syms., *Ballad*, *Solemn Ovt.*, Polonaise & symph. poem *Hashish* for orch.; 2 pf. concs., Rhapsody on Ukrainian themes for pf. & orch.; numerous pf. pieces, incl. suite *Christmas Songs*, &c.; folksong settings, &c.

Liatoshinsky, Boris Nikolaievitch (b. Kiev, 4. I. 1895), Rus. comp. He played pf. & v. and attempted comp. as a child and in 1913 was sent to the Kiev Cons., where he studied with Glière, remaining until 1918, having studied law at the Univ. at the same time. From 1920 he was prof. of comp. at Kiev and Moscow.

Works incl. operas *The Golden Hoop* and *Shtchors*; film m.; Solemn Cantata for chor. & orch. for Stalin's 60th birthday; 3 syms., Ovt. on Ukrainian themes, *Fantastic March* & other orch. works; 3 stg. 4tets, pf. Trio; v. & pf. So.; 2 pf. sos. and other pf. works; songs, Ukrainian folksong arrs., &c.

Lib. (abbr.)=Libretto.

Liberati, Antimo (b. Foligno, ?; d. ?, after 1685), It. singer, orgst. & comp. Pupil of Allegri and Benevoli in Rome, where in 1661 he became a singer in the Papal Chapel and orgst. at 2 churches. He wrote a letter giving particulars for Palestrina's biog. and another defending a passage in Corelli.

Works incl. orats., madrigals, arias, &c.

Libert, Henri (b. Paris, 15. XII. 1869; d. Paris, 14. I. 1937), Fr. orgst. & comp. Studied at the Paris Cons., where Franck, Widor and Massenet were among his masters. He was app. orgst. at the church of Saint-Denis and prof. at the Amer. Cons. at Fontainebleau.

Works incl. motets; *Variations symphoniques*, *Chorals*, *Préludes et Fugues* & many other org. works; pf. pieces, &c.

Librettist. The author of a lib.

Libretto (It. = booklet). The term, generally current as Eng., for the text of an opera or other voc. work in dramatic form. The It. plur. is *libretti*, but if the word is accepted as Eng. 'librettos' is permissible.

Libst. (abbr.)=Librettist.

Libuše, opera by Smetana (lib., in Ger., by Joseph Wenzig, Cz. trans. by Ervín Špindler), prod. Prague, Cz. Theatre, 11. VI. 1881.

Licenza (It., plur. *licenze*)=licence, freedom, liberty, e.g. the direction *con alcune licenze*='with some freedom' (in form, style or perf.); up to the 18th cent., a cadenza or ornament inserted at the perf.'s discretion and not written down by the comp.; also, in 17th-cent. opera, esp. in Vienna, a mus. epilogue to a stage perf. with special ref. to the occasion (royal birthday, wedding, &c.).

Lichard, Milan (b. Uherska Skalice, Slovakia, 24. II. 1853), Cz. comp. While under Hung. rule he worked as a railway official, but cultivated m. as best he could. Later took to comp. and folksong collecting. For a time he was imprisoned as a rebel.

Works incl. *The Lark*, *Praise to Thee*, 2 funeral odes, &c. for chor.; Rhapsody for orch.; songs; folksong arrs. incl. *Garlands of Popular Song*, &c.

Lichfild, Henry (b. ?; d. ? nr. Luton, ?), Eng. 16th-17th cent. (? amateur) comp. He was in some capacity in the household of Lord, and later Lady, Cheney at Toddington House nr. Luton. Wrote madrigals.

Lickl, Johann Georg (b. Korneuburg, 11. IV. 1769; d. Pécs, 12. V. 1843), Aus. comp. Was chapel master in Vienna from 1806 and wrote several mus. plays for Schikaneder's theatre.

Works incl. plays with m.; masses, motets; chamber m., &c.

Lidarti, Cristiano Giuseppe (b. Pisa, ?; d. ?), It. 18th-cent. cst. & comp. Lived at Pisa and Bologna, and may have visited Vienna and London.

Works incl. stage work *La tutela contrastata*; chamber m.; catches & glees. &c.

Lidl, Andreas (b. Vienna, *c.* 1740; d. ? London, ?), Aus. barytone virtuoso and comp. He increased the stgs. on his inst., travelled much on the Continent and 1st appeared in London in 1778.

Works incl. chamber m.; pieces for the barytone, &c.

Lie, Sigurd (b. Drammen, 23. V. 1871; d. Drammen, 29. IX. 1904), Norw. cond., vst. & comp. Studied at the Leipzig Cons. and in 1894 became chor. and theatre cond. at Bergen.

After further study in Berlin he became chor. cond. at Christiania.

Works incl. Sym. in A min., *Orientalisk Suite, Marche symphonique* for orch.; cantatas & other chor. works; pf. 5tet; songs, &c.

Lie-Nissen, Erika (b. Kongsvinger, 17. I. 1845; d. Christiania, 27. X. 1903), Norw. pfst. Pupil of Kjerulf at Oslo, Kullak in Berlin and Tellefsen in Paris. She was app. prof. of pf. at the Copenhagen Cons. in 1870, but 4 years later married Dr. Oscar Nissen and settled at Christiania.

Liebe der Danae, Die (R. Strauss). *See* **Kuss der Danae.** The opera was 1st reported under the title of this entry, but apparently changed later.

Liebe im Narrenhaus, Die (*Love in the Madhouse*), opera by Dittersdorf (lib. by Gottlieb Stephanie, jun.), prod. Vienna, Kärntnertor Theatre, 12. IV. 1787.

Liebenthaler, Marie. *See* **Wilt.**

Liebeslieder (*Love Songs*), a set of waltzes by Brahms for pf. duet with solo voc. quartet *ad lib.*, Op. 52, comp. in 1869. There is a 2nd set of *Neue Liebeslieder*, Op. 65, written in 1874.

Liebesverbot, Das, oder Die Novize von Palermo (*The Love-Prohibition, or The Novice of P.*), opera by Wagner (lib. by comp., based on Shakespeare's *Measure for Measure*), prod. Magdeburg, 29. III. 1836.

Lieblich Flute (½ Ger. = lovely, sweet). A 4-ft. org. stop, the upper range of Lieblich gedackt.

Lieblich gedackt (Ger. lit. 'lovely and covered,' earlier *gedact* or *gedakt*; modern [but not used in this connection] *gedeckt*). An old name for an 8-ft. org. stop, used in Eng. as well as Ger., governing a range of stopped diapason pipes.

Lied (Ger.) = Song. A *Lied* is nothing more nor less than a song with Ger. words. In other languages the term has acquired the significance of a special type of Ger. song, as cultivated partic. by Schubert, Brahms, Schumann, Wolf, R. Strauss and others, but Gers. themselves called any songs *Lieder* long before the earliest of these masters appeared.

Lied von der Erde, Das (*The Song of the Earth*), sym. for m.-sop., ten. & orch. by Mahler (so called by the comp., but not numbered among his other syms.). The words are from Hans Bethge's anthol. of Ger. transs. of Chin. poetry, *Die chinesische Flöte*: 1. (Li-Tai-Po). *Das Trinklied vom Jammer der Erde* (*The Drinking-Song of Earth's Misery*); 2. (Tchang-Tsi) *Der Einsame im Herbst* (*The Lonely One in Autumn*); 3. (Li-Tai-Po) *Von der Jugend* (*Of Youth*); 4. (do.) *Von der Schönheit* (*Of Beauty*); 5. (do.) *Der Trunkene im Frühling* (*The Toper in Spring*); 6. (Mong-Kao-Yen & Wang-Wei) *Der Abschied* (*The Farewell*). Comp. in 1908; 1st perf. Munich, 20. XI. 1911, after M.'s death.

Lieder ohne Worte. 36 pf. pieces by Mendelssohn in the form and character of songs exploiting the principle of accompd. melody rather than polyphonic textures. Vol. I, Op. 19, Nos. 1–6 (1830–2); II, Op. 30, 7–12 (1833–7); III, Op. 38, 13–18 (1836–7); IV, Op. 53, 19–24 (1841); V, Op. 62, 25–30 (1842–3); VI, Op. 67, 31–6 (1843–5). The only titles which are M.'s own are those of the 3 *Venezianische Gondellieder* (*Venetian Barcarolles*), Nos. 6, 12 & 29, the *Duetto*, No. 18, and the *Volkslied*, No. 23.

Liederkreis (Ger.). *See* **Song Cycle.**

Liederspiel (Ger. lit. 'song-play'). A play with songs similar to the *Singspiel*. The term was 1st used by Reichardt in 1800. It may also mean 'song cycle,' e.g. Schumann's *Spanisches L.*

Liedertafel (Ger. lit. 'song-table' or 'singing-table'). A male-voice chor. assocn. doubtless deriving its name from early gatherings seated round a table drinking and singing.

Lier, Bertus van (b. Utrecht, 10. IX. 1906), Dutch cst., cond., critic & comp. Studied at the Amsterdam Cons., Pijper being his comp. master, and later learnt cond. from Scherchen at Strasburg. Became m. critic at Amsterdam, cond. of amateur orchs. and prof. at the Utrecht Cons.

Works incl. incid. m. to Sophocles' *Ajax*; 3 syms.; Concertino for co. & chamber orch.; chamber m.; unaccomp. chors.; declamation with orch. *The D*[illegible], &c.

Life for the Tsar, A (*Zhizn za Tsaria*; now *Ivan Sussanin*), opera by Glinka (lib. by Georgy Fedorovitch Rosen), prod. St. Petersburg, 9. XII. 1836.

Ligata (It. fem. = bound). A fugue was said to be a *fuga ligata* if the answer was so exact a reproduction of the subject that it needed not even to be fully written out, but could be merely indicated by the comp. and was then perf. according to strict rules or a strict 'canon'—hence the word Canon still in use.

Ligature(s). A group of 2 or more notes in voc. m., esp. Plainsong, sung to a single syllable. Also the var. signs in plainsong notation by which such groups are indicated.

Lilac Time. The Eng. version, made by Clutsam in 1923, of the operetta *Das Dreimäderlhaus* by Berté (lib. by Willner & Reichert), prod. (Ger. orig.) Vienna, Raimund-Theater, 15.

I. 1916; *L. T.* prod. London, 22. XII. 1922. The lib. is a gross perversion of the life of Schubert and the m. consists of a choice of Schubertian material, much of it badly distorted.

Lilien, Ignaz (b. Limburg, 29. V. 1897), Dutch comp. Studied in Hol. and with Suk in Prague.

Works incl. operas *Beatrix* (in Flem.) & *Die grosse Katharina* (in Ger., based on Shaw's *Great Catherine*); Sym.; pf. Conc.; chamber m.; songs, &c.

Liliencron, Rochus, von, Freiherr (b. Plön, Holstein, 8. XII. 1820; d. Coblenz, 5. III. 1912), Ger. theologian, philologist & mcolst. He was successively prof. at Kiel and Jena, later lived at Munich and afterwards became prelate of the St. John's foundation at Schleswig. His mus. writings incl. studies of old Ger. song, Lutheran church m. & 16th-cent. Ger. settings of Horace's odes.

Lilliburlero. A satirical song sung in Ir. after the appt. of General Talbot to the lord-lieutenancy in 1687. It is not likely that the attribution of the tune to Purcell is justified: it was prob. a popular melody merely arr. by him, much as *The Prince of Denmark's March* was arr. by J. Clarke as the *Trumpet Voluntary.*

Lily of Killarney, The, opera by Benedict (lib. by John Oxenford and Dion Boucicault, based on the latter's play, *The Colleen Bawn*), prod. London, Covent Garden Theatre, 8. II. 1862.

Lima, Bras Francisco de (b. Lisbon, *c.* 1745; d. Lisbon, 1813), Port. comp. Wrote orats., &c.

Lima, Jeronymo Francisco de (b. Lisbon, 30. IX. 1743; d. Lisbon, 19. II. 1822), Port. comp., brother of prec. He was elected to the Brotherhood of St. Cecilia, visited It., and in 1798 became cond. of the Royal Opera at Lisbon.

Works incl. opera *Le nozze d'Ercole e d'Ebe* and 5 others (all It.); church m.; cantatas, &c.

Lincke, Josef (b. Trachenberg, Prus. Silesia, 8. VI. 1783; d. Vienna, 26. III. 1837), Ger. cst. & comp. He settled in Vienna in 1808, becoming a member of Rasumovsky's quartet. He wrote concs., vars., &c. for the co.

Lincoln, Abraham (1809–65), Amer. statesman & president. *See* **Copland** (speeches), **Damrosch (W.), Goldmark (R.)** (address at Gettysburg).

Lind, Jenny (b. Stockholm, 6. X. 1820; d. Malvern, 2. XI. 1887), Swe. sop. singer. 1st appeared at Stockholm, 1838; studied with García in Paris; sang much in Ger.; went to Eng. in 1847 and settled in London permanently. Distinguished in opera in her early years, but afterwards mainly as concert singer. She made many extensive tours. Married Otto Goldschmidt in 1852. She was called ' The Swe. Nightingale.'

Linda di Chamounix, opera by Donizetti (lib. by Gaetano Rossi, after a vaudeville, *La Grâce de Dieu*), prod. Vienna, Kärntnertor Theatre, 19. V. 1842.

Lindberg, Oskar Fredrik (b. Gagnef, 23. II. 1887), Swe. orgst. & comp. Studied at the Stockholm Cons. and at Sondershausen. In 1914 he was app. orgst. at a Stockholm church and in 1919 prof. at the Cons.

Requiem & cantata for solo voices, chor. & orch.; Sym. in F maj.; *3 Pictures from Dalarne,* 3 ovts., symph. poems *Wilderness, Flor and Blancheflor* & *From the Great Forests,* suite *Travel Memories* for orch.; pf. pieces; songs with orch. & with pf., &c.

Lindblad, Adolf Fredrik (b. nr. Stockholm, 1. II. 1801; d. Linköping, 28. VIII. 1878), Swe. comp. and singing-teacher. Studied with Zelter in Berlin and in 1827 settled at Stockholm as teacher of singing. Jenny Lind was among his pupils.

Works incl. opera *Frondörerna*; Sym. in C maj.; Duo for v. & pf.; voc. duets, trios & 4tets; numerous songs. &c.

Lindblad, Otto Jonas (b. Karlstorp, 31. III. 1809; d. Ny Mellby, 26. I. 1864), Swe. comp. Learnt the org. while studying theology, which he afterwards abandoned in order to study m., mainly by himself, though he had a few lessons at Copenhagen. Having learnt the v. he joined a touring opera company, took part in a mus. festival at Hamburg in 1841 and founded a students' chor soc. at Lund.

Works incl. numerous chors., voc. 4tets, trios & duets, songs, &c.

Lindeman, Ludvig Mathias (b. Trondhjem, 28. XI. 1812; d. Christiania, 23. V. 1887), Norw. orgst. & comp. Studied theol. at first and m. afterwards. App. orgst. at Our Saviour's church at Christiania in 1840, teacher of singing at the Theol. Seminary in 1849 and estab. a m. school with his son Peter L. (b. 1858) in 1883. Collected Norw. folksongs and ed. a book of them, also a hymn-book.

Works incl. *Dream Chant* for chor.; hymn-tunes; org. fugues, &c.

Lindley, Robert (b. Rotherham, 4. III. 1776; d. London, 13. VI. 1855), Eng. cst. & comp. Learnt v. & cc. from his father, then studied the latter under Cervetto, played at the Brighton theatre, and in 1794–1851 was principal cst. at the Opera in London. He wrote concs. & other works for co.

Lindner, Friedrich (b. Liegnitz, Silesia, c. 1540; d. Nuremberg, 15. IX. 1597), Ger. comp. & ed. He was a choirboy in the electoral chapel at Dresden and later studied at Leipzig Univ., became musn. to the Margrave of Brandenburg and in 1574 cantor at St. Giles's church at Nuremberg. He ed. several books of It. church m. and madrigals, and comp. 2 Passions.

Lindpaintner, Peter Joseph von (b. Coblenz, 9. XII. 1791; d. Nonnenhorn, Lake of Constance, 21. VIII. 1856), Ger. cond. & comp. Studied at Augsburg and (?) with Winter at Munich, where in 1812 he became cond. at a minor theatre. In 1819 he went to Stuttgart as cond. of the royal orch. In 1853–4 he visited London to cond. the New Phil. Soc.'s concerts.

Works incl. operas *Der Bergkönig, Der Vampyr, Die Genueserin, Lichtenstein* & 24 others; ballet *Joko* & 2 others; incid. m. to Goethe's *Faust*; *Stabat Mater*, 6 masses; orats. *Abraham* & others; cantatas *The Widow of Nain*, Schiller's *Lied van der Glocke*; syms. & ovts.; concs.; chamber m.; over 50 songs, &c.

Lindsay, (Nicholas) Vachel (1879–1931), Amer. author. *See* **Gruenberg** (*Daniel Jazz*), **Kubik** (*In Praise of Johnny Appleseed*), **Palmer (R.)** (*Abraham Lincoln Walks at Night*).

Linear Counterpoint. A term for a new kind of ctpt. in 20th-cent. m. of certain schools. It aims, not in the 1st place at euphony in the collaboration of parts, but at satisfactory lines traced by each part individually, often apparently regardless of the way in which they clash, though of course this cannot be left altogether to chance. A principle usually followed in the writing of L. C. is that each part should be given to a medium of different tone-colour, so that they more easily strike the ear as separate strands in the fabric of sound.

Lingual Stops. *See* **Reed Stops.**

Linke, Joseph. *See* **Lincke.**

Linklater, Eric (b. 1899), Sco. novelist. *See* **Gerhard** (*Adventures of Don Quixote*).

Linko, Ernst (b. Tammerfors, 14. VII. 1889), Fin. comp. Studied at Helsinki Cons. and Stern's Cons. in Berlin, also in Paris & St. Petersburg. In 1915 he became prof. at and in 1936 dir. of the Helsinki Cons.

Works incl. 3 sonatinas & other works for pf.; songs, &c.

Linley. Eng. family of musns.:

1. Thomas L. (b. Badminton, 17. I. 1773; d. London, 19. XI. 1795), singing-master & comp. Studied with Thomas Chilcot, orgst. of Bath Abbey, and with Paradisi in London; settled at Bath as singing-teacher and concert promoter. From 1774 he managed the orats. at Drury Lane Theatre in London jointly with Stanley and from 1786 with Arnold. Sheridan having become his son-in-law in 1773, he and his son Thomas (3) wrote m. for S.'s play *The Duenna* in 1775. In 1776 he moved to London and bought Garrick's share in Drury Lane Theatre, where he managed the m. and wrote m. for var. pieces.

Works incl. opera *The Royal Merchant*; m. for Sheridan's *Duenna* & *School for Scandal* (the song 'Here 's to the maiden'), *Tom Jones* (after Fielding), *The Carnival of Venice, The Gentle Shepherd, Robinson Crusoe* (after Defoe), *The Triumph of Mirth, The Spanish Rivals, The Strangers at Home, Love in the East* & other plays; adaptations from Grétry: *Selima and Azor* & *Richard Cœur de Lion*; accomps. for *The Beggar's Opera*; m. for Sheridan's monody on the death of Garrick; 6 Elegies for 3 voices; 12 ballads; cantatas, madrigals, &c.

2. Elizabeth Ann L. (b. Bath, 5. IX. 1754; d. Bristol, 28. VI. 1792), sop. singer, daughter of prec. Pupil of her father. She sang at Bath as a child and 1st appeared in London and at the Worcester Festival in 1770. Married Sheridan on 13. IV. 1773, was painted by Reynolds as St. Cecilia and d. of consumption.

3. Thomas L. (b. Bath, 5. V. 1756; d. Grimsthorpe, Lincs., 5. VIII. 1778), vst. & comp., brother of prec. Studied with his father, appeared as a child prodigy and was sent to Boyce in London for further study and to Nardini at Florence, where he met Mozart, his exact contemp., in 1770. On his return to Eng. he led his father's concerts at Bath and London, in 1773 wrote an anthem for the Worcester Festival and in 1775 assisted his father in providing m. for his brother-in-law Sheridan's *Duenna*. He was drowned while boating on the Duke of Ancaster's estate.

Works incl. opera *The Cady of Bagdad*; incid. m. for Shakespeare's *Tempest* & Sheridan's *Duenna*, festival anthem *Let God arise*; orat. *The Song of Moses*; *Ode on the Witches and Fairies of Shakespeare*; madrigals, songs, &c.

4. Mary L. (b. Bath, 4. I. 1758; d. Clifton, Bristol, 27. VII. 1787), singer, sister of prec. Pupil of her father, sang at festivals, orats., &c., but retired on her marriage to Richard Tickell, commissioner of stamps & dramatist (wrote *The*

Carnival of Venice for his father-in-law & altered Ramsay's *Gentle Shepherd* for him).

5. Maria L. (b. Bath, autumn 1763; d. Bath, 5. IX. 1784), singer, sister of prec. Pupil of her father, sang at concerts & orats., but d. young, (?) of consumption.

6. Ozias Thurston L. (b. Bath, summer 1765; d. London, 6. III. 1831), clergyman & orgst., brother of prec. Pupil of his father, entered the church, but resigned on becoming fellow & orgst. at Dulwich Coll. in 1816.

7. William L. (b. Bath, II. 1771; d. London, 6. V. 1835), govt. official & comp., brother of prec. Pupil of his father and of Abel. He went to Madras in an official capacity in 1796 and again in 1800, but in between joined his brother-in-law Sheridan in the management of Drury Lane Theatre in London. Having held posts elsewhere in India, he returned in 1806 and settled in London as novelist, poet and comp.

Works incl. pantomimes & mus. comedies *Harlequin Captive*, *The Pavilion*, *The Honey Moon*, &c.; m. for W. H. Ireland's *Vortigern* (a Shakespeare forgery), songs for Shakespeare's plays, &c.

'Linz' Symphony. Mozart's Sym. in C maj., K. 425, comp. at the house of Count Thun at Linz, where M. and his wife stayed on their return from Salzburg to Vienna, X–XI. 1783, and where it was 1st perf. by the domestic orch. on 4. XI.

Lionel and Clarissa, opera by Dibdin (lib. by Isaac Bickerstaffe), prod. London, Covent Garden Theatre, 25. II. 1768.

Lipinski, Karl Joseph (b. Radzyn, 30. X. 1790; d. Orlow nr. Lwów, 16. XII. 1861), Pol. vst. & comp. Travelled much and became leader of the court orch. at Dresden, 1839. Ed. a collection of Galician folksongs with the poet Zalewski.

Works incl. opera *The Siren of the Dnieper*; *Polonaise guerrière* for orch.; 4 v. concs.; stg. Trio; v. pieces, &c.

Lipp, Maria Magdalena (b. ?; d. ?), Aus. 18th-cent. singer. Married Michael Haydn at Salzburg in 1768.

Lipsius, Marie. *See* **La Mara.**

Lira (It.). A generic name given to var. old bowed stg. insts., such as the Rebec and Crwth in earlier times and later, *c.* 16th & 17th cents., the viols with extra (sympathetic) stgs. vibrating in accord with those actually touched by the bow, e.g. *lira da braccio* and *lira da gamba*.

Lisinski, Vatroslav (b. Zagreb, 8. VII. 1819; d. Zagreb, 31. V. 1854), Yslv. comp. Studied at Zagreb and with Kittl in Prague. Although he comp. much, he lived in obscurity and d. in poverty, only his 1st opera having been perf., in 1846, at Zagreb in a half-amateurish way.

Works incl. operas *Love and Malice* & *Porin* (in Croatian); *Evening* for small orch., 7 orch. ovts.; numerous dances, chors., songs, &c.

Lisle, Charles Leconte de. *See* **Leconte de Lisle.**

Lisle, Rouget de. *See* **Rouget de Lisle.**

Lisley, John (b. ?; d. ?), Eng. 16th–17th-cent. comp. One of the contribs. to the madrigal coll. *The Triumphes of Oriana* of 1601, of whom nothing is otherwise known.

Lissenko, Nikolai Vitalievitch (b. Grinsky, Govt. Poltava, 22. III. 1842; d. Kiev, 6. XI. 1912), Rus. comp. Studied natural science, but while making researches in ethnog. he became interested in Ukrainian folksong, specimens of which he began to collect. He then studied at the Leipzig Cons. and with Rimsky-Korsakov at St. Petersburg. He settled at Kiev.

Works incl. operas *Taras Bulba* (after Gogol), *Sappho*, *The Aeneid* (after Virgil) & others; operettas; cantatas & other chor. works; *Ukrainian Rhapsody* for v. & pf.; pf. pieces; songs, settings of Ukrainian folksongs, &c.

Listov, Constantin (b. ?, 1900), Rus. comp. Although of poor parentage and without advantages, he showed mus. talent as a child and in 1914 was sent to the Tsaritsin (Stalingrad) Cons.; but left in 1917 to join the army, for which he wrote songs. Severely wounded, he was enabled by the army command to continue his mus. studies at Saratov, 1919–21.

Works incl. mus. comedies, m. for reviews, incid. m. for plays incl. Molière's *Bourgeois gentilhomme*; many army and battle songs, &c.

Liszt, Ferencz (more commonly Franz) (b. Raiding, Hung., 22. X. 1811; d. Bayreuth, 31. VII. 1886), Hung. pfst. & comp. His father, a steward of the Esterházy family's property, was Hung., his mother Aus. At the age of 9 he gave a concert at Sopron and in 1823 he had advanced so amazingly that his father took him to Vienna and Paris, where he had an immense success. In Vienna he studied briefly with Salieri and Czerny. In 1824–5 he paid 2 visits to Eng. and another in 1827. At 14 he came out as a comp. as well, prod. his opera *Don Sanche* in Paris. His father d. in 1827 and he was taken to Paris by his paternal grandmother, who looked after his educ. there. He remained there and after a period of religious mysticism under the influence of Lamennais and great successes as a pfst., he began a love affair with the Comtesse d'Agoult in 1833. They went to live at Geneva in 1835, where a daughter, Blandine, was b., followed by another, Cosima (later Wagner's 2nd wife) at Como in 1837. A son, Daniel, was b. in Rome, 1839. Not so much from ambition as to please the countess and provide for his children, he travelled widely as pfst. and made much money; but in 1840 he collected funds for the Beethoven memorial at Bonn, and he often played for charitable purposes organized on a large scale. In 1840–1 he paid further visits to Eng., playing before Queen Victoria, and in 1842–4 he toured in Rus., Turkey, Den., &c. After a break with the countess in the latter year, he went to Spa. and Port. in 1845; 2 years later, at Kiev, he met Princess Caroline Sayn-Wittgenstein, the wife of a wealthy Rus. landowner, who fell violently in love with him and in 1848 left with him for Weimar, where he was engaged as cond. and mus. dir. to the grand-ducal court for certain periods of the year. He prod. many new operas there, incl. Wagner's *Lohengrin* and Berlioz's *Béatrice et Bénédict*, and settled down to cultivate comp. of a var. of works, some on a very large scale, having previously confined himself almost exclusively to pf. m. The princess long tried unsuccessfully to obtain a divorce, but failed, even in 1861, when at last she was on the point of marrying L. in Rome, where both had retired after his resignation of the Weimar post in 1859. But he was perhaps secretly relieved, for after his 2 great and innumerable minor love affairs, he had once more turned to religion, and in 1865 was made a secular priest, being thereafter known as the Abbé L. Even after that, in 1869, when he took up residence at Weimar again for some part of the year, and had a great following of pf. pupils, spending the other months alternately at Rome and Budapest, where he was hon. dir. of the Cons., he became involved in some melodramatically romantic episodes with a girl of 19, Olga Janina. He taught and travelled much to the end of his life, which came in a way quite unsuited to his spectacular career. He had gone to the Wagner festival at Bayreuth, where he caught a chill, but his daughter Cosima was so busy attending to the prod. of her husband's works that she allowed her father's death to pass almost unnoticed.

Works incl. a vast number of pf. comps. incl. 3 vols. of *Années de pèlerinage*, 12 *Études d'exécution transcendante*, 2 *Légendes* (*Saint François d'Assise prédicant aux oiseaux* & *Saint François de Paule marchant sur les flots*), *Liebesträume* (3 nocturnes, orig. songs), So. in B min., 20 Hung. Rhapsodies; innumerable transcriptions for pf. incl. *c.* 50 operatic pieces and fantasies, *c.* 40 works by var. comps. (Beethoven's syms., Berlioz's *Symph. fantastique*, 6 Caprices by Paganini, 9 waltzes by Schubert [*Soirées de Vienne*], &c., *c.* 150 songs incl. many by Schubert); *Faust* and *Dante* syms.; 14 symph. poems for orch.; other orch. works incl. 2 Episodes from Lenau's *Faust*; 2 pf. concs., Hungarian Fantasy, *Malédiction*, *Totentanz* and Fantasy on Beethoven's *Ruins of Athens* for pf. & orch.; orats. *St. Elizabeth* & *Christus*; *Gran Mass* for solo voices, chor. & orch., Hung. Coronation Mass & 2 other masses, 3 Psalms and a number of other chor. works; 55 songs; 6 recitations with pf.; Fugue on B. A. C. H., fantasy and fugue on *Ad nos, ad salutarem undam* & a few other org. works, &c.

Lit. (abbr.). Literally.

Litaniae Lauretanae (Lat. = Litanies of Loreto). A litany sung in honour of the Virgin Mary in the Rom. church, dating prob. from the 13th cent. It has its own plainsong melody, but has also been set by comps., incl. Palestrina, Lassus and Mozart.

Literes, Antonio (b. ?; d. Madrid, after 1752), Spa. orgst., vst. & comp. Attached to the court as vst. and 2nd orgst. in the royal chapel at the time of his death. After the fire at the royal palace on 24. XII. 1734, he and Nebra were engaged to arrange the m. that had survived and to write new works as required by the services.

Works incl. operas *Jupiter y Danae*, *Accis y Galatea*, *Los elementos*, *Dido y Eneas*; zarzuela *Coronis*; orat. *San Vicente*; vesper psalms, hymns & other church m., &c.

Lithuanian Composers. *See* **Baltic Composers.**

Litinsky, Heinrich (b. Lipovets, Ukraine, 17. III. 1901), Rus. comp. Studied with Glière at the Moscow Cons.

Works incl. 2 syms.; pf. Conc., v. Conc.; 5 stg. 4tets; unaccomp. sos. for v., va. & co., &c.

Litolff, Henry (Charles) (b. London, 6. II. 1818; d. Bois-les-Combes nr. Paris, 6. VIII. 1891), Anglo-Alsat. comp., pfst. & m. pub. His father was Alsat., his mother Eng. As a boy of 13 he became a pupil of Moscheles for pf., made his 1st appearance in 1732 and at 17 left for Fr., having married against his parents' wish. He travelled widely as concert pfst. until 1851, when he acquired a m. pub. business at Brunswick, marrying as his 2nd wife the widow of the former owner. But he soon left his adopted son Theodor L. in charge and settled in Paris, where later he married again, a Comtesse de la Rochefoucauld. He prod. his best opera at Brussels in 1886.

Works incl. opera *Les Templiers* & several others; orat. *Ruth and Boaz*; pf. concs., v. Conc.; ovt. *Robespierre* & others; chamber m.; pf. works, &c.

' Little - Russian ' Symphony. Tchaikovsky's 2nd Sym., in C min., Op. 17, also called ' Ukrainian ' Sym., comp. VI.–X. 1872, prod. Moscow, 18. I. 1873.

Liturgical Music-Drama. *See* **Sepulchre Music.**

Lituus (Lat.). The Rom. forerunner of the tpt.

Litvinne, Felia (real name Litvinova) (b. St. Petersburg, 1861; d. Paris, 12. X. 1936), Rus. sop. singer. Studied with Maurel and others in Paris and made her 1st appearance there in 1880.

Liuto (It.) = Lute.

Liuzzi, Fernando (b. Senigallia, 19. XII. 1884; d. Florence, 6. X. 1940), It. mcolst. & comp. Studied with Fano and later with Reger and Mottl at Munich. He became prof. of harmony at the Conss. of Parma and of Florence successively, also prof. of mus. hist. at Rome Univ. He ed. old It. *laudi*, arranged perfs. of Vecchi's *Amfiparnaso* and of Sophocles' *Oedipus Rex* with A. Gabrieli's m., wrote books on the *laude*, on It. musns. in Fr. & a vol. of critical studies *Estetica della musica*, also numerous learned articles.

Works incl. puppet opera *L'augellin bel verde* (after Gozzi); incid. m. to Pirandello's *Scamandro*; orats. *La Passione, Laudi Francescane* & *Le vergini savie e le vergini folli*; Neapol. impression *Giaola e Marecchiaro* for orch.; v. & pf. So. & 2 pieces; org. m.; 5 sets of songs, incl. It., Gr. & Serbian folksongs, &c.

Livietta e Tracollo, intermezzi by Pergolesi (lib. by Tommaso Mariani), prod. Naples, Teatro San Bartolommeo, between the acts of Pergolesi's serious opera *Adriano in Siria*, 25. X. 1734.

Livonian Composers. *See* **Baltic Composers.**

Lizard. *See* **Lyzarden.**

Lloyd, Charles Harford (b. Thornbury, Glos., 16. X. 1849; d. Slough, 16. X. 1919), Eng. orgst. & comp. Educ. at Oxford; Mus.D. there in 1892. App. orgst. at Gloucester cath., 1876, and Christ Church, Oxford, 1882; precentor at Eton Coll., 1892–1914, then orgst. at Chapel Royal, London.

Works incl. services & anthems; motet *The Souls of the Righteous*; cantatas *Hero and Leander, Song of Balder, Andromeda, The Longbeards' Saga, A Song of Judgment, Sir Ogie and Lady Elsie*; incid. m. to Euripides' *Alcestis*; So., Conc. & other works for org.; madrigals & partsongs, &c.

Lloyd, Edward (b. London, 7. III. 1845; d. Worthing, 31. III. 1927), Eng. ten. singer. Choir-boy at Westminster Abbey in London until 1860 and Gentlemen of the Chapel Royal from 1869. 1st important public appearance at Gloucester Festival, 1871.

Lloyd, George (b. St. Ives, Cornwall, 28. VI. 1913), Eng. comp. Studied v. with Albert Sammons and comp. with Harry Farjeon, then briefly attended the Trinity Coll. of M. in London. His father wrote the libs. for his 2 operas, the 1st of which was prod. at Penzance in 1934 and the 2nd in London in 1938.

Works incl. operas *Iernin* & *The Serf*; 3 syms., &c.

Lloyd, Ll(ewlyn). S(outhworth). (b. Cheadle Hulme, Ches., 20. IV. 1876), Brit. physicist & writer on acoustics. Educ. at King William's Coll., Isle of Man, and Christ's Coll., Cambridge. He became an inspector of schools and later asst. sec. to the Dept. of Scientific and Industrial Research. He has written articles on acoustics, esp. intonation, for scientific and mus. periodicals and pub. books *The Mus. Ear, M. and Sound*, &c.

Lloyd, Robert (1733–64), Eng. poet & dramatist. *See* **Giordani, (T. G.)** (*Capricious Lovers*), **Stanley** (*Arcadia & Tears and Triumphs of Parnassus*).

Lobe, Johann Christian (b. Weimar, 30. V. 1797; d. Leipzig, 27. VII. 1881), Ger. flst., comp. & writer on m. Studied at the expense of the Grand Duchess of Weimar, Maria Pavlovna, appeared as fl. soloist at Leipzig in 1811, and then joined the court orch. at Weimar, where his 5 operas were prod. He left in 1842 and 4 years later became ed. of the *Allgemeine Musik-Zeitung* at Leipzig; he also pub. several books on m.

Works incl. operas *Wittekind, Die Flibustier, Die Fürstin von Granada, Der rote Domino* & *König und Pächter*; 2 syms., ovts.; pf. 4tets, &c.

Lobgesang. *See* **Hymn of Praise.**

Lobo (also called **Lopez** or **Lupus**), **Duarte** (b. ?, 1540; d. ? Lisbon, 1643), Port. comp. Studied under Mendes at Evora and later became choirmaster there. Afterwards he went to Lisbon with an appt. to the Royal Hosp. and became chapel master at the cath. *c.* 1590. Living to the age of 103, he disappears from hist. long before his death.

Works incl. masses, offices for the dead, canticles, motets & much other church m.

Locatelli, Pietro (b. Bergamo, 3. IX. 1693; d. Amsterdam, 1. IV. 1764), It. vst. & comp. Pupil of Corelli in Rome. Travelled widely as a virtuoso and settled down at Amsterdam, where he estab. public concerts.

Works incl. concs., sos., studies, caprices, &c. for v.

Locke (or Lock), Matthew (b. Exeter, *c.* 1630; d. London, VIII. 1677), Eng. comp. He learnt m. as a choir-boy at Exeter cath. under Edward Gibbons, and (?) was afterwards a pupil of Wm. Wake there. He went to London *c.* 1650, and in 1653 collab. in Shirley's masque *Cupid and Death* perf. before the Port. ambassador. In 1656 Wake, who had become a Gentleman of the Chapel Royal, asked him to write the *Little Consort* for viols in 3 parts for his pupils and the same year he was one of the comps. who took part in the setting of Davenant's *Siege of Rhodes*. For Charles II's coronation in 1661 he wrote inst. m. for the procession and was app. Comp. in Ordinary to the King. In 1663, having turned Rom. catholic, he became orgst. to Queen Catherine. He was a vigorous and acrimonious defender of 'modern m.,' writing in 1666 a pamphlet defending his church m. and in 1672 opening a controversy with Thomas Salmon. Purcell wrote an Elegy on his death.

Works incl. operas, Davenant's *The Siege of Rhodes* (with Colman, Cooke, Hudson & H. Lawes), *Psyche* (with G. B. Draghi); masque, Shirley's *Cupid & Death* (with C. Gibbons); incid. m. to Stapylton's *The Stepmother*, (?) Shakespeare's *Macbeth* altered by Davenant and containing material from Middleton's *The Witch*, and for Shadwell's version of Shakespeare's *Tempest*, song in Durfey's *The Fool turned Critic*; Kyrie, Credo, anthems, Lat. hymns; consorts for viols in 3 and 4 parts (the latter in 6 suites); songs in 3 parts, duets; airs and songs for 1 voice with accomp., &c.

Lockey, Charles (b. Thatcham nr. Newbury, 23. III. 1820; d. Hastings, 3. XII. 1901), Eng. ten. singer. Made his 1st important appearance in the prod. of Mendelssohn's *Elijah* at Birmingham Festival, 1846.

Lockspeiser, Edward (b. London, 21. V. 1905), Eng. critic. Studied with Nadia Boulanger in Paris and at the R.C.M. in London. Author of a book on Debussy and trans. of Prunières's hist.

Loco (It. = place, sometimes *al loco* = to the place). A direction indicating that a passage is to be played in the normal position indicated by the written notes, often given for greater safety after a passage shown to be played an 8ve higher or lower.

Locrian Mode. The ecclesiastical mode theoretically covering the octave B to B on a keyboard, but rejected in mus. practice.

Loder, Edward (James) (b. Bath, 1813; d. London, 5. IV. 1865), Eng. comp. He 1st learnt m. from his father, John David L. (1788–1846), a vst. & m. pub., and in 1826–8 studied with F. Ries at Frankfort o/M. After a 2nd period of study there he settled in London and was induced by Arnold to set an opera, *Nourjahad*, for the New Eng. Opera House, under which name the Lyceum Theatre opened with it in 1834. He was theatre cond. in London and later at Manchester, but about 1856 began to suffer from a disease of the brain.

Works incl. operas & plays with m. *Nourjahad*, *The Dice of Death*, *Francis I* (a concoction from his songs), *The Foresters*, *The Deerstalker*, *The Night Dancers*, *Robin Goodfellow*, *The Sultana*, *The Young Guard*, *Raymond and Agnes*, &c.; masque *The Island of Calypso*; stg. 4tets; numerous songs, incl. *12 Sacred Songs*, *The Diver*, *The Brave old Oak*, *Invocation to the Deep* & *The Brooklet* (a trans. of Wilhelm Müller's *Wohin* set by Schubert in *The Fair Maid of the Mill*).

Loder, Kate (Fanny) (b. Bath, 21. VIII. 1825; d. Headley, Surrey, 30. VIII. 1904), Eng. pfst. & comp. Studied at the R.A.M. in London, where she became prof. of harmony later; made her 1st appearance in 1844, playing Mendelssohn in his presence; married the surgeon Henry Thompson in 1851; gave the 1st perf. of Brahms's Requiem at her house in 1871, playing with Potter an arr. for 2 pfs. made by herself.

Works incl. opera *L'elisir d'amore*, &c.

Lodizhensky, Nikolai Nikolaievitch (b. St. Petersburg, 1. I. 1843; d. St. Petersburg, 15. II. 1916), Rus. comp. Studied for a diplomatic career, but comp. as an amateur and about 1866 joined the Balakirev circle. He went to the Balkans and later to N.Y. in the diplomatic service, but returned to Rus. in 1907.

Works incl. opera *Dimitri the Usurper*; cantata *Russalka*; several syms. (all unfinished); 6 songs, &c.

Lodoïska, opera by Cherubini (lib. by Claude François Fillette-Loraux), prod. Paris, Théâtre Feydeau, 18. VII. 1791

Opera by R. Kreutzer (lib. by Jean Claude Bédéno Dejaure), prod. Paris, Comédie-Italienne, 1. VIII. 1791.

Lodoiska, opera by Mayr (lib. by Francesco Gonella), prod. Venice, Teatro La Fenice, 26. I 1796.

Loeffler, Charles Martin (b. Mulhouse, 30. I. 1861; d. Medfield, Mass., 19. V. 1935), Alsat.-Amer. comp. Before Alsace was lost to Fr. in the 1870–1 war, L., whose father was an agricultural chemist and an author who wrote under the name of ' Tornow,' was taken to Smela nr. Kiev, and it was there that he was 1st given v. lessons. The family later moved to Debreczin in Hung. and about 1873 to Swi. There he decided to become a vst. and went to Berlin to study with Rappoldi, Kiel, Bargiel and lastly Joachim. Later he had a period of study with Massart and Guiraud in Paris, joined the Pasdeloup Orch. and that of a wealthy amateur, where he remained until 1881. That year he went to U.S.A., played in Damrosch's orch., in 4tets and with touring opera companies. In 1882 he joined the Boston Sym. Orch., where he remained, sharing the 1st desk with the leader, until 1903. In 1887 he became a naturalized Amer.

Works incl. psalm *By the waters of Babylon* for women's voices & insts., *Beat! Beat! Drums!* (from Whitman's *Drum Taps*) for male voices & orch., *Evocation* for women's voices & orch., *For one who fell in battle* for unaccomp. chor.; dramatic poem for orch. & va. d'amore *La Mort de Tintagiles* (after Maeterlinck), fantasy for orch. & org. *La Villanelle du Diable, A Pagan Poem* (after Virgil) for orch. with pf., Eng. hn. & 3 tpts., *Poem* & *Memories of my Childhood* for orch.; *Canticum Fratris Solis* (St. Francis) & 5 Ir. Fantasies for voice & orch.; 2 Rhapsodies for ob., va. & pf., 5tet for 3 v., va. & co., M. for stg. 4tet; Partita for v. & pf., v. studies; 4 songs with va. & pf.; 3 sets of songs, incl. *The Wind among the Reeds* (Yeats), &c.

Loeffler-Tornov. A pseud. used by C. M. Loeffler for his earliest, now discarded works, derived from the pseud. ' Tornow ' used by his father as an author.

Lœillet, Jean-Baptiste (b. Ghent, 18. XI. 1680; d. London, 19. VII. 1730), Flem. flst., obst. & comp. He made an early success as a perf., went to Paris in 1702 and to London in 1705, where he joined the orch. of the King's Theatre in the Haymarket. Later he was at one time chamber musn. to the elector of Bavaria at Munich, but he returned to London some time after 1825.

Works incl. sos. for 1, 2 and 3 fls., for ob. or v., &c.

Loeschhorn, Albert (b. Berlin, 27. VI. 1819; d. Berlin, 4. VI. 1905), Ger. pfst., teacher & comp. Studied in Berlin, where he taught from 1851 and became prof. in 1858.

Works incl. 4tets; sos. & esp. studies & other instructive works for pf., &c.

Loewe, Ferdinand (b. Vienna, 19. II. 1865; d. Vienna, 6. I. 1925), Aus. cond. Studied at the Vienna Cons. and taught there, 1883–96. In 1897 he became cond. of the Kaim Orch. at Munich and in 1898–1900 was dir. of the Vienna Opera. Later he was a concert cond. in Vienna, Munich, Budapest & Berlin.

Loewe, Johann Jakob (b. Vienna, 1628; d. Lüneburg, IX. 1703), Ger. orgst. & comp. Pupil of Schütz at Dresden; held appts. at Brunswick from 1655 and Zeitz from 1663, became orgst. of St. Nicholas's church at Lüneburg in 1682.

Works incl. operas *Amelinde, Andromeda* & *Orpheus aus Thracien*; ballets; syms., &c.

Loewe, Johanna Sophie (b. Oldenburg, 24. III. 1816; d. Pest, 28. XI. 1866), Ger. sop. singer. Began her career in Vienna and Berlin, later sang in It.

Loewe, (Johann) Karl (Gottfried) (b. Loebejuen nr. Halle, 30. XI. 1796; d. Kiel, 20. IV. 1869), Ger. comp. He was 1st taught m. by his father, but at the age of 10 became a choirboy at Cöthen, and in 1809 went to the grammar-school at Halle. There was a good choir there, which was heard by Mme de Staël and Jérôme Bonaparte, then king of Westphalia, and the latter gave L. an annuity at the headmaster's suggestion. He devoted himself to comp., to further mus. studies, to the learning of Fr. and It. and later, at Halle Univ., the study of theol. The flight of Jérôme in 1813 deprived him of his income, but he managed to make a living and in 1820 became prof. and cantor at Stettin, and in 1821 mus. dir. and orgst. In later years, when his songs had begun to be popular, he travelled much, going as far as Vienna in 1844 and London in 1847, where he appeared at court. He visited Swe. and Norw. in 1851 and Fr. in 1857. In 1864 he suffered from a 6 weeks' trance and was asked to resign in 1866, when he went to live at Kiel. He d. there after a similar attack.

Works incl. opera *Die drei Wünsche* & 4 others; orats. *Die Zerstörung Jerusalems, Palestrina, Hiob, Die Auferweckung des Lazarus* & 12 others; syms.; concs.; pf. solos and duets; numerous songs & ballads, incl. Goethe's *Erlkönig*, Herder's Ger. versions of *Edward, Archibald Douglas, Tom the Rhymer*, &c.

Loewenberg, Alfred (b. Berlin, 14. V. 1902), Ger. mcolst. Studied at Jena Univ. and graduated D.Phil. there in 1925. The Nazi régime drove him from Ger. in 1934, and he settled in London, where he compiled, in Eng., *Annals of Opera*, containing details of *c.* 4,000 operas in chronol. order.

Loewenstern (orig. **Loewe**), **Matthaeus (Apelles)** (b. Neustadt, Silesia, 20. IV. 1594; d. Bernstadt nr. Breslau, 16. IV. 1648), Ger. poet & comp. Studied (?) at the Univ. of Frankfort o/O. Having been schoolmaster and cantor at Neustadt and Leobschütz, the 30 Years War obliged him to move, and he went into the service of the Duke of Oels-Bernstadt.

Works incl. chors. for Opitz's tragedy *Judith*; Lat. & Ger. motets; sacred concs.; book of 30 sacred songs to words of his own entitled *Frühlings-Mayen*, &c.

Logier, Johann Bernhard (b. Cassel, 9. II. 1777; d. Dublin, 27. VII. 1846), Ger. musn. of Fr. descent. Pupil of his father. He settled in Eng. as a boy after his parents' death and soon went to Ir., settling finally at Dublin in 1809 as bandmaster and m. dealer. He invented the Chiroplast, an appliance used in learning the pf., spent 3 years in Berlin, returned to Dublin, and comp. and arr. pf. m. In 1809 he prod. an ode on the 50th year of George III's reign.

Logroscino, Nicola (b. Bitonto, 1698; d. Palermo, after 1765), It. comp. Studied with Durante at Naples. In 1738 he appeared as collab. in the opera *Demetrio* with Leo and others and prod. his 1st comic opera at the Teatro dei Fiorentini there. About 1747 he went to Palermo to teach ctpt. at the Cons.

Works incl. operas *L'inganno per inganno, L'inganno felice, La ciommettella correvata, Il governadore, Giunio Bruto, Il Leandro, Le zite, Don Paduano, La Griselda, Le finte magie* & many others (lost) as well as operas shared with other comps.; 2 *Stabat Mater*, psalms & other church m., &c.

Lohengrin, opera by Wagner (lib. by comp.), prod. Weimar, Court Theatre, by Liszt, 28. VIII. 1850.

Lohet, Simon (b. ?; d. ? Stuttgart, VII. 1611), Ger. orgst. & comp. App. orgst. to the court of Württemberg at Stuttgart in 1571.

Works incl. pieces in fugal style, canzoni & hymn-tune fantasies for org., &c.

Lolli, Antonio (b. Bergamo, *c.* 1730; d. Palermo, 10. VIII. 1802), It. vst. & comp. Prob. almost wholly self-taught on the v. He was at the court of Württemberg at Stuttgart with Nardini in 1762 and remained till 1773, when he went to St. Petersburg, where he remained in Catherine II's service till 1779. Later he lived by turns in Paris, London, Vienna and Naples. He seems to have written only the v. parts of his concs. and sos.

Lombardi alla prima crociata, I (*The Lombards at the First Crusade*), opera by Verdi (lib. by Temistocle Solera, founded on a romance by Tommaso Grassi), prod. Milan, Teatro alla Scala, 11. II. 1843.

Lombardini, Maddalena. *See* **Sirmen.**

London Philharmonic Orchestra. Founded in 1931 by Sir Thomas Beecham and assoc. with the Royal Phil. Soc. for its concerts in London, also with the Covent Garden Opera. During the 2nd world war it became a self-governing company.

London Symphony. Haydn's Sym. No. 104, in D min. & maj. (No. 7 of the 'Salomon' syms.), written in 1795. Actually all the 12 syms. comp. for Salomon's concerts are 'London syms.,' for they were all perf. there.

London Symphony, A. The 2nd Sym. by Vaughan Williams, prod. London, 27. III. 1914; revised version, London, Queen's Hall, 4. V. 1920.

London Symphony Orchestra. Founded in 1904 from the bulk of players of the 1st Queen's Hall Orch., which left Henry J. Wood, who insisted on abolishing the system of sending deputies to rehearsals and concerts.

Long. The name of a note-value in the old mensural notation, where it was shorter than the 'Large' but longer than the 'Breve,' the value of which it could either double or treble, according to the time-signature.

Long, John Luther (1861–1927), Amer. novelist. *See* **Madama Butterfly** (Puccini).

Longfellow, Henry Wadsworth (1807–82), Amer. poet. *See* **Black Knight** (Elgar), **Boughton** (*Skeleton in Armour*), **Buck (D.)** (*Golden Legend*), **Cellier** (*Masque of Pandora*), **Coerne** (*Hiawatha*), **Coleridge-Taylor** (do. & *Chor. Ballads*), **Foote** (*Hiawatha. Wreck of the Hesperus* & *Skeleton in Armour*), **Golden Legend** (Sullivan), **Goldmark (R.)** (*Hiawatha*), **Hiawatha** (Coleridge-Taylor), **Holbrooke**

(*Skelcton in A.*), **Kaun** (*Hiawatha*), **King Olaf** (Elgar), **Lahee** (*Building of the Ship*), **MacCunn** (*Wreck of the H.*).

Longo, Alessandro (b. Amantea, 30. XII. 1864), It. pfst. & ed. He became prof. of pf. at the Naples Cons., but later moved to Bologna, where he founded the Cercolo Scarlatti and the Società del Quartetto. He ed. the journal *L'arte pianistica* and has brought out eds. of old It. keyboard m., incl. the complete sos. of D. Scarlatti.

Longus (5th cent.), Gr. author. *See* **Cythère assiégée (Gluck).**

Loosemore, George (b. Cambridge, ?; d. ? Cambridge, ? 1682), Eng. orgst. & comp. Studied under his father, Henry L. as a chorister at King's Coll. chapel, Cambridge, and in 1660 became orgst. of Trinity Coll. there.

Works incl. anthems, &c.

Loosemore, Henry (b. ?; d. Cambridge, 1670), Eng. orgst. & comp., father of prec. He learnt m. as a choir-boy at Cambridge and became orgst. of King's Coll. chapel there in 1627.

Works incl. Service in D min., anthems, 2 Lat. litanies; a piece for 3 viols & org., &c.

Lopatnikov, Nikolai Lvovitch (b. Reval, 16. III. 1903), Estonian-Rus. pfst. & comp. Studied at the St. Petersburg Cons., left for Fin. during the 1917 Revol. and in 1920 settled in Ger., studying pf. with Willi Rehberg and comp. with Toch in Berlin. In 1933 he returned to Fin. and sought the advice of Sibelius. Settled in U.S.A.

Works incl. opera *Danton* (after Rolland's play); 2 syms., Vars. Concertino & *Introd. and Scherzo* for orch.; 2 pf. concs., v. Conc.; 2 stg. 4tets; v. & pf. So. (with side-drum *ad lib.*), 3 pieces for v. & pf.; co. So., &c.

Lope de Vega. *See* **Vega.**

López de Velasco, Sebastián (b. Segovia, ?; d. ? Madrid, after 1628), Spa. comp. He may have been a pupil of Victoria, whose post as chapel master he was given later by the Infanta Juana at the convent of the Descalzas Reales in Madrid.

Works incl. masses, motets, psalms, magnificats & other church m.

Lopez, Duarte. *See* **Lobo.**

Loreley. *See also* **Lurline.**

Opera by Bruch (lib. by Emanuel Geibel, orig. written for Mendelssohn), prod. Mannheim, 14. VI. 1863.

Unfinished opera by Mendelssohn (lib. by Emanuel Geibel). Only the 1st-act finale, an *Ave Maria* and a chor. of vintners exist.

Lorenz, Alfred (Ottokar) (b. Vienna, 11. VII. 1868; d. Munich, 20. XI. 1939), Aus. cond. & writer on m. After var. other appts. he became cond. at Coburg-Gotha in 1898; but he retired, took a degree in 1922, became lecturer at Munich Univ., 1923, and prof., 1926. He ed. Wagner's literary works and Weber's early operas, and wrote several books on the form of Wagner's m.-dramas, on the hist. of western m. and on A. Scarlatti's early operas.

Lorenzani, Paolo (b. Rome, 1640; d. Rome, 28. X. 1713), It. comp. Pupil of Benevoli in Rome, whom, after serving as chapel master elsewhere (? Turin), he wished to succeed as chapel master of the Vatican in 1672. The post was given to Bernabei in preference, but L. was app. to a similar one at the Jesuit Coll. In 1675 he went to Sicily and became chapel master at the cath. of Messina. In 1678 the Fr. viceroy, Marshal de Vivonne, induced him to go to Paris, and his sister, Mme. de Montespan, exerted her influence on his behalf with Louis XIV. In 1679 he bought from Boësset one of the posts of m.-master to the queen. After a visit to It. to engage singers, he became very successful as a comp. at court and was upheld by the *Mercure de France* against Lully; but the queen's death in 1683 deprived him of his court appt. and he sought refuge as chapel master at the Theatine monastery, where his motets were very successful, but did not reach the court. He never again had access there even after Lully's death in 1687, but was able to prod. his Fr. opera *Orontée* at Chantilly by order of the Prince de Condé. More and more unsuccessful, he again tried for the post of chapel master to the Vatican, which he succeeded in obtaining in 1694, when he returned to Rome.

Works incl. operas *Nicandro e Fileno* & *Orontée*; motets and magnificats; cantatas; It. & Fr. airs, &c.

Loris, Heinrich. *See* **Glareanus.**

Lortzing, (Gustav) Albert (b. Berlin, 23. X. 1801; d. Berlin, 21. I. 1851), Ger. cond., singer, comp. & libst. He had some lessons with Rungenhagen in Berlin as a child, but his parents being wandering actors, he had to obtain his general and mus. educ. as best he could. He learnt the pf., v. & co. and studied such theoret. works as he could pick up. He married in 1823 and found it very difficult to make a living in a travelling opera co. But in 1828 that co. prod. his 1st stage work, *Ali Pascha von Janina*, at Münster and repeated it at Cologne, Detmold and Osnabrück. In 1833–4 he was able to lead a more settled life, being engaged as 1st ten. at the Leipzig munic. theatre. The 1st 2 comic operas he wrote there were very successful, and so was his adapt. from Kotzebue, *Der Wildschütz*, in 1842, when he gave up acting. 2 short terms as cond. at Leipzig and Vienna were unsuccessful. He had a large family by this time and fell upon more and more difficult times. The cond.-ship at a suburban theatre in Berlin in 1850 merely humiliated him without doing much to relieve the situation.

Works incl. operas *Die beiden Schützen*, *Zar und Zimmermann*, *Hans Sachs*, *Casanova*, *Der Wildschütz*, *Undine* (after de la Motte Fouqué), *Der Waffenschmied*, *Zum Grossadmiral*, *Rolandsknappen*, *Regina* & others; operettas *Ali Pascha von Janina*, *Die Opernprobe, oder Die vornehmen Dilettanten*; orat. *Die Himmelfahrt Christi*; incid. m. for plays incl. Goethe's *Faust*, Grabbe's *Don Juan und Faust*, Scribe's *Yelva*; plays with m. *Der Pole und sein Kind*, *Der Weihnachtsabend*, *Szenen aus Mozarts Leben* (with m. adapted from Mozart); partsongs, songs, &c.

Lotario, opera by Handel (lib. by ?, based on Antonio Salvi's *Adelaide*, not, as Burney says, on Matteo Noris's *Berengario*), prod. London, King's Theatre, Haymarket, 2. XII. 1729.

Lothar, Mark (b. Berlin, 23. V. 1902), Ger. comp.

Works incl. operas *Tyll*, *Lord Spleen* (after Ben Jonson's *Epicoene*), *Münchhausen* & *Schneider Wibbel*; incid. m. for Eichendorff's *Der Freier* & other plays; *Narrenmesse* for male chor.; *Orchesterstücke* & Suite for orch.; Serenade for chamber orch.; pf. Trio; pf. pieces; songs, &c.

Loti, Pierre (Julien Viaud) (1850–1923), Fr. novelist. *See* **Lambert (L.)** (*Spahi*), **Messager** (*Mme Chrysanthème*), **Préludes** (Debussy, II. 7), **Ropartz** (*Pêcheur d'Islande*), **Taylor (D.)** (Ramuntcho).

Lottchen am Hofe (*Lottie at Court*), opera by J. A. Hiller (lib. by Christian Felix Weisse, after Goldoni and Charles Simon Favart), prod. Leipzig, 24. IV. 1767.

Lotti, Antonio (b. ? Venice, *c.* 1667; d. Venice, 5. I. 1740), It. comp. Studied (?) under his father, chapel master to the court of Hanover, where he may possibly have been b.; but he spent at least some of his boyhood at Venice, where he prod. his 1st opera at the age of 16 and studied under Legrenzi. He entered the doge's chapel, where he became successively singer and orgst. In 1692 he was app. 2nd orgst. at St. Mark's, and became 1st orgst. in 1704, remaining till his death. After competing first with Pollarolo and Porpora and then with the former and Porta, he obtained in 1737 the post of chapel master in addition. In 1717–9, with his wife, the singer Santa Stella, he was at the Saxon court at Dresden, where he prod. 3 operas. He also wrote the opera *Costantino* and 2 orats. for Vienna, Fux writing the ovt. for the former.

Works incl. operas *Giove in Argo*, *Alessandro severo*, *Teofane*, *Costantino*, *Gl' odi delusi del sangue*, *Sidonio*, *Polidoro* & *c.* 20 others; masses, Requiem, Miserere, motets & other church m.; orats. *Il voto crudele*, *L'umilità coronata*, *Gioa, rè di Giuda*, *Giuditta*; madrigals & cantatas, &c.

Loud Pedal. The popular but misleading name for the Sustaining Pedal of the pf.

Louis Ferdinand of Prussia, Prince (b. Friedrichsfelde nr. Berlin, 18. XI. 1772; d. Saalfeld, 13. X. 1806), Ger. amateur comp. Studied under var. masters, was heard and praised by Beethoven in Berlin, 1796, visited It. in 1804, again met Beethoven in Vienna, who ded. the C min. pf. Conc. to him, and during the last years of his life made an intimate friend of Dussek, from whom he learnt much in comp. He fell in the battle of Saalfeld.

Works incl. Rondo for pf. & orch.; 4 pf. trios, 2 pf. 4tets, 2 pf. 5tets, 8tet for pf., cl., 2 hns. & stgs. & other chamber m.; Rondo, Fugue & other works for pf., &c.

Louise, opera by G. Charpentier (lib. by comp.), prod. Paris, Opéra-Comique, 2. II. 1900.

Loure (Fr.). Orig. a special type of bagpipe, found esp. in Normandy, but later the name of a dance in fairly slow 6–8 time.

Louré (Fr.). Adj. der. from above, used as a direction to play in the manner of bagpipe m.

Lourer (Fr.). Verb der. from above, indicating a *legato* style of playing with a slight accent or *sostenuto* effect on the 1st note of each phrase.

Lourié, Arthur (Vincent) (b. St. Petersburg, 14. V. 1892), Rus. comp. of Fr. descent. Studied for a short time at the St. Petersburg Cons., but was self-taught later. App. dir. of the m. section of the Ministry of Public Instruction in 1918, but left in 1921 and settled in Fr.

Works incl. opera *A Feast in Time of Plague* (after Pushkin); ballet *Le Masque de neige* & others; *Symphonie dialectique* for orch.; *Sonate liturgique* for orch., pf. & chor.; *Ave Maria*, *Salve Regina* & other church m.; *Regina coeli* for con., ob. & tpt., *Improperium* for bar., 4 v. & db.; *Canzona di Dante* for chor. & stgs.;

Japanese Suite for voice & orch.; 3 stg. 4tets; So. for v. & db.; 3 pf. sonatinas; song-cycles *Elysium* (Pushkin) & *Alphabet* (A. Tolstoy), &c.

Louÿs, Pierre (1870–1925), Fr. novelist & poet. *See* **Conchita** (Zandonai), **Dandelot** (*Bilitis*), **Debussy** (do.), **Dupuis (A.)** (do.), **Maciejewski** (do.).

Love in a Village, opera by Arne (lib. by Isaac Bickerstaffe), prod. London, Covent Garden Theatre, 8. XII. 1762. Partly a ballad opera & pasticcio, A. having introd. popular songs & airs by Handel, Galuppi, Geminiani & others.

Love of Three Kings (Montemezzi). *See* **Amore di tre re.**

Love of Three Oranges, The (*Liubov k trem Apelsinam*), opera by Prokofiev (lib. by comp., based on Gozzi's comedy *Fiaba dell' amore delle tre melarancie*), prod., in Fr. trans., Chicago, Auditorium, 30. XII. 1921. The March from it has become one of the most popular modern pf. pieces.

Lowe, Edward (b. Salisbury, *c.* 1610; d. Oxford, 11. VII. 1682), Eng. orgst. & comp. Boy chorister at Salisbury cath.; became orgst. of Christ Church, Oxford, about 1630. App. one of the orgsts. at the Chapel Royal in London, 1660. Wrote on the perf. of cath. m. and comp. anthems.

Lowe, Thomas (b. ?; d. London, 1. III. 1783), Eng. ten. singer. Made his 1st stage appearance at Drury Lane Theatre, London, in 1740.

Lualdi, Adriano (b. Larino, 22. III. 1887), It. comp. & m. critic. Studied with Wolf-Ferrari at Venice, became critic to the *Secolo* at Milan and in 1936 to the *Giornale d'Italia* in Rome. Later he became dir. of the Naples Cons.

Works incl. operas *Le nozze di Haura, La figlia del rè, Le furie di Arlecchino, Il diavolo nel campanile* (after Poe), *La Granceola*; ballet *Lumawig e la Saetia*; choral pieces; *La leggenda del vecchio marinaio, Suite adriatica*, colonial rhapsody *Africa*, 3 folk-tunes *Samnium* for orch.; *Sire Halewyn* for sop. & orch., *La rosa di Saron* for ten. & orch.; stg. 4tet in E maj.; v. & pf. So.; Passacaglia for org.; songs, &c.

Lübeck, Vincenz (b. Padingbüttel, Hanover, IX. 1654; d. Hamburg, 9. II. 1740), Ger. orgst. & comp. Orgst. at Stade until 1702, when he was app. orgst. to St. Nicholas's church at Hamburg.

Works incl. cantatas, chorale-preludes & other org. m., &c.

Lucas, Charles (b. Salisbury, 28. VII. 1808; d. London, 30. III. 1869), Eng. cst., orgst., cond. & comp. Choirboy at Salisbury cath., 1815–23 studied co. & comp. at the R.A.M. in London, of which, after a number of appts. as cond., cst. & orgst., he became principal in 1859, succeeding Potter.

Works incl. opera *The Regicide*; anthems; 3 syms.; stg. 4tets; songs, &c.

Lucas, Leighton (b. London, 5. I. 1903), Eng. dancer, cond. & comp. He studied m. by himself while engaged in the career of a dancer and at 19 became a theatre cond.

Works incl. ballet *Orpheus*, masques (tragic) *The Wolf's Bride* & (Japanese) *Kanawa, the Incantation*; film m. for *Target for To-night*; *Missa pro defunctis* for solo voices, chor. & orch.; *Masque of the Sea* for chor. & orch.; Passacaglia & Chaconne for orch.; Sonnets for pf. & orch.; *La Goya* 2 dance impressions for chamber orch.; Partita for pf. & chamber orch., *Eurhythmy* for v. & stgs., 4 Divertissements for v. & chamber orch.; pf. Trio in F maj.; songs, &c.

Lucca, Pauline (b. Vienna, 25. IV. 1841; d. Vienna, 28. II. 1908), It.-Aus. sop. singer. Studied in Vienna, joined the Opera chor. and made her 1st stage appearance at Olomouc in 1859, being engaged for Prague, 1860, and Berlin, 1861. In 1863 she 1st visited London.

Lucia di Lammermoor, opera by Donizetti (lib. by Salvatore Cammarano, based on Scott's *Bride of Lammermoor*), prod. Naples, Teatro San Carlo, 26. IX. 1835.

Lucia, Fernando de (b. Naples, 11. X. 1860; d. Naples, 21. II. 1925), It. ten. singer. Studied at Naples and made his 1st stage appearance there in 1883. His 1st visit to Eng. was in 1887. Later in life he was prof. of singing at the Naples Cons.

Lucio Papirio, opera by Caldara (lib. by Apostolo Zeno), prod. Vienna, 4. XI. 1719.

Opera by Hasse (lib. do.), prod. Dresden, at court, 18. I. 1742.

Lucio Silla, opera by J. C. Bach (lib. by Giovanni de Gamerra, with alterations by Metastasio), prod. Mannheim, at court, 4. XI. 1774.

Opera by Mozart (lib. do.), prod. Milan, Teatro Regio Ducal, 26. XII. 1772.

Lucio Vero, opera by Pollarolo (lib. by Apostolo Zeno), prod. Venice, Teatro San Giovanni Crisostomo, 1700.

Opera by Sacchini (lib. do.), prod. Naples, Teatro San Carlo, 4. XI. 1764.

Lucrezia Borgia, opera by Donizetti (lib. by Felice Romani, based on Victor Hugo's tragedy), prod. Milan, Teatro alla Scala, 26. XII. 1833.

Ludford, Nicholas (b. ?; d. ?), Eng.

15th–16th-cent. comp., (?) member of the Chapel Royal in London.
Works incl. masses, motets & other church m.

Ludovic, opera by Hérold, left unfinished and completed by Halévy (lib. by Jules Henri Vernoy de Saint-Georges), prod. Paris, Opéra-Comique, 16. V. 1833. Chopin wrote pf. Vars. on an air from it, Op. 12.

Ludwig, Otto (1813–65), Ger. novelist & dramatist. *See* Mottl (*Agnes Bernauer*), **Rubinstein (A.)** (*Maccabees*).

Ludwig (actually Ledwidge), William (b. Dublin, VII. 1847; d. London, 25. XII. 1923), Ir. bar. singer. Studied at Dublin, joined the Gaiety Theatre in London as a chorister, gradually appeared in small parts and made his 1st important stage appearance with the Carl Rosa Opera Co. in 1877.

Lugg (or Lugge), John (b. ?; d. ?), Eng. 17th-cent. orgst & comp. He was (?) vicar-chor. and orgst. at Exeter and perhaps later at Oxford.
Works incl. services, anthems, motets; org. voluntaries; canons; jig for hpchd., &c.

Lugg (or Lugge), Robert (b. ?; d. ?), Eng. 17th-cent. orgst. & comp., (?) related to prec. Mus.B., Oxford, 1638, and later orgst. at St. John's Coll. there. He (?) became a Rom. Catholic and went abroad.
Works incl. services, anthems, &c.

Luigini, Alexandre (Clément Léon Joseph) (b. Lyons, 9. III. 1850; d. Paris, 29. VII. 1906), Fr. vst., cond. & comp. Studied at the Paris Cons., became leader at the Grand Théâtre of Lyons in 1869 and cond. in 1877. In 1897 he became cond. of the Opéra-Comique in Paris.
Works incl. operas *Faublas* & *Les Caprices de Margot*; ballets; cantata *Gloria victis*; *Ballet égyptien*, *Ballet russe*, *Carnaval turc* & other light works for orch., &c.

Luineag or **Luinig** — A Gaelic labour song sung in chor., mainly by women.

Luisa Miller, opera by Verdi (lib. by Salvatore Cammarano, based on Schiller's drama *Kabale und Liebe*), prod. Naples, Teatro San Carlo, 8. XII. 1849.

Lully, Jean Baptiste (orig. Giovanni Battista Lulli) (b. Florence, 29. XI. 1632; d. Paris, 22. III. 1687), It.-Fr. comp. Son of a miller, he had little educ. and learnt guitar and v. without much guidance. At first joined strolling players, but in 1646 was discovered by the Chevalier de Guise and taken to Fr., where he entered the household of Mlle de Montpensier, the king's cousin, as a scullion; but when she found that he was mus. she made him a personal servant and leader of her stg. band. In 1652 he passed into the service of Louis XIV, who was then 14. L. became ballet dancer, vst. in the king's '24 vs.' and comp. In 1658 he began to comp. ballets of his own, having contrib. to some since 1653, in which the king himself danced, and in 1664 he began to collaborate with Molière in comedy-ballets. In 1661 he became a naturalized Frenchman and Comp. to the King's Chamber Music, and in 1662 M. Master to the Royal Family; and that year he married Madeleine Lambert, the daughter of a court musn., who brought him a good dowry. His ballets, pastorals, &c. became more and more substantial and like operas, and his 1st full opera, *Cadmus et Hermione*, appeared in 1673, when he obtained a royal patent granting him the monopoly of operatic prod. and annulling a previous patent given to Perrin and Cambert, who had mismanaged the opera estab. or were alleged to have done so. The Académie Royale de Musique, as the Opéra was 1st called, was opened in 1672 with a pasticcio from earlier works of his, *Les Festes de l'Amour et de Bacchus*. Quinault became his libst. His last complete opera was *Acis et Galathée* in 1686. In 1687 he injured his foot with the stick with which he cond. a Te Deum to celebrate the king's recovery and d. of blood poisoning. The opera *Achille et Polyxène*, left unfinished by him, was completed by Colasse.
Works incl. operas *Cadmus et Hermione*, *Alceste*, *Thésée*, *Atys*, *Isis*, *Psyché*, *Bellérophon*, *Proserpine*, *Persée*, *Phaéton*, *Amadis de Gaule*, *Roland*, *Armide et Renaud*, *Acis et Galatée*, *Achille et Polyxène*; comedy-ballets (all with Molière) *Les Fâcheux*, *Le Mariage forcé*, *L'Amour médecin*, *La Princesse d'Élide*, *Le Sicilien*, *George Dandin*, *Monsieur de Pourceaugnac*, *Les Amants magnifiques*, *Le Bourgeois gentilhomme*; pastorals & divertissements *Les Plaisirs de l'île enchantée*, *La Pastorale comique*, *Les Festes de l'Églogue de Versailles*, *Idylle de Sceaux ou de la Paix*; ballets (some poss. by Boësset & others) *Ballet d'Alcidiane*, *B. de la raillerie*, *B. de Xerxès* (for Cavalli's opera), *B. de l'impatience*, *B. des saisons*, *B. de l'Ercole amante*, *B. des arts*, *B. des noces de village*, *B. des amours déguisés*, *La Naissance de Vénus*, *B. des gardes*, *Le Triomphe de Bacchus dans les Indes*, *B. des Muses*, *Le Carnaval ou Mascarade de Versailles*, *B. de Flore*, *B. des ballets*, *Le*

Triomphe de l'Amour, Le Temple de la paix; incid. m. to Corneille's *Œdipe*; church m. Miserere, *Plaude laetare*, Te Deum, *De profundis, Dies irae* & Benedictus, 5 *Grands Motets*, 12 *Petits Motets*, motets for double chor.; dances for var. insts., *Suites de trompettes, Suites de symphonies et trios*, &c.

Lulu, unfinished opera by Berg (lib. by comp., based on Frank Wedekind's plays *Erdgeist* and *Die Büchse der Pandora*), Acts I & II and a fragment of III prod., Zürich, 2. VI. 1937.

Lumby, Herbert (Horace) (b. Birmingham, 8. X. 1906), Eng. vst., violist, pfst. & comp. Studied with Bantock and others at the Birmingham & Midland Institute School of M. and joined the City of Birmingham Orch. as va. Later studied comp. with Edmunds and left the orch. in 1944.

Works incl. Sym. in A min., *Ankerdine* & *Summer Pastoral* for orch., *The Lovely Rosalind* & *Pastoral* for stg. orch.; 2 pf. trios; v. & pf. So. in E min.; pieces for va. & pf.; Prelude & Rondo for 2 pfs.; Vars., *Rhapsody-Ballade* & other works for pf.; songs, &c.

Lumbye. Dan. family of musns.:

1. Hans Christian L. (b. Copenhagen, 2. V. 1810; d. Copenhagen, 20. III. 1874), cond. & comp. Cond. a light orch. at the Tivoli in Copenhagen from 1848 and wrote much dance and other light m. for it.

2. Karl L. (b. Copenhagen, 9. VII. 1841; d. Copenhagen, 10. VIII. 1911), cond. & comp., son of prec. He succeeded his father in 1865 and also comp. dances, marches, &c.

3. Georg L. (b. Copenhagen, 26. VIII. 1843; d. ?), cond. & comp., brother of prec. Wrote chiefly for the stage, incl. the opera *The Witch's Flute*.

Lund, Signe (b. Christiana, 15. IV. 1868), Norw. comp. Studied with W. Berger in Berlin and later in Copenhagen and Paris. She then lived in U.S.A. for *c*. 20 years.

Works incl. Norw.-Amer. cantata, m. for the Bjørnson memorial at Chicago, 1910, and *The Road to France* for Amer.'s entry into the 1st world war; orch. pieces; pf. works; songs, &c.

Lunga pausa (It. = long pause, long rest). A direction indicating that such a pause is to be made at the perf.'s discretion, not according to rests indicating its precise length shown by the comp.

Lunn, Louisa Kirkby (b. Manchester, 8. XI. 1873; d. London, 17. II. 1930), Eng. m.-sop. singer. Studied under the org. J. H. Greenwood at Manchester and with Visetti at the R.C.M. in London. In 1893-4 she appeared at the R.C.M.'s students' perfs. of Schumann's *Genoveva* and Delibes's *Le Roi l'a dit*, and in the latter year she was engaged by Augustus Harris to begin her career in opera. Later she appeared with the Carl Rosa Opera Co., at concerts and from 1901 in important parts at Covent Garden.

Lunssens, Martin (b. Brussels, 16. IV. 1871; d. Brussels, 1. II. 1944), Belg. comp. Studied with Gevaert and others at the Brussels Cons., gained the Belg. Prix de Rome in 1895, travelled for 3 years in Fr., It. and Ger., and became leader of the orch. at the Lyric Theatre of Antwerp in 1901. In 1911 he was app. prof. of harmony at the Brussels Cons. and in 1924 dir. of that of Ghent.

Works incl. incid. m. for *Saint Amand* (Delbeke); cantatas *Callirhoë* & *Jubilaire, Ode to M.* for chor. & orch.; 4 syms., symph. poems on Shakespeare's *Romeo and Juliet, Timon of Athens* & *Julius Caesar* and on Corneille's *Cid*, ovt. to Racine's *Phèdre*, Concert Ovt. for orch.; chamber m.; songs with orch., &c.

Lupo. Eng. 16th-17th family of musns. of It. orig., all active at the Eng. court between 1540-1640:

1. Ambroso da Milano.
2. Mark Anthony.
3. Joseph, violist.
4. Peter, violist.
5. Thomas, son of 3, violist, lutenist, singer & comp.
6. Thomas, son of 4, vst.
7. Theophil, vst.
8. Horatio, vst.

Luprano, Filippo de (b. ?; d. ?), It. 15th-16th-cent. comp.

Works incl. frottole, &c.

Lupus, Eduardus. *See* Lobo.

Lupus, Joannes. *See* Hellinck.

Lur or **Lure** — A primitive hn. found among prehistoric remains in Scand.

Lurline, opera by V. Wallace (lib. by Edward Fitzball), prod. London, Covent Garden Theatre, 23. II. 1860. The subject is that of the Ger. legend of the Loreley.

Luscinius, Othmar (real name Nachtgall or Nachtigall) (b. Strasburg, 1487; d. Freiburg i/B., 1537), Ger. orgst. & comp. Pupil of Hofhaimer. He was orgst. at Strasburg, but left for Freiburg in 1523, owing to the Reformation, and settled at a Carthusian monastery. He wrote mus. treatises and comp. org. m., &c.

Lusingando or **Lusinghiero** (It. = wheedling, coaxing). A direction to perf. a piece or passage in a charming, alluring manner.

Lusitano, Vicente (b. Olivença, ?; d. Rome, after 1553), Port. theorist & comp. He was known as Vicente de Olivença in Port., but was called L. ('the Port.') in Rome, where he settled about 1550. In 1551 he had a learned dispute with Vicentino, which was settled in his favour, with Danckerts and Escobedo as judges. He pub. a treatise on *cantus firmus* in 1553.

Works incl. motets *Epigrammata*, &c.

Lustige Krieg, Der (*The Merry War*), operetta by J. Strauss, jun. (lib. F. Zell & Richard Genée), prod. Vienna, Theater an der Wien, 25. XI. 1881.

Lustige Witwe, Die (*The Merry Widow*), operetta by Lehár (lib. by Victor Léon & Leo Stein), prod. Vienna, Theater an der Wien, 30. XII. 1905.

Lustigen Weiber von Windsor, Die (*The Merry Wives of W.*), comic opera by Nicolai (lib. by Salomon Hermann Mosenthal, after Shakespeare), prod. Berlin, Opera, 9. III. 1849.

Lute. A stg. inst. now obs. but still having descendants in the guitar, mandoline, balalaika, ukelele, &c. Its orig. is eastern and very remote, and it gained currency in Eur. in medieval times and was still very popular in the 17th cent., but declined in the 18th. Its stgs. were plucked and the notes were determined on a fingerboard with frets by the left hand. There were usually 6 pairs of stgs., 2 to each note, and they were tuned in rising 4ths, but with an interval of a 3rd between 3 and 4. It was not played from ordinary mus. notation, but from a Tablature.

Lute-Harpsichord. A hpchd. made for Bach in 1740, called *Lautenclavicymbel*, with stops imitating the sound of a lute.

Lutenist. A lute-player, usually also a singer to the lute and often a comp. for the inst.

Luther, Martin (b. Eisleben, 10. XI. 1483; d. Eisleben, 18. II. 1546), Ger. reformer & amateur musn. The mus. relevant facts of his biog. are that his reforms of the church service, begun in 1522, incl. the much greater scope given to singing by the congregation and the consequent necessity to sing in the vernacular, instead of in Lat. He arranged a Ger. Mass in 1524 and he had the assistance of Walther and of Conrad Rupff, mus. dir. to the Elector of Saxony, in compiling a Ger. hymn-book, with tunes selected by him, adapted from formerly secular songs, and some possibly invented by himself. He sang bass and played the fl. and the lute.

For literary works set by other comps. *see* **Burkhard** (*Musikalische Uebung*), **Otto** (hymn 'Ein' feste Burg'), **Walther (J.)** (sacred songs).

Luthier (Fr.). Now the Fr. word for a maker of vs. and other insts. of the v. family, though obviously derived from what was orig. the term for a lute-maker.

Lutyens, Elisabeth (b. London, 9. VII. 1906), Eng. comp. Daughter of the architect Sir Edwin Lutyens. Studied va. & comp. at the R.C.M. in London, the latter with Harold Dark, and later with Caussade in Paris. She married the B.B.C. cond. Edward Clark.

Works incl. ballet *The Birthday of the Infanta* (after Oscar Wilde); 3 orch. pieces in 12-tone technique, 3 symph. preludes, march *Bustle for the W.A.A.F.s*, *Divertissement*, ovt. *Proud City* (London) for orch.; *Suite gauloise* for small orch. or wind octet, Conc. for 9 insts., Conc. for cl., saxophone, pf. & stgs., bn. Conc. with stgs.; *The Dying of Tanneguy du Bois* (Austin Dobson) for ten., 4 hns. & stgs., 3 Salutes (Milton) for ten., chor. & orch.; 2 stg. 4tets, Fantasy for stg. 5tet, stg. Trio; chamber cantata *Winter the Huntsman* for chor., hn., tpt. co. & pf. (Osbert Sitwell), 4 songs for ten. & stg. 4tet; va. solo So., Partita for 2 vs., 9 Bagatelles for co. & pf.; *The Check Book* (for children), 5 Intermezzi & ovt. (for *Hommage à la France*) for pf.; Eng. & Fr. songs, &c.

Lux, Friedrich (b. Ruhla, 23. XI. 1820; d. Mainz, 9. VII. 1895), Ger. cond. & comp. Pupil of his father and of F. Schneider at Dessau, where he cond. the Court Opera in 1841–50. He then became opera cond. at Mainz and also cond. chor. socs.

Works incl. operas *Käthchen von Heilbronn* (on Kleist's play), *Der Schmied von Ruhla* & *Die Fürstin von Athen*; chor. sym. *Durch Nacht zum Licht* & other chor. works; scene from Shakespeare's *Coriolanus* for voices & orch.; orch. works; stg. 4tets, pf. Trio; org. & pf. pieces; songs, &c.

Luyton, Carl (b. Antwerp, ?; d. Prague, VIII. 1620), Flem. orgst. & comp. He was in the service of the Emperor Maximilian II at Prague in 1576, when that monarch d., and was app. to the Emperor Rudolf II in the same capacity.

Works incl. masses, motets, lamentations, *Sacrae cantiones*; It. madrigals; *Fuga suavissima* & *Ricercare* for org., &c.

Luzzaschi, Luzzasco (b. Ferrara, 1545; d. Ferrara, 11. IX. 1607), It. orgst. & comp. Pupil of Rore at Ferrara and afterwards orgst. and chapel master to Duke Alfonso II. Among his org. pupils was Frescobaldi.

Works incl. motets, *Sacrae cantiones*; madrigals; org. m., &c.

Lvov, Alexis Feodorovitch (b. Reval, 5. VI. 1798; d. Romano nr. Kovno, 28. XII. 1870), Rus. comp. Studied with his father, Feodor L., an authority on church m. and folksong, who succeeded Bortniansky as dir. of the Imp. Chapel in 1825. His son, who rose to high rank on the army and became adjutant to Nicholas I, succeeded him there in 1836. He was a good vst. and founded a stg. 4tet at St. Petersburg. He became deaf and retired in 1867.

Works incl. operas *Bianca e Gualtiero, Undine* (after Fouqué) & *The Bailiff*; much church m.; v. Conc.; fantasy *The Duel* for v. & co.; Rus. Imp. hymn ' God save the Tsar,' &c.

Lydian Mode. One of the old ecclesiastical modes with semitones between the 4th & 5th and 7th & 8th notes of the scale, represented by the scale beginning on F on the white notes of the pf. keyboard.

Lyne, Felice (b. Slater, Mo., 1891; d. Allentown, Pa., 1. IX. 1935), Amer. sop. singer. Studied in Paris and made her 1st appearance in opera in London, 1911.

Lyon, James (b. Manchester, 25. X. 1872), Eng. comp. He was mainly self-taught, but took the Mus.D. degree in 1905 and later taught comp. at the Midland Institute School of M. at Birmingham.

Works incl. operas *The Palace of Cards, Stormwreck, Fiammetta, La sirena*; melomimes *Toinette, The Necklace, Madame s'amuse*; 4 suites, *Gwalia, Poem on Manx Tunes*, prelude *Aucassin and Nicolette* for orch.; *Idyll* for stgs.; Ballade for v. & orch.; Fantasy stg. 4tet, pf. Trio; org. & pf. pieces; songs, &c.

Lyons. The name often given to lute bass stgs. in the 17th cent., from their place of supply.

Lyra. A percussion inst. with tuned steel bars or plates which are played with hammers, similar to the Stahlspiel, used in Eng. military bands and made for them in the shape of a lyre.

Lyra Viol. This is not a specific inst., but a term for the Viola da gamba when played from a Tablature instead of from mus. notation. This was in use in Eng. *c.* 1650–1700 and also variously called ' Lero Viol,' ' Leero Viol ' or ' Viol Lyra Way.'

Lyre. The most important inst. of ancient Gr., but doubtless of eastern orig. It had 4, 7 or 10 stgs. stretched on a framework with a hollow soundbox at the bottom. The stgs. were plucked, like those of a hp., with both hands, but only the left used the finger-tips, while the right played with a Plectrum. The large inst. of the type was called Cithara, a name from which the modern word ' guitar ' derives.

Lyre-Guitar, or **Apollo Lyre.** A stg. inst. prod. in Fr. near the end of the 18th cent., built to suggest the shape of the ancient Gr. lyre, but with a fretted finger-board. It had 6 stgs.

Lysard. *See* **Lyzarden.**

Lysberg, Charles Samuel. *See* **Bovy-Lysberg.**

Lytton, Edward George Earle Lytton Bulwer-, Baron Lytton (1803–73), Eng. novelist. *See* **Fry** (*Lady of Lyons*), **Ione** (Petrella), **Joncières** (*Dernier Jour de Pompéi*), **Kashpirov** (*Rienzi*), **Leila** (Bendl), **Pauline** (Cowen), **Perosi (M.)** (*Pompei*), **Rienzi** (Wagner).

Lyzarden or **Lyzardyne**. The old Eng. name for the bass Cornett or Corno torto, the predecessor of the Serpent, which latter came into use in the 17th cent. Also sometimes called **Lizard** or Lysard.

(Mark reference p. 306)

Lady of the Lake, The, songs by Schubert set to Ger. transs. from Scott's poem by P. A. Storck in 1825 and pub. in 1826 as Op. 52. 1. Ellen's 1st song, 'Soldier, rest!'; 2. Ellen's 2nd song, 'Huntsman, rest!'; 3. Ellen's 3rd song, 'Ave Maria'; 4. Norman's song, 'The heath this night'; 5. Lay of the Imprisoned Huntsman, 'My hawk is tired.' The trans. is often so free that the m. will not fit the orig. Eng. metres. These 5 are S.'s only 'L. o. t. L.' songs for solo voice and pf., but Op. 52 contained 2 more poems from Scott's work, *Boating Song* for male chor. and *Coronach* for female chor.

(Mark reference p. 326)

Linstead, George (**Frederick**) (b. Melrose, 24. I. 1908), Sco. critic, orgst. & comp. Studied with F. H. Shera at Sheffield, also comp. with Sir Edward Bairstow & pf. with James Ching. He took the D.Mus. degree at Durham. App. orgst. & choirmaster at Walker Parish Church, Sheffield, in 1933, and m. critic to the *Sheffield Daily Telegraph* in 1940.

Works incl. opera *Eastward in Eden*; Symph. Mvt., Suite *Cadmus et Hermione* (after Lully) & In Nomine for orch.; 2 Concertinos for pf. & orch.; folksong arrs. for orch. & for milit. band; stg. 4tet; v. & pf. So.; Sonatina, *4 Moods, Le Babil, Une Brioche,* 5 2-part Inventions for pf., &c.

(Mark reference p. 328)

Livy (Titus Livius) (59 B.C.–A.D. 17), Rom. historian. *See* **Rape of Lucretia** (Britten), p. 519.

M

M. (abbr.) = Music.

M'. For names with this prefix *see* **Mac . . .**

M. The Mediant note in any key in Tonic Sol-fa notation, pronounced Me.

M.D. (abbr. Fr. *main droite*, It. *mano destra*) = Right Hand, often used in pf. m.

M.G. (abbr. Fr. *main gauche*) = Left Hand, often used in pf. m.

M.S. (abbr. It. *mano sinistra*) = Left Hand, often used in pf. m.

M.-sop. (abbr.) = Mezzo-soprano.

Ma Mère l'Oye (*Mother Goose*), suite by Ravel, written for pf. duet in 1908 and pub. in 1910, scored for orch. and prod. as a ballet, Paris, Opéra, 11. III. 1915, scen. by Louis Laloy, chgph. by L. Staats. The mvts. are based on tales by Perrault: 1. *Pavan of the Sleeping Beauty*; 2. *Hop-o'-my-Thumb*; 3. *Little Ugly, Empress of the Pagodas*; 4. *Colloquy between the Beauty and the Beast*; 5. *The Fairy Garden*.

Má Vlast (*My Country*), cycle of 6 symph. poems by Smetana, comp. 1874–9 and containing programme works on var. aspects of Cz. hist. and geog.: 1. *Vyšehrad* (the citadel of Prague); 2. *Vltava* (the river); 3. *Šarka* (the Cz. Amazon); 4. *From Bohemia's Fields and Groves*; 5. *Tabor* (the city); 6. *Blaník* (the mountain).

Maas, Joseph (b. Dartford, 30. I. 1847; d. London, 16. I. 1886), Eng. ten. singer. He was a choir-boy at Rochester cath. and after working as a clerk in Chatham dockyard, he went to Milan in 1869 to study singing under San Giovanni. He 1st appeared at a concert in London, taking Sims Reeves's place, in 1871, and on the stage in 1872.

Mabellini, Teodulo (b. Pistoia, 2. IV. 1817; d. Florence, 10. III. 1897), It. cond. & comp. Studied at the Istituto Reale Musicale at Florence and prod. his 1st opera there at the age of 19. After further study with Mercadante at Novara, he settled at Florence, became cond. of the Società Filarmonica in 1843 and of the Teatro della Pergola in 1848. In 1859–87 he was prof. at the Istituto.

Works incl. operas *Matilda a Toledo, Rolla, Ginevra degli Almieri, Il conte di Lavagna, I Veneziani a Constantinopoli, Maria di Francia, Il venturiero, Baldassare* & *Fiammetta*; orats. *Eudossio e Paolo* & *L'ultimo giorno di Gerusalemme*; cantatas *La caccia, Il ritorno, Elegiaca, Rafaelle Sanzio* & *Lo spirito di Dante*; much church m., &c.

Macbeth, incid. m. by (?) Locke for Davenant's version of Shakespeare's play, prod. London, Dorset Gardens Theatre, summer 1674. There were later prods. with m. by Purcell, Eccles, Leveridge & others.

Opera by Bloch (lib. by Edmond Fleg, after Shakespeare), prod. Paris, Opéra-Comique, 30. XI. 1910.

Opera by Chelard (lib. by Rouget de Lisle, after Shakespeare), prod. Paris, Opéra, 29. VI. 1827.

Opera by Collingwood (lib. by comp., chosen from Shakespeare), prod. London, Sadler's Wells Theatre, 12. IV. 1934.

Opera by Taubert (lib. by Friedrich Eggers, after Shakespeare), prod. Berlin, Royal Opera, 16. XI. 1857.

Opera by Verdi (lib. by Francesco Maria Piave & Andrea Maffei, after Shakespeare), prod. Florence, Teatro della Pergola, 14. III. 1847; revised version (Fr. lib. by Charles Nuitter & A. Beaumont) prod. Paris, Théâtre Lyrique, 21. IV. 1865.

Ovt. by Spohr, Op. 75.

Symph. poem by R. Strauss, 1st perf. Weimar, 13. X. 1890.

Macbeth, Allan (b. Greenock, 13. III. 1856; d. Glasgow, 25. VIII. 1910), Sco. cond., orgst., teacher & comp. Studied at the Leipzig Cons., and was cond. of the Glasgow Chor. Union in 1880–7. He was orgst. at var. churches at Glasgow and Edinburgh, and in 1890 became dir. of the m. school of the Glasgow Athenaeum.

Works incl. operetta *The Duke's Doctor*; incid. m. for *Bruce, Lord of the Isles*, a dram. adapt. from Scott; cantata *The Land of Glory* & others; orch. pieces; chamber m.; many pf. pieces; songs; partsongs, &c.

McBride, Robert (b. Tucson, Arizona, 1911), Amer. comp. Studied and took the Mus.B. at Arizona Univ. and obtained the Guggenheim Fellowship in 1937. Later he joined the faculty of Bennington Coll.

Works incl. ballet *Show Piece*; *Mexican Rhapsody* & *Prelude to a Tragedy* for orch.; Fugato for 25 insts., *Workout* for 15 insts.; Prelude & Fugue for stg. 4tet; So. *Depression* for v. & pf.; *Workout* for ob. & pf., *Swing Music* for cl. & pf.; Dance Suite for pf., &c.

McCormack, John, Count (b. Athlone, 14. VI. 1884; d. Dublin, 16. IX. 1945), Ir. ten. singer. Began as chorister in Dublin Rom. Catholic cath. and in 1905 went to It. to study with Sabbatini at Milan. Made his 1st concert appearance in London in II. 1907 and was engaged for opera by Covent Garden in the autumn. He soon sang in It., U.S.A., &c. and made a great reput., but in later years made popularity rather than serious mus. interest his chief concern. His title was a papal one.

MacCunn, Hamish (b. Greenock, 22. III. 1868; d. London, 2. VIII. 1916), Sco. cond. & comp. Studied with Parry at the R.C.M. in London and had an ovt. *Cior Mhor* perf. at the Crystal Palace at the age of 17. He married a daughter of the painter John Pettie in 1888 and soon afterwards cond. the Carl Rosa Opera Co. for some time, also German's light operas at the Savoy Theatre.

Works incl. operas *Jeanie Deans* (after Scott), *Diarmid & Breast of Light* (unfinished), light operas *The Golden Girl* & *Prue*; m. for *The Masque of War and Peace* & *Pageant of Darkness and Light*; cantatas *The Moss Rose, Lord Ullin's Daughter, The Lay of the Last Minstrel* (after Scott), *Bonny Kilmeny, The Cameronian's Dream, Queen Hynde of Caledon, The Death of Parcy Reed, The Wreck of the Hesperus* (Longfellow) & others; Psalm viii for chor. & org.; ovt. *The Land of the Mountain and the Flood*; ballads *The Ship o' the Fiend* & *The Dowie Dens o' Yarrow*, 3 descriptive pieces *Highland Memories* for orch.; 3 pieces for co. & pf.; *Scotch Dances* & other pieces for pf.; c. 80 songs; partsongs, &c.

McDonald, Harl (b. nr. Boulder, Colorado, 27. VII. 1899), Amer. pfst., scientist & comp. Studied at home, at California Univ. and the Leipzig Cons. He toured as a pfst. in Eur. & U.S.A., settled at Philadelphia as teacher and cond. and in 1930–3 studied physics in relation to acoustic problems with a Rockefeller grant and wrote a book on *New Methods of Measuring Sound*.

Works incl. 84th Psalm & *Missa ad Patrem* for chor. & orch.; 4 syms. (No. 1 *The Santa Fé Trial*, No. 2 *Rhumba*), 2 Suites & 3 Poems on Aramaic Themes for orch.; 2 pf. concs.; stg. 4tet on Negro themes, pf. Trio; pf. works; songs, &c.

MacDowell, Edward (Alexander) (b. New York, 18. XII. 1861; d. New York, 23. I. 1908), Amer. comp. & pfst. Learnt the pf. at home at first, was taken to the Paris Cons. in 1876, where he studied pf. under Marmontel and theory under Savard; afterwards worked with Louis Ehlert at Wiesbaden, 1878, and entered the Frankfort Cons. in 1879, where Raff taught him comp. In 1881 he became pf. prof. at the Darmstadt Cons. and the next year played his 1st pf. Conc. at Zürich at Liszt's invitation. Returned to U.S.A. in 1884 and married Marian Nevins, who had been his pupil at Frankfort, 21. VII. After another period at Frankfort and Wiesbaden, he went home for good and settled at Boston in 1888, making his 1st public appearance in U.S.A. there, 19. XI. He now began to comp. much and to give many pf. recitals from 1891. In 1896 he was app. head of the new m. dept. at Columbia Univ. in N.Y. and became hon. Mus.D. at Princeton Univ. Resigned in 1904, but continued to teach and comp. In 1905 his mind became affected and soon broke down completely.

Works incl. symph. poems *Hamlet and Ophelia* (after Shakespeare), *Lancelot and Elaine, Lamia* (after Keats), 2 Suites (No. 2 *Indian*) for orch.; 2 pf. concs.; 6 orch. works; 26 op. nos. of pf. solos, incl. 4 sos., 2 *Modern Suites*, 24 studies, *Woodland Sketches, Sea Pieces, Fireside Tales, New England Idyls*, also 2 books of techn. exercises; 2 sets of pieces for pf. duet; 42 songs; 26 partsongs, &c.

Mace, John (b. ?; d. ?), Eng. 16th–17th-cent. comp. Nothing is known of his life.

Works incl. anthem *Let Thy merciful ears.*

Mace, Thomas (b. Cambridge, *c.* 1619; d. ? Cambridge, ? 1709), Eng. writer on m., (?) son of prec. Clerk of Trinity Coll., Cambridge; pub. *Musick's Monument* in 1676. He invented a 'table org.' for use with a consort of viols and in 1672 a lute with 50 stgs. he called the 'Dyphone,' designed to serve him when he was becoming deaf. His comps. incl. an anthem 'I heard a voice.'

McEwen, John (Blackwood) (b. Hawick, 13. IV. 1868), Sco. mus. educst. & comp. Studied at Glasgow Univ. and after being choirmaster at 2 churches there, entered the R.A.M. in London, 1893. In 1895 he returned to Sco. to become choirmaster at Greenock and prof. of pf. at the school of m. attached to the Glasgow Athenaeum; but he came back to the R.A.M. as prof. of harmony & comp. in 1898 and succeeded Mackenzie as its principal in 1924, retiring in 1936.

He received the hon. Mus.D. from Oxford Univ. in 1926 and was knighted in 1931.

Works incl. incid. m. for Empire Pageant (1910); syms. (incl. *Solway Sym.*); border ballad *Grey Galloway* & Prelude for orch.; va. Conc.; stg. 4tets (incl. *Biscay* 4tet), stg. 5tet; chor. works; pf. pieces, &c.

Macfarren, George (Alexander) (b. London, 2. III. 1813; d. London, 31. X. 1887), Eng. mus. educst. & comp. Pupil of Lucas from 1827, entered the R.A.M. in 1829, of which he became a prof. in 1834 and principal in 1876. In 1845 he married the Ger. con. singer and translator Natalia Andrae (1828–1916). He ed. works by Purcell and Handel. In the 1870s his eyesight began to fail and he eventually became blind, but he continued to work at comp. and to teach. Knighted in 1883.

Works incl. operas *The Devil's Opera, The Adventures of Don Quixote* (after Cervantes), *King Charles II, Robin Hood, Jessy Lea, She Stoops to Conquer* (after Goldsmith), *The Soldier's Legacy, Helvellyn*; masque *Freya's Gift*; orats. *St. John the Baptist, The Resurrection, Joseph, King David*; cantatas *Emblematical Tribute on the Queen's Marriage* (1840), *The Sleeper Awakened, Lenora, May Day, Christmas, The Lady of the Lake* (after Scott); much church m.; Sym. in F min. & others, ovts. to Shakespeare's *Hamlet, Romeo and Juliet* & *The Merchant of Venice*, Schiller's *Don Carlos*, ovt. *Chevy Chase* & other orch. works; v. Conc.; stg. 4tets & other chamber m.; sos. for var. insts.; pf. sos. & pieces; *Shakespeare Songs* for 4 voices; *Songs in a Cornfield* & numerous other songs, incl. settings of Tennyson & Kingsley, &c.

Macfarren, Walter (Cecil) (b. London, 28. VIII. 1826; d. London, 2. IX. 1905), Eng. pfst., cond. & comp., brother of prec. Choir-boy at Westminster Abbey and student at the R.A.M., where he became prof. of pf. in 1846.

Works incl. Sym. in B♭ maj., ovts. to Shakespeare's *Winter's Tale, Taming of the Shrew, Henry V* & *Othello* & other ovts.; pf. Conc.; sos. for var. insts.; pf. sos. & pieces; church m.; madrigals & partsongs; songs, &c.

M'Gibbon, William (b. Edinburgh, *c.* 1695; d. Edinburgh, 3. X. 1756), Sco. vst. & comp. 1st learnt m. from his father, the obst. Matthew M'G., and was sent to London early, studying v. under Wm. Corbett. On his return to Edinburgh he became leader of the Gentlemen's Concerts orch. He collected Sco. tunes, pub. in 3 vols., 1742–55.

Works incl. sos. for v. or fl., for 2 fls., &c.

M'Guckin, Barton (d. Dublin, 28. VII. 1852; d. Stoke Poges, Bucks., 17. IV. 1913), Ir. ten. singer. Choir-boy at Armagh cath., became a singer at St. Patrick's cath., Dublin, and made his 1st concert appearance there in 1874. The next year he came out in London, then studied briefly at Milan, and afterwards took to opera In 1887–8 he appeared in U.S.A.

Machado, Augusto (b. Lisbon, 27. XII. 1845; d. Lisbon, 28. III. 1925), Port. comp. Dir. of the Lisbon Cons. in 1900–10.

Works incl. It. operas *Lauriana, I Doria, Mario Wetter* (lib. by Leoncavallo) & *La Borghesina*, Port. operettas; cantata *Camões e os Lusiadas*, &c.

Machaut (or **Machault**), **Guillaume de** (b. at or nr. Rheims, *c.* 1300; d. Rheims, 1377), Fr. priest & comp. He became secretary, *c.* 1323, to John of Luxemburg, king of Boh., and went with him to Pol., Lithuania & It. On the king's death in 1346 M. went into the service of his daughter, the Duchess of Normandy, and on her death in 1349 into that of Charles, king of Navarre; later into that of the dauphin (afterwards Charles V) and his brother Jean, Duc de Berry. He became canon of Rheims cath. in 1333. His Mass was (?) perf. at the coronation of Charles V at Rheims in 1364. An exponent of the *Ars nova* in Fr.

Works incl. Mass for 4 voices, motets, voc. ballades & rondeaux, chansons balladées, lais, &c.

Maciejewski, Roman (b. Berlin, 1910), Pol. pfst. & comp. Studied pf. at the Poznan Cons. and comp. with Sikorski at the Warsaw Cons. He went to live in Paris in 1934 and in Eng. in 1938.

Works incl. Conc. for 2 pfs. & orch.; mazurkas, *Dances of the Highlander* &c. for pf.; *Songs from Kurpie, Songs of Bilitis* (Pierre Louÿs), &c.

Machiavelli, Niccolo (1469–1527), It. politician & author. *See* **Mandragola** (Castelnuovo-Tedesco), **Ullrich** (*Mandragola*), **Waghalter** (do.).

Machicotage (Fr.) or **Macicotatico** (It.) or **Macicotaticum** (Lat.) — A kind of ornamentation used in plainsong, now largely discredited, extraneous notes being inserted between those prescribed by the notation.

Macintyre, Margaret (b. India, *c.* 1865; d. ?, IV. 1943), Brit. sop singer. Made her 1st appearance in London, at Covent Garden, in 1888.

Mackay, Angus (b. ?; d. nr. Dumfries, 21. III. 1859), Sco. bagpiper and folk-song collector. Piper to Queen Victoria. Pub. a collection of old bagpipe tunes and a book on bagpipe playing.

Mackenzie, Alexander (Campbell) (b. Edinburgh, 22. VIII. 1847; d. London, 28. IV. 1935), Sco. comp. Studied in Ger. and at the R.A.M. in London, of which, after 14 years as vst. and teacher at Edinburgh and some years at Florence, he became principal in 1888. Knighted 1895.

Works incl. operas *Colomba*, *The Troubadour*, *The Cricket on the Hearth* (after Dickens) and *The Eve of St. John*; incid. m. *Marmion* & *Ravenswood* (plays based on Scott), Shakespeare's *Coriolanus*, Byron's *Manfred* and Barrie's *The Little Minister*; orats. *The Rose of Sharon*, *Bethlehem*, *The Temptation* (after Milton); cantatas *The Bride*, *Jason*, *The Story of Sayid*, *The Witch's Daughter*, *The Sun-God's Return*; *The Cottar's Saturday Night* (Burns) for chor. & orch.; Suite, Sco. Rhapsody, Canadian Rhapsody, ballad *La Belle Dame sans merci* (after Keats), *Tam o' Shanter* (after Burns), ovts. *Cervantes*, *Twelfth Night* (Shakespeare), *Britannia* & *Youth*, *Sport and Loyalty* for orch.; Conc., Sco. Conc., Suite & *Pibroch* suite for v. & orch.; stg. 4tet, pf. 4tet, pf. Trio; v. & pf. pieces; org. & pf. m.; songs, partsongs, &c.

Mackintosh, Robert (b. ? Tullymet, Athole, ? 1745; d. London, II. 1807), Sco. vst. & comp. Settled at Edinburgh as v. teacher and concert organizer, but went to live in London in 1803. He comp. & arr. reels, strathspeys, minuets, gavottes, &c.

Maclean, Alick (Alexander Morvaren) (b. Eton, 20. VII. 1872; d. London, 18. V. 1936), Eng. cond. & comp. Educ. at Eton. Coll. He became cond. at Wyndham's Theatre in 1899 and of the Scarborough orch. in 1911.

Works incl. operas *Petruccio* (after Shakespeare's *Taming of the Shrew*), *Die Liebesgeige*, *Maitre Seiler*, *Quentin Durward* (after Scott), *The King's Prince*, *Die Waldidylle*; incid. m. for Rostand's *Cyrano de Bergerac*, &c.

Maclean, Charles (Donald) (b. Cambridge, 27. III. 1843; d. London, 23. VI. 1916), Eng. mus. scholar & comp., father of prec. Educ. at Shrewsbury School and Exeter Coll., Oxford, studied m. with Hiller at Cologne and was mus. dir. at Eton Coll., 1871–5. After 22 years in the Ind. Civil Service, he ed. the pubs. of the I.M.C. and became its gen. secretary in 1908. Comp. a large number of works, esp. for orch.

Macleod, Fiona (William Sharp) (1856–1902), Sco. poet. *See* **Immortal Hour** (Boughton).

M'Leod, Peter (b. West Calder, 8. V. 1797; d. Bonnington nr. Edinburgh, 10. II. 1859), Sco. comp. Pub. several vols. of songs to words by Sco. poets.

McNaught, William (Gray) (b. London, 30. III. 1849; d. London, 13. X. 1918), Eng. mus. educst. & ed. Studied at the R.A.M., became a chor. cond., an inspector of m. for the Board of Educ., adjudicator at mus. festivals and in 1909 ed. of the *Mus. Times*.

McNaught, William (b. London, 1. IX. 1883), Eng. m. critic & ed., son of prec. Educ. at Univ. Coll. School and Worcester Coll., Oxford. He was critic to var. London newspapers, assisted his father and Harvey Grace in ed. the *Mus. Times* and followed the latter as ed. in 1944.

Maçon, Le (*The Mason*), opera by Auber (lib. by Scribe & Germain Delavigne), prod. Paris, Opéra-Comique, 3. V. 1825.

Maconchy, Elizabeth (b. Broxbourne, Herts., 19. III. 1907), Eng. comp. of Ir. descent. Studied comp. under Vaughan Williams and pf. under Arthur Alexander at the R.C.M. in London; later in Prague. Several of her works were perf. at the I.S.C.M. festivals abroad and were successful in Belg., Cz., Hung. & Pol. She married Wm. Le Fanu, who trans. poems by Anacreon for her.

Works incl. ballet *Great Agrippa* (from *Shock-headed Peter*); 2 motets for double chor. (Donne); suites for orch. *The Land* (on a poem by V. Sackville-West) & *Puck*; pf. Conc., va. Conc.; *Samson at the Gates of Gaza* for voice & orch.; 2 stg. 4tets, stg. Trio, *Prelude, Interlude & Fugue* for 2 vs.; song-cycle *The Garland* (Anacreon), &c.

Macpherson, Charles (b. Edinburgh, 10. V. 1870; d. London, 28. V. 1927), Sco. orgst. & comp. At the age of 9 he became a choir-boy at St. Paul's cath. in London and in 1890 he entered the R.A.M. there. After holding 2 private appts., he became sub-orgst. in 1895 and orgst. in 1916 of St. Paul's.

Works incl. Psalm cxxxvii for chor. & orch.; anthems & other church m.; *Highland* and *Hallowe'en* suites & ovt. *Cridhe an Ghaidhil* for orch.; pf. 4tet; *Gaelic Melodies* for voice, stgs. & hp., &c.

Macpherson, James (1736–96), Sco. poet, alleged trans. of 'Ossian.' For mus. works *see* **Ossian.**

Macpherson, Stewart (b. Liverpool, 29. III. 1865; d. London, 27. III. 1941), Eng. mus. educst. & comp. Studied at the R.A.M. in London and later became a prof. there. He also held orgst.'s and cond.'s posts, acted as examiner and wrote a number of theoret. books.

Works incl. Mass in D maj.; Sym. in C maj., 2 ovts. & other orch. works; *Concerto alla fantasia* for v. & orch.; church m.; pf. pieces; songs, &c.

Macque, Jean de (b. ?; d. Naples, 1614), Flem. comp. Pupil of Philippe de Monte. He went to It., living in Rome, 1576–82, and at Naples from 1586, where he was choirmaster of the royal chapel.

Works incl. motets, madrigals, &c.

Madama Butterfly, opera by Puccini (lib. by Giuseppe Giacosa and Luigi Illica, based on David Belasco's dramatic version of a story by John Luther Long), prod. Milan, Teatro alla Scala, 17. II. 1904.

Mademoiselle Fifi, opera by Cuí (lib. by ?, in Rus., based on Maupassant's story), prod. Moscow, 15. XII. 1903.

Madetoja, Leevi (Antti) (b. Uleaaborg, 17. II. 1887), Fin. cond., critic & comp. Studied at the Cons. of his native town and later with Järnefelt and Sibelius at Helsingfors; afterwards with d'Indy in Paris and Fuchs in Vienna. In 1912–4 he cond. the Helsingfors orch., afterwards that of Viborg; became m. critic at Helsingfors in 1916 and teacher at the Cons., and in 1926 at the Univ.

Works incl. operas *Pohjalaisia* & *Juha*; ballets; 3 syms., symph. poems & ovts.; *Stabat Mater*; 8 cantatas; pf. Trio; v. & pf. So.; *Lyric Suite* for co. & pf.; pf. pieces; songs, &c.

Madrigal. A comp. for several voices (most usually 5) dating from the 14th cent. and continuing until the early 17th, though there have been artificial revivals of it at later periods. Among its special features are a richly polyphonic style and its assoc. with poetry of high literary value, always in the vernacular of the comp.'s country, not in Lat. The texts were secular, except where they were otherwise designated (e.g. *madrigali spirituali*), and the m. showed a tendency to keep a definite melody in the top part: indeed Ms. were often sung by a single voice, the lower parts being played by insts,; and sometimes the whole perf. was inst. The M. was cultivated partic. by the Flem., It. & Eng. schools.

Madrileña. A Spa. dance from the city or province of Madrid. In Fr. m. it appears as Madrilène.

Maestoso (It. lit. ' majestic ') = Stately, dignified, also usually moderate in tempo.

Maestrale. *See* **Stretto maestrale.**

Maestro (It. = master). In mus. parlance the word is often given by Its., deservedly or otherwise, to some creative or executive musn. who has won a prominent place for himself in the mus. world by superior ability, good fortune or diplomatic skill.

Maestro al cembalo (It. lit. ' master at the harpsichord '). The post of hpchd. player in the late 17th and whole 18th cent. The M. a. c. not only played the keyboard parts in orch. or operatic m. from the figured bass, filling in the harmony from the figures and elaborating the texture by improvisation, but also acted as cond. Where the post survived into the 19th cent. (e.g. at Covent Garden Theatre in London) it became virtually that of a coach, charged with teaching the singers their parts, and it retained its name long after the *cembalo* had disappeared.

Maestro de capilla (Spa.). *See* **Chapel Master.**

Maestro di cappella (It.). *See* **Chapel Master.**

Maestro di musica, Il, intermezzi by Pergolesi (lib. unknown), prod. Naples, summer 1731.

Maeterlinck, Maurice (b. 1862), Belg. dramatist & essayist. *See* **Abrányi (E.)** (*Monna Vanna*), **Alexandrov (A. N.)** (*Ariane et Barbe-bleue*), **Ariane et Barbe-bleue** (Dukas), **Boulanger (L.)** (*Princesse Maleine*), **Bréville** (do. & *Sept Princesses*), **Burian (E.)** (*Aladina und Palomid*), **Chlubna** (do.), **Davis (J. D.)** (*Intruse*), **Février** (*Monna Vanna*), **Gibbs (C. A.)** (*Betrothal*), **Gretchaninov** (*Sœur Béatrice*), **Humperdinck** (*Blue Bird*), **Křička** (do.), **Liadov** (*S. Béatrice*), **Loeffler** (*Mort de Tintagiles*), **Marqués** (*Sor Beatriz*), **Monna Vanna** (Février), **Netchaiev** (*Seven Princesses*), **Nougués** (*Mort de T.*), **Oiseau bleu** (Wolff), **O'Neill** (*Blue Bird*), **Pelléas et Mélisande** (Debussy, Fauré, Schoenberg & Sibelius), **Salmhofer** (*Intruse*), **Santoliquido** (*Morte di Tintagiles*), **Séverac** (songs), **Steinberg** (*Princesse Maleine*), **Szeligowski** (*Blue Bird*), **Tocchi** (*Destino*), **Tovey** (*Aglavaine et Sélysette*).

Magadis. An ancient Gr. inst. about which no precise information has come down to us, but which was evidently capable of prod. sounds in 8ves. It was prob. of the Dulcimer or Psaltery type.

Magadizing (der. from above) = playing or singing in 8ves.

Magalhães, Filippe de (b. Azeitão nr. Lisbon, ?; d. ?), Port. 16th–17th cent. comp. Pupil of Mendes at Evora. Chapel master of the Misericordia at Lisbon and from 1614 of the royal chapel there under the Spa. king, Philip III.

Works incl. masses, canticles to the Blessed Virgin, chants, &c.

Mage, Pierre du. *See* **Du Mage.**

Magelone Romances. A cycle of 15 songs by Brahms, settings of poems from Ludwig Tieck's *Story of the Fair Magelone*, Op. 33, comp. in 1861–6.

Maggiore (It.) = major. The word is sometimes explicitly stated at a point in a comp. where the maj. key returns after a prolonged section in min., esp. in vars., to prevent the perf. from overlooking the change of key.

Magic Flute (Mozart). *See* **Zauberflöte.**

Magic Opal, The, opera by I. Albéniz (lib. by Arthur Law), prod. London, Lyric Theatre, 19. I. 1893.

Magic Opera, a species of opera not unlike the Eng. pantomime, popular partic. on the Viennese stage at the end of the 18th and opening of the 19th cent., where it was called *Zauberoper.* It consisted of dialogue and mus. numbers, had a fairy-tale subject with incidents of low comedy, and contained numerous scenic effects. The outstanding ex. is Mozart's *Zauberflöte*; others are Müller's *Zauberzither*, Wranitzky's *Oberon*, Süssmayr's *Spiegel von Arkadien*, Schubert's *Zauberharfe*; the Eng. work nearest to it in character is Weber's *Oberon.*

Magnard, (Lucien Denis Gabriel) Albéric (b. Paris, 9. VI. 1865; d. Baron, Oise, 3. IX. 1914), Fr. comp. Studied at the Paris Cons. and in 1888 became a private pupil of d'Indy. As the son of Francis M., ed. of *Le Figaro*, he was comfortably off and never held any official posts. He retired to Baron to devote himself to comp., pub. his works himself and never took any trouble to have them performed, though some were brought out by enthus. friends. During the very last days of the 1914–8 war he fired on the Gers. from his window, was killed as a sniper, and his house, incl. several of his MSS., was burnt down.

Works incl. operas *Yolande* (destroyed), *Guercœur* (partly destroyed) & *Bérénice*; 4 syms., *Suite dans le style ancien, Chant funèbre*, Ovt. *Hymne à la Justice* & *Hymne à Vénus* for orch.; stg. 4tet, pf. Trio, pf. & wind 5tet; v. & pf. So., co. & pf. So.; pf. pieces; songs, &c.

Magnetton (Ger. = Magnet Tone). An electrophonic inst. invented by Stelzhammer of Vienna in 1933, prod. its notes by means of electro-magnets and capable of imitating var. insts.

Magnificat. The song of the Blessed Virgin, often set to m. as a Vesper canticle in the Rom. Catholic and as part of the Evening Service in the Ang. church; also, more rarely, in a form better suited to concert perf.: e.g. Bach, Vaughan Williams, &c.

Mahabharata, The, Hindu epic, in Sanskrit. *See* **Sāvitri (Holst), Zumpe** (*Sawitri*).

Mahillon, (Charles) Victor (b. Brussels, 10. III. 1841; d. Saint-Jean, Cap Ferrat, 17. VI. 1924), Belg. mus. scholar. Son of the inst. maker Charles M. (1813–87). Studied at the Brussels Cons., where he became curator of the museum of mus. insts. He wrote on acoustics & insts.

Mahler, Gustav (b. Kališt, Boh., 7. VII. 1860; d. Vienna, 18. V. 1911), Cz.-Aus. comp. & cond. Son of a Jewish shopkeeper, but later embraced Rom. Catholicism. He showed great talent as a pfst. in his childhood, and in 1875 his family, who had removed to Jihlava (Iglau) soon after his birth, succeeded in entering him at the Vienna Cons. His pf. prof., Julius Epstein, seeing his real gifts, advised him to study comp. and cond. He remained at the Cons. until 1878 and also attended Bruckner's lectures at the Univ. He tried his luck in a competition for an opera in 1880 with *Das klagende Lied* (later turned into a cantata), but being unsuccessful he took to cond., 1st at a small summer theatre at Hall, in 1881 at Ljubljana and in 1882–3 at Olomouc. His outstanding gifts advanced him to more and more important posts: Cassel, 1884; Prague, 1885; Leipzig, 1886–8; Budapest, 1888–91; Hamburg, 1891–7; and Vienna, Imp. Opera, 1897–1907, where he became artistic dir. after a few months. But he hated the intrigues of theat. life and always longed to give himself up entirely to comp., for the concert-room, not the stage. In 1902 he married Alma Maria Schindler, 10. III. In 1892 he cond. Ger. opera at Covent Garden, London, and in 1907, when he was already suffering from heart disease, at the Metrop. Opera in N.Y. From 1908 to his death he was cond. of the N.Y. Phil. Soc., but spent the summers in Aus. composing.

Works incl. 10 syms. (the last unfinished), some with voc. parts; *Das Lied von der Erde*, sym. for m.-sop. & ten. solo & orch.; cantata *Das klagende Lied*; song-cycles *Lieder eines fahrenden Gesellen, Kindertotenlieder*; 3 books of early songs, 5 songs to words by Rückert, many other songs, incl. settings from *Des Knaben Wunderhorn*, &c.

Maichelbeck, Franz Anton (b. Reichenau

nr. Constance, 6. VII. 1702; d. Freiburg i/B., 14. VI. 1750), Ger. priest & comp. Studied in Rome and became prof. of It. & prebendary at the collegiate church at Freiburg.

Works incl. sos., suites, preludes, fugues, &c. for hpchd.

Maid Marian, or The Huntress of Arlingford, opera by Bishop (lib. by James Robinson Planché, based on Thomas Love Peacock's novel), prod. London, Covent Garden Theatre, 3. XII. 1822.

Maid of Artois, The, opera by Balfe (lib. by Alfred Bunn), prod. London, Drury Lane Theatre, 27. V. 1836. Written for Malibran.

Maid of Honour, The, opera by Balfe (lib. by Edward Fitzball, based on the same subject as Flotow's *Martha*), prod. London, Drury Lane Theatre, 20. XII. 1847.

Maid of Orleans, The (*Orleanskaya Dieva*), opera by Tchaikovsky (lib. by comp., based on Vassily Andreievitch Zhukovsky's trans. of Schiller's drama), prod. St. Petersburg, 25. II. 1881.

Maid of the Mill, The, opera by Arnold (lib. by Isaac Bickerstaffe, based on Richardson's *Pamela*), prod. London, Covent Garden Theatre, 31. I. 1765.

Maiden's Prayer, The. The most popular of tasteless and sentimental pf. drawing-room pieces ever written, by the Pol. comp. Thekla Badarczewska (1838–62).

Maikov, Apollon Nikolaievitch (1821–97), Rus. poet & dramatist. *See* **Judith** (Serov).

Maillard, Jean (b. ?; d. ?), Fr. 16th-cent. comp. Pupil (?) of Josquin des Prés. Wrote masses, motets, magnificats, chansons, &c.

Maillart, (Louis) Aimé (b. Montpellier, 24. III. 1817; d. Moulins, Alliers, 26. V. 1871), Fr. comp. Studied v. and comp. at the Paris Cons., Halévy being among his masters. He gained the Prix de Rome in 1841.

Works incl. operas *Gastibelza* (on Hugo's ballad *Guitare*), *Le Moulin des tilleuls, La Croix de Marie, Les Dragons de Villars, Les Pêcheurs de Catane* & *Lara* (after Byron); cantatas *Lionel Foscari, La Voie. sacrée* & *Le 15 Août*, &c.

Maine, Basil (b. Norwich, 4. III. 1894), Eng. critic, novelist & biog. Studied at Cambridge, and after schoolmastering and acting became m. critic to the *Daily Telegraph* in London, 1921, and the *Morning Post*, 1926. Later in his career he joined the Church of Eng. His mus. books incl. a large biog. of Elgar, *The Glory of Eng. M.*, var. essays, &c.

Maio, Gian Francesco di (old spelling Majo) (b. Naples, 24. III. 1732; d. Rome, 18. I. 1771), It. comp. Pupil of his father, Giuseppe di M. (1698–1771), chapel master to the king of the 2 Sicilies, and later of G. B. Martini at Bologna.

Works incl. operas *Ricimero, rè dei Goti, Caio Fabricio, Astrea placata, L'Almeria, Artaserse, Ipermestra, Alcide negli orti Esperidi, Adriano in Siria, Ifigenia in Tauride, Eumene* (unfinished, completed by Insanguine and Errichelli); contributions to other operas; orats., cantatas, &c.

Maison à vendre (*House for Sale*), opera by Dalayrac (lib. by Alexandre Duval), prod. Paris, Opéra-Comique, 23. X. 1800.

Maistre, Matthieu Le. *See* **Le Maistre.**

Maître de Chapelle (Fr.). *See* **Chapel Master.**

Maîtrise (Fr. = mastership). The former Fr. name for the whole estab. of the choir at caths. and collegiate churches, incl. not only all that appertained to their perf. in church, but also to their accommodation and maintenance. The Ms. were actually schools of m.

Maj. (abbr.) = Major.

Major. One of the 2 predominant scales (the other being Minor) of the tonal system superseding that of the Modes. The M. scale was identical with the late 16th-cent. Ionian mode (C–C on the white keys of the pf.), with semitones between the 3rd & 4th and 7th & 8th notes of the ascending scale. Its chief characteristics, as distinct from those of the modes, are the maj. 3rd and more esp. the maj.-7th leading-note, which is not present in any of the old modes except the Lydian. The modern M. scale, unlike the Ionian mode, may begin on any note of the chromatic scale.

Major Bass. A 32-ft. open pedal org. stop.

Major Intervals. Those Intervals in the mus. scale which by being lowered a semitone become Minor, not Diminished intervals, i.e. 2nds, 3rds, 6ths and 7ths; also 2nds, 3rds, &c. carried beyond the 8ve, i.e. 9ths, 10ths, &c.

Makarova, Nina (b. Yurin-on-Volga, 12. VIII. 1908). Rus. comp. She studied at the School of M. at Gorky (Nizhny-Novgorod) from 1923 and at the Moscow Cons. from 1927–35.

Works incl. opera *Courage*; m. for films; Sym. in D min.; cantata for Molotov for solo voices, chor. & orch.; v. & pf. So.; inst. pieces; pf. So. & pieces; song cycles (Pushkin, &c), chor. songs, &c.

Maklakiewicz, Jan Adam (b. Chojnata nr. Warsaw, 24. XI. 1899), Pol. orgst. & comp. Studied at the Chopin High School of M. and the Cons. at War-

saw, later with Dukas in Paris. In 1932 he became orgst. at the church of the Holy Cross at Warsaw and gained the Pol. State M. Prize for comp. He is also a teacher & critic.
Works incl. m. for plays & films; church m.; sym. *Holy God* and Prelude to *Lilla Weneda* for solo voices, chor. & orch.; Symph. Vars., *Lyric Poem, Song of the Daily Bread, Spanish Impressions,* suite of Pol. dances, *The Last Drum in memory of Marshal Pilsudski* for orch. (some with voices); Conc. for pf., voice & orch., v. & co. concs.; v. & co. pieces; 4 Japanese songs with orch.; *Les Vierges au crépuscule* for 2 voices, fl., va. & hp.; 7 songs *Preludes,* other songs; folksong arrs., &c.

Makropulos Case, The (*Več Makropulos*), opera by Janáček (lib. based on Karel Čapek's play), prod. Brno, 18. XII. 1926.

Malagueña. A Spa. (Andalusian) song whose place of orig. is Málaga. It also appears often as an inst. piece. It begins and ends on the dominant of its key.

Malczewski, Antoni (1793–1826), Pol. poet. *See* **Melcer** (*Maria*), **Opienski** (do.), **Soltys** (do.), **Statkowski** (do.).

Malder(e), Pierre van (b. Brussels, 13. V. 1724; d. Brussels, 3. XI. 1768), Flem. vst. & comp. He became vst. in the Duke of Lorraine's orch. and went to Paris, whence his fame spread through the chief mus. countries.
Works incl. operas *La Bagarre* & others; syms.; chamber m., &c.

Male Alto. An artificial extension of the highest male-voice register, prod. by Falsetto, used in Angl. church choirs and in male-voice 4tets & chor. socs., partic. in glees and partsongs.

Male Contralto
Male Soprano } *See* **Castrati.**

Maleingreau, Paul de (b. Trélon-en-Thiérache, 23. XI. 1887), Belg. orgst. & comp. Entered the Brussels Cons. in 1905, studying comp. under Tinel. He became prof. of harmony there and acquired fame as an org. recitalist.
Works incl. *Symphonie de Noël, Symphonie de la Passion,* Suite, 2 *Opus sacrum, Préludes à l'Introit, Triptyque pour la Noël,* &c. for org.; *Prélude, Choral et Fugue,* Suite, Sonatina, *Les Angelus de printemps,* &c. for pf.; co. & pf. So., &c.

Maler, Wilhelm (b. Heidelberg, 21. VI. 1902), Ger. comp. Studied with var. masters, incl. Jarnach, and was influenced by Hindemith. He was app. prof. of comp. at Cologne Cons. in 1925 and later also taught at Bonn Univ.
Works incl. orat. *Der ewige Strom,* cantata on poems by Stefan George; *Concerto grosso* & *Rondo on an Old Flem. Dance Ballad* for orch.; pf. Conc., hpchd. Conc.; stg. 4tet; m. for Youth Movement, games, &c.

Malherbe, Charles (Théodore) (b. Paris, 21. IV. 1853; d. Corneilles, Eure, 5. X. 1911), Fr. mcolst. Studied law and literature in Paris, but turned to m. and became asst. archivist at the Opéra in 1895 and archivist, in succession to Nuitter, in 1898. He made a great collection of mus. autographs, which he left to the Paris Cons. His books incl. studies of opéra comique, Wagner, Donizetti (catalogue), Auber, Tchaikovsky, &c.

Malheurs d'Orphée, Les (*The Miseries of Orpheus*), opera by Milhaud (lib. by Armand Lunel), prod. Brussels, Théâtre de la Monnaie, 7. V. 1926.

Malibran (*née* **García**), **Maria Felicita** (b. Paris, 24. III. 1808; d. Manchester, 23. IX. 1836), Spa. sop. singer. Studied under her father, Manuel García. After much travelling in It., &c., and appearing in a child's part in Paer's *Agnese* at Naples in 1813, she made her 1st concert appearance in Paris in 1824, and on the stage in London in 1825. In 1826 she married Malibran, an elderly Frenchman, but left him when he went bankrupt in 1827, and in 1830 she formed an attachment to Bériot, whom she married as soon as she had obtained her divorce shortly before her sudden death.

Malipiero, (Gian) Francesco (b. Venice, 18. III. 1882), It. comp. Studied under Rossi at the Bologna Liceo Musicale and became prof. of comp. at the Parma Cons. in 1921. Later he held a similar position at the Liceo Benedetto Marcello at Venice and in 1936 became prof. of mus. hist. at Padua Univ. He is the ed. of the complete ed. of Monteverdi's works.
Works incl. operatic trilogy *L'Orfeide* (*La morte delle maschere, Sette canzoni, Orfeo*), operas *Tre commedie goldoniane* (Goldoni's plays *La bottega da caffè, Sior Todero Brontolon, Le baruffe chiozzotte*), *Filomela e l'infatuato, Merlino mastro d'organi, Il mistero di Venezia* (*Le aquile Aquileia, Il finto Arlecchino, I corvi di San Marco*), *Torneo notturno, La favola del figlio cambiato* (lib. by Pirandello), *Giulio Cesare* & *Antonio e Cleopatra* (both after Shakespeare), *Ecuba, I capricci di Callot*; ballets *La mascherata delle principesse prigioniere, Pantea*; for orch.: *Sinfoniadel mare, Sinfonia del silenzio e della morte, Ditirambo tragico, Impressioni dal vero* (3 sets), *Per una favola cavalleresca, Pause del silenzio, Concerti, Inni, Invenzioni, Sinfonia in quattro tempi come le quattro stagioni, Sinfonia*

elegiaca & others; 2 pf. concs., *Variazioni senza tema* for pf. & orch., v. Conc., co. Conc.; *Il commiato* (Leopardi) for bar. & orch.; orats. *San Francesco d'Assisi, La cena, La passione, Missa pro mortuis*; 2 stg. 4tets, *Rispetti e strambotti, Stornelli e ballate* & *Canzoni alla madrigalesca* for stg. 4tet, *Sonata a tre* for v., co. & pf., *Sonata a cinque* for fl., hp., v., va. & co., *Ricercari* & *Ritrovari* for 11 insts. & other chamber m.; many pf. works: *Preludi autunnali, Poemi asolani, Barlumi, Maschere che passano*, &c.; songs *Tre poesie di Angelo Poliziano, Quattro sonetti del Burchiello, Due sonetti del Berni, Le stagioni italiche*, &c.

Malishevsky. Though often so translit. from Rus., the proper Pol. spelling is

Maliszewski, Witold (b. Mohylew, Podolia, 20. VII. 1873; d. ?, 1939), Pol. vst., pfst. & comp. In his youth the family lived in the Caucasus and he studied at Tiflis, but in 1891 went to St. Petersburg to study medicine; however, he later entered the Cons. as a pupil of Rimsky-Korsakov, and in 1908–21 was dir. of the Odessa school of m. He then left for Warsaw, where he taught at the Cons. and the Chopin School of M. In 1931 he became dir. of the art dept. of the Ministry of Educ. and gained the State M. Prize.

Works incl. opera-ballets *Syrena* & *The Legend of Boruta*; Requiem & *Missa Pontificalis Papae Pii XI*; 4 syms., 2 symph. pictures, *Merry Ovt.* and ovt. on themes by Schubert; pf. Conc., Fantasy for pf. & orch., Suite for co. & orch.; 3 stg. 4tets, stg. 5tet; pf. pieces; songs, &c.

Mallapert, Robin (b. ?; d. ?), Fr. 16th-cent. musn. Master of the children at Santa Maria Maggiore in Rome for some time before 1538, when he was app. chapel master at San Luigi dei Francesi there. He (?) returned to Santa Maria about 1550.

Mallarmé, Stéphane (1842–98), Fr. poet. *See* **Cartan, Debussy** (3 poems), **Hindemith** (*Mirror before me*), **Prélude à l'Après-midi d'un faune** (Debussy), **Ravel** (3 poems).

Mallet (orig. **Malloch**), **David** (1705–65), Sco. poet & essayist. *See* **Alfred** (Arne, incl. 'Rule, Britannia').

Malling, Otto (Valdemar) (b. Copenhagen, 1. VI. 1848; d. Copenhagen, 5. X. 1915), Dan. comp. Studied in Copenhagen and abroad, became chor. cond. in Copenhagen in 1872, church orgst. in 1878 and dir. of the Cons. in 1899.

Works incl. Sym. & other orch. comps.; pf. Conc.; chor. works; chamber m.; songs, &c.

Mallinger (*née* **Lichtenegger**), **Mathilde** (b. Zagreb, 17. II. 1847; d. Berlin, 19. IV. 1920), Ger.-Croat. sop. singer. Studied 1st with her father, then at the Prague Cons. and in Vienna; made her 1st stage appearance at Munich in 1866 and created the part of Eva in Wagner's *Meistersinger* in 1868.

Mallinson, (James) Albert (b. Leeds, 13. XI. 1870), Eng. orgst. & comp. He studied mainly abroad and married the Ger. singer Anna Steinhauer, who sang his songs on her tours with him in Ger. and Den. In 1904 he was app. orgst. of the Eng. church at Dresden.

Works incl. over 300 songs, &c.

Malten, Therese (real name Müller) (b. Insterburg, 21. VI. 1855; d. Neu-Zschieren nr. Dresden, 2. I. 1930), Ger. sop. singer. Studied with Gustav Engel in Berlin and made her 1st stage appearance at Dresden in 1873, remaining attached to the Court Opera there.

Mälzel, Johann Nepomuk (b. Ratisbon, 15. VIII. 1772; d. at sea, 21. VII. 1838), Ger. inventor. Settled in Vienna in 1792 and invented var. mechan. insts., also, in 1814, the Metronome. Later he lived in Paris and from 1826 in U.S.A. Beethoven's *Battle of Victoria* was orig. written for M.'s 'Panharmonion.'

Manchicourt, Pierre de (b. Béthune, ?; d. ?), Fr. or Flem. 16th-cent. comp. He worked at Tournai *c.* 1740, at Arras *c.* 1755 and (?) at Antwerp later.

Works incl. masses, motets; chansons, &c.

Mancinelli, Luigi (b. Orvieto, 5. II. 1848; d. Rome, 2. II. 1921), It. cond. & comp. Studied at Florence, incl. the co., and joined the orch. at the Teatro della Pergola there. In 1874 he went to the Teatro Apollo in Rome, where he deputized for a cond. so successfully that he made operatic cond. his future career. In 1876 he appeared as comp. of incid. m. and in 1884 prod. his 1st opera. In 1881 he became dir. of the Liceo Musicale at Bologna, as well as chapel master at San Petronio cath. and cond. of the Teatro Comunale there, and he organized orch. and chamber m.

Works incl. operas *Isora di Provenza, Ero e Leandro, Paolo e Francesca* (after Dante), *Tizianello, Sogno di una notte d'estate* (after Shakespeare); incid. m. to Pietro Cossa's *Messalina* & *Cleopatra*; orat. *Isaias*, cantata *St. Agnes*; 2 masses, &c.

Mancini, Francesco (b. Naples, 1679; d. Naples, 11. VI. 1739), It. comp. Pupil at the Cons. di San Loreto, Naples, afterwards a teacher there and from 1728 its principal.

Works incl. operas *Gli amanti generosi* (later *L'Idaspe fedele*) and *c.* 20 others; orats., &c.

Mancinus, Thomas (real name Mencken) (b. Schwerin, 1550; d. Wolfenbüttel, *c.* 1620), Ger. comp. Cantor at the cath. school of Schwerin, 1572–8, and then in the service of the Duke of Brunswick at Wolfenbüttel.
Works incl. Passions according to St. Matthew & St. John, Lat. & Ger. motets and madrigals, secular Ger. songs for several voices, &c.

Mandoline (or Mandolin). A stg. inst. descending from the lute, but with a more rounded back and metal instead of gut stgs., which are played with a plectrum. The fingerboard is fretted to facilitate fingering and intonation.

Mandore. A stg. inst. of the lute type, now obs., but surviving in a slightly different form in the Mandoline.

Mandragola, La (*The Mandrake*), opera by Castelnuovo-Tedesco (lib. based on Machiavelli's comedy), prod. Venice, Teatro La Fenice, 4. V. 1926.

Mandyczewski, Eusebius (b. Czernowitz [Cernauti], 18. VIII. 1857; d. Vienna, 15. VII. 1929), Aus. mcolst. Studied at the Vienna Cons. In 1880 he became keeper of the archives of the Vienna Phil. Soc. and in 1897 prof. at the Cons. Ed. of the complete Schubert ed. and of that of Haydn's works (now abandoned).

Manelli, Francesco (b. Tivoli, 1595; d. Parma, IX. 1667), It. bass singer & comp. Singer at Tivoli cath., 1605–24, and chapel master there, 1627–9. He then went to Rome, married a singer, Maddalena ?, and about 1636 settled at Venice, where his wife ed. his collected non-operatic works. From about 1645 he was in the service of the Duke of Parma, Ranuccio II.
Works incl. operas *L'Andromeda*, *La maga fulminata*, *L'Alcate*, *La Licaste* & others; cantatas, canzonets, chaconnes, &c.

Manén, Joan (b. Barcelona, 14. III. 1883), Spa. vst. & comp. Studied with his father and later with Jean Alard in Paris. He toured widely and eventually settled in Berlin. Ed. of complete works of Paganini.
Works incl. operas *Giovanna di Napoli*, *Neron y Acte*, *Cami del sol*, *Der Fackeltanz*; symph. poem *Nova Catalonia*; Spa. v. Conc., Catalan Caprices & *Scherzo fantastique* for v. & orch., Concerto grosso *Juventus* for 2 vs., pf. & orch.; stg. 4tet; suites for v. & pf., &c.

Manfred, incid. m. for Byron's drama by Schumann, Op. 115, comp. 1849; 1st concert perf. of the ovt., Leipzig, Gewandhaus, III. 1852. The whole prod. with Byron's play, Weimar, 13. VI. 1852.
Sym. by Tchaikovsky, Op. 58, based on the same, comp. 1885 and prod. Moscow, 6. IV. 1886.

Manfredina. A corruption of the name of the Monferrina which became current in Eng. when that dance was introd.

Mangold. Ger. family of musns.:
1. August Daniel M. (b. Darmstadt, 25. VII. 1775; d. Darmstadt, 1842), cst. 1st at the Frankfort theatre and from 1814 in the Grand-Ducal orch. at Darmstadt.
2. Wilhelm M. (b. Darmstadt, 19. XI. 1796; d. Darmstadt, 23. V. 1875), vst. & comp., nephew of prec. Studied with Vogler and under Méhul and Cherubini at the Paris Cons. In court service at Darmstadt from 1819. Comp. operas, ovts., chamber m., &c.
3. Karl Ludwig Amand M. (b. Darmstadt, 8. X. 1813; d. Oberstdorf, Allgäu, 5. VIII. 1889), cond. & comp., brother of prec. Studied with his father & brother, and later at the Paris Cons. Court mus. dir. at Darmstadt from 1848.
Works incl. opera *Tannhäuser* & others; cantatas; orch. pieces; male voice chors., &c.

Manicorde (Fr.) = Clavichord.

Manieren (Ger. plur., lit. 'manners'). In its now obs. mus. sense the word was used for 'Ornaments.'

Mann, Arthur Henry (b. Norwich, 16. V. 1850; d. Cambridge, 19. XI. 1929), Eng. orgst., choirmaster & comp. Choir-boy at Norwich cath. under Z. Buck. He held var. orgst.'s posts, took the Mus.D. degree at Oxford in 1882, and in 1876 was app. orgst. & choirmaster at King's Coll. Chapel, Cambridge.
Works incl. orat. *Ecce Homo*; Te Deum, services, anthems & other church m., &c.

Männergesangverein (Ger. lit. 'men's singing-association'). A male-voice chor. soc.

Manners, Charles (real name Southcote Mansergh) (b. London, 27. XII. 1857; d. Dundrum, Co. Dublin, 3. V. 1935), Ir. singer and impresario. Studied at the R. Ir. A.M. at Dublin and the R.A.M. in London; later in It. After joining an opera chor. he made his 1st solo stage appearance in 1882. Having married Fanny Moody in 1890 he estab. the Moody-Manners Opera Co. in 1897.

Mannheim School. A group of comps., early exponents of the sym., so named for having their centre at the electoral court of Mannheim, middle of 18th cent. Its chief members are, in order of age, F. X. Richter, Holzbauer, J. Stamitz, Toeschi (the only It.), Filtz and Cannabich.

Manns, August (Friedrich) (b. Stolzenberg nr. Stettin, 12. III. 1825; d. London, 1. III. 1907), Ger. cond. At first clst. and vst. in var. bands and orchs. in Ger.; later bandmaster. Went to London as sub-cond. at Crystal Palace, 1854, becoming full cond. in 1855, when he enlarged the orch. Began popular Saturday concerts in 1856 and cond. the Handel Festival, 1883–1900. Knighted 1904.

Manon, opera by Massenet (lib. by Henri Meilhac and Philippe Gille, based on Prévost's novel *Manon Lescaut*), prod. Paris. Opéra-Comique, 19. I. 1884.

Manon Lescaut, ballet by Halévy (scen. by Scribe, based on Prévost's novel, chgph. by Jean-Pierre Aumer), prod. Paris, Opéra, 3. V. 1830.

Opera by Auber (lib. by Scribe, based on Prévost's novel), prod. Paris, Opéra-Comique, 23. II. 1856.

Opera by Puccini (lib., in It., by Marco Praga, Domenico Oliva & Luigi Illica, based on Prévost's novel), prod. Turin, Teatro Regio, 1. II. 1893.

Mansergh, Southcote. *See* **Manners, Charles.**

Manual (from Lat. *manus* = hand). A keyboard played by the hand, esp. the keyboards of the org. as distinct from the pedals.

Manualiter (Lat. corrupt.). A direction in org. m., esp. Bach's, indicating that a passage is to be played on a manual or manuals.

Manuel Venegas, unfinished opera by H. Wolf (lib. by Moritz Hoernes based on Alarcón's *El niño de la bola*), begun 1897.

Manzoni, Alessandro (1785–1873), It. poet & novelist. *See* **Bianca e Falliero** (Rossini), **Bryllupet ved Como-Søen** (Gläser), **Promessi sposi** (Petrella & Ponchielli).

Manzoni Requiem. The name often given to Verdi's Requiem, comp. in 1873 for the anniversary of the death of Alessandro Manzoni, on which it was 1st perf. at Milan, church of San Marco, 22. V. 1874; repeated at the Teatro alla Scala on 25. V. The 'Libera me' is adapted from that contrib. by V. to the collective Requiem he suggested should be written by var. It. comps. on the death of Rossini in 1868, a plan which did not materialize. That the 'Libera me' was not merely taken over as it stood is proved by the fact that it contains allusions to material occurring earlier in the M. R.

Manzuoli, Giovanni (b. Florence, *c.* 1725; d. Florence, *c.* 1780), It. male sop. singer. Made an early success in It.; went to Madrid in 1763 and to London in 1764.

Maometto Secondo (*Mahomet II*), opera by Rossini (lib. by Cesare della Valle, Duke of Ventignano), prod. Naples, Teatro San Carlo, 3. XII. 1820. A Fr. version entitled *Le Siège de Corinthe,* prod. Paris, 9. X. 1826.

Mara (*née* **Schmeling**), **Gertrud Elisabeth** (b. Cassel, 23. II. 1749; d. Reval, 20. I. 1833), Ger. sop. singer. She was taken to London by her father, a poor musn., as child prodigy on the v., but he was persuaded to have her taught singing by Paradisi there. Later she studied at F. Hiller's m. school at Leipzig and made her 1st appearance as a singer in 1771 at the Dresden court opera. She went to Berlin into the service of Frederick II and married the cst. Johann Baptist Mara there. In 1781 she 1st appeared in Vienna and in 1784 in London.

Mara, La (Marie Lipsius). *See* **La Mara.**

Maraca. A perc. inst. used mainly in jazz and swing bands, a rattle made of a dried gourd containing beads, dried seeds or shot.

Marais, Marin (b. Paris, 31. III. 1656; d. Paris, 15. VIII. 1728), Fr. bass violist and comp. Pupil of Chaperon at the Sainte-Chapelle and of viol masters; later member of the royal band and the orch. at the Opéra, where he studied comp. under Lully. In 1725 he retired to devote himself to gardening, but continued to teach. He added a 7th stg. to the bass viol.

Works incl. operas *Idylle dramatique, Alcide* & *Pantomime des pages* (both with Lully's son Louis), *Ariane et Bacchus, Alcyone, Sémélé*; Te Deum; concs. for v. & bass; trios for fl., v. & bass; pieces for 1 & 2 viols; *La Gamme* pieces for v., viol & hpchd., &c.

Marais, Roland (b. Paris, ?; d. ?), Fr. violist & comp., son of prec. Studied with his father, who had 18 other children by his wife Catherine (*née* Damicourt), and joined the royal band in 1725, when his father retired. He wrote a *Nouvelle Méthode de musique* and pub. 2 books of viol pieces.

Marazzoli (or **Marazzuoli**), **Marco** (b. Parma, ?; d. Rome, 24. I. 1662), It. singer, hpst. & comp. Sang in the Papal Chapel in Rome in the 1630s and was in the service of Christina of Swe. there.

Works incl. operas *Chi soffre speri* (with V. Mazzocchi), *Dal male il bene* (with Abbatini), *La vita umana* & others; orats., cantatas; songs, &c.

Marbeck, John. *See* **Merbecke.**

Marcando (It. = marking, accentuating) or

Marcato (It. = marked, accentuated). A direction indicating that a piece or mvt. is to be played in a decided, energetic manner, or that a part is to be brought out strongly above the accomp. or surrounding parts in a passage.

Marcello, Benedetto (b. Venice, 24. VII. 1686; d. Brescia, 24. VII. 1739), It. vst., singer & comp. Pupil of Lotti and Gasparini in Venice. Of noble birth, he was sent to Rome to study law, his father regarding a mus. career as undignified. He never held any mus. posts, but filled important gvt. appts. at Venice. He was also a writer and poet, pub. the satirical pamphlet *Il teatro alla moda,* writing the lib. for Ruggieri's opera *Arato in Sparta* and transl. Dryden's *Timotheus* for a cantata.

Works incl. operas & serenatas *La fede riconosciuta, Arianna*; orats. *Giuditta, Gioas; Il trionfo della poesia e della musica*; solo cantatas *Timoteo, Cassandra, Clori e Daliso, La stravaganza*; 50 psalms *Estro poetico-armonico* as paraphrased by Girolamo Giustiniani for several voices & insts., &c.

March. A piece of m. in strongly emphasized regular metre, usually in 4–4 or 2–4 time, but sometimes in 6–4 (equiv. to a dual rhythm of triplets), primarily intended for use at military parades to keep marching soldiers in step, but also the m. most often used at processionals of var. kinds, incl. esp. those occurring on the stage in operas and other theatre pieces. Funeral Ms. also have primarily a processional purpose, and they are considerably slower in pace. Ms. of all kinds, however, can be used by comps. in a purely mus. way, merely as mvts. in some work in so. or suite form. Mvts. of this kind which are not so much actual Ms. as pieces of M. character, are often labelled *alla marcia* or *alla marcia funebre.*

Marchand de Venise, Le (*The Merchant of Venice*), opera by Hahn (lib. by Miguel Zamaçoïs, after Shakespeare), prod. Paris, Opéra, 25. III. 1935.

Marchand, Louis (b. Lyons, 2. II. 1669; d. Paris, 17. II. 1732), Fr. orgst. & comp. Studied with his father, a m. master, made a reputation as an org. concert performer in Paris and became court orgst. at Versailles, also at var. Paris churches. He was sent into exile in 1717 for insubordination and went to Dresden and nearly obtained the post of Saxon court orgst.; but being challenged to compete with Bach at the org., he disappeared and returned to Paris, where he set up as org. teacher.

Works incl. opera *Pyrame et Thisbé*; several books of org. pieces; 2 of hpchd. pieces, &c.

Marchant, Stanley (Robert) (b. London, 15. V. 1883), Eng. orgst., teacher & comp. Studied at the R.A.M. in London, of which he became principal in 1936, succeeding McEwen. He held var. orgst.'s post, incl. those of asst. and sub-orgst. at St. Paul's cath., took the Mus.D. degree at Oxford in 1914 and became 1st orgst. at St. Paul's in 1927. In 1937 he became prof. of m. at London Univ. Knighted in 1943.

Works incl. Te Deum for the re-opening of St. Paul's (1930), Te Deum for George V's jubilee (1935), &c.

Marchesi (de Castrone). It. family of singers:

1. Salvatore M. (b. Palermo, 15. I. 1822; d. Paris, 20. II. 1908), bar. singer & teacher. He came of a noble family, succeeding later to the title of Marchese della Raiata. Studying law and philos. at Palermo, he took singing and comp. lessons from Raimondi and later studied at Milan under Lamperti & others. Having fled to Amer. as a political refugee from the 1848 revols., he made his 1st stage appearance there. On his return to Eur. he settled in London for a time. He married Mathilde Graumann in 1852. Wrote books on singing, voc. exercises, a number of songs and made It. transs. of var. opera libs.

2. Mathilde M. (*née* Graumann) (b. Frankfort o/M., 24. III. 1821; d. London, 18. XI. 1913), m.-sop. singer & teacher, wife of prec. Began to study singing when her father, a wealthy merchant, lost his fortune in 1843. In 1845 she went to Paris to continue her studies with García, whose pupils she took over when he was incapacitated by an accident. Settled in London in 1849, she sang much at concerts. Soon after her marriage to M. she became prof. of singing at the Vienna Cons., 1854–61; later taught mainly in Paris.

3. Blanche M. (b. Paris, 4. IV. 1863; d. London, 15. XII. 1940), sop. singer & teacher, daughter of prec. Studying the v. at first, she took to singing in 1881, appeared in Berlin and Brussels in 1895, in London in 1896, and settled there as teacher and concert singer.

Marchesi, Luigi (or Lodovico) (b. Milan, 1755; d. Milan, 18. XII. 1829), It. male sop. Studied 1st under his father, a hn. player, and then at Bergamo and Milan; made his 1st stage appearance in Rome, 1774. He travelled widely, incl. St. Petersburg in 1785 and London in 1788.

He comp. some songs and was painted by Cosway.

Marchetti, Filippo (b. Bolognola, Macerata, 26. II. 1831; d. Rome, 18. I. 1902), It. comp. Studied at the Collegio di San Pietro a Maiella at Naples, settled in Rome and later at Milan. Having prod. several successful operas, he ceased to comp. in 1880, became president of the Accademia di Santa Cecilia in Rome, 1881, and dir. of the Liceo Musicale there, 1885.

Works incl. operas *Gentile da Verano, La demente, Il paria, Romeo e Giulietta* (after Shakespeare), *Ruy Blas* (after Hugo), *Gustavo Wasa, Don Giovanni d'Austria*, &c.

Marchettus (b. Padua, ?; d. ?), It. 13th–14th-cent. theorist. Lived at Cesena and Verona at some time and was in the service of Rainier, Prince of Monaco. He wrote 2 treatises on the division of the scale and on notation, which aroused much opposition.

Marcia (It.) = March.

Maréchal, (Charles) Henri (b. Paris, 22. I. 1842; d. Paris, 10. V. 1924), Fr. comp. Studied at the Paris Cons., where he gained the Prix de Rome in 1870. In 1896 he became inspector of mus. educ.

Works incl. operas *Les Amours de Cathérine, La Taverne des Trabans, L'Étoile, Déidamie, Calendal, Ping-Sin, Daphnis et Chloé*; ballet *Le Lac des aulnes*; incid. m. for a stage version of Erckmann - Chatrian's *L'Ami Fritz*, of Dostoievsky's *Crime and Punishment*, &c.; orats. *La Nativité, Le Miracle de Naïm*; cantata *Le Jugement de Dieu*; *Esquisses vénitiennes* & *Antar* for orch.: *Les Vivants et les morts* for voc. 4tet & orch,. &c.

Marek, Czeslaw (b. Přžemysl, 16. IX. 1891), Pol. pfst. & comp. Studied at Lwów, at the Acad. of M. in Vienna and was also a pf. pupil of Leschetizky there. In 1913–4 he studied comp. with Pfitzner at Strasburg. He travelled widely as pfst. in 1916–28, taught at Lwów and later at Zürich, where he settled.

Works incl. Suite & *Sinfonia* for the Schubert centenary, Scherzo for orch.; Pol. folksongs with chamber orch.; *Little Suite* for 3 recorders or vs. & pf. & other school and home m.; So. & pieces for v. & pf.; 2 *Romantic Pieces* for hp.; *Triptych, Pieces for Children* & other pf. works; chor. works; songs, incl. 5 to words by Lenau, &c.

Marenzio, Luca (b. Coccaglio nr. Brescia, 1553; d. Rome, 22. VIII. 1599), It. singer & comp. Studied with Giovanni Contini, orgst. at Brescia cath., pub. his 1st work in 1581, went to Rome soon afterwards, where he became chapel master to Cardinal d'Este, served under Sigismund III in Pol. for 2 years some time between 1588–93, returned to Rome, where he became a singer or (?) orgst. in the Papal Chapel and came under the patronage of Cardinal Aldobrandini. His madrigals were introd. into Eng. through Yonge's *Musica transalpina* in 1588 and he was in correspond. with Dowland in 1595.

Works incl. Mass, motets, *Sacri concenti*; madrigals (9 vols.), *Villanelle ed arie alla napolitana* (5 vols.), &c.

Marescotti, André (b. Geneva, 30. IV. 1902), Swi. orgst. & comp. Studied at Geneva and with Roger-Ducasse in Paris. App. orgst. & choirmaster at the Sacré-Cœur at Geneva in 1924 and prof. at the Cons. there.

Works incl. *Messe Saint-André*, 2 motets; Ovt., *Prélude au Grand Meaulnes* & *Aubade* for orch.; pf. pieces; songs, &c.

Margaret at the Spinning-Wheel (Schubert). *See* **Gretchen am Spinnrade.**

Margherita d'Anjou, opera by Meyerbeer (lib., in It., by Felice Romani, based on a play by René Charles Guilbert de Pixérécourt), prod. Milan, Teatro alla Scala, 14. XI. 1820.

Maria Antonia Walpurga (or **Walpurgis**) (b. Munich, 18. VII. 1724; d. Dresden, 23. IV. 1780), Ger. comp. Daughter of the Elector of Bavaria, afterwards Emperor Charles VII. Pupil of Giovanni Ferrandini, Porpora and Hasse; married Frederick Augustus II, Elector of Saxony (Augustus III of Pol.). She was a member of the Arcadian Acad. in Rome under the name of Ermelinda Talèa Pastorella Arcada (pseud. E. T. P. A.).

Works incl. operas *Il trionfo della fedeltà* (with add. m. by Hasse) & *Talestri, regina delle Amazoni*, &c.

Maria di Rohan, opera by Donizetti (lib. by Salvatore Cammarano), prod. Vienna, Kärntnertor Theatre, 5. VI. 1843.

Maria di Rudenz, opera by Donizetti (lib. by Salvatore Cammarano), prod. Venice, Teatro La Fenice, 30. I. 1838.

Maria Theresa (actually *Maria Theresia*), the nickname of a Sym. by Haydn, No. 48, C maj., comp. in 1773 for a visit of the Empress M. T. to Prince Esterházy at Esterház.

Maria Tudor, opera by Gomes (lib. by Marco Praga, based on Victor Hugo's tragedy), prod. Milan, Teatro alla Scala, 27. III. 1879.

Mariages samnites, Les, opera by Grétry (lib. by Barnabé Farmian de Rozoy, based on a story by Marmontel), prod. Paris, Comédie-Italienne, 12. IV. 1776.

Mariani, Angelo (b. Ravenna, 11. X. 1822; d. Genoa, 13. VI. 1873), It. cond. & comp. Studied at home, at Rimini and under Rossini at the Liceo Filarmonico of Bologna; came out as vst.-cond. at Messina in 1844 and was cond. of the court theatre at Copenhagen, 1847–8. After fighting in the revol. army in 1848, he went to the sultan's court at Constantinople, 1849–52, and then became cond. at the Teatro Carlo Felice at Genoa. He appeared in many places in It. and abroad as guest cond. and gave the 1st It. perf. of Wagner's *Lohengrin* at Bologna in 1871.

Works incl. Requiem; hymn for the Sultan of Turkey, cantatas *La fidanzata del guerriero* & *Gli esuli*; orch. m.; songs, &c.

Mariazell Mass. The familiar name of Haydn's Mass in C maj. comp. in 1782 for the Benedictine monastery at M.

Marie, opera by Hérold (lib. by François Antoine Eugène de Planard), prod. Paris, Opéra-Comique, 12. VIII. 1826.

Mariés de la Tour d'Eiffel, Les (*The Wedded Pair of the Eiffel Tower*), ballet by 5 of 'Les Six': Auric, Honegger, Milhaud, Poulenc & Tailleferre (scen. by Jean Cocteau), Prod. Paris, Théâtre des Champs-Élysées, 18. VI. 1921.

Mariette, Auguste Édouard (Mariette Bey) (1821–81), Fr. Egyptologist. Founder of the museum at Cairo. He outlined the lib. for Verdi's *Aida,* drafted in Fr. by Camille du Locle and written in It. by Ghislanzoni.

Marimba. A Mex. perc. inst. of African origin, made of wood, similar to the Xylophone, but larger and with resonance-boxes to each note.

Marimba Gongs. A perc. inst. similar to the Marimba, but with metal plates instead of wooden strips to prod. the notes.

Marin de La Guerre. *See* **La Guerre.**

Marin, José (b. Madrid, 1619; d. Madrid, 17. III. 1699), Spa. ten. singer & comp. He sang in the Encarnación convent at Madrid in his younger years, became a priest and a highwayman, fled to Rome after committing murder, was imprisoned, but at the end of his life had a great reputation as a musn.

Works incl. songs with continuo, songs with guitar accomp., &c.

Marin, Marie-Martin Marcel de, Viscount (b. Saint-Jean-de-Luz, 8. IX. 1769; d. ?, after 1861), Fr. hpst., vst. & comp., (?) of It. descent. In 1783 he became a member of the Arcadian Acad. in Rome and during the Fr. Revol. settled in London; later at Toulouse.

Works incl. chamber m., hp. sos. & pieces, v. sos., &c.

Marine Trumpet. *See* **Tromba marina.**

Marini, Biagio (b. Brescia, before 1597; d. Venice, 1665), It. vst. & comp. He was employed successively as vst. at Venice, as mus. dir. at the church of Sant' Eufemia at Brescia, at the courts of Parma and Munich, at Düsseldorf, Ferrara and Milan.

Works incl. psalms, vespers & other church m.; syms.; sos., dances, &c. for stg. insts.; voc. & inst. chamber m.; madrigals, canzonets, &c. for several voices; sacred songs for several voices, &c.

Marino Faliero, opera by Donizetti (lib. by Emanuele Bidera, based on Byron's drama), prod. Paris, Théâtre Italien, 12. III. 1835.

Marinuzzi, Gino (b. Palermo, 24. III. 1882; d. Milan, 17. VIII. 1945), It. cond. & comp. Studied at the Palermo Cons. 1st appeared as cond. at Catania, later worked at Palermo, Madrid, Trieste, Buenos Aires and Chicago. On his return to It. he cond. opera in all the large cities and he was dir. of the Liceo Musicale at Bologna, 1915–9.

Works incl. operas *Barberina, Jacquerie, Palla de' Mozzi*; suites *Siciliana* & *Romana,* symph. poem *Sicania, Elegia, Rito nuziale* for orch.; *Andantino all' antica* for fl., stgs. & hp., &c.

Mario (Giovanni Matteo), Cavaliere di Candia (b. Cagliari, 17. X. 1810; d. Rome, 11. XII. 1883), It. ten. singer. 1st appearance, Paris, 1838; 1st visit to London the following year. Married Giulia Grisi.

Mariotte, Antoine (b. Avignon, 22. XII. 1875), Fr. comp. A naval officer at first, he left the Navy in 1897 and became a student at the Schola Cantorum in Paris as a pupil of d'Indy. He cond. at Saint-Étienne and then at Lyons, and became dir. of the Orleans Cons. in 1920. In 1935–9 he was dir. of the Opéra-Comique in Paris. He was accused of having plagiarized R. Strauss in his *Salomé,* but the work was written before S.'s was prod.

Works incl. operas *Salomé* (Oscar Wilde), *Le Vieux Roi, Esther: Princesse d'Israël, Léontine Sœurs, Nele Dooryn, Gargantua* (after Rabelais); *Avril, Pâques françaises* & *Toujours* for unaccomp. chor.: *Impressions urbaines* & *Kakemonos* for pf. & orch.; *En montagne* for 3 wind or stg. insts. with stg. 5tet or pf.; So., *50 Canons expressifs,* suite *Marine, Sonatines d'automne* for pf.; *Intimités, Poème de pitié, Le Vieux Chemin* & other songs, &c.

Maritana, opera by V. Wallace (lib. by

Edward Fitzball, based on the play *Don César de Bazan* by Adolphe Philippe d'Ennery & Philippe François Dumanoir), prod. London, Drury Lane Theatre, 15. XI. 1845.

Marivaux, Pierre de (1688–1763), Fr. novelist and dramatist. *See* **Poise** (*Surprise de l'amour*).

Markevitch, Igor (b. Kiev, 27. VII. 1912), Rus. comp. His parents emigrated and lived in Swi., but he went to Paris at the age of 15 as a pupil of Nadia Boulanger. He owed his 1st public appearances to Sergey Diaghilev.

Works incl. ballets *Rébus* & *L'Envoi d'Icare*; cantata on Milton's *Paradise Lost* and others, *Cantique d'Amour*, *Nouvel Age*, cantata for sop. and male-voice chor. (Jean Cocteau); *Hymnes*, Concerto grosso and Sinfonietta for orch.; Conc. and Partita for pf. & orch.; *Galop* for small orch.; Psalm for sop. & orch.; Serenade for v., cl. & bn., &c.

Markull, Friedrich Wilhelm (b. Reichenbach nr. Elbing, Prus., 17. II. 1816; d. Danzig, 30. IV. 1887), Ger. pfst., orgst. & comp. Studied with Schneider at Dessau and was app. orgst. at St. Mary's church at Danzig in 1836.

Works incl. operas *Maja und Alpino*, *Der König von Zion*, *Das Walpurgisfest*; orats. *Johannes der Täufer*, *Das Gedächtnis der Entschlafenen*; Psalm lxxxvi and hymn-tunes: syms.; org. & pf. works; songs, &c.

Marlowe, Christopher (1564–93), Eng. dramatist. *See* **Bowles** (*Dr. Faustus*, **Heming** (*Tamburlaine*).

Marmontel, Antoine François (b. Clermont-Ferrand, 18. VII. 1816; d. Paris, 15. I. 1898), Fr. pfst. and teacher. Studied under Zimmermann at the Paris Cons. and became prof. of pf. there in 1848. He wrote several books on the pf. and its m. and comp. instructive pf. works.

Marmontel, Jean François (b. Bort, Limousin, 11. VII. 1723; d. Abloville, Eure, 31. XII. 1799), Fr. author. Libst. for Grétry, Piccinni, Cherubini and others; defender of Piccinni against Gluck and author of an *Essai sur les révolutions de la musique en France*.

See also **Amitié à l'épreuve** (Grétry), **Antigone** (Zingarelli), **Atys** (Piccinni), **Céphale et Procris** (Grétry), **Clari** (Bishop, from *Laurette*), **Démophon** (Cherubini), **Didon** (Piccinni), **Mariages samnites** (Grétry), **Zémire et Azor** (Grétry), **Zemire und Azor** (Spohr).

Mârouf, savetier du Caire (*M., the Cobbler of Cairo*), opera by Rabaud (lib. by Lucien Népoty, based on a story in the *Arabian Nights*), prod. Paris, Opéra-Comique, 15. V. 1914.

Marpurg, Friedrich Wilhelm (b. nr. Seehausen, Brandenburg, 21. XI. 1718; d. Berlin, 22. V. 1795), Ger. writer on m. He held a secretary's appt. in Paris in 1746 and met Voltaire, Rameau and others, later lived at Hamburg and Berlin, being dir. of the govt. lottery at the latter place from 1763. He wrote a number of theoret. works, incl. *Der critische Musicus*, *Die Kunst das Clavier zu spielen*, *Historisch-critische Beyträge*, works on thorough-bass, voc. comp., fugue, temperament, hist. of m. & of the org., &c.; also comp. some works for the hpchd.

Marqués y García, Pedro Miguel (b. Palma de Mallorca, 20. V. 1843; d. Palma, 25. II. 1918), Spa. vst. & comp. Studied at the Paris Cons. and with Berlioz and later in Madrid.

Works incl. zarzuela *El anillo de hierro* & many others; 4 syms., &c.

Marqués Puig, Antonio (b. Barcelona, 1897), Spa. pfst. & comp. Pupil of Pedrell and others. In 1913 he became m. critic at Barcelona.

Works incl. opera *Sor Beatriz* (after Maeterlinck); stg. 4tet; co. & pf. So.; pf. So.; songs, &c.

Marquise de Brinvilliers, La, comic opera by Auber, Batton, Berton, Blangini, Boïeldieu, Carafa, Cherubini, Hérold & Paer (lib. by Scribe & Castil-Blaze), prod. Paris, Opéra-Comique, 31. X. 1831.

Marriage of Figaro (Mozart). *See* **Nozze di Figaro**.

Marriage, The (*Zhenitba*), unfinished opera by Mussorgsky (lib. taken from Gogol's comedy), comp. 1864; never perf. in M.'s lifetime; prod. with pf. accomp., St. Petersburg, 1. IV. 1909; with orch., Petrograd, 26. X. 1917, with M.'s *Sorotchintsy Fair*.

Marschner, Heinrich (August) (b. Zittau, 16. VIII. 1795; d. Hanover, 14. XII. 1861), Ger. comp. As a boy he played the pf., sang sop. and comp. tentatively without much instruction. In 1813 he was sent to Leipzig to study law, but met Rochlitz, who induced him to take to m. In 1816 he went to Vienna and Pressburg with a Hung., Count de Varkony, and settled in the latter place, comp. several operas, until 1823, when he became asst. cond. to Weber and Morlacchi at Dresden. In 1827 he became cond. of the Leipzig theatre and in 1831 court cond. at Hanover.

Works incl. operas *Der Kyffhäuserberg*, *Saidar*, *Heinrich IV und Aubigné*, *Der Holzdieb*, *Lucretia*, *Der Vampyr*, *Der Templer und die Jüdin* (after Scott's *Ivanhoe*), *Des Falkners*

Braut, Hans Heiling, Der Bäbu, Das Schloss am Aetna, Kaiser Adolf von Nassau, Austin, Sangeskönig Hiarne; incid. m. to Kleist's *Prinz Friedrich von Homburg* & other plays; ovt. on 'God save the King' & other orch. works; male-voice chors.; sos.; songs, &c.

Marseillaise. *See* **National Anthems: France** & **Rouget de l'Isle.**

Marsick, Martin Pierre Joseph (b. Jupille nr. Liége, 9. III. 1848; d. Paris, 21. X. 1924), Belg. vst. Studied at the Liége Cons., later with Léonard and with Massart at the Paris Cons., succeeding the latter as v. prof. there in 1892. He was also a pupil of Joachim and 1st appeared in 1873 in Paris, where he formed a stg. 4tet.

Marson, George (b. ?; d. Canterbury, II. 1632), Eng. orgst. & comp. He became orgst. & choirmaster at Canterbury cath. *c.* 1598.

Works incl. services, anthem, psalms & other church m.; madrigal contrib. to *The Triumphes of Oriana*, &c.

Marteau, Henri (b. Rheims, 31. III. 1874; d. Lichtenberg, Franconia, 4. X. 1934), Fr. vst. & comp. Studied v. with Léonard and others, and appeared in Vienna, Ger. & Swi. at the age of 10. He then continued his studies at the Paris Cons., where Dubois was his comp. master, travelled much as a vst. later and became prof. of v. at the Geneva Cons., 1900, at the Berlin Hochschule für Musik, 1908, and at the Prague Cons., 1921.

Works incl. opera *Meister Schwalbe*; cantata *La Voix de Jeanne d'Arc*; v. Conc., co. Conc.; chamber m., &c.

Martelé (Fr.) / **Martellato (It.)** } lit. 'hammered.' Detached, strongly accentuated playing or singing, used esp. for a stroke of the bow prod. such an effect on stg. insts.

Martellement (Fr.) = Mordent. Also the repetition of a single note on the hp.

Martelli, Henri (b. Bastia, Corsica, 1895), Fr. comp. Studied at the Paris Cons., Widor being among his masters.

Works incl. opera *La Chanson de Roland*; symph. poem *Sur la vie de Jeanne d'Arc, Bas-reliefs assyriens* & Conc. for orch.; stg. 4tet; pf. pieces; songs, &c.

Martenot, Maurice (b. Paris, 14. X. 1898), Fr. scientist & musn. Studied pf. & co. at the Paris Cons. and comp. with Gédalge. After var. appts. as cond. and teacher he opened the École d'Art Martenot at Neuilly. Inventor of the radio-elect. inst. Ondes Musicales, a development of Theremin's, which he prod. in 1928.

Martha, oder Der Markt von Richmond (*M., or The Market at R.*), comic opera by Flotow (lib. by Friedrich Wilhelm Riese, pseud. 'W. Friedrich,' based on a ballet-pantomime, *Lady Henriette, ou La Servante de Greenwich*, by Jules Henri Vernoy de Saint-Georges, prod. Paris, 21. II. 1844, with m. by F., Burgmüller and Deldevez), prod. Vienna, Kärntnertor Theatre, 25. XI. 1847.

Martin. The Fr. name of a type of bar. voice of exceptional range, der. from the bar. Jean Blaise Martin (1768–1837).

Martin, Frank (b. Geneva, 15. IX. 1890), Swi. pfst. & comp. Studied with Joseph Lauber at Geneva and in 1928 became prof. at the Institut Jaques-Dalcroze there.

Works incl. ballet *Die blaue Blume*; incid. m. for Sophocles' *Oedipus Coloneus* & *Oedipus Rex* and Shakespeare's *Romeo and Juliet*; Mass for double chor., orat. *In terra pax, Cantate pour la Nativité*; Sym., suite *Rhytmes, Esquisse* for orch.; pf. Conc.; 4 monologues from *Everyman* for voice & orch.; *Cornet* (Rilke) for con. & orch.; pf. 5tet, Rhapsody for stg. 4tet, stg. Trio, pf. Trio on Ir. tunes; *Le Vin herbé* for 12 voices, stgs. & pf. (on the subject of Tristram and Yseult); 2 v. & pf. sos., &c.

Martin, George (Clement) (b. Lambourne, Berks., 11. IX. 1844; d. London, 23. II. 1916), Eng. orgst. & comp. Pupil of Stainer and others. After holding var. org. appts. & becoming org. prof. at the R.C.M. in London, he became org. of St. Paul's cath. in succession to Stainer in 1888. Knighted 1897, Mus.D., Oxford, 1912.

Works incl. Te Deum for Queen Victoria's Diamond Jubilee; services, anthems & other church m.; songs, partsongs, &c.

Martín y Soler, Vicente (b. Valencia, 2. V. 1754; d. St. Petersburg, 15. III. 1806), Spa. comp. Began his career as orgst. at Alicante, but took to comp. It. operas, went to It. in the 1770s and to Vienna in 1785, where Lorenzo da Ponte wrote libs. for him. In 1788 he left for St. Petersburg to succeed Sarti as cond. at the court of Catherine II. In 1794–5 he was in London, having gone there at Da Ponte's request to prod. 2 more joint works, but he returned to Rus.

Works incl. operas *Ifigenia in Aulide, Ipermestra, Andromaca, Astartea, Partenope, L'amor geloso, In amor si vuol destrezza* (*L'accorta cameriera*), *Vologeso, Le burle per amore, La vedova spiritosa, Il burbero di buon cuore, Une cosa rara, o Bellezza ed onestà, L'arbore di Diana,*

Gore Bogatyr Kosometovitch, Melomania (Rus.), *Fedul and his Children* (Rus. libs. of these 3 by Catherine II), *Il castello d'Atlante, La scola de' maritati, L'isola del piacere, Le nozze de' contadini spagnuoli, La festa del villaggio*; prologue *La Dora festeggiante* for *Vologeso*; several ballets; church m.; cantatas *La deità benefica* & *Il sogno*, canzonets, canons, &c.

Martinez, Marianne (b. Vienna, 4. V. 1744; d. Vienna, 13. XII. 1812), Aus. comp. and clav. player of Spa. descent. Daughter of the master of ceremonies to the pope's nuncio in Vienna; pupil of Metastasio, Porpora and Haydn.

Works incl. orats. *Isacco* & *Santa Elena al Calvario*, psalms trans. by Metastasio, Mass, motets, cantatas; syms., ovts.; concs.; sos., &c.

Martini, Giovanni Battista (or **Giambattista**) (b. Bologna, 24. IV. 1706; d. Bologna, 4. X. 1784), It. priest, ctptst., teacher & comp. Studied under his father, Antonio Maria M., also v., hpchd. & singing with other masters; also studied philos. & theol. with the monks of St. Philip Neri, entering the Franciscan monastery at Lago and being ordained in 1722. He returned to Bologna in 1725, became chapel master at the church of San Francesco, and studied further with Perti at San Petronio cath. He also devoted himself to maths. and collected a vast mus. and scientific library. He became the most famous mus. theorist and teacher of the time in Eur. and taught many famous pupils, incl. Mozart. He engaged in var. controversies, e.g. with Eximeno, and wrote a hist. of m. and a treatise on ctpt.

Works incl. masses, Requiem, motets & other church m.; orats. *San Pietro, Il Sacrifizio d'Abramo, L'assunzione di Salomone*; stage intermezzi *La Dirindina, L'impresario delle Canarie, Don Chisciotte* (after Cervantes), *Il maestro di musica*; sos. for org. & hpchd., var. sos.; keyboard pieces; arias, canons, &c.

Martini (Giovanni Paolo or Jean Paul) (actually Johann Paul Aegidius Schwartzendorf) (b. Freistadt, Upper Palat., 1. IX. 1741; d. Paris, 10. II. 1816), Ger. orgst. & comp. Played the org. at the Jesuit seminary at Neustadt at the age of 10, in 1758 began to study m. at Freiburg i/B. and became orgst. at the Franciscan monastery there. His father having married again, he left for Fr. and at Nancy found a friend in the org. builder Dupont, who advised him to adopt the It. name of M. In 1761–6 he was in the service of the Pol. king Stanislas at Lunéville, then went to Paris and became known as a comp. for military band. Inspector of the Cons., 1798–1802, and superintendent of the court m. after the Restor. of 1814.

Works incl. operas *L'Amoureux de quinze ans, Le Fermier cru sourd, Le Rendez-vous nocturne, Henri IV, Le Droit du seigneur, L'Amant sylphe, Annette et Lubin, Sapho, Ziméo* & others; masses, Requiem for Louis XVI & others, psalms & other church m.; cantata for the marriage of Napoleon I to Marie-Louise; syms. & other inst. works; march for the Swi. Guard & other military band m.; songs, incl. 'Plaisir d'amour,' &c.

Martini il tedesco (It. = M. the Ger.). The It. nickname given to the above.

Martini, Padre. *See* **Martini, Giovanni Battista.**

Martini, Vincenzo (*see* **Martín y Soler, Vicente**). The It. form of the Spa. comp.'s name.

Martinů, Bohuslav (b. Policka, 8. XII. 1890), Cz. comp. Pupil of Suk at Prague and Roussel in Paris. He was for a time a vst. in the Cz. Phil. Orch., but attracted attention as a comp. at the I.S.C.M. festival at Siena in 1928.

Works incl. operas *The Soldier and the Dancer, Les Lames du couteau, Les Vicissitudes de la vie, Journée de bonté, The Miracle of Our Lady, The Suburban Theatre, Alexandre bis, Juliette*; radio operas *The Voice of the Forest, Comedy on a Bridge*; ballets *Istar, Who is the Most Powerful in the World?, Revolt, On tourne, La Revue de cuisine, Échec au roi, The Butterfly that Stamped, Špalíček, Le Jugement de Paris, Cz. Rhapsody, Bouquet of Flowers*; *Field Mass* for solo voices, chor. & orch.; madrigals for 6 voices; 2 syms., Sinfonia for 2 orchs., symph. poem *Vanishing Midnight*, symph. pieces *Half-time, La Bagarre, La Rapsodie*, Ovt. for the Sokol Festival, *Memorial to Lidice*, Inventions for grand orch., Concerto grosso, *Tre Ricercari, Les Sérénades* & *Les Rondes* for chamber orch., Partita for stg. orch.; 2 pf. concs. and Concertino, Conc. for 2 pfs.; 3 v. concs., co. Conc., hpchd. Conc. and var. other works for insts. & orch., stg. 4tet & pf. trio with orch.; 5 stg. 4tets, stg. 5tet, wind 5tet, pf. 4tet & other chamber m.; 2 v. & pf. sos., 2 co. & pf. sos.; var. inst. pieces; *Film en miniature, 3 Danses tchèques, Préludes, Esquisses de danse, Ritournelles, Train-Fantôme*, &c. for pf.; 2 Preludes for hpchd., &c.

Martucci, Giuseppe (b. Capua, 6. I. 1856; d. Naples, 1. VI. 1909), It. pfst., cond. & comp. Was 1st taught by his father, a bandmaster, and appeared as pfst. in his childhood. He then studied at the Naples Cons., 1867–72, and became prof. there in 1874. He travelled widely as pfst., founded the Quartetto Napoletano for the cultivation of chamber m. and became an orch. cond. In 1886 he was app. dir. of the Liceo Musicale at Bologna and there prod. the 1st It. perf. of Wagner's *Tristan* in 1888. In 1902 he returned to Naples as dir. of the Cons.

Works incl. orat. *Samuele*; 2 syms., *4 piccoli pezzi* for orch.; pf. Conc. in B♭ min.; pf. 5tet, 2 pf. trios; co. & pf. So.; var. inst. pieces; Vars. & Fantasy for 2 pfs.; songs, *Pagine sparse, Due sogni* & others, &c.

Marty, (Eugène) Georges (b. Paris, 16. V, 1860; d. Paris, 11. X. 1908), Fr. cond. & comp. Studied at the Paris Cons., where he gained the Prix de Rome in 1882. He became successively chor.-master at the Théâtre Eden and the Opéra, dir. of the voc, ensemble classes at the Cons. and cond. at the Opéra-Comique. In 1901–8 he cond. the Cons. concerts and from 1906 he also gave classical orch. concerts at Vichy.

Works incl. operas *Le Duc de Ferrare* & *Daria*; pantomime *Lysis*; *Ballade d'hiver*, ovt. *Balthasar*, suite *Les Saisons*, symph. poem *Merlin enchanté* for orch.; pf. pieces; songs, &c.

Martyre de Saint Sébastien, Le (*The Martyrdom of St. Sebastian*), incid. m. by Debussy for the mystery play, written in Fr., by Gabriele d'Annunzio, comp. for solo voices, chor. & orch. in 1911 and 1st perf., Paris, Théâtre du Châtelet, 22. V. 1911, in 5 acts, and Opéra, 17. VI. 1922, in 4 acts.

Martyrs, Les, opera by Donizetti (lib. by Scribe, based on Corneille's *Polyeucte*), prod. Paris, Opéra, 10. IV. 1840.

Marvell, Andrew (1621–78), Eng. poet. *See* **White (F.)** (*Nymph's Complaint*).

Marx, Adolph Bernhard (b. Halle, 15. V. 1795; d. Berlin, 17. V. 1866), Ger. mcolst. & comp. Studied law, but gave it up for m., to which he devoted himself in Berlin, where in 1824 he founded the *Berliner allgemeine musikalische Zeitung*. In 1830 he became prof. of m. and in 1850 founded a m. school with Kullak and Stern (later Stern Cons.). He wrote books on the hist. of m. teaching, on Gluck, Handel, Beethoven, comp., tone-painting, &c.

Works incl. opera *Jery und Bätely* (Goethe); melodrama *Die Rache wartet*; orats. *Johannes der Täufer, Moses, Nahid und Omar;* inst. works, &c.

Marx, Joseph (b. Graz, 11. V. 1882), Aus. comp. Studied in Vienna and in 1922 became dir. of the Acad. of M. there in succession to Ferdinand Loewe.

Works incl. *Autumn Sym.*: Romantic Conc. for pf. & orch.; several chor. pieces; pf. 4tet, Fantasy for pf. trio; v. & pf. So., co. & pf. So.; *c.* 120 songs, &c.

Marx, Karl (b. Munich, 12. XI. 1897), Ger. comp. Studied natural science at first, but met Carl Orff during the 1914–8 war and later studied m. with him. App. prof. of the Munich Acad. in 1924 and cond. of the Bach Soc. there in 1928.

Works incl. Passacaglia for orch.; concs. for pf., v., 2 vs., va. & fl.; var. chor. works, some to words by Rilke; Divertimento for wind insts., stg. 4tet & other chamber m; songs, some to words by Rilke, &c.

Marxsen, Eduard (b. Nienstädten nr. Altona, 23. VII. 1806; d. Altona, 18. XI. 1887), Ger. pfst., orgst., teacher & comp. Assisted his father, an orgst., until 1830, then studied comp. with Seyfried and pf. with Bocklet in Vienna, returning to settle at Hamburg in 1834 and devoting himself mainly to teaching. Among his pupils was Brahms.

Works incl. *Beethoven's Schatten* for orch.; pf. m.; songs, &c.

Marziale (It.) = martial, warlike.

Masagniello furioso, oder Die neapolitanische Fischer-Empörung (*M. enraged, or The Neapolitan Fishermen's Revolt*), opera by Keiser (lib. by Barthold Feind), prod. Hamburg, Theater am Gänsemarkt, VI. 1706.

Masaniello (Auber). *See* **Muette de Portici.**

Masaniello, ou Le Pêcheur napolitain (*M., or The Neapolitan Fisherman*), opera by Carafa (lib. by C. Moreau & A. M. Lafortelle), prod. Paris, Opéra-Comique, 27. XII. 1827. Auber's *Muette de Portici* was prod. at the Opéra 2 months later.

Mascagni, Pietro (b. Leghorn, 7. XII. 1863; d. Rome, 2. VIII. 1945), It. comp. His father, a baker, wished him to study law, but he managed to take lessons in secret at the Istituto Cherubini. On being discovered, he was adopted by an uncle, and soon reconciled his father by having 2 works perf. at the Istituto. Later Count Florestano de Larderel paid for his further mus. educ. at the Milan Cons., where Ponchielli was among his masters. But he deserted, not wishing to apply himself to solid study, and joined a travelling opera co. After many wanderings and a marriage that forced him to settle at Cerignola nr.

Foggia to make a precarious living by teaching, he won the 1st prize in an operatic competition with *Cavalleria rusticana* in 1889, and after its prod. in Rome, 17. V. 1890, he began to accumulate a great fortune, though his many later operas never repeated its success.

Works incl. operas *Cavalleria rusticana, L'amico Fritz, I Rantzau* (both based on Erckmann-Chatrian), *Guglielmo Ratcliff* (after Heine), *Silvano* (Coppée), *Zanetto, Iris, Le maschere, Amica, Isabeau, Parisina* (d'Annunzio), *Lodoletta, Il piccolo Marat, Pinotta, Nerone*; operetta *Si*; incid. m. for Hall Caine's *The Eternal City*; *Kyrie*, Requiem in memory of King Humbert; cantata for Leopardi centenary (1898), setting of It. trans. of Schiller's *Ode to Joy* for chor. & orch., cantata *In Filanda*; Sym. in C min., symph. poem for a film *Rapsodia satanica*, &c.

Mascheroni, Edoardo (b. Milan, 4. IX. 1857; d. Milan, 4. III. 1941), It. cond. & comp. Studied maths. and literature in his youth and did not take to m. until he joined a group of enthusiasts, when he began to study under Boucheron at Milan, and soon comp. a good deal. But he discovered that his real vocation was cond., and in 1883 secured an engagement at the Teatro Goldoni at Leghorn. Not long after he advanced to the Teatro Apollo in Rome, and in 1893 he was chosen by Verdi to cond. the prod. of his *Falstaff* at Milan.

Works incl. operas *Lorenza & La Perugina*; 2 Requiems, for solo voices, chor. & orch. and for voices alone (both on the death of Victor Emmanuel I); chamber m.; album of pf. pieces, &c.

Maschinist Hopkins, opera by Brand (lib. by comp.), prod. Duisburg, 13. IV. 1929.

Mascotte, La (*The Mascot*), operetta by Audran (lib. by Alfred Duru & Henri Charles Chivot). Prod. Paris, Bouffes-Parisiens, 28. XII. 1880.

Masefield, John (b. 1878), Eng. poet & novelist. *See* **Gardiner (H. B.)** (*News from Wydah*), **Ireland (J.)** (*Sea Fever*), **Shaw (M.)** (*Seaport & Easter*).

Masini, Angelo (b. Terra del Sole nr. Forli, 28. XI. 1844; d. Forli, 29. IX. 1926), It. ten. singer. His studies were retarded by poverty, but he appeared in opera for the 1st time in 1857, at Modena.

Mask. *See* Masque.

Masked Ball, The (Verdi). *See* **Ballo in maschera.**

Masnadieri, I (*The Brigands*), opera by Verdi (lib. by Andrea Maffei, based on Schiller's drama *Die Räuber*), prod. London, Her Majesty's Theatre, 22. VII. 1847. The only opera commissioned by London from V. Jenny Lind and Lablache appeared in it.

Mason, Daniel Gregory (b. Brookline, Mass., 20. XI. 1873), Amer. comp. & writer on m., grandson of Lowell Mason and son of a member of the firm of pf. makers Mason & Hamlin. Graduated from Harvard and studied m. in N.Y., later with d'Indy in Fr. He wrote a number of books on m.

Works incl. Sym. in C min.; Prelude & Fugue for pf. & orch.; stg. 4tet on Negro themes, Intermezzo for stg. 4tet, pf. 4tet, 3 pieces for fl., hp. & stg. 4tet, *Pastorale* for v., cl. & pf.; v. & pf. So., cl. & pf. So.; pf. pieces incl. Vars. on *Yankee Doodle* in the style of var. comps.; songs, &c.

Mason, Lowell (b. Medfield, Mass., 8. I. 1792; d. Orange, N.J., 11. VIII. 1872), Amer. hymnologist, grandfather of prec. Self-taught in m. and a bank clerk at Savannah from 1812. He practised any inst. he could lay hands on and with F. L. Abel adapted Gardiner's *Sacred Melodies*, mainly themes from the classics, to the psalms, with the result that in 1827 he was called to Boston to supervise church m. there; but a more important service was his introd. of m. teaching into schools.

Mason, William (b. Boston, Mass., 24. I. 1829; d. New York, 14. VII. 1908), Amer. pfst., son of prec. Studied at Boston, later at the Leipzig Cons. and under Liszt at Weimar. On his return to U.S.A. he appeared much in public and in 1854, with Theodore Thomas and others, he founded chamber m. concerts.

Mason, William (1724–97), Eng. poet & dramatist. *See* **Arne (T. A.)**, **Caractacus** (Arne), **Giardini** (*Elfrida*), **Paisiello** (do.), **Sacchini** (*Arvire et Evelina*), **Wesley (C.)** (*Caractacus*).

Masque. A stage entertainment cultivated in Eng. in the 17th cent. and laying great stress on spectacular presentation, but also making a feature of m. to some extent, so that the M. became the direct forerunner of Opera. Dancing being also indispensable to it, the Ballet too is in a direct line of descent from it: the Eng. M., indeed, closely resembled the Fr. *opéra-ballet*. Pantomimes and harlequinades of the 19th cent. also retain some connection with it. The subjects, mainly based on It. models, were mythological, heroic or allegorical.

Masques et bergamasques, m. by Fauré, Op. 112, for an entertainment by René Fauchois prod. Monte Carlo, 10. IV. 1919; Paris, Opéra-Comique, 4. III. 1920, with a Watteau setting and inspired by Verlaine's poetry.

It incl. an ovt. and 3 dances, newly comp., as well as the Pavane, Op. 50, of 1887 and an orch. version of the Verlaine song *Clair de lune*, Op. 46 No. 2, of the same year, in which the words ' masques et bergamasques ' occur.

Mass. The chief ritual of the Rom. Catholic church service, i.e. the celebration of the Eucharist. Only High M. is concerned with m., Low M. being spoken, not sung. Formerly assoc. with Organum or Plainsong, the M. has from the 14th cent. onwards been treated as a form of mus. comp., as a rule primarily for the purpose of relig. service, but sometimes more elaborately for concert use; also, Ms. orig. written, esp. in the 18th & 19th cents., for church use with orch. accomp. are now usable only as concert works, Pius X's *Motu proprio* of 1903 having forbidden orchs. in church. The ordinary of the M. falls into 5 main sections: Kyrie, Gloria, Credo, Sanctus with Hosanna & Benedictus and Agnus Dei with Dona nobis pacem; these remain invariable throughout the year and are usually all that is set to m. by comps. The proper of the M. consists of additional matter, such as Introits and Offertories, and these are far more rarely found as parts of a M. comp. The early Ms. written in parts were polyphonic in treatment, and at first the ten. part retained the old plainsong melody, around which the other parts spun a ctptl. texture. But in the 15th cent. the plainsong tunes were often abandoned and this *cantus firmus* in the ten. was often the tune of a secular song, sometimes even a very frivolous one. *L'Homme armé* on the Continent and *The Western Wind* in Eng., for ex., were esp. favoured for this purpose. Even in later times the treatment of the M. remained essentially polyphonic, though not necessarily throughout. Certain portions, e.g. ' Et vitam venturi saeculi ' at the end of the Credo, are almost invar. the basis of fugues.

Mass in B minor (Bach). *See* **B minor Mass.**

Mass of Life, A, setting of words from Nietzsche's *Also sprach Zarathustra* for solo voices, chor. & orch. by Delius, comp. 1904–5, prod. (2nd part only, in Ger.) Munich Mus. Festival, 1908; 1st complete perf. (in Eng.), London, 1909.

Massart, Joseph (Lambert) (b. Liége, 19. VII. 1811; d. Paris, 13. II. 1892), Belg. vst. & teacher. Studied under Auguste Kreutzer (1778–1832) in Paris and in 1843 became v. prof. at the Cons. there.

Massé, Victor (actually Félix Marie) (b. Lorient, 7. III. 1822; d. Paris, 5. VII. 1884), Fr. comp. Studied at the Paris Cons. where Halévy was his comp. master, and gained the Prix de Rome in 1844. He travelled in It. & Ger. after his stay in Rome; in 1860 became chor.-master at the Paris Opéra and in 1866 prof. of comp. at the Cons.

Works incl. operas and operettas *La Chambre gothique, La Chanteuse voilée, Galathée, Les Noces de Jeannette, La Reine Topaze, La Fiancée du Diable, Miss Fauvette, Les Saisons, La Fée Carabosse, Mariette la promise, La Mule de Pedro, Fior d'Aliza* (after Lamartine), *Le Fils du brigadier, Paul et Virginie* (after Saint-Pierre), *La favorita e la schiava, Le Cousin de Marivaux, Les Chaises à porteurs, Le Prix de famille, Une Loi somptuaire, Les Enfants de Perrette, La Petite Sœur d'Achille, La Trouvaille, Une Nuit de Cléopâtre; Messe solennelle*; cantata *Le Renégat*; songs, &c.

Massenet, Jules (Émile Frédéric) (b. Montaud nr. Saint-Étienne, 12. V. 1842; d. Paris, 13. VIII. 1912), Fr. comp. Entered the Paris Cons. at the age of 11, studying comp. with A. Thomas and gaining the Prix de Rome in 1863. On his return from Rome in 1866 he married a pf. pupil of his, Mlle. Sainte-Marie, and had his 1st opera, *La Grand'tante*, prod. at the Opéra-Comique the next year. The 1st really successful opera, *Hérodiade*, was prod. at Brussels in 1881 and *Manon* at the Opéra-Comique in 1884. Prof. of comp. at the Cons., 1878–96.

Works incl. operas *Don César de Bazan, Le Roi de Lahore, Hérodiade, Manon* (after Prévost), *Le Cid* (after Corneille), *Esclarmonde, Le Mage, Werther* (after Goethe), *Le Portrait de Manon, La Navarraise, Sapho* (after Daudet), *Cendrillon Grisélidis, Le Jongleur de Notre-Dame, Thaïs* (both after A. France), *Chérubin, Ariane, Thérèse, Bacchus, Don Quichotte* (after Cervantes), *Roma, Panurge* (after Rabelais), *Cléopatre, Amadis*; ballets *Le Carillon, La Cigale, Espada*; incid. m. to Leconte de Lisle's *Les Erynnies*, Racine's *Phèdre* & other plays; orats. *Marie-Magdeleine, Ève, La Vierge, La Terre promise*; cantatas *David Rizzio, Narcisse, Biblis*; 13 orch. works incl. *Scènes pittoresques, Scènes napolitaines* and 3 other similar suites, symph. poem *Visions*; pf. Conc., Fantasy for cl. & orch.; *c.* 200 songs; duets; chors., &c.

Mässig (Ger.) = Moderate.

Massimilla Doni, opera by Schoeck (lib. by Armin Rüeger, based on Balzac's novel), prod. Dresden, 2. III. 1937.

Masson, Paul (Marie) (b. Cette, Herault, 19. IX. 1882), Fr. mcolst. & comp. Studied mus. hist. & aesthetics under Rolland and comp. with d'Indy and Koechlin. App. prof. of mus. hist. at the Institut Français at Florence in 1910 and that of Naples in 1919. Lecturer at Grenoble Univ., 1910, and prof. at the Sorbonne in Paris, 1931. His books incl. studies of Florentine carnival songs, Rameau and Berlioz.

Works incl. *Chant des peuples unis* for solo voices, chor. & orch.; *Chants sans paroles, Le Val de Terzolle*, suite *Printemps guerrier, Prélude et Berceuse* for orch., &c.

Master-Note. The old name of the Leading-note, also sometimes given to the Semibreve.

Master Peter's Puppet Show (Falla). *See* **Retablo de Maese Pedro.**

Master-Singers. *See* **Meistersinger.**

Mastersingers of Nuremberg, The (Wagner). *See* **Meistersinger von Nürnberg.**

Matassins (Fr.). An old dance of armed men, sometimes called *Mattachins.*

Matelotte (Fr., from *matelot* = sailor). A Dutch sailors' dance similar to the Hornpipe, danced in clogs with the sailors' arms linked behind their backs.

Materna, Amalie (b. St. Georgen, Styria, 10. VII. 1845; d. Vienna, 18. I. 1918), Aus. sop. singer. 1st appeared on the stage at Graz in 1864, then married the Ger. actor Karl Friedrich, with whom she was engaged at one of the minor theatres in Vienna; but in 1869 she came out at the Imp. Opera. She was Wagner's 1st Brünnhilde and Kundry at Bayreuth in 1876 and 1882.

Mathias, Georges (Amédée Saint-Claire) (b. Paris, 14. X. 1826; d. Paris, 14. X. 1910), Fr. pfst. & comp. Studied at the Paris Cons. and was a private pupil of Kalkbrenner and Chopin. In 1862–93 he was pf. prof. at the Cons.

Works incl. Sym., 2 ovts.; chor. works; 2 pf. concs.; 5 pieces for pf. & stgs. 6 pf. trios; pf. studies and pieces; songs. &c.

Mathieu, Émile Louis Victor (b. Lille, 16. X. 1844; d. Ghent, 22. VIII. 1932), Belg. comp. Studied at the Brussels Cons. Dir. of a school of m. at Louvain, where his mother had taught singing, 1881–96, and then until 1924 dir. of the Ghent Cons.

Works incl. operas *George Dandin* (after Molière), *L'Échange, La Bernoise, Richilde, L'Enfance de Roland*; biblical opera *La Reine Vasthi*; ballet *Les Femmes de Kiff*; Te Deum & 3 cantatas *Le Hoyoux, Freyir* & *Le Sorbier* for solo voices, chor. & orch.; 6 ballads by Goethe for voice & pf., &c.

Mathis der Maler (*Matthew the Painter*), opera by Hindemith (lib. by comp.), prod. Zürich, 28. V. 1938. The painter is Matthias Grünewald (16th cent.).

Matilde di Shabran, ossia Bellezza e cuor di ferro (. . ., *or Beauty and Heart of Iron*), opera by Rossini (lib. by Jacopo Ferretti), prod. Rome, Teatro Apollo, 24. II. 1821.

Matin, Le (*The Morning*), the name of 1 of 3 syms. by Haydn, comp. c. 1761. It is No. 6 of H.'s complete syms., in D maj.; the others are No. 7, in C maj., *Le Midi*, and No. 8, in G maj., *La Soir et la tempête.*

Matinsky, Mikhail (b. ?; d. c. 1820), Rus. comp. & libst. B. as a serf, he was liberated by his master and sent to It. for study. In 1777 he wrote the lib. for Fomin's *The Renaissance* and in 1782 that of Pashkevitch's *The Pasha of Tunis.* His own operas incl. *The St. Petersburg Bazaar.*

Matrimonio segreto, Il (*The Clandestine Marriage*), opera by Cimarosa (lib. by Giovanni Bertati, based on George Colman and David Garrick's play of that name), prod. Vienna, Burg Theatre, 7. II. 1792.

Mattachins. *See* **Matassins.**

Mattei, Filippo, called Pippo, the supposed comp. of the 1st act of the opera *Muzio Scevola* (often attrib. to Ariosti), the others being Bononcini & Handel, is prob. no other than Filippo Amadei.

Mattei, Stanislao (b. Bologna, II. 1750; d. Bologna, 12. V. 1825), It. priest, theorist & comp. Pupil of G. B. Martini, for whom he often deputized after his ordination and whom he succeeded as chapel master at the church of San Francesco. Later chapel master at San Petronio cath. and from 1804 prof. of ctpt. at the Liceo Musicale, founded that year. Rossini was among his pupils. He wrote a work in 3 vols. on playing from figured bass.

Works incl. masses & other church m., a Passion; intermezzo *La bottega del libraio.* &c.

Matteis, Nicola (b. ?; d. ?), It. 17th-cent. vst. Went to Eng. about 1672; pub. 3 collections of v. m., 1 of songs and a treatise, *The False Consonances of Musick.*

Mattheson, Johann (b. Hamburg, 28. IX. 1681; d. Hamburg, 17. IV. 1764), Ger. writer on m., orgst. & comp. 1st sang female parts at the Hamburg Opera, then comp. 2 operas (1699 & 1704), went to Lübeck with Handel to investigate the chances of succeeding to Buxtehude's orgst.'s post, which they both refused, B.'s condition being marriage with his daughter. M. became cantor at Hamburg cath. in 1715; wrote several books on m., the most important being *Das neu eröffnete Orchester* (*The Newly Inaugurated Orchestra*, 1713), *Der vollkommene Capellmeister* (*The Perfect Conductor*, 1739) and *Grundlage einer Ehrenpforte* (*Sketch for a Portal of Honour*, 1740).

Works incl. operas *Die Pleyades*, *Cleopatra*, *Henrico IV* & 5 others; 24 orats. & cantatas; wedding & funeral pieces; inst. sos.; suites for hpchd.; arias, &c.

Matthisson, Friedrich von (1761–1831), Ger. poet. Remembered chiefly by Beethoven's setting of his *Adelaïde*; Schubert set 26 of his poems. *See also* **Schröter (C.)** (songs).

Mattinata (It.). A morning song, similar to the Fr. *aubade* and the Spa. *alborada*.

Mauduit, Jacques (b. Paris, 16. IX. 1557; d. Paris, 21. VIII. 1627), Fr. lutenist & comp. He was, like his father before him, registrar to the courts of justice in Paris, but became famous as a musn. In 1581 he gained the 1st prize at the annual Puy de Musique at Évreux, and he was assoc. with Baïf in his experiments with *Musique mesurée*, though after B.'s death in 1590 he relaxed the rigid subordination of mus. to verbal rhythm in his settings of verse. In 1588 he (?) saved the MSS. of the Huguenot Le Jeune from destruction by the Catholic soldiers, though he was himself a Catholic.

Works incl. Requiem on the death of Ronsard (1585), motets, chansons, *Chansonnettes mesurées* for 4 voices, &c.

Maugars, André (b. ?; d. ?), Fr. 16th–17th-cent. violist, politician and trans. He lived in Eng. for 4 years *c.* 1620, on his return entered the service of Cardinal Richelieu, became interpreter in Eng. to Louis XIII and trans. Bacon's *Advancement of Learning*. In 1639 he visited Rome and wrote a pamphlet on It. m. He comp. viol m. (lost).

Maugham, W(illiam). Somerset (b. 1874), Eng. novelist & dramatist. *See* **Goossens** (*East of Suez*).

Maultrommel (Ger. lit. mouth [vulg.] drum) = Jew's Harp. The inst. is neither a drum nor a hp.

Maupassant, Guy de (1850–93), Fr. novelist. *See* **Glière** (*Mam'zelle Fifi*), **Mademoiselle Fifi** (Cui), **Senilov** (*Wild Geese*).

Maurel, Victor (b. Marseilles, 17. VI. 1848; d. New York, 22. X. 1923), Fr. bar. singer. Went to the school of m. at Marseilles, after studying architecture, and later to the Paris Cons. Made his 1st appearance in 1867, at the Paris Opéra, but was later devoted more to It. opera. The 1st Iago in Verdi's *Otello*.

Maurer, Ludwig (Wilhelm) (b. Potsdam, 8. II. 1789; d. St. Petersburg, 25. X. 1878), Ger. vst. & comp. Studied under Haak, the leader of Frederick the Great's orch.; made his 1st appearance at a concert given by Mara in Berlin, 1802. In 1824–33 he led the theatre orch. at Hanover & later lived in Rus., mainly at Moscow and St. Petersburg. He was inspector-general of the imp. orchs., 1841–62.

Works incl. 3 Ger. operas *Der neue Paris*, *Eloise* & *Die Runenschrift*, & several in Rus. & Fr.; v. concs.; stg. 4tets, &c.

Mavra, opera by Stravinsky (lib., in Rus., by Boris Koshno, based on Pushkin's *The Little House at Kolomna*), prod., in Fr. trans. by Jacques Larmanjat, Paris, Opéra, 2. VI. 1922.

Maximilien, opera by Milhaud (lib. by Armand Lunel, trans. from a Ger. lib. by Rudolf Stephan Hoffmann, based on Franz Werfel's play, *Juarez und Maximilian*), prod. Paris, Opéra, 4. I. 1932.

Maxixe. A Braz. dance similar to the Tango which had some vogue in Eur. in the 1910s.

May-horn. *See* **Whithorn.**

May Night (*Maïskaya Notch*), opera by Rimsky-Korsakov (lib. by comp., based on a story by Gogol), prod. St. Petersburg, 21. I. 1880.

Mayer, Charles (b. Königsberg, 21. III. 1790; d. Dresden, 2. VII. 1862), Ger. pfst. & comp. Was taken to Rus. as a child and became a pupil of Field at Moscow, and after the fire of 1812 in St. Petersburg. He travelled in Fr., Swe., Ger., &c. and in 1850 settled at Dresden. He wrote an enormous number of pf. works, incl. a Mazurka in F♯ maj. that was for some time thought to be by Chopin.

Maynard, John (b. ?; d. ?), Eng. 16th–17th-cent. lutenist & comp. He was connected with the school of St. Julian in Herts., and at some time in the service of Lady Joan Thynne at Cause Castle in Salop.

Works incl. pavans and galliards for the lute; (?) org. pieces; lessons for lute & bass viol and for lyra-viol; 12 songs *The XII Wonders of the World*, describing var. characters, for voice, lute and va. da gamba, &c.

Mayr, Richard (b. Henndorf nr. Salzburg, 18. XI. 1877; d. Vienna, 1. XII. 1935), Aus. bass-bar. singer. Studied medicine at Vienna Univ., but left it for the Cons. and made his 1st stage appearance at the Wagner festival theatre at Bayreuth in 1902.

Mayr, Simone (Johann Simon) (b. Mendorf, Bav., 14. VI. 1763; d. Bergamo, 2. XII. 1845), Ger. (Italianized) comp. Studied m. with his father, a village orgst., and at the Jesuit Coll. at Ingolstadt, where later he studied law, until he entered the service of a nobleman, Thomas de Bessus, in Swi., who sent him to study with Lenzi, chapel master at Bergamo. Thence he went to Bertoni at Venice, where he began to make a success with orats. until 1794, when he prod. his 1st opera, written at the suggestion of Piccinni. In 1802 he was app. chapel master to Santa Maria Maggiore at Bergamo, and in 1805 prof. at the m. school there.

Works incl. operas *Saffo, ossia I riti d'Apollo, Leucadio, Lodoiska, Che originali, Adelaïda di Guesclino, Il carretto del venditore d'aceto, Ginevra di Scozia, I misteri eleusini, Alonso e Cora, Elisa, Adelasia ed Aleramo, La rosa rossa e la rosa bianca, Medea in Corinto* & c. 60 others; orats. *Jacob a Labano fugiens, David, Tobiae matrimonium, Sisara, Jephte*; Passion; masses, motets, psalms & other church m., &c.

Mayrhofer, Johann (1787–1836), Aus. poet. *See* **Freunde von Salamanka** (Schubert).

47 of his poems were set by Schubert.

Mayseder, Joseph (b. Vienna, 26. X. 1789; d. Vienna, 21. XI. 1863), Aus. vst. & comp. 1st appeared in Vienna, 1800, and later held several important appts., incl. that of chamber musn. to the emperor.

Works incl. Mass; v. concs.; 8 stg. 4tets, 5 stg. 5tets, pf. trios & other chamber m.; v. duets; pieces and studies for v., &c.

Mazas, Jacques (Féréol) (b. Béziers, 23. IX. 1782; d. ?, 1849), Fr. vst. & comp. Studied under Baillot at the Paris Cons., appeared with a v. conc. written for him by Auber, travelled widely, lived in Paris 1829–37 and was dir. of the m. school at Cambrai, 1837–41.

Works incl. opera *Le Kiosque*; 2 v. concs.; stg. 4tets; v. duets; many v. pieces, &c.

Mazeppa, opera by Tchaikovsky (lib. by comp. & Victor Petrovitch Burenin, based on Pushkin's *Poltava*), prod. Moscow, 15. II. 1884.

Symph. poem by Liszt, comp. in 1854 on Victor Hugo's poem and on the basis of one of the *Grandes Études pour le piano* of *c.* 1838 and their new version, the *Études d'exécution transcendante* of 1851. 1st perf. Weimar, 16. IV. 1854.

Mazur or Mazurka A Pol. nat. dance dating at least as far back as the 16th cent. and originating in the old palat. of Masovia. It was at first accomp. with voc. m. The dance-figures are complicated and subject to much var., not excluding improvisation. The m. is in moderate 3–4, orig. in 2 parts of 8 bars each, both repeated; there is a tendency to accentuate the 2nd beat. Its treatment by comps. (e.g. Chopin) often extends and develops it.

Mazzaferrata, Giovanni Battista (b. Como or Pavia, ?; d. Ferrara, 26. II. 1691), It. comp. Chapel master at the Accademia della Morte at Ferrara. His orat. was perf. at Siena in 1684.

Works incl. orat. & cantatas; *Salmi concertati* for 3–4 voices; madrigals & canzonets; cantatas for solo voices; 12 sos. for 2 v. & bass, &c.

Mazzinghi, Joseph (b. London, 25. XII. 1765; d. Downside nr. Bath, 15. I. 1844), Eng. pfst., cond. & comp. of It. descent. Pupil of J. C. Bach. At the age of 10 he succeeded his father as orgst. of the Port. Chapel in London. He then studied further with Bertoni, Sacchini and Anfossi during their stays in Eng. and in 1787 became cond. & comp. to the King's Theatre. He taught much and was m. master to the Princess of Wales (later Queen Caroline).

Works incl. operas *La bella Arsena* & *Il tesoro*; plays with m. *A Day in Turkey, Paul and Virginia* (with Reeve, after Saint-Pierre), *The Wife of Two Husbands, The Exile, The Free Knights* & others; several ballets; Mass for 3 voices; 6 hymns; many keyboard sos.; glees, arias, songs, &c.

Mazzocchi, Domenico (b. Veia nr. Civita Castellana, 8. XI. 1592; d. Rome, 20. I. 1665), It. comp. Was in the service of the Aldobrandini Borghese family for 20 years.

Works incl. operas *La catena d' Adone* & *L'innocenza difesa*; orats. *Querimonia di S. Maria Maddalena, Il martirio dei SS. Abbundia ed Abbundanzio*; *Musiche sacre*; madrigals, *Dialoghi e sonetti*; &c.

Mazzocchi, Virgilio (b. Veia, 22. VII. 1597; d. Veia, 3. X. 1646), It. comp., brother of prec. Chapel master at St. John Lateran in Rome, 1628–9, and then at St. Peter's until his death.

Works incl. opera *Chi soffre speri* (with Marazzoli); psalms for double chor.; *Sacre flores* for 2–4 voices, &c.

Mazzucato, Alberto (b. Udine, 28. VII. 1813; d. Milan, 31. XII. 1877), It. vst., teacher & comp. Studied at Padua. He became leader of the

Scala orch. at Milan in 1859, taught v. at the Cons. there and became its dir. in 1872. Ed. of the *Gazzetta musicale*.

Works incl. operas *La fidanzata di Lammermoor* (after Scott). *Esmeralda* (after Hugo) & 6 others, &c.

Mc (for names with this prefix *see* **Mac . . .**).

Mcol. (abbr.) = Musicological; Musicology.

Mcolst. (abbr.) = Musicologist.

Me. The name for the Mediant note in any key in Tonic Sol-fa, so pronounced, but in notation represented by the symbol m.

Meadows White, Alice. *See* **Smith, Alice Mary.**

Mean(e). In the old sense of 'middle' the word was formerly used in var. ways: i.e. for voice-parts in voc. comps. lying between the treble and the bass; for the 2nd inst. in a consort of viols; for the 2nd & 3rd stgs. on the viol (small & great meane).

Meantone. In tuning the M. system was used for keyboard insts. before Equal Temperament came into general use. It provided for the pure intonation of the key of C maj. and those lying near it at the expense of the more extreme sharp and flat keys; which is the reason why remote keys were so rarely used in keyboard comps. before Bach showed in *The Well-tempered Clavier* that they could all be used by the compromise of Equal Temp. There was, for ex., a pure F♯ and B♭, but these notes were out of tune when used as G♭ or A♯.

Meares, Richard (b. ?; d. London, ?), Eng. 17th-cent. inst. maker. Made lutes, viols, &c. in London in the 2nd half of the cent.

Meares, Richard (b. London, ?; d. London, *c.* 1743), Eng. inst. maker & m. pub., son of prec. He succeeded to his father's business, but enlarged it by selling not only insts., but m., books and cutlery, and he began to pub. m. *c.* 1714, incl. several operas by Handel.

Measure (Amer.) = Bar. In Eng. (poet.) a 'measure' is a regularly rhythmic piece of m., esp. a dance.

Measured Music. *See* **Musique mesurée.**

Medea, play with m. (melodrama) by G. Benda (text by Friedrich Wilhelm Gotter), prod. Leipzig, 1. V. 1775.

Médecin malgré lui, Le (*Doctor against his Will*), opera by Gounod (lib. a small alteration of Molière's comedy by comp., Jules Barbier & Michel Carrée), prod. Paris, Théâtre Lyrique, 15. I. 1858.

Médée, opera by Marc-Antoine Charpentier (lib. by Thomas Corneille), prod. Paris, Opéra, 4. XII. 1693.

Opera by Cherubini (lib. by François Benoît Hoffman), prod. Paris, Théâtre Feydeau, 13. III. 1797.

Opera by Milhaud (lib. by Madeleine Milhaud, the comp.'s wife), prod., in Flem. trans., Antwerp, 7. X. 1939.

Meder, Johann Valentin (b. Wasungen o/Werra, V. 1649; d. Riga, VII. 1719), Ger. singer & comp. After var. appts. he became cantor at Reval in 1674 and at Danzig in 1687, later mus. dir. at Königsberg & Riga cath.

Works incl. operas *Nero* & others; orat., motets; trios; org. m., &c.

Mederitsch, Johann (called Gallus) (b. Nymburk [Nimburg o/Elbe], *c.* 1755; d. Lwów, 1835), Boh. cond. & comp. He was a theatre cond. at Olomouc and Pest, and later for many years a private m. teacher in Vienna, Grillparzer being among his pupils.

Works incl. operas *Babylons Pyramiden* (with Winter), *Orkatastor und Illiane, Der redliche Verwalter* & others; incid. m. for Shakespeare's *Macbeth*; masses; chamber m., &c.

Medesimo tempo (It. = 'same time'). A direction indicating that a change of metre does not imply a change of pace. The more usual term is *l'istesso tempo* (formerly *lo stesso tempo*).

Mediant. The 3rd degree of the rising modern maj. or min. scale, so called because it stands half-way between Tonic and Dominant. The names of the degrees of the whole scale are Tonic, Supertonic, M., Subdominant, Dominant, Submediant and Leading-note.

Medinš, Janis (b. Riga, 9. X. 1890), Latv. comp. Studied at Riga, joined the orch. and after 2 years in Rus. became cond. at the Nat. Opera at Riga and prof. at the Cons.

Works incl. operas *Fire and Night, Gods and Men* & *Tom Thumb*; cantata; Sym. in E min., symph. poems & suites for orch.; co. Conc.; inst. pieces; songs, &c.

Medtner, Nikolai Raslovitch (b. Moscow, 5. I. 1880), Rus. comp. Studied pf. under Safonov at the Moscow Cons., gained the Rubinstein prize there and toured Eur. as pfst. in 1901–2, becoming prof. at the Cons. for a year on his return, but then retiring to devote himself to comp. After the Revol. he taught at a school in Moscow and in 1922 went on another tour in the west, but found himself unable to return. He settled in Paris for a time and later in London, which he left temporarily for Warwickshire in 1940.

Works incl. 3 pf. concs.; 3 sos. & 3 Nocturnes for v. & pf.; 12 pf. sos. and a great number of pieces for pf.

incl. *Fairy Tales* Opp. 8, 9, 14, 20, 26, 34, 35, 42, 48, 51, *Forgotten Melodies* Opp. 38–40, *Dithyrambs*, *Novels*, *Lyric Fragments*, *Improvisations*, *Hymn in Praise of Toil*, &c.; So.-Vocalise for voice & pf.; 17 op. nos. of songs to words by Pushkin, Tiutchev, Goethe, Heine, Nietzsche & others, &c.

Meeresstille und glückliche Fahrt (*Calm Sea and Prosperous Voyage*). A poem by Goethe, set by Beethoven as a cantata for chor. & orch. in 1815, Op. 112, and ded. to the poet; and used by Mendelssohn as the subject for a concert ovt., Op. 27, in 1828. Elgar quotes from the latter in the Romance of the ' Enigma ' Vars.

Mefistofele, opera by Boito (lib. by comp., based on Goethe's *Faust*), prod. Milan, Teatro alla Scala, 5. III. 1868.

Méhul, Étienne (Henri Nicolas) (b. Givet nr. Mézières, 22. VI. 1763; d. Paris, 18. X. 1817), Fr. comp. His father, a cook, could give him no adequate mus. educ., but he learnt the org. and obtained appts. at relig. institutions very early, eventually learning much from the orgst. Wilhelm Hauser at the neighbouring La Val-Dieu. In 1778 an amateur took him to Paris, and there he studied pf. and comp. under Edelmann, supporting himself by giving lessons at the same time. He met Gluck during his visit to Paris in 1779 and was encouraged by him to write for the stage. He wrote several stage works for practice and *Cora et Alonzo* was accepted by the Opéra but not prod. The Comédie-Italienne, however, accepted *Euphrosine* in 1790, and thereafter he had many successes, the greatest being *Joseph* in 1807. On the foundation of the Cons. in 1795 he became one of its inspectors. Suffering from consumption, he went to Provence in I. 1817, but the disease had gone too far and he returned to Paris to die.

Works incl. operas *Euphrosine et Coradin, ou Le Tyran corrigé*, *Cora*, *Stratonice*, *Le Jeune Sage et le vieux fou*, *Le Pont de Lodi*, *Horatius Coclès*, *Mélidore et Phrosine*, *La Caverne*, *Doria*, *Le Jeune Henri*, *Adrien*, *Ariodant*, *Épicure* (with Cherubini), *Bion*, *L'irato, ou L'Emporté*, *Une Folie*, *Le Trésor supposé*, *Joanna*, *L'Heureux malgré lui*, *Héléna*, *Le Baiser et la quittance* (with Kreutzer, Boïeldieu & Isouard), *Les Deux Aveugles de Tolède*, *Uthal* (without vs.), *Gabrielle d'Estrée*, *Joseph*, *Le Prince Troubadour*, *L'Oriflamme* (with Paer, Berton & Kreutzer), *La Journée aux aventures*, *Valentine de Milan* (unfinished, completed by his nephew Louis Joseph Daussoigne-M. 1790–1875); ballets *La Dansomanie*, *Le Jugement de Paris* (with adds. from Haydn & Pleyel), *Daphnis et Pandrose*, *Persée et Andromède*, *Les Amazones*; incid. m. to Joseph Chénier's *Timoléon*; Mass for the coronation of Napoleon I (not perf.); cantatas *Chanson de Roland*, *Le Pont de Lodi*, *Chant lyrique* (for the unveiling of Napoleon's statue at the Institut); patriotic songs *Chant national du 14 juillet*, *Chant du départ*, *Chant du retour*; syms.; 2 pf. sos., &c.

Meiland, Jacob (b. Senftenberg, Saxony, c. 1542; d. Frankfort o/M., 31. XII. 1577), Ger. comp. He learnt m. as a choir-boy in the Saxon court chapel at Dresden, studied at Leipzig Univ., travelled, and was app. chapel master to the Margrave of Ansbach, whose chapel was dissolved in 1574, when M. retired to Frankfort in ill health.

Works incl. Lat. & Ger. motets; *Cantiones sacrae* for 5–6 voices; Ger. songs for 4–5 voices, &c.

Meinardus, Ludwig Siegfried (b. Hooksiel, Oldenburg, 17. IX. 1827; d. Bielefeld, 10. VII. 1896), Ger. pfst., cond. & comp. Pupil of Schumann at Leipzig and of Liszt at Weimar. Taught at Dresden from 1865 and was critic at Hamburg, 1874–87.

Works incl. operas *Bahnesa* & *Doktor Sassafras*; orats. *Simon Petrus*, *Gideon*, *König Salomo*, *Luther in Worms* & *Odrun*; chor. ballad; syms.; chamber m., &c.

Meistersinger (Ger. = Master-Singers). 14th–16th-cent. guilds of poets & musns. who cultivated poetry and singing in var. Ger. towns., prob. founded at Mainz in 1311 by Heinrich von Meissen (Frauenlob). The members passed through var. stages from apprenticeship to mastery, and they were middle-class burghers, merchants, tradesmen and artisans, not nobles like the Minnesinger.

Meistersinger von Nürnberg, Die (*The Mastersingers of Nuremberg*), m.-drama by Wagner (lib. by comp.), prod. Munich, Court Theatre, 21. VI. 1868.

Mel (or Mell), Gaudio (b. ?; d. ?), 16th-cent. musn., who, if he existed at all under that name, may or may not have taught Palestrina in Rome c. 1540. He has been variously but uncertainly identified with Arcadelt, Firmin Le Bel and even (on account of the similarity in names) Goudimel, who however was not in Rome.

Mel, Rinaldo del (b. Malines, c. 1554; d. ?, after 1596), Flem. comp. He went to Rome in 1580 after serving at the Port. court, entered the service of Cardinal Gabriele Paleotto and (?)

studied under Palestrina. About 1587–91 he was at Liége in the household of Ernst, Duke of Bavaria, but he rejoined Paleotto at Bologna, who app. him chapel master to Magliano cath.

Works incl. motets, *Sacrae cantiones*, a litany; madrigals, &c.

Melani, Jacopo (b. Pistoia, 6. VII. 1623; d. Pistoia, 1676), It. comp. His father was a sexton at Pistoia and had 7 other mus. sons. He went to Rome at some time and became one of the exponents of comic opera there.

Works incl. operas *Il potestà di Colognole, Il girello, Il pazzo per forza, Il vecchio burlato, Enea in Italia, Ercole in Tebe, Il ritorno d'Ulisse*, &c.

His brothers were: Atto M. (1626–1714), singer; Francesco Maria M. 1628–?), singer & later a monk; Bartolomeo M. (1634–?), singer; Alessandro M. (?–1703), chapel master at Bologna & Rome, comp. of 5 operas, motets, orats., cantatas, &c.; Antonio M. (?–?), comp. of inst. m.; Domenico M. (?–1693), singer; Nicola M. (?–?), singer.

Melartin, Erkki (b. Käkisalmi, 7. II. 1875; d. Helsinki, 14. II. 1937), Fin. comp. Studied at the Helsinki Cons., Wegelius being his comp. master; later in Ger. He became prof. of comp. at the Cons. in 1901, and cond. at Viipuri in 1906. He was dir. of the Cons. in 1911–22.

Works incl. opera *Aino*; ballet *Sininen helmi*; 7 syms., 5 orch. suites, symph. poems; v. Conc.; 4 stg. 4tets; v. & pf. sos.; pf. So. and *c.* 400 pieces; *c.* 300 songs, &c.

Melba, Nellie (real name Helen Mitchell) (b. Burnley nr. Melbourne, 19. V. 1861; d. Sydney, 23. II. 1931), Austral. sop. singer. Studied singing at an early age, but was not allowed to take it up professionally until her marriage to Captain Charles Armstrong in 1882 enabled her to do so. She appeared in London in 1886, went to Paris for further study with Mathilde Marchesi and made her 1st stage appearance at the Théâtre de la Monnaie in Brussels, 1887, coming out at Covent Garden, London, in 1888. She 1st visited Paris in 1889, Rus. in 1891, It. in 1892 and N. Amer. in 1903.

Melcer, Henryk (b. Kalisz, 21. IX. 1869; d. Warsaw, 18. IV. 1928), Pol. pfst. & comp. Studied comp. with Noskowski at Warsaw and pf. with Leschetizky in Vienna, having already appeared in public at the age of 8. He travelled widely as a pfst. and in 1895 became prof. at the Helsingfors Cons. Later he taught at Lwów, Warsaw and Vienna and in 1922 became dir. of the Warsaw Cons.

Works incl. operas *Maria* (Malczewski) & *Protesilaus and Laodamia* (lib. by Wyspianski); *3 Mus. Thoughts* & *Vars. on a Folk Theme* for orch.; 2 pf. concs.; chor. ballad *Pani Twardowska*; pf. Trio; v. & pf. So.; songs with orch. to words by Dehmel, &c.

Melgunov, Julius Nikolaievitch (b. Vetluga, Gvt. Kostroma, 11. IX. 1846; d. Moscow, 31. III. 1893), Rus. pfst. & mcolst. Studied at the Moscow Cons. and with private teachers, toured in Ger. and Rus., but later devoted himself mainly to folksong research, on which he wrote several treatises.

Melisma (from Gr. =song, plur. *melismata*). An ornament: in plainsong a group of notes sung to a single syllable; in modern m. any short passage of a decorative nature.

Mell, Davis (b. Wilton nr. Salisbury, 15. XI. 1604; d. London, 1662), Eng. vst. & clockmaker. Became a member of the King's Band at the Restor. (1660) and joint master. Wrote viol m., &c.

Mell, Gaudio. *See* **Mel.**

Mellers, Wilfrid (Howard) (b. Leamington, 26. IV. 1914), Eng. critic & comp. Studied at Cambridge and began to write criticism in the revue *Scrutiny* there, of which he became mus. asst. ed. He has written many critical essays, mainly on modern comps.

Works incl. *Ricercare* for orch., do. (No. 2) for chamber orch., do. (No. 3) for stg. orch., *Concerto grosso* for chamber orch.; stg. 4tet, pf. 4tet, *Eclogue* for stg. trio; sos. for v. & pf., co. & pf.; So. & *Epithalamium* for pf.; 3 songs for sop., 6 poems for ten., &c.

Melodic Minor Scale. *See* **Minor.**

Melodic Scale. A scale, as for ex. that of the bagpipes, in which the intervals are not in tune according to either Just Intonation or the Tempered Scale, and can thus not be harmonized according to the existing harmonic system and do not even suggest any such harmonization to the ear.

Mélodie (Fr.). Lit. a melody or tune, but the word is now generally current in Fr. as an exact equivalent of the Eng. 'Song' or the Ger. 'Lied.'

Melodram(a) (Ger.). In m. the term is used in a different sense from that current in Eng., It applies to a spoken play or spoken passages in an opera accomp. by a mus. background. Rousseau's *Pygmalion* and Benda's *Ariadne* and *Medea* are early instances of the former, and the 1st version of Humperdinck's *Königskinder* and works by Fibich are later ones; familiar exs. of the latter occur in Beethoven's *Fidelio* and Weber's *Freischütz*.

Melodramma (It. = melodrama). A term for 'opera' current in It. from the end of the 18th cent. onwards.

Melody. A succession of notes making a design in pitch and rhythm to prod. a satisfactory mus. effect; but not necessarily in itself a completely organic mus. line, since even a part of such an organism (a tune or air) may be called a M. The chief decisive elements of M. are tempo, rhythm and the distribution of intervals; harmony forms no part of it; yet from the point of view of western mus. art only such Ms. can be regarded as successful which call for or at least imply a satisfying harmonic assoc.

Melville, Herman (1819–91), Amer. novelist. *See* **Claflin** (*Moby Dick* Suite), **Moore (D.)** (*Moby Dick*).

Mendelssohn, Arnold (b. Ratibor, 26. XII. 1855; d. Darmstadt, 19. II. 1933), Ger. comp., son of a cousin of Felix M.-Bartholdy. Studied law at Tübingen and m. in Berlin, and held teaching and cond. appts. at Bonn, Bielefed, Cologne & Darmstadt, where he became prof. in 1917.

Works incl. operas *Elsi, die seltsame Magd* (after Jeremias Gotthelf), *Der Bärenhäuter* & *Die Minneburg*; cantatas; madrigals to words from Goethe's *Werther*; much church m.; Sym. in E♭ maj.; v. Conc.; 2 stg. 4tets; sos. for v. & pf., co. & pf. and pf.; songs, partsongs, &c.

Mendelssohn, Fanny. *See* **Hensel.**

Mendelssohn (-Bartholdy, Jakob Ludwig) Felix (b. Hamburg, 3. II. 1809; d. Leipzig, 4. XI. 1847), Ger. comp. Son of the banker Abraham M. and grandson of the Jewish philos. Moses M. M.'s branch of the family embraced Christianity and moved to Berlin in 1812. At 6 M. had pf. lessons from his mother and at 7 from Marie Bigot in Paris. In 1817, back in Berlin, he learnt comp. from Zelter, whose friend Goethe he visited at Weimar in 1821. Before that, in 1818, aged 9, he appeared at a public chamber concert, and before he was 13 he had written many works, incl. the pf. 4tet Op. 1. His father was wealthy enough to enable him to cond. a private orch. and he wrote his 1st Sym. at 15, when he also had pf. lessons from Moscheles during a visit. By 1825 he had ready the short opera *Gamacho's Wedding*, prod. at the family's expense in 1827, and at 17 he had written the ovt. to Shakespeare's *Midsummer Night's Dream* (the rest of the incid. m. folowed in 1842). In 1829 he cond. Bach's forgotten St. Matthew Passion at the Voc. Acad. and paid the 1st of his 10 visits to Eng., cond. the Phil. Soc. in London and taking a holiday in Sco., where he gathered impressions for the *Hebrides* ovt. and the 'Scottish' Sym., at which he worked in It. in 1830–1. The 'It.' Sym. he finished in 1833, the year he cond. the Lower Rhine Festival at Düsseldorf, where he was engaged to stay as general mus. dir. But he left for Leipzig, where he was app. cond. of the Gewandhaus concerts in 1835. During a visit to Frankfort o/M. he met Cécile Jeanrenaud, a girl about 10 years his junior, descendant of a Fr. Huguenot family, whom he married on 28. III. 1837. In IX of the same year he cond. *St. Paul* at the Birmingham Festival. In 1841 he left for Berlin, having been app. dir. of the m. section of the Acad. of Arts, and there he furnished incid. m. for several classical plays, Gr., Eng. and Fr. But he returned to Leipzig late in 1842 and founded the Cons. there in XI, opening it in IV. 1843. He was still living in Berlin, however, but resumed his cond.-ship at Leipzig in IX. 1845 and taught pf. and comp. at the Cons. But he was in poor health, and his visit to Eng. to conduct *Elijah* at the Birmingham Festival on 26. VIII. 1846 was his last but one. After the last, in the spring of 1847, the death of his sister Fanny Hensel greatly depressed him, and he went to Swi. too ill to do any work, returning to Leipzig in IX., completely exhausted.

Works incl. operas *Die Hochzeit des Gamacho, Die Heimkehr aus der Fremde* (*Son and Stranger*) & *Loreley* (unfinished); incid. m. to Sophocles' *Antigone* & *Oedipus at Colonos*, Shakespeare's *Midsummer Night's Dream*, Racine's *Athalie* & ovt. to Hugo's *Ruy Blas*; orats. *St. Paul* & *Elijah*, many chor. settings of psalms & other sacred voc. works, *Lobgesang* (*Hymn of Praise*: the 2nd sym. followed by a short cantata), cantata *Lauda Sion*, Goethe's *Erste Walpurgisnacht* for solo voices, chor. & orch.; 5 syms.; 6 concert ovts. and some misc. orch. works; 2 concs. and 3 shorter works for pf. & orch.; v. Conc. in E min.; chamber m. incl. 7 stg. 4tets, 3 pf. 4tets, 2 stg. 5tets, 2 pf. trios, stg. Octet, 6tet, 4 pieces for stg. 4tet, &c.; v. & pf. So., 2 co. & pf. sos.; a large amount of pf. m. incl. 48 *Songs without Words*, 3 sos., fantasies, characteristic pieces, capriccios, vars., preludes & fugues, studies, &c.; 6 sos., 3 preludes & fugues and other pieces for org.; over 80 songs; 12 sets of voc. duets and partsongs; 44 vols. of misc. works left in MS., &c.

Mendès, Catulle (1841–1909), Fr. writer, poet & dramatist. He wrote libs. for several comps., incl. Chabrier, Messager, Pierné, Pessard, Massenet and Debussy. D.'s work, *Rodrigue et Chimène*, was never finished. Married Judith Gautier (1850–1917), with whom he visited Wagner at Triebschen in Swi., 1869. *See also* **Bruneau** (*Chansons à danser & Lieds de France*), **Gwendoline** (Chabrier), **Indy** (*Médée*), **Leroux** (*Reine Fiammette*), **Vidal (P.)** (do.).

Ménestrel (Fr.) = Minstrel.

Ménétrandise (Fr., formerly *Ménestrandise*). In 17th- & 18th-cent. Paris a corporation of *Ménétriers* protected by an official privilege against the encroachment of other musns. on their exclusive right to play for dancing. Couperin wrote a satirical hpchd. suite on it entitled *Les Fastes de la Grande Mxnxstrxndxsx.*

Ménétrier (Fr. formerly *Ménestrier*). A player of dance-m., esp. a fiddler.

Mengelberg, (Kurt) Rudolf (b. Crefeld, 1. II. 1892), Dutch comp., cousin of the cond. Willem M. Studied with var. masters, incl. Riemann at Leipzig, and in 1915 became dir. of the Concertgebouw at Amsterdam. In 1945 he was, like his cousin, denounced as a Nazi collaborator. He wrote a book on Mahler.

Works incl. *Missa pro pace*, hymn *Op Amstelredam* (Vondel) & other chor. & orch. works; *Symph. Elegy* for orch.; v. Conc., Capriccio for pf. & orch., Symph. Vars. for co. & orch.; v. & pf. So. numerous songs incl. settings of Verlaine, &c.

Mengozzi, Bernardo (b. Florence, 1758; d. Paris, III. 1800), It. ten singer & comp. Studied at Florence and Venice, visited London in 1786 and settled in Paris soon after, becoming prof. of singing on the estab. of the Cons. in 1795. Wrote opera *Pourceaugnac* (after Molière) & *c*. 15 others, operettas, &c.

Meno mosso (It. = less moved). A direction indicating that the pace of a comp. or mvt. is to be slowed down somewhat.

Menotti, Gian Carlo (b. Cadigliano, 7. VII. 1911), It.-Amer. comp. Studied comp. with Scalero at the Curtis Inst., Philadelphia.

Works incl. opera *Amelia al ballo*; radio opera *The Old Maid and the Thief*; *Pastorale* for pf. & stg. orch.; 4 pieces for stg. 4tet, *Trio for a House-warming Party* for fl., co. & pf.; *Poemetti*, pf. pieces for children; pieces for carillon, &c.

Mensurable Music. Measured or measurable m. divided into bars and grouped according to regular successions of beats, as distinct from plainsong, which has no measured rhythmic pulse.

Mensural Notation. The mus. notation which, as distinct from Modal N., came into use during the 13th cent. and for the 1st time began to indicate the exact value of notes and rests by its symbols.

Menter, Joseph (b. Deutenkofen, Bavaria, 19. I. 1808; d. Munich, 18. IV. 1856), Ger. vst. & cst. Played in the orch. of the Royal Opera at Munich most of his life.

Menter, Sophie (b. Munich, 29. VII. 1848; d. Stockdorf nr. Munich, 23. II. 1918), Ger. pfst. & teacher, daughter of prec. Studied at the Munich Cons., toured 1st at the age of 15, resumed studies with Tausig and Liszt, married Popper in 1872 and became pf. prof. at St. Petersburg, 1883.

Menu, Pierre (b. Paris, 1896; d. Paris, 16. X. 1919), Fr. comp. Studied with Roger-Ducasse at the Paris Cons., but his career was cut short by his early death.

Works incl. Sonatina for stg. 4tet, pf. 4tet; *Dans l'ambiance espagnole* for chrom. hp.; songs, &c.

Menuet (Fr.) = Minuet. The word is a diminutive of *menu* = small.

Menuetto (Ger.-It.). The Ger. classics often labelled their minuets thus under the impression that they were using an It. term. The correct It. is *minuetto*, the Ger. *Menuett.*

Mer, La (*The Sea*). 3 symph. sketches by Debussy, *De l'aube à midi sur la mer, Jeux de vagues & Dialogue du vent et de la mer*, comp. in 1903–5 and 1st perf. Paris, 15. X. 1905.

Merbecke (or **Merbeck, Marbeck, Marbecke**), **John** (b. ?; d. Windsor, *c*. 1585), Eng. singer, orgst. & comp. He was lay-clerk and orgst. at St. George's Chapel, Windsor, from *c*. 1540. In 1543 he was arrested and in 1544 tried and condemned for heresy, but he was pardoned and allowed to retain his office.

Works incl. Mass & 2 motets (prob. early); carol *A Virgine and Mother*; *The Booke of Common Praier noted* (i.e. set to notes), being the 1st mus. setting of the Angl. prayer book (1st version authorized by Edward VI).

Mercadante, (Giuseppe) Saverio (**Raffaele**) (b. Altamura nr. Bari, 17. IX. 1795; d. Naples, 17. XII. 1870), It. comp. Studied at the Collegio di San Sebastiano at Naples, and having learnt the fl. and v., became leader of the orch. there. On being dismissed he began to earn his living as a stage comp. After several successes in It. he won favour in Vienna, visited Spa.

in 1827–9, and in 1833 became chapel master at Novara cath. in succession to Generali and in 1840 dir. of the Naples Cons. While at Novara he lost an eye and in 1862 he became totally blind.

Works incl. *c.* 60 operas, e.g. *Violenza e costanza, Elisa e Claudio, Caritea, regina di Spagna, Gabriella di Vergy, I Normanni a Parigi, I briganti, Il giuramento, I due illustri rivali, Elena da Feltre, Il bravo, La Vestale, Leonora, Gli Orazi ed i Curiazi, Virginia*; 20 masses, motets, psalms, &c.; cantatas *L'apoteosi d'Ercole* & others; inst. pieces; songs, &c.

Mercante di Venezia, Il (*The Merchant of Venice*), opera by Pinsuti (lib. by Giorgio Tommaso Cimino, after Shakespeare), prod. Bologna, Teatro Comunale, 9. XI. 1873.

Mercury, the nickname of a Sym. by Haydn, No. 43, in E♭ maj., comp. *c.* 1771.

Mereaux, Nicolas (Jean Le Froid) de (b. Paris, 1745; d. Paris, 1797), Fr. orgst. & comp. Orgst. at the Paris churches of Saint-Sauveur and Petits Augustins as well as of the royal chapel.

Works incl. operas *La Ressource comique, Le Retour de tendresse, Le Duel comique* (adapted from Paisiello), *Laurette, Alexandre aux Indes, Œdipe et Jocaste, Fabius, Les Thermopyles, Scipion à Carthage*; orats. *Samson* & *Esther*; ode on the birth of the dauphin, &c.

Méric-Lalande, Henriette-Clémentine (b. Dunkirk, 1798; d. Chantilly, 7. IX. 1867), Fr. sop. singer. As the daughter of a provincial opera manager she picked up enough experience to appear on the stage at Naples in 1814, but after a good deal of success she decided in 1822 to take lessons from García and appeared in 1823 at the Opéra-Comique in Paris, marrying the hn. player Méric there. She studied further in It., sang there and 1st appeared in London in 1830.

Merighi, Antonia (b. ?; d. ?), It. 18th-cent. con. singer. 1st appeared in London in 1720.

Merikanto, Aarre (b. Helsingfors, 29. VII. 1893), Fin. comp. Studied with Reger and others at Leipzig and with Vassilenko at Moscow. Later became prof. at the Helsingfors Cons.

Works incl. ballet *The Abduction of Kylliki* (on a subject from the *Kalevala*); 3 syms. Vars. and Fugue & several suites for orch.; 3 v. concs., 2 pf. concs., co. Conc., Conc. for v., cl. hn. & stgs.; Partita for woodwind & hp.; folksong arrs. &c.

Merikanto, (Frans) Oscari (b. Helsingfors, 5. VIII. 1868; d. Helsinki, 17. II. 1924), Fin. comp., father of prec. Studied at the Helsingfors Cons. and at Leipzig and Berlin.

Works incl. operas *Pohjan neiti, Elinan surma, Regina von Emmeritz*; incid. m. for plays; cantatas, songs, &c.

Mérimée, Prosper (1803–70), Fr. novelist. *See* **Büsser** (*Carrosse du Saint-Sacrement* & *Colomba*), **Carmen** (Bizet), **Carrosse du Saint-Sacrement** (Berners), **Colomba** (Mackenzie), **Cui** (*Matteo Falcone*), **Durey** (*L'Occasion*), **Halévy** (*Dame de Pique*), **Périchole** (Offenbach), **Schoeck** (*Don Ranudo*), **Venus** (Schoeck), **Wetzler** (*Basque Venus*).

Merk, Joseph (b. Vienna, 18. I. 1795; d. Vienna, 16. VI. 1852), Aus. cst. Studied in Vienna, where he became cst. at the Opera in 1818 and prof. at the Cons. in 1823. Wrote m. for his inst.

Merkel, Gustav (b. Oberoderwitz, Saxony, 12. XI. 1827; d. Dresden, 30. X. 1885), Ger. orgst. & comp. Studied at Dresden and became orgst. at the orphanage church there in 1858, the Kreuzkirche in 1860 and court orgst. in 1864. He also cond. the Voc. Acad. and was prof. at the Cons.

Works incl. 9 sos., preludes & fugues, fantasies, studies, &c. for org.; inst. pieces with org.; pf. works; songs, &c.

Merker (Ger. lit. marker = judge, adjudicator, umpire). One of the masters among the Ger. Meistersinger who was elected to judge the competitions for mastership and prizes. Beckmesser is the M. in Wagner's *Meistersinger*.

Merlo, Alessandro (called Alessandro Romano or A. della Viola) (b. Rome, *c.* 1530; d. ?), It. ten.-bass singer, violist & comp. Pupil of Willaert and Rore. Singer in the Papal Chapel in Rome.

Works incl. motets; madrigals, Canzoni alla Napolitana, villanelle, &c.

Merlotti, Claudio. *See* **Merulo.**

Mermet, Auguste (b. Brussels, 5. I. 1810; d. Paris, 4. VII. 1889), Belg. comp. Pupil of Lesueur and Halévy.

Works incl. operas *La Bannière du roi, Le Roi David, Roland à Roncevaux* & *Jeanne d'Arc*.

Merope, opera by Gasparini (lib. by Apostolo Zeno), prod. Venice, Teatro San Cassiano, 26. XII. 1711.

Opera by Graun (lib. in Fr., by Frederick II of Prus.), prod. Berlin, Opera, 27. III. 1756.

Opera by Jommelli (lib. by Zeno), prod. Venice, Teatro San Giovanni Crisostomo, 26. XII. 1741.

Opera by Terradellas (lib. do.), prod. Rome, Teatro delle Dame, Carnival 1743.

Merrie England, operetta by German (lib. by Basil Hood), prod. London, Savoy Theatre, 2. IV. 1902.

Merry Widow (Lehàr). *See* **Lustige Witwe.**

Merry Wives of Windsor. *See* **Falstaff, Lustigen Weiber, Sir John in Love.**

Mersenne, Marin (b. Oizé, Maine, 8. IX. 1588; d. Paris, 1. IX. 1648), Fr. monk & mus. theorist. Educ. at Le Mans and La Flèche, he became a Minorite friar, being ordained in 1613. He taught philosophy at Nevers and then studied maths. and m. in Paris, Descartes and the elder Pascal being among his colleagues. He corresponded with scholars in Eng., Hol. and It., the last of which he visited 3 times. His treatises incl. *Harmonie universelle, Questions harmoniques, De la nature des sons,* &c.

Mersmann, Hans (b. Potsdam, 6. X. 1891), Ger. mclst. & cond. Studied at Munich, Leipzig & Berlin, last under Kretzschmar. He held var. appts. in Berlin as lecturer, prof. at the Technical Univ., on the staff of the broadcasting organization and as ed. of the magazine *Melos.* His books incl. *Angewandte Musikaesthetik, Musik der Gegenwart* and others on modern m., 3 works on folksong, &c.

Merula, Tarquinio (b. ? Cremona, ?; d. ?), It. 17th-cent. comp. Held appts. alternately at Bergamo and Cremona, and was court and church orgst. at Warsaw in 1624. In 1628 he was at Cremona again and was chapel master at the cath. there in 1652, having held a similar appt. at Bergamo from *c.* 1640. Later he was at court at Florence.

Works incl. masses, motets, psalms, *Concerti spirituali* & other church m.; madrigals, canzoni for voices and/or insts.; church sos., &c.

Merulo, Claudio (also called Claudio da Correggio; real name Merlotti) (b. Correggio, 8. IV. 1533; d. Parma, 4. V. 1604), It. orgst., teacher & comp. App. orgst. at Brescia in 1556 and 2nd orgst. at St. Mark's, Venice, in 1557, advancing to 1st orgst. in 1566. In 1584 he left Venice, visited the court of Mantua and became orgst. to the ducal chapel at Parma.

Works incl. intermezzi for Dolce's *Le Troiane* & Cornelio Frangipani's *La tragedia*; masses, motets, *Sacrae cantiones,* litanies; madrigals; toccatas and ricercari for org., &c.

Méry, Joseph (1798–1865), Fr. poet. *See* **Franck (C.)** (songs).

Mésangeau, René (b. Paris, ?; d. Paris, *c.* 1639), Fr. lutenist & comp. Wrote pieces for his inst.

Messa di voce (It. setting or placing of the voice). Sustained singing of notes or phrases; but *messa* may also mean 'growth,' i.e. *crescendo.*

Messager, André (Charles Prosper) (b. Montluçon, 30. XII. 1853; d. Paris, 24. II. 1929), Fr. cond. & comp. Studied at Niedermeyer's school in Paris and later under Saint-Saëns. In 1876 he won prizes for a sym. and a cantata, and in 1883 he prod. a completion of an operetta *François les Bas-bleus* left unfinished by Firmin Bernicat. He became cond. of the Opéra-Comique and in 1898 its general dir.; and in 1906–13 he was joint dir. of the Opéra. He was also a concert cond. His wife was the Ir. comp. Hope Temple (Dotie Davies, 1859–1938), who had been a pupil of his.

Works incl. operas and operettas *La Fauvette du Temple, La Béarnaise, Le Bourgeois de Calais, Isoline, Le Mari de la reine, La Basoche, Madame Chrysanthème* (after Pierre Loti's novel), *Miss Dollar, Mirette, Le Chevalier d'Harmental, Le P'tites Michu, Véronique, Les Dragons de l'impératrice, Fortunio, Béatrice, Monsieur Beaucaire* (in Eng.), *La Petite Fonctionnaire, L'Amour masqué, Passionnément, Coup de roulis*; ballets *Les Deux Pigeons, Scaramouche, Le Chevalier aux fleurs, Une Aventure de la Guimard* & others; inst. pieces; pf. duets; songs, &c.

Messanza (It. = mixture). *See* **Quodlibet.**

Messchaert, Johannes (b. Hoorn, 22. VIII. 1857; d. Zürich, 9. IX. 1922), Dutch bass-bar. singer. Studied with Stockhausen. He sang much in Hol., Ger. and elsewhere and toured as interpreter of songs with Julius Röntgen as pfst.

Messe (Fr. & Ger.) = Mass.

Messe solennelle. *See* **Missa solemnis.**

Messiaen, Olivier (Eugène Prosper Charles) (b. Avignon, 10. XII. 1908), Fr. orgst. & comp., son of the poetess Cécile Sauvage. Studied org. under Marcel Dupré, theory under Maurice Emmanuel and comp. under Dukas at the Paris Cons. App. orgst. of the Trinité in Paris, 1931, and prof. at the École Normale de Musique and the Schola Cantorum. With Baudrier, Jolivet and Lesur he formed the group 'La Jeune France.' In 1940, he was taken prisoner by the Gers. but repatriated later and app. prof. of harmony at the Cons. in 1941. His wife, Claire Delbos, is a comp. of songs.

Works incl. *O sacrum convivium* & 2 Liturgies for chor.; *Les Offrandes oubliées* for orch.; *Trois petites liturgies de la Présence Divine* for women's chor., celesta, vibraphone, ondes Martenot, pf., perc. & stgs.; *Poèmes pour Mi* & *La Mort du nombre* for voice & orch.; *Diptyque, Le Banquet céleste, L'Ascension, La Nativité du Seigneur* (4 vols.), *Apparition de l'église éternelle, Les Corps glorieux* for org.; *Quatuor pour le fin du temps* for cl., v., co. & pf.; Theme & Vars. for v. & pf.; *Fantaisie burlesque, Vingt regards sur l'Enfant Jésus* & 8 Preludes for pf; *Les Visions de l'Amen* for 2 pfs.; *3 Mélodies* & *Vocalise* for voice & pf., &c.

Messiah (not *The Messiah*), orat. by Handel (words selected from the Bible ostensibly by Charles Jennens, but more probably by his chaplain, Pooley, with suggestions from the comp.), prod. Dublin, Music Hall in Fishamble Street, 13. IV. 1742; 1st perf. in Eng., Covent Garden Theatre, London, 23. III. 1743.

Messidor, opera by Bruneau (lib. by Émile Zola), prod. Paris, Opéra, 19. II. 1897. B. had already written operas on subjects from Zola's works (*L'Attaque du moulin* and *Le Rêve*), but this was the 1st for which Z. himself wrote the lib.

Messner, Joseph (b. Schwaz, Tyrol, 27. II. 1893), Aus. orgst., cond. & comp. Studied in Munich and was app. orgst. to Salzburg cath. in 1922. He also conds. there, incl. the m. in the cath. during the Salzburg Festival.

Works incl. operas *Hadassa, Das letzte Recht, Ines, Agnes Bernauer*; 6 masses, Te Deum & other church m.; orats. *Das Leben* & *Die vier letzten Dinge*; 2 syms., *Symphonische Festmusik* for orch.; *Sinfonietta* for pf. & orch., &c.

Mesto (It.) = sad, gloomy.

Mesuré (Fr.). *See* **Musique mesurée.**

Metamorphosis. The transformation of a theme or motif, esp. rhythmically while the same notes are retained, as for ex. the *idée fixe* of Berlioz, the themes in Liszt's symph. poems, &c. and the *Leitmotive* in Wagner's operas.

Metaphor Aria. *See* **Parable Aria.**

Metastasio, Pietro (real name Trapassi) (1698–1782), It. poet & libst. Operas on his libs. *see* **Achille in Sciro, Adriano in Siria, Alessandro nell' Indie, Antigono, Artaserse, Cinesi, Clemenza di Tito, Cleofide, Contesa dei numi, Demetrio, Demofoonte, Démophon, Didone abbandonata, Eroe cinese, Ezio, Galatea, Innocenza giustificata, Ipermestra, Isola disabitata, Lucio Silla, Olimpiade, Partenope, Rè pastore, Ruggiero, Semiramide riconosciuta, Siface, Siroe, Sogno di Scipione, Tito Vespasiano, Trionfo di Clelia.**

See also **Araia, Arne** (T. A.), **Bioni** (*Pace fra virtù e bellezza*), **Frederick II, Gluck, Martinez** (psalms), **Morlacchi** (Passion orat.), **Poissl, Poro** (Handel), **Reichardt, Rota** (N.), **Wellesz** (*Amor timido*).

Metre. The rhythmic patterns prod. in m. by notes of varying length combined with strong and weak beats (*arsis* and *thesis*), similar to the different 'feet' (spondees, dactyls, anapaests, trochees, iambics, &c.) in poetry.

Metronome. An inst. invented by Mälzel in 1814 and designed to determine and prescribe the pace of any mus. comp. by the beats of a pendulum. The tempo is indicated by the comp., who prescribes how many time-units of a certain note-value are to occupy 1 minute: e.g. ♩ = 60 shows that there are to be 60 crotchets to the minute. The M., however, can only set the pace, which can never be strictly maintained in accordance with the beats of its pendulum, since all m. that is alive and breathing must be subject to slights vars. in pace. It is a fallacy to suppose that any musn. should play or sing to the metronome, and teachers who encourage this are to be regarded with suspicion.

Mexican Composers. *See* **Ayala, Carrillo, Chávez, Morales** (M.), **Pomar, Ponce, Revueltas, Rolón.**

Mey, Lev Alexandrovitch (1822–62), Rus. dramatist & trans. *See* **Pskovitianka** (Rimsky-K.), **Servilia** (do.), **Tsar's Bride** (do.).

Meyer, Bernard van den Sigtenhorst. *See* **Sigtenhorst Meyer.**

Meyer, Conrad Ferdinand (1825–98), Swi. poet & novelist. *See* **Kaminski** (*Jürg Jenatsch*), **Kunz** (*Huttens letzte Tage*).

Meyer, Ernst Hermann (b. Berlin, 8. XII. 1905), Ger. mcolst. & comp. Settled in London from 1933. His books incl. studies of 17th-cent. inst. m. & Eng. chamber m. from the Middle Ages to Purcell.

Works incl. film & chamber m., &c.

Meyer, Gregor (b. ?; d. ?), Swi. 16th-cent. orgst. & comp. He was orgst. at Solothurn cath. and supplied Glareanus with comps. exemplifying the correct use of the modes.

Works incl. motets, kyries, antiphons, &c.

Meyer-Helmund, Erik (b. St. Petersburg, 25. IV. 1861; d. Berlin, 4. IV. 1932), Ger. singer & comp. Studied under his father and later in Berlin: comp. with Kiel and singing with Stockhausen. He wrote his own words for many of his songs.

Works incl. operas and operettas *Margitta, Der Liebeskampf, Trischka, Lucullus* & *Heines Traumbilder, Tag-*

lioni; ballets *Münchener Bilderbogen*, *Rübezahl*; numerous songs, &c.

Meyer-Lutz, Wilhelm (b. Männerstadt nr. Kissingen, 1822; d. London, 31. I. 1903), Ger. pfst., orgst. & comp. Pupil of his father, an orgst. and theorist. He 1st appeared in public as a pfst., at the age of 12, and later, the family having moved to Würzburg, went to the grammar-school and the Univ. there. In 1848 he settled in Eng., becoming orgst. to St. Chad's Rom. Catholic cath. at Birmingham and later to St. Ann's church at Leeds and St. George's cath. in London. He also cond. for many years at the Surrey and Gaiety Theatres there.

Works incl. operas and operettas *Faust and Marguerite* (after Goethe), *Blonde and Brunette*, *Zaïda*, *Miller of Milburg*, *The Legend of the Lys*; cantata *Herne the Hunter*; theatre & orch. m.; stg. 4tet and other chamber m., &c.

Meyer von Schauensee, Franz (Joseph Leonti) (b. Lucerne, 10. VIII. 1720; d. Lucerne, 2. I. 1789), Swi. orgst. & comp. Studied at Lucerne and Milan, served in Sardinia and Aus. as a mercenary, but returned to Lucerne in 1745 as a civil servant and musn., took holy orders in 1752 and became orgst. of the collegiate church, founding a coll. of m. in 1760.

Works incl. comic operas *Hans Hüttenstock* & others; masses, offertories & other church m.; syms.; concs.; arias, &c.

Meyerbeer, Giacomo (real name Jakob Liebmann Beer) (b. Berlin, 5. IX. 1791; d. Paris, 2. V. 1864), Ger. comp. His father, Herz Beer, a Jewish banker, gave him every facility to develop his precocious mus. gifts. He was at first trained as a pfst. and had some lessons from Clementi during the latter's stay in Berlin. He played in public at the age of 7, but afterwards studied theory and comp. under Zelter, B. A. Weber and Vogler, to whose house at Darmstadt he moved in 1810, being a fellow-student with C. M. von Weber there. His 1st opera was prod. at Munich in 1812 and the 2nd at Stuttgart in 1813. He then went to Vienna, and hearing Hummel play, he retired for further pf. studies, after which he appeared again as a virtuoso. On Salieri's advice he went to It. to study voc. writing in 1815, and prod. his 1st It. opera at Padua in 1817. In 1823 he tried his luck in Berlin, but without much success, and having prod. *Il crociato* at Venice in 1824, went to Paris for its 1st perf. there in 1826. He settled and spent much time there for the rest of his life. He wrote no new work between 1824–31, among the reasons being his father's death, his marriage and the loss of 2 children. In 1831 *Robert le Diable* made him sensationally fashionable in Paris. In 1842 the King of Prus. app. him General Mus. Dir. in Berlin. He visited Vienna and London in 1847 and the latter again in 1862, when he represented Ger. m. at the Internat. Exhib. His health began to fail about 1850.

Works incl. operas *Jephthas Gelübde*, *Alimelek, oder Die beiden Kalifen*, *Romilda e Costanza*, *Semiramide riconosciuta*, *Emma di Resburgo*, *Margherita d'Anjou*, *L'esule di Granata*, *Das Brandenburger Tor*, *Il crociato in Egitto*, *Robert le Diable*, *Les Huguenots*, *Ein Feldlager in Schlesien*, *Le Prophète*, *L'Étoile du Nord*, *Le Pardon de Ploërmel* (*Dinorah*), *L'Africaine*, *Judith* (unfinished); monodrama *Thevelindens Liebe*; incid. m. to Michael Beer's (his brother's) drama *Struensee*, Blaze de Bury's *Jeunesse de Goethe* & Aeschylus's *Eumenides*; masque *Das Hoffest von Ferrara*; ballet *Der Fischer und des Milchmädchen*; orat. *Gott und die Natur*; *Stabat Mater*, Te Deum, psalms & other church m.; several cantatas, incl. 2 for the Schiller centenary, 1859; March for do., 3 Torch Dances, Coronation March, *Ovt. in the Form of a March* for the London Exhib.; pf. works; songs, &c.

Meynell, Alice (1849–1922), Eng. poetess. *See* **Davies (Walford)** (*Christ in the Universe*).

Meyrowitz, Selmar (b. Bartenstein, E. Prus., 18. IV. 1875; d. Toulouse, V. 1941), Ger. cond. Studied at the Leipzig Cons. and with Bruch in Berlin. His appts. as opera cond. incl. Carlsruhe, N.Y., Prague and Berlin, and later he was a concert cond. in Berlin, Hamburg, Vienna, Rome, &c. In 1933 he emigrated to Paris.

Mezari, Maddalena (called Casulana) (b. Vicenza, ?; d. ?), It. 16th-cent. comp. She seems to have lived in Venice, where she pub. madrigals.

Mezza (It. fem.) = half, as in *mezza voce* = half-voice, a special way of prod. the voice as if under the breath, resulting not only in a soft tone, but in a different quality from that of the full voice.

Mezzo (It. masc.) = half, as in *mezzo-soprano*, a voice half-way between sop. and con. in range.

mf (abbr.) = *mezzo forte* (half-loud).

Mi. The old name for the note E (*see* **Solmization**), still used in Lat. countries, and in Tonic Sol-fa the Mediant note in any key, repres. by the symbol m, pronounced Me.

Mi contra Fa. A medieval designation of the Tritone (the forbidden interval of the augmented 4th), the Mi being the mediant of the hard hexachord beginning on G.

Miaskovsky, Nikolai Yokovlevitch (b. Novogeorgievsk nr. Warsaw, 20. IV. 1881), Rus. comp. Son of a Rus. military engineer stationed in Pol., whence the family moved successively to Orenburg, Kazan and Nizhny-Novgorod, where M. joined the cadet corps. Intended to follow his father's career, he did not finally take to m. until 1907, when he resigned his commission, though he had comp. many pf. preludes, studied with Glière and Krizhanovsky and entered the St. Petersburg Cons. in 1906, where he studied with Rimsky-Korsakov, Liadov and Wihtol. In 1914–7 he fought on the Aus. front and was badly wounded; in 1921 he became comp. prof. at the Moscow Cons.

Works incl. orat. *Kirov is with us*; 25 syms., 2 sinfoniettas, symph. poems *Silence* (after Poe) & *Alastor* (after Shelley), Serenade & *Lyric Concertino* for small orch.; v. Conc.; 9 stg. 4tets; co. & pf. So.; 4 pf. sos. & other pf. pieces; 13 op. nos. of songs, &c.

Michael, Rogier (b. Mons, *c.* 1550; d. Dresden, *c.* 1619), Flem. ten. singer & comp. Studied under his father, Simon M., a musn. to the Emperor Ferdinand I. He became a ten. in the electoral chapel at Dresden in 1575 and chapel master in 1587, being succeeded in the latter post by Schütz in 1619.

Works incl. introits in the motet style, settings of hymn-tunes in 4 parts & other sacred m.

Michael, Tobias (b. Dresden, 13. VI. 1592; d. Leipzig, 26. VI. 1657), Ger. comp., son of prec. Studied as a boy chorister under his father in the Dresden court chapel and became mus. dir. at Sondershausen in 1619. In 1631 he succeeded Schein as cantor of St. Thomas's church at Leipzig.

Works incl. *Musikalische Seelenlust* containing sacred madrigals for voices and sacred concs. for voices and insts., other church m., &c.

Michelangelo (Michelagnolo Buonarroti) (1475–1564), It. painter, sculptor & poet. *See* **Britten** (7 sonnets), **Dallapiccola** (chors.), **Valen** (*Sonetto*).

3 sonnets set by Hugo Wolf.

Micheli, Romano (b. Rome, *c.* 1575; d. Rome, *c.* 1660), It. comp. Studied under Soriano, travelled widely in It., became a priest, held appts. at Modena and Aquileia, and returned to Rome in 1625 as chapel master of the church of San Luigi de' Francesi. In 1647 he refuted the assertion made by the Danzig orgst. Paul Syfert that It. m. was flimsy by sending works of his own.

Works incl. masses, motets, psalms; madrigals, canons, &c.

Micinski, Tadeusz (1873–1919), Pol. poet. *See* **Szymanowski** (*Prince Potemkin* & songs).

Mickiewicz, Adam (1798–1855), Pol. poet. *See* **Chopin** (Ballades), **Cui** (songs), **Moniuszko** (ballads), **Rytel** (*Grazyna*).

Microcosm (Bartok). *See* **Mikrokosmos.**

Microphone. The receiver which transmits and amplifies the sounds of a broadcast perf. It can also be used for other than wireless purposes, e.g. in theatres and public halls for the relaying of speech and song to amplifiers placed at var. points of the building. One of its modern uses, unfortunately, is that made by popular singers of light m., whom it enables to prod. on undiscriminating listeners an effect of huge voc. powers without compelling them to acquire any adequate voc. technique; an effect, too, which is wholly artificial and crude in the extreme. The worst achievement of the M., which is in itself an admirable and valuable invention, is that it has made Crooning possible.

Microtones. The small fractional notes into which the mus. scale was divided by the Mex. comp. Julián Carrillo, who invented special insts. for the purpose and wrote m. on the M. system.

Middle C. The note C designated by the sop., alto & ten. clefs on the line of the stave on which the clef is placed and lying in the centre of the pf. keyboard. It is shown in a kind of mirror picture by the treble and bass clefs, standing on the 1st leger line below the stave in the former and on the 1st leger line above the stave in the latter.

Middleton, Thomas (1570–1627), Eng. dramatist. *See* **Johnson (R. ii)** (*Witch*), **Locke** (do.).

Midi, Le (*Noon*), the name of 1 of 3 syms. by Haydn, comp. *c.* 1761. It is No. 7 of H.'s complete syms., in C maj.; the others are No. 6, in D maj., *Le Matin*, and No. 8, in G maj., *Le Soir et la tempête.*

Midsummer Night's Dream, A. *See also* **Songe d'une nuit d'été.**

Incid. m. by Mendelssohn to Shakespeare's play. Ovt. comp. in VII—VIII. 1826 and 1st perf. at Stettin in II. 1827; the rest of the m. comp. in 1842 and used for a stage prod. at Potsdam on 14. X. 1843.

Mighty Handful, The. *See* **Kutchka.**

Mignon, opera by A. Thomas (lib. by Jules Barbier & Michel Carré, based on Goethe's *Wilhelm Meister*), prod. Paris, Opéra-Comique, 17. XI. 1866.

Mignone, Francisco (b. São Paulo, 3. XI. 1897), Brazil. comp.

Works incl. operas *El inocente* & *El contratista de diamantes*; sym. *Maxixe*; songs, &c.

Migot, Georges (Elbert) (b. Paris, 27. II. 1891), Fr. comp. Studied with var. masters, incl. Widor, and made a speciality of medieval m. In 1917 he made himself known in Paris by giving a concert of his own, and, holding no official post, he relied on his own efforts to keep before the public.

Works incl. operas *Hagoromo, Le Rossignol en amour, Bérénice éternelle*; ballets *La Fête de la bergère, Le Paravent de laque, Les Aveux et les promesses*; Psalm xix for chor. & orch., *The Sermon on the Mount* for solo voices, chor., org. & stgs.; *Les Agrestides, 3 Guirlandes sonores* for orch.; *La Jungle* for org. & orch.; *Le Livre des danseries* for v., fl. & pf. & other chamber m.: *Dialogues* for v. & pf. and co. & pf.; *Ad usum Delphini, Le Zodiaque, Le Calendrier du petit berger* (for children) & other pf. works; *Les Poèmes de Brugnon, Le Cortège d'Amphitrite* & other songs, &c.

Mihalovich, Ödön (b. Fericsancze, 13. IX. 1842; d. Budapest, 22. IV. 1929), Hung. comp. Studied with Mosonyi at Budapest, Hauptmann at Leipzig and Bülow in Munich. In 1887 he succeeded Liszt as dir. of the Mus. Acad. at Budapest, and remained there until 1919.

Works incl. operas *Hagbarth und Signe* & *Wieland der Schmied* (Wagner's lib.) (both in Ger.), *Toldi Szerelme* (*Toldi's Love*) & *Eliána* (after Tennyson's *Idylls of the King*) (both in Hung.); Sym. in D min., *Faust* ovt. (after Goethe), 4 Ballads for orch., &c.

Mihalovici, Marcel (b. Bucharest, 22. X. 1898), Rum. comp. Studied with d'Indy in Paris and joined a group of advanced Fr. and Rus. comps. there after the Eur. war of 1914–8.

Works incl. opera *L'Intransigeant Pluton*; ballets *Karagueuz, Divertissement* & others; *Cortège des divinités infernales* (from the opera), *Introduction au mouvement, Notturno* & Fantasy for orch.; stg. Trio; v. & pf. So., Sonatina for ob. & pf., &c.

Mikado, The, or The Town of Titipu, operetta by Sullivan (lib. by W. S. Gilbert), prod. London, Savoy Theatre, 14. III. 1885.

Mikrokosmos (*Microcosm*), a set of 153 small pf. pieces by Bartók, arr. in progressive order and pub. in 6 vols., setting the player var. problems of modern technique, each piece being written on a particular principle or system (special rhythms, time-signatures, chords, intervals, atonal or bitonal combs., &c.), comp. 1926–37, pub. 1940.

Milán, Luis (b. ? Valencia, *c.* 1500; d. Valencia, after 1561), Spa. lutenist & comp. He was the son of a nobleman, Don Luis de M., played the vihuela, (?) visited It. and Port.

Works incl. fantasies and pavans for lute, Spa. and Port. villancicos, Spa. ballads & It. sonnets for voice & lute, &c.

Milanollo, Domenica Maria Teresa (b. Savigliano nr. Turin, 28. VIII. 1827; d. Paris, 25. X. 1904), It. vst. Her father, a poor carpenter, succeeded in having her taught at Turin and in taking her to Paris in 1837, where she had a great success, as later in Hol., Eng., &c. Later still she appeared with her sister, after whose early death she retired for a time, and again for good after her marriage to the military engineer Charles Parmentier. She also prod. some comps., mainly for v.

Milanollo, Maria (b. Savigliano nr. Turin, 19. VII. 1832; d. Paris, 21. X. 1848), It. vst., sister of prec. She was taught by her sister and appeared with her on tour until her early death.

Milder-Hauptmann, (Pauline) Anna (b. Constantinople, 13. XII. 1785; d. Berlin, 29. V. 1838), Aus. sop. singer. The daughter of a courier in the Aus. diplomatic service, she was brought to Vienna as a child and on the recommendation of Schikaneder studied singing under Tomaselli and Salieri, making her 1st stage appearance in 1803. Beethoven wrote the part of Leonore in *Fidelio* for her and she early became interested in Schubert's songs. In 1810 she married the jeweller Hauptmann.

Milford, Robin (Humphrey) (b. Oxford, 22. I. 1903), Eng. comp. Educ. at Rugby and studied m. at the R.C.M. in London, where his masters were Holst, Vaughan Williams and R. O. Morris.

Works incl. orat. *A Prophet in the Land*; cantata *Wind, Rain and Sunshine, Bemerton Cantatas, 5 Songs of Escape* for unaccomp. chor.; Sym., Concerto grosso, Double Fugue for orch.; v. Conc., *The Dark Thrush* (on Hardy's poem) for v. & small orch.; pf. works; songs; partsongs, &c.

Milhaud, Darius (b. Aix-en-Provence, 4. IX. 1892), Fr. comp. Studied v. and comp. at the Paris Cons. from 1910, under Gédalge, Widor and d'Indy. In 1917–9 he was attaché to the Fr. Legation at Rio de Janeiro, where he met Paul Claudel, who collab. freqently with him as libst. About 1920 he became a member of 'Les Six,' and in 1922 he was repres. for the 1st time at the festival of the I.S.C.M. He emigrated to U.S.A. in 1940.

Works incl. operas *La Brebis égarée, Les Malheurs d'Orphée, Esther de Carpentras, Le Pauvre Matelot, Christophe Colomb, Maximilien, Bolivar*, minute - operas *L'Enlèvement d'Europe, L'Abandon d'Ariane, La Délivrance de Thésée*; ballets *L'Homme et son désir, Le Bœuf sur le toit* (*The Nothing-doing Bar*), *Les Mariés de la Tour d'Eiffel* (with others), *La Création du monde, Salade, Le Train bleu, La Bien-aimée* (after Schubert & Liszt), *Jeux de printemps*; incid. m. for works by Claudel: *Protée, L'Annonce faite à Marie* and *Oreste* trans. from Aeschylus (*Agamemnon, Les Choëphores* & *Les Euménides*) & for Rolland's *14 Juillet* (with 6 others); orch. works incl. 2 symph. suites, *Suite provençale, Sérénade, Saudades do Brazil*; 5 syms. for small orch.; 5 Études, *Ballade, Le Carnaval d'Aix* & Conc. for pf. & orch.; Conc. & *Concertino de printemps* for v. & orch., va., co. & cl. concs. & Conc. for percussion & small orch.; 9 stg. 4tets; 2 v. & pf. sos.; So. for 2 vs. & pf.; So. for pf., fl., ob. & clar.; sonatinas for fl. & pf. and clar. & pf.; some smaller inst. pieces; Sonatina for org.; 6 pf. works incl. Suite, So., *Printemps* (2 vols.), *Saudades do Brazil* (2 vols)., *3 Rag Caprices*; suite *Scaramouche* for 2 pfs.; 14 books of songs incl. *Poèmes de Léo Latil, Poèmes de Paul Claudel, Poèmes juifs, Poèmes de Cocteau, Les Soirées de Pétrograde*; *Machines agricoles* for voice & 7 insts., *Catalogue des fleurs* for voice & chamber orch.; 2 Psalms for bar. & orch.; Psalm cxxi for male voices; cantata *Cain and Abel*; 4 *Poèmes* for voice & v., &c.

Military Band. A wind band attached to military regiments and used by them for their ceremonial occasions, but also often allowed to play for the entertainment of the general public in parks, at the sea-side, &c. The M.B. is often confused with the Brass Band, from which it differs by incl. in its constitution woodwind as well as brass and perc. insts.

Military Symphony. Haydn's Sym. in G maj., No. 100 (No. 12 of the 'Salomon' syms.), comp. for London in 1794. The military m. in it is that of the barracks and parade-ground rather than that of warfare.

Millay, Edna St. Vincent (b. 1892). Amer. poetess. *See* **Bliss** (*5 Amer. Songs*), **King's Henchman** (Deems Taylor), **Wagenaar** (B.) (songs).

Millico, Giuseppe (b. Terlizzi, Modena. 1739; d. Naples, 1802), It. male sop. and comp. Had an immense success in It. and went to Eng. in 1772 and to the court opera in Vienna, returning to Eng. again and later retiring to It.

Works incl. operas *L'isola disabitata, Ipermestra* (Calzabigi's lib. written for Gluck and the orig. of Salieri's *Danaïdes*), *L'avventura benefica, La Zelinda, La pietà d'amore*; cantatas, &c.

Millöcker, Karl (b. Vienna, 29. V. 1842; d. Baden nr. Vienna, 31. XII. 1899), Aus. cond. & comp. Studied at the Vienna Cons. and became cond. at Graz in 1864 and at the Harmonie-Theater in Vienna, 1866. In 1869 he was app. cond. at the Theater an der Wien there and prod. operettas for it.

Works incl. operettas *Der tote Gast, Die beiden Binder, Diana, Die Frauen-insel, Ein Abenteuer in Wien, Das verwunschene Schloss, Gräfin Dubarry, Apajune der Wassermann, Der Bettelstudent, Der Feldprediger, Der Vice-Admiral, Die sieben Schwaben, Der arme Jonathan, Das Sonntagskind, Gasparone* and many others; numerous pf. pieces, &c.

Mills, Charles (b. Ashville, N.C., 8. I. 1914), Amer. comp. Studied with a 6 years' scholarship under Copland, Sessions and Roy Harris, 2 years with each, and later devoted himself entirely to comp.

Works incl. m. for solo dance *John Brown*; 3 syms., slow mvt. for stg. orch.; Concertino for fl. & orch., Prelude for fl. & stgs.; Festival Ovt. for chor. & orch.; *Ars poetica* for unaccomp. chor.; chamber sym. for 11 insts., chamber conc. for 10 insts., chamber concertino for woodwind 5tet, 3 stg. 4tets, pf. Trio in D min.; *Sacred Suite* for 2 vs. & pf., 2 v. & pf. sos., 2 co. & pf. sos., 2 sos. for solo v., fl. & pf. So., Dance-So. & So. for solo fl., ob. & pf. So., *Chant and Hymn* for solo ob.; 2 sos., 2 suites, 10 sonatinas for pf.; 4 Sacred Canticles for voice & pf., &c.

Milojević, Miloje (b. Belgrade, 15. X. 1884), Serb. comp. Studied at Belgrade and Munich. Lecturer in mus. aesthetics at Belgrade Univ.

Works incl. symph. poem *Death of the Mother of Jugovich* & *Antique Legend* for solo voices, chor. & orch.; *Serbian Dance* for v. & pf., *Legend* for co. & pf.; pf. pieces; songs, folk-song settings, partsongs, &c.

Milton, opera by Spontini (lib. by Victor Joseph Étienne de Jouy & Michel Dieulafoy). prod. Paris, Opéra-Comique, 27. XI. 1804. A 2nd Milton opera was planned by S. in 1838, when he visited Eng. in the summer to study the environment. It was to be entitled *Miltons Tod und Busse* *für den Königsmord* (*M.'s Death and Expiation for the King's Murder*) (lib. by Ernst Raupach), but turned into *Das verlorene Paradies* (*Paradise Lost*); but it remained unfinished.

Milton, John (b. Stanton St. John nr. Oxford, *c.* 1563; d. London, III., 1647), Eng. comp., father of John M., the poet. Educ. (?) at Christ Church Coll., Oxford. He received a gold medal from a Pol. prince for an In Nomine in 40 parts, was cast out by his father as a Protestant, went to London and in 1600 became a member of the Scriveners' Co., marrying Sarah Jeffrey about that time. Having made a fair fortune as a scribe, he retired to Horton (Bucks.) in 1632, but after his wife's death moved to Reading, *c.* 1640 and back to London in 1643, where he lived with his son John.

Works incl. In Nomine in 40 parts; var. sacred pieces for several voices; madrigal contrib. to *The Triumphes of Oriana*, 4 voc. pieces contrib. to Leighton *Teares or Lamentacions*; 2 tunes for Ravenscroft's Psalter; 5 fancies for viols, &c.

Milton, John (1608–74), Eng. poet, son of prec. *See* **Allegro, il Pensieroso . . . L'** (Handel), **Bossi (E.)** (*Paradiso perduto*), **Comus** (H. Lawes & T. A. Arne), **Creation** (Haydn, *Paradise Lost*), **Darke** (*Ring out, ye crystal spheres*), **Davies (Walford)** (*Ode on Time*), **Festing** (*Song on May Morning*), **Finzi** (sonnets), **Galliard** (*P. Lost*), **Gatty** (*Ode on Time*), **Georges** (*Paradis perdu*), **Harris (C.)** (*Paradise L.*, *Il Pensieroso & L'Allegro*), **Harwood** (*Ode on a May Morning*), **Horsley (C. E.)** (*Comus*), **Jackson (W. i)** (*Lycidas*), **Lutyens** (Salutes), **Mackenzie** (*Temptation*), **Markevitch** (*Paradise L.*), **Nabokov** (*Samson Agonistes*), **Occasional Oratorio** (Handel), **Paine** (*Nativity*), **Parry (H.)** (*Blest Pair of Sirens & L'Allegro ed il Pensieroso*), **Reichardt** (*Morning Hymn*), **Ritter (P.)** (*Verlorene Paradies*), **Rootham** (*Ode on Christ's Nativity*), **Rubinstein (A)**. (*Paradise L.*), **Samson**) Handel), **Schneider (F.)** (*Verlorene Paradies*), **Scott (C.)** (*Nativity Hymn*), **Smith (J. C.** (*Paradise (L.)*, **Wood (C.)** (*Ode on Time*).

Mimodrama. One of the names for a play without words accomp. by inst. m., often called on the continent of Eur. by the equivalents of 'pantomime' or 'melodrama,' which however have other connotations in Eng.

Min. (abbr.) = Minor.

Minacciando (It.) = menacing, threatening.

Mingotti (*née* **Valentini**), **Regina** (b. Naples, 16. II. 1722; d. Neuburg o/Danube, 1. X. 1808), Aus.-It. sop. singer, who became an orphan as a child, was sent to a convent by an uncle at Graz, but had to leave on his death and married the It. musn. Pietro M. attached to the Dresden Opera, who had her taught singing by Porpora. She made her 1st stage appearance at Dresden in 1747. She appeared in It., Spa., Eng. and Fr.

Miniature Scores. Full scores of orch. and chamber m., operas, orats., &c., pub. in pocket size of usually *c.* $5\frac{1}{4} \times 7\frac{1}{2}$ in. Most of the current non-copyright works have by this time been issued in this convenient form in series of which several pubs. have made a speciality; many pubs. also prod. their own more important copyright works in M. S. form. M. Ss. are extremely useful for ref. and study, they can easily be taken to perfs., and libraries of them can be accumulated compar. rapidly owing to their usually reasonable and in the case of non-copyright works very cheap prices. The practice of following M. Ss. at concerts is not to be recommended in all circumstances, but it helps listeners who have acquired sufficient skill in it to form more complete 1st impressions of works new to them and up to a point makes excellent practice in score-reading.

Minim. In modern notation the white note with a tail to it, with the value of half a semibreve or 2 crotchets.

Minima (Lat.). The minim rest.

Minnesinger or **Minnesänger** (Ger. plur.). The guilds of singers in 12th- and 13th-cent. Ger. who cultivated minstrelsy on the lines of that of the Troubadours in Fr., and preceded the Meistersinger, but unlike them were aristocrats, not middle-class merchants and artisans.

Minor. 1 of the 2 predominant scales (the other being Maj.) of the tonal system superseding that of the Modes. The M. scale was identical with the late 16th-cent. Aeolian mode (A—A on the white keys of the pf.), except for certain semitonal alterations requiring that there should be a maj.-7th leading-note, which is not present in any of the old modes except the Lydian (the Ionian being regarded as the maj. scale, not as a genuine mode). There are 2 forms of the M. scale: the harmonic and the melodic. In the former the only change from the mode is the sharpened 7th, or Leading-note; in the latter the 6th as well as the 7th is sharpened in the ascending scale, but the 7th as well as the 6th is flattened when the scale descends.

Minor Intervals. Those Intervals in the mus. scale which by being widened by a semitone become Maj., not

Augmented intervals: i.e. 2nds, 3rds, 6ths and 7ths; also 2nds, 3rds, &c. carried beyond the 8ve, i.e. 9ths, 10ths, &c.

Minore (It.) = Minor. In older m. the word is often used as a kind of signal showing the beginning of a section in min. occurring during the course of a comp. in a maj. key, espec. in vars., to prevent the perf. from overlooking the change of key.

Minstrel. Orig. the Eng. equivalent of the Fr. *Troubadour* and the Ger. *Minnesinger*, but in a wider sense any travelling singer, usually one who accomp. himself on some inst.

Minuet. A dance of Fr. orig. (*menuet*, der. from *menu*—small) 1st appearing in artistic m. about the time of Lully. It is in moderately animated 3–4 time and in its later developments always has a contrasting trio section, after which the 1st section is repeated. It was not a regular feature of the suite, but appeared in many of its examples; on the other hand it was the only dance form retained by the So. form, where it remained as 1 of 2 middle mvts. in 4-mvt. sos., syms., 4tets, &c. until it was displaced by the scherzo, round about 1800. But scherzos could appear much earlier (e.g. Haydn's 4tets Op. 33 of 1781) and Ms. were sometimes restored by later comps.

Minuetto (It.). This, not 'Menuetto,' is the correct It. name for the Minuet.

'Minute Waltz.' The nickname sometimes given to Chopin's Waltz in D♭ maj., Op. 64 No. 1, though unless taken much too fast it takes more than a minute to play.

Miolan-Carvalho, Marie. *See* **Carvalho.**

Miracle, The. The nickname of a Sym. by Haydn, No. 96, in D maj. (No. 6 of the 'Salomon' syms.), written for London in 1791.

Mireille, opera by Gounod (lib. by Michel Carré, based on the poem *Mirèio* by Frédéric Mistral), prod. Paris, Théâtre Lyrique, 19. III. 1864.

Mirliton (Fr.). A toy inst. consisting of a simple pipe covered at one end with parchment or tissue-paper, into which the player sings, thus prod. a reedy tone not unlike that of a primitive ob. It is similar to the Eunuch fl. and was also known as Kazoo in Eng.

Mirror Canon / **Mirror Fugue** } A Canon or Fugue in which 2 or more voices are so inverted that the intervals appear simultaneously upside down as well as right side up, looking on paper like a reflection in water.

Misón, Luis (b. ? Barcelona, ?; d. Madrid, 13. II. 1766), Spa. woodwind player & comp. He entered the royal orch. at Madrid in 1748 as flst. and obst., became cond. there in 1756 and prod. his 1st *tonadilla* on the stage in 1757.

Works incl. numerous *tonadillas*, 3 operas *La festa cinese*, *El tutor enamorado* & *El amor a todos vence*; 6 sos. for fl. & bass, &c.

Missa (It. & Lat.) = Mass.

Missa, Edmond (Jean Louis) (b. Reims, 12. VI. 1861; d. Paris, 29. I. 1910), Fr. comp. Pupil of Massenet at the Paris Cons., where he took the Prix de Rome in 1881.

Works incl. operas *Juge et partie*, *Lydia*, *Le Chevalier timide*, *La Princesse Nangara*, *Mariage galant*, *Dinah* (after Shakespeare's *Cymbeline*), *Ninon de Lenclos*, *L'Hôte*, *Babette*, *Muguette*, *Maguelone*; operetta *La Belle Sophie* & others; pantomimes; orch. works; chors.; pf. pieces; songs, &c.

Missa parodia (Lat. = parody Mass). A type of 16th-cent. mass the material of which was based on a motet previously written by the same or another comp. There was no 'parody' in the modern derogatory sense. The practice began with a similar treatment of chansons in the 15th cent. Only a single melody might be borrowed from the model or all its parts could be used and imitated in the mass.

Missa pro defunctis (Lat. = Mass for the dead). *See* **Requiem.**

Missa solemnis (or solennis) (Lat.) = Solemn Mass. A title sometimes used by comps. for a mass of a particularly festive or elaborate kind, e.g. Beethoven's Op. 123. Schubert also used it, and it occurs in Fr. as *Messe solennelle* (e.g. Gounod). The title is now used partic. for Beethoven's work, comp. in 1818–23 and 1st perf. in part, Vienna, 7. V. 1824.

Misticanza (old It. = mixture). *See* **Quodlibet.**

Mistral, Frédéric (1830–1914), Fr. (Provençal) poet. *See* **Mireille** (Gounod), Widor (*Nerto*).

Mitford, Mary Russell (1787–1855), Eng. novelist & dramatist. *See* **Rienzi** (Wagner).

Mitjana y Gordon, Rafael (b. Málaga, 6. XII. 1869; d. Stockholm, 15. VIII. 1921), Spa. diplomat, mcolst. & comp. Studied with Pedrell and Saint-Saëns. While on diplom. service in var. countries, esp. in Swe., he was able to find Spa. material scattered in foreign libraries to help his researches, and he wrote on 16th-cent. Spa. m., on Morales, Victoria, Infantas, Guerrero, &c. and contrib. the vol. on Spa. m. to the *Encyclopédie du Conservatoire* pub. in Paris. His comps. incl. operas, e.g. *La buena guarda.*

Mitridate Eupatore, Il (*Mithradates Eupator*), opera by A. Scarlatti (lib. by Girolamo Frigimelica Roberti), prod. Venice, Teatro San Giovanni Crisostomo, Carnival 1707.

Mitridate, Rè di Ponto (*Mithradates, King of Pontus*), opera by Mozart (lib. by Vittorio Amadeo Cigna-Santi), based on a tragedy by Racine, prod. Milan, Teatro Regio Ducal, 26. XII. 1770. M.'s 1st opera for an It. stage.

Mixolydian Mode. One of the old ecclesiastical modes with semitones between the 3rd & 4th and 6th & 7th notes of the ascending scale, repres. by the scale beginning on G on the white notes of the pf. keyboard.

Mixture Stops. Org. stops controlling a range of pipes with more than 1 note to each key, sounding not only the fundamental note but some of its harmonics.

Mizler (von Kolof), Lorenz Christoph (b. Heidenheim, Württemberg, 25. VII. 1711; d. Warsaw, III. 1778), Ger. mus. writer and ed. One of Bach's pupil's at St. Thomas's school, Leipzig; founded the Assoc. for Mus. Science there in 1738 and ed. a periodical, *Neu eröffnete musikalische Bibliothek*, 1736–54.

Mlada, opera-ballet commissioned from Borodin, Cui, Mussorgsky & Rimsky-Korsakov by the Rus. Imp. Theatres in 1872, but never completed (lib. by Stepan Alexandrovitch Gedeonov); the 1st 3 comps. afterwards used their m. in other works.

Opera by Rimsky-Korsakov (lib. as above), prod. St. Petersburg, 1. XI. 1892. R.-K. rewrote the whole work in 1889.

Mlynarski, Emil (b. Kibarty, 18. VII. 1870; d. Warsaw, 5. IV. 1935), Pol. vst., cond. & comp. Studied at St. Petersburg. Cond. of the Warsaw Phil. Orch. from 1901 and dir. of the Cons. there from 1904. Cond. of the Sco. Orch., 1911–6.

Works incl. opera *A Summer Night*; *Polonia* Sym.; v. Conc. in D min., &c.

Mocke, Marie Félicité Denise. *See* **Moke.**

Modal. Of the Modes.

Modal Notation. A kind of notation in use for voc. m. up to the 13th cent., where, as in plainsong, the notes had no definite time-values, the rhythm being determined by the metre of the words alone.

Moderato (It. = moderate). A direction either used singly, in which case it indicates a tempo neither very fast nor very slow, or in comb. with another word, when it modifies the prescribed pace to a slower time in the case of fast tempos and a quicker time in the case of slow ones.

Moderne, Jacques (b. ? Pinguento, Istria, ?; d. Lyons, ?), Fr. 16th-cent. musn. and pub., (?) of It. stock. He became chapel master at the church of Notre-Dame du Confort at Lyons and about 1530 estab. a printing-press there, pub. books of masses, motets and chansons between 1532–67, with contribs. by var. comps., incl. himself.

Modes. The scales in use for m. before the estab. of the modern maj. and min. scales towards the end of the 16th cent., both in ancient Gr. and in the Middle Ages. They are named after the old Gr. provinces, but unfortunately the names were exchanged later. After var. complicated changes the system, which is best understood by ref. to the pf. keyboard, settled down as follows:

Gr. Ms.: starting from
A = Mixolydian
G = Lydian
F = Phrygian
E = Dorian
D = Hypolydian
C = Hypophrygian
B = Hypodorian

Medieval Ms.: starting from
D = Dorian
D = Hypomixolydian (final on G)
E = Phrygian
E = Hypoæolian (final on A)
F = Lydian
F = Hyperphrygian or Hypolocrian } (final on B) (rejected)
G = Mixolydian
G = Hypoionian (final on C)
A = Æolian (16th cent.)
A = Hypodorian (final on D)
B = Hyperæolian or Locrian } (rejected)
B = Hypophrygian (final on E)
C = Ionian (16th cent.)
C = Hypolydian (final on F)

The Ms. with the Gr. prefix 'Hypo' (below) have their finals or tonics on other notes than those on which the scales begin and end; but the suffixes correspond in each case with the names of those Ms. which have their tonics on the starting-note. These latter are called the Authentic Modes; those with the 'Hypo' prefix are Plagal Modes.

In modern m. where the use of a M. is desired by the comp., it need not be retained throughout a piece or mvt.; it may also be transposed: e.g. the scale of C with a B♭ will be Mixolydian, with an F♯ Lydian, and so on.

Modes, Rhythmic. The rhythms, all in triple time, of m. between *c.* 1150 and 1350 were classified into 6 different R. Ms. corresponding to the feet in poetry.

Modulation. The art of changing from one key to another in the course of a comp. in such a way that the transition makes grammatical sense and also adds to the formal and logical progress of the m.

Moeran, E(rnest). J(ohn). (b. London, 31. XII. 1894), Eng. comp. of Ir. descent. He lived in Norfolk in his childhood, his father, a clergyman, holding a living there. Educ. at Uppigham School and later studied m. at the R.C.M. in London. After serving in the 1914–8 war, he continued his studies with Ireland. In 1923 he came before the public with a concert of his works given in London, but after some years spent there he retired to a country residence in Herefordshire.

Works incl. Magnificat and Nunc dimittis, Te Deum and Jubilate, 2 anthems; *Nocturne* for bar., chor. & orch., *Songs of Springtime* & suite *Phyllida and Corydon* for unaccomp. chor., *Blue-eyed Spring* for bar. and chor., madrigals, partsongs & folksong arrs.; Sym. in G min., Sinfonietta, 2 Rhapsodies, symph. impression *In the Mountain Country*, suite *Farrago* for orch., 2 pieces for small orch. *Whythorne's Shadow* & *Lonely Waters*; concs. for pf., v. & co.; stg. 4tet in A min., stg. Trio in G maj., pf. Trio in D maj., So. for 2 vs., v. & pf. So. in E min.; Prelude for co. & pf., pf. Vars. & pieces *On a May Morning*, *Stalham River*, *Windmills*, *Bank Holiday*, *Summer Valley*, &c.; songs incl. cycles *Ludlow Town* (A. E. Housman), *7 Poems by James Joyce*; Norfolk, Suffolk & other folksong arrs., &c.

Moeschinger, Albert (b. Basle, 10. I. 1897), Swi. comp. Studied at Berne, Leipzig & Munich, in the latter place under Courvoisier. In 1927 he settled at Berne as prof.

Works incl. motet *Gottes Pfad*, cantata *Angelus Silesius*, *Das Posthorn* for male chor. & orch., partsongs & other chor. works; Suite for orch., Vars. on a theme by Purcell for stgs. & perc., Divertimento for stgs., *Fantasia 1944* for chamber orch.; 3 pf. concs., v. Conc.; 6 stg. 4tets, pf. 5tet, wind 5tet on Swi. folksongs, 2 pf. trios; So., *Esquisses valaisannes*, Vars. & Humoresques for v. & pf., co. & pf. So., Sonatine for cl. & pf.; 2 Sonatinas, Toccata, Rondo & other works for pf.; *Vision und Verinnerlichung* for 2 pfs.; Vars. & Fugue on a theme by Purcell, Introd. and Double Fugue, *Fuga mystica* & Studies in Canon for org.; songs, &c.

Moffat, Alfred (b. Edinburgh, 4. XII. 1866), Sco. comp. & ed. Studied in Berlin and worked there for a time. settled in London in the 1890s and ed. a large collection of old stg. m., incl. many Eng. and Fr. works, also several vols. of Sco., Welsh and Ir. folksongs.

Moissonneurs, Les (*The Reapers*), opera by Duni (lib. by Charles Simon Favart, based on an incident in Thomson's *Seasons*), prod. Paris, Comédie-Italienne, 27. I. 1768.

Mojsisovics, Roderich von (b. Graz, 10. V. 1877), Aus. comp. of Hung. descent. Studied at Graz, Cologne and Munich (with Thuille there), but took a degree in law and became a civil servant. Reger, however, persuaded him to devote himself to m. He cond. a male chor. at Brno in 1903–5, returned to Styria, became head of the Styrian Mus. Soc. at Graz in 1912 and settled at Munich in 1935.

Works incl. operas *Tantchen Rosmarin*, *Messer Ricciardo Minutolo*, *Der Zauberer*, *Die Locke*, *Anno domini*, *Die roten Dominos*, *Norden in Not*, *Much Ado about Nothing* (after Shakespeare); incid. m. for Sophocles' *Oedipus Rex* & other plays; ballets *Phantastisches Tanzspiel*, *Chorisches Tanzspiel*; incid. m. to plays; Mass for the Dead, cantata *Eine Weihnachtskantilene*; 5 syms., 2 ovts., 2 serenades; 2 pf. concs., v. Conc.; 3 stg. 4tets, stg. Trio; 2 v. & pf. sos., va. So.; 2 org. sos., *Festmusik* for org. & brass; *Waldphantasie* for 2 pfs.; org. & pf. pieces, &c.

Moke (or **Mocke** or **Mooke**), **Marie Félicité Denise** (b. Paris, 4. VII. 1811; d. Saint Josseten Noode nr. Brussels, 30. III. 1875), Fr. pfst. Studied under Herz, Moscheles and Kalkbrenner, and toured very successfully. Berlioz fell in love with her before he went to Rome in 1830 and she became engaged to him, but married Camille Pleyel, as whose wife she made an international reputation. Pf. prof. at the Brussels Cons. for 24 years until 1872.

Mokrussov, Boris (b. Nizhny-Novgorod, 27. II. 1909), Rus. comp. Pupil of Miaskovsky at the Moscow Cons.

Works incl. opera *Tchapaiev*; incid. m. for plays; *Song of Stalin* for chor. & orch.; *Anti-Fascist Sym.* & tone poem for orch; Suite for brass band; tromb. Conc.; stg. 4tet; *Pioneer Suite* for pf., &c.

Molière (Jean - Baptiste Poquelin) (1622–73), Fr. dramatist. *See* **Ariadne auf Naxos** (*Bourgeois gentilhomme*, R. Strauss), **Auric** (*Les Fâcheux*), **Austin (R.)** (*Malade imaginaire*), **Bourgeois gentilhomme** (R. Strauss), **Charpentier (M.-A.)** (*Comtesse d'Escarbagnas* & *Malade i.*), **David (K. H.)** (*Sicilien*), **Festes de l'Amour** (Lully), **Grétry** (*Amphitryon*), **Grosz** (*Sganarell*), **Haug** (*Tartuffe*), **Joncières** (*Sicilien*), **Lattuada** (*Preziose* *ridicole*), **Listov** (*Bourgeois g.*), **Lully** (*Mariage forcé, Amour médecin, Princesse d'Élide, Sicilien, George Dandin, M. de Pourceaugnac, Amants magnifiques* & *Bourgeois g.*), **Mathieu** (*George Dandin*), **Médecin malgré lui** (Gounod), **Mengozzi** (*Pourceaugnac*), **Mortari** (*Scuola delle mogli*), **Ollone** (*George Dandin*), **Poise** (*Amour médecin*), **Purcell** (*Female Virtuosos*), **Quinault (J. B.)** (*Bourgeois g.* & *Princess d'Élide*), **Roger-Ducasse** (*Madrigal*), **Sauguet** (*Sicilien*), **Sauzay** (*George Dandin* & *Sicilien*), **Schulhoff (E.)** (*Bourgeois g.*), **Schweitzer** (do.), **Shaporin** (*Tartuffe*), **Signor di Pourceaugnac** (Franchetti), **Sor** (*Sicilien*), **Szymanowski** (*Bourgeois g.*), **Wagner-Régeny** (*Sganarelle*), **Wolf-Ferrari** (*Amor medico*), **Wolfurt** (*Tanz um den Narren*), **Zich** (*Précieuses ridicules*).

Molinaro, Simone (b. Genoa, ?; d. ? Genoa, ?), It. 16th–17th-cent. lutenist, ed. & comp. Pupil of Gostena, his uncle, whom he succeeded as chapel master of Genoa cath. in 1599. In 1613 he ed. the madrigals of Gesualdo.

Works incl. masses, motets, magnificats, sacred concertos; madrigals, canzonets; lute pieces, &c.

Molique, (Wilhelm) Bernhard (b. Nuremberg, 7. X. 1802; d. Cannstadt nr. Stuttgart, 10. V. 1869), Ger. vst. & comp. Pupil of Spohr and of Rovelli at Munich, succeeding him in 1820 as leader of the orch.; after some time in the orch. of the Theater an der Wien in Vienna, he toured widely, became leader in the royal orch. at Stuttgart in 1826, settled in London in 1849 and returned to Ger. in 1866.

Works incl. 2 masses; orat. *Abraham*; Sym.; 6 v. concs.; 8 stg. 4tets, 2 pf. trios, duets for vs. and fl. & v.; v. studies and pieces, &c.

Moll (Ger., from Lat. *mollis* = soft). The Ger. word for Minor.

Molteni, Benedetta Emilia (b. Modena, 1722; d. c. 1780), It. sop. singer. App. to the court of Frederick II of Prus. in Berlin, 1742–74, where she married J. F. Agricola in 1751.

Molto (It.) = Much, very.

Moments musicals. The title, which in correct Fr. should be *Moments musicaux*, of Schubert's 6 pf. pieces Op. 94, written prob. in 1828.

Mompou, Federico (b. Barcelona, 16. IV. 1893), Spa. pfst. & comp. Studied at the Barcelona Cons. and later in Paris, where I. Philipp was his pf. master and Samuel Rousseau taught him comp. He lived at Barcelona again in 1914–21, but then settled in Paris.

Works incl. pf. pieces *6 Impresiones intimas, Scènes d'enfants, Suburbis, 3 Pessebres, Canço i dansa, Cants magics, Fêtes lointaines, 6 Charmes, Dialogues, 3 Variations, 4 Préludes*; songs *L'hora grisa, Cançoneta incerta, 4 Mélodies, Le Nuage, 3 Comptines*, &c.

Monckton, Lionel (b. London, 18. XII. 1861; d. London, 15. II. 1924), Eng. comp. Educ. at Charterhouse School and Oxford. He began his mus. career by writing some numbers for mus. comedies prod. by George Edwardes, and even after prod. his 1st complete piece of the kind he continued to write songs for others.

Works incl. mus. comedies *The Quaker Girl, The Dancing-Mistress, The Cingalee, The Country Girl*, &c.

'Monday Pops' (Monday Popular Concerts). Chamber concerts held at St. James's Hall, London, until its demolition in 1905. Artists of internat. fame appeared and the series was widely celebrated. It is alluded to as a familiar topic by W. S. Gilbert in Sullivan's *Mikado*.

Mondo alla roversa, Il, o sia Le donne che comandano (*The World Upside Down, or Women in Command*), opera by Galuppi (lib. by Goldoni), prod. Venice, Teatro San Cassiano, 14. XI. 1750.

Mondo della luna, Il (*The World of the Moon*), opera by Galuppi (lib. by Goldoni), prod. Venice, Teatro San Moisè, 29. I. 1750.

Opera by Haydn (lib. do.), prod. Esterház, 3. VIII. 1777.

Mondonville, Jean (Joseph Cassanea) de (b. Narbonne, 25. XII. 1711; d. Belleville nr. Paris, 8. X. 1772), Fr. vst. & comp. His parents were aristocrats in reduced circumstances, but he succeeded in studying the v. He settled in Paris in 1733, made his name as a perf. and comp. and appeared at the Concert spirituel in 1737, for which he wrote motets until 1770. In 1744 he became superintendent of the royal chapel and in 1755–62 he was dir. of the Concert spirituel. During the *guerre des bouffons* in 1752 he was chosen as the represent. of the Fr. nat. school opposing the Its. under the patronage of Mme. de Pompadour.

Works incl. operas and opera-ballets *Isbé, Le Carnaval du Parnasse, Titon et l'Aurore, Daphnis et Alcimaduro* (in Provençal), *Les Fêtes de Paphos, Thésée, Psyché, Érigone, Vénus et Adonis, Les Projets de l'Amour*; mus. dialogue *Les Titans*; orats. *Les Israélites au Mont Oreb, Les Fureurs de Saül, Les Titans*; the *Privilège du Roi* set as a cantata; trio sos. for 2 vs. or fls. & bass; sos. incl. *Les Sons harmoniques* for v. & bass; sos. and pieces for hpchd. with v. or voice;

hpchd. works incl. *Pièces de clavecin en sonates*; org. pieces, &c.

Monferrina (It.). A Piedmontese country dance introd. into Eng. early in the 19th cent.

Monfreda
Monfrina }. Corrupt versions of the name of the above word in Eng.

Mong Kao-Yen (689–740), Chin. poet. *See* **Lied von der Erde** (Mahler).

Moniuszko, Stanislaw (b. Ubiel, Lithuania, 5. V. 1819; d. Warsaw, 4. VI. 1872), Pol. comp. After studying at home, he went to Berlin as a pupil of Rungenhagen, 1837–9, and on his return settled down at Wilno as m. teacher and orgst., prod. the opera *Halka* there in 1854. In 1858 he became cond. at the Opera in Warsaw and later prof. at the Cons.

Works incl. opera *Halka*, *Flis*, *Hrabina* (*The Countess*), *Verbum nobile*, *Straszny Dwór* (*The Haunted Mansion*), *Paria*, *Beata*; incid. m. for Shakespeare's *Hamlet* & *Merry Wives of Windsor* and other plays; cantatas *Spectres*, *Crimean Sonnets*, &c.; 5 masses, litanies and other church m.; ovt. *Bajka* (*Fairy Tale*); 270 songs, incl. ballads by Adam Mickiewicz, &c.

Monn, Georg (Matthias) (b. ?, 1717; d. Vienna, 3. X. 1750), Aus. orgst. & comp. He became orgst. of the Karl church in Vienna.

Works incl. syms.; stg. 4tets, trio sos., &c.

Monna Vanna, opera by Février (lib. Maeterlinck's play with alterations), prod. Paris, Opéra, 13. I. 1909.

Monnikendam, Marius (b. Haarlem, 28. V. 1896), Dutch critic & comp. Studied at the Amsterdam Cons., at Dresden and the Schola Cantorum in Paris. He became a m. critic in Amsterdam.

Works incl. Mass, Te Deum, psalms for chor. & org.; symph. mvt. *Arbeid* (*Labour*); chamber m.; pf. & org. works, &c.

Monochord. A primitive inst., not for playing, but for measuring the vibration of stgs. It has a single stg. (hence its name) stretched over a long, narrow box. It is at least as old as the 6th cent. B.C., when it was used by Pythagoras, and it was mentioned by Euclid *c.* 300 B.C., but it still occupied scientists in the Middle Ages. It was found that if the stg. was stopped exactly in the centre, it gave out the higher 8ve on each side, and other intervals were found to sound at proportional points.

Monocorde (Fr.)
Monocordo (It.) } =Single String). A direction used in v. m. where the comp. wishes a passage to be played on 1 stg.

Monodrama. A mus. stage work for a single singer, an opera with a cast of 1, as for ex. Meyerbeer's *Tevelindens Liebe*, Gomis's *Sensibilidad y prudencia* or Schoenberg's *Erwartung*. *See also* **Lélio** (Berlioz).

Monody (from Gr. for 'single song'). A term used to describe m. making its effect with a single melodic part, accomp. or not, instead of a collab. of var. parts as in Polyphony.

Monophonic. M. in a single melodic part, without harmony, as distinct from Homophonic, which is melodic m. accomp. by harmony, or Polyphonic, which is m. in a number of melodic parts moving simultaneously.

Monopoli. *See* **Insanguine.**

Monothematic. An adj. used for a work based throughout, esp. in the course of more than one mvt., on a single dominating theme, not as prominent as a motto theme but more persistent. All chaconnes and passacaglias are single M. mvts.; exs. of M. m. in more than one mvt. are the old pavans and galliards based on the same melody and, in modern times, such a work as Mahler's *Song of the Earth*, where a figure of 3 notes is used in each mvt. All m. based on the 12-note system is necessarily M.

Monpou, (François Louis) Hippolyte (b. Paris, 12. I. 1804; d. Orleans, 10. VIII. 1841), Fr. comp. He became a choir-boy at the church of Saint-Germain-l'Auxerrois in Paris at the age of 5, and at Notre-Dame at 9. In 1817 he entered Choron's school of m., became orgst. at Tours cath. in 1819, but being unsuccessful there returned to Choron as accompst. He picked up more instruction at the school, but never became a good technician, and he took to opera from sheer necessity when Choron's school was closed. But he had already made a name for himself by settings of verses by the new poets, who approved of them.

Works incl. operas *Les Deux Reines*, *Le Luthier de Vienne*, *Piquillo*, *Un Conte d'autrefois*, *Perugina*, *Le Planteur*, *La Chaste Suzanne*, *La Reine Jeanne*, *L'Orfèvre*, *Lambert Simnel* (unfinished, completed by Adam); Nocturne for 3 voices *Si j'étais petit oiseau* (Béranger); songs to words by Hugo (*Guitare*), Musset & others, &c.

Monro, George (b. ?; d. London, ? 1731), Eng. orgst. & comp. He was orgst. at St. Peter's, Cornhill, in London and played hpchd. at the theatre in Goodman's Fields.

Works incl. incid. m. to Fielding's *The Temple Beau*; a great number of songs, incl. 'My lovely Celia,' &c.

Monsigny, Pierre Alexandre (b. Fauquembergue nr. Saint-Omer, 17. X. 1729; d. Paris, 14. I. 1817), Fr. comp.

He received a classical educ., but his father d. when he was 20 and he went to Paris to take an official post to help his family, which, being a noble one, afforded him good connections, so that he was soon able to become steward to the Duke of Orleans. Being thus able to study m., he took lessons from Gianotti, a db. player at the Opéra, under whom he advanced so rapidly that he very soon finished his 1st opera, which was prod. in 1757. His assoc. with Sedaine as libst. soon afterwards consolidated his success and he made a fortune, which he lost during the Revol.; but the Opéra-Comique granted him an annuity.

Works incl. operas *Les Aveux indiscrets, Le Maître en droit, Le Cadi dupé, On ne s'avise jamais de tout, Le Roi et le fermier, Rose et Colas, Aline, reine de Golconde, L'Île sonnante* (after Rabelais), *Le Déserteur, Le Faucon, La Belle Arsène, Félix, ou L'Enfant trouvé, Pagamin de Monègue, Philémon et Baucis*, &c.

Montagnana, Domenico (b. ?, *c.* 1700; d. Venice, *c.* 1740), It. v. maker. Pupil of Antonio Stradivari at Cremona, where he 1st set up a workshop, afterwards moving to Venice.

Monte, Philippe de (b. Malines, *c.* 1521; d. Prague, 4. VII. 1603), Flem. comp. He lived (?) at Antwerp in the 1550s and (?) made friends there with Lassus. In 1568 he went to Vienna as chapel master to the Emperor Maximilian II, after whose death in 1576 he followed the next emperor, Rudolph II, to Prague. He was made a canon of Cambrai cath., but (?) did not reside there.

Works incl. masses, motets; over 30 books of madrigals, &c.

Montéclair, Michel (Pinolet) de (b. Chaumont-en-Bassigny, *c.* 1666; d. Saint-Denis, IX. 1737), Fr. comp. Studied m. as a chorister at Langres cath., later sang in other churches and went to It. in the service of the Prince de Vaudémont. After 1702 he settled in Paris and he was db. player at the Opéra in 1707–37. He was also a va. player and taught the inst.

Works incl. operas and opera-ballets, e.g. *Les Festes de l'été* & *Jephté*, ballet m. for C. F. Pollaroli's opera *Ascanio*; chamber m., &c.

Montemezzi, Italo (b. Vigasio nr. Verona, 4. VIII. 1875), It. comp. Learnt the pf. as a child, then went to Milan to be trained for engineering, but wished to take to m. He entered the Cons. with some difficulty, but obtained a diploma there in 1900. After the prod. of his 1st opera in 1905 he was able to give all his time to comp.

Works incl. operas *Giovanni Gallurese, Hellera, L'amore di tre rè, La Nave* (d'Annunzio), *La notte di Zoraima, La principessa lontana* (after Rostand's *Princesse lointaine*); *The Song of Songs* for chor. or orch.; symph. poem *Paolo e Virginia* (after Saint-Pierre); Elegy for co. & pf., &c.

Montesquieu, Charles (Louis), Baron de La Brède et de Secondat (1689–1755), Fr. philosopher & historian. *See* **Otesco** (*Temple de Gnide*).

Monteverdi, Claudio (b. Cremona, V. 1567; d. Venice, 29. XI. 1643), It. comp. Son of a doctor; went to Cremona cath. as a choir-boy and a pupil of Ingegneri; became an orgst. and violist and at 16 pub. sacred madrigals, 1583. Entered the service of the Duke of Mantua, Vincenzo Gonzaga, as violist and singer, and there married the hpst. Claudia Cataneo. He was in Gonzaga's retinue in the war against the Turks on the Danube and again in Flanders in 1599. He prob. heard Peri's *Euridice* at Florence in 1600, and in 1602 was made m. master to the court of Mantua. His wife d. after a long illness on 10. IX. 1607, the year M. finished his 1st opera, *Orfeo*. The next, *Arianna*, made him widely famous. When Francesco Gonzaga succeeded his brother in the dukedom in 1612 he quarrelled with M., who left for his native Cremona to wait for a new appt., which came from Venice in 1613, where he was made master of m. to the republic and worked at St. Mark's. He had by this time written much church m. and numerous madrigals. In 1630 he took holy orders after escaping the plague at Venice. In 1639 the 2nd public opera theatre in Venice, the Teatro dei SS. Giovanni e Paolo, was opened with M.'s *Adone*, and *Arianna* was revived the same year when the Teatro di San Moisè was inaugurated.

Works incl. operas *Orfeo, Arianna* (lost except the *Lament*), *Il combattimento di Tancredi e Clorinda* (after Tasso), *Il ritorno d'Ulisse in patria, L'incoronazione di Poppea* & about a dozen lost stage works; ballets *Ballo delle ingrate* and *Tirsi e Clori*; 29 masses, magnificats and psalms; *Sancta Maria* for voice & 8 insts.; 40 sacred madrigals; 21 canzonette for 3 voices; 9 books of secular madrigals cont. 250; 26 madrigals published in var. collections; 25 *Scherzi musicali* for 1–3 voices, &c.

Monticelli, Angelo Maria (b. Milan, *c.* 1714; d. Dresden, 1764), It. male sop. singer. 1st appearance in Rome, 1730; later sang in Venice, London, Naples, Vienna and Dresden.

Montigny-Rémaury, Fanny (Marcelline Caroline) (b. Pamiers, 22. I. 1843; d. Pamiers, 29. VI. 1913), Fr. pfst. Pupil of her sister Elvire Rémaury, who married A. Thomas, and of Le Couppey at the Paris Cons. She made her 1st appearance in 1862 and married the journalist Léon Montigny in 1866.

Mood. The specific mus. meaning of the word is connected with the time-signature of the old mensural notation, where a longer note could be equal in value to either 2 or 3 shorter notes, according to the signature. The mood could be Maj. Perfect with a Large equalling 3 Longs or Maj. Imperfect with a Large equalling 2 Longs; or Min. Perfect with a Long equalling 3 Breves or Min. Imperfect with a Long equalling 2 Breves.

Moodie, Alma (b. Brisbane, 12. IX. 1900; d. Cologne III. 1943), Austral. vst. Studied with César Thomson at Brussels and travelled widely, making her reput. esp. in Ger., where she married a lawyer at Cologne.

Moody, Fanny (b. Redruth, Cornwall, 23. XI. 1866; d. Dundrum, Co. Dublin, 21. VII. 1945), Eng. sop. singer. Studied with Charlotte Sainton-Dolby and made her 1st stage appearance at Liverpool in 1887. In 1890 she married Charles Manners and in 1897 became his partner in the Moody-Manners Opera Co.

Mooke, Marie Félicité Denise. *See* **Moke.**

Moonie, William (Walter Beaton) (b. Stobo, Peeblesshire, 29. V. 1883), Sco. comp. Studied at Edinburgh Univ. and at the Hoch Cons. at Frankfort o/M. In 1908 he settled at Edinburgh and occupied himself with teaching, lecturing and org. playing.

Works incl. opera *The Weird of Colbar*; *A Deeside Sym.*, symph. poem *The Riders of the Sidhe*, *Springtime-on-Tweed* for orch.; chor. works; chamber m.; inst. pieces, &c.

Moonlight Sonata. The nickname of Beethoven's pf. So. in C♯ min., Op. 27 No. 2, not invented by the comp., but prob. due to a description of the 1st mvt. by Rellstab. It does not fit the other 2 mvts. in the least.

Moór, Emanuel (b. Kecskémet, 19. II. 1863; d. Vevey, Swi., 21. X. 1931), Hung. pfst., comp. & inventor. Studied at Budapest and Vienna, and toured in Eur. & Amer. as pfst. and cond. Inventor of the Duplex-Coupler pf. Married the Eng. pfst. Winifred Christie.

Works incl. operas *La Pompadour* (after Musset), *Andreas Hofer*, *Hochzeitsglocken*; 7 syms.; 4 v. concs.; chamber m.; pf. works, &c.

Moore, Douglas (Stuart) (b. Cutchogue, N.Y., 10. VIII. 1893), Amer. comp. Studied at Yale Univ. and with Horatio Parker, Bloch, d'Indy, Tournemire and Nadia Boulanger. He served in the U.S. Navy in the 1914–8 war, was orgst. & lecturer at Cleveland, 1921–5, and became assoc. prof. of m. at Columbia Univ. in N.Y. in 1926.

Works incl. opera *The Devil and Daniel Webster*, operetta *The Headless Horseman*, chamber opera *White Wings*; motet *Dedication* for 6 voices, *Simon Legree* for male chor., *Perhaps to dream* for female chor.; *A Sym. of Autumn*, Ovt. on an Amer. Tune, *Pageant of P. T. Barnum*, *Moby Dick* (after Herman Melville) for orch.; stg. 4tet; So. & *Down East* Suite for v. & pf.; *Ballad of William Sycamore* for bar., fl., tromb. & pf., &c.

Moore, George (1852–1933), Ir. novelist, essayist & critic. *See* **Grania and Diarmid** (Elgar).

Moore, Thomas (1779–1852), Ir. poet. From about 1802 he began to pub. songs with words and occasionally m. by himself, and between 1807–34 he prod. collections of Ir. tunes with new words of his own. He also prod., in 1811, an opera *M.P., or The Blue Stocking* with m. by himself and C. E. Horn. He wrote the tune as well as the words of 'The Last Rose of Summer,' used by Flotow in *Martha*. For works used by comps. *see* **Barnett (J. F.)** (*Paradise and the Peri*), **Bennett (W. S.)** (do.), **Bishop** (nat. melodies), **Clay** (*Lalla Rookh*), **David (Fél.)** (do.), **Feramors** (A. Rubinstein), **Horn (C. E.)** (do. & *M.P., or The Blue Stocking*), **Jensen** (songs), **Jongen** (*Lalla R.*), **Kashin** (*Nourmahal*), **Kelly** (*Gypsy Prince*), **Knight (J. P.)** (songs), **Krizhanovsky** (*Paradise and the P.*), **Lalla-Roukh** (F. David), **Paradise and the Peri** (Schumann), **Spontini** (*Nurmahal* & *Lalla Rookh*), **Stevenson (J.)** (Ir. songs ed.), **Thomas (G.)** (*Light of the Harem*), **Veiled Prophet** (Stanford), **Zolotarev** (*Paradise and the P.*).

Moore (or More), William. *See* **More.**

Moorehead, John (b. Ir., ?; d. nr. Deal, III. 1804), Ir. vst. & comp. Studied in Ir., went to Eng. as a youth and played at var. provincial theatres, va. at Sadler's Wells Theatre in London from 1796, and v. at Covent Garden from 1798. He had already prod. his 1st stage work in 1796 and wrote several more for Covent Garden. In 1802 he became insane and was confined, entered the Navy on being released, but hanged himself in a fit of madness.

Works incl. stage pieces *Birds of a Feather*, *Harlequin's Tour* (with Attwood), *Perouse* (with Davy), *The*

Cabinet (with Braham, Davy & others), *Family Quarrels* (with Braham & Reeve), *The Naval Pillar*, Morton's *Speed the Plough* & others; pantomimes, &c.

Morales, Cristobal (b. Seville, c. 1500; d. Málaga, 14. VI. 1553), Spa. comp. Studied at Seville under the cath. chapel master Fernández de Castilleja. Was chapel master at Avila, 1526–30, and some time later went to Rome, where he was ordained a priest and became cantor in the Pontifical Chapel, 1535. In 1545 he was given leave to visit Spa., but did not return, living at Toledo, Málaga and Marchena, app. chapel master at the former 2 places and serving in the household of the Duke of Arcos at the last.

Works incl. masses, magnificats, motets, lamentations & other church m.; cantatas for the peace conference at Nice (1538) and for Ippolito d'Este; madrigals, &c.

Morales, Melesio (b. Mexico City, 1838; d. Mexico City, 1908), Mex. comp. Studied in his native city, founded several mus. socs. there and in 1880 became dir. of the Cons.

Works incl. operas *Romeo e Giulietta* (after Shakespeare), *Ildegonda, Gina Corsini* & *Cleopatra* (all in It.); *Missa di Gloria* & other church m.; 2 cantatas, &c.

Morales, Olallo (Juan Magnus) (b. Almería, 15. X. 1874), Spa. comp. He studied in Swe., his mother's country, and in Berlin. After appts. at Lausanne and Göteborg, he went to Stockholm in 1909 and became dir. of the Cons. He has written criticism and mus.-hist. studies.

Works incl. Sym. in G min., ovt. *Försommar* & other orch. works; stg. 4tet, *Berceuse* for fl. & stgs., &c.

Morales, Pedro (García) (b. Huelva, 1879; d. Huelva, 9. XII. 1938), Spa. poet & comp. Studied at Seville and the R.C.M. in London, where he remained for most of his life.

Works incl. *Esquisse andalouse* for v. & orch.; *Bagatelle* for v. & pf.; songs to his own poems, &c.

Moravian Composers. *See* **Bohemian Composers,** where the older names are listed, not with strict historical accuracy, but for convenience of reference, just as modern Slovak comps. are shown under the head of **Czech Composers.**

Morawski, Eugeniusz (b. Warsaw, 1. XI. 1876), Pol. comp. & painter. Studied m. with Noskowski at the Warsaw Cons. and painting at the Acad. of Art. He lived in Paris as a political refugee in 1905–29, when he returned and in 1930 became dir. of the Warsaw Cons.

Works incl. ballet *The Merchant of Switez*; symph. poems *Vae victis, Fleurs du mal* (after Baudelaire), *Don Quixote* (after Cervantes), *Nevermore* & *Ulalume* (both after Poe), dance poem *Love* for orch.; hymns for con. with org., &c.

Mordent. An ornament which, when placed over a note, indicates that this note should be struck twice in rapid succession with a note a degree higher or lower in between, according to the sign: 𝆗 in the former case, 𝆘 in the latter. Double Ms. 𝆗𝆗 or 𝆘𝆘 repeat the same process.

Mordente (It.) = **Mordent.**

More, Hannah (1745–1833), Eng. philanthropist, religious writer & poetess. *See* **Hook** (*Search after Happiness*), **Latrobe** (airs).

More (or Moore), William (b. ?; d. ?, 1565), Eng. hpst. & comp. He was in the service of Henry VIII, Edward VI and (?) Elizabeth, and comp. motets, (?) &c.

Moreau, Jean-Baptiste (b. Angers, 1656; d. Paris, 24. VIII. 1733), Fr. comp. He learnt m. as a boy chorister at Angers cath. and comp. motets as a youth. App. choirmaster at the cath. of Langres, where he married, and later that of Dijon; and went to Paris during the 1680s. He found his way into the court, for which he began to write stage pieces, and in 1688 he was commissioned to write m. for Racine's *Esther* for perf. at the young ladies' acad. of Saint-Cyr. This earned him a pension for life and an appt. at Saint-Cyr jointly with the orgst. Nivers and later with Clérambault. He remained under the patronage of the king and Mme de Maintenon. He taught both singing and comp., among his pupils for the former being his daughter Claude-Marie M. and for the latter Clérambault, Dandrieu and Montéclair.

Works incl. Requiem, motet *In exitu Israel, Cantiques spirituels* (Racine), Te Deum for the king's recovery (1687) & other church m.; stage divertissements incl. *Les Bergers de Marty*; *Athalie*; *Idylle sur la naissance de Notre Seigneur*; drinking-songs, &c.

Morendo (It.) = dying. A direction used where a phrase is intended to die away. It may mean, not only a decrease in tone, but in pace as well.

Morera, Enric (b. Barcelona, 22. V. 1865; d. Barcelona, II. 1942), Spa. comp. Lived in Argentine in his youth and studied m. at Barcelona and Brussels. He did much work to further interest in Catalan folksong, which influenced his comps.

Works incl. operas *Emporium,*

Bruniselda, Don Joan de Serralonga, Titayna, Tassarba. La nit de St. Joan, La font de l'Albera, La fada; chor. works; arrs. of Catalan songs, &c.

Moresca. A Moorish dance of remote antiquity, 1st introd. by the Moors into Spa. and popular all over Eur. by the 15th–16th cent. Allied to the Eng. Morris Dance, 'morys' being an obs. Eng. variant of 'Moorish'; at any rate one of the latter's features—bells or jingles tied to the legs—belonged to the M. also.

Moreto y Cavana, Augustín (1618–61), Spa. dramatist. *See* **Donna Diana** (Rezniček), **Ferreira, Hofmann (H.)** (*Donna D.*), **Laserna, Turina** (*Margot*), **Woyrsch** (*Donna D.*).

Morhange, Charles Henri Valentin. *See* **Alkan.**

Mori, Nicholas (b. London, 24. I. 1796 or 1797; d. London, 14. VI. 1839), Eng. vnst. and m. pub. of It. descent. Pupil of Barthélemon, at whose concerts he played at the age of 8, and later of Viotti. He appeared as soloist of the Phil. Soc.'s concerts and became leader of its orch. In 1819 he married the widow of the m. pub. Lavenu and became a partner with her son.

Moriani, Napoleone (b. Florence, 10. III. 1808; d. ?, 4. III. 1878), It. ten. singer. Made his 1st appearance at Pavia in 1833.

Mörike, Eduard (Friedrich) (1804–75), Ger. poet. *See* **Dieren (van)** (songs), **Schoeck** (songs), **Sutermeister** (*Jorinde*), **Trapp** (*Letzte König von Orplid*).
2 songs by Brahms, 3 by Schumann, 57 (incl. 4 early) by H. Wolf.

Morisco. An Eng. corruption of the name of the Moresca.

Morlacchi, Francesco (b. Perugia, 14. VI. 1784; d. Innsbruck, 28. X. 1841), It. cond. & comp. Studied with his father, then at Perugia cath., later with Zingarelli at Loreto and finally with Mattei at Bologna. In 1810 he was app. mus. dir. of the It. opera at Dresden, where he remained to the end of his life, when he set out on a visit to It., but d. on the way. He intrigued unobtrusively against Weber when the latter was app. cond. of Ger. opera at Dresden in 1817.
Works incl. operas *Il ritratto, Enone e Paride, Oreste, Le Danaidi, Raoul de Crequi, La capricciosa pentita, Il barbiere di Siviglia* (after Beaumarchais), *Boadicea, Gianni di Parigi, Il Simoncino, Donna Aurora, Tebaldo ed Isolina, La gioventù di Enrico V, Il Colombo, Francesca da Rimini* (after Dante, unfinished) & *c.* 10 others; *c.* 12 masses, Requiem for the King of Saxony (1827), Miserere for 16 voices, unaccomp. Mass for the Gr. service & other church m.; orats. *Gli angeli al sepolcro, La morte di Abele & Il sacrifizio d'Abramo*, Passion orat. (words by Metastasio); cantatas for the coronation of Napoleon as king of It. (1805) & for the taking of Paris (1814); Narration of Ugolino from Dante's *Inferno* for bar. & pf., &c.

Morley, Thomas (b. ? London, 1557; d. ? London, ? 1603), Eng. comp. Pupil of Byrd, took his B.Mus. degree at Oxford in 1588 and about that time became (?) orgst. of St Giles's church, Cripplegate, in London. Soon afterwards he was orgst. of St. Paul's cath. and in 1592 became a Gentleman of the Chapel Royal. In 1598 both M. and Shakespeare, who were prob. acquainted, appealed against the assessment for taxes, and in 1599 M. contrib. the setting of 'It was a lover and his lass,' if not more m., to the prod. of *As You Like It.* M. obtained a patent for the printing of m. and m. paper in 1598, but he had already pub. his treatise, *A Plaine and Easie Introduction to Practicall Musick*, in 1597. He resigned from the Chapel Royal in 1602, (?) owing to ill health.
Works incl. services, anthems and responses, 10 Lat. motets; madrigals (incl. 2 in *The Triumphes of Oriana*), canzonets and balletts for voices; 4 tunes contrib. to *The Whole Booke of Psalmes*; fancies for viols; virginal pieces, &c.

Morning Heroes, sym. for orator, chor. & orch. by Bliss (words by Homer, Li-Tai-Po, Whitman, Robert Nichols & Wilfred Owen), 1st perf. Norwich Festival, IX. 1930.

Morris Dance. An old Eng. folk dance, deriving its name from the Moorish *Moresca* (obs. Eng. 'morys' = 'Moorish'), introd. into Eng. about the 15th cent. It partook of a pageant in character and was danced in var. kinds of fancy dress, with jingles tied to the dancers' legs. In some districts elements of the Sword Dance were introd. into it. The m., a great variety of tunes, was played by a pipe and tabor, or more rarely by a bagpipe or v.

Morris, Harold (b. San Antonia, Texas, 17. III. 1890), Amer. pfst. & comp. Studied at Texas Univ. and the Cincinnati Cons. He lectured at the Rice Institute at Houston, Texas, and later became a teacher at the Juillard School of M. in N.Y.
Works incl. 2 syms. (No. 2 on Browning's *Prospice*), symph. poem on Tagore's *Gitanjali*, Vars. on a Negro spiritual, Suite for small orch.; pf. Conc., v. Conc.; 2 stg. 4tets, pf. 5tet, 2 pf. trios, Suite for fl., v., co. & pf.; v. & pf. So., &c.

Morris, R(eginald). O(wen). (b. York, 3. III. 1886), Eng. teacher & comp. Educ. at Harrow, New Coll., Oxford, and the R.C.M. in London, where later he became prof. of ctpt. and comp. In 1926 he was app. to a similar post at the Curtis Institute at Philadelphia, but soon returned to Eng. His books incl. *Contrapuntal Technique in the 16th Century, Foundations of Practical Harmony and Counterpoint, The Structure of Music.*
Works incl. Sym. in D maj.; v.Conc.in G min., *Concerto piccolo* for 2 vs. & stgs.; Fantasy for stg. 4tet, Motets for stg. 4tet; songs with 4tet accomp., &c.

Mors et Vita (*Death and* [*New*] *Life*), orat. by Gounod, a sequel to *The Redemption*, prod. Birmingham Festival, 26. VIII. 1885.

Morselli, Ercole Luigi (1882–1921), It. dramatist. *See* **Belfagor** (Respighi).

Mortari, Virgilio (b. Passirana di Lainate nr. Milan, 6. XII. 1902), It. comp. Pupil of Pizzetti.
Works incl. operas *Secchi e sberlecchi, La scuola delle mogli* (after Molière); Rhapsody for orch.; chamber m.; Partita for v.; children's songs *Giro, giro, tondo*, &c.

Mortimer, Philip. *See* **Knight, J. P.**

Morton (Mourton in Fr.), **Robert** (b. ?; d. ?), Eng. 15th-cent. musn. He was in the service of the dukes of Burgundy, Philip the Good and Charles the Bold at Dijon, *c.* 1464–78, and had a great reput. as a learned musn. Later in the cent. he may have been a singer at St. Peter's in Rome, named Robertus Anglicus. His works incl. chansons for several voices.

Morton, Thomas (1764–1838), Eng. playwright. *See* **Moorehead** (*Speed the Plough*).

Moscheles, Ignaz (b. Prague, 30. V. 1794; d. Leipzig, 10. III. 1870), Boh. pfst. & comp. Studied under Dionys Weber at the Prague Cons., played a conc. in public at the age of 14, was sent to Vienna and there took lessons in ctpt. from Albrechtsberger and comp. from Salieri. He made Beethoven's acquaintance when he arr. the voc. score of *Fidelio* in 1814. He then began to travel widely, and in 1821 appeared in Hol., Paris and London. In 1824 he taught Mendelssohn in Berlin; in 1826 he married Charlotte Embden at Hamburg and settled permanently in London. He appeared all over the country, had a vast number of pupils and comp. a great deal, esp. for the pf. In 1846 he went to Leipzig at Mendelssohn's invitation to become 1st pf. prof. at the new Cons., but still visited Eng.
Works incl. pf. concs., e.g. G min. & *Concerto pathétique*; a great number of pf. works incl. *Sonate mélancolique, Characteristic Studies, Allegro di bravura* & endless sos., vars. fantasies, studies, &c.; *Hommage à Handel* for 2 pfs., &c.

Mosè in Egitto (*Moses in Egypt*). *See also* **Moïse.**
Opera by Rossini (lib. by Andrea Leone Tottola), prod. Naples, Teatro San Carlo, 5. III. 1818.

Moser, Franz (Joseph) (b. Vienna, 20. III. 1880; d. Vienna, VI. 1939), Aus. pfst., cond. & comp. Studied at the Vienna Cons. and after var. appts. became prof. at the State Acad. there, chor. master at the Opera and lecturer at the Univ.
Works incl. a Mass; incid. m.; 3 syms. & other orch. works; 4 stg. 4tets & other chamber m.; pf. m.; songs. &c.

Moser, Hans Joachim (b. Berlin, 25. V. 1889), Ger. singer, mcolst. & comp., son of Andreas M. (1859–1925), vst. and writer on m., biog. of Joachim. Studied with his father and later at Berlin, Marburg & Leipzig, and became prof. of mcol. at Halle, Heidelberg and later Berlin. His lit. works incl. a hist. of Ger. m., studies of medieval stg. m., Luther's songs, Ger. song, &c., biogs. of Hofhaimer, Schütz & Bach, &c.

Moser, Rudolf (b. Niederzuwil, St. Gall, 7. I. 1892), Swi. comp. Studied at Basle, later with Reger, Sitt and Klengel at the Leipzig Cons. and finally under Huber, Suter and others at Basle again, where he became cond. of the Orch. Soc. and the cath. choir and prof. at the Cons.
Works incl. operetta *Die Fischerin* (Goethe), radio opera *Pereander und Lykophron*; Odes by Horace for bar., chor. & orch.; motets & other chor. works; Suite, Conc. grosso & other orch. works; pf. Conc., 3 v. concs., va. Conc., org. Conc., Triple Conc. for v., va. & co.; 4 stg. 4tets, pf. Trio, stg. 6tet; inst. sos. & pieces; pf. works; songs, &c.

Mosonyi, Mihaly (real name Michael Brand) (b. Frauenkirchen, Wieselburg, 2. IX. 1815; d. Budapest, 31. X. 1870), Hung. comp. Studied at Poszony (Pressburg) and was m. master in a noble family in 1835–42, when he settled at Budapest. He changed his Ger. name of Brand in 1859, when he began to aim at writing Hung. nat. m.
Works incl. operas *Kaiser Max auf der Martinswand, The Fair Ilonka* & *Almos* (both in Hung.); 3 masses; syms., symph. poems *Mourning for Széchényi* & *Festival Music* & other orch. works; 20 pf. pieces in the Hung. manner; 25 Hung. folksong arrs., &c.

Mosso (It.) = moving, in motion, animated.

Mossolov, Alexander Vassilievitch (b. Kiev, 10. VIII. 1900), Rus. pf. & comp. His family, which cultivated var. branches of art, moved to Moscow in 1904 and in 1921 he entered the Cons. there, studying under Glière until 1925. He travelled much as pfst. and to study folk m. in central Asia.

Works incl. operas *The Dam*, *The Hero*, *The Signal*; cantatas *Sphinx* (Oscar Wilde) & *Kirghiz Rhapsody*; 4 syms., symph. poem *The Iron Foundry* (*Music of Machines*), *Turcomanian Suite* & *Uzbek Dance* for orch.; 2 pf. concs., hp. Conc., co. Conc.; stg. 4tet, *Dance Suite* for pf. trio; va. & pf. So.; songs to words by Pushkin, Lermontov & Blok; massed chors., battle songs, &c.

Mosto, Giovanni Battista (b. Udine, ?; d. ?), It. 16th-cent. comp. Pupil of Merulo, chapel master of Padua cath., 1580–9, and then in the service of Prince Bathori of Transylvania.

Works incl. church m.; madrigals, &c.

Moszkowski, Moritz (b. Breslau, 23. VIII. 1854; d. Paris, 4. III. 1925), Pol.-Ger. pfst. & comp. Studied at Dresden and Berlin, where he became prof. at Kullak's acad. later on. He lived mainly in Paris from 1879, being at first successful as pfst. & comp., but in the end dying in poverty.

Works incl. opera *Boabdil*; ballet *Laurin*; sym. *Jeanne d'Arc*, 2 Suites, *Phantastischer Zug* & other pieces for orch.; pf. Conc. in E maj., 2 concert pieces for pf. & orch., v. Conc.; Scherzo for v. & pf., 3 pieces for co. & pf.; 3 Concert Studies, Barcarolle & many other pieces for pf.; Spa. Dances & *Aus aller Herren Landen* for pf. duet; songs, &c.

Motet. A form of sacred voc. comp. for several voices arising out of the Conductus and the Trope in the 13th cent. It was at first an elaboration of a given melody with words by the ctptal. addition of other melodies with different words. There were usually 3 voices at first, *triplex* (treble), *motetus* (alto or a 2nd sop.)—hence the name of the species—and *tenor* or *pes* (tenor or high bass), which was the lowest part; and the *motetus* sang the chief words. In the 15th cent. it became more independent, and it gradually developed into an elab. form of polyphonic sacred comp. set to any words (nearly always in Lat.) not incl. in the Mass. Its place in the Rom. liturgy was that of a perf. additional to the regular service, like that of the Anthem in the Angl. church.

Motetus. *See* **Motet.**

Mother Goose (Ravel). *See* **Ma Mère l'Oye.**

Motif (Fr.) *See* **Motiv, Motive.**

Motion. The succession of notes of different pitch. The word is used only with some adjectival qualification or other:

Conjunct M.: a single part moving by steps of adjoining notes.

Contrary M.: 2 or more parts moving together in different directions.

Disjunct M.: a single part moving by larger than stepwise intervals.

Oblique M.: one part moving when another stands still.

Similar M.: 2 or more parts moving together in the same direction.

Motiv (Ger.)
Motive (Eng. by adoption) } A brief melodic or rhythmic figure, too short to be called a theme, sometimes used as a purely abstract subject, sometimes in programme m. or opera in assoc. with a character, object or idea, in which case it becomes a Leading Motive like the *idée fixe* of Berlioz or the *Leitmotiv* of Wagner.

Moto (It.) = motion, pace.

Moto perpetuo (It. = perpetual motion). A piece proceeding at length in a series of uniform rapid figuration; also called by the Lat. name of *perpetuum mobile*.

Motta, José Vianna da. *See* **Vianna da Motta.**

Motteux, Peter Anthony (1663–1718), Eng. playwright and trans. *See* **Arsinoe** (? Clayton), **Finger** (*Loves of Mars and Venus* & *Anatomist*), **Franck (J. W.)** (masque for *Timon of Athens*), **King (R.)** (*Ode for John Cecil*), **Thomyris** (Pepusch, &c.).

Mottl, Felix (b. Unter-St.-Veit nr. Vienna, 24. VIII. 1856; d. Munich, 2. VII. 1911), Aus. cond. & comp. Studied at a choir-school and at the Cons. in Vienna, became cond. of the Wagner Soc. there and in 1876 was engaged by Wagner to cond. the m. on the stage in the prod. of the *Ring*. In 1881–1903 he was cond. at the ducal court of Carlsruhe, where he dir. the sym. concerts and the opera, prod. many unfamiliar works.

Works incl. operas *Agnes Bernauer* (after Hebbel), *Rama* & *Fürst und Sänger*; festival play *Eberstein*; m. for O. J. Bierbaum's play *Pan im Busch*; stg. 4tet; songs, &c.

Motto. In m. a short and well-defined theme usually occurring at the opening of a comp. and used again during its course, in its 1st form or altered, in the manner of a quotation or an allusion to some definite idea. The opening themes in Tchaikovsky's 4th and 5th syms. are familiar exs. The *idée fixe* in Berlioz's *Fantastic Sym.* may also be called a M., although it approximates to a *Leitmotiv.*

Motu proprio (Lat. lit. of one's own motion). A decree issued by the Pope personally, esp. that issued by Pius X setting down the principles of and introd. reforms into the singing of Rom. Catholic church m.

Moulu, Pierre (b. ?; d. ?), Flem. or Fr. 15th-16th cent. comp. Pupil of Josquin des Prés. Wrote masses, motets & other church m.

Mounsey, Ann Sheppard (b. London, 17. IV. 1811; d. London, 24. VI. 1891), Eng. orgst. & comp. She held var. org. appts. in London churches and in 1843 began a series of Classical Concerts. In 1853 she married the painter and trans. William Bartholomew (1793–1867), who was also a vst.

Works incl. orat. *The Nativity*; pf. & org. m.; many songs, partsongs, &c.

Mounsey, Elizabeth (b. London, 8. X. 1819; d. London, 3. X. 1905), Eng. orgst. & comp., sister of prec. She was app. orgst. of St. Peter's church, Cornhill, in 1834, aged 14, and remained there until 1882. She also appeared in public as pfst. and guitar player.

Works incl. m. for org., pf. & guitar.

Mount-Edgcumbe, Earl of (Richard Edgcumbe) (b. Plymouth, 13. IX. 1764; d. Richmond, Surrey, 26. IX. 1839), Eng. mus. amateur & comp. Known chiefly by his *Musical Reminiscences*, pub. in 1823, mainly of operatic singing in London between 1773–1823.

Works incl. opera *Zenobia.*

Mount of Olives, The (Beethoven). *See* **Christus am Oelberge.**

Mouret, Jean Joseph (b. Avignon, 16. IV. 1682; d. Charenton, 22. XII. 1738), Fr. comp. He entered the service of the Duchess of Maine in Paris about 1707 and in 1714 began to write for the stage. He was dir. of the Concert spirituel in 1728–34, also for a time cond. of the Comédie-Italienne. In 1736 he became insane and was taken to the lunatic asylum of Charenton.

Works incl. operas and opera-ballets *Les Festes de Thalie, Ragonde, Ariane, Les Amours des dieux, Le Triomphe des sens,* &c.; Mass, 2 books of motets; cantatas *Cantatilles*; 2 *Suites de Symphonies*, 47 divertissements for orch.; 2 books of *Concerts de chambre*; fanfares, &c.

Mourning Symphony (Haydn). *See* **Trauer-Sinfonie.**

Mourning Waltz (Schubert). *See* **Trauerwalzer.**

Mourton, Robert. *See* **Morton.**

Moussorgsky. *See* **Mussorgsky.**

Mouton, Charles (b. ?, 1626; d. ?), Fr. lutenist & comp. Lived at Turin in 1670–1700, twice visited Paris, and in 1700 settled there. Wrote lute pieces, &c.

Mouton, Jean (b. ? Hollingue nr. Metz, *c.* 1475; d. Saint-Quentin, 30. X. 1522), Fr. comp. Pupil of Josquin des Prés. He was in the service of Louis XII and François I, became canon of Thérouanne, which he left prob. on its being taken by the Eng. in 1513 and afterwards of the collegiate church of Saint-Quentin.

Works incl. masses, motets, psalms, *Alleluia* & *In illo tempore* for Easter, *Noe, noe, psallite* for Christmas, &c.

Movable Doh. The Tonic or Keynote in the Tonic Sol-fa system which shifts the tonal centre at each modulation into another Key instead of prescribing Accidentals.

Mouvement (Fr.) = tempo, pace; not the Fr. equiv. of the following.

Movement. In m. the term is reserved for the separate pieces in a comp. consisting of several detached parts, such as a sym. or so. with, for ex., 1st movt., slow mvt., minuet or scherzo, and finale. But it may also serve for the dance pieces in a suite or detachable piece in any other kind of work, though it is rarely used for voc. pieces.

Mozart and Salieri, opera by Rimsky-Korsakov (lib. Pushkin's dramatic poem, set as it stands), prod. Moscow, 7. XII. 1898.

Mozart, (Johann Georg) Leopold (b. Augsburg, XI. 1719; d. Salzburg, 28. V. 1787), Ger. vst. & comp. Studied theol. at Salzburg Univ., but forsook it for m., becoming vst. and chamberlain to one of the canons there, Count Thurn und Taxis, in 1740. In 1743 he joined the archbishop's orch. and remained at his court, where in 1757 he became court comp. and in 1763 2nd mus. dir. In 1747 he married Anna Maria Pertl and had 6 children by her, of whom 2 survived: Maria Anna and Wolfgang Amadeus. In 1756 he pub. a v. school, *Versuch einer gründlichen Violinschule.*

Works incl. church m.; syms. & divertimenti (incl. pieces descriptive of sledge parties, &c.); concs., sos. for var. insts., &c.

Mozart, Maria Anna (fam. Nannerl) (b. Salzburg, 30. VII. 1751; d. Salzburg, 29. X. 1829), Aus. pfst. & teacher, daughter of prec. Like her brother Wolfgang Amadeus she developed very early as a clavier player, though not as a comp., and was taken on tour with him by Leopold. Later she taught at Salzburg, in 1784 married Baron von Berchtold zu Sonnenberg, a court councillor at Salzburg and warden of St. Gilgen, where she lived. She returned to Salzburg as teacher on his death in 1801 and in 1820 became blind.

Mozart, Wolfgang Amadeus (b. Salzburg, 27. I. 1756; d. Vienna, 5. XII. 1791). Aus. comp., brother of prec. His father, Leopold M., taught him from the age of 3 or 4 and found that the boy could play almost at once and invent little pieces when he was 5. He and his sister, then 11, were taken to Munich in 1762 to show off before the Elector of Bavaria and then to Vienna to play at court. By the next year M. had begun to play the v. too, and Leopold decided to take his family on a long tour to exploit the children's gifts. They went through southern Ger. to Brussels and Paris, played at court at Versailles and then went on to London in IV. 1764. They made a sensation at concerts and before royalty and M. came under the influence of J. C. Bach, under which he wrote his first syms. and v. sos. They left for Hol. in the summer of 1765, and after another visit to Paris in 1766 and to Swi., they returned to Salzburg in XI. M. comp. an orat. and a Lat. comedy, but they were off to Vienna again in IX. 1767 and did not get back home until I. 1769. M. had written his 1st It. comic opera, *La finta semplice*, in Vienna at the age of 12, but its prod. was frustrated by intrigues; the Ger. operetta, *Bastien und Bastienne* was given in the private theatre of the hypnotist Mesmer. Much of the next 4 years was taken up by 3 journeys to It. on which Leopold took his son alone. The first was much the longest and most important. Between XII. 1769 and III. 1771 they visited Verona, Mantua, Milan, Parma, Bologna, Florence, Rome, Naples, Turin, Venice and some other places. In Rome M. wrote down Allegri's *Miserere* from memory, at Bologna he took ctpt. lessons from Martini and was elected a member of the Phil. Soc. and at Milan he prod. the opera *Mitridate* with great success. Back home, M. was busy comp. some church m., a sym. and a 2nd opera, *Ascanio in Alba*, commissioned by Milan, the prod. there in X. 1771 occasioning the 2nd journey, which lasted only some 2 months. The 3rd was undertaken for the prod. of the 3rd Milan opera, *Lucio Silla*, on 26. XII. 1772: it lasted no longer and did not take them far. A visit to Vienna in 1773 to secure a post at court proved fruitless, and much as M. disliked his servitude at Salzburg, he had to remain there until he obtained leave in 1777 for another journey. But Leopold could not release himself, and M. went in his mother's company. Their 1st important halt was at Mannheim, where they met many good musns. and M. fell in love with the daughter of one of them, Fridolin Weber, the young singer Aloysia W., a girl of 16. But Leopold, hearing of this, insisted on their going off to Paris at once, and they arrived there in III. 1778. This time the Fr. were lukewarm in their interest, and the visit was not fruitful in important works and turned into a tragedy when M.'s mother d. on 3. VII. He left in IX., returned to Mannheim, and on finding that the court had left for Munich, went there to see Aloysia again, only to find that she had jilted him. Back at Salzburg in I. 1779, he wrote much m., incl. the serious opera *Idomeneo*, prod. at Munich on 29. I. 1781. He was now 25 and had found that whenever he was properly appreciated it was always outside Salzburg, which he now decided to leave. On resigning he was ignominiously dismissed, and he decided to settle in Vienna. There he lodged with the Weber family, Fridolin's widow and her 3 remaining daughters. He now fell in love with the next below Aloysia in age, Constanze, who was then 18, and by the time Leopold had protested by letter M. was already engaged to her. He succeeded in prod. the opera *The Elopement from the Harem* on 16. VII. 1782, and in making himself known by a series of concerts for which he wrote pf. concs. to play himself. During a visit to Salzburg to introd. Constanze in 1783 he began the Mass in C min. as a thanksgiving, but left it unfinished. A visit to Count Thun at Linz on the return journey prod. the Sym. named after that place (C maj. K. 425). Many important inst. works appeared during these years, and on 1. V. 1786 *The Marriage of Figaro* was prod. in Vienna, followed by *Don Giovanni* in Prague on 29. X. 1787. The group of the last great 3 syms. (K. 543, 550, 551) was written in an incredibly short time in the summer of 1788. The following year M. visited Berlin, staying at Dresden and Leipzig on the way, discussing Bach with his successor, Doles, at the latter place. In Berlin Frederick William II of Prus. welcomed him and ordered a set of 6 stg. 4tets from him, of which only 3 were eventually written (K. 575, 589, 590). The 3rd of the great It. operas, *Cosi fan tutte*, was prod. on 26. I. 1790, and the following year M. was busy with the greatest Ger. opera he wrote, *The*

Magic Flute, prod. in Vienna on 30. IX. 1791. It was interrupted by another visit to Prague, for which *La clemenza di Tito* was hastily written and by the mysterious commission of the Requiem by a stranger, whom M. did not know as the steward of a nobleman who hoped to pass off the work as his own. But M. was unable to finish it, for he was suffering from some disease like uraemia which led to serious illness, partial paralysis and death.

Works incl. 19 operas: *Bastien und Bastienne, La finta semplice, Mitridate, rè di Ponto, Ascanio in Alba, Il sogno di Scipione, Lucio Silla, La finta giardiniera, Il rè pastore, Zaide* (unfinished), *Idomeneo, Die Entführung aus dem Serail, L'oca del Cairo* (unfinished), *Lo sposo deluso* (unfinished), *Der Schauspieldirektor, Le nozze di Figaro, Don Giovanni, Così fan tutte, Die Zauberflöte, La clemenza di Tito*; plays with m. *Die Schuldigkeit des ersten Gebotes, Apollo et Hyacinthus, Thamos: König in Aegypten*; over 50 church works, incl. 17 Masses and the Requiem (finished by Süssmayr); 55 solo arias with orch.; 36 songs (Ger., Fr. & It.); 8 chor. works with orch.; 45 misc. voc. works; over 50 syms.; over 100 misc. orch. works, incl. serenades, divertimenti, cassations, marches, minuets, country dances, Ger. dances, &c.; 21 pf. concs. & 1 each for 2 & 3 pfs., also other works for pf. and orch., e.g. 2 rondos, &c., *c.* 30 other works for solo insts. & orch., incl. 6–8 v. concs., 4 for hn., 2 for fl., 1 each for cl. and bn., 1 for fl. & hp., 1 *Sinfonia concertante* for v. & va. and another for 4 wind insts.; 6 stg. 5tets; 23 stg. 4tets & 2 arrs.; *Divertimento* for stg. trio; 2 duets for v. & va.; 2 pf. 4tets; 8 pf. trios (1 with clar. & va.); 15 misc. chamber works, incl. 5tet for pf. & wind and 5tet for cl. & stgs.; 40 v. & pf. sos. and vars.; over 60 pf. works, incl. 18 sos. and 14 sets of vars.; 5 sos., a Fugue, *Andante and Vars.* for pf. duet and 2 works orig. written for a mechanical org.; Fugue & So. for 2 pfs., &c.

Mozart, (Franz Xaver) Wolfgang (he added his father's name of Amadeus, but it is not a baptismal one) (b. Vienna, 26. VII. 1791; d. Carlsbad, 29. VII. 1844), Aus. pfst. & comp., son of prec. Pupil of Hummel, Salieri and Vogler. He settled as m. master at Lwów in 1808, but toured in Aus. and Ger. in 1819–22.

Works incl. orch. & chamber m., &c.

Mozartiana. Tchaikovsky's 4th Suite for orch., Op. 61, comp. in 1887. It consists of 4 works by Mozart scored for orch. by T.: Jig & Minuet for pf., K. 475 & 355, motet *Ave, verum corpus*, K. 618, and Vars. on a theme by Gluck for pf., K. 455. 1st perf. Moscow, 26. XI. 1887.

mp (abbr.) = *mezzo piano* (half soft).

Mraczek, Joseph Gustav (b. Brno, 12. III. 1878; d. Dresden, *c.* 1944), Morav. vst. & comp. Studied at Brno and Vienna, led the theatre orch. at Brno in 1897–1902 and taught the v. there in 1898–1918. In 1919 he became prof. at the Dresden Cons.

Works incl. operas *Der gläserne Pantoffel, Der Traum* (after Grillparzer), *Herrn Dürers Bild* & others; symph. poem *Rustans Traum*, symph. burlesque *Max und Moritz* (after Wilhelm Busch), symph. poems *Eva & Variété, Oriental Dance Rhapsody*, &c. for orch.; *Oriental Sketches* for chamber orch.; stg. 4tet, pf. 5tet; pf. pieces; songs, &c.

Much Ado about Nothing. *See also* **Béatrice et Bénédict.**

Opera by Stanford (lib. by Julian Russell Sturgis, after Shakespeare), prod. London, Covent Garden Theatre, 30. V. 1901.

Muck, Karl (b. Darmstadt, 22. X. 1859; d. Stuttgart, 3. III. 1940), Ger. cond. Studied at Heidelberg Univ. and at the Leipzig Univ. & Cons. In 1880 he began a pfst.'s career, but became cond. at Salzburg, Brno and Graz in succession, at Prague in 1886, and finally in Berlin, at the Royal Opera, in 1892. He cond. Wagner in London and from 1901 at Bayreuth, also the Phil. concerts in Vienna. From 1906–14, with an interruption, he cond. the Boston Sym. Orch., and after the 1914–8 war worked at Munich, Hamburg and Amsterdam.

Mudarra, Alonso de (b. ?; d. ?), Spa. 16th-cent. lutenist & comp. He became (?) a canon of Seville cath. and pub. a book of lute pieces and songs to the lute incl. vars. and dances, settings of passages from Virgil and Ovid and sonnets by Petrarch and Sannazaro.

Mudd, John (b. ?; d. ? Peterborough, ? 1629), Eng. orgst. & comp. Orgst. at Peterborough cath. from 1583 to (?) 1629. Wrote services, anthems, &c.

Mudd, Thomas (b. ? London, *c.* 1560; d. ? Cambridge, ?), Eng. comp. He went to St. Paul's School in London and in 1578 to Cambridge as a sizar for the sons of London mercers.

Works incl. services, anthems; dances for 3 viols, &c.

Mudie, Thomas (Molleson) (b. London, 30. XI. 1809; d. London, 24. VII. 1876), Eng. pfst. & comp. Entered the R.A.M. in London in 1823, studying pf. with Potter, comp. with Crotch and cl. with Willman, and was pf. prof. there in 1832–44. In

1844–63 he taught at Edinburgh and also gave pf. recitals there, returning to London in the latter year.

Works incl. syms., ovts. & other orch. works; pf. 5tet, pf. Trio; pf. pieces; songs; settings of Sco. folksongs, &c.

Muette de Portici, La (*The Dumb Girl of Portici*), opera by Auber (lib. by Scribe and Germain Delavigne), prod. Paris, Opéra, 29. II. 1828. Carafa's *Masaniello*, on the same subject, had been prod. at the Opéra-Comique 2 months earlier. A.'s work is often called *Masaniello*.

Muffat, Georg (b. Schlettstadt, c. 1645; d. Passau, 23. II. 1704), Ger. orgst. & comp. of Sco. descent. Studied in Paris, with Lully or members of his school, and became orgst. of Strasburg cath. until 1675. In 1678 he was app. orgst. to the Archbishop of Salzburg, and after visiting Vienna and Rome went to Passau to become orgst. to the bishop in 1690 and mus. dir. in 1695.

Works incl. chamber sos. *Armonico tributo, Auserlesene mit Ernst und Lust gemengte Instrumental-Musik, Apparatus musico-organisticus* for org. (12 toccatas, chaconne & passacaglia), *Suaviores harmoniae*, 2 vols. for hpchd., &c.

Muffat, Gottlieb (Theophil) (b. Passau, IV. 1690; d. Vienna, 10. XII. 1770), Ger. orgst. & comp., son of prec. Studied with Fux in Vienna, became orgst. to the Emperor Charles VI in 1717, then to the dowager-empress, and m. master to the imp. children, retiring with a pension in 1763.

Works incl. 72 fugues & 12 toccatas for church service; *Componimenti musicali* for hpchd., &c.

Müglin, Heinrich von (b. ?; d. ?), Ger. 14th-cent. song comp.

Mühlfeld, Richard (b. Salzungen, 28. II. 1856; d. Meiningen, 1. VI. 1907), Ger. clst. In the grand-ducal orch. at Meiningen from 1873. Brahms wrote the 4 late chamber works with cl. parts, Opp. 114, 115, 120 (i & ii), for him.

Mulè, Giuseppe (b. Termini, Sicily, 28. VI. 1885), It. cst. & comp. Studied at the Palermo Cons., of which he was dir. in 1922–5, when he became dir. of the Santa Cecilia Cons. in Rome. He also became secretary to the Fascist syndicate of musns. He studied Sicilian folksong and found that its roots went back to Gr. m.; and he wrote much incid. m. for the perfs. of Gr. plays in the open-air theatre at Syracuse.

Works incl. operas *La Baronessa di Carini, Al lupo!, La monacella della fontana, Dafni, Liolà* (on Pirandello's play), *Taormina*; m. for Gr. plays: Aeschylus's *Choephorae, Seven against Thebes*, Euripides' *Bacchae, Medea, The Cyclops, Hippolytus, Iphigenia in Aulis, Iphigenia in Tauris*, Sophocles' *Antigone*; incid. m. for Corradini's *Giulio Cesare*; orat. *Il cieco di Gerico*; symph. poems *Sicilia canora* & *Vendemmia*; *Tre canti siciliani* for voice & orch.; stg. 4tet; v. & co. pieces, &c.

Mulgrave, Earl of (John Sheffield), later Marquess of Normanby and Duke of Buckingham (1684–1721), Eng. poet & playwright. *See* **Galliard** (*Julius Caesar*).

Müller, August Eberhard (b. Northeim, Hanover, 13. XII. 1767; d. Weimar, 3. XII. 1817), Ger. orgst. & comp. Held appts. at Magdeburg, Berlin and Leipzig, where he became cantor of St. Thomas's church in 1804. App. court chapel master at Weimar in 1810.

Works incl. 2 operettas; 3 cantatas; 2 pf. concs., 11 fl. concs.; pf. Trio; 2 v. & pf. sos.; pf. sos., vars., &c.; So., suites, chorale vars., &c. for org.; fl. duets & pieces, &c.

Müller-Blattau, Josef (b. Colmar, 21. V. 1895), Ger. mcolst. Studied at Strasburg, Pfitzner being among his masters. After serving in the 1914–8 war, he finished his studies with Willibald Gurlitt at Freiburg i/B., became lecturer at Königsberg Univ. in 1922 and prof. in 1928. Later he held a similar post at Frankfort o/M., 1935–7 and then at Freiburg. His books incl. works on Schütz, Handel, baroque m., Ger. folksong and a hist. of Ger. m.

Müller-Hartmann, Robert (b. Hamburg, 11. X. 1884), Ger. critic & comp. He was lecturer in mus. theory at Hamburg Univ. in 1923–33 and settled in London in 1937.

Works incl. incid. m. to Büchner's *Leonce und Lena* & other plays; Vars. on a Pastoral Theme & other works for orch.; chamber m.; songs, &c.

Müller-Hermann, Johanna (b. Vienna, 15. I. 1878), Aus. comp. She studied with Karel Navrátil, Josef Labor, Zemlinsky and J. B. Foerster, and in 1918 became teacher of theory at the New Vienna Cons.

Works incl. orat. *Song of Remembrance* (after Whitman) and other chor. works, *Deutscher Schwur, Der sterbende Schwan, Von Minnelob und Glaubenstreu*; Sym. in D maj. with chor.; *Heroic Ovt.*, symph. fantasy *Brand* & other orch. works; stg. 4tet, pf. 5tet; v. & pf. So.; pf. pieces; songs, &c.

Müller von Kulm, Walter (b. Basle, 31. VIII. 1899), Swi. comp. Studied under Werner Wehrli at Aarau and at the Basle and Zürich Cons. He was a school teacher until 1928, when he devoted himself entirely to m., teaching at the Basle Cons. and cond. male chor. socs. there.

Works incl. opera *Die Probe*, festival opera *Mutterland*; ballet *Die blaue Blume*; Sym., *Ovt. in the Old Style*, m. with hpchd. & other orch. works; chamber conc. for v., Concertino for fl.; 2 stg. 4tets, pf. Trio, Serenade for 5 wind insts. & other chamber m.; org. & pf. works; songs, partsongs, &c.

Müller, Wenzel (b. Trnava, Moravia, 26. IX. 1767; d. Baden nr. Vienna, 3. VIII. 1835), Aus. cond. & comp. Pupil of Dittersdorf, became cond. at the Brno theatre in 1783, aged 16, and in 1786 at Marinelli's theatre in Vienna, where he settled until 1808, and again in 1813, being dir. at the Prague Opera during those years, when his daughter Therese was engaged there. On his return to Vienna he became cond. of the Leopoldstadt Theatre.

Works incl. nearly 200 operas and mus. plays, e.g. *Das Sonnenfest der Braminen, Die Zauberzither, oder Kaspar der Fagottist, Das Neusonntagskind, Die Schwestern von Prag, Die Teufelsmühle auf dem Wienerberge, Die travestierte Zauberflöte* (a parody of Mozart's *Magic Flute*); masses; syms., &c.

Müller, Wilhelm (1794–1827), Ger. poet. *See* **Loder** (*Brooklet*), **Schöne Müllerin** (Schubert), **Winterreise** (do.).

Munday, Eliza. *See* **Salmon.**

Mundy, John (b. ?; d. Windsor, 1630), Eng. orgst. & comp. Studied under his father, William M., became a Gentleman of the Chapel Royal in London and succeeded Merbecke as one of the orgsts. of St. George's Chapel, Windsor, about 1585.

Works incl. anthems, *Songs and Psalmes* for 3–5 voices; madrigals (one in *The Triumphes of Oriana*); virginal pieces incl. the 'Weather' Fantasia, &c.

Mundy, William (b. ?; d. ? London, *c.* 1591), Eng. singer & comp., father of prec. He was a vicar-choral at St. Paul's cath. in London and became a Gentleman of the Chapel Royal in 1564.

Works incl. services, anthems, Lat. motets, &c.

Munkittrick, Richard Lansdale. *See* **Talbot, Howard.**

Munzinger, Karl (b. Balstal, Ct. Solothurn, 23. IX. 1842; d. Berne, 16. VIII. 1911), Swi. comp. & cond. Studied at the Leipzig Cons. and became cond. of the Solothurn *Liedertafel* in 1867. He went to Berne 2 years later to take up a similar post, and later became cond. of the Cecilia Soc. & the sym. concerts and dir. of the M. School. In 1909 he retired and was succeeded in all these posts by Brun.

Works incl. m. for the festival of the 700th anniversary of the foundation of Berne (1891); Mass; pf. 4tet; chor. works with orch.; inst. pieces; partsongs, &c.

Muradeli, Vano (b. Gori nr. Tiflis, 6. IV. 1908), Rus. comp. Studied with Shtcherbatchev at the Tiflis Cons. and with Shekhter and Miaskovsky at that of Moscow. He made a special study of Caucas. folksong, on which some of his work is based.

Works incl. a Sym., &c.

Murciana. A Spa. dance from Murcia allied to the Fandango.

Murdoch, William (David) (b. Bendigo, Austral., 10. II. 1888; d. Holmbury St. Mary, Surrey, 9. IX. 1942), Austral. pfst. Studied at Melbourne and the R.C.M. in London. He began his concert career in 1910.

Murger, Henri (1822–61), Fr. novelist. *See* **Bohème** (Leoncavallo & Puccini).

Muris, Johannes de (b. ?; d. ?), 14th-cent. theorist of unknown nationality. He lived for some time in Paris and worked also as mathematician and astronomer. The chief among the mus. treatises attrib. to him is the *Speculum musices*.

Murray, (George) Gilbert (Aimé) (b. 1866), Eng. prof. of Gr. & translator. *See* **Alkestis** (Boughton), **Drysdale** (*Hippolytus*).

Murrill, Herbert (Henry John) (b. London, 11. V. 1909), Eng. comp. Studied at the R.A.M. in London and at Worcester Coll., Oxford. After holding var. orgst.'s posts from 1926, he became prof. of comp. at the R.A.M. in 1933 and joined the m. staff of the B.B.C. in 1936.

Works incl. opera *Man in Cage*; 3 Hornpipes for orch.; Conc. & 3 pieces for co. & orch.; stg. 4tet; Capriccio for co. & pf., *Prelude, Cadenza and Fugue* for cl. & pf.; Sonatina, 2 Impromptus, 4 Studies, *Presto alla giga*, Toccatina and Canzone, &c. for pf.; *Suite française* for hpchd. or pf.; song-cycle *Self Portrait*, 2 songs (Herrick), &c.; partsongs, &c.

Murschhauser, Franz Xaver Anton (b. Zabern, VI. 1663; d. Munich, 6. I. 1738), Alsat. comp. Pupil of Kerl at Munich, where he became chapel master at the church of Our Lady. In 1721, by a remark made in his treatise on comp., *Academia musico-poetica*, he came into conflict with Mattheson.

Works incl. *Vespertinus latriae* for 4 voices & stgs.; org. books *Octitonium novum organum, Prototypon longobreve organicum, Opus organicum tripartitum*, &c.

Murska, Ilma de (b. Zagreb, 1836; d. Munich, 14. I. 1889), Croat. sop. singer. Studied with Mathilde

Marchesi in Paris and made her 1st appearance at Florence in 1862. After singing in Vienna she came out in London in 1865.

Mus. (abbr.) = Musical.

Mus.B.
Mus.Bac. } (Lat. *baccalaureus musices*, der. (?) from *Lauri bacca* = the fruit [berry] of the laurel or bay-tree). The degree of Bachelor of M. conferred by Eng. univs. since the 15th cent., and later by those of U.S.A.

Mus.D.
Mus.Doc. } (Lat. *doctor musices*). The degree of Doctor of M. conferred by Eng. univs., the 1st being Cambridge 1463, and later by those of U.S.A. The Eng. degrees of Mus.B. and Mus.D., the latter being the higher (Mus.M., where it exists, is intermediate), were adopted by the whole of Great Brit., Ireland and the colonies, but not by the continent of Eur., where m. is treated as a branch of philos. and the higher degree is equiv. to the Eng. Ph.D.

Mus.M. (Lat. *musices magister*). The degree of Master of M., conferred by Amer. univs., but in Brit. only by Cambridge, Birmingham & Wales.

Musard, Philippe (b. Tours, 1793; d. Auteuil, 31. III. 1859), Fr. vst. & cond. Studied privately with Reicha in Paris, played at masked balls and instituted a series of promenade concerts in the bazaar in the Rue Saint-Honoré. Having come into competition with J. Strauss, jun., as a dance musn. during the Viennese master's visit to Paris, he began to devote himself to classical m., and in 1840 was invited to London to give promenade concerts at Drury Lane Theatre, and afterwards at the Lyceum Theatre. He specialized in Quadrilles.

Muscadin. An old dance used by Eng. virginal comps., allied to the Hornpipe.

Muset, Colin (b. ?; d. ?), Fr. 12th-cent. trouvère & juggler. The poems of 15 and the m. of 8 of his songs are extant.

Musette (Fr.). A piece on a drone bass imitating more or less faithfully the m. of a bagpipe (Fr. *cornemuse*). It often took the place of a trio section alternating with a Gavotte in classical suites. Also the Fr. name for the Shawm or Shepherd's Pipe, sometimes provided with a wind reservoir in the shape of a small bag. Also an 8-ft. org. stop of metal pipes with free reeds reprod. bagpipe tone.

Music Drama. A neologism for 'opera' used by comps., notably Wagner, who felt that the older term implies obs. methods and forms for which they had no use.

Music Makers, The, ode for con. solo, chor. & orch. by Elgar, Op. 69 (poem by Arthur O'Shaughnessy), prod. Birmingham Festival, 1. X. 1912. The work contains a number of mus. quotations from earlier works by E.

Musica colorata (It. = coloured m.). *See* **Musica ficta.**

Musica falsa (It. = false m.). *See* **Musica ficta.**

Musica ficta (Lat. = shaped m.). The art of inserting accidentals into early modal polyphonic m. They were not prescribed by comps. because their use was guided by certain conventions with which every singer was conversant. In order to make harmonic sense between the parts or to avoid awkward intervals such as the Tritone between F and B, the leading-note of the scale was often sharpened and the B often flattened, the latter esp. in the Lydian mode. In It. the process was called *musica falsa* or *musica colorata.*

Musica figurata (Lat. & It. = figured or decorated m.). The ornamenting of Plainsong by auxiliary notes or the addition of a Descant sung against a fundamental melody.

Musica mensurata. *See* **Mensurable Music.**

Musica Transalpina. The title of a collection of It. (transalpine) madrigals with Eng. words pub. in London by Nicholas Yonge in 1588, containing 75 pieces, incl. 2 by Byrd, *La verginella*, set to a trans. of 2 stanzas from Ariosto. The It. contribs. incl. Palestrina and Marenzio, and there are also It. madrigals by Flem. comps., incl. Lassus, de Vert and Verdonck. A 2nd vol. followed in 1597, containing 24 works, this time all by It. comps.

Musical Box. A toy inst. made in var. shapes of fancy boxes and containing a cylinder with pins which, turning round by clockwork, twangs the teeth of a metal comb prod. the notes of a mus. scale. The pins are so arranged as to make the pattern of a piece of m., and several sets of pins can be set in the barrel, only one touching the teeth at a time, a choice of more than one piece being thus producible by the simple device of shifting the barrel slightly sideways. The M. B. industry centres mainly in Swi.

Musical Comedy. The term current in Eng. for a type a light mus. stage entertainment in no way different in kind from the Operetta, though often inferior to it in quality. As a non-specific term, however, it appears as early as 1765 in a title of a Covent Garden pasticcio, *The Summer's Tale.*

Musical Glasses. *See* **Harmonica.**

Musical Offering (Bach). *See* **Musikalisches Opfer.**

Musical Snuffbox. A special kind of Mus. Box made espec. in the 18th cent., with a double bottom concealing a mechanical mus. apparatus beneath its normal contents.

Musicians' Company. *See* **Worshipful Company of Musicians.**

Musicology; Musicologist. Mus. scholarship; mus. scholar. A neologism, but so useful that its adoption is desirable.

Musikalischer Spass, Ein (*A Musical Joke*), a work for stgs. & 2 hns. by Mozart, K. 522, comp. in VI. 1787, as a parody of a work in symph. or serenade form written in the clumsy manner of a bad comp. It is sometimes called by some such name as 'The Village Band,' &c., but M.'s jest is not written at the expense of rustic m., but at that of incompetence in professional mus. circles.

Musikalisches Opfer (*Musical Offering*). A late work by Bach containing 2 ricercari, a fugue in canon, 8 canons and 5 sos. for fl., v. & continuo, all based on a theme given to B. by Frederick II of Prus. during the comp.'s visit to Potsdam in 1747.

Musikwissenschaft (Ger. = mus. science) = Musicology.

Musique mesurée (Fr. = measured m.). A special method of setting words to m. cultivated in 16th-cent. Fr. by Baïf, Le Jeune, Mauduit and others. The metrical rhythm of the words furnished the basis for the mus. rhythm, which was not written out in longer and shorter note-values, but determined by the verbal declamation, which it followed closely.

Musn. (abbr.) = Musician.

Musset, Alfred de (1810–57), Fr. poet & playwright. *See* **Beydts** (*Il ne faut jurer de rien*), **Djamileh** (Bizet), **Edgar** (Puccini), **Fantasio** (Smyth), **Février** (*Carmosine*), **Franck** (**C.**) (songs), **Gnecchi** (*Rosiera*), **Huré** (*Fantasio*), **Messager** (*Fortunio*), **Monpou** (songs), **Moór** (*Pompadour*), **Nottara** (*On ne badine pas avec l'amour*), **Pierné** (do.), **Poise** (*Carmosine*).

Mussorgsky, Modest Petrovitch (b. Karevo, Gvt. of Pskov, 21. III. 1839; d. St. Petersburg, 28. III. 1881), Rus. comp. The son of well-to-do landowners, he was sent to St. Petersburg at the age of 10 to prepare for a military school, which he entered in 1851. He joined a regiment in 1856 and often entertained his comrades by singing and pf. playing; but he did not seriously think of a mus. career until he met Dargomizhsky and Balakirev in 1857 and began to study under the latter. He resigned his commission in 1858, but not caring to study systematically, he remained an amateur and forged a technique of his own. His family's fortune waned after the liberation of the serfs in 1861, but he was in sympathy with that movement and content to live on the small pay he obtained for a gvt. employment. His interest in the common people led him to write realistic songs following the inflections of their speech, and he endeavoured to do the same with his operatic characters. He finished *Boris Godunov* in its 1st form in 1869, but it was rejected by the Imp. Opera and he recast it in 1871–2, this 2nd version being prod. in 1874; but few people even among his set, except Stassov, understood it. He sank more and more into poverty and ruined his health with drink. He earned a little money by accomp. at the singing-school of Daria Leonova and he went on a tour with her, but he grew steadily worse and d. in hospital from a spinal disease.

Works incl. operas *Salammbô* (after Flaubert, unfinished), *The Marriage* (Gogol, unfinished), *Boris Godunov* (after Pushkin), *Khovanshtchina*, *Sorochintsy Fair* (after Gogol, unfinished); an act for a collective opera, *Mlada* (with Borodin, Cui and Rimsky-Korsakov, afterwards used for other works); incid. m. for Ozerov's *Oedipus Rex*; *The Destruction of Sennacherib* (after Byron) and *Jesus Navin* for chor. & orch.; 4 Rus. folksongs for male chor.; *Night on the Bare Mountain* for orch. (orig. with chor., from *Mlada*) and 3 small orch. pieces; suite *Pictures at an Exhibition* and 12 small pieces for pf.; over 60 songs incl. cycles *The Nursery*, *Sunless* & *Songs and Dances of Death*, &c.

Mustafà, Domenico (b. Fellano nr. Spoleto, 14. IV. 1829; d. Montefalco nr. Perugia, 18. III. 1912), It. male sop. singer & comp. He was the last male sop. of the Sistine Chapel, which he entered in 1848. He was later chapel master there in 1902, when he was succeeded by Lorenzo Perosi.

Works incl. Miserere, *Tu es Petrus*, *Dies irae* for 7 voices, *Laudate* & other church m.

Mustel Organ. An inst. invented by Victor Mustel (1815–90) of Paris. It is of the Harmonium type, but contains some improvements, incl. a device by which the top and bottom halves of the range of pipes can be separately controlled for dynamic expression.

Muta (It. imper. = change). A direction used in scores where a change is to be made between insts. (e.g. A and B♭

cl. or different hn. crooks) or in tunings (e.g. kettledrums, stgs. of insts. of the v. family temporarily tuned to abnormal notes), &c. The plur. is *mutano*.

Mutation. *See* **Gamut.**

Mutation Stops. A range of org. stops sounding notes either a 12th or a 17th above those of the key pressed down. They are not played alone, but only with other stops which sound their own proper notes, and they fulfil, together with those normal keys, the function of Mixture Stops.

Mute. The name of var. devices of different kinds but all serving to damp the tone of an inst. The 'soft pedal' of the pf. is a M., but is never so called. Ms. of stg. insts. are a kind of fork whose prongs are made to grip the bridge and lessen its vibration, and with it the vibration of the stgs. Brass wind insts. have cone-shaped Ms. inserted into the bell. Drums can be muted without any special mechanical device, merely by a cloth spread over the head.

Müthel, Johann Gottfried (b. Mölln, Lauenburg, 17. I. 1718; d. Riga, 17. I. 1788), Ger. orgst., hpchdst. & comp. Pupil of Kuntzen at Lübeck, became chamber musn. and court orgst. at Schwerin in 1738. Went to Leipzig in 1750 to study under Bach, but being in time only to be present at his deathbed, went to Altnikol at Naumburg. Orgst. at the Lutheran church at Riga from 1753 to his death.

Works incl. concs. for hpchd.; sos., ariosi with vars. &c. for hpchd.; Duetto for 2 claviers, &c.

Muzio, Claudia (b. Pavia, 1892; d. Rome, 24. V. 1936), It. sop. singer. Studied pf. & hp. at first, but her teachers discovered great voc. gifts, and she made her 1st stage appearance at Arezzo in 1912. Soon afterwards she 1st visited London and in 1916 N.Y.

Muzio Scevola, Il (*Mutius Scaevola*), opera by Filippo Mattei (or Amadei), Giovanni Bononcini and Handel (lib. by Paolo Antonio Rolli), prod. London, King's Theatre, Haymarket, 15. IV. 1721.

Mvt. (abbr.) = Movement.

My Country (Smetana). *See* **Má Vlast.**

Mysliveček, Josef (b. Prague, 9. III. 1737; d. Rome, 4. II. 1781), Boh. comp. His father, a miller, gave him a good educ. and he devoted himself to m. after his father's death. He travelled much in search of instruction and success, and studied with Pescetti at Venice in the 1760s, prod. his 1st opera at Naples in 1767. After that he was very successful as an opera comp., mainly at Milan, Venice and Naples, and the Its. called him *Il divino Boemo*. He also prod. works at Munich, where Mozart, who already knew him at Bologna in 1772, met him again in 1777. Catterina Gabrielli made a speciality of his arias.

Works incl. operas *Il Bellerofonte*, *Motezuma*, *Ezio*, *L'Olimpiade*, *Armida* & c. 15 others; orat. *Abramo ed Isacco* & 3 others; syms.; concs.; sos.; arias, &c.

Mystic Chord. A harmonic invention by Skriabin about half-way through his career, when he began to use this chord as a tonic basis instead of the maj. or min. triad. It consists of a series derived from 6 of the natural harmonics, arranged in 4ths in the following order beginning at the bottom: 2nd, 11th, 7th, 5th, 13th, 9th. Thus, if the fundamental note from which these upper partials are selected is C below the stave in the bass clef, Skriabin's chord consists of the C an octave higher with the following notes rising in 4ths above it: F♯, B♭, E, A, D.

(Mark reference p. 344)

Madrigal Opera. *See also* **Amfiparnaso.** A kind of grouping of a succession of madrigals in a quasi-dramatic form, said to be a 16th-cent. forerunner of opera in It. and long supposed to have been perf. in dumb-show while the madrigals were sung behind the scenes, a view no longer held by mcolsts. The most famous but not the earliest ex. is Orazio Vecchi's *L'Amfiparnaso*, and similar works of his are *La selva di varie ricreazioni* (*The Forest of Multifarious Delights*), *Il convito musicale* (*The Musical Banquet*) and *Le veglie di Siena* (*The Vigils of S.*). A similar work, Simone Balsamino's *Novellette*, based on Tasso's *Aminta*, appeared the same year as *L'Amfiparnaso* (1594), but there were earlier ones, notably Striggio's *Il cicalamento delle donne al bucato* (*The Cackling of Women at the Wash*), and later Vecchi was imitated by Banchieri and others.

(Mark reference p. 360)

Matthay, Tobias (b. London, 19. II. 1858; d. Haslemere, Surrey, 14. XII. 1945), Eng. pfst., teacher & comp. of Ger. descent. Studied at the R.A.M. in London, where he became sub-prof. in 1876 and full prof. of pf. in 1880, remaining until 1925, although he had opened his own school of pf. playing in 1900. In 1893 he married Jessie Kennedy, daughter of David K. and sister of Marjorie K.-Fraser. He wrote several books on his own method of pf. playing and comp. much pf. m., mainly of educ. value.

(Mark reference p. 384)

Morillo, Roberto Garcia (b. Buenos Aires, 22. I. 1911), Arg. comp. Studied at home with Aguirre, J. J. Castro and others, also in Paris in 1927–9. On his return he devoted himself to comp. and criticism.

Works incl. ballet *Harrild*; Poem for orch.; pf. Conc. and ovt. *Bersarks* for pf. & small orch.; suite *Las pinturas negras de Goya* for pf., v., co., fl., cl. & bn., 4tet for v., cl., co. & pf.; suite *Conjuros* & other pf. works, &c.

N

N.Y. (abbr.) = New York.

Nabokov, Nikolai (b. St. Petersburg, 17. IV. 1903), Rus. comp. Studied in Berlin and Stuttgart. He became attached to Diaghilev's Rus. Ballet in the 1920s. and later he settled in U.S.A.

Works incl. ballets *Ode on seeing the Aurora Borealis* & *Union Pacific*; incid. m. to a dramatic version of Milton's *Samson Agonistes*; Sym., *Sinfonia biblica* for orch.; pf. Conc.; cantata *Collectionneur d'échos* for sop., bass, chor. & perc., &c.

Nabucco. *See* below.

Nabucodonosor (*Nebuchadnezzar*: colloquially *Nabucco*), opera by Verdi (lib. by Temistocle Solera), prod. Milan, Teatro alla Scala, 9. III. 1842.

Nacchera (It. = naker[s]). A kettledrum. *Nacchere* are esp. the military drums used on horseback, the orch. ones being more commonly called *timpani*.

Naccherone (It., as above, with augment. suffix). A kettledrum of unusually large size.

Nachbaur, Franz (b. Giessen nr. Friedrichshafen, 25. III. 1835; d. Munich, 21. III. 1902), Ger. ten. singer. Studied with Lamperti at Milan and others, sang at var. Ger. opera houses and became attached to the Munich Court opera in 1866, creating the part of Walther in Wagner's *Meistersinger* there in 1868.

Nachez, Tivadar (b. Budapest, 1. V. 1859; d. Lausanne, 29. V. 1930), Hung. vst. Studied at Budapest, with Joachim in Berlin and with Léonard in Paris, where he settled, living in London from 1889. Ed. much v. m. and wrote a v. Conc., a stg. 4tet & v. pieces.

Nachschlag (Ger.). *See* **Ornaments.**

Nachspiel (Ger. = afterpiece). *See* **Postlude.**

Nacht in Venedig, Eine (*A Night in Venice*), operetta by J. Strauss, jun. (lib. by F. Zell & Richard Genée), prod. Berlin, Friedrich-Wilhelmstädtisches Theater, 3. X. 1883. Written for the opening of that theatre. 1st Vienna perf. Theater an der Wien, 9. X. 1883.

Nachtanz (*see also* **Proporz**; Ger. lit. after-dance). The quicker dance following a slower one, often with the same m. in different rhythm in the 15th–16th cents., esp. the Galliard following the Pavan.

Nachtgall, Othmar. *See* **Luscinius.**

Nachtlager von Granada, Das (*The Night-Camp at Granada*), opera by C. Kreutzer (lib. by Karl Johann Braun von Braunthal, based on a play by Friedrich Kind), prod. Vienna, Josefstadt Theatre, 13. I. 1834.

Nachtmusik (Ger. = night m.). A serenade. Mozart's *Eine kleine Nachtmusik* is simply *A little Serenade.*

Naderman, François Joseph (b. Paris, c. 1773; d. Paris, 2. IV. 1835), Fr. hpst. & comp. Son of a hp. maker, he became hpst. at the Paris Opéra and in the royal chapel, also hp. prof. at the Cons. from 1825.

Works incl. hp. concs.; chamber m. with hp. parts; hp. solos; also, with Duport, Nocturnes for co. & hp.

Nadeshda, opera by G. Thomas (lib. by Julian Russell Sturgis), prod. London, Drury Lane Theatre, 16. IV. 1885.

Naenia (Lat.). A funeral dirge. There is an ode by Schiller (*Nänie*) set to m. as a cantata for chor. & orch. by Brahms, Op. 82, and by Goetz, Op. 10.

Nagel, Wilibald (b. Mühlheim o/Ruhr, 12. I. 1863; d. Stuttgart, 17. X. 1929), Ger. mcolst. Studied in Berlin, taught mus. hist. at Zürich and settled for a time in Eng. to collect materials for a 2-vol. hist. of Eng. m. and annals of Eng. court m., both written in Ger. He returned to Ger. in 1896. He also wrote a study of Beethoven's pf. scs. & other works.

Nägeli, Hans Georg (b. Wetzikon nr. Zürich, 26. V. 1773; d. Zürich, 26. XII. 1836), Swi. comp., teacher, author & m. pub. Studied at Zürich and Berne and began to pub. m. at Zürich in 1792. In 1803 he began a series entitled *Répertoire des clavecinistes* and incl. in it Beethoven's Sos. Op. 31 Nos. 1 & 2, adding 4 bars to the former, much to the comp.'s annoyance. He estab. the *Schweizerbund* chor. soc., which soon formed branches, and reformed m. teaching in schools on the lines of Pestalozzi's educ. system. He also wrote on mus. educ. and lectured on m. in Swi. & Ger.

Works incl. church & school m.; toccatas & other pf. pieces; 15 books of pop. songs, incl. 'Freut euch des Lebens' & 'Lied vom Rhein,' &c.

Naich, Hubert (b. ?; d. ?), Flem. 16th-cent. comp. Lived in Rome, where he was a member of the Accademia degli Amici and pub. a book of madrigals there *c.* 1540.

Nail Violin. An 18th-cent. inst. also called N. Fiddle or N. Harmonica, invented by a Ger. vst. Johann Wilde, living at St. Petersburg. It was a semicircular sound-board studded with nails along the rounded edge, whic hwere scraped with a bow.

Nairne (*née* **Oliphant), Carolina,** Lady (1766–1845), Sco. poetess. *See* **Gow** (4) (*Caller Herrin'*).

Nakers (from Arabic through old Fr. *nacaires*). An old Eng. name for the Kettledrums, which were then much smaller and therefore higher in pitch, and could not have their tuning altered. In cavalry regiments they were played on horseback, hung on each side of the horse's neck.

Nakhabin, Vladimir Nikolaievitch (b. Kharkov, 1910), Rus. comp. Studied under Bogatirev at Kharkov.

Works incl. ballet *The Burgess of Tuscany* (after Boccaccio); *Dnieprostrov* for chor. & orch.; Sym., tone-poems *Lenin's Death* & *The Factory*, suite *Springtime* for orch., &c.

Naldi, Giuseppe (b. Bologna, 2. II. 1770; d. Paris, 15. XII. 1820), It. bar. singer. Studied law at Bologna and Pavia Univs., but turned to m. and made his 1st stage appearance at Milan at an early age. He sang in London each year in 1806–19.

Namouna, ballet by Lalo (scen. by Charles Nuitter; chgph. by Lucien Petipa), prod. Paris, Opéra, 6. III. 1882.

Nanini, Giovanni Bernardino (b. Vallerano, *c.* 1560; d. Rome, 1623), It. comp. Studied under his brother, went to Rome, and in 1599 became chapel master at the church of San Luigi de' Francesi there, later at that of San Lorenzo in Damaso.

Works incl. motets, psalms & other church m., some with org. accomp.; madrigals, &c.

Nanini, Giovanni Maria (b. Tivoli, *c.* 1545; d. Rome, 11. III. 1607), It. ten. singer & comp., brother of prec. After learning m. as a choir-boy at Vallerano, he went to Rome as a pupil of Mel, became a singer at the church of Santa Maria Maggiore, chapel master at the church of San Luigi de' Francesi in 1575, singer in the Papal Chapel, 1577, and chapel master at Santa Maria Maggiore, 1579. He opened a m. school with the assistance of his brother and Palestrina, supplied m. to the Sistine Chapel and became chapel master there in 1604.

Works incl. motets (e.g. 2 for Christmas, *Hodie nobis caelorum rex* & *Hodie Christus natus est*), psalms & other church m.; madrigals, canzonets, &c.

Nantier-Didiée, Constance (Betsy Rosabella) (b. Saint-Denis, Île de Bourbon [Réunion], 16. XI. 1831; d. Madrid, 4. XII. 1867), Fr. sop. singer. Studied with Duprez at the Paris Cons. and made her 1st stage appearance at Turin, and in Paris in 1851. Married a singer named Didiée and 1st visited London in 1853.

Napolitana. A light song for several voices, allied to the *Villanella* and cultivated at Naples esp. in the 16th and 17th cents.

Nápravnik, Eduard Franzevitch (b. Beišt nr. Hradeckrálove, 24. VIII. 1839; d. Leningrad, 23. XI. 1916), Cz. cond. & comp. Studied m. precariously as a child, being the son of a poor teacher, and was left an orphan and destitute in 1854, but succeeded in entering the Org. School in Prague, where he studied with Kittel and others, and became an asst. teacher. In 1861 he went to St. Petersburg as cond. of Prince Yussipov's private orch., became orgst. and asst. cond. at the imp. theatres in 1863, 2nd cond. in 1867 and chief cond., succeeding Liadov, in 1869, holding the post until his death. He also cond. concerts of the Rus. Mus. Soc.

Works incl. operas *The Nizhni-Novgorodians, Harold, Dubrovsky* & *Francesca da Rimini* (on Stephen Phillips's play); incid. m. for Alexei Tolstoy's *Don Juan*; ballads for voices & orch. *The Voyevode, The Cossack* & *Tamara* (after Lermontov); 4 syms., symph. poems *The Demon* (after Lermontov) & *The East*, Suite, *Solemn Ovt.*, marches & nat. dances for orch; Conc. & Fantasy on Rus. themes for pf. & orch., Fantasy & Suite for v. & orch.; 3 stg. 4tets, stg. 5tet, 2 pf. trios, pf. 4tet; v. & pf. So., 2 suites for co. & pf.; stg. inst. & pf. pieces, &c.

Narciso, Il (*Narcissus*), opera by D. Scarlatti (lib. by Apostolo Zeno), prod. Rome, private theatre of Queen Maria Casimira of Pol., Carnival 1714. Perf. in London, 31. V. 1720, with add. m. by T. Roseingrave.

Nardini, Pietro (b. Leghorn, 12. IV. 1722; d. Florence, 7. V. 1793), It. vst. & comp. Studied at Leghorn and later with Tartini at Padua. Solo vst. at the ducal court of Württemberg at Stuttgart, 1752–67, when he settled at Leghorn and in 1770 at Florence as mus. dir. to the ducal court of Tuscany.

Works incl. 6 v. concs.; 6 stg. 4tets; sos. for v., 2 vs., solo & duets for vs.; trios for fl., v. & bass, &c.

Nares, James (b. Stanwell, Mdx., IV. 1715; d. London, 10. II. 1783), Eng. orgst. & comp. Studied with Gates, Croft and Pepusch as a chorister at the Chapel Royal in London, became deputy orgst. at St. George's Chapel, Windsor, and in 1734 was app. orgst. of York Minster. D.Mus. Cambridge, 1756, in which year he returned to the Chapel Royal as orgst. & comp., becoming Master of the Children in succession to Gates, 1757. He pub. treatises on singing and on hpchd. & org. playing.

Works incl. services & anthems; dramatic ode *The Royal Pastoral*; catches, glees & canons; hpchd. lessons; org. fugues, &c.

Narvaez, Luis de (b. ? Granada, ?; d. ?), Spa. 16th-cent. lutenist & comp. Wrote lute pieces, motets, &c.

Nascimbeni, Maria Francesca (b. ?; d. ?), It. 17th-cent. comp. She was a pupil of Scipione Lazarini. Comp. motets, madrigals, canzoni, &c.

Nascimbeni, Stefano (also known as Nasimbeni) (b. Mantua, ?; d. ?), It. 17th-cent. comp. Wrote masses, psalms, *Concerti ecclesiastici*, songs, &c.

Nasco, Giovanni (b. ?; d. ?, before 1560), It. comp. He was master of a mus. acad. at Verona in the 1540s and chapel master at Treviso cath. in the 1550s. Comp. lamentations, madrigals, canzoni, &c.

Nash, Thomas (1567–1601), Eng. poet & satirist. *See* **Dieren (van)** (songs), **Lambert (C.)** (*Summer's Last Will*).

Nasimbeni. *See* **Nascimbeni, Stefano.**

Nasolini, Sebastiano (b. Piacenza, *c.* 1768; d. ? Venice, before 1806), It. hpchdst. & comp. Studied at the Cons. dei Mendicanti at Venice, was cembalist at the San Pietro theatre at Trieste and chapel master at the cath. there in 1787–90, after which time he seems to have lived entirely on his operatic successes.

Works incl. operas *Nitteti, Andromaca, La morte di Cleopatra, Eugenia, Le feste d'Iside, Merope, La morte di Mitridate, Il medico di Lucca, Gli umori contrari, Il ritorno di Serse* & *c.* 20 others, &c.

Nat. (abbr.) = National.

Nathan, Isaac (b. Canterbury, 1790; d. Sydney, 15. I. 1864), Eng. singer & comp. Studied Hebrew &c. at Cambridge, being intended for a Jewish relig. career, but turned to m., studying with D. Corri in London and appearing as a singer at Covent Garden Theatre. He made friends with Byron and in 1841 went to Austral., settling at Sydney as a singing-master.

Works incl. stage pieces with m. *Sweethearts and Wives, The Alcaid, The Illustrious Stranger, Merry Freaks in Troublous Times*; *Hebrew Melodies* & other songs to words by Byron, &c.

National Anthems. The following are the titles (if any), 1st lines (in the orig. language), with names of the author of the words (W.) and comps. of the tunes (T.) and dates, where known, of the N.As. of var. countries:

Abyssinia: 'Etiopia hoy, des yibalish'; (W.) by a group of Abyssinian scholars, 1930; (T.) M. K. Nalbandian, 1925.

Albania: 'Alla bandiera' (W.) ?; (T.) E. A. Mario (Giovanni Gaeta), 1937.

Argentine: 'Oid, mortales, el grito sagrado Libertad'; (W.) Vicente López y Planes, 1813; (T.) José Blas Parera, revised by Juan P. Esnaola.

Armenia: (W.) Sarmen; (T.) Khatchaturian, 1945.

Australia: 'Advance, Australia fair'; (W. & T.) Peter Dodd McCormick, before 1916 (broadcast, but not actually adopted as a N. A.).

Austria (imp.): 'Gott erhalte Franz den (or unsern) Kaiser'; (W.) Leopold Haschka; (T.) Haydn, 1797.

— (repub.): *Oesterreichische Bundeshymne*, 'Sei gesegnet ohne Ende'; (W. & T.) do.

— (do. 1920–9): 'Deutsch-Oesterreich, du herrliches Land, wir lieben dich'; (W.) Karl Renner; (T.) Kienzl, 1920.

— (Nazi): *Lied der Jugend*, 'Ihr Jungen schliesst die Reihen gut'; (W. & T.) Hermann Leopoldi, *c.* 1933.

Bavaria: 'Bayern, mein Heimatland'; (W.) F. Beck; (T.) F. Lachner, 1848; also 'Gott mit dir, du Land der Bayern'; (W.) Michael Öchsner; (T.) F. M. Kunz.

Belgian Congo. *See* Congo.

Belgium: *La Brabançonne*, 'Qui l'aurait dit de l'arbitraire'; (W.) Jenneval, 1830; (T.) François van Campenhout, 1830 (real name, Louis Alexandre Hippolyte Dechez).

— (Flem.); *De Vlaamsche Leeuw*; (W.) H. van Peene; (T.) Karel Miry.

Bolivia: 'Bolivianos, el hado propicio'; (W.) Ignacio de Sanjinés; (T.) Benedetto Vincenti.

Brazil: 'Ouviram do Ypiranga as margens placidas'; (W.) Joaquin Osorio Duque Estrada; (T.) Francisco Manoel da Silva.

— (earlier): 'Seja um pallio luz'; (W.) M. Albuquerque; (T.) Léopold Miguez.

Bulgaria; *Shoumi Maritza*; (W.) Mereček; (T.) Gabriel Šebek.

Canada: *The Maple Leaf for ever*, 'In days of yore, from Britain's shore'; (W. & T.) Alexander Muir, 1867.

— (Fr.): 'O Canada: Terre de nos aïeux'; (W.) Adolphe Basile Routhier, 1880; (T.) C. Lavallée (adapted from the priests' march in Mozart's *Magic Flute*).

Chile; *Dulce patria*, 'Ha cesado la lucha sangrienta'; (W.) Eusebio Lillo, 1847; (T.) Carnicer, 1828.

China: 'Tsung-kuoh hiung li jüh dschou tiän'; (W. & T.) unknown, 1912.

— (democratic): *The Song of Kuomintang*; (W.) Sun Yat-Sen; (T.) Ch'eng Mao-Yün, 1928.

Colombia: *Oh! Gloria inmarcesible*, 'Cesó la horrible noche'; (W.) Rafael Núnez; (T.) Orestes Sindici, *c.* 1905.

Congo (Belg.): *Vers l'avenir*: *Naar wijden zijd*, 'Le siècle marche': 'De tijd spoedt heen'; (W.) Gentil Théodore Antheunis; (T.) Gevaert, 1908.

Costa Rica: 'Noble patria, tu hermosa bandera'; (W.) José Maria Zeledón; (T.) Manuel Maria Gutiérrez, 1821, in use from 1853.

Cuba: *Himno Bayamés*, 'Al combate corred bayameses'; (W. & T.) Pedro Figueredo, 1868.

Czechoslovakia: Combination of 'Kde domov muj'; (W.) Josef Kajetán Tyl; (T.) Škroup, 1834, and 'Nad Tatrou sa blyska'; (W.) Janko Matúska, 1844; (T.) traditional; 1st officially used 1919.

Denmark: 'Kong Kristian stod ved højen mast'; (W.) Johannes Ewald; (T.) J. E. Hartmann (from opera *Fiskerne*), 1780; also 'Der er et yndigt land'; (W.) Adam Oehlenschläger; (T.) H. E. Krøyer, 20th cent., and 'Dengang jog drog afsted'; (W.) F. Faber; (T.) J. O. E. Horneman, 20th cent.

Dominican Republic: 'Quisqueyanos valientes, alcemos'; (W.) Emilio Prud'homme; (T.) José Reyes, 1900.

Ecuador: *Salve! Oh patria, mil veces*, 'Indignados tus hijos del yugo'; (W.) Juan Léon Mera; (T.) Antonio Neumann, 1866.

Egypt: March, 'Ha ni an bé au da to samil ma kam'; (W.) ?; (T.) ? Verdi.

Eire: 'Let Erin remember the days of old'; (W.) Thomas Moore; (T.) traditional, *The Red Fox*.

England. *See* Great Britain.

Esthonia: 'Mu isamaa, mu önn ja röön'; (W.) J. Jannsen, 1865; (T.) Pacius, 1848.

Finland: *Maamme*, 'Oi maamme suomi synnyiumaa'; (W.) J. L. Runeberg (orig. in Swe.), 1843; (T.) Pacius, as for Esthonia. A 2nd tune by Pacius was also adopted.

France: *La Marseillaise*, 'Allons, enfants de la patrie' (W. & T.) Rouget de Lisle, 1792.

Germany (imp.): 'Heil dir im Siegerkranz'; (W.) Heinrich Harries, 1790, adapted by B. G. Schumacher, 1793; (T.) as for Great Britain; also, after 1870, *Die Wacht am Rhein*, 'Es braust ein Ruf wie Donnerschall'; (W.) M. Schneckenburger, 1840; (T.) Carl Wilhelm, 1854.

— (repub.): 'Deutschland, Deutschland über alles'; (W.) H. A. Hoffmann von Fallersleben, 1841; (T.) Haydn, as for Aus.

— (Nazi): *Horst Wessel Lied*, 'Die Fahne hoch, die Reihen dicht geschlossen'; (W.) Horst Wessel; (T.) ? Boh. comic song; in use 1933–45.

Great Britain: 'God save the King'; (W. & T.) unknown, 1744–5.

Greece: 'Se gnorizo apo ten kopsi tu spatjiu ten tromere'; (W.) Dionysius Solomos, 1824; (T.) N. Mántzarios; in use since 1873.

Guatemala: 'Guatemala feliz!'; (W.) J. Joachin Palma; (T.) Rafael Alvarez, in use from 1896.

Haiti: *La Dessalinène*, 'Pour le pays, pour les ancêtres'; (W.) Justin Lhérisson; (T.) Nicolas Geffard, 1903.

Hawaii: 'Hawaii ponoi'; (W. & T.) ? Kalakana, king of H., *c.* 1880.

Holkar's Dominions. *See* Indore.

Holland: 'Wilhelmus van Nassouwe'; (W.) Philip van Marnix, *c.* 1570; (T.) unknown, 1st pub. 1626; also 'Wien Neerlandsch bloed door de aderen vloeit'; (W.) Hendrik Tollens; (T.) Jan Wilms, 1820.

Honduras: 'Compatriotas, de Honduras los fueros'; (W.) Augusto C. Coello; (T.) Carlos Hartling.

Hungary: *Himnusz*, 'Ysten áldd meg a Magyart'; (W.) Kölcsey, 1823; (T.) Erkel, 1845; usually followed by *Szózat*, 'Hazádnak rendületlenül légy hive óh magyar'; (W.) Michael Vörösmarty, 1836; (T.) Benjamin Egressy, 1844.

Iceland: 'O Gud vors land'; (W.) Mathias Jochumsen, 1874; (T.) Sveinbjørn Sveinbjørnsson.

Indore: 'Prabho prarth ana parisa amuchi'; (W.) ?; (T.) Jad.

Iran: 'Shāhanshān—a mā Zandah bādā'; (W.) S. Afsar; (T.) Najmi Moghaddam, *c.* 1934.

Iraq: Royal Salute (march); (W.) none; (T.) A. R. Murray.

Ireland. *See* Eire.

Italy: *La marcia reale*; (W.) none; (T.) Giuseppe Gabetti, 1831; sung in southern It.: *Inno di Garibaldi*, 'All' armi, all' armi, si scopron le tombe'; (W.) L. Mercantini; (T.) A. Olivieri, 1858.

— (Fascist): *La Giovinezza*, 'Sù, compagni in forti schiere'; (W.) Marcello Manni; (T.) G. Castaldo after Giuseppe Blanc, 1921.

Japan: *Kimagayo*; (W.) 9th cent.; (T.) Hayashi Hirokami, revised by F. Eckert, 1880.

Jewish. *See* Palestine.

Jugoslavia. *See* Yugoslavia.

Latvia: 'Dievs, sveti Latviju'; (W. & T.) Karlis Baumanis.

Liberia: 'Salve, Liberia, salve!'; (W.) President Warner; (T.) Olmstead Luca, 1860.

Lichtenstein: 'Oben am deutschen Rhein lehnet sich Lichtenstein'; (W.) H. H. Jauch, 1850; (T.) as for Great Britain.

Lithuania: 'Lietuva, tévyné mūsu'; (W. & T.) Vincas Kudirka, 1918.

Luxemburg: *Ons Hémecht*, 'Wò d'Uolzécht duréch d'Wisen zēt'; (W.) Michel Lentz, 1859; (T.) J. A. Zinnen.

Malta: *Tifhira lil Mâlta*, 'Int sabīha, Mâlta tâna'; (W.) Giovanni Antonio Vassalla; (T.) Bersaglieri song adapted, 20th cent. After 1942: 'Lil din l'art Helwa'; (W.) C. Psaila; (T.) R. Samut.

Mexico: 'Mexicanos, al grito guerra'; (W.) Francisco Gonzáles Bocanegra; (T.) Jaime Nunó, 1854.

Montenegro: (W.) John Soundechitch; (T.) ?; also 'Onam', onamo! za brda ona'; (W.) King Nikola, 1867; (T.) Davorin Jenko.

New Zealand: 'God defend New Zealand'; (W.) Thomas Bracken; (T.) R. A. Horne, not consistently used until 1940.

Newfoundland: 'When sun rays crown thy pine-clad hills'; (W.) Sir Chas. Cavendish Boyle; (T.) Hubert Parry. (This does not displace 'God save the King.')

Nicaragua: 'Hermosa soberana'; (W.) Blas Villatas; (T.) A. Cousin; after 1917 (W.) Salomón Ibarra Mayorga; (T.) unknown.

Norway: 'Ja, vi elsker dette landet'; (W.) Bjørnson; (T.) Nordraak, 1859.

Orange Free State: 'Heft, Burgers, 't lied der vrijheid aan'; (W. & T.) Hamelberg.

Palestine: *Hatikvoh* (*Hope*), 'While even yet unchanged'; (W.) Hebrew: N. H. Imber; Eng.: Nina Salaman; (T.) ?, 1936.

Panama: 'Alcanzamos por fin la victoria'; (W.) Gerónimo de la Osa; (T.) Santos Jorge, 1903.

Paraguay: 'Paraguayos, Republica ó muerte:'; (W.) Francisco Acuna de Figueroa; (T.) Francés Dupey.

Persia. *See* Iran.

Peru: 'Somos libres, seámos lo siempre'; (W.) José de la Torre Ugarte; (T.) José Bernardo Alcedo, 1821.

Philippine Islands: 'Tierra adorata (*Marcha nacional filipina*); (W.) José Palma; (T.) Julian Felipe, *c.* 1898.

Poland: 'Jeszcze Polska nie zgineta'; (W.) Josef Wybicki; (T.) ? Kleofas Oginski, 1795.

Portugal (royal): 'O patria, O rei, O povo'; (W. & T.) Pedro I of Brazil, formerly Pedro IV of Port., 1822.

— (repub.): 'Heiros do mar'; (W.) Lopez de Mendoça 1890; (T.) Alfredo Keil; used since 1910.

Prussia: 'Borussia'; (W.) G. R. Duncker; (M.) Spontini, 1818; also 'Ich bin ein Preusse'; (W.) Bernhard Thiersch; (T.) A. H. Neithardt, 1826.

Rumania: 'Trăeasca Regele in pace si onor'; (W.) V. Alexandri; (T.) E. A. Hübsch, 1861.

Russia (imp.): 'Bozhe Tsarya khrani'; (W.) W. A. Zhukovsky, 1833; (T.) Lvov, 1833.

— (Soviet to 1944): *L'Internationale*, 'Debout, les damnés de la terre'; (W.) Eugène Pottier (trans. into Rus., last in 1932); (T.) Pierre Degeyter.

— (Soviet, after 1944): *Gymn Sovietskogo Soiusa*; (W.) Sergey Mikhalkov & I. Registan; (T.) A. V. Alexandrov, *c.* 1942.

Salvador: 'Saludemos la patria orgullosos'; (W.) Juan J. Cañas; (T.) Juan Aberte.

Scotland: 'Scots wha ha'e wi' Wallace bled'; (W.) Burns, 1793; (T.) traditional.

Serbia: *Srpska Himna*, 'Bože pravde, ti što spase'; (W.) J. Djordjewić; (T.) Davorin Jenko, 1872.

Siam: 'Taurasoen Barami'; (W. & T.) unknown.

South Africa (Union): 'Die Stem van Suid-Afrika'; (W.) unknown; (T.) M. L. Villiers.

Spain (royal): *Marcha real*; (W.) none; (T.) unknown Ger. comp., 1770; also *Hymno de Riego*; (W.) unknown; (T.) Herta.

— (repub.): *Marcha grandera*, adapted, and Ger. Nazi & It. Fascist songs also used.

Sweden: 'Du gamla, du fria, du fjällhöga Nord'; (W.) R. Dybeck; (T.) traditional, 1844.

Switzerland: 'Rufst du, mein Vaterland'; (W.) J. H. Wyss, 1811, with Fr. & It. transs.; (T.) as for Great Britain; also *Schweizerpsalm*, 'Trittst im Morgenrot daher'; (W.) L. Widmer; (T.) Josef (Father Alberik) Zwyssig, 1841.

Transvaal: 'Kentgij dat volk vol heldenmoed'; (W. & T.) Catherine Félicie van Rees.

Tunisia: *Marche beylicale*; (W.) none; (T.) by an It. comp., 1881–3, adapted by Sidi-Sadock.

Turkey: *Istiklal marsi* (March of Independence); (W.) none; (T.) Vittorio Radaglia, 1921.

U.S.A.: *The Star-spangled Banner*, 'Oh, say, can you see, by the dawn's early light'; (W.) Francis Scott Key,

1814; (T.) John Stafford Smith; officially adopted 1931; earlier 'Hail Columbia'; (W.) J. Hopkinson; (T.) Fyls, *c.* 1800.

Uruguay: 'Orientales, la patria ó la tumba!'; (W. & T.) Juan Coppetti.

Venezuela: 'Gloria al bravo pueblo'; (W.) Vicente Salias; (T.) Juan Landaeta, after 1810.

Wales: 'Mae hen wlad fy nhadan' ('Land of my fathers'); (W.) Evan James, Eng. John Owen; (T.) J. James.

Westphalia: 'Ihr mögt den Rhein, den stolzen, preisen'; (W.) ?; (T.) Johann Peters.

Württemberg: 'Preisend mit viel schönen Reden'; (W.) J. Kerner, 1826; (T.) Traditional.

Yugoslavia: A compound of the Serbian hymn 'Bože pravde' (*see* Serbia), the Croatian hymn 'Lijepa naša domovino'; (W.) Antun Mihanoic; (T.) Lichtenegger, and the Slovene hymn 'Naprej zastava Slav'; (W.) Simon Jenko; (T.) Davorin Jenko.

Zanzibar: An unidentifiable tune.

National Composers. For refs. to comps. of var. countries *see* **Argentine, Austalian, Belgian,** &c. (No such refs. are given, however, for the larger schools, i.e. Aus., Eng., Fr., Ger., It., Rus., Spa. & U.S.A.)

Nationalism. In m. N. manifests itself through the endeavour of individual comps. or schools to find some sort of mus. idiom that may be said to express their countries' characteristics, either idiomatically or spiritually. Idiomatic expression of this kind is most usually and easily attained through the adoption, imitation or adaptation of folksong and nat. dances, which however may become more or less strongly coloured by each comp.'s individuality and will certainly be much elaborated in the process of sustained comp. (e.g. Smetana in Cz., Grieg in Norw., Balakirev in Rus., Falla in Spa., Bartók in Hung., &c.). The reflection of a country's spirit in m. is less definite, more subtle and not so easily perceptible, but there is no doubt that certain comps. have achieved this without consciously resorting to folk m.; and those who sometimes do so may remain just as strongly nat. when they happen to refrain (e.g. Tchaikovsky & Mussorgsky in Rus. [in different ways], Elgar in Eng., Fauré & Ravel in Fr., Sibelius in Fin., &c.).

Natural. The sign ♮, which restores to its normal position a note previously raised by a ♯ or lowered by a ♭.

Naturale (It. = natural). A direction indicating that a voice or inst., after perf. a passage in some unusual way (*mezza voce*, muted, &c.), is to return to its normal manner).

Naumann, Johann Gottlieb (b. Blasewitz nr. Dresden, 17. IV. 1741; d. Dresden, 23. X. 1801), Ger. comp. Was educ. at Dresden to become a schoolmaster, but studied m. assiduously and at the age of 14 was taken on a tour by a Swe., Weeström, 1st to Hamburg and then to It. There, badly treated by his patron, he freed himself at Padua, obtained free lessons from Tartini and help from an Eng. musn. named Hunt, and made the acquaintance of Hasse. In 1761 he went to Naples to study dramatic m. and soon afterwards to Bologna for lessons in ctpt. from Martini. At Venice he prod. his 1st opera, with more to follow in 1765–8, when he returned to It. after an app. as court comp. for church m. at Dresden. A 3rd visit followed in the early 1770s, whereupon he declined an invitation to the court of Frederick II of Prus. 2 long visits to Stockholm followed, where he prod. 3 operas in Swe., and 1 in Dan. for Copenhagen brought him an invitation to that court, which he declined, being rewarded for this by the Saxon court with the post of supreme mus. dir.

Works incl. operas *Achille in Sciro, La clemenza di Tito, Solimano, Le nozze disturbate, Armida, Ipermestra, Amphion, Cora och Alonzo, Gustaf Vasa* (all 3 in Swe.), *Orpheus og Euridice* (in Dan.), *Protesilao* (with Reichardt), *La dama soldato, Aci e Galatea* & others; 21 masses & other church m.; 13 orats., &c.

Navarraise, La (*The Girl of Navarre*), opera by Massenet (lib. by Jules Claretie & Henri Cain, based on the former's story *La Cigarette*) prod. London, Covent Garden Theatre, 20. VI. 1894.

Navarro, Juan (b. Seville, *c.* 1530; d. Palencia, 25. IX. 1580), Spa. comp. After the death of Morales in 1553 he competed unsuccessfully for the post of chapel master at Málaga cath., but he later obtained a similar post in Salamanca. He (?) visited Rome in 1590, where his nephew Fernando Navarro Salazar arr. for the pub. of some of his church m. After his death Passions and Lamentations in plainsong were pub. in Mex., but he probably never lived there.

Works incl. psalms, hymns, magnificats & other church m.; madrigals, &c.

Nave, La (*The Ship*), incid. m. by Pizzetti for Gabriele d'Annunzio's tragedy, prod. Rome, 11. I. 1908.

Opera by Montemezzi (lib. by Tito Ricordi, based on d'Annunzio), prod. Milan, Teatro alla Scala, 1. XI. 1918.

Navrátil, Karel (b. Prague, 24. IV. 1867; d. Prague, 23. XII. 1936), Cz. vts. & comp. Studied in Prague, theory under Guido Aller and v. under Ondříček.

Works incl. operas *Hermann* and *Salammbô* (after Flaubert); Mass in D maj., 2 Psalms for chor.; Sym. in G min., 5 symph. poems; v. Conc., pf. Conc.; stg. 4tet in D min., 2 pf. trios, 2 pf. 5tets; v. So., va. So.; pf. m.; songs, &c.

Naylor, Edward (Woodall) (b. Scarborough, 9. II. 1867; d. Cambridge, 7. V. 1934), Eng. orgst., mcolst. & comp. Studied at Cambridge and the R.C.M. in London, and after 2 orgst.'s apps. there he returned to Cambridge in 1897 to become orgst. at Emmanuel Coll., taking the Mus.D. degree at the Univ. He lectured and wrote on m., pub. a book on *Shakespeare and Music*.

Works incl. opera *The Angelus*; cantata *Arthur the King*; partsongs; pf. Trio in D maj., &c.

Neapolitan Sixth. In cadences in m. written in min. keys the harmony on the Subdominant, preceding progressions to the Dominant and Tonic, normally includes a maj. 6th, that 6th being the Supertonic of the scale, which is a maj. 2nd away from the Tonic. Thus in C min., for ex., the supertonic is D♮, making a maj. 6th over the subdominant of F. But by a kind of extra depression a min. key can be made even more 'minorish' if the supertonic over the subdominant root is flattened: in C min. the min. instead of maj. 6th over the subdominant thus becomes D♭, and such a min. 6th is, in that position in the scale, called a N. S.

Neate, Charles (b. London, 28. III. 1784; d. Brighton, 30. III. 1877), Eng. pfst. & cst. He became a pupil of Field, who learnt the co. with him under Wm. Sharp, and made his 1st public appearance at Covent Garden Theatre in 1800. He also studied comp. with Woelfl. In 1815 he spent 8 months in Vienna and made friends with Beethoven, and then 5 at Munich for ctpt. lessons with Winter. He taught and perf. for many years in London with much success and wrote m., mainly for pf.

Nebra, José de (b. ?; d. Madrid, 11. VII. 1768), Spa. orgst. & comp. He became orgst. at the Convent of the Descalzas Reales in Madrid and 2nd orgst. at the royal chapel in 1724. After the destruction of the library there in the fire of 24. XII. 1734, he and Literes were commissioned to replace the lost church m. and to restore what had survived. In 1751 he was made vice chapel master under Corselli, who neglected his duties for the comp. of It. operas, and by 1757 he had completely reorganized the court m. In 1758 he comp. a Requiem for 8 voices, fl. & stgs. for the funeral of Queen Barbara of Braganza, who had been D. Scarlatti's patroness.

Works incl. *c.* 20 operas; Requiem, Miserere, psalms & other church m.; villancico for 4 voices, &c.

Neckniz. *See* **Sommer, Hans.**

Nedbal, Oskar (b. Tábor, 26. III. 1874; d. Zagreb, 24. XII. 1930), Cz. cond., va. player and comp. Pupil of Dvořák, member of the Boh. Stg. 4tet and from 1896 cond. of the Cz. Phil. Soc. in Prague. From 1906 he cond. concerts and opera mainly in Vienna. He comp. light opera *Polenblut* & others; ballets *Pohádko o Honzovi*, *Princezna Hyacinta*, *Andersen*, &c.

Neefe, Christian Gottlob (b. Chemnitz, 5. II. 1748; d. Dessau, 26. I. 1798), Ger. cond. & comp. Although of poor parentage, he was sent to Leipzig Univ. to study law, but took to m., met J. A. Hiller and deputized for him as cond. of a travelling opera co. in 1777. He married at Frankfort and settled at Bonn in 1779, where in 1781 he became orgst. at court. Beethoven became his pupil that year, aged 11. Later the court m. declined and finally N. lost his place in 1794, served as an official under the Fr. and finally went to Dessau as theatre cond.

Works incl. operas *Die Apotheke*, *Adelheid von Veltheim*, *Amors Guckkasten*, *Der Einspruch*, *Heinrich und Lyda*, *Sophonisbe*, *Zemire und Azor* & others; incid. m. for Shakespeare's *Macbeth*; church m.; chamber m., &c.

Nef, Karl (b. St. Gall, 22. VIII. 1873; d. Basle, 9. II. 1935), Swi. mcolst. Studied at the Leipzig Cons. and became lecturer at Basle Univ. in 1901, was critic of the *Basler Nachrichten* in 1897–1925 and ed. of the *Schweizerische Musikzeitung* in 1898–1909. He wrote a number of books on mus. hist., the sym. and the suite, mus. insts., Beethoven's syms., &c.

Neidhart von Reuental (b. Bavaria, ?; d. ?, *c.* 1240), Ger. minnesinger. Went on a crusade in 1217–9 and settled in Aus. on his return. Songs in 2 & 3 parts of his are preserved.

Nejedlý, Zdeněk (b. Litomšl, 10. II. 1878), Cz. mcolst. Lecturer at Prague Univ. and prof. from 1905. His books incl. a hist. of m. in Boh., works on Fibich, Mahler, Foerster,

Novák and Smetana, on Beethoven's 4tets and on Wagner.

Nekrasov, Nikolai Alexeievitch (1821–77), Rus. poet & journalist. *See* **Cui** (songs), **Koval** (songs).

Nelson Mass. The nickname given to Haydn's Mass in D min., written in 1798 after Nelson's visit to Eisenstadt, during which he had asked H. for his pen and presented him with his gold watch in return.

Němcová, Božena (1820–62), Cz. novelist. *See* **At the Old Bleaching-Ground** (Kovařovic & Horák).

Nenia. *See* **Naenia.**

Nenna, Pomponio (b. Bari nr. Naples, *c.* 1560; d. ?, before 1618), It. comp. Lived (?) mainly at Naples and was the teacher of Gesualdo, Prince of Venosa.

Works incl. responsoria & other church m.; madrigals, &c.

Neo - Bechstein Piano. An electrophonic pf. invented by Vierling of Berlin in 1928–33 and further developed by Franco and Nernst, prod. its notes by the conversion of electrical waves into audible sounds.

Neo-Modal. Modern m. using new derivations from the modes, harmonized, transposed or otherwise altered, is called N.-M.

Nepomuceno, Alberto (b. Fatalya, 6. VII. 1864; d. Rio de Janeiro, 16. X. 1920), Brazil. comp. Studied in It., with Herzogenberg at Leipzig and with Guilmant in Paris. He returned to Brazil *c.* 1895 and later became dir. of the Cons. at Rio.

Works incl. operas *Arthemis* & *Abul*; orch. works; concs. for var. insts.; *National Hymn*; pf. pieces; songs; arrs. of Brazil. folksongs. &c.

Neri, Filippo (St. Philip Neri) (b. Florence, 21. VII. 1515; d. Rome, 26. V. 1595), It. monk & saint. Of importance to m. for his foundation of the Soc. of Oratorians in 1564, which cultivated m. at the oratory of San Girolamo in Rome, for which among others Animuccia and Palestrina worked in his lifetime and which in 1600 prod. Cavalieri's *Rappresentazione di anima e di corpo.* It was from this soc. that the Oratorio received its name as a mus. form.

Neri, Massimiliano (b. ?; d. ?), It. 17th-cent. orgst. & comp. He was the 1st orgst. of St. Mark's, Venice, in 1644, was ennobled by the Emperor Ferdinand II in 1651 and became court orgst. to the Elector of Cologne in 1664.

Comp. motets; sos. & inst. canzoni, &c.

Nero. *See also* **Nerone.**

Opera by Rubinstein (lib., in Fr. [*Néron*], by Jules Barbier), prod., in Ger., Hamburg, Municipal Theatre, 1. XI. 1879.

Nerone (*Nero*), opera by Boito (lib. by comp.), begun 1879, but left unfinished at B.'s death in 1918. Prod., ed. by Tommasini & Arturo Toscanini, Milan, Teatro alla Scala, 1. V. 1924.

Neruda, Wilma (Wilhelmina) (Norman-Neruda; Lady Hallé) (b. Brno, 21. III. 1839; d. Berlin, 15. IV. 1911), Morav. vst. Studied under her father, Josef N. (1807–75) and with Jansa, and made her 1st appearance in Vienna with her sister Amalie, a pfst., in 1846. She then went on tour in Ger. and appeared in London in 1849. Afterwards she appeared all over Eur., often with her brother, the cst. Franz N. (1843–1915). In 1864 she played in Paris and married the Swe. comp. Ludvig Norman. In 1888 she became the 2nd wife of Charles Hallé and settled at Manchester.

Nesle, Blondel de. *See* **Blondel.**

Nessler, Viktor (Ernst) (b. Baldenheim, Alsace, 28. I. 1841; d. Strasburg, 28. V. 1890), Ger. comp. Studied theol. at Strasburg, but took to m. and prod. a Fr. opera there in 1864. He went to Leipzig, became chor. and afterwards operatic cond.

Works incl. operas *Fleurette, Die Hochzeitsreise, Dornröschens Brautfahrt, Nachtwächter und Student, Am Alexandertag, Irmingard, Der Rattenfänger von Hameln, Der wilde Jäger, Der Trompeter von Säckingen* (after Scheffel's poem), *Otto der Schütz, Die Rose von Strassburg*; partsongs, &c.

Nešvera, Josef (b. Praskolesice, 24. X. 1842; d. Olomouc, 12. IV. 1914), Cz. comp. Choirmaster at Olomouc cath.

Works incl. operas *Perdita* (on Shakespeare's *Winter's Tale*), *The Forest Breeze, The Cousin, Mlynarski* & *Radhošt*; Mass, Passion, *De profundis* & other church m.; pf. & v. pieces, &c.

Netchaiev, Vassily Vassilievitch (b. Moscow, 28. IX. 1895), Rus. comp. Studied pf. with Goldenweiser and comp. with Vassilenko at the Moscow Cons.

Works incl. operas *Seven Princesses* (after Maeterlinck) & *Ivan Bolotnikov*; incid. m. to Shakespeare's *Macbeth*, Sophocles' *Ajax* & other plays; stg. 4tet, &c.

Neue krumme Teufel, Der (*The New Crooked Devil*), opera by Haydn (lib. by Johann Joseph Felix von Kurz, based on Le Sage's *Le Diable boiteux*), prod. Vienna, Kärntnertor Theatre, spring 1752.

Neue Sachlichkeit (Ger. = new objectivity). A term coming into use after the 1914–8 world war in Ger. and used to describe m. of a purely extrinsic nature, detached from all sentiment or descriptiveness.

Neues vom Tage (*News of the Day*), opera by Hindemith (lib. by Marcellus Schiffer), prod. Berlin, Kroll's Opera, 8. VI. 1929.

Neukomm, Sigismund von (b. Salzburg, 10. VII. 1778; d. Paris, 3. IV. 1858), Aus. comp. As a chorister at Salzburg cath. he was a pupil of M. Haydn, who in 1798 sent him to his great brother in Vienna. In 1806 he went to Swe. and Rus., becoming cond. at the tsar's Ger. theatre in St. Petersburg; but he returned to Vienna in 1809 and went to live in Paris soon after, succeeding Dussek in 1812 as pfst. to Talleyrand. From 1816–21 he was chapel master to Pedro I of Brazil, with whom he returned to Lisbon after the revol., afterwards travelling with Talleyrand. In 1829 he visited London, meeting Mendelssohn, and he lived there and alternately in Paris for the rest of his life.

Works incl. opera *Alexander in Indien* & others; many masses & Requiem for Louis XVI; orats. *Mount Sinai*, *David* & 6 others; incid. m. for Schiller's *Braut von Messina*; songs, &c.

Neumann, František (b. Přerov, Moravia, 16. VI. 1874; d. Brno, 24. II. 1929), Cz. comp. & cond. After starting a commercial and military career he went to study m. at the Leipzig Cons. After filling var. chor.-master's and cond.'s posts at Ger. & Cz. theatres, he went to Brno as chief cond. at the Nat. Theatre.

Works incl. operas *Idalka*, *Die Brautwerbung*, *Liebelei* (on Schnitzler's play), *Herbststurm*, *Beatrice Caracci*; melodrama *Pan*; ballets *In Pleasant Pastures*, *The Peri*, *Pierrot*; masses & motets; symph. poem *Infernal Dance*, suite *The Sunken Bell*, *Morav. Rhapsody*, ovts., &c. for orch.; Octet, pf. Trio; chors., songs, &c.

Neumark, Georg (b. Mühlhausen, Thuringia, 16. III. 1621; d. Weimar, 8. VII. 1681), Ger. poet & musn. He pub. a collection of sacred and secular songs, *Musikalisch-poetischer Lustwald* in 1657, some set to m. by himself, incl. the hymn 'Wer nur den lieben Gott lässt walten.'

Neumes. The signs in old mus. notation indicating the single notes or groups of notes to which each syllable was to be sung, still surviving in plainsong notation, orig. not set on staves, but merely marked above the words and showing neither precise length nor exact pitch. They were only rough reminders of tunes already known to the singers.

Neusidler, Hans (b. Poszony [Pressburg], 1508/9; d. Nuremberg, 2. II. 1563), Hung. or Ger. lutenist. Settled at Nuremberb, where he pub. books of pieces arr. for lute in tablature in 1533, 1540 and 1544.

Neusidler, Melchior (b. Poszony, 1507; d. Nuremberg, 1590), Hung. or Ger. lutenist, brother of prec. Visited It. and pub. 2 books of lute m. at Venice in 1566. On his return to Ger. he went to live at Augsburg, partly in the service of Anton Fugger and partly as purveyor of domestic m. to the city. In 1574 he pub. at Strasburg a book of m. by Josquin, Lassus, Arcadelt, Rore & others arr. for the lute.

Nevada, Emma (real name Wixom) (b. Alpha nr. Nevada City, Cal., 7. II. 1859; d. Liverpool, 20. VI. 1940), Amer. sop. singer. Studied with Mathilde Marchesi in Vienna and made her 1st stage appearance in London in 1880, later singing in It., Paris, the Eng. festivals, &c.

Nevin, Arthur (Finlay) (b. Edgeworth, Pa., 27. IV. 1871; d. Pittsburgh, 10. VII. 1943), Amer. comp. Studied at Pittsburgh, Boston and Berlin. He taught and cond. in var. Amer. cities, studied Amer.-Indian m., and on 23. X. 1910 his *Poia* was the 1st Amer. opera prod. in Berlin.

Works incl. operas *Poia* & *A Daughter of the Forest*, masque *A Night in Yaddo Land*; cantatas; suites for orch. incl. *Lorna Doone* (after Blackmore); stg. 4tet, pf. Trio; suites & pieces for pf.; songs, &c.

Nevin, Ethelbert (Woodbridge) (b. Edgeworth, Pa., 25. XI. 1862; d. New Haven, Conn., 17. II. 1901), Amer. comp., brother of prec. Studied pf. & comp. at Boston and Berlin. Later taught at Boston and between 1884–92 in Eur.

Works incl. pantomime *Lady Floriane's Dream*; numerous pf. pieces incl. *Narcissus*; many songs, incl. *The Rosary*, &c.

New Objectivity. *See* **Neue Sachlichkeit.**

'New World' Symphony. Dvořák's 9th Sym., but called 'No. 5,' in E min., Op. 95, with the subtitle *From the New World* given it because it was written in U.S.A. and uses material inspired by but not directly derived from Negro songs heard by him there. Comp. 1893 and 1st perf. N.Y., Phil. Soc., XII. 1893.

Newark, William (b. Newark-on-Trent, *c.* 1450; d. ? London, XI. 1509), Eng. comp. Became a Gentleman of the Chapel Royal in

London, 1477 and, after var. other appts., Master of the Children there in 1493. Comp. madrigals, &c.

Newbolt, Henry (John) (1862–1938), Eng. poet. *See* **Travelling Companion** (Stanford).

Newman, Ernest (b. Liverpool, 30. XI. 1868), Eng. critic & writer on m. Educ. at Liverpool. Became critic of the *Manchester Guardian*, 1905, the *Birmingham Post*, 1906, the *Observer*, 1919, and the *Sunday Times*, 1920. Books incl. *Gluck and the Opera, Hugo Wolf, A Musical Critic's Holiday* and several works on Wagner, incl. the largest modern biog.

Newman, John Henry (1801–90), Eng. cardinal & poet. *See* **Dream of Gerontius** (Elgar).

Newmarch (*née* **Jeaffreson**), **Rosa (Harriet)**, (b. Leamington, 18. XII. 1857; d. Worthing, 9. IV. 1940), Eng. writer on m. Wrote programme notes for London Queen's Hall concerts, 1908–27. Made special studies of Rus. and Cz. m. Her books incl. *The Rus. Opera* & *The M. of Czechoslovakia.*

Nibelung Saga (*Nibelungenlied*), ancient Teutonic epic in the Middle High Ger. dialect. *See* **Dorn** (*Nibelungen*), **Draeseke** (*Gudrun*), **Ring des Nibelungen** (Wagner), **Sigurd** (Reyer).

Nibelung's Ring, The (Wagner). *See* **Ring des Nibelungen.**

Niccolini, Giuseppe (b. Piacenza, 29. I. 1763; d. Piacenza, 18. XII. 1842), It. comp. Studied at the Cons. di Sant' Onofrio, Naples, under Insanguine. Was at first very successful in opera, but was eventually driven from the stage by Rossini. Chapel master at Piacenza cath. from 1819.

Works incl. operas *I baccanti di Roma, Traiano in Dacia, Coriolano* & c. 40 others; masses & other church m., &c.

Niccolo or Nicolo. *See* **Isouard.**

Nichelmann, Christoph (b. Treuenbrietzen, Brandenburg, 13. VIII. 1717; d. Berlin, 20. VII. 1762), Ger. hpchdst. & comp. Pupil of Bach at St. Thomas's school, Leipzig; lived at Hamburg and Berlin, being app. hpchdst. to Frederick II of Prus. in 1744.

Works incl. opera (serenata) *Il sogno di Scipione*; hpchd. concs.; hpchd. sos., &c.

Nichols, Robert (Malise Bowyer) (1893–1944), Eng. poet. *See* **Darnton** (*Swan-song*), **Dieren (van)** (*Tailor*), **Morning Heroes** (Bliss), **Pastoral** (Bliss).

Nicholson, Richard (b. ?; d. ? Oxford, 1639), Eng. orgst. & comp. Became choirmaster and (?) orgst. at Magdalen Coll., Oxford, in 1595, took the Mus.B. there, 1596, and became the 1st Prof. of M. there in 1627.

Works incl. anthems, madrigals (1 in *The Triumphes of Oriana*), m. for viols, 'dialogue' (or song-cycle) for 3 voices 'Joane, quoth John,' &c.

Nicholson, Sydney H(ugo). (b. London, 9. II. 1875), Eng. orgst. & church educst. Studied at the R.C.M. in London and under Knorr at Frankfort o/M. Orgst. of Manchester cath., 1908–18, and Westminster Abbey, 1918–27, when he founded the School of Eng. Church M. at Chislehurst, now transferred to Canterbury. Knighted 1938. His comps. incl. church m. and a comic opera *The Mermaid* (lib. by George Birmingham).

Nicodé, Jean Louis (b. Jerczyce nr. Poznan, 12. VIII. 1853; d. Langebrück nr. Dresden, 5. X. 1919), Ger.-Pol. cond. & comp., ? of Fr. descent. The family having moved to Berlin in 1856, N. studied there, 1st under his father and from 1869 at the Neue Akademie der Tonkunst. Afterwards he taught there and arr. concerts at which he appeared as pfst., toured in the Balkans with Désirée Artôt and in 1878 became prof. at the Dresden Cons. From 1885 he devoted himself to cond. and comp.

Works incl. symph. ode *Das Meer* for solo voices, male chor., orch. & org.; symph. poems *Maria Stuart* (after Schiller), *Die Jagd nach dem Glück, Gloria*, Symph. Vars. &c. for orch.; Romance for v. & orch.; co. & pf. So.; So. and numerous pieces for pf.; songs, incl. cycle *Dem Andenken an Amarantha*; male-voice chors., &c.

Nicolai, Johann Michael (b. ?; d. ? Stuttgart, ?), Ger. 17th-cent. comp. Chamber musn. at the court of Württemberg at Stuttgart.

Works incl. sacred songs for 3 voices with 2 vs.; sos. for 2 vs. and var. continuos (va. da gamba, bassoon), &c.

Nicolai, (Carl) Otto (Ehrenfried) (b. Königsberg, 9. VI. 1810; d. Berlin, 11. V. 1849), Ger. cond. & comp. Studied the pf. as a child, but was so unhappy at home that in 1826 he ran away and was sent to Berlin for study under Zelter and Klein by a patron the following year. In 1833 another patron sent him to Rome as orgst. in the Prus. Embassy chapel, and there he studied under Baini. He returned there after a year at the Kärntnertor Theatre in Vienna, 1837–8, where he became 1st cond. in 1841–7, and he founded the Phil. concerts there in 1842. In 1847 he became dir. of the cath. choir and the Court Opera in Berlin, where he

d. of a stroke, 2 months after the prod. of his *Merry Wives of Windsor.*

Works incl. operas *Enrico II* (later *Rosmonda d'Inghilterra*), *Il templario, Odoardo e Gildippe, Il proscritto* (later *Die Heimkehr des Verbannten*), *Die lustigen Weiber von Windsor* (after Shakespeare); Mass for Frederick William IV of Prus., Requiem, Te Deum; Sym. Festival Ovt. on 'Ein' feste Burg' for the jubilee of Königsberg Univ., &c.

Nicolai, Philipp (b. Mengeringhausen, 10. VIII. 1556; d. Hamburg, 26. X. 1608), Ger. pastor, poet & amateur musn. In 1599 he pub. a hymn-book, *Freudenspiegel des ewigen Lebens,* containing the tunes of 'Wachet auf' and 'Wie schön leucht' uns der Morgenstern.'

Nicolai, Willem (Frederik Gerard) (b. Leyden, 20. XI. 1829; d. The Hague, 25. IV. 1896), Dutch teacher & comp. Studied at the Leipzig Cons. and from 1852 taught at The Hague Cons., becoming dir. in 1865.

Works incl. orat. *Bonifacius,* chor. works *The Song of the Bell* (Schiller), *The Swedish Nightingale, Jehovah's Wrath & Hanske van Gelder*; sym. & ovts.; songs, &c.

Nicolau, Antonio (b. Barcelona, 8. VI. 1858; d. Barcelona, 26. II. 1933), Spa. teacher, cond. & comp. Studied with Pujol and others, cond. the Sociedad de Conciertos at Barcelona and had a number of distinguished pupils.

Works incl. operas *Costanza & El rapto,* chor. works *La mort del Escolà, Captant, Entre flors, La Mare de Deu*; symn. poems *El triunfo de Venus & Spes*; songs, &c.

Nicolini (Nicola Grimaldi) (b. Naples, III. 1673; d. Naples, before 31. XII. 1731), It. male sop. singer, later con. 1st appearance in Rome, about 1694. 1st went to Eng. in 1708.

Nicolo or Niccolo. The name under which Isouard prod. most of his operas.

Niecks, Frederick (Friedrich) (b. Düsseldorf, 3. II. 1845; d. Edinburgh, 24. VI. 1924), Ger. mcolst. Studied at Düsseldorf and appeared as a vst. there, later went to Leipzig Univ. and in 1868 was invited by Mackenzie to join his stg. 4tet at Edinburgh. He lectured there and in 1901 was app. Reid Prof. of M. at the Univ. He wrote books on Chopin, Schumann, the hist. of programme m., &c.

Niedermeyer, (Abraham) Louis (b. Nyon, Vaud, 27. IV. 1802; d. Paris, 14. III. 1861), Swi. comp. & educst. Studied in Vienna, Rome and Naples, settled as m. teacher at Geneva and went to Paris in 1823, settling there after a brief teaching period at Brussels. In Paris he took over Choron's school of m. and called it École de Musique Religieuse Classique.

Works incl. operas *Il reo per amore, La casa nel bosco, Stradella, Marie Stuart* (after Schiller), *La Fronde*; mass with orch., low masses, motets & anthems; songs to words by Lamartine (e.g. *Le Lac*), Hugo, Deschamps, &c.

Nielsen,* Carl (August) (b. Nørre-Lyndelse nr. Odense, 9. VI. 1865; d. Copenhagen, 3. X. 1931), Dan. cond. & comp. Being poor as a youth, he joined a military band at the age of 14, but at 18 succeeded in entering the Copenhagen Cons. as a pupil of Gade. In 1891 he entered the royal orch. and was its cond. in 1908–14. He also became cond. of the Mus. Soc. and dir. of the Cons.

Works incl. operas *Saul og David, Maskarade* (after Holberg) & others; incid. m. for Oehlenschläger's *Aladdin*; 6 syms. (II. *The Four Temperaments,* III. *Espansiva,* VI. *Sinfonia semplice*), *Saga-Dream* for orch.; v. & pf. So., &c.

Nielsen, Hans (b. ? Roskilde, c. 1585; d. ? Copenhagen, ?), Dan. lutenist & comp. After learning m. as choirboy in the royal chapel at Copenhagen, he studied with G. Gabrieli at Venice between 1599 and 1606, and in 1606–8 with the Eng. lutenist Richard Howett at Wolfenbüttel. After that he was lutenist at the Dan. court until 1611, when he was dismissed and went to Heidelberg Univ. In 1623 he was app. vice-dir. of the royal chapel in succession to Pederson.

Nielsen, Ludolf (b. Nørre Tvede, 29. I. 1876), Dan. cond. & comp. Studied at the Copenhagen Cons., became cond. at the Tivoli and the Palace until 1909.

Works incl. operas *The Clock, Lola* (after Victor Hugo) & *Isabella*; ballet *Lakschmi*; 2 syms., 3 symph. poems, 2 suites and concert ovt. for orch.; 2 stg. 4tets; pf. pieces; songs, &c.

Nielsen, Riccardo (b. Bologna, 3. III. 1908), It. comp. of Scand. descent. Studied at the Liceo Musicale of Bologna and at Salzburg, and was infl. by Casella.

Works incl. incid. m. for *Maria ed il Nazzareno*; Psalms for male voices & orch.; Conc. for orch., Sym., for small orch.; Capriccio & *Sinfonia concertante* for pf. & orch., v. Conc.; Divertimento for bn., tpt., v., va. & co., Trio for ob., bn. & hn., Adagio & Allegro for co. & 11 insts.; sos. for v. & pf. and co. & pf.; *Musica* for 2 pfs.; So. & Ricercare, Chorale and

Toccata on B.A.C.H. for pf.; *Laude di Jacopone da Todi* & *Tre satire di Giusti* for voice & pf., &c.

Niemann, Albert (b. Erxleben, Magdeburg, 15. I. 1831; d. Berlin, 13. I. 1917), Ger. ten. singer. After a precarious beginning on the stage at Dessau, he was discovered by F. Schneider, the court mus. dir. and given some lessons, and was also taught by a singer. He gradually obtained better engagements and was sent to Paris by the King of Hanover to study under Duprez. In 1866–88 he was court opera singer in Berlin and in 1876 Wagner chose him to create the part of Siegmund in the *Ring* at Bayreuth.

Niemann, Walter (b. Hamburg, 10. X. 1876), Ger. comp. & writer on m. Studied under his father, the pfst. & comp. Rudolph Friedrich N. (1838–98) and at Leipzig Univ. & Cons. His books include studies of Scand. m., virginal & pf. m., Brahms, Grieg, Sibelius, &c.

Niente (It.=nothing). The word is generally used in conn. with *quasi* (so to speak, almost) when extreme softness of tone is required.

Nietzsche, Friedrich (1844–1900), Ger. philosopher & author. *See* **Also sprach Zarathustra** (R. Strauss), **Ingenhoven** (do.), **Mass of Life** (Delius), **Medtner** (songs), **Rezniček** (*Ruhm und Ewigkeit*).

Niewiadomski, Stanislaw (b. Soposzyn nr. Lwów, 4. XI. 1859; d. Lwów, 16. VIII. 1936), Pol. critic & comp. Studied with Chopin's pupil Karol Mikuli at Lwów and later in Vienna and Leipzig. He became prof. at the Lwów Cons. and dir. of the Opera, later prof. at the Cons. and critic in Warsaw. He wrote books on Chopin, Moniuszko, &c. and his comps. are mainly songs and chors.

'Nigger' Quartet. A stg. 4tet in F maj. by Dvořák, Op. 96, the material of which is inspired by but not directly derived from Negro songs heard by him in U.S.A.; comp. 1893.

Night in May, A (Rimsky-Korsakov). *See* **May Night.**

Night on the Bare Mountain, a work in var. forms by Mussorgsky, more properly called *St. John's Night on the B. M.*, based on the incident of the witches' sabbath in Gogol's story *St. John's Eve*: comp. as a symph. poem for orch. in 1866–7; later used in a version for chor. & orch. and called *Night on Mount Triglav* in 1872 as part of the opera *Mlada* commissioned from M., Borodin, Cui and Rimsky-Korsakov, but never completed; revised version of this used as introd. to Act III of the unfinished opera *Sorotchintsy Fair*, begun in 1875; this last version revised and arranged as an orch. piece by Rimsky-Korsakov after M.'s death.

Nightingale. A toy inst. *See* **Toy Symphony.**

Nightingale, The, opera by Stravinsky (lib. by comp. & Stepan Nikolaievitch Mitusov, from Hans Andersen's fairy-tale), prod. Paris, Opéra, 26. V. 1914; revived in the form of a ballet (chgph. by Leonid Massin), Paris, Opéra, 2. II. 1920.

Nights in the Gardens of Spain (Falla). *See* **Noches en los jardines de España.**

Nikisch, Artur (b. Lébényi Szent Miklos, 12. X. 1855; d. Leipzig, 23. I. 1922), Hung.-Ger. cond. Studied in Vienna and made his 1st appearance there in 1874. Held important appts. at Leipzig, Boston, Budapest and Berlin, and toured widely in Eur. and Amer.

Nikisch, Mitja (b. Leipzig, 21. V. 1899; d. Venice, 5. VIII. 1936), Hung.-Ger. pfst., son of prec. Studied at the Leipzig Cons. and made his 1st appearance there in 1912.

Nilsson, Kristina (Christine) (b. Sjöabol nr. Wexiö, 20. VIII. 1843; d. Stockholm, 22. III. 1921), Swe. sop. singer. Studied at Stockholm and Paris, and after several appearances in Swe. received her 1st important stage engagement in Paris in 1864, and 1st went to London in 1867, where she married Auguste Rouzeaud in 1872. In 1887 she married Count Casa Miranda.

Nin (y Castellanos), Joaquín (b. Havana, 29. IX. 1883), Spa. pfst., mcolst. & comp. Studied at Barcelona and in Paris, where in 1906 he became pf. prof. at the Schola Cantorum. After short periods in Berlin and Cuba, he settled in Brussels & later in Paris again. He has ed. much old Spa. m. and written 3 books.

Works incl. mimodrama *L'Autre*, ballet *L'Écharpe bleue*; v. pieces; pf. works; songs, &c.

Nina, o sia La pazza per amore (*Nina, or the Lunatic from Love*), opera by Paisiello (lib. by Giovanni Battista Lorenzi, based on the Fr. lib. by Benoît Joseph Marsollier), prod. Naples, Caserta Palace, for the visit of Queen Maria Carolina of Sicily, 25. VI. 1789; 1st publ. perf. Naples, Teatro Fiorentino, 1790.

Nina, ou La Folle par amour (do.), ballet by Persuis, partly based on Dalayrac's m. (chgph. by Louis Milon), prod. Paris, Opéra, 23. XI. 1813.

Opera by Dalayrac (lib. by Marsollier), prod. Paris, Comédie-Italienne, 15. V. 1786.

Ninth. The interval a whole tone larger than an 8ve. (maj. N.) or a semitone larger (min. N.). It is actually a maj. or min. 2nd enlarged beyond the 8ve, but being thus capable of var. harmonic fillings-in between its 2 notes, its use can have an entirely different effect.

Ninth Symphony (Beethoven). *See* **'Choral' Symphony.**

Nissen, Erika. *See* **Lie-Nissen.**

Nissen, Georg Nicolaus (b. Haderslev, 27. I. 1765; d. Salzburg, 24. III. 1826), Dan. diplomat & author, 2nd husband of Constanze Mozart, whom he married in 1809, and author of one of the earliest biogs. of Mozart.

Nivers, Guillaume (Gabriel) (b. Melun, 1617; d. Paris, XII. 1714), Fr. orgst., hpchdst., theorist & comp. Pupil of Chambonnières in Paris and orgst. of the church of Saint-Sulpice there, also app. orgst. to the king and m. master to the queen in 1667. He wrote a treatise on singing and others.

Works incl. motets & other church m.; org. pieces, &c.

No Song, No Supper, opera by Storace (lib. by Prince Hoare), prod. London, Drury Lane Theatre, 16. IV. 1790.

Noces (Stravinsky). *See* **Wedding.**

Noces de Jeannette, Les (*Jenny's Wedding*), operetta by Massé (lib. by Jules Barbier & Michel Carré), prod. Paris, Opéra-Comique, 4. II. 1853.

Noches en los jardines de España (*Nights in the Gardens of Spain*), symph. impressions for pf. & orch. by Falla, begun in 1909, finished in 1916, 1st perf. Madrid, IV. 1916. There are 3 mvts.: 1. *En el Generalife*; 2. *Danza lejana* (*Dance in the distance*); 3. *En los jardines de la Sierra de Córdoba.*

Nocturne (Fr.). A 'night piece' or inst. serenade, gen. of a quiet, lyrical character, but sometimes (as in Chopin) with a more agitated middle section. As a pf. piece it originated, not with Chopin, but with Field, but it existed already as the It. Notturno in the 18th cent., when however it was similar to the Serenade or Divertimento in several mvts. The N. in the modern sense is not necess. slow, soft and sentimental. Even Field's are not all so, and one is in the curious form of a voc. operatic scene; Chopin's may have agitated middle sections; *Fêtes* in Debussy's work below is a very animated piece; in Vaughan Williams's *London Sym.* the scherzo is a N., i.e. a piece suggesting London's gaiety by night.

Nocturnes. 3 orch. pieces by Debussy, *Nuages, Fêtes & Sirènes,* the last with fem. chor., comp. in 1893–9 and 1st perf. Paris, 9. XII. 1900 (Nos. 1 & 2); 27. X. 1901 (complete).

Node (from Lat. *nodus* = knot). The point in a vibrating stg. at which the vibration becomes cut into segments.

Noël (Fr.). *See* **Carol.**

Noël, Victoire. *See* **Stoltz, Rosine.**

Nola, Domenico da (Joan Domenico del Giovane) (b. Nola, Naples, ?; d. ?), It. 16th-cent. comp. Chapel master of the church of the Annunciation at Naples. Comp. motets, madrigals, villanelle, &c.

Non nobis Domine. A canon for voices, ? by Byrd, often sung in Eng. for 'grace' after public dinners. It was a Riddle C. capable of being sung with the entries in var. positions, also in Inversion.

Nonet. A comp. for 9 insts., usually in several mvts. and in some kind of so. or suite form.

Nonnengeige (Ger. = nun's fiddle). *See* **Tromba marina.**

Noordt, Anthony van (b. ?; d. ? Amsterdam, ?), Dutch 17th-cent. orgst. & comp. Orgst. of the Nieuwe Kerk at Amsterdam in 1659, when he pub. a book of org. works in tablature, incl. vars. on Fr. psalm tunes and fugal fantasies.

Norcome, Daniel (b. Windsor, 1576; d. ? Brussels, before 1626), Eng. singer & comp. He went to the Dan. court in his early 20s, but fled from Copenhagen to Ger., Hung. and Venice *c.* 1600. Later he became a lay-clerk at St. George's chapel, Windsor, but lost that post on turning Rom. Catholic and went to Brussels as an inst. player to the viceregal chapel.

Works incl. viol pieces; madrigal contrib. to *The Triumphes of Oriana,* &c.

Nordica, Lilian (Lillian Norton) (b. Farmington, Me., 12. V. 1859; d. Batavia, 10. V. 1914), Amer. sop. singer. Studied at Boston and, after successful appearances in U.S.A. and Eng., at Milan, making her 1st stage appearance at Brescia in 1879.

Nordraak, Rikard (b. Christiania, 12. VI. 1842; d. Berlin, 20. III. 1866), Norw. comp. Studied pf. & comp. in Berlin and on his return to Norw. made friends with Grieg and became an enthusiastic exponent of nat. m.

Works incl. incid. m. for Bjørnson's *Mary Stuart* and *Sigurd Slembe*; songs incl. a setting of Bjørnson's 'Ja, vi elsker dette landet,' now the Norw. nat. anthem.

Noren, Heinrich (Gottlieb) (b. Graz, 5. I. 1861; d. Rottach, 6. VI. 1928), Aus. vst. & comp. Studied in Paris and was orch. leader in Belg., Spa., Rus. & Ger. Later taught at Crefeld, Cologne and Berlin.

Works incl. *Kaleidoskop* vars. and

Vita sym. for orch.; v. Conc; chamber m.; inst. sos., &c.

Norma, opera by Bellini (lib. by Felice Romani, based on Louis Alexandre Soumet's tragedy), prod. Milan, Teatro alla Scala, 26. XII. 1831.

Norman, John (b. ?; d. ?), Eng. 15th–16th-cent. orgst. & comp. In the early 16th cent. he was orgst. and choirmaster at St. David's cath.

Works incl. masses, motets, &c.

Norman, (Fredrik Vilhelm) Ludvig (b. Stockholm, 28. VIII. 1831; d. Stockholm, 28. III. 1885), Swe. pfst., cond. & comp. Pub. a book of songs at the age of 11, was left a poor orphan, but enabled by patrons, incl. Jenny Lind, to study at the Leipzig Cons. In 1851 his 1st pf. work was pub. at Schumann's instigation. Returning to Stockholm in 1861, he became cond. of the royal orch., which he cond. until 1879, and was cond. of the sym. concerts to his death. In 1864 he married the vst. Wilma Neruda.

Works incl. incid. m. to Shakespeare's *Antony and Cleopatra*; 3 syms., 4 ovts.; chamber m.; inst. sos.; pf. works; songs, &c.

Norman-Neruda, Wilma. *See* **Neruda.**

Norris, William (b. ?, *c.* 1675; d. ? Lincoln, *c.* 1710), Eng. singer & comp. Choir-boy in the Chapel Royal in London, later a singer there and choirmaster at Lincoln cath. from 1691.

Works incl. services & anthems; Ode for St. Cecilia's Day, &c.

North, Roger (Hon.) (b. Tostock, Suffolk, 3. IX. 1653; d. Rougham, 1. III. 1734), Eng. lawyer & amateur musn., brother of Francis N., Lord Guilford (1637–85), who was also a musn. and pub. *A Philosophical Essay on Musick* in 1677. R. N. wrote *Memoires of Musick* incl. the treatise *The Musicall Gramarian.*

Northcote, Sydney (b. Deri, Glam., 3. IX. 1897), Eng. educst., comp. & writer on m. Studied at the R.C.M. in London and New Coll., Oxford, where he took the D.Mus. in 1932. Prof. at the G.S.M., examiner and festival adjudicator. He has written a book on *The Ballad in M.* and his comps. incl. chor. works, folksong arrs., &c.

Norton, Lillian. *See* **Nordica.**

Norw. (abbr.) = Norway, Norwegian.

Norwegian Composers. *See* **Alnaes, Backer - Grøndahl, Backer - Lunde, Brustad, Grieg, Haberbier, Halvorsen, Johansen, Kjerulf, Lie, Lindeman, Lund (Signe), Nordraak, Saeverud, Schjelderup, Sinding, Svendsen, Thrane, Valen.**

Norwich Festival. A triennial mus. festival estab. at Norwich in 1824, but preceded by festivals held at irregular intervals between 1770–1817. It continued regularly into the 1st world war of 1914–8 and was revived between that and the 2nd.

Noskowski, Zygmunt (b. Warsaw, 2. V. 1846; d. Wiesbaden, 23. VII. 1909), Pol. comp. Studied with Moniuszko in Warsaw and with Kiel in Berlin, and after cond. at Constance, he returned to Pol. in 1881, teaching and cond. at Warsaw, where he became prof. of comp. at the Cons.

Works incl. operas *Livia Quintilla, The Judgment, The Quarrel about a Frontier Wall*; ballet *The Fire Feast*; *Return* suite for solo voices, chor. & orch., cantata *The Mermaid, Veni Creator* for chor.; 3 syms., Vars. on a Chopin Prelude & 3 ovts. for orch.; songs, children's songs, &c.

Nota cambiata (It. = changed note). A passing-note placed on the strong beat of a bar; or in ctpt., where Fux calls it *cambita*, a 2nd passing-note following one that should be resolved from above by 1st descending below the note of resolution.

Notation. The act of writing down m. by means of special symbols, as by letters or numbers in ancient m., by neumes in the Middle Ages, in tablature for old lute and org. m., in notes according to the present system, or in the special syllable form of the Tonic Sol-fa system.

Note sensible (Fr., or **Sensible** [noun]) = Leading-note.

Notes. The symbols which in modern mus. notation represent each tone prod. by the voices or insts. for which the m. is written; but the word is used also for the tones as they are heard.

Notker (Balbulus = 'The Stammerer') (b. ? Swi., *c.* 840; d. St. Gall, 6. IV. 912), Swi. monk and musn. at the monastery of St. Gall. He wrote on mus. notation, the org. and the perf. of plainsong, and as a comp. contrib. to the development of the Sequences.

Notot, Joseph (b. Arras, 1755; d. Eng., ?), Fr. orgst. & comp. Was sent to Paris as a child for his educ., but was discovered as a wonderful extempore player on the org. by Leclerc, the orgst. of the church of Saint-Germain-des-Prés, who undertook to teach him. Later he became orgst. at Arras, but the Revol. drove him to Eng. and he gave up m.

Works incl. 4 syms.; 3 pf. concs.; pf. sos., &c.

Nottara, Constantine (b. Bucharest, 1890), Rum. vst. & comp. Studied at the Bucharest Cons. and later in Paris and Berlin. After playing v. in the Charlottenburg opera orch. he returned to Bucharest as a member of the Phil. Orch., formed a stg. 4tet for the queen and became prof. at the Cons.

Works incl. operas *On the Highway* (after Tchekhov) and *On ne badine pas avec l'amour* (after Musset); ballet *Iris*; incid. m. to Euripides' *Hecuba* and Corneille's *Polyeucte*; *Hymn to Peace* for chor. & orch.; Rum. & Cz. suites, *Saudades de Portugal*, Dramatic Ovt., 5 Preludes for orch.; Poem for v. & orch.; *Mircea and Baiazid* for bar. & orch.; inst. sos. & pieces; songs, &c.

Nottebohm, (Martin) Gustav (b. Lüdenscheid, Westphalia, 12. XI. 1817; d. Graz, 29. X. 1882), Ger. writer on m. Friend of Mendelssohn and Schumann at Leipzig; settled in Vienna, 1846. He compiled thematic catalogues of Beethoven's and Schubert's works, wrote a book on the former's sketches, &c.

Notturno (It. = night piece). The 18th-cent. forerunner of the Nocturne, not then a single lyrical inst. piece, but a comp. in several mvts. similar to the Serenade or Divertimento. In the 19th cent. it became simply the It. equivalent of the Nocturne, as for ex. in Mendelssohn's *Midsummer Night's Dream* m.

Nouguès, Jean (b. Bordeaux, 25. IV. 1875; d. Paris, 28. VIII. 1932), Fr. comp. Worked and prod. operas at Bordeaux at first, later in Paris.

Works incl. operas *Le Roy du Papagey*, *Thamyris*, *La Mort de Tintagiles* (after Maeterlinck), *Chiquito*, *Quo vadis?* (after Sienkiewicz), *L'Auberge rouge*, *La Vendetta*, *L'Aigle*, *L'Éclaircie*, *Dante*, *Jeanne de France*, *Le Scarabée bleu*, *Une Aventure de Villon*; ballets *La Danseuse de Pompéi* & *Narcisse*; incid. m., for Rostand's *Cyrano de Bergerac*; film m., &c.

Nourrit, Adolphe (b. Paris, 3. III. 1802; d. Naples, 8. III. 1839), Fr. ten. singer. Made his 1st appearance at the Paris Opéra 1821, remaining attached to that theatre for 16 years.

Nováček, Ottokar (b. Fehertemplom, 13. V. 1866; d. New York, 3. II. 1900), Hung. vst. & comp. Studied with his father, later in Vienna and Leipzig. In the latter city he joined the stg. 4tet of his teacher, Brodsky, as 2nd v. and then as va. In 1892 he went to N.Y. and became va. leader in Damrosch's orch. In 1899 he retired for reasons of health and took to comp.

Works incl. pf. Conc., *Perpetuum mobile* for v. & orch.; 3 stg. 4tets; 8 Caprices and other works for v. & pf.; pf. m.; 6 songs to words by Tolstoy, &c.

Novák, Vítězslav (b. Kamenice, 5. XII. 1870), Cz. comp. He was the son of a doctor, but lost his father early and had to support the family by teaching. While studying law at Prague Univ. he attended the Cons., studying pf with Jiránek and comp. with Dvořák, who persuaded him to devote himself wholly to m. He soon made a career as a distinguished teacher of comp. and in 1909 was app. prof. at the Cons. After the 1914–8 war, which regained his country's independence, he became prof. of the 'Master School' and was its dir. in 1919–22.

Works incl. operas *The Imp of Zvíkov*, *A Night at Karlstein*, *The Lantern*, *The Grandfather's Will*, *The Wood Nymph*; ballets *Signorina Gioventù* & *Nikotina*; cantatas *The Storm*, *The Spectre's Bride* & chor. ballads; symph. poems *In the Tatra*, *Eternal Longing*, *Toman and the Wood Nymph*, ovts. *The Corsair* (after Byron), *Maryša*, *Lady Godiva*, Serenade for small orch.; pf. Conc.; 2 stg. 4tets, 2 pf. trios, pf. 4tet, pf. 5tet; *So. eroica*, *Manfred* (ballad after Byron), *Songs of Winter Nights*, *Pan*, *Exoticon*, 6 Sonatinas, *Youth* (children's pieces) &c. for pf.; song cycles *Gypsy Songs*, *Melancholy*, *In the Valley of a New Kingdom*, *Melancholy Songs of Love*, *Nocturnes*, *Eroticon*, & other songs; partsongs, &c.

Novelletten (Ger. lit. 'short stories'). A category title used by Schumann for his 8 pf. pieces Op. 21, comp. in 1838, also for No. 9 of the *Bunte Blätter* for pf., Op. 99.

Novello, Clara (Anastasia) (b. London, 10. VI. 1818; d. Rome, 12. III. 1908), Eng. sop. singer. Studied at the Paris Cons. and 1st appeared at Windsor in 1833. Lived in London but had many successes abroad, esp. in It.* and Ger. Married Count Gigliucci in 1843.

Novello, Vincent (b. London, 6. IX. 1781; d. Nice, 9. VIII. 1861), Eng. comp., orgst., ed. & pub., father of prec. Founder of the m. pub. firm of Novello & Co. in London, 1811. Ed. valuable collections of m. and comp. church m., cantatas, &c.

November Woods, symph. poem by Bax, comp. 1917, 1st perf. Manchester, Hallé Orch., 18. XI. 1920.

Novotný, Jaroslav (b. Jičín, 28. III. 1886; d. Ural district, 1. VI. 1918), Cz. comp. Studied in Prague, joined the Aus. army during the 1st world war, was a prisoner in Rus., where he wrote much in camp, and was released and killed near the end of the war fighting on the other side with the Cz. legion.

Works incl. stg. 4tet; chors.; pf. So.; song cycles *The Eternal Wedding* & *Ballads of the Soul*, &c.

Nowell (from Fr. *Noël*). *See* **Carol.**

Nowowiejski, Feliks (b. Wartenburg, E. Prus., 7. II. 1877), Pol. cond. & comp. Studied in Berlin and church m. at Ratisbon, afterwards in Fr., Belg. and It. In 1909 he returned to Pol., cond. the Cracow Mus. Soc. until 1914 and in 1919 became dir. of the Poznan Cons. and cond. orch. concerts there.

Works incl. operas *Baltic Legend*, *The Mountain Goblin*; opera-ballet *Leluja*; ballets *Tatra*, *Polish Wedding*; masses, motets & psalms; orats. *Quo vadis?*, *Beatum scelus*, *Missa pro pace*, &c.; cantata *Upper Silesian Folk Scene*; symph. poems, *Beatrix*, *Nina*, ovt. *Polish Wooing*, *The Prodigal Son*, *Jerusalem*; 9 syms. &c. for org., &c.

Noyes, Alfred (b. 1880), Eng. poet. *See* **Coleridge-Taylor** (*Tale of Old Japan*), **Gibbs (C. A.)** (*Highwayman*), **Wood (T.)** (*40 Singing Men*).

Nozze d'Ercole e d'Ebe, Le (*The Nuptials of Hercules and Hebe*). Opera by Gluck (lib. by ?), prod. Pillnitz nr. Dresden, at the double wedding of Max Joseph, Elector of Bavaria, and Maria Anna, Princess of Saxony, and Frederick Christian, Prince of Saxony, and Maria Antonia Walpurgis, Princess of Bavaria, 29. VI. 1747.

Opera by Porpora (lib. as above), prod. Venice, 18. II. 1744.

Nozze di Figaro, Le (*The Marriage of Figaro*), opera by Mozart (lib. by Lorenzo da Ponte, based on Beaumarchais's comedy, *La Folle Journée, ou Le Mariage de Figaro*), prod. Vienna, Burg Theatre, 1. V. 1786.

Nozze di Teti e di Peleo, Le (*The Nuptials of Thetis and Peleus*), opera by Cavalli (lib. by Orazio Persiani), prod. Venice, Teatro San Cassiano, prob. 24. I. 1639.

Nthlds. (abbr.) = Netherlands.

Nuances (Fr., also used in Eng.). Light and shade of expression, of dynamic intensity, &c.

Nucius, Joannes (or **Nux** or **Nucis**) (b. Görlitz, *c.* 1556; d. Himmelwitz, Silesia, 25. III. 1620), Ger. monk & comp. Entered the Cistercian abbey of Rauden, Upper Silesia, and in 1591 became abbot of its offshoot at Himmelwitz. Comp. masses, motets, &c.

Nuitter, Charles (Louis Étienne) (real name Truinet) (b. Paris, 24. IV. 1828; d. Paris, 24. II. 1899), Fr. libst. & writer on m. A lawyer at first, he later devoted himself to the writing and trans. of libs. and of books on opera. In 1865 he became archivist of the Paris Opéra.

Nunc dimittis (Lat. = 'Now lettest thou [thy servant] depart [in peace]'). Part of the Evening Service of the Angl. church and often set by comps. as a 2nd part following the Magnificat.

Nursery, The, song cycle by Mussorgsky (words by comp.), comp. 1868–72: 1. *With Nurse*; 2. *In the Corner*; 3. *The Cockchafer*; 4. *With the Doll*; 5. *Going to sleep*; 6. *On the Hobby-Horse*; 7. *The Cat 'Sailor.'*

Nut. The contrivance at the heel of a v. or other bow at which the hairs are attached and can be stretched by the turn of a screw; also the strip, usually of ebony, at the end of the fingerboard of a stg. inst. near the pegs, serving to raise the stgs. clear of the board.

Nutcracker (*Casse-Noisette*), ballet by Tchaikovsky (chgph. by Lev Ivanovitch Ivanov, based on a tale by E. T. A. Hoffmann), prod. St. Petersburg, Maryinsky Theatre, 17. XII. 1892.

Nux, Joannes. *See* **Nucius.**

Nystroem, Gösta (b. Silfberg, 13. X. 1890), Swe. comp. & painter. Son of a headmaster who taught him m. and painting, which he afterwards studied at Stockholm, Copenhagen and Paris, where he lived for 12 years and where d'Indy and Sabaneiev were among his masters for comp. and he came under the influence of Picasso, Braque, Chirico and other modern painters. After some further studies in It. and Spa. he settled at Göteborg and in 1933 became m. critic of the *Göteborgs Handelstidning*.

Works incl. ballet-pantomime *Maskerade*; incid. m. to var. plays incl. Shakespeare's *Merchant of Venice* & *The Tempest*; 3 syms. (*Sinfonia breve*, *S. espressiva*, *S. concertante*), symph. poems *The Arctic Sea*, *The Tower of Babel*, Lyric Suite & Festival Ovt. for orch., Conc. for stg. orch.; Rondo for v. & orch., va. Conc., Co. Conc.; pf. suites & pieces; songs, &c.

O

Oakeley, Herbert (Stanley) (b. London, 22. VII. 1830; d. Eastbourne, 26. X. 1903), Eng. orgst., educst. & comp. Educ. at Rugby and Oxford, studied m. in London, Dresden and Leipzig. He became Prof. of M. at Edinburgh Univ. in 1865 and Mus.D. (Cantuar.) in 1871. Knighted 1876.

Works incl. services & anthems; Jubilee Cantata (1887) & other chor. works, partsongs; Festal & Funeral Marches for orch.; org. & pf. m.; songs, &c.

Ob. (abbr.) = Oboe.

Obbligato (It. = obligatory, compulsory). An inst. part in a work that is 'essential' in the sense that it performs an important soloistic function is said to be O.

Oberon, König der Elfen (*Oberon, King of the Fairies*), opera by Wranitzky (lib. by Karl Ludwig Gieseke, based on Wieland's poem and Friederike Sophie Seyler's lib. *Hüon und Amande*), prod. Vienna, Theater auf der Wieden, 7. XI. 1789.

Oberon, or The Elf King's Oath, opera by Weber (lib. by James Robinson Planché, based on Wieland's poem and farther back on the medieval Fr. romance *Huon de Bordeaux*), prod. London, Covent Garden Theatre, 12. IV. 1826.

Obertas. A Pol. dance perf. in figures by couples following a leader. The m. is in 3–4 time, not unlike that of the Mazurka, but wilder in character.

Oberthür, Charles (b. Munich, 4. III. 1819; d. London, 8. XI. 1895), Ger. hpst. & comp. After var. orch. engagements in Ger. & Swi. he settled in London in 1844 as perf. and teacher.

Works incl. opera *Floris von Namur*; Mass *St. Philip Neri*; cantatas *The Pilgrim Queen, The Red Cross Knight, Lady Jane Grey*; ovt. *Rübezahl*, ovt. for Shakespeare's *Macbeth* & others; *Loreley* & Concertino for hp. & orch.; trios for hp., v. & co., 4tets for hps.; many hp. solos, &c.

Oberto, Conte di San Bonifacio, opera by Verdi (lib. by Antonio Piazza, altered by Bartolommeo Merelli and Temistocle Solera), prod. Milan, Teatro alla Scala, 17. XI. 1839. V.'s 1st opera.

Obertus, Jacobus. *See* **Obrecht.**

Obligato. *See* **Obbligato,** of which this is the wrong spelling.

Oblique Motion. *See* **Motion.**

Oboe. A woodwind inst., formerly called hautboy, held vertically and played with a double reed. It descended from the Cromorne and was in full use by the 16th cent., though it remained primitive until the 18th and was not wholly perfected until the 19th. 2 Os., together with 2 bns., were the most constant insts. in the orch., apart from the stgs., in the 18th cent. The O. has a compass of not quite 3 8ves above B♭ below middle C.—Also an 8-ft. reed org. stop sometimes called Hautboy and reprod. the tone of the O.

Oboe d'amore (It. = love ob.). An obs. inst. of the ob. type, tuned a min. 3rd lower and transposing a min. 3rd down. It has not been in normal use since the time of Bach, who often wrote for it.

Oboe da caccia (It. = hunting ob.). An obs. inst. of the ob. type, tuned a 5th lower and transposing a 5th down. It fell out of use after Bach's time, and its parts in old m. are now generally played on the Eng. hn., whose pitch is the same.

Obrecht (or **Hobrecht**), **Jacob** (or Jacobus Obertus) (b. Bergen-op-Zoom, *c.* 1450; d. Ferrara, 1505), Nthlds. comp. Studied at Leuven Univ. and in 1479 became choirmaster at Bergen-op-Zoom. Dir. of the singing-school at Cambrai, 1484–5, and teacher at Bruges, 1491–6, though he must have resided at Antwerp, where he was app. chapel master at the cath. in 1491. Towards the end of his life he went to It. and was for a time at the court of Lorenzo de' Medici at Florence.

Works incl. masses, motets, (?) a Passion, chansons, &c.

Obs. (abbr.) = Obsolete.

Obst. (abbr.) = Oboist.

Obukhov, Nikolai (b. Moscow, 22. IV. 1892), Rus. comp. Pupil of N. Tcherepnin and Steinberg at the St. Petersburg Cons. He settled in Paris in 1918 and made further studies with Ravel and others.

Works incl. mystery *Le Livre de la vie, Poèmes liturgiques*, &c.

Oca del Cairo, L' (*The Goose of Cairo*), unfinished opera by Mozart (lib. by Giovanni Battista Varesco). Prod. in a version completed with other Mozartian fragments (lib. by Victor Wilder), Paris, Fantaisies-Parisiennes, 6. VI. 1867; new version by Virgilio Mortari (lib. by L. Cavicchioli), Salzburg, 22. VIII. 1936;

another by Hans Redlich, London, Sadler's Wells Theatre, 30. V. 1940.

Ocarina. A primitive inst. of the fl. type with finger-holes, approx. pear-shaped, with a mouthpiece protruding like a fish's fin, and usually made of terracotta.

Occa, Sophie dall'. *See* **Schoberlechner.**

Occasional Oratorio, orat. by Handel (lib. from Milton's Psalms completed by ? Thomas Morell), comp. to celebrate the suppression of the Jacobite rebellion, prod. London, Covent Garden Theatre, 14. II. 1746.

Occasione fa il ladro, L' (*Opportunity makes a Thief*), opera by Rossini (lib. by Luigi Prividali), prod. Venice, Teatro San Moisè, 24. XI. 1812.

Ochelly. *See* **Kelly, Michael.**

Ochetto (It.) } *See* **Hocket.**
Ochetus (Lat.) }

Ochs, Siegfried (b. Frankfort o/M., 19. IV. 1858; d. Berlin, 6. II. 1929), Ger. cond. & comp. After a general educ. at Darmstadt and at Heidelberg Univ., he studied m. in Berlin and founded a chor. soc. in 1882, which in assoc. with the Phil. Orch. became the Philharmonische Chor in 1888. In the 1920s he became prof. of the Hochschule für Musik and cond. the orats. and other chor. concerts there.

Works incl. opera *Im Namen des Gesetzes*; songs, &c.

Ochsenkuhn, Sebastian (b. ?, 6. II. 1521; d. Heidelberg, 20. VIII. 1574), Ger. lutenist. In the service of Otto Heinrich, Elector Palatine of the Rhine, and his successors. He pub. in 1558 a book of arrs. of motets and Fr. & Ger. songs in lute tablature.

Ockeghem } *See* **Okeghem.**
Ockenheim }

Octava. Another name for the Principal org. stop.

Octave. An interval embracing 8 notes of a diatonic scale. The upper note having exactly twice the number of vibrations of the lower, the phenomenon—the most astonishing in acoustics, scientif. accountable but in the last resort inexplicable—prod. itself that the 2 appear to be the same, although different in pitch. Thus an O. does not prod. the effect of an interval, but of a unison.

Octave Flute. *See* **Piccolo.**

Octave Keys. *See* **Speaker Keys.**

Octave Unison. Passages perf. in bare 8ves, without harmony, although not strictly speaking in unison, are correctly said to be in O. U.

Octet. A comp. for 8 insts., usually in several mvts. and in some kind of so. or suite form. An O. may also be voc., but in that case it would not be given the name O. as a title, and it would prob. be merely an incidental section for 8 voices in a larger comp.

Octo Basse (Fr.) } A 3-stged. db. of
Octobass (Eng.) }
huge size invented in 1849 by J. B. Vuillaume in Paris, which never became current and is now obs. It was capable of playing extremely low notes, the range being from C below the stave in the bass clef with a perfect 4th and a further perfect 5th below. It was extremely unwieldy and its stgs. were so thick and heavy that they had to be stopped by means of levers and pedals.

Odak, Krsto (b. Siverić, 20. III. 1888), Yslv. comp. Studied at Munich and with Novák in Prague. In 1922 he was app. prof. at the Acad. of M. at Zagreb.

Works incl. opera *Dorrit Dances*; m. for a Christmas play & other incid. m.; 2 Slav masses; madrigal & other chors.; Symph. Ovt. for orch.; Rhapsodies for v. & orch.; 2 stg. 4tets; v. & pf. So.; 3 Psalms for bar. & pf., songs, &c.

Ode. The term used in poetry was adopted by Eng. mus. terminology for cantata-like settings of Os., usually in several mvts., with alternating solos and chors., often of a dedicatory or congratulatory character.

Ode for St. Cecilia's Day, setting by Handel of Dryden's poem, prod. London, Theatre in Lincoln's Inn Fields, 22. XI. 1739.

Odes for St. Cecilia's Day by Purcell: 1. *Laudate Ceciliam* (1683); 2. *Welcome to all the pleasures* (Fishburn; 1683); 3. *Hail, bright Cecilia* (Brady; 1692); 4. *Raise, raise the voice* (?).

Odington, Walter de (or W. of Evesham) (b. ? Oddington, Glos., ?; d. ? Evesham, ?), Eng. 13th-cent. monk, musn. & astron. He entered the Benedictine monastery at Evesham and wrote a treatise *De speculatione musices*.

Odo (b. ?, 879; d. Tours, 18. XI. ? 942), Fr. monk & musn. Educ. at the court of Guillaume, Duke of Aquitaine, took holy orders, joined the monastery of Saint-Martin at Tours, and after studying dialectics and m. in Paris, returned there, then entered the Benedictine monastery of Beaume nr. Besançon, became abbot of that of Cluny nr. Macon, 927–42, but returned to Tours to die. He comp. hymns and antiphons and wrote treatises on m., incl. (?) a *Dialogus de musica*.

Odzmek. A Slovak dance in quick 2–4 time with a more moderately paced middle section. The 9th of Dvořák's *Slavonic Dances* for pf. duet is an O.

Œdipe, opera by Enesco (lib. by Edmond Fleg, after Sophocles), prod. Paris, Opéra, 10. III. 1936.

Œdipe à Colone (*Oedipus Coloneus*), opera by Sacchini (lib. by Nicolas François Guillard, after Sophocles), prod. Versailles, at court, 4. I. 1786; 1st Paris perf. Opéra, 1. II. 1787.

Oedipus auf Kolonos, incid. m. by Mendelssohn for Sophocles' tragedy, Op. 93, for male chor. & orch., prod. Potsdam, 1. XI. 1845.

Oedipus Rex, stage orat. by Stravinsky (lib., in Lat., by J. Daniélou, trans. from Fr. by Jean Cocteau, after Sophocles), prod. Paris, Théâtre Sarah Bernhardt, 30. V. 1927. The parts are sung in costume but without action, and the words are in Lat. in order not to distract the ordinary listener by verbal associations.

Oedipus Tyrannus, incid. m. by Mendelssohn for Sophocles' tragedy, never perf. & now lost.

Incid. m. for do. by Stanford, prod. Cambridge, 22–6. XI. 1887.

Oehlenschläger, Adam (1779–1850), Dan. poet & dramatist. *See* **Danning** (*Aladdin*), **Gyrowetz** (do.), **Hartmann** (**J. P. E.**) (*Golden Horns*), **Heise** (*Palnatoke*), **Horneman** (*Aladdin*), **Nielsen** (**C.**) (do.).

Offenbach, Jacques (real name Jakob Levy Eberst) (b. Offenbach o/M., 20. VI. 1819; d. Paris, 5. X. 1880), Ger.-Fr. comp. His father was cantor at the synagogue of Cologne, but he was sent to Paris early in his youth, studying at the Cons. in 1833–7, perfecting himself in co. playing and then playing in the orch. of the Opéra-Comique even before he left the Cons. In 1849 he became cond. at the Théâtre Français. In 1853 he prod. his 1st operetta, *Pepito*, and during a quarter of a century he turned out nearly 100 light stage pieces. In 1855 he took over the management of the Théâtre Comte and renamed the Bouffes-Parisiens. This lasted until 1861, whereafter he had no theatre of his own until 1873, when he managed the Théâtre de la Gaîté until 1875. In 1876–7 he was in U.S.A., but returned to Paris, where alone he found that his success was permanent. His only large-scale opera, *Les Contes d'Hoffmann*, occupied him for many years, but he left it not quite finished at his death, and it was revised and partly scored by Guiraud.

Works incl. opera *Les Contes d'Hoffmann*, 89 operettas incl. *Barbebleue, Ba-ta-clan, La Belle Hélène, Chanson de Fortunio, Le Docteur Ox* (after Jules Verne), *La Fille du tambour-major, La Foire de Saint-Laurent, Geneviève de Brabant, La Grande-Duchesse de Gérolstein, L'Île de Tulipatan, La Jolie Parfumeuse, Madame Favart, Orphée aux enfers, La Périchole, Princesse de Trébizonde, Robinson Crusoé* (after Defoe), *Vert-Vert, La Vie Parisienne, Voyage dans la lune* (after Verne), *Whittington and his Cat*; ballet *Le Papillon*; incid. m. for Barrière's *La Gascon* & Sardou's *La Haine*, &c. A 2nd opera, *The Goldsmith of Toledo* (after a tale by E. T. A. Hoffmann) is a pasticcio from var. operettas, esp. *Le Corsaire noir*, prod. Mannheim, 1919.

Offertorium (Lat.) / **Offertory** (Eng.) A setting of a passage from the Bible, esp. the Psalms, often sung during mass in the Rom. Catholic church, but not forming part of the order of that service. When used it is inserted after the Credo while the priests prepare the Eucharist. Formerly, at var. times, antiphonal psalms in plainsong, motets or org. voluntaries were used, as the last still frequently are.

Oiseau bleu, L' (*The Blue Bird*), opera by A. Wolff (lib. taken from Maeterlinck's play), prod. N.Y., Metrop. Opera, 27. XII. 1919.

Okeghem, Jean de (Joannes) (or Ockeghem, Ockenheim, Hoquegan), (b. ? Termonde, *c.* 1420; d. Tours, *c.* 1495), Flem. comp. Pupil (?) of Binchois, chorister at Antwerp cath. until 1444, in the service of Charles, Duke of Bourbon, at Moulins in 1446–8, and in the service of the Fr. court from c. 1452, where he became 1st chapel master. Louis XI app. him treasurer of Saint-Martin at Tours, where he lived during the latter part of his life, though he visited Spa. in 1469. He had many distinguished pupils, incl. Josquin des Prés and Pierre de La Rue.

Works incl. masses, motets; Fr. chansons, &c.

Olav Trygvason, unfinished opera by Grieg (lib. by Bjørnson), 3 scenes only, perf. in concert form, Christiania, 19. X. 1889; never staged in G.'s lifetime, but prod. Christiania, 8. X. 1908.

Old Hall Manuscript. A collection of 15th-cent. church m. (c. 1415–80) copied in 4 different hands and kept at St. Edmund's Coll., Old Hall nr. Ware (Herts.), pub. in 1933–5.

Oldman, C(ecil). B(ernard). (b. London, 2. IV. 1894), Eng. bibliog. & mcolst. Educ. at City of London School and Exeter Coll., Oxford. He joined the staff of the British Museum library in 1920, where he was app. Deputy Keeper of Printed Books in 1943, and became interested in mus. research, specializing partic. in Mozart, on whom he has written var. learned studies.

Olé. *See* **Polo.**

Oleg. *See* **Early Reign of Oleg.**

Olimpia vendicata (*Olympia revenged*), opera by A. Scarlatti (lib. by Aurelio Aureli), prod. Naples, Palazzo Reale, 23. XII. 1685.

Olimpiade, L' (*The Olympiad*). *See also* **Olympie.** Lib. by Metastasio.

Opera by Caldara, prod. Vienna, 28. VIII. 1733.

Opera by Cimarosa, prod. Vicenza, 17. VII. 1784.

Opera by Ignazio Fiorillo (1715–87), prod. Venice, Teatro San Samuele, V. 1745.

Opera by Galuppi, prod. Milan, Teatro Regio Ducal, 26. XII. 1747.

Opera by Hasse, prod. Dresden, at court, 16. II. 1756.

Opera by Jommelli, prod. Stuttgart, at court, 11. II. 1761.

Opera by Leo, prod. Naples, Teatro San Carlo, 19. XII. 1737.

Opera by Mysliveček, prod. Naples, Teatro San Carlo, 4. XI. 1778.

Opera by Pergolesi, prod. Rome, Teatro Tordinona, 8. I. 1735.

Opera by Sacchini, prod. Padua, VI. 1763.

Opera by Traetta, prod. Verona, autumn 1758.

Opera by Vivaldi, prod. Venice, Teatro Sant' Angelo, Carnival 1734.

(There are at least 30 other settings of this lib. O. is prob. the most frequently comp. work by Metastasio or by any other libst.)

Oliphant (from old Eng. ' olifaunt ' = elephant). A bugle-like hn. made of an elephant's tusk, used for signalling and hunting in old times, often beautifully carved.

Olivieri-Sangiacomo, Elsa. *See* **Respighi.**

Ollone, Max d' (b. Besançon, 13. VI. 1875), Fr. cond. & comp. Studied under Massenet and Lenepveu at the Paris Cons. and gained the Prix de Rome in 1897. After cond. at Angers, Geneva and Paris (Opéra-Comique, concerts, &c.), and touring as cond., he became prof. at the Cons. in 1939.

Works incl. operas *Le Retour, Les Amants de Rimini* (after Dante), *Les Uns et les autres* (on a comedy by Verlaine), *L'Arlequin, George Dandin* (after Molière) & *La Samaritaine* (after Rostand); ballet *Le Peuple abandonné*; pantomime *Bacchus et Silène*; orat. *François d'Assise*, cantatas *Frédégonde, Jeanne d'Arc à Domrémy*; Fantasy for pf. & orch., *Le Ménétrier* for v. & orch.; stg. 4tet, pf. Trio; songs, &c.

Olmeda de San José, Federico (b. Burgo de Osma, 1865; d. Madrid, 11. II. 1909), Spa. mcolst., orgst. & comp. After 2 other orgst.'s appts. he became orgst. to the convent of the Descalzas Reales in Madrid, 1893. He wrote on early Spa. polyphony and Castilian folksong.

Works incl. church m.; 4 syms.; stg. 4tet; pf. pieces, &c.

Olsen, Ole (b. Hammerfest, 4. VII. 1850; d. Oslo, 10. XI. 1927), Norw. orgst., cond. & comp. Studied engineering at Trondhjem, but took to m., taking any appt. as orgst. and travelling theatre cond. he could secure. In 1870–4 he consolidated his studies at the Leipzig Cons. and then settled at Christiania, where he taught cond. and wrote criticism.

Works incl. operas *Stig Hvide, Laila, Klippeøerne* & *Stallo*; incid. m. to Nordahl Rolfsen's *Svein Uroed*; orat. *Nideros*, cantatas *Ludwig Holberg, Griffenfeld, Broderbud, Tourist Cantata*; Sym. in G maj., symph. poems *Aasgaardsreien, Elf-dans*, &c.

Olthoff, Statius (b. Osnabrück, 1555; d. Rostock, 28. II. 1629), Ger. comp. Became cantor at St. Mary's church at Rostock in 1579 and there comp. 4-part settings of George Buchanan's Lat. verse paraphrase of the Psalms.

Olympie, opera by Spontini (lib. by Michel Dieulafoy & Charles Brifaut, based on Voltaire's tragedy), prod. Paris, Opéra, 22. XII. 1819.

Omar Khayyám (?–1123), Persian scholar & poet. *See* **Bantock, Cadman, Ettinger, Lehmann (L. ii), Levidis, Respighi (E.).**

O'Mara, Joseph (b. Limerick, 16. VII. 1866; d. Dublin, 5. VIII. 1927), Ir. ten. singer. Studied at Milan and made his 1st appearance in London, 1891.

Ombra di Don Giovanni, L' (*Don Juan's Shade*), opera by Alfano (lib. by Ettore Moschino), prod. Milan, Teatro alla Scala, 2. IV. 1914.

Omphale, opera by Destouches (lib. by Antoine Houdar de la Motte), prod. Paris, Opéra, 10. XI. 1700.

On Hearing the First Cuckoo in Spring, 1 of 2 pieces for small orch. by Delius (the other being *Summer Night on the River*), comp. 1912, 1st perf. Leipzig, Gewandhaus, 2. X. 1913. The cuckoo call is heard unobtrusively on the cl. and the main theme is a Norw. folksong previously used by Grieg.

Ondes Musicales. An electrophonic inst. invented by Maurice Martenot of Paris in 1929, prod. notes from the air graded according to the chromatic scale by a special device, not indeterminate in pitch like those of the Aetherophone or Theremin.

Ondříček, František (b. Prague, 29. IV. 1859; d. Milan, 13. IV. 1922), Cz. vst. Pupil of his father and at the Prague and Paris Conss. 1st appeared in Paris in 1882 and then went on tour. Prof. at the Vienna Cons., 1911–9, and then at that of Prague.

Onegin (*née* **Hoffmann**), **Sigrid** (b. Stockholm, 1. VI. 1891; d. Magliaso, Swi., VI. 1934), Swe. con. singer of Ger. and (?) Rus. descent. Studied in Swe. & Ger. and appeared frequently in both countries, also in Eng.

O'Neill, Eugene (Gladstone) (b. 1888), Amer. dramatist. *See* **Gruenberg** (*Emperor Jones*), **Whithorne** (*Marco Millions*).

O'Neill, Norman (b. London, 14. III. 1875; d. London, 3. III. 1934), Anglo-Ir. cond. & comp. Great-grandson of Callcott. Studied with Somervell in London and with Knorr at the Hoch Cons. at Frankfort o/M. In 1899 he married the Fr. pfst. Adine Rückert and in 1908 became cond. at the Haymarket Theatre, for which he wrote much incid. m. In 1919 he became treasurer of the Royal Phil. Soc. and in 1924 prof. at the R.A.M.

Works incl. incid. m. for Shakespeare's *Hamlet, Henry V, Julius Caesar, King Lear, Macbeth, Measure for Measure* & *The Merchant of Venice*, Maeterlinck's *Blue Bird*, Barrie's *Mary Rose* & *A Kiss for Cinderella*, Ibsen's *Pretenders*, Stephen Phillips's *The Lost Heir*: dramatic adapts. of Dickens's *Pickwick* & Scott's *Bride of Lammermoor*, &c.; *Swinburne Ballet* & *Punch and Judy* ballet; concert ovts., Vars., *Miniatures* & other works for orch.; chor. works; pf. 5tet, 2 pf. trios; Vars. & Fugue on an Ir. Air for 2 pfs.; pf. pieces; many songs, &c.

Onomatopoeia (from Gr., lit. 'word-making'). In m. the direct imitation of sounds in nature, e.g. the birds in Beethoven's *Pastoral* Sym., the sheep in Strauss's *Don Quixote* or the gramophone record of a nightingale used in Respighi's *Pines of Rome*.

Onslow, George (or **Georges**) (b. Clermont-Ferrand, 27. VII. 1784; d. Clermont-Ferrand, 3. X. 1853), Fr. comp. of Eng. descent. Grandson of the 1st Lord Onslow. He studied pf. with Hüllmandel, Dussek & Cramer while living in London for some years as a young man, but settled at Clermont-Ferrand as a country squire, held regular chamber m. practices there, studied the co. and went for 2 years to Vienna to study comp. In the 1820s, wishing to write operas, he made further studies with Reicha in Paris, where he lived alternatively.

Works incl. operas *L'Alcalde de la Vega, Le Colporteur* & *Le Duc de Guise*; 4 syms.; 36 stg. 4tets, 36 stg. 5tets, 2 pf. 6tets, pf. 7tet, Nonet for stgs. & wind, 6 pf. trios; v. & pf. and co. & pf. sos.; sos. for pf. duet; pf. pieces, &c.

Op. (abbr.) = Opus (Lat. = work). A prefix used for the enumeration of a comp.'s works. It was at first a pub.'s rather than a comp.'s device and in the early 18th cent. (e.g. Handel) was used only for inst. comps. Later in that cent. it began to become more general, being used for Haydn but not for Mozart, and from Beethoven onward it began to be used by comps.

Open. Org. pipes of which the upper end is left open and which, unlike the Stopped pipes, prod. notes corresponding to their full length.

Open Diapason. *See* **Diapason.**

Open Notes. On wind insts. the notes prod. naturally as harmonics as distinct from Stopped Notes prod. by valves, keys or other mechanical means, or sometimes by the hand in hn. playing; on stg. insts. any notes prod. by the stgs. without being stopped by a finger.

Open Strings. The stgs. of stg. insts. as played without being stopped by the left hand on the fingerboard.

Oper (Ger.) = Opera. Plur. *Opern.*

Opera (It. = work: the same as the Lat. *opus* and orig. used in the same sense). A mus. work for the stage of varying types, originating in the 1st years of the 17th cent. in It. The dramatic foundation of it is a Libretto, which is set to m. in var. ways that may be divided into 3 main types: (1) recitative carrying on the action and set mus. numbers such as arias, concerted pieces for several voices, chors., &c. forming mus. climaxes; (2) similar mus. numbers, but with the action carried on in spoken dialogue instead of recit.; (3) the text comp. continuously throughout, but often with traces of separate mus. numbers still apparent. The treatment of the voices showed a tendency from the beginning to create a variety of definite dramatic types; the inst. share in an O. is almost always orchestral.

See also **Action musicale; Azione teatrale; Ballad Opera; Burlesque; Burletta; Comédie lyrique; Commedia per musica; Dramma giocoso; Dramma per musica; Extravaganza; Favola per musica; Festa teatrale; Handlung; Intermezzi; Melodrama; Melodramma; Music Drama; Musical Comedy; Opera-Ballet; Opéra bouffe; O. buffa; Opéra comique; O. seria; Operetta; Pastorale; Singe-Spiel; Singspiel; Tragédie lyrique; Vaudeville.**

Opera-Ballet. A combination of O. and B. orig. in 17th-cent. Fr. and there called *opéra-ballet* from the beginning.

Opéra bouffe (Fr. = comic opera, der. from It. *opera buffa*). A type of Fr.

comic opera, or rather operetta, lighter in tone and flimsier in mus. workmanship than an *opéra comique*.

Opera buffa (It. =comic opera). A light type of opera with a comedy lib., partic. of the 18th cent. in It., with dialogue in Recitative (accomp. by the hpchd.) and mus. numbers: arias, duets, &c. and (more rarely) chors.

Opéra comique (Fr. lit. comic opera). An exclusively Fr. type of opera, not always comic and often by no means light, but orig. always with spoken dialogue, though that is now sometimes replaced by recitatives (e.g. Bizet's *Carmen*).

Opera seria (It. =serious opera). A type of 18th-cent. O., esp. that cultivated by the libsts. Zeno and Metastasio, treating mytholog. or heroic-histor. subjects. The mus. treatment is mainly by recitative and arias, more rarely duets & other concerted numbers or chors.

Operetta (It. =little opera). A type of very light opera or mus. comedy, often in 1 act, but normally in 3 acts in some types (e.g. the Viennese), always with spoken dialogue except sometimes in It.

Opernball, Der (*The Opera Ball*), operetta by Heuberger (lib. by Victor Léon & Heinrich von Waldberg), prod. Vienna, Theater an der Wien, 5. I. 1898.

Ophicleide. An obs. wind inst. of the bn. type, but more closely related to the Serpent, whose coarse tone it had. It was prob. invented by a Fr. musn. named Frichot settled in London, *c.* 1790, and called Bass Horn. This, however, was actually the Rus. Bassoon, whereas the O. descended from the Cornett family. It resembled the bassoon in shape, but was thicker and more uncouth, had 11 or 12 keys, a mouthpiece like that of the tromb. and a compass of *c.* 3 8ves.—Also a 16-ft. reed org. pedal stop of powerful tone.

Opie (*née* **Alderson**), **Amelia** (1769–1853), Eng. novelist, wife of the painter John O. *See* **Agnese di Fitz-Henry** (Paer).

Opienski, Henryk (b. Cracow, 13. I. 1870; d. Morges nr. Lausanne, 21. I. 1942), Pol. mcolst., cond. & comp. Studied pf. with Paderewski, comp. with d'Indy at the Schola Cantorum in Paris and cond. and mcol. with Nikisch and Riemann at Leipzig. He formed a voc. soc. at Lausanne in 1918 and lived in Swi. until his death, except when he was dir. of the Poznan Cons. in 1920–6. He ed. Chopin's letters and wrote on him, on Paderewski, on Pol. m. in general, &c.

Works incl. operas *Maria* (Malczewski) & *Jacob the Lutenist*; incid. m. for Calderón's *El principe constante*; orat. *The Prodigal Son*; cantata *Mickiewicz*; symph. poems *Zymunt August i Barbara* & *Lilla Weneda*; stg. 4tet; inst. pieces; songs, &c.

Opitz (von Boberfeld), Martin (1597–1639), Ger. poet. *See* **Dafne** (Schütz), **Loewenstern** (*Judith*).

Oppure (It. =or rather). *See* **Ossia.** A more rarely used word for the same thing.

Opus (Lat. =work). Its abbr., **Op.,** is used as a prefix to enumerations of a comp.'s works. Its It. equiv., *opera*, at first had the same meaning, but is now used almost exclusively in its later specific sense.

Orat. (abbr.) =Oratorio.

Oratorio. A voc. work, usually for solo voices and chor. with some kind of inst. accomp. and generally set to sacred words, often direct from the Bible or paraphrased from it, and at any rate nearly always treating subject of a sacred character (such notable exceptions as Handel's *Hercules* and Haydn's *Seasons* not being strictly speaking Os.). It originated vaguely in the medieval mystery and miracle plays and such things as the 12th-cent. Fr. *Prose de l'âne*, and more clearly in the congregation of the Oratorians founded by St. Philip Neri in the 16th cent., where scenes from Scripture were enacted with m. in Rome. In the 17th cent. the O. developed side by side with Opera and was indistinguishable from it in some of its features, except that greater prominence was nearly always given to the chor.; and this is still true of the operas and Os. of Handel. Settings of one of the Evangelists' narratives of the Passion developed a special type of O., esp. in Ger. In 19th-cent. Eng. the O. became fashionable as the preferred type of festival work.

Orazi ed i Curiazi, Gli (*The Horatii and the Curiatii*), opera by Cimarosa (lib. by Antonio Simone Sografi), prod. Venice, Teatro La Fenice, 26. XII. 1796.

Opera by Mercadante (lib. by Salvatore Cammarano), prod. Naples, Teatro San Carlo, 10. XI. 1846.

Orch. (abbr.) =Orchestra, Orchestral.

Orchestra (from Gr.: dancing-place). Orig. the space in the Gr. theatre equivalent to that now occupied by the O. in an opera-house; now the name for the assembly of inst. players itself. The modern O. as a choric body, distinct from chamber-m. consorts of individual perfs., originated in the 1st operas of the early 17th cent. It then contained a number of insts. now obs., such as lutes, viols, hpchds., regals, &c. and was not standardized. In the 18th cent. pairs of obs. and hns. were the insts. most frequently used apart from stgs., with tpts. and drums, often brought in from the military estabs. of the O.'s patrons. Trombs. were used only for solemn occasions, bns. if they happened to be available. The fl. dropped in and out, often exchanged by the same players with obs. The cl. appeared in the 2nd half of the 18th cent.; picc., Eng. hn., bass cl., double bn., hp. and extra perc. not normally till the 19th, when also natural hns. and tpts. gave way to valve insts. Until the end of the 18th cent., and sometimes later, the cond. sat at the hpchd. or played 1st v.

Orchestration (or Scoring). The art of setting out a comp. for the insts. of an orch. The comp. may score his m. fully as he invents it or 1st write it down in some kind of a sketchy short score or even in a pf. version; but this last is unlikely unless he is so limited technically as to be constrained to comp. at the pf. The art of O. has developed enormously since the early 17th cent., but not necessarily always improved, for good O. depends on the proper use of the resources available at any given time, not on the discovery of new ones, which may or may not have artistic results. Methods of O. have also changed vastly. Monteverdi (*c.* 1610) roughed out his scores approximately, and they were played by such insts. as happened to be available; Bach (*c.* 1720) chose a partic. set of insts. prod. a partic. tone-colour and retained it throughout a whole work; Berlioz (*c.* 1830) used a great range of insts. with endless variety from point to point and may be said to have been the originator of modern O., since this is still the normal procedure.

Orchn. (abbr.) = Orchestration.

Ordoñez, Pedro (b. Palencia, *c.* 1500; d. Rome, 1550), Spa. singer & comp. In 1539 he went to Rome as a singer in the Pontifical chapel and remained there to his death, attending the Council of Trent in 1545 and again in 1547, when it had moved to Bologna. Comp. church m.

Ordre (Fr.). The old Fr. name for the Suite, now obs.

Orefice, Giacomo (b. Vicenza, 27. VIII. 1865; d. Milan, 22. XII. 1922), It. comp. Studied at the Bologna Liceo Musicale, Mancinelli being among his masters. He later became prof. of comp. at the Milan Cons.

Works incl. operas *Consuelo* (after George Sand), *Chopin* (on m. by C.), *Cecilia, Mosè, Pane altrui, Radda, Il castello del sogno* & others; Sym. in D min., *Sinfonia del bosco, Anacreontiche* for orch.; Suite for co. & orch.; *Riflessioni ed ombre* for 5tet, pf. Trio; 2 v. & pf. sos., co. & pf. So.; *Preludi del mare, Quadri di Böcklin, Crepuscoli, Miraggi,* &c. for pf.

Orel, Alfred (b. Vienna, 3. VII. 1889), Aus. mcolst. A lawyer and civil servant at first, he studied m. with Adler when nearly 30. Later app. prof. at Vienna Univ. and head of the m. dept. of the munic. library. Author of works on Bruckner and co-ed. with Robert Haas of the ed. of the orig. versions of B.'s works.

Orel, Dobroslav (b. Ronov, 15. XII. 1870), Cz. mcolst. Studied theol. and taught church m. at the Prague Cons., later studied comp. with Novák and mcol. with Adler. App. prof. at the Komensky Univ. at Bratislava, 1921. Author of studies of old Boh. m., &c.

Oresteia, trilogy of short operas by Taneiev (lib. by A. A. Venkstern, after Aeschylus), prod. St. Petersburg, 29. X. 1895.

Orestes. *See also* **Leben des Orest.**

Opera by Weingartner (lib. by comp., after Aeschylus), prod. Leipzig, 15. II. 1902.

Orfeide, L', cycle of operas by Malipiero (lib. by comp.), prod. complete, in Ger. trans., Düsseldorf, 30. X. 1925.

I. **La morte delle maschere** (*The Death of the Masques*).

II. **Sette canzoni** (*Seven Songs*), prod., in Fr. trans., Paris, Opéra, 10. VII. 1920.

III. **L'Orfeo, ossia L'ottava canzone** (*Orpheus, or the Eighth Song*).

Orfeo (Monteverdi). *See* **Favola d'Orfeo.**

Orfeo ed Euridice (*Orpheus and Eurydice*), opera by Bertoni (lib. by Ranieri da Calzabigi, written for Gluck), prod. Venice, Teatro San Benedetto, I. 1776.

Opera by Gluck (lib. do.), prod. Vienna, Burg Theatre, 5. X. 1762. (For Fr. version *see* **Orphée.**)

Orfeo, L' (*Orpheus*), opera by Luigi Rossi (lib. by Francesco Buti), prod. Paris, Palais Royal, 2. III. 1647.

Orff, Carl (b. Munich, 10. VII. 1895), Ger. comp. & teacher. Studied at Munich and became prof. of comp. at the Günther School there. He is also a cond. and ed. of old m.

Works incl. mainly chor. comps., e.g. *Carmina Burana* (scenic cantata: settings of medieval poetry), cantata *Des Turmes Auferstehung* (Franz Werfel); ballet *Der Feuerfarbene*;

Schulwerk for combs. of popular insts. and similar comps. intended for use by amateurs; incid. m. for Shakespeare's *Midsummer Night's Dream*, &c.

Org. (abbr.) = Organ.

Organ. The most elaborate inst. playable by a single perf. Its origin lies in remote antiquity, e.g. the syrinx or pan-pipe. Later the wind was no longer supplied by the player's breath, but by bellows; the pipes were opened and closed by an action of keys and a keyboard of pedals, played by the feet, was added to control the largest bass pipes. The number of pipes, ranging from 2 ft. to 32 ft. in size, was enormously increased, and they were made in a growing variety of shapes from different materials and with different speaking-mechanisms, each range being controlled by stops which could bring it into action or shut it off at the player's will. 2 or more manuals (hand keyboards) were added to the formerly only one, whereby a greater number of stops drawn before the perf. could be controlled and varied. From the late 19th cent. the bellows, formerly blown by hand, were worked by electricity and in the 20th devices by which whole ranges of stops could be brought into action in var. combs. were invented, still further increasing the resources already enlarged by the couplers, by which the registration controlled by 2 manuals or by a manual and the pedals could be mechanically united. Expression was added by swell pedals prod. *crescendo* and *diminuendo*, but beyond that the player's hands and feet have no power to vary the tone either in strength or in quality.

Organ-Point (from Ger. *Orgelpunkt*). Another term, used mainly in Amer., for Pedal-Point.

Organ Stops. *See* **Acoustic Bass, Acute Mixture, Bass Flute, Bassoon, Bell Gamba, Bombarde, Bombardon, Bourdon, Carillons, Claribel, Claribel Flute, Clarinet, Clarion, Clarion Mixture, Clarionet Flute, Closed Horn, Cor anglais, Cor-de-Nuit, Cor-Oboe, Cornet, Corno di Bassetto, Corno dolce, Cornopean, Cremona, Cymbal, Diapason, Diaphone, Dolcan, Dulciana, Dulcina Mixture, Echo, Fagotto, Fifteenth, Flageolet, Flautina, Flauto traverso, Flute, Flûte à cheminée, Flute Bass, Flûte d'amour, Flute Harmonic, Furniture, Gamba, Gedackt, Geigen Principal, Gemshorn, Grave Mixture, Hautboy, Hohl Flute, Hohlflöte, Horn, Horn Diapason, Keraulophon, Lieblich Flute, Lieblich Gedackt, Major Bass, Mixture, Oboe, Octave, Ophicleide, Piccolo, Posaune, Principal, Quint, Quintaton, Rohr Flute, Rohrflöte, Salicional, Sesquialtera, Sharp Mixture, Suabe Flute, Sub Bass, Sub Bourdon, Super Octave, Tremulant, Tromba, Trombone, Trumpet, Tuba, Twelfth, Unda Maris, Viol, Viol d'amour, Viol da Gamba, Viol d'orchestre, Viola, Violin Diapason, Violoncello, Violone, Voix céleste, Vox angelica, Vox humana, Wald Flute.**

Organistrum. *See* **Hurdy-Gurdy.**

Organo pieno (It.) or **Organo pleno (Lat.)** = full org. A direction indicating that an org. passage is to be played with the use of the full extent of the inst.'s power.

Organum (Lat.). An old term for Measured or Mensural M. as distinct from Plainsong; also another name for Diaphony and for var. forms of Descant.

Orgatron. An electrophonic org. invented by Everett of Michigan in 1934, prod. its notes by the conversion of electrical waves into audible sounds.

Orgelpunkt (Ger. = organ-point). *See* **Pedal-Point.**

Orgeni (or **Orgenyi**, actually **Görger St. Jorgen**), **Anna Maria Aglaia** (b. Rima Szombat, 17. XII. 1841; d. Vienna, 15. III. 1926), Hung. sop. singer. Pupil of Pauline Viardot-García. Made her 1st stage appearance in Berlin, 1865.

Orgst. (abbr). = Organist.

Orgue expressif (Fr.) = Harmonium.

Orlandi, Santi (b. Florence, ?; d. Mantua, VII. 1619), It. comp. He was chapel master to Ferdinando Gonzaga at Florence and succeeded Monteverdi as chapel master to the ducal Gonzaga family at Mantua in 1612.

Works incl. opera *Gli amori di Aci e Galatea*; 5 books of madrigals, &c.

Orlandini, Giuseppe Maria (b. Bologna, 4. II. 1688; d. Florence, *c.* 1750), It. comp. Chapel master to the Duke of Tuscany at Florence.

Works incl. operas *Amore e maestà, Antigona, Il marito giocatore, Nerone* & 40 others; orats., cantatas, &c.

Orlando (*Roland*), opera by Handel (lib. by Grazio Braccioli, based on Ariosto's *Orlando furioso*), prod. London, King's Theatre, Haymarket, 27. I. 1733.

Orléans, Charles Duc de (1391–1465), Fr. prince & poet. *See* **Debussy** (*Chansons de France*), **Dieren (van)** (songs).

Ornaments. *See also* **Acciaccatura, Appoggiatura, Arpeggio, Mordent, Shake, Turn, Tremolo, Vibrato.**

Apart from the main ornaments discussed under the above headings, the following are some of the terms found in old treatises on the subject. Some are now obs., either because the fashion of highly ornamented singing and playing is dead or because great elaboration is not suited to modern insts. Some of the embellishments that were indispensable to the hpchd., for ex., because of its inability to give prominence to certain notes by accentuation, sound merely fussy on the pf.

Eng.:

Acute = Springer.

Backfall = Appoggiatura (from above).

Battery = Arpeggio.

Beat = Appoggiatura (from below).

Cadent. 3 notes rising or falling consecutively, the middle of which is a Turn following by a Shake.

Close Shake = Vibrato.

Forefall = Appoggiatura (from below).

Half Fall. A semitonal Appoggiatura from below on the lute.

Lead (imper.). Perform with an Appoggiatura.

Passing Appoggiatura. An unaccented A. inserting a note between 2 notes of a falling 3rd.

Prepare (imper.). Perform with an Appoggiatura.

Prepared Shake. A Shake beginning with an Appoggiatura.

Relish = Turn.

Shake = Trill.

Sigh = Springer.

Slide. 2 notes below a principal note leading up to it.

Springer. A short auxiliary note inserted after a main note, the reverse of an Appoggiatura.

Turned Shake. A Shake followed by a Turn.

Unprepared Shake. A Shake beginning at once on the main note, without an Appoggiatura.

Fr.:

Accent. An Appoggiatura inserting a grace-note between a rising or falling 3rd or repeating the 1st note of a rising or falling 2nd.

Appuyer (verb). Perf. with an Appoggiatura.

Aspiration = Springer.

Battement = Mordent.

Cadence = Shake.

Cadence appuyée = Prepared Shake.

Cadence sans tremblement = Turn.

Chevroté (goaty). The description of a too rapid Shake.

Chute or Traînée = Appoggiatura (from above or below).

Coulé or Coulade = Appoggiatura (from below) or Slide, in which all the intermediate notes are not clearly articulated.

Doublé = Turn.

Double Cadence = Turn.

Flatté = Slide.

Frappé = Passing Appoggiatura.

Harpègement = Arpeggio, which could be upwards or downwards according to the sign used.

Jeté = Port de voix double.

Martellement = Mordent with note above.

Pincé = Mordent with note below.

Pincé étouffé = Acciaccatura.

Pincé renversé = Shake.

Pincement = Mordent.

Plainte = Springer.

Port de voix = Appoggiatura (from below).

Port de voix double or jeté. A double Appoggiatura with 1 note below and 1 above the principal note.

Roulade. A general term for extended ornamental voc. phrases; more specifically an O. consisting of a descending scale with intermed. notes rising by 1 degree.

Suspension. The delaying of a note a fraction of time.

Tacté = Acciaccatura.

Tour de gosier = Turn.

Trainée = Chute.

Trait. A slide similar to the Coulé, but with all the intermediate notes articulated.

Tremblement = Shake.

Tremblement appuyé = Prepared Shake.

Trille = Shake.

Ger.:

Abzug. An Appoggiatura inserting a grace-note between a rising or falling 3rd or repeating the 1st note of a rising or falling 2nd.

Anschlag = Port de voix double.

Anschlagend (adj.). Of Passing Appoggiatura.

Bebung = Vibrato.

Beisser = Mordent.

Brechung = Arpeggio.

Doppelschlag = Turn.

Nachschlag = Springer.

Pralltriller = Mordent.

Schleifer = Slide.

Schneller = Mordent with note above.

Triller = Shake.

Vorschlag = Appoggiatura.

Zusammenschlag = Mordent or Acciaccatura.

It.

Circolo mezzo = Turn.

Groppo = Shake.

Mordente = Mordent.

Portamento = Appoggiatura (for another meaning *see* main entry).

Ribattuta (from *ribattere* = to strike again). The Eng. name of this O. might lit. be 'Rebound.' It consists of a repetition of 2 alternating adjacent notes several times with increasing speed, the note-values being progressively doubled, until a shake is worked up.

Tatto = Acciaccatura.
Tremoletto = Shake.
Trillo = Shake. *See also* Vibrato.
Lat.:
Tremor pressus = Vibrato.

Ornithoparcus, Andreas (actually Vogelgesang or Vogelsang) (b. Meiningen, ?; d. ?), Ger. 15th–16th-cent. mus. scholar. Studied (?) at Tübingen Univ., travelled in many countries and (?) held some post at Wittenberg Univ. Author of the Lat. treatise *Musicae activae micrologus*, which was trans. into Eng. by J. Dowland.

Ornstein, Leo (b. Krementchug, 11. XII. 1895), Rus. pfst. & comp., naturalized in U.S.A. Studied at the St. Petersburg Cons., where he appeared as a child prodigy, settled in N.Y. in 1906, studying further at the Inst. of Mus. Art, and made his 1st concert appearance there in 1911.

Works incl. pantomime *Lima Beans*, pantomime ballet; incid. m. to Aristophanes' *Lysistrata*; Sym., 2 Nocturnes, *Nocturne and Dance of the Fates*, symph. poem *The Fog* for orch.; 2 pf. concs.; stg. 4tet, pf. 5tet; 2 v. & pf. sos., So. for co. & pf.; chor. works; pf. m., &c.

Orpharion. *See* **Orpheoreon.**

Orphée, opera by Gluck (lib. by Pierre Louis Moline, trans. from Calzabigi's *Orfeo ed Euridice*, of G.'s 1st setting of which it is a revised version), prod. Paris, 2. VIII. 1774.

Orphée aux enfer (*Orpheus in the Underworld*), operetta by Offenbach (lib. by Hector Crémieux & Ludovic Halévy), prod. Paris, Bouffes-Parisiens, 21. X. 1858.

Orphéon (Fr.). A Fr. male-voice chor. soc. similar to the Ger. *Liedertafel*.

Orpheoreon (or **Orpharion**). An obs. inst. of the Cittern type. It had 6 or 7 pairs of stgs. played with a plectrum.

Orpheus. *See also* **Favola d'Orfeo; Malheurs d'Orphée; Orfeide; Orfeo; Orfeo ed Euridice; Orphée; Orphée aux enfers; Orpheus og Euridice; Orpheus und Eurydike.**

Opera by Keiser (lib. by Friedrich Christian Bressand), prod. Brunswick (Part I: *Die sterbende Eurydice*) ? II. 1699. Hamburg (Part II: *Die verwandelte Leyer des Orpheus*), 1709.

Symph. poem by Liszt, comp. 1853–4, 1st perf. as an introd. to Gluck's *Orfeo*, Weimar, 16. II. 1854, with closing m. on the same themes after the opera.

Orpheus Britannicus. A collection of voc. m. by Purcell begun soon after P.'s death by Henry Playford, who pub. a 1st vol. in 1698 and a 2nd in 1702; also a collection of P.'s songs pub. by John Walsh in 1735.

Orpheus og Euridice, opera by Naumann (lib. by Charlotte Dorothea Biehl, based on Calzabigi), prod. Copenhagen, 31. I. 1786. The 1st grand opera on a Dan. lib.

Orpheus und Eurydike, opera by Krenek (lib. by Oskar Kokoschka), prod. Cassel, 27. XI. 1926.

Orr, C(harles). W(ilfred). (b. Cheltenham, 31. VII. 1893), Eng. comp. Educ. at Cheltenham Coll. He suffered much from ill-health in his youth and did not begin to study m. at the G.S.M. in London until 1917. He has lived most of his life quietly at Painswick, Glos., and has never held any official mus. posts; but he did war-work in London during the 1939–45 world war.

Works incl. *A Cotswold Hill Tune* for stg. orch.; numerous songs, esp. settings of A. E. Housman, also D. G. Rossetti, James Joyce, &c.

Orr, Robin (b. Brechin, 1909), Sco. comp. Studied at the R.C.M. in London and with E. J. Dent at Cambridge, also with Casella at Siena and Nadia Boulanger in Paris. In 1938 he was app. orgst. and dir. of studies at St. John's Coll., Cambridge, but joined the R.A.F. in 1941.

Works incl. Divertimento for chamber orch.; 3 Lat. Psalms for voice & stg. 4tet; Sonatina for v. & pf.; pf. pieces; songs, &c.

Ortigue, Joseph Louis, d' (b. Cavaillon, 22. V. 1802; d. Paris, 20. XI. 1866), Fr. writer on m. & authority on church m. Succeeded Berlioz as critic of the *Journal des Débats*, having already contrib. to many other papers since 1829.

Ortiz, Diego (b. Toledo, ?; d. ?), Spa. 16th-cent. comp. He went to Naples about the 1550s to become chapel master to the viceroy, the Duke of Alva, where he worked with many other Spa. musns., incl. Salinas.

Works incl. motets; vars. for bass viol, &c.

Orto, Marbriano de (b. ?; d. ?), Flem. 15th–16th-cent. singer & comp. His name may have been Dujardin, the It. form being taken when he went to Rome, where he was a singer in the Papal chapel in 1484–94, with Josquin des Prés. Early in the 16th cent. he became chaplain and singer at the court of Philip the Fair of Burgundy.

Works incl. masses, motets & other church m.; chansons, &c.

Osborne, (George) Alexander (b. Limerick, 24. IX. 1806; d. London, 16. XI. 1893), Ir. pfst. Studied in Belg. and afterwards taught pf. in Brussels. In 1826 he went to Paris, making further studies with Pixis and Kalkbrenner and becoming a friend of

Chopin, Berlioz and Rossini. He settled in London in 1843, where he taught and championed Chopin's work.

O'Shaughnessy, Arthur (William Edgar) (1844–81), Eng. poet of Ir. descent. *See* **Music Makers** (Elgar).

Ossia (It., from *o sia* = or be it, or else). A word shown with an alternative passage, usually easier and sometimes more difficult, which may be perf. at will instead of that orig. written down by the comp. Such passages are usually shown in smaller notes above or below the stave. The word may also be used for alternatives where a comp. clearly wrote a passage of pf. m. for a short keyboard and where it is clear that he would have written it otherwise for a modern pf. It also occurs, like the older *ovvero*, in 2nd alternative titles of mus. works (e.g. 'Così fan tutte, ossia La scuola degli amanti,' &c.).

Ossian. *See* **Macpherson, James.**

Works based on 'Ossian' *see* **Bainton** (*Oithona*), **Coquard** (symph. poem), **Davie, Dupuis (S.)** (*Moïna*), **Gade** (ovt.), **Goossens** (symph. prelude), **Ippolitov - Ivanov** (symph. poem), **Kunzen** (*O.'s Harfe*), **Lesueur** (opera), **Pavesi** (*Fingallo e Comala*), **Rust (F. W.)** (*Colma*), **Sobolevsky** (*Komala*), **Uthal** (Méhul), **Whyte** (*Comala*), **Zumsteeg** (*Kolma*), 9 songs by Schubert.

Osterc, Slavko (b. Veržej, 17. VI. 1895), Yslv. comp. Studied with Jirák and Novák at the Prague Cons., also quarter-tone m. with Hába. Later he became prof. at the Ljubljana Cons.

Works incl. 3 miniature operas; ballet; children's cantata; 2 stg. 4tets, Trio for wind insts., Nonet; So. for saxophone & pf.; pf. m.; songs; quarter-tone comps., &c.

Ostinato (It. = obstinate). A persistently repeated figure in a comp. If, as is most often the case, it is in the bass, it is called *basso o.* A rhythm also can be called O., and so can some inst. device, like Tchaikovsky's *pizzicato o.* in the 4th Sym.

Ostrčil, Otakar (b. Smichov nr. Prague, 25. II. 1879; d. Prague, 20. VIII. 1935), Cz. cond. & comp. Studied at Prague Univ. and became prof. of modern languages at the Commercial Acad. there. But he had already studied m., esp. with Fibich, and in 1909 he became cond. of an amateur orch. and in 1914 at the Vinohrady Theatre. He succeeded Kovařovic as cond. of the Nat. Theatre in 1920.

Works incl. operas *The Death of Vlasta, Kunala's Eyes, The Bud, Legend of Erin* & *John's Kingdom*; incid. m. for Jaroslav Kvapil's play *The Orphan*; *The Legend of St. Zita* for ten., chor., orch. & org. and other chor. works; Sym. in A maj., Sinfonietta, 2 Suites, symph. poem *The Tale of Šemik, Rustic Festival* & *Impromptu* for orch.; *Ballad of the Dead Cobbler* & *Cz. Ballad* for declamation & orch.; stg. 4tet in B maj., Sonatina for v., va. & pf.; songs, &c.

Ostrovsky, Alexander Nikolaievitch (1823–86), Rus. dramatist. *See* **Blaramberg** (*Tushino* & *Voyevoda*), **Dzerzhinsky** (*Storm*), **Kashperov** (do.), **Káta Kabanová** (Janáček), **Serov** (*Power of Evil*), **Snow Maiden** (Rimsky-Korsakov), **Tchaikovsky** (*Snegurotchka*), **Tcherepnin (N.)** (*Poverty no Crime*), **Voyevoda** (Tchaikovsky).

O'Sullivan, Denis (b. San Francisco, 25. IV. 1868; d. Columbus, Ohio, 1. II. 1908), Amer. bar. singer of Ir. descent. Studied in Florence, London and Paris. Made his 1st concert appearance in London and his 1st on the stage at Dublin in 1895.

Otello, opera by Verdi (lib. by Boito, after Shakespeare), prod. Milan, Teatro alla Scala, 5. II. 1887.

Otello, ossia Il Moro di Venezia (*Othello, or The Moor of Venice*), opera by Rossini (lib. by Marchese Francesco Berio di Salsa, after Shakespeare), prod. Naples, Teatro Fondo, 4. XII. 1816.

Otesco, I. Nonna (b. Bucharest, 3. XII. 1888; d. Bucharest, 25. III. 1940), Rum. cond. & comp. Studied at Bucharest and at the Cons. and Schola Cantorum in Paris. On his return he founded what became the Royal Opera at Bucharest, and cond. this as well as the Phil. Orch. He became dir. of the Royal Acad. of M. and of the Opera.

Works incl. operas *Ilderim* (after Carmen Sylva) & *De la matei cetire*; ballets *Ileana Cosânzeana* & *Le Rubis enchanté*; symph. poems *Le Temple de Gnide* (after Montesquieu), *Narcisse* & others, &c.

Otger (b. ?, d. ?) ? Fr. medieval cleric & mus. scholar, abbot of (?) monastery; prob. author of several mus. treatises incl. *Musica enchiriadis* & *Scolica enchiriadis*.

Othello. *See also* **Otello.**

Concert ovt. by Dvořák, Op. 93, ref. to Shakespeare's tragedy, comp. 1892 and forming, with *Amid Nature* and *Carnival*, a cycle with thematic connections orig. called *Nature, Life and Love.*

Othmayr, Kaspar (b. Amberg, 12. III. 1515; d. Nuremberg, 7. II. 1553), Ger. clergyman & musn. Studied at Heidelberg Univ. and was a pupil of Lemlin for m. there. He held church appts. at Heilbronn and Ansbach, but *c.* 1550 retired to Nuremberg on account of relig. controversies, himself being a Lutheran.

Works incl. Lat. motets, Ger. hymns & other sacred m.; an Epitaph on Luther's death; 26 secular songs contrib. to Georg Forster's collection, &c.

Ottava (It.) = Octave.

Ottavino (It. from *ottava* = 8ve). The current It. name of the 8ve fl. elsewhere called Piccolo (from *flauto piccolo* = little fl.).

Otterloo, Jan Willem van (b. Winterswijk, 27. XII. 1907), Dutch cond. & comp. Studied at the Amsterdam Cons. under Dresden and others. App. 2nd cond. of the Utrecht Munic. Orch. in 1933 and 1st in 1937.

Works incl. Sym., 3 Suites & Passacaglia for orch,; chamber m.; pf. & org. works, &c.

Otto, Stephan (b. Freiberg, Saxony, *c.* 1594; d. ? Schandau, *c.* 1650), Ger. comp. Studied at Freiberg under Christoph Demantius, and after an appt. at Augsburg he became cantor at his home-town in 1632 and at Schandau in 1633. Hammerschmidt was among his pupils.

Works incl. *Kronen-Krönlein*, a coll. of sacred voc. pieces in a mixed motet and madrigal style for 3–8 voices, setting of Luther's hymn 'Ein' feste Burg' for 19 voices, &c.

Ottobi, Giovanni. *See* **Hothby.**

Ottone, rè di Germania (*Otho, King of Germany*), opera by Handel (lib. by Nicola Franceso Haym), prod. London, King's Theatre, Haymarket, 12. I. 1723.

Otway, Thomas (1652–85), Eng. dramatist. *See* **Lenton** (*Venice Preserved*).

Oudin, Eugène (Espérance) (b. New York, 24. II. 1858; d. London, 4. XI. 1894), Amer. bar. singer of Fr. descent. Studied law at Yale Univ. and practised it for a time, but during a holiday in London in 1886 decided to turn to m. He made his 1st stage appearance in New York that year, with Louise Parker, who became his wife on 4. XII. In 1891 he 1st appeared in opera in London as the Templar in Sullivan's *Ivanhoe*.

Oulibicheff. *See* **Ulibishev.**

Ours, L' (*The Bear*), the nickname of a sym. by Haydn, No. 82, in C maj. (No. 1 of the 'Paris' syms.), comp. in 1786.

Ouseley, Frederick (Arthur) Gore (b. London, 12. VIII. 1825; d. Hereford, 6. IV. 1889), Eng. orgst., comp. & divine. Studied at Oxford, where he took the Mus.D. in 1854 and was app. Prof. of M. in 1855. Founder of St. Michael's Coll., Tenbury. He succeeded to his father's baronetcy in 1844.

Works incl. 11 services, *c.* 70 anthems; orats. *The Martyrdom of St. Polycarp* & *Hagar*; over 30 preludes & fugues, 2 sos. and other works for org.; 2 stg. 4tets; partsongs, glees; songs, &c.

Ouverture (Fr.). *See* **Overture.**

Overblowing. A special way of playing wind insts. so that the upper harmonics are prod. instead of the fundamental notes. It is in this way that wind insts. greatly increase their natural compass. O. may occur by accident in org. pipes by too great a pressure of wind, but safety-valve devices have been invented to prevent this.

Overspun. The lower stgs. of insts. of the v. family and also those of the pf. are O., i.e. spun round with wire.

Overstrung. Stgs. in pfs. which are made in 2 ranges crossing each other diagonally to save space and to secure greater length in the stgs.

Overtones. *See* **Harmonics.**

Overture (from Fr. *Ouverture* = opening). An inst. introductory comp. preceding some other large work, esp. an opera or orat. in modern times; but also sometimes an independent comp. for concert use, though that use at first arose from the insertion of Os. to larger works into concert programmes. Thus, for ex., Handel's *Occasional Ovt.* and Weber's *Oberon* O. may be detached for concert use from the works to which they belong, but Mendelssohn's *Hebrides* and Brahms's *Tragic* Os. were specially written for concert use. From the time of Lully to that of Handel the O. in its Fr. form had a slow introd. and a fugal *allegro*, often followed by a return to the slow section or by a new slow portion, also sometimes by one or more independent pieces in dance form, in which case it resembled the Suite; hence Bach's Os. are in fact suites with 1st mvts. in Fr. O. form. The It. O. form differed from the Fr. in the 17th & 18th cents. by being in several mvts. approximating more to the early sym., so that the 1st syms., even Haydn's and Mozart's early ones, were sometimes called Os. In opera the m. of the O. had no special relevance to the works itself up to the time of Gluck, and sometimes not afterwards (e.g. Rossini except that to *Guillaume Tell*). Gluck's mature Os. foreshadow the character and atmosphere of the operas to which they belong, and from his time on the actual mus. material of the O. was more often than not drawn from the opera itself to a greater or smaller extent.

Ovid (Publius Ovidius Naso) (43 B.C.–

A.D. 17), Rom. poet. *See* **Dittersdorf** (*Metamorphoses*), **Monsigny** (*Philémon et Baucis*), **Mudarra, Philémon et Baucis** (Gounod), **Rebikov** (*Metamorphoses*), **Steinberg** (do.),

Ovvero (It. = or rather, or else, lit. from *o vero*, or truly). An earlier word for *ossia*; also found in front of 2nd, alternative titles of mus. works.

Owen, Wilfred (1893–1918), Eng. poet. *See* **Morning Heroes** (Bliss).

Ox Minuet. This is often believed to be the nickname of one of Haydn's minuets, but it is the title of a *Singspiel* by Seyfried, *Die Ochsenmenuette*, prod. in Vienna in 1823 as a pasticcio with m. arranged from Haydn's works. It was based on 2 earlier Fr. pieces, *Le Menuet du Bœuf, ou Une Leçon de Haydn*, prod. at Verdun in 1805, with m. selected from H., and *Haydn, ou Le Menuet du Bœuf*, prod. in Paris, 1812, with 5 numbers from H.

'Oxford' Symphony, the nickname of a Sym. by Haydn, No. 92, in G maj., comp. in 1788 (before H.'s 1st visit to Eng.) and perf. at Oxford in VII. 1791, when the Univ. conferred the hon. degree of D.Mus. on him.

Ozaneaux, Jean Georges (1795–1852), Fr. historian & author. *See* **Hérold** (*Dernier Jour de Missolonghi*).

Ozerov, Vladislav Alexandrovitch (1769–1816), Rus. dramatist. *See* **Mussorgsky** (*Oedipus in Athens*).

P

P. (abbr.). Used in m. for *piano* = soft, in this form: *p*; sometimes also for the pedal in pf. m., in this: *P.* In the latter case, however, it is more often *Ped.*

Pabst. Ger. family of musns.:

1. **August P.** (b. Elberfeld, 30. V. 1811; d. Riga, 21. VII. 1885), orgst. & comp. He became orgst. at Königsberg and later dir. of the M. School at Riga. Comp. operas, &c.

2. **Louis P.** (b. Königsberg, 18. VII. 1846; d. ?), pfst. & comp., son of prec. Studied under his father, made his 1st appearance as pfst. in 1862, lived at Liverpool, Riga, Melbourne, founding m. schools in the latter 2 places, and finally held a prof.-ship in Moscow. Comp. melodramas, pf. works, songs, &c.

3. **Paul P.** (b. Königsberg, 27. V. 1854; d. Moscow, 9. VI. 1897), pfst. & comp., brother of prec. Studied under his father and brother, later under Liszt. Settled in Moscow as prof. at the Cons. Comp. pf. m., incl. operatic paraphrases.

Pacchierotti, Gasparo (b. Fabriano nr. Ancona, 1744; d. Padua, 28. X. 1821), It. male sop. singer. Was a choirboy either at St. Mark's, Venice, or more prob. at Forli cath., sang at Venice, Vienna and Milan from the age of 16 and made his 1st important stage appearance at Milan in 1769. In 1778 he 1st visited London.

Pacchioni, Antonio Maria (b. Modena, 5. VII. 1654; d. Modena, 16. VII. 1738), It. priest & comp. Studied at Modena cath., where he became chaplain at the ducal court and later asst. choirmaster. In 1733 he and Pitoni settled a dispute between Martini and Redi about the solution of a canon by Animuccia.

Works incl. masses & other church m., orats., &c.

Pace, Pietro (also called Pacius) (b. Loreto, 1559; d. Loreto, IV. 1622), It. comp. Was orgst. at Pesaro in 1597 and of the Santa Casa at Loreto, 1591–2, and again, 1611–22.

Works incl. magnificats, motets (with accomp.) & other church m.; *Arie spirituali* & madrigals with & without accomp., &c.

Pacelli, Asprilio (b. Varciano nr. Narni, Umbria, *c.* 1570; d. Warsaw, 4. V. 1623), It. comp. Choirmaster of the Ger. Coll. and later of the Vatican basilica in Rome until 1603, when he went to the court of Sigismund III of Pol. at Warsaw, succeeding Marenzio.

Works incl. motets, psalms, *Sacrae cantiones*; madrigals, &c.

Pachelbel, Johann (b. Nuremberg, *c.* VIII. 1653; d. Nuremberg, 6 or 7. III. 1706), Ger. orgst. & comp. Studied under Heinrich Schwemmer at home and after holding brief appts. at Altdorf and Ratisbon, went to Vienna *c.* 1671–2 and studied under Kerl from 1674. Between 1677–95 he was orgst. successively at Eisenach, Erfurt, Stuttgart and Gotha, and in the latter years was app. orgst. at St. Sebaldus's church at Nuremberg.

Works incl. 94 org. fugues on the Magnificat, org. vars. & preludes on chorales; suites for 2 vs. *Musikalisches Ergötzen*; 6 sets of vars. for hpchd. *Hexachordum Apollinis*, &c.

Pachelbel, Wilhelm Hieronymus (b. Erfurt, 1685; d. Nuremberg, 1764), Ger. orgst. & comp., son of prec. Pupil of his father and prob. his successor at St. Sebaldus's church, Nuremberg. Comp. org. & hpchd. m., &c.

Pachmann, Vladimir de (b. Odessa, 27. VII. 1848; d. Rome, 6. I. 1933), Rus. pfst. of Aus. descent. Studied 1st under his father, a univ. prof., and later in Vienna, and made his 1st concert appearance in Rus. in 1869. In 1882 he 1st visited London. He became a famous but somewhat eccentric exponent of Chopin.

Pacific 231, symph. mvt. by Honegger, named after a railway engine and depicting its start and progress, not merely realistically, but, the comp. claims, 'lyrically.' 1st perf. Paris, at a Kussevitsky concert, 8. V. 1924.

Pacini, Giovanni (b. Catania, 17. II. 1796; d. Pescia, 6. XII. 1867), It. comp. Studied 1st under his father, a famous ten., and later at Bologna and Venice. At the age of 17 he prod. his 1st opera at Milan. He became chapel master to Napoleon's widow, the Empress Marie Louise, and in 1834 settled at Viareggio, where he opened a m. school, later transferred to Lucca. For this he wrote some theoret. treatises.

Works incl. operas *Annetta e Lucindo*, *La sacerdotessa d'Irminsul*, *La schiava in Bagdad*, *La gioventù di Enrico V* (after Shakespeare's *Henry IV*), *L'ultimo giorno di Pompei* (not based on Bulwer-Lytton), *Gli Arabi nelle Gallie*, *Saffo*, *Medea*, *Lorenzino de' Medici*, *La regina di Cipro*, *Il saltimbanco* & over 60 others; incid. m. for Sophocles' *Oedipus Rex*; masses, orats., cantata for Dante anniversary & others; stg. 4tet in C maj., &c.

Paciotti, Pietro Paolo (b. ?; d. ? Rome, ?), It. 16th-cent. comp. Choirmaster of the Seminario Romano in Rome, 1591. Wrote masses, motets, madrigals, &c.

Pacius. *See also* **Pace.**

Pacius, Frederik (b. Hamburg, 19. III. 1809; d. Helsingfors, 8. I. 1891), Ger. vst. & comp., naturalized Finn. Pupil of Spohr and Hauptmann at Cassel, vst. in the court orch. at Stockholm, 1828–34, when he became m. teacher at Helsingfors Univ. He remained in the Fin. capital, estab. orch. concerts there in 1845 and became prof. of m. at the Univ. in 1860.

Works incl. operas *Kung Karls Jakt* & *Loreley*; incid. m. for Topelius's *Princess of Cyprus*; v. Conc.; cantatas; songs incl. *Suomis Saang* and *Vaart Land*, both adopted as Fin. nat. anthems.

Packe, Thomas (b. ?; d. ?), Eng. 15th–16th-cent. comp. He was a knight and prob. held no official mus. post.

Works incl. masses, motets & a Te Deum.

Paderewski, Ignacy (Jan) (b. Kuryłówka, Podolia, 18. XI. 1860; d. New York, 29. VI. 1941), Pol. pfst., comp. & statesman. Studied at the Warsaw Cons. and went on his 1st concert tour in 1876. After teaching in 1879–81 at the Cons. he went to Berlin for further study, finishing with Leschetizky in Vienna, reappearing there and in Paris in 1887. In 1890 he paid his 1st visit to Eng. and in 1891 to U.S.A. During the 1st world war he collected large sums for the Pol. relief fund and in 1919 became the 1st president of the Pol. Repub.

Works incl. operas *Manru* & *Sakuntala* (after Kalidasa); Sym. in B min.; Conc. in A min. and Pol. Fantasy for pf. & orch.; v. & pf. So.; So. in E♭ min. & many other pf. works; songs, &c.

Padilla y Ramos, Mariano (b. Murcia, 1842; d. Auteuil nr. Paris, 21. XI. 1906), Spa. bar. singer. Studied in It. and toured Eur. extensively. Married Désirée Artôt in 1869.

Padlock, The, opera by Dibdin (lib. by Isaac Bickerstaffe, based on a story by Cervantes, *El celoso extremeño*), prod. London, Drury Lane Theatre, 3. X. 1768.

Padmâvati, opera by Roussel (lib., in Fr., by Louis Laloy), prod. Paris, Opéra, 1. VI. 1923.

Padovana (It., i.e. of Padua). The It. name of the Pavan.

Paer, Ferdinando (b. Parma, 1. VI. 1771; d. Paris, 3. V. 1839), It. comp. Studied with Gasparo Ghiretti at Padua and at the age of 20 became chapel master at Venice. Having married the singer Riccardi, he was invited to Vienna in 1798, where she was engaged at the court opera, and he prod. *Camilla* there. In 1803 he went to Dresden, remaining as opera cond. until 1806 and there prod. *Leonora*, a setting of an It. version of Gaveaux's opera on which Beethoven's *Fidelio* was also based later. In 1807, after accomp. Napoleon to Warsaw and Posen, he was app. his chapel master and settled in Paris.

Works incl. *Circe*, *Il tempo fa giustizia a tutti*, *Il nuovo Figaro* (after Beaumarchais's *Mariage de F.*), *Il matrimonio improvviso*, *Idomeneo*, *Eroe e Leandro*, *L'intrigo amoroso*, *Il principe di Taranto*, *Camilla, o Il sotterraneo*, *La sonnambula*, *Achille*, *Leonora, o L'amore conjugale*, *Sofonisba*, *Numa Pompilio*, *Agnese di Fitz-Henry*, *Didone abbandonata*, *Le Maître de chapelle*, *La Marquise de Brinvilliers* (with Auber, Batton, Berton, Blangini, Boïeldieu, Carafa, Cherubini & Hérold) & over 20 others; orats. *Il santo sepolcro* & *La passione*, masses & motets; *c.* 12 cantatas (It., Fr. & Ger.); Bacchanalian Sym. for orch., Bridal March for the wedding of Napoleon and Joséphine, &c.

(The spelling 'Paër' is incorrect, diaereses not being used in It.; it was used in Fr. & Ger., in the latter to prevent the name from being pronounced 'Pär.')

Paesiello. *See* **Paisiello.**

Paganini, Niccolò (b. Genoa, 27. X. 1782; d. Nice, 27. V. 1840), It. vst. & comp. Learnt guitar and v. from his father, afterwards with the theatre vst. Servetto and the cath. chapel master Giacomo Costa. At the age of 9 he made his 1st appearance as a vst. at Genoa, playing his own vars. on *La Carmagnole*. As a comp. he profited by the advice of Gnecco, and in 1795 his father sent him to the vst. Alessandro Rolla at Parma. While there he also studied comp. with Gasparo Ghiretti, and in 1797 made his 1st professional tour. After that he became increasingly famous, travelled widely, beginning with Vienna and Paris in 1828–31, and in the latter year he went to Eng. for the 1st time. In 1834 he invited Berlioz in Paris to write a concert work for viola, and *Harold en Italie* was the result; but he never played it.

Works incl. 2 v. Concs. (Op. 7 with the *Rondo alla campanella*), vars. (e.g. on 'God save the King') & concert pieces for v. & orch.; 3 stg. 4tets with a guitar part; 12 sos. for v. & guitar; 24 *Capricci* (studies) for v. solo, &c.

Paganini Rhapsody, a work by Rakhmaninov for pf. & orch. entitled *Rhapsody on a Theme by P.*, but actually a set of vars., without opus number, comp. in 1934. The theme, in A min., from P.'s *Capricci* for unaccomp. v., is the same as that used by Brahms for the Vars. below.

Paganini Studies, a set of 6 studies for pf. by Liszt, transcribed from P.'s v. *Capricci* (except No. 3, which is another version of *La Campanella*), ded. to Clara Schumann. There is an orig. version, *Études d'exécution transcendante d'après P.*, written in 1838, and a revised one, *Grandes Études de P.*, written in 1851.

2 sets of studies for pf. (6 each) by Schumann on themes from P.'s v. *Capricci*: Op. 3, written in 1832, and Op. 10, written in 1833.

Paganini Variations, 2 sets of studies for pf. in var. form by Brahms, Op. 35, comp. in 1866, on a theme in A min. from P.'s v. *Capricci.*

Pagliacci (*Clowns*), opera by Leoncavallo (lib. by comp.), prod. Milan, Teatro dal Verme, 21. V. 1892.

Pagliardi, Giovanni Maria (b. Florence, ?; d. ?), It. 17th-cent. comp. Chapel master to the Duke of Tuscany at Florence and in the 1660s at 2 churches in Rome.

Works incl. operas *Caligula delirante, Lisimaco, Numa Pompilio, Attilio Regolo, Il pazzo per forza* & *Il tiranno di Colco*; motets, sacred songs; voc. duets, &c.

Pahissa, Jaime (b. Barcelona, 7. X. 1880), Spa. comp. Pupil of Morera.

Works incl. operas *La presó de Lleida, Canigó, Gala Placidia, La Morisca, Marianela, La Princesa Margarida*; orch. works; pf. pieces, &c.

Paine, John Knowles (b. Portland, Me., 9. I. 1839; d. Cambridge, Mass., 25. IV. 1906), Amer. orgst., comp. & teacher. Studied at home and at the Hochschule für Musik in Berlin, gave org. recitals in Ger. and returned to U.S.A. in 1861. He became instructor in m. at Harvard Univ. in 1862, asst. prof. in 1872 and full prof. in 1875. Hon. D.Mus. of Yale, 1890.

Works incl. opera *Azara*; incid. m. for Sophocles' *Oedipus Tyrannus* and Aristophanes' *Birds*; Mass in D maj.; orat. *St. Peter*; cantatas *A Song of Promise, Phoebus arise, The Realm of Fancy* (Keats), *The Nativity* (Milton); syms. in C min. & A maj. (*Spring*), symph. poems *An Island Fantasy* & *The Tempest* (after Shakespeare), ovt. for Shakespeare's *As You Like It*; stg. 4tet, pf. Trio; v. & pf. So.; inst. pieces, &c.

Paintings, &c., Music based on:

Fibich, *Malirske Studie* for pf. (Ruysdael, Brueghel, sen., Fra Angelico, Correggio & Watteau).

Frank, duets from Kate Greenaway's *At the Window.*

Gasco, var. works (Besnard, Carpaccio, Giorgione & Rossetti).

Granados, *Goyescas* for pf. & opera (Goya).

Hahn, *Portraits de peintres* for pf. (Cuyp, Potter, van Dyck, Watteau).

Hallén, *The Isle of the Dead* for orch. (Böcklin).

Honegger, *Danse des morts* (Holbein).

Huber, Böcklin Sym. (No. 2).

Kazanly, *Villa by the Sea* for orch. (Böcklin).

Liszt, *Il sposalizio* (Raphael) in *Années de pèlerinage* for pf.

—, *The Battle of the Huns*, symph. poem (Kaulbach).

—, *Totentanz* for pf. & orch. (Orcagna).

Morillo, *Pinturas negras de Goya.*

Mussorgsky, *Pictures at an Exhibition* for pf. (Victor Hartmann).

Orefice, *Quadri di Böcklin* for pf. (6 pictures).

Rakhmaninov, *The Isle of the Dead*, symph. poem (Böcklin).

Reger, Böcklin Suite for orch. (4 pictures).

Respighi, *Trittico Botticelliano* for orch.

Rózycki, orch. prelude *Mona Lisa Gioconda* (on Leonardo da Vinci's portrait).

Schulz-Beuthen, *The Isle of the Dead* for orch. (Böcklin).

Tcherepnin (N.), *The Rus. Alphabet*, pf. pieces on Benois's picture-book.

Vaughan Williams, *Job*, masque for dancing (based on Blake's illustrations for the Book of Job); settings by Gwendolen Raverat.

Walton, *Portsmouth Point* ovt. (Rowlandson).

Weingartner, *Die Gefilde der Seligen*, symph. poem (Böcklin).

White (Felix), *Astarte Syriaca* for orch. (D. G. Rossetti).

Wood (Haydn), *3 Pictures* for orch. (2 by Luke Fildes & Hals's *Laughing Cavalier*).

Woyrsch, Böcklin Suite for orch. (4 pictures).

Zandonai, *Quadri di Segantini* for orch.

In opera the finale in Auber's *Marco Spada* reprod. Horace Vernet's 'La Confession du bandit'; Rheinberger's *Die sieben Raben* founded on Schwind's cycle of paintings; Schillings's *Mona Lisa*, introd. the subject of Leonardo da Vinci's portrait; Mraczek's *Herrn Dürers Bild* deals with that master's 'Madonna "am Weisenzaun"'; Hindemith's *Mathis der Maler* is based on Matthias Grünewald's altar-piece at Colmar; R. Strauss's *Friedenstag* on Velazquez's 'Surrender of Breda' (*see also* **Gasco**). In ballet there is A. Tcherepnin's *Ajanta Frescoes*; Inghelbrecht's *El Greco* uses that master's 'Burial of Count Orgaz'; *The Rake's Progress* by Gavin Gordon is based on Hogarth settings by Rex Whistler.

Paisible (or **Peasable**), **James** (b. ? Fr., *c.* 1650; d. London, 1721), Eng. musn., ? of Fr. extraction. Member of the King's Band in London.

Works incl. incid. m. for Shakespeare's *Henry IV* (*The Humours of Sir John Falstaff*), Southerne's adapt. of Aphra Behn's *Oroonoko*, Bancroft's *King Edward III*, Cibber's *She wou'd and she wou'd not* & *Love's Last Shift* & Mme La Roche Guilhen's *Rare en tout*; duets, sos. & pieces for fl., &c.

Paisiello, Giovanni (b. Taranto, 9. V. 1740; d. Naples, 5. VI. 1816), It. comp. Educ. at the Jesuit school of Taranto with a view to a legal career, but was taught m. by a priest, Carlo Presta, and allowed in 1754 to enter the Cons. of Sant' Onofrio at Naples as a pupil of Durante, and later of Cotumacci and Abos. He prod. a dramatic intermezzo there and wrote his 1st opera for Parma when he was little more than 20. Settling at Naples after some successes at Bologna, Florence, &c., he was greatly worried by the rivalry of Piccinni and later of Cimarosa, and in 1776 accepted an invitation to the court of Catherine II at St. Petersburg, where he wrote his opera on Beaumarchais's *Barbier de Séville*. In 1784 he returned home after a stay in Vienna and became chapel master to Ferdinand IV at Naples. In 1799 he accommodated himself to the Repub., but was reinstated into royal favour at the Restor., only to be called to Paris by Napoleon. He finally returned to Naples in 1804, but fell out of favour with the Bourbon régime.

Works incl. operas *Il Ciarlone* (after Goldoni's *La pupilla*), *Il Marchese Tulipano*, *L'idolo cinese*, *Don Chisciotte della Mancia* (after Cervantes), *Il tamburo* (after Addison), *La Frascatana*, *Socrate immaginario*, *La serva padrona*, *Il barbiere di Siviglia* (after Beaumarchais), *Il Rè Teodoro in Venezia*, *Pirro*, *Nina, o La pazza per amore*, *La molinara* (containing 'Nel cor più non mi sento'), *I zingari in fiera*, *La locanda*, *Elfrida* (after Mason's tragedy), *Proserpine* (Quinault) & *c.* 70 others; *c.* 12 scenic cantatas; masses & other church m.; orat. *La passione di Gesù Cristo* & others; syms. & other inst. works, Funeral March for General Hoche, &c.

Paladilhe, Émile (b. Montpellier, 3. VI. 1844; d. Paris, 8. I. 1926), Fr. comp. Studied at the Paris Cons. and gained the Prix de Rome in 1860.

Works incl. operas *Le Passant* (lib. by François Coppée), *L'Amour africain*, *Suzanne*, *Diana*, *Patrie* (after Sardou); orat. *Saintes Maries de la mer*; 2 masses; Sym. & *Fragments symphoniques* for orch.; songs, &c.

Palester, Roman (b. Sniatyn, 28. XII. 1907), Pol. comp. Studied at Lwów and under Kasimierz Sikorski in Warsaw. For some years he lived in Paris, later settled in Warsaw.

Works incl. ballets *Song of the Earth* & *The End of the World*; Psalm for bar., chor., orch. & org.; Sym. in D maj., symph. suite, *Symph. Music*, *Wedding Celebration* & other orch. works; Concertino for saxophone, pf. Conc.; Divertimento for 6 insts., 2 stg. 4tets, Sonatinas for 3 cls. & for v. & co.; org. Toccata; pf. pieces; songs, &c.

Palestrina, Giovanni Pierluigi da (b. Palestrina, (?) 17. XII. (?) 1525; d. Rome, 2. II. 1594), It. comp. Son of Sante Pierluigi, a well-to-do citizen. Became a choir-boy at the cath. of St. Agapit in his native town. When the bishop of Palestrina went to the church of Santa Maria Maggiore in Rome in 1534, he took P. with him, and he remained there until he was 14, when his voice broke. After a stay at home he returned to Rome in 1540 and (?) became a pupil of Firmin Le Bel. At 19 he was app. orgst. and singing-master at St. Agapit's at home. On 12. VI. 1547 he married Lucrezia Gori, who inherited money and property from her father. P. was app. chapel master of the Julian choir in Rome, 1551, and pub. a madrigal and a 1st book of masses in 1554. Pope Julius III made him a member of the Pontifical Choir in 1555, in spite of the resentment of members at his having been elected without examination. Pope Marcellus II, who succeeded that year, to whom P. ded. the *Missa Papae Marcelli*, intended to reform the church m. with P.'s help, but d., and under his successor, Paul IV, P. retired from the choir with a pension, becoming chapel master at the church of San Giovanni in the Lateran. When under Pius IV in 1560 that church wished to make economies, P.

resigned and was app. the next year chapel master at Santa Maria Maggiore. Before the accession of Pius V in 1566, P. was made dir. of the new Roman seminary in 1565. The Council of Trent having already laid down some reforms in church m. in 1563, the new pope, Gregory XIII, in 1577 directed P. and Zoilo to revise the Gradual. P.'s wife having d. in VII. 1580, he applied for admission to the priesthood, but having been made a canon, he renounced his vows and was married again on 28. III. 1581 to Virginia Dormuli, the widow of a prosperous furrier, in whose business he now took a considerable interest. After the accession of the next pope, Sixtus V, there was a scheme to app. P. chapel master of the Pontifical Choir, but it was defeated, 1585. Much of P.'s m. was pub., partic. in the last 10 years of his life, incl. 4 vols. of motets and 6 of masses; the 7th of the latter was sent to press in I. 1594 when P. was seized with the illness from which he d.

Works incl. 39 masses for 4 voices, 29 for 5 voices, 22 for 6 voices, 4 for 8 voices; 67 motets for 4 voices, 108 for 5 voices, 34 for 6 voices, 2 for 7 voices, 56 for 8 voices, 6 for 12 voices; 45 hymns for 4 voices; 68 offertories for 5 voices; 12 lamentations; 7 litanies; 4 psalms for 12 voices; 1 antiphon; 35 magnificats; 7 *Cantiones sacrae*; 61 spiritual madrigals; 95 secular madrigals; 12 *Cantiones profanae*, &c.

Palestrina, opera by Pfitzner (lib. by comp.), prod. Munich, 12. VI. 1917.

Paliashvili, Zakharia Petrovitch (b. Kutais, 1872; d. Kutais, XII. 1933), Rus. (Georgian) comp. Studied at the Moscow Cons. under Taneiev, later taught at Tiflis, cond. the orch. and made excursions into eastern Georgia to study its folk m., on which his work is based.

Works incl. operas, *Absalom and Eteri*, *Twilight* & *Latavra*; chor. works; folksong arrs., &c.

Palindrome. Lit. a word or poem reading the same backwards as forwards. In m. a piece constructed in the same way, more or less loosely, as e.g. the prelude and postlude in Hindemith's *Ludus tonalis*, the same comp.'s 1-act opera *Hin und zurück* or the prelude to Lambert's ballet *Horoscope*. The procedure is that of *Recte et retro* or *Rovescio* on a larger scale.

Pallavicini, Carlo (b. Brescia or Salò, *c*. 1630; d. Dresden, 29. I. 1688). He lived at Salò at first, married Giulia Rossi at Padua and settled there, prod. operas at Venice between 1666–87, where he also lived for a time. In 1667–73 he was at the Saxon court at Dresden; 1st as asst. and later as 1st mus. dir. In 1674 he was back at Venice, but was recalled to Dresden in 1685 to reorganize the It. opera.

Works incl. *Demetrio*, *Diocletiano*, *Enea in Italia*, *Vespasiano*, *Nerone*, *Le amazoni nell' isole fortunate*, *Messalina*, *Bassiano, ovvero Il maggior impossibile*, *Penelope la casta*, *Massimo Puppieno*, *Didone delirante*, *L'amazone corsara*, *La Gerusalemme liberata* (after Tasso), *Antiope* (finished by Strungk) & 9 others; a mass & an orat.; arias and canzoni with insts.; stg. fantasies, &c.

Pallavicini, Vincenzo (b. ?; d. ?), It. 18th-cent. comp., (?) related to prec. Chapel master at the Cons. degl' Incurabili at Venice.

Works incl. opera *Lo speziale* (with Fischietti, lib. by Goldoni), &c.

Pallavicino, Benedetto (b. Cremona, ?; d. Camaldoli, after 1616), It. comp. Towards the end of the 16th cent. he was in the service of the Duke of Mantua, succeeded Wert as chapel master there in 1596, but was in turn succeeded in 1601, when he retired to the monastery of Camaldoli in Tuscany.

Works incl. masses, psalms & other church m.; madrigals, &c.

Palma, Silvestro (b. Palermo, 1762; d. Naples, 8. VIII. 1834), It. comp. Studied at Naples and was a pupil of Paisiello.

Works incl. operas *La pietra simpatica*, *Il geloso di se stesso* and *c*. 15 others; church m., &c.

Palmer, Elizabeth (or **Bessie**) (b. London, 9. VIII. 1831; d. London, 1. IX. 1910), Eng. con. singer. Studied at the R.A.M. in London, and made her 1st appearance in 1854.

Palmer, Geoffrey (Molyneux) (b. Staines, Middlesex, 8. X. 1882), Ir. orgst. & comp. Educ. at Oxford and studied m. at the R.C.M. in London, Stanford being among his masters. He settled in Ir. in 1910 and became orgst. of several churches.

Works incl. opera *Sruth na Maoile* (*The Sea of Moyle*); cantatas; songs, &c.

Palmer, Henry (b. ?; d. ?), Eng. 17th-cent. comp. He may have worked at Durham cath. Comp. services & anthems.

Palmer, Robert (b. Syracuse, N.Y., 2. VI. 1915), Amer. comp. Studied at the Eastman School of M. at Rochester, N.Y., where he took degrees in 1938–9, also privately with Roy Harris. In 1943 he became asst. prof. of m. at Cornell Univ., Ithaca, N.Y.

Works incl. ballet *Ir. Legend* with chamber orch.; elegy *K. 19* and Conc.

for orch.; Conc. for chamber orch.; *Abraham Lincoln Walks at Midnight* (Vachel Lindsay) for chor. & orch.; 2 stg. 4tets, pf. 4tet, 2 stg. trios, Conc. for fl., v., cl., Eng. hn. & bn.; va. & pf. So.; So. for 2 pfs.; So. & 3 Preludes for pf., &c.

Palmgren, Selim (b. Björneborg, 16. II. 1878), Fin. pfst., cond. & comp. Studied at the Helsingfors Cons., where Wegelius was among his masters, and later with Ansorge in Ger. and Busoni in It. On his return he became cond. of the Fin. Students' Chor. Soc. and later of the Mus. Soc. at Aabo. He also frequently appeared as pfst. Married the singer Maikki Järnefelt, toured Eur. and U.S.A. with her and in 1923 settled as prof. of comp. at the Eastman School of M. at Rochester, N.Y.

Works incl. operas *Daniel Hjort* & *Peter Schlemihl* (after Chamisso); incid. m. to Kyösti's *Tukhimo* (*Cinderella*); chor. works; 2 pf. concs. *Metamorphoses* & *The River*; numerous pf. pieces, &c.

Palotta, Matteo (b. Palermo, 1680; d. Vienna, 28. III. 1758), It. comp., priest & mus. scholar. Studied at Naples, returned to Sicily after being ordained, but was app. one of the court comps. in Vienna in 1733. He wrote treatises on solmization and the modes and comp. masses, motets & other church m.

Paminger, Leonhard (b. Aschau, Upper Aus., 29. III. 1495; d. Passau, 3. V. 1567), Aus. comp. Educ. at the monastery of St. Nicholas at Passau, studied in Vienna afterwards, but returned to Passau to become a teacher and later secretary at the monastery. He became a Lutheran.

Works incl. Lat. motets, Ger. hymns, psalms, &c.

Pammelia. The 1st part of a collection of canons, rounds and catches pub. by Ravenscroft in 1609, the 2nd being *Deuteromelia*.

Pan (or Pandean) Pipe. A very primitive wind inst., also called Syrinx, consisting of a bundle of reeds of graded lengths made into pipes giving out a scale of different notes. It still survives in some countries, but is of no artistic value in comp., its nearest approach to that being Mozart's use of an inst. of the type playing 5 notes from G to D in *The Magic Flute*.

Pan Tvardovsky, opera by Verstovsky (lib. by Konstantin Sergeievitch Aksakov), prod. Moscow, 5. VI. 1828.

Pan Voyevoda, opera by Rimsky-Korsakov (lib. by I. F. Tiumenev), prod. St. Petersburg, 16. X. 1904.

Pandean Pipe. *See* **Pan Pipe.**

Pandero (Spa.) = Timbrel. A Tambourine (for which the Eng. word is properly 'timbrel'). The word is not generally used in mus. terminol., but must be mentioned here for its occurrence in one of Wolf's Spa. songs: 'Klinge, klinge, mein Pandero.'

Pandora (from Gr.; also, from Arab. *tanbur*, Tamboura). An obs. stg. inst. of the lute type with a long neck and a small body, surviving in var. forms only in the Balkans, Turkey, Egypt and the East.

Pandore (or **Bandora**). An obs. stg. inst. of the Cittern type, with 6 or 7 metal stgs. plucked by the fingers and with a flat back.

Pandorina. An obs. stg. inst.; a small lute.

Pane, Domenico del (b. Rome, ?; d. ? Rome, ?), It. 17th-cent. singer & comp. Pupil of Abbatini in Rome, went to Vienna in 1650 as a singer in the imp. chapel, but returned to Rome to join the Papal Chapel in 1654 and became choirmaster there in 1669.

Works incl. masses on motets by Palestrina, motets of his own; sacred concs.; madrigals, &c.

Panizza, Ettore (b. Buenos Aires, 12. VIII. 1875), Arg. cond. & comp. of It. descent. Studied at the Milan Cons. and 1st appeared as cond. in Rome, 1899, 1st visiting London (Covent Garden) in 1907.

Works incl. operas *Il fidanzato del mare, Medio Evo Latino, Aurora, Bisanzio*, &c.

Pankiewicz, Eugeniusz (b. Siedlce, 1857; d. Warsaw, 1898), Pol. pfst. & comp. Began to study privately, then at Warsaw and finally at St. Petersburg, where Leschetizky was his pf. master and Rubinstein and Rimsky-Korsakov taught him comp. He finished his studies with Szopski and Zelenski at the Warsaw Cons., where he became prof. in succession to Paderewski, 1880.

Works incl. *Ballet-Waltzes* for male chor.; Vars. & other works for pf.; song cycles *Love Stories*, &c., single songs; &c.

Pannain, Guido (b. Naples, 17. XI. 1891), It. m. critic. Studied at the Naples Cons., where he became prof. later. He also studied philos. under the influence of Benedetto Croce. App. m. critic to *Il mattino* at Naples. His books incl. studies of Tinctoris, old It. keyboard m., the Neapol. school, Bellini & modern m.

Panny, Joseph (b. Kolmitzberg, 23. X. 1794; d. Mainz, 7. IX. 1838), Aus. vst. & comp. Studied at home and with Eybler in Vienna, made friends with Paganini during his visits there, appeared in Ger., Norw., Paris and

London, founded a school of m. at Weisserling in Alsace and another at Mainz.

Works incl. 3 masses, Requiem; 3 stg. 4tets, pf. trios; *Scène dramatique* for the v. G stg. (for Paganini) & other solos; chors.; songs, &c.

Panofka, Heinrich (b. Breslau, 3. X. 1807; d. Florence, 18. XI. 1887), Ger. vst., singing-teacher & comp. Studied at home and with Mayseder in Vienna, where he 1st appeared in public in 1827. After living in Munich and Berlin, he settled by turns in Paris, London and Florence, teaching singing and pub. treatises on the subject. Comp. works for v. with pf. and with orch.

Panseron, Auguste (Matthieu) (b. Paris, 26. IV. 1796; d. Paris, 29. VII. 1859), Fr. comp. & singing-teacher. Studied at the Paris Cons. and took the Prix de Rome in 1813, making further studies in It. under Mattei. As accompst. at the Opéra-Comique in Paris, he gained much experience in singing and he became prof. at the Cons. in 1826, writing treatises on solfège and singing.

Works incl. operas *La Grille du parc, Le Mariage difficile* & *L'École de Rome*; 2 masses for treble voices, motets & canticles *Mois de Marie*; numerous songs, &c.

Pantaleon. An inst. of the Dulcimer type invented by Pantaleon Hebenstreit in the 18th cent. and called P. after him by Louis XIV.

Pantchenko. *See* **Pashtchenko.** The name has frequently appeared wrongly transliterated.

Pantomime (from Gr. = 'all - imitating'). Actually a play in dumbshow, and so understood anywhere but in Eng., where the term has come to be applied to a spectacular and far from 'dumb' type of adaptation of familiar fairy-tales showing many traces of its direct descent from 18th-cent. opera, though in a debased form: e.g. the male sop., still perpetuated in the 'pantomime boy' always interpreted by an actress. Formerly the Eng. P., with a harlequinade at the end, was more closely connected with the *commedia dell' arte* and retained some of its conventional stock characters.

Pantonality. A term less frequently used, but preferred by Schoenberg and others, for Atonality, and referring to m. not written in any definite key.

Pantoum (Fr. & Eng. from Malay *pantun*). The title of a mvt. in Ravel's pf. Trio, the form of which is based on the type of Malay verse named P., which has been adopted by Fr. and Eng. poets. A P. is a quatrain, and in Fr. or Eng. poems where more than one such stanza occurs the 2nd and 4th line of each reappear as the 1st and 3rd of the next.

Panum, Hortense (b. Kiel, 14. III. 1856; d. Copenhagen, 26. IV. 1933), Dan. mcolst. She pub. studies of mus. hist. & insts., a m. lexicon, &c.

Panzacchi, Enrico (1840–1904), It. poet, libst. & writer on m. *See* **Scontrino** (*Intima vita*).

Paolo e Francesca, opera by Mancinelli (lib. by Arturo Colautti, after Dante), prod. Bologna, Teatro Comunale, 11. XI. 1907.

Paolo e Virginia, opera by P. C. Guglielmi (lib. by Giuseppe Maria Diodati, based on Bernardin de Saint-Pierre's novel), prod. Naples, Teatro Fiorentino, 2. I. 1817.

Papandopulo, Boris (b. Honef, 25. II. 1906), Yslv. cond. & comp. Studied at Zagreb and Vienna, and became chor. & orch. cond. at Zagreb, returning there after teaching at the M. School of Split in 1935–8.

Works incl. opera *The Sun Flower* & *Amphitryon*; ballet *Gold*; orat. for unaccomp. chor. *The Torments of Our Lord Jesus Christ, Laudamus* for solo voices, chor. & orch.; Sym., symph. picture *The Overflowing*; pf. Conc.; 2 stg. 4tets & other chamber m.; pf. m.; songs, &c.

Papillons (*Butterflies*). A set of short pf. pieces by Schumann, Op. 2, with a finale suggesting the end of a ball in the early morning, with a clock striking 6 and a quotation of the *Grossvatertanz* or *Kehraus*, which also appears in the *Carnival*, for which this smaller work might almost be a kind of preliminary sketch. There is a further connection between the 2, the opening of *Papillons* being quoted in the *Florestan* piece in *Carnival*. The 1st part of Op. 2 was comp. (before Op. 1) in 1829, the end in 1831.

Papini, Guido (b. Camagiore nr. Florence, 1. VIII. 1847; d. London, 3. X. 1912), It. vst. & comp. Made his 1st public appearance at Florence at the age of 13, became leader of the Società del Quartetto there, travelled and 1st visited London in 1874, became v. prof. at the R. Ir. A.M. at Dublin in 1893 and retired to London in 1896.

Works incl. v. conc., co. conc.; v. duets & trios; many v. studies & pieces; co. pieces; songs, &c.

Pâque, Guillaume (b. Brussels, 24. VII. 1825; d. London, 2. III. 1876), Belg. cst. Studied at the Brussels Cons. and after working in Paris and Madrid settled in London in 1851.

Parable Aria (esp. Ger. *Gleichnisarie*)

or Metaphor Aria. A type of mainly operatic aria cultivated in the early 18th cent., esp. by Zeno and Metastasio in their libs., where certain abstract conceptions are illustrated by concrete ideas resembling them, e.g. fidelity by a rock in a stormy sea, love by cooing turtle-doves, &c. ' As when the dove ' in Handel's *Acis and Galatea* is a P. A. and 'Come scoglio' (' Like a rock ') in Mozart's *Così fan tutte* is both verbally and musically a parody of the type. The m. of a P. A. was usually illustrative of the image chosen by the libst.

Paradies, Domenico. *See* **Paradisi.**

Paradis, Marie Therese von (b. Vienna, 15. V. 1759; d. Vienna, 1. II. 1824), Aus. pfst., orgst., singer & comp. She was blind from childhood, but had a great success, which she extended to Paris and London. Mozart wrote the pf. Conc. in B♭ maj. (K. 456) for her.

Works incl. operas *Der Schulcandidat, Rinaldo und Alcina*; melodrama *Ariadne und Bacchus*; cantata *Deutsches Monument* (on the death of Louis XVI); pf. trios; sos. and vars. for pf.; songs incl. a setting of Bürger's *Lenore*, &c.

Paradise and the Peri (*Das Paradies und die Peri*), a setting for solo voices, chor. & orch. of one of the poems in Thomas Moore's *Lalla Rookh*, trans. into Ger. with alterations, by Schumann, Op. 50; comp. 1st contemplated in 1841, begun II. 1843; 1st perf., Leipzig, 4. XII. 1843.

Paradisi (or **Paradies**), (**Pietro**) **Domenico** (b. Naples, 1710; d. Venice, 1792), It. hpchdst. & comp. Pupil of Porpora, lived for many years in London as a teacher.

Works incl. operas *Alessandro in Persia, Il decreto del fato, Fetonte, La forza d'amore*; cantata *Le Muse in gara*; hpchd. sos., toccatas, &c.

Parallel Motion. 2 or more parts in ctpt. moving up or down in unchanging intervals.

Paray, Paul (Charles) (b. Tréport, 24. V. 1886), Fr. cond. & comp. Studied with Leroux and others at the Paris Cons. and took the Prix de Rome in 1911. Returning to Paris from imprisonment during the 1914–8 war he became asst. and later successor to Chevillard, whose concerts he continued to cond. until 1933, when he succeeded Pierné as cond. of the Colonne Orch.

Works incl. orat. *Jeanne d'Arc*; ballet *Artémis troublée*; Mass for the 500th anniv. of the death of Joan of Arc; Sym. in C maj.; Fantasy for pf. & orch.; stg. 4tet; v. & pf. So., &c.

Pardon de Ploërmel, Le, opera by Meyerbeer (lib. by Jules Barbier & Michel Carré), prod. Paris, Opéra-Comique, 4. IV. 1859. The work is also known as *Dinorah*.

Parepa-Rosa, Euphrosyne (b. Edinburgh, 7. V. 1836; d. London, 21. I. 1874), Sco. sop. singer of Wallachian descent. She was taught by her mother, the singer Elizabeth Seguin, and by several famous masters, and made her 1st appearance at Malta at the age of 16, and in London in 1857. Married Carl Rosa in 1867 and was the leading sop. of his opera company.

Paride ed Elena (*Paris and Helen*), opera by Gluck (lib. by Ranieri Calzabigi), prod. Vienna, Burg Theatre, 3. XI. 1770.

Paris and Helen (Gluck). *See above.*

Paris Symphonies. A set of 6 syms. by Haydn, Nos. 82–7, in C maj., G min., E♭, B♭, D & A maj., comp. in and about 1786 for the Concert de la Loge Olympique in Paris. It incl. 3 nicknamed works: 1. *L'Ours*, 2. *La Poule*, 3. *La Reine* (*de France*).

' Paris ' Symphony. Mozart's Sym. in D maj., K. 297, written in Paris for perf. at the Concert spirituel in 1778. After the 1st perf. M. replaced the slow mvt. by another.

Parish-Alvars, Elias (b. Teignmouth, 28. II. 1808; d. Vienna, 25. I. 1849), Eng.-Jewish hpst. & pfst. Studied under Bochsa and others, 1st went on tour, in Ger., in 1831, and later visited It., Aus. and the East. In 1847 he settled in Vienna as chamber musn. to the court.

Works incl. hp. concs., fantasies for hp and for hp. & pf., &c.

Parisina, opera by Donizetti (lib. by Felice Romani, based on Byron's poem), prod. Florence, Teatro della Pergola, 17. III. 1833.

Opera by Mascagni (lib. by Gabriele d'Annunzio), prod. Milan, Teatro alla Scala, 15. XII. 1913.

Parker, Clifton (b. London, 5. II. 1905), Eng. comp. He was made to go into business, but being anxious to become a musn., he began by copying m. and laboriously taught himself. In 1936 he joined the Folkestone Munic. Orch. as copyist, arranger, &c., then became pfst. to the Ballet Jooss school at Dartington Hall, Totnes, where he married the dancer Yoma Saburgh. In 1941 he settled in London as theatre and film comp.

Works incl. opera *Aucassin and Nicolette*; incid. m. for Shakespeare's *Othello*, for an adapt. of Tolstoy's *War and Peace* & other plays; m. for film *Western Approaches* & others, &c.

Parker, Horatio (William) (b. Auburndale, Mass., 15. IX. 1863; d. Cedarhurst, New York, 18. XII. 1919), Amer. orgst. & comp. Studied at

Boston and Munich, where he was a pupil of Rheinberger. In 1884 he returned to N.Y. and became an orgst. and choirmaster, and taught at the Nat. Cons. directed by Dvořák. Later he became orgst. at Trinity Church, Boston, and in 1894 prof. of m. at Yale Univ. He visited Eng. several times for perfs. of his works at the festivals and to receive the Mus.D. from Cambridge in 1902.

Works incl. operas *Mona* & *Fairyland*; orats. *Hora novissima, The Legend of St. Christopher, Morven and the Grail*; *The Holy Child, The Dream of Mary* & other cantatas, chor. ballads and songs; church services; Sym. in C min., ovts. & other orch. works; org. Conc.; stg. 4tet in F maj.; org. So.; pf. pieces; songs, &c.

Parlando or **Parlante** (It. =speaking). A direction indicating, in inst. m., that a passage is to be perf. in a 'speaking' manner, expressively but not sustained or 'sung'; in voc. m. that the tone is to be reduced to something approximating speech.

Parodies. *See* **Imitations.**

Parody Mass. *See* **Missa parodia.**

Parratt, Walter (b. Huddersfield, 10. II. 1841; d. Windsor, 27. III. 1924), Eng. orgst. Held var. appts. from childhood. Orgst. of St. George's Chapel, Windsor, 1882–1924. Mus.D. Oxford, 1892; Cambridge, 1910. Prof. of M. at Oxford, 1908–18. Knighted 1892.

Parry, (Charles) Hubert (Hastings) (b. Bournemouth, 27. II. 1848; d. Rustington, 7. X. 1918), Eng. comp. & writer on m. Son of Thomas Gambier P., a distinguished amateur painter and squire at Highnam Court nr. Gloucester. Educ. at Eton and Oxford, studied m. with Elvey at Eton and with Macfarren and Sterndale Bennett later, also during vacation with Pierson at Stuttgart. Although an amateur at first, he decided to pursue m. professionally. A piece for stgs. had been prod. at the Gloucester Festival of 1868, but he did not make his mark in public until his pf. Conc. was played by Dannreuther at the Crystal Palace in 1880 and his chor. Scenes from Shelley's *Prometheus Unbound* appeared at the Gloucester Festival the same year. Hon. Mus.D., Cambridge 1883, Oxford 1884 and Dublin 1891. After examining for London Univ. and teaching at the R.C.M., he was app. dir. of the latter in succession to Grove in 1894, remaining until his death. Knighted in 1898 and app. Prof. of M. at Oxford in 1900, a post hd resigned in 1908. He wrote several learned books on m., incl. a volume of the *Oxford History of Music*.

Works incl. opera *Guinevere*; incid. m. to Aristophanes' *The Birds, The Frogs, The Clouds* & *The Acharnians*, Aeschylus's *Agamemnon*, Ogilvy's *Hypatia*, Pearl Mary Theresa Craigie's *A Repentance* & Keats's *Proserpine*; orats. *Judith, Job, King Saul*; 6 motets, 4 *Songs of Farewell* & 2 other motets for chor.; chor. works: Scenes from Shelley's *Prometheus Unbound*, ode *The Glories of our Blood and State* (Shirley), ode *Blest Pair of Sirens* (Milton), *Ode on St. Cecilia's Day* (Pope), *L'Allegro ed il Pensieroso* (Milton), ode *Eton* (Swinburne), Choric song from Tennyson's *Lotos-Eaters, Invocation to Music* (Bridges), *A Song of Darkness and Light* (Bridges), *The Pied Piper of Hamelin* (Browning), *Ode on the Nativity* (Dunbar), *The Chivalry of the Sea* & *Eton Memorial Ode* (both Bridges). ode *Persicos odi* (Horace); Magnificat in F maj., 3 Te Deums (the last for George V's coronation), anthem and processional m. for Edward VII's coronation; 2 madrigals; *c.* 50 part-songs; services, anthems and hymn tunes; 5 syms., 3 concert ovts., symph. poem *From Death to Life* and *Suite Moderne* for orch., *Lady Radnor's Suite* and *An English Suite* for stg. orch.; pf. Conc. in F♯ min.; stg. 5tet, 3 stg. 4tets, pf. 4tet, Nonet for wind insts., 4 pf. trios; sos. for v. & pf. and co. & pf., 2 suites and many smaller pieces for v. & pf.; org. m.: *Grand Fugue* in G maj., *Fantasy and Fugue, Wanderer Toccata and Fugue*, 2 sets of chorale preludes, 3 chorale fantasies, Elegy; pf. m. incl. 2 sos., Vars. on an air by Bach, suite *Hands across the Centuries*, Theme & Vars. in D min., suite *Shulbrede Tunes*; Ovt. in B min., So. in F min. & 2 books of *Popular Tunes of the British Isles* for pf. duet; *Grand Duo* for 2 pfs.; over 100 songs incl. 74 in 12 books of *English Lyrics*, &c.

Parry, John (b. ?; d. Ruabon, 7. X. 1782), Welsh hpst. Appeared at Dublin in 1736 and in London and Cambridge in 1746. Handel admired him and Gray wrote his poem *The Bard* on him. He pub. collections of Welsh & other Brit. nat. melodies.

Parry, John (b. Denbigh, 18. II. 1776; d. London, 8. IV. 1851), Welsh clst., bandmaster & comp. Settled in London in 1807 and in 1809 was engaged to comp. songs for Vauxhall Gardens. Later he became a theatre comp. and m. critic to the *Morning Post* in 1834–48. In the 1820s he cond. Welsh festivals at Wrexham and Brecon.

Works incl. stage pieces *Harlequin Hoax* (lib. by T. Dibdin), *Oberon's Oath, Fair Cheating, The Sham Prince*, &c.; songs & ballads; arrs. of Welsh songs, &c.

Parry, John Orlando (b. London, 3. I. 1810; d. East Molesey, 20. II. 1879), Welsh hpst., pfst., singer & comp., son of prec. Studied with his father and later in It. under Lablache. In 1836 he began a career in London as stage singer, mus. entertainer and mimic of singers. He wrote and arr. comic songs, glees, &c.

Parry, Joseph (b. Merthyr Tydvil, 21. V. 1841; d. Penarth, 17. II. 1903), Welsh comp. In spite of the poorest circumstances, he picked up a mus. educ. and after 2 visits to U.S.A. entered the R.A.M. in London at the age of 27, was app. prof. of m. at Aberystwyth, took the Mus.D. at Cambridge in 1878.

Works incl. operas *Blodwen, Virginia, Arianwen, Sylvia, King Arthur*; orats. *Emmanuel, Saul of Tarsus & The Maid of Cefu Idfa, The Prodigal Son, Nebuchadnezzar*; cantata *Cambria* & others; Ballad, ovts. & other works for orch.; stg. 4tet; Welsh hymn-tunes; songs, &c.

Parry, Joseph Haydn (b. Pennsylvania, V. 1864; d. London, 29. III. 1894), Welsh pfst. & comp., son of prec. Studied under his father and in 1890 became prof. at the G.S.M. in London.

Works incl. operas *Cigarette, Miami, Marigold Farm*; cantata *Gwen*; pf. So., &c.

Parsifal, m.-drama by Wagner (lib. by comp.), prod. Bayreuth, Wagner Festival Theatre, 26. VII. 1882.

Parsley, Osbert (b. ?, 1511; d. Norwich, 1585), Eng. singer & comp. Attached to Norwich cath. for 50 years. Comp. services, motets, &c.

Parsons, John (b. ?; d. London, VII. 1623), Eng. orgst. & comp. Became parish clerk and orgst. at St. Margaret's church, Westminster, in 1616, and in 1621 orgst. & choirmaster of Westminster Abbey. He wrote a Burial Service, which Purcell used in 1685 for the funeral of Charles II.

Parsons, Robert (b. Exeter, ?; d. Newark-on-Trent, 25. I. 1570), Eng. comp., (?) father of prec. He became a Gentleman of the Chapel Royal in London, 1563. He was drowned in the Trent.

Works incl. services, anthems, motets; madrigals; In Nomines for viols or virginal; song *Pandolpho* for a stage play, &c.

Part. The m. perf. by any single singer or player in a work for a number of perfs.; a single strand of melody in a polyphonic or other comp. in a number of voices, whether perf. by several people or by a single player on a keyboard inst.; also the copy of the m. from which a single singer or player perfs. in a work for a number of people.

Part du diable, La (*The Devil's Share*), opera by Auber (lib. by Scribe), prod. Paris, Opéra-Comique, 16. I. 1843. The work is sometimes called *Carlo Broschi*, the real name of Farinelli, who is the chief character, sung by a sop.

Part-Playing. The art of playing polyphonic m. on keyboard insts. in such a way that the separate ctptal parts are clearly heard.

Part-Writing. In comp. the way of managing the satisfactory progress of each single part or voice in a texture of any number of parts. In good P.-W. not only the total effect of the comp. is pleasant and rational, but each strand pursues its own course in a way that is interesting to perf.

Partbooks. Books containing printed or MS. m. to be sung or played by 1 or 2 perfs. in a work written for a larger number.

Parte (It.). *See* **Colla parte.**

Partenope, opera by Handel (lib. by Silvio Stampiglia), prod. London, King's Theatre, Haymarket, 24. II. 1730.

Opera by Hasse (lib. by Metastasio), prod. Vienna, Burg Theatre, 9. IX. 1767.

Parthenia. The title of the 1st collection of virginal m. to be printed in Eng., pub. in 1611 and containing 21 pieces by Byrd, Bull and O. Gibbons.

Parthenia inviolata. A companion vol. to the prec. containing 20 virginal pieces with bass viol *continuo*.

Partials. In acoustics the separate constituents (overtones) of a mus. note sounding above the fundamental note, but not perceived as separate notes by the ear.

Partimenti (It. = divisions). Exercises in playing more or less elaborate ctptal parts over a figured bass.

Partita (*see also* **Suite**). The It. word, now obs. in that sense, for Suite. Among its lit. meanings are 'order,' so that it may have been ident. with the Fr. word *Ordre* for the Suite, and 'departure,' which may have indicated its difference from that species, which was that it admitted a freer choice of dances and characteristic mvts. It may also have been connected with the Ger. *Partien* (parties) = Consorts.

Partition (Fr.) } = Score.
Partitur (Ger.) }

Partsong. A voc. comp. for severa voices or chor., for mixed, female or male voices, usually less polyphonic than madrigals or even glees and cultivated mainly in the 19th cent.

Pasdeloup Jules (Étienne) (b. Paris, 15. IX. 1819; d. Fontainebleau, 13. VIII. 1887), Fr. cond. Studied at the Paris Cons. Founder of the Societé des Jeunes Artistes du Cons., 1851, and the Concerts Pasdeloup, 1861, at which he prod. many works previously unknown in Fr.

Pashkeevitch, Vassily Alexeievitch (b. ?; d. ?), Rus. 18th-cent. vst. & comp. Entered the service of Catherine II in 1763 and became cond. & court comp.

Works incl. operas *The Mishap in the Carriage, Fevey, Our Own Load is Light, The Two Anthonys, The Miser, Fedul and his Children* (with Martín y Soler), *The Early Reign of Oleg* (with Sarti & Canobbio), *The Pasha of Tunis*, &c.

Pashtchenko, Andrey Filipovitch (b. Rostov-on-Don, 15. VIII. 1883), Rus. comp. Entered the St. Petersburg Cons. in 1914, after receiving private mus. instruction, and studied comp. under Steinberg and Wihtol. He has been active as teacher and mus. organizer, but devoted most of his time to comp. During the 2nd world war he remained at Leningrad all through the siege.

Works incl. operas *The Revolt of the Eagles, Emperor Maximilian, The Black Cliff, The Pompadours* (after Saltikov-Shtchedrin's story); film m.; orats. *The Liberation of Prometheus & Lenin*, Requiem in memory of the heroes of the great war; 7 syms., *Solemn Polonaise & Festive Overture*, symph. poems *The Giants & The Bacchantes*, scherzo *Harlequin and Columbine*, Suite in the Classical Style, *Legend* for orch.; 3 pieces for a band of folk insts.; stg. 4tet; songs, &c.

Pasino (called Ghizzolo Stefano) (b. Brescia, ?; d. ? Salò, ?), It. 17th-cent. comp. Became town orgst. at Lonato *c.* 1640 and chapel master at Salò in 1651.

Works incl. masses & motets: sos. for 2–4 insts., inst. ricercari, &c.

Paso doble (or Pasodoble; Spa. = double step, two-step). A modern Spa. dance.

Paspy (Eng. obs.). The old Eng. word for the Passepied, unfortunately no longer current.

Pasquali, Francesco (b. Cosenza, ?; d. ? Rome, ?), It. 16th–17th-cent. comp. Studied and worked in Rome.

Works incl. sacred & secular songs, madrigals, &c.

Pasquali, Niccolò (b. ?; d. Edinburgh, 13. X. 1757), It. vst. & comp. Settled at Edinburgh *c.* 1740, lived at Dublin in 1748–51, but returned to Edinburgh, visiting London in 1752. Wrote treatises on thorough-bass and hpchd. playing.

Works incl. opera *The Triumph of Hibernia*; dirge in Shakespeare's *Romeo & Juliet*; orat. *Noah*; 12 ovts. for (or with) hns.; sos. for v. or 2 vs. & bass; songs contrib. to var. collections, &c.

Pasquini, Bernardo (b. Massa di Valdinievole, Tuscany, 7. XII. 1637; d. Rome, 22. XI. 1710), It. hpchdst., orgst. & comp. Studied with Loreto Vittori and Cesti. As a young man he settled in Rome and became orgst. of the church of Santa Maria Maggiore. His *Accademia per musica* was perf. at the Rom. palace of Queen Christina of Swe. in 1687 to celebrate the accession of James II, Corelli leading a stg. orch. of 150 players.

Works incl. operas *La donna ancora è fedele, Dov' è amore e pietà, La forza d'amore* & 8 others, dramatic work *Accademia per musica*; many orats.; sos. & other works for hpchd., &c.

Passacaglia. Orig. an It. or Spa. dance, but now an inst. comp. based on a Ground, i.e. a tune continuing throughout, usually but not necessarily in the bass, as it always does in the Chaconne. The best-known ex. actually called P. is Bach's for org.; but the finale of Brahms's 4th Sym., although not so entitled, is also a familiar P. The name is derived from Spa. *pasar* (to walk) and *calle* (street).

Passage. Any melodic or decorative feature in a comp., esp. if it is conspicuous or calls for brilliant perf.

Passaggio (It.). As above, but used in more specialized senses for Modulations (i.e. passing from key to key) and for florid voc. or inst. decorations.

Passamezzo (It. from *passo e mezzo* = a step and a half). An old It. dance at least as early as the 16th cent. The m. was in common time and a charact. rhythm was 2 bars of minims followed by 3 of crotchets. There were var. Eng. corruptions of its name, now obs., e.g. Passa-measure, Passemeasures paven, Passing Measure, Passy measures pavyn (*Twelfth Night*), &c.

Passecaille (Fr.) = Passacaglia.

Passepied (Fr. lit. pass-foot). A Fr. (prob. Breton) dance at least as old as the 16th cent. The m. is in 3–4 or 3–8 time taken at a moderately running pace. It sometimes occurs in suites, but is not an obligatory part of them.

Passing Appoggiatura. *See* **Ornaments.**

Passing Notes. In harmonic progressions any notes which form part of the melodic or polyphonic material but are not integral parts of the harmony, to which they make discords, are called P. Ns.

Passingalia (Old Eng.) = Passacaglia.

Passion Music. The story of the Passion of Christ, taken from one of the Gospels, was musically presented in church during Holy Week in var. extracts and 1st sung in plainsong. 4-part settings of the passages for the crowd (*turba*) were interpolated and polyphonic Ps. in motet form had already appeared in the late 15th cent. The Lutheran reformation in the 16th cent. introd. a more dramatic form and the use of Ger. instead of Lat., the Evangelist's narrative being given to a ten., but still in plainsong. This gradually developed into Bach's recitative, and other personages in the story, notably Christ (a bass part), began to utter the direct speech of their parts through solo voices. Schütz in the 17th cent. retained these traditions, combined with the It. orat. style, and treated the chor. more elaborately. The 18th cent. developed the orch. and introd. reflective arias with words by contemp. poets, as in Bach's Ps.

Passione, La (*The Passion*), the nickname of a Sym. by Haydn, No. 49, in F min., comp. *c.* 1772.

Pasta (*née* **Negri**) **Giuditta** (b. Saronno nr. Milan, 9. IV. 1798; d. Blevio nr. Como, 1. IV. 1865), It. sop. singer. Studied at home, at the Milan Cons. and in Paris, made her 1st appearance in 1815 and went to London in 1816. In Paris she was 1st heard at the Théâtre Italien in 1821.

Pasterwitz, Georg von (b. Bierhütten nr. Passau, 7. VI. 1730; d. Kremsmünster, 28. I. 1803), Aus. monk, orgst. & comp. Studied at Kremsmünster Abbey, where he was ordained in 1755, and with Eberlin at Salzburg. In 1767–82 he was chapel master at the Abbey, but later lived chiefly in Vienna.

Works incl. opera *Samson*; masses, Requiem; numerous fugues and other pieces for keyboard insts., &c.

Pasticcio (It. lit. pie or pasty). A mus. stage entertainment for which the m. was not written by a single comp. but put together from var. earlier works by any number of comps. who happened to be popular. The words were therefore written to the m., not the reverse, as in opera, &c. In 18th-cent. It., however, words as well as m., esp. from Metastasio's works, were often taken over by a P. The P. was esp. fashionable in the 18th cent. The Ballad Opera and the Vaudeville were both Ps. of a kind.

Pastor fido, Il (*The Faithful Shepherd*), opera by Handel (lib. by Giacomo Rossi after Guarini's pastoral play), prod. London, Queen's Theatre, Haymarket, 22. XI. 1712.

Pastoral, an anthology by Bliss for m.-sop. solo, chor., fl., drums & stgs. (words by Theocritus, Poliziano, Ben Jonson, John Fletcher & Robert Nichols), 1st perf. London, 8. V. 1929.

'Pastoral' Sonata. Beethoven's pf. So. in D maj., Op. 28, comp. in 1801 and ded. to Joseph, Edler von Sonnenfels. The nickname was not B.'s own, but was later invented by the Hamburg pub. Cranz. It suits only the finale.

'Pastoral' Symphony. Beethoven's 6th Sym., in F maj., Op. 68, comp. in 1807–8, 1st perf. Vienna, 22. XII. 1808. The title-page bears B.'s own heading of *Symphonie pastorale*, and on the 1st v. part is the inscription 'Pastoral-Sinfonie oder Erinnerung an das Landleben (mehr Ausdruck der Empfindung als Mahlerey).' (P. S. or Recollection of Country Life [Expression of Emotion rather than Painting].)

Pastoral Symphony, A. The 3rd Sym. by Vaughan Williams, for orch. with a sop. voice (without words), prod. London, Queen's Hall, 26. I. 1922.

Pastorale. A type of Fr. 17th-cent. opera, or opera-ballet, with recitatives, airs & chors., often prod. on special festive occasions and treating pastoral subjects in a courtly and artificial manner, often allegorically. In modern times P. has been often used as a title for all kinds of comps. of a pastoral character.

Pastorale (called *La Pastorale d'Issy*), opera by Cambert (lib. by Pierre Perrin), prod. at Issy nr. Paris, IV. 1659. Long regarded as the 1st Fr. opera (but *see* **Triomphe de l'Amour**).

Pastorella nobile, La (*The Noble Shepherdess*), opera by P. Guglielmi (lib. by Saverio Zini), prod. Naples, Teatro Nuovo, 19. IV. 1788.

Pastourelle (Fr.). A light Fr. song of, as the name suggests, a pastoral character, dating as far back as the 12th cent., but cultivated mainly in the 18th.

Patey (*née* **Whytock**), **Janet** (**Monach**) (b. London, 1. V. 1842; d. Sheffield, 28. II. 1894), Sco. con. singer. Studied with John Wass, Mrs. Sims Reeves and Pinsuti, made an early appearance at Birmingham and went on tour in Eng. in 1865, marrying John P. the following year.

Patey, John (George) (b. Stonehouse, Devon, 1835; d. Falmouth, 4. XII. 1901), Eng. bar. singer, husband of prec. Studied medicine at first, but went to Paris and Milan to learn singing and made his 1st stage appearance in London. 1858. He married Janet Whytock in 1866.

Pathetic Sonata (*Sonate pathétique*). Beethoven's pf. So. in C min., Op. 13, comp. *c.* 1798 and ded. to Prince Carl von Lichnowsky. The title (in Fr.) is, exceptionally, the comp.'s own.

'Pathetic' Symphony. Tchaikovsky's 6th Sym., in B min., Op. 74, comp. 1893 and 1st perf. under the comp., St. Petersburg, 28. X. 1893. The title 'Tragic' Sym. was suggested by the comp.'s brother Modest, but rejected by T., who afterwards agreed to the adj. 'Pathétique.'

Pathétique. *See* **Pathetic Sonata** (Beethoven).

Patience, or Bunthorne's Bride, operetta by Sullivan (lib. by W. S. Gilbert), prod. London, Opera Comique, 25. IV. 1881.

Patiño, Carlos (b. Galicia, ?; d. Madrid, 1683), Spa. comp. Was (?) in the service of John IV of Port. early in the cent. and in 1633 became choirmaster in the royal chapel at Madrid.

Works incl. masses, Benedictus for the funeral of Philip II (1599) & other church m.; incid. m. for plays; villancicos, &c.

Paton, Mary Ann (b. Edinburgh, X. 1802; d. Chapelthorpe, Yorks., 21. VII. 1864), Sco. sop. singer. Appeared as a child playing the harp, pf. and v. and made her 1st stage appearance in London in 1822. Married Lord William Pitt Lennox in 1824, but they separated later. She was the 1st Rezia in Weber's *Oberon* in 1826.

Patter Song. A type of song, usually comic, the effect of which depends on a rapid, syllabic delivery of the words to quick m. Many familiar exs. occur in Sullivan's operettas.

Patti, Adelina (Adela Juana Maria) (b. Madrid, 10. II. 1843; d. Craig-y-Nos, Wales, 27. IX. 1919), It. sop. singer. Made her 1st appearance in N.Y. at the age of 7, and after a period of study reappeared there in 1859. She went to London in 1861 and sang at Covent Garden, and in Paris in 1862. She sang for the last time in 1914.

Patti, Carlotta (b. Florence, 1840; d. Paris, 27. VI. 1889), It. sop. singer, sister of prec. Studied pf. with Herz in Paris, but turned to singing and made her 1st appearance in N.Y. in 1861.

Pauke (Ger.; plur. *Pauken*) = Kettledrum.

Paukenmesse ('Drum Mass,' 'Mass with Drums'). The nickname given to Haydn's Mass in C maj. comp. in 1790 because it makes unusually persistent use of the kettledrums, e.g. in the 'Agnus Dei,' where both sense and tradition dictates that they should be silent.

Paukenschlag, Sinfonie mit dem (Haydn). *See* **Surprise Symphony.**

Paukenwirbel, Sinfonie mit dem (Haydn). *See* **Drum-Roll Symphony.**

Paul et Virginie. *See also* **Paolo e Virginia.**

Opera by R. Kreutzer (lib. by Étienne Guillaume François de Favières, based on Bernardin de Saint-Pierre's novel), prod. Paris, Comédie-Italienne, 15. I. 1791.

Opera by Massé (lib. by Jules Barbier & Michel Carré, after Saint-Pierre), prod. Paris, Opéra National Lyrique, 15. XI. 1876.

Paulin et Virginie, opera by Lesueur (lib. by Alphonse Du Congé Dubreuil, after Saint-Pierre), prod. Paris, Théâtre Feydeau, 13. I. 1794.

Pauline, opera by Cowen (lib. by Henry Hersee, based on Bulwer-Lytton's *The Lady of Lyons*), prod. London, Lyceum Theatre, 22. XI. 1876.

Paulli, Holger (Simon) (b. Copenhagen, 22. II. 1810; d. Copenhagen, 23. XII. 1891), Dan. vst., cond. & comp. Made the v. his principal study, became vst. in the royal orch., leader in 1849 and cond. in 1864, also cond. orch. & chor. socs. In 1866, with Gade and J. P. E. Hartmann, he became one of the dirs. of the Cons.

Works incl. opera *Lodsen* (*The Pilot*); 13 ballets; ovt. & other orch. works; v. pieces; songs, &c.

Paulus. The Ger. title of Mendelssohn's orat. *St. Paul.*

Paumann, Conrad (b. Nuremberg, *c.* 1410; d. Munich, 24. I. 1473), Ger. orgst. & comp. Although blind from birth, he was educ. by the Grundherr family of Nuremberg, learnt the org. & comp. and became orgst. at St. Sebald's church in the early 1440s. In 1467 he was app. orgst. to Duke Albrecht III at Munich. He travelled as org. perf. and also played other insts., incl. lute and fl.

Works incl. org. pieces; songs in 3 parts, &c.

Paumgartner, Bernhard (b. Vienna, 14. XI. 1887), Aus. mcolst. & comp. Studied 1st with his parents, the critic Hans P. and the singer Rosa P., *née* Papier, and afterwards with Bruno Walter. He was dir. of the Mozarteum at Salzburg, 1917–38, cond. a Mozart orch. there and was one of the organizers of the Salzburg festivals. He has written mainly on Mozart.

Works incl. operas *Das heisse Eisen* (after Hans Sachs), *Die Hölle von Salamanca* (after Cervantes), *Rossini in Neapel*, *Aus dem Leben eines Taugenichts* (after Eichendorff's novel); ballet *Pagoden*; incid. m. to Shakespeare's *King Lear* & *Twelfth Night* (on old Eng. tunes), Goethe's *Faust*, Gozzi's *Turandot*, &c.; *Eine deutsche Weihnachtsmusik* for chor. & orch.; Suite in G min., *Ovt. for a Chivalric Play*, Divertimento, &c. for orch.; chors., songs, &c.

Pause. The Fermata, indicated by the sign 𝄐, which means that a note or rest over which it is placed is to be longer than its nominal time-value requires; but the exact length is left to the perf.'s discretion. P. may also mean a complete temporary cessation of the m. for the time specified by rests and often indicated by the abbr. G.P. (General Pause).

Pause (Ger.) = Rest.

Pause del silenzio (*Pauses of Silence*), 7 symph. expressions by Malipiero, prod. Rome, Augusteo, 27. I. 1918.

Pavan (Eng.) }
Pavane (Fr.) } An old dance, prob. of It. orig., since one of its It. names is Padovana (i.e. 'from Padua'), dating back to at least the 16th cent. But the name may also come from Lat. *pavo* (peacock), and the real orig. of the dance may be Spa. It was in common time and went at a moderate pace, usually with a rhythm based on a semibreve followed by 2 minims, to which the same notes succeeded in reverse order. It was often followed by a Galliard on the same tune, but transformed into its own rhythm.

Pavane pour une infante défunte. A pf. piece by Ravel (1899), later orch. (1912). The 'infante défunte' in the title is not a defunct female infant, as is still sometimes supposed, and even stated in print, but a Spa. princess (infanta) of the royal house.

Pavesi, Stefano (b. Casaletto Vaprio nr. Crema, 22. I. 1779; d. Crema, 28. VII. 1850), It. comp. Studied at the Cons. dei Turchini, Naples, 1795–9, and became very popular as an opera comp.

Works incl. operas *Un avvertimento ai gelosi*, *Fingallo e Comala* (after Ossian), *Ser Marcantonio* & more than 60 others.

Pavillon (Fr.). In the mus. sense the bell of a hn., tpt. or tromb. The dir. *pavillon en l'air* occurs in scores where the comp. wishes the bell to be raised to increase the power of tone.

Pavillon chinois (Fr. = Chin. pavilion). The inst. hung with bells, &c. known in Eng. as Turkish Crescent or Jingling Johnny.

Pavin (old Eng.) = Pavan, Pavane.

Paz, Juan Carlos (b. Buenos Aires, 5. VIII. 1897), Arg. comp. Studied in Buenos Aires and was one of the founders of the Grupo Renovación of progressive comps. in 1929, also founded a soc. for the perf. of new m.

Works incl. incid. m. for Ibsen's *Julian the Emperor*; *Canto de Navidad*, *Movimiento sinfónico*, Polytonal Vars., 3 Jazz Mvts. & Passacaglia for orch.; ovt. for 12 solo insts.; 4tet for v., cl., bass cl. & saxophone; sonatinas for cl. & pf., fl. & cl., and ob. & bn.; 3 sos., 9 Ballads, 3 Inventions & other works for pf.; var. works in 12-note technique, &c.

Peacock, Thomas Love (1785–1866), Eng. novelist. *See* **Maid Marian** (Bishop).

Pearsall, Robert (Lucas) (b. Clifton, Bristol, 14. III. 1795; d. Wartensee, 5. VIII. 1856), Eng. comp. Studied law and was called to the bar in 1821, but had already comp. In 1825 he settled at Mainz and studied with Panny there, devoting himself entirely to m. Another year in Eng., 1829–30, was his last, except for visits: he settled in Ger. for good, although he inherited a property at Willsbridge, Glos., in 1836. He sold this and bought Wartensee castle on Lake Constance.

Works incl. church m. (Angl. & Catholic), Requiem; ovt. & chor. for Shakespeare's *Macbeth*; madrigals, partsongs, &c.

Pearson, Henry Hugh. *See* **Pierson, Henry Hugo.**

Pearson, Martin. *See* **Peerson.**

Peasable, James. *See* **Paisible.**

Peasant a Rogue, The (*Selma Sedlák*), comic opera by Dvořák (lib. by Josef Otakar Veselý), prod. Prague, Cz. Theatre, 27. I. 1878.

Peasant Cantata (*Mer hahn en neue Oberkeet* = *We have a new magistracy*). A secular cantata by Bach for solo voices, chor. & orch., comp. in 1742, to words in Saxon dialect. The m. is noticeably rustic and comes as near to the manner of folksong as anything Bach ever wrote.

Pêcheurs de perles, Les (*The Pearl Fishers*), opera by Bizet (lib. by Eugène Cormon & Michel Carré), prod. Paris, Théâtre Lyrique, 30. IX. 1863.

Pêcheurs, Les (*The Fishermen*), opera by Gossec (lib. by Adrien Nicolas de La Salle d'Offémont), prod. Paris, Comédie-Italienne, 7. VI. 1766.

Ped. An abbr. used in the notation of pf. m. to indicate the use of the sustaining Pedal. (The use of the damping pedal is indicated by the words *una corda* [one stg.], or sometimes its abbr. *u.c.*).

Pedal. A device in comp., esp. in the

climax of a fugue, whereby a single note in the mus. texture, most often but not always the bass, is held on for a considerable time while the other parts continue to move. A bass pedal on the dominant gives the ear an overwhelming desire for resolution in the tonic, but the effect is so obvious as easily to become cheap, and it is often a sign of helplessness in a comp., whom it appears to show as unable to keep his m. going in any other way or to prod. a grandiose effect by more orig. means (e.g. Bruckner's syms.).

Pedal Board. The keyboard of pedals on an org. or Pedal Piano.

Pedal Harp. The ord. hp. in current use, as distinct from the chromatic hp.

Pedal Notes. The fundamental notes of trombs. & other brass wind insts., the normal compass of which consists of the upper harmonics. These low notes beyond the normal range, though usable in most of these insts., are difficult to obtain.

Pedal Organ. The portion of the org. controlled by the pedals and the stops connected with them.

Pedal Piano. A pf. specially constructed with a keyboard of pedals and used mainly for org. practice at home, very little m. having been written expressly for it except by Schumann.

Pedal-Point. Another name for the Pedal, as applied to comp.

Pedalflügel (Ger.). The Ger. name for the Pedal (grand) pf., used for ex. by Schumann for his works for that inst.

Pédalier (Fr.). The Fr. name for the pedal keyboard and also for the Pedal Piano.

Pedals. Mechanical devices in certain insts. which require manipulation by the feet. Ps. may actually prod. notes, as in the org.; they may be means of obtaining certain effects of tone, as in the sustaining and damping pf. Ps.; or they may be used to alter the length, and thus the tuning, of stgs., as in the hp.

Pedersøn, Mogens (b. ?, *c.* 1585; d. ? Copenhagen, 1623), Dan. singer & comp. Pupil of Melchior Borgrevinck in the royal chapel of Christian IV. After a visit to Venice, 1599–1603, he became a singer in the chapel. In 1605–9 he was at Venice again studying with G. Gabrieli. In 1611–4 he was in Eng., but returned to Den. and became vice-dir. of the chapel in 1618.

Works incl. madrigal for 5 voices, *Pratum spirituale* for voices, &c.

Pedrell, Carlos (b. Minas, 16. X. 1878), Uruguayan comp. of Spa. descent. Studied at Montevideo, with his uncle Felipe P. at Barcelona in 1898–1900 and then with d'Indy and Bréville at the Schola Cantorum in Paris. In 1906 he went to Buenos Aires, where he held var. official mus. posts and founded the Sociedad Nacional de Música in 1915. Later he settled in Paris.

Works incl. operas *Ardid de amor* & *Cuento de abril*; ballet *Alleluia*; *Une Nuit de Schéhérazade*, *Danza y canción de Aixa*, *En el estrado de Beatriz*, *Fantasia Argentina* & *Ouverture catalane* for orch.; chors.; songs with orch. & with pf., &c.

Pedrell, Felipe (b. Tortosa, 19. II. 1841; d. Barcelona, 19. VIII. 1922), Spa. comp. & mcolst., uncle of prec. Studied m. at home and as a choirboy at Tortosa cath., but had otherwise little systematic instruction. He began to pub. works in 1871 and prod. his 1st opera in 1874, at Barcelona. From that time he taught mus. hist. and aesthetics at the Madrid Cons., but he settled at Barcelona in 1894, where he worked for the revival of old and the spread of new Spa. m., ed. the complete works of Victoria and a collection of old Spa. church m., also old stage & org. m., &c.

Works incl. operas *El último Abencerraje* (after Chateaubriand), *Quasimodo* (on Victor Hugo's *Notre-Dame de Paris*), *Cleopatra*, *Los Pirineos*, *La Celestina*, *El Conde Arnau*, *Visión de Randa* & 4 early light operas; indic. m. for Shakespeare's *King Lear*; Mass, Requiem & Te Deum; *Mazeppa*, *Il Tasso a Ferrara*, *La Canço Llatina*, *In captivitatem comploratio*, *Glosa* & other voc. works; *Festa*, *Lo cant de los montanyes*, *Excelsior*, *I trionfi*, symph. poems *Marcha de la coronación a Mistral*, *Motinada*, *Otger* for orch.; stg. 4tet; *Escenas de niños* for pf. duet; songs *Orientales*, *Consolations*, *Canciones arabescas*, &c.

Pedrollo, Arrigo (b. Montebello Vicentino, 5. XII. 1878), It. cond. & comp. Studied under his father and at the Milan Cons.

Works incl. operas *Juana*, *La veglia* (after Synge's *The Shadow of the Glen*), *L'uomo che ride* (after Victor Hugo), *Delitto e castigo* (after Dostoievsky's *Crime and Punishment*), *L'amante in trappola* & 5 others, 3 mimodramas; 2 *Poemetti* for chor. & orch.; Sym.; chamber m., &c.

Pedrotti, Carlo (b. Verona, 12. XI. 1817; d. Verona, 16. X. 1892), It. cond. & comp. Studied under Domenico Foroni at Verona and prod. his 1st opera there in 1840. From that time until 1845 he was cond. at the It. Opera of Amsterdam, and in 1845–68 he directed the Nuovo and Filarmonico theatres at Verona. In the latter year he settled at Turin, where he became dir. of the Liceo Musicale, cond. at the Teatro Regio and founded popular orch. concerts for classical m.

Works incl. operas *Lina, Matilde, La figlia dell' arciere, Romea di Montfort, Fiorina, Il parrucchiere della reggenza, Gelmina, Genoveffa del Brabante, Tutti in maschera, Isabella d'Aragona, Mazeppa, Guerra in quattro, Marion Delorme* (after Hugo), *Il favorito, Olema la schiava*, &c.

Peel, (Gerald) Graham (b. nr. Manchester, 9. VIII. 1877; d. Bournemouth, 16. X. 1937), Eng. comp. Ed. at Harrow and Oxford, where he remained to study m. with Ernest Walker.

Works incl. over 100 songs, many on words by **A. E. Housman.**

Peer Gynt, incid. m. for Ibsen's drama by Grieg, prod. Christiana, 24. II. 1876. G. afterwards arr. 2 orch. suites from it, Opp. 46 & 55.

Peerson, Martin (b. ? Dunnington nr. Ely, *c.* 1580; d. London, XII. 1650–I. 1651), Eng. orgst. & comp. He took the B.Mus. at Oxford and was soon afterwards app. orgst. and choirmaster at St. Paul's cath. in London.

Works incl. church m. (3 contribs. to Leighton's *Teares or Lamentacions*), airs and dialogues for voices, *Mottects or Grave Chamber Musique* for voices & insts. on sonnets from Fulke Greville's *Caelica*, also an elegy on Greville's death; fancies and almains for viols, virginal pieces, &c.

Peintre amoureux de son modèle, Le (*The Painter in Love with his Model*), opera by Duni (lib. by Louis Anseaume), prod. Paris, Opéra-Comique, 26. VII. 1757.

Pèlerins de la Mecque (Gluck). *See* **Rencontre imprévue.**

Pelléas et Mélisande, incid. m. for Maurice Maeterlinck's play by Fauré, prod. London, Prince of Wales Theatre, 21. VI. 1898.

Incid. m. for do. by Sibelius, Op. 46, comp. 1905.

Opera by Debussy (lib. Maeterlinck's play, slightly altered), prod. Paris, Opéra-Comique, 30. IV. 1902.

Symph. poem on do. by Schoenberg, Op. 5, prod. Berlin, 1911.

Pellegrini, Valeriano. *See* **Valeriano.**

Pellegrini, Vincenzo (b. Pesaro, ?; d. ? Milan, ?), It. 16th–17th-cent. cleric & comp. He was a canon at Pesaro early in the 17th cent. and chapel master at Milan cath. in 1611–31.

Works incl. masses & other church m.; org. canzonets; inst. pieces in 3–4 parts; secular canzonets for voices, &c.

Peñalosa, Francisco (b. ?, *c.* 1470; d. ?, 1535), Spa. comp. He was (?) choirmaster to Ferdinand the Catholic after 1504 and (?) singer in the Julian Chapel in Rome under Leo X.

Works incl. church m.; secular songs for several voices, &c.

Peñalosa, Juan (b. ?; d. ?), Spa. 16th-cent. comp. He became orgst. of Toledo cath. in 1549. Comp. motets & other church m.

Penelope. *See* **Circe** for Keiser's opera.

Opera by Galuppi (lib. by Paolo Antonio Rolli), prod. London, King's Theatre, Haymarket, 12. XII. 1741.

Pénélope, opera by Fauré (lib. by René Fauchois), prod. Monte Carlo, 4. III. 1913; 1st Paris perf., Théâtre des Champs-Élysées, 10. V. 1913.

Penet, Hilaire (b. ?; d. ?), Fr. 16th-cent. singer & comp. He held some clerical post at Poitiers and in 1514 became a singer in the Papal Chapel in Rome, also chamber musn. to Leo X. Comp. masses, motets, &c.

Penillion. An old form of Welsh song to the hp. which was improvised (often the words as well as the m.) as a ctpt. or descant to the hp. part. It is still cultivated, but now tends to rely on tradition rather than improv.

Penna, Lorenzo (b. Bologna, 1613; d. Imola, 20. X. 1693), It. monk & comp. Entered the Carmelite order at Mantua and in 1669 became chapel master at the Carmelite church of Parma, also a prof. of theology. Later he was app. to Imola cath. He wrote treatises on ctpt. and figured bass.

Works incl. masses & other church m.; Fr. courantes for 4 insts., &c.

Penny Whistle. A small and rudimentary pipe of the Fife or Recorder type, also known as 'tin whistle,' played vertically and having a small range of treble notes controlled by 6 finger-holes.

Penorcon. A 17th-cent. inst. of the Cittern type.

Pentatone (from Gr. = 5 notes). Another name for the Pentatonic Scale.

Pentatonic Scale. A scale of 5 notes; actually any 'gapped' scale that cuts out 2 of the normal 7 notes of the ordinary diatonic scales, but more partic. that represented by the black notes of the pf.

Penthesilea, opera by Schoeck (lib. by comp., based on Kleist's drama), prod. Dresden, 8. I. 1927.

Symph. poem on do. by H. Wolf, comp. 1883–5.

Pepita Jiménez, opera by I. Albéniz

(lib., in Eng., by Francis Burdett Money-Coutts, based on a story by Juan Valera), prod. in Spa., Barcelona, Liceo, 5. I. 1896.

Pepping, Ernst (b. Duisburg, 12. IX. 1901), Ger. comp. Studied at the Hochschule für Musik in Berlin and devoted himself chiefly to the cultivation of Protestant church m., being app. prof. at the Kirchenmusikschule at Spandau.

Works incl. setting of the 90th Psalm, unaccomp. motets, *Spandauer Chorbuch* containing voc. pieces for 2–6 voices for the whole eccles. year; Partita, var. concs. and Vars. on a theme by Senfl for orch.; 3 pf. sos., &c.

Pepusch, Johann Christoph (John Christopher) (b. Berlin, 1667; d. London, 20. VII. 1752), Ger. comp. & theorist. App. to the Prus. court at the age of 14; emigrated 1st to Hol. and went to Eng. about 1700, where he settled in London for the rest of his life. Married Margherita de l'Épine in 1718. He arranged the m. of *The Beggar's Opera* for John Gay in 1728.

Works incl. recitatives and songs for a pasticcio opera *Thomyris* & prob. others; incid. m. for Colley Cibber's *Myrtillo*; m. for masques *Apollo and Daphne*, *The Death of Dido*, *The Union of the Sister Arts*, *Venus and Adonis*; dramatic ode for the Peace of Utrecht; ovt. for *The Beggar's Opera* & arrs. for it and its sequel, *Polly*, and another ballad opera, *The Wedding*; services, anthems & Lat. motets; cantatas to words by John Hughes (incl. *Alexis*) and others; odes, concs., sos., &c.

Pepys, Samuel (b. Brampton, Huntingdon, or London, 23. II. 1633; d. London, 25. V. 1703), Eng. official, diarist & amateur musn. Educ. at Huntingdon, St. Paul's School in London and Cambridge Univ. He held several govt. posts and was last secretary to the Admiralty. He kept his diary from I. 1660 to V. 1669. It testifies to his interest in mus. perfs. of all kinds and to his cultivation of m. in his home. In 1665 he made a setting of the song 'Beauty retire' from Davenant's *Siege of Rhodes*, prod. in 1656 with m. by H. Lawes, Locke & others.

See also **Coates (A.)**.

Perabo, Ernest (b. Wiesbaden, 14. XI. 1845; d. Boston, Mass., 29. X. 1920), Ger. pfst. & comp. A very gifted pfst. as a child, he was taken to N.Y. in 1852, studied there and from 1858 in Ger., finishing at the Leipzig Cons. He returned to U.S.A. in 1865 and soon afterwards settled at Boston.

Works incl. studies and pieces for pf., e.g. *Pensées* containing an impression of the soliloquies in *Hamlet*, 10 transcriptions from Sullivan's *Iolanthe*, concert Fantasies on Beethoven's *Fidelio*, &c.

Perc. (abbr.) = Percussion Instruments.

Percussion. A term used in harmony for the actual incident of a discord, after its Preparation and before its Resolution.

Percussion Instruments. All insts. played by being beaten are called P. I., incl. all varieties of drums, bells, cymbals, triangles, gongs, &c. also some in which the perc. is prod. by the intermediary of a keyboard, such as the **Celesta.** These last insts., as also bells, xylophone and kettledrums, prod. notes of definite pitch; others prod. sound without pitch and thus strictly speaking merely a kind of refined and organized noise.

Perdendosi (It. accent on 2nd syll.; *perdendo* = losing, *si* = itself). A direction indicating that the sound of a note or passage is to become gradually weaker until it fades away. The effect may be assoc. with slowing down, but this is not necessarily intended by the comp.

Peregrine Tone. *See* **Tonus peregrinus.**

Perez, Davidde (b. Naples, 1711; d. Lisbon, 1778–9), Spa. comp. Studied at the Cons. di Santa Maria di Loreto at Naples and prod. his 1st opera, *La nemica amante*, there in 1735. He became chapel master to Prince Naselli at Palermo and in 1752 went to Lisbon, where he became attached to the royal chapel and the new Opera opened in 1755.

Works incl. operas *Siroe*, *I travestimenti amorosi*, *L'eroismo di Scipione*, *Astartea*, *Medea*, *L'isola disabitata*, *La clemenza di Tito*, *Semiramide*, *Alessandro nell' Indie*, *Demetrio*, *Demofoonte*, *Solimano*, *Ezio* & others, many to libs. by Metastasio; *Mattutino de' morti*, Credo & other church m.; orat. *Il martirio di San Bartolommeo*, &c.

Perf. (abbr.) = Performance, performed, performer.

Perfall, Karl von, Freiherr (b. Munich, 29. I. 1824; d. Munich, 14. I. 1907), Ger. comp. Studied at Leipzig with Moritz Hauptmann, returned to Munich in 1850 and founded an orat. soc. in 1854. Became intendant of the court m. in 1864 and also of the court theatres in 1867, and was one of Wagner's opponents there.

Works incl. operas *Sakuntala* (after Kalidasa), *Das Konterfei*, *Raimondin* (*Melusine*) & *Junker Heinz*; incid. m. for Shakespeare's *Pericles*; fairy tales for solo voices, chor. & orch. *Dorn-*

röschen, *Undine* (after Fouqué) & *Rübezahl*; chors., songs, &c.

Perfect Cadence. A C. which conclusively leads to the common chord of the tonic, either by a step from the Dominant to the Tonic in the bass (Authentic C.) or from the Subdominant to the Tonic (Plagal C.).

Perfect Fool, The, opera by Holst (lib. by comp.), prod. London, Covent Garden Theatre, 14. V. 1923. A parody, both verbal and mus., of operatic conventions.

Perfect Intervals. Those Is. which do not possess alternative maj. and min. forms, but become Augmented or Diminished by being enlarged or reduced by a semitone, viz. 4ths, 5ths and 8ves, also their repetitions beyond the 8ve, i.e. 11ths, &c.

Pergolesi, Giovanni Battista (b. Jesi nr. Ancona, 3. I. 1710; d. Pozzuoli, 16. III. 1736), It. comp. Studied at Jesi under Francesco Santini and v. under Francesco Mondini, but in 1725 was sent to Naples, where he entered the Cons. dei Poveri di Gesù Cristo, studying under Greco and later Durante and Feo. He also contd. the v. under Matteis. In 1731 he made his 1st appearance as a stage comp. with a serious work and a comic intermezzo, and through the influence of the Prince of Stigliano he began to make his mark at the court theatre. He went into the service of the Duke of Maddaloni abt. 1733 and in 1734 his patron took him on a visit to Rome. Soon afterwards he was app. orgst. at the Neapol. royal chapel. In I. 1735 his opera *L'Olimpiade* failed in Rome and he decided to devote himself only to sacred m. But he was already suffering from consumption, and a visit to Pozzuoli for his health in II. 1736 did not restore him.

Works incl. operas *La Salustia*, *Lo frate nnamorato* (in Neapol. dialect), *Il prigionier superbo*, *Adriano in Siria*, *L'Olimpiade*, *Il Flaminio*; intermezzi *Il maestro di musica*, *L'amor fa l'uomo cieco* (*Nerina e Nibbio*), *Il geloso schernito*, *La serva padrona*, *Livietta e Tracollo*; orats. *San Guglielmo d'Aquitania* & *Il transito di San Giuseppe* (doubtful); 4 masses, *Stabat Mater* for female voices, 4 Misereres, 5 settings of *Salve Regina* & other church m.; *c.* 12 cantatas; Sym. in G maj.; v. & fl. concs.; 26 sos. for 2 vs. & bass, So. for co. & bass; lessons for hpchd., &c.

Peri, Jacopo (b. Rome, 20. VIII. 1561; d. Florence, 12. VIII. 1633), It. comp. Pupil of Cristoforo Malvezzi, a canon at the church of San Lorenzo at Florence and chapel master to the Medici family. P. himself became attached to their court, later as chapel master and chamberlain. He became a member of the progressive artists grouped round Count Giovanni Bardi with Caccini, Corsi, V. Galilei and the poet Ottavio Rinuccini, and in their mistaken endeavour to revive Gr. drama with the kind of m. they imagined to be genuine Gr., they stumbled on the invention of modern opera.

Works incl. operas *Dafne*, *Euridice*, *Tetide*, *Adone*, tournament with m. *La precedenza delle dame*; recitatives for *Arianna* (arias by Monteverdi); parts of operas (with others) *La guerra d'amore* & *Flora* (with Gagliano); several ballets; *Lamento d'Iole* for sop. and insts., madrigals, &c.

Péri, La, ballet (*poème dansé*) by Dukas, prod. Paris, Théâtre du Châtelet, 22. IV. 1912.

Périchole, La, operetta by Offenbach (lib. by Henri Meilhac & Ludovic Halévy, based on Mérimée's *Le Carrosse du Saint-Sacrement*), prod. Paris, Théâtre des Variétés, 6. X. 1868.

Périgourdine. A Fr. country dance from the region of Périgord, known to musns. from at least the 18th cent. Its m. is in quick 6–8 time.

Perkowski, Piotr (b. Ukraine, 17. XI. 1902), Pol. comp. Studied with Statkowski and Szymanowski at the Warsaw Cons. and later with Roussel in Paris, where in 1927 he founded a soc. of young Pol. comps. with Czapski, Labunski and Wiechowicz. He returned to Pol. and in 1935 became dir. of the Torun Cons.

Works incl. ballet *Swantewit*; Sinfonietta for small orch.; v. Conc.; stg. 4tet; inst. pieces; songs, &c.

Perle du Brésil, La (*The Pearl of Brazil*), opera by Fél. David (lib. by Jules Joseph Gabriel & Sylvain Saint-Étienne), prod. Paris, Théâtre Lyrique, 22. XI. 1851.

Perne, François Louis (b. Paris, 4. X. 1772; d. Paris, 26. V. 1832), Fr. comp. and mus. scholar. Although he began humbly as a chor. singer and later db. player at the Paris Opéra, he made a career as a serious comp. and made a close study of Gr. m. In 1813 he succeeded Catel as prof. of harmony at the Cons. and became inspector in 1816 and librarian in 1819.

Works incl. masses & other church m.; chors. for Racine's *Esther*, &c.

Perosi, Lorenzo (b. Tortona, 20. XII. 1872), It. priest & comp. Studied at Milan and Ratisbon, and among other appts. became choirmaster at St. Mark's, Venice, 1894, and mus.

dir. of the Sistine chapel in Rome, 1898. In 1905 he was nominated perpetual master of the Pontifical Chapel.

Works incl. 25 masses, Requiem, *Stabat Mater*, a Te Deum & much other church m.; orats. *The Transfiguration, The Raising of Lazarus, The Resurrection, Moses, Leo the Great, The Last Judgment* & *Il sogno interpretato*; *Florence, Rome, Venice* & *Bologna* from 10 syms. on the names of It. cities planned; org. works, &c.

Perosi, Marziano (b. Tortona, 20. X. 1875), It. comp., brother of prec. Pupil of Haberl at Ratisbon and of Riemann at Leipzig. Church musn. at Zürich and Vienna, 1906–12, and orgst. at the Basilica di Valle di Pompei in Rome, 1912–21.

Works incl. opera *Pompei* (after Bulwer-Lytton); orat. *L'addolorata*; cantata *Spes nostra*, symph. poem *Notte e giorno* for solo voices, chor. & orch.; 3 syms. for org. & orch., &c.

Pérotin (Perotinus Magnus) (b. ?; d. ? Paris, ?), Fr. 12th-cent. comp. & scholar. Chapel master of the church of the Blessed Virgin Mary (later Notre-Dame cath.). Revised the *Liber organi de graduali* of Leoninus, improved mus. notation and comp. church m.

Perotti, Giovanni Agostino (b. Vercelli, 11. IV. 1769; d. Venice, 28. VI. 1855), It. comp. Studied under his brother G. D. P. and Mattei, visited Vienna in 1795 and London in 1798, settled in Venice *c.* 1800, became 2nd chapel master at St. Mark's, 1812, and 1st in succession to Furlanetto, 1817.

Works incl. operas, ballets; church m., orats.; pf. sos., &c.

Perotti, Giovanni Domenico (b. Vercelli, *c.* 1750; d. ? Vercelli, 1824), It. comp., brother of prec. Pupil of G. B. Martini and chapel master of Vercelli cath. until 1820 or later. Comp. operas, church m., &c.

Perpetual Canon. A C. in which each part begins again as soon as it is finished, the other parts being at that moment at other stages of their progress. Since even a P. C. must finish sooner or later, however, it is broken off at a point agreed to by the perfs.

Perpetuum mobile (Lat. = perpetually in motion). *See* **Moto perpetuo.**

Perrault, Charles (1628–1703), Fr. poet & fairy-tale writer. *See* **Cendrillon** (4 operas), **Cenerentola** (2 operas), **Forêt bleue** (Aubert), **Fourdrain** (opera), **Hérold** (*Belle au bois dormant*), **Hüe** (*Riquet à la Houppe*), **Ma mère l'Oye** (Ravel).

Perrin, Pierre (1620–75), Fr. author, who in 1669–72 prec. Lully in holding the patent for the management of the Académie de Musique (Opéra) in Paris. Libst. for Cambert & others. *See also* **Boësset (J.-B.)** (*Mort d'Adonis*), **Pomone** (Cambert).

Perry, George Frederick (b. Norwich, 1793; d. London, 4. III. 1862), Eng. vst., orgst., cond. & comp. Learnt m. as a choir-boy at Norwich cath. and later became vst. at the theatre there. Settled in London as cond. of the Haymarket Theatre, 1822, was orgst. at Quebec Chapel and became leader and later cond. of the Sacred Harmonic Soc.

Works incl. opera *Morning, Noon and Night*; orats. *The Death of Abel, Elijah and the Priests of Baal, The Fall of Jerusalem, Hezekiah*, cantata *Belshazzar's Feast*; church m.; ovt. *The Persian Hunters*; songs for var. plays, &c.

Persée (*Perseus*), opera by Lully (lib. by Quinault), prod. Paris, Opéra, 18. IV. 1682.

Perseleye, Osbert. *See* **Parsley.**

Perséphone, melodrama for the stage or concert-room by Stravinsky (lib. by André Gide), prod. Paris, Opéra, 30. IV. 1934.

Persiani (*née* **Tacchinardi**) **Fanny** (b. Rome, 4. X. 1812; d. Neuilly nr. Paris, 3. V. 1867), It. sop. singer. Studied under her father, Niccolo T., and appeared at his private pupils' theatre near Florence at the age of 11. Married the comp. Giuseppe P. in 1830 and made her 1st public stage appearance at Leghorn in 1832. She 1st went to Paris in 1837 and to London in 1838.

Persiani, Giuseppe (b. Recanati, 1804; d. Paris, 14. VIII. 1869), It. comp., husband of prec. He settled as singing-master in Paris.

Works incl. operas *Inez di Castro, Eufemio di Messina* & 8 others.

Persuis, Louis (Luc Loiseau) de (b. Metz, 4. VII. 1769; d. Paris, 20. XII. 1819), Fr. vst. & comp. Studied under his father, member of the mus. staff at Metz cath., became a vst. in the theatre orch. and went to Avignon following an actress with whom he had fallen in love. There he studied further, went to Paris, appeared at the Concert spirituel in 1787, again became a theatre vst., in 1793 at the Opéra. In 1795–1802 he was v. prof. at the Cons., in 1810–5 court cond. to Napoleon, inspector of m. in 1814 and manager of the Opéra in 1817.

Works incl. operas *La Nuit espagnole, Estelle, Phanor et Angéla, Fanny Morna, Le Triomphe de Trajan* (with Lesueur), *Jérusalem délivrée* (after Tasso), *Les Dieux rivaux* (with Berton, R. Kreutzer & Spontini) & others; ballets *Nina, ou La Folle par amour* & 5 others (some with R. Kreutzer); church m.; cantatas *Chant de victoire, Chant français* & others, &c.

Persymfans (abbr. of Pervyi Symfonitchesky Ansamble = Rus. for 1st symph. ensemble). A conductorless orch. organized in Moscow and making its 1st appearance there on 13. II. 1922. It was later discontinued, not from any lack of success, but because it was found that its principle involved an enormous amount of discussion and rehearsing.

Perti, Giacomo (Antonio) (b. Bologna, 6. VI. 1661; d. Bologna, 10. IV. 1756), It. comp. Studied with his uncle Lorenzo P., a priest at San Petronio cath. at Bologna, and later with Petronio Franceschini. After visits to Venice and Modena in the 1680s, he became chapel master at San Pietro at Bologna in 1690 and of San Petronio cath. in 1696.

Works incl. operas *Oreste, Marzio Coriolano, L'incoronazione di Dario, Teodora, Il furio Camillo, Pompeo, Nerone fatto Cesare, Penelope la casta, Fausta, Rodelinda, Lucio Vero* & 17 others; *Missa solemnis* for solo voices, chor. & orch., other masses, motets, &c.; orat. *Abramo*, 4 Passion orats. & several others, &c.

Peruvian Composer. *See* Sas.

Pes (Lat. = foot). In old m. the lowest part of a voc. comp. in several parts; meaning the same as *tenor* (holder), but not necessarily sung by ten. voices, being more often in a high bass register.

Pesante (It. = heavy, weighty). A direction indicating that a passage is to be played very firmly.

Pesca (It. noun = fishing). A light It. madrigal the subject of the words of which is fishing.

Pescatrici, Le (*The Fisher Girls*), opera by Bertoni (lib. by Goldoni), prod. Venice, Teatro San Samuele, 26. XII. 1751.

Pescetti, Giovanni Battista (b. Venice, *c.* 1704; d. Venice, *c.* 1766), It. comp. Studied with Lotti at Venice and prod. his 1st opera, *Nerone detronato*, there in 1725. He lived in London from *c.* 1737 to the early 1750s, being for a time mus. dir. both of the Covent Garden and King's Theatres. He was app. to a post at St. Mark's, Venice.

Works incl. operas *Gli odi delusi del sangue, Dorinda* (both with Galuppi), *Demetrio, Diana ed Endimione, La conquista del vello d'oro, Tamerlano* (with Cocchi) & *c.* 20 others; orat. *Gionata*; church m.; hpchd. sos., &c.

Pesenti, Michele (b. Verona, ?; d. ?), It. 15th–16th-cent. priest & comp. Wrote frottole, &c.

Pessard, Émile (Louis Fortuné) (b. Paris, 29. V. 1843; d. Paris, 10. II. 1917), Fr. comp. & teacher. Studied at the Paris Cons., where he gained the Prix de Rome in 1866. He later became prof. of harmony there and also inspector of singing in the Paris munic. schools.

Works incl. operas *La Cruche cassée, Don Quichotte* (after Cervantes), *Le Capitaine Fracasse, Tartarin sur les Alpes* (after Daudet), *Les Folies amoureuses* (after Regnard), *Une Nuit de Noël, La Dame de trèfle, Mamzelle Carabin* & others; church m.; orch. works; chamber m.; songs, &c.

Peter Grimes, opera by Britten (lib. by Montagu Slater, based on part of Crabbe's poem *The Borough*), prod. London, Sadler's Wells Opera, 7. VI. 1945.

Peter Ibbetson, opera by Deems Taylor (lib. by comp. & Constance Collier, based on George du Maurier's novel), prod. N.Y. Metrop. Opera, 7. II. 1931.

Peter Schmoll und seine Nachbarn (*P. S. and his Neighbours*), opera by Weber (lib. by Joseph Türk), prod. Augsburg, (?) III. 1803.

Peter the Shipwright (Lortzing). *See* **Zar und Zimmermann**, of which it was the 1st Eng. title.

Peterkin, Norman (b. Liverpool, 21. XII. 1886), Eng. comp. of Sco. & Ir. descent. He is self-taught in m. He joined the m. dept. of the Oxford Univ. Press and in 1941 became its head in succession to Foss.

Works incl. chamber m.; Rhapsody & *Twilight Tune* for v. & pf.; 2 Suites & many pieces for pf.; numerous songs, &c.

Peterson-Berger, (Olof) Vilhelm (b. Ullaanger, 27. II. 1867), Swe. m. critic, poet & comp. Studied at the Stockholm Cons. and at Dresden, where he taught at the M. School for a time. Later he settled at Stockholm as critic.

Works incl. operas *Sveagaldrar, Ran, Arnljot, Domedags profeterna* & *Adils och Elisiv*; syms. *The Banner* & *Sunnanfärd*, intermezzo *Carnival in Stockholm* for orch.; ballad *Florez and Blanzeflor* for voice & orch.; many songs, &c.

Petit Chaperon Rouge, Le (*Little Red Riding-Hood*), opera by Boieldieu (lib. by Emmanuel Guillaume Théaulon de Lambert), prod. Paris, Opéra-Comique, 30. VI. 1818.

Petit Faust, Le, operetta by Hervé (lib. by Hector Crémieux & Adolphe Jaime, a parody of Goethe's drama and esp. of Gounod's opera), prod.

Paris, Fantaisies-Parisiennes, 29. IV. 1869.

Petits Riens, Les (*The Little Nothings*), ballet by Mozart, K. App. 10 (chgph. by Jean Noverre), written in Paris and prod. there, Opéra, 11. VI. 1778.

Petrarch (Francesco Petrarca) (1304–74), It. poet. *See* **Balmer** (Sonnet 103), **Mudarra** (sonnets), **Tommasini** (chor. work). There are also 3 *Sonetti di Petrarca* in Liszt's *Années de Pèlerinage* for pf., arr. in 1846 from earlier settings of the poems for voice & pf.

Petrassi, Goffredo (b. Zagarolo nr. Rome, 16. VII. 1904), It. comp. Learnt m. as a child in the singing-school of the church of San Salvatore in Lauro at Rome, but did not study systematically until the age of 21, when he entered the Cons. di Santa Cecilia, gaining comp. and org. prizes there. He also had advice from Casella, and in 1933 he came out as a comp. by a perf. of his orch. Partita at the Augusteo, which was later given at the S.I.M.C. festival in Amsterdam.

Works incl. incid. m. for A. Aniante's play *Carmen*; Psalm ix for chor. & orch.; *Il coro dei morti* for chor.; Magnificat for voice & orch.; Partita, Passacaglia, Conc. & Concert Ovt. for orch.; *Tre Cori* for chamber orch.; *Lamento d'Arianna* (Rinuccini) for voice & chamber orch., *Introduzione ed Allegro* for v. & 11 insts.; *Sinfonia, Siciliana e Fuga* for stg. 4tet; *Preludio, Aria e Finale* for co. & pf.; Toccata for pf., *Siciliana e Marcetta* for pf. duet; song cycle *Colori del tempo* & other songs, &c.

Petrella, Enrico (b. Palermo, 1. XII. 1813; d. Genoa, 7. IV. 1877), It. comp. Studied at Naples with Zingarelli and others and prod. his 1st opera, *Il diavolo color di rosa*, there in 1829.

Works incl. operas *Le precauzioni, Elena di Tolosa, La contessa d'Amalfi, Ione, Marco Visconti, Giovanni II di Napoli, I promessi sposi* (after Manzoni), *Bianca Orsini* & many others, &c.

Petridis, Petro (b. Nigdé, Asia Min., 23. VII. 1892), Gr. comp. Studied at Constantinople and with Roussel in Paris.

Works incl. opera *Zamphyra*; ballet; 4 syms., dramatic sym. *Digenis Afrikas*, Gr. & Ionian Suites, Elegiac Ovt., *Prelude, Aria and Fugue* for orch.; 2 pf. concs., co. Conc.; Conc. grosso for wind insts.; pf. Trio; 2 *Modal Suites* for pf.; songs, &c.

Petronius (?–?), Lat. author. *See* **Durey** (*3 Poèmes de Pétrone*).

Petrov, Ossip Afanassievitch (b. Elisavetgrad, 15. XI. 1807; d. St. Petersburg, 14. III. 1878), Rus. bass singer. Discovered singing in the market at Kursk in 1830, he was brought to St. Petersburg and made his 1st stage appearance there that year. In 1836 he created the part of Ivan Sussanin in Glinka's *Life for the Tsar*.

Petrucci, Ottaviano dei (b. Fossombrone nr. Ancona, 18. VI. 1466; d. Fossombrone, 7. V. 1539), It. m. printer. He estab. himself at Venice *c.* 1491 and held a patent for the pub. of m. in tablature and notes in 1498–1511, when he returned to Fossombrone to continue business there. He issued many famous collections of masses, motets, frottole, &c.

Petrushka, ballet by Stravinsky (scen. by comp. & Alexander Benois; chgph. by Mikhail Mikhailovitch Fokin), prod. Paris, Théâtre du Châtelet, 13. VI. 1911.

Petrželka, Vilém (b. Královo Pole, 10. IX. 1889), Cz. comp. He studied with Novák in Prague and Janáček at Brno, became a cond. at Pardubice and in 1919 went to Brno as prof. at the Cons.

Works incl. symph. drama *Sailor Nicholas*; *Hymn to the Sun* for chor. & orch.; *Eternal Return*, 2 suites, Dramatic Ovt. for orch.; 2 stg. 4tets, Fantasy and Suite for stg. 4tet; So. & *Intimate Hours* for v. & pf.; pf. pieces; songs; partsongs, &c.

Petto (It.). Chest. Hence *voce di petto* = Chest Voice.

Petyrek, Felix (b. Brno, 14. V. 1892), Cz. pfst. & comp. Studied with his father, an orgst. & cond. and with Adler in Vienna for theory, with Godowsky and Sauer for pf. and with Schreker for comp. Later he taught at Salzburg, Berlin, Athens and Stuttgart.

Works incl. operas *Die arme Mutter und der Tod, Der Garten des Paradieses*; pantomime *Comedy*; incid. m. for Hans Reinhart's *Der Schatten*; *Das heilige Abendmahl, Litanei* & other cantatas, 3 sacred madrigals; 6tet; *Kammerlieder* for voice and chamber m.; v. & pf. So.; pieces for 2 fls.; Conc., *Toccata and Fugue* (Mixolydian), *Dreikönigsmusik* (Dorian) & 6 concert studies for 2 pfs.; Chorale Vars. & Sonatina, 6 Gr. Rhapsodies, Vars. on an Aus. soldier's song, 24 Ukrainian folksongs, &c. for pf., &c.

Pevernage, André (b. Courtrai, 1543; d. Antwerp, 30. VII. 1591), Flem. comp. After holding an appt. at Courtrai, he moved to Antwerp *c.* 1577 and became choirmaster at the cath., holding the post until his early death. Apart from cultivating church m., he held weekly concerts at his house.

Works incl. *Cantiones sacrae* & other church m.; madrigals & chansons; ode to St. Cecilia, &c.

Peyro, José (b. ?; d. ?), Spa. 17th-cent. comp.

Works incl. incid. m. to Calderón's *El jardín de Falerina* & (?) Lope de Vega's *Selva sin amor.*

Pezzo (It., plur. *pezzi*). A piece of m.

Pf. (abbr.) = Pianoforte.

Pfeifertag, Der (*The Pipers' Day*), opera by Schillings (lib. by Ferdinand von Sporck), prod. Schwerin, 26. XI. 1899.

Pfeiffer, Marianne. *See* **Spohr.**

Pfitzner, Hans (Erich) (b. Moscow, 5. V. 1869), Ger. cond. & comp. The family moved to Frankfort o/M., where P.'s father, a vst., became mus. dir. of the munic. theatre. He studied pf. with Kwast and comp. with Knorr at the Cons. there. In 1893 he gave a 1st concert of his own works in Berlin, and after some teaching and cond. appts. he became prof. at Stern's Cons. there in 1897, 1st cond. at the Theater des Westens in 1903. He also cond. the Kaim orch. at Munich and the Opera at Strasburg. After the success of his *Palestrina* in 1917 he devoted himself mainly to comp., but wrote many essays and pamphlets attacking modern m., esp. Busoni, and defending romantic and Germanic ideals.

Works incl. operas *Der arme Heinrich, Die Rose vom Liebesgarten, Christelflein, Palestrina, Das Herz*; incid. m. to Ibsen's *Feast at Solhaug* & Kleist's *Käthchen von Heilbronn*; cantatas *Von deutscher Seele* (Eichendorff), *Das dunkle Reich* & others; Scherzo for orch.; pf. Conc., v. Conc., ballads & songs for voice & orch.; 2 stg. 4tets, pf. 5tet, pf. Trio; v. & pf. So., co. & pf. So.; numerous songs, &c.

Pfst. (abbr.) = Pianoforte player, pianist.

Phaedra. *See* **Fedra.**

Phaéton, opera by Lully (lib. by Quinault), prod. Versailles, 9. I. and 1st perf. Paris, 27. IV. 1683.

Symph. poem by Saint-Saëns, 1st perf. Paris, 7. XII. 1873.

Phagotus (= It. *fagotto* = faggot, bundle). A curious inst., long obs., developed from the Serbian bagpipe by Afranio Albonese of Pavia early in the 16th cent. It consisted of 2 pipes like those of an org., supplied with wind from hand bellows, but their pitch was variable by their being fingered on holes.

Phalèse. Flem. family of m. printers:

1. Pierre P. (b. Louvain, *c.* 1510; d. Louvain, 1573–4), began to pub. m. at Louvain *c.* 1545.

2. Corneille (or Cornelius) P. (b. Louvain, ?; d. ?), son of prec., who gave up his share in the business to his brother (3) at an early date.

3. Pierre P. (b. Louvain, ?; d. Antwerp, 13. III. 1629), brother of prec., who moved to Antwerp to join his father's partner, Jean Bellère, there.

4. Madeleine P. (b. Antwerp, 1586; d. Antwerp, 30. V. 1652), daughter of prec., who continued her father's business in partnership with her sister (5).

5. Marie P. (b. Antwerp, 1589; d. Antwerp, *c.* 1674), sister of prec., with whom she continued in partnership and after her death ran the business under her married name of de Meyer.

Phantasy. *See* **Fantasy.**

Phil. Soc. (abbr). = Philharmonic Society.

Philémon et Baucis, opera by Gounod (lib. by Jules Barbier & Michel Carré, after Ovid), prod. Paris, Théâtre Lyrique, 18. II. 1860.

Philharmonic Pitch. *See* **Pitch.**

Philharmonic Society. London, *see* **Royal Philharmonic Society**: Vienna, *see* **Gesellschaft der Musikfreunde.**

Philidor. Fr. family of musns.:

1. Jean P. (b. ? Dauphiné, *c.* 1620; d. Paris, 8. IX. 1679), fifer, obst., cromorne & tromba marina player, brother of Michel Danican, which was the orig. family name (for reasons of the change of name *see* **Danican**). He entered the service of Louis XIII about the time of his brother's death, *c.* 1659. Comp. dance m.

2. André P. (b. ? Dauphiné, *c.* 1647; d. Dreux, 11. VIII. 1730), bnst., obst. &c. & comp., son of prec. Entered the royal service as a boy, played all sorts of insts. there, competed with Lully in writing fanfares, marches, &c. and was soon commissioned to provide dances and stage diversions. In 1684 he became librarian of the king's mus. library and made a huge MS. collection of court and church m.

Works incl. divertissements *Le Carnaval de Versailles, Le Mariage de la Couture avec la grosse Cathos, La Princesse de Crète, La Mascarade du vaisseau marchand, Le Jeu d'échecs,* &c.

3. Jacques P. (b. Paris, 5. V. 1657; d. Versailles, 27. V. 1708), obst., bnst., &c. & comp., brother of prec. Entered court service *c.* 1670, the royal chapel in 1683 and the chamber m., as bnst., in 1690. Comp. marches, airs for ob., dance m., &c.

4. Alexandre P. (b. Paris, *c.* 1660; d. ?), cromorne & tromba marina player, brother of prec. He too was in service at court.

5. Anne P. (b. Paris, 11. IV. 1681

d. Paris, 8. X. 1728), obst. & comp., son of 2. by his 1st wife, Marguerite Mouginot. Entered court service as obst. in the chamber m. and the royal chapel, founded the Concert spirituel in Paris, 1725, and later in life superintended the Duchesse de Maine's and the Prince de Conti's private concerts.

Works incl. pastorals *L'Amour vainqueur, Diane et Endymion, Danaé*, &c.

6. Michel P. (b. Versailles, 2. IX. 1683), drummer, brother of prec. In service at court.

7. François P. (b. Versailles, 17. III. 1689; d. ? Versailles, 1717–8), ob., cromorne, tromba marina & bass viol player & comp., brother of prec. In court service, comp. fl. pieces, &c.

8. François André (Danican) P. (b. Dreux, 7. IX. 1726; d. London, 24. VIII. 1795), comp. and chess player, step-brother of prec., being the son of 2 by his 2nd wife, Élisabeth Le Roy. As a page in royal service he showed an amazing gift for chess and played with the courtiers, at the same time studying m. with Campra in the royal chapel. Leaving the court as an adolescent, he tried to make his way in Paris by giving m. lessons and copying, but got into debt. In 1745 he went on a tour to display his genius for chess, visiting Hol., Ger. and Eng. In London he pub. his *Analyze des échecs* in 1749, and perf. feats of playing several simultaneous games blindfold, &c. In 1754 Diderot and other friends induced him to return to Paris and to take up m. seriously, which he did, writing 1st motets in the manner of Handel and then operas, the 1st of which was prod. in 1759. After a long series of prods. he returned to London in 1777, going back to Paris some 2 years later to bring out another series of stage works. In 1792 he took refuge from the Revol. in London, whence he had for some time derived a pension from the Chess Club. His family tried to obtain permission for his return, but he d. before it could take effect.

Works incl. operas *Blaise le savetier, L'Huître et les plaideurs, Le Quiproquo, Le Soldat magicien, Le Jardinier et son seigneur, Le Maréchal ferrant, Sancho Pança dans son île* (after Cervantes), *Le Bûcheron, Les Fêtes de la paix, Le Sorcier, Tom Jones* (after Fielding), *Le Jardinier de Sidon, L'Amant déguisé, La Nouvelle école des femmes, Mélide, ou Le Navigateur, Le Bon Fils, Les Femmes vengées, Ernelinde, Persée* (Lully's old lib.), *Thémistocle, L'Amitié au village, La Belle Esclave, ou Valcour et Zeïla, Bélisaire* & others; Requiem for Rameau, motet *Lauda Jerusalem* & others; settings of Horace's *Carmen saeculare* & Congreve's *Ode on St. Cecilia's Day*, &c.

9. Pierre P. (b. Paris, 22. VIII. 1681; d. ?, 1. IX. 1731), flst., violist & comp., son of 3. Was in the royal bands, comp. a pastoral, *L'Églogue de Marly* & another, fl. suites, &c.

10. Jacques P. (b. ? Paris, 7. IX. 1686; d. Pamplona, 25. VI. 1709), obst. & drummer, brother of prec. Succeeded his father in the royal service.

11. François P. (b. ? Paris, 21. I. 1695; d. ? Paris, 27. X. 1726), obst., brother of prec. Member of the royal chamber m.

12. Nicolas P. (b. Versailles, 3. XI. 1699; d. ? Paris, 1769), obst. & violist, brother of prec. In service at court.

Philip, Saint. *See* **Neri.**

Philippe de Vitry. *See* **Vitry.**

Philips, Peter (b. ?; d. Brussels, ? 1634), Eng. orgst. & comp. He left Eng. *c.* 1590, prob. because he was a Rom. Catholic, (?) visited It., settled at (?) Antwerp, became a canon at the collegiate church of Soignies and *c.* 1611 was app. orgst. at the royal chapel in Brussels. In 1621 he became chaplain of the church of Saint-Germain at Tirlemont and *c.* 1623 canon of Béthune, but may not have resided at either place. He was famous as an orgst. throughout the Nthlds.

Works incl. masses, motets, hymns, *Sacrae cantiones*; madrigals; fantasies, pavans & galliards for var. insts.; org. & virginal pieces, &c.

Phillipps, Adelaide (b. Stratford-on-Avon, 1833; d. Carlsbad, 3. X. 1882), Eng. con. singer. The family settled in N. Amer. in 1840, where she 1st appeared as a dancer. But she studied singing with García in London and in 1854 made her 1st appearance in opera at Milan. Later she sang chiefly in U.S.A.

Phillips. *See* **Wilder, Philip van,** who was sometimes misleadingly called by that name.

Phillips, Burrill (b. Omaha, Nebraska, 9. XI. 1907), Amer. comp. Pupil of Howard Hanson at the Eastman School of M. at Rochester, N.Y., where he joined the teaching staff later.

Works incl. 1-act opera; ballet *Princess and Puppet*; *Grotesque Dance, Selections from Guffey's Reader* & *Courthouse Square* for orch.; Conc. for pf. & chamber orch.; 4tet for ob. & stgs.; Trio for tpts.; pf. suite *A Set of Informalities*, &c.

Phillips, Henry (b. Bristol, 13. VIII.

1801; d. London, 8. IX. 1876), Eng. bar. singer. Appeared on the stage as a boy, sang in the chor. at Drury Lane Theatre in London and gradually worked his way up as a concert singer.

Phillips, Montague (Fawcett) (b. London, 13. IX. 1885), Eng. comp. Studied at the R.A.M. in London.

Works incl. operettas *The Rebel Maid* & *The Golden Triangle*; Sym. in C min., Sinfonietta, ovts. & suites, symph. poem *Boadicea* for orch.; 2 pf. concs., Fantasy for v. & orch.; songs, &c.

Phillips, Stephen (1868–1915), Eng. poet & dramatist. *See* **Coleridge-Taylor** (4 plays, incid. m.), **Francesca da Rimini** (Nápravnik), **O'Neill** (*Lost Heir*), **Pitt** (*Paolo and Francesca*).

Philosopher, The. The nickname of a Sym. by Haydn, No. 22, in E♭ maj., comp. in 1764 and containing, very exceptionally, parts for 2 Eng. hns.

Philtre, Le (*The Love Potion*), opera by Auber (lib. by Scribe), prod. Paris, Opéra, 20. VI. 1831. *See also* **Elisir d'amore.**

Phinot (or Finot), Dominique (b. ?; d. ?), Fr. 16th-cent. comp.

Works incl. masses, motets, magnificats, psalms & other church m.; chansons, &c.

Phoebus and Pan (Bach). *See* **Streit zwischen Phöbus und Pan.**

Phonetics. The science of the physical conditions of speech and song.

Phonograph. *See* **Gramophone.**

Phonology. The science of voc. sound.

Phrase. A small group of notes forming a definite melodic or thematic feature in a comp.

Phrasing. The proper perf. of a Phrase, delivered according to the comp.'s prescriptions and, where these are not sufficiently definite, according to the perf.'s taste and feeling. Good P. incl. the observance of tied or detached grouping of notes, the distribution of stresses and inflections, bowing on stg. insts., breath control in wind playing and singing and choice of the best fingering in inst. m. The problems of breathing also affect, by analogy, the delivery on other than wind insts., where minute breaks between the phrases are an important element of expressive P.

Phrygian Cadence. A Cadence in the P. mode proceeding from Subdominant to Tonic in the bass and from C to B in the treble, the G in the final chord being sharpened to form the maj. Triad. The P. C. can, however, be used in non-modal, diatonic m., transposed into any key, and has been so used mainly in 2 ways: (1) by progressing in the way described above out of the key of C maj., ending on the chord of E. G♯, B (e.g. in some chorale tunes set by Bach), this procedure being, of course, admissible in transpositions into any key; (2) by progressing with subdominant-tonic bass to the final maj. chord on the dominant of the prevailing key, the leading-note before that final chord being flattened, the effect being that of a half-close, not a full close, the dominant triad leaving the ear to expect a further progression towards the tonic (e.g. at the end of many of Handel's conc. mvts. other than final mvts.).

Phrygian Mode. The 3rd ecclesiastical mode, represented on the pf. by the scale beginning with the note E played on the white notes.

Physharmonica. A small inst. of the org. type invented by Anton Hackel of Vienna in 1818; a forerunner of the Harmonium.

Piacere (It. = pleasure). *See* **A piacere.**

Piacevole (It., accent on 2nd syll.). Pleasantly, agreeably.

Pianette (corrupt Fr.). A name used in Eng. for a tiny upright pf., similar to the Pianino, but even smaller. It is called Bibi, orig. Bébé, in Fr.

Piangendo (It.). Weeping, wailing, plangent.

Pianino. A small upright pf.

Pianissimo (It., superlative = most softly). A direction rarely written out in full, but indicated by the sign *pp* or a multiplication thereof.

Piano (It. adj. = soft). This too is as a rule repres. by a symbol: *p*. The compar. 'softer' for a dynamic direction between *p* and *pp*, &c. has no symbol, but is expressed by the words *più piano* (or *più p*).

Piano (noun). The current abbr. name of the Pianoforte, still only reluctantly admitted into literary Eng. on account of its being absurd to call an inst. 'the soft.' It is, however, nearly as absurd to call it 'the soft-loud,' and failing the acceptance of a good Eng. word, the shorter name may as reasonably be used as the longer.

Piano-Organ (or Handle-Piano). A mech. inst. similar to the Barrel Org., in the shape of an upright pf., prod. its notes in the same way by a studded cylinder, but from stgs. struck by hammers instead of pipes. It was widely used by street musns. in the larger Eng. cities in the late 19th and early 20th cent., esp. in London, of which it was long part of the atmosphere. It was often wrongly called 'barrel org.' and even more incorrectly 'hurdy-gurdy.'

Piano Quartet. The techn. term for a 4tet for pf., v., va. & co.

Piano Quintet. A 5tet for pf. and stg. 4tet.

Piano Trio. A trio for pf., v. & co.

Piano Score. *See* **Score.**

Pianoforte (It. lit. soft-loud). This domestic inst. in universal use in the western world needs no detailed description. It is a devel. of but not a direct descendant from the hpchd., the method of tone-prod. being entirely different, the hpchd. stgs. being plucked whereas those of the P. are struck by hammers. In that respect the P. was more closely related at first to the Dulcimer. Its beginnings go back to It. at the end of the 16th cent., but the 1st inventor who prob. consolidated it in its present form was Bartolommeo Cristofori of Padua, settled at Florence, about the 1st decade of the 18th cent. Its 1st form was the wing shape of the hpchd., corresponding roughly to the modern grand pf.; the table-shaped square pf. came later in the cent. and the upright pf. followed last in the 19th cent. The hammer action was improved by very gradual processes, and Eng. makers contrib. the invention of the iron frame, which was capable of supporting a much greater tension of stgs. resulting in more powerful tone.

Pianola. A mech. device attached to an ordinary pf. whereby the hammers are made to touch the stgs. not by action of the hand on the keyboard but by air-pressure. This is regulated by a roll of perforated paper running over a series of slits corresponding with the mus. scale and releasing the air only where the holes momentarily pass over the slits. The mechanism is set in motion by pedals like those of a harmonium. Dynamics were at first controlled by action of the player's hands, more or less roughly, according to his skill, but they were later reprod. mechanically exactly as played by the recording artist. This, however, left the manipulator with nothing of any interest to do, and no doubt for that reason the P., after enjoying a great vogue in the early 20th cent., has now fallen into neglect.

Pianotron. An electrophonic upright pf. evolved from the Neo-Bechstein grand pf. by Selmer of London in 1938, prod. its notes by the conversion of electrical waves into audible sounds.

Piatti (It. = plates) = Cymbals.

Piatti, Alfredo (Carlo) (b. Bergamo, 8. I. 1822; d. Crocetta di Mozzo, 18. VII. 1901), It. cst. Studied m. under his father, a vst., and co. under his great-uncle Zanetti. He soon entered a theatre orch., came under the notice of Mayr and was sent to study at the Milan Cons., making his 1st public appearance in 1837. He travelled widely later and lived much of his life in London, where he became assoc. with Joachim and played frequently at the Popular Concerts at St. James's Hall. He wrote 2 concs. and a number of pieces & studies for co.

Pib-Corn or **Pibgorn** (from Welsh = pipe-horn). A primitive wind inst. made of wood or bone with a bell made of an animal's horn, formerly used by the Welsh and other Celts.

Pibrac (du Faur), Guy (1529–86), Fr. poet. *See* **Boni** (quatrains).

Pibroch. Vars. for the bagpipe played elaborately on a type of theme called the Urlar.

Picardy Third. *See* **Tierce de Picardie.**

Piccinni, Louis-Alexandre, **Piccinni, Luigi** *See* end of par. below.

Piccinni, Nicola (b. Bari, Naples, 16. I. 1728; d. Passy nr. Paris, 7. V. 1800), It. comp. Studied at the Cons. di Sant' Onofrio at Naples, Leo and Durante being among his masters. He prod. his 1st opera at Naples in 1754. In spite of Logroscino's exclusive success it was well received and soon followed by other operas, both comic and serious. In 1756 he married the singer Vincenza Sibilla, his pupil. In 1760 he made an enormous success in Rome with *La buona figliuola*. After some years of success there, he was ousted by Anfossi and returned to Naples in 1773. In 1776 he was invited to Paris, where he was at first in great difficulties, but was helped by Marmontel, who taught him Fr. and wrote the lib. of his 1st Fr. opera, *Roland*, for him, which was prod. in I. 1778. By this time he had been artificially made into an opponent to Gluck by those who were determined to organize a partisan feud, though neither he nor G. had any desire to take a share in this and liked and respected each other. The quarrel of their adherents was heightened by their being both given an *Iphigénie en Tauride* to set to m. P. became dir. of an It. opera company and singing-master to Marie-Antoinette, and received a pension, which however he lost when the Revol. broke out in 1789. Having got into trouble politically, he left for It., visited Venice and then returned home to Naples, where however he was placed under close surveillance and lived in great poverty. In 1798 he at last succeeded in returning to Paris. After a period of comparative affluence, he again fell into poverty, was relieved by a gift from Bonaparte and an inspector's post at the Cons., but became paralysed and finally d. in distress. His son Luigi (1766–1827) and his natural grandson Louis-Alexandre (1779–1850) were both comps. The former wrote operas for Paris and Stockholm, the latter ballets, melodramas, &c. for the Paris theatres.

Works incl. operas *Le donne dispettose, Le Gelosie, Zenobia, Alessandro nell' Indie* (2 versions), *Madama Arrighetta, La buona figliuola, La buona figliuola maritata* (both after Richardson's *Pamela*), *Il cavaliere per amore, Le contadine bizarre, Gli stravaganti, L'Olimpiade, I viaggiatori, La pescatrice, Le finte gemelle, Vittorina* (Goldoni), *Roland, Atys, Iphigénie en Tauride, Didon, Le Faux Lord, Pénélope, Endymion* & *c.* 85 others; orat. *Jonathan* & 2 others; mass, psalms & other church m., &c.

Picco Pipe. A woodwind inst. of the recorder or flageolet type which became fashionable in Eng. on being introd. to London in 1856 by a Sardinian player named Picco.

Piccolo (It., abbr. for *flauto piccolo* = little flute). The small 8ve fl., more usually called *ottavino* in It., similar in shape and technique to the ordinary fl., but smaller in size and standing an 8ve higher in pitch. It transposes up an 8ve, its m. being written an 8ve below the actual sound. Also a 2-ft. org. stop reprod. P. tone.

Piccolomini, Marietta (b. Siena, 15. III. 1834; d. Florence, 23. XII. 1899), It. sop. singer. Made her 1st appearance at Florence in 1852 and 1st visited Eng. in 1856.

Pichl, Vaclav (b. Bechin, Tábor, 25. IX. 1741; d. Vienna, 23. I. 1805), Boh. vst. & comp. Studied in Prague and became 1st v. in Dittersdorf's orch. at Grosswardein. Later played in Count Hartig's orch. in Prague and at the Court Opera in Vienna, whence the empress sent him to It., where he made further v. studies with Nardini and worked at the theatre at Monza *c.* 1789–95. In 1796 he returned to Vienna with the Archduke Ferdinand.

Works were said by him to incl. 25 operas; 14 masses & other church m.; 88 syms., 13 serenades & other orch. works; concs. for v. & for wind insts.; chamber m.; v. pieces; pf. sos.; 148 pieces for barytone; ariettas, &c.

Pick-Mangiagalli, Riccardo (b. Strakonice, 10. VII. 1882), Cz.-It. comp. Studied in Prague, Vienna and Milan. In 1936 he succeeded Pizzetti as dir. of the Milan Cons.

Works incl. operas *Basi e bote, L'ospite inatteso* & *Notturno romantico*; ballets *Salice d'oro, Il carillon magico, Casanova a Venezia, La Berceuse* & *Variazioni choreografiche*; mime dramas *Sumitra* & *Mahit*; *Sortileggi* for pf. & orch.; stg. 4tet; v. & pf. So.; pf. works, &c.

Pickwick, opera by Albert Coates (lib. by comp., based on Dickens), prod. London, Covent Garden Theatre, 20. XI. 1936.

Pictures at an Exhibition, a suite of pf. pieces by Mussorgsky, comp. in 1874 in memory of the painter and architect Victor Alexandrovitch Hartmann (d. 1873) and illustrating pictures and designs by him shown at a memorial exhibition, organized by V. V. Stassov. Orch. versions of the work have been made by Henry J. Wood, Ravel and Walter Goehr. The Rus. title is lit. *P. from an E.*, but there is no harm in using a better Eng. one.

Pictures, Music based on. *See* **Paintings.**

Pieno (It. = full). A direction used esp. in org. m. in comb., *organo pieno*, meaning either that a figured bass is to be filled with ample harmony or that the inst. is to be played with full registration.

Pierluigi, Giovanni. *See* **Palestrina.**

Pierné, (Henri Constant) Gabriel (b. Metz, 16. VIII. 1863; d. Ploujean, Côtes du Nord, 17. VII. 1937), Fr. cond. & comp. Studied at the Paris Cons. and gained the Prix de Rome in 1882. In 1890 he succeeded Franck as orgst. of the church of Sainte-Clotilde, became 2nd cond. of Colonne's orch. in 1903 and at Colonne's death in 1910 succeeded him as chief cond.

Works incl. operas *Les Elfes, Pandore, La Coupe enchantée* (after La Fontaine), *La Nuit de Noël, Vendée, La Fille de Tabarin, On ne badine pas avec l'amour* (after Musset), *Fragonard, Sophie Arnould*; ballets *Les Joyeuses Commères de Paris, Bouton d'or, Cydalise et Chèvre-pied, Impressions de Music-Hall, Girations, Images, La Grisi*; pantomimes *Le Collier de saphirs, Le Docteur Blanc, Salomé*; incid m. to Shakespeare's *Hamlet*, Rostand's *Princesse lointaine* & other plays; orats. *Les Enfants de Bethléem, Les Fioretti de Saint François d'Assise*; symph. poem for chor. & orch. *L'An mil*; *La Croisade des enfants* for children's chor. & orch.; Suites, *Ouverture symphonique, Paysages franciscains, Divertissement sur un thème pastoral,*

Gulliver au pays de Lilliput (after Swift), &c. for orch.; Conc. in C min., *Fantaisie-ballet, Scherzo-caprice, Poème symphonique,* &c. for pf. & orch.; pf. 5tet, pf. Trio, *3 Pièces en trio* for v., va. & co., & other chamber m.; pf. works; songs, &c.

Pierrot lunaire, song-cycle with chamber orch. by Schoenberg, Op. 21, consisting of 21 poems by Albert Giraud trans. into Ger. by Otto Erich Hartleben, comp. 1912 and 1st perf. Berlin, 16. X. 1912. The treatment of the voice-part is one of the outstanding exs. of the use of Speech-song (*Sprechgesang*).

Pierson (orig. **Pearson**), **Henry Hugh** (or **Heinrich Hugo**) (b. Oxford, 12. IV. 1815; d. Leipzig, 28. I. 1873), Eng. comp. Educ. at Harrow and Cambridge, studied m. with Attwood & Corfe, and interrupted a medical course to continue mus. studies at Leipzig, where he met Mendelssohn, Schumann & others. He became Reid Prof. of M. at Edinburgh in 1844 in succession to Bishop, but soon resigned and returned to Ger., where he remained, married Caroline Leonhardt and changed the spelling of his name.

Works incl. operas *Der Elfensieg, Leila* & *Contarini* (*Fenice*); incid. m. to Goethe's *Faust* (Part II); orat. *Jerusalem*; *Macbeth* sym., ovts. to Shakespeare's *Twelfth Night, Julius Caesar* & *Romeo and Juliet,* funeral march for *Hamlet*; numerous songs; partsongs, &c.

Pierson, Martin. *See* **Peerson.**

Piéton, Loyset (b. Bernay, Normandy, ?; d. ?, after 1545), Fr. comp. often confused with Compère, both being usually called only by their Christian names. Comp. masses, motets, psalms, &c.

Pietoso (It. from *pietà* = pity) = pityingly, compassionately.

Pietra del paragone, La (*The Touchstone*), opera by Rossini (lib. by Luigi Romanelli), prod. Milan, Teatro alla Scala, 26. IX. 1812.

Pifa. *See* below.

Pifferari (It.). Players on the inst. below.

Piffero (It. = fife). A small fl.-like pipe, also a shepherd's pipe akin to the ob. or bagpipe. It was often played in It. cities, esp. Rome and Naples, at Christmas time, by pipers from the hills, who seem to have played tunes of the Siciliana type akin to that of the *Pastoral Symphony* in Handel's *Messiah*, which bears the word ' Pifa ' in the MS., evidently in reference to the P.

Piggott, Richard. *See* **Pygott.**

Pigheaded Peasants, The (*Tvrdé Palice*), opera by Dvořák (lib. Josef Štolba), prod. Prague, Cz. Theatre, 2. X. 1881.

Pigott, Richard. *See* **Pygott.**

Pijper, Willem (b. Zeist, 8. IX. 1894), Dutch comp. Studied with Wagenaar and was app. prof. of comp. at the Amsterdam Cons. in 1925; dir. of the Rotterdam Cons. in 1930.

Works incl. opera *Halewijn*; incid. m. for Euripides' *The Cyclops* & *The Bacchantes,* Sophocles' *Antigone* & Shakespeare's *Tempest*; 3 syms., 6 Symph. Epigrams for orch.; pf. Conc., v. Conc.; 4 stg. 4tets, 2 pf. trios, 6tet for wind & pf.; v. & pf. sos.; pf. m.; chors.; songs, &c.

Pilati, Mario (b. Naples, 16. X. 1903; d. Naples, 10. XII. 1938), It. comp. Studied at the Naples Cons. Taught at Cagliari and Milan for some time and then returned to Naples, where he was app. prof. at the Cons. S. Pietro a Maiella.

Works incl. pf. Conc. in C maj., Suite for pf. & stgs.; pf. 5tet; v. & pf. sos., &c.

Pilgrims to Mecca, The (Gluck). *See* **Rencontre imprévue.**

Pilkington, Francis (b. ? Lancashire, ?; d. Chester, 1638), Eng. comp. Took the Mus.B. at Oxford in 1595 and was soon after app. to some post at Chester cath., where he remained to his death, becoming a minor canon in 1612.

Works incl. anthems (1 in Leighton's *Teares or Lamentacions*); madrigals & pastorals for 3–6 voices; lute pieces; songs to the lute, &c.

Pimmaglione (*Pygmalion*), **opera by** Cimador (lib. by Antonio Simone Sografi, based on Rousseau's *Pygmalion*), prod. Venice, Teatro San Samuele, 26. I. 1790.

Pimmalione (*Pygmalion*), **opera by** Cherubini (lib. by Stefano Vestris), prod. Paris, Tuileries, at Napoleon's private theatre, for which it was written, 30. XI. 1809.

Pinafore (Sullivan). *See* **H.M.S. Pinafore.**

Pincé (Fr.) = Mordent.

Pincé étouffé (Fr.) = Acciaccatura.

Pincé renversé (Fr.) = Shake.

Pincement (Fr.) = Mordent.

Pincherle, Marc (b. Constantine, Algeria, 13. VI. 1888), Fr. mcolst. Prof. at the École Normale de Musique in Paris and ed. successively of *Le Monde musical* and *Musique.* His works incl. studies of Corelli, Vivaldi, the v. and v. m.

Pinelli, Ettore (b. Rome, 18. X. 1843; d. Rome, 17. IX. 1915), It. vst. & cond. Studied in Rome and with Joachim at Hanover, organized chamber concerts in Rome and with Sgambati founded the Liceo Musicale there, became v. prof. and cond.

orch. & chor. concerts. Comp. an ovt., a stg. 4tet, &c.

Pinello di Gherardi, Giovanni Battista (b. Genoa, 1544; d. Prague, 15. VI. 1587), It. comp. After an appt. at Vicenza cath. he went to Innsbruck in the 1570s as musn. to the archduke, to the imp. chapel in Prague soon afterwards and to the Saxon court at Dresden in 1580 in succession to Scandello, but was dismissed because of differences with other musns. and returned to Prague.

Works incl. motets, Ger. magnificats & other church m.; madrigals & canzone napoletane; Ger. songs for several voices, &c.

Pini-Corsi, Antonio (b. Zara, VI. 1859; d. Milan, 22. IV. 1918), It. bar. singer. Made his 1st appearance at the age of 19 at Cremona and became one of the leading interpreters of comic parts, Verdi choosing him for Ford in his *Falstaff* in 1893.

Pinsuti, Ciro (b. Sinalunga, Siena, 9. V. 1829; d. Florence, 10. III. 1888), It. pfst., singing-teacher & comp. Studied with his father and played the pf. in public as a child, was taken to Eng., studying comp. with Potter, returning to It. in 1845 and becoming a pupil of Rossini at Bologna. From 1848 he was in Eng. again, teaching singing for many years in London and Newcastle-on-Tyne and becoming prof. at the R.A.M. in 1856.

Works incl. operas *Il mercante di Venezia* (after Shakespeare), *Mattia Corvino* & *Margherita*; Te Deum for the annexation of Tuscany to It. (1859); hymn for the Internat. Exhib. in London (1871); 30 pf. pieces; 230 songs; many voc. duets & trios, partsongs, &c.

Pinto, George Frederic (b. London, 25. IX. 1786; d. London, 23. III. 1806), Eng. vst. & comp. His real name was Saunders, but he adopted that of his maternal grandfather. Studied with Salomon and others and appeared at S.'s concerts from 1796. He then toured in Eng. & Sco. and visited Paris.

Works incl. v. & pf. sos., v. duets, pf. sos., canzonets, &c.

Pinto, Thomas (b. ?, 1714; d. ? Dublin, 1783), Eng. vst. of It. descent, grandfather of prec. through his 1st wife. In 1766 he married the singer Charlotte Brent as his 2nd wife. He played in London at an early age, later at the Three Choirs Festival, &c., failed in a speculation with Arnold to run Marylebone Gardens and last lived in Sco. and Ir.

Piozzi, Gabriel(e) (b. Florence, ?; d. Brynbela, Denbighshire, III. 1809), It.-Eng. m.-master & comp. He settled in Eng. before 1780 and taught at Bath. In 1784 he married Samuel Johnson's friend, Mrs. Hester Thrale, who defied the objections of her circle to her marrying a musn. younger than herself.

Works incl. stg 4tets; sos. for pf. with v.; canzonets, songs, voc. duets, &c.

Pipe and Tabor. A comb. of 2 insts. of a primitive kind, a small pipe of the recorder type, but held with one hand only while the other beats the T., a small drum without snares hung round the player's shoulder or strapped to his waist. The insts. are obs., but have been revived for folk-dancing.

Pipo or **Pippo** } Nicknames sometimes given, even in print, to Filippo Mattei.

Pique Dame. The name sometimes given in Eng. to Tchaikovsky's opera *The Queen of Spades* (*Pikovaya Dama*), with a Fr. pronunciation. It is the Ger. title, not the correct Fr. trans. There is no such term in Fr., the correct words being *dame de pique*.

Pirame et Thisbé (*Pyramus and Thisbe*), opera by Rebel and Francœur (lib. by Jean Louis Ignace de La Serre), prod. Paris, Opéra, 17. X. 1726.

Pirandello, Luigi (1867–1936), It. dramatist. *See* **Casella** (*Giara*), **Liuzzi** (*Scamandro*), **Malipiero** (*Favola del figlio cambiato*), **Mulè** (*Liolà*).

Pirata, Il (*The Pirate*), opera by Bellini (lib. by Felice Romani), prod. Milan, Teatro alla Scala, 27. X. 1827.

Pirates of Penzance, The, or The Slave of Duty, operetta by Sullivan (lib. by W. S. Gilbert), prod. Paignton, Bijou Theatre, 30. XII. 1879; pirated perf., N.Y., Fifth Avenue Theatre, 31. XII. 1879; 1st London perf., Opera Comique, 3. IV. 1880.

Piron, Alexis (1689–1773), Fr. poet & dramatist. *See* **Fernand Cortez** (Spontini), **Rameau** (m. for 5 plays).

Pirro, André (b. Saint-Dizier, 12. II. 1869; d. ? Paris, 1943), Fr. mcolst. Studied law and literature in Paris and at the same time picked up as much mus. educ. as he could, attending the org. classes of Franck and Widor. In 1896 he became prof. and a dir. of the newly opened Schola Cantorum. In 1904 he began to lecture at the École des Hautes Études Sociales and in 1912 succeeded Rolland as prof. of mus. hist. at the Sorbonne. His books incl. studies of Schütz, Buxtehude, Bach (general & org. works), the Fr. clavecinists, Descartes & m., old Ger. church & secular m., &c.

Pirro e Demetrio (*Pyrrhus and Demetrius*), opera by A. Scarlatti (lib. by

Adriano Morselli), prod. Naples, Teatro San Bartolommeo, prob. 28. I. 1694.

Pisador, Diego (b. Salamanca, 1508–9; d. ?, after 1557), Spa. lutenist. Son of a notary attached to the household of the Archbishop of Santiago. He took holy orders but did not enter the church. In 1552 he pub. a book of transcriptions of old Spa. songs, portions of masses by Josquin des Prés, motets by Morales & others, &c. for vihuela.

Pisari, Pasquale (b. Rome, 1725; d. Rome, 27. III. 1778), It. singer & comp. Although the son of a poor mason, he was able to learn m. thanks to the possession of a good voice, which later developed into a bass. From 1752 to his death he was a singer in the Papal Chapel in Rome. In 1775 he comp. a *Dixit Dominus* in 16 parts for the papal jubilee for perf. at the court of Port., which also ordered services for all the days in the year; but the payment, which he hoped would relieve his great poverty, did not arrive until after his death.

Works incl. masses, motets, Te Deums, Miserere, psalms & other church m.

Pisaroni, Benedetta (Rosamunda) (b. Piacenza, 6. II. 1793; d. Piacenza, 6. VIII. 1872), It. con. singer. Studied under Marchesi and others and made her 1st appearance at Bergamo in 1811, as a sop., but she changed to con. on Rossini's advice in 1813.

Pischek (or Pišek), Johann Baptist (b. Melnik, 14. X. 1814; d. Stuttgart, 16. II. 1873), Cz. bar. singer. Made his 1st stage appearance at the age of 21 and in 1844 was app. court singer to the King of Württemberg. Paid his 1st visit to Eng. in 1845.

Pisendel, Georg Johann (b. Cadolzburg, Bavaria, 26. XII. 1687; d. Dresden, 25. XI. 1755), Ger. vst. Studied the v. under Corelli while he was a choir-boy at the chapel of the Margrave of Ansbach and theory under Pistocchi. After studying at Leipzig Univ. he went to Dresden to enter the service of the king of Pol. there in 1712, travelled in Fr., Ger., It. and Aus. with the king, became concert master in 1730 on the death of Volumier and led the opera orch. under Hasse. Wrote concs. and pieces for the v.

Pisk, Paul A(madeus). (b. Vienna, 16. V. 1893), Aus. mcolst. & comp. Studied under Adler at Vienna Univ. and comp. with Schreker and Schoenberg. After cond. at var. Ger. theatres, he returned to Vienna, cond. and broadcasting, and became dir. of the m. dept. of the Volkshochschule, but left for U.S.A. in 1936 and became head of the m. dept. at Redlands Univ. He has ed. old m. and written on modern Ger. m.

Works incl. ballet *Der grosse Regenmacher*; cantata *Die neue Stadt*; Partita for orch., Suite for small orch. & other orch. works; stg. 4tet & other chamber m.; pf. m.; songs with org., &c.

Pistocchi, Francesco (Antonio Mamiliano) (b. Palermo, 1659; d. Bologna, 13. V. 1726), It. singer & comp. The family moved to Bologna in 1661, where he began to comp. at a very early age, entered San Petronio cath. as a choir-boy in 1670 and in 1675 began to appear in opera. In 1679 his 1st opera, for puppets, *Il Leandro* (*Gli amori fatali*), was prod. at Venice. In 1687–94 he was a singer at the ducal court of Parma, and he then became mus. dir. to the Margrave of Ansbach, returning to Bologna in 1701, founding a singing-school there.

Works incl. operas *Il girello, Narciso, Le pazzie d'amore, Le risa di Democrito* & *Il Leandro*, &c.; orats. *Il martirio di Sant' Adriano, Maria Vergine addolorata, La fuga di Santa Teresa*; church m.; voc. duets & trios; airs *Scherzi musicali* to It., Fr. & Ger. words, &c.

Piston (Fr.) = Valve. Also sometimes the colloquial name for the Cornet, abbr. from *cornet à pistons*.

Piston, Walter (b. Rockland, Me., 20. I. 1894), Amer. comp. Studied at the École Normale de Musique in Paris and at Harvard Univ., also with Nadia Boulanger & others. App. asst. prof. at Harvard in 1932 and prof. in 1938.

Works incl. ballet *The Incredible Flutist*; Sym., Suite, Conc., Symph. Piece, Prelude & Fugue for orch.; Concertino for pf. & chamber orch.; *Carnival Song* for male chor. & brass insts.; 2 stg. 4tets, pf. Trio, 3 pieces for fl., cl. & bn.; v. & pf. So., fl. & pf. So., Suite for ob. & pf., Partita for v., va. & org., &c.

Pistons. Another name for the Valves of brass insts.

Pitch. The exact height (or depth) of any mus. sound according to the number of vibrations that prod. it; also the standard by which notes, with the A above middle C as a starting-point, are to be tuned, a standard which determines at how many vibrations to the second that A is to be taken, as well as every other note in relation to it. P. varied at different times and in different countries. Early in the 19th cent. it was gradually raised, esp. by makers of wind insts., to secure more brilliant effect, but with results dangerous to singers, and in Eng. 2 Ps. were in use, the higher for orch. perf. and the lower Classical or Fr. P. for church and purely voc. m. The new Philharmonic P., with 439 vibrations per second at 68° Fahr. is now in general use, even by military bands, which until 1927 used the old Phil. P., which was slightly higher.

Pitoni, Giuseppe (Ottavio) (b. Rieti, 18. III. 1657; d. Rome, 1. II. 1743), It. comp. Studied with Pompeo Natale from early childhood and became a choir-boy at the churches of San Giovanni dei Fiorentini and SS. Apostoli in Rome, where Foggia taught him ctpt. After a 1st appt. he became chapel master at Assisi and held a similar post at the Collegio di San Marco in Rome from 1677 to his death, working also at var. other churches there, incl. the Lateran and St. Peter's.

Works incl. masses, *Dixit Dominus* (sung at St. Peter's during Holy Week), complete services for the whole year, Requiem, motets & other church m., some for 6 & 9 choirs, &c.

Pitt, Percy (b. London, 4. I. 1870; d. London, 23. XI. 1932), Eng. cond. & comp. Educ. in Fr. and studied m. there and at Leipzig with Reinecke and Jadassohn, and at Munich with Rheinberger. In 1896 he became orgst. at Queen's Hall in London and in 1902 adviser and cond. at Covent Garden Opera, later dir. of the Grand Opera Syndicate there, of the B.N.O.C. and in 1922 mus. dir. of the B.B.C.

Works incl. incid. m. to Stephen Phillips's *Paolo and Francesca*, Alfred Austin's *Flodden Field* & Shakespeare's *Richard II*; suites *Fêtes galantes* (after Verlaine), *Cinderella*, *Dance Rhythms* & others, ovt. to Shakespeare's *Taming of the Shrew*, symph. prelude *Le Sang des crépuscules*, Sinfonietta & other works for orch.; Ballade for v. & orch., Conc. for cl. & orch.; songs with orch., &c.

Pittore e Duca (*Painter and Duke*), opera by Balfe (lib. by Francesco Maria Piave), prod. Trieste, 21. XI. 1854.

Pittore parigino, Il (*The Parisian Painter*), opera by Cimarosa (lib. by Giuseppe Petrosellini), prod. Rome, Teatro Valle, 4. I. 1781.

Più (It. = more). Used for var. mus. directions in combinations such as *più allegro* (faster), *più lento* (slower), *più mosso* (more animated), *un poco più* (a little more [of whatever has been happening before]), &c.

Piuttosto (It.) = somewhat, rather. A word used with directions where the comp. wishes to make sure that an indication of tempo or expression is obeyed in moderation.

Piva (It.) = Bagpipe.

Pixérécourt, René Charles Guilbert de (1773–1844), Fr. dramatist & librst., biog. of Dalayrac, author of melodramas with m. *See* **Margherita d'Anjou** (Meyerbeer).

Pixis, Johann Peter (b. Mannheim, 1788; d. Baden-Baden, 22. XII. 1874), Ger. pfst. & comp. Studied with his father, Friedrich Wilhelm P. (*c.* 1760–*c.* 1810), and began to appear as pfst. with his brother Friedrich Wilhelm P. (1786–1842), a vst., settled at Munich in 1809 and in Paris in 1825, where he became a noted pf. teacher. In 1845 he bought a villa at Baden-Baden and continued to train pupils there. He adopted and trained the singer Franzilla Göhringer (1816–?).

Works incl. operas *Almazinde*, *Bibiana* & *Die Sprache des Herzens*; pf. concs.; sos. & pieces for pf., &c.

Pizz. (abbr.). *See* **Pizzicato**, for which this abbr. is very commonly used.

Pizzetti, Ildebrando (b. Parma, 20. IX. 1880), It. comp. Son of a pf. teacher. He entered the Parma Cons. in 1895 and wrote several orch., chor. and chamber works before he left in 1901, when he received a diploma for comp. In 1905 he returned to the Cons. to take a course in mus. hist., and in 1908 he was app. prof. of harmony and ctpt. at the Istituto Musicale at Florence, of which he became dir. in 1917. He removed to Milan in 1924 on his appt. as dir. of the Cons. Giuseppe Verdi there, and in 1933 he went to Rome to succeed Respighi as prof. of advanced comp. at the Accademia di Santa Cecilia.

Works incl. operas *Fedra*, *Debora e Jaele*, *Lo straniero*, *Fra Gherardo*, *Orseolo*, *L'oro* & some early unfinished; incid. m. for *La nave* and *La Pisanella* (both by d'Annunzio) Feo Belcari's *Sacra rappresentazione di Abraam ed Isacco*, Sophocles' *Trachiniae*, Corrado d'Errico's *Rappresentazione di Santa Uliva*, *Le Panateatiche*, Shakespeare's *As You Like It*; orch. works: dances for Tasso's *Aminta*, 3 symph. preludes for Sophocles' *Oedipus Rex* & *Coloneus*, *Ouverture per una farsa tragica*, *Concerto dell' estate*, *Rondo veneziano*; chor. & orch. works: *L'ultima caccia di Sant' Uberto*, introd. to Aeschylus's *Agamemnon* & *Epithalamium*; film m.; *Sinfonia del fuoco* for d'Annunzio's *Cabirio* and orch. & chor. m. for *Scipione l'Africano*; Conc. for co. & orch.; *Missa di Requiem* and *De profundis* for unaccomp. chor., also some smaller sacred and secular works; 2 stg. 4tets, pf. Trio; sos. for

v. & pf. and for co. & pf.; So., *Foglio d'album* and suite *Da un autunno già lontano* for pf.; 2 songs for bar. and pf. 4tet, 3 with stg. 4tet and 21 with pf., &c.

Pizzicato (It. = pinched). A direction indicating that the stgs. on insts. of the v. family are to be played, not with the bow, but by being plucked with a finger of the right hand, or occasionally with fingers of the left hand between bowed notes.

Pizzicato tremolando (It. = pinched and trembling). An effect 1st used by Elgar in the accomp. cadenza of his v. Conc., where the orch. stgs. play chords by thrumming the stgs. both ways across with the fingers of the right hand.

Plagal Cadence. A C. the bass of which does not progress in the most usual way from the Dominant to the Tonic, but from the Subdominant (5th below or 4th above) to the Tonic. The 'Amen' at the end of a hymn sung in the Angl. church is a familiar ex. of P. C. of the simplest kind.

Plagal Modes. *See* Modes.

Plaidy, Louis (b. Wermsdorf, Saxony, 28. XI. 1810; d. Grimma, Saxony, 3. III. 1874), Ger. pfst., vst. & teacher. Studied at Dresden, worked 1st as vst. but later turned to the pf., appeared with success and was app. by Mendelssohn as prof. at the Leipzig Cons. in 1843. Wrote technical studies for pf.

Plainchant or **Plainsong** The medieval church m., still surviving in the services of the Rom. Catholic church, sung in unison, without harmony and with no definitely measured rhythms. Its groupings of notes have, however, a strongly rhythmic character, but it resembles the free rhythm of prose, whereas that of measured m. is comparable to the rhythm of verse. The old notation on a stave of 4 lines, with square notes, is still used for P. The notes, although they have the appearance of representing different values, do not indicate the duration of the sounds, which is a matter of tradition and sense, the different strokes being merely matters of penmanship. Notes set above each other are not sung simultaneously, the m. being entirely monodic, but successively with the lower coming first.

Plainte. *See* Ornaments.

Planché, James Robinson (b. London, 27. II. 1796; d. London, 30. V. 1880), Eng. dramatist, libst. & critic of Fr. descent. Lived in London and wrote a number of libs. incl. *Maid Marian* for Bishop, *Oberon* for Weber and *The Surrender of Calais*, intended for Mendelssohn and later offered to H. Smart, who left it unfinished.

Plançon, Pol (Henri) (b. Fumay, Ardennes, 12. VI. 1854; d. Paris, 11. VIII. 1914), Fr. bass singer. Studied with Duprez and Sbriglia in Paris and made his 1st stage appearance at Lyons in 1877. He came out in Paris in 1880 and 1st visited London in 1891.

Planets, The, suite by Holst for orch. with org. and (in final section) fem. chor. 1. *Mars, the Bringer of War*; 2. *Venus, the Bringer of Peace*; 3. *Mercury, the Winged Messenger*; 4. *Jupiter, the Bringer of Jollity*; 5. *Saturn, the Bringer of Old Age*; 6. *Uranus, the Magician*; 7. *Neptune, the Mystic.* 1st perf. London, Queen's Hall, 1918. The idea of writing m. on the Ps. was not new: Buxtehude wrote a hpchd. suite on them; but H. dealt with them from the astrolog. aspect.

Planquette, (Jean) Robert (b. Paris, 31. VII. 1848; d. Paris, 28. I. 1903), Fr. comp. Studied briefly at the Paris Cons. and then began to make a success with songs perf. at café-concerts. From this he passed on to operettas, the 4th of which, *Les Cloches de Corneville*, made an immense hit in 1877.

Works incl. operettas *Valet de cœur, Le Serment de Mme. Grégoire, Paille d'avoine, Les Cloches de Corneville, Le Chevalier Gaston, Les Voltigeurs de la 32me* (*The Old Guard*), *La Cantinière, Rip van Winkle* (after Washington Irving), *Nell Gwynne, La Crémaillère, Surcouf* (*Paul Jones*), *Capitaine Thérèse, La Cocarde tricolore, Le Talisman, Panurge* (after Rabelais), *Mam'zelle Quat' Sous, Le Paradis de Mahomed*, &c.

Plantade, Charles Henri (b. Pontoise, 14. X. 1764; d. Paris, 18. XII. 1839), Fr. pfst., hpst., cst. & comp. Learnt singing and co. as one of the royal pages and later studied comp. with Langlé, pf. with Hüllmandel and hp. with Petrini. Having set up as a teacher of singing and hp., he began to write duets and they gained him access to the stage. He taught singing to Queen Hortense, became chapel master at court and prof. at the Cons., and held other posts and distinctions.

Works incl. operas *Palma, ou Le Voyage en Grèce, Zoé, ou La Pauvre Petite, Le Mari de circonstance* & many others; masses, Requiem, Te Deum, motets, &c.; romances & nocturnes for 2 voices, &c.

Planté, Francis (b. Orthez, Basses Pyrénées, 2. III. 1839; d. Mont-de-Marsan, 19. XII. 1934), Fr. pfst. Appeared as an infant prodigy, studied with Marmontel at the Paris Cons. and reappeared with brilliant success, taking part in Alard and Franchomme's chamber concerts. In 1863–72 he lived retired in the Pyrenees, having been offended by the inattention of the Parisian public, but he began playing again and continued until the war of 1914–8.

Platée (*Plataea*), comic ballet by Rameau (lib. by Jacques Autreau and Adrien Joseph Le Valois d'Orville), prod. Versailles, at court, 17. III. 1745, 1st Paris perf., Opéra, 4. II. 1749.

Platel, Nicolas Joseph (b. Versailles, 1777; d. Brussels, 25. VIII. 1835), Fr. cst. As the son of a royal chamber musn. he was educ. as a page at court, learning the co. from Duport. After some orch. appts. in Paris and Lyons, he toured in Belg. and Eng., settled at Antwerp and then at Brussels, where he became prof. at the Cons. in 1831. Comp. 5 co. concs.; duets for v. & co.; co. sos., &c.

Plato (*c.* 428–*c.* 348 B.C.), Gr. philos. He outlined a system of 'harmony,' as understood by the Grs., in *Timaeus* and discussed the nature of the modes, from their supposed moral aspect, in *The Republic*. *See also* **Socrate** (Satie).

Plautus, Titus Maccius (*c.* 252–184 B.C.), Rom. playwright. *See* **Emmanuel** (*Amphitryon*).

Player-Piano. *See* **Pianola.**

Playford Henry (b. London, 5. V. 1657; d. London, *c.* 1706), Eng. bookseller & m. pub. Succeeded to his father's business in 1684; estab. regular concerts, held 3 times a week at a London coffee-house from 1699, and another series at Oxford in 1701.

Playford, John (b. Norfolk, 1623; d. London, XI. 1686), Eng. bookseller & m. pub., father of prec. Estab. in London about 1648. His 1st mus. pub., *The English Dancing Master*, appeared in 1650, dated 1651.

Playford, John (b. Stanmore Magna, 1655; d. London, 1685), Eng. printer, nephew of prec. Was apprenticed to the printer William Godbid in London and in 1679 went into partnership with his widow, Anne G. He printed the mus. works issued by his cousin Henry.

Plectrum (Lat.). A hard spike of quill or metal with which the stgs. of certain insts. were made to sound. In the virginals, spinet and hpchd. the P. was attached to the jack, and when used for insts. of the lute type, such as the cittern (and still at present the mandoline) it projected from a metal ring placed on the thumb.

Plein jeu (Fr. = full play). The Fr. equivalent of *Organo pleno* (or *pieno*).

Pleno (Lat. = full). *See* **Pieno** & **Organo pleno.**

Pleyel, Camille (b. Strasburg, 18. XII. 1788; d. Montmorency nr. Paris, 4. V. 1855), Fr. pf. maker, m. pub. & pfst., husband of Marie Moke. He succeeded to his father's business in 1824 and assoc. himself with Kalkbrenner. Studied m. with his father and Dussek and pub. some pf. pieces.

Pleyel, Ignaz (Joseph) (b. Rupperstal, Lower Aus., 1. VI. 1757; d. Paris, 14. XI. 1831), Aus. pfst., vst., comp. & pf. maker, father of prec. Pupil of Vanhal and Haydn in Vienna, became chapel master to Count Erdödy in 1777, went to It., was at Strasburg cath. in 1783–91, when he visited London, invited to appear as rival to Haydn, with whom however he remained on friendly terms. Early in the 19th cent. he settled in Paris and in 1807 founded his pf. manufacture.

Works incl. opera *Ifigenia in Aulide*, puppet opera *Die Fee Urgele* (after Voltaire, from Chaucer); 29 syms.; many concs. and sinfonie concertanti; numerous stg. 5tets & 4tets, 4tets with fl., pf. trios, duets for vs.; v. & pf. sos.; pf. scs.; songs; Sco. songs arr. for George Thomson, &c.

Pleyel, Marie. *See* **Moke.**

Plica (Lat. = fold or plait). A special sign in old mus. notation the var. forms of which, unlike the square notes of Plainsong notation, indicated different note-values; but the P. also asked for a special kind of voc. ornament at the end of the note, the secret of which is now lost.

Plockflute (Eng., obs.). An old altern. name for the Recorder, a corruption of the Ger. *Blockflöte*.

Plugging. A popular term for the persistent use of a theme-song or other melodic feature in the course of a mus. comedy, operetta, film, &c.

Plunkett, Catherine (b. Dublin, 1725; d. ?), Ir. vst. Pupil of Dubourg in Dublin, where she made her 1st appearance in 1740.

Pneuma (from Gr. = 'breather'). Voc. ornaments in Plainsong inserting long cadential phrases on the syllables of certain words, notably 'Alleluia.' The P. were also called by the Lat. name of Jubili, and they developed later into Tropes and Sequences.

Pneums. The Eng. word sometimes used for the prec.

Pochette (Fr.). A small pocket v. used by dancing-masters in the 17th and 18th cents., similar to the Kit.

Pochettino (It.). The diminutive of *poco* ('a very little'), sometimes used as a direction.

Pochissimo (It.). The superlative of *poco* (' extremely little ').

Poco (It. =a little). A qualifying direction used where any indication of tempo or expression is to be applied in moderation.

Poe, Edgar Allan (1809–49), Amer. poet & novelist. *See* **Caplet** (2 works), **Chute de la Maison Usher** (Debussy), **Claflin** (*Fall of Usher*), **Diable dans le beffroi** (Debussy), **Gilbert (H. F.)** (*Island of Fay*), **Gnessin** (*Conqueror Worm*), **Hawley** (*Bells & Raven*), **Holbrooke** (*Red Mask, Bells, Raven, Ulalume, Masque of Red Death*), **Kelley** (*Sleeper*), **Lualdi** (*Diavolo nel campanile*), **Miaskovsky** (*Silence*), **Morawski** (*Nevermore & Ulalume*), **Rakhmaninov** (*Bells*), **Schmitt (F.)** (*Palais hanté*), **Séverac** (songs), **Shapleigh** (*Raven*), **Tcherepnin (N.)** (*Masque of the R.D.*), **Vactor** (do.).

Poet's Love (Schumann). *See* **Dichterliebe.**

Poglietti, Alessandro (b. ?; d. Vienna, VII. 1683), It. orgst. & comp. His early career is unknown; he became orgst. of the imp. chapel in Vienna, 1661, and was killed during the Turkish siege of the Aus. capital.

Works incl. sacred voc. comps. with inst. accomp.; modal ricercari, toccatas & other works for org.; hpchd. suites incl. *Rossignolo, Sopra la ribellione di Ungheria*, another containing a Capriccio on the cries of cocks and hens, &c.

Pohjola's Daughter, symph. poem by Sibelius, Op. 49, comp. 1906 and based on an incident in the *Kalevala*; 1st perf. St. Petersburg, Siloti concerts (cond. by comp.), 29. XII. 1906.

Pohl, Carl Ferdinand (b. Darmstadt, 6. IX. 1819; d. Vienna, 28. IV. 1887), Ger. orgst., bibliog. & writer on m. Studied with Sechter in Vienna, was orgst. at the Protestant church in the Gumpendorf suburb, 1849–55, lived in London, 1863–6, and in the latter year became librarian to the Phil. Soc. in Vienna. He wrote on this, on Haydn and Mozart in London, the standard biog. of Haydn (finished by Botstiber), &c.

Pohl, Richard (b. Leipzig, 12. IX. 1826; d. Baden-Baden, 17. XII. 1896), Ger. critic & author. Studied at Göttingen and Leipzig, and was for a time ed. of the *Neue Zeitschrift für Musik.* Wrote mainly on Wagner, also on Berlioz, Liszt, &c.

Pohl, Vladimir (b. Kiev, 17. I. 1880), Rus. comp. Studied at the Kiev and Moscow Conss., became one of the dirs. of the Rus. Mus. Soc. in Moscow, 1905–10, and in 1911 succeeded Rakhmaninov as dir. of the Empress Maria Mus. Inst. there. Later settled in Paris.

Works incl. ballet *Trois Ballets sur des thèmes de Beethoven*; incid. m. for plays, &c.

Pohlenz, Christian August (b. Sallgast, Lusatia, 3. VII. 1790; d. Leipzig, 10. III. 1843), Ger. orgst., teacher & cond. Studied at Leipzig, where he became orgst. at St. Thomas's church, cond. of the Gewandhaus concerts before Mendelssohn, &c.

Poi (It. =then). Used in directions where some mus. section is to follow another in a way not made immediately obvious by the notation: e.g. after a repeat of an earlier section, *poi la coda* or *e poi la coda.*

Point d'Orgue (Fr. =org.-point). The same as Pedal or Pedal-Point in comp.; also the Pause on a $\frac{6}{4}$ chord marking the traditional place for the insertion of a Cadenza; also the Pause or Fermata.

Pointing. The distribution of the syllables of the Psalms in Angl. chant, formerly (and still in churches where the old tradition prevails) according to rules by which the mus. accent often overrode the verbal stress; more recently more in accordance with the latter.

Poise, (Jean Alexandre) Ferdinand (b. Nîmes, 3. VI. 1828; d. Paris, 13. V. 1892), Fr. comp. Studied with Adam and others at the Paris Cons. and in 1853 prod. his 1st opera.

Works incl. operas *Bonsoir Voisin, Les Charmeurs, Polichinelle, Le Roi Don Pèdre, Le Jardinier galant, Les Absents, Corricolo, Les Trois Souhaits, La Surprise de l'amour* (after Marivaux), *L'Amour médecin* (after Molière), *Les Deux Billets, Joli Gilles, Carmosine* (after Musset); orat. *Cécile,* &c.

Poisoned Kiss, The, or The Empress and the Necromancer, opera by Vaughan Williams (lib. by Evelyn Sharp), prod. Cambridge Arts Theatre, 12. V. 1936. Much of the score is a satire on var. mus. styles.

Poissl, Johann Nepomuk, von, Freiherr (b. Haukenzell, Bavaria, 15. II. 1783; d. Munich, 17. VIII. 1865), Ger. comp. Studied with Danzi at Munich and became intendant of the royal orch. and dir. of the royal opera there.

Works incl. operas *Athalia* (after Racine), *Der Wettkampf zu Olympia* and *Nittetis* (transs. of Metastasio's *Olimpiade & Nitteti*), *Zayde* and c. 10 others; Mass, *Stabat Mater*, Psalm xcv; orat. *Der Erntetag,* &c.

Pokrass, Dimitri (b. Kiev, 1899), Rus. comp. The son of a poor cattle drover, he early played the pf. in cinemas to earn a living. In 1914 he was heard by the dir. of the St. Petersburg Cons., who took him there for study, and he lived on his earnings there playing in restaurants and cinemas. In 1917 he returned to Kiev and in 1919 joined the Red Army, for which he wrote many songs, incl. the *Budenny March.* He attracted the attention of Marshal Voroshilov, who advised him to go to Moscow, where he appeared as cond. and pfst. and wrote m. for var. occasions. In 1926–36 he was mus. dir. of the Moscow M. Hall and of the jazz-band in the railway workers' house of culture, and in 1941 he gained the Stalin prize for film m.

Works incl. m. for many films; popular chors., army and battle songs, m.-hall songs, &c.

Pol. (abbr). = Poland, Polish.

Polacca (It. = Polonaise). Although P. is the exact It. equivalent of the Polonaise, the word is often more loosely used for pieces in polonaise rhythm, but not necessarily in polonaise form, in which case they are actually, as indeed they are often designated, *alla polacca.*

Polaroli. Another form of the surname of Antonio & Carlo Francesco Pollarolo.

Poldini, Ede (b. Budapest, 13. VI. 1869), Hung. comp. Studied at Budapest and with Mandyczewski in Vienna.

Works incl. operas *The Vagabond and the Princess, Wedding in Carnival-Time* (*Love Adrift*), *Himfy*; ballet *Night's Magic*; *Marionettes* for orch. (orig. pf.); numerous pf. suites & pieces incl. *Arlequinades, Morceaux pittoresques, Épisodes à la Cour, Images, Moments musicaux, Poupée valsante,* &c.

Poldowski (Irene Regine Wieniawska, later Lady Dean Paul) (b. Brussels, before 1880; d. London, 28. I. 1932), Pol.-Eng. comp. Daughter of H. Wieniawski. After some private mus. tuition she studied at the Brussels Cons., where Gevaert was her comp. master. Later she went to London and continued studying under Percy Pitt, married Sir Aubrey Dean Paul, and after her marriage she studied in Paris, 1st under Gédalge and later, after the death of her 1st child, with d'Indy at the Schola Cantorum.

Works incl. operetta *Laughter*; *Nocturnes* & *Tenements* for orch.; *Pat Malone's Wake* for pf. & orch.; *Suite miniature de chansons à danser* for woodwind; v. & pf. So.; *Berceuse de l'enfant mourant* & *Tango* for v. & pf.; suite *Caledonian Market* for pf.; Fr. & Eng. songs to words by Verlaine, Samain, Blake, &c.

Polidori, John William (1795–1821), Eng. novelist, Byron's secretary & physician. *See* **Vampyr** (Lindpaintner & Marschner).

Polifemo, opera by Giovanni Bononcini (lib. by Attilio Ariosti), prod. Berlin, Lietzenburg Palace, summer 1702.

Poliphant. An obs. stg. inst., also called Polyphon, of the lute or cittern type but with anything from 25 to 40 stgs., invented *c.* 1600 by Daniel Farrant and played by Queen Elizabeth.

Polish Composers. *See* **Brzezinski, Chopin, Durand** (**Duranowski**), **Elsner, Felszynski, Fitelberg** (2), **Gorczynski, Joteyko, Kamienski, Karlowicz, Kassern, Kazuro, Koffler, Kolberg, Kondracki, Kurpinski, Labunski, Lipinski, Maciejewski, Maklakiewicz, Maliszewski, Marek, Melcer, Mlynarski, Moniuszko, Morawski, Niewiadomski, Noskowski, Nowowiejski, Paderewski, Palester, Pankiewicz, Perkowski, Poldowski, Poniatowski, Poradowski, Radziwill, Rathaus, Rogowski, Rózycki, Rytel, Scharwenka** (2), **Sikorski, Soltys, Statkozski, Stojowski, Surzynski, Szalowski, Szamotulski, Szeligowski, Szulc, Szymanowski, Tansman, Tausig, Wallek-Walewski, Wiechowicz, Wieniewski** (3), **Woytowicz, Zarebski, Zarzycki, Zelenski, Zielenski.**

'Polish' Symphony. Tchaikovsky's 3rd Sym., in D maj., Op. 29, finished VIII. 1875 and prod. Moscow, 19. XI. 1875. The finale is in polonaise rhythm.

Politian. *See* **Poliziano.**

Poliuto (later *Les Martyrs* & *I martiri*), opera by Donizetti (lib. devised by Adolphe Nourrit & written by Salvatore Cammarano, based on Corneille's tragedy *Polyeucte*), finished 1838 for prod. at Naples, but forbidden by censor; prod. in Fr. (trans. by Scribe), Paris, Opéra, 1. IV. 1840.

Poliziano (real name Angelo Ambrogini) (1454–94), It. poet. *See* **Favola d'Orfeo** (Casella), **Isaac** (Monody on Lorenzo de' Medici), **Malipiero** (3 songs), **Pastoral** (Bliss), **Vatielli** (*Favolo di Orfeo*).

Polka. A dance dating from *c.* 1830 and prob. originating in Boh., though the story of its being invented there by a servant-girl, the tune being written down by a musn. named Neruda, is not authenticated. It is danced in couples and the m. is in 2–4 time and divided into regular 2-bar patterns grouped into periods of 8 bars.

Pollarolo, Antonio (b. Venice, 1680; d. Venice, 4. V. 1746), It. comp. Pupil of his father, became asst. chapel master at St. Mark's in Venice, 1723, and chapel master in 1740.

Works incl. operas *Aristeo, Leucippo e Teonoe, Cosroe, I tre voti* & 10 others, &c.

Pollarolo, Carlo Francesco (b. Brescia, 1653; d. Venice, 1722), It. orgst. & comp., father of prec. Pupil of Legrenzi at Venice, became a singer at St. Mark's there in 1665, 2nd orgst. in 1690 and asst. chapel master in 1692. Later taught m. at the Cons. degli Incurabili.

Works incl. operas *Roderico, La forza della virtù, Ottone, Faramondo, Semiramide, Marsia deluso, Ariodante, Le pazzie degli amanti Gl' inganni felici, Santa Genuinda* (with Violone & A. Scarlatti) & *c.* 70 others; org. m., &c.

Polledro, Giovanni Battista (b. Piovà nr. Turin, 10. VI. 1781; d. Piovà, 15. VIII. 1853), It. vst., Pupil of Pugnani. Made his 1st appearance at Turin in 1797 and, after touring widely, was concert master at Dresden, 1814–24.

Pollini, Francesco (Giuseppe) (b. Ljubljana, 1763; d. Milan, 17. IX. 1846), It. pfst. & comp. Pupil of Mozart in Vienna and later of Zingarelli at Milan, where he was app. pf. prof. at the Cons. in 1809.

Works incl. *Stabat Mater*; m. for the stage; many pf. studies & pieces, &c.

Polly, ballad opera, sequel to *The Beggar's Opera* (words by John Gay), pub. 1729, but not allowed to be perf. Prod. London, with the m. arr. by Arnold, Little Haymarket Theatre, 19. VI. 1777. Modern version by F. Austin, prod. London, Kingsway Theatre, 30. XII. 1922.

Polo (or **Olé**). A Spa. dance with song, native to Andalusia but prob. of Moorish orig.

Polonaise. A Pol. dance of a stately, processional character, dating back to at least the 16th cent. The m. is in 3–4 march-time and is characterized by feminine cadences at the end of each section, also often by dotted rhythms. The more primitive exs. were in binary form: 2 sections, each repeated; but later (e.g. Chopin) a trio section developed, after which the main section is repeated.

Polonia, symph. prelude for orch. by Elgar, Op. 76, written for a concert given for the Pol. Relief Fund, London, 6. VII. 1915, and ded. to Paderewski, a quotation from whose *Polish Fantasy* it contains as well as one from Chopin and the Pol. Nat. Anthem.

Polovinkin, Leonid Alexeievitch (b. Kurgan, Siberia, 13. VIII. 1894), Rus. comp. Son of a railway engineer, who moved to Moscow in 1896 with his family. P. was educ. for law at the Univ. there, but in spite of many other cultural interests he wished to devote himself to m. and entered the Cons. in 1915. He taught there later, but devoted himself mainly to comp.

Works incl. operas *The Irish Hero* (after Synge's *Playboy of the Western World*), *The Fisherman and his Wife, The Mirror*; ballet *The Gypsy*; m. for children's plays; 6 syms., *Telescopes* (4 parts), ovt. *1st May* & *Dance-Riddle* for orch.; pf. Conc.; suite for woodwind 4tet, pf. Trio; inst. pieces; 5 sos., 5 suites *Magnets, Happenings* & others, 24 preludes & other pf. pieces, &c.

Polska. A Swe. folk dance whose m. is in a brisk 3–4 time and usually in min. keys.

Polyeucte. *See also* **Poliuto.**

Opera by Gounod (lib. by Jules Barbier & Michel Carré, based on Corneille's drama), prod. Paris, Opéra, 7. X. 1878.

Polyphon. *See* **Poliphant.**

Polyphony. The comb. of 2 or more melodies or melodic strands in such a way that they make mus. sense. Essentially the same as Counterpoint, but the latter term is used more specifically for the scientific way of writing P. and applying it to mus. comp.

Polytonality. A system of comp. of the 20th cent. the principle of which is that m. may be written in several keys at once.

Polytone. A keyboard inst. invented by the Amer. comp. Arthur Fickenscher and patented in Ger. in 1912, prod. 60 notes to the 8ve in 'pure' intonation.

Pomar, José (b. Mexico City, 18. VI. 1880), Mex. comp. He did not begin to study until he was 48, and then at once experimented in var. modern techniques.

Works incl. ballets *Ocho horas* & *Bestia parda* (*The Brown Beast,* a satire on Hitler); Mex. dance *Huapengo* for orch.; Prelude & Fugue for perc. insts., &c.

Pommer (Ger.) = Bombard.

Pomo d'oro, Il (*The Golden Apple*), opera by Cesti (lib. by Francesco Sbarra), prod. Vienna, Carnival 1667, for the wedding of the Emperor Leopold I and the Infanta Margherita of Spa. Probably the most elaborate operatic prod. ever staged. The subject is the judgment of Paris.

Pomone, opera by Cambert (lib. by Pierre Perrin), prod. Paris, Opéra, 3. III. 1671. An altered version by Grabu was prod. in London, at the Theatre in Whitehall, in Fr., VII. 1674.

Pomp and Circumstance. 5 military marches by Elgar, orig. intended as a set of 6, Op. 39. 1–4 comp. 1901–7, 5 in 1930. 1 contains, as a trio, the tune afterwards used in the *Coronation Ode* with the words 'Land of hope and glory.' The title of the set comes from *Othello*, III. iii: 'Pride, pomp and circumstance of glorious war.'

Pomposo (It. = pompous, stately). A direction occasionally used for m. of a sumptuous character.

Ponce, Manuel (b. Fresnillo, 8. XII. 1886), Mex. comp. Learnt m. from his sister at first, became cath. orgst. at Aguas Calientes and at 14 comp. a Gavotte which was later made famous by the dancer Argentina. At 15 he entered the Nat. Cons. at Mexico City and at 18 went to Eur. for further study with Bossi at Bologna and Martin Krause in Berlin. In 1908 he returned home and became prof. at the Nat. Cons. In 1915–8 he lived at Havana and at the age of 40 he went to Paris to take a comp. course with Dukas.

Works incl. symph. triptych *Chapultepec, Canto y danza de los antiguos Mexicanos, Poema elegiaco, Ferial* for orch.; pf. Conc., v. Conc., Conc. for guitar & chamber orch.; 3 Tagore songs with orch.; *Sonata en duo* for v. & va.; 2 Mex. Rhapsodies & many other pf. works, numerous songs, &c.

Ponchielli, Amilcare (b. Paderno Fasolaro nr. Cremona, 1. IX. 1834; d. Milan, 17. I. 1886), It. comp. Studied at the Milan Cons. and prod. his 1st opera, on Manzoni's *Promessi sposi*, at Cremona in 1856. In 1881 he was app. chapel master at Bergamo cath.

Works incl. operas *I promessi sposi, La Savoiarda* (*Lina*), *Roderico, Bertrand de Born, Il parlatore eterno, I Lituani* (*Aldona*), *Gioconda* (after Hugo's *Angelo*), *Il figliuol prodigo, Marion Delorme* (on Hugo's play), *I Mori di Valenza*; ballets *Le due gemelle* & *Clarina*; cantatas for the reception of the remains of Donizetti and Mayr at Bergamo & in memory of Garibaldi, &c.

Poniatowski, Józef Michal Xawery Franciszek Jan, Prince of Monte Rotondo (b. Rome, 20. II. 1816; d. Chislehurst, 3. VII. 1873), Pol. amateur comp. Studied at the Liceo at Florence and under Ceccherini. He appeared as ten. at the Teatro della Pergola there and prod. his 1st opera at Lucca in 1838, singing the title-part. After the 1848 Revol. he settled in Paris, but after the Franco-Prussian war he followed Napoleon III to Eng. 1871.

Works incl. operas *Giovanni da Procida, Don Desiderio, Ruy Blas* (after Hugo), *Bonifazio de' Geremei* (*I Lambertazzi*), *Malek Adel, Esmeralda* (after Hugo's *Notre-Dame de Paris*), *La sposa d'Abido* (after Byron's *Bride of Abydos*), *Pierre de Médicis, Gelmina* & others; Mass in F maj.; songs incl. *The Yeoman's Wedding Song*, &c.

Poniridy, Georges (b. Constantinople, 26. IX. 1892), Gr. comp. Studied with Gilson and others at Brussels and with d'Indy and Gastoué in Paris. Later settled in Athens and studied plainsong and Byzantine m.

Works incl. 3 Byzantine chants for female voices & orch., cantata *Kassiani*; *Symph. Triptych* for orch.; Prelude and Fugue for stgs.; poems for voice, fl., cl., stg. 4tet & pf.; v. & pf. So.; So., 3 Attic Suites, preludes & fugues, Prelude and Gigue, &c. for pf.; songs, &c.

Pons, José (b. Gerona, Catalonia, 1768; d. Valencia, 1818), Spa. comp. Studied at Córdoba, became chapel master at Gerona and later at Valencia.

Works incl. misereres & other church m.; villancicos for Christmas with orch. or org., &c.

Ponsard, François (1814–67), Fr. dramatist. *See* **Gounod** (*Ulysse*).

Ponsin, Marie. *See* **Roze.**

Pont-neuf (Fr. lit. new bridge). A satirical song of the 18th cent. similar to the Vaudeville, sung in public mainly on the P.-N. in Paris.

Ponte, Lorenzo da (real name Emmanuele Conegliano) (b. Ceneda, Venetia, 10. III. 1749; d. New York, 17. VIII. 1838), It. poet, adventurer and libst. Worked in Vienna, lived for a time in London and Hol. about the turn of the cent., and in 1805 escaped his London creditors by going to N.Y. Wrote the libs. of *Le nozze di Figaro, Don Giovanni* and *Così fan tutte* for Mozart, others for Bianchi, Martín y Soler, Winter, &c. *See also* **Burbero di buon cuore** (Martín y Soler), **Ratto di Proserpina** (Winter), **Scuola de' maritati** (Martín y Soler), **Una cosa rara** (do.).

Ponticello (It. = little bridge). The bridge of stg. insts. over which the stgs. are stretched to keep clear of the body of the inst. The direction *sul ponticello* (on the bridge) indicates that the bow is to be drawn close to the bridge, which results in a peculiar nasal tone.

Poole, Elizabeth (b. London, 5. IV. 1820; d. Langley, Bucks, 14. I. 1906), Eng. sop. singer & actress. Appeared as a child actress at the Olympic Theatre and made her 1st appearance in opera at Drury Lane in 1834.

Pope, Alexander (1688–1744), Eng. poet. *See* **Acis and Galatea** (Handel), **Busby** (*Prophecy* & odes), **Greene (M.)** (*Ode on St. Cecilia's Day*),

Jackson (W. i) (*Dying Christian*), (?) **Semele** (Handel).

Popov, Gavriel Nikolaievitch (b. Novotcherkask, 12. IX. 1904), Rus. comp. Studied at the School of M. at Rostov-on-Don and from 1922 at the St. Petersburg Cons., where Steinberg and Shtcherbatchev were his comp. masters.

Works incl. operas *The Slow Horseman* (after Pushkin) & *Alexander Nevsky*; film m.; *Heroic Intermezzo* for solo voice, chor. & orch., based on the 2nd opera; Sym., 2 suites for orch.; v. Conc.; 7tet for fl., cl., bn., tpt., v., va. & db.; Suite & pieces for pf., &c.

Popper, David (b. Prague, 9. XII. 1843; d. Baden nr. Vienna, 7. VIII. 1913), Ger.-Cz. cst. & comp. Studied m. in general at the Prague Cons. and the co. under Goltermann at Frankfort o/M., and made his 1st concert tour in Ger. in 1863. In 1867 he became 1st cst. at the Court Opera in Vienna, in 1872 he married Sophie Menter, but the marriage was dissolved in 1886, and in 1896 he became co. prof. at the Budapest Cons.

Works incl. *Requiem* for 3 cos., numerous pieces for co., &c.

Poradowski, Stefan Boleslaw (b. Wloclawek, 16. VIII. 1902), Pol. comp. Studied at the Cons. and Univ. of Poznan and in 1930 became prof. at the former and m. critic.

Works incl. cantatas *Triumph*, *The Song of Spring*, *The Horse of the Swiatowid*; 5 syms., Sinfonietta on folk themes, *Lyrical Ovt.* & other orch. works; *Antique Suite* for stgs.; db. Conc., *Concerto antico* for va. d'amore & stg. orch.; stg. 4tet & *Metamorphoses* for stg. 4tet, 3 stg. trios, duets for 2 vs.; Prelude & Pol. Dance for pf.; songs, partsongs, &c.

Poro, rè dell' Indie (*Porus, King of the Indies*), opera by Handel (lib. by ?, altered from Metastasio's *Alessandro nell' Indie*), prod. London, King's Theatre, Haymarket, 2. II. 1731.

Porpora, Niccola (Antonio) (b. Naples, 19. VIII. 1686; d. Naples, II. 1766), It. comp., theorist and singing-teacher. Studied under Mancini and others at the Cons. di Santa Maria di Loreto at Naples, became chapel master to the Port. ambassador there and began to prod. operas soon after his 20th year. About 1720 he became a master at the Cons. di Sant' Onofrio. In 1724 Hasse became his pupil, but incurred his lasting enmity by deserting him for A. Scarlatti. Soon afterwards he began a wandering life, working by turns at Venice, Vienna (where Haydn was his pupil), Dresden and London, rivalling Hasse in the Saxon capital and Handel in the Eng. one. In 1760 he at last settled at Naples again as chapel master at the cath. and prof. at the Onofrio Cons.

Works incl. operas *Basilio*, *Berenice*, *Flavio Anicio Olibrio*, *Faramondo*, *Eumene*, *Amare per regnare*, *Semiramide*, *Semiramide riconosciuta*, *L'Imeneo*, *Adelaide*, *Siface*, *Mitridate*, *Annibale*, *Il trionfo di Camilla*, *Arianna e Teseo*, *Temistocle*, *Filandro* & *c.* 20 others; orats. *La martiria di Santa Eugenia* & 5 others; masses, motets, duets on the Passion & other church m.; cantatas; v. sos.; fugues for clavichord, &c.

Porporino. *See* **Uberti.**

Porrino, Ennio (b. Cagliari, Sardinia, 20. I. 1910), It. comp. Studied in Rome with Respighi and others and won a competition at the Accademia di Santa Cecilia.

Works incl. 2 chor. comps., symph. poem *Sardegna*, ovt. *Tartarin de Tarascon* (after Daudet), &c.

Porsile, Giuseppe (b. Naples, *c.* 1672; d. Vienna, 29. V. 1750), It. comp. Was successively assistant chapel master at Naples, chapel master to Charles II at Barcelona until 1711, then singing-master to the Empress Amalia in Vienna, and in 1720–40 comp. to the Aus. court there.

Works incl. opera *Meride e Selinunte*, *Spartaco* & some others; 12 orats.; 13 occasional stage pieces; cantatas, canzonets, partitas for stgs., &c.

Port. (abbr.) = Portugal, Portuguese.

Port. A Sco. term for an inst. comp., esp. for the hp.

Port de voix
Port de voix double } (Fr. *see* **Ornaments**). The term P. de v. is also used for Portamento in singing, i.e. passing from 1 note to the next with a very slight effect of scooping.

Porta, Costanza (b. Cremona, *c.* 1530; d. Padua, 26. V. 1601), It. monk & comp. Pupil of Willaert at Venice. He took orders and became choirmaster at Osimo nr. Ancona, 1552–64, when he went to Padua to take up a similar post at the Cappella Antoniana, the church of the Minorite order to which he belonged, which he left for a time to work at Ravenna and Loreto by turns.

Works incl. masses, motets, psalms, hymns, introits & other church m.; madrigals, &c.

Porta, Ercole (b. Bologna, ?; d. Capri, 30. IV. 1630), It. orgst. & comp. Orgst. at the coll. of San Giovanni in Persiceto in 1609.

Works incl. sacred voc. concs.; inst. 'syms.'; So. for v., cornett & 2 trombs.; secular songs, &c.

Porta, Francesco della (b. Monza, *c.* 1590; d. Milan, I. 1666), It. orgst. & comp. Studied with the orgst. Ripalta at Monza and became orgst. and chapel master of 2 or 3 churches at Milan.

Works incl. motets, psalms; inst. ricercari; villanelle for 1–3 voices with insts., &c.

Porta, Giovanni (b. Venice, *c.* 1690; d. Munich, 21. VI. 1755), It. comp. Was in the service of Cardinal Ottoboni in Rome, lived in London in 1720–36 and in 1737 became mus. dir. to the court at Munich.

Works incl. operas *Numitore, Farnace* & 30 others; masses & other church m., &c.

Portamento (It.). The ornament called P. is synonymous with Appoggiatura. In another sense the word means the carrying on from 1 note to another with a very slight effect of scooping, esp. in singing and stg. playing.

Portative Organ. *See* **Positive Organ** & **Regal.**

Porter, Anna Maria (1780–1832), Eng. novelist & playwright. *See* **Busby** (*Fair Fugitives*).

Porter, Quincy C. (b. New Haven, Conn., 7. II. 1897), Amer. comp. Studied at Yale Univ. & School of M. with H. Parker and D. S. Smith, later with Bloch and with d'Indy in Paris. He taught at the Cleveland Inst. of M. for 2 periods in 1922–32, at Vassar Coll., Poughkeepsie, in 1932–8 and at the New Eng. Cons. at Boston from 1938. He also has played va. in var. stg. 4tets.

Works incl. incid. m. for Shakespeare's *Antony and Cleopatra* and T. S. Eliot's *Sweeney Agonistes*; Sym., *Poem and Dance* for orch.; *Ukrainian Suite* for stgs.; *Dance in Three Time* for chamber orch., *3 Gr. Mimes* for voices, stg. 4tet & perc.; 7 stg. 4tets; 2 v. & pf. sos., Suite for va. solo, &c.

Porter, Walter (b. ?, *c.* 1595; d. London, XI. 1659), Eng. comp. He became a Gentleman of the Chapel Royal in London in 1617 and (?) some time later went to It. to become a pupil of Monteverdi. In 1639 he became choirmaster at Westminster Abbey and when the chor. service was suppressed in 1644 came under the patronage of Sir Edward Spencer.

Works incl. motets for 2 voices and insts., psalms (George Sandys's paraphrases) for 2 voices & org.; madrigals and airs for voices & insts., &c.

Portman, Richard (b. ?; d. ? London, 1655), Eng. orgst. & comp. Pupil of O. Gibbons, succeeded Thomas Day as orgst. of Westminster Abbey in London, 1633. Like W. Porter, who was choirmaster, he lost this post in 1644 and became a m. teacher.

Works incl. services, anthems; *Dialogue of the Prodigal Son* for 2 voices and chor., meditations *The Soules Life*; hpchd. m., &c.

Portogallo. *See* below.

Portugal, Marcos Antonio da Fonseca (called Portogallo in It.) (b. Lisbon, 24. III. 1762; d. Rio de Janeiro, 7. II. 1830), Port. comp. Educ. at the Patriarchal Seminary at Lisbon, where later he became cantor and orgst., and he learnt m. from João de Sousa Carvalho. He was also a theatre cond. and in 1787 prod. his 1st stage work. In 1792 he went to Naples and began to comp. It. operas in great numbers. In 1800 he returned to Lisbon to become dir. of the San Carlos Theatre, where he continued to prod. It. operas. In 1807 the Fr. invasion drove the court to Brazil, and he followed it in 1810, but was unable to return with it in 1821, being incapacitated by a stroke.

Works incl. *Licença pastoril, A Castanheira* and 20 other Port. operas; *La confusione nata della somiglianza, Demofoonte, Lo spazzacamino principe, La donna di genio volubile, Fernando nel Messico, Alceste, La morte di Semiramide, Non irritare le donne, L'oro non compra amore, Il trionfo di Clelia, Il diavolo a quattro, La pazza giornata* (on Beaumarchais's *La Folle Journée* [*Figaro*]) & c. 25 other It. operas; church m.; cantata *La speranza*; songs, &c.

Portuguese Composers. *See* **Arneiro, Arroyo, Bomtempo, Branco** (2), **Cardoso, Carvalho, Coelho, Cruz, Escobar, Freitas, Kastner, Keil, Lima** (2), **Lobo, Lusitano, Machado, Magalhães, Portugal, Rebello, Seixas, Silva Leite, Vianna da Motta.**

Posaune (Ger.) = Trombone. Also an 8-ft. & 16-ft. org. stop powerfully reprod. tromb. tone.

Positions. In the playing of stg. insts. the left hand moves to var. Ps. to reach the higher notes. Thus on the v. only the open note G, with A, B, C (with their accidentals) and D above it can be played in the 1st P. on the G stg.; 5 similar notes then follow in the same P. on the D stg., and 5 each on the E and A stgs., finishing with B above the stave on the E stg. Beyond that the Ps. have to be shifted to incl. the higher reaches. The term is also used for the var. degrees of extension of the tromb. tubes by means of the slide, each P. yielding a different fundamental note and harmonics above it.

Positive Organ (*see also* **Regal**). In its early sense the term denoted a small chamber org. and later it was also used for the part of the org. controlled by the manual called 'choir org.' By frequent confusion with the portative or portable org., however, it has now become too indeterminate to be useful.

Postans, Mary. *See* **Shaw.**

Posthorn. A primitive brass inst. akin to the bugle rather than the hn., used by postilions in the 18th and early 19th cent. It had no valves and could therefore prod. only the natural harmonics, which were coarse and penetrating in tone. It was hardly ever used in serious m., but Bach imitated it in his Capriccio on his brother's departure for hpchd. and Mozart scored parts for 2 in his Ger. Dances, K. 605.

Postillon de Longjumeau, Le, opera by Adam (lib. by Adolphe de Leuven & Léon Lévy Brunswick), prod. Paris, Opéra-Comique, 13. X. 1836.

Postlude or **Postludium** } The opposite of Prelude or Praeludium: a final piece, esp. an org. piece played after service in Ger. churches, where it is called *Nachspiel*, perf. while the congregation is leaving.

Pot-Pourri (Fr. lit. rotten pot). A medley of preserves, identical with the Spa. *olla podrida*, the name of which is applied to selections of themes from var. mus. works, esp. operas or operettas, dished up for pf. or other insts., for military band or orch. as a light and easy entertainment and to awaken memories of works previously heard in their entirety. Unlike fantasies on such themes P.-Ps. are very loosely strung together and have no artistic value apart from the material they use, which indeed they often considerably depreciate.

Potter, (Philip) Cipriani (Hambly) (b. London, 2. X. 1792; d. London, 28. IX. 1871), Eng. pfst. & comp. Studied under Attwood, Callcott and Crotch, and had finishing pf. lessons from Woelfl in 1805–10. He became an assoc. of the Phil. Soc. on its foundation in 1813 and a member when he reached majority, and in 1816 wrote an ovt. for it, also playing the pf. there that year in a 6tet of his own. In 1817 he went to Vienna, studied with Aloys Förster and made friends with Beethoven. After visiting Ger. and It. he returned to London in 1821, became prof. of pf. at the R.A.M. the next year and principal in succession to Crotch in 1832, but resigned in 1859. In 1855 Wagner cond. one of his syms. with the Phil. Soc.

Works incl. cantata *Medora e Corrado*, Ode to Harmony; 9 syms., 4 ovts. for orch.; 3 pf. concs., Concertante for co. & orch.; 3 pf. trios, 6tet for pf. & stgs.; hn. & pf. So., Duo for v. & pf.; 2 sos., *The Enigma* ('Vars. in the style of 5 eminent artists'), studies, rondos, toccatas, &c. for pf.; Sym. & other works for pf. duet; Fantasy & Fugue for 2 pfs., &c.

Poueigh, (Marie Octave Géraud) Jean (b. Toulouse, 24. II. 1876), Fr. critic & comp. Studied at the Toulouse Cons. and at that of Paris with Caussade and Lenepveu, later with Fauré, and also had advice from d'Indy. He became m. critic to *L'Ère nouvelle* and pub. a book on *Musiciens français d'aujourd'hui* under the name of Octave Séré.

Works incl. operas *Le Meneur de louves* & *Perkain*; ballets *Fünn* & *Frivolant*; *La Ronde du Blé-d'Amour* for chor. & orch.; *Marche triomphante* for orch.; v. & pf. So.; *Pointes sèches* for pf.; songs; arrs. of Languedocian & Gascon folksongs, &c.

Pougin, (François Auguste) Arthur (Eugène Paroisse-) (b. Châteauroux, 6. VIII. 1834; d. Paris, 8. VIII. 1921), Fr. mcolst. He had little general educ., but studied v. with Alard and theory with Réber at the Paris Cons. After working at var. theatres as vst. and cond., he began to write biog. articles on 18th-cent. Fr. musns. and gradually made his way by writing for var. mus. papers, contrib. to dictionaries and writing mus. criticism for several newspapers. He wrote biogs. of Verdi, Campra, Meyerbeer, V. Wallace, Bellini, Rossini, Auber, Adam, Méhul, &c. and studies of Fr. mus. hist., the v., Rus. m., &c.

Poule, La (*The Hen*), the nickname of a Sym. by Haydn, No. 83, in G min., (No. 2 of the 'Paris' syms.), comp. in 1786.

Poulenc, Francis (b. Paris, 7. I. 1899), Fr. comp. Received a classical educ., but was able to take pf. lessons from Ricardo Viñes and to pick up technical knowledge in var. ways. When he was called up for war service in 1918 he had already written 1 or 2 works under the influence of Satie, and on being demobilized he joined the group of 'Les Six' with Auric, Durey, Honegger, Milhaud and Tailleferre, and thus came for a time under the influence of Jean Cocteau. His success was from that time sufficient to enable him to devote all his time to comp.

Works incl. comic operas *Le Gendarme incompris* & *Les Mamelles de Tirésias*; ballets *Les Biches* (*The House-Party*) & *Les Animaux modèles* (after La Fontaine); Mass in G min.

and cantata for double chor. *Figure humaine* (Paul Éluard), cantata *Le Bal masqué* (Max Jacob); *2 Marches et un Intermède* for orch.; *Concert champêtre* for hpchd. & orch., *Marches militaires* for pf. & orch., Conc. in D min. for 2 pfs. & orch.; *Aubade* for pf. & 18 insts.; *Rapsodie nègre* for fl., cl. & stg. 4tet, Trio for ob., bn. & pf.; sos. for 2 cls., for cl. & bn. and for hn., tpt. & tromb.; v. & pf. and co. & pf. sos.; song cycles with chamber insts. *Le Bestiaire* (G. Apollinaire) & *Cocardes* (Cocteau); *Mouvements perpétuels, Suite, Impromptus, Feuillets d'album, Nocturnes, Suite française, Villageoises,* &c. for pf.; So. for pf. duet; *5 Poèmes de Ronsard,* 8 Pol. Songs, *Banalités* (Apollinaire), *Chansons villageoises* (Éluard), *Fiançailles pour rire* & other songs, &c.

Pound, Ezra (b. 1885), Amer. poet, *See* **Diamond** (*Night Litany*).

Poupée de Nuremberg, La (*The Nuremberg Doll*), opera by Adam (lib. by Adolphe de Leuven & Léon Lévy Brunswick), prod. Paris, Théâtre Lyrique, 21. II. 1852.

Poupée, La (*The Doll*), operetta by Audran (lib. by Maurice Ordonneau), prod. Paris, Théâtre de la Gaîté, 21. X. 1896.

Poupelinière, Alexandre de la. *See* **La Poupelinière.**

Poussé (Fr. = pushed). The upstroke of the bow in the playing of stg. insts., the opposite of *tiré* (= drawn).

Powell, John (b. Richmond, Virginia, 6. IX. 1882), Amer. pfst. & comp. Studied at Virginia Univ. and with Leschetizky and Navrátil in Vienna. Made his 1st appearance in Berlin in 1907 and toured in Eur. and U.S.A.

Works incl. *The Babe of Bethlehem* for chor. & orch.; Sym. in A maj., *Natchez on the Hill, A Set of Three,* &c. for orch.; Conc. & *Rapsodie nègre* for pf. & orch., v. Conc.; stg. 4tet; 3 v. & pf. sos.; pf. So. and pieces; songs, &c.

Powell, Maud (b. Peru, Ill., 22. VIII. 1868; d. Uniontown, Pa., 8. I. 1920), Amer. vst. Studied with Schradieck at Leipzig and Dancla in Paris and made her 1st appearance in Eng. in 1883.

Power, Lionel (b. ?; d. ?), Eng. 15th-cent. comp. & theorist. He wrote 1 or 2 treatises on the gamut, singing of descant, faburden, &c. and comp. masses, motets & other church m.

Praeger, Ferdinand (Christian Wilhelm) (b. Leipzig, 22. I. 1815; d. London, 2. IX. 1891), Ger. pfst. & comp. Studied under his father and settled in London in 1834; wrote a book *Wagner as I knew him* in 1885 and comp. a symph. prelude to Byron's *Manfred,* an ovt. *Abellino,* a pf. Trio, pf. pieces, &c.

Praeludium. *See* **Prelude.**

Praetorius (real name Schulz, Schulze, Schultz or Schultze), Ger. 16th–17th-cent. musns. not of the same family, except 3 & 5:

1. Godescalcus P. (b. Salzwedel, 28. III. 1524; d. ? Wittenberg, 8. VII. 1573), scholar. Prof. of philos. at Wittenberg Univ. Pub. in 1557 a vol. *Melodiae scholasticae* in which he was assisted by M. Agricola.

2. Bartholomaeus P. (b. ?; d. ?), comp. Pub. pavans and galliards in 5 parts in 1616.

3. Hieronymus P. (b. Hamburg, 10. VIII. 1560; d. Hamburg, 27. I. 1629), orgst. & comp. Pupil of his father, Jacob P. (or Schultz), orgst. at St. James's church, Hamburg, whom he succeeded in 1582. He wrote in the Venetian antiphonal chor. style.

Works incl. masses, motets, magnificats, *Cantiones sacrae,* hymn-tunes; Lat. & Ger. songs in 5–20 parts, &c.

4. Michael P. (b. Kreuzburg, Thuringia, 15. II. 1571; d. Wolfenbüttel, 15. II. 1621), orgst., comp. & author. He was mus. dir. at Lüneburg until 1604, when he was app. orgst. to the Duke of Brunswick, who later made him his mus. dir. He wrote the voluminous treatise on m. & insts. entitled *Syntagma musicum* and comp. a number of vols. of Lat. & Ger. sacred and secular songs for several voices, one entitled *Musae Sionae* and others named after separate Muses, &c.

5. Jacob P. (b. Hamburg, 8. II. 1586; d. ? Hamburg, 21. X. 1655), orgst. & comp., son of 3. Pupil of Sweelinck at Amsterdam; app. orgst. of St. Peter's church, Hamburg, in 1603. Wrote motets, &c.

'Prague' Symphony. Mozart's Sym. in D maj. (without a minuet), K. 504, comp. in Vienna, XII. 1786 and prod. in Prague, 19. I. 1787, during a visit for the perf. there of *Le nozze di Figaro,* which led to the commission of a new opera esp. for the Boh. capital, which was to be *Don Giovanni.*

Pralltriller (Ger.) = Mordent.

Pratella, Francesco (Balilla) (b. Lugo, Romagna, 1. II. 1880), It. comp. Studied at the Liceo Musicale of Pesaro, where Mascagni was among his masters. He settled at Milan, where in 1910 he began to make propaganda for futurist m., on which he lectured and wrote in the more progressive periodicals.

Works incl. operas *Il regno lontano, Lilia, La Sina d'Vargöun, L'aviatore Dro, Il dono primaverile, Fabiano;* children's opera *La ninna nanna della bambola*; incid. m. to plays; symph. poems on Carducci's ode *La chiesa di Polenta,* 5 symph. poems *Romagna, Inno alla vita* (musica futuristica), 3 dances *La guerra,* &c. for orch.; pf. Trio; v., org. & pf. pieces; songs, &c.

Prati, Alessio (b. Ferrara, 19. VII. 1750; d. Ferrara, 17. I. 1788), It. comp. Studied at the Cons. di Loreto at Naples, went to Paris in 1779, to St. Petersburg in 1781 and to Vienna in 1783, returning to Ferrara the next year.

Works incl. operas *L'École de la jeunesse, Ifigenia in Aulide* & 5 others; church m.; sos. for v., hpchd. & hp.; duet for 2 sops.; voc. arias and rondos, &c.

Pré aux clercs, Le (*The Scholars' Meadow*), opera by Hérold (lib. by François Antoine Eugène de Planard), prod. Paris, Opéra-Comique, 15. XII. 1832.

Préambule (Fr. } = preamble).
Preambulum (Lat. }
Other names for Prelude.

Prec. (abbr.) = preceding.

Precentor. A dignitary in an Angl. cath., orig. the leading singer in the choir, but also in charge of the voc. church m. and superior to the orgst. His seat is opposite that of the dean (who takes the Decani side) on the Cantoris side of the chancel.

Preciosa, play with m. by Weber (lib. by Pius Alexander Wolff, based on Cervantes's story *La Gitanella*), prod. Berlin, Opera House, 15. III. 1821.

Precipitando (It. = precipitately). A direction indicating that an *accelerando* is to be made to increase in pace very rapidly.

Predieri, Luc' Antonio (b. Bologna, 13. IX. 1688; d. Bologna, 1767), It. comp. Chapel master of the cath. at Bologna; went to the court chapel in Vienna, 1739, and became chief chapel master there in 1746; but returned to It. in 1751.

Works incl. operas *Il sogno di Scipione* & others, serenades and festival plays for the stage; orats., &c.

Preindl, Joseph (b. Marbach o/Danube, 30. I. 1756; d. Vienna, 26. X. 1823), Aus. orgst., comp. & teacher. Studied with Albrechtsberger in Vienna, became orgst. of St. Peter's church there and in 1809 chapel master of St. Stephen's cath. He wrote treatises on singing and on comp.

Works incl. 5 masses, Requiem, lamentations & other church m.; settings of hymns with inst. elaborations; org. & pf. m., &c.

Prelude (from Lat. *praeludium*). An introd. piece played for ex., before a church service or a mus. perf., or forming the 1st mvt. of a suite or other sectional work; also one paired with a fugue, to which it forms an introd.; from the 19th cent. onward sometimes a separate concert work, esp. for pf. (Chopin, &c.) or orch.; and from Wagner onwards the orch. introd. to an opera where it does not take the form of a detached ovt. and leads straight into the 1st act.

Prélude à l'Après-midi d'un faune (*Prelude to 'The Afternoon of a Faun'*). An orch. piece by Debussy intended as a mus. introd. to Stéphane Mallarmé's poem of that name, comp. in 1892–4 and 1st perf. in the latter year by the Société Nationale in Paris.

Ballet on this work (chgph. by Vaslav Nizhinsky), prod. Paris, Théâtre du Châtelet, 29. V. 1912.

Préludes, 2 sets of pf. pieces, 12 in each, by Debussy, comp. in 1910–3. Their contents are: I. 1. *Danseuses de Delphes*; 2. *Voiles* (*Sails,* not *Veils*); 3. *Le Vent dans la plaine*; 4. *Les Sons et les parfums tournent dans l'air du soir* (*Sounds and scents whirl in the evening air*: a quotation from Baudelaire); 5. *Les Collines d'Anacapri*; 6. *Des Pas sur la neige* (*Footprints in the snow*); 7. *Ce qu'a vu le vent d'Ouest* (*What the West Wind saw*); 8. *La Fille aux cheveux de lin* (*The Flaxen-haired Girl*: based on a Sco. song by Leconte de Lisle); 9. *La Sérénade interrompue*; 10. *La Cathédrale engloutie* (*The Submerged Cathedral*: on the old Breton tale of the sunken city of Ys); 11. *La Danse de Puck* (on Shakespeare's *Midsummer Night's Dream*); 12. *Minstrels* (m.-hall artists, not troubadours). II. 1. *Brouillards* (*Mists*); 2. *Feuilles mortes* (*Dead Leaves*); 3. *La Puerta del Vino* (a gate at Granada); 4. *Les Fées sont d'exquises danseuses* (*The Fairies are exquisite Dancers*); 5. *Bruyères* (*Heather*); 6. *General Lavine —eccentric* (a m.-hall character); 7. *La Terrasse des audiences du clair de lune* (*The Terrace of the Moonlight Audiences*: a phrase that occurs in Pierre Loti's *L'Inde sans les Anglais*; the piece contains a quotation of the folksong 'Au clair de la lune'); 8. *Ondine*; 9. *Hommage à S. Pickwick, Esq., P.P.M.P.C.* (after Dickens; the piece quotes 'God save the King' in the bass); 10. *Canope* (a Canopic jar holding the ashes of a dead lover); 11. *Les Tierces alternées* (*Alternating Thirds*); 12. *Feux d'artifice* (*Fireworks*; quoting a few notes of the *Marseillaise* at the end).

Préludes, Les, symph. poem by Liszt, based on the title of a poem by

Lamartine, comp. 1848, revised early 1850s, 1st perf. Weimar, 28. II. 1854.

Preparation. A term used in harmony for a chord that anticipates a discord by the introd. of a note foreign to the P. The discord following is then called Percussion and its passing into the next concord Resolution.

Prepare. *See* **Ornaments.**

Prepared Shake. *See* **Ornaments.**

Prés, Josquin des. *See* **Josquin.**

Presa (It. = the taking). A sign used for Canons not written in score, but in one continuous melodic line showing the places where the later voices are to enter. Riddle Canons are distinguished by the absence of any such signs, the leads for each voice having to be discovered.

Presle, Jacques de la. *See* **La Presle.**

Prestissimo (It.) = extremely fast.

Presto (It. = quick, fast). The direction most commonly used to indicate the fastest speeds in m. P. is quicker than *allegro*.

Preston, Thomas (b. ?; d. ?), Eng. 15th–16th-cent. orgst. & comp. Nothing of his life is known, but he left a MS. book of 91 motets arr. for a keyboard inst., written by him and Redford, many of the originals being prob. their own work. Comp. motet *O Lux* & other church m.

Prévost (d'Exiles), Antoine François (1697–1763), Fr. novelist. For works based on *Manon Lescaut see* **Kleinmichel** (*Schloss de l'Orme*), **Manon** (opera, Massenet), **Manon Lescaut** (ballet, Halévy; operas, Auber & Puccini).

Prévost, Eugène (Prosper) (b. Paris, 23. VIII. 1809; d. New Orleans, 30. VIII. 1872), Fr. comp. and singing-teacher. Studied at the Paris Cons. with Lesueur and others and gained the Prix de Rome in 1831. After prod. some works in Paris, he became cond. at the theatre of Le Havre for a time, but left for New Orleans in 1838, where he cond. at the Fr. theatre and taught singing. On the outbreak of the Amer. Civil War he returned to Paris, but went again to New Orleans in 1867.

Works incl.. operas *L'Hôtel des Princes, Le Grenadier de Wagram, Cosimo, Le Bon Garçon, Esmeralda* (after Hugo's *Notre-Dame de Paris*), *L'Illustre Gaspard*; Mass with orch.; cantata *Bianca Capello*, &c.

Prick-Song. About the time of Shakespeare ' pricking ' meant writing m. A P.-S. was therefore primarily a song written down as distinct from one extemporized or sung from memory. More specif. the term referred to vars. or descants sung upon a ground, usually a familiar tune or plainsong that could be sung from memory, whereas the vars. or descant had to be written down.

Priestley, J(ohn). B(oynton). (b. 1894), Eng. novelist & dramatist. *See* **Britten** (*Johnson over Jordan*).

Prigione d'Édimburg, La (*Edinburgh Gaol*), opera by F. Ricci (lib. by Gaetano Rossi, based on Scribe & Planard's *Prison d'Édimbourg* and farther back on Scott's *Heart of Midlothian*), prod. Trieste, 13. III. 1838.

Prima donna (It. = 1st lady). The singer of the leading sop. part in a partic. opera or the leading sop. in an opera co.

Prima vista (It. = 1st sight). A term used for sight-reading.

Prima volta (It. = 1st time). A direction sometimes given where a repeated portion of a comp. takes a new turn after the repetition. The join leading to the repeat is then called *P. v.*, while the different one taking the m. on to its continuation is marked *Seconda volta*.

Primavera, Giovanni Leonardo (b. Barletta, Naples, ?; d. ?), It. comp. Chapel master to the Spa. governor of Milan in 1573. Palestrina used his madrigal ' Nasce la gioia mia ' as a *cantus firmus* for a mass, called by that name.

Works incl. madrigals, *Canzoni napoletàne* for 3 voices, villotte for 3 voices, &c.

Primo (It. = first). P. is often written over the top part in pf. duets, the bottom one being *Secondo*; the word also appears in orch. scores where the comp. wishes to make sure that a passage is played by only the 1st of a pair or groups of similar insts. It may also take the place of *Prima volta*, as explained above, to indicate the treatment of repeats, and there the terms are often abbr. 1° and 2°.

Primo uomo (It. = 1st man). The singer of the leading male sop. part in a partic. opera or the leading male sop. in an opera co. in the 18th cent.

Prince Ferelon, or The Princess's Suitors, opera by Gatty (lib. by comp.), prod. London, Old Vic. Theatre, 21. V. 1921.

Prince Igor (*Kniaz Igor*), opera by Borodin (lib. by comp. based on a sketch by Stassov), comp. between 1871 & 1887 and left unfinished at B.'s death in the latter year. Completed and scored by Rimsky-Korsakov and Glazunov. Prod. St. Petersburg, 4. XI. 1890.

Princess Ida, or Castle Adamant, operetta by Sullivan (lib. by W. S. Gilbert, a parody of Tennyson's *Princess*), prod. London, Savoy Theatre, 5. I. 1884.

Princesse jaune, La (*The Yellow*

Princess), opera by Saint-Saëns (lib. by Louis Gallet), prod. Paris, Opéra-Comique, 12. VI. 1872.

Principal. An open Diapason org. stop transposing an 8ve higher, 4 ft. in the manuals and 8 ft. in the pedals. Also, in old m., the lowest tpt. part, written for a large inst. of which high and florid notes were not demanded. In modern terminology a P. is the leading player of any group of orch. insts., except 1st vs., which are headed by the Leader.

Prior, Matthew (1664–1721), Eng. poet. *See* **Arne (T. A.)** (*Henry and Emma*), **Travers** (canzonets).

Prioris, Johannes (b. ?; d. ?), 15th–16th-cent. orgst. & comp. Orgst. at St. Peter's in Rome in 1490 and chapel master to Louis XII of Fr. in 1507. Wrote masses, motets, magnificats, &c.

Prise de Troie, La (Berlioz). *See* **Troyens.**

Prison d'Édimbourg, La (*Edinburgh Gaol*), opera by Carafa (lib. by Scribe & François Antoine Eugène de Planard, based on Scott's *Heart of Midlothian*), prod. Paris, Opéra-Comique, 20. VII. 1833.

Prisoner in the Caucasus, The (*Kavkasky Plennik*), opera by Cui (lib. by Victor Alexandrovitch Kruilov, based on Pushkin's poem), prod. St. Petersburg, 16. II. 1883.

Priuli, Giovanni (b. ?; d. ? Vienna, 1629), It. comp. Chapel master to the Archduke Ferdinand of Aus. at Graz early in the 17th cent.; remained in his service when he became the Emperor Ferdinand II.

Works incl. motets, psalms & other church m.; madrigals, *Musiche concertate*, *Delicie musicali* for several voices, &c.

Prix de Rome (Fr. Prize of Rome; officially Grand Prix de Rome). A prize instituted in 1803 and offered annually in Paris by the Académie des Beaux-Arts, a branch of the Institut de France, to var. artists, that for m. going to the successful competitor at the Cons. The holder is entitled to 3 years' study at the Fr. Acad. housed in the Villa Medici in Rome. The work required was formerly a dramatic cantata, but is now a 1-act opera. Belg. has a similar prize, but without obligatory residence in Rome.

Procopé, Hjalmar (b. 1868), Fin. dramatist. *See* **Sibelius** (*Belshazzar's Feast*).

Prod. (abbr.) = Produced, Production.

Prodaná Nevěstá (Smetana). *See* **Bartered Bride.**

Prod'homme, J(acques). G(abriel). (b. Paris, 28. XI. 1871), Fr. mcolst. Studied in Ger. and lived at Munich in 1897–1900, where he founded a periodical in Fr. and Ger. After his return to Paris he founded the Fr. section of the S.I.M., became its secretary and performed var. other mus. administrative functions, succeeding Bouvet in 1931 as librarian and archivist at the Opéra, and Expert in 1934 as Cons. librarian. He has written several works both on Beethoven and on Berlioz, also on Mozart, Schubert, Wagner, &c.

Programme Music. Any kind of inst. m., esp. orch., based on a literary, pictorial, histor., biog., autobiog., descriptive or other extra-mus. subject and not intended to appeal only as m. pure and simple.

Progression. The mvt. from 1 chord into the next, either harmonically with all the notes moving simultaneously or polyphonically with each one being part of a continuously moving horizontal melodic line.

Prohaska, Carl (b. Mödling nr. Vienna, 25. IV. 1869; d. Vienna, 28. III. 1927), Aus. comp. Studied pf. with d'Albert and comp. with Mandyczewski and Herzogenberg, being also befriended by Brahms. He taught at the Strasburg Cons. in 1894–5 and cond. the Warsaw Phil. Orch. in 1901–5. In 1908 he became prof. at the Cons. of the Vienna Phil. Soc.

Works incl. opera *Madeleine Guimard*; orat. *Frühlingsfeier*, motet *Aus dem Buch Hiob*, *Lebensmesse*, *Der Feind*, *Infanterie* & other chor. works; Vars. on a theme from Rousseau's *Devin du village*, symph. prelude to Anzengruber's *Das vierte Gebot*, Symph. Fantasy, Serenade, Passacaglia and Fugue for orch.; stg. 4tet, stg. 5tet, pf. Trio; So. and *Allegro con spirito* for v. & pf.; songs, duets, &c.

Prokofiev, Sergey Sergeyevitch (b. Sontsovka, Ekaterinoslav, 23. IV. 1891), Rus. comp. Began to comp. almost before he could write and tried his hand at an opera at the age of 9. He was sent to Glière for lessons, wrote 12 pf. pieces in 1902 as well as a Sym. for pf. duet, and at 12 he set Pushkin's play *A Feast in Time of Plague* as an opera. At the St. Petersburg Cons., which he left in 1914, he studied pf. with Anna Essipova, comp. with Rimsky-Korsakov and Liadov, and cond. with N. Tcherepnin. By that time he had written many works, incl. the 1st pf. Conc., and he then set to work on the *Scythian Suite* for orch. During the war of 1914–8 he lived in London for a time and at its close he went to the U.S..A. by way of Japan. The opera *The Love for Three Oranges* was prod.

at Chicago in 1921, and the next year he went to live in Paris and became connected with Diaghilev's Rus. Ballet, which prod. several of his works. In 1934 he settled in Moscow and was induced by the Soviet gvt. to simplify and popularize his style, a tendency which is very noticeable in such works as *Peter and the Wolf* and the quantities of film m. he wrote there.

Works incl. operas *Magdalene, The Gambler* (after Dostoievsky), *The Love for Three Oranges* (after Gozzi), *The Flaming Angel, War and Peace* (after Tolstoy), *Betrothed in a Monastery* (after Sheridan's *Duenna*), *The Unknown Boy*; ballets *The Buffoon, La Pas d'acier, L'Enfant prodigue, Sur le Borysthène, Romeo and Juliet* (after Shakespeare), *Cinderella*; orch. works incl. *Symphonie classique* and 4 other syms., *Sinfonietta, Scythian Suite, Symphonic Song*, Rus. Ovt. *Toast to Stalin*: incid. m. for *Egyptian Nights* (after Shakespeare & Shaw), *Boris Godunov* & *Eugene Onegin* (both Pushkin); film m. for *Lieutenant Kizhe, The Queen of Spades* (after Pushkin), *Ivan the Terrible*, &c.; 5 pf. concs., 2 v. concs., co. Conc.; stg. 4tet, 5tet for wind & pf., So. for 2 vs., *Ovt. on Hebrew Themes* for cl., stg. 4tet & pf.; So. in D maj. for v. & pf., Ballade for co. & pf.; 8 pf. sos., *c.* 25 other op. nos. of pf. pieces, incl. 3 studies, Toccata, *Sarcasms, Visions fugitives, Contes de la vieille grand'-mère* & 2 sonatinas; 8 sets of songs (1 without words, 1 to words by Pushkin); *Seven, they are Seven*, for ten., chor. & orch. & some other chor. works; Cantata for the 29th anniversary of the Oct. Revol. (words by Stalin, Lenin & Marx) for orch., military band, accordion band, percussion & double chor., &c.

Prolation. The division of the Semibreve into Minims in old notation, where according to the time-signature a semibreve could be equal to 2 minims (min. P.) or to 3 (maj. P.).

Promenade Concerts. A special type of popular orch. concert, cultivated espec. at the London Queen's Hall from 1895 until its destruction in 1941, under the dir. of Sir Henry Wood, and continued at the Albert Hall. The programmes gradually improved until they contained all the best orch. m. and modern novelties, and a special feature is that the floor of the hall is left bare for people to stand, not to walk about, for which they have neither room nor inclination. P. C. were not new to London in 1895: they were started by Musard at Drury Lane in 1840 and by Jullien at Covent Garden about the same time.

Promessi sposi, I (*The Betrothed*). *See also* **Bryllupet ved Como-Søen.**

Opera by Petrella (lib. by Antonio Ghislanzoni, based on Manzoni's novel), prod. Lecco, 2. X. 1869; 1st perf. Milan, X. 1872. The prod. at Lecco was given there because it is the scene of Manzoni's book.

Opera by Ponchielli (lib. by ?, based on Manzoni's novel), prod. Cremona, 30. VIII. 1856.

Prométhée (*Prometheus*), open-air spectacle by Fauré (lib. by Jean Lorrain & André Ferdinand Hérold, based on Aeschylus), prod. Béziers, Arènes, 27. VIII. 1900; 1st Paris perf., Hippodrome, 5. XII. 1907.

Prometheus (Beethoven). *See* **Geschöpfe des Prometheus.**

Symph. poem by Liszt, comp. 1850 as an ovt. to the chors. from Herder's *Prometheus*, perf. Weimar, 28. VIII. 1850; revised 1855 and 1st perf. Brunswick, 18. X. 1855.

Prometheus, the Poem of Fire, symph. work for pf. & orch. by Skriabin, prod. Moscow, 15. III. 1911. The score contains a part for an inst. projecting coloured lights, called *Tastiera per luce*, which was however never perfected.

Prometheus Unbound, setting of Shelley's poem for solo voices, chor. & orch. by Parry, prod. Gloucester Festival, 1880.

Prometheus Variations (Beethoven). *See* **'Eroica' Variations.**

Proms. (abbr.). The popular name by which the Promenade Concerts in London are affectionately called by the mus. public.

Prophète, Le, opera by Meyerbeer (lib. by Scribe), prod. Paris, Opéra, 16. IV. 1849.

Prophetess, The, or The History of Dioclesian, m. by Purcell for the play adapted from Beaumont and Fletcher by Thomas Betterton, prod. London, Dorset Gardens Theatre, IV. or V. 1690. Pepusch wrote new m. for its revival, London, Lincoln's Inn Fields Theatre, 28. XI. 1724.

Proportio (Lat.). *See* **Saltarello.**

Proportion. The math. relationship between the numbers of vibrations of different notes, which are exactly in tune with each other when the ratios between these vibrations are math. correct, e.g. a perfect 5th stands in the relation of 2 : 3 in the number of vibrations of its 2 notes. But the term P. was also used in old m. to designate the rhythmic relationships between different note-values, e.g. where according to the time-signature a semibreve was equal to 2 minims or to 3, &c.

Proporz (Ger.). *See* **Saltarello.**

Proposta (It. = proposal, suggestion). Another term for the 1st statement of a fugue subject, which is rather like a question calling for an answer. The 2nd statement of the subject is, in fact, called the Answer or, in contradistinction to the P., the *Risposta*. The Lat. terms *Dux* and *Comes* also correspond to the P. and R., or subject and answer.

Proscritto, Il (*The Outlaw*), opera by Nicolai (lib., orig. written for Verdi, by Gaetano Rossi), prod. Milan, Teatro alla Scala, 13. III. 1841.

Prose. Another name, chiefly Fr., for the Sequence in the medieval sense of the term meaning an ornamental interpolation into the m. of the mass. After the 9th cent. words began to be added to the sequences, and this is the reason for their being called Ps.

Prose de l'âne, La. A Fr. 12th-cent. ex. of the above, taking the form of a processional with m., repres. the Flight into Egypt and held annually at Beauvais on 1. I.

Proserpine, opera by Lully (lib. by Quinault), prod. Saint-Germain, 3. II. 1680, 1st Paris perf., 15. XI. 1680.

Opera by Paisiello (lib. by Quinault, revised by Nicolas François Guillard), prod. Paris, Opéra, 29. III. 1803. P.'s only Fr. opera.

Proske, Karl (b. Gröbnig, Silesia, 11. II. 1794; d. Ratisbon, 20. XII. 1861), Ger. priest & mus. ed. Studied medicine and practised for a time, but was ordained priest in 1826 and became attached in a mus. capacity to Ratisbon cath. There and in It. he made his great collection of church m. entitled *Musica Divina*.

Prout, Ebenezer (b. Oundle, 1. III. 1835; d. London, 5. XII. 1909), Eng. theorist & comp. Studied pf. & org. and began to make a career as orgst., pf. teacher, mus. ed. and critic. In 1876 he became prof. at the Nat. Training-School for M. in London and 3 years later at the R.A.M. He wrote a number of books on harmony, ctpt., form, orchn., &c. and comp. cantatas, syms., org. concs., chamber m., &c.

Provenzale, Francesco (b. Naples, ? 1627; d. Naples, IX. 1704), It. comp. Studied (?) at Naples and in 1663–74 taught at the Cons. Santa Maria di Loreto there, and in 1673–1701 at that of the Turchini. He was also chapel master at the church of San Gennaro and in the royal chapel.

Works incl. operas *Lo schiavo di sua moglie, Difendere l'offensore* & 6 others; church m.; 9 cantatas, &c.

Prudent, Émile (Racine Gauthier) (b. Angoulême, 3. II. 1817; d. Paris, 14. V. 1863), Fr. pfst. & comp. Having no parents, he was adopted by a pf. tuner, entered the Paris Cons. at the age of 10 and afterwards had a hard struggle to make a living, but eventually made his way successfully.

Works incl. conc.-sym. *Les Trois Rêves* and Conc. in B♭ maj. for pf. & orch.; pf. Trio; *Étude de genre* and many pieces, fantasies and transcriptions for pf., &c.

Prunières, Henry (b. Paris, 24. V. 1886; d. Paris, 1942), Fr. mcolst. & ed. Studied with Rolland at the Sorbonne, founded the *Revue musicale* in 1920 and was app. ed. of the complete ed. of Lully's works. He wrote books on that master, on Monteverdi, Cavalli, Fr. & It. opera and ballet, &c., also a hist. of m. (unfinished).

Prus. (abbr.) = Prussia, Prussian.

'Prussian' Quartets, a set of stg. 4tets by Mozart, so called (not by himself) because they are ded. to the King of Prus., Frederick William II. The plan to write 6 4tets for the king, who was a good amateur cst., was conceived during M.'s visit to Berlin in the spring of 1789, and the 1st work, in D maj., K. 575, was finished in Vienna the following VI. The 2nd and 3rd, in B♭ maj. and F maj., K. 589–90, followed in V and VI. 1790; the remaining 3 were never written. The co. parts are unusually elaborate and evidently intended to please the king.

Psalms. The Ps. form part of the offices of the Rom. Catholic church and of the Angl. morning and evening services; in the former they are chanted in Plainsong, in the latter to Chants. Ps. have also been set by comps. as concert works, more or less elaborately, most often for solo voices, chor. and orch.

Psaltery. An obs. inst. of the Dulcimer type, triangular in shape and with stgs. stretched across its frame hp.-wise, which were played with the bare fingers or with a plectrum. It became extinct during the 17th cent.

Pskovitianka (*The Maid of Pskov*, also known as *Ivan the Terrible*), opera by Rimsky-Korsakov (lib. by comp. based on a play by Lev Alexandrovitch Mey), prod. St. Petersburg, 13. I. 1873. Revived with a new prologue-opera, *Boyarina Vera Sheloga*, Moscow, 27. CXII. 1898.

Psyche, opera by Locke (lib. by Shadwell), prod. London, Dorset Gardens Theatre, 27. II. 1675.

Psyché, opera by Lully (lib. by Thomas Corneille & Bernard de Fontenelle), prod. Paris, Opéra 19. IV. 1678.

Suite by Franck for orch. with chor. interpolations, comp. 1887–8.

Pub. (abbr.) = Published, publisher.

Puccini. It. family of musns. & opera comps.:
1. Giacomo P. (1712–81).
2. Antonio P. (1747–1832), son of prec.
3. Domenico P. (1771–1815), son of prec.
4. Michele P. (1813–64), son of prec.

Puccini, Giacomo (Antonio Domenico Michele Secondo Maria) (b. Lucca, 22. XII. 1858; d. Brussels, 29. IX. 1924), It. comp., son of prec. He came of a mus. family and his father was church orgst. at Lucca. Although the father d. early, P. was given a mus. educ. and at the age of 19 was orgst. and choirmaster at the church of San Martino and had written a motet. Being poor, he once walked to Pisa to hear Verdi's *Aida* and was fired with a desire to write for the stage. In 1880 his mother managed with the aid of a less poverty-stricken relative and a grant from the queen to send him to the Milan Cons., where he studied comp. 1st under Bazzini and later under Ponchielli. He wrote a *Capriccio sinfonico* for orch., but Ponchielli urged him to take part in a competition for a 1-act opera advertised by the m. pub. Sonzogno, and he wrote *Le Villi*; but the prize was won by Mascagni's *Cavalleria rusticana.* It was, however, prod. at Milan in 1884 and drew Ricordi's attention to P., whom he commissioned to write a 2nd opera. This was *Edgar*, prod. in 1889. It failed, but P. had his 1st great success with *Manon Lescaut* at Turin in 1893. The same city brought out *La Bohème* in 1896. His successes now made him immensely wealthy and he bought an estate at Torre del Lago near Lucca, where he lived with Elvira Bonturi, who had left her husband for him, but whom he was unable to marry until much later, when she became a widow. In the last years of his life he suffered from cancer of the throat and he d. after an operation undergone at Brussels.

Works incl. operas *Le Villi, Edgar, Manon Lescaut, La Bohème, Tosca, Madama Butterfly, La fanciulla del West, La rondine, Trittico: Il tabarro, Suor Angelica* & *Gianni Schicchi, Turandot* (unfinished, completed by Alfano); *Scherzo sinfonico* for orch. (later used in *La Bohème*); cantata *Juno*; 2 minuets for stgs.; a Mass and a motet; *Inno a Roma* for chor., &c.

Pugnani, Gaetano (b. Turin, 27. XI. 1731; d. Turin, 15. VII. 1798), It. vst. & comp. Pupil of Somis, became 1st v. to the Sardinian court in 1752 and began to tour in 1754, visiting Paris and London for some considerable time, but finally settling at Turin again as cond., orch. leader and teacher.

Works incl. operas *Nanetta e Lubino, Issea, Tamas, Kouli-Kan, Aurora, Adone, Achille in Sciro, Demofoonte, Demetrio a Rodi* & others; ballets; orat. *La Betulia liberata*; Sym. on Goethe's *Werther*; v. concs.; chamber m.; v. sos., &c.

Pugno, (Stéphane) Raoul (b. Paris, 23. VI. 1852; d. Moscow, 3. I. 1914), Fr. pfst. & comp. Studied at the Paris Cons. where after some orgst.'s & choirmaster's posts he became prof. of harmony and pf. in 1892 & 1896. He 1st appeared in London in 1894.

Works incl. operas *Ninetta, La Sosie, Le Valet de cœur, Le Retour d'Ulysse, La Vocation de Marius, La Petite Poucette,* &c.; ballets *Les Papillons, Viviane, Le Chevalier aux fleurs* (with Messager); fairy-plays, pantomimes & mimo-drama; incid. m. for d'Annunzio's *Città morte* (with Nadia Boulanger); orat. *La Résurrection de Lazare*; So. and *Les Nuits* for pf.; songs, &c.

Puits d'amour, Le (*The Well of Love*), opera by Balfe (lib. by Scribe & Adolphe de Leuven), prod. Paris, Opéra-Comique, 20. IV. 1843. B.'s 1st Fr. opera.

Pujol, Joan (b. Barcelona, 1573; d. Barcelona, 1626), Spa. priest & comp. He was chapel master at Tarragona, 1593–95, Saragossa cath., 1595–1612, and Barcelona, 1612–26.

Works incl. masses and other church m.; secular songs, &c.

Pulcinella, ballet by Stravinsky with m. adapted from Pergolesi (chgph. by Leonid Fedorovitch Massin), prod. Paris, Opéra, 15. V. 1920. The settings were designed by Picasso.

Puns. Punning in m. is rare and can be done only by allusions to m. which in some way suggests words or ideas outside strictly mus. concepts, as for ex. Fauré's beginning the melody of the song *Lydia* in the Lydian mode or Stanford's accomp. the words ' O, cursèd parry ' in *The Critic* (Sheridan) with the opening of Parry's *Blest Pair of Sirens.* Occasionally the sound of some particular inst. can be used punningly: the use of the horns at the end of the aria ' Aprite un po' quegl' occhi ' in Mozart's *Figaro*, in which Figaro declares that all women deceive their menfolk, may or may not be a pun on the traditional symbol for the betrayed male.

Punto. *See* **Stich.**

Puppo, Giuseppe (b. Lucca, 12. VI. 1749; d. Florence, 19. IV. 1827), It. vst. Studied at the Naples Cons. and made a great success as a youth;

visited Paris in 1775, then Spa., Port. & Eng. Wrote v. concs., studies, duets, &c.

Purcell, Daniel (b. ? London, *c.* 1660; d. London, XI. 1717), Eng. orgst. & comp. Studied (?) under his father Thomas P. and was orgst. at Magdalen Coll., Oxford, 1688–95, when he came to London and added m. to his dead brother Henry's *Indian Queen* and *Pausanias*. After a busy career as comp. of m. for plays, he became orgst. of St. Andrew's church, Holborn, in 1713. For the opening of the Queen's Theatre in 1705 he began an opera on Ariosto's *Orlando furioso*, but it was (?) not perf.

Works incl. masque *Orpheus and Eurydice*; opera *Brutus of Alba*; incid. m. for Cibber's *Love's Last Shift* & *Love makes a Man*, Durfey's *Cynthia and Endymion*, Lacy's *Sawny the Scot* (based on Shakespeare's *Taming of the Shrew*), Steele's *Funeral* and *Tender Husband*, Farquhar's *The Beaux's Stratagem*, *The Inconstant* & (with Leveridge) *The Constant Couple*, Vanbrugh's *The Relapse* & (with Finger) *The Pilgrim*, an adapt. of Shakespeare's *Macbeth*, and many others; odes for St. Cecilia's Day; m. for Congreve's *Judgment of Paris* (3rd prize in competition with Eccles, Finger and Weldon); sos. for v. or fl. & bass; cantatas for 1 voice, &c.

Purcell, Henry (b. ? London, VI.–20. XI. 1659; d. London, 21. XI. 1695), Eng. comp., brother of prec. Son of Thomas P., musn. attached to the court after the Restor. of 1660; nephew of Henry P. previously said to be his father. He showed genius in early childhood and became a choir-boy at the Chapel Royal (?) in 1669 under Cooke, from 1672 under Humfrey. Left in 1673 and became asst. to the keeper of the king's insts. and the following year, on Humfrey's death, pupil of Blow; tuned the org. and copied parts for Westminster Abbey; app. Composer in Ordinary for the Violins, IX. 1677. Songs of his were pub. since the age of 16, (?) one when he was 8. In 1679 Blow resigned the orgst.'s post at the Abbey in his favour; the next year he wrote stg. fantasies in the old polyph. style and his 1st theatre m., for Lee's *Theodosius*. Married in (?) 1681 and became a very successful church and theatre comp.; also, in 1683, pub. his 1st inst. sos. Made a speciality of welcome-songs for royalty and odes for official occasions. Coronation anthem for James II, 1685, and played at that of William and Mary, 1689. Prod. the opera *Dido and Aeneas* at a girls' school at Chelsea, (?) 1689, and collab. with Dryden in *King Arthur*, prod. 1690. Anthem for the funeral service of Queen Mary comp. 1695, the year of his own death, said to have been caused by a cold caught while locked out of his house at night.

Works incl. operas and quasi-operas: *Dido and Aeneas*, *The Fairy Queen* (adapt. from Shakespeare's *Midsummer Night's Dream*), *King Arthur*, *The Prophetess*, *The Tempest* (adapt. from Shakespeare); incid. m. and songs for plays: Bancroft, *Henry II*, Beaumont & Fletcher, *Bonduca*, *The Double Marriage*, Behn, *Abdelazer*, Congreve, *The Double Dealer*, *The Old Bachelor*, Crowne, *The Married Beau*, *Regulus*, Chas. Davenant, *Circe*, Dryden, *Amphitryon*, *Aureng-Zebe*, *Cleomenes*, *Love Triumphant*, *The Spanish Friar*, *Tyrannic Love*, Dryden & Howard, The *Indian Queen*, Dryden & Lee, *Oedipus*, Durfey, *Don Quixote*, *A Fool's Preferment* (adapt. from Fletcher), *The Marriage-Hater Matched*, *The Richmond Heiress*, *Sir Barnaby Whigg*, *The Virtuous Wife*, Fletcher, *Rule a Wife and Have a Wife*, Gould, *The Rival Sisters*, Lee, *The Massacre of Paris*, *Sophonisba*, *Theodosius*, Molière (adapt. Wright), *The Female Vertuosos* (*Les Femmes savantes*), Norton, *Pausanias*, Ravenscroft, *The Canterbury Guests*, Thomas Scott, *The Mock Marriage*, Settle, *Distressed Innocence*, Shadwell, *Epsom Wells*, *The Libertine*, Shakespeare (adapt. Tate) *King Richard II*, (adapt. Shadwell) *Timon of Athens*, Southerne, *The Fatal Marriage*, *The Maid's Last Prayer*, *Oroonoko* (adapt. from Behn), *Sir Anthony Love*, *The Wives' Excuse*, ?, *The Gordian Knot Untied*; 15 odes for voices & orch.; 9 welcome-songs for voices & orch.; *Yorkshire Feast Song* for voices & orch.; 9 secular cantatas; 66 anthems; 3 services; 26 hymns, psalms, chants and sacred canons; 22 sacred songs; 53 catches; 4 3-part songs; 42 voc. duets; over 100 songs (not counting *c.* 150 in the plays); 13 fantasies & 4 other works for stgs.; 22 sos. for 2 vs. & bass & some other misc. chamber works; 8 suites (lessons) & *c.* 30 other pieces for hpchd.; 3 or 4 voluntaries for org., &c.

Puritani di Scozia, I (*The Puritans of Scotland*), opera by Bellini (lib. by Carlo Pepoli, based on a play by Jacques Ancelot & Xavier Boniface Saintine, *Têtes rondes et Cavaliers*, and farther back on Scott's *Old Mortality*), prod. Paris, Théâtre Italien, 25. I. 1835.

Puschmann, Adam Zacharias (b. Görlitz, 1532; d. Breslau, 4. IV. 1600),

Ger. mastersinger. Pupil of Hans Sachs at Nuremberg. He pub. in 1574 a treatise on master-singing, containing songs of his own as well as by Sachs, Behaim and others.

Pushkin, Alexander (1799–1837), Rus. poet, dramatist & novelist. *See* **Aleko** (Rakhmaninov), **Assafiev** (*Feast in Time of Plague*, *Brass Horseman* & *Fountain of Bakhchissarai*), **Boris Godunov** (Mussorgsky), **Cui** (*Captive in the Caucasus*, *Feast in Time of Plague* & songs), **Dargomizhsky** (*Bacchus' Feast*), **Eugene Onegin** (Tchaikovsky), **Feinberg** (songs), **Francesca da Rimini** (Rakhmaninov), **Gaigerova** (songs), **Golden Cockerel** (Rimsky-K.), **Ilyinsky** (*Fountain of B.*), **Khrennikov** (songs), **Koval** (*Manor House* & songs), **Legend of Tsar Saltan** (Rimsky-K.), **Leoncavallo** (*Zingari*), **Lourié** (*Feast in T. of P.* & songs), **Makarova** (songs), **Mavra** (Stravinsky), **Mazeppa** (Tchaikovsky), **Medtner** (songs), **Mossolov** (songs), **Mozart and Salieri** (Rimsky-K.), **Popov** (*Slow Horseman*), **Prisoner in the Caucasus** (Cui), **Prokofiev** (*Feast in T. of P.*, *Boris Godunov*, *Eugene Onegin*, *Egyptian Nights*, *Queen of Spades* & songs), **Queen of Spades** (Tchaikovsky), **Russalka** (Dargomizhsky), **Russlan and Ludmilla** (Glinka), **Shaporin** (*Boris Godunov* & songs), **Shebalin** (*Mozart and Salieri*, *Stone Guest* & songs), **Shostakovitch** (songs), **Stone Guest** (Dargomizhsky), **Tcherepnin** (N.) (*Golden Fish*), **Vassilenko** (*Gypsies*), **Verstovsky** (*Black Shawl*).

Püttlingen, Johann Vesque von. *See* **Vesque von Püttlingen.**

Puy (Fr.). A competitive festival held in Fr. in the Middle Ages by literary and mus. guilds, incl. the Troubadours of the 11th cent. Ps. continued to the 16th cent. and the most famous was that of Évreux, held annually on St. Cecilia's Day (22. XI), 1570–1614. Prizes were given and the laureate was called *roy de puy*.

Puy, Jean du. *See* **Du Puy.**

Pygott, Richard (b. ?; d. ?), Eng. 15th–16th-cent. comp. He was in Wolsey's private chapel in 1517 as master of the children and in 1524 became a Gentleman of the Chapel Royal. Later he was given a corrody at Coggeshall monastery in Essex and a canonry at Tamworth, but lost some of the benefits at the dissolution of the monasteries. Henry VIII, however, and after him Edward VI, retained his services.

Works incl. masses, motets, *Salve Regina*; carols, &c.

Pythagoras (b. ?; d. ?), Gr. 6th-cent. (B.C.) philos. He contrib. to the science of m. by working out by maths. the intervals of the scale accord. to the number of vibrations to each note and by helping to systematize the **Tetrachords.**

Q

Quadrille. A dance originating from the figured displays of mounted squadrons at tournaments, introd. into the ballet in the 18th cent., where dancers perf. similar figures and in the 19th cent. passing into the ballroom for the perf. of country dances, 5 in number and each calling for different figures and different m. Its m., like that of the Lancers, which evidently had a military orig., soon ceased to use the orig. country-dance tunes and was made up of arrs. of popular songs or more esp. fashionable operatic tunes.

Quadruple Counterpoint. Ctpt. in 4 parts or voices.

Quadruplets. Groups of 4 notes occurring abnormally in m. written in a time in which the regular units are divisible by 3.

Quagliati, Paolo (b. Chioggia, *c.* 1555; d. Rome, 16. XI. 1628), It. comp. He was orgst. at the church of Santa Maria Maggiore in Rome, 1608.

Works incl. dramatic cantata *Carro di fedeltà d'amore*; motets; spiritual and secular madrigals & canzonets; org. & hpchd. works, &c.

Quail. A toy inst. *See* **Toy Symphony.**

Quantz, Johann Joachim (b. Oberscheden nr. Göttingen, 30. I. 1697; d. Potsdam, 12. VII. 1773), Ger. flst. & comp. Studied at Dresden and Vienna, entered the chapel of the King of Pol. (Elector of Saxony), which was alternately at Warsaw and Dresden; later travelled in It., Fr. and Eng. Taught Frederick II of Prus. the fl. and became his chamber musn. at Berlin and Potsdam in 1741, remaining to his death. He wrote a treatise on fl. playing.

Works incl. *c.* 300 concs. for 1 or 2 fls., *c.* 200 fl. pieces, sos. and duets for fls.; 22 hymns to words by Gellert; songs, &c.

Quart-Geige (Ger. = quarter v.). *See* **Violino piccolo.**

Quarter Note (Amer. = crotchet). The Amer. use of the term is obviously derived from the Ger. *Viertel*, but although serviceable, it is not strictly accurate, since a crotchet, although always a quarter of a semibreve (if that is to be the norm), does not necessarily perform the function of a quarter unit in a comp., e.g. a piece in 2–4, 3–4 or 6–4 time. There is also the possibility of confusion with 'quarter-tone,' and the disadvantage of using 2 words where one will do.

Quarter-Tones. Notes half-way between 2 semitones in pitch; not used in western m. until the 20th cent. and producible on few insts. except stgs. The chief exponent of quarter-tone m. is Alois Hába; others, e.g. Bartók and Bloch, have used the device, but not systematically.

Quartet. Any work or mus. number in a work written for 4 voc. or inst. parts; more partic. a chamber work in so. form for 2 vs., va. & co. (stg. 4tet) or v., va., co. & pf. (pf. 4tet). The use of the word Q. without further specification usually suggests a stg. 4tet.

Quartettsatz (Ger. = quartet mvt.). The 1st movt. of Schubert's unfinished stg. 4tet in C min., comp. in XII. 1820 and not perf. until 1. III. 1867, in Vienna. The work was clearly intended to be completed, for S wrote 41 bars of a slow mvt. in A♭ maj. The Ger. word Q. is still frequently used as a title in Eng., although it might describe any separate 4tet mvt.

Quasi (It. = as it were, so to speak). A qualifying word used in directions suggesting an approximate manner of perf. (e.g. *quasi allegro*) or an apparent contradiction of a time signature by the m.'s actual effect (e.g. *andante quasi allegro*, meaning that although the beats are moderately slow, the figuration is rapid and will give an effect of quickness). Q. is also used for titles of mus. comps. approximating to some partic. style, e.g. 'Quasi Scherzo,' Beethoven's sos. 'quasi una fantasia,' &c.

Quatorze Juillet, Le (*The Fourteenth of July*), play by Romain Rolland, forming part of the trilogy *Le Théâtre de la Révolution* with *Danton* & *Les Loups*, pub. and perf. *c.* 1900–2, collectively pub. 1909. It was prod. in the open air, Paris, Arènes de Lutèce, 14. VII. 1936, with m. by Auric, Honegger, Ibert, Koechlin, Lazarus, Milhaud and Roussel.

Quatrible (Eng., obs.). A descant added a 4th above a tune according to the practice of Organum.

Quattro rusteghi, I (*The Four Boors*), opera by Wolf-Ferrari (lib. by Giuseppe Pizzolato, based on Goldoni's comedy), prod., in Ger., Munich, 19. III. 1906.

Quatuor (Fr.). Quartet.

Quaver. The black note of half the time-value of a crotchet or an eighth of a semibreve, symbolized by the figure 8 in time-signatures, e.g. 3–8 indicates bar-lengths of 3 Qs.

Queen of Cornwall, The, opera by Boughton (lib. Thomas Hardy's play, with alterations), prod. Glastonbury, 21. VIII. 1924. The subject is Tristram and Iseult.

Queen of Sheba. *See* **Königin von Saba; Reine de Saba.**

Queen of Spades, The (*Pikovaya Dama*), opera by Tchaikovsky (lib. by Modest Ilitch Tckaikovsky, T.'s brother, based on Pushkin's story), prod. St. Petersburg, 19. XII. 1890.

Quentin Durward, opera by Gevaert (lib. by Eugène Cormon & Michel Carré, based on Scott's novel), prod. Paris, Opéra-Comique, 25. III. 1858.

Opera by A. Maclean (lib. by Sheridan Ross, based on Scott), prod. Newcastle-on-Tyne, 13. I. 1920.

Querstand (Ger. lit. 'oblique-standing'). False Relation.

Quest, The, ballet by Walton (chgph. by Frederick Ashton, based on Spenser's *Fairy Queen*), prod. London, Sadler's Wells Ballet, 1943.

Quiet Don, The (*Tikhi Don*), opera by Dzerzhinsky (lib. by comp., based on Mikhail Sholokhov's novel), prod. Leningrad, 22. X. 1935.

Quilter, Roger (b. Brighton, 1. XI. 1877), Eng. comp. Educ. at Eton and studied m. with Knorr at Frankfort o/M. He has never held any official mus. posts.

Works incl. opera *Julia*, radio opera *The Blue Boar*; incid. m. for Shakespeare's *As You Like It* and the children's fairy-play *Where the Rainbow ends*; *Children's Ovt.* on nursery tunes, Serenade, *3 Eng. Dances*, &c. for orch.; song-cycle *To Julia* (Herrick), songs to words by Shakespeare, Tennyson & others, &c.

Quinault, Jean Baptiste (Maurice) (b. ?; d. Gien, 1744), Fr. singer, actor & comp. Sang at the Théâtre Français in Paris, 1712–8, and was an actor at the Comédie-Française, 1718–23.

Works incl. ballet *Les Amours des déesses* & others, stage divertissements, incid. m. for Molière's *Bourgeois gentilhomme* & *La Princesse d'Élide* & many other plays, &c.

Quinault, Philippe (1635–88), Fr. poet & librst. *See* **Alceste** (Lully), **Amadis** (Lully), **Amadis de Gaule** (J. C. Bach), **Armida** (Mysliveček), **Armide** (Gluck & Lully), **Atys** (Lully & Piccinni), **Cadmus et Hermione** (Lully), **Festes de l'Amour** (Lully), **Floquet** (*Nouvelle Omphale* & *Alceste*), **Isis** (Lully), **Persée** (Lully), **Phaéton** (Lully), **Proserpine** (Lully & Paisiello), **Roland** (Lully & Piccinni), **Thésée** (Lully).

Quincuplum. *See* **Quintus.**

Quinet, Fernand (b. Charleroi, 29. I. 1898), Belg. cst., cond. & comp. Studied at the Brussels Cons., where he was awarded the Belg. Prix de Rome in 1921. Later became dir. of the Charleroi Cons.

Works incl. *Esquisses symphoniques*, *Mouvements symphoniques*, &c. for orch.; suite *L'École buissonière* & Fantasy for stg. 4tet, *Charade* for pf. trio, suite for 2 cls. & bass cl.; *Moralités non légendaires* for voice & 18 insts.; va. & pf. So.; song-cycle *La Bonne Aventure* & other songs, &c.

Quinible (Eng., obs.). A descant added a 5th above a tune in the manner of the Organum or Diaphony.

Quint. A 5⅓-ft. org. stop transposing a 5th upwards; also called Great Q.

Quint de Loup (Fr. = wolf's 5th). *See* **Wolf.**

Quinta falsa (Lat. = false 5th). Another name for the Tritone when it appears as a diminished 5th, not an augmented 4th.

Quintadena or **Quintaton** } An org. stop governing wood or metal pipes with labial openings sounding the 12th together with the fundamental note.

Quinte (Fr.). The word is now used for the interval of the 5th, but was formerly also the name of a stg. inst. of the viol family, the ten. viol with 5 stgs.; also later of the va., another Fr. name of which was Taille.

Quintero, Joaquín Alvarez (1873–1944) & **Serafín Alvarez** (b. 1871), Spa. dramatists. *See* **Vittadini** (*Anima allegro*).

Quintet. Any work or mus. number in a work written in 5 voc. or inst. parts; more partic. a chamber work in so. form for 5 insts., most usually pf. & stg. 4tet (pf. 5tet) or 5 stg. insts. (stg. 5tet).

Quintoles. Another name for Quintuplets.

Quinton (Fr.). The Fr. name of the now obs. 5-stged treble viol.

Quintoyer (Fr. = old Eng. Quinible). An old term for singing in 5ths in the manner of the Organum or Diaphony.

Quintuple Time. M. with 5 beats to the bar, the time-signature of which is 5–4, 5–8, &c., is said to be in Q. T.

Quintuplets. Groups of 5 notes occupying a beat or the space of a note of normal duration.

Quintus (Lat. = the fifth). The 5th part in a comp. for 5 voices in old m. It was so called because its range was always equal to that of one of the other 4 parts, so that it could not be described as sop., alto, ten. or bass. It was also called Quincuplum.

Quire. The old Eng. spelling of Choir.

Quiterne (Fr. & old Eng.) = Cittern.

Quittard, Henri (b. Clermont-Ferrand, 13. V. 1864; d. Paris, 21. VII. 1919), Fr. mcolst. Studied with Franck in Paris, but soon began to specialize in mus. hist. He wrote many learned articles for the mus. papers and his books incl. studies of the Fr. lutenists, Machaut, the Couperin family, &c.

Quo vadis?, opera by Nouguès (lib. by Henri Cain, based on Sienkiewicz's novel), prod. Nice, 9. II. 1909.

Quodlibet (Lat. *quod libet* = as it pleases). A comp. made up of a medley of tunes, usually familiar songs, in polyphonic combs. Some of Obrecht's masses are elaborate Qs., containing combs. of portions of plainsong and popular songs with his own m., each tune being sung to a different text. A more familiar ex. is the Q. in Bach's Goldberg Vars. Leslie Heward's Q. for orch. is not a Q. in this sense, but simply a piece entitled in Lat. 'As you like it.'

Quotations. Short passages in mus. works taken from other m. (*a*) by the same comp., (*b*) by another, or (*c*) traditional, folk or popular tunes, e.g.:

(*a*) Brahms, *Regenlied* in finale of D min. v. So.;

Elgar, a number of themes from earlier works in *The Music Makers*; demons' chor. from *The Dream of Gerontius* in *The Fourth of August* (as a theme for the enemy);

Haydn, theme from slow mvt. of 'Surprise' Sym. in the bass aria in *Spring* section of *The Seasons*;

Mozart, 'Non più andrai' from *Figaro* in 2nd finale of *Don Giovanni*;

Rimsky - Korsakov, theme from *Pskovitianka* (*Ivan the Terrible*) in *The Tsar's Bride* (ref. to Ivan);

Saint-Saëns, theme from *Danse macabre* in *Fossils* section of *Le Carnaval des animaux*;

Schumann, opening of *Papillons*, Op. 1, in *Florestan* piece in *Carnival*, Op. 9.

Smetana, theme assoc. with the Vysehrad citadel of Prague in *My Country* symph. poem of that name ref. to in the later one entitled *Vltava*;

Smyth, *March of the Women* in the ovt. to *The Boatswain's Mate*;

Strauss, theme from *Guntram* in 'Childhood' section of *Tod und Verklärung*; a number of themes from earlier works in the 'Hero's Works' section of *Heldenleben* and in the dinner m. in the *Bourgeois gentilhomme* incid. m.;

Wagner, theme from *Tristan* in *Meistersinger*, III. i; swan motive from *Lohengrin* in *Parsifal*, I; themes from *Siegfried* in *Siegfried Idyll* (some going back to a projected stg. 4tet;

Wolf, song, 'In dem Schatten meiner Locken' from *Spanish Song-Book* in opera *Der Corregidor*, I.

(*b*) Bax, theme from Wagner's *Tristan* in symph. poem *Tintagel*;

Beethoven, 'Notte e giorno faticar' from Mozart's *Don Giovanni* in Vars. on a theme by Diabelli, Op. 120;

Berg, theme from Wagner's *Tristan* in Suite for stg. 4tet;

Brahms, 'Batti, batti' from Mozart's *Don Giovanni* in song *Liebe und Frühling*, Op. 3 No. 2;

Bréville, 'Tarnhelm' motive from Wagner's *Ring* in *Portraits de Maîtres* for pf., indicating a transformation between the pieces imitating var. comps.;

Charpentier, theme from Wagner's *Ring* in *Louise*, II;

Debussy, theme from Wagner's *Tristan* in *Golliwog's Cake-Walk* (*Children's Corner*);

Elgar, theme from Mendelssohn's ovt. *Calm Sea and Properous Voyage* in 'Enigma' Vars. (*Romance*); Chopin's G min. Nocturne & Paderewski's *Polish Fantasy* for pf. & orch. in symph. prelude *Polonia*;

Falla, opening motive from Beethoven's 5th Sym. ('Fate knocking at the door') in ballet *The Three-cornered Hat*;

Fibich, var. themes from Mozart's *Don Giovanni* in opera *Hedy* (based on Byron's *Don Juan*);

Handel, opening of Arne's *Rule, Britannia* (1740) in the *Occasional Orat.* of 1746, at the words 'War shall cease, welcome peace.'

Mozart, tunes from Martín y Soler's *Una cosa rara* and Sarti's *Fra due litiganti* in 2nd finale of *Don Giovanni*;

Mussorgsky, Handel's 'See, the conquering hero' and themes from Serov's opera *Rogneda* in satirical song *The Peep-Show*; sea motive from Rimsky-Korsakov's *Sadko* in song *The Classicist*;

Noren, 2 themes from Strauss's *Heldenleben* in *Kaleidoskop* suite for orch.;

Offenbach, 'Notte e giorno faticar' from Mozart's *Don Giovanni* in *Tales of Hoffmann*, prologue;

Parry, Chopin's Funeral March from B♭ min. So. in cantata *The Pied Piper of Hamelin*; var. Qs. in incid. m. for Aristophanes' *Frogs*;

Rimsky-Korsakov, themes from Mozart's Requiem in opera *Mozart and Salieri*;

Saint-Saëns, themes from ovt. to Offenbach's *Orphée aux enfers* in *Tortoises* section of *Le Carnaval des animaux* (because Orpheus's lute was made of tortoise-shell), also a phrase from Rossini's *Barber of Seville* in *Fossils* in the same work;

Schumann, chor. from Marschner's *Der Templer und die Jüdin* in finale of *Études symphoniques*, Op. 13.

Smyth, opening motive from Beethoven's 5th Sym. (' Fate knocking at the door ') in *The Boatswain's Mate*; song from Méhul's *Joseph* in *Entente cordiale*;

Stanford, a number of themes in opera *The Critic* (incl. opening of Parry's *Blest Pair of Sirens* at the words ' O, cursèd parry ');

Strauss, Denza's song *Funiculi, funiculà* in Sym. *Aus Italien* (under the impression that it was an It. folksong); giants' motive in Wagner's *Ring* in *Feuersnot*; themes by Bull, Legrenzi, Monteverdi and Peerson in *Die schweigsame Frau*;

Stravinsky, waltz by Lanner (played on a barrel-organ) in ballet *Petrushka*;

Sullivan, Bach's great G min. org. Fugue in song ' A more humane Mikado never ' in *The Mikado*;

Vaughan Williams, opening theme from Debussy's *L'Après-midi d'un faune* in incid. m. for Aristophanes' *Wasps*.

Walton, 2 themes from Rossini's *William Tell* ovt. in *Façade* (*Swiss Yodelling Song*).

(*c*) Beethoven, ' God save the King' and ' Malbrouk s'en va-t-en guerre ' in *The Battle of Victoria*; Rus. folksong ' Slava ' in Rasumovsky 4tets, Op. 59 Nos. 2 & 3;

Brahms, ' God save the King ' (as ' Heil Dir im Siegerkranz ') & hymn ' Now thank we all our God ' in *Triumphlied*; Ger. students' songs in *Acad. Festival* ovt.;

Debussy, ' Au clair de la lune ' in *Préludes*, II. 7; ' God save the King ' in *Hommage à S. Pickwick, Esq.* & *Marseillaise* in *Feux d'artifice* (both in *Préludes*, II); ' Nous n'irons plus au bois ' in *Jardins sous la pluie* for pf. & *Rondes de printemps* for orch.

Elgar, Pol. nat. anthem in symph. prelude *Polonia*;

Glazunov, Volga boatmen's song in symph. poem *Stenka Razin*;

Litolff, *Marseillaise* in *Robespierre* ovt.

Puccini, Amer. nat. anthem in *Madama Butterfly*, I;

Saint-Saëns, Fr. folksongs in *Fossils* section of *Le Carnaval des animaux*;

Schumann, *Marseillaise* in *Faschingsschwank aus Wien* for pf. & in song *Die beiden Grenadiere*; old Ger. 'Grossvatertanz' (or 'Kehraus') at the end of *Papillons* & *Carnaval* for pf.

Smyth, 2 Fr. folksongs in *Entente cordiale*, later pub. as *Two Interlinked Fr. Melodies* for fl., ob. & pf.

Stravinsky, Fr. popular song ' Ell' avait une jamb' en bois ' in ballet *Petrushka*;

Suppé, Ger. students' songs in ovt. *Flotte Bursche*.

Tchaikovsky, Rus. nat. anthem and Marseillaise in ovt. *The Year 1812*; Dan. & Rus. nat. anthems in *Danish Ovt.*; Rus. nat. anthem in *Slav March*, *Coronation March* & *Jurists' March*;

Vaughan Williams, song *Greensleeves* in opera *Sir John in Love*;

Wagner, Marseillaise in Fr. song *Les Deux Grenadiers* (trans. from Heine); Ger. folksong ' Schlaf, Kindlein, schlaf ' in *Siegfried Idyll*;

Weber, ' God save the King ' at close of *Jubilee Ovt.*;

(*See also* Dies irae for var. Qs. of the plainsong tune.)

R

Ř. In Cz., **Ř** or **ř** is pronounced like R followed by a soft 'zh' sound similar to S in 'leisure' (e.g. Dvořák = Dvorzhák).

r. The Supertonic note in any key in Tonic Sol-fa notation, pronounced Ray.

R.A.M. (abbr.) = Royal Academy of Music (London).

R.C.M. (abbr.) = Royal College of Music (London).

R.H. (abbr.) = Right Hand.

R. Ir. A.M. (abbr.) = Royal Irish Academy of Music (Dublin).

Raaff, Anton (b. Gelsdorf nr. Bonn, 6. V. 1714; d. Munich, 27. V. 1797), Ger. ten. singer. Studied and sang in It., returned to Ger. in 1742, but continued to travel; entered the service of the Elector Palatine of Mannheim in 1770.

Rabaud, Henri (Benjamin) (b. Paris, 10. XI. 1873), Fr. comp. Studied under his father, the cst. Hippolyte R. (1839–1900), and with Gédalge and Massenet at the Paris Cons., where he gained the Prix de Rome in 1894. After his stay in Rome he visited Vienna and travelled elsewhere, and after his return to Paris he became harmony prof. at the Cons. and cond. at the Opéra. In 1920 he succeeded Fauré as dir. of the Cons., and was in turn succeeded in that post by Delvincourt in 1941.

Works incl. operas *La Fille de Roland, Le Premier Glaive, Mârouf, savetier du Caire, L'Appel de la mer* (after Synge's *Riders to the Sea*), *Rolande et les mauvais garçons*; incid. m. for Shakespeare's *Merchant of Venice* & *Antony and Cleopatra*; m. for films *Joueurs d'échecs* & *Le Miracle des loups*; Psalm iv for chor.; 2 syms., symph. poem *Andromède, La Procession nocturne* (after Lenau's *Faust*), *Le Sacrifice d'Isaac, La Flûte de Pan, Divertissement grec, Divertissement sur des airs russes, Poème sur le livre de Job*, &c. for orch.; stg. 4tet; songs, &c.

Rabelais, François (c. 149?–1553), Fr. novelist. *See* **Dieren (van)** (*Propous des Beuveurs*), **Fanelli** (suite), **Ganne** (operetta), **Gargantua** (Mariotte), **Grétry** (*Panurge*), **Massenet** (do.), **Monsigny** (*Île sonnante*), **Planquette** (*Panurge*), **Terrasse** (*Pantagruel*).

Rachmaninoff. *See* **Rakhmaninov.**

Racine, Jean (1639–99), Fr. poet and dramatist. *See* **Andromaque** (Grétry), **Athalie** (Mendelssohn & others), **Boïeldieu** (*Athalie*), **Clément (F.)** (*Athalie* & *Esther*), **Cohen** (do., do.), **Coquard** (*Esther*), **Esther** (Handel), **Fauré** (*Cantique*), **Hervé** (*Nouvel Aladin*), **Honegger** (*Phèdre*), **Ifigenia in Aulide** (Graun), **Iphigénie en Aulide** (Gluck), **Lemoyne** (*Phèdre*), **Lunssens** (do.), **Massenet** (do.), **Mitridate** (Mozart), **Moreau** (*Cantiques spirituels* & *Esther* & *Athalie*), **Perne** (*Esther*), **Poissl** (*Athalia*), **Rossini** (*Ermione*), **Rousseau (M.)** (*Bérénice*), **Saint-Saëns** (*Andromaque*), **Schulz** (*Athalie*), **Thomson (V.)** (*Air de Phèdre*), **Vogler** (*Athalie*).

Racket. An obs. inst. of the bn. type, also called Rackett, Ranket or Sausage Bn. Its long tube was folded many times, so that the actual size of the inst. seemed small.

Radamisto, opera by Handel (lib. by Nicola Francesco Haym), prod. London, King's Theatre, Haymarket, 27. IV. 1720.

Radcliffe (*née* **Ward**), **Ann** (1764–1823), Eng. novelist. *See* **Arneiro.**

Raddoppiamento (It. = redoubling) = Augmentation.

Radford, Robert (b. Nottingham, 13. V. 1874; d. London, 3. III. 1933), Eng. bass singer. Studied at the R.A.M. in London and made his 1st appearance at the Norwich Festival in 1899, and in opera at Covent Garden Theatre in London in 1904.

Radical Bass. *See* **Root Bass.**

Radicati, Felice (Alessandro) (b. Turin, 1775; d. Bologna, 19. III. 1820), It. vst. & comp. Pupil of Pugnani, began to tour in It., visited Fr. and Eng., played in It. opera at Dublin in 1811, entered the service of Victor Emmanuel V in Rome and in 1815 went to Bologna, where he became leader of the town and cath. orchs. and v. prof. at the Liceo Filarmonico.

Works incl. operas *Riccardo Cuor di Leone, Fedra, Coriolano, Castore e Polluce, Zaira* & some others; v. concs.; v. pieces; arias, &c.

Radiciotti, Giuseppe (b. Jesi, 25. I. 1858; d. Tivoli, 4. IV. 1931), It. mcolst. Studied with his uncle G. Faini, worked in Rome for a time and in 1881 became prof. of mus. hist. at the Liceo at Tivoli. His books incl. studies of Pergolesi, of the mus. hist. of Rome, Senigallia, Urbino & Tivoli, a biog. of Rossini, &c.

Radino, Giovanni Maria (b. ?; d. ?), It. 16th-cent. orgst. & comp. He was orgst. at the church of San Giovanni in Verdara at Padua.

Works incl. madrigals for 4 voices; dances for hpchd. or lute, &c.

Radio-Synthetic Organ. An electrophonic org. invented by Abbé Puget of Paris in 1934, prod. its notes by the conversion of electrical waves into audible sounds.

Radnai, Miklós (b. Budapest, 1. I. 1892; d. Budapest, 4. XI. 1935), Hung. comp. Studied at Budapest and Munich, became a prof. at the Budapest Cons., 1919–25, and then dir. of the Opera there.

Works incl. opera *The Former Lovers*; ballet *The Infanta's Birthday* (after Wilde); Hung. Sym., *Mosaic* Suite, 5 Poems, *Fairy Tale, Orcan the Hero,* for orch.; pf. Trio; inst. sos.; pf. works; songs, &c.

Radoux, Charles (Jean Édouard Firmin Paul) (b. Liége, 30. VII. 1877), Belg. comp. Studied under his father at the Liége Cons. and gained the Belg. Prix de Rome in 1907. He became prof. there in 1911, having acted as asst. since 1905.

Works incl. operas *Oudelette, Le Sanglier des Ardennes, Œdipe à Colone* (after Sophocles) & *Le Poème de Roseclaire*; incid. m.; Te Deum; *Geneviève de Brabant, Cantate à Grétry* & other chor. works; *Danse tzigane, Burlesque, Triptyque champêtre* for orch.; Vars. for pf. & orch., *Fantaisie* & *Dans les fagnes* for v. & orch., *Scènes grecques* & *Choral varié* for co. & orch.; pf. pieces; songs, &c.

Radoux, Jean Théodore (b. Liége, 9. XI. 1835; d. Liége, 20. III. 1911), Belg. comp., father of prec. Studied at the Liége and Paris Conss. and obtained the Belg. Prix de Rome in 1859. He taught bn. at the Liége Cons. from 1855 and became its dir. in 1872.

Works incl. operas *Le Béarnais, La Coupe enchantée* & *André Doria* (unfinished); Te Deum; orat. *Cain* and cantatas; symph. poems *Ahasvère, Le Festin de Balthasar* & *Godefroid de Bouillon*; ovt. *Épopée nationale*; chors.; songs, &c.

Radziwill, Anton (Heinrich), Prince (b. Vilna, 13. VI. 1775; d. Berlin, 7. IV. 1833), Ger.-Pol. amateur cst., singer & comp. He married the sister of another amateur musn., Prince Louis Ferdinand of Prus., and became Prus. governor of the duchy of Posen.

Works incl. incid. m. to Goethe's *Faust*; *Complaint of Mary Stuart* for voice, pf. & co., songs with guitar and co., duets and songs with pf.; partsongs, &c.

Raff, (Joseph) Joachim (b. Lachen, Ct. Zürich, 27. V. 1822; d. Frankfort o/M., 24–5. VI. 1882), Swi. comp. Studied to become a schoolmaster, but took to m. and in 1843 had some comps. pub. on Mendelssohn's recommendation. He met Liszt, and at Cologne in 1846 Mendelssohn, who invited him to become his pupil at Leipzig, but d. before this was done. He then wrote criticism at Cologne, studied further at Stuttgart and in 1850 settled at Weimar to be near Liszt. In 1856 he went to Wiesbaden, where he wrote incid. m. for a drama by Wilhelm Genast and married his daughter Doris, an actress. In 1877 he became dir. of the Hoch Cons. at Frankfort.

Works incl. operas *König Alfred, Dame Kobold* (on Calderón's *Dama duende*) & others; incid. m. for Genast's *Bernhard von Weimar* & other plays; orat. *Weltende* and other chor. works; programme syms. *An das Vaterland, Im Walde, Lenore* (on Bürger's ballad), *Gelebt, gestrebt . . ., In den Alpen, Frühlingsklange, Im Sommer, Zur Herbstzeit, Der Winter* (unfinished), 2 suites, 3 ovts. for orch.; Sinfonietta for wind insts.; Conc., Suite & *Ode au printemps* for pf. & orch., 2 v. concs., co. Conc.; 8 stg. 4tets, stg. 6tet, stg. 8tet, 4 pf. trios, 2 pf. 4tets, pf. 5tet; 5 v. & pf. sos.; numerous pf. works; v. pieces, &c.

Ragtime. An Amer. form of syncopated dance m. of Negro orig. and coming into fashion *c.* 1910, the forerunner of Jazz and Swing.

Raimann, Rezsö (b. Veszprém, 7. V. 1861; d. Vienna, 26. IX. 1913), Hung. comp., mus. dir. to Prince Esterházy at Totis Castle.

Works incl. operas *Enoch Arden* (after Tennyson), *Imre Kiraly* & others, operettas; incid. m. to plays; pf. pieces; songs, &c.

Raimondi, Ignazio (b. Naples, *c.* 1773; d. London, 14. I. 1813), It. vst. & comp. Went to Amsterdam in 1760, was dir. of the concerts there, 1762–80, when he settled in London, where he taught and gave concerts.

Works incl. opera *La Muette* (prod. Paris); programme syms. *The Adventures of Telemachus, The Battle,* &c.; stg. 4tets, trios for 2 vs. & bass; var. sos., &c.

Raimondi, Pietro (b. Rome, 20. XII. 1786; d. Rome, 30. X. 1853), It. comp. Studied at the Cons. di Pietà de' Turchini at Naples and wandered all over It. in great poverty until he succeeded in prod. an opera at Genoa in 1807. Prod. operas at Rome, Milan, Naples and in Sicily until 1824, became dir. of the royal theatres there until 1832, when he became prof. of comp. at the Palermo Cons. In 1852 he was app. chapel master at St. Peter's in Rome in succession to Basili.

Works incl. operas *Le bizzarrie d'amore*, *Il ventaglio* & 60 others incl. a serious and a comic one which could be perf. together; 21 ballets; 8 orats. incl. trilogy *Giuseppe* (incl. *Putifar*, *Farao* & *Giacobbe* performable separately or together); masses, Requiems, psalms & other church m., much of it in very numerous parts; voc. fugues, one in 64 parts and incl. others in 4 parts, 4 of which could be sung together in 16 parts, &c.

Raimund, Ferdinand (1790–1836), Aus. actor & playwright. *See* **Alpenkönig und Menschenfeind** (Blech), **Kreutzer (C.)** (*Verschwender*), **Reiter** (*Bauer als Millionär*).

Raindrop Prelude. Chopin's pf. Prelude in D♭ maj., Op. 28 No. 15, written at Valdemosa, Majorca, in 1839 and said to have been suggested by the dripping of raindrops from the roof; hence the continuously repeated A♭=G♯, which is the dominant both of the main key and of the C♯ min. middle section.

Rainforth, Elizabeth (b. ?, 23. XI. 1814; d. Bristol, 22. IX. 1877), Eng. sop. singer. Studied under George Perry and T. Cooke and made her 1st stage appearance in London in 1836, and in orat. the following year.

Raison, André (b. ?; d. ? Paris, ?), Fr. 17th–18th-cent. orgst. & comp. He was orgst. at the Sainte-Geneviève and Jacobin churches in Paris. Comp. org. pieces.

Raitio, Väinö (b. Sortavala, 15. IV. 1891), Fin. comp. Studied the pf. with his mother, later comp. with Melartin and Furuhjelm and in 1916–7 with Ilyinsky at Moscow. Taught comp. at Viipuri in 1932–8, but settled at Helsinki and devoted himself entirely to comp.

Works incl. operas *Jephtha's Daughter*, *Princess Cecilia* & 2 others; ballet *Waterspout*; Sym., 10 symph. poems; pf. Conc., Conc. for v. & co., Poem for co. & orch.; stg. 4tet, pf. 5tet; v. & pf. So.; songs, &c.

Rake's Progress, The, ballet by Gavin Gordon (chgph. by Ninette de Valois, setting by Rex Whistler based on Hogarth), prod. London, Sadler's Wells Theatre, 20. V. 1935. *See also* **Whitaker.**

Rakhmaninov, Sergey Vassilievitch (b. Oneg, Novgorod, 1. IV. 1873; d. Beverley Hills, Cal., 28. III. 1943), Rus. pfst. & comp. Son of a captain in the Imp. Guards and descendant of a wealthy and noble family. The family fortune was gravely impaired during his childhood and his parents separated in 1882, R. living with his mother in St. Petersburg. There he continued m. lessons in a desultory way until Siloti, who was his cousin, advised his mother to send him to Moscow to study under Nikolai Sverev. He went to the Moscow Cons. and lived in Sverev's house for 4 years. Later he went to live with his aunt, whose daughter, Natalia Satin, was later to become his wife. He wrote the 1-act opera *Aleko* while still a student, and the pf. pieces Op. 3, containing the notoriously popular C♯ min. Prelude, at the age of 20. In 1895 he wrote his 1st (unpub.) Sym. and in 1898 he was invited by the Phil. Soc. in London to appear as pfst. and to cond. his orch. fantasy *The Rock*. In 1905–6 he became cond. of the Imp. Grand Opera at Moscow and in 1909 he visited the U.S.A. for the 1st time, writing the 3rd pf. Conc. for the occasion and playing it himself. He had by this time developed into one of the finest pfsts. of the time and he remained pre-eminent in that respect throughout his life. He lived in Moscow again from 1910–7 and cond. the Phil. concerts there, 1911–3. During the war of 1914–8 he played much for charity, and at the death of Skriabin, who had been his fellow-pupil under Arensky, he decided to make a tour playing that comp.'s works only. It was from that time on that he became a much-travelled pfst., and finding himself out of sympathy with the Revol. in Rus., he took the opportunity of a concert journey to Scandinavia in 1917 to leave his country for ever. He lived in Paris for a time and then spent most of the rest of his life in Amer., touring there each year from I to IV and visiting Eur. as pfst. in X and XI, spending some of the summer months at a small property he had acquired in Swi. on the lake of Lucerne.

Works incl. operas *Aleko*, *The Miserly Knight*, *Francesca da Rimini*; chor. sym., *The Bells* (Poe), for solo voices, chor. & orch.; cantata, *The Spring*; *Liturgy of St. John Chrysostom* and Vesper Mass; 3 Rus. folk-songs for chor.; 4 pf. concs. and *Rhapsody on a Theme by Paganini* for pf. & orch.; 3 syms.; fantasy *The Rock*, *Caprice bohémien* and symph. poem, *The Isle of the Dead* (after Böcklin's picture) for orch.; *Elegiac Trio* for v., co. & pf., stg. 5tet and pf. Trio (unpub.); co. & pf. So., 2 pieces for v. & pf. and 2 for co. & pf.; a dozen works for pf. solo, incl. 2 sos., vars. on themes by Chopin & Corelli and 57 smaller pieces (preludes, *Études-Tableaux*, &c.); 4 works for 2 pfs.; 77 songs, &c.

Rakoczy March (the usual but incorrect spelling). A Hung. nat. tune named after Prince Ferencz Rákóczi, the leader of the revolt against Aus. in 1703–11. The orig. of the tune is unknown. The Hung. March in Berlioz's *Damnation of Faust* is an orch. arr. of it and Liszt's 15th Hung. Rhapsody for pf. is based on it. L. also made a symph. arr. for orch. and himself transcribed this for pf. duet.

Rallentando (It. = slowing down). The same direction is also expressed by *ritenuto* (holding back) or *ritardando* (retarding).

Rameau, Jean Philippe (b. Dijon, IX. 1683; d. Paris, 12. IX. 1764), Fr. comp. & theorist. He picked up mus. knowledge from his father, a church orgst., although the latter was against his taking up m. and gave him a classical educ. at a Jesuit coll., which however he neglected. He was very precociously gifted and somehow learnt the hpchd., org. and v. At 17 he fell in love with a young widow, but his father sent him to It. in 1701, where he visited Milan and other places. In 1702 he returned to Fr., visiting var. southern towns, teaching for a short time at Avignon and then settling at Clermont-Ferrand as orgst., 1702–5. He lived in Paris as orgst. at a Jesuit convent in 1705–8, but the following year succeeded his father as orgst. of Notre-Dame at Dijon, 1709–14. He then went to Lyons for a year, and in 1715 became cath. orgst. at Clermont-Ferrand, where he wrote the *Traité de l'harmonie*, which was later followed by other important theoret. works. In 1722 he settled in Paris, began to make his mark on the stage in 1723 and in 1726 married a girl of 18, Marie Louise Mangot. He became clavecinist and cond. to the wealthy art patron La Poupelinière, who obtained for him the lib. of *Samson* from Voltaire. In the 1730s he became orgst. to a church and to the Jesuit coll. In later life he had many successes as a operatic comp. and during the Guerre des Bouffons he was the central figure repres. Fr. m. against the It. party.

Works incl. operas & opera-ballets *Hippolyte et Aricie*, *Les Indes galantes*, *Castor et Pollux*, *Les Fêtes d'Hébé*, *Dardanus*, *Les Fêtes de Polyhymnie*, *Le Temple de la gloire*, *Zaïs*, *Pygmalion*, *Les Fêtes de l'Hymen et de l'Amour*, *Platée*, *Naïs*, *Zoroastre*, *Acante et Céphise*, *Les Surprises de l'amour*, *Les Paladins*, *Abaris, ou Les Boréades*, *Lysis et Délie*, *Daphnis et Églé*, *Les Sybarites*, *La Naissance d'Osiris*, *Anacréon*, *La Princesse de Navarre* (lib. by Voltaire), *La Guirlande* & others; incid. m. for *L'Endriague* & 4 other plays by Piron; cantatas; *Pièces en concert* for v. or fl. & hpchd.; hpchd. pieces, some adapted from the operas, &c.

Ramin, Günther (b. Carlsruhe, 15. X. 1898), Ger., orgst., cond. & comp. Studied at the Leipzig Cons. and in 1918 succeeded Straube as orgst. of St. Thomas's church there, the post once held by Bach.

Works incl. motet in 4 parts; v. & pf. So.; much org. m., &c.

Ramis, Bartolomé. *See* **Ramos.**

Ramler, Karl Wilhelm (1725–98), Ger. poet. *See* **Bach (J. C. F.)** (*Tod Jesu*), **Graun (K. H.)** (do.), **Kreusser** (do.), **Reihardt** (*Cephalus und Procris*), **Telemann** (*Tod Jesu* & *Auferstehung Christi*, **Veichtner** (*Cephalus und Procris*), **Vogler** (*Ino*).

Ramondon, Lewis (b. ?; d. London, *c.* 1720), Eng. or Fr. bass singer and comp. He sang in opera in London until *c.* 1711 and then made a success as a comp. of songs, some contrib. to var. plays.

Ramos (or Ramis) de Pareja, Bartolomé (b. Baeza, *c.* 1440; d. ? Rome, after 1491), Spa. theorist & comp. He lectured at Salamanca, went to It., living at Bologna in 1480–2 and later in Rome. He wrote a theoret. work in which he advocated equal temperament and comp. church m.

Ramsay, Allan (1686–1758), Sco. poet. *See* **Gentle Shepherd.**

Ramsey, Robert (b. ?; d. ? Cambridge, ?), Eng. 17th-cent. orgst. & comp. He took the Mus.B. at Cambridge in 1616 and became orgst. and master of the children at Trinity Coll. there, 1628–44.

Works incl. services, anthems, motets; madrigals, canons; dialogue between Saul and the Witch of Endor; songs, &c.

Randall, John (b. ? London, 1715; d. Cambridge, 18. III. 1799), Eng. orgst., scholar & comp. He was a choir-boy under Gates at the Chapel Royal in London; orgst. of King's Coll., Cambridge, from 1743 and prof. of m. there in succession to Greene from 1755, taking the Mus.D. in 1756; also orgst. of Trinity Coll. later.

Works incl. church m., hymn tunes, setting of Gray's ode for the installation of the Duke of Grafton as Chancellor of the Univ., &c.

Randegger, Alberto (b. Trieste, 13. IV. 1832; d. London, 18. XII. 1911), It. cond., singing-master & comp. Studied at Trieste with L. Ricci, became known locally as a comp. for the church and stage, and in the 1850s settled in London, where he became prof. of singing at the R.A.M. in 1868. He also cond. opera, orch.

& chor. concerts and in 1881–1905 the triennial Norwich Festival.

Works incl. operas *Il lazzarone*, *Werthers Schatten* (after Goethe), *Bianca Capello*, *The Rival Beauties*; masses & other church m.; cantata *Fridolin*, 150th Psalm, Funeral Anthem for the Prince Consort & other chor. works; scena for ten. *The Prayer of Nature*; songs with orch. & with pf., &c.

Randhartinger, Benedikt (b. Ruprechtshofen, Lower Aus., 27. VII. 1802; d. Vienna, 22. XII. 1893), Aus. ten. singer, cond. & comp. Fellow-pupil of Schubert's at the Seminary in Vienna; sang in the court chapel from 1832 and in 1862 became cond. there.

Works incl. opera *König Enzio*; *c.* 20 masses, *c.* 600 motets; chors.; chamber m.; *c.* 400 songs, &c.

Range. *See* **Compass.**

Rangström, Ture (b. Stockholm, 30. XI. 1884), Swe. cond., critic & comp. Studied with Lindgren at Stockholm and Pfitzner at Munich, also in Berlin. He settled in Stockholm as critic in 1907 and in 1922–5 cond. the Göteborg Sym. Orch.

Works incl. *Kronbruden* (after Strindberg) & *Medeltida* (after Drachman); incid. m. to Ibsen's *Brand* and Strindberg's *Til Damascus*; syms. *August Strindberg in memoriam*, *Mitt land*, *Sang under stjärnorna*, symph. poems *Dityramb*, *Et Midsommernattstycke*, *En höstsang*, *Havetsjunger*; chamber m.; songs, &c.

Rank. A set of org. pipes prod. a whole scale of notes of the same quality.

Ranket. *See* **Racket.**

Ranks. The pairs of stgs. tuned to the same note on insts. of the lute type.

Rant. An old Eng. dance the precise character of which is not known.

Ranta, Sulho (Veikko Juhan) (b. Peräseinäjoki, 15. VIII. 1901), Fin. comp. Studied with Melartin and Krohn at the Helsingfors Cons., with Arthur Willner in Vienna, and in Paris. Became prof. at Viipuri Cons. and in 1933 at that of Helsinki. He wrote books on harmony and mus. hist.

Works incl. a ballet *Kirsikankukkia*; *Sinfonia programmatica*, *Sinfonia piccola* for orch.; pf. Conc.; chamber m.; pf. pieces; songs, &c.

Ranz des Vaches. A Swi. cowherds' song or Alphorn signal by which the cattle is called in June from the valleys to the mountain pastures. There are many different tunes, varying according to the cantons or even districts. They are metrically very irregular and use a limited scale of the natural notes of the alphorn, as do the voc. Yodels which are obviously derived from the R. d. V. The Ger. is Kuhreigen or Kuhreihen.

Raphael, Günther (b. Berlin, 30. IV. 1903), Ger. comp. Studied under his father, a church orgst., and later with Trapp, R. Kahn and others at the Berlin Hochschule für Musik. In his early 20s he succeeded in having works pub., played by the Busch 4tet, cond. by Wilhelm Furtwängler and others, and in 1926 he became prof. at the Cons. and church m. institute at Leipzig.

Works incl. Requiem, Te Deum, cantata *Vater unser*; 3 motets, Psalm civ & other unaccomp. sacred chor. works; 3 syms., Sinfonietta, *Theme, Vars. and Rondo*, Divertimento, Smetana Suite for orch.; v. Conc., org. Conc.; chamber Conc. for co. with wind & stgs., other chamber m.; org. & pf. works, &c.

Rapimento di Cefalo, Il (*The Abduction of Cephalus*), opera by Caccini (lib. by Gabriele Chiabrera), prod. Florence, Palazzo Vecchio, 9. X. 1600.

Rappresentativo. *See* **Stile rappresentativo.**

Rappresentazione (It. = representation). A species of acted orat. or mus. drama in the *stile rappresentativo*, the direct forerunner of the opera. The immediate link with the latter, as well as the most famous ex. of R., is the

Rappresentazione di anima e di corpo (*Representation of Soul and Body*) by Emilio de' Cavalieri, prod. Rome, oratory of St. Philip Neri, II. 1600.

Rapsodie (Fr.). *See* **Rhapsody.**

Rapsodie espagnole (*Spa. Rhapsody*). An orch. work by Ravel in a Spa. manner as cultivated by a typically Fr. comp. with a strong taste for and leanings towards Spa. m.; comp. 1907, 1st perf. Paris, 15. III. 1908.

Raselius (orig. **Rasel**), **Andreas** (b. Hahnbach nr. Amberg, Upper Palatinate, *c.* 1563; d. Heidelberg, 6. I. 1602), Ger. clergyman, theorist & comp. Studied at the Lutheran Univ. at Heidelberg, became cantor at Ratisbon, 1584–1600, and then mus. dir. to the Elector Palatine at Heidelberg. Wrote a treatise on the hexachord, set hymn and psalm tunes in 5 parts and comp. Ger. motets.

Rasi, Francesco (b. Arezzo, *c.* 1575; d. Mantua, after 1620), It. singer, poet & comp. He came of a noble family and was a pupil of Caccini at Florence. Musn. at the court of Mantua, *c.* 1600–20.

Works incl. *Musica di camera e di chiesa*; madrigals, songs, &c.

Rasumovsky Quartets. Beethoven's 3 stg. 4tets, Op. 59, in F maj., E min. & C maj., comp. in 1806 and ded. to the Rus. ambassador to Vienna, Count (later Prince) Andrey Kyrillovitch Rasumovsky (1752–1836), by whose domestic 4tet, led by Schuppanzigh, they were 1st perf.

Rataplan (Fr. onomat. = Eng. rub-a-dub). A word imitating the sound of the side-drum and used for mus. pieces, esp. in opera, of a military-march character, containing drum parts or suggesting them by the word R. sung.

Ratcliff, opera by Andreae (lib. taken from Heine's tragedy *William R.*), prod. Duisburg, 25. V. 1914.

Rathaus, Karol (b. Tarnopol, Galicia, 16. IX. 1895), Pol. comp. Studied with Schreker in Vienna and followed him to Berlin when S. became dir. of the Hochschule für Musik, where R. taught in 1925–33. In 1934 he took refuge from the Nazi régime in London and later settled in U.S.A.

Works incl. opera *Strange Soil*; ballets *The Last Pierrot* & *Lion amoureux*; incid. m. to Shakespeare's *Merchant of Venice*, Gutzkow's *Uriel Acosta*, Hebbel's *Herodes und Mariamne*, &c.; chor. works; 2 syms., Ovt., Serenade, suites, *4 Dance Pieces*, *Kontrapunktisches Triptychon*, *Jacob's Dream*, *Polonaise symphonique* for orch.; Concertino for pf. & orch., Suite for v. & orch., *Little Prelude* for tpt. & stgs.; 3 stg. 4tets, Trio for v., cl. & pf., *Little Serenade* for wind insts. & pf.; 2 v. & pf. sos.; pf. & org. works, &c.

Ratswahlkantate (Council Election Cantata), cantata by Bach (No. 71 of complete ed.), written for the election of the town council of Mühlhausen, where Bach was orgst. of St. Blasius's church in 1707–8, and perf. there at St. Mary's church, 4. II. 1708.

Ratto di Proserpina, Il (*The Rape of Proserpine*), opera by Winter (lib. by Lorenzo da Ponte), prod. London, King's Theatre, Haymarket, 3. V. 1804.

Rauchfangkehrer, Der (*The Chimney-Sweep*), play with m. by Salieri (lib. by Leopold von Auenbrugger), prod. Vienna, Burg Theatre, 30. IV. 1781.

Raugel, Félix (Alphonse) (b. Saint-Quentin, 27. XI. 1881), Fr. cond. & mcolst. Studied at the Schola Cantorum in Paris with d'Indy, Roussel & others, founded a Handel Soc. in 1908 and cond. this as well as the Société Chorale Française later, and was chapel master at the church of Saint-Eustache, 1911–28, later of Saint-Honoré-d'Eylau, and founded a Mozart Soc. and a choir of his own in 1930–1. Wrote books on orgs. and their m., Palestrina, Bruckner, &c.

Raupach, Christoph (b. Tondern, Slesvig, 5. VII. 1686; d. Stralsund, 1744), Ger. orgst. & writer on m. Lived at Hamburg for a time and in 1703 became orgst. at Stralsund.

Raupach, Hermann Friedrich (b. Stralsund, 1728; d. ? St. Petersburg, after 1786), Ger. hpchd. player & comp., son of prec. Pupil of his father; went to St. Petersburg in 1755 as cond. of the Imp. Opera.

Works incl. operas *Alceste* & *Good Soldiers* (Rus.) & *Siroe* (It.); ballet *Love's Sanctuary* & some others, ballet m. for Traetta's *Lucio Vero*; sos. for hpchd. with v. accomp., &c.

Rauzzini, Matteo (b. Camerino, 1754; d. Dublin, 1791), It. comp. and singing-master. Brought out his 1st opera at Munich in 1772, went to Eng. and then to Ir., settling in Dublin as singing-master.

Works incl. operas *Le finte gemelle*, *L'opera nuova*, *Il rè pastore*, &c.

Rauzzini, Venanzio (b. Camerino, 19. XII. 1746; d. Bath, 8. IV. 1810), It. male sop. singer & comp., brother of prec. Made his 1st stage appearance in Rome, 1765, then sang at Munich until 1772, when he went to Milan and appeared in Mozart's *Lucio Silla*. In 1774 he settled in London, where he gave concerts and taught singing, but about 1780 he moved to Bath, where he took a prominent part in the mus. life of what was then almost a 2nd capital. Many famous singers were his pupils.

Works incl. operas *Piramo e Tisbe*, *Le ali d'amore*, *Creusa in Delfo*, *Alina* (*La regina di Golconda*), *L'Amore protettore dal cielo* (*La Vestale*), *L'eroe cinese*; incid. m. to Frederick Reynolds's tragedy *Werther* (after Goethe); Requiem; cantata *La sorpresa* & others; stg. 4tets; hpchd. sos.; It. arias & duets, Eng. songs, &c.

Raval, Sebastián (b. ?, *c.* 1560; d. ? Palermo, *c.* 1603), Spa. comp. He went to It. early in his career and served var. patrons at (?) Naples, Urbino, Rome and Palermo. In Rome in 1593 he was challenged through his boastfulness to a contest with Nanini and Soriano, and defeated by them. His last post was that of chapel master to the Spa. Duke of Maqueda at Palermo.

Works incl. motets, lamentations; madrigals, canzonets for 4 voices, &c.

Ravel, (Joseph) Maurice (b. Ciboure, Basses-Pyrénées, 7. III. 1875; d. Paris, 28. XII. 1937), Fr. comp. His father was of Swi. and his mother of Basque descent. They moved to Paris the year of his birth and after some preliminary teaching he entered the Cons. in 1889, studying pf. with Anthiome and later with Bériot, also theory under Pessard from 1891. He comp. a good deal and in 1897 passed to Fauré's class for comp. and to that of Gédalge for ctpt. In 1899 he had an ovt. *Schéhérazade* (unpub. and unconnected with the later song-cycle) and the *Pavane pour une infante défunte* in the orig. pf. version perf. by the Société Nationale. During the next 10 years he wrote some of his best works, but his 1st great public success came in 1909, when Diaghilev's Rus. Ballet prod. *Daphnis et Chloé*, and the 2nd in 1910, when the Opéra-Comique brought out *L'Heure espagnole*. During the war of 1914–8 he served in an ambulance corps at the front, but was demobilized owing to ill-health in 1917. In the 1920s he visited London more than once with great success, and in 1928 he paid a visit to U.S.A. In 1935, after a car accident, he began to suffer from a kind of mental paralysis, and he d. after an operation on his brain.

Works incl. opera, *L'Heure espagnole*; opera-ballet, *L'Enfant et les sortilèges*, ballet *Daphnis et Chloé* (& 2 others arr. from pf. works: *Ma Mère l'Oye* and *Adélaïde, ou Le Langage des fleurs*=*Valses nobles et sentimentales*, also *La Valse* & 2 from orch. works; *Boléro*; *Rapsodie espagnole* for orch.; Conc. for pf. & orch.; pf. Conc. for the left hand with orch.; stg. 4tet, *Introduction et Allegro* for hp., fl., clar. & stg. 4tet, pf. Trio in A min.; So. for v. & co., So. and *Tzigane* for v. & pf.; 15 pf. works incl. *Menuet antique*, *Pavane pour une infante défunte*, *Jeux d'eau*, *5 Miroirs*, Sonatina, *Gaspard de la nuit* (3 pieces), suite *Le Tombeau de Couperin*; suite *Ma Mère l'Oye* for pf. duet; 29 songs incl. cycles *Schéhérazade*, *Cinq Mélodies populaires grecques*, *Histoires naturelles*; *3 Poèmes de Mallarmé* for voice, 2 fls., 2 clars., stg. 4tet & pf.; *Chansons madécasses* for voice, fl., co. & pf.; *Don Quichotte à Dulcinée* (after Cervantes) for bar. & small orch.; 3 partsongs, &c.

Ravenscroft, Edward (17th cent.), Eng. playwright. *See* **Purcell** (*Canterbury Guests*).

Ravenscroft, Thomas (b. ? London, *c.* 1590; d. ? London, *c.* 1633), Eng. comp. He was a chorister at St. Paul's cath. under Edward Pearce, took the B.Mus. at Cambridge in 1607 and in 1618–22 was m. master at Christ's Hospital.

Works incl. anthems, 48 hymn-tune settings in his Psalter containing 100; madrigals; some of the 4-part songs *The Pleasures of 5 usuall Recreations* in his treatise on notation *A Briefe Discourse*, are by himself; some of the rounds and catches in the collections *Pammelia*, *Deuteromelia* & *Melismata* are prob. of his own comp.

Ravvivando (It. =reviving). A direction sometimes used to indicate a return to an orig. faster tempo after a slowing-down.

Rawsthorne, Alan (b. Haslingden, Lancs., 2. V. 1905), Eng. comp. He studied dentistry at first, but turned to m. at the age of 20 and in 1926–9 studied at the R. Manchester C.M. In 1932–4 he taught at Dartington Hall, Totnes, but settled in London in 1935 and married the vst. Jessie Hinchliffe. In 1938–9 he had works perf. at the I.S.C.M. festivals in London and Warsaw.

Works incl. *Symph. Studies*, ovt. *Street Corner* & fantasy-ovt. *Cortèges* for orch., film m. *Burma Victory*; pf. Conc.; Theme & Vars. for stg. 4tet; va. & pf. So., Theme & Vars. for 2 vs.; 4 Bagatelles for pf.; *The Creel* suite for pf. duet based on Izaak Walton's *Compleat Angler*; songs *The Enemy Speaks* (C. Day Lewis), *Away Delights* & *God Lyaeus* (John Fletcher), *3 Fr. Nursery Songs*, &c.

Ray. The name for the Supertonic note in any key in Tonic Sol-fa, so pronounced, but in notation represented by the symbol r.

Rayl(e). An old Eng. dance the precise character of which is not known.

Raymond, ou Le Secret de la Reine (*R., or The Queen's Secret*), opera by A. Thomas (lib. by Adolphe de Leuven & Joseph Bernard Rosier), prod. Paris, Opéra-Comique, 5. VI. 1851.

Raymonda, ballet by Glazunov (chgphy. by Marius Petipa), prod. St. Petersburg, Maryinsky Theatre, 19. I. 1898.

'Razor' Quartet (*Rasiermesser*). The nickname of a stg. 4tet by Haydn, Op. 55 No. 2, in F min. & maj., comp. in or shortly before 1787, when the London m. pub. Bland visited him at Esterház. H., shaving, declared that he would give his best 4tet for a good razor, whereupon Bland presented him with one, and this was the 4tet.

Re. The old name for the note D in Solmization, still used in Lat. countries, and in Tonic Sol-fa notation the Supertonic in any key, represented by the symbol r, pronounced Ray.

Re Lear (*King Lear*), opera by Alberto Ghislanzoni (b. 1897), (lib. by comp., based on Shakespeare), prod. Rome, Teatro Reale, 24. IV. 1937.

For Verdi *see* **King Lear.**

Re pastore, Il (*The Shepherd King*), opera by Bonno (lib. by Metastasio), prod. Vienna, Schönbrunn Palace, 13. V. 1751.

Opera by Gluck (lib. do.), prod. Vienna, Burg Theatre, 8. XII. 1756.

Opera by Mozart (lib. do.), prod. Salzburg, 23. IV. 1775.

Re Teodoro in Venezia, Il (*King Theodore at Venice*), opera by Paisiello (lib. by Giovanni Battista Casti), prod. Vienna, Burg Theatre, 23. VIII. 1784.

Reading Rota. *See* **Sumer is icumen in.**

Real Fugue. *See* **Fugue.**

Real Sequence. *See* **Rosalia** & **Sequence.**

Realism. Strictly realistic repres. in m. is neither desirable nor easily attainable. Exs. of the nearest comps. have come to it are such things as the anvils in Wagner's *Rheingold*, the sheep and wind machine in R. Strauss's *Don Quixote* and the nightingale (gramophone record of the bird's song) in Respighi's *Pini di Roma*. (There is said to be a pistol shot in Pugnani's sym. on Goethe's *Werther* to signify the hero's death.) Imitations of bells, birds, &c. are, of course, very frequent in m., but usually the more mus. the less they approach R. More generally, a realistic style of It. opera is known as *Verismo*.

Rebab or **Rebec(k)** An obs. stg. inst. of the v. type of Arab orig., the immediate forerunner of the viol family and the ancestor of the v. family, though its shape was more like that of the mandoline, which is prob. one of its descendants. It had 3 gut stgs. and was played with a bow. In Fr. it survived until the 18th cent., but only as a street inst.

Rebel. Fr. family of musns.:

1. Jean R. (b. ? ; d. ? Versailles or Paris, 1692), singer. Was in the service of the court from 1661.

2. Jean-Féry R. (b. Paris, IV. 1661; d. Paris, 2. I. 1747), vst. & comp., son of prec. Pupil of Lully, entered the Opéra orch. as a vst. *c.* 1700 and prod. his 1st opera there in 1703. It failed, but a v. solo, *Le Caprice*, was so successful that it was long afterwards used as a test piece for ballet dancers. He then wrote similar pieces for a number of ballets, became one of the 24 vs. at court in 1717 and chamber musn. to the king in 1720.

Works incl. opera *Ulysse*; ballet pieces for v.; v. sos., &c.

3. Anne-Renée R. (b. ? Paris, 1662; d. ? Paris, 1722), singer, sister of prec. Appeared in stage pieces at court from the age of 11, became one of the best singers there and married Lalande in 1684.

4. François R. (b. Paris, 19. VI. 1701; d. Paris, 7. XI. 1775), vst. & comp., son of 2. Studied under his father and entered the Opéra orch. at an early age, meeting there Francœur, with whom he was to collaborate extensively. They both visited Prague for the coronation of Charles VI in 1723. In 1733–44 they were joint leaders of the Opéra orch. and in 1749 they became managers there, but retired about 4 years later, to return in III. 1757 with a privilege enabling them to manage the Opéra without interference until 1767, when Berton and Trial succeeded them. In 1749 R. was made 'Surintendant de la Musique du Roi.'

Works incl. *Pyrame et Thisbé*, *Tarsis et Zélie*, *Scanderbeg*, *Les Augustales*, *Le Retour du roi*, *Zélindor*, *Le Trophée*, *Ismène*, *Les Génies tutélaires*, *Le Prince de Noisy*, *Ballet de la Paix* (all with Francœur), *Pastorale héroïque*; Te Deum, De Profundis, cantatas, &c.; sym. *Les Éléments*; v. So. *La Terpsichore* & others; sos. in 2 or 3 parts with continuo; v. & va. pieces, &c.

Rebello, João Soares (or **João Lourenço**) (b. Caminha, 1609; d. S. Amaro nr. Lisbon, 16. XI. 1661), Port. comp. A fellow-student of King John IV, who promoted him on his accession.

Works incl. psalms, Magnificat, lamentations, Miserere, &c.

Reber, Napoléon-Henri (b. Mulhouse, 21. X. 1807; d. Paris, 24. XI. 1880), Fr. comp. Studied at the Paris Cons. with Lesueur and others. He was app. prof. of harmony there in 1851 and of comp. in 1862 in succession to Halévy.

Works incl. operas *La Nuit de Noël*, *Le Père Gaillard*, *Les Papillotes de M. Benoît*, *Les Dames capitaines*; 2nd act of ballet *Le Diable amoureux*; cantata *Roland*; 4 syms., ovts. to unpub. operas *Le Ménétrier à la cour* & *Naïm*; 3 stg. 4tets, stg. 5tet, pf. 4tet, 7 pf. trios; duets for v. & pf.; pf. pieces & duets, &c.

Rebhuhn, Paul (b. ? Saxony, ?; d. ?), 16th-cent. Ger. poet & comp. Wrote dramas, *Susanna* & others, for which he wrote his own incid. m.

Rebikov, Vladimir Ivanovitch (b. Krasnoiarsk, 1. VI. 1866; d. Yalta, 1. XII. 1920), Rus. comp. Studied at Moscow and Berlin and later settled in the south of Rus. and founded mus. socs. at Odessa and Kishinev.

Works incl. operas & dramatic

scenes *The Storm*, *The Christmas Tree*, *Thea*, *The Woman with the Dagger* (based on Schnitzler's play), *Alpha and Omega*, *The Abyss* (after Andreiev), *Narcissus* (after Ovid's *Metamorphoses*), *Fables* (after Krylov); ballet *Snow-White*; suites for orch. & stg. orch.; numerous sets of pf. pieces incl. *Rêveries d'automne*, *Mélomimiques*, *Aspirer et attendre*, *Chansons blanches* (on the white keys), &c.

Reboul, Jean (1796–1864), Fr. poet. *See* **Franck (C.)** (songs).

Recapitulation. *See* **Sonata.**

Recherché (Fr. = searched out). The Fr. equivalent of *ricercato*, from which the Ricercare is derived. Beethoven still used this old term, as meaning strict fugal writing, in his *Great Fugue* for stg. 4tet, Op. 133, which he called a fugue 'tantôt libre, tantôt recherchée.'

Recital. A mus. perf., usually with a misc. programme, given by a single perf. or by one singing or playing an inst. with a pf. accompst.

Recitation. Works to be recited to a mus. background for orch., pf. or var. inst. combs. include the following (stage-works [melodramas] by Benda, Rousseau, &c. are not cited here):

Badings, Rs. with orch.
Bemberg, *La Ballade du désespéré.*
Copland, *Portrait of Abraham Lincoln.*
Corder, var. poems with pf.
Dieren (van), Baudelaire & Villon poems.
Foerster (J. B.), var. poems with pf.
Gilson, *La Mer.*
Goossens, *The Cowl.*
Grieg, *Bergliot* (Bjørnson).
Hawley, poems by Poe & others.
Hauer, R. with voices & chamber orch.
Klose, *Wallfahrt nach Kevlaar* (Heine).
Lier, *The Dyke.*
Liszt, Bürger's *Lenore* & Lenau's *Der traurige Mönch* (Ger.), Jókai's *The Dead Poet's Love* (Hung. & Ger.) & A. Tolstoy's *The Blind Singer* (Rus. & Ger.), all with pf. accomp.
Ostrčil, Ballads with orch.
Prokofiev, *Peter and the Wolf.*
Schillings, Wildenbruch's *Hexenlied.*
Schoenberg, Ode to Napoleon (Byron).
Schumann, Hebbel's *Schön Hedwig* & *Ballade vom Heideknaben*; Shelley's *The Fugitives.*
Sibelius, Rydberg's *Skograaet* & Runeberg's *Nights of Jealousy.*
Strauss (R.), Tennyson's *Enoch Arden* & Uhland's *Das Schloss am Meer*, with pf.
Vaughan Williams's *Thanksgiving for Victory* (1945) contains a part for a speaker.

Recitative. Declamation in singing, with fixed notes but without definite metre or time, comparable to prose inserted into verse drama. But although the notes are fixed by notation, they are not always, or should not always be, sung with full tone or even very definite intonation; on the other hand, although the time is free, in mus. notation R. is generally written down by convention in 4–4 time, with bar-lines. There are, broadly speaking, 2 kinds of R., as follows:

Recitativo accompagnato. A type of recitative accomp. by the orch., as distinct from R. secco, which in the 18th cent. was accomp. by a hpchd. R. a. served to modulate to or near the key of the set mus. number, usually an aria, that followed it, and also to give the singer an opportunity for dramatic declamation.

Recitativo secco. A type of recitative accomp. by the hpchd., mainly in 18th-cent. It. or Italianate opera. The comp.'s score showed only the voice-part and a figured or unfigured bass; the harmony was supplied by the player according to conventional rules and Rs. was never intended to be of mus. interest, but merely to advance the action without letting the m. drop out altogether and give place to spoken dialogue. It also served to modulate from the key of one set mus. number to the next.

Recitativo stromentato (It. = instrumentated recitative). Another term for the *R. accompagnato.*

Record (noun). A gramophone disc.

Recorder. A woodwind inst., the forerunner of the fl., from which it differs by being held vertically and blown into through a mouthpiece in which the air is diverted by an obstructive block called the 'fipple' and prod. a milder tone than that of the fl. Rs. were made in 4 different sizes prod. ranges corresponding roughly to the sop., con., ten. & bass voices. In modern times the R. has been revived, mainly for amateur perf., esp. in Eng. and Ger. (*Blockflöte*).

Recte et retro (Lat. = right way and backwards). A form of canon, also called, in It., *al rovescio*, in which a 2nd entry brings in the tune sung or played backwards, R. & r. is similar to Cancrizans, except that there the theme, although used backwards, does not necessarily combine with its orig. form in canon. Retrograde motion alone is thus common to both R. & r. and Cancrizans.

Redemption, The, Eng. orat. by

Gounod (words compiled by the comp.), prod. Birmingham Festival, 1882.

Redford, John (b. ? London, *c.* 1485; d. ? London, *c.* 1545), Eng. orgst., comp., poet & dramatist. He learnt m. (?) in the choir-school of St. Paul's cath. in London and later became orgst. and choir-master there. He also supervised the choir-boys in their prod. of plays with m., one of which in Lat. and Fr. was prod. at Greenwich in 1527 for the entertainment of Fr. nobles, and a morality of his own, *Wyt and Science*, *c.* in the 1540s.

Works incl. motets & anthems; prob. m. for plays, incl. *Wyt and Science*; org. voluntaries (? arrs. of motets), &c.

Redi, Tommaso (b. Siena, *c.* 1675; d. Montelupone nr. Loreto, 20. VII. 1738), It. comp. App. chapel master of the church of the Santa Casa at Loreto in 1731. In 1733 he had a dispute with Martini of Bologna about the solution of a canon by Animuccia, which was settled by Pacchioni and Pitoni in Martini's favour.

Works incl. masses & other church m., &c.

Redman, Reginald (b. London, 17. IX. 1892), Eng. comp. After an attempt to make a career in banking, he studied m. at the G.S.M. in London, became orgst. at Stanmore parish church and m. master at Harrow prep. school. 3 years later he went to the B.B.C. as pfst. & chor. master, became mus. dir. of the Welsh region and later of that of the West of Eng. at Bristol.

Works incl. opera *The Ring of Jade*; m. for many radio plays; *The Hills of Dream* & *The Dancers of Huai-Nan* for chor. & orch.; Nocturne, *Moods*, suite *The West Countree* for orch.; *Away on the Hills*, *Introduction and Folk Tune* & Serenade for stg. orch.; co. Conc., Conc. for pf. & stgs.; *Pan's Garden* for chamber orch.; Chin. songs to transs. by Arthur Waley and L. Cranmer-Byng; ed. of Chin. folksongs, &c.

Redoute (Fr., used also in Ger., and derived from It. *ridotto*). A kind of public ball, partic. in the 18th cent.; but carried on into the 19th in Aus. and Ger., where dancers gathered haphazard from all classes of society, usually at assembly halls called *Redoutensäle* in Ger. Comps. of note, esp. in Vienna, often wrote dances for Rs.

Redova or **Redowa** } A Boh. dance of unknown age, but not introd. in western Eur. until near the middle of the 19th cent. The name seems to be a corrupt. of Rejdovák, a dance in moderate triple time, to which var. exs. used by comps. conform; but there is also a Rejdovacka in 2–4 time.

Reed Stops. Org. stops which control pipes resembling obs., cls. & other reed insts. in having vibrating metal tongues, as distinct from Flue Stops, which are tubes with open mouthpieces. They are also called lingual S.

Reed, W(illiam). H(enry). (b. Frome, Somerset, 29. VII. 1876; d. Dumfries, 2. VII. 1942), Eng. vst. & comp. Studied v. with Sauret and comp. with F. Corder and Prout at the R.A.M. in London. He joined the London Sym. Orch., on its foundation in 1904 and became its leader in 1912; also v. prof. at the R.C.M. He wrote 2 books on Elgar.

Works incl. symph. poems *The Lincoln Imp* & *Aesop's Fables*, 2 *Somerset Idylls* for small orch., Sym. & Vars. for stg. orch.; Conc. in A min. & Rhapsody for v. & orch.; chamber m., &c.

Reed, William Leonard (b. London, 16. X. 1910), Eng. comp. Studied at Oxford and at the R.C.M. in London, with Howells for comp. and Lambert for cond. After travelling in Scand. and the Baltic states he was sent on a mus. mission there by the Brit. Council, 1937–9.

Works incl. *Recitative and Dance*, Scherzo, *3 Dance Mvts.*, *2 Short Pieces* for orch., *Idyll* for small orch.; Fantasy for fl., va. & hp.; *Pavane Caprice* & *Child Portrait* for pf., &c.

Reeds. The vibrating tongues prod. the tone of certain woodwind insts. (except fls., for ex.) and of org. pipes, though in the latter case they are often made of other materials than reed. These insts. use so-called 'beating R.,' and these are single for cls., saxophones and org. pipes and double for obs., bns. and bagpipes. There are also 'free R.,' used in harmoniums and insts. of the concertina and mouth-org. type.

Reel. A Sco., Ir. & Scand. dance, either of Celtic or Scand. orig. It is perf. with the dancers standing face to face and the m. is in quick 2–4 or 4–4, occasionally 6–8, time and divided into regular 8-bar phrases. A mus. characteristic of many Rs. is a drop into the triad of the subdominant unprepared by modulation.

Reese, Gustave (b. New York, 29. XI. 1899), Amer. mcolst. Studied at N.Y. Univ. and became lecturer in m. there 1927–39, assoc. ed. of *The Mus. Quarterly* and its ed. on the death of Carl Engel in 1944, but resigned in 1945 and was succeeded by Paul H. Láng. His work incl. a book on *M. in the Middle Ages.*

Reeve, William (b. ? London, 1757; d. London, 22. VI. 1815), Eng. comp. Studied with Richardson, the orgst. at St. James's church, Westminster, and was orgst. at Totnes, Devon, 1781–3. After var. engagements at London theatres, he joined the Covent Garden chor., and there was asked to complete the ballet-pantomime *Oscar and Malvina* (after Ossian) left unfinished by Shield in 1791 on account of differences with the management. He then became comp. to that theatre and in 1802 part-owner of Sadler's Wells Theatre.

Works incl. pieces for the stage, *The Apparition, Hercules and Omphale, Merry Sherwood, Harlequin and Oberon, Harlequin and Quixote* (after Cervantes), *Joan of Arc, Paul and Virginia* (with Mazzinghi, based on Saint-Pierre), *Out of Place* (with Braham), *The Corsair, Rokeby Castle* & many others (some with Braham, Davy, Mazzinghi or Moorehead); m. for Sadler's Wells pantomimes, &c.

Reeves, John Sims (b. Woolwich, 26. IX. 1818; d. Worthing, 25. X. 1900), Eng. ten. singer. Learnt m. from his father, a musn. in the Royal Artillery, studied singing and made his 1st stage appearance at Newcastle-on-Tyne, as a bar. After further study, incl. Paris and Milan, he came out at the Teatro alla Scala there as a ten. and as such made his 1st London appearance in 1847.

Refice, Licinio (b. Patrica, Rome, 12. II. 1885), It. priest & comp. He became prof. of church m. at the Scuola Pontifica in Rome in 1910 and in 1911 cond. at the church of Sante Maria Maggiora.

Works incl. masses, motets, Requiem, *Stabat Mater* & other church m.; 2 orats., 3 sacred cantatas, 3 chor. symph. poems, &c.

'Reformation' Symphony. Mendelssohn's 5th Sym., Op. 107, in D min., comp. in 1830 for the tercentenary of the Augsburg Conference. It was not perf. there owing to Rom. Catholic opposition, but prod. Berlin, XI. 1832.

Refrain (from Fr.). The burden of a song, more familiarly known in m.-hall songs as the 'chorus,' a recurrent strain returning with the same words at the end of each verse with m. different from but relevant to the 1st strain.

Regal. A small portable org., said to have been invented about 1460 by Heinrich Traxdorff of Nuremberg, but existing in var. forms much earlier as the Portative or Positive Org., which could be held by a band slung round the player's neck, one hand playing the keys and the other working the small bellows, or placed on a table, with the bellows worked by the feet or by another person.

Reger, Max (b. Brand, Bavaria, 19. III. 1873; d. Leipzig, 11. V. 1916), Ger. comp. 1st learnt m. from his mother and das so precocious that at the age of 13 he became orgst. at the Catholic church of Weiden in Bavaria, where his parents had moved in 1874. After 3 years there Riemann was consulted about his gifts and invited him to become his pupil at Sondershausen. R. went there in 1890 and the next year followed his master to Wiesbaden, where he soon became a teacher at the Cons. A period divided between hard work and dissipation led to a serious breakdown, and he lived with his parents at Weiden again in 1898–1901, writing vast quantities of m. In the latter year he went to Munich in the hope of making his way as a comp., but posing as a progressive and being in reality a conservative, he made enemies all round and had some success only with his pf. playing. But he began to tour Ger. and also visited Prague and Vienna, and gradually he made his work known; he also made a reputation as a remarkable comp. teacher. In 1907 he settled at Leipzig as mus. dir. to the Univ. and prof. at the Cons., soon resigning the former post as uncongenial, but retaining the latter for the rest of his life. In 1911 he became cond. of the ducal orch. at Meiningen, with which he went on tour, but this came to an end in 1913, when he went to live at Jena, travelling to Leipzig each week to carry out his duties at the Cons.

Works incl. *Gesang der Verklärten* & *Psalm c* for chor. & orch.; Sinfonietta, Serenade, Vars. on themes by J. A. Hiller & by Mozart, Symph. Prologue to a Tragedy, Comedy Ovt., Conc. in the Old Style, Romantic Suite, 4 tone-poems on pictures by Böcklin, &c. for orch.; pf. Conc., v. Conc., 2 Romances for v. & orch.; 5 stg. 4tets, stg. 6tet, cl. 5tet, 2 pf. 4tets, stg. Trio, 2 pf. trios, pf. 5tet; 7 v. & pf. sos., 4 co. & pf. sos., 3 cl. & pf. sos.; 2 sos., 2 suites, Fantasy & Fugue on B.A.C.H., Vars. & Fugue on orig. theme, chorale preludes, preludes & fugues, Introduction, Passacaglia & Fugue, Symph. Fantasy & Fugue, &c. for org.; Introduction, Passacaglia & Fugue for 2 pfs.; 2 sos., Vars. & Fugue on theme by Bach & numerous smaller works for pf.; pf., duets; many songs incl. *Schlichte Weisen*; partsongs, &c.

Reggio, Pietro (b. Genoa, ?; d. London, 23. VII. 1685), It. singer, comp. & lutenist. In the service of Queen Christina of Swe. in Rome; later settled at Oxford, where he pub. *A Treatise to sing well any Song whatsoever*, 1677. Comp. motets, song for Shadwell's adapt. of Shakespeare's *Tempest*, songs, duets, &c.

Regis, Jean (b. ?; d. ?), Flem. 15th-cent. comp. He was choirmaster at Antwerp cath. and (?) was at some time connected with Dufay. Wrote masses, incl. one on *L'Homme armé*, songs in parts, &c.

Register. A certain set of pipes brought into action in org. playing to prod. a particular kind of tone and dynamics; also the different parts of the range of the human voice according to the manner, or supposed manner, of its prod. as 'head R.' or 'chest R.'

Registration. The use of the org. stops by means of which the qualities and power of the inst., over which the manuals and pedals have no dynamic control, can be altered according to the comp.'s prescription or the perf.'s skill and taste.

Regnard, Jean François (1655–1709), Fr. playwright. *See* **Distratto** (Haydn), **Lattuada** (*Follie d'amore*), **Pessard** (*Folies amoureuses*).

Regnart, Francis (b. ?; d. ?), Flem. 16th-cent. comp. Learnt m. at Tournai cath. and studied at Douai Univ.

Works incl. motets; chansons *Poésies de Ronsard et autres* for 4–5 voices, &c.

Regnart, Jacob (b. ?; d. Prague, 1600), Flem. comp., brother of prec. Went to Vienna and Prague as a pupil in the imp. chapel at an early age, became a ten. there in the 1560s, and in the 1570s choirmaster and vice chapel master. In 1582–95 he was in the service of the Archduke Ferdinand at Innsbruck, but lived in Prague for the last 5 years of his life.

Works incl. masses, motets; *Canzone italiane* and Ger. songs for 5 voices, &c.

There were 2 other brothers, Charles and Paschasius, who contrib. motets to a collection in which Francis and Jacob also appeared, ed. by a 5th brother, Augustin, a canon at Lille.

Régnier, Henri de (1864–1936), Fr. poet. *See* **Roussel (A.)** (songs), **Witkowski** (songs with orch.).

Reich, Willi (b. Vienna, 27. V. 1898), Aus. mus. author & ed. Studied at Vienna Univ. and m. with Berg and Webern. He founded and ed. the review *23* in 1932, but in 1938 went to Swi., settling at Basle. He pub. a study of Berg's *Wozzeck* and worked with Křenek and Theodor Wiesengrund-Adorno on a biog. of the same comp.

Reicha, Anton (b. Prague, Feb. 27, 1770; d. Paris, 28. V. 1836), Boh. theorist, teacher & comp., naturalized Fr. Studied at Wallerstein, Bavaria, under his uncle Joseph R. (1746–95), from whose wife he learnt Fr. In 1788 he went to Bonn with his uncle, who became mus. dir. there and worked at the electoral court, where he made friends with Beethoven. In 1799–1802 he had some success as comp. in Paris, but went to Vienna, where he remained until 1808 and was patronized by the empress. He then settled in Paris for the rest of his life and became prof. at the Cons. in 1818.

Works incl. operas *Godefroid de Montfort, Oubouaidi, ou Les Français en Égypte, Cagliostro* (with Dourlen), *Natalie, Sapho*; 2 syms., *Scènes italiennes* for orch.; 20 stg. 4tets, 6 stg. 5tets, Diecetto & Octet for stgs. & wind, 24 wind 5tets, 6 stg. trios, duets for vs. and for fls.; 12 v. & pf. sos.; pf. sos. & pieces, &c.

Reichardt, Johann Friedrich (b. Königsberg, 25. XI. 1752; d. Giebichenstein nr. Halle, 26. VI. 1814), Ger. comp. Studied at Königsberg Univ. and picked up a rather haphazard mus. educ. He travelled widely in 1771–4 and pub. his experiences in *Vertraute Briefe*. After working as a civil servant at Königsberg, he obtained the post of mus. dir. at the Prus. court in 1776, lived at Berlin and Potsdam, prod. operas and in 1783 founded a Concert spirituel. He also pub. collections of m. and wrote criticism. After the death of Frederick II he made himself disliked more and more and in 1794 he was dismissed, ostensibly for his sympathy with the Fr. Revol. He retired to Giebichenstein, only briefly holding a post at the court of Jérôme Bonaparte at Cassel in 1808. He wrote several books on m., was a forerunner of Schubert in song comp., married Juliane Benda (1752–83), a singer, pfst. & comp., daughter of F. Benda, and had a daughter, Louise (1780–1826), who became a singer and also wrote songs.

Works incl. operas and plays with m. *Hänschen und Gretchen, Amors Guckkasten, Cephalus und Procris, Le feste galanti, Claudine von Villa Bella* (Goethe), *Erwin und Elmire* (Goethe), *L'Olimpiade* (Metastasio), *Tamerlan* (in Fr.), *Jery und Bätely* (Goethe), *Der Taucher* (after Schiller's ballad), *Brenno*, *Die Geisterinsel* (after Shakespeare's *Tempest*) and *c.* 12 others; incid. m. to Shakespeare's *Macbeth*, several plays by Goethe and Kotzebue's *Die Kreuzfahrer*; cantatas *Ariadne auf Naxos*, *Ino*, *Morning Hymn* (Milton, trans. Herder) & others; inst. works; numerous songs, &c.

Reicher - Kindermann, Hedwig (b. Munich, 15. VII. 1853; d. Trieste, 2. VI. 1883), Ger. m.-sop. singer, daughter of the bar. Kindermann. Studied with her father, made var. small stage appearances in her youth, 1st appeared as a concert singer at Leipzig in 1871 and on the stage in Berlin in 1874.

Reichmann, Theodor (b. Rostock, 15. III. 1849; d. Marbach, Lake of Constance, 22. V. 1903), Ger. bass singer. Studied in Ger. and with Lamperti at Milan and made his 1st appearance at Magdeburg in 1869.

Reigen (Ger.) = Roundelay.

Reinach, Théodore (b. Saint-Germain-en-Laye, 3. VII. 1860; d. Paris, 30. X. 1928), Fr. archaeologist & hist. Author of several works on Gr. m. and of the libs. of Maurice Emmanuel's *Salamine* (after Aeschylus' *Persae*) and Roussel's *La Naissance de la lyre*.

Reincken. *See* **Reinken.**

Reine de Chypre, La (*The Queen of Cyprus*), opera by Halévy (lib. by Jules Henri Vernoy de Saint-Georges), prod. Paris, Opéra, 22. XII. 1841.

Reine (de France), La (*The Queen of Fr.*), the nickname of a Sym. by Haydn, No. 85, in B♭ maj. (No. 4 of the 'Paris' syms.), comp. *c.* 1786.

Reine de Saba, La (*The Queen of Sheba*), opera by Gounod (lib. by Jules Barbier & Michel Carré), prod. Paris, Opéra, 28. II. 1862.

Reinecke, Carl (Heinrich Carsten) (b. Altona, 23. VI. 1824; d. Leipzig, 10. III. 1910), Ger pfst., cond. & comp. Settled at Leipzig from 1843; cond. of the Gewandhaus concerts and prof. of comp. at the Cons. from 1860. App. pfst. to the Dan. court and several times visited Copenhagen.

Works incl. operas *König Manfred* (after Byron), *Der vierjährige Posten* (after Körner), *Ein Abenteuer Händels*, *Auf hohen Befehl*, *Der Gouverneur von Tours*; incid. m. for Schiller's *Wilhelm Tell*; orat. *Belsazar*; 2 masses; cantatas *Haakon Jarl*, *Die Flucht nach Aegypten*, fairy-tale cantatas for female voices *Schneewittchen*, *Dornröschen*, *Aschenbrödel* & others; 3 syms., ovts. *Dame Kobold* (Calderón's *Dama duende*), *Aladdin*, *Friedensfeier*, *Zenobia* & other orch. works; 3 pf. concs., concs. for v. & for co.; 4 stg. 4tets, wind 8tet, 7 pf. trios & other chamber m.; 3 pf. sos. & many pieces; songs, &c.

Reiner, Jacob (b. Altdorf, Württemberg, *c.* 1560; d. Weingarten, 12. VIII. 1606), Ger. singer & comp. Learnt m. at the monastery of Weingarten and later studied with Lassus at Munich. He returned to Weingarten about 1585 and remained there as singer and choirmaster to his death.

Works incl. masses, motets, magnificats, 3 Passions; Ger. songs for 3–5 voices, &c.

Reinhold, Frederick Charles (b. London, 1737; d. London 29. IX. 1815), Eng. bass singer, son of the Ger. singer Thomas R. (*c.* 1690–1751). who had followed Handel to London. Pupil of his father and chorister at St. Paul's cath. and the Chapel Royal. Made his 1st stage appearance, at Drury Lane Theatre, 1755.

Reinken (or **Reincken**), **Johann Adam** (b. Wilshausen, Alsace, 27. IV. 1623; d. Hamburg, 24. XI. 1722), Ger. orgst. & comp. Pupil of Heinrich Scheidemann. App. orgst. of the church of St. Catherine at Hamburg, 1654, where he remained to his death. Bach walked from Lüneburg as a youth and later came from Cöthen to hear him play and was influenced by him.

Works incl. chorale preludes, toccatas, fugues, &c. for org.; *Hortus musicus* for 2 vs., va. da gamba & bass; keyboard pieces, &c.

Reinthaler, Karl (Martin) (b. Erfurt, 13. X. 1822; d. Bremen, 13. II. 1896), Ger. cond. & comp. After some early mus. training he went to Berlin to study theol., but turned to m., studying under A. B. Marx. With a grant from Frederick William IV he then studied further in Paris and It.; in 1853 he joined the staff of the Cologne Cons. and in 1858 became cath. orgst. and chor. cond. at Bremen.

Works incl. operas *Edda*, *Das Käthchen von Heilbronn* (after Kleist); orat. *Jephtha*, cantata *In der Wüste*; hymns & other church m.; Sym.; partsongs, &c.

Reissiger, Karl (Gottlieb) (b. Belzig nr. Wittenberg, 31. I. 1798; d. Dresden, 7. XI. 1859), Ger. cond. & comp. Studied under his father, the cantor and comp. Christian Gottlieb R., and with Schicht at St. Thomas's School, Leipzig. Later he studied in Vienna and with Winter at Munich, toured in Hol., Fr. & It. in 1824, succeeded Marschner as cond. of the Dresden opera on his return and Weber as cond. of the Ger. opera in 1827.

Works incl. operas *Dido*, *Libella*,

Turandot (after Gozzi), *Die Felsenmühle zu Estalières* & others; melodrama *Yelva*; orat. *David*; masses, motets & other church m.; pf. Conc.; pf. trios & other chamber m.; pf. pieces incl. *Danses brillantes* (with that known as *Webers letzter Gedanke*), &c.

Reiter, Josef (b. Braunau, Upper Aus., 19. I. 1862; d. Vienna, 2. VI. 1939), Aus. comp. Studied with his father, an orgst. Taught and cond. in Vienna, 1886–1907, and was dir. of the Mozarteum at Salzburg, 1908–11.
Works incl. operas *Klopstock in Zürich*, *Der Bundschuh*, *Totentanz* & *Der Tell*; incid. m. for Raimund's *Bauer als Millionär*; masses & Requiem; chor. works; 6 stg. 4tets, 2 stg. 5tets & other chamber m.; part-songs; *c.* 120 songs, &c.

Réjouissance (Fr. = enjoyment). A sprightly mvt. sometimes found as one of the accessory pieces in old suites.

Relative. The connection between maj. and min. keys with the same key-signature is said to be R. Thus E♭ maj. is the R. maj. of C min. (3 ♭s), B min. the R. min. of D maj. (2 ♯s), &c.

Relative Pitch. A person who does not possess the sense of Absolute Pitch i.e. who cannot name any note on hearing it, but who is capable of deducing what any note is from its relationship with any other note already ascertained, is said to have R. P.

Reliquie (Ger. from Lat. = the relic). A nickname sometimes given to Schubert's unfinished C maj. pf. So. begun in 1825, of which only the 1st and slow mvts. were completed. The fragmentary minuet and finale have been completed by Ludwig Stark, by Ernst Křenek and by Willi Rehberg.

Relish (obs.) { (noun). An ornament, a special kind of Turn. (verb) = to ornament.

Rellstab, (Heinrich Friedrich) Ludwig (b. Berlin, 13. IV. 1799; d. Berlin, 27. XI. 1860), Ger. critic, novelist & poet, son of the pub. & critic Johann Karl Friedrich R. (1759–1813). He studied with Ludwig Berger and Bernhard Klein, and followed his father as m. critic of the *Vossische Zeitung* and ed. the mus. periodical *Iris* in 1830–42. He was imprisoned for libelling Henriette Sontag and attacking Spontini. His books incl. var. mus. studies and several novels on mus. themes. Schubert set 10 of his poems to m., incl. *Ständchen*, *see* **Schwanengesang**.

Rémaury, Fanny. *See* **Montigny-Rémaury.**

Reményi, Eduard (real name Hoffmann) (b. Heves or Miskolcz, 1830; d. San Francisco, 15. V. 1898), Hung. vst. Studied at the Vienna Cons. with Joseph Böhm and others. He took part in the 1848 Revol., toured with Brahms in 1852–3 and introd. Hung. gypsy (not folk) m. to him, made friends with Liszt at Weimar and afterwards toured widely in Eur. and U.S.A.

Renard (Stravinsky). *See* **Fox.**

Renaud, Maurice (Arnold) (b. Bordeaux, 24. VII. 1865; d. Paris, 16. X. 1933), Fr. bar. singer. Studied at the Conss. of Paris and Brussels, and in 1883 made his 1st stage appearance at the Théâtre de la Monnaie there. In 1890 he 1st sang in opera in Paris and in 1897 in London.

Rencontre imprévue, La (*The Unforeseen Meeting*), later known as *Les Pèlerins de la Mecque* (*The Pilgrims to Mecca*), opera by Gluck (lib. by L. H. Dancourt, based on a vaudeville by Lesage and d'Orneval), prod. Vienna, Burg Theatre, 7. I. 1764.

Rendano, Alfonso (b. Carolei nr. Cosenza, 5. IV. 1853; d. Rome, 10. IX. 1931), It. pfst. & comp. Studied at Naples and Leipzig, also with Thalberg. Appeared at the Leipzig Gewandhaus in 1872, then in Paris and London, where he remained some time, afterwards becoming pf. prof. at the Naples Cons.
Works incl. opera *Consuelo* (after George Sand); pf. m., &c.

Renié, Henriette (b. Paris, 18. IX. 1875), Fr. hpst. & comp. She studied hp. at the Cons., also comp. with Lenepveu, appearing with great success at an early age.
Works incl. Conc. & *Élégie* for hp. & orch.; Trio for hp., v. & co.; co. & pf. So.; pieces for v. & hp.; many hp. solos and transcriptions of hpchd. pieces; songs, &c.

Rennes, Catharina van (b. Utrecht, 2. VIII. 1858), Dutch singer & comp. Studied singing with Richard Hol and Messchaert, also abroad, taught at Utrecht, Hilversum and The Hague, and comp. children's cantatas, many songs, &c.

Renvoysy, Richard de (b. Nancy, *c.* 1530; d. Dijon, 6. III. 1586), Fr. cleric, lutenist & comp. Canon and choirmaster at the Sainte Chapelle of Dijon. He was condemned to death by fire for immorality.
Works incl. psalms; Anacreontic odes for 4 voices, &c.

Repeat. The restatement of a section of a mus. comp., not written out a 2nd time, but indicated by a special sign of dots placed next to a double bar-line on the side of that part of the m. which is to be repeated. That section itself is given the name of R. In classical m. the expositions of mvts. in so. form are nearly always marked for repetition, and more rarely the working-out and recapitulation also, with or without the coda. Such Rs. are, however, by no means always observed, and indeed need not necessarily be if the R. is just a bare restatement. On the other hand, in cases where different joins at the end of the exposition lead to the R. and to the continuation respectively, a vital incident (the 1st of these joins) may be lost if the R. is not made.

Répétiteur (Fr., but in use elsewhere =coach). The musn. at an opera-house whose function it is to take the singers through their parts, explaining to and teaching them, before they gather for rehearsal with the conductor. He also helps the freak singers—not yet extinct even to-day —who are unable to read m. to memorize their parts.

Repetizione (It.) = Repeat.

Reports (Eng., obs.). An old Eng. term for Imitation.

Reprise (Fr. lit. re-taking = Repetition). Although the Fr. meaning is simply that of Repeat, in Eng. the word is sometimes used in a special sense, indicating the reappearance of the 1st subject in a so.-form mvt. at the point where the recapitulation begins.

Requiem. The Mass for the Dead in the Rom. Catholic church service, used generally on All Souls' Day (2. XI) and specifically at funeral services at any time. It may be sung to plainsong or in more or less elaborate mus. settings. Some of the greatest settings, although orig. written to order (Mozart) or intended for a special religious occasion (Berlioz, Verdi), are now fit mainly or solely for concert use, and some were actually written for that purpose (e.g. Dvořák). The general plan of the R. has been transferred to purely inst. m. by Britten in his *Sinfonia da Requiem.*

Requiem (Brahms). *See* **German Requiem.**

Requiem (Verdi). *See* **Manzoni Requiem.**

Requiem for Rossini. A Mass for the Dead planned by Verdi for perf. in memory of Rossini's death in 1868, his suggestion being that each portion should be written by a different It. comp. of eminence. He himself comp. the 'Libera me' in 1869, and the other contribs. were Bazzini, Cagnoni, Coccia, Mabellini, Pedrotti, Petrella and Ricci. Mercadante was also invited, but was unable to comply on account of blindness and infirmity. The work was never perf. and the comps. all withdrew their contribs. Verdi's was later used, with some alterations, for the Manzoni Requiem of 1873–4.

Rescue Opera. A type of Fr. opera the lib. of which is based on plots, often taken from true happenings (the words *fait historique* sometimes appear in the sub-title), in which the hero or heroine are saved after fearful trials and tribulations. The taste for such works arose during the Revol. The most familiar exs. are Cherubini's *Deux Journées* and Beethoven's *Fidelio,* both with libs. by Bouilly, the latter a Ger. trans. of *Léonore* written for Gaveaux.

Resin. *See* **Rosin.**

Resolution. A term used in harmony for the process by which a discord is made to pass into a concord.

Respighi (*née* **Olivieri-Sangiacomo**), **Elsa** (b. Rome, 24. III. 1894), It. singer & comp. Pupil of Ottorino R. at the Accademia di Santa Cecilia in Rome and later (1919) his wife. She finished the orchn. of his opera *Lucrezia* and wrote one of her own, *Fior di neve,* also a symph. poem, a dance suite for orch, songs from the *Rubáiyát* of Omar Khayyám and many others.

Respighi, Ottorino (b. Bologna, 9. VII. 1879; d. Rome, 18. IV. 1936), It. comp., husband of prec. He entered the Liceo Musicale of Bologna as a v. student in 1891 and received a diploma for v. in 1899. The previous year he began to study comp. under Luigi Torchi and later on under Martucci. In 1900 he became 1st va. in the Opera orch. at St. Petersburg and the next year studied comp. and orchn. with Rimsky-Korsakov. In 1902 he took an additional comp. course with Bruch in Berlin, but returned home in 1903 to join the Mugellini 5tet, of which he remained a member until 1908, when Bologna prod. his 1st opera. In 1913 he was app. prof. of comp. at the Accademia di Santa Cecilia in Rome and toured It. as cond. of his own works. In 1919 he married his pupil Elsa Olivieri-Sangiacomo, a comp. and singer, and from about that time he began to take a keen interest in old It. m. and the church modes. App. dir. of the Accademia in 1923, but resigned in 1925, though retaining the comp. professorship.

Works incl. operas *Re Enzo, Semirama, Belfagor, Marie Victoire, La campana sommersa* (after Gerhard Hauptmann), *La bella addormentata nel bosco, Maria Egiziaca, La fiamma,*

Lucrezia (orchn. finished by his wife), also a transcription of Monteverdi's *Orfeo*; ballets *Scherzo veneziano*, *La Boutique fantasque* (m. adapted from Rossini), *Belkis, regina di Saba*, *Il ponticello dei sospiri* & *Gli uccelli* (adapt. from the orch. suite to form a trilogy with *Maria E.* & *Lucrezia*; 17 orch. works incl. the suites *Fontane di Roma*, *Pini di Roma*, *Vetrate di chiesa*, *Trittico Botticelliano*, *Gli uccelli* (bird pieces by old masters), *Feste romane* & *Sinfonia drammatica*, 2 sets of old lute airs and dances arr., Conc. in the Mixolydian mode, also 3 works by Bach arr.; Fantasy & Toccata for pf. & orch., Conc. in the old style and *Concerto gregoriano* for v. & orch., Adagio with vars. for co. & orch.; Conc. for ob., hn., v., db., pf. & stgs.; 2 stg. 4tets (2nd in the Dorian mode), pf. 5tet; So. in B min. & 5 pieces for v. & pf.; 3 Preludes on a Gregorian melody for pf.; *Aretusa* for m.-sop. & orch.; *La primavera*, for solo voices, chor. & orch.; eds. of Monteverdi's *Lamento d'Arianna* and Marcello's *Didone* for voice & orch.; *Il tramonto* and *La sensitiva* for voice & stg. 4tet; 52 songs, &c.

Respond. The Eng. term for the Responsorium of the Rom. Catholic church service, a later development of Responsorial Psalmody.

Responses. In Angl. church m. the chor. and congregat. cadences answering the versicles read or chanted in monotone by the priest, e.g. the 'Amens' or 'have mercy upon us . . .' at the end of each verse of the Litany.

Responsorial Psalmody. The orig. source of the modern Rom. Catholic Respond and the Angl. Responses: chor. cadences inserted into the psalms sung in monotone or plainsong by a single perf.

Responsorium (Lat.). *See* **Respond.**

Rest. All organized m. consists not only of notes, but also of Rs., which, like the notes, take part of the measured scheme of a comp. and thus have definite time-values in the same way as the notes. Special signs are used to indicate the exact length of the Rs., equivalent to breves, semibreves, crotchets, quavers, and so on. If, for ex., a bar of 4–4 time consists of a crotchet, followed by a silence and 2 other crotchets, that silence filling the 2nd beat must be shown by the symbol of a crotchet rest.

Resta, Natale (b. Milan, ?; d. ?), It. 18th-cent. comp.

Works incl. opera *Gli tre cicisbei ridicoli*, 1748 (containing the song 'Tre giorni son che Nina' usually ascribed to Pergolesi and later said to be by Ciampi, under whose direction R.'s opera was prod. in London, 1749).

Resultant Tones. The secondary sounds prod. by certain intervals of 2 notes struck at the same time, in the nature of inverted Harmonics, since they sound (all but inaudibly) below instead of above the generating notes. There are 2 kinds of R. T.: Differential, prod. by the difference between the 2 generating notes, and Summational, prod. by the sum of these 2 notes, i.e. in both cases the vibrations of these notes.

Resurrection (Alfano). *See* **Risurrezione.**

Reszke, Édouard de (b. Warsaw, 23. XII. 1855; d. Garnek, 25. V. 1917), Pol. bass singer. Pupil of his brother Jean de R. & others. Made his 1st appearance in Verdi's *Aida* at the Théâtre Italien in Paris, 1876.

Reszke, (Jan Mieczyslaw) Jean de (b. Warsaw, 14. I. 1850; d. Nice, 3. IV. 1925), Pol. ten. singer, brother of prec. Sang at Warsaw cath. as a child, studied there and in It. and made his 1st appearance in 1874, at the Teatro La Fenice, Venice.

Retablo de Maese Pedro, El (*Master Peter's Puppet Show*), marionette opera by Falla (lib. by comp., based on a chapter from Cervantes's *Don Quixote*), prod. Seville, 23. III. 1923, in concert form; 1st stage perf. Paris, 25. VI. 1923.

Retardation. A term sometimes used for a process of harmonic resolution similar to that of the Suspension, but with the discordant note going to a concordant one by an upward instead of a downward step.

Retrograde Motion. *See* **Cancrizans** & **Recte et retro.**

Reubke, Julius (b. Hausniendorf nr. Quedlinburg, 23. III. 1834; d. Pillnitz, 3. VI. 1858), Ger. pfst. & comp. Son of the org.-builder Adolf R. (1805–75). Pupil of Liszt at Weimar. His early death cut short a very promising career.

Works incl. org. So. *The 94th Psalm*; So. & pieces for pf.; songs, &c.

Reusner, Esajas (b. ?; d. ?), Ger. 17th-cent. lutenist. Pub. a book of sacred songs arr. for the lute in 1645.

Reusner, Esajas (b. Löwenberg, Silesia, 29. IV. 1636; d. Berlin, 1. V. 1679), Ger. lutenist & comp., son of prec. Studied with a Fr. lutenist at the court of the Pol. Princess Radziwill, became lutenist at the court of Liegnitz-Brieg in 1655 and at that of Brandenburg in 1674.

Works incl. 4 books of lute suites, lute arrs. of 100 sacred tunes, &c.

Reuss, August (b. Liliendorf nr. Znaim, Moravia, 6. III. 1871; d. Munich, 18. VI. 1935), Ger.-Morav.

comp. Pupil of Thuille at Munich, where he became prof. at the Acad. of M. in 1929.

Works incl. opera *Herzog Philipps Brautfahrt*; 2 pantomimes; orch. prologue to Hofmannsthal's *Der Tor und der Tod*; *Johannisnacht*, *Judith*, *Sommer Idylle*, Ballet Suite for orch.; pf. Conc., Serenade for v. & orch.; 2 stg. 4tets, pf. 5tet, stg. Trio; inst. sos.; chors.; songs & duets, &c.

Reutter, (Johann Adam Karl) Georg von (b. Vienna, *c.* III. 1708; d. Vienna, 11. III. 1772), Aus. orgst. & comp., son of the cath. orgst. & comp. Georg R. (1656–1738). Studied under his father, whom he succeeded as orgst. at St. Stephen's cath. in Vienna, 1738, having already become court comp. in 1731. Haydn became his pupil as a cath. choir-boy. He was app. 2nd court mus. dir. in 1746 and 1st on Predieri's retirement in 1751. He married the singer Therese Holzhauser (?–1782) in 1731 and was ennobled in 1740.

Works incl. operas *La pazienza di Socrate* (with Caldara) & *c.* 30 others, shorter stage works; masses with orch., Requiem; orats.; syms., &c.

Reutter, Hermann (b. Stuttgart, 17. VI. 1900), Ger. comp. Studied under Courvoisier and others at Munich. In 1932 he became prof. at the Musikhochschule of Stuttgart and later became dir. of the State Hochschule at Frankfort o/M.

Works incl. operas *Saul*, *Doktor Johannes Faust* (on the old Ger. puppet play) & *Odysseus*; ballet *Die Kirmes von Delft*; incid. m. for *Der verlassene Sohn* (Gide, trans. by Rilke); orats. *Volks-Seele* & *Der grosse Kalender*, cantata *Gesang vom Tode*; chamber m.; pf. works; song cycle *Weise von Liebe und Tod* (Rilke), &c.

Rêve, Le (*The Dream*), opera by Bruneau (lib. by Louis Gallet, based on Zola's novel), prod. Paris, Opéra-Comique, 18. VI. 1891.

Reverse. The Eng. term equivalent to *Rovescio*.

Revolutionary Study. The nickname of Chopin's Study in C min., Op. 10 No. 12, for pf., written at Stuttgart in IX. 1831, where, on his way to Paris, he heard of the taking of Warsaw by the Russ.

Revueltas, Silvestre (b. Santiago Papasquiaro, 31. XII. 1899; d. Mexico City, 5. X. 1940), Mex. vst. & comp. Studied at Mexico City and at St. Edward's Coll., Austin, Texas, also comp. with Felix Borowski at Chicago. App. at Mexico as vst. in 1920, but continued to study the inst. in 1922 under Kochansky and Ševčik. Later he gave recitals of modern m. with Chávez as pfst., whom after some theatre appts. he went to assist in cond. the Orquesta Sinfónica at Mexico, where he also became prof. at the Cons.

Works incl. m. for numerous films; *Cuauhnahuac*, *Esquinas*, *Ventanas*, *Alcancías*, *Colorines*, *Planos*, *Caminos*, *Janitzio*, *homenaje a García Lorca*, *El renacuajo paseador*, *Sensemaya* &c. for orch.; Toccata for v. & small orch.; 3 stg. 4tets, *Feria* for stg. 4tet; pieces for v. & pf.; *Siete canciones* & other songs, &c.

Revutsin, Lev Nikolaievitch (b. Iriovets nr. Poltava, 20. II. 1889), Rus. comp. Pupil of Glière at the Kiev Cons.; began to teach at Kiev in 1924.

Works incl. incid. m. for plays; film m.; cantata *Song to Stalin*; 2 syms.; 2 pf. concs.; war songs, Ukrainian folksong arrs., &c.

Rey, Jean-Baptiste (b. Lauzerte, 18. XII. 1734; d. Paris, 15. VII. 1810), Fr. cond. & comp. Studied at Toulouse, where he became opera cond.; later cond. at var. provincial theatres until 1776, when he went to Paris to assist Gluck at the Opéra. In 1779 he became master of Louis XVI's private m. and in 1787 cond. at the Opéra in succession to Francœur. In 1799–1802 he was prof. at the Cons.

Works incl. operas *Apollon et Coronis* (with his brother, the cst. Louis R., 1737–1811), *La Halte des Savoyards*, *Le Double Mariage* & completion of Sacchini's *Arvire et Evelina*; motets with orch.; solfèges, &c.

Rey, Louis Ernest. *See* **Réyer.**

Reyer, Ernest (Louis Ernest Étienne Rey) (b. Marseilles, 1. XII. 1823; d. Le Lavandou, Hyères, 15. I. 1909), Fr. comp. Learnt m. at the Free School of M. at Marseilles, but showed no exceptional promise. At the age of 16 he was sent to live with an uncle at Algiers and there began to comp. songs, &c., and succeeded in having a Mass perf. at the cath. In 1848 he went to Paris and studied with his aunt, the comp. Louise Farrenc. He met Flaubert, Gautier and others, with whom he had an interest in oriental subjects in common, and they provided him with subjects for comps. He became a critic in the 1850s and in 1871 succeeded d'Ortigue as m. critic to the *Journal des Débats*, becoming a champion of Wagner and the new Fr. school.

Works incl. operas *Maître Wolfram*, *La Statue*, *Érostrate*, *Sigurd* (on the Nibelung Saga), *Salammbô* (after Flaubert); ballet-pantomime *Sacountala* (after Kalidasa); symph. ode

Le Sélam (words by Gautier), dramatic cantata *Victoire*; *L'Hymne du Rhin* for sop., chor. & orch., hymn *L'Union des Arts*; *Ave Maria*, *Salve Regina* & *O Salutaris*; *La Madeleine au désert* for bar. & orch.; male-voice chors.; pf. pieces; songs, &c.

Rezniček, E(mil). N(ikolaus). von (b. Vienna, 4. V. 1860; d. Berlin, 5. VIII. 1945), Aus. cond. & comp. Studied law at Graz, but at 22, when he was already married to Milka Thurn, a kinswoman of Weingartner's, he went to the Leipzig Cons. to study with Reinecke and Jadassohn. He gained stage experience as theatre cond. in var. towns and finally became military cond. at Prague. In 1906 he was app. prof. at the Klindworth-Scharwenka Cons. in Berlin, where he founded a chamber orch., and later he cond. the Warsaw Opera and the Komische Oper in Berlin.

Works incl. operas *Die Jungfrau von Orleans* (after Schiller), *Satanella*, *Emmerich Fortunat*, *Donna Diana* (after Moreto), *Till Eulenspiegel*, *Ritter Blaubart*, *Holofernes* (after Hebbel's *Judith*), *Satuala*, *Spiel oder Ernst?*, *Der Gondoliere des Dogen*; incid. m. for Strindberg's *Dream Play*; Mass in F maj., Requiem in D min., *Vater unser* for chor.; 4 syms. (incl. *Schlemihl* [after Chamisso], 'Tragic' & 'Ironic'), 2 symph. suites, Comedy & Idyllic Ovts., Fugue in C♯ min. for orch.; Serenata for stgs.; v. Conc., Introd. & Valse-Caprice for v. & orch.; *Ruhm und Ewigkeit* (Nietzsche) for ten. & orch.; stg. 4tet in C♯ min., &c.

Rfz. An abbr. used in mus. notation for *Rinforzando*.

Rhapsodie (so-called 'Alto Rhapsody'), a setting of a fragment from Goethe's *Harzreise im Winter* for con. solo, male chor. & orch. by Brahms, Op. 53, comp. in 1869 and 1st perf. Jena, 3. III. 1870.

Rhapsody (from Gr. *rhapsōidos* = reciter; in Fr. *rapsodie*). A R. is thus orig. a recited or chanted poem, esp. an epic one, but the term became adapted to m. of a declamatory character and later, by derivation therefrom, to comps. of an eloquent kind cast in no definite form. The temptation thus arose to call any shapeless work, or any work whose form could not be classified, a R., but good comps. of that kind have, like all good works of art, a satisfactory form of their own, though it may not lend itself to classification.

Rhau, Georg (or Rhaw) (b. Eisfeld, Franconia, *c.* 1488; d. Wittenberg, 6. VIII. 1548), Ger. comp. & pub. Cantor at St. Thomas's School, Leipzig, until 1520, then schoolmaster at Eisleben and printer at Wittenberg, where he pub. var. mus. collections incl. works of his own. Wrote voc. works incl. (?) hymn-tunes.

Rheinberger, Josef (Gabriel) (b. Vaduz, Liechtenstein, 17. III. 1839; d. Munich, 25. XI. 1901), Ger. orgst., teacher & comp. He was so precociously gifted that he was app. orgst. at the parish church of his native place at the age of 7. After some lessons at Feldkirch, he went to the Munich Cons. in 1850, continued to study with F. Lachner on leaving in 1854, supported himself by teaching and in 1859 became pf. prof. at the Cons. He also for a time worked at the Court Opera, and became a church orgst. and chor. cond. When the Cons. was reorganized by Bülow in 1867 he was app. org. and comp. prof. In 1877 he became dir. of the court church m. in succession to Wüllner.

Works incl. operas *Die sieben Raben*, *Der Türmers Töchterlein* & *Das Zauberwort*; incid. m. for Calderón's *Mágico prodigioso*; numerous masses, 3 Requiems, *Stabat Mater*, motets; cantatas & chor. ballads; syms. *Wallenstein* (after Schiller) and 'Florentine,' ovts. to Shakespeare's *Taming of the Shrew* and Schiller's *Demetrius*, *Academic* (*fugal*) *Ovt.* for orch.; 2 org. concs., pf. Conc.; 2 stg. 4tets, 2 pf. trios, pf. 5tet, pf. 4tet,, stg. 5tet; sos. for v. & pf., co. & pf., hn. & pf.; 20 org. sos. and many other org. works; numerous pf. works; songs, partsongs, &c.

Rheingold, Das (*The Rhinegold*, Wagner). *See* **Ring des Nibelungen.**

Rhené-Baton (real name René Baton) (b. Courseulles-sur-Mer, Calvados, 5. IX. 1879; d. Chatou, Seine-et-Oise, 9. X. 1940), Fr. cond. & comp. Studied at the Paris Cons. and worked in Paris, Bordeaux and Angers; in 1916 he returned to Paris as cond. of the Pasdeloup concerts.

Works incl. Suite for orch.; Vars. for pf. & orch.; *Suite bretonne* & var. pieces for pf.; songs, &c.

'Rhenish' Symphony. The name of Schumann's 3rd Sym., in E♭ maj., Op. 97, begun after a Rhine excursion in IX. 1850. The 4th of the 5 mvts. is an impression of Cologne cath. 1st perf. Düsseldorf, 6. II. 1851.

Rhythm. In a larger sense the word means all that is concerned in m. with matters dependent on time, such as the metre, the proper division of the m. into bars, the distribution and balance of phrases, &c. But it also implies the proper perf. of m. in a natural, living and breathing way, as distinct from a merely mechanical accuracy. What is often called R. in modern dance m., which is rigidly accurate in time, is therefore not R., but merely a strict application of Time.

Rhythmic Modes. *See* **Modes, Rhythmic.**

Rhythmicon. An inst. invented by Lev Theremin and Henry Cowell for the artificial prod. of rhythms and cross-rhythms.

Riadis, Emil (b. Salonika, 13. V. 1890; d. Salonika, 17. VII. 1935), Gr. comp. Studied with Mottl and others at Munich and with Ravel in Paris.

Works incl. operas *Le Chant sur le fleuve, Galatea* & *La Route verte*; incid. m. for Euripides' *Hecuba* & Wilde's *Salome*; Byzantine Mass; symph. poem *Arel* & other orch. works; chamber m.; pf. pieces, &c.

Ribattuta. *See* **Ornaments.**

Ribeca (It.) = Rebec.

Ribible (Eng., obs.). Another old word for the Rebec, or for a slightly different inst. of the same type.

Riccardo I, rè d'Inghilterra (*Richard I, King of England*), opera by Handel (lib. by Paolo Antonio Rolli), prod. London, King's Theatre, Haymarket, 11. XI. 1727.

Ricci, Federico (b. Naples, 22. X. 1809; d. Conegliano, 10. XII. 1877), It. comp. Studied with Bellini and Zingarelli at the Naples Cons. In 1835 he prod. his 1st opera with his brother at Naples and the 1st of his own at Venice and in 1853, after several stage successes, he became mus. dir. at the imp. theatres in St. Petersburg.

Works incl. operas *Monsieur de Chalumeaux, Le prigione d'Edimburgo, Un duello sotto Richelieu, Luigi Rolla e Michelangelo, Corrado d'Altamura, Vallombra, Isabella de' Medici, Estella di Murcia, Griselda, I due ritratti, Il marito e l'amante, Il paniere d'amore, Une Folie à Rome, Le Docteur rose* & 4 others in collab. with L. R.; 2 masses; cantata for the marriage of Victor Emmanuel; songs, &c.

Ricci, Luigi (b. Naples, 8. VII. 1805; d. Prague, ? 21. XII. 1859), It. comp., brother of prec. Studied under Zingarelli at the Naples Cons., where he and Bellini became subprofs. in 1819. His 1st opera was prod. there in 1823. In 1835, after a number of successful prods., he became cond. of the Opera and mus. dir. of the cath. at Trieste. In 1844 he married Lidia Stoltz of Prague, where he was confined in an asylum in 1859, having become hopelessly insane.

Works incl. opera *L'impresario in angustie, Il diavolo condannato, Il Colombo, L'orfanella di Ginevra, Chiara di Rosemberg, Il nuovo Figaro, Un' avventura di Scaramuccia, Gli esposti* (*Eran due ed or son tre*), *Chi dura vince, Chiara di Montalbano, La serva e l'ussaro, Le nozze di Figaro* (after Beaumarchais), *Il birraio di Preston, La festa di Piedigrotta, Il diavolo a quattro* & 14 others incl. 4 in collab. with F. R.; church m.; song-books *Mes Loisirs* & *Les Inspirations du thé*, &c.

Operas written jointly by the 2 brothers: *Il colonello, Il disertore per amore, L'amante di Richiamo* & *Crispino e la comare.*

Ricciardo e Zoraide, opera by Rossini (lib. by Marchese Francesco Berio di Salsa), prod. Naples, Teatro San Carlo, 3. XII. 1818.

Riccio, (Antonio) Teodoro (b. Brescia, *c.* 1540; d. Ansbach, after 1594), It. comp. Choirmaster at a church at Brescia, app. mus. dir. by the Margrave of Brandenburg-Ansbach, settled there and followed the margrave to Königsberg in 1579, having become a Lutheran, and returned to Ansbach with his patron in 1586. Eccard served under him there from 1581 and succeeded him at his death.

Works incl. motets & other church m.; madrigals, *Canzoni alla napoletana*, &c.

Ricercare (It. = to search out). A fugal comp., also called *ricercar* or *ricercata*, the inst. counterpart of the motet or madrigal in the 17th cent., played on keyboard insts. or by a consort of stg. of wind insts. and using the fugal devices in a strictly scientific way (in the way of 'research'), but not introd. independent episodes.

Ricercata. *See* **Ricercare.**

Richafort, Jean (b. ?; d. ?), Flem. 16th-cent. comp. Pupil of Josquin des Prés. He was choirmaster at the church of Saint-Gilles at Bruges in the 1540s. Wrote masses, motets, chansons, &c.

Richard I (Cœur de Lion) (b. ?., IX. 1157; d. ?, 6. IV. 1199), King of Eng. & Fr. trouvère. He was the son of Henry II, and his mother was Eleanor of Aquitaine. He introd. the art of the Troubadours to the north of Fr. and this estab. the school of the Trouvères to which he belonged both as poet & musn. According to legend another trouvère, Blondel de Nesle, discovered his place of imprisonment in Aus. in 1192, when he is said to have sung outside the castle of Dürenstein and to have been answered by R. in song from within, a story which furnished the plot for the following opera:

Richard Cœur-de-Lion, opera by Grétry (lib. by Jean Michel Sedaine), prod. Paris, Comédie-Italienne, 21. X. 1784. Beethoven wrote pf. vars. on the song 'Une fièvre brûlante' from it.

Richards, Henry Brinley (b. Carmarthen, 13. XI. 1817; d. London, 1. V. 1885), Welsh pfst. & comp. Studied at the R.A.M. in London and with Chopin in Paris. Settled in London, where he taught the pf. and lectured on Welsh m.

Works incl. Ovt. in F min.; add. songs for Auber's *Diamants de la couronne*; pf. pieces; songs, incl. 'God bless the Prince of Wales'; partsongs, &c.

Richardson, Ferdinand(o) (real surname Heybourne) (b. ?, *c.* 1558; d. Tottenham, 4. VI. 1618), Eng. comp. Pupil of Tallis. Groom of the Privy Chamber, 1587–1611. Comp. virginal pieces, &c.

Richardson, Samuel (1689–1761), Eng. novelist. *See* **Buona figliuola** (Piccinni), **Generali** (*Pamela nubile*), **Maid of the Mill** (Arnold), **Traetta** (*Buona figliuola maritata*).

Richardson, Vaughan (b. London, ?; d. ? Winchester, 26. VI. 1729), Eng. orgst. & comp. Pupil of Blow in the Chapel Royal. App. orgst of Winchester cath. in 1692.

Works incl. services, anthems *O Lord God of my salvation, O how amiable* & others; *Song in Praise of St. Cecilia*; *Entertainment for the Peace of Ryswick*; songs for 1–3 voices with insts., &c.

Richepin, Jean (1849–1926), Fr. poet & dramatist. *See* **Chemineau** (Leroux), **Cui** (*Flibustier* & songs), **Dupont** (*La Glu*), **Georges** (*Miarka*), **Leroux** (*Xantho chez les courtisanes*).

Richter, Ferdinand (Tobias) (b. Würzburg, 1649; d. Vienna, 1711), Ger. orgst. & comp. App. court orgst. in Vienna, succeeding Poglietti, in 1683, and m. teacher to the imp. children.

Works incl. serenatas *L'istro ossequioso* & *Le promesse degli dei*; sacred dramas for the Jesuit Coll.; so. for 7 insts. & others in 8 parts, balletti in 4 & 5 parts; org. toccatas & other works; suites for hpchd., &c.

Richter, Franz Xaver (b. Holešov, Moravia, 1. XII. 1709; d. Strasburg, 12. IX. 1789), Morav. bass singer & comp. Mus. dir. at the abbey of Kempten, 1740–7, singer and vst. at Mannheim, 1749–69, when he went to Strasburg as mus. dir. to the cath. At Mannheim his work made him a prominent member of that school of symphonists.

Works incl. 28 masses, 2 Requiems, 38 motets, 16 psalms; 64 syms.; 6 stg. 4tets, &c.

Richter, Hans (b. Györ, Hung., 4. IV. 1843; d. Bayreuth, 5. XII. 1916), Aus.-Hung. cond. Studied in Vienna, where he played hn. at the Kärntnertor Theatre, 1862–6. Asst. to Wagner, opera cond. at Budapest and Vienna; 1st to cond. Wagner's *Ring* at Bayreuth, 1876; cond. much in London between 1877 and 1910. Cond. of the Hallé Orch., Manchester, 1900–11.

Richter, Johann Paul Friedrich (called Jean Paul) (1763–1825), Ger. novelist. *See* **Heller.**

Ricochet (Fr. = rebound). A special kind of *staccato* in V. m., prod. by letting the bow bounce on the stgs., whereas in ord. *staccato* it remains on the stg. and is moved in rapid jerks.

Ricordi, Giovanni (b. Milan, 1785; d. Milan, 15. III. 1853), It. m. pub. Founded the pub. house at Milan *c.* 1808.

Ricordi, Giulio (b. Milan, 19. XII. 1840; d. Milan, 6. VI. 1912), It. m. pub., grandson of prec. Became head of the Milan firm on his father's death in 1888. He was also a comp. under his own name and that of J. Burgmein.

Ricordi, Tito (b. Milan, 29. X. 1811; d. Milan, 7. IX. 1888), It. m. pub., father of prec. Succeeded his father, Giovanni R., in 1853.

Riddle Canon. A form of canon, in which esp. the 15th-cent. Flems. delighted, written in a single part with no indication where the subsequent entries of the parts are to occur, the perfs. being left to guess how the m. fits or to find it out by experiment.

Riders to the Sea, opera by Vaughan Williams (lib. John Millington Synge's play), prod. London, R.C.M., 1. XII. 1937; 1st public perf. Cambridge, Arts Theatre, 22. II. 1938.

Ridotto. *See* **Redoute.**

Riedel, Carl (b. Kronenberg nr. Elberfeld, 6. X. 1827; d. Leipzig, 3. VI. 1888), Ger. chor. cond. Studied at the Leipzig Cons. after starting life in commerce and founded a chor. soc. there.

Rieder, Ambrosius (b. Döbling nr. Vienna, 10. X. 1771; d. Perchtoldsdorf nr. Vienna, 19. XI. 1855), Aus. comp. Pupil of Albrechtsberger in Vienna, where he became a choirmaster later on.

Works incl. masses & other church m.; chamber m.; org. works, &c.

Riegger, Wallingford (b. Albany, Ga., 29. IV. 1885), Amer. comp. Studied in N.Y. and Berlin, with Goetschius, Stillman - Kelley and others. After cond. in Ger., he returned to U.S.A., where he held var. teaching appts.

Works incl. *Amer. Polonaise*—

Triple Jazz, Rhapsody, Fantasy & Fugue, Lyric Suite, 2 Dance Suites, Canon & Fugue, &c. for orch.; var. works for dancers; *La Belle Dame sans merci* (Keats) for 4 voices & chamber orch.; *Dichotomy* & *Scherzo* for chamber orch.; *Study in Sonority* for 10 vs.; stg. 4tet in G min., pf. Trio, *Divertissement* for hp., fl. & co., 3 Canons for woodwind & other chamber m.; Suite for solo fl., &c.

Riemann, (Karl Wilhelm Julius) Hugo (b. Grossmehlra nr. Sondershausen, 18. VII. 1849; d. Leipzig, 10. VII. 1919), Ger. mcolst. Studied law at Berlin and Tübingen, m. at the Leipzig Cons. and later became lecturer at the Univ. there, 1878–80, and again, after var. appts. elsewhere, in 1895–1901, when he became prof. Among his many mus. - literary works are a *Musiklexikon, Handbuch der Musikgeschichte, Opernhandbuch*, works on notation, harmony, phrasing, hist., &c. He ed. many standard works.

Rienzi, der letzte der Tribunen (*R., the Last of the Tribunes*: first called *Cola Rienzi, . . .*), opera by Wagner (lib. by comp., based on Bulwer-Lytton's novel and, farther back, on Mary Russell Mitford's play), prod. Dresden, 20. X. 1842.

Ries. Ger. family of musns.:

1. Johann R. (b.Benzheim o/Rhine, 1723; d. Cologne, 1784), vst. & tpt. player. Worked at the court of the Elector of Cologne at Bonn.

2. Anna R. (b. ?; d. ?), sop. singer, daughter of prec. Also active at Bonn.

3. Franz (Anton) R. (b. Bonn, 10. XI. 1755; d. Bonn, 1. XI. 1846), vst., brother of prec. Studied v. with Salomon, began to play in the Bonn orch. at 11 and at 19 was app. with a salary, receiving a better post in 1779, when he paid a visit to Vienna. Beethoven was his pupil.

4. Ferdinand R. (b. Bonn, XI. 1784; d. Frankfort o/M., 13. I. 1838), pfst., vst. & comp., son of prec. Pupil of his father, of B. Romberg for co. and of Beethoven, whose friend he remained. After a short course in comp. with Winter at Munich in 1801, he went to Vienna that year, remaining, in close touch with Beethoven, until 1805, studying with Albrechtsberger and becoming pfst. to Counts Browne and Lichnowsky. Later he lived by turns in Paris, Vienna, Cassel, Stockholm and St. Petersburg. In 1813–24 he lived in London, where he married an Englishwoman and played, taught and comp. much. He bought a property at Godesberg nr. Bonn, but in 1826 went to live at Frankfort, where he returned again after 2 years as cond. at Aachen, 1834–6. He cond. several of the Lower Rhine Festivals.

Works incl. operas *Die Räuberbraut, Liska* (*The Sorceress*) & *Eine Nacht auf dem Libanon*; orats. *Der Sieg des Glaubens* & *Die Könige Israels*; 6 syms., 4 ovts.; 9 pf. concs.; 14 stg. 4tets, 6 stg. 5tets, 3 pf. 4tets, 5 pf. trios, Octet, 7tet & other chamber m.; 20 duets for v. & pf.; 10 sos. and many other works for pf., &c.

5. Peter Joseph R. (b. Bonn, 6. IV. 1791; d. London, 6. IV. 1882), pfst., brother of prec. He lived in London, was a friend of Charles Lamb and worked for a time in Broadwood's pf. manufacture, also taught the pf.

6. Hubert R. (b. Bonn, 1. IV. 1802; d. Berlin, 14. IX. 1886), vst., brother of prec. Pupil of his father and Spohr. Held var. appts. in Berlin from 1824.

7. Louis R. (b. Berlin, 30. I. 1830; d. London, 3. X. 1913), vst., son of prec. Studied under his father and Vieuxtemps, and lived in London from 1853.

8. Adolph R. (b. Berlin, 20. XII. 1837; d. London, IV. 1899), pfst. & comp., brother of prec. Studied pf. with Kullak and comp. with Boehmer. Settled in London as pf. teacher. Comp. pf. works & songs.

9. Franz R. (b. Berlin, 7. IV. 1846; d. Naumburg, 20. VI. 1932), vst. & ed., brother of prec. Pupil of his father and of Massart and Vieuxtemps in Paris. Appeared in London in 1870, but later gave up playing and took to m. pub. and ed.

Rieti, Vittorio (b. Alexandria, 28. I. 1898), It. comp. Studied with Frugatta at Milan and Respighi in Rome, but destroyed all his works written up to 1920.

Works incl. opera *Teresa nel bosco*; ballets *Noah's Ark, Barabau, Waltz Academy, The Sleep-walker, Robinson and Friday* (after Defoe) & *David's Triumph*; incid. m. for Pierre Corneille's *L'Illusion comique* & Giraudoux's *Électre*; Sym.; Conc. for wind insts. & orch., v. Conc., clavichord Conc.; *Madrigal* for 12 insts., So. for fl., ob., bn. & pf.; pf. pieces, &c.

Rietz, Eduard (b. Berlin, 17. X. 1802; d. Berlin, 23. I. 1832), Ger. vst. Pupil of his father and of Rode. He joined the royal orch. in Berlin and founded an orch. of his own, but suffered from consumption and had to give up work.

Rietz, Julius (b. Berlin, 28. XII. 1812; d. Dresden, 12. IX. 1877), Ger. comp. & cond., brother of prec. Studied under his father, co. under B. Romberg and others, and comp. under Zelter. In 1835 he succeeded Mendelssohn as cond. of the opera at Düsseldorf, but the next year became town mus. dir. and cond. the orch. and chor. concerts. In 1847–60 he was cond. of the Voc. Academy and the Gewandhaus orch. at Leipzig and taught comp. at the Cons. In 1860 he was app. cond. of the Royal Opera, dir. of the church chapel and of the Cons. at Dresden.

Works incl. operas *Der Corsar, Das Mädchen aus der Fremde* & *Georg Neumark*, operetta *Jery und Bätely* (Goethe); incid. m. for Shakespeare's *Hamlet* & *As You Like It*, Holtei's *Lorbeerbaum und Bettelstab* and plays by Goethe, Calderón, Immermann, &c.; 2 syms. & 3 ovts.; *Altdeutscher Schlachtgesang* & *Dithyrambe* for male chor. & orch., &c.

Rigadoon (Eng.)
Rigaudon (Fr.) } A Fr. dance, prob. from the south (Provence or Languedoc), dating back to the 17th cent. at the latest. It is in lively common or 2–4 time and consists of 3 or 4 parts, each repeated, the 3rd being the shortest.

Rigby, George Vernon (b. Birmingham, 21. I. 1840; d. ?), Eng. ten. singer. Made his 1st appearance in London, in 1861, later studied at Milan, where he sang in opera, as also in Berlin and Copenhagen.

Righetti-Giorgi, Geltrude (not Maria Brighenti). *See* **Giorgi-Righetti.**

Righini, Vincenzo (b. Bologna, 22. I. 1756; d. Bologna, 19. VIII. 1812), It. singer & comp. Having been a choir-boy at Bologna cath., he studied with Martini there, later sang in opera in Prague and Vienna, and prod. his 1st stage works. In 1788–92 he was at the court of Mainz and in 1793 he was app. mus. dir. at the It. Opera in Berlin and married the singer Henriette Kneisel (1767–1801). The Opera gradually deteriorated in favour of Ger. opera, and in 1812 he returned to Bologna in poor health.

Works incl. operas *La vedova scaltra, Il Demogorgone, Il convitato di pietra* (*Don Giovanni*), *Alcide al Bivio, Eneo nel Lazio, Il trionfo d'Arianna, Armida, Tigrane, Gerusalemme liberata* (after Tasso), *La selva incantata* & others; ballet *Minerva belebt die Statuen des Dädalus*; Requiem, Missa solemnis, Te Deum & other church m.; cantatas; songs, &c.

Rigoletti (It., plur.). Old It. round dances.

Rigoletto, opera by Verdi (lib. by Francesco Maria Piave, based on Victor Hugo's play *Le Roi s'amuse*), prod. Venice, Teatro la Fenice, 11. III. 1851.

Riisager, Knudaage (b. Port Kunda, Estonia, 6. III. 1897), Dan. comp. Studied polit. economy at Copenhagen Univ., but later turned to m., studying comp. with Peder Gram and Otto Malling, later with Roussel and Le Flem in Paris and finally with Hermann Grabner at Leipzig.

Works incl. ballets *Benzin, Cocktail Party* & *Slaraffenland* (*Land of Cockaigne*); incid. m. to Johannes Jensen's fairy play *Darduse*; chor. works; 3 syms., Vars. *Poème mécanique, Jabiru T—DOXC* & ovt. to Holberg's *Erasmus Montanus* for orch.; Conc. for tpt. & stgs.; 5 stg. 4tets, So. for fl., cl., v. & co., Serenade for fl., v. & co.; v. & pf. So.; So. & var. pieces for pf.; songs, &c.

Rilke, Rainer Maria (1875–1926), Ger. poet. *See* **Beck** (*Lyric Cantata*), **Burkhard** (song cycle), **Hindemith** (*Marienleben*), **Klenau, Martin (F.)** (*Cornet*), **Marx (K.)** (chors. & songs), **Reutter (H.)** (*Weise von Liebe & Tod* & play trans. from Gide), **Webern** (songs), **Weill** (songs with orch.).

Rimbaud, (Jean) Arthur (1854–91), Fr. poet. *See* **Britten** (*Illuminations*).

Rimbault, Edward Francis (b. London, 13. VI. 1816; d. London, 26. IX. 1876), Eng. mus. historian & antiquarian. After beginning his career as an orgst. he took part in the foundation of the Mus. Antiquarian Soc. in 1840 and became its secretary, also of the Percy Soc., and he ed. old Eng. m. for both. He also ed. much old church, oratorio &c. m. independently, collected a library and wrote several learned books on the org., the pf., old Eng. voc. m., &c. Comp. an operetta *The Fair Maid of Islington*, incid. m., a cantata *Country Life*, songs, &c.

Rimington, A(lexander). Wallace (1854–1918), Eng. painter and prof. of fine arts. Inventor of a 'Colour Organ' first shown in London in 1895.

Rimonte. *See* **Ruimonte.**

Rimsky-Korsakov, Andrey Nikolaievitch (b. St. Petersburg, 17. X. 1878; d. Leningrad, 23. V. 1940), Rus. critic & mus. hist. Studied at the Univs. of St. Petersburg, Strasburg and Heidelberg, and did not turn to m. until 1913, after his father's death. In 1915 he founded a monthly mus. journal and in 1922 he became ed. of another. He ed. his father's and Glinka's memoirs, Mussorgsky's letters and documents, Cui's critical writings, his father's correspondence with Tchaikovsky; wrote on Mussorgsky's *Boris Godunov*, the mus.

MSS. in the Leningrad Public Library, of which he was curator, &c. He married the comp. Julia Lazarevna Weissberg (b. 1878).

Rimsky-Korsakov, Nikolai Andreievitch (b. Tikhvin, Gvt. Novgorod, 18. III. 1844; d. Liubensk, 21. VI. 1908), Rus. comp., father of prec. He came of a naval family and his ambition was to become a sailor, though he showed great interest in the Rus. folksongs and church m. he heard in his childhood, as well as in the operas he knew from pf. selections. In 1856 he was sent to the Naval Coll. at St. Petersburg, where he remained until 1862. He had more pf. lessons during that time and learnt a little theory, but was not taught anything systematic even when in 1861 he met Balakirev and his circle, and came under their influence. He began a Sym. in E♭ min., but in 1862 was ordered on a 3-years' cruise. He wrote the slow mvt. of the Sym. off Gravesend and heard opera in London and N.Y., but did not take up m. again until his return to St. Petersburg in 1865, when he worked more seriously under Balakirev, who cond. the Sym. The 1st important works were the symph. poem *Sadko* (1867) and the programme sym. *Antar* (1868). In 1868 he also began his 1st opera, *The Maid of Pskov*, finished in 1872. Meanwhile he had been app. prof. of comp. at the Cons., though in theor. knowledge he was always little more than 1 lesson ahead of his pupils, and in 1872 he married the pfst. Nadezhda Purgold. App. inspector of naval bands in 1873 and dir. of the Free School of M. in 1874, in succession to Balakirev, until 1881, when he became the latter's asst. in the dir. of the Imp. Chapel. He became rather pedantically scholastic during those years, in reaction against his earlier amateurism, but this tendency was counteracted by his interest in Rus. folk m. and by the influence of Wagner. In 1892–3 he had a serious nervous breakdown and temporarily took a dislike to m., but his interest revived. In 1905, when he had sided with the 'wrong' party during political disturbances, he was dismissed from the Cons., but there was such a storm of protest that he was reinstated later; but his last opera, based on Pushkin's *Golden Cockerel* (comp. 1906–7), was a satire on official stupidity and its perf. was forbidden. He cond. a festival of Rus. m. in Paris at Diaghilev's invitation in 1907. In 1908 he suffered from angina and d. 4 days after the marriage of his daughter Nadia to his pupil M. Steinberg.

Works incl. operas *The Maid of Pskov* (*Ivan the Terrible*), *A Night in May*, *The Snow Maiden* (*Snegurotchka*), *Mlada* (based on the collective opera commissioned earlier from him, Borodin, Cui and Mussorgsky), *Christmas Eve*, *Sadko*, *Mozart and Salieri*, *Boyarina Vera Sheloga* (prologue to *The Maid of Pskov*), *The Tsar's Bride*, *The Legend of Tsar Saltan*, *Servilia*, *Kashtchey the Immortal*, *Pan Voievoda*, *The Legend of the Invisible City of Kitezh*, *The Golden Cockerel*; 3 syms. (2nd *Antar*); symph. poem *Sadko*, concert ovts. on Rus. themes & *Russian Easter*, Fantasy on Serbian themes, Sinfonietta on Rus. themes, symph. suite *Shahrazad*, *Spanish Capriccio*, *Fairy-Tale*, *On the Tomb* (Belaiev's) & *Dubinushka* for orch.; pf. Conc. & fantasy for v. & orch. (both on Rus. themes); 2 stg. 4tets (2nd unpub.) & 3 movts. for stg. 4tet contrib. to collective sets by var. comps., stg. 6tet, 5tet for pf. & wind insts.; 4 cantatas; pf. pieces; many partsongs, songs, voc. duets, 2 collections of Rus. folksongs, &c.

Rinaldo, cantata for ten. solo, male chor. & orch. by Brahms, Op. 50, on a ballad by Goethe, prod. Vienna, 28. II. 1869.

Opera by Handel (lib. by Giacomo Rossi, from a sketch based on Tasso by Aaron Hill), prod. London, Queen's Theatre, Haymarket, 24. II. 1711. H.'s 1st London opera.

Rinaldo di Capua (b. Capua or Naples, c. 1715; d. ? Rome, after 1771), It. comp. Being (?) the natural son of an exalted personage in the Kingdom of Naples, he made himself known only under his assumed name when he took to m. professionally. He prod. his 1st opera in Rome in 1737. Numerous operas and intermezzi of his were prod. thereafter in It., and the pasticcio-intermezzo *La zingara* in Paris in 1753. But nearly all his work is lost, having been sold as waste paper by his son. Burney met him in Rome in 1770 in poor circumstances and recommended him to William Parsons as teacher of comp.

Works incl. operas *Ciro riconosciuto*, *Vologeso rè de' Parti*, *Mario in Numidia*, *La forza della pace*, *Adriano in Siria* & c. 7 others; intermezzi *Il bravo burlato*, *La donna superba*, *Le donne ridicole*, *I finti pazzi per amore* & c. 15 others; *Cantata per la natività della Beata Vergine* & others, &c.

Rinck, Johann Christian Heinrich (b. Elgersburg, Saxe-Gotha, 18. II. 1770; d. Darmstadt, 7. VIII. 1846), Ger. orgst., comp. & teacher. Studied at Erfurt under the Bach pupil Kittel. In 1805 he settled at Darmstadt, where he became prof., court orgst. and ducal chamber musn.

Works incl. *Practical Org. School* and many other works for org.; motets and *Pater noster* for voices & org.; sos. for pf., v. & pf., co. & pf.; pf. duets, &c.

Rinf. An abbr. often used in mus. notation for

Rinforzando (It. = reinforcing). A sudden *crescendo* made on a short phrase, similar to the *sforzando*, which is made on a single note or chord.

Ring des Nibelungen, Der (*The Nibelung's Ring*), trilogy of m.-dramas, with a prologue, by Wagner (lib. by comp. based on the Nibelung Saga):

Das Rheingold (*The Rhinegold*), prod. Munich, Court Opera, 22. IX. 1869.

Die Walküre (*The Valkyrie*), prod. Munich, Court Opera, 26. VI. 1870.

Siegfried, prod. Bayreuth, Wagner Festival Theatre, 16. VIII. 1876.

Götterdämmerung (*The Dusk of the Gods*), prod. Bayreuth, Wagner Festival Theatre, 17. VIII. 1876.

The whole cycle prod. Bayreuth, Wagner Festival Theatre, 13–17. VIII. 1876.

Rinuccini, Ottavio (1562–1621), It. poet & libst. *See* **Arianna** (Monteverdi), **Bonini** (*Lamento d'Arianna*), **Camerata, Dafne** (Gagliano, Peri & Schütz), **Euridice** (Caccini & Peri), **Petrassi** (*Lamento d'Arianna*).

Rios, Alvaro de los (b. ?; d. ? Madrid, 1623), Spa. comp. App. chamber musn. to the queen, Margaret of Aus., in 1607.

Works incl. incid. m. to Tirso de Molina's play *El vergonzoso en palacio*, &c.

Riotte, Philipp Jacob (b. Trèves, 16. VIII. 1776; d. Vienna, 20. VIII. 1856), Ger. cond. & comp. Studied with André at Offenbach, became theatre cond. at Gotha and in 1809 went to Vienna, where he settled, being app. cond. at the Theater an der Wien in 1818.

Works incl. operas & operettas *Mozarts Zauberflöte, Nureddin, Der Sturm* (on Shakespeare's *Tempest*) & many others; ballets; incid. m.; cantata *Der Kreuzzug*; Sym.; 3 cl. concs.; 6 v. & pf. sos.; 9 pf. sos., pf. piece *The Battle of Leipzig*, &c.

Ripieno (It. = replenished, supplementary). The name of the passages in works of the *concerto grosso* type in which the whole orch. takes part, as distinct from the *concertino* played by the solo insts.

Ripresa (It. = re-taking, repetition). A refrain, esp. in the 14th–15th-cent. It. ballata and frottola.

Riquier, Guiraut (b. ?; d. ?, 1292), Fr. troubadour. He was the last great exponent of this particular minstrel art. 48 tunes of his songs are extant.

Riseley George (b. Bristol, 28. VIII. 1845; d. Bristol, 12. IV. 1932), Eng. orgst. & cond. Held var. orgst.'s posts at Bristol, incl. Colston Hall and the cath., started orch. concerts in 1877, founded the Bristol Chor. Soc. in 1889 and began a triennial Bristol Festival in 1896.

Risler, (Joseph) Édouard (b. Baden-Baden, 23. II. 1873; d. Paris, 22. VII. 1929), Fr. pfst. of Ger. descent. Studied at the Paris Cons. and later. in Ger. with d'Albert, Klindworth and others. He was pf. prof. at the Cons. in 1907–9 and toured widely as a recitalist, esp. an exponent of Beethoven's sos.

Rispetto. A type of old It. improvised folk poem of 6–10 (usually 8) inter-rhyming lines, sung to popular tunes.

Risposta (It. = response, answer). Another term for the 2nd statement of a fugue subject, which is rather like an answer to a question and is, in fact, technically called the Answer, or R. in contradistinction to the *Proposta*. The Lat. terms *Dux* and *Comes* also correspond to the P. and R., or subject and answer.

Rist, Johann (b. Ottensen nr. Hamburg, 8. III. 1607; d. Wedel o/Elbe, 31. VIII. 1667), Ger. clergyman, poet and musn. He founded a song school at Hamburg and wrote words for a great number of songs and hymns, some of which he comp. himself.

Ristori, Giovanni Alberto (b. Bologna, 1692; d. Dresden, 7. II. 1753), It. comp. Settled at Dresden in 1715, having gone there with an It. theatrical co. directed by his father. In 1717 he was app. comp. to the It. Opera and dir. of the Pol. chapel, and in 1733 court orgst.

Works incl. operas *Calandro, Le fate* & 15 others; 3 orats.; 15 masses, 3 Requiems, *Stabat Mater*, motets & other church m., &c.

Risurrezione (*Resurrection*), opera by Alfano (lib. by Cesare Hanau, based on Tolstoy's novel), prod. Turin, Teatro Vittorio Emanuele, 30. XI. 1904.

Ritardando (It.) = retarding. The same direction is also expressed by *rallentando* (slowing down) or *ritenuto* (holding back).

Rite of Spring, The, ballet by Stravinsky (scen. by comp. & Nikolay Roerich, chgph. by Vaslav Fomitch Nizhinsky), prod. as *Le Sacre du printemps*, Paris, Théâtre des

Champs-Élysées, 29. V. 1913. There was a riot between partisans and opponents on the first night.

Ritenuto (It.) = holding back. The same direction is also expressed by *rallentando* (slowing down) or *ritardando* (retarding).

Ritmo di . . . battute (It. = rhythm of . . . beats). An indication that the metrical scheme of a piece or mvt. is to be accented in groups of as many bars as may be shown in this direction between the 2nd & 3rd word, e.g. in the scherzo of Beethoven's 9th Sym., where the metre changes between *ritmo di tre battute* and *ritmo di quattro battute.*

Ritornello (It. lit. 'little return'). Orig. a refrain and thence, in the early 17th cent., a recurrent inst. piece played in the course of a mus. stage work; later the inst. passages between voc. portions of an anthem or aria, from which in turn is derived the meaning of the word R. as applied to the orch. *tutti* in concs., esp. in rondos where the same theme returns several times. *See also* **Stornello.**

Ritorno d'Ulisse in patria, Il (*Ulysses' Return to his Country*), opera by Monteverdi (lib. by Giacomo Badoaro), prod. Venice, Teatro San Cassiano, II. 1641.

Ritter, Alexander (b. Narva, Rus., 27. VI. 1833; d. Munich, 12. IV. 1896), Ger. vst., cond. & comp. Studied v. with Franz Schubert of Dresden and later went to the Leipzig Cons. Married Wagner's niece, Franziska W., in 1854, became an ardent Wagnerian, cond. at Stettin in 1856, settled at Würzburg in 1863, ran a m. shop there in 1875–82 and then joined the ducal orch. at Meiningen under Bülow, whose retirement caused him to move to Munich in 1886.

Works incl. operas *Der faule Hans* & *Wem die Krone?*; symph. poems, &c.

Ritter Blaubart (*Knight Bluebeard*), opera by Rezniček (lib. by Herbert Eulenberg), prod. Darmstadt, 29. I. 1920.

Ritter, Christian (b. ?; d. ?), Ger. 17th–18th-cent. comp. Worked (?) at Dresden, Stockholm and Hamburg.

Works incl. Te Deum for double chor.; cantatas incl. *O amantissime sponse, Jesu* for sop. & stgs.; inst. works, &c.

Ritter, Peter (b. Mannheim, 2. VII. 1763; d. Mannheim, 1. VIII. 1846). Ger. cst. & comp. Studied co. with Filtz and Danzi, comp. with Vogler, succeeded Danzi in the Manheim orch. in 1784 and became cond. in 1803.

Works incl. operas *Der Eremit auf Formentara* (Kotzebue), *Die lustigen Weiber* (after Shakespeare's *Merry Wives*) & *c.* 20 others; plays with m.; church m.; orat. *Das verlorene Paradies* (after Milton); co. concs.; chamber m.; co. & pf. sos., &c.

Ritter, Théodore (real name Bennet) (b. nr. Paris, 5. IV. 1841; d. Paris, 6. IV. 1886), Fr. pfst. & comp. Pupil of Liszt.

Works incl. operas *Marianne* & *La dea risorta*; pf. pieces, incl. *Chant du braconnier*, *Sylphes*, &c.

Rivarde, (Serge) Achille (b. New York, 31. X. 1865; d. London, 31. III. 1940), Spa.-Amer. (Anglicized) vst. Studied in U.S.A. and with Dancla at the Paris Cons. After a return to U.S.A., when he gave up playing, he entered the Lamoureux Orch. in Paris, 1885, as leader, leaving in 1891. He made his 1st appearance in London in 1894, settled there and in 1899 became v. prof. at the R.C.M.

Rivas, Duke of (Angel Pérez de Saavedra) (1791–1865), Spa. poet & dramatist. *See* **Forza del destino** (Verdi).

Rivolgimento (It. = revolution, turning, upsetting). The inversion of the parts in double ctpt.

Rizzio, Davidde (b. Turin, ?; d. Holyrood Palace, Sco., 9. III. 1566), It. bass singer & diplomat. In service at the court of Savoy, he visited Sco. in 1561 in the ambassador's suite and remained in the service of Queen Mary with his brother Giuseppe. He arr. masques at court and became her foreign secretary in 1564, but her favour aroused jealousies and he was stabbed to death. Comp. (?) several tunes now regarded as traditional Sco.

Roberday, François (b. ?; d. Paris, *c.* 1695), Fr. orgst. & comp. He held appts. under the Queens Anne of Aus. and Marie-Thérèse, taught Lully and was orgst. at the church of the Petits-Pères in Paris.

Works incl. *Fugues et Caprices* for org., &c.

Robert le Diable (*Robert the Devil*), opera by Meyerbeer (lib. by Scribe), prod. Paris, Opéra, 21. XI. 1831.

Roberto Devereux, Conte d'Essex, opera by Donizetti (lib. by Salvatore Cammarano, based on Jacques Ancelot's tragedy *Élisabeth d'Angleterre*), prod. Naples, Teatro San Carlo, 2. X. 1837.

Opera by Mercadante (lib. by Felice Romani, based on Corneille's *Comte d'Essex*), prod. Milan, Teatro alla Scala, 10. III. 1833.

Roberts, John Henry (b. Bethesda, 31. III. 1848; d. Liverpool, 30. VII. 1924). Welsh orgst., educst. & comp.

Played the org. as a child, was offered a post at Gloucester cath. by S. S. Wesley and in 1870–3 studied at the R.A.M. in London. He then held org. appts. at Bethesda and Carnarvon and later became dir. of the Cambrian School of M. at Liverpool.
Works incl. hymn tunes, partsongs, &c.

Roberts, Juliane. *See* **Walter, Ignaz.**

Robertson, Alec (b. Southsea, 3. VI. 1892), Eng. mcolst. Studied at the R.A.M. in London and became an orgst. & choirmaster in 1913. After serving in the 1914–8 war he lectured at L.C.C. evening institutes and in 1920 became lecturer and later head of the Gramophone Co.'s educ. dept. Lived in Rome for 4 years to study plainsong and in 1940 joined the B.B.C. in charge of the m. talks in the home service. His books incl. *The Interpretation of Plainchant, Art and Religion, Dvořák* and a chapter on Schubert's songs. He is writing a book on Handel's m.

Robertus Anglicus. *See* **Morton.**

Robin Hood, opera by Macfarren (lib. by John Oxenford), prod. London, Her Majesty's Theatre, 11. X. 1860.

Robin Hood, or Sherwood Forest, opera by Shield (lib. by Leonard MacNally), prod. London, Covent Garden Opera, 17. IV. 1784.

Robinson, Anastasia (b. ? It., *c.* 1695; d. Berris Mount nr. Southampton, IV. 1755), Eng. sop. singer. Studied with Croft and others, made her 1st appearance in London, 1714, and retired 10 years later, having married the Earl of Peterborough in 1722.

Robinson Crusoé, operetta by Offenbach (lib. by Eugène Cormon & Hector Crémieux, based distantly on Defoe's novel), prod. Paris, Opéra-Comique, 23. XI. 1867.

Robinson, Elizabeth (b. ? London, *c.* 1700; d. ?), Eng. singer, sister of Anastasia R. She was intended to follow her father as a miniature painter, but studied m. with Bononcini in London and Rameau in Paris; retired on making a favourable marriage.

Robinson, John (b. ? London, 1682; d. London, 30. IV. 1762), Eng. orgst. & comp. Pupil of Blow at the Chapel Royal, became orgst. of St. Lawrence, Jewry, and St. Magnus, London Bridge, and in 1727 succeeded Croft as orgst. of Westminster Abbey. In 1716 he married Wm. Turner's daughter Ann (?–1741), a singer at the It. Opera.
Works incl. Double Chant in E♭ maj., &c.

Robinson, Joseph (b. Dublin, 20. VIII. 1816; d. Dublin, 23. VIII., 1898), Ir. singer, cond. & educst. Studied under his father, Francis R. (?–?), appeared in voc. 4tets with his brothers Francis (*c.* 1799–1872), John (*c.* 1812–44) and William (?–?), founded an Antient Concert Soc. at Dublin in 1834, married the Eng. pfst. Fanny Arthur (1831–79) and in 1856 revived the Ir. Acad. of M. founded in 1848. Comp. anthems, songs, &c.

Robledo, Melchior (b. ?; d. Saragossa, 1587), Spa. comp. Spent some time in Rome, but returned to Spa. in 1769 and became choirmaster at the old cath. of Saragossa, where, as at the new one, his work alone was sung with that of Morales, Victoria and Palestrina.
Works incl. masses, motets, &c.

Rocca, Lodovico (b. Turin, 29. XI. 1895), It. comp. Pupil of Orefice.
Works incl. operas *La morte di Frine, La corona del re Gaulo, Il Dibuc, In terra di leggenda* & *Monte Ivnor*; symph. poems *Contrasti, Aurora di morte, L'alba del malato* & *La foresta delle Samodive,* also *La cella azzurra, Chiaroscuri* & *Interludio epico* for orch.; chamber m., &c.

Rochlitz, Johann Friedrich (b. Leipzig. 12. II. 1769; d. Leipzig, 16. XII. 1842), Ger. m. critic & poet. Studied under Doles at the St. Thomas School, Leipzig, later theol. at the Univ. In 1798 he founded the *Allgemeine musikalische Zeitung,* which he ed. until 1818. He also comp., wrote libs. and poems, 3 of which were set by Schubert.

Rockstro, William (Smith) (orig. Rackstraw) (b. North Cheam, Surrey, 5. I. 1823; d. London, 2. VII. 1895), Eng. orgst., comp., theorist & teacher. Studied with Sterndale Bennett and at the Leipzig Cons. From the early 1860s to 1891 he lived at Torquay. He wrote books on hist. and theory, and biogs. of Handel, Mendelssohn and Jenny Lind.
Works incl. orat. *The Good Shepherd*; madrigal 'O too cruel fair'; songs, &c.

Rode, (Jacques) Pierre (Joseph) (b. Bordeaux, 16. II. 1774; d. Château de Bourbon nr. Damazon, 25. XI. 1830), Fr. vst. & comp. After making great progress as a child, he was sent to Paris in 1788 and became a pupil of Viotti's, making his 1st public appearance in 1790. He joined the orch at the Théâtre Feydeau and in 1794 began to tour abroad, visiting Hol., Ger. & Eng. On his return to Paris he became prof. at the new Cons. and leader at the Opéra. In 1799 he visited Spa., when (?) Boccherini orch. some of his concs. In 1800 he became vst.

to Napoleon and in 1803 went to St. Petersburg with Boïeldieu, remaining until 1808. In 1811–3 he travelled in Ger. again, going to Vienna in the latter year, where Beethoven finished the So. Op. 96 for him. In 1814 he settled in Berlin, married, but soon afterwards went to live in retirement near Bordeaux.

Works incl. 13 v. concs.; many stg. 4tets; v. duets; 24 Caprices, vars. &c. for v., &c.

Rodelinda, opera by Handel (lib. by Antonio Salvi, adapted by Nicola Francesco Haym), prod. London, King's Theatre, Haymarket, 13. II. 1725.

Rodelinda, regina de' Longobardi, opera by Graun (lib. Giovanni Gualberto Bottarelli, altered from Antonio Salvi), prod. Berlin, at court, 13. XII. 1741.

Rodenbach, Georges (1855–98), Belg. dramatist. *See* **Tote Stadt** (Korngold).

Rodolphe, Jean Joseph (orig. Johann Joseph Rudolph) (b. Strasburg, 14. X. 1730; d. Paris, 18. VIII. 1812), Fr. hn. & v. player & comp. Studied hn. & v. with his father, and from 1746 v. with Leclair in Paris. In 1754 he went to Parma, in 1761 to Stuttgart and in 1767 back to Paris. He studied comp. under Traetta and Jommelli. In later years he taught, from 1798 at the Cons.

Works incl. operas *Le Mariage par capitulation, L'Aveugle de Palmyre* & *Isménor*; ballets; hn. concs.; v. duets; hn. pieces, &c.

Rodríguez de Hita, Antonio (b. ?; d. Madrid, 21. II. 1787), Spa. comp. In the 1750s he was chapel master at Palencia and later went to Madrid, (?) as mus. dir. of the Convent of the Incarnation. He met the dramatist Ramón de La Cruz and with him prod. operas.

Works incl. operas *Briseida, Las segadoras de Vallecas, Las labradoras de Murcia*; hymns for 4 & 8 voices, &c.

Rodwell, George (Herbert Bonaparte) (b. London, 15. XI. 1800; d. London, 22. I. 1852), Eng. cond., author & comp. Studied with V. Novello and Bishop and became mus. dir. at the Adelphi Theatre, under his brother's management, to which he succeeded in 1825. In 1828 he became prof. at the R.A.M. and in 1831 mus. dir. at Covent Garden Theatre. He also wrote plays and novels.

Works incl. stage pieces *The Flying Dutchman, The Cornish Miners, The Bottle Imp, The Earthquake, The Devil's Elixir, The Lord of the Isles* (after Scott), *The Sexton of Cologne, The Seven Sisters of Munich* and a number of others; *Songs of the Sabbath Eve, Songs of the Birds*, &c.

Rogel, José (b. Orihuela, Alicante, 24. XII. 1829; d. Cartagena, 25. II. 1901), Spa. cond. & comp. Studied under the cath. orgst. at Alicante, but was sent to Valencia to study law. There he pursued further mus. studies under Pascual Pérez, and after taking his degree in law, became a theatre cond. He wrote or collab. in over 80 stage works, some with Barbieri.

Works incl. operas & zarzuelas *Loa a la libertad, El jovén Telémaco, Revista de un muerto, Un viage de mil demonios, El General Bumbum*, &c.

Roger-Ducasse (Jean Jules Aimable Roger Ducasse) (b. Bordeaux, 18. IV. 1873), Fr. comp. Studied at the Paris Cons., where he was a comp. pupil of Fauré. App. inspector of singing in the Paris city schools in 1909, and in 1935 succeeded Dukas as comp. prof. at the Cons.

Works incl. opera *Cantegril*, mimed drama *Orphée*; *Au Jardin de Marguerite* & *Ulysse et les Sirènes* for voices & orch.; motets and secular voc. works incl. *Sur quelques vers de Virgile, Madrigal sur des vers de Molière*; *Suite française, Le Joli Jeu de furet, Prélude d'un ballet, Nocturne de printemps, Épithalame, Poème symphonique sur le nom de Fauré* for orch; *Variations plaisantes* for hp. & orch.; pf. works; inst. pieces; songs, &c.

Roger, Gustave Hippolyte (b. Paris, 17. XII. 1815; d. Paris, 12. IX. 1879), Fr. ten. singer. Studied at the Paris Cons. and made his 1st appearance, at the Opéra-Comique, in 1838. In 1849 he transferred to the Opéra. In 1868 he became prof. at the Cons.

Rogers, Benjamin (b. Windsor, V. 1614; d. ? Oxford, VI. 1698), Eng. orgst. & comp. Learnt m. from his father, Peter R., a lay-clerk at St. George's Chapel, Windsor, and from the orgst., Giles. He became himself a lay-clerk, but in 1639 went to Dublin as orgst. of Christ Church cath. He returned to Windsor in 1641, but in 1644 the choir was disbanded and he taught m. privately. B.Mus., Cambridge, 1658, and in 1669 D.Mus., Oxford, where he had become orgst. and choirmaster at Magdalen Coll., in 1664, being dismissed for irregularities in 1685, but given a pension.

Works incl. services & anthems, *Hymnus Eucharisticus* (sung on Magdalen tower at 5 a.m. on 1. V. each year); inst. pieces; org. works, &c.

Rogers, Bernard (b. New York, 4. II. 1893), Amer. comp. Studied at the

N.Y. Institute of Mus. Art and with Bloch at Cleveland. He gained several prizes and distinctions and for a time did mus. journalism. In 1938 he became prof. of comp. at the Eastman School of M. at Rochester, N.Y.

Works incl. operas *The Marriage of Aude* & *Samson*; cantatas *The Raising of Lazarus* & *The Exodus, Passion* with org. accomp.; 3 syms., ovt. *The Faithful, 3 Eastern Dances, 2 Amer. Frescoes, 4 Fairy Tales, The Supper at Emmaus, The Colours of War, The Dance of Salome, The Song of the Nightingale, The Plains, The Sailors of Toulon, Invasion* & *Characters from Hans Andersen* for orch.; Soliloquies for fl. & stgs. and bn. & stgs., Fantasy for fl., va. & orch.; *Pastorale* for 11 insts., stg. 4tet; *M. for an Industrial Film* for 2 pfs.; songs, &c.

Rogier, Philippe (b. Arras, ? 1563; d. Madrid, 29. II. 1596), Fr. comp. He must have been sent to Spa. as a child, being a choir-boy at Madrid in 1572; member of the royal chapel from 1586, chapel master from 1587.

Works incl. masses, motets, &c.

Rogneda, opera by Serov (lib., in Rus., by Dmitry Vassilievitch Averkiev), prod. St. Petersburg, 8. XI. 1865.

Rogowski, Ludomir (Michal) (b. Lublin, 3. X. 1881), Pol. comp. Studied at the Warsaw Cons. and with Riemann and Nikisch at Leipzig. On his return to Pol. he founded a sym. orch. at Vilna, lived in Paris in 1914–21 and withdrew to a monastery in Yugoslavia in 1926.

Works incl. opera *Tamara* (after Lermontov) & *Prince Marco*; film opera *Un Grand Chagrin de la Petite Ondine*; ballets *St. John's Eve* & *Fairy Tale*; 2 syms., suites *Pictures of my Daughter, The Seasons, Les Sourires, Villafranca, Phantasmagoria, Sporting Scene, Fantasy Pictures* for orch.; 4tet for 4 cos., suites for 6 and for 9 insts. & other chamber m.; inst. pieces; pf. works; chor. songs with & without accomp., &c.

Rohr Flute. A stopped Diapason org. stop of metal pipes prod. 8-ft. tone.

Rohrflöte (Ger. lit. tube flute). The name sometimes used in Eng. for the Rohr F. org. stop.

Roi David, Le, dramatic Psalm by Honegger (lib. by René Morax), prod. Mézières, Swi., open-air Théâtre du Jorat, 11. VI. 1921.

Roi de Lahore, Le (*The King of L.*), opera by Massenet (lib. by Louis Gallet). prod. Paris, Opéra, 27. IV. 1877.

Roi des Violons (Fr. = King of the Violins). The title of the head of the guild of v. players, the Ménétriers, founded in Paris in 1321. It was not abolished until 1773.

Roi d'Ys, Le, opera by Lalo (lib. by Édouard Blau), prod. Paris, Opéra-Comique, 7. V. 1888. Ys is the submerged city of Debussy's pf. prelude *La Cathédrale engloutie.*

Roi et le fermier, Le (*King and Farmer*), opera by Monsigny (lib. by Jean Michel Sedaine), prod. Paris, Comédie-Italienne, 22. XI. 1762.

Roi l'a dit, Le (*The King has said it*), opera by Delibes (lib. by Edmond Gondinet), prod. Paris, Opéra-Comique, 24. V. 1873.

Roi malgré lui, Le (*King against his Will*), opera by Chabrier (lib. by Émile de Najac & Paul Burani, based on a comedy by Ancelot), prod. Paris, Opéra-Comique, 18. V. 1887.

Rokitansky, Hans von, Freiherr (b. Vienna, 6. III. 1835; d. Laubegg Castle, Styria, 2. XI. 1909). Aus. bass singer. Studied at Bologna and Milan, made his 1st appearance in Eng. in 1856, in Prague, 1862, and in Vienna, 1863. In 1894 he became prof. at the Vienna Cons.

Rokseth (*née* **Rihouet**), **Yvonne** (b. Maisons-Laffitte, 18. VII. 1890), Fr. mcolst. & comp. Studied v. at the Paris Cons., also org. with Abel Decaux and comp. with d'Indy at the Schola Cantorum. Later she became a private pupil of Roussel. She took degrees in science and letters, and in 1937 was app. Prof. of M. at Strasburg Univ. She ed. old Fr. org. m. for the Société Française de Musicologie and the Montpellier MS. of 13th-cent. polyph. m. Her books incl. studies of 15th–16th-cent. org. m. and of Grieg; her comps. a Te Deum for chor., stgs. & org., a Fantasy for pf. & orch. & a stg. 5tet.

Roland. *See also* **Orlando.**

Opera by Lully (lib. by Quinault), prod. Versailles, at court, 8. I. 1685, 1st Paris perf., 8. III. 1685.

Roland-Manuel (real name Roland Alexis Manuel Lévy) (b. Paris, 22. III. 1891), Fr. comp. & critic. Pupil of Roussel at the Schola Cantorum in Paris and of Ravel. He has written much criticism and books on Ravel and Falla.

Works incl. operas *Isabelle et Pantalon, Le Diable amoureux*; ballets *Le Tournoi singulier, L'Écran des jeunes filles, Elvire* (on m. by D. Scarlatti); film m. *L'Ami Fritz* (after Erckmann-Chatrian), *La Bandéra* & others; orat. *Jeanne d'Arc*; symph. poems *Le Harem du vice-roi, Tempo di ballo*, suite *Pena de Francia* for orch.; Suite in the Spa. style for hpchd., ob., bn. & tpt., stg. Trio; partsongs; songs, &c.

Roldán, Amadeo (b. Paris, 9. VII. 1900; d. Havana, 2. III. 1939), Cuban mulatto comp. Studied v. in Madrid and comp. at Havana, where in 1924 he became leader and in 1932 cond. of the Phil. Orch. He studied Cuban folk m., on which all his works are based.

Works incl. ballets *La Rebambaramba* & *El Milagro de Anaquillé*; *Oberture sobre temas cubanos* & *Tres pequeños poemas* for orch.; *3 Toques* for chamber orch.; *Danza negra* for sop. & 7 insts., *Poema negra* for stg. 4tet; 6 *Rítmicas* for var. insts., &c.

Rolfsen, Johan Nordahl (Brun) (1848–1928), Norw. dramatist. *See* **Olsen** (*Svein Uroed*).

Roll. A very rapid succession of notes on drums prod. by quick alternating strokes of the 2 sticks.

Rolla, Alessandro (b. Pavia, 22. IV. 1757; d. Milan, 15. IX. 1841), It. vst., cond. & comp. 1st studied pf. but took to the v. and va. He led the ducal orch. at Parma in 1782–1802 and Paganini was his pupil there for a short time. From 1802 he was leader and cond. at the Scala in Milan and in 1805 he became prof. at the Cons. there.

Works incl. ballets *Adelasia, Marte e la Pace* & 5 others; v. & va. concs.; stg. 4tets & 5tets & other chamber m.; v. duets; songs, &c.

Rolland, Romain (b. Clamecy, Nièvre, 29. I. 1866; d. Vézelay, Nièvre, 30. XII. 1944), Fr. mcolst. & author. He had a 1st-rate general educ., but devoted himself much to mus. and other artistic studies. In 1901 he became president of the mus. section of the École des Hautes Études Sociales and lectured on m. 1st at the École Normale Supérieure and from 1903 at the Sorbonne. He also contrib. essays on m. to var. periodicals and wrote plays and other lit. works. From 1913 he lived in Swi., having retired owing to bad health. He returned to Fr. in 1938 in order not to evade the war, was interned in a concentration camp by the Gers. and released only when he was mortally ill. His works incl. books on Handel and Beethoven, on early opera, *Musiciens d'autrefois, Musiciens d'aujourd'hui, Voyage musical au pays du passé*, the novel *Jean-Christophe* (10 vols.) with a musn. as hero, &c.

For incid. m. to his plays *see* **Honegger** (*Danton*), **Kabalévsky** (*Craftsman of Clamecy*), **Lopatnikov** (*Danton*), **Quatorze Juillet** (7 comps.), **Tcherepnin (A.)** (*Esprit troimphant*).

Rolle, Johann Heinrich (b. Quedlinburg, 23. XII. 1718; d. Magdeburg, 29. XII. 1785), Ger. orgst. & comp. Studied under his father, Christian Friedrich R. (?–1751), town musn. of Quedlinburg and later of Magdeburg. He became a church orgst. at the age of 14 and afterwards went to Leipzig Univ. to study law. Having failed to secure a legal post, he became chamber musn. to Frederick II *c.* 1740, as va. player, but in 1746 became orgst. and town musn. at Magdeburg.

Works incl. dramatic orats. *Saul, Samson, David and Jonathan, The Labours of Hercules, Orestes and Pylades, The Death of Abel* & 15 others; several cycles of church m. for the whole year, 5 Passions, Easter, Whitsun and Christmas cantatas and numerous other church works; inst. m.; songs, &c.

Rolltrommel (Ger.) = Tenor Drum (more often called *Rührtrommel*).

Rolón, José (b. Ciudad Guzmán, Jalisco, 22. VI. 1883), Mex. comp. Studied with his father and later with Moszkowski in Paris, where however he came under the influence of the modern school. He returned to Mex. in 1907 and founded a m. school at Guadalajara, but at the age of 44 he returned to Paris to study with Dukas and Nadia Boulanger.

Works incl. Sym., Ovt., *El festín de los enanos, Scherzo sinfónico, Baile Michoacana, Zapotlán, Cuauhtémoc* for orch.; pf. Conc., &c.

Roman, Johan Helmich (b. Stockholm, 26. X. 1694; d. Haraldsmaala nr. Kalmar, 19. X. 1758), Swe. comp. He was in London in 1714, studying with Ariosti and Pepusch, and entered the service of the Duke of Newcastle. In 1720 he returned to Swe. and became mus. dir. at Stockholm in 1729. He visited It., Fr. and Eng. in 1735–7, became a member of the Swe. Acad. in 1740 and retired in 1745.

Works incl. Mass, motets, over 80 psalms; 21 syms., 6 ovts.; concs.; over 20 v. sos., 12 fl. sos., *Assaggio* for solo v., &c.

Romance (Eng. & Fr.). A piece or song of a 'romantic' nature, usually moderate in tempo and emotional, sometimes sentimental in style. There is no prescribed form, but it is as a rule fairly short and in the character of a song, generally contemplative and sometimes narrative in tone.

Romance (Fr.). As above, but more often and more specifically a song. In Fr. the R. was one of the species of medieval song for several voices, but single-voice songs were called *romances* from about the end of the 18th cent. onward until recently, and the term is still in use, though the more general one now is *mélodie*.

Romanesca. *See* **Galliard.**

Romanticism. A term capable of as vague an application as are Classicism and Modernism; indeed any classification of m. into categories whose names end in -ism are to be regarded with suspicion. Broadly speaking, however, R. defines with fair accuracy the greater part of m. of the 19th cent., beginning with Beethoven and Schubert, and ending with Wagner and Brahms, though many composers alive in the 1940s are still romantics. The most useful and reasonably accurate definition of R. is that it describes m. which is not self-sufficing as such, but attempts to express or describe things lying beyond its immediate scope: the comp.'s state of mind, a mood of place, season or time of day, the feeling or content of some other work of art (e.g. a poem or a picture), &c.

Romanze (Ger.) = Romance, in the 1st sense defined above.

Romberg, Andreas (Jakob) (b. Vechta nr. Münster, 27. IV. 1767; d. Gotha, 10. XI. 1821), Ger. vst. & comp. Pupil of his father, Gerhard Heinrich R. (1745–1819). He appeared in stg. duets with his cousin Bernhard R. at the age of 7 and at 17 played at the Concert spirituel in Paris. In 1790 he joined the electoral orch. at Bonn and in 1793–6 he was in It., Spa. and Port. with Bernhard, whom he joined again in Paris in 1800 after visits to Vienna and Hamburg. He returned to the latter place, married and remained for 15 years, after which he became court mus. dir. at Gotha.

Works incl. operas *Don Mendoce, ou Le Tuteur portugais* (with Bernhard R.), *Das blaue Ungeheuer, Der Rabe* (both after Gozzi), *Die Ruinen zu Paluzzi, Die Grossmut des Scipio* & others; Te Deum, Magnificat, psalms & other church m.; setting of Schiller's *Lied von der Glocke* for solo voices, chor. & orch., & other cantatas *The Transient and the Eternal, The Harmony of the Spheres, The Power of Song,* &c.; 6 syms. & Toy Sym.; stg. 4tets & 5tets, &c.

Romberg, Bernhard (b. Dinklage, Oldenburg, 12. XI. 1767; d. Hamburg, 13. VIII. 1841), Ger. cst. & comp., cousin of prec. Pupil of his father Anton R. (1742–1814), appeared at the age of 7 with his cousin and in Paris at 14. In 1790–3 he was in the electoral orch. at Bonn, together with Andreas, also Beethoven, Reicha and F. A. Ries; then, until 1796, he was in It., Spa. and Port. with Andreas. After visits to Vienna and Hamburg he taught the co. at the Paris Cons., 1801–3, and in 1804–6 he was cst. in the royal orch. in Berlin, where he was court mus. dir. in 1815–9, after a tour in Rus., retiring to Hamburg in 1819. In the meantime he had visited London, Paris, Vienna, St. Petersburg, Moscow, &c.

Works incl. operas *Don Mendoce, ou Le Tuteur portugais* (with Andreas R.), *Die wiedergefundene Statue* (after Gozzi), *Der Schiffbruch, Alma, Ulysses und Circe, Rittertreue*; many co. concs., Conc. for 2 cos.; funeral sym. for Queen Louise of Prus.; stg. 4tets, pf. 4tets & other chamber m.; co. pieces, &c.

Romeo and Juliet. *See also* **Giulietta e Romeo, Capuleti e Montecchi.**

Fantasy-ovt. by Tchaikovsky, based on Shakespeare's tragedy, comp. at Balakirev's suggestion, 1869–70; prod. Moscow, 16. III. 1870; revised X. 1870.

Opera by John Edmund Barkworth (1858–1929) (lib. by comp. adapted from Shakespeare), prod. Middlesbrough, 7. I. 1916; 1st London perf. Surrey Theatre, 10. IV. 1920.

Roméo et Juliette, opera by Gounod (lib. by Jules Barbier & Michel Carré, after Shakespeare), prod. Paris, Théâtre Lyrique, 27. IV. 1867.

Opera by Steibelt (lib. by Joseph Alexandre Pierre de Ségur, after Shakespeare), prod. Paris, Théâtre Feydeau, 10. IX. 1793.

Sym. by Berlioz, Op. 17, for solo voices, chor. & orch., based on Shakespeare's tragedy, comp. in 1839, 1st perf. Paris Cons., 24. XI. 1839.

Romeo und Julia auf dem Dorfe (*A Village Romeo and Juliet*), opera by Delius (lib. by comp., in Ger., based on a story by Gottfried Keller), prod. Berlin, 21. II. 1907. First perf. in Eng., London, Covent Garden Theatre, 22. II. 1910.

Romeo und Julie, opera by G. Benda (lib. by Friedrich Wilhelm Gotter), prod. Gotha, at court, 25. IX. 1776. The 1st opera on Shakespeare's tragedy and the only Ger. one.

Romer, Emma (b. ? London, 1814; d. Margate, 11. IV. 1868), Eng. sop. singer. Pupil of George Smart, made her 1st appearance in London, at Covent Garden Theatre, in 1830.

Romero, Mateo (? orig. Rosmarin) (b. Flanders, ?; d. Madrid, 10. V. 1647), Flem.-Spa. singer, comp. & priest. He joined the royal chapel at Madrid in 1594. He was a pupil of Rogier and belonged to the Flem. section of the choir. In 1598 he succeeded Rogier as chapel master. He was ordained priest and retired with a pension in 1633, but was sent on a mus. mission to Port. in 1638.

Works incl. motets & other church m.; secular songs for 3 & 4 voices, incl. settings of poems by Lope de Vega, &c.

Romilda e Costanza, opera by Meyerbeer (lib. by Giacomo Rossi), prod. Padua, 19. VII. 1817. M.'s 1st It. opera.

Ronald, Landon (real name Russell) (b. London, 7. VI. 1873; d. London, 14. VIII. 1938), Eng. cond., pfst. & comp., son of Henry Russell. Studied at the R.C.M., made his 1st public appearance as pfst. in Wormser's *L'Enfant prodigue* and gained experience as asst. cond. to Mancinelli at Covent Garden and accompst. to Melba. Later he cond. sym. concerts and visited Ger., Aus. and It. as cond. In 1910 he was app. principal of the G.S.M. in London. Knighted 1922.

Works incl. incid. m. to dramatic version of Robert Hichens's *Garden of Allah*; *Birthday Ovt.* for orch.; *Adonais* (Shelley) for voice & orch.; pf. pieces; songs, &c.

Ronconi. It. family of singers:

1. Domenico R. (b. Lendinara nr. Rovigo, 11. VII. 1772; d. Milan, 13. IV. 1839), made his 1st appearance, at the Teatro La Fenice in Venice, in 1797, later worked at St. Petersburg, Vienna, Paris and Munich. He founded a school of singing at Milan in 1829.

2. Giorgio R. (b. Milan, 6. VIII. 1810; d. Madrid, 8. I. 1890), bar., son of prec. Pupil of his father, made his 1st appearance at Pavia in 1831. Travelled all over It. and 1st visited London in 1842. Married the singer Elguerra Giannoni and visited many Eur. countries as well as the U.S.A. In 1874 he became prof. of singing at the Madrid Cons.

3. Felice R. (b. Venice, 1811; d. St. Petersburg, 10. IX. 1875), brother of prec. Pupil of his father, taught at Würzburg, Frankfort, Milan, London and St. Petersburg.

4. Sebastiano R. (b. Milan, 1810; d. Milan, I. 1900), bar., brother of prec. Pupil of his father and made his 1st appearance at Lucca in 1836, and in London later that year. He travelled widely and in 1849 settled at Milan as singing-master.

Rondeau (Fr.). *See* **Rondo.**

Rondelet (Fr.) = Roundelay.

Rondeña. A Spa. folksong type of Andalusia, resembling the Fandango, with words in stanzas of 4 lines of 8 syllables.

Rondine, La (*The Swallow*), operetta by Puccini (lib. by Giuseppe Adami, trans. from the Ger. of Alfred Maria Willner & Heinrich Reichert), prod. Monte Carlo, 27. III. 1917. Orig. intended to be set to the Ger. words for the Carl Theater in Vienna, but It. being at war with Aus., this fell through.

Rondo. The most important mus. form since the 18th cent., next to so. form, and frequently forming part of a so.-form work, esp. as the finale. Its general principle is that of a return to an initial theme, as to a refrain, with different episodes between. The Fr. *rondeau* of the 18th cent. was merely a matter of detached sections, the 1st of them recurring after each of the incidental ones, which were called *couplets*. Later the episodes became linked to the principal theme by transitions, and the highest devel. of the R. was, esp. in Mozart's hands at first, the so-called so.-R. form, where one of the episodes appeared at first in a key related to the tonic and returned as another episode in the tonic key, exactly like a 2nd so. subject. Like a so. mvt., a R. may have a coda; much more rarely one of the episodes may be in the nature of a thematic working-out. The recurrences of the theme are often saved from monotony by (e.g. Mozart) abbrev. or (e.g. Beethoven) var.

Ronga, Luigi (b. Turin, 19. VI. 1901), It. mcolst. Studied at Turin Univ. and at Dresden, became prof. of mus. hist. at the Palermo Cons. in 1926 and later at the Univ. and Accademia di Santa Cecilia in Rome. His works incl. studies of Frescobaldi, Rossini and Wagner, a treatise on mus. hist., &c.

Ronsard, Pierre de (1524–85), Fr. poet. *See* **Boni** (sonnets), **Dieren (van)** (songs), **Dukas** (*Sonnet de R.*), **Honegger** (songs), **Poulenc** (songs), **Regnart (F.)** (chansons), **Roussel (A.)** (songs), **Séverac** (songs), **Witkowski** (songs with orch.).

Röntgen, Engelbert (b. Deventer, 30. IX. 1829; d. Leipzig, 12. XII. 1897), Dutch vst. Studied at the Leipzig Cons. and became a member of the Opera and Gewandhaus orchs. there, and in 1869 v. prof. at the Cons. In 1873 he succeeded David as leader at the Gewandhaus. He married a daughter of a former leader, Moritz Klengel.

Röntgen, Julius (b. Leipzig, 9. V. 1855; d. Utrecht, 13. IX. 1932), Ger. pfst., cond. & comp. of Dutch descent, son of prec. Studied at the Leipzig Cons., but reverted to Hol., living at Amsterdam in 1877–1924 as teacher and cond., becoming dir. of the Cons. in 1914. He was a great friend of Grieg's, of whom he wrote a biog.

Works incl. operas *Agnete, The Laughing Cavalier, Samûm*; film m.; 12 syms.; 3 pf. concs.; chamber m.; arrs. of old Dutch songs and dances, &c.

Rooke, William Michael (real name Rourke or O'Rourke) (b. Dublin, 29. IX. 1794; d. London, 14. X. 1847), Ir. vst., pfst. & comp. He was largely self-taught, and after an appt. at the Crow Street Theatre, Dublin, and prod. his 1st opera in London, he settled there in 1821, working at Drury Lane Theatre and Vauxhall and cond. orats. at Birmingham.

Works incl. operas *Amilie, or The Love Test, Henrique, or The Love Pilgrim, Cagliostro, The Valkyrie,* &c.

Root. The bottom note of a chord when set out in its 1st and fundamental position, e.g., in the case of common chords (Triads), A in a chord of A min., C in a chord of C maj., &c. Chords so used are said to be in R. position and their basses are called R. basses. In old m., where a great deal of the harmonic basis rested on common chords, it was essential that many of these chords should appear in their var. inversions and that progressions of R. basses should thus be avoided, since m. progressing by chords in R. positions is both resourceless and clumsy.

Rootham, Cyril B(radley). (b. Bristol, 5. X. 1875; d. Cambridge, 18. III. 1938), Eng. orgst., educst. & comp. Studied under his father, the singer, orgst. & cond. Daniel R. (1837–1922), later at St. John's Coll., Cambridge, where he took the Mus.B. in 1900, and the R.C.M. in London. In 1901 he went back to Cambridge as orgst. and mus. dir. at St. John's Coll. and took the Mus.D. in 1910. He cond. many interesting perfs. with the Cambridge Univ. Mus. Soc. and at festivals in the town.

Works incl. opera *The Two Sisters*; chor. & orch. works *Andromeda, Coronach, For the Fallen* (Binyon), *Brown Earth, Ode on the Morning of Christ's Nativity* (Milton), *City in the West,* Psalm ciii; 2 syms. (2nd with chor. finale), rhapsodies *Pan* & on the tune *Lazarus* (stgs.), *Miniature* & *St. John's* suites for orch.; stg. 4tet, stg. 5tet, pf. Trio, 7tet for va., wind & hp.: v. & pf. So., Suite for fl. & pf.; partsongs, &c.

Rooy, Anton(ius Maria Josephus) van (b. Rotterdam, 1. I. 1870; d. Munich, 28. XI. 1932), Dutch bar. singer. Orig. engaged in commerce, he went to Frankfort o/M. to study singing with Stockhausen, sang at concerts in Ger. and obtained his 1st stage engagement at the Wagner festival theatre at Bayreuth in 1897. He 1st visited London as a Wagner singer at Covent Garden in 1898.

Ropartz, (Joseph) Guy (Marie) (b. Guingamp, Côtes du Nord, 15. VI. 1864), Fr. comp. He 1st studied literature, but went to the Paris Cons. as a pupil of Dubois, Massenet and Franck. In 1894 he became dir. of the Nancy Cons. and in 1919 of that of Strasburg. Later he retired to Brittany, where he was b. and to which he belonged by race.

Works incl. operas *Le Diable couturier, Marguerite d'Écosse, Le Miracle de Saint-Nicolas, Le Pays*; incid. m. to a stage version of Pierre Loti's *Pêcheur d'Islande* and for Sophocles' *Oedipus at Colonus*; *Messe de Sainte-Odile, Messe de Saint-Anne,* Requiem, Psalm cxxxvi, motets & other church m.; 4 syms., *Paysage de Bretagne, Les Landes, Dimanche breton, La Cloche des morts, Concert en ré majeur* & other orch. works; *Rhapsodie* for v. & orch.; 4 stg. 4tets, stg. Trio, pf. Trio; 2 v. & pf. sos., 2 co. & pf. sos.; *Ouverture, Variations et Final, Choral varié, Dans l'ombre de la montagne, Musique au jardin,* 3 Nocturnes, *Croquis d'été, Croquis d'automne, Jeunes Filles* & other works for pf.; org. works; songs *4 Poèmes, Veilles de départ, Le Rêve sur le sable, 4 Odelettes,* &c.

Rore, Cyprien de (b. Mechlin or Antwerp. *c.* 1516; d. Parma, 1565), Flem. comp. Studied under his fellow-countryman Willaert at Venice, where he was (?) a singer, and began to pub. madrigals in 1542. He left Venice *c.* 1550 to enter the service of Ercole II, Duke of Ferrara. In 1558 he visited his parents at Antwerp and the court of Margaret of Aus. in the Nthlds., into the service of whose husband, Ottavio Farnese, Duke of Parma, he passed. He succeeded Willaert as chapel master of St. Mark's, Venice, in 1563, but returned to Parma in VII. 1564.

Works incl. masses, motets, 2 Passions & other church m.; madrigals; inst. fantasies & ricercari, &c.

Rosa, Carl (August Nikolaus) (real name Rose) (b. Hamburg, 22. III. 1842; d. Paris, 30. IV. 1889), Ger. vst. & cond. Studied at the Leipzig and Paris Conss., became orch. leader at Hamburg and visited Eng. in 1866 and afterwards the U.S.A., where he met and in II. 1867 married Euphrosyne Parepa, with whom he formed an opera co. which incl. Santley and G. Ronconi. This he took to Eng. and although his wife d. in 1874 carried on as the C. R. Opera Company.

Rosa, Salvator(e) (b. Arenella nr. Naples, 21. VI. 1615; d. Rome, 15. III. 1673), It. painter, lutenist, comp. & writer. Studied m. before painting, but worked seriously at the latter in Rome and Naples, and in 1640 became court painter to the Medici family at Florence. He left in 1647 and lived at var. places, incl. Rome, Naples, Pisa, Siena and Florence, writing poetry, satires on m., painting, poetry, &c., painting and comp. some of his own verses, others of which were set by his comp.-friends, Cesti, Bandini and Cavalli.

Works incl. cantatas, songs, incl. 'Vado ben spesso,' 'Star vicino,' 'Selve, voi che,' &c.

Rosalia. The usual name for the Real Sequence repeating a phrase higher or lower, not within the scale of the same key, as in the Tonal Sequence, but by so changing the key that its steps retain exactly the same succession of whole tones and semitones. The name derives from an It. popular song, 'Rosalia, mia bella,' in which this device occurs.

Rosalie. *See* **Levasseur.**

Rosamond, opera by Arne (lib. by Joseph Addison), prod. London, Theatre in Lincoln's Inn Fields, 7. III. 1733.

Opera by Clayton (lib. do.), prod. London, Drury Lane Theatre, 4. III. 1707.

Rosamunde. Incid. m. by Schubert for a play by Helmina von Chézy, *Rosamunde, Prinzessin von Cypern,* prod. Vienna, Theater an der Wien, 20. XII. 1823. The m. consists of 3 entr'actes, 2 ballet tunes, a romance for con., a chor. of spirits, a shepherd's melody & shepherds' chor. & a hunting-chor. No ovt. was specially written for the piece. At the 1st perf. that to the opera *Alfonso und Estrella* was used; later that to the melodrama *Die Zauberharfe* was pub. as *Rosamunde* ovt. and is still so played.

Rose. The ornamental fretwork sound-hole of many flat-bellied stg. insts. of the lute and guitar type, also of dulcimers, hpchds., &c., sometimes serving as the makers' trade-mark. Another name for it is Knot.

Rose Cavalier (R. Strauss). *See* **Rosenkavalier.**

Rose et Colas, opera by Monsigny (lib. by Jean Michel Sedaine), prod. Paris, Comédie-Italienne, 8. III. 1764.

Rose of Castille (*sic*), **The,** opera by Balfe (lib. by Augustus Glossop Harris and Edmund Falconer, based on a Fr. lib., *Le Muletier de Tolède,* by Adolphe Philippe d'Ennery & Clairville, set by Auber and prod. 1854), prod. London, Lyceum Theatre, 29. X. 1857.

Rose of Persia, The, or The Story-Teller and the Slave, operetta by Sullivan (lib. by Basil Hood); prod. London, Savoy Theatre, 29. XI. 1899.

Roseingrave. Eng. family of musns.:

1. Daniel R. (b. ? London, *c.* 1650; d. Dublin, V. 1727), orgst. & comp. Educ. in m. as a boy chorister in the Chapel Royal in London, under Cook or Humfrey, and (?) as a pupil of Blow and Purcell. In 1679–98 he was successively orgst. of Gloucester, Winchester and Salisbury caths., and was then app. to St. Patrick's and Christ Church caths., Dublin.

Works incl. services, anthems, &c.

2. Thomas R. (b. Winchester, *c.* 1690; d. Dunleary nr. Dublin, 23. VI. 1766), Eng. orgst. and comp., son of prec. Pupil of his father at Dublin, where he was educ. at Trinity Coll. In 1710 he went to It. where he met A. and D. Scarlatti, making great friends with the latter and travelling with him. He went to London before 1720, when he prod. D. Scarlatti's opera *Narciso* with interpolations of his own. In 1725 he was app. orgst. of St. George's Church, Hanover Square. He fell in love with a pupil, whose father forbade her marriage to him, and his mind was affected. He retired in 1737 and the next year moved to Dublin, living prob. with his nephew William R. (1725–?), a son of 3.

Works incl. opera *Phaedra and Hippolytus*; services & anthems; org. voluntaries & fugues; suites for hpchd. & an introd. pieces for his ed. of Scarlatti's sos.; 12 solos for fl. & hpchd.; 6 It. cantatas, &c.

3. Ralph R. (b. Salisbury, *c.* 1695; d. Dublin, 1747), Eng. orgst. & comp., brother of prec. Studied with his father, who petitioned for him to succeed him as orgst. of St. Patrick's cath., Dublin, in 1719; but he was app. vicar-chor., and not orgst. till 1726. He also became orgst. of Christ Church cath. on his father's death.

Works incl. services, anthems, &c.

Rosenberg, Hilding (Constantin) (b. Bosjökloster, 21. VI. 1892), Swe. cond. & comp. Studied at the Stockholm Cons., and at Dresden, Berlin, Vienna and Paris. On his return to Swe. he was app. cond. of the Stockholm Opera.

Works incl. operas *Journey to America* & *Marionettes*; 2 ballets; incid. m. to Gr. tragedies & other plays; Christmas & Good Friday orats.; 4 syms., *Sinfonia concertante,* Suite, &c. for orch.; v. Conc., tpt. Conc.; 3 stg. 4tets, stg. Trio, Trio for fl., v. & va.; Suite for v. & pf.; So. for solo v.; 4 pf. sos., &c.

Rosenhain, Jacob (b. Mannheim, 2. XII. 1813; d. Baden-Baden, 21. III. 1894), Ger. pfst. & comp. Studied with Kalliwoda, Schnyder von Wartensee and others, and made his 1st appearance as a pfst. at Frankfort o/M. in 1832. He visited London in 1837 and then settled in Paris, where he played and taught.

Works incl. operas *Der Besuch im Irrenhause*, *Liswenna* (*Le Démon de la Nuit*), *Volage et jaloux*; 3 syms.; pf. Conc.; 3 stg. 4tets, 4 pf. trios; 2 co. & pf. sos.; So., studies & pieces for pf.; songs, &c.

Rosenkavalier, Der (*The Rose Cavalier*), opera by R. Strauss (lib. by Hugo von Hofmannsthal), prod. Dresden, Royal Opera, 26. I. 1911.

Rosenmüller, Johann (b. Oelsnitz, Saxony, *c.* 1619; d. Wolfenbüttel, 10–11. IX. 1684), Ger. comp. Studied at Leipzig Univ. and in 1642 became asst. master at St. Thomas's School there, studying m. with the cantor, Tobias Michael, for whom he deputized when he (M.) became infirm. He was marked out for the succession and in 1651 became orgst. of St. Nicholas's church; but in 1655 he was imprisoned for a moral offence, escaping to Hamburg and later fleeing to Venice, where he settled and was influenced as a comp. by the local style. There J. P. Krieger became his pupil. In 1674 he was recalled to Ger. by an appt. to the court of Duke Anton Ulrich of Brunswick at Wolfenbüttel.

Works incl. masses, motets, vesper psalms & lamentations, Lat. & Ger. motets *Kernsprüche* for 3–7 voices & insts., Ger. motets & cantatas, hymns, hymn by Albinus ' Straf mich nicht'; *Sonate da camera* for 5 insts., sos. for 2–5 insts., suites of inst. dances, &c.

Rosenthal, Manuel (orig. Emmanuel) (b. Paris, 18. VI. 1904), Fr. cond. & comp. Studied at the Paris Cons., with Ravel and others. He became leader of var. orchs. and in 1939 2nd cond. of the nat. wireless orch.

Works incl. comic opera *Rayon des soieries*, operettas *Les Bootleggers* & *La Poule noire*; ballet *Un Baiser pour rien*; orat. *Saint François d'Assise*; suite *Jeanne d'Arc*, *Fête du vin*, *Les Petits Métiers*, Serenade for orch.; Sonatina for 2 vs. & pf.; pf. pieces; songs, &c.

Rosetti, Francesco Antonio. *See* **Rössler.**

Rosin (also called Resin). A preparation made of gum of turpentine applied to the hair of the bows of stg. insts. to prod. the required friction on the stgs.

Rosina, ballad opera by Shield (lib. by Frances Brooke, based on an episode in Thomson's *Seasons* and Favart's *Les Moissonneurs* with Duni's m.), prod. London, Covent Garden Theatre, 31. XII. 1782.

Roslavets, Nikolai Andreievitch (b. Surai, Gvt. of Tchernigov, 5. I. 1881), Rus. comp. He came of peasant stock, but studied m. at the Moscow Cons. and attracted attention by his advanced tendencies.

Works incl. cantata *Heaven and Earth* (after Byron); Sym., 2 symph. poems; 5 stg. 4tets, 5tet for ob., 2 vs., co. & hp., 2 pf. trios; 5 v. & pf. sos., 2 co. & pf. sos.; many pf. pieces; songs, &c.

Rosmene, La, ovvero L'infedeltà fedele (*R., or Faithful Faithlessness*), opera by A. Scarlatti (lib. by Giuseppe Domenico de Totis), prod. Naples, Palazzo Reale, Carnival 1688.

Rossellini, Renzo (b. Rome, 2. II. 1908), It. comp. Pupil of Sallustio, Settacioli and Molinari.

Works incl. operas *Alcassino e Nicoletta* & *Ljhadéh*; ballets *La danza di Dassine* (m. adapt. from *Hoggar* Suite) & *Gli amanti di Siviglia*; *Suite in tre tempi*, rhapsodic suite *Hoggar*, *Preludio all' Aminta del Tasso*, *Canti di marzo* & *Ditirambo a Dioniso* for orch.; pf. Trio, &c.

Rossello, Francesco. *See* **Roussel, François.**

Rosseter, Philip (b. ?, *c.* 1575; d. London, 5. V. 1623), Eng. lutenist & comp. Worked in London and was assoc. with R. Jones, Kingham and Reeve in the training of the children for the queen's revels; also with Campion, with whom he was on terms of friendship and pub. a book of songs to the lute, some if not all of the words by C. and half of the m. by R.

Works incl. *A Booke of Ayres* with lute, orpheoreon & bass viol; *Lessons for the Consort* for 6 insts. by var. comps., &c.

Rossetti, Christina (Georgina) (1830–94), Eng. poetess of It. descent. *See* **Finzi** (Children's Songs), **Ireland (J.)** (*Mother and Child*).

Rossetti, Dante Gabriel (1828–82), Eng. poet & painter of It. descent, brother of prec. *See* **Bainton** (*Blessed Damozel*), **Damoiselle élue** (Debussy), **Gasco** (*Sette torri*), **Orr (C. W.)** (songs), **Vaughan Williams** (*Silent Noon* & *House of Life*), **Wallace (W.)** (*Sister Helen*), **White (F.** (*Astarte Syriaca*).

Rossetto, Steffano (b. Nice, ?; d. ?). It. 16th-cent. orgst. & comp. He lived at Florence in the 1560s as musn. to Cardinal de' Medici, was court orgst. at Munich in 1579–80 and later (?) orgst. at Novara.

Works incl. motets in 5–6 parts for

voices & insts. in diff. combs.; madrigal cycle *Il lamento di Olimpia*, other madrigals for 4–6 voices, &c.

Rossi, Giovanni Gaetano (b. Borgo San Donnino nr. Parma, 5. VIII. 1828; d. Genoa, 30. III. 1886), It. cond. & comp. Studied at the Milan Cons. App. leader of the theatre orch. and orgst. at the court chapel of Parma; dir. of the Cons. there in 1864–73; cond. of the Teatro Carlo Felice at Genoa, 1873–9.

Works incl. operas *Elena di Taranto, Giovanni Giscala, Nicolò de' Lapi, La Contessa d'Altemberg*; 3 masses, Requiem; orat.; sym. *Saul*, &c.

Rossi, Lauro (b. Macerata, 19. II. 1810; d. Cremona, 5. V. 1885), It. comp. Studied at Naples with Zingarelli and others, and began to prod. operas at the age of 18. He had much success in It. cities until 1835, when he left for Mexico in disgust after a failure. Thence he went as far as India, but returned to Eur. in 1843 and again prod. many operas. In 1870 he succeeded Mercadante as dir. of the Naples Cons.

Works incl. operas *Le contesse villane, Il casino di campagna, Costanza ed Oringaldo, La casa disabitata, Amelia, Leocadia, Cellini a Parigi, Azema di Granata, Il borgomastro di Schiedam, Il domino nero, Bianca Contarini, La Contessa di Mons, La figlia di Figaro, Biorn* (after Shakespeare's *Macbeth*) & 15 others; orat. *Saul*; mass; 6 fugues for stgs.; elegies on the deaths of Bellini and Mercadante, &c.

Rossi, Luigi (b. Torre Maggiore, 1598; d. Rome, 19. II. 1653), It. singer & comp. He was in the service of Cardinal Barberini in Rome *c.* 1620. In 1647 he was called to Paris at the instigation of Mazarin and prod. his *Orpheus* as one of the 1st It. operas to be given there.

Works incl. operas *Il palagio d'Atlante* (or *Il palazzo incantato*), *Le nozze d'Orfeo e d'Euridice*; orat. *Giuseppe*, cantatas, &c.

Rossi, Michele Angelo (b. ? Rome, *c.* 1600; d. ? Rome, *c.* 1660), It. orgst. & comp. Pupil of Frescobaldi. His opera, to a lib. by Giulio Rospigliosi, later Pope Clement IX, was given in Rome in 1633.

Works incl. operas *Erminia sul Giordano* (after Tasso) & *Andromeda*; toccatas and correnti for org. or hpchd., &c.

Rossi, Salomone (b. ?, *c.* 1560; d. ? Mantua, *c.* 1630), It. comp. He worked at the court of Mantua and enjoyed the privilege of dispensing with the wearing of the yellow badge that stigmatized the Jews in It.

Works incl. m. for Guarini's *Idropica* & orat. *Maddalena* (both with Monteverdi & others); 28 Hebrew psalms for 4–8 voices; madrigals & canzonets; inst. works *Sinfonie e gagliarde* & *Sonate*, &c.

Rossignol, Félix Ludger. *See* **Joncières.**

Rossignol, Le (Stravinsky). *See* **Nightingale.**

Rossini, Gioacchino (Antonio) (b. Pesaro, 29. II. 1792; d. Paris, 13. XI. 1868), It comp. His father was a hn. and tpt. player, his mother a singer in a small way. He learnt pf., singing and harmony early and at 10 sang in churches; at 13 he was cembalo and hn. player at the theatre and at 15, when he had already tried his hand at an opera and other works, he entered the Bologna Liceo Musicale, studying ctpt. and co. In 1808 he won a prize with a cantata and in 1810 had his 1st comic opera, *La cambiale di matrimonio*, prod. at Venice. From that time he went from success to success, the 1st great one being *Tancredi* at Venice in 1813, but *Il barbiere di Siviglia* was at first a failure in Rome in 1816. His 1st great foreign success came during a visit to Vienna in 1822, soon after his marriage to the Spa. sop. Isabella Colbran, 16. III. *Semiramide*, prod. at Venice in 1823, was his last opera written for the It. stage: he and his wife went to Paris and to London that year, remaining in Eng. until VII. 1824, being well received at court. He wrote a lament on the death of Byron for 8 voices. On returning to Paris he was app. dir. of the Théâtre Italien, where he prod. a new and 2 revised works, followed by a Fr. comic opera, *Le Comte Ory* and finally *Guillaume Tell* (1829) at the Opéra. After that, although only 37, he gave up opera and lived alternately at Bologna and Paris. In 1832, at Aix-les-Bains, he met Olympe Pélissier, a demimondaine, and entered into a liaison with her; his separation from Isabella was legalized in 1837, she d. in 1845, and he married Olympe on 21. VIII. 1846. He wrote very little and took 10 years to complete the *Stabat Mater* (1831–41). In 1839 he was commissioned to reform the Liceo Musicale at Bologna, where he had once been a pupil, and he worked there at intervals until 1848, when he left for Florence, to remain until 1855, leaving It. for the last time for Paris that year. In his retirement he wrote many small pieces for the entertainment of his friends and in 1863 the *Petite Messe solennelle*; and his dinner parties, for which he cooked the food himself, were much sought after.

Works incl. operas *La cambiale di matrimonio, L'equivoco stravagante, L'inganno felice, Ciro in Babilonia, La scala di seta, La pietra del paragone, L'occasione fà il ladro, Il signore Bruschino, Tancredi, L'Italiana in Algeri, Aureliano in Palmira, Il Turco in Italia, Sigismondo, Elisabetta, regina d'Inghilterra, Torvaldo e Dorliska, Il barbiere di Siviglia* (after Beaumarchais), *La gazzetta, Otello* (after Shakespeare), *La Cenerentola, La gazza ladra, Armida, Adelaida di Borgogna, Mosè in Egitto, Adina, Ricciardo e Zoraide, Ermione* (on Racine's *Andromaque*), *Edoardo e Cristina, La donna del lago* (after Scott), *Bianca e Falliero, Maometto secondo, Matilda di Shabran, Zelmira, Semiramide, Il viaggio a Reims, Le Siège de Corinthe* (Fr. rev. version of *Maometto secondo*), *Moïse* (Fr. rev. version of *Mosè in Egitto*), *Le Comte Ory, Guillaume Tell* (after Schiller); 15 cantatas; *Missa solenne, Stabat Mater, La Foi, l'Espérance, la Charité, Petite Messe solennelle* & some shorter sacred pieces; *Soirées musicales* (songs & duets); *Péchés de vieillesse* (small pf. pieces, songs, &c.); a number of works written in his youth incl. the opera *Demetrio e Polibio*, a Mass for male voices, duets for hns., 2 ovts. & 5 stg. 4tets. 6 pasticcios with m. from his works were prod. in his lifetime, and a modern one is the ballet *La Boutique fantasque* arr. by Respighi from *Péchés de vieillesse* &c.

Rössler, Franz Anton (b. Litoměřice, 1750; d. Ludwigslust, Mecklenburg-Schwerin, 30. VI. 1792), Boh. comp. Destined for the priesthood, he attended the Jesuit Coll. of Olomouc, but in 1773 entered the service of the Prince of Öttingen as db. player and later became cond. He left for Ludwigslust in 1789 and was court mus. dir. there to his death. He wrote under the name of Francesco Antonio Rosetti.

Works incl. opera *Das Winterfest der Hirten*; orats. *Der sterbende Jesus & Jesus in Gethsemane*; Requiem for Mozart; 34 syms.; chamber m.; v. sos., &c.

Rostand, Edmond (1868–1918), Fr. poet & dramatist. *See* **Addinsell** (*Aiglon*), **Aiglon** (Honegger & Ibert), **Cyrano de Bergerac** (Alfano & W. Damrosch), **Gipps** (*Chantecler*), **Hahn** (*Bois sacré*), **Hüe** (*Romanesques*), **Jacobson** (*Woman of Samaria*), **Maclean (A.)** (*Cyrano de B.*), **Montemezzi** (*Princesse lointaine*), **Nouguès** (*Cyrano de B.*), **Ollone** (*Samaritaine*), **Pierné** (*Princesse l.*), **Stoessel** (*Cyrano de B.*), **Tcherepnin (A.)** (*Princesse l.*), **Wagenaar (J.)** (*Cyrano de B.*), **Witkowski** (*Princesse l.*).

Rota. Another form of the name of the Rote or Rotte; also an old term for a Round, e.g. *Sumer is icumen in*, known as the Reading R.

Rota, Andrea (b. Bologna, c. 1553; d. Bologna, VI. 1597), It. comp. He became choirmaster at San Petronio cath. at Bologna in 1583.

Works incl. masses, motets, *Agnus Dei* (with double canon), *Dixit Dominus* for 8 voices & other church m.: madrigals, &c.

Rota, Nino (b. Milan, 3. XII. 1911), It. comp. Studied with Pizzetti, Casella and in U.S.A. On his return to Milan he obtained a degree with a treatise on Zarlino and It. Renascence m.

Works incl. operas *Il principe porcaro* (after Hans Andersen) & *L'isola disabitata* (Metastasio); orat. *L'infanzia di San Giovanni Battista*; Sym., Serenade, *Balli & Canzona* for orch.; *Invenzioni* for stg. 4tet, 5tet for fl., ob., va., co. & hp., *Il presepio* for voice, stg. 4tet & pf.; sos. for v. & pf., va. & pf. and fl. & hp.; songs *Liriche di Tagore, Tre liriche infantili*, &c.

Rote. An obs. inst. of the lyre type, also called Rota or Rotte, and similar to the Crwth. It was in use up to medieval times.

Rotte. *See* **Rote.**

Rouget de Lisle, Claude Joseph (b. Lons-le-Saulnier, 10. V. 1760; d. Choisy-le-Roi, 26–7. VI. 1836), Fr. soldier, author & musn. After starting a military career, he settled at Strasburg in 1791 and made a name as poet, vst. & singer. He wrote the *Hymne à la liberté*, set by I. Pleyel, that year and words and m. of the *Marseillaise* in 1792. Similar later pieces of the kind were *Hymne dithyrambique, Le Chant des vengeances, Le Chant des combats, Hymne à la Raison, Hymne du 9 Thermidor* and *Les Héros du Vengeur*. He also wrote libs., incl. *Bayard dans Bresse* for Champein and *Macbeth* (based on Shakespeare) for Chelard.

Roulade. *See* **Ornaments.**

Round. A kind of Canon best defined by saying that its successive entries consist of complete melodies rather than mere phrases. The entries are thus apt to lie farther apart. Unlike canons, Rs. are always sung with the theme in its orig. position or in the octave, never at other intervals. An older name for the R. was Rota: *Sumer is icumen in*, known as the 'Reading Rota,' is a typical early R. A familiar later ex. is in the 2nd finale of Mozart's *Così fan tutte*.

Roundelays. Country songs of the 14th cent., so called, from the Fr. *rondelet*, because their words returned to the opening lines again and again; also round dances.

Rounds. Round dances, i.e. dances perf. in circles, and hence tunes intended for such dances.

Rousseau, Jean Baptiste (1669–1741), Fr. poet. *See* **Floquet** (*Gloire du Seigneur*), **Vénus et Adonis** (Desmarets).

Rousseau, Jean Jacques (b. Geneva, 28. VI. 1712; d. Ermenonville nr. Paris, 2. VII. 1778), Swi. author, philosopher & musn. Studied m. with a chapel master, was (?) musn. at Chambéry in 1735–7 and settled in Paris in 1742, when he gave a lecture to the Académie des Sciences, pub. in 1743 as *Dissertation sur la musique moderne*, advocating a new system of notation. In 1745 he prod. his opera *Les Muses galantes* at La Poupelinière's house and soon afterwards contrib. mus. articles to the *Encyclopédie*, which were unsatisfactory owing to his defective knowledge. In the Guerre des Bouffons he sided with the Its. and aroused great indignation with his *Lettre sur la musique française* in 1753. In 1764 he finished a *Dictionnaire de musique*. He pub. a number of controversial essays and open letters, incl. 2 in defence of Gluck. In his comps. he had the help of Francœur and the advice of the ten. Jélyotte.

Works incl. operas *Iphis et Anaxarète*, *La Découverte du nouveau monde*, *Les Fêtes de Ramire*, *Les Muses galantes*, *Le Devin du village* & *Daphnis et Chloé* (unfinished); monodrama *Pygmalion*; c. 100 songs and pieces pub. as *Consolations des misères de ma vie*, &c.

For literary works used by comps. *see* **Bastien und Bastienne** (Mozart), **Favart** (*Devin du village*), **Heller** (*Promenades d'un solitaire*), **Pimmaglione** (Cimadoro).

Rousseau, Marcel (Auguste Louis; called **Marcel Samuel-R.)** (b. Paris, 18. VIII. 1882), Fr. comp. Pupil of his father and of Lenepveu. He took the Prix de Rome in 1905.

Works incl. operas *Tarass-Boulba* (after Gogol), *Le Hulla*, *Le Bon Roi Dagobert* & *Yamilé sous les cèdres*; ballet *Promenade dans Rome*; incid. m. for Racine's *Bérénice*, &c.

Rousseau, Samuel (Alexandre) (b. Neuve-Maison, Aisne, 11. VI. 1853; d. Paris, 1. X. 1904), Fr. comp., father of prec. Studied at the Paris Cons., gaining the Prix de Rome in 1878. He became chapel master at the church of Sainte-Clotilde and held other mus. offices.

Works incl. operas *Dianora*, *La Cloche du Rhin*, *Mérowig*, *Milia* & *Leone*; masses, motets & other church m.; symph. poems *Sabinus*, *Kaddir*, *La Florentine*; cantata *La Fille de Jephté* & other chor. works; org. & pf. works; inst. pieces, &c.

Roussel, Albert (b. Tourcoing, 5. IV. 1869; d. Royan, 23. VIII. 1937), Fr. comp. Educ. in Paris for the Navy, but took pf. lessons at the same time. Wrote his 1st comps. while engaged in naval service and voyaging to the East, but he resigned in 1893 to devote himself to m., studying with Gigout and d'Indy. In 1902 he became prof. at the Schola Cantorum, where he had studied. In the 1914–8 war he served with the Red Cross and later with the transport service, in 1918 retired, broken in health, to Perros - Guirec in Brittany and in 1920 to a villa nr. Varengeville.

Works incl. operas *Padmâvati*, *La Naissance de la lyre*; operetta *Le Testament de Tante Caroline*; ballets *Le Festin de l'araignée*, *Bacchus et Ariane*, *Énée*, *Les Enchantements d'Alcine* & contrib. to *L'Éventail de Jeanne*; incid. m. to Jean-Aubry's *Le Marchand de sable qui passe*; prelude to Act II of Rolland's *14 Juillet* (with 6 others); Psalm lxxx for ten., chor. & orch. (in Eng.); 4 syms. (No. 1 *Le Poème de la forêt*), *3 Évocations* (3rd with chor.), *Pour une fête de printemps*, *Suite en Fa*, *Concert*, *Petite Suite*, *Rapsodie flamande* for orch.; Sinfonietta for stgs.; *A Glorious Day* for milit. band; pf. Conc., Concertino for co. & orch.; stg. 4tet, *Divertissement* for wind & pf., Serenade for fl., v., va., co. & hp., stg. Trio, trios for v., cl. & pf. and fl., v. & cl.; 2 v. & pf. sos., *Joueurs de flûte* for fl. & pf.; Impromptu for hp.; *Segovia* for guitar; Suite *Des heures passent*, *Rustiques*, *Suite*, Sonatina, Prelude & Fugue (*Hommage à Bach*) &c. for pf.; songs *6 Odes anacréontiques*, *2 Poèmes chinois*, 8 poems by Henri de Régnier, 2 poems by Ronsard, *A Flower given to my Daughter* (James Joyce), &c.

Roussel, François (Francesco Rossello) (b. ? ; d. ?), Fr. 16th-cent. musn. Succeeded Ferrabosco as master of the children at Santa Maria Maggiore in Rome, 1548–50. In 1572–3 he was chapel master at San Giovanni in Laterano there.

Works incl. church m., &c.

Roux, Gaspard Le. *See* **Le Roux.**

Rovescio. *See* **Cancrizans, Palindrome & Recte et retro.**

Rovetta, Giovanni (b. Venice, ?; d. Venice, VIII. 1668), It. priest & comp. Learnt m. as a choir-boy at

St. Mark's in Venice and in 1623 was app. a bass singer there. He was ordained priest, became vice chapel master at St. Mark's in 1627 and 1st chapel master on Monteverdi's death in 1644, being himself succeeded by Cavalli.

Works incl. masses, motets, psalms, operas, madrigals, &c.

Rowe, Nicholas (1674–1718), Eng. dramatist. *See* **Conti (C.)** (*Giovanna Shore*), **Eccles** (*The Biter*), **Lenton** (*Tamerlane* & *Fair Penitent*).

Rowe, Walter (b. ?; d. ?), Eng. 16th–17th-cent. violist & comp. He was at Hamburg before 1614, when he was app. violist at the court chapel in Berlin. He had a son of the same name and occupation (d. Berlin, 1671).

Works incl. m. for va. da gamba.

Rowley, Alec (b. London, 13. III. 1892), Eng. pfst., teacher & comp. Studied at the R.A.M. in London and became prof. and examiner at Trinity Coll. of M. there in 1920.

Works incl. mimed ballet *The Princess who lost a Tune*; *Burlesque Quadrilles* for orch.; 2 pf. concs. (1st with milit. band), Rhapsody for va. & orch., ob. Conc.; Suite for chor. (without words); stg. 4tet, 2 trios for fl., ob. & pf.; many pf. pieces, mainly educ., &c.

Roxolane, La. The nickname of a Sym. by Haydn, No. 63, in C maj., comp. in 1777.

Roy, Adrien Le. *See* **Le Roy.**

Royal Academy of Music. Founded in London in 1822 and opened in III. 1823 with Crotch as principal, who was followed by Potter (1832), Charles Lucas (1859), Sterndale Bennett (1866), Macfarren (1875), Mackenzie (1888), McEwen (1924) and Stanley Marchant (1936).

Royal College of Music. Founded in London in 1882 and opened on 7. V. 1883 with Grove as dir., who was followed by Parry (1894), Hugh Allen (1918) and George Dyson (1938).

Royal Philharmonic Society. A soc. formed in London for the cultivation of good orch. m. in 1813 by J. B. Cramer, P. A. Corri and W. Dance. The 1st concert was given at the Argyll Rooms, 8. III. 1813, cond. by Clementi (at the pf.) and led by J. P. Salomon. Among the 1st members were Attwood, Ayrton, Bishop, Horsley, Knyvett, V. Novello, Potter, Shield, G. Smart, Viotti & Webbe, jun. It has continued uninterruptedly until the present day. Among later conds. were Weber, Mendelssohn, Spohr, Wagner, Sullivan, Mackenzie, H. J. Wood, Nikisch, Chevillard, Elgar, Safonov, Bruno Walter, Beecham, Mengelberg, Stanford, Hamilton Harty, Furtwängler, Weingartner & Monteux. Beethoven figured in the programmes from the first and when he was on his deathbed the P. S. sent him the sum of £100.

Roze (*née* **Ponsin**), **Marie (Hippolyte)** (b. Paris, 2. III. 1846; d. nr. Paris, 21. VI. 1926), Fr. sop. singer. Studied at the Paris Cons. and made her 1st appearance, at the Opéra-Comique, in 1865. Later she also sang at the Opéra and in Brussels, and in 1872 she 1st visited London. She remained in Eng. as a member of the Carl Rosa Opera Co. until 1890, when she returned to Paris to settle down as a teacher.

Rozkošný, Josef Richard (b. Prague, 21. X. 1833; d. Prague, 3. VI. 1913), Cz. pfst. & comp. Studied in Prague and toured as pfst. in Aus., Hung., It., Serbia and Rum. Later had a great success as a popular opera comp.

Works incl. operas *Nicholas, The Rapids of St. John, Cinderella, Stoja, Zavis of Falkenstein, Krakonos, The Poacher, Satanella, The Black Lake*; pf. pieces; songs, &c.

Rózycki, Ludomir (b. Warsaw, 6. XI. 1883), Pol. cond. & comp. Studied with Noskowski at the Warsaw Cons. and with Humperdinck in Berlin. In 1912 he became cond. at Lwów, and later lived by turns in Warsaw and Berlin.

Works incl. operas *Boleslaw the Bold, Medusa, Eros and Psyche, Casanova, Beatrice Cenci, The Devil's Mill*; ballet *Pan Twardowski*; symph. poems *Boleslaw the Bold, Anhelli* & others, Prelude *Mona Lisa Gioconda* & Ballad for orch.; pf. Conc. in G min.; stg. 4tet, pf. 5tet, Rhapsody for pf. trio; co. & pf. So.; pf. pieces; songs, &c.

Rub-a-dub. *See* **Rataplan.**

Rubato (It. lit. 'robbed'). A manner of perf. m. without adhering strictly to time. Var. rules have been estab. at different times, e.g. that what is taken away by hurrying from the time properly occupied by a comp. as written, must be given back elsewhere by slackening, or that in pf. m. the right hand only may play R. while the left keeps strict time; but R. should be subject, not to rules, but to feeling, and it cannot be taught to those who have either no sense or an exaggerated notion of it.

Rubbra, Edmund (Duncan) (b. Northampton, 23. V. 1901), Eng. comp. Studied at Reading Univ. and the R.C.M. in London, Holst, Vaughan Williams and R. O. Morris being among his masters. Married the Fr. vst. Antoinette Chapin in 1933.

Works incl. opera *Beebee-bei*; *La Belle Dame sans merci* (Keats) & 2 Poems for chor. & orch.; 5 syms., Double Fugue & Triple Fugue for orch.; Conc. and *Sinfonia concertante* for pf. & orch., Fantasy & Rhapsody for v. & orch., *Soliloquy* for co. & stg. orch., 2 hns. & timp.; 4 Medieval Lat. Lyrics, 5 Motets & *The Revival* (Henry Vaughan) for unaccomp. chor.; stg. 4tet, Fantasies for pf. 5tet and for 2 vs. & pf.; 2 v. & pf. sos.; *Ballad of Tristram* for voice & chamber orch., 10 *Amoretti* (Spenser) for voice & stg. 4tet; 3 songs for children, many other songs, &c.

Rubebe or **Rubible** (Eng., obs.). Other old words for the Rebec, or for a slightly different inst. of the same type.

Rubinelli, Giovanni Battista (b. Brescia, 1753; d. Brescia, 1829), It. singer. Made his 1st stage appearance at Stuttgart in 1771, where he remained in the ducal chapel of the court of Württemberg, but from 1774 he sang much in It. and in 1786 visited London.

Rubini, Giovanni Battista (b. Romano nr. Bergamo, 7. IV. 1795; d. Romano, 2. III. 1854), It. ten. singer. He began with small engagements, but made his way to Venice, Naples and Rome, where his successes in opera increased steadily. In 1819 he married the Fr. singer Chomel at Naples, visited Paris for the 1st time in 1825 and London in 1831. In 1843 he toured Hol. and Ger. with Liszt, and went on alone to St. Petersburg.

Rubinstein, Anton Grigorevitch (b. Vekhvotinets, Volhynia, 28. XI. 1829; d. Peterhof, 20. XI. 1894), Rus. pfst. & comp. of Ger.-Pol. descent. Learnt the pf. from his mother and from a teacher named Villoing at Moscow. He appeared in public at the age of 9 and in 1840 went on tour with his teacher, who took him to Paris and placed him under Liszt for further instruction. He afterwards went to Eng., Hol., Ger. and Swe. and in 1845 studied comp. with Dehn in Berlin. After teaching in Vienna and Pressburg he returned to Rus. in 1848, becoming chamber virtuoso to the Grand Duchess Helena Pavlovna. From 1856 onward he again travelled widely as a pfst. and in 1858 he was app. imp. mus. dir. at St. Petersburg, founding the Cons. in 1862.

Works incl. operas & stage orats. *Dimitry Donskoy*, *The Siberian Hunters*, *Children of the Heath*, *Feramors* (from Moore's *Lalla Rookh*), *The Tower of Babel*, *The Demon* (after Lermontov), *The Maccabees* (after Otto Ludwig), *Paradise Lost* (after Milton), *Nero*, *The Merchant of Moscow*, *The Shulamite*, *Moses*, *Christus* & others; Songs and Requiem for Mignon from Goethe's *Wilhelm Meister* for solo voices, chor. & pf.; 6 syms. (2. *Ocean*, 4. *Dramatic*), 4 concert ovts. (1 on Shakespeare's *Antony and Cleopatra*), mus. portraits *Faust* (after Goethe), *Ivan the Terrible*, *Don Quixote* (after Cervantes), Suite in E♭ maj. for orch.; 5 concs. and *Conzertstück* for pf. & orch.; v. Conc., 2 co. concs.; 10 stg. 4tets, stg. 5tet & 6tet, Octet for pf., stgs. & wind, 5 pf. trios, pf. & wind 5tet, pf. 5tet & 4tet; 3 v. & pf. sos., va. & pf. So., 2 co. & pf. sos.; inst. pieces; 4 sos., Theme & Vars. and many other works for pf.; *Bal costumé* for pf. duet; numerous songs, &c.

Rubinstein, Nikolai Grigorevitch (b. Moscow, 2. VI. 1835; d. Paris, 23. III. 1881), Rus. pfst. & comp., of Ger.-Pol. descent, brother of prec. Studied under Kullak and Dehn in Berlin and after his return to Rus. settled at Moscow, where he founded the Rus. M. Soc. in 1859 and the Cons. in 1864, to which he invited Tchaikovsky as prof.

Rubsamen, Walter (b. New York, 21. VII. 1911), Amer. mcolst. Studied at Columbia Coll., N.Y. and at Munich Univ., later joined the m. dept. of his coll. and in 1938 became lecturer in mus. hist. at the Univ. of California at Los Angeles. His works incl. studies of Pierre de La Rue, old It. secular m., &c.

Ruckers. Flem. family of hpchd. makers:

1. Hans R. (b. ?, *c.* 1550; d. Antwerp, *c.* 1625).

2. Joannes R. (b. Antwerp, I. 1578; d. Antwerp, 1642), son of prec.

3. Andries R. (b. Antwerp, VIII. 1579; d. Antwerp, *c.* 1652), brother of prec.

4. Andries R. (b. Antwerp, 1607; d. Antwerp, *c.* 1670, son of prec.

5. Christophel R. (b. Antwerp, *c.* 1620; d. ?), son of ?.

Rückert, Friedrich (1788–1866), Ger. poet. *See* **Kindertotenlieder** (Mahler), **Rudorff** (*Gesang an die Sterne*), also 5 other songs by Mahler, 5 by Schubert, 18 by Schumann, 2 by Brahms.

Ruddigore, or The Witch's Curse, operetta by Sullivan (lib. by W. S. Gilbert), prod. London, Savoy Theatre, 22. I. 1887.

Rudersdorff, Hermine (b. Ivanovsky, Ukraine, 12. XII. 1822; d. Boston, 26. II. 1882), Ger. sop. singer. Learnt m. from her father, the vst-

Joseph R., and singing in Paris, Milan and London. She made her 1st appearance in Ger. at the age of 18, sang in the prod. of Mendelssohn's *Hymn of Praise* at Leipzig in 1840 and then appeared in opera at Carlsruhe and Frankfort o/M. In 1854 she 1st visited London, where she remained for a number of years, but settled at Boston in the 1870s.

Rudhyar, Dane (b. Paris, 23. III. 1895), Fr.-Amer. comp. Studied in Paris and settled in U.S.A. in 1916, receiving a comp. prize in 1920.

Works incl. ballet *Dance Poem*; symph. poem *Surge of Fire* & other orch. works; pf. pieces, m. for 2 pfs.; songs, &c.

Rudolph (Johann Joseph Rainer) of Habsburg, Archduke (b. Florence, 8. I. 1788; d. Baden nr. Vienna, 24. VII. 1831), Aus. amateur musn. Pupil of Anton Teyber, mus. instructor of the imp. children, and later, by his own choice, of Beethoven, who wrote the *Missa solemnis* for his installation as Archbishop of Olomouc (1820), though he finished it 3 years too late.

Works incl. So. for cl. & pf.; Vars. for pf. on themes by Beethoven and Rossini, &c.

Rudorff, Ernst (b. Berlin, 18. I. 1840; d. Berlin, 31. XII. 1916), Ger. pfst., teacher & comp. Pupil of Bargiel, Clara Schumann and others, later studied at the Leipzig Univ. and Cons. In 1865 he became prof. at the Cologne Cons. and in 1869–1910 at the Hochschule für Musik in Berlin. He also cond. Stern's Voc. Acad. in 1880–90.

Works incl. *Der Aufzug der Romanze* (Tieck) for solo voices, chor. & orch., *Gesang an die Sterne* (Rückert) for chor. & orch.; 2 syms., 2 sets of vars., Ballad, Serenade, 3 ovts. for orch.; Romance for co. & orch.; stg. 6tet; Vars. for 2 pfs.; pieces for pf. solo & duet; songs, partsongs, &c.

Rue, Pierre de la. *See* **La Rue.**

Ruffo, Vincenzo (b. Verona, *c.* 1510; d. Sacile nr. Udine, 9. II. 1587), It. male sop. singer & comp. App. chapel master at Verona cath. in 1554 and in 1563 at that of Milan. He occupied a similar post at Pistoia in 1574–9, but returned to Milan.

Works incl. masses, motets, Magnificat, psalms & other church m.; madrigals, &c.

Rugby. Honegger's 2nd symph. mvt. for orch., following *Pacific 231* and succeeded by *Mouvement symphonique No. 3.* It is an impression of a game of football. 1st perf. Paris, Orchestre Symphonique, 19. X. 1928.

Ruggieri. It. family of v. makers at Cremona and Brescia:

1. Francesco R. (b. ?; d. ?), worked *c.* 1668–1720.

2. Giovanni Battista R. (b. ?; d. ?), ? son of prec., worked *c.* 1700–25.

3. Pietro R. (b. ?; d. ?), ? brother of prec., worked c. 1700–20.

4. Guido R. (b. ?; d. ?)
5. Vincenzo R. (b. ?; d. ?) } Worked early 18th cent.

Ruggiero, o vero L'eroica gratitudine (*R., or Heroic Gratitude*), opera by Hasse (lib. by Metastasio), prod. Milan, Teatro Regio Ducal, 16. X. 1771. H.'s last opera.

Ruggles, Carl (b. Marion, Mass., 11. III. 1876), Amer. comp. & painter. Studied at Harvard Univ., with Walter Spalding and others. Afterwards he cond. the Sym. Orch. at Winona, Minnesota, for a time.

Works incl. opera *The Sunken Bell*; *Men and Angels*, *Men and Mountains*, *Portals*, *The Sun Treaders*, *Evocations* for orch.; Concertino for pf. & orch.; *Vox clamans in deserto* for voice & chamber orch.; *Polyphonic Comps.* for 3 pfs., &c.

Rührtrommel (Ger.) = Tenor Drum.

Ruimonte, Pedro (b. Saragossa, ?; d. ?), Spa. 16th–17th-cent. comp. The Infanta Isabella took him to the Nthlds. on her marriage to the Archduke Albert, governor of the Nthlds., at whose court at Brussels he became chamber musn. in 1603. He returned to Spa. in 1614, but was in Brussels again 4 years later.

Works incl. masses & *Cantiones sacrae*; madrigals & villancicos, &c.

Ruins of Athens, The. Incid. m. by Beethoven, Op. 113, for a play by Kotzebue written for the opening of the Ger. theatre at Pest, 9. II. 1812. It comprises an ovt. and 8 numbers, incl. the *Turkish March*, already comp. by B. for his pf. Vars., Op. 76, in 1809.

Rule, Britannia, a patriotic song by Arne, now almost a 2nd Brit. nat. anthem, orig. part of the masque *Alfred* prod. 1. VIII. 1740, at Cliefden (now Clivedon) House nr. Maidenhead, the residence of Frederick, Prince of Wales.

Rule of the Octave. The harmonic rule according to which a scale is properly accompanied by chords in correct progressions.

Rules. The 16th–17th-cent. term for Stave.

Rum. (abbr.) = Rumania, Rumanian.

Rumanian Composers. *See* **Alessandrescu, Andrico, Constantinescu, Cuclin, Dima, Enesco, Golestan, Mihalovici, Nottara, Otesco.**

Rumba. A Cuban dance of African Negro origin, in quick 2–4 time and making much use of Syncopation. It was introd. in Jazz in the 1920s.

Runeberg, Johan Ludvig (1804–77),

Swe. poet. *See* **Sibelius** (*Nights of Jealousy*).

Rung, Frederik (b. Copenhagen, 14. VI. 1854; d. Copenhagen, 22. I. 1914), Dan. cond. & comp. Pupil of his father Henrik R. (1807–71), of Gade and others. He went to the Royal Opera as coach, became asst. cond. in 1884 and succeeded Svendsen as 1st cond. in 1911. He also taught at the Cons. and Horneman's m. school and cond. chor. socs., incl. a madrigal choir founded by him.

Works incl. operas *The Secret Society* & *The Three-Cornered Hat* (after Alarcón's story); ballet *Aditi* & *A Carnival Jest in Venice*; incid. m. to Holger Drachman's *1001 Nights* & other plays; Sym. in D min., Rhapsody, *Suite in the Old Style* & *Danse des papillons* for orch.; Suite for tpt. & stgs., Nonet for woodwind, pf. 5tet, 2 stg. 4tets; pf. pieces; songs, &c.

Rungenhagen, Carl Friedrich (b. Berlin, 27. IX. 1778; d. Berlin, 21. XII. 1851), Ger. comp. & cond. Worked in Berlin, where he became asst. cond. to Zelter of the Voc. Acad. in 1815 and succeeded to the post of 1st cond. in 1833.

Works incl. 4 operas, 3 orats., mass, *Stabat Mater* for female voices & other church m.; orch. works; chamber m.; songs, &c.

Rus. (abbr.) = Russia, Russian.

Russalka (*The Water-Sprite*), opera by Dargomizhsky (lib. by comp., from Pushkin's dramatic poem), prod. St. Petersburg, 16. V. 1856.

Opera by Dvořák (lib. by Jaromir Kvapil), prod. Prague, Cz. Theatre, 31. III. 1901.

Russell, Ella (b. Cleveland, Ohio, 1864; d. Florence, 16. I. 1935), Amer. sop. singer. Studied in Paris and Milan, made her 1st appearance at Prato in Sicily and 1st visited London in 1885.

Russell, Henry (b. Sheerness, 24. XII. 1812; d. London, 8. XII. 1900), Eng. singer, orgst. & comp. Studied at Bologna and with Rossini at Naples, appeared as singer in London in 1828, lived in Canada and U.S.A. (orgst. at Rochester, N.Y.) in 1833–41 and then gave entertainments in London with Charles Mackay for which he wrote many popular songs. He was the father of Landon Ronald.

Works incl. songs 'Cheer, boys, cheer,' 'There 's a good time coming,' 'A life on the ocean wave' (march of the Royal Marines), &c.

Russian Bassoon. An obs. brass wind inst. not related to the bn., but to the bass hn. and the ophicleide.

'Russian' Quartets. One of the nicknames given to the 6 stg. 4tets, Op. 33, by Haydn, the others being *Gli scherzi* and *Jungfern Quartette.* They were written in 1772.

Russlan and Ludmilla, opera by Glinka (lib. by Valerian Fedorovitch Shirkov & Constantin Alexandrovitch Bakhturin, based on Pushkin's poem), prod. St. Petersburg, 9. XII. 1842.

Rust, Friedrich Wilhelm (b. Wörlitz nr. Dessau, 6. VII. 1739; d. Dessau, 28. II. 1796), Ger. pfst., orgst., vst. & comp. Pupil of his elder brother at first, then of C. P. E. and W. F. Bach, and F. Benda for v.; in 1765 of G. Benda, Tartini and Pugnani in It. He returned to Dessau in 1766 and worked much on behalf of m., using his influence to have a new theatre estab., which opened in 1774, and he became its mus. dir. He married his pupil, the singer Henriette Niedhart.

Works incl. monodrama *Inkle und Yariko* (after Steele), duodrama *Colma* (after Ossian), some prologues & other stage works; Psalm for solo voice, chor. & orch.; church cantatas; pf. and v. concs.; 48 pf. sos., many pf. vars.; 3 v. solo sos., &c.

Rust, Wilhelm (b. Dessau, 15. VIII. 1822; d. Leipzig, 2. V. 1892), Ger. pfst., vst. & comp., grandson of prec. Studied with his uncle W. K. R. and F. Schneider and settled in Berlin as pfst., orgst. and teacher. In 1870 he became prof. at Stern's Cons. there and in 1878 orgst. and 2 years later cantor at St. Thomas's church, Leipzig. He ed. his grandfather's pf. sos., much modernizing them, on the strength of which ed. d'Indy declared F. W. R. to be a prophetic forerunner of Beethoven.

Works incl. pf. & voc. m.

Rust, Wilhelm Karl (b. Dessau, 29. IV. 1787; d. Dessau, 18. IV. 1855), Ger. pfst. & teacher, uncle of prec. and son of F. W. R. Pupil of his father and of Türk at Halle. In 1807 he went to Vienna, made friends with Beethoven and remained there as teacher until 1827, when he returned to Dessau.

Rutini, Ferdinando (b. Modena, 1767; d. Terracina, XI. 1827), It. comp. Son and pupil of Giovanni Maria R., later chapel master at Macerata and Terracina.

Works incl. over 20 operas; cantatas; sos., &c.

Rutini, Giovanni Maria (also called G. Marco & G. Placido) (b. Florence, 25. IV. 1723; d. Florence, 7. XII. 1797), It. comp., father of prec. Studied at the Cons. di Sant' Onofrio at Naples. Travelled in central & eastern Eur. *c.* 1748–58, visiting Prague, Dresden, St. Petersburg, &c. His 1st opera was prod. at Bologna in 1762. From 1766 to *c.* 1772 he was in the service of the Duke of Modena and later lived chiefly at Florence.

Works incl. operas *Il caffè di campagna, Il matrimonio in maschera* & c. 12 others; cantatas; many hpchd. sos., &c.

Rutscher (Ger. lit. glider). *See* **Galop.**

Ruy Blas, opera by William Howard Glover (1819–75) (lib. by comp., based on Victor Hugo's drama), prod. London, Covent Garden Theatre, 24. X. 1861.

Opera by Marchetti (lib., in It., by Carlo d'Ormeville, based on Hugo), prod. Milan, Teatro alla Scala, 3. IV. 1869.

Ovt. and chor. for Hugo's drama by Mendelssohn, Op. 95 & Op. 77 No. 3, comp. for a prod. at Leipzig, 9. III. 1839.

Ruygrok, Leonard (b. Utrecht, 8. V. 1889), Dutch cst. & comp. Pupil of Wagenaar for comp. He became 1st cst. in the royal orch. at The Hague and in 1924 was app. 2nd cond.

Works incl. incid. m. for plays; film m. for *Forty Years, 1898–1938* for Queen Wilhelmina's jubilee; 2 syms., 4 ovts.; Poem for va. & orch., &c.

Ruyneman, Daniel (b. Amsterdam, 8. VIII. 1886), Dutch comp. He was trained for commerce and self-taught in m. He has made many experiments with comp. and insts. and invented cup-bells with a rich and long-sustained sonority, which he used in several of his works.

Works incl. psycho-symbolic play with voc. & inst. orch. *The Clown*; *Hieroglyphs* for chamber orch.; So. in G maj. & *Klaaglied van een Slaaf* for v. & pf.; 3 *Pathemologies* & Sonatina for pf.; 2 Sacred Songs (Tagore) and several other sets, &c.

Rydberg, Abraham Viktor (1828–95), Swe. poet. *See* **Sibelius** (*Skogsraaet*).

Ryelandt, Joseph (b. Bruges, 7. IV. 1870), Belg. comp. Pupil of Tinel.

Works incl. opera *Sainte Cécile*; orats. *La Parabole des vierges, Purgatorium, De Komst des Heeren, Maria, Agnus Dei & Christus Rex*, cantatas *Le Bon Pasteur & L'Idylle mystique*; 4 syms., symph. poem *Gethsémani*, 2 ovts. for orch.; chamber m.; 8 pf. sos.; numerous songs, &c.

Rytel, Piotr (b. Wilno, 16. V. 1884), Pol. comp. Studied at the Warsaw Cons. He became a prof. there in 1911 and was also engaged in criticism.

Works incl. opera *Ijola*; ballet *Faun and Psyche*; Sym., symph. poems *The Corsair* (Byron), *Grazyna* (Mickiewicz), *Dante's Dream, The Holy Grove, The Legend of St. George, An Introduction to a Drama*, &c.

(Mark reference p. 482)

Rape of Lucretia, The, opera by Britten (lib. by Ronald Duncan, after Livy and Shakespeare), prod. Glyndebourne Opera House, Sussex, VII. 1946.

S

Š. In Cz., Š or š is pronounced 'sh.'

s. The Dominant note in any key in Tonic Sol-fa notation, pronounced Soh.

S.I.M. (abbr.) = Société Internationale de Musique.

Sabaneiev, Leonid Leonidovitch (b. Moscow, 19. XI. 1881), Rus. critic & comp. Studied with Taneiev at the Moscow Cons. and at the Univ. there. He wrote esp. on Skriabin.

Sabata, Victor De (b. Trieste, 10. IV. 1892), It. cond. & comp. Studied under his father, a chor. master at the Teatro alla Scala, Milan, and at the Cons. there, with Orefice and others.

Works incl. operas *Lisistrata* (after Aristophanes), *Il macigno, Mille e una notte*; incid. m. for Shakespeare's *Merchant of Venice*; symph. poems *Juventus, La notte di Platon, Gethsemane*, Suite for orch., &c.

Sabatier, Caroline. *See* **Unger.**

Sabbatini, Galeazzo (b. ? Pesaro, *c.* 1590; d. ? Pesaro, 1662), It. comp. He was chapel master at Pesaro in the 1620s and dir. of chamber m. to the Duke of Mirandola in the 1630s. He was also at Bergamo some time. In 1628 he pub. a treatise on thorough-bass.

Works incl. masses, motets, lauds & other church m.; madrigals, &c.

Sabbatini, Luigi Antonio (b. Albano Laziale nr. Rome, 1739; d. Padua, 29. I. 1809), It. comp. Pupil of Martini at Bologna, later of Vallotti at Padua, and became chapel master of the church of the Santi Apostoli in Rome. In 1786 he was app. chapel master of Sant' Antonio at Padua, a post that had been offered him in 1780, but for which he then recommended Agostino Ricci. He pub. several treatises, on fugue, canon, &c., and a life of Vallotti.

Works incl. masses, motets, psalms, vespers & other church m.

Sabbatini, Pietro Paolo (b. Rome, *c.* 1600; d. ? Rome, *c.* 1660), It. comp. He was chapel master in Rome, from 1630 of the church of San Luigi de' Francesci, and prof. of m. from 1650, when he pub. a treatise on thorough-bass, &c.

Works incl. psalms, spiritual songs; villanelle and canzonette for 1–3 voices, &c.

Sacchini, Antonio (Maria Gasparo) (b. Florence, 14. VI. 1730; d. Paris, 6. X. 1786), It. comp. Studied at the Cons. Santa Maria di Loreto at Naples, incl. v. and singing, and comp. with Durante. In 1754 he prod. the intermezzo *Fra Donato* there and on leaving the school earned a living by teaching singing and writing small theatrical pieces, but in 1761 he prod. his 1st serious opera, *Andromaca*, at Naples. In 1768 he succeeded Traetta as dir. of the m. school of the Ospedaletto at Venice, but left in 1770, visiting Ger. that year and London in 1773. He remained there until 1781, again travelled on the Continent, and in 1784 went to Paris, where he came under the protection of Marie Antoinette, but she was unable to enforce the prod. of his last Fr. opera, having been accused of showing too much favour to foreigners. The disappointment is said to have hastened his death.

Works incl. operas *Alessandro nell' Indie, Scipione in Cartagena, L'eroe cinese, Calliroe, Tamerlano, Lucio Vero, Nitteti, Perseo, Motezuma, Didone abbandonata, L'Olimpiade, Armida* (*Renaud*, after Tasso), *Il Cidde* (*Chimène*, after Corneille), *Dardanus, Œdipe à Colone* (after Sophocles), *Arvire et Evelina* (after Mason, unfinished) & *c.* 25 others; *c.* 8 orats.; masses, motets & other church m.; 2 syms.; 6 stg. 4tets, 6 trios for vs. & bass; 12 v. & hpchd. sos.; 12 hpchd. sos., &c.

Sachlichkeit. *See* **Neue Sachlichkeit.**

Sachs, Curt (b. Berlin, 29. VI. 1881), Ger. mcolst. Studied hist. at Berlin Univ. and comp. with Hugo Schrattenholz, later theory with Kretzschmar and Johannes Wolf. In 1919 he became head of the State collection of old mus. insts. in Berlin. In 1933 he left Ger., settled in Paris and later in U.S.A., where he became prof. at N.Y. Univ. His books incl. studies of the hist. of the dance, ancient m., mus. insts., the hist. of m. in Berlin, &c., and he is the ed. of the Fr. collection of gramophone records of old m., *Anthologie sonore.*

Sachs, Hans (1494–1576), Ger. cobbler, mastersinger, poet & playwright. *See* **Forster** (*Dot Mon*), **Paumgartner** (*Heisse Eisen*), **Wehrli** (do.).

Sackbut. The old Eng. name for the tromb.

Sackville-West, Victoria (b. 1892), Eng. poetess & novelist. *See* **Maconchy** (*The Land*).

Sacountala, ballet by Reyer (scen. by Théophile Gautier, based on Kalidasa's drama; chgph. by Lucien Petipa), prod. Paris, Opéra, 14. VII. 1858.

Sacr(a)(e) Rappresentazion(e)(i) (It. = sacred representation[s]). *See* **Rappresentazione.**

Sacrae Cantiones. *See* **Cantiones sacrae.**

Sacre du printemps, Le (Stravinsky). *See* **Rite of Spring**: there is no reason why in Eng.-speaking countries a Fr. title should be used for a work written by a Rus. comp. and prod. by the Rus. Ballet. It was so called merely because it happened to be brought out in Paris.

Sadko, opera by Rimsky-Korsakov (lib. by comp. & Vladimir Ivanovitch Bielsky), prod. Moscow, 7. I. 1898. The m. is partly based on R.-K.'s symph. poem of the same name comp. 1867, 1st perf. St. Petersburg, 21. XII. 1867.

Sadler's Wells Opera. The S. W. theatre was built in the 18th cent., when Islington was a village outside London and S. W. a watering-place and pleasure-garden dating back to the end of the 17th cent. It was used for plays and pantomime into the 19th cent., then became a m.-hall and later fell into disuse, but was acquired as a northern branch of the Old Vic. Theatre for the alternate prod. of classical drama and opera, rebuilt and opened on 6. I. 1931. From 1935 plays were confined exclusively to the O. V. and opera to S. W., which has become the only permanent repertory opera-house in Brit. for the prod. of opera in Eng. A ballet, at first attached to the opera, later developed independently, but a nucleus of it remains available for opera when required.

Saeta (Spa.). An unaccomp. Andalusian folksong sung during a halt in a relig. procession.

Sæverud, Harald (b. Bergen, 17. IV. 1897), Norw. cond. & comp. Studied at Bergen and Berlin, cond. under Clemens Krauss. He returned to Bergen as cond. and received a state pension for comp. in 1933.

Works incl. *Cantata ostinata* & *Lucretia Suite* (after Shakespeare's *Rape of Lucrece*); 50 vars. for chamber orch.; pf. pieces, &c.

Saffo (*Sappho*), opera by Pacini (lib. by Salvatore Cammarano), prod. Naples, Teatro San Carlo, 29. XI. 1840.

Safonov, Vassily Ilitch (b. Itsuiursk, Terek, 6. II. 1852; d. Kislovodsk, Caucasus, 13. III. 1918), Rus. cond. & pfst. Studied at St. Petersburg; prof. at the Cons. there, 1881, and at Moscow, 1885. Became dir. of Moscow Cons., 1889. Estab. popular concerts there and was cond. of the Moscow branch of the Rus. Mus. Soc., 1890–1905. Appeared frequently in London and N.Y.

Saga, A. Symph. poem by Sibelius, Op. 9, comp. in 1892, revised in 1901. It depicts no partic. incident, but has a distinctly narrative, ballad-like tone. It is usually called *En Saga* on programmes, as on the score, but there is no reason for retaining the Swe. title in Eng.-speaking countries.

Sagbut. Another spelling of Sackbut.

Sagittarius. The Lat. form of the name of Schütz, sometimes used on his title-pages.

Sainete (Spa.). A type of comedy with m.

'St. Anne's' Fugue. The fugue of Bach's E♭ maj. Prelude and Fugue for org., so named in Eng. because its subject is identical with the opening of Croft's (?) hymn-tune *St. Anne.*

'St. Anthony' Variations (Brahms). *See* **'Haydn' Variations.**

St. Elizabeth (Liszt). *See* **Legende von der heiligen Elisabeth.**

Saint-Foix, (Marie Olivier) Georges (du Parc Poullain) de, Count (b. Paris, 2. III. 1874), Fr. mcolst. Studied law, and m. at the Schola Cantorum in Paris. He has written on var. subjects, incl. Beethoven and Boccherini, but mainly on the classification and analysis of Mozart's works in a large 5-vol. work, the 1st 2 vols. in collab. with Théodore de Wyzewa.

Saint-Huberty, Antoinette (Cécile) (real name Clavel) (b. Toul, *c.* 1756; d. London, 22. VII. 1812), Fr. sop. singer. Studied with the cond. Lemoyne at Warsaw and made her 1st appearance there, then sang in Berlin and Strasburg, and 1st appeared in Paris in 1777. In 1790 she married the Comte d'Entraigues, a royalist, with whom she escaped to Lausanne. In 1797 she rescued her husband from prison at Milan. They went 1st to St. Petersburg and then to London, where they settled and were murdered by a servant.

St. James's Hall. A concert hall in London, between Regent Street and Piccadilly (the site of the present Piccadilly Hotel), opening on 25. III. 1858 and sold for demolition in 1905, when the last concert took place on 11. II. It was large enough for an orch., but used also for chamber m., partic. the Monday Popular Concerts ('Monday Pops'), at which artists of internat. fame appeared.

St. John Passion. A setting by Bach of the Passion narrative as related in the Gospel of St. John, for solo voices, chor. & orch., 1st perf. at St. Thomas's church, Leipzig, Good

Friday, 26. III. 1723, as a trial before B.'s election as cantor.

Saint-Lambert, (? Michel) de (b. ?; d. ? Paris, ?), Fr. 17th–18th-cent. hpchd. player, teacher & author. He lived and taught in Paris, and wrote 2 books, *Les Principes du clavecin* and *Nouveau Traité de l'accompagnement.*

St. Ludmilla, orat. by Dvořák, Op. 71 (Cz. words by Jaroslav Vrchlický), comp. 1886 and prod. in the autumn at the Leeds Festival, in an Eng. trans.

St. Matthew Passion. A setting by Bach of the Passion narrative as related in the Gospel of St. Matthew, for solo voices, chor. & orch., 1st perf. at St. Thomas's church, Leipzig, Good Friday, 15. IV. 1729.

St. Paul, orat. by Mendelssohn, Op. 36, prod. Düsseldorf, Lower Rhine Festival, 22. V. 1836; in Eng., Liverpool, 7. X. 1836.

St. Philip. *See* **Neri.**

Saint-Pierre, (Jacques Henri) Bernardin de (1737–1814), Fr. naturalist & novelist. For works based on *Paul et Virginie see* **Gavazzeni** (opera), **Lesueur** (do.), **Mazzinghi** (do.), **Montemezzi** (symph. poem), **Paolo e Virginia** (P. C. Guglielmi), **Paul et Virginie** (R. Kreutzer & Massé), **Reeve** (opera).

Saint-Saëns, (Charles) Camille (b. Paris, 9. X. 1835; d. Algiers, 16. XII. 1921), Fr. comp. He began to comp. at the age of 5 and played the pf. well at that age. Gave a public recital in 1846 and entered the Cons. as an org. scholar in 1848, gaining a 1st prize in 1851, when he entered Halévy's class for comp. App. orgst. at the church of Saint-Merry in Paris, 1853, the Madeleine, 1857, and pf. prof. at the École Niedermeyer in 1861. His 1st 2 syms. were perf. in 1853 and 1857, he played his 2nd pf. Conc. in 1868 and founded the Société Nationale de Musique with Romain Bussine in 1871. He played in Eng. several times from 1871 and toured Spa. and Port. in 1880. The biblical opera *Samson et Dalila,* begun in 1868 and prohibited on the Fr. stage on account of its subject, was prod. by him at Weimar in 1877; but allowed in Paris from 1892, the year he received the hon. Mus.D. at Cambridge. In 1906 he visited the U.S.A., and again in 1916, together with S. Amer.

Works incl. operas *La Princesse jaune, Le Timbre d'argent, Étienne Marcel, Samson et Dalila, Henri VIII, Proserpine, Ascanio, Phryné, Les Barbares, Hélène, L'Ancêtre, Déjanire*; ballet *Javotte*; incid. m. for Sophocles' *Antigone,* Racine's *Andromaque* & 6 other plays; 3 syms. (the 3rd with org. & pf. duet), symph. poems *Le Rouet d'Omphale, Phaëton, Danse macabre* (orig. a song), *La Jeunesse d'Hercule,* Suite & *Suite algérienne* for orch., other orch. pieces incl. *Une Nuit à Lisbonne, Jota aragonesa, Ouverture de fête*; 5 pf. concs., *Allegro appassionato, Rapsodie d'Auvergne* & *Africa* for pf. & orch., 3 v. concs. & *Introduction et Rondo capriccioso,* Romance, *Morceau de concert* & *Caprice andalou* for v. & orch., 2 co. concs., var. pieces for wind insts. & orch.; *Le Carnaval des animaux* for chamber orch.; 2 stg. 4tets, pf. 5tet & 4tet, 2 pf. trios, 7tet for pf., stgs. & tpt.; 2 v. & pf. sos., 2 co. & pf. sos., Suite for co. & pf., sos. for ob., clar. and bn. & pf.; fantasies for hp. and for v. & hp.; many smaller inst. pieces with pf.; 24 op. nos. of pf. m., 6 op. nos. for pf. duet, 5 op. nos. for 2 pfs. incl. Vars. on a theme by Beethoven; 7 org. works; Mass, Requiem, 2 Psalms and other church m. for chor. & orch. (some with solo voices); *Ode à Sainte Cécile* & *La Fiancée du timbalier* for voice & orch.; orat. *Le Déluge*; several cantatas; many songs, &c.

Saintine, Xavier (Boniface) (1798–1865), Fr. novelist & playwright. *See* **Puritani di Scozia** (Bellini).

Sainton-Dolby, Charlotte (Helen) (b. London, 17. V. 1821; d. London, 18. II. 1885), Eng. con. singer & comp. Studied at the R.A.M. in London and made her 1st appearance at a Phil. concert there in 1842. In 1845 Mendelssohn invited her to sing with Jenny Lind at Leipzig, and later she had a success in Fr. and Hol. In 1860 she married Prosper Sainton.

Works incl. cantatas *The Legend of St. Dorothea* & *The Story of a Faithful Soul,* cantata for female voices *Florimel,* &c.

Sainton, Prosper (Philippe Cathérine) (b. Toulouse, 5. VI. 1813; d. London, 17. X. 1890), Fr. vst. & comp., husband of prec. Studied v. under Habeneck at the Paris Cons., played at the Société des Concerts and the Opéra there, then travelled widely in Eur. and in 1840 became prof. at the Toulouse Cons. In 1844 he visited London and played under Mendelssohn, returning in 1845 to settle down as member of the Beethoven 4tet Soc., orch. leader and teacher.

Works incl. 2 v. concs. & other solos with orch.; vars., romances, operatic fantasies, &c. for v. & pf., &c.

Saite(n) (Ger.) = string(s).

Saiteninstrumente (Ger.) = stg. insts.

Sakuntala. *See also* **Leggenda di Sakuntala, Sacountala.**

Opera by Weingartner (lib. by comp., based on Kalidasa's drama), prod. Weimar, 23. III. 1884.

Sala, Nicola (b. Tocco-Gaudio nr. Benevento, 7. IV. 1713; d. Naples, 31. VIII. 1801), It. comp. & theorist. Studied with Fago, Abos and Leo at the Cons. de' Turchini at Naples and later became a master there, principal in 1787, succeeding Cafaro. In 1794 he pub. *Regole del contrappunto prattico* in 3 vols.

Works incl. operas *Vologeso, Zenobia, Merope* & *Demetrio*; orat. *Giuditta*; mass, litany & other church m.; Prologues for the birth of kings of Naples, &c.

Salaman, Charles (Kensington) (b. London, 3. III. 1814; d. London, 23. VI. 1901), Eng. pfst., comp., cond. & lecturer. Studied at the R.A.M. in London and under Neate, made his 1st appearance in 1828 and went to Paris for further studies with Herz. On his return to London he played much at concerts and helped to found chamber m. & chor. socs. He also lectured and contrib. to mus. papers. In 1846–8 he cond. in Rome.

Works incl. anthems & Hebrew services; Ode for the Shakespeare commem. at Stratford-on-Avon (23. IV. 1830); *Rondeau brillant* for pf. & orch.; pf. works; songs in Eng., Hebrew, Gr. and Lat., incl. 'I arise from dreams of thee' (Shelley), &c.

Salammbô, opera by Reyer (lib. by Camille du Locle, based on Flaubert's novel), prod. Brussels, Théâtre de la Monnaie, 10. II. 1890.

Unfinished opera by Mussorgsky (lib. by comp., based on Flaubert), partly comp. in the 1860s.

Salazar, Adolfo (b. Madrid, 6. III. 1890), Spa. mcolst. & comp. Pupil of Pérez Casas and Falla. He ed. the *Revista Musical Hispano-Americana* in 1914–8 and from 1918–36 was m. critic to *El Sol* in Madrid. He emigrated to Buenos Aires after the Spa. Civil War and has lived in Mex. since 1939. His books incl. studies of modern m., Spa. m., sym. & ballet, &c.

Works incl. symph. poem *Don Juan en los infiernos, Paisajes* & *Tres preludios* for orch.; stg. 4tet, *Arabia* for pf. 5tet; v. & pf. So.; pf. pieces; *Romancilla* for guitar, &c.

Salcional. Another name for the Salicet or Salicional org. stop.

Sales, Pietro Pompeo (b. Brescia, 1729; d. Hanau, 1797), It. violist & comp. He was driven to Ger. by an earthquake at Brescia and held var. appts. there, esp. at the court of the Prince-Bishop of Augsburg. In 1763 he went to Padua to prod. an opera and between 1765–8 to London, after which he became mus. dir. to the Elector of Coblenz, where Burney visited him in 1772.

Works incl. operas *Le nozze di Amore e di Norizia, Antigono, Achille in Sciro, Il rè pastore*, &c.; orats. *La Betulia liberata, Gioas, Giuseppe riconosciuto*; church m.; 2 syms.; concs.; hpchd. sos., &c.

Salicet or **Salicional** } An 8-ft. open metal org. stop. prod. a moderately powerful tone.

Salieri, Antonio (b. Legnago nr. Verona, 19. VIII. 1750; d. Vienna, 7. V. 1825), It. comp. & teacher. Studied m. with his brother Francesco S., a pupil of Tartini's. On the death of his parents a member of the Mocenigo family took him to Venice, where he made further studies. In 1766 he there met Gassmann, who took him to Vienna, saw to his further educ., introd. him to Metastasio and to the court. Having comp. a comic opera, *Le donne letterate*, he was app. court comp. in 1774 and on Bonno's death in 1788 court mus. dir. In 1778–9 he prod. 5 operas at Venice, Milan and Rome, and in 1784 *Les Danaïdes* in Paris at Gluck's instigation; otherwise he worked in Vienna all his life, celebrating his 50th anniv. there in 1816, his pupils, incl. Schubert, taking part. He took a share in the foundation of the Cons. in 1817 and retired in 1824. He intrigued against Mozart (but the story that he poisoned M. is an absurd fabrication) and taught Beethoven voc. writing, esp. with regard to It. prosody.

Works incl. It. operas *Armida, La fiera di Venezia, La locandiera, Europa riconosciuta, La scuola de' gelosi, La dama pastorella, La grotta di Trofonio, Il talismano, Palmira, regina di Persia, Falstaff* (after Shakespeare). *Angiolina* & c. 20 others, Fr. operas *Les Danaïdes, Tarare* (*Axur*) & *Les Horaces*, Ger. opera *Der Rauchfangkehrer*; incid. m. for Kotzebue's *Die Hussiten von Naumburg*; 5 masses, Requiem, 3 Te Deums & other church m.; 4 orats. incl. *La Passione di Gesù Cristo*; 6 cantatas incl. *La riconoscenza* for the 25th anniv. of the Tonkünstler-Societät and *Zu Ehren Joseph Haydns*; inst. works; arias, partsongs, chors. and canons *Scherzi armonici*, &c.

Salimbeni, Felice (b. Milan, *c.* 1712; d. Ljubljana, VIII. 1751), It. male sop. singer. Pupil of Porpora, made his 1st appearance in Rome in 1731 and afterwards sang in It., Vienna, Berlin and Dresden, and was one of Hasse's chief interpreters.

Salinas, Francisco de (b. Burgos, 1. III. 1513; d. Salamanca, 13. I. 1590), Spa. orgst., theorist and folksong investigator. He was the son of an official in the treasury of Charles V and became blind at the age of 10, whereupon his parents decided to let him study m. He was taken to Rome in 1538, where he met the lutenist Francesco da Milano and became a great admirer of Lassus. In 1558 he became orgst. to the Duke of Alba, viceroy of Naples, under Ortiz. In 1561 he returned to Spa., became orgst. at León in 1563 and prof. of m. at Salamanca Univ., 1567. There he made friends with the poet Luis de León, who wrote a poem on his org. playing. In his treatise *De musica libri septem* he quotes the tunes of many Spa. folksongs.

Salmhofer, Franz (b. Vienna, 22. I. 1900), Aus. cond. & comp. Having learnt m. as a choir-boy, he studied at the Vienna Acad. under Schreker and others, later taught at Horak's m. school and in 1929–39 was cond. at the Burg Theatre, for which he wrote incid. m. to over 100 plays.

Works incl. operas *Dame im Traum, Ivan Sergeievitch, Tarassenko, Das Werbekleid* & several others; ballets *Das lockende Phantom, Der Taugenichts in Wien, Weihnachtsmärchen, Oesterreichische Bauernhochzeit*; incid. m. for Shakespeare's *The Tempest, King Lear, Romeo and Juliet, Othello, The Merry Wives of Windsor*, Goethe's *Faust* (pts. I & II), &c.; ovt. to Maeterlinck's *L'Intruse* & others, *Der geheimnisvolle Trompeter, Fairy-Tale* for orch.; Suite for chamber orch.; concs. for co., v. & co. and tpt.; stg. 4tet in F min., pf. 4tet in F min., Serenade for stg. trio, Slavonic Rhapsody and Dance Suite for v., va. & guitar; sos. for va. & pf. and co. & pf.; songs, &c.

Salmo (It., plur. *salmi*) = psalm.

Salmon (*née* **Munday), Eliza** (b. Oxford, 1787; d. London, 5. VI. 1849), Eng. sop. singer. Studied with John Ashley and made her 1st appearance in orat. at Covent Garden Theatre in London, 1803. She married James Salmon in 1806 and they settled at Liverpool. But she continued to sing in London and at the festivals until she lost her voice through intemperance in 1825.

Salmon, James (b. ?; d. West Indies, *c.* 1813), Eng. orgst., husband of prec. Studied with his father, James S. (?–1827), vicar-chor. at St. Paul's cath. in London and lay-clerk at St. George's Chapel, Windsor, and in 1806, after his marriage, settled at Liverpool as orgst. of St. Peter's church. In 1813 he enlisted and went to the W. Indies.

Salmon, Thomas (b. London, 24. VI. 1648; d. Mepsal, Beds., VII. 1706), Eng. clergyman & writer on m. Wrote on notation and temperament, and his *Essay on the Advancement of Musick* in 1672 involved him in a controversy with Locke.

Salò, Francesco da (b. Brescia, 1565; d. ?), It. v. maker. Succeeded his father, whose business however he sold after his death, and he seems to have left Brescia in 1614.

Salò, Gasparo da (real name G. di Bertoletti) (b. ? Salò, 1542; d. Brescia, 14. IV. 1609), It. v. maker, father of prec. He began working at Brescia in the 1560s.

Salomé, opera by Mariotte (lib. Oscar Wilde's orig. in Fr.), prod. Lyons, 3. X. 1908. Comp. earlier than R. Strauss's opera, although prod. later.

Salome, opera by R. Strauss (lib. Hedwig Lachmann's Ger. trans. of Oscar Wilde's play, written in Fr.), prod. Dresden, Royal Opera, 9. XII. 1905.

See also **Tragédie de Salomé.**

Salomon, Johann Peter (b. Bonn, I. 1745; d. London, 28. XI. 1815), Ger. vst., cond. & comp. Studied at Bonn and joined the electoral orch. in 1758. After a tour in 1765 he became court musn. at Rheinsberg to Prince Henry of Prus., who however dissolved his orch. *c.* 1780, when S. went to Paris and thence to London, where he settled as concert vst., 4tet player and cond. He gave sub. concerts at the Hanover Square Rooms and invited Haydn to London in 1790 and again in 1794. He wrote 4 Fr. operas and an Eng. one, *Windsor Castle*, for the marriage of the Prince of Wales in 1795, an orat. *Hiskias*, v. sos., &c.

Salomon Symphonies. The 12 syms. written by Haydn in 1791–5 for the concerts given by Johann Peter Salomon in London during H.'s 2 visits to Eng. in 1790–2 and 1794–5. They are Nos. 93–104.

Saltando (It. = springing, bounding). A spec. way of playing the v. & other stg. insts. in such a manner that the bow is made to rebound from the stgs.

Saltarello. An It. dance, obviously incl. jumps (*salti*) and in the 16th cent. a kind of after-dance in common time, also called by the Lat. name of *proportio* and the Ger. one of *Proporz*, the name being due to its using the same m. as the **1st**

dance (Passamezzo), but with the 'proportions' (i.e. time) altered; later a Rom. dance in animated 3–4 or 6–8 time, not unlike the Neapol. Tarantella, but using jerky instead of even mus. figuration. In perf. by dancers it gradually increased its pace towards the end.

Saltato (It.) = Saltando.

Saltikov-Shtchedrin, Mikhail (1826–89), Rus. novelist & satirist. *See* **Pashtchenko** (*Pompadour*).

Salvayre, Gaston (actually Gervais Bernard) (b. Toulouse, 24. VI. 1847; d. Saint-Ague nr. Toulouse, 16. V. 1916), Fr. orgst. & comp. Studied at the Paris Cons., A. Thomas being among his masters, and gained the Prix de Rome in 1872. After his stay in Rome he was app. chor. master at the popular opera at the Théâtre du Châtelet and later he became m. critic to *Gil Blas*.

Works incl. operas *Salah-el-Din, Egmont, Sainte Geneviève, Myrto, Le Bravo, Richard III, La Dame de Monsoreau* (after Dumas) & *Solange*; ballets *La Fontaine des fées, L'Odalisque* & *Fandango* and ballet m. for Grisar's *Amours du Diable*; *Stabat Mater* & Psalm cxiii for solo voices, chor. & orch.; sym. *Le Jugement dernier* (later called *Le Résurrection* & *La Vallée de Josaphat*), *Ouverture symphonique*, Air & Vars. for stg. orch., &c.

Salviucci, Giovanni (b. Rome, 28. X. 1907; d. Rome, 5. IX. 1937), It. comp. & teacher. Giving up legal studies, he studied m. under Boezi, dir. of the Cappella Giulia at St. Peter's, and the Accademia di Santa Cecilia, also with Casella and Respighi. He afterwards taught at the Istituto Muzio Clementi in Rome and the Liceo Musicale at Pescara.

Works incl. episode from *Alcestis* (Euripides) for chor. & orch.; symph. poems & suites *Samarith, Saul, Campagna romana, Serena, La Tentazione e la preghiera*, 2 sketches *Villavecchia*, Ovt. in C♯ min., *Sinfonia italiana, Introduzione, passacaglia e finale*; *Sinfonia da camera* for 17 insts., *Serenata* for 9 insts.; *Salmo di Davidde* for ten. & chamber orch.; stg. 4tet; inst. pieces; songs, &c.

Salzburg Festivals. Summer festivals of m. and drama begun at Salzburg in 1920, mainly at the instigation of the poet Hugo von Hofmannsthal, the producer Max Reinhardt, the cond. Franz Schalk and the comp. Richard Strauss. The mus. perfs. incl. opera, church m., orch. concerts, chamber m. and serenades, a festival opera-house being built in 1926. Being Mozart's birthplace, Salzburg gave prominence to his works, but cultivated old and modern m. of many kinds. In 1938 the Nazis took charge of the S. Fs. and made them a centre of exclusively Ger. culture. They were interrupted by the 1939–45 world war.

Salzedo, Carlos (b. Arcachon, Gironde, 6. IV. 1885), Fr.-Amer. hpst. & comp. Studied pf. & hp. at the Paris Cons. and went to N.Y. at Toscanini's invitation to become 1st hp. at the Metrop. Opera. Much interested in modern m., he founded the Internat. Comps.' Guild with Varèse, ed. *Eolus* and cond. many concerts. Prof. of hp. at the Juillard School in N.Y. and the Curtis Inst. at Philadelphia.

Works incl. *The Enchanted Isle* for hp. & orch., Conc. for hp. & 7 wind insts., *Préambule et Jeux* for hp. & chamber orch.; So. for hp. & pf.; many pieces and arrs. for hp., &c.

Samain, Albert (1858–1900), Fr. poet. *See* **Bernard** (*Polyphème*), **Cras** (do.), **Poldowski** (songs).

Samara, Spiro (b. Corfu, 29. XI. 1861; d. Athens, 25. III. 1917), Gr. comp. Studied at Athens, later with Delibes and others at the Paris Cons. The It. pub. Sonzogno procured him his 1st operatic prod. at Milan. He subsequently prod. other works at Rome, Naples, Florence, Milan and Genoa, with no more than ephemeral success, and the last came out at Athens in 1914.

Works incl. operas *Flora mirabilis, Medgé, Lionella, La martire, La furia domata* (after Shakespeare's *Taming of the Shrew*), *Storia d'amore, Mademoiselle de Belle-Isle, Rhea, La guerra in tempo di guerra, The Princess of Saxony* (in Gr.); Suite for pf. duet, pf. pieces; songs, &c.

Samazeuilh, Gustave (Marie Victor Fernand) (b. Bordeaux, 2. VI. 1877), Fr. comp. & critic. Pupil of Chausson and after his master's death of d'Indy and Dukas at the Schola Cantorum. His lit. works incl. studies of Rameau and Dukas, translations of Wagner's *Tristan* and Schumann's *Genoveva*, songs by Wagner and Liszt, &c. He also made many pf. arrs. of modern Fr. m.

Works incl. *Étude symphonique pour 'La Nef'* (Élémir Bourges), *Nuit, Naïades au soir, Le Sommeil de Canope* for orch.; the last also for voice & orch.; stg. 4tet; So. & *Fantaisie élégiaque* for v. & pf.; *Le Chant de la mer* & Suite for pf.; Serenade for guitar; songs, &c.

Saminsky, Lazare (b. nr. Odessa, 27. X. 1882), Rus.-Amer. comp., cond. & writer on m. Pupil of Liadov and Rimsky-Korsakov at St. Petersburg

Cons. Cond. at Tiflis in 1915–8 and then dir. of the People's Cons. there. After a period in London, he went to the U.S.A., where he became naturalized. He was one of the founders of the League of Comps. in 1924, became m. dir. of the Jewish Temple of Emanu-El, and has done much cond. in Amer. and Eur. Author of *M. of Our Day* & *M. of the Ghetto*.

Works incl. opera-ballets *The Vision of Ariel, Lament of Rachel* & *The Daughter of Jephtha*, chamber opera *Gagliarda of the Merry Plague*; 5 syms., symph. poems *Three Shadows, Pueblo, a Moon Rhapsody* & *Ausonia*, *2 Images* for orch.; *By the Rivers of Babylon* for chor.; *Litanies of Women* for m.-sop. and small orch.; Sabbath Morning Service & Holiday Service for the synagogue, &c.

Sammarco, Mario (b. Palermo, 13. XII. 1873; d. Milan, 24. I. 1930), It. bar. singer. Pupil of Antonio Cantelli; made his 1st appearance at Milan and 1st visited London in 1904.

Sammartini (or San Martini), Giovanni Battista (b. Milan, 1701; d. Milan, 15. I. 1775), It. comp. Studied at Milan and worked there all his life, his posts incl. those of chapel master to a number of churches. Gluck was among his pupils.

Works incl. operas *L'ambizione superata* & *L'Agrippina*, serenate *La gara del genio* & *La reggia dei fati*; masses, motets; syms., ovts.; trio-sos. for 2 vs. & bass, &c.

Sammartini (or San Martini), Giuseppe (b. Milan, *c.* 1693; d. ? London, *c.* 1750), It. obst. & comp., brother of prec. He settled in London in the 1720s, became obst. at the opera and in 1732 gave concerts with Arrigoni. He left the Opera to become dir. of the chamber m. to Frederick, Prince of Wales.

Works incl. setting of Congreve's masque *The Judgment of Paris*; orat. *La calunnia delusa*; Concerti grossi; concs. for hpchd. & for v.; sos. for 2 fls., 2 vs., &c. with bass, fl. solos (? all fl. works intended also for ob.), &c.

Samori, opera by Vogler (lib. by Franz Xaver Huber), prod. Vienna, Theater an der Wien, 17. V. 1804. Weber wrote a set of pf. Vars., Op. 6, on a theme from it.

Samson, orat. by Handel (lib. by Newburgh Hamilton, based on Milton's *Samson Agonistes, Hymn on the Nativity* & *At a Solemn Musick*), prod. London, Covent Garden Theatre, 18. II. 1743.

Samson et Dalila, opera (orig. orat.) by Saint-Saëns (lib. by Ferdinand Lemaire), prod. Weimar, in Ger., 2. XII. 1877; not perf. in Paris until 31. X. 1890, and at the Opéra 23. XI. 1892, having been at first forbidden on account of its biblical subject.

Samuel, Harold (b. London, 23. V. 1879; d. London, 15. I. 1937), Eng. pfst. Studied under Dannreuther and Stanford at the R.C.M. in London, where he became pf. prof. later. He made a speciality of Bach and knew the whole of that master's clavier works by heart, often giving serial recitals of them; but he also excelled as a chamber m. player.

Samuel - Rousseau, Marcel. *See* **Rousseau, Marcel.**

San Martini. *See* **Sammartini.**

Sances, Giovanni Felice (b. Rome, *c.* 1600; d. Vienna, 24. XI. 1679), It. ten. singer & comp. He went to Vienna as a singer in the imp. chapel in 1637, became vice mus. dir. in 1649 and 1st mus. dir. in 1669.

Works incl. operas *Apollo deluso* (with the Emperor Leopold I), *Aristomene Messenio* & others; orats.; cantatas for solo voice, *Capricci poetici, Trattenimenti musicali per camera*, &c.

Sánchez de Fuentes y Peláez, Eduardo (b. Havana, 3. IV. 1876; d. Havana, 7. IX. 1944), Cuban comp. & mus. historian. He is the author of several books on the hist. of Cuban folk m.

Works incl. operas *Dolorosa, Doreya* & 3 others, operettas and zarzuelas; orat. *Novidad*; suite *Bocetos cubanos*, symph. prelude *Temas del Patio* for orch.; voc. habanera *Tú espera*, &c.

Sancho Pança dans son île (*Sancho Panza on his Island*), opera by Philidor (lib. by Antoine Alexandre Henri Poinsinet, based on Cervantes's *Don Quixote*), prod. Paris, Comédie-Italienne, 8. VII. 1762.

Sancho Panza, opera by Jaques-Dalcroze (lib. by Robert Yve-Plessis, based on Cervantes's *Don Quixote*), prod. Geneva, 13. XII. 1897.

Sancio Panza, governatore dell' isola Barattaria (*Sancho P., Governor of the Isle of Barataria*), opera by Caldara (lib. by Giovanni Claudio Pasquini, based on Cervantes's *Don Quixote*), prod. Vienna, Burg Theatre, 27. I. 1733. W. S. Gilbert borrowed the name of the island for Sullivan's *Gondoliers*.

Sancta Civitas (*The Holy City*), orat. by Vaughan Williams (words from the Bible, &c.) for solo voices, chor. & orch., 1st perf. Oxford, 7. V. 1926.

Sand, George (Aurore Dudevant, *née* Dupin) (1804–76), Fr. novelist. *See* **Fourdrain** (*Claudie* & *Mare au Diable*), **Hillemacher** (*Claudie*), **Kashperov** (*Consuelo*), **Orefice** (do.), **Rendano** (do.).

Sandberger, Adolf (b. Würzburg, 19. XII. 1864; d. ? Munich, summer 1942), Ger. mcolst. & comp. Studied in a number of Eur. centres and in 1894 became lecturer in m. at Munich Univ. and was prof. in 1900–29, being at the same time curator of the m. dept. of the State Library. He ed. the complete ed of Lassus and the *Denkmäler der Tonkunst in Bayern*, and his books incl. studies of the Bavarian court chapel under Lassus, of Cornelius, &c.

Works incl. operas *Ludwig der Springer* & *Der Tod des Kaisers*; symph. poem *Viola* (on Shakespeare's *Twelfth Night*), symph. prologue *Riccio*; chamber m.; pf. works; songs, &c.

Sanderson (or Saunderson), James (b. Workington, Cumberland, 1769; d. ? London, 1841), Eng. vst. & comp. He was self-taught and in 1783 obtained an engagement as vst. at the Sunderland theatre. Later he taught at Shields, became leader at the Newcastle-on-Tyne theatre, 1787, and at Astley's Amphitheatre in London, 1788. He began to write stage pieces and in 1793 went as mus. dir. and comp. to the Royal Circus (Surrey Theatre).

Works incl. stage pieces and pantomimes *Harlequin in Ireland, Blackbeard, Cora, Sir Francis Drake, The Magic Pipe, Hallowe'en* & many others; inst. interludes for Collins's *Ode to the Passions*; v. pieces; many popular songs, &c.

Sanderson, Sibyl (b. Sacramento, Cal., 7. XII. 1865; d. Paris, 16. V. 1903), Amer. sop. singer. Studied at the Paris Cons. and made her 1st stage appearance at The Hague in 1888, in Massenet's *Manon*. She was later chiefly assoc. with that comp.'s operas, making her 1st Paris appearance in his *Esclarmonde* in 1889.

Sandys, George (1578–1644), Eng. trans. *See* **Porter (W.)** (psalms).

Sannazaro, Jacopo (1458–1530), It. poet. *See* **Mudarra** (sonnets).

Santa Cruz, Domingo (b. La Cruz, 5. VII. 1899), Chilean comp., teacher & critic. Studied at Santiago de Chile and Madrid. In 1918 he founded a Bach Soc. at Santiago and in 1932 became dean of the Fine Arts Dept. at the Univ. of Chile.

Works incl. *5 Piezas brevas* for stg. orch.; 3 v. & pf. pieces; pf. works; songs, &c.

Santa Maria, Tomás de (b. Madrid, ?; d. ?, 1570), Spa. monk & orgst. He joined a Dominican monastery and in 1565 pub. a treatise on playing polyphonic fantasies on keyboard insts. and lutes.

Santi, Angelo De (b. Trieste, 12. VII. 1847; d. Rome, 28. I. 1922), It. priest and mus. scholar. He entered the Jesuit Order as a youth and graduated at Innsbruck. He advocated reforms in Rom. church m. to the Popes Leo XIII and Pius X, and it was owing to his recommendations that the latter issued the *Motu proprio* of 1903.

Santini, Fortunato (b. Rome, 5. I. 1778; d. Rome, 1862), It. priest, mus. scholar & comp. He studied m. with Jannaconi and after being ordained in 1801 began to make an immense collection of old m., scoring it from parts in var. mus. libraries. He made friends with Mendelssohn and through him introd. many works by Bach into It., as well as other Ger. sacred m.

Works incl. Requiem for 8 voices, masses & other church m., &c.

Santley, Charles (b. Liverpool, 28. II. 1834; d. London, 22. IX. 1922), Eng. bass-bar. singer. Learnt m. as a choir-boy and at first appeared as an amateur singer, but went to Milan in 1855 to study with Gaetano Nava, made a stage appearance at Pavia and in 1857 returned to Eng., continuing his studies with Manuel García in London, where he 1st appeared on 16. XI. He soon sang in opera, orat. and at the great festivals with enormous success. He toured the U.S.A. in 1871 and Austral. in 1890. In 1907 he celebrated his 50th anniversary as a singer and was knighted.

Santoliquido, Francesco (b. San Giorgio a Cremano, Naples, 6. VIII. 1883), It. comp. Studied at the Liceo di Santa Cecilia in Rome, cond. his student work, *Crepuscolo sul mare*, at Nuremberg in 1909 and prod. his 1st opera at Milan in 1910. He then went to live in Tunisia, in the small Arab village of Hammamek, where he became interested in the study of native m.

Works incl. operas *La favola di Helga, Ferhuda, L'ignota* & *La porta verde*, mimed drama *La ballata della maschera gialla*; Sym. in F maj., *Crepuscolo sul mare, Il profumo delle oasi sahariane, La morte di Tintagiles* (after Maeterlinck), *Paesaggi, Acquarelle* for orch.; *Due acqueforti tunisine, Ex humo ad sidera*, &c. for pf.; songs on Japanese and Persian poetry, &c.

Sapho, opera by Gounod (lib. by Émile Augier), prod. Paris, Opéra, 16. IV. 1851. G.'s 1st opera.

Opera by Massenet (lib. by Henri Cain & Arthur Bernède, based on Daudet's novel), prod. Paris, Opéra-Comique, 27. XI. 1897. The heroine is not the Gr. poetess Sappho.

Sappho. *See also* **Saffo, Sapho.**
Opera by **Hugo Kaun** (1863–1932) (lib. by comp., based on Grillparzer's play), prod. Leipzig, 27. X. 1917.

Saraband (Eng.) } **Sarabande** (Fr.) } A dance, poss. orig. in Spa. in the 16th cent. Its name was formerly supposed to be derived from a dancer called Zarabanda, but it is very likely of more remote eastern orig. It was introd. to the Fr. court in 1588 and in 17th-cent. Eng. became a country dance. The m. is in slow 3–2 time with, as a rule, a peculiar rhythm of a minim, dotted minim and crotchet in the 1st bar followed by 2 minims and a minim rest in the 2nd. The S. is one of the 4 regular mvts. in the Suite, together with the Allemande, Courante and Gigue (Jig).

Sarasate (y Navascues), Pablo (Martín Melitón) (b. Pamplona, 10. III. 1844; d. Biarritz, 20. IX. 1908), Spa. vst. & comp. Pupil of Alard at the Paris Cons. He soon began to make a remarkable career as a virtuoso, at first in Fr. and Spa., later all over Eur. and Amer. He 1st appeared in London in 1861.
Works incl. romances, fantasies, 4 books of Spa. Dances, &c. for v.

Sardana. A Spa. dance of Catalonia revived in the middle of the 19th cent. and perf. to pipe and drum.

Sardou, Victorien (1831–1908), Fr. playwright. *See* **Duchess of Dantzic** (Caryll), **Fedora** (Giordano), **Giordano** (*Mme Sans-Gêne*), **Leroux** (*Cléopâtre & Théodora*), **Offenbach** (*Haine*), **Paladilhe** (*Patrie*), **Saint-Saëns** (*Barbares*), **Soloviev** (*Cordelia*), **Strauss (J. ii)** (*Karneval in Rom*), **Tosca** (Puccini), **Webber** (*Fiorella*).

Šárka (Smetana). *See* **Má Vlast.**
Opera by Fibich (lib. by Anežka Schulzová), prod. Prague, Cz. Theatre, 28. XII. 1897.

Saroyan, William (b. 1908), Armenian-Amer. playwright & novelist. *See* **Bowles** (*My Heart's in the Highlands* & *Love's Old Sweet Song*).

Sarro, Domenico (b. Trani, Naples, 1679; d. Naples, 1744), It. comp. Studied at the Cons. de' Turchini at Naples and in 1712 became vice chapel master at the royal chapel there, later 1st chapel master.
Works incl. operas *Didone abbandonata, Achille in Sciro* & *c.* 50 others; masses & other church m.; orats. & cantatas; Conc. for 2 vs., fl., va., co. & bass, &c.

Sarrusophone. A brass wind inst. with a double-reed mouthpiece invented in 1863 by Sarrus, a bandmaster in the Fr. army, intended to be made in var. sizes to cover a whole range of tone replacing obs. and bns. in milit. bands. Only the bass types have been used by some Fr. comps., incl. Saint-Saëns and Massenet, but have not taken a regular place in the orch. They are, however, part of jazz and swing bands.

Sarselli, Elisabeth. *See* **Wendling.**

Sarti, Giuseppe (b. Faenza, 1. XII. 1729; d. Berlin, 28. VII. 1802), It. comp. He 1st learnt m. from his father, a jeweller who played the v., and later from Vallotti or Martini at Padua or Bologna. He was orgst. at Faenza cath. in 1748–50, prod. his 1st opera at the theatre there in 1751 and in 1752 became its dir. The following year he went to the Dan. court at Copenhagen, where Frederick V made him dir. of the opera and mus. dir. to the crown prince. The opera was closed for a time, but reopened in 1765, S. going to It. in search of singers. But he was delayed by the king's death and that of his own mother. He returned to Copenhagen to serve under Christian VII, married Camilla Pasi and was dismissed in 1775, when the queen-mother's party gained the upper hand. He became dir. of the Ospedaletto school of m. at Venice and in 1779 chapel master of Milan cath., where Cherubini became his pupil and asst. In 1784 he was invited to the court of Catherine II at St. Petersburg and on his way there visited Vienna, being well received by Joseph II and meeting Mozart, who wrote vars. on 'Come un agnello' from his *Fra due litiganti* and later used the theme in *Don Giovanni*. He prod. a number of operas in Rus., incl. *Oleg*, the lib. of which was by the empress, and remained there until 1802, living at a village in the Ukraine while temporarily out of favour at court and founding a school of singing there. He stayed in Berlin on his way to It., met the court mus. dir. Natale Mussini (1765–1837), who married his daughter Giuliana, and d. before he could proceed on his journey.
Works incl. operas *Pompeo in Armenia, Il rè pastore, I contrattempi, Didone abbandonata, Deucalion og Pyrrha* (Dan.), *Le gelosie villane, Farnace, Medonte, Achille in Sciro, Giulio Sabino, Fra due litiganti il terzo gode, I finti eredi, Armida, Oleg* (Rus., with Pashkevitch and Canobbio) & *c.* 60 others (9 in Dan., 4 in Fr.); masses, Requiem, Miserere, Te Deum, motets & other church m.; Rus. orat. 'Lord, I beseech Thee'; hpchd. sos., &c.

Sartorio, Antonio (b. Venice, *c.* 1620; d. Venice, *c.* 1681), It. comp. He was mus. dir. at the court of Brunswick until 1676 and then chapel master at St. Mark's, Venice, preceding Legrenzi.

Works incl. operas *Seleuco, La prosperità di Elio Seiano, La caduta di Elio Seiano, Adelaide, Orfeo* & 9 others; psalms & motets; cantatas for chor. & for solo voices, canzonets, &c.

Sartorius, Paul (? actually Schneider) (b. ?; d. ?), Ger. 16th–17th-cent. orgst. & comp. He was orgst. to the Archduke Maximilian of Aus. in 1599 and lived at Nuremberg.

Works incl. masses, *Sonetti spirituali* for 6 voices, motets, madrigals, *Neue teutsche Liedlein*, &c.

Sas, André (b. Paris, 6. IV. 1900), Belg.-Fr.-Peruv. comp. Studied in Brussels and went to Peru in 1924 as v. teacher at the Nat. Acad. of M. at Lima. He married the Peruv. pfst. Lily Rosay and with her founded a private m. school in 1929.

Works incl. *Himno al sol, Himno y danza* & *Poema Indio* for orch.; *Rapsodia peruana* for v. & orch.; *Quenas* for voice, fl. & hp.; *Sonatina india* for fl. & pf.; works for v. & pf.; pf. pieces; songs, &c.

Sass, Marie (Constance) (actually Saxe) (b. Ghent, 26. I. 1838; d. Auteuil nr. Paris, 8. XI. 1907), Belg. sop. singer. Pupil of Mme Ugalde, had her 1st stage perf. in Paris in 1859 and went to the Opéra in 1860, where the following year she sang Elisabeth in the Fr. version of Wagner's *Tannhäuser*. She d. insane.

Satanella, or The Power of Love, opera by Balfe (lib. by Augustus Glossop Harris and Edmund Falconer, based on Lesage's *Diable boiteux*), prod. London, Covent Garden Theatre, 20. XII. 1858.

Satie, Erik (Alfred Leslie) (b. Honfleur, 17. V. 1866; d. Paris, 1. VII. 1925), Fr. comp. He was brought up in a mus. home, his father being a comp. and m. pub. in Paris and his mother, of Sco. orig., a minor comp. of pf. pieces under the name of Eugénie Satie-Barnetsche. He spent only a year at the Paris Cons. and later made a precarious living by playing at cafés, writing m. for the Montmartre song-writer Hypsa and the m.-hall singer Paulette Darty. But he made friends with Debussy, whom he influenced to some extent, *c.* 1890, and came into contact with intellectual circles, made further studies at the Schola Cantorum under d'Indy and Roussel at the age of 40. He continued to pub. small pf. works under eccentric titles. In later years he came into touch with Jean Cocteau and estab. a school at Arcueil where he exercised some influence on younger comps.

Works incl. symph. drama *Socrate*; incid. m. for Péladan's *Le Fils de l'étoile*; ballets *Parade, Relâche* & *Mercure*; operettas *Geneviève de Brabant* (for marionettes), *Pousse-l'Amour* & *Le Piège de Méduse*; pantomime *Jack in the Box* (orch. by Milhaud); *Messe des pauvres* for voices & org.; pf. pieces *Ogives, 3 Sarabandes, 3 Gymnopédies, 3 Gnossiennes, Danses gothiques, Sonneries de la Rose-Croix, Pièces froides, Préludes en tapisserie, 3 Préludes flasques, Descriptions automatiques, Embryons desséchés, Croquis et agaceries d'un gros bonhomme en bois, Chapitres tournés en tous sens, Vieux Sequins et vieilles cuirasses, Heures séculaires et instantanées, 3 Valses du précieux dégoûté, Avant-dernières pensées*, &c.; *3 Morceaux en forme de poire, Aperçus désagréables* & *En habit de cheval* for pf. duet; 4 sets of songs, &c.

Satz (Ger. lit. 'setting') = Movement; also texture, lay-out or general contrivance in comp. *Tonsatz* is a Ger. word for comp.

Saudades (Port. = regrets for things of the past, nostalgias). The word has been used by Warlock for a set of songs & by Milhaud for 2 vols. of pf. pieces, *S. do Brasil.*

Sauer, Emil (b. Hamburg, 8. X. 1862; d. Vienna, 27. IV. 1942), Ger. pfst. & comp. Studied with N. Rubinstein at the Moscow Cons. and later with Liszt. Began to tour Eur. in 1882 and 1st visited Eng. in 1894. In 1901 he became head of the pf. branch at the Vienna Cons.

Works incl. 2 pf. concs.; 2 sos., 24 concert studies, *Suite moderne* & many pieces for pf.

Sauguet, Henri (actually Jean Pierre Poupard) (b. Bordeaux, 18. V. 1901), Fr. comp. & critic. Studied pf. & org. at Bordeaux, then became a pupil of J. Canteloube at Montauban and in 1921 of Koechlin in Paris. Introd. by Milhaud to Satie, he joined the latter's school at Arcueil. In 1936 he succeeded Milhaud as m. critic to *Le Jour-Écho de Paris.*

Works incl. operas *La Chartreuse de Parme* (after Stendhal) & *La Gageure imprévue* (Sedaine), operettas *Le Plumet du colonel* & *La Contrebasse*; ballets *La Chatte, David, La Nuit, Fastes*; incid. m. for Molière's *Le Sicilien*, Roger Ferdinand's *Irma* & other plays; pf. Conc. in A min.; Sonatina for fl. & pf.; So. in D maj. & other works for pf.; songs to poems by Tagore, &c.

Saul, orat. by Handel (lib. ? by Charles Jennens or Thomas Morell), prod. London, King's Theatre, 16. I. 1739.

Saunders, John (b. London, 23. XII.

1867; d. London, 7. X. 1919), Eng. vst. Studied at the G.S.M. in London, became an orch. player and in 1910 leader of the Royal Phil. Soc.; but he chiefly cultivated chamber m., esp. at the South Place Concerts, where he played regularly from 1891 to 1919.

Saunderson, James. *See* **Sanderson.**

Sauret, Émile (b. Dun-le-Roi, 22. V. 1852; d. London, 12. II. 1920), Fr. vst. & comp. Pupil of Bériot. He began to travel at an early age, 1st visited London in 1862, played much at the Fr. court in the last years of the 2nd Empire, visited the U.S.A. twice in 1872–6, studied comp. with Jadassohn at Leipzig and appeared with Liszt. In 1872 he married Teresa Carreño, but they were divorced before long. In 1890 he succeeded Sainton as v. prof. at the R.A.M. in London and in 1903 he took up a similar post at Chicago.

Works incl. 2 concs., *Ballade*, *Légende*; Serenade for v. & orch.; many v. pieces, studies and arrs., &c.

Sausage Bassoon. *See* **Racket.**

Sautillé (Fr.=springing, bounding). A spec. way of playing the v. and other stg. insts. in such a manner that the bow is made to rebound from the stgs.

Sauzay, Charles Eugène (b. Paris, 14. VII. 1809; d. Paris, 24. I. 1901), Fr. vst. & comp. Studied at the Paris Cons., Baillot and Reicha being among his masters. He joined Baillot's 4tet and married his daughter, became court vst. in 1840 and prof. at the Cons. in 1860.

Works incl. incid. m. for Molière's *George Dandin* & *Le Sicilien*; stg. Trio, pf. Trio; v. & pf. pieces; *Études harmoniques* for solo v.; songs, &c.

Savart, Félix (b. Mézières, 30. VI. 1791; d. Paris, 17. III. 1841), Fr. scientist. Orig. a physician, he gave up practice in order to investigate sound-waves, becoming a lecturer in physics at the Collège de Fr. in Paris in 1819. He made inventions in connection with vibrations and wrote a number of treatises.

Savile, Jeremy (b. ?; d. ?), Eng. 17th-cent. comp. Contrib. songs to *Select Musicall Ayres and Dialogues* in 1653. Comps. incl. partsong *The Waits*, song 'Here's a health unto His Majesty,' &c.

Sāvitri, opera by Holst (lib. by comp., based on an episode in the *Mahabharata*), prod. London, Wellington Hall, 5. XII. 1916; 1st public perf. London, Lyric Theatre, Hammersmith, 23. VI. 1921.

Savonarola, opera by Stanford (lib. by Gilbert Arthur à Beckett), prod., in Ger. (trans. by Ernst Frank), Hamburg, 18. IV. 1884.

Savorini, Eugenia. *See* **Tadolini.**

Sax. Belg. family of inst. makers:

1. Charles Joseph S. (b. Dinant, 1. II. 1791; d. Paris, 26. IV. 1865). He set up in business at Brussels, made wind insts. and prod. several inventions, esp. in connection with hns. & other brass insts.

2. Adolphe (actually Antoine Joseph) S. (b. Dinant, 6. XI. 1814; d. Paris, 4. II. 1894), son of prec. Studied fl. and cl. at the Brussels Cons. and worked with his father, made several improvements in wind insts. and estab. himself in Paris in 1842. His chief inventions are the Saxhorn and the Saxophone.

3. Alphonse S. (b. ?; d. ?), brother of prec. He made some inventions in connection with the valves of brass insts. and estab. himself independently in Paris, but did not succeed.

Saxe, Marie. *See* **Sass.**

Saxhorn. A brass wind inst. allied to the Bugle, but with valves, invented by Adolphe Sax and patented by him in 1845. It is played with a cup mouthpiece and made in 7 different pitches covering between them a range of some 5 octaves: sop. in E♭, alto in B♭ (both also called Flügelhorns), ten. in E♭, bar. in B♭ (both also called Althorns), bass in B♭ (Euphonium), bass tuba in E♭ (Bombardon) and contrabass in B♭. They are rarely if ever used in the orch., but are regular constituents of milit. and brass bands.

Saxophone. A wind inst. made of brass, but with woodwind characteristics, invented by Adolphe Sax *c.* 1840. It is played through a mouthpiece with a single reed of the cl. type and the notes are controlled by keys. It is made in 5 or 6 pitches: sopranino in E♭ (rare), sop. in B♭, alto in E♭, ten. in B♭ (these 2 the most common), bar. in E♭ and bass in B♭. It is rarely used in the orch. (most often by Fr. comps.), but is a regular member of milit. bands and an indispensable one of jazz and swing bands.

Saynète (Fr.)=Spa. **Sainete.**

Sbriglia, Giovanni (b. Naples, 1840; d. ?), It. ten. singer & teacher. Made his 1st appearance at Naples in 1861, travelled widely in Eur. and U.S.A. and eventually settled in Paris as a singing-master, where he had the de Reszke brothers among his pupils.

Scacchi, Marco (b. Rome, *c.* 1600; d. Gallese nr. Rome, before 1685), It. comp. Pupil of Anerio. In 1623 he succeeded Pacelli as chapel master and court cond. at Warsaw, whence he returned to It. in 1648. He introd. It. opera to Warsaw, Danzig and Vilna. He wrote some theoret. tracts.

Works incl. operas *Il ratto di Helena, Narciso trasformato, Armida abbandonata, Enea, Le nozze d'Amore e di Psiche* & *Circe delusa*; masses; orat. *S. Cecilia*; madrigals, &c.

Scala di seta, La (*The Silken Ladder*), opera by Rossini (lib. by Gaetano Rossi, based on Planard's lib. *L'Échelle de soie* set by Gaveaux), prod. Venice, Teatro San Moisè, 9. V. 1812.

Scala enigmatica (It. = enigmatic scale; also *enimmatica*). Verdi's term for the curious scale on which he constructed his *Ave Maria* for 4 voices comp. *c.* 1889. Its notes are C, D♭, E, F♯, G♯, A♯, B, C, i.e. degrees of ½, 1½, 1, 1, 1, ½, ½ tones.

Scala Theatre (Teatro alla Scala). The great opera-house at Milan, built after the destruction by fire of the Teatro Regio Ducal in 1776 on the site of the church of Santa Maria alla Scala and opened 3. VIII. 1778. It was reconstructed in 1867 and the stage was re-equipped in 1921. During the 1939–45 war it was damaged, but not irreparably.

Scalabrini, Paolo (b. Bologna, 1713; d. Lucca, 23. II. 1806), It. comp. He travelled in Aus. and Ger. with Pietro Mingotti's opera company and settled at Copenhagen in 1748, succeeding Scheibe as court cond. He remained until 1753 and held the post again in 1775–81, when he returned to It. He was the 1st to set an opera to Dan. words.

Works incl. Dan. operas *Love rewarded, or The Faithful Lovers, Oraklet*, &c., *c.* 20 It. operas; incid. m.; orat. *Giuseppe riconosciuto*; inst. m., &c.

Scalchi, Sofia (b. Turin, 29. XI. 1850; d. ?), It. con. singer. Studied with Boccabadati and made her 1st stage appearance at Mantua in 1866. She 1st visited Eng. in 1868 and sang regularly in London until 1890; also travelled widely in Eur. and 1st went to U.S.A. in 1882.

Scale (from Lat. *scalae* & It. *scala* = ladder). A succession of adjoining notes proceeding in ascent or descent, most commonly in some spec. order of alternating semitones and whole tones, in which case they form either Diatonic (maj. or min.) Ss. or Modal Ss. But there are also the Chromatic S., proceeding entirely by semitones, and Gapped Ss. of var. kinds, such as Pentatonic or Whole-tone Ss. In the old system of the Gamut Ss. consisted of Tetrachords (Ss. of 4 successive notes only) which could be rearranged with the interval between the 3rd and 4th degree made variable as either a whole tone or a semitone, in the latter case the 3rd one becoming a Leading-note.

Scand. (abbr.) = Scandinavia, Scandinavian.

Scandello, Antonio (or **Scandelli**) (b. Brescia, 1517; d. Dresden, 18. I. 1580), It. comp. He is 1st heard of as a member of the Saxon court chapel at Dresden in 1553, but he often returned to Brescia for visits, as in 1567, when he and his family took refuge there during the plague at Dresden. Among the court musns. was his brother Angelo S., and also employed at the court was the It. painter Benedetto Tola, whose daughter Agnese became S.'s 2nd wife in 1568, in which year he was app. chapel master in place of Matthieu Le Maistre, whose asst. chapel master he had been for 2 years. He became involved in quarrels with the Ger. court musns. and the Flem. singers because the Its. received higher pay.

Works incl. masses, motets, setting for voices of the Passion and Resurrection narrative according to St. John, hymn-tunes for several voices & other church m.; madrigals, epithalamia, *canzoni napoletane* for 4 voices, sacred and secular Ger. songs for several voices & insts.; lute m., &c.

Scandinavian Composers. *See* **Danish, Norwegian, Swedish.**

Scaria, Emil (b. Graz, 18. IX. 1838; d. Blazewitz nr. Dresden, 22. VII. 1886), Aus. bass singer. Studied at the Vienna Cons. and made his 1st stage appearance at Budapest. In 1862 he visited London to study under Manuel García and sang at the Crystal Palace. In 1876 he sang Wotan in the prod. of Wagner's *Ring* at Bayreuth and in 1882 Gurnemanz in that of *Parsifal* there.

Scarlatti. It. family of musns.:

1. Alessandro S. (b. Palermo, 2. V. 1660; d. Naples, 24. X. 1725), comp. His parents, Pietro and Eleonora (*née* d'Amato) S., went to live in Rome in 1672, taking all but the 2 youngest children, Francesco and Tommaso, with them. He (?) studied with Carissimi before he was 15, when that master d., and possibly with Legrenzi or Stradella, if not both. In 1678 he married Antonia Anzalone, of whom he had many children. He became chapel master to Queen Christina of Swe. there, but moved to Naples some time in the early 1680s. On 17. II. 1684 he was app. chapel master to the viceroy of Naples. But his salary fell into

arrears and he was dissatisfied with the mus. life of Naples, so that in 1702 he left with his son Domenico for Florence, where they found a patron in Ferdinando (III) de' Medici, for whose theatre at Pratolino he wrote several operas; but he left before long for Rome, where he was given the small post of asst. chapel master at the church of Santa Maria Maggiore. In 1706 he joined the Arcadian Acad., together with Corelli and Pasquini, and in 1707 he succeeded Foggia as 1st chapel master of his church, and it was only then that he left off writing operas for the Florentine prince, who dropped him in favour of Perti. He went to Venice that year to prod. 2 operas, returning some months later and staying at Urbino with the Albani family, relatives of Pope Clement XI, and prob. at Ferrara. In 1713 he returned to Naples as master of the viceregal chapel. He was knighted (title of *Cavaliere*) soon afterwards and returned to Rome, only to make Naples his last home *c.* 1723, after which time he lived there in retirement, though accepting Hasse as pupil in 1724.

Works incl. operas *L'errore innocente, ovvero Gli equivoci nel sembiante, L'honestà negli amori, Il Pompeo, Olimpia vendicata, La Rosmene, La Statira, Gli equivoci in amore, Pirro e Demetrio, La caduta de' decemviri, Il prigioniero fortunato, L'Eraclea, Il Mitridate Eupatore, Il trionfo della libertà, L'amore volubile e tiranno, La principessa fedele, Il Tigrane, Carlo, rè d'Alemagna, Cambise, Il Telemaco, Il trionfo dell' onore, Marco Attilio Regolo, Tito Sempronio Gracco, Turno Aricino, La Griselda* and nearly 100 others (*c.* 80 known by titles & *c.* 40 preserved); masses (10 preserved, but many more comp.), *Ave Maria*, motets for double chor. *Tu es Petrus, O magnum mysterium, Volo, Pater* & other church m.; orat. *San Filippo Neri* & others; cantatas & serenades; 12 syms.; 4 stg. 4tets (*Sonate a quattro*); org. pieces; vars. on Corelli's *Follia* and other hpchd. pieces, &c.

2. Francesco S. (b. ? Palermo, 1668; d. ?), vst. & comp., brother of prec. He was one of the children left in Sicily when his parents went to Rome, and he became a vst. in the royal orch. at Naples in 1684. In 1691 he went back to Palermo, prob. only on a visit, and in 1715 he was in Vienna, recommended by Fux for a post at court, which he did not obtain.

Works incl. operas; masses, *Dixit Dominus* & other church m.; cantatas, &c.

3. Tommaso S. (b. Palermo, *c.* 1670; d. Naples, 1. VIII. 1760), ten. singer, brother of prec. He was another of the children left in Sicily by his parents; later sang in opera at Naples, incl. his brother Alessandro's (1) works.

4. Pietro Filippo S. (b. Rome, 5. I. 1679; d. Naples, 22. II. 1750), orgst., nephew of prec., son of 1. Studied with his father and others in Rome and returned with him to Naples in 1708, where he was app. a supernumerary orgst. in the viceregal chapel, and became 1st orgst. in succession to Vignola in 1712. In 1744 he was refused an application for Leo's former post as chapel master, and he left his wife and children destitute on his death.

Works incl. opera *Chitarco*, &c.

5. (Giuseppe) Domenico S. (b. Naples, 26. X. 1685; d. Madrid, 23. VII. 1757), hpchdst. & comp., brother of prec. Studied with his father (1) and later with Gasparini, prob. also with Greco and poss. with Pasquini. He became a supremely gifted hpchd. player, but was not appreciated by his countrymen in that capacity. In 1704 he remodelled Pollarolo's opera *Irene* for perf. and in 1705 his father sent him to Venice in the company of Nicolini by way of Florence, where he visited Alessandro's former patron, Ferdinando de' Medici. It was in Venice that he studied with Gasparini and he met Handel there in 1708, going to Rome with him and engaging there in a friendly contest with him at the hpchd., which remained undecided, H. however being victor at the org. In 1709 he went into the service of the Queen of Pol., Maria Casimira, for whose private theatre in Rome he wrote operas. In 1715 he became chapel master at St. Peter's, in succession to Bai. In 1720 one of the operas, *Narciso*, was prod. in London, but whether he went there in person is doubtful. But he did go to Lisbon that year and was well received at the Port. court. In 1724–5 he was at Naples with his family, but in 1729 he accepted an invitation to the Spa. court and left for Madrid. There is no evidence that he visited Dublin in 1740 or London in 1741–2, when m. of his was used in 2 pasticcios.

Works incl. operas *Silvia, Orlando, Tetide in Sciro, Ifigenia in Aulide, Ifigenia in Tauride, Amor d'un' ombra, Narciso, Amleto* (based on the sources of Shakespeare's *Hamlet*) & others; masses, *Stabat Mater* for 10 voices & other church m.; over 500 *Esercizi* for hpchd. (now called sos., being in a terse binary form distinctly foreshadowing 1st-mvt. so. form).

6. Giuseppe S. (b. Naples, 24. VI. 1723; d. Vienna, 17. VIII. 1777), comp., cousin of prec. Pupil of (?) Leo at Naples. He began writing operas at 16 and settled in Vienna in 1757.

Works incl. operas *Merope*, *Dario*, *I portentosi effetti della Madre Natura* (lib. by Goldoni), *L'isola disabitata*, *L'amor geloso* & 23 others, &c.

Scarlet Letter, The, opera by W. Damrosch (lib. by George Parsons Lathrop, based on Hawthorne's novel), prod. Boston, 10. II. 1896.

Scarron, Paul (1610–60), Fr. author & poet. *See* **Lächerliche Prinz Jodelet** (Keiser).

Sce. (abbr.) = Scenario.

Scena (It. = stage, or scene, i.e. the subdivision of an act in a dram. piece). The It. word is not used in these senses in Eng., which has its own words for them; but S. is a technical term for operatic solo numbers on a large scale, usually a recit. followed by one or more aria-like sections; also similar pieces designed for concert perf.

Scenario (It.). The sketch or rough draft for the plot of an opera lib. or for the story of a ballet, &c.

Scenes from Goethe's 'Faust' (Schumann). *See* **Szenen aus Goethe's 'Faust.'**

Schack (orig. **Žak**), **Benedict** (b. Miřovice, 1758; d. Munich, 11. XII. 1826), Boh. ten. singer, flst. & comp. 1st heard of as a singer of minor parts in Vienna, 1787; afterwards attached to Schikaneder's theatre, where he was the 1st Tamino in Mozart's *Magic Flute* and played the fl. part himself. M. wrote pf. vars. on his song 'Ein Weib ist das herrlichste Ding' (K. 613).

Works incl. operas & mus. plays (some with Gerl & others) *Der dumme Gärtner* (with 6 sequels), *Der Stein der Weisen*, *Der Fall ist noch weit seltner* (sequel to Martín y Soler's *Una cosa rara*) & others; Mass; songs, &c.

Schaeffner, André (b. Paris, 7. II. 1895), Fr. mcolst. Studied at the Schola Cantorum in Paris and after 1920 became m. critic to var. periodicals. His books incl. studies of the origin of mus. insts. and of Stravinsky. He is the ed. of the Fr. ed. of Riemann's Dict. of M.

Schäfer, Dirk (b. Rotterdam, 25. XI. 1873; d. Amsterdam, 18. II. 1931), Dutch pfst. & comp. Studied at the Cologne Cons. and in Berlin. He 1st settled at The Hague and in 1904 at Amsterdam.

Works incl. *Suite pastorale* & *Javaansche Rhapsodie* for orch.; stg. 4tet, pf. 5tet; v. & pf. sos.; pf. works, &c.

Schaffrath, Christoph (b. Hohenstein nr. Dresden, 1709; d. Berlin, 17. II. 1763), Ger. hpchdst., orgst. & comp. In 1733, when in the service of a Pol. prince, he competed unsuccessfully with W. F. Bach for the post of orgst. at St. Sophia's church at Dresden, but in 1735 he became chamber musn. to the crown prince of Prus. and remained with him when he acceded as Frederick II.

Works incl. syms. & ovts. for orch.; hpchd. & v. concs.; chamber m., &c.

Schale, Christian Friedrich (b. Brandenburg, 10. III. 1713; d. Berlin, 2. III. 1800), Ger. cst., orgst. & comp. Pupil of Christian Friedrich Rolle (?–1751), became royal Prus. chamber virtuoso in 1742 and orgst. at Berlin cath. in 1764.

Schalk, Franz (b. Vienna, 27. V. 1863; d. Edlach, 2. IX. 1931), Aus. cond. Pupil of Bruckner and, after var. engagements, chief cond. at the Vienna Court Opera in succession to Ferdinand Löwe, with whom he suggested var. revisions in Bruckner's syms. to the comp. He visited London in 1907 and 1911.

Schalmei (Ger.) = Shawm.

Schantz, Johan Filip von (b. Ulvila, 17. I. 1835; d. Helsingfors, 24. VII. 1865), Fin. cond. & comp. Studied law at Helsingfors Univ. and, after involving himself in political demonstrations during the Crimean War in 1855, at Stockholm and at the Leipzig Cons. In 1860 he returned home as cond. of the orch. attached to the new theatre, but left for Stockholm in 1863 with part of the orch. after a disagreement with the management. He cond. concerts also at Göteborg and Copenhagen, but later returned to Helsingfors in poor health.

Works incl. symph. poem *Kullervo* (on the *Kalevala*); partsongs, songs, folksong settings, &c.

Scharwenka, (Ludwig) Philipp (b. Szamotuly, Poznania, 16. II. 1847; d. Bad Nauheim, 16. VII. 1917), Ger.-Pol. comp. & teacher. On the family's removal to Berlin he studied m. at Kullak's school there and remained as teacher until 1881, when he joined his brother's newly opened Cons., which he dir. in 1891 on the latter's departure for Amer., together with Hugo Goldschmidt. In 1880 he married the vst. Marianne Stresow (?–1918).

Works incl. 2 syms., *Sinfonia brevis*, Serenade, Festival Ovt., *Liebesnacht*, *Arcadian Suite*, symph. poems *Frühlingswogen* & *Traum und*

Wirklichkeit; v. Conc.; *Herbstfeier* & *Sakuntala* (after Kalidasa) for solo voices, chor. & orch.; pf. Trio in C♯ min.; 3 concert pieces for v. & pf., v. & co. studies; *Album polonais*, 3 sos. and many other works for pf., &c.

Scharwenka, (Franz) Xaver (b. Szamotuly, Poznania, 6. I. 1850; d. Berlin, 8. XII. 1924), Ger.-Pol. pfst., comp. & teacher, brother of prec. Studied at Kullak's school of m. in Berlin, where the family had settled in 1865, and made his 1st appearance as a pfst. there in 1869. Later he travelled widely, paying his 1st visit to Eng. in 1879. In 1881 he opened a Cons. of his own in Berlin, which in 1893 became amalgamated with Klindworth's. In 1891–8 he lived mainly in N.Y., where he had opened a branch of his school.

Works incl. opera *Mataswintha* (on Felix Dahn's novel *Ein Kampf um Rom*); Sym. in C min.; 4 pf. concs.; pf. 4tet, 2 pf. trios; 2 co. & pf. sos.; Theme & Vars., Pol. dances & numerous other works for pf., &c.

Schauspieldirektor, Der (*The Impresario*), play with m. by Mozart (lib. by Gottlieb Stephanie, jun.), prod. Vienna, Schönbrunn Palace, at court, 7. II. 1786; 1st Vienna perf., Kärntnertor Theatre, 18. II. 1786.

Schechner, Nanette (b. Munich, 1806; d. Munich, 29. IV. 1860), Ger. sop. singer. Pupil of Weber and studied in It. 1st appeared in Munich and in 1826 in Vienna.

Scheffel, Joseph Victor von (1826–86), Ger. poet & novelist. *See* **Henschel** (*Trompeter von Säckingen*), **Jensen** (*Gaudeamus*), **Scholz** (*Trompeter von S.*), **Schreker** (*Ekkehard*), **Trompeter von Säckingen** (Nessler).

Scheherazade (Ravel & Rimsky-Korsakov). *See* **Shéhérazade** & **Shahrazad.**

Scheibe, Johann Adolph (b. Leipzig, V. 1708; d. Copenhagen, 22. IV. 1776), Ger. writer on m., critic & comp. Studied law at Leipzig and in 1736 settled at Hamburg as m. teacher. In 1740 he became chapel master to the Margrave of Brandenburg-Culmbach and in 1742 settled in Copenhagen as cond. of the Court Operá, 1744–8. He ed. the periodical *Der critische Musikus*, in which he attacked Bach.

Works incl. pastoral opera *Il giudizio di Paride*; incid. m.; 2 orats.; masses & other church m.; cantatas; many syms. & concs.; 4tets, trios; sos., &c.

Scheidemann. Ger. family of orgsts. & comps.:

1. David S. (b. Hamburg, ?; d. Hamburg, ?), orgst. at St. Michael's church, Hamburg. Pub. a hymn-book with H. J. Praetorius and Joachim Decker in 1604, with the tunes in the sop. part, not, as earlier, in the ten.

2. Hans S. (b. Hamburg, ?; d. Hamburg, 1625), ? brother of prec. Orgst. at St. Catherine's church, Hamburg.

3. Heinrich S. (b. Hamburg, *c.* 1596; d. Hamburg, 1663), son of prec. Pupil of his father and later of Sweelinck at Amsterdam. On his father's death he succeeded to the post of orgst. at St. Catherine's church, Hamburg, where on his death he was himself succeeded by Reinken, his pupil, as were Fabricius and Weckmann. He contrib., with J. Praetorius, to Rist's hymn-book *Himmlische Lieder*, pub. in 1641–2.

Works incl. church m.; org. pieces, &c.

Scheidemantel, Karl (b. Weimar, 21. I. 1859; d. Weimar, 26. VI. 1923), Ger. bar. singer. Studied with Bodo Borchers and made his 1st stage appearance at Weimar in 1878. After further study with Stockhausen he became famous, mainly as a Wagner singer. He 1st visited London in 1884 and was 1st engaged at the Bayreuth Wagner theatre in 1886.

Scheidler, Dorette. *See* **Spohr.**

Scheidt, Samuel (b. Halle, 1587; d. Halle, 30. III. 1654), Ger. orgst. & comp. Pupil of Sweelinck at Amsterdam. He returned to Halle *c.* 1609 and became orgst. at St. Maurice's church. In or before 1620 he also received the appt. of orgst. and chapel master to the Margrave of Brandenburg in his capacity as Protestant administrator of the archbishopric of Magdeburg, but S.'s appt. was to the court church at Halle, where he remained all his life. His activities at that church ceased in 1625, though he remained in touch with the Brandenburg court until the Margrave Christian William abdicated in 1638. In 1637 the Maurice church was burnt down. He abolished the old Ger. org. tablature in favour of modern staff notation and did away with extemporized embellishments.

Works incl. *Cantiones sacrae* for 8 voices; sacred concs. for 2–12 voices with insts.; pavans and galliards for 4–5 voices; *Liebliche Krafft-Blümlein* for 2 voices & insts.; org. accomps. for or transcriptions of 100 hymns and psalms; *Tabulatura nova* containing a great variety of org. pieces in 3 vols., &c.

Schein, Johann Hermann (b. Grünhain, Saxony, 20. I. 1586; d. Leipzig, 19. XI. 1630), Ger. comp. After the death of his father, a Lutheran pastor, he went to Dresden as a choir-boy in the court chapel in 1599, to the grammar-school at Schulpforta in 1603 and to Leipzig Univ. in 1607. In 1613–5 he was chapel master at the court of Weimar and in XI. 1615 he became cantor at St. Thomas's School, Leipzig, on the death of Calvisius, remaining there until his death.

Works incl. *Cantiones sacrae* for 5–12 voices; 2 vols. of sacred concs. for 3–5 voices with insts.; *Fontana d'Israel* containing biblical words set for 4–5 voices and insts.; *Cantional* hymn-book with *c.* 80 tunes of his own; songs for 5 voices, *Venus-Kränzlein, Studenten-Schmaus* & *Diletti pastorali*; inst. dances *Banchetto musicale*; songs with insts. *Musica boscareccia*; wedding & funeral cantatas, &c.

Schelble, Johann Nepomuk (b. Hüfingen, Black Forest, 16. V. 1789; d. Frankfort o/M., 7. VIII. 1837), Ger. singer, teacher & cond. Studied with Vogler and others, lived and sang in Vienna in 1813–6 and then settled at Frankfort, where he taught and founded the Caecilian Soc. in 1818.

Schelle, Johann (b. Geising nr. Meissen, 6. IX. 1648; d. Leipzig, 10. III. 1701), Ger. orgst. & comp. Studied at Leipzig, became cantor at Eilenburg and in 1676 cantor at St. Thomas's church, Leipzig.

Works incl. cantatas, songs, &c.

Schellen (Ger.) = Jingles.

Schellenbaum (Ger. lit. jingle-tree) = Chinese Pavilion, Jingling Johnny, Turkish Crescent.

Schellentrommel (Ger. lit. drum with jingles) = Tabor or tambourine.

Schelling, Ernest (b. Belvidere, New Jersey, 26. VII. 1876; d. New York, 8. XII. 1939), Amer. pfst. & comp. After coming out as a wonder child at Philadelphia at the age of 4, he studied at the Paris Cons., also in Vienna with Leschetizky for pf. and Bruckner for comp., as well as elsewhere with Paderewski, Moszkowski and others. He toured widely, joined the Amer. army in 1918 and later lectured on the orch. to children.

Works incl. Sym. in C min., *Symph. Legend*, fantasy *A Victory Ball* & *Morocco* for orch.; *Fantastic Suite* & *Impressions from an Artist's Life* for pf. & orch., v. Conc.; *Divertimento* for pf. 5tet & other chamber m.; pf. pieces; songs, &c.

Schelomo, rhapsody for co. & orch. by Bloch, comp. 1915, 1st perf. N.Y., 3. V. 1916.

Schemelli, Georg Christian (b. Herzberg, 1676; d. ?), Ger. musn. & mus. ed. Pupil at St. Thomas's school, Leipzig, cantor at the palace of Zeitz. His *Musicalisches Gesang-Buch*, ed. by Bach, was pub. in 1736. On some of the hymns in it Bach wrote chorale-preludes.

Schenck, Johan(n) (b. ?; d. ?), Ger. or Dutch va. da gamba player & comp. He worked at the electoral court at Düsseldorf, later in Amsterdam.

Works incl. opera *Ceres en Bacchus*; chamber sos. for 2 vs., va. da gamba & bass, va. da gamba sos. & suites, &c.

Schenk, Johann (b. Wiener Neustadt, 30. XI. 1753; d. Vienna, 29. XII. 1836), Aus. comp. Learnt m. as a child in the archbishop's choir in Vienna and later became a pupil of Wagenseil. He prod. his 1st mass in 1778 and his 1st stage piece in 1785. In 1794 he became mus. dir. to Prince Carl von Auersperg and in 1793 Beethoven became his pupil for a short time.

Works incl. operas & mus. plays *Die Weinlese, Die Weihnacht auf dem Lande, Achmet und Almanzine, Der Dorfbarbier, Die Jagd, Der Fassbinder* & others; masses; cantatas *Die Huldigung* & *Der Mai*; syms.; concs.; stg. 4tets; songs, &c.

Schenker, Heinrich (b. Wisniowczyk, 19. VI. 1868; d. Vienna, 14. I. 1935), Pol.-Aus. theorist. Studied with Bruckner at the Vienna Cons. and on Brahms's recommendation pub. some early comps. He taught a number of pupils privately and in his literary works, incl. *Neue musikalische Theorien und Phantasien* and *Das Meisterwerk in der Musik,* laid down his extremely minute method of analysing masterpieces.

Scherer, Sebastian Anton (b. Ulm, X. 1631; d. Ulm, 26. VIII. 1712), Ger. orgst. & comp. He rose through var. posts to that of orgst. of Ulm cath. in 1671. In the 1680s (?) he was orgst. at St. Thomas's church, Strasburg.

Works incl. masses, motets & psalms; sos. for 2 vs. & bass; org. pieces; suites for lute, &c.

Schering, Arnold (b. Breslau, 2. IV. 1877; d. Berlin, 1941), Ger. mcolst. Studied at Leipzig Univ., where in 1907 he became lecturer and later prof. of m. From 1909 he also lectured at the Cons. and in 1920 he became prof. at Halle Univ. His books incl. studies of the early v. conc., the develop. of the orat. and so., the perf. of old m., early org. and chamber m. and a series of attempts to prove that Beethoven's sos. and 4tets are based on Shakespeare's plays and other dramatic works.

Scherz, List und Rache (*Jest, Cunning*

and Revenge), operetta by Bruch (lib. by Goethe, altered by Ludwig Bischoff), prod. Cologne, 14. I. 1858.

Opera by Philipp Christoph Kayser (1755–1823) (lib. do.), comp. 1785–6, not perf.

For other settings *see* **Goethe.**

Scherzando (It. = playful, humorous, skittish). A direction written by comps. over passages intended to be perf. in that manner. It may also be used as an adj. in tempo directions, e.g. *allegretto scherzando.*

Scherzevole (It., accent on 2nd syll.). The same as the prec., but less frequently used.

Scherzetto. A small Scherzo.

Scherzi, Gli (*The Jokes*). One of the nicknames given to Haydn's 6 stg. 4tets, Op. 33, the others being *Russian Quartets* and *Jungfern Quartette.* They were written in 1772 and described by H. as being 'in a new style.' 3 of them also have separate nicknames: No. 2 *The Joke,* No. 3 *The Bird* (or *Birds*), No. 5 *How do you do?*

Scherzino. A small Scherzo. This term, like Scherzetto, is used only for short inst. pieces of the scherzo type, not for mvts. in Scherzo form.

Scherzo. One of the 2 middle mvts., more usually the 3rd, of a 4-mvt. sym., so. or other so.-form work, where it displaced the Minuet. It does not occur regularly before the early 19th cent., being estab. mainly by Beethoven and Schubert; but the term S. dates back to the 17th cent., when It. canzonets were often called 'scherzi musicali' and inst. pieces were also sometimes pub. under that title. (For an early use of the name *see* Haydn's work above.) The S., having arisen from the minuet, is normally in triple time, generally 3–4, and it has as a rule a contrasting trio section. But exs. in duple or quadruple time occur, e.g. in Beethoven's E♭ maj. pf. So., Op. 31 No. 3, in Mendelssohn and Schumann. The 5–4 mvt. in Tchaikovsky's 'Pathetic' Sym. is also in the nature of a S. Sometimes the trio occurs twice, e.g. in Beethoven's 7th Sym., or there may be, esp. in Schumann, 2 different trios. A coda, often based on the trio, is neither normal nor unusual. There are very successful Ss. which do not conform to the classical pattern, e.g. Chopin's.

Scherzoso (It.) = Scherzando, but less frequently used.

Scheurleer, Daniel (François) (b. The Hague, 13. XI. 1855; d. The Hague, 6. II. 1927), Dutch mcolst. A banker by profession, he made a collection of m., mus. books and insts. and was a member of several important Dutch mus. socs. His writings incl. learned articles and prefaces, and books on Nthld. m., Mozart, Berlioz, Liszt, &c.

Schibler, Armin (b. Kreuzlingen, Lake Constance, 1920), Swi. comp. Studied m. while at school at Aarau and then at the Zürich Cons. In 1942 he became a pupil of Burkhard.

Works incl. cantatas *Marignano* & *Vision des Mittelalters*; Toccata and Fugue for stg. orch.; v. Conc., pf. Conc., Conc. for v., co. & stgs.; Toccata, Interlude and Fugue for wind insts.; pf. 4tet; v. & pf. So.; Toccata for org.; *Circulus Fugae* for pf.; songs, &c.

Schicht, Johann Gottfried (b. Reichenau nr. Zittau, 29. IX. 1753; d. Leipzig, 16. II. 1823), Ger. hpchd. player & comp. Studied law at Leipzig Univ. but turned to m. and was engaged as hpchdst. by **J. A. Hiller** for his concerts, whom he succeeded as their cond. In 1810 he was app. cantor at St. Thomas's church.

Works incl. 3 orats., church m. chamber works, &c.

Schick, Ernst (b. The Hague, 1756; d. Berlin, 10. XII. 1815), Dutch or Ger. vst. Married the singer Margarete Luise Hamel in 1791 and was engaged for the Berlin Court Opera in 1793. He estab. chamber concerts there with Bohrer.

Schick (*née* **Hamel**), **Margarete Luise** (b. Mainz, 26. IV. 1773; d. Berlin, 29. IV. 1809), Ger. sop. singer. Studied at Würzburg and with Righini at Mainz, where she made her 1st stage appearance in 1788. In 1791 she married Ernst Schick and in 1793 they were both engaged by Frederick William II of Prus. and went to Berlin.

Schicksalslied (*Song of Destiny*), a setting by Brahms for chor. & orch. of a poem in Hölderlin's *Hyperion,* Op. 54, comp. in 1871.

Schiedermair, Ludwig (b. Ratisbon, 7. XII. 1876), Ger. mus. scholar. Studied with Sandberger and Beer-Walbrunn at Munich, where he took a degree in 1901. After further studies with Riemann and Kretzschmar in Berlin he became lecturer at Marburg and in 1914 prof. of m. at Bonn Univ. There he became dir. of the Beethoven Archives, and among his books are bibliog. works on Beethoven and an ed. of Mozart's letters with an iconog. vol.

Schikaneder, (Johann) Emanuel (b. Ratisbon, 3. I. 1748; d. Vienna, 21. IX. 1812), Ger. actor, singer, playwright and theat. manager. Settled in Vienna in 1784. Author (or ? part-author with Ludwig Gieseke) of the lib. of Mozart's *Magic Flute,* which he prod. with himself as

Papageno. He also wrote libs. for Schack, Gerl, Süssmayr, Woelfl, Seyfried, Winter, Diabelli and others.

Schiller, Friedrich (1759–1805), Ger. poet & dramatist. *See* **Assafiev** (*Fiesco* & *Don Carlos*), **Balfe** (*Joan of Arc*), **Berneker** (*Bride of Messina*), **Boughton** (*Invincible Armada*), **Bride of Messina** (Fibich), **Briganti** (Mercadante), **Bruch** (*Lied von der Glocke* & *Macht des Gesanges*), **Carafa** (*Jeanne d'Arc*), **Costa** (*Don Carlos*), **'Choral' Symphony** (Beethoven), **Denza** (*Wallenstein*), **Don Carlos** (Verdi), **Faisst** (*Macht des Gesanges*), **Foerster (J. B.)** (*Maria Stuart*), **Giovanna d'Arco** (Verdi), **Guillaume Tell** (Rossini), **Hellmesberger** (3) (*Bürgschaft*), **Hiller (F.)** (*Demetrius*), **Holstein** (*Braut von M.*), **Ideale** (Liszt), **Indy** (*Piccolomini: Wallenstein*), **Joachim** (*Demetrius*), **Lachner (F.)** (*Bürgschaft*), **Lachner (V.)** (*Turandot*), **Lalo** (*Fiesque*), **Liadov** (*Bride of M.*), **Lindpaintner** (*Lied von der Glocke*), **Luisa Miller** (Verdi), **Macfarren (G.)** (*Don Carlos*), **Maid of Orleans** (Tchaikovsky), **Mascagni** (*Ode to Joy*), **Masnadieri** (Verdi), **Mermet** (*Jeanne d'Arc*), **Naenia** (Brahms & Goetz), **Neukomm** (*Braut von M.*), **Nicodé** (*Maria Stuart*), **Nicolai (W.)** (*Song of the Bell*), **Niedermeyer** (*Marie Stuart*), **Reichardt** (*Taucher*), **Reinecke** (*Wilhelm Tell*), **Rezniček** (*Jungfrau von Orleans*), **Rheinberger** (*Wallenstein* & *Demetrius*), **Romberg (A.)** (*Lied von der Glocke*), **Schillings** (*Verklärten*), **Scholz** (*Lied von der Glocke*), **Schröter (C.)** (*Taucher* & *Würde der Frauen*), **Schulz-Beuthen** (*Wilhelm Tell*), **Sechter** (*Braut von M.*), **Seyfried** (*Räuber* & *Jungfrau von O.*), **Shaporin** (*Robbers*), **Shebalin** (*Robbers* & *Mary Stuart*), **Smetana** (*Wallenstein's Camp*), **Söderman** (*Maid of Orleans*), **Suppé** (*Wallensteins Lager*), **Tomašek** (*Wallenstein*, *Maria Stuart*, *Braut von M.* & songs), **Vaccai** (*Giovanna d'Arco* & *Sposa di Messina*), **Vierling** (*Maria S.*), **Weber (B. A.)** (*W. Tell*), **Weber (C. M. v.)** (*Turandot*), **Weinberger** (*Wallenstein*), **White (M. V.)** (*Ich habe gelebt*), **Zajc** (*Amelia*), **Zumsteeg** (*Räuber*, *Wallensteins Lager* & *Ritter Toggenburg*).

42 songs by Schubert.

Schillings, Max von (b. Düren, Rhineland, 19. IV. 1868; d. Berlin, 24. VII. 1933), Ger. cond. & comp. Studied at Bonn and Munich, where he settled, taking part in the Wagner perfs. at Bayreuth. In 1908 he went to Stuttgart, where he gradually rose to the post of general mus. dir. of the Court Opera. In 1919 he went to Berlin as dir. of the State Opera.

Works incl. operas *Ingwelde*, *Der Pfeifertag*, *Moloch* (after Hebbel) & *Mona Lisa*; incid. m. for Aeschylus's *Orestes* & Goethe's *Faust*; symph. fantasies *Meergruss* & *Seemorgen*, symph. prologue, *Oedipus* (after Sophocles) for orch.; recitations with orch. incl. Wildenbruch's *Hexenlied*; v. Conc., *Zwiegespräch* for v., co. & small orch.; *Hochzeitslied* for solo voices, chor. & orch.; *Dem Verklärten* (Schiller) & *Glockenlieder* for solo voice & orch.; stg. 4tet in E min., stg. 5tet in E♭ maj.; Improvisation for v. & pf., &c.

Schindler, Anton (b. Meedl nr. Neustadt, Moravia, 13. VI. 1796; d. Bockenheim nr. Frankfort o/M., 16. I. 1864), Aus. vst. & writer on m. Studied in Vienna, met Beethoven in 1814, played at his concerts and later became his factotum and early biog.

Schira, Francesco (b. Malta, 21. VIII. 1809; d. London, 15. X. 1883), It. cond. & comp. Studied at the Cons. of Milan and prod. his 1st opera there in 1832, on the strength of which he was engaged as cond. & comp. for the Opera at Lisbon, where he also taught at the Cons. In 1842 he left for Paris in the hope of obtaining a Fr. lib., but met the manager of the Princess's Theatre in London, who engaged him as cond. In 1844 he went to Drury Lane as Benedict's successor and in 1848 to Covent Garden. Several other changes occurred, but he remained in London to his death. In 1873 the Birmingham Festival commissioned a cantata from him.

Works incl. operas *Elena e Malvina*, *I cavalieri di Valenza*, *Il fanatico per la musica*, *Kenilworth* (in Eng., after Scott), *Mina*, *Theresa, the Orphan of Geneva*, *Niccolo de' Lapi*, *Selvaggia*, *Lia*, operetta *The Ear-Ring*; cantata *The Lord of Burleigh* (after Tennyson); voc. trios and duets; songs, &c.

Schjelderup, Gerhard (Rosenkrone) (b. Christiansand, 17. XI. 1859; d. Benediktbeuren, Bav., 29. VII. 1933), Norw. comp. Studied comp. with Massenet and co. with Franchomme in Paris and later with Mottl at Carlsruhe. He prod. his operas in Ger. and Prague, and only later brought them to Norw. He wrote a hist. of Norw. m. and biogs. of Grieg and Wagner.

Works incl. operas *Sunday Morning*, *Norwegian Wedding*, *Spring Night*, *Storm Birds* & others; incid. m. to Gjellerup's *Offerildene* & other plays; Sym., symph. poem *Brand* (after Ibsen), Christmas & Norw. Suites for orch.; stg. 4tet, pf. Trio; songs, &c.

Schläger (Ger. lit. beaters). Sometimes used in scores, &c. as an abbr. for the word overleaf.

Schlaginstrumente (Ger. lit. beaten insts.) = Percussion insts.

Schlagobers (*Whipped Cream* in Viennese dialect), ballet by R. Strauss (chgph. by Heinrich Kröller), prod. Vienna, Opera, 9. V. 1924.

Schlagzither (Ger. lit. striking-zither). A zither the stgs. of which are struck with hammers, i.e. a dulcimer rather than a Z.

Schlegel, August Wilhelm von (1767–1845), Ger. poet, critic & trans. *See* **Fierrabras** (Schubert), **Hark, hark, the lark** (Schubert).

7 poems by S. set as songs by Schubert.

Schleifer (Ger.). *See* **Ornaments.**

Schleppen (Ger. = to drag). Sometimes used by Ger. comps. as a negat. imper., *nicht schleppen* = 'do not drag.'

Schlesinger, Kathleen (b. Hollywood nr. Belfast, 27. VI. 1862), Brit. mus. research scholar. Made a special study of insts. and contrib. articles on them to the *Ency. Brit.* and a chapter to the *Oxford Hist. of M.* Her original scientific investigations into the pipe insts. of ancient Gr. resulted in the book *The Greek Aulos.*

Schlick, Arnolt (b. Boh., *c.* 1460; d. Heidelberg, after 1517), Ger.-Boh. orgst., lutenist and author. The 1st known fact of his career is that he was in the service of the court chapel at Heidelberg as orgst. to the Count Palatine before 1511, except that he visited Worms in 1495 during his travels in Ger. and Hol. He wrote a kind of guide-book on org. builders and orgsts., *Spiegel der Orgelmacher und Organisten.* He became blind, prob. *c.* 1510.

Works incl. org. pieces, lute pieces & songs to the lute (all pub. in a vol. entitled *Tabulaturen*).

Schlick, Johann (Conrad) (b. Münster, *c.* 1759; d. Gotha, 1825), Ger. cst. & comp. He worked in the episcopal chapel at Münster and in 1776 became court musn. at Gotha. In 1785 he married the vst. Regina Strinasacchi.

Works incl. syms.; co. concs.; 3 stg. 4tets & other chamber m.; co. sos., &c.

Schloezer, Boris Feodorovitch de (b. Vitebsk, 8. XII. 1884), Rus. m. critic. His sister Tatiana married Skriabin, on whom he wrote at first. In 1920 he settled in Paris and wrote criticism both in Rus. and Fr. His books incl. works on Skriabin and Stravinsky.

Schlüssel (Ger. lit. key) = Clef.

Schmedes, Erik (b. Gjentofte nr. Copenhagen, 27. VIII. 1868; d. Vienna, 23. III. 1931), Dan. ten. singer. Studied in Ger. and Aus. and with Padilla in Paris; made his 1st stage appearance at Wiesbaden in 1891. In 1899 he was 1st engaged for the Wagner theatre at Bayreuth.

Schmeltzel, Wolfgang (b. Kemnat, Upper Palatinate, *c.* 1500; d. ?, *c.* 1560), Ger. comp. He became cantor at Amberg and married there, but later became a Catholic priest and left his family. He was a schoolmaster in Vienna in 1540.

Works incl. a book of songs, quodlibets and folksong settings for 4–5 voices, &c.

Schmelzer (von Ehrenruff), Andreas (Anton) (b. Vienna, 26. XI. 1653; d. Vienna, 13. X. 1701), Aus. vst. & comp. He was in the service of the Aus. court in 1671–1700.

Works incl. ballet m. for more than 30 of Draghi's operas.

Schmelzer, (Johann) Heinrich (b. Vienna, *c.* 1623; d. Vienna, *c.* II. 1680), Aus. comp., father of prec. He was chamber musn. at the Aus. court in Vienna from 1649, asst. cond. from 1671 and 1st cond. from 1679.

Works incl. ballet m. for *c.* 40 operas by Draghi & others; *Missa nuptialis* & other church m.; inst. sos.; tpt. fanfares, &c.

Schmetternd (Ger. = brassy, brazen, clanging). The term is prescribed, like the Fr. *cuivré,* when that kind of tone is required of brass insts.

Schmidt, Bernhard. *See* **Smith, Bernard.**

Schmidt, Franz (b. Bratislava, 22. XII. 1874; d. Perchtoldsdorf, 11. II. 1939), Morav.-Aus. cst., pfst. & comp. Studied at the Vienna Cons. and in 1896 became cst. in the Court Opera orch. He left in 1910 to become pf. prof. at the Vienna M. Acad., of which he became dir. in 1925. He also appeared as concert pfst.

Works incl. operas *Notre-Dame* (after Hugo) & *Fredegundis*; orat. *Das Buch mit den sieben Siegeln*; 4 syms., Chaconne & *Vars. on a Hussar's Song* for orch.; Vars. on a theme by Beethoven for pf. & orch.; stg. 4tet, pf. 5tet; 7 org. works, &c.

Schmidt, Gustav (b. Weimar, 1. IX. 1816; d. Darmstadt, 11. II. 1882), Ger. cond. & comp. Studied with Hummel and others at Weimar and with Mendelssohn at Leipzig. He began as opera cond. at Brno and then served in the same capacity in several Ger. towns, last at Darmstadt.

Works incl. operas *Prinz Eugen der edle Ritter, Weibertreue, La Réole, Alibi*; incid. m. for a play based on Dickens's *Christmas Carol*; male-voice chors.; songs, &c.

Schmidt, Johann Christoph, sen. & jun. *See* **Smith, John Christopher.**

Schmitt, (Georg) Aloys (b. Hanover, 2. II. 1827; d. Dresden, 15. X. 1902), Ger. cond., pfst. & comp. Pupil of his father, the pfst. & comp. Aloys S. (1788–1866). He toured widely in Eur. as pfst. and after var. cond.'s posts settled at Dresden in 1893 as dir. of the Mozart Soc. He married the singer Cornelia Czanyi (1851–1906) and completed and ed. Mozart's unfinished C min. Mass.

Works incl. opera *Trilby* (adapt. from Nodier by Scribe), *Das Wunderwasser* & *Maienzauber*; incid. m. for plays; ovts. & other orch. works; concert piece for ob. & orch.; stg. 4tets, pf. trios; pf. pieces; songs, &c.

Schmitt, Florent (b. Blamont, 28. IX. 1870), Fr. comp. Studied m. at Nancy from 1887 and in 1889 was sent to the Paris Cons., where he was 1st a pupil of Dubois and Lavignac and afterwards of Massenet and Fauré for comp. Won the Prix de Rome in 1900 and wrote his 1st mature works during his 3 years in Rome. Dir. of the Lyons Cons., 1922–4.

Works incl. ballets *La Tragédie de Salomé, Le Petit Elfe Ferme-l'œil, Reflets, Ourvasi* & *Oriane et le Prince d'Amour*; incid. m. for Shakespeare's *Antony and Cleopatra* (trans. by Gide); film m. for an adapt. of Flaubert's *Salammbô*; Psalm xlvi for sop. solo, chor., org. & orch.: symph. study *Le Palais hanté* (after Poe), *3 Rapsodies, Ronde burlesque, Çançunik, Kermesse-Valse, Symphonie concertante* & *Suite sans esprit de suite* for orch.; *Légende* for saxophone & orch., *Final* for co. & orch.; pf. 5tet, *Lied et Scherzo* for double wind 5tet, *Andante et Scherzo* for chrom. hp. & stg. 4tet, *Suite en Rocaille* for stgs., fl. & hp., *Sonatine en trio* for fl., cl. & hpchd. (or pf.), stg. Trio; *Sonate libre* for v. & pf.; inst. pieces; *c.* 25 works for pf.; 6 works for pf. duet; *3 Rapsodies* for 2 pfs.; partsongs; 8 op. nos. of songs, &c.

Schmittbaur, Joseph Aloys (b. Bamberg, 8. XI. 1718; d. Carlsruhe, 24. X. 1809), Ger. comp. Pupil of Jommelli. App. chapel master at Carlsruhe in 1772.

Works incl. operas *Lindor und Ismene, Herkules auf dem Oeta, Der Betrug aus Liebe* & others; masses; syms.; chamber m., &c.

Schmuck, Margarete. *See* **Stockhausen.**

Schnabelflöte (Ger. lit. beak fl., from Fr. *flûte à bec*) = Recorder.

Schnadahüpfeln (Aus. dialect). Folk dances, often sung with words, of the *Ländler* or slow waltz type as a rule, belonging to the Tyrol or other Aus. mountain regions.

*S

Schneeweiss, Amalie. *See* **Weiss.**

Schneider, (Johann Christian) Friedrich (b. Alt-Waltersdorf nr. Zittau, 3. I. 1786; d. Dessau, 23. XI. 1853), Ger. cond., teacher & comp. Studied at Zittau and at Leipzig while a student at the Univ. He advanced through several posts there to that of orgst. at St. Thomas's church and cond. at the munic. theatre. In 1821 he moved to Dessau, where he was app. chapel master to the ducal court. There he founded a voc. acad. and a m. school.

Works incl. operas; orats. *Die Höllenfahrt des Messias, Das Weltgericht, Die Sündflut, Das verlorene Paradies* (after Milton), *Das befreite Jerusalem, Gethsemane und Golgatha* & several others; 14 masses & other church m.; 25 cantatas; 23 syms., ovt. on 'God save the King'; 6 concs.; 60 sos.; 400 male-voice partsongs; 200 songs, &c.

Schneider, Johann Gottlob (b. Alt-Gersdorf, 28. X. 1789; d. Dresden, 13. IV. 1864), Ger. orgst. & comp., brother of prec. Studied at Leipzig and became orgst. to the Univ. there, remaining until 1825, when he became court orgst. at Dresden. His fame was enormous and he had many distinguished pupils, incl. Mendelssohn, Schumann and Liszt.

Works incl. Fantasy & Fugue in D min., and others for org.

Schneider, Max (b. Eisleben, 20. VII. 1875), Ger. mcolst. Studied with Kretzschmar and Riemann at Leipzig Univ. and comp. with Jadassohn. After a cond. app. at Halle and a teaching post in Berlin, he became prof. of m. at Breslau, returning to Halle in the same capacity in 1928. In 1935 he succeeded Einstein as ed. of the *Zeitschrift für Musikwissenschaft.* His writings are mainly on the Bach family and he has ed. works by Schütz, Keiser, Telemann and others.

Schneider, Paul. *See* **Sartorius.**

Schneider-Trnavský, Mikuláš (orig. Schneider [of Trnava]) (b. Trnava, 24. V. 1881), Slovak comp. Studied at the Budapest, Vienna and Prague Conss. and became m. inspector at Trnava.

Works incl. church m.; *Dumka and Dance* for orch.; pf. 5tet; v. & pf. So.; chors.; songs; arrs. of Slovak folksongs, &c.

Schneller (Ger. noun). *See* **Ornaments.**

Schnitzler, Arthur (1862–1931), Aus. novelist. *See* **Neumann** (*Liebelei*). **Rebikov** (*Woman with the Dagger*).

Schnorr von Carolsfeld, Ludwig (b. Munich, 2. VII. 1836; d. Dresden, 21. VII. 1865), Ger. ten. singer. Studied at Dresden, Leipzig and Carlsruhe, where he was engaged at the Opera and married the sop. Malwina Garrigues. In 1860 they were engaged by the Dresden Court Opera. He was Wagner's 1st Tristan at the Munich prod. in 1865.

Schnorr von Carolsfeld, Malwina. *See* **Garrigues.**

Schnyder von Wartensee, (Franz) Xaver (Joseph Peter) (b. Lucerne, 18. IV. 1786; d. Frankfort o/M., 27. VIII. 1868), Swi. pfst. & comp. He appeared early as a pfst. at Lucerne and although intended for the civil service, studied assiduously, visiting Zürich to be in touch with Nägeli in 1810–1 and in 1812 Vienna, where he met Beethoven and others. Finding himself disappointed in the expectation of a good heritage in 1815, he went to teach at Pestalozzi's model school at Yverdon and in 1817 went to Frankfort as pf. teacher at an institute for young ladies. He remained there for the rest of his life, except for visits to Swi., founded a chor. soc. and periodically attended the Swi. mus. festivals.

Works incl. opera *Fortunat*, operetta *Heimweh und Heimkehr*; 4 syms. (1 unfinished), Ovt. in C min. & other orch. works; Vars. for pf. & orch., Conc. for 2 cls.; chor. works; many pf. works; partsongs; songs, &c.

Schoberlechner, Franz (b. Vienna, 21. VII. 1797; d. Berlin, 7. I. 1843), Aus. pfst. & comp. He played a pf. conc. by Hummel, comp. for him, at the age of 10 and was sent to Vienna by Prince Esterházy to study with Förster. In 1814 he went to It. and in 1823 to Rus., marrying the singer Sophie dall' Occa there in 1824. After 4 years in St. Petersburg they retired to a villa near Florence in 1831.

Schoberlechner (*née* dall' Occa), Sophie (b. St. Petersburg, 1807; d. St. Petersburg, I. 1864), Rus. singer of It. descent, daughter of a singing-master, with whom she studied. She married Schoberlechner in 1824, sang at concerts at first, but in 1827 was engaged by the Imp. Opera in St. Petersburg. She retired with her husband in 1831, but returned to Rus. later.

Schobert, Johann (b. ? Silesia or Nuremberg, *c.* 1720; d. Paris, 28. VIII. 1767), Ger. hpchdst. & comp. Studied at Strasburg and became orgst. at Versailles, whence he was dismissed for negligence. He lived in Paris from 1760, where he played and taught successfully. He, his family, a friend and a servant were all killed by poisonous fungi.

Works incl. operetta *Le Gardechasse et le braconnier*; 6 hpchd. concs.; 6 syms. for hpchd., v. & 2 hns., 3 pf. 4tets (with 2 vs.), 11 pf. trios; 17 hpchd. sos. with v.; 4 books of hpchd. solo sos., &c.

Schoeck, Othmar (b. Brunnen, 1. IX. 1886), Swi. comp. He was at first undecided whether to follow his father's calling of a painter, but at 17 went to the Zürich Cons. to study with Niggli and others, finishing with Reger at the Leipzig Cons. In 1907–17 he cond. chor. socs. at Zürich and remained there when app. cond. of the St. Gall sym. concerts that year. The Univ. conferred an hon. doctor's degree on him in 1928.

Works incl. operas *Don Ranudo* (after Holberg), *Venus* (after Mérimée), *Penthesilea* (after Kleist), *Vom Fischer und syner Fru* (after Grimm), *Massimilla Doni* (after Balzac), *Das Schloss Dürande* (after Eichendorff), operetta *Erwin und Elmire* (Goethe), scena & pantomime *Das Wandbild*; *Der Postillon* (Lenau) for ten. solo, chor. & orch., *Dithyrambe* (Goethe) for double chor. & orch.; *Trommelschläge* (Whitman's *Drum Taps*) for chor. & orch., *Für ein Gesangfest im Frühling* (Keller) for male voices & orch.; Serenade for small orch., Praeludium for orch.; *Lebendig begraben* (Keller) song-cycle for bar. & orch.; v. Conc.; 2 stg. 4tets; 2 v. & pf. sos., So. for bass cl. & pf.; song-cycles *Elegie* with chamber orch., *Gaselen* (Keller) with 6 insts., *Wandersprüche* (Eichendorff) with 4 insts., *Notturno* with stg. 4tet; pf. pieces; song-cycles *Wandsbecker Liederbuch* (Matthias Claudius), *Unter Sternen* (Keller) & numerous sets of songs to words by Eichendorff, Goethe, Hafiz, Hebbel, Heine, Keller, Lenau, Mörike, Uhland & others, &c.

Schoelcher, Victor (b. Paris, 21. VII. 1804; d. Harville, Seine-et-Oise, 24. XII. 1893), Fr. politician & writer on m. He lived in exile in London during the reign of Napoleon III and did great work in Handel research, part of the result of which he published in an Eng. biog. in 1857. He also made a great collection of m. which he presented to the Paris Cons.

Schoenberg, Arnold (b. Vienna, 13. IX. 1874), Aus. comp. He played v. as a boy and co. as a youth, and at 16 decided to become a musn., studying ctpt. with Zemlinsky, but being otherwise self-taught. About the turn of the century he earned his living by scoring operettas, but his own comps. of that period were the stg. 6tet *Verklärte Nacht* and the *Gurrelieder*. He married Mathilde von Zemlinsky, his teacher-friend's sister, and in 1901 became cond. of an artistic cabaret in Berlin and a little later teacher at Stern's Cons. there. Back in Vienna in 1903, he gradually changed his style and his Chamber Symphony created a riot in 1906, but Mahler took his part. In 1911 he returned to Berlin, and by that time he had reached atonality and also took to painting in a futurist manner. After the war of 1914–8, during which he did garrison duty, he settled at Mödling nr. Vienna, but in 1920 taught at Amsterdam, where he had begun to attract attention. In 1923 his wife d. and the next year he was recalled to Berlin to teach at the Prus. Acad. of Arts, where he remained until 1933 and married a sister of the vst. Rudolf Kolisch. The Nazi régime drove him from Ger. and he settled in U.S.A., first teaching in Boston and N.Y., 1933–6, and then becoming prof. at the Univ. of California at Los Angeles.

Works incl. opera *Von heute auf morgen*, monodrama *Erwartung*, drama with m. *Die glückliche Hand*; symph. poem *Pelleas und Melisande* (after Maeterlinck), 5 Pieces for orch., Vars. for orch.; 2 pf. concs., v. Conc.; *Gurre-Lieder* (to words trans. from Jacobsen) for solo voices, chor. & orch.; Byron's *Ode to Napoleon* for reciter, pf. & stg. orch.; *Pierrot lunaire* for speech-song & chamber orch.; *Friede auf Erden* for chor.; *Verklärte Nacht* for stg. 6tet; 4 stg. 4tets (2nd with a voice part); 2 Chamber Syms.; Serenade for low voice & chamber orch.; 5tet for wind insts.; So. for v. or cl. & pf.; Vars. for org.; 16 pf. pieces & Suite for pf.; 10 songs with orch. & 39 with pf. incl. cycle *Das Buch der hängenden Gärten* (Stefan George); *Herzgewächse* for sop. with celesta, harmonium & hp.; books: *Harmonielehre* and a treatise on ctpt.

Scholes, Percy A(lfred). (b. Leeds, 24. VII. 1877), Eng. critic, mus. author and ed. He became m. critic to the *Evening Standard* and the *Observer* in London, founded and ed. the *Music Student* and *Music and Youth*, in 1923 became m. critic to the B.B.C., but later settled in Swi., where he lived until the outbreak of the 1939–45 war, being made an hon. Litt.D. of Lausanne Univ. He has written many books to further the popularity and appreciation of m. and ed. a dictionary *The Oxford Companion to M.*

Scholz, Bernhard (b. Mainz, 30. III. 1835; d. Munich, 26. XII. 1916), Ger. cond. & comp. Pupil of Ernst Pauer for pf. and of S. W. Dehn for theory. He was app. teacher at the Royal school of M. at Munich in 1854, was cond. at the Hanover Court Theatre in 1859–65, then worked at Berlin and Breslau, and in 1883 succeeded Raff as dir. of the Hoch Cons. at Frankfort o/M.

Works incl. operas *Carlo Rosa*, *Zietensche Husaren*, *Morgiane*, *Golo* (after Tieck), *Der Trompeter von Säckingen* (after Scheffel), *Die vornehmen Wirte*, *Ingo*, *Anno 1757* & *Mirandolina* (Goldoni); Requiem; setting of Schiller's *Lied von der Glocke* for solo voices, chor. & orch.; sym. *Malinconia*, ovt. to Goethe's *Iphigenie*, ovt. *Im Freien* & other orch. works; pf. Conc.; 2 stg. 4tets, pf. 5tet; songs, &c.

Schönberg. *See* **Schoenberg**, the spelling adopted by the comp. when he settled in U.S.A. in 1933.

Schöne Melusine, Die (*The Fair Melusina*), concert ovt. by Mendelssohn, Op. 32, comp. in 1833 after a perf. in Berlin of K. Kreutzer's opera *Melusina*, with a lib. by Grillparzer orig. written for Beethoven.

Schöne Müllerin, Die (*The Fair Maid of the Mill*), song cycle by Schubert (poems by Wilhelm Müller), comp. 1823.

Schoolmaster, The. The nickname of a Sym. by Haydn, No. 55, in E♭ maj., comp. in 1774.

Schop, Johann (b. ?; d. ?, *c.* 1665), Ger. lutenist, vst., trombst. & comp. Court musn. at Wolfenbüttel and Copenhagen; became dir. of the town council m. at Hamburg and later orgst. there.

Works incl. hymn tunes, sacred concs.; occasional odes; inst. pavans, galliards and almains, &c.

Schöpfungsmesse (Creation Mass). The nickname of Haydn's Mass in B♭ maj. of 1801, where a theme from *The Creation* is used in the 'Qui tollis.'

Schott, Anton (b. Castle Staufeneck, Suabia, 24. VI. 1846; d. Stuttgart, 6. I. 1913), Ger. ten. singer. Pupil of Pischek and Agnes Schebest, made his 1st stage appearance at Frankfort o/M. in 1870.

Schottisch (Ger. = Scottish). A ballroom dance fashionable in the 19th cent. introd. to Eng. in 1848, not ident. with the *Écossaise*. In Eng. it is usually called by its plur., *Schottische*. The m. is in 2–4 time, much like that of the Polka, but played rather slower.

Schreider-Trnavský. *See* **Schneider-Trnavský** (the name is wrongly spelt in some refs.).

Schreker, Franz (b. Monaco, 23. III. 1878; d. Berlin, 21. III. 1934), Aus. cond. & comp. Studied under Fuchs in Vienna, founded the Phil. Choir there in 1911 and taught at the Imp. Acad. of M. until his app. as dir. of the Acad. of M. in Berlin in 1920.

Works incl. operas *Flammen, Der ferne Klang, Das Spielwerk und die Prinzessin, Die Gezeichneten, Der Schatzgräber, Irrelohe, Der singende Teufel, Der Schmied von Gent*; ballets *Der Geburtstag der Infantin* (after Wilde), *Der Wind* & *Rokoko*; Romantic Suite, Fantastic Ovt., ovt. *Ekkehard* (after Scheffel), Dance Suite for orch.; Chamber Sym. for 23 insts.; Psalm cxvi & *Swan Song* for chor. & orch.; v. & pf. pieces; songs, &c.

Schröder - Devrient, Wilhelmine (b. Hamburg, 6. XII. 1804; d. Coburg, 26. I. 1860), Ger. sop. singer. She learnt much from her parents, the bar. singer Friedrich S. and the actress Antoinette Sophie Bürger, and when still in her teens appeared as a classical actress at the Burg Theatre in Vienna, where she made her 1st operatic appearance in 1821. In 1822 she greatly pleased Beethoven as Leonore in the revival of *Fidelio*. In 1823 she was engaged by the Dresden Court Opera and soon afterwards married the actor Karl Devrient, but they separated in 1828. In 1830 she 1st sang in Paris and in 1832 in London. She worked long enough to appear in the early Wagner operas.

Schroeter, Christoph Gottlieb (b. Hohnstein, Saxony, 10. VIII. 1699; d. Nordhausen, XI. 1782), Ger. musn. He was educ. in theol. as well as m. and in 1721 invented a hammer action to apply to the hpchd., but was anticipated in the actual invention of the pf. by Cristofori.

Schroeter, Leonhard (b. Torgau, *c.* 1540; d. Magdeburg, 1595), Ger. comp. Succeeded Gallus Dressler as cantor of Magdeburg cath. in 1564.

Works incl. Ger. Te Deum for double choir, *Hymni sacri* for 4–5 voices, *Weihnachts - Liedlein* for several voices, &c.

Schröter, Corona (Elisabeth Wilhelmine) (b. Guben, 14. I. 1751; d. Ilmenau, 23. VIII. 1802), Ger. singer, actress & comp. She learnt m. from her father, the obst. Johann Friedrich S., lived in Warsaw and Leipzig as a child, appeared in the latter town at the age of 14. Between 1772–6 she was in London with her family, but Goethe invited her to the court of Weimar in 1776, where she appeared in his plays and comp. the m. for his play *Die Fischerin*, which incl. a setting of *Erl King* by her. She retired in 1786 to teach, painting and comp.

Works incl. play with m. *Die Fischerin*; songs, incl. settings of Goethe's *Der neue Amadis* & *Erlkönig*, Schiller's *Der Taucher* & *Würde der Frauen*, poems by Herder, Klopstock, Mathisson, &c.

Schröter, Johann (Samuel) (b. Warsaw, 1750; d. London, 2. XI. 1788), Ger. pfst. & comp., brother of prec. Pupil of his father, went to Leipzig with his family *c.* 1763, and visited London with them in 1772, appearing with his sister at the J. C. Bach and Abel concerts, another brother, Johann Heinrich, playing the v. On J. C. Bach's death he became m. master to the queen, 1782. He secretly married one of his pupils, a young woman of fortune and good birth, and her family made much trouble for him. It was his widow who fell in love with Haydn later.

Works incl. hpchd. or pf. concs.; trios & other chamber m.; hpchd. or pf. sos., &c.

Schubart, (Christian Friedrich) Daniel (1739–91), Ger. author, ed. & musn. Author of the poems of Schubert's songs *Die Forelle, An den Tod* & *Grablied auf einen Soldaten*. He wrote many prologues, &c. set by Zumsteeg. His own comps. incl. pf. pieces, songs, &c.

Schubart, Mark (b. New York, 24. V. 1918), Amer. comp. Educ. in Fr. & Amer. He became a comp. pupil of Sessions, later a m. critic and afterwards m. ed. for the N.Y. *Times*.

Works incl. opera *Etched in Moonlight* (after James Stephens); concert ovt. & 4 pieces for orch.; Concertino for fl., stgs., 2 hns. & timp.; stg. 4tet; pf. So., &c.

Schubaur, Johann Lukas (b. Lechfeld, Suabia, XII. 1749; d. Munich, 15. XI. 1815), Ger. comp. Studied medicine as well as m., but made his living by teaching the latter.

Works incl. plays with m. (*Singspiele*) *Die Dorfdeputierten, Die treuen Köhler* & others; Psalm cvii (trans. by Moses Mendelssohn); cantatas, &c.

Schubert, Franz (Peter) (b. Vienna, 31. I. 1797; d. Vienna, 19. XI. 1828), Aus. comp. Son of a schoolmaster who cultivated m. in his household. Began to learn pf. and v. early and received lessons from Michael Holzer at the age of 9, learning also org. and ctpt. Admitted to the Seminary for choristers in the Imp. Chapel in 1808, played v. in the orch. there and sometimes cond. as deputy. At 13 wrote a Fantasy for pf. duet and sketched other works, and in 1811 comp. his 1st song. Played va. in the stg. 4tet at home. His mother d. in 1812 and the father married again in 1813, when S. wrote the 1st Sym. and left the Seminary, continuing studies under Salieri. At 17 he became asst. teacher in his father's school, but disliked teaching; wrote the song *Margaret at the Spinning-Wheel* from Goethe's *Faust* that year and set the same poet's *Erl King* in 1815, also wrote the G maj. Mass, the 2nd and 3rd Syms. and several dramatic pieces. In 1816 he left the school and joined his friend Schober in rooms, gathering a circle of literary and artistic rather than mus. friends round him and in 1817 meeting the singer Michael Vogl, who took a great interest in his songs and succeeded in getting his play with m., *The Twin Brothers*, prod. in VI. 1820. His reputation grew beyond his own circle, but pubs. failed to recognize him until his friends had 20 songs pub. at their own expense in 1821. He lived in Vienna all his life, except for some summer excursions and 2 visits to Hung. as domestic musn. to the Esterhàzy family on their country estate at Zséliz, 1818 and 1824. He never held an official appt. and failed to stabilize his financial position, but earned enough casually to lead a modest if improvident and bohemian existence. His industry was phenomenal, for although he d. at 31 he left more m. than almost any other master. His death was prob. purely accidental, its immediate cause being typhus.

Works incl. operas *Alfonso und Estrella, Fierrabras* [*sic*], *Des Teufels Lustschloss, Die Verschworenen* (*Der häusliche Krieg*), operettas *Die Freunde von Salamanka, Fernando, Der Spiegelritter, Der vierjährige Posten, Die Zwillingsbrüder*, melodrama *Die Zauberharfe*, incid. m. *Rosamunde*; 7 masses and c. 20 other church works; over 70 chor. works with orch., pf. or without accomp.; 9 syms. (2 unfinished) & var. misc. orch. works, incl. 2 ovts. in the It. style; Octet, pf. 5tet (*Trout*), stg. 5tet, 15 stg. 4tets (1 unfinished), 2 pf. trios & var. other chamber works; Fantasy, *Rondo brillant*, So. & 3 sonatinas for v. & pf.; over 30 works for pf. duet; 21 pf. sos. (some unfinished) & numerous other pf. works incl. 8 Impromptus, *Moments musicaux* & many dances; 606 songs incl. cycles *Die schöne Müllerin* and *Die Winterreise* (the 3rd, *Schwanengesang*, was so named by the pub.), 71 settings of Goethe, 42 of Schiller, 8 trans. of Scott, 3 trans. of Shakespeare, &c.

Schuch, Ernst von (b. Graz, 23. XI. 1846; d. Dresden, 10. V. 1914), Aus. cond. Studied at Graz and Vienna, had his 1st cond. engagement at Breslau, and after several others went to Dresden in 1872 and was made court mus. dir. the next year. He also cond. the sym. concerts of the Royal (later State) Orch.

Schuch-Proska, Clementine (b. Vienna, 12. II. 1853; d. Kötzschenbroda nr. Dresden, [illegible]1. VI. 1932), Aus. sop. singer, wife of prec. Pupil of Mathilde Marchesi at the Vienna Cons., was engaged by the Dresden Court Opera in 1873 and married Schuch there in 1875.

Schuh, Willi (b. Basle, 12. XI. 1900), Swi. mcolst. Studied under Courvoisier and Sandberger at Munich and Ernst Kurth at Berne, where he took a doctor's degree in 1927. He became a critic at Zürich and in 1930 prof. of mus. hist. at the Univ. His works incl. studies of Schütz, Swi. folk and early m., Schoeck, &c.

Schulhoff, Erwin (b. Prague, 8. VI. 1894), Cz. pfst. & comp. Studied at the Prague, Vienna, Leipzig and Cologne Conss.

Works incl. operas *Don Juan's Destination* & *Flames*; ballets *Ogelala* & *Moonstruck*; incid. m. to Molière's *Bourgeois gentilhomme*; 2 syms.; pf. Conc.; chamber m.; pf. works, &c.

Schulhoff, Julius (b. Prague, 2. VIII. 1825; d. Berlin, 13. III. 1898), Cz. pfst. & comp., great-granduncle of prec. Settled in Paris from 1842 until the 1848 Revol., then toured, and finally lived at Dresden and Berlin. Comp. drawing-room m. for his inst., also a So. in F min. & 12 studies.

Schuloper (Ger. = school opera). A Ger. work of a special type of the 20th cent. with a didactic purpose; the same as a *Lehrstück*, but invariably intended for the stage.

Schultheiss, Benedict (b. ?, c. 1650; d. Nuremberg, 1. III. 1693), Ger. orgst. & comp. Pupil of his father, Hieronymus S. (1600–69). He was app. orgst. of the church of St. Giles at Nuremberg.

Works incl. hymn-tunes; hpchd. pieces, &c.

Schultz (or **Schulz**). Prob. the Ger. form of the name of the musns. calling themselves Praetorius.

Schultz, Helmut (b. Frankfort o/M., 2. XI. 1904), Ger. mus. scholar. Studied with Theodor Kroyer at Leipzig and took a doctor's degree in 1930. He became lecturer at Leipzig Univ. in 1932 and prof. in 1933. He ed. works by Haydn and the early works of Hugo Wolf, and his literary works incl. studies of the madrigal, old insts., &c.

Schulz-Beuthen, Heinrich (b. Beuthen, Silesia, 19. VI. 1838; d. Dresden, 12. III. 1915), Ger. comp. Studied at the Leipzig Cons., taught at Zürich in 1866–80, at Dresden in 1880–93, in Vienna in 1893–5, and at the Dresden Cons. from 1895.

Works incl. operas *Aschenbrödel*, *Die Verschollene* & others; Christmas play *Die Blume Wunderhold*; Requiem, 6 Psalms & other chor. works; 8 syms. (No. 6 on Shakespeare's *King Lear*), symph. poems on Schiller's *Wilhelm Tell*, on Böcklin's picture 'The Isle of the Dead,' on Grillparzer's *Des Meeres und der Liebe Wellen* & others, 2 suites, 2 scenes from Goethe's *Faust*, Serenade & other works for orch.; pf. Conc.; wind Octet, stg. 5tet & trio; 2 sos. & pieces for pf.; numerous songs, &c.

Schulz-Evler, Adolf (b. Warsaw, 1854; d. Cracow, 1905), Pol. pfst. & comp. Pupil of Tausig. Wrote many virtuoso pieces for pf., incl. a transcription of J. Strauss's *Blue Danube* waltz.

Schulz, Johann Abraham Peter (b. Lüneburg, 31. III. 1747; d. Schwedt, 10. VI. 1800). Ger. cond. & writer on m. & comp. Studied with Kirnberger in Berlin, having run away from home at the age of 15, travelled in Ger., Fr. and It. in 1768, returned to Berlin in 1773, collab. in Kirnberger and Sulzer's encyc., cond. at the Fr. theatre in 1776–8 and at that of the crown prince of Prus. at Rheinsberg in 1780–7. In 1787–95 he was at the Dan. court in Copenhagen. He wrote a treatise on harmony.

Works incl. operas (Fr.) *Clarisse*, *La Fée Urgèle* (after Voltaire), *Le Barbier de Séville* (after Beaumarchais) & *Aline, reine de Golconde* (Dan.), *The Harvest Home*, *The Entry & Peter's Wedding*; Ger. melodrama *Minona*; incid. m. for Racine's *Athalie* & other plays; *Christi Tod*, *Maria und Johannes* & other sacred works; chamber m., *Lieder im Volkston* and many other songs, in which he is a forerunner of Schubert.

Schuman, William H(oward). (b. New York, 1910), Amer. comp. Studied at Columbia Univ. and at the Mozarteum, Salzburg. In 1936 he was app. teacher at the Columbia Univ. summer school and in 1938 at the Sarah Lawrence Coll. in N.Y. In 1945 he succeeded Carl Engel as dir. of mus. pubs. in the house of Schirmer in N.Y. and Ernest Hutcheson as president of the Juillard Graduate School of M.

Works incl. ballet *Choreographic Poem*; incid. m. for Shakespeare's *Henry VIII*; film m. for *Steeltown*; 2 secular cantatas for chor. & orch.; 4 syms., *Amer. Festival* and *William Billings* ovts., *Prayer in Time of War* & *Side-Show* for orch.; Sym. for stg. orch.; *Newsreel* for milit. band; pf. Conc.; *4 Canonic Choruses*, *Pioneers*, *Requiescat* (without words), &c. for unaccomp. chor.; 3 stg. 4tets, Canon and Fugue for pf. trio, Sym. for 18 insts., Quartettino for 4 bns.; *Three-Score Set* for pf., &c.

Schumann (*née* **Wieck**), **Clara** (**Josephine**), (b. Leipzig, 13. IX. 1819; d. Frankfort o/M., 20. V. 1896), Ger pfst. & comp. Pupil of her father, Friedrick Wieck, made her 1st public appearance at the age of 9 in 1828 and gave her own 1st concert at the Leipzig Gewandhaus on 8. XI. 1830. In 1837 she was in Vienna for some time. Her engagement to Schumann was violently opposed by her father, but they married after many difficulties on 12. IX. 1840. She appeared less frequently during her married life, but after S.'s death in 1856 she was obliged to do so continuously and to teach. She went to live in Berlin with her mother, who had married Bargiel, but in 1863 she settled at Baden-Baden and in 1878 became chief pf. prof. at the Hoch Cons. at Frankfort.

Works incl. pf. Conc. in A min.; pf. Trio in G min.; Vars. on a theme by Robert S. & *c*. 12 other op. nos. for pf.; several sets of songs, &c.

Schumann, Georg (**Alfred**) (b. Königstein o/Elbe, 25. X. 1866), Ger. vst., orgst., cond. & comp. Studied with his father, later at Dresden and at the Leipzig Cons. After var. appts. at Danzig and Bremen, he became prof. and dir. of the Voc. Acad. in Berlin, 1900. In 1913 he succeeded Bruch as prof. of comp. at the Acad. of Arts.

Works incl. orat. *Ruth*; *Amor und Psyche*, *Totenklage* & *Sehnsucht* for chor. & orch.; Sym. in F min., Vars. & Double Fugue on a Merry Theme, Serenade, ovt. *Liebesfrühling* for orch.; Symph. Vars. on a Chorale for org. & orch.; pf. 5tet, 2 pf. trios; 2 v. & pf. sos., co. So.; Vars. & Fugue on a theme by Beethoven for 2 pfs., &c.

Schumann - Heink (*née* **Rössler**), **Ernestine** (b. Lieben nr. Prague, 15. VI. 1861; d. Hollywood, Cal., 17. XI. 1936), Cz.-Ger.-Amer. con. singer. Studied with Marietta Leclair at Graz and made her 1st stage appearance at Dresden in 1878. In 1892 she paid her 1st visit to London and in 1896 made her 1st appearance at the Wagner theatre at Bayreuth. Soon after a visit to U.S.A. in 1898 she settled there and was naturalized in 1905.

Schumann, Robert (**Alexander**) (b. Zwickau, Saxony, 8. VI. 1810; d. Endenich nr. Bonn, 29. VII. 1856), Ger. comp. Son of a bookseller and pub. Began to learn the pf. from a schoolmaster and orgst. at the age of 8 and played well by the time he was 11, besides studying all the m. found at his father's shop, where he also developed a literary taste. He played at school concerts and private houses and made such progress in improv. and comp. that in 1825 Weber was approached to teach him, but could not, being busy preparing *Oberon* for London and expecting to go there. His father d. in 1826, and in 1828 he was sent to Leipzig Univ. to study law. There he met Wieck, from whom he took pf. lessons, neglecting his legal studies, as he did again when in 1829 he moved to Heidelberg Univ., where he came under the infl. of Thibaut. Back at Leipzig in 1830, he lodged at Wieck's house, wrote his 1st pub. works (Opp. 1 & 7) and the next year went to the St. Thomas cantor, Weinlig, for instruction, but left him for the younger Dorn. In 1832 he permanently injured his hand by a mechanical contrivance he had invented for finger-development and thus had to give up a pfst.'s career for that of a comp. With a circle of young intellectuals he founded the *Neue Zeitschrift für Musik* in 1833, and the circle calling itself the 'Davidsbündler.' He fell in love with Ernestine von Fricken in 1834, but the engagement was broken off next year. In 1836 Wieck's daughter Clara, already a remarkable pfst., was 17 and she and S. fell seriously in love. The father violently opposed a match and in 1839 they took legal proceedings against him; he failed to yield, but they married on 12. IX. 1840, the day before she came of age. In 1843 S. suffered a crisis of mental exhaustion and he had a more serious breakdown after a tour in Rus. with Clara in 1844, at the end of which year they settled at Dresden. Although his nervous complaint grew more marked after periods of recovery, he accepted the cond.-ship at Düsseldorf, incl. subscription concerts, chor. practices and church m., in 1850, a post for which he proved quite unfit. The committee tactfully suggested his resignation in 1852, but with Clara's injudicious support he obstinately refused to withdraw. Signs of a mental collapse grew more and more alarming and his creative work progressively less convincing, and in II. 1854 he threw himself into the Rhine. On being rescued he was sent at his own request to a private asylum at Endenich, where he d. more than 2 years later.

Works incl. opera *Genoveva*; incid. m. to Byron's *Manfred*; 15 works for chor. & orch. with or without solo voices, incl. *Das Paradies und die Peri, Vom Pagen und der Königstochter* (Geibel); *Das Glück von Edenhall* (Uhland); *Requiem für Mignon* & scenes from Goethe's *Faust*; 4 syms.; *Overture, Scherzo and Finale* for orch.; 5 concert ovts.; concs. for pf., v. & co., 2 short works for pf. & orch., Fantasy for v. & orch. & *Concertstück* for 4 hns. & orch.; 3 stg. 4tets, 3 pf. trios, pf. 4tet, pf. 5tet, *Fantasiestücke* & *Märchenerzählungen* for pf. trio (the latter with cl. & va.); 2 v. & pf. sos.; sets of pieces for hn., cl., ob., va. & co. with pf.; 36 op. nos. of pf. m. incl. *Papillons*, 6 *Intermezzi, Davidsbündlertänze, Carnaval*, 3 sos., *Fantasiestücke* (2 sets), *Études symphoniques, Kinderscenen, Kreisleriana, Humoreske, Nachtstücke, Faschingsschwank aus Wien*, 3 Romances, *Album für die Jugend, Waldscenen, Bunte Blätter, Albumblätter*; 4 works for pf. duet (33 pieces); *Andante and Variations* for 2 pfs.; Studies and Sketches for pedal pf.; 6 org. fugues; 35 op. nos. of songs (some containing numerous pieces), incl. the cycles *Frauenliebe und Leben* & *Dichterliebe*, also *Liederkreise* (Heine & Eichendorff) and *Myrthen*; 3 pieces for declamation & pf.; 4 op. nos. of voc. duets, 1 of voc. trios, 4 of voc. 4tets; 14 op. nos. of partsongs, &c.

Schünemann, Georg (b. Berlin, 13. III. 1884; d. ?, I. 1945), Ger. mcolst. & flst. Studied at Stern's Cons. in Berlin and with Kretzschmar at the Univ., where he took a doctor's degree in 1907. He was 1st active as fl. virtuoso and critic, but in 1919 became lecturer and in 1923 prof. in Berlin Univ., and in 1932 dir. of the Hochschule für Musik. In 1933 he succeeded Curt Sachs, who resigned under the Nazi régime, as dir. of the collection of ancient insts. and in 1935 became head of the Prus. State Library's m. dept. Among his works are studies of the hist. of cond., Ger. chor. m., mus. autographs and a biog. of Zelter.

Schunke, Ludwig (b. Cassel, 21. XII. 1810; d. Leipzig, 7. XII. 1834), Ger. pfst. Pupil of Kalkbrenner and Reicha in Paris. At Leipzig at the end of his short life and an intimate friend of Schumann's. Left some promising work for pf.

Schuppanzigh, Ignaz (b. Vienna, 1776; d. Vienna, 2. III. 1830), Aus. vst. Worked in Vienna; dir. of the Augarten concerts, founder of a 4tet of his own and that of Prince Rasumovsky. He was the 1st to lead 4tets by Beethoven and Schubert.

Schürmann, Georg Caspar (b. Hanover, *c.* 1672; d. Wolfenbüttel, 25. II. 1751), Ger. singer & comp. He was 1st engaged at the Hamburg opera in 1693–7, then at Wolfenbüttel, entered the service of the Duke of Brunswick, who sent him to It. for further study and gave him leave in 1702–7 to enter the service of the Duke of Meiningen, after which he remained at Wolfenbüttel to his death.

Works incl. operas *Télémaque* (after Fénelon), *Heinrich der Vogler*, *Die getreue Alceste* (after Euripides), *Ludovicus Pius* & *c.* 16 others; New Year cantata, &c.

Schusterfleck (Ger. cobbler's patch). A playful Ger. description of a technical device, esp. the Rosalia, used as an easy subterfuge in comp. Beethoven called Diabelli's waltz, on which he wrote the Vars. Op. 120, a S.

Schütt, Eduard (b. St. Petersburg 22. X. 1856; d. Obermais nr. Meran, 26. VII. 1933), Ger. pfst. & comp. Studied at the St. Petersburg and Leipzig Conss. and settled in Vienna in 1878.

Works incl. opera *Signor Formica*; Serenade for stg. orch.; 2 pf. concs.; Vars. for 2 pfs.; many pf. pieces and arrs.; songs, &c.

Schütz, Heinrich (b. Köstritz, Saxony, 8. X. 1585; d. Dresden, 6. XI. 1672), Ger. comp. Learnt m. as a choir-boy in the chapel of the Landgrave of Hesse-Cassel, studied law at Marburg Univ. and m. under G. Gabrieli at Venice, 1609–12. He returned to Cassel as court orgst., but left for Dresden in 1614, with an appt. as mus. dir. to the Elector Johann Georg of Saxony. He did much there to estab. the fashion for It. m. and musns., but although he had written It. madrigals at Venice, he set his own works to Ger. or Lat. words. In 1627 he wrote the 1st Ger. opera, *Dafne*, on a trans. of Rinuccini's lib. by Martin Opitz, for the marriage of the elector's daughter to the Landgrave of Hesse-Darmstadt. After the death of his wife in 1628, he again went to It. in 1629. In 1633, the 30 Years War having disorganized the Dresden court chapel, he obtained leave to go to Copenhagen, and he spent the years until 1641 there and at other courts. Returning to Dresden, he did not succeed in reorganizing the court m. satisfactorily until the later 1640s. In the 1650s he became much dissatisfied with the new tendencies among the It. court musns. and had many quarrels with Bontempi, but did not succeed in obtaining his release, and after some improvements later on he remained at the Saxon court for the rest of his life.

Works incl. opera *Dafne* (lost); ballet *Orpheus und Euridice* (lost); motets, *Cantiones sacrae*, psalms, sacred syms. & concs. for voices & insts. & other church m.; Christmas, Passion and Resurrection orats., *The 7 Words of Christ*; It. madrigals; *Exequien* (funeral pieces) for 6–8 voices, Elegy on the death of the electress of Saxony, &c.

Schwanberg (Schwanenburger), Johann Gottfried (b. Wolfenbüttel, 28. XII. 1740; d. Brunswick, 5. IV. 1804), Ger. comp. Pupil of Hasse. He was app. court cond. at Brunswick in 1762.

Works incl. operas *Romeo e Giulia* (after Shakespeare), *Adriano in Siria*, *Solimano*, *Zenobia* & *c.* 10 others; syms.; pf. concs.; pf. sos., &c.

Schwanda (Švanda) the Bagpiper. *See* **Švanda Dudák.**

Schwanengesang (*Swan Song*), song cycle by Schubert, containing the last songs written by him in 1828, incl. 7 settings of Rellstab, 6 of Heine (his only settings of that poet) and Seidl's *Pigeon Post* (*Die Taubenpost*). The idea of a cycle was actually Schubert's, but not, of course, the title, which was invented by the pub. as an allusion to the comp.'s death, and the inclusion of Seidl's song was also the pub.'s afterthought.

Schwartzendorf, Johann Paul. *See* **Martini, Giovanni Paolo.**

Schwarz, Joseph (b. Riga, 1880; d. Berlin, 10. XI. 1926), Baltic bar. singer. He was a member of the Vienna Volksoper and later of the Berlin Court (afterwards State) Opera; also sang in London and N.Y.

Schweigsame Frau, Die (*The Silent Woman*), opera by R. Strauss (lib. by Stefan Zweig, based on Ben Jonson's *Epicoene*), prod. Dresden, 24. VI. 1936.

Schweitzer, Albert (b. Günsbach, Upper Alsace, 14. I. 1875), Fr. theologian, medical missionary, orgst. & mus. scholar. Studied org. at Strasburg and with Widor in Paris. He became lecturer in theol. at Strasburg Univ. in 1913 and later undertook medical missions in Central Africa, where he has spent most of his life, visiting Eur. periodically and giving org. recitals of Bach's works. Author of a work on Bach pub. in Fr. in 1905 and in an enlarged Ger. ed. in 1908.

Schweitzer, Anton (b. Coburg, VI. 1735; d. Gotha, 23. XI. 1787), Ger. cond. & comp. Studied with Kleinknecht at Bayreuth under the patronage of the Duke of Coburg and went to Hildburghausen as cond. at the court and at a theatre. After further studies in It. he became mus. dir. at the court theatre of Weimar and in 1778 succeeded J. A. Benda at the court of Saxe-Coburg-Gotha.

Works incl. operas & operettas *Alceste, Rosamund, Aurora, Die Wahl des Herkules* (libs. by Wieland), *Die Dorfgala, Walmir und Gertraud, Das wütende Heer, Erwin und Elmire* (Goethe), &c., monodramas *Polyxena* & *Pygmalion*, dram. prologues *Apollo unter den Hirten, Elysium*, &c.; ballet *Die neuen Amazonen*; incid. m. to Goethe's *Clavigo*, Gozzi's *Il segreto pubblico*, Molière's *Bourgeois gentilhomme* & other plays; cantata *Minerva e Marte*, &c.

Schweizerfamilie, Die (*The Swiss Family*), opera by Weigl (lib. by Ignaz Franz Castelli), prod. Vienna, Kärntnertor Theatre, 14. III. 1809.

Schwemmer, Heinrich (b. Gumbertshausen, Franconia, 28. III. 1621; d. Nuremberg, 26. V. 1696), Ger. comp. Studied with Kindermann at Nuremberg, where he became a master at a school in 1650 and soon after choirmaster at the church of Our Lady. Among his pupils were J. Krieger and Pachelbel.

Works incl. wedding and funeral anthems, motets, hymn-tunes & other church m., &c.

Schwencke, Christian Friedrich Gottlieb (b. Wachenhausen, Harz, 30. VIII. 1767; d. Hamburg, 27. X. 1822), Ger. hpchdst. & comp. Studied under his father, the bnst. Johann Gottlieb S. (1744–1823) at Hamburg, where he 1st appeared in a conc. by his father in 1779. Through the influence of C. P. E. Bach he was sent to study with Kirnberger in Berlin, 1782, and later studied at Leipzig and Halle Univs. In 1788 he became town cantor at Hamburg. His sons, Johann Friedrich S. (1792–1852) and Karl S. (1797–?), as well as the former's son, Friedrich Gottlieb S. (1823–96), were also musns. He was a friend of C. P. E. Bach and of Klopstock.

Works incl. opera *Theseus auf Kreta*; incid. m. to plays; cantatas for solo voices, chor. & orch., odes *Vater unser* & *Der Frohsinn* by Klopstock; ob. Conc.; 6 org. fugues; hpchd. sos., &c.

Schwindl, Friedrich (b. Amsterdam, 3. V. 1737; d. Carlsruhe, 7. VIII. 1786), Dutch or Ger. vst., flst., hpchdst. & comp. He was at The Hague when Burney stayed there in 1770, later at Geneva and Mulhouse, and finally at Carlsruhe as mus. dir. to the Margrave of Baden. As a symst. he belonged to the Mannheim school.

Works incl. operas *L'Astronome, Das Liebesgrab* & *Die drei Pächter*; Mass in E min.; syms.; 4tets, trios, &c.

Schytte, Ludvig Theodor (b. Aarhus, Jutland, 28. IV. 1848; d. Berlin, 10. XI. 1909), Dan. pfst. & comp. He was in business as a chemist, but took to m. in 1870, studying with Gade and others in Copenhagen and later with Taubert in Berlin and Liszt at Weimar. In 1887 he settled in Vienna as concert pfst. and teacher.

Works incl. monodrama *Hero*, operettas *Der Mameluk* & *Der Student von Salamanca*; pf. Conc.; numerous pf. works, incl. a So. and *Naturstimmungen*; *Pantomimen*, &c. for pf. duet; song-cycle *Die Verlassene* & other songs, &c.

Scioltezza (It.) = Freedom, independence, looseness.

Sciolto (It.) = Free, independent, unfettered.

Scipione (*Scipio*), opera by Handel (lib. by Paolo Antonio Rolli, based on on Apostolo Zeno's *Scipione nelle Spagne*), prod. London, King's Theatre, Haymarket, 12. III. 1726.

Sco. (abbr.) = Scotland, Scottish.

Scola de' maritati, La (*The School for the Married*), opera by Martín y Soler (lib. by Lorenzo da Ponte), prod. London, King's Theatre, Haymarket, 27. I. 1795.

Scontrino, Antonio (b. Trapani, Sicily, 17. V. 1850; d. Florence, 7. I. 1922), It. db. player & comp. Although the son of a poor carpenter, he was brought up in a mus. atmosphere, his father running a primitive but enthusiastic amateur orch. in which he played db. parts on an adapted co. In 1861 he went to the Palermo Cons. and in 1870 began to tour as a db. virtuoso, and in 1876 he prod. his 1st opera, having studied for another 2 years at Munich. In 1891 he became prof. at the Palermo Cons. and in 1892 at the Reale Istituto Musicale at Florence.

Works incl. operas *Matelda, Il progettista, Il sortilegio, Gringoire* & *La cortigiana*; incid. m. for d'Annunzio's *Francesca da Rimini*; motet *Tota pulchra, O Salutaris, Salve Regina* & other church m.; *Sinfonia marinesca* & *Sinfonia romantica* for orch.; 3 stg. 4tets & Prelude and Fugue for stg. 4tet; pieces for v., co. and db.; pf. pieces; song cycles *La Vie intérieure* (Sully-Prud'homme) & *Intima vita* (Panzacchi) & many other songs, &c.

Scooping. The bad habit of gliding from one note to another in singing, or of attacking a note uncertainly by gliding to its proper pitch from below.

Scordatura (It. =mistuning). Tuning of the v. or other stg. insts. temporarily to other intervals than the normal perfect 5ths, &c. for the purpose of facilitating the playing of chords with certain intervals or altering the inst.'s tone-quality. The m. is still written as for the normal tuning (and fingering), so that the inst. becomes to that extent a transposing inst.

Score. The copy of any m. written in several parts on separate staves, with the coincident notes appearing vertically over each other, so that the work can be read with comparative ease in a way that would be quite impossible with parts written out or printed separately for each participant. Complete orch. or chor. Ss. showing all the parts are given the name of Full S.; arrs. of operas, orats., &c. for voices and pf. are Voc. Ss.; arrs. for pf. only are Piano Ss.; comps.' sketches reduced to a few staves, to be elaborated and fully written out later, are known as Short Ss. The usual lay-out of orch. Ss. is in groups of var. types of insts., with the treble insts. of each group at the top and the bass insts. at the bottom, and the order is as a rule woodwind at the top, brass in the middle and stgs. at the bottom. Hps., perc. and any other extras are placed between brass and stgs.

Scoring. *See* **Orchestration.**

Scorrevole (It., accent on 2nd syll.) = scurrying, fluent.

Scotch Snap. The technical name for rhythmic figures inverting the order of dotted notes, the short note coming 1st instead of last, e.g. a semiquaver followed by a dotted quaver. Its name in Eng., which is also Scots Catch, is no doubt due to the fact that the S. S. is a feature in the Sco. Strathspey. But the device is also frequent in Eng. voc. m. because it perfectly fits the rhythms of certain words with short 1st and longer 2nd syllables, such as 'never.' In inst., esp. orch., m. the S. S. is all too often heard badly interpreted, as though it were 2 short notes followed by a pause of twice their length: it is very important that the 2nd note should be held to its full extent of 3 times the length of the 1st.

'Scotch' Symphony. *See* **'Scottish' Symphony.**

Scots Catch. *See* **Scotch Snap.**

Scott, Cyril (Meir) (b. Oxton, Ches., 27. IX. 1879), Eng. comp. & poet. He played the pf. and began to comp. as a child and was sent to the Hoch Cons. at Frankfort o/M. at the age of 12. Later he studied pf. under Steudner-Welsing at Liverpool and returned to Frankfort for comp. studies with Iwan Knorr. Grainger, O'Neill and Quilter were there at the same time. In 1898 he settled at Liverpool as pfst. and gave some lessons, and soon after the turn of the cent. he began to become known as a comp. in London, having some works perf. and soon afterwards a number of songs & pf. pieces pub. In 1913 Alma Mahler, the comp.'s widow, invited him to Vienna, where he gave some perfs. During the 1914–8 war some works were prod. in Eng. and in 1925 the opera *The Alchemist* was given, in Ger., at Essen.

Works incl. opera *The Alchemist* & others (unpub.); ballet *The Incompetent Apothecary*; *La Belle Dame sans merci* (Keats), *Nativity Hymn* (Milton), *Let us now praise famous men* for chor. & orch.; *Aubade*, *Christmas Ovt.*, 2 *Passacaglias on Ir. Themes*, *Rhapsody*, 3 *Symph. Dances* for orch.; pf. Conc., v. Conc.; *Fair Helen of Kirkconnel* for bar. & orch.; Suite for stg. 4tet, pf. 5tet, pf. 4tet, pf. Trio; So., *Tallahassee* Suite & var. pieces for v. & pf.; pieces for va., co. & fl. with pf.; So., 4 suites, *Impressions from the Jungle Book* (after Kipling) & *c.* 100 pieces for pf.; *Idyll* for voice & fl., *Idyllic Fantasy* for voice, ob. & co.; *c.* 80 songs, &c.

Scott, Francis George (b. Hawick, 25. I. 1880), Sco. comp. Educ. at Hawick and Edinburgh Univ., took the Mus.B. at Durham Univ. and later studied with Roger-Ducasse in Paris. In 1925 he became lecturer in m. at the Jordanhill Training-Coll. for Teachers.

Works incl. ovt. *Renaissance*, dance suite *The Seven Deidly Sins* (after Dunbar) for orch., *Lament for the Heroes* for stg. orch.; *The Ballad of Kynd Kittok* (Dunbar) and Sco. ballad *Edward* for bar. & orch.; 55 songs in 5 vols. of *Scottish Lyrics* (poems by Dunbar, Wm. Drummond, Burns, Allan Cunningham & others), *c.* 50 other songs (Sco. & Eng. poets), 4 Fr. & 4 Ger. songs; 14 partsongs, &c.

Scott, Lady John Douglas (*née* Alicia Ann Spottiswoode) (b. Spottiswoode, Berwick, 1810; d. Spottiswoode, 12. III. 1900), Sco. amateur musn. Married Lord John Montagu-Douglas-Scott in 1836, but in 1870, 10 years after his death, wrote under her maiden name again. She comp. some songs, among which *Annie Laurie* became extremely popular.

Scott, Marion M(argaret). (b. London), Eng. mcolst. Studied at the R.C.M.

in London, 1896–1904, with which she afterwards remained assoc. as sec. of the R.C.M. Union and ed. of the *R.C.M. Magazine*. She has written criticism for var. periodicals and many articles, notably on Haydn, in whose work she has specialized and on whom she is engaged in writing a large work. She has also written a book on Beethoven.

Scott, Thomas (b. Campbellsburgh, Kentucky, 28. V. 1912), Amer. comp. Although obliged to earn his living in commerce and radio, he studied comp. privately with Harrison Kerr in N.Y.

Works incl. Sym. & *Horn and Chantey* for orch.; *Appalachian Suite* for stg. orch.; stg. 4tet; Sonatina for pf.; songs; var. Amer. folk-song arrs., &c.

Scott, Walter (1771–1832), Sco. poet & novelist. *See* **Amy Robsart** (de Lara), **Attwood** (*Guy Mannering*), **Bishop** (do., *Heart of Midlothian, Montrose, Kenilworth* & *Waverley*), **Bruch** (*Feuerkreuz*), **Bruden fra Lammermoor** (Bredal), **Buck (D.)** (*Marmion*), **Carafa** (*Fiancée de Lammermoor*), **Corder** (*Bridal of Triermain*), **Costa** (*Kenilworth*, ballet), **Dame blanche** (Boïeldieu: *Guy Mannering* & *Monastery*), **Donizetti** (*Castello di Kenilworth*), **Donna del lago** (Rossini), **Eve of St. John** (Mackenzie), **Flotow** (*Rob Roy*), **Gomis** (*Revenant*), **Grisar** (*Sarah*), **Holstein** (*Waverley*), **Horn (C. E.)** (*Peveril of the Peak*), **Ivanhoe** (Sullivan), **Jeanie Deans** (MacCunn), **Jensen** (*Donald Caird* & songs), **Jolie Fille de Perth** (Bizet), **Koven** (*Robin Hood* & *Rob Roy*), **Lady of the Lake** (Schubert), **Leicester** (Auber), **Macbeth** (*Bruce* [*Lord of the Isles*]), **MacCunn** (*Lay of the Last Minstrel*, 'Land of (the mountain and the flood'), **Macfarren (G.)** (*Lady of the Lake*), **Mackenzie** (*Marmion*), **Mazzucato (A.)** (*Fidanzata di Lammermoor*), **O'Neill** (*Bride of L.*), **Prigione d'Edimburg** (F. Ricci), **Prison d'Edimbourg** (Carafa), **Puritani** (Bellini), **Quentin Durward** (Gevaert & A. Maclean), **Rodwell** (*Lord of the Isles*), **Schira** (*Kenilworth*), **Sullivan** (do., & *Marmion*), **Talismano** (Balfe), **Templario** (Nicolai), **Templer und die Jüdin** (Marschner), **Vesque von Püttlingen** (*Donna del lago*), **Weyse** (*Feast at Kenilworth*), **Whitaker** (*Guy Mannering*), **Whyte (I.)** (*Marmion*).

8 songs by Schubert (in Ger. trans.).

Scotti, Antonio (b. Naples, 25. I. 1866; d. Naples, 26. II. 1936), It. bar. singer. Pupil of Signora Trifari-Payanini (?–1908). Made his 1st appearance at Malta in 1889 and 1st visited London, after successful tours in It., Spa. and S. Amer., in 1899.

Scottish Composers. *See* **Carver, Chisholm, Costeley (?), Davie, Drysdale, Gordon, Gow, Holden (J.), Johnson (R.), Linstead, Macbeth, MacCunn, McEwen, M'Gibbon, Mackenzie, Mackintosh, M'Leod, Macpherson, Moffat, Scott (F. G.), Scott (Lady), Skinner, Smith (R. A.), Stephen, Wallace (W.), Whyte.**

'Scottish' Symphony. Mendelssohn's 3rd Sym., Op. 56, in A min. & maj., begun in It. in 1831 and finished in Berlin, 20. I. 1842; prod. Leipzig, Gewandhaus, 3. III. 1842.

Scriabine. *See* **Skriabin.**

Scribe, Eugène (1791–1861), Fr. playwright & libst. *See* **Adriana Lecouvreur** (Cilèa), **Africaine** (Meyerbeer), **Alexandrov (A. N.)** (*Adrienne Lecouvreur*), **Ali Baba** (Cherubini), **Ballo in maschera** (Verdi), **Châlet** (*Adam*), **Cheval de bronze** (Auber), **Comte Ory** (Rossini), **Dame blanche** (Boïeldieu), **Diamants de la Couronne** (Auber), **Domino noir** (Auber), **Don Sébastien** (Donizetti), **Elisir d'amore** (do.), **Étoile du Nord** (Meyerbeer), **Favorite** (Donizetti), **Fra Diavolo** (Auber), **Gustave III** (do.), **Huguenots** (Meyerbeer), **Juive** (Halévy), **Leicester** (Auber), **Lortzing** (*Yelva*), **Maçon** (Auber), **Manon Lescaut** (Auber), **Marquise de Brinvilliers** (8 comps.), **Martyrs** (Donizetti), **Muette de Portici** (Auber), **Part du diable** (Auber), **Philtre** (Auber), **Prigione d'Edimburg** (F. Ricci), **Prison d'Édimbourg** (Carafa), **Prophète** (Meyerbeer), **Puits d'Amour** (Balfe), **Robert le Diable** (Meyerbeer), **Schmitt (A.)** (*Trilby*), **Setaccioli** (*Adrienne L.*), **Shebalin** (*Glass of Water*), **Vêpres siciliennes** (Verdi).

Scrittura (It. lit. scripture). In It. operatic circles the term is used for a commission to comp. an opera.

Scudo, Pietro (Pierre) (b. Venice, 8. VI. 1806; d. Blois, 14. X. 1864), It. critic who wrote in Fr. Educ. in Ger. but settled in Paris in boyhood and unsuccessfully tried to become a singer. Later became a critic and joined the *Revue des Deux Mondes*.

Scucla. *See* **Scola.**

Scylla et Glaucus, opera by Leclair (lib. by d'Albaret), prod. Paris, Opéra, 4. X. 1746.

Sea Drift, setting of a poem by Walt Whitman for bar. solo, chor. & orch. by Delius, comp. 1903, 1st perf., in Ger., Essen Mus. Festival, 1906; in Eng., Sheffield Festival, 1908.

Sea Pictures, song cycle for con. & orch. by Elgar, Op. 37: 1. *Sea Slumber Song* (Roden Noel); 2. *In Haven* (Alice Elgar); 3. *Sabbath Morning at Sea* (Elizabeth Barrett Browning); 4. *Where Corals lie* (Richard Garnett); 5. *The Swimmer*

(A. L. Gordon); 1st perf., Norwich Festival, 1899.

Sea Symphony, A. The 1st Sym. by Vaughan Williams, for solo voices, chor. & orch. (words by Walt Whitman), prod. Leeds Festival, 1910.

Seal Woman, The, opera by Bantock (lib. by Marjorie Kennedy Fraser), prod. Birmingham, Repertory Theatre, 27. IX. 1924. A Celtic folk opera containing many trad. Hebridean tunes.

Seasons, The, ballet by Glazunov (chgph. by Marius Petipa), prod. St. Petersburg, Maryinsky Theatre, 20. II. 1900.

Orat. (*Die Jahreszeiten*) by Haydn (Ger. words by Gottfried van Swieten, based on Thomson's poem), comp. 1798–1801; prod. Vienna, Schwarzenberg Palace, 24. IV. 1801.

Sebastiani, Johann (b. Weimar, 30. IX. 1622; d. Königsberg, spring 1683), Ger. comp. Studied prob. in It., went to Königsberg c. 1650, where he became cantor in 1661 and mus. dir. at the electoral church in 1663, retiring in 1679.

Works incl. a Passion for voices and stgs.; sacred concs. for voices & insts. & other church m.; wedding and funeral cantatas; sacred & secular songs *Parnass-Blumen*, &c.

Sec (Fr. = dry). A term used by modern Fr. comps., esp. Debussy, where a note or chord is to be struck and released again abruptly without any richness of tone.

Secco (It. = dry). *See* **Recitativo secco.**

Sechter, Simon (b. Friedberg, Boh., 11. X. 1788); d. Vienna, 10. IX. 1867), Boh.-Aus. theorist, orgst. & comp. Settled in Vienna in 1804 and continued mus. studies there, wrote pf. accomps. for Dragonetti's db. concs. in 1809, while the It. player took refuge in Vienna, and in 1810 became teacher of pf. and singing at the Inst. for the Blind. In 1825 he succeeded Worzischek as court orgst. In 1850 he became prof. at the Cons. He wrote several theoret. works.

Works incl. opera *Ali Hitsch-Hatsch*; masses, Requiem & other church m.; orats. & cantatas; chor. from Schiller's *Braut von Messina*; chorale preludes, fugues, &c. for org.; vars., fugues & other works for pf., &c.

Second. The interval of 1 tone between 2 notes, either a whole tone (maj. S.) or a semitone (min. S.); but theoret. and in notation there can also be augmented Ss., if they are written as 2 adjacent notes, e.g. C–D♯ or B♭–C♯, although in practice they have the sound of min. 3rds.

Second Subject. *See* **Sonata.**

Secondo (It. = second). The part of the 2nd player in a pf. duet, that of the 1st being called Primo.

Sedaine, Michel Jean (1719–97), Fr. playwright & libst. *See* **Aline, Reine de Golconde** (Berton & Monsigny), **Aucassin et Nicolette** (Grétry), **Blaise le savetier** (Philidor), **Déserteur** (Monsigny), **Diable à quatre** (Philidor), **Félix** (Monsigny), **Grétry** (*Raoul Barbe-bleue*), **Guillaume Tell** (Grétry), **Jagd** (J. A. Hiller), **Richard Cœur de Lion** (Grétry), **Roi et le fermier** (Monsigny), **Rose et Colas** (do.).

Sedie, Enrico delle. *See* **Delle Sedie.**

Sedley, Charles (? 1639–1701), Eng. poet & dramatist. *See* **Clarke (J.)** (*Antony and Cleopatra*).

Seeger, Charles (Louis) (b. Mexico City, 14. XII. 1886), Amer. cond., teacher & comp. Studied at Harvard Univ. After cond. at the Cologne Opera in 1910, he was Prof. of M. at California Univ., 1912–9, and then in N Y. He was among the founders of var. mcol. socs. in U.S.A., and wrote theoret. books.

Works incl. masques *Dedra* & *The Queen's Masque*; ovt. *Shadowy Waters* for orch.; chamber m.; v. & pf. So.; numerous songs, &c.

Seegr, Joseph (Ferdinand Norbert) (b. Řepin nr. Melnik, 21. III. 1716; d. Prague, 22. IV. 1782), Boh. orgst. & comp. Studied in Prague and became singer, vst. & orgst. at several churches there. On hearing him play, Joseph II offered him a court appt. in Vienna, but he d. before he could take it up.

Works incl. masses, psalms, litanies & other church m.; toccatas & fugues for org., &c.

Seger or **Segert** } *See* **Seegr.**

Segno (It. = sign). *See* **Dal segno.**

Segreto di Susanna, Il (*Susanna's Secret*), opera by Wolf-Ferrari (lib. by Enrico Golisciani), prod. Munich, Court Opera, in Ger. trans. by Max Kalbeck, 4. XII. 1909.

Segue (It. = follows). An indication, like *attacca*, that a piece, number or section is to be played or sung immediately after another one. In MSS. the word is sometimes used instead of *V.S.* (*volti subito*) where a blank space is left at the bottom of a page to avoid turning over during the perf. of what follows on the next.

Seguidilla. A Spa. dance dating back to at least the 16th cent. and 1st heard of in La Mancha, though poss. of earlier Moorish orig. The orig. form was the S. Manchega, but when the dance spread over Spa. others developed: the S. Bolera—slow and stately; the S. Gitana—slow and sentimental; and the S. Teleada—in combined 3–4 and 3–8 rhythm, and related to the Cachucha. The S. is usually played on guitars, often with castanet accomp. and sometimes with v. or fl. Frequently popular verses are sung to the S. consisting of *coplas* (couplets) of 4 lines followed by *estrevillos* (refrains) of 3 lines.

Seguin, Arthur (b. London, 7. IV. 1809; d. New York, 9. XII. 1852), Eng. bass singer. Studied at the R.A.M. in London and made his 1st appearance at the Exeter Festival in 1829, 1st came out in opera at Covent Garden Theatre in London in 1833 and visited U.S.A. in 1838, settling later in N.Y. He married the sop. Ann Childe (1814–88).

Sehnsuchtswalzer (attrib. to Beethoven). *See* **Trauerwalzer.**

Seiber, Mátyás (b. Budapest, 4. V. 1904), Hung. cst., cond. & comp. Studied with Kodály at the Budapest Acad. of M. Travelled abroad, incl. N. and S. Amer., from 1925 and in 1928–33 was prof. at the Frankfort o/M. Cons., also cst. in a stg. 4tet there and cond. at a theatre and of a workers' chor. In 1935 he settled in London, as chor. cond. & film comp., and joined the teaching staff at Morley Coll.

Works incl. light operas; incid. m. for plays; film & radio m.; *Missa brevis* for unaccomp. chor.; 2 Besardo Suites (from 16th-cent. lute tablatures), *Transylvanian Rhapsody* for orch.; *Pastorale & Burlesque* for fl. & stgs., *Fantasia concertante* for v. & stgs., *Notturno* for hn. & stgs., 4 Gr. Songs for voice & stgs.; 2 stg. 4tets, wind 6tet, 5tet for cl. & stgs., Duo for v. & co.; Fantasy for co. & pf., v. pieces; pf. works; songs, chors., folksong arrs., &c.

Seidl, Anton (b. Budapest, 7. V. 1850; d. New York, 28. III. 1898), Hung.-Ger. cond. Studied at the Leipzig Cons. from 1870 and 2 years later went to Bayreuth as Wagner's asst. Cond. at the Leipzig Opera, 1879–82, afterwards toured and cond. Ger. opera at the Metrop. Opera House in N.Y. from 1885 to his death.

Seiffert, Max (b. Beeskow o/Spree, 9. II. 1868), Ger. mcolst. Studied with Spitta in Berlin and took a doctor's degree in 1891. In 1904–14 he was ed. of the pubs. of the I.M.S. and in 1918 became ed. of the *Archiv für Musikwissenschaft.* He held 2 professorships in Berlin and in 1935 became dir. of the State Institute for Ger. Mus. Research. He has ed. much old m., some vols. of the *Denkmäler deutscher Tonkunst* and the complete ed. of Sweelinck.

Seixas, José Antonio Carlos de (b. Coimbra, 11. VI. 1704; d. ? Lisbon, 25. VIII. 1742), Port. orgst., hpchdst. & comp. Studied under his father, an orgst., and became orgst. at Coimbra cath. at an early age, later going to Lisbon as orgst. to the patriarchate. He also taught hpchd. there and (?) met D. Scarlatti, whose work influenced his.

Works incl. church m.; Conc. for hpchd. & stgs.; many toccatas & sos. for hpchd., &c.

Séjan, Nicolas (b. Paris, 19. III. 1745; d. Paris, 16. III. 1819), Fr. orgst. & comp. He became an orgst. in Paris in his teens and in 1772 succeeded Daquin as orgst. at Notre-Dame and in 1789 Pierre Louis Couperin in the royal chapel. He also taught at the École Royale du Chant until deprived of the post by the Revol. In 1806 he was orgst. at the Invalides and in 1814 was restored to the royal chapel.

Works incl. 3 pf. trios; 6 v. & pf. sos.; hpchd. & org. pieces, &c.

Sekles, Bernhard (b. Frankfort o/M., 20. VI. 1872; d. Frankfort, 15. XII. 1934), Ger. comp. Studied at the Hoch Cons. at Frankfort, under Knorr and others, cond. for a time at Heidelberg and Mainz and then joined the teaching-staff at his former school.

Works incl. operas *Schahrazade* (after the *Arabian Nights*) & *Die zehn Küsse*, burlesque *Die Hochzeit des Faun*, dance play *Der Zwerg und die Infantin* (after Wilde); symph. poem *Aus den Gärten der Semiramis, Kleine Suite, Die Temperamente* for orch.; Passacaglia and Fugue for org. & orch.; Serenade for 11 insts.; Passacaglia and Fugue for stg. 4tet; co. & pf. So.; pf. pieces; songs, &c.

Selection. *See* **Pot-Pourri.**

Selle, Thomas (b. Zörbig, Saxony, 23. III. 1599; d. Hamburg, 2. VII. 1663), Ger. comp. Was rector and cantor at var. places, finally at the Johanneum in Hamburg from 1637, and town cantor there from 1641, also minor canon and mus. dir. at the cath.

Works incl. motets, sacred concs.; madrigals; sacred & secular songs, &c.

Selneccer, Nikolaus (b. Hersbruck nr. Nuremberg, 6. XII. 1528; d. Leipzig, 24. V. 1592), Ger. theol. and orgst. Court preacher at Dresden, 1557–61, later held var. posts at Jena, Leipzig and Wolfenbüttel. Wrote words and m. of many chorales, of which he pub. an important book, containing the work of others and his own, in 1587.

Sembrich, Marcella (real name Praxede Marcelline Kochanska) (b. Wisniewczyk, Galicia, 15. II. 1858; d. New

York, 11. I. 1935), Pol. sop. singer. Pupil of her father, Kasimir Kochanski (S. being her mother's name), and appeared at the age of 12 as pfst. & vst. When she went to Vienna for further study, she found she had a voice and studied singing there with Rokitansky and then with Lamperti at Milan and Richard Lewy in Ger. In 1878 she made her 1st stage appearance at Dresden. In 1880 she 1st visited London and later sang mainly at the Metrop. Opera in N.Y., where she settled.

Semele, serenata by Handel (lib. by Congreve with alterations (?) by Pope), prod. London, Covent Garden Theatre, 10. II. 1744.

Semellum. *See* **Gemellum.**

Semet, Théophile (b. Lille, 6. IX. 1824; d. Corbeil nr. Paris, 15. IV. 1888), Fr. comp. Studied at the Lille and Paris Conss., Halévy being among his masters. In 1850 he prod. his 1st stage piece, a vaudeville on George Sand's *La Petite Fadette*, but in 1857 began to have operatic successes. He was a perc. player in the Paris Opéra orch.

Works incl. operas *Nuits d'Espagne*, *La Demoiselle d'honneur*, *Gil Blas* (after Le Sage), *Ondine* & *La Petite Fadette* (a new operatic version); ballet *Les Pirates de la Savane*; songs for the play *Constantinople*; cantata; partsongs; songs, &c.

Semi-Chorus. A group of singers detached from a chor. for the purpose of obtaining antiphonal effects or changes of tone-colour. It does not often lit. consist of half the voices, but is more usually a much smaller contingent.

Semibreve. The largest note-value now in current use, and therefore called 'whole note' in Ger. and Amer.; but it is actually half the value of the old Breve, and therefore quite correctly described by its Eng. name.

Semicroma (It.). The It. term for the Semiquaver in modern usage, but earlier sometimes used to denote the Quaver.

Semiquaver. The note-value of half a Quaver, as the name implies, and therefore of one 16th of a Semibreve.

Semiramide (*Semiramis*), opera by Rossini (lib. by Giacomo Rossi, based on Voltaire's tragedy), prod. Venice, Teatro La Fenice, 3. II. 1823.

Semiramide riconosciuta (*Semiramis Recognized*), opera by Gluck (lib. by Metastasio), prod. Vienna, Burg Theatre, 14. V. 1748.

Opera by Hasse (lib. do.), prod. Venice, Teatro San Giovanni Crisostomo, 26. XII. 1744.

Opera by Vinci (lib. do.), prod. Rome, Teatro delle Dame, 6. II. 1729.

Sémiramis, opera by Catel (lib. by Philippe Desriaux, after Voltaire), prod. Paris, 4. V. 1802.

Semiseria (It. fem. = half-serious). The term for a hybrid between *opera seria* and *opera buffa*.

Semitone. The smallest interval normally used in occidental m. Except for adjustments of leading-notes (*see* **Musica ficta**) only 2 S. intervals occur in any of the Modes and in the Diatonic Scales, the others being whole tones; in the chromatic scales all the intervals are Ss.

Semplice (It. = simple, accent on 1st syll.). A direction indicating that a passage or whole comp. is to be perf. in an unaffected or not over-expressive manner.

Sempre (It.) = Always, ever.

Senaillé, Jean Baptiste (b. Paris, 23. XI. 1687; d. Paris, 8 or 15. X. 1730), Fr. vst. & comp. Studied under his father, Jean S., a member of the royal orch. and with the latter's colleague there, Queversin; later with Corelli's pupil Anet and with Vitali at Modena, where he was app. to the ducal court. He returned to Paris in 1720 and received an appt. at court under the regent, the Duke of Orleans, later confirmed under Louis XV.

Works incl. sos. for unaccomp. v.; v. sos. with bass; pieces for v. & hpchd., &c.

Senesino (i.e. the Sienese). The nickname of the singer below was sometimes also given to Tenducci, another native of Siena.

Senesino (real name Francesco Bernardi) (b. Siena, *c.* 1680; d. ?, *c.* 1750), It. male sop. singer. Studied with Bernacchi at Bologna. Attached to the court opera at Dresden in 1719 and there invited by Handel to London, where he 1st appeared in 1720.

Senfl, Ludwig (b. Zürich, *c.* **1490**; d. Munich, *c.* 1555), Swi. comp. Pupil of Isaac in Vienna and his successor as chapel master to Maximilian I, which post he held until the emperor's death in 1519. In 1520 he went to Augsburg and some time after that to Munich, where he settled, (?) in some connection with the ducal court. In 1530 he was in correspondence with Luther.

Works incl. masses, magnificats, motets & other church m.; odes by Horace for voices; *c.* 150 Ger. songs, &c.

Senilov, Vladimir Alexeievitch (b. Viatka, 9. VII. 1875; d. St. Petersburg, 18. IX. 1918), Rus. comp. Studied law at first, but went to Leipzig for mus. studies under Riemann and later worked under

Glazunov and Rimsky-Korsakov at the St. Petersburg Cons.

Works incl. operas *Vassily Buslaiev* & *Hippolytus* (after Euripides), mus. action *George the Bold*; Sym. in D maj., ovt. *In Autumn*, symph. poems *The Wild Geese* (after Maupassant), *The Mtsyrs* (after Lermontov), *Pan*, *The Scythians* & *Vars. on a Chant of the Old Believers* for orch.; *Chloe forsaken* for voice & orch.; cantata *John of Damascus*; Poem for co. & pf., Scherzo for fl. & pf., &c.

Sennet (Eng., obs.). A word found in stage-directions of Eng. plays of the Elizabethan period where the author asks for a fanfare to be played on or off the stage. It has been said to be derived from ' seven ' and to denote a phrase of 7 notes; also to come from ' sonata,' just as ' tucket ' was poss. connected with ' toccata.' But it is prob. a variant of ' signet ' = ' sign.'

Sensible (Fr. noun, or *note sensible*) = Leading-note.

Senza (It.) = without.

Septave. An org. builders' term for the diatonic notes counted upwards from the keynote of a scale, excl. that note.

Septet. Any work, or number in a work, written in 7 parts for voices or insts.

Septimole or **Septuplet** } A group of 7 notes to be fitted into a beat or other time-unit in which its number is irregular.

Sepulchre Music. A medieval kind of mus. drama or mystery play perf. in church as a Trope in the Easter Mass and sung in plainsong. It dealt with the story of the Resurrection and was enacted by priests and choristers. In so far as it was a dramatic perf. it may be regarded as the earliest beginnings of Opera, just as the spoken mystery and miracle plays were the beginnings of the drama. It goes back to the end of the 10th cent. Early exs. of it occurred at Limoges, St. Gall, Winchester and elsewhere, and it was spread over most of Eur., incl. esp. Ger. and Spa. as well as Fr. and Eng.

Sequence. A hymn of the 12th–15th cents., deriving from the older Trope and Prose. Its name is due to its following the Gradual and Alleluia in the Mass, of which, like these, it never formed a regular part. Numerous Ss. in plainsong were in use up to the time of the Council of Trent, which however disallowed all but 5 of them: the *Victimae paschali* for Easter Sunday, the *Veni Sancte Spiritus* for Whitsun, the *Lauda Sion* for Corpus Christi, the *Stabat Mater* for Good Friday and 3rd Sunday in IX, and the *Dies irae* in the Mass for the Dead (Requiem).

Sequences. A device whereby a melodic figure is repeated rising, or more rarely falling, by a degree of the scale, at least twice in succession. It is called S. only in cases where the comp. retains the same key throughout, regardless of changes in the intervals; where the key changes with each step up or down the scale, so that all the intervals remain the same, the technical term is not S. but Rosalia.

Serafino, Giorgio (b. ?; d. ?), It. 18th-cent. v. maker, who worked at Venice.

Serafino, Santo (b. ?; d. ?), It. 17th–18th-cent. v. maker, uncle of prec. He worked at Udine, *c.* 1678–98, and then at Venice until *c.* 1735.

Seraglio, The (Mozart). *See* **Entführung aus dem Serail.**

Serbian Composers. *See* **Yugoslav Composers.**

Séré, Octave. *See* **Poueigh, Jean.**

Serenade. Evening song or evening m., esp. perf. in the open air either to woo a girl, to do homage to some person or to create a general atmosphere of festivity. On these lines the S. gradually developed into organized comps. for accomp. voice, for several voices or for var. combs. of insts., and in the 18th cent. the S. became an inst. work in several mvts., with the 1st in so. form and containing one or more minuets (which may have been actually danced at times), of the type of the Divertimento.

' Serenade ' Quartet. The nickname of a stg. 4tet by Haydn, Op. 3 No. 5, in F maj., comp. *c.* 1768. The name derives from the slow mvt., which is a 1st-v. tune over a *pizzicato* accomp. for the other insts.

Serenata (It.). Actually the It. word for Serenade (as above), but used in Eng. with a spec. meaning for 18th-cent. works, often of an occasional or congratulatory type, either prod. on the stage as small topical and allegorical operas or in concerts (and even then sometimes in costume) in the manner of a secular cantata.

Serf, The, opera by G. Lloyd (lib. by William Lloyd, the comp.'s father), prod. London, Covent Garden Theatre, 20. X. 1938.

Seria (It. fem. = serious). *See* **Opera seria.**

Sérieyx, Auguste (b. Amiens, 14. VI. 1865), Fr. comp. Studied with Gédalge and d'Indy, in the writing of the latter's *Cours de Composition* he assisted. In 1900 he became prof. of comp. at the Schola Cantorum in Paris.

Works incl. masses & motets; cantata *Salvete cedri Libani*; *La Voie lactée* for voice & orch.; v. & pf. So.; org. & pf. pieces; songs, &c.

Serious Songs (Brahms). *See* **Vier ernste Gesänge.**

Sermisy, Claude de (b. ?, c. 1490; d. ? Paris, 1562), Fr. comp. In 1508–14 he was attached to the Sainte-Chapelle in Paris and in 1515 became a singer in Louis XII's royal chapel, just before that king's death, and later he succeeded Antoine de Longueval as master of the choir-boys. In 1533 he was made a canon of the Sainte-Chapelle, with a living and a substantial salary attached to it; but his duties there were light and he remained in the royal chapel, with which, under François I, he visited Bologna, where his choir competed with the Papal choir before Leo X, in 1515. In 1520, with the same king, he met Henry VIII at the Field of the Cloth of Gold, a similar meeting following in 1532 at Boulogne; and on both occasions the Fr. and Eng. choirs sang together.

Works incl. masses, motets; over 200 chansons for several voices, &c.

Serov, Alexander Nikolaievitch (b. St. Petersburg, 23. I. 1820; d. St. Petersburg, 1. II. 1871), Rus. comp. & critic. Studied law, but found time to cultivate m., which eventually, after a career as civil servant, he took up professionally. He studied co. and theory from c. 1840, met Glinka in 1842, began an opera on Shakespeare's *Merry Wives* in 1843, but was reduced to a correspondence course of mus. instruction when transferred to Simferopol. He began to write criticism and in 1858, when he returned from a visit to Ger. as an ardent admirer of Wagner, he began to attack the Rus. nat. school of comps., but found a powerful opponent in Stassov. He was over 40 when he began his 1st opera. He married the comp. Valentina Semionovna Bergman (1846–1927), who wrote some operas of her own, incl. *Uriel Acosta* (based on Gutzkow's play). When he d. from heart disease, he had just begun a 4th opera on Gogol's *Christmas Eve Revels*.

Works incl. operas *Judith*, *Rogneda*, *The Power of Evil* (after Ostrovsky's play; orchn. finished by Soloviev); incid. m. to Nikolai Pavlovitch Zhadr's tragedy *Nero*; *Stabat Mater* & *Ave Maria*; *Gopak*, *Dance of the Zaporogue Cossacks* & other orch. works, &c.

Serpent. An obs. wind inst., formerly the bass of the Cornett family, with a long winding wooden tube covered with leather and played with a cupped brass mouthpiece. Sometimes the whole was made of brass or copper. It prob. orig. late in the 16th cent. and was used both in bands and in churches, but fell out of use in the 19th cent.

Serpentone (It.) = Serpent.

Serpette, (Henri Charles Antoine) Gaston (b. Nantes, 4. XI. 1846; d. Paris, 3. XI. 1904), Fr. comp. He was orig. a lawyer, but studied with A. Thomas at the Paris Cons. and took the Prix de Rome in 1871. Returning from Rome in 1874, he hoped to prod. a work at the Opéra-Comique, but failed and took to writing light pieces for the Bouffes-Parisiens.

Works incl. operettas *La Branche cassée*, *La Petite Muette*, *Cendrillonnette*, *La Demoiselle du téléphone*, *La Dot de Brigitte*, *Le Capitole*, *Le Carnet du diable*, *Shakespeare* and others; cantata *Jeanne d'Arc*, &c.

Serrano y Ruiz, Emilio (b. Victoria, Alava, 15. III. 1850; d. Madrid, 9. IV. 1939), Spa. pfst. & comp. He became court pfst. to the Infanta Isabella, dir. of the Royal Opera in Madrid and prof. at the Cons.

Works incl. operas *Mitridate*, *Giovanna la pazza*, *Irene de Otranto*, *Gonzalo de Córdoba* & *La maja de Rumbo*; symph. poem *La primera salide de Don Quijote* (after Cervantes), &c.

Serrao, Paolo (b. Filadelfia, Catanzaro, 1830; d. Naples, 17. III. 1907), It. comp. Studied at the Naples Cons. and became a prof. there in 1863.

Works incl. operas *Pergolesi*, *La duchessa di Guisa*, *Il figliuol prodigo*, *L'impostore*, *Leonora de' Bardi*; orat. *Gli Ortonesi in Scio*, Passion *Le tre ore d'agonia*; mass, Requiem & other church m.; funeral sym. for Mercadante; ovt. for orch.; pf. pieces, &c.

Serré (Fr. = tightened). A direction sometimes used by Fr. comps. for *stringendo*.

Serres, (Marie) François (Louis Arnal) de (b. Lyons, 8. X. 1864), Fr. orgst. & comp. Studied at the Paris Cons., Franck being his org. master. After studying with him privately for another 5 years, he became org. prof. at the Schola Cantorum and orgst. at the Ir. Chapel.

Works incl. Fr. & Lat. motets, *Ave, verum corpus* & other church m.; *Nuits d'été*, *Le Jour des morts*, &c. for chor. & orch.; *Les Caresses*, &c. for orch.; *Les Heures claires* for voice & orch.; songs, &c.

Serse (*Xerxes*). *See also* **Xerse.**

Opera by Handel (lib. do., altered), prod. London, King's Theatre, Haymarket, 15. IV. 1738. It contains the famous so-called *Largo*, 'Ombra mai fù.'

Serva padrona, La (*The Maid as Mistress*), intermezzi by **Paisiello** (lib. by Gennaro Antonio Federico), prod. St. Petersburg, Hermitage, at court, 10. IX. 1781.

Intermezzi by Pergolesi (lib. do.), prod. Naples, Teatro San Bartolommeo, between the acts of P.'s serious opera *Il prigionier superbo*, 28. VIII. 1733.

Servais, (Adrien) François (b. Hal nr. Brussels, 6. VI. 1807; d. Brussels, 26. XI. 1866), Belg. cst. & comp. Studied with Platel at the Brussels Cons., visited Paris and London, later toured all over Eur. and in 1848 became prof. at the Cons.

Works incl. 6 co. concs. & 16 fantasies for co. & orch.; duets for v. & co.; many co. studies & pieces, &c.

Servais, Joseph (b. Hal nr. Brussels, 28. XI. 1850; d. Brussels, 29. VIII. 1885), Belg. cst., son of prec. Pupil of his father, with whom he travelled afterwards. In 1868–70 he was at the court of Weimar, in 1875 made his 1st appearance in Paris, and eventually settled at Brussels.

Servetta (It. lit. servant-girl). A stock figure in opera given to a singer with a light sop. voice. *See* **Soubrette.**

Service. As a mus. term the word implies the setting of those parts of the services of the Angl. church which lend themselves to mus. treatment, esp. the Morning Prayer and the Evening Prayer (Magnificat and Nunc dimittis).

Servilia, opera by Rimsky-Korsakov (lib. by comp., based on a play by Lev Alexandrovitch Mey), prod. St. Petersburg, 14. X. 1902.

Sesquialtera. An org. mixture stop.

Sessions, Roger (b. Brooklyn, New York, 28. XII. 1896), Amer. comp. Studied at Harvard Univ. and later at Yale Univ. with H. Parker, also with Bloch in N.Y. and Cleveland. In 1917–21 he taught at Smith Coll., Northampton, Mass. and in 1921–5 was head of the theoret. dept. of the Cleveland Inst. of M. He lived in It. and Ger. in 1925–33, then taught for 2 years at Boston Univ. and afterwards at var. places until he became asst. prof. at Princeton Univ. in 1937.

Works incl. incid. m. for Andreiev's *The Black Maskers*; 3 syms., 3 *Dirges* for orch.; v. Conc.; stg. 4tet; So. & 3 Chorale Preludes for org.; pf. So.; songs to words by James Joyce & others, &c.

Sestet. In m. an obs. form of the word Sextet.

Sestina (It., derived from *sesto* = sixth, with diminutive suffix). In m. the term is used for a maj. common chord of 6 notes so distributed as to represent the ratios of the 1st 6 harmonics: i.e. built up, from the bass upwards, in an octave, a perfect 5th, a perfect 4th, a maj. 3rd and a min. 3rd.

Set. An old Eng. name for the Suite.

Setaccioli, Giacomo (b. Corneto Tarquinia, 8. XII. 1868; d. Siena, 5. XII. 1925), It. comp. Studied at the Accademia di Santa Cecilia in Rome and became a prof. there in 1922, but moved to Florence in 1925 on being app. dir. of the Cherubini Cons. there.

Works incl. operas *La sorella di Mark*, *L'ultimo degli Abenceragi*, *Il mantellaccio* & *Adrienne Lecouvreur* (after Scribe); Requiem for Humbert I, *Cantica* for solo voices, chor. & orch., motets, *Quadro sinfonico* for chor., org. & orch.; Sym. in A maj., symph. poems, Fugue, &c. for orch.; Concert Allegro for pf. & orch., Suite for hp. & stgs.; stg. 4tet, Nonet for wind insts.; So. for cl. & pf.; org. Prelude & Fugue; pf. pieces; songs, &c.

Sett. An old Eng. name for the Suite.

Sette canzoni (*Seven Songs*), opera by Malipiero (lib. by comp.), prod., in Fr. version by Henry Prunières, Paris, Opéra, 10. VII. 1920. Part II of the operatic cycle *L'Orfeide*.

Settle, Elkanah (1648–1724), Eng. poet & dramatist. *See* **Clarke (J.)** (*World in the Moon*, with D. Purcell), **Fairy Queen** (Purcell), **Finger** (*Virgin Prophetess*), **Purcell** (*Distressed Innocence*), **Turner** (*Pastor fido*, from Guarini).

Ševčík, Ottokar (b. Horazdovice, 22. III. 1852; d. Pisek, 18. I. 1934), Cz. vst. & teacher. Studied at the Prague Cons. and became leader at the Mozarteum at Salzburg and gave concerts in Prague, but in 1873 he settled in Vienna, was prof. at the M. School at Kiev in 1875–92 and then became chief v. prof. at the Prague Cons. He wrote a v. method in 4 vols. and in 1903 formed a stg. 4tet.

Seven Words of the Saviour on the Cross, The. A work by Haydn in 7 slow mvts. for orch., commissioned by the cath. of Cadiz in 1785 and perf. there during Lent, when the 'Words' were read and a sermon was preached on them. In 1787 H. arr. the work for stg. 4tet and in 1797 he perf. it at Eisenstadt with a chor. arr. of the words.

Seventh. Any one of 3 intervals lying 7 notes of a mode or diatonic scale apart: i.e. the maj. S., a semitone short of an Octave; the min. S., a whole tone short of an 8ve; the diminished S., a semitone less than the min. S., actually the same as a maj. 6th in the tempered scale, but so written as to look like a 7th, e.g. C♯ with B♭ above it.

Séverac, (Joseph Marie) Déodat de (b. Saint-Félix de Caraman-Lauraguais, 20. VII. 1873; d. Céret, Pyrénées Orientales, 24. III. 1921), Fr. comp. Studied at the Toulouse Cons. and the Schola Cantorum in Paris, with Magnard and d'Indy. He returned to the S. of Fr. and devoted himself entirely to comp., neither his health nor his taste permitting him to hold any official mus. position.

Works incl. opera *Le Cœur du moulin*; ballet *La Fête des vendanges*; incid. m. for Sicard's *Héliogabale* & for Verhaeren's *Hélène de Sparte*; *Ave, verum corpus* & other church m.; *Chant de vacances* for chor.; *Nymphes au crépuscule* (unpub.), *Didon et Énée* (lost) & other unpub. orch. works; *Sérénade au clair de lune* for fl., stg. 5tet & pf. & unpub. chamber m.; Suite for org.; *Le Soldat de plomb* for pf. duet; *Le Chant de la terre, En Languedoc, Baigneuses au soleil, Cerdaña, En vacances* for pf.; 19 songs to poems by Ronsard, Verlaine, Maeterlinck, Poe & others, and poems in *langue d'oc*, &c.

Sevillana (Spa.). An Andalusian folk-song type similar to the Seguidilla and orig. confined to Seville.

Sextet. Any work, or number in a work, written in 6 parts for voices or insts.

Sextolet. A group of 6 notes, or double Triplet, when used in a comp. or mvt. whose time-unit is normally divisible into 2, 4 or 8 note-values.

Sextus. In old voc. m. the 6th part in a composition for 6 voices, always equal in compass to one of the voices in a 4-part comp.: sop., alto, ten. or bass.

Seyfried, Ignaz (Xaver) von (b. Vienna, 15. VIII. 1776; d. Vienna, 27. VIII. 1841), Aus. cond., teacher & comp. Studied law in Vienna, but on the advice of Winter he took to m. and became a pupil of Kozeluch and Haydn. In 1797 he became cond. at Schikaneder's Theater auf der Wieden and remained there in 1801 when it became the Theater an der Wien. He wrote theoret. articles and taught many distinguished pupils.

Works incl. operas, operettas and plays with m. *Der Löwenbrunnen, Preciosa* (P. A. Wolff), *Der Wundermann am Rheinfall* & *c.* 150 others, 5 biblical dramas, operetta *Die Ochsenmenuette* with m. arr. from Haydn's works; incid. m. for Shakespeare's *Julius Caesar*, Calderón's *Vida es sueño*, Schiller's *Räuber* & *Jungfrau von Orleans*, Grillparzer's *Ahnfrau* & *König Ottokar*, &c.; masses, Requiems, motets, offertories & other church m.; *Libera* for men's voices for Beethoven's funeral, &c.

Sf. (abbr.) = *Sforzando*.

Sfogato (It. = vaporous, evaporated). Sometimes used as a direction by comps., e.g. Chopin, to indicate a delicate and rather indistinct perf. of certain passages; also as an adj., esp. 'soprano s.,' meaning a thin and rather veiled voice.

Sforzando or **Sforzato** (It. = forced, reinforced). A direction indicating that a note or chord is to be strongly emphasized by an accent.

Sfumato (It.). Dissolved, blended, stumped.

Sfz. (abbr.) = *Sforzando*.

Sgambati, Giovanni (b. Rome, 28. V. 1841; d. Rome, 14. XII. 1914), It. pfst. & comp. Studied at Trevi in Umbria and in Rome and was a pupil of Liszt; later estab. important orch. and chamber concerts for the cultivation of serious m. in the It. capital. In 1869 he visited Ger. and 1st heard works by Wagner, whom he met in Rome in 1876 and who induced his pub., Schott, to bring out some of S.'s works. In 1882 he 1st visited Eng.

Works incl. Requiem; Syms. in D & E♭ maj., *Epitalamio sinfonico*, ovt. *Cola di Rienzi* & Festival Ovt. for orch.; pf. Conc. in G min.; stg. 4tet, 2 pf. 5tets; Prelude and Fugue, *Fogli volanti, Pièces lyriques, Mélodies poétiques*, Suite, studies & other works for pf.; songs, &c.

Shadwell, Thomas (*c.* 1642–92), Eng. poet & playwright. *See* **Franck (J. W.)** (masque for *Timon of Athens*), **Grabu** (*Timon of A.*), **King (R.)** (*Ode on St. Cecilia's Day*), **Locke** (*Tempest*), **Psyche** (Locke), **Purcell** (*Epsom Wells* & *Libertine*), **Reggio** (song 'Arise ye subterranean winds,' *Tempest*), **Smith (R.)** (*Epsom W.*), **Steggins** (do.), **Turner** (*Libertine*).

Shagbut. Another spelling of Sackbut.

Shahrazad (usually *Scheherazade*, though in Eng. the name is preferable in the form shown), symph. suite by Rimsky-Korsakov on the subject of the story-teller in the *Arabian Nights* and of some of the tales, Op. 35, finished summer 1888 and prod. St. Petersburg, 3. XI. 1888. Ballet based on it (chgph. by Mikhail Fokin, settings by Leon Bakst), prod. Paris, Opéra, 4. VI. 1910.

Shake. One of the principal mus. orna-

ments, consisting of the rapid alternation of the note written down with that a whole tone or semitone above, according to the key in which the piece is written, or according to the comp.'s notation. Where nothing is indicated to the contrary, the key determines whether the upper note is a whole or a semitone: i.e. the S. is perf. according to the key-signature. A S. may begin with the note below the principal note, if it is intended to do so with a Turn; more frequently it will end with a Turn and take in the lower note there before returning to the main note. But far too frequently this end-turn is perf. where it is not indicated by the comp., a habit to be avoided, Ss. being often very effective without the turn, except where the next principal note is the higher note actually incl. in the S.

Shakespeare, William (1564–1616), Eng. poet & dramatist. *See:*

All 's Well that Ends Well: **Linley (W.)** (song ' Was this fair face ').

Antony and Cleopatra: **Amours d'Antoine et de Cléopatre** (ballet, R. Kreutzer), **Antonio e Cleopatra** (opera, Malipiero), **Come, thou monarch of the vine** (Schubert [also set by Bishop & W. Linley]), **Jacobson** (incid. m.), **Klenovsky** (do.), **Norman (L.)** (do.), **Porter (Q.)** (do.), **Prokofiev** (play, *Egyptian Nights*), **Rabaud** (incid. m.), **Rubinstein (A.)** (ovt.), **Schmitt (F.)** (incid. m.), **Smyth** (ovt.).

As You Like It: **Arne** (songs), **Bishop** (incid. m.), **Castéra** (2 chors.), **German** (incid. m.), **Morley** (? do.), **Paine** (ovt.), **Pizzetti** (incid. m.), **Quilter** (do.), **Rietz** (do.), **Toch** (do.), **Veracini** (opera *Rosalinda*), **Walton** (song ' Under the greenwood tree '), **Wetzler** (incid. m.).

Comedy of Errors, The: **Bishop** (incid. m.), **Equivoci** (opera, Storace), **Fogg** (ovt.), **Shaporin** (incid. m.).

Coriolanus: **Lux** (scene), **Mackenzie** (incid. m.). (Beethoven's ovt. [not for Shakespeare], *see* **Coriolan**.)

Cymbeline: **Arne** (incid. m.), **Aylward** (do.), **Boyce** (do.), **Dietrich (A.)** (do.), **Hark, hark, the lark** (Schubert [also set by Aylward, Thomas Chilcot, B. Cooke, Kücken, G. Macfarren, &c.]), **Missa** (opera *Dinah*), **Sobolewski** (opera *Imogene*), **Tiessen** (incid. m.), **Vaughan Williams** (*Dirge for Fidele*).

Hamlet: **Ambleto** (operas, Gasparini & D. Scarlatti), **Amleto** (opera, Faccio), **Berlioz** (funeral march), **Bishop** (incid. m.), **Bourgault-Ducoudray** (*Enterrement d'Ophélie* for orch.), **Bridge** (Lament for stgs.), **Ferrari (G.)** (incid. m.), **Gade** (ovt.), **German** (symph. poem), **Hamlet** (operas, **Hignard** & A. Thomas; incid. m., Tchaikovsky; symph. poem, Liszt), **Haydn** (incid. m.), **Henschel** (do.), **Jacobson** (do.), **Joachim** (ovt.), **Joncières** (incid. m.), **Lambert (C.)** (do.), **Lazzari** (*Ophélie* for orch.), **Lekeu** (symph. study), **MacDowell** (symph. poem), **Macfarren (G.)** (ovt.), **Moniuszko** (incid. m.), **O'Neill** (do.), **Perabo** (pf. pieces), **Pierné** (incid. m.), **Pierson (H. H.)** (funeral march), **Rietz** (incid. m.), **Shostakovitch** (do.), **Stenhammar** (do.), **Taneiev (A. S.)** (ovt.), **Thomson (V.)** (incid. m.), **Tiessen** (do.), **Tuczek** (travesty), **Vogler** (incid. m.), **Weigl** (melodrama), **Weyrsch** (ovt.), *Zumsteeg* (incid. m.). 5 songs for Ophelia set by Brahms in 1873; ' To be or not to be ' noted for Pepys by one Cesare Morelli, prob. ordered by P. from some comp., (?) Locke.

Henry IV, 1 & 2: **At the Boar's Head** (opera, Holst), **Bishop** (incid. m.), **Corbett** (do.), **Falstaff** (symph. study, Elgar), **Gioventù di Enrico V** (opera on *Henry IV*, Pacini), **Joachim** (ovt.), **Paisible** (incid. m.), **Williams (G.)** (symph. impressions *Owen Glendower*).

Henry V: **Boughton** (Agincourt scene), **Falstaff** (symph. study, Elgar), **Macfarren (W.)** (ovt.), **O'Neill** (incid. m.), **Smith (D. S.)** (ovt. *Prince Hal*), **Walton** (film m.).

Henry VI, 1, 2 & 3: —

Henry VIII: **German** (incid. m.), **Henry VIII** (opera, Saint-Saëns), **Schumann** (incid. m.), **Sullivan** (do.).

Julius Caesar: **Blitzstein** (incid. m.), **Castelnuovo-Tedesco** (ovt.), **Doret** (incid. m.), **Falchi** (ovt.), **Galliard** (incid. m. for Mulgrave's adapt.), **García Roblez** (opera), **Giulio Cesare** (opera, Malipiero), **Jacobson** (incid. m.), **Lunssens** (symph. poem), **O'Neill** (do.), **Pierson (H. H.)** (ovt.), **Seyfried** (incid. m.).

King John: **Castelnuovo-Tedesco** (ovt.).

King Lear: **André (J.)** (incid. m.), **Balakirev** (ovt.), **Bazzini** (do.), **Berlioz** (do.), **Dukas** (do.), **King Lear** (incid. m., Haydn; sketched opera, Verdi), **O'Neill** (incid. m.), **Paumgartner** (do.), **Pedrell (F.)** (do.), **Re Lear** (opera, Ghislanzoni), **Salmhofer** (incid. m.), **Schulz-Beuthen** (sym.), **Shaporin** (incid. m.), **Shostakovitch** (do.), **Stegmann** (do.), **Weingartner** (symph. poem).

Love's Labour 's Lost: **Bishop** (incid. m.), **Cusins** (ovt.), also songs by Arne, Braham, Thomas Chilcot, Leveridge, G. Macfarren, H. Parry, J. C. Smith, &c.

Macbeth: **Asplmayr** (pantomime), **Assafiev** (incid. m.), **Bantock** (do.),

Braunfels (do.), **Brüll** (ovt.), **Dupuis (S.)** (symph. poem), **Eccles (J.)** (incid. m.), **Fisher (J. A.)** (do.), **Gatty** (opera), **Jacobson** (incid. m.), **Kelley** (do.), **Khatchaturian** (do.), **Le Flem** (chgph. drama), **Leveridge** (incid. m.), **Macbeth** (incid. m., Locke; operas, Bloch, Chelard, Collingwood, Taubert, Verdi; ovt., Spohr; symph. poem, R. Strauss), **Mederitsch** (incid. m.), **Neefe** (do.), **Netchaiev** (do.), **Oberthür** (ovt.), **O'Neill** (incid. m.), **Pearsall** (chors.), **Pierson (H. H.)** (sym.), **Purcell (D.)** (incid. m.), **Reichardt** (do.), **Rossi (Lauro)** (opera *Biorn*), **Smetana** (pf. pieces), **Stegmann** (incid. m.), **Sullivan** (do.), **Sutor** (do.), **Tcherepnin (N.)** (witches' scene for orch.), **Walton** (incid. m.). **Zumsteeg** (do.).

Measure for Measure: **Kabalevsky** (incid. m.), **Liebesverbot** (Wagner), **O'Neill** (incid. m.), **Wilson (J.)** (song 'Take, O take' [also set by Bishop, Galliard, G. Giordani, W [illegible]ley, G. Macfarren H. [illegible]arry, &c.]).

Merchant of Venice, The: **Arne (T. A.)** (incid. m.), **Assafiev** (do.), **Castelnuovo-Tedesco** (ovt.), **Fauré** (incid. m. *Shylock*), **Foerster (J. B.)** (opera *Jessica*), **Greenwood** (incid. m.), **Humperdinck** (do.), **Macfarren (G.)** (ovt.), **Marchand de Venise** (opera, Hahn), **Mercante di Venezia** (opera, Pinsuti), **Nystroem** (incid. m.), **O'Neill** (do.), **Rabaud** (do.), **Rathaus** (do.), **Sabata** (do.), **Simon (A.)** (do.), **Sullivan** (do.), **Taubmann** (opera *Porzia*), **Vaughan Williams** (*Serenade to Music*), **White (F.)** (ovt. *Shylock*).

Merry Wives of Windsor, The: **Adam** (opera *Falstaff*), **Dittersdorf** (opera), **Falstaff** (operas, Balfe, Salieri & Verdi), **Horn (C. E.)** (songs), **Kaun** (opera *Falstaff*), **Lustigen Weiber von Windsor** (opera, Nicolai), **Moniuszko** (incid. m.), **Ritter (P.)** (opera), **Salmhofer** (incid. m.), **Serov** (opera sketch), **Sir John in Love** (opera, Vaughan Williams), **Sullivan** (incid. m.).

Midsummer Night's Dream, A: **Aylward** (incid. m.), **Bishop** (do.), **Castelnuovo-Tedesco** (ovt.), **Cooke (T.)** (songs), **Fairies** (opera, J. C. Smith), **Fairy Queen** (Purcell), **Greenwood** (incid. m.), **Hüe** (opera *Titania*), **Křenek** (incid. m.), **Lampe** (*Pyramus and Thisbe*), **Leigh** (incid. m.), **Leveridge** (*Pyramus and T.*), **Mancinelli** (opera *Sogno di una notte d'estate*), **Midsummer N. D.** (incid. m., Mendelssohn), **Orff** (do.), **Préludes** (Debussy, I. 11), **Suppé** (incid. m.), **Vreuls** (opera), **Wolf (E. W.)** (opera *Zauberirrungen*), **Wolf (H.)** (*Elfenlied*).

Much Ado about Nothing: **Béatrice et Bénédict** (opera, Berlioz), **German** (incid. m.), **Godard** (do.), **Hahn** (do.), **Khrennikov** (incid. m.), **Korngold** (incid. m.), **Mojsisovics** (opera), **Much Ado** (opera, Stanford), **Stransky** (opera *Beatrice and Benedick*). Settings of 'Sigh no more' by Arne, Balfe, W. Linley, G. Macfarren, J. C. Smith, Sullivan, &c.

Othello: **Ambros** (ovt.), **Assafiev** (incid. m.), **Bortkievitch** (symph. poem), **Coleridge-Taylor** (do.), **Esposito** (ovt.), **Fibich** (symph. poem), **Hadley (H.)** (ovt.), **Krein (A.)** (ballet), **Krug** (prelude), **Lenton** (incid. m.), **Macfarren (W.)** (ovt.), **Otello** (operas, Rossini & Verdi), **Othello** (ovt., Dvořák), **Parker (C.)** (incid. m.), **Salmhofer** (do.), **Shostakovitch** (do.), **Zumsteeg** (do.). Settings of Drinking Song by Humfrey & W. Linley; of Willow Song by Bishop, Giordani, J. Hook, W. Linley, Shield, Sullivan, &c.

Pericles: **Perfall** (incid. m.).

Rape of Lucrece, The: **Rape of Lucretia** (Britten), **Sæverud** (suite).

Richard II: **Ames** (incid. m.), **Pitt** (do.), **Purcell** (do.).

Richard III: **German** (incid. m.), **Smetana** (symph. poem), **Volkmann** (incid. m.).

Romeo and Juliet: **Arne (T. A.)** (incid. m.), **Bedford** (love scene), **Boyce** (incid. m.), **Campo** (opera), **Capuleti ed i Montecchi** (opera, Bellini), **Dalayrac** (opera *Tout pour l'amour*), **German** (incid. m.), **Giulietta e Romeo** (operas, Vaccai, Zandonai & Zingarelli), **Holbrooke** (symph. poem *Queen Mab*), **Holmes (A.)** (sym.), **Ivry** (opera *Amants de Vérone*), **Lambert (C.)** (ballet), **Lunssens** (symph. poem), **Macfarren (G.)** (ovt.), **Marchetti** (opera), **Martin (F.)** (incid. m.), **Morales (M.)** (opera), **Pasquali (N.)** (dirge), **Pierson (H. H.)** (incid. m.), **Prokofiev** (ballet), **Romeo and Juliet** (opera, Barkworth; fantasy-ovt., Tchaikovsky), **Roméo et Juliette** (operas, Gounod & Steibelt; sym., Berlioz), **Romeo und Julie** (opera, G. Benda), **Salmhofer** (incid. m.), **Schwanberg** (opera), **Stenhammar** (incid. m.), **Sutermeister** (opera), **Svendsen** (ovt.), **Thomé** (incid. m.).

Songs: **Castelnuovo-Tedesco** (all the songs in the plays), **Finzi**, **Macfarren (G.)**, **Quilter**, **Schubert** (3 songs in Ger. trans.), **Strauss (R.)**.

Sonnets: **Cooke (A.)**, **Dieren (van)**, **Ketting**.

Taming of the Shrew, The: **Addinsell** (incid. m.), **Bossi (R.)** (opera *Volpino il calderaio*), **Braham**, **Castelnuovo-Tedesco** (ovt.), **Macfarren (W.)** (do.), **Maclean (A.)** (opera), **Pitt** (ovt.), **Purcell (D.)** (incid. m.), **Rheinberger** (ovt.), **Samara** (opera *Furia domata*), **Sly** (opera, Wolf-Ferrari), **Wagenaar (J.)** (ovt.), **Widerspänstigen Zähmung** (opera, Goetz).

Tempest, The: **Arensky** (incid. m.), **Arne** (do.), **Asplmayr** (play with m.), **Bliss** (incid. m.), **Boyce** (do.), **Chausson** (do.), **Corder** (ovt. *Prospero*), **Davy (J.)** (incid. m.), **Farwell** (masque *Caliban*), **Fibich** (opera & symph. poem), **Fisher** (incid. m.), **Frank** (opera *Sturm*), **Gatty** (opera), **Halévy** (do.), **Honegger** (incid. m.), **Humfrey** (do.), **Humperdinck** (do.), **Johnson (R. ii)** (songs), **Kunzen** (opera *Stormen*), **Lattuada** (opera), **Linley (3)** (incid. m.), **Locke** (do.), **Nystroem** (do.), **Paine** (symph. poem), **Pijper** (incid. m.), **Reichardt** (opera *Geisterinsel*), **Riotte** (opera), **Salmhofer** (incid. m.), **Smith (J. C.)** (opera), **Stucken** (incid. m.), **Sullivan** (do.), **Sutermeister** (opera *Zauberinsel*), **Taubert** (incid. m.), **Tempest** (do., Sibelius; operas, Fibich, Gatty, Purcell, &c.; symph. fantasy, Tchaikovsky), **Tempesta** (opera, Halévy), **Tiessen** (incid. m.), **Unger (H.)** (do.), **Vierling** (ovt.), **Weingartner** (incid. m.), **Wellesz** (suite *Prosperos Beschwörungen*), **Wessely (C. B.)** (incid, m.), **Zumsteeg** (opera *Geisterinsel*).

Timon of Athens: **Franck (J. W.)** (masque), **Grabu** (incid. m.), **Lunssens** (symph. poem), **Purcell** (do.), **Sullivan** (ovt.), **Trapp** (incid. m.).

Titus Andronicus: **Clarke (J.)** (incid. m.).

Troilus and Cressida: Song ' O heart, heavy heart ' set by Matthew King.

Twelfth Night: **Arne** (songs), **Bishop** (incid. m.), **Bowles** (do.), **Braunfels** (do.), **Castelnuovo-Tedesco** (ovt.), **Clay** (incid. m.), **Dale** (songs), **Filippi** (opera *Malvolio*), **Humperdinck** (incid. m.), **Koreshtchenko** (do.), **Mackenzie** (ovt.), **Paumgartner** (incid. m.), **Pierson (H. H.)** (ovt.), **Sandberger** (symph. poem *Viola*), **Stenhammar** (incid. m.), **Taubert** (opera *Cesario*), **Tausch** (incid. m.), **Vernon** (songs), **Viola** (Holenia & Smetana), **Weiss (K.)** (opera *Viola = The Twins*), **Widor** (incid. m.). ' Come away, death ' set for 3 female voices by Brahms; ' She never told her love ' set for 1 voice by Haydn.

Two Gentlemen of Verona: **Bishop** (incid. m.), **Vernon** (songs), **Who is Silvia?** (Schubert [also set by Leveridge, W. Linley, G. Macfarren, S. Webbe, &c.]).

Winter's Tale, A: **Barnett (J. F.)** (ovt.), **Boyce** (incid. m.), **Castelnuovo-Tedesco** (ovt.), **Ehlert** (do.), **Flotow** (incid. m.), **Hermione** (opera, Bruch), **Humperdinck** (incid. m.), **Larsson** (do.), **Macfarren (W.)** (ovt.), **Nešvera** (opera *Perdita*), **Sokolov** (incid. m.), **Suk** (ovt.), **Wilson (J.)** (song ' Lawn as white as driven snow '), **Wintermärchen** (opera, Goldmark).

See also **Jirák** (ovt. to a comedy), **Linley (3)** (ode on the witches), **Speaight** (fairy characters for stg. 4tet), **Zilcher** (incid. m. for var. plays).

Shakespeare, William (b. Croydon, 16. VI. 1849; d. London, 1. XI. 1931), Eng. ten. singer, teacher & comp. Studied under Molique in London and later at the R.A.M. with Sterndale Bennett, afterwards with Reinecke at the Leipzig Cons., where he prod. his Sym. Mendelssohn, on discovering his voice, sent him to study singing with Lamperti at Milan. In 1875 he returned to London and made his name as a concert singer, and in 1878 became prof. of singing at the R.A.M.

Works incl. Sym. in C min., 2 ovts. for orch.; Conc. & *Capriccio* for pf. & orch.; 2 stg. 4tets, pf. Trio; pf. pieces; songs, &c.

Shaliapin, Feodor Ivanovitch (b. Kazan, 11. II. 1873; d. Paris, 12. IV. 1938), Rus. bass-bar. singer. After a childhood spent in poverty, he joined a provincial opera co. and in 1892 studied singing at Tiflis. In 1894 he made his 1st appearance at St. Petersburg and he began to become famous when he was engaged for Mamontov's Private Opera at Moscow in 1896. He sang at Milan in 1901 & 1904 and was engaged for Paris and London by Diaghilev in 1913.

Shalm. *See* **Shawm.**

Shamus O'Brien, opera by Stanford (lib. by George H. Jessop, based on a poem by Joseph Sheridan Le Fanu), prod. London, Opera Comique, 2. III. 1896.

Shanewis (*The Robin Woman*), opera by Cadman (lib. by Nelle Richmond Eberhart), prod. N.Y., Metrop. Opera, 23. III. 1918.

Shanty (correctly but less familiarly Chanty, from ' chant ' or Fr. *chanter*, but always pronounced Shanty). A sailors' song with the quite definite character of a labour song, sung to lighten some hard manual task by aiding the rhythmic motions in the act of pumping, hauling ropes, hoisting sails and the like. It is only in recent years that these songs have been pub. and ed. in var. ways for home and concert perf. for the sake of the often high quality of their tunes; but they lose much of their character on being sung out of their proper surroundings.

Shapleigh, Bertram (b. Boston, 15. I. 1871; d. Washington, 4. VII. 1940), Amer. comp. Studied medicine, but was a pupil of Chadwick, MacDowell & others for m. He bought an estate in Eng., but returned to U.S.A. in 1915 after its destruction by fire.

Works incl. 2 operas, 5 1-act operas;

Mass in D maj. & other church m.; Cantata on the Song of Solomon, *The Raven* (Poe) & *Mirage* for chor. & orch.; works for unaccomp. chor.; 2 syms., 2 suites, Symph. Prelude, 3 Consolations, &c. for orch.; Poem for co. & orch.; inst. pieces; pf. works, &c.

Shaporin, Yuri Alexandrovitch (b. Glukhov, 8. XI. 1889), Rus. comp. Educ. at St. Petersburg, where he graduated in law at the Univ. In 1913 he entered the Cons. there, studying under Sokolov, Steinberg and N. Tcherepnin. On leaving he became interested in stage m. and founded the Great Dramatic Theatre with Gorky and Blok. In 1937 he moved to Moscow.

Works incl. opera *The Decembrists* (lib. by Alexey Tolstoy); incid. m. for Shakespeare's *King Lear* & *Comedy of Errors*, Schiller's *Robbers*, Molière's *Tartuffe*, Pushkin's *Boris Godunov*, Beaumarchais's *Marriage of Figaro*, Turgenev's *The Nest of Gentlefolk* (*Liza*), Labiche's *The Italian Straw Hat*, &c.; film m. incl. *General Suvarov*; symph. cantata *On the Kulikov Field*; Sym. in E min., suite *The Flea* for orch.; 2 suites for pf.; song cycles to words by Pushkin & Tiutchev, & other songs, &c.

Sharp. The sign ♯, which raises a note by a semitone. Also an adj. describing out-of-tune intonation on the S. side.

Sharp, Cecil (James) (b. London, 22. XI. 1859; d. London, 23. VI. 1924), Eng. folksong collector. Educ. at Uppingham and Clare Coll., Cambridge. After living in Austral. in 1889–92, he returned to London and in 1896 became principal of the Hampstead Cons. In 1899 he began to collect folksongs and dances, later he joined the Folksong Soc. and in 1911 founded the Eng. Folk-Dance Soc. During the 1914–8 war he visited the U.S.A. to collect songs in the Appalachian mountains, where many Eng. songs were still preserved in the primitive form by descendants of the 17th-cent. emigrants.

Sharp Mixture. An org. Mixture stop sounding the higher harmonics with the fundamental notes.

Shaw, Geoffrey (Turton) (b. London, 14. XI. 1879; d. London, 14. IV. 1943), Eng. church musn. & educst. He was a choir-boy at St. Paul's cath. in London and later studied with Stanford and Chas. Wood at Cambridge. After some years as orgst. in London, he became Staff Inspector of M. to the Board of Educ., and he did much adjudicating at mus. festivals.

Shaw, George Bernard (b. Dublin, 26 VII. 1856), Ir. critic, dramatist, novelist & polit. author. Settled in London early in his career and wrote mus. criticism for the *Star* and the *World*, 1890–4. *See also* **Auric** (*Caesar and Cleopatra*), **Bliss** (do.), **Chocolate Soldier** (Straus), **Lilien** (*Grosse Katharina*), **Prokofiev** (*Egyptian Nights* [*Caesar and C.*]).

Shaw, Martin (Fallas) (b. London, 9. III. 1876), Eng. orgst. & comp., brother of Geoffrey S. Studied at the R.C.M. in London, was orgst. at several London churches, founded the Purcell Operatic Soc. in 1900, ed. var. voc. pubs., incl. the hymn-book *Songs of Praise* with Vaughan Williams, and in 1935 became mus. dir. to the diocese of Chelmsford.

Works incl. opera *The Thorn of Avalon*, ballad operas *Mr. Pepys* & *Waterloo Leave* (Clifford Bax), operetta *Philomel*; pageant *Judgment at Chelmsford*; Lenten orat. *The Redeemer*, chor. works *The Seaport* & *Easter* (Masefield), *Sursum corda* (Binyon), *The Rock* (T. S. Eliot), 2 motets for double chor.; *The Ungentle Guest* for bar., stg. 4tet & hp., *Water Folk* for bar., stg. 4tet & pf.; So. for fl. & pf.; *c.* 100 songs, part-songs, incl. *Budmouth Dears* (Hardy), &c.

Shaw (*née* Postans), Mary (called Mrs. Alfred Shaw) (b. Lee, Kent, 1814; d. Hadleigh Hall, Suffolk, 9. IX. 1876), Eng. con. singer. Student at the R.A.M. in London and then pupil of G. Smart. She made her 1st appearance in 1834 and the following year married the painter Alfred S. In 1838 she sang at the Gewandhaus, Leipzig, under Mendelssohn, and the next year she appeared at the Scala, Milan.

Shawm (or Shalm). A primitive woodwind inst., the forerunner of the ob., with a double-reed mouthpiece and a wide bell. The largest types had bent tubes to their mouthpieces and thus approximated more to the bn.

Shcherbatchev. *See* **Shtcherbatchev.**

She Stoops to Conquer, opera by Macfarren (lib. by Edward Fitzball, based on Goldsmith's comedy), prod. London, Covent Garden Theatre, 11. II. 1864.

Shebalin, Vissarion Yakovlevitch (b. Omsk, 11. VI. 1902), Rus. comp. Son of a teacher; received his 1st mus. training at the Omsk School of M., entered the Moscow Cons. as a pupil of Miaskovsky in 1923 and stayed there as a prof. in 1928, as well as teaching at the Gnessin School of M.

Works incl. comic opera *The Embassy Bridegroom*; incid. m. for Schiller's *Robbers* and *Mary Stuart*,

Pushkin's *Mozart and Salieri* & *The Stone Guest* (Don Juan), Lermontov's *Masquerade*, Scribe's *A Glass of Water*, &c.; film m.; symph. cantata *Lenin* for solo voices, chor. & orch.; 5 syms., 2 suites and 2 ovts. for orch.; v. Conc., concertinos for v. & stgs. & for hn. & small orch.; 6 stg. 4tets, stg. Trio; Sonatina for v. & va., Suite for solo v.; 2 pf. sos. & 3 sonatinas; songs (Pushkin, Heine, &c.), popular chors. and war songs, &c.

Shedlock, John S(outh). (b. Reading, 29. IX. 1843; d. London, 9. I. 1919), Eng. mus. scholar & critic. Studied at London Univ., with Lalo in Paris and elsewhere abroad. He settled in London and taught, and in 1879 he became m. critic to the *Academy* and in 1901 to the *Athenaeum.* He wrote works on Beethoven's sketch-books and pf. sos. and another on *The Pianoforte Sonata.*

Sheffield, John. *See* **Mulgrave, Earl of.**

Sheffield Musical Festival. Founded in 1895, cond. by Henry Coward, held triennially from 1896–1911, but interrupted by the 1st world war in 1914; revived in 1933, but again stopped by the 1939–45 war.

Sheherazade (Rimsky-Korsakov). *See* **Shahrazad.**

Shéhérazade, song-cycle with orch. by Ravel (poems by Tristan Klingsor), comp. 1903 on the basis of an unpub. ovt. of the same name of 1898. There are 3 songs: *Asie, La Flûte enchantée* & *L'Indifférent.*

Shekhter, Boris Semionovitch (b. Odessa, 20. I. 1900), Rus. comp. Pupil of Miaskovsky at the Moscow Cons. Later he made a close study of Turcomanian folk m., and based some of his works on it.

Works incl. operas *The Year 1905* (with Davidenko) & *The Son of the People*; suite *Turkmenia* for orch., symph. Dithyramb for the celebrations of the 20th anniv. of the Rus. Revol.; pf. Conc.; song cycles, &c.

Shelley, Percy Bysshe (1792–1822), Eng. poet. *See* **Barber** (scene for orch.), **Chadwick** (*Adonais*), **Coke** (*Cenci*), **Davis (J. D.)** (do.), **Dieren (van)** (do. & songs), **Gatty** (odes), **Gnessin** (symph. fragment), **Miaskovsky** (*Alastor*), **Prometheus Unbound** (H. Parry), **Ronald** (*Adonais*), **Salaman** ('I arise from dreams'), **Tiersot** (*Hellas*), **White (M. V.)** (songs).

Shenshin, Alexander Alexeievitch (b. Moscow, 18. XI. 1890), Rus. comp. Studied philology in Moscow and became a teacher of hist. and Lat. Only then did he begin to study m. with Gretchaninov and Glière, and in 1912 he pub. his 1st work.

Works incl. opera *O'Tao* & other works for the stage; song cycles *From Japanese Anthologies* & other songs, &c.

Shepherd, Arthur (b. Paris, Idaho, 19. II. 1880), Amer. cond. & comp. Studied at the New. Eng. Cons. at Boston, where after a period of teaching at Salt Lake City he was prof. in 1908–20, when he became cond. of the Cleveland Sym. Orch. In 1938 he joined the staff of the Western Reserve Univ.

Works incl. sym. *Horizons* & *Choreographic Suite* for orch.; Fantasy for pf. & orch.; 2 stg. 4tets; *Triptych* (from Tagore's *Gitanjali*) for voice & stg. 4tet; v. & pf. So.; 2 pf. sos. & pieces; songs, &c.

Shepherd, John (b. ? London, ?; d. ?, ? 1563), Eng. comp. Learnt m. as a choir-boy at St. Paul's cath. in London under Thomas Mulliner. In 1542 he became orgst. & choirmaster at Magdalen Coll., Oxford, and later was in Queen Mary's Chapel Royal.

Works incl. masses *The Western Wynde, The French Masse, Be not afraide* & *Playn Song Mass for a Mene*, motets, 2 Te Deums, 2 magnificats, anthems, &c.

Shepherd's Pipe. A rustic wind inst. akin to the ob., the Fr. Musette, played with a double reed, like the chanter of a bagpipe, but usually used separately.

Shepherds of the Delectable Mountains, The, opera by Vaughan Williams (lib. by comp., based on Bunyan's *Pilgrim's Progress*), prod. London, R.C.M., 11. VII. 1922.

Sheppard or **Shepperd** } *See* **Shepherd, John.**

Shera, F(rank). H(enry). (b. Sheffield, 4. V. 1882), Eng. mus. scholar. Studied at the R.C.M. in London and after taking var. degrees was dir. of m. at Malvern Coll. in 1916–28, when he became prof. of m. at Sheffield Univ. He has pub. studies of Debussy and Ravel, Elgar's inst. works and a book on *Mus. Groundwork.*

Sheridan, Richard Brinsley (1751–1816), Eng. dramatist. *See* **Barber** (*School for Scandal*), **Critic** (Stanford), **Duenna** (Linley), **Dussek** (*Pizarro*), **Giordani (T.)** (*Critic*), **Kabalevsky** (*School for S.*), **Kelly** (*Pizarro*), **Klenau** (*School for S.*), **Linley (1 & 3)** (*Duenna*), **Linley (1)** (*School for S.* & *Monody on the Death of Garrick*), **Prokofiev** (*Betrothed in a Monastery*).

Sherrington, Helen. *See* **Lemmens-Sherrington.**

Sheryngham, ? (b. ?; d. ?), Eng. 15th–16th-cent. comp.

Works incl. 6 carols for 4 voices 2-part madrigal 'My wofull hart,' &c,

Shield, William (b. Whickham, Durham, 5. III. 1748; d. London, 25. I. 1829), Eng. vst. & comp. Pupil of his father, a singing-master, who d. when he was 9. Having lost his mother as well, he was apprenticed to a shipbuilder at South Shields, but allowed to study with Avison at Newcastle-on-Tyne. Later he became leading vst. at the subscription concerts there and then removed to Scarborough as leader of the theatre orch. In 1772 he went to London with an engagement from Giardini as 2nd v. in the Opera orch., and in 1773–91 he was principal va. there. He was also comp. to Covent Garden Theatre in 1778–91, when he met Haydn and visited Fr. and It. He resumed his Covent Garden post in 1792–7. In 1817 he was app. Master of the King's M.

Works incl. operas & other stage pieces *The Flitch of Bacon*, *Rosina*, *The Shamrock*, *Robin Hood*, *Richard Cœur de Lion*, *The Highland Reel*, *Marian*, *Oscar and Malvina* (with Reeve), *The Travellers in Switzerland*, *Netley Abbey*, *The Italian Villagers* & many others; anthems; trios for 2 vs. & bass, v. duets; canzonets, rounds, glees, songs, &c.

Shift. The change from one position to another in stg. and tromb. playing, in the former case by moving the left hand to a different position on the fingerboard, in the latter by lengthening or shortening the slide to alter the length of the tube.

Shifting Pedal. *See* **Damping Pedal.**

Shimmy. An Amer. ballroom dance that became pop. after the 1914–8 war and was accomp. by jazz m.; a fast mvt. of the Foxtrot type.

Shirinsky, Vassily Petrovitch (b. Ekaterinodar, 4. I. 1901), Rus. vst. & comp. Studied at the Moscow Cons. and became a member of that institution's stg. 4tet.

Works incl. Sym. & suite for orch.; 3 stg. 4tets, pf. 5tet; v. & pf. So., va. & pf. So.; So. & pieces for pf.; songs, &c.

Shirley, James (1596–1666), Eng. dramatist. *See* **Coleman (E.)** (*Ajax and Achilles*), **Cupid and Death** (Locke & C. Gibbons), **Parry (H.)** (*Glories of our Blood and State*), **Triumphs of Peace** (H. & W. Lawes & Ive).

Shofar. An ancient Jewish wind inst. made of a ram's horn, still used in the synagogue.

Sholokhov, Mikhail Alexandrovitch (b. 1905), Rus. novelist. *See* **Dzerzhinsky** (*Ploughing the Fallows*, also called *Virgin Soil Upturned*), **Quiet Don** (Dzerzhinsky).

Shore. Eng. family of musns.:

1. Matthew S. (b. ?; d. London, 1700), tptr. In the service of the court of James II and William and Mary in the post of Sergeant Trumpeter.

2. William S. (b. London, *c.* 1665; d. London, XII. 1707), tptr., son of prec. Succeeded his father in his post.

3. Catherine S. (b. London, *c.* 1668; d. London, *c.* 1730), singer & hpchdst., sister of prec. Pupil of Purcell; married Colley Cibber in 1693.

4. John S. (b. London, *c.* 1670; d. London, 20. XI. 1752), tptr. & lutenist, brother of prec. Succeeded in his brother's post in 1707. He invented the Tuning-fork in 1711.

Short Octave. On old keyboard insts. the notes governed by the extreme bottom keys were sometimes not tuned to the ordinary scale, but to a selection of lower notes more likely to be frequently required. The bottom octave so tuned was called the S. O.

Short Score. *See* **Score.**

Shostakovitch, Dmitri (b. St. Petersburg, 25. IX. 1906), Rus. comp. Entered the Cons. there in 1919 and studied with Nikolaiev, Steinberg and Glazunov. He left in 1925, having already written a great many works. The 1st Sym., which dates from that year, was prod. in 1926. He quickly made his mark, but came into conflict with Soviet authority in 1930, when his opera, *The Nose*, based on a story by Gogol, was denounced as bourgeois and decadent. The next, *A Lady Macbeth of Mtsensk*, prod. in 1934, was even more violently attacked in 1935 and had to be withdrawn. Thereafter, however, he suited his manner to the gvt.'s requirements, which in turn became somewhat modified, and established himself as the leading comp. of the day, gaining the Stalin Prize with his pf. 5tet in 1941.

Works incl. operas *The Nose* & *A Lady Macbeth of Mtsensk*; ballets *The Golden Age*, *The Bolt*, *The Limpid Stream* & *The Golden Key*; incid. m. to several plays incl. Shakespeare's *Hamlet*, *King Lear* & *Othello*, Piotrovsky's *Rule, Britannia* and an adapt. from Balzac's *Human Comedy*; m. to *c.* 14 films; 9 syms. (No. 7 *Leningrad Sym.*); Conc. for pf., tpt. & orch.; 2 pieces for stg. 8tet, 2 stg. 4tets, pf. 5tet; co. & pf. So.; 2 sos., 24 Preludes & many pieces for pf.; songs incl. cycle to Japanese poems, 4 poems by Pushkin, &c.

Shtcherbatchev, Andrey Vladimirovitch (b. Gvt. of Poltava, 29. I. 1869), Rus. comp. Studied under Blumenfeld, Liadov and Rimsky-Korsakov at the St. Petersburg Cons.

Works incl. March for orch.; pf. So. and pieces; songs, &c.

Shtcherbatchev, Nikolai Vladimirovitch (b. St. Petersburg, 24. VIII. 1853), Rus. pfst. & comp., (?) brother of prec. Spent some of his youth in Rome, but on returning to Rus. studied at the St. Petersburg Cons. and joined the Balakirev circle. Some of his orch. & chor. comps. remained unfinished.

Works incl. Serenade & 2 Idylls for orch.; 25 op. nos. of pf. pieces; songs to words to Alexey Tolstoy and Heine, &c.

Shtcherbatchev, Vladimir Vassilievitch (b. Warsaw, 24. I. 1889), Rus. comp. Studied with Steinberg, Liadov and Wihtol and the St. Petersburg Cons. and later became prof. at the Moscow Cons.

Works incl. opera *Anna Kolossova*; film m. *The Tempest*; 4 syms. (No. 4 chor.), suite & other orch. works; Nonet for voice and insts. & other chamber m.; 2 pf. sos. & other pf. works, &c.

Shudi, Burkat (Burkhardt Tschudi) (b. Schwanden, Glarus, 13. III. 1702; d. London, 19. VIII. 1773), Swi. (anglicized) hpchd. maker. He settled in London as a cabinet maker in 1718, joined the hpchd. maker Tabel and set up on his own account in the 1730s.

Si. The old name for the note B (*see* **Solmization**), still used in Lat. countries, and in Tonic Sol-fa the leading note in any key, represented by the symbol t, pronounced Te.

Si j'étais roi (*If I were King*), opera by Adam (lib. by Adolphe Philippe d'Ennery & Jules Brésil), prod. Paris, Théâtre Lyrique, 4. IX. 1852.

Sibelius, Jean (Johan Julian Christian) (b. Tavastehus, 8. XII. 1865), Fin. comp. Son of a surgeon. Having been given a classical educ., he was intended for the law, entering Helsingfors Univ. But he learned pf. and v. as a child and tried comp. long before he had any theoret. instruction. While studying law he managed to take a special course under Wegelius at the Cons. and in 1885 went there altogether, giving up the Univ. He left in 1889 and had a stg. 4tet and a suite for stg. orch. perf. in public. With a gvt. grant he went to study ctpt. with A. Becker in Berlin and later orch. with Fuchs in Vienna, where he also consulted Goldmark. When he returned home he became a passionate nationalist, studying the *Kalevala* and other Fin. literature for subjects for his works, the 1st being *Kullervo*, prod. at Helsingfors on 28. IV. 1892, the year in which he married Aino Järnefelt, sister of the comp. of that name, and was asked by Kajanus to write an orch. work for perf. at the Cons., a request to which he responded with *A Saga*. His only opera, *The Maiden in the Tower*, had a single perf. in 1896, but like *Kullervo* remained unpub. An annual grant was voted to S. by the gvt. in 1897 and increased in 1926, and he was thus enabled to devote himself entirely to comp. without having to fill any official or administrative post. He gradually made his way abroad, but not in every country. Much of his work was pub. in Ger., but not widely perf. there; in Eng. he became much better known after the perf. of the 4th Sym. at the Birmingham Festival in 1912, and in Amer. after his visit in 1914, when Yale Univ. conferred a doctor's degree on him. During the Rus. Revol. after the 1914–8 war there was much unrest in Fin., and S.'s country home at Järvenpää was invaded; but he spent most of his life there quietly, devoted wholly to comp.

Works incl. opera, *The Maiden in the Tower* (unpub.); incid. m. to Adolf Paul's *King Christian*, Arvid Järnefelt's *Kuolema* (incl. *Valse triste*), Maeterlinck's *Pelléas et Mélisande*, Hjalmar Procopé's *Belshazzar's Feast*, Strindberg's *Svanevhit*, Paul Knudsen's *Scaramouche*, Hofmannsthal's version of *Everyman*, Shakespeare's *Tempest*; 7 syms., *Kullervo*, with solo voices & chor. (unpub.), symph. poem *A Saga*, *Karelia* ovt. & suite, *Rakastava* for stgs. & timp., *Spring Song*, 4 Legends (2 unpub. & *The Swan of Tuonela* & *Lemminkainen's Homefaring*), 2 suites of *Scènes historiques*, tone-poem *Finlandia*, 2 pieces *The Dryads* & *Dance Intermezzo*, symph. fantasy *Pohjola's Daughter*, dance intermezzo *Pan and Echo*, tone-poem *Night-Ride and Sunrise*, funeral march *In Memoriam*, tone-poems *The Bard* & *Luonnotar*, symph. poems *The Oceanides* & *Tapiola*, a number of smaller orch. pieces; v. Conc.; stg. 4tet *Voces intimae*; Sonatina & many smaller pieces for v. & pf.; *Malinconia* & 2 *Serious Pieces* for co. & pf.; 18 op. nos. of pf. works incl. So. in F maj., *Pensées lyriques*, *Kyllikki*, 3 sonatinas; 2 org. pieces; chor. works with orch. (with or without solo voices): *Impromptu* (fem. chor.), *The Origin of Fire*, *The Ferryman's Bride*, *The Captive Queen*; a number of part-songs; 85 songs; Rydberg's *Skogsraet* & Runeberg's *Nights of Jealousy* for recitation & inst. accomp.; a large number of misc. works, many unpub., &c.

Siboni, Erik (Anton Valdemar) (b. Copenhagen, 26. VIII. 1828; d. Copenhagen, 22. II. 1892), Dan. pfst., orgst. & comp. Studied at Copenhagen, J. P. E. Hartmann being among his masters, and with Moscheles and Hauptmann at Leipzig, but he fought on the Dan. side in the war of Slesvig-Holstein in 1848. In 1851–3 he continued his studies with Sechter in Vienna. After his return to Copenhagen he settled as a m. teacher, among his pupils being Princess Alexandra. In 1864–83 he was prof. of the Royal Acad. of M. at Sorø, but retired to Copenhagen.

Works incl. operas *Loreley* & *Carl den Andens Flugt*; Psalm cxi, *Stabat Mater*, cantatas *The Battle of Murten* & *The Assault of Copenhagen* for solo voices, chor. & orch.; 2 syms. & other orch. works; pf. Conc.; stg. 4tets, pf. 4tet, pf. Trio; v. & pf. and co., & pf. sos.; Duet for 2 pfs.; pf. pieces; songs, &c.

Siboni, Giuseppe (b. Forli, 27. I. 1780; d. Copenhagen, 29. III. 1839), It. ten. singer, father of prec. He made his 1st appearance at Florence in 1797, and having appeared elsewhere in It., went to Prague, London, Vienna and St. Petersburg, settling at Copenhagen in 1819, where he became dir. of the Royal Opera and the Cons.

Siccardi, Honorio (b. Buenos Aires, 13. IX. 1897), Argentine comp. Studied at Buenos Aires and in It. with Malipiero. After his return home he took part in the foundation of the Grupo Renovación in 1933.

Works incl. Symph. Suite for orch., Ballet Suite for wind & perc.; 3 cantatas on Aeschylus's *Prometheus*; pf. pieces; songs, &c.

Sicilian Vespers (Verdi). *See* **Vespri siciliani.**

Siciliana or **Siciliano** (It.). A piece or song in dotted 6–8 rhythm derived from a Sicilian dance. It is rather slow, and indeed may form the slow mvt. of so. or suite. Arias in S. rhythm were common in the 18th cent.

Sicilienne (Fr.) = Siciliana, Siciliano.

Side Drum. The military drum, which is the smallest drum used in the orch., covered with a skin at either end and having a snare of catgut string stretched over the lower one, to produce a rattling sound when the upper one is struck by a pair of hard wooden drumsticks. Single strokes on the S. D. are ineffective: it is usually made to prod. small patterns of repeated notes or more or less prolonged rolls. Its tone is bright and hard, without definite pitch. It can be muted by relaxing the tension of the snare.

Sidney, Philip (1554–86), Eng. poet. *See* **Tessier (C.)** (*Astrophel and Stella*).

Siefert, Paul (b. Danzig, 1586; d. Danzig, 6. V. 1666), Ger. orgst. & comp. Pupil of Sweelinck at Amsterdam. After serving in the royal chapel of Sigismund III at Warsaw, he became orgst. at St. Mary's church, Danzig, *c.* 1620.

Works incl. Te Deum, psalms for 4–8 voices & other church m.; org. pieces, &c.

Siège de Corinthe (Rossini). *See* **Maometto II.**

Siege of Belgrade, The, opera by Storace (lib. by James Cobb), prod. London, Drury Lane Theatre, 1. I. 1791.

Siege of Rhodes, The, opera by Locke, H. Lawes, H. Cooke, Coleman and Hudson (lib. by William Davenant), prod. London, Rutland House, IX. 1656. The 1st Eng. opera.

Siege of Rochelle, The, opera by Balfe (lib. by Edward Fitzball, based on the Comtesse de Genlis's novel), prod. London, Drury Lane Theatre, 29. X. 1835.

Siegel, Rudolf (b. Berlin, 12. IV. 1878), Ger. cond. & comp. Pupil of Humperdinck and of Thuille at Munich. He cond. at Berlin, 1912–4, Königsberg, 1914–7 and Crefeld, 1919–30.

Works incl. opera *Herr Dandolo*; *Heroische Tondichtung* & other works for orch.; chors.; *Deutsche Volkslieder* & other songs, &c.

Siegfried (Wagner). *See* **Ring des Nibelungen.**

Siegfried Idyll, a symph. piece for small orch. by Wagner, comp. at Triebschen on the Lake of Lucerne in XI. 1870 and perf. on Cosima W.'s birthday, 25. XII, on the staircase of the villa. It was therefore at first entitled *Triebschener Idyll* and called ' Treppenmusik ' in the family circle. The thematic material is taken from *Siegfried*, except the Ger. cradle song ' Schlaf, Kindlein, schlaf,' but some of it, even though incl. in *Siegfried*, dates back to a stg. 4tet of 1864.

Siegl, Otto (b. Graz, 6. X. 1896), Aus. vst., cond. & comp. Studied v. with E. Kornauth and comp. with Mojsisovics in Vienna. Joined the Vienna Sym. Orch. as a vst., worked at the Graz Opera and then went to Ger., becoming mus. dir. at Paderborn, at the same time cond. and teaching at

Bielefeld and Essen. In 1933 he became comp. prof. at the Cologne Cons.

Works incl. fairy opera *Der Wassermann*; m. for 2 puppet plays; orats. *Das Grosse Halleluja* (Claudius), *Eines Menschen Lied*, *Klingendes Jahr*, *Trostkantate*, *Mutter Deutschland*; *Missa Mysterium Magnum*; *Verliebte alte Reime* for chor.; Sinfonietta, *Lyrische Tanzmusik*, *Festliche Ouvertüre*, *Pastoralouvertüre*, *Concerto grosso antico*, *Galante Abendmusik*, *Festmusik und Trauermusik* for orch.; pf. Conc., v. Conc., Conc. for stg. 4tet & stg. orch.; chamber m.; songs, &c.

Sienkiewicz, Henryk (1846–1916), Pol. novelist. *See* **Quo vadis?** (Nouguès).

Sierra, Gregorio Martínez (b. 1882), Spa. dramatist. *See* **Turina** (*Margot*, *Jardin de oriente* & *Navidad*).

Siface (**Giovanni Francesco Grossi**) (b. La Chiesina nr. Pescia, 12. II. 1653; d. Uzzanese nr. Ferrara, 29. V. 1697), It. male sop. singer. Became singer at the Papal Chapel in Rome, 1675 and went to Eng. about 1679. Sang at the court of James II, but soon returned to It. Purcell wrote a hpchd. piece, *Sefauchi's Farewell*, on his departure. He was murdered on a journey.

Siface (*Syphax*), opera by Feo (lib. by Metastasio), prod. Naples, Teatro San Bartolommeo, 13. V. 1723.

Opera by Porpora (lib. do.), prod. Milan, Teatro Regio Ducal, 26. XII. 1725.

Sigh. *See* **Ornaments.**

Signature. *See* **Key Signature**; **Time Signature.**

Signature Tune. A favourite song or dance tune of a popular kind by which perfs., esp. dance bands & light orchs., identify themselves, partic. when they broadcast and are invisible to their audiences.

Signor Bruschino, Il, ossia Il figlio per azzardo (*Mr. B., or The Son by Accident*), opera by Rossini (lib. by Giuseppe Maria Foppa), prod. Venice, Teatro San Moisè, I. 1813.

Signor di Pourceaugnac, Il, opera by Franchetti (lib. by Ferdinando Fontana, based on Molière's comedy, *Monsieur de P*)., prod. Milan, Teatro alla Scala, 10. IV. 1897.

Sigtenhorst Meyer, Bernhard van den (b. Amsterdam, 17. VI. 1888), Dutch pfst. & comp. Studied with Zweers, D. de Lange & others and later in Paris, afterwards travelling to Java and the Far East. He returned to Amsterdam.

Works incl. incid. m. to Tagore's play *The King's Letter*; orat. *The Temptation of Buddha*, *Stabat Mater*; stg. 4tet; v. & pf. So.; So. and c. 12 other op. nos. of pf. pieces; several op. nos. of songs, &c.

Sigurd, opera by Reyer (lib. by Camille du Locle & Alfred Blau, based on the Nibelung Saga), prod. Brussels, Théâtre de la Monnaie, 7. I. 1884.

Sikorski, Kazimierz (b. Zürich, 28. VI. du Locle & Alfred Blau, based on the Nibelung Saga), prod. Brussels, prof. at the Poznan Cons., and in 1927 at the Warsaw Cons. In 1936 he was one of the founders of the Soc. for the Pub. of Pol. M.

Works incl. Psalm vii for chor. & orch.; 2 syms. & symph. poem for orch.; 3 stg. 4tets, stg. 6tet; songs; partsongs, &c.

Silas, Édouard (b. Amsterdam, 22. VIII. 1827; d. London, 8. II. 1909), Dutch pfst., orgst. & comp. Studied at Amsterdam, made his 1st appearance there at the age of 10, took further lessons with Lacombe and Kalkbrenner in Paris, where he entered the Cons. to study org. with Benoist and comp. with Halévy. In 1850 he settled in London as church orgst., concert pfst. & teacher.

Works incl. opera *Nitocris*; orat. *Joash*; Mass for voices & org.; Sym. in A maj. & *Mythological Pieces* for orch.; Conc. in D min., Fantasy & Elegy for pf. & orch.; org. pieces; Suite in A min. & pieces for pf., &c.

Silbermann. Ger. family of org. builders & hpchd. makers:

1. Andreas S. (b. Kleinbobritzsch nr. Frauenstein, Saxony, 16. V. 1678; d. Strasburg, 16. III. 1734), son of the carpenter Michael S. He began to travel in 1700, learnt org. building and in 1703 settled at Strasburg, where he built the cath. org. in 1714–6.

2. Gottfried S. (b. Kleinbobritzsch, 14. I. 1683; d. Dresden, 4. VIII. 1753), brother of prec. Apprenticed to a bookbinder, he joined his brother at Strasburg, but returned home in 1707, building the org. at Frauenstein, then lived at Freiberg from 1709, building the cath. org. there in 1714, and d. while building the org. at the Dresden court. He also made clavichds. & hpchds. and was the 1st in Ger. to make a pf. after the model of Cristofori.

3. Johann Andreas S. (b. Strasburg, 26. VI. 1712; d. Strasburg, 11. II. 1783), son of 1. He built 54 orgs.

4. Johann Daniel S. (b. Strasburg, 31. III. 1717; d. Leipzig, 6. V. 1766), brother of prec. Worked with his uncle, 2, whose org. at Dresden he finished.

5. Johann Heinrich S. (b. Strasburg, 24. IX. 1727; d. Strasburg, 15. I. 1799), brother of prec. He made hpchds. and pfs., some with pedal boards.

6. Johann Friedrich S. (b. Strasburg, 21. VI. 1762; d. Strasburg, 8. III. 1817), son of prec. He was also an orgst. (at St. Thomas's, Strasburg) and a comp. of songs, &c.

Silcher, Friedrich (b. Schnait nr. Schorndorf, Württemberg, 27. VI. 1789; d. Tübingen, 26. VIII. 1860), Ger. cond. & comp. Pupil of his father and others. He became a schoolmaster, but in 1815 went to Stuttgart as cond. and in 1817 to the Univ. of Tübingen in the same capacity. Some of his songs have become what in Ger. are called folk-songs.

Works incl. 2 hymn-books (3 & 4 voices), collections of songs, some arr., some comp. by himself, incl. *Aennchen von Tharau, Loreley* (Heine), *Morgen muss ich fort, Zu Strassburg auf der Schanz*, &c.

Silent Woman (R. Strauss). *See* **Schweigsame Frau.**

Silk, Dorothy (b. Birmingham, 1884; d. Alvechurch, Worcs., 30. VII. 1942), Eng. sop. singer. Studied at Birmingham and in Vienna, giving her 1st recital in London in 1920. She specialized in Bach and earlier comps., but also studied modern works.

Silva, Andreas de (Silvanus or Sylvanus) (b. ?; d. ?), ? Flem. 15th–16th-cent. singer & comp. Sang in the Papal Chapel in Rome early in the 16th cent. and later was prob. in the service of the Duke of Mantua.

Works incl. masses, motets; madrigals, &c.

Silva Leite, Antonio da (b. Oporto, 23. V. 1759; d. Oporto, 10. I. 1833), Port. comp. Studied (?) with Girolamo Sartori, an It. musn. settled at Oporto, where he was chapel master at the cath. from 1814.

Works incl. It. operas *Le astuzie delle donne* & *I puntigli per equivoco*; *Tantum ergo* with orch.; sos. & studies for guitar, &c.

Silvana, opera by Weber (lib. by Franz Karl Hiemer, altered from Steinsberg's *Waldmädchen*), prod. Frankfort o/M., 16. IX. 1810. W.'s 2nd version of *Das Waldmädchen* of 1800.

Silvani, Giuseppe Antonio (b. Bologna, 21. I. 1672; d. Bologna, before 1727), It. comp. & m. pub. Chapel master at the church of San Stefano at Bologna, 1702–25. He inherited Marino S., his father's, m. pub. business.

Works incl. masses, motets, lamentations, *Stabat Mater*, litanies, sacred cantatas & other church m. for voices with stg. or org. accomp.

Simes, William. *See* **Simmes.**

Similar Motion. *See* **Motion.**

Simile (It. =like). An abbr. often used to indicate that certain passages are to be perf. in the same way as similar passages occurring before, to save repetitions of troublesome notation.

Simmes (or **Simes** or **Sims**), **William** (b. ?; d. ?), Eng. 16th–17th-cent. comp.

Works incl. anthems; fantasies for viols, &c.

Simon, Antoine (**Antony Yulievitch**) (b. Fr., 1851; d. ?), Fr. cond. & comp. Studied at the Paris Cons. and in 1871 settled at Moscow, where he became cond. of the Théâtre-Bouffe. In the 1890s he was app. pf. prof. at the Phil. M. School and superintendent of the orch. of the imp. theatres.

Works incl. operas *Rolla, The Song of Love Triumphant* (after Turgenev), *The Fishers* (after Hugo); mimed drama *Esmeralda* (after Hugo's *Notre-Dame*); ballets *The Stars & Living Flowers*; incid. m. for Shakespeare's *Merchant of Venice*; Mass; Suite, *Triumphal Ovt.* on Rus. themes, ovt.-fantasy on Malo-Rus. themes, symph. poems *The Midnight Review* & *La Pêcheresse* for orch.; concs. for pf. & for cl.; stg. 4tets, 2 pf. trios & other chamber m.; v. & pf. pieces; pieces for 1 & 2 pfs.; *c.* 80 songs, &c.

Simon Boccanegra, opera by Verdi (lib. by Francesco Maria Piave, based on a Spanish drama by Antonio García Gutiérrez), prod. Venice, Teatro La Fenice, 12. III. 1857; revised version, with the lib. altered by Boito, prod. Milan, Teatro alla Scala, 24. III. 1881.

Simon, Simon (b. Vaux-de-Cernay nr. Rambouillet, *c.* 1720; d. ? Versailles, after 1780), Fr. hpchdst. & comp. Pupil of Dauvergne. He was app. hpchd. master to the queen and the royal children at Versailles.

Works incl. 3 books of hpchd. pieces, pieces & sos. for hpchd. with v., &c.

Simonetti, Achille (b. Turin, 12. VI. 1859; d. London, 19. XI. 1928), It. vst. & comp. Pupil of Pedrotti for comp. and later of Sivori at Genoa for v. Having appeared as a concert artist, he went to Paris for further study with Dancla and Massenet. Later he settled in London as concert artist, teacher and member of the London Trio.

Works incl. 2 stg. 4tets; 2 v. & pf. sos., v. pieces, &c.

Simoutre, Nicolas Eugène (b. Mirecourt, 19. IV. 1839; d. Geneva, I. 1908), Fr. v. maker. After working with var. masters in Paris and Strasburg, he settled in business at Basle in 1859.

Simple Intervals. Any Intervals not larger than an 8ve, those exceeding that width being called Compound I. S. I. might be better called 'essential' I., those exceeding an 8ve differing from them only in width, not in character; e.g. a perfect 12th is essentially the same as a perfect 5th, &c.

Simple (or Duple) Time. Any mus. metre governed by a time signature prescribing 2 or 4 beats, i.e. having a multiple of 2 as its unit.

Simpson, Christopher (b. Yorkshire, ?; d. ? Scampton, Lincs. or London, 1669), Eng. va. da gamba player, theorist & comp. He joined the royalist army under the Duke of Newcastle in 1643 and endured much hardship, but later came under the patronage of Sir Robert Bolles, at whose residences at Scampton and in London he lived in comfort, teaching the children of the family and taking charge of the domestic m.-making. He wrote an instruction book for the v. da gamba, *The Division Violist.* He bought a house and farm at Pickering, Yorks., but d. (?) at one of Sir John Bolles's houses. He wrote another treatise, *The Principles of Practicle Musick* and annotations to Campion's *Art of Descant.*

Works incl. *Months and Seasons* for a treble and 2 bass viols, fancies and consorts for viols, Suite in 3 parts for viols, divisions (vars.) and pieces for va. da gamba, &c.

Simpson, Thomas (b. ?; d. ?), Eng. 16th–17th-cent. violist & comp. Settled in Ger. early in the 17th cent., was in the service of the Elector Palatine in 1610, in that of the Prince of Holstein-Schaumburg in 1617–21, and afterwards at the Dan. court in Copenhagen.

Works incl. pavans, galliards & other dances for viols.; songs with insts., &c.

Sims, William. *See* **Simmes.**

Sin' (It. abbr.). *See* **Sino.**

Sinclair, John (b. nr. Edinburgh, 9. XII. 1791; d. Margate, 23. IX. 1857), Sco. ten. singer. Studied at Aberdeen and 1st appeared in London in 1810. In 1819 he visited Paris, studied in It. and sang there with success until 1823.

Sinding, Christian (b. Kongsberg, 11. I. 1856; d. Oslo, XII. 1941), Norw. pfst. & comp. Studied at Leipzig, Berlin and Munich. He settled at Oslo as pfst. and comp.

Works incl. opera *The Holy Mountain*; 3 syms. & *Rondo infinito* for orch.; pf. Conc. in D♭ maj., 2 v. concs.; stg. 4tet, pf. 5tet, pf. Trio; sos. & Suite for v. & pf.; Vars. for 2 pfs.; Suite, studies and numerous pieces for pf.; songs, &c.

Sinfonia (Lat. & It.) = Symphony. In the 18th cent. the S. was simply an inst. piece in an opera or other voc. work, esp. the Overture; it is in fact out of the latter that the sym. developed.

Sinfonia concertante. A work in symph. form with 1 or more solo insts., but in no way different from a conc. Familiar exs. are Mozart's K. 364 for v., va. & orch. of 1779 and K. App. 9 for ob., cl., hn. & bn. with orch. of 1778.

Sinfonia domestica (R. Strauss). *See* **Symphonia domestica.**

Sinfonietta (It. = little sym.). A work in sym. form, but of smaller dimensions & usually lightly scored.

Singakademie (Ger. lit. singing-academy = voc. academy). The special name of certain chor. socs. in Ger. and Aus.

Singe-Spiel (Ger. = song-play or singing-play). A term for the earliest type of Ger. opera, as cultivated at Hamburg by Keiser, Mattheson, Handel & others, not to be confused with the following.

Singspiel (Ger. = song-play). Orig. the Ger. equivalent of the Ballad Opera, by which it was in fact directly influenced (esp. Coffey's *The Devil to Pay*). Popular songs were used as interpolations into the dialogue in the same way; later comps. took up the type and wrote m. specially for it, but it always retained spoken dialogue and continued to include simple songs, many of which became what the Gers. call folksongs.

Sinigaglia, Leone (b. Turin, 14. VIII. 1868), It. comp. Studied at the Turin Cons. and with Mandyczewski in Vienna. After his return home he settled down to comp. and folksong collecting.

Works incl. suite *Piemonte*, ovt. to Goldoni's *Le baruffe chiozzote*, *Danze piemontesi* for orch.; Conc., *Rapsodia piemontese* & Romance for v. & orch.; stg. 4tet in D maj., Concert Study & Vars. on a theme by Brahms for stg. 4tet; Vars. on Schubert's *Heidenröslein* for ob. & pf., 2 pieces for hn. & pf., pieces for v., co., &c.; settings of Piedmontese folksongs, &c.

Sinkapace. *See* **Cinquepace.**

Sino (It. = till, until, or abbr. *sin'* when followed by a vowel). A word used in such directions as that indicating a repeat *sin' al fine* (until the end) or *sin' al segno* . . . (to the sign . . .), &c.

Siqueira, José (b. Conceição, 24. VI. 1907), Braz. comp. Pupil of his father, a bandmaster, and studied at Rio de Janeiro. In 1940 he became dir. of the Braz. Orch. and cond. of broadcast concerts.

Works incl. Sym. in D min., 2 ovts., 3 symph. poems, 3 symph. preludes, Suite for orch., 5 pieces for stgs., *Frevo* for brass band; *Elegia* for co. & orch.; stg. 4tet, pf. Trio; v. & pf. So.; inst. pieces; pf. m.; songs, &c.

Sir John in Love, opera by Vaughan Williams (lib. selected by comp. from Shakespeare's *Merry Wives of Windsor*), prod. London, R.C.M., 21. III. 1929.

Sirmen (*née* **Lombardini**), **Maddalena** (b. Venice, ? 1735; d. ?), It. vst., singer & comp. Studied at the Cons. dei Mendicanti at Venice and v. with Tartini at Padua. In 1760 she began to tour in It. and at Bergamo she met Ludovico Sirmen, a vst. and cond. at the church of Santa Maria Maddalena there, and married him. They visited Paris in 1768 and in 1771 she 1st appeared in London, where she also played the hpchd. But she gave up the v. in 1772 and revisited London as a singer.

Works incl. 6 v. concs.; 6 stg. 4tets, 6 trios for 2 vs. & co.; 6 duets & 6 sos. for 2 vs., &c.

Siroe, rè di Persia (*Cyrus, King of Persia*), lib. by Metastasio.

Opera by Handel, prod. London, King's Theatre, Haymarket, 17. II. 1728.

Opera by Hasse, prod. Bologna, Teatro Malvezzi, 2. V. 1733.

Opera by Pérez, prod. Naples, Teatro San Carlo, 4. XI. 1740.

Opera by Vinci, prod. Venice, Teatro San Giovanni Crisostomo, I. 1726.

Sirola, Božidar (b. Žakanj, 20. XII. 1889), Yslv. comp. Studied at Zagreb and in Vienna, where he took a doctor's degree. Later he was app. dir. of the Mus. Acad. at Zagreb.

Works incl. operas *A Story from Stanac* & *The Wandering Scholar*; ballet *Shadows*; incid. m. to plays; orat.; symph. poem *Notturno*, Suite & 2 ovts. for orch.; 2 stg. 4tets, pf. 4tet, pf. Trio; songs, &c.

Sirvente (Prov.). A Provençal Troubadour song the words of which were in *terza rima*.

Sistrum. An ancient inst. prob. orig. in Egypt, played like a rattle. It had a metal frame fitted to a handle and metal bars or loops were loosely hung on the frame and made to strike against it by shaking the inst.

Sitt, Hans (b. Prague, 21. IX. 1850; d. Leipzig, 10. III. 1922), Cz.-Ger. vst., teacher and ed. Studied at the Prague Cons., became leader in more than one orch. and settled at Leipzig, where he joined Brodsky's 4tet as violist. App. prof. of v. at the Leipzig Cons. He has ed. much v. m.

Works incl. chamber m., v. studies & pieces, songs, &c.

Sitwell, Edith (b. 1887), Eng. poetess & essayist. *See* **Façade** (Walton), **Walton** (3 songs).

Sitwell, Osbert (b. 1892), Eng. poet, essayist & novelist, brother of prec. *See* **Belshazzar's Feast** (Walton), **Lutyens** (*Winter the Huntsman*).

Sitwell, Sacheverell (b. Scarborough, 1897), Eng. poet & essayist, brother of prec. Educ. at Eton and Balliol Coll., Oxford. Mentioned here as the author of biog. books on D. Scarlatti, Mozart, Liszt and Offenbach. *See also* **Triumph of Neptune** (Berners).

Sivori, (Ernesto) Camillo (b. Genoa, 25. X. 1815; d. Genoa, 19. II. 1894), It. vst. & comp. Pupil of Paganini, who wrote his works for 4tet with guitar for him and, going on tour, sent him to another master, Giacomo Costa, and later to Dellepiane, with whom he went on tour, making his 1st appearance at Turin in 1827. They went on to Fr. and London, but in 1829 S. returned to Genoa to study comp. with Giovanni Serra. He then travelled widely in Eur. and N. & S. Amer. until 1870.

Works incl. 2 concs., *Tarantelle napolitaine*, &c., for v. & orch.; Duet for v. & db. (with Bottesini); 2 *Duos concertants* for v. & pf.; 3 *Romances sans paroles*, *Andante spianato* & numerous other pieces and fantasies on operatic airs for v. & pf.; v. studies, &c.

Six-Four Chord. *See* **Sixth.**

Six, Les. A group of Fr. comps. who in their youth gathered together, under the leadership of Satie and Jean Cocteau, for the furtherance of their interests and to some extent those of modern m. in general. It was formed in Paris in 1917 and its active comp. members were Auric, Durey, Honegger, Milhaud, Poulenc and Tailleferre; the chief perfs. were the singer Jane Bathori and the pfst. Andrée Vaurabourg, the latter becoming Honegger's wife. The group gradually lost its solidarity during the 1920s.

Sixth. The interval between the 2 notes of which lie 6 degrees of a diatonic scale. Ss. can be maj., min. or augmented, in the last case being equal to min. 7ths on the pf., but written to look like 6ths, e.g. C♯–B being a min. 7th, but D♭–B an augm. 6th. Min. 6ths are inverted maj. 3rds (e.g. C–A♭), maj. 6ths inverted min. 3rds (e.g. C–A). The most common 'chord of the 6th' (maj. or min.), and so called, consists of a 3rd with a 4th above it; but scarcely less usual is the ' 6–4 chord,' which consists of a 4th with a 3rd above it. Chords of the augm. 6th are known in 3 forms, *see* **French Sixth, German Sixth, Italian Sixth.**

Sjögren, Emil (b. Stockholm, 16. VI. 1853; d. Stockholm, 1. III. 1918), Swe. comp. Studied at the Stockholm Cons. and later in Berlin, also came under the influence of Lange-Müller during a stay of 6 months at Meran. In 1891 he became orgst. at St. John's church, Stockholm, but devoted most of his time to teaching and comp.

Works incl. 3 v. & pf. sos.; org. works; 2 pf. sos., *Erotikon, Novellettes* & numerous other works for pf.; songs, &c.

Skelton, John (? 1460–1529), Eng. poet. *See* **Cornyshe, Five Tudor Portraits** (Vaughan Williams).

Skilton, Charles Sanford (b. Northampton, Mass., 16. VIII. 1868; d. Lawrence, Kans., 12. III. 1941), Amer. comp. Studied at Yale Univ. and in Ger. In 1903 he was app. Prof. of M. at Kansas Univ. and there made a study of Indian tribal tunes.

Works incl. operas *Kalopin, The Sun Bride, The Day of Gayomair*; incid. m. for Sophocles' *Electra* & Barrie's *Mary Rose*; orat. *The Guardian Angel* & cantatas; *Primeval Suite* & other suites & ovts. for orch.; *2 Indian Dances* for stg. 4tet; v. & pf. So.; org. & pf. works, &c.

Skinner, James Scott (b. Banchory-Ternan, 5. VIII. 1843; d. Aberdeen, 17. III. 1927), Sco. vst. & comp. He joined an orch. for orphaned children, studied with Charles Rougier at Manchester, then settled at Aberdeen as a dancing-master and wrote popular dance m., mainly based on Sco. reels, strathspeys and other nat. dances and airs.

Skjöldebrand, Anders Fredrik (1757–1834), Swe. dramatist. *See* **Vogler** (*Hermann von Unna*).

Skočná. A Cz. dance in quick 2–4 time in which 3-bar phrases are a feature. The 5th, 7th and 11th of Dvořák's *Slavonic Dances* for pf. duet are Ss.

Skolie (Ger. from Swe.). A drinking-song, the title given to 2 of Schubert's songs (words by Deinhardstein & Mathisson). The word is der. from the Scand. word used for a drinking-pledge, *skol* in Swe. and *skaal* in Dan. & Norw.

Skriabin, Alexander Nikolaievitch (b. Moscow, 6. I. 1872; d. Moscow, 27. IV. 1915), Rus. pfst. & comp. Giving up a military career, he studied pf. with Safonov and comp. with Taneiev at the Moscow Cons., where he became prof. of pf. in 1898 after touring successfully in western Eur. He gave up that post in 1904 to devote himself entirely to comp. and occasional appearances as pfst. He visited Eng. in 1913.

Works incl. 3 syms, *Rêverie & Poem of Ecstasy* for orch.; pf. Conc. in F♯ min., *Prometheus: a Poem of Fire* for orch., pf. & org. (and a projected colour org.); 10 pf. sos. & 58 op. nos. of other pf. works, incl. Preludes, Impromptus, Studies, Mazurkas, Nocturnes, *Tragic Poem, Satanic Poem, Vers la flamme*, Prelude & Nocturne for the left hand, &c.

Škroup, František Jan (b. Vosice nr. Pardubice, 3. VI. 1801; d. Rotterdam, 7. II. 1862), Boh. comp. Studied law, but was from 1827 2nd and in 1837–57 1st cond. at the Nat. Theatre in Prague; from 1860 cond. at the Opera of Rotterdam. Comp. the 1st Cz. opera and the nat. anthem.

Works incl. operas *Drátenik* (*The Tinker*), *The Marriage of Libuša, Oldřich and Božena, Drahomíra* & some other Cz. and Ger. operas; incid. m. to Tyl's *Fidlovačka*, &c.

Skuherský, František Zdenko (b. Opočno, 31. VII. 1830; d. Budějovice, 19. VIII. 1892), Boh. comp. & teacher. He gave up medical studies for m., which he studied under Kittl and Pitsch, the dirs. of the Prague Cons. and Org. School respectively. In 1854–65 he was cond. at Innsbruck, but returned to Prague as dir. of the Org. School in the latter year. He was also active as pfst. and as lecturer at the Cz. Univ., and he took part in the reform of church m. after studying it in Rome and Ratisbon. He wrote several theoret. treatises.

Works incl. operas *Samo, Vladimir: God's Chosen, Lora, Rector and General* & *The Love Ring*; symph. poem *May* & 3 fugues for orch.; stg. 4tet, pf. 5tet, pf. Trio, &c.

Skyscrapers, ballet by Carpenter (chgph. by Heinrich Kröller), prod. Monte Carlo, Rus. Ballet, 1925; 1st Amer. perf. N.Y., Metrop. Opera, 19. II. 1926.

Sleeping Princess, The, ballet by Tchaikovsky (chgph. by Marius Petipa), prod. St. Petersburg, Maryinsky Theatre, 15. I. 1890; new version, with add. orchns. by Stravinsky and adds. to the chgph. by Bronislava Nizhinska, London, Alhambra Theatre, 2. XI. 1921.

Slentando (It.) = Gradually decreasing in pace.

Slezak, Leo (b. Šumperk, 18. VIII. 1873; d. Vienna, IX. 1943), Morav. ten. singer. He studied engineering, but had his voice trained at the same time and in 1896 made his 1st stage appearance at Brno. **After engagements** at the court operas in Berlin and Vienna, and a visit to London in 1900, he made further studies with J. de Reszke in Paris in 1908.

Slide (*see* **Ornaments**). Also the device of passing from one note to another on stg. insts. by moving the finger along the stg. instead of lifting it to make way for another finger; also the movable part of the tube of the tromb. by which the positions, and therefore the notes, are altered, as well as mechanisms on other wind insts. by which the pitch can be adjusted by a change in the length of the tube.

Slide Trumpet. *See* **Tromba da tirarsi.**

Sliwinski, Josef (b. Warsaw, 15. XII. 1865; d. Warsaw, 4. III. 1930), Pol. pfst. Studied with Strobl at Warsaw, Leschetizky in Vienna and A. Rubinstein in St. Petersburg. Made his 1st public appearance in 1890 and 1st visited Eng. in 1892.

Slonimsky, Nicolas (orig. Nikolai) (b. St. Petersburg, 27. IV. 1897), Rus. mus. author & comp. Studied at the St. Petersburg Cons. and in 1923 settled in U.S.A., becoming a naturalized Amer. in 1931. He compiled a survey *M. since 1900.*

Works incl. *Fragment from Orestes* (Euripides) for orch. (in quarter-tones); *Suite in Black and White* for pf., &c.

Slovak Composers. *See* **Czech** (for **Czechoslovak**) **Composers.**

Slow Movement. The slowest of the mvts. in a mus. comp. in several parts, esp. a sym., so. or chamber work in so. form. It may, however, be slow only relatively to the other mvts.

Slur. An arching stroke in mus. notation drawn over a group of notes and indicating that they are to be played *legato*. It may also be used between single notes of the same pitch or pairs of such notes in chords to prevent their being struck a 2nd time; in that case, however, it is called Tie.

Sly (i.e. Christopher Sly), opera by Wolf-Ferrari (lib. by Giovacchino Forzano, based on the prologue of Shakespeare's *Taming of the Shrew*), prod. Milan, Teatro alla Scala, 29. XII. 1927.

Smareglia, Antonio (b. Pola, Istria, 5. V. 1854; d. Grado nr. Trieste, 15. IV. 1929), It. comp. He was sent to Vienna to study engineering, but on hearing works by the great masters there he left for Milan in 1872 and studied comp. under Faccio at the Cons. He prod. his 1st opera there in 1879, but he never had any real success, in spite of the good quality of his work, and in 1900 he went blind.

Works incl. operas *Preziosa, Bianca da Cervia, Rè Nala, Der Vasall von Szigeth, Cornelius Schutt, Nozze istriane, La Falena, Oceàna, L'Abisso*; symph. poem *Leonore*, songs, &c.

Smart, George (Thomas) (b. London, 10. V. 1776; d. London, 23. II. 1867), Eng. orgst., comp. & cond. He was sent by his father, George S., a m. pub., to become a choir-boy at the Chapel Royal under Ayrton, and later became a comp. pupil of Arnold. He became an orgst., teacher and cond., was one of the orig. members of the Phil. Soc. in 1813 and succeeded Charles Knyvett as orgst. of the Chapel Royal in 1822. In 1825 he went to Dresden with Charles Kemble to engage Weber to write *Oberon* for Covent Garden, and it was at his house that Weber stayed during the prod. in 1826 and d. in the night of 4–5. VI. S. was knighted in 1811, and became a favourite festival cond.

Works incl. anthems, chants & other church m.; canons & glees, &c.

Smart, Henry (Thomas) (b. London, 26. X. 1813; d. London, 6. VII. 1879); Eng. orgst. & comp., nephew of prec. Learnt m. from his father, the vst. Henry S. (1778–1823) and later under W. H. Kearns; but was largely self-taught. After an orgst.'s appt. at Blackburn in 1831–6 he returned to London and was successively orgst. at several churches until he became blind in 1864.

Works incl. operas *Berta, or The Gnome of the Hartzberg, Undine & The Surrender of Calais* (last 2 unfinished); cantatas *The Bride of Dunkerron, King René's Daughter* (after Herz), *The Fishermaidens & Jacob*; festival anthems *Sing to the Lord & Lord, thou hast been our refuge*; org. works; partsongs, &c.

Smert, Richard (b. ? Devonshire; d. ?), Eng. 15th–16th-cent. comp. Carols of his for 2 voices and 3-part chor., some written with John Truelove, are preserved.

Smetana, Bedřich (Frederick) (b. Litomyšl, Boh., 2. III. 1824; d. Prague, 12. V. 1884), Cz. comp. Son of a brewer. He played pf. and v. at a very early age and was soon able to play in the domestic stg. 4tet. He was educ. in Ger. and all his life, in spite of his mus. nationalism, spoke and wrote Cz. like a foreigner. He was sent to school 1st in Prague and then at Pilsen, and his father opposed a mus. career, but he was in the end allowed to study m. in Prague, though with a very small allowance; but in 1844 he obtained the post of m. master in Count Thun's family, which helped to support him till 1847. In 1848 he took part in the revol. against Aus., married the pfst. Katharina Kolař, estab. a school of m. for which Liszt supplied funds, and was recommended by the latter to the Leipzig pub. Kistner. In 1856 he went to Göteborg in Swe., where at first he taught but later became cond. of the new Phil. Soc. and gave pf. and chamber m. recitals. But he returned to Prague in 1859 because the northern climate did not suit his wife, who however d. at Dresden on the way back, 19. IV. He married Betty Ferdinandi in VII. 1860 and returned to Swe. in the autumn, but finally returned to Prague in the spring of 1861. After a long tour in Ger., Hol. and Swe. to collect funds, he settled in the Cz. capital in 1863 and opened another school of m., this time with distinctly nat. tendencies, and became cond. of the chor. soc. Hlahol. His work too was now becoming thoroughly Cz. in character, and he began to prod. Cz. operas in the nat. theatre estab. in 1864, of which he became cond. in IX. 1866. He overworked and suffered much from headaches, and in 1874 he suddenly became totally deaf, but still comp. operas as well as the stg. 4tet *From my Life* and the cycle of symph. poems *My Country*. In 1883 he became insane and in IV. 1884 he had to be taken to an asylum, where he d.

Works incl. operas *The Brandenburgers in Bohemia*, *The Bartered Bride*, *Dalibor*, *Libuše*, *Two Widows*, *The Kiss*, *The Secret*, *The Devil's Wall*, *Viola* (based on Shakespeare's *Twelfth Night*, unfinished); 3 concert ovts.; symph. poems *Richard III* (after Shakespeare), *Wallenstein's Camp* (after Schiller), *Haakon Jarl*; cycle of symph. poems *My Country* containing *Vyšehrad*, *Vltava*, *Šárka*, *In the Bohemian Woods and Fields*, *Tábor*, *Blaník*; Festival March for orch.; pf. Trio in G min., 2 stg. 4tets (1st *From my Life*); 8 op. nos. of pf. works & many misc. pf. pieces incl. *Wedding Scenes*, *Scenes from Macbeth*, Cz. dances, &c.; a cantata and a number of partsongs; 3 books of songs, &c.

Smijers, Albert (Anton) (b. Raamsdonksveer, 19. VII. 1888), Dutch mcolst. Pupil of Anton Averkamp at Amsterdam and of Adler in Vienna, where he took a doctor's degree. He taught mus. hist. at the Amsterdam Cons., 1929–34, and became prof. of mus. science at Utrecht Univ. in 1930. His works incl. a catalogue of Dutch m. in It. libraries and he ed. the complete works of Josquin des Prés as well as old Dutch and Flem. m.

Smith, Alice Mary (b. London, 19. V. 1839; d. London, 4. XII. 1884), Eng. comp. Pupil of Sterndale Bennett and Macfarren. Married Frederick Meadows White, Q.C., in 1867.

Works incl. masque *Pandora*; cantatas on Kingsley's *Ode to the North-East Wind*, *Song of the Little Baltung & Red King*, Collins's *Ode to the Passions*; 2 syms., 4 ovts., for orch.; cl. Conc., *Introduction and Allegro* for pf. & orch.; 3 stg. 4tets, 4 pf. 4tets, pf. Trio; songs, duets, partsongs, &c.

Smith, Bernard (Bernhard Schmidt) (b. Ger., *c.* 1630; d. London, 1708), Ger. org. builder. Settled in Eng. from 1660. His 1st Eng. org. was at the Chapel Royal in London. App. orgst. at St. Margaret's church, Westminster, after building the org. there. He was known as Father Smith.

Smith, Carleton Sprague (b. New York, 8. VIII. 1905), Amer. critic, mcolst. & flst. Studied at Harvard Univ. and in Vienna. After a year as critic to the *Boston Transcript*, he became chief librarian of the m. section of the N.Y. Public Library and lecturer in mus. hist. at Columbia Univ. In 1938 he was elected president of the Amer. Mcol. Soc.

Smith, David Stanley (b. Toledo, Ohio, 6. VII. 1877), Amer. comp., cond. & teacher. Studied with H. Parker at Yale Univ. and later in London, Munich and Paris. In 1903 he became instructor and later prof. of m. at Yale.

Works incl. *Rhapsody of St. Bernard* for solo voices, chor. & orch., *The Fallen Star* for chor. & orch., *The Vision of Isaiah* for chor.; anthems; partsongs; 4 syms., *A Poem of Youth*, suite *Impressions*, *Epic Poem*, *1929—A Satire*, ovts. *Prince Hal* (on Shakespeare's *Henry IV*) & *Tomorrow*, &c. for orch.; *Fête galante* for fl. & orch., *Cathedral Prelude* for org. & orch., *Rondo appassionato* for v. & orch.; 9 stg. 4tets, pf. 5tet; sos. for v. & pf. and co. & pf., *Sonata pastorale* for ob. & pf.; songs, &c.

Smith, John Christopher (b. Ansbach, 1712; d. Bath, 3. X. 1795), Ger. (anglicized) orgst. & comp., son of Johann Christoph Schmidt of Ansbach, who went to London as Handel's treasurer and copyist. J. C. S. became a pupil of Handel, and later of Pepusch and T. Roseingrave. In 1745–8 he travelled on the Continent and in 1754 became orgst. of the Foundling Hospital. He acted as

Handel's amanuensis during that master's blindness.

Works incl. operas *Teraminta, Ulysses, Dario, Issipile, Ciro riconosciuto, The Fairies* (from Shakespeare's *Midsummer Night's Dream*), *The Tempest* (after Shakespeare); *Rosalinda, The Enchanter, or Love and Magic* (Garrick) & *The Happy Captive*; incid. m. for Buckingham's (George Villiers) *The Chances*; orats. *David's Lamentation over Saul and Jonathan, Paradise Lost* (after Milton), *Rebecca, Judith, Jehoshaphat, Redemption*; Burial Service; inst. works, &c.

Smith, John Stafford (b. Gloucester, 1750; d. London, 21. IX. 1836), Eng. orgst., ten. singer & comp. Pupil of his father, Martin S., orgst. at Gloucester cath., and later of Boyce and Nares in London, where he was a chorister in the Chapel Royal. He became a Gentleman of the Chapel Royal in 1785, orgst. at Gloucester cath. in 1790 and in 1802 of the Chapel Royal in succession to Arnold, succeeding Ayrton as Master of the Children in 1805. He assisted Hawkins in his *History of Music*.

Works incl. anthems, glees, catches, canons, madrigals, partsongs; songs incl. *Anacreon in Heaven* (now *The Star-spangled Banner*), &c.

Smith, Robert (b. ?, *c.* 1648; d. London, 22. XI. 1675), Eng. comp. Chorister at the Chapel Royal in London under Cooke; became Musician in Ordinary to the King on the death of Humfrey in 1674.

Works incl. incid. m. for numerous plays (some with Staggins & others); m. for stgs.; hpchd. pieces; songs, duets, &c.

Smith, Robert Archibald (b. Reading, 16. XI. 1780; d. Edinburgh, 3. I. 1829), Sco. comp. & pub. Although b. in Eng., he was the son of a Sco. silk-weaver, who returned to Paisley in 1800. In 1807 he became precentor at the Abbey church there and in 1823 leader of the psalmody at St. George's church, Edinburgh. He pub. from 1820 *The Scottish Minstrel* ed. by Lady Nairn and others, to which he contrib. tunes of his own. He also pub. other collections, incl. *Select Melodies of All Nations* & *Sacred Harmony of the Church of Scotland*.

Works incl. anthems; songs, duets, &c.

Smith, (Edward) Sydney (b. Dorchester, 14. VII. 1839; d. London, 3. III. 1889), Eng. pfst. & comp. Studied at Leipzig and settled as pf. teacher in London in 1859. He wrote numerous drawing-room pieces for pf.

Smolensky, Stepan Vassilievitch (b. Kazan, 1848; d. Kazan, 6. VIII. 1909), Rus. mcolst. He made a special study of Rus. church m. and in 1889 became dir. of the Synodal school and choir and prof. of his subject at the Cons. in Moscow. In 1901–3 he was dir. of the imp. court chapel. He collected MSS. of old church m. and wrote several works on the subject.

Smollett, Tobias (George) (1721–71), Eng. novelist & playwright. *See* **Alceste** (Handel).

Smorzando (It. = extinguished, smothered). A direction indicating that a passage is to be perf. with an effect of calming down or fading away.

Smyth, Ethel (Mary) (b. London, 23. IV. 1858; d. Woking, 8. V. 1944), Eng. comp. Studied at the Leipzig Cons. and then privately there with Herzogenberg. She had some works perf. there and after her return to Eng. one or two appeared in London, incl. the Mass in 1893. Her earlier operas were prod. in Ger. She lived much abroad, but in 1910 received the hon. Mus.D. degree from Durham Univ. and about that time joined actively in the movement for women's suffrage. In her later years she lived at Woking in Surrey and, regarding herself as neglected on account of her sex, comp. less and less, but wrote a number of autobiog. books. She received the honour of a D.B.E. in 1922. During her last years she suffered much from deafness and distorted hearing.

Works incl. operas *Fantasio* (after Musset), *The Forest, The Wreckers, The Boatswain's Mate* (after W. W. Jacobs), *Fête galante, Entente cordiale*; Mass in D maj.; *The Prison* for solo voices, chor. & orch.; *Sleepless Dreams, Hey Nonny No!* & *March of the Women* for chor. & orch; ovt. to Shakespeare's *Antony and Cleopatra*, Serenade, &c. for orch.; Conc. for v., hn. & orch.; 3 Anacreontic Odes for voice & orch.; stg. 5tet, stg. 4tet; sos. for v. & pf. and co. & pf.; 3 songs with fl., hp., stg. & perc.; songs, &c.

Snap. *See* **Scotch Snap.**

Snares. Gut stgs. stretched over one of the heads of some types of drum, esp. the Side-drum, adding brilliance to their tone by vibrating against the skin as the drum is struck. If that effect is not required, the Ss. can be temporarily slackened.

Snow Maiden, The (*Snegurotchka*), opera by Rimsky-Korsakov (lib. by comp. based on a play by Alexander Nikolaievitch Ostrovsky), prod. St. Petersburg, 10. II. 1882.

Snow, Valentine (b. ? London, ?; d. London, XII. 1770), Eng. tpt. player.

Son of (?) Moses S., a Gentleman of the Chapel Royal in London and lay-vicar at Westminster Abbey. In 1753 he succeeded John Shore as Sergeant Trumpeter to the King. Handel wrote the tpt. obbligato parts in his orats. for him.

So. (abbr.) = Sonata.

Soave (It.) = Sweet, tender.

Sob. A trick in lute-playing prod. a peculiar effect of deadening the tone by immediately lightening the pressure of the finger on the stg. after it had been struck.

Sobolewski, Eduard (b. Königsberg, 1. X. 1808; d. St. Louis, 23. V. 1872), Ger. cond. & comp. He was cond. at the Königsberg Theatre in succession to Dorn, 1830–6. Later he lived at Weimar and in 1859 he emigrated to U.S.A., where he became cond. to the St. Louis Phil. Soc.

Works incl. operas *Komala* (after Ossian), *Imogene* (after Shakespeare's *Cymbeline*), *Velleda*, *Salvator Rosa* & *Mohega*; orat. *The Saviour*; syms., symph. poems, &c.

Sobrino, Carlos (b. Pontevedra, 25. II. 1861; d. London, 17. I. 1927), Spa. pfst. Studied at the Madrid Cons. and with A. Rubinstein, later toured widely in Eur., sometimes in partnership with Sarasate or Ysaÿe. He settled in London and in 1905 became pf. prof. at the G.M.S.

Soc. (abbr.) = Society.

Socrate (*Socrates*), symphonic drama by Satie (lib. taken from Victor Cousin's Fr. trans. of Plato's *Dialogues*), prod. Paris, 14. II. 1920 & perf. Prague, festival of the I.S.C.M., V. 1925.

Söderman, Johan August (b. Stockholm, 17. VII. 1832; d. Stockholm, 10. II. 1876), Swe. comp. Learnt m. from his father, a theatre cond., at 18 went to Fin. as instructor to a Swe. co. of musns., in 1856 prod. his 1st operetta at Stockholm and then went to finish his studies at Leipzig. After holding the appt. of chor. master at the Royal Opera at Stockholm, he went again to Ger. in 1865 to study further with the help of Jenny Lind. He afterwards held var. official posts and was elected a member of the Swe. Acad. of M.

Works incl. operetta *The Devil's First Lesson* & others; incid. m. to Schiller's *Maid of Orleans*, Topelius's *Regina* & other plays; Mass for solo voices, chor. & orch.; *Swe. Wedding* for fem. voices, cantatas & partsongs; voc. settings of Bellman's rhapsodies; *Circassian Dance* & concert ovt. for orch.; sacred songs & hymns with org.; ballads & songs for voice & pf., &c.

Sofonisba, La, opera by Caldara (lib. by Francesco Silvani), prod. Venice, Teatro S. Giovanni Crisostomo, XII. 1708.

Opera by Gluck (lib. do., with airs from different libs. by Metastasio), prod. Milan, Teatro Regio Ducal, I. 1744.

Soft Pedal. The popular name for the Damping Pedal of the pf.

Soggetto (It.) = Subject, in the mus. sense, esp. the subject of a fugue.

Sogno di Scipione, Il (*Scipio's Dream*), dramatic serenade by Mozart (lib. by Metastasio), prod. Salzburg, at the installation of the new archbishop, Hieronymus von Colloredo, 1. V. 1772.

Dramatic serenade by Predieri (lib. do.), prod. Vienna, Favorita palace, 1. X. 1735.

Soh. The name for the Dominant note in any key in Tonic Sol-fa, so pronounced, but in notation represented by the letter s.

Soir et la Tempête, Le (*Evening and the Storm*), the name of one of 3 syms. by Haydn, comp. *c.* 1761. It is No. 8, in G maj.; the others are No. 6, in D maj., *Le Matin*, and No. 7, in C maj., *Le Midi*.

Sokalsky, Peter Petrovitch (b. Kharkov, 26. IX. 1832; d. Odessa, 11. IV. 1887), Rus. scholar, author & comp. Studied at Kharkov Univ., collected folksongs, was sec. to the Rus. Consulate in N.Y., 1857–60, and then became a newspaper ed. at Odessa.

Works incl. operas *Maria* (*Mazeppa*), *A Night in May* (after Gogol), *The Siege of Dubno* (after Gogol's *Taras Bulba*), &c.

Sokalsky, Vladimir Ivanovitch (b. Heidelberg, 6. V. 1863), Rus. comp., nephew of prec. Studied law at Kharkov Univ., but turned to m.

Works incl. children's opera *The Turnip*; Sym. in G min., Dramatic Fantasy & Eastern March for orch.; *Andante elegiaco* for co. & orch.; *Impressions musicales* & suite *In the Meadows* for pf.; songs, &c.

Sokolov, Nikolai Alexandrovitch (b. St. Petersburg, 26. III. 1859; d. Leningrad, 27. III. 1922), Rus. comp. Studied with Rimsky-Korsakov and others at the St. Petersburg Cons., where he became prof. in 1896.

Works incl. ballet *The Wild Swans*; incid. m. to Shakespeare's *Winter's Tale* & A. Tolstoy's *Don Juan*; Elegy for orch.; 3 stg. 4tets; v. & co. pieces with pf.; partsongs; *c.* 80 songs, &c.

Sol. The old name for the note G (*see* **Solmization**), still used in Lat. countries, and in Tonic Sol-fa notation the Dominant note in any key represented by the symbol s, pronounced Soh.

Sol-fa. *See* **Solmization** & **Tonic Sol-fa.**

Soléa (Spa., plur. *soléares*). A Spa. folksong of Andalusia with words in 3-line stanzas.

Soler, Antonio (b. Olot, Catalonia, 3. XII. 1729; d. Escurial Palace, 20. XII. 1783), Spa. friar & comp. Studied m. at the Escolanía at Montserrat, became chapel master at Lérida cath. and, after being ordained, a monk at the Escurial, where he acted as orgst. He wrote a mus. treatise.

Works incl. incid. m. for plays by Calderón and other 17th-cent. Spa. playwrights; Requiem & other church m.; 5tets for org. & stgs.; hpchd. sos., &c.

Solerti, Angelo (b. Savona, 20. IX. 1865; d. Massa Carrara, 10. II. 1907), It. mcolst. He wrote several works on the origins of dramatic m. in the early 17th cent.

Solfège (Fr.) / **Solfeggio** (It.) } An elementary method of teaching sight-reading and of ear, training, practised mainly in Fr. and It. The names of the notes ('Do, re, mi,' &c.) are pronounced while the notes are sung unaccomp. and the intervals have thus to be learnt by ear.

Soli (It. plur. of **Solo**). The word designates a group of solo perfs. as distinct from the whole voc. or orch. body employed in a work.

Solié (orig. Soulier), **Jean Pierre** (b. Nîmes, 1755; d. Paris, 6. VIII. 1812), Fr. ten. singer, cst. & comp. Learnt the co. from his father, played in the orch. at Nîmes and 1st appeared as singer in 1778, failed in Paris in 1782, went to Lyons and in 1787 succeeded in gaining admission to the Paris Opéra-Comique, where he remained, turned into a bar. and wrote 33 operas for the theatre.

Works incl. operas *Jean et Geneviève, Le Jockey, Le Secret, Le Chapitre second, Le Diable à quatre, Mademoiselle de Guise, Les Ménestrels* & many others.

Solmization (from Lat. *solmisatio*). The designation of the mus. scales by means of syllables, at the same time indicating Mutation according to the Gamut. The Gr. Tetrachords were already designated by letters, but Guido d'Arezzo in the 11th cent. replaced them by the Hexachords and used the Lat. syllables Ut, Re, Mi, Fa, Sol, La for their 6 notes, Si being added later for the 7th and Ut being replaced by Do in It. and elsewhere, though still largely retained in Fr. These syllables, as in modern Tonic Sol-fa with movable Doh, were not immutably fixed to C, D, E, F, G, A, but could be transferred by **Mutation** to other degrees of the scale, so long as the semitone always occurred between Mi and Fa. The so-called 'natural hexachord' beginning on C could thus be changed to the 'hard hexachord' beginning on G, in which case Mi–Fa corresponded with B–C, or to the 'soft Hexachord' beginning on F (hence Fa–Ut, *see* **Gamut**), in which case Mi–Fa fell on A–B, the B having to be flattened in order to put the semitone into the right place. S. allowed for changes to different scales on certain notes, as for ex. hard to natural changing on C (hence the term C fa-ut), soft to hard changing on C (hence C sol-fa), hard to natural changing on E (hence E la-mi), &c. The syllables were derived from a hymn of the year 770 for the festival of St. John the Baptist, the lines of the plainsong of which began on the successive notes of the hexachord:

UT queant laxis
REsonare fibris
MIra gestorum
FAmuli tuorum
SOLve polluti
LAbii reatum
Sancte Ioannes.

Solo (It. = alone). A piece or part of a comp. sung or played by a single perf., though it may be accomp. by others. The word, although an adj., has thus become a noun and is accepted in this form as an Eng. word; but it is also used adjectivally in directions given in It., e.g. *violino solo* (to be played by one v. alone), *voce sola* (voice unaccomp.), &c.

Solo Organ. One of the manuals of an org. governing mainly Solo Stops.

Solo Stops. Org. stops controlling a range of pipes of strikingly characteristic tone generally used for single melodic lines rather than in chords.

Sologub, Feodor Kuzmitch (real name Teternikov) (1863–1927), Rus. poet, novelist & playwright. *See* **Dukelsky** (*Triolets of the North*), **Gnessin** (songs), **Tcherepnin (N.)** (*Vanka the Chancellor*).

Solomon, orat. by Handel (lib. ? by Thomas Morell), prod. London, Covent Garden Theatre, 17. III. 1749.

Soloviev, Nikolai Feopemptovitch (b. Petrozadovsk, 9. V. 1846; d. Petrograd, 14. XII. 1916), Rus. comp. Began by studying medicine, but turned to m. and entered the St. Petersburg Cons., Zaremba being among his masters. He became prof. there in 1874. In 1871 Serov, when dying, charged him with the orchn. of his opera *The Power of*

Evil. He was also a critic and collector of folksongs.

Works incl. operas *Cordelia* (after Sardou's *La Haine*), *Vakula the Smith* (on Gogol's *Christmas Eve*) & *The Cottage at Kolomua*; cantata for the bicentenary of Peter the Great; symph. poem *Russians and Mongols* & Fantasy on a Folksong for orch.; pf. pieces; songs, &c.

Soltys, Mieczyslaw (b. Lwów, 7. II. 1863; d. Lwów, 12. XI. 1929), Pol. cond. & comp. Studied in Vienna and Paris. He returned to Lwów in 1901 and became dir. of the Cons. and cond. of the Mus. Assn.

Works incl. operas *The Republic of Babin*, *Maria* (on Antoni Malczewski's poem), *Panie Kochanku* & others; orats.; Sym., symph. poem *The Fugitive*, &c.

Sombrée (Fr. = darkened). The Fr. adj. for the term Veiled Voice (*voix s.*).

Sombrero de tres picos, El (*The Three-cornered Hat*), ballet by Falla (scen. by Martínez Sierra, based on Alarcón's story; chgph. by Leonid Fedorovitch Massin), prod. London, Alhambra Theatre, 22. VII. 1919. The setting and dresses were designed by Picasso.

Somervell, Arthur (b. Windermere, 5. VI. 1863; d. London, 2. V. 1937), Eng. cond. & educst. Educ. at Uppingham School and King's Coll., Cambridge, where he studied comp. with Stanford, going later to Kiel in Berlin, to the R.C.M. in London in 1885 and to Parry as a private pupil in 1887. In 1894 he became prof. at the R.C.M. and in 1901 an inspector of m. in schools, which led to his appt. as official Inspector of M. to the Board of Educ., which he resigned in 1928. Knighted 1929.

Works incl. Masses in C min. & D min. (the latter for male voices), anthem *Let all the world*, orat. *The Passion of Christ*, cantatas *A Song of Praise*, *The Power of Sound*, *The Forsaken Merman* (Matthew Arnold), *Ode to the Sea* & others; Sym. in D min. *Thalassa*, ballad *Helen of Kirkconnell*, suite *In Arcady* for orch.; symph. vars. *Normandy* for pf. & orch., Conc. in G min. and *Concertstück* for v. & orch.; cl. 5tet; v. & pf. So.; Vars. on an Original Theme for 2 pfs.; v. pieces; pf. pieces; song cycles *Maud* (Tennyson), *A Shropshire Lad* (A. E. Housman), *James Lee's Wife*, *A Broken Arc* (both Browning) & *Love in Springtime*, & other songs; partsongs, &c.

Somis, Giovanni Battista (b. Turin, 25. XII. 1686; d. Turin, 14. VIII. 1763), It. vst. & comp. Pupil of Corelli in Rome and (?) Vivaldi at Venice. Returning to Turin, he was app. vst. to the King of Piedmont and leader of the royal orch. About 1733 he lived in Paris for a time. He taught many famous pupils, incl. Leclair, Giardini and Pugnani.

Works incl. v. concs.; sos., &c.

Somis, Lorenzo (b. Turin, 11. XI. 1688; d. Turin, 29. XI. 1775), It. vst. & comp., brother of prec. Lived in Turin as vst. in the royal orch. Comp. v. sos., &c.

Sommeils (Fr., plur. of *sommeil* = sleep). Quiet airs in old Fr. operas supposed to induce sleep.

Sommer, Hans (real name Hans Friedrich August Zincken, sometimes anag. 'Neckniz') (b. Brunswick, 20. VII. 1837; d. Brunswick, 28. IV. 1922), Ger. comp. Studied at Göttingen Univ. and became prof. of physics there. Later he became dir. of the Technical High School at Brunswick, settled in Berlin in 1885, at Weimar in 1888, and in 1898 returned to Brunswick. He had been comp. as an amateur since before 1865, when he prod. his 1st opera.

Works incl. operas *Der Nachtwächter*, *Loreley*, *Saint-Foix*, *Der Meermann*, *Augustin*, *Münchhausen*, *Rübezahl*, *Riquet mit dem Schopf* & *Der Waldschratt*; song cycles from Julius Wolff's *Der Wilde Jäger* (*Mädchenlieder*), *Hunold Singuf* & *Tannhäuser*, from Carmen Sylva's *Sappho* & many other songs, &c.

Son and Stranger (Mendelssohn). *See* **Heimkehr aus der Fremde.**

Sonata (It. & Eng.). A term designating both a type of comp. and a mus. form. The S. as a type is now normally a comp. in 3 or 4 mvts., only the 1st of which is with few exceptions in S. form, and often the last, though that is at least as frequently a Rondo. The word is derived from *suonare* or *sonare* = 'to sound': a S. is thus orig. simply 'a thing sounded,' i.e. played, as distinct from a Cantata (from *cantare*), 'a thing sung.' But in the 17th cent. the S. developed into the two types described hereunder, the S. da camera and the S. da chiesa. In the 18th the 1-mvt. S. of D. Scarlatti began to approximate to the modern 1st-mvt. form, while other works of the kind, esp. in Ger., still approximated to the Suite, from which indeed the mature S. borrowed the minuet, which it later developed into the Scherzo, but often dropped in favour of a 3-mvt. comp.: 1st mvt. in S. form, slow mvt., & finale in S. or rondo form. The modern 1st-mvt. form developed through C. P. E. Bach and some of his contemps., reached full maturity in the hands of Haydn, Mozart and others, and was greatly strained by the innovations of Beethoven, e.g. in his type of S. quasi una fantasia and his late works of the species, which admitted fugal developments and made much of the var. form. But it was only after Beethoven in the 19th cent. that the S. became often so much modified as to lose its shape, e.g. in the hands of Schumann and Chopin, to whom it was uncongenial, or in those of Liszt, who introd. his principle of thematic transformation (as distinct from development) into it. The S. form in its fully matured but not sophisticated manifestations shows the following main outlines: a single mvt. in 2 principal sections, the 1st called the Exposition, ending in another key than that of the tonic. Two main thematic groups make up its material, with room for subsidiary themes and connecting bridge passages, and these groups are not very accurately but conveniently described as First and Second Subjects. The 1st is in the tonic key, the 2nd usually in the dominant in a mvt. in a maj. key and in the relative maj. in one in a min. key. The 2nd section begins with a Development or Working-out, which, as its names suggest, develops some of the foregoing material in new ways, but may also partly or even exclusively introd. new matter (e.g. Mozart), which however in the hands of a master will be relevant to the principal material. This development leads to the Recapitulation, where the opening of the mvt., i.e. the 1st subject, returns as before, though possibly with new embellishments; the 2nd subject, however, now also appears in the tonic key, maj. or min., and in the latter case it is normally in min. even if in the 1st section it appeared in maj. All this necessitates a new modulatory transition between 1st and 2nd subjects, and it is often here rather than in the Working-out that the greatest point of interest or surprise of a S. mvt. lies. The mvt. may end in the tonic exactly as the 1st section ended in another key; but there may be a Coda added, either a very brief tail-piece of a merely ceremonial nature or a more developed section which may further work upon the foregoing material, as often in the case of Beethoven. Not only works so called are Ss., but also chamber m. of the normal classical type and syms.

Sonata da camera (It. = chamber so.). An inst. work of the late 17th and early 18th cent. of the Suite or Partita type in several mvts., mainly in dance forms, but always for more than 1 inst., most usually 2 vs. with continuo for bass viol or co. with a keyboard inst., generally hpchd. Unlike the So. da chiesa, the S. d. c. usually had a quick 1st mvt.

Sonata da chiesa (It. = church so.). An inst. work of the late 17th and early 18th cent. in 4 mvts. (slow introd., fugal *allegro*, slow *cantabile* mvt. and finale in a binary dance-form) always written for more than 1 inst., most usually 2 vs. with continuo for bass viol or co. with a keyboard inst., which if played in church must have been generally the org. But such works were quite often perf. elsewhere.

Sonata quasi una fantasia (It. = so., as it were a fantasy). A term invented by Beethoven for some of his sos. in which he began to modify the form freely, the 2 works of Op. 27 for pf. being the 1st of the kind.

Sonate (Fr. & Ger.) = Sonata.

Sonate pathétique (Beethoven). *See* **Pathetic Sonata.**

Sonatina (It. dim. of sonata = little so.). A work of the so. type in a condensed form or easy to play. The 1st mvt. of a S. usually contains the normal 1st and 2nd subjects, though as a rule they are less extended, but it may have only a rudimentary working-out section and coda or none at all. The key-scheme for the reappearance of the 2 subjects in the 2nd section, however, will be similar to that in a so. Ss. have often been written for teaching purposes, esp. for the pf.

Song. Strictly speaking any poem set to m. for a single voice, with or without an accomp., is a S., but the species is distinct from other forms of voc. comp. such as the aria, the ballad, the couplet, &c. The most distinctive type of S. is the strophic S., where each verse of a póem is set to a repetition of the same tune, which is usually either in Binary or in Ternary form, as are also folksongs. But Ss. may also be set continuously, the m. developing throughout in a manner calculated to illustrate the progress of the words. It may be said that such a S. is distinguished from an Aria by shaping itself according to the form and the meaning of the words, whereas the latter subjects its words to a more specifically mus. structure.

Song Cycle. A series of songs set as a rule to a number of poems with a connected narrative or some other unifying feature. Schubert's *Fair Maid of the Mill* and *Winter Journey*, for ex., are thus S. Cs. properly speaking, while his *Swan Song* is not, being merely a set of his last songs posthumously brought out together under a collective title by a pub.

Song Form. According to a theoret. superstition slow mvts. in so.-form works are still sometimes said to be in S. F. if they happen to approximate in some way to Ternary Form. There is no justification for this, since songs are not bound to be particularly in ternary or any other specific form. Songs of a popular type, it is true, are frequently ternary, but minuets and scherzos in so.-form works are almost invariably so, while slow mvts. may take other forms, e.g. rondo, vars., &c. Yet it never occurs to anybody to say that minuets and scherzos are in S. F.

Song of Destiny (Brahms). *See* **Schicksalslied.**

Song of the Earth (Mahler). *See* **Lied von der Erde.**

Song of Triumph (Brahms). *See* **Triumphlied.**

Songe d'une nuit d'été, Le (*The Dream of a Midsummer Night*), opera by A. Thomas (lib. by Joseph Bernard Rosier & Adolphe de Leuven, not based on Shakespeare's play), prod. Paris, Opéra-Comique, 20. IV. 1850. Shakespeare, Queen Elizabeth and Falstaff appear in it as characters.

Songs and Dances of Death, song cycle by Mussorgsky (poems by A. A. Golenishtchev-Kutuzov), comp. 1875–7: 1. *The Peasant's Lullaby*; 2. *Serenade*; 3. *Trepak*; 4. *The Field Marshal.*

Songs without Words (Mendelssohn). *See* **Lieder ohne Worte.**

Sonnambula, La (*The Sleepwalker*), opera by Bellini (lib. by Felice Romani), prod. Milan, Teatro Carcano, 6. III. 1831.

Sonneck, Oscar (George Theodore) (b. Jersey City, N.J., 6. X. 1873; d. New York, 30. X. 1928), Amer. mcolst. of Ger. descent. Educ. at Frankfort o/M. and Heidelberg and Munich Univs. Head of the m. division of the Library of Congress at Washington, 1902–17, and ed. of the *Musical Quarterly* from 1915 to his death. Pub. a catalogue of early opera libs. and lists of Stephen Foster's and MacDowell's works, wrote books on Beethoven and a number on early Amer. m.

Sonore (Fr. =sonorous). This word is not It., but often used by non-It. comps. as if it were, prob. because it sometimes appears abbr. as *sonor^{e}*, for *sonoramente*, which is the proper It. term.

Sons, Maurice (b. Amsterdam, 13. IX. 1857; d. London, 28. IX. 1942, Dutch vst. Studied at the Brussels Cons. with Wieniawski and others, and with Rappoldi at Dresden. After an appt. in Swi. he settled in Sco. as leader of the Sco. Orch. and in 1904 removed to London to become leader of the Queen's Hall Orch., where he remained until 1927. He was v. prof. at the R.C.M., 1903–37.

Sontag, Henriette (Gertrud Walpurgis) (b. Coblenz, 3. I. 1806; d. Mexico City, 3. VI. 1854), Ger. sop. singer. The daughter of actors, she appeared on the stage as a child, but in 1815 entered the Prague Cons. as a singing-student, and in 1821 made a very successful stage appearance as an understudy. She was then taken to Vienna for further study and at once appeared there in It. and Ger. opera, Weber choosing her to sing the title-part in *Euryanthe* in 1823. She 1st visited Paris in 1826 and London in 1828. She married Count Rossi, a diplomat of the Sardinian court, and retired, living with him at var. courts in Hol., Ger. & Rus., but after the 1848 revols. she reappeared on the stage, esp. in Eng. and U.S.A.

Sop. (abbr.) =Soprano.

Sophocles (497 or 495–405 B.C.), Gr. dramatist. *See* **Antigone** (incid. m., Mendelssohn; operas, Honegger, Zingarelli), **Assafiev** (*Oedipus Rex*), **Bantock** (*Electra*), **Bennett (W. S.)** (*Ajax*), **Champein** (*Electra*), **Commer** (do.), **Diepenbrock** (do.), **Dupuis (A.)** (*Oedipus Coloneus*), **Elektra** (R. Strauss), **Gabrieli (A.)** (*Oe. Tyrannus*), **Glière** (*Oe. Rex*), **Gnessin** (do. & *Antigone*), **Hadley (P.)** (do.), **Hauer, Honegger** (*Antigone*), **Hüttenbrenner (A.)** (*Ödipus auf Kolonos*), **Ilynsky** (*Oe. Rex* & *Philoctetes*), **Krejči** (*Antigone*), **Lassen** (*Oe.*), **Lemoyne** (*Électre*), **Leoncavallo** (*Edipo rè*), **Lier** (*Ajax*), **Martin (F.)** (*Oe. Rex*), **Mojsisovics** (*Oe. Rex*), **Mulè** (*Antigone* & *Satyr*), **Œdipe** (Enesco), **Œdipe à Colone** (Sacchini), **Oedipus Coloneus** (Mendelssohn), **Oedipus Rex** (Stravinsky), **Oedipus Tyrannus** (Mendelssohn & Stanford), **Pacini** (*Oe. Rex*), **Paine** (*Oe. Tyrannus*), **Pijper** (*Antigone*), **Pizzetti** (*Trachiniae* & *Oe. Rex* & *Coloneus*), **Radoux (C.)** (*Œdipe à Colone*), **Ropartz** (*Oe. Col.*), **Saint-Saëns** (*Antigone*), **Schillings** (*Oe.*), **Skilton** (*Electra*), **Tiessen** (*Antigone*), **Zingarelli** (*Edipo a Colono*).

Sopranino. The highest of the 6 ranges of Saxophones, standing in E♭.

Soprano. The highest female voice, extending normally from about B♭ below middle C to the C 2 octaves above that, but occasionally extended to the F (Mozart) or F♯ (R. Strauss) above that. Up to the end of the 18th cent. there were also artificial male Ss., prod. by castration, and boys can also sing S., though their range is smaller than that of women. Some insts. made in var. ranges use the word S. as a prefix for those types which roughly equal the compass of the S. voice (e.g. S. Saxophone).

Soprano Clef. The C clef so used as to indicate that middle C stands on the bottom line of the stave; now obs.

Sor (or **Sors**), **Fernando** (b. Barcelona, 14. II. 1778; d. Paris, 8. VII. 1839). Spa. guitarist and comp. Educ. at the Escolanía of Montserrat, prod. his opera at the age of 19, went to Paris and in 1809 to London, where he played and taught the guitar.

Works incl. opera *Telemaco nell' isola di Calipso*; songs for an (anon.) operatic drama *Gil Blas*; ballets *Cendrillon, Le Sicilien* (after Molière) & others; guitar pieces & studies, &c.

Sorabji, Kaikhosru Shapurji (b. Chelmsford, Essex, 14. VIII. 1895), Parsee pfst. & comp. He has lived in London all his life and has Eur. blood in him through a Spa. mother. Except for the pf., he was mainly self-taught, but was fortunate enough to be able to give all his time to mus. studies. He appeared as pfst. in his own works in London, Paris and Vienna, and has also written criticism, incl. a book *Around Music*.

Works incl. 2 syms. for orch., pf., org. & chor.; *Chaleur* & *Opusculum* for orch.; 5 pf. Concs., Symph. Vars. for pf. & orch.; 2 syms. for org.; 2 pf. 5tets; 5 sos., *Opus clavicembalisticum, Le Jardin parfumé, Fantaisie espagnole, In the Hothouse*, Toccata, *Prelude, Interlude and Fugue, Valse-Fantaisie, Fantasia Hispanica*, 3 Toccatas, Sym., Vars. on *Dies irae* for pf.; *3 Poèmes* (Verlaine & Baudelaire), *Fêtes galantes* (Verlaine) for voice & pf., &c.

Sorcerer, The, operetta by Sullivan (lib. by W. S. Gilbert), prod. London, Opera Comique, 17. XI. 1877.

Sordino (It. from *sordo* = deaf). *See* **Mute.** Also the It. name for the Kit.

Soriano, Francesco (b. Soriano sul Cimino, 1549; d. Rome, after 1621), It. comp. Became a choir-boy at St. John Lateran in Rome and studied with var. masters incl. G. B. Nanini and Palestrina. After a 1st app. he went to the court of Mantua, 1583–6, and then became chapel master in Rome, by turns at Santa Maria Maggiore, St. John Lateran and in 1603 St. Peter's.

Works incl. masses, motets, psalms, magnificat, a Passion & other church m.; madrigals, &c.

Sorotchintsy Fair (*Sorotchinskaya Yarmarka*), unfinished opera by Mussorgsky (lib. by comp., based on Gogol's *Evenings on a Farm near Dakanka*), comp. begun 1875; revised by Liadov for concert perf., 1904; perf. in orig. form, St. Petersburg, Comedia Theatre, 30. XII. 1911; a version by Sakhnovsky prod. Moscow, Free Theatre, 3. XI. 1913; version by Cui with m. of his own added prod. St. Petersburg, Musical Drama Theatre, 26. X. 1917; version by N. Tcherepnin prod. Monte Carlo, 17. III. 1923 (in Fr.); another version made by Shebalin in 1931 was prod. Leningrad, Little Opera Theatre, 21. XII. 1931.

Sors, Fernando. *See* **Sor.**

Sortita (It. from *sortire* = to come out). A principal character's aria to which the 1st entry is made in an opera of the 18th cent.

Sos. (abbr.) = Sonatas.

Sosarme, rè di Media (*Sosarmes, King of the Medes*), opera by Handel (lib. by ?, based on Matteo Noris's *Alfonso primo*), prod. London, King's Theatre, Haymarket, 15. II. 1732.

Sostenendo
Sostenente } (It.). Less frequently used forms of

Sostenuto (It. = sustained). A direction which may mean either that a note or notes are to be held to their full value (as with *tenuto*) or that a passage is to be played broadly, though not exactly slowed down (as with *ritenuto*). The term is best reserved for the latter meaning alone, since another serves perfectly for the former: i.e. S. applies to a phrase or passage, while *tenuto* is used for a note or chord.

Soto de Langa, Francisco (b. Langa nr. Osma, 1539; d. Rome, 25. IX. 1619), Spa. priest, male sop. singer and arranger. He entered the Papal choir in Rome in 1562, joined the Oratory of St. Philip Neri and continued to sing to the end of his long life. He adapted 5 books of *laudi spirituali* for 3 & 4 voices, using It. folksongs and var. It. and Spa. comps.

Sotto voce (It. = under the voice). A direction indicating that a passage is to be perf. in an undertone. As the term indicates, it was orig. applied to voc. m., but it became current for inst. m. also.

Soubies, Albert (b. Paris, 10. V. 1846; d. Paris, 19. III. 1918), Fr. mcolst. After studying law, he entered the Paris Cons., became a critic and contrib. to mus. journals, and pub. a number of books incl. a hist. of m. divided into a number of vols. for var. countries, studies of opera in Paris, of Wagner (with Malherbe), &c.

Soubrette (Fr. from old Fr. *soubret* = cunning, sharp). A stock figure in opera given to a singer with a light sop. voice and impersonating characters of the type of servants, young confidantes, girls usually connected with the sub-plot, &c. (e.g. Despina in Mozart's *Così fan tutte*, Aennchen in Weber's *Freischütz*, Micaela in Bizet's *Carmen*, &c.). Occasionally the S. may assume a principal part (e.g. Serpina in Pergolesi's *Serva padrona*, Susanna in Mozart's *Figaro*, &c.).

Soulier, Jean Pierre. *See* **Solié.**

Soumet, Alexandre (1788–1845), Fr. poet & dramatist. *See* **Norma** (Bellini).

Sound-Board. A resonant wooden part of var. insts., incl. org., pf., dulcimer, cimbalom, &c. which adds to the volume of tone by vibrating with the notes.

Sound-Holes. The holes in the tables of stg. insts., also in the sound-boards of hpchds., &c. In insts. of the v. family they take the shape of *f* holes or something approximating to them; in keyboard insts. as well as lutes, guitars, &c., usually the shape of a ' Rose.'

Sound-Post. The piece of pine wood standing upright between the table and the back of stg. insts., inserted partly to support the pressure of the stgs. on the bridge, but mainly to act as the chief distributor of the vibrations.

Sounding-Board. *See* **Sound-Board.**

Soupir (Fr. =sigh) =crotchet rest. The name is borrowed by confusion from the Lat. *suspirium*, which was, however, a minim rest.

Sourdine (Fr. from *sourd* =deaf). *See* **Mute.** Also an obs. inst. of the bn. type.

Šourek, Otakar (b. Prague, 1. X. 1883), Cz. m. critic. Although an engineer by profession, he became critic to 2 Prague newspapers and has pub. important works, mainly on Dvořák, incl. a thematic catalogue and a large 2-vol. life and study of the works.

Souris, André (b. Marchienne-au-Pont, 10. VII. 1899), Belg. comp. He worked under the infl. of Fr. impressionism at first, but from 1926 endeavoured to prod. in m. some equivalent to the surrealist painters.

Works incl. incid. m. for *Le Dessous des cartes*; *Musique* for orch.; fanfare *Hommage à Babeuf*; *Petite Suite* for 4 brass insts.; *Quelques airs de Clarisse Juranville* for con. & pf., &c.

Sousa, John Philip (b. Washington, 6. XI. 1854; d. Reading, Pa., 6. III. 1932), Amer. bandmaster & comp. In 1880 he became master of the U.S. Marine Corps band and in 1892 formed a band of his own.

Works incl. operetta *El Capitan* & others; military marches, dances, incl. *The Washington Post*, &c.

Sousaphone. A brass inst. of the Tuba type made for Sousa's band in 1899 in a different shape from that with a bell opening towards the audience, well-known as a constituent of the jazz and swing bands.

Sousedská. A Boh. country dance in slow triple time. The 3rd, 4th and 16th of Dvořák's *Slavonic Dances* for pf. duet are Ss.

Souter Liedenkens (Dutch = psalter songlets). Hymns introd. into Hol. with Protestantism in the 16th cent., sung to metrical versions of the Psalms.

South American Composers. *See* **Argentine, Brazilian, Chilean, Colombian, Uruguayan.**

South Place Concerts. *See* **Walthew.**

Southerne, Thomas (1660–1746), Ir. playwright. *See* **Courteville** (2) (*Oroonoko*), **Paisible** (do.), **Purcell** (*Fatal Marriage, Maid's Last Prayer, Sir Anthony Love* & *Wives' Excuse*), **Stanley** (*Oroonoko*).

Southey, Robert (1774–1843), Eng. poet. *See* **Bantock** (*Processional* & *Jaga-Naut*).

Sowerby, Leo (b. Grand Rapids, Mich., 1. V. 1895), Amer. pfst. & comp. Studied at the Amer. Cons. of Chicago, where he taught later. He served as bandmaster in Eur. during the 1914–8 war and in 1922 won the Amer. Prix de Rome. He has appeared as pfst. in U.S.A., Eng., It. & Aus.

Works incl. cantata *Great is the Lord* & Te Deum for mixed chor. & org.; 2 syms., suite *From the Northland*, ovt. *Comes Autumn Time*, *Irish Washerwoman*, *Money Musk*, *Set of Four*, symph. poem *Prairie*, *Theme in Yellow* for orch.; Sinfonietta for stgs.; Rhapsody for chamber orch.; *Sinconata* for jazz orch.; 2 pf. concs., org. Conc., co. Conc., ballad *King Estmere* for 2 pfs. & orch., *Medieval Poem* for org. & orch.; 2 stg. 4tets, wind 5tet, Serenade for stg. 4tet; So. & Suite for v. & pf.; Sym., So. & Suite for org.; *Florida Suite* & other pf. works; songs, &c.

Spa. (abbr.) =Spain, Spanish.

Spagnoletti, Paolo (real surname? Diana) (b. Cremona, 1768; d. London, 23. IX. 1834), It. vst. Studied at Naples and settled in London in 1802 as orch. leader, teacher and soloist. He wrote some v. pieces and songs.

Spagnoletto (or **Spagnoletta**). An It. dance of Spa. orig.

Spalding, Albert (b. Chicago, 15. VIII. 1888), Amer. vst. & comp. Studied at Bologna and Paris and made his 1st appearance at the latter in 1905. After touring widely in Eur. he 1st appeared in N.Y. in 1908.

Works incl. Suite for orch.; 2 v. concs.; stg. 4tet in E min.; So. and Suite for v. & pf., *Etchings* & other works for v. & pf.; pf. pieces; songs, &c.

Spanisches Liederbuch (*Spa. Song Book*). H Wolf's settings of Spa. poems in Ger. trans. by Emanuel Geibel and Paul Heyse, comp. X. 1889–IV. 1890. There are 10 sacred and 34 secular poems in his set.

Spanish Lady, The, unfinished opera by Elgar (lib. by Barry Jackson, based on Ben Jonson's play *The Devil is an Ass*). Begun 1932–3; only a number of sketches are left.

Spanish Viol (or Vial) = Cittern.

Špasírka. A Cz. dance in alternating slow and quick 4–8 time. The 13th of Dvořák's *Slavonic Dances* for pf. duet is a S.

Speaight, Joseph (b. London, 24. X. 1868), Eng. pfst. & comp. Studied with Ernst Pauer and Orlando Morgan at the G.S.M. in London, became a prof. there in 1894 and at Trinity Coll. of M. in 1919.

Works incl. 2 syms., 3 symph. poems, 3 suites for orch.; pf. Conc.; 5 stg. 4tets, 3 stg. 5tets, *Shakespeare Fairy Characters* for stg. 4tet; inst. pieces; pf. works; partsongs; songs, &c.

Speaker Keys. Extra keys fitted to reed wind insts. to facilitate the prod. of harmonic notes: e.g. 2 on the ob. prod. octaves (also known as Octave Keys) and 1 on the cl. prod. 12ths.

Speaking-Length. That portion of an org. pipe in which the air vibrates to prod. the note.

Specht, Richard (b. Vienna, 7. XII. 1870; d. Vienna, 18. III. 1932), Aus. writer on m. Studied architecture, but encouraged by Brahms and others took up mus. criticism, joined the staff of *Die Zeit* and in 1909 founded *Der Merkur* with Bittner and Richard Batka. His books incl. studies of Brahms, J. Strauss, R. Strauss, Mahler, Puccini, Bittner, Rezniček, the Vienna Opera, &c.

Species. The var. types of Counterpoint taught in academic ctptal instruction.

Specification. The detailed list of the pipes, stops, keyboards and mechanisms of an org. given to the builder or used to describe the inst.

Spectre's Bride, The (actually *The Wedding-Shift*), dramatic cantata by Dvořák, Op. 69 (Cz. words by K. J. Erben), comp. 1884, prod. in Eng., Birmingham Festival, VIII. 1885.

Speech-Song (Ger. Sprechgesang). A term for a kind of singing that approximates to speech and touches the notes, indicated by special signs, without intoning them clearly at the proper pitch. It is used esp. by Schoenberg (e.g. in *Pierrot lunaire*) and his disciples (e.g. Berg in *Wozzeck* and *Lulu*).

Spelman, Timothy Mather (b. Brooklyn, New York, 21. I. 1891), Amer. comp. Studied in N.Y., at Harvard Univ. and with Courvoisier at the Munich Cons.

Works incl. operas *La Magnifica, The Sea Rovers, Babakan* & *The Sunken City*; pantomimes *The Romance of the Rose* & *Snowdrop*; *Litany of the Middle Ages* for sop., women's chor. & orch., *Pervigilium Veneris* for sop., bar., chor. & orch.; Sym. in G min., symph. poem *Christ and the Blind Man*, suites *Barbaresques* & *Saints' Days* for orch.; *Dawn in the Woods* for v. & orch.; *Eclogue* & *In the Princess's Garden* for chamber orch.; 5 *Whimsical Serenades* for stg. 4tet, *Le Pavillon sur l'eau* for 5 insts.; Sp. and *Barbaresques* suite for pf., &c.

Spender, Stephen (b. 1909), Eng. poet. *See* **Barber** (chors.).

Spendiarov, Alexander Afanasievitch (b. Khakovka, Crimea, 1. XI. 1871; d. Erivan, 7. V. 1928), Rus. comp. Studied with Klenovsky at Moscow and with Rimsky-Korsakov in St. Petersburg. In 1924 he settled at Erivan, Armenia, and began to write m. based on Armenian folksong.

Works incl. opera *Almast*; memorial cantata for Stassov; *Crimean Sketches*, symph. poem *The Three Palm Trees* (after Lermontov), *Erivan Sketches* for orch., &c.

Spenser, Edmund (? 1552–99), Eng. poet. *See* **Darke** (*Hymn of Heavenly Beauty*), **Davies (Walford)** (*High Heaven's King*), **Dieren (van)** (*Fayre eies*), **Greene (M.)** (*Amoretti*), **Quest** (Walton), **Rubbra** (*Amoretti*).

Speyer, Wilhelm (b. Frankfort o/M., 21. VI. 1790; d. Frankfort, 5. IV. 1878), Ger. vst. & comp. Studied at Offenbach with Thieriot and André and with Baillot in Paris. He became a merchant at Frankfort, but continued to comp.

Works incl. stg. 4tets & 5tets; v. duets; numerous songs, &c.

Speziale, Lo (*The Apothecary*), opera by Haydn (lib. by Goldoni), prod. Esterház, autumn 1768.

Sphaerophon (Ger. from Gr.). An electrophonic inst. invented by Jörg Mager in 1921, prod. notes from the air graded according to the chromatic scale, not indeterminate in pitch like those of the Aetherophone or Theremin. In 1928 Mager improved it by applying a keyboard to it and called it *Klaviatur Sphaerophon*.

Spianato (It.) = Smooth, even, level.

Spiccato (It. = separated, distinct). A

direction indicating a special kind of bowing on insts. of the v. family, possible only in rapid passages of notes of equal duration, which are played with the middle of the bow and a loose wrist, allowing the bow to rebound off the stgs. after each note.

Spies, Hermine (b. Löhnberg nr. Weilburg, Nassau, 25. II. 1857; d. Wiesbaden, 26. II. 1893), Ger. con. singer. Studied at the Wiesbaden Cons., in Berlin and with Stockhausen at Frankfort o/M. She made her 1st appearance at the Mannheim Festival in 1880, later travelled widely and visited London in 1889. Brahms is said to have been in love with her, but she married a lawyer at Wiesbaden in 1892.

Spinaccino, Francesco (b. ? Fossombrone, ?; d. ?), It. 15th–16th-cent. lutenist. Pub. 4 books of arrs. of songs, ricercari and dances in lute tablature.

Spindler, Fritz (b. Wurzbach, Lobenstein, 24. XI. 1817; d. Niederlössnitz nr. Dresden, 26. XII. 1905), Ger. pfst. & comp. Pupil of Schneider at Dessau, settled at Dresden as concert perf. and teacher.

Works incl. 2 syms.; pf. Conc.; pf. trios; studies and numerous drawing-room pieces for pf.

Spinelli, Nicola (b. Turin, 29. VII. 1865; d. Rome, 17. X. 1906), It. pfst., cond. & comp. Studied at Florence, Rome and Naples, pupil of Mancinelli and Sgambati. His 1st opera gained a Sonzogno prize in 1889. He suffered from a mental complaint during his last years.

Works incl. operas *Labilia, A basso porto*, &c.

Spinet. A keyboard inst. often confused with the square pf., but actually a hpchd. of square shape like the Virginal, or wing-shaped like the hpchd., but smaller in size and often without legs, to be placed on a table or stand. Its name prob. derives from the It. *spina* = thorn, ref. to the plectra with which the stgs. were plucked; but there was also a 16th-cent. Venetian maker named Giovanni Spinetti.

Spirit of England, The, 3 cantatas for sop. solo, chor. & orch. by Elgar, Op. 80, *The Fourth of August, To Women & For the Fallen* (poems by Laurence Binyon), comp. in 1916–7 and prod. (II & III) London, 7. V. 1916 and (I—III) London, 24. XI. 1917.

'Spirit' Trio (Beethoven). *See* **'Ghost' Trio.**

Spiritoso (It. = spiritedly). A direction indicating that a comp., mvt. or passage is to be perf. briskly and energetically.

Spiritual. A Negro song of the southern states of U.S.A., with religious but not ecclesiastical words and folksong tunes. One of the chief influences from which jazz and swing have sprung, where it has however become either debased or sophisticated. On the other hand it has influenced many serious Amer. comps. and even Eur. ones, from Dvořák's 'New World' Sym. and 'Nigger' 4tet to Tippett's orat. *A Child of our Time.*

Spitta, (Julius August) Philipp (b. Wechold, Hanover, 27. XII. 1841; d. Berlin, 13. IV. 1894), Ger. mcolst. Studied at Göttingen Univ. and in 1875 became prof. of mus. hist. at Berlin Univ. He also taught the subject at the Hochschule für Musik, of which he became dir. in 1882. He was joint ed. with Adler and Chrysander of the *Vierteljahrsschrift für Musikwissenschaft*, and ed. the complete works of Schütz and the org. works of Buxtehude. His chief lit. work is his book on Bach in 2 vols.

Spitteler, Karl (1845–1924), Swi. poet. *See* **Courvoisier.**

Spitzflöte (Ger. = point-fl.). A 2-ft., 4-ft. (most usually) and 8-ft. org. stop governing tapering pipes with a thin, fl.-like but rather reedier tone.

Spofforth, Reginald (b. Southwell, 1770; d. London, 8. IX. 1827), Eng. comp. Pupil of his uncle Thomas S., orgst. of Southwell minster and of B. Cooke in London, where he settled. He gained several of the Glee Club's prizes.

Works incl. farce with m. *The Witch of the Wood, or The Nutting Girls*, adds. to Salomon's *Windsor Castle*; many glees, incl. 'Hail, smiling morn,' &c.

Spohr, Louis (b. Brunswick, 5. IV. 1784; d. Cassel, 22. X. 1859), Ger. vst. & comp. He 1st learnt m. from his parents, who were both mus., although his father was a physician. They lived at Seesen in his childhood, and he was afterwards taught by 2 amateurs, but sent to school and for further mus. studies to Brunswick. He played a v. conc. of his own at a school concert and at 14 went to Hamburg trying to gain a hearing. He failed and on his return petitioned the duke for assistance and was sent to Franz Eck for lessons, the duke paying half the expenses for his accompanying that vst. on his travels. They went to Rus. in 1802, where he met Clementi and Field. He practised and comp. much at that time, returned to Brunswick in 1803, heard Rode there and entered the ducal orch. In 1804 he visited Berlin and played there with Meyerbeer, aged 13. In 1805 he became leader in the Duke of Gotha's orch. and married the hpst. Dorette Scheidler, with whom he toured much. After playing the hn. in the orch. before Napoleon at the Congress of Erfurt in 1808 and prod. his 3rd opera at Hamburg in 1811, he visited Vienna in 1812, becoming leader at the Theater an der Wien and staying until 1815. After prod. *Faust* in Prague, he travelled in It., 1816–7 and then became cond. at the Frankfort o/M. opera, 1818–20, when he 1st visited London and Paris, meeting Cherubini, R. Kreutzer, Viotti and others. After a visit to Dresden he became court mus. dir. at Cassel on 1. I. 1822, having accepted the post declined by Weber. who had recommended him in his place. He remained there for the rest of his life, but continued to travel. In 1831 he finished his *V. School*, in 1834 his wife d., and in 1836 he married the pfst. Marianne Pfeiffer. In 1839 he revisited Eng. for the prod. of *Calvary* at the Norwich Festival, and was commissioned to write an Eng. orat. *The Fall of Babylon* for the next festival of 1842, in which year he prod. Wagner's *Flying Dutchman* at Cassel. He was not allowed leave to go to Eng. for the orat., but went during his summer vacation in 1843, when he appeared before Queen Victoria and Prince Albert and toured Eng. and Wales. During the 1848 Revols. he showed liberal leanings and so annoyed the elector that he was refused leave of absence, and having taken his vacations without leave, he became involved in a long law-suit, which he lost after 4 years. In 1852 he adapted *Faust* with recits. for a prod. in It. in London and in 1863 he prod. Wagner's *Tannhäuser* at Cassel. He was pensioned off against his will in 1857.

Works incl. operas *Die Prüfung, Alruna, Der Zweikampf mit der Geliebten, Faust, Zemire und Azor, Jessonda, Der Berggeist, Pietro von Albano, Der Alchymist, Die Kreuzfahrer*; orats. *Das jüngste Gericht, Die letzten Dinge* (both *The Last Judgment*), *Des Heilands letzte Stunden* (*Calvary*), *The Fall of Babylon*; Mass, psalms, hymn *St. Cecilia*, cantata *Vater unser* (Klopstock); 9 syms. (4. *Die Weihe der Töne*, 6. Histor. Sym., 9. *The Seasons*), 5 ovts. (incl. one on Shakespeare's *Macbeth*); 17 v. concs. (8. *In modo d'una scena cantante*) & concertinos, concert pieces for v. & orch.; 4 cl. concs.; 33 stg. 4tets, 4 double stg. 4tets, 8 stg. 5tets, 2 stg. 6tets, 7tet for pf. stgs. & wind, Octet for stgs. & wind, Nonet for do., 5 pf. trios; pieces, vars. potpourris &c. for v.; v. duets; sos. for v. & hp.; hp. pieces; songs; part-songs, &c.

Sponga or **Spongia** } *See* **Usper.**

Spontini, Gasparo (Luigi Pacifico) (b. Maiolati nr. Jesi, 14. XI. 1774; d. Maiolati, 24. I. 1851), It. comp. His parents, who were poor peasants, and an uncle destined him for the priesthood, but he ran away to Monte San Vito, where another uncle allowed him to study m., and when he had advanced sufficiently, he returned home and was allowed to study at the Cons. de' Turchini at Naples from 1791, Sala and Tritto being among his masters. In 1795 he became a pupil-teacher. In 1796 he prod. his 1st opera in Rome, having run away from the Cons., but he was readmitted at the intercession of Piccinni, from whom he learnt much. He now prod. one opera after another, and in 1798 went to Palermo with the Neapol. court, which took refuge there and app. him mus. dir. in the place of Cimarosa, who refused to leave Naples. In 1803 he left for Paris, where he taught singing and tried his hand at Fr. comic opera, but made his 1st real success with the serious opera *La Vestale* in 1807. He was app. comp. to the Empress Joséphine and in 1810 became dir. of the It. opera at the Théâtre de l'Impératrice. In 1812 he was dismissed, but the Bourbon restor. in 1814 reinstated him. He soon sold his post to Angelica Catalani, however. In 1820 he was summoned to the court of Frederick William III in Berlin as general mus. dir. to the Prus. court. He was not on good terms with the intendant, Count Brühl, but nevertheless succeeded in introd. excellent reforms at the court opera; but his success was obscured in 1821 by that of Weber's *Freischütz*, which aroused an appetite for Ger. opera, as distinct from foreign opera set to Ger. words. In 1822–3 he visited Dresden, where he met Weber, also Vienna and Paris. In 1838 he spent the summer in Eng. to study Eng. hist. and local colour for a new opera on the subject of Milton, differing from his early one, which however was never finished; neither was an earlier work, *Les Athéniennes*. On the king's death in 1840 his position became more and more difficult, partly through his own fault, for he quarrelled with the new intendant, Count Redern, and became involved in a law-suit, and after much trouble and threatened imprisonment he left Berlin in VII. 1842. He went to live in Paris, visited Dresden in 1844 to cond. a perf. of *La Vestale* rehearsed for him by Wagner, became deaf in 1848 and returned to his birthplace, founding a m. school at Jesi.

Works incl. operas *I puntigli delle donne, Adelina Senese, L'eroismo ridicolo, Il finto pittore, La finta filosofa, La fuga in maschera* & 8 other It. operas, *La Petite Maison, Julie, ou Le Pot de fleurs, Milton* (in Fr.), *La Vestale, Fernand Cortez, Olympie* (Fr., rev. in Ger. as *Olympia*), *Pélage, ou Le Roi de la paix, Nurmahal* (Ger., after Moore's *Lalla Rookh*), *Alcidor, Agnes von Hohenstaufen, Les Dieux rivaux* (with Berton, R. Kreutzer and Persuis); festival play with m. on Moore's *Lalla Rookh* (orig. version of the opera); ballet for Salieri's *Les Danaïdes*; *Domine salvum fac* & other church m.; cantata *L'eccelsa gara* for the victory of Austerlitz, coronation cantata for Nicholas I of Rus.; voc. duets & trios; songs with pf. or hp. *Sensations douces*, &c.

Spontone, Bartolommeo (b. Bologna, *c.* 1529; d. Bergamo, after 1586), It. comp. Pupil of Nicola Mantovano and Morales, singer and in 1577–83 chapel master at San Petronio cath. at Bologna, and in 1584–6 at Santa Maria Maggiore, Bergamo. Comp. masses, madrigals, &c.

Sponza. *See* **Usper.**

Sporer, Thomas (b. ?, *c.* 1534; d. Strasburg, ?), Ger. comp. Wrote songs with accomp., then rare, but cultivated by Isaak, Hofhaimer, Senfl and others beside S.

Spottiswoode, Alicia Ann. *See* **Scott, Lady.**

Spourni, Dorothea. *See* **Wendling.**

Sprechgesang (Ger.). *See* **Speech-Song.**

'Spring' Sonata. The familiar nickname given to Beethoven's v. & pf. So. in F maj., Op. 24, comp. 1801.

'Spring' Symphony. A nickname sometimes given to Schumann's 1st Sym., in B♭ maj., Op. 38, finished II. 1841 and 1st perf. at Leipzig by Mendelssohn, 31. III. 1841.

Springdan or **Springer** (Norw.). A folk dance of Norw. in animated 3–4 time with a tune over a drone bass. The melody was often sung as well as played.

Springer (Ger.). *See* **Ornaments.**

Springer, Max (b. Schwendi, Württemberg, 19. XII. 1877), Ger. orgst., comp. & writer on church m. Educ. at Benedictine monasteries in Cz. and Aus. and later studied m. in Prague. App. prof. of church m. at the Vienna Acad. Author of books on plainsong and other church subjects.

Works incl. Christmas Mass, Easter Mass, Crescenzia Mass, Te Deum, *Lauda Sion*, Psalm cl, *Resurrection, Evening at Golgotha* & other sacred voc. works; 3 org. sos., 3 Pastorals, 4 Preludes, 8 Postludes & other org. works; 2 syms.; stg. 5tets, pf. 5tet; pf. pieces; songs, &c.

Sprung Rhythm. A term invented by Gerard Manley Hopkins for displacements of metrical stresses in poetry, not new to his verse, but exploited by him consciously and with great persistence and variety; and transferred to mus. terminology by Michael Tippett in the prefatory notes to his 2nd stg. 4tet, where S. R. is used with a deliberation similar to Hopkins's in the finale. It is no new thing to m., where it may be said to incl. such devices as syncopation, transference of stresses to weak beats or by tying notes over bar-lines or beats, the omission of rhythmic units by rests or the addition of them by triplets, &c.; but the new term may become useful to describe such rhythmic subtleties.

Squarcialupi, Antonio (b. ?; d. Florence, *c.* 1475), It. orgst. & comp. He lived at Siena in 1450 and at Florence, as orgst. of the church of Santa Maria, in 1467, when he was in correspondence with Dufay. All his works are lost.

Squire, W(illiam). Barclay (b. London, 16. X. 1855; d. London, 13. I. 1927), Eng. mcolst. Educ. at Frankfort o/M. and Pembroke Coll., Cambridge, where he took the M.A. in 1902. In 1885 he took charge of the dept. of printed m. in the British Museum. He was also a critic and the author of the lib. of Stanford's opera *The Veiled Prophet*, hon. sec. of the Purcell Soc. and one of the hon. secs. of the I.M.S. He pub. catalogues for the British Museum and the R.C.M., ed. Purcell's hpchd. m. and other works, and with Fuller-Maitland the *Fitzwilliam Virginal Book*.

St. *See* **Saint** for names comb. with it, e.g. Saint-Saëns.

Stabat Mater. A medieval Lat. sacred poem, prob. by Jacopone da Todi, not orig. liturgical, but increasingly used for devotional purposes until it was admitted as a Sequence to the Rom. missal in 1727.

Stabile, Annibale (b. Rome, *c.* 1540; d. ? Cracow, ?), It. comp. Pupil of Palestrina in Rome, where he became chapel master at the Lateran. In 1576–90 he held a similar post at the Ger. Coll. there, in 1592 at the church of Santa Maria Maggiore, and before 1604 he became chapel master to the King of Pol. at Cracow.

Works incl. motets, litanies & other church m.; madrigals, &c.

Staccato (It. = detached). A special manner of perf. mus. phrases without slurring the notes together, articulating each separately. The S. actually shortens the value of each note as written by the insertion of a minute pause, so that for ex. crotchets marked S. become something like dotted quavers followed by a semiquaver rest. The notation of S. is a series of dots placed over each note or chord to be so perf.

Staden, Johann (b. Nuremberg, 1581; d. Nuremberg, 15. XI. 1634), Ger. orgst. & comp. He was in the service of the Margrave of Kulmbach and Bayreuth in 1603–16, but became orgst. of St. Lorenz's church at Nuremberg and soon afterwards of St. Sebald's church.

Works incl. motets for voices alone, motets with inst. thorough-bass, sacred concertos for voices and insts.; *Hausmusik* for voices and insts. with Ger. words; sacred and secular songs with continuo for org. or lute; secular songs for 4–5 voices; inst. pavans, galliards, canzoni, &c.

Staden, Sigmund Gottlieb (or Theophilus) (b. ? Bayreuth, 1607; d. Nuremberg, 30. VII. 1655), Ger. orgst., violist & comp., son of prec. Pupil of his father, then of Jacob Baumann at Augsburg, 1620, and for va. bastarda of Walter Rowe in Berlin, 1626. In 1627 he became town musn. at Nuremberg and in 1634 orgst. of St. Lorenz's church, whose orgst., Valentin Dretzel, succeeded his father at St. Sebald's. In 1648 he pub. a book on singing.

Works incl. opera *Seelewig*; hymn-tunes for 4 voices; *Seelenmusik* containing hymn-tunes for 4 voices with thorough-bass for domestic use; songs with figured bass, &c.

Stadler, Maximilian (b. Melk, 7. VIII. 1748; d. Vienna, 8. XI. 1833), Aus. priest, orgst. & comp. Learnt m. as a choir-boy in the Lilienfeld monastery and finished his educ. at the Jesuit Coll. in Vienna. He joined the Benedictine order at the monastery of Melk in 1766, was a parish priest and prof. until 1786, when he became abbot of Lilienfeld and in 1789 of Kremsmünster monastery. Later he lived at var. country houses, at Linz and in Vienna, and became a parish priest again at Alt-Lerchenfeld and then in Boh. He completed several of Mozart's unfinished works.

Works incl. masses, 2 Requiems, misereres, Te Deum & other church m.; orat. *Die Befreiung von Jerusalem*; chor. for Collin's tragedy *Polyxena*; cantata *Die Frühlingsfeier* (Klopstock); org. sos. & fugues; pf. sos., &c.

Stadlmayr, Johann (b. Freising, Bavaria, 1560; d. Innsbruck, 12. VII. 1648), Ger. comp. He was in the service of the Archbishop of Salzburg early in the 17th cent., and chapel master of the Archdukes Maximilian and Leopold in 1610 and 1625 and of the Archduchess Claudia in 1636, at Innsbruck.

Works incl. masses, magnificats, Marian canticles, introits, hymns, psalms & other sacred m., some with insts., &c.

Staempfli, Eduard (b. Berne, 1. II. 1908), Swi. comp. Studied medicine at first but gave it up for m., which he studied with Jarnach at Cologne and with Dukas in Paris.

Works incl. ballets *Das Märchen von den zwei Flöten* & *Le Pendu*; cantata *Filles de Sion* for solo voices, chor. & orch.; 4 *Sinfonie concertanti* & other orch. works; 2 pf. concs., v. Conc., Conc. for 2 pfs. & stgs.; m. for 11 insts., Conc. for pf. & 8 insts., 2 stg. 4tets, 5tet for wind, 4tet for fl. & stgs., pf. Trio, stg. Trio & other chamber m.; pf. pieces; songs, &c.

Staff Notation. The ordinary mus. notation, so called to distinguish it from the notation used for Tonic Sol-fa.

Staggins, Nicholas (b. ? London, ?; d. London, 1705), Eng. comp. Pupil of his father. Charles II app. him Master of the King's Band in 1674 and he took the Mus.D. degree at Cambridge that year, becoming prof. of m. there in 1684. He advanced to the post of Master of the King's M., but was succeeded in it by Eccles in 1698.

Works incl. masque *Calisto, or The Chaste Nimph* (Crowne); incid. m. for Etheredge's *The Man of Mode*, Lee's *Gloriana*, Dryden's *Conquest of Granada* & *Marriage à la Mode* & Shadwell's *Epsom Wells* (last 2 with Robert Smith); odes for the birthdays of William III and Queen Anne; songs, &c.

Stagione (It. = season). The term is used esp. for an opera season.

Stahlspiel (Ger. lit. steel-play). A perc. inst. with tuned steel plates or bars which are played with hammers. It is known in Eng. milit. bands as Lyra, being made for them in the shape of a lyre. The modern Glockenspiel being also made of steel bars, and no longer of actual bells, is now to all intents and purposes the same inst. There is also an org. stop controlling steel bars named S.

Stainer, Jacob (b. Absam nr. Hall, 14. VII. 1621; d. Absam, 1683), Aus. v. maker. He learnt his craft at Innsbruck and (?) with one of the Amati family at Cremona or (?) with Vimercati at Venice. He began to work on his own account at Absam in 1641 and was later assisted by his brother Marcus (b. *c.* 1625), who afterwards worked on his own account at Laufen.

Stainer, John (b. London, 6. VI. 1840; d. Verona, 31. III. 1901), Eng. orgst. & comp. He became a choir-boy at St. Paul's cath. at the age of 7 and before long was able to deputize at the org. After working under var. masters and receiving an orgst.'s appt. in the City of London, he was app. by Ouseley orgst. of St. Michael's Coll., Tenbury, in 1856. In 1860 he went to Oxford as an undergraduate and orgst. to Magdalen Coll., then became orgst. to the Univ. in succession to Elvey and in 1865 took the D.Mus. degree. In 1872 he returned to London, having succeeded Goss as orgst. at St. Paul's cath. He held many posts, incl. those of univ. examiner and prof. at the Nat. Training School for M., where he succeeded Sullivan as principal in 1881. In 1888 he was knighted and in 1889 became Prof. of M. at Oxford. He wrote books on m. in the Bible, *Dufay and his Contemporaries*, &c.

Works incl. orats. *Gideon* & *The Crucifixion*; *Sevenfold Amen*, services & anthems; cantatas *The Daughter of Jairus* & *St. Mary Magdalen*, &c.

Stamaty, Camille (Marie) (b. Rome, 13. III. 1811; d. Paris, 19. IV. 1870), Fr. pfst. & comp. of Gr. descent. After the death of his father, his mother returned to Fr., taking him 1st to Dijon and then to Paris and teaching him m. In 1828 he became a civil servant, but continued to cultivate m., studying the pf. with Kalkbrenner and others, and comp. when he was attacked by rheumatism. He taught successfully, but sought further study with Mendelssohn at Leipzig in 1836–7. He had many disting. pupils, incl. Saint-Saëns.

Works incl. pf. Conc.; sos., Vars. on an orig. theme, numerous studies (one set on Weber's *Oberon*), exercises, transcriptions for pf., &c.

Stamitz (Stamic). Boh. family of musns.:

1. Johann Wenzel Anton S. (b. Německý-Brod, 19. VI. 1717; d. Mannheim, *c.* 27. III. 1757), vst. & comp. Studied v. and in 1742 played at the coronation of the Emperor Charles VII, where the Elector of Mannheim was struck by his gifts and invited him to his court. He was made mus. dir. there in 1745 and became the founder of the Mannheim school of early symsts.

Works incl. 45 syms., 10 orch. trios; many v. concs., hpchd. concs.; 18 v. sos., exercises for solo v.; hpchd. sos., &c.

2. Anton Thaddaeus S. (b. Německý-Brod, 1721; d. Altbunzlau, 22. VIII. 1768), cst., brother of prec. He entered the orch. at Mannheim under his brother, but later became a priest.

3. Carl S. (b. Mannheim, 7. V. 1746; d. Jena, XI. 1801), vst. & comp., son of 1. Pupil of his father. He became 2nd v. in the Mannheim orch. in 1762, but left for Paris in 1770 and became known there esp. as violist. He visited London in 1778. Later he lived in Ger., Prague and St. Petersburg, and from 1794 at Jena as mus. dir. to the Univ.

Works incl. operas *Der verliebte Vormund* & *Dardanus*; 70 syms.; concs.; chamber m., &c.

4. Anton S. (b. Mannheim, XI. 1754; d. ?, *c.* 1820), comp., brother of prec. He went to Paris with 3 in 1770.

Works incl. 13 syms.; 3 pf. concs., v. Conc., co. Conc.; chamber m., &c.

Ständchen (Ger.) = Serenade.

Standfuss, J. C. (b. ?; d. Hamburg, 1756), Ger. vst. & comp. He was attached to Koch's opera co. He was the 1st to prod. Ger. *Singspiele* by adapting Coffey's *The Devil to Pay* and *The Merry Cobbler*, the 1st of which had been given with the Eng. m. in Berlin in 1743.

Works incl. plays with m. *Der Teufel ist los, oder Die verwandelten Weiber*, *Der lustige Schuster*, *Der stolze Bauer Jochen Tröbs*; motets, &c.

Stanford, Charles Villiers (b. Dublin, 30. IX. 1852; d. London, 29. III. 1924), Ir. comp. In 1870 he became chor. scholar at Queen's Coll., Cambridge, and in 1873 orgst. of Trinity Coll., where he took classical honours the next year; also cond. of the Cambridge Univ. Mus. Soc. In 1874–6 he studied with Reinecke at Leipzig and Kiel in Berlin, and in the latter year Tennyson suggested him as comp. of incid. m. for his *Queen Mary*. Mus.D. at Oxford 1883 and Cambridge 1888, where he had succeeded Macfarren as Prof. of M. in 1887. He was also cond. of the Bach Choir in London and prof. of comp. at the R.C.M., where he cond. the orch. and opera classes. Knighted 1901.

Works incl. operas *The Veiled Prophet of Khorassan*, *Savonarola*, *The Canterbury Pilgrims* (after Chaucer),

Shamus O'Brien (after Le Fanu), *Much Ado About Nothing* (on Shakespeare), *The Critic* (on Sheridan), *The Travelling Companion*; incid. m. for Tennyson's *Queen Mary* & *Becket*, Aeschylus's *Eumenides*, Sophocles' *Oedipus Tyrannus*, Binyon's *Attila* and Louis N. Parker's *Drake*; 7 syms.; 5 Ir. Rhapsodies, 3 concert ovts., Serenade and Ir. dances for orch.; 3 pf. concs., 2 v. concs., co. Conc., cl. Conc., Suite for v. & orch., Vars. on an Eng. Theme for pf. & orch.; 8 stg. 4tets, 2 stg. 5tets, 2 pf. trios, 2 pf. 4tets, pf. 5tet, Serenade for 9 insts.; 2 sos. for v. & pf., 2 sos. for co. & pf., cl. & pf. So., some smaller inst. pieces with pf.; pf. works incl. Suite, Toccata, So., 3 *Dante Rhapsodies*; 11 org. works incl. 5 sos.; orats. *The Three Holy Children*, *Eden*; Mass, Requiem, Te Deum, *Stabat Mater*, Magnificat; 2 Psalms, 6 services, 3 anthems; chor. ballads *The Revenge*, *Phaudrig Crohoore*, *The Last Post*, &c.; works for solo voice and chor. (with or without orch.): *3 Cavalier Songs*, *The Bard*, *Songs of the Sea*, *Songs of the Fleet*; a number of partsongs; 20 op. nos. of songs (c. 100), incl. Heine's *Die Wallfahrt nach Kevlaar* and cycles *A Child's Garland* (Stevenson), poems by Robert Bridges, *An Irish Idyll*, *Songs of Faith*, *Cushendall*; voc. 4tets from Tennyson's *Princess*; 5 collections of Ir. folksongs ed., incl. the Petrie Collection in 3 vols., &c.

Stanley, Charles John (b. London, 17. I. 1713; d. London, 19. V. 1786), Eng. orgst. & comp. He was blind from the age of 2, but became a pupil of Greene and held var. orgst.'s appts. in London later. In 1760 he joined John Christopher Smith to continue Handel's orat. concerts, and when Smith retired in 1774, he continued with T. Linley. In 1779 he succeeded Boyce as Master of the King's M.

Works incl. opera *Teraminta*; dramatic cantata *The Choice of Hercules*; m. for Lloyd's *Arcadia, or The Shepherd's Wedding* & *Tears and Triumphs of Parnassus* & Southerne's *Oroonoko*; orats. *Jepthah*, *Zimri* & *The Fall of Egypt*; 12 cantatas to words by John Hawkins; 6 concs. for stgs.; solos for fl. or v.; cantatas and songs for voice & insts., &c.

Stanton, W(alter). K(endall). (b. Dauntsey, Wilts., 29. IX. 1891), Eng. comp. & educst. Learnt m. as choir-boy at Salisbury cath. and was educ. at Lancing Coll. and Merton Coll., Oxford, where he took the Mus.D. degree in 1935. In 1924 he succeeded Dyson as dir. of m. at Wellington Coll. and in 1927–37 he also dir. the m. at Reading Univ. and cond. perfs. in that town. In 1937 he became dir. of m. to the Midland Region of the B.B.C. at Birmingham, resigning in 1945.

Works incl. motets for double choir *The Spacious Firmament* (Addison) & *Sing we Triumphant Hymns*, &c.

Stapylton, Robert (1599–1669), Eng. playwright. *See* **Locke** (*Stepmother*).

Starck, Ingeborg (b. St. Petersburg, 24. VIII. 1840; d. Munich, 17. VI. 1913), Swe. pfst. & comp. Pupil of Henselt at St. Petersburg and of Liszt at Weimar. She made a long concert tour in 1858–9 and in 1862 married Hans von Bronsart, who later became intendant of the court theatre at Hanover.

Works incl. operas *Die Göttin von Sais*, *Jery und Bätely* (Goethe), *König Hiarne*, *Manfred* (after Byron), *Die Sühne*; pf. Conc.; *Kaiser Wilhelm Marsch*; chamber m.; pf. pieces; songs, &c.

Starokadomsky, Mikhail (b. Brest-Litovsk, 13. VI. 1901), Rus. comp. Studied at the Moscow Cons. under Vassilenko, Miaskovsky and Catoire.

Works incl. opera *Sot*; orat. *Simon Proshakov*; Sym., Conc. & 2 suites for orch.; org. Conc., v. Conc.; 2 stg. 4tets; pf. So., &c.

Starzer, Josef (b. ?, 1726; d. Vienna, 22. IV. 1787), Aus. vst. & comp. Began his career as leader in the Vienna court chapel and vst. at the Fr. theatre. In 1760–8 he was leader in the court orch. at St. Petersburg, but resumed his activities in Viennese mus. life on his return. He became assoc. with Noverre, for whose ballets he comp. m.

Works incl. play with m. *Die Wildschützen*; ballet m. for Raupach's *Alcesta*; ballets *Flora und Boreas*, *Apollo und Daphne*, *Die Horazier und die Curazier*, *Theseus auf Creta*, *Adelheid von Ponthieu* & others; orat. *La passione di Gesù Cristo*; syms., divertimenti, &c. for orch.; v. Conc.; stg. 4tets & other chamber m., &c.

Stassov, Vladimir Vassilievitch (b. St. Petersburg, 14. I. 1824; d. St. Petersburg, 23. X. 1906), Rus. scholar & art critic. Educ. at the School of Jurisprudence and studied for 3 years in It., joined the Imp. Public Library on his return in 1854 and in 1872 became dir. of the dept. of fine arts there. He was the 1st literary champion of the Rus. nationalist school of comps.

Statkowski, Roman (b. Szczypiorno nr. Kalisz, 5. I. 1860; d. Warsaw, 12. XI. 1925), Pol. comp. Studied with Zelenski at Warsaw and with Soloviev at St. Petersburg. On the death of Noskowski in 1909 he was app. prof. of comp. at the Warsaw Cons.

Works incl. operas *Philaenis* & *Maria* (after Malczewski); Fantasy, Polonaise & other works for orch.; 6 stg. 4tets; v. & pf. pieces; *Krakowiak* & other works for pf.; songs, &c.

Staudigl, Joseph (b. Wöllersdorf, 14. IV. 1807; d. Döbling nr. Vienna, 28. III. 1861), Aus. bass singer. Learnt m. as a novice at the monastery of Melk, but ran away to Vienna in 1827 and entered the chor. of the Kärntnertor Theatre, where he soon rose through small parts to a position of eminence. He 1st visited Eng. in 1846, when he created the title part in Mendelssohn's *Elijah* at the Birmingham Festival. He d. insane.

Stave. The 5 horizontal lines on which m. is written.

Stavenhagen, Bernhard (b. Greiz, Reuss, 25. XI. 1862; d. Geneva, 26. XII. 1914), Ger. cond. & pfst. Studied with Kiel and Rudorff in Berlin and with Liszt at Weimar, where he became court pfst. in 1890 and mus. dir. in 1895. After a similar post in Munich, he returned to Weimar, but in 1907 went to Swi. and settled at Geneva as cond. He wrote a Conc. and pieces for pf.

Stcherbatchev. *See* **Shtcherbatchev.**

Steele, Richard (1672 – 1729), Ir. essayist & dramatist. *See* **Croft** (*Lying Lover*), **Inkle and Yarico** (Arnold), **Purcell (D.)** (*Funeral* & *Tender Husband*), **Rust (F. W.)** (*Inkle und Yariko*).

Stefan, Paul (real name P. S. Gruenfeldt) (b. Brno, 25. XI. 1879; d. New York, 12. XI. 1943), Aus. writer on m. Studied at Brno, at Vienna Univ. and with Graedener & Schoenberg. Settled in Vienna as m. critic and correspondent and in 1921 founded the *Musikblätter des Anbruch*. In 1938 he left Aus. owing to the Nazi régime and went to Swi., later to U.S.A. He wrote books on m. in Vienna, Schubert, Dvořák, Mahler, Schoenberg, Toscanini, Bruno Walter, &c.

Steffani, Agostino (b. Castelfranco, 25. VII. 1654; d. Frankfort o/M., 12. II. 1728), It. diplomat & comp. Learnt m. as a choir-boy at Padua and was taken to Munich, where he studied m. under Kerl at the expense of the Elector Ferdinand Maria. After further studies in Rome, 1673–4, he returned to Munich and became court orgst. in 1675; having also studied maths., philos. and theol., he was ordained priest in 1680. He was made dir. of the court chamber m., but in 1688 the younger Bernabei was app. general mus. dir. on the death of his father, and S., disappointed of the post, left Munich. After a visit to Venice he went to the court of Hanover, where the post of mus. dir. was offered him, and there he also filled other posts, incl. diplomatic ones. The philos. Leibniz, who was also at the court, sent him on a diplomatic mission to var. Ger. courts in 1696; in 1698 he was ambassador to Brussels, and on the death of the Elector Ernest Augustus transferred his services to the Elector Palatine at Düsseldorf. In 1706 he was made a nominal bishop. In 1708–9 he was on a diplomatic mission in It., where he met Handel, who went into service at the Hanoverian court at his suggestion. In 1722–5 he lived at Padua and in 1724 he was elected hon. president of the London Acad. of Ancient M. In 1727 he went to It. for the last time. He d. at Frankfort during a diplomatic visit.

Works incl. operas *Marco Aurelio, Solone, Servio Tullio, Alarico il Baltha, Niobe, Enrico Leone, La lotta d'Hercole con Achelao, La superbia d'Alessandro, Orlando generoso, Le rivali concordi, La libertà contenta, I trionfi del fato, Baccanali, Briseide, Arminio, Enea* & *Tassilone*; m. for a tournament *Audacia e rispetto*; motets, vesper psalms for 8 voices, *Stabat Mater* for 6 voices, stgs. & org., *Confitebor* for 3 voices & stgs. & other church m.; madrigals; voc. chamber duets with bass; chamber sos. for 2 vs., va. & bass, &c.

Steffkins. Family of lutenists & violists of unknown nationality settled in London in the 17th cent.:

1. Theodore S. (b. ?; d. ? London), teacher of the lute & va. da gamba.

2. Dietricht S. (b. ?; d. ? London), brother of prec., member of Charles I's band.

3. Frederick S. (b. London, ?; d. ? London), son of prec.

4. Christian S. (b. London, ?; d. ? London), brother of prec.

Stèg (Ger.). The bridge of a stg. inst.

Steggall, Reginald (b. London, 17. IV. 1867; d. London, 16. XI. 1938), Eng. orgst. & comp. Studied with his father, Charles S. (1826–1905), and at the R.A.M., where he became org. prof. in 1895. In 1886 he was app. orgst. at St. Anne's church, Soho, and in 1905 succeeded his father as orgst. of Lincoln's Inn chapel.

Works incl. Mass, services & anthems; Sym., Vars on an Orig. Theme, Fantasy Ovt. for orch.; voc. scenas with orch. *Elaine* & *Alcestis*; org. pieces, &c.

Stegmann, Carl David (b. Dresden, *c.* 1751; d. Bonn, 27. V. 1826), Ger. ten. singer, cond. & comp. Studied with Homilius and others at Dresden, and after singing and cond. at var. opera houses in Ger., he became cond. at the Hamburg theatre in 1798, retiring to Bonn in 1811.

Works incl. operas *Heinrich der Löwe, Der Triumph der Liebe, Erwin und Elmire* (Goethe) & many others; incid. m. for Shakespeare's *King Lear* & *Macbeth* & other plays; concs., &c.

Steibelt, Daniel (b. Berlin, 22. X. 1765; d. St. Petersburg, 2. X. 1823), Ger. pfst. & comp. He learnt much about keyboard insts. in his childhood, being the son of a hpchd. & pf. maker, and studied m. with Kirnberger. After serving in the army, he made his 1st appearance as pfst. & comp. in Paris during the late 1780s. At the end of 1796 he visited London, where he remained until 1799 and married an Englishwoman. He visited Hamburg, Dresden, Prague, Berlin and Vienna, where he had an encounter with Beethoven at the pf., and in VIII. 1800 again settled in Paris, but spent as much of his time in London. In 1808 he left for the court at St. Petersburg, where he became chapel master to the tsar on the departure of Boïeldieu in 1810.

Works incl. operas *Roméo et Juliette* (after Shakespeare), *La Princesse de Babylone, Cendrillon, Sargines* & *Le Jugement de Midas* (unfinished); ballets *Le Retour de Zéphyr, Le Jugement du berger Paris, La Belle Laitière, La Fête de l'empereur*; intermezzo *La Fête de Mars* for the victory at Austerlitz; incid. m.; 5 pf. concs.; 50 studies and numerous pieces and transcriptions for pf., &c.

Steigleder, Hans Ulrich (b. Schwäbisch-Hall, III. 1593; d. Stuttgart, 10. X. 1635), Ger. orgst. & comp. After an appt. as orgst. at Lindau on Lake Constance, he became orgst. at a monastery at Stuttgart in 1617 and musn. to the court of Württemberg.

Works incl. ricercari and vars. on a Lord's Prayer hymn-tune for org., &c.

Stein. Ger. family of pf. makers:

1. Johann Andreas S. (b. Heidesheim, 1728; d. Augsburg, 29. II. 1792), orgst. & pf. & org. maker. Learnt his craft in Paris and settled at Augsburg.

2. Maria Anna (Nanette) S. (b. Augsburg, 2. I. 1769; d. Vienna, 16. I. 1833), pfst. & pf. maker, daughter of prec. She played to Mozart as a child during his visit to Augsburg in 1777, and on her father's death in 1792 carried on the business with her brother, 3, but married Andreas Streicher in 1793 and moved with him to Vienna, where they estab. a new manufacture, jointly with 3. Later she and her husband became friends of Beethoven.

3. Matthäus Andreas S. (b. Augsburg, 12. XII. 1776; d. Vienna, 6. V. 1842), pf. maker, brother of prec. He accompanied his sister and her husband to Vienna in 1793 and joined their firm, but estab. himself independently in 1802.

4. Friedrich S. (b. Augsburg, 26. V. 1784; d. Vienna, 5. V. 1809), pfst. & comp., brother of prec. Went to Vienna as a child with his sister and brother, and studied pf. playing, also comp. with Albrechtsberger. He appeared in public frequently, esp. with Mozart's concs.

Works incl. 3 operettas; pantomime *Die Fee Radiante*; v. Conc.; pf. Trio; pf. So; songs, &c.

5. Karl Andreas S. (b. Vienna, 4. IX. 1797; d. Vienna, 28. VIII. 1863), comp. & pf. maker, nephew of prec., son of 3. Pupil of Forster. He 1st devoted himself to comp., but later mainly to his father's factory, to which he succeeded.

Works incl. comic opera *Die goldene Gans*; 2 ovts.; 2 pf. concs., &c.

Stein, Erwin (b. Vienna, 7. XI. 1885), Aus. mcolst. Pupil of Schoenberg. After cond. at var. places, he joined the Universal Ed. in Vienna, but settled in London after the Anschluss. He has written much on Schoenberg and his school.

Stein, Gertrude (b. 1874), Amer. authoress. *See* **Berners** (*Wedding Bouquet*), **Bowles** (*Letter to Freddy*), **Thomson (V.)** (*4 Saints in 3 Acts* & *Capital, Capitals*).

Steinbach, Emil (b. Lengenrieden, Baden, 14. XI. 1849; d. Mainz, 6. XII. 1919), Ger. cond. & comp. Studied at the Leipzig Cons. and became cond. and theatre dir. at Mainz. Comp. orch. works, chamber m., songs, &c.

Steinbach, Fritz (b. Grünsfeld, Baden, 17. VI. 1855; d. Munich, 13. VIII. 1916), Ger. cond. & comp., brother of prec. Studied with his brother and at the Leipzig Cons. After working as 2nd cond. at Mainz in 1880–6, he went to the court of Meiningen, with whose orch. he visited London in 1902, when he succeeded Wüllner as munic. cond. and dir. of the Cons. at Cologne. His works incl. a 7tet and a co. So.

Steinberg, Maximilian Osseievitch (b. Vilna, 4. VII. 1883), Rus. comp. Studied at St. Petersburg Univ. and Cons. Pupil (and later son-in-law) of Rimsky-Korsakov, also of Liadov and Glazunov. He became prof. at the Leningrad Cons.

Works incl. ballets *Midas* (after Ovid) & *Till Eulenspiegel*; incid. m.; orat. *Heaven and Earth* (after Byron); 4 syms., dramatic fantasy on Ibsen's *Brand*, ovt. to Maeterlinck's *La*

Princesse Maleine & other orch. works; 2 stg. 4tets; songs incl. 2 Tagore cycles, folksong arrs., &c.

Steinway (orig. Steinweg). A firm of pf. makers in N.Y., founded in 1849 by Heinrich Engelhard Steinweg at Brunswick, who emigrated with 5 sons and estab. himself in 1853.

Stem. The stroke attached to the heads of all notes of smaller value than a semibreve.

Stendhal (Henri Beyle) (1783–1842), Fr. critic & novelist. Wrote a biog. of Rossini, letters on Haydn (partly plagiarized from Carpani), &c. *See* **Chartreuse de Parme** (Sauguet).

Stenhammar, Vilhelm (Eugen) (b. Stockholm, 7. II. 1871; d. Stockholm, 20. XI. 1927), Swe. pfst., cond. & comp. Pupil of his father, the comp. Per Ulrik S., and later of Sjögren and others; also studied in Berlin. He became cond. of the royal orch. at Stockholm and also cond. at Göteborg.

Works incl. operas *The Feast at Solhaug* (based on Ibsen) & *Tirfing*; incid. m. to Shakespeare's *Twelfth Night*, *Hamlet* & *Romeo and Juliet*, Strindberg's *Ett dromspel*, Gozzi's *Turandot*, Tagore's *Chitra* & other plays; cantatas *The Princess and the Page*, *Snöfrid*, *Hemmarschen* & *Saangen*; 2 syms., symph. ovt. *Excelsior*, *Prelude and Bourrée*, Serenade in F maj., for orch.; 2 pf. concs., *2 Sentimental Romances* for v. & orch.; 6 stg. 4tets, pf. 4tet; v. & pf. So.; 4 sos. & Fantasy for pf.; partsongs incl. *Sverige*; songs, &c.

Stentando (It. = toiling, labouring). A direction indicating a dragging delivery of a passage.

Štěpán, Vaclav (b. Pečky, 12. XII. 1889), Cz. pfst., critic & comp. Studied with Novák and others and became prof. of mus. aesthetics at the Prague Cons. His literary works incl. a study of *Mus. Symbolism of Programme M.* and his comps. a poem *Life's Halcyon Days* for co. & pf.

Stepanian, Aro (b. Elisabetopol, 1897), Rus, comp. He began to teach m. in the Armenian school of his native town and later of Alexandropol before he was 20; then studied at the Moscow School of M. under Glière and Gnessin and at the Leningrad Cons. under Shtcherbatchev. Settled as prof. of m. at Everan in Rus. Armenia, the folksongs of which he studied.

Works incl. operas *Nazar the Brave*, *David Sassunsky* & *The Dawn*; symph. poem *To the Memory of Twenty-six Commissars*; chamber m.; inst. pieces; songs, &c.

Stephan, Rudi (b. Worms, 29. VII. 1887; d. Gorlice, Galicia, 29. IX. 1915), Ger. comp. Studied at Worms, with Sekles at Frankfort o/M. and at Munich. He fell in battle near Gorlice.

Works incl. opera *Die ersten Menschen*; ballad *Liebeszauber* (Hebbel) for bar. & orch.; *Music for Orch.*; *Music for Fiddle and Orch.*; *Music for 7 Stringed Insts.* (incl. pf. & hp.); pf. pieces; songs, &c.

Stephen, David (b. Dundee, 25. VIII. 1869), Sco. pfst., orgst. & comp. Studied in London, returned to Sco. and became orgst. at Dundee and then at Glasgow, and was mus. dir. to the Carnegie Trust at Dunfermline, 1903–27. Ed. of a *Collection of Sco. Songs*.

Works incl. cantata *The Abbot's Bell*, ballad for chor. & orch. *Sir Patrick Spens*; Sym., Sinfonietta, *Hebridean Rhapsodie* & *Coronach*; Fantasy pf. 5tet; v. & pf. So., &c.

Stephens, Catherine (b. London, 18. IX. 1794; d. London, 22. II. 1882), Eng. sop. singer. 1st appeared in It. opera in 1812, in London, and at Covent Garden in 1813.

Stephens, James (b. 1882), Ir. novelist & poet. *See* **Barber** (chors.), **Busch** (songs), **Schubart** (M.) (*Etched in Moonlight*).

Sterkel, Johann Franz Xaver (b. Würzburg, 3. XII. 1750; d. Würzburg, 21. X. 1817), Ger. priest, pfst. & comp. Educ. at Würzburg Univ., he took holy orders and in 1778 became chaplain and pfst. to the Elector of Mainz at Aschaffenburg. After a visit to It. he became famous as a teacher and pfst., esp. as an improviser. In 1791 the court was visited by the musns. attached to the Elector of Cologne, incl. Beethoven, whom he induced to play, and in 1793 he succeeded Righini as mus. dir. In 1805–13 he was chapel master at Ratisbon.

Works incl. opera *Farnace*; 10 syms., 2 ovts. for orch.; 6 pf. concs.; stg. 5tet, pf. 4tet, 6 stg. trios; sos. for pf. solo & duet, pf. pieces, vars., &c.; Ger. songs, It. canzonets; voc. duets, &c.

Sterling, Antoinette (b. Sterlingville, N.Y., 23. I. 1850; d. London, 9. I. 1904), Amer. con. singer. Studied in N.Y. and made her 1st appearance in Eng. in 1868. After a visit to Ger. and further studies with Pauline Viardot-García and Manuel García, she sang in U.S.A. and London, where she settled and married John MacKinlay. Mother of the folksong singer Jean Sterling MacKinlay and the bar. Sterling MacKinlay.

Stern, Julius (b. Breslau, 8. VIII. 1820; d. Berlin, 27. II. 1883), Ger. cond. & educst. Studied in Berlin,

Dresden and Paris, and after a career as chor. cond. opened a Cons. in Berlin with Kullak and Marx, who later withdrew from it.

Stern, Leo(pold Lawrence) (b. Brighton, 5. IV. 1862; d. London, 10. IX. 1904), Eng. cst. After beginning a career as chemist, he studied at the R.A.M. in London and with J. Klengel and Davidov at Leipzig, making his 1st appearance in London in 1886.

Sterndale Bennett. *See* **Bennett, William Sterndale.**

Sterne, Laurence (1713–68), Eng. novelist. *See* **Arne (M.)** (*Tristram Shandy*).

Stesso tempo, Lo (It., obs., now *l'istesso tempo*). A direction given where a change is indicated in the time-signature, but the comp. wishes the m. to continue at the same pace or beat. The change is thus merely one of metre, not of motion.

Stevens, Bernard (b. London, 1916), Eng. comp. Studied at Cambridge with E. J. Dent and Rootham and at the R.C.M. in London with R. O. Morris.

Works incl. Mass for unaccomp. choir, chor. work to words by Blake; Sym.; v. Conc.; stg. 4tet, pf. Trio; Vars. for pf., &c.

Stevens, Richard (John Samuel) (b. London, 27. III. 1757; d. London, 23. IX. 1837), Eng. orgst. & comp. Learnt m. as a choir-boy at St. Paul's cath. and became orgst. of the Temple church in 1786, also at Charterhouse school in 1796, and was app. Gresham Prof. of M. at London Univ. in 1801.

Works incl. hpchd. sos.; glees; songs, &c.

Stevenson, John (Andrew) (b. Dublin, XI. 1761; d. Kells, Co. Meath, 14. IX. 1833), Ir. orgst. & comp. Learnt m. as a chorister at Christ Church and St. Patrick's caths. at Dublin and later became vicar-choral at both. In 1814 he was app. orgst. and mus. dir. at the Castle Chapel. Knighted in 1803.

Works incl. operas *The Contract* (with Cogan) & *Love in a Blaze*; m. for O'Keeffe's farces *The Son-in-Law, The Dead Alive* & *The Agreeable Surprise*, m. for other stage pieces; orat. *Thanksgiving*; services & anthems; glees, canzonets & duets; songs; accomps. for Ir. songs ed. with words by Thomas Moore, &c.

Stevenson, Robert (b. ?; d. ? Chester, ?), Eng. 16th-cent. comp. Took the Mus.B. and Mus.D. degree at Oxford in 1587 and 1596 and was orgst. at Chester cath., 1570–99.

Works incl. services, anthems, Miserere for 6 voices, &c.

Stevenson, Robert Louis (1850–94), Sco. poet, novelist & essayist. *See* **Gilbert (H. F.)** (*Pirate Song*), **Hill (E. B.)** (suites), **Hughes (G.)** (songs), **Stanford** (*Child's Garland*), **Vaughan Williams** (*Songs of Travel*).

Stewart, Robert (Prescott) (b. Dublin, 16. XII. 1825; d. Dublin, 24. III. 1894), Ir. orgst. & comp. Learnt m. as chorister at Christ Church cath., Dublin, and became orgst. there and at Trinity Coll. in 1844; also cond. of the chor. soc. at Dublin Univ. in 1846, where he became prof. of m. in 1861. Knighted in 1872. Ed. the Ir. *Church Hymnal* in 1876.

Works incl. Fantasy on Ir. Airs for chor., org. & orch., cantata *A Winter Night's Wake* & *The Eve of St. John, Ode on Shakespeare* and Ode for Cork Exhib.; org. works; glees, &c.

Stg(s). (abbr.) = String, strings.

Stiastný, Johann (b. Prague, 1764; d. ?, *c.* 1820), Cz. cst. & comp. Studied at Prague, together with his brother, Bernard Wenzel S. (1760–1835), also a cst., later lived by turns at Frankfort o/M., Nuremberg and Mannheim, and became known both in London and Paris.

Works incl. Concertino & Andante for co. with fl. & stgs.; Trio for co. with va. & 2nd co.; duets for 2 cos.; co. pieces and studies, &c.

Sticcado-Pastrole. An 18th-cent. name for an inst. of the xylophone type.

Stich, Johann Wenzel (called Punto) (b. Žehušice nr. Časlav, 1746; d. Prague, 16. II. 1803), Boh. hn. player and comp. for his inst. Studied at Dresden. Travelled much under the name of Punto and settled for a time in Paris, also appeared in London and in Vienna, where Beethoven wrote his hn. So. for him.

Stiehl, Heinrich (Franz Daniel) (b. Lübeck, 5. VIII. 1829; d. Reval, 1. V. 1886), Ger. orgst., cond. & comp. Studied with his father, Johann Dietrich S. (1800–73), orgst. at Lübeck, and at Weimar and Leipzig. He lived by turns in Rus., Aus., It., Eng., Ir., and Eng. and Rus. again, working as orgst., cond. and teacher. His brother Karl Johann Christian S. (1826–1911) was an orgst. and cond.

Works incl. operas *Der Schatzgräber* & *Jery und Bätely* (Goethe); *The Vision* & other orch. pieces; stg. 4tets, 3 pf. trios; co. & pf. So.; *Sonata quasi fantasia* & other pf. works, &c.

Stierhorn (Ger. = bull hn.) A primitive wind inst., made of a bull or cow horn, sounding a single note of rough quality. Wagner uses it for the watchman in *The Mastersingers*.

Stiffelio, opera by Verdi (lib. by Francesco Maria Piave), prod. Trieste, 16. XI. 1850.

Stile rappresentativo (It. =representative style). A neologism used by It. musns. of the new monodic school in the early years of the 17th cent. to describe the new voc. style of declamatory, recitative-like dramatic m. which tried to imitate human speech as closely as possible and thus endeavoured to 'represent' dramatic action in a naturalistic way.

Still, William Grant (b. Woodville, Miss., 11. V. 1895), Amer. Negro comp. Educ. at Wilberforce Univ. and studied m. at Oberlin Cons., later with Chadwick at Boston and with Varèse.

Works incl. opera *Blue Steel*; ballets *La Guiablesse* & *Sahdji*; *Lenox Avenue* for radio announcer, chor. & orch.; *Afro-Amer. Sym.*, *Africa*, *Poem* & other orch. works; *Kaintuck* for pf. & orch.; *From the Black Belt* & *Log Cabin Ballads* for chamber orch., &c.

Stimme (Ger. =voice & part). Not only the human voice, but also any part, voc. or inst., in a comp., esp. a polyphonic one; also the copy of an orch., voc. or chamber m. part used for perf.

Stimmführung (Ger. lit. voice-leading) =Part-writing.

Sting. An old term describing the effect of Vibrato in lute playing.

Stirling, Elizabeth (b. Greenwich, 26. II. 1819; d. London, 25. III. 1895), Eng. orgst. & comp. Studied with Macfarren and others and in 1839, having given very successful org. recitals, she was app. orgst. at All Saints' church, Poplar, later going to St. Andrew's Undershaft, 1858–60. She married the orgst. Frederick Albert Bridge in 1863.

Works incl. Psalm for 5 voices & orch.; org. fugues & other pieces; songs, duets, partsongs, &c.

Stivori, Francesco (b. ?; d. ?), It. 16th–17th-cent. orgst. & comp. Pupil of Merulo. He became town orgst. at Montagnana in 1579 and was later in the service of the Archduke Ferdinand of Aus. until 1605.

Works incl. masses, magnificat, *Sacrae cantiones*; madrigals; inst. ricercari, &c.

Stobaeus, Johann (b. Graudenz, W. Prus., 6. VII. 1580; d. Königsberg, 11. IX. 1646), Ger. bass singer & comp. While attending the Univ. at Königsberg, he studied m. with Eccard, and after holding var. minor appts. there he became chapel master to the Elector of Brandenburg in 1626.

Works incl. *Cantiones sacrae* for 5–10 voices, magnificats for 5–6 voices, 5-part settings of hymn-tunes; Prus. Festival Songs for 5–8 voices (with Eccard); sacred & secular occasional comps., &c.

Stock and Horn. *See* **Stockhorn.**

Stock, Frederick (Friedrich August) (b. Jülich, 11. XI. 1872; d. Chicago, 20. X. 1942), Ger.-Amer. vst., cond. & comp. Studied with his father, a bandmaster, and at the Cologne Cons., later with Humperdinck, Jensen and Wüllner. He joined the Cologne orch. as a vst. in 1890, but settled at Chicago in 1895 in the same capacity, becoming asst. cond. to Theodore Thomas and succeeding him as cond. in 1905.

Works incl. *Psalmic Rhapsody* for solo voice, chor. & orch.; 2 syms., symph. poem *Life*, Vars., *Symph. Sketches* & 3 ovts. for orch.; v. Conc.; chamber m.; v. pieces; pf. pieces; songs, &c.

Stockflöte (Ger. =stick fl.). *See* **Czakan.**

Stockhausen, Julius (b. Paris, 22. VII. 1826; d. Frankfort o/M., 22. IX. 1906), Ger. bar. singer. Pupil of his mother and later of Manuel García in Paris for singing and Halié and Stamaty for pf. He made his 1st important concert appearance at Basle in 1848, visited Eng. the next year and then divided his attention between Fr. opera and Ger. song. In 1869 he became chamber singer to the King of Württemberg, but left Stuttgart in 1874, teaching by turns at Berlin and Frankfort.

Stockhausen (*née* **Schmuck**), **Margarete** (b. Gebweiler, 1803; d. Colmar, 6. X. 1877), Ger. sop. singer, mother of prec. & wife of the hpst. & comp. Franz S. (1792–1868). Studied with Catrufo in Paris and 1st toured with her husband in 1825.

Stockhorn. A primitive Sco. inst. similar to the Pibgorn, made of wood or bone fitted with a cow horn, hence orig. 'stock and horn.' It was played like the chanter of a bagpipe, with a single reed.

Stockmarr, Johanne (b. Copenhagen, 21. IV. 1869; d. Copenhagen, I. 1944), Dan. pfst. Studied in Copenhagen and Paris; app. court pfst. to the King of Den.

Stodart. A firm of Eng. 18th–19th-cent. hpchd. and pf. makers, founded *c.* 1776 by Robert S., carried on by his son William S., whose workman William Allen invented the metal frame for the pf., and later by his grandson Malcolm S.

Stoelzel, Gottfried Heinrich (b. Grünstädtl, Saxony, 13. I. 1690; d. Gotha, 27. XI. 1749), Ger. comp. Studied at Leipzig, where he joined Telemann's Collegium Musicum. He taught at Breslau in 1710–2, went to It. in 1713, and then lived at Prague,

Bayreuth and Gera, becoming chapel master to the Duke of Saxe-Coburg-Gotha in 1719.

Works incl. opera *Narcissus* & *c.* 15 others; masses; 14 orats.; concs.; trio-sos., &c.

Stoessel, Albert (Frederic) (b. St. Louis, 11. X. 1894; d. New York, 12. V. 1943), Amer. vst., cond. & comp. Studied at home and later at the Hochschule für Musik in Berlin. On his return to Amer. he appeared as solo vst., served as a bandmaster during the 1914–8 war and in 1922 succeeded W. Damrosch as cond. of the Orat. Soc. of N.Y. and dir. of m. at the Chautauqua Institution. In 1930 he became dir. of the opera and orch. at the Juillard Graduate School there.

Works incl. opera *Garrick*; *Hispania* & *Early Americana* suites, *Suite antique*, symph. portrait *Cyrano de Bergerac* (after Rostand), Concerto grosso, &c. for orch.; *Suite antique* arr. for 2 vs. & pf.; v. & pf. So. & pieces, &c.

Stojowski, Sigismond (Denis Antoine) (b. Strzelce, 14. V. 1870), Pol. pfst. & comp. Studied with Zelenski at Cracow, then with Diémer, Dubois, Delibes and Massenet in Paris, and finally, on his return, with Gorski and Paderewski. He toured Eur. as a pfst. in 1905–11 and then became head of the pf. dept. at the Inst. of Mus. Art in N.Y., where he remained.

Works incl. *A Prayer for Poland* for chor., org. & orch., cantata; Sym. in D min.; 2 pf. concs., *Symph. Rhapsody* for pf. & orch., Conc. & Romanza for v. & orch., co. Conc.; chamber m.; inst. sos.; pf. pieces; songs, &c.

Stollen (Ger. = props). The songs of the Ger. Minnesinger and Meistersinger were usually divided into 3 sections: 2 S. of equal length often sung to the same and always to very similar m., and an *Abgesang* (after-song) forming a concluding section of unspecified length and with different though relevant m. The 2 S. together were called the *Aufgesang* (fore-song).

Stoltz, Rosine (real name Victorine Noeb) (b. Paris, 13. II. 1815; d. Paris, 28. VII. 1903), Fr. sop. singer. Studied at Choron's school, became a chor. singer after the 1830 Revol., made a 1st appearance at Brussels in 1832 and in 1837 came out at the Paris Opéra.

Stöltzel, Gottfried Heinrich. *See* **Stoelzel.**

Stoltzer, Thomas (b. Schweidnitz, Silesia, ?; d. ?), Ger. 16th-cent. comp. Became chapel master to King Louis of Boh. and Hung. at Buda, but left after the battle of Mohács in 1526 (if he was not killed in it) and (?) took up a post in the service of Duke Albert of Prus. at Königsberg.

Works incl. Lat. motets & psalms, Lat. hymns for 4–5 voices, Psalm xxxvii in Luther's Ger. trans. for 3–7 voices in motet form & 4 others; Ger. sacred & secular songs, &c.

Stolz, Teres(in)a (b. Kostelec nad Labem, 1836; d. Milan, 22–3. VIII. 1902), Boh.-It. sop. singer. Studied under Lamperti at Milan and made her 1st stage appearance in 1860. She was Verdi's 1st Aida at Milan and the sop. in the 1st perf. of his Requiem.

Stölzel, Gottfried Heinrich. *See* **Stoelzel.**

Stonard, William (b. ?; d. Oxford, 1630), Eng. orgst. & comp. In 1608 he took a degree at Oxford and became orgst. of Christ Church cath. there, retaining the post until his death.

Works incl. services, anthems; catch ' Ding dong bell,' &c.

Stone Guest, The (*Kamennyi Gost*), opera by Dargomizhsky (lib. Pushkin's drama set unaltered), not perf. in the comp.'s lifetime; prod. St. Petersburg, 28. II. 1872.

Stone, Robert (b. Alphington, Devon, 1516; d. London, 2. VII. 1613), Eng. comp. He learnt m. as a chorister at Exeter cath., but *c.* 1543 went to London to enter the Chapel Royal, of which he became a Gentleman. Comp. a setting of the Lord's Prayer, &c.

Stonerd or **Stonnard**, **William.** *See* **Stonard.**

Stopped. Org. pipes the upper end of which is closed are said to be S. pipes. They prod. notes similar in pitch to those of Open pipes of half their length.

Stopped Diapason. *See* **Diapason.**

Stopped Notes. On wind insts. the Ns. not prod. naturally as harmonics, but by valves, keys or other mechanical means, or sometimes by the hand in hn. playing. On stg. insts. any Ns. not prod. on open stgs.

Stopping. The placing of the left-hand fingers on the stgs. of stg. insts. to change the pitch of the notes of the open stgs. The playing of 2 notes in this way simultaneously is called Double S., but the term is also used loosely for the playing of chords with more than 2 notes. S. is also a device in hn. playing: the placing of the hand in the bell to prod. a special quality of sound and formerly, before the invention of the valves, to change the pitch of some notes.

Stops. The devices by which the registration of the org. can be regulated and altered. *See* **Organ Stops** for ref. to their names to be found under separate headings. The larger kinds of hpchds. also had Ss. prod. different qualities of tone by governing softer or harder plectra to pluck the stgs.

Storace, Ann Selina (Nancy) (b. London, 1766; d. London, 24. VIII. 1817), Eng. sop. singer of It. descent. Pupil of Rauzzini. Made her 1st appearance in London, 1777, later went to It. and was engaged for the It. opera in Vienna, 1784. There she was the 1st Susanna in Mozart's *Nozze di Figaro*, 1786.

Storace, Stephen (b. London, 4. I. 1763; d. London, 19. III. 1796); Eng. comp. of It. descent, brother of prec. Studied hpchd., v. and comp. at the Cons. di Sant' Onofrio at Naples, became a pupil of Mozart in Vienna, where he prod. his 1st It. opera in 1785. Returned to Eng. with his sister, Attwood and Kelly in 1787.

Works incl. operas *Gli sposi malcontenti*, *Gli equivoci* (after Shakespeare's *Comedy of Errors*), *La cameriera astuta*, *The Haunted Tower*, *No Song, No Supper*, *The Siege of Belgrade*, *The Pirates*, *Dido: Queen of Carthage*, *The Cherokee*, *The Iron Chest* (Colman), *Mahmoud, or The Prince of Persia* (unfinished, completed by Kelly and Ann S.) & others; ballet *Venus and Adonis*, &c.

Storm, Theodor (1817–88), Ger. poet & novelist. *See* **Vrieslander** (songs).

Stornello (It., prob. corruption of *Ritornello*, which is also used in the same sense). An old It. form of popular song set to verses of 3 lines, the 1st and 3rd of which rhyme, as in *terza rima*.

Strada del Pò, Anna (b. Bergamo, ?; d. ?), It. 18th-cent. sop. singer. 1st appeared in London in 1729.

Stradal, August (b. Teplitz-Schönau, 17. V. 1860; d. Schönlinde, 13. III. 1930), Sudeten-Ger. pfst. Studied pf. with Anton Door and Leschetizky and theory with Nottebohm and Bruckner in Vienna. In 1884 he took a finishing course with Liszt and in 1893 he joined the staff of Horak's Cons. in Vienna, later touring extensively. He made *c.* 250 arrs. of important classical works.

Stradella (Flotow). *See* **Alessandro Stradella.**

Stradella, Alessandro (b. Naples, *c.* 1645; d. Genoa, II. 1682), It. singer, vst. & comp. Of noble birth, he never held any official posts, and most of what is known of his career seems to be based on legend rather than fact. But he taught singing at Venice at some time and eloped with a young patrician lady (?) to Rome or Turin, and (?) an attempt at assassinating him was made. He (?) entered the service of the Duchess of Savoy and regent of Piedmont, Marie de Nemours, at Turin. He was murdered on the Wed. before 28. II. 1682.

Works incl. operas *La forza dell' amor paterno*, *Doriclea*, *Il trespolo tutore balordo*, *Il barcheggio*; motets & other church m.; orat. *San Giovanni Battista* & others; sacred & secular cantatas; serenade *Qual prodigio ch' io miri* & others; madrigals; Conc. for stgs., &c.

Stradivari (Latinized Stradivarius), It. family of v. makers:

1. Antonio S. (b. ?, ? 1644; d. Cremona, 18. XII. 1737), founder of the workshop at Cremona in the 1660s, after (?) serving an apprenticeship to Nicolo Amati.

2. Francesco S. (b. Cremona, 1. II. 1671; d. Cremona, 11. V. 1743), son of prec. He carried on his father's craft with

3. Omobono S. (b. Cremona, 14. XI. 1679; d. Cremona, 8. VI. 1742), brother of prec.

Straeten, Edmond van der (b. Oudenarde, 3. XII. 1826; d. Oudenarde, 25. XI. 1895), Belg. mcolst. Studied law at Alost and Ghent, but on returning home cultivated mus. science and in 1849 prod. an opera, *Le Proscrit*. He became sec. to Fétis for the purpose of studying with him and contrib. to his Dictionary. He also acted as critic and wrote books on Flem. m., incl. *La Musique aux Pays-bas* in 8 vols.

Straeten, Edmund (Sebastian Joseph) van der (b. Düsseldorf, 29. IV. 1855; d. London, 17. IX. 1934), Ger. cst. and writer on m. He settled in London in 1881 and wrote and lectured much on old stg. insts. His works incl. a *History of the Violoncello*.

Strambotto (It.). A form of verse used by the comps. of frottole in the 15th–16th cents. It had 8 lines (*ottava rima*), the 1st 6 rhyming alternately and the last 2 consecutively.

Strangways, A. H. Fox. *See* **Fox Strangways.**

Straniera, La (*The Stranger*), opera by Bellini (lib. by Felice Romani), prod. Milan, Teatro alla Scala, 14. II. 1829.

Stransky, Josef (b. Hupoleč, 9. IX. 1872; d. New York, 6. III. 1936), Cz. cond. & comp. Studied medicine at first, but turned to m., studying under Fibich and Dvořák in Prague and Fuchs and Bruckner in Vienna. He became cond. of the Ger. Opera in Prague, then of the Hamburg Opera, 1909, and in 1911–22 cond. the N.Y. Philh. Soc., following Mahler.

Works incl. opera *Beatrice and Benedick* (after Shakespeare's *Much Ado*), operetta *The General*; syms.; chamber m.; songs, &c.

Strascinando (It.). Dragging, slurring.

Strathspey. A Sco. folk dance in quick common time, similar to the Reel, but with dotted rhythms. The name derives from the strath (valley) of Spey and is 1st heard of in 1780, though dances of the kind are much older.

Straus, Ludwig (b. Pozsony, 28. III. 1835; d. Cambridge, 23. X. 1899), Hung. vst. Studied at the Vienna Cons. and made his 1st appearance there in 1850. In 1855 he made a tour incl. It. and in 1857 another in Ger. and Swe., with Piatti. In 1860 he 1st visited Eng. and in 1864 settled in Manchester as leader of the Hallé Orch., and in 1888 in London.

Straus, Oscar (b. Vienna, 6. IV. 1870), Aus. cond. & comp. Studied with Graedener and Bruch in Berlin and became theatre cond. at var. towns. He then settled in Berlin and in 1927 in N.Y.

Works incl. operas *Die Waise von Cordova* & *Das Tal der Liebe*; operettas *Ein Walzertraum* (*A Waltz Dream*), *Der tapfere Soldat* (*The Chocolate Soldier*, after Shaw's *Arms and the Man*), *Love and Laughter*, *The Last Waltz*, *Riquette* & others; ovt. to Grillparzer's *Der Traum ein Leben*, Serenade for stg. orch., &c.

Strauss. Aus. family of musns.:

1. Johann S. (b. Vienna, 14. III. 1804; d. Vienna, 25. IX. 1849), vst., cond. & comp. His parents were innkeepers and apprenticed him to a bookbinder, but he learnt the v. and va. and was eventually allowed to study with Seyfried. He played va. in private stg. 4tets, at 15 managed to join Pamer's orch. at the Sperl, a place of entertainment, m. and dancing, then Lanner's band, in which he became deputy cond. In 1825 he and Lanner parted and he began a rival band, for which he comp. dances, esp. waltzes, which had by that time become fashionable. He was invited to return to the Sperl, which had enlarged the orch., and in 1833 began travelling abroad with a visit to Pest. By 1837 he had been to Ger., Hol., Belg., Fr., Eng. and Sco. He added the quadrille to the m. of the Viennese ballrooms, having picked it up in Paris, and made a great hit with the *Radetzky Marsch*. He toured again and was then made cond. of the court balls.

Works incl. 152 waltzes (*Täuberl*, *Kettenbrücken*, *Donaulieder* Walzer, &c.), 32 quadrilles, 24 galops, 18 marches, 13 polkas, &c.

2. Johann S. (b. Vienna, 25. X. 1825; d. Vienna, 3. VI. 1899), vst., cond. & comp., son of prec. He was not allowed to follow his father's profession, but learnt the v. and studied secretly with Drechsler. In 1844 he appeared as cond. at Dommayer's hall in the Hietzing suburb, and his father capitulated. After the latter's death he amalgamated his orch. with his own, toured in Aus., Pol. and Ger. and in 1855–65 visited St. Petersburg in the summer. In 1863 he became cond. of the court balls.

Works incl. operettas *Indigo und die vierzig Räuber*, *Der Karneval in Rom*, *Die Fledermaus*, *Cagliostro in Wien*, *Prinz Methusalem*, *Blindekuh*, *Das Spitzentuch der Königin*, *Der lustige Krieg*, *Eine Nacht in Venedig*, *Der Zigeunerbaron*, *Simplizius*, *Ritter Pázmán*, *Fürstin Ninetta*, *Jabuka*, *Waldmeister*, *Die Göttin der Vernunft*; ballet *Aschenbrödel*; *Traumbilder* for orch.; a large number of waltzes (*An der schönen blauen Donau*, *Tausend und eine Nacht*, *Wiener Blut*, *Künstlerleben*, *Man lebt nur einmal*, *Morgenblätter*, *Geschichten aus dem Wiener Wald*, &c.), polkas, galops & other dances, &c.

3. Joseph S. (b. Vienna, 22. VIII. 1827; d. Vienna, 22. VII. 1870), cond. & comp., brother of prec. He became an architect at his father's wish, but secretly studied m. and during an illness of 2 cond. his band with success. He then formed his own band and wrote 283 dances for it. He d. after a visit to Warsaw, where he was ill-treated by Rus. officers for refusing to play for them.

4. Eduard S. (b. Vienna, 15. III. 1835; d. Vienna, 28. XII. 1916), cond. & comp., brother of prec. Studied hp. & comp. and appeared as cond. in 1862. After 1865 he took 2's place at the summer concerts in St. Petersburg and in 1870 became cond. of the court balls. He toured much, appearing at the Inventions Exhib. in London in 1885. His works incl. over 200 dances.

Strauss, Christoph (b. Vienna, *c.* 1580; d. Vienna, VI. 1631), Aus. orgst. & comp. He entered the service of the court in 1594 and in 1601 became orgst. at the church of St. Michael. In 1617–9 he was court cond. and afterwards chapel master at St. Stephen's cath.

Works incl. masses, Requiems, motets for voices and insts., &c.

Strauss, Richard (b. Munich, 11. VI. 1864), Ger. comp. His father, Franz S. (1822–1905), was hnst. at the Court Opera in Munich, but had married into the wealthy brewers' family of Pschorr. S. began to comp. at the age of 6 and at 10 wrote his 1st two pub. works, the *Festival March* and the Serenade for wind insts. In 1880 he finished a Sym. in D min. and the next year his A maj. stg. 4tet was perf. in public. He entered Munich Univ. in 1882, but left it in 1883, went to Berlin for a short period of study, but became asst. cond. to Bülow at Meiningen very soon after. A member of the orch., Alexander Ritter, turned his classical leanings into admiration for Berlioz, Wagner and Liszt. In 1885 Bülow resigned and S. became 1st cond. at Meiningen. In spring 1886 he visited It. and afterwards wrote the sym. *Aus Italien*, prod. at Munich in spring 1887, when he became sub-cond. at the Opera there. *Macbeth*, his 1st symph. poem, was comp. that year. In 1889 he became asst. cond. to Lassen at the Weimar Court Opera and in 1891 Cosima Wagner invited him to conduct *Tannhäuser* at Bayreuth. Under Wagner's influence he wrote his 1st opera, *Guntram*, most of it during a tour in the Mediterranean undertaken to counteract threatening lung trouble. It was prod. at Weimar on 10. V. 1894. The heroine was sung by Pauline de Ahna, whom he married in VI, and he was that year app. cond. of the Berlin Phil. Orch. in succession to Bülow. After the prod. of *Salome* at Dresden in 1905 S. began his series of operas written with Hugo von Hofmannsthal as libst. with *Elektra*, prod. there in 1909, and about that time he bought a country house at Garmisch in the Bavarian highlands, where all his later works were written. After Hofmannsthal's death in 1929 S., who had already written a lib. of his own for *Intermezzo*, prod. at Dresden, 1924, worked with Stefan Zweig on *Die schweigsame Frau* (based on Ben Jonson's *Epicoene*), which was prod. at Dresden in 1935 but quickly withdrawn on a trumped-up excuse because Zweig, as a Jew, had to be boycotted by the Nazi party. Strauss thereupon resigned his appt. as president of the Reichs-Musikkammer and was himself under a cloud for a time, but had long been too important a figure in Ger. mus. life to be ignored.

Works incl. operas *Guntram*, *Feuersnot*, *Salome*, *Elektra*, *Der Rosenkavalier*, *Ariadne auf Naxos*, *Die Frau ohne Schatten*, *Intermezzo*, *Die ägyptische Helena*, *Arabella*, *Die schweigsame Frau*, *Friedenstag*, *Daphne*, *Midas*, *Die Liebe der Danae*, *Capriccio*; ballets *Josephs - Legende*, *Schlagobers*; incid. m. to Molière's *Le Bourgeois gentilhomme* (orig. connected with *Ariadne auf Naxos*); 2 syms., F min. & *Aus Italien*; symph. poems *Macbeth*, *Don Juan*, *Tod und Verklärung*, *Till Eulenspiegels lustige Streiche*, *Also sprach Zarathustra*, *Don Quixote*, *Ein Heldenleben*, *Symphonia domestica*, *Eine Alpensinfonie*; other orch. works: *Festival March*, 2 Serenades for wind insts., 2 military marches, *Festliches Praeludium*, *Japanische Festmusik*, Divertimento on pieces by Couperin; v. Conc., ob. Conc., 2 hn. concs., *Burleske* for pf. & orch., *Parergon zur Symphonia domestica* for pf. left hand & orch.; stg. 4tet in A maj., pf. 4tet in C min.; sos. for v. & pf. and co. & pf.; 11 songs with orch. incl. 3 Hymns by Hölderlin; 26 op. nos. of songs (*c.* 150) incl. cycles *Schlichte Weisen* (Felix Dahn), *Mädchenblumen*, *Krämerspiegel* & 6 songs by Shakespeare and Goethe; pf. So., 9 pf. pieces; Tennyson's *Enoch Arden* and Uhland's *Das Schloss am Meer* for recitation & pf.

Stravaganza (It. = extravagance). A word sometimes used for a comp. of a freakish nature.

Stravinsky, Igor (b. Oranienbaum nr. St. Petersburg, 17. VI. 1882), Rus. comp. His father was a bass singer at the Imp. Opera. In 1903 S. met Rimsky-Korsakov at Heidelberg and played him his early comps., but did not become his pupil until 1907, by which time he had finished a pf. So., begun a Sym. and married his 2nd cousin, Nadezhda Sulima, 11. I. 1906. In 1908 he had the Sym. perf. and wrote *Fireworks* for orch. for the marriage of Nadia Rimsky-Korsakov and M. Steinberg, and a *Funeral Chant* on R.-K.'s death. The perf. of the *Fantastic Scherzo* in 1909 drew Diaghilev's attention to S., who was commissioned to write *The Fire-Bird* for the Rus. Ballet. It was prod. in Paris in 1910, and S. began to become known in western Eur. *Petrushka* followed in 1911 and *The Rite of Spring* in 1913, both prod. in Paris, where the latter provoked a riot of protest and fanatical partisanship. In 1914 S. went to Rus. for the last time: he never returned after the 1914–8 war and the Revol. He settled in Swi., on the Lake of Geneva. From 1914 he became as well known in London as in Paris, and in 1925 he 1st made a tour in U.S.A. In 1934 he became a Fr. citizen, but from 1937 he has lived mostly in Amer.

Works incl. operas *The Nightingale* (afterwards a ballet), *Mavra*; opera-orat. *Oedipus Rex*; ballets *Fire-Bird*, *Petrushka*, *The Rite of Spring*, *The Fox*, *The Bees*, *The Wedding*, *Pulcinella*, *Apollo Musagetes*, *The Fairy's Kiss*, *Card-Party*; play with

m. *The Soldier's Tale*; melodrama *Persephone*; cantata *Babel*; orch. works: Sym. in E♭ maj., Sym. in C maj. (1943), *Fantastic Scherzo*, *Fireworks*, *Symphonies for Wind Instruments*, *4 Études*, *Scènes de ballet*, *Ode*; *4 Norw. Moods*; 2 suites for small orch., *Ragtime* & *Danses concertantes* for chamber orch, Polka for circus elephants; Conc. for 16 insts. (*Dumbarton Oaks*); Conc. for pf. & wind insts., *Capriccio* for pf. & orch., v. Conc.; songs for m.-sop. & orch. *Le Faune et la bergère*, cantata for voice & orch. *The King of the Stars*; *Funeral Chant on the Death of Rimsky-Korsakov* for chor. & orch., *Symphony of Psalms* for chor. & orch.; 3 pieces & Concertino for stg. 4tet, Octet for wind insts., *Duo concertant* for v. & pf.; 3 pieces for cl. solo, *Elegy* for va. solo; 3 poems from the Japanese for sop. and 9 insts., *Pribaoutki* for voice & 8 insts., *The Cat's Cradle-Songs* for voice & 3 cls.; 2 sos., 4 études, Serenade, *Piano Rag-Music* and *The Five Fingers* for pf.; 2 sets of easy pieces for pf. duet; Conc. & So. for 2 pfs.; Étude for pianola; *The Saucer*, 4 Rus. peasant songs for fem. voices; 14 songs, &c.

Straw Fiddle. *See* **Strohfiedel.**

Streicher (Ger., plur.). Stgs., as in Eng. for stg. insts.

Streicher. Ger. family of pf. makers:

1. Johann Andreas S. (b. Stuttgart, 13. XII. 1761; d. Vienna, 25. V. 1833), m. teacher in Vienna and founder there of a pf. manufacture after 1793, when he married

2. Maria Anna (Nanette) S. (*née* Stein) (b. Augsburg, 2. I. 1769; d. Vienna, 16. I. 1833. *See* **Stein, 2**).

3. Johann Baptist S. (b. Vienna, 3. I. 1796; d. Vienna, 28. III. 1871), son of above. He succeeded his parents in business, and from him it descended to his son Emil.

Streicher, Theodor (b. Vienna, 7. VI. 1874; d. nr. Graz, 28. V. 1940), Aus. comp. Studied in Vienna and at Bayreuth.

Works incl. *Mignons Exequien* (after Goethe's *Wilhelm Meister*) for chor., children's chor. & orch., *Die Schlacht bei Murten* for chor. & orch.; *Kleiner Vogel Kolibri* for chamber orch.; *Um Inez weinten* for sop. & orch.; *Die Monologe des Faust* (after Goethe) for stg. 6tet; many songs, &c.

Streichinstrumente (Ger.). Stg. insts.

Streichzither (Ger. lit. stroke-zither). A var. of Zither played with a v. bow instead of being plucked with the fingers or with a plectrum.

Streit zwischen Phöbus und Pan, Der (*The Strife between Phoebus and Pan*), secular cantata by Bach, written in 1731 and (?) satirizing Johann Adolf Scheibe, ed. of *Der critische Musikus*, in the part of Midas; prod. as an opera, (lib. by Michael Diack, London, Aldwych Theatre, 22. VI. 1916.

Strepitoso (It. = noisy). A direction suggesting a forceful and spirited perf., but more often used in the sense of a climax growing in force and speed.

Strepponi, Giuseppina (b. Lodi, 8. IX. 1815; d. Busseto, 14. XI. 1897), It. sop. singer. Studied at the Milan Cons. and made her 1st appearance in 1835, at Trieste. Verdi's 2nd wife.

Stretta (It. lit. pressure, tightening, squeezing). A passage, usually at the end of a comp., esp. an operatic finale, in which the tempo is accelerated either gradually or by sections and so makes a climax.

Stretto (It. lit. narrow, tightened, squeezed). A device in fugal writing whereby the entries of the subject are drawn more closely together in time. Instead of following each other voice by voice, each waiting until the last has been fully stated, in S. they are made to overlap, the 2nd coming in before the end of the 1st, and so on. Strictly speaking the term S. applies only to such statements of the whole subject; but it is often loosely used for mere overlapping entries of part of the subject.

Stretto maestrale (It. lit. magisterial S.). A S. in which the fugal subject not only appears in close, overlapping entries, but is carried through from beginning to end at each entry, which need not happen consistently in an ord. S., where entries of the opening notes of the subject are sufficient.

Strict Counterpoint. The application of ctpt. to comp., or its use for exercise, according to the rules of the Species.

Striggio, Alessandro (b. Mantua, *c.* 1535; d. Mantua, *c.* 1595), It. orgst., lutenist, violist & comp. He was in the service of Cosimo de' Medici at Florence, *c.* 1560–70. He returned to Mantua, (?) to the court of Duke Guglielmo Gonzaga.

Works incl. masses, motet in 40 parts for voices & insts.; madrigal opera *Il cicalamento delle donne al bucato*; intermezzi for perf. between the acts of plays; madrigals; var. works for voices & insts. in many parts, &c.

Striggio, Alessandro (b. ?; d. ? Mantua, after 1628), It. vst., violist & author, son of prec. In service at the court of Mantua. Libst. of Monteverdi's *Orfeo*.

Strinasacchi, Regina (b. Ostiglia nr. Mantua, 1764; d. Gotha, *c.* 1823),

It. vst. & guitar player. Educ. in Venice and Paris. She began to travel in 1780 and visited Vienna in 1784. Mozart wrote the v. Sc. in B♭ maj. (K. 454) for her. In 1785 she married J. C. Schlick.

Strindberg, August (1849–1912), Swe. novelist & dramatist. *See* **Foerster (J. B.)** (*Journey of Fortunate Peter*), **Rangström** (*Kronbruden* & *Til Damascus*), **Rezniček** (*Dream Play*), **Sibelius** (*Svanevhit*), **Stenhammar** (*Dromspel*), **Tiessen** (*Advent*), **Vladigerov** (*Dream Play*), **Weismann** (3 operas).

Stringendo (It. from verb *stringere* = to tighten). A direction indicating that a passage is to be perf. with increasing speed and mounting excitement.

String Quartet. The most usual, normal and satisfactory inst. combination for chamber m., consisting of 2 vs., va. and co. Works in so. form for stg. 4tet began to be written from *c.* the middle of the 18th cent.

Strings. The cords, usually of gut (v. family, hps., &c.) or wire (lute & guitar families, pfs., &c.) by means of which the notes are prod. on such insts. The term Ss. is also used to designate stg. insts. collectively, esp. those of the v. family in the orch.

Strisciando (It. lit. sliding). The proper It. term for that generally used elsewhere in the mock-It. *glissando*.

Strogers, E. (b. ?; d. ?), Eng. 16th-cent. comp.

Strogers, Nicholas (b. ?; d. ?), Eng. 16th–17th-cent. orgst. & comp., (?) son of prec.

Works (many uncertainly attrib. to either) incl. motets, services & other church m.; madrigals; In Nomines for stgs.; org., lute & virginal pieces, &c.

Strohfiedel (Ger. lit. straw fiddle). A perc. inst. similar to the xylophone.

Stromentato (It. = instrumented, orchestrated, scored). The word is assoc. mainly with recitative (*recitativo stromentato*), where it has the same meaning as *recitativo accompagnato*, but is more accurately descriptive of a recitative accomp. by the orch., as distinct from a *recitativo secco* accomp. from a figured bass on the hpchd.

Strong, G(eorge). Templeton (b. New York, 26. V. 1856), Amer. comp. Studied at the Leipzig Cons., became a member of the Liszt circle, was in close touch with MacDowell while living at Wiesbaden in 1886–9, and after teaching at Boston in 1891–2 settled in Swi. on the Lake of Geneva, living 1st at Vevey and later in Geneva.

Works incl. *Knights and Dryads* for solo voices, chor. & orch.; 2 cantatas for solo voices, male chor. & orch.; 3 syms.: *Sintram* (after Fouqué), *In the Mountains* & *By the Sea*, symph. poem *Undine* (after Fouqué); *2 Amer. Sketches* for v. & orch.; Trio for 2 vs. & va. *A Village Music-Director* & other chamber m., &c.

Strophic Bass. An inst. bass part used without change throughout a series of verses of a song or chor. the upper parts of which vary at each occurrence; or a similar device in inst. m.

Strophic Song. The simplest form of song, structurally considered, in which each verse of a poem is set to the same m.

Strowger. *See* **Strogers.**

Strozzi, Barbara (b. Venice, ?; d. ?), It. 17th-cent. singer & comp. Adopted daughter of the poet Giulio S. Comp. madrigals, cantatas, sacred songs with continuo, duets, ariettas, &c.

Strungk (or **Strunck**), **Delphin** (b. ?, 1601; d. Brunswick, 1694), Ger. orgst. & comp. He was, after 1630, successively orgst. at Wolfenbüttel, Celle and Brunswick.

Works incl. m. for the Duke of Brunswick in 5 voc. and 8 inst. parts; var. voc. works with insts.; chorale preludes & other works for org., &c.

Strungk, Nikolaus Adam (b. Brunswick, XI. 1640; d. Dresden, 23. IX. 1700), Ger. vst., orgst. & comp., son of prec. Pupil of his father, for whom he deputized at the org. at Brunswick from the age of 12. While at Helmstadt Univ. he learnt the v. at Lübeck during vacations. In 1660 he joined the court orch. at Wolfenbüttel, then that at Celle, and in 1665 went to the court of Hanover. After a period at Hamburg from 1678, two visits to Vienna and one to It., he returned to Hanover, 1682–6, but in 1688 he went to Dresden as chamber orgst. and 2nd chapel master to the Saxon court in succession to Pallavicini, and succeeded Bernhard as 1st chapel master in 1692. In 1693 he opened an opera-house at Leipzig, where he prod. his later stage works and where his daughters Philippine and Elisabeth sang.

Works incl. operas *Der glückselig-steigende Sejanus*, *Der unglücklich-fallende Sejanus*, *Esther*, *Doris*, *Semiramis*, *Nero*, *Agrippina* & others, completion of Pallavicini's *L'Antiope*; orat. *Die Auferstehung Jesu*; Ricercare on the death of his mother; sos. & chaconnes for v. or va. da gamba; sos. for 2 vs. & va. and for 6 stgs.; airs and dances for recorders, &c.

Strunz, Jacob (b. Pappenheim, 1783;

d. Munich, 23. V. 1852), Ger. comp. Pupil of Winter at Munich. He travelled all over Eur. in 1798–1845 and also visited Egypt; then settled at Munich for the rest of his life. He was a friend of Meyerbeer, Berlioz and Balzac, who ded. his story *Massimilla Doni* to him.

Works incl. operas *Le Maître de chapelle* & *Les Courses de Newmarket*; several ballets; incid. m. (the 1st) for Hugo's *Ruy Blas*; 3 stg. 4tets; songs, &c.

Stuart, Leslie (real name Thomas Barrett) (b. Southport, 15. III. 1866; d. Richmond, Surrey, 27. III. 1928), Eng. comp.

Works incl. operettas *Florodora, The Silver Slipper, The School Girl, The Belle of Mayfair, Havana, Captain Kidd, The Slim Princess, Peggy*, &c.

Stück (Ger.)=Piece, a piece of m.

Stuck, Batistin (usually called Batistin) (b. Florence, *c.* 1680; d. Paris, 9. XII. 1755), It. cst. & comp. (?) of Ger. origin. He went to Fr. at an early age and was the 1st cst. in the Paris Opéra orch., also court musn. to the Duke of Orleans.

Works incl. operas *Rodrigo in Algieri* (with Albinoni), *Méléagre, Mantho la fée* & *Polidore*; many court ballets; cantatas, airs, &c.

Stucken, Frank (Valentin) van der (b. Fredericksburg, Texas, 15. X. 1858; d. Hamburg, 18. VIII. 1929), Amer. cond. & comp. of Ger. & Belg. descent. Studied in Eur. with Benoît, Reinecke, Grieg and others. In 1884–95 he cond. a male-voice choir in N.Y., where he also cond. orch. concerts. In 1895–1903 he was dir. of the Cincinnati Coll. of M. and from the same year to 1907 he cond. the Sym. Orch. there. After 1908 he lived much in Eur.

Works incl. opera *Vlasda*; incid. m. to Shakespeare's *Tempest*; prologue to Heine's *William Ratcliff*, symph. prologue *Pax triumphans*, *Louisiana* festival march & other orch. works; chor. works; songs, &c.

Study. An inst. piece, usually for a single inst., written mainly for the purpose of technical exercise and display, but not necessarily devoid of expression and high artistic quality. The Fr. word *étude* is more often used for it.

Stump. An obs. stg. inst. of the Cittern type invented *c.* 1600 by Daniel Farrant. No details of it are known.

Stumpf, Carl (b. Wiesentheid, 21. IV. 1848; d. Berlin, 29. XII. 1936), Ger. mus. scientist & psychol. Studied at Göttingen Univ. and held professorships at Würzburg, Prague, Halle, Munich, and from 1893 in Berlin. He collab. with Hornbostel in ed. the *Beiträge zur Akustik und Musikwissenschaft* and wrote much on the psychól. aspects of acoustical phenomena.

Stuntz, Joseph (Hartmann) (b. Arlesheim nr. Basle, 25. VII. 1793; d. Munich, 18. VI. 1859), Swi. cond. & comp. Studied with Winter at Munich and Salieri in Vienna. He spent 3 years in It. and in 1825 succeeded Winter as 1st cond. of the Royal Opera at Munich.

Works incl. operas *La rappresaglia, Costantino, Argene e Dalmiro, Elvira e Lucindo, Heinrich IV zu Givry* (after Voltaire's *Charlot*) & *Maria Rosa*; ballets; church m.; cantatas & partsongs, Sym. in D min. & concert ovts.; songs, &c.

Styrienne (Fr.). In drawing-room m. what is supposed to be a Styrian dance, but not more genuinely so that the Écossaise is a Sco. one. It is usually in moderate 2–4 time and in a min. key.

Suabe Flute. A 4-ft. org. stop similar in tone to the Claribel, but smaller in scale and with the lips of its pipes inverted.

Sub. A prefix denoting transposition an 8ve lower, like Contra or Double, used for certain org. stops.

Sub Bass. Another name for the Bourdon org. stop.

Sub Bourdon. A Bourdon org. stop prod. 32-ft. tone.

Subdiapente (*see also* **Diapente**; from Lat. & Gr.). A 5th lower. The term is used esp. for canons at the 5th.

Subdiatessaron (from Lat. & Gr.). A 4th lower.

Subdominant. The 4th degree of the rising modern maj. or min. scale, harmonically important because a common chord based on it leads back to the Tonic common chord by means of a Plagal Cadence.

Subito (It., accent on 1st syll.)=at once, immediately.

Subject. A theme used as a principal feature in a mus. comp., esp. in a Fugue, where it is brought in a number of times, voice by voice, or in a Rondo, where it is a recurrent main theme returning after a series of episodes. In so. form 1st and 2nd Ss. are the main structural features, but there they are thematic groups more often than single themes.

Submediant. The 6th degree of the rising maj. or min. scale, so called because it is the opposite of the Mediant: a 3rd below instead of above the Tonic. The names of the degrees of the whole scale are Tonic, Supertonic, Mediant, Subdominant, Dominant, S. and Leading-note.

The S. of a maj. scale is the tonic of its relative min.

Subsemitonium (Lat. = under-semitone). The old name for the Leading-note, esp. when used in the Modes by sharpening the 7th of the scale.

Subtonium (Lat. = under-[whole] tone). The old name for the 7th of the Modes, esp. the Lydian (and later the Ionian), which was always a whole tone below the Tonic, but was often sharpened in perf. according to the principle of Musica ficta.

Subtonic. The Eng. term for the above, which might also usefully be applied to the Leading-note.

Sucher, Josef (b. Döbör, Eisenburg, 23. XI. 1844; d. Berlin, 4. IV. 1908), Aus.-Hung. cond. & comp. Learnt m. as choir-boy of the Aus. court chapel at the Löwenburg seminary in Vienna and later studied with Sechter. After var. cond. appts. at Viennese theatres, incl. the Court Opera, he went to Leipzig as cond. of the munic. theatre in 1876. In 1877 he married Rosa Hasselbeck.

Works incl. opera *Ilse*; masses & cantatas, ovts. for orch.; song cycle *Ruheort*, &c.

Sucher (*née* **Hasselbeck**), **Rosa** (b. Velburg, Bav., 23. II. 1849; d. Eschweiler nr. Aachen, 1927), Ger. sop. singer, wife of prec. She made her 1st appearance at Trèves and advanced rapidly to more important opera houses, going with her husband to Hamburg in 1879, where he became cond. of the Opera. They visited Eng. in 1882 and in 1886 she sang Isolde at the Wagner Theatre at Bayreuth.

Suckling, Norman (Charles) (b. Forest Gate, Essex, 24. X. 1904), Eng. scholar, pfst., comp. & writer on m. Educ. at Bancroft's School and Queen's Coll., Oxford. He taught at Liverpool and later became lecturer in Fr. at King's Coll., Newcastle-on-Tyne. His writings incl. a book on Fauré and his comps. a chamber opera *Avalon*, a Mass for 8 voices and an Introd. and Scherzo for stg. 4tet.

Sue, Eugène (1804–57), Fr. novelist. *See* **Halévy** (*Juif errant*).

Suite. *See also* **Overture.** A form of inst. m., in some sense the forerunner of the so., although it continued independently. The governing principle of the S. is the stringing together of a number of mvts., orig. dances, but now any pieces the comp. desires, incl. chosen numbers from operas, ballets, &c. From the 16th to the 18th cent. the dances in a S. consisted of 4 obligatory pieces: Allemande, Courante, Sarabande and Gigue (to give the Fr. names as the most freq. used). These were almost invariably in the same key, prob. because Ss. were often written for lutes, which had to be newly tuned for each key and where it was desirable to avoid retuning between mvts. Other dances could be added at will, such as the Gavotte, Minuet, Bourrée, Rigaudon, Hornpipe, &c., and the whole could be preceded by a Prelude (e.g. Purcell, Bach's Eng. Ss., &c.). There could also be fancy pieces with a var. of titles, as in Bach's Partitas (*partita* being only another name for S.) and more esp. in the Ss. by Fr. comps., among whom Couperin and others often went to fantastic lengths in the invention of curious titles. The chief features inherited from the S. by the so. are the binary form of the dances, which became the exposition, working-out & recapitulation of the so. form, and the minuet, which was retained partic. in syms. and in the 19th cent. turned into the scherzo.

Suivez (Fr. imper. = follow). A direction used in two senses: (1) to indicate that one movt. of a comp. is to follow the preceding one immediately (equiv. to It. *Attacca*); (2) to indicate that accompanying parts are to follow a voc. or other solo part moving independently of the prescribed rhythm or tempo (equiv. to It. *Colla parte*).

Suk, Josef (b. Křečovice, 4. I. 1874; d. Benešov nr. Prague, 29. V. 1935), Cz. vst., violist & comp. Studied with Dvořák in Prague and in 1898 became his son-in-law. In 1892 he formed the Boh. Stg. 4tet with Karel Hofmann, Oscar Nedbal and Otto Berger, playing 2nd v. He began to comp. early and in 1922 became prof. of comp. at the Prague Cons., of which he was dir. in 1924–6. Much of his m. was influenced by personal experiences, esp. the death of his wife in 1905, e.g. the pf. pieces *About Mother* written for his infant son, and by that of Dvořák, e.g. the *Asrael* Sym., which refers to those 2 deaths.

Works incl. Mass in B♭ maj.; incid. m. for Julius Zeyer's *Radúz and Mahulena*; *Epilogue* for bar. solo, women's chor. & orch.; Syms. in E maj. & *Asrael*, symph. poems *Prague*, *A Summer Tale* and *Maturity*, Dramatic Ovt. & ovt. to Shakespeare's *Winter's Tale*, *A Tale* & *Under the Apple-trees* for orch.; Serenade & Meditation on a Chorale for stg. orch.; Fantasy for v. & orch.; 2 stg. 4tets, pf. 4tet, pf. Trio, Elegy for v. & co. with stg. 4tet, harmonium & hp.; *Ballade and Serenade* for co. & pf.; inst pieces; sets of pf. pieces

Moods, Spring, Summer Impressions, About Mother, Things Lived and Dreamed, Slumber Songs, Pol. Fantasy & other pf. pieces; partsongs with & without pf., &c.

Suk, Váša (b. Kladno, XI. 1861; d. Moscow, 13. I. 1933), Cz. vst., cond. & comp. Studied at the Prague Cons. and became vst. and cond. successively at Warsaw, Kiev and Moscow.

Works incl. opera *The Forest King*; symph. poem *Jan Hus*; Serenade for stg. orch., &c.

Sul ponticello (It.) = on the bridge. A direction in m. for bowed stg. insts. to play a passage very near (not actually on) the bridge to prod. a peculiar nasal and rustling sound.

Sul tasto (It.). A direction indicating that a passage of stg. m. is to be played with the bow over the fingerboard.

Sullivan, Arthur (Seymour) (b. London, 13. V. 1842; d. London, 22. XI. 1900), Eng. comp. Son of a bandmaster and prof. at the Royal Military School of M., entered the Chapel Royal in 1854 and was taught by Helmore. The following year he wrote an anthem, which was pub., and in 1856 he gained the Mendelssohn scholarship at the R.A.M., where he studied under Sterndale Bennett, Goss and O'Leary. The scholarship entitled him to a course of study at the Leipzig Cons., where he studied comp., cond. and pf., returning in 1861 to London, where he became orgst. at St. Michael's church, Chester Square. He 1st made his mark as comp. with incid. m. to Shakespeare's *Tempest*. His 1st operetta, *The Sapphire Necklace*, was prod. in 1864 and the 1st for which Gilbert wrote the libretto in 1871. After that he and Gilbert repeated their joint triumphs until 1889, when they reached their climax in *The Gondoliers*; but although they quarrelled, two works were still prod. by them half-heartedly, in 1893 and 1896. S. taught and cond. intermittently; he had been app. prof. of comp. at the R.A.M. in 1866. The following year he and Grove went to Vienna and discovered a pile of forgotten MSS. of Schubert's works. S. was knighted in 1883.

Works incl. opera *Ivanhoe*; operettas (with Gilbert as libst.) *Thespis, or The Gods Grown Old, Trial by Jury, The Sorcerer, H.M.S. Pinafore, The Pirates of Penzance, Patience, Iolanthe, Princess Ida, The Mikado, Ruddigore, The Yeomen of the Guard, The Gondoliers, Utopia Limited, The Grand Duke*; other operettas: *The Sapphire Necklace, Cox and Box, The Contrabandista, The Zoo, Haddon Hall, The Chieftain* (adapted from *The Contrabandista*), *The Beauty Stone, The Rose of Persia, The Emerald Isle* (unfinished, completed by German); ballets *L'Île enchantée* & *Victoria and Merrie England*; incid. m. to Shakespeare's *Tempest, Merchant of Venice, Merry Wives of Windsor, Henry VIII* & *Macbeth*, Tennyson's *The Foresters* and Comyns Carr's *King Arthur*; chor. works: *Kenilworth* (after Scott), *The Prodigal Son, On Shore and Sea, The Light of the World, The Martyr of Antioch, The Golden Legend, Festival Te Deum, Exhibition Ode, Imperial Institute Ode*; Te Deum, Jubilate and Kyrie in D; ode 'I wish to tune my quiv'ring lyre' for bar. & orch.; services, anthems and hymn-tunes (incl. 'Onward, Christian soldiers'; Sym. in E maj.; Ovts. *In Memoriam, Di ballo*, to Shakespeare's *Timon of Athens* & *Marmion* (after Scott); *Procession March, Princess of Wales March, Imperial March*; co. Conc.; Romance for stg. 4tet; var. pf. pieces; song cycle *The Window* (Tennyson), a number of songs incl. 'Orpheus with his lute,' *The Lost Chord* & Kipling's *The Absent-minded Beggar*, &c.

Sully-Prudhomme, Armand (1839–1907), Fr. poet. *See* **Franck (C.)** (songs), **Scontrino** (*Vie intérieure*). 3 songs by Fauré.

Sulzer, Salomon (b. Hohenems, Vorarlberg, 30. III. 1804; d. Vienna, 18. I. 1890), Aus. bar. singer, Jewish cantor & ed. He was placed in charge of the m. at the new Vienna synagogue in 1825 and studied with Seyfried. He ed. a collection of Jewish hymns and commissioned var. comps. to contribute to it. Schubert's setting of Psalm xcii in Moses Mendelssohn's trans. for bar. and male chor. orig. in this way. In 1844–7 S. was prof. of singing at the Vienna Cons.

Sumer is icumen in. An Eng. song in parts long thought to be dating from *c.* 1240, but after re-examination of the MS. found to be not earlier than 1280, known as the Reading Rota (round) and previously conjectured to be either comp. or copied by John of Fornsete, a monk at Reading Abbey, for whose dates it is however too late. Even so, it is one of the oldest comps. in harmony still preserved and sung, as distinct from Plainsong and from primitive harmonizations based on it, such as Conductus, Descant and Organum. It is a canon for 4 voices and there are 2 additional bass voices adding a Pes or Ground-bass, itself in canon.

Summational Tones. *See* **Resultant Tones.**

'Sun' Quartets. The nickname of the 6 stg. 4tets Op. 20 by Haydn, comp. in 1772.

Sunderland (*née* **Sykes**), **Susan** (b. Brighouse, Yorks, 30. IV. 1819; d. Brighouse, 6. V. 1905), Eng. sop. singer. The daughter of a gardener, she was discovered by accident, induced to join the Halifax Chor. Soc. and, after a 1st appearance at Bradford in 1838, given a few months' training in London. She at first sang in Yorkshire only, but in 1849 came out in London.

Sunless, song cycle by Mussorgsky (words by A. A. Golenishtchev-Kutuzov), comp. 1874: 1. *Between four walls*; 2. *Thou didst not know me in the crowd*; 3. *The idle, noisy day is ended*; 4. *Boredom*; 5. *Elegy*; 6. *On the River*.

Suor Angelica (Puccini). *See* **Trittico.**

Super. A prefix denoting transposition an 8ve higher, used for certain org. stops.

Super Octave. An org. term denoting transposition an 8ve higher in the case of Couplers and 2 8ves higher in the case of pipes.

Supertonic. The 2nd degree of the rising modern maj. or min. scale, so called because it stands above the Tonic. The names of the degrees of the whole scale are Tonic, S., Mediant, Subdominant, Dominant, Submediant and Leading-note.

Supervia, Conchita (b. Barcelona, 6. XII. 1899; d. London, 30. III. 1936), Spa. m.-sop. singer. She 1st appeared in London in the 1920s as a concert singer, excelling in Spa. songs as well as in arias from the parts written by Rossini for his wife, Isabella Colbran; later she appeared in some of these parts, as well as in *Carmen*, at Covent Garden. She became Eng. by marriage.

Suppé, Franz von (full name Francesco Ezechiele Ermenegildo Suppe Demelli) (b. Spalato [Split], 18. IV. 1819; d. Vienna, 21. V. 1895), Aus. (Dalmat.) cond. & comp. of Belg. descent. He showed a talent for comp. early, prod. a Mass and a comic opera *Der Apfel* at Zara in 1834; but he was sent to Padua Univ. by his father to study medicine. On his father's death, however, he settled in Vienna with his mother, studied with Seyfried and cond. at var. Viennese and provincial theatres, incl. the Josephstadt, Wieden and Leopoldstadt Theatres in Vienna from 1841 to his death.

Works incl. operettas *Das Mädchen vom Lande*, *Das Pensionat*, *Paragraph 3*, *Zehn Mädchen und kein Mann*, *Flotte Bursche* (with an ovt. on students' songs), *Die schöne Galatee*, *Leichte Kavallerie* (*Light Cavalry*), *Fatinitza*, *Boccaccio*, *Donna Juanita*, *Die Afrikareise* & several others; farces; ballets; incid. m. to Elmar's *Dichter und Bauer* (*Poet and Peasant*), Shakespeare's *Midsummer Night's Dream*, Schiller's *Wallensteins Lager* & others (more than 200 stage works); Mass, Requiem (*L'estremo giudizio*), &c.

Supprimez (Fr. imper. = suppress). A direction in org. m. indicating the putting out of action of stops.

Suriani / **Suriano** / **Surianus** — Alternative spellings of the name of Francesco Soriano.

Surprise Symphony. Haydn's Sym. in G maj., No. 94 (No. 3 of the 'Salomon' syms), written for London in 1791 and so called because of the sudden loud chord that bursts into the slow mvt., of which H. said 'That will make the ladies jump.' It is reinforced by a loud drum-tap: hence the Ger. nickname of the work is 'Sinfonie mit dem Paukenschlag.'

Surzynski, Józef (b. Szrem nr. Poznan, 15. III. 1851; d. Koscian, 5. III. 1919), Pol. priest & comp. Studied at Ratisbon and Leipzig, later taking holy orders in Rome. In 1882 he became dir. of the cath. choir at Poznan and in 1894 provost at Koscian. He ed. the *Monumenta Musices Sacrae in Polonia* and *Musica Ecclesiastica*.

Works incl. numerous masses, hymns & other church m., *Pol. Songs of the Catholic Church*, &c.

Susanna, orat. by Handel (lib. by ?), prod. London, Covent Garden Theatre, 10. II. 1749.

Susanna's Secret (Wolf-Ferrari). *See* **Segreto di Susanna.**

Susato, Tylman (b. Cologne, ?; d. Antwerp, before 1564), Ger. musn. & pub. He settled at Antwerp in the 1520s as m. copyist and tptr., and in 1543 began to print m. The books he issued contained masses, motets, psalm-tunes, madrigals and chansons, nearly all of which incl. some comps. of his own.

Suspension (Eng.). A device in harmony by which a note, usually but not invar. in the top part, is anticipated or retarded to appear, before or after the chord to which it properly belongs. The S. was formerly also used in voc. m., esp. in recitative cadences, where an Appoggiatura, as it is more often called in that connection, was inserted by the singer, though conventionally the phrase was written by the comp. as though the notes on the strong beats belonged to the chord. Some modern scholars, although aware of this tradition, now discredit it as not according with the comps.' intentions. Notes foreign to chords on strong beats written by 18th-cent. comps. as if they were appoggiaturas, though they are meant to be played as notes of full value, are in the nature of Ss.

Suspension (Fr.). *See* **Ornaments.**

Suspirium (Lat. = sigh). The old name for the Minima (the minim rest).

Süssmayr, Franz (Xaver) (b. Schwanenstadt, Upper Aus., 1766; d. Vienna, 16. IX. 1803), Aus. comp. Educ. at the monastery of Kremsmünster and pupil of Salieri and Mozart in Vienna. He assisted Mozart with *La clemenza di Tito* (prob. the recitatives) and completed his unfinished Requiem. In 1795 he became cond. of the Kärntnertor Theatre.

Works incl. operas *Moses, L'incanto superato, Der Spiegel von Arkadien, Il Turco in Italia, Idris und Zenide, Die edle Rache, Die Freiwilligen, Der Wildfang* (after Kotzebue), *Der Marktschreier, Soliman II* (after Favart), *Gulnare, Phasma* & others; 2 ballets; masses & other church m.; cantatas *Der Retter in Gefahr* & *Der Kampf für den Frieden*; cl. Conc.; Serenades for fl., va. & hn. and for v., guitar & Eng. hn.; inst. pieces, &c.

Sustaining Pedal. The so-called 'loud' P. of the pf., not used to prod. greater volume of tone, but to sustain any notes struck after it has been depressed, even after the fingers have left the keys, until it is released again.

Suter, Hermann (b. Kaiserstuhl, Aargau, 28. IV. 1870; d. Basle, 22. VI. 1926), Swi. cond. & comp. Studied with Huber and others at Basle and at the Conss. of Stuttgart and Leipzig. In 1892 he became cond. of a male chor. soc. at Zürich, was invited to several other posts of the kind, and in 1896 became prof. at the Cons. In 1902 he moved to Basle, where he cond. the mixed and male chor. socs. as well as the orch. concerts. In 1918–21 he was dir. of the Cons.

Works incl. *Die erste Walpurgisnacht* (Goethe) & *Le Laudi di San Francesco d'Assisi* for solo voices, chor. & orch.; Sym. in D min.; v. Conc.; 3 stg. 4tets., stg. 6tet; chor. works with & without accomp.; songs, &c.

Sutermeister, Heinrich (b. Feuerthalen, Ct. Zürich, 12. VIII. 1910), Swi. comp. Studied philol. at Paris and Basle, where he entered the Cons., later studying with Courvoisier, Pfitzner and others at Munich. In 1934 he settled at Berne, at first as operatic coach at the munic. theatre.

Works incl. operas *Romeo und Julia* & *Die Zauberinsel* (*The Tempest*) (both based on Shakespeare), radio opera *Die scharze Spinne* (after Jeremias Gotthelf); ballet *Das Dorf unter dem Gletscher*; chamber orat. *Jorinde und Jorindel* (after Mörike); *Baroque Songs* for ten., women's chor. & insts., songs for chor.; *7 Liebesbriefe* for ten. & orch.; Divertimento for stg. orch.; pf. Conc.; 3 stg. 4tets, stg. Trio & other chamber m.; pf. & org. pieces; songs, &c.

Sutor, Wilhelm (b. Edelstetten, Bav., c. 1774; d. Linden nr. Hanover, 7. IX. 1828), Ger. ten. singer & comp. Studied singing with Valesi and others, settled at Stuttgart in 1800 and from 1818 was mus. dir. at the court of Hanover.

Works incl. opera *Apollos Wettgesang* & 4 others; incid. m. to Shakespeare's *Macbeth*; orat. & cantatas; partsongs; songs, &c.

Švanda Dudák (*Shvanda the Bagpiper*), opera by Adalbert Hřimalý (1842–1908) (lib. by Karel Želenský, based on a folk-tale by Josef Kajetán Tyl), prod. Pilsen, 20. I. 1896.

Opera by Weinberger (lib. by Miloš Kareš, source as above), prod. Prague, Cz. Theatre, 27. IV. 1927.

Svendsen, Johan (Severin) (b. Christiania, 30. IX. 1840; d. Copenhagen, 14. VI. 1911). Norw. comp. Learnt m. from his father, a bandmaster, and at first adopted that profession himself. But, playing several insts., he joined the orch. at the Christiania theatre, began extensive travels in Swe. and Ger. in 1861 and in 1863 finished his studies at the Leipzig Cons. After travelling in Scand. and Sco. in 1867, he settled in Paris in 1868. In 1870–1 he was in Ger. again, mainly at Leipzig and Weimar, and in 1872–7 he taught and cond. at Christiania. After visits to Munich, Rome, London and Paris, he became court cond. at Copenhagen.

Works incl. incid. m. to Coppée's *Le Passant*; 2 syms., Ovt. to Bjørnson's *Sigurd Slembe, Carnaval à Paris, Carnaval des artistes norvégiens*, 4 Norw. Rhapsodies, legend *Zorahayde*, ovt. to Shakespeare's *Romeo and Juliet*, &c. for orch.; v. Conc. & Romance, co. Conc.; stg. 4tet, stg. 5tet, stg. Octet; Marriage Cantata; songs, &c.

Swain, Freda (b. Portsmouth, 31. X. 1902), Eng. pfst. & comp. Studied at the Tobias Matthay Pf. School in London and at the R.C.M., comp. with Stanford and pf. with Arthur

Alexander, to whom she was married in 1921. She also learnt v. from Rivarde there and played fl. in the Coll. orch. In 1924 she became prof. at the R.C.M. In 1940, when her husband was held up by the war in S. Africa, where he had been examining, she sent him her pf. Conc. by airmail; later she joined him, and they toured in S. Africa and Australia, broadcasting and giving 2-pf. recitals, returning to Eng. in 1943.

Works incl. opera *The Shadowy Waters* (Yeats, unfinished); *Pastoral Fantasy* for orch.; pf. Conc. (*Airmail*), *The Harp of Aengus* (after Yeats) for v. & orch.; stg. 4tet *Norfolk*; v. & pf. sos. in C min. & *The River*, co. & pf. So., duets for 2 vs., *Danse barbare* for v. & co.; Scherzo for 3 pfs., so.-poem *The Sea*, So. in F min., *So.-Saga*, *Tetrad*, sonatina *The Skerries* & a number of pieces for pf.; songs to poems by Burns, Bridges, Housman, Coppard & others, &c.

Swan Lake, The, ballet by Tchaikovsky (chgph. by Marius Petipa & L. I. Ivanov), prod. St. Petersburg, Maryinsky Theatre, 27. I. 1895.

Swan of Tuonela, The, symph. legend by Sibelius, Op. 22, one of 4 on subjects from the *Kalevala* only 2 of which were pub., the other being *Lemminkainen's Home-Faring*. S. was comp. in 1895.

Swan Song (Schubert). *See* **Schwanengesang.**

Swe. (abbr.) = Sweden, Swedish.

Swedish Composers. *See* **Agrell, Ahlström, Alfvén, Aulin, Atterberg, Berg (N.), Berwald, Björkander, Broman, Buxtehude, Düben, Frumerie, Geijer, Hallén, Hallström, Hyllester, Koch, Larsson, Lindberg, Lindblad** (2), **Norman, Nystroem, Peterson-Berger, Roman, Sjögren, Söderman, Starck, Stenhammar, Wennerberg, Wiklund, Wirén.**

'Swedish Nightingale, The.' The nickname given to Jenny Lind.

Sweelinck, Jan Pieterszoon (b. Deventer, 1562; d. Amsterdam, 16. X. 1621), Dutch orgst., hpchdst. & comp. Studied under his father, Pieter S., who became orgst. at the Old Church at Amsterdam in 1566, and others (not with Zarlino and Gabrieli at Venice, as earlier biogs. asserted). His father d. in 1573 and he succeeded to his post between 1577 and 1580, holding it to his death. He had many famous pupils, some from foreign countries, and his org. playing was celebrated; he was also a highly skilled hpchdst. The poet Vondel wrote an epitaph on his death.

Works incl. 4 books of psalms for 4–8 voices, *Cantiones sacrae* for several voices; org. fugues & other works; hpchd. pieces; Chansons for 5 voices, *Rimes françoises et italiennes*, &c.

Swell. A device on the hpchd. and the org. for the artificial prod. of *crescendo* and *diminuendo*, which these insts. are incapable of prod. by touch. It took var. forms, the most successful being a contrivance in the form of a slatted blind (hence the name Venetian S.), which, opening and shutting by means of a pedal, increased or reduced the volume of tone.

Swell Box. A box enclosing a number of org. pipes and fitted with a Venetian S. device.

Swell Organ. One of the manuals of the org. controlling the S. Box.

Swell Pedal. A special org. pedal, not prod. notes, but controlling the S.

Swi. (abbr.) = Swiss, Switzerland.

Swieten, Gottfried van, Baron (b. Leyden, 1734; d. Vienna, 29. III. 1803), Dutch diplomat and mus. amateur. He was brought to Vienna in 1745, when his father, Gerhard v. S., became physician to Maria Theresa. In 1769 he was in Paris and comp. songs for Favart's *Rosière de Salency*; in 1771 he became ambassador at the court of Frederick II of Prus. He returned to Vienna in 1778, held var. official posts and gave private Sunday morning concerts at his house. It was for these that Mozart prod. the additional accomps. for 4 works by Handel, incl. *Messiah*. S. was also a patron of Haydn and later of Beethoven.

Swift, Jonathan (1667–1745), Anglo-Ir. novelist & satirist. *See* **Kelley** (*Gulliver*), **Pierné** (do.).

Swinburne, Algernon Charles (1837–1909), Eng. poet. *See* **Bainton** (*Before Sunrise*), **Bantock** (*Atalanta in Calydon*), **Grainger** (*Bride's Tragedy*), **Parry (H.)** (*Eton*), **Wood (C.)** (*Ode on Music*).

Swing. A development of Jazz which became known during the 1930s. It relies on improvisation on the part of individual members of a dance band to a much greater extent than jazz did.

Swinstead, Felix (Gerald) (b. London, 25. VI. 1880), Eng. pfst., teacher & comp. Studied at the R.A.M. in London, where he became pf. prof. in 1910. He gave recitals and toured in the Dominions in 1902–12, wrote a treatise on pf. playing and became an examiner to the Assoc. Board of the Royal Schools of M.

Works incl. Scarlatti Suite for pf. & stgs.; pieces for v. & pf.; c. 250 studies & pieces for pf., &c.

Swiss Composers. *See* **Albicastro, Andreae, Attenhofer, Bachofen, Balmer, Barblan, Baumgartner, Beck, Bernard, Binet, Blanchet, Bloch, Bovy-Lysberg, Brun, Burkhard, Courvoisier, David (K. H.), Doret, Du Puy, Egli, Ferrari, Haug, Hegar, Honegger, Huber (2), Jaques-Dalcroze, Klose, Kunz, Lang, Marescotti, Martin (F.), Meyer (G.), Meyer von Schauensee, Moeschinger, Munzinger, Nägeli, Niedermeyer, Raff, Schnyder von Wartensee, Schoeck, Senfl, Staempfli, Stuntz, Suter, Sutermeister, Vogler (C.), Vuatez, Wannenmacher, Wehrli, Zwyssig.**

Syberg, Franz (Adolf) (b. Kerteminde nr. Odense, 5. VII. 1904), Dan. orgst. & comp. His father, the painter Fritz S., sent him to study at the Leipzig Cons., and later he became a private pupil of Karg-Elert. In 1930 he returned to Den. to study org. with Peder Thomsen in Copenhagen, and in 1933 he became orgst. at Kerteminde.

Works incl. incid. m. to Büchner's *Leonce and Lena* and the marionette comedy *Uffe hin Spage*; Sym.; Concertino for ob. & stgs.; stg. 4tet, stg. Trio, 5tet for fl., cl., v., va. & co.; Suite for org., &c.

Sykes, Susan. *See* **Sunderland.**

Sylphides, Les, ballet with m. adapted from Chopin (chgph. by Mikhail Mikhailovitch Fokin), prod. Paris, Théâtre du Châtelet, 2. VI. 1909.

Sylva, Carmen. *See* **Carmen Sylva.**

Sylvana (Weber). *See* **Silvana.**

Sylvia, ou La Nymphe de Diane, ballet by Delibes (scen. by Jules Barbier & Baron de Reinach; chgph. by Louis Mérante), prod. Paris, Opéra, 14. VI. 1876.

Sym. (abbr.) = Symphony.

Symonds, John Addington (1840–93), Eng. essayist & poet. *See* **Griffes** (*These Things shall be*), **Ireland** (do.).

Sympathetic Resonance. An acoustical phenomenon observed in resonant bodies, such as a stg., a glass, a tuning-fork, &c., which will vibrate and give forth a faint sound without being touched, if their fundamental note is sung or played on an inst. near them.

Sympathetic Strings. A set of stgs. in certain types of bowed insts. vibrating in accord with those actually touched by the bow. Among the insts. having S. Ss. were the Viola d'amore, the Lira da braccio and the Lira da gamba.

Sympathetic Tone
Sympathetic Vibration } *See* **Sympathetic Resonance.**

Symph. (abbr.) = symphonic.

Symphonia (from Lat. *sinfonia*). Lit. = Symphony, esp. in the earlier sense of any piece of m. in which insts. play together in consort; also an obs. inst., possibly a kind of Bagpipe and, in a later sense, a Clavichord.

Symphonia domestica (*Domestic Sym.*), a sym. by R. Strauss, 1st perf. N.Y., 31. III. 1904. Like *Heldenleben* the work is autobiog., but describes the comp.'s private life, while the earlier work showed him as a public figure.

Symphonic Poem. A type of orch. work coming under the category of Programme M., i.e. descriptive of some literary or other subject and not purely self-sufficient in mus. content and form. Both content and form, in fact, are dictated or at least influenced by the subject in ways that could not be achieved by Absolute M.; but m. being incapable of doing more than suggesting concrete objects and ideas, even a S. P. cannot be literally understood by the hearer without the aid of a descriptive programme. Such a programme is therefore provided in a literary form by the comp. or by a programme annotator, or it may be outlined simply by quotation of or from a literary work on which the S. P. is based. Other than literary subjects of S. P.s may include actual events in hist. or contemporary life, landscapes and natural phenomena, paintings, &c. The term S. P. was the invention of Liszt, who wrote 13 works of the kind.

Symphonic Study. A category term invented by Elgar for his *Falstaff*, prob. because, although it is a Symphonic Poem to all intents and purposes, it is intended to be as much an outline of Falstaff's character as a description of the events surrounding him.

Symphonie fantastique. A sym. by Berlioz, Op. 14, comp. in 1830 and 1st perf., with its sequel, *Lélio*, Paris, 9. XII. 1832. It has a programme arising out of B.'s disappointed love for Henrietta Smithson and represents the crazy dreams of a poet crossed in love who has taken poison.

Symphonie funèbre et triomphale. A sym. by Berlioz, Op. 15, for military band, stgs. & chor., comp. in 1840 by order of the Fr. gvt. and perf. at the 10th anniversary of the 1830 Revol., Paris, 28. VII. 1840.

Symphony. The most important form of orch. m., in its most usual form a so. comp. for orch. instead of for 1 or 2 insts. (sos. for more than 2 insts. are now called trios, 4tets, &c.). Orig., until the middle of the 18th cent., the term S. was used vaguely for a variety of inst. works, and also for the inst. introds. and interludes of arias and other voc. pieces; also for operatic and other ovts., which were identical with the early 18th-cent. Ss. The modern S. as we know it emerged indefinitely from such other forms of inst. m. as the Suite, from which it inherited the Minuet (later replaced by the Scherzo), the Concerto grosso, the Divertimento, &c. Among its earliest exponents are G. B. Sammartini in It. and C. P. E. Bach and the Mannheim School (which was partly Boh.) in Ger. Haydn's early Ss. resembled those of these exemplars, but later developed into the mature modern form, which Mozart, mainly after the ex. of J. C. Bach in London, cultivated from the first. Beethoven greatly expanded the species without fundamentally changing it, except that he introd. voices into it in No. 9. Schubert further cultivated the purely classical form, but impressed the S. with his own individuality. Berlioz and Spohr (like Raff, Rubinstein and others later) introd. programmatic elements into it and thus began to approach the Symph. Poem, and so to a smaller extent did Mendelssohn (' It.' & ' Sco.' Ss.). In Schumann's and Franck's hands the form began to disintegrate, but it was reconsolidated by Brahms, Dvořák and even Tchaikovsky, later still by Elgar. Bruckner brought Wagnerian influences to bear on it, but lacked the gift of development and transition; Mahler reintroduced voices and could not keep out the literary element showing the inspiration of the song-writer rather than the symphonist. Vaughan Williams also began with words (*Sea S.*) and pictorial suggestions (*London* & *Pastoral* Ss.), but in his 4th & 5th Ss. returned to absolute m. The normal form of the S. (from which there are many departures) need not be described: it is that of the so., the main, but never fundamental differences being, apart from the orch. medium, that Ss. are often on a larger scale and more usually retain the minuet or scherzo, i.e. that they are as a rule in 4 mvts., whereas sos. are more often in 3.

Sympson, Christopher. *See* **Simpson.**

Syncopation. A displacement of the mus. accent to weak beats or off-beats in the bar, where they are normally expected to lie on the 1st beat and, less pronounced, on the other main divisions of the bar. The effect is that of a syncope (i.e. missing a heart-beat): hence the name. According to a popular superstition S. is the invention, or at least the sole property, of Ragtime, Jazz and Swing comps.; actually it goes as far back as folksong, i.e. to unfathomable antiquity, and classical as well as serious romantic and modern m. is full of exs. of it.

Synge, John Millington (1871–1909), Ir. dramatist. *See* **Gilbert (H. F.)** (*Riders to the Sea*), **Pedrollo** (*Veglia*), **Polovinkin** (*Irish Hero*), **Rabaud** (*Appel de la mer*), **Riders to the Sea** (Vaughan Williams).

Syrinx. *See* **Pan Pipe.**

Syrmen, Maddalena (sometimes so spelt). *See* **Sirmen.**

System. In Eng. (not in Ger., where it means a Stave) a S. is a number of m. staves required for the scoring of a comp., e.g. 2 for a pf. work, 1–2 for a song, 4 for a 4tet, &c., up to any number needed for an orch. full score. Such a S. is connected on the left-hand side of the page by var. kinds of braces or brackets; an open space between these shows that the next S. begins lower down on the same page.

Szábados, Béla (b. Budapest, 3. VI. 1867; d. Budapest, 15. IX. 1936), Hung. comp. Studied with Volkmann, became leader in the orch. of the Budapest Acad. of M. and was from 1927 to his death dir. of the Nat. Cons. there.

Works incl. operas *Aunt is asleep, The Simpleton, Mária* (with Szendy), *Fanni*, operettas; chamber m.; songs, &c.

Szábo, Ferencz (b. Budapest, 27. XII. 1902), Hung. comp. Pupil of Bartók and Kodály at the Budapest Cons. Settled in Rus. in 1932.

Works incl. *Song Sym.*, symph. poems *Class Struggle* & *November 7th*, suite *The Collective Farm*; 2 stg. 4tets, 3 pf. trios; mass songs incl. *A Song of Voroshilov*; songs, &c.

Szalowski, Antoni (b. Warsaw, 1907), Pol. comp. Studied with his father, a v. prof. at the Warsaw Cons., also pf. with 2 masters and comp. with Sikorski; later with Nadia Boulanger in Paris, where he stayed for some years from 1930.

Works incl. Sym., Symph. Vars.; Capriccio & Ovt. for stg. orch.; pf. Conc.; 3 songs with orch.; 3 stg. 4tets; Trio for ob., cl. & bn.; Suite for v. & pf., Sonatina for cl. & pf.; v. & pf. pieces; Partita for solo co.; So., Sonatina & other works for pf. &c.

Szamotulski, Waclaw (b. Szamotuly, Poznania, *c.* 1525; d. Cracow, 1572), Pol. comp. He was attached to the Coll. of Roratists at Cracow.

Works incl. masses, motets, psalms & other church m.; songs, &c.

Szántó, Tivadar (or **Theodor**) (b. Vienna, 3. VI. 1877; d. Budapest, 7.

I. 1934), Hung. pfst. & comp. Studied in Vienna and Budapest, and with Busoni in Berlin. Lived in Paris in 1905–14, in Swi. in 1914–21 and then settled at Budapest. He revised Delius's C min. pf. Conc., which is dedicated to him.

Works incl. opera *Typhoon* (after Lengyel's play); sym. *Land and Sea, Japan Suite* & other suites, Symph. Rhapsody for orch.; v. & pf. So.; Vars. on a Hung. Folksong, *Essays in Japanese Harmony* & other works for pf., &c.

Székely, Zoltán (b. Kocs, 8. XII. 1903), Hung. vst. & comp. Studied v. with Hubay and comp. with Kodály at Budapest. After touring as soloist he formed the Hung. Stg. 4tet in 1935.

Works incl. stg. 4tet; So. for unaccomp. v., Duet for v. & co., &c.

Szeligowski, Tadeusz (b. Lwów, 13. IX. 1896), Pol. comp. Studied at Lwów and Cracow, later with Nadia Boulanger in Paris. In 1932 he became prof. of comp. at the Vilna Cons. He made special studies of folksong and old church m.

Works incl. incid. m. for plays, e.g. Maeterlinck's *Blue Bird*; 2 Psalms for solo voices, chor. & orch.; Conc., *Phantaisie rapsodique*, suite *St. Casimir Fair* for orch.; cl. Conc.; 2 stg. 4tets; *Lithuanian Song* for v. & pf.; *Children's Album* for pf.; *Green Songs, Flower Allegories* & other songs, &c.

Szendy, Arpád (b. Szarvas, 11. VIII. 1863; d. Budapest, 10. IX. 1922), Hung. pfst. & comp. Studied under Liszt and others at the Budapest Acad. of M., where he became prof. of pf. later.

Works incl. *Mária* (with Szábados); Fantasy for pf. & orch.; 2 stg. 4tets; So. in B min., *Aphorisms on Hung. Folksongs* & other works for pf., &c.

Szenen aus Goethes ' Faust,' a setting of a number of scenes from Goethe's drama for solo voices, chor. & orch. by Schumann; comp. begun with a setting of the final chor., VIII. 1844, resumed 1849, completed without the ovt. 1850, ovt. added 1853.

Szulc, Joseph (Sigismond) (b. Warsaw, 4. IV. 1875), Pol. pfst. & comp. Studied with Noskowski at the Warsaw Cons. and later with Moszkowski in Paris. On the advice of Paderewski he began a career as concert pfst., but later devoted himself to comp. He settled in Paris.

Works incl. Fr. operettas *Une Nuit d'Ispahan, Flup!, Divin Mensonge, Flossie, Le Garçon de chez Prunier, Le Coffre-fort vivant* & others; Ovt. for orch.; v. & pf. So.; songs, &c.

Szymanowska (*née* **Wolowska**), **Maria** (b. Warsaw, 1795; d. St. Petersburg, VIII. 1831), Pol. pfst. Pupil of Field at Moscow. In 1821 she met Goethe, who fell in love with her, and later she introd. to him the Pol. poet Adam Mickiewicz, who married one of her daughters. She comp. some pf. pieces and songs.

Szymanowski, Karol (b. Timashovka, Ukraine, 21. IX. 1883; d. Lausanne, 29. III. 1937), Pol. comp. Learnt m. privately as a child and comp. a set of pf. Preludes, Op. 1, in 1900. In 1903 he entered the Warsaw Cons., studying with Noskowski and at the Lwów Chopin Festival he won a 1st prize with a C min. pf. Sonata in 1905. Lived in Berlin for a time from 1907 and worked on behalf of Pol. m. As an aristocrat he lost his property in the 1914–8 war and was imprisoned in Rus., but escaped to Warsaw, where in 1922 he became prof. of comp. and dir. of the State Cons. His last years were marred by illness and he had to go to a sanatorium in Swi., where he d.

Works incl. operas *Hagith* & *King Roger*; ballets *Mandragora* (also incid. m. to Molière's *Le Bourgeois gentilhomme*) & *Harnasie*; incid. m. to Micinski's *Prince Potemkin*; 3 syms.; *Sinfonia concertante* for pf. & orch.; 2 v. concs.; *Penthesilea* (Wyspianski) for sop. & orch.; *Hafiz Love Songs* for voice & orch.; *Stabat Mater, Veni Creator* & *Litany* for solo voices, chor. & orch.; 2 stg. 4tets; pf. Trio; numerous v. & pf. pieces; 3 sos. & many other works for pf.; many songs incl. cycles *Songs of the Infatuated Muezzin* (J. Iwaszkiewicz), *Slopiewnie* (Julian Tuwim), *Children's Rhymes* (J. Illakowicz) and settings of poems by Kasprowicz, Micinski, Kurpie, James Joyce, Tagore & others, &c.

T

t. The leading-note in Tonic Sol-fa notation, pronounced Te.

Tabarro, Il (Puccini). *See* **Trittico.**

Tablature. Var. old systems of writing down m., esp. for org. and for lute, without notes, but by means of letters, numbers or other signs. The only modern insts. for which a T. notation is now normally in use are the Ukelele and similar guitar types, but Tonic Sol-fa notation may be said to be a kind of T. (For the old Ger. Mastersingers' T. *see* **Tabulatur.**)

Table Entertainment. An 18th-cent. Eng. entertainment, only partly mus. in character, given by a single perf. sitting at a table and telling stories and jokes, giving displays of mimicry, singing songs, &c. The 1st T. Es. on record are those of George Alexander Steevens at Dublin in 1752. Dibdin began a series in London in 1789 and continued for 20 years, introd. most of his songs in this way.

Tableau parlant, Le (*The Speaking Picture*), opera by Grétry (lib. by Louis Anseaume), prod. Paris, Comédie-Italienne, 20. IX. 1769.

Tabor. A small drum with a high, narrow body and small drum-heads made of animal skin, sounding an indefinite pitch and struck with drum-sticks. It is almost obs. and was rarely used alone, but accomp. a pipe of a primitive Fife or Recorder type, similar to the modern Tin Whistle. It is occasionally used in the modern orch. to prod. a dry, dull percussive sound, and has been revived for folk-dancing.

Tabor (Smetana). *See* **Má Vlast.**

Taboret. A small Tabor.

Tabourin (Fr.) = Tabor.

Tabourot, Jehan (anag.). *See* **Arbeau.**

Tabrete (Eng., obs.) = Drum.

Tabulatur (Ger. = Tablature). In one sense the Ger. word differs from the Eng., meaning the table of rules for the instruction and guidance of the Mastersingers.

Tacchinardi, Niccolò (b. Leghorn, 3. IX. 1772; d. Florence, 14. III. 1859), It. ten. singer. He studied literature and art at first, but learnt the v., joined the orch. at the Florence Opera in 1789, and in 1794 began to appear as a singer. He soon sang in the principal theatres of It. and in 1811–4 visited Paris, then settling at Florence in the service of the Grand Duke of Tuscany.

Tacet (Lat. = is silent). An indication in old voc. part-books and later in orch. parts to show that a voice or inst. has finished its part in a work, although the work itself is still continuing. In that case the wording is usually *tacet al fine* (T. to the end). But the word T. alone may also stand below a certain number or section of a work to show that the voice or inst. in question does not perform during that portion of the m., though it will come in again later.

Taci / **Taciasi** (accent on 1st syll.) } (It.) = Tacet.

Tacté (Fr.) = Acciaccatura.

Tadolini, Giovanni (b. Bologna, *c.* 1793; d. Bologna, 29. XI. 1872), It. singer & comp. Studied comp. with Martini and singing with Babini, and in 1811 was engaged by Spontini as accompst. & chor. master at the Théâtre des Italiens in Paris, leaving in 1814, but going there again in 1830–9, after living in It. and comp. operas in between. He married the sop. Eugenia Savorini (1809–after 1848).

Works incl. operas *Le bestie in uomini, La principessa di Navarra, Il credulo deluso* (*Il finto molinaro*), *Tamerlano, Moctar, Mitridate, Almanzor*; canzonets, incl. *Eco di Scozia* with hn. obbligato, &c.

Tafel - Musik (Ger. = table m.). M., usually voc., perf. at convivial gatherings round a table at or after dinner.

Taffanel, Claude Paul (b. Bordeaux, 16. IX. 1844; d. Paris, 22. XI. 1908), Fr. flst. Studied at the Paris Cons. and was 1st fl. at the Opéra in 1864–90. In 1879 he founded the Société des Instruments à Vent, and in 1890 became one of the conds. of the Opéra and the Concerts du Cons.

Tag, Christian Gotthelf (b. Bayerfeld, Saxony, 1735; d. Niederzwönitz nr. Zwickau, 19. VI. 1811), Ger. comp. Pupil of Homilius at Dresden. In 1755 he became cantor at Hohenstein, Saxony.

Works incl. 11 masses, motets; 72 cantatas; syms. for org. & orch., songs, &c.

Tageweisen (Ger. = day tunes). Songs formerly used in Ger. to announce the break of day from church towers or by night-watchmen in the streets. They were often folksongs and some have passed into currency as hymns for the Lutheran church.

Tagliapietra, Gino (b. Lubiana, 30. V. 1887), It. pfst. & comp. Studied with Julius Epstein in Vienna and with Busoni in Berlin. Later became prof. of pf. at the Liceo Benedetto Marcello at Venice.

Works incl. ballet *La bella addormentata nel bosco*; Requiem & other chor. works; pf. Conc.; pf. pieces & studies, &c.

Tagliapietra, Giovanni (b. Venice, 24. XII. 1846; d. New York, 11. IV. 1921), It. bar. singer. Studied architecture at Venice and Padua, but later took to singing, toured in It. and S. Amer. and in 1874 settled in N.Y. He was one of Teresa Carreño's husbands.

Tagliato (It. = cut). A term, now obs., for the vertical stroke through the time-signature C, indicating *Alla breve* time.

Täglichsbeck, Thomas (b. Ansbach, 31. XII. 1799; d. Baden-Baden, 5. X. 1867), Ger. vst. & comp. Studied in Munich and became deputy cond. to Lindpaintner there in 1820. Soon after he began to travel as a vst. in Ger., Hol. and Den., and in the 1830s settled in Paris. He became mus. dir. to the Prince of Hohenzollern-Hechingen until the 1848 Revol.

Works incl. operas *Webers Bild, König Enzio*; Mass, Psalm; syms.; v. concs.; pf. Trio; partsongs, &c.

Taglietti, Giulio (b. Brescia, *c.* 1660; d. ?), It. comp. Chapel master of the Jesuit coll. of Sant' Antonio at Brescia. Comp. numerous works for 2 vs. & bass with org. or hpchd., v. sos. with bass, &c.

Tagore, Rabindranath (1861–1941), Indian poet. *See* **Carpenter** (*Gitanjali*), **Cras, Durey, Fogg** (*Hillside & Songs of Love and Life*), **Fourestier, Janáček** (*Wandering Madman*), **Morris (H.)** (*Gitanjali*), **Ponce** (3 songs), **Rota (N.)** (songs), **Ruyneman** (sacred songs), **Sauguet** (songs), **Shepherd (A.)** (*Triptych*), **Sigtenhorst Meyer** (*King's Letter*), **Stenhammar** (*Chitra*), **Szymanowski** (songs), **Tiessen** (*Post Office*).

Taille (Fr. = cut, edge). Orig. the Fr. word for the ten. voice, but in 18th-cent. scores a ten. part played by an unspecified inst., usually the ten. viol or va., but also the Eng. hn. (*oboe da caccia*), &c.

Tailleferre, Germaine (b. Pau-Saint-Maur nr. Paris, 19. IV. 1892), Fr. comp. Studied in Paris and joined the group of 'Les Six,' 1st appearing as a comp. in public in 1920. She emigrated to U.S.A. in 1942.

Works incl. ballet *Le Marchand d'oiseaux*; *Pastorale* for small orch.; pf. Conc. & Ballade for pf. & orch.; stg. 4tet; v. & pf. So.; *Jeux de plein air* for 2 pfs.; songs, &c.

Talbot, Howard (real name Richard Lansdale Munkittrick) (b. Yonkers, N.Y., 9. III. 1865; d. Reigate, 12. IX. 1928), Amer. (anglicized) comp. Studied with Parry at the R.C.M. in London.

Works incl. mus. comedies *Wapping Old Stairs, Three Little Maids, The Girl behind the Counter, The Belle of Brittany, The Arcadians, The Mousmé, The Pearl Girl, A Lucky Miss, My Lady Frayle, Mr. Manhattan* & others.

Tales of Hoffmann (Offenbach). *See* **Contes d'Hoffmann.**

Talismano, Il, unfinished opera by Balfe, completed by Macfarren (lib. *The Knight of the Leopard,* based on Scott's *Talisman,* by Arthur Matthison; It. trans. by Giuseppe Zaffira), prod. London, Her Majesty's Theatre, 11. VI. 1874.

Tallis, Thomas (b. ? Leicestershire, *c.* 1505; d. Greenwich, 23. XI. 1585), Eng. orgst. & comp. He may have been educ. in the Chapel Royal or at St. Paul's cath. in London, and held a post at Waltham Abbey before its dissolution in 1540, prob. as choirmaster or orgst. He became a Gentleman of the Chapel Royal *c.* 1537. In 1557 Queen Mary granted him, jointly with Richard Bowyer, Master of the Children in the Chapel Royal, a lease of the manor of Minster, Thanet, and at her death he passed into the service of Elizabeth, who in 1575 granted him, jointly with Byrd, a patent for the sole right to print m. and m. paper in Eng.; but 2 years later, not finding this immediately profitable, they petitioned for an annual grant, which was sanctioned. The 2 masters were then joint orgsts. at the Chapel Royal. In his last years he and his wife Joan, whom he had married in 1552, lived at their own house at Greenwich.

Works incl. 2 masses, 2 Lat. magnificats, lamentations for 5 voices, over 50 Lat. motets, incl. *Spem in alium* in 40 parts; services, psalms, litanies, *c.* 30 anthems & other Eng. church m.; secular voc. pieces; 2 In Nomines for stgs., 1 for lute; org. & virginal pieces, &c.

Talon (Fr.). The heel of a bow.

Tam-Tam (onomat., used in Ger. and some other languages) = Gong.

Tamagno, Francesco (b. Turin, 1851; d. Varese, 31. VIII. 1905), It. ten. singer. At first a baker's apprentice and locksmith, he studied at the Turin Cons., sang in the opera chor. there studied further with Pedrotti at Palermo and made his 1st appearance there in 1873. Verdi's 1st Othello.

Tamara, symph. poem by Balakirev, based on a poem by Lermontov (sometimes called *Thamar* in Eng.), begun 1866, finished 1882. Ballet on this work (chgph. by Mikhail Fokin, setting by Leon Bakst), prod. Paris, Théâtre du Châtelet, 20. V. 1912.

Tamberlik, Enrico (b. Rome, 16. III. 1820; d. Paris, 13. III. 1889), It. ten. singer, (?) of Turkish descent. At first intended for a lawyer, he made his 1st stage appearance at Naples in 1841, sang in Port. and Spa. and in 1850 1st appeared in London.

Tambour (Fr.) = Drum.

Tambour de Basque (Fr.) = Timbrel.

Tamboura. *See* **Pandora.**

Tambouret (Fr.) = Timbrel.

Tambourin (Fr.). An old Provençal dance with a drone-bass imitating a drum.

Tambourine (corrupt. from Fr.). The word, neither good Fr. nor good Eng., is current in mus. terminol. for an inst. for which there is a perfectly good Eng. word that might well be restored to use. *See* **Timbrel.**

Tamburini, Antonio (b. Faenza, 28. III. 1800; d. Nice, 9. XI. 1876), It. bar. singer. Was at first taught the hn., but appeared in opera at the age of 18, at Bologna. 1st appeared in London and Paris in 1832.

Tamburino (It.) = Timbrel.

Tamburo (It. = drum). The term is used in scores, with var. adjectival qualifications for any kind of drum except the Kettle-drums, which are called *timpani* (not *tympani*) in It.

Tamerlano (*Tamburlane*), opera by Handel (lib. by Agostino Piovene, adapted by Nicola Francesco Haym), prod. London, King's Theatre, Haymarket, 31. X. 1724.

Taming of the Shrew, The. *See* **Sly; Widerspänstigen Zähmung.**

Tampon (Fr.). A drum mallet with 2 heads, one at each end of the stick, sometimes used, esp. by 19th-cent. Fr. comps., to prod. rolls on the Bass Drum, the 2 heads being made to hit the drum-head alternately by rapid rotary motions of the wrist.

Tampur. A Caucasian inst. of the lute type, but played with a bow. It has 3 stgs.

Tancredi (*Tancred*), opera by Rossini (lib. by Gaetano Rossi, based on Tasso's *Gerusalemme liberata* and Voltaire's tragedy *Tancrède*), prod. Venice, Teatro La Fenice, 6. II. 1813. Rossini's 1st serious opera.

Taneiev, Alexander Sergeievitch (b. St. Petersburg, 17. I. 1850; d. Petrograd, 7. II. 1918), Rus. comp. Entered state service after studies at St. Petersburg Univ., but also studied m. there and at Dresden, and came under the influence of the Balakirev circle.

Works incl. operas *Cupid's Revenge* & *The Snowstorm*; 3 syms., symph. poem *Alesha Popovitch*, ovt. to Shakespeare's *Hamlet*, 2 suites for orch.; 2 stg. 4tets; pieces for v. & pf. and for pf.; songs, partsongs, &c.

Taneiev, Sergey Ivanovitch (b. Gvt. of Vladimir, 25. XI. 1856; d. Moscow, 19. VI. 1915), Rus. comp. Studied at the Moscow Cons., intending at first to became a pfst., but also studying comp. with Tchaikovsky. In 1876 he toured Rus., in 1877–8 he visited Paris, and after playing in the Baltic Provinces became prof. of orchn. at the Moscow Cons., in 1881 chief prof. of pf. on N. Rubinstein's death and in 1885 dir., succeeding Hubert. He was followed by Safonov in 1889 and became a great teacher of ctpt.

Works incl. operatic trilogy *Oresteia* (based on Aeschylus); cantata *John of Damascus* for solo voices, chor. & orch.; 4 syms., Ovt. on Rus. Themes for orch.; Concert Suite for v. & orch.; 6 stg. 4tets, pf. 4tet, 2 stg. trios, pf. Trio; Prelude and Fugue for 2 pfs.; *c.* 40 songs to words by Tiutchev & others; partsongs, &c.

Tañer (Spa. = to touch). A 16th-cent. lute prelude with which the stgs. were 'touched,' or tried; equiv. to a Toccata.

Tangents. The screwdriver-shaped pins striking the wire stgs. in the Clavichord. The stgs. continued to sound while the Ts. touched them, and their tone could thus be to a certain extent influenced by the player's fingers, which was impossible on the hpchd., and made to vibrate like a v. *vibrato* by shaking the finger on the key.

Tango. A dance of Central African orig., imported by Negro slaves into Cuba, Haiti and Mex. and thence taken with them when they migrated to the Arg. and Urug. shores of the river Plate, where it became indigenous. It is thus not of Arg. orig., but became mainly Arg. during the 19th cent. until, *c.* 1910, it came into the Eur. ballrooms and was taken up by the jazz bands. It is in 2–4 time, like the Spa. Habanera, but faster in pace, and is accomp. with a rhythm of 4 quavers, the 1st of which is dotted.

Tannhäuser und der Sängerkrieg auf der Wartburg (*Tannhäuser and the Singers' Contest at the Wartburg*), opera by Wagner (lib. by comp.), prod. Dresden, 19. X. 1845.

Tansman, Alexander (b. Lodz, 12. VI. 1897), Pol. comp. Studied at home and then at Warsaw, and in 1919 took 2 prizes for comp. He settled in Paris, but travelled extensively as pfst. & cond.

Works incl. operas *La Nuit Kurde* & *La Grande Ville*; ballet *Sextuor*; Sym. in A min., Sinfonietta, *Danse de la sorcière*, Symph. Ovt., *Toccata, Sonatine transatlantique, 4 Danses polonaises, Triptyque, Partita, Deux Pièces* for orch.; 2 concs. & Concertino for pf. & orch.; 4 stg. 4tets, Mazurka for 9 insts., *Danse de la sorcière* for 5 wind insts. & pf.; *Sonata quasi una fantasia* for v. & pf.; pf. works; songs, &c.

Tanto (It.) = as much, so much, or 'so' (e.g. *tanto bello* = 'so beautiful').

Tapiola, symph. poem by Sibelius, Op. 112, comp. in 1926 for the Symph. Soc. in N.Y. The title is the old mythol. name of Fin., der. from the forest god Tapio, who appears in the *Kalevala*. 1st perf. N.Y., 26. XII. 1926.

Tapissier, Jean (b. ?; d. ?), Fr. 15th-cent. comp. He (?) lived in It. for some time. Comp. church m.

Tappert, Wilhelm (b. Ober-Thomaswaldau, Silesia, 19. II. 1830; d. Berlin, 27. X. 1907), Ger. mus. scholar. Studied with Dehn and Kullak in Berlin and after 8 years as teacher and critic at Glogau settled in Berlin in 1866, where he taught at Tausig's pf. school and wrote numerous mus.-literary works, incl. a Wagner Lexicon & other works on Wagner, studies of notation, old lute m., the settings of Goethe's *Erl King* (51), &c. He also comp. pf. pieces, incl. 50 Studies for the left hand, songs, &c.

Tarantella. An It. dance deriving its name from Taranto, formerly sometimes sung, but now purely inst. It is in quick 6–8, increasing its speed progressively towards the end, and consists of alternating maj. and min. sections. It was danced by a couple, or in couples, who often accompanied the m. with timbrels. 2 superstitions were connected with it: (1) that the bite of the tarantula caused a kind of madness which made people dance it; (2) that the dance was a remedy against such madness.

Tarantino, Il. *See* **Fago.**

Tarare, opera by Salieri (lib. by Beaumarchais), prod. Paris, Opéra, 8. VI. 1787. It became known later under the It. title of *Axur, rè d'Ormus*.

Tarchi, Angelo (b. Naples, 1760; d. Paris, 19. VIII. 1814), It. comp. Studied at the Cons. dei Turchini at Naples with Fago and Sala. He visited London in 1789 and wrote the operas *Il disertore* and *La generosità d'Alessandro* for the King's Theatre. Later he lived in Paris.

Works incl. over 40 It. & 7 Fr. operas, &c.

Tardando (It. = delaying). A direction indicating that a passage is to be played in a lingering manner.

Tarditi, Orazio (b. Rome, ?; d. Faenza, *c.* 1670), It. monk, orgst. & comp. He was orgst. at var. It. towns after 1622, became a monk at Calmaldoli and in 1647 abbot at Ravenna; the following year he was chapel master at Faenza cath.

Works incl. masses, motets, madrigals, canzonets, &c.

Tarenghi, Mario (b. Bergamo, 10. VII. 1870; d. Milan, 21. IX. 1938), It. pfst. & comp. Studied at the Milan Cons. and later became dir. of a school of m. there.

Works incl. operas *Marcella, Gara antica, La notte di Quarto, Piero Vidal*; *Stabat Mater*; chor. works; stg. 4tet in G min.; Vars. on themes by Chopin & Schumann for 2 pfs., Vars. on *Santa Lucia* for pf. duet; numerous works for pf. solo, &c.

Tarogato. A Hung. inst., formerly a wooden tpt. with a scale confined to the natural harmonics; now a woodwind inst. akin to the Saxophone with a cl. mouthpiece.

Tartaglione, Ippolito (b. Modena, *c.* 1539; d. Naples, *c.* 1580), It. comp. He was successively chapel master at Santa Maria Maggiore in Rome and, from *c.* 1576, at Naples cath.

Works incl. masses & motets for 3 and 4 chors., &c.

Tartini, Giuseppe (b. Pirano, Istria, 8. IV. 1692; d. Padua, 26. II. 1770), It. vst. & comp. He learnt v. and m. at school at Capo d'Istria and in 1709 went to Padua Univ. as a law student, although his father had wished him to enter the priesthood. At 20 he made a runaway marriage with Elisabetta Premazone, either a relative or a dependent of Cardinal Cornaro, who ordered T.'s arrest, with the result that he was obliged to flee from Padua, leaving his wife there. He (?) went to Rome and then was offered refuge at the monastery of Assisi, where he studied with Černohorsky, discovered the acoustical phenomenon of Resultant Tones and began to comp. In 1715 he was accidentally discovered by some pilgrims from Padua, who gave him news of his wife, and he obtained pardon and returned to her. On being invited to a contest with Veracini at Venice, he discovered that he was insufficiently equipped and went to Ancona for further technical study. In 1721 he was app. 1st v. at the Cappella del Santo at Padua. In 1723 he went to Prague at the invitation of Count Kinsky to attend the coronation of Charles VI, and he remained there as a member of Kinsky's orch. until 1726, visiting Venice on his way home. In 1728 he estab. a school of v. playing at Padua, where he remained, refusing invitations to London and Paris, but *c.* 1739–41 he visited many It. cities, incl. Naples and Rome, where he wrote a *Miserere* at the request of Pope Clement XII. He wrote a number of theoret. treatises.

Works incl. *Miserere* & *Salve Regina*; over 100 v. concs.; numerous trio-sos. for 2 vs. & bass; many sos. for v. & bass; canzoni for 2 & 3 voices, &c.

Taschengeige (Ger., lit. pocket fiddle). *See* **Kit.**

Taskin, Émile Alexandre (b. Paris, 18. III. 1853; d. Paris, 5. X. 1897), Fr. bar. singer. Studied at the Paris Cons. and was a member of the Opéra-Comique in 1879–94. Grandson of the orgst. & comp. Henri Joseph T. (1779–1852), great-grandson of Pascal Joseph T. (1750–1829), keeper of the royal insts., and great-great-grandson of the inst. maker Pascal T. (1723–93).

Tasso, lamento e trionfo (*Tasso's Lament and Triumph*), symph. poem by Liszt, based on a poem by Byron, comp. 1849, perf. Weimar, 28. VIII. 1849, as an ovt. to Goethe's drama *Torquato Tasso*, revised 1850–1 with a new middle section and 1st perf. Weimar, 19. IV. 1854.

Tasso, Torquato (1544–95), It. poet. *See* **Armida & Armide** (11 operas on *Gerusalemme liberata*), **Belli (D.)** (*Aminta*), **Caccini (F.)**, **Campra** (*Tancrède*), **Gavazzeni** (*Aminta*), **Lenepveu** (*Renaud dans les jardins d'Armide*), **Madrigal Opera** (*Aminta*), **Monteverdi** (*Combattimento di Tancredi e Clorinda*), **Pallavicini (C.)** (*Gerus. lib.*), **Persuis** (*Jérusalem délivrée*), **Pizzetti** (*Aminta*), **Righini** (*Gerus. lib.*), **Rinaldo** (Handel), **Rossellini** (*Aminta*), **Rossi (M. A.)** (*Erminia sul Giordano*), **Sacchini** (*Armida*), **Tancredi** (Rossini).

Tastar (It., from *tastare* = to touch). A 16th-cent. lute prelude with which the stgs. were 'touched,' or tried; equiv. to a Toccata.

Tasten (Ger.) = Keys (of a keyboard).

Tastiera per luce (It. = keyboard for light). An inst. appearing in the score of Skriabin's *Prometheus*, designed to throw differently coloured lights. It was never perfected for practical use.

Tasto (It.). Key (of keyboard insts.); also fingerboard (of stg. insts.).

Tasto solo (It. = key alone). A direction indicating that in a comp. with a thorough-bass the bass notes are for the moment to be played alone on the keyboard inst. used, without any harmony above them.

Tate, Nahum (1652–1715), Ir. poet. *See* **Dido and Aeneas** (Purcell).

Tatto (It. obs.) = Acciaccatura.

Taubert, (Karl Gottfried) Wilhelm (b. Berlin, 23. III. 1811; d. Berlin, 7. I. 1891), Ger. pfst., cond. & comp. Pupil of Ludwig Berger for pf. and of Klein for comp., and student at Berlin Univ. He became Prus. court pfst., in 1841 cond. of the Royal Opera and in 1845 court mus. dir.

Works incl. operas *Die Kirmess*, *Der Zigeuner*, *Marquis und Dieb*, *Joggeli*, *Macbeth* (after Shakespeare) & *Cesario* (on Shakespeare's *Twelfth Night*); incid. m. to *Medea* (Euripides), *The Tempest* (Shakespeare) & other plays; 3 Psalms & other church m.; 4 cantatas; 3 syms., ovt. to Tieck's *Blaubart*, Festival Ovt. for orch.; 3 stg. 4tets, 2 pf. trios; 6 v. & pf. sos.; 6 pf. sos. & many pieces; *c.* 300 songs incl. *Kinderlieder*; duets, partsongs, &c.

Taubmann, Otto (b. Hamburg, 8. III. 1859; d. Berlin, 8. VII. 1929), Ger. cond., critic & comp. Studied at the Dresden Cons. and became cond. and critic in several towns, settling in Berlin in 1895 as prof. at the Hochschule für Musik.

Works incl. opera *Porzia*; *Deutsche Messe* & other chor. works; Sym., stg. 4tet, &c.

Tausch, Julius (b. Dessau, 15. IV. 1827; d. Bonn, 11. XI. 1895), Ger. cond. & comp. Pupil of Schneider at Dessau and at the Leipzig Cons. Successor of J. Rietz at Düsseldorf in 1847, where he displaced Schumann.

Works incl. incid. m. to Shakespeare's *Twelfth Night*; Festival Ovt. for orch.; pf. pieces; songs, &c.

Tausig, Carl (b. Warsaw, 4. XI. 1841; d. Leipzig, 17. VII. 1871), Pol. pfst. & comp. Pupil of his father, the pfst. Aloys T. (1820–85), and of Liszt at Weimar. In 1858 he made his 1st appearance at a concert cond. by Bülow in Berlin, then toured, settled at Dresden and in 1862 in Vienna, where he gave concerts with programmes of modern m. In 1865 he married, settled in Berlin and opened a school of advanced pf. playing.

Works incl. symph. poems; pf. Conc.; concert studies, exercises, bravura pieces & numerous transcriptions for pf., &c.

Taverner, John (b. ? Boston or Tattershall, Lincs., *c.* 1495; d. Boston, 25. X. 1545), Eng. orgst. & comp. In

1526 he was app. master of the choristers at Wolsey's new coll. (Cardinal Coll., later Christ Church) at Oxford and orgst. at St. Frideswide's church (later cath.) attached to it. In 1528 he was imprisoned for heresy and in 1530 he left the Coll. or was dismissed, the rest of his career being devoted to the activities of an agent in Thomas Cromwell's pay. He gave up m., settled at Boston and there took part in the fanatical destructions of church property.

Works incl. 8 masses (*The Western Wind*, &c.), 28 Lat. motets 3 magnificats & other church m.; In Nomines for stgs.; 3 songs for Wynkyn de Worde's book, &c.

Tayber, Anton & Franz. *See* **Teyber.**

Taylor, (Joseph) Deems (b. New York, 22. XII. 1885), Amer. comp. & critic. Studied at the Ethical Culture School and the Univ. in N.Y., received pf. lessons, but was self-taught in other mus. subjects. Having done a good deal of mus. editing, he became m. critic to the *N.Y. World* in 1921, but from 1925 devoted himself to comp.

Works incl. operas *The King's Henchman, Peter Ibbetson* (after George du Maurier) & *Ramuntcho* (after Loti); incid. m. for Thornton Wilder's *Lucrece* & other plays; symph. poems *The Siren Song* & *Jurgen* (after J. Branch Cabell), suites *Through the Looking-Glass* (after Lewis Carroll) & *Circus Day*; *Lucrece* suite for stg. 4tet; chor. works. &c.

Taylor, Samuel Coleridge. *See* **Coleridge-Taylor.**

Tchaikovsky, Peter Ilyitch (b. Kamsko-Votinsk, 7. V. 1840; d. St. Petersburg, 6. XI. 1893), Rus. comp. His father, an inspector of mines, allowed him to have m. lessons from the age of 4, and at 6 he played well. The family moved to St. Petersburg in 1848; he received more systematic teaching there and in 1850 was sent to the School of Jurisprudence, which he left in 1859 to become a clerk in the Ministry of Justice. He approached m. as an amateur, but in 1862 entered the newly opened Cons., having already studied with Zaremba, and had lessons in orchn. from A. Rubinstein. N. Rubinstein, having opened a similar Cons. at Moscow, engaged him as prof. of harmony in 1865, and there he began to comp. seriously and professionally. In 1868 he met Balakirev and his circle of nationalist comps. in St. Petersburg, but remained aloof from them. He became engaged to Désirée Artôt that year, but she married Padilla early in 1869. His operas gained him recognition, and the 2nd Sym., a distinctly nationalist work, was prod. in 1873, and the B♭ min. pf. Concerto, already done abroad by Bülow, was 1st played by Taneiev at Moscow in 1875. In 1876 began a correspondence with Nadezhda von Meck, the widow of a wealthy engineer, who greatly admired his work and made him an allowance to free him from financial anxiety, but never met him face to face. In 1877 he married Antonina Ivanovna Miliukov, who had sent him a declaration of love, although he did not return her feelings, and he left her for ever less than a month after the wedding, on the verge of a mental collapse. After some months in Swi. and It., he resigned the post at the Moscow Cons. and lived in the country, wholly devoted to comp. In 1888 he made a 1st internat. tour as cond. of his own works, which became known in many countries. In 1890 he had a misunderstanding with Nadezhda von Meck which brought their friendship by correspondence to an end; but he was by that time quite able to earn his own living. He visited the U.S.A. in 1892 and London in the summer of 1893, when the Mus.D. degree was conferred on him by Cambridge Univ. On his return to Rus., where the 6th Sym. ('Pathetic') was perf. at St. Petersburg on 28. X, he rashly (? intentionally) drank a glass of unboiled water and developed cholera, from which he d.

Works incl. operas *The Opritchnik, Vakula the Smith* (afterwards *Tcherevitchki* or *Oxana's Caprices*), *Eugene Onegin, Joan of Arc, Mazeppa, The Sorceress, The Queen of Spades, Iolanta* & 3 partly lost early works; incid. m. to Ostrovsky's *Snegurotchka* and Shakespeare's *Hamlet*; ballets, *The Swan Lake, The Sleeping Beauty* & *The Nutcracker*; 6 syms.; 4 suites for orch.; misc. orch. works incl. fantasy-ovt. *Romeo and Juliet*, symph. fantasies *The Tempest* & *Francesca da Rimini*, *Capriccio italien*, Serenade for stg. orch., ovt. *The Year 1812*, fantasy-ovt. *Hamlet*, symph. ballad *The Voyevoda*; 3 pf. concs. (3rd unfinished), v. Conc., *Vars. on a Rococo Theme* for co. & orch. & some smaller pieces for solo insts. & orch.; stg. 6tet *Souvenir de Florence*, 3 stg. 4tets, pf. Trio; 17 op. nos. of pf. comps. incl. 6 pieces on 1 theme, So. in G maj., *The Seasons*; 50 Rus. folksongs for voc. duet; 13 op. nos. of songs (nearly 100); 6 voc. duets; 3 cantatas; some church m.; partsongs, &c.

Tchang-Tsi (*c.* 11th cent.), Chin. poet. *See* **Lied von der Erde** (Mahler).

Tchekhov, Anton Pavlovitch (1860–1904), Rus. dramatist & novelist. *See* **Nottara** (*On the Highway*).

Tcherepnin, Alexander Nikolaievitch (b. St. Petersburg, 20. I. 1899), Rus. comp. Studied under his father, Nikolai T., Sokolov and others, learning the pf. from Anna Essipova. He appeared as a boy pfst. and began to pub. his works, but in 1921 settled in Paris with his father, studying comp. with Gédalge and pf. with Philipp at the Cons. In 1935 he left for Shanghai.

Works incl. operas *Ol-Ol* (after Andreiev) & *Die Hochzeit der Sobeide* (after Hofmannsthal); ballet *The Frescoes of Ajanta*; incid. m. for Wilde's *Salome*, Rolland's *L'Esprit triomphant* & Hauptmann's *Hannele*; Sym., 3 pieces for chamber orch.; 3 pf. concs., *Rapsodie géorgienne* for co. & pf., *Concerto da camera* for fl., v. & small orch.; 2 stg. 4tets, pf. Trio; v. & pf. So., 2 co. & pf. sos.; So., studies and many pieces for pf., &c.

Tcherepnin, Nikolai Nikolaievitch (b. St. Petersburg, 14. V. 1873), Rus. cond. & comp. He gave up a legal career at the age of 22 and studied at the St. Petersburg Cons. with Rimsky-Korsakov and others. Having appeared as pfst., he became cond. of the Belaiev concerts in 1901, and then became cond. of opera at the Maryinsky Theatre. In 1908 he joined Diaghilev and cond. Rus. opera and ballet in Paris and elsewhere, remaining with the company until 1914, when he returned to Petrograd, to become dir. of the Cons. at Tiflis in 1918. In 1921 he settled in Paris.

Works incl. operas *Vanka the Chancellor* (after Sologub) & *Poverty no Crime* (after Ostrovsky); ballets *Armida's Pavilion*, *Narcissus*, *A Russian Fairy-Tale*, *The Romance of a Mummy* (after Gautier), *The Masque of the Red Death* (after Poe), *The Tale of the Princess Ulyba*, *Dionysius*; Sym., Sinfonietta, symph. poems *Narcissus and Echo* & *The Enchanted Kingdom*, witches' scene from *Macbeth*, suite *The Enchanted Garden*, ovt. to Rostand's *La Princesse lointaine*, 6 pieces on Pushkin's *The Golden Fish* for orch.; pf. Conc. in C♯ min., Lyric Poem for v. & orch.; stg. 4tet in A min.; pf. pieces on Benois's picture-book *The Rus. Alphabet* & other pf. works; songs, &c.

Tcherevitchki (Tchaikovsky). *See* **Vakula the Smith.**

Tchishko, Oles (b. nr. Kharkov, 2. VII. 1895), Rus. singer, cond. & comp. Son of a peasant, he learnt m. mainly in the choir-school and picked up Ukrainian folksongs. He studied briefly at the Kharkov Cons. Working mainly as singer and cond., he nevertheless comp. an opera, *Judith*, which he went to Leningrad to show to Glazunov, who approved of it. In 1927 he sang in popular opera at Odessa, but returned to Leningrad in 1931 to continue his comp. studies.

Works incl. operas *Judith*, *Imprisoned by Apple Orchards*, *Mutiny on the Battleship Potemkin*; ovt. *Red Army Days*, *Ukrainian Capriccio*, *Suite for Dancing*, suite *Youth*, &c. for orch.; Ukrainian songs arr. for chor. & orch., &c.

Te. The name for the leading-note in any key in Tonic Sol-fa, so pronounced, but in notation represented by the symbol t.

Teares and Lamentacions of a Sorrowfull Soul, The. *See* **Leighton.**

Tedesca (fem.), **Tedesco** (masc.) (It.) = German. The term *alla tedesca* means 'in the Ger. manner,' but more partic. indicates a piece or mvt. in rather slow waltz time, in the character of the *Deutscher* or *Ländler*.

Tegnér, Esias (1782–1846), Swe. poet. *See* **Bruch** (*Frithjof*), **Dubois** (do.), **Hofmann (H.)** (do,), **Zöllner** (do.).

Telemaco, Il, ossia L'isola di Circe (*Telemachus, or Circe's Island*), opera by Gluck (lib. by Marco Coltellini), prod. Vienna, Burg Theatre, 30. I. 1765.

Telemann, Georg Philipp (b. Magdeburg, 14. III. 1681; d. Hamburg, 25. VI. 1767), Ger. comp. Studied languages and science at Leipzig Univ. and was mainly self-taught in m., but in 1704 secured the appt. of orgst. at the New Church there and founded a students' mus. soc., the Collegium Musicum. After var. appts. at Sorau, Eisenach, Frankfort and Bayreuth, he became mus. dir. of the Johanneum at Hamburg in 1721 and orgst. at the 5 principal churches. He travelled a good deal, several times visited Berlin and in 1737 Paris.

Works incl. operas *Der gedultige Socrates*, *Der neu-modische Liebhaber Damon*, *Die ungleiche Heyrath*, *Miriways*, *Flavois Bertaridus* & 35 others; orats. *Der Tag des Gerichts*, *Die Tageszeiten*, *Der Tod Jesu* & *Die Auferstehung Christi* (words of both by Ramler), Passion (words by Brockes), Scenes from the Gospels, 43 other Passions & other sacred works; 12 sets of services for the whole year, motets, psalms & other church m.; cantatas for funerals, weddings & other occasions; many inst. comps.; org. fugues, &c.

Telharmonium. An electrophonic inst. invented by the Amer. scientist

Thomas Cahill early in the 20th cent., prod. its notes by means of electro-magnets and capable of imitating var. insts.

Tellefsen, Thomas (Dyke Acland) (b. Trondhjem, 26. XI. 1823; d. Paris, 7. X. 1874), Norw. pfst., (?) godson of Thomas Dyke Acland, M.P. for N. Devon, who travelled much in Norw. He was a pupil of Chopin in Paris and visited Eng. with him in 1848. He frequently played there later and ed. Chopin's works in Paris.

Tema (It.) = Theme.

Temistocle (*Themistocles*), opera by Porpora (lib. by Apostolo Zeno), prod. Vienna, 1. X. 1718.

Temperament. *See also* **Equal Temperament.** A term used to designate the tuning of the mus. scale in such a way as to prod. satisfying intonation in some way not according to the natural harmonics, some of which are not in accord with the requirements of mus. comp. or perf.

Tempest, The, incid. m. by Sibelius, Op. 109, comp. for prod. of Shakespeare's play at the Theatre Royal, Copenhagen, 1926.

Opera by Fibich (lib. by Jaroslav Vrchlický, based on Shakespeare), prod. Prague, Cz. Theatre, 1. III. 1895.

Opera by N. Gatty (lib. by Reginald Gatty, based on Shakespeare), prod. London, Surrey Theatre, 17. IV. 1920.

Symph. Fantasy by Tchaikovsky, after Shakespeare, suggested by Stassov, begun VIII. 1873, 1st perf. Moscow, XII. 1873.

Tempest, The, or The Enchanted Island, opera adapted from Shakespeare by Thomas Shadwell, with m. by (?) Locke, Humfrey, Reggio, James Hart, G. B. Draghi and Banister, prod. London, Dorset Gardens Theatre, 30. IV. 1674.

Opera adapted from Shakespeare and from Dryden and Davenant's previous adapt. by ?, with m. by Purcell, comp. (?) 1695.

Tempesta, La, opera by Halévy (lib. by Scribe, orig. written in Fr. for Mendelssohn, based on Shakespeare's *Tempest* and trans. into It.), prod. London, Her Majesty's Theatre, 8. VI. 1850.

Templario, Il (*The Templar*), opera by Nicolai (lib by Girolamo Maria Marini, based on Scott's *Ivanhoe*), prod. Turin, Teatro Regio, 11. II. 1840.

Temple Block. *See* **Chinese Block.**

Temple, Hope. *See* **Messager.**

Templer und die Jüdin, Der (*The Templar and the Jewess*), opera by Marschner (lib. by Wilhelm August Wohlbrück, based on Scott's *Ivanhoe*), prod. Leipzig, 22. XII. 1829.

Templeton, John (b. Riccarton, Kilmarnock, 30. VII. 1802; d. New Hampton, 2. VII. 1886), Sco. ten. singer. Appeared as a child singer at Edinburgh, studied there and in London, and made his 1st stage appearance at Worthing in 1828. In 1831 he became known in London and in 1833 Malibran engaged him as her ten. partner.

Tempo (It. lit. time) = Pace. The speed of any mus. comp., determined, not by the note-values used by the comp., which are relative, but by the directions set above the stave at the opening of a piece or section (e.g. *allegro, andante, adagio*, &c.). These words cannot fix the exact pace required by the comp.; this can only be done by means of Metronome marks (e.g. ♩ = 96, i.e. 96 crotchets to the minute, &c.). The word T., although It., may be said to have become Eng. by adoption; there is no reason, therefore, for not using the plur. 'tempos' instead of the rather pedantic *tempi*.

Tempo giusto (It.) = Strict time, also another term for

Tempo ordinario (It. = common time, ordinary pace). One of the directions mentioned above, sometimes used by old comps., esp. Handel, to indicate not only 'common time' in the present sense of 4 beats to the bar, but that kind of time taken at a moderate pace.

Tempo primo (It. lit. 1st time = 1st tempo). After a change of tempo the direction *t. p.* means that the pace 1st indicated is to be resumed.

Tempo rubato. *See* **Rubato.**

Tempus imperfectum
Tempus perfectum } (Lat. = imperfect & perfect time). *See* **Time Signature.**

Ten. (abbr.) = Tenor, for the purpose of this book; in mus. terminology it is used for *tenuto*.

Tenaglia, Antonio Francesco (b. Florence, ?; d. ?), It. 17th-cent. comp. Studied and lived in Rome.

Works incl. opera *Clearco*; madrigals; arias & duets, &c.

Tenducci, Giusto Ferdinando (b. Siena, *c.* 1736; d. ?), It. male sop. singer & comp. He 1st appeared in It. in 1753 and 1st went to London in 1758, remaining until after 1791, but for occasional visits to It. and some years spent at Edinburgh and Dublin. He pub. a treatise on singing, compiled pasticcios for the stage, wrote songs for other comps.' operas, ovts., hpchd. sos., &c.

Tenendo (It. = holding) = Sustained, without hurrying.

Teneramente (It.) = Tenderly.

Tenerezza (It.) = Tenderness.

Tenero (It.) = Tender, gentle.

Tenete (It. imper.). Hold, sustain.

Tennyson, Alfred, Lord (1809–92), Eng. poet. *See* **Bennett (W. S.)** (*May Queen*), **Clutsam** (*Lady of Shalott*), **Delius** (*Maud*), **Hadley (P.)** (*Mariana*), **Jacobson** (*Lady of Shalott*), **Jensen** (songs), **Lahee** (*Sleeping Beauty*), **Lehmann (L. ii)** (*In Memoriam*), **Macfarren (G.)** (songs), **Mihalovich** (*Eliána*), **Novák** (*Lady Godiva*), **Parry (H.)** (*Lotos-Eaters*), **Quilter** (songs), **Raimann** (*Enoch Arden*), **Schira** (*Lord of Burleigh*), **Somervell** (*Maud*), **Stanford** (*Queen Mary, Becket, Revenge & Princess*), **Strauss (R.)** (*Enoch Arden*), **Sullivan** (*Foresters & The Window*).

Tenor. The highest male voice prod. naturally, i.e. not in falsetto, like the male alto. It is so called (from Lat. *teneo* = 'I hold') because it 'held' the plainsong theme in early polyphonic comps. using a *Cantus firmus*. The compass is usually about 2 8ves on either side of middle C. The word T. is also sometimes used for the va.

Tenor Clef. The C clef so used as to indicate that middle C stands on the 4th line (from below) of the stave; now obs. for the ten. voice, but still used for some insts., e.g. co. and bn.

Tenor Cor. A milit.-band brass inst. invented *c.* 1860 by Henry Ditsin to provide a better substitute for the hn. than had been found in the Saxhorn. It is in the circular form of a hn. and has valves, generally made to stand in the key of F, with an extra slide to change it to E♭.

Tenor Drum. A drum with 2 skins stretched over either end, similar in shape to the side drum and bass drum, but of intermediate size. It prod. a duller sound than that of the side drum, having no snares, but gives out clearer notes, though of indefinite pitch, than the bass drum.

Tenor Horn. A brass valve wind inst. of the Saxhorn type, made in var. tunings and compasses.

Tenor Tuba. Another name for the Euphonium.

Tenor Viol. *See* **Viola da braccio.**

Tenor Violin. An obs. inst. of the v. family, the 4 stgs. of which were tuned like the 3 lower ones of the va. with one another 5th lower, the compass thus starting from F below the stave in the bass clef. It fell into disuse about the middle of the 18th cent.

Tenore (It.) = Tenor (voice).

Tenore robusto (It. = robust ten.). One of the categories of operatic voices: a ten. capable of sustaining parts of a heroic type; equiv. to the Ger. *Heldentenor.*

Tenoroon. An obs. inst. of the bn. type, smaller and tuned higher than the bn.

Tenson. A Troubadour, Trouvère or Minnesinger song the words of which took the form of a dispute.

Tenuta (It.) = Fermata.

Tenuto (It. = held). A direction usually marked *ten.*, indicating that the note or notes to which it applies are to be sustained to their full value, or even an almost imperceptible fraction beyond, but not so much so as to give the different effect of *ritenuto*: the meaning is 'held,' not 'held back.'

Ternary. A voc. or inst. piece in 3 distinct sections, the 3rd of which is a repetition of the 1st, is said to be in T. form. The middle section is usually a contrast, sometimes based on similar but more often on different thematic material, but always relevant in style if not in mood. In voc. m. *da capo* arias and in inst. m. minuets or scherzos with trios are outstanding exs. of T. form.

Ternina, Milka (b. Vezisce, Croatia, 19. XII. 1864; d. Zagreb, IV. 1940), Yslv. sop. singer. Studied at home from the age of 12 and in 1880–2 in Vienna. She appeared at Agram when still a student, then sang light parts at Leipzig, rising gradually through greater parts at Graz and Bremen to the Court Opera at Munich, to which she was attached in 1890–9. In 1895 she 1st sang in London, making her 1st appearance at Covent Garden in 1898, and the next year, having become one of the great Wagner singers, she was engaged for Bayreuth.

Terpander (7th cent. B.C.), Gr. poet & musn. He won a prize at the mus. festival in Sparta between 676–2 B.C. His contribs. to m. are uncertain, but are said to have incl. the comp. of drinking-songs, the increase of the lyre-stgs. from 4 to 7 and the introd. of new metres into poetry and consequently into m.

Terradeglias, Domenico. The It. form of the name of

Terradellas, Domingo (Miguel Bernabé) (b. Barcelona, II. 1713; d. Rome, 20. V. 1751), Spa. comp. Began to study m. at a Catalan monastery, but succeeded in being taken to It. by a merchant as a child, and with the aid of the Spa. ambassador was sent to study with Durante at the Cons. di Sant' Onofrio at Naples. In 1746–7 he was in London, prod. 2 operas, and he then settled in Rome, having visited Paris on the way. He became chapel master at the church of San Giacomo dei Spagnuoli. He was drowned in the Tiber, (?) by suicide owing to the failure of his last opera.

Works incl. operas *Astarto, Gli intrighi delle cantarine, Artemisia, Cerere, Romolo* (with Latilla), *Merope, Artaserse, Semiramide riconosciuta, Mitridate, Bellerofonte, Imeneo in Atene, Didone, Sesostri, rè d'Egitto*; orats. *Giuseppe riconosciuto* & *Ermenegildo martire*; (?) masses, motets & other church m., &c.

Terrasse, Claude (Antoine) (b. Grand Lamps nr. Grenoble, 27. I. 1867; d. Paris, 30. VI. 1923), Fr. orgst. & comp. He studied at the Lyons Cons. and then at Niedermeyer's school in Paris, afterwards privately with Gigout. After living obscurely as an orgst. at Auteuil and a pf. teacher at Arcachon, he began to comp. and settled in Paris in 1895.

Works incl. opera *Pantagruel* (after Rabelais), operettas *La Fiancée du scaphandrier, Chonchette, Le Sire de Vergy, Monsieur de la Palisse, L'Ingénu libertin, Le Coq d'Inde, Le Mariage de Télémaque, Les Transatlantiques, La Petite Femme de Loth* (Tristan Bernard), *Les Travaux d'Hercule, Cartouche, Le Cochon qui sommeille, Faust en ménage, Le Manoir enchanté* & several others; incid. m. for var. comedies; m. for Théophile Gautier's and Théodore de Banville's *Matinées poétiques*; *Trio bouffe* for stgs., *Sérénade bouffe* for pf. & stgs.; songs, &c.

Terry, Charles Sanford (b. Newport Pagnell, Bucks., 24. X. 1864; d. Westerton of Pitfodels nr. Aberdeen, 5. XI. 1936), Eng. historian and mus. biographer. He was app. prof of hist. at Aberdeen Univ., but did invaluable work for m. by writing the most authoritative biog. of Bach in existence, as well as numerous detailed studies of var. aspects of his work, and a biog. of J. C. Bach.

Terry, Richard (Runciman) (b. Ellington, Northumberland, 3. I. 1865; d. London, 18. IV. 1938), Eng. orgst. & mcolst. After var. appts. he became orgst. & choirmaster at Downside Abbey in Somerset in 1896 and at Westminster cath. in London in 1901, where he remained until 1924. He did great work there in enforcing services of the Rom. church according to the highest mus. standards and traditions, and he wrote on and ed. much church m. He also had a specialist's knowledge of sea shanties and carols. Knighted in 1922.

Terzet (Eng.) / **Terzetto** (It.) } A comp. for 3 voices or for insts. in 3 parts. Both terms are obs. in Eng. usage, and are better replaced by Trio.

Terzina (It.) = Triplet.

Teseo (*Theseus*), opera by Handel (lib. by Nicola Francesco Haym), prod. London, Queen's Theatre, Haymarket, 10. I. 1713.

Tesi-Tramontini, Vittoria (b. Florence, 13. II. 1700; d. Vienna, 9. V. 1775), It. con. singer. Made her 1st appearance at a very early age. In 1719 she was at Dresden, later in Vienna. It is one of the well-known and purely fictitious Handel stories that he fell in love with her at Florence when his *Rodrigo* was prod. there in 1707: the date of her birth refutes it effectively.

Tess, opera by F. d'Erlanger (lib., in It., by Luigi Illica, based on Thomas Hardy's *Tess of the D'Urbervilles*), prod. Naples, Teatro San Carlo, 10. IV. 1906.

Tessarini, Carlo (b. Rimini, 1690; d. ?), It. vst. & comp. Pupil of Corelli or a master of his school. He became vst. at St. Mark's, Venice, in 1729 and later at the church of SS. Giovanni e Paolo there. He visited Amsterdam in 1762 and at the end of his life was in the service of Cardinal Wolfgang Hannibal at Brno.

Works incl. concertini & concerti grossi for stgs.; trio-sos.; duets & 3-mvt. sos. for v., &c.

Tessier, André (b. Paris, 8. III. 1886; d. Paris, 2. VII. 1931), Fr. mcolst. Studied law, literature and art, and after attending Rolland's lectures took to mcol. in 1919. He wrote mainly on old Fr. m., incl. a book on Couperin, and took part in the complete eds. of Lully and Couperin.

Tessier, Charles (b. Pézénas, Hérault, c. 1550; d. ?), Fr. lutenist & comp. He may have been at the court at Cassel and visited Eng. for some time in the 1590s, dedicating a book of Chansons to Lady Penelope Rich (Sidney's Stella).

Works incl. Chansons for 4–5 voices, *Airs et villanelles* for 3–5 voices, setting of the 8th song in Sidney's *Astrophel and Stella*, &c.

Tessitura (It. lit. texture). The disposition of a voice and the region of its compass within which it can sing most normally and comfortably, inside which most passages intended for it had better be written, though it is capable of going higher or lower.

Testudo (Lat. = tortoise). A Lat. name for the Gr. lyre, which was often made of tortoiseshell; transferred to the lute in 16th-cent. Lat.

Tetrachord (from Gr. = 4 sounds). A scale of 4 notes comprising 2 whole tones and a semitone (in any order) and thus taking up the space of a perfect 4th.

Tetrazzini, Luisa (b. Florence, 29. VI.

1871; d. Milan, 28. IV. 1940), It. sop. singer. Studied with Ceccherini at the Florence Liceo Musicale and with her sister Eva (1862–1938), the wife of the cond. Cleofante Campanini. She made her 1st appearance at Florence in 1895, then toured, 1st in It. and later in Eur., Mexico and S. Amer. In 1907 she 1st appeared in London, in 1908 in U.S.A.

Teufel ist los, Der, oder Die verwandelten Weiber (*The Devil to pay, or The Women metamorphosed*), musical play by J. C. Standfuss (lib. by Christian Felix Weisse, based on Coffey's *Devil to pay*), prod. Leipzig, 6. X. 1752. *See also* **Verwandelten Weiber** (J. A. Hiller).

Teufels Lustschloss, Das (*The Devil's Pleasaunce*), opera by Schubert (lib. by August von Kotzebue), comp. in 1814 but not perf.

Teutsche (Ger., obs.). *See* **Deutsche Tänze.**

Texture. In m. terminol. the word is usefully applied to the disposition of parts in comp.

Teyber, Anton (b. Vienna, 8. IX. 1756; d. Vienna, 18. XI. 1822), Aus. comp. App. court comp. to the Imp. Chapel in 1793 and later m. teacher to the archdukes.

Works incl. play with m. *Zermes und Mirabella*; orat. *Joas*; Passion, masses & other church m.; syms.; chamber m., &c.

Teyber, Franz (b. Vienna, 15. XI. 1756; d. Vienna, 22. X. 1810), Aus. cond., orgst. & comp., brother of prec. Cond. of Schikaneder's company and late in his life app. court orgst.

Works incl. operas & plays with m. *Adelheid von Veltheim, Laura Rossetti, Die Dorfdeputierten, Alexander, Der Schlaftrunk* & others; orat.; church m.; songs, &c.

Thaïs, opera by Massenet (lib. by Louis Gallet, based on the novel by Anatole France), prod. Paris, Opéra, 16. III. 1894. It contains the popular *Méditation* as an orch. interlude.

Thalberg, Sigismond (b. Geneva, 7. I. 1812; d. Posilipo, 27. IV. 1871), Aus. pfst. & comp. Natural son of Count Moritz Dietrichstein and Baroness Wetzlar. When he was 10 his father sent him to school in Vienna, where he later studied pf. with Hummel and theory with Sechter. He soon played at private parties, appeared at Prince Metternich's house in 1826 and in 1830 made his 1st tour, in Ger., having by this time begun to pub. comps. In 1835 he made further studies with Pixis and Kalkbrenner in Paris, and in 1836 1st appeared in London.

Works incl. operas *Florinda* & *Cristina di Suezia*; pf. Conc.; pf. So., studies, nocturnes, romances & numerous other pieces for pf., operatic fantasies & other transcriptions for pf.; over 50 Ger. songs, &c.

Thalberg, Zaré (real name Ethel Western) (b. Derbyshire, 16. IV. 1858; d. London, 1915), Eng. sop. singer & actress. Pupil of Thalberg, whose name she adopted; also studied in Paris and Milan, and made her 1st London appearance at Covent Garden Theatre in 1875. She soon lost her voice, after some successful appearances on the Continent, and became an actress under her own name.

Thamar (Balakirev). *See* **Tamara.**

Thamos, König von Aegypten (*T., King of Egypt*), incid. m. by Mozart (3 chors. & 5 interludes) comp. in 1773 for the play by Tobias Philipp von Gebler, pub. in 1772. In M.'s lifetime the m. was used only for another play, Plümicke's *Lanassa*, at Cologne, Cassel & Frankfort o/M., *c.* 1783–90. A modernized version of the orig. play by Gisbert von Vincke was prod. at Frankfort, 5. I. 1867.

Thayer, Alexander Wheelock (b. South Natick, Mass., 22. X. 1817; d. Trieste, 15. VII. 1897), Amer. biog. Studied law at Harvard Univ. and in 1849 went to Ger., living at Bonn and Berlin, also to Prague and Vienna, collecting material for a Beethoven biog. After some journalistic activities in N.Y. and Boston, he again went to Eur. in 1854–6 and for a 3rd time in 1858, eventually becoming U.S. consul at Trieste. The 4th vol. of his biog. was left unfinished, but completed by Hermann Deiters in a Ger. ed. of the work, and the whole was afterwards pub. in Eng. by Krehbiel.

Théâtre de la Révolution (Rolland). *See* **Quatorze Juillet.**

Theile, Johann (b. Naumburg, 29. VII. 1646; d. Naumburg, VI. 1724), Ger. comp. Learnt m. as a youth at Magdeburg and Halle, and later studied at Leipzig Univ., where he took part in the students' perfs. as singer and va. da gamba player. He then became a pupil of Schütz at Weissenfels, taught m. at Stettin and Lübeck, and at the latter place (?) studied with Buxtehude or (?) taught him the va. da gamba. In 1673–5 he was chapel master to the Duke of Holstein at Gottorp, but fled to Hamburg during the Dan. invasion. In 1676 he competed unsuccessfully for the post of cantor at St. Thomas's church, Leipzig. In 1678 the opera at Hamburg was opened and he was the 1st comp. to contrib. to its repertory. In 1685 he succeeded Rosenmüller as mus. dir. at Wolfenbüttel and in 1689 he was app. to a similar post at Merseburg. In his last years he lived in retirement at his birthplace.

Works incl. operas *Adam und Eva* & *Orontes*; 23 masses, 8 magnificats, 12 psalms for 4–11 voices; Passion according to St. Matthew, church cantatas, &c.

Theme. A principal melodic feature in a comp., differing from a Subject by greater length and more self-contained completeness, a subject being usually susceptible to development, e.g. in a fugue or so.-form work, whereas a T. may be said more often to undergo restatement or decorative elaboration, espec. in var. form. Sets of vars. are always based on a T.

Theme-Song. A song in a mus. stage work reappearing several times as a kind of motto. It is a trick of sentimental reminiscence often employed in modern mus. comedy, but there is an early instance of it in Bishop's *Clari*, where the T.-S. is 'Home, sweet home.' The prize song in Wagner's ***Mastersingers*** is also, strictly speaking, a T.-S.

Theocritus (3rd cent. B.C.), Gr. poet. *See* **Durey** (*Épigrammes de Théocrite*), **Pastoral** (Bliss).

Theodora, orat. by Handel (lib. by Thomas Morell), prod. London, Covent Garden Theatre, 16. III. 1750.

Theorbo. An obs. inst. of the lute type, actually a kind of bass lute of large size with a double neck on which only the upper stgs. are stretched over a fingerboard, the bass stgs. being at the side of it and not capable of prod. different notes, except by retuning. The inst. came orig. from Padua, but there were other exs., incl. the Eng. one also called Archlute. The It. Chitarrone was a similar inst., but orig. from Rome. The number of stgs. varied from *c.* 11–17.

Theremin. *See also* **Aetherophone.** An electrophonic inst. invented by Lev Theremin (b. 1896) of Leningrad in 1924.

Theresienmesse (Theresa's Mass). The nickname of Haydn's Mass in B♭ maj., comp. in 1799. The origin of the title is not known; the work cannot have been written for Maria Theresa, who d. in 1780.

Thésée (*Theseus*), opera by Lully (lib. by Quinault), prod. at Saint-Germain, 12. I. 1675; 1st Paris perf., IV. 1675.

Thesis. *See* **Metre.**

Thespis, or The Gods Grown Old, operetta by Sullivan (lib. by W. S. Gilbert), prod. London, Gaiety Theatre, 26. XII. 1871. S.'s 1st work comp. in assoc. with Gilbert.

Thétis et Pélée (*Thetis and Peleus*), opera by Colasse (lib. by Bernard de Fontenelle), prod. Paris, Opéra, 11. I. 1689.

Thibaut IV (b. Troyes, 1201; d. Pamplona, 8. VII. 1253), king of Navarre and a trouvère, 63 of whose songs are still extant.

Thibaut, Anton Friedrich Justus (b. Hameln o/Weser, 4. I. 1774; d. Heidelberg, 28. III. 1840), Ger. scholar & mcolst. Studied law at Göttingen and became prof. of jurisprudence at Kiel, Jena and in 1805 at Heidelberg. He founded a soc. for the study and practice of Palestrina and other old It. church m., collected folksongs of all nations and pub. a treatise *Ueber Reinheit der Tonkunst.*

Thillon (*née* **Hunt**), **Sophie Anne** (b. ? Calcutta or London, 1819; d. Torquay, 5. V. 1903), Anglo-Fr. sop. singer. She was taken to Fr. for study at the age of 14 and married one of her masters, the Havre cond. Claude Thomas T. After appearing in the provinces she came out in opera in Paris, 1838, studied with Auber and sang with great success in his and other comps.' operas. In 1844 she made her stage début in London and sang much there during the next 10 years, also at Brussels and in U.S.A.

Thiman, Eric (Harding) (b. Ashford, Kent, 12. IX. 1900), Eng. orgst. & comp. Studied m. privately, obtained the F.R.C.O. in 1921 and the London Mus.D. in 1927. In 1930 he was app. prof. at the R.A.M. He also became orgst. & choirmaster at a congregational church.

Works incl. anthems & other church m.; org. accomps. in varied harmony and free part-writing to hymns; partsongs, &c.

Third. The interval between the 2 notes of which lie 3 degrees of a diatonic scale. Ts. can be maj., min. or diminished, in the last case being equal to maj. 2nds on the pf., but written to look like 3rds, e.g. C♯–E♭. A diminished 3rd is the inversion of an augmented 6th. The 3rd of a diatonic scale is the most characteristic interval determining the difference between maj. and min.

Thirion, Louis (Marie Joseph) (b. Baccarat, Meurthe-et-Moselle, 18. II. 1879), Fr. orgst., pfst. & comp. Pupil of Ropartz at the Nancy Cons., where he became prof. of org. & pf. in 1898.

Works incl. 2 syms.; stg. 4tet, pf. Trio; sos. for v. & pf. and co. & pf.;

So., Impromptu, *Rêves* & other works for pf.; inst. pieces, &c.

Thoma, Therese. *See* **Vogl.**

Thomas, (Charles Louis) Ambroise (b. Metz, 5. VIII. 1811; d. Paris, 12. II. 1896), Fr. comp. Learnt m. from his father as a child and in 1828 entered the Paris Cons., where he gained the Prix de Rome in 1832. He also privately studied pf. with Kalkbrenner and comp. with Lesueur. Soon after his return from Rome he began to make operatic successes in Paris. In 1852 he became prof. at the Cons. and in 1871 dir. in succession to Auber.

Works incl. operas *La Double Échelle, Le Perruquier de la Régence, Le Panier fleuri, Carline, Le Comte de Carmagnola, Le Guerillero, Angélique et Médor, Mina, Le Caïd, Le Songe d'une nuit d'été* (not Shakespeare), *Raymond, La Tonelli, La Cour de Célimène, Psyché, Le Carnaval de Venise, Le Roman d'Elvire, Mignon* (after Goethe's *Wilhelm Meister*), *Gille et Gillotin, Hamlet* (after Shakespeare), *Françoise de Rimini* (after Dante); ballets *La Gipsy, Betty* & *La Tempête*; *Messe solennelle, Messe de Requiem*, motets; cantata *Hermann et Ketty*, cantatas for the unveiling of a Lesueur statue & for the Boïeldieu centenary; Fantasy for pf. & orch.; stg. 4tet, stg. 5tet, pf. Trio; pf. pieces; 6 It. songs; partsongs, &c.

Thomas and Sally, or The Sailor's Return, opera by Arne (lib. by Isaac Bickerstaffe), prod. London, Covent Garden Theatre, 28. XI. 1760.

Thomas, Arthur Goring (b. Ratton Park, Sussex, 20. XI. 1850; d. London, 20. III. 1892), Eng. comp. Educ. for the civil service, but studied m. after he came of age, with Émile Durand in Paris and with Sullivan and Prout at the R.A.M. in London. Later he went to Bruch in Berlin for orchn. He began to work on an opera to a lib. by his brother, *Don Braggadocio*, and although he did not finish it, he persevered and eventually received a commission from the Carl Rosa Opera Co. He became insane in 1891.

Works incl. operas *The Light of the Harem* (after Thomas Moore), *Esmeralda* (after Hugo's *Notre-Dame de Paris*), *Nadeshda* & *The Golden Web*; anthem *Out of the Deep* for sop., chor. & orch.; cantatas *The Sun Worshippers* & *The Swan and the Skylark*; *Suite de Ballet* for orch.; songs, duets, &c.

Thomas, John (b. Bridgend, Glam., 1. III. 1826; d. London, 19. III. 1913), Welsh hpst., cond. & comp. Studied at the R.A.M. in London and later became hp. prof. there, hpst. at the opera in Her Majesty's Theatre and in 1872 hpst. to Queen Victoria. But he took great interest in m. in Wales and in 1861, at the Aberdare Eisteddfod, was nominated chief of the Welsh minstrels.

Works incl. cantatas *Llewelyn* & *The Bride of Neath Valley*; Sym., ovts.; 2 hp. concs.; many hp. studies & pieces, &c.

Thomas, Kurt (b. Tönning, Schleswig-Holstein, 25. V. 1904), Ger. comp. Studied at Barmen, at the Leipzig Cons. and privately with Arnold Mendelssohn; he was also influenced by Karl Straube at Leipzig. In 1925 he became prof. at the Cons. there.

Works incl. Mass in A min.; Psalm cxxxvii for double chor.; pf. Trio in D min.; v. & pf. So. in E min., &c.

Thomas, Theodore (b. Esens, Hanover, 11. X. 1835; d. Chicago, 4. I. 1905), Ger.-Amer. cond. Was taken to U.S.A. in 1845; appeared in N.Y., with an orch. formed by himself, in 1862; organized the Cincinnati Mus. Festival in 1873 and became cond. of the N.Y. Phil. Soc. in 1877 and of the Chicago Sym. Orch. in 1891.

Thomé, Francis (actually Joseph François Luc) (b. Port Louis, Mauritius, 18. X. 1850; d. Paris, 16. XI. 1909), Fr. comp. Studied at the Paris Cons. He afterwards settled down as a private teacher of m.

Works incl. operas & operettas *Martin et Frontin, Barbe-Bleuette, Endymion et Phœbé, Le Caprice de la reine, Le Papillon, Le Trottin, Mademoiselle Pygmalion*; ballets *Djemmah, La Folie parisienne, La Bulle d'amour*; incid. m. to plays, incl. Shakespeare's *Romeo and Juliet*, & mystery *L'Enfant Jésus*; *Hymne à la nuit* for chor.; *Simple Aveu* for pf. with many arrs., &c.

Thompson, Herbert (b. Leeds, 11. VIII. 1856; d. Leeds, 6. V. 1945), Eng. m. & art critic. Educ. at Wiesbaden and St. John's Coll., Cambridge, where he came under the infl. of Stanford. In 1886–1936 he was m. and art critic to the *Yorkshire Post* at Leeds.

Thompson, Oscar (b. Crawfordsville, Ind., 10. X. 1887; d. New York, 3. VII. 1945), Amer. m. critic. In 1937 he succeeded W. J. Henderson as m. critic of the *New York Sun*. He was the author of several books on m. and the ed. of the *International Cyclopedia of M.*

Thompson, Randall (b. New York, 21. IV. 1899), Amer. comp. He studied at Harvard Univ. and among his m. masters was Bloch. He lived in Rome in 1922–5, was asst. prof. of m.

at Wellesley Coll. and was later app. to study mus. conditions at the Amer. colls., becoming prof. of m. at California Univ. in 1937 and dir. of the Curtis Inst. at Philadelphia in 1939.

Works incl. opera *Solomon and Balkis* (after Kipling's *Just So Stories*); incid. m. for Labiche's *The It. Straw Hat*; 2 syms. *Pierrot and Cothurnus* & *The Piper at the Gates of Dawn* for orch.; *Jazz Poem* for pf. & orch.; *Odes of Horace* for unaccomp. chor., *Rosemary* for women's chor., *Americana* for mixed chor. & pf.; 2 stg. 4tets, one on Kenneth Grahame's *The Wind in the Willows*, So. & Suite for pf.; songs, &c.

Thomson, César (b. Liége, 17. III. 1857; d. Lugano, 21. VIII. 1931), Belg. vst. Studied at the Liége Cons., where in 1882 became v. prof., after a career as virtuoso that took him to It., Ger., &c. In 1897 he succeeded Ysaÿe at the Brussels Cons.

Thomson, George (b. Limekilns, Dunfermline, 4. III. 1757; d. Leith, 18. II. 1851), Sco. official & mus. collector. Pub. collections of nat. Sco., Welsh and Ir. airs arr. by Haydn, Beethoven, Kozeluch, Weber, Bishop and others.

Thomson, James (1700–48), Sco. poet. *See* **Alfred** (Arne), **Moissonneurs** (Duni), **Rosina** (Shield), **Seasons** (Haydn).

Thomson, Virgil (b. Kansas City, 25. XI. 1896), Amer. comp. Studied at Harvard Univ. and among his m. masters were Scalero and Nadia Boulanger. He was asst. m. instructor at Harvard in 1920–5 and cond. the Glee Club there, then lived in Paris until 1932, when he became orgst. of King's Chapel at Boston and critic to several papers and periodicals.

Works incl. opera *Four Saints in Three Acts* (lib. by Gertrude Stein); ballet *The Filling-Station*; incid. m. to Shakespeare's *Hamlet* & other plays; film m.; 2 syms., suite *The Plough that Broke the Plains*, *2 Sentimental Tangoes*, *Portraits*, Sym. on a Hymn-Tune; *So. da Chiesa* for orch.; *Oraison funèbre* (Bossuet) for ten. & orch.; 2 *Missae breves*, 3 Psalms for women's voices, *Capital, Capitals* (Gertrude Stein) for men's chor. & pf.; 2 stg. 4tets, *5 Portraits* for 4 cls.; *Stabat Mater* for sop. & stg. 4tet, *5 Phrases from the Song of Solomon* for sop. & percussion; *The 40 Portraits* for v. & pf., So. for v. & pf.; *Gospel Hymns*, variations & fugues for org.; 3 pf. sos., 5 Inventions for pf.; *Synthetic Waltzes* for 2 pfs.; *Air de Phèdre* (Racine) & other Fr. songs, &c.

Thomyris, Queen of Scythia, pasticcio arranged by Pepusch from m. by A. Scarlatti, G. Bononcini, Steffani, Gasparini and Albinoni (lib. by Peter Anthony Motteux), prod. London, Drury Lane Theatre, 1. IV. 1707.

Thorne, John (b. ?; d. York, 7. XII. 1573), Eng. comp. Prob. orgst. at York Minster, 1550–73. Comp. Lat. motets, &c.

Thorough-Bass (actually the old spelling of Through-B.). A system of shorthand notation that came into use during the early part of the 17th cent. and persisted until *c.* the middle of the 18th. Comps., instead of writing out the full harmony they required, often contented themselves with setting out only the chief melodic parts over a single bass-line, under which they wrote figures indicating what the harmony above that bass was to be, but not how it was to be spaced or distributed, much less giving any indication as to how it might be broken up into figuration or made more interesting by such devices as suspensions or passing-notes, all of which was left to the ingenuity of the player at the hpchd. or org., who was expected to improvise an interesting part to amplify the m. with a background of texture and harmony. T.-Bs. were not always completely figured, and sometimes not at all, which made the *continuo* player's task more difficult.

Thousand and One Nights. *See* **Arabian Nights.**

Thrane, Valdemar (b. Christiania, 8. X. 1790; d. Christiania, 30. XII. 1828), Norw. comp. Learnt m. at home, his parents being keen amateurs at whose house many musns. met. Although intended for commerce, T. continually exercised himself in m. and wrote the 1st Norw. opera, which however was not staged until 1850. He also studied Norw. folk m.

Works incl. opera *Fjeldeventyret* (*A Mountain Adventure*); ovts. for orch.; chor. works, &c.

Three Choirs Festival. An annual mus. festival held at the 3 cath. towns of Gloucester, Worcester and Hereford, with the 3 choirs, formed on a nucleus of the cath. choirs, gathering together in one of the towns alternately. The T.C.F. was founded in 1724, but meetings date back to *c.* 1716. The perfs. begin with a cath. service on the 1st Sunday of IX and continue from Tues. to Sat. of the same week, being devoted mainly to orats. & other (not always sacred) chor. works, but also incl. orch. & other m., all held in the cath. except 1 orch. and 1 chamber concert. New works from eminent comps. of the day, mainly but not exclus. Brit., have always been a feature of the T.C.F. The proceeds go to cath. charities.

Three-Cornered Hat. *See* **Sombrero de tres picos**; *also* **Corregidor.**

Three Musketeers, The (I. de Lara). *See* **Trois Mousquetaires.**

Thuille, Ludwig (b. Bozen, 30. XI. 1861; d. Munich, 5. II. 1907), Aus. comp. Learnt m. from his father, an amateur, on whose death he was sent as a choir-boy to the monastery of Kremsmünster. At the age of 15 he began to study with Joseph Pembaur of Innsbruck, and in 1879 he went to the M. School at Munich, where Rheinberger was among his masters. In 1883 he became prof. at the Munich school, and there was influenced by R. Strauss and Alexander Ritter, who wrote the lib. for his 1st opera, the 2 later ones being by Otto Julius Bierbaum. Apart from teaching and comp., he also cond. the male-voice choir Liederhort.

Works incl. operas *Theuerdank, Lobetanz* and *Gugeline*; *Romantic Ovt.* (orig. for *Theuerdank*) for orch.; *Weihnacht im Walde* for male chor., *Traum Sommernacht* & *Rosenlied* for female chor.; pf. 5tet, 6tet for wind & pf.; co. & pf. So.; pf. pieces; songs, &c.

Thump (old Eng.) = plucking of stgs. (*pizzicato*); also a piece employing *pizz.*

Thus spake Zarathustra (R. Strauss). *See* **Also sprach Zarathustra.**

Thyl Uylenspiegel. *See* **Till Eulenspiegel.**

Tichatschek (Tichaček), Joseph (Aloys) (b. Ober-Weckelsdorf, Boh., 11. VII. 1807; d. Blasewitz nr. Dresden, 18. I. 1886), Cz. ten. singer. Studied medicine at first, but learnt singing and in 1830 joined the chor. at the Kärntnertor Theatre in Vienna, then sang small parts, and in 1837 made his 1st important stage appearance, at Dresden. He remained there until he retired in 1870 and was Wagner's 1st Rienzi and Tannhäuser.

Tie. An arching stroke, or Slur, used to connect 2 notes of the same pitch or a group of such notes in chords, indicating that the 2nd note of the pair is not to be struck again.

Tieck, (Johann) Ludwig (1773–1853), Ger. poet, novelist, critic & trans. *See* **Magelone Romances** (Brahms), **Genoveva** (Schumann), **Rudorff** (*Aufzug der Romanze*), **Scholz** (*Golo*), Taubert (*Blaubart*).

Tied Notes. *See* **Tie.**

Tiefland (*The Lowland*), **opera** by d'Albert (lib. by Rudolf Lothar based on a Catalan play, *Terra baixa*, by Angel Guimerá), prod. Prague, Ger. Theatre, 15. XI. 1903.

Tiento (Spa.). A 16th-cent. type of org. piece similar to the Ricercare.

Tierce. The interval of the 3rd, and more specifically the 4th Harmonic, which is the maj. 3rd above the fundamental note 2 octaves higher; also an org. stop sounding that harmonic as well as the fundamental note.

Tierce de Picardie (Fr. = Picardy 3rd). The maj. 3rd introd. into the final chord of a comp. in a min. key. The maj. 3rd corresponds to a natural harmonic, the Tierce (*see above*), but the min. 3rd does not: it was therefore for a long time considered, if not an actual dissonance, at any rate not a finally satisfactory ingredient in a concluding chord, for which reason the T. d. P. was often substituted. The orig. of the name is not known.

Tiersot, (Jean Baptiste Élisée) Julien (b. Bourg-en-Bresse, 5. VII. 1857; d. Paris, 10. VIII. 1936), Fr. mcolst. & comp. Studied at the Paris Cons., Massenet and Franck being among his masters. He became asst. librarian there in 1883 and librarian in 1910. He wrote many books and articles on Fr. and other folksongs, Rouget de Lisle, Berlioz, Gluck, J. J. Rousseau, Smetana, m. in Molière's works, Bach, &c., and collected folksongs, some with d'Indy. He was prof. at the École des Hautes Études Sociales and president of the Société Française de Musicologie.

Works incl. incid. m. to Corneille's *Andromède*; *Hellas* (Shelley) & *Chansons populaires françaises* for chor. & orch.; Rhapsody on Bresse folksongs, symph. legend *Sire Halewyn* & *Danses populaires françaises* for orch., &c.

Tiessen, Heinz (b. Königsberg, 10. IV. 1887), Ger. cond. & comp. Studied in Berlin, was critic to the *Allgemeine Musikzeitung* in 1912–7, in 1918 became cond. of the Berlin Volksbühne and in 1920 to the Univ. concerts. He also did chor. cond. and in 1925 became prof. at the Hochschule für Musik.

Works incl. ballet *Salammbo* (after Flaubert); incid. m. to Sophocles' *Antigone*, Shakespeare's *Tempest*, *Hamlet* & *Cymbeline*, Grabbe's *Don Juan und Faust*, Immermann's *Merlin*, Tagore's *Post Office*, Strindberg's *Advent* & other plays; 3 *Liebeslieder* for chor.; Sym. in F min.; *Totentanz* for v. & orch.; stg. 5tet, *Spring M.* for fl., cl., hn. & stg. 4tet, *Kleine Schularbeit* for wind insts.; Little Suite for 2 vs., Duo for v. & pf.;

Nature Trilogy, Kleine Schularbeit & other pieces for pf.; songs, &c.

Tietjens, Therese (Cathline Johanna Alexandra) (b. Hamburg, 17. VII. 1831; d. London, 3. X. 1877), Hung. sop. singer of Ger. birth and Belg. descent. Made her 1st appearance at Hamburg in 1849; paid her 1st visit to Eng. in 1858, remaining there for good except for her appearances abroad.

Tigrane, Il (*Tigranes*), opera by Gluck (lib. by Francesco Silvani, altered by Goldoni), prod. Crema, 9. IX. 1743.

Opera by Hasse (lib. by Francesco Silvani), prod. Naples, Teatro San Bartolommeo, 4. XI. 1723.

Opera by A. Scarlatti (lib. by Domenico Lalli), prod. Naples, Teatro San Bartolommeo, 16. II. 1715.

Till Eulenspiegel (*Tyl Owlglass*). A 15th-cent. Low Ger. folk-tale of unknown authorship. For operas on the subject *see* **Blockx, Braunfels, Kistler, Lothar** & **Rezniček**; for a ballet *see* **Steinberg**; for a symph. poem (R. Strauss) *see* below, for a cantata *see* **Vogel (V.)**.

Till Eulenspiegels lustige Streiche (*Tyl Owlglass's Merry Pranks*), symph. poem by R. Strauss, Op. 28, based on the old Low Ger. folk-tale. 1st perf. Cologne, 5. XI. 1895.

Tillyard, Henry (Julius Wetenhall) (b. Cambridge, 18. XI. 1881), Eng. mus. scholar. Studied at Cambridge Univ. in 1900–4 and at the Eng. schools in Athens and Rome in 1904–7. He specialized in the study of Byzantine m., on which he wrote a good deal, and was prof. successively at Johannesburg, Birmingham and Cardiff.

Timbal(l)es (Fr.) = Kettle-drums.

Timbre (Fr. lit. Chime-bell). In m. the word is used, in Eng. as well as Fr., for Tone-colour, which however has become equally current and may quite reasonably be used.

Timbrel. The proper Eng. word for the inst. more generally known as the Tambourine, a small, shallow drum with a single skin stretched over the edge of one side of its rim, into which jingles are loosely set to add their noise to that of the drum-head when it is struck by the hand or to be made to resound separately by shaking the inst.

Time. The physical conditions in which all the arts have their existence, so far as they become communicable to the human senses, are either space (painting, sculpture, &c.) or T., or both (drama and in a sense all literature). M. exists in T., and has therefore to be written down in symbols repres. certain divisions of T. in which it is to be made audible. T. must not be confused with Tempo or pace, which determines the speed at which a comp. should go; the T. of a comp. is its division into units of notes or rests, and their subdivisions. A piece in 3–4 T., for ex., has 3 crotchets to a Bar and normally a metrical stress on the 1st Beat after the bar-line; and it makes no difference to this fundamental T. whether 2 crotchets are replaced by a Minim, or whether one is displaced by a rest or divided into smaller fractions in any pattern of notes. The T. of a piece or mvt. remains fixed until the comp. changes the Time Signature.

Time Signature. The sign at the beginning of a comp. indicating the time-divisions governing the rhythm of the piece. The T. S. is shown in the shape of a fraction, but does not represent a mathematical fraction: it is a symbol showing in the upper figure the unit of the note-values into which each bar is divided and in the lower the number of such note-values contained in a bar: e.g. $\frac{3}{4}$ means that there are 3 crotchets to the bar and that the time is beaten in 3's; $\frac{6}{8}$ is 6 quavers to the bar; $\frac{2}{2}$ is 2 minims to the bar, &c. There are also 2 conventional abbrevs., which are signs surviving from the old notation, where the T. Ss. were full circles for Perfect Time (*tempus perfectum*) and broken circles resembling letter C for Imperfect Time (*tempus imperfectum*). The broken circle has survived as indicating $\frac{4}{4}$ time and as ₵ indicating *alla breve* time, i.e. $\frac{4}{4}$ taken at double speed and beaten in 2's.

Timmermans, Armand (b. Antwerp, 20. I. 1860; d. Antwerp, 12. VII. 1939), Belg. comp. Studied under P. Benoît and later devoted himself to comp. and criticism.

Works incl. operas *Marguerite, Misères de la guerre* & *Vae victis*; cantatas *21 Juillet* & *Van Dyck*; inst. works; songs, &c.

Timpan (or Timpe, from Lat. *tympanum*). A kind of Psaltery, now obs., but used in the Brit. isles in medieval times. It had wire stgs. stretched on a frame and they were plucked by the fingers or a plectrum, later struck with a rod.

Timpani (It., not *tympani*) = Kettle-drums.

Timpe. *See* **Timpan.**

Tin Whistle. A small and rudimentary pipe of the Fife or Recorder type, also called 'penny whistle,' played vertically and having a small range of high notes controlled by 6 finger-holes.

Tinctor, John, or
Tinctoris, Joannes de (b. Poperinghe, *c.* 1446; d. Nivelles, before 12. X. 1511), Flem. priest & mus. scholar. Studied both law and theol., was ordained priest and became a canon of Poperinghe. He went to It. and in 1476 was in the service of the king of Naples, Ferdinand of Aragon. He founded a school of m. and between 1484–1500 was in the Papal Chapel in Rome. He wrote a number of important theoret. works and comp. masses.

Tinel, Edgar (b. Sinay, 27. III. 1854; d. Brussels, 28. X. 1912), Belg. comp. Studied with Gevaert and others at the Brussels Cons. and gained the Belg. Prix de Rome in 1877. In 1881 he became dir. of the institute of church m. at Malines in succession to Lemmens, in 1889 mus. inspector of the state schools and in 1896 prof. of ctpt. at the Brussels Cons. in succession to H. Kufferath.

Works incl. sacred m.-dramas *Godoleva* & *Katharina*; incid. m. to Corneille's *Polyeucte*; orat. *Franciscus*; 2 Te Deums, Mass for the Holy Virgin of Lourdes, Alleluia for chor. & org.; sacred songs for mixed chor.; cantatas *Klokke Roeland*, *Kollebloemen* & *De drie Ridders*; 4 Nocturnes for voices & pf., &c.

Tintore, Giovanni del. *See* **Tinctoris.**

Tiorba (It.) = Theorbo.

Tippett, Michael (Kemp) (b. London, 2. I. 1905), Eng. comp. Studied with C. Wood and R. O. Morris at the R.C.M. in London. He became cond. of educational organizations under the London County Council and mus. dir. at Morley Coll., a post formerly held by Holst.

Works incl. orat. *A Child of our Time* for solo voices, chor. & orch., *A Song of Liberty* (from Blake's *Marriage of Heaven and Hell*) for chor. & orch.; anthem *Plebs angelica* for double chor.; Sym. in B♭ maj., *Sym. 1945*, Conc. for double stg. orch.; Fantasy on a Theme by Handel for pf. & orch.; 2 stg. 4tets; pf. So.; *Boyhood's End* cantata for ten. & pf. (from W. H. Hudson's *Far Away and Long Ago*); partsongs *The Source* & *The Windhover* (Hopkins), &c.

Tirade (Fr. = a sliding or dragging). An ornamental scale passage between 2 notes of a melody or 2 chords.

Tirana. A Spa. dance of Andalusia in 6–8 time, usually danced to guitar m. and accomp. by words in 4-lined *coplas*.

Tirarsi (It. = to draw itself, to pull itself). A *tromba da tirarsi* is a tpt. with a slide like that of the tromb.

Tirasse (Fr.) = (Org.) Coupler.

Tirata (It.) = Fr. *Tirade*.

Tiré (Fr. = drawn). The downstroke of the bow in the playing of stg. insts., the opposite of *poussé* (= pushed).

Tirso de Molina (Gabriel Tellez) (1571–1648), Spa. dramatist. *See* **Assafiev** (*Don Juan*), **Braunfels** (*Don Gil*), **Don Giovanni Tenorio** (Gazzaniga), Rios (*Vergonzoso en palacio*).

Titelouze, Jean (b. Saint-Omer, 1563; d. Rouen, 25. X. 1633), Fr. priest, orgst. & comp. He became a canon at Rouen cath. in the 1580s, often visited Paris to inaugurate new orgs., incl. that at Notre-Dame in 1610.

Works incl. magnificats & other church m.; hymns arr. for org., fugues and ricercari on plainsong tunes for org., &c.

Titiens, Therese. *See* **Tietjens.**

Tito Vespasiano, ovvero La clemenza di Tito (*Titus Vespasian, or The Clemency of Titus*), opera by Caldara (lib. by Metastasio, partly based on Corneille's *Cinna*), comp. 1734.

Opera by Hasse (lib. do.), prod. Pesaro, Teatro pubblico, 24. IX. 1735.

Titov. Rus. family of amateur musns.:

1. Alexey Nikolaievitch T. (b. St. Petersburg, 24. VI. 1769; d. St. Petersburg, 20. XI. 1827), managed the Imp. Opera for some time before the death of Catherine the Great in 1796 and became a major-general in the cavalry guards. Comp. *c.* 20 operas, vaudevilles, melodramas and other stage works. He is sometimes confused with his brother,

2. Sergey Nikolaievitch T. (b. ?, 1770; d. ?), who wrote incid. m. for 2 or 3 plays.

3. Nikolai Alexeievitch T. (b. St. Petersburg, 10. V. 1800; d. ?, 22. XII. 1875), son of 1. Like his father, he was in the cavalry guard and rose to the rank of lieut.-gen. He came under the infl. of Glinka and Dargomizhsky. Comp. popular marches, pf. m. and *c.* 60 songs.

Tiutchev, Feodor Ivanovitch (1803–73), Rus. poet. *See* **Medtner** (songs), **Shaporin** (songs), **Taneiev (S.)** (songs).

Toccata (from It. *toccare* = lit. to touch, fig. to play). Orig., in the 17th cent., simply 'a thing to play,' as distinct from *cantata*, 'a thing to sing.' But it soon acquired a sense of touching an inst. for the purpose of trying or testing it, which meant that it usually contained scales, shakes and other brilliant figuration, often interspersed with slow chordal passages. Modern Ts. usually lay stress on brilliance and rapid execution alone, and are often more or less uniform in figuration throughout: there is in fact little or nothing to distinguish them from concert Studies.

Tocchi, Gianluca (b. Perugia, 10. I. 1901), It. comp. Studied with Respighi in Rome, where in 1930 he gained a comp. prize.

Works incl. symph. poem *Il destino* (after Maeterlinck), *Rapsodia romantica*, *Quadro sonoro*, impressions *Record*, suite *Film* for orch.; Conc. for jazz orch.; *Tre canzoni alla maniera popolare italiana* for voice & pf., &c.

Toch, Ernst (b. Vienna, 7. XII. 1887), Aus. pfst. & comp. Studied medicine and philos. at first and was self-taught in m., but in 1909 was awarded the Frankfort o/M. Mozart prize and studied there under Willy Rehberg, being app. pf. prof. at the Mannheim Hochschule für Musik in 1913. He served in the 1914–8 war, settled in Berlin in 1929, but emigrated in 1932, visiting the U.S.A., then London for a time, to settle permanently in U.S.A. in 1934, 1st teaching in N.Y. for 2 years and then moving to Hollywood as film comp. & teacher.

Works incl. operas *Wegwende*, *Die Prinzessin auf der Erbse*, *Egon und Emilie*, *Der Fächer*; incid. m. for Euripides' *Bacchantes*, Shakespeare's *As You Like It*, Zweig's *Die Heilige aus U.S.A.* & other plays; m. for radio play *The Garden of Jade* & others; film m. for *Catherine the Great*, *The Private Life of Don Juan*, &c.; Passover Service; cantata *Das Wasser*; *Der Tierkreis* for unaccomp. chor.; *Bunte Suite*, *Kleine Theater Suite*, *Big Ben*, *Pinocchio* ovt. for orch.; *Spiel* for wind band; Conc. & Sym. for pf. & orch.; 6 stg. 4tets, pf. 5tet, stg. Trio, Divertimento for v. & va.; 2 v. & pf. sos.; So., 50 studies & c. 12 op. nos. of pf. pieces, &c.

Tod und Verklärung (*Death and Transfiguration*), symph. poem by R. Strauss, Op. 24, comp. 1888–9, 1st perf. Eisenach, 21. VI. 1890.

Todi, Jacopone da (?–1306), It. poet, prob. author of the Lat. verses of the *Stabat Mater*. *See* **Nielsen (R.)** (*Laude*).

Todi (*née* **d'Aguiar**), **Luiza Rosa** (b. Setubal, 9. I. 1753; d. Lisbon, 1. X. 1833), Port. m.-sop. singer. Made her 1st appearance as an actress at Lisbon at the age of 15, studied m. with David Perez, and 1st came out as an opera singer in London in 1777. She married Francesco Saverio T., appeared in Paris and at Versailles in 1778, was engaged by the Berlin Court Opera in 1782, but the next year went to Paris again and was engaged by the Rus. court, where she so far influenced Catherine the Great as to secure Sarti's dismissal. In 1786 she returned to Berlin until 1789, again visiting Rus. and Paris, also singing in It. and at Lisbon, where she retired.

Toeschi, Carlo Giuseppe (b. Romagna, c. 1724; d. Munich, 12. IV. 1788), It. comp. & vst. Attached to the Mannheim school of early symsts., and its only It. member. He became vst. in the court orch. there in 1752 and leader in 1759; later he followed the court to Munich.

Works incl. ballet m. for var. operas by other comps.; syms.; chamber m., &c.

Tofts (*née* **?**), **Catherine** (b. ?; d. Venice, 1756), Eng. sop. singer. She 1st (?) appeared at concerts in Lincoln's Inn Fields Theatre, London, in 1703, and on the stage at Drury Lane Theatre in 1704, when a disturbance arose against her rival, Margherita de l'Épine, which she was accused of having instigated. When It. opera became estab. in London, she became one of its finest exponents, but she lost her reason in 1709. Recovering partly, she married Joseph Smith, who became Eng. consul at Venice, but she had to be periodically confined to a part of the house.

Toinon et Toinette, opera by Gossec (lib. by Jean Auguste Julien Des Boulmiers), prod. Paris, Comédie-Italienne, 20. VI. 1767.

Tolomeo, Rè di Egitto (*Ptolemy, King of Egypt*), opera by Handel (lib. by Nicola Francesco Haym), prod. London, King's Theatre, Haymarket, 30. IV. 1728.

Tolstoy, Alexey Constantinovitch, Count (1817–75), Rus. poet & dramatist. *See* **Ilyinsky** (*Tsar Feodor*), **Kalinnikov** (*Tsar Boris*), **Lourié** (*Alphabet*), **Nápravnik** (*Don Juan*), **Shaporin** (*Decembrists*), **Shtcherbatchev (N. V.)** (songs), **Sokolov** (*Don Juan*).

Tolstoy, Lev Nikolaievitch, Count (1828–1910), Rus. novelist & social reformer, distant relative of prec. *See* **Anna Karenina** (Hubay), **Janáček** (*Kreutzer Sonata*), **'Kreutzer' Sonata** (Beethoven), **Novaček** (songs), **Parker (C.)** (*War and Peace*), **Risurrezione** (Alfano), **Vassilenko** (*3 Bloody Battles*), **War and Peace** (Prokofiev).

Tom Jones, opera by Philidor (lib. by Antoine Alexandre Henri Poinsinet, based on Fielding's novel), prod. Paris, Comédie-Italienne, 27. II. 1765.

Operetta by Ed. German (lib. by Alexander M. Thompson & Robert Courtneidge, lyrics by Charles H. Taylor, based on Fielding's novel), prod. Manchester, 30. III, and London, Apollo Theatre, 17. IV. 1907.

Tomašek, Jan Vaclav (b. Skuč, 17. IV. 1774; d. Prague, 3. IV. 1850), Boh. orgst., pfst. & comp. His father having been reduced to poverty, he was educ. at the expense of 2 elder brothers, learning v. and singing with one Wolf at Chrudin, practising a spinet sent him by his priest brother and then becoming a choir-boy at the monastery of Jihlava, which he left in 1790 to study law and philos. in Prague. But he studied the great theoret. treatises assiduously, as well as any m. he could lay hands on, and estab. a reputation as teacher and comp. before the end of the cent. Count Bucquoi von Longueval offered him a well-paid post in his household, to which he remained attached even after his marriage to Wilhelmine Ebert in 1823, though he kept his own house, which he kept open for mus. visitors, esp. from Eng. He often visited Vienna and met Beethoven in 1814, and he played his settings of Goethe's poems to the poet at Eger.

Works incl. opera *Seraphine* & 2 not prod.; 3 masses, 2 Requiems & other church m.; voc. scenes from Goethe's *Faust* & Schiller's *Wallenstein*, *Maria Stuart* & *Die Braut von Messina*; Sym.; pf. Conc.; stg. 4tets, pf. Trio; 5 pf. sos., *Elegie auf eine Rose* (after Hölty), 7 sets of *Eclogues* & 2 of *Dithyrambs* & many other works for pf.; numerous songs to words by Goethe, Schiller & others, &c.

Tomasi, Henri (b. Marseilles, 17. VIII. 1901), Fr. cond. & comp. Studied at the Paris Cons. and in 1927 gained the Prix de Rome. On his return from Rome in 1930 became cond. of the nat. wireless station.

Works incl. ballets *La Grisi*, *La Rosière du village* & *Les Santons*; *Scènes municipales*, *Chants laotiens*, *Petite Suite médiévale*, *Deux Danses cambodgiennes*, *Danses brésiliennes* for orch.; Capriccio for v. & orch.; *Ajax* & *Chants de Cyrnos* for chor. & orch., &c.

Tomasini. It.-Aus. family of musns.:

1. Luigi T. (b. Pesaro, 1741; d. Esterház, 25. IV. 1808), vst. & comp. Member of the orch. at Eisenstadt, from 1757, and later at Esterház, where he became leader. Wrote v. concs., stg. 4tets, divertimenti for barytone, v. & co., &c.

2. Anton(io) T. (b. Eisenstadt, 1775; d. Eisenstadt, 12. VI. 1824), violist, son of prec. He played in Esterházy's orch. as an amateur from 1791 and became a regular member in 1796.

3. Luigi T. (b. Esterház, 1779), vst., brother of prec. He became a member of the Esterházy orch. in 1796, was several times dismissed for insubordination, once for marrying the singer Sophie Groll without the prince's consent, but taken on again at Haydn's request. He and his wife appeared in Berlin in 1812 and in Vienna in 1814.

Tombeau (Fr. = tomb[stone]). A commemorative comp., esp. in 17th-cent. Fr. m.

Tombeau de Couperin, Le (*C.'s Tomb*), suite for pf. by Ravel in the form of a suite such as C. might have written, but resembling him in spirit rather than in style, R.'s idiom being as modern as that of any of his works. It was comp. in 1914–7 and consists of 6 mvts.: *Prélude*, *Fugue*, *Forlane*, *Menuet*, *Rigaudon* & *Toccata*. The comp. orch. it in 1919, without the fugue and toccata; 1st perf. in that version, Paris, 28. II. 1920.

Tombelle, Antoine de la. *See* **La Tombelle.**

Tomkins. Eng. family of musns.:

1. Thomas T. (b. Lostwithiel, Cornwall, *c.* 1545; d. Gloucester, *c.* 1627), orgst. He became orgst. and choirmaster at St. David's cath., later lived at Gloucester in var. church posts and in 1625 became precentor at the cath. He married 1st Margaret Poher (or Pore), mother of 2 & 3, and later Ann Hargest, mother of 4–6.

2. Thomas T. (b. St. David's, *c.* 1570; d. at sea, 1591), singer, son of prec. He became a lay-clerk, but was expelled for misdemeanour and went to sea, losing his life in Grenville's action in the *Revenge*.

3. Thomas T. (b. St. David's, 1572; d. Martin Hussingtree nr. Worcester, VI. 1656), orgst. & comp., brother of prec. Pupil of Byrd, app. orgst. of Worcester cath. *c.* 1596. He married a widow, Alice Pattrick (*née* Hassard) and in 1607 took the B.Mus. at Oxford. Although remaining at Worcester until the 2nd siege of 1646, he became one of the orgsts. in the Chapel Royal in 1621 and in 1625 wrote m. for Charles I's coronation. His last 10 years were spent at Martin Hussingtree, where the manor house was the property of the wife of his son Nathaniel (1599–1681).

Works incl. 7 services, *c.* 100 anthems; madrigals & balletts for 3–6 voices; m. for viols; virginal pieces, &c.

4. John T. (b. ?, *c.* 1586; d. London, 27. IX. 1638), orgst. & comp., half-brother of prec. Educ. at King's Coll., Cambridge, where he became orgst. in 1606. In 1619 he went to London as orgst. of St. Paul's cath., and in 1625 he became a Gentleman Extraordinary of the Chapel Royal,

with a reversion of the next vacant orgst.'s post.

Works incl. anthems; vars. on 'John come kiss me now' for virginal, &c.

5. Giles T. (b. ?; d. Salisbury, 1668), orgst. and virginalist, brother of prec. In 1624 he succeeded Matthew Barton in his brother's former post as orgst. of King's Chapel, Cambridge, but in 1629 went to Salisbury cath. as orgst. and choirmaster, and in 1630, though remaining at Salisbury, he succeeded Dering as Musician for the Virginals to Charles I.

6. Robert T. (b. ?; d. ?), comp., brother of prec. He became a musn. to Charles I in 1633 and remained in the royal household until 1641 or later. Comp. anthems, &c.

Tommasini, Vincenzo (b. Rome, 17. IX. 1880), It. comp. Studied at the Liceo di Santa Cecilia in Rome and became an associate of the Accademia di Santa Cecilia. He travelled much before 1910 and then settled down to comp.

Works incl. operas *Medea* & *Uguale Fortuna*; ballet *The Good-humoured Ladies* (on m. by D. Scarlatti); chor. works on Dante, Petrarch & others; ovt. to Calderón's *Life is a Dream*, *Poema erotico*, prelude to Baudelaire's *Hymne à la beauté*, Suite, *Chiari di luna*, *Il beato regno*, *Paesaggi toscani* for orch.; 2 stg. 4tets; v. & pf. So., &c.

Ton (Ger. lit. tone, sound). In its obs. sense the word was used by the Ger. Minnesinger for the words and melody of their songs, and by the Meistersinger for the melody alone. The latter used all kinds of adjectives, sometimes of extreme oddity, to differentiate the numerous tunes. (Specimens of such names appear in Wagner's *Meistersinger*, where a T. is also called a *Weis* (= *Weise* = tune).)

Tonada (Spa.). A type of Castilian ballad at least as old as the 16th cent.

Tonadilla (Spa., der. from above). A stage interlude for a few singers introd. in the 18th cent. and 1st cultivated by Misón and others.

Tonal Fugue. *See* **Fugue.**

Tonal Sequence. *See* **Sequence.**

Tonality. Synon. with Key, but also meaning, more specif., the feeling of a definite key suggested by a comp. or passage. In modern mus. terminology 2 antithetical derivatives of the word have appeared. *See* **Atonality** & **Polytonality.**

Tonart (Ger. = tone species). Key, tonality or mode.

Tondichtung (Ger.) = Tone - poem, symph. poem.

Tone. In Eng. the term is used for pure mus. notes not charged with harmonics, each harmonic being itself a T.; also for the quality of a mus. sound, esp. with ref. to perf. The word T. does not imply pitch; but in Amer. it is often used confusingly as synon. with 'note,' doubtless under the infl. of the Ger. *Ton*, and it is said in U.S.A. that 'note' should be reserved for the written symbol. But a 'word' is a word, whether it is written or spoken, and there is no reason why a difference should be made between a note seen and a note heard.

Tone-Colour. T.-C., or timbre, is a convenient term for the sound of an inst. or voice as regards the peculiar quality prod. by it; also for combs. of such sounds. It has nothing to do with pitch or duration. High and low or long and short notes do not differ in T.-C. in any one medium; but the same note has a different T.-C. according to the medium that prod. it.

Tone-Poem. *See* **Symphonic Poem.**

Tone-Quality. The word is sometimes used with the same meaning as that of Tone-Colour, but strictly it indicates not so much the nature of a sound as the degree of satisfaction it offers to the ear.

Tone-Row. A neologism introd. from the Ger. *Tonreihe*, to designate the 'rows' of 12 notes on which comps. in Twelve-note m. are based.

Tonelli, Antonio (b. Carpi, 19. VIII. 1686; d. Carpi, 25. XII. 1765), It. cst. & comp. Learnt m. from his parents, who were both good amateurs, then studied with the choirmaster of Carpi cath. and at Bologna and Parma, where the duke became his patron. He spent 3 years at the Dan. court, returned to his home town and became choirmaster at the cath. in 1730, but resigned in the 1740s and spent some of his time in other towns and on tour. At the age of 76 he fell in love with his pupil, Rosa Parteggotti, whom he had taught from the age of 6 and who was then 15 and determined to become a nun.

Works incl. operas *L'enigma disciolto* & *Lucio Vero*; intermezzi *Canoppo e Lisetta*; orat. *Il trionfo dell' umiltà di S. Filippo Neri* & others; church m.; cantatas; a *Canzoniere* against nuns, &c.

Tongattung (Ger. = tone species, t. genus) or

Tongeschlecht (Ger. = tone gender). The species of tonality, maj. or min., or else modal, in which a comp. is written.

Tonguing. The act of using the tongue in the playing of wind insts.

Tonic. The Keynote: the note on which the scale begins and ends which determines the key of a piece of m., either in maj. or min. or in one of the modes (in the latter case, however, it is not called 'keynote'). F, for ex., is the tonic of a piece in the Lydian mode or in F maj. or min. A Lydian piece, which is normally unharmonized, will end on the note F, which is therefore also called the Final; one in F maj. or min. will usually end on the maj. or min. common chord of its tonic, F. The names of the degrees of the whole modern scale are T., Supertonic, Mediant, Subdominant, Dominant, Submediant and Leading-note.

Tonic Sol-fa. A system of mus. notation without staves and notes, invented by John Spencer Curwen in the middle of the 19th cent. on a basis of the principles of Solmization and Solfeggio, and now widely used in Brit. and the dominions by chor. singers, for whom it simplifies the sight-reading of m., though greatly limiting the scope of their mus. cultivation because only single parts (not harmony) can be conveniently written in it. A pf. piece or a full score in T. S.-f. would be more difficult to read than the old org. or lute tablatures, and far more so than modern staff notation, even if they were possible to write. The T. S.-f. notation is based on the old syllabic system of Do (Ut), Re, Mi, &c. and takes the following form: d, r, m, f, s, l, t, the names of the notes being Doh, Ray, Me, Fah, Soh, Lah, Te. The substitution of 'Te' for the old 'Si' was made to avoid the duplication of the letter 's' in the abbrs. The range of voices being limited, upper and lower 8ves can be sufficiently indicated by a simple stroke placed behind the letters in a higher or lower position, thus: $d^{|}$ and $d_{|}$. Accidentals are indicated by the addition of a letter 'a' (da, ra, &c.) for flats and 'e' (de, re, &c.) for sharps. But accidentals appear comparatively rarely now that the system of the 'movable Doh' has been adopted. This is a system of transposition according to which everything is, except for some very short incidental modulations, sung from a notation that looks as though the m. were always in C maj. or A min. But the actual key is indicated at the beginning of a piece, so that singers know at once, for ex., if the comp. is in A maj., that their d is to be read as A, their r as B, &c. If the piece modulates to another key, a change is indicated, so that temporarily d may become any other note of the scale, &c.; but in maj. keys it will always remain the tonic, in whatever key the m. moves, s always the dominant, f always the subdominant, &c., while in min. keys l will be the tonic, m the dominant, r the subdominant, &c. (A special syllable, 'ba,' is used for the sharp 6th in the melodic min. scale.) The time divisions are indicated by short bar-lines, and there are subdivisions between these. The way in which the notes fill these spaces determines their time-values, though there are special signs for dotted notes, triplets, &c. A blank space means a rest, dashes after a note mean that it is to be held beyond the space it occupies over one or more of the following time-divisions. The merits of T. S.-f. have always been subject to controversy, no doubt because there is much to be said on either side. Its great defect is that for any general study of m. it is obviously useless, and that it is apt to keep chor. singers from expanding their mus. experience. Its advantages to inst. players, even where it might be applicable, as in the case of non-harmonic insts., are very slight, because it is not after all so much easier to learn than staff notation, nor so flexible in picturing the comp.'s intentions; but for choralists it has not only the merit of simplicity, but the greater one of teaching them a sense of Relative Pitch.

Tonkunst (Ger.) = the art of m.

Tonleiter (Ger. lit. tone-ladder) = Scale.

Tonos (Spa. plur.). Short voc. pieces for several voices sung at the opening of plays in 17th-cent. Spa.

Tonreihe. *See* **Tone-Row.**

Tonsatz (Ger. lit. 'tone-setting') = Composition. *See also* **Satz.**

Tonstück (Ger. = tone-piece). A comp., a piece of m.

Tonus lascivus (Lat. = playful, frolicsome, wanton tone). The medieval name for what later became the Ionian mode and the maj. scale, not recognized as a proper mode at the time, but used for secular songs by minstrels, though only exceptionally and without the approval of professional musicians.

Tonus peregrinus (Lat. = foreign tone). The medieval name for what later became the Aeolian Mode and the natural min. scale (without the sharp leading-note, e.g. the scale of A on the white notes of the pf.), called 'foreign' because not recognized as a proper mode at the time by musns. and used only exceptionally by wandering musns., &c. The name T. p. was also given specifically to the chant in plainsong, dating back beyond the 9th cent., sung to the psalm *In exitu Israel*, which was in that mode.

Topelius, Zakris (1818–98), Fin. novelist & dramatist. *See* **Merikanto (O.)** (*Regina von Emmeritz*), **Pacius** (*Princess of Cyprus*), **Söderman** (*Regina*).

Torchi, Luigi (b. Mondano, 7. XI. 1858; d. Bologna, 18. IX. 1920), It. mcolst. Pupil of Serrao at Naples and of Jadassohn and Reinecke at Leipzig. Returning to It. in 1884, he became prof. of mus. hist. and aesthetics at the Liceo Rossini at Pesaro. In 1891 he took up a similar post at the Liceo musicale of Bologna. He wrote much on Wagner, also on old It. inst. and voc. m., and ed. *L'arte musicale in Italia*, a collection of 14th–18th-cent. m.

Tordion. *See* **Cinquepace.**

Torelli, Giuseppe (b. Verona, *c.* 1658; d. Bologna, 1708), It. vst. & comp. He went to Bologna as leader of the cath. orch. in 1686, and in 1695 left for Ger., to become leader of the orch. at the court of the Margrave of Brandenburg-Ansbach until *c.* 1700, when he returned to It.

Works incl. Concerti grossi, Concerto da camera & other works for stgs. with solo vs., &c.

Tornada (Spa.). The refrain which is a feature of many old Catalan songs.

Törne, Bengt de (b. Helsingfors, 22. XI. 1891), Fin. comp. Studied with Furuhjelm at the Helsingfors Cons. and later privately with Sibelius, on whom he wrote a book. Kajanus allowed him to try out his orch. works with the Fin. State Orch.

Works incl. 2 syms., Sinfonietta, 2 symph. poems; v. Conc., pf. Conc.; chamber m.; pf. pieces, &c.

Tornov. A pseud. used by C. M. Loeffler for his earliest, now discarded works, der. from the pseud. 'Tornow' used by his father as an author.

Torquato Tasso, opera by Donizetti (lib. by Jacopo Ferretti), prod. Rome, Teatro Valle, 9. IX. 1833.

Torrance, George William (b. Rathmines, Dublin, 1835; d. Kilkenny, 20. VIII. 1907), Ir. clergyman, orgst. & comp. Learnt m. as a choir-boy in Christ Church cath., Dublin, became an orgst. and after prod. church m. and an orat. before he was 20 went for further study to Leipzig in 1856. In 1859 he entered Dublin Univ. to study theol. and was ordained in 1865–6. In 1869–97 he lived in Australia, but took the Mus.D. at Dublin in 1879.

Works incl. opera *William of Normandy*; orats. *Abraham, The Captivity* (words by Goldsmith) & *The Revelation*; 2 settings of Te Deum & Jubilate, hymn-tunes & other church m.; madrigal 'Dry be that tear.' &c.

Torrefranca, Fausto (b. Monteleone Calabro, 1. II. 1883), It. mcolst. Studied at Turin and in Ger., became lecturer in hist. at Rome Univ. in 1915 and from that year to 1923 was librarian of Naples Cons. In 1924 he took up a similar post at the Milan Cons. and in 1939 became prof. of mus. hist. at the Univ. there. He wrote studies of the It. origins of mus. romanticism, of Verdi, Puccini and Strauss, and of more general aesthetic subjects.

Torri, Pietro (b. Peschiera, Lago d'Iseo, *c.* 1655; d. Munich, 6. VII. 1737), It. comp. Pupil of Steffani. He became chamber orgst. at Munich in 1689, chapel master at Hanover in 1696, and returned to Munich in 1703 as dir. of the chamber m., becoming mus. dir. in 1715. Like Abaco, he followed the Elector Max Emanuel into exile at Brussels.

Works incl. operas *Merope, Lucio Vero, Griselda* & c. 20 others; orat. *Les Vanités du monde*; chamber conc.; chamber duets, &c.

Torvaldo e Dorliska, opera by Rossini (lib. by Cesare Sterbini), prod. Rome, Teatro Valle, 26. XII. 1815.

Tosca, La, opera by Puccini (lib. by Giuseppe Giacosa & Luigi Illica, based on Sardou's drama), prod. Rome, Teatro Costanzi, 14. I. 1900.

Toselli, Enrico (b. Florence, 15. III. 1883; d. Florence, 15. I. 1926), It. pfst. & comp. Studied with Sgambati and Martucci. He made his name chiefly with the song *Serenata* and in 1907 created a sensation by his marriage to the former Crown Princess Luisa of Saxony.

Works incl. operetta *La principessa bizzarra* (lib. by his wife) & some others; symph. poem *Fuoco* (after d'Annunzio); chamber m.; pf. pieces; songs, &c.

Tosi, Giuseppe Felice (b. Bologna, *c.* 1620; d. ?), It. comp. Orgst. at San Petronio cath. at Bologna, and later chapel master at San Giovanni in Monte and the cath. of Monte di Ferrara.

Works incl. operas; *salmi concertati* & other church m.; chamber cantatas, &c.

Tosi, Pier Francesco (b. Bologna, 1646; d. London, 1727), It. singer, teacher & comp., son of prec. He learnt m. from his father and travelled much until 1693, when he settled as singing-master in London. He pub. a book on florid singing and comp., cantatas for voice & hpchd., &c.

Tosti, (Francesco) Paolo (b. Ortona

sul Mare, Abruzzi, 9. IV. 1846; d. Rome, 2. XII. 1916), It. singing-master & comp. Studied at Naples under Mercadante and others from 1858 and was app. a student-teacher, remaining until 1869. During a long illness at home he wrote his 1st songs. He then went to Rome, where Sgambati helped him to give a concert and Princess Margherita of Savoy (afterwards queen of It.) app. him her singing-master. In 1875 he 1st visited London, returning each year until 1880, where he remained as singing-master to the royal family. Knighted in 1908.

Works incl. It., Eng. & Fr. songs, e.g. *Non m'ama più, Lamento d'amore, Aprile, Vorrei morire, Forever, Good-bye, Mother, At Vespers, That Day, Mattinata, Serenata*; *Canti popolari abruzzesi* for voc. duet, &c.

Tote Stadt, Die (*The Dead City*), opera by Korngold (lib. by Paul Schott, based on Georges Rodenbach's play *Bruges-la-morte*), prod. **Hamburg & Cologne**, 4. XII. 1920.

Toten Augen, Die (*The Dead Eyes*), opera by d'Albert (lib. orig. Fr. by Marc Henry, Ger. trans. by Hanns Heinz Ewers), prod. Dresden, 5. III. 1916.

Touch (modern). The way of approaching the keys in pf. playing to prod. good, varied and significant tone. Scientists have recently denied the possibility of varying the quality of tone by anything but weight, since it is obviously impossible to transmit to the hammers and stgs. anything but degrees of strength by the intermediary of the action, which is not susceptible to any but a mechanical response to the player's hand. This is quite true so long as it is said of single notes only, but not of combinations of notes, which are capable of varying enormously in quality in countless different ways by the slightest inequalities in the strength of the constituent notes or by the minutest inaccuracies of synchronization. It is these infinitesimal inequalities and inaccuracies which account for subtleties of T., and although they too are in the last resort mechanical, they do express the player's interpretative intentions and translate themselves into aesthetic values.

Touch (old). As a verb the word, up to *c.* the early 17th cent., meant simply to 'sound' an inst., exactly as *toccare* still does in It.; as a noun ('a touch' or 'touche') it was equiv. to Toccata.

Touche (Fr.) = Key (of pf. &c.); Fingerboard (of stg. insts.).

Tour de gosier (Fr. = turn of the gullet). A voc. ornament resembling the Turn.

Tourdion. *See* **Cinquepace.**

Tournemire, Charles (Arnould) (b. Bordeaux, 22. I. 1870; d. Arcachon, 3. XI. 1939), Fr. orgst. & comp. Studied at the Paris Cons. and later with d'Indy. In 1898 he was app. to Franck's former orgst.'s post at the church of Sainte-Clotilde. Later he became prof. of chamber m. at the Cons. and travelled much as org. recitalist on the Continent.

Works incl. operas *Les Dieux sont morts* & *Nittetis*; *Le Sang de la Sirène* for solo voices, chor. & orch.; Sym.; pf. 4tet, pf. Trio & other chamber m.; *Pièces symphoniques, Triple Choral, L'Orgue mystique, Petites Fleurs musicales* & other org. works; pf. pieces; songs, &c.

Tourte, François (b. Paris, 1747; d. Paris, IV. 1835), Fr. bowmaker. He learnt his craft from his father and set up in business with his elder brother Xavier, but they quarrelled and set up each for himself. He made great improvements in the v. bow, esp. after 1775.

Tovey, Donald Francis (b. Eton, 17. VII. 1875; d. Edinburgh, 10. VII. 1940), Eng. mus. scholar, pfst. & comp. He was privately educ. and taught the pf. early, playing it astonishingly as a child and memorizing Bach and other classics. Before he was 10 he had begun to comp. and was allowed to study ctpt. with Parratt, and at 13 he was a pupil of Parry. He went to Balliol Coll., Oxford, in 1894, after giving a concert with Joachim at Windsor, and there he distinguished himself by brilliant scholarship and by taking a leading part in the Univ.'s mus. life. In 1900–1 he gave pf. recitals at St. James's Hall in London, and in 1901–2 in Berlin and Vienna. In 1914 he was app. Reid Prof. of M. at Edinburgh Univ., a post he held to his death, and also cond. the Reid orch. concerts there. He wrote many of the mus. articles in the *Encyc. Brit.* and several books, incl. 6 vols. of *Essays in Mus. Analysis*. Knighted in 1935.

Works incl. opera *The Bride of Dionysus*; incid. m. for Maeterlinck's *Aglavaine et Sélysette*; Sym. in D maj.; Suite for wind band; pf. Conc., co. Conc.; 2 stg. 4tets, *Aria and Vars.* for stg. 4tet, 2 pf. trios, pf. 4tet, pf. 5tet, *Vars. on a Theme by Gluck* for fl. & stg. 4tet; *Sonata eroica* for v. solo, So. for co. solo, v. & pf. So., co. & pf. So., cl. & pf. So., Divertimento for ob. & pf., So. for 2 cos.; pf. pieces; *Balliol Dances* for pf. duet; songs; conjectural completion of Bach's *Art of Fugue*, &c.

Toy Symphony. A freak sym. by Haydn, comp. in 1788, for a set of toy insts. bought by him at a fair at Berchtesgaden—hence his title *Sinfonia Berchtoldsgadensis*. It is in C maj. and scored for 1st & 2nd vs., db., cuckoo, quail, nightingale, toy tpt., toy drum, rattle & triangle. A similar work was later comp. by A. Romberg.

Toye (old Eng.). A piece of light, playful character.

Toye, (John) Francis (b. Winchester, 27. I. 1883), Eng. m. critic & comp. Studied with S. P. Waddington and Edward J. Dent, and after a varied journalistic experience became critic to the *Morning Post* in 1925. He became dir. of the Brit. Institute at Florence in 1936, returned to Eng. at the outbreak of war with It. and later went to Rio de Janeiro as representative of the Brit. Council. His books incl. critical biogs. of Rossini and Verdi.

Works incl. masque *Day and Night* (with his brother); songs, &c.

Toye, Geoffrey (b. London, 17. II. 1889; d. London, 11. VI. 1942), Eng. cond. & comp., brother of prec. Studied at the R.C.M. in London and became a theatre cond.; later also cond. orch. concerts and founded Lloyd's Choir, being a member of the Stock Exchange.

Works incl. opera *The Fairy Cup*; masque *Day and Night* (with his brother); ballet *The Haunted Ballroom*; radio opera *The Red Pen* (A. P. Herbert); Sym.; Chin. songs *The Sad Heart* & other songs, &c.

Tpt. (abbr.) = Trumpet.

Tptr. (abbr.) = Trumpeter.

tr (abbr). = Trill, Shake. Used in mus. notation.

Trabaci, Giovanni Maria (b. Montepeloso nr. Potenza, ?; d. Naples, after 1634), It. orgst. & comp. He was orgst. in the royal chapel at Naples early in the 17th cent. and later chapel master.

Works incl. masses, motets, psalms; madrigals; toccatas, ricercari & other org. pieces, &c.

Traetta, Tommaso (Michele Francesco Saverio) (b. Bitonto, Bari, 30. III. 1727; d. Venice, 6. IV. 1779), It. comp. Pupil of Durante at the Naples Cons. di Santa Maria di Loreto, which he left in 1748 to become a teacher of singing and comp. of church m. But in 1751 he prod. his 1st opera and thereafter continued to be a theatre comp., successful all over It. In 1758 he secured Goldoni as libst. and was one of the many who set Metastasio's *Olimpiade*. In 1759 he went to Parma as chapel master and domestic m. teacher at the ducal court of the Infante Felipe of Spa. In the early 1760s he paid successful visits to Vienna and in 1765, on the death of the Duke of Parma, he settled at Venice, where he became dir. of the Cons. dell' Ospedaletto; but in 1768 he went to St. Petersburg to succeed Galuppi at the court of Catherine II. In 1775 he left Rus. with his health impaired by the climate and went to London, where he wrote 3 new operas; but Sacchini's success hindered his own. He retired to Naples, but d. at Venice.

Works incl. operas *Farnace*, *I pastori felici*, *Le nozzi contrastate*, *L'incredulo*, *La fanta furba*, *Nitteti*, *Didone abbandonata*, *Ezio*, *Buovo d'Antona* (Goldoni), *L'Olimpiade*, *Solimano*, *Ippolito ed Aricia*, *Demofoonte*, *Le feste d'Imeneo*, *Enea nel Lazio*, *I Tindaridi*, trilogy *Enea e Lavinia*, *Armida*, *Sofonisba*, *La Francese a Malghera*, *Alessandro nell' Indie*, *Zenobia*, *Ifigenia in Tauride*, *Antigono*, *La buona figliuola maritata* (after Richardson's *Pamela*), *Semiramide*, *Le serve rivali*, *Siroe*, *Amor in trappola*, *Il tributo campestre*, *L'isola disabitata*, *Antigona*, *Amore e Psiche*, *Lucio Vero*, *Merope*, *Germondo*, *Telemacco*, *I capricci del Sesso*, *La disfatta di Dario*, *Il cavaliere errante*, *Gli eroi dei Campi Elisi* (finished by Astaritta); *Stabat Mater* & other church m.; orat. *Salomone*; cantata for sop. & orch., *Hymn to the Creator* for voices & orch.; divertimento for 4 orchs. *Le quattro stagioni e i dodici mesi dell' anno*; arias & duets, &c.

Tragédie de Salomé, La, ballet by Florent Schmitt (chgph. by Guerra), prod. Paris, Théâtre des Arts, 9. XI. 1907.

Tragédie lyrique (Fr.). A 17th-cent. term for Fr. opera of a tragic or at any rate serious character.

Tragic Overture (*Tragische Ouvertüre*). An ovt. by Brahms, Op. 81, comp. in 1880 as a companion-piece to the *Academic Festival Ovt.*, written as an acknowledgment of the hon. degree of doctor of philos. conferred on him by Breslau Univ. in 1879. 1st perf., Breslau, 4. I. 1881.

'Tragic' Symphony. Schubert's 4th Sym., in C min., comp. in 1816.

Traherne, Thomas (? 1636–74), Eng. theol. writer and poet. *See* **Finzi** (*Farewell to Arms*).

Traînée (Fr.). Another name for the *chute*. *See* **Ornaments.**

Trait. *See* **Ornaments.**

Tranquillo (It.) = Quiet, calm, tranquil. The adv., more rarely used as a direction, is *tranquillamente*.

Trans. (abbr.) = Translated, translation, translator.

Transcription. An arrangement of a mus. comp. for some other medium than that intended by the comp. Strictly speaking, a T. differs from an arr. by not merely reprod. the orig. as closely as possible, but by introd. more or less imaginative changes which may be supposed to conform to the comp.'s own procedure if he had written for the different medium.

Transitions. Subordinate passages in a mus. comp. between 2 salient thematic features, more often than not modulating from one key to another. A T. has not in itself any thematic significance, but it may nevertheless, in the hands of a master, be of great interest, esp. in m. in so. form, where apart from the Working-out section the crux of the comp. often lies in the Ts. between 1st and 2nd subjects and in the different turns they take in the Exposition and Recapitulation. The term should not be confused with Modulation, which may occur anywhere in a comp. and does not in itself constitute a T.

Transposing Instruments. Many wind insts. are built in fundamental tunings in which the maj. scale without key signature, written as C maj., actually sounds higher or lower. A cl. in B♭, for ex., will automatically play the scale of that key when the m. is written in C maj.; or, conversely stated, if it is to play a piece in F maj., the m. must be written in G maj., and so on. A hn. in F will transp. a 5th down, a tpt. in F a 4th up, and both will play, for ex., in E♭ if their m. is written in B♭, but the former an octave lower than the latter. Among the most common orch. insts. Eng. hns., cls., hns. and tpts. are T. Is.; fls., obs., bns. and trombs. are not. In milit. bands the variety of T. Is. is bewildering to the uninitiated.

Transposing Keyboards. Contrivances of var. sorts to shift the manuals of keyboard insts. so that the m. played becomes automatically higher or lower, saving the players from acquiring the art of transposing at sight, which is particularly difficult on such insts. owing to the great number of notes and chords employed. Such keyboards appeared on some orgs. as early as the 16th cent. and several inventions of the kind were made for the pf. late in the 18th and throughout the 19th cents.

Transposition. The process, either in comp. or perf., of turning a piece or passage from one key into another in such a way that the m. remains exactly the same except for the change in pitch. All melodic and chordal intervals thus remain of the same size, whatever the new key may be, so that a Sequence, which merely shifts a passage up or down in the same key and thus changes its intervals, does not amount to T., whereas a Rosalia does. The difficulties of T., both in writing and in playing, are somewhat mitigated by the beautifully mathematical fact that, owing to the change in key signature, all Accidentals arising incidentally in the course of the m. (i.e. not contained in the key signature) still remain accidentals. In a piece transp. from E maj. up to F maj., for ex., an incidental A♯ will become B♮, and incidental F♮ will be G♭, and so on. Accompsts. are often required to transpose at sight when a song is too high or low for a singer's voice, and occasionally the inst. parts of a whole orch. have to be transposed in the same way for similar reasons. A special kind of double T. is sometimes made by hn. players when they wish to play on the usual hn. in F a part written for a hn. in some other tuning (for ex. the note C written for an E hn., and expected to sound E, would have to be played as B on the F hn. to prod. the required note, and so on).

Transverse Flute. The modern fl. held horizontally, as distinct from the earlier fls. of the Recorder type, which were held vertically.

Trapassi. *See* **Metastasio.**

Trapp, Max (b. Berlin, 8. XI. 1889), Ger. comp. Studied comp. with Juon and pf. with Dohnányi at the Berlin Hochschule für Musik, became pf. prof. there in 1920 and prof. of advanced comp. in 1934.

Works incl. marionette play *Der letzte König von Orplid* (after Mörike); incid. m. to Shakespeare's *Timon of Athens*; 5 syms., 2 concs., 2 divertimenti, symph. suite, *Notturno* for orch.; pf. Conc., v. Conc., co. Conc.; stg. 4tets, pf. 5tet, 3 pf. 4tets; Vars. for 2 pfs.; Sonatina for pf., &c.

Traquenard (Fr. lit. trap, snare; also racking-pace [of horses]). A 17th-cent. dance the dotted rhythm of which refers to the 2nd sense of the word.

Trascinando (It.) = Dragging.

Trattenuto (It.) = Held back (in pace).

Trauer-Ode (*Funeral Ode*). A cantata by Bach written on the death of the Electress Christiane Eberhardine of Saxony and perf. at the memorial ceremony at Leipzig, 17. X. 1727.

Trauer-Sinfonie (*Mourning Sym.*). The

nickname of a Sym. by Haydn, No. 44, in E min., comp. *c.* 1771.

Trauermarsch (Ger.) = Funeral March.

Trauerwalzer (*Mourning Waltz*). The title given by the pub. to Schubert's waltz for pf., Op. 9 No. 2, in 1821, a piece later wrongly attrib. to Beethoven. Schubert, who wrote it in 1816, disapproved of the title. The attrib. to Beethoven occurred in 1826, when Schott of Mainz brought out a *Sehnsuchtswalzer* (also called *Le Désir*) under his name, although it was a compound of Schubert's piece and Himmel's *Favoritwalzer*.

Trautonium. An electrophonic inst. invented by Friedrich Trautwein of Berlin in 1930, prod. notes from the air graded according to the chromatic scale by means of a special device, not indeterminate in pitch like those of the Aetherophone or Theremin.

Travelling Companion, The, opera by Stanford (lib. by Henry Newbolt, based on a story by Hans Andersen), pub. 1919, but not perf. in S.'s lifetime; prod. Liverpool, 30. IV. 1925.

Travers, John (b. ?, *c.* 1703; d. London, VI. 1758), Eng. orgst. & comp. Learnt m. as a choir-boy at St. George's Chapel, Windsor, and later studied with Greene and Pepusch in London, where in his early 20s he became orgst. at St. Paul's church, Covent Garden, and later at Fulham church. In 1737 he succeeded Jonathan Martin as orgst. in the Chapel Royal.

Works incl. services, anthems, Te Deum; *The Whole Book of Psalms* for 1–5 voices with continuo; 18 canzonets for 2–3 voices to words by Matthew Prior and others; org. voluntaries; hpchd. pieces, &c.

Traversière (Fr. fem. = transverse). The *flûte traversière* was the inst. that came into use in the 18th cent., played horizontally.

Traverso (It. = transverse). An abbr. sometimes used in old scores for the *flauto traverso*, the modern fl. played sideways, as distinct from fls. of the Recorder type, which were held vertically.

Traviata, La (*The Lady Gone Astray*), opera by Verdi (lib. by Francesco Maria Piave, based on the younger Dumas's *La Dame aux camélias*), prod. Venice, Teatro La Fenice, 6. III. 1853.

Traybenraiff, Peter. *See* **Tritonius.**

Traynour. The grouping of notes in odd and even number against each other in 14th-cent. m.

Tre corde (It. = 3 stgs.). A direction in pf. m. indicating that after the use of the left pedal (*una corda*) normal playing is to be resumed.

Tre giorni son che Nina (' Three days it is since Nina '), song previously attrib. to Pergolesi, later to Ciampi, but now known to be by Natale Resta.

Trebelli, Zelia (real name Gilbert) (b. Paris, 1838; d. Étretat, 18. VIII. 1892), Fr. m.-sop. singer. She began serious mus. studies, incl. pf., at the age of 6, and at 16 was allowed to take a course in singing. She made her 1st stage appearance at Madrid in 1859, travelled in Ger. in 1860–1 with Merelli's It. co. and 1st visited London in 1862.

Treble. The highest voice in a voc. comp. in several parts, derived from the Lat. *triplus*, which was the top part of the earliest 3-part Motets. T. is now often taken as the synon. of sop., but strictly it is so only if it denotes the sop. part in a comp. for several voices.

Treble Clef. The G clef (being a modif. of that letter and indicating the position of the note G on the stave), the higher of the 2 clefs used for pf. m., also replacing the former different C clefs used for sop., alto and ten. voices. If used for the ten., it is understood that the voice sounds an 8ve lower. It was formerly used (rarely) in other positions, to indicate that G stood on another than the 2nd line from the bottom, as now. The T. C. is also called the v. clef, being used for that inst.

Treble Viol. The smallest of the viols, also called descant viol. It had 6 stgs. and was tuned an 8ve above the Va. da gamba, viz. D below middle C, with rising above this, G. C, E, A, D.

Tree, Ann Maria (b. London, VIII. 1801; d. London, 17. II. 1862), Eng. m.-sop. singer & actress. Studied singing with Lanza and T. Cooke, joined the chor. at Drury Lane Theatre and made her 1st important stage appearances at Bath in 1818 and in London in 1819. Later she became a good Shakespearian actress as well as a stage singer.

Treibenreif, Peter. *See* **Tritonius.**

Tremando, **Tremante** (It.) = trembling, quivering; played with *tremolo*.

Tremblement (Fr.) = Shake.

Tremblement appuyé (Fr.). *See* **Ornaments.**

Tremolando (It. = trembling). A direction sometimes used instead of the conventional notation for stg. Tremolo, or for a passage to be sung in a tremulous voice.

Tremoletto (It., obs.) = Shake.

Tremolo (It. noun = trembling, shaking, shivering). In It. terminology the word was formerly synonymous with Vibrato; it is now used in var languages for the bad habit in singing vulgarly called 'wobbling,' due to faulty technique of breathing. As a legitimate effect it came into use during the development of m. for insts. of the v. family, where Ts. are prod. by a rapid oscillating movement of the bow and have a striking dramatic effect, differing entirely in quality from the Vibrato, which is prod. by the left hand on the fingerboard. Stg. insts. also use another kind, the fingered T., which is the rapid alternation of 2 notes in double stopping, prod. by the raising and pressing down again in rapid succession of the finger controlling the upper note. A similar T. between 2 or more notes can be easily prod. on the pf.

Tremor pressus (Lat.) = Vibrato.

Tremulant. *See* **Vibrato.** Also the name of an org. stop prod. *vibrato* effects.

Trench, (Frederick) Herbert (1865–1923), Eng. poet. *See* **Holbrooke** (*Apollo and the Seaman*).

Trenchmore. An Eng. country dance 'longways for as many as will,' known in the 16th & 17th cents. and introd. into the court and noble houses as a kind of democratic dance in which masters and servants could take part together and strict class distinctions were temporarily relaxed.

Trend, J(ohn). B(rande). (b. Southampton, 17. XII. 1887), Eng. scholar. Educ. at Charterhouse and Cambridge. He specialized in Spa. and became prof. of the subject at Cambridge Univ. in 1933. He has written learned articles and books on Spa. mus. subjects.

Trent, Council of. *See* **Council of T.**

Trento, Vittorio (b. Venice, 1761 or 1765; d. ? Lisbon, 1833), It. comp. Pupil of Bertoni. In the last decade of the 18th cent. he visited London and in the 1st of the 19th became impresario at Amsterdam, going to Lisbon in the same capacity soon after. He returned to Venice before his death.

Works incl. operas *La finta ammalata, Quanti casi in un giorno, Teresa vedova, Ifigenia in Aulide, Climene* & c. 35 others; ballet *Mastino della Scala* & more than 50 others; orats. *The Deluge, The Maccabees* & others, &c.

Trepak. A Rus. dance of Cossack origin in animated 2–4 time.

Treu, Daniel Gottlieb (b. Stuttgart, 1695; d. Breslau, 7. VIII. 1749), Ger. vst. & comp. Pupil of Cousser and from 1716 of Vivaldi in Venice, where he was called by a lit. trans. of his name, Fedele. In 1725 he went to Breslau as cond. of an It. opera company, in 1727 to Prague as mus. dir. and in 1740 into the service of Count Schaffgotsch at Hirschberg.

Works incl. operas *Astarto, Ulisse, Don Chisciotte* & some others; cantatas; orch. m., &c.

Triad. The common chord of 3 notes based on the tonic note and normally concluding a comp. in a definite maj. or min. key; also its inversions (i.e. chords of the 6th and $\frac{6}{4}$) and chromatic alterations (e.g. the augmented T. containing 2 maj. 3rds).

Trial. A Fr. term for a special type of operatic ten. voice of a high, thin, rather nasal quality suited to comic parts derived from Antoine T. below.

Trial. Fr. family of musns.:

1. Jean Claude T. (b. Avignon, 13. XII. 1732; d. Paris, 23. VI. 1771), comp. Studied v. with Garnier at Montpellier, settled in Paris, where he became a friend of Rameau's, was app. cond. at the Opéra and later of the private orch. of the Prince de Conti, whose influence procured him the joint directorship of the Opéra with Berton.

Works incl. operas *Ésope à Cythère* (with Vachon), *La Fête de Flore, Silvie* (with Berton), *Théonis* (do.) & *Renaud d'Ast* (with Vachon); cantatas; ovt. and divertissements for orch., &c.

2. Antoine T. (b. Avignon, 1736; d. Paris, 5. II. 1795), ten. singer, brother of prec. He was educ. as a church singer, but went on the stage, toured in the provinces and in 1764 appeared for the 1st time in Paris. He took part in the Revol., lost his reason and poisoned himself.

3. Marie Jeanne T. (*née* Milon) (b. Paris, 1. VIII. 1746; d. Paris, 13. II. 1818), sop. singer, wife of prec. Made her 1st stage appearance in 1766.

4. Armand (Emmanuel) T. (b. Paris, 1. III. 1771; d. Paris, 9. IX. 1803), pfst. & comp., son of 2 & 3. He began to comp. at an early age, married Jeanne Méon, an actress at the Théâtre Favart, and d. from the effects of a wild life.

Works incl. operas *Julien et Colette, Adélaïde et Mirval, Les Deux Petits Aveugles*; revol. pieces *La Cause et les effets, Les Congrès des rois* (with other comps.) & *Le Siège de Lille*.

Trial by Jury, dramatic cantata by Sullivan (lib. by W. S. Gilbert), prod. London, Royalty Theatre, 25. III. 1875.

Triangle. A perc. inst. consisting of a simple steel bar in 3-cornered form, with an open end hooked so that it can be suspended to hang freely. It is struck with a short steel rod and prod. a bright tinkling sound of no definite pitch.

Tricinium (Lat.) = A song in 3 parts (the term is obs.).

Tridentine Council. *See* **Council of Trent.**

Trihoris. An old Fr. dance of Lower Brittany, also called Trihory, Triori or Triory, allied to the Branle.

Trill. *See* **Shake.**

Trille (Fr.) }
Triller (Ger.) } = Shake.

Trillo (It.) = Shake. *See also* **Vibrato.**

Trillo del diavolo, Il (*The Devil's Trill*). Tartini's v. So. written at Assisi *c.* 1714, said to have been inspired by a dream in which he bargained with the devil for his soul in return for mus. inspiration, the devil playing the v. to him. He related that on waking he immediately wrote down what he had heard, but that the m. as written fell far short of the dream devil's perf. The work is in 4 mvts., written for v. & continuo; the famous trill is in the finale. An opera on the story of the So. was written by Falchi.

Trinona. An 8-ft. org. stop governing open pipes with tone akin to that of the Gamba stop.

Trio. A comp. or mvt. for 3 voc. or inst. parts; more partic. a chamber work for 3 insts., esp. v., co. & pf. (pf. T.) or v., va. & co. (stg. T.); also the alternative section in a minuet, scherzo, march or sometimes other kinds of mvt. in a so.-form work, so called because orig. such sections were by convention written in 3 parts.

Trio Sonata. The medium predominantly used for chamber m. with a keyboard Continuo part in the later 17th and early 18th cent. T. Ss. were most usually written for 2 vs. and bass viol or co. and thus strictly in 3 parts, but harmonic and ctptal fillings were supplied by a hpchd. or other keyboard inst. played from the figured bass part. In another sense Bach's org. Trios were, strictly speaking, T. Ss., being written in 3 single melodic parts, 1 in each hand and 1 in the pedals.

Triomphe de l'Amour sur des bergers et bergères, Le (*The Triumph of Love over Shepherds and Shepherdesses*), opera by La Guerre (lib. by Charles de Beys), prod. Paris, Louvre, 22. I. 1655. The 1st Fr. opera.

Trionfi del fato, I, ovvero Le glorie d'Enea (*The Triumphs of Fate, or The Glories of Aeneas*), opera by Steffani (lib. by Ortensio Mauro), prod. Hanover, Court Opera, XII. 1695.

Trionfo dell' onore, Il (*The Triumph of Honour*), opera by A. Scarlatti (lib. by Francesco Antonio Tullio), prod. Naples, Teatro dei Fiorentini, autumn 1718.

Trionfo di Camilla, Il (*Camilla's Triumph*), opera by M. A. Bononcini (lib. by Silvio Stampiglia), prod. Naples, Teatro San Bartolommeo, (?) XII. 1696.

Opera by Leo (lib. do.), prod. Rome, Teatro Capranica, 8. I. 1726.

Trionfo di Clelia, Il (*Clelia's Triumph*), opera by Gluck (lib. by Metastasio), prod. Bologna, Teatro Comunale, 14. V. 1763.

Opera by Hasse (lib. do.), prod. Vienna, Burg Theatre, 27. IV. 1762.

Opera by Jommelli (lib. do.), prod. Lisbon, Teatro d'Ajuda, 6. VI. 1774.

Trionfo di Dori, Il (*The Triumph of Doris*), collection of It. madrigals pub. by Gardano of Venice in 1592. It contains 29 6-part madrigals on var. poems all ending with the line 'Viva la bella Dori,' which suggested the similar uniform final line in the Eng. collection modelled on this, *The Triumphes of Oriana.* The comps., all represented by 1 piece only, incl. Anerio, Asola, Baccusi, Croce, G. Gabrieli, Gastoldi, Marenzio, Palestrina, Striggio & Vecchi.

Triori }
or } *See* **Trihoris.**
Triory }

Tripla. An old term for triple time in old Mensurable m., but also the figure 3 shown in the time-signature and later, when the device of the Triplet came into use, the figure 3 set over a group of notes.

Triple Concerto. A conc. with 3 solo parts, e.g. Bach's 2 concs. for 3 hpchds. & stgs. or Beethoven's Conc. for v., co. & pf. & orch.

Triple Counterpoint. Ctpt. in which 3 parts are reversible, each being capable of appearing at the top, in the middle or at the bottom without ill effect.

Triple Time. *See* **Compound Time.**

Triplet. A group of 3 notes occupying a beat or other fraction of a bar normally filled by a time-unit of 1 note or its subdivisions into 2, 4 or more notes in even numbers. Rests instead of notes may form part of Ts.

Triplex (Lat. = threefold, triple). An old term for Compound Time.

Triplus (Lat. = the third). The highest of the orig. 3 voices in the Motet, and thus the origin of the Eng. word Treble.

Tristan und Isolde, m.-drama by Wagner (lib. by comp., based on the Tristram and Iseult legend), prod. Munich, Court Opera, 10. VI. 1865.

Tristitiae remedium (*The Remedy for Sadness*). A collection of motets, anthems and madrigals by Eng. and It. comps. (Byrd, Croce, Milton, Peerson, Tallis, Tye, &c.) made by the clergyman Thomas Myriell of Barnet and pub. in 1616.

Tristram and Iseult. *See* **Queen of Cornwall; Tristan und Isolde.**

Tritone. The interval of the augmented 4th or diminished 5th (e.g. C–F♯ or B–F, progressing upwards). *See* **Diabolus in Musica.**

Tritonius, Petrus (actually Peter Treibenreif or Traybenraiff) (b. Bozen or Sterzing, ?; d. ?), Aus. 15th–16th-cent. comp & scholar. Studied at Padua Univ. and later became teacher of Lat. and (?) m. at the cath. school of Brixen. He was invited to settle in Vienna by Conrad Celtes, a prof. there whom he had met in It., and joined the literary and humanist soc. founded by that scholar, making his setting of Horatian odes for it. Senfl later took the ten. parts of these as a *cantus firmus* for his own settings, and Hofhaimer imitated T.'s settings. On the death of Celtes in 1508 T. returned to the Tyrol and became dir. of the Lat. school at Bozen; but in 1521 he retired to Schwatz nr. Innsbruck.

Works incl. hymns in 4 parts; odes by Horace and other Lat. poems set in 4 parts, &c.

Trittico (*Triptych*), cycle of 3 1-act operas by Puccini, prod. New York, Metrop. Opera, 14. XII. 1918.

I. **Il Tabarro** (*The Cloak*) (lib. by Giuseppe Adami, based on Didier Gold's *Houppelande*).

II. **Suor Angelica** (*Sister A.*) (lib. by Giovacchino Forzano).

III. **Gianni Schicchi** (lib. by do., based on the story of a rogue who is mentioned in Dante's *Divina commedia*).

Tritto, Giacomo (b. Altamura nr. Bari, 2. IV. 1733; d. Naples, 16. IX. 1824), It. comp. Pupil of Cafaro and Sala at the Cons. dei Turchini, Naples, where he taught from 1780 and became co-dir. with Paisiello in 1798, succeeding Sala as prof. in 1800. He wrote several theoret. books.

Works incl. opera *Le avventure amorose*, *Gli Americani* & c. 50 others; church m., &c.

Triumph of Neptune, The, ballet by Lord Berners (scen. by Sacheverell Sitwell, chgph. by George Melitonovitch Balanshin), prod. London, Lyceum Theatre, 3. XII. 1926. The settings were based on B. Pollock's 'penny plain, twopence coloured' toy theatre designs.

Triumphes of Oriana, The. An Eng. coll. of madrigals written in honour of Queen Elizabeth, ed. by Morley and pub. in 1603 (with the date 1601). It was modelled on the It. collection of *Il Trionfo di Dori* of 1592 and contains a similar series of different poems all ending with the same line, 'Long live fair Oriana.' There were 25 pieces by 23 Eng. comps. in the 1st ed.: Benet, Carlton, Cavendish, Cobbold, Este, Farmer, E. Gibbons (2), Hilton, Holmes, Hunt, E. Johnson, R. Jones, Kirby, Lisley, Marson, Milton, Morley (2), Mundy, Nicolson, Norcome, T. Tomkins, Weelkes, Wilbye, with the addition of a trans. of a madrigal by Croce taken from *Musica transalpina*; 2 pieces by Bateson and 1 by Pilkington were added to later eds.

Triumphlied (*Song of Triumph*), a setting by Brahms of words from the Revelation of St. John for 8-part chor., orch. & org. *ad lib.*, Op. 55, comp. in spring 1871 to celebrate the Ger. victory in the Franco-Prus. war; 1st perf. Carlsruhe, 1872.

Triumphs of Oriana. *See* **Triumphes of Oriana.**

Triumphs of Peace, The, masque by James Shirley with m. by H. & W. Lawes and Simon Ive, prod. at the Banqueting House in Whitehall, 3. II. (Candlemas) 1634.

Trois Fermiers, Les (*The Three Farmers*), opera by Dezède (lib. by Jacques Marie Boutet de Monvel), prod. Paris, Comédie-Italienne, 24. V. 1777.

Trois Mousquetaires, Les (*The Three Musketeers*), opera by Isidore de Lara (lib. by Henri Cain & Louis Payen, based on Dumas, sen.), prod. Cannes, 3. III. 1921.

Tromb. (abbr.) = Trombone.

Tromba (It.) = Trumpet. Also one of the names for the Trumpet org. stop (8 ft.). *See also* **Clarino.**

Tromba da tirarsi (It. lit. tpt. to draw itself [out] = tpt. to be drawn). The Slide tpt., an obs. inst. of the tpt. type with a slide similar to that of the tromb. It was used in Ger. in the 18th cent. and had the advantage before the invention of the valves of being capable of prod. more notes than the fundamental harmonics by the temporary changes in the length of the tuba, exactly as in the tromb. But it never attained a wide currency.

Tromba marina (It. = Marine tpt.). An obs. and primitive stg. inst. with a single stg. and thus allied to the Monochord, played with a bow. It was used mainly for popular m.-making, esp. in Ger., but also in nunneries, as the Ger. name *Nonnengeige* (nun's fiddle) indicates. It was also called *Trummscheit* (trumpet [*tromba*] wood) or *Brummscheit* (humming wood), and the It. & Eng. names connecting it with a tpt. were doubtless due to its penetrating tone. The adj. 'marine' is said (uncertainly) to have come either from It. because of the inst.'s resemblance to the speaking-tpt. on It. ships or from Fr. because a 15th-cent. tptr. named Marin or Maurin improved the inst. The inst. prod. harmonics very easily and, like the old tpt., often restricted itself to them, its normally prod. notes being very poor and coarse in quality.

Tromba spezzata (It. = broken-up tpt.). An obs. It. peasant inst. of the tpt. type with a slide: actually a variant of the Slide Tpt. or Tromba da tirarsi.

Trombetti, Ascanio (b. ? Bologna, ?; d. ? Bologna, ?), It. 16th–17th-cent. comp. In the service of the Signoria of Bologna.

Works incl. motets in 5–12 parts for voices & insts.; madrigals for 4–5 voices, Napolitane for 3 voices, &c.

Tromboncino, Bartolommeo (b. ? Verona, ?; d. ? Ferrara, ?), It. 15th–16th-cent. comp. At the ducal court of Mantua, 1487–95, then at Venice, Vicenza, Casale, at Mantua again in 1501–13, and then at Ferrara.

Works incl. Benedictus for 3 voices, 9 lamentations & other church m.; frottole for 4 voices, &c.

Trombone. A brass wind inst., developed from the medieval Sackbut, made in 4 sizes apart from some freaks: alto, ten., bass and contrabass, the 1st of which is now very rarely used, parts written for it being played on the ten. T., while the last hardly ever appears in the orch., except in Wagner's *Ring*. The inst.'s most characteristic feature is the slide, by means of which the tube can be adjusted to different lengths in 7 positions, so that all the notes of the chromatic scale can be prod. as natural harmonics. The T. was thus a chrom. inst. long before the hn. and tpt. became so by the invention of the valves. The intonation, as in stg. insts., is not fixed, but depends entirely on the player's ear and skill. Many notes are, of course, available in more than one position (as different harmonics), so that the player often has the choice between an easier and a more difficult way of passing from note to note. A strict *legato* between notes in different positions is not possible, as the breath has to be interrupted during the change of the slide to avoid an unpleasant scoop; but this scoop, usually designated by the hybrid term *glissando*, can be used as a special effect, though, having been exploited by the m.-halls as a comic vulgarity, it rarely appears in serious scores. The range of the ten. tromb. is from E below the stave in the bass clef to B♭ above middle C, with 2 or 3 possible but dangerous notes higher and 3 pedal notes (B♭, A & A♭) below the bass E. The alto T. has the same range a perfect 5th higher, the bass T. an augmented 4th lower and the contrabass T. an 8ve lower. In the 19th cent. valve Ts. were invented and gained favour in military and brass bands as being easier to play, though even there it is admitted that their tone is inferior to that of the slide T. The valve T. never gained a firm footing in the orch.

Trombone Stop. A 16-ft. org. reed stop of powerful tone, the bass of the Trumpet Stop.

Trombst. (abbr.) = Trombonist, trombone player.

Trommel (Ger.) = Drum.

Trommelbass (Ger. lit. drum bass). A techn. term for the notes of a bass part divided up into groups of repeated even quavers, a device used espec. in the 18th cent. to give a kind of artificial animation to m.

Trompeter von Säckingen, Der (*The Trumpeter of S.*), opera by Nessler (lib. by Rudolf Bunge, based on Scheffel's poem), prod. Leipzig, 4. V. 1884.

Tronco (It. = truncated, cut off, interrupted). A direction indicating that a note or chord is to cease abruptly.

Trope. The verb 'to trope' meant to insert Tropes into ecclesiastical chanting. The process was also called 'farcing' (i.e. larding).

Tropen (Ger. = tropes). The term, which does not refer to the old Tropes, is used by Josef Hauer for his own variant of the system of Twelve-Note M. He divides the possible combs. of the 12 notes of the chromatic scale, which run into hundreds of millions, into 44 main groups, and these are what he calls T., and he further divides each row of 12 notes into 2 halves of 6, which form 2 fundamental chords, whatever the order in which each 6 may appear. The T. for him are equivalent to keys in the diatonic system, and a change from one T. to another is equivalent to modulation.

Troper. A book or collection containing Tropes, e.g. the 13th-cent. Winchester T., which contains tropes used at Winchester cath.

Tropes. Interpolations into liturgical chants dating from the 8th or 9th cent. and prob. of Byzantine orig. They were at first vocalized as purely mus. ornamentations or sung on syllables of certain words, esp. 'Alleluia,' but later they became so important that special words were newly written for them. Sometimes new words came 1st and demanded new m.: thus the Sequence arose, being merely a special kind of trope.

Troppo (It. =too much). The word is often used in the negative in mus. directions: *non troppo* = not too much, or *ma non troppo* = but not too much.

Troubadour (Fr., from old Provençal musn. or *trobador*). A poet-minstrel of southern Fr. in the 11th–13th cents. Ts. always wrote their own poems as well as the tunes for them. The names of 460 Ts. are known, over 2,500 poems have been preserved and 259 melodies are still extant. The poems were usually *poésies courtoises* (mainly love-songs, but also incl. satires, &c.), while story-telling *chansons à personnages*, though also cultivated by them, belonged chiefly to the northern Trouvères. Only the melodies were written down in a notation showing the pitch but not the rhythm of the notes, the latter being either committed to memory or determined (if the notation is modal) by the poetic metre, a question that has never been solved beyond controversy. Neither is it known how the songs were accomp.: prob. on insts. of the hp. or lute type, either by the Ts. themselves or by attendants, for the Ts. were not poor wandering musns. but gentlemen whose audiences were at courts and noble houses.

Troubadour, The (Verdi). *See* **Trovatore.**

'Trout' Quintet. A 5tet in A maj. for v., va., co., db. & pf. by Schubert, Op. 114, comp. summer 1819 during an excursion to Upper Aus.; so called because the 4th of the 5 mvts. is a set of vars. on his song *The Trout* (*Die Forelle*).

Trouvère (Fr., from old Fr. *trovere* or *troveur*). A minstrel of northern Fr. in the 12th & 13th cents. The Ts. cultivated an art similar to that of the southern Troubadours, and their name is prob. exactly the same, derived from old Fr. as theirs was from old Provençal. The art was brought to the north by Eleanor of Aquitaine, who married Louis VII in 1137. The names of *c.* 200 Ts. are known and *c.* 2,000 songs have been preserved. They were usually *chansons à personnages* (narrative songs), while *poésies courtoises* (courtly poems, mainly love-songs), though also cultivated by them, belonged chiefly to the Troubadours; but 2 types belonging to the Ts. alone are the Pastourelles and dancing-songs. The notation and manner of perf. of the songs was similar to that of the Troubadours.

Trovatore, Il (*The Troubadour* or *The Minstrel*), opera by Verdi (lib. by Salvatore Cammarano, based on a Spa. play, *El trovador*, by Antonio García Gutiérrez), prod. Rome, Teatro Apollo, 19. I. 1853.

Troyens, Les (*The Trojans*), opera by Berlioz in 2 parts (lib. by comp., after Virgil): I. **La Prise de Troie** (*The Taking of Troy*), prod. Carlsruhe (in Ger.), 6. XII. 1890; II. **Les Troyens à Carthage**, prod. Paris, Théâtre-Lyrique, 4. XI. 1863.

Trugschluss (Ger. =deceptive ending in m. (false conclusion in logic)). The Ger. term for Interrupted Cadence.

Truinet, Charles. *See* **Nuitter.**

Trummscheit, also **Trumbscheit** or **Trumscheit** (Ger., prob. from *tromba* =trumpet and *Scheit* =a piece of wood). *See* **Tromba marina.**

Trumpet. A brass wind inst. tracing its descent through the Bugle to the Rom. Lituus or Tuba. Until the invention of the valves in the 19th cent. the tpt. was capable of prod. only the natural harmonic notes, for which reason, combined with that of its incisive and carrying tone, it was found useful for fanfares, and for military purposes was often comb. with kettledrums, a practice clearly reflected in the scores of classical orch. works up to the early 19th cent. The valves made the T. a chromatic inst., 1st made in the pitch of F, transposing a perfect 4th up. The Ts. in modern use, however, are usually in B♭ or A, transp. a maj. 2nd or a min. 3rd down, respectively, the written compass being from F♯ below middle C to C above the stave in the treble clef, sounding respectively E–B♭ and D–A. There are also Ts. in C, and the T. in F is still in use. *See also* **Bach Trumpet, Bass Trumpet, Clarino, Principal** & **Tromba da tirarsi.**

Trumpet Marine (more usually Marine Trumpet). *See* **Tromba marina.**

Trumpet Stop. An 8-ft. reed org. stop reprod. tpt. tone.

Trumpet Voluntary. In the late 17th cent. a piece, not for tpt., but an org. voluntary the tune of which was played on the tpt. stop. The ex. still familiar is that by J. Clarke, long wrongly attrib. to Purcell, popularized by Sir Henry Wood's orch. arr. The tune was also known as *The Prince of Denmark's March*: it is therefore unlikely to have been C.'s own, but was prob. merely arr. by him for such an org. piece, evidently from a tune favoured by Queen Anne's consort, Prince George of Denmark.

Trumscheit. *See* **Trummscheit.**

Trunk, Richard (b. Tauberbischofsheim, Baden, 10. II. 1879), Ger. comp. Studied with Knorr at the Hoch Cons., Frankfort o/M., and with Rheinberger at the Munich Acad. He settled there as chor. cond. and critic, but spent 1912–4 in N.Y. as cond. of the Arion chor. soc. In 1925–34 he was dir. of the Rheinische Musikschule at Cologne, but he returned to Munich as president of the Akademie der Tonkunst, succeeding Hausegger.

Works incl. operetta *Herzdame*; male-voice chors., e.g. cycle from *Des Knaben Wunderhorn*, poems by Goethe, &c.; Serenade for stg. orch.; pf. 5tet; Romance for v. & pf.; several sets of songs, &c.

Tsar and Carpenter (Lortzing). *See* **Zar und Zimmermann.**

Tsar Saltan (Rimsky-Korsakov). *See* **Legend of Tsar Saltan.**

Tsar's Bride, The (*Tsarskaya Nevesta*), opera by Rimsky-Korsakov (lib. by I. F. Tumenev, based on a play by Lev Alexandrovitch Mey), prod. Moscow, Imp. Opera, 3. XI. 1899.

Tschaikowski. *See* **Tchaikovsky,** the usual Eng. translit. of the name. The Ger. translit., although used by the comp. himself when he wrote in Latin script, has no justification in Eng.-speaking countries.

Tschudi, Burkhardt. *See* **Shudi, Burkat.**

Tsigane (Fr., or tzigane). A gypsy or musn. of the bohemian world of Paris.

Tuba. An ancient Rom. military inst. of the hn. type; now the bass inst. of the hn. family, used in the orch. as the bass of the brass insts. and more often assoc. in 4-part harmony with the trombs. than with the hns., though its tone is nearer the latter. The inst., owing to its 3 or 4 valves, controls a complete chromatic scale from F an 8ve below the bass-clef stave to *c*. F an 8ve above it (i.e. 3 8ves. *See also* **Bombardon, Euphonium** & **Wagner Tubas.**

Tuba major or **Tuba mirabilis** (or **Tuba** for short). An 8-ft. org. reed stop of great power, but prod. a higher range of notes than the orch. T.

Tubular Bells. Metal tubes tuned to the mus. scale and used for bell effects in the orch., real bells being cumbersome and difficult to play with precision.

Tubuphone. A perc. inst. of the bell variety the notes of which are prod. by metal tubes set in rows like a pf. keyboard, but struck with hammers.

Tuck (old Eng.). The sound of a drum, drum-tap.

Tucker, William (b. ?; d. London, 28. II. 1679), Eng. comp. Gentleman of the Chapel Royal in London, and minor canon and precentor of Westminster Abbey from 1660.

Works incl. services, anthems, &c.

Tucket (Eng., obs.). A word found in stage directions of Eng. plays of the Elizabethan period where the author asks for a fanfare to be played on or off the stage (' tucket within '). It was connected with Fr. *toquer* and It. *toccare* =to touch, and thus prob. with ' toccata,' just as ' sennet,' which meant much the same thing, may have been ' sonata.'

Tuczek (or Tuček or Dušek), Vincent (František) (b. ? Prague, *c.* 1755; d. Pest, 1820), Boh. singer, cond. & comp. He was a singer and accompst. at Prague theatres, mus. dir. to the Duke of Courland at Sagan, and then cond. at Breslau, Vienna and Budapest.

Works incl. operas *Dämona, Lanassa, Der Zauberkuss* & others; mus. travesty of *Hamlet*; orats. *Moses' Tod* & *Simson*; masses; cantatas; pf. & guitar pieces, &c.

Tuczek-Herrenburg, Leopoldine (b. Vienna, 11. XI. 1821; d. Baden nr. Vienna, 20. X. 1883), Aus. sop. singer. Pupil of Josephine Fröhlich at the Vienna Cons. and of It. masters. She appeared on the stage as a child and made her 1st important operatic appearance *c.* 1840. In 1841–61 she was at the Berlin Court Opera.

Tudway, Thomas (b. ?, *c.* 1650; d. ? Cambridge, 23. XI. 1726), Eng. comp., orgst. & mus. ed. Became chorister in the Chapel Royal in London soon after the Restor. (1660) and lay vicar at Windsor in 1664; app. orgst. at King's Coll., Cambridge, 1670, and Prof. of M. in the Univ. there, 1705, in succession to Staggins. In 1714–20 he compiled a large collection of Eng. cath. m. in 6 vols.

Works incl. services, anthems, &c.

Tulou, Jean Louis (b. Paris, 12. IX. 1786; d. Nantes, 23. VII. 1865), Fr. flst. & comp. 1st learnt m. from his father, Jean Pierre T. (1749–99), a bnst., and studied at the Paris Cons. He played successively in the orchs. of the Théâtre Italien and the Opéra and in 1829 became fl. prof. at the Cons., leaving in 1856 to take to fl. manufacture.

Works incl. fl. concs., fl. duets & trios, vars., fantasies & other pieces for fl. & pf., test pieces for fl., &c.

Tuma, Franz (b. Kostelec, 2. X. 1704; d. Vienna, 30. I. 1774), Boh. violist & comp. Pupil of Černohorsky in Prague and of Fux in Vienna. In 1741 he became mus. dir. to the Dowager Empress Elisabeth until her death in 1750. In 1768 he retired to a monastery at Gera, but later returned to one in Vienna.

Works incl. masses & other church m., &c.

Tunder, Franz (b. Lübeck, 1614; d. Lübeck, 5. XI. 1667), Ger. orgst. & comp. Pupil of Frescobaldi in Rome; became in 1641 orgst. of St. Mary's church at Lübeck, where he prec. Buxtehude, who had to marry his daughter in order to secure the post. He greatly improved the church m. and also instituted the 'Evening M.' (*Abendmusiken*) which soon became famous beyond the town.

Works incl. church cantatas, sacred arias with stgs. & org.; chorale vars. for org., &c.

Tune. Another word for Melody, more colloquial and therefore often considered vulg., but a perfectly good Eng. term for its purpose. 'In tune,' however, means in pure intonation, 'out of tune' the opposite. 'To tune' is to adjust the intonation of an inst.

Tuning-Fork. A small and simple inst. in the form of a fork with 2 long prongs, invented by the tptr. John Shore in 1711. It not only retains pitch very accurately, but gives out a very pure sound free from harmonic upper partials. It is tuned to the A above middle C used by orchs. as their fundamental tuning-note.

Tunstead, Simon (b. Norwich, ?; d. Bruisyard, Suffolk, 1369), Eng. priest & mus. scholar. He took his name from his father's birthplace in Norfolk, became a minor friar of the Franciscan Order at Oxford, studied theol., m. and astronomy, became regent of the Minorites, and head of their order in 1360. In 1351 he wrote the mus. treatise *De quatuor principalibus musice*.

Tuotilo (or Tutilo) (b. ?; d. St. Gall, ?), 9th–10th-cent. monk & musn. at the Swi. monastery of St. Gall. He played and taught all the insts. of the period and comp. church m., incl. the Christmas trope *Hodie cantandus est nobis puer*.

Turanda, opera by Bazzini (lib. by Antonia Gazzoletti, based on Gozzi's play *Turandot*), prod. Milan, Teatro alla Scala, 13. I. 1867.

Turandot. *See also* **Turanda.**

Incid. m. for Schiller's Ger. version of Gozzi's play by Weber, Op. 37, comp. in 1809 and incl. the *Overtura chinese* (*Chinese Ovt.*), comp. on a Chin. theme in 1805.

Opera by Busoni (Ger. lib. by comp. based on Gozzi's play), prod. Zürich, 11. V. 1917, together with another short opera *Arlecchino*. The m. of *Turandot* was elaborated from incid. m. for Max Reinhardt's prod. of Karl Vollmöller's version of Gozzi's play, prod. Berlin, Deutsches Theater, 27. X. 1911.

Opera by Herman Severin Løvenskjold (1815–70) (Dan. lib. by Hans Haagen Nyegaard, based on Gozzi's play), prod. Copenhagen, 3. XII. 1854.

Opera by Puccini (It. lib. by Giuseppe Adami & Renato Simoni, based on Gozzi's play), left unfinished by P. and completed by Alfano; prod. Milan, Teatro alla Scala, 25. V. 1926.

See also **Danzi, Jensen, Reissiger & Vesque von Püttlingen.**

Turba (Lat. = crowd). The chor. in settings of the Passion representing priests, people, disciples, &c.

Turca (It. fem. = Turkish). The word is used in the comb. *alla turca* (in the Turkish manner) by Mozart for the finale of the A maj. pf. So. (K. 331) and by Beethoven for the *Marcia a. t.* in *The Ruins of Athens*, which is the theme of the pf. Vars. Op. 76.

Turco in Italia, Il (*The Turk in Italy*), opera by Rossini (lib. by Felice Romani), prod. Milan, Teatro alla Scala, 14. VIII. 1814.

Turgenev, Ivan (1818–83), Rus. novelist & dramatist. *See* **Ippolitov-Ivanov** (*Assia*), **Kastalsky** (*Clara Militch*), **Shaporin** (*Gentlefolk*), **Simon (A.)** (*Song of Love Triumphant*), **Viardot-García** (operettas).

Turges, Edmund (b. ?; d. ?), Eng. 15th–16th-cent. comp. Son of (?) John T., harper to Queen Margaret. He was at King's Coll., Cambridge, in 1522, not as a student, but prob. as a master of some kind, for he had already written a partsong for the marriage of Prince Arthur and Catherine of Aragon in 1501.

Works incl. masses, magnificats, anthems, partsongs, &c.

Turina, Joaquín (b. Seville, 9. XII. 1882), Spa. comp. Studied at Seville and Madrid, later with d'Indy at the Schola Cantorum in Paris. He has devoted much time to teaching as well as comp. and has written a small treatise, *Enciclopedia abreviada de la música*.

Works incl. operas *Margot* & *Jardín de oriente* (libs. by G. Martínez Sierra); incid. m. for Moreto's *La adúltera penitente*, Martínez Sierra's *Navidad* & other plays; *La procesión del Rocío*, *Danzas fantásticas*, *Sinfonía sevillana*, *Ritmos* & other works for orch.; stg. 4tet, pf. 5tet, *Escena andaluza* for va., pf. & stg. 4tet; *Poema de una Sanluqueña* for v. & pf.; suites *Rincones sevillanos* & *Sevilla* & other works for pf.; songs. &c.

Turini, Francesco (b. Prague, *c.* 1595;

d. Brescia, 1656), It. comp. His father Gregorio T. was cornet player & comp. to the Emperor Rudolph II in Prague, but d. early, whereupon the emperor sent T. to Venice and Rome to study m. and later made him his chamber orgst. He left Prague to become cath. orgst. at Brescia.

Works incl. masses & motets; madrigals, canons, &c.

Türk, Daniel Gottlob (b. Clausnitz nr. Chemnitz, 10. VIII. 1756; d. Halle, 26. VIII. 1813), Ger. theorist & comp. Studied under his father and under Homilius at Dresden. Later he went to Leipzig Univ., where he became a pupil and friend of J. A. Hiller, who procured him appts. as vst. at the Opera and the orch. concerts. In 1776 he became orgst. at St. Ulric's church at Halle, in 1779 mus. dir. of the Univ. and in 1787 orgst. at the church of Our Lady. He wrote treatises on org. & clavier playing, thorough-bass & temperament.

Works incl. duodrama *Pyramus und Thisbe*; cantata *Die Hirten bei der Krippe in Bethlehem*; 2 syms.; pf. sos. & pieces, &c.

Turkish Crescent. *See* **Chinese Pavilion.**

Turn. An ornament connecting 2 adjacent notes with a rapidly executed group of 4 notes beginning on the note above the 1st of these 2 notes, which it takes in on passing to the note below and returning to it before passing on to the next principal note written down. The T. normally remains within the prescribed key, retaining its proper whole tones and semitones, but departures from this rule may be indicated by the comp. by marking accidentals above and below it, as he desires the upper or lower note to be altered.

Turned Shake. *See* **Ornaments.**

Turner, Ann. *See* **Robinson, John & Turner, William.**

Turner, W(alter). J(ames). (b. Shanghai, 13. X. 1889), Eng. poet, novelist & m. critic. Studied m. with his father, became orgst. at Melbourne and later studied at Dresden, Munich and Vienna. He has pub. books of misc. mus. essays, works on Mozart, Beethoven, Berlioz and Wagner, *Eng. M.* for the *Britain in Pictures* series ed. by him, &c.

Turner, William (b. Oxford, 1651; d. London, 13. I. 1740), Eng. ten. singer & comp. Chorister at Christ Church, Oxford, and later in the Chapel Royal in London, where he joined Blow and Humfrey in comp. the so-called 'club anthem.' Later became singer successively at Lincoln cath., St. Paul's cath. and Westminster Abbey. Mus.D., Cambridge, 1696. The singer Ann T. (?–1741), wife of John Robinson, was his youngest daughter.

Works incl. services, anthems (1 for Queen Anne's coronation); masque *Presumptuous Love*; songs for Durfey's *A Fond Husband* & *Madam Fickle*, Shadwell's *The Libertine*, Settle's *Pastor fido* & other plays; catches, songs, &c.

Turnhout, Gérard de (real name Gheert Jacques) (b. Turnhout, *c.* 1520; d. Madrid, 15. IX. 1580), Flem. singer & comp. He became a church singer at Antwerp in 1545 and chapel master of the cath. in 1562. In 1572 he was called into the service of Philip II at Madrid.

Works incl. masses & motets; chansons, &c.

Turnhout, Jean de (real name Jean Jacques) (b. ? Antwerp, ?; d. ?), Flem. 17th-cent. comp. son of prec. He became 2nd master in the royal chapel at Brussels *c.* 1610 and chapel master in 1618.

Works incl. motets, madrigals, &c.

Tusch (Ger.) = Fanfare. The word is prob. derived from Fr. *touche* (with the same source as the It. *toccare* and *toccata*) and is thus related to the Eng. Tucket.

Tut. A device in lute-playing: the damping of a note by a finger not used for stopping.

Tutchev. *See* **Tiutchev.**

Tutilo. *See* **Tuotilo.**

Tutti (It. = all). A term used, in the 1st place, to designate the singing and playing together of all the forces engaged in a mus. perf.; but it is also used for the purely orch. passages in a conc., where the solo inst. is silent, whether the whole orch. happens to be playing or only part of it. Used as a noun, the word means any passage in an orch. work in which the whole force is employed, esp. when playing at full strength.

Tvisöngur (Icelandic = twin songs). Ancient songs of Iceland, dating back beyond the 15th cent., sung in 2 parts in a primitive kind of ctpt. akin to Organum.

Twelfth. A $2\frac{2}{3}$-ft. org. stop prod. notes 12 diatonic degrees above those played.

Twelfth Mass. A mass long attrib. to Mozart and pub. as No. 12 by Novello in London; previously as No. 7 by Simrock of Mainz, who had received a MS. from a m. teacher named Carl Zulehner. It is unquestionably spurious.

Twelve-Note Music. The new system of comp. on which the later works by

Schoenberg and the m. of some of his disciples (e.g. Berg, Hauer, Křenek, Pisk, Webern, Wellesz) are based. It abolishes keys and with them the predominance of certain notes in a scale (tonic, dominant, subdominant and mediant), using instead the 12 notes of the chromatic scale, each of which has exactly the same importance as any other. This rules out any feeling of tonality and also discards the resource of modulation, so important to mus. structure in the classical sense. In order to make sure that no note assumes an even temporary predominance, the rule has been established that a mus. theme must invariably consist of all the 12 notes of the chromatic scale, and that each note must appear only once in its course (transposition into any 8ve being allowed); but this does not mean that all melodic patterns of T.-N. M. are necessarily of the same length, for they may be given any rhythmic shape the comp. desires, and these shapes may be varied throughout a work, though the order of the notes, once determined at his desire, may not. By way of change, however, 2 or more of the 12 notes may appear simultaneously instead of successively. Moreover, 3 ways of achieving melodic as distinct from rhythmic or harmonic variety are open to the comp.: he may (1) restate his theme inverted (i.e. turned upside down), (2) in reverse or *cancrizans* (i.e. turned backwards) or (3) inverted and reversed at the same time. That this very severely limits the comp. is not disputed by the advocates of T.-N. M., but they contend that some rules must be imposed if m. is not to become merely chaotic. Adversaries hold that to estab. new rules more tyrannical than those which are rejected can only result in some kind of mus. mathematics, to which the defence would retort that there is much beauty in mathematics. It is too early to decide whether T.-N. M. is likely to estab. itself permanently, but it seems certain that it will never do so exclusively, as the maj.-min. diatonic system did estab. itself in Eur. for at least 3 cents. For the moment one may reasonably decide that, while obviously bad T.-N. M. is no better than any other bad m., the best exs. of it so far have shown that the system imposes some kind of mental discipline on a comp. that may result in work of character and power, in spite of the evident fact that its ingenious devices, fascinating to the eye on paper, remain quite undiscoverable to the ear in perf. The final test. then, as in all m., must be sought, not in technique but in a comp.'s inspiration, and whether many comps. in the future will be inspired by this system remains to be seen.

Twilight of the Gods, The (Wagner, better *Dusk of the Gods*). *See* **Ring des Nibelungen.**

Twin Songs. *See* **Tvisöngur.**

Two Sisters, The, opera by **Rootham** (lib. by Marjorie Fausset, based on the ballad *The Twa Sisters o' Binnorie*), prod. Cambridge, 14. II. 1922.

Two Widows (*Dvě Vdovy*), opera by **Smetana** (lib. by Emanuel Züngel, based on a Fr. comedy by Pierre Jean Félicien Mallefille), prod. Prague, Cz. Theatre, 27. III. 1874.

Tye, Christopher (b. ? Ely or Cambridge, *c.* 1500; d. ? Doddington, ? III. 1573), Eng. comp. & poet. Learnt m. (?) as a choir-boy in King's Coll. chapel, Cambridge, and was certainly a lay-clerk there in 1537. In 1541 or 1542 he was app. choirmaster at Ely cath. and in 1545 he took the Mus.D. at Cambridge. He may have been m. master to Edward VI in 1544–50, and he was made a Gentleman of the Chapel Royal. In 1561 he resigned his post at Ely and was succeeded by R. White, (?) his son-in-law, and, having been ordained accepted the living at Doddington-cum-Marche in the Isle of Ely, and for some time later he held 2 other livings in the neighbourhood, but had to resign them, as well as Doddington, on account of carelessness in the matter of payments due. But he was at the latter place until the year before his death. He wrote a good deal of verse in his later years.

Works incl. masses, motets, services, anthems, *The Actes of the Apostles* in Eng. metrical versions set for 4 voices; In Nomines for insts., &c.

Tyl, Josef Kajetan (1808–56), Cz. dramatist. *See* **Kovařovic** (*Wood Nymph*), **Škroup** (*Fidlovačka*), **Švanda Dudák** (Hřimalý & Weinberger).

Tyl Owlglass. *See* **Till Eulenspiegel.**

Tymbal (from Fr. *timbale*). An early Eng. name for the kettledrum.

Tympani. *See* **Timpani,** which is correct It., where the letter Y is not used.

Tympanon (Fr.) = Dulcimer.

Tympanum (Lat.). *See* **Timpan.**

Tyndall, John (b. Leighlin Bridge, Co. Carlow, 2. VIII. 1820; d. London, 4. XII. 1893), Ir. physicist. His contrib. to m. is a book containing acoustical investigations and entitled *Sound.*

Typophone (Fr.) = Dulcitone.

Tyrolienne (Fr. fem. = Tyrolese). A

country dance similar to the *Ländler* or slow waltz, supposed to be native of the mountain regions of the Tyrol, but really an artificial growth introd. into ballets and operas and loosely based on melodic figurations imitating var. forms of Yodel. Ts. also became fashionable in the form of pf. pieces & songs, &c.

Tyrwhitt, Gerald. *See* **Berners, Lord.**

Tzigane (Fr., or tsigane). As gypsy or musn. of the bohemian world of Paris. The title of a rhapsody for v. & pf. by Ravel comp. in 1924.

U

U. C. An abbr. occasionally used for *una corda* (one stg.), indicating the use of the damping Pedal in pf. m.

Uberti, Antonio (real name Anton Hubert) (b. Verona, 1697; d. Berlin, 20. I. 1783), Ger. singer. Pupil of Porpora and known as Porporino. He sang in It. opera in Ger. and became chamber singer to Frederick II of Prus. Among his pupils was Mara.

Uccellatori, Gli (*The Birdcatchers*), opera by Gassmann (lib. by Goldoni), prod. Venice, Teatro San Moisè, Carnival 1759.

Uccellini, Marco (b. Modena, *c.* 1610; d. Modena, ?), It. vst. & comp. Master of inst. m. at the ducal court of Modena in the 1640s and chapel master at Modena cath. then or later.

Works incl. opera *Gli eventi di Filandro ed Edessa*; prologues *La nave d'Enea* & *Giove di Elide fulminato*; psalms & litanies for voices & insts.; *Composizioni armoniche* & *Sinfonici concerti* for v. & other insts., *Sinfonie boscarecie* & sos. for v. & bass, &c.

Ugalde (*née* **Beaucé**), **Delphine** (b. Paris, 3. XII. 1829; d. Paris, 19. VII. 1910), Fr. sop. singer. Pupil of her mother, of Moreau-Sainti and prob. of Laure Cinti-Damoreau. Married the Spa. musn. Ugalde and made her 1st stage appearance at the Paris Opéra-Comique in 1848.

Ugarte, Floro (b. Buenos Aires, 15. IX. 1884), Arg. comp. Studied with Fourdrain in Paris and became a private m. teacher on his return in 1913 and prof. at the Nat. Cons. at Buenos Aires in 1924. He also became mus. dir. of the Teatro Colón, resigning in 1943.

Works incl. opera *Saika* & others; symph. poems & suites for orch.; inst. pieces, &c.

Ugolini, Vincenzo (b. Perugia, *c.* 1570; d. Rome, 6. V. 1638), It. comp. Pupil of Bernardino Nassini. Chapel master at the church of Santa Maria Maggiore in Rome, 1592–1603. He then retired after a severe illness, but in 1609 became chapel master at Benevento cath. and returned in 1616 to Rome, where after some other appts. he became Soriano's successor in the Julian Chapel in 1620 and chapel master of San Luigi dei Francesi in 1631, a post he had held in 1616–20.

Works incl. masses, motets, psalms & other church m.; madrigals, &c.

Uhland, Johann Ludwig (1787–1862), Ger. poet. *See* **Black Knight** (Elgar), **Humperdinck** (*Glück von Edenhall*), **Schoeck** (songs), **Schumann** (*Glück von E.*), **Strauss** (R.) (*Schloss am Meer*).

Uhlig, Theodor (b. Wurzen nr. Leipzig, 15. II. 1822; d. Dresden, 3. I. 1853), Ger. vst., author and comp. of theoret. works. Pupil of Schneider at Dessau. He entered the royal orch. at Dresden in 1841 and became an intimate friend of Wagner there.

Uilleann Pipes (Ir. =elbow pipes). Ir. bagpipes, wrongly known as 'Union Pipes,' the bellows of which are worked by the elbow.

Ukelele (lit. 'the jumping flea'). The Hawaiian guitar, introd. to the Sandwich Islands by the Port. in 1877 and more recently into Eur. as a popular inst. It has 4 gut stgs. and can be played from a notation resembling the old lute tablature.

'Ukrainian' Symphony (Tchaikovsky). *See* **'Little-Russian' Symphony.**

Ulibishev, Alexander Dimitrievitch (b. Dresden, 2. IV. 1794; d. nr. Nizhny-Novgorod, 2. II. 1858), Rus. writer on m. and amateur musn. As the son of a nobleman he served in the army and then lived in retirement on his estate, but was a good vst. and 4tet player. He made a special study of Mozart and pub. a work in 3 vols. on him, but disliked the late works of Beethoven and attacked Lenz's book on that master.

Ullmann, Viktor (b. Těšín, 1. I. 1898), Sudeten-Ger. comp. Pupil of Schoenberg in Vienna, later theatre cond. at Aussig and m. teacher in Prague.

Works incl. operas *Peer Gynt* (after Ibsen) & *Der Sturz des Antichrist*; Vars. & Double Fugue on a theme by Schoenberg for orch.; Octet, 2 stg. 4tets, &c.

Ullrich, Hermann (b. Mödling nr. Vienna, 15. VIII. 1888), Aus. comp. Studied in Vienna and at the Mozarteum at Salzburg.

Works incl. ballet-pantomime *Der erste Ball*; Sym. in F maj., symph. prologue to Machiavelli's *Mandragola*, symph. poem on Hauptmann's *Hanneles Himmelfahrt*, Little Suite in the Old Style for orch.; Vars. on a Romantic Theme for chamber orch.;

m. for stg. 4tet, Fantasy for v., hn. & pf., &c.

Ulrich, Hugo (b. Oppeln, Silesia, 26. XI. 1827; d. Berlin, 23. V. 1872), Ger. comp. & teacher. He lost his parents at the age of 12 and was sent to school at Breslau and Glogau. In 1846 he went to Berlin and was helped by Meyerbeer to study with Dehn. He had some success with his comps., lived in It. for some years from 1855, but was driven back to Berlin by poverty, taught there at Stern's Cons., but soon preferred to lead a precarious existence by making arrs. and picking up other casual work.

Works incl. opera *Bertrand de Born* (unfinished); Sym. in B min., *Symphonie triomphale* & 3rd Sym. (unfinished), 2 ovts. for orch.; stg. 4tet, pf. Trio; pf. pieces, &c.

Ultimo giorno di Pompei, L' (*The Last Day of Pompeii*), opera by Pacini (lib. by Andrea Leone Tottola, not founded on Bulwer-Lytton's novel, which was not then pub.), prod. Naples, Teatro San Carlo, 19. XI. 1825. Perf. London in 1831, it may have been heard by Bulwer-Lytton.

Ulysses (*see also* **Circe & Penelope**), opera by Keiser (lib. by Friedrich Maximilian Lersner), prod. (in Ger.) Copenhagen, at court, XI. 1722.

Umbreit, Karl Gottlieb (b. Rehstedt nr. Gotha, 9. I. 1763; d. Rehstedt, 28. IV. 1829), Ger. orgst. & comp. Pupil of Kittel. He was app. orgst. at Sonneborn, Coburg, and became a famous org. teacher.

Works incl. chorales, chorale-preludes, preludes and fugues, &c. for org.

Umělecká Beseda (Cz. =Society of Arts). An assoc. founded in Prague in 1863, for the encouragement of the arts, esp. nat. Cz. m.

Umlauf, Ignaz (b. Vienna, 1746; d. Mödling nr. Vienna, 8. VI. 1796), Aus. comp. He became a vst. in the orch. of the court theatres in 1772, cond. of the Ger. opera in 1778 and in 1789 2nd mus. dir. under Salieri at court, later 2nd cond. under Weigl at the Court Opera. In 1790 he accomp. Salieri to Frankfort o/M. for the coronation of Leopold II and must have met Mozart there.

Works incl. operas and plays with m. *Die Insel der Liebe*, *Welches ist die beste Nation?*, *Die Bergknappen*, *Die Apotheke*, *Die pucefarbenen Schuhe, oder Die schöne Schusterin*, *Das Irrlicht*, *Die glücklichen Jäger*, *Der Ring der Liebe* (sequel to Grétry's *Zémire et Azor*); incid. m. for *Der Oberamtmann und die Soldaten* (after Calderón's *L'alcalde de Falamea*). &c.

Umlauf, Michael (b. Vienna, 9. VIII. 1781; d. Baden nr. Vienna, 20. VI. 1842), Aus. cond. & comp., son of prec. Pupil of his father, became a vst. at the Opera and was cond. of the 2 court theatres in 1810–25 and again from 1840. On and after the revival of *Fidelio* in 1814 he assisted Beethoven, who was then too deaf to hear the orch., to conduct some of his maj. works.

Opera *Das Wirtshaus in Granada*, play with m. *Der Grenadier*; 12 ballets; church m.; pf. sos., &c.

Un ballo in maschera (Verdi). *See* **Ballo in maschera**, *also* **Gustave III** (Auber).

Un giorno di regno (Verdi). *See* Giorno di regno.

Una corda (It. =one stg.). A direction used by Beethoven and others in pf. m. to indicate the use of the Damping Pedal, which so shifts the hammers that they touch only a single stg. for each note, instead of 2 or 3.

Una cosa rara, o sia Bellezza ed onestà (*A Rare Thing, or Beauty and Honesty*), opera by Martín y Soler (lib. by Lorenzo da Ponte, based on a story by Luis Vélez de Guevara), prod. Vienna, Burg Theatre, 17. XI. 1786. Mozart quotes an air from it in the finale of the 2nd act of *Don Giovanni*.

Unda Maris (Lat. lit. sea-wave). An org. stop similar to the Voix céleste.

Undina, opera by Lvov (lib., in Rus., by Count Vladimir Alexandrovitch Sollogub, based on a Fr. lib. *La Marquise*, by Jules Henri Vernoy de Saint-Georges), prod. St. Petersburg, 20. IX. 1848.

Undine, opera by Karl Friedrich Girschner (1794–1860) (lib. by Friedrich de la Motte Fouqué, based on his own story of that name), prod. Danzig, 20. IV. 1837.

Opera by E. T. A. Hoffmann (lib. do.), prod. Berlin, Schauspielhaus, 3. VIII. 1816.

Opera by Lortzing (lib. by comp., based on Fouqué), prod. Magdeburg, 21. IV. 1845.

Unequal Temperament. A system of tuning, esp. on old keyboard insts., in which some of the accidentals were treated as sharps according to Just Intonation and some as flats (e.g. F♯, not G♭; B♭, not A♯). An attempt was thus made to make some of the more frequently used keys come nearer to just intonation than is possible in the tempered scale of the modern pf., but the result was also that the more extreme sharp and flat keys were out of tune. This is one of the reasons why these keys were rarely used by old comps.

Unequal Voices. A comp. for several voices which do not lie within the same compass is said to be for U. V.

Unfinished Symphony. Schubert's Sym. in B min., of which 2 mvts. only were completed, but which he clearly intended to carry on, since he sketched a few bars of a scherzo. He wished to dedicate a work to the Graz Mus. Soc. in 1822, and prob. desiring to do so quickly, he sent off the 2 mvts. to Anselm Hüttenbrenner there, doubtless intending to let 2 more follow. Only pressure of work or other preoccupations can have deterred him from completing it, or quite possibly he simply forgot to do so; the reason was certainly not, as is sometimes supposed, that he felt incapable of matching the 2 finished mvts. with 2 equally great ones. He was quite able to do this, and on the other hand there are finished works of his in which the later mvts. do fall off in quality. Hüttenbrenner kept the MS. to himself until his death in 1868 and it was pub. only after that date.

Other U. Ss. are Schubert's in E min. of 1821, Bruckner's No. 9, Borodin's No. 3 & Mahler's No. 10.

Unger, Caroline (b. Vienna, 28. X. 1803; d. nr. Florence, 23. III. 1877), Aus. con. singer. Pupil of Aloysia Lange, Mozart's sister-in-law, and Vogl in Vienna, where she made her 1st stage appearance in 1821. She sang the con. part, with Sontag as sop., in the 1st perf. of Beethoven's *Missa solemnis* in 1824. Later she sang in It. and Paris. In 1840 she married a Florentine named Sabatier and retired in 1843.

Unger, Georg (b. Leipzig, 6. III. 1837; d. Leipzig, 2. II. 1887), Ger. ten. singer. Studied theol. at first, but took to singing and made his 1st stage appearance at Leipzig in 1867. He was Wagner's 1st Siegfried in the prod. of the *Ring* at Bayreuth in 1876.

Unger, (Gustav) Hermann (b. Kamenz, Saxony, 26. X. 1886), Ger. comp. Studied in Munich and later with Reger at Meiningen.

Works incl. operas *Richmodis* & *Der Zauberhandschuh*; incid. m. for Shakespeare's *Tempest*, Kleist's *Penthesilea*, Hofmannsthal's *Der Tod und der Tor*, Hauptmann's *Hannele*, Unruh's *Heinrich aus Andernach* & many other plays; *Der Gott und die Bajadere* (Goethe) & *Old Ger. Songs* for chor. & orch.; 2 syms., Symph. Suite, suites *Night* & *Rustic Scenes*, *Pictures from the Orient* for orch.; Divertimento for stg. 4tet, stg. Trio, Trio for cl., va. & pf.; Vars. for 2 pfs.; pf. pieces; songs, partsongs, &c.

Unger, Max (b. Taura, Saxony, 28. V. 1883), Ger. cond., painter & mcolst. Studied at Chemnitz and at the Leipzig Cons., also attending Riemann's lectures at the Univ. After a visit to London to collect material for a work on Clementi, he ed. the *Neue Zeitschrift für Musik* in 1919–20 and in 1932 visited Zürich to study Hans Bodmer's Beethoven collection, of which he pub. a catalogue. He also wrote var. works on Beethoven research and one on Mendelssohn's relations with Eng.

Ungherese (It.) = Hungarian. 'All' u.' = in the Hung. manner.

Unichord. Another name for the Monochord.

Union Pipes. *See* **Uileann Pipes.**

Unison. 2 notes sounding together at the same pitch, or successions of notes so perf. Passages in 8ves are not in U., although they sound so; but they are quite correctly described as being in Octave U.

Univ. (abbr.) = University.

Unprepared Shake. *See* **Ornaments.**

Unruh, Fritz von (b. 1885), Ger. dramatist. *See* **Unger (H.)** (*Heinrich aus Andernach*).

Unterbrochene Opferfest, Das (*The Interrupted Sacrificial Feast*), opera by Winter (lib. by Franz Xaver Huber), prod. Vienna, Kärntnertor Theatre, 14. VI. 1796.

Up Bow. The motion of the bow in the playing of stg. insts. in the direction from the point to the heel.

Upbeat. An unstressed note or group of notes beginning a comp. and standing before the 1st bar-line, which indicates the 1st main accent. An old rule was that in notation a beat thus anticipated at the beginning should be cut off the final bar (e.g. a mvt. in common time beginning on the 4th beat would have only 3 beats in its last bar); but this is no longer strictly observed. The word U. derives, of course, from the act of beating time in cond., where opening notes before the bar-line are indicated by an upward motion; but a note or notes forming an anacrusis, i.e. an unstressed metrical limb beginning a comp. before the 1st bar accent, is called an U. even in m where the time is not actually beaten by a cond.

Upper Partials. *See* **Partials.**

Upright Piano. The ord. domestic pf. with its stgs. placed vertically, not horizontally as in the grand pf.

Urbani, Pietro (b. Milan, 1749; d. Dublin, XII. 1816), It. singer, m. pub. & comp. After a period in London he went to Glasgow in 1780 and to Edinburgh in 1784, singing Sco. songs and later pub. them with his own accomps., with words by Burns, with whom he made friends, and others. Towards the end of the cent. he became a m.-seller & pub., but *c.* 1810 he failed and went to Dublin, where he d. in poverty.

Works incl. operas *Il Farnace, Il trionfo di Clelia* & others; Sco. songs with accomps., &c.

Urbani, Valentino. *See* **Valentini.**

Urhan, Chrétien (b. Montjoie nr. Aix-la-Chapelle, 16. II. 1790; d. Belleville nr. Paris, 2. XI. 1845), Belg. vst., violist & comp. Learnt the v. from his father, was heard by the Empress Joséphine and sent by her to Paris with a recommend. to Lesueur. He joined the Opéra orch. in 1816 and in 1831 succeeded Baillot as leader. He played much in public, incl. the va. and va. d'amore, also in chamber m.

Works incl. 2 stg. 5tets, 2 5tets for 3 vas., co. & db. (with drums *ad lib.*) & other chamber m.; v. & pf. pieces; pf. works, incl. duets; songs & duets, &c.

Uribe-Holguin, Guillermo (b. Bogotá, 17. III. 1880), Colombian comp. Studied at home and with d'Indy at the Schola Cantorum in Paris. In 1910 he became dir. of the Nat. Cons. at Bogotá, where he founded and cond. sym. concerts.

Works incl. Requiem; Sym. in F min., *Sinfonía del terruño, 3 Danzas, Carnavalesca, Marche funèbre, Marche de fête, Suite típica* for orch.; Conc. & *Villanesca* for pf. & orch., v. Conc.; 3 stg. 4tets, pf. 4tet, 2 pf. 5tets; 5 v. & pf. sos., 2 co. & pf. sos.; pf. pieces, incl. 300 folk dances; songs, &c.

Urio, Francesco Antonio (b. Milan, ?; d. ?), It. 17th–18th-cent. comp. Worked at (?) Bologna, later in Rome and as chapel master of the Frari church at Venice. Handel used passages from his Te Deum in the Dettingen Te Deum, *Saul, Israel in Egypt* & *L'Allegro*.

Works incl. Te Deum, motets for 2–4 voices and insts., psalms for 3 voices & insts., *Tantum ergo* for sop. & insts., orats., &c.

Urlar. The name of the themes on which the bagpipe vars. of the Pibroch are founded.

Urlus, Jacques (b. Hergenrath, 9. I. 1867; d. Noordwijk-aan-Zee, 6. VI. 1935), Dutch ten. singer. Studied at the Amsterdam Cons. and made his 1st appearance at Utrecht in 1887. He then studied opera and made his stage début there in 1894. Becoming a Wagnerian singer, he was soon invited to Bayreuth, and in 1910 he 1st visited London.

Uruguayan Composers. *See* **Broqua, Pedrell (C.).**

Usandizaga, José María (b. San Sebastián, 31. III. 1887; d. Yanthi, 5. X. 1915), Basque comp. Studied at the Schola Cantorum in Paris.

Works incl. operas *Mendy-Mendiyan, Las Golondrinas* & *La Llama*; works for chor. & orch.; stg. 4tet, &c.

Usiglio, Emilio (b. Parma, 8. I. 1841; d. Milan, 7. VII. 1910), It. cond. & comp. Pupil of Mabellini.

Works incl. operas *Le educande di Sorrento, Le donne curiose* (after Goldoni) & 6 others; many ballets; chamber m., &c.

Usper, Francesco (real name Spongia, Sponga or Sponza) (b. Parenzo, ?; d. Venice, ?), It. 16th–17th-cent. priest, orgst. & comp. Pupil of Monteverdi. In the 1610s he became orgst. at the church of San Salvatore at Venice, in 1621 he deputized for Grillo as orgst. at St. Mark's and in the 1620s he became principal of the school of St. John the Evangelist.

Works incl. masses, motets, psalms, &c. for voices with insts., vesper psalms for 4–8 voices & bass, some for double choir; *La battaglia* for voices & insts.; madrigals; ricercari and arie francesi in 4 parts, &c.

Ut. The old name for the note C, still used in Fr., but elsewhere replaced by Do. For its origin *see* **Solmization.**

Uthal, opera by Méhul (lib. by Jacques Maximilien Benjamin Bins de Saint-Victor, based on Ossian), prod. Paris, Opéra-Comique, 17. V. 1806. The work is scored without violins.

Utility Music. *See* **Gebrauchsmusik,** the Ger. term having been adopted by Eng. musns.

Utopia (Limited), or The Flowers of Progress, operetta by Sullivan (lib. by W. S. Gilbert), prod. London, Savoy Theatre, 7. X. 1893.

Utrecht Te Deum and Jubilate, a T. D. and J. by Handel, comp. for the celebration of the Peace of Utrecht and perf. London, St. Paul's cath., 7. VII. 1713.

Uttendal, Alexander (b. ?; d. Innsbruck, 8. V. 1581), Flem. comp. Learnt m. as a choir-boy in the Archduke Ferdinand's chapel in Prague, and in 1568 became a singer in his chapel at Innsbruck. In 1573 he received the title of court comp. and soon afterwards became 2nd chapel master. On the death of Scandello at Dresden in 1580 he was offered the post of chapel master to the Saxon court, but declined it.

Works incl. masses, motets, *Sacrae cantiones*; secular Fr. & Ger. songs for voices & insts., &c.

Uttini, Francesco (Antonio Baldassare) (b. Bologna, 1723; d. Stockholm, 25. X. 1795), It. singer &

comp. Pupil of Sandoni and Perti at Bologna, where he became a member of the Philh. Acad. in 1743. In 1753 he was at the Dan. court in Copenhagen, gave a concert at Hamburg in 1754, and in 1767 became court mus. dir. at Stockholm.

Works incl. *Il rè pastore* & several other It., Fr. and Dan. operas, Swe. operas *Thetis and Peleus*, *Aline*; incid. m. to Racine's *Athalie* & *Iphigénie* & other plays; 3 syms.; sos. for 2 vs. & bass, co. So.; hpchd. So., &c.

V

V. (abbr.) = Violin.

V.S. (abbr.) = *volti subito* (It. = turn at once). This is often written in MS. m. where a blank space is left at the bottom of a page to avoid turning over during the perf. of what follows on the next.

Va. (abbr.) = Viola.

Vaccai, Nicola (old spelling Vaccaj) (b. Tolentino, 15. III. 1790; d. Pesaro, 5. VIII. 1848), It. comp. He went to school at Pesaro, then studied law in Rome, but at the age of 17 or 18 gave it up for m. and studied ctpt. with Jannaconi. In 1811 he went to Paisiello at Naples for dramatic comp. and in 1815 prod. his 1st opera there. He then lived at Venice for 7 years, prod. 2 operas there, afterwards taught singing at Trieste and Vienna, in 1824 prod. 2 operas at Parma and Turin and in 1825 had his greatest success, at Milan, with a work on Shakespeare's *Romeo and Juliet*. In 1829–31 he lived in Paris and afterwards briefly in London, which he visited again in 1833–4. In 1838 he succeeded Basili as dir. of the Milan Cons., retiring to Pesaro in 1844.

Works incl. operas *I solitari di Scozia, Pietro il grande, La pastorella feudataria, Giulietta e Romeo, Marco Visconti, Giovanna Grey, Virginia, Giovanna d'Arco, La sposa di Messina* (both after Schiller) & others; church m.; cantata on the death of Malibran & others; *Ariette per camera* for voice & pf., &c.

Vaccari, Francesco (b. Modena, 1773; d. Lisbon, after 1823), It. vst. Pupil of Nardini at Florence. He soon began to play with great success all over It., then went to Spa., and later appeared in Paris, Ger., London, Spa. and Port. Wrote v. m., incl. vars. on 'God save the King.'

Vachon, Pierre (b. Arles, 1731; d. Berlin, 1802), Fr. vst. & comp. Studied at the Paris Cons. and 1st appeared there in 1758, at a Concert spirituel, with a conc. of his own. He visited London in 1772 and toured Ger. in 1784, when he was app. dir. of the court m. in Berlin.

Works incl. operas *Les Femmes et le secret, Sara, ou La Fermière écossaise, Hippomène et Atalante, Ésope à Cythère, Renaud d'Ast* (both with J. C. Trial); v. concs.; chamber m.; sos. for v. & bass, &c.

Vacqueras, Beltrame (also known as Bertrandus or Bernardus de Crassia) (b. ?; d. ?), Spa. 15th–16th-cent. singer & comp. He was in the Papal Chapel in Rome in 1483–1507. Comp. masses, motets, psalms, chansons, &c.

Vactor, David van (b. Plymouth, Indiana, 1906), Amer. flst. & comp. Studied at the North Western Univ. School of M., later fl. with Moyse and comp. with Dukas in Paris. On his return to Amer. he joined the teaching staff of his univ.

Works incl. ballet *The Play of Words*; symph. prelude to Poe's *Masque of the Red Death*, Ovt. *Cristobal Colón*, Ovt. to a Comedy, 5 small pieces, Passacaglia and Fugue for orch.; Chaconne for stg. orch.; *Concerto grosso* for 3 fls. & hp., fl. Conc.; 5tet for fl. & stgs., Suite for 2 fls., *Nachtlied* for sop. & stg. 4tet, &c.

Vaet, Jacobus (b. ?; d. Vienna, 8. I. 1567), Flem. comp. He was choirmaster to Maximilian, King of Boh., in the 1560s and in 1564 became chief mus. dir. in Vienna, a post formerly held by Jachet Buus, when his patron became the Emperor Maximilian II.

Works incl. masses, motets, magnificats, Te Deum for 8 voices & other church m.; chansons, &c.

Vagans (Lat. = wandering, vagrant). A *cantus firmus* consisting of a short phrase continually repeated while a polyphonic fabric of other voices develops round it. Its name is due to the fact that it did not necessarily keep to the ten. part.

Vagierender Akkord. *See* **Vagrant Chord.**

Vagrant Chord. A term coined in Ger. (as above) by Schoenberg to describe chromatic chords which confuse or lead away from any definite key-centre.

Vaisseau-fantôme, Le (*The Phantom Vessel*), opera by Dietsch (lib. by Bénédict Henri Révoil and Paul Henri Foucher, founded on Wagner's scenario for *The Flying Dutchman*, intended for an opera of his own to be prod. at the Opéra, which however accepted the lib. only and had it set by D.), prod. Paris, Opéra, 9. XI. 1842.

Vakula the Smith (*Vakula Kuznets*), opera by Tchaikovsky (lib. by

Yakov Petrovitch Polonsky, based on Gogol's *Christmas Eve*), prod. St. Petersburg, 6. XII. 1876; revised version entitled *Tcherevitchki* (*The Little Shoes*), prod. Moscow, 31. I. 1887. It is also known as *Oxana's Caprices*.

Valen, Fartein Olav (b. Stavanger, 25. VIII. 1887), Norw. comp. Studied languages at Oslo Univ., but later entered the Cons., finishing his studies with Reger at the Hochschule für Musik in Berlin. In 1925–35 he was in the m. dept. of the library of Oslo Univ., but was then made the recipient of a govt. grant for comp.

Works incl. *Pastorale, Sonetto di Michelangelo, To Hope* (after Keats) for orch.; motets for mixed chor.; 2 stg. 4tets, pf. Trio; v. & pf. So.; songs for sop. & orch.; pf. So. & pieces; songs to words by Goethe, &c.

Valentini (Valentino Urbani) (b. ?; d. ?), It. 17th–18th-cent. male con. singer, later a counter-ten. 1st went to London in 1707.

Valentini, Giovanni (b. ?; d. ? Vienna, IV. 1649), It. orgst. & comp. Early in the cent. he was orgst. to the Archduke Ferdinand at Graz, and on his patron's succession to the title of Emperor Ferdinand II in 1619 remained in his service. He was later in that of Ferdinand III.

Works incl. masses, motets & other church m.; madrigals, *Musiche a 2 voci*, &c.

Valentini, Giuseppe (b. ? Rome, 1681; d. ?), It. comp. In the service of the Grand Duke of Tuscany at Florence from *c.* 1735.

Works incl. opera *La costanza in amore*; orats. *Absalone* & *S. Alessio*; Concerti grossi; syms., *Bizzarrie*, 12 fantasies, *Idee per camera* & 12 sos. for 3 stg. insts. & bass; chamber sos. and *Alletamenti* for v., co. & bass, &c.

Valentini, Pietro Francesco (b. Rome, *c.* 1570; d. Rome, 1654), It. comp. Pupil of G. M. Nanini in Rome.

Works incl. operas (*favole*) *La mitra* & *La trasformazione di Dafne*; motets, litanies & other church m.; *Canzonetti spirituali* & *Musiche spirituali* for the Nativity; madrigals & canons; canzoni & arias for 1–2 voices, &c.

Valenzuela, Pedro (b. ?; d. ?), Spa. 16th-cent. comp. He lived in It., was cantor at St. Mark's, Venice, and cond. to the Phil. Acad. at Verona.

Works incl. madrigals, &c.

Valera y Alcalá Galiano, Juan (1824–1905), Spa. novelist. *See* **Pepita Jiménez** (Albéniz).

Valeriano (surname Pellegrini) (b. ?; d. ?), It. 17th–18th-cent. counter-ten. singer. Attached to the court of the Elector Palatine in Ger. before 1712, when he visited London, leaving the following year.

Valéry, Paul (1871–1945), Fr. poet. *See* **Fourestier** (*Orchestique*), **Honegger** (*Amphion*).

Valesi, Johann Evangelist (real name Wallishauser) (b. Unterhattenhofen, Bavaria, 28. IV. 1735; d. Munich, 1811), Ger. singer. Chamber singer to the Elector of Bavaria from 1756, later studied in It. and sang there with success. Weber was his pupil for a short time in 1798.

Valkyrie, The (*Die Walküre*, Wagner). *See* **Ring des Nibelungen.**

Vallas, Léon (b. Roanne, Loire, 17. V. 1879), Fr. mcolst. Studied medicine and literature at Lyons Univ. and in 1903 founded a mus. paper there which in 1912 became the *Revue française de musique*, and in 1920 he started the *Nouvelle Revue musicale*. He lectured on mus. hist. at Lyons Univ. in 1908–11, at the Cons. there in 1912–31 and at the Sorbonne in Paris in 1929–30. In 1939 he became mus. dir. of the wireless station at Lyons and president of the Société Française de Musicologie. His books incl. studies of the hist. of m. at Lyons and 2 works on Debussy.

Valledor, Jacinto (b. Cadiz, *c.* 1744; d. Madrid, 1809), Spa. comp. Settled in Madrid and wrote tonadillas & other works for the stage, incl. *La decantada vida y muerte del General Malbrú*, &c.

Vallotti, Francesco Antonio (b. Vercelli, 11. VI. 1697; d. Padua, 10. I. 1780), It. orgst., teacher & comp. He became 3rd orgst. at the church of Sant' Antonio at Padua in 1722 and chief orgst. in 1730. He wrote a learned treatise, *Della scienza teoretica e pratica della moderna musica*.

Works incl. motets, Requiem for Tartini & other church m., &c.

Valls, Josep (b. Barcelona, 1904), Spa. comp. Educ. at the Orfeo Català. In 1920 he decided to make m. his career, studied under Joan Salvat, then at the Barcelona Cons. and finally with d'Indy at the Schola Cantorum in Paris.

Works incl. sym. *The Song of Deborah*; Conc. for stg. 4tet & orch., Vars. for pf. & orch.; st. Trio, *La inutil ofrena* for voice, fl. & co.; Sonatina for pf.; songs, &c

Valse. *See* **Waltz.**

Valse à deux temps (Fr. = waltz in two-time). The term is not strictly accurate, since a waltz must always be in triple time; but it describes a type of waltz in which each note of the melody takes the time of 2 beats, each 3 notes thus occupying 2 bars and falling alternately on beats 1, 3 and 2 in cross-rhythm. Familiar examples occur in the waltz in Gounod's *Faust*, many of Tchaikovsky's waltzes (*Eugene Onegin*, the ballets and *Christmas* in *The Seasons* for pf.), Liadov's *Musical Box*, &c. The finale of Schumann's pf. Conc., though not a waltz, contains a famous passage of that kind of augmented triple rhythm, with some additional complications. This rhythm is a special feature of the Bohemian dance known as the Furiant, such as that in Smetana's *Bartered Bride* (Act II) and Dvořák's *Slavonic Dance* in G min., Op. 46 No. 8. The name of V. à d. t. might be much more properly applied to a waltz with a tune of 2 dotted crotchets to the bar, e.g. Chopin's Op. 42.

Valse, La, chgph. poem for orch. by Ravel, finished 1920 and 1st perf. Paris, 12. XII. 1920. It imitates or parodies the style of J. Strauss's waltzes and has several times served for ballets, as its description shows that it was intended to do.

Valses nobles et sentimentales. A set of waltzes by Ravel, comp. in 1911 and afterwds. scored for orch. The title is derived from Schubert, who pub. 2 sets: *Valses nobles*, Op. 77, and *Valses sentimentales*, Op. 50. R.'s work was turned into a ballet, *Adélaïde, ou Le Langage des fleurs*, prod. Paris, 22. IV. 1912.

Valverde, Joaquín (b. Badajoz, 27. II. 1846; d. Madrid, 17. III. 1910), Spa. flst., cond. & comp. He played the fl. in theatre orchs., became theatre cond. at Madrid in 1871 and fl. prof. at the Cons. in 1879.

Works incl. operettas *La gran via* (with Chueca), *Cadiz*, &c.

Valves. The keys added to brass wind insts., invented early in the 19th cent. to make it possible for hns., tpts., cornets, &c. to prod. the complete chromatic scale instead of only the natural harmonics. Trombs. alone, already prod. this scale by means of their slides, need no Vs., although they have been exceptionally and not very successfully added to facilitate perf.

Vamping. A colloq. term for the practice of accomp. in the most primitive way by improvisation, more partic. the playing of introds. to popular or m.-hall songs with stereotyped figures of accomp. until the singer is ready to fall in. The direction for this is 'vamp till ready.'

Vampyr, Der (*The Vampire*), opera by Lindpaintner (lib. by Cäsar Max Heigel, based on John William Polidori's story, pub. in 1819 and thought to be by Byron, and more directly on a Fr. melodrama by Charles Nodier, Pierre François Adrien Carmouche & Achille de Jouffroy), prod. Stuttgart, 21. IX. 1828.

Opera by Marschner (lib. by Wilhelm August Wohlbrück, based on the sources above), prod. Leipzig, 29. III. 1828.

Van; van den; van der. Dutch & Flem. names with these prefixes appear under the initials of the principal names.

Vanbrugh, John (1664–1726), Eng. dramatist & architect of Flem. descent. *See* **Carey** (*The Provoked Husband*), **Finger** (*Pilgrim*), **Leveridge** (*Aesop*), **Purcell (D.)** (*Pilgrim* & *Relapse*).

Vanhall. *See* **Wanhal.**

Var. (abbr.) = Varied, various.

Varèse, Edgar (b. Paris, 22. XII. 1885), Fr. (Americanized) comp. Pupil of d'Indy and Roussel at the Schola Cantorum in Paris and of Widor at the Cons. He cond. chor. & orch. m. in Paris, Berlin and Prague until 1914, when he joined the Fr. army to take part in the 1st world war; but he was discharged for reasons of health in 1915 and settled in U.S.A. in 1916. He did much to advance the cultivation of modern m. in N.Y. and joined Salzedo in 1921 to found the Internat. Comps. Guild.

Works incl. Sym. with chor.; *Amériques*, *Arcana* & *Espaces* for orch.; *Hyperprism* for wind & perc., *Ionisation* for perc.; *Intégrales* for chamber orch.; *Metal* for sop. & orch.; *Equatorial* for bar., brass, org., perc. and theremin, &c.

Varesi, Felice (b. Calais, 1813; d. Milan, 13. III. 1889), It. bar. singer. Studied at Milan. He was Verdi's 1st Macbeth in 1847, 1st Rigoletto in 1851 and 1st Germont, père, in 1853, and did not visit London until 1864.

Variations. One of the important mus. forms, the principle of which is the statement of a theme followed by varied treatments of it, sometimes with a restatement of the theme in its 1st form at the end (e.g. Bach's 'Goldberg' Vars.), sometimes with a more elaborate final section, such as a fugue (e.g. Beethoven's 'Eroica' Vars. for pf. or Brahms's Handel Vars. for pf.), a passacaglia (e.g. Brahms's Haydn Vars. for 2 pfs. or orch.). There is at least one instance (d'Indy's *Istar*) where the theme does not appear in its primitive form until the end. Historically the V. principle goes back as for as inst. m., but sets of Vs. 1st emerge towards the end of the 16th cent., esp. in Eng. and Spa. The Eng. virginal masters wrote sets on popular tunes for their inst. and another favoured medium for Vs. was the lute. In 17th-cent. Eng. Vs. were called Divisions, because they split up the theme into smaller rhythmic patterns, and they could be based on a Ground, i.e. an unchanging bass. The later hist. of the form continues to show the 2 different tendencies of (1) varying the tune and (2) maintaining the foundation of the same bass, with greater or lesser incidental changes while the superstructure can be handled very freely and need not keep to the melodic line of the theme at all. Mozart's Vs., for ex., are predominantly melodic, and so are Beethoven's earlier sets, but the latter reverts to the 'ground' type by keeping chiefly to the harmonic framework in such a work as the 'Diabelli' Vs., and in the 32 Vs. for pf. he keeps so close to the bass that the work is more like a Passacaglia, which is true also of the finale of Brahms's 4th Sym. In Elgar's 'Enigma' Vs. for orch., each of which represents a portrait of one of the comp.'s friends, and in R. Strauss's *Don Quixote*, the form is complicated by an element of Programme M.

Variations on a Russian Theme. A set of pf. vars. on a Rus. folksong by Blumenfeld, Glazunov, Liadov, Rimsky-Korsakov, Sokolov, Wihtol & Winkler.

Variations on a Theme by Handel (Brahms). *See* **'Handel' Variations.**

Variations on a Theme by Haydn (Brahms). *See* **'Haydn' Variations.**

Varlamov, Alexander Igorovitch (b. Moscow, 27. XI. 1801; d. St. Petersburg, X. 1848), Rus. comp. Learnt m. as a choir-boy in the court chapel at St. Petersburg, where Bortniansky became interested in his mus. educ. He left in 1819 and went to The Hague as mus. dir. of the Rus. embassy chapel and became attached to the court of the Princess of Orange, Anna Pavlovna, who was a Rus. Returning home in 1823, he settled at Moscow, where he taught, and he spent his last years alternately there and at St. Petersburg.

Works incl. 223 songs, e.g. *The Red Sarafan*, &c.

Varney, Louis (b. Paris, 1844; d. Cauterets, 20. VIII. 1908), Fr. comp. Pupil of his father.

Works incl. operettas *Les Mousquetaires au couvent*, *Les Forains*, *Le Pompier de service*, *Les Demoiselles de Saint-Cyr* & over 30 others, &c.

Varney, Pierre (Joseph Alphonse) (b. Paris, 1. XII. 1811; d. Paris, 7. II. 1879), Fr. cond. & comp., father of prec. Studied at the Paris Cons. and became cond. at var. theatres there, also at different times at The Hague, Ghent, Rouen and Bordeaux. In 1848 he set Dumas's words for the Chant des Girondins, 'Mourir pour la patrie.' He also wrote operas and operettas.

Vars. (abbr.) = Variations.

Varsoviana (It.) or **Varsovienne** (Fr.), An alleged Pol. dance, but prob. of Fr. orig., appearing 1st in Paris in the middle of the 19th cent. It is in 3-4 time and resembles the Mazurka. The name is, of course, der. from Warsaw.

Vasquez, Juan (b. Badajoz, ?; d. ?), Spa. 16th-cent. comp. Studied at Seville and (?) became chapel master at Burgos. Comp. service for the dead, villancicos for 3-5 voices (1 part being often a folksong), &c.

Vassilenko, Sergey Nikiforovitch (b. Moscow, 30. III. 1872), Rus. comp. After receiving private lessons from Gretchaninov and Konius, and studying law, he entered the Moscow Cons. in 1895, studying comp. with Taneiev and Ippolitov-Ivanov. In 1905 he taught there and was soon app. full prof. He organized and cond. histor. concerts.

Works incl. operas *The Legend of the Holy City of Kitezh*, *The Son of the Sun*, *Christopher Columbus*, *Suvarov*, &c.; ballets *Joseph the Beautiful*, *The Gypsies* (after Pushkin), &c.; 2 syms., *Epic Poem*, symph. poem on Oscar Wilde's *The Garden of Death* & others & suite *In the Sun* & others, *Three Bloody Battles* (after Tolstoy) & other orch. works; v. Conc.; cantata for the 20th anniversary of the Oct. Revol.; 4 stg. 4tets, woodwind 4tet, pf. Trio & other chamber m.; va. & pf. So.; songs, folksong arrs., &c.

Vaterländischer Künstlerverein (Ger. = *Patriotic Artists' Association*). The title of Part II of the Vars. commissioned by Cappi & Diabelli of Vienna to be written by Beethoven and others on a waltz by Diabelli. Beethoven eventually wrote 33 vars. instead of 1, and they were pub. separately as Part I in 1824, Part II following with contribs. by Czerny, Hummel, Kalkbrenner, C. Kreutzer, Liszt (aged 11), Moscheles, W. A. Mozart, jun., the Archduke Rudolph, Schubert, Sechter & *c.* 40 others.

Vatielli, Francesco (b. Pesaro, 1. I. 1877), It. mcolst. & comp. Studied philosophy at Bologna Univ., but took a private course in m. as well, later entered the Pesaro Cons. and became a pupil of Mascagni. In 1905 he joined the staff of the Liceo Musicale of Bologna. His books incl. hist. studies of m. at Pesaro and

Bologna, 1 of 16th-cent. song-books, &c. He has ed. much old It. m.

Works incl. incid. m. for Poliziano's *Favola di Orfeo*; pf. pieces; songs, &c.

Vaudeville (Fr.). A term with var. meanings and of uncertain origin. Le Roy, in his *Airs de Cour* of 1571, says that such songs were formerly called 'voix de ville' (town voices); but the form 'vau de Vire' is also known, which may have referred to the valley of Vire in Normandy, the home of Olivier Basselin (*c.* 1400–50), a comp. of such songs. In 18th-cent. Fr. Vs. were at first satirical songs, then songs with words set to popular tunes used in comedies with m. (*comédies mêlées de vaudevilles*), as in the Eng. ballad opera (songs specially comp. being called *ariettes*). In time Vs. in Fr. became songs sung at the end of spoken stage pieces, taken up verse by verse by all the characters and sometimes by the chor., and this device was sometimes introd. into opera, in Fr. and elsewhere, as for ex. at the end of Rousseau's *Devin du village* and Mozart's *Entführung aus dem Serail*. The next step from this was to call a whole light mus. stage entertainment a V.

Vaughan, Henry (1622–95), Anglo-Welsh poet. **Rubbra** (*Revival*).

Vaughan Williams, Ralph (b. Down Ampney, Glos., 12. X. 1872), Eng. comp. Son of a clergyman, he was educ. at Charterhouse School in London, 1887–90, and Trinity Coll., Cambridge, 1892–5, the intervening years being devoted to study at the R.C.M. in London, where he returned for another year after Cambridge. He learnt pf. and org. for the sake of usefulness, but was from the 1st determined to be a comp. But on leaving the R.C.M. in 1896 he became orgst. at South Lambeth church in London and saved enough money to gain further experience by study abroad, 1st at the Akademie der Künste in Berlin, under Bruch, and in 1909 with Ravel in Paris, though the Fr. comp. was younger than himself. In 1901 he took the Mus.D. at Cambridge. In 1904 he joined the Folk-Song Society and began to take an active share in the recovery and study of old country tunes, collecting some in Norfolk. His 1st great public success he made with *Toward the Unknown Region* at the Leeds Festival in 1907. In the 1914–8 war he first served as a private in Macedonia and Fr., but later rose to officer's rank, and after the declaration of peace he was app. prof. of comp. at the R.C.M. He was often represented at the festivals of the I.S.C.M. and in 1935 he had the Order of Merit conferred on him.

Works incl. operas *Hugh the Drover*, *The Shepherds of the Delectable Mountains* (after Bunyan), *Sir John in Love* (on Shakespeare's *Merry Wives*), *The Poisoned Kiss*, *Riders to the Sea* (Synge); masque for dancing *Job*, ballet *Old King Cole*; incid. m. to Ben Jonson's *Pan's Anniversary* & Aristophanes' *The Wasps*; film m. incl. *The People's Land*, *The Story of a Flemish Farm*; chor. & orch. works (some with solo voices): *Willow Wood*, *Toward the Unknown Region* (Whitman), *A Sea Symphony* (Whitman) (Sym. No. 1), *5 Mystical Songs* (George Herbert), *Fantasy on Christmas Carols*, orat. *Sancta Civitas*, *Benedicite*, *Magnificat*, *Dona nobis pacem*, *Five Tudor Portraits* (Skelton), *Flourish for a Coronation*, *Thanksgiving for Victory* (1945) for sop., speaker, chor. & orch.; *Serenade to Music* for 16 solo voices & orch. (from Shakespeare's *Merchant of Venice*); unaccomp. chor. works; *A London Symphony* (No. 2), *A Pastoral Symphony* (No. 3), syms. No. 4 in F min. & No. 5 in D maj., Serenade for small orch., *Bucolic Suite*, 2 orch. Impressions, 3 *Norfolk Rhapsodies*, *Fantasy on a Theme by Tallis*, for stgs.; *Flos campi*, for va. & orch., *Concerto accademico* & *The Lark Ascending* for v. & orch., *Fantasy on Sussex Folk Tunes* for co. & orch., pf. Conc., ob. Conc., Suite for va. & orch.; pf. 5tet in C min., 2 stg. 4tets, fantasy 5tet for stgs.; *On Wenlock Edge* (Housman) for ten., stg. 4tet & pf.; *The Lake in the Mountains* for pf. & Introduction & Fugue for 2 pfs.; some org. & pf. pieces; many songs incl. *Silent Noon* (Rossetti) and cycles, *The House of Life* (Rossetti) & *Songs of Travel* (Stevenson); some hymns incl. 'For all the Saints,' &c.

Vaurabourg, Andrée (b. Toulouse, 8. IX. 1894), Fr. comp. Studied at the Toulouse Cons. and in Paris, with Widor, Nadia Boulanger & others, also pf. with Pugno in 1908–13. She became attached as perf. to the group of 'Les Six' and married Honegger.

Works incl. *Prélude & Intérieur* for orch.; v. & pf. So.; songs, &c.

Vautor, Thomas (b. ? Leicestershire, ?; d. ?), Eng. 16th–17th-cent. comp. Educ. at Lincoln Coll., Oxford, where he took the B.Mus. in 1616. He was for many years in the service of Sir George Villiers, father of the later Duke of Buckingham, at Brooksby, and later of his widow at Goadby. Comp. madrigals.

Vavrinecz, Mauritius (b. Czegléd, 18. VII. 1858; d. Budapest, 5. VIII. 1913), Hung. comp. Studied at the

Budapest Cons. and with Volkmann and in 1886 became mus. dir. of Budapest cath.

Works incl. operas *Ratcliff* (after Heine) & *Rosamunde*; 5 masses, Requiem, *Stabat Mater*; orat. *Christus*; Sym., ovt. to Byron's *Bride of Abydos*, Dithyramb for orch., &c.

Vecchi, Lorenzo (b. Bologna, 1566; d. ? Bologna, ?), It. comp. He was a pupil at San Petronio cath. at Bologna, where he became chapel master in 1605. Comp. masses, Requiem & other church m.

Vecchi, Orazio (b. Modena, XII. 1550; d. Modena, 19. II. 1605), It. comp. He took holy orders and was made a canon at Correggio in 1586 and archdeacon in 1591; but he deserted to Modena and was deprived of his office in 1595. In 1596 he became chapel master of Modena cath. and in 1598 at the ducal court. He became famous, being summoned to the court of the Emperor Rudolph II at one time and invited to comp. m. for the king of Pol. In 1604 his pupil Geminiano Capi-Lupi intrigued successfully against him and supplanted him in his post.

Works incl. madrigal opera *L'Amfiparnaso*; masses, motets, lamentations & other church m.; madrigals, canzonets, &c.

Vecchi, Orfeo (b. Milan, *c.* 1540; d. Milan, before 1604), It. comp. Chapel master of the church of Santa Maria della Scala at Milan.

Works incl. masses, motets, psalms, magnificats, *Cantiones sacrae* & other church m.; madrigals, &c.

Veccia, Cesare (b. Palestrina, ?; d. Palestrina, 1593), It. musn. Pupil and prob. a kinsman of Palestrina, whose mother's family name he bore. He became orgst. at the church of St. Agapit at Palestrina.

Vecsey, Franz von (b. Budapest, 23. III. 1893; d. Rome, 6. IV. 1935), Hung. vst. Studied with Hubay and Joachim, and made a concert tour at the age of 10. He lived mainly in Ger.

Veerbecke di Fiandra (=of Flanders). *See* **Weerbecke.**

Vega (Carpio), Félix Lope de (1562–1635), Spa. poet & dramatist. *See* **Casal y Chapí, Khatchaturian** (*Widow of Valencia*), **Krein (A.)** (*Laurencia*), **Laserna, Peyra** (*Selva sin amor*), **Romero** (songs), **Vives** (*Doña Francisquita*), **Wolf-Ferrari** (*Dama boba*).

Veichtner, Franz Adam (b. Ratisbon, 1741; d. St. Petersburg, 1822), Ger. vst. & comp. Studied v. with F. Benda and comp. with Riepel. In the 1760s he went into the service of Count Kaiserling at Königsberg, in the 1770s he was leader of the Duke of Courland's orch. at Mitau, and after a visit to It. he became chapel master at St. Petersburg.

Works incl. opera *Scipio*; orat.; cantata *Cephalus und Procris* (words by Ramler); *c.* 60 syms.; v. Conc.; 3 stg. 4tets; 24 fantasies and 24 sos. for v. & bass, &c.

Veilchen, Das (*The Violet*), song by Mozart, K. 476: his only setting of a poem by Goethe, comp. 8. VI. 1785.

Veiled Prophet of Khorassan, The, opera by Stanford (lib. by William Barclay Squire, based on Moore's *Lalla Rookh*), prod., in Ger., Hanover, Court Theatre, 6. II. 1881; 1st London perf., in It., Covent Garden Theatre, 26. VII. 1893.

Veiled Voice. An affection of the throat in singers resulting in dullness of voc. tone, but sometimes an advantage, if not too pronounced, because it imparts an interesting quality of slight pathos to the voice. It may be temporary or permanent and due to var. causes, incl. fatigue, illness or faulty voice-prod.

Velasco Maidana, José Maria (b. La Paz, 4. VII. 1899), Boliv. comp. Studied v. and comp. at Buenos Aires and investigated Boliv. folk m. after his return home and became cond. of the Nat. Sym. Orch.

Works incl. ballet *Amerindia*; symph. legend *Cory Wara*, ovt. *Los hijos del sol*, symph. poem *Vida de Cóndores, Los Huacos, Los Khusillos* & *Cuento brujo* for orch., &c.

Velato (It. = veiled). Used in the fem. for above, *voce velata*.

Velluti, Giovanni Battista (b. Montolino [now Pausula] nr. Ancona, 28. I. 1780; d. Bruson o/Brenta, II. 1861), It. male sop. singer (one of the last). Made his 1st stage appearance at Forli in 1800. In 1812 he visited Vienna and in 1825 London.

Veloce (It. = quick, swift, rapid, fluent). The direction does not so much indicate increased speed, though it may include that meaning, as smoothness of rapid figuration.

Venatorini. The name sometimes given by the Its. to Mysliveček.

Vendemmia, La (*The Vintage*), opera by Gazzaniga (lib. by Giovanni Bertati, partly based on an earlier lib. of the same name by Goldoni), prod. Florence, Teatro della Pergola, 15. V. 1778.

Venegas de Henestrosa, Luys (b. ?; d. ?), Spa. 16th-cent. lutenist & comp. He pub. a book of vars. & transcriptions in a special tablature suitable for keyboard insts., hps., lutes & guitars.

Venetian Swell. Nothing to do with Venice or with the waters of the Adriatic: it is the term used for a device in the org. resembling a Venetian blind, the slats of which can be opened and shut more or less gradually and thus, letting through a greater or smaller volume of tone, create an artificial *crescendo* or *diminuendo*.

Venosa, Prince of. *See* **Gesualdo.**

Ventadorn, Bernart de (b. ?; d. ?, 1195), Fr. troubadour. 45 of his poems and 19 of his melodies have been preserved.

Ventil (Ger.) = Valve.

Vento, Ivo de (b. ?; d. Munich, 1575), (?) Flem. comp. In *c.* the 1560s he was app. chapel master to Duke William of Bavaria at Landshut and in 1569 he became orgst. in the ducal chapel at Munich under Lassus.

Works incl. motets; Ger. sacred & secular songs for several voices, &c.

Vento, Matteo (b. Naples, *c.* 1735; d. London, 22. XI. 1776), It. comp. At the invitation of Giardini he settled in London *c.* 1763.

Works incl. operas *L'Egiziana, Demofoonte, La conquista del Messico, Leucippo, Sofonisba, Il bacio, La vestale* & some others; cantata *Threnodia Augustalis* (Goldsmith) on the death of George III's mother; hpchd. lessons; songs & duets, &c.

Venturi (del Nibbio), Steffano (b. ? Venice, ?; d. ? Venice, ?), It. 16th-cent. comp. Wrote part of the chors. in Caccini's *Rapimento di Cefalo*, motets, madrigals, &c.

Venturini, Franciscus (b. ?; d. Hanover, 18. IV. 1745), (?) Fr. or It. vst. & comp. Pupil of J. B. Farinelli at Hanover, where he joined the electoral chapel in 1698 and succeeded his master as head of the inst. m. in 1713, later becoming court chapel master. He is said also to have been at the court of Württemberg at Stuttgart.

Works incl. chamber concs., 4 v. concs., ovts. for 8 & for 5 insts., v. sos., &c.

Venus, opera by Schoeck (lib. by Armin Rüeger, on Mérimée's story *La Vénus d'Ille*), prod. Zürich, 10. V. 1922.

Venus and Adonis, masque by Blow (lib. unknown), prod. London, at court, *c.* 1684.

Vénus et Adonis, opera by Desmarets (lib. by Jean Baptiste Rousseau), prod. Paris, Opéra, 17. III. 1697.

Vêpres siciliennes, Les (*The Sicilian Vespers*), opera by Verdi (lib. by Scribe & Charles Duveyrier), prod. Paris, Opéra, 13. VI. 1855. V.'s 1st Fr. opera, the only other set to Fr. words being *Don Carlos*. Prod. in It., as *Giovanna de Guzman*, Milan, Teatro alla Scala, 4. II. 1856, but later called *I vespri siciliani* there.

Veprik, Alexander Moiseievitch (b. Balta, 23. VII. 1899), Rus. comp. Studied with Reger at Leipzig, with Kalafati and Zhitomirsky at St. Petersburg and with Miaskovsky at Moscow. He also had some lessons from Janáček.

Works incl. 5 Episodes for chor. & orch.; *Songs and Dances of the Ghetto, A Song of Mourning, A Song of Joy* for orch.; *Songs of Death* for va. & pf.; 2 pf. sos., &c.

Vera costanza, La (*True Constancy*), opera by Anfossi (lib. by Francesco Puttini), prod. Rome, Teatro delle Dame, 2. I. 1776.

Opera by Haydn (lib. do., altered by Pietro Travaglia), prod. Esterház, spring 1779.

Vera Sheloga (Rimsky-Korsakov). *See* **Pskovitianka.**

Veracini, Antonio (b. Florence, *c.* 1650; d. ? Florence, ?), It. vst. & comp. Was in the service of the Grand Duchess Vittoria of Tuscany at Florence.

Works incl. *Sonate da chiesa* for v., co. & continuo, *Sonate da camera* for v. & violone or archlute & continuo, sos. for 2 vs. & do., &c.

Veracini, Francesco (Maria) (b. Florence, 1. II. 1690; d. nr. Pisa *c.* 1750), It. vst. & comp., nephew of prec. Studied with his uncle, settled at Venice, which Tartini left, dissatisfied with his own style of v. playing after comparing it with V.'s. He 1st visited Eng. in 1714, playing at concerts and leading the Opera orch. In 1717 he left for Dresden, where he was app. solo vst. to the Elector of Saxony. He threw himself out of a window there, prob. on account of a trick played on him by Pisendel, against whom he had intrigued, and lamed himself for life. In 1723 he left for Prague and returned to It. In 1735 he was in London again, prod. some operas, but as a vst. was overshadowed by Geminiani. He returned to It. *c.* 1745.

Works incl. operas *Adriano in Siria, La clemenza di Tito, Partenio, Rosalinda* (after Shakespeare's *As You Like It*), *L'errore di Salomone*; cantatas *Nice e Tirsi* & *Parla al ritratto dell' amante*; v. sos.; canons, arias, &c.

Verbonnet, Jean (b. ?; d. ?), Flem. 15th–16th-cent. comp.

Works incl. masses, *Salve Regina* & other church m.; *Dulces exuviae* from Virgil's *Aeneid* for 4 voices; songs for several voices, &c.

Verbunko. An 18th-cent. Hung. dance for soldiers, who perf. it in full uniform with swords and spurs. Like the later Csárdás, to which it is related, it contained a slow (*lassú*) and quick (*friss*) section.

Verdelot, Philippe (b. ?; d. ? Florence, ? 1567), Flem. singer & comp. He went to It., prob. at an early age, lived at Rome and was a singer at St. Mark's, Venice, and between 1530–40 m. master at the church of San Giovanni at Florence.

Works incl. masses, motets; *c.* 100 madrigals, &c.

Verdi, Giuseppe (Fortunino Francesco) (b. Le Roncole nr. Busseto, 10. X. 1813; d. Milan, 27. I. 1901), It. comp. Son of a poor innkeeper and grocer. He heard his 1st m. from strolling musns. in the village and at the local church, where he became a choir-boy at the age of 7 and was taught by the orgst., in whose place he was app. in 1823. At 11 he was sent to Busseto and went to school there, walking home twice a week to carry on the orgst.'s duties. Barezzi, a friend of V.'s father at Busseto, took him into his house in 1826, and he learnt much from the cath. orgst. Provesi. He had an ovt. perf. and comp. for military band in 1828, and the next year he wrote a Sym. and deputized for Provesi. In 1831 he was sent to Milan with a scholarship and some financial help from Barezzi, but rejected by the Cons. as over entrance age. He studied with Lavigna, the *maestro al cembalo* at the Scala Theatre. When Provesi d. in 1833 he tried for the post of cath. orgst., and when it was given to an inferior musn. the Phil. Soc. made him an allowance. In 1836 he married Barezzi's daughter, Margherita, by whom he had 2 children, but the whole family d. between 1838–40. Meanwhile he had comp. his 1st opera, *Oberto*, prod. at the Scala, 17. XI. 1839. A 2nd (comic) opera, *Un giorno di regno*, was a failure, having been comp. at the time of his bereavements; but *Nabucco*, prod. there in 1842, had a great success. In the cast was Giuseppina Strepponi, who became a great and loyal friend, and later on V.'s 2nd wife. He now went from strength to strength as an operatic comp. and his fame spread beyond Milan: *Ernani* was prod. at Venice in 1844, *I due Foscari* in Rome, 1844, *Alzira* at Naples, 1845 and *Macbeth* at Florence, 1847. Meanwhile *Ernani* had gone to Paris in 1846 and London commissioned *I masnadieri*, prod. there on 22. VII. 1847. Operas growing in mastery followed almost annually until 1871 and in his old age, after a long interval, he prod. his 2 great Shakespearian masterpieces. Apart from these prods. and frequent travels to var. Eur. countries V.'s life was uneventful, spent mostly at his estate of Sant' Agata nr. Busseto, which he bought in 1848. An opera on Shakespeare's *King Lear*, at which he worked intermittently, was never completed; otherwise all his plans materialized once they had taken definite shape. Fr., Rus. and Egypt offered him special commissions and his fame spread all over the world. He repres. It. at the Internat. Exhib. in London in 1862 and wrote a *Hymn of the Nations*. In 1868 he suggested a Requiem for Rossini, to be written by var. It. comps., but the plan came to nothing. He used his contrib. in 1873 for a Requiem of his own commemorating the death of Manzoni. *Otello* was prod. at the Scala, Milan, 5. II. 1887, and *Falstaff* at the same theatre, 9. II. 1893, when he was in his 80th year. Giuseppina d. in 1897 and he was himself growing very weak, but still wrote some sacred pieces for chor. & orch. in 1898–9.

Works incl. operas: *Oberto: Conte di San Bonifacio, Un giorno di regno, Nabucodonosor* (*Nabucco*), *I Lombardi alla prima crociata, Ernani, I due Foscari, Giovanna d'Arco, Alzira, Attila, Macbeth, I masnadieri, Jérusalem* (Fr. revised version of *I Lombardi*), *Il corsaro, La battaglia di Legnano, Luisa Miller, Stiffelio, Rigoletto, Il trovatore, La traviata, Les Vêpres siciliennes, Simon Boccanegra*; *Araldo* (revised as *Stiffelio*), *Un ballo in maschera, La forza del destino, Don Carlos, Aida, Otello, Falstaff*; chor. works *Inno delle nazioni*, Requiem, *Pater noster, Ave Maria, Stabat Mater, Laudi alla Vergine Maria*, Te Deum; *Ave Maria* for sop. & stgs.; 16 songs; 1 partsong; stg. 4tet, &c.

Verdi, Giuseppina. *See* **Strepponi.**

Verdonck, Cornelius (b. Turnhout, 1563; d. Antwerp, 4. VII. 1625), Flem. singer & comp. In the service of Corneille Pruenen, treasurer and later sheriff of Antwerp until 1598, when on the death of his patron he served 2 of his nephews. He (or ? a relative) was singer at the Spa. court in Madrid for a time.

Works incl. Magnificat, *Ave Maria* & other church m.; madrigals for 4–9 voices, *Poésies françoises* for 5–10 voices, &c.

Verecoren. *See* **Werrekoren.**

Veress, Sándor (b. Kolozsvár, Transylvania, 1. IX. 1907), Hung. pfst. & comp. Learnt the pf. from his mother and later entered the Budapest Cons. He also studied with Bartók and Kodály. In 1929 he studied at the Ethnological Museum and went collecting folksongs. He settled at Budapest as teacher of pf.

& comp. and asst. to Bartók at the Scientif. Acad. of Folk M.

Works incl. ballet *The Magic Flute*; 2 Partitas & Divertimento for orch.; v. Conc.; cantata & folksong arrs. for unaccomp. chor.; 2 stg. 4tets, stg. Trio, Trio for ob., cl. & bn.; v. & pf. So., co. & pf. So.; 2 pf. sos., &c.

Verga, Giovanni (1840–1922), It. novelist & playwright. *See* **Cavalleria rusticana** (Mascagni).

Verhaeren, Émile (1855–1916), Belg. poet & dramatist. *See* **Dobroven** (*Philip II*), **Goossens** (do.), **Séverac** (*Hélène de Sparte*).

Verheyen, Pierre (b. Ghent, 1750; d. Ghent, 11. I. 1819), Belg. ten. singer. & comp. Learnt m. from his father, a singer at the church of St. Bavon, Ghent. Having had lessons from another master, he sent to Maestricht for a preparatory Univ. course, but took to m., became a singer at Bruges cath., then went on the stage, and in 1786 became sole ten. at Ghent cath. After further vicissitudes, complicated by the Fr. Revol., he returned there early in the 19th cent.

Works incl. operas *Arlequin magicien*, *Les Chevaliers, ou Le Prix de l'arc* & *De Jachtpartij van Hendrik IV*; masses, psalms, Requiem for Haydn, Te Deum & other church m.; cantata *La Bataille de Waterloo*, &c.

Verhulst, Johannes (Josephus Herman) (b. The Hague, 19. III. 1816; d. The Hague, 17. I. 1891), Dutch comp. & cond. Studied at The Hague Royal School of M. and after some work as vst. at the Opera at Cologne, went to Leipzig in 1838, became cond. of the Euterpe concerts and made friends with Mendelssohn and Schumann. In 1842 he returned to The Hague as court mus. dir. and also cond. important mus. socs. at Amsterdam and Rotterdam.

Works incl. Requiem for male voices & other church m.; syms., ovts., intermezzo *Greetings from Afar* for orch.; stg. 4tets; songs; part-songs, &c.

Verismo (It. = realism). A term used to classify It. opera of a supposedly 'realistic' order, incl. the works of Puccini, Mascagni, Leoncavallo, Giordani, Zandonai, &c.

Verklärte Nacht (*Transfigured Night*), stg. 6tet by Schoenberg, Op. 4, comp. IX. 1899, arr. for stg. orch. *c.* 1920, revised 1943. It was inspired by a poem in Richard Dehmel's *Weib und die Welt*.

Verlaine, Paul (1844–96), Fr. poet. *See* **Fauré** (*Bonne Chanson*), **Charpentier** (*Impressions fausses*), **Debussy** (*Ariettes oubliées* & *Fêtes galantes*), **Dieren (van)** (songs), **Durey** (songs), **Fauré** (songs), **Lazzari** (*Effet de nuit*), **Mengelberg (R.)** (songs), **Ollone** (*Les Uns et les autres*), **Pitt** (*Fêtes galantes*), **Poldowski** (songs), **Séverac** (songs), **Sorabji** (songs).

18 songs by Debussy, 17 by Fauré.

Vermont, Pierre (b. ?; d. ?), Flem. 16th-cent. singer & comp. He sang in the Papal Chapel in Rome until 1530, then in the royal chapel in Paris. Comp. motets, chansons for several voices, &c.

Verne, Jules (1828–1905), Fr. novelist. Wrote 3 libs. for Hignard in collab. with Michel Carré. *See* **Offenbach**, (*Docteur Ox* & *Voyage dans la lune*).

Verne, Mathilde (real name Wurm) (b. Southampton, 25. V. 1868; d. London, 4. VI. 1936), Eng. pfst. of Ger. descent. Pupil of Clara Schumann at Frankfort o/M. She taught and played much in London, organized midday chamber concerts, and in 1909 opened a school for pf. playing.

Vernizzi, Ottavio (b. Bologna, *c.* 1580; d. Bologna, IX. 1649), It. orgst. & comp. Orgst. at San Petronio cath. at Bologna from *c.* 1603 to his death.

Works incl. *Intermezzi della coronazione di Apollo per Dafne* & 4 other intermezzi for plays by Silvestro Branchi; motets, *Concerti spirituali*, &c.

Vernon, Joseph (b. Coventry, *c.* 1738; d. London, 19. III. 1782), Eng. actor, ten. singer & comp. He was a choir-boy at St. Paul's cath. in London and 1st appeared on the stage as a boy sop. in 1751, and as a ten. in 1754. Later he became famous chiefly as a singing actor in Shakespeare, Sheridan's *Duenna* & *School for Scandal*, where Linley's song was comp. for him, &c.

Works incl. pantomime *The Witches*; songs for Shakespeare's *Two Gentlemen of Verona* & *Twelfth Night* and for Garrick's *The Irish Widow* & *Linco's Travels*; ballads, &c.

Véronique, operetta by Messager (lib. by Albert Vanloo & Georges Duval), prod. Paris, Bouffes-Parisiens, 10. XII. 1898.

Vers mesurés (Fr. = measured verses). The words of Musique mesurée.

Verschiebung (Ger. lit. displacement) = Damping pedal: the left (called 'soft') pedal of the pf.

Verschworenen, Die, oder Der häusliche Krieg (*The Conspirators, or Domestic Warfare*), operetta by Schubert (lib. by Ignaz Franz Castelli, based on Aristophanes' *Lysistrata*), never perf. in S.'s lifetime; prod. Frankfort o/M., 29. VIII. 1861. An Eng. version of the lib., *War in the Household*, by Marian Miller, was set by Henry Hiles (1826–1904) and pub. in 1884.

Verse Anthem. *See* **Anthem.**

Verset (Fr.) / **Versetto** (It.) } A short org. piece, normally fugal. The name is derived from the practice in the Rom. Catholic service in the 16th–18th cents. of replacing every other sung verse of psalms, &c. by interludes on the org., to relieve the supposed monotony of plainsong.

Verstovsky, Alexey Nikolaievitch (b. Govt. of Tambov, 2. III. 1799; d. Moscow, 17. XI. 1862), Rus. comp. Studied civil engineering at St. Petersburg, but picked up mus. training at the same time, studying theory, singing, v. & pf., the latter with Field and Steibelt. As a rich man's son he remained an amateur, but prod. his 1st operetta at the age of 19. In 1824 he was app. inspector of the Imp. Opera at Moscow, where in 1828 he prod. his 1st opera. In 1842 he married the famous actress Nadezhda Repin.

Works incl. *Pan Tvardovsky, Vadim, Askold's Tomb, Homesickness, The Valley of Tchurov* & *Gromoboy* (after Zhukovsky); 22 operettas; cantatas, melodramas & dramatic scenas; 29 songs, incl. Pushkin's *The Black Shawl*, &c.

Versunkene Glocke, Die (*The Submerged Bell*), opera by Respighi (lib., in It. [*La campana sommersa*], by Claudio Guastalla, based on Gerhart Hauptmann's play), prod. in Ger., Hamburg, 18. XI. 1927.

Opera by Zöllner (lib. by comp., based on Gerhart Hauptmann's play), prod. Berlin, Theater des Westens, 8. VII. 1899.

Vert, Jacques de. *See* **Wert.**

Vertical. Harmonic as distinct from ctptal m. is said to be written in a V. manner, the harmony being prod. in blocks of chords which in a score the eye reads from top to bottom, not horizontally as a network of melodic lines.

Verwandelten Weiber, Die, oder Der Teufel ist los, mus. play by J. A. Hiller (lib. by Christian Felix Weisse, based on Coffey's *The Devil to Pay*), prod. Leipzig, 28. V. 1766. *See also* **Teufel ist los** (Standfuss).

Vespri siciliani, I (Verdi). *See* **Vêpres siciliennes.**

Vesque von Püttlingen, Johann (pseud. J. Hoven) (b. Opole, Rus., 23. VII. 1803; d. Vienna, 29. X. 1883), Aus. comp. of Belg. descent. He was b. at the residence of Prince Alexander Lubomirsky. The family moved to Vienna in 1815 and he studied m. there with Leidesdorf, Moscheles and Worzischek. In 1822 he entered Vienna Univ. and in 1827 the civil service. But in 1829 he exercised himself in opera by setting the lib. of Rossini's *Donna del lago* (based on Scott) and in 1833 he studied ctpt. with Sechter.

Works incl. operas *Turandot* (after Gozzi), *Jeanne d'Arc, Liebeszauber* (after Kleist's *Käthchen von Heilbronn*), *Ein Abenteuer Carl des Zweiten, Der lustige Rat* & 2 unfinished; 2 masses, &c.

Vestale, La, opera by Mercadante (lib., in It., by Salvatore Cammarano), prod. Naples, Teatro San Carlo, 10. III. 1840.

Opera by Spontini (lib., in Fr., by Victor Jacques Étienne de Jouy), prod. Paris, Opéra, 16. XII. 1807.

Vestris (*née* **Bartolozzi**), **Lucia Elizabeth** (or **Eliza Lucy**) (b. London, 3. I. or 2. III. 1797; d. London, 8. VIII. 1856), Eng. actress & sop. singer of It. descent, daughter of Gaetano B. and granddaughter of the engraver Francesco B. Studied singing with Domenico Corri, married the dancer Auguste Armand V. (1788–1825) in 1813 and in 1815 made her 1st stage appearance in London. She was Fatima in the prod. of Weber's *Oberon* in 1826.

Vezzoso (It.) = Charming, graceful.

Via (It. imper. = away). A direction to remove pedals, mutes (*via sordini*), &c.

Viadana (real name **Lodovico Grossi**) (b. Viadana, *c.* 1564; d. Gualtieri o/Po, 2. V. 1645), It. comp. Pupil of Porta and before 1590 app. chapel master at Mantua cath. In 1596 he joined the Franciscan order, in 1609 became chapel master at Concordia, in 1612 at Fano cath.; in 1615 went to live at Piacenza, whence he retired to the Franciscan monastery at Gualtieri.

Works incl. masses, psalms & other church m.; 100 *Concerti ecclesiastici* for 1–4 voices with org. continuo; madrigals, canzonets, &c.

Viaggiatori felici, I (*The Happy Travellers*), opera by Anfossi (lib. by Filippo Livigni), prod. Venice, Teatro San Samuele, X. 1780.

Viaggio a Reims, Il, ossia L'albergo del giglio d'oro (*The Journey to Rheims, or the Golden Lily Inn*), opera by Rossini (lib. by Giuseppe Luigi Balochi), prod. Paris, Théâtre-Italien, 19. VI. 1825.

Vial / **Viall** } Alternative old names of the Viol.

Vianna da Motta, José (b. São Thomé, 22. IV. 1868), Port. pfst. & comp. Studied at the Lisbon Cons. and with the Scharwenka brothers in Berlin, later with Liszt at Weimar and Bülow at Frankfort o/M. He began to tour Eur. and S. Amer. in 1902, was app. Prus. court pfst. and taught at Geneva in 1915–7, after which he became dir. of the Cons. and cond. of the sym. orch. at Lisbon.

Works incl. *Lusiads* (Camoens) for chor. & orch.; Sym.; stg. 4tet; *Port. Scenes, Port. Rhapsodies*, &c. for **pf.**; songs, &c.

Viardot-García, (Michelle Ferdinande) Pauline (b. Paris, 18. VII. 1821; d. Paris, 17–18. V. 1910), Fr. m.-sop. singer & comp. of Spa. descent, daughter of Manuel García and sister of Maria Malibran. Pupil of her father, also studied pf. Made her 1st appearance as a singer at Brussels in 1837 and 1st visited London in 1839. In 1841 she married the opera manager and critic Louis V. (1800–83). She comp. operettas, *Le Dernier Sorcier, L'Ogre* & *Trop de femmes*, to libs. by Turgenev, songs, &c.

Viardot, Louise. *See* **Héritte-Viardot.**

Vibraphone. An electrophonic inst. the resonators of which are kept vibrating by an electric current, so that the notes struck give out an oscillating sound.

Vibrato (It. = vibrating, oscillating). A special mus. effect prod. on a single note, though often with minute alterations in pitch. In voc. m. of the early 17th cent. it was called *trillo* in It., which did not mean a trill or Shake in the modern sense, but a rapid repeating of one and the same note on one syll., with a bleating effect. On the Clavichord a V. effect was possible by a shaking of the finger on the key without releasing it, much as it is still in use by stg. players, who prod. a warmer and more vibrant tone by shaking their left hand on the fingerboard while pressing down the stg. On the org. a similar effect is made possible by special 'tremulant' stops, but it has been deplorably over-exploited by builders and players of cinema orgs.; and so has the V. in singing, commonly called the 'wobble.'

Vicente de Olivença. *See* **Lusitano.**

Vicente, Gil (1470–1540), Port. dramatist. *See* **Badajoz** (*Dom Duardos*).

Vicentino, Nicola (b. Vicenza, *c.* 1511; d. Rome, 1572), It. keyboard player & theorist. Pupil of (?) Willaert at Venice. He entered the service of Ippolito d'Este, cardinal of Ferrara, with whom he went to live in Rome. He sought to revive the Gr. modes in his madrigals, invented an inst. he called the archicembalo and pub. a treatise, *L'antica musica ridotta alla moderna prattica*, which involved him in a controversy with Lusitano, in which he was defeated. He returned to Ferrara with his patron and became his chapel master.

Victoria, Tomás Luis de (not Vittoria, which is merely the It. form of the name) (b. Avila, *c.* 1535–40; d. Madrid, 27. VIII. 1611), Spa. comp. Studied (?) with Escobedo at Segovia. He may have been in touch with St. Teresa, also a native of Avila. In 1565 he received a grant from Philip II and the following year went to Rome, where he became a priest and singer at the Ger. Coll. He became choirmaster there in 1571. In 1578 he resigned, having been app. chaplain to the dowager empress Maria, Philip II's sister, who returned to Spa. in 1581 and was followed there by V. in (?) 1583. In 1586 he became choirmaster at the convent of the Descalzas Reales in Madrid, where the empress lived and her daughter, the Infanta Margaret, became a nun. On the death of the empress in 1603 he wrote an *Officium defunctorum* (Requiem mass) for 6 voices.

Works incl. 18 masses, 2 Requiems, 44 motets, office for Holy Week, 18 magnificats, 34 hymns, 10 psalms, 10 antiphons, &c.

Victorinus, Georgius (b. Huldschön, Bavaria, ?; d. Munich, 1624), Ger. monk and comp. He became mus. prefect at the Jesuit monastery of St. Michael, where a sacred play with m. by him was perf. in 1597. Other works incl. Magnificat for 6 voices, 3 litanies, *c.* 20 sacred songs, &c.

'Victory' Symphony. The new nickname recently acquired by Beethoven's 5th Sym., in C min., Op. 67, comp. in 1805–7 and 1st perf. Vienna, 22. XII. 1808. It was invented during the 2nd world war in Eng., where the rhythm of the opening, corresponding to the 'V' sign in Morse code (. . . —) was used, on the radio and elsewhere, as victory signal.

Vida breve, La (*Life is Short*), opera by Falla (lib., in Spa., by Carlos Fernández Shaw), prod. Nice, in Fr., trans. by Paul Milliet, 1. IV. 1913.

Vidal, Louis (Antoine) (b. Rouen, 10. VII. 1820; d. Paris, 7. I. 1891), Fr. cst. & mus. historian. Studied co. with Franchomme in Paris and became a friend of Vuillaume, from whom he learnt much about stg. insts. His literary works incl. studies of the hist. of stg. insts., the old Paris corporations of musns., the bibliog. of chamber m., &c.

Vidal, Paul (Antonin) (b. Toulouse, 16. VI. 1863; d. Paris, 9. IV. 1931), Fr. cond. & comp. Studied at the Paris Cons., where he took the Prix de Rome in 1883. In 1893 he became asst. chor. master at the Opéra and in 1898 cond., leaving in 1906. He also became a prof. at the Cons.

Works incl. operas *Burgonde* &

Guernica, operetta *Eros*; ballets *La Maladetta* & *Fête russe*, also one on m. by Chopin, orch. with Messager; pantomimes *Pierrot assassin* & *Colombine pardonnée*; mystery plays *Noël* & *Les Mystères d'Éleusis*; incid. m. for Banville's *Le Baiser*, Mendès's *La Reine Fiammette* & other plays; motets; cantata *Ecce sacerdos magnus*; old dances arr. for orch., &c.

Vidal, Peire (b. ?; d. ?, *c.* 1215), Fr. troubadour, 50 of whose poems and 12 of whose tunes are preserved.

Vie parisienne, La (*Life in Paris*), operetta by Offenbach (lib. by Henri Meilhac and Ludovic Halévy), prod. Paris, Théâtre du Palais-Royal, 31. X. 1866.

Vielle (Fr.) = Hurdy-gurdy.

Vier ernste Gesänge (*Four Serious Songs*), settings by Brahms for bar. & pf. of words from the Bible, Op. 121, comp. V. 1896. The corresponding passages in Eng. are *One thing befalleth, So I returned, O death, how bitter is thy sting, Though I speak with the tongues of men and of angels.*

Vierdanck, Johann (b. ?, *c.* 1610; d. ? Stralsund, ?), Ger. 17th-cent. orgst. & comp. Learnt m. as a choir-boy in the court chapel at Dresden and was sent to Vienna in 1628 to study under Sansoni. From 1641–56 he was orgst. at St. Mary's church, Stralsund.

Works incl. sacred concs. for 2–9 voices; dances for 2 vs., viol and continuo, capriccios, canzonets & sos. for 2–5 insts. with and without continuo, &c.

Vierjährige Posten, Der (*The Four Years' Sentry*), comic opera by Schubert (lib. by Theodor Körner), comp. 1815, but never perf. in S.'s lifetime. Prod. Dresden, Opera, 23. IX. 1896.

Vierling, Georg (b. Frankenthal, Bavaria, 5. IX. 1820; d. Wiesbaden, 1. V. 1901), Ger. orgst. & cond. Studied under his father, a schoolmaster and orgst., later at Darmstadt and Berlin. In 1847 he became orgst. and chor. cond. at Frankfort o/Oder. Later he went to Mainz for a short time and then settled in Berlin, where he became royal mus. dir. in 1859 and prof. of the Acad. in 1882.

Works incl. cantatas for chor. & orch. *Hero and Leander, The Rape of the Sabines, Alaric's Death* & *Constantine*; Sym., ovts. to Shakespeare's *Tempest*, Schiller's *Maria Stuart* & others; pf. Trio; *O Roma nobilis* for unaccomp. chor.; part-songs; pf. pieces; songs, &c.

Vierling, Johann Gottfried (b. Metzels nr. Meiningen, 25. I. 1750; d. Schmalkalden, 22. XI. 1813), Ger. orgst. & comp. Studied with the orgst. Fischer at Schmalkalden, whom he succeeded as church orgst. there, but interrupted his office to study further with C. P. E. Bach at Hamburg and Kirnberger in Berlin. He wrote treatises on thorough-bass and on preluding to hymns.

Works incl. play with m., *Empfindung und Empfindelei*; Magnificat 4-part hymns, Harvest Festival M. & other church m.; Psalm cxxvii for chor. & orch.; *c.* 40 cantatas for solo voices, chor. & orch.; pf. 4tet, 2 pf. trios; org. m.; 6 pf. sos.; songs, &c.

Vierne, Louis (b. Poitiers, 8. X. 1870; d. Paris, 2. VI. 1937), Fr. orgst. & comp. Pupil of Franck and Widor at the Paris Cons. Although blind, he became asst. orgst. to Widor at the church of Saint-Sulpice and later orgst. at Notre-Dame, where he d. at his post.

Works incl. Mass with orch.; Sym.; stg. 4tet; sos. for v. & pf. and co. & pf.; 6 syms., 24 *Pièces en style libre*, 24 *Pièces de fantaisie* & other works for org., &c.

Vieuxtemps, Henri (b. Verviers, 20. II. 1820; d. Mustapha-lez-Alger, Algiers, 6. VI. 1881), Belg. vst. & comp. Learnt the v. at home and at the age of 6 was able to play a conc. by Rode. At 7 he was taken on tour by his father and heard by Bériot, who offered to teach him at Brussels. In 1828 his master took him to Paris and prod. him there. In 1833 he went on tour in Ger. and Aus., remaining in Vienna to study ctpt. with Sechter. In 1834 he 1st visited London, where he met Paganini, and the following year he studied comp. with Reicha in Paris. He afterwards. travelled long and extensively in Eur. and in 1844 went to U.S.A. In 1845 he married the Viennese pfst. Josephine Eder. In 1846–52 he was v. prof. at the St. Petersburg Cons. In 1871–3 he taught at the Brussels Cons., but was lamed by a stroke.

Works incl. 6 v. concs., *Fantaisie-Caprice* & *Ballade et Polonaise*, &c. for v. & orch.; v. & pf. So.; cadenzas for Beethoven v. Conc., &c.

Vigny, Alfred de (1797–1863), Fr. poet, novelist & dramatist. *See* **Gounod** (*Cinq-Mars*), **Leoncavallo** (*Chatterton*).

Vihuela (Spa.). The Spa. lute, but made in the shape of a guitar. It dates back to at least the 13th cent., but became obs. about the 16th. It usually had 6 stgs. tuned in 4ths, but with an interval of a 3rd between the 2 middle ones.

Vihuela de arco (Spa. = bowed V.). Actually an inst. of the viol rather than strictly the V. type.

Vihuela de Flandes (Spa. = Flem. V.). The Spa. name for the ord. lute, which was an outlandish inst. in Spa., played by foreigners.

Vihuela de mano (Spa. = hand V.). A V. plucked with the fingers. The most commonly used type.

Vihuela de pédola (Spa. = plectrum V.). A V. the stgs. of which were plucked with a plectrum.

Vila, Pedro Alberto (b. ? Barcelona, 1517; d. Barcelona, 16. XI. 1582), Spa. orgst. & comp. Became a priest and canon of Barcelona cath.

Works incl. madrigals, org. m., &c.

Vilar, José Teodor (b. Barcelona, 10. VIII. 1836; d. Barcelona, 21. X. 1905), Spa. cond. & comp. Studied with the cath. orgst. Ramón Vilanova (1801–70) at Barcelona and in 1859 went to Paris with study pf. with Herz and comp. with Bazin and Halévy. Returning home in 1863, he became cond. at one of the minor theatres and later at the principal theatre. He also did much teaching.

Works incl. zarzuelas *La romeria de Racasens, L'ultim rey de Magnolia, El pescador de San Pol, Una prometensa, La rambla de las flores, Pot mes qui piuta, La lluna en un cove, L'esca del pecat, La torre del amor*, &c.

Vilbac, Alphonse (Charles Renaud) de (b. Montpellier, 3. VI. 1829; d. Brussels, 19. III. 1884), Fr. orgst., pfst. & comp. Studied at the Paris Cons., Halévy being among his masters, and gained the Prix de Rome in 1844. After an early success he was unfortunate, made a precarious living by arrs. and other hack-work, became almost blind and d. in poverty.

Works incl. operettas *Au Clair de la lune* & *Don Almanzor*; *Messe solennelle*; cantata *Le Renégat de Tanger*; *Pompadour Gavotte, Chant cypriote, Marche serbe*, &c. for orch.; pf. pieces, &c.

Vilda, Maria. *See* **Wilt, Marie.**

Villa-Lobos, Heitor (b. Rio de Janeiro, 5. III. 1881), Braz. comp. His father, a cst., gave him his 1st lessons, but he became a pfst. and for some time as a young man toured Brazil as a concert artist. In 1912 he began to explore his country's folk m. and in 1915 gave the 1st concert devoted to his own works at Rio de Janeiro. A gvt. grant enabled him to live in Paris for a few years from 1922, but on his return he did much useful work as cond. and mus. educst., being app. dir. of mus. educ. for the schools in the capital in 1931. In 1929 he pub. a book on Braz. folk m., *Alma de Brasil.*

Works incl. operas *Aglaia, Izaht, Femina, Zoé, Malazerte* & *Jesus*; ballets *Amozona* & *Juripary*; orat. *Vida pura*; 13 works entitled *Choros* cast in a new form and consisting of 3 for orch., 2 for pf. & orch., 1 for 2 pfs. & orch., 1 for chor. & orch. and 6 for var. chamber combs.; var. orch. works incl. *Bachianas Brasileiras* (5 suites in the spirit of Bach); *Momopercoce* fantasy for pf. & orch., concs. for v. and co. & orch.; Nonet for wind, hp., perc. & chor., 5tet for wind insts.; 5 stg. 4tets, 3 pf. trios; 3 so.-fantasies for v. & pf.; a very large number of pf. works; songs, &c.

Village Coquettes, The, opera by Hullah (lib. by Dickens), prod. London, St. James's Theatre, 6. XII. 1836.

Village Romeo and Juliet (Delius). *See* **Romeo und Julia auf dem Dorfe.**

Villalba Muñoz, Luis (b. Valladolid, 22. IX. 1873; d. Madrid, 9. I. 1921), Spa. mus. historian. He entered the Augustinian order and was ordained priest, retiring as a monk to the Escurial, but renounced the order not long before his death and went to live in Madrid. He wrote a book on Spa. 15th–16th-cent. org. m., ed. old lutenist songs and org. works, and transcribed much other old Spa. m.

Villancico (Spa.). A type of verse with a refrain and a complex rhyme-scheme; also the m. to which such poems were set, at first tunes without harmony, later pieces similar to madrigals; sometimes a comp. for solo voices, stgs. & org. to sacred words, esp. connected with the Nativity.

Villanella (It. lit. country girl). An It. partsong of the late 15th to the earlier 17th cent., set to rustic words and light in character, differing little from the canzona and the ballet except by the greater freedom it allows the comp. in the matter of rules of harmony and ctpt., the bucolic nature of the songs being deemed to warrant greater licence. The best comps., however, rarely cared to sacrifice elegance of workmanship.

Villanella rapita, La (*The Ravished Country Girl*), opera by Bianchi (lib. by Giovanni Bertati, based on Jean Michel Favart's *Le Caprice amoureux*), prod. Venice, Teatro San Moisè, autumn 1783. Mozart wrote an additional 4tet and a trio for the Vienna perf., 25. XI. 1785.

Villanelle (Fr.). In Fr. m. a V. is not the equivalent of the It. Villanella and the Spa. Villancico, but a voc. setting of a poem in V. form, which consists of stanzas of 3 lines, the 1st and 3rd lines of the opening stanza being repeated alternately as the 3rd line of the succeeding stanzas.

Villi, Le (*The Witches*), opera by Puccini (lib. by Ferdinando Fontana), prod. Milan, Teatro dal Verme, 31. V. 1884.

Villiers de l'Isle Adam, Auguste, Count (1840–89), Fr. poet. *See* **Dieren (van)** (songs), **Georges** (*Nouveau Monde* & *Axël*), **Wieniawski (A.)** (*Évasion*).

Villiers, George, Duke of Buckingham (1628–87), Eng. courtier & author. *See* **Smith (J. C.)** (*Chances*).

Villon, François (1431–*c.* 1489), Fr. poet. *See* **Cartan, Debussy** (3 ballads), **Dieren (van)** (recitations), **Hubeau** (songs).

Villota or **Villotta**. A Venetian folksong, so popular that it was sung to many different words.

Vinacesi, Benedetto (b. Brescia, *c.* 1670; d. Venice, 1719), It. comp. He was chapel master to Prince Francesco Gonzaga di Castiglione, but in 1704 was app. 2nd orgst. at St. Mark's, Venice, in 1706 taking on the addit. duties of choirmaster at the girls' Cons. dell' Ospedaletto.

Works incl. operas *L'innocenza giustificata*, *Gli amanti generosi* & *Gli sfoghi di giubilo*; 2 orats.; motets & other church m.; *Sonate da chiesa*, *Sfere armoniche* for 2 vs., co. & org. continuo, &c.

Vincent, Thomas (b. ? London, *c.* 1720; d. London, ? 10. V. 1783), Eng. obst. & comp. Pupil of Sammartini. He entered the king's band as obst. in 1735.

Works incl. solo for ob., fl. or v. with hpchd. continuo; hpchd. lessons, &c.

Vinci, Leonardo (b. Strongoli, Calabria, 1690; d. Naples, 28. V. 1730), It. comp. Pupil of Greco at the Cons. dei Poveri di Gesù Cristo at Naples. He prod. his 1st opera there in 1719 and became chapel master to A. Scarlatti's patron, the Prince of Sansevero. On Scarlatti's death in 1725 he was app. deputy chapel master of the royal chapel and in 1728 he (?) entered a monastic order, but continued to write for the stage. He was an inveterate gambler and d. in utter poverty.

Works incl. operas *Lo cecato fauzo*, *Le zite 'n galera* (both in Neapol. dialect), *La Stratonice*, *Silla dittatore*, *La mogliera fedele*, *Astianatte*, *Siroe*, *La caduta dei decemviri*, *Artaserse* & *c.* 30 others.

Vinci, Leonardo da (b. Vinci nr. Empoli, 1452; d. Amboise nr. Paris, 2. V. 1519), It. painter, scientist, inventor & musn. In this last capacity he excelled as singer, lutenist and violist, made improvements in the viols and invented a new kind of lute.

Vinci, Pietro (b. Nicosia, *c.* 1540; d. Nicosia or Palermo, *c.* 1584), It. comp. He became chapel master at the church of Santa Maria Maggiore at Bergamo in the 1570s and in 1581 took on a similar post at his birthplace.

Works incl. masses, motets; madrigals, &c.

Viner, William (b. ?; d. Dublin, XI. 1716), Ir. vst. & comp. He was master of the State M. at Dublin in 1703–16. Comp. solos for v. & bass, &c.

Vingt-quatre Violons du Roy (Fr. = The King's 24 Vs.). The Fr. court stg. band of the 17th cent. under Henri IV and Louis XIII—XIV, used for ballets, court balls, dinners, &c. Its 24 players were not, of course, all vsts., but all the insts. of the v. family were repres. A similar stg. orch. was founded, on the Fr. model, by Charles II in London after his restoration in 1660.

Vinning, Louisa (b. Kingsbridge, Devon, 10. XI. 1836; d. London, 1904), Eng. sop. singer & hpst. She sang on the stage at Plymouth as a small child and appeared as singer & hpst. in 1840–2 under the name of 'The Infant Sappho.' Having studied singing with Frank Mori, she made her 1st appearance in London in 1856, when she took an indisposed singer's part in *Messiah* at a moment's notice.

Viol. The generic name of the chief family of bowed stg. insts. preceding that of the v. Vs. 1st appeared in the 15th cent. and were in vogue until near the end of the 17th, disappearing completely in the 18th. The main representatives were the treble or descant, the ten. (Viola da braccio) and the bass (Viola da gamba), but there were others, incl. the db. (Violone); also an 8-ft. org. stop, the full name of which is Viol d'orchestre.

See also names below, **Treble Viol & Violone.**

Viol d'amour. An 8-ft. open Diapason org. stop, similar to the Violin Diapason, prod. an imitation of stg. tone.

Viol de Gamboys (old Eng.) = Viola da gamba.

Viol di Gamba. An 8-ft. org. stop reprod. stg. tone.

Viol d'orchestre. An 8-ft. org. stop of the Gamba type prod. an imitation of energetic stg. tone.

Viol Lyra Way. *See* **Lyra Viol.**

Viola, opera by Hans Holenia (b. 1890) (lib. by Oskar Widowitz, based on

Shakespeare's *Twelfth Night*), prod. Graz, 17. XI. 1934.

Unfinished opera by Smetana (lib. by Eliška Krasnohorská, on Shakespeare's *Twelfth Night*), begun 1883.

Viola. The ten. inst. of the modern v. family which superseded the Viols in the 18th cent. It has 4 stgs. tuned from C an 8ve below middle C with 3 perfect 5ths above. It is the regular middle part in the stg. section of the orch. and in the stg. 4tet, &c.; also an 8-ft. open Diapason org. stop similar to the Violin Diapason.

Viola, Alfonso della (b. Ferrara, ?; d. Ferrara, ? after 1567), It. comp. Chapel master at the court of Ercole d'Este (II), Duke of Ferrara, where he prod. plays with m. on the stage almost amounting to operas. He remained in the service of the next duke, Alfonso II.

Viola alta (It. = high va.). A special va. made by Hörlein of Würzburg in the 1870s for use in the orch. at the Wagner festivals at Bayreuth. It is of exceptionally large size and in 1898 a 5th stg. was added, tuned to the E of the highest v. stg.

Viola bastarda (It. lit. bastard viol). A bass viol of a special type with 6 stgs. variously tuned and ranging from about C below the stave in the bass clef to D above middle C, and sympathetic stgs. not touched by the bow but vibrating with those actually played. The name of the inst. was due to its being a hybrid, capable of playing at any pitch from treble to bass. It later developed into the Barytone.

Viola Clef. Another name sometimes given to the Alto Clef.

Viola da braccio (It. = arm viol). The ten. of the Viol family. It was the largest of those played held in the arm, the Va. da gamba being held between the knees. It supplied the middle parts in consorts and had 6 stgs. ranging from G on the bottom line in the bass clef to G above middle C.

Viola da gamba (It. = leg viol). The bass of the Viol family, and also, on account of its being capable of playing both bass and treble, the most frequently used as a solo inst. Having 6 stgs. tuned in 4ths, with a 3rd between the 2 middle ones, ranging from D below the stave in the bass clef to D above it, it was capable, like the Lute, of prod. chords and was therefore much used as an accomp. inst. It also served for Continuo playing, either filling in the harmony from the figured bass or following the bass line only while the harmony was supplied by a keyboard inst.

Viola da spalla (It. = shoulder va.). A bowed stg. inst. of the v. family used mainly by wandering musns. in the 17th & 18th cents., held by a shoulder strap.

Viola d'amore (It. lit. love viol). A ten. viol of a special variety with 7 stgs. and from 7–14 sympathetic stgs. not touched by the bow but vibrating with those actually played. The stgs. were variously tuned, but usually ranged from D below middle C to D a 9th above it.

Viola di bordone (It. = drone viol). *See also* **Barytone.**
Viola di fagotto (It. = bassoon viol).
} Alternative names of the Viola bastarda.

Viola, Francesco della (b. Ferrara, ?; d. ? Ferrara, ?), It. 16th-cent. comp., (?) relative of Alfonso d. V. Pupil of Willaert and later chapel master to Alfonso d'Este (II), Duke of Ferrara, with whom he visited Venice in 1562.

Works incl. masses, motets, madrigals, songs, &c.

Viola pomposa. A special type of bowed stg. inst. of the v. family, very rarely used. It has 4 stgs. tuned in irregular intervals from D below middle C to C an 8ve above it.

Violet. The Eng. name sometimes given to the Viola d'amore.

Violet, The (Mozart). *See* **Veilchen.**

Violetta marina (It. lit. little marine viol). A special type of Viol, allied to the Viola d'amore, like which it has sympathetic stgs.

Violetta piccola (It. small little viol). A rare kind of Viol made in var. shapes, with 3–6 stgs. and capable of taking both treble and middle parts.

Violin. The principal modern bowed stg. inst., to whose family belong also the Viola, Violoncello and Double Bass. The V. has 4 stgs. tuned in perfect 5ths from G below middle C upwards. It began to displace the Viol in the 17th cent. and completely superseded it in the 18th. *See also* **Basse-contre, Cellone, Cinquième, Dessus de viole, Double Bass, Hardanger Fiddle, Haute-contre, Kit, Quinton, Taille, Tenor Violin, Viola, Viola alta, Viola da spalla, Viola pomposa, Violino piccolo, Violon d'amour, Violoncello, Violoncello piccolo, Violotta.**

Violin Clef. Another name, more rarely used, for the Treble Clef.

Violin Diapason. An 8-ft. open Diapason org. stop prod. an imitation of stg. tone.

Violino piccolo (It. = little v.). A small stg. inst. of the v. family with 4 stgs.

tuned in perfect 5ths from middle C upwards and thus standing a 4th above the v. in pitch.

Violon d'amour (Fr. lit. love violin). The member of the modern stg. family representing the Viola d'amore of the Viol family, used in the 18th cent., but now obs. It had 5 stgs. ranging from G below middle C tuned in 2 5ths and 2 4ths from below, and 6 sympathetic stgs., not touched by the bow but vibrating with those actually played.

Violoncello. The inst. of the modern v. family which superseded the Viola da gamba in the 18th cent. It has 4 stgs. tuned C below the stave in the bass clef and in 3 perfect 5ths above that. It has thus a bass range, though it is not the lowest of the family, the db. going a min. 6th below it and exceptionally even an 8ve or 9th; and it is also somewhat freakishly capable of extending its range upwards to heights abnormal for its size and relatively far exceeding the range of any other inst. in the family. However, it normally plays bass parts in the orch., in classical m. often in 8ves with the db., and it is the regular bass of the stg. 4tet. Also an 8-ft. org. stop prod. an imitation of stg. tone an octave above that of the Violone.

Violoncello piccolo. An abnormal member of the v. family, a smaller co. on which the playing of high passages was easier than on the normal co. because its top stg. was tuned a 5th higher: E above middle C. The lower stgs. were tuned in perfect 5ths below this, so that on the 4-stgd. V. p. the lowest note was G on the bottom line in the bass clef. But there was also a 5-stgd. V. p., which added the bottom C of the normal co.

Violone. The db. of the Viol family, similar to the Va. da gamba, with 6 stgs. similarly tuned an 8ve lower. Also a 16-ft. org. stop prod. an imitation of bass stg. tone.

Violotta. A modern stg. inst. of the v. family invented by Alfred Stelzner of Dresden. It has 4 stgs. tuned so as to stand in pitch between the va. and the co.: G on the bottom stave of the bass clef, with 3 perfect 5ths above.

Viotti, Giovanni Battista (b. Fontanetto nr. Crescentino, Piedmont, 23. V. 1753; d. London, 3. III. 1824), It. vst. & comp. Learnt the elements of m. from his father, a blacksmith who played the hn., could play the v. at the age of 8, studied at 11 with a wandering lute player, Giovannini. In 1766 he was sent to Turin for serious study, and with the aid of a patron, the Marchese de Vogliera, had lessons from Pugnani, who took him on tour in 1780. (At Geneva he is said to have met Voltaire, who d. in 1778.) They visited Swi., Ger. (incl. the court of Frederick II of Prus.), Pol. and Rus. In 1781 V. 1st visited Paris and played in public in 1782. At first he appeared much at the Concert spirituel and elsewhere, but later he withdrew from the public and in 1784, receiving a pension from Marie Antoinette, decided to serve only the court. In 1788 he took part in the revival of It. opera at the Théâtre de Monsieur, but the venture was interfered with by the Revol. He joined the National Guard, determined to remain in Paris, but in VII. 1792 he left for London just before the arrest of the king and queen. He settled there for good, but visited his birthplace in VII. 1793, when his mother d., and paid other visits abroad, esp. to Paris. He played often at Salomon's concerts, took a share in the management of the It. opera at the King's Theatre and led the orch. there. But in 1798 he was exiled on suspicion of revol. activities and lived for nearly 3 years at Schönfeld nr. Hamburg. But the suspicion was unfounded, and in 1801 he was allowed to return to London. His mus. success was no longer the same, and he became a wine merchant, with disastrous financial results. In 1813 he returned to mus. activities. In 1818–22 he was in Paris again, where his former patron, now Louis XVIII, app. him dir. of the It. opera, but this failed after the assassination of the Duc de Berry at the theatre in 1820 and he returned to London in 1822 completely ruined.

Works incl. 29 v. concs., 2 *Symphonies concertantes* for 2 vs. & orch., 10 pf. concs.; many stg. 4tets & trios for 2 vs. & bass; 12 sos. for v. & pf.; Serenades & other duets for 2 vs.; 9 pf. sos.; 3 divertimenti for co. & pf.; duets for 2 cos.; songs, &c.

Virdung, Sebastian (b. Amberg, Upper Palatinate, ?; d. ?), Ger. 15th–16th-cent. cleric & writer on m. He was a priest at Eichstätt and in 1511 pub. at Basle his book on mus. insts., *Musica getutscht und auszgezogen*, ded. to the Bishop of Strasburg.

Virelai (Fr. = a lay from Vire in Normandy). A type of medieval Fr. song.

Virgil (Publius Vergilius Maro) (70–19 B.C.), Rom. poet. *See* **Dido and Aeneas** (Purcell), **Énée et Lavinie** (Colasse & Dauvergne), **Freitas** (eclogue), **Lissenko** (*Aeneid*), **Loeffler** (*Pagan Poem*), **Mudarra, Roger-**

Ducasse, Troyens (Berlioz), **Verbonnet** (*Dulces exuviae*).

Virginal. The Eng. stgd. keyboard inst. of the 16th & 17th cents., often called 'virginals' or 'a pair of virginals' when it had 2 keyboards. Except in shape, which was rectangular, it did not differ essentially from the hpchd., and still less from the spinet, save that the latter more often had its own legs, whereas the V. usually had none and was placed on a table or a suitable stand. Various explanations of its name are that it was the inst. most often played by girls, that it was the favourite inst. of the 'virgin queen' Elizabeth, who indeed played it well, and that it was used to accomp. the hymn *Angelus ad Virginem*.

Virginia, opera by Mercadante (lib. by Salvatore Cammarano, based on Alfieri's tragedy), prod. Naples, Teatro San Carlo, 7. IV. 1866.

Virtuosity (der. from Virtuoso, below). The manner of perf. with complete technical mastery; but the term is often used in a derogatory sense, suggesting that no other quality of interpretation is displayed by the perf.

Virtuoso (It., from Lat. *virtus* = excellence, ability). In m. an executive artist who has achieved complete mastery over the medium in which he perfs.

Visé, Jean Donneau de (1640–1710), Fr. dramatist. *See* **Charpentier (M.-A.)** (3 plays, 2 with Corneille).

Visée, Robert de (b. ?, *c.* 1650; d. ?, *c.* 1725), Fr. lutenist, guitarist & comp. He was guitar and ob. player to the dauphin and chamber musn. to the king from near the end of the 17th cent. to 1721.

Works incl. guitar pieces, trios for lute, theorbo and bass, songs, &c.

Vitali, Angelo (b. Modena, ?; d. ?), It. 17th-cent. comp. Chapel master at Orvieto.

Works incl. opera *Tomiri*.

Vitali, Filippo (b. Florence, ?; d. Florence, after 1653), It. priest, ten. singer & comp. He worked at Florence until 1631, when he was called to Rome as singer in the Papal chapel. While there he became attached to the household of Cardinal Francesco Barberini; but in 1642 he returned to Florence to become chapel master to the Duke of Tuscany and at San Lorenzo cath. In 1653 he became a canon there.

Works incl. m.-drama *L'Aretusa*; incid. m. to Jacopo Cicognini's comedy *La finta Mora*; psalms for 5 voices, hymns, *Sacrae cantiones* & other church m.; madrigals; var. works for voices & insts. in several parts, &c.

Vitali, Giovanni Battista (b. Cremona, *c.* 1640; d. Modena, 12. X. 1692), It. violist & comp. Pupil of Maurizio Cazzati, chapel master of San Petronio cath. at Bologna, where V. himself was a violist from 1666. In the 1670s he became chapel master of the Santissimo Rosario, and in 1674 he went to Modena as master of the ducal chapel. His opera on Monmouth was prod. there in 1686, the year after M.'s execution.

Works incl. psalms for 2–5 voices and insts.; orats. *Agar, Gefte, Il Giona* & *L'ambizione debellata, ovvero La caduta di Monmouth*; cantata *L'alloro trionfante*; numerous dances for several insts.; sos. for 2 vs. & continuo and others for var. inst. combs., &c.

Vitali, Tommaso (Antonio) (b. Bologna, *c.* 1665; d. ? Modena, after 1735), It. vst. & comp., son of prec. Pupil of his father, later member of the court chapel at Modena under him and app. its dir. towards the end of the 17th cent., prob. on his father's death. He taught the v. to distinguished pupils, incl. Abaco and Senaillé.

Works incl. pf. trios; sos. for 2 vs. & continuo; *Ciacona* in G min. for v. & bass, &c.

Vitry, Philippe de (b. Champagne, 31. X. 1291; d. Paris, 9. VI. 1361), Fr. diplomat, priest, mus. theorist, poet & comp. He was secretary to Charles IV and Philip VI of Fr., in 1350 arr. a meeting between the king and the pope at Avignon and was soon afterwards created Bishop of Meaux. His poetry was much esteemed, Petrarch writing him a letter of appreciation. His m. is lost. He wrote treatises on the change from the old modal (*ars antiqua*) to the new mensural notation (*ars nova*) and was the 1st in Fr. to allow duple rhythm, triple alone having been permitted before.

Vittadini, Franco (b. Pavia, 9. IV. 1884), It. cond. & comp. Studied at the Milan Cons., became cond. at Varese and later settled at Pavia, where he became dir. of the Istituto musicale.

Works incl. operas *Il mare di Tiberiade, Anima allegra* (after the Quintero brothers), *Nazareth* (after Lagerlöf), *La Sagredo* & *Caracciolo*; ballets *Vecchia Milano, Le dame galanti* & *Fiordisole*; 10 masses & motets; orat. *Il natale di Gesù, Le sette parole di Cristo* for chor.; symph. poem *Armonie della notte*; org. works, &c.

Vittori, Loreto (b. Spoleto, 16. I. 1604; d. Rome, 23 or 27. IV. 1670), It. male sop. singer & comp. Studied with Sorto, Nanini and Soriano in Rome and lived for a time at the court of Cosimo II de' Medici at Florence, but returned to Rome and entered the Papal Chapel in 1622. Among his pupils were Queen Caroline of Swe., during her residence in Rome, and Pasquini.

Works incl. opera *La Galatea*; plays with m. *La fiera di Palestrina* & *Le zitelle canterine*; orats. *Santa Irene, la pellegrina costante* & *Sant' Ignazio di Loiola*; cantatas, arias, &c.

Vittoria, Tommaso Lodovico da. *See* **Victoria, Tomás Luis de.**

Vitzthumb, Ignaz (b. Baden nr. Vienna, 20. VII. 1723; d. Brussels, 23. III. 1816), Aus. cond. & comp. Studied in Vienna and settled in Brussels in the service of Prince Charles of Lorraine. He cond. at Ghent, Amsterdam and at the Théâtre de la Monnaie in Brussels, but lost his posts and pension during the Revol. and d. in poverty.

Works incl. comic operas *Le Soldat par amour, La Foire de village*, &c.; masses, motets & other church m.; Fr. cantatas; syms., &c.

Vivace (It.) = lively, animated.

Vivacissimo (It. superl.) = most lively, &c.

Vivaldi, Antonio (b. ? Venice, *c.* 1675; d. Vienna, VII. 1741), It. vst. & comp. Learnt m. from his father, Gian-Battista V., a vst. in the chapel of St. Mark's at Venice. He received minor orders in 1693 and was ordained priest in 1703, but did not actually enter the church. Before that he had also been a pupil of Legrenzi. In 1704 he became a teacher at the Cons. of the Ospedale della Pietà, to which he remained attached until 1740. But *c.* 1720 he was absent at Mantua for 3 years as chapel master to Prince Philip of Hesse-Darmstadt. He was, however. required to furnish concs. for the Venice Cons. even during his absence, sending them by post, and during Gasparini's absence, when he acted also as choirmaster, he was required to furnish motets and other church m. He seems to have gone to Ger. for a year in 1729 with his father; indeed there is no sign that he was in Venice again before 1735, and in 1740 or earlier he visited Vienna, where he d. in poverty, although he had made much money during his career. He was nicknamed 'Il prete rosso' ('the red priest') from the colour of his hair.

Works incl. operas *L'Olimpiade, Dorilla in Tempe, Tito Manlio, Il Giustino, Griselda, Armida, Catone, Orlando finto pazzo, L'incoronazione di Dario, Il Farnace, Tamerlano, Orlando furioso* (after Ariosto) & c. 35 others; Lat. orat. *Juditha*; 33 cantatas; 8 motets, *Stabat Mater, Salve Regina* & other church m.; numerous sacred concs. with & without voices; 124 concs. for v., stgs. & continuo, 39 bn. concs., 30 fl. concs., numerous other concs. for 2–4 vs., 1 or 2 obs. and var. other insts. & orch., &c.

Vives, Amadeo (b. Collbató nr. Barcelona, 18. XI. 1871; d. Madrid, 1. XII. 1932), Spa. comp. Prof. of comp. at the Madrid Cons.

Works incl. operas & zarzuelas *Don Lucas del Cigarral, Euda d'Uriach, Maruxa, Balada de carnaval, Doña Francisquita* (on Lope de Vega's *La discreta enamorada*) & c. 60 others; *Canciones epigramáticas* for voice & pf., &c.

Vivo (It.) = Lively, animated. The same as *vivace*, but more rarely used.

Vladigerov, Panchu (b. Sofia, 18. III. 1899), Bulg. comp. Studied with Juon and Georg Schumann in Berlin and at the Sofia Cons.

Works incl. opera *Tsar Kaloyan*; incid. m. for Strindberg's *A Dream Play*; Bulg. Rhapsody *Vardar*; v. Conc.; pf. Trio; v. & pf. So.; pf. pieces; songs, &c.

Vltava (Smetana). *See* **Má Vlast.**

Vocal Score. *See* **Score.**

Vocalise (Fr.) / **Vocalizzo** (It.) } Any kind of voc. exercise without words, also sometimes in recent years a comp. for voice without words for concert perf. (the most ambitious being Medtner's *Sonata-V.*); also used as a synonym for Solfège and Solfeggio.

Voce di gola (It.) = Throat voice; voice of a guttural quality.

Voce di petto (It.) = Chest Voice.

Voce di testa (It.) = Head Voice.

Vogel, Charles (Louis Adolphe) (b. Lille, 17. V. 1808; d. Paris, 11. IX. 1892), Fr.-Belg. comp. of Ger. descent. Studied at the Paris Cons.

Works incl. operas *Le Podestat, Le Siège de Leyde, La Moissonneuse, Rompons, Le Nid de cigognes, Gredin de Pigoche, La Filleule du roi*; orat. *Le Jugement dernier*; syms.; stg. 4tets, stg. 5tets; songs incl. *Les Trois Couleurs*, &c.

Vögel, Die (*The Birds*), opera by Braunfels (lib. by comp., based on the comedy by Aristophanes), prod. Munich, 4. XII. 1920.

Vogel, Johann Christoph (b. Nuremberg, 1756; d. Paris, 26. VI. 1788), Ger. comp. Pupil of Riepel at Ratisbon. He went to Paris in 1776 to join the household of the Duc de Montmorency and later that of the Comte de Valentinois. He was an enthusiastic partisan of Gluck, whose work he imitated and who accepted the ded. of his *Toison d'or*.

Works incl. operas *La Toison d'or* & *Démophon*; syms.; var. concs.; chamber m., &c.

Vogel, Vladimir Rudolfovitch (b. Moscow, 29. II. 1896), Rus. comp. of Ger. descent. Studied in Rus., later with Tiessen and Busoni in Berlin.

Works incl. cantatas *Thyl Claes* (after *Till Eulenspiegel*) & *The Fall of Wagadu* for solo voices, chor. & 5 saxophones; *Sinfonia fugata*, *2 Studies*, *Devise*, *Tripartita* for orch.; v. Conc.; stg. 4tets, *Composition* & *Chaconne*, *Étude and Toccata* for pf.; *Composition* for 2 pfs., &c.

Vogelgesang. *See* **Ornithoparcus.**

Vogelhändler, Der (*The Bird Dealer*), operetta by Zeller (lib. by Moritz West & Ludwig Held), prod. Vienna, Theater an der Wien, 10. I. 1891.

Vogelsang. *See* **Ornithoparcus.**

Vogelweide, Walther von der (b. ? Tyrol or Swi., *c.* 1165; d. ? Würzburg, *c.* 1230), Ger. poet, minnesinger & comp. Pupil of Reinmar von Hagenau in Aus. He was in service at the Aus. court in Vienna, then led a wandering life in Ger. and after 1220 prob. lived at an estate given to him at Würzburg. Only a few of his tunes have been preserved.

Vogl, Heinrich (b. Au nr. Munich, 15. I. 1845; d. Munich, 21. IV. 1900), Ger. ten. singer. Began his career as a schoolmaster, but learnt singing from F. Lachner at Munich, also studied acting. He made his 1st stage appearance there in 1865. He married the sop. Therese Thoma in 1868. He appeared in the 1st 2 parts of Wagner's *Ring* at Munich in 1869–70 and in the prod. of the whole work at Bayreuth in 1876.

Vogl, Johann Michael (b. Steyr, 10. VIII. 1768; d. Vienna, 19. XI. 1840), Aus. bar. singer. Educ. at the monastery of Kremsmünster and Vienna Univ., he was engaged by Süssmayr in 1794 and made his 1st appearance as a court opera singer in 1795. He met Schubert in 1816 and was the 1st important artist to sing his songs in public. He retired from the stage with a pension in 1822 and devoted himself to songs.

Vogl (*née* **Thoma**), **Therese** (b. Tutzing, Bavaria, 12. XI. 1845; d. Munich, 29. IX. 1921), Ger. sop. singer. Studied at the Munich Cons. and made her 1st stage appearance at Carlsruhe in 1865. In 1868 she married Heinrich V.

Vogler, Carl (b. Oberrohrdorf, Aargau, 26. II. 1874), Swi. comp. Studied at Lucerne, with Hegar and others at Zürich and with Rheinberger and others at Munich. In 1915 he became prof. at the Zürich Cons. and in 1919 joint dir. with Andreae. Many official mus. posts were conferred on him.

Works incl. operas *Rübezahl* & *Fiedelhänschen*, play with m. *Mutter Sybille*; org. works; songs & part-songs, &c.

Vogler, Georg Joseph (b. Würzburg, 15. VI. 1749; d. Darmstadt, 6. V. 1814), Ger. pfst. & comp. Showed great mus. gifts as a child, esp. at the org., but received a relig. educ. at a Jesuit coll. Later he studied law at Bamberg Univ., but in 1771 left for Mannheim. In 1773 the elector sent him to It. to study with Martini at Bologna, but he did not get on with him, nor with Vallotti at Padua; he went on to Rome, where he received holy orders as a secular priest at the end of the year (hence being known as Abbé V.). After some lessons from Mysliveček he returned to Mannheim in 1775, where he became court chaplain and 2nd mus. dir. There in 1777 he met Mozart, who disliked him. He followed the court to Munich in 1780. In 1783 he succeeded Holzbauer as chief mus. dir., but he had frequent leave of absence for his travels as pf. virtuoso, which took him all over Eur. and beyond. In 1786–99 he was mus. dir. at the Swe. court at Stockholm, but during these years he again travelled extensively and frequently. At the end he received a large pension, went to live in Copenhagen until 1800 and then returned to Ger. In 1802–4 he was in Vienna and in 1807 he was invited by the Duke of Hesse-Darmstadt to settle near his court. He opened a school of m. at Darmstadt, where Meyerbeer and Weber became his pupils.

Works incl. operas *Albert III von Bayern*, *Erwin und Elmire* (Goethe), *La Kermesse*, *Castore e Polluce*, *Gustav Adolph och Ebba Brahe*, *Samori* & others, operetta *Der Kaufmann von Smyrna*; ballet *Rendezvous de chasse*; incid. m. to Shakespeare's *Hamlet*; chors. for Racine's *Athalie* & Skjöldebrand's *Hermann von Unna*; 7 masses, motets, psalms & other church m.; cantata *Ino* (Ramler), 4 syms.; several pf. concs., vars. for pf. & orch.; 18 pf. trios & much other chamber m.; pf. & v. sos.; pf. sos. & vars., &c.; 6 sos. for 2 pfs.; chor. works, &c.

Voices. The parts in a polyphonic comp., even one for insts.

Voicing. The prod. of particular qualities of tone by mechanical means in org. construction, and more partic. the control of the tone of a whole range of pipes governed by a single stop in such a way that the tone-colour is exactly the same throughout.

Voix céleste (Fr. = heavenly voice). An 8-ft. org. stop with 2 pipes to each note, one tuned slightly sharper than the other, so that they prod. a quivering effect.

Voix sombrée (Fr.) = Veiled Voice.

Volata (It. lit. flight). A run or other rapid passage.

Volbach, Fritz (b. Wippelfürth, Rhineland, 17. XII. 1861; d. ? Münster, 1941), Ger. cond. & comp. Studied at the Cologne Cons. He went on the staff of the Royal Inst. of Church M. in Berlin, 1886, became mus. dir. at Mainz in 1892 and prof. of m. at Tübingen Univ. in 1907, moving to that of Münster in 1919.

Works incl. opera *Die Kunst zu lieben*; ballads for male voices & orch. *Der Troubadour, Am Siegfrieds-Brunnen, König Laurins Rosengarten*; *Raffael* for chor., orch. & org., *Hymne an Maria* (Dante) for chor., solo insts. & org.; Sym. in B min., symph. poems *Es waren zwei Königskinder* & *Alt Heidelberg*; *Easter* for org. & orch.; pf. 5tet, 5tet for wind & pf.; song cycle *Vom Pagen und der Königstochter* (Geibel), &c.

Volkert, Franz (b. Friedland nr. Bunzlau, 2. II. 1767; d. Vienna, 22. III. 1845), Aus. orgst., cond. & comp. Settled in Vienna as orgst. and became cond. at the Theater an der Wien.

Works incl. *c.* 150 mus. pieces for the stage (farces, melodramas, pantomimes, &c.); graduals & other church m.; pf. trios; vars. for pf.; songs, &c.

Volkmann, (Friedrich) Robert (b. Lommatzsch, Saxony, 6. IV. 1815; d. Budapest, 29. X. 1883), Ger. comp. Pupil of his father, a schoolmaster and cantor, and of another local musn. for stg. insts. In 1836 he went to Leipzig for further study, was a private m. tutor in Prague, 1839–41, lived and taught at Budapest in 1841–54 and in Vienna in 1854–78, when he became prof. of comp. at the Nat. Mus. Acad. in Budapest.

Works incl. incid. m. for Shakespeare's *Richard III*; 2 masses for male voices; 2 syms., 2 Serenades, Festival Ovt. for orch.; *Concertstück* for pf. & orch., co. Conc., Serenade for co. & stgs.; 6 stg. 4tets, 2 pf. trios & other chamber m.; 2 sonatinas for v. & pf., v. & pf. pieces, co. & pf. pieces; So. & *c.* 20 other op. nos. for pf.; several pf. duet works; 9 op. nos. of songs, &c.

Volkslied (Ger. = Folksong). Although Ger. possesses a treasury of old folksongs, many of which became hymns for the Lutheran church, the term V. no longer exclusively or even principally designates them: what Gers. now mean by V. is a type of popular song, such as Silcher's *Loreley*, the comps. of which are known (which is not the case with genuine folksongs), and which have passed into general currency, often for sentimental rather than artistic reasons.

Volkstümlich (Ger. adj. from *Volkstum* = folk matters, folklore). A word used in Ger. to describe popular m. that has become or is likely to become part of the nation's mus. heritage, without actually belonging to folk m. What Gers. commonly call *Volkslied* (*see above*) would thus more properly be described by them as *volkstümliches Lied*.

Vollerthun, Georg (b. Fürstenau nr. Danzig, 29. IX. 1876), Ger. cond. & comp. Pupil of Tappert, Gernsheim and others. He cond. at var. towns, lived in Paris in 1908–10 and in 1933 became prof. at the Hochschule für Musik in Berlin.

Works incl. operas *Veeda, Islandsaga* & *Der Freikorporal* (after Gustav Freytag); songs & duets, &c.

Volta (It. = time, turn, jump). The word is used in such mus. directions as *prima volta* (first time), *seconda volta* (second time), *ancora una volta* (once again). It is also the name of an old dance incl. a characteristic jump. *See* **Lavolta.**

Voltaire, François Marie Arouet de (1694–1778), Fr. man of letters, philosopher & dramatist. *See* **Alzira** (Verdi), **Fée Urgèle** (Duni), **Knipper** (*Candide*), **Lefèbvre** (*Zaïre*), **Olympie** (Spontini), **Pleyel (I.)** (*Fée Urgèle*), **Rameau** (*Samson* & *Princesse de Navarre*), **Schulz** (*Fée U.*), **Semiramide** (Rossini), **Sémiramis** (Catel), **Stuntz** (*Heinrich IV*), **Tancredi** (Rossini), **Woelfl** (*Alzire*).

Volte (Fr. for the It. dance). *See* **Lavolta.**

Volti subito. *See* **V.S.**

Volumier, Jean Baptiste (b. ? Spa., *c.* 1670; d. Dresden, 7. X. 1728), Flem. vst., dulcimer player & comp. Educ. at the Fr. court and in 1692 transferred to that of Prus. in Berlin, where he became leader of the orch. and dir. of the dance m. In 1709 he went to Dresden as mus. dir. to the Saxon court, where in 1717 he arr. the contest between Bach and Marchand.

Works incl. ballets, divertissements, dances, &c.

Voluntary. An org. piece intended for use in church, but not part of the service. In modern practice it is used only at the beginning and esp. at the end of a service, in the latter case often serving to play the congregation out.

Vom Blatt (lesen, spielen) (Ger. lit. [read, play] from the leaf or sheet = at sight). Sight-reading.

Vomáčka, Boleslav (b. Mlada Boleslav, 28. VI. 1887), Cz. critic & comp. Studied law, and m. with Novák at the Prague Cons. He was a solicitor until 1919, when he entered the Ministry of Social Welfare. He also worked as critic with 2 newspapers and is ed. of the monthly *Listy Hudební Matice.*

Works incl. opera *The Waterman*; symph. poem *Mládí* (*Youth*) & Chaconne for orch.; v. & pf. So.; So. and cycle *The Quest* for pf.; song cycle; partsongs, &c.

Vondel, Joost van den (1587–1679), Dutch poet & dramatist. *See* **Diepenbrock, Mengelberg (R.), Zweers** (*Gysbrecht van Amstel*).

Voormolen, Alexander (b. Rotterdam, 3. III. 1895), Dutch critic & comp. Studied in Paris and was much influenced by Ravel. On his return home he became m. critic to the *Nieuwe Rotterdamsche Courant.*

Works incl. melodrama *Beatrijs*; ballets *Baron Hop*, *Le Roi Grenouille* & *Diana*; Sinfonietta; Vars. for v. & orch., Conc. for 2 obs. & orch.; chamber m., &c.

Vopelius, Gottfried (b. Herwigsdorf nr. Zittau, 28. I. 1635; d. Leipzig, 3. II. 1715), Ger. comp. App. cantor of St. Nicholas's church, Leipzig, 1675. Compiled a book of chorales (1682) and harmonized many, beside writing tunes for some.

Vorhalt (Ger.) = Suspension.

Vörösmarty, Mihály (1800–55), Hung. poet & dramatist. *See* **Weiner** (*Csongor and Tünde*).

Vorschlag. *See* **Ornaments.**

Vorspiel (Ger. lit. foreplay) = Prelude.

Vortrag (Ger.) = Delivery, performance, interpretation.

Vortragsbezeichnungen or **Vortragszeichen** } Ger. Indications of perf., directions, expression marks.

Vos, Laurent de. *See* **Voz.**

Vox angelica or **Vox coelestis** } An 8-ft. open metal org. stop of very delicate tone. The term is also sometimes used for the Voix céleste stop where one of the 2 sets of pipes is tuned slightly flat instead of sharp.

Vox humana. An 8-ft. reed org. stop prod. an imitation of the human voice. Its effect is so striking as to prod. a sensation in an audience whenever it is used, as it is by cinema orgsts. in and out of season. Serious concert orgsts. have learnt to avoid it.

Voyevoda, opera by Tchaikovsky (lib. by comp. & Alexander Nikolaievitch Ostrovsky, based on a play by the latter), prod. Moscow, 11. II. 1869.

Voz (or Vos), Laurent de (b. Antwerp, 1533; d. Cambrai, I. 1580), Flem. comp. Brother of the painter Martin de Vos. Worked at Antwerp cath. and was app. mus. dir. and choirmaster at Cambrai cath. by the archbp. Louis de Berlaymont. When the latter's place was usurped by Inchy, V. comp. a motet compiled from words from the Psalms in such a way as to attack the latter, who had him hanged without a trial.

Works incl. motets, chansons, &c.

Vrchlický, Jaroslav (1853–1912), Cz. poet & playwright. *See* **Fibich** (*Night at Karlstein*), **Foerster (J. B.)** (*Samson*), **St. Ludmilla** (**Dvořák**).

Other mus. works based on his writings are: Dvořák, opera *Armida*; Fibich, operatic trilogy *Hippodamia* & melodramas *Haakon* & *Queen Emma*; Foerster (J. B.), melodramas *The Three Riders* & *The Legend of St. Julia*; Janáček, chor. work *Amarus*; Novák, opera *A Night at Karlstein.*

Vreuls, Victor (b. Verviers, 4. II. 1876; d. Brussels, 27. VII. 1944), Belg. cond., violist & comp. Studied at the Verviers school of m. and the Liége Cons., later with d'Indy in Paris. He became prof. of va. and harmony at the Schola Cantorum there and in 1906 dir. of the Luxembourg Cons.

Works incl. operas *Olivier le simple* & *Un Songe d'une nuit d'été* (after Shakespeare); Sym. with solo v., 3 symph. poems, Ovt. & Prelude for orch.; cantata & *Triptyche* for chor.; songs & inst. pieces with orch.; stg. 4tet, pf. 4tet, 2 pf. trios; 2 sos. for v. & pf., So. & *Poème* for co. & pf.; songs, &c.

Vrieslander, Otto (b. Münster, 18. VII. 1880), Ger. mcolst. & comp. Studied at the Cologne Cons. Settled at Munich in 1906 and went to live at Locarno in Swi. in 1920. As a mcolst. he was a pupil of Schenker, whose unfinished *Harmonielehre* he completed, and he has written much on C. P. E. Bach and ed. some of his works.

Works incl. songs from *Des Knaben Wunderhorn*, on Giraud's *Pierrot lunaire* & to words by Goethe, Keller, Theodor Storm, &c.

Vst. (abbr.) = Violinist.

Vuataz, Roger (b. Geneva, 4. I. 1898) Swi. comp. Studied at the Geneva

Cons., Barblan and Jaques-Dalcroze being among his masters. In 1918 he became orgst. to the Fr. Protestant church there. He was cond. of several choirs and prof. at the Acad. de Musique. In 1928–34 he was also m. critic to the *Journal de Genève*.

Works incl. stage works *Mil-six-cent-deux* & *Le Mystère d'Abraham*; orat. *Abraham*; motets, psalms; *Le Rhône* for ten. and chor., *La Flûte de roseau* for chor.; *Deux pièces brèves* & *Petit Concert* for orch.; *Suite sur deux thèmes populaires anciens* for 15 insts., *Géométrie & Musique* for 5 insts. & other chamber m.; org. & pf. works, &c.

Vuert, Giaches. *See* **Wert.**

Vuillaume, Jean Baptiste (b. Mirecourt, Vosges, 7. X. 1798; d. Paris, 19. II. 1875), Fr. v. maker. Estab. independently in Paris, 1828.

Vuillermoz, Émile (b. Lyons, 23. V. 1878), Fr. m. critic & author. Studied law and literature at Lyons Univ. and m. at the Paris Cons., where Fauré was among his masters. He gave up comp. to become critic to the *Mercure musical* and from 1911 ed. the journal of the Société Musicale Indépendante. Among his books are studies of modern m., 50 years of Fr. m. and Ravel.

Vulpius, Melchior (b. Wasungen, Henneberg, *c.* 1560; d. Weimar, VIII. 1615), Ger. comp. He became cantor at Weimar in 1602 and remained there to his death. He harmonized many hymn-tunes not his own and wrote a treatise, *Musicae compendium*. Goethe's wife was prob. a descendant of his.

Works incl. *Sacrae cantiones* for 5–8 voices, canticles, hymns for 4–5 voices & other sacred m.; Passion orat. according to St. Matthew, &c.

Vuota (It. fem. adj. = empty). A direction to stg. players to play a note or notes on an open stg.

Vycpálek, Ladislav (b. Vršovice nr. Prague, 23. II. 1882), Cz. comp. Studied philos. at Prague Univ., took a doctor's degree in it, and became secretary to the Univ. library. He also studied comp. with Novák at the Cons.

Works incl. cantata *The Last Things of Man*; song-cycles *Quiet Reconcilement*, *Visions*, *In God's Hands*, Moravian ballads & folk-songs; pf. pieces; chors. for mixed & male voices, &c.

Vyšehrad (Smetana). *See* **Má Vlast.**

W

Wächterlieder (Ger. = watchmen's songs). Songs formerly used in Ger. by night watchmen in the streets to announce the hours and by fire-watchers on church towers to proclaim festival days, &c. They were often folksongs and some have passed into currency as hymns for the Lutheran church.

Waddell, Helen (b. 1889), Ir. poetess & playwright. *See* **Barber** (chors.).

Waelrant, Hubert (b. Tongerloo, N. Brabant, *c.* 1518; d. Antwerp, 19. XI. 1595), Flem. comp. He (?) went to study with Willaert at Venice, and by 1544 was a singer at Notre-Dame, Antwerp, where 3 years later he estab. a school of m. In *c.* 1554–8 he was assoc. with J. de Laet as m. pub.

Works inc. motets, madrigals, chansons, &c.

Waffenschmied (von Worms), Der (*The Armourer* [*of Worms*]), opera by Lortzing (lib. by comp., based on Friedrich Julius Wilhelm Ziegler's comedy *Liebhaber and Nebenbuhler in einer Person*), prod. Vienna, Theater an der Wien, 31. V. 1846. Weigl's opera *Il rivale di se stesso* (*His Own Rival*), prod. Milan 1808, was based on the same play.

Wagenaar, Bernard (b. Arnhem, 18. VII. 1894), Dutch-Amer. comp. Studied with his father, Johan W., and at the Utrecht Cons. and learnt the v. and keyboard insts. In 1921 he settled in N.Y. and joined the N.Y. Phil. Orch. and from 1927 taught at the Juillard Graduate School there.

Works incl. chamber opera *Pieces of Eight*; 3 syms., Sinfonietta, Divertimento, *Feuilleton*, &c. for orch.; v. Conc., Triple Conc. for fl., hp. & co.; 3 stg. 4tets, Concertino for 8 insts.; v. & pf. So., Sonatina for co. & pf.; 3 Chinese songs for voice, fl., hp. & pf.; pf. So.; Eclogue for org.; songs, incl. settings of Edna St. Vincent Millay, &c.

Wagenaar, Johan (b. Utrecht, 1. XI. 1862), Dutch comp., father of prec. Studied with Richard Hol and with Herzogenberg in Berlin. App. orgst. at Utrecht cath. in 1888 and dir. of the Cons. there in 1904, also cond. of a chor. soc. In 1918 he became dir. of the Royal Cons. at The Hague, retiring in 1937 in favour of S. Dresden.

Works incl. operas *The Doge of Venice, The Cid* (after Corneille) & *Jupiter amans*; ovts. to Shakespeare's *Taming of the Shrew*, Goldoni's *Philosophical Princess*, Kleist's *Amphitryon* and Rostand's *Cyrano de Bergerac*, ovt. *Saul and David*, Funeral March & Waltz Suite for orch.; Fantasy on Dutch folksongs for male chor. & orch., female chors. with pf.; v. & pf. pieces; pf. pieces; songs, &c.

Wagenseil, Georg Christoph (b. Vienna, 15. I. 1715; d. Vienna, 1. III. 1777), Aus. comp. Studied in Vienna with Fux and others and in 1736, on that master's recommendation, received a court scholarship, becoming court comp. in 1739. In 1741–50 he was also orgst. to the dowager empress and he was app. m. master to the Empress Maria Theresa and her daughters. Mozart at the age of 6 played one of W.'s concs. at court and he turned pages for him.

Works incl. operas *I lamenti d'Orfeo, Ariodante, Le cacciatrici* & c. 10 others; orats. *La redenzione* & *Gioas, rè di Giuda*; 2 masses, Requiem, motets & other church m.; syms.; pf. concs.; divertimenti for pf. solo, &c.

Wagenseil, Johann Christoph (b. Nuremberg, 26. XI. 1633; d. Altdorf, 9. X. 1708), Ger. historian and librarian. Wrote a book on the art of the Meistersinger, pub. in 1697, which served Wagner as a source for *The Mastersingers*.

Waghalter, Ignaz (b. Warsaw, 15. III. 1882), Pol.-Ger. cond. & comp. Pupil of Gernsheim. He cond. opera in Berlin and Essen, 1907–23, and for some years from 1925 cond. the State Sym. Orch. in N.Y., returning to Berlin later and going to Prague in 1933.

Works incl. operas *Der Teufelsweg, Mandragola* (after Machiavelli), *Jugend, Der späte Gast* & *Sataniel*, operettas; v. Conc.; stg. 4tet; v. & pf. So., &c.

Wagner, Johanna (b. Seelze nr. Hanover, 13. X. 1826; d. Würzburg, 16. X. 1894), Ger. sop. singer, niece of Richard W., who engaged her for the Royal Opera at Dresden, where she was the 1st Elisabeth in his *Tannhäuser* in 1845. In 1847 she went to Paris to study with García. In 1859 she married an official named Jachmann.

Wagner, Peter (Josef) (b. Kürenz nr. Trèves, 19. VIII. 1865; d. Fribourg, Swi., 17. X. 1931), Ger. mcolst. Studied at Strasburg Univ. and later in Berlin. In 1897 he became prof. at the Univ. of Fribourg, where he founded a Gregorian coll. in 1901. His works incl. a hist. of the mass and studies of medieval and Gregorian m.

Wagner-Régeny, Rudolf (b. Szasz-Régen, 28. VIII. 1903), Hung. comp. of Ger. descent. Studied at Leipzig and Berlin.

Works incl. operas *Der Günstling, Mary Tudor* (after Hugo), *Der nackte König* (on Andersen's *The Emperor's New Clothes*), *Maschopulos, Sganarelle* (after Molière), *Esau und Jakob, La Sainte Courtisane* & *Die Bürger von Calais* (Georg Kaiser); ballet *Der zerbrochene Krug* (after Kleist's comedy), &c.

Wagner, (Wilhelm) Richard (b. Leipzig, 22. V. 1813; d. Venice, 13. II. 1883), Ger. comp. & author. Son of a clerk to the city police, who d. 6 months after W.'s birth. His mother removed to Dresden and married the actor and painter Ludwig Geyer in 1815, who in turn d. in 1821. W. learnt the pf. but tried to read voc. scores of operas instead of practising and also acquired knowledge of opera from 2 elder sisters who were both stage singers. He wrote poems and a tragedy at the age of about 13 and at 14 went to school at Leipzig, where the family had returned. There he heard Beethoven's works and tried to imitate them in comps. of his own. In 1830 Dorn perf. an ovt. of his in the theatre, but it was received with scorn as a very crude work. He then studied harmony and ctpt. with Weinlig at St. Thomas's school and entered the Univ. in 1831. At 19 he began an opera, *Die Hochzeit*, but on the advice of his sister abandoned it for *Die Feen*. The libs., as always later on, were written by himself. He became chor. master at the theatre of Würzburg in 1833 and cond. of a summer theatre at Lauchstädt, the company of which was at Magdeburg in winter, where he went with it. Minna Planer (b. 1809) was there as an actress, and he married her on 24. XI. 1836, at Königsberg, where she had a new engagement. The Magdeburg company had been dissolved soon after a disastrous prod. of W.'s 3rd opera, *Das Liebesverbot*, on 29. III. 1836. The Königsberg theatre also went into liquidation just after W. had been app. cond., but in the summer of 1837 he became cond. at Riga. In I. 1839 his post was given to Dorn and he decided to go to Paris by sea. A very stormy voyage took them as far as the coast of Norway and then to Eng., and they did not reach Paris until IX, in desperate straits. They spent nearly all the time until IV. 1842 there in wretched poverty, but W., in such time as he could spare from hack-work, had managed to finish both *Rienzi* and *The Flying Dutchman*, the former of which had been accepted by Dresden and was prod. there on 20. X. 1842, the latter work following on 2. I. 1843, W. being app. 2nd cond. at the court opera. *Tannhäuser* was finished in IV. 1845 and prod. on 19. X. When the Fr. Revol. of 1848 spread its influence across Eur., W. showed sympathy with liberal ideas, and when the revolt at Dresden failed in V. 1849 he had to fly and a warrant for his arrest was issued, should he be found in Saxony. Not deeming the rest of Ger. safe, he went to Swi. There, at Zürich, he worked on the lib. and m. for the *Nibelung's Ring* cycle, which was interrupted by *Tristan and Isolde*, written under the influence of Mathilde Wesendonk, the wife of a friend and benefactor with whom he was more and more deeply in love. In 1858 Minna created a scene and Mathilde decided to stay with her husband, W. going to Venice and later to Lucerne, where *Tristan* was finished in VIII. 1859. In 1860 a revised version of *Tannhäuser*, with a ballet, was commissioned by the Paris Opéra, and W. complied so far as his artistic conscience would let him, which was not enough for the patrons, who saw to it that after the prod. on 13. III. 1861 the work should fail disastrously. W. next went to Vienna, where he heard *Lohengrin* for the 1st time, though it had been prod. by Liszt at Weimar in 1850. In 1862 he settled at Biebrich on the Rhine to work on *The Mastersingers*, but was in Vienna again by the end of the year, staying there until III. 1864, when he was pursued by his creditors and threatened with imprisonment. At the critical moment he was invited by Ludwig II of Bavaria to join his court at Munich as friend and artistic adviser, and he saw to it that Hans von Bülow was app. cond. Bülow's wife, Cosima (1837–1930), was Liszt's daughter, and she and W. soon fell deeply in love. This created a scandal which was fully exploited by his enemies, the courtiers and officials who feared his influence on the youthful and idealistic king, and soon after the prod. of *Tristan*, 10. VI. 1865, W. was obliged to go into exile once more. He chose Triebschen on the lake of Lucerne in Swi., where Cosima joined him in III. 1866. Bülow divorced her in 1870 and on 25. VIII she married W., whose 1st wife had d. 25. I. 1866. After the prod. of *The Mastersingers*, 21. VI. 1868, at Munich, W. quietly continued work on the *Ring* cycle, dropped so many years before, and planned a festival theatre to be erected by subscription at Bayreuth in Bavaria. The family took a house there in 1874; rehearsals began the following year, and the four works were prod. on 13–7. VIII. 1876. *Parsifal* followed, after a slow process of comp. much interrupted by illness and by holidays in It. for his health, on 26. VII. 1882. W. left for Venice in IX, greatly exhausted and subject to frequent heart attacks, from one of which he d. there.

Works incl. operas *Die Hochzeit* (unfinished), *Die Feen*, *Das Liebesverbot*, *Rienzi*, *Der fliegende Holländer*, *Tannhäuser*, *Lohengrin*, *Tristan und Isolde*, *Die Meistersinger von Nürnberg*, *Der Ring des Nibelungen* (comprising *Das Rheingold*, *Die Walküre*, *Siegfried* & *Götterdämmerung*), *Parsifal*; Sym., 9 concert ovts. (2 unpub.), incl. *Eine Faust Ouvertüre* (after Goethe), 3 marches for orch., *Siegfried Idyll* for small orch.; several chor. works; a number of songs, incl. 7 from Goethe's *Faust*, 5 poems by Mathilde Wesendonk & 6 settings of Fr. poems; a So. and some smaller pf. works; *Albumblatt* for v. & pf.; stg. 4tet (unpub.), &c.

For settings of his libs. by other comps. *see* **Bella** (*Veland the Smith*), **Bianca und Giuseppe** (Kittl), **Mihalovich** (*Wieland der Schmied*), **Vaisseau-fantôme** (Dietsch).

Wagner, (Helferich) Siegfried (Richard) (b. Triebschen, Swi., 6. VI. 1869; d. Bayreuth, 4. VIII. 1930), Ger. cond. & comp., son of prec. Although intended for an architect, he studied m. with Humperdinck and Kneise, and gained much experience by assisting at the Wagner festival perfs. at Bayreuth, some of which he cond. after 1896. When his mother, Cosima W., became too old to manage the affairs of the theatre, he took its dir. in hand.

Works incl. operas *Der Bärenhäuter*, *Herzog Wildfang*, *Der Kobold*, *Bruder Lustig*, *Sternengebot*, *Banadietrich*, *An allem ist Hütchen schuld*, *Schwarzschwanenreich*, *Sonnenflammen*, *Der Schmied von Marienburg*, *Der Friedensengel*, *Der Heidenkönig* & 3 others not perf. or pub.; symph. poem *Sehnsucht*, &c.

Wagner Tubas. Brass wind insts. of the hn. var. devised by Wagner for his *Ring des Nibelungen*, which requires 5, but only 3 different kinds: 2 ten. Ts. not unlike the Euphonium, but with funnel-shaped mouthpieces, ranging from B♭ on the 2nd line of the bass stave to F on the top line of the treble stave; 2 bass Ts. ranging from B♭ an 8ve lower to F 2 8ves lower; and a db. T. ranging an 8ve lower than the ordinary orch. T.

Wailly, (Louis Auguste) Paul (Warnier) de (b. Amiens, 16. V. 1854; d. Paris, 18. VI. 1933), Fr. comp. He studied law, but became a pupil of Franck for comp.

Works incl. dramatic orat. *L'Apôtre*; *Hylas, idylle antique* for voices & orch.; church m.; 3 syms.; pf. 5tet, Octet & other chamber m.; inst. sos.; 26 harmonium pieces; songs, &c.

Waisenhaus, Das (*The Orphanage*), opera by Weigl (lib. ? by Georg Friedrich Treitschke), prod. Vienna, Kärntnertor Theatre, 4. X. 1808.

Wait. An obs. inst. of the ob. type, similar to the Shawm, used in Eng. by the Christmas Waits and, in the 13th cent., by the keepers of the City of London gates and other town gates for the purpose of signalling 'All 's well,' &c.

Waits. Orig. the keepers of town gates, in the 15th-16th cents. salaried bands employed to play at var. functions, afterwards amateur singers and players perf. outside the houses of the more substantial citizens for rewards in money and refreshment at Christmas-tide; also the name of pieces sung and played on these occasions.

Wakefield, (Augusta) Mary (b. Sedgwick nr. Kendal, 19. VIII. 1853; d. Grange-over-Sands, Lancs., 16. IX. 1910), Eng. amateur con. singer, pfst. & comp. In 1885 she started the 1st competitive festival at her home at Sedgwick, which was later transferred to Kendal and became the Westmorland Mus. Festival.

Wald, Der (*The Forest*), opera by Ethel Smyth (lib. by comp.), prod. Berlin, Opera, 9. IV. 1902.

Wald Flute. A 4-ft. & 8-ft. org. stop similar to the Claribel, but with the mouths of the pipes inverted.

Waldhorn (Ger. =forest hn.). The Ger. name for the hunting-hn. without valves, prod. only the natural harmonics; but still sometimes used loosely to describe the orch. hn.

Waldmädchen, Das (*The Woodland Maid*), opera by Weber (lib. by Carl Franz von Steinsberg), prod. Freiberg, Saxony, 23. XI. 1800. The 1st version of *Silvana*.

Waldmann, Maria (b. Vienna, 1844;

d. Ferrara, 6. XI. 1920), Aus.-It. m.-sop. singer. The 1st Amneris in the Milan prod. of Verdi's *Aida* and the m.-sop. in the 1st perf. of his Requiem. She married the Duke Galeazzo Massari of Ferrara and retired from the stage.

Waldstein, Ferdinand (Ernst Gabriel), Count (b. Duchcov, Boh., 24. III. 1762; d. Vienna, 29. VIII. 1823), Boh. mus. amateur. Patron of Beethoven, whom he met in the early days at Bonn and knew later in Vienna.

'Waldstein' Sonata. Beethoven's pf. So. in C maj., Op. 53, comp. in 1804, so called (not by B.) because it is ded. to the above.

Waldteufel, Emil (b. Strasburg, 9. XII. 1837; d. Paris, 16. II. 1915), Fr. (Alsat.) pfst. & comp. Studied at the Paris Cons. He joined a pf. factory and was later app. pfst. to the Empress Eugénie.

Works incl. many hundreds of waltzes & other dances, incl. a waltz on Chabrier's *España*.

Waley, Simon (Waley) (b. London, 23. VIII. 1827; d. London, 30. XII. 1875), Eng. pfst. & comp. Studied with Moscheles, Sterndale Bennett and others and began to comp. as a boy. He often perf. in public, but was also a member of the Stock Exchange.

Works incl. Psalms cxvii & cxviii for the synagogue; pf. Conc.; 2 pf. trios; many studies & pieces for pf.; pf. duets; songs & duets, &c.

Walker, Ernest (b. Bombay, 15. VII. 1870), Eng. pfst., teacher, mcolst. & comp. Educ. at Balliol Coll., Oxford, where he took the D.Mus. in 1898 and remained as teacher at the Univ., examiner and, in 1900–25, mus. dir. at Balliol. His books incl. *A History of M. in Eng.*

Works incl. incid. m. to Euripides' *Rhesus*; *Stabat Mater, Ode to a Nightingale* (Keats) for solo voice, chor. & orch., *Hymn to Dionysus* (Euripides) & *Neptune's Empire* (Campion) for chor. & orch.; Concert Ovt. in F min., *Fantasy on a Norfolk Folksong* for orch.; Fantasy for stg. 4tet, pf. 5tet, 5tet for hn. & stgs., 2 pf. 4tets, pf. Trio; Vars. for pf. (left hand), cl. & stg. trio; Vars. on a theme by Joachim for v. & pf., Vars. for va. & pf., co. & pf. So.; Waltzes for 2 pfs.; songs from *England's Helicon* for voc. 4tet & pf.; pf. pieces; songs, &c.

Walker, Frank (b. Gosport, Hants., 10. VI. 1907), Eng. writer on m. Educ. at Portsmouth Grammar School, engaged in an electro-techn. career and during the 2nd world war served in the Army P.O. in It., where he made researches in Verdi's biog., which resulted in his 2nd book, *The Man Verdi*, the 1st being a biog. of Hugo Wolf.

Walküre, Die (*The Valkyrie*, Wagner). *See* **Ring des Nibelungen.**

Wallace, Lewis (1827–1905), Amer. general, politician & novelist. *See* **Kelley** (*Ben Hur*).

Wallace, (William) Vincent (b. Waterford, 11. III. 1812; d. Château de Bagen, Pyrenees, 12. X. 1865), Ir. comp. Pupil of his father, a bandmaster and bn. player, who moved to Dublin, where W. played the org. & v. in public as a boy. In 1831 he married Isabella Kelly, but they separated in 1835 and he lived with the pfst. Hélène Stoepel, by whom he had 2 sons. In 1834 he appeared at Dublin with a v. Conc. of his own. Between 1835–45 he was in Australia and elsewhere abroad, but went to London in the latter year and was induced to comp. *Maritana*. After a successful operatic career, incl. a visit to S. Amer. in 1849 and 14 years in Ger., a commission from the Paris Opéra which he was unable to finish owing to failing eyesight, and another visit to S. & N. Amer. in 1850–3, his health broke down and he was ordered to the Pyrenees.

Works incl. operas *Maritana, Matilda of Hungary, Lurline, The Maid of Zürich* (unpub.), *The Amber Witch, Love's Triumph, The Desert Flower, Estrella* (unfinished), operettas *Gulnare & Olga*; cantata *Maypole*; v. Conc.; pf. m., &c.

Wallace, William (b. Greenock, 3. VII. 1860; d. Malmesbury, Wilts., 16. XII. 1940), Sco. ophthalmic surgeon, mus. author & comp. Educ. at Edinburgh & Glasgow Univs. and in Vienna as an eye specialist, began to practice in 1888, but gave up his profession for m. except during the war of 1914–8. In 1889 he entered the R.A.M. in London for a brief course in comp. and later he became successively secretary and trustee of the Phil. Soc. His books incl. *The Threshold of M., The Mus. Faculty, A Study of Wagner & Liszt, Wagner and the Princess.*

Works incl. opera *Brassolis*; sym. *Koheleth* for chor. & orch.; sym. *The Creation*, symph. poems *The Passing of Beatrice* (after Dante's *Paradiso*), *Anvil or Hammer* (after Goethe's *Koptisches Lied*), *Sister Helen* (after D. G. Rossetti), *To the New Country, Wallace, A.D. 1305–1905, Villon*, suite *The Lady from the Sea* (after Ibsen), symph. prelude to Aeschylus's *Eumenides*, ovt. *In Praise of Scottish Poesie, A Scots Fantasy* for orch., 2 suites for small orch.; pf. Trio in A maj.; *Spa. Songs* for voc. 4tet; song cycles *Freebooter Songs, Jacobite Songs, Lords of the Sea* & other songs, &c.

Wallek-Walewski, Boleslaw (b. Lwów, 1885), Pol. cond. & comp. Studied at his home town, at Cracow with Zelenski and Szopski, and with Riemann at Leipzig. On returning to Lwów he became chor., orch. and operatic cond. and dir. of the Cons.

Works incl. operas *Destiny* & *Jontek's Revenge* (a sequel to Moniuszko's *Halka*); orat. *Apocalypse*; masses, Requiem, motets, psalms and other church m.; scherzo *Bawel and Gawel* for orch.; male-voice chors.; folksong arrs., &c.

Waller, Edmund (1606–87), Eng. poet & dramatist. *See* **Grabu** (*Maid's Tragedy*).

Walliser, Christoph Thomas (b. Strasburg, 17. IV. 1568; d. Strasburg, 26. IV. 1648), Ger. comp. Pupil of Vulpius and others. In 1599 he became dir. of the Mus. Acad. and mus. dir. of 2 churches at Strasburg.

Works incl. incid. m. for Aristophanes' *The Clouds* & other plays; *Ecclesiodae* containing psalms for 4–6 voices or insts., *Ecclesiodae novae* incl. Te Deum, litany, &c. for 4–7 voices, Ger. psalms for 5 voices & other church m.

Wallishauser. *See* **Valesi.**

Wally, La, opera by Catalani (lib. by Luigi Illica, based on Wilhelmine von Hillern's novel *Die Geyer-Wally*), prod. Milan, Teatro alla Scala, 20. I. 1892.

Walmisley, Thomas (Attwood) (b. London, 21. I. 1814; d. Hastings, 17. I. 1856), Eng. orgst. & comp. Learnt m. from his father, the glee comp. and teacher, Thomas Forbes W. (1783–1866), and studied with his godfather, Attwood. After 3 years as orgst. at Croydon, he became orgst. of Trinity and St. John's Colls., Cambridge, in 1833, where he also devoted himself to the study of mathematics and wrote poetry. In 1836 he became Prof. of M., but did not take the Mus.D. degree until 1848.

Works incl. services & anthems; 3 odes for the installation of Univ. chancellors; madrigal *Sweete Floweres*; duets for ob. & pf.; org. works; songs, &c.

Walsh, John (b. ?; d. London, 13. III. 1736), ? Ir. m. pub. Estab. in London early in the 18th cent. Handel was among the comps. whose works he pub.

Walsh, John (b. ? London, ?; d. London, 15. I. 1766), Eng. m. pub., son of prec. Succeeded his father.

Walter, Gustav (b. Bilin, 11. II. 1834; d. Vienna, 30. I. 1910), Boh.-Aus. ten. singer. Studied at the Prague Cons., appeared there and at Brno, and in 1856 made his 1st appearance in Vienna, where he settled down.

Walter, Ignaz (b. Radovice, 1759; d. Ratisbon, IV. 1822), Boh. ten. singer & comp. Pupil of Starzer in Vienna. He made his 1st stage appearance at Prague in 1783 and later took over a company appearing at Frankfort o/M. and Ratisbon. He married the singer Juliane Roberts.

Works incl. opera *Doktor Faust* (based on the orig. version of Goethe's drama); play with m. *Der Spiegelritter* (Kotzebue) & c. 12 others; coronation cantata for the Emperor Leopold; memorial m. for Schiller, &c.

Walter of Evesham. *See* **Odington.**

Waltershausen, Hermann (Wolfgang Sartorius) von (b. Göttingen, 12. X. 1882), Ger. comp. and mus. author. Studied at Strasburg, lost his right arm and foot in a game and learnt to play the pf. and cond. with the left hand. He further studied at Munich from 1901 and attended Sandberger's lectures at the Univ., founded a m. school in 1917 and in 1920 became prof. at the Munich State Acad. of M., being app. dir. in 1922. His books incl. works on mus. style, opera, modern comps., R. Strauss, &c. He also wrote all his opera libs.

Works incl. operas *Oberst Chabert, Pellegrino, Else Klapperzehen, Richardis, Die Rauensteiner Hochzeit, Die Gräfin von Tolosa*; *Apocalyptic Sym., Hero and Leander, Partita on 3 Hymn-tunes*, Comedy Ovt., *Passion and Resurrection M.* for orch.; *Krippenmusik* for hpchd. & chamber orch.; pf. works; songs, &c.

Walther, Johann (b. Thuringia, 1496; d. Torgau, 24. IV. 1570), Ger. bass singer & comp. He sang in the service of the Elector of Saxony and in 1548 organized and dir. the singers of the court chapel at Dresden. In 1554 he retired to Torgau with a pension. He was a friend of Luther's and in 1524 went to Wittenberg to assist him in framing the Ger. Protestant mass.

Works incl. Magnificat, Ger. hymns for 4 voices, sacred songs, some with words by Luther; inst. pieces, &c.

Walther, Johann Gottfried (b. Erfurt, 18. IX. 1684; d. Weimar, 23. III. 1748), Ger. comp., orgst. & lexicographer. Pupil of J. B. Bach (*see* Bach, No. 21) at Erfurt, where in 1702 he became orgst. at St. Thomas's church. In 1707 he was app. town orgst. at Weimar, where he was in close touch with J. S. Bach, his kinsman. He pub. a *Musicalisches Lexicon* in 1732.

Works incl. much ogr. m., incl.

preludes & fugues, vars. of chorales, &c.; Conc. for hpchd. solo, &c.

Walther, Johann Jakob (b. Witterda nr. Erfurt, 1650; d. ?), Ger. vst. & comp. In the service of the Elector of Saxony and later that of Mainz. Comp. *Scherzi* for v. and continuo & *Hortulus Chelicus* for solo v. & stgs. containing realistic effects.

Walther von der Vogelweide. *See* **Vogelweide.**

Walthew, Richard (Henry) (b. London, 4. XI. 1872), Eng. pfst. & comp. Studied at the G.S.M. and later at the R.C.M. in London, Parry being his comp. master at the latter. He became much interested in cond. amateur mus. socs. and esp. in the South Place Concerts held on Sunday evenings in the City of London, where the finest chamber m. could be heard free (with a collection) and where he often appeared as pfst.

Works incl. operettas *The Enchanted Island* & *The Gardeners*; cantatas *Ode to a Nightingale* (Keats), *The Pied Piper* (Browning) & others; Vars. in B maj. and ovt. to Erckmann-Chatrian's *Friend Fritz* for orch.; pf. Conc., *Caprice-Impromptu* for v. & orch.; 3 stg. 4tets, pf. Trio, Trio for v., cl. & pf., pf. 5tet, pf. 4tet, 5tet for cl. & stgs., 5 *Diversions* & *Prelude, Sarabande and Fugue* for stg. trio & other chamber m.; So. & Serenade-So. for v. & pf., co. & pf. So.; songs, voc. duets & 4tets; partsongs, &c.

Walton, Izaak (1593–1683), Eng. author. *See* Rawsthorne (*Creel*).

Walton, William (Turner) (b. Oldham, Lancs., 29. III. 1902), Eng. comp. Showed great precocity of talent at home and was sent to Christ Church cath., Oxford, as a choir-boy, later becoming an undergraduate at Christ Church Coll. He had some comp. lessons from Hugh Allen, but after the age of 16 was self-taught, though he later received some advice from Busoni and others. In 1923 he appeared for the 1st time at the I.S.C.M. festival, at Salzburg, where his 1st stg. 4tet was perf. He settled in London and was in close touch with the literary family Edith, Osbert and Sacheverell Sitwell. In 1934 his Sym. in B♭ min. was perf. in London before it was completed and the finale was added the next year. In 1938 he went to U.S.A. to confer with Yasha Heifetz about the solo part of the v. Conc., which is ded. to him. During the 1939–45 war he was commissioned by the Ministry of Labour to write m. for official films.

Works incl. ballet *The Quest* (on Spenser's *Faery Queen*); incid. m. to Shakespeare's *Macbeth*; film m. for *Escape me never*, *The First of the Few* (incl. *Spitfire* Prelude and Fugue), *Next of Kin*, *King Henry V* (Shakespeare) & others; *Belshazzar's Feast* for bar. solo, chor. & orch., *In Honour of the City of London* (Dunbar) for chor. & orch.; Sym. in B♭ min., ovts. *Dr. Syntax* (on Combe and Rowlandson) & *Portsmouth Point* (on Rowlandson's drawing), coronation march *Crown Imperial*; *Siesta* for chamber orch.; *Sinfonia concertante* for pf. & orch., v. Conc., va. Conc.; *The Passionate Shepherd* for ten. & chamber orch.; *Façade* (words by Edith Sitwell) for declamation & chamber orch. (later arr. as 2 orch. suites and as a ballet); 2 stg. 4tets, pf. 4tet; Toccata for v. & pf.; song cycles *Bucolic Comedies*, 3 songs (Edith Sitwell) in the Eng., Spa. & Amer. manner, songs *The Winds*, *Tritons* & ' Under the greenwood tree ' (Shakespeare), &c.

Waltz (*see also* **Valse à deux temps**). A ballroom dance coming into fashion in the earlier 19th cent. and developing from the Ger. dances (*Deutsche*) and the Aus. *Ländler*, Beethoven, Weber and Schubert being among the 1st masters to cultivate it seriously and the elder J. Strauss and Lanner among the 1st ballroom comps. to develop its vogue in Vienna, whence it rapidly spread all over Eur. It is in 3–4 time, varying in pace at different times and in different countries, but usually rather leisurely, and its most typical feature is a bass note on the 1st beat followed by 2 repeated chords of the upper harmony belonging to that bass on the 2nd and 3rd.

Waltz Dream (Straus). *See* **Walzertraum.**

Waltz, Gustavus (b. ?; d. ? London, *c.* 1753), Ger. bass singer and minor comp. He is said, without evidence, to have been for a time Handel's cook in London. In 1732 appeared as Polypheme in his master's *Acis and Galatea* and then, until 1751, in many operas and orats.

Walzer (Ger.) = Waltz.

Walzertraum, Ein (*A Waltz Dream*), operetta by Straus (lib. by Felix Dörmann & Leopold Jacobson), prod. Vienna, Carl Theatre, 2. III. 1907.

Wand of Youth, The. 2 orch. suites by Elgar, Opp. 1a & b, which are all that remains of m. written for a play in his childhood, 1869, revised and scored in the present form in 1907.

' Wanderer ' Fantasy. Schubert's Fantasy in C maj. for pf., Op. 15, comp. in 1822. It is so called because it contains material from his song *The Wanderer* written in 1816.

Wang-Wei (699–759), Chin. poet &

painter. *See* **Lied von der Erde** (Mahler).

Wanhal (or **Vanhall** in Eng. eds.), **Johann Baptist** (b. Nechanice, 12. V. 1739; d. Vienna, 26. VIII. 1813), Boh. comp. of Dutch descent. He studied at home with local musns. and then taught and played the v. at var. small neighbouring towns. In 1760 he was taken to Vienna to study under Dittersdorf. He found var. patrons and was sent to It. In 1772 he met Burney in Vienna and he paid visits several times to noble houses in Hung. and Croatia.

Works incl. 2 operas; 25 masses, 2 Requiems, *Stabat Mater* & over 60 smaller pieces of church m.; *c.* 100 syms.; *c.* 100 stg. 4tets; inst. sos., &c.

Wanless, Thomas (b. ? Lincoln, *c.* 1640; d. ? York, 1721), Eng. orgst. & comp. Pupil (?) of John W., (?) his father, orgst. of Lincoln cath. He became orgst. of York minster in 1691, remaining until 1715.

Works incl. anthems, funeral anthem 'I am the resurrection,' York litany in 4 parts, psalm tunes in 4 parts, &c.

Wannenmacher, Johannes (b. Neuenburg o/Rhine, ?; d. Interlaken, 1551), Swi. priest & comp. He was app. cantor of the collegiate foundation of St. Vincent at Berne in 1510, but left in 1514 after a dispute and went to Ger. as canon and cantor at Freiburg, Baden. After a brief return to Swi., in 1519, when he went to Sion (Valais), he went back to Freiburg, but having come under the influence of the Swi. reformer Zwingli, embraced Protestantism in 1530, was tortured and banished, returned to Berne and, finding no employment there, became town clerk at Interlaken.

Works incl. Psalm cxxxvii for 3–6 voices, motets; Ger. sacred & secular songs, &c.

War and Peace, opera by Prokofiev (lib. by Mira Mendelson, based on Tolstoy's novel), perf. in concert, Moscow, 17. X. 1944.

Ward, John (b. ?; d. ?, before 1641), Eng. 16th–17th-cent. comp. He was in the service of Sir Henry Fanshawe, Remembrancer of the Exchequer, at Ware Park, Herts., and in London.

Works incl. services & anthems; madrigals; fantasies for viols, &c.

Warlich, Reinhold von (b. St. Petersburg, 24. V. 1879; d. New York, XI. 1939), Ger. bar. singer. Studied m. generally at the Hamburg Cons. and singing at Florence and Cologne. Made his 1st appearance at Florence in 1899.

Warlock, Peter. For biog. *see* **Heseltine, Philip.**

Works incl. *3 Dirges by Webster* & other chor. works; *An Old Song* & *Serenade* for stg. orch.; *The Curlew* for ten., fl., Eng. hn. & stg. 4tet, *Corpus Christi* & *Sorrow's Lullaby* (Beddoes) for sop., bar. & stg. 4tet; *Capriol* suite for full or stg. orch. on dances from Arbeau's *Orchésographie*; *c.* 90 songs, many on Elizabethan & Jacobean poems, &c.

Warner, H(arry). Waldo (b. Northampton, 4. I. 1874), Eng. violist. & comp. He went to London with his family in 1880 and entered the G.S.M. in 1888, later became a prof. there, but resigned in order to be able to travel with the London Stg. 4tet, which he had joined as va. in 1907. He was also principal va. in 2 of the great London orchs.

Works incl. opera *The Royal Vagrants*; *3 Elfin Dances* & other suites for orch.; stg. 4tet in C min., 3 fantasy stg. 4tets, *The Pixy Ring* for stg. 4tet, Rhapsody for va. & stg. 4tet, 3 pf. trios; v. & pf. So., va. & pf. So.; pieces for v., va. & co. with pf.; numerous songs & part-songs, &c.

Warsaw Concerto. The pf. Conc. played by the comp.-airman hero in the film *Dangerous Moonlight*, specially written for that purpose by Richard Addinsell. It is, intentionally or not, an excellent parody of Rakhmaninov's concs. and was never intended for concert perf. Its success in the concert-room, as dangerous as that of the 'Moonlight' So., because attained for the wrong reasons, is said to have surprised none more than the comp. himself.

Warton, Joseph (1722–1800), Eng. critic & poet. *See* **Callcott, Crotch.**

Wasielewski, Joseph von (b. Gross Leesen nr. Danzig, 17. VI. 1822; d. Sondershausen, 13. XII. 1896), Ger.-Pol. vst., cond. & writer on m. Pupil of Mendelssohn at Leipzig, then living at Düsseldorf, Bonn, Dresden and Sondershausen. His books incl. a biog. of Schumann, works on the v. & its masters, the co., the hist. of inst. m., mus. princes &c.

Wassermann, Jakob (1873–1934), Ger. novelist & essayist. *See* **Wellesz** (*Prinzessin Girnara*).

Water Carrier, The (Cherubini). *See* **Deux Journées.**

Water Music, a set of inst. pieces by Handel, comp. *c.* 1715 and perf. that year, London, 22. VIII, on a boat following the royal barge on the Thames. The m. is said to have reconciled George I to H. after the latter's desertion from the court of Hanover, but the story is doubtful.

Water Organ. *See* **Hydraulus.**

Watkin-Mills, Robert (b. Painswick, Glos., 5. III. 1856; d. Toronto, XII. 1930), Eng. bar. singer. Studied in London and Milan, and made his 1st appearance at the Crystal Palace in London in 1884. He had much success at concerts and festivals, visited the colonies and U.S.A. in 1894 and finally settled at Toronto.

Webbe, Samuel (b. ?, 1740; d. London, 25. V. 1816), Eng. comp. He was apprenticed to a cabinet-maker, but contrived to learn m. and 6 languages, appearing as a voc. comp. *c.* 1763. In 1766 he for the 1st time gained a prize from the Catch Club, which was followed by many others until 1794. He became sec. of that club in 1784 and held the office until his death, and in 1787 he also became librarian to the Glee Club. He was moreover orgst. of the Sardinian and (?) Port. embassy chapels.

Works incl. masses, motets & antiphons; glees, catches & canons; songs, &c.

Webbe, Samuel (b. London, *c.* 1770; d. Liverpool, 25. XI. 1843), Eng. pfst., orgst. & comp., son of prec. Pupil of his father. He obtained the Catch Club prize in 1794 and others later. He settled at Liverpool in 1798, returning briefly to London in 1817 to teach jointly with Logier and became orgst. of the Spa. embassy chapel, but he returned to Liverpool, where he held several church orgst.'s posts.

Works incl. operatic farce *The Speechless Wife*; motets, glees, songs, &c.

Webber, Amherst (b. Cannes, 25. X. 1867), Eng. comp. Studied with Nicodé at Dresden and with Guiraud at the Paris Cons. Later he became cond. at Covent Garden Opera in London and the Metrop. Opera in N.Y.

Works incl. opera *Fiorella* (lib. by Sardou); Sym.; Eng. & Fr. songs, &c.

Weber, Aloysia (b. Zell, Baden, 1760; d. Salzburg, 1839), Ger. sop. singer, 2nd daughter of Fridolin Weber & sister of Constanze Mozart. 1st appeared at the electoral court of Mannheim, where Mozart fell in love with her in 1778. She left for Munich during his visit to Paris and jilted him there; engaged to sing in Vienna in 1779, where she married the actor Josef Lange in 1780.

Weber, Bernhard Anselm (b. Mannheim, 18. IV. 1766; d. Berlin, 23. III. 1821), Ger. pfst., cond. & comp. After studying law and theol., and managing theatre companies, toured with Vogler, his master, in 1790, and became court cond. in Berlin, 1793.

Works incl. operas *Mudarra, Die Wette* & others; incid. m. to Schiller's *Wilhelm Tell* & many other plays; songs, &c.

Weber, Bernhard Christian (b. Wolferschwenda, Thuringia, 1. XII. 1712; d. Tennstedt nr. Erfurt, 5. II. 1758), Ger. orgst. & comp. App. orgst. at Tennstedt in 1732. It was long claimed that he anticipated Bach by writing a set of preludes and fugues for clavier in all the keys, entitled *Das wohltemperierte Clavier*, but he actually was an imitator, the work, wrongly dated 1689 (23 years before his birth), being in fact written *c.* 1745–50.

Weber, Carl Maria (Friedrich Ernst) von (b. Eutin nr. Lübeck, 18. XII. 1786; d. London, 4–5. VI. 1826), Ger. comp. Son of a town and travelling theatre musn. of good family but in poor circumstances. He was taken about the country in his childhood and received a desultory educ., but his father, anxious to make a wonder-child of him, taught him all the m. he knew. When at last they settled down at Salzburg, the boy, aged 10, became a pupil of Michael Haydn. But his mother d. in III. 1798, and he was taken to Vienna and Munich. There he studied under Valesi (Wallishauser) and Kalcher, and at 13 he was a good enough pfst. to appear at concerts. By 1800 he had comp. a good deal of juvenile m. and learned lithography with Senefelder; but the wandering life was resumed and W. was reduced to continuing his studies with the aid of theoretical books. At Augsburg in 1803 he succeeded in having his opera *Peter Schmoll und seine Nachbarn* prod. In Vienna again in 1803–4, he became Vogler's pupil for a time, and his master recommended him for a cond.-ship at Breslau, where he went in the autumn of 1804. In 1806 he became domestic musn. to Duke Eugen of Württemberg, who, on being obliged to dismiss his musns., recommended W. as private secretary to his younger brother Ludwig. He settled at Stuttgart in VII. 1807, where he lead a rather dissolute life, and incurred the displeasure of the king, his patron's elder brother. In 1810 he was banished from the kingdom on a trumped-up charge and went to Mannheim and later to Darmstadt, where he resumed his studies with Vogler more seriously. After much travelling he secured the cond.-ship at the Ger. theatre in Prague in 1813. In XII. 1816 he was app. cond. of the Dresden court opera, where he did much to estab. Ger. opera in the face of the strong opposition of Morlacchi and other Its. On 4. XI. 1817 he married the opera singer Caroline Brandt, who was still at Prague, and took her to Dresden after a concert tour. On 4. V. 1821 his most famous opera, *Der Freischütz,* was prod. in Berlin, and *Euryanthe* followed in Vienna on 25. X. 1823. In 1824 the Covent Garden Theatre in London commissioned an Eng. opera from him, and he took Eng. lessons to make a success of *Oberon.* He suffered badly from a severe disease of the throat and felt unfit to visit London, but in order to keep his family from want he took the risk in II. 1826, visiting Paris on the way. He arrived in London on 5. III., cond. works of his own at a Phil. concert and prod. *Oberon* on 12. IV. Although he felt increasingly ill, he still cond. the succeeding perfs. and appeared at several concerts. Utterly worn out early in VI. he made preparations for a hasty return home, but d. during the night at the house of his host, George Smart.

Works incl. operas *Die Macht der Liebe und des Weins* (lost), *Das Waldmädchen* (fragment, early version of *Silvana*), *Peter Schmoll und seine Nachbarn, Rübezahl* (fragments only), *Silvana, Abu Hassan, Der Freischütz, Die drei Pintos* (fragment, later finished by Mahler), *Euryanthe, Oberon*; 32 other works for the stage incl. incid. m. to Schiller's trans. of Gozzi's *Turandot,* P. A. Wolff's *Preciosa* and extra songs, arias and other interpolations for plays; 7 cantatas; 3 masses & 2 offertories; 13 orch. works, incl. ovts., &c.; 22 works for solo insts. & orch., incl. 2 pf. concs., *Concertstück* for pf. & orch., Concertino for cl. & orch., 2 cl. & 1 bn. concs.; 5tet for cl., 2 v., va. & co., pf. 4tet; Trio for pf., fl. & co.; 27 pf. works incl. 8 sets of vars., 4 sos., *Momento capriccioso, Rondo brillante, Aufforderung zum Tanz* (*Invitation to the Dance*); 64 songs, partsongs & similar voc. pieces, &c.

Weber, Constanze. *See* **Mozart.**

Weber, (Friedrich) Dionys(us) (b. Velichov, 9. X. 1766; d. Prague, 25. XII. 1842), Boh. teacher & comp. Pupil of Vogler. He was one of the founders and the 1st dir. of the Prague Cons. and wrote several theoret. treatises.

Works incl. operas; military band m., &c.

Weber, Fridolin (b. ?, 1733; d. Vienna, 23. X. 1779), Ger. singer & vst., father of Aloysia, Constanze (Mozart) and Josefa W. Member of the electoral chapel at Mannheim from 1765, before which date he was an official at Zell (Baden). Married Maria Cäcilie Stamm in 1756.

Weber, Gottfried (b. Freinsheim nr. Mannheim, 1. III. 1779; d. Kreuznach, 21. IX. 1839), Ger. comp. & theorist. Settled at Mannheim from 1802 as lawyer and government employee. In 1810 his family provided refuge for their namesakes, C. M. v. Weber and his father, after the former's banishment from Stuttgart, and they formed a mus. and cultural soc. W. wrote a number of theoretical books.

Works incl. 3 masses & other church m.; inst. sos. & pieces; songs with pf. & guitar, &c.

Weber, Josefa (b. Zell, Baden, 1758; d. Vienna, 29. XII. 1819), Ger. sop. singer, eldest daughter of Fridolin W. She does not appear to have sung in public until after 1780 in Vienna, where she joined Schikaneder's theatre in 1788, in which year she married the vst. Franz de Paula Hofer (1755–96). Mozart, her brother-in-law, wrote the part of the Queen of Night in *The Magic Flute* for her.

Webern, Anton (von) (b. Vienna, 3. XII. 1883; d. Mittersill, Salzburg, 15. IX. 1945), Aus. comp. Studied mcol. with Adler and took the Ph.D. degree at Vienna Univ. in 1906. He became a pupil of Schoenberg for comp. He cond. for a time at Ger. provincial theatres and in Prague. After the war of 1914–8 he settled at Mödling nr. Vienna and devoted himself to teaching and comp., though he still cond., esp. the modern perfs. of the Verein für musikalische Privataufführungen and the workers' sym. concerts. In the 1920s he emigrated to U.S.A., but returned to Aus. later. His death was due to a stray shot.

Works incl. *Das Augenlicht* for chor. & orch.; 2 songs (Goethe) for chor. & chamber orch.; 2 syms., Passacaglia, 6 Pieces, 5 Pieces for orch.; Conc. for 9 insts.; stg. 4tet, 5 mvts. & *6 Bagatelles* for stg. 4tet, 4tet for v., cl., saxophone & pf., stg. Trio; 2 songs (Rilke) for voice & chamber m., 4 & 6 songs for do., 5 canons for voice, cl., & bass cl., *3 geistliche Volkslieder* for voice, v., cl. & bass cl., 3 songs with cl. & guitar, *5 geistliche Lieder* for voice & 5 insts.; 4 pieces for v. & pf., 3 little pieces for co. & pf.; Vars. for pf.; songs to words by Rilke, Stephan George & others; 'Entflieht auf leichten Kähnen' (George) for unaccomp. chor., &c.

Webers letzter Gedanke (known in Eng. as *Weber's Last Waltz*). *See* **Reissiger.**

Webster, John (? 1580–? 1625), Eng. dramatist. *See* **Warlock** (*3 Dirges*).

Wechseldominante (Ger. = change dominant). The Ger. techn. term for the dominant of the dominant of any key: e.g. E maj. or min. as related to the key of D maj. or min., A being dominant to D, and E to A.

Wechselnote (Ger. lit. change note, changing note). *See* **Nota cambiata.**

Wecker, Georg Kaspar (b. Nuremberg, 2. IV. 1632; d. Nuremberg, 20. IV. 1695), Ger. orgst. & comp. Pupil of his father, an inst. perf., and Erasmus Kindermann. He was orgst. at var. Nuremberg churches from the age of 19 and in 1686 was app. to the principal one, St. Sebald's. J. Krieger and Pachelbel were among his pupils.

Works incl. 18 sacred concs. (church cantatas) for voices & insts.; org. m., &c.

Weckerlin, Jean Baptiste (Théodore) (b. Guebwiller, Alsace, 29. XI. 1821; d. Trottberg nr. Guebwiller, 20. V. 1910), Fr. comp. & ed. Studied at the Paris Cons. Although unsuccessful, he was determined to make his way as a musn., collected much old Fr. m. and in 1863 became archivist of the Société des Compositeurs de Musique, whose library he estab. In 1869 Auber invited him to the Cons. library, of which he became head librarian in 1876. He ed. many collections of old Fr. songs & other m.

Works incl. opera *L'Organiste dans l'embarras* & 5 others (some in Alsat. dialect); *Roland* for solo voices, chor. & orch.; Mass & motets; Sym. & Suite for orch.; chamber m.; songs, &c.

Weckmann, Matthias (b. ? Oppershausen, Thuringia, 1621; d. Hamburg, 1674), Ger. orgst. & comp. He became a pupil of Schütz as a choirboy in the electoral chapel at Dresden and in 1637 was sent at the elector's expense to study further with J. Praetorius at Hamburg. In 1640 he became court orgst. at Dresden, where he remained until 1655, except for a visit to Nykjøbing in the service of the crown prince of Den., some time before 1647. He then became orgst. at St. James's church, Hamburg. He organized a concert soc. (*Collegium musicum*) with Scheidemann, Selle, Schop and other Hamburg musns. and during a visit to Dresden competed as an orgst. with Froberger.

Works incl. sacred concs. for voices & insts.; org. m., &c.

Wedding, The, ballet by Stravinsky (chgph. by Bronislava Nizhinska), prod. Paris, Théâtre Gaité-Lyrique, 14. VI. 1923. The work is scored for chor. (Rus. words), 4 pfs. and perc. It is more generally known as *Les Noces*, but as it is not Fr. in any way, there is no justification for this title outside France.

Wedekind, Frank (1864–1918), Ger. dramatist. *See* **Ettinger** (*Frühlingserwachen*), **Lulu** (Berg).

'Wedge, The.' The nickname given in Eng. to Bach's greater E min. Fugue for org. because its subject has the appearance of a wedge on paper, its alternating intervals widening gradually.

Weelkes, Thomas (b. ?, c. 1575; d. London, 30. XI. 1623), Eng. comp. He may have been in the service of George Phillpot at Thruxton nr. Andover in his early years and then was in that of Edward Darcye, Groom of the Privy Chamber. In 1600 he was orgst. at Winchester Coll. and in 1602 he took the B.Mus. at Oxford, soon afterwards becoming orgst. of Chichester cath. He remained there to the end, but d. during a visit to London.

Works incl. services & numerous anthems; 2 books of madrigals, balletts, *Ayeres or Phantasticke Spirites* for 3 voices; 2 voc. pieces contrib. to Leighton's *Teares or Lamentacions*; In Nomines for 4–5 viols & other pieces for 5 viols.

Weerbecke, Gaspard (b. Oudenarde, *c.* 1440; d. ? Milan, ?), Flem. singer, priest & comp. Pupil of the maîtrise at Oudenarde and of Okeghem. He took holy orders at Tournai and went to It. in the 1470s and became chapel master at Milan cath. and a singer at the ducal court. He was in Rome as a singer at the Papal Chapel in 1481–9, but in 1488 prod. m. for allegorical plays given at the marriage of Galeazzo Sforza, Duke of Milan, to Isabella of Aragon. He visited his home-town in 1490 and was received with honours.

Works incl. masses, motets, *Stabat Mater* & other church m.; m. for plays, &c.

Wegelius, Martin (b. Helsingfors, 10. XI. 1846; d. Helsingfors, 22. III. 1906), Fin. teacher & comp. Studied at Helsingfors Univ. and also had m. lessons there, later studied m. in Vienna, Leipzig and Munich. Returning home in 1878, he took an active part in the mus. life of the Fin. capital as critic and lecturer, and in 1882 founded the Cons., of which he became the 1st dir. Among his pupils there were Sibelius, Melartin, Järnefelt & others.

Works incl. cantata in memory of Runeberg; orch. works; songs, &c.

Wehrli, Werner (b. Aarau, 8. I. 1892), Swi. comp. Studied natural science at Munich Univ., but turned to m.

and joined the Zürich Cons. Later became a pupil of Knorr at the Hoch Cons. at Frankfort o/M. In 1920 he settled in his native town as teacher & cond.

Works incl. operas *Das heiss Eisen* (Hans Sachs), *Das Vermächtnis*, festival operas *Die Schweizer, Die Brücke, Das Weltgericht*, play with m. *Der Märchenspiegel*; orats. *Ein weltliches Requiem*; Sinfonietta & Vars. for orch.; *Pantomime* for chamber orch.; 3 stg. 4tets, 2 pf. trios & other chamber m.; pf. & org. works; songs, partsongs, &c.

Weichsel, Carl & Elizabeth. *See* **Billington.**

Weideman(n), Carl Friedrich (Charles Weideman) (b. ?; d. London, 1782), Ger. flst. & comp. Settled in London *c.* 1726. He was concerned with Festing in the foundation of the Royal Soc. of Musns. in 1739 and in 1778 became cond. of the royal orch. He comp. concs., solos, duets, trios & 4tets for fl.

Weigl, Joseph (Franz) (b. Bavaria, 19. III. 1740; d. Vienna, 25. I. 1820), Ger. cst. He joined Prince Esterházy's orch. at Eisenstadt under Haydn in 1761, but left in 1769 for the Vienna Court Opera and joined the Imp. Chapel there in 1792.

Weigl, Joseph (b. Eisenstadt, 28. III. 1766; d. Vienna, 3. II. 1846), Aus. comp., son of prec. Haydn was his godfather and he was taken to Vienna at the age of 3, where later he studied with Albrechtsberger and Salieri. When he was 16, Gluck secured the prod. of his 1st Ger. opera. In 1788 he prod. his 1st It. opera. He was very successful and after acting as asst. cond. to Salieri at the Opera, he was app. comp. to the Opera in 1792, later mus. dir. and 1st cond.

Works incl. operas *Die betrogene Arglist, Il pazzo per forza, La principessa d'Amalfi, L'amore marinaro, Das Dorf im Gebürge, Die Uniform, Vestas Feuer, Cleopatra, Il rivale de se stesso, Kaiser Hadrian, Adrian von Ostade, Das Waisenhaus, Die Schweizerfamilie, Der Bergsturz, Nachtigall und Rabe, Baals Sturz* & 15 others; melodrama on Shakespeare's *Hamlet*; 17 ballets; orat. *La passione di Gesù Cristo* & another; 9 masses & other church m.; 19 cantatas; voc. scenas & arias; songs, duets, &c.

Weigl, Karl (b. Vienna, 6. II. 1881), Aus. comp. Studied mcol. at Vienna Univ., worked as asst. cond. under Mahler at the Vienna Opera, became a teacher at the New Vienna Cons. in 1918 and later lecturer at the Univ.

Works incl. cantata *Weltfeier* for solo voices, chor., orch. & org.; syms.; var. concs.; stg. 4tet; co. & pf. So.; songs with pf. & with chamber accomp., &c.

Weigl, Thaddäus (b. Vienna, 1776; d. Vienna, 10. II. 1844), Aus. comp. & pub., son & brother of J. Weigl I & II. Pupil of his father, was for a time cond. at the court theatres, but in 1801 became a m. pub.

Works incl. opera *Der Jahrmarkt zu Grünewald* & others; ballet *Cyrus und Thomyris* & others, &c.

Weihe des Hauses, Die (*The Consecration of the House*), ovt. by Beethoven, Op. 124, written in 1822 for the opening of the Josefstadt Theatre in Vienna, and perf. there in 3. X.

Weill, Kurt (b. Dessau, 2. III. 1900), Ger. comp. Studied locally at first, later with Humperdinck and Busoni in Berlin. He had his 1st stage success at the age of 26 and his modern version of Gay's *Beggar's Opera* (*Die Dreigroschenoper*) made an enormous hit in 1928, but the Nazi régime condemned his works in 1933 as both Jewish and decadent, and he left Ger., taking refuge at Louveciennes nr. Paris. He visited London in 1935 for the prod. of an Eng. operetta, *A Kingdom for a Cow*, but went the same year to settle in U.S.A.

Works incl. operas & operettas *Der Protagonist, Der Silbersee, Der Zar lässt sich photographieren* (libs. by Georg Kaiser), *Royal Palace, Die Dreigroschenoper, Happy End, Mahagonny, Der Jasager, Die Bürgschaft* (several on libs. by Bert Brecht), *Marie galante, A Kingdom for a Cow, Johnny Johnson, Knickerbocker Holiday*; biblical m.-drama *The Eternal Road*; ballet *Die sieben Todsünden* (*Anna Anna*); cantatas *Der neue Orpheus* & *Der Lindberghflug*; Sym., *Fantasia, Passacaglia und Hymnus, Divertimento* & *Quodlibet* for orch.; Conc. for v. & wind band; stg. 4tet; works for voices & chamber orch., songs (Rilke) with orch., &c.

Weinberger, Jaromír (b. Prague, 8. I. 1896), Cz. comp. Studied with Hofmeister and Křička in Prague and with Reger in Ger. Prof. of comp. at the Cons. of Ithaca, N.Y., 1922–6; returned to Eur. to cond. and teach in var. places.

Works incl. operas *Švanda the Bagpiper, The Beloved Voice, The Outcasts of Poker Flat* (after Bret Harte) & *Wallenstein* (after Schiller); pantomime *The Abduction of Eveline*; incid. m. for Shakespeare & other plays; *Don Quixote* (after Cervantes), *Scherzo giocoso*, Vars. on the Eng. folksong 'Under the spreading chestnut tree,' for orch., &c.

Weiner, Leo (b. Budapest, 16. IV. 1885), Hung. comp. Studied at the

Nat. Acad. of M. in Budapest, where he became a prof. in 1913.

Works incl. ballet on & incid. m. for Vörösmarty's *Csongor and Tünde*; Scherzo, Serenade & humoresque *Carnival* for orch.; 2 stg. 4tets, stg. Trio; v. & pf. So.; Passacaglia & other pf. works, &c.

Weingartner (Paul) Felix (von) (b. Zara, Dalmatia, 2. VI. 1863; d. Winterthur, Swi., 7. V. 1942), Aus. cond. & comp. Studied at Graz, at the Leipzig Cons. and under Liszt at Weimar, where he prod. his 1st opera in 1884. He became cond. at Königsberg, Danzig, Hamburg and Mannheim before 1891, when he was app. cond. of the Court Opera in Berlin and cond. of the sym. concerts. In 1898 he left for Munich to become cond. of the Kaim orch. and in 1907 he succeeded Mahler as chief cond. at the Vienna Court Opera. After 1910 he frequently changed his sphere of activity, cond. much abroad, esp. in Fr., Eng. and U.S.A. The last years of his life he spent, still actively, in Swi., esp. at Basle. He wrote books on cond., on Beethoven's syms., &c.

Works incl. operas *Sakuntala* (after Kalidasa), *Malawika, Genesius, Orestes* trilogy (after Aeschylus), *Kain und Abel, Dame Kobold* (after Calderón), *Die Dorfschule, Meister Andrea, Der Apostat*; incid. m. for Shakespeare's *Tempest* & Goethe's *Faust*; 6 syms., symph. poems *King Lear* (after Shakespeare) & *Die Gefilde der Seligen* (after Böcklin's picture), *Lustige Ouvertüre*, ovt. *Aus schwerer Zeit*; Serenade for stg. orch.; v. Conc.; 3 stg. 4tets, stg. 5tet, 5tet for cl. & stgs., 6tet for stgs. & pf.; 2 v. & pf. sos.; pf. pieces; numerous songs, &c.

Weinlig, Christian Theodor (b. Dresden, 25. VII. 1780; d. Leipzig, 6. III. 1842), Ger. theorist & comp. Pupil of his uncle, Christian Ehregott W. (1743–1813), cantor of the Kreuzschule at Dresden. He succeeded Schicht as cantor of St. Thomas's school at Leipzig in 1823. Schumann and Wagner were his pupils for a short time. He wrote a treatise on fugue and comp. a Ger. Magnificat, &c.

Weis, Karel (b. Prague, 13. II. 1862; d. Brno, 25. IX. 1938), Cz. cond. & comp. Studied at the Prague Cons. and with Skuherský and Fibich at the Org. School. After var. posts as orgst., teacher and orch. player (v. & hn.), he became cond. at the Nat. Theatre at Brno in 1886, but later devoted himself to comp.

Works incl. operas *Viola* (after Shakespeare's *Twelfth Night*; later called *The Twins*), *The Polish Jew* (after Erckmann-Chatrian), *The Attack on the Mill* (after Zola), *The Blacksmith of Lesetin*, operettas *The Village Musicians* & *The Revisor* (after Gogol's comedy); chor. scene *Triumfator*; symph. poem *Helios and Selene*; stg. 4tet; v. & pf. So.; pf. pieces; folksong arrs., &c.

Weismann, Julius (b. Freiburg i/B., 26. XII. 1879), Ger. comp. Studied at Munich, with Herzogenberg in Berlin and again at Munich with Thuille.

Works incl. operas *Schwanenweiss, Traumspiel, Gespenstersonate* (all after Strindberg), *Leonce und Lena* (Georg Büchner), *Landsknechte, Regina del Lago, Die pfiffige Magd* (after Holberg); Sym. in B min., 3 Pieces for orch.; Conc. & Vars. and Fugue on an old *Ave Maria* for pf. & orch., co. Conc.; stg. 4tet in F maj., 2 pf. trios; So. for v. solo, 2 co. sos., Vars. for ob. & pf.; chor. works; Vars. for 2 pfs.; 7 op. nos. of pf. pieces; 15 op. nos. of songs, &c.

Weiss, Amalie (real name Schneeweiss) (b. Marburg, Styria, 10. V. 1839; d. Berlin, 3. II. 1898), Aus. con. singer. Made her 1st stage appearance at Troppau in 1853, was later engaged in Vienna and Hanover, and at the latter place married Joachim in 1863. She then appeared only as a concert singer. They separated in 1884.

Weiss, Franz (b. Silesia, 18. I. 1788; d. Vienna, 25. I. 1830), Aus. violist & comp. Settled in Vienna and became the va. player in Prince Rasumovsky's 4tet founded in 1808.

Works incl. Sym. for fl., bn. & tpt. with orch., Vars. for v. & orch.; stg. 4tet; duets for vs. & for fls.; pf. sos., &c.

Weiss, Sylvius Leopold (b. Breslau, 12. X. 1686; d. Dresden, 15. X. 1750), Ger. lutenist & comp. He was in the service of the Pol. Prince Alexander Sobieski, with whom he went to Rome c. 1708, later at the courts of Hesse-Cassel, Düsseldorf, and from 1718 Dresden, where he worked with Lotti, Hasse, Porpora, Hebenstreit, Pisendel and others, and was sent to Vienna with a visiting Saxon orch. that year. In 1723 he played in Prague with Quantz and H. Graun in Fux's coronation opera *Costanza e fortezza*. Comp. lute m.

Weissberg, Julia Lazarevna (b. Orenburg, 23. XII. 1878), Rus. comp. Studied at the St. Petersburg Cons., under Krizhanovsky, Rimsky-Korsakov and Glazunov, but was expelled for taking part in a demonstration against the dir., Bernard. In 1907–12 she made further studies in Ger. She married Andrey Rimsky-Korsakov.

Works incl. operas *The Little Mermaid* (after Hans Andersen) & *Gulnara* (from the *Arabian Nights*); cantata *The Twelve* (Alex. Blok); Sym., Fantasy, symph. poem *In the Night*, *Ballad* & *A Tale* for orch.; songs with orch. *Rautendelein* (from Hauptmann's *The Sunken Bell*); *Chinese Songs* & others for voice & pf.; folksong arrs., &c.

Weissenburg, Hainz. *See* **Albicastro.**

Weissensee, Friedrich (b. Schwerstedt, Thuringia, *c.* 1560; d. Altenweddingen, 1622), Ger. clergyman & comp. Studied (?) at Venice and became rector of a Lat. coll. at Gebesee, *c.* 1590, and of the town school of Magdeburg in 1596. About 1602 he became rector at Altenweddingen.

Works incl. motets, &c.

Weisshan (or Winsheim), Abraham (b. ?; d. ?), Ger. 16th–17th-cent. lutenist & comp. In 1568 he went into service at the Saxon court at Dresden, where he still was in 1611.

Works incl. a collection of lute preludes, fantasies and dances *Silvae musicalis libri VII*, &c.

Weissmann, Adolf (b. Rosenberg, Silesia, 15. VIII. 1873; d. Haifa, 23. IV. 1929), Ger. m. critic & author. Studied in Cz., Ger., Aus. and Swi. He became m. critic to several Berlin papers and periodicals, but d. on a lecturing-tour in Palestine. His books incl. studies of Bizet, Chopin, Puccini & Verdi, the virtuoso, the prima donna & the cond., the hist. of m. in Berlin, modern mus. conditions, &c.

Welcome Odes or **Welcome Songs** } Cantatas by Purcell for the return to London of Charles II and James II on var. occasions. One, of 1682, is addressed to James as Duke of York, before his accession.

Weldon, John (b. Chichester, 19. I. 1676; d. London, 7. V. 1736), Eng. orgst. & comp. Educ. at Eton, where he studied m. under the coll. orgst. John Walton, and later became a pupil of Purcell in London. In 1694 he was app. orgst. of New Coll., Oxford, and in 1700 gained the 1st prize for the setting of Congreve's masque *The Judgment of Paris* against Eccles, Finger and D. Purcell. In 1701 he became a Gentleman of the Chapel Royal and in 1708 orgst. there on the death of Blow; he also became orgst. of St. Bride's and (1726) St. Martin's-in-the-Field churches.

Works incl. masque *The Judgment of Paris*; songs for Cibber's *She would and she would not* & other plays; anthems; songs, &c.

Well-tempered Clavier. *See* **Wohltemperierte Clavier, Das.**

Wellesz, Egon (b. Vienna, 21. X. 1885), Aus. mcolst. & comp. Studied with Schoenberg, Bruno Walter & others in Vienna, also mcol. with Adler at the Univ., where he graduated Ph.D. in 1908. In 1913 he became lecturer in mus. hist. there. He specialized in Byzantine and modern m., ed. and wrote on the former and pub. works on Schoenberg, Cavalli and the Venetian opera, modern orchn., &c. In 1932 he received the hon. Mus.D. from Oxford Univ. and in 1938, exiled from Aus., he settled there with a special research fellowship.

Works incl. operas *Die Prinzessin Girnara* (Jacob Wassermann), *Alkestis* & *Die Bacchantinnen* (both after Euripides), *Opferung des Gefangenen*, *Scherz, List und Rache* (Goethe's lib.); ballets *Das Wunder der Diana*, *Persian Ballet*, *Achilles auf Skyros* & *Die Nächtlichen*; unaccomp. chors. to old Eng. poems; *Gebete der Mädchen zu Maria* for sop., chor. & orch.; Sym. in C maj., symph. poem *Vorfrühling*, symph. suite *Prosperos Beschwörungen* (after Shakespeare's *Tempest*), Festival March for orch.; *Amor timido* (Metastasio) & *Lied der Welt* (Hofmannsthal) for sop. & orch., *Leben, Traum und Tod* (Hofmannsthal) for con. & orch.; Dance Suite for v. & chamber orch.; 2 masses, motets, cantata *Mitte des Lebens*; 5 stg. 4tets, *Geistiges Lied* for pf. 4tet; *The Leaden Echo and the Golden Echo* (Gerard Manley Hopkins) for sop., cl., va., co. & pf.; sos. for v. solo & co. solo, Suite for v. & pf., Suite for fl. solo; *Epigrams*, *Idylls* & other sets of pf. pieces; song cycle *Kirschblütenlieder* & other songs with pf., unaccomp. song *Aurora*, &c.

Wellingtons Sieg (Beethoven). *See* **Battle of Vittoria.**

Wells, H(erbert). G(eorge). (b. 1866), Eng. novelist. *See* **Bliss** (*Things to come*).

Welsh Composers. *See* **Parry** (4), **Richards, Roberts, Thomas, Williams (G.).**

Wendling (*née* **Spourni**), **Dorothea** (b. Stuttgart, 1737; d. Munich, 20. VIII. 1811), Ger. sop. singer. Worked at the court of Mannheim and Munich; wife of J. B. Wendling.

Wendling (*née* **Sarselli**), **(Augusta) Elisabeth** (b. ?, 1746; d. Munich, 1794), Ger. sop. singer, sister-in-law of prec. Attached to the Mannheim and Munich courts; married to the vst. and singer Carl Wendling.

Wendling, Johann Baptist (b. Alsace,

c. 1720; d. Munich, 27. XI. 1797), Ger. flst. Attached to the electoral court of Mannheim from 1754, brother-in-law of prec. Married the singer Dorothea Spourni.

Wennerberg, Gunnar (b. Linköping, 2. X. 1817; d. Leckö, 22. VIII. 1901), Swe. poet & comp. Educ. at Upsala Univ. He became a lawyer and was self-taught in m.

Works incl. orat. *The Birth of Christ, Stabat Mater*, Psalms for solo voices, chor. & orch.; *Gluntarne* (students' songs) for male-voice duet, *Songs of Freedom*, &c.

Werckmeister, Andreas (b. Beneckenstein, 30. XI. 1645; d. Halberstadt, 26. X. 1706), Ger. orgst. and theorist. Orgst. at Brunswick, Quedlinburg and Halberstadt in succession. Wrote theor. works, esp. on the tuning of orgs. and claviers.

Werfel, Franz (b. Prague, 1891; d. Beverly Hills, Cal., 26. VIII. 1945), Aus. novelist & playwright. Studied at Prague and Leipzig Univ. His works incl. a novel on Verdi and transs. of many of Verdi's operas. *See* **Grosz** (*Spiegelmensch*), **Maximilien** (Milhaud), **Orff** (*Turmes Auferstehung*).

Werner, Gregor Joseph (b. ?, 1695; d. Eisenstadt, 3. III. 1766), Aus. cond. & comp. App. mus. dir. to the Esterházy family in 1728; predecessor of Haydn there and his superior for 5 years from 1761.

Works incl. 40 masses, 3 Requiems & other church m.; 18 orats.; syms.; stg. 4tet, 6 fugues for stg. 4tet (arr. by Haydn, who added introds.); sos., &c. for 2 vs. & bass, &c.

Werrekoren (or **Verecoren**), **Hermann Matthias** (b. ?; d. ?), Flem. 16th-cent. comp. He was in service in It., prob. Milan or Pavia (but the biog. is very uncertain, and there may have been more than 1 comp. of the name).

Works incl. motets for 5 voices, 4-part song on the battles of Bicocca and Pavia, in which Francesco Sforza gained the mastery of Milan, motets, &c.

Wert, Giaches (or **Jaches**) **de** (b. ? Antwerp, *c*. 1536; d. Mantua, 6. V. 1596), Flem. comp. Was sent to It. as a choir-boy when a small child and at 9 became a member of the choir of the Novellara at Reggio. He began to pub. madrigals towards the end of the 1550s and *c*. 1560 went into service at the ducal court of Mantua under Guglielmo Gonzaga. He was also attached to the church of Santa Barbara, where he succeeded Giovanni Contino as chapel master in 1565. In 1566 he accomp. the duke to Ausgburg and there declined an offer from the Emperor Maximilian II. In 1567 he visited Venice with the court and later Ferrara under Alfonso (II) d'Este. About that time he suffered much from the intrigues of the It. musns., who disliked him as a foreigner, and in 1570 one of them, Agostino Bonvicino, was dismissed for a love-affair with his wife. In 1580 he and his family were given the freedom of the city of Mantua in perpetuity.

Works incl. motets, 11 books of madrigals for 5 voices, 1 for 4 voices, canzonets, villanelle, &c.

Werther, opera by Massenet (lib. by Édouard Blau, Paul Milliet & Georges Hartmann, based on Goethe's novel), prod., in Ger., Vienna, Opera, 16. II. 1892; 1st Paris perf., Opéra-Comique, 16. I. 1893.

Wesley, Charles (b. Bristol, 11. XII. 1757; d. London, 23. V. 1834), Eng. orgst. & comp. Pupil of Kelway and Boyce in London and later orgst. at var. churches and chapels. He also appeared in public a hpchdst.

Works incl. incid. m. for Mason's *Caractacus*; Concerto grosso; org. or hpchd. concs.; stg. 4tets; anthems, hymn 'Father of heroes' & others; hpchd. pieces; songs, &c.

Wesley, Samuel (b. Bristol, 24. II. 1766; d. London, 11. X. 1837), Eng. orgst., cond. & comp., brother of prec. and nephew of John W. Like his brother he showed precocious mus. gifts at a very early age. At 6 he was taught by an orgst. at Bath, at 8 he finished the orat. *Ruth* and soon after appeared at the org. as a prodigy. In 1784 he became a Rom. Catholic and in 1787 injured his head in an accident, with the result that he periodically fell into strange behaviour for the rest of his life. He did much work to spread a knowledge of Bach in Eng. and ed. some of his works. He cond. the Birmingham Festival in 1811, lectured at the Royal Institution and gave frequent org. recitals, but had periodically to retire for several years. Shortly before his death he met Mendelssohn and they played the org. to each other.

Works incl. orats. *Ruth* & *The Death of Abel*; 4 masses, numerous Lat. & Eng. anthems incl. 'In exitu Israel,' 'Exultate Deo,' 'Dixit Dominus,' 'All go unto one place,' 'Behold how good,' 'Hear, O thou shepherd' (some with org.), Morning & Evening Service in F maj. & other church m.; Ode on St. Cecilia's Day; 4 syms. (1 unfinished) & ovts.; 9 org. concs.; 3 stg. 4tets & other chamber m.; org. fugues, voluntaries,

&c.; numerous pf. works; glees, songs & duets, &c.

Wesley, Samuel Sebastian (b. London, 14. VIII. 1810; d. Gloucester, 19. IV. 1876), Eng. orgst. & comp., natural son of prec. and great-nephew of John W. Pupil of his father and choir-boy in the Chapel Royal from 1820. In 1826 he was app. orgst. of a London church and by 1830 he held similar posts at 2 more. In 1832 he became orgst. of Hereford cath., in 1835, when he married, of Exeter cath.; in 1842–9 he was orgst. of Leeds parish church, in 1849–65 of Winchester cath. and then until his death of Gloucester cath. He took the Mus.D. at Oxford in 1839 and became org. prof. at the R.A.M. in London in 1850.

Works incl. 5 services, 24 anthems, Psalm c, 2 settings of ' By the waters of Babylon ' with sop. and with con. solo, chants & hymn-tunes; org. works; *Ode to Labour* & *The Praise of Music* for chor.; 3 glees; 9 songs (2 with co. *ad lib.*); pf. pieces, &c.

Wessely Carl Bernhard (b. Berlin, 1. IX. 1768; d. Potsdam, 11. VII. 1826), Ger. cond. & comp. Pupil of J. A. P. Schulz. He was cond. at the Berlin Nat. Theatre, 1788–95, and in 1796–1802 at Prince Heinrich's private theatre at Rheinsberg. After the prince's death he became a civil servant at Potsdam, where he founded a soc. for the perf. of classical m.

Works incl. operas *Psyché, Louis XI* & *L'Ogre*, prologue *Die Freuden des Herbstes*; ballet *Die Wahl des Helden*; incid. m. to Shakespeare's *Tempest*, Kotzebue's *Sonnenjungfrau* & other plays; cantatas on the deaths of Moses Mendelssohn & Prince Henry of Prus.; stg. 4tets; songs, &c.

Wessely, Hans (b. Vienna, 23. XII. 1862; d. Innsbruck, 29. IX. 1926), Aus. vst. Studied at the Vienna Cons. and made his 1st appearance at the age of 21. In 1888 he visited Eng., becoming prof. at the R.A.M. in London in 1889 and remaining for almost the rest of his life. He formed a stg. 4tet.

Western, Ethel. *See* **Thalberg, Zaré.**

Westrup, J(ack). A(llan). (b. London, 26. VII. 1904), Eng. mcolst., critic & comp. Educ. at Dulwich Coll. and Balliol Coll., Oxford, where as an undergraduate he ed. Monteverdi's *Orfeo* and *Incoronazione di Poppea* for perf. by the Oxford Univ. Opera Club. He became classics master at Dulwich Coll. for a time, but went to the *Daily Telegraph* as m. critic until the outbreak of war in 1939, when he returned to teaching, at St. Paul's School. In 1942–4 he was lecturer in m. at King's Coll., Newcastle-on-Tyne, and in 1945 succeeded Hely-Hutchinson as prof. of m. at Birmingham Univ. He became general ed. of the *Oxford Hist. of M.* in 1946, and his literary work incl. the chapter on *Song* in that work & books on Purcell, Handel, Eng. m. and m. in 17th-cent. soc.

Works incl. motet ' When Israel came out of Egypt ' for unaccomp. double chor.; partsong *Weathers*; Divertimento for bn., co. & pf., &c.

Wetz, Richard (b. Gleiwitz, 26. II. 1875; d. Erfurt, 16. I. 1935), Ger. comp. He was very precociously gifted, began to comp. at the age of 8 and was almost wholly self-taught, though he studied a little with Alfred Apel and Thuille at Munich. In 1906 he settled at Erfurt, where he became cond. of orch. and chor. socs. and prof. at the Thüringische Musikakademie. From 1916 he also taught at Weimar.

Works incl. operas *Das ewige Feuer* & *Judith*; Christmas Orat., Requiem, Psalm iii & other chor. works; 3 syms. & *Kleist Ovt.* for orch.; v. Conc.; 2 stg. 4tets; v. & pf. So.; 21 op. nos. of songs, &c.

Wetzler, Hermann Hans (b. Frankfort o/M., 8. IX. 1870; d. New York, 29. V. 1943), Ger.-Amer. cond. & comp. Spent his childhood in U.S.A., but in 1882 went to study at the Hoch Cons. at Frankfort under Scholz, Knorr, Humperdinck, Clara Schumann & others. In 1897–1901 he was orgst. at a N.Y. church. In 1903 he organized sym. concerts there, but in 1905 returned to Ger. and became cond. at var. opera houses. About 1930 he retired to Ascona, Swi., and later settled in U.S.A.

Works incl. operas *The Basque Venus* (after Mérimée); incid. m. to Shakespeare's *As You Like It*; Magnificat for sop., chor. & org.; *Symph. Fantasy, Visions, Assisi* for orch.; *Symphonie concertante* for v. & orch.; Easter m. for wind insts. & org.; Vars. for ob., cl. & stgs.; *Sco. Songs* & 6 other op. nos. of songs, &c.

Weyse, Christoph Ernst Friedrich (b. Altona, 5. III. 1774; d. Copenhagen, 8. X. 1842), Ger.-Dan. comp. Pupil of Schulz at Copenhagen from 1789 He settled there as orgst. and m. teacher. He also collected and ed. Dan. folksongs.

Works incl. operas *The Sleeping-Draught, Faruk, The Cave of Adullam, An Adventure in Rosenborg Gardens, Floribella, The Feast at Kenilworth* (after Scott), operettas; 4 syms.; *c.* 30 cantatas; org. & pf. works; Dan. folksongs, &c.

Whichello, Abiell (b. ?; d. ? London, *c.* 1745), Eng. orgst. & comp. He was orgst. at the church of St. Edmund the King in London, taught the hpchd. and appeared at Thomas Britten's concerts.
Works incl. cantatas *Apollo and Daphne* & *Vertumnus and Pomona*; hpchd. lessons; songs, &c.

Whiffle (old Eng.) = Fife.

Whiffler (old Eng.). A piper, esp. on the Fife.

Whitaker, John (b. ?, 1776; d. London, 4. XII. 1847), Eng. orgst., comp. & m. pub. He was orgst. at the church of St. Clement, Eastcheap, in London and a partner in the m. pub. firm of Button & W. He was in request as a comp. of m. for the Sadler's Wells Theatre pantomimes, incl. the song 'Hot Codlins' sung by the clown Grimaldi.
Works incl. stage pieces *The Outside Passenger* (with Corri & Reeves), *A Chip of the Old Block*, *A Friend indeed*, *Three Miles from Paris*, *A Figure of Fun*, *The Apprentice's Opera*, *The Rake's Progress* & others; songs for a stage adaptation of Scott's *Guy Mannering*; anthem & other sacred m.; settings of Eng. transs. of Anacreon's Odes and Aesop's Fables; 12 pedal exercises for org., &c.

Whitbroke, William (b. ?; d. ?), Eng. 16th-cent. cleric & comp. He was educ. at Cardinal (later Christ Church) Coll., Oxford, where he was ordained priest in 1529. In 1531 he was app. sub-dean at St. Paul's cath. in London and soon afterwards also vicar of All Saints' church at Stanton, Suffolk, where he may have retired on leaving St. Paul's in 1535.
Works incl. Mass for 4 voices, Magnificat & other church m.

White, Alice Meadows. *See* **Smith, Alice Mary.**

White, Felix (Harold) (b. London, 27. IV. 1884; d. London, 31. I. 1945), Eng. pfst. & comp. Learnt the pf. from his mother, but was otherwise self-taught. He was almost wholly devoted to comp., but in 1931 he joined the London Phil. Orch. as celesta & pf. player, and he also did transs. of mus. works, editing, &c.
Works incl. anthems; symph. poems *Astarte Syriaca* (D. G. Rossetti's picture) & *The Deserted Village* (after Goldsmith), ovt. *Shylock* (after Shakespeare's *Merchant of Venice*), Serenade for stg. orch.; *The Nymph's Complaint for the Death of her Fawn* (Marvell) for voice, ob., va. & pf., *Four Proverbs* for fl., ob., v., va. & co., *Arietta* for stg. trio; pieces for var. insts. & pf.; *A Dickens Note-book* for pf.; many songs; partsongs, &c.

White, Maude Valerie (b. Dieppe, 23. VI. 1855; d. London, 2. XI. 1937), Eng. comp. After some preliminary lessons from Rockstro and others, she entered the R.A.M. in London and became a comp. student under Macfarren. After a period spent in S. America for her health, she finished her studies in Vienna.
Works incl. Mass for solo voices, chor. & orch.; 'Ich habe gelebt' (Schiller) for sop. & orch.; voc. 5tet 'Du bist wie eine Blume' (Heine); pf. pieces, numerous Eng., Fr. & Ger. songs to words by Herrick, Shelley, Byron, Hugo, Heine, &c.

White, Paul (b. Bangor, Maine, 22. VIII. 1895), Amer. vst., cond. and comp. Studied at the New Eng. Cons., also comp. with Chadwick, v. with E. Ysaÿe and cond. with Goossens, whose orch. at Cincinnati he joined. Later became cond. of the Civic and Eastman School orchs. at Rochester, N.Y., and in 1938 became a member of the faculty of the latter.
Works incl. *Voyage of the Mayflower* for chor. & orch.; Sym. in E min., *Lyric Ovt.*, *Pagan Festival* & *To Youth* ovts., *Feuilles symphoniques*, *5 Miniatures* for orch.; Sinfonietta & *Old-fashioned Suite* for stgs.; Poem for v. & orch.; *Little Romance* & *Tune and Vars.* for chamber orch., *Fantastic Dance* for woodwind; stg. 4tet; v. & pf. So., &c.

White (or **Whyte**), **Robert** (b. ? London, *c.* 1530; d. London, XI. 1574), Eng. comp. He was prob. the son of a London org. builder, also named Robert W., and took the Mus.B. degree at Cambridge in 1560. In 1561 he succeeded Tye as choirmaster at Ely cath. He married Ellen Tye, prob. a daughter of that master, in 1565 and left Ely in 1566, succeeded by John Farrant, to become choirmaster of Chester cath. until *c.* 1570, when he went to London to take up a similar post at Westminster Abbey. Nearly the whole of his family succumbed to the plague of 1574, himself incl.
Works incl. 20 Lat. motets & services; Eng. anthems; In Nomines for viols and arr. for lute; org. piece *Ut re mi fa sol la*; secular songs for several voices, &c.

White, Terence (d'Olbert) (b. London, 22. V. 1913), Eng. critic, orgst., cond. & comp., partly of Ir., Fr. & Afr. descent. Studied at the R.C.M. and became a solo orgst. and contrib. to mus. periodicals. He now (from 1946) writes under the matronymic of Gervais.

Works incl. 3 operas; ballets; relig. works for chor. & orch.; 2 syms.; 3 stg. 4tets; org. & pf. works; songs, &c.

White, William (b. ?; d. ?), Eng. 16th–17th-cent. singer & comp. He was a singer at Westminster Abbey in London.

Works incl. verse anthem in 2 parts, 'Almighty Lord' and 'Bend down'; fantasies & pavans for viols, &c.

Whitehill, Clarence (b. Marengo, Iowa, 5. XI. 1871; d. New York, 19. XII. 1932), Amer. bass-bar. singer. Studied at Chicago and Paris and made his 1st stage appearance at Brussels in 1899. After 1st singing in N.Y. in 1900 he made further studies with Stockhausen at Frankfort o/M. and learnt Wagnerian parts with Cosima Wagner at Bayreuth.

Whitehouse, W(illiam). E(dward). (b. London, 20. V. 1859; d. London, 12. I. 1935), Eng cst. Studied at the R.A.M. in London, Piatti being among his masters, and he joined the teaching-staff there in 1882. He travelled with Joachim and became a member of several chamber-m. organizations.

Whithorn. A primitive Eng. inst. of the ob. type, also called May-horn, made of willow bark with a double reed of material from the same tree. It was formerly used in Oxfordshire for the Whit-Monday hunt.

Whithorne, Emerson (real name Wittern) (b. Cleveland, Ohio, 6. IX. 1884), Amer. pfst. & comp. Studied at Cleveland and began to appear a pfst. at the age of 15, but later had further lessons from Leschetizky in Vienna, where he also studied comp. with Fuchs. He lived in London in 1907–15, then returned to U.S.A., settled at St. Louis in 1915–20, then in N.Y.

Works incl. ballet *Sooner or later*; incid. m. for Eugene O'Neill's *Marco Millions*; 2 syms., symph. poems *The Rain, La Nuit, The Aeroplane, Fata Morgana, The Dream Pedlar, The Moon Trail*, suite *New York Days and Nights, Fandango* for orch.; Poem for pf. & orch., v. Conc.; *Saturday's Child* for 2 voices & orch.; stg. 4tet, pf. 5tet, *Greek Impressions* for stg. 4tet; *The Grim Troubadour* for voice & stg. 4tet; v. & pf. So.; suites *New York Days and Nights* & *El camino real* & other works for pf.; songs, &c.

Whitlock, Percy (William) (b. Chatham, 1. VI. 1903; d. Bournemouth, 1. V. 1946), Eng. orgst. & comp. Learnt m. as a choir-boy at Rochester cath. and later studied at the G.S.M. and the R.C.M. in London. Asst. orgst. at Rochester cath., 1921–30 and orgst. at Chatham and Borstal, from 1932 borough orgst. at Bournemouth.

Works incl. services, anthems, motets & hymn-tunes; m. for a Rochester pageant; Sym. for org. & orch.; So. in C min., *Plymouth Suite* & other works for org., &c.

Whitman, Walt(er) (1819–92), Amer. poet. *See* **Bell** (Sym.), **Bonner** (*Whispers of Heavenly Death*), **Bryson** (*Drum Taps*), **Carpenter** (*Sea Drift*), **Coleridge-Taylor** (do.), **Converse** (*Mystic Trumpeter* & *Night and Day*), **Farwell** (symbolistic study), **Harris (R.)** (suite), **Harty** (*Mystic Trumpeter*), **Holst** (*Ode to Death*), **Kelley** (*My Captain*), **Loeffler** (*Beat! Beat! Drums!*), **Morning Heroes** (Bliss), **Müller-Hermann** (*Song of Remembrance*), **Schoeck** (*Trommelschläge*), **Sea Drift** (Delius), **Sea Symphony** (Vaughan Williams), **Vaughan Williams** (*Toward the Unknown Region*), **Wood (C.)** (*Dirge for 2 Veterans* & *Ethiopia Saluting the Colours*).

Whittaker, W(illiam). G(illies). (b. Newcastle-on-Tyne, 23. VII. 1876; d. Orkney Isles, 5. VII. 1944), Eng. educst., cond., ed. & comp. Taught and cond. choirs at Armstrong and King's Colls., Newcastle-on-Tyne, and founded a Bach Choir there. In 1929 he was app. prof. of m. at Glasgow Univ. and principal of the Sco. Acad. of M. there. He ed. much old m. and pub. books incl. misc. essays and a work on Bach's cantatas.

Comps. incl. ovt. & chors. for Aeschylus's *Choephorae, A Lykewake Dirge* for chor. & orch.; pf. 5tet *Among the Northumbrian Hills*; partsongs & folksong arrs., &c.

Whittle and Dub. An old Eng. name for the Pipe and Tabor.

Who is Silvia?, song by Schubert from Shakespeare's *Two Gentlemen of Verona*, trans. by Eduard von Bauernfeld as *An Silvia* and comp., in Ger., in 1826.

Whole-tone Scale. A mus. scale progressing by steps of nothing but whole tones. Only 2 such scales are possible, i.e. C, D, E, F♯, G♯, A♯, C and C♯, D♯, F, G, A, B, C♯, but they can of course begin at any point, there being no feeling of tonality or of any keynote; neither is there, consequently, any possibility of modulation, and the chances of harmonizing whole-tone m. are limited. The accidentals may, of course, be equally well written as D♭, E♭, G♭, A♭, B♭.

Whytbroke. *See* **Whitbroke**.

Whyte, Ian (b. Dunfermline, 13. VIII

1901), Sco. cond. & comp. Studied at the Carnegie Dunfermline Trust school of m. and later at the R.C.M. in London, where Stanford and Vaughan Williams were his comp. masters. In 1923 he became mus. dir. to Lord Glentanar at Aboyne, Aberdeenshire, where he prod. operas, and in 1931 he was app. Sco. regional mus. dir. by the B.B.C.

Works incl. opera *Comala* (after Ossian); ballet *Goblin Ha*; incid. m. for broadcast plays incl. an adapt. of Scott's *Marmion*; 6 Psalms for chor. & orch.; 2 operettas *The Forge* & *The Tale of the Shepherds* for solo voices, chor. & stgs., *The Beatitudes* and sonnet by Wordsworth for chor. & stgs.; 2 syms., ovts. *The Treadmill* & *Bassoon Factory*, Festival March for orch.; pf. Conc.; pf. 5tet; v. & pf. sos., &c.

Whyte, Robert. *See* **White.**

Whythorne, Thomas (b. ?, 1528; d. ?, after 1590), Eng. comp. Nothing is known of his biog., except that he travelled in It. and elsewhere on the Continent and pub. his 1st book of m. in 1571 and his 2nd in 1590.

Works incl. psalms & secular songs for 2–5 voices or solo voice with insts., &c.

Wichello, Abiell. *See* **Whichello.**

Widerspänstigen Zähmung, Der (*The Taming of the Shrew*), opera by Götz (lib. by Johann Viktor Widmann, after Shakespeare), prod. Mannheim, 11. X. 1874.

Widor, Charles Marie (Jean Albert) (b. Lyons, 24. II. 1845; d. Paris, 12. III. 1937), Fr. orgst., teacher & comp. Studied under his father, an orgst. at Lyons, and later with Lemmens and Fétis in Brussels. In 1870 he became orgst. of the church of Saint-Sulpice in Paris, and in 1890 succeeded Franck as org. prof. at the Cons., where he also became prof. of comp. in succession to Dubois.

Works incl. operas *Maître Ambros*, *Les Pêcheurs de Saint-Jean*, *Nerto* (after Mistral); ballet *La Korrigane*; pantomime *Jeanne d'Arc*; incid. m. to *Conte d'Avril* (adapt. of Shakespeare's *Twelfth Night*) & Coppée's *Les Jacobites*; Mass for double chor. & 2 orgs., Psalm cxii for chor., orch. & org.; 2 syms., symph. poem *Une Nuit de Valpurgis*; Sym. for org. & orch., concs. for pf., v., & co.; pf. 5tet, pf. Trio; v. & pf. So., Suite for fl. & pf.; 6 duets for pf. & org.; 10 syms. & pieces for org.; pf. works; songs, &c.

Wiechowicz, Stanislaw (b. Kroczyce, 27. XI. 1893), Pol. cond., critic & comp. Studied at Cracow, Dresden, Leningrad and Paris and settled at Poznan as cond. & critic. He was awarded the Pol. State prize for m. in 1939.

Works incl. opera *Chmiel*; Children's Cantata & Romantic Cantata for chor. & orch.; *Slavonic Apotheosis* for chor. & wind band; symph. poems *Indian Summer*, Symph. M., Rhapsody & other orch. works; *Pastoralki* (Pol. Christmas songs) & other songs; partsongs, folksong arrs., &c.

Wieck, Clara. *See* **Schumann.**

Wieck, Friedrich (b. Pretzsch nr. Torgau, 18. VIII. 1785; d. Dresden, 6. X. 1873), Ger. pfst. & teacher of his inst., father of Clara Schumann. Worked at Leipzig and Dresden, and had Schumann and Bülow among his pupils.

Wiegand, Carl Friedrich (1877–1942), Swi. dramatist. *See* **Jelmoli** (*Marignano*).

Wiegenlied (Ger. = cradle song). A title often given by Ger. comps. to voc. lullabies or to inst. pieces in their manner; there is a notorious voc. ex. long attrib. to Mozart ('Schlafe, mein Prinzchen') and still too frequently sung under his name, although, except quite superficially, it is obviously un-Mozartian in style. It was 1st pub. about 4 years after Mozart's death (*c.* 1795) in Berlin, and it was perfectly clear at that time that the words were by Friedrich Wilhelm Gotter and the m. by one Bernhard Flies. There is no evidence whatever that Flies had stolen the comp. from Mozart.

Wieland, Christoph Martin (1733–1813), Ger. poet. *See* **Oberon** (Weber & Wranitzky), **Schweitzer (Anton)** (4 operas), **Wolf (E. W.)** (*Seraphina*), **Zelter** (do.).

Wieniawski, Adam (Tadeusz) (b. Warsaw, 27. XI. 1879), Pol. comp. Studied with Noskowski and others at Warsaw, later with Bargiel in Berlin and d'Indy and Fauré in Paris. He served at the Fr. front in the 1914–8 war, returned to Warsaw and in 1928 became dir. of the Mus. Soc. and the Chopin High School of M.

Works incl. operas *Megae* & *Escape* (on Villiers de l'Isle-Adam's *L'Évasion*); ballets *A Celebration at Herod's*, *Acté in Jerusalem* & *Lalita*; suite for orch.; Concertino for pf. & orch.; 2 stg. 4tets; songs; folksong arrs., &c.

Wieniawski, Henryk (b. Lublin, 10. VII. 1835; d. Moscow, 2. IV. 1880), Pol. vst. & comp., uncle of prec., father of Poldowski. Was sent to the Paris Cons. at the age of 8 and in 1846 allowed to make his 1st tour, in Pol. and Rus. From 1850 he travelled with his brother **Józef**

and in 1860 was app. solo vst. to the tsar, living in St. Petersburg most of his time until 1872, when he toured the U.S.A. with A. Rubinstein. In 1874 he succeeded Vieuxtemps as 1st v. prof. at the Brussels Cons. But he travelled again towards the end of his life, in spite of serious ill-health, which caused his sudden death in Rus.

Works incl. 2 v. Cons.; *Souvenir de Moscou*, *Le Carnaval russe*, *Légende* & numerous other pieces, fantasies & studies for the v., &c.

Wieniawski, Józef (b. Lublin, 23. V. 1837; d. Brussels, 11. XI. 1912), Pol. pfst. & comp., brother of prec. Studied at the Paris Cons. and with Liszt at Weimar. He began to tour Eur. with his brother Henryk in 1850 and became prof. of pf. successively at Moscow and Brussels.

Works incl. chamber m., pf. pieces, &c.

Wihan, Hanuš (b. Police, 5. V. 1855; d. Prague, 3. V. 1920), Cz. cst. Studied at the Prague Cons. and made his 1st appearance in Berlin, 1876. Solo cst. in the Munich court orch., 1880, and prof. at Prague Cons., 1887. Founded the Cz. Stg. 4tet in 1892. Dvořák's co. Conc. is ded. to him.

Wihtol, Joseph (b. Wolmar, 26. VII. 1863), Latvian comp. Studied with Rimsky-Korsakov and others at the St. Petersburg Cons., where in 1886 he became prof. of theory. In 1918 he returned to Latvia and took an important share in its mus. independence as a separate nation, becoming dir. of the Nat. Opera at Riga and dir. of the Latvian Cons.

Works incl. m. for fairy play *King Brussubard*; Sym., symph. poem *The Feast of Ligo*, Latv. ovt. *Spriditis*, dramatic ovt. for orch.; Fantasy of Latv. folksongs for co. & orch.; stg. 4tet; 5 pf. sos.; partsongs, folksong arrs., &c.

Wiklund, Adolf (b. Langserud, Vermeland, 5. VI. 1879), Swe. pfst., cond. & comp. Studied at the Stockholm Cons. and later travelled in Fr., It. and Ger., becoming a pupil of Kwast in Berlin. After cond. opera in Ger., he became 2nd cond. at the Stockholm Opera in 1911 and was app. court cond. in 1923.

Works incl. Sym., symph. poem *Sommar*, concert ovt. for orch.; 2 concs. & *Conzertstück* for pf. & orch.; stg. 4tet; 2 v. & pf. sos.; pf. pieces; songs, &c.

Wilbye, John (b. Diss, Norfolk, III. 1574; d. Colchester, IX. 1638), Eng. comp. His father, a tanner and landowner, seems to have given him a good educ. His was patronized by the Cornwallis family at Brome Hall and *c.* 1595 he went into the service of their son-in-law, Sir Thomas Kytson, at Hengrave Hall nr. Bury St. Edmunds, and he was frequently in London with the family. After the death of his patron he remained in the service of his widow, who d. in 1628, whereupon he went to Colchester to join the household of her daughter, Lady Rivers. He never married and was well-to-do, having been granted a lease of a sheep-farm by Kytson and gradually acquiring property at Diss, Bury St. Edmunds and elsewhere.

Works incl. 2 sacred voc. pieces contrib. to Leighton's *Teares and Lamentacions*; 2 books of (64) madrigals, madrigal *The Lady Oriana* contrib. to *The Triumphes of Oriana*; 3 fantasies for viols (incomplete); lute lessons (lost), &c.

Wilcken, Anna Magdalena. *See* **Bach** family, 29.

Wilde, Oscar (O'Flaherty) (1856–1900), Ir. poet, dramatist & novelist. *See* **Bantock** (*Salome*), **Bossi (R.)** (*Rosa rossa*), **Carpenter** (*Birthday of the Infanta*), **Glazunov** (*Salome*), **Ibert** (*Ballad of Reading Gaol*), **Krein (A.)** (*Salome*), **Křička** (*Gentleman in White*), **Lutyens** (*Birthday of the I.*), **Mossolov** (*Sphinx*), **Radnai** (*Birthday of the I.*), **Riadis** (*Salome*), **Salome** (R. Strauss), **Salomé** (Mariotte), **Schreker** (*Geburtstag der Infantin*), **Sekles** (*Zwerg und die Infantin*), **Tcherepnin (A.)** (*Salome*), **Vassilenko** (*Garden of Death*), **Zemlinsky** (*Florentinische Tragödie* & *Zwerg*).

Wildenbruch, Ernst von (1845–1909), Ger. poet & dramatist. *See* **Hummel (F.)** (incid. m. for plays), **Schillings** (*Hexenlied*), **Zöllner** (*Überfall*).

Wilder, Philip van (b. ?; d. ?), Flem. lutenist & comp. App. lutenist to Henry VIII in 1538 and later became gentleman of the privy chamber to Edward VI. Comp. motets, In Nomines for 5–8 voices and/or insts., &c.

Wilder, Thornton (Niven) (b. 1897), Amer. playwright. *See* **Taylor (Deems)** (*Lucrece*).

Wilder, (Jérôme Albert) Victor (van) (b. Wetteren nr. Ghent, 21. VIII. 1835; d. Paris, 8. IX. 1882), Belg. poet, m. critic & trans. Studied law and philosophy at Ghent Univ. and m. at the Cons. Later settled in Paris as critic, made many Fr. transs. of great works, incl. Handel's *Messiah* and Wagner's later operas, and pub. books on Mozart and Beethoven.

Wildroe, Philip de. Another form of the name of Philip van Wilder.

Wildschütz, Der, oder Die Stimme der

Natur (*The Poacher, or The Voice of Nature*), opera by Lortzing (lib. by comp. based on a play by Kotzebue), prod. Leipzig, 31. XII. 1842.

Wilhelm, Carl (b. Schmalkalden, 5. IX. 1815; d. Schmalkalden, 26. VIII. 1873), Ger. cond. & comp. He cond. a male-voice chor. soc. at Crefeld in 1840–65, and in 1854 set the words of Max Schneckenburger's *Die Wacht am Rhein* as a patriotic song, for which he received a pension in 1871.

Wilhelmj, August (Daniel Ferdinand) (b. Usingen, Nassau, 21. IX. 1845; d. London, 22. I. 1908), Ger. vst. Made his 1st public appearance in 1854 and in 1861 was sent by Liszt to Leipzig to study with David at the Cons. In 1865 he began to travel and in 1866 1st visited London, where in 1893 he settled as v. prof.

Wilkinson, Robert (b. ?; d. ?), Eng. 15th–16th-cent. comp. Comp. 2 settings of *Salve Regina* for 5 & 9 voices, 'Jesus autem transiens' (Apostles' Creed) for 13 voices in canon, 'O virgo prudentissima,' &c.

Wilkinson, Thomas (b. ?; d. ?), Eng. 16th–17th-cent. comp. He may have been a singer at Durham cath. and he contrib. 3 anthems to Myriell's *Tristitiae remedium* in 1616.

Works incl. services, 18 anthems, madrigals, pavans for viols, &c.

Willaert, Adrian (b. ? Bruges, *c.* 1480; d. Venice, 7. XII. 1562), Flem. comp. Educ. for law, he was sent to Paris for further study, but turned to m. and became a pupil of Mouton or Josquin des Prés. After a return home he went to It., visiting Venice, Rome and Ferrara, then went into the service of King Lewis of Boh. & Hung, who d. in 1526, when W. returned to It., becoming chapel master at St. Mark's, Venice, in 1527, and founding a singing-school there. He revisited Flanders in 1542 and 1556.

Works incl. masses, motets, Magnificat, set of motets on the hist. of Susanna, psalms, hymns; madrigals, canzoni, villanesche; inst. fantasies and ricercari, &c.

Willan, Healey (b. London, 12. X. 1880), Eng.-Canad. orgst. & comp. Began his career as church orgst. in London, but emigrated to Toronto, where he became lecturer at the Univ. in 1914 and mus. dir. to the Hart House Players in 1919. In 1920 he became vice-principal of the Cons. and later prof. at the Univ.

Works incl. incid. m. to plays; church m.; war elegy *Why they so softly sleep, Apostrophe to the Heavenly Hosts* & *Coronation Te Deum* for chor. & orch.; Sym. in D min., *Marche solennelle* for orch.; Preludes and Fugues, *Epilogue, Introduction, Passacaglia and Fugue* & other works for org.; songs to words by Yeats & others, &c.

William of Newark (b. Newark-on-Trent, ?; d. ? London, 1509), Eng. comp. Predecessor of Cornyshe as Master of the Children in the Chapel Royal. A madrigal and 7 songs are preserved.

William Ratcliff. *See also* **Guglielmo Ratcliff** & **Ratcliff.**

Opera by Cui (lib. by Alexey Nikolaievitch Fleshtcheiev, based on Heine's drama), prod. St. Petersburg, 26. II. 1869.

Opera by Dopper (lib. by ?, based on Heine), prod. Weimar, 19. X. 1909.

Opera by Emilio Pizzi (1861–1931) (lib. by Angelo Zanardini, based on Heine), prod. Bologna, Teatro Comunale, 31. X. 1889.

William Tell. *See* **Guillaume Tell** for Rossini's opera; **Schiller** for other works.

Williams, Alberto (b. Buenos Aires, 23. XI. 1862), Arg. pfst., cond., poet & comp. of Eng. & Spa. descent. Studied at the Buenos Aires Cons. and later in Paris, where he studied pf. with the Chopin pupil Mathias, harmony with Durand, ctpt. with Guiraud and comp. with Franck. In 1889 he returned home, where he gave pf. recitals and cond. sym. concerts.

Works incl. 2 syms. (No. 2 *La bruja de las montañas*) & other orch. works; chors.; works for v. & pf. and co. & pf.; *El rancho abandonado* & other pf. pieces; songs, &c.

Williams, Anna (b. London, 6. VIII. 1845; d. London, 3. IX. 1924), Eng. sop. singer. Studied in London, took a prize at the Crystal Palace in 1872, went to Naples to finish her studies with Scafati and in 1874 made her 1st important appearance in London.

Williams, (John) Gerard (b. London, 10. XII. 1888), Eng. comp. Studied architecture at first, but picked up any mus. experience he could in choirs and orchs., &c. He began as a self-taught comp. in 1911, but in 1913 had some lessons from Walthew.

Works incl. ballad opera *Kate, the Cabin Boy*, operetta *The Story of the Willow-pattern Plate* & others; ballet *The Wings of Horus*; suites *Pot Pourri* & *Miniatures* for orch.; 2 stg. 4tets; Preludes, *Side-shows*, &c. for pf.; many songs, &c.

Williams, Grace (b. Barry, Glam., 19. II. 1906), Welsh comp. Educ. at Cardiff Univ., where she took the B.Mus. in 1926; studied with Vaughan Williams at the R.C.M. in

London, 1926–30, and with Wellesz in Vienna, 1930–1.

Works incl. *Hymn of Praise* (*Gogonedawg Arglwydd* from 12th-cent. Black Book of Carmarthen) for chor. & orch.; Welsh ovt. *Hen Walia*, legend *Rhiannon*, Fantasy on Welsh Nursery Rhymes, symph. impressions *Owen Glendower* (after Shakespeare's *1 Henry IV*); 2 Psalms for sop. & orch., *The Song of Mary* (Magnificat) for sop. & orch.; *Sinfonia concertante* for pf. & orch.; Elegy & *Sea Sketches* for stg. orch.; songs to words by Herrick, Byron, Belloc, D. H. Lawrence, &c.; arrs. of Welsh folk-songs, &c.

Williams, Ralph Vaughan. *See* **Vaughan Williams.**

Willner, Arthur (b. Teplice, 5. III. 1881), Ger.-Cz. comp. Studied at the Leipzig Cons. and later with Rheinberger and Thuille at Munich. In 1903 he joined the staff of the Stern Cons. in Berlin, of which he became deputy dir.; in 1924 he settled in Vienna and in 1938 in London.

Works incl. Sym. in A min., Suite of Fugues, *The Insts. present themselves* for orch.; pf. Conc., co. Conc., *Bagpipes* & Suite for pf. & stgs., Conc. for 2 vs. & stgs.; 5 stg. 4tets, 12 fugues *Circle of Life* for stg. 4tet; 4 sos., 3 sonatinas & Suite for v. & pf.; var. inst. pieces; pf. duets, 4 sos., Vars., *Tanzweisen*, *A travers les siècles*, *Sketches*, *Neues Notenbuch*, *La Voix du piano* & other works for pf.; songs, &c.

Wilm, Nikolai von (b. Riga, 4. III. 1834; d. Wiesbaden, 20. II. 1911), Latvian comp. Studied at the Leipzig Cons. and in 1857 became 2nd cond. at the Riga munic. theatre and in 1860 went to St. Petersburg as prof. at the Nikolai Institute. He lived at Dresden in 1875–8 and then at Wiesbaden.

Works incl. motets; stg. 4tet, stg. 6tet; 2 sos. & 2 suites for v. & pf., So. for co. & pf.; numerous pf. pieces; songs; partsongs, &c.

Wilson, John (b. ? Faversham, 5. IV. 1595; d. London, 22. II. 1674), Eng. lutenist, singer & comp. Contrib., (?) with Coperario and Lanier, to *The Maske of Flowers*, perf. at Whitehall in 1614. After being (?) a singing actor, he became one of the king's musns. in 1635. Lived at Oxford during the Civil War and took the D.Mus. there in 1645; soon afterwards was in private service in Oxfordshire, but in 1656–61 was Prof. of M. at Oxford Univ.; then returned to London to be at or near the restored court and became a Gentleman of the Chapel Royal in 1662 in succession to H. Lawes.

Works incl. m. for Brome's *The Northern Lass*, songs for *The Maske of Flowers*; anthem 'Hearken, O God'; *Psalterium Carolinum* for 3 voices & continuo; Elegy on the Death of Wm. Lawes; *Cheerful Ayres* for 3 voices; airs & dialogues with lute; songs incl. Shakespeare's 'Take, O take those lips away' & 'Lawn as white as driven snow'; catches, &c.

Wilson, Thomas (b. ?; d. ?), Eng. 17th-cent. orgst. & comp. He was a singer at Ripon cath., where in 1670–7 he played the org. in place of the orgst. Wanless, who had become deaf but retained his post. He may also have been at some time orgst. of Peterhouse Coll., Cambridge.

Works incl. anthems, Te Deums, settings of Magnificat & Nunc dimittis, &c.

Wilt (*née* **Liebenthaler**), **Marie** (b. Vienna, 30. I. 1833; d. Vienna, 24. IX. 1891), Aus. sop. singer. An orphan, she was brought up by foster-parents and married the architect Franz Wilt. After singing at concerts, she was advised by Désirée Artôt to go on the stage, studied with Gänsbacher and Wolf, and made her 1st stage appearance at Graz in 1865. In 1866 she sang in It. opera in London as Maria Vilda.

Winchester Troper. *See* **Troper.**

Wind Machine. Although used by R. Strauss in *Don Quixote*, this is a stage property, not a mus. inst. It is a barrel covered with silk, the friction of which on being turned prod. a sound like a whistling wind.

Winkler, Alexander Adolfovitch (b. Kharkov, 3. III. 1865; d. Leningrad, X. 1935), Rus. pfst. & comp. Studied at Kharkov, with Duvernoy in Paris and with Leschetizky in Vienna. After teaching at the Kharkov School of M. he became prof. at the St. Petersburg Cons. in 1896.

Works incl. ovt. *En Bretagne*, Vars. on Rus. & Fin. folksongs for orch.; 3 stg. 4tets, stg. 5tet, pf. 4tet, pf. Trio; va. & pf. So.; Vars. & Fugue on a theme by Bach for 2 pfs.; Vars. & Fugue on an orig. theme & other works for pf.; songs, &c.

Winsheim, Abraham. *See* **Weisshan.**

Winter Journey (Schubert). *See* **Winterreise.**

Winter, Peter von (b. Mannheim, 2. V. 1755; d. Munich, 17. X. 1825), Ger. comp. Played v. in the electoral orch. at Mannheim at the age of 11, became a pupil of Vogler, but was largely self-taught as a comp. In 1776 he became mus. dir. of the court theatre and met Mozart during his visit to Mannheim, but the two disliked each other. When the court moved to Munich he followed it and in 1798 became court mus. dir. He remained to his death, but frequently had prolonged leave of absence to visit Vienna, It., Prague, Paris and London.

Works incl. operas *Helena und Paris, Der Bettelstudent, I fratelli rivali, Das unterbrochene Opferfest, Das Labyrinth* (sequel to Mozart's *Magic Flute*), *Maria von Montelban, Tamerlan, La grotta di Calipso, Il trionfo dell' amor fraterno, Il ratto di Proserpina, Zaira, Colmal, Maometto II, Scherz, List und Rache* & *Jery und Bätely* (both libs. by Goethe) & c. 20 others; ballets *Heinrich IV, Inez de Castro, La Mort d'Hector* & 6 others; 26 masses, 2 Requiems, 3 *Stabat Maters* and other church m.; orats. *Der Sterbende Jesus, La Betulia liberata* & others; cantata *Timoteo, o Gli effetti della musica* & others; syms. & ovts.; concerted pieces for var. insts.; songs, partsongs, &c.

'Winter Wind' Study. The nickname sometimes given to Chopin's pf. Study in A min., Op. 25 No. 11.

Wintermärchen, Ein (*A Winter's Tale*), opera by Goldmark (lib. by Alfred Maria Willner, after Shakespeare), prod. Vienna, Opera, 2. I. 1908.

Winterreise, Die (*The Winter Journey*), song cycle by Schubert (poems by Wilhelm Müller), comp. Part i, II. 1827; Part ii, X. 1827.

Winter's Tale. *See* **Hermione; Wintermärchen.**

Wirbel (Ger.). A roll on any kind of drum.

Wirbeltrommel (Ger. = rolling-drum) = Tenor Drum (more often called *Rührtrommel*).

Wirén, Dag (b. Örebro, 1905), Swe. critic & comp. Studied at the Stockholm Cons. In 1932 he received a stage grant and continued his studies with Sabaneiev in Paris. On his return he became a m. critic at Stockholm.

Works incl. Sym., Sinfonietta; Serenade for stgs.; co. Conc.; stg. 4tet, 2 pf. trios; 2 sonatinas for co. & pf.; pf. pieces; songs, &c.

Wise, Michael (b. ? Salisbury, c. 1648; d. Salisbury, 24. VIII. 1687), Eng. singer & comp. Choir-boy at the Chapel Royal in London in 1660. In 1663 he became a lay-clerk at St. George's Chapel, Windsor, and in 1668 orgst. & choirmaster of Salisbury cath. He was admitted a Gentleman of the Chapel Royal in 1676, but retained his post at Salisbury until 1685, when at the time of the coronation of James II he was suspended, probably for some political opposition to the new king. In I. 1687 he became almoner and choirmaster at St. Paul's cath. in London, but he still visited Salisbury, where his wife had remained. After a dispute with her at night, he left the house and was challenged by a watchman and killed in a dispute with him.

Works incl. services & anthems; catches; duet *Old Charon*, &c.

'Witch' or 'Witches' Minuet (Ger. *Hexenmenuett*). The nickname sometimes given to the minuet in Haydn's D min. stg. 4tet, Op. 76 No. 2.

Witkowski, Georges (Martin) (b. Mostagneux, Algeria, 6. I. 1867; d. Paris, VIII. 1943), Fr. comp. (?) of Pol. descent. Educ. for a military career, but turned to m. and studied with d'Indy. Leaving the army, he cond. chor. & orch. concerts at Lyons and later became dir. of the Cons. there.

Works incl. operas *Le Maître à chanter, La Princesse lointaine* (after Rostand's play); *Poème de la maison* for solo voices, chor. & orch.; 2 syms.; prelude, vars. & finale *Mon lac* for pf. & orch., 4 *Poèmes* & *Introduction et Danses* for v. & orch.; songs with orch. on poems by Ronsard, H. de Régnier & others; stg. 4tet, pf. 5tet; song cycle *Poèmes de l'amour*, &c.

Witt, Christian Friedrich (b. Altenburg, 1660; d. Altenburg, 13. IV. 1716), Ger. comp. Court mus. dir. at Altenburg.

Works incl. *Psalmodia sacra*, cantatas; Fr. ovts. & suites for orch.; org. & hpchd. works, &c.

Woelfl, Joseph (b. Salzburg, 24. XII. 1773; d. London, 21. V. 1812), Aus. pfst. & comp. Pupil of L. Mozart and M. Haydn at Salzburg, where he was a choir-boy at the cath. In 1790 he went to Vienna and c. 1792 made his 1st public appearance, at Warsaw. He soon made his name as a virtuoso and after prod. some stage works in Vienna married the actress Therese Klemm in 1798 and went on a long tour in Boh. and Ger. In 1801–5 he lived in Paris, where he prod. 2 more operas, and he then settled in London.

Works incl. operas *Der Höllenberg, Das schöne Milchmädchen, Der Kopf ohne Mann, Liebe macht kurzen Prozess* (with others), *L'Amour romanesque, Fernanda, ou Les Maures*; ballets *La Surprise de Diane* & *Alzire* (on Voltaire's play); Sym.; *The Calm* & other pf. concs.; chamber m.; *Non plus ultra* & other pf. sos., var. pf. works, &c.

Wohltemperierte Clavier, Das (*The Well-tempered Clavier, see also* **Weber, B. C.**). A collection of 48 preludes and fugues by Bach, in 2 parts, finished in 1722 and 1744 resp. and comprising 2 cycles going through all the maj. and min. keys (excl. of enharmonic keys: e.g. F♯ maj. is present, but not G♭ maj.), designed to prove the utility of tuning keyboard insts. in Equal Temperament, so that they could play in all the keys without the extreme sharp and flat tonalities being less in tune than the others, though all were slightly out of tune according to Just Intonation. This applied to all keyboard insts., even the org., so that there is no justification in supposing that Bach thought only of the clavichord, or in calling the work *The W.-t. Clavichord* in Eng. It was doubtless intended to be played on any suitable inst. that happened to be available.

Wolf. A techn. term for certain harsh and grating sounds prod. between certain intervals on keyboard insts. not tuned in Equal Temperament, or on stg. insts. by defective vibration on a certain note or notes.

Wolf, Ernst Wilhelm (b. Grossenbehringen nr. Gotha, II. 1735; d. Weimar, XI. 1792), Ger. comp. He was leader and from 1761 court cond. at Weimar.

Works incl. operas *Das grosse Los, Die Dorfdeputierten* (after Goldoni), *Erwin und Elmire* (Goethe), *Der Eremit auf Formentara* (Kotzebue), *Die Zauberirrungen* (after Shakespeare's *Midsummer Night's Dream*) & others; monodrama *Polyxena*; cantata *Seraphina* (Wieland); church m.; orats., Easter cantatas (Herder); syms.; stg. 4tets & other chamber m.; songs, &c.

Wolf-Ferrari, Ermanno (b. Venice, 12. I. 1876), It.-Ger. comp. He was sent to Rome to study art by his Ger. father, a painter, but turned to m. and studied with Rheinberger at Munich. In 1899 he went to Venice and succeeded in having his orat. perf. and in 1900 brought out his 1st opera, after which his stage successes were frequently repeated. Many of his operas were 1st prod. in Ger. In 1902–12 he was dir. of the Liceo Benedetto Marcello at Venice.

Works incl. operas *Cenerentola, Le donne curiose, I quattro rusteghi, Il segreto di Susanna, I gioielli della Madonna, Amor medico* (after Molière), *Gli amanti sposi, Das Himmelskleid, Sly* (after Shakespeare's *Taming of the Shrew*), *La vedova scaltra, Il campiello, La dama boba* (after Lope de Vega), *Gli dei a Tebe*; cantatas *La Sulamita* & *La vita nuova* (after Dante); v. Conc.; Chamber Sym. for stgs., woodwind, pf. & hn.; pf. 5tet, pf. Trio; 2 v. & pf. sos.; org. pieces; co. pieces; *Rispetti* for sop. & pf., &c.

Wolf, Hugo (b. Windischgraz, 13. III. 1860; d. Vienna, 22. II. 1903), Aus. comp. His father, a leather merchant, encouraged his early gifts by teaching him pf. and v. After visiting var. schools, he was allowed to enter the Vienna Cons. in 1875, but left it the following year, preferring to pick up his own instruction where he could. From 1877, his father having incurred great losses in business, he was obliged to earn his own living by teaching. He often lived in great poverty, but when his pride would allow, he was befriended by var. mus. families, while Schalk and Mottl took a professional interest in him. In 1880 he was engaged as 2nd cond. at Salzburg under Muck, but was found to be temperamentally so unfitted for the post that the engagement was terminated within 3 months. From 1884–7 he was m. critic for the Vienna *Salonblatt*, but here again he offended many people by his irascibility and his intolerance, which saw no fault in Wagner and no good at all in Brahms, for ex. In 1897 his mind became unhinged and he was sent to a sanatorium. He was discharged as cured in I. 1898, but had a relapse and was taken to an asylum in a hopeless condition in X, remaining there until his death.

Works incl. operas *Der Corregidor* & *Manuel Venegas* (unfinished); incid. m. to Ibsen's *The Feast at Solhaug*; 48 early songs, 53 songs to words by Mörike, 20 to words by Eichendorff, 51 to words by Goethe, *Italian Song-Book* (46 songs), *Spanish Song-Book* (44 songs), 31 songs to words by var. poets, incl. 6 by Gottfried Keller & 3 sonnets by Michelangelo; symph. poem *Penthesilea* (after Kleist); *Italian Serenade* for small orch. or stg. 4tet; stg. 4tet in D min.; *Christnacht* for solo voices, chor. & orch., *Elfenlied* from Shakespeare's *Midsummer Night's Dream* for sop., chor. & orch., *Der Feuerreiter* & *Dem Vaterland* for chor. & orch.; 6 partsongs, &c.

Wolf, Johannes (b. Berlin, 17. IV. 1869), Ger. mcolst. Studied with Spitta in Berlin and took a doctor's degree at Leipzig in 1893. In 1908 he became prof. of m. at Berlin Univ. and in 1915 librarian of the m. section of the Prus. State Library, where he succeeded Altmann as dir. in 1928. He has specialized in and written on early m., old mus. treatises and old notations.

Wolfe, Humbert (1885–1940), Eng. poet. *See* **Holst** (songs).

Wolff, Albert (Louis) (b. Paris, 19. I. 1889), Fr. cond. & comp. Studied at the Paris Cons., became chor. master at the Opéra-Comique in 1908 and cond. in 1911, succeeded Messager as chief cond. in 1922. In 1928–34 he cond. the Lamoureux concerts and later the Pasdeloup concerts.

Works incl. opera *L'Oiseau bleu* (after Maeterlinck), &c.

Wolff, Erich (b. Vienna, 3. XII. 1874; d. New York, 20. III. 1913), Aus. pfst. & comp. Studied at the Phil. Soc. Cons. in Vienna and became an accompst.

Works incl. ballet *Zlatorog*; v. Conc.; stg. 4tet; numerous songs, &c.

Wolff, Pius Alexander (1784–1826), Ger. actor & playwright. *See* **Eberwein** (*Preciosa*), **Preciosa** (Weber), **Seyfried** (*Preciosa*).

Wolfrum, Philipp (b. Schwarzenbach, Bavaria, 17. XII. 1854; d. Samaden, Swi., 8. V. 1919), Ger. orgst. & comp. Studied at Munich with Rheinberger and others, later became orgst. and mus. dir. to Heidelberg Univ., and also cond. chor. perfs.

Works incl. orat. *Weihnachtsmysterium*, *Das grosse Hallelujah* (Klopstock) for male chor., hymns *Der evangelische Kirchenchor* for chor., *Festmusik* for bar. & male chor.; stg. 4tet, pf. 5tet, stg. Trio; co. & pf. So.; 3 sos., 57 preludes, *3 Tondichtungen*, &c. for org.; pf. pieces; songs, &c.

Wolfurt, Kurt von (b. Lettin, Latvia, 7. IX. 1880), Ger.-Baltic comp. Studied at the Leipzig Cons. and privately with Reger. After cond. at var. places, he lived in Rus. during the 1914–8 war and then in Berlin, where he taught m. He wrote a book on Mussorgsky.

Works incl. operas *Der Tanz um den Narren* (after Molière) & *Dame Kobold* (after Calderón); Christmas Orat., Rhapsody from Goethe's *Faust* & other chor. works; Triple Fugue, Conc. grosso, Divertimento, Serenade, Vars. & Characteristic Pieces on a theme by Mozart for orch.; M. for stgs. & drums; pf. Conc.; Suite for v. & chamber orch.; stg. 4tet; pf. pieces; songs, &c.

Wolkenstein, Oswald von (b. Gröden nr. Brixen, *c.* 1377; d. Hauenstein castle, 2. VIII. 1445), Aus. Minnesinger. Led a very adventurous life, travelled much, even as far as Asia and Africa. From 1415 he was in the service of King (later Emperor) Sigismund and was sent to Spa. and Port. on diplomatic missions. In 1421–7 he involved himself in much strife and was twice imprisoned in his endeavour to extend his land by encroaching on that of his neighbours.

Works incl. songs of love, spring, travel, &c. for 1–3 voices (to his own words).

Wolowska, Maria. *See* **Szymanowska.**

Wolstenholme, William (b. Blackburn, 24. II. 1865; d. London, 23. VII. 1931), Eng. orgst. & comp. Precociously gifted, although blind, he was trained in m. at the Coll. for the Blind at Worcester, where Elgar taught him the v. But he cultivated the org. & pf. especially, became church orgst. at Blackburn in 1887, and from 1902 at var. churches in London. In 1908 he toured the U.S.A. as a recitalist.

Works incl. church m.; orch. and military band works; chamber m.; *c.* 100 works for the org., incl. sos., Fantasy, Prelude & Fugue, &c.; pf. pieces, &c.

Wolzogen, Hans (Paul) von (b. Potsdam, 13. XI. 1848; d. Bayreuth, 2. VI. 1938), Ger. writer on m. He was called to Bayreuth by Wagner in 1877 to become ed. of the *Bayreuther Blätter*, and he wrote several works of analysis and propaganda on Wagner's m.-dramas.

Woman's Life and Love (Schumann). *See* **Frauenliebe und Leben.**

Women Composers. Most of the following will be found entered in detail in their proper alphabetical places:

Andrée, Elfrida (1841–1929), Swe.

Backer-Grøndahl, Agathe (1847–1907), Norw.

Beach, Amy Marcy (1867–1944), Amer.

Bergman, Valentina Semenovna (wife of Serov) (1846–1927), Rus.

Bertin, Louise Angélique (1805–77), Fr.

Boulanger, Lili (1893–1918), Fr.

Boulanger, Nadia (b. 1887), Fr.

Bourges, Clémentine de (?–*c.* 1561), Fr.

Bright, Dora (b. 1864), Eng.

Bronsart, Ingeborg von. *See* Starck.

Caccini, Francesca (1581–?), It.

Candeille, Amélie Julie (1767–1834), Fr.

Chaminade, Cécile (1857–1944), Fr.

Clarke, Rebecca (b. 1886), Eng.

Coccia, Maria Rosa (1759–1833), It.

Coleridge-Taylor, Avril (b. ?), Eng.

Delbos, Claire (wife of Messiaen) (b. *c.* 1910), Fr.

Farrenc, Louise (1804–75), Fr.

Gaigerova, Varvara (b. 1903), Rus.

Gipps, Ruth (b. 1921), Eng.

Glanville-Hicks, Peggy (b. 1912), Austral.

Grétry, Lucile (1773–93), Fr.

Harvey, Mary (Lady Dering) (1629–1704), Eng.

Hensel (*née* Mendelssohn), Fanny (1805–47), Ger.

Héritte-Viardot, Louise (1841–1918), Fr.

Holmès, Augusta (1847–1903), Ir.-Fr.

Holst, Imogen (b. 1907), Eng.
Hopekirk, Helen (1856–1945), Sco.-Amer.
Howell, Dorothy (b. 1898), Eng.
Kaprálová, Vitězslava (1915–40), Cz.
La Guerre (*née* Jacquet), Elisabeth de (*c.* 1666–1729), Fr.
Lebrun, Francesca (1756–91), Ger.
Lehmann, Liza (1862–1918), Eng.
Loder, Kate (1825–1904), Eng.
Lund, Signe (b. 1868), Norw.
Lutyens, Elisabeth (b. 1906), Eng.
Maconchy, Elizabeth (b. 1907), Eng.
Makarova, Nina (b. 1908), Rus.
Maria Antonia Walpurgis, Electress of Saxony (1724–80), Ger.
Martinez, Marianne (1744–1812), Aus.
Mezari, Maddalena (16th cent.), It.
Mounsey, Ann Sheppard (1811–91), Eng. } sisters.
Mounsey, Elizabeth (1819–1905), Eng. }
Müller-Hermann, Johanna (b. 1878), Aus.
Nascimbeni, Maria Francesca (17th cent.), It.
Paradies, Marie Therese von (1759–1824), Aus.
Poldowski (Lady Dean Paul) (1870s–1932), Pol.-Eng.
Renié, Henriette (b. 1875), Fr.
Rennes, Catherina van (b. 1858), Dutch.
Respighi (*née* Olivieri-Sangiacomo), Elsa (b. 1894), It.
Rokseth, Yvonne (b. 1890), Fr.
Sainton-Dolby, Charlotte (1821–85), Eng.
Schröter, Corona (1751–1802), Ger.
Schumann (*née* Wieck), Clara (1819–96), Ger.
Scott, Lady John Douglas (*née* Alicia Ann Spottiswood) (1810–1900), Sco.
Sirmen (*née* Lombardini), Maddalena (? 1735–?), It.
Smith, Alice Mary (1839–84), Eng.
Smyth, Ethel (1858–1944), Eng.
Starck, Ingeborg (1840–1913), Swe.
Stirling, Elizabeth (1819–95), Eng.
Strozzi, Barbara (17th cent.), It.
Swain, Freda (b. 1902), Eng.
Tailleferre, Germaine (b. 1892), Fr.
Temple, Hope (wife of Messager) (1859–1938), Ir.-Fr.
Vaurabourg, Andrée (wife of Honegger) (b. 1894), Fr.
Viardot-García, Pauline (1821–1910), Spa.-Fr.
Wakefield, Mary (1853–1910), Eng.
Weissberg, Julia Lazarevna (wife of Andrey Rimsky-Korsakov) (b. 1878), Rus.
White, Maude Valérie (1855–1937), Eng.
Williams, Grace (b. 1906), Welsh.
Wurm, Mary (1860–?), Anglo-Ger.

Wood, Anthony (à) (b. Oxford, 17. XII. 1632; d. Oxford, 25. XI. 1695), Eng. mus. historian. Educ. at Merton Coll., Oxford, where he took the M.A. in 1655. He wrote several works on the hist. of Oxford, incl. biog. particulars of musns.

Wood, Charles (b. Armagh, 15. VI. 1866; d. Cambridge, 12. VII. 1926), Ir. mus. scholar, teacher & comp. Learnt m. from the orgst. of Armagh cath., where his father was lay vicar, and in 1883–7 studied at the R.C.M. in London, where he became prof. in 1888, from which year until 1894 he also cond. the Univ. Mus. Soc. at Cambridge, where he became an orgst.-scholar at Caius Coll. and took the Mus.D. In 1897 he became m. lecturer to the Univ. and in 1924 succeeded Stanford of Prof. of M.

Works incl. opera *The Pickwick Papers* (after Dickens); incid. m. to Euripides' *Ion* & *Iphigenia in Tauris*; *Ode to the West Wind* & *The Song of the Tempest* for solo voices, chor. & orch.; *Ode on Music* (Swinburne), *Ode on Time* (Milton), *Dirge for Two Veterans* (Whitman), *Ballad of Dundee* for chor. & orch.; Passion according to St. Mark; services, motets, anthems, psalm-tunes; Symph. Vars. on *Patrick Sarsfield*; 3 stg. 4tets; 16 org. preludes; songs incl. *Ethiopia saluting the Colours* (Whitman), &c.

Wood, Henry J(oseph). (b. London, 3. III. 1869; d. Hitchin, Herts., 19. VIII. 1944), Eng. cond. He showed precocious gifts, esp. as an orgst., and gave recitals and held church appts. as a boy. In 1889 he had his 1st experience as a cond., in opera, in which he toured for the next few years. In 1895 he was engaged by Robert Newman to take charge of the Promenade Concerts at the newly-built Queen's Hall, and he remained in charge of them for 50 years to the end of his life, celebrating their half-centenary just before his death. He began modestly with popular programmes, but soon perf. almost all the important orch. m. ever written, always incl. many of the latest foreign and Eng. novelties as soon as they appeared. He also cond. many mus. festivals. In 1898 he married the Rus. sop. Olga Urussov, who d. in 1909, and in 1911 Muriel Greatorex. Knighted in 1911.

Wood, Thomas (b. Chorley, Lancs., 28. XI. 1892), Eng. comp. & author. As the son of a master mariner he spent much of his youth at sea; but he was passionately interested in m., was sent to Exeter Coll., Oxford, in 1913 and to the R.C.M., London, in 1918, where Stanford was his comp.

master. He was mus. dir. at Tonbridge School in 1918–24, took the Mus.D. at Oxford in 1920 and in 1924–8 was lecturer and precentor at Exeter Coll. there. Owing to poor eyesight he retired to Essex in the latter year and has since devoted his time to comp., authorship & travel. These last 2 preoccupations have produced 2 books, *Cobbers* & *True Thomas*.

Works incl. cantatas *Forty Singing Men* (Alfred Noyes), *Master Mariners, Merchantmen, The Ballad of Hampstead Heath* (Flecker); c. 30 part-songs; *In the Hill Country* for org.; pf. pieces, &c.

Woods, Michael (b. ?; d. ?), Eng. 16th-cent. orgst. & comp. Was orgst. of Chichester cath. in the middle of the cent. and wrote motets.

Woodson, Leonard (b. Winchester, ?; d. Eton, 1641), Eng. orgst., singer & comp. He was in the choir at St. George's Chapel, Windsor, early in the 17th cent. and became orgst. of Eton Coll. in 1615.

Works incl. Te Deum & other church m.; m. for viols; songs, &c.

Woodward, Richard (b. Dublin, 1744; d. Dublin, 22. XI. 1777), Ir. orgst. & comp. Learnt m. as a choir-boy at Christ Church cath., Dublin, where his father, Richard W., was vicar-choral, and in 1765 he was app. orgst. there. He took the Mus.D. at Trinity Coll., Dublin, in 1771.

Works incl. services, anthems, chants & other church m.; catches & canons; songs, &c.

Wooldridge, H(arry). E(llis). (b. Winchester, 28. III. 1845; d. London, 13. II. 1917), Eng. painter & mus. scholar. He was Slade Prof. of Fine Arts at Oxford, but made a special study of medieval m. His chief works are the 1st 2 vols. of the *Oxford History of M.*

Wooldridge, John (b. Japan, 18. VII. 1911), Eng. comp. Educ. at St. Paul's School in London and Magdalen Coll., Oxford, later studied m. and in IX. 1939 joined the R.A.F., in which he served through the 2nd world war.

Works incl. *A Solemn Hymn for Victory* for orch., &c.

Wordless Songs. Unlike Mendelssohn's *Songs without Words*, which are pf. pieces, W. S. are here understood as songs with voice and accomp. to be sung merely on vowels. Exs. are Medtner's *Sonata-Vocalise*, Ravel's *Vocalise en forme d'Habanera*, Cyril Scott's *Pastorale*, Stravinsky's *Pastorale*, &c.

Wordsworth, William (1770–1850), Eng. poet. *See* **Davies (Walford)** (orch. suite), **Whyte (I.)** (sonnet),

Worgan, John (b. ? London, 1724; d. London, 24. VIII. 1790), Eng. orgst. & comp. Pupil of T. Roseingrave. App. orgst. of the church of St. Andrew Undershaft c. 1749 and of Vauxhall Gardens c. 1751 in succession to his brother James W. (c. 1720–53), to which he was also attached as comp. until 1761, and again in 1770–4. He took the Mus.D. in 1775. He became famous as an org. recitalist.

Works incl. orats. *The Chief of Maon, Hannah, Manasseh* & *Gioas* (unfinished); anthem for a victory, psalm-tunes; serenata *The Royal Voyage*, dirge in memory of Frederick, Prince of Wales; ode on the rebellion of 1745; org. pieces; hpchd. lessons; glees; songs, &c.

Working-Out (or Development). The 2nd section of a mvt. in so. form, following the exposition, where the thematic material is subjected to var. developments, according to the comp.'s fancy. The usual procedure is to develop the 1st or 2nd subjects or both, but subsidiaries may be used as well, or instead, and new matter may be introd. at will.

Wormser, Andre (Alphonse Toussaint) (b. Paris, 1. XI. 1851; d. Paris, 4. XI. 1926), Fr. comp. Studied at the Paris Cons. and obtained the Prix de Rome in 1875.

Works incl. operas *Adèle de Ponthieu* & *Rivoli*; pantomimes *L'Enfant prodigue* & *L'Idéal*; ballet *L'Étoile*; cantata *Clytemnestre*; symph. poems *Lupercale* & *Diane et Endymion*, *Suite tzigane* for orch.; *Gigue* for v. & orch.; *Amour* poem for voice & orch.; pf. pieces; songs, &c.

Worshipful Company of Musicians of London, The. An assoc. dating back to the Middle Ages, but not formally incorporated by royal charter until 1604, under James I. But minstrels had already been allowed to form themselves into guilds by Edward IV in 1469. Among its present function is the bestowal of prizes and scholarships.

Worzischek (or **Worzišek**), **J(oh)an(n) (Hugo)** (b. Wamberg, 11. V. 1791; d. Vienna, 19. XI. 1825), Boh. pfst. & comp. Pupil of his father, a schoolmaster, and later of Tomašek. He went to Vienna in 1813 and when Hummel left he recommended him as pf. teacher to all his pupils. He became pfst. and cond. to the Phil. Soc. and in 1822 court orgst.

Works incl. church m.; Sym.; duet for co. & pf.; Divertissement for 2 pfs.; pf. works, &c.

Wotquenne, Alfred (b. Lobbes, Hainault, 25. I. 1867), Belg. mus. bibliog. Studied at the Brussels Cons. and became its librarian in 1894. He pub. its catalogue, bibliogs. of C. P. E. Bach, Galuppi, Gluck & Luigi Rossi, &c.

Woyrsch, Felix (b. Troppau, 8. X. 1860), Ger.-Cz. cond. & comp. He is self-taught in m. and went to Altona as chor. & orch. cond.

Works incl. operas *Der Pfarrer von Meudon, Der Weiberkrieg, Wikingerfahrt*; incid. m. to Moreto's *Donna Diana*; motets & other church m.; Passion Orat.; works for male chor. & orch.; 5 syms., prologue to Dante's *Divina commedia*, Böcklin Suite, Theme & Vars., ovt. to Shakespeare's *Hamlet* for orch.; v. Conc.; 4 stg. 4tets, stg. 6tet, pf. 5tet, 2 pf. trios & other chamber m.; org. & pf. pieces; numerous songs, &c.

Woytowicz, Boleslaw (b. Dunajowce, Podolia, 5. XII. 1899), Pol. pfst. & comp. Began by studying maths. and philology at Kiev Univ. and law at Warsaw Univ., but coming of a mus. family, turned to the pf., which he studied at the Chopin High School at Warsaw, where he later became a teacher. He next took to comp., studying 1st with Szopski, Maliszewski & others, and in 1930 with Nadia Boulanger in Paris.

Works incl. Concertino, Concert Suite, *Poème funèbre* on the death of Pilsudski, Vars. in the form of a sym. for orch.; pf. Conc.; stg. 4tet, Trio for fl., cl. & bn., *Cradle Song* for sop., cl., bn. & hp.; Vars. & other works for pf., &c.

Wozzeck, opera by A. Berg (lib. by comp., from Georg Büchner's drama of 1836), prod. Berlin, Opera, 14. XII. 1925.

Opera by M. Gurlitt (lib. do.), prod. Bremen, 22. IV. 1926.

Wranitzky, Paul (b. Neureisch, Moravia, 30. XII. 1756; d. Vienna, 28. IX. 1808), Morav. cond. & comp. Educ. at a monastery, later at Jihlava (Iglau) and Olomouc, went to Vienna in 1776 and studied theol. and comp. In 1780 he was app. cond. to the court theatres, a post he held to his death, and he was also for some time mus. dir. to Prince Lobkowitz. He was secretary of the Phil. Soc.

Works incl. operas & mus. plays *Oberon: König der Elfen* (after Wieland), *Die gute Mutter, Der Schreiner*; ballets *Die Weinlese, Das Urteil des Paris, Der Sabinerraub*; incid. m. for plays by Gustav III of Swe., Kotzebue & others; 12 syms.; Concs. for fl. & for co.; stg. 4tets, stg. 5tets, pf. trios, 3 trios for 2 fls. & co., &c.

Wreckers, The, opera by Ethel Smyth (lib. orig. in Fr., *Les Naufrageurs*, by Henry Brewster), prod., in Ger., as *Strandrecht*, Leipzig, 11. XI. 1906; 1st perf. in Eng., London, His Majesty's Theatre, 22. VI. 1909.

Wrest (noun). The old Eng. term for a tuning-key, from the verb meaning to twist or wrench. The tuning-pins of the pf. are still called wrest-pins and the board into which they are inserted is the wrest-plank.

Wulfstan (b. ?; d. ?), Eng. 11th-cent. monk & musn. Precentor at St. Swithin's, Winchester. Prob. the author of the treatise *De tonorum harmonia*.

Wüllner, Franz (b. Münster, 28. I. 1832; d. Braunsels o/Lahn, 7. IX. 1902), Ger. pfst., cond. & comp. Studied at home and at Frankfort o/M., and appeared as pfst. at Brussels in 1852–3, where he enlarged his experience by meeting Fétis, Kufferath & other musns. He then made a tour in Ger., settled at Munich in 1854 and in 1856 became pf. prof. at the Cons. In 1858–64 he was mus. dir. at Aachen, where he did much chor. & orch. cond., but he returned to Munich as court mus. dir., reorganized the court church m. and became cond. of the court opera in 1869 in succession to Bülow. In 1877–82 he was court mus. dir. at Dresden, succeeding Rietz, and from 1884 dir. of the Cons. at Cologne in succession to F. Hiller and cond. of the Gürzenich concerts.

Works incl. masses, motets, *Stabat Mater*, Miserere; Psalm cxxv for chor. & orch.; chor. works with & without orch.; cantata *Heinrich der Finkler* for voice & orch.; chamber m.; pf. pieces & duets; songs, &c.

Wurm, Mary (b. Southampton, 18. V. 1860; d. Munich, 21. I. 1938), Eng. pfst. & comp. of Ger. descent. Studied at the Stuttgart Cons., also with Clara Schumann and Raff at Frankfort o/M., and made her 1st appearance in London in 1882.

Works incl. ovt. for orch.; pf. Conc.; stg. 4tet; co. & pf. So.; pf. pieces, &c.

Wurm, Mathilde. *See* **Verne.**

Wycherley, William (? 1640–1716), Eng. dramatist. *See* **Banister** (*Gentleman Dancing-Master*), **Humfrey** (*Love in a Wood*).

Wyck, Arnold van (b. nr. Calvinia, Cape Province, 26. IV. 1916), S. Afr. comp. Began to learn the pf. at 12 and after working in an insurance office at Capetown, entered Stellenbosch Univ. in 1936. In 1937 he was commissioned to write m. for the centenary of the Voortrekkers and in 1938 he went to live in London, having gained the Performing Right Soc.'s scholarship. He studied comp. with Theodore Holland and pf. with Harold Craxton at the R.A.M., joined the B.B.C. for a short time and later devoted himself to comp.

Works incl. Sym. in A min., Suite for small orch. on Afr. tunes *Southern Cross*; *Saudade* for v. & orch.; 5 Elegies for stg. 4tet; 3 Improvisations on a Dutch folksong for pf. duet, &c.

Wynne, Sarah (Edith) (b. Holywell, Flintshire, 11. III. 1842; d. London, 24. I. 1897), Welsh sop. singer. Studied at Liverpool, at the R.A.M. in London and at Florence. Made her 1st London appearance in 1862.

Wyspianski, Stanislaw (1869–1907), Pol. painter & dramatist. *See* **Melcer** (*Protesilaus and Laodamia*), **Szymanowski** (*Penthesilea*).

Wyzewa, Teodor de (orig. Wyzewski) (b. Kaluszik, 12. IX. 1862; d. Paris, 17. IV. 1917), Pol.-Fr. mcolst. Settled in Paris in 1889, where he founded the *Revue Wagnérienne* with Édouard Dujardin and the Société Mozart with Boschot. He became a political and literary journalist, but also wrote articles on m. and trans. var. lit. works from Eng. and Rus. His chief work is the great study of Mozart in the 1st 2 vols. of which he collab. with Georges de Saint-Foix.

X

Xerse (*Xerxes*). *See also* **Serse**.

Opera by Cavalli (lib. by Niccolò Minato), prod. Venice, Teatro dei SS. Giovanni e Paolo, 12. I. 1654.

Xylophone. A perc. inst. with a series of wooden sticks or plates tuned in a chromatic scale ranging from middle C about 3 8ves upwards in foreign insts., but in Eng. ones often only from B♭ flat above middle C. It is played with hammers and makes a dry, rattling but perfectly clear and richly sonorous sound.

Xylorimba. A perc. inst., a small Marimba made in Amer.

Xyndas, Spiridion (b. Corfu, 1812; d. Athens, 25. XI. 1896), Gr. comp.

Works incl. It. operas *Anna Winter*, *I duo rivali*, *Il Conte Giuliano*, *Il candidato al parlamento* & others; pf. pieces; many songs, &c.

Y

Yaniewicz. *See* **Janiewicz.**

Yasser, Joseph (b. Lodz, 16. IV. 1893), Pol.-Amer. orgst. & mcolst. Studied at the Moscow Cons. and became org. prof. there, also orgst. at the chief theatres. Later he lectured, cond. and gave many org. recitals in Rus., China and U.S.A., where he settled in 1927 as orgst. to the N.Y. synagogue and became a naturalized citizen. He made a special study of the mus. scales and the harmonic implications of the old and exotic ones. His books incl. *A Theory of Evolving Tonality* & *Medieval Quartal Harmony*.

Year 1812, The, festival ovt. by Tchaikovsky, Op. 49, written for the commemoration of the 70th anniversary of Napoleon's retreat from Moscow and 1st perf. during the Moscow Arts and Industrial Exhib., 20. VIII. 1882, at the consecration of the Cath. of the Redeemer in the Kremlin.

Yeats, W(illiam). **B**(utler). (1865–1939), Ir. poet. *See* **Barber** (songs), **Berger** (*Words for Music, Perhaps*), **Bryson** (*Cloak, Boot and Shoes*). **Dunhill** (*Cloths of Heaven*), **Edwards (J.)** (*Land of Heart's Desire*), **Grania and Diarmid** (Elgar), **Hadley (P.)** (*Ephemera*), **Loeffler** (*Wind among the Reeds*), **Swain** (*Shadowy Waters* & *Harp of Aengus*).

Yeomen of the Guard, The, or The Merryman and his Maid, operetta by Sullivan (lib. by W. S. Gilbert), prod. London, Savoy Theatre, 3. X. 1888.

Yodel. A peculiar, primitive but elaborate form of song in Swi., usually sung by men in Falsetto, very free in rhythm and metre and using as a rule the restricted scale of the natural harmonics of insts. like the Alphorn. The Y. is thus very prob. derived or copied from the Ranz des Vaches.

Yonge, Nicholas (b. Lewes, ?; d. London, X. 1619), Eng. singer & mus. ed. Worked in London and pub. in 1588 a vol. of It. madrigals with Eng. trans. entitled *Musica transalpina.*

Yorkshire Feast Song, The. An ode or cantata by Purcell, 'Of old when heroes,' for 2 altos, ten., 2 basses, 5-part chor., fls., obs. tpts. & stgs., words by Thomas Durfey, written in 1690 for the annual reunion of Yorkshiremen in London, intended to be held that year on 14. II, but postponed to 27. III owing to parliamentary elections.

Youll, Henry (b. ?; d. ?), Eng. 16th–17th-cent. comp. Pub. a book of canzonets and balletts for 3 voices in 1608.

Young, Cecilia (b. London, 1711; d. ? London, 6. X. 1789), Eng. singer. Learnt m. from her father, Charles Y., orgst. of the church of All Hallows, Barking, in London. She married Arne in 1736.

Young, Isabella (b. London, *c.* 1710; d. ?), Eng. singer, sister of prec. Pupil of her father. She married Lampe.

Young, Mary (b. London, *c.* 1745; d. London, 20. IX. 1799), Eng. singer, niece of the 2 prec. She appeared in opera in London and married Barthélemon in 1766.

Young, Percy M(arshall). (b. Northwich, Ches., 17. V. 1912), Eng. mus. educst., cond. & writer on m. Educ. at Christ's Hospital and Cambridge, where he was org. scholar at Selwyn Coll. and took the M.A. and Mus.B. degrees. Mus.D. at Trinity Coll., Dublin. In 1934 he became dir. of m. at the Teachers' Training Coll., Belfast, in 1937 mus. adviser to the Stoke-on-Trent Educ. Committee, in 1945 dir. of mus. studies at Wolverhampton Techn. Coll. Pub. part-songs and var. collections for children, articles in mus. periodicals and books *Pageant of England's Music* & *Handel.*

Young, Thomas (b. Canterbury, 1809; d. London, 12. VIII. 1872), Eng. alto singer. Educ. as a choir-boy at Canterbury cath. where he became an alto in 1831. In 1836 he went to London to join the choir of Westminster Abbey and in 1848 he became 1st alto at the Temple church. He also frequently sang at concerts.

Young, William (b. ?; d. London, 1672), Eng. violist, vst., flst. & comp. He was in the service of the imp. court at Innsbruck, in the middle of the 17th cent., but returned to Eng. to join the king's band in 1660. From 1664 he and others were also allowed to play for Killigrew at the theatre.

Works incl. 21 sos. for 3–5 insts.

with appended dances, 3-part fantasies for viols, pieces for lyra viol, for va. da gamba; airs for 2 treble viols & bass, &c.

Yradier, Sebastián (b. Sauciego, Alva, 20. I. 1809; d. Vitoria, 6. XII. 1865), Spa. comp. He was in Paris for a time as singing-master to the Empress Eugénie and later lived in Cuba for some years. Wrote popular Spa. songs, incl. *La Paloma*, and is said to be the comp. of the Habanera in Bizet's *Carmen*.

Yriarte, Tomás de (b. Teneriffe, 18. IX. 1750; d. Santa Maria nr. Cadiz, 17. IX. 1791), Spa. poet & comp. Sec. to the Madrid archives. He wrote poems under the anagram of Tirso Imareta, the most important being *La Música*, a didactic poem on mus. theory and on comps., pub. in 1779.

Comps. incl. monodrama *Guzman el bueno*; syms.; stg. 4tets; songs, &c.

Yrvid, Richard. *See* **Ivry.**

Ysaÿe, Eugène (b. Liége, 16. VII. 1858; d. Brussels, 12. V. 1931), Belg. vst., cond. & comp. Studied with his father, Nicolas Y., then at the Liége Cons. and later with Wieniawski and Vieuxtemps. Having already appeared in public in 1865, he played at Pauline Lucca's concerts at Cologne and Aachen, where he met F. Hiller and Joachim, and later, at Frankfort o/M., he came into touch with Raff and Clara Schumann. In 1886–98 he was v. prof. at the Brussels Cons. and founded and cond. orch. concerts in the Belg. capital. He toured extensively, 1st visiting Eng. in 1889 and U.S.A. in 1894.

Works incl. opera *Piér li Houïeu* (in Walloon dialect); v. concs.; *Poème élégiaque*, mazurkas & other pieces for v. & pf., &c.

Ysaÿe, Théo(phile). (b. Verviers, 2. III. 1865; d. Nice, 24. III. 1918), Belg. pfst. & cond., brother of prec. Studied at the Liége Cons., with Kullak in Berlin and with Franck in Paris. He often appeared at concerts with his brother and also gave recitals of his own.

Works incl. Requiem; Sym. in F min., symph. poems, Fantasy, *Suite wallonne* for orch.; pf. Conc.; pf. 5tet, &c.

Yslv. (abbr.) = Yugoslav, Yugoslavia.

Yugoslav Composers. *See* **Baranovic, Gostovec, Hirschler, Lhotka, Lisinski, Miloyevich, Odak, Osterc, Papandopulo, Sirola, Zajc.**

Yurovsky, Vladimir Mikhailovitch (b. Tarastcha, Uzbekistan, 20. III. 1915), Rus. comp. Pupil of Miaskovsky at the Moscow Cons.

Works incl. opera *Concerning Opanas*; Sym., symph. suite *Moscow Carnival* for orch.; v. Conc.; songs, &c.

Yussupov, Nikolai Borisovitch, Prince (b. St. Petersburg, 1827; d. Baden-Baden, 3. VIII. 1891), Rus. amateur vst. & comp. Studied v. with Vieuxtemps and later kept a private orch. in his palace, wrote a book on the v. and planned another on mus. hist. with special reference to Rus.

Works incl. ballet *Ballet d'Espagne*; sym. with v. solo *Gonzalvo de Córdova*; v. Conc., &c.

Yvain, Maurice (Pierre Paul) (b. Paris, 12. II. 1891), Fr. comp. Studied at the Paris Cons. He served in the army during the 1914–8 war, resuming his studies later, devoting his whole attention to the comp. of operettas, the 1st of which, *Ta bouche*, was an immediate success in 1921 and was followed by 16 others, also a ballet *Vent*.

Z

Ž. In Cz., **Ž** or **ž** has a soft 'zh' sound, like *s* in 'leisure.'

Zacconi, Lodovico (b. Pesaro, 11. VI. 1555; d. Venice, 23. III. 1627), It. priest & mus. theorist. He went to live at Venice, joined the monastic order of St. Augustine and was chapel master at its church. In 1593, at the invitation of the Archduke Charles, he went to Vienna, where he became court mus. dir. and remained until 1619, when he returned to Venice. He wrote a great treatise in 4 vols., *Prattica di musica.*

Zachau, Friedrich Wilhelm (b. Leipzig, 19. XI. 1663; d. Halle, 14. VIII. 1712), Ger. orgst. & comp. Pupil of his father, a town musn., under whom he learnt to play all the current insts. The family moved to Eilenburg in 1673 and in 1684 he was app. orgst. at the church of Our Lady at Halle, where Handel became his pupil at the age of 7 or so.

Works incl. church cantatas, org. pieces, &c.

Zador, Jenö (b. Bátaszék, 5. XI. 1894), Hung. comp. Studied with Heuberger in Vienna and Reger at Leipzig, also took a course in mcol. and graduated with the Ph.D. in 1921. In 1922 he became prof. at the new Vienna Cons. and in 1935 at the Budapest Acad. of M.

Works incl. operas *Diana, The Island of the Dead, Asra* & others; Romantic Sym., Dance Sym., Vars. on a Hung. folksong, Carnival Suite, Hung. Capriccio, &c.; chamber m.; pf. works; songs, &c.

Zagwijn, Henri (b. Nieuwer-Amstel nr. Amsterdam, 17. VII. 1878), Dutch comp. He was mainly self-taught, settled at Rotterdam and became a teacher at the Cons. there.

Works incl. *The Sorcerer's Apprentice* (Goethe) & *The Course of the Year* for chor. & orch.; ovts. *Wijdingsnacht* & *Opstanding* for orch.; chamber m.; songs, &c.

Zaide, unfinished opera by Mozart (lib., in Ger., by Johann Andreas Schachtner), begun 1779, 1st prod. Frankfort o/M., 27. I. 1866.

Zajc, Ivan (better known as Giovanni von Zaytz) (b. Fiume, 21. I. 1832; d. Zagreb, 17. XII. 1914), Yslv. (Croatian) cond. & comp. Pupil of his father, a bandmaster in the Aus. army & of Lauro Rossi at the Milan Cons. He lived at Fiume and Vienna and was from 1870 cond. at the theatre and dir. of the Cons. at Zagreb.

Works incl. 15 Croatian operas, It. opera *Amelia* (after Schiller's *Räuber*) & others, 15 Ger. & Croatian operettas; orat. *The Fall of Man*; church m.; songs, &c.

Žak, Benedict. *See* **Schack.**

Zambra. A Moorish dance introd. into Spa. and danced to m. for scabebas (fls.) and dulzianas (? obs.).

Zampa, ou La Fiancée de marbre (*Z., or The Marble Betrothed*), opera by Hérold (lib. by Anne Honoré Joseph Mélesville), prod. Paris, Opéra-Comique, 3. V. 1831.

ampogna (It.). The Calabrian bagpipe.

andonai, Riccardo (b. Sacco, Trentino, 28. V. 1883; d. Pesaro, VI. 1944), It. comp. Studied at Roveredo and later at the Liceo Musicale of Pesaro, where Mascagni was dir. He left in 1902 and at Milan met Boito, who introd. him to the pub. Ricordi, by whom his 1st opera was commissioned.

Works incl. operas *Il grillo sul focolare* (after Dickens's *Cricket on the Hearth*), *Conchita* (after Louÿs's *La Femme et le pantin*), *Melenis, La via della finestra, Francesca da Rimini* (on d'Annunzio's play), *Giulietta e Romeo* (after Shakespeare), *I cavalieri di Ekebù* (after Selma Lagerlöf), *Giuliano, La farsa amorosa, Una partita*; film m. for *Princess Tarakanova*; Requiem, *Pater noster* for chor., org. & orch.; *Ballata eroica, Fra gli alberghi delle Dolomiti,)uadri di Segantini, Rapsodia trenina,* ovt. *Colombina* for orch.; *Concerto romantico* for v. & orch., erenade & *Concerto andaluso,* for co. & orch.; stg. 4tet; songs, &c.

Zanella, Amilcare (b. Monticelli d'Ongina nr. Piacenza, 26. IX. 1873), It. pfst., cond. & comp. Studied at Cremona and Parma. After cond. an opera company in S. Amer. he became dir. of the Parma Cons. in 1903 and 2 years later succeeded Mascagni as dir. of the Liceo Musicale at Pesaro.

Works incl. operas *Aura, Sulamita, Il revisore* (after Gogol) & others; Requiem; symph. poem *Vita* & other orch. works; chamber m.; pf. works; songs, &c.

Zanetti, Francesco (b. Volterra, c. 1740; d. ?), It. singer & comp. He was chapel master at Perugia cath. but was dismissed in 1770 for his connections with the stage, married a singer and travelled with an operatic company.

Works incl. opera *Le lavarandine* & c. 10 others; church m.; 6 stg. 5tets;

sos. for 2 vs. & bass; hpchd., fl. & v. sos.; songs, &c.

Zanettini. *See* **Gianettini.**

Zapateado. A Spa. dance for a single perf., in 3–4 time and with the rhythmic accents marked by stamping of the heels.

Zapfenstreich (Ger.) = Tattoo.

Zar und Zimmermann, oder Die zwei Peter (*Tsar and Carpenter, or The Two Peters*), opera by Lortzing (lib. by comp., based on a Fr. play by Anne Honoré Joseph Mélesville, Jean Toussaint Merle and Eugène Cantiran de Boirie), prod. Leipzig, 22. XII. 1837.

See also **Borgomastro di Saardam.**

Zarathustra (R. Strauss). *See* **Also sprach Zarathustra.**

Zaremba, Nikolai Ivanovitch (b. Gvt. of Vitebsk, 15. VI. 1821; d. St. Petersburg, 8. IV. 1879), Rus. theorist. Prof. at the St. Petersburg Cons. from its foundation in 1861; succeeded A. Rubinstein as dir. from 1867 to 1871.

Works incl. orat. *St. John the Baptist*, &c.

Zarembski, Juliusz (b. Zytomierz, 28. II. 1854; d. Zytomierz, 15. IX. 1885), Pol. pfst. & comp. He appeared in public at the age of 10 with works of his own, studied later at the Vienna and St. Petersburg Conss., and with Liszt in Rome. He travelled widely and became pf. prof. at the Brussels Cons. in 1879, but had to leave shortly afterwards because he suffered from consumption.

Works incl. pf. 5tet in G min.; polonaises, mazurkas, studies, waltzes, Pol. Suite, &c. for pf.; Pol. folk dances for pf. duet *A travers Pologne*, &c.

Zarlino, Gioseffe (b. Chioggia, 22. III. 1517; d. Venice, 14. II. 1590), It. theorist & comp. Studied theol. and received minor orders in 1539, but was learned also in philos., sciences and languages. He settled at Venice in 1541, became a fellow-student with Rore under Willaert and in 1565 became 1st chapel master at St. Mark's. In 1583 he was offered the bishopric of Chioggia, but declined it, preferring to remain at St. Mark's. He wrote 2 great treatises, the 3-vol. *Istitutioni armoniche* and *Dimostrationi armoniche*, for which he was attacked by V. Galilei, whereupon he issued another vol., *Sopplimenti musicali*, a 4th, non-mus., being added to the complete ed. later.

Comps. incl. dramatic piece *Orfeo*; Mass for the foundation of the church of Santa Maria della Salute & other church m.; pageant for the victory of Lepanto, &c.

Zarzuela (Spa.). A light Spa. mus. stage play or comic opera, usually in 1 act but sometimes in 2, generally of a satirical but occasionally tragic nature, and often a skit on a spoken play. The m. is as a rule strongly national. The libs. have spoken dialogue and allow improvised interpolations, in which even the audience sometimes joins.

Zarzycki, Alexander (b. Lwów, 21. II. 1834; d. Warsaw, 13. X. 1895), Pol. vst. & comp. He became dir. of the Warsaw Cons.

Works incl. pf. Conc.; numerous v. pieces, &c.

Zauberflöte, Die, opera by Mozart (lib. by Emanuel Schikaneder, ? with the aid of Karl Ludwig Giesecke), prod. Vienna, Theater auf der Wieden, 30. IX. 1791. Winter's opera *Das Labyrinth* is a sequel to it. There is also an unfinished lib. by Goethe intended for a sequel.

Zauberharfe, Die (*The Magic Harp*), magic play with m. by Schubert (lib. by Georg Ernst von Hofmann), prod. Vienna, Theater an der Wien, 19. VIII. 1820.

Zauberoper (Ger.). *See* **Magic Opera.**

Zauberzither, Die, oder Caspar der Fagottist (*The Magic Zither, or Jasper the Bassoonist*), play with m. by Wenzel Müller, prod. Vienna, Leopoldstadt Theatre, 8. VI. 1791. The plot shows close resemblances to that of Schikander's lib. for Mozart's *Magic Flute*, which may have been borrowed from it or based on the same source.

Zaytz, Giovanni von. *See* **Zajc.**

Zecchi, Adone (b. Bologna, 23. VII. 1904), It. comp. Pupil of Alfano. He founded a chamber orch. in 1930 and began to tour It. with it.

Works incl. *Partita* & *Due preludi* for orch.; *Giovane pastore* & *Arpège* for sop. & orch.; *Dittico campestre* for ob. & stgs.; 2 v. & pf. sos.; songs, &c.

Zeckert, Joseph. *See* **Seegr.**

Zelenka, Johan Dismas (b. Launovice 16. X. 1679; d. Dresden, 23. XII. 1745), Boh. comp. Studied at Prague, was db. player in the court band at Dresden from 1710 and went to Vienna to study under Fux in 1716; then went to It. but returned to Dresden to collaborate with Heinichen, whom he succeeded as dir. of the church m. in 1729.

Works incl. Lat. *Melodrama de Sancto Wenceslao*; orats. *I penitenti al sepolcro, Il serpente di bronzo* & *Gesù al Calvario*; 21 masses, motets, 108 psalms & other church m.; Lat. cantatas, &c.

Zelenski, Wladyslaw (b. Grodkowice, 6. VII. 1837; d. Cracow, 23. I. 1921), Pol. teacher & comp. Studied at

Prague Univ., also m. with Krejči there and later in Paris. He became prof. at the Warsaw Cons. in 1872 and dir. of the Cracow Cons. in 1887.
Works incl. operas *Konrad Wallenrod, Goplana, Janek, Balandina* & *An Old Story*; masses & motets; cantatas; *Woodland Echoes*, concert ovt. *In the Tatra* & other orch. works; pf. Conc.; 2 stg. 4tets, pf. 4tet, Vars. for stg. 4tet, 6tet for stgs. & pf., pf. Trio; v. & pf. So.; pf. pieces, &c.

Zeller, Karl (b. St. Peter-in-der-Au, 19. VII. 1842; d. Baden nr. Vienna, 17. VIII. 1898), Aus. comp.
Works incl. operettas *Der Vogelhändler, Der Obersteiger, Der Vagabund* & many others.

Zelmira, opera by Rossini (lib. by Andrea Leone Tottola, based on a Fr. tragedy by Pierre Laurent Buirette de Belloy), prod. Naples, Teatro San Carlo, 16. II. 1822.

Zelter, Carl Friedrich (b. Berlin, 11. XII. 1758; d. Berlin, 15. V. 1832), Ger. cond., teacher & comp. 1st learnt m. at a school kept by an orgst. He was intended to follow his father's calling of mason, but at 18 made such an impression with a cantata that Marpurg advised him to study with Kirnberger and K. F. C. Fasch. He assisted the latter as accompst. at the Voc. Acad. in 1782–1800, when he succeeded him as cond. He began to set poems by Goethe as songs, which won the poet's approval and led to a correspondence and subsequent friendship between them. In 1809 he founded a *Liedertafel* for male-voice chor. singing and in 1819 the Royal Institute for Church M. Mendelssohn became his pupil and was allowed by him to conduct the 1st perf. within living memory of Bach's St. Matthew Passion in 1829, which led to a revival of Bach's all but forgotten m.
Works incl. incid. m. to Goethe's *Pandora*; Requiem, Te Deum & other church m.; cantata *Seraphina* (Wieland), cantata on the death of Frederick II of Prus. & others; male-voice 4tets & partsongs; songs to words by Goethe, &c.

Zémire et Azor, opera by Grétry (lib. by Marmontel), prod. Fontainebleau, at court, 9. XI. 1771; 1st Paris perf., Théâtre Italien, 16. XII. 1771.

Zemire und Azor, opera by Spohr (lib. by Johann Jakob Ihlee, based on that by Marmontel), prod. Frankfort o/M., 4. IV. 1819. The familiar song 'Rose, softly blooming' is in this work.

Zemlinsky, Alexander von (b. Vienna, 4. X. 1872; d. Larchmont, New York, 16. III. 1942), Aus. cond. & comp. Studied at the Vienna Cons. He became cond. at the Vienna Volksoper in 1906 and at the Court Opera in 1908, later at Mannheim and in Prague, where he cond. the Ger. Opera; finally, in 1927–32, he was one of the conds. at the Berlin State Opera. But he returned to Vienna in 1933 and later emigrated to the U.S.A. Schoenberg was among his pupils and married his daughter.
Works incl. operas *Sarema, Es war einmal, Kleider machen Leute* (Gottfried Keller), *Eine florentinische Tragödie, Der Zwerg* (both after Oscar Wilde), *Der Kreidekreis*; Lyric Sym., &c.

Zeno, Apostolo (1668–1750), It. poet & libst. Operas on his libs. *see* **Alessandro Severo** (Lotti), **Ambleto** (Gasparini & D. Scarlatti), **Astarto** (G. B. Bononcini), **Faramondo** (Handel), **Ifigenia in Aulide** (Caldara), **Lucio Papirio** (do. & Hasse), **Lucio Vero** (Pollarolo & Sacchini), **Merope** (Gasparini, Jommelli & Terradellas), **Narciso** (D. Scarlatti), **Scipione** (Handel), **Temistocle** (Porpora).

Zenta, Hermann. *See* **Holmès, Augusta.**

Zeyer, Julius (1841–1901), Cz. poet & dramatist. *See* **Janáček** (*Šarka*), **Ostrčil** (*Kunala's Eyes*), **Suk** (*Radúz and Mahulena*).

Zhelobinsky, Valery Viktorovitch (b. Tambov, 12. III. 1912), Rus. pfst. & comp. He played the pf. extremely well as a child and taught it; was sent to the School of M. at Tambov, which he left at 15 for the Leningrad Cons., where he was a pupil of Shtcherbatchev.
Works incl. operas *The Peasant from Kamarinsk, Her Name-day* & *Mother* (based on Gorky's novel); ballet *Party Ticket*; incid. and film m.; syms.; 3 pf. concs.; chamber m.; 24 Preludes for pf.; songs, &c.

Zhiganov, Nazib Gaiazovitch (b. Uralsk, 15. VIII. 1911), Rus. comp. He lost his parents during the Revol. and was brought up in an orphanage, later studying comp. with Litinsky.
Works incl. operas *A Fugitive* & *Irik*; cantata for the 15th anniversary of the Tartar Soviet Repub. estab. in 1920; chamber m.; pf. pieces, &c.

Zhivotov, Alexey Semionovitch (b. Kazan, 14. XI. 1904), Rus. comp. Pupil of Shtcherbatchev at the Leningrad Cons.
Works incl. opera *Enny*; Symph. Suite & Jazz Suite for orch.; Symph. Cycle for voice & orch.; Nonet, &c.

Zhukovsky, Vassily Andreievitch (1783–1852), Rus. author and trans. *See* **Maid of Orleans** (Tchaikovsky), **Verstovsky** (*Gromoboy*).

Ziani, Marc' Antonio (b. Venice, *c.* 1653; d. Vienna, 22. I. 1715), It. comp. Chapel master at the church of Santa Barbara and cond. at the theatre at Mantua until 1686, when he was dismissed. He went to Vienna, where he became vice mus. dir. in 1700 and 1st mus. dir. in 1712.

Works incl. operas *Alessandro magno in Sidone, Damira placata, Meleagro, Chilonida* & 41 others; masses, motets & other church m.; orats., cantatas, &c.

Ziani, Pietro Andrea (b. Venice, c. 1620; d. Naples, 12. II. 1684), It. comp., uncle of prec. He was orgst. at Venice, then at Santa Maria Maggiore, Bergamo, visited Vienna and Dresden in 1660–7 and became 2nd orgst. at St. Mark's, Venice, in succession to Cavalli in 1669. But he went to Naples on failing to get the 1st post in 1676, becoming a teacher at the Cons. di Sant' Onofrio and in 1680 royal chapel master.

Works incl. operas *Le fortune di Rodope e di Damira, L'Antigona delusa da Alceste* & 21 others; masses, psalms, orats.; inst. sos.; org. pieces, &c.

Zich, Otakar (b. Kralové Městic, 25. III. 1879; d. Ouběnice nr. Benešova, 9. VII. 1934), Cz. comp. He was at first a secondary schoolmaster, but took a degree at the Univ. of Brno and was app. prof. of aesthetics there. He also collected folksongs.

Works incl. operas *The Painter's Whim, The Sin* & *Les Précieuses ridicules* (after Molière); *The Ill-fated Marriage* & *Polka Rides* for chor. & orch.; songs, &c.

Zichy, Géza, Count (b. Sztára Castle, 23. VII. 1849; d. Budapest, 14. I. 1924), Hung. pfst., poet & comp. Pupil of Volkmann and Liszt at Budapest. He lost his right arm as a boy of 14 in a hunting accident and wrote much pf. m. for the left hand. He became president of the Hung. Acad. of M. and the Nat. Cons.

Works incl. operas *Castle Story, Alár, Master Roland,* trilogy *Rákóczi* (*Nemo, Rákóczi Ferenc* & *Rodostó*); ballet *Gemma*; pf. Conc. for the left hand; So., 6 Studies, &c. for the left hand & other pf. m.; songs, &c.

Ziehharmonika (Ger. lit. draw-harmonica) = Accordion.

Zielenski, Mikolaj (b. ?; d. ?), Pol. 17th-cent. orgst. & comp. Comp. offertories and communions for the service of the whole year.

Zigeunerbaron, Der (*The Gypsy Baron*), operetta by J. Strauss, jun. (lib. by Ignaz Schnitzer, based on another by Mór Jókai founded on his own story *Saffi*), prod. Vienna, Theater an der Wien, 24. X. 1885.

Zilafone (It.) = Xylophone.

Zilcher, Hermann (b. Frankfort o/M., 18. VIII. 1881), Ger. comp. Studied at the Hoch Cons. at Frankfort, became prof. at the Acad. of M. at Munich in 1908 and in 1920 dir. of the Würzburg Cons.

Works incl. opera *Doktor Eisenbart*; incid. m. for plays by Shakespeare, Dehmel's children's play *Fitzebutze* and Hauptmann's *Die goldene Harfe*; orat. *Liebesmesse*; 2 syms., *Tanzphantasie* & other works for orch.; pieces for solo insts. & orch.; chamber m.; pf. pieces; songs, &c.

Zimbalon (incorrect spelling). *See* **Cimbalom.**

Zimmermann, Pierre Joseph Guillaume (b. Paris, 17. III. 1785; d. Paris, 29. X. 1853), Fr. pfst., teacher & comp. Studied at the Paris Cons., where he became a pupil-teacher in 1811, asst. master in 1817 and prof. of pf. in 1820. Gounod married a daughter of his. He wrote a treatise, *Encyclopédie du pianiste.*

Works incl. operas *L'Enlèvement* & *Nausicaa*; pf. works, &c.

Zincken, Hans Friedrich August. *See* **Sommer, Hans.**

Zingara, La (*The Gypsy*), intermezzo by Rinaldo di Capua (lib. by ?), prod. (prob. not for the 1st time) Paris, Opéra, 19. VI. 1753.

Zingarelli, Niccolò Antonio (b. Naples. 4. IV. 1752; d. Torre del Greco, 5 V. 1837), It. comp. His father, a singer and teacher, d. in 1759 and left the family very poor, but Z. was admitted to the Mus. Coll. of Santa Maria di Loreto and prod. the intermezzo *I quattro pazzi* there in 1768. In 1769 he left, taught the v. to a wealthy family nr. Naples and later came under the patronage of the Duchess of Castelpagano, for whom he wrote the cantata *Pimmalione* at Naples in 1779. The San Carlo theatre there accepted his 1st opera in 1781. He soon afterwards went to Milan with a recommendation to the Archduchess Beatrice of Aus. and prod. most of his operas at La Scala there. In 1789 he went to Paris to prod. a Fr. opera to a lib. by Marmontel. In 1792 he was app. chapel master of Milan cath.; but in 1794 he went to a similar post at Loreto, where he remained until 1804, when he became chapel master of the Sistine Chapel in Rome in succession to Guglielmi. When Napoleon ordered a Te Deum to be sung to celebrate his son's title of King of Rome, Z. refused to have anything to do with it and was arrested and taken to Paris for trial; but Napoleon, being very fond of his m., released him. In 1813 he became dir. of the Royal Cons. at Naples and in 1816 succeeded Paisiello as chapel master of the cath. there.

Works incl. operas *Montesuma, Armida, Antigono, Ifigenia in Aulide, Antigone, Il mercato di Monfregoso, Artaserse, Quinto Fabio, Gli Orazi e Curazi, Giulietta e Romeo* (after Shakespeare), *Andromeda, La morte di Mitridate, I veri amici, Il ratto delle Sabine, Edipo a Colono* (after Sophocles), *Inez di Castro, Berenice in Armenia* & c. 20 others; orats. *La Passione, La distruzione di Gerusalemme, La riedificazione di Gerusalemme* & others; many cantatas (incl. *Isaiah* for the Birmingham Festival of 1829); numerous masses, 2 Requiems & other church m.; canon for 8 voices; *Partimenti* & *Solfeggi* for voc. exercise, &c.

Zingaresa (It. noun) } **Zingarese** (It. adj.) } Words used to describe m. in or supposed to be in a gypsy manner. The adj. is used in the form of *alla z.*

Zingari (*Gypsies*), opera by Leoncavallo (lib. by Enrico Cavacchioli & Guglielmo Emanuel, after Pushkin), prod. London, Hippodrome, 16. IX. 1912.

Zinke (Ger.) =Cornett.

Zipoli, Domenico (b. Nola, Naples, *c.* 1675; d. ?), It. comp. Studied at the Cons. dei Turchini at Naples and became orgst. at the Jesuit church in Rome in 1696. He seems to have been in Eng. some time.

Works incl. orat. *Santa Caterina*; sos. & dances for org. or hpchd.; org. toccatas, voluntaries & fugues; hpchd. lessons, &c.

Zitek, Otakar (b. Prague, 5. XI. 1892), Cz. critic & comp. Pupil of Novák and Adler. Prof. at the Brno Cons. He wrote a book on modern opera.

Works incl. operas *The Sublime Heart* & *The Fall of Peter Králenec*; song cycles, &c.

Zither (Ger. from Gr. *kithara*). A stg. inst. of the Dulcimer type, although etymolog. connected with the Cittern, which it does not resemble. It has many stgs. (27–40) stretched over a flat sound-box and is played with the tips of the finger, the bass stgs. alone being struck with a plectrum fixed to the thumb by a ring. It has little artistic value and the m. played on it, mainly in the mountain regions of Aus. and Bavaria, is of a primitive kind akin to inferior types of folk-song and dance.

Znamenny Chant (from Rus. *znamia* =neume). The chant of the Rus. Orthodox church in use from the 12th to the 17th cent., when it began to decline.

Zoilo, Annibale (b. Rome, ?; d. Loreto, 1592), It. singer & comp. Chapel master at the churches of St. John Lateran and San Luigi in Rome, singer in the Papal Chapel from 1570 to *c.* 1582, and chapel master of the Santa Casa at Loreto in 1584–92.

Works incl. masses; madrigals; songs, &c.

Zoilo, Cesare (b. Rome, ?; d. ?), It. 17th-cent. comp., (?) son of prec. Comp. motets, madrigals, &c.

Zola, Émile (1840–1902), Fr. novelist. *See* **Attaque du moulin** (Bruneau, *Soirées de Médan*), **Bruneau** (*Kérim, Ouragan, Enfant-roi, Lazare, Naïs Micoulin, 4 Journées* & *Faute de l'Abbé Mouret*), **Gurlitt (M.)** (*Nana*), **Messidor** (Bruneau), **Rêve** (do.), **Weiss (K.)** (*Attack on the Mill*).

Zöllner, Heinrich (b. Leipzig, 4. VII. 1854), Ger. cond. & comp. Studied at the Leipzig Cons. App. teacher at Dorpat Univ. (Tartu, Estonia) in 1878, cond. at Cologne, lived in U.S.A. in 1890–8, became mus. dir. of Leipzig Univ. in succession to Kretzschmar until 1906, cond. the Flem. Opera at Antwerp from 1907 and retired to Freiburg i/B. in 1914.

Works incl. operas *Frithjof* (after Tegnér), *Faust* (on part of Goethe's orig. text), *Der Überfall* (on a story by Wildenbruch), *Die versunkene Glocke* (on Hauptmann's play) & others; festival cantata *The New World* & others; 5 syms., ovt. *Under the Starry Banner*, &c.

Zolotarev, Vassily Andreievitch (b. Taganrog, 7. III. 1879), Rus. comp. He was a choir-boy in the court chapel at St. Petersburg, learnt the v., but had to give it up because of an injury to his hand, also studied comp. with Liadov and Balakirev, later with Rimsky-Korsakov at the Cons. Later he became prof. at the Moscow Cons., but in 1925 went to live in the Caucasus.

Works incl opera *The Decembrists*; cantata *Paradise and the Peri* (after Thomas Moore); Sym., ovt. *A Rustic Festival*; 4 stg. 4tets, stg. 5tet, pf. 4tet, pf. Trio; pf. So. & pieces; songs, &c.

Zopfstil (Ger. = pigtail style). The formal, courtly 18th-cent. style in m.; but the term is always used contemptuously, not for the m. of the masters of that period, but for the work of later comps. who imitated it when it no longer suited their period or who used it merely dryly and academically.

Zoppa (It. =limp). A strong accent on a 2nd note off the beat or a long note following a short one, as in the Scotch snap. The motion of a mus. piece in such a rhythm is called *alla z.*

Zoroastre, opera by Rameau (lib. by

Louis de Cahusac), prod. Paris, Opéra, 5. XII. 1749.

Zorrilla y Moral, José (1817–93), Spa. poet & dramatist. *See* **Don Giovanni** (Lattuada).

Zortziko (Basque) } **Zorzico** (Spa.) } A Basque dance-song of remote orig., now in 5–8 time, but prob. in 6–8 before the 19th cent.

Zuccalmaglio, Anton Wilhelm Florentin von (b. Waldbröl, 12. IV. 1803; d. Nachrodt, Westphalia, 23. III. 1869), Ger. critic & folksong collector (?) of It. descent. He was a contributor to Schumann's *Neue Zeitschrift für Musik* and with A. Kretschmer ed. 2 vols. of Ger. folksong, or what passes for such in Ger., although some were comp. by himself.

Zuffolo (It.). A whistle or pipe of a primitive fl., flageolet or ob. type.

Zumpe, Hermann (b. Taubenheim, Saxony, 9. IV. 1850; d. Munich, 4. IX. 1903), Ger. cond. & comp. Educ. at a seminary at Bautzen to become a schoolmaster, but he was so taken up with m. that he went to Leipzig in 1871 to join the opera orch. as a subordinate perc. player in order to gain experience. In 1873–6 he assisted Wagner at Bayreuth, and then succeeded in securing one post as theatre cond. after another, until in 1891 he became court mus. dir. at Stuttgart. In 1895–7 he cond. the Kaim orch. at Munich and then became court cond. at Schwerin, from 1900 at Munich.

Works incl. operas *Anahra, Die verwunschene Prinzess, Das Gespenst von Horodin* & *Sawitri* (from the Mahabharata, unfinished), operettas *Farinelli, Karin* & *Polnische Wirtschaft*, &c.

Zumsteeg, Johann (Rudolf) (b. Sachsenflur, Baden, 10. I. 1760; d. Stuttgart, 27. I. 1802), Ger. comp. As the son of a valet at the ducal court of Württemberg he was educ. at the Carl School nr. Stuttgart, where Schiller was his fellow-pupil and became his friend. He was intended to become a sculptor, but took to m. and studied the co. and theory with Poli, the court mus. dir., whom he succeeded in 1792. He also became cond. of the Court Opera.

Works incl. operas *Die Geisterinsel* (after Shakespeare's *Tempest*), *Das Pfauenfest, Elbondocani, Der Betrug aus Liebe* & *Zalaor*; incid. m. for Shakespeare's *Hamlet, Macbeth* & *Othello*, Goethe's *Clavigo*, Schiller's *Die Räuber* & *Wallensteins Lager* & other plays; 18 church cantatas; co. Conc.; ode *Die Frühlingsfeier* (Klopstock) & others; songs & ballads *Lenore* (Bürger), *Kolma* (Ossian), *Die Büssende, Ritter Toggenburg* (Schiller), *Elwina, Die Entführung*, &c.

Zur Mühlen, Raimund von (b. Livonia, 10. XI. 1854; d. Steyning, Sussex, 9. XII. 1931), Ger. bar. singer. Educ. in Ger., he began to learn singing at the Hochschule für Musik in Berlin, later went to Stockhausen at Frankfort o/M. and Bussine in Paris. He 1st visited London in 1882, frequently returned and finally settled in Eng., where he was much sought after as a teacher of singing.

Zusammenschlag (Ger.) = Acciaccatura or Mordent.

Zvonař, Josef (Leopold) (b. Kublov nr. Prague, 22. I. 1824; d. Prague, 23. XI. 1865), Cz. theorist & comp. He became dir. of the Org. School in Prague and in 1861 was one of the founders of the Hlahol chor. soc. He wrote several educ. treatises and a vol. on early Cz. m.

Works incl. opera *Záboj*; masses, 2 Requiems; humorous chors; songs, &c.

Zweers, Bernard (b. Amsterdam, 18. V. 1854; d. Amsterdam, 9. XII. 1924), Dutch comp. Self-taught at first and later a pupil of Jadassohn at Leipzig. On his return to Amsterdam he cond., later became prof. at the Cons.

Works incl. incid. m. to Vondel's *Gysbrecht van Amstel*; chor. works; 3 syms. (3rd *To my Fatherland*), &c.

Zweig, Stefan (1881–1942), Aus. novelist & dramatist. *See* **Schweigsame Frau** (R. Strauss), **Toch** (*Heilige aus U.S.A.*).

Z. intended to write the lib. for R. Strauss's *Friedenstag*, suggested to him by Joseph Gregor; but the Nazi régime making his appearance on any Ger. stage impossible after 1933, this was afterwards undertaken by Gregor himself.

Zwillingsbrüder, Die (*The Twin Brothers*), play with m. by Schubert (lib. by Georg Ernst von Hofmann), prod. Vienna, Kärntnertor Theatre, 14. VI. 1820.

Zwischenspiel (Ger.) = Interlude.

Zwyssig, Joseph (Father Alberik) (b. Bauen, Uri, 17. XI. 1808; d. Mehrerau nr. Bregenz, 18. XI. 1854), Swi. priest, orgst. & comp. Educ. at the monastery school of Wettingen, ordained priest and became m. teacher and cath. orgst. & cond. After the dissolution of the monastery he led a precarious existence, but was in demand as an authority on the org.

Works incl. masses, offertories & other church m.; chors. incl. the patriotic *Schweizerpsalm* 'Trittst im Morgenrot daher'; songs, &c.